D0475357

The Reader's Adviser

The Reader's Adviser
14th EDITION

Marion Sader, Series Editor

Volume 1
The Best in Reference Works, British Literature, and American Literature

David Scott Kastan and Emory Elliott, Volume Editors

Books About Books • Bibliography • Reference Books: General • Reference Books: Literature • Medieval Literature • Renaissance Literature • Shakespeare • Restoration and Eighteenth-Century Literature • The Romantic Period • The Victorian Period • Modern British and Irish Literature • British Literature: Popular Modes • Early American Literature: Beginnings to the Nineteenth Century • Early Nineteenth-Century American Literature • Middle to Late Nineteenth-Century American Literature • Early Twentieth-Century American Literature • Middle to Late Twentieth-Century American Literature • Modern American Drama • American Literature: Some New Directions • American Literature: Popular Modes

Volume 2
The Best in World Literature

Robert DiYanni, Volume Editor

Introduction to World Literature • Hebrew Literature • Yiddish Literature • Middle Eastern Literatures • African Literatures • Literature of the Indian Subcontinent • Chinese Literature • Japanese Literature • Korean Literature • Southeast Asian Literatures • Greek Literature • Latin Literature • Italian Literature • French Literature • Spanish Literature • Portuguese Literature • German Literature • Netherlandic Literature • Scandinavian Literatures • Russian Literature • East European Literatures • Latin American Literatures • Canadian Literature • Literature of the Caribbean • Australian Literature • New Zealand Literature • Comparative Literature

Volume 3
The Best in Social Sciences, History, and the Arts

John G. Sproat, Volume Editor

Social Sciences and History: General Reference • Anthropology • Economics • Geography • Political Science • Psychology • Sociology • Education • World History • Ancient History • European History • African History • Middle Eastern History • History of Asia and the Pacific • United States History • Canadian History • Latin American History • Music and Dance • Art and Architecture • Mass Media • Folklore, Humor, and Popular Culture • Travel and Exploration

Volume 4

The Best in Philosophy and Religion

Robert S. Ellwood, Volume Editor

Philosophy and Religion: General Reference • General Philosophy • Greek and Roman Philosophy • Medieval Philosophy • Renaissance Philosophy • Modern Western Philosophy, 1600–1900 • Twentieth-Century Western Philosophy • Asian and African Philosophy, 1850 to the Present • Contemporary Issues in Philosophy • Ancient Religions and Philosophies • Eastern Religions • Islam • Judaism • Early and Medieval Christianity • Late Christianity, 1500 to the Present • The Bible and Related Literature • Minority Religions and Contemporary Religious Movements • Contemporary Issues in Religious Thought

Volume 5

The Best in Science, Technology, and Medicine

Carl Mitcham and William F. Williams, Volume Editors

Science, Technology, and Medicine: General Reference • A General View: Science, Technology, and Medicine • History of Science, Technology, and Medicine • Philosophy of Science, Technology, and Medicine • Ethics in Science, Technology, and Medicine • Science, Technology, and Society • Special Issues in Science, Technology, and Society • Engineering and Technology • Agriculture and Food Technology • Energy • Communications Technology • Medicine and Health • Illness and Disease • Clinical Psychology and Psychiatry • Mathematics • Statistics and Probability • Information Science and Computer Science • Astronomy and Space Science • Earth Sciences • Physics • Chemistry • Biological Sciences • Ecology and Environmental Science

THE

The Reader's Adviser®

14th EDITION

Volume 2

The Best in World Literature

Robert DiYanni, Volume Editor

Marion Sader, Series Editor

R. R. Bowker®

A Reed Reference Publishing Company

New Providence, New Jersey

Published by R. R. Bowker
A Reed Reference Publishing Company

Printed and bound in the United States of America

International Standard Book Numbers
0-8352-3320-0 (SET)
0-8352-3321-9 (Volume 1)
0-8352-3322-7 (Volume 2)
0-8352-3323-5 (Volume 3)
0-8352-3324-3 (Volume 4)
0-8352-3325-1 (Volume 5)
0-8352-3326-X (Volume 6)
International Standard Serial Number 0094-5943
Library of Congress Catalog Card Number 57-13277

The paper used in this publication meets the minimum requirements of American National Standard for Information Sciences—Permanence of Papers for Printed Library Materials, ANSI Z39.48-1984.

ISBN 0-8352-3320-0

Contents

Preface

> Libraries are busy places and rarely is there time for the reader and the librarian to sit down, discuss and analyze the reader's book problem, direct his interest or locate the book he wants. . . . In answer to this demand readers' advisers are appearing on many library staffs.
>
> —JENNIE M. FLEXNER

When Jennie M. Flexner, founder of the New York Public Library's famous Reader's Advisory service, wrote those words in *Library Journal* in 1938, R. R. Bowker's own *Reader's Adviser* had already been a Baedeker for overwhelmed library patrons for nearly a generation. Known then as *The Bookman's Manual*, it had, as its name suggests, actually been conceived, not by a librarian, but by a bookseller, Bessie Graham. Graham's first edition, published in 1921, was based on an enormously popular bookselling course she had recently taught at the William Penn Evening High School in Philadelphia. Just over 400 pages, that first *Bookman's Manual* was intended to give novice book retailers a basic inventory of essential in-print titles, both to stock and to recommend to customers. (It did, admittedly, fail to mention Shakespeare—a shortcoming that so appalled Mildred C. Smith, the young Bowker employee who had been asked to organize Graham's material, that more than four decades later, as editor of *Publishers Weekly*, Smith still vividly recalled the omission.) Not surprisingly, however, *The Bookman's Manual* was quickly adopted by librarians facing much the same task with their own patrons—and through 13 editions the work, in its various guises, has been successfully matching good books with grateful readers for more than 70 years.

Because of its roots in bookselling, *The Reader's Adviser* has always been far more than a guide to "the classics"—those time-honored treasures that, as Mark Twain once insisted, "everybody talks about but nobody reads." From the very first edition, its chapters reflected current literary, social, and political trends, embracing not only such mainstream categories as "Great Names in English Poetry" and "Essays and Letters" but also, as befitted the new era of universal suffrage, "American Fiction—Contemporary *Men* Writers" and "American Fiction—Contemporary *Women* Writers." Modern British authors experienced the same sexual differentiation in the second edition, published three years later, by which time Shakespeare had returned from exile and books on such extraliterary subjects as "Nature," "Music," and "Travel" had also been added.

Throughout the 1920s and 1930s, *The Bookman's Manual* continued to grow explosively—so much so that, by the time Bessie Graham bid farewell to her "lifework" (as she called it in her preface to the fifth edition of 1941), it had nearly doubled in size. "I commend its future editions to my unknown successor," she wrote, "and take leave of a task that holds only pleasant associations for me now that I pass 'Out of the stress of the doing, Into the peace of the done.'" Sadly, the United States's entry into World War II would soon interrupt that peace as well as the arrival of "future editions."

With the war near an end in June 1945, Bowker's Mildred Smith recommended Hester R. Hoffman, a bookseller with nearly 30 years' experience at the Hampshire Bookshop in Northampton, Massachusetts, to compile the next peacetime edition of Graham's *The Bookman's Manual.* Unfortunately, Hoffman's start was frustrated by more than a wartime paper shortage; Bowker's proposal reached her (as she later put it) while she was "lying flat in a room in a South Boston Hospital recovering from, of all things, a broken neck." Undaunted by her predicament, by the dearth of current titles on publishers' lists, and even by her typesetter's utter lack of foreign accents for the chapter on French literature, she succeeded in pulling together the sixth edition of *The Bookman's Manual* by 1948. The war, though, had taken its toll: despite a seven-year hiatus between editions, Hoffman's first effort was 62 pages *shorter* than Graham's last.

As the 1950s unfolded and the nuclear age cast a lengthening shadow, Hester Hoffman strove to keep *The Bookman's Manual* at the forefront of breaking literary and nonliterary events worldwide. A new chapter on science in the seventh edition of 1954 helped readers make sense of the profound legacy of such diverse theorists as Einstein and Freud. Thanks to Russian literature editors Helen Muchnic and Nicolai Vorobiov, anyone searching for contemporary Soviet novelists could have discovered the great Boris Pasternak (then known in the West only as a poet) fully three years before *Doctor Zhivago* made him an international sensation. In the eighth edition of 1958, the chapter on bibles updated readers who were eager to learn more about one of the seminal discoveries in Judeo-Christian history: a tattered collection of Hebrew and Aramaic parchments, concealed in pottery jars in caves near Qumran, that soon became known as the Dead Sea Scrolls.

Renamed *The Reader's Adviser and Bookman's Manual,* in 1960, the work continued to grow precipitously—struggling to reward the newfound postwar affluence, leisure, and cosmopolitan curiosity of American readers. With the baby boom at that time came a publishing boom, and, as Americans opened the New Frontier, they hungered for books about everything from rockets and space travel to parapsychology to segregation and the South. Indeed, just a glimpse of the new reading lists added during this heady and tumultuous era recaptures a time when readers were discovering ideas, arts, peoples, and places as perhaps they never had discovered before. There were books on the North American Indian and the opening of the West, Soviet history and policy, and the Civil War (as it reached its centenary); there were books by authors from Africa, Japan, China, India, Latin America, and, at long last, black America, as well as books about the lively arts of jazz, cinema, children's theater, and, yes, McLuhan's "cool medium," television.

By 1968, when Winifred F. Courtney guided the eleventh edition to press, one volume could no longer hold it all: It took two. The twelfth edition, published from 1974 to 1977, then blossomed to three volumes. As Bowker's own *Books in Print* continued to document a book market that was all but doubling in size every 10 years (from 245,000 titles in 1967 to 750,000 in 1987), the thirteenth edition, published in two installments, in 1986 and 1988, swelled to five volumes (plus a separately bound index). *The Reader's Adviser,* which always had been a reference tool built on the contributions of subject specialists, now had become virtually an encyclopedia—requiring separate editors for the set, for the individual volumes, for the sections . . . and even for the chapters!

As little as today's *Reader's Adviser* may resemble Bessie Graham's once modest *Bookman's Manual*, the work still adheres to tradition. More than ever the essential starting point for anyone who is setting out to read about the world of literary, artistic, philosophical, or scientific endeavor, the work's individual volumes are designed to carry users from the general to the specific—from overarching reference guides, critical histories, and anthologies about a genre or a field to the lives and works of its leading exemplars. As always, booksellers, reference and acquisitions librarians, lay readers, teachers, academics, and students alike can readily use it to identify the best of nearly everything available in English in the United States today, from the poetry of the ancients to Renaissance philosophy to meditations on the ethics of modern medicine.

Choosing what to include and what to leave out is never easy. As specialists, the volume and chapter editors know their field's most noted and popular figures, current and historic, and the body of literature on which the reputations of those individuals stand. Although I have asked each editor, when possible, to revise an "out of vogue" author's profile and bibliography rather than simply to eliminate it, paring is inevitable with any new edition. Then, too, the mere availability of an author's work can play its own editorial role. Although it is customary to list only titles published as books and (according to the latest monthly release of *Books in Print* on CD-ROM) currently for sale in the United States, exceptions are made for invaluable out-of-print works deemed likely to appear in the stacks of an established, modest-sized municipal library.

Revisions to the fourteenth edition have been judicious. Most noticeably, the set itself is longer and has a larger trim size—up from 6″ x 9″ to 7″ x 10″—to give the pages a more open look. As the heart of *The Reader's Adviser*, the bibliographies have been more extensively annotated than ever before, and the lists of "books by" that accompany each profiled author in Volumes 1 and 2 are now helpfully subcategorized into genres (fiction, nonfiction, poetry, plays, etc.). Furthermore, ISBNs have been added to the usual bibliographic data (again, drawn from the latest monthly release of *Books in Print* on CD-ROM) of publisher, price, and year of publication. In addition, on the sensible assumption that the author profiles preceding bibliographies should be a tantalizing appetizer for the entrée to come, the editors have done their best to season them all with rich, lively biographical detail. Finally, the reader should be aware that not all in-print editions of a work are necessarily listed but, rather, only those editions selected because of their quality or special features.

Another change in this edition is the addition of a "Chronology of Authors" section before the alphabetical arrangement of profiled authors in each chapter—a complement to the chronology that appears at the outset of each volume and a quick and easy means of placing each chapter's profiled entrants in historical perspective. Finally, to boost *The Reader's Adviser's* reference utility, the subject index of each volume has been greatly expanded, and the chapters on "Books about Books," "General Bibliography," and "General Reference" (which were previously split between Volumes 1 and 2) have been brought together and now appear at the beginning of Volume 1.

Of course, much about this new edition of *The Reader's Adviser* remains uniquely similar to the previous edition. The six-volume organization begun with the thirteenth edition continues: Volume 1 encompasses general reference works and American and British literature; Volume 2, world literature in translation; Volume 3, the social sciences, history, and the arts; Volume 4, the literature of philosophy and world religions; and Volume 5, the literature of science, technology, and medicine. Similarly, Volume 6 incorporates the name, title, and subject indexes of each of the previous volumes. Also retained are convenient cross-references throughout, which guide inquiring readers to related authors, chapters, sections, or volumes. A "see" reference leads the reader to the appropriate volume and chapter for information on a specific author. "See also" refers the reader to additional information in another chapter or volume. Within any sections of narrative, the name of an author who appears as a main listing in another chapter or volume is printed in large and small capital letters. If the chapter cross-referenced is to be found in a different volume from the one being consulted, the volume number is also given. Furthermore, to make basic research easier, the annotated bibliographies accompanying profiled individuals separately list works "by" and "about" those authors.

To assure that all volumes of the fourteenth edition are compiled concurrently and arrive together, I have relied on the contributions of countless authorities. Special thanks are due to both *The Reader's Adviser's* team of volume editors and the chapter contributors, whose names are listed in each volume. The book production experts at Book Builders Incorporated directed the almost Herculean task of coordinating the 110 chapters by 120 authors through numerous editing and production stages; to everyone's satisfaction, the system succeeded, as the reader can affirm from a glance at these six volumes. In particular, I must recognize Book Builders' Lauren Fedorko, president and guiding spirit, for her unfailing good spirits and intelligent decisions; Diane Schadoff, editorial coordinator; and Paula Wiech, production manager. Many thanks to them and their staffs for the extra hours and care that they lavished on our "magnum opus." Very special appreciation is due to Charles Roebuck, managing editor *extraordinaire*, whose concerns for accuracy, detail, and style made perfection almost attainable. Charles's contributions are countless, and much of the success of this edition is due to his tact and diplomacy in managing many people, many deadlines, and many pages of manuscript. Here at Bowker, I am especially grateful to my assistant, Angela Szablewski, who has had the monumental responsibility of coordinating all stages of the books' production.

In her 1938 article, Ms. Flexner wrote that "libraries are made up of good, old books as well as good, new books." In agreement with her view, I have continued in the *Reader's Adviser* tradition by including in this new fourteenth edition titles that are timeless, as well as those that are timely; the aim is to provide the user with both a broad and a specific view of the great writings and great writers of the past and present. I wish you all satisfaction in your research, delight in your browsing, and pleasure in your reading.

Marion Sader
Publisher
Professional & Reference Books
R.R. Bowker
September 1993

Contributing Editors

Sangita Advani, LITERATURE OF THE INDIAN SUBCONTINENT
Formerly of Columbia University

Chukwuma Azuonye, AFRICAN LITERATURES
Associate Professor and Chair of Black Studies Department, University of Massachusetts, Boston

Martinus A. Bakker, NETHERLANDIC LITERATURE
Professor of Germanic Languages, Calvin College

Henryk Baran, RUSSIAN LITERATURE
Associate Professor of Russian, University at Albany, State University of New York

Henry J. Baron, FRISIAN LITERATURE
Professor of English, Calvin College

Susan C. Brantly, SCANDINAVIAN LITERATURES
Associate Professor of Scandinavian Literature, University of Wisconsin, Madison

Robert DiYanni, VOLUME EDITOR, INTRODUCTION TO WORLD LITERATURE
Professor of English and Director of Interdisciplinary Studies, Pace University, Pleasantville, New York

David William Foster, LATIN AMERICAN LITERATURES
Regents' Professor of Spanish, Arizona State University

Gale Fox, JAPANESE LITERATURE
Graduate Assistant, Department of English and Comparative Literature, San Diego State University

Meryle Gaston, MIDDLE EASTERN LITERATURES
Near East Librarian, E. H. Bobst Library, New York University

Timothy Hampton, FRENCH LITERATURE
Associate Professor of French and Comparative Literature, University of California at Berkeley

David G. Hirsch, HEBREW LITERATURE, YIDDISH LITERATURE
Jewish and Near Eastern Studies Bibliographer, University Research Library, University of California at Los Angeles

Marshall Hurwitz, GREEK LITERATURE
Professor of Classical Languages, The City College of the City University of New York

Priya Joshi, LITERATURE OF THE INDIAN SUBCONTINENT
Lecturer in English and Comparative Literature, Columbia University

Helane Levine-Keating, COMPARATIVE LITERATURE
Professor of English, Director of Women's Studies, Pace University, New York City

Frances LaFleur, CHINESE LITERATURE
Chinese Curator, East Asia Library, Columbia University

Robin Lewis, LITERATURE OF THE INDIAN SUBCONTINENT
Associate Dean and Director of the International Affairs Program, School of International and Public Affairs, Columbia University

Michael McGaha, SPANISH LITERATURE
Professor of Romance Languages, Pomona College, Claremont, California

Dan McLeod, JAPANESE LITERATURE
Program Director, Literature; California State University, San Marcos

Vasa Mihailovich, EAST EUROPEAN LITERATURES
Professor of Slavic Literature, University of North Carolina at Chapel Hill

Carol L. Mitchell, SOUTHEAST ASIAN LITERATURES
Southeast Asian Bibliographic Services Librarian, Memorial Library, University of Wisconsin, Madison

Fred J. Nichols, LATIN LITERATURE
Professor of Comparative Literature, French, German, and Classical Literature, CUNY (City University of New York) Graduate Center

Noêl Ortega, PORTUGUESE LITERATURE
Associate Professor of Modern Languages, Pace University, Pleasantville, New York

Marshall R. Pihl, KOREAN LITERATURE
Associate Professor of Korean Literature, University of Hawaii

Ruby S. Ramraj, LITERATURE OF THE CARIBBEAN
Professor of English, University of Calgary, Alberta, Canada

Robert Ross, AUSTRALIAN LITERATURE, CANADIAN LITERATURE, AND NEW ZEALAND LITERATURE
Research Associate, Edward A. Clark Center for Australian Studies, The University of Texas at Austin

Boria Sax, GERMAN LITERATURE
Adjunct Full Professor of German, Pace University, Pleasantville, New York

Adelia Williams, ITALIAN LITERATURE
Assistant Professor of French and Italian, Pace University, Pleasantville, New York

Abbreviations

abr.	abridged
A.D.	in the year of the Lord
annot(s).	annotated, annotator(s)
B.C.	before Christ
B.C.E.	before the common era
B.P.	before the present
Bk(s)	Book(s)
c.	circa
C.E.	of the common era
Class.	Classic(s)
coll.	collected
comp(s).	compiled, compiler(s)
ed(s).	edited, editor(s), edition(s)
fl.	flourished
fwd.	foreword
gen. ed(s).	general editor(s)
ill(s).	illustrated, illustrator(s)
intro.	introduction
Lit.	Literature
o.p.	out-of-print
Pr.	Press
pref.	preface
pt(s).	part(s)
repr.	reprint
rev. ed.	revised edition
Ser.	Series
Supp.	Supplement
trans.	translated, translator(s), translation
U. or Univ.	University
Vol(s).	Volume(s)

Throughout this series, publisher names are abbreviated within bibliographic entries. The full names of these publishers can be found listed in Volume 6, the Index to the series.

Chronology of Authors

Main author entries appear here chronologically by year of birth. Within each chapter, main author entries are arranged alphabetically by surname.

1. Introduction to World Literature

2. Hebrew Literature

Ibn Gabirol, Solomon ben Judah. c.1021–1058

Judah Ha-Levi. 12th century

Ahad Ha-Am. 1856–1927

Berdichevsky, Micah Joseph. 1865–1921

Bialik, Hayyim Nahman. 1873–1934

Feierberg (Feuerberg), Mordecai Ze'ev. 1874–1899

Tchernichovski (Tchernichowsky), Saul. 1875–1943

Brenner, Joseph Hayyim. 1881–1921

Agnon, Shmuel Yosef. 1888–1970

Barash, Asher. 1889–1952

Vogel, David. 1891–1944

Hazaz, Haim. 1898–1973

Goldberg, Leah. 1911–1970

Gilboa, Amir. 1917–

Tammuz, Benjamin. 1919–

Megged, Aharon. 1920–

Shamir, Moshe. 1921–

Gouri, Haim. 1923–

Amichai, Yehuda. 1924–

Kishon, Ephraim. 1924–

Carmi, T. 1925–

Shaham, Nathan. 1925–

Michael, Sami. 1926–

Shahar, David. 1926–

Bartov, Hanokh. 1928–

Kaniuk, Yoram. 1930–

Pagis, Dan. 1930–

Zach, Nathan. 1930–

Hareven, Shulamith. 1931–

Appelfeld, Aron. 1932–

Yehoshua, A(braham) B. 1936–

Oz, Amos. 1939–

Goor, Batya. 1947–

Shammas, Anton. 1951–

Grossman, David. 1954–

3. Yiddish Literature

Jacob ben Isaac of Janow. d. 1620?

Gluckel of Hameln. 1645–1724

Nahman of Bratslav. 1772–1811

Zunser, Eliakum. 1835–1913

Mendele Mokher Seforim. 1836–1917

Linetski, Isaac Joel. 1839–1915

Peretz, Yitskhok Leybush. 1852–1915

Sholom Aleichem. 1859–1916

Cahan, Abraham. 1860–1951

Rosenfeld, Morris. 1862–1923

Ansky, S. 1863–1920

Pinsky, David. 1872–1959

Reisin, Avraham. 1876–1953

Shapiro, Lamed. 1878–1948

Blinkin, Meir. 1879–1915

Asch, Sholem. 1880–1957

Mani-Leib. 1883–1953

Bergelson, David. 1884–1952

Der Nister. 1884–1950

Halpern, Moyshe-Leyb. 1886–1932
Opatoshu, Joseph. 1886–1954
Kreitman, Esther. 1891–1954
Singer, I(srael) J(oshua). 1893–1944
Glatstein, Jacob. 1896–1971
Korn, Rokhl. 1898–1982
Rontsh, Isaac Elchonon. 1899–1985
Rabon, Israel. 1900–1941
Khaver-Paver. 1901–1964
Manger, Itzik. 1901–1969
Singer, I(saac) B(ashevis). 1904–1991
Tsanin, Mordekhai. 1906–
Grade, Chaim. 1910–1982
Bryks, Rachmil. 1912–1964
Sutzkever, Abraham. 1913–

4. Middle Eastern Literatures

David of Sassoun. Late medieval period
Abu Nuwas. c.756–810
al-Jahiz. d. 868 or 869
Al-Mutanabbi, Abu al-Tayyib Ahmad ibn al-Husayn. 915?–965
Firdawsī. c.934–c.1020
Abu al-'ala' al-Ma'arri. 973–1057
'Aṭṭār, Farīd al-Dīn. 1142–c.1229
Omar Khayyam. c.1021–1122
Rūmī, Jalāl al-Dīn. 1207–1273
Sa'di. d. c.1292
Yunus, Emre. d. c.1320
al-Hafiz. 14th century
Kouchag, Nahabed. d. 1592
Baronian, Hagop. 1842–1891
Shirvanzadeh. 1858–1935
Zohrab, Krikor. 1861–1915
Shawqi, Ahmad. 1868–1932
Odian, Yervant. 1869–1926
Issahakian, Avedick. 1875–1957
Tekeyan, Vahan. 1878–1948
Yessayan, Zabel. 1878–1943
Jubran, Kahlil. 1883–1931
Edip, Halide. 1884–1964
Zarian, Gostan. 1885–1969
Taha Husayn. 1889–1973
Karaosmanoğlu, Yakup Kadri. 1889–1974
Jamalzadah, Muhammad 'Ali. 1892–
Yushij, Nima. 1895–1960
Charents, Eghishe. 1897–1937
Al-Hakim, Tawfiq. 1902–1976?
Hikmet, Nazim. 1902–1963
Hidāyat, Sādiq. 1903–1951
Haqqi, Yahya. 1905–
'Alavī, Bezorg. 1907–
I'tisami, Parvin. 1907–1941
Sabahattin Ali. 1907–1948
Antreassian, Antranig. 1908–
Mahfuz, Najib. 1911–
Zaroukian, Antranik. 1913–
Dağlarca, Fazil Hüsnü. 1914–
Kanik, Orhan Veli. 1914–1950
Anday, Melih Cevdat. 1915–
Nesin, Aziz. 1915–
Chubak, Sadiq. 1916–
Taner, Haldun. 1916–1986
'Abd al-Qaddus, Ihsan. 1919–1990
Gaboudigian, Sylva. 1920–
Dānishvār, Sīmīn. 1921–
Kemal, Yaşar. 1922–
Āl-i Aḥmad, Jalāl. 1923–1969
Qabbani, Nizar. 1923–
Al-Bayati, 'Abd al-Wahab. 1926–
al-Sayyab, Badr Shakir. 1926–1964
Idrīs, Yūsuf. 1927–
Salih, al-Tayib. 1929–
Adonis. 1930–
'Abd al-Ṣabūr, Ṣalāh. 1931–1981
al-Sa'dawi, Nawal. 1931–
Tamir, Zakariya. 1931–
al-Munif, 'Abd al-Rahman. 1933–
Farrokhzad, Forough. 1935–1967
Fürūzan. 1935–
Sa'idi, Ghulam Husayn. 1935–1985
Kanafani, Ghassan. 1936–1972
Ibrahim, Sun' Allah. 1937–
Behrangi, Samad. 1939–1968

5. African Literatures

Equiano, Olaudah. 1745–1797

Dan Fodio, Shehu Usman. 1754–1817
Mofolo, Thomas. 1876–1948
Paton, Alan. 1903–
Senghor, Leopold Sedar. 1906–
Mahfouz, Najib. 1911–
Ranaivo, Flavien. 1914–
Abrahams, Peter. 1919–
Mphahlele, Es'kia. 1919–
Dib, Mohammed. 1920–
Tutuola, Amos. 1920–
Ekwensi, Cyprain. 1921–
Okara, Gabriel. 1921–
Gordimer, Nadine. 1923–
Brutus, Dennis. 1924–
Fanon, Franz. 1925–1961
La Guma, Alex. 1925–1984
Chraibi, Driss. 1926–
Idris, Yusuf. 1927–1992
Laye, Camara. 1928–1980
Ba, Mariama. 1929–1981
Munonye, John. 1929–
Ousmane, Sembene. 1929–
Oyono, Ferdinand. 1929–
Salih, al-Tayib. 1929–
Yacine, Kateb. 1929–1989
Achebe, Chinua. 1930–
Kunene, Mazisi. 1930–
Ogot, Grace Akinye. 1930–
Tlali, Miriam. c.1930–
Nwapa, Flora. 1931–
Okot p'Bitek. 1931–1980
al-Sa'dawi, Nawal. 1931–
U Tam'si, Tchikiya. 1931–1990
Beti, Mongo. 1932–
Okigbo, Christopher. 1932–1967
Peters, Lenrie. 1932–
Mazrui, Ali al Amin. 1933–
Amadi, Elechi. 1934–
Clark, J. P. 1934–
Soyinka, Wole. 1934–
Awoonor, Kofi. 1935–
Brink, André. 1935–
Fugard, Athol. 1935–
Gabre-Medhin, Tsegaye. 1935–
Ogali, Ogali A. 1935–
Djebar, Assia. 1936–
Head, Bessie. 1937–1986
Echervo, Michael. 1937–
Khatibi, Abdelkebir. 1938–
Lo Liyong, Taban. 1938?–
Ngugi wa Thiong'o. 1938–
Sofola, Zulu. 1938–
Armah, Ayi Kwei. 1939–
Serumaga, Robert. 1939–
Coetzee, J(acobus) M. 1940–
Mapanje, Jack. c.1940?–
Ouologuem, Yambo. 1940–
Boudjedra, Rachid. 1941–
Okpewho, Isidore. 1941–
Aidoo, Ama Ata. 1942–
Omotoso, Kole. 1943–
Ben Jelloun, Tahar. 1944–
Emecheta, Buchi. 1944–
Farah, Nuruddin. 1945–
Marechera, Dambudzo. 1952–1987
Onwueme, Tess. 1955–
Okri, Ben. 1960–

6. Literature of the Indian Subcontinent

Tagore, Sir Rabindranath. 1861–1941
Gandhi, Mohandas. 1869–1948
Premchand. 1880–1936
Nehru, Jawaharlal. 1889–1964
Narayan, R. K. 1906–
Sahgal, Nayantara. 1927–
Desai, Anita. 1937–
Rushdie, Salman. 1947–

7. Chinese Literature

Book of Songs. Compiled c.600 B.C.
Ch'ü Yüan. 343?–277 B.C.
Yang Hsiung. 53 B.C.–A.D. 18
Chang Heng. 79–139
Ts'ao Chih. 192–232
Juan Chi. 210–263
Hsi K'ang. 223–262
Lu Chi. 261–303
T'ao Ch'ien. 365–427
Hsieh Ling-yün. 385–433

Hsiao Kang. 505–555
Yü Hsin. 513–581
Meng Hao-jan. 689–740
Wang Ch'ang-ling. 698?–756
Han Shan. fl. early 8th century?
Li Po. 701–762
Wang Wei. 701–761
Tu Fu. 719–770
Han Yü. 768–824
Po Chü-i. 772–846
Li Ho. 791–817
Li Shang-yin. 813–858
Wei Chuang. 836–910
Li Yü. 937–978
Mei Yao-ch'en. 1002–1060
Ou-yang Hsiu. 1007–1072
Wang An-shih. 1021–1086
Su Shih. 1037–1101
Li Ch'ing-chao. 1084–c.1151
Yang Wan-li. 1124–1206
Lu Yu. 1125–1210
Fan Ch'eng-ta. 1126–1193
Kuan Han-ch'ing. c.1220–c.1300
Wang Shih-fu. fl. 13th century
Lo Kuan-chung. c.1330–1400
Kao Ch'i. 1336–1374
Shih Nai-an. fl. before 1400
Wu Ch'eng-en. 1500–1582
Wang Shih-chen. 1526–1590
T'ang Hsien-tzu. 1550–1617
Feng Meng-lung. 1574–1646
Li Yü. 1611–1680?
P'u Sung-ling. 1640–1715
Wu Ching-tzu. 1701–1754
Ts'ao Chan. 1715–1763
Shen Fu. 1763–after 1809?
Liu E. 1857–1909
Liang Ch'i-ch'ao. 1873–1929
Lu Hsün. 1881–1936
Hu Shih. 1891–1962
Kuo Mo-jo. 1892–1978
Mao Tse-tung. 1893–1976
Lin Yü-t'ang. 1895–1976
Mao Tun. 1896–1981
Lao She. 1899–1966
Ping Hsin. 1902–1968
Shen Ts'ung-wen. 1902–1988
Feng Hsüeh-feng. 1903–1976
Pa Chin. 1904–
Ting Ling. 1904–1986
Ts'ao Yü. 1905–
Chang T'ien-i. 1906–1985
Hsiao Chun. 1907–1988
Ai Ch'ing. 1910–
Ch'ien Chung-shu. 1910–
Hsiao Hung. 1911–1941
Yang Chiang. 1911–
Ho Ch'i-fang. 1912–1977
Chang Ai-ling. 1921–
Ju Chih-chüan. 1925–
Liu Pin-yen. 1925–
Kao Hsiao-sheng. 1928–
Wang Meng. 1934–
Chang Hsien-liang. 1936–
Chang Chieh. 1937–
Ch'en Ying-chen. 1937–
Pai Hsien-yung. 1937–
Ch'en Jo-hsi. 1938–
Tai Hou-ying. 1938–
Huang Ch'un-ming. 1939–
Chiang Tzu-lung. 1941–
Feng Chi-ts'ai. 1942–
Ku Hua. 1942–
Liu Hsin-wu. 1942–
Ch'eng Nai-shan. 1946–
A-ch'eng. 1949–
Pei Tao. 1949–
Chia P'ing-wa. 1952–
Li Ang. 1952–
Ts'an Hsüeh. 1953–
Chang Hsin-hsin. 1954–
Wang An-i. 1954–
Mo Yen. 1956–

8. Japanese Literature

Ki no Tsurayuki. c.868–c.945
The Mother of Fujiwara Michitsuna. d.955
Izumi Shikibu. c.976
Murasaki Shikibu. c.978–c.1030
Sei Shōnagon. fl. late 10th century
Nijō, Lady. b.1257

Kenkō Yoshida. 1283–1352
Zeami. 1363–c.1493
Ihara Saikaku. 1642–1693
Bashō. 1644–1694
Chikamatsu Monzaemon. 1653–1724
Yosa Buson. 1716–1783
Ueda Akinari. 1734–1809
Kobayashi Issa. 1763–1827
Mori Ōgai. 1862–1922
Futabatei Shimei. 1864–1909
Masaoka Shiki. 1867–1902
Natsume Sōseki. 1867–1917
Higuchi Ichiyō. 1872–1896
Shimazaki Tōson. 1872–1943
Yosano Akiko. 1878–1942
Nagai Kafū. 1879–1959
Shiga Naoya. 1883–1971.
Ishikawa Takuboku. 1886–1912
Tanizaki Jun'ichirō. 1886–1965
Kawabata Yasunari. 1889–1972
Akutagawa Ryūnosuke. 1892–1927
Uno Chiyo. 1897–
Ibuse Masuji. 1898–
Yokomitsu Riichi. 1898–1947
Enchi Fumiko. 1905–1986
Inoue Yasushi. 1907–
Dazai Osamu. 1909–1948
Matsumoto Seicho. 1909–
Endō Shūsaku. 1923–
Abe Kōbō. 1924–
Mishima Yukio. 1925–1970
Tachihara Masaaki. 1926–1980
Ariyoshi Sawako. 1931–
Tanikawa Shuntaro. 1931–
Ōe Kenzaburō. 1935–
Tsushima Yuko. 1947–
Murakami Haruki. 1949–

9. Korean Literature

Kim Man-jung. 1637–1692
Lady Hong of Hyegyông Palace. 1735–1815
Han Yong-un. 1879–1944
Kim So-Wôl. 1902–1934
Kim Tong-ni. 1913–
O Yông-su. 1914–1979
Sô Chông-ju. 1915–
Hwang Sun-wôn. 1915–
Kang Shin-jae. 1924–
Kim, Richard. 1932–
Choi In-hoon. 1936–
Kim Chi-ha. 1941–
Yun Heung-gil. 1942–
Yi Mun-yôl. 1948–

10. Southeast Asian Literatures

Sunthorn Phu. 1786–1856.
Rizal, José. 1861–1896
Ho Chi Minh. 1890–1969
Alisjahbana, S. Takdir. 1908–
Khukrit Pramoj. 1911–
Santos, Bienvenido N. 1911–
Joaquin, Nick. 1917–
Anwar, Chairil. 1922–1949.
Lubis, Mochtar. 1922–
José, F. Sionil. 1924–
Toer, Pramoedya Ananta. 1925–
Usman Awang. 1929–
Shahnon Ahmad. 1933–
A. Samad Said. 1935–
Rendra, W. S. 1935–
Aung San Suu Kyi. 1945–

11. Greek Literature

Hesiod. c.700 B.C.
Homer. c.700 B.C.
Sappho. fl. c.610–c.580 B.C.
Aesop. fl. 570 B.C.
Aeschylus. 525–456 B.C.
Pindar. c.518–c.438 B.C.
Sophocles. c.496–406 B.C.
Euripides. c.485–c.406 B.C.
Aristophanes. c.450–c.385 B.C.
Demosthenes. 385?–322 B.C.
Theophrastus. c.371–287 B.C.
Menander. c.342–c.292 B.C.
Theocritus. c.310–c.250 B.C.
Callimachus. c.305–c.240 B.C.
Apollonius Rhodius. 3rd century B.C.
Longinus. c.1st century A.D.
Longus. fl. 2nd or 3rd century A.D.?

Lucian. c.120-c.185?
Heliodorus of Emesa. fl. 220–250
Makriyannis, John. 1797–1864
Palamas, Kostes. 1859–1943
Cavafy, Constantine P. 1863–1933
Drakopoulou, Theone. 1883–1968
Sikelianos, Angelos. 1884–1951
Kazantzakis, Niko. 1885–1957
Seferis, George. 1900–1971
Ritsos, Yannis. 1909–
Elytis, Odysseus. 1911–
Vakalo, Eleni. 1921–

12. Latin Literature

Terence. c.190 B.C.–159 B.C.
Plautus, Titus Maccius. d. c.184 B.C.
Cicero. 106 B.C.–43 B.C.
Caesar, Julius. 100 B.C.–44 B.C.
Lucretius. c.94 or 99 B.C.–55 B.C.
Catullus. 84? B.C.–54? B.C.
Virgil. 70 B.C.–19 B.C.
Horace. 65 B.C.–8 B.C.
Livy. c.59 B.C.–C.A.D. 17
Propertius. c.50 B.C.–c.16 B.C.
Tibullus. 48? B.C.–19 B.C.
Ovid. 43 B.C.–A.D. 17
Seneca, Lucius Annaeus. c.3 B.C.–A.D. 65
Petronius. d. 65
Persius. 34–62
Quintilian. c.35–c.95
Lucan. 39–65
Martial. 40?–104
Statius, Publius Papinius. c.45–c.96
Tacitus, Cornelius. c.56–c.112
Juvenal. 60?–140?
Pliny the Younger. c.61–c.112
Suetonius. c.69–c.140
Apuleius, Lucius. 114–?

13. Italian Literature

Cavalcanti, Guido. c.1254–1300
Dante Alighieri. 1265–1321
Petrarch. 1304–1374
Boccaccio, Giovanni. 1313–1375
Alberti, Leon Battista. 1404–1472
Poliziano, Angelo. 1454–1494
Bembo, Pietro. 1470–1547
Ariosto, Ludovico. 1474–1533
Castiglione, Baldassare. 1478–1529
Aretino, Pietro. 1492–1556
Tasso, Torquato. 1544–1595
Bruno, Giordano. 1548–1600
Vico, Giambattista. 1668–1744
Goldoni, Carlo. 1707–1793
Baretti, Giuseppe. 1719–1789
Parini, Giuseppe. 1729–1799
Alfieri, Count Vittorio. 1749–1803
Foscolo, Ugo. 1778–1827
Manzoni, Alessandro. 1785–1873
Belli, Giuseppe Gioacchino. 1791–1863
Leopardi, Giacomo. 1798–1837
De Sanctis, Francesco. 1817–1883
Carducci, Giosuè. 1835–1907
Pascoli, Giovanni. 1835–1912
Verga, Giovanni. 1840–1922
Svevo, Italo. 1861–1928
D'Annunzio, Gabriele. 1863–1938
Croce, Benedetto. 1866–1952
Pirandello, Luigi. 1867–1936
Deledda, Grazia. 1871–1936
Marinetti, Filippo Tommaso. 1875–1944
Papini, Giovanni. 1881–1956
Ungaretti, Giuseppe. 1888–1970
Gramsci, Antonio. 1891–1937
Betti, Ugo. 1892–1953
Lampedusa, Giuseppe Tomasi, Prince of. 1896–1957
Montale, Eugenio. 1896–1981
De Filippo, Eduardo. 1900–1984
Silone, Ignazio. 1900–1978
Quasimodo, Salvatore. 1901–1968
Levi, Carlo. 1902–1975
Buzzati, Dino. 1906–1972
Moravia, Alberto. 1907–1990
Pavese, Cesare. 1908–1950
Vittorini, Elio. 1908–1966
Pratolini, Vasco. 1913–1991
Bassani, Giorgio. 1916–
Ginzburg, Natalia Levi. 1916–1991

Morante, Elsa. 1918–1985

Levi, Primo. 1919–1987

Sciascia, Leonardo. 1921–1989

Pasolini, Pier Paolo. 1922–1975

Calvino, Italo. 1923–1985

Fo, Dario. 1926–

Fallaci, Oriana. 1930–

Eco, Umberto. 1932–

Maraini, Dacia. 1936–

14. French Literature

The Song of Roland. 11th century

Tristan and Iseult. c.1160–c.1170

Chrétien de Troyes. c.12th century

Aucassin and Nicolette. 13th century

Romance of the Rose. 13th century

Villon, François. 1431–1465?

Navarre, Marguerite de. 1492–1549

Rabelais, François. 1494–1553?

Ronsard, Pierre de. 1524–1585

Montaigne, Michel Eyquem de. 1533–1592

Corneille, Pierre. 1606–1684

La Rochefoucauld, François, Duc de. 1613–1680

La Fontaine, Jean de. 1621–1695

Molière. 1622–1673

Sévigné, Mme de. 1626–1696

La Fayette, Marie M. de la Verge, Comtesse de. 1634–1693

Racine, Jean. 1639–1699

Marivaux, Pierre de. 1688–1763

Voltaire. 1694–1778

Diderot, Denis. 1713–1784

Beaumarchais, Pierre A. C. de. 1732–1799

Sade, Comte de. 1740–1814

Laclos, Pierre A. F. C. de. 1741–1803

Staël, Mme de. 1766–1817

Chateaubriand, Francois Rene, Vicomte de. 1768–1848

Stendhal. 1783–1842

Balzac, Honoré de. 1799–1850

Dumas, Alexandre (père). 1802–1870

Hugo, Victor. 1802–1885

Sand, George. 1804–1876

Baudelaire, Charles. 1821–1867

Flaubert, Gustave. 1821–1880

Dumas, Alexandre (fils). 1824–1895

Zola, Émile. 1840–1902

Mallarmé, Stéphane. 1842–1898

France, Anatole. 1844–1924

Verlaine, Paul. 1844–1896

Maupassant, Guy de. 1850–1893

Rimbaud, Arthur. 1854–1891

Rolland, Romain. 1866–1944

Claudel, Paul. 1868–1955

Gide, André. 1869–1951

Proust, Marcel. 1871–1922

Valéry, Paul. 1871–1945

Colette. 1873–1954

Apollinaire, Guillaume. 1880–1918

Giraudoux, Jean. 1882–1944

Mauriac, François. 1885–1970

Romains, Jules. 1885–1972

Perse, Saint-John. 1887–1975

Bernanos, Georges. 1888–1948

Cocteau, Jean. 1889–1963

Celine, Louis-Ferdinand. 1894–1961

Éluard, Paul. 1895–1952

Giono, Jean. 1895–1970

Artaud, Antonin. 1896–1948

Breton, André. 1896–1966

Bataille, Georges. 1897–1962

Ponge, Francis. 1899–1988

Green, Julien. 1900–

Prévert, Jacques. 1900–1977

Saint-Exupéry, Antoine de. 1900–1944

Malraux, André. 1901–1976

Aymé, Marcel. 1902–1967

Sarraute, Nathalie. 1902–

Queneau, Raymond. 1903–1976

Radiquet, Raymond. 1903–1923

Yourcenar, Marguerite. 1903–

Sartre, Jean-Paul. 1905–1980

Beckett, Samuel. 1906–1989

Char, René. 1907–1988

Leduc, Violette. 1907–1971

Beauvoir, Simone de. 1908–1986

Simenon, Georges. 1909–1989
Weil, Simone. 1909–1943
Anouilh, Jean. 1910–
Genet, Jean. 1910–1986
Blanchot, Maurice. 1911–
Ionesco, Eugene. 1912–
Camus, Albert. 1913–1960
Simon, Claude. 1913–
Duras, Marguerite. 1914–
Barthes, Roland. 1915–1980
Pinget, Robert. 1919–
Robbe-Grillet, Alain. 1922–
Bonnefoy, Yves. 1923–
Tournier, Michel. 1924–
Butor, Michel. 1926–
Foucault, Michel. 1926–1984
Cixous, Hélène. 1937–

15. Spanish Literature

The Cid, Poem of. c.1175–1200
Ruiz, Juan. 1283?–1350?
Rojas, Fernando de. 1475?–1541
Teresa of Jesus, St. 1515–1582
John of the Cross, St. 1542–1591
Alemán, Mateo. 1546–1614
Cervantes Saavedra, Miguel de. 1547–1616
The Life of Lazarillo de Tormes. 1554
Góngora y Argote, Luis de. 1561–1627
Vega Carpio, Lope Félix de. 1562–1635
Quevedo y Villegas, Francisco Gómez de. 1580–1645
Tirso de Molina. 1584–1648
Calderón de la Barca, Pedro. 1600–1681
Valera y Alcalá Galiano, Juan. 1827–1905
Bécquer, Gustavo Adolfo. 1836–1870
Castro, Rosalía de. 1837–1885
Pérez Galdós, Benito. 1843–1920
Alas, Leopoldo. 1852–1901
Pardo Bazán, Emilia. 1852–1921
Unamuno y Jugo, Miguel de. 1864–1936
Benavente, Jacinto. 1866–1945
Valle-Inclán, Ramón del. 1866–1936
Baroja y Nessi, Pío. 1872–1956
Machado y Ruiz, Antonio. 1875–1939
Jiménez, Juan Ramón. 1881–1958
Pérez de Ayala, Ramón. 1881–1962
Salinas, Pedro. 1891–1951
Guillén, Jorge. 1893–1984
Aleixandre, Vicente. 1898–1984
García Lorca, Federico. 1898–1936
Alberti, Rafael. 1902–
Hernández, Miguel. 1910–1942
Buero Vallejo, Antonio. 1916–
Cela, Camilo José. 1916–
Delibes, Miguel. 1920–
Matute, Ana María. 1926–
Goytisolo, Juan. 1931–

16. Portuguese Literature

Vicente, Gil. 1465–1537?
Pinto Fernão Mendes. c.1510–1583
Camões, Luís Vaz De. 1524?–1580
Quental, Anthero Tarqüínio De. 1842–1891
Eça De Queiróz, José Maria. 1843–1900
Pessoa, Fernando. 1888–1935
Miguéis, José Rodrigues. 1901–1980
Andrade, Eugénio De. 1923–
Lobo Antunes, Antonio. 1942–

17. German Literature

Hartmann von Aue. c.1160–c.1220
Walther von der Vogelweide. c.1168–1228
Gottfried von Strassburg. 1170?–1210?
Wolfram von Eschenbach. 1170?–1220?
Johannes von Saaz. c.1350–c.1414
Brant, Sebastian. 1457?–1521
Sachs, Hans. 1494–1576
Grimmelshausen, Johann Jakob Christoffel von. 1620?–1676

Lessing, Gotthold Ephraim. 1729–1781
Herder, Johann Gottfried von. 1744–1803
Goethe, Johann Wolfgang von. 1749–1832
Schiller, Friedrich von. 1759–1805
Paul, Jean. 1763–1825
Schlegel, August, 1767–1845, and Friedrich Schlegel. 1772–1829
Hölderlin, Friedrich. 1770–1843
Novalis. 1772–1801
Tieck, Ludwig. 1773–1853
Hoffmann, E(rnst) T(heodor) A(madeus). 1776–1822
Kleist, Heinrich von. 1777–1811
Chamisso, Adelbert von. 1781–1838
Grimm, Jacob, 1785–1863, and Wilhelm Grimm. 1786–1859
Eichendorff, Joseph, Freiherr von. 1788–1857
Grillparzer, Franz. 1791–1872
Droste-Hülshoff, Annette von. 1797–1848
Heine, Heinrich. 1797–1856
Mörike, Eduard. 1804–1875
Hoffman, Heinrich. 1809–1894
Büchner, Georg. 1813–1837
Hebbel, Friedrich. 1813–1863
Fontane, Theodor. 1819–1898
Keller, Gottfried. 1819–1890
Busch, Wilhelm. 1832–1908
Hauptmann, Gerhart. 1862–1946
Schnitzler, Arthur. 1862–1931
Wedekind, Frank. 1864–1918
George, Stefan. 1868–1933
Mann, Heinrich. 1871–1950
Hofmannsthal, Hugo von. 1874–1929
Mann, Thomas. 1875–1955
Rilke, Rainer Maria. 1875–1926
Hesse, Hermann. 1877–1962
Döblin, Alfred. 1878–1957
Kaiser, Georg. 1878–1945
Musil, Robert. 1880–1942
Zweig, Stefan. 1881–1942
Kafka, Franz. 1883–1924
Feuchtwanger, Lion. 1884–1958
Benn, Gottfried. 1886–1956
Broch, Hermann. 1886–1951
Trakl, Georg. 1887–1914
Werfel, Franz. 1890–1945
Sachs, Nelly. 1891–1970
Toller, Ernst. 1893–1939
Jünger, Ernst. 1895–
Brecht, Bertolt. 1898–1956
Remarque, Erich Maria. 1898–1970
Seghers, Anna. 1900–1983
Canetti, Elias. 1905–
Frisch, Max. 1911–1991
Heym, Stefan. 1913–
Kirst, Hans Hellmut. 1914–
Weiss, Peter. 1916–1982
Böll, Heinrich. 1917–1985
Celan, Paul. 1920–1970
Borchert, Wolfgang. 1921–1947
Dürrenmatt, Friedrich. 1921–
Bachmann, Ingeborg. 1926–1973
Grass, Günter. 1927–
Lind, Jakov. 1927–
Müller, Heiner. 1929–
Wolf, Christa. 1929–
Bernhard, Thomas. 1931–
Hochhuth, Rolf. 1931–
Johnson, Uwe. 1934–1984
Kirsch, Sarah. 1935–
Biermann, Wolf. 1936–
Handke, Peter. 1942–
Rathenow, Lutz. 1952–

18. Netherlandic Literature

Reynard the Fox. 12th Century
Hadewijch. c.1200–1250
Bredero, Gerbrand A. 1580–1617
Revius, Jacobus. 1586–1658
Vondel, Joost van den. 1587–1679
Multatuli. 1820–1887
Emants, Marcellus. 1848–1923
Eeden, Frederik van. 1860–1932
Fan Hichtum, Nynke. 1860—1939
Van Schendel, Arthur. 1874–1946
Ellsschot, Willem. 1882–1960
Ostaijen, Paul van. 1896–1928

Vestdijk, Simon. 1898–1971
Brouwer, Abe. 1901—1984
Alberts, A. 1905–
Boon, Louis Paul. 1912–1979
Haasse, Hella S. 1912–
Schierbeek, Bert. 1918–
Lampo, Hubert. 1920–
Hermans, Willem F. 1921–
Wolkers, Jan. 1925–
Mulisch, Harry. 1927–
Claus, Hugo. 1929–
Ruyslinck, Ward. 1929–
Herzberg, Judith. 1934–
Hart, Martin. 1944–

19. Scandinavian Literatures

The Poetic Edda. 12th or 13th century
Sturluson, Snorri. 1179–1241
Völsunga Saga. 13th century
Eyrbyggja Saga. c.1230–1280
Laxdaela Saga. c.1250
Njál's Saga. c.1280
Sturlunga Saga. c.1300
Holberg, Ludvig. 1684–1754
Almqvist, Carl Jonas Love. 1793–1866
Andersen, Hans Christian. 1805–1875
Ibsen, Henrik. 1828–1906
Bjørnson, Bjørnstjerne. 1832–1910
Lie, Jonas. 1833–1908
The Kalevala. 1835–1849
Skram, Amalie. 1846–1905
Jacobsen, Jens Peter. 1847–1885
Strindberg, August. 1849–1912
Bang, Herman. 1857–1912
Lagerlöf, Selma. 1858–1940
Hamsun, Knut. 1859–1952
Nexø, Martin Andersen. 1869–1954
Jensen, Johannes V(ilhelm). 1873–1950
Rølvaag, Ole Edvart. 1876–1931
Sandel, Cora. 1880–1974
Undset, Sigrid. 1882–1949
Dinesen, Isak. 1885–1962
Sillanpää, Frans Eemil. 1888–1964
Gunnarsson, Gunnar. 1889–1975
Thórdarson, Thorbergur. 1889–1974
Lagerkvist, Pär. 1891–1974
Södergran, Edith. 1892–1923
Vesaas, Tarjei. 1897–1970
Munk, Kaj. 1898–1944
Moberg, Vilhelm. 1898–1973
Heinesen, William. 1900–
Jacobsen, Jørgen-Frantz. 1900–1938
Johnson, Eyvind. 1900–1976
Brú, Hedin. 1901–
Laxness, Halldór Kiljan. 1902–
Branner, Hans Christian. 1903–1966
Martinson, Harry. 1904–1978
Scherfig, Hans. 1905–1979
Ekelöf, Gunnar. 1907–1968
Lindgren, Astrid. 1907–
Schoultz, Solveig von. 1907–
Waltari, Mika Toimi. 1908–1979
Hansen, Martin A. 1909–1955
Jansson, Tove. 1914–
Ditlevsen, Tove. 1918–1976
Carpelan, Bo. 1926–
Andersen, Benny Allen. 1929–
Sørensen, Villy. 1929–
Kihlman, Christer. 1930–
Rifbjerg, Klaus. 1931–
Tranströmer, Tomas. 1931–
Enquist, P(er) O(lov). 1934–
Jersild, P(er) C(hristian). 1935–
Vik, Bjørg. 1935–
Gustafsson, Lars. 1936–
Saarikoski, Pentti. 1937–
Faldbakken, Knut. 1941–
Thorup, Kirsten. 1942–
Nordbrandt, Henrik. 1945–

20. Russian Literature

Karamzin, Nikolai. 1766–1826
Aksakov, Sergei. 1791–1859
Griboyedov, Aleksandr. 1795–1829
Pushkin, Aleksandr. 1799–1837
Tyutchev, Fyodor. 1803–1873
Gogol, Nikolai. 1809–1852
Goncharov, Ivan. 1812–1891

Herzen, Aleksandr. 1812–1870
Lermontov, Mikhail. 1814–1841
Turgenev, Ivan. 1818–1883
Pisemsky, Aleksei. 1820–1881
Dostoyevsky, Fyodor. 1821–1881
Nekrasov, Nikolai. 1821–1878
Ostrovsky, Aleksandr. 1823–1886
Saltykov-Shchedrin, Mikhail. 1826–1889
Chernyshevsky, Nikolai. 1828–1889
Tolstoy, Leo. 1828–1910
Leskov, Nikolai. 1831–1895
Korolenko, Vladimir, 1853–1921
Garshin, Vsevolod. 1855–1888
Chekhov, Anton. 1860–1904
Sologub, Fedor. 1863–1927
Gorky, Maxim. 1868–1936
Hippius (Gippius). 1869–1945
Bunin, Ivan. 1870–1953
Kuprin, Aleksandr. 1870–1938
Andreyev, Leonid. 1871–1919
Bryusov, Valery. 1873–1924
Prishvin, Mikhail. 1873–1954
Kuzmin, Mikhail. 1875–1936
Remizov, Aleksei. 1877–1957
Bely, Andrei. 1880–1934
Blok, Aleksandr. 1880–1921
Chukovsky, Kornei. 1882–1969
Gladkov, Fyodor. 1883–1958
Zamyatin, Yevgeny. 1884–1937
Khlebnikov, Velimir. 1885–1922
Akhmatova, Anna. 1889–1966
Pasternak, Boris. 1890–1960
Bulgakov, Mikhail. 1891–1940
Ehrenburg, Ilya. 1891–1967
Furmanov, Dmitry. 1891–1926
Mandelstam, Osip. 1891–1938
Fedin Konstantin. 1892–1977
Paustovsky, Konstantin. 1892–1968
Tsvetaeva, Marina. 1892–1941
Mayakovsky, Vladimir. 1893–1930
Babel, Isaac. 1894–1941
Pilnyak, Boris. 1894?–1937?
Tynyanov, Yury. 1894–1943
Esenin, Sergei. 1895–1925
Ivanov, Vsevolod. 1895–1963
Zoshchenko, Mikhail. 1895–1958
Ilf, Ilya. 1897–1937
Kataev, Valentin. 1897–1986
Leonov, Leonid. 1899–
Nabokov, Vladimir. 1899–1977
Olesha, Yury. 1899–1960
Platonov, Andrei. 1899–1951
Berberova, Nina. 1901–
Kaverin, Veniamin. 1902–1989
Petrov, Yevgeny. 1903–1942
Grossman, Vasily. 1905–1964
Panova, Vera. 1905–1973
Sholokhov, Mikhail. 1905–1984
Chukovskaya, Lydia. 1907–
Grekova, Irina. 1907–
Shalamov, Varlam. 1907–1982
Rybakov, Anatoly. 1911–
Simonov, Konstantin. 1915–1979
Galich, Aleksandr. 1918–1977
Solzhenitsyn, Aleksandr. 1918–
Okudzhava, Bulat. 1924–
Soloukhin, Vladimir. 1924–
Sinyavsky, Andrei. 1925–
Strugatsky, Arkady. 1925–
Trifonov, Yury. 1925–1981
Aitmatov, Chingiz. 1928–
Aleshkovsky, Yuz. 1929–
Iskander, Fazil. 1929–
Shukshin, Vasily. 1929–1974
Vladimov, Georgy. 1931–
Aksyonov, Vassily. 1932–
Gorenstein, Friedrich. 1932–
Voinovich, Vladimir. 1932–
Strugatsky, Boris. 1933–
Voznesensky, Andrei. 1933–
Yevtushenko, Yevgeny. 1933–
Gladilin, Anatoly. 1935–
Kushner, Aleksandr. 1936–
Akhmadulina, Bella. 1937–
Bitov, Andrei. 1937–
Rasputin, Valentin. 1937–
Erofeev, Venedikt. 1938 or 1939–
Brodsky, Joseph. 1940–
Dovlatov, Sergei. 1941–1990
Limonov, Edward. 1943–
Sokolov, Sasha. 1943–

Tolstaya, Tatyana. 1951–
Ratushinskaya, Irina. 1954–

21. East European Literatures

Pasek, Jan Chryzostom. 1630–1701
Donelaitis, Kristijonas. 1714–1780
Fredro, Alexander. 1793–1876
Mickiewicz, Adam Bernard. 1798–1855
Prešeren, France. 1800–1849
Krasiński, Zygmunt. 1812–1859
Njegoš, Petar Petrović. 1813–1851
Ševčenko, Taras. 1814–1861
Kuliš, Pantelejmon. 1819–1897
Madách Imre. 1823–1864
Petöfi, Sándor. 1823–1849
Jókai, Mór. 1825–1904
Baranauskas, Antanas. 1835–1902
Šenoa, August. 1838–1881
Prus, Bolesław. 1845–1912
Sienkiewicz, Henryk. 1846–1916
Botev, Khristo. 1847–1876
Eminescu, Mihail. 1850–1889
Vazov, Ivan. 1850–1921
Franko, Ivan. 1856–1916
Reymont, Wladyslaw Stanislaw. 1867–1925
Ukrajinka, Lesja. 1871–1913
Dučić, Jovan. 1874–1943
Cankar, Ivan. 1876–1918
Ady, Endre. 1877–1919
Pelin, Elin. 1877–1949
Župančič, Oton. 1878–1949
Moricz, Szigmond. 1879–1942
Yovkov, Yordan. 1880–1937
Arghezi, Tudor. 1880–1967
Sadoveanu, Mihail. 1880–1961
Krėvė, Vincas. 1882–1954
Hašek, Jaroslav. 1883–1923
Under, Marie. 1883–1980
Lukács, György. 1885–1971
Witkiewicz, Stanisław Ignacy. 1885–1939
Rebreanu, Liviu. 1885–1944
Čapek, Karel. 1890–1938
Andrić, Ivo. 1892–1975
Kuliš, Mykola. 1892–1942
Krleža, Miroslav. 1893–1981
Tuwim, Julian. 1894–1953
Parandowski, Jan. 1895–1978
Cíger-Hronský, Jozef. 1896–1960
Lengyel, Jozsef. 1896–1975
Németh, László. 1901–1975
Pidmohylny, Valerian. 1901–1941
Seifert, Jaroslav. 1901–1986
Illyés, Gyula. 1902–1983
Stancu, Zaharia. 1902–1974
Gombrowicz, Witold. 1904–1969
József, Attila. 1905–1937
Gliauda, Jurgis. 1906–
Vaičiulaitis, Antanas. 1906–
Eliade, Mircea. 1907–1986
Kangro, Bernard. 1910–
Djilas, Milovan. 1911–
Miłosz, Czesław. 1911–
Marinković, Ranko. 1913–
Dygat, Stanislaw. 1914–
Hrabal, Bohumil. 1914–
Rannit, Aleksis. 1914–1985
Honchar, Oleksander. 1918–
Herling, Gustaw. 1919–
Mňačko, Ladislav. 1919–
Ćosić, Dobrica. 1921–
Koneski, Blaže. 1921–
Lem, Stanislaw. 1921–
Różewicz, Tadeusz. 1921–
Białoszewski, Tadeusz. 1922–1984
Borowski, Tadeusz. 1922–1951
Dimitrova, Blaga. 1922–
Parun, Vesna. 1922–
Popa, Vasko. 1922–1991
Holub, Miroslav. 1923–
Janevski, Slavko. 1923–
Bykaŭ, Vasil. 1924–
Dumitriu, Petru. 1924–
Herbert, Zbigniew. 1924–
Landsbergis, Algirdas. 1924–
Škvorecký, Josef. 1924–
Konwicki, Tadeusz. 1926–
Vaculík, Ludvík. 1926–
Juhász, Ferenc. 1928–
Kohout, Pavel. 1928–
Mihalić, Slavko. 1928–

Pavlović, Miodrag. 1928–
Kundera, Milan. 1929–
Pavić, Milorad. 1929–
Mrożek, Sławomir. 1930–
Hlasko, Marek. 1934–1969
Kiš, Danilo. 1935–1989
Havel, Václav. 1936–
Kadare, Ismail. 1936–
Šalamun, Tomaž. 1941–
Stefanovski, Goran. 1952–

22. Latin American Literatures

Cruz, Sor Júana Inés de la. 1648–1695
Sarmiento, Domingo Faustino. 1811–1888
Alencar, José de. 1829–1877
Hernández, José. 1834–1866
Machado de Assis, Joaquim Maria. 1839–1908
Martí, José. 1853–1895
Cunha, Euclydes da. 1866–1909
Darío, Rubén. 1867–1916
Azuela, Mariano. 1873–1952
Quiroga, Horacio. 1878–1937
Bandeira, Manuel. 1886–1968
Rivera, José Eustasio. 1888–1928
Mistral, Gabriela. 1889–1957
Andrade, Oswald de. 1890–1954
Ramos, Graciliano. 1892–1953
Vallejo, César. 1892–1938
Andrade, Mário de. 1893–1945
Huidobro, Vicente. 1893–1948
Asturias, Miguel Angel. 1899–1974
Borges, Jorge Luis. 1899–1986
Arlt, Roberto. 1900–1942
Freyre, Gilberto de Mello. 1900–1987
Gorostiza, José. 1901–1973
Guillén, Nicolas. 1902–1989
Mallea, Eduardo. 1903–1983
Carpentier, Alejo. 1904–1980
Neruda, Pablo. 1904–1973
Yáñez, Agustin. 1904–1980
Veríssimo, Érico. 1905–1975
Rosa, João Guimarães. 1908–1967
Onetti, Juan Carlos. 1909–
Queirós, Raquel de. 1910–
Arguedas, José María. 1911–1969
Sábato, Ernesto. 1911–
Amado, Jorge. 1912–
Bioy Casares, Adolfo. 1914–
Cortázar, Julio. 1914–1984
Parra, Nicanor. 1914–
Paz, Octavio. 1914–
Roa Bastos, Augusto. 1917–
Arreola, Juan José. 1918–
Rulfo, Juan. 1918–1986
Marqués, René. 1919–1979
Garro, Elena. 1920–
Ribeiro, Darcy. 1922–
Telles, Lygia Fagundes. 1923–
Lispector, Clarice. 1924–1977
Carballido, Emilio. 1925–
Cardenal, Ernesto. 1925–
Castellanos, Rosario. 1925–1974
Donoso, José. 1925–
Wolff, Egon. 1926–
García Márquez, Gabriel. 1928–
Cabrera Infante, Guillermo. 1929–
Fuentes, Carlos. 1929–
Lihn, Enrique. 1929–
Méndez-M., Miguel. 1930–
Padilla, Heberto. 1932–
Puig, Manuel. 1932–1991
Sánchez, Luis Rafael. 1932–
Dalton, Roque. 1935–1975
Ângelo, Ivan. 1936–
Brandão, Ignácio de Loyola. 1936–
Pizarnik, Alejandra. 1936–1972
Vargas Llosa, Mario. 1936–
Medina, Enrique. 1937–
Sarduy, Severo. 1937–
Scliar, Moacyr. 1937–
Valenzuela, Luisa. 1938–
Pacheco, José Emilio. 1939–
Aridjis, Homero. 1940–
Ribeiro, João Ubaldo. 1940–
Skármeta, Antonio. 1940–
Allende, Isabel. 1942–
Arenas, Reinaldo. 1943–1990
Dorfman, Ariel. 1943–
Goldemberg, Isaac. 1945–

Souza, Márcio. 1946–
Zapata, Luis. 1951–

23. Canadian Literature

Haliburton, Thomas Chandler. 1796–1865
Moodie, Susanna. 1803–1885
Roberts, Charles G. 1860–1943
Carman, Bliss. 1861–1929
Scott, Duncan Campbell. 1862–1947
Pratt, E(dwin) J(ohn). 1882–1964
Leacock, Stephen. 1896–1944
Callaghan, Morley. 1903–1990
Birney, Earle. 1904–
Ross, Sinclair. 1908–
Klein, A(braham) M(oses). 1909–1972
Lowry, Malcolm. 1909–1957
Layton, Irving. 1912–
Davies, Robertson. 1913–
Waddington, Miriam. 1917–
Purdy, Al. 1918–
Gallant, Mavis. 1922–
Laurence, Margaret. 1926–1987
Kroetsch, Robert. 1927–
Hood, Hugh. 1928–
Findley, Timothy. 1930–
Macpherson, Jay. 1931–
Munro, Alice. 1931–
Richler, Mordecai. 1931–
Joe, Rita. 1932–
Cohen, Leonard. 1934–
Wiebe, Rudy. 1934–
Hodgins, Jack. 1938–
Atwood, Margaret. 1939–
Ondaatje, Michael. 1943–
Mistry, Rohinton. 1952–

24. Literature of the Caribbean

De Lisser, Herbert George. 1878–1944
Rhys, Jean. 1890–1979
Mais, Roger. 1905–1955
Roumain, Jacques. 1907–1944
Mittelholzer, Edgar. 1909–1965
Gomes, Albert M. 1911–1978
Reid, V(ictor) S(tafford). 1913–
Harris, Wilson. 1921–
Selvon, Samuel. 1923–
Lamming, George. 1927–
Salkey, Andrew. 1928–
Braithwaite, Edward Kamau. 1930–
Walcott, Derek. 1930–
Anthony, Michael. 1932–
Naipaul, V(idiadhar) S(urajprasad). 1932–
Clarke, Austin. 1934–
Kincaid, Jamaica. 1949–
Bissoondath, Neil. 1955–

25. Australian Literature

Furphy, Joseph. 1843–1912
Richardson, Henry Handel. 1870–1946
Franklin, Miles (Stella Maria). 1879–1954
Boyd, Martin. 1893–1972
Shute, Nevil. 1899–1960
Slessor, Kenneth. 1901–1971
Herbert, Xavier. 1901–1984
Stead, Christina. 1902–1983
Hope, A. D. 1907–
White, Patrick. 1912–1990
Wright, Judith. 1915–
McAuley, James. 1917–1976
Anderson, Jessica. 1920s?–
Jolley, Elizabeth. 1923–
Astley, Thea. 1925–
Hazzard, Shirley. 1931–
Malouf, David. 1934–
Keneally, Thomas. 1935–
Stow, Randolph. 1935–
Murray, Les. 1938–
Narogin, Mudrooroo. 1939–
Williamson, David. 1942–
Carey, Peter. 1943–

26. New Zealand Literature

Mansfield, Katherine. 1888–1923
Sargeson, Frank. 1903–1982
Brasch, Charles Orwell. 1909–1973
Curnow, Allen. 1911–
Frame, Janet. 1924–

Baxter, James Keir. 1926–1972
Gee, Maurice. 1931–
Grace, Patricia. 1937–
Wendt, Albert. 1939–
Ihimaera, Witi. 1944–
Hulme, Keri. 1947–

27. Comparative Literature

Introduction

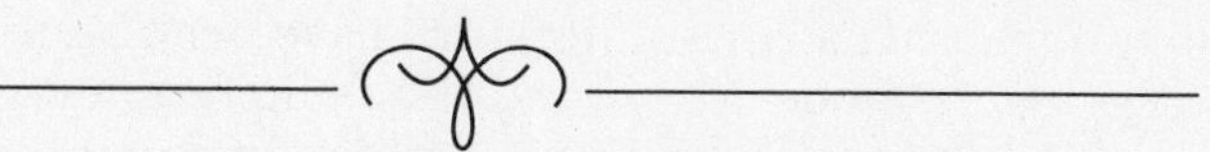

This second volume of the fourteenth edition of *The Reader's Adviser* appears seven years after the last edition, which was published in 1986. In more than 1,000 pages, this volume contains clear and concise chapter introductions, tens of thousands of updated and new bibliographic entries, and biographical profiles of more than 1,100 authors. The changes in this volume represent a major effort, and the contributors to each chapter should be commended for their scholarship and diligence.

Compared to the thirteenth edition, this volume has undergone substantial changes in both organization and content. In the previous edition, the subject of world literature shared space with several chapters on British and American drama. The present volume, in contrast, is devoted solely to world literature (the drama chapters having been moved to Volume 1 with the rest of British and American literature). This shift in emphasis has allowed for the inclusion of several new chapters and the expansion of old ones.

Among the new chapters in this volume are those on the national literatures of Korea, the Netherlands, Australia, Canada, New Zealand, and the Caribbean. Previously, Korean and Netherlandic literatures were combined with Southeast Asian and German literatures, respectively. Providing new chapters for them accords each a language-specific chapter of its own to reflect its cultural distinctiveness. The Netherlandic chapter, moreover, now includes a section on Frisian literature, a distinct and growing literature of its own. In the case of the literatures of Australia, Canada, and New Zealand, these literatures were combined in the thirteenth edition into one chapter on Commonwealth literature, which appeared in the old Volume 1 within British literature. Their separation in this edition and their inclusion in this volume reflect the growing importance of these national literatures as well as their countries' increasing cultural independence from Great Britain. Further, the new chapter on the literature of the Caribbean has been separated from a previous chapter on Spanish American literature to signify its growing importance and to allow for the treatment of authors from former British Commonwealth nations in the region, those whose cultural heritage is not Spanish.

Several chapters in this edition have been greatly expanded to reflect the growing importance of a particular national literature or to acknowledge political or cultural changes. Thus, the chapter on Southeast Asian literatures has had new sections added on Cambodian and Laotian literature and now includes a number of author profiles in a chapter that previously had none. The chapter on Scandinavian literatures has been expanded with a new section on Faroese literature, including author profiles. The chapter on East European literatures, reflecting the political changes in that volatile region, has had added a number of new sections: The section on Czechoslovak literature has been split into separate sections on Czech and Slovak literatures, and the section on Yugoslav literature has been divided into the literatures of Croatia, Macedonia, Serbia, and Slovenia. The chapter on African literatures has been both reorganized and expanded. This chapter is now divided into four major geographic sections representing the literatures of Northern, Western, Eastern, and Southern Africa, with a significant number of new profiles added to each region's literature.

Several other chapters should also be cited for their changes. The chapters on Chinese literature and Japanese literature have been restructured and expanded. The classical and modern periods of each literature now appear as separate sections, each with many new bibliographic entries and new author profiles. Finally, this edition contains a more focused and discriminating discussion of "World Literature," which is the opening chapter, as well as a separate and more expansive consideration of "Comparative Literature," the concluding chapter.

Throughout this volume, contributors have been quite successful in presenting a wide range of authors and works, building upon the base established in the thirteenth edition and adding greatly to it. As in the past, both major and minor authors have been included, but contributors have also given considerably more attention in this edition to women and contemporary writers and to writers previously marginalized. As a result, this new edition presents a greater diversity of literary voices and perspectives.

This volume lives up to its title, *The Best in World Literature*, with its extensive coverage of the major literatures of every continent and its more than a thousand profiles. Its clarity, organization, and wealth of information make it an invaluable reference tool, as well as a useful adviser to many types of readers, as the title of the series proclaims. Perhaps, above all, this volume reveals the splendid diversity of the world's literatures.

Robert DiYanni

The Reader's Adviser

CHAPTER 1

Introduction to World Literature

Robert DiYanni

> I think of the literature of the world, of the literature of Europe, of the literature of a single country, not as a collection of the writings of individuals, but as "organic wholes," as systems in relation to which, and only in relation to which, individual works of literary art, and the works of individual artists, have their significance. . . . A common inheritance and a common cause unite artists consciously or unconsciously. . . . Between the true artists of any time there is, I believe, an unconscious community.
>
> — T. S. Eliot, "The Function of Criticism"

The most common sense of the term *world literature* is simply the sum total of literature produced in the multitude of languages throughout the world. This aggregate notion of an encyclopedic literary compendium extends vertically backward in time as well as horizontally around the globe. Within such an all-encompassing conception of world literature, furthermore, exists a second inclusive notion: that everything associated with imaginative literature is part of the literary corpus. Biographical and critical works thus join novels, stories, poems, plays, and essays as elements in the universe of literature. All works in these genres, moreover, regardless of literary merit or value, assume their proper places, with popular fiction and film scripts standing beside serious poetry, fiction, and drama.

A second and narrower sense of the term *world literature* reflects a distinction between works designed for popular consumption, such as detective novels and romances, and works of enduring literary value. Admitting of inherent problems in changing literary fashion, this second, narrower conception of world literature restricts the definition to works judged to be of serious intent and of lasting quality. In addition, this more exclusive sense of the term also invites consideration of the relations among various national literatures based on the linguistic and cultural relationships that link them. The emphasis thus falls on world literature as it ranges across geographic boundaries and as it echoes through the centuries.

These two different yet compatible senses of the term are reflected in the coverage and organization of this World Literature volume of *The Reader's Adviser.* While the volume attempts to range as widely as possible in the sweep of its coverage, it also groups discussions of the various national literatures to emphasize their internal historical development and their external links with other literatures both synchronically, through space, and diachronically, across time. The influence of Greek literature on Latin, for example, and of Latin literature on the literatures written in Romance languages, provides one example of such developmental influences and connections. Similar patterns of conjunction and relationship emerge among the various Scandinavian national literatures with their common origin in Old Norse–Icelandic literature, and analogously among some of the East Asian languages and literatures, with Chinese the antecedent influence on Japanese, Korean, and other Southeast Asian literatures. The connections, however, should not be pressed too far, for the impulse toward the formation of individual national literatures was grounded in a splitting off from the older entrenched literature to develop a national literature that reflects an independent social, political, and cultural identity. This type of literary fission has occurred all over the globe, with the result that individual differences among national literatures are sometimes emphasized over the common historical elements that connect them. Currently, at the end of the twentieth century, one of the most pervasive features of the literatures of the world is their shifting national identities. The political map of Eastern Europe, for example, has been radically redrawn, so much so that what had only recently been characterized as Czechoslovak and Yugoslav literatures have splintered into independent and individual literatures reflecting the linguistic and political differences that divide Czechs from Slovaks, and Serbs from Croats, Macedonians and other formerly united Yugoslavs. Even so, however, these independent literatures form part of a larger and greater historical literary continuum.

Changing political realities accompanied by cultural shifts among the world's ethnic groups are not the only complicating factor to consider in determining what constitutes world literature. Recent modern critical approaches to literary works, including feminist criticism, structuralism and semiotics, and various forms of cultural analysis, have brought with them new ways of mapping and evaluating literature. Fueled by modern philosophical and theoretical ideas and ignited by broadly based cultural and political changes, literary categories that formerly seemed impervious to alteration have been affected to the point of redefinition. Changes in the canons of various national literatures continue to emerge. Writers and works previously neglected or simply considered unworthy of inclusion in the literary canon have found their way to acceptability.

Amidst changes in how the term *literature* is defined and understood, and along with shifting reconfigurations among national borders, two things remain clear. One is that our understanding of world literature will continue changing to reflect shifting cultural and political realignments. The other is that important literary works will continue to be created in the world's living languages. Moreover, these individual works will take their place in the vast literary universe as parts of particular constellations of nation, language, and genre, each work standing on its own, independent, yet related both to works in its own language, reflecting a set of national values and, more broadly, united with literary works that transcend boundaries of nation, language, genre, and culture.

It remains a paradox that the greatest works of world literature reflect the particular time, place, and culture of their creation while simultaneously transcending them. For regardless of language and nationality, literary works of real imaginative splendor transcend their local settings, national origin, and language of composition to become works of artistic imagination, inhabiting a glorious world of their own. This world of artistic excellence perhaps best expresses the ultimate meaning of the term *world literature*.

GENERAL REFERENCE

Beacham, Walton, ed. *Research Guide to Biography and Criticism: Literature*. 2 vols. Beacham Pub. 1985 $129.00. ISBN 0-933833-00-8

______, ed. *Research Guide to Biography and Criticism: World Drama.* Beacham Pub. 1986 $69.00. ISBN 0-933833-06-7. A one-volume guide to research and criticism of 146 world dramatists. Companion volume to Beacham's *Research Guide to Biography and Criticism: Literature.*

Bédé, Jean-Albert, and William Edgerton, eds. *Columbia Dictionary of Modern European Literature.* Col. U. Pr. 1980 $155.00. ISBN 0-231-03717-1. Includes entries on 1,853 late nineteenth- and twentieth-century European authors and 36 European literatures. Author entries include biographical and critical discussions of principal works along with brief bibliographies.

Benet, William R., ed. *Benet's Reader's Encyclopedia.* HarpC 1987 $39.95. ISBN 0-06-181088-6. Contains 9,000 brief entries on such categories as authors, national literatures, individual works, and literary characters; particularly valuable for students.

Berthold, Margot. *A History of World Theater.* Trans. by Edith Simmons. Continuum 1972 o.p. A scholarly encyclopedic survey of theater from antiquity to the present with emphasis on both historical periods and cultural contexts of theatrical works.

Colby, Vineta, ed. *World Authors 1975–1980.* Wilson 1985 $78.00. ISBN 0-8242-0715-7

______, ed. *World Authors 1980–1985.* Wilson 1990 $80.00. ISBN 0-8242-0797-1. Both volumes follow the principles and format established by *Twentieth-Century Authors.*

Gassner, John, and Edward Quinn, eds. *The Reader's Encyclopedia of World Drama.* T. Y. Crowell 1969 o.p. Covers plays from all five continents; concentrates on plays as literary works rather than on theatrical productions.

Hochman, Stanley, ed. *McGraw-Hill Encyclopedia of World Drama.* 5 vols. McGraw 1984 $395.00. ISBN 0-07-079169-4. Includes signed articles on national, regional, and ethnic drama and biographies of playwrights among the many and varied entries.

Klein, Leonard S., ed. *Encyclopedia of World Literature in the Twentieth Century.* 5 vols. Continuum rev. ed. 1983–1984. Vol. 1 $100.00. ISBN 0-8044-3135-3. Vol. 2 $100.00. ISBN 0-8044-3136-1. Vol. 3 $100.00. ISBN 0-8044-3137-X. Vol. 4 $130.00. ISBN 0-8044-3131-8. Vol. 5 $40.00. ISBN 0-8044-3131-0. Includes carefully researched, informative articles on the literatures of most of the nations of the world, including major and minor authors and literary movements.

Kunitz, Stanley J., and Howard Haycraft, eds. *Twentieth-Century Authors: A Biographical Dictionary of Modern Literature.* Wilson 1942 $80.00. ISBN 0-8242-0049-7. The first of a series of biographical dictionaries that summarizes the lives and achievements of twentieth-century world authors.

Kunitz, Stanley J., and Vineta Colby, eds. *European Authors, One Thousand to Nineteen Hundred: A Biographical Dictionary of European Literature.* Wilson 1967 $63.00. ISBN 0-8242-0013-6. The second in a series of biographical dictionaries that includes nearly 1,000 writers of 31 different literatures; authors in this volume were born after 1000 and died before 1925.

Lang, D. M., and D. R. Dudley, eds. *The Penguin Companion to Classical, Oriental and African Literature.* Viking Penguin rev. ed. 1971 o.p. Like its companion, *The Penguin Companion to European Literature,* this volume includes entries on individual authors and works as well as more extensive general articles on national literatures and special topics.

Preminger, Alex, and others, eds. *The Princeton Encyclopedia of Poetry and Poetics.* Princeton U. Pr. rev. ed. 1974 $24.50. ISBN 0-691-01317-9. Includes more than 800 signed articles by more than 240 contributors. Includes articles on the major bodies of world poetry, on the history of national and international movements in poetry and technique, and on the relationship of poetry to the other arts.

Seymour-Smith, Martin. *The New Guide to Modern World Literature.* 4 vols. P. Bedrick Bks. o.p. Reprint of Seymour-Smith's *Funk and Wagnalls Guide to Modern World Literature,* 1970. An introduction to the literature of the modern world with 35 extensive essays on more than 50 different literatures; excludes authors who died before the beginning of the twentieth century.

Shipley, Joseph T. *The Crown Guide to the World's Greatest Plays: From Ancient Greece to Modern Times.* Crown Pub. Group rev. ed. 1984 $24.95. ISBN 0-517-55392-9. Devoted chiefly to 750 classics of world drama, considering drama less as literature than as theater.

Stade, George, and William T. Jackson, eds. *European Writers.* 7 vols. Macmillan 1983–1985. $80.00 ea. ISBNs 0-684-16594-4 (Vols. 1-2), 0-684-17914-8 (Vols. 3-4), 0-684-17915-6 (Vols. 5–7). Comprises 261 extended essays on continental authors and their works, arranged chronologically from Prudentius to Milan Kundera. Includes bibliographies of works by and about each author.

Steinberg, S. H., ed. *Cassell's Encyclopedia of World Literature.* 3 vols. Morrow rev. ed. 1973 o.p. Contains 650 articles on the histories of national literatures and on literary subjects such as literary genres and schools; also includes biographies of authors from all periods and continents.

Thorlby, Anthony, ed. *The Penguin Companion to European Literature.* Viking Penguin rev. ed. 1971 o.p. A companion volume to *The Penguin Companion to Classical, Oriental and African Literature.* Includes articles on 40 national literatures and entries on major and minor writers. Eight additional general articles appear on such topics as Dada, Expressionism, and Marxist views on Art and Literature.

Vinson, James, and Daniel L. Kirkpatrick, eds. *Great Foreign Language Writers.* St. Martin $49.95. ISBN 0-312-34585-2

______, eds. *Contemporary Foreign Language Writers.* St. Martin 1984 $39.95. ISBN 0-312-16663-X. Includes collections of critical articles on major world writers prefaced by a brief biographical summary, a chronological list of the writer's published works, and a listing of bibliographical and critical studies.

Wakeman, John, ed. *World Authors, 1950–1970.* Wilson 1975 $95.00. ISBN 0-8242-0419-0

Wakeman, John, and Stanley J. Kunitz, eds. *World Authors 1970-1975.* Wilson 1980 $78.00. ISBN 0-8242-0641-X. Both volumes follow the principles and format of *Twentieth-Century Authors.*

Ward, A. C., ed. *Longman Companion to Twentieth-Century Literature.* Longman 3rd ed. 1981 o.p. Includes biographical and bibliographical entries on writers of international repute whose books have appeared in English, as well as entries on literary categories, summaries of important literary works, discussions of literary terms, topical phrases, and various literary allusions.

Wilson, Katharina, ed. *An Encyclopedia of Continental Women Writers.* 2 vols. Garland 1991 o.p. Contains essays and bibliographies on a wide range of women writers previously omitted from such books. An important and much needed resource.

COLLECTIONS

Barnstone, Aliki, and Willis Barnstone, eds. *A Book of Women Poets from Antiquity to Now.* Schocken rev. ed. 1992 $18.00. ISBN 0-8052-0997-2. Contains a rich selection of poems from 50 languages, beginning with the Sumerian poet Enheduanna (c. 2300 B.C.) and continuing to contemporary times.

Block, Haskell M., and Robert G. Shedd, eds. *Masters of Modern Drama.* McGraw 1962 $43.00. ISBN 0-07-55355-6. Contains 45 plays by 35 playwrights, lucid and informed introductions to authors and works, photographs of productions, and brief critical bibliography for each author.

Clark, Barrett H., ed. *World Drama.* 2 vols. Dover 1933. $11.95 ea. ISBNs 0-486-20057-4, 0-486-20059-0. Contains a broad selection of plays from around the world. Volume 1: the Orient, medieval Europe, England, ancient Greece and Rome, and India. Volume 2: Italy, Spain, France, Germany, Denmark, Norway, and Russia.

DiYanni, Robert, and Kraft Rompf, eds. *The McGraw-Hill Book of Poetry.* McGraw 1993 $29.95. ISBN 0-07-016944-6. Provides an extensive selection of poems in English along with a special section of more than 200 poems by 100 poets in 20 languages, as well as a full representation of women poets.

Halpern, Daniel, ed. *The Art of the Tale: An International Anthology of Short Stories.* Viking Penguin 1987 $12.95. ISBN 0-14-007949-1. Presents an excellent selection of short fiction, including novellas from numerous cultural traditions, thereby avoiding a Eurocentric emphasis.

Mack, Maynard, and others, eds. *The Norton Anthology of World Masterpieces.* 2 vols. Norton 1992 $37.95. ISBN 0-393-96140-0. Classic anthology of world literary masterpieces set in historical contexts.

Nims, John Frederic. *Sappho to Valery: Poems in Translation.* U. of Ark. Pr. 1990 $19.95. ISBN 1-55728-141-6. Translations of poetry from antiquity to the early twentieth century. Includes original language versions of poems included on facing pages.

Tomlinson, Charles, ed. *The Oxford Book of Verse in English Translation.* OUP 1980 o.p. Extensive selection of world poetry translated by celebrated writers from the Renaissance to the present.

Wilkie, Brian, and James Hurt, eds. *Literature of the Western World.* 2 vols. Macmillan 1988. $24.75 ea. ISBNs 0-02-427800-9, 0-02-427810-6. Contains literary selections, predominantly European, from influential authors of the western tradition; biographical and critical headnotes precede the work of each writer.

CHAPTER 2

Hebrew Literature

David G. Hirsch

> Literature responds to the demands of life, and life reacts to the guidance of literature. The function of literature is to plant the seed of new ideas and new desires; the seed once planted, life does the rest. The tender shoot is nurtured and brought to maturity by the spontaneous action of men's minds, and its growth is shaped by their needs.
>
> —AHAD HA-AM, *The Eternal Light*

Hebrew literature encompasses more than 2,000 years of creativity, functioning as the literary outlet and creative expression of the Jewish people from the biblical period to the present. When Hebrew ceased to be the spoken language toward the end of the biblical period, it was maintained chiefly in religious literature. By the Middle Ages, Hebrew was known as *leshon hakodesh,* the sacred tongue. The Hebrew language was used primarily for liturgical works, codes, and legal texts (e.g., commentaries, glosses, decisions, judgments), prophetic and wisdom literature, and responsa.

Tenth-century Spain, Provence, and Italy witnessed a growth in Hebrew secular or quasi-secular literature. The poetry of SOLOMON IBN GABIROL, Moses Ibn Ezra, and JUDAH HA-LEVI are based on biblical and secular themes. Their works are the primary fruits of the renaissance of Hebrew literature during the Golden Age of Spain.

Modern Hebrew literature arose from the secular literature of Ashkenazi Jewry, the Jewish populations of Northern and Eastern Europe. The exact beginning of the modern Hebrew literary era is disputed by two prominent schools of thought. There are those who adhere to GERSHOM SCHOLEM's (see Vol. 4) view that the close of the seventeenth century is the starting point, which coincides with the disruption of medieval authority following Shabbtai Zvi's messianic proclamation and downfall; others view the German *Haskalah* (Enlightenment) movement in the latter part of the eighteenth century as the impetus for the modern period.

Historians also debate the periodization of modern Hebrew literature. In the *Encyclopaedia Judaica,* Professor Ezra Spicehandler offers the following generally accepted schema. The European Period (1781–1921), including *Haskalah* literature in Europe (1781–1881) and modern Hebrew literature in Russia and Poland (1881–1920); the Palestinian-Halutzic Period (1905–1948), which comprises the Ottoman Period (1905–17) and the Mandate Period (1920–48); and, lastly, the Israel Period (1948 to the present).

The *Haskalah,* from the Hebrew root meaning "understanding" or "intelligence," was a movement committed to reason. Followers called *maskilim* chose those practices and beliefs in Judaism that were in accord with reason, and the purpose of their literature was to advance moral, social, and aesthetic goals through rational means.

Except for the poems of Ephraim Luzzatto, no Hebrew lyric poetry or Hebrew narrative prose of this period was especially noteworthy. The major emphasis of the Haskalah was in the area of modern Jewish scholarship, known as *Wissenschaft des Judenthums*.

In the Russian Haskalah, the greatest literary figure was the poet, short story writer, and journalist, Judah Leib Gordon. He dominated the literary scene until the 1880s. Abraham Mapu, the first modern Hebrew novelist, wrote in Russia during the mid-1800s.

Political and social events of the 1880s in Europe influenced literary critics, who began to demand a more realistic form of literature and the development of social criticism. Hebrew critics voiced similar attitudes and thus an empathy for people—their hopes and life-styles—became the focus of writings. AHAD HA-AM is considered the most influential intellectual figure of the Modern European Period and is also the father of the modern Hebrew essay.

The Yiddish writer MENDELE MOKHER SEFORIM bridges the period between the Haskalah (1781–1881) and the beginning of the twentieth century, when nationalistic feelings became more prominent among European Jewry. While he is perhaps better known as the first serious Yiddish writer, he wrote in a new Hebrew literary style that established a standard of imaginative complexity and command of Hebrew prose.

In contrast to Mendele's style of realism, the works of David Frischmann, I. L. PERETZ, and MICAH JOSEPH BERDICHEVSKY, all from Warsaw, were neoromantic and impressionistic. Berdichevsky is considered the most skillful proponent of this style. He challenged Ahad Ha-Am's views that a mainstream, unified Judaism existed and also opposed his efforts toward a nationalistic culture. Berdichevsky was a proponent of individualism and secularism rather than traditionalism, themes he reiterated throughout his works. M. Z. FEUERBERG'S writings, also of the same period, never cross into secularism but remain much like the author was, caught between the loss of faith and reason.

The high point in literary form and content of this European Period is found in the poetry of HAYYIM NAHMAN BIALIK. His works, written between 1892 and 1917, masterfully strike the balance between the old traditionalist culture and the new European culture. His style and command of the vast resources of the Hebrew literary tradition cast a strong influence over most other Hebrew writers of this period.

There were few exceptions to the dominance of Bialik's style, SAUL TCHERNICHOVSKI being the most significant. He introduced a more European style of poetry that stressed individualism, humanism, and universalism.

Hebrew literature in Palestine found its literary voice with the writers who emigrated during the 1880s. Best known among these was Eliezer Ben-Yehuda, the great lexicographer and journalist. Moshe Smilansky wrote realistic stories of Palestinian life and was the first to write about Arab life in Hebrew fiction. The ancient divinely promised land of *Eretz Israel* became the focus of many writers. Hebrew, as a language, was also developing and the literature reflects a growing flexibility in the vocabulary and stylistic use of language.

Following the upheavals of World War I and the Russian Revolution, Palestine became the new center of Hebrew literature as writers like Bialik continued to emigrate. The emigration of 1920–24 brought a new radical expression of literary leadership. Eliezer Steinman and Abraham Shlonsky founded a new literary journal called *Ketuvim* (Writings), which became a principal vehicle for the modernists. These new writers included Yaakov Horowitz, Nathan Alterman, and LEAH GOLDBERG. The leading poets of this period were Shlonsky, his disciples Alterman and Goldberg, and Uri Zvi Greenberg. They experimented with new rhythms and the spoken idiom. The leading prose writers of this period were SHMUEL YOSEF AGNON and HAIM HAZAZ. Agnon's achievements are considered second only to Bialik's. Typical themes were an idealistic attitude toward Zionism and nostalgic recollections of European childhoods.

The latest period of modern Hebrew literature began with the establishment of the State of Israel. Many writers of this generation were native speakers of Hebrew, most having been born in Palestine or emigrating there as young children. As a result, they were less affected by Yiddish and European linguistic and cultural styles. Many were members of the *kibbutzim* (collective settlements) and favored the collective ideology rather than an individualistic one. By the late 1950s, some writers began to question the collective ideology and expressed their disillusionment through a new individualism and existentialism.

Many of these Israeli writers spoke of the alienation of modern life and of a world becoming more secularized. The Holocaust, whether dealt with directly or appearing on a more subconscious level, became one of the major themes in modern Hebrew literature. It is the major source of spiritual struggle found in the works of ARON APPLEFELD, Yonat Sened and Alexander Sened, MOSHE SHAMIR, HANOKH BARTOV, AMOS OZ, A. B. YEHOSHUA, and YEHUDA AMICHAI. In recent years, several new themes have emerged. One such theme focuses on the Palestinian problem and the Intifada, which are highlighted in the works of writers like DAVID GROSSMAN. Sephardic themes have also become more prevalent. Another change in Hebrew literature is that women writers, particularly novelists, are becoming more prominent. Although Israel has long had a number of noted women poets, there were relatively few novelists until recently. Among those who have achieved high standing are SHULAMITH HAREVEN, Ruth Almog, and BATYA GOOR.

Only a small part of Hebrew literature has been translated into book length form in English. Most of the English translations appear either in anthologies or in periodical literature.

HISTORY AND CRITICISM

Aschkenasy, Nehama. *Eve's Journey: Feminine Images in Hebraic Literary Tradition*. U. of Pa. Pr. 1987 $40.95. ISBN 0-8122-8033-4. Examines the use of feminine themes and imagery.

Benjamin, Anne Myra Goodman. *Decadence in Thirteenth Century Provencal and Hebrew Poetry. Medieval and Renaissance monograph ser.* VIII. MARC Publ. Co. 1987 $10.00. ISBN 0-941107-01-9

Brann, Ross. *The Compunctious Poet: Cultural Ambiguity and Hebrew Poetry in Muslim Spain. Johns Hopkins Jewish Studies.* Johns Hopkins 1991 $36.50. ISBN 0-8018-4073-2. A study of Jewish cultural tradition as expressed in Hebrew poetry in Moorish Spain.

Chomsky, William. *Hebrew: The Eternal Language*. JPS Phila. 1975 $9.95. ISBN 0-8276-0077-1

Cohen, Joseph. *Voices of Israel: Essays on and Interviews with Yehuda Amichai, A. B. Yehoshua, T. Carmi, Aharon Appelfeld, and Amos Oz*. State U. NY Pr. 1990 $59.50. ISBN 0-7914-0243-6

Goell, Yohai. *Bibliography of Modern Hebrew Literature in English Translation*. Transaction Bks. 1968 $28.95. ISBN 0-87855-187-5. An annual supplement is published by the Institute for the Translation of Hebrew Literature.

Halkin, Simon. *Modern Hebrew Literature: From the Enlightenment to the Birth of the State of Israel.* Shocken 1975 o.p. An excellent guide to trends and values in Hebrew literature from its beginnings to the 1940s.

Pagis, Dan. *Hebrew Poetry in the Middle Ages and the Renaissance. The Traubman Lectures in Jewish Studies.* U. CA Pr. 1991 $26.95. ISBN 0-5200-6547-6. Critical study of medieval and Renaissance Hebrew poetry.

Posner, R., and I. Ta-Shema. *The Hebrew Book: An Historical Survey.* Keter 1975 o.p.

Ramraz-Ravich, Gilah. *The Arab in Israeli Literature.* Ind. U. Pr. 1989 $29.95. ISBN 0-2533-4832-3. Examines depictions of Arab-Israeli conflicts and writers' relation to Arabs in their literature.

Shaked, Gershon. *The Shadows Within: Essays on Modern Jewish Writers.* JPS Phila. 1987 $19.95. ISBN 0-8276-0295-2. Focuses primarily on Shmuel Yosef Agnon and interpretations of his work.

Silberschlag, Eisig. *From Renaissance to Renaissance: Hebrew Literature.* 2 vols. Ktav 1971–77 $25.00 ea. ISBN 0-87068-184-2. Encyclopedic in its survey of Hebrew literature from the end of the medieval Spanish period through modern times. See also Leon I. Yudkin's *Escape into Siege* below.

Stern, David, and Mark Jay Mirsky, eds. *Rabbinic Fantasies: Imaginative Narratives from Classic Hebrew Literature.* Trans. by Norman Bronznick and others. JPS Phila. 1990 $27.50. ISBN 0-8276-0363-0. Anthology of 16 works from classical Hebrew literature, arranged chronologically.

Yudkin, Leon I. *Escape into Siege.* Bnai Brith Bk. 1974 $18.50. ISBN 0-19-710016-3. A survey of contemporary Israeli literature from the 1940s to the early 1970s.

Zinberg, Israel. *A History of Jewish Literature.* 12 vols. Trans. and ed. by Bernard Martin. Ktav $315.00. ISBN 0-685-53636-X. A monumental work tracing the development of Jewish literature from tenth-century Spain to nineteenth-century Russia. Includes major Jewish writers of poetry, fiction, and drama, as well as contributors to other fields such as philosophy, history, the Bible, religious law, folklore, and legend.

COLLECTIONS

Bargad, Warren, and Stanley F. Chyet, eds. and trans. *Israeli Poetry: A Contemporary Anthology. Jewish Literature and Culture Ser.* Ind. U. Pr. 1986 $29.95. ISBN 0-253-33140-4. Includes a bibliography and index.

Burnshaw, Stanley, ed. *The Modern Hebrew Poem Itself.* Shocken 1960 $14.95. ISBN 0-674-57925-9. Contains 69 transliterated Hebrew poems; the original Hebrew and literal English translations together with commentaries.

Burnshaw, Stanley, T. Carmi, and Ezra Spicehandler, eds. *The Modern Hebrew Poem Itself: From the Beginnings to the Present.* HUP 1989 $14.95. ISBN 0-674-57925-9. Addressed to people who know no Hebrew but wish to experience modern Hebrew poetry.

Carmi, T., ed. *The Penguin Book of Hebrew Verse.* Viking Penguin 1981 $15.95. ISBN 0-14-042197-1. Winner of the Kenneth B. Smilen/Present Tense Literary Award (1982). A collection spanning 4,000 years of Hebrew poetry from biblical verse and poems from the Talmud to the modern poets.

Davidson, Israel. *Thesaurus of Medieval Hebrew Poetry. Lib. of Jewish Class.* 4 vols. Ktav rev. ed. 1970 $150.00. ISBN 0-87068-003

Frank, Bernhard, trans. *Modern Hebrew Poetry.* Bks. Demand repr. of 1980 ed. $65.40. ISBN 0-7837-1623-0. Completed as part of a master's thesis project.

Glazer, Myra, ed. *Burning Air and a Clear Mind: Contemporary Israeli Women Poets.* Ohio U. Pr. 1981 $17.95. ISBN 0-8214-0572-1. A collection of works by 18 poets, who range in age from their twenties to their eighties, expressing a remarkably similar vision.

Kravitz, Nathaniel. *Three Thousand Years of Hebrew Literature: From the Earliest Time through the 20th Century.* Ohio U. Pr. 1971 o.p. Discussions of the origin, history, and translation of Hebrew literature.

Lasker-Schuler, Else. *Hebrew Ballads and Other Poems. Jewish Poetry Ser.* JPS Phila. 1981 $10.95. ISBN 0-8276-0179-4. Collection of lyrical German-Jewish poetry.

Lelchuk, Alan, and Gershon Shaked, eds. *Eight Great Hebrew Short Novels.* New Amer. Lib. 1983 o.p. A display of the versatility of modern Hebrew literature. Included are works of U. N. Gnessin, Y. C. Brenner, Y. Shami, S. Y. Agnon, D. Fogel, Amos Oz, J. Knaz, and A. B. Yehoshua.

Leviant, Curt. *Masterpieces of Hebrew Literature: A Treasury of Two Thousand Years of Jewish Creativity.* Ktav 1969 $14.95. ISBN 0-87068-079-X. A comprehensive introduction to the mainstream of postbiblical literature.

Mezey, Robert, ed. *Poems from the Hebrew. Poems of the World Ser.* Crowell 1973 $12.95. ISBN 0-690-63685-7. Includes ancient poems, the poems of Moorish Spain (e.g., Samuel the Prince, Solomon Ibn Gabirol, Moses Ibn Ezra, Judah Halevi), and the modern poets (e.g., Bialik, S. Tchernichovski, Y. Fichman, N. Alterman, L. Goldberg, A. Gilboa, and Y. Amichai).

Michener, James A. *First Fruits: A Harvest of 25 Years of Israeli Writing.* Jewish Pubns. 1975 o.p. Foreword by Chaim Potok. Fifteen tales representing the first 25 years of Israel's existence as a state, including stories by A. Barash, H. Hazaz, S. Y. Agnon, Amos Oz, and A. Megged.

Millgram, Abraham E. *An Anthology of Medieval Hebrew Literature.* Telegraph Bks. 1982 o.p. Divided into the following categories: Poetry of Spain; Prayers; Hymns; Dirges; Ethical Literature; Zohar; Legal Literature; Travelers' Accounts; and Folk Tales.

Mintz, Ruth F., ed. *Modern Hebrew Poetry: A Bilingual Anthology.* U. CA Pr. 1982 $12.95. ISBN 0-520-4781-8. "Excellent representatives of the Hebrew Literature of the late 19th and 20th centuries" (*LJ*).

Penueli, S. Y., and A. Ukhmani, eds. *Anthology of Modern Hebrew Poetry.* 2 vols. Keter Pub. IS 1975 o.p. A fine selection made under the auspices of the Institute for the Translation of Hebrew Literature.

Scheindlin, Raymond P. *The Gazelle: Medieval Hebrew Poems on God, Israel, and the Soul.* JPS Phila. 1991 $24.95. ISBN 0-8276-0384-3. Profound study of Hebrew literature in medieval Spain. Focuses on religious poetry.

———, comp. *Wine, Women and Death: Medieval Hebrew Poems on the Good Life.* JPS Phila. 1986 $15.95. ISBN 0-8276-0266-9. Discusses the emergence of secular love poetry and examines innovations in medieval poetry.

Schwartz, Howard, and Anthony Rudolf, eds. *Voices within the Ark: The Modern Jewish Poets.* Avon 1983 $15.95. ISBN 0-380-76109-2. A one-volume work of selections from the finest poetry written by Jewish poets since the turn of the century; approximately a fifth of the volume contains translated Hebrew poems.

CHRONOLOGY OF AUTHORS

Ibn Gabirol, Solomon ben Judah. c.1021–1058
Judah Ha-Levi. 12th century
Ahad Ha-Am. 1856–1927
Berdichevsky, Micah Joseph. 1865–1921
Bialik, Hayyim Nahman. 1873–1934
Feierberg (Feuerberg), Mordecai Ze'ev. 1874–1899
Tchernichovski (Tchernichowsky), Saul. 1875–1943
Brenner, Joseph Hayyim. 1881–1921
Agnon, Shmuel Yosef. 1888–1970
Barash, Asher. 1889–1952
Vogel, David. 1891–1944
Hazaz, Haim. 1898–1973
Goldberg, Leah. 1911–1970
Gilboa, Amir. 1917–
Tammuz, Benjamin. 1919–
Megged, Aharon. 1920–
Shamir, Moshe. 1921–
Gouri, Haim. 1923–
Amichai, Yehuda. 1924–
Kishon, Ephraim. 1924–
Carmi, T. 1925–
Shaham, Nathan. 1925–
Michael, Sami. 1926–
Shahar, David. 1926–

Bartov, Hanokh. 1928–
Kaniuk, Yoram. 1930–
Pagis, Dan. 1930–
Zach, Nathan. 1930–
Hareven, Shulamith. 1931–
Appelfeld, Aron. 1932–
Yehoshua, A(braham) B. 1936–
Oz, Amos. 1939–
Goor, Batya. 1947–
Shammas, Anton. 1951–
Grossman, David. 1954–

AGNON, SHMUEL YOSEF (pseud. of Samuel Josef Czaczkes). 1888–1970 (NOBEL PRIZE 1966)

Born in Galicia, in a home influenced by rabbinic and Hasidic traditions and the reviving spirit of European culture, Agnon began writing Hebrew and Yiddish at the age of eight. He contributed poetry and prose to periodicals, such as *Ha-Mizpeh* and *Der Juedische Wecker*. After he immigrated to Palestine in 1907, he no longer wrote in Yiddish. He chose the pen name "Agnon" from the title of his first novel, *Agunot* (*Forsaken Wives*); its meaning is "cut off" in Hebrew. From 1912 to 1914 Agnon lived in Germany, where, in 1914 he met Salman Schocken and convinced him that someone should undertake the publishing of Hebrew books. Many years later four volumes of Agnon's collected works in Hebrew were published by Berlin Schocken Verlag in 1931. Agnon was awarded the Bialik Prize for literature in 1934, and in 1936 he was made an honorary Doctor of Hebrew Letters by the Jewish Theological Seminary of America. Other honors followed, including the Israel Prize in 1954 and 1958. In 1966 he became the first Israeli to win the Nobel Prize for literature, which was awarded jointly to the Swedish writer NELLY SACHS.

Agnon often deals with philosophical and psychological problems in a miraculous or supernatural manner. Reality is colored in a dreamlike atmosphere. Agnon is concerned with contemporary problems of a spiritual nature—the disintegration of traditional life, loss of faith and identity, and loneliness. At the center of his work is the Jew in various manifestations: a person of faith, a nihilist, a victim of pogroms and the Holocaust, a pioneer, and a saint.

Creating a unique Hebrew prose style, his works link historic Jewish piety and martyrdom with longing for Israel, and yet they have universal appeal to the modern reader. Agnon himself has said: "I am not a modern writer. I am astounded that I even have one reader. I don't see the reader before me . . . . No, I see before me only the Hebrew letter saying 'write me thus and not thus.' I, to my regret, am like the wicked Balaam. It is written of him that 'the word that God putteth in my mouth, that shall I speak'" (*N.Y. Times*).

NOVELS BY AGNON

Betrothed (and *Edo and Enam*). 1965. Trans. by Walter Lever. Schocken 1975 o.p. Two tales.

The Bridal Canopy. 1931. Trans. by I. M. Lask. Schocken 1967 o.p. Recognized as one of the cornerstones of modern Hebrew literature; established Agnon as a central writer.

A Guest for the Night. 1968. Trans. by Misha Louvish. Schocken 1968 o.p. Written after Agnon revisited his home in Galicia in 1930; describes the desolation time has wrought. Originally published in serial form in the magazine *Haaretz* from October 18, 1938 to April 7, 1939.

In the Heart of the Seas: A Story of a Journey to the Land of Israel. 1947. Trans. by I. M. Lask. Schocken 1980 repr. of 1948 ed. o.p. The story of the pilgrimage to Palestine of Polish Jews in the early nineteenth century.

Shira. Trans. by Zeva Shapiro. Schocken 1989 $24.95. ISBN 0-8052-4043-8. Agnon's last major novel; follows the love affair of a university professor with a free-spirited woman in Jerusalem during the 1930's. Afterword by Robert Alter.

A Simple Story. 1935. Trans. by Hillel Halkin. Schocken 1985 $14.95. ISBN 0-8052-3999-5

Works by Agnon

Days of Awe. 1948. Schocken 1965 $9.95. ISBN 0-8052-0100-9. Introduction by Judah Goldin. A collection of traditions, legends, and learned commentaries concerning the Jewish High Holy Days.

Twenty-one Stories. 1970. Ed. by Nahum N. Glatzer. Schocken 1971 $8.95. ISBN 0-8052-0318-3

Books about Agnon

Aberbach, David. *At the Handles of the Lock*. OUP 1985 o.p. Discusses the love triangle theme that appears throughout Agnon's work.

Band, Arnold J. *Nostalgia and Nightmare: A Study in the Fiction of S. Y. Agnon*. U. CA Pr. o.p. Includes a bibliography.

Fisch, Harold. *S. Y. Agnon. Lit. and Life Ser.* Continuum 1975 $18.95. ISBN 0-8044-2197-8. An overview and informative critique of some of Agnon's work.

Hochman, Baruch. *The Fiction of S. Y. Agnon*. Cornell Univ. Pr. 1970 o.p. Important overview of Agnon's work.

Hoffman, Anne Golomb. *Between Exile and Return: S. Y. Agnon and the Drama of Writing*. State U. NY Pr. 1991 $59.50. ISBN 0-7914-0540-0. Inquiry into Agnon as a modern Jewish writer, focusing on his modernist sensibilities and his sacred language.

Shaked, Gershon. *Shmuel Yosef Agnon: a Revolutionary Traditionalist*. Trans. by Jeffrey M. Green. *Modern Jewish Master Series*. NYU Pr. 1989 $35.00. ISBN 0-814-77894-1. Biography of Agnon discussing how he departs from traditional themes while using traditional sacred language in his writings.

AHAD HA-AM (pseud. of Asher Hirsch Ginzberg). 1856–1927

A self-taught thinker and Hebrew essayist, Ahad Ha-Am (meaning "One of the People") received a traditional Jewish education in his Hasidic home in Skvira, Kiev. Not being able to reconcile his modern rationalist thinking with Hasidism, he first abandoned that way of life and eventually all religious faith. Settling in Odessa in 1884, he became one of the leading members of the *Hibbat Zion* (Lovers of Zion) movement in Russia. Ahad Ha-Am developed an idea of Zionism that was not rooted in completely political ideals. While he did not agree with those who urged the establishment of a national Jewish homeland for the sake of obtaining the survival of many desperate Jews who suffered under the severity of czarist Russia, Ahad Ha-Am placed more emphasis on the need to create a national consciousness by cultural preparation through education. "Cultural Zionism" developed around the idea of a Jewish state as the "spiritual center" for all Jews. As editor of *Ha-Shilo'ah* (1896), the predominant monthly of Hebrew literature and Zionism in Eastern Europe, Ahad Ha-Am contributed to the development of Hebrew literature. After he settled in Palestine in 1922, Ahad Ha-Am continued to expound his ideas of spiritual and cultural revitalization. It was there that he published his correspondence and memoirs.

Works by Ahad Ha-Am

Essays, Letters, Memoirs. Trans. and ed. by Leon Simon. East & West Lib. 1946 o.p. Selection of writings geared toward the political commitment of Ahad Ha-Am's works.

Nationalism and the Jewish Ethic. Trans. by Leon Simon. Ed. by Hans Kohn. Schocken 1962 o.p. Introduction by Hans Kohn.

Selected Essays of Ahad Ha-Am. Ed. by Leon Simon. Atheneum 1970 repr. of 1912 ed. o.p. First volume in a series of modern Hebrew texts.

Ten Essays on Zionism and Judaism. Ayer repr. of 1922 ed. $26.50. ISBN 0-405-05267-7. Examines Jewish history, religion, and literature in the context of Zionism and world Jewry.

BOOKS ABOUT AHAD HA-AM

Ahad Ha-Am, Asher Ginzberg: A Biography. Jewish Pubns. 1960 o.p. Deals primarily with Ahad Ha-Am's public work and personal philosophy.

Kornberg, Jacques, ed. *At the Crossroads: Essays on Ahad Ha'am. Modern Jewish History Ser.* State U. NY Pr. 1984 $59.50. ISBN 0-87395-739-3. Collection of essays analyzing Ahad Ha-Am's views of Jewish distress in the world.

AMICHAI, YEHUDA. 1924–

Yehuda Amichai was born in Germany and immigrated to Palestine in 1936. His novels and poetry are innovative in their use of Hebrew terms. Following World War II and Israel's War of Independence in 1948, Amichai began to introduce new words of technical, legal, and administrative meaning into his poetry to replace sacral phrases. His poetry reflects the modernizing of the Hebrew language within the last 45 years. "One of Amichai's most characteristic effects in his poetry is the mingling of past and present, ancient and modern, person and place: the here and now for him inevitably recalls the past" (*Judaica Book News*). One of Israel's most highly regarded poets, Amichai shared the Israel Prize for Literature with AMIR GILBOA in 1981.

POETRY BY AMICHAI

Amen. Trans. by Yehuda Amichai and Ted Hughes. HarpC 1977 $7.95. ISBN 0-915443-22-0. Third volume of poetry. Includes poems from a cycle, "Patriotic Songs."

The Early Books of Yehuda Amichai. Trans. by Ted Hughes and Assia Gutman. Sheep Meadow 1988 $12.95. ISBN 0-9353-9675-1. Includes "Songs of Jerusalem and Myself."

Even a Fist Was Once an Open Palm with Fingers: Recent Poems. Ed. and trans. by Barbara and Benjamin Harshav. HarpC 1991 $21.95. ISBN 0-0605-5297-2. Intense study of the subject of love.

Great Tranquility: Questions and Answers. Trans. by Glenda Abramson and Tudor Parfitt. HarpC 1983 $7.95. ISBN 0-06-091085-2. Poetry reflecting the insights of a man coming to terms with his past.

Love Poems. HarpC 1981 $11.95. ISBN 0-06-090873-4. Poems of longing and separation gathered from earlier collections of the poet's work already published in English. Bilingual edition.

Not of This Time, Not of This Place. 1963. Trans. by Shlomo Katz. Biblio Dist. 1973 o.p. Poems centered on Amichai's struggle with the unforgiving landscape of Jerusalem.

Poems. Trans. by Assia Gutman. HarpC 1969 o.p. Introduction by Michael Hamburger.

Selected Poetry of Yehuda Amichai. Ed. and trans. by Chana Bloch and Stephen Mitchell. HarpC 1986 $10.00. ISBN 0-0609-6062-0. Love poems and poetry based in Jerusalem. Bilingual with original Hebrew text.

Songs of Jerusalem and Myself. 1973. Trans. by Harold Schimmel. HarpC 1975 o.p. Received the Jewish Book Council's Kovner Award for Poetry in 1974.

Time. Trans. by Yehuda Amichai. HarpC 1979 o.p. Poems reflecting Amichai's present life as a Jew in Jerusalem.

Travels. Trans. by Ruth Nevo. Sheep Meadow 1986 $13.95. ISBN 0-9352-662-X. English and Hebrew text of *Mas'ot Binhyamin ha-Aharon mi-Tudelah*.

Short story collection by Amichai

The World Is a Room. Trans. by Elinor Grumet and others. Jewish Pubns. 1984 $13.95. ISBN 0-8276-0234-0. A collection of some of the author's most poignant short stories, all written in the 1950s. Included are stories that expose conflicts in Israeli society and the struggle for humanity.

APPELFELD, ARON. 1932–

Born to a wealthy Jewish family in Chernovtsy, Romania, Appelfeld and his father were deported to a concentration camp shortly after the Nazis shot and killed his mother in 1940. Appelfeld, however—only eight years old—managed to escape, and he hid out in the Ukranian countryside, camouflaged by his blondness. After the war, he made his way to refugee camps in Yugoslavia and Italy before finally immigrating to Palestine in 1947. Still only a teenager, he worked on a kibbutz and studied Hebrew. Fourteen years later, he was reunited with his father, who survived the Holocaust.

Upon reaching adulthood, Appelfeld began to write. Considered one of Israel's foremost novelists, Appelfeld's fame reached the United States with the publication of *Badenheim 1939* in 1980. His sparse style is often devoid of descriptive detail, dreamy like a fairy tale, and full of a sense of heaviness and lurking evil. Although he never writes directly about the Holocaust itself in his novels, his work describes the experiences of the survivors. He exposes the outlines of that apocalypse, often comparing it to a very bright flame, like the sun, that one cannot look at directly. His literary work transcends historical retelling in a remarkable fusion of despair and hope, weakness and strength, cowardice and courage.

Novels by Appelfeld

The Age of Wonders. Trans. by Dalya Bilu. Godine 1981 $11.95. ISBN 0-87923-798-7

Badenheim 1939. Trans. by Dalya Bilu. Godine 1980 $9.95. ISBN 0-87923-799-6. A novelization of the author's earlier story with the same title. "A novel rich in perception, clarity, and understanding of this difficult period" (*Judaica Book News*).

For Every Sin. Trans. by Jeffrey M. Green. Random 1989 $9.95. ISBN 0-67972758-2. The story of a Holocaust survivor who trudges through Europe after four years in concentration camps and finds that other survivors are his best companions.

The Healer. Trans. by Jeffrey M. Green. Grove Pr. 1990 $16.95 ISBN 0-80211223-4. An irreligious Jewish family in prewar Vienna makes a pilgrimage to a small Jewish village in the Carpathians to visit a healer.

The Immortal Bartfuss. Trans. by Jeffrey M. Green. Weidenfeld & Nicolson 1988 o.p. A Holocaust survivor living in Israel tries to forget his experiences during the war despite his need to remember.

Katerina: A Novel. Random 1992 $17.50. ISBN 0-67940610-7. Story of an aging peasant woman who identifies with Jews during the Holocaust.

To the Land of the Cattails. Trans. by Jeffrey M. Green. Weidenfeld & Nicolson 1986 o.p.

The Retreat. Trans. by Dalya Bilu. NAL-Dutton 1984 o.p. A story about a hotel retreat near Vienna established to relieve Jews of their ethnic characteristics to enable them to assimilate into the general population. Demonstrates that escape from the world and one's identity is an experiment in futility.

Tzili: The Story of a Life. Trans. by Dalya Bilu. NAL-Dutton 1983 o.p. A surreal novel about the Jewish spirit. A collective symbol of exile "particularly as it is expressed in the figure of a woman symbolic of the Jewish people betrothed to God" (*Judaica Book News*).

BARASH, ASHER. 1889–1952

Asher Barash is a major Hebrew novelist and short story writer of historical fiction. His works illustrate the traditional life of Galician Jewry, combining realism and a certain heartiness with a touch of mysticism. Like other authors who immigrated to Israel, his works exhibit the tension of living on two planes, the Diaspora and the land of Israel.

SHORT STORY COLLECTIONS BY BARASH

A Golden Treasury of Jewish Tales. Trans. by Murray Rosten. Massada 1965 o.p. A collection of folklore.

Though He Slay Me. Trans. by Murray Rosten. Massada 1963 o.p. A collection of short stories.

NOVEL BY BARASH

Pictures from a Brewery. Trans. by Katie Kaplan. Bobbs 1974 o.p. A family saga set in a twentieth-century East Galician town in Poland. "The prose in translation is almost poetic; the style tends to offer the reader 'pictures' of people and places" (*AJL Bulletin*).

BARTOV, HANOKH. 1928–

Combining his journalistic skills with his talents as a novelist, Bartov's fiction reflects the traumatic experience of the Holocaust. The Israeli novelist also has written stories of his travels. He was a cultural attaché at the Israeli Embassy in London from 1966 to 1968.

NOVELS BY BARTOV

The Brigade (Wounds of Maturity). 1965. Trans. by David S. Segal. H. Holt & Co. 1969 o.p. A portrait of a soldier, a member of the Jewish Brigade of the British Army in World War II, who confronts both the victims and victimizers of the Holocaust. Received the Shlonsky Prize and additional critical acclaim.

Whose Little Boy Are You? 1970. Trans. by Hillel Halkin. Jewish Pubns. 1979 o.p. A story of a boy growing up in Palestine during the British Mandate Period. "Imbued with the mysticism of childhood—it is also full of the color of a small village distinctly resembling the author's own Petah Tikvah" (*AJL Bulletin*).

BERDICHEVSKY, MICAH JOSEPH (also known as Bin-Gorion). 1865–1921

The revolutionary figure in modern Hebrew literature rebelled against his Hasidic family of Medzibezh, in the former Soviet Union, and advocated aestheticism and extreme secularism in Jewish life. He called for a "transvaluation," in the Nietzschean sense, of Judaism and Jewish history that led Hebrew contemporary critics to attach the name "Aher" ("the alien" or "the apostate") to him. Berdichevsky, in turn, showed little appreciation for outstanding contemporary literary figures. His prolific writings can be divided into four groups: essays, fiction, folklore anthologies, and scholarship. Berdichevsky's works embody the ambivalent attitudes of his time toward traditional Judaism and the European culture of the Jewish intellectuals.

SHORT STORY COLLECTION BY BERDICHEVSKY

Mimekor Yisrael: Classical Jewish Folktales. Trans. by I. M. Lask. Ed. by Micha J. Bin-Gorion and Emanuel Bin-Gorion. Ind. U. Pr. 1990 $57.50. ISBN 0-253-31158-6. Abridged and annotated edition. A collection of national, religious, folk, and oriental tales collected by Berdichevsky. Introduction by Dan Ben-Amos.

BIALIK, HAYYIM NAHMAN (also Chaim). 1873–1934

Born of humble parentage in the Ukraine, Bialik went to Odessa in 1891, where he was a teacher and a publisher. He was influenced by early Zionist ideas, particularly those of AHAD HA-AM, and lived in various places in Europe, writing and teaching. By the time he settled in Tel Aviv in 1924, his fame had become legendary. Bialik brought about a revolution in Hebrew poetry, avoiding European trends and drawing inspiration from early Hebrew literature. In prophetic, rhetorical poems of national revival, Bialik identified himself with the fate of his people and called upon Jews to express pride in their heritage and to resist the Russian pogroms. The crises of his generation were not his only themes, however; he wrote many lyric poems of a personal character and about nature. He also wrote short stories, translated into Hebrew works by such authors as CERVANTES, SHAKESPEARE (see Vol. 1), HEINRICH HEINE, and others, and wrote a variety of essays on Hebrew literature, language, style, and culture. Israel's highest literary prize and an Israeli publishing house are named for Bialik.

POETRY BY BIALIK

Selected Poems. 1926. Ed. by I. Efros. Trans. by Maurice Samuel. Bloch 1965 o.p. Reissue of translations that originally appeared in *New Palestine.*

SHORT STORY COLLECTIONS BY BIALIK

And It Came to Pass. Hebrew Publ. 1938 o.p. A collection of retold legends and stories of Kings David and Solomon.

The Book of Legends. Trans. by William G. Braude. Pantheon 1992 $74.50. ISBN 0-80524113-2. Translation of *Sefer Haggadah.*

Shirot Bialik. Trans. by Steven L. Jacobs. *Hebraica/Judaica Bookshelf Ser.* Alpha Pub. Co. 1987 $22.95. ISBN 0-93377103-7. New and annotated translation; illustrations by Richard Russell.

BOOKS ABOUT BIALIK

Aberbach, David. *Bialik. Jewish Thinkers Ser.* Grove Pr. 1988 $15.95. ISBN 0-802110-62-2. Explores the social, literary, and historical background of the poet.

Breslaver, S. Daniel. *The Hebrew Poetry of Hayyim Nahman Bialik and Modern Jewish Theology. Jewish Studies Ser.* E. Mellen 1991 Vol. 10 $59.95. ISBN 0-7734-9627-0. Includes a discussion of Bialik's theological thinking.

Kurzweil, Baruch. *Bialik and Tshernichovsky.* Schocken 1971 o.p.

BRENNER, JOSEPH HAYYIM. 1881–1921

A novelist and short story writer, Brenner drew upon his years of wandering after leaving his traditional home in Novi Mlini (Ukraine) to focus on the problem of the uprooted fugitives from traditional Judaism. He exposed the anxieties, self-probing, and despair of the self-doubting Jewish intelligentsia. Such despair, ironically, infused his readers with a new creative life. Brenner is viewed as exercising powerful personal influence on his generation and the succeeding one. He was killed during the riots in the spring of 1921 near Tel Aviv.

NOVELS BY BRENNER

Breakdown and Bereavement. Trans. by Hillel Halkin. Jewish Pubns. 1975 o.p. Brenner's last novel. The story of Hefez, who searches for a spiritual home in Palestine. Set in an agricultural settlement prior to World War I, where many of Brenner's uprooted generation attempted to create a new life for themselves, having left their European ties behind.

Out of the Depths. Trans. by David Patterson. Westview Pr. 1992 $12.95. ISBN 0-81331427-5. A novel that focuses on a group of Russian immigrants in London who work for a Yiddish daily newspaper.

BOOK ABOUT BRENNER

Fleck, Jeffrey. *Character and Context: Studies in the Fiction of Abramovitsh, Brenner and Agnon.* Scholars Pr. GA 1984 $14.00. ISBN 0-685-09565-7

CARMI, T. (pseud. of Carmi Charny). 1925–

Born in New York City, Carmi grew up in a home where Hebrew was the mother tongue. Having lived as a child in Palestine, he immigrated in 1947. He has taught at Brandeis, Oxford, and Stanford, and was poet-in-residence at the Hebrew University of Jerusalem. Carmi has published 10 volumes of poetry in Hebrew. Thus, far, three of these works have appeared in English translation. In Israel he was awarded the Shlonsky Prize for Poetry, the Brenner Prize for Literature, and the Prime Minister's Award for Creative Writing. He was also awarded the 1982 Irving and Bertha Neuman Literary Award of New York University's Institute of Hebrew Culture and Education and the 1982 Kenneth B. Smilen/Present Tense Literary Award for his translation and editing work for *The Penguin Book of Hebrew Verse.*

POETRY BY CARMI

At the Stone of Losses. Trans. by Grace Schulman. *Jewish Poetry Ser.* U. CA Pr. bilingual ed. 1983 $11.95. ISBN 0-520-05107-6. Poems marked by Carmi's ideas of loss and Jewish tradition.

The Brass Serpent. Trans. by Dom Moraes. Ohio U. Pr. 1964 o.p.

The Penguin Book of Hebrew Verse. Viking Penguin 1981 $15.95. ISBN 0-14-042197-1. Spans the full range of Hebrew poetry from the Bible to contemporary works.

Selected Poems of T. Carmi and Dan Pagis. Trans. by Stephen Mitchell. Viking Penguin 1976 o.p. Carmi's imagery of passion coupled with Pagis's savage chaos.

FEIERBERG (FEUERBERG), MORDECAI ZE'EV. 1874–1899

Born in Russia, Feierberg wrote essays and novels in Hebrew. *Whither?* is regarded as one of the outstanding achievements in Hebrew fiction.

SHORT STORY COLLECTION BY FEIERBERG

Whither? and Other Stories. Trans. by Hillel Halkin. Jewish Pubns. 1973 o.p. Relates the struggles of Eastern European Jewish youths who are disappointed with the Enlightenment, yet not content with being traditional Jews.

GILBOA, AMIR. 1917–

Born in Radzywilow, Volhynia (Russia), Gilboa immigrated to Palestine in 1937. His poetry was first published while he was serving in the Jewish Brigade during World War II. His verse blends personal and national motifs reminiscent of BIALIK. In his poems Gilboa is able to use various levels of language to create a freshness in ancient words through the wonder of new experiences. He is considered a leading Israeli poet. In 1981 he shared the Israel Prize for Literature with YEHUDA AMICHAI.

POETRY BY GILBOA

The Light of Lost Sons. Trans. by Shirley Kaufman with Shlomith Rimmon. Persea Bks. 1979 o.p. Anthology of selected poems.

GOLDBERG, LEAH. 1911–1970

A Lithuanian-born poet and critic, Goldberg arrived in Tel Aviv in 1935. Shortly afterward, she published her first volume of poetry with the assistance of Abraham Shlonsky, her mentor, and the mentor of a circle of other modernist authors. A prolific writer, Goldberg primarily wrote poetry, but she also wrote several children's works, translated European classics into Hebrew, and was the author of a novel and a play. Her approach to writing was universal and only after the Holocaust did she write from within a Jewish framework.

Poetry by Goldberg

Lady of the Castle. Trans. by T. Carmi. Inst. for the Translation of Hebrew Lit. 1974 o.p. A revision of *Lady of the Manor* (1957), also translated by T. Carmi.

Selected Poems of Leah Goldberg. 1976. Trans. by Robert Friend. Panjandrum 1977 $6.00. ISBN 0-915572-273

Nonfiction by Goldberg

Russian Literature in the Nineteenth Century. Trans. by Hillel Halkin. Humanities 1976 o.p.

GOOR, BATYA. 1947–

Batya Goor teaches literature at a Jerusalem high school and is a book critic for the Israeli newspaper *Ha-Aretz.* She has written several murder mysteries, only one of which has been translated into English.

Novel by Goor

Saturday Morning Murder: A Psychoanalytic Case. HarpC 1992 $20.00. ISBN 0-06-019024-8. Story of a murder in the Jerusalem Psychoanalytic Institute. Focuses on the relationship between an isolationist Ashkenazi elite group and a Sephardic police inspector and the ethics of relationships between psychoanalysts and their patients.

GOURI, HAIM. 1923–

Haim Gouri is a novelist, poet, and journalist who was born in Tel Aviv and educated at the Kadoorie Agricultural School. He later studied at Hebrew University in Jerusalem and the Sorbonne in Paris. He served in the Palmah from 1942 to 1947 and was an officer during the War of Independence. In 1987 he received the Israel Prize for Literature. Gouri has published over 20 works of fiction and poetry, but only one, *The Chocolate Deal,* has been translated into English. He has also made several full-length documentary films.

Novel by Gouri

The Chocolate Deal. Trans. by Seymour Simckes. HR&W Schl. Div. 1968 o.p.

GROSSMAN, DAVID. 1954–

Born in Jerusalem, Grossman obtained a B.A. in philosophy and theater at Hebrew University and worked as a news editor and broadcaster for Kol Yisrael (Israel Radio). His concern with the Palestinian problem is reflected in his novels, *The Smile of the Lamb* and *The Yellow Wind,* and have helped to make him one of the most acclaimed Israeli writers of his generation. He was awarded the Prime Minister's Prize for Hebrew literature (1984) and the Israeli Publishers Association Prize for best Hebrew novel (1985).

NOVELS BY GROSSMAN

See Under Love. Trans. by Betsy Rosenberg. FS&G 1990 $27.95. ISBN 0-37425731-0. Set during and immediately after the Holocaust, focusing on an individual's struggle against meaninglessness.

Smile of the Lamb. Trans. by Betsy Rosenberg. FS&G 1990 $22.95. ISBN 0-67175025-9. The relationship between an Israeli soldier and an elderly half-blind half-crazy Arab who captures the imagination of the soldier with historical tales.

The Yellow Wind. Trans. by Haim Watzman. FS&G 1989 $17.95. ISBN 0-37429345-7. Reflects Grossman's impressions of the West Bank before the Intifada. Depicts the no-win situation of both Palestinians and Israelis.

HAREVEN, SHULAMITH. 1931–

Shulamith Hareven, who lives in Jerusalem, is one of the best-known writers in Israel and the only woman member of the Academy of Hebrew Language. In her work, she often brings the biblical past to life.

NOVELS BY HAREVEN

City of Many Days. Trans. by Hillel Halkin. Doubleday 1977 o.p.

The Miracle Hater. Trans. by Hillel Halkin. N. Point Pr. 1988 o.p.

Prophet. Trans. by Hillel Halkin. N. Point Pr. o.p.

SHORT STORY COLLECTION BY HAREVEN

Twilight and Other Stories. Trans. by Hillel Halkin and others. Mercury Hse. Inc. 1992 $10.95. ISBN 1-56279-012-9. Seven stories detailing the sorrow and loneliness that is life.

HAZAZ, HAIM. 1898–1973

Born in Kiev, Russia, Haim Hazaz moved to Palestine in 1921. His early works are based on themes of village life among European Jews during crucial changes that uprooted Jewish life. However, he is not restricted in era or location in his writings. His fiction encompasses wide geographic, historic, and ethnographic variations, from stories on the biblical period to works dealing with Yemenite and other Jewish settlers who came to Israel from Europe and non-European countries. Hazaz is ranked among the greatest Hebrew authors. He was awarded the Israel Prize for Literature in 1953.

NOVELS BY HAZAZ

The End of Days. Trans. by Dalya Bilu. Inst. for the Translation of Hebrew Lit. 1982 o.p.

Gates of Bronze. Jewish Pubns. 1975 o.p. A novel set in a fictional village in Russia during the crisis faced by the Jews who experienced the Bolshevik Revolution. Introduction by Robert Alter.

Mori Sa'id. Trans. by Ben Halpern. Abelard-Schuman 1956 o.p.

BOOK ABOUT HAZAZ

Bargad, Warren. *Ideas in Fiction: The Works of Hayim Hazaz.* Scholars Pr. GA 1982 $13.50. ISBN 0-89130-518-1. An intertextual analysis of Hazaz's work.

IBN GABIROL, SOLOMON BEN JUDAH. c.1021–1058

Solomon ben Judah ibn Gabirol, also known as Avicebron, was a Spanish poet and philosopher. He is thought to have been born in Málaga and later moved to Zaragoza (Saragossa). Orphaned at an early age, he wrote a number of elegies on the death of his parents. He devoted his life to philosophy and poetry and was dependent on the support of patrons. His most generous protector was

Jekuthiel ben Isaac ibn Hassan. Upon Jekuthiel's death, Gabirol composed a 200-verse elegy, which is considered to be one of the finest examples of secular medieval Jewish poetry. He was one of the earliest poets to use Arabic meter. All of his poems, regardless of length, are rhymed and end with the same syllable. He is believed to have died in Valencia.

POETRY BY IBN GABIROL

Selected Religious Poems of Solomon Ibn Gabirol. 1952. Trans. by Israel Zangwill. JPS Phila. 1974 $3.95. ISBN 0-8276-0060-7. From a critical text edition by Israel Davidson.

BOOK ABOUT IBN GABIROL

Loewe, Raphael. *Ibn Gabirol. Jewish Thinkers Ser.* Grove Pr. 1991. $9.95. ISBN 0-8021-3254-5. Analyzes the historical context of Ibn Gabirol's writings.

JUDAH HA-LEVI. 12th century

Poet and philosopher Judah Ha-Levi is thought to have been born in Toledo or Tudela, Spain. He came from a wealthy and cultured family and was educated in both Hebrew and Arabic. Ha-Levi's own poetry is one of the most important sources of information on his life. He was a physician to the rulers and nobles in Toledo. Ha-Levi strongly believed that the only place that Jews could have an ideal existence was in their own land of Israel, and he resolved eventually to emigrate there. In 1140, accompanied by his son-in-law Isaac ibn Ezra, he arrived in Alexandria, Egypt, and later traveled to Cairo. He enjoyed the scenery and friends there so much that he prolonged his stay. But, fearing he would never reach his homeland, he finally boarded a ship in Alexandria. Unfortunately, its departure was delayed by severe weather, and he is believed to have died before the ship left and then been buried in Egypt.

Ha-Levi is known to have written about 800 poems, including love poems, lyric poems, eulogies, and laments, and is noted for his poems of longing for the Land of Israel.

POETRY BY JUDAH HA-LEVI

Selected poems of Jehudah Halevi. Ed. by Heinrich Brody. Trans. by Nina Salaman. Ayer repr. of 1924 ed. $32.00. ISBN 0-405-05268-5. Poems describing the Jewish peoples' place in history and illuminating their religion.

Selected poems of Jehuda Halevi. Gordon Pr. 1972 $59.95. ISBN 0-8490-1019-5

BOOK ABOUT JUDAH HA-LEVI

Kayser, Rudolf. *The Life and Time of Jehudah Halevi.* Trans. by Frank Gaynor. Philosophical Library 1949 o.p.

KANIUK, YORAM. 1930–

A native Israeli, Kaniuk served in the Haganah and later in the War of Independence. He was in the United States from 1950 to 1961, sharpened his artistic abilities, and developed a nostalgic vision of Tel Aviv and a deep attachment for Jerusalem.

NOVELS BY KANIUK

Confessions of a Good Arab. 1984. Trans. by Dalya Bilu. Braziller 1988 $17.50. ISBN 0-8076-1210-3. A novel about a man who is part Jewish and part Arab who leaves Israel because of the pressures associated with his identity.

Himmo, King of Jerusalem. Trans. by Yosef Schacter. Atheneum 1969 o.p.

His Daughter. Trans. by Seymour Simckes. P. Halban UK 1988 o.p. The story of a retired general who reassesses his life after his daughter disappears.

Rockinghorse. Trans. by Richard Flantz. HarpC 1977 o.p. "Eloquent in its descriptive passages" (*AJL Bulletin*).

The Story of Great Aunt Shlomzion. 1978. Trans. by Zeva Shapiro. HarpC 1979 o.p.

SHORT STORY COLLECTIONS BY KANIUK

The Acrophile. 1960. Trans. by Zeva Shapiro. Atheneum 1961 o.p. A collection of short stories.

Adam Resurrected. 1971. HarpC 1978 o.p. Seven short vignettes and characterizations.

KISHON, EPHRAIM (formerly Ferenc Kishont). 1924–

An Israeli satirist, playwright, film writer, and director, Kishon is best known in the English-speaking world for his feuilletons, or political pamphlets. Born in Budapest, Kishon first began publishing humorous essays there. In 1949 he immigrated to Israel and began writing his columns for the Hebrew daily newspaper *Omer* and later for the daily *Ma'ariv* and the *Jerusalem Post.* Kishon is considered Israel's national humorist. He has been awarded the Israeli Nordau Prize, the Herzl Prize for Literature, and the Sokolov Prize for outstanding journalistic achievement.

WORKS BY KISHON

Blow Softly in Jericho. Trans. by Yohanan Goldman. Atheneum 1970 o.p.

The Funniest Man in the World: The Wild and Crazy Humor of Ephraim Kishon. Shapolsky Pubs. 1989 $12.95. ISBN 0-944007-47-3

Look Back, Mrs. Lot! 1960. Trans. by Yohanan Goldman. Viking Penguin 1964 o.p.

New York Ain't America. Trans. by Miriam Arad and Yohanan Goldman. Bantam 1982 o.p.

Wise Guy, Solomon. Trans. by Yohanan Goldman. Atheneum 1973 o.p. Kishon's "private war with the telephone, TV, taxes, traffic, politics, and women's fashions, to name a few of the targets of his freewheeling, wildly improbable response to the late twentieth century" (Jacket notes).

MEGGED, AHARON. 1920–

Megged's family immigrated to Palestine from Wloclavek, Poland, in 1926. Until 1950 he worked on a kibbutz in Haifa. His first short story collection, *Sea Winds,* was inspired by his life on kibbutz Sedot Yam. His prose often shows strong autobiographical emphasis. Megged's stories and novels have been translated into many languages.

NOVELS BY MEGGED

Asahel. 1980. Trans. by Robert Whitehill and Susan C. Lilly. Taplinger 1982 o.p. "Superb characterizations of the three main characters" and "many beautifully drawn surrounding portraits" (*Judaica Book News*).

Fortunes of a Fool. 1960. Trans. by Aubrey Hodes. Random 1962 o.p. The story of an antihero, tortured by thoughts of his shortcomings and terrified of ridicule, who perceives himself the only "good man" among a society of "wicked."

The Living on the Dead. 1970. Trans. by Misha Louvish. McCall 1971 o.p. Describes modern Israeli society in unflattering terms as the unfulfilled society of the first pioneers.

The Short Life: A Novel. Trans. by Miriam Arad. Taplinger 1980 o.p.

MICHAEL, SAMI. 1926–

Born in Baghdad, Sami Michael was active in the leftist underground in Iraq. In 1948 he fled to Iran, where he continued his fight against the Iraqi regime. He later emigrated to Israel, where he is a graduate of the departments of Psychology and Arabic at Haifa University. *Refuge* is the first of his novels to be translated into English.

Novel by Michael

Refuge. Trans. by Edward Grossman. JPS Phila. 1988 $19.95. ISBN 0-8276-0308-8. Chronicles the activities of various Jewish and Arab members of Israel's Communist Party during the first days of the 1973 war.

OZ, AMOS. 1939–

A native Israeli, Oz was born in Jerusalem. At age 14 he went to live in a kibbutz, where he eventually taught school. After taking up writing, Oz became the first contemporary Israeli author to earn an international reputation through his writing. His stories and novels are rooted in the rich life of Israel, frequently revealing a fondness for realistically conveyed history handled with graceful manipulation of plot, character, style, and mood. His work has been widely translated, and he has won numerous awards.

Novels by Oz

Black Box. Trans. by Nicholas de Lange. HarBraceJ 1988 $19.95. ISBN 0-15-112888-X. A novel dealing with the disintegration of a family in Jerusalem. Separated parents exchange letters dealing with their son.

Elsewhere Perhaps. 1966. Trans. by Nicholas de Lange. HarBraceJ 1973 $9.95. ISBN 0-15-628475-8. Captures the essence of kibbutz life in Metsudat Ram, near the Syrian border in the Golan Heights. "Portrays human relationships movingly, yet with detached, unsentimental realism" (*AJL Bulletin*).

The Hill of Evil Counsel. 1976. HarBraceJ 1991 $7.95. ISBN 0-15-640275-0. Recreates the fading days of the British Mandate in Jerusalem as the plot advances to the planning for the future and the anticipated revolt leading to the State of Israel. The title story along with the two other stories, *Mr. Levi* and *Longing*.

My Michael. 1972. Trans. by Nicholas de Lange. Random 1975 o.p. Focuses on the interplay between characters in the urban landscape of Jerusalem.

A Perfect Peace. 1984. Trans. by Hillel Halkin. HarBraceJ 1985 $16.95. ISBN 0-15-171696-X. Set on a kibbutz in the mid-1960s, focusing on the immigrant generation that built the country and the following generation making their lives there. "An excellent picture of life in Israel on the kibbutz" (*AJL Newsletter*).

Soumchi. Trans. by Penelope Farmer. HarpC 1981 o.p.

To Know a Woman. Trans. by Nicholas de Lange. HarBraceJ 1991 $19.95. ISBN 0-15-190499-5. A novel that focuses on a retired Mossad officer traumatized by his wife's sudden death in a highway accident, and his attempts to console himself by repairing things around the house.

Unto Death: "Crusade" and "Late Love." HarBraceJ 1978 $3.95. ISBN 0-15-693170-2. These novellas depict the atmosphere of hate in which Jews live today and as they did in the Middle Ages.

Short Story Collection by Oz

Where the Jackals Howl and Other Stories. Trans. by Nicholas de Lange and Philip Simpson. HarBraceJ 1981 o.p. The first collection of Oz's stories with the jackal symbolic of the dispenser of death.

WORKS BY OZ

In the Land of Israel. 1983. Trans. by Maurie Goldberg-Bartura. Random 1984 $9.00. ISBN 0-394-72728-2. Interviews conducted by Oz with people in all echelons of Israel's society accompanied by his observations and reflections.

The Slopes of Lebanon. Trans. by Maurie Goldberg-Bartura. HarBraceJ 1990 $18.95. ISBN 0-15-183090-8. A collection of Oz's writings in Israeli newspapers between 1982 and 1987 relating to the war in Lebanon and Israeli politics.

PAGIS, DAN. 1930–

Born in Rumania in 1930, Dan Pagis survived three years in a concentration camp before arriving in Israel in 1946. He now lives in Jerusalem, where he is a professor of medieval Hebrew literature at Hebrew University. As a scholar, Pagis has established himself by publishing distinguished editions of medieval Hebrew poetry. One of the leading poets of this generation, he has mastered and applied the tools of textual criticism to medieval Hebrew poetry. The mastery of the idiom shows itself in his own poems that echo the poets of Spain's Golden Age, such as JUDAH HA-LEVI, SOLOMON IBN GABIROL, and MOSES IBN EZRA. The Holocaust is the outstanding influence in his work. Imaginatively, "his art mirrors the agony of the survivor, resounds with the pangs and poetry of Jewish history, and grapples with genocide, grief, survival, and an attempt to perceive redemption" (*Judaica Book News*).

POETRY BY PAGIS

Points of Departure. 1981. Trans. by Stephen Mitchell. *Jewish Poetry Ser.* JPS Phila. 1982 $8.95. ISBN 0-8276-0201-4. More than 50 poems with English and Hebrew on facing pages.

Selected Poems. Trans. by Stephen Mitchell. Small Pr. Dist. repr. of 1972 ed. o.p.

Selected Poems of T. Carmi and Dan Pagis. Trans. by Stephen Mitchell. Penguin 1976 o.p. Introduction by W. L. Rosenthal.

Variable Directions. Trans. by Stephen Mitchell. N. Point Pr. 1989 o.p. Selected poetry.

WORK BY PAGIS

Hebrew Poetry of the Middle Ages and the Renaissance. U. CA. Pr. 1991 $22.50. ISBN 0-520-06547-6. With a foreword by Robert Alter.

SHAHAM, NATHAN. 1925–

Born in Tel Aviv, Shaham served in the Palmah and later in the War of Independence. He joined kibbutz Bet Alfa in the 1950s. He has written fiction, plays, and children's stories.

SHORT STORY COLLECTION BY SHAHAM

The Other Side of the Wall: Three Novellas. Trans. by Leonard Gold. JPS Phila. 1983 $13.95. ISBN 0-8276-0223-5. "The three tales in the present collection, *S/S Cairo City, The Other Side of the Wall,* and *The Salt of the Earth,* offer vivid refractions of Israeli society as experienced through the prism of the kibbutz" (*Judaica Book News*).

NOVEL BY SHAHAM

The Rosendorf Quartet: A Novel. Trans. by Dalya Bilu. Grove Pr. 1991 $19.95. ISBN 0-80211234-X. Set in Tel Aviv in the 1930s in the shadow of Arab uprisings and on the eve of World War II.

SHAHAR, DAVID. 1926–

A fifth-generation native of Israel, Shahar is rooted in the sights and sounds of Jerusalem. Few writers can capture as well the multiple ethnicity of the inhabitants of that ancient city. As a writer he is compelling. He has published 15 books, 5 of which have appeared in English or French translation. Shahar received the coveted Prix Médicis for the best foreign literature of the year in 1981 for *Day of the Countess*, the third volume in his trilogy *The Palace of Shattered Vessels*.

Novels by Shahar

His Majesty's Agent. Trans. by Dalya Bilu. HarBraceJ 1980 o.p. A compelling love story as well as an evocation of life in Mandate Palestine and the new State of Israel.

The Palace of Shattered Vessels. Trans. by Dalya Bilu. HM 1975 o.p.

Summer in the Street of the Prophets and A Voyage to Ur of Chaldees. Trans. by Dalya Bilu. Weidenfeld & Nicolson 1988 o.p.

Short Story Collection by Shahar

News From Jerusalem. Trans. by Dalya Bilu and others. HM 1974 o.p. Stories recreating city life in Jerusalem and its people during the past 60 years.

SHAMIR, MOSHE. 1921–

Born in Safed and raised in Tel Aviv, Shamir is a writer of novels, plays, short stories, and contemporary comment. His early works showed strong interest in the human concerns of social and national problems. As he begins to criticize his heroes' motives, he turns his attention to the psychological and social issues facing Israeli society. At one point, Shamir declared that history had usurped the place of religion in Jewish life, so, although committed to Israeli life, he frequently returns to the times of the first and second commonwealth. He shows strong narrative talent, writing in a high literary style with elaborate descriptions and dialogues.

Novels by Shamir

The Fifth Wheel. Benmir Bks. 1986 repr. of 1961 ed. $8.95. ISBN 0-917883-02-0

The Hittite Must Die. Trans. by Margaret Benaya. Hebrew Pub. 1978 repr. of 1964 ed. $5.95. ISBN 0-85222-231-9

The King of Flesh and Blood. Trans. by David Patterson. Hebrew Pub. 1958 $5.95. ISBN 0-85222-220-3. The original Hebrew version was issued in ten editions.

My Life with Ishmael. Biblio Dist. 1970 o.p.

SHAMMAS, ANTON. 1951–

Shammas is a Christian Arab citizen of Israel who writes novels, poetry, and nonfiction works in Hebrew. He draws heavily upon his heritage and the cultural distinctions among Arabs and Israelis in his work. His narrative style, with its epic scope and multiple levels of plot and theme, has been compared to that of Gabriel García Marquez.

Novel by Shammas

Arabesques. Trans. by Vivian Eden. HarpC 1989 repr. of 1988 ed. $8.95. ISBN 0-06-091-583-8. The story of a Christian Arab family in the Galilee. Begins in the nineteenth century in Syria and ends in Iowa City in the twentieth century.

TAMMUZ, BENJAMIN. 1919–

A native of Kharkov, Russia, Tammuz immigrated to Palestine in 1924. He attended a yeshiva in Tel Aviv while also studying at the Herzlia secondary school. He worked as a laborer in the British army camps and was a member of the Palmah. His work as a journalist involved assignments as a press censor for the Mandatory Government, as a reporter for a political party newspaper, and later as the editor of the weekend literary supplement of *Ha'aretz*. His earliest works were short stories of his childhood, focusing on the roots of Israeli life. His subsequent novels often reflect themes that are critical of modern society.

NOVELS BY TAMMUZ

Castle in Spain. Trans. by Joseph Schacter. Bobbs 1973 o.p. Story of the love affair and escapades of a Jewish man in Spain.

Minotaur. Trans. by Kim Parfitt and Mildred Budny. NAL-Dutton 1981 o.p. "The writing is spare and evocative of another era, a tribute to the translators. A beautiful work" (*AJL Newsletter*).

Requiem for Na'aman. Trans. by Mildred Budny and Yehuda Safran. New Amer. Lib. 1982 o.p. Spanning the years from 1895 to 1974, the novel dramatizes the counterpoint between sensitive individuals coming to terms with reality and the political emergence of the modern Israeli state.

TCHERNICHOVSKI (TCHERNICHOWSKY), SAUL. 1875–1943

The great modern Hebrew poet grew up in a pious home that was open to the influences of the *Haskalah* (Enlightenment) and *Hibbat Zion* (Lovers of Zion). The religious and secular education he received in his native village of Mikhailovka, Russia, was a source of inspiration to him. His further education in Odessa included the works of the great contemporary poets of his time and also Hebrew literary circles. Tchernichovski published his first poems in 1892, which were characterized by a variety of classical poetic forms. Tchernichovski's poetic works show the strong influences of various periods of his life. From 1905 to 1922, he was strongly influenced by the works of GOETHE and NIETZSCHE (see Vol. 4) and then earlier romantic tendencies of his poetry were replaced by outspoken and univeralistic views of life. His experiences during World War I and the Bolshevik Revolution left a deep impression on him. He left for Berlin, where his literary work provided a meager living. The Zionist General Council published a 10-volume jubilee edition of his works (1928–34) as a mark of appreciation to him. The years from 1931 to 1943 are considered his Eretz Israel Period. It was there that his lifelong relationship with Schocken Publishing developed. He later moved from Tel Aviv to Jerusalem, where he lived the remainder of his life. While Tchernichovski's earlier works tended toward universalism and humanism, his later works proved him to be the poet of the historic Jewish tragedy, the simplicity of Jewish folk life, and the Jewish national rebirth.

POETRY BY TCHERNICHOVSKI

Poems. Trans. by David Kuselewitz. Eked 1978 o.p.

BOOK ABOUT TCHERNICHOVSKI

Silberschlag, Eisig. *Saul Tschernichovsky: Poet of Revolt*. Cornell Univ. Pr. 1968 o.p. The most important study of Tchernichovski produced in English. Contains translations by Sholom J. Kahn and others as well as a bibliography.

VOGEL, DAVID. 1891–1944

David Vogel was a Hebrew poet and writer whose early years were spent in Vilnius and Lwow. In 1912 he settled in Vienna. His poems were printed individually in Hebrew-language journals long before they were published as an anthology. Although his poetry has not yet been translated, one of his two novels is available in English.

Novel by Vogel

Married Life: A Novel. Trans. by Dalya Bilu. BDD Promo Bk. 1988 $3.98. ISBN 0-7924-8318-9. Portrays the difficult marriage of a young Jewish writer and an Austrian baroness in prewar Vienna.

YEHOSHUA, A(BRAHAM) B. 1936–

Born in Jerusalem, Yehoshua served in the Israeli army and eventually settled in Haifa. Like Amos Oz, his fiction and dramatic works show a subtlety of portraiture and semisurrealist style that place them in the forefront of modern Israeli literature and his popularity among the English reading public continues to grow. He has been called a visionary in writer's garb.

Novels by Yehoshua

Five Seasons. Trans. by Hillel Halkin. NAL-Dutton 1990 $9.95. ISBN 0-525-48555-4. Describes a year in the life of Solomon Molho, a Sephardic Jew from Haifa, and his relations with five different women in specific locations and seasons of the year.

A Late Divorce. Doubleday 1984 o.p. A novel about nine days in the lives of the turbulent Kaminka family. An allegory of the modern Israeli condition.

The Lover. Doubleday 1978 o.p. Written against the background of the Yom Kippur War; tells of a husband's search for his wife's lover. Main characters fully developed and the scenes of Israel vividly portrayed.

Mr. Mani. Trans. by Hillel Halkin. Doubleday 1992 $22.50. ISBN 0-385-26792-4. Five generations of a Sephardic family and their journey from Greece to Jerusalem.

A Night in May. Trans. by Miriam Arad. Inst. for the Translation of Hebrew Lit. 1974 o.p. Confronts the fates of individuals with the fate of the nation on the eve of the Six Day War.

Short Story Collections by Yehoshua

The Continuing Silence of the Poet: The Collected Stories of A. B. Yehoshua. Viking Penguin 1991 $9.95. ISBN 0-14-014844-2. A collection of novellas and short stories.

Early in the Summer of 1970. Doubleday 1977 o.p. A collection of short stories focusing on the emotional violence that pervades the life of the people in Israel. "A very thoughtful picture of life in a beleaguered land" (*AJL Bulletin*).

Three Days and a Child. Trans. by Miriam Arad. Doubleday 1970 o.p. A collection of short stories including "A Poet's Continuing Silence," "Three Days and a Child," "Facing the Forests," "Flood Tide," and "A Long Hot Day, His Despair, His Wife, and His Daughter."

Work by Yehoshua

Between Right and Right. Doubleday 1981 o.p. Examines the old myths and new realities of Israel in this collection of essays on Zionism. "A thought-provoking and challenging book" (*Judaica Book News*).

ZACH, NATHAN. 1930–

Originally from Berlin, Zach's family immigrated to Palestine in 1935. He has been known since the mid-1950s as the leader of a Hebrew modernistic revolution. Although he is a major Israeli poet and has received the Bialik Prize, he is not as widely known as YEHUDA AMICHAI. The majority of his works have yet to appear in English.

POETRY BY ZACH

The Static Element, Selected Poems. Trans. by Nathan Zach and Shulamit Yasny-Starkman. Atheneum 1982 o.p. Zach's personal responses to World War II. Written between 1955 and 1979.

CHAPTER 3

Yiddish Literature

David G. Hirsch

> The Yiddish language—a language of exile, without a land, without frontiers, not supported by any government, a language which possesses no words for weapons, ammunition, military exercises, war tactics. . . . In a figurative way, Yiddish is the wise and humble language of us all, the idiom of frightened and hopeful humanity.
>
> —Isaac Bashevis Singer, *The Nobel Lecture*

Yiddish had its origins in the Middle Ages as the spoken vernacular of Ashkenazic Jews who settled in the Rhineland after migrating there from France and northern Italy. By 1750 the geographical spread of Yiddish encompassed Jews residing throughout northern, central, and eastern Europe. At its apogee, before 1939, an estimated 11 million people, spread over 6 continents, were native Yiddish speakers. Now only 2–3 million people worldwide speak Yiddish.

The sharp decline of the language can be attributed above all to the gradual linguistic assimilation of Yiddish speakers to prevailing national languages, and to the tragic Nazi onslaught, which eliminated about half of all Yiddish-speaking Jews, including more than a million children. In recent years Yiddish has shown signs of some vitality, particularly among Hasidic Jews and among university students returning to their ancestral language.

Linguists describe Yiddish as a complex "fusion language," composed of elements deriving from Middle High German, Hebrew, and Aramaic, and from various Romance and Slavic languages. Naturally, Yiddish is a product of the culture that nurtured it and is steeped in the rhythms of traditional Jewish prayer, talmudic study, and Hasidic storytelling—what Max Weinreich labeled "The Way of the Shas" (rabbinically steeped culture). With the onset of industrialization, urbanization, and massive emigration, the Yiddish language and its burgeoning secular literature could not help but be affected by the translation of Eastern European Jewry from an insular, small-town group to a socially and linguistically diversified population with offshoots the world over.

Yiddish literature is commonly divided into two periods: early and modern. Early Yiddish literature was largely produced and almost exclusively printed in Western Europe from the sixteenth to the eighteenth centuries. Although many of the works written during this period were religious in nature, this was not universally the case, as is demonstrated by one of the very oldest extant Yiddish books, the *Bove-bukh*, by Elye Bohur Levita Ashkenazi, published in Venice in 1540. This epic poem was a translation from the Italian *Buovo d'Antona*, which, in turn, was based on the Middle English romance *Sir Bevis of Hampton*.

Nevertheless, the most widely disseminated Yiddish book of the early period was the *Tsene-urene* collection of Bible stories and commentaries, written by Jacob ben Isaac, Ashkenazi of Janow, at the end of the sixteenth century. Much religious literature in Yiddish was aimed explicitly at a female readership, because it was assumed that women (unlike men) were not literate in Hebrew. Indeed, Yiddish literature did not entirely lose its stigma as a literature of women and unlettered men until the end of the nineteenth century.

The groundwork for modern Yiddish literature was laid in part by the early Hasidim, whose leaders preached, sang, and spun their stories in the everyday language of their followers. The symbolistic *Tales* of NAHMAN OF BRATSLAV, published in 1815, are the outstanding example of this Hasidic literature, and they enjoy a sizable audience to this day.

Half a century after Rabbi Nahman's *Tales* were first published, a new, secular literature arose, under the influence of the *Haskalah* (Enlightenment) movement. There were popular "dime novelists" like I. M. Dik and N. M. Shaykevitsh; at the same time, the three great Yiddish literary pioneers, S. Y. Abramovitsh, who adopted the pen name MENDELE MOKHER SEFORIM (Mendele the Book Peddler), I. L. PERETZ, and S. Rabinovitsh, better known as SHOLOM ALEICHEM, now flourished. All three of these Yiddish "classicists" began their literary careers in Hebrew, with Peretz writing in Polish as well.

Peretz was the only one of this literary trio to raise a generation of disciples. From the 1890s until his death, Peretz held court in Warsaw, and many writers who achieved fame after his death visited him for words of advice and encouragement. One such writer was SHOLEM ASCH, who until the emergence of I. B. SINGER was the Yiddish author whose works were by far the most widely available in English.

Twentieth-century Yiddish literature includes realism, naturalism, neoromanticism, symbolism, futurism, expressionism, stream-of-consciousness, proletarian fiction, and socialist realism. One circle of New York-based modernist poets known as *Di Yunge* (The Young Ones), active during and shortly after World War I, was succeeded by the introspective *In Zikh* group, one of whose leading exponents was JACOB GLATSTEIN.

The unfolding tragedy of European Jewry (the Holocaust) put an end to much avant-garde experimentation among the surviving Yiddish authors, who were suddenly deprived of a younger generation of readers. Nevertheless, the post-Holocaust period witnessed a last great flowering of Yiddish fiction and poetry, much of it devoted to an exploration of the catastrophe theme. It was during the two decades after the end of World War II that ABRAHAM SUTZKEVER, ROKHL KORN, CHAIM GRADE, and I. B. Singer were at the peak of their powers, creating enduring poems, short stories, and novels.

The first Yiddish author to have his works translated into English was the New York "sweatshop poet" MORRIS ROSENFELD, whose *Songs from the Ghetto* was published in 1898. Since then the quantity of translations and authors translated has steadily increased—a trend that has greatly accelerated during the past decade. The recent growth of academic interest in Yiddish studies has seen the emergence of critical editions in translation, aimed at a university-based audience. Students of Yiddish literature, as well as general readers, will clearly benefit, should the current proliferation of translations continue. It is to be devoutly desired, moreover, that publishers will see fit to reissue important titles that have gone out of print all too soon after their initial appearance.

GENERAL READING

Coldoff, Harry. *A Yiddish Dictionary in Transliteration*. Proclaim 1988 o.p. Includes some of the most essential Yiddish idioms, as well as basic vocabulary.

Dawidowicz, Lucy S. *From That Place and Time: A Memoir, 1938–1947.* Norton 1989 $21.95. ISBN 0-393-02674-4. About the murdered Jews of Vilna. Reconstructs the past through personal recollections.

Dobroszycki, Lucjan, and Barbara Kirshenblatt-Gimblett. *Image Before My Eyes: A Photographic History of Jewish Life in Poland, 1864–1939.* Schocken 1979 $19.95. ISBN 0-685-04524-2. A richly illustrated photo album, including an informative introduction on Polish-Jewish history and culture during the period covered.

Dubnow, Simon. *History of the Jews in Russia and Poland from the Earliest Times Until the Present Day.* 3 vols. Ktav o.p. Classic survey of the history of Eastern European Jewry by one of its pioneer historians. Reprinted from the 1916 Jewish Publication Society of America edition.

Fein, Richard J. *The Dance of Leah: Discovering Yiddish in America.* Assoc. Univ. Prs. 1986 $22.50. ISBN 0-8453-4803-5. A melange of memory, meditation, and commentary based on the specter of Yiddish in Fein's life.

Fishman, Joshua A. *Yiddish: Turning to Life.* Benjamins North Am. 1991 $110.00. ISBN 1-55619-111-1

Galvin, Herman. *The Yiddish Dictionary Sourcebook.* Ktav 1983 $25.00. ISBN 0-87068-715-8. A transliterated guide to the Yiddish language.

Howe, Irving. *The World of Our Fathers.* 1976. HarBraceJ 1989 $34.95. ISBN 0-15-146353-0. The story of Eastern European Jews in the United States, their struggles, achievements, and contributions to American life. Combines a thorough knowledge of the American scene with an intimate familiarity with American Jewish life and letters.

Katz, David. *Grammar of the Yiddish Language.* Duckworth 1987 $30.00. ISBN 0-715-62161-0. Basic sourcebook of the Yiddish language.

Mason, Jackie, and Ira Berkow. *How to Talk Jewish.* St. Martin 1990 $13.95. ISBN 0-312-05445-9. Humorous account of learning English as a native Yiddish speaker.

Prager, Leonard. *Yiddish Culture in Britain: A Guide.* P. Lang Pubs. 1990 $103.80. ISBN 3-631-41978-3. Attempts to place Yiddish culture in Britain within a historical context.

Rosten, Leo Calvin. *The Joys of Yinglish. An Exuberant Dictionary of Yiddish Words, Phrases, and Locutions.* McGraw 1989 $29.95. ISBN 0-07-053987-1. Built upon *The Joys of Yiddish* (1968) and *Hooray for Yiddish* (1982).

Sanders, Ronald. *The Downtown Jews: Portraits of an Immigrant Generation. Dover Books on New York City Ser.* Dover 1987 $10.95. ISBN 0-486-25510-7

Steinmetz, Sol. *Yiddish and English: A Century of Yiddish in America.* U. of Ala. Pr. 1986 $17.55. ISBN 0-8173-0258-1. Examines the interaction of Yiddish and English in America.

Stenberg, Peter. *Journey to Oblivion: The End of the East European Yiddish and German Worlds.* U. of Toronto Pr. 1991 $35.00. ISBN 0-8020-5861-2. Considers the decline of the close relation between Yiddish and German in Eastern Europe.

Vishniac, Roman. *Polish Jews: A Pictorial Record.* Schocken 1968 $7.95. ISBN 0-8052-0360-5. Some 31 photographs, many of which are reproduced in the author's 1983 album, *A Vanished World,* published by FS&G.

Wisse, Ruth R. *A Little Love in Big Manhattan: Two Yiddish Poets.* HUP 1988 $25.00. ISBN 0-674-53659-2

Zborowski, Mark, and Elizabeth Herzog. *Life Is with People: The Culture of the Shtetl.* Schocken 1962 $9.95. ISBN 0-8052-0020-7. Introduction by Margaret Mead. A classic anthropological study of the now-disappeared small-town life of Eastern European Jewry.

HISTORY AND CRITICISM

Aaron, Frieda W. *Bearing the Unbearable: Yiddish and Polish Poetry in the Ghettos and Concentration Camps. SUNY Ser. in Modern Jewish Literature and Culture.* State U. NY Pr. 1990 $34.50. ISBN 0-7914-0247-9. In-depth survey of Yiddish poetry by Polish authors written between 1939 and 1945.

Abramowicz, Dina, ed. *Yiddish Literature in English Translation: Books Published 1945–1967*. YIVO Inst. 1968 $5.00. ISBN 0-914512-11-0

———. *Yiddish Literature in English Translation: List of Books in Print*. YIVO Inst. 1976 $7.50. ISBN 0-914512-36-6. With the above, two essential tools for the compilation of a comprehensive bibliography of Yiddish works in English translation.

Birnbaum, S. A. *Yiddish: A Survey and a Grammar*. Bks. Demand repr. of 1979 ed. $107.90. ISBN 0-8357-6357-9. Based in part on lectures delivered at the University of London in 1934 and 1938, this work includes a topical overview of Jewish languages, along with a history and a grammar of Yiddish.

Bluestein, Gene. *Anglish-Yinglish: Yiddish in American Life and Literature*. U. of Ga. Pr. 1989 $20.25. ISBN 0-8203-1083-2. Analyzes the process of linguistic assimilation between the Yiddish and English languages.

Dawidowicz, L. S., ed. *For Max Weinreich on His Seventieth Birthday: Studies in Jewish Language, Literature and Society*. Mouton 1964 $110.00. ISBN 0-686-22430-2. Contributions to Yiddish linguistics and literature and Jewish sociology, by scholars paying tribute to a major figure in Yiddish studies.

Doroshkin, Milton. *Yiddish in America: Social and Cultural Foundations*. Fairleigh Dickinson 1975 $32.50. ISBN 0-8386-7453-4. Covers the period 1880–1920 and concentrates on two major institutions of Eastern European Jewry: the Yiddish press and the *landsmanshaftn*, or fraternal organizations.

Feinsilver, Lillian M. *The Taste of Yiddish*. A. S. Barnes 1980 o.p. Includes observations on the general characteristics of the language, lists of idiomatic expressions with their translations, and a study of mutual influences between Yiddish and English.

The Field of Yiddish: Studies in Yiddish Language, Folklore, and Literature. Ed. by Uriel Weinreich. Lexik Hse. repr. of 1954 ed. $12.50. ISBN 0-936368-02-0. Scholarly contributions dealing with the Yiddish language in its historical development, dialects, and onomastics, as well as with Yiddish literature and folklore.

Fishman, Joshua A. *Ideology, Society and Language: The Odyssey of Nathan Birnbaum*. Karoma 1987 $45.00. ISBN 0-89720-082-9

———, ed. *Never Say Die: A Thousand Years of Yiddish in Jewish Life and Letters. Contributions to the Sociology of Language Ser.* Mouton 1981 $63.35. ISBN 90-279-7978-2. Includes articles on the history of Yiddish and the sociology, culture, and political status of Yiddish-speaking Jews. Most articles in English, but some in Yiddish.

———, ed. *Yiddish in America: Socio-Linguistic Description and Analysis*. Res. Inst. Inner Asian Studies 1965 $8.00. ISBN 0-87750-110-6. Sociocultural background, periodization, and statistical data on Yiddish in the United States.

Fried, Lewis, ed. *Handbook of American-Jewish Literature: An Analytical Guide to Topics, Themes, and Sources*. Greenwood 1988 $75.00. ISBN 0-313-24593-2. Index of Jewish authors in the United States.

Geipel, John. *Mame-Loshn: The Making of Yiddish*. Flatiron 1982 o.p. Brief survey of the Yiddish language, its history, and its idioms.

Goldberg, Judith. *Laughter through Tears: The Yiddish Cinema*. Fairleigh Dickinson 1983 $26.50. ISBN 0-8386-3074-X. Research on the condition, content, and background of Yiddish film throughout the world.

Goldman, Eric A. *Visions, Images and Dreams: Yiddish Film Past and Present*. Ed. by Diane Kirkpatrick. UMI Res. Collect 1983 $39.95. ISBN 0-962204-0-1. Two academic surveys of Yiddish-language films with extensive bibliographies and filmographies.

Goldsmith, Emanuel S. *Architects of Yiddishism at the Beginning of the Twentieth Century: A Study in Jewish Cultural History*. Fairleigh Dickinson 1976 $32.50. ISBN 0-8386-1384-5. The Yiddish language and cultural movement and its significance for Jewish life.

Hadda, Janet. *Passionate Women, Passive Men: Suicide in Yiddish Literature. SUNY Series in Modern Jewish Literature and Culture*. State U. NY Pr. 1988 $59.50. ISBN 0-88706-595-3. Scholarly analysis of suicide in Yiddish literature. Attempts to describe the ethos of Jewish society in literature.

Harshav, Benjamin. *The Meaning of Yiddish.* U. CA Pr. 1990 $29.95. ISBN 0-520-05947-6. Discusses the origins and derivations of the Yiddish language and the history of Yiddish literature. Includes bibliographic references.

Kahn, Yitzhak. *Portraits of Yiddish Writers.* Vantage 1979 o.p. Essays on 22 writers including M.S. Mendele, I. L. Peretz, Sholom Aleichem, D. Bergelson, J. Opatoshu, H. Leivick, C. Grade, A. Sutzkever, I. Manger, J. Glatstein, R. Korn, E. Greenberg, and others.

Kumove, Shirley. *Words like Arrows: A Collection of Yiddish Folk Sayings.* Bks. Demand $74.90. ISBN 0-8357-6883-8. Representative collection of Eastern European Jewish proverbs. Bilingual edition (original and transliterated Yiddish, English translations).

Liptzin, Sol. *A History of Yiddish Literature.* Jonathan David 1985 $12.95. ISBN 0-8246-0307-9. Historical survey, covering the development of Yiddish literature from medieval times through the post-World War II period.

Madison, Charles A. *Yiddish Literature: Its Scope and Major Writers.* Continuum 1968 o.p. A historical survey of the development of Yiddish literature from the beginning to Mendele with individual treatment of "the work of fourteen major writers. . . . Major novels, plays and poems are outlined and discussed critically" (Publisher's note).

Mirror of a People: Canadian Jewish Experience in Poetry and Prose. Jewish Educational Publishers of Canada 1985 $9.95. ISBN 0-9206-5700-7. Significant body of poetry, fiction, and prose narrative formed through the assimilation of Jewish culture into Canadian culture.

Pinsker, Sanford. *Schlemiel as Metaphor: Studies in the Yiddish and American Jewish Novel.* S. Ill. U. Pr. 1991 $29.95. ISBN 0-8093-1581-5. A study of a comic figure who is conceived as a metaphor of the Jewish and human condition. The works of Mendele, Sholom Aleichem, I. B. Singer, and American-Jewish writers are analyzed.

Roback, A. A. *The Story of Yiddish Literature.* Gordon 1972 $300.00. ISBN 0-87968-084-9. The first comprehensive survey in English since 1899. Includes a bibliography of translations and other works in English on the subject.

Rosten, Leo. *Hooray for Yiddish.* S & S 1984 $10.00. ISBN 0-671-43026-2. Dictionary of Yiddish-English hybrids, phrasings, and Yinglish expressions.

______. *The Joys of Yiddish.* S & S 1991 $5.95. ISBN 0-671-72813-X. Lexicons of common Yiddish expressions, aimed at a popular readership, that also seek to illuminate.

Rubin, Ruth. *Voices of a People: The Story of Yiddish Folksong.* JPS Phila. 1979 repr. of 1973 ed. $12.95. ISBN 0-8276-0121-2. Covers historical development from the sixteenth century to the present. Provides content analysis and music to selected songs.

Sandrow, Nahma. *Vagabond Stars: A World History of Yiddish Theater.* Limelight Edns. 1986 $13.95. ISBN 0-87910-060-5. "A lively, vital chronicle of the life and times of Yiddish theater, through five continents and more than 300 years" (Publisher's note).

Schulman, Elias. *The Holocaust in Yiddish Literature.* Workmen's Circle 1983 $4.00. ISBN 0-318-20364-2. Brief survey of a central motif in post-World War II Yiddish literature.

Soltes, Mordecai. *The Yiddish Press: An Americanizing Agency.* Ayer 1969 repr. of 1925 ed. $15.00. ISBN 0-405-01474-0. Thorough study based on an analysis of primary sources.

Waxman, Meyer. *A History of Jewish Literature.* 6 vols. Cornwall Bks. $50.00. ISBN 0-8453-8640-9. Historical survey of Jewish literature in several languages, from biblical times to the twentieth century. Deals extensively with Yiddish literature.

Weinreich, Max. *History of the Yiddish Language.* Trans. by Shlomo Noble and Joshua A. Fishman. YIVO Inst. 1993 $45.00. ISBN 0-914512-39-0. A seminal work that treats the vocabulary, phonology, and grammar of Yiddish, their historical development, and the symbiotic relationship of the language with the traditional religious culture of Ashkenazic Jewry. Based on the first two volumes of the four-volume Yiddish original, published in 1973, it includes the complete narrative and an exhaustive index, but omits the footnotes and bibliography.

Weinreich, Uriel, and Beatrice Weinreich. *Yiddish Language and Folklore: A Selective Bibliography for Research.* Mouton 1959 o.p. Includes works both in English and Yiddish, and covers books as well as contributions to journals.

Wiener, Leo. *The History of Yiddish Literature in the Nineteenth Century.* Hermon 1973 repr. of 1899 ed. o.p. Introduction by Elias Schulman. "The first introduction to Yiddish literature for the English reader. . . . Though now slightly dated [it] remains a classic handbook" (Publisher's note).

Wisse, Ruth R. *The Schlemiel as Modern Hero.* U. Ch. Pr. 1980 $3.95. ISBN 0-226-90312-5. Study of a representative motif in modern Yiddish fiction, which reappears in a different disguise in contemporary American literature.

Zinberg, Israel. *A History of Jewish Literature.* 12 vols. Ktav $315.00. ISBN 0-685-53782-X. Volume 7, *Old Yiddish Literature from Its Origins to the Haskalah Period.* "An account of the rich literature produced in this language from its origins in the eleventh century to the dawn of the era of Enlightenment" (Publisher's note). With valuable bibliographic notes, a glossary of Hebrew and other terms, and an index.

COLLECTIONS

Ausubel, Nathan, ed. *A Treasury of Jewish Folklore.* Crown 1989 $17.95. ISBN 0-517-50293-3. Comprehensive treatment of Jewish folklore, its origins, and its significance to the Jewish religion.

______, ed. *A Treasury of Jewish Humor.* M. Evans 1988 $14.95. ISBN 0-87131-546-7. A rich selection of material from Yiddish sources.

Betsky, Sarah Z., ed. and trans. *Onions and Cucumbers and Plums: Forty-six Yiddish Poems in English. Granger Index Repr. Ser.* Ayer repr. of 1958 ed. $29.95. ISBN 0-8143-1080-X. Selections from modern Yiddish poets, with Yiddish and English on opposite pages.

Cooperman, Jehiel B., and Sara H. Cooperman, trans. *America in Yiddish Poetry: An Anthology.* Exposition Pr. 1967 o.p. Poems about the United States and American life.

Frank, Helena, trans. and comp. *Yiddish Tales.* Ed. by Moses Rischin. Ayer 1975 repr. of 1912 ed. $47.50. ISBN 0-405-06755-0. Includes stories by 20 Yiddish writers.

Gaster, Moses, trans. *Ma'aseh Book: Book of Jewish Tales and Legends.* JPS Phila. 1981 o.p. A popular collection of talmudic and midrashic tales from early Yiddish literature.

Glatstein, Jacob. *Anthology of Holocaust Literature.* Temple Bks. Atheneum 1972 repr. of 1968 ed. $11.95. ISBN 0-689-70343-0. Most of the materials included are translations from the Yiddish.

Goldberg, Isaac, ed. *Six Plays of the Yiddish Theatre.* Gordon Pr. 1977 $59.95. ISBN 0-8490-2611-3.

Harshav, Benjamin, and Barbara Harshav, eds. *American Yiddish Poetry: a Bilingual Anthology.* U. CA Pr. 1986 $60.00. ISBN 0-520-04842-3. Contains twentieth century poetry written between 1918 and 1974. Also examines the background and achievements of Yiddish poets.

Howe, Irving, and Eliezer Greenberg, eds. *Ashes out of Hope: Fiction by Soviet Yiddish Writers.* Schocken 1987 $4.95. ISBN 0-8052-0605-1. Includes D. Bergelson, "Joseph Schur," "The Hole through Which Life Slips," "Civil War"; Moyshe Kulbak, "Zelmenyaner"; and Der Nister, "Under a Fence."

______. *A Treasury of Yiddish Poetry.* H. Holt & Co. 1972 o.p. An important effort, making outstanding Yiddish poets available to the English reader.

______. *A Treasury of Yiddish Stories.* Viking Penguin 1990 $17.00. ISBN 0-14-014419-6. Comprehensive selection, covering Yiddish writers of the nineteenth and twentieth centuries, with a valuable introduction by Irving Howe.

______. *Voices from the Yiddish: Essays, Memoirs, Diaries.* Schocken 1975 o.p. An anthology arranged by topics, such as "The Founding Fathers," "East European Scene," "A Few Central Themes and Figures," "Jewishness in America," "The Holocaust," "Yiddish: Language and Literature."

______. *Yiddish Stories Old and New.* Avon 1977 o.p. Selection of stories by Sholom Aleichem, I. L. Peretz, A. Reisen, I. D. Berkowitz, I. Metzker, I. Manger, J. Opatoshu, and I. B. Singer.

Howe, Irving, Ruth R. Wisse, and Khone Shmeruk, eds. *The Penguin Book of Modern Yiddish Verse.* Viking Penguin 1988 $14.00. ISBN 0-14-009472-5. Traces the development of modern Yiddish poetry. Includes the original Yiddish texts as well as brief biographical sketches.

Kramer, Aaron, ed. and trans. *A Century of Yiddish Poetry.* Cornwall Bks. 1989 $24.95. ISBN 0-8453-4815-9. Study of pre-twentieth century poets. Includes the works of minor poets, left-wing socialists, and labor zionists.

Landis, Joseph C., ed. and trans. *The Great Jewish Plays.* Horizon Pr. AZ 1972 o.p. Contains S. Ansky, *The Dybbuk;* Hirshbein, *Green Fields;* D. Pinsky, *King David and His Wives;* H. Leivick, *The Golem.*

Leftwich, Joseph, ed. *An Anthology of Modern Yiddish Literature.* Mouton 1974 $22.70. ISBN 90-2793-496-7. Includes stories, essays, plays, and poems of 42 Yiddish writers of the pre- and post-1939 period. With an introduction, biographical notes, glossary, and bibliography.

______, trans. and ed. *The Golden Peacock: A Worldwide Treasury of Yiddish Poetry.* A. S. Barnes 1961 o.p. A comprehensive edition, with an introduction by Leftwich.

Lifson, David S., trans. and ed. *Epic and Folk Plays of the Yiddish Theater.* Fairleigh Dickinson 1975 $32.50. ISBN 0-8386-1082-X. Contains P. Hirshbein, *Farvorfn vinkl;* H. Leivick, *Hirsh Lekert;* L. Kobrin, *Yankel Boyla;* Y. Aksenfeld, *Recruits.*

Metzker, Isaac, ed. *A Bintel Brief.* Trans. by Bella S. Metzker and Diana S. Levy. Shocken 1990 $10.00. ISBN 0-8052-0980-8. A collection of letters that reflect the life and problems of Yiddish-speaking immigrants from Eastern Europe.

Neugroschel, Joachim, trans. *The Shtetl.* Overlook Pr. 1990 $25.00. ISBN 0-87951-356-X. Includes 20 stories and novellas, in 4 parts: "The Religious Roots," "The Jewish Enlightenment," "Tradition and Modernism," "War, Revolution, Destruction."

______, trans. *Yenne Velt: The Great Works of Jewish Fantasy and Occult.* Pocket Bks. 1978 o.p. Includes works ranging from the medieval *Ma'aseh Book* to the stories of I. B. Singer. Among other authors represented are A. B. Gotlober, Mendele Mokher Seforim, I. L. Peretz, S. Ansky, Der Nister (Pinkhes Kahanovitsh), M. Kulbak, and D. Bergelson, plus tales of Rabbi Nahman of Bratslav.

Schwartz, Howard, and Anthony Rudolf, eds. *Voices within the Ark: The Modern Jewish Poets.* Avon 1980 $15.95. ISBN 0-380-76109-2. Authors active on all continents and in many languages represented in this anthology are 44 Yiddish poets.

Whitman, Ruth. *An Anthology of Modern Yiddish Poetry.* Workmen's Circle 1979 repr. of 1966 ed. $4.00. ISBN 0-686-29291-X. Included in this collection are works by 14 Yiddish poets.

Wisse, Ruth R. *A Shtetl and Other Yiddish Novellas.* Wayne St. U. Pr. 1986 $34.95. ISBN 0-8143-1848-7. Contains five novels by masters of Yiddish letters. I. M. Weissenberg, *A Shtetl;* D. Bergelson, *At the Depot;* S. Ansky, *Behind a Mask;* J. Opatoshu, *Romance of a Horse Thief;* Mendele Mokher Seforim, *Of Bygone Days.* Translated for the first time into English, with an introduction that traces the development of modern Yiddish literature in the late nineteenth and early twentieth centuries.

CHRONOLOGY OF AUTHORS

Jacob ben Isaac of Janow. d. 1620?
Gluckel of Hameln. 1645–1724
Nahman of Bratslav. 1772–1811
Zunser, Eliakum. 1835–1913
Mendele Mokher Seforim. 1836–1917
Linetski, Isaac Joel. 1839–1915
Peretz, Yitskhok Leybush. 1852–1915
Sholom Aleichem. 1859–1916
Cahan, Abraham. 1860–1951
Rosenfeld, Morris. 1862–1923
Ansky, S. 1863–1920
Pinsky, David. 1872–1959
Reisin, Avraham. 1876–1953
Shapiro, Lamed. 1878–1948

Blinkin, Meir. 1879–1915
Asch, Sholem. 1880–1957
Mani-Leib. 1883–1953
Bergelson, David. 1884–1952
Der Nister. 1884–1950
Halpern, Moyshe-Leyb. 1886–1932
Opatoshu, Joseph. 1886–1954
Kreitman, Esther. 1891–1954
Singer, I(srael) J(oshua). 1893–1944
Glatstein, Jacob. 1896–1971
Korn, Rokhl. 1898–1982
Rontsh, Isaac Elchonon. 1899–1985
Rabon, Israel. 1900–1941
Khaver-Paver. 1901–1964
Manger, Itzik. 1901–1969
Singer, I(saac) B(ashevis). 1904–1991
Tsanin, Mordekhai. 1906–
Grade, Chaim. 1910–1982
Bryks, Rachmil. 1912–1964
Sutzkever, Abraham. 1913–

ANSKY, S. (pseud. of Shloyme Zaynvil Rapaport). 1863–1920

Born in a small town in Belorussia, Ansky studied in traditional Jewish schools and was also self-educated. His writing reflects his democratic ideas and love for the poor and underprivileged, which also prompted his interest in folk psychology and its artistic reflection—folklore. Ansky gave a highly poetic and symbolic interpretation to a popular folk belief in his play *The Dybbuk*. The story of a dead soul that enters the body of a living person as a malevolent spirit, the play is a classic of Yiddish theater.

PLAY BY ANSKY

The Dybbuk: A Play. Trans. by S. Morris Engel. Regnery Gateway 1979 repr. of 1974 ed. $8.95. ISBN 0-89526-904-X

WORK BY ANSKY

The Dybbuk and Other Writings. Ed. by David G. Roskies. Trans. by Golda Werman. Pantheon 1992 $24.50. ISBN 0-8052-4111-6. With an introduction by David G. Roskies.

ASCH, SHOLEM. 1880–1957

Asch, one of the major figures in Yiddish letters, was born in Kutno, near Warsaw, Poland. He began writing in 1901, first in Hebrew, then in Yiddish. His early, quietly humorous stories of Jewish small-town life brought Yiddish literature to international notice. His epic novels and plays dealt with the contemporary scene and the Jewish experience on a worldwide scale. The range and reach of his talent were wide; his collected works appeared in Yiddish in 29 volumes. Much of it was translated into English, but some translations are now out of print.

NOVELS BY ASCH

East River. Trans. by A. H. Gross. Carroll & Graf 1983 repr. of 1946 ed. $8.95. ISBN 0-88184-280-X. A novel about life in New York.

Kiddush ha-Shem: An Epic of 1648. Trans. by Rufus Learsi. *Modern Jewish Experience Ser.* Ayer 1975 repr. of 1926 ed. $21.00. ISBN 0-405-06691-0

Mary, The Nazarene, The Apostle. 1949. Carroll & Graf 1985 $10.95. ISBN 0-88184-141-2. A trilogy; *The Nazarene* is part 1, *The Apostle* part 2, and *Mary* part 3.

Mother. 1925. Trans. by Nathan Ausubel. AMS Pr. repr. of 1930 ed. $12.50. ISBN 0-404-00408-3.

The Nazarene (Der Man fun Natseres). 1939. Carroll & Graf 1984 $21.95. ISBN 0-88184-048-3. Part 1 of a trilogy; see above for other tales (*Mary* and *The Apostle*).

Three Cities: Petersburg, Warsaw, Moscow. Trans. by Edwin Muir. Carroll & Graf 1983 repr. of 1933 ed. $10.50. ISBN 0-88184-009-2

Short Story Collections by Asch

In the Beginning: Stories from the Bible. 1914. Trans. by Caroline Cunningham. Schocken 1966 o.p.

Children of Abraham: The Short Stories of Sholem Asch. 1939. Trans. by Maurice Samuel. Irvington 1982 repr. of 1942 ed. $27.50. ISBN 0-8369-3792-9

Tales of My People. Trans. by Meyer Levin. *Short Story Index Repr. Ser.* Ayer repr. of 1948 ed. $20.00. ISBN 0-8369-3609-4

Play by Asch

Mottke the Thief. 1916. Trans. by Willa Muir and Edwin Muir. Greenwood repr. of 1935 ed. $38.50. ISBN 0-8371-2953-2

Works by Asch

Sabbatai Zevi. Trans. by Florence Whyte and George R. Noyes. Greenwood 1974 repr. of 1930 ed. $55.00. ISBN 0-8371-7449-X

Salvation (Der tilim yid). 1934. Trans. by Willa Muir and Edwin Muir. Schocken 1968 o.p. A glorification of Jewish ethical striving published on the eve of Hitler's rise to power.

Book about Asch

Siegel, Ben. *The Controversial Sholem Asch: An Introduction to His Fiction*. Bowling Green Univ. 1976 $13.95. ISBN 0-87972-170-2. Critical biography of Asch discussing his literary contribution and including plot summaries of various works.

BERGELSON, DAVID. 1884–1952

One of the masters of modern Yiddish prose, Bergelson was born in Okhrimova, the Ukraine. His works deal with the decline of the small-town Ukrainian Jewish shtetl before and during the Russian Revolution. He left Soviet Russia for Western Europe in 1921, returning there in 1934. On August 12, 1952, along with 23 other notable Soviet Jewish personalities, Bergelson was executed in Moscow. Although some of his shorter works have appeared in anthologies of Yiddish fiction in English translation, only one of his longer novels has been translated.

Novel by Bergelson

When All Is Said and Done (Nokh Alemen). 1913. Trans. by Bernard Martin. Ohio U. Pr. 1971 o.p. Traces the decay of the Jewish bourgeoisie in pre-revolutionary Russia.

BLINKIN, MEIR. 1879–1915

A member of the literary group *Di Yunge* (The Young Ones), Blinkin's career was cut short when he died at 36. The stories contained in the slim volume listed below describe life in the shtetl and on the lower east side of New York City.

Short Story Collection by Blinkin

Stories. Trans. by Max Rosenfeld. *Modern Jewish Lit. and Culture Ser.* State U. NY Pr. 1984 $10.95. ISBN 0-87395-818-7. With an introduction by Ruth R. Wisse. Tales reflecting the life of the Jewish population on New York's Lower East Side at the end of the nineteenth century.

BRYKS, RACHMIL. 1912–1964

Born in a small town near Lodz, Poland, Bryks survived the terrible experience of the ghetto in Lodz and the concentration camp at Auschwitz. After his liberation, he settled in the United States and began to write works of fiction dealing almost exclusively with the Holocaust period.

NOVEL BY BRYKS

Kiddush Hashem: Cat in the Ghetto. Trans. by S. Morris Engel. Behrman 1977 o.p. Deceptively simple narrative detailing life in Poland under the Nazis.

CAHAN, ABRAHAM. 1860–1951

Cahan was the founder and influential editor of the *Jewish Daily Forward.* He was the author of several important immigrant-era novels in English, including *Yekl* (1896) and *The Rise of David Levinsky* (1917). His Yiddish-language memoirs offer insight on American-Jewish literature, Yiddish journalism, and the immigrant scene in New York.

NOVELS BY CAHAN

The Rise of David Levinsky. Peter Smith $12.00. ISBN 0-8446-1794-6

The White Terror and the Red: A Novel of Revolutionary Russia. Modern Jewish Experience Ser. Ayer repr. of 1905 ed. $34.50. ISBN 0-405-06699-6. A story of Jewish experiences during the revolutionary era.

SHORT STORY COLLECTIONS BY CAHAN

The Imported Bridegroom and Other Stories of the New York Ghetto. Irvington 1972 repr. of 1898 ed. $36.50. ISBN 0-8422-8021-9. "The Imported Bridegroom" is the story of a rich Jew who returns to his village in Poland to find a husband for his daughter. Other stories reflect the longings and visions of Russian Jewish immigrants in America.

Yekl and the Imported Bridegroom and Other Stories of the New York Ghetto. Peter Smith $11.25. ISBN 0-8446-0048-2. Stories of Russian Jewish immigrants in New York City.

WORKS BY CAHAN

The Education of Abraham Cahan. Trans. and intro. by Leon Stein. Schocken 1969 o.p. Translated from vols. 1 and 2 of his *Bleter fun mayn lebn.*

Grandma Never Lived in America: The New Journalism of Abraham Cahan. Ed. and intro. by Moses Rischin. Ind. U. Pr. 1985 o.p. Series of essays and lectures about the social life and customs of Jews in New York City.

DER NISTER (pseud. of Pinkhes Kahanovich). 1884–1950

Born in Berdichev, Ukraine, Der Nister ("the concealed one" in Yiddish) received a traditional Jewish education but also read secular Russian works at an early age. His spiritual and literary growth were greatly influenced by his older brother Aaron, a Bratzlaver Hasid. To avoid serving in the Russian army, Der Nister left Berdichev in 1905. He lived mainly in Zhitomir, eking out a meager existence giving private Hebrew lessons. In 1921 Der Nister left the Soviet Union and settled first in Kaunas (Kovno), Lithuania, and then Berlin, which had become a center for literary exiles and emigrants. In 1926 he returned to the Soviet Union, this time settling in Kharkov. He revived NAHMAN OF BRATSLAV's Hasidic symbolic tales, and his own writing is also characterized by folk fantasy and modern Kabbalistic symbolism. His most famous work, *Di Mishpokhe Mashber* (*The Family Crisis*), is considered by many to be the greatest achievement of Soviet Yiddish literature. It combines the fantasy of the author's earlier works with modern realism. However, only two of the originally projected three volumes have been published.

Novel by Der Nister

The Family Mashber. Trans. by Leonard Wolf. Summit Bks. 1987 o.p. Novel set in the late nineteenth century portraying a family in crisis (or *mashber*).

Book about Der Nister

Bechtel, Delphine. *Der Nister's Work, 1907–1929: A Study of a Yiddish Symbolist.* P. Lang Pubs. 1990 $52.80. ISBN 3-261-04239-7. Criticism and interpretation of symbolism as a literary movement and Der Nister's place in it.

GLATSTEIN, JACOB. 1896–1971

Born in Lublin, Poland, Glatstein emigrated to the United States in 1914 and lived there until his death. One of the major figures in modern Yiddish poetry, Glatstein cultivated free verse and poetry closely related to the reality of contemporary events and society. A master of the Yiddish language, he created poems that became classic expressions of Jewish attitudes and reactions to the tragic events of the Holocaust. He also wrote brilliant prose; especially remarkable are two accounts of a trip to Europe on the eve of World War II.

Poetry by Glatstein

Homecoming at Twilight (Ven Yash iz gekumen). 1940. Trans. by Norbert Guterman. A. S. Barnes 1962 o.p. Foreword by Maurice Samuel.

The Selected Poems of Jacob Glatstein. Trans. by Ruth Whitman. October 1973 $9.50 ISBN 0-8079-0176-8. Weighted toward Glatstein's love poems.

Book about Glatstein

Hadda, Janet. *Yankev Glatshteyn.* Twayne 1980 o.p. Analyzes fifty years of Glatstein's poetry in the context of their original volumes.

GLUCKEL OF HAMELN. 1645–1724

Gluckel of Hameln was a writer and businesswoman who lived in Hamburg, Germany. Her memoirs were first published by her family in 1896 and are considered a classic of early Yiddish literature. They provide a rare inside look at everyday life during the late seventeenth and early eighteenth centuries, a period of great turmoil for European Jews.

Work by Gluckel of Hameln

The Memoirs of Gluckel of Hameln. Trans. by Marvin Lowenthal. Schocken 1987 $14.00. ISBN 0-8052-0572-1. With an introduction by Robert Rosen. Remarkable diary of Jewish life in Europe during the end of the seventeenth century and beginning of the eighteenth.

GRADE, CHAIM. 1910–1982

Grade was born in Vilna, Poland, where he received a thorough education in the talmudic academies of the region. He began writing poetry in 1932 and soon won literary recognition. He escaped the Nazi onslaught as a refugee in the Soviet Union, only to return to Poland after the war to find his mother and wife killed and his hometown destroyed. His later work, both poetry and prose, reflect the tragic Holocaust theme and is dedicated to the re-creation of a world that is no more. His characters are deeply rooted in Jewish tradition and the lore of his native land; his poetry is forceful and dramatic, with the pathos of national and personal tragedy.

WORKS BY GRADE

The Agunah. Trans. and intro. by Curt Leviant. Menorah Pub. 1978 $5.95. ISBN 0-932232-00-0. Details Jewish life in Vilna and its surroundings.

My Mother's Sabbath Days: A Memoir (Der Mames Shabosim). Trans. by Channa Kleinerman Goldstein and Inna Hecker Grade. Schocken 1986 $9.95. ISBN 0-8052-0839-9. Story of Jewish society during World War II.

Rabbis and Wives. Trans. by Harold Rabinowitz and Inna Hecker Grade. Knopf 1982 o.p. Contains the stories "Rebbetzin," "The Courtyard," and "The Oath."

The Well. Trans. by Ruth R. Wisse. JPS Phila. 1967 o.p.

The Yeshiva (Tsemakh Atlas). 2 vols. Trans. by Curt Leviant. Menorah Pub. repr. of 1979 ed. $15.95. ISBN 0-932232-05-1

HALPERN, MOYSHE-LEYB. 1886–1932

Halpern was born in Zloczow (Galicia) and came to the United States in 1908, where he joined up with the group of New York Yiddish poets known as *Di Yunge* (The Young Ones). His work conveys vivid images of his European childhood home and the modern American urban scene.

POETRY BY HALPERN

In New York: A Selection. Trans. and ed. by Kathryn Hellerstein. *Jewish Poetry Ser.* JPS Phila. 1982 $14.95. ISBN 0-8276-0209-1. Contains some of the best of Halpern's early poems.

JACOB BEN ISAAC OF JANOW. d.1620?

Very little is known about the author of the seventeenth-century bestseller that has had more than 200 editions since its first known printing in 1622. The book is a collection of rabbinical commentaries and legends on the Bible and reflects faithfully the Jewish folk psyche, its naive piety, its absolute identification with the word of God as transmitted in the Bible, and its stern adherence to the moral principles of its religious tradition. Its influence on later Yiddish literature has been significant.

WORK BY JACOB BEN ISAAC

Tz'enah ur'enah: The Classic Anthology of Torah Lore and Midrashic Comment. 3 vols. Trans. by Miriam Stark Zakon. *ArtScroll Judaica Ser.* Menorah Pubns. 1983–84 $49.95. ISBN 0-89906-931-2. With an introduction by Meir Holder.

KHAVER-PAVER (pseud. of Gershon Einbinder). 1901–1964

Born in Bershad, Bessarabia, Khaver-Paver (also spelled Chaver-Paver) emigrated to the United States in 1924, living first in New York and then in Los Angeles. His first published works were children's stories but the bulk of his writings are stories and novels for adults.

SHORT STORY COLLECTION BY KHAVER-PAVER

Clinton Street, and Other Stories. Trans. by Henry Goodman. YKUF 1974 o.p. Collection of short stories and autobiographical sketches of life on the Lower East Side in New York during the early part of the twentieth century.

KORN, ROKHL (RACHEL). 1898–1982

Born in Galicia, Rokhl Korn wrote her first poems in Polish, before switching to Yiddish. She published several books in Poland before World War II, and her postwar writing is regarded as some of the finest poetry produced in Yiddish during that period. She received numerous literary prizes for her work. After the war she settled in Montreal.

POETRY BY KORN

Generations: Selected Poems. Ed. by Seymour Mayne. Trans. by Rivka Augenfeld. Flatiron 1982 o.p. Forty-one poems focusing on the themes of exile and nostalgia.

KREITMAN, ESTHER. 1891–1954

The older sister of I. B. and I. J. SINGER, Esther Kreitman was a notable Yiddish author in her own right. "What distinguished her fiction . . . is her portrayal of the woman's, particularly the free thinking woman's, point of view. . . . [Her] works record a young woman's passionate struggle for identity and autonomy" (Joshua A. Fogel, *The Yale Review*). Among her translations is a Yiddish version of *A Christmas Carol* by CHARLES DICKENS (see Vol. 1).

NOVEL BY KREITMAN

Deborah: A Novel. Trans. by Maurice Carr. St. Martin 1984 o.p. Novel about a female writer fighting madness. Introduction by Clive Sinclair.

LINETSKI, ISAAC JOEL. 1839–1915

The author, a contemporary of the great Yiddish writer MENDELE MOKHER SEFORIM, earned his fame with a single book, *Dos poylishe yingl* (*The Polish Lad;* also called *Dos Khsidishe yingl*, or *The Hasidic Lad*), which first appeared in 1867. It is a biting satire on what the author portrayed as the backwardness, fanaticism, ignorance, and superstitions of shtetl life during the mid-nineteenth century.

NOVEL BY LINETSKI

The Polish Lad. Trans. by Moshe Spiegel. JPS Phila. 1975 o.p. With an introduction by Milton Hindus.

MANGER, ITZIK. 1901–1969

Manger, a noted poet, playwright, and novelist, was born in Czernowitz, Romania. The son of a master tailor, he began writing poetry at an early age with his father's encouragement. His first book of poetry was published when he was 29 years old. Several of his poetry anthologies have been translated into English, as has his best-known novel, *The Book of Paradise*.

NOVEL BY MANGER

Book of Paradise: The Wonderful Adventures of Shmuel Aba-Abervo. Trans. by Leonard Wolf. Hill & Wang 1986 o.p. Describes the adventures of a prodigious child who emerged from the womb able to recall life in paradise.

MANI-LEIB, (Pseud. of Mani-Leib Brahinsky). 1883–1953

At the age of 18, Mani-Leib had to flee Russia as a result of his participation in the 1905 Revolution. He settled in the United States, where he wrote original poems for the *Jewish Daily Forward* (*Forverts*) and other Yiddish periodicals. He is also the author of many children's books and songs, only one of which, *Yingl, Tsingl Khvat,* has been translated into English.

Work by Mani-Leib

Yingl, Tsingl Khvat. Trans. by Jeffrey Shandler. Moyer Bell Limited 1986 $11.95. ISBN 0-9188-2552-0. The story of a young boy, Yingl Tsingl, who brings winter to his village. Illustrated by El Lissitzky.

MENDELE MOKHER SEFORIM (pseud. of Sholem Yankev Abramovitsh). 1836–1917

The grandfather of Yiddish literature, Mendele Mokher Seforim won fame under the pen name Mendele the Book Peddler. A novelist and essayist, he was reared in a small town not far from Minsk, Belorussia, and received a traditional orthodox Jewish education. After his father's death, when he was 14, he set out as a wandering scholar and gained a great fund of experience and insight into Russian Jewish folkways, at the same time falling under the influence of the secularizing trends of the *Haskalah* (Enlightenment) movement. His first works were in Hebrew, but for his popular tales he turned to Yiddish as a more suitable vehicle. Later, he translated most of his Yiddish works into Hebrew. He has been called the creator of classical Yiddish, and he was a master of early modern Hebrew prose as well.

Novels by Mendele Mokher Seforim

Fishke the Lame. 1869. Trans. by Gerald Stillman. Yoseloff 1960 o.p.

The Nag (Di klyatshe). 1873. Trans. by Moshe Spiegel. Beechhurst 1955 o.p. Satiric allegory telling of the adventures of an impoverished scholar and his battered workhorse, symbol of the Jewish people.

The Parasite (Dos kleyne mentshele). 1866. Trans. by Gerald Stillman. Yoseloff 1956 o.p.

The Travels and Adventures of Benjamin the Third. 1878. Schocken 1987 $5.50. ISBN 0-8052-0176-9. "This early classic of Yiddish literature tells the story of two small town innocents who wander out into the world in search of the legendary Red Jews and of the rock-hurling, Sabbath-observing river Sambatyon" (*Judaica Book News*).

Work by Mendele Mokher Seforim

Selected Works. Ed. by Marvin Zuckerman, Gerald Stillman, and Marion Herbst. J. Simon 1991 $34.50. ISBN 0-934710-23-6. Collection of novels, short stories, and memoirs. The first volume of a three volume work, *Three Great Classic Writers of Modern Yiddish Literature.*

Books about Mendele Mokher Seforim

Miron, Dan. *A Traveler Disguised: A Study in the Rise of Modern Yiddish Fiction in the 19th Century.* Schocken 1973 o.p. About the contribution of Abramovitsh/Mendele to the development of Yiddish fiction.

Steinberg, Theodore L. *Mendele Mocher Seforim. Twayne's World Authors Ser.* G. K. Hall 1977 $16.95

NAHMAN OF BRATSLAV. 1772–1811

The grandson of Israel ben Eliezer (Baal Shem Tov), founder of Hasidism, Rabbi Nahman of Bratslav was renowned for his storytelling. After his death a number of his moralistic and symbolic tales were published in a bilingual Yiddish and Hebrew book. These tales had an important impact on later Yiddish writing and, thanks largely to the efforts of the philosopher Martin Buber (see Vol. 4), were eventually made known to a far wider public. Several English translations of *The Tales* exist, one of them published by Rabbi Nahman's disciples.

WORKS BY NAHMAN OF BRATSLAV

The Aleph-Bet Book: Sefer Hamiddot. Trans. by Moshe Mykoff. Breslov Res. Inst. 1986 $13.00. ISBN 0-930213-15-7

Beggars and Prayers: Adin Steinsaltz Retells the Tales of Rabbi Nachman of Bratslav. Ed. by Jonathan Omer-Man. Trans. by Yehuda Hanegbi and others. Basic 1979 $9.95. ISBN 0-465-00581-0. Six religious parables.

Rabbi Nachman's Stories. Trans. by Aryeh Kaplan. Breslov Res. Inst. 1983 o.p. Stories from Nachman's interpretation of the *Torah.*

The Tales. 1815. Trans. by Arnold J. Band. Paulist Pr. 1978 o.p. Collection of sermons and homilies.

BOOKS ABOUT NAHMAN OF BRATSLAV

Kaplan, Aryeh. *Until the Mashiach: Rabbi Nachman's Biography.* Ed. by David Shapiro. Breslov Res. Inst. 1985 $17.05. ISBN 0-930213-08-4. Annotated chronology.

Schwartz, Howard. *The Captive Soul of the Messiah: New Tales about Reb Nachman.* Schocken 1983 $20.95. ISBN 0-8052-3873-5. Comprehensive collection of Jewish tales and parables.

OPATOSHU, JOSEPH. 1886–1954

One of the greatest Yiddish novelists, Opatoshu was born in Poland and came to the United States in 1907. His first writings were naturalistic stories of contemporary life. He was especially interested in the lower strata of society and underworld characters, and he described life in the New York ghetto. Later he became a historical novelist par excellence, dealing with such varied periods and places as the Roman Empire, medieval Germany, and nineteenth-century Poland. Several of his historical novels have been translated into English but are now out of print.

NOVELS BY OPATOSHU

A Day in Regensburg: Short Stories. 1933. Trans. by Jacob Sloan. JPS Phila. 1968 o.p. Set in the sixteenth-century German Jewish community of Regensburg.

In Polish Woods. 1922. Trans. by Isaac Goldberg. JPS Phila. 1938 o.p. Set in and around the nineteenth-century Hasidic rabbinical court of Kotsk.

PERETZ, YITSKHOK LEYBUSH (I. L.). 1852–1915

One of the three founding fathers of Yiddish literature, "I. L. Peretz stands at the intellectual center of Yiddish culture and literature. Born in Poland he was exposed . . . to that conflict of ideas and impulses which was to dominate his . . . life as a writer and intellectual leader: the conflict between traditionalism as embodied in a powerful Hasidic inheritance, and modernism, the new trend of secular-progressivist thought that was beginning to sweep through the world of East European Jewry" (Irving Howe, *A Treasury of Yiddish Stories*). His work has had a significant influence on many Jewish writers in Yiddish, especially SHOLEM ASCH. Peretz wrote short stories, plays, and essays. A bibliography of translations of Peretz's works into English was compiled by Uriel Weinreich and appeared in Volume 1 of *The Field of Yiddish.* Unfortunately, many important Peretz translations are now out of print.

SHORT STORY COLLECTIONS BY PERETZ

Bontshe the Silent. Trans. by A. S. Rappoport. *Short Story Index Repr. Ser.* Ayer repr. of 1927 ed. $16.00. ISBN 0-8369-4055-5. Collection of twenty-five stories.

Book of Fire: Stories. Trans. by Joseph Letwich. Yoseloff 1960 o.p.

Selected Stories. Ed. by Irving Howe and Eliezer Greenberg. Schocken 1987 $6.95. ISBN 0-8053-0496-2. Retelling of old stories handed down through Yiddish oral tradition.

The Seven Good Years and Other Stories. Trans. and adapted by Esther Hautzig. JPS Phila. 1984 $10.95. ISBN 0-8276-0244-8. Includes 10 stories and a biographical sketch.

Stories and Pictures. Gordon Pr. $250.00. ISBN 0-87968-376-7. Stories based on the lore of the Talmud and the Kabbalah.

WORKS BY PERETZ

The I. L. Peretz Reader. Ed. and intro. by Ruth R. Wisse. Pantheon 1992 $16.00. ISBN 0-8052-1001-6. Includes 26 short stories, some translated into English for the first time.

In This World and the Next: Selected Writings. Trans. by Moshe Spiegel. Yoseloff 1958 o.p.

My Memoirs. Trans. by Fred Goldberg. Citadel Pr. 1964 o.p.

Peretz. Ed. and trans. by Sol Liptzin. *Biography Index Repr. Ser.* Ayer repr. of 1947 ed. $21.25. ISBN 0-8369-8137-5. Bilingual English/Yiddish edition.

BOOKS ABOUT PERETZ

Adler, Ruth. *Women of the Shtetl: Through the Eye of Y. L. Peretz.* Fairleigh Dickinson 1980 $22.50. ISBN 0-8386-2336-0. Feminist overview of women's life in the Shtetl through literary sources.

Samuel, Maurice. *Prince of the Ghetto.* U. Pr. of Amer. *Brown Classics in Judaica Ser.* 1987 $26.50. ISBN 0-8191-5784-8. Skillful retelling of Peretz's folk and Hasidic tales.

PINSKY, DAVID. 1872–1959

Born in Mogilev, the Ukraine, Pinsky early became involved in the Labor Zionist movement. In 1898 he emigrated to the United States. His works include novels, short stories, and plays, many of which have been translated into English but are no longer in print. "It is the earliest stories that seem most fresh. . . . The young Pinsky was able to communicate compassionate tenderness in writing about the Jewish poor" (Irving Howe, *A Treasury of Yiddish Stories*).

PLAYS BY PINSKY

Ten Plays. 1920. Trans. by Isaac Goldberg. Core Collection 1977 o.p. Collection of one-act plays.

Three Plays. Trans. by Isaac Goldberg. *Modern Jewish Experience Ser.* Ayer repr. of 1918 ed. $21.00. ISBN 0-405-06739-9. Includes *Isaac Sheftel, The Last Jew, The Dumb Messiah.*

SHORT STORY COLLECTION BY PINSKY

Temptations: A Book of Short Stories. Trans. by Isaac Goldberg. *Short Story Index Repr. Ser.* Ayer repr. of 1919 ed. $20.00. ISBN 0-8369-3959-X

WORK BY PINSKY

King David and His Wives. Trans. by Isaac Goldberg. B. W. Huebsch 1923 o.p.

RABON, ISRAEL. 1900–1941

Rabon was born in Lodz, Poland, to an impoverished, slum-dwelling family. His literary output was meager, consisting of two volumes of prose fiction and one book of poems. Nevertheless, these works have become recognized for the light they shed on the urban *lumpenproletariat* of pre-Holocaust Poland, as well as for their purely literary qualities. In both style and subject matter, Rabon's fiction is influenced by the works of the Norwegian novelist KNUT HAMSUN.

Novel by Rabon

The Street. 1928. Trans. by Leonard Wolf. FWEW 1990 $9.95. ISBN 0-941423-45-X. A novel about a Jewish soldier who, returning to Lodz at the end of World War I, joins the ranks of unemployed transients in the large city, and becomes a street person. "A surrealistic and bizarre novel written in the style of avant-garde German expressionism of the 1920's" (*Judaica Book News*).

REISIN, AVRAHAM. 1876-1953

The son of a Hebrew-Yiddish poet, Reisin was born in Koidanov, Minsk. After emigrating to New York in 1908, he wrote dozens of short stories and poems for the Yiddish press. He is considered a master of the Yiddish short story. Many of his writings are compassionate portrayals of the poor and uneducated.

Short Story Collection by Reisin

The Heart-Stirrring Sermon and Other Stories. Ed. and trans. by Curt Leviant. Overlook Pr. $23.95. ISBN 0-8795-1436-1. The first English-language collection of Reisin's short stories.

RONTSH, ISAAC ELCHONON. 1899-1985

Rontsh was a Yiddish poet, novelist, essayist, and journalist. Born in Poland, he emigrated to New York and later moved to Los Angeles. He published numerous works of poetry and prose in Yiddish.

Novel by Rontsh

The Awakening of Motek. Bunting 1953 o.p.

Poetry by Rontsh

Poems. Trans. by Marc Chagall. I. E. Ronch, 1981 o.p. Drawings by Marc Chagall.

ROSENFELD, MORRIS. 1862-1923

Born in the Ukraine, Rosenfeld settled in the United States in 1886, where he put in long hours at the needle trades. His famous "sweatshop poems" made him the champion of the immigrant working masses, and he was one of the pioneers of American-Yiddish literature.

Poetry by Rosenfeld

Songs from the Ghetto. Trans. by Leo Wiener. Irvington repr. of 1898 ed. $19.00. ISBN 0-8398-1766-5. The first Yiddish book to be translated into English. The translator was professor of Slavic languages at Harvard and author of a history of Yiddish literature.

SHAPIRO, LAMED. 1878–1948

Lamed Shapiro was born and lived in the Ukraine. He visited the United States in 1905 and again in 1911. One of the most important short story writers in Yiddish, he was "a successor to the first generation of Yiddish writers . . . but after some early influence he departed radically from their style and subject matter. . . ." (Publisher's note)

Short Story Collection by Shapiro

The Jewish Government and Other Stories. Trans. and ed. by Curt Leviant. Twayne 1971 o.p. Tales focusing on the theme of conflict.

SHOLOM ALEICHEM (pseud. of Sholem Rabinovitsh). 1859–1916

Sholom Aleichem (Hebrew greeting meaning "Peace be unto you!") was born near Pereyaslav, the Ukraine, and settled in the United States two years before his death. The most popular and beloved of all Yiddish writers, he wrote with humor and tenderness about the Yiddish-speaking Jews of Eastern Europe and won the title "the Jewish MARK TWAIN" (see Vol. 1). "He is the passer-by, the informal correspondent, the post office into which Jews drop their communications to the world. All he does, you understand, is to write down stories people bring him. He invents nothing" (Alfred Kazin, *Contemporaries*). One of his creations, Tevye the Dairyman, has become world famous, thanks to the highly successful Broadway musical *Fiddler on the Roof*, which is based on Sholom Aleichem's Tevye stories. Although he also wrote plays and novels, it is for his short stories and his humorous monologues that Sholom Aleichem is best remembered.

SHORT STORY COLLECTIONS BY SHOLOM ALEICHEM

The Adventure of Menahem-Mendl. 1892–1913. Trans. by Tamara Kahana. Putnam 1979 $4.95. ISBN 0-399-50396-X. Stories of Menahem-Mendl, the clever but perpetually poor man always trying to make a deal.

The Adventures of Mottel, the Cantor's Son. 1907–16. Trans. by Tamara Kahana. Macmillan 1961 o.p.

Favorite Tales of Sholom Aleichem. Trans. by Julius Butwin and Frances Butwin. Avenel 1983 o.p. Reprint of *The Old Country,* published in 1946, and *Tevye's Daughters,* published in 1949.

Holiday Tales of Sholom Aleichem. Trans. by Aliza Shevrin. Macmillan 1985 $5.95. ISBN 0-689-71034-8. "Seven stories, two available for the first time in English, capture the essence of the Jewish holidays of Passover, Purim, Chanukah or Sukkot" (*Judaica Book News*).

Selected Stories. Modern Lib. 1956 o.p. Introduction by Alfred Kazin.

Some Laughter, Some Tears: Tales from the Old World and New. Trans. by Curt Leviant. Putnam 1979 o.p. Stories of Aleichem's personal experiences.

Tevye the Dairyman and the Railroad Stories. Schocken 1988 $15.00. ISBN 0-8052-0905-0. Tales reflect Tevye's good humor which helps him and his five daughters survive tragedy and misfortune.

PLAYS BY SHOLOM ALEICHEM

The Jackpot: A Folk-Play in Four Acts. Trans. by Kobi Weitzner and Barnett Zumoff. Workmen's Circle 1989 $7.50. ISBN 1-8779-0940-8

Sholom Aleichem's Wandering Star, and Other Plays of Jewish Life. Trans. by David S. Lifson. Cornwall Bks. 1988 $19.95 ISBN 0-8453-4810-8

NOVELS BY SHOLOM ALEICHEM

Hanukah Money. Trans. and adapted by Uri Shulevitz and Elizabeth Shub. Morrow 1991 $3.95. ISBN 0-688-10993-4. A tale of two boys yearning for holiday gelt (money).

In the Storm. 1907. Trans. by Aliza Shevrin. NAL-Dutton 1985 o.p. Story of social and political upheaval and Jewish-gentile conflict in Russia at the turn of the nineteenth century.

The Nightingale, or The Saga of Yosele Solovey the Cantor (Yosele Solovey). 1889. Trans. by Aliza Shevrin. Putnam 1985 o.p. Travails of a young singer and his struggle for fame.

Wandering Star. 1912. Trans. by Frances Butwin. Crown 1952 o.p. Novel about an itinerant Yiddish theatrical troupe.

Works by Sholom Aleichem

The Best of Sholom Aleichem. Ed. by Irving Howe and Ruth R. Wisse. Walker & Co. 1991 $14.95. ISBN 0-8027-2645-3. Humorous views of Jewish culture.

The Bloody Hoax. Trans. by Aliza Shevrin. Ind. U. Pr. 1991 $29.95. ISBN 0-2533-0401-6. Translation of *Der Blutiger shpas,* with an introduction by Maurice Friedberg.

From the Fair: The Autobiography of Sholom Aleichem (Funem yarid). 1916-17. Trans. by Curt Leviant. Viking Penguin 1985 o.p. New, expanded edition of a work earlier translated by Tamara Kahana, under the title *The Great Fair: Scenes from My Childhood* (1955).

Inside Kasrilevke. Trans. by Isidore Goldstick. Schocken 1968 o.p.

Marienbad. 1913. Trans. by Aliza Shevrin. Putnam 1982 o.p.

Stories and Satires. Trans. by Curt Leviant. Macmillan 1970 o.p.

Why Do Jews Need a Land of Their Own? (Oyf vos badarfn yidn a land?). Trans. by Joseph Leftwich and Mordecai S. Chertoff. Cornwall Bks. 1984 o.p. "Contains nearly everything that Sholom Aleichem wrote on Zion, Zionism and Palestine as a homeland for the Jews" (*AJL Newsletter*).

Books about Sholom Aleichem

Aarons, Victoria. *Author as Character in the Works of Sholom Aleichem.* E. Mellen 1985 $69.95. ISBN 0-88946-553-3. Study of Sholom Aleichem's literary techniques and the way his changing attitude toward Eastern European Jewish community life influenced those techniques.

Butwin, Joseph, and Frances Butwin. *Sholom Aleichem. Twayne's World Authors Ser.* G. K. Hall 1977 o.p.

Falstein, Louis. *The Man Who Loved Laughter: The Story of Sholom Aleichem. Covenant Ser.* JPS Phila. 1968 o.p.

Gittleman, Sol. *Sholom Aleichem: A Non-Critical Introduction.* Mouton 1974 $22.70. ISBN 90-2792-606-9

Halberstam-Rubin, Anna. *Sholom Aleichem: The Writer as Social Historian.* P. Lang Pubs. 1989 $23.95. ISBN 0-8204-0675-9. Biography that draws on the original stones of the Yiddish humorist Sholom Aleichem and vividly portrays the situation of Jews in czarist Russia.

Miron, Dan A. *Sholom Aleykhem: Person, Persona, Presence.* YIVO Inst. 1972 $5.00. ISBN 0-914512-02-1. About Sholom Aleichem's pseudonyms and their meaning in his work.

Samuel, Maurice. *World of Sholom Aleichem.* Knopf 1943 o.p. "A pilgrimage through . . . the townlets and villages of the famous Pale of Settlement, recounting the adventures of the chief characters in the works of Sholom Aleichem and recreating the folklore, the outlook and the memories which were in part transplanted to America" (Publisher's note).

Sholom Aleichem in America: the Story of a Culture Hero. Trans. by Paul Glasser. YIVO Inst. 1990 $3.00. ISBN 0-685-33403-1. Catalog of an exhibit on Sholom Aleichem held at the YIVO Institute in New York in 1990–1991.

Waife-Goldberg, Marie. *My Father, Sholom Aleichem.* Pocket Bks. o.p.

SINGER, I(SAAC) B(ASHEVIS). 1904–1991 (Nobel Prize 1978)

The first Yiddish writer to be awarded the Nobel Prize for literature (1978), I. B. Singer is also the most widely translated of Yiddish authors. Born in Leoncin, Poland, he had a traditional Jewish education and, as the son of a rabbi, attended a rabbinical seminary in Warsaw, concentrating on the study of talmudic law and the Kabbalah (oral traditions). Rather than becoming a rabbi, however, he chose the life of a writer. His first fiction was written in Hebrew, but most of his work has been in Yiddish. Before coming to the United States in 1935, he worked as a proofreader and translator in Warsaw. His work was not translated into English until he was 46. After his arrival in the United States he settled in New York City and joined the staff of the *Jewish Daily Forward,* where most of his work was serialized. His books are often marked by elements of fantasy and are distinguished for their lustiness, philosophical insight, and humor. Singer has written a large number of children's books, some of which are listed here. In recent years, stage productions and films have been made of several of his works, including *The Magician of Lublin* and *Yentl.*

In 1964 Singer was elected to the National Institute of Arts and Letters. Eleven years later he received an honorary doctoral degree from the Hebrew University of Jerusalem and the S. J. Agnon Golden Medal Award from the American Friends of the Hebrew University. After receiving the Nobel Prize, he continued an active literary career until his death in 1991. Singer's older brother, ISRAEL JOSHUA SINGER, is also a well-known Yiddish writer, as is his sister, ESTHER (Singer) KREITMAN.

SHORT STORY COLLECTIONS BY I. B. SINGER

The Collected Stories of Isaac Bashevis Singer. FS&G 1983 $16.95. ISBN 0-374-51788-6. Anthology including 47 previously published stories.

A Crown of Feathers. FS&G 1981 $7.95. ISBN 0-374-51624-3. Winner of a National Book Award.

A Day of Pleasure: Stories of a Boy Growing Up in Warsaw. FS&G 1969 o.p. Episodes from the author's childhood.

The Death of Methuselah and Other Stories. FS&G 1988 $17.95. ISBN 0-374-13563-0

A Friend of Kafka and Other Stories. FS&G 1970 $5.95. ISBN 0-374-51538-7. Stories of an Americanized Singer reflecting on his past.

Gifts. Author's Workshop Ser. JPS Phila. 1985 o.p. "New, previously unpublished stories with an introductory essay that describes the author's early passion for writing" (*Judaica Book News*).

Gimpel the Fool and Other Stories. Trans. by Saul Bellow and others. FS&G 1978 $11.00. ISBN 0-374-50052-5

The Image and Other Stories. FS&G 1985 $18.95. ISBN 0-374-52079-8. "The master's new stories range from the old days in Warsaw to recent years in America" (*Judaica Book News*).

Old Love and Other Stories. FS&G 1979 o.p. Eighteen stories about love and middle age.

Passions and Other Stories. FS&G 1975 o.p. Stories about Yiddish-speaking Jews in Eastern Europe.

The Reaches of Heaven: A Story of the Baal Shem Tov. FS&G 1980 $15.00. ISBN 0-374-24733-1

The Safe Deposit and Other Stories about Grandparents, Old Lovers, and Crazy Old Men. Ed. by Kerry M. Olitzky. *Masterworks of Modern Jewish Writing Ser.* Wiener Pub. Inc. 1989 $19.95. ISBN 1-55876-013-X. Preface by Claude Pepper and afterword by Olitzky.

The Séance and Other Stories. FS&G 1968 $6.95. ISBN 0-374-50832-1

Short Friday and Other Stories. FS&G 1964 o.p. Sixteen tales that "penetrate life, depth, reality, the supernatural, and have an earthy quality that makes for enjoyable reading" (*LJ*).

The Spinoza of Market Street. 1961. Trans. by Elaine Gottlieb and others. Fawcett 1980 o.p. An anthology of 11 short stories.

Stories for Children. FS&G 1984 $22.95. ISBN 0-374-37266-7. Includes 36 previously published stories and an essay: "Are Children the Ultimate Literary Critics?"

Zlateh the Goat and Other Stories. Trans. by I. B. Singer and Elizabeth Shub. HarpC 1966 $16.00. ISBN 0-06-025698-2. "Seven short stories coming out of the author's background as a young Jewish boy in Poland before World War I" (Library of Congress card).

Novels by I. B. Singer

Enemies: A Love Story. NAL-Dutton 1989 $4.95. ISBN 0-451-16663-9. A tale of Holocaust victims and how they have also become victims of their own personalities.

The Estate. 1969. FS&G 1979 o.p.

The Family Moskat. 1950. FS&G 1988 $16.00. ISBN 0-374-50392-3. The first novel by the author, this is the history of a Polish-Jewish family from the early 1900s to World War II.

The King of the Fields. FS&G 1988 $18.95. ISBN 0-3741-8128-4. Translation of *Der Kenig fun di Felder*.

The Magician of Lublin. 1960. Fawcett 1985 $2.95. ISBN 0-449-20966-0. A novel of nineteenth-century Poland.

The Manor. FS&G 1987 o.p. The first volume of a planned trilogy, set in nineteenth-century Poland.

Satan in Goray. 1935. Trans. by Jacob Sloan. FS&G 1955 o.p. A story of religious hysteria among persecuted Jews in a small Polish town in the seventeenth century; portrays the messianic longing for redemption among Jews in the wake of the Chmielnicki massacres of 1648–54.

Scum. Trans. by Rosaline D. Schwartz. FS&G 1991 $19.95. ISBN 0-37425-511-3. Tale of deception and depression about a secularized Jew living in Buenos Aires in the early part of the century.

Shosha. FS&G 1978 o.p. About Jews in Poland before the Nazi era.

The Slave. 1962. Trans. by I. B. Singer and Cecil H. Femley. FS&G 1962 $11.00. ISBN 0-374-50680-9. Novel set in a seventeenth-century Carpathian village.

Yentl the Yeshiva Boy. Trans. by Marion Magid and Elizabeth Pollet. FS&G 1983 $10.95. ISBN 0-374-29347-3. An orphaned young woman who longs to study at a Yeshiva disguises herself as a man in order to continue her work.

Works by I. B. Singer

The Golem. FS&G 1982 o.p. Story of a giant miraculously brought to life by a saintly rabbi.

In My Father's Court. 1956. Trans. by Channah Kleinerman-Goldstein, Elaine Gottlieb, and Joseph Singer. Fawcett 1980 $2.50. ISBN 0-449-24074-6. Memoir of the author's childhood in Poland, offering a glimpse of Hasidic life and of his rabbinical family.

An Isaac Bashevis Singer Reader. FS&G 1971 o.p. Collected works, including stories from five collections.

Joseph and Koza, or The Sacrifice to the Vistula. FS&G 1970 o.p. Winner of the 1970 National Book Award for children's literature.

Lost in America. Trans. by Joseph Singer. Doubleday 1981 o.p. Memoirs.

Love and Exile: The Early Years—A Memoir. FS&G 1986 o.p. Contains "A Little Boy in Search of God," "A Young Man in Search of Love," "Lost in America," and a new introduction, "The Beginning"—Singer's autobiography covering his childhood through his immigration to the U.S.

The Penitent. 1974. FS&G 1983 $13.95. ISBN 0-374-23064-1

A Young Man in Search of Love. Trans. by Joseph Singer. Doubleday 1978 o.p. Memoirs.

Books about I. B. Singer

Allentuck, Marcia, ed. *Achievement of Isaac Bashevis Singer*. *Cross-currents Modern Critiques Ser.* S. Ill. U. Pr. 1969 o.p. Examines Singer's contribution to Jewish culture.

Buchen, Irving H. *Isaac Bashevis Singer and the Eternal Past*. *Gotham Lib.* NYU Pr. 1968 o.p.

Farrell Lee, Grace. *From Exile to Redemption: The Fiction of Isaac Bashevis Singer*. S. Ill. U. Pr. 1987 $18.95. ISBN 0-8093-1330-8. Shows the links between the imagery and metaphors of Singer's writing and those of the sacred books.

Friedman, Lawrence S. *Understanding Isaac Bashevis Singer*. *Understanding Contemporary Amer. Lit. Ser.* U. of SC Pr. 1988 $24.95. ISBN 0-8724-9543-4

Kresh, Paul. *Isaac Bashevis Singer: The Magician of West 86th Street.* Doubleday 1979 o.p. Biography based on interviews.

______. *Isaac Bashevis Singer: The Story of a Storyteller. Jewish Biography Ser.* NAL-Dutton 1984 $13.95. ISBN 0-525-67156-0. A very readable biography.

Malin, Irving, ed. *Critical Views of Isaac Bashevis Singer. Gotham Lib.* NYU Pr. 1969 o.p. Diverse viewpoints on the contextual analysis of Singer's works.

______. *Isaac Bashevis Singer. Lit. and Life Ser.* Continuum 1972 o.p.

Miller, David Neal. *Fear of Fiction: Narrative Strategies in the Works of Isaac Bashevis Singer.* State U. NY Pr. 1985 $57.50. ISBN 0-88706-009-9. Investigates the way Singer experimented with literary genre between fiction and reportage.

______, ed. *Recovering the Canon: Essays on Isaac Bashevis Singer. Studies in Judaism in Modern Times Ser.* E. J. Brill 1986 $35.50. ISBN 9-0040-7681-6

Siegel, Ben. *Isaac Bashevis Singer. Pamphlets on Amer. Writers Ser.* U. of Minn. Pr. 1969 o.p. Overview of Singer's works translated into English.

Sinclair, Clive. *The Brothers Singer.* Schocken 1987 $14.95. ISBN 0-8052-8145-2. Literary biography of Israel Joshua Singer and Isaac Bashevis Singer.

Singer, Isaac Bashevis, and Richard Burgin. *Conversations with Isaac Bashevis Singer.* Doubleday 1985 o.p. By the author of *Conversations with Jorge Luis Borges.*

SINGER, I(SRAEL) J(OSHUA). 1893–1944

I. J. Singer, the older brother of Isaac Bashevis Singer, was born in Bilgoraj, Poland, came to the United States in 1934, and was naturalized in 1939. His works include novels, short stories, and plays, and have enjoyed both critical acclaim and widespread popularity.

NOVELS BY I. J. SINGER

The Brothers Ashkenazi. 1936. Trans. by Joseph Singer. Carroll & Graf 1985 $9.95. ISBN 0-88184-192-7. A panoramic novel about the rise and fall of a family of Jewish industrialists in prewar Poland.

East of Eden. 1938. Trans. by Maurice Samuel. Vanguard 1974 o.p. The deceived hopes and expectations of Jewish Communists in the Soviet Union.

The Family Carnovsky. 1943. Trans. by Joseph Singer. HarpC 1973 o.p. Tragedy of assimilated Jewish families in Nazi Germany.

Yoshe Kalb. 1932. Trans. by Maurice Samuel. Schocken 1988 $8.95. ISBN 0-8052-0860-7. Introduction by I. B. Singer. A portrayal of Hasidic life in nineteenth-century Poland.

SHORT STORY COLLECTION BY I. J. SINGER

The River Breaks Up. 1938. Trans. by Maurice Samuel. Vanguard 1976 o.p. Short stories.

WORKS BY I. J. SINGER

Of a World That Is No More. 1946. Vanguard 1970 o.p. Childhood memoirs, worth comparing with I. B. Singer's *In My Father's Court,* which deal with the same household.

Steel and Iron. 1927. Trans. by Joseph Singer. Crowell 1969 o.p. The impact of World War I and the Russian Revolution on Jewish life.

BOOK ABOUT I. J. SINGER

Norich, Anita. *The Homeless Imagination in the Fiction of Israel Joshua Singer. Jewish Lit. and Culture Ser.* Ind. U. Pr. 1991. $29.95. ISBN 0-2533-4109-4. Examines cultural tensions that influence Singer's writings.

SUTZKEVER, ABRAHAM. 1913–

Sutzkever is a towering figure among Yiddish poets of all ages. He started to write in his native city of Vilna in the 1930s and endured the Nazi occupation of that city. He joined the partisans in 1943 and was called as a witness at the

Nuremberg trials of 1946. He now lives in Israel, where he edits the prestigious Yiddish literary journal *Di Goldene Keyt* (The Golden Chain). A great master of word and image, he has found his own way of extracting beauty from the somber realities of Jewish life, and his writing eloquently expresses the tragedy and heroism of the Holocaust period.

Poetry by Sutzkever

Burnt Pearls: Ghetto Poems. Trans. by Seymour Mayne. Mosaic Pr. OH 1981 o.p.

The Fiddle Rose: Poems, 1970–1972. Ed. and trans. by Ruth Whitman. Wayne St. U. Pr. 1990 $24.95. ISBN 0-8143-2001-5. Large collection of more modern poems. Drawings by Marc Chagall; introduction by Ruth R. Wisse.

Siberia: A Poem. Trans. and intro. by Jacob Sonntag. Abelard-Schuman 1961 o.p. Includes drawings by Marc Chagall.

Work by Sutzkever

Selected Poetry and Prose. Trans. by Barbara Harshav and Benjamin Harshav. U. CA Pr. 1991 $40.00. ISBN 0-5200-6539-5. Introduction by Benjamin Harshav.

Book about Sutzkever

Leftwich, Joseph. *Abraham Sutzkever: Partisan Poet.* A. S. Barnes 1971 o.p. Examines Sutzkever's personal convictions through his writings.

TSANIN, MORDEKHAI. 1906–

Tsanin, born in Sokolow-Podlaski, Poland, settled in Israel, where he has served as editor-in-chief of the Yiddish daily *Letste nayes.* In addition to his distinguished journalistic activities, he has devoted himself to producing a multivolume fictional panorama of Jewish history, one volume of which has been translated into English.

Novel by Tsanin

Artapanos Comes Home. Trans. by I. M. Lask. A. S. Barnes 1980 o.p. Historical novel.

ZUNSER, ELIAKUM. 1835–1913

Zunser was a famous wedding bard, composing couplets so popular that they passed into the realm of folk poetry and folk song. Both before and after his emigration to the United States in 1889, collections of his rhymes were frequently published, some of which were later translated into English.

Poetry by Zunser

Selected Songs of Eliakum Zunser. Modern Jewish Experience Ser. Ayer 1975 repr. of 1928 ed. $24.50. ISBN 0-405-06757-7

Book about Zunser

Liptzin, Sol. *Eliakum Zunser: Poet of His People.* Behrman 1950 o.p.

CHAPTER 4

Middle Eastern Literatures

Meryle Gaston

The old Levant must go on living. Ancient land of symbiosis, with its frictions, its injustices but also its wealth. Mosaic of cultures and creeds, precious for its diversity.

—NICOLAS SOUDRAY, *The House of the Prophets*

ANCIENT NEAR EASTERN LITERATURE

Middle Eastern literature includes a variety of linguistic traditions in the region that includes southwestern Asia and northern Africa. This chapter will focus on the literature of the four major languages of that region: Arabic, Armenian, Persian, and Turkish. These language traditions, for the most part, overlap the boundaries of a number of modern nations, yet reflect cultural traditions going back a thousand or more years.

Whereas the term "Middle East" is a fairly modern usage, the term "Near East" is a somewhat older term reflecting a more Eurocentric perspective. As a regional designation, the term "Near East" usually refers to the lands that border the eastern Mediterranean; that is, northeastern Africa, southwestern Asia, Asia Minor, and occasionally the Balkan Peninsula. For the purposes of this section, the ancient Near East is defined as the area consisting of Egypt, Nubia, Palestine and Syria, Armenia, Asia Minor, Mesopotamia, and the adjoining areas of northeastern Africa, the Aegean, Iran (Persia), and the Indus Valley during the era between 9000 B.C. and the fourth century B.C., when the course of history was changed by the conquests of Alexander the Great.

The literature of the ancient Near East comprises works from three mainstreams of culture: the Mesopotamian-Anatolian, which includes the Sumerians, the Elamites, the Babylonians, the Assyrians, and the Hittites; the Syro-Palestinian, which takes in the writings of the Canaanite and Hebrew peoples; and the Egyptian, which was inscribed on stone and papyrus in what was the earliest written language.

Apart from these alignments in time, place, and language, what justifies the concept of an ancient Near Eastern literature is its characteristic clustering around some half dozen major genres and a number of lesser genres. The former include myth, epic, historical narrative, such "wisdom" literature as proverbs and sayings, and meditations, hymns, prayers, omens, and incantations. The latter include fables, folk tales and legends, lamentations, songs, autobiography, satire, riddles, and dialogue-debates.

As a rule, a literary work in the ancient Near East was not the creation of a single individual, but a collective effort, preserved, modified, and recopied. The original author faded into obscurity and the work entered the public realm to serve a social purpose.

Because this literature was produced before literary theory was invented, it defies easy definition by accepted genres. Thus, the reader does not have the benefit of literary criticism or theory validated by criteria produced internally by the cultures in question. Finally, the line between sacred and secular literature is far from clear.

General Background

The following list should serve as an introduction to a literature now perceived as vital to an understanding of society's origins and early heritage.

Chiera, Edward. *They Wrote on Clay: The Babylonian Tablets Speak Today*. Ed. by George G. Cameron. U. Ch. Pr. 1956 $9.95. ISBN 0-226-10425-7. A sensitive introduction to the world of clay tablets and the environment from which they emanate. For the general reader.

Frankfurt, Henri. *The Intellectual Adventure of Ancient Man: An Essay on Speculative Thought in the Ancient Near East*. U. Ch. Pr. 1977 repr. of 1946 ed. $13.50. ISBN 0-226-26009-7. The single comprehensive book clarifying first principles of ancient Near Eastern thought, especially Egyptian and Babylonian. Indispensable for literary study.

Kirk, G. S. *Myth: Its Meaning and Functions in Ancient and Other Cultures*. U. CA Pr. 1970 $14.95. ISBN 0-520-02389-7. A wide-ranging, unconventional exploration of the nature and meaning of myth; especially interesting chapters on Mesopotamia and Greek-Hurrian-Hittite connections.

Kramer, Samuel N., ed. *Mythologies of the Ancient World*. Doubleday 1961 o.p. An essential volume. All essays superb, especially Rudolf Anthes's essay on mythology in Ancient Egypt.

Sasson, Jack, ed. *Studies in Literature from the Ancient Near East. American Oriental Ser.* Am. Orient. Soc. 1984 $25.00. ISBN 0-940490-65-X. Wide–ranging study of ancient Near Eastern literature.

Collections

Breasted, James H., trans. and ed. *Ancient Records of Egypt*. 5 vols. in 3. Russell Sage 1906–07 o.p. Although dated, still a useful introduction to Egyptian historical writing.

Ceadel, Eric B., ed. *Literatures of the East*. Grove Pr. 1959 o.p. Succinct and authoritative essays on Canaanite, early Arab, Hebrew, and Iranian writings.

Erman, Adolf, ed. *The Ancient Egyptians: A Sourcebook of Their Writings*. 1927. HarpC 1966 o.p. "Remains by far the best selection and translation of Egyptian belles-lettres which has appeared so far" (William F. Albright). Translations employing archaic English but still enjoyable. Introduction by William K. Simpson.

Faulkner, R. O., trans. *The Ancient Egyptian Pyramid Texts*. OUP 1969 o.p. Designed for use by philologists and students of ancient religion.

Gaster, Theodor H., ed. *The Oldest Stories in the World*. Beacon Pr. 1958 o.p. A very elementary retelling of a number of myths and legends designed for the general reader but probably more appropriate to the young. With useful index of motifs.

______, ed. *Thespis: Ritual, Myth, and Drama in the Ancient Near East*. Foreword by Gilbert Murray. Gordian 2d rev. ed. 1975 $75.00. ISBN 0-87752-188-3. Lively, imaginative, but controversial.

Jacobsen, Thorkild. *The Harps That Once: Sumerian Poetry in Translation*. Yale U. Pr. 1987 $40.00. ISBN 0-300-03906-9. By an established scholar in the field of Sumerian studies.

Kramer, Samuel N. *From the Poetry of Sumer: Creation, Glorification, Adoration*. U. CA Pr. 1979 $37.50. ISBN 0-520-03703-0. Study of ancient Sumerian poetry by one of the most outstanding scholars in the field.

Lambert, Wilfred G. *Babylonian Wisdom Literature.* OUP 1960 o.p. Although specifically limited to wisdom literature, includes translations of many texts.

Lichtheim, Miriam. *Ancient Egyptian Literature: a Book of Readings, Vol 3.* U. CA Pr. 1973–1980 $37.50. ISBN 0-520-03882-7. Decrees, funerary and monument inscriptions, treatises, prayers, hymns, songs, tales, excerpts from the Book of the Dead, instructional literature, and poems.

Luckenbill, D. D. *Ancient Records of Assyria and Babylonia.* 2 vols. Greenwood 1969 repr. of 1926–27 ed. o.p. Still useful as a basic introduction to Assyro-Babylonian historical writing, but with outdated translations. See Pritchard volume following.

Parkinson, R. B. *Voices from Ancient Egypt: an Anthology of Middle Kingdom Writings.* U. of Okla. Pr. 1991 $19.95. ISBN 0-8061-2362-1

Pritchard, James B., ed. *Ancient Near Eastern Texts Relating to the Old Testament.* Princeton U. Pr. 3rd ed. 1955 o.p. Includes most major works of the ancient Near East. Translations by major scholars. All periods and principal genres; many lesser genres. Scholarly, readable, indispensable.

Reiner, Erica. *Your Thwarts in Pieces, Your Mooring Rope Cut: Poetry from Babylonia and Assyria.* U. of Mich. Pr. 1985 $10.00. ISBN 0-936534-04-4. Nine pieces, each preceded by introductory and critical material. The author worked on the Univ. of Chicago Assyrian Dictionary project.

Simpson, William K., ed. *The Literature of Ancient Egypt: An Anthology of Stories, Instructions and Poetry.* Yale U. Pr. 1973 o.p. Modern translations by foremost Egyptologists.

Individual Texts

In addition to James B. Pritchard's collection, *Ancient Near Eastern Texts*, the reader should consult appreciations and criticisms of regional ancient Near Eastern literature cited previously. In this section only easily procurable translations and studies of a few well-known individual works are noted.

Atra-Hasis: The Babylonian Story of the Flood. Trans. and ed. by Wilfred G. Lambert and A. R. Millard. OUP 1969 o.p. The Babylonian flood story, related to the Hebrew account in Genesis, was first known only in fragments and a summarized version within the *Gilgamesh Epic*. This is the first translation of fuller material uncovered in the sixties. The edition also includes the other Babylonian fragments and a revised version of the *Sumerian Flood* story.

The Babylonian Genesis. Trans. by Alexander Heidel. U. Ch. Pr. 1963 $6.50. ISBN 0-226-32399-4. Heidel's translation and interpretation of the Babylonian creation story, the *Enuma-Elish*, and associated texts. An extensive chapter covers parallels between the Akkadian creation texts and the Old Testament.

The Book of the Dead: The Papyrus of Ani in the British Museum. 1895. Trans. and ed. by E. A. Wallis Budge. Dover 1967 o.p. Almost a century old, and since publication technically refined, this book remains an accessible introduction to the burial ritual texts of the Middle Kingdom Egyptians and their successors.

The Epic of Gilgamesh. Trans. by Maureen Gallery. Stanford U. Pr. 1989 $29.95. ISBN 0-8047-1589-0. A somewhat literal translation based on sources and texts available through 1988. Includes a glossary of proper names, critical material, reading suggestions.

The Epic of Gilgamesh. Trans. by N. K. Sanders. Viking Penguin 1960 $4.95. ISBN 0-14-044100-X. A prose version aesthetically less satisfying than the translation into poetry that Pritchard includes in his collection cited above.

Gilgamesh. Trans. from the Sin-legi-unninni version by John Gardner and John Maier. Random 1985 $13.00. ISBN 0-394-74089-0

The Gilgamesh Epic and Old Testament Parallels. Ed. by A. Heidel. U. Ch. Pr. 1963 $10.95. ISBN 0-226-32398-6. The first two chapters contain fully annotated translations of the Gilgamesh Epic, the Sumerian account of the deluge from Nippur, the Atra-Hasis Epic, Berossus's account of the deluge, the story of Ishtar's descent into the underworld, the myth about Nergal and Ereshkigal, and an Assyrian prince's vision of the underworld (probably the origin of the Greek Hades and the Christian Hell).

The Ugaritic Poem of AGHT: Text, Translation, Commentary. Trans. and ed. by Baruch Margalit. De Gruyter 1989 $132.00. ISBN 0-89925-472-1. With text and commentary by Margalit.

ARABIC LITERATURE

Arabic is the major living language of the five-branched Hamido-Semitic family and the primary tongue of more than 100 million people. The vehicle of MUHAMMAD (see Vol. 4) the Prophet's message, it was carried and spread by civilization over a vast area stretching from Morocco and Spain in the West through India and Indonesia in the East. Since Muslims believe that the Koran was revealed in Arabic, it has also been the language of religious education wherever Islam has prevailed.

Literary Arabic differs from the spoken language, and is a unifying element in the Arab world and in Islamic civilization. Arabic literature is unparalleled in extent, perhaps because all writings in the Arabic language, whether composed by Arabs or non-Arabs, are considered part of Arabic literature.

According to most Arabists, Arabic literature falls into six periods, but for the reader's purposes it may be divided into two broad categories: the classical and the modern. The classical is characterized by the proverbs and poetry (or *qasidah,* a highly formalized form of ode) of the Arabs of the northern Arabian Peninsula. The modern opens with the nineteenth-century renaissance (*al-Nahdah al-adabiyah*) in Syria, Lebanon, and Egypt. It was stimulated by growing contacts with the West and fed by a renewed interest in the great classical past. Since the sixteenth century, the freer environment of Egypt has made that country the focus of the renaissance. When the Ottoman Empire crumbled after World War I, the movement spread to other Arab lands and came to a full flowering as the Arab countries gained their independence during the years following World War II.

The novel and the drama, literary forms largely unfamiliar to the Arab world, took shape under the impact of European works made available by nineteenth-century translations into Arabic, but the short story, the essay, and the new verse forms had their roots in classical Arabic literature. The confrontation between Arab tradition and modern attitudes put Arabic literature as well as Arab society on a new course. To some extent, the anti-Western sentiment that has prevailed as a consequence of the Palestinian disaster has led to a conscious discarding of Western themes. The romanticism of the earlier poetry is all but gone, and the younger poets have turned increasingly to free verse to convey their concern with social and political issues. Current practitioners of the art have dropped all the technical restraints of prosody and have been expressing themselves in prose poetry. An important development is the emergence since 1948 of at least a dozen dazzling poets and fiction writers who are carrying on the Arab woman's 1,300-year-old tradition of self-expression within the male-dominated culture.

History and Criticism

Accad, Evelyne. *Sexuality and War: Literary Masks of the Middle East.* NYU Pr. 1990 $40.00. ISBN 0-8147-0595-2. A critical study of both male and female Arab writers on the Lebanese war.

Allen, Roger. *The Arabic Novel: An Historical and Critical Introduction.* Syracuse U. Pr. 1982 $16.00. ISBN 0-8156-2276-7. A general introduction to the novel in Arabic. Analysis of eight novels by Mahfuz, Kanafani, Barakat, Qasim, Munif, Salih, Jabra, and Isma'il. Older, but very important.

______. *Modern Arabic Literature.* Continuum 1987 $75.00. ISBN 0-8044-3024-1. A collection of literary criticism on major writers. Essays from both books and journals, including translated Arabic criticism invaluable for non-Arabic readers.

Altoma, Salih. *Modern Arabic Literature: A Bibliography of Articles, Books, Dissertations and Translations in English.* Asian Studies Research Inst. 1975 o.p. A useful bibliography of 850 items. No annotations, but an essential starting point for researchers.

Ashtiany, Julia. *Abbasid Belles-lettres.* Cambridge U. Pr. 1990 $99.95. ISBN 0-521-24016-6. The second volume in the new *Cambridge History of Arabic Literature.* Destined to become a basic reference source.

Badawi, M. M. *A Critical Introduction to Modern Arabic Poetry.* Cambridge U. 1975 o.p. By a scholar of modern Arabic literature. All of his works are important.

______. *Early Arabic Drama.* Cambridge U. Pr. 1988 $54.95. ISBN 0-521-34427-1. Attempts to trace the development of Arabic drama from its beginnings in the middle of the nineteenth century until the early decades of the twentieth century. Particular emphasis on Egyptian and Syrian writers.

______. *Modern Arabic Drama in Egypt.* Cambridge U. Pr. 1988 $54.95. ISBN 0-521-24222-3. A study beginning with the works of Tawfiq al-Hakim. Also includes Yūsuf Idrīs and Ahmad Shawqi.

______. *Modern Arabic Literature and the West.* OUP 1985 o.p. A collection of essays, some published previously, which focus on the relation of Arabic literature to the West and its relation to its own tradition and its own past.

Beeston, A. F. L. *Arabic Literature to the End of the Umayyad Period.* Cambridge U. Pr. 1984. $105.00. ISBN 0-521-24015-8. The first volume in the definitive reference series, the *Cambridge History of Arabic Literature.*

Boullata, Issa. *Critical Perspectives in Modern Arabic Literature.* Three Continents 1980 o.p. Arab and Western criticism on various topics and authors.

Gibb, Hamilton A. *Arabic Literature: An Introduction.* OUP 1974 o.p. By perhaps the outstanding English Arabist of the twentieth century. Although dated in some respects, the best brief account of Arabic literature from pre-Islamic times through the 'Abbāsid era.

______. *Studies on the Civilization of Islam.* Ed. by Stanford J. Shaw and William R. Polk. Princeton U. Pr. 1982 repr. of 1962 ed. $19.95. ISBN 0-691-00786-1. Contains excellent articles on interpretation of Islamic history, political thought, religion, and Arabic literature.

Hamori, Andras. *On the Art of Medieval Arabic Literature.* Princeton U. Pr. 1974 o.p. Applies modern literary criticism to poetry and the *Arabian Nights.* Innovative on poetry. Useful to advanced students of Arabic.

al-Jayyusi, Salma al-Khadra. *Trends and Movements in Modern Arabic Poetry.* 2 vols. Humanities 1977 o.p. A comprehensive study intended for the specialist, but suitable for the general reader as well.

Khouri, Mounah A. *Poetry and the Making of Modern Egypt (1882–1922).* E. J. Brill 1971 o.p. Examines the role of Arabic poetry in reflecting and directing social and intellectual currents in Egypt during the British occupation.

______. *Studies in Contemporary Arabic Poetry and Criticism.* Jahan Bk. Co. 1987 $12.00. ISBN 0-317-65709-7. Essays on contemporary poetry and poets such as Gibran, Adonis, and Nu'aymah.

Kilpatrick, Hilary. *The Modern Egyptian Novel.* Intl. Lrn. Syst. 1974 o.p. Studies and traces specific topics in Egyptian prose from Haykal's "Zaynab" up to 1968. Can serve as a reference work for biographical and bibliographic information.

Lichtenstadter, Ilse. *Introduction to Classical Arabic Literature.* Twayne 1974 o.p. Notable for its discussion of "polite letters" (correspondence) and "how-to-do-it" manuals that gave rise to a bureaucratic secretarial class known as *kuttab* (scribes) in the eighth and ninth centuries.

Malti-Douglas, Fedwa. *Critical Pilgrimages: Studies in the Arabic Literary Tradition.* U. of Tex. Pr. 1989 o.p. Part of the series *Literature East & West.* Eight essays by various contributors including one by the editor of Yūsuf Idrīs.

______. *Woman's Body, Woman's Word: Gender and Discourse in Arabo-Islamic Writing.* Princeton U. Pr. 1992 $37.50. ISBN 0-691-06856-9. Women in Arabic literature and Arab women writers from Shahrazad to Nawal Sa'dawi.

Mernissi, Fatima. *Beyond the Veil: Male-Female Dynamics in a Modern Muslim Society.* Ind. U. Pr. 1987 $25.00. ISBN 0-253-31162-4. Useful as background to novels of contemporary Arab life.

Moosa, Matti. *The Origins of Modern Arabic Fiction.* Three Continents 1992 $32.00. ISBN 0-89410-684-X. Traces the evolution of Arabic fiction from the Egyptian and Syrian drama of the 1840s to the novels of Mahfouz.

Moreh, Shmuel. *Modern Arabic Poetry 1800–1970: The Development of Its Forms and Themes under the Influence of Western Literature.* E. J. Brill 1976 o.p.

Naddaff, Sandra. *Arabesque: Narrative Structure and the Aesthetics of Repetition in the 1001 Nights.* Northwestern U. Pr. 1991 $24.95. ISBN 0-8101-0976-X

Nicholson, R. A. *A Literary History of the Arabs.* Bks. Demand repr. of 1969 ed. $134.50. ISBN 0-317-27312-4. The standard in-depth work (English) on classical Arabic belles-lettres up to the fall of Baghdad in 1258. Contains a wealth of information not found in other surveys.

Pinault, David. *Story-telling Techniques in the Arabian Nights.* E. J. Brill 1992 $68.75. ISBN 90-04-09530-6. An important new study by a recognized scholar of *1001 Nights.*

Stetkevych, Suzanne. *Abu Tammam and the Poetics of the 'Abbasid Age.* E. J. Brill 1991 $103.00. ISBN 90-04-09340-0. Concerning an important figure in the classical age of Arabic poetry.

Zwettler, Michael. *The Oral Tradition of Classical Arabic Poetry.* Ohio St. U. Pr. 1978 o.p. Argues persuasively that early Arabic poetry represents the culmination of a long tradition of transmission from poet to reciter to eventual recording in written form. Also important because it foreshadowed another oral phenomenon, the Koran itself.

Collections

Abdel Wahab, Farouk W. *Modern Egyptian Drama: An Anthology. Studies in Middle Eastern Lit.* Bibliotheca 1974 $25.00. ISBN 0-88297-005-4. A good 40-page introduction. Includes *The Sultan's Dilemma* by Tawfiq al-Hakim, *The New Arrival* by Mikhail Roman, *A Journey Outside the Wall* by Rashad Rushdi, and *The Farfoors* by Yūsuf Idrīs.

Algosaibi, Ghazi A. *Lyrics from Arabia.* Three Continents 1983 $15.00. ISBN 0-89410-379-2. Bilingual selections from classical poetry, selected and translated by a well-known Saudi poet.

Arberry, A. J., trans. *Arabic Poetry: A Primer for Students.* Cambridge U. Pr. 1965 o.p. Includes translation of the famous elegy written by the poetess al-Khansa for her brother Sakhr slain in battle. Classical poets through early twentieth century. Bilingual.

Azrak, Michel G. *Modern Syrian Short Stories.* Three Continents 1988 $22.00. ISBN 0-89410-440-3. Eighteen short stories translated by the author.

Bagader, Abu Bakr. *Assassination of Light: Modern Saudi Short Stories.* Three Continents 1990 $24.00. ISBN 0-89410-598-1. Includes biographical information as well as selected stories.

Bennani, Ben. *Bread, Hashish, and Moon: Four Modern Arab Poets.* Unicorn Pr. 1982 $17.50. ISBN 0-87775-134-X. Six poems by Qabbani, three by al-Sayyab, five by Adonis, and six by Mahmud Darwish. Includes bio-bibliographical notes.

Boullata, Issa J., ed. *Modern Arab Poets, 1950–1975.* Three Continents 1976 o.p. Representative modern poets.

______, ed. *Women of the Fertile Crescent: An Anthology of Arab Women's Poems.* Three Continents 1978 o.p. Modern poetry by thirteen Arab women.

Compton, Linda Fish, ed. *Andalusian Lyrical Poetry and Old Spanish Love Songs.* NYU Pr. 1976 o.p. Poetry exhibiting many of the features associated with the tradition of courtly love and troubadours (a word of Arabic origin meaning "singers").

Elmessiri, A. M. *The Palestinian Wedding: A Bilingual Anthology of Contemporary Palestinian Resistance Poetry.* Three Continents 1982 $28.00. ISBN 0-89410-095-5. Poems by major Palestinian poets such as Salma al-Jayyusi, Fadwa Tuqan, Mahmud Darwish, and Samih al-Qasim.

Hamalian, Leo, and John D. Yohannan, eds. *New Writing from the Middle East.* A collection of stories, poems, and plays from Armenia, Egypt, Iran, Israel, Jordan, Lebanon, Syria, and Turkey, all written after World War II. An exciting, unique anthology.

Haywood, John, ed. *Modern Arabic Literature, 1800–1970.* St. Martin 1971 o.p. Extracts in translation, with an editor's introduction. Many nonliterary sections.

Johnson-Davies, Denys, trans. *Egyptian Short Stories.* Three Continents 2nd ed. 1990 $9.50. ISBN 0-89410-702-X. "Partly because they have had one of the longest cultural and intellectual connections with the West, it is the Egyptians who have given form and structure to story-telling as an Arab literary art." Seventeen short stories.

______, trans. *Modern Arabic Short Stories.* Col. U. Pr. 1985 o.p. Contains 20 translations of such high quality that they give the reader the impression that the stories were originally written in English. Indicates the way Arab men and women view the modern world.

Hutchins, Williams M. *Egyptian Tales and Short Stories of the 1970's and 1980's.* Col. U. Pr. 1987 o.p. Includes selections by Nawal al-Sa'dawi, Sabri Musa, and many more.

Jayyusi, Salma K., ed. *The Literature of Modern Arabia: An Anthology.* U. of Tex. Pr. 1988 $24.95. ISBN 0-292-74662-8. The author, an established scholar of Modern Arabic literature, is a poet in her own right.

______, ed. *Modern Arabic Poetry: An Anthology.* Col. U. Pr. 1991 $15.00. ISBN 0-231-05273-1

Johnson-Davies, Denys, trans. *Arabic Short Stories.* Interlink Pub. 1983 o.p.

______, ed. and trans. *Egyptian One-act Plays.* Three Continents 1981 $6.00. ISBN 0-89410-237-0. Includes Tawfiq al-Hakim's *The Donkey Market.*

Kassen, Ceza, ed. *Flights of Fantasy: Arabic Short Stories.* Elias Pubs. Cairo 1985 o.p. An important collection of surrealistic stories, including selections by Mahfuz, Kanafani, and Īdris.

Khouri, Mounah A., and Hamid Algar, eds. *An Anthology of Modern Arabic Poetry.* U. CA Pr. 1974 o.p. A short, excellent introduction. Chronological selections (text and translation). Short biographical sketches. Essential for tracing and understanding modern poetry.

Kritzeck, James, ed. *Anthology of Islamic Literature.* NAL-Dutton 1975 $10.95. ISBN 0-452-00783-6. Covers the period between the rise of Muhammad and the Age of the Caliphs to the Ottoman poetry at the end of the eighteenth century. Geared to the general reader, not to the specialist.

______, ed. *Modern Islamic Literature.* H. Holt & Co. 1970 o.p. Selections from the outstanding Muslim writers from 1800 to present. Off-beat excerpts from Agha Khan, the Shah of Iran, Abdul Nasser, King Abdullah of Jordan (on Lawrence of Arabia).

Manzalaoui, Mahmoud, ed. *Arabic Short Stories, 1945–1965.* Col. U. Pr. 1985 $20.00. ISBN 977-424-121-5

______, ed. *Arabic Writing Today.* 2 vols. Eisenbrauns 1968–1977 o.p. Important collection. Vol. 1 covers the short story; Vol. 2, drama.

Nicholson, Reynold A., trans. *Translations of Eastern Poetry and Prose.* Humanities 1987 o.p.

al-Udhari, Abdullah, ed. and trans. *Modern Poetry of the Arab World.* Viking Penguin 1986 o.p. The translator is also a poet.

______. *Victims of a Map.* Humanities 1984 o.p. Bilingual selections with short biographical notices. Selections from the poets Mahmud Darwish, Samih al-Qasim, and Adonis.

Wightman, G. B. H., and A. Y. al-Udhari, trans. *Birds through a Ceiling of Alabaster: Three Abbasid Poets. Penguin Class. Ser.* Viking Penguin 1976 o.p. A brief but interesting introduction to Arabic poetry and the difficulties of translation. Present-day English used to convey the poetic tone of Ibn al-Ahnaf, Ibn al-Mu'tazz, and al-Ma'arri. For popular, nonscholarly reading. With an introduction by the translators.

General Reading

Abu Zayd, Layla. *Year of the Elephant: A Moroccan Woman's Journey Toward Independence and Other Stories.* Trans. by Barbara Parmenter. U. of Tex. Pr. Ctr. Mid. East. Stud. 1989 $8.95. ISBN 0-292-79603-X. Eight short stories and a novella, *The Year of the Elephant,* which first appeared in serialized form in 1983. All have a Moroccan setting. Includes an introduction and a glossary.

The Arabian Nights. Trans. by Husain Haddawy. Ed. by Muhsin Mahdi. Norton 1990. $27.95. ISBN 0-393-02707-4. A new translation, edited by one of the most highly respected scholars of Arabic literature. Already the definitive edition.

Awwad, Tewfiq Yussef. *Death in Beirut.* Trans. by Leslie McLoughlin. Three Continents 1978 $10.00. ISBN 0-914478-87-7. A novel about a young Shi'ah woman from the south. Love against the background of the tragic civil war.

Badi al-Zaman al-Hamdhani. *The Maqamat of Badi' al-Zaman al-Hamadhani.* Trans. by W. J. Prendergast. Humanities 1973 o.p. The only complete translation of the two collections of Maqamat. Classical Arabic's great prose form, related to the European picaresque novel.

Badr, Liyanah. *A Balcony over the Fakihani.* Trans. by Peter Clark and Christopher Tingley. Interlink Pub. 1992 $19.95. ISBN 1-56656-104-3. Three novellas by an important Palestinian woman writer.

______. *A Compass for the Sunflower.* Interlink Pub. 1990 $19.95. ISBN 0-7043-5037-8. By a Palestinian woman novelist. The story "moves backwards and forwards in time and space between several episodes of recent Palestinian history" (p. vii).

Bakr, Salwa. *The Wiles of Men and Other Stories.* Trans. by Denys Johnson-Davies. Interlink Pub. 1992 o.p.

Barakat, Halim. *Days of Dust.* Trans. by Trevor J. Le Gassick. Three Continents 1983 repr. of 1974 ed. $8.00. ISBN 0-89410-360-1. A novel set at the time of the 1967 war. Includes an introduction by Edward W. Said.

______. *Six Days.* Trans. by Bassam Frangieh and Scott McGehee. Three Continents 1990 $22.00. ISBN 0-89410-661-9

Bogary, Hamza. *The Sheltered Quarter: a Tale of a Boyhood in Mecca.* Trans. by Olive Kenny and Jeremy Reed. U. of Tex. Ctr. Mid. East. Stud. 1992 $8.95. ISBN 0-292-72752-6. Originally published in 1983. A novel based on the author's boyhood in Mecca in the "days before oil" (p. 2). The author, born in 1932, died in 1984.

Darwish, Mahmud. *The Music of Human Flesh.* Trans. by Denys Johnson-Davies. Three Continents 1980 o.p. Selections from the poetry of one of the best-known Palestinian poets. Twenty-two poems by a Palestinian who worked as a journalist in Haifa for many years before going to Lebanon and Europe.

______. *Sand and Other Poems.* Trans. by Rana Kabbani. Routledge 1986 $19.95. ISBN 0-7103-0062-X

Desert Tracings: Six Classical Arabian Odes. Trans. by Michael A. Sells. U. Pr. of New Eng. 1989 $22.50. ISBN 0-8195-2157-4. A new translation of the earliest known Arabic poetry, called the Mu'allaqat.

Ghanim, Fathi. *The Man Who Lost His Shadow.* Trans. by Desmond Stewart. Three Continents 1980 $14.00. ISBN 0-89410-206-0. Novel about an ambitious journalist.

Ghitani, Jamal. *Zayni Barakat.* Trans. by Farouk Abdel Wahab. Viking Penguin 1990 $8.95. ISBN 0-14-009346-X. A novel.

Habibi, Emile. *The Secret Life of Saeed, the Ill-Fated Pessimist: The Ill-Fated Pessoptimist (A Palestinian Who Became a Citizen of Israel).* Trans. by Salma Jayyusi. Humanities

1985 $7.95. ISBN 0-86232-399-1. Combining fact and fantasy, this comic novel depicts the life of a Palestinian who becomes a citizen of Israel. Habibi, an Arab Christian and a founding member of the Israeli Community party, has been elected to the Knesset three times.

Hawi, Khalil. *Naked in Exile: Khalil Hawi's Threshing Floors of Hunger*. Trans. by Adnan Haydar and Michael Beard. Three Continents 1984 $22.00. ISBN 0-89410-366-0. Poems by a Lebanese poet who died in 1982. Includes extensive analysis.

Hussein, M. Kamal. *City of Wrong*. Trans. by Kenneth Cragg. Harper SF 1959 o.p. A novel set in Jerusalem on Good Friday.

Jabra, Jabra Ibrahim. *The Ship*. Trans. by Adnan Haydar and Roger Allen. Three Continents 1985 $24.00. ISBN 0-89410-328-8. A novel by a well-known Palestinian writer of fiction and criticism who also writes in English.

Jurji, Nabil Na''um. *The Slave's Dream and Other Stories*. Trans. by Denys Johnson-Davies. Interlink Pub. 1991 $19.95. ISBN 0-7043-2776-7. Short stories by an Egyptian writer. Somewhat unique in that these "writings are devoid of any political or social content . . ." (p. viii).

Khalifah, Sahar. *Wild Thorns*. Trans. by Trevor LeGassick and Elizabeth Fernea. Interlink Pub. 1989 repr. of 1985 ed. $9.95. ISBN 0-940793-25-3. A novel about a Palestinian living in the Gulf region.

Kharrat, Idwar. *City of Saffron*. Trans. by Frances Liardet. Interlink Pub. 1990 $19.95. ISBN 0-7043-2693-0. A collection of pieces by an important Egyptian writer about a Coptic boy in Alexandria in the 1930s and 1940s.

Khuri, Ilyas. *Little Mountain*. Trans. by Maia Tabet. U. of Minn. Pr. 1989 $24.95. ISBN 0-8166-1769-4. Poetry by a Palestinian.

Maghut, Muhammad. *Fans of Swords*. Trans. by May Jayyusi. Three Continents 1991 $16.00. ISBN 0-89410-685-6. Thirty poems.

Mazini, Ibrahim 'Abd al-Qadir. *al-Mazini's Egypt*. Trans. by William Hutchins. Three Continents 1983 $18.00. ISBN 0-89410-332-6. Two novellas and a short story by a pioneer of the fiction genre in modern Arabic literature. Historically important.

Musa, Sabri. *Seeds of Corruption*. Trans. by Mona Mikhail. HM 1980 o.p. An important novel by an Egyptian writer.

Naimy, Mikhail. *A New Year: Stories, Autobiography and Poems*. E. J. Brill 1974 o.p. Selections from the work of a Lebanese author who was also prominent in the American immigrant movement; a colleague of Jubran.

Nasr Allah, Ibrahim. *Prairies of Fever*. Trans. by May Jayyusi. Interlink Pub. 1992 $22.95. ISBN 1-56656-103-5. A novel about a teacher in an isolated area of Saudi Arabia, "A negation of chronology and sequence, a cohesive relationship between form and content, and a temporal parallelism of events, memories and dreams . . ." (the publisher).

Qu'ayd, Muhammad Yusuf. *War in the Land of Egypt*. Trans. by Olive and Lorne Kenny and Christopher Tingley. Interlink Pub. 1986 o.p. The son of a poor villager stands in as a soldier for the son of a leader. Set immediately before the October 1973 war.

Rifaat, Alita. *Distant View of a Minaret and Other Stories*. Heinemann ed. 1985 $9.95. ISBN 0-435-90912-6. Tales depicting lives of futility, isolation, and unsatisfied desire.

Salmawi, Muhammad. *Come Back Tomorrow and Other Plays*. Trans. by Amira el-Maghraby. Three Continents 1984 $7.50. ISBN 0-89410-559-0. Three plays in the style of theater of the absurd by an Egyptian writer.

Sharqawi, 'Abd al-Rahman. *Egyptian Earth*. U. of Tex. Pr. 1990 $24.95. ISBN 0-292-72071-8. One of the most important novels in modern Arabic literature, previously long out of print. A sensitive and moving portrait of the tough life of the Egyptian peasant.

Shaykh, Hanan. *The Story of Zahra*. Interlink Pub. 1986 o.p. A novel by one of the Arab world's most important women writers.

______. *Women of Sand and Myrrh*. Doubleday 1992 $9.00. ISBN 0-385-42358-6. Eloquent story of four friends struggling to live in Middle Eastern society.

Tuqan, Fadwa. *A Mountainous Journey: A Poet's Autobiography*. Trans. by Olive Kenny and Naomi Shihab Nye. Graywolf 1990 $8.95. ISBN 1-55597-138-5. An essential document on women writers and Palestinian literature by an important Palestinian poet. Her brother, Ibrahim, is also an important poet.

CHRONOLOGY OF AUTHORS

Abu Nuwas. c.756–810
al-Jahiz. d. 868 or 869
Al-Mutanabbi, Abu al-Tayyib Ahmad ibn al-Husayn. 915?–965
Abu al-'ala' al-Ma'arri. 973–1057
Shawqi, Ahmad. 1868–1932
Jubran, Kahlil. 1883–1931
Taha Husayn. 1889–1973
Al-Hakim, Tawfiq. 1902–1976?
Haqqi, Yahya. 1905–
Mahfuz, Najib. 1911–
'Abd al-Qaddus, Ihsan. 1919–1990
Qabbani, Nizar. 1923–
Al-Bayati, 'Abd al-Wahab. 1926–
al-Sayyab, Badr Shakir. 1926–1964
Idrīs, Yūsuf. 1927–
Salih, al-Tayib. 1929–
Adonis. 1930–
'Abd al-Ṣabūr, Ṣalāh. 1931–1981
al-Sa'dawi, Nawal. 1931–
Tamir, Zakariya. 1931–
al-Munif, 'Abd al-Rahman. 1933–
Kanafani, Ghassan. 1936–1972
Ibrahim, Sun' Allah. 1937–

'ABD AL-QADDUS, IHSAN. 1919–1990

At his death in 1990, Ihsan 'Abd al-Qaddus was probably the most popular writer of short stories in the Arabic-speaking world. He was born in Cairo to an important artistic family. His mother—the famous Lebanese actress-turned-journalist Fatimah "Ruz" (Rose) al-Yusuf—was the founder of the popular weekly *Ruz al-Yusuf,* which is still published today. Like many Arab writers in general, and Egyptian writers in particular, 'Abd al-Qaddus was trained in the law, although his active vocation throughout his life was journalism. He was the editor of *Ruz al-Yusuf* for many years. Like his contemporary NIZAR QABBANI, he has often been perceived as a champion of women's issues exemplified in his most famous work, the novella *Ana Hurrah (I Am Free)*. Later he turned to other social, political, and religious themes and in 1952 published "a collection of two novellas and one short story which amazed, delighted, and shocked the Egyptian public by his daring exploration of sexual themes" (Mahmoud Manzalaoui, *Arabic Writing Today*). He has also written novels, but his shorter fiction is generally considered more satisfactory. Trevor LeGassick in his introduction to *I am Free* has stated that "he powerfully evokes situation, character, and mood in pleasing brevity. His work demonstrates a steady progression in his sensitivity, maturity and artistic skill and sheds fascinating light on many facets of Egyptian life in the mid-twentieth century."

SHORT STORY COLLECTION BY 'ABD AL-QADDUS

I Am Free and Other Stories. Trans. and ed. by Trevor LeGassick. General Egyptian Book Organization 1978 o.p. Twelve short stories and the novella *I Am Free.*

'ABD AL-ṢABŪR, ṢALĀH. 1931–1981

Born in Cairo, Ṣalāh 'Abd al-Ṣabūr studied at Cairo University, graduating in 1951 with a degree in literature. Following in the tradition of many Egyptian writers, he pursued a career as a bureaucrat to support his literary career. He began publishing in the 1960s and is considered by the critic M. M. Badawi to have been the leading Egyptian poet in his lifetime. According to Badawi, "although he began as a social realist his later development reveals an increasing concern with spiritual and metaphysical issues" (*An Anthology of Modern Arabic Verse*). Although known primarily as a poet, 'Abd al-Ṣabūr wrote several plays in verse and was also a literary critic. His best-known work in the West is probably his play *Ma'sāt al-Ḥallāj* (The Tragedy of al-Ḥallāj), which has been translated into English as *Murder in Baghdad*. Although no longer in print, it is probably the most readily available of all his translated works. The eminent poet and literary critic Salma al-Jayyusi states that "'Abd al-Ṣabūr succeeds in reproducing the rhythms of common speech, where the single word is characterized by simplicity, the tone often intimate and the structure often conventional" (*Trends and Movements in Modern Arabic Poetry*).

PLAYS BY 'ABD AL-ṢABŪR

Murder in Baghdad. Trans. and intro. by Khalil I. Semaan. E. J. Brill 1972 o.p. A verse play which deals with the very political death of the ninth-century mystic al-Hallaj.

Night Traveller. Trans. by M. M. Enani. General Egyptian Book Organization 1980 o.p.

Now the King is Dead. Trans. by Nehad Selaiha. General Egyptian Book Organization 1986 o.p.

The Princess Waits. Trans. by Shafik Megally. General Egyptian Book Organization 1975 o.p.

ABU AL-'ALA' AL-MA'ARRI. 973–1057

Although he is today considered one of the greatest poets in the Arabic language and was greatly admired in his own time, al-Ma'arri was much neglected until he was "rediscovered" by TAHA HUSAYN in the early part of this century. He was born in the village of Ma'arrat al-Nu'man in northern Syria. In spite of being blind, he became an educated man and traveled extensively throughout Syria, even journeying to the caliph's court in Baghdad. However, he rejected the capital and returned to his village in 992 to settle down to a rather ascetic life of writing and lecturing. Pupils flocked to him, a sign of the high esteem in which he was held.

This very philosophical and moralistic poet's work can be divided into two periods. In the first he indulged in a quite conventional and ordinary style. In the second the more individual and philosophical style upon which his fame rests emerged. Al-Ma'arri has the reputation of being a melancholy and supremely pessimistic poet, a stance that is not surprising in view of his life. He lived in a period of great turmoil: the breakup of centralized rule, heavy taxation, growing disparity between rich and poor and Arabs and non-Arabs. This atmosphere, plus his own handicap, greatly influenced the poet. His poetry insists on encompassing the complete spectrum of life, but especially its baser aspects and its ultimate end in death. The poet often refers to the vileness of the body and human wickedness, particularly in actions toward others. Society is an illness, learning is extinct, the "wisdom of man" is a joke, and organized religion is an invention of mind control. In sum, life is constantly viewed as painful and the world as cruel, wicked, and capricious. In such a world, death is a release from pain, inevitable and peaceful.

In spite of al-Ma'arri's negative view of religion, however, he frequently invokes, prays, or complains to God. And on the positive side, he paradoxically has a deep sense of humanity and a strong belief in people's innate goodness. Al-Ma'arri's poetry shows him to be a keen, though cynical, observer of life. His poetry is not culture-bound and, in spite of its overwhelming sadness, reaches a universal audience. His most famous works are the poetry collections *Luzumiyat* (Necessities) and *Saqt al-Zand* (Sparks of Flint), and the prose *Risalat al-Ghufran* (Letter of Forgiveness). Al-Ma'arri is well represented in all anthologies of Arabic poetry, but only his collected letters have been translated into English.

Works by Al-Ma'arri

Birds Through a Ceiling of Alabaster: Three Abbasid Poets. Trans. by G. B. H. Wightman and A. Y. al-Udhairi. *Penguin Class. Ser.* Viking Penguin 1976 o.p. A brief but interesting introduction to Arabic poetry and the difficulties of translation. For popular, nonscholarly reading, with an introduction by the translators.

The Letters of Abu'l-'Ala. Trans. by D. S. Margoliouth. OUP 1898

ABU NUWAS. c.756–810

Al-Hasan ibn Hani' al-Hakami, known as Abu Nuwas, was born in either Ahvaz or Shiraz in southern Iran, sometime around the middle of the eighth century (his birthdate has been given variously as 747 or 756). Of mixed parentage, with an Arab father and a Persian mother, he was born and lived in a region and time that saw the mixture of the two cultures as well as the tensions between them. This may, in part, explain Abu Nuwas's break with the old traditional desert school of poetry that had produced the form known as the *qasidah,* rapidly ossifying by his time. Clearly a part of the social class known as *mawali* (client), Abu Nuwas has been called the voice of this group. Critics suggest that his antagonism toward traditional Arabic forms also results from their representing to him the "patrician" Arab society and its values.

Many consider Abu Nuwas to be the apogee of the writers—especially the poets—of the 'Abbasid period, which takes its name from the 'Abbasid caliphs, centered in Baghdad from 750 to 1250, who heavily patronized all art and learning. Abu Nuwas's career flourished in Baghdad, where he wrote poetry in the form known as the *ghazal,* or ode. He has come down to the present time known particularly as the poet of wine and love.

Abu Nuwas's *Diwan,* his complete works of poetry, is not readily available in English translation. A large number of his poems were translated into French by Vincent Monteil and published in 1979. However, virtually every collection or anthology of English translations covering the classical poets includes examples of his poetry.

Poetry by Abu Nuwas

Classical Arabic Poetry. Charles G. Tuetey, trans. Routledge Chapman & Hall 1985 $39.50. ISBN 0-7103-0110-3. Excellent anthology of classical Arabic poetry from pre-Islamic, Omayyad, and Abbasid periods. Includes representative works by Abu Nuwas.

ADONIS (ALI AHMED SA'ID). 1930–

Ali Ahmed Sa'id was born near Tartus in northern Syria, not far from the mythical birthplace of the god whose name he adopted as a pen name. He moved to Beirut in 1956 and became the editor of *Sh'ir,* the poetry review he helped to found. Educated at the Sorbonne and the author of a two-volume anthology of classical Arabic poetry, he was, until Lebanon went up in flames, an influential voice in the social and intellectual life of the Arab world. He has been a critic and editor of the journal *Mawaquif.* Among his published collections not yet translated into English are *The Book of Changes* and *The Stage and the Mirrors.*

Poetry by Adonis

The Blood of Adonis. Trans. by Samuel Hazo. U. of Pittsburgh Pr. 1971 o.p. Thirty-nine "transpositions" of Adonis's poems by a recognized American poet.

Transformation of the Lover. Trans. by Samuel Hazo. International Poetry Forum 1982 o.p.

NONFICTION BY ADONIS

An Introduction to Arab Poetics. Trans. by Catherine Cobham. U. of Tex. Pr. 1991 $22.50. ISBN 0-292-73859-5. Adonis's view of poetics. An important document in modern Arabic literary criticism.

AL-BAYATI, 'ABD AL-WAHAB. 1926–

'Abd al-Wahab al-Bayati, one of the most popular poets in the Arab world, is a leader of the social-realist school of poetry. Born in poverty in Baghdad, he writes poetry of strong political content. An avowed Communist and antiroyalist, he lived in exile during the years of the monarchy in Iraq. After graduation from university, he became a teacher and after that moved into the field of journalism. His work first began to appear in the early 1950s.

A proponent of the new poetry movement, his verse employs simple language and regular rhyme. Some critics have commented that his technique is loose, but Salma Jayyusi has stated that, in spite of technical weakness, "the enduring attraction of his poetry is its sincere, enthusiastic and often tender approach to life, its rare ability to portray human reality in its simple, but paradoxical qualities of hope and despair, love and hate, pride and disdain, compassion and cruelty. Despite . . . [his] . . . outlook as a Communist, his poetry shows a sustained involvement with the true human condition existing in his own part of the world" (*Trends and Movements in Modern Arabic Poetry*). Desmond Stewart has said that "perhaps more than any other Arab poet al-Bayati has broken down the walls which divide the speakers of Arabic from the outside world" (*Gazelle*).

POETRY BY AL-BAYATI

Love, Death, and Exile. Trans. by Bassam K. Frangieh. Georgetown U. Pr. 1991. $29.95. ISBN 0-87840-217-9. Fifty-four poems from collections originally published between 1969 and 1989. Texts in Arabic and English. Includes an introduction.

AL-HAKIM, TAWFIQ. 1902–1976?

Tawfiq al-Hakim was the undisputed pioneer of dramatic writing in Arabic: "With his natural talent, his wide reading in French, his close study of the techniques of European theatre . . . his interest in the problems of language—most pertinent in a culture where the written language differs so much from the spoken—with these attributes he gave to the Egyptian theatre the foundations of respectability it needed" (Denys Johnson-Davies). Born in Alexandria, he studied law in Paris and spent time with writers there. In 1928 he was appointed an attorney to the public prosecutor in the provinces of Egypt, and his experiences there inspired his novel *The Maze of Justice.* He resigned from government service and devoted himself completely to writing. Among his works widely read in Europe, particularly in France, are *The Return of the Spring* (1933) and *The Tree Climber* (1962), considered his masterwork.

PLAYS BY AL-HAKIM

Conversation with the Planet Earth: the World as a Comedy. General Egyptian Book Organization 1985 o.p. Two plays.

Fate of a Cockroach and Other Plays. Trans. by Denys Johnson-Davies. Three Continents 1992 $15.00. ISBN 0-89410-196-X. Representative of al-Hakim's writing, these plays range from romance to domestic comedy.

Plays, Prefaces and Postscripts of Tawfiq al-Hakim. 2 vols. Trans. by William H. Hutchins. Three Continents 1981 $38.00. ISBN 0-89410-280-X. Vol. 1: "Theater of the Mind"; Vol. 2: "Theater of Society."

The Tree Climber. Trans. by Denys Johnson-Davies. Three Continents 1985 o.p. Humorous avant-garde play about "murder and philosophy . . . in a suburb of modern Cairo" (publisher's introduction). One of al-Hakim's best-known works.

Novels by al-Hakim

Bird of the East. 1937. Trans. by R. Bayly Winder. Khayats 1966 o.p. A somewhat autobiographical novel concerning an Egyptian student in Paris.

The Maze of Justice: Diary of a Country Prosecutor, An Egyptian Novel. Trans. by Abba Eban. U. of Tex. Pr. 1989 $22.50. ISBN 0-2927-5112-5

The Return of Consciousness. Trans. by Bayly Winder. NYU Pr. 1985 o.p.

Return of the Spirit: Tawfiq al-Hakim's Classic Novel of the 1919 Revolution. Trans. by William M. Hutchins. Three Continents 1990 $38.00. ISBN 0-89410-425-X. "For some critics, this is still al-Hakim's greatest novel . . ." (the publisher).

Book about al-Hakim

Long, Richard. *Tawfiq al-Hakim, Playwright of Egypt.* Ithaca UK 1979 o.p. An illustrated biography of al-Hakim, with background and analysis of 32 plays.

HAQQI, YAHYA. 1905–

Egyptian short story writer and literary critic Yahya Haqqi is considered to be one of the greatest stylists in modern Arabic literature. In fact, his scrupulous craftsmanship directly accounts for his relatively modest output. Haqqi was born in Cairo into a literary family in 1905. Trained in the law, he served in various governmental posts within Egypt and abroad. His first work was published in 1925, but he is best known for his story *"Qindil Umm Hashim"* (The Lamp of Umm Hashim), which has been translated into English as "The Saint's Lamp." In this moving prose poem, Haqqi deals with a theme pervading modern Arabic literature, particularly fiction: the dilemma of Arab intellectuals caught between East and West.

Haqqi's words are carefully chosen, his tone sympathetic, and his themes socially relevant. Mahmoud Manzalaoui has said, "He has a genuinely sympathetic, if ironic, humanism of outlook as a thinker, which, in many of his stories, emerges in a sharply wry form" (*Arabic Writing Today*). M. M. Badawi in his introduction to *The Saint's Lamp* has referred to the collected stories as "classic[s] displaying a peculiar mixture of realism and fantasy . . . humour and poetry, . . . [with a] strange and haunting note of mysticism that runs through them, and not least because of the impassioned and artistically faultless style. . . ." As a writer and also an editor of the Egyptian cultural journal *al-Majallah* (the Journal), Haqqi has had a tremendous influence on writers who followed him.

Short Story Collections by Haqqi

Good Morning! and Other Stories. Trans. by Miriam Cooke. Three Continents 1987 $20.00. ISBN 0-89410-334-2. Stories set in Upper Egypt and based on the author's experiences as a provincial administrator. Includes an introduction by Miriam Cooke.

The Saint's Lamp and Other Stories. Trans. by M. M. Badawi. E. J. Brill 1973 o.p. With an introduction by the translator.

Book about Haqqi

Cook, Miriam. *The Anatomy of an Egyptian Intellectual, Yahya Haqqi.* Three Continents 1984 o.p. Biographical and critical treatment of Haqqi and his work.

IBRAHIM, SUN' ALLAH. 1937–

Born in Cairo and trained as a lawyer, Ibrahim chose a career of journalism. He was imprisoned for five years (1959–64) because of his political activities. In 1968 he went to Lebanon, then to East Berlin, and later to Moscow, where he studied cinema.

Short Story Collection by Ibrahim

The Smell of It. Trans. by Denys Johnson-Davies. Three Continents 1971 o.p. Five short stories. The title story was published in 1966 after Ibrahim's release from prison and was promptly banned in Egypt.

IDRĪS, YŪSUF. 1927–

Idrīs was born in an Egyptian village, practiced medicine for a while, was imprisoned several times for political activism during the 1950s, and then devoted himself entirely to writing. Although recently he has been writing for the stage, he is regarded as Egypt's foremost craftsman in the short story. In his psychologically penetrating tales, death and forbidden erotic love are handled in a poetic, almost surrealistic style.

Short Story Collections by Idrīs

The Cheapest Nights. Trans. by Wadida Wassef. Three Continents 1978 $22.00. ISBN 0-89410-665-1. Fifteen short stories from five of the author's collections representing "every stage of Idrīs's development . . ." (p. vii).

In the Eye of the Beholder: Tales of Egyptian Life from the Writings of Yūsef Idrīs. Bibliotheca 1978 $20.00. ISBN 0-88297-019-4. Fourteen short stories from a number of collections by various translators. Introduction by Roger Allen.

A Leader of Men. Trans. by Saad Elkhadem. York Pr. 1988 o.p. Bilingual edition of a short story originally published in the Egyptian weekly *Uktubar* (October) in 1987.

The Piper Dies and Other Short Stories. Trans. by Dalya Cohen-Mor. Sheba Pr. 1992 $15.95. ISBN 1-880613-03-4

Rings of Burnished Brass. Trans. by Catherine Cobham. Col. U. Pr. 1992 $9.00. ISBN 977-424-248-3. Four stories.

The Sinners. Trans. by Kristin Peterson-Ishaq. Three Continents 1984 $20.00. ISBN 0-89410-393-8

Three Egyptian Short Stories. Trans. by Saad El-Gabalawy. York Pr. 1991 o.p. Bilingual edition.

Books about Idrīs

Cohen-Mor, Dalya. *Yūsuf Idrīs: Changing Visions.* Sheba Pr. 1992 $39.95. ISBN 1-880613-00-X

Kurpershoek, P. M. *The Short Stories of Yūsuf Idrīs: A Modern Egyptian Author.* E. J. Brill 1981 o.p. Discusses "the short stories of Yūsuf Idrīs, taking into account their literary and historical context . . ." (p. vii).

Mikhail, Mona. *Mafouz & Idrīs: Studies in Arabic Short Fiction.* NYU Pr. 1992 $35.00. ISBN 0-8147-5474-0. An excellent new study by one of the foremost specialists on modern Arabic fiction.

AL-JAHIZ (Pseud. of 'AMR IBN BAHR). d. 868 or 869

Al-Jahiz, born in Basrah in the early 800s, is one of the most important writers in the whole of Arabic literature and considered by many its greatest prose writer. His pseudonym derives from his abnormally protruding eyes. Al-Jahiz flourished as a writer in Baghdad after 817 or 818, when he caught the attention of the 'Abbasid caliph al-Ma'mun. A rarity among classical Arabic authors, al-Jahiz wrote prose in a time when poetry was the signature form of literature. He wrote essays or epistles (*risalat*) and important linguistic and religious treatises, but the genre upon which a great deal of his fame rests is *adab*, meaning "manners" (in contemporary language, it also means "literature"). *Adab*'s initial purpose was the education and edification of princes and rulers, but it further developed into instructional works, especially using anecdotes, for essay writers. Considered the beginning of Arabic *belles-lettres*, it is associated with the rise of the *kuttab*, or secretarial class.

A work such as al-Jahiz's *Kitab al-Bukhala'* (The Book of Misers) is a pure delight in terms of both content and style—charming, humorous, and still relevant. Most important, perhaps, among his *adab* collections is the quasi-zoological work *Kitab al-Hayawan* (The Book of the Animals), which makes use of animal anecdotes. In *Kitab Fakhr al-Sudan 'ala al-Bidan* (*The Book of the Glory of the Black Race*), al-Jahiz, thought to be of African heritage, extols the virtues of the black race and heritage. Another important work is *Risalat al-Qiyan* (The Essay of the Songstresses). However, his exemplar of character traits, the *Kitab al-Bukhala'*, is probably his best-known work.

Charles Pellat, an eminent Jahiz scholar, has translated many of al-Jahiz's works into French. Some are available in English, but the most important volume is *The Life and Works of Jahiz*, which is a translation of one of Pellat's French works.

Nonfiction by al-Jahiz

The Book of the Glory of the Black Race. F. Preston 1981 $6.95. ISBN 0-939222-00-0

The Epistle on Singing Girls, Vol. 2: Approaches to Arabic Literature. Ed. and trans. by A. F. L. Beeston. David Brown 1980 $49.95. ISBN 0-85668-165-2. A translation of *Risalat al-Qiyan*, with a commentary by an outstanding scholar of Arabic literature and language.

The Life and Works of Jahiz. Trans. by Charles Pellat. U. CA Pr. 1969 o.p. Includes selections from all of the major texts plus a 27-page essay on al-Jahiz's life and works and critical introductions to the various selections.

Nine Essays of al-Jahiz. Trans. by William M. Hutchins. P. Lang Pubs. 1989 $39.95. ISBN 0-8204-0821-2

JUBRAN (GIBRAN), KHALIL. 1883–1931

Poet, philosopher, and artist, Jubran was born near the Cedars of Lebanon. In 1895 he emigrated with his family to the United States, but returned to Lebanon at age 14 to enter college. He later studied with Rodin in Paris. The millions of Arabic-speaking peoples familiar with his writings regard him as the foremost poet of his age. His fame and influence spread beyond the Middle East, and *The Prophet* (1923), his masterpiece, has sold more than 4 million copies in the United States alone. In the United States, where he lived during the last 20 years of his life, he began to write in English.

Works by Jubran

Blue Flame: The Love Letters of Kahlil Gibran to May Ziadeh. Intl. Bk. Ctr. 1983 $25.00. ISBN 0-86685-387-1. Ziadeh was an important figure in modern Arabic literature.

The Broken Wings. Carol Pub. Group 1965 $3.95. ISBN 0-8065-0190-1

The Prophet. 1923. Walker & Co. 1986 $7.95. ISBN 0-8027-2532-5. Jubran's most famous work. Originally written in English.

Prose Poems. Trans. by Andrew Ghareeb. Knopf 1934 o.p. Twelve poems with illustrations by the author.

Secrets of the Heart. Trans. by Anthony Ferris. Carol Pub. Group 1978 $5.95. ISBN 0-8065-0062-X. A collection of poems, stories, and meditations that convey the heart of Jubran's spiritual vision.

Spirit Rebellious. Trans. by A. Ferris. Philosophical Lib. 1947 o.p.

A Tear and a Smile. Trans. by H. M. Nahmad. Knopf 1950 $20.00. ISBN 0-394-44804-9

BOOKS ABOUT JUBRAN

Gibran, Jean. *Kahlil Gibran: His Life and World.* Rev. and updated ed. Interlink Pub. 1991 $35.00. ISBN 0-940793-79-2. Written by the son of Gibran's cousin and fellow traveler.

Naimy, Mikhail. *Kahlil Gibran: A Biography.* Philosophical Lib. 1985 o.p. By a Lebanese compatriot and fellow writer in the immigrant literary movement in North America.

KANAFANI, GHASSAN. 1936–1972

Kanafani was born in Acre and worked for a time in Kuwait as a teacher. He edited a daily newspaper in Beirut until he was blown up by a bomb placed in his car. His novels, short stories, and one play are interwoven with the tragedy of the Palestinian refugees.

SHORT STORY COLLECTIONS BY KANAFANI

All That's Left to You: A Novella and Other Stories. Trans. by May Jayyusi and Jeremy Reed. U. of Tex. Pr. 1990 $8.95. ISBN 0-292-70418-6. A novella and 10 short stories. With an important introduction by Roger Allen.

Men in the Sun and Other Palestinian Stories. Three Continents 1978 $8.50. ISBN 0-89410-392-X. In the title story three Palestinians try to reach Kuwait by crossing the desert in a water tanker. Introduction by Denys Johnson-Davies.

Palestine's Children. Trans. by Barbara Harlow. Three Continents 1984 o.p.

BOOK ABOUT KANAFANI

Siddiq, Muhammad. *"Man Is a Cause": Political Consciousness and the Fiction of Ghassan Kanafani.* U. of Wash. Pr. 1984 $9.95. ISBN 0-295-96154-5

MAHFUZ, NAJIB. 1911– (NOBEL PRIZE 1988)

The son of a Cairo merchant, Najib Mahfuz studied philosophy at Cairo University. He spent many years in government posts, retiring from that career in 1971. His writing career began with several historical novels, the first of which appeared in 1939. In 1945 he completed the first of his novels depicting the life of Cairo's Egyptian middle class, and during the 1950s, he gained fame with the publication of his "Cairo trilogy." The three volumes, which follow the 'Abd al-Jawad family through the first half of the twentieth century, are *Bayna al-Qasrayn* (Between the Two Palaces) (1990) (translated as *Palace Walk*), *Qasr al-Shawq* (*Palace of Desire*) (1991), and *Sukkariyah* (*Sugar Street) (1992).*

Mahfuz's earlier work is realistic but later work shows a more abstract or allegorical style, as well as exploration of new ideas. The later work also makes heavier use of dialogue and omniscient narration. While most famous as a novelist (he has written more than 30 novels), Mahfuz has written over 100 short stories, as well as some plays. Winning the Nobel Prize for literature in 1988 only reinforced the primary place Mahfuz already held among Arabic speakers. It did have the effect, however, of stimulating him to new work after a period of producing very little. Even now, past 80, he is active.

Even before he was awarded the Nobel Prize, Najib Mahfuz was better represented in English and other translations than any other Arab writer.

American University in Cairo (AUC) Press has been issuing his complete corpus in English translation. The number of titles is growing, and almost all are available. Three Continents Press has also issued many of Mahfuz's works over the years in readily available and inexpensive editions. Also, since 1989 Doubleday has been regularly issuing hardcover editions of his work, which are usually the same as those issued by AUC Press.

Novels by Mahfuz

Autumn Quail. Trans. by Roger Allen. Doubleday 1990 $7.95. ISBN 0-385-26454-2. About a civil servant during the 1952 Egyptian Revolution.

The Beggar. Trans. by Kristin Walker Henry and Nariman Khales Naili al-Warraki. Doubleday 1990 $19.95. ISBN 0-385-26455-0. Also concerns the Egyptian Revolution.

The Beginning and the End. Trans. by Ramses H. Awad. Doubleday 1989 $10.00. ISBN 0-385-26458-5. The problems of a Cairo family during World War II.

Children of Gebelawi. Trans. by Philip Steward. Three Continents 1990 o.p. A translation of *Awlad Haritina* (The Children of Our Neighborhood), an allegorical novel banned in Egypt for its political views. Possibly Mahfuz's most famous work, the only one never published in Egypt.

The Day the Leader Was Killed. Trans. by Malak Hashem. General Egyptian Book Organization 1989 o.p. A novel originally published in Arabic.

Fountain and Tomb. Trans. by Soad Sobhy, Essam Fattouh, and James Kenneson. Three Continents 1988 $22.00. ISBN 0-89410-580-9. A translation of *Hikayat Haritina* (Stories of Our Neighborhood), several stories woven together to form a novel.

The Journey of Ibn Fattouma. Trans. by Denys Johnson-Davies. Doubleday 1992 $20.00. ISBN 0-385-42323-3. The most recently published translation of Mahfuz's novels.

Midaq Alley. Trans. by Trevor LeGassick. Doubleday 1992 $8.50. ISBN 0-385-26476-3. One of Mahfuz's earliest works, about a young woman who tries to escape from her harsh life in an impoverished Cairo neighborhood.

Miramar. Trans. by Fatma Moussa Mahmoud. Three Continents 1978 $10.00. ISBN 0-89410-693-7. A journalist and the woman who owns the pension in which they live ponder the new Egypt. Set in Alexandria in the early 1960s.

Mirrors. Trans. by Roger Allen. Bibliotheca 1977 o.p.

Palace of Desire. Trans. by William M. Hutchins, Lorne M. Kenny, and Olive E. Kenny. Doubleday 1991 $22.95. ISBN 0-385-26467-4. Part II of the Cairo trilogy.

Palace Walk. Trans. by William M. Hutchins and Olive E. Kenny. Doubleday 1990 $22.95. ISBN 0-385-26465-8. Part I of the Cairo trilogy.

Respected Sir. Trans. by Rasheed El-Enany. Doubleday 1990 $19.95. ISBN 0-385-26479-8. The story of an ambitious civil servant.

The Search. Trans. by Mohamed Islam. Doubleday 1991 $20.00. ISBN 0-385-26459-3. "A young man, hoping to escape a sordid background and an impoverished future, sets out to find the father he has never known" (the publisher).

Sugar Street. Trans. by William M. Hutchins and Angele Botros Samaan. Doubleday 1992 $22.50. ISBN 0-385-26469-0. Part III of the Cairo trilogy.

The Thief and the Dogs. Trans. by Trevor LeGassick and M. M. Badawi. Doubleday 1989 $7.95. ISBN 0-385-26462-3. A thriller with strong political themes about a thief bent on revenge on his betrayers.

Wedding Song. Trans. by Olive E. Kenny. Doubleday 1989 $7.95. ISBN 0-385-26464-X. About a Cairo theater family; the same story related by four different characters.

Short Story Collections by Mahfuz

God's World: An Anthology of Short Stories. Trans. by Akef Abadir and Roger Allen. Bibliotheca 1973 o.p.

The Time and the Place and Other Stories. Trans. by Denys Johnson-Davies. Doubleday 1991 $19.50. ISBN 0-385-26471-2

Plays by Mahfuz

Naguib Mahfouz, One-act Plays. Trans. by Nehad Selaiha. General Egyptian Book Organization 1989 o.p. A collection of four one-act plays.

Books about Mahfuz

Gordon, Hayim. *Naguib Mahfouz's Egypt: Existential Themes in His Writings.* Greenwood 1990 $39.95. ISBN 0-313-26876-2. English bibliography of works.

LeGassick, Trevor, ed. *Critical Perspectives on Naguib Mahfouz.* Three Continents 1991 $25.00. ISBN 0-89410-659-7. A collection of essays from many sources.

Mikhail, Mona. *Mahfouz & Idris: Studies in Arabic Short Fiction.* NYU Pr. 1992 $35.00. ISBN 0-8147-5474-0. An excellent new study by one of the foremost specialists on modern Arabic fiction.

Peled, Matityahu. *Religion, My Own: The Literary Works of Najib Mahfuz.* Transaction Pubs. 1983 o.p. An analysis of Mahfuz's works with particular emphasis on their Islamic context.

Somekh, Sasson. *The Changing Rhythm: A Study of Najib Mahfuz's Novels.* E. J. Brill 1973 o.p. Introduction to Mahfuz's fiction published before 1967. Four of the six chapters deal with the novels, especially *Awlad Haritina.* Includes an appendix of plot outlines of 17 novels published between 1935 and 1966.

AL-MUNIF, 'ABD AL-RAHMAN. 1933–

'Abd al-Rahman al-Munif is a highly respected and popular novelist of the second generation of Arab fiction writers. He was born in 1933 in Jordan but was a Saudi citizen. Because he has never lived there—he is not permitted to do so—he is something of a *cause celèbre* among Arab intellectuals. As with many modern Arab writers, al-Munif was educated and has worked in fields that are not unrelated to his literary activities. Initially he studied law in Cairo and Baghdad and later took a Ph.D. in petroleum economics. He occupied posts in this field for many years before devoting his full attention to writing. For a period of time, he edited the journal *Naft wa-al-Tanmiyah* (Oil and Development).

Al-Munif's first novel, *al-Nihayat* (*Endings*), was published in 1978. Nature—the proper appreciation and proper use of it—is a central theme in this story of the adverse conditions facing a village located at the edge of the desert. The theme is common to his work, as is the desert setting, which Roger Allen notes is unique in modern Arabic literature. Al-Munif's fame rests on his multivolume novel cycle *Mudun al-Milh* (Cities of Salt). To date the work is comprised of five volumes, but only the first two volumes have been translated into English.

Novels by al-Munif

Cities of Salt. Trans. by Peter Theroux. Random 1989 $16.00. ISBN 0-394-75526-X. A translation of the first volume of the Cities of Salt cycle (*Mudun al-Milh*). The volume title in Arabic is *al-Tih* (The Desert).

Endings. Trans. by Roger Allen. Interlink Pub. 1988 o.p.

The Trench. Trans. by Peter Theroux. Pantheon 1991 $25.00. ISBN 0-394-57672-1. Volume Two, *al-Ukhdud*, of *Mudun al-Milh.*

AL-MUTANABBI, ABU AL-TAYYIB AHMAD IBN AL-HUSAYN. 915?–965

Al-Mutanabbi is one of the best Arabic poets of the classical period. He was born in Kufa in what is now southern Iraq during the early tenth century—a place and time of great importance because of the proliferation of petty kingdoms in the central Muslim lands. A product of his time, he was patronized by the Hamdanid ruler in Aleppo, Sayf al-Dawlah, for whom he wrote many panegyrics. Because he was educated among the Bedouin, he was well versed in the traditional poetry of Arabia, and many critics and literary historians now consider him as representing the peak of patronized poetry. He was, however, quite unorthodox in his views, which landed him in prison. During his lifetime he was accused not only of blasphemy but also of plagiarism. His pen name, al-Mutanabbi, means "one who pretends to be a prophet."

Although he used some of the oldest forms of the Arabic language, he combined them with new poetic elements and wrote with great clarity. The intensity of his language often gives his poetry a heroic quality. In spite of all the criticisms leveled against him, his poetry is of a moralistic nature. According to the literary scholar Arthur Arberry, "He is accounted the most sublime of classical poets, and many of his phrases have become proverbs" (*Arabic Poetry*). True to the rather unorthodox life he lived, al-Mutanabbi died at the hands of highwaymen.

POETRY BY AL-MUTANABBI

Poems of al-Mutanabbi. Trans. by A. J. Arberry. Bks. Demand repr. of 1967 ed. $40.30. ISBN 0-317-09928-0. Bilingual selections from al-Mutanabbi's *diwan.* Critical material by Arberry, an established scholar.

BOOKS ABOUT AL-MUTANABBI

Bonebakker, S. A. *Hatimi and His Encounter with Mutanabbi: A Biographical Sketch.* North-Holland 1984 o.p. A short treatise by an important literary historian.

Hamori, Andras. *The Composition of Mutanabbi's Panegyrics to Sayf al-Dawla.* E. J. Brill 1992 $40.00. ISBN 90-04-09366-4. An important new study by a leading scholar of classical Arabic literature.

QABBANI, NIZAR. 1923–

Nizar Qabbani is perhaps the most popular poet in the Arab world today with works published in many countries and in numerous editions. Born in 1923 into a merchant-class Damascene family, he was trained in the law and worked for some time in government and diplomatic posts in Asia and Europe. His first collection of poetry was published in 1944. While Qabbani is representative of the modernist movement and writes in free verse, he is also characterized as a romantic poet.

His themes and his use of colloquial language are the major factors in his popularity. In theme, Qabbani's work falls into two distinct periods: pre-June 1967 and post-June 1967. In his earlier period, one of his major themes is love, and he had the reputation of being a voice for women. Salma Jayyusi, however, takes exception to this view and states that his "attitude often reflected a rather conventional outlook towards women and love. He began his career . . . [singing] the praises of playful, coquettish women" (*Trends and Movements in Modern Arabic Poetry*). Nevertheless, Qabbani definitely breaks down sexual barriers with his work.

After the Six Day War in 1967 between the Arab nations and Israel, Qabbani, like many Arab writers and intellectuals, turned his attention to the social and political dilemmas brought to the fore by the defeat. His work tended to become more revolutionary and, as Jayyusi has said, somewhat rhetorical in tone as well. Perhaps his most famous postwar poem is "Khubz" (Bread), one of the first works really critical of Arab society. Qabbani, not surprisingly, is especially popular with Palestinians, although he himself is Syrian.

Like many of his countrypeople, he was influenced by French literature. His literary "manifesto" is that "poetry is justified by the pleasure it gives." Jayyusi states that more than any other modern Arab poet, Qabbani has attempted "to bring the language of poetry as near as possible to the level of current language, both the written and the vernacular."

POETRY COLLECTION BY QABBANI

Qabbani, Nizar. *Arabian Love Poems.* Trans. and ed. by Bassam K. Frangieh and Clementina R. Brown. Three Continents 1992 $28.00. ISBN 0-89410-744-5. Bilingual edition.

AL-SA'DAWI, NAWAL. 1931–

Nawal al-Sa'dawi is one of the most published Arab women writers in the West and in the Arab world, yet she has received scant critical acclaim in her homeland, especially among more conservative readers. Her outspoken feminist and political views have even led to her imprisonment in the past.

She was born in the Nile Delta village of Kafr Tahla in 1931 and was trained as a medical doctor, although in recent years she has not pursued that vocation on a full-time basis. For a brief time, she was the Director of Public Health. This medical background has figured in some of her works of fiction, most notably *Mudhakkirat Tabibah* (*Memoirs of a Woman Doctor*), which first appeared in serialized form in the popular Egyptian weekly *Ruz al-Yusuf*. In recent years she has held academic posts and, continuing to be politically active, helped found the Arab Women's Solidarity Association. She was editor of its journal *Nashrat Tadamun al-Mar'ah al-'Arabiyah* for its brief four-issue run before it was suspended in 1991.

Although al-Sa'dawi is primarily known for her novels, she has also written short stories, memoirs, travel essays, and social criticism. The most notable example of the last genre is *The Hidden Face of Eve*, which deals with women's issues in the Arab world. Fedwa Malti-Douglas states that "more than any other Arab woman writer . . . [al-Sa'dawi] has broken the barriers. She is conscious of the literary tradition weighing on her . . ." (*Woman's Body, Woman's Word*). Malti-Douglas charactierizes al-Sa'dawi's first novel, *Memoirs of a Woman Doctor*, as an angry retort to TAHA HUSAYN's *al-Ayyam* (The Days) because of its negative view of women.

NOVELS BY AL-SA'DAWI

The Circling Song. 1973. Humanities 1989 $15.00. ISBN 0-86232-816-0. A translation of *Ughniyat al-Atfal al-Da'iriyah.*

The Fall of the Imam. Trans. by Sherif Hetata. S. Asia 1989 o.p. A translation of *Suqut al-Imam.*

God Dies by the Nile. Trans. by Sherif Hetata. Humanities 1985 $15.00. ISBN 0-86232-294-4

Memoirs of a Woman Doctor. Trans. by Catherine Cobham. City Lights 1989 $6.95. ISBN 0-87286-223-2

Searching. Trans. by Shirley Eber. Humanities 1991 $15.00. ISBN 1-85649-008-4. A translation of *al-Gha'ib.*

Two Women in One. Trans. by Osman Nusairi and Jana Gough. Women Translation 1991 $9.95. ISBN 1-879679-01-9. A translation of *Imra'atan fi Imra'a.*

Woman at Point Zero. Trans. by Sherif Hetata. Humanities 1983 o.p. Set in a women's prison. A translation of *Imr'ah 'inda Nuqtat al-Sifr.*

SHORT STORY COLLECTIONS BY AL-SA'DAWI

Death of an Ex-minister. Trans. by Shirley Eber. Heinemann Ed. 1992 $9.95. ISBN 0-7493-9950-3. Stories written between 1969 and 1979.

She Has No Place in Paradise. Trans. by Shirley Eber. S. Asia 1992 o.p.

Nonfiction by al-Sa'dawi

The Hidden Face of Eve: Women in the Arab World. Trans. and ed. by Sherif Hetata. Beacon Pr. 1982 $11.95. ISBN 0-8070-6701-6

Memoirs from the Women's Prison. Trans. by Marilyn Booth. Interlink Pub. 1986 o.p. Autobiographical.

Book about al-Sa'dawi

Tarabishi, Georges. *Women against her Sex: A Critique of Nawal el-Saadawi with a Reply by Nawal el-Saadawi.* Saqi Books UK 1990 $39.95. ISBN 0-86356-143-8. Highly critical of al-Sa'dawi, with claims that her heroines undermine women's emancipation. A reply by Sa'dawi that accuses the author of outmoded thinking and reliance on Freudian analysis.

SALIH, AL-TAYIB. 1929–

Salih was born in northern Sudan and was educated in Khartoum and London. He originally intended to follow a career in agriculture but instead has worked in broadcasting, for a time as head of drama for the BBC's Arabic Service.

Short Story Collection by Salih

The Wedding of Zein. Trans. by Denys Johnson-Davies. Three Continents 1978 $19.00. ISBN 0-89410-201-X. "These stories are interesting . . . because they show what happens when a considerable sophistication and resourcefulness of technique is applied to traditional storytelling material" (*The Guardian*).

Novel by Salih

Season of Migration to the North. Trans. by Denys Johnson-Davies. Three Continents 1991 $10.00. ISBN 0-89410-199-4. About a brilliant Sudanese student who is seduced and ultimately destroyed by his obsession with the values and freedom of British life.

AL-SAYYAB, BADR SHAKIR. 1926–1964

Al-Sayyab is one of the elite in modern Arabic poetry, a founder of the movement known as *al'shi'r al'jadid* (new poetry). His birthplace, which figures prominently in his poetry, was Jaykur, a town located near Basra in southern Iraq. Al-Sayyab came from an extremely modest background and led a brief life, full of suffering because of his health, his political ideas, and his poverty. After completing his higher education, al-Sayyab taught for a while, but his political ideas led to his dismissal. His first works were published in 1947; his last work was published posthumously. Death is a frequent theme in his poetry, especially in his later work as he became aware of his own impending death, but politics also figure strongly.

Most critics consider al-Sayyab, as well as his contemporary, Nazik al-Mala'ikah, to have "led the revolution in form in modern Arabic poetry" (Salma Jayyusi, *Trends and Movements in Modern Arabic Poetry*). Although his early poems may be considered to be of a more romantic nature, he broke away to a more avant-garde style and politically and socially aware themes. He is a symbolist and a master of metaphor. Influenced by such English poets as T. S. Eliot (see Vol. 1) and Edith Sitwell (see Vol. 1), he himself had a tremendous influence on later Arab poets. Mounah Khouri has said that "his poetry mirrored the contending political currents in the Arab world, and although his affiliations changed more than once, his abiding concern was the effective poetic expression of his loyalties. He . . . is, without doubt, the greatest of the contemporary Arab poets" (*An Anthology of Modern Arabic Poetry*).

In spite of his importance in modern Arabic poetry, few English translations of his work exist. Two collections have been translated into French, including the "Jaykur poems." Al-Sayyab is represented, however, in all of the anthologies and collections of modern Arabic poetry.

POETRY BY AL-SAYYAB

Selected Poems. Trans. by Nadia Bishai. Third World Centre for Research and Publishing 1986 o.p.

SHAWQI, AHMAD. 1868–1932

Salma Jayyusi has written "the emergence of Shawqi on the literary scene was the greatest poetic event of the late nineteenth and early twentieth centuries" (*Trends and Movements in Modern Arabic Poetry*). Yet in spite of his importance as a cofounder of the literary neoclassical movement and of a revolution in Arabic poetry, none of Ahmad Shawqi's corpus of poetry has been translated into English except for a few representative pieces in anthologies.

Born in Cairo of a literary family, Shawqi began his career as a court poet under the Khedive 'Abbas Hilmi II (1892–1914). His early work fits the traditional classical model, although by 1898 there was a glimmer of the originality which was to make him a leader of the modern movement. In 1914 he was exiled to Spain because of his criticism of the new ruling Khedive. During this exile, he truly broke away from Arabic poetic conventions. His fame and popularity rest upon the work done during this fertile period. In 1920 he returned to Egypt, and in 1927 at a celebration in his honor, he received the title, albeit unofficial, of Amir al-shu'ara, "prince of poets." Part of Shawqi's high esteem results from the fact that, while revolutionary, he was able to retain the vigor and mastery of expression of earlier Arabic poetry. Shawqi's most important work is *al-Shawqiyat,* a four-volume collection of his poems published between 1898 and 1932.

Shawqi was also a pioneer in verse drama, though his plays "are generally regarded as more lyrical and poetic than dramatic" (M. M. Badawi, *An Anthology of Modern Arabic Verse*) and are rarely performed. One of his most famous plays is *Sitt Huda* (Lady Huda).

POETRY BY SHAWQI

An Anthology of Modern Arabic Poetry. Ed. by Mounah Khouri and Hamid Algar. U. CA Pr. 1974 $23.75. ISBN 0-520-02234-3. Includes representative works by Shawqi.

TAHA HUSAYN. 1889–1973

Taha Husayn, if not the most influential force in modern Arabic literature, is certainly a major one. His numerous publications in literary and cultural criticism, and particularly his autobiography, have variously inspired, proselytized, annoyed, or angered a host of Arab writers and others. Born to a traditional village family near Maghaghah in Upper Egypt in 1889, he was stricken as a young boy with blindness. This did not, however, prevent him from receiving the traditional education of the village *kuttab* school, which centered on learning the Qur'an by heart. In spite of his handicap and modest background, becasue of his talent and promise he was sent to Cairo at age 13 to attend the great mosque school of al-Azhar. From there he went on to the Egyptian University (now Cairo University), where he wrote his thesis on the classical poet ABU AL-'ALA' AL-MA'ARRI. He continued his studies at the Sorbonne between 1915 and 1919, receiving a doctorate. Upon returning to Egypt, Taha occupied a number of high academic and administrative posts at the Egyptian University and Alexandria University. From 1951 to 1952, he was Minister of Culture.

His chief fame in the Arab world—and certainly in the West—rests on his autobiography *al-Ayyam* (The Days), published in three parts from 1929 to 1967. In English, the first part has been translated as *An Egyptian Childhood*, the second part as *The Stream of Days*, and the last part as *A Passage to France*. Although this work clearly is an account of Taha Husayn's life from childhood in his village through his years at al-Azhar and then in France, it does not read strictly as autobiography. The first two volumes are narrated in the third person, with Taha always referred to as "our friend." The language is clear, concise, and very moving.

Perhaps the next most influential, and also very controversial, of Taha's works was *Fi al-Shi'r al-Jahili* (Concerning Pre-Islamic Poetry), which appeared in 1926. Aimed at breaking traditional approaches to Arabic literature and at stimulating serious literary criticism, the work suggested that the entire corpus of pre-Islamic literature was a forgery. Needless to say, this provoked strong criticism. Another seminal book is *Mustaqbal al-Thaqafah al-Misriyah* (*The Future of Culture in Eqypt*), published in 1938, which used new analytic techniques to make classical Arabic literature accessible and relevant to the twentieth century.

Taha's best-known works of fiction are *Du'a al-Qayrawan* (*The Call of the Curlew*) and *al-Adib* (The Writer).

Nonfiction by Taha Husayn

An Egyptian Childhood: The Autobiography of Taha Hussein. Trans. by E. H. Paxton. Col. U. Pr. 1992 $9.95. ISBN 977-424-246-7

The Future of Culture in Egypt. Trans. by Sidney Glazer. Hippocrene Bks. 1975 o.p. Reprint of the 1954 edition of the American Council of Learned Societies.

A Passage to France: The Third Volume of the Autobiography of Taha Husain. Trans. by Kenneth Cragg. E. J. Brill 1976 o.p.

The Stream of Days: A Student at the Azhar. Trans. by Hilary Wayment. Longman 2nd rev. ed. 1948 o.p.

Novels by Taha Husayn

The Call of the Curlew. Trans. by A. B. as-Safi. E. J. Brill 1980 o.p. A novel more famous for its style than its content. Considered to have a highly elevated poetic style.

The Dreams of Scheherazade. Trans. by Magdi Wahba. General Egyptian Book Organization 1974 o.p.

Books about Taha Husayn

Cachia, Pierre. *Taha Husayn: His Place in the Egyptian Literary Renaissance*. Luzac 1956 o.p.

Malti-Douglas, Fedwa. *Blindness & Autobiography: al-Ayyam of Taha Husayn*. Princeton U. Pr. 1988 $30.00. ISBN 0-691-06733-3

TAMIR, ZAKARIYA. 1931–

Zakariya Tamir, one of the Arab world's leading short story writers and children's writers, was born in 1931 in Damascus, Syria. Largely self-educated, he worked as a laborer but published his first short story in 1956, with his first collection, *Sahil al-Jawad al-Abyad* (The Neighing of the White Steed), appearing in 1960. Eventually, he also followed careers in journalism and television.

From August 1978 to May 1980, Tamir was the editor of *al-Ma'rifah* (Knowledge), the monthly cultural journal issued by the Ministry of Culture. He was also a founder of the Arab Writers Union in Syria, serving, among many positions, as editor of the union's journal, *al Mawqif al-Adabi* (Literary Attitude).

Like many modern writers in the Arab world, Tamir leans heavily toward political and social themes. And, like many writers of his generation, his works show a marked response to the 1967 Six Day War. Expressionist in style, his writing is clear and spare. Denys Johnson-Davies has characterized his stories as "political and social fables and allegories," with characters drawn from the common people and the oppressed.

SHORT STORY COLLECTION BY TAMIR

Tigers on the Tenth Day and Other Stories. Interlink Pub. 1985 o.p. A collection of 24 of the author's stories. The title story and "What Happened to Muhammad Mahmoud" are among his most famous political commentaries.

ARMENIAN LITERATURE

Armenian literature is one of the most distinctive in the Middle East. Having begun as the independent expression of a nation newly converted to Christianity, it flourishes today in such different environments as the former Soviet Union, the Middle East, France, and the United States, where there has been a literary renaissance inspired to a large extent by the literary quarterly *Ararat.*

Geographically, Armenia is a tiny republic in the former Soviet Union, the Caucasian remnant of a once-mighty empire. Elsewhere in the Middle East, Armenians constitute a significant cultural minority. Beyond geography, Armenia is a state of thousands of people who fled the Turkish terror of 1915 and who put down new roots in Europe, Latin America, Canada, and the United States.

Armenian literature has an impressive heritage, based on Armenia's adoption of Christianity as a state religion in A.D. c.301, and the invention of the Armenian alphabet (based on the Greek) a century later. Not unexpectedly, Armenian oral literature is older than the written, and folk poetry had flourished among proto-Armenians for at least 300 years before Mashtots (c.400). Perhaps the most remarkable piece of oral literature to survive is the epic of DAVID OF SASSOUN, "discovered" in 1873 by an Armenian clergyman, Garegin Servantstian.

After the political collapse of Greater Armenia in the eleventh century, the literature divided itself into eastern and western branches based on dialect. This split has persisted into modern times. Following a period of literary decadence in the fifteenth century, recovery began in the sixteenth century with the rise of popular bards or troubadours. By the eighteenth century, the spoken language—and secular themes—emerged alongside the *grapar* (church language) and theological or classical themes. By the first decade of the twentieth century, Armenian literature had become secularized.

In 1915, the Ottoman Empire's decision to deport the entire Armenian population of Turkey to the desert of Syria resulted in the death of countless Armenians, among them the writers responsible for the literary renaissance at the turn of the century. The novel became a vehicle for moral, social, and political aspirations of a newly awakened nationalism among Armenians. During the Stalinist purges of the 1930s, a number of Armenian writers were arrested for political "deviationism" and either jailed or deported to Siberia.

Despite this setback, Armenian literature flowered for a third time in the twentieth century. Although the publication of books in Armenia has flourished, perhaps as never before, Armenian writers are reluctantly leaving their Middle Eastern roots for a more secure life elsewhere.

General Background

Baliozian, Ara, ed. *Armenia Observed.* Ararat Pr. 1979 $10.95. ISBN 0-933706-10-3. An anthology of the experiences and impressions of noted writers from Pushkin to Michael Arlen, gathered during visits to Armenia, both Turkish and Russian.

Bedrosian, Robert. *Armenia in Ancient and Medieval Times.* Armenian Natl. Educ. 1985 $9.95. ISBN 0-685-37410-6. Comprehensive look at early Armenian history.

Chahin, M. *The Kingdom of Armenia.* Routledge Chapman & Hall 1987 $52.50. ISBN 0-7099-4800-X. Excellent historical background on Armenia.

Emin, Gevorg. *Land, Love, Century: New and Selected Poems.* Trans. by Martin Robbins and Tatul Sonentz-Papazian. Three Continents 1988 $22.00. ISBN 0-89410-625-2. By a very popular contemporary poet.

Hamalian, Leo. *Burn after Reading.* Ararat Pr. 1979 $8.95. ISBN 0-933706-02-2. A collection of personal essays that provide an appreciation of the Middle Eastern temperament.

Khrakhuni, Zareh. *Selected Poems of Zareh Khrakhouni.* Trans. by A. J. Hacikyan Arsene Mamourian. E. Mellen 1990 $29.95. ISBN 0-88946-745-5. Selections from 10 of the author's works published between 1964 and 1987.

Mavian, Vahram. *Selected Writings of Vahram Mavian (1926–1983): A Unique Voice in Armenian Diaspora Literature.* Trans. by Agop J. Hacikyan. E. Mellen 1992 o.p.

History and Criticism

Baliozian, Ara. *The Armenians: Their History and Culture.* Ararat Pr. 1980 $6.95. ISBN 0-933706-22-7. Perhaps the best introduction for the general reader. A concise and readable study of Armenian history and culture (religion, language, all arts).

Etmekjian, James. *History of Armenian Literature: Fifth to Thirteenth Centuries.* DOAC 1988 $19.00. ISBN 0-934728-19-4

Hamalian, Leo. *As Others See Us: The Armenian Image in Literature.* Ararat Pr. 1980 $9.95. ISBN 0-933706-17-0. A study of the image of the Armenian in Western fiction and travel literature. Contains a concise history of Armenia and a bibliography.

______. *The View from Ararat: Twenty-five Years of Armenian-American Writing.* Ararat Pr. o.p. Includes reviews and criticism of books about Armenia by Armenians. Well-written articles on every phase of Armenian history and cultural life, both in Armenia and in the diaspora.

Hovannisian, Richard G., ed. *The Armenian Image in History and Literature.* Undena Pubns. 1981 o.p.

Oshagan, Vahe, ed. *Armenia.* Griffon Hse. 1984 o.p. Eleven articles on Armenian literature, early to modern. Includes essays on drama, poetry, specific writers, and Armenian and Western literary relations.

Collections

Boyajian, Zabelle C. *Armenian Legends and Poems.* Col. U. Pr. 1959 o.p. Includes early legends in prose and a wide range of translations in verse of medieval and modern poetry. Valuable essay on Armenian epics, folk songs, and medieval poetry by Aram Raffi (son of the famous novelist).

Der Hovanessian, Diana, and Marzbed Margossian, eds. *Anthology of Armenian Poetry.* Col. U. Pr. 1978 $50.00. ISBN 0-231-04564-6. Spans more than 20 centuries, includes pagan fragments. An extraordinary collection hitherto unavailable in English, including works by Grigor Naregatsi, Nahabed Kouchag, and Sayat Nova.

Downing, Charles. *Armenian Folk-Tales and Fables*. Ed. by William Papas. OUP o.p. Also includes proverbs.

Etmekjian, James, ed. *Anthology of Western Armenian Literature*. Caravan Bks. 1980 $30.00. ISBN 0-88206-026-0

Hoogasian-Villa, Susie. *One Hundred Armenian Tales and Their Folkloristic Significance*. Wayne St. U. Pr. 1982 $39.95. ISBN 0-8143-1282-9. A valuable collection of folk tales as told by Armenian immigrants to the United States.

Issahakian, Avedick. *Scent, Smile and Sorrow: Selected Verse*. Library of Armenian 1984 $6.00. ISBN 0-910154-02-3. Well-rounded collection of poetry.

Samuelian, Thomas J., ed. *Classical Armenian Culture: Influences and Creativity*. Scholars Pr. GA 1982 $13.00. ISBN 0-89130-566-1. Essays.

Samuelian, Thomas J., and Michael E. Stone. *Medieval Armenian Culture*. Scholars Pr. GA 1983 $23.50. ISBN 0-89130-642-0. Fifteen essays on Armenian literature of the period.

Surmelian, Leon. *Apples of Immortality: Folk Tales of Armenia*. Greenwood 1983 repr. of 1968 ed. o.p. A collection of charming folk tales that reveal the folk wisdom of the Armenian peasantry.

Tolegian, Aram. *Armenian Poetry Old and New*. Wayne St. U. Pr. 1979 o.p. Bilingual text sampling the richness of 16 centuries of the Armenian poetic tradition. Contains the complete text of the Hovhannes Toumanian version of "David of Sassoun."

______. *We of the Mountains*. Progressive Pubns. 1972 o.p. A collection of short stories by 19 writers of different generations, outlook, and style. Translated from Russian.

CHRONOLOGY OF AUTHORS

David of Sassoun. Late medieval period
Kouchag, Nahabed. d. 1592
Baronian, Hagop. 1842–1891
Shirvanzadeh. 1858–1935
Zohrab, Krikor. 1861–1915
Odian, Yervant. 1869–1926
Issahakian, Avedick. 1875–1957
Tekeyan, Vahan. 1878–1948
Yessayan, Zabel. 1878–1943
Zarian, Gostan. 1885–1969
Charents, Eghishe. 1897–1937
Antreassian, Antranig. 1908–
Zaroukian, Antranik. 1913–
Gaboudigian, Sylva. 1920–

ANTREASSIAN, ANTRANIG. 1908–

Now residing in California, Antreassian is among the few Armenian writers in the United States who has created a corpus of work in his own language.

SHORT STORY COLLECTION BY ANTREASSIAN

The Cup of Bitterness. Trans. by Jack Antreassian. Ashod Pr. 1979 $4.95. ISBN 0-935102-01-9. A collection of eight stories concerned with survivors of Turkish persecution who, though they escaped death, bear the psychic damage of the holocaust all their lives.

BARONIAN, HAGOP 1842–1891

Armenia's foremost satirist, Baronian was born and educated in Edirne but was active mainly in Istanbul. Although both his family and health were poor, he managed to write hugely popular plays, such as *Brother Balthazar*, and satiric sketches before he died of tuberculosis at age 50.

WORKS BY BARONIAN

The Perils of Politeness. Trans. by Jack Antreassian. Ashod Pr. 1983 $7.50. ISBN 0-935102-10-8. A satire on the torments people suffer in the name of politeness. Set in

Constantinople a century ago, the episodes are disquieting reflections of experiences today. Introduction by Michael Kermian.

The Honorable Beggars. Trans. by Jack Antreassian. Ashod Pr. 1979 $4.95. ISBN 0-935102-01-9. A satire on avarice, about a man who visits Constantinople and finds himself the target of endless schemes to separate him from his money.

CHARENTS, EGHISHE. 1897–1937

Modern Armenia's most brilliant poet, Charents was caught up in the Communist Revolution until he fell out of favor in the 1930s. He died in a Soviet prison.

Poetry by Charents

Land of Fire. Trans. by Diana Der Hovanessian and Marzbed Margossian. Ardis Pubs. 1985 o.p.

Work by Charents

Across Two Worlds: Selected Prose of Eghishe Charents: Letters, Excerpts from "Erkir Nayiri" and "Erevan's House of Correction," Essays, and Pages from His Diary. Trans. by Jack Antreassian and Marzbed Margossian. Ashod Pr. 1985 $10.00. ISBN 0-935102-17-5

DAVID OF SASSOUN. Late medieval period

The deeds of David of Sassoun were repeated orally in the Armenian countryside but were not written down until the late nineteenth century. The complete epic consists of four cycles in rhythmic prose, each describing the exploits of a succeeding generation of legendary heroes from the wild regions of Sassoun, southwest of Lake Van (near Iran), who defend their homeland against foreign tyrants. David is the hero of the third generation and became, especially in Soviet Armenia, a symbol of patriotic valor.

Books about David of Sassoun

Daredevils of Sassoun. Trans. by Leon Surmelian. Swallow Pr. 1954 o.p. The Armenian saga of the twelfth century rendered into stirring prose by a skilled novelist, with a substantial introduction setting the epic in its historical and political context.

David of Sassoun: The Armenian Folk Epic in Four Cycles. Trans. and ed. by Artin K. Shalian. Ohio U. Pr. 1964 o.p. A translation of the Armenian text by the poet Hovhannes Toumanian. Covers the third cycle only, of which David is the hero.

GABOUDIGIAN, SYLVA. 1920–

One of Armenia's most famous contemporary poets, Gaboudigian has been translated into more than 20 languages. She survived revolution and terror to write more than 500 lyric poems, which stand as an intimate autobiography.

Poetry by Gaboudigian

Lyrical Poetry of Sylva Gaboudigian. Dorrance 1981 o.p. The first English translation of poems celebrating the love of country and compatriots.

ISSAHAKIAN, AVEDICK. 1875–1957

Issahakian's work includes legends, short stories, political essays, an unfinished novel, prose cameos, and memoirs, but he is best known for his poems recited as popular songs. In 1895 he was imprisoned for political activities. *Songs and Hurts*, his first book, appeared in 1896. Again accused of conspiring against the czar, he was exiled to Odessa and jailed. He escaped to Paris, then returned to Armenia for four years. After another absence, he returned again in 1936, remaining there until his death. He is one of Armenia's best-loved poets.

POETRY BY ISSAHAKIAN

Scent Smile and Sorrow: Selected Verse, 1891–1957. Ed. by E. B. Chrakian. Library of Armenian 1984 $6.00. ISBN 0-910154-02-3

NONFICTION BY ISSAHAKIAN

Notebooks of a Lyric Poet, Avetik S. Isahakian, 1875–1957. Trans. by Leon D. Megrian. U. Pr. of Amer. 1991 $42.50. ISBN 0-8191-8051-3

KOUCHAG, NAHABED. d. 1592

A tombstone in an Armenian village (Karagonis) gives the date of Kouchag's death. Nothing more is known about him except that he wrote poetry. (Until scholars recently settled the question, it was thought that the work attributed to him was anonymous folk poetry.) His lyricism, simplicity, and candor illuminate a dark period in Armenian history. Kouchag's verse is not overburdened with grief like that of most modern Armenian poets, nor do all his poems always praise God, like the work of his religious contemporaries. He knows pathos and love, and mixes them gracefully in his verse.

POETRY BY KOUCHAG

Come Sit Beside Me and Listen to Kouchag. Trans. by Diana Der Hovanessian. Ashod Pr. 1984 $7.50. ISBN 09-35102-14-0. Medieval poems marvelously rendered into idiomatic English by an outstanding poet.

ODIAN, YERVANT. 1869–1926

Sickly as a child, Odian was educated at home. He established his reputation with a novella, *The Victim of Love* (1892), at age 23. He barely escaped the murderous persecutions of 1896 and fled to exile, memorably recounted in *Twelve Years Away from Constantinople.* In other books and in articles, he exposed the abuses of the political parties, criticized Turkish policies, and attacked the oppressive influence of landlords and *pashas.* A survivor of the 1915 death marches, he spent his last disillusioned days in Egypt.

NOVEL BY ODIAN

Comrade Panchoonie. Trans. by Jack Antreassian. DOAC 1977 o.p. A rollicking satire of a would-be revolutionary who bungles almost everything. *Panchoonie* literally means "has nothing [upstairs]." Excellent illustrations by Alexander Saroukhian.

SHIRVANZADEH (pseud. of Alexander Movsessian). 1858–1935

Regarded as the father of eastern Armenian realism, both fiction and drama, Shirvanzadeh was born in Shirvan, Azerbaijan, and had little formal education. He worked as an accountant in the oil city of Baku, and his novel *Chaos* describes the early days of the oil industry. He lived in Paris (1905–10), in the United States for seven years, and returned to Russia in 1926, where he died of alcoholism. His plays, adapted from his novels, are still widely performed and have been turned into successful films and operas. He had a bitter vision of society, depicting it as dominated by greed, superstition, puritanism, and gossip.

PLAY BY SHIRVANZADEH

Evil Spirit. Trans. by Nishan Parlakian. DOAC 1980 $4.95. ISBN 0-934728-01-1. A competent, idiomatic, and witty translation by a playwright and professor of theater.

For the Sake of Honor. DOAC 1976 o.p.

TEKEYAN, VAHAN. 1878–1948

Born and educated in Constantinople, Tekeyan developed into the outstanding poet of his milieu. Besides his own books, he published translations of French symbolist poetry and Shakespearean sonnets (the sonnet remained his favorite form). During the 1896 persecutions, he escaped to Europe. He returned briefly to Turkey but left again to settle in Egypt, where he was active in Armenian political life and editor of the Armenian newspaper *Arev* (Sun).

Poetry by Tekeyan

Sacred Wrath: The Selected Poems of Vahan Tekeyan. Trans. by Diana Der Hovanessian and Marzbed Margossian. Ashod Pr. 1982 $12.50. ISBN 0-935102-08-6. Brilliant translations of a brilliant poet.

YESSAYAN, ZABEL. 1878–1943

Zabel Yessayan was born in Constantinople to a prosperous family who educated her at the Sorbonne. She lived and worked in Arab-speaking countries and Europe before settling permanently in Yerevan, the capital of Armenia. An erudite scholar, influential teacher, and versatile author, she wrote in French and Armenian an autobiography of her early life, eyewitness accounts of the 1909 massacres of Armenians, literary criticism, and travel impressions (the last reveals a full commitment to the Soviet regime). For her passionate defense of the writers accused of deviationism and antigovernment agitation in the mid-thirties, she too was arrested and banished. She died amid mysterious circumstances. Her unfinished *magnum opus,* a long novel about her Zorba-like uncle, awaits translation into English.

Work by Yessayan

The Gardens of Silihdar and Other Writings. Trans. by Ara Baliozian. Ashod Pr. 1982 $7.50. ISBN 0-935102-07-8. Selections from the fiction, satire, autobiography, and travel impressions of a woman much admired in her own time and still avidly read by Armenians.

ZARIAN, GOSTAN. 1885–1969

Lawrence Durrell (see Vol. 1) called Zarian "a wild and roguish literary man of almost mythological quality." Picasso (see Vol. 3) and Marc Chagall illustrated his books and the Italian composer Respighi set his poems to music. Born in the Caucasus and educated in France and Italy, he became a noted poet, editor, teacher, journalist, and storyteller. Multilingual, he produced a body of various work unmatched by any Armenian writer, except possibly his friend William Saroyan (see Vol. 1).

Nonfiction by Zarian

The Traveller & His Road. Trans. by Ara Baliozian. Ashod Pr. 1981 $5.95. ISBN 0-935102-04-3. Sparkling encounters with the people of the Caucasus, based on a diary covering the critical years 1922–25. Informative introduction, historical and literary notes useful to the general reader, and swift, crisp, and graceful translation.

Bancoop and the Bones of the Mammoth. Trans. by Ara Baliozian. Ashod Pr. 1982 $7.50. ISBN 0-935102-06-X. Further travels through Turkey and Europe, brimming over with penetrating meditations on the role of the artist in society, the decline of the West, and the Armenian "situation" in diaspora. Also provocative portraits of eminent writers.

ZAROUKIAN, ANTRANIK. 1913–

Zaroukian grew up in an Armenian orphanage and received his schooling in Aleppo and Beirut. As a young man, he worked as editor and teacher. In 1942 he began publishing *Nayiri,* a journal on Armenian letters and public life. After the outbreak of the Lebanese civil war, the journal appeared irregularly, ceasing altogether in 1983. Zaroukian now lives in Paris with his wife and daughter. His books include *Tragic Writers, The Astray,* a satiric novel, and *Sails,* a collection of poetry.

NONFICTION BY ZAROUKIAN

Men without Childhood. Trans. by Elise Bayizian and Marzbed Margossian. Ashod Pr. 1985 $10.00. ISBN 0-935102-15-9. The story of thousands of children who were orphaned by the massacres, haunted forever by the bitter past, and effectively denied a normal childhood.

ZOHRAB, KRIKOR. 1861–1915

Author, lawyer, and statesman, Krikor Zohrab was a prominent and respected figure in both Turkish and Armenian life of the late nineteenth and early twentieth centuries. When he fiercely opposed the Ottoman plan to deport Armenians into the desert, he was murdered by the police along with 200 other leaders of the Armenian community as a prelude to mass killings. Although born in affluent circumstances, he knew how poor people lived their wretched lives, and his stories touch on their tragedies and occasional pleasures with sympathy and sensitivity.

SHORT STORY COLLECTION BY ZOHRAB

Voice of Conscience. Trans. by Jack Antreassian. DOAC 1983 $10.00. ISBN 0-934728-09-7. Stories of ordinary people of Turkey, immersed in their fears, conflicts, and small joys. Excellent introduction by Michael Kermian that makes clear Zohrab's virtues as a man and a writer.

WORK BY ZOHRAB

Zohrab: An Introduction. Trans. by Ara Baliozian. NAASR 1985 $3.95. ISBN 0-920553-00-1

PERSIAN (IRANIAN) LITERATURE

Like Armenian, Persian is an Indo-European language. It is the official language of Iran and widely spoken in Afghanistan. Beginning with the Achaemenid Dynasty (559–529 B.C.), the Persians have made brilliant contributions to the progress of world civilization, and their achievements in the areas of lyric poetry, epic narrative, and mystical imagery are no less impressive. (The term "Persian literature" is usually restricted to the prose and poetry written after the Islamic conquest of Iran in the seventh century.)

The Middle Persian period of the third to the ninth centuries had a varied literature. The Arab conquest of Iran caused profound shifts in Persian language and literature. Arabic script replaced the ideograms of Aramaic, many Arabic words passed into the new language, and certain forms of literature underwent modification. The most far-reaching change, however, was the defeat of Zoroastrian fire worship by Islam. Iran came to identify itself with the Shi'ite branch of Islam, which regards Ali as MUHAMMAD's (see Vol. 4) successor and ignores the first three caliphs.

One of the Iranian dynasties to arise after the collapse of the Abbāsid Caliphate was the Ghaznavids (rulers of what today is Afghanistan), who were great patrons of literature. Poets were encouraged, and the greatest was FIRDAWSĪ, whose tenth-century *Shahnamah (Books of Kings)* is accepted without question as *the* Iranian epic. MATTHEW ARNOLD (see Vol. 1) drew upon it for his "Sohrab and Rustum." During the reign of the Ghaznavids, significant cultural exchange took place between the Indian and the Islamic worlds, and Persian became the court language of most of India until the British came.

Under the patronage of the Seljuk Turks in the eleventh century, many great authors flourished. By this time, Persian poetry had been colored with the tenets and images of Islamic mysticism known as Sufism, which provided the background and imagery of the greatest Persian poetry of the following two centuries.

The nineteenth century witnessed a quickening tempo of changes in society and literary expression, but it was not until 1920 that the truly modern turn in prose and poetry was taken. Prose, relegated to a secondary role in the past, now became the dominant medium of literary expression.

The modern revolt against classical Persian poetry was somewhat retarded by a more persistent strength in the tradition. Like prose, modern poetry has been perhaps too self-conscious. In the opinion of some critics, it has been a literature of ideas rather than of experience, but there are signs that this trend may now be reversing itself.

Although the Persian branch of Islam produced a very powerful religious drama, the *ta'ziyah,* serious drama has come to Iran through translations of European works. On the other hand, a long tradition of comic and satiric theater, originating in puppetry and court entertainments known as *tamash,* was revived during the constitutional struggle in the late nineteenth century and reasserted itself in the wake of Reza Shah's abdication in 1941. With the resurgence of the monarchy after 1953, censorship curtailed much of this activity except in the bland versions performed in the *chai-khanehs* (teahouses).

The future of all Iranian literature will depend on the degree of independence granted to literary artists by the intensely religious regime. Free-thinking Iranians may have to develop their art in diaspora. The first year of the Islamic Republic saw a flourish of literary activity before censorship was again imposed.

History and Criticism

Baraheni, Reza. *The Crowned Cannibals: Writings on Repression in Iran.* Random 1977 o.p. Once a prisoner of the secret police, the leading critic and novelist of Iran writes about the situation of writers in his country and the problems of nationality groups and women, and chronicles the nation's "torture industry." A stunning and shattering book. Introduction by E. L. Doctorow.

Bosworth, Clifford E. *The Later Ghaznavids: Splendor and Decay—The Dynasty in Afghanistan and Northern India.* Mazda Pubs. 1977 $19.95. ISBN 0-231-04428-3. About the fertile artistic period that produced Firdawsī and a flowering of Persian culture.

Browne, Edward G. *A Literary History of Persia.* 4 vols. Cambridge U. Pr. 1920. Vol. 1 o.p. Vol. 2 $94.95. ISBN 0-521-04345-X. Vol. 3 $94.95. ISBN 0-521-04346-8. Vol. 4 o.p. Among the most valuable works in English by a sensitive interpreter of Persian life and literature. Includes numerous texts and translations, to 1924, with the Islamic era receiving most attention.

Chelkowski, Peter J. *Ta'ziyeh, Ritual and Drama in Iran.* NYU Pr. 1979 o.p. An important work on a form of great literary, religious, and cultural significance to Iran.

Proceedings of a conference by Western and Middle Eastern scholars in Middle East studies, drama, and anthropology.

Ghanoonparvar, M. R. *Prophets of Doom: Literature as a Socio-political Phenomenon in Modern Iran.* U. Pr. of Amer. 1985 $47.25. ISBN 0-8191-4292-1

Green, John. *Iranian Short Story Authors: a Bio-bibliographic Survey.* Mazda Pubs. 1989 $29.95. ISBN 0-939214-64-4. Includes profiles on many modern Persian writers, some not readily available in English. Citations of works in both Persian and translation.

Hekmat, Forough, and Yann Lovelock. *Folk Tales of Ancient Persia.* Caravan Pr. 1974 o.p. One of the UNESCO Collection of Representative Works, Asian Series. Contains eight folk tales from ancient Persia, preserving part of the oral storytelling tradition of present-day Iran.

Javadi, Hasan. *Satire in Persian Literature.* Fairleigh Dickinson 1988 $39.50. ISBN 0-8386-3260-2. Covers classical and modern authors, including journalists, and includes political cartoons. A postscript on the situation since the 1979 revolution.

Kamshad, Hassan. *Modern Persian Prose Literature.* Cambridge U. Pr. 1966 $54.95. ISBN 0-521-05464-8. The best discussion in English. Kamshad gives a good historical background, settles the identity of the Persian translator of Morier's *Hajji Baba,* and analyzes the principal authors of the twentieth century. The second part analyzes the life and work of Sādiq Hidāyat. An excellent general bibliography and an extensive list of Hidāyat's work.

Levy, Reuben. *An Introduction to Persian Literature.* Col. U. Pr. 1969 o.p. A still-useful survey (excellent for its small compass) up to the modern period, where the coverage is weak. Several brief translations.

Meisami, Julie Scott. *Medieval Persian Court Poetry.* Princeton U. Pr. 1987 o.p. "Discusses previously neglected stylistic qualities and ethical purposes in medieval Persian court poetry, and shows that court poets were also moral instructors . . . " (the publisher).

Milani, Farzaneh. *Veils and Words: The Emerging Voices of Iranian Women Writers.* Syracuse U. Pr. 1992 $34.95. ISBN 0-8156-2557-X. "Examines a long line of pioneering women who unveiled both their bodies and their voices" (the publisher).

Ricks, Thomas M., ed. *Critical Perspectives on Modern Persian Literature.* Three Continents 1984 $40.00. ISBN 0-914478-95-8. A collection of essays from various sources.

Rypka, J. *History of Iranian Literature.* Trans. by Hope P. Van Popta. Ed. by Karl Jahn. Kluwer Ac. rev. & enl. ed. 1968 $142.50. ISBN 90-277-0143-1. A work originally written in Czech by one of the most accomplished of Iranologists, with the collaboration of many scholars. English edition translated from the German, with revisions. An excellent, in-depth account that uses Russian research not usually available to English readers. Also covers Tajik literature, folk literature, Persian literature in India, and Judeo-Persian literature. A good index and bibliography.

Schimmel, Annemarie. *Two-colored Brocade: The Imagery of Persian Poetry.* U. of NC Pr. 1992 $59.95. ISBN 0-8078-2050-4. By a leading scholar of Persian poetry. "Provides the first comprehensive introduction to the . . . system of rhetoric used by the poets of Iran, Ottoman Turkey, and Muslim India" (the publisher).

Storey, Charles A. *Persian Literature: A Bio-Bibliography Survey.* Verry 1970 o.p. A monumental work, not completed by the time of Storey's death, intended to be the essential reference work for advanced researchers. To be continued by G. M. Meridith-Owens.

Yohannan, John D. *Persian Poetry in England and America: A Two Hundred Year History. Persian Studies Ser.* Caravan Bks. 1977 $40.00. ISBN 0-88206-006-6. A detailed study of the interpretation of Persian and English literatures.

Collections

Arberry, A. J. *Immortal Rose: An Anthology of Persian Lyrics.* Gordon Pr. 1976 $59.95. ISBN 0-8490-2039-5. Originally published in 1948. Contains examples from classical Persian poetry.

Bowen, J. C. *Poems from the Persian.* Humanities 1964 repr. of 1948 ed. o.p. Good translations of the classical Persian poets from Firdawsī to Qulzum, with useful introductions to the life and work of each.

Ghanoonparvar, M. R., and John Green. *Iranian Drama: an Anthology*. Mazda Pubs. 1989 $24.95. ISBN 0-939214-63-6. Ten plays by seven authors including Sa'idi and Chubak. Contains critical introductory material.

Hamalian, Leo, and John D. Yohannan. *New Writing from the Middle East.* NAL-Dutton 1978 o.p. Previously unpublished (in English) works of Alavī, Baraheni, Farzan, Golshiri, Shamlu, and Saedi, with an excellent introduction by Yohannan.

Kapuscinski, Gisele, trans. *Modern Persian Drama: An Anthology*. U. Pr. of Amer. 1987 $45.50. ISBN 0-8191-6578-6. Plays by Bahram Bayza'i, Gawhar Murad (Ghulam Husayn Sa'idi), and 'Abbas Nalbandian.

Karimi-Hakkak, Ahmad, trans. *An Anthology of Modern Persian Poetry*. Mazda Pubs. 1978 $19.50. ISBN 0-89158-181-2. Representative selections from major modern poets.

Moayyad, Heshmat, ed. *Stories from Iran 1921–1991: A Chicago Anthology*. Mage Pubs. Inc. 1991 $35.00. ISBN 0-934211-28-0. Thirty-three short stories by major modern writers translated by many scholars. Includes a glossary and some portraits.

Sullivan, Soraya Paknazar, trans. *Stories by Iranian Women since the Revolution*. U. of Tex. Pr. 1991 $8.95. ISBN 0-292-77649-7. Thirteen authors, including Dānishvār, with biographical information about each, plus an essay by Farzaneh Milani.

Pound, Omar. *Arabic and Persian Poems*. New Dir. Pr. 1970 $7.50. ISBN 0-8112-0385-1. Excellent translations by the son of Ezra Pound. Mostly classical poems.

Sharma, Nasira, ed. *Echoes of Iranian Revolution: Poems of Revolt and Liberation, 1979*. Advent text ed. 1979 o.p. Poems of revolt and liberation ably translated.

Southgate, Minoo, ed. and trans. *Modern Persian Short Stories*. Three Continents 1980 o.p. Includes 15 works by Chubak, Sadiqi, Sa'idi, Dānishvār.

General Reading

Baraheni, Reza. *God's Shadow*. Bks. Demand repr. of 1976 ed. $25.80. ISBN 0-317-27949-1. A collection of poems translated by the poet himself. A haunting and harrowing reflection on his incarceration in an Iranian prison during the reign of the late shah.

Fasih, Isma'il. *Sorraya in a Coma*. Humanities 1985 $14.95. ISBN 0-86232-525-0. A novel set in Paris with Iranian exiles and in Iran during the war with Iraq. Originally published in 1984.

Irani, Mauchehr. *King of the Benighted*. Trans. by Abbas Milani. Mage Pubs. Inc. 1990 $29.95. ISBN 0-934211-26-4. A novella "superimposed" on Nizami's *The Black Dome* (thirteenth century). Milani states, "The story epitomizes what can be considered a budding cultural and artistic revolution in [contemporary] Iranian society." Written after the revolution by an author using a pseudonym.

Nadirpur, Nadir. *False Dawn: Persian Poems (1951–1984)*. Trans. by Michael C. Hillman. Three Continents 1986 $7.00. ISBN 0-89410-606-6. Forty poems from an important modernist poet. Includes two long essays on Nadirpur by Hillman and Leonardo Alishan.

Sholevar, Bahman. *The Night's Journey; and, The Coming of the Messiah*. Trans. by the author. Concourse Pr. 1984 o.p. Two novels. *Night Journey* was first published in 1967, although it was completed in 1961 after being censored for a number of years. The author also writes in English.

Sipihri, Suhrab. *The Expanse of Green*. Trans. by David L. Martin. Kalimat 1988 $24.95. ISBN 0-933770-42-1. Mystical poems in a bilingual edition. Sipihri, who died in 1980, is considered one of modern Iran's greatest poets.

Ubayd Zakani, Nizam al-Din. *The Ethics of the Aristocrats and Other Satirical Works*. Trans. by Hasan Javadi. Jahan Bk. Co. 1986 $16.00. ISBN 0-936665-000-9. A translation of the satirical poetry of a fourteenth-century author.

Vajdi, Shadab. *Closed Circuit*. Trans. by Lotfali Khonji. Dufour 1990 $16.95. ISBN 0-948259-78-7

CHRONOLOGY OF AUTHORS

Firdawsī. c.934–c.1020
Omar Khayyam. c.1021–1122
'Aṭṭār, Farīd al-Dīn. 1142–c.1229
Rūmī, Jalāl al-Dīn. 1207–1273
Sa'di. d. c.1292
al-Hafiz. 14th century
Jamalzadah, Muhammad 'Ali. 1892–
Yushij, Nima. 1895–1960
Hidāyat, Sādiq. 1903–1951
'Alavī, Bezorg. 1907–
I'tisami, Parvin. 1907–1941
Chubak, Sadiq. 1916–
Dānishvār, Sīmīn. 1921–
Āl-i Aḥmad, Jalāl. 1923–1969
Farrokhzad, Forough. 1935–1967
Sa'idi, Ghulam Husayn. 1935–1985
Behrangi, Samad. 1939–1968

ĀL-I AḤMAD, JALĀL. 1923–1969

Born in Tehran in 1923, Jalāl Āl-i Aḥmad is considered to be one of Iran's major modern prose writers, distinguished in both fiction and nonfiction. His first works of fiction began to appear in 1945. His seminal work, *Mūdīr-i Madrasah* (*The School Principal*) (1958) is social criticism as much as a novel—a blend that has led to many of Āl-i Aḥmad's works, especially his later ones, being banned.

His political affiliations changed markedly during his life. The son of a Shi'ah cleric, he eventually came to have a strong belief in Islamic government and the importance of Shi'ah Islam in Iranian life, but earlier in his life he was active in the Tudeh (Communist) party and a strong supporter of Muhammad Musaddiq. Unquestionably, though, he was a nationalist with a strong dislike of Western culture and its pervasive intrusion in Iran. These feelings are particularly evident in his best-known nonfiction work in both Iran and the West, *Gharbzadigi* (Struck by the West). Originally published in serialized form in 1962, only a part appeared before it was banned. The first uncensored edition was published in 1978.

Yet Āl-i Aḥmad was not solely an angry voice. H. Kamshad has said that in his fiction one always finds "cynicism and disillusionment . . . mingled with humour . . ." (*Modern Persian Prose Literature*). His last novel, *Nafrīn-i Zamīn* (*Cursing of the Land*), was published in 1968 shortly before he died of a heart attack. He was married to the well-known fiction writer Sīmīn Dānishvār, and his brother, Shams Āl-i Aḥmad, is also a writer.

Novels by Āl-i Aḥmad

By the Pen. 1961. Trans. by M. R. Ghanoonparvar. U. of Tex. Ctr. Mid. East. Stud. 1988 o.p. The novel *Nūn va al-Qalam.* "About Iranian intellectuals. Set in an imaginary time and place." Introduction and glossary by Michael C. Hillmann.

Lost in the Crowd. Three Continents 1985 $20.00. ISBN 0-89410-442-X

The School Principal: A Novel. 1958. Trans. by John K. Newton. Bibliotheca 1983 $12.00. ISBN 0-88297-032-1. Introduction and notes by Michael C. Hillmann.

Nonfiction by Āl-i Aḥmad

Gharbzadegi = Weststruckness. Trans. by John Green and Ahmad Alizadeh. Mazda Pubs. 1982 $16.95. ISBN 0-939214-08-3. One of several English translations under various titles (see below).

Occidentosis: A Plague from the West. Trans. by R. Campbell. Ed. by Hamid Algar. Mizan Pr. 1984 o.p. Another translation of *Gharbzadigi,* edited by an eminent scholar of modern Iran.

Plagued by the West. Trans. by Paul Sprachman. Center for Iranian Studies, Col. U. Pr. 1982 $18.00. ISBN 0-88206-047-3. *Gharbzadigi.*

Work by Āl-i Aḥmad

Iranian Society: An Anthology of Writings. Comp. and ed. by Michael Hillmann. Mazda Pubs. 1982 $6.95. ISBN 0-939214-03-2. Includes both fiction and nonfiction, especially a wonderful autobiographical piece written with much humor.

'ALAVĪ, BEZORG (or BOZORG). 1907–

Cofounder of the Tudeh (Communist party) in Iran, 'Alavī was jailed during the 1930s for his political views. Since 1941 he has lived in the former East Germany, where he had both literary and academic standing. He has written three volumes of short stories, a novel (*Her Eyes*), and, in German, a history of Persian literature. "*The Lead Soldier*" is considered one of the best short stories written in Persian.

Novel by 'Alavī

Her Eyes. Trans. by John O'Kane. U. Pr. of Amer. 1989 $34.75. ISBN 0-8191-7344-4. A work that caused some controversy among leftist writers for being too soft on the upper class.

Nonfiction by 'Alavī

The Prison Papers of Bozorg Alavī: A Literary Odyssey. Syracuse U. Pr. 1985 $28.00. ISBN 0-8156-0195-6. Translations of the five short stories comprising 'Alavī's collection *Scrap Papers from Prison.* Includes extensive critical material on 'Alavī's life in Iran, his years of exile in Berlin, and his return to Iran in 1979. Based on 10 years of interviews.

'AṬṬĀR, FARĪD AL-DĪN. 1142-c.1229

Little accurate information is known about 'Aṭṭār, one of the great Sufi poets of Iran. An apothecary and physician, he had many works attributed to him; the two best known are *The Conference of the Birds* and *Muslim Saints and Mystics.*

Poetry by 'Aṭṭār

The Conference of the Birds. 1917. Trans. by C. S. Nott. Viking Penguin 1984 $8.95. ISBN 0-14-044434-3. An allegory in rhymed couplets in which birds on a pilgrimage undergo the seven stages of the mystic's path to the truth.

Nonfiction by 'Aṭṭār

Muslim Saints and Mystics. Viking Penguin 1990 $9.95. ISBN 0-14-019264-6

BEHRANGI, SAMAD. 1939–1968

Behrangi was born in Tabriz (Azerbaijan) and taught in the rural village schools of the Turkish North before devoting himself wholly to writing stories that would honestly portray the inhuman plight of the poor and their children. He drowned at age 29 while swimming in a swift river. His pioneering stories, his strong social consciousness, and his sympathy for the downtrodden place him in the forefront of contemporary Persian writers.

SHORT STORY COLLECTION BY BEHRANGI

The Little Black Fish and Other Modern Persian Stories. Trans. by Mary Hooglund and Eric Hooglund. Three Continents 1987 $9.00. ISBN 0-89410-621-X. Five stories. Realistic stories rendered more poetic by the simple and everyday language, an innovation in Persian prose. An illuminating commentary by Thomas Ricks.

CHUBAK, SADIQ. 1916–

Sadiq Chubak is one of the leading fiction writers in modern Persian, both in the critical and the popular sense. He was born into a merchant family in Bushihr on the Persian Gulf, an area that figures prominently in some of his stories. Later he moved to Shiraz. Although he was a protegé of SADIQ HIDAYAT, Chubak has not imitated his mentor but is an innovator in his own right. His influences are both Eastern and Western, from the classical epics and poetry of Persia to European and American novelists such as JAMES JOYCE (see Vol. 1) and WILLIAM FAULKNER (see Vol. 1). His writings include short stories, novels, and plays—full of satire, but possessing a stark and gloomy tone. Favoring characters from the rural and urban underclasses, he is a master of colloquial language and has upset conservative readers and critics by his use of vulgarities. His social criticism is also strong. As Hasan Javadi notes, "the burden of misery and corruption" is never alleviated in his stories (*Satire in Persian Literature*).

Chubak is a modernist writer who uses a minimum of description and places himself in the role of detached observer. Yet, while he "keeps his picture balanced and spare . . . a whole pattern of emotion and situation is revealed within it. The result is generally convincing and shows a moving insight into human nature" (Hassan Kamshad, *Modern Persian Prose Literature*). Sadiq Chubak's first story collection appeared in 1945. He is perhaps best known for his novel *Sang-i Sabur* (*The Patient Stone*), published in 1966. (Interestingly, his mentor Hidayat wrote a collection of short stories with the same title.) Two other works for which he is especially well known are the novella *Tangsir* (translated as *One Man and His Gun*), based on an actual incident that took place in his hometown during his youth, and the one-act play *Tup-i Elastik* (*The Rubber Ball*), an extremely biting political satire.

NOVEL BY CHUBAK

The Patient Stone. Trans. by M. R. Ghanoonparvar. Mazda Pubs. 1989 $24.95. ISBN 0-939214-62-8. "A misunderstood girl who, in her struggle to earn a living to support her small child, has resigned herself to temporary marriages. . ." (Hassan Kamshad). Introduction, annotations.

WORK BY CHUBAK

Sadeq Chubak, an Anthology. Ed. by F. R. C. Bagley. Col. U. Pr. 1981 o.p. Examples of work in all genres, translated by several hands. Includes the novel *Tangsir* and the play *The Rubber Ball.* Includes an introduction by Bagley.

DĀNISHVĀR, SĪMĪN. 1921–

Sīmīn Dānishvār is one of the most distinguished and popular women writers in Persian. Dānishvār was born in 1921 in Shiraz, in the south of Iran, into a middle-class educated family; her father was a physician and her mother an artist. In 1942 she entered the University of Tehran but left briefly for a career in journalism.

Although she was on the faculty of the University of Tehran for many years, she was never granted tenure because of her opinions and activism. While she has always maintained a nonpolitical stance, never joining a political party, she has been outspoken. She was a founder of the Writers' Association, which was formed as an alternative to the state-sponsored association and which fought long and hard against the intellectual and artistic censorship of the Shah's era. One of her cofounders was the leading writer JALĀL ĀL-I AḤMAD, whom she married in 1952.

Her first work, a collection of short stories, was published in 1948, the first such collection ever published by a woman. Her novel *Savushun* (*A Persian Requiem*), first published in 1969, continues to be the single best-selling book in Iran, and some literary historians view it as the highest peak of novel writing in Persian. Yet, in spite of this popularity and high scholarly regard, the literary establishment still neglects her.

Although Dānishvār is strongly identified with women's concerns and experiences, she shows concern for a broader spectrum of the Iranian people as well. According to some critics, Dānishvār's work is a true mirror of Iranian society.

NOVELS BY DĀNISHVĀR

A Persian Requiem. 1969. Trans. by Roxane Zand. Braziller 1992 $22.50. ISBN 0-8076-1273-1. The most recent translation of *Savushun.* Set in Shiraz during World War II and the British occupation.

Savushun: A Novel about Modern Iran. Trans. by M. R. Ghanoonparvar. Mage Pubs. Inc. 1990 $29.95. ISBN 0-934211-24-8. Introduction by Brian Spooner.

SHORT STORY COLLECTION BY DĀNISHVĀR

Dāneshvār's Playhouse: A Collection of Short Stories. Trans. by Maryam Mafi. Mage Pubs. Inc. 1989 $21.95. ISBN 0-934211-19-1. Five short stories, the author's "letter to the reader," and "Ghurub-i Jalāl" (Jalāl's Sunset)—her remembrance of her husband Jalāl Āl-i Aḥmad.

FARROKHZAD, FOROUGH. 1935–1967

Before her untimely death at age 32, Forough Farrokhzad published five volumes of poetry that made her a major figure in modern Persian letters, one who defied social restraint and taboo to express her innermost feelings about love, sex, society, and self with a candor unprecedented in the history of Persian literature. Her style and thought developed from the personal and often introspective to a broader social vision and transcendental view of universal questions.

Born in Tehran to an upper-middle-class family, she was married at age 16 to a man she did not love. A year later she gave birth to a son, her only child, of whom she lost custody when she was divorced in 1954. She was killed in an automobile accident in 1967.

WORK BY FARROKHZAD

Another Birth. Three Continents 1981 $11.00. ISBN 0-89410-3610-X. Selections from each of her five collections. Includes excerpts from interviews and letters, analytical essays on two of her major poems by A. Davaran and H. Javadi, and a bibliography of criticism.

POETRY BY FARROKHZAD

Bride of Acacias: Selected Poems of Forough Farrokhzad. Trans. by Jascha Kessler and Amin Banani. Mazda Pubs. 1982 $19.50. ISBN 0-88206-050-3

A Rebirth: Poems. Trans. by David Martin. Mazda Pubs. 1985 $9.95. ISBN 0-939214-30-X. Includes a critical essay by Farzaneh Milani. Bilingual edition.

BOOKS ABOUT FARROKHZAD

Forough Farrokhzad a Quarter-Century Later: Essays, Reviews and Translations. Literature East & West 1988 o.p. A collection of essays from many sources.

Hillmann, Michael C. *A Lonely Woman: Forugh Farrokhzad and Her Poetry.* Three Continents 1987 $22.00. ISBN 0-89410-543-4. Analysis by a leading scholar of Persian literature who believes Farrokhzad's "days of confinement in the prison of 'women's poetry' are numbered because her total commitment to art and life is the stuff of which a great poet . . . is made" (the publisher).

FIRDAWSĪ. c.934–c.1020

Firdawsī was born to a family of landowners near Tus, where his tomb is now a national shrine. Beyond that, little is known about the author of the greatest epic of Persia. He won immortality through his *Shahnamah,* an epic of unique literary and historic importance in Iran. Composed of more than 50,000 couplets, it is a vast collection of Indo-European and Iranian legends and history strung together by the poet's skill. Rustum's exploits are central to this work, and MATTHEW ARNOLD's (see Vol. 1) poem "Sohrab and Rustum" is based on the tragic encounter between the warrior hero and his son. The most complete edition of the *Shahnamah* in a Western language is the seven-volume critical French edition by Jules Mohl, *Le Livre des Rois* (1976).

POETRY BY FIRDAWSĪ

The Epic of Kings: Shah-nama. Routledge 1973 o.p. The standard translation in English.

The Tragedy of Sohrab and Rostam. Trans. by Jerome W. Clinton. U. of Wash. Pr. 1988 $25.00. ISBN 0-295-96577-0. A portion of the *Shah-namah* translated by a well-known Persian literary scholar.

AL-HAFIZ (Pseud. of Muhammed Shams al-Din). 14th century

Al-Hafiz, along with his near contemporary and fellow Shirazi SA'DI, has always been regarded by Persian speakers as the most beloved and sublime of poets. He was famous in his own lifetime. For centuries his tomb in Shiraz in southern Iran has been a shrine, and his poems are still quoted by the broadest spectrum of Iranians. Although his birthdate is widely disputed, scholars believe that Muhammad Shams al-Din died in 1389 or 1390. His pen name, al-Hafiz, means "memorizer," particularly one who has committed the Qur'an to memory. This would seem to indicate that he received a traditional religious education at the very least.

Typical of the time in which he lived, al-Hafiz was a court poet, excelling in the *ghazal,* or ode, although he also wrote in many other forms, including *ruba'iyat* (quatrains).

Al-Hafiz loved Shiraz, and it appears often in his works, particularly the quarter in which he lived. His other themes are those common to his times: youth, love, beauty. His poems are always moralistic. Although he frequently uses Sufi language and images, many of his poems cannot be read allegorically. His *diwan* (complete works) contains close to 700 poems and has been translated into English several times and in several styles. In Persian, editions of the *diwan* are innumerable, and literally hundreds of books have been written about al-Hafiz and his works by the great and the nongreat alike.

Poetry by Hafiz

The Divan, Written in the Fourteenth Century. Trans. by H. Wilberforce Clarke. 2 vols. Weiser 1970 o.p. The first translation into English, with critical and explanatory remarks.

Fifty Poems of Hafiz. Trans. by Arthur J. Arberry. Cambridge U. Pr. 1947 $59.95. ISBN 0-521-04039-6. Introduction and annotations by Arberry.

Thirty Poems. Trans. by Peter Avery and John Heath-Stubbs. Trafalgar 1952 o.p.

Books about Hafiz

Hillmann, Michael C. *Unity in the Ghazals of Hafez.* Bibliotheca 1976 $20.00. ISBN 0-88297-010-0. A fairly recent critical study by a leading American scholar of Persian literature.

HIDĀYAT, SĀDIQ. 1903–1951

Critics regard Sādiq Hidāyat as one of the outstanding writers of the twentieth century. Known primarily for his short stories, he was influenced by Poe (see Vol. 1) and Kafka. His stories plumb the depth of human motivation and seek out the meaning of life. Many critics regard his novel *The Blind Owl* (1937) as the masterpiece of all Persian fiction. His work evidences a deep pessimism, which eventually led him to suicide.

Novels by Hidāyat

The Blind Owl. 1937. Trans. by D. P. Costello. Grove Pr. 1989 $8.95. ISBN 0-8021-3180-8. *Būf-i Kūr* was first published in India. Most readers find the translation morbid and depressing, but agree that Hidāyat's work of self-analysis is a masterpiece.

Haji Agha: Portrait of an Iranian Confidence Man. 1945. Trans. by G. M. Wickens. U. of Tex. Ctr. Mid. East. Stud. 1979 o.p. A "bitingly satirical" novel set in Tehran about a corrupt, self-centered, and self-serving local official and businessman.

The Patient Stone: A Persian Folktale. Retold by M. Batmanglij and N. Batmanglij. Mage Pubs. Inc. 1986. ISBN 0-934211-02-7

The Pearl Canon. Ed. by Iraj Bashiri. Mazda Pubs. 1986 $9.95. ISBN 0-685-11886-X

Short Story Collection by Hidāyat

Sadeq Hedayat, an Anthology. Westview 1979 o.p. Seventeen short stories by several translators. Introduction by the preeminent scholar Ihsan Yarshater.

Books about Hidāyat

Bashiri, Iraj. *The Fiction of Sādiq Hidāyat.* Mazda Pubs. 1984 $17.95. ISBN 0-939214-22-9. A revision of *Hidāyat's Ivory Tower* (1974) that stresses the importance of the covert details in Hidāyat's life and points out his debt to Indian sources as well as the Bible.

Beard, Michael. *Hedayat's Blind Owl as a Western Novel.* Princeton U. Pr. 1990 $35.00. ISBN 0-691-03137-1. Beard, a leading scholar of Persian literature, analyzes Hidāyat's major work as a piece of western literature.

Hillman, Michael C., ed. *The Blind Owl Forty Years After.* U. of Tex. Pr. 1978 $8.95. ISBN 0-292-73006-3. Sixteen essays ranging from the structure of the novel to the influence of Freud and Buddhism on Hidāyat.

Katouzian, Homa. *Sadeq Hedayat: The Life and Literature of an Iranian Writer.* St. Martin 1991 o.p.

I'TISAMI, PARVIN. 1907–1941

Persian literature over its long history has produced few women poets. Parvin I'tisami is to be counted among the most important of them, even though today she is often eclipsed by her younger compatriot, Forough Farrokhzad, a proponent of the new poetry. I'tisami's poetry is written in the traditional classical style, although, paradoxically, she came from a background that mixed the traditional and modern. Her father especially held modern views. He allowed Parvin to be educated away from the home, took her along on his travels, and included her in his (male) literary gatherings. He was a forward-looking intellectual who edited and published the important cultural journal *Bahar,* in which I'tisami's first poems were published, anonymously, when she was a young teenager.

I'tisami herself was a founder of the Women's Center in Tehran, an institution seeking women's emancipation, including unveiling. Yet she sometimes veiled, and she kept public contact to the barest minimum. After a brief unhappy marriage, she worked for a short time in the library at the University of Tehran, but most of her life was spent within the family home. Farzaneh Milani, in her book *Veils and Words,* has claimed, however, that publication of I'tisami's *diwan,* the first ever by a woman, was an act of unveiling.

I'tisami wrote in a variety of forms, including fables. Unlike other traditional poets, she did not write about love. Her poems have a great sadness about them, often bordering on the melancholy, and reveal her intense concern with the conditions of Iran's poor and disenfranchised. Yet, although the language of her poetry is simple, she did not use the colloquial language. Her translator, Margaret Madelung, calls I'tisami "a cultural and historical philosopher" and says that, because of the social issues that appear in I'tisami's work, "she is a reformer and belongs to the future, though her formal poetry may appear as a thing of the past."

WORK BY I'TISAMI

A Nightingale's Lament: Selections from the Poems and Fables of Parvin E'tesami, 1907–1941. Trans. by Heshmat Moayyad and A. Margaret Arent Madelung. Mazda Pubs. 1985 $17.95. ISBN 0-93921-421-0. Presents somewhat less than half of her poems.

JAMALZADAH, MUHAMMAD 'ALI. 1892–

Short story writer and novelist M. A. Jamalzadah has the distinction of having spent his entire writing career outside of Iran, while being considered the father of the modern Persian short story. Jamalzadah was born in 1892 in Isfahan into the family of a Shi'ah cleric. His father, Jamal al-Din Isfahani, was a reform-minded mullah who ended his days in prison. Jamalzadah left Iran at the age of 12 to attend school in Beirut. He continued his studies in Germany, remaining there after graduation to pursue a career in journalism, particularly as a writer for *Kava.* Even abroad he was, in the tradition of his father, an ardent nationalist.

In 1921 he published a short story collection *Yaki Bud, Yaki Nabud* (*Once upon a Time*). This collection of six pieces was the first of the genre in Persian to achieve any measure of success. The characters are the common folk, and the language is their language. Full of humor, critical of much of Iranian society, it drew criticism from the conservative elements within Iran. His use of the colloquial language, particularly slang, also outraged conservatives. His introduction to *Yaki Bud, Yaki Nabud* is an important document in its own right, as it sets out Jamalzadah's views on the short story in Persian. Although he was opposed to the traditional school of Persian literature, he believed in developing distinctively Persian forms rather than simply importing styles. To be this sort of innovator, Jamalzadah had to educate himself in Persian. He succeeded, for Hassan Kamshad has called him "the most absolutely Persian of writers," noting that "the striking thing about . . . [Jamalzadah] is that in his compositions one senses the life, spirit, and atmosphere of Persia more than in those of any other writers now living in the land" (*Modern Persian Prose Literature*). As an innovator in form and especially language, Jamalzadah has influenced all twentieth-century Persian writers.

Short Story Collection by Jamalzadah

Once Upon a Time: Yeki Bud, Yeki Nabud. Trans. by Heshmat Moayyad and Paul Sprachman. Mazda Pubs. 1985 $19.50. ISBN 0-933273-00-2

Nonfiction by Jamalzadah

Isfahan is Half the World: Memories of a Persian Boyhood. Trans. by W. L. Heston. Princeton U. Pr. 1983 $50.00. ISBN 0-691-06563-2. The first part is the author's recollections of his boyhood in Isfahan; the second part is a story about a friend.

OMAR KHAYYAM. c.1021–1122

Known in Iran as a leading mathematician, Omar gained literary importance through certain quatrains that were translated by Edward FitzGerald. The *Rubā'iyāt* is justly famous in English translation. Others besides FitzGerald have tried their hand at translating it, not all with admired results. Bowens's is a good example of competent and pleasing work.

Poetry by Omar Khayyam

A New Selection from the Rubaiyat of Omar Khayyam. Trans. and ed. by John Bowen. Humanities 1976 o.p. Rendered into English verse by Bowen, with a literal translation of each Persian quatrain by A. J. Arberry.

The Ruba'iyat of Omar Khayyam. Trans. by Edward FitzGerald. Outlet Bk. Co. 1992 $7.99. ISBN 0-517-07232-7. Numerous paperback editions are available.

Ruba'iyat of Omar Khayyam. Trans. by Ahmad Saidi. Jain Pub. Co. 1991 $60.00. ISBN 0-89581-897-3

Books about Omar Khayyam

Dashti, Ali. *In Search of Omar Khayyam.* Trans. by L. P. Elwell-Sutton. Col. U. Pr. 1971 o.p. By an eminent author and critic who wrote on many of the classical poets. Important as a Persian literary figure's views on another Persian literary figure.

Shahid, Irfan. *Omar Khayyam: The Philosopher-Poet of Medieval Islam.* Georgetown U. Pr. 1982 o.p. A short analytical lecture by a distinguished scholar who is professor of Arabic and Islamic literature at Georgetown University.

RŪMĪ, JALĀL AL-DĪN. 1207–1273

The greatest Sufi poet, Rūmī was born in Balkh and settled in Anatolia (Turkey) after years of travel. His major work, the *Masnavi*, stands as one of the great complete expressions of Islamic mysticism. There are countless studies of his work in Persian.

Poetry by Rūmī

Discourses of Rūmī. Trans. by A. J. Arberry. Weiser 1972 o.p. Rūmī's famous poetic treatise on Sufism, the *Fihi Ma Fihi.*

Mystical Poems of Rumi: First Selection, Poems 1-200. Trans. by A. J. Arberry. U. Ch. Pr. 1968 o.p.

Mystical Poems of Rūmī: Second Selection—Poems 201–400. Trans. by A. J. Arberry. *Persian Heritage Ser.* Mazda Pubs. 1983 $19.50. ISBN 0-89158-477-3. A stream of rapturous lyric poems, many written in the name of a wandering dervish, Shams al-Din of Tabriz, who aroused Rūmī's passionate devotion.

Unseen Rain: Quatrains of Rumi. Trans. by John Moyne and Coleman Barks. Threshold VT 1986 $8.00. ISBN 0-939660-16-4. Translated by a professor of linguistics and a poet. Quatrains from Rūmī's complete works (eight volumes in Persian).

BOOKS ABOUT RŪMĪ

Schimmel, Annemarie. *I Am Wind, You Are Fire: the Life and Work of Rumi.* Shambhala Pubns. 1992 $16.00. ISBN 0-87773-611-1. By one of the most important scholars of mysticism. A free form discussion of Rūmī's life and works. Includes a bibliography.

SA'DI (pseud. of Muslih al-Din). d. c.1292

Much beloved by Persian-speaking people from his own time to the present day, Sa'di is second, if not equal, to his near-contemporary AL-HAFIZ. Like Hafiz, Sa'di was born in the city of Shiraz. He spent many years wandering throughout the Muslim world before returning to Shiraz at the age of 50. His great writings date from this period. His best work is the *Bustan* (the Orchard), a long poem of an extremely moralistic flavor that appeared in 1257. Tradition says that a year later he produced his *Gulistan* (Rose Garden), a collection of anecdotes, primarily in prose. Critics consider it inferior to *Bustan.* Sa'di's other major work is his *Kulliyat,* which contains several forms of poetry, including *ghazals* in both Persian and Arabic. Living as he did in an age of court patronage (his pen name was taken from that of his patron Sa'd ibn Zangi), Sa'di's work is full of moralistic advice and direction, yet is also realistic and satiric. In his fables, Sa'di made great use of animals to represent, or to contrast with, human characteristics. An innovation was his reversal of the traditional order of Persian fables: He first told the tale; then he gave its moral.

WORKS BY SA'DI

The Gulistan, or Rose Garden, of Sa'di. Trans. by Edward Rehatsek. Ed. by W. G. Archer. Paul & Co. Pubs. AT 1964 o.p.

Morals Pointed and Tales Adorned: The Bustan of Sa'di. Trans. by G. M. Wickens. U. of Toronto Pr. 1974 o.p. A readable and up-to-date translation with valuable critical introductory material.

BOOKS ABOUT SA'DI

Yohannan, John D. *The Poet Sa'di: A Persian Humanist.* U. Pr. of Amer. 1987 $17.75. ISBN 0-8191-5740-6. On Sa'di's life and works. Includes chapters on *Bustan* and *Gulistan,* Sa'di in the East and the West, and many fragments (in translation) from his poetry.

SA'IDI, GHULAM HUSAYN. 1935–1985

In his short lifetime, Ghulam Husayn Sa'idi established himself firmly in two genres: short stories and plays. Born in Tabriz in the Azerbaijan province of northwestern Iran, Sa'idi was a physician by training. Because of his outspoken political views, he was often imprisoned during the period of Pahlavi rule. He was also one of the founders of the Writers' Association of Iran, a group that was outspoken and relentless in its criticism of the government's censorship. In 1982 Sa'idi left the Islamic Republic of Iran for self-imposed exile in Paris, where he published and edited the important journal *Alifba.*

Sa'idi's first play appeared in 1961. Many of his plays are political allegories, written in the style of the theater of the absurd; most were published under the pseudonym of Gawhar Murad. Some critics consider Sa'idi's drama superior to his fiction and praise him as one of Iran's great playwrights, exploring such themes as rebellion versus freedom and conformity versus control.

Sa'idi's first short story collection, published in 1964, contains his famous "Dandil." His novel *Tars va Larz* (*Fear and Trembling*) was published in 1968. Sa'idi's fiction, like his plays, often contains satirical, black humor. It focuses on the common folk, often from the seamier side of life, such as the red light district in "Dandil." Sa'idi is considered a master of dialogue, not surprising for a playwright, and his work has been a popular source for films, a form in which he was quite interested. His story "Gav" (The Cow) became one of the most successful and acclaimed films produced in Iran.

In style Sa'idi fluctuates from the allegorical and surrealistic to an often depressing realism. Unfortunately, some of his work is marred by regrettable stereotypes.

Novel by Sa'idi

Fear and Trembling. 1968. Trans. by Minoo Southgate. Three Continents 1984 $18.00. ISBN 0-89410-287-7. "Paints a portrait of the 'people of the wind' of the southwestern Iranian coast, who eke out a living in a desolate landscape. . ." (the publisher). Introduction and bibliography by Southgate.

Short Story Collection by Sa'idi

Dandil: Stories from Iranian Life. Trans. by Robert Campbell, Hasan Javadi, and Julie Scott Meisami. Random 1981 o.p. Four short stories. The title story, dealing with local Iranians and an American soldier, "clearly indicates the growing resentment toward American involvement in Iran" (Hasan Javadi).

YUSHIJ, NIMA (pseud. of 'Ali Isfandiyari). 1895–1960

Although he is not well known in the West and only one of his works, a children's book, has been translated into English, Yushij is important in any listing of Persian writers. As one of the founders of the *shi'r-i naw* (new poetry) movement, he has influenced succeeding generations of Persian poets. Forough Farrokhzad, for example, has acknowledged his impact on her own development as a poet.

Yushij was born in Yush, a town in Mazandaran Province on the Caspian Sea. Politically active, he believed social and political change was a necessity for Iran and was a member of Iran's Tudeh (Communist) party. His period of great literary production was in the 1920s and 1930s. Reza Baraheni, himself a poet as well as a literary critic, has said: "Nima gave a multi-sided dimension to the construction of Persian poetry; a construction in content, . . . in the subjective form of a complete poem and . . . in the apparent form. New poetry or the poetry of Nima was formed by these three [things] . . . ."

Novel by Yushij

When the Elephants Came. Retold by Mariam Evans. Mage Pubs. Inc. 1988 $18.50. ISBN 0-934211-15-9. A children's story.

TURKISH LITERATURE

Turkish is one of the languages spoken from Sinkiang to Skopje. By convention, the word *Turkish* is applied most properly to the language and literature of the Ottoman Turks and their descendants in modern Turkey. Thus, one may speak of Ottoman Turkish literature (c.1400–1920) and modern Turkish literature from 1920 to the present.

The native traditions that fed contemporary Turkish literature were threefold: the classical or *diwan* poetry of the Ottomans, modeled on Arab and Persian forms and intended for a court elite; religious literature connected with the *tekkes,* or cells of practicing mystics; and oral folk tradition, nationalistic and democratic in its impulse, which antedated the first two.

The republic of Kemal Ataturk, by at once ridding the country of both the caliphate and the sultanate in the 1920s, paved the way for the ascendancy of the folk tradition. Under the reform government, the new Turkish culture had no quarrel with a return of poetry to its native syllabic meters and away from the quantitative meters of Arabo-Persian verse that had shaped the *diwan* tradition. It did not oppose, either, the attempt to purify the Turkish language of its foreign borrowings.

The nineteenth-century dominance of French literature has been shared, perhaps displaced, in the twentieth century by British and American influences. But from the West came not only the winds of ideological change, but also the concept of the writer as an autonomous agent who has the right to create a literature of no social significance whatsoever. These antithetical forces give contemporary Turkish literature a pendular movement between elitist and populist poles.

The outstanding figure in Turkish poetry of this century is NAZIM HIKMET, who brought to Turkish literature both the free-style verse of the Soviet poet MAYAKOVSKY and the revolutionary doctrines of the Marxist thinkers, but it was left to FAZIL HÜSNÜ DAĞLARCA, the most talented poet of the post-World War II period, to effect a kind of synthesis of these popular trends.

The criticism of society has been perhaps even stronger in contemporary fiction than in poetry, and many novelists and short-story writers have run afoul of the government for their political views. The preeminence of the "committed" writers of fiction has been challenged, though not successfully thus far, by a more cosmopolitan school concerned mainly with avant-garde techniques of narration adapted from JOYCE (see Vol. 1) and other Western writers given to experiment.

The traditional drama of Turkey is the *karagöz,* or shadow play, a genre imported from Egypt during the sixteenth century. An analogous theater of unknown origin, the *Orta Oyunu* (sometimes called the Turkish *commedia dell' arte*) used human actors instead of puppets, but like the *karagöz,* relied heavily on broad humor. These two traditions have barely survived into the modern era, but their absurd and nonrealistic elements have to some extent been embodied in the drama that has developed under Western influence. Contemporary theater emerged during the nineteenth century, first with successful translations of MOLIÈRE into the Turkish vernacular, then with adaptations of Western forms to native themes and situations. But the fact remains in modern Turkey that no playwright, native or foreign, has enjoyed as wide a fame as SHAKESPEARE (see Vol. 1) in translation.

History and Criticism

Andrews, Walter G. *Poetry's Voice, Society's Song: Ottoman Lyric Poetry.* U. of Wash. Pr. 1985 $25.00. ISBN 0-295-96153-8. A unique study of an important aspect of Ottoman literature by a professor of Turkish at the University of Washington.

Bombaci, Alessio. *The History of Turkish Literature.* Trans. by Kathleen Burrill. Col. U. Pr. 1975 o.p. The only reliable, detailed survey of Turkish literature up to World War II.

Durrell, Lawrence. *Prospero's Cell.* Viking Penguin 1978 o.p. Contains a marvelous account of a *karagöz* performance.

Even, Ahmet O. *Origins and Development of the Turkish Novel.* Bibliotheca 1983 o.p.

Gibb, E. J. W. *A History of Ottoman Poetry. Gibb Memorial, 1963–1984.* 6 vols. o.p. Although Gibb died in 1901, still the standard work on Ottoman poetry.

Mitler, Louis. *Contemporary Turkish Writers: A Critical Bio-bibliography of Leading Writers of the Turkish Republican Period up to 1980.* Ind. U. Res. Inst. 1988 $29.50. ISBN 0-933070-14-4. The only work on modern Turkish writers in a western language.

______. *Ottoman Turkish Writers: A Bibliographical Dictionary of Significant Ottoman Literature.* P. Lang. Pubs. 1988 $31.50. ISBN 0-8204-0633-3. With the previous work, forms a concise but thorough bio-bibliographic record of Turkey's major writers.

Rathbun, Carole. *The Village in the Turkish Novel and Short Story, 1920 to 1955.* Mouton 1972 $49.35. ISBN 90-2792-327-2. A scholarly but readable analysis of a most important theme in recent fiction. The work of Turkish authors form the basis of this excellent study.

Walker, Barbara K. *The Art of the Turkish Tale.* Tex. Tech. Univ. Pr. 1990 $25.00. ISBN 0-89672-28-7. Only Vol. 1 has appeared to date.

Collections

Downing, Charles, ed. *Tales of the Hodja.* OUP 1970 o.p. Tales about the celebrated Nareddin (or Nasr-ed-Din, meaning "Helper of Faith") that will entertain both young and old. Delightfully illustrated by William Paps.

Halman, Talât, ed. *Contemporary Turkish Literature: Fiction and Poetry.* Fairleigh Dickinson 1982 $45.00. ISBN 0-8386-1360-8. First truly representative anthology of modern Turkish writing in English translation, from 1923 until the late 1970s. An illuminating introduction.

______. *Modern Turkish Drama: an Anthology of Plays in Translation.* Bibliotheca $20.00. ISBN 0-88297-007-0. Four plays including Haldun Taner's *Ballad of Ali of Keshan.*

Iz, Fahir. *An Anthology of Modern Turkish Short Stories.* Bibliotheca 1978 o.p. Thirty-six short stories written between 1900 and 1975.

General Reading

Lewis, Geoffrey, trans. *The Book of Dede Korkut.* Viking Penguin 1974 $6.95. ISBN 0-14-044298-7. Turkey's classical epic collection.

Menemencioglu, Nermin, and Fahir Iz, eds. *The Penguin Book of Turkish Verse.* Viking Penguin 1978 o.p. An important collection.

Ozakin, Aysel. *The Prizegiving.* Trans. by Celia Kerslake. Interlink Pub. 1988 o.p. A novel.

Pamuk, Orhan. *The White Castle: A Novel.* Trans. by Victoria Holbrook. Braziller 1991 $17.50. ISBN 0-8076-1264-2. Translation of *Beyoz Kale* originally published in 1979.

Sinasi, Ibrahim. *The Wedding of a Poet: A One-Act Comedy (1859).* Trans. by Edward Allworth. Griffon Hse. 1981 o.p. A short play, only 31 pages, that has historic importance as the first modern Turkish play.

CHRONOLOGY OF AUTHORS

Yunus, Emre. d. c.1320
Edip, Halide. 1884–1964
Karaosmanoğlu, Yakup Kadri. 1889–1974
Hikmet, Nazim. 1902–1963
Sabahattin Ali. 1907–1948
Dağlarca, Fazil Hüsnü. 1914–
Kanik, Orhan Veli. 1914–1950
Anday, Melih Cevdat. 1915–
Nesin, Aziz. 1915–
Taner, Haldun. 1916–1986
Kemal, Yaşar. 1922–
Fürüzan. 1935–

ANDAY, MELIH CEVDAT. 1915–

Poet, playwright, novelist, essayist, translator, and critic, Anday has been published extensively in Europe and the former Soviet Union, as well as in England. In 1971, UNESCO referred to him as "one of the world's foremost literary figures" and published a volume of his selected poems in French.

POETRY BY ANDAY

Rain One Step Away. Trans. by Talât Halman and Brian Swann. Charioteer 1980 $7.50. ISBN 0-910350-00-0

DAĞLARCA, FAZIL HÜSNÜ. 1914–

Born in Istanbul and educated in military schools, Dağlarca pursued a military career until 1950. He then worked in various ministries through 1959, when he left government service to found a publishing house and devote himself to literature.

Dağlarca's poems have appeared in all of the leading Turkish journals, and he has published more than 40 books, including at least 27 volumes of poetry. His poems are distinguished by a skillful and unusual use of language. His style seems to be genuinely Turkish, not revealing direct foreign influences. His style and themes have gradually evolved, but since 1950, with the work "Toprak Ana" ("Mother Earth"), he has pursued social realism.

POETRY BY DAĞLARCA

Selected Poems. Trans. by Talât Halman. U. of Pittsburgh Pr. 1969 o.p. Good translations.

EDIP, HALIDE. 1884–1964

Halide Edip was born in Istanbul and educated at the American Girls College. She taught in various capacities from 1903 to 1917 and entered political and cultural affairs during World War I. She was an active participant in the Struggle for National Independence.

After a sojourn in England (1936–39), Edip returned to Turkey and served as professor of English literature at Istanbul University from 1940 to 1950. She was the first Turkish woman to hold professional rank. From 1950 to 1954 she was a member of the National Assembly.

Edip, the outstanding Turkish woman of the twentieth century, is known primarily for her novels and memoirs. Of her 20-odd volumes, the most popular deal with the events of the War for Independence. Several have been translated into foreign languages and some have been the basis of motion pictures.

WORKS BY EDIP

Memoirs of Halide Edip. Ayer 1972 repr. of 1926 ed. o.p. Essential reading because so much of twentieth-century Turkey is reflected in the life of this leading female personality.

Turkey Faces West. Ayer repr. of 1930 ed. $21.00. ISBN 0-405-05320-7

FÜRÜZAN (FÜRÜZAN YERDELEN). 1935–

Fürüzan is one of contemporary Turkey's major writers and certainly one of its most famous women writers. But in spite of her importance, her work appears in English translation only in anthologies. Born Fürüzan Yerdelen in Istanbul in 1931, she comes from a modest background. Forced to leave school after the eighth grade, she later pursued a career in the theater before turning to literature. Her first story collection was published in 1971.

Her corpus of work, while not large, includes short stories, novellas, and novels, and her critical acclaim is great. Her stories are not without low-key humor as she portrays the disenfranchised elements of society and their situations without offering any reforms or solutions. Her work displays strong psychological insights and a great facility with the Turkish language. Fürüzan has won two prestigious literary awards, the Turkish Linguistic Association's novel award in 1975 and the Sait Faik Abasiyanik short story award in 1972.

SHORT STORY COLLECTIONS BY FÜRÜZAN

An Anthology of Modern Turkish Short Stories. Bibliotheca $12.00. ISBN 0-88297-039-9. Includes "The River," translated by Louis Mitler.

Contemporary Turkish Literature. Ed. by Talât Halman. Fairleigh Dickinson 1982 $45.00. ISBN 0-8386-1360-8. Includes "Knowing How to Play the Piano," translated by Ellen Wrvin.

HIKMET, NAZIM. 1902–1963

Nazim Hikmet was born in Salonika. After participating in the Struggle for National Independence, he taught school for a brief period and then studied economics and sociology in Moscow (1922–34). After returning to Turkey, he worked as a journalist and in a film studio. He was in continual trouble with the Turkish authorities during the thirties because of his adherence to communism, and in 1938 he was sentenced to a 20-year term in prison. Released in 1950—partly because of world opinion—he left Turkey and lived in exile until his death in 1963.

Hikmet's poetry (he also wrote plays) represents a complete break with the traditional heritage and a full acceptance of occidental models. Much of his work was inspired outside of Turkey and reached a universal dimension; nevertheless, the land and people of Turkey figure prominently as sources of inspiration. He has been especially well received in France via translation. Ironically, most of his work has appeared in Turkey only since his death.

POETRY BY HIKMET

The Epic of Sheik Beddreddin and Other Poems. Trans. by Randy Blasing and Mutlu Konuk. Persea Bks. 1980 $5.95. ISBN 0-892550-24-4

Human Landscapes. Trans. by Randy Blasing and Mutlu Konuk. Persea Bks. 1982 $9.95. ISBN 0-89255-068-6. An epic novel in verse, a wonderful read. Foreword by Denise Levertov.

Rubaiyat. Trans. by Randy Blasing and Mutlu Konuk. Copper Beech 1985 $4.95. ISBN 0-914278-48-7

Selected Poems. Trans. by Taner Baybars. Grossman 1967 o.p. A representative selection from Nazim's work.

Selected Poetry. Trans. by Randy Blasing and Mutlu Konuk. Persea Bks. 1987 $9.95. ISBN 0-89255-101-1. Sixty poems covering all periods of Nazim's literary activity. Includes some of his prison poetry.

Things I Didn't Know I Loved. Trans. by Randy Blasing and Mutlu Konuk. Persea Bks. o.p. Without question, one of the most important books of this century. The title poem is one of the great statements in any language, in any form.

KANIK, ORHAN VELI. 1914–1950

Orhan Veli, as he is known in the world of literature, was an important part of the new poetry movement in Turkey. In 1941 he, Oktay Rifat, and MELIH CEVDAT ANDAY published their joint poetry collection *Garip* (Stranger) and became leaders of the movement that took its name from their volume.

Born in Istanbul into an artistic middle-class family, Orhan Veli initially pursued a career as a bureaucrat. However, he soon left this vocation to follow a "free" and dissipated lifestyle. He died at age 36, his very brief life ended by a brain tumor. In the last years of his life, he published and edited the important literary journal *Yaprak* (Leaf). In all, he produced only five poetry collections and some prose pieces.

Orhan Veli broke with the old poetic traditions, writing in free verse and using colloquial language. His images are quick, his repetition is striking, and his flowing lines are powerful, lyrical, evocative, and engaging. A prime example of his prosody is his well-known poem "Istanbul'u Dinliyorum" ("I Am Listening to Istanbul"). Critics claim that he broke the conventional mold of polite Turkish verse by discarding rhyme and meter and expressing an almost nihilistic world view that placed him firmly within much modern thought. Yet Orhan Veli's poetry is not humorless. His translator Murat Nemet-Nejat describes its "ordinariness," its "clarity and transparency." These qualities have helped to make his poetry much loved by the people.

POETRY BY ORHAN VELI

I Am Listening to Istanbul: Selected Poems of Orhan Veli Kanik. Trans. by Talat Sait Halman. Corinth Bks. 1971 o.p. Introduction by Halman.

I, Orhan Veli. Trans. by Murat Nemet-Nejat. Hanging Loose 1989 $15.00. ISBN 0-914610-65-1

KARAOSMANOĞLU, YAKUP KADRI. 1889–1974

Karaosmanoğlu is one of those important twentieth-century figures who actually spanned the two worlds of the Ottoman Empire and Republican Turkey. He wrote in a wide variety of genres but is especially well known as a novelist. Born in Cairo in the last years of the Ottoman Empire, Karaosmanoğlu grew up in Istanbul. He was appointed to government posts and even served as a diplomat in Europe. He served twice in the Turkish parliament. Prominent also in literary movements, he wrote nine novels, two short story collections, two poetry collections, journalism, and memoirs. Critics have characterized Karaosmanoğlu this way: his work as revolutionary, pessimist and religious mystic at the same time, and comprising all the contradictions that typified the intelligentsia of his day.

WORK BY KARAOSMANOĞLU

Contemporary Turkish Literature. Ed. by Talat Halman. Fairleigh Dickinson 1982 $45.00. ISBN 0-8386-1360-8. Includes an excerpt from Karaosmanoğlu's novel *Kiralik Konak* (The Rented Mansion).

KEMAL YAŞAR. 1922–

Yaşar Kemal was born in the Turkish village of Gokceli. After finishing his secondary education, he worked in various jobs in southern Anatolia, gaining a deep knowledge of the folklore of the region. Kemal's first volume of short stories was issued in 1952, and since then more than 15 volumes have appeared. His novels, short stories, and reportage deal with Anatolian themes.

NOVELS BY KEMAL

The Birds Have Also Gone: A Novel. Trans. by Thilda Kemal. Minerva 1989 o.p.

To Crush the Serpent. Trans. by Thilda Kemal. HarperC 1992 $10.00. ISBN 0-00-271111-7. Stark tale of cruelty and vendetta told in a tense narrative reminiscent of Greek tragedy.

The Legend of Ararat. Trans. by Thilda Kemal. Collins and Harvill 1975 o.p.
The Legend of the Thousand Bulls. Trans. by Thilda Kemal. Collins and Harvill 1976 o.p.
Memed, My Hawk. Trans. by Edouard Roditi. British Bk. Ctr. 1961 o.p. Probably his most popular novel; it has been translated into at least 23 languages. A translation of Vol. 1 of the original (1955) edition, titled *Ince Memed (They Burn the Thistles).*
Murder in the Ironsmiths' Market. Trans. by Thilda Kemal. Morrow 1980 o.p.
The Sea-Crossed Fisherman: A Novel. Trans. by Thilda Kemal. Braziller 1985 o.p.
Seagull. Pantheon 1981 o.p.
The Undying Grass. Trans. by Thilda Kemal. Morrow 1978 o.p. Volume 2 of the trilogy *The Wind from the Plain.*
The Wind from the Plain. Trans. by Thilda Kemal. HarperC 1992 $12.00. ISBN 0-00-271029-3. English translation of Volume 3 of the trilogy of the same name. All volumes set in Turkish villages.

Play by Kemal

Iron Earth, Copper Sky. Trans. by Thilda Kemal. British Bk. Ctr. 1974 o.p. A prize-winning drama, originally titled *Yer Demir, Gok Baker.* Volume 2 of *The Wind from the Plain* trilogy.

Short Story Collection by Kemal

Anatolian Tales. Trans. by Thilda Kemal. British Bk. Ctr. 1969 o.p.

NESIN, AZIZ. 1915–

After serving as a career officer for several years, Turkey's most popular humorist became a columnist in 1944 and edited a series of satiric publications. He was jailed several times for his political views.

Nonfiction by Nesin

Istanbul Boy: The Autobiography of Aziz Nesin. 3 vols. Trans. by Joseph S. Jacobson. U. of Tex. Pr. 1977–1990. Vol. 1 o.p. Vol. 2 o.p. Vol. 3 $9.95. ISBN 0-292-73864-1

Short Story Collection by Nesin

Turkish Stories for Four Decades. Trans. by Louis Mitler. Three Continents 1991 $24.00. ISBN 0-89410-687-2. Twenty-one stories, with a critical essay.

SABAHATTIN ALI. 1907–1948

Although he wrote some poetry (published in 1934), Sabahattin Ali is known primarily for his short stories and novels. Between 1935 and 1947, he produced three novels and five short story collections. He is perhaps best known for his 1937 novel *Kuyucakli Yusuf* (Joseph of Kiuyujak), which has been translated into French as *Youssouf le taciturne.*

Born in Greece, Sabahattin Ali studied in Germany and taught German upon his return to Turkey. He was, however, fired because of his leftist political views and eventually imprisoned. He edited several journals, including the satirical review *Marko Pasa.* He died at the age of 41 under very mysterious circumstances while crossing the Bulgarian border.

An early socialist realist writer in Turkey, he created a combination of social realism and psychological insight that makes his works compelling reading.

Short Stories by Sabahattin Ali

An Anthology of Modern Turkish Short Stories. Bibliotheca 1978 $12.00. ISBN 0-88297-039-9. Includes two stories by Sabahattin.

TANER, HALDUN. 1916–1986

Haldun Taner is perhaps contemporary Turkish literature's most popular and outstanding playwright, also intimately involved in all aspects of the theater. The son of a lawyer and professor, Taner was born in Istanbul. After receiving his secondary education at the famous Galataysaray Lycee, he pursued advanced study and degrees in Heidelberg and Vienna. Among his many endeavors, he has taught drama at Istanbul University and worked as a journalist for the newspapers *Milliyet* and Tercümen. In all, Taner published 7 short story collections, 10 plays, and 6 cabaret pieces. One of his most famous plays is *Kesanli Ali Destani* (*The Ballad of Ali of Keshan*), which appeared in 1964. A political satire that includes incidental music, Talat Halman refers to it as "Brechtian epic theater" (*Modern Turkish Drama*). Taner's realistic short stories, however, are his primary achievement, and many regard him as Turkey's finest writer in this form.

Short Story Collection by Taner

Thickhead and Other Stories. Trans. by Geoffrey Lewis. Dufour 1991 $21.00. ISBN 0-948259-59-0

Play by Taner

Modern Turkish Drama. Bibliotheca 1976 $20.00. ISBN 0-88297-033-X. Includes Taner's complete play *The Ballad of Ali of Keshan*, which was translated and published in English in Turkey (1970).

YUNUS EMRE. d. c.1320

Yunus Emre is one of classical Turkish literature's most beloved poets. Brother Yunus [Jonah] was the greatest of the mystical poets, a Sufi, as his title and poetry indicate. Little is known of his early life. He is believed to have been born c.1238–50 in Eskisehir in the western part of Anatolia. Tradition says that he knew the great Persian mystic Jalāl al-Dīn Rūmī, but for how long or in what capacity is unknown. His works comprise his *diwan* (poetical works) and *Risalet-i nushiyye* (Book of Good Counsel).

Yunus Emre used the vernacular language and simple, traditional Turkish meters. The respected writer Ahmet Tanpinar has called him "the door of Turkish" because "it was Yunus who established Turkish as a literary language. . . ." The critic Talat Halman has called him "the most significant folk poet in . . . Islamic literature" because he "expressed humanistic ethics in forthright and easily communicable verse. . . . assimilate[d] the teachings of Islam and . . . forge[d] a synthesis of Islam's primary values and mystic folk poetry."

Poetry by Yunus Emre

The City of the Heart: Yunus Emre's Verses of Wisdom and Love. Trans. by Süha Faiz. Element MA 1992 $14.95. ISBN 1-85230-333-6. Preface by John D. Norton. Includes introductory notes, glossary, and an index of first lines in Turkish.

The Drop That Became the Sea: Lyric Poems of Yunus Emre. Trans. by Kabir Helminski and Refik Algan. Threshold VT 1989 $8.00. ISBN 0-939660-30-X

The Wandering Fool: A Sufi Poem of a Thirteenth-century Turkish Dervish. Trans. by Edouard Roditi and Guzin Dino. Cadmus Eds. 1987 $25.00. ISBN 0-932274-39-0

Yunus Emre: Secme Siirler = Selected Poems = Poèmes choisis = ausgewählte Gedichte. Trans. by Talat Halman. Eskisehir Valiligi 1991 o.p. A quatra-lingual edition of Yunus's poems published in Turkey. Translations by highly regarded scholars.

Book about Yunus Emre

Halman, Talat. *Yunus Emre and His Mystical Poetry.* Ind. U. Pr. 1981 $11.95. ISBN 0-685-29319-X. A compilation of six essays on a variety of topics, by important scholars such as Talat Halman, Annemarie Schimmel, Mehmet Kaplan, Andreas Tietze, and Ilhan Basgöz.

CHAPTER 5

African Literatures

Chukwuma Azuonye

. . . twentieth-century African literature is not a fledgling offspring of European literature; rather, it is a continuation (partly but only partly) in European languages, of a 5,000 year-old indigenous African tradition.
—CHINWEIZU, *Voices from Twentieth-Century Africa*

Most discussions of African literature have focused on the relatively new body of works written in European languages during the past few decades as an expression of the colonial experience. However, a more catholic view of African literature is rapidly emerging from recent scholarship. There is now a growing feeling, championed by writers like NGUGI WA THIONG'O of Kenya, that only by writing in African languages can African writers reach an indigenous audience without the cultural ambiguity inherent in the use of the colonial languages. This feeling has been reinforced by the new Afrocentric poetics, which opposes Eurocentric aesthetic canons in favor of traditional African principles of art as exemplified in oral performances. Through the Afrocentric challenge, a radical revision of African literary history is now in process. This revision sees African literature as the totality of the oral and written expressions, in all languages and scripts, that have been used by Africans of all races and ethnic origins ever since human culture originated in the rift valley of East Africa.

Very little is known about the character of early human cultures in Africa; but it might be supposed that, through diffusion and contacts going back to prehistoric times, certain modes of oral expression have established themselves firmly in both ritual and secular contexts. The ritual forms, rooted in magic and religion, include prayers; hymns (or praises addressed to deities and other supernatural forces); magical incantations for healing, rainmaking, and the like; and various forms of mantic performances, such as divination, oracle, possession, and spirit-mediumship chants. In the secular domain—chiefly in relation to hunting, war, work, family and communal relationships, and leadership in society—there emerged such forms as panegyric poetry (praises addressed to human heroes); odes (praises addressed to remarkable animals and inanimate objects); self-praises and boasts; folk tales; folk songs; and rhetorical forms, such as proverbs, riddles, tongue twisters, and oratory. Traversing the ritual and the secular domains are tales of the land or historical tales (including myths, legends, and personal narratives) and elegiac poems, including general laments and dirges.

Among the recurring themes of these forms of African oral expression are the eternal flow of life between the spirit world and the physical world; the recognition of the existence of a supreme deity and of elemental deities representing the divine essence in every aspect of nature; the idea of duality and balance in gender and other forms of human relations; a strong emphasis on the family values of love, loyalty, and reciprocity; the veneration of ancestors; a heroic view of life associated with public celebrations of heroes; and the culture of subjecting social deviants and failures to public ridicule. These themes continue to assert themselves through age-old forms in contemporary oral traditions, despite the destabilizing effects of centuries of alien cultural disturbance. It is in these recurring themes, images, and thought patterns that we can discern the unity of the many different—at times mutually contradictory—traditions of verbal expression that constitute African literature.

The written literatures of Africa, rooted in the age-old traditions of oral literature, are among the oldest in human culture. As we will see in the discussion of North African literatures, the classical literatures that flourished in Egypt and Nubia for nearly 4,000 years bear the unmistakable imprint of the forms, genres, and stylistic conventions of the oral traditions that continue to sustain artistic verbal expression in Africa today. The millenia during which these classical African literatures flourished were essentially Africa's Golden Age. In contrast to subsequent African literatures, these early literatures were preoccupied with the celebration of life and of the power of the divine forces; the contemplation of the soul's journey toward immortality; and the projection of African achievements in science, technology, religion, and philosophy. But as Africa became colonized and dominated by European and Arab powers over the centuries, the great traditions of literacy and literature that date back to ancient Egypt were eclipsed. During the subsequent Dark Ages in African cultural development, overseas slavery and alien domination unsettled much of the social and cultural life of African peoples. The successful domination of African peoples gave rise throughout Europe to feelings of racial superiority over the black world—feelings that found their way into classical European literatures, as well as into philosophical writings, traveler's tales, missionary literature, and anthropological studies of Africa and Africans. These racist stereotypes, which portrayed the African as subhuman or at best a "Noble Savage," became a great burden. Much of what Europeans consider "African literature" was born in reaction to this burden, during the period of the most recent European colonialism in Africa.

The precursors of the nationalist and protest literature of the colonial and postcolonial periods in Africa were late eighteenth-century ex-captive writers. For example, OLAUDAH EQUIANO, whose *Interesting Narrative of the Life of Olaudah Equiano or Gustavus Vassa, the African, Written by Himself* was first published in London in 1789, strikes a note that reverberates through the writings of CHINUA ACHEBE and other modern African writers, namely, that "the African did not hear of culture for the first time with the coming of the Europeans." Equiano paints an idyllic picture of his Igbo hometown, which he calls Essaka, in a romantic rebuttal of the negative images of Africa in European writings. Achebe and his contemporaries have been less romantic. In representing the conflict between Western and African cultures in *Things Fall Apart* (1958) and *Arrow of God* (1964), Achebe—the chief exemplar of the culture-conflict strain of postcolonial African literature—takes pains to represent both the ugliness and the beauty of African traditional, precolonial culture, in keeping with his dictum that "our past was not one technicolor idyll."

The Negritude Movement, championed by such Francophonic poets as LEOPOLD SEDAR SENGHOR, created a mystique around blackness, turning the celebration of black cultural heritage into a romantic philosophy of self-pity and, at times, of retaliatory racism. Nobel Prize winner WOLE SOYINKA's remark that "the tiger does not proclaim its tigritude" is generally considered to be representative of the critical response of the great majority of other African writers to the romantic rhetoric of negritude. Continuing the tradition of realism established by Achebe, many Anglophonic writers evoked less romanticized images of the "African personality" without sacrificing the opportunity for a critical review of the past, as in Soyinka's Nigerian independence play, *A Dance of Forests.* Nevertheless, there is an unalloyed tone of celebration and affirmation in these authors' exploration of the idea of returning to the past; that is, of a symbolic reclamation of traditional African modes of worship in repudiation of what the poet sees as the spiritual emptiness of the imported religions of Islam and Christianity. This theme reverberates with vitriolic passion in the anti-Islamic novels of YAMBO OUOLOGUEM, AYI KWEI ARMAH, and MONGO BETI.

Since the end of World War II, the Algerian Revolution, the liberation struggles of Portuguese-controlled African states (Angola, Mozambique, and Guinea-Bissau), and the antiracism struggles in Kenya, Zimbabwe, Namibia, and South Africa, have forced vicarious modes of revolutionary black consciousness that continue to feed literary expression in these regions. But, elsewhere in Africa, as African nations attained independence from European colonists, there has been a somber tone of disillusionment in African literature. Much of the romantic cultural nationalism and revolutionary fervor of the colonial era has given way to sober self-criticism. In their novels, poems, and plays, writers have portrayed the betrayal of the promises of independence, and they have also frequently probed the tragic distance between the African leadership elite and the masses.

Four ideological tendencies have established themselves as a consequence of this situation. The first is a revolutionary aesthetic, founded largely on Marxist ideology, in which a younger generation of writers like KOLE OMOTOSHO and Festus Iyayi in Nigeria are seeking to create role models for revolutionary changes in postcolonial society. The second is an Afrocentric philosophy that advocates the replacement of Eurocentric sensibilities with an Afrocentric aesthetic. Advocates hold that only this aesthetic can guarantee the decolonization of the African mind and the emergence of African literature as an unambiguous mirror of African consciousness and history. The third tendency is feminism. It has grown in importance with the emergence of such female writers as ASSIA DJEBAR of Algeria, FLORA NWAPA of Nigeria, AMA ATA AIDOO of Ghana, MARIAMA BA and Aminata Sow Fall of Senegal, BESSIE HEAD of South Africa, and BUCHI EMECHETA of Nigeria. The fourth ideological tendency is modernist and postmodernist ideas. These first asserted themselves through dense poetic universes like that of Christopher Okigbo, and they are now reasserting themselves in such novels as the Booker prize-winning masterpiece, *The Famished Road,* by BEN OKRI of Nigeria.

Today, African literature is at a crossroads, between the Eurocentric canons of the past and the burgeoning Afrocentric canons of the present. Afrocentrism insists on greater recognition of African languages and on a redefinition of the boundaries of African literature. These new literary boundaries reflect facts about African history and civilization revealed through recent research. Such a broadening of perspective will ultimately result in the recognition of African literature, not as a recent phenomenon, but as a complex artistic development of more than 5,000 years, bolstered by continuity and change in a powerful oral tradition, and including literatures in African languages and indigenous scripts, in colonial languages and scripts, in African languages and colonial scripts.

Readers who want to see African literature in its totality will seek out materials from all three of these streams and must go as far back in antiquity as possible.

HISTORY AND CRITICISM

Abrash, Barbara, ed. *Black African Literature in English Since 1952.* Johnson Repr. $9.00. ISBN 0-382-00201-3. Listing of literature in English by black Africans; includes relevant criticism, starting with *Palm-wine Drinkard.*

Adams, Anne V., and Janis Mayers, eds. *African Literature and Africa's Development.* Three Continents 1992 $22.00. ISBN 0-89410-734-8. Discusses the current development of African literature.

Alvarez-Pereyre, Jacques. *The Poetry of Commitment in South Africa.* Trans. by Clive Wake. *Studies in African Literature.* Heinemann Ed. 1985 o.p. Discusses poetry of protest against apartheid in South Africa.

Angoff, Charles, and John Povey, eds. *African Writing Today.* Manyland 1969 $10.00. ISBN 0-87141-029-X. A literary review of a new generation of African writers; focuses on the quality of African writing.

Anyidoho, Kofi, and others, eds. *Interdisciplinary Dimensions of African Literature. African Literature Association Annuals Ser.* Three Continents 1985 $14.00. ISBN 0-89140-457-8. Essays on the history and criticism of English and French African literature selected by the African Literature Association.

Arnold, Stephen, ed. *African Literature Studies: The Present State—L'Etat Present. African Studies Association Annuals Ser.* Three Continents $26.00. ISBN 0-89410-435-7. Essays selected by the African Literature Association; criticism of, and discussion on, twentieth-century African writers.

Awoonor, Kofi. *The Breast of the Earth: A Survey of the History, Culture and Literature of Africa South of the Sahara.* 1975. Nok 1983 $19.95. ISBN 0-685-03583-2. Ghanaian author Awoonor's "comments on contemporary African writing are often brilliant, and his characterization of the modern African intellectual is certain to be provocative" (*Choice*).

Barkan, Sandra, and others, eds. *African Literatures: Retrospective Assessments. African Literature Association Annuals Ser.* Three Continents 1989 $22.00. ISBN 0-89410-588-4

Beier, Ulli. *An Introduction to African Literature: An Anthology of Critical Writing from Black Orpheus.* Bks. Demand repr. of 1967 ed. $70.50. ISBN 0-317-10051-3. Insightful essays by major African and non-African authors that examine African novels, drama, poetry, and the oral tradition.

Bishop, Rand. *African Literature, African Critics: The Forming of Critical Standards, 1947–1966.* Greenwood 1988 $39.95. ISBN 0-313-25918-6. Identifies empirically and non-evaluatively the standards by which African critics judged African literature between 1947 and 1966.

Bjornson, Richard. *The African Quest for Freedom and Identity: Cameroonian Writing and the National Experience.* Ind. U. Pr. 1991 $29.95. ISBN 0-253-31194-2. Authoritative study that reflects exacting and thorough scholarship, direct contact with African writers and scholars, and masterful treatment of a very complex subject.

Blair, Dorothy S. *African Literature in French: A History of Creative Writing in French from West and Equatorial Africa.* Cambridge U. Pr. 1981 $18.95. ISBN 0-521-28403-1. A scholarly assessment of the effects of French language on African writing; history and criticism of French cultural influences on African culture.

Brown, Lloyd W. *Women Writers in Black Africa: Contributions in Women's Studies.* Greenwood 1981 $38.50. ISBN 0-313-22540-0. A pioneering work, focusing on five of Africa's most popular female novelists: Ama Ata Aidoo, Buchi Emecheta, Bessie Head, Flora Nwapa, and Efua Sutherland.

Burness, Donald, ed. *Critical Perspectives on Lusophone Literature from Africa.* Three Continents 1981 $25.00. ISBN 0-89410-015-7. Covers writing from Angola, Mozambique, Guinea-Bissau, Cape Verde, and Sao Tome-Principe; includes essays on specific writers and general literary movements; important literary journals also noted.

______, ed. *Wanasema: Conversations with African Writers. CIS African Ser.* Ohio U. Pr. 1985 $11.00. ISBN 0-89680-129-2. Includes conversations with 12 authors, all recommended both in and of themselves and for the variety that they bring to a continuing understanding of the varieties of African experience.

Chinweizu, and others. *Towards the Decolonization of African Literature*, Vol. 1. Howard U. Pr. 1982 o.p. "The attacks on Eurocentric writers and critics are free-swinging . . . , but the basic thesis has much validity, . . . a healthy antidote to the often second-rate writing about contemporary African literature . . ." (*Choice*).

Cook, Mercer, and Stephen E. Henderson. *Militant Black Writer in Africa and the United States.* U. of Wis. Pr. 1969 $9.95. ISBN 0-299-05394-6. Compares black African consciousness in the writings of black Africans with those of black writers in the United States.

Dathorne, O. R. *The Black Mind: A History of African Literature.* Bks. Demand repr. of 1974 ed. $134.80. ISBN 0-8357-7293-4. A comprehensive account of the development of African literature from its beginnings in oral tradition to its contemporary expression in writings of Africans in various African and European languages.

______. *African Literature in the Twentieth Century.* Univ. of Minn. Pr. 1976 o.p. An extensive survey of African literature in French, English, and Portuguese, as well as in several indigenous languages.

Davies, Carole B., and Anne A. Graves, eds. *Ngambika: Studies of Women in African Literature.* Africa World 1986 $125.00. ISBN 0-86543-017-9. A helpful source of criticism on African women's perspectives and characterizations.

Dorsey, David F., and others, eds. *Design and Intent in African Literature.* Three Continents 1982 $22.00. ISBN 0-89410-354-7. Essays discussing the intertextual structure of selected writings by a number of authors.

Echeruo, Michael J. C., and E. N. Obiechina, eds. *Igbo Traditional Life, Culture and Literature. Africa in Transition Ser.* Conch Mag. 1971 $17.50. ISBN 0-914970-25-9. An attempt to authenticate the experience and writings of the Igbo people by dissecting their life-style and literature.

Egejuru, Phanuel A. *Black Writers, White Audiences: A Critical Approach to African Literature. Exposition-University Book Ser.* Bks. Demand repr. of 1978 ed. $63.80. ISBN 0-8357-7303-5

______. *Towards African Literary Independence: A Dialogue with Contemporary African Writers.* Greenwood 1980 $42.95. ISBN 0-313-22310-6. Interviews with selected authors; examines the effects of French and English culture on black writers.

Egudu, Romanus. *Modern African Literature and the African Predicament.* B&N Imports 1978 o.p.

Elimimian, Isaac I. *Theme and Style in African Poetry.* E. Mellen 1991 $69.95. ISBN 0-7734-9675-0. A critical study of the art and craft of African verse.

Etherton, Michael. *The Development of African Drama.* Holmes & Meier 1983 $35.00. ISBN 0-8419-0812-5. Analyzes the way in which African drama is developing within the context of African society.

Fritshi, Gerhard. *Africa & Gutenberg: Exploring Organic Structures in the Modern African Novel.* P. Lang Pubs. 1983 $27.70. ISBN 3-261-03322-3

Gakwandi, Shatto A. *The Novel & Contemporary Experience in Africa.* Holmes & Meier 1978 $35.00. ISBN 0-8419-0306-9. Discusses African fiction in the context of history and criticism; includes a bibliography.

Gerard, Albert S. *Four African Literatures: Xhosa, Sotho, Zulu, Amharic.* U. CA Pr. 1971 o.p. Covers a neglected area of African literature; "an admirable literary history and critical study . . ." (*LJ*).

______. *African Language Literatures: An Introduction to the Literary History of Sub-Saharan Africa.* Three Continents 1981 $35.00. ISBN 0-914478-65-6. Traces linguistic and literary development in sub-Saharan Africa; discusses writing within this area in a historical context.

Giguere, Ronald G. *Écrivains Noirs. American University Studies Ser.* P. Lang Pubs. 1989 $41.00. ISBN 0-8204-0990-1

Gikandi, Simon. *Reading the African Novel. African Writers Ser.* Heinemann Ed. 1987 $16.50. ISBN 0-435-08018-0. Useful commentary on established African fiction.

Graham-White, Anthony. *The Drama of Black Africa.* French 1925 $9.95. ISBN 0-573-69024-3. A thorough investigation of the total spectrum of sub-Saharan African drama, with an emphasis on that of West Africa.

Griffiths, Gareth. *Double Exile: African and West Indian Writing Between Two Cultures.* M. Boyars Pubs. 1980 $7.95. ISBN 0-7145-2623-1. History and criticism of Commonwealth and West Indian literature.

Gugelberger, Georg M., ed. *Marxism & African Literature.* Africa World 1985 $29.95. ISBN 0-86543-030-6. An anthology of Marxist criticism.

Gunner, Elizabeth. *A Handbook for Teaching African Literature.* Heinemann Ed. 1985 $17.50. ISBN 0-435-92260-2. Guidelines for secondary study and teaching of African literature in Great Britain.

Hale, Thomas, and Richard Priebe, eds. *The Teaching of African Literature. African Literature Association Annuals Ser.* Three Continents 1989 repr. of 1976 ed. $24.00. ISBN 0-89410-472-1. Study and teaching papers in higher education selected from the second annual meeting of the African Literature Association; includes bibliography and references.

Harrow, Ken, ed. *Faces of Islam in African Literature. Studies in African Literature.* Heinemann Ed. 1991 $17.50. ISBN 0-435-08025-3. Addresses the much varied role of Islam in Africa.

Harrow, Ken, and others, eds. *Criss-Crossing Boundaries in African Literatures 1986.* Three Continents 1991 $22.00. ISBN 0-89410-718-8. Essays on history and criticism, selected by the African Literature Association.

Harvard University Library Staff. *African History and Literatures. Widener Library Shelflist Ser.* HUP 1971 $37.50. ISBN 0-674-00780-8. Covers 10,000 titles; classified by call number, chronologically, alphabetically.

Haynes, John. *The Poetry of Africa: An Introduction for Students.* Three Continents repr. of 1989 ed. $12.00. ISBN 0-333-48901-2. Introduces students to reading and comprehending African poetry in English.

Herdeck, Donald E., ed. *African Authors: A Companion to Black African Writing, 1300–1973,* Vol. 1. Gale 1973 $70.00. ISBN 0-8103-0076-1. A pioneering work that includes lengthy biographies of more than 500 authors and critical discussions of their writings.

Heywood, Christopher, ed. *Papers on African Literature: Given at the Seminar on African Art & Literature, Sheffield University, 1975.* Bks. Demand repr. of 1976 ed. $33.80. ISBN 0-685-10878-3. Criticism, as well as analysis of earlier criticism, of African literature.

______. *Perspectives on African Literature.* Holmes & Meier 1972 $29.50. ISBN 0-8419-0093-0

Holloway, Karla F. *Moorings and Metaphors: Figures of Culture & Gender in Black Women's Literature.* Rutgers U. Pr. 1992 $36.00. ISBN 0-8135-1745-1. Advances the study of black women's fiction in two specific and important directions.

Hord, Fred. *Reconstructing Memory: Black Literary Criticism.* Third World 1991 $12.95. ISBN 0-88378-144-1. Proposes a pedagogical model for African American literature emphasizing its social and political contexts.

Irele, Abiola. *The African Experience in Literature & Ideology.* Ind. U. Pr. 1990 $29.95. ISBN 0-253-33124-2. Describes political ideology in African literature.

Jablow, Alta. *Yes and No: The Intimate Folklore of Africa.* Greenwood 1973 repr. of 1961 ed. $39.75. ISBN 0-8371-6757-4. "Particularly delightful and relatively little known to non-Africans are the dilemma stories, which pose ethical and moral . . . problems . . . . Jablow has selected excellent examples from the oral traditions of many peoples of Africa's western bulge. Her book will not only instruct scholars and specialists but also entertain general readers" (*LJ*).

Jahn, Janheinz. *Neo-African Literature: A History of Black Writing*. Grove Pr. 1961 o.p. *Die Neoafrikanische Literatur*. Kraus 1990 repr. of 1965 ed. $32.00. ISBN 0-262-007669-2. Jahn was a pioneer and leading critic in the introduction of African literature to an international audience.

Jahn, Janheinz, and P. Claus Dressler. *Bibliography of Creative African Writing*. Kraus 1971 $45.00. ISBN 0-527-45150-9. List of African literature available in Germany.

James, Adeola, ed. *In Their Own Voices: African Women Writers Talk*. Heinemann Ed. 1990 $17.50. ISBN 0-435-08043-1. Included are Aidoo, Alkali, Emecheta, Kola, Kuzwayo, Likimani, Ogundipe-Leslie, Mlama, Mugo, Njau, Nwapa, Ochieng, Odega, Okoye, and Sofola.

Johnson, Lemuel, ed. *Toward Defining the African Aesthetic*. Three Continents 1983 $22.00. ISBN 0-89410-356-3. Essays on the history and criticism of artistic structure.

Jones, Eldred, ed. *African Literature Today: Omnibus Edition, Nos. 1–4*. Holmes & Meier 1972 $24.50. ISBN 0-8419-0124-4. Intended to be a forum for examining contemporary African literature.

———. *African Literature Today, No. 5: The Novel in Africa*. Holmes & Meier 1975 $24.50. ISBN 0-8419-0227-0. Essays on literary criticism of the novel in Africa.

———. *African Literature Today, No. 6: Poetry in Africa*. Holmes & Meier 1972 $24.50. ISBN 0-8419-0133-3. Essays on, and reviews of, poetry in Africa, with special dedicatory essays on Okigbo's poetry.

———. *African Literature Today, No. 7: Focus on Criticism*. Holmes & Meier 1975 $19.50. ISBN 0-8419-0168-6. General critical questions about African literature and discourse.

———. *African Literature Today, No. 8: Drama in Africa*. Holmes & Meier 1976 $18.50. ISBN 0-8419-0261-5. Focuses on discussion and criticism of modern African drama.

———. *African Literature Today, No. 9: Africa, America and the Caribbean*. Holmes & Meier 1978 $24.50. ISBN 0-8419-0335-2. Ideas of black unity from three different geographical perspectives.

———. *African Literature Today, No. 10: Retrospect and Prospect*. Holmes & Meier 1979 $32.95. ISBN 0-8419-0397-2. A reassessment of African writing and criticism.

———. *African Literature Today, No. 11: Myth, History and the Contemporary Writer*. Holmes & Meier 1980 $39.50. ISBN 0-8419-0577-0. Examination of the nature of myth in African literature.

Jones, Eldred D., and Eustace Palmer, eds. *African Literature Today, No. 12: New Writing, New Approaches*. Holmes & Meier 1982 $37.50. ISBN 0-8419-0719-6. A cumulative index, dedicated to the work of newer African writers, which has not received much attention.

———. *African Literature Today, No. 13: Recent Trends in the Novel*. Holmes & Meier 1983 $35.00. ISBN 0-8419-0804-4. Compares the latest developments in the African novel with more established works.

———. *African Literature Today, No. 14: Insiders and Outsiders*. Holmes & Meier 1983 $32.50. ISBN 0-8419-0968-7. Discussion of non-African writers since the days of Herodotus's representation of Africa.

———. *Oral and Written Poetry in African Literature Today*. *African Literature Today Ser*. Africa World 1989 $29.95. ISBN 0-86543-125-6. History and criticism of African poetry—past, present, and future.

Jones, Eldred Durosimi, Eustace Palmer, and Majorie Jones, eds. *Women in African Literature Today*. *AWP African Literature Today Ser*. Africa World 1991 $29.95. ISBN 0-86543-056-X. A thorough, critical examination of the works of some women who are writing in Africa today.

———. *Oral and Written Poetry*. *AWP African Literature Today Ser*. Africa World 1991 $29.95. ISBN 0-86543-125-6

———. *The Question of Language*. *AWP African Literature Today Ser*. Africa World 1991 o.p.

Julien, Eileen, and others, eds. *African Literature in Its Social and Political Dimensions*. *African Literature Association Annuals Ser*. Three Continents 1986 $22.00. ISBN 0-

89410-458-6. A collection of essays examining the ideological commitment and effect of "belief" in African literature.

Killam, G. D., ed. *African Writers on African Writing*. Heinemann Ed. *Studies in African Literature* 1973 o.p. "A collection of sixteen previously published essays by fourteen of Africa's best-known creative writers . . ." (*Choice*).

Klima, Vladimir, and others, eds. *Black Africa*. Kluwer Ac. 1975 $93.00. ISBN 90-277-0531-3. A survey of English, French, and Portuguese literary efforts in Senegal, Kenya, and Lake Chad.

Kotei, S. I. *The Book Today in Africa*. UNIPUB 1981 $9.00. ISBN 92-3-101876-0

Kubayanda, Josaphat B. *The Poet's Africa: Africanness in the Poetry of Nicolas Guillen and Aimé Cesaire*. Greenwood 1990 $42.95. ISBN 0-313-26298-5. Criticism and interpretation of Guillen and Cesaire's work; examines their views of women in their work; includes a bibliography.

Larson, Charles R. *The Emergence of African Fiction*. Three Continents 1972 rev. ed. $15.00. ISBN 0-253-31945-5. A broad survey of the African novel, with a strong concentration on Nigerian novelists; judges African literature from a Eurocentric perspective; contains an extensive bibliography.

Lazarus, Neil. *Resistance in Postcolonial African Fiction*. Yale U. Pr. 1990 $27.50. ISBN 0-300-04553-0. Provides a provocative and convincing argument.

Lindfors, Bernth. *Folklore in Nigerian Literature*. Holmes & Meier 1974 $35.00. ISBN 0-8419-0134-1. A group of essays focusing on the critical interpretive aspects of folklore in modern African writing.

______. *Black African Literature in English: A Guide to Information Sources. American Literature, English Literature & World Literature in English Information Guide Ser.* Gale 1978 $68.00. ISBN 0-8103-1206-9. A guide to sources on the history and criticism of African literature in English by black authors; includes bibliography and indexes.

______. *Black African Literature in English: 1977–1981*. Holmes & Meier 1986 $45.00. ISBN 0-8419-0962-8. A supplement to Lindfors's *Guide to Information Sources;* includes bibliography, indexes, and some annotated sources and reviews.

______. *Black African Literature in English: 1982–1986*. K. G. Saur 1989 $85.00. ISBN 0-905450-75-2. History and criticism of black authors; discussion of black African intellectual life; includes bibliography and indexes.

Lindfors, Bernth, and Ulla Schild, eds. *Neo-African Literature & Culture: Essays in Memory of Janheinz Jahn*. Irvington 1982 $49.50. ISBN 3-593-32821-6. Addresses, essays, and lectures discussing the life and work of Janheinz Jahn, a German writer who was very influential in introducing black literature in Germany.

Little, Kenneth. *Sociology of Urban Women's Image in African Literature*. Rowman 1980 $35.50. ISBN 0-8476-6290-X. Discusses the development and incorporation of social conditions for black women in English African literatures; discusses the context and history of African literature.

Maja-Pearce, Adewale. *A Mask Dancing: Nigerian Novelists of the Eighties. New Perspectives on African Literature Ser.* K. G. Saur 1992 $70.00. ISBN 0-90540-92-2. A group of essays analyzing twentieth-century Nigerian novelists.

Miller, Christopher L. *Theories of Africans: Francophone Literature and Anthropology in Africa. Black Literature & Culture Ser.* U. Ch. Pr. 1990 $49.95. ISBN 0-226-52801-4. Engaging and provocative book that challenges the Western reader to become engaged in a better understanding of francophone African literature.

Mlama, Penina Muhando. *Culture and Development: The Popular Theatre Approach in Africa*. Scandinavian Inst. of African Studies o.p.

Moore, Gerald. *Twelve African Writers*. Ind. U. Pr. 1980 o.p. An excellent introduction to 12 of Africa's most significant contemporary authors from French-speaking and English-speaking countries; an updated and extended edition of Moore's *Seven African Writers*.

Mortimer, Mildred. *Journeys Through the French African Novel. Studies in African Literature*. Heinemann Ed. 1990 $17.50. ISBN 0-435-08042-3. Fascinating and scholarly examination of six comparative studies.

Mortimer, Mildred, and others, eds. *The Literature of Africa and the African Continuum. African Literature Association Annuals Ser.* Three Continents 1988 $22.00. ISBN 0-89410-460-8. Papers selected by the African Literature Association, edited by Jonathan Peters, Mildred Mortimer, and Russell V. Linnemann.

Mutloatse, Mothobi, ed. *Reconstruction: Ninety Years of Black Historical Literature. Staffrider Ser.* Ohio U. Pr. 1981 $8.95. ISBN 0-86975-207-3

Nasta, Susheila, ed. *Motherlands: Black Women's Writings from Africa, Caribbean, & South Asia.* Rutgers U. Pr. 1992 $36.00. ISBN 0-8135-1781-8. A collection of stories centered around black women's struggle in a patriarchal society.

Ngara, Emmanuel. *Art and Ideology in the African Novel. Studies in African Literature.* Heinemann Ed. 1985 $17.50. ISBN 0-435-91721-8. Presents the ideological and esthetic situation in Africa today.

Ngate, Jonathan. *Francophone African Fiction: Reading a Literary Tradition.* Ed. by Stephen H. Arnold and George Lang. *Comparative Studies in African-Caribbean Literature Ser.* Africa World 1988 $32.00. ISBN 0-86543-087-X. Critical study of francophone African fiction from the 1920s to the 1980s.

Ngugi wa Thiong'o. *Decolonizing the Mind: The Politics of Language in African Literature.* Heinemann Ed. 1986 $14.50. ISBN 0-435-08016-4. Essays on ideology and language in African literature.

Nichols, Lee. *African Writers at the Microphone.* Three Continents 1984 $25.00. ISBN 0-89410-164-1. Radio interviews with 83 African authors.

Nkosi, Lewis. *Tasks and Masks: Themes and Styles of African Literature. African Literature Studies.* Bks. Demand repr. of 1982 ed. $55.00. ISBN 0-685-20311-5. A highly readable, perceptive review of the growth of sub-Saharan literature within its social, historical, and ideological context; topics explored are language, negritude, and South African protest writings.

Obiechina, Emmanuel. *Language and Theme: Essays on African Literature.* Howard U. Pr. 1990 $26.95. ISBN 0-88258-045-0. Collection of previously published essays that examines general problems in the development of contemporary African literature.

Ojo-Ade, Femi. *Analytical Index of Presence Africaine: 1948–1972.* Three Continents 1977 $22.00. ISBN 0-914478-92-3

Okpaku, Joseph O., ed. *New African Literature and the Arts*, vol. 3. Okpaku Communications 1973 $29.95. ISBN 0-685-29060-3. Essays by African scholars and critics on the relationship between African culture and literature and criticism.

Okpewho, Isidore. *The Epic in Africa: Towards a Poetics of the Oral Performance.* Col. U. Pr. 1979 $40.50. ISBN 0-231-04401-1. Discussion of epic poetry in African history; examines the influence of songs, African languages, and oral tradition on modern literature.

———. *Myth in Africa: A Study of Its Cultural and Aesthetic Relevance.* Cambridge U. Pr. 1983 $54.95. ISBN 0-521-24554-0. History and criticism of oral traditions; discussion of African myths in modern literature.

———. *African Oral Literature: Backgrounds, Character and Continuity.* Ind. U. Pr. 1992 $45.00. ISBN 0-253-34167-1. Evocative intertextual studies of recorded African songs, myths, and histories of literature; includes bibliography and indexes.

Olafioye, Tayo. *Politics in African Poetry.* PCA Enterp. 1984 $15.00. ISBN 0-916765-00-8

Olney, James. *Tell Me, Africa: An Approach to African Literature.* Princeton U. Pr. 1973 $47.50. ISBN 0-691-06254-4. Examination of social life and customs in African literature.

Owomeyela, Oyeka. *Visions and Revisions: Essays on African Literature and Criticism.* P. Lang Pubs. 1991 $41.95. ISBN 0-8204-1471-9. A collection of essays published for scholarly interest about European influence on African literature; includes bibliography and index.

Owusu, Martin. *Drama of the Gods: A Study of Seven African Plays.* Omemana 1983 $8.95. ISBN 0-685-06783-1

Parker, Carolyn, and Stephen Arnold, eds. *When the Drumbeat Changes.* Three Continents 1981 $22.00. ISBN 0-89410-242-1

Paulitschke, P. V. *Die Afrika-Literatur in der Zeit von 1500–1750*. Kraus 1990 repr. of 1882 ed. $30.00. ISBN 0-8115-3873

Petersen, Kirsten H., ed. *Criticism and Ideology: Second African Writers' Conference, Stockholm*. Coronet Bks. 1988 $46.50. ISBN 91-7106-276-9. Contains 16 lectures and several brief dialogues that offer invaluable insight into the consensus and concerns that eminent African authors share.

Pieterse, Cosmo, and Dennis Duerden, eds. *African Writers Talking*. Holmes & Meier 1972 $39.50. ISBN 0-8419-0118-X. Interviews with famous African writers over a period of six years.

Pieterse, Cosmo, and Donald Munro, eds. *Conflict in African Literature*. Holmes & Meier 1969 $24.50. ISBN 0-8419-0004-3. Collection of essays on various topics, from politics of negritude to protest against apartheid.

Priebe, Richard K. *Myth, Realism and the African Writer*. Ed. by Stephen H. Arnold and George Lang. *Comparative Studies in African-Caribbean Literature Ser*. Africa World 1988 $35.00. ISBN 0-86543-097-7. Divides African literature into two categories—ethical and mythical—and fits all African writing along a continuum between these two extreme rhetorical categories.

Priebe, Richard, and Thomas Hale, eds. *Artist and Audience: African Literature as a Shared Experience*. Three Continents 1979 $22.00. ISBN 0-89410-122-6. Collection of essays discussing issues of a white audience and its effects on African literature.

Schipper, Mineke. *Beyond the Boundaries: Text and Context in African Literature*. I. R. Dee 1990 $24.95. ISBN 0-929587-36-7. Intelligent discussion of theoretical questions that form the basis of any just, comparative critical analysis.

Schmidt, Nancy J. *Children's Books on Africa and Their Authors: An Annotated Bibliography*. *African Bibliography Ser*. Holmes & Meier 1975 $32.50. ISBN 0-8419-0166-X. A highly recommended text, containing more than 8,000 annotated entries arranged by author, along with subject, title, and series index.

Sellin, Eric, ed. *Africana Journal, Vol. XII*. Holmes & Meier 1985 $65.00. ISBN 0-8419-1216-5

Senkoro, F. E. *The Prostitute in African Literature*. Three Continents 1985 $8.50. ISBN 0-89410-617-1. Discusses the role of prostitutes in African literature.

Shreve, G. M., and E. Ojo-Arewa. *Genesis of Structures in African Narrative, Dahomean Narratives: Vol. 2. Studies in African Semiotics*. Conch Mag. 1984 $35.00. ISBN 0-914970-01-1. Analyzes selections from *The Zande Trickster* by E. E. Evans-Pritchard.

Smith, Roland, ed. *Exile and Tradition: Studies in African and Caribbean Literature. Dalhousie African Studies*. Holmes & Meier 1976 $34.50. ISBN 0-8419-0263-1. Essays on the differences between indigenous reflections in literature and the imposed values of others.

Soyinka, Wole. *Myth, Literature and the African World. A Canto Book Ser*. Cambridge U. Pr. 1990 $7.95. ISBN 0-521-39834-7. Collection of addresses, lectures, and essays dealing with African civilization and its creative writings.

Tibble, Anne, ed. *African English Literature*. October 1969 $7.95. ISBN 0-8079-0139-30. Brief historical outline of African English literature; discussion of significant African writers—both English and French speaking.

Wilkinson, Jane, ed. *Talking with African Writers: Interviews with African Poets, Playwrights and Novelists. Studies in African Literature*. Heinemann Ed. 1992 $17.50. ISBN 0-435-08065-2. Interviews with twentieth-century authors—from Ghana to South Africa: Awoonor, Achebe, Ngugi, and others.

Wylie, Hal, and others, eds. *African Literature, 1988: New Masks*. Three Continents 1990 $22.00. ISBN 0-89410-698-8

Wylie, Hal, and Eileen Julien, and others, eds. *Contemporary African Literature*. Three Continents 1983 $22.00. ISBN 0-89410-369-5

Zell, Hans M., ed. *A New Reader's Guide to African Literature*. Holmes & Meier 1983 $44.50. ISBN 0-8419-0639-4. Lists 3,091 works by black African authors south of the Sahara writing in English, French, and Portuguese, along with criticisms and essays; the most comprehensive book available on the subject.

COLLECTIONS

Beier, Ulli, and Gerald Moore, eds. *The Penguin Book of Modern African Poetry.* Viking Penguin 1989 $9.95. ISBN 0-14-058573-7. Poems from major African states, with notes and sources.

Burness, Don, ed. *Fire: Six Writers from Angola, Mozambique, & Cape Verde.* Three Continents 1977 $18.00. ISBN 0-914478-51-6. Works by six writers, including eight poems by Victor Bessa (with translations by D. Burness); includes bibliography and index.

Chinweizu, ed. *Voices from Twentieth Century Africa: Griots and Town-Criers.* Faber & Faber 1989 $14.95. ISBN 0-571-14930-8. Consists of short stories, parables, songs, among other things.

Classic Black African Poems. Eakins 1966 $11.95. ISBN 0-87130-024-9. A selection of songs of black Africans; examines their lyrics.

Maja-Pearce, Adewale, ed. *The Heinemann Book of African Poetry in English. African Writers Ser.* Heinemann Ed. 1991 $9.95. ISBN 0-435-91323-9. Consists of poets from the second generation of African writers.

Okpewho, Isidore. *The Heritage of African Poetry.* Longman 1985 $17.95. ISBN 0-582-72704-9. One hundred poems grouped by such themes as love, praise, war and death.

Roth Publishing Inc. Editorial Board Staff, ed. *World's Best Poetry, Supplement VI: Twentieth Century African & Latin American Verse.* Roth Pub. Inc. 1989 $49.95. ISBN 0-8960-271-2. An expansive collection of twentieth-century poetry from Africa and Latin America.

Senanu, K. E., and Theo Vincent, eds. *Selection of African Poetry.* Longman 1990 $6.36. ISBN 0-582-01683-5. A selection of twentieth-century African poetry, including translations from African languages.

Stefaniszyn, B., ed. *African Lyric Poetry 1974.* Hapi Pr. 1974 $6.95. ISBN 0-913244-07-4. Poems based on songs from Zambia.

Zimunya, Musaemura, and others, eds. *The Fate of Vultures: New Poetry from Africa. African Writers Ser.* Heinemann Ed. 1989 $9.95. ISBN 0-435-90550-3. An anthology of poems by new African writers, from the 1988 BBC Arts and African poetry award competition.

CHRONOLOGY OF AUTHORS

North African Literature
Mahfouz, Najib. 1911–
Dib, Mohammed. 1920–
Fanon, Franz. 1925–1961
Chraibi, Driss. 1926–
Idris, Yusuf. 1927–1992
Salih, al-Tayib. 1929–
Yacine, Kateb. 1929–1989
al-Sa'dawi, Nawal. 1931–
Gabre-Medhin, Tsegaye. 1935–
Djebar, Assia. 1936–
Khatibi, Abdelkebir. 1938–
Boudjedra, Rachid. 1941–
Ben Jelloun, Tahar. 1944–
Farah, Nuruddin. 1945–

West African Literature
Equiano, Olaudah. 1745–1797
Dan Fodio, Shehu Usman. 1754–1817
Senghor, Leopold Sedar. 1906–
Tutuola, Amos. 1920–
Ekwensi, Cyprain. 1921–
Okara, Gabriel. 1921–
Laye, Camara. 1928–1980
Ba, Mariama. 1929–1981
Munonye, John. 1929–
Ousmane, Sembene. 1929–
Oyono, Ferdinand. 1929–
Achebe, Chinua. 1930–
Nwapa, Flora. 1931–
U Tam'si, Tchikiya. 1931–1990
Beti, Mongo. 1932–
Okigbo, Christopher. 1932–1967
Peters, Lenrie. 1932–
Amadi, Elechi. 1934–
Clark, J. P. 1934–
Soyinka, Wole. 1934–
Awoonor, Kofi. 1935–
Ogali, Ogali A. 1935–
Echeruo, Michael. 1937–

Sofola, Zulu. 1938–
Armah, Ayi Kwei. 1939–
Ouologuem, Yambo. 1940–
Okpewho, Isidore. 1941–
Aidoo, Ama Ata. 1942–
Omotoso, Kole. 1943–
Emecheta, Buchi. 1944–
Onwueme, Tess. 1955–
Okri, Ben. 1960–

East African Literature
Ranaivo, Flavien. 1914–
Ogot, Grace Akinye. 1930–
Okot p'Bitek. 1931–1980
Mazrui, Ali al Amin. 1933–
Ngugi wa Thiong'o. 1938–
Lo Liyong, Taban. 1938 or 1939–
Serumaga, Robert. 1939–

South African Literature
Mofolo, Thomas. 1876–1948
Paton, Alan. 1903–
Abrahams, Peter. 1919–
Mphahlele, Es'kia. 1919–
Gordimer, Nadine. 1923–
Brutus, Dennis. 1924–
La Guma, Alex. 1925–1984
Kunene, Mazisi. 1930–
Tlali, Miriam. c.1930–
Brink, André. 1935–
Fugard, Athol. 1935–
Head, Bessie. 1937–1986
Coetzee, J(acobus) M. 1940–
Mapanje, Jack. c.1940?–
Marechera, Dambudzo. 1952–1987

NORTH AFRICAN LITERATURE

In their historical development, the literatures of North Africa fall into three main traditions: pre-Arabic, Arabic, and non-Arabic.

The pre-Arabic literatures of North Africa are among the oldest and most varied literatures of the world, going back to the hieroglyphic writings of the ancient civilizations of Egypt and Nubia in the Nile Valley, and including later developments in other languages and scripts within and outside the Nile Valley.

Most discussions of the classical literatures of ancient Egypt and Nubia are subsumed in discussions of oriental or Middle-Eastern traditions; but it is important to recognize vital links between these ancient African literary traditions and parallel and latter-day traditions of oral and written literatures south of the Sahara. This essentially Afrocentric perspective is supported by evidence of cross-fertilization of ideas across the Sahara long before and long after its desertification.

The culture of the early people of Africa seems to have dispersed from its East African epicenter toward all cardinal points throughout the continent. It flourished in the Nile Valley, where it gave rise to the earliest fully documented human civilization in ancient pharaonic Egypt. This civilization, together with others in the fertile crescent, was seminal to contemporary Western culture. However, prior to its dispersal to Europe and Asia, ancient Egyptian civilization had been intermeshed with cultural developments in the rest of black Africa for several millennia. Ancient Egyptian literature retains much evidence, both in the themes and in the features of its major genres, of having drawn from the same pool of oral traditions that are still active in Africa today. The self-praises of the pharaohs are remarkably reminiscent of the heroic recitations of the Bahima of Ankole and similar boasts elsewhere in Africa, while the hymns to the great deities of the ancient Egyptian and Nubian pantheons are closely comparable to hymns recorded across Africa, especially the paradoxical hymns of the Yoruba to their *orishas*. In the same vein, the odes to the Nile and to many other objects strike a note of identity with similar African praises to animals, forces of nature, and other inanimate objects. The greatest pinnacle of ancient

Egyptian and Nubian literature, *The Book of the Dead*, is a complex work comprised of hymns, odes, praises, and magical chants designed to be performed as talismans to assist the dead in their passage through the spirit world to the passageway of rebirth in a cyclical order of existence—a passage and order shared with the rest of the African continent. Paremiologists will find in the ancient Egyptian maxims attributed to such scribes as Ani and in the lyric poems a further opportunity for studying landscapes of identity in the recreation of African culture through literature. Furthermore, although Eurocentric scholarship for centuries denied the existence of writing in Africa south of the Sahara, it has long been known that scripts of various levels of development have flourished in the region. These scripts, discussed further in the relevant subsections of this chapter, share more or less identical inspiration and design with the scripts in which the literature of ancient Egypt and Nubia were written.

Following the successive conquests of ancient Egypt by the Assyrians, Greeks, and Romans and the emergence of the Christian era, the classical literatures of the ancient "black lands" of Egypt and Nubia were succeeded by three different traditions of African Christian literature. The first centered around the Coptic church in Egypt and was dominated by the works of Clement of Alexandria and other Christian fathers, through whose efforts orthodox Christianity seeped into the ancient empire of Ethiopia in the Horn of Africa where the Coptic metropolitan, Abba Salama, was largely responsible for laying the foundations of Ethiopian Christian literature. Later, when the Roman church became established in Northern Africa on the heels of Roman colonization of the Maghreb, the emergent North African Christian literature in Latin was dominated by black writers of Berber origins, such as St. Augustine of Hippo, whose *Confessions* is the precursor of the genre of that name. These early traditions of Christian literature are forerunners, both to African Islamic literatures in Arabic and African languages (the *ajami* tradition), which dominated the subsequent centuries, and to the missionary-sponsored literatures in African languages that emerged in the middle of the nineteenth century and have continued to flourish as a pedagogic undergrowth in a modern literary scene dominated by European-language writings. By and large, both the Christian and the Islamic traditions in African literature have functioned as iconoclastic traditions of cultural alienation and displacement. By displacing African world views with the world views of the great Middle Eastern religions (largely through the deliberate replacement of African myths, legends, and ritual chants with Christian or Islamic mythologies, hagiography, and hymns, or other liturgical forms), they succeeded in forging, in most parts of Northern, Eastern and Western Africa, a new African consciousness completely deracinated of its ancient values.

The sweep of Islam throughout North Africa, from the Horn of Africa through the Maghreb to the Atlantic littoral zone of the western bulge of Africa, dealt a more devastating blow to indigenous African traditions than had been accomplished in the preceding Christian centuries. In the Maghreb, for example, the Arabs not only proscribed indigenous African scripts, such as the Berber script of the pre-Arabic black populations of the region, but also succeeded in erasing most traces of the people's traditions—a tendency that was to repeat itself across the savannah belt of the western Sudan and along the Indian Ocean coastline of East Africa from Mombasa to Zanzibar. The impact of the emergent Arab Islamic traditions on the development of West and East African literatures during the Islamic centuries is discussed further in the subsections of this chapter.

Fuller details regarding the progress of the Arabic literatures of North Africa will be found in Chapter 4 in this volume, where they have been treated as part of the wider Arab Islamic literatures of the Middle East. It is, however, noteworthy that, in more recent years, largely through the writings of such feminist women authors as AL-SA'DAWI, such anti-Israel writers as playwright YUSUF IDRIS, and writers with a universal vision such as Nobel Prize winner NAJIB MAHFOUZ, the Arabic literatures of North Africa have begun to address issues of wider social and political dimensions and to participate with modern non-Arabic literatures of the region in the criticism of Islamic orthodoxy, especially with regard to such questions as the continued subjugation of women. With these tendencies, visible points of congruence are beginning to emerge in the concerns of the Arabic and non-Arabic literatures of North Africa, as well as between them and the literatures of the rest of the continent.

The history of the non-Arabic literatures of North Africa goes back to what Albert Gerard has described as "the Golden Age of Ge'ez," when a pre-Christian literature written in a script introduced from across the Red Sea flourished around Axum, the capital of what later became the kingdom of Ethiopia. Originally preoccupied with the praise of kings, royal genealogies, and the prescription of codes of behavior for princes and rulers, the classical Axumite tradition ultimately merged with the new tradition of Christian literature that established itself with the Christianization of the region. Eventually, Ge'ez receded from popular use into a liturgical literary lect, with the emergence of Amharic as the main medium of literary expression. Today, Amharic in Ethiopia, Somali in Somalia, and Berber in the Maghreb continue to flourish as popular media for non-Arabic literatures in North Africa. These literatures have a grass-roots appeal, imbued with the freedom to explore values and traditions outside those conduced by the avant-garde Arabic Islamic and modern European language traditions.

Beyond their nativistic impulses, the non-Arabic literatures in the indigenous languages of North Africa share more or less the same thematic concerns with modern North African literatures in French (Algeria, Morocco, Libya, Tunisia, and Mauritania) and English (Sudan, Ethiopia, Eritrea, Somalia, and, to a lesser extent, Egypt). Exhibiting similar postcolonial concerns with nationalism in the face of alienating Western values and allegedly decadent indigenous traditions, these literatures belong to the wider postcolonial corpus of African literature. Some writers, like DRISS CHRAIBI (Morocco), are as critical of their native Arabic Islamic heritage as they are of the colonial overculture; female writers like ASSIA DJEBAR (Algeria) pitch their protest against the subjugation of women under Islamic culture but are, at the same time, critical of Arab women's acceptance of their condition, and, in noncommitted writers like AL-TAYIB SALIH (Sudan), the poetic celebration of seasonal rhythms (as in *Season of Migration to the North)* overshadows any discontent over the impact of Western traditions on traditional life and customs.

With the growing recognition of patterns of continuity and commonality between North African literatures and sub-Saharan literatures, the current tendency to isolate North African literature for separate attention as part of oriental, Middle Eastern, or Arab Islamic traditions will gradually give way to a broader frame of literary history. The contextual, thematic, stylistic, and historical interconnections among the literatures of all parts of Africa will be more fully explored, enriching the reader's perception of African literature in its complex, varied, yet unified totality.

History and Criticism

(See Chapter 4 for additional listings)

Abdulrazak, Fawzi, et al. *Arabic Literature in North Africa: Critical Essays and Annotated Bibliography*. Cambridge U. Pr. 1982 o.p. Well-respected and well-rounded work. Bibliography is especially useful.

Geesey, Patricia, ed. *North African Literatures*. Ind. U. Pr. 1992 o.p. Scholarly approach to the Arabic literatures of North Africa.

Kaye, Jacqueline, and Abdelhamid Zoubir. *The Ambiguous Compromise: Language, Literature, and National Identity in Algeria and Morocco*. Routledge 1990 $66.00. ISBN 0-415-03055-2. Focuses on language and literature as a major unifying force in North African culture.

Monego, Joan. *Maghrebian Literature in French*. Twayne 1984 o.p. Examines the French literary tradition of the Maghreb region of North Africa.

Collections

Abokor, Axmed Cali. *The Camel in Somali Oral Traditions*. Red Sea Pr. 1987 o.p. Includes translations from poems and proverbs that use folklore of the camel, with brief biographies of poets quoted in the original texts.

Hanghe, Ahmed Artan. *Folktales from Somalia*. Red Sea Pr. 1978 o.p. Translation of oral and written traditional folklore.

Ortzen, Len, ed. *North African Writing*. *African Writers Ser.* Heinemann Ed. 1970 o.p. North African French fiction—selections and translations—with an introduction by Len Ortzen.

BEN JELLOUN, TAHAR. 1944–

Controversial winner of the prestigious French Prix Goncourt (1987), Tahar Ben Jelloun is a Moroccan writer who has not found much favor at home, despite his growing popularity abroad. According to some North African critics, Ben Jelloun intentionally sets out to please foreign readers. They contend that his writing reinforces European stereotypes by pandering to Western tastes for quaint folklore and traditions, and exotic scenery. Moroccan critics have accused Ben Jelloun of creating artificial, fabricated stories that fail to convey a true picture of Morocco. They have also been offended by his criticism of Morocco, and the fact that he reveals sides of Moroccan life that are usually kept hidden. Ben Jelloun's story of a girl dressed as a boy, *L'Enfant du Sable* (*The Sand Child*) (1985), was scandalous in their eyes. Since Ben Jelloun won the Prix Goncourt, a number of critics changed their minds and have begun to praise his work.

NOVELS BY BEN JELLOUN

Harrouda. Schoenhof 1988 $7.95. ISBN 2-07-038069-6

The Sacred Night. HarBraceJ 1989 $18.95. ISBN 0-15-197150-3. Sequel to *The Sand Child*.

The Sand Child. 1985. Trans. by Alan Sheridan. HarBraceJ 1987 $17.95. ISBN 0-15-179287-9

BOUDJEDRA, RACHID. 1941–

Born in Algeria, Rachid Boudjedra has been described as "the greatest living writer from the Maghreb." A journalist, teacher, lecturer, and militant leftist who has served in the Algerian resistance movement, Boudjedra established himself as a leading writer of the French language with the publication of his first novel, *La Répudiation*, in 1969. However, like NGUGI WA THIONG'O of Kenya, he was driven by nationalist fervor and dissatisfaction with the colonial language and its literature to renounce the use of French in 1981 and to turn to his native Arabic as his primary medium of expression.

Boudjedra's work is perhaps best understood in terms of his identification with questions about Arab adaptation to, and identity in, the modern world. The novel *La Répudiation* marked a turning point in Algerian literature by breaking with the past and transgressing against such taboos as politics, sex, and religion. The themes introduced by *La Répudiation* were intensified in his subsequent novels. *Topographie Idéale pour une Aggression Caracterisée* (1975) confronts two cultures by reversing the Western perspective and denouncing the violence of modern life. *L'Escargot Entêté* (1977) presents a political fable on the nature of bureaucracy while bringing to light societal prejudices, the small-mindedness of Islam, and the arbitrariness of patriarchal values. *Les 1001 Annes de la Nostalgie* (1979) adopts a fantastic, parodistic mode to reexamine the myths of Arab-Muslim society and culture when faced with the intrusion of the modern world. And *Le Vainqueur de Coupe* (1981) and *Le Demantelement* (1982) are an intense meditation on the mysteries of history and the demand for subjectivity as a fundamental expression of freedom and truth.

NOVEL BY BOUDJEDRA

Insolation. Schoenhof 1987 $8.95. ISBN 2-07-037871-3

CHRAIBI, DRISS. 1926–

Born in 1926 to a rich Moroccan businessman, Driss Chraibi is one of the most distinct voices in modern North African literature. His upper-middle-class background exposed him to a thoroughly French education of the type usually reserved for "assimilated" Africans. From a French grammar school in Casablanca, he went to Paris, where he studied chemistry. Twice married, in both cases to French women, he has lived most of his life in France, where he has worked in various chemical laboratories and as a freelance journalist. But, despite his "assimilated" status in France, Chraibi has remained largely alienated intellectually and spiritually from France. A nonconformist, almost nihilistic in his younger days, Chraibi lets his novels reflect his deep antipathies, not only to France and to Western values, but also to Islam and to his own Arabic heritage. This crisis of dual alienation may be responsible for the violence that critics perceive in his works. *Les Boucs* (*The Butts*) (1955), named for a racist French epithet for North African Arabs settled in Paris, is widely seen as a counterracist call for Arab vengeance against the French. Chraibi's works are by no means uniformly tendentious. His more recent works reflect a sober appreciation of the emotional and spiritual distance between the colonizer (the French) and the colonized (North African Arabs), and he has developed more balanced artistic attitudes, at times creating characters that function as viable role models for resolving the deep tensions that he perceives between the West and the Orient, and between the past and the present. His well-established international standing is reflected in the growing number of his works that have been translated into English and other languages.

NOVELS BY CHRAIBI

Birth at Dawn (*Le Noussance de l'Aube*). Trans. by Ann Woollcombe. Three Continents 1990 $22.00. ISBN 0-89410-576-0

The Butts. 1955. Trans. by Hugh Harter. Three Continents 1983 $18.00. ISBN 0-89410-324-5

Civilisation, Ma Mère! Schoenhof 1972 $7.95. ISBN 2-07-037902-7

Flutes of Death. Trans. by Rubin Roosevelt. Three Continents 1985 $22.00. ISBN 0-89410-326-1. Two Arabic-speaking policemen, searching for a rebel, find themselves in the Atlas mountains among the Berber peoples of Morocco.

Heirs to the Past. 1962. *African Writers Ser.* Heinemann Ed. 1972 $8.95. ISBN 0-435-90079-X. A prodigal son returns home, tired and empty, to claim his inheritance, and his family revolts against him.

Inspector Ali. Three Continents 1992 $26.00. ISBN 0-89410-746-1

Mother Comes of Age. Trans. by Hugh Harter. Three Continents 1989 $18.00. ISBN 0-89410-401-2. A mother's son is liberated by modernization and education, and she chooses to join him on his journey.

The Mother Spring. Trans. by Hugh Harter. Three Continents 1989 $18.00. ISBN 0-89410-401-2. Discusses political standing of a small Moroccan community.

The Simple Past. Trans. by Hugh Harter. 1953. Three Continents 1990 $22.00. A story of revolt against the oppressive customs of Islam, incarnated in a father.

DIB, MOHAMMED. 1920–

Described by Len Ortzen in *North African Writing* as "the doyen of North African writers in French," Mohammed Dib, who emigrated from his native Algeria to southern France in 1959, was born in 1920 at Tlemcen, near the Algerian-Moroccan border. After leaving high school, he worked successively as a primary school teacher, a carpet weaver, and a railway worker until he became a reporter for a small local newspaper. It was at this point that he began to develop his literary talents. His first novel, *La Grande Maison* (1952), the first volume of a trilogy, *Algerie*, was followed by *L'Incindie* (1954) and *Le Métier à Tisser* (1957). This trilogy set the tone for his early writings, which are characterized by their realistic and semiautobiographical focus on the problems and crises of individual adjustment to a French-dominated Arab social and cultural environment. But, since the 1960s, there has been a tremendous shift in his style and commitments. According to Len Ortzen, the techniques employed by Dib from the late 1960s and early 1970s "are reminiscent of abstract painting. Indeed, *Qui Se Souvient de la Mer* [first published in 1962 and translated into English as *Who Remembers the Sea*] was inspired by Picasso's painting *Guernica.*" Among Dib's most dominant themes is the futility of war, a concern grounded in his experience of the Algerian War of Independence, which he handles with passion, humanity, and universality of vision in *Le Dance du Roi* (1968). Given his high standing among contemporary North African writers of the French expression, it is somewhat surprising that only a few of his works are available in English.

NOVELS BY DIB

Omneros. Trans. by Carol Lettieri and Paul Vangelisti. Invisible-Red Hill 1978 $3.00. ISBN 0-88031-050-2

Who Remembers the Sea. Trans. by Louis Tremaine. Three Continents 1985 $18.00. ISBN 0-89410-444-6

DJEBAR, ASSIA. 1936–

One of the earliest feminist writers of modern Africa, Assia Djebar was born in 1936 into a middle-class conservative family in Algeria. She read history at the Sorbonne in Paris, and, after teaching at Tunis and Rabat universities, emigrated to France with her husband and children. A modestly successful writer, from the artistic point of view, she began advocating militant feminism (for which her works are mostly valued) even before the Algerian War of Independence. Her main concern is with the submissiveness of Arab women and the tenacity and egoism with which the men have clung to age-old male-chauvinist values. But she is sufficiently balanced in her judgments to hold the women answerable for aspects of their subjugation, by reason of inaction and self-degradation.

NOVELS BY DJEBAR

A Sister to Scheharazade. Interlink Pub. $19.95. ISBN 0-7043-2670-1. A group of vignettes representing the liberation and subjugation of women in a patriarchal system.

Women of Algiers in their Apartment. Trans. by De Jager Marjolijn. U. Pr. of Va. 1992 $19.95. ISBN 0-8139-142-7

AL-SA'DAWI, NAWAL. 1931–

Described by the London *Guardian* as "the leading spokeswoman on the status of women in the Arab world," Nawal al-Sa'dawi is the best-known female Arabic-language novelist and short story writer in Egypt. Trained as a medical practitioner, al-Sa'dawi has devoted her life to fighting the oppression of women by the Islamic and colonialist establishments—a cause reflected in most of her novels. Her own accomplishments and setbacks exemplify the enormity of the problems that women in her society frequently encounter. Although she achieved the position of Egypt's director of public health, antipathy generated by the publication of the nonfiction work *Women and Sex* (1972) was enough to force the Ministry of Health to dismiss her from her post. Under similar pressures, she was later dismissed as chief editor of an Egyptian health journal and as assistant general secretary of the Egyptian Medical Association. Subsequently, al-Sa'dawi worked as a researcher on women and neurosis at Ain Shams University, and as UN advisor for the Women's Program in Africa and the Middle East. However, antagonism over her feminist activism continued to dog her career. Imprisoned for her activism in 1980, al-Sa'dawi has since devoted herself to writing and to speaking to various national and international forums on women's issues.

NOVELS BY AL-SA'DAWI

The Circling Song. Humanities 1989 $15.00. ISBN 0-86232-816-0. Powerful example of the kind of anger and desperation Arab women writers are beginning to express.

Death of an Ex-Minister. Heinemann Ed. 1992 $9.95. ISBN 0-7493-9950-3

The Fall of the Imam. Heinemann Ed. 1989 o.p.

God Dies by the Nile. Humanities 1985 $15.00. ISBN 0-86232-294-4

Searching. Humanities 1991 $15.00. ISBN 1-85649-008-4

Two Women in One. Trans. by Osman Nusairi and Jana Gough. Women Translation 1991 $9.95. ISBN 1-879679-01-9

Woman at Point Zero. 1984. Trans. by Sherif Hetata. Humanities 1983 $15.00. ISBN 0-86232-517-X

SHORT STORY COLLECTION BY AL-SA'DAWI

She Has No Place in Paradise. Heinemann Ed. 1987 o.p. A selection of short stories describing life for women in Arab culture.

NONFICTION BY AL-SA'DAWI

The Hidden Face of Eve: Women in the Arab World. 1980. Trans. by Sherif Hetata. Beacon Pr. 1982 $11.95. ISBN 0-8070-6701-6. A startling representation of woman's role as victim in an Arab patriarchal society and the abuses inflicted upon them.

GABRE-MEDHIN, TSEGAYE. 1935–

Tsegaye Gabre-Medhin is a distinguished modern Ethiopian playwright, novelist, and poet who writes in both his native language, Amharic, and in English. A 1960 graduate of the Blackstone School of Law in Chicago, Illinois, Gabre-Medhin branched into professional theater after intensive training in Europe in the early 1960s. In 1966, he became the acting director of the Haile Salassie I Theatre in Addis Ababa. In that same year, Gabre-Medhin also made his debut as a playwright with his plays *Tewodros* (1966) and *Azmari* (1966). His first poetry appeared in 1965 in the *Ethiopian Observer*. But it was his novel, *Oda Oak Oracle* (1965), described by Donald Herdeck in *African Authors* as "probably the best fiction in English to come from Ethiopia," that established him as an important modern voice from the Horn of Africa. In general, his works deal with the clash between age-old Ethiopian traditions and Western values.

NOVEL BY GABRE-MEDHIN

Oda Oak Oracle. 1965. *Three Crowns Ser.* OUP o.p.

FANON, FRANZ. 1925–1961

A Martinique Islander by birth and a psychiatrist by training, Franz Fanon is better known as a pan-African revolutionary ideologue. His treatises on colonialism call for revolutionary confrontation with malignant colonial regimes, where necessary on the battlefield, and, more important, for the eradication of the most invidious form of colonialism, namely, colonial mentality. Fanon holds that this mentality prevents the African and the black person everywhere even from being aware of the seriousness of the social and personal deprivations of his or her colonized status. Fanon found his voice when he worked for the Algerian revolutionaries during the Algerian War of Independence against the French. He not only became deeply involved in the Algerian struggle but also emerged as its principal ideologue and formulated his anticolonial writings from the Algerian experience.

NONFICTION BY FANON

Black Skin, White Masks. 1967. Trans. by Charles Markman. Grove Pr. 1989. $8.95. ISBN 0-8021-5084-5

A Dying Colonialism. Trans. by Haakon Chevalier. Grove Pr. 1988 $12.50. ISBN 0-8021-5027-6. Examines Algerian social conditions and the collapse of colonialism.

Sociologie d'une Révolution. Fr. & Eur. $9.95. ISBN 0-685-35634-5. Discussion of Algerian social conditions, written in French.

Towards the African Revolution. Trans. by Haakon Chevalier. Grove Pr. 1988 $7.95. ISBN 0-8021-3090-9. Examines the politics and government of both Africa and Algeria in 1945.

The Wretched of the Earth. 1965. Trans. by Constance Farrington. Grove Pr. 1988 $48.95. ISBN 0-8021-5083-7. An account of offenses against people in the French colonies of Africa.

FARAH, NURUDDIN. 1945–

Born in Baidoa, Somalia, Nuruddin Farah, who is now an exile in the United States, is widely recognized as one of the finest writers of English-language works from the Horn of Africa. His achievement is all the more impressive considering the fact that English is a fourth language to him. Farah also writes in his native Somali and translates children's stories into Somali from Arabic, English, Italian, and French.

Educated at the University of Chandigarh in India, Farah taught in high schools in Somalia and lived and worked for brief periods in England, Rome, and Nigeria before coming to the United States. He now teaches literature at Brown University in Rhode Island.

Farah made his literary debut with the novel *From a Crooked Rib* (1970). This book revisits the old theme of conflict between the traditional and modern in the story of Ebla, a nomadic girl who flees her parents' desert home and eventually faces the corrupting influences of the city of Mogadishu. Successive works have successfully exploited a wide range of social, cultural, and political themes in a confident, yet still evolving, style. Farah has a keen eye for detail. His work has a colloquial flavor that blends a cosmopolitan outlook with authentic Somali subject matter. In 1979 Farah won the English-Speaking Union Literary Award for his third novel, *Sweet and Sour Milk*.

Novels by Farah

Close Sesame. 1983. Graywolf 1992 $12.00. ISBN 1-55597-162-8. The final book of a trilogy depicting the traditions and struggles of African characters.

From a Crooked Rib. Heinemann Ed. 1970 o.p. A country girl moves to the city and encounters life.

Maps. Pantheon 1987 o.p.

A Naked Needle. 1976. Heinemann Ed. 1976 o.p. A young man African struggles to come to terms with his marriage to a European woman.

Sardines. 1981. Graywolf 1992 $12.00. ISBN 1-55597-161-X. Focuses on relationships among Somali women.

Sweet and Sour Milk. 1980. Graywolf 1992 $12.00. ISBN 1-55597-159-8. Follows Loyaan's investigation of his brother's apparent murder.

IDRIS, YUSUF. 1927–1991

Yusuf Idris, an Arab fundamentalist known for his anti-Israel ideas and commitments, was one of the most outstanding of modern Egyptian writers. The author of 9 plays and 11 collections of short stories that have been translated into 24 languages, Idris was rated by many critics in the Arab world as highly as the 1988 Nobel Prize winner Najib Mahfouz. He, himself, however, saw his artistic accomplishments as superior to Mahfouz's and protested vehemently when the Nobel Prize was awarded to Mahfouz rather than to himself. Idris, who was for some time a patient at the Egyptian National Hospital for Nervous Diseases, died of heart failure in London late in July 1991.

Short Story Collections by Idris

The Cheapest Nights: Short Stories. Trans. by Wadida Wassef. Three Continents 1991 $10.00. ISBN 0-89410-666-X. Fifteen short stories, representing Idris's work at every stage of his development as a writer.

Rings of Burnished Brass and Other Stories. Trans. by Catherine Cobham. Col. U. Pr. 1992 $9.95. ISBN 977-424-248-3. Stories about the struggles of the poor against oppression; includes "The Stranger," "The Black Policeman," "The Siren," and "Rings of Burnished Brass."

KHATIBI, ABDELKEBIR. 1938–

Primarily a novelist, Abdelkebir Khatibi of Morocco is one of the most philosophically engaging and stylistically innovative Maghrebian writers of the French language. Drawing upon his native Arab-Berber oral traditional and cultural heritage, his writings trace the journey of a man constantly in search of a new identity. This search is reflected in such works as *La Mémoire Tatouée*

(1971), *Le Livre du Sang* (1983), and *Un Été à Stockholm* (1990). Combining the autobiographical and the fictional, as well as the poetic and the philosophical, Khatibi's fiction has frequently been compared to the works of Dostoyevski, Proust, Faulkner (see Vol. 1), and Joyce (see Vol. 1). In his work, Khatibi has created a fictional world in which elements such as character and setting anticipate and complement each other. Together with a skillful use of inchoate patterns and themes, Khatibi's style is characterized by a subtle use of language with which he conveys a sense of otherness or difference in a world where individual identity is constantly threatened by *sameness.*

Khatibi's major fictional writings include *La Mémoire Tatouée* (1971), *Amour Bilingue* (1983), *Le Livre du Sang* (1983), *Maghreb au Pluriel* (1983), *Figures de l'Étranger* (1987), *Par-dessus l'Épaule* (1988), and *Un Été à Stockholm* (1990). Of these, only one work (*Amour Bilingue*) has been translated into English as *Love in Two Languages.*

Novel by Khatibi

Love in Two Languages. Trans. by Richard Howard. U. of Minn. Pr. 1990 $19.95. ISBN 0-8166-1779-1. His English-language debut.

MAHFOUZ, NAJIB. 1911–

[See Chapter 4 in this volume.]

SALIH, AL-TAYIB. 1929–

[See Chapter 4 in this volume.]

YACINE, KATEB. 1929–1989

The son of an Algerian Islamic lawyer of Berber origins, Kateb Yacine is one of the most enigmatic Maghrebian writers in the French language. Better known for his ambivalent and often contradictory public roles—a Communist ideologue, yet opponent of orthodox communism and a Berber ethnic nationalist—his fame as an author rests on his mythical-autobiographical novel, *Nedjima* (1955). This epic work was begun in 1946 and completed in 1955 after the outbreak of the Algerian War of Independence. *Nedjima* means "star" in Arabic; but the star is also the symbol of nationhood in many national banners, and the word also alludes to the name of the first Algerian national party, *Étoile Nord-Africaine* (the North African Star). In this novel, the author's subtle interweaving of situations and relationships transforms the story of a woman into a parable touching upon many of the struggles for national, racial, ethnic, and personal identity that have dominated postcolonial Algerian consciousness. Although Yacine began his writing career as a poet and went on to distinguish himself primarily as a playwright, scholarly interest in his writings has continued to focus on the novel *Nedjima.* Because of the reappearance of the same characters, settings, and situations from *Nedjima* in his plays, critics tend to see his works as constituting an epic cycle.

Two years before his death in 1989, Yacine was awarded the Grand Prix National des Lettres. English translations of the works of this controversial author, who contributed greatly to the establishment of Francophonic African literature in the Maghreb, are not yet widely available.

Novel by Yacine

Nedjima: Kateb Yacine. U. Pr. of Va. 1991 $35.00. ISBN 0-8139-1312-8

Book about Yacine

Bonn, Charles. *Kateb Yacine: "Nedjma"*. P.U.F. 1990 o.p.

WEST AFRICAN LITERATURE

If there are any traditions of written literatures in West Africa before the advent of Islam and its subsequent spread during the Almoravid *jihad,* such traditions are yet to be discovered. Recent scholarship has, however, called attention to the existence of well over 30 different indigenous systems of writing in West Africa, ranging from the pictographic and ideographic to the syllabic and even phonetic. But, apart from the Vai script of Liberia and Sierra Leone and, especially, the more recently discovered Nwagu Aneke Igbo syllabary of southeastern Nigeria, in which there is an abundant corpus of literature, no pre-Arabic or pre-Islamic corpus of literature in any of the scripts has been discovered. The impression gained from a study of the known indigenous scripts of West Africa is that, whereas some of them may be of some antiquity, literature in them is a postcolonial development, instigated by nativistic or cultural nationalist impulses arising from the colonial experience. For example, in the Nwagu Aneke script, literature turns out to be an ideological instrument for the restatement of traditional African values that are considered superior to the European social, philosophical, and cultural values that displaced them. In these circumstances, any survey of the written literatures of West Africa must begin with the Arabic literatures of the Islamic West African empires—Mali, Songhay, Ghana, Sokoto, Kanem-Bornu—that flourished between 700 A.D. and the turn of the nineteenth century. Before their eclipse in the nineteenth century, these early Arabic literatures of West Africa had been displaced by missionary-sponsored literatures in African languages, namely the *ajami* traditions of Islamic literatures in African languages written in the Arabic script in the savannah belt and a parallel corpus of Christian literatures in the Roman script in the forest belts across the region.

Timbuktu, the seat of Islamic learning in the medieval empire of Mali, was known throughout the cultured world of the age, not only for its learning, but also for its writers. The best-known literary figures of the Timbuktu school include Muhammad Kati (1468–1597) and Ahmad Baba (1556–1627), whose histories and redactions of Islamic legends were valued for their powerful restatements of Islamic orthodoxy in the face of skepticism arising from the tenacity of traditional African values. Celebrated literary events of the period include literary exchanges on the problems of Islamic penetration into animistic African society and writings against the upsurge of "innovation." These literary events reveal that indigenous world views, religious ideas, myths, and traditions of heroism persisted and continued to challenge generations of often violent assaults from Islam. Not surprisingly, the Arabic-Islamic literatures of this period centered on providing countermyths, counterhagiographies and counterliturgies based on Islamic traditions. With the collapse of the great West African empires, these literary battles continued to be waged from five main centers: Futa Jalon, Futa Toro (what is now northern Ghana), the Sokoto Caliphate, and the Kanem-Bornu empire on Lake Chad.

It was the tenacity of indigenous culture in the face of centuries of Arabic Islamic literary assaults that gave birth to the *ajami* tradition of writing African language in Arabic script. The nomadic Fula purveyors of the Islamic faith, on discovering that the message of the Prophet was more readily acceptable when presented to the people in their own languages, hit upon the expedient of creating Islamic literatures in African languages, written in the Arabic script. A similar strategy was subsequently followed by the Christian missionaries. In each case, Arab–Islamic or European–Christian classics, folk tales, and scriptures were translated, imitated, adapted, or copied, and the resultant African-language literatures were largely allegorical, fabular, and didactic. In West Africa, as in other parts of Africa, allegorical works like JOHN BUNYAN's (see Vol. 1) *Pilgrim's Progress* (1678) were translated into practically every major language and became the models for early prose works by such writers as D. O. Fagunwa and Pita Nwana. Similar influences from Islam gave birth to allegorical fiction in Hausa, as in the work of Abubakar Tafawa Balewa. Not surprisingly, these derivative writings in African languages remain largely uncritical of the European and Arab presence in Africa and, in many cases, reveal acceptance of the power and role of Europeans, Arabs, and their religions.

Prior to the emergence of Christian missionary literature in West Africa, a new phase of West African writing, inspired by European contacts with precolonial West Africa, was born. The capture of Africans for labor in the Americas was followed by explorations, trade, missionary activity, wars of conquest, and colonial rule. After a succession of defeats, the Golden Age of Africa was forgotten, and, in European writings, Africans came to be represented as inferior beings who needed to be rescued from primitiveness and savagery. It was against these images, and against the experience of slavery, that West African protest writing emerged in precolonial times in the works of liberated slaves like Juan Latino, OLAUDAH EQUIANO, Ignatius Sancho, Ottombah Cugoano, and PHILLIS WHEATLEY (see Vol. 1). Writing from Europe and America, and voicing their protests through autobiographies, letters, and poetry, these pioneers of modern West African writing not only established protest writing as a powerful weapon for the liberation struggle but also laid the foundations for the major intellectual movements that are still active in postcolonial Africa, including pan-Africanism, negritude, African personality, black consciousness, and even Afrocentricity. Today, the crude early formulations of these ideas in the poetry of early political nationalists like Nnamdi Azikiwe and Dennis Osadebay have given way to the more subtle cultural nationalism, historical reconstructions, and postindependence self-criticism of avant-garde West African writers like CHINUA ACHEBE, WOLE SOYINKA, AYI KWEI ARMAH, YAMBO OUOLOGUEM, and SEMBENE OUSMANE, among others.

The growth of popular literature in West Africa has been associated with the emergence of the working and petty-trader classes in the postcolonial African urban environment. Steeped in the colonial mentality of their readers (the semiliterate urban masses committed to moneymaking and the acquisition of possessions), the works of West African popular writers pitch their art against traditional African values. One example is the caricaturing of the ideas of the heroine's father in OGALI OGALI's *Veronica, My Daughter* (1956), a play that also reveals the popular writers' fetishization of the language of the colonizer as the gateway to high status, power, and respectability. Not surprisingly, given readers' postindependence disillusionment with an elite deemed to have brought ruin on their nations, this type of writing has virtually disappeared, giving way to pulp fiction of the kind found in Western societies.

In many respects, West African literatures are by far the most varied and most copious of contemporary African literatures. This variety and prolixity reflect not only the demographic and linguistic variety of the region but also the great variety of social, political, and cultural experiences of the people in the various phases of their contacts with the Arab Islamic and the European Christian worlds. West African literature also reflects the relatively greater freedom of individuals and groups in the region to participate fully in the debate over their own future.

History and Criticism

Fraser, Robert. *West African Poetry: A Critical History*. Cambridge U. Pr. 1986 $59.95. ISBN 0-521-30993-X. Primarily concerned with verse in English.

Lindfors, Bernth. *Critical Perspectives on Nigerian Literatures*. Three Continents 1976 $25.00. ISBN 0-914478-27-3. Presents a sampling of scholarly views of Nigerian literature.

Nyamndi, George. *The West African Village Novel*. P. Lang Pubs. 1983 $34.60. ISBN 3-261-05077-2. Examines the novel in West African literature and its historical social context.

Obiechina, Emmanuel. *Culture, Tradition and Society in the West African Novel*. Cambridge U. Pr. 1975 $47.50. ISBN 0-521-09876-9. Concentrating on twentieth-century prose, this valuable study examines the effects of the mass media, the rise of the middle class, and cultural nationalism on the works of such African authors as Achebe, Soyinka, and Okara.

Ogungbesan, Kolawole. *New West African Literature. African Writers Ser.* Heinemann Ed. 1980 $16.50. ISBN 0-435-91761-7

Roscoe, Adrian. *Mother Is Gold: A Study in West African Literature*. Cambridge U. Pr. 1971 o.p. "The book attempts a broad historical perspective and sets the writing into both its socio-linguistic and aesthetic contexts" (*Choice*).

Collections

Ajuwon, Bade. *Funeral Dirges of Yoruba Hunters. Traditional African Literature Ser.* NOK Pubs. 1982 $18.95. ISBN 0-88357-075-0. A collection of Yoruba poetry and funeral rites describing the ceremonials of Yoruba hunters.

Awoonor, Kofi, and G. Adali-Mortty, eds. *Messages: Poems from Ghana. African Writers Ser.* Heinemann Ed. 1982 $8.95. ISBN 0-435-90042-0. A full complement of modern poetry from Ghana.

Berry, Jack, and Richard A. Spears. *West African Folk-Tales*. Northwestern U. Pr. 1991 $24.95. ISBN 0-8101-0979-4. Collection of folk tales representing an important contribution spanning 35 years of collection and translation.

Biebuyck, Daniel. *Hero and Chief: Epic Literature from the Banyangoa (Zaire Republic)*. U. CA Pr. 1978 $49.95. ISBN 0-520-03386-8. Presents three epics sung by Nyanga bards and a comprehensive study of Nyanga epic literature.

Bird, Charles, and Mamadou Koita, eds. *The Songs of Seydou Camara, Vol. I: Kambili*. Ohio U. Pr. 1974 $7.00. ISBN 0-941934-12-8

Roscoe, Adrian, and Hangson Msika. *Quiet Chameleon: Modern Poetry from Central Africa. New Perspectives on African Literature Ser.* K. G. Saur 1991 $75.00. ISBN 0-905450-52-3

Soumaoro, Bourama, and Charles S. Bird, eds. *Seyidu Kamara: Ka Donkiliw*. Indiana Africa 1976 $7.50. ISBN 0-941934-18-7

Walker, Barbara K., and Warren S. Walker, eds. *Nigerian Folk Tales*. Shoe String 2nd rev. ed. 1980 o.p. A collection of Yoruba folk tales, with commentaries by the authors.

ACHEBE, CHINUA. 1930–

Chinua Achebe of Nigeria achieved international recognition with his first novel, *Things Fall Apart* (1958). Since then, his name has been in the forefront of modern African literature. A recipient of numerous awards and fellowships, Achebe has also been considered for the Nobel Prize for Literature and, in 1987, was on the Booker Prize short list for his most recent novel, *Anthills of the Savannah* (1987). To date he has published five novels, a book of short stories, children's books, a book of poetry, and many literary and critical essays.

Achebe began writing during his student days at the University College, Ibadan, and contributed short stories and essays to the institution's *University Herald,* a magazine that also carried the early works of a number of other major Nigerian authors. By the time his first novel, *Things Fall Apart,* appeared, he had already achieved a confident and controlled style, although he has stated in an interview that he regards writing as one of the most difficult of human undertakings. In *Things Fall Apart,* Achebe realistically portrays the traditional aspects of his native Igbo culture. He is also the acknowledged doyen of the culture-conflict theme, a subject on which he has written so vividly that his name is almost synonymous with it. *No Longer at Ease* (1960), a sequel to *Things Fall Apart,* takes up the plight of what was then referred to as the "been-to" African, a term used to describe Africans who had lived abroad and then returned home, generally with Western ways. Until the publication of *Anthills of the Savannah, Arrow of God* (1964), Achebe's third novel, was considered his most complex because of the paradoxes that emerge in his treatment of the multifaceted conflicts between religion and politics, both within the traditional Igbo society and in its collision with Christianity and colonial power.

Achebe's fourth novel, *A Man of the People* (1966), is set in the decadent and corrupt political atmosphere of an imaginary African country that closely resembles Nigeria. The novel is harshly critical of the political leadership of postindependence Africa. Hailed as prophetic, the novel was published just as the first postindependence civilian government in Nigeria was overthrown, in situations paralleling those evoked at the end of the novel. The crisis engendered by the coup of January 1966 eventually led to civil war, following the massacre of Igbo people in northern Nigeria and the attempted secession from Nigeria, under the name Biafra, of eastern Nigeria (the Igbo homeland). Because he was an active participant in the war, Achebe lacked the extended time needed for narrative writing, so he chose poetry as a more expedient mode of expression. In 1972 he was awarded the Commonwealth Poetry Prize for *Beware, Soul Brother and Other Poems* (1972), a poignant reflection on the human tragedies of the civil war. He also contributed to *The Insider: Stories of War and Peace from Nigeria* (1971) and shortly after published his own book of short stories, *Girls at War and Other Stories* (1971), the title story of which is concerned with the impact of corruption on the ideals of the Biafran revolt among soldiers and civilian officers.

In his fifth novel, *Anthills of the Savannah,* Achebe draws together, in a brutal portraiture of the fortunes of a visionless and corrupt military leader, his concerns about the complexity and symbolism of traditional culture and postindependence political corruption. He creates a broad canvas, revealing the frightening failure of political and moral leadership in Africa today.

Achebe's works have been translated into more than 25 languages, and his books are required in many African, African American, and comparative literature courses and in many other humanities courses in Africa, Europe, and the United States. Considered to be among Africa's first generation of writers (those published in the 1950s and 1960s), Achebe is best known for his appealingly simple, though memorable, novels rooted in Igbo traditions and folklore, especially proverbs. According to Achebe's English rendering of an Igbo adage, "proverbs are the palm oil with which words are eaten."

Born in Ogidi, Achebe proceeded from Government College, Umuahia, to the University College, Ibadan, where he received his B.A. in English, history, and religious studies in 1953. After graduation, he pursued a successful broadcasting career and served as director of external broadcasting for Nigeria from 1961 to 1966. During the civil war, he undertook many trips abroad to canvass for the recognition of Biafra. At the end of the war, he joined the faculty of the University of Nigeria, Nsukka, as a Senior Research Fellow in the Institute of African Studies. After a three-year leave of absence from the University of Massachusetts at Amherst, he was appointed professor and head of the Department of English at Nsukka. But, in 1980, he retired to devote his time to writing, and occasional lecturing and literary publishing. One of his first major undertakings after his retirement was to found the Association of Nigerian Writers (1982), which has since set up prizes, publications, and other activities to stimulate and encourage new writers. An international symposium to mark Achebe's sixtieth birthday brought more than 300 scholars from all over the world to Nsukka; but shortly after this, Achebe was involved in an automobile accident that has left him confined to a wheelchair. Nevertheless, he remains professionally active and is currently the Charles P. Stevenson Professor of Literature at the Department of English at Bard College, Annandale-on-Hudson, New York.

Novels by Achebe

Anthills of the Savannah. Doubleday 1989 $8.95. ISBN 0-385-26045-8

Arrow of God. 1964. Doubleday 1989 $8.95. ISBN 0-385-01480-5

A Man of the People. 1966. Doubleday 1989 $7.95. ISBN 0-385-08616-4

No Longer at Ease. 1960. *African Writers Ser.* Heinemann Ed. 1987 $7.95. ISBN 0-435-90528-7

Things Fall Apart. 1958. Knopf 1992 $15.00. ISBN 0-679-41714-1

Short Story Collections by Achebe

Chike and the River. Cambridge U. Pr. 1966 $3.50. ISBN 0-521-04003-5. A story for children focusing on nature and discovery.

Girls at War and Others Stories. 1971. Doubleday 1991 $8.00. ISBN 0-385-41896-5

Nonfiction by Achebe

Hopes and Impediments: Selected Essays. Doubleday 1990 $9.95. ISBN 0-385-41479-X. Selected essays addressing his concerns in literature and the arts, relating them to larger issues of race and social justice.

The Trouble with Nigeria. Heinemann Ed. 1984 $7.50. ISBN 0-435-90698-4. Discussion of politics and government, social conditions, national characteristics, and ethnic relations in Nigeria.

Poetry by Achebe

Beware, Soul Brother. African Writers Ser. Heinemann Ed. 1972 $8.95. ISBN 0-435-90120-6

Books about Achebe

Anderson, M., and M. J. Arnoldi. *Art in Achebe's* Things Fall Apart *and* Arrow of God. Indiana Africa 1978 $2.00. ISBN 0-941934-25-X

Carroll, David. *Chinua Achebe.* St. Martin 1980 $16.95. ISBN 0-312-13386-3. Discusses Achebe's work in the context of problems of present-day Africa; examines particular characters in Achebe's novels.

Gikandi, Simon. *Reading Chinua Achebe: Language and Ideology in Fiction*. Heinemann Ed. 1991 $17.50. ISBN 0-435-08057-1. Places Achebe's writing in a wider context than many books about him. Integrates his critical and theoretical writing.

Innes, C. L. *Chinua Achebe. Cambridge Studies in African and Caribbean Literature*. Cambridge U. Pr. 1990 $44.95. ISBN 0-521-35623-7. Comprehensive chronological account of the whole oeuvre of Achebe's writings, lectures, and activities.

Innes, Catherine L., and Bernth Lindfors, eds. *Critical Perspectives on Chinua Achebe*. Three Continents 1978 $25.00. ISBN 0-914478-45-1. A group of critical essays examining the best and most illuminating of Achebe's works.

Killam, G. D. *The Novels of Chinua Achebe*. Holmes & Meier 1969 $12.50. ISBN 0-8419-0023-X. Lucid exposition on *Things Fall Apart, No Longer at Ease, Arrow of God*, and *A Man of the People*.

Njoku, Benedict C. *The Four Novels of Chinua Achebe: A Critical Study*. P. Lang Pubs. 1984 $20.00. ISBN 0-8204-0154-4. Critical study of Africa's foremost novelist by one of Africa's newest critics.

Ogbaa, Kalu. *Gods, Oracles and Divination: Folkways in Chinua Achebe's Novels*. Africa World 1992 $49.95. ISBN 0-86543-256-2

Omotoso, Kole. *Achebe or Soyinka? A Re-interpretation and a Study in Contrasts. New Perspectives on African Literature Ser*. K. G. Saur 1992 $70.00. ISBN 0-905450-38-8

Peters, Jonathan A. *A Dance of Masks: Senghor, Achebe, Soyinka*. Three Continents 1978 $18.00. ISBN 0-914478-23-0

Rutherford, A., and K. H. Peterson, eds. *Chinua Achebe: A Celebration. Studies in African Literature*. Heinemann Ed. $17.50. ISBN 0-435-08060-1

Wren, Robert M. *Achebe's World: the Historical and Cultural Context of Chinua Achebe's Novels*. Three Continents 1980 $22.00. ISBN 0-89410-005-X. Discusses in depth the background and cultural and historical context of Achebe's novels.

AIDOO, AMA ATA (Aidoo, Christine). 1942–

Born near Dominase, in Central Ghana, Aidoo is today the leading Ghanaian woman writer. Educated at the University of Ghana at Legon, where she graduated in 1964 with a B.A. in English, Aidoo worked as a Research Fellow at the Institute of African Studies in Legon before proceeding to Stanford University at Palo Alto, California, for a creative writing course. She made her debut as writer with a short story, "No Sweetness Here" (1965); the story had previously won a prize in a short story competition. This story provides the title of Aidoo's first collection of stories; however, she is better known as a playwright, and her two earliest plays, *Anowa* (first published in 1970) and *The Dilemma of a Ghost* (first published in 1965) remain popular. Aidoo now lives and teaches in Harare, Zimbabwe.

SHORT STORY COLLECTIONS BY AIDOO

No Sweetness Here. 1965. Doubleday 1970 o.p.
Our Sister Kill Joy. NOK Pubs. $9.95. ISBN 0-88357-064-5

NOVEL BY AIDOO

Changes: A Love Story. Interlink Pub. 1992 o.p. A woman separates from her husband and confronts society and the near impossibility of finding a man to love.

PLAYS BY AIDOO

Anowa. Longmans 1970 o.p.
The Dilemma of a Ghost. Longman 1965 o.p.

AMADI, ELECHI. 1934–

An Ikwerre Igbo, Elechi Amadi was educated at the elite Government College, Umuahia, and at the University College, Ibadan. After working briefly as a secondary school teacher, he was commissioned into the Nigerian army and remained at the Nigerian Defense Academy in Kaduna until his voluntary retirement and return to the teaching profession on the eve of the Nigerian civil war in 1965. During the war, Amadi opposed the Biafran cause. His unpleasant encounters with the Biafran authorities are recorded in *Sunset in Biafra*, a memoir in which he portrays not only himself but also his Ikwerre people as having been coerced into a sad and senseless war against Nigeria by their ambitious and overbearing Igbo neighbors. Since the end of the civil war, however, Amadi has come to be cynical and critical about the divisive social developments in Nigeria. His portrait of Nigerian society in his first post-civil war novel, *Estrangement* (1986), vividly evokes the image of the total destruction of time-honored individual and community bonds in the prewar society. Amadi now lives in retirement near Port Harcourt, the setting of his first novels—*The Concubine* (1958) and *The Great Ponds* (1969)—in which Igbo cultural ambience remains unmistakable, despite the author's earlier politically motivated attempts to redefine his ethnolinguistic identity.

Novels by Amadi

The Concubine. 1958. *African Writers Ser.* Heinemann Ed. 1966 $9.95. ISBN 0-435-90556-2

Estrangement. 1986. *African Writers Ser.* Heinemann Ed. 1986 $9.95. ISBN 0-435-90564-3

The Great Ponds. 1969. *African Writers Ser.* Heinemann Ed. 1970 $9.95. ISBN 0-435-90044-7

ARMAH, AYI KWEI. 1939–

Ayi Kwei Armah was born in Takoradi, Ghana. He was educated at the elite Achimota College, near Accra, and received a degree in sociology from Harvard University in 1963. He has taught at several universities in Africa and the United States. But his first choice on leaving Harvard University was to become actively involved in the struggle for African liberation. This decision took him to Algeria, which had just emerged from its armed struggle for independence from France. In Algeria, Armah worked as a translator for the magazine *Révolution Africaine* until his health broke down toward the end of 1963, leading to a five-month hospitalization in Boston, Massachusetts. He returned to Ghana in 1964. However, since 1970 he has been living and traveling in other parts of Africa, beginning with Tanzania, where he learned Swahili and where he was able to find a publisher, East African Publishing House, for his second, third, and fourth novels. He currently lives in Dakar, Senegal.

Armah's first novel, *The Beautiful Ones Are Not Yet Born* (1968), deals with political corruption in a newly independent African nation, which looks unquestionably like his home country, Ghana. The capital of this nation, which looks like Accra, is the setting for this symbolic novel, which is generally felt to be about the last years of Nkrumah's government. In his largely autobiographical second novel, *Fragments* (1970), Armah illustrates the difficulties of an intellectual in a culture oriented toward material possessions. His third novel, *Why Are We So Blest?* (1972), has been called by Edward Lobb in *Critical Perspectives on Ayi Kwei Armah* "an ambitious and largely successful attempt to probe the complex relation of colonizer and colonized—a relation which is seen as historically past but psychologically present in any relationship between the African and a European." But by far the most ambitious novel published so far is his fourth, *Two Thousand Seasons* (1973), a complex mythical and highly polemical work described by Simon Simonse in *Research in African Literature*, as "a reconstruction of two thousand years of African history, organized around the question 'What happened to the Way?' The Way is the rule of reciprocity: of giving, receiving and returning the gift." In his fifth novel, *The Healers* (1978), Armah revisits the same theme within his own Akan society. He portrays a dispiriting social decay, reflecting in microcosm the wider malaise of the black world. To deal with this grave social trauma, the novel invokes the idealistic image of a group of saintly healers whose goal is to instill an awareness of the need for correcting society and re-create a new life for the Black race.

NOVELS BY ARMAH

The Beautiful Ones Are Not Yet Born. Heinemann Ed. 1989 $8.95. ISBN 0-435-90540-6
Fragments. 1970. Heinemann Ed. 1974 o.p.
The Healers. 1978. Heinemann Ed. 1979 o.p.
Two Thousand Seasons. 1973. Third World 1980 o.p.
Why Are We So Blest? 1972. Heinemann Ed. 1974 o.p.

BOOKS ABOUT ARMAH

Fraser, Robert. *The Novels of Ayi Kwei Armah: A Study in Polemical Fiction*. Heinemann Ed. 1980 o.p. A comprehensive view of all of Armah's works; examines his political stand and the political policies that influenced his writing.

Wright, Derek. *Ayi Kwei Armah's Africa: The Sources of His Fiction*. K. G. Saur 1989 $60.00. ISBN 0-905450-95-7. Offers an indispensable elucidation of Armah's corpus to date.

———, ed. *Critical Perspectives on Ayi Kwei Armah*. Three Continents 1992 $30.00. ISBN 0-89410-640-6. Broad and representative selection of critical responses to Ayi Kwei Armah's writings.

AWOONOR, KOFI (Awooner-Williams, George). 1935–

Born in Wheta, Ghana, Kofi Awoonor, who is now his country's ambassador to the United Nations, is an internationally recognized poet whose work has been widely translated and anthologized. He also writes novels and plays and is a keen collector and translator of oral literature from his mother tongue, Ewe, as well as a critic of modern African literature in the colonial languages. In 1979 the Ghanaian government jailed Awoonor for political reasons. At the time of his arrest, he was visiting home from the United States, where he was on a one-year sabbatical from the State University of New York at Stony Brook. His arrest raised an international protest. During his incarceration, Awoonor wrote *The House by the Sea* (1978), a piercing collection of poetry in which he reflects on his ten months in jail. His first novel, *This Earth, My Brother* (1971), is a highly acclaimed allegorical work set in postindependence Africa. It recounts a lawyer's search for identity and meaning in life.

NOVELS BY AWOONOR

Comes the Voyager at Last. A Tale of Return to Africa. Africa World 1992 $24.95. ISBN 0-86543-262-7

This Earth, My Brother. 1971. *African Writers Ser*. Heinemann Ed. 1972 $8.95. ISBN 0-435-90108-7

POETRY BY AWOONOR

The House by the Sea. 1978. Greenfld. Rev. Lit. 1978 o.p.

Until the Morning After: Selected Poems 1963–1985. Greenfld Rev. Lit. 1987 $10.95. ISBN 0-912678-69-0. Consists of poems from his earliest volume to his most recent work.

Nonfiction by Awoonor

The Breast of the Earth: A Survey of the History, Culture and Literature of Africa South of the Sahara. NOK Pubs. 1983 $19.95. ISBN 0-685-03583-2

Fire in the Valley: Ewe Folktales. NOK Pubs. $10.00. ISBN 0-88357-079-3

Guardians of the Sacred Word: Ewe Poetry. NOK Pubs. 1974 $11.95. ISBN 0-88357-007-6. Exhaustive study of Akpalu and Dunyo poetry.

BA, MARIAMA. 1929–1981

The promising but short literary career of Mariama Ba ended with her death in 1981 at the age of 52, just before the publication of her second novel, *Le Chant Écarlate* (*The Scarlet Song*) (1981), a poetic drama of a love affair between a Senegalese student and the daughter of a French diplomat. Like the works of other feminist African women writers, Ba's writing challenges many prevalent stereotypes that reinforce the African woman's acceptance of her "place" in society. Her first novel, *So Long a Letter* (1979), which revealed her clarity of vision and persuasive rhetoric, is written in an epistolary style. This long letter from one female friend to another is a deeply moving account of a Muslim woman's innermost feelings and emotional survival following her husband's decision to take a second, and much younger, wife. The novel has been translated into more than 15 languages and has received international acclaim. In 1980 Mariama Ba received the Noma Award for the best novel published in Africa.

Novels by Ba

So Long a Letter. 1979. Trans. by Modupe Bode-Thomas. *African Writers Ser.* Heinemann Ed. 1981 o.p.

The Scarlet Song. 1981. *African Classics Ser.* Dearborn Trade $9.95. ISBN 0-582-78595-2

BETI, MONGO. 1932–

Mongo Beti was born in Yaounde, the capital of Cameroon. He received his early education in local schools, which was followed by studies at the Sorbonne in Paris. Now a French citizen, he lives and teaches in Paris, where he is the editor of the journal *Peuples Noirs, Peuples Africains,* founded in 1978.

Beti wrote his first novel, *Ville Cruelle* (1954), under the pseudonym Eza Boto. A favorite theme of Beti is the failure of colonial missionary efforts in Africa. He speaks not so much against Christianity as against the futile Europeanization of Africans in the name of religion. *The Poor Christ of Bomba* (1956), his best-known work, is written as a diary. The novel is a satire of Christian religion in precolonial Cameroon.

Novels by Beti

Lament for an African Pol. Trans. by Richard Bjornson. Three Continents 1985 $18.00. ISBN 0-89410-304-0. Introduction by Bjornson.

Mission to Kala. 1958. *African Writers Ser.* Heinemann Ed. 1964 $8.95. ISBN 0-435-90013-7. Bawdy satire about a scholar who returns to the countryside to continue his studies.

Le Pauvre Christ de Bomba. Kraus 1956 $29.00. ISBN 0-8115-2978-9. Local churchmen use Christian girls at a church camp for their own purposes.

Perpetua & the Habit of Unhappiness. African Writers Ser. Heinemann Ed. 1978 $10.95. ISBN 0-435-90181-8. Essola comes out of a 10-year detention, determined to find out why his sister Perpetua died.

The Poor Christ of Bomba. 1956. *African Writers Ser.* Heinemann Ed. 1971 $9.95. ISBN 0-435-90088-9

Remember Ruben. 1974. Trans. by Gerald Moore. *African Writers Ser.* Heinemann Ed. 1988 $9.95. ISBN 0-435-90214-8. Study of a political protestor set against a documentary portrayal of the political evolution of the colony.

BOOK ABOUT BETI

Drame, Kandioura. *The Novel as Transformation Myth: A Study of the Novels of Mongo Beti and Ngugi wa Thiong'o. Foreign & Comparative Studies—African Ser.* Syracuse U. Pr. 1990 $14.00. ISBN 0-915984-68-7. A cross-cultural comparative study between the two authors.

CLARK, J. P. (Clark-Bekederemo, J. P.). 1934–

One of the leading first generation postcolonial writers in Nigeria, Clark (who recently changed his surname to Clark-Bekederemo) was born in Kiagbodo, near Warri, in the Delta State of Nigeria, to Ijaw and Urhobo parents. A poet, playwright, and folklorist, he was educated at the University College, Ibadan, where he read English and edited the seminal student literary magazine, *The Horn.* After graduating from the university, Clark worked as a newspaper editor, and, after studying briefly at Princeton University, he joined the Institute of African Studies at the University of Ibadan as a research fellow. Clark's dissatisfaction with the condition of human rights in American society was partly responsible for his sudden withdrawal from his studies at Princeton; his bitterness is recorded in his memoir, *America, Their America* (1965). Soon after his return to Nigeria, to a mixed reception as an outspoken radical writer, Clark joined the faculty of the Department of English at the University of Lagos, from which he retired in 1979. Since his retirement, he has been living in Lagos, where he runs his own theater company—Pec Repertory Theatre.

An early contributor to the journal *Black Orpheus* and the Mbari publications of the early 1960s, Clark is best known for his early plays, *The Song of a Goat* (1961), *The Raft* (1964), *The Masquerade* (1964), and *Ozidi* (1966) and for his performance-oriented edition and translation of the magnificent oral epic of his native Ijaw people, *The Ozidi Saga,* on which he based his first play, *Ozidi.* Together with his early poetry, gathered in *A Reed in the Tide* (1965), these early plays deal with the myths, legends, and traditional life of Clark's hometown in the river fishing communities of the Niger Delta. The language of his work pulsates with the rhythm of his native Ijaw. References to events of the day were already beginning to assert themselves in allegorical form in *The Raft.* In his later writings, these references emerged to dominate his creative concerns: first in his collection of civil war poetry, *Casualties* (1970), and then in most of his subsequent writings—*The State of the Union* (1985), *A Decade of Tongues, Mandela and Other Poems,* and *The Birodoa Plays.* In 1991 Howard University Press released his *Collected Plays and Poems,* which offers the entire corpus of his writings from 1958 to 1988.

NONFICTION BY CLARK

America, Their America. Holmes & Meier 1969 $17.50. ISBN 0-8419-0012-4

POETRY BY CLARK

Casualties, Poems 1966–1968. 1970. Holmes & Meier 1970 $14.50. ISBN 0-8419-0096-5. Poems written during the Nigerian Civil War.

Work by Clark

Collected Plays and Poems by J. P. Clark-Bekederemo. Howard U. Pr. 1991 o.p. Introduction by Abiola Irele. Covers the whole oeuvre of Clark's writings, and tries to represent them in a cohesive, chronological fashion.

DAN FODIO, SHEHU USMAN. 1754–1817

Leader of the Fulani *jihad,* which transformed the Hausa states of northern Nigeria into a bastion of Islam in West Africa, Usman Dan Fodio, whose ancestors came from Futa Toro, was born in Gobir and was educated at Agades. A pious Muslim, he was the first Sultan of Sokoto, the Islamic Caliphate that he established after the great Islamic Revolution of 1804. In his efforts to ensure the survival of Islam in the Caliphate and elsewhere in West Africa, he not only patronized Islamic writing but also produced a large corpus of poetry and prose in Arabic, all of which was concerned with the propagation of the Islamic faith and the defense of its orthodoxy against all forms of innovation. He was among the pioneers of *ajami* writing (the writing of African languages in the Arabic script), and his *ajami* writings in both Hausa and his native Fula are still highly influential in northern Nigeria.

Book about Dan Fodio

Hiskett, Melville. *The Life and Times of Shehu Usman dan Fodio*. London 1973 o.p.

ECHERUO, MICHAEL. 1937–

Currently Professor of Modern Letters at Syracuse University, Michael Echeruo was born in Umunumo in the Imo State of Nigeria. Best known as a scholar and university administrator, he was the first African professor of English literature and head of the Department of English at both the University of Nigeria and the University of Ibadan. By and large, Echeruo's accomplishments in such diverse scholarly fields as Shakespearean drama, African literature, the English novel, cultural history, and Igbo studies have tended to overshadow his status as a writer. But he is undoubtedly one of the most powerful voices among his generation of Nigerian poets. In the early 1960s, he won the first prize in the first poetry competition organized by the Mbari Artists and Writers Club with poems that eventually formed the core of his first poetry collection, *Mortality* (1968). His second book of poetry, *Distanced* (1971), was one of the first of its kind to be published at the end of the Nigerian civil war. In an interview with Chukwuma Azuonye, Echeruo says of his first book of poems that "*Mortality* is about the vulnerability of all existence: intellectual, moral, physical, cultural, and political." Of his second book, he says in the same interview that "*Distanced* is 'distanced'. . . . some of the poems were actually first drafted during the [Nigerian] war. It was after the war that some of those poems came to be re-made in their kind of form and I thought that they were distanced from the original experience. . . . But *Distanced* also is the experience explored in the poems and the question was: will it, years from now, tell what had happened? I was so distanced from it that the telling could only be surreal. So, that's *Distanced*. . . . there is no disillusionment, only agony at the . . . losses of both fatherlands."

Poetry by Echeruo

Distanced. IK Imprints o.p.
Mortality. Longman 1968 o.p.

EKWENSI, CYPRAIN. 1921–

Born in Minna in the Niger State of Nigeria, Cyprain Ekwensi, an Igbo from Nkwelle Ezunaka in the Anambra State, was educated in Nigeria, Ghana, and at the Chelsea School of Pharmacy in London. After quitting the pharmaceutical profession for writing and cultural pursuits, he served as director of Nigeria's Federal Information Services, and during the civil war (1967–70) he was director of Biafra's external publicity. At the end of the war, he briefly traded in plastics and subsequently served as a commissioner in the government of Anambra State (1983). He now lives in retirement at Enugu, the state capital, writing and traveling to give occasional lectures or to attend literary meetings.

A popular novelist, Ekwensi has frequently stated that he writes for the masses. One of his earliest works was a highly successful romantic novella, *When Love Whispers*, published in 1948. Filled with moralistic and sentimental overtones, it typifies Onitsha market literature, a genre that was until recently very popular among the masses, especially in Nigeria and Ghana.

Ekwensi's reputation as a novelist was established with *People of the City* (1953). Urban decay (political corruption, squalor, and overcrowding) is the dominant theme running through this and many of Ekwensi's other works. Consequently, Ekwensi earned the reputation of being Africa's foremost "city novelist."

In Ekwensi's best-known city novel, *Jagua Nana* (1961), he skillfully weaves into the story of a high class, middle-aged prostitute vivid scenes of Lagos high life, against the backdrop of political intrigue. This book earned praise in Africa and abroad, and has been translated into more foreign languages than any of his other books, but it also elicited considerable controversy, especially in Nigeria. Some prudish critics were incensed by the graphic descriptions of explicit sexual encounters in the book and called for a ban. Others, however, considered it a timely portrayal of the realities of Nigerian city life and awaited eagerly a projected but unsuccessful attempt to release a feature film based on it.

Although Ekwensi is known as a chronicler (as well as critic) of city life, he is by no means one-dimensional. *Burning Grass* (1962), for example, is a sensitive look at migratory patterns of the Fulani cattlemen of Northern Nigeria. Ekwensi's firsthand knowledge of the traditional rural areas of the Muslim north of Nigeria surfaces in this work, as well as in *An African Night's Entertainment* (1962). He has also produced numerous children's books, the best known of which is *The Drummer Boy* (1960), based on the life of a blind beggar in Lagos.

Ekwensi is undoubtedly a pioneer and a major influence in contemporary African literature. His strengths are reflected in his social commitment to the topics on which he has chosen to write, coupled with the relevance of these topics to modern Africa. Indeed, his impact seems broader than one might at first suspect, as evidenced by his being awarded the Dag Hammarskjold International Prize for Literature in 1968.

NOVELS BY EKWENSI

Beautiful Feathers. 1963. *African Writers Ser.* Heinemann Ed. 1971 o.p. A young man endeavors to found a political party in an attempt to promote Pan-Africanism.

Jagua Nana. *African Writers Ser.* Heinemann Ed. 1987 $8.95. ISBN 0-435-90678-X. "Unlike *People of the City*, where even the most developed character, Amusa Sango, still remains a shadowy figure, Jagua is very well developed, and the great difference in characterization between the two books is evidence of Ekwensi's growing mastery of the novel" (Ernest Emenyonu, *Cyprain Ekwensi*).

The Passport of Malam Ilia. Cambridge U. Pr. 1960 o.p.

People of the City. 1953. *African Writers Ser.* Heinemann Ed. 1963 o.p.

Nonfiction by Ekwensi

Burning Grass. 1962. Heinemann Ed. 1962 $7.95. ISBN 0-435-90669-0

Short Story Collection by Ekwensi

Lokotown and Other Stories. African Writers Ser. Heinemann Ed. 1966 o.p. Nine short stories reflecting the glitter and seediness of Nigerian city life.

Children's Fiction by Ekwensi

The Drummer Boy. 1960. Cambridge U. Pr. 1960 o.p.
King Forever! Junior African Writers Ser. Heinemann Ed. 1992 $4.00. ISBN 0-435-89295-9
Masquerade Time. Junior African Writers Ser. Heinemann Ed. 1992 $2.50. ISBN 0-435-89165-0

EMECHETA, BUCHI. 1944–

Buchi Emecheta is probably West Africa's most prolific woman novelist, having published more than 12 books, including novels and children's books, as well as numerous articles on African women. The primary focus of her work is the contemporary African woman, torn between traditional and modern social roles.

Her first novel, *In the Ditch,* was published in London in 1972. Largely autobiographical, it recounts the struggle of Adah, a Nigerian mother of five, who is separated from her husband, living in London, and trying simultaneously to raise a family and earn an advanced degree. In her next book (a prequel), *Second-Class Citizen* (1975), Emecheta takes her readers back in time to Lagos, where she acquaints us with Adah's early years, marriage, and eventual move to London with her husband and two children. The novel's title derives from the dual discrimination that Adah experiences in London, both as a black and as a woman.

Emecheta's subsequent novels are all set in her Igbo hometown, Ibusa, in the Delta State of Nigeria, and usually revolve around a female protagonist who challenges cultural traditions. Emecheta has earned a reputation as an outspoken opponent of African patriarchal customs. However, some critics condemn as shallow her understanding of the paradoxes and complexities of gender relationships in the Igbo culture about which she writes. They cite her one-sided handling of such issues as arranged marriages, polygyny, the abuse of women as child-breeding machines, and the maltreatment of widows as evidence that she panders to Western stereotypes by exaggerating Igbo cultural shortcomings while ignoring their sociohistorical bases. Critics also maintain that Emecheta ignores evidence of the exercise of real power by women in what is essentially a dual system of social organization that allows each gender enormous freedoms within its own domain. Emecheta gave up a job as a lecturer at the University of Calabar in the mid-1980s and returned to Great Britain, where she had been living on and off since the early 1960s and where she is now a permanent resident.

Novels by Emecheta

The Bride Price: Young Ibo Girl's Love; Conflict of Family and Tradition. Braziller 1976 $7.95. ISBN 0-8076-0951-X. A tragic story of a modern Nigerian girl.
Destination Biafra. Schocken 1988 $14.95. ISBN 0-8052-8119-3. A story about the struggles of a man during the Nigerian civil war of 1967–1970.

Double Yoke. 1982. Braziller 1983 $7.95. ISBN 0-8076-1128-X. On-campus story of a young woman who overcomes society's resistance to the education of females.

The Family. Braziller 1990 $17.95. ISBN 0-8076-1245-6. A touching portrait of a Jamaican teenager.

Head Above Water. 1986. Kayode Pubns. 1991 $10.95. ISBN 1-879831-06-6

In the Ditch. 1972. Schocken 1987 $4.95. ISBN 0-8052-8010-3

The Joys of Motherhood. African Writers Ser. Heinemann Ed. 1989 $8.95. ISBN 0-435-90684-4. A compassionate story of an extended Ibo family struggling to survive and to adapt to a bewildering change of values.

The Moonlight Bride. 1980. Braziller 1983 $6.95. ISBN 0-8076-1063-1. Two young girls overhear their elders arranging a marriage in their traditional village and watch the preparations.

Nowhere to Play. 1979. Schocken 1981 o.p. Juvenile fiction about vacation, based on a story by the author's 12-year-old daughter.

Rape of Shavi. Braziller 1985 $6.95. ISBN 0-8076-1118-2

Second-Class Citizen. Braziller 1983 $7.95. ISBN 0-8076-1066-6

The Slave Girl. 1977. Braziller 1977 $7.95. ISBN 0-8076-0952-8. Follows the fortunes of Objebeta, a young girl who is sold into slavery.

The Wrestling Match. Braziller 1983 $4.95. ISBN 0-8076-1061-5. Sixteen-year-old Okei is left orphaned after the Nigerian civil war and engages in a wrestling match in order to prove to his critical uncle and aunt that he is not as idle and worthless as they think.

EQUIANO, OLAUDAH. 1745–1798

One of the most remarkable figures in the history of African literature, Olaudah Equiano (or Gustavus Vassa) was born in an Igbo community that he called Essaka (most probably Isieke, in what is now the Ihiala local government area of the Anambra State of Nigeria). Captured and sold into slavery at the age of 12, he was taken to the West Indies. There he was resold to a British naval officer who helped him acquire an education and some nautical experience. But, when he was beginning to consider himself a free man, he was unexpectedly sold again to a Philadelphia trader, for whom he undertook business trips to the West Indies. These trips enabled him to make enough money to buy his freedom. As a free man, Equiano continued his vocation as a sailor and traveled extensively in Europe, Africa, and the Americas. He eventually joined the abolitionist movement in Great Britain, where he settled down as a respectable African European, married an English woman, and had two children. Equiano moved in high social circles, wrote and spoke frequently in various public media on abolition issues, and petitioned the British Parliament on the evils of slavery. But by far his most important contribution to the abolition movement was his autobiography, *The Interesting Narrative of the Life of Olaudah Equiano or Gustavus Vassa, the African, Written by Himself,* which was first published in London in 1789. *The Interesting Narrative* is not only an eloquent diatribe against the evils of slavery; its early chapters also present a thoroughly idyllic picture of the culture, social life, and geographical environment of his Igbo home, which he describes as "a charming, fruitful vale." In the autobiography, Equiano refutes the detractions of African peoples in European and oriental literatures, religious dogmas, and philosophical and ethnographic writings; he emerges as the first spokesperson of pan-African nationalism, black consciousness, negritude, and a whole range of other contemporary African and African American intellectual movements. *The Interesting Narrative* is a mixture of factual ethnographic and historical details, debatable assertions, and outright fallacies and is as mystifying as it is revealing. But so powerful is its eighteenth-century rhetorical style that, despite the assertion in its title that it was "written by himself," few of his white contemporaries were convinced that such elegant prose and humane sentiments could be written by an African.

NONFICTION BY EQUIANO

Equiano's Travels. Ed. by Paul Edwards. *African Writers Ser.* Heinemann Ed. 1967 $9.95. ISBN 0-435-90010-2

The Life of Olaudah Equiano, or Gustavus Vassa, the African, Written by Himself. 1789. Ed. by Paul Edwards. *Longman African Classics.* Longman 1988 $9.95. ISBN 0-582-03070-6. New abridged version of Equiano's autobiography by the foremost Equiano scholar, the late Paul Edwards. Includes much of the original text.

BOOKS ABOUT EQUIANO

Acholonu, Catherine Obianuju. *The Igbo Roots of Equiano (Gustavus Vassa).* Afa Pr. o.p. An anthropological study of slaves' biographies. Includes bibliography.

Constanza, Angelo. *Surprising Narrative: Olaudah Equiano and the Beginnings of Black Autobiography.* Greenwood Pr. 1987 o.p.

LAYE, CAMARA. 1928–1980

Camara Laye, a pioneer in modern African literature and one of the continent's major novelists, died in exile in 1980. Since the late 1960s, he had been living in Senegal as the guest of President LEOPOLD SEDAR SENGHOR, who is himself one of Africa's foremost poets. Born in the Guinean city of Kouroussa, Laye was raised in an African rural environment in which Islam and traditional African folkways had become so harmoniously interwoven that they were completely indistinguishable from one another—a situation recaptured vividly in his first novel, *L'Enfant Noir* (*The Dark Child*) (1953). After completing technical school in Conakry, Laye continued his education in France. In between odd jobs, and as a way of coping with loneliness, Laye began writing remembrances of his childhood days in Guinea. The result was *L'Enfant Noir* (1953), an autobiographical novel considered by many to be one of the most remarkable portraits ever written of the assimilation of Islamic culture into traditional African life. The wide appeal of the book has survived, despite criticism from African nationalists that it glamorizes the alien religion of a colonial power and ignores the struggle for national independence that was underway at the time of its publication.

Laye's next book, *Le Regard du Roi* (1954), is much more ambitious and complex. Full of symbolism, the novel is generally regarded as an ingenious allegory about a man's search for God. Laye cleverly weaves humor and mysticism throughout the book. Reviewers often compare the white protagonist's wandering throughout Africa to the quest for the Holy Grail. In 1966, Laye published *Dramouss* (*A Dream of Africa*), a sequel to *L'Enfant Noir,* which explores the postindependence politics of Guinea. This work was viewed as politically provocative and was the cause of Laye's exile to Senegal.

While living in exile, Laye worked with the Dakar-based Institut Français d'Afrique Noire (I.F.A.N.), collecting and editing folk tales and songs of his Malinke people. His last work, *Le Maître de la Parole: Kouma Lafolo Kuoma* (*The Guardian of the Word*), is about the great Mali emperor, Sundiata. At his death, Laye was working on a political novel called *The Exiles,* which has not yet been published.

NOVELS BY LAYE

The Dark Child. 1953. Trans. by James Kirkup and others. FS&G 1954 $8.95. ISBN 0-8090-1548-X. Classic autobiography.

L'Enfant Noir. 1953. Trans. by Joyce Hutchison. Cambridge U. Pr. 1966 o.p.

The Guardian of the Word. Trans. by James Kirkup and others. Random 1984 o.p. Story of the warrior-hero Sundiata and the ancient empire of Mali that he founded.

MUNONYE, JOHN. 1929–

John Munonye emerged on the Nigerian literary scene in 1966 with his first novel, *The Only Son.* Since then, he has published six novels, including *Obi* (1969), *The Oil Man of Obange* (1970), *A Wreath for the Maidens* (1973), and *A Dancer of Fortunes,* all widely acclaimed by critics for their mature realism and close attention to ironic details of social relationships in the traditional and modern Igbo social environment in which they are set. Born in Akokwa in the Imo State of Nigeria, Munonye studied at Christ the King College, Onitsha, before he enrolled at the University College, Ibadan, where he studied Latin, Greek, and history. After obtaining a diploma in education from the University of London, Munonye joined the Eastern Nigerian Ministry of Education at Enugu as an inspector of education, where he attained the rank of deputy permanent secretary. He later served as the principal of the Advanced Teacher Training College (now Alvan Ikoku College of Education), Owerri. He retired in the early 1970s.

NOVELS BY MUNONYE

A Bridge to a Wedding. Africa Writers Ser. Heinemann Ed. 1978 $8.95. ISBN 0-435-90195-8

Obi. African Writers Ser. Heinemann Ed. 1969 $8.95. ISBN 0-435-90045-5

Oil Man of Obange. African Writers Ser. Heinemann Ed. 1971 $8.95. ISBN 0-435-90094-3

The Only Son. African Writers Ser. Heinemann Ed. 1966 $8.95. ISBN 0-435-90021-8

NWAPA, FLORA. 1931–

A pioneer among contemporary African authors, Flora Nwapa is the first Nigerian woman to publish a novel, *Efuru* (1966). This landmark book explores a subject that is quite important in Nwapa's writing, although very unusual in African literature as a whole—the unconventional African woman. Nwapa's heroines are generally independent-minded women who often flout traditional customs. In *Efuru,* the protagonist agrees to marry without waiting for the customary premarital investigations of the groom's family background and the payment of the bride price—two extremely important traditions in Igbo culture.

Marital compatibility, a secondary theme in *Efuru,* is the main theme of Nwapa's second novel, *Idu* (1970). By skillfully using traditional Igbo dialogue, she gives dimension and credibility to her fundamentally stereotypical folk characters. Simultaneously, she sensitizes her readers to the importance of love and mutual understanding in traditional African society by depicting suffering and hardworking wives who bear the brunt of family responsibilities and tragically grow apart from their truant and irresponsible husbands.

Born in 1931 at Oguta (Ugwuta), the setting of her works, Nwapa was educated at the Archdeacon Crowther Memorial Girls High School, near Port Harcourt, and at the University College, Ibadan, after which she worked as an education officer. After the Nigerian civil war, she served as a commissioner for education in the government of East Central Nigeria. She then retired to a publishing business, Tana Press, which specializes in publishing children's literature and to which she has contributed numerous titles. Her post-civil war titles include works set during and after the Nigerian civil war, notably *This Is Lagos and Other Stories* (1971) and *Wives at War and Other Stories* (1975). She continues to appear regularly at African literature and African women's meetings and, during the 1991–92 academic year she accepted an appointment as visiting professor of African literature at the University of Maiduguri, Nigeria.

Novels by Nwapa

Efuru. 1966. *African Writers Ser.* Heinemann Ed. 1966 $8.95. ISBN 0-435-900026-9
Idu. 1970. *African Writers Ser.* Heinemann Ed. 1970 $8.95. ISBN 0-435-90056-0
Never Again. Africa World 1992 $24.95. ISBN 0-86543-318-6
One is Enough. Africa World 1992 $24.95. ISBN 0-86543-322-4
Women are Different. Africa World 1992 $24.95. ISBN 0-86543-325-5

Short Story Collections by Nwapa

This is Lagos and Other Stories. 1971. Africa World 1992 $24.95. ISBN 0-86543-320-8
Wives at War and Other Stories. 1975. Africa World 1992 $24.95. ISBN 0-86543-327-5

OGALI, OGALI A. 1935–

Ogali is perhaps the best known and most internationally visible of Nigerian popular writers of the Onitsha market school. Born in Item in the Abia State of Nigeria, he studied at the Hope Waddell Training Institution, Calabar, and received a diploma in journalism from the Ghana School of Journalism. Ogali is best known for his fictional social comedies, such as *Eddie the Coal City Boy* (1955), *Okeke, the Magician* (1958), *Long, Long Ago* (1957), and *Smile Awhile* (1957), and for farcical plays about postcolonial politics and urban social relationships, among which the most popular include *Patrice Lumumba* (1961), *Veronica, My Daughter* (1956), *Adelabu* (1958), *Mr. Rabbit is Dead* (1958), and *The Ghost of Lumumba* (1961). Soon after the Nigerian civil war, Ogali (who worked in the Biafran information and propaganda complex during the war years) issued a devastatingly bitter tirade against the corrupt practices of priests and Christian workers in Biafran relief centers, entitled *No Heaven for Priests* (1970). Since then Ogali has been mostly silent, but his works continue to be the subject of academic study, and at least one major collection of his writings has appeared in the United States.

Works by Ogali

Veronica, My Daughter and Other Onitsha Plays and Stories. Ed. by Reinhard W. Sander and Peter K. Ayers. Three Continents 1980 $18.00. ISBN 0-914478-61-3

OKARA, GABRIEL. 1921–

Gabriel (Imomotimi Gbaingbain) Okara was born in Bomadi State, Nigeria, and was educated at the Government College, Umuahia, and the Higher College, Yaba. During World War II, he worked in the British Overseas Airways Corporation after a heart problem prevented him from becoming a pilot in the British Royal Air Force. After the war, he was trained as a bookbinder and worked at the Government Printer, Enugu. From there he went to the United States to study journalism at Northwestern University. He returned to Nigeria in the early 1960s as an information officer in the Eastern Nigeria Ministry of Information at Enugu.

Okara began writing poetry seriously during the mid-1950s after winning the first prize for poetry in the 1953 Nigerian Festival of Arts. Since then he has contributed regularly to major African poetry magazines and anthologies. To

Black Orpheus, in particular, he has contributed not only poetry but also an Ijaw creation myth, short stories, and the first chapter of his first and only novel, *The Voice* (1965).

During the Nigerian civil war (1967–70), Okara embraced the Biafran cause. He articulated its principles of justice and morality powerfully in his poem, "Leave Us Alone," and, in defense of that cause, he toured the United States with CHINUA ACHEBE in 1969. Ordinarily a nonpolitical and withdrawn man, Okara was the director of the Biafran Cultural Center at Ogwa for most of the civil war. After the war he served as a commissioner for information in the Rivers State, as well as a writer-in-residence in the Rivers State Council of Arts and Culture in Port Harcourt, where he now lives in quiet retirement.

Okara has been accused of being extremely careless about the preservation of his poems. But the truth is that he is essentially a modern Mbari artist who appears to be more interested in the poetic process itself than in the finished artifact. Nigerian author Michael Echeruo observes that "Okara [is] not a poet, as this season knows it. Like other poets before him, within our tradition of impermanence, his 'poems' [are] 'thoughts,' 'words,' not 'texts' or 'monuments' but memories."

NOVEL BY OKARA

The Voice. 1965. Holmes & Meier 1970 $11.50. ISBN 0-8419-0015-9

POETRY BY OKARA

The Fisherman's Invocations and Other Poems. Ed. by Theo Vincent. *African Writers Ser.* Heinemann Ed. 1978 o.p. Introduction by Vincent.

OKIGBO, CHRISTOPHER. 1932–1967

Christopher Okigbo, an Igbo, was strongly committed to the Biafran cause during the Nigerian civil war and was killed in action in August 1967 while serving as a major at the Nsukka front. During his brief literary career, lasting from 1957 (when his *Four Canzones* appeared in the journal *Black Orpheus*) to his death, he distinguished himself as one of Africa's leading poets. His reputation rests primarily on the densely allusive, symbolic, and verbal complexity of the mythic universe he created in the poetry sequences—*Heavensgate, Limits, Silences,* and *Distances*—which he collected under the title *Labyrinths* (1971). These were published posthumously together with his more openly prophetic swan song, *Path of Thunder* (1971), in which he predicted the outbreak of the Nigerian civil war and envisioned aspects of the postwar social wounds still festering in Nigeria today. In 1987 Heinemann issued his *Collected Poems,* including *Labyrinths, Path of Thunder,* and the previously uncollected earlier sequences: *Four Canzones, Lament of the Masks, A Dance of the Painted Maidens,* and two earlier fragments, "On the New Year" and "Moonglow." During the period immediately after the civil war, there was an explosion of Okigbo scholarship, as critics attempted to unravel the meaning of his poetry and to reconstruct aspects of what was perceived as its "organic unity." Scholarly attention also focused on what was seen as a spiritual vein in his poetry. As Okigbo himself said in his introduction to *Labyrinths, "Heavensgate* was originally conceived as an Easter sequence and . . . the various sections of the poem represent the celebrant at various stations of his cross."

Commenting on the difficulty of comprehending Okigbo's poetry, his biographer, S. O. Anozie, writes: "You feel [at every stage] that a final comprehension is just around the corner, but it is a corner you never reach. . . . Okigbo's poetry is constantly exploring two regular dimensions of myth. . . . myth as a privileged mode of cognition. . . . [and] myth and totem. . . seen as not merely cognitive but affective and even evaluative in a given cultural context—that, for example, of the Ibo [Igbo]-speaking people of Nigeria." More than anything else, it is this combination of mythical charm and elusiveness that has endeared Okigbo to the younger generation of African poets, many of whom have continued to imitate his style. Poems written in his memory and collected by CHINUA ACHEBE and Dubem Okafor under the title, *Don't Let Him Die*, reveal the depth of the indebtedness felt by his contemporaries and the younger generation of poets who regard themselves as inheritors of his richly embroidered poetic legacy.

Okigbo was indeed a complex individual, not one who readily gave in to tradition and conformity. He was awarded the first prize for poetry in 1966 at the First Festival of Negro Arts held in Dakar, Senegal. But he rejected the prize on the grounds that he did not subscribe to the terms "negro art" or "African literature." There are numerous oral accounts, of legendary proportions, by his relatives, friends, and casual acquaintances about his eccentricities.

POETRY BY OKIGBO

Christopher Okigbo: Collected Poems. Ed. by Adewale Maja-Pearce. Heinemann Ed. o.p.
Labyrinths and Path of Thunder. Holmes & Meier 1971 o.p.

BOOKS ABOUT OKIGBO

Anozie, S. O. *Christopher Okigbo: Creative Rhetoric.* Holmes & Meier 1972 $35.00. ISBN 0-8419-0086-8. Critical analysis of Okigbo's work, arranged chronologically.

Nwoga, Donatus, ed. *Critical Perspectives on Christopher Okigbo. Critical Perspectives Ser.* Three Continents 1985 $25.00. ISBN 0-89410-258-3 Brings together the appraisals of both African and non-African critics as well as provides useful bibliographic material.

OKPEWHO, ISIDORE. 1941–

A novelist, poet, and oral literary scholar, Isidore Okpewho is currently a professor of African-American Studies and Comparative Literature at the State University of New York at Binghamton. Born at Asaba in the Delta State of Nigeria, he was educated at St. Patrick's College, Asaba, and later at the University of Ibadan, where he earned a first class Honors B.A. degree. For six years after his graduation, he worked as an editor for Longman publishers, but he then opted for an academic career. After obtaining his Ph.D. in comparative literature at the University of Colorado in 1974, he joined the University of Ibadan, where he rose to the rank of full professor. As a scholar, Okpewho is well known for challenging and demolishing, through forceful arguments backed by textual and contextual evidence, several Eurocentric preconceptions about oral literature in Africa. His first book, *Epic in Africa* (1979), effectively ended the Eurocentric view that the epic does not exist in Africa. In his second book, *Myth in Africa* (1982), he offers incisive, aesthetically grounded, redefinitions of "myth" against the prevailing ritual-based definitions of the old European schools of anthropological inquiry. His radical redirections of perspective have culminated in his most recent book, *African Oral Literature: Backgrounds, Character and Continuity* (1992). Okpewho has also published a collection of poetry, *Heritage of African Poetry*, and a collection of essays, *Oral Performance in Africa* (1990). His creative output includes several poems published in *Okike* and other literary journals and three novels. His first novel, *The Victims* (1970), is a tragedy of domestic conflicts. His Second, *The Last Duty*

(1976), which is set in the Nigerian civil war, won the African Arts Prize for Literature. His third novel, *Tides*, is his most recent publication.

Novels by Okpewho

The Victims. Dearborn Trade 1988 $12.95. ISBN 0-582-00241-9
The Last Duty. Dearborn Trade 1988 $12.95. ISBN 0-582-78535-9

OKRI, BEN. 1960–

The youngest of the leading Nigerian writers today, Ben Okri completed his first novel, *Flowers and Shadows*, and his first collection of short stories, *Stars of a New Curfew* (1988), before he turned 21. In 1991, he won the Booker Prize for his postmodernist novel, *The Famished Road* (1991), in which the socially and culturally disturbed post-civil war world of the ordinary rural and urban-dwelling masses of Nigeria are presented through the equally disturbed perceptions and subconscious memories of an *abiku*, a child born to die and to be reborn again and again, who lives simultaneously in the spirit world and the human world. Okri, who has lived in England for most of his adult life, is now a fellow at Cambridge University, England.

Novels by Okri

The Famished Road. 1991. Doubleday 1992 $22.50. ISBN 0-385-42476-0
Flowers and Shadows. *African Classics Ser*. Dearborn Trade 1989 $9.95. ISBN 0-582-035336-8

Short Story Collection By Okri

Stars of the New Curfew. 1991. Viking Penguin 1989 $17.95. ISBN 0-670-82520-4. Collection of powerful short stories.

OMOTOSO, KOLE. 1943–

Born in Akure, Nigeria, Kole Omotoso is one of the most visible and prolific of Africa's new generation of radical writers. His publications include two novels—*The Combat* (1972), which uses the Nigerian civil war as a backdrop, and *The Edifice* (1971), which concerns the marriage of an African student and an English woman—and a piece on recent Nigerian history, *Just Before Dawn*, which attracted much public attention because of threats of civil action against him for misrepresentations of the roles of some of the people in the account.

Described by critics as a revolutionary writer, Omotoso is concerned with the political and social problems facing contemporary Africa. He therefore strives to write for the masses, using a simple and direct style. Many of his characters are contrived and predictable.

Novels by Omotoso

The Combat. 1972. *African Writers Ser*. Heinemann Ed. 1972 $8.95. ISBN 0-435-90122-2
The Edifice. 1971. *African Writers Ser*. Heinemann Ed. 1971 $8.95. ISBN 0-435-90102-8

ONWUEME, TESS. 1955–

One of the most prolific of the younger generation of African female writers, Tess Onwueme (also known as Tess Akaeke Onwueme) was criticized as "a writer too soon" when she suddenly burst into prominence during the late 1970s as Nigeria's second female playwright with her play, *A Hen Too Soon* (1983). But since that immature beginning, Onwueme has written, produced, and published more than 12 plays and has won several national and international prizes for her works, including the United States' Martin Luther King

Distinguished Writers' Award. Earlier awards include the Distinguished Authors Award at the 1988 Ife International Book Fair and the 1985 Association of Nigerian Authors Award in Drama for her play, *The Desert Encroaches* (1988). Born in Ogwashi-Uku in the Delta State of Nigeria, Onwueme was educated at Mary Mount Secondary School, Agbor, Delta State, and University of Ife (now Obafemi Awolowo University), Ile-Ife, Oyo State, where she majored in English literature. She later earned an M.A. in drama from Ife and a Ph.D. at the University of Benin, Edo State. Married to Professor Innocent Onwueme of the Federal University of Technology, Owerri, Imo State, Nigeria, with whom she has five children, Onwueme has, since 1980, combined her family responsibilities and her dramatic productions with teaching at various universities in Nigeria and the United States. Her most recent work is a feminist epic, *Go Tell It To Women* (1992), a humorous and provocative work exploring women's power, empowerment, and marginality in a diverse and changing world.

PLAYS BY ONWUEME

The Broken Calabash. 1988. Heinemann Nigeria 1988 o.p.
The Desert Encroaches. Heinemann Nigeria o.p.
Go Tell It To Women: A Play. Afri. Her. Pr. 1992 $10.00. ISBN 0-9628864-3-2
A Hen Too Soon. Heins Nigeria 1983 o.p.
Legacies. Ibadan: Heinemann Nigeria 1989 o.p.
Mirror for Campus. Heinemann Nigeria 1991 o.p.
Parable for a Season. 1991. Heinemann Nigeria 1991 o.p.
The Reign of Wazobia. Heinemann Nigeria 1988 o.p.
Riot in Heaven. Heinemann Nigeria 1991 o.p.
A Scent of Onions. Totan Nigeria 1986 o.p.
Three Plays: Broken Calabash, The Reign of Wazobia, and Parables for a Season. Wayne St. U. Pr. 1992 o.p.

OUOLOGUEM, YAMBO. 1940–

Yambo Ouologuem is one of the most radical of contemporary African writers. His only published novel to date, *Bound to Violence* (1968), is a powerful, vituperative, and controversial assault on Islam and Arabs. It presents Islam as a vicious, destabilizing, and culturally alienating system whose unholy alliance with state power has resulted over the years in barbaric slave raids, the creation of male-chauvinist harems, and the ruthless exploitation of the masses and the countryside. In the novel, Ouologuem reveals a commitment to the crusade for the total decolonization of the African mind by Islam (long accepted as a way of life in many parts of Africa), as well as Christianity. He views the two as antithetical alien religions whose dogmas inhibit African self-expression and freedom.

NOVEL BY OUOLOGUEM

Bound to Violence. 1968. *African Writers Ser.* Heinemann Ed. 1971 $9.95. ISBN 0-435-90099-4

OUSMANE, SEMBENE (Sembene, Ousmane). 1929–

Born in Senegal and recognized primarily as Africa's premier filmmaker, Sembene Ousmane first gained recognition as a novelist. His books and films are characteristically political, reflecting his keen sense of social commitment. Ousmane often writes from personal experience. Before embarking on a writing career, he worked as a manual laborer in Senegal and France, where he was very active in the dock workers' union. Union activities are the backdrop for his third book, *God's Bits of Wood* (1962), which established his reputation as an important literary figure. In it he recounts the 1947–48 strike of African railroad workers in Senegal, highlighting the effects of the strike on traditional African customs.

As a way of reaching a more popular audience, Ousmane turned to filmmaking. He has adapted several of his novels into films. *Xala* (1976) is perhaps the best known. This film, and others by Ousmane, have been either censored or banned in Senegal because of their political sentiments. His most recent novel, *The Last of the Empire* (1983), is a political novel set in Senegal.

NOVELS BY OUSMANE

The Black Docker (*Le Docker Noir*). Trans. by Ros Schwartz. *African Writers Ser.* Heinemann Ed. 1987 $8.95. ISBN 0-435-90896-0. A semi-autobiographical work.

God's Bits of Wood. 1962. Trans. by Francis Price. *African Writers Ser.* Heinemann Ed. 1987 $8.95. ISBN 0-435-90896-0

The Last of the Empire (*Le Dernier de L'Empire*). Trans. by Adrian Adams. *African Writers Ser.* Heinemann Ed. 1983 $9.95. ISBN 0-435-90250-4

The Money-Order with White Genesis. 1972. Trans. by Clive Wake. *African Writers Ser.* Heinemann Ed. 1987 $7.95. ISBN 0-435-90894-4. *Money-Order* deals with the colonial bureaucracy, while *White Genesis* is a story about the decline of village life and traditional morality.

Niiwam and Taaw. Heinemann Ed. 1992 $8.95. ISBN 0-435-90671-2

Tribal Scars and Other Stories. *African Writers Ser.* Heinemann Ed. 1987 $8.95. ISBN 0-435-90142-7. Twelve short stories about African village life.

Xala. Trans. by Clive Wake. L. Hill Bks. 1976 $8.95. ISBN 1-55652-070-0

BOOK ABOUT OUSMANE

Peters, Jonathan A. *Ousmane Sembene: Contemporary Griot*. Three Continents 1992 $26.00. ISBN 0-89410-068-8

OYONO, FERDINAND. 1929–

Born in Cameroon, Ferdinand Oyono was educated in local schools and in France, where he studied law and administration. Since 1960 he has served in the Cameroonian diplomatic corps. His international reputation for humorous, satiric writing rests on his 1956 publication of *The Houseboy*, which has been widely translated. The novel, written as a diary of an African houseboy, bitterly attacks French colonialism in Africa.

NOVELS BY OYONO

Boi. Heinemann Ed. 1978 o.p.

The Houseboy. 1956. Trans. by John Reed. *African Writers Ser.* Heinemann Ed. 1991 $7.95. ISBN 0-435-90532-5

The Old Man and the Medal. 1956. Trans. by John Reed. *African Writers Ser.* Heinemann Ed. repr. of 1969 ed. $8.95. ISBN 0-435-90039-0

PETERS, LENRIE. 1932–

Educated at the Prince of Wales School, Freetown, Sierra Leone, and at Cambridge University, England, where he studied medicine, Lenrie Peters was born at Bathurst (now Banjul) in The Gambia, where he now lives and practices medicine after having practiced for several years in Great Britain. A highly versatile and energetic man, Peters first established himself in modern African letters as a poet, with two poems published in several leading journals and anthologies and two poetry collections, *Satellites* (1967) and *Katchikali* (1971), before turning to the novel with *The Second Round* (1965).

Poetry by Peters

Satellites. 1967. *African Writers Ser.* Heinemann Ed. 1967 $9.95. ISBN 0-435-90037-4
Selected Poetry. *African Writers Ser.* Heinemann Ed. $10.95. ISBN 0-435-90238-5

Novel by Peters

The Second Round. 1965. *African Writers Ser.* Heinemann Ed. o.p.

SENGHOR, LEOPOLD SEDAR. 1906–

Poet, scholar, and politician, Leopold Senghor personifies the ideals of black writers of the French expression. World renowned as the chief apostle of negritude (a literary ideology that extols the cultural values of Africa), he is one of Africa's most famous and revered poets and has often been mentioned as a candidate for the Nobel Prize in literature. Among his many literary honors and degrees, including an honorary doctorate from Oxford University, is his election in 1983 into the Académie Française. Senghor is the first black member in the 349-year history of the academy. An architect of Senegalese independence, Senghor reached the pinnacle of his political career in 1960, when he was elected the first president of the Republic of Senegal, a position that he held until his retirement in 1981.

Born in the small village of Joal, Senegal, Senghor received a government scholarship in 1928 and left to study in France, first at the Lycée Louis-le-Grande and then at the Sorbonne. A teacher in the *lycées* until World War II, Senghor joined the French army and was captured by the Germans, who held him prisoner from 1940 to 1942.

Senghor remained in France after the war, and in 1945 his first collection of poems, *Chants d'Ombre*, was published. Written mostly during his student days in Paris, the poems have a noticeable negritude tone and reflect Senghor's feelings of cultural alienation and physical isolation from his homeland. Three years later, the landmark volume, *Anthologie de la Nouvelle Poésie Nègre et Malagache de la Langue Française*, edited by Senghor and including JEAN-PAUL SARTRE's (see also Vol. 4) well-known and somewhat controversial preface, was published. The works of many then obscure, yet highly talented, Caribbean and African writers, like Birago Diop, Leon Damas, and JACQUES ROUMAIN, among others, were celebrated for the first time in this now famous collection.

Senghor's poetry is the quintessential expression of love and respect for traditional African culture. He draws heavily on his African roots to create strikingly visual and, in many cases, highly sensual poems, often focusing on the themes of nature, woman, Africa, and blood. Unfortunately, few of Senghor's works are now available in English.

Poetry by Senghor

Ethiopiques. Trans. by Jessica Harris. Okpaku Communications. ISBN 0-89388-210-0

Leopold Sedar Senghor: The Collected Poetry. Trans. by Melvin Dixon. *Caribbean & African Literature Ser.* U. Pr. of Va. 1991 $40.00. ISBN 0-8139-1275-X. With this, Senghor's entire poetic work is accessible to the English reader.

Nocturnes. 1961. Trans. by John Reed and Clive Wake. Okpaku Communications 1971 $15.95. ISBN 0-89388-014-0. A group of elegies that reflect Senghor's theory of poetics.

Senghor: Prose and Poetry. Ed. by John Reed and Clive Wake. *African Writers Ser.* Heinemann Ed. 1976 o.p.

NONFICTION BY SENGHOR

The Foundations of "Africanité" or "Negritude" and "Arabité". Fr. & Eur. 1967 $9.95. ISBN 0-685-35636-1. Translation of *Les Fondements de l'Africanité ou Negritude et Arabité.*

Negritude & Humanism. Trans. by Wendell Jeanpierre. Okpaku Communications. ISBN 0-89388-197-X. A translation of *Liberté I: Negritude et Humanisme.* Essays about socialism in Africa.

BOOKS ABOUT SENGHOR

Ba, Sylvia. *The Concept of Negritude in the Poetry of Leopold Sedar Senghor.* Bks. Demand repr. of 1973 ed. $82.20. ISBN 0-8357-4039-0

Mezu, Okechukwu S. *The Poetry of Leopold Sedar Senghor.* Fairleigh Dickinson 1973 $14.50. ISBN 0-8386-1391-8. Examines Senghor's poetry from a historical and chronological viewpoint.

Peters, Jonathan A. *A Dance of Masks: Senghor, Achebe, Soyinka.* Three Continents 1978 $18.00. ISBN 0-914478-23-0. Critical interpretation of the three authors, with attention paid to their most accomplished and successful works.

Spleth, Janice. *Critical Perspectives on Leopold Sedar Senghor.* Three Continents 1993 $25.00. ISBN 0-89410-548-5

———. *Leopold Sedar Senghor.* Macmillan 1985 $29.95. ISBN 0-8057-6616-2. Examines in detail the breadth of Senghor's poetry as well as the relationship between African literature in French and Continental literature.

SOFOLA, ZULU. 1938–

A playwright, musician, and theater director, Zulu Sofola was born at Ogwashi-Uku in the Delta State of Nigeria. A graduate of Virginia Union University, she earned an M.A. in drama from the Catholic University in Washington, D.C., and a Ph.D. in theater arts from the University of Ibadan, Nigeria, where she taught for several years before accepting a position at the University of Ilorin, Nigeria. Sofola's plays are mainly on the order of popular drama, and are largely concerned with conventional social and domestic issues. They include *Wedlock of the Gods* (1970), *Wizard of Law, The Sweet Trap* (1977) *Old Wines are Tasty, Fantasies in Moonlight, Song of a Maiden,* and *The Operators.* In addition, she has produced at least one historical tragedy, *King Emene* (1974). Sofola manages to flavor her work with local idioms and folkways.

PLAY BY SOFOLA

King Emene. 1974. Heinemann Ed. 1974 o.p.

SOYINKA, WOLE. 1934– (NOBEL PRIZE 1986)

The first African writer to win the Nobel Prize for Literature (1986), Wole Soyinka, a Yoruba from western Nigeria, is a distinguished playwright, poet, novelist, essayist, social critic, political activist, and literary scholar. Although his literary oeuvre is varied, Soyinka is best known internationally for his politically provocative plays, which invariably are social commentaries on the day-to-day problems of Nigeria and the wider African world. In a recent interview with Henry Louis Gates, Jr., with whom he revived *Transition* magazine as an intellectual medium for a wider African and African-diasporic expression and readership, Soyinka said, "I cannot conceive of my existence without political involvement" (*N.Y. Times Book Review*).

Soyinka's political commitment resulted in his imprisonment during the Nigerian civil war. Accused of treason, he was held in solitary confinement during most of this period. Two of his works, *The Man Died: Prison Notes of Wole Soyinka* (1988) and *Poems from Prison* (1969), were secretly written on toilet paper and smuggled out of prison.

Soyinka's pioneering efforts and creative talents have been a major influence on the development of Nigerian drama. In the 1960s, he founded two Nigerian theater groups: the 1960 Masks and the Orisun Theatre. Since then, his plays have been widely performed in university and public theaters in Nigeria, elsewhere in Africa, as well as in Europe and the United States. Some of the most widely staged of his plays have been his adaptation of *The Bacchae of Euripides* (1973), his parody of African dictators, *A Play for Giants* (1984), and his topical and symbolic recreation of the political intrigues in a typical Yoruba kingdom, *Death and the King's Horsemen* (1976).

To date Soyinka has published two stylistically challenging novels, *The Interpreters* (1965), winner of the 1968 Jock Campbell Literary Award, and *Season of Anomy* (1973). The former is about a group of young Nigerian intellectuals frustrated by their society, and the latter is an allegory on the Nigerian civil war.

More stylistically challenging but far less opaque than his novels is Soyinka's poetry, which is deeply rooted in Yoruba mythology. While most of his poems are symbolic reflections on universal philosophical questions about human and transhuman existence, others, like those collected in *A Shuttle in the Crypt* (1972) and more recently in *Mandela's Earth and Other Poems* (1988), deal with the more pressing issues in Nigerian and pan-African politics in much the same vein as his plays.

When his autobiography *Ake: The Years of Childhood* was published in 1982, it was hailed by the *New York Times* as one of the 12 best books of the year. A charming memoir of Soyinka's first 11 years, the book offers insights into Yoruba culture and its influence on his childhood.

Born in Abeokuta, Ogunm State of Nigeria, Soyinka was educated at the University College, Ibadan, and at the University of London and Leeds University in England, where he moved in 1954. He has held research and teaching appointments in several universities both at home and abroad, including the University of Ibadan, the University of Ife (now Obafemi Awolowo University) at Ile-Ife, and Cornell University. Just before he won the Nobel Prize for literature, he had retired as professor of comparative literature at Ife to devote himself to writing, occasional lecturing, and voluntary public service. His first voluntary public service was as chairman of the National Road Safety Commission, from which he was recently forced to resign because he disagreed with the constant change of direction of Babanginda's military government.

Plays by Soyinka

The Bacchae of Euripides: A Communion Rite. 1973. Norton 1975 $5.95. ISBN 0-393-00789-8

Camwood on the Leaves and Before the Blackout: Plays. 1974. Okpaku Communications $8.95. ISBN 0-89388-150-3. Play about the rites of childhood passage in which a young man rebels against his father's beliefs.

A Dance of the Forest. OUP 1963 $7.95. ISBN 0-19-911082-4. Satire of the myth of Africa's glorious past.

Death and the King's Horsemen: A Play. 1976. *Noonday Ser*. FS&G 1990 $8.95. ISBN 0-374-52210-3

Kongi's Harvest. OUP 1967 $7.95. ISBN 0-19-911085-9. Comic depiction of a man trying to build power and self-image through any means necessary.

The Lion and the Jewel. OUP 1963 $6.95. ISBN 0-19-911083-2. Classic comedy of village life and folklore.

Madmen and Specialists. 1972. *Mermaid Dramabook Ser.* Hill & Wang 1987 $16.95. ISBN 0-8090-6708-0. About a man's desire to consume others.

Opera Woyonsi. Ind. U. Pr. 1981 o.p.

A Play for Giants. 1984. Methuen 1984 o.p.

The Road. OUP 1965 $7.95. ISBN 0-19-911084-0. Story of a man who is dedicated to the search for a new religion.

Three Short Plays. OUP 1969 $6.95. ISBN 0-19-911086-7. Includes *The Strong Breed, The Swamp Dweller,* and *The Trials of Brother Zero.*

POETRY BY SOYINKA

Idanre and Other Poems. Hill & Wang 1987 $7.95. ISBN 0-8419-0121-X. Group of Soyinka's more mature poems.

Poems of Black Africa. Hill & Wang 1975 o.p. Poems focusing on the modern and historic experiences of black Africans.

A Shuttle in the Crypt. 1972. Hill & Wang 1987 $7.95. ISBN 0-8090-1364-9

NOVEL BY SOYINKA

The Interpreters. 1965. *African Writers Ser.* Heinemann Ed. 1984 $7.95. ISBN 0-435-90076-5

NONFICTION BY SOYINKA

Ake: The Years of Childhood. 1982. *Vintage International Ser.* Random 1989 $11.00. ISBN 0-679-72540-7

Isara: A Voyage Around "Essay." Vintage International Ser. Random 1990 $9.95. ISBN 0-679-73246-2. Rich with sights and sounds of his native land under colonial rule.

The Man Died: Prison Notes of W. S. Noonday Ser. FS&G 1988 $9.95. ISBN 0-374-52127-1

Myth, Literature and the African World. A Canto Book Ser. Cambridge U. Pr. 1990 $7.95. ISBN 0-521-39834-7. Lectures about African literature and the world view.

Palaver: Three Dramatic Discussion Starters. Bks. Demand repr. of 1971 ed. $25.00. ISBN 0-7837-1954-X

TRANSLATION BY SOYINKA

Forest of a Thousand Demons: A Hunter's Saga. Random 1983 o.p. D. O. Fagunwa's fantastic story of beings who inhabit their creator's hunting ground. Explores the theme of the human search for happiness and peace.

BOOKS ABOUT SOYINKA

Gibbs, James. *Critical Perspectives on Wole Soyinka. Critical Perspectives Ser.* Three Continents 1980 $25.00. ISBN 0-914478-49-4. Essays analysing Soyinka's plays, poetry, and prose.

Jones, Eldred. *The Writing of Wole Soyinka. Studies in African Literature.* Heinemann Ed. 1987 $16.50. ISBN 0-435-08021-4

Maduakor, Obi. *Wole Soyinka: An Introduction to His Writing. Critical Studies in Black Life and Culture.* Garland 1987 $43.00. ISBN 0-8240-9141-8. Attempts to reveal larger patterns in Soyinka's work.

Moore, Gerald. *Wole Soyinka.* Holmes & Meier 1972 $24.50. ISBN 0-8419-0095-7. Examines Soyinka's entire literary output in an attempt to expose new elements of structure.

Omotoso, Kole. *Achebe or Soyinka? A Re-Interpretation and a Study in Contrasts. New Perspectives on African Literature Ser.* K. G. Saur 1992 $70.00. ISBN 0-905450-38-8

Peters, Jonathan A. *A Dance of Masks: Senghor, Achebe, Soyinka.* Three Continents 1978 $18.00. ISBN 0-914478-23-0 Critical examination of the three authors focusing on their most well-known works.

Rajeshwar, M. *The Novels of Wole Soyinka.* Advent NY 1990 $17.95. ISBN 81-85218-21-8. Analysis of intertextual development in characterization, narrative, and structure.

TUTUOLA, AMOS. 1920–

Amos Tutuola was born in Abeokuta, Nigeria. He received his elementary education at a Salvation Army school and has lived mostly at Ibadan, where he was for a long time a messenger. His highly controversial reputation as a writer is based on his unique style, a type of pidgin English. Tutuola's most popular work so far is his romance, *The Palm-Wine Drinkard* (1952), an extremely imaginative tall tale drawn from Yoruba legends and myths about a journey into the land of the dead. Despite the controversy surrounding Tutuola's "wrong" use of English, his historical significance as a writer cannot be disputed. Among the first black African writers to be published and win some degree of international recognition, he was also the first writer to see the possibilities of translating African mythology into English in an imaginative way. For all the controversy, Tutuola is highly popular and his books have been translated into many languages.

Novels by Tutuola

Feather Woman of the Jungle. City Lights 1988 $6.95. ISBN 0-87286-215-1. The people of a Yoruba village gather every night in the moonlight to hear stories and lore from their chief.

My Life in the Bush of Ghosts. 1962. Grove Pr. 1988 $10.95. ISBN 0-8021-3105-0. Story of a young boy who wanders into the mythical "Bush of Ghosts" and relates his fantastic adventure.

The Palm-Wine Drinkard. 1952. Grove Pr. 1954 $7.95. ISBN 0-8021-3105-0

The Palm-Wine Drinkard and His Dead Palm-Wine Tapster in Dead's Town. 1953. Greenwood repr. of 1970 ed. $38.75. ISBN 0-8371-4044-7

Pauper, Brawler and Slanderer. Faber & Faber 1987 $8.95. ISBN 0-571-14765-8. Recounts the intertwined adventures of three people born with unfortunate innate characters.

Simbi and the Satyr of the Dark Jungle. City Lights 1988 $6.95. ISBN 0-87286-214-3. A young girl who journeys into the world experiences poverty and punishment.

Wild Hunter in the Bush of Ghosts. Ed. by Bernth Lindfors. Three Continents 1982 $20.00. ISBN 0-89410-452-7. Continues the saga in the mythical "Bush of Ghosts."

The Witch Herbalist of the Remote Town. Faber & Faber 1982 $8.95. ISBN 0-571-11704-X

Short Story Collection by Tutuola

The Village Witch Doctor and Other Stories. Faber & Faber 1990 $7.95. ISBN 0-571-14215-X. Stories revolving around real and imagined images from Yoruban folklore.

Book about Tutuola

Lindfors, Bernth, ed. *Critical Perspectives on Amos Tutuola.* Three Continents 1975 $25.00. ISBN 0-914478-05-2. Traces the ups and downs of Tutuola's literary reputation and provides critical perspectives on his work.

U TAM'SI, TCHIKIYA (TCHIKIYA, GERALD FELIX). 1931–1990

Tchikiya U Tam'si, the most outstanding poet to come out of the Republic of Congo, was born in M'Pili, the son of a deputy at the French National Assembly in Paris. From 1946 he lived with his father in Paris, attending school at a *lycée* in Orleans and later at the Lycée Janson de Sailly. Largely "assimilated" and out of touch with traditional African life and culture, he made serious efforts to reintegrate himself into the world of his ancestors through intensive study of Congolese folklore and oral traditions. The results of his efforts show through his collections and adaptations of African folk tales and the ancestral imagery that dominates his poetry. Before his death in 1990, U Tam'si, who worked as a diplomat throughout his adult life, had published six volumes of poetry—*Le Mauvais Sang* (*Bad Blood*) (1955), *Feu de Brousse* (*Brush Fire*) (1957), *A Triche-Coeur* (*The Tricky Heart*) (1958), *Épitomé* (*Epitome*) (1962), *Le Ventre* (*The Belly*) (1964), *L'Arc Musical* (1969)—and a collection of African folk tales—*Légendes Africaines* (1968). In addition to other French and Congolese prizes, he won the first prize in the Festival of African Arts held in Dakar in 1965, a prize that the late Nigerian poet, CHRISTOPHER OKIGBO, had rejected.

POETRY BY U TAM'SI

The Glorious Destiny of Marshal Nnikon Nnika. Trans. by Timothy John. Ubu Repertory Theater Pubns. 1986 $7.95. ISBN 0-913745-18-9. Set in a fictional African republic, the story recounts the dramatic rise and fall of a megalomaniacal leader.

EAST AFRICAN LITERATURE

Early East African literatures followed more or less the same pattern of development as the literatures of West Africa. An early phase of Arabic Islamic literature was succeeded by *ajami* writing in Swahili, through which various Arabic genres were introduced into African literature; however, unlike its counterpart in West Africa, this *ajami* tradition boasts classical texts dating back to the sixteenth and seventeenth centuries. It also includes such innovative developments as the *utendi* epic, which combines Arabic epic conventions with traditions of African heroic narrative poetry going back to the legendary Fumo Liyong, widely acknowledged to be the founder of Swahili poetry. As in West Africa, a parallel to Islamic *ajami* writing in the form of African-language writing in the Roman script (notably Swahili) has continued to flourish side by side with contemporary literature in the colonial languages. But, remarkably, in East Africa—where centuries of literacy in Swahili have confirmed the potency of African languages as a medium of addressing the masses—avant-garde writers like Uganda's OKOT P'BITEK and NGUGI WA THIONG'O of Kenya have participated fully in the development of literature in African languages. In fact, Ngugi wa Thiong'o now writes solely in Swahili or his native Gikuyu. Not surprisingly, African-language literatures in East Africa have emerged not only as a medium for communicating directly with the masses but also as a major weapon in the Afrocentric crusade for the decolonization of the African mind.

By and large, modern East African literatures have been concerned with political issues: institutionalized racism manifested in confrontations between indigenous East Africans and white settlers as represented in Ngugi's *Weep Not, Child* (1964) and *The River Between* (1965); political nationalism manifested in the Mau Mau revolutionary movement; and postindependence corruption and disillusionment, the staple of the great majority of the plays and novels that have brought their authors detention and exile. The white-settler problem and the passions that it has aroused against the trappings of the white world appear to have preempted the development of popular literature of the Onitsha market type. The tone of East African literature is thus serious and confrontational, except in the writings of bourgeois authors like Kenya's GRACE OGOT, whose writings can be seen as reflecting an admiration of the benefits of European colonization.

Although Madagascar has been included in this survey of East African literatures, its contemporary literary relations are more with Anglophone literature of West and North Africa, as can be seen from the writings of FLAVIEN RANAIVO. Madagascar's traditional roots are largely Asiatic, the great majority of the people having come to the island from the Indian subcontinent. However, its distinctive blend of Asiatic and African heritage is part of the variety and complexity that must be noted in any survey of the literature of any region of Africa.

History and Criticism

Killam, G. D. *The Writing of East and Central Africa. Studies in African Literature.* Heinemann Ed. 1985 $17.50. ISBN 0-435-91671-8. Collection of essays that gives access to information that so far is available only to the specialist researcher.

Maughan-Brown, David. *Land, Freedom and Fiction: History and Ideology in Kenya.* Humanities 1985 $17.50. ISBN 0-86232-408-4. Examines the relationship among fiction, ideology, propaganda, and racial prejudice.

Collections

Allen, J. W., ed. *Tendi: A Swahili Classical Verse Form.* Holmes & Meier 1971 $75.00. ISBN 0-8419-0075-2. Discusses Swahili poetry through the use of various poems.

Maina wa Kinyatti, ed. *Thunder from the Mountains: Poems and Songs from the Mau Mau.* Afri. World Pr. o.p. Includes a number of patriotic and nationalistic poems and songs of Kenya.

LO LIYONG, TABAN. 1938?–

Taban Lo Liyong is one of the most eccentric of modern African writers, both in his writing style and in his personal style; even the titles of his works—*Fixions* (1969), *Eating Chiefs* (1970), *Franz Fanon's Uneven Ribs* (1971), *Another Nigger Dead* (1972)—catch the reader's attention. Born of southern Sudanese and Ugandan parents somewhere between 1938 and 1939, Lo Liyong grew up and was educated in Uganda. He then went to the United States to complete his education at Howard University and Iowa University. A widely traveled man, Lo Liyong joined the faculty of the Makerere University in Kampala, Uganda, on his return from the United States and then went on to teach at the University of Nairobi, Kenya, following the breakdown of law and order after Idi Amin's takeover of Uganda in the early 1970s. Political repression in Kenya, however, drove him to seek new climes in the University of Papua and New Guinea. He has since settled in southern Sudan, where, after serving as director of cultural affairs in Juba, he now teaches at the university located in the city. As a folklorist, Lo Liyong has researched Luo and Masai oral traditions and has published two collections of folk tales: *Fixions* and *Eating Chiefs*. He is, however, best known for his poetry collections—*Franz Fanon's Uneven Ribs*, *Another Nigger Dead*, *The Last Word*, and *Another Last Word*. A strong advocate of the use of African languages for creative writing and for the grounding of African writing in traditional African thought patterns and aesthetics, he creates his eccentric writings in order to measure up to his Afrocentric standards.

POETRY BY LO LIYONG

Another Nigger Dead. 1972. *African Writers Ser.* Heinemann Ed. 1972 $7.00. ISBN 0-435-90116-8

Work by Lo Liyong

Eating Chiefs. 1970. *African Writers Ser.* Heinemann Ed. 1970 $7.00. ISBN 0-435-90074-9

MAZRUI, ALI AL AMIN. 1933–

Currently professor of global cultural studies at the State University of New York, Ali Mazrui was born in Mombasa, Kenya. After obtaining his B.A. from the University of Manchester, England, he proceeded to obtain his M.A. from Columbia University, and his Ph.D. in political science from Oxford University, England. He then returned to East Africa to teach at Makerere University, Kampala, where he headed the Department of Political Science. Known as an academic and a critic, he is also the author of a novel, *The Trial of Christopher Okigbo*, in which he places on trial the Nigerian poet who died in 1967 while fighting for Biafra. In the novel, Okigbo is tried for betraying the larger issues of African freedom and unity in the service of a narrow sectional struggle. Although the charges are left "unproven" at the end of the novel, it can be seen quite clearly that the author's sympathies are with the preservation of the cause of one Nigeria. Mazrui taught at the University of Jos, Nigeria, before joining the faculties of various universities in the United States.

Novel by Mazrui

The Trial of Christopher Okigbo. African Writers Ser. Heinemann Ed. 1971 $8.95. ISBN 0-435-90097-8

NGUGI WA THIONG'O (NGUGI, JAMES). 1938–

Ngugi is one of several African writers who have been imprisoned and forced into exile because of the political nature of their writings. Novelist, playwright, essayist, and critic, he is Kenya's best-known writer and, according to Bernth Lindfors, "East Africa's most articulate social commentator." An outspoken nationalist with a decidedly Marxist perspective, Ngugi consistently focuses on colonial and postcolonial issues in Kenya since the advent of white settlers, Christian missionaries, and the British colonial regime.

His first novel, *Weep Not, Child* (1964), is set against the Mau Mau uprising. It offers a penetrating account of the socially destabilizing impact of white settlers' appropriation of the ancestral lands of poor Kenyans, who were consequently forced either to eke out a living by laboring on the land for white owners or to move to the newly emerging cities to seek employment. This was the first English-language novel by an East African. Two subsequent works—*The River Between* (1965) (actually written earlier than *Weep Not, Child*) (1964) and *A Grain of Wheat* (1967)—are sensitive novels about Kenya's Gikuyu people, caught between traditional values and the traumatic transformation of their land and culture by the combined forces of Christianity, colonialism, and institutionalized racism.

One of Ngugi's prime concerns is the liberation of his people, and of Africa, in general. He demonstrates this concern by persistently attacking colonial and neocolonial institutions, including the postindependence leaders, whom he perceives as surrogates for colonial power. In this crusade, he has found a powerful medium in African languages, not only because they liberate the writer from addressing issues of freedom through a colonial linguistic medium, but also because he believes that "an African writer should write in a language that will allow him to communicate effectively with peasants and workers in Africa—in other words, he should write in an African language." In 1977 Ngugi took a major step in this direction by writing and producing a play in Gikuyu, his mother tongue. The play, *Ngaahika Ndeenda* (*I Will Marry When I Want*) depicts the social, economic, and religious exploitation of workers in the Gikuyu highlands. The government, fearful that the play would encourage grass-roots political criticism, banned it in 1978 and sentenced Ngugi to one year in prison—a ruling that provoked an international outcry.

Ngugi's imprisonment did not stop him from writing politically provocative pieces, as his later novel, *Petals of Blood* (1977), attests. Critics gave it mixed reviews, complaining that the work was difficult to follow. Its underlying theme is political unrest in postindependence Kenya and the failure of the black political and business elite to live up to expectations.

Born in Limuru, Kenya, Ngugi attended missionary and Gikuyu schools. In 1964 he graduated from Uganda's Makerere University and pursued advanced work at the University of Leeds in England. He later taught in the United States for a brief period. From 1973 until his detention in 1978, he headed the Department of Literature at the University of Nairobi. After his release, Ngugi remained in Kenya briefly, devoting his time to writing, including children's books. But continuing political repression has kept him away from Kenya since the 1980s. He now lives partly in London and teaches periodically at Yale University.

Novels by Ngugi

Devil on the Cross. African Writers Ser. Heinemann Ed. 1982 $8.95. ISBN 0-435-90844-8

A Grain of Wheat. 1967. *African Writers Ser.* Heinemann Ed. 1968 $8.95. ISBN 0-435-90836-7

Matigari. 1989. Trans. by Wangui wa Goro. *African Writers Ser.* Heinemann Ed. 1989 $17.95. ISBN 0-435-90654-2. A historical fable with an ideological message for social justice in Ngugi's native Gikuyu-speaking Kenya.

Mtawa Mweusi. Heinemann Ed. 1978 o.p.

Nyamba Nene and the Flying Bus. Trans. by Wangui wa Goro. *AWP Young Readers Ser.* Africa World $12.95. ISBN 0-86543-079-9

Nyamba Nene's Pistol. Trans. by Wangui wa Goro. *AWP Young Readers Ser.* Africa World $12.95. ISBN 0-86543-08-0

Petals of Blood. 1977. NAL-Dutton 1978 $10.95. ISBN 0-525-48235-0

The River Between. 1965. *African Writers Ser.* Heinemann Ed. 1965. $7.95. ISBN 0-435-90548-1

Weep Not, Child. 1964. *African Writers Ser.* Heinemann Ed. 1988 $8.95. ISBN 0-435-90830-8

Plays by Ngugi

The Black Hermit. African Writers Ser. Heinemann Ed. 1968 $8.95. ISBN 0-435-90051-X. Story of a young man who is considered a hermit because he leaves his village for the University.

I Will Marry When I Want. African Writers Ser. Heinemann Ed. 1982 $9.95. ISBN 0-435-90246-6

The Trial of Dedan Kimathi. African Writers Ser. Heinemann Ed. 1977 $9.95. ISBN 0-435-90191-5. Relates the circumstances surrounding the trial of one of the celebrated leaders of the Mau Mau revolution.

Nonfiction by Ngugi

Barrel of a Pen: Resistance to Repression in Neo-Colonial Kenya. Africa World 1983 $15.95. ISBN 0-86543-001-2. Collection of essays, concerned with the history of Kenya and its resistance to Great Britain.

Decolonizing the Mind: The Politics of Language in African Literature. Heinemann Ed. 1986 $14.50. ISBN 0-435-08016-4. Essays on the cultural politics and egalitarian ideology of Africa in the 1950s.

Writers in Politics. Studies in African Literature. Heinemann Ed. 1981 o.p. Collection of essays valuable for their insight into Ngugi's political beliefs. Includes a bibliography and index.

WORK BY NGUGI

Detained: A Writer's Prison Diary. African Writers Ser. Heinemann Ed. 1981 $10.95. ISBN 0-435-08016-4. Autobiographical description of the degradation and humiliations of political prisoners.

BOOKS ABOUT NGUGI

Drame, Kandioura. *The Novel as Transformation Myth: A Study of the Novels of Mongo Beti and Ngugi wa Thiong'o. Foreign & Comparative Studies—African Ser.* Syracuse U. Pr. 1990 $14.00. ISBN 0-915984-68-7. Offers a cross-cultural comparative study.

Killam, G. D. *An Introduction to the Writings of Ngugi. Studies in African Literature.* Heinemann Ed. 1981 $16.50. ISBN 0-435-91669-6

______, ed. *Critical Perspectives on Ngugi wa Thiong'o.* Three Continents 1984 $25.00. ISBN 0-89410-064-5. A valuable consolidation of work on Ngugi.

Robson, Clifford B. *Ngugi Wa Thiong'o.* St. Martin 1980 $18.95. ISBN 0-312-57245-X

OGOT, GRACE AKINYE. 1930–

Born in Butere, Central Nyanza District, in Kenya, Grace Akinye Ogot was educated in Butere High School before training as a nurse and midwife in Kenya and England. The first, and still the most important, female writer to emerge from Kenya, she is married to B. A. Ogot, a former Kenyan professor of history, now a businessman. Her medical training is reflected in the close attention paid to health care issues in her novels, while her Westernized, largely upper-middle-class life is reflected in her ambivalent attitude toward the colonial experience. More conservative than feminist in outlook, she seems to admire the modernity and progress lent by the colonial experience to such fields as medicine and education. However, this apparent admiration stands in sharp contrast to the poverty pervading the rural environment that she portrays in her first novel, *The Promised Land* (1966).

NOVELS BY OGOT

The Promised Land. 1966. East African Pub. Hse. 1966 o.p.

Strange Bride. 1983. East African Pub. Hse. 1989 o.p. first published in Luo under the title, *Miaha,* 1983.

SHORT STORY COLLECTIONS BY OGOT

The Island of Tears. 1980. East African Pub. Hse. o.p.

Land Without Thunder. East African Pub. Hse. 1968 o.p. Respectable collection.

The Other Woman. 1976. East African Pub. Hse. o.p. Interesting collection.

OKOT P'BITEK. 1931–1980.

One of the most eloquent crusaders for the decolonization of the African mind through confrontations with all manifestations of colonial mentality in African manners, fashion, spiritual values, and use of language, Okot p'Bitek wrote his only novel, *Lak Tar Miyo Kinyero We Lobo* (*Are Your Teeth White, If So, Laugh*) (1953), and his long satirical and humorous poems or "poetic novels"—*Song of Lawino* (1966), *Song of Ocol* (1970), *The Song of a Prisoner* (1971), and *The Revelations of a Prostitute*—in his native Luo. He then produced English translations of the songs in order to be able to reach a wider audience. Born in Gulu, northern Uganda, Okot was educated at Gulu High School and King's College in Budo, Uganda, before proceeding to England in the mid-

1950s, where he earned degrees from Bristol University, the University of Wales at Aberystwyth, and Oxford University. Before his premature death in 1980, Okot served as the director of the Uganda National Theatre, professor at the Makerere University at Kampala, writer-in-residence at the University of Iowa, and visiting professor at the University of Ife (now the Obafemi Awolowo University) at Ile-Ife, Nigeria.

Novels by Okot

Song of a Prisoner. 1971. Okpaku Communications 1971 $15.95. ISBN 0-89388-004-3
Song of Lawino & Song of Ocol. Heinemann Ed. 1984 repr. of 1966 ed. $9.95. ISBN 0-435-90266-0

Book about Okot

Heron, G. A. *The Poetry of Okot p'Bitek.* Holmes & Meier 1976 $29.50. ISBN 0-8419-0280-1

RANAIVO, FLAVIEN. 1914–

Flavien Ranaivo is one of the leading Anglophonic African poets. The sixth son of the governor of Arivonimamo, the Imerina District of Malagasy, Ranaivo had a privileged upbringing. He studied at the French military school Saint Cyr and spent one year at the University of Paris. He later held cabinet positions both in France and in his home country, and served on the French National Commission for UNESCO. Despite the travels from his home, Ranaivo's intensely lyrical poetry retains the popular Malagasy *hainteny* ballad form and is rooted in the folklore and traditional rhetoric of his people. His poetry collections include *L'Ombre et le Vent* (*Shadow and Wind*) (1947), *Mes Chansons de Toujours* (*My Songs of Always*) (1955), and *Le Retour au Bercail* (*Return to the Fold*) (1970), which were reissued in one volume in 1970. The last two, in turn, won the Madagascar Grand Prize for Literature.

Poetry by Ranaivo

The Poetic Works of Flavien Ranaivo: L'Ombre et le Vent, Mes Chansons de Toujours, Le Retour au Bercail. B.E. Ser. Kraus 1962 $18.00. ISBN 0-8115-2980-0

SERUMAGA, ROBERT. 1939–

Educated at Makrere University, Kampala, and Trinity College, Dublin, Serumaga founded the Ugandan Theatre Limited on his return to Kampala. He had first discovered his interest in drama while working in London as producer of the BBC program "Africa Abroad." Although primarily a dramatist, he is best known outside Uganda for his first novel, *Return to the Shadows* (1969), and for the interviews with African writers that he conducted with Dennis Duerden and published regularly during the 1960s in *Cultural Events from Africa.*

Novel by Serumaga

Return to the Shadows. 1969. *African Writers Ser.* Heinemann Ed. 1969 $6.50. ISBN 0-435-90054-4

SOUTH AFRICAN LITERATURE

In the absence of Arab Islamic penetration of southern Africa, the literature of the region comprises a powerful oral tradition, dominated by clan histories and praise poetry. These preserve the great heroic traditions of the indigenous Zulu,

Tsana, Sotho, Xhosa, and other nations, which, since the end of World War II, have been condemned to a bitter struggle for their freedom and humanity in their own land. In the Republic of South Africa, this struggle continues against the Afrikaners, who displaced the English colonial power as the leading European elite in the region. Bolstered by superior arms, a ruthless police force, and the policy of separate development (*apartheid*), the racist social order of the Afrikaner elite is doubly ironic. Not only does it marginalize the indigenous black majority in favor of the minority white settlers, it also seeks to turn the indigenous people into aliens in their own ancestral lands through the creation of the so-called African homelands.

In the face of this unusual social order, modern South African literature is preoccupied with the pains of racism and the ineluctable goals of the creation of a just, nonracial society, and the institution of majority rule. This literature is essentially protest literature of a different texture and tone from the anticolonial protest literature of the rest of Africa. The more intense urgency, radicalism, and even ideological extremism of its tone arise from the ever-present depredations of society by the forces of racial bigotry and from the constant attempt at muffling the voices of protest through the censoring and banning of new works, and the imprisonment and exiling of writers.

Today, three categories of antiapartheid writing flourish side by side: first the writings of exiles like DENNIS BRUTUS and LEWIS NKOSI, who have left South Africa in order to freely and fully articulate their protests without the encumbrances of censorship, bans, and detention; second, the works of defiant underground writers like OSWALD MBUYISENI MTSHALI and MIRIAM TLALI, who operate from black townships within South Africa itself, pitching their artistic reflections against the emergent issues of the day; and third, the works of white liberal writers like ALAN PATON and Nobel Prize winner NADINE GORDIMER.

Side by side with this dominant antiapartheid literature exists a growing corpus of Afrikaans literature by white South African writers like J. M. COETZEE and ANDRE BRINK, who, although concerned with the problems of the institutionalized racism and the black struggle for liberation, are more overtly concerned with universal issues in human relationships.

While the current racial and political concerns of South African literature distinguish it from the literature of the rest of Africa, a look at its preapartheid development reveals identical patterns with East and West Africa, especially with regard to missionary-sponsored writing in African languages. The early twentieth-century writings of THOMAS MOFOLO, for example, represent the use of African-language literatures as a medium for the propagation of Christian values, often to the detriment of traditional customs and beliefs. But in the poetry of Dlomo, who wrote between World Wars I and II, the seeds of the latter-day protest literature can be discerned. This perceptive, but rhetorically conservative, writer attempts to make sense of the first signs of apartheid and related changes that were beginning to take place in his country.

In this survey, the literatures of the so-called front-line states—Botswana, Zimbabwe, Namibia, Malawi, Zambia, Swaziland, and Lesotho—have been grouped together with South African literature in view of the close identity between their historical experience and that of the whole of South Africa.

History and Criticism

Bright, David F. *The Miniature Epic in Vandal Africa*. U. of Okla. Pr. 1987 $34.95. ISBN 0-8061-2075-4. Includes an excellent bibliography.

Brown, Duncan, and Bruno Van Dyk, eds. *Exchanges: South African Literature in Translation*. Intl. Spec. Bk. 1991 $22.50. ISBN 0-86980-789-7. Considers recent South African literature.

Gray, Stephen. *Southern African Literature: An Introduction*. B&N Imports 1977 $40.00. ISBN 0-06-492530-7. Insightful look at the Commonwealth literature of Southern Africa.

Heywood, Christopher. *Aspects of South African Literature*. Holmes & Meier 1976 $35.00. ISBN 0-8419-0292-5. Interesting collection of articles by well-known writers and literary critics from Europe, America, and Africa.

Jordan, A. C. *Towards an African Literature: The Emergence of Literary Form in Xhosa*. *Perspectives on Southern Africa Ser.* U. CA Pr. 1973 $24.00. ISBN 0-520-02079-0. Xhosa folk tales and proverbs, along with commentaries on their origins and social functions, by a prominent Xhosa scholar.

Mutswairo, Solomon. *Zimbabwe Prose and Poetry*. Three Continents 1979 $18.00. ISBN 0-914478-82-6. Seventeenth-century Shona prose and poetry from the area of the Zambezi Valley.

Nethersole, Reingard, ed. *Emerging Literatures*. P. Lang Pubs. 1990 $58.00. ISBN 3-261-04308-3. Focuses on newer literatures within the entire South African region.

Parker, Kenneth, ed. *The South African Novel in English: Essays in Criticism and Society*. Holmes & Meier 1979 $39.50. ISBN 0-8419-0425-1. Collection of essays presenting a historical overview of South African English-language novels.

Trump, Martin, ed. *Rendering Things Visible: Essays on South African Literary Culture of the 1970s and 1980s*. Ohio U. Pr. 1991 $19.95. ISBN 0-8214-0993-X. Critical essays on literature and its social and political context.

Collections

Brink, Andre, and J. M. Coetzee, eds. *A Land Apart: A South African Reader*. Viking Penguin 1987 $9.95. ISBN 0-14-010004-0. An anthology of contemporary South African writing.

Couzens, Tim, and Essop Patel, eds. *The Return of the Amasi Bird: Black South African Poetry, 1891–1981*. Ohio U. Pr. 1982 $12.95. ISBN 0-86975-195-6. Broad overview of South African poetry, with short works by influential poets.

Gray, Stephen, ed. *The Penguin Book of Southern African Verse*. Viking Penguin 1989 $8.95. ISBN 0-14-058510-9. A multicultural historical collection bringing together 120 poets.

Hodge, Norman, ed. *To Kill a Man's Pride & Other Stories from Southern Africa*. Ohio U. Pr. 1984 $14.95. ISBN 0-86975-146-8

Lefanu, Sarah, and Stephen Hayward, eds. *Colors of a New Day: Writing for South Africa*. Pantheon 1990 $12.95. ISBN 0-679-73094-X. A collection of 38 short stories and poems to benefit the African National Congress.

ABRAHAMS, PETE. 1919–

Born in Johannesburg, South Africa, Abrahams emigrated to England at the age of 20, a refugee from apartheid. His best-selling autobiography, *Tell Freedom* (1954), one of the earliest books by an African published in England, focuses on his years in South Africa and recaptures his experiences as a mulatto in a racist environment. Critics generally agree that Abrahams's novel, *Mine Boy* (1946), a vivid picture of the life of an African miner, is his finest work. Other important books are *Wild Conquest* (1950), about the Great Boer Trek, and *A Wreath for Udomo* (1956), a *roman à clef*, in which Abrahams foretells, with sophisticated narrative skill, the downfall of a hero generally thought to be Ghana's Kwame Nkrumah. *This Island, Now* (1967), a critically acclaimed work, is set against the backdrop of a black-ruled Caribbean island seething with political and racial tensions. Abrahams currently lives with his family in Jamaica, West Indies.

NOVELS BY ABRAHAMS

The Fury of Rachel Monette. PB 1982 o.p.
Mine Boy. 1946. *African Writers Ser.* Heinemann Ed. 1988 $8.95. ISBN 0-435-90562-7
Path of Thunder. Chatham 1975 repr. of 1948 ed. $8.95. ISBN 0-911860-43-6. A romance about a black boy and white girl confronting segregationist policies.
Pressure Drop. NAL-Dutton 1992 $4.95. ISBN 0-451-40235-9. A New York PR executive searches for her kidnapped infant son.
Revolution, No. 9. Mysterious Pr. 1992 $18.95. ISBN 0-89296-481-2. A longtime fugitive is forced to track down his former comrades-in-arms.
Tongues of Fire. PB 1985 o.p.
The View from Coyaba. Faber & Faber 1985 $8.95. ISBN 0-571-13289-8
A Wreath for Udomo. AMS Pr. 1971 repr. of 1956 ed. $32.00. ISBN 0-404-20001-X

SHORT STORY COLLECTION BY ABRAHAMS

Dark Testament. 1942. *B.E. Ser.* Kraus 1992 $18.00. ISBN 0-8115-3018-3. A volume of short stories containing his earliest published works.

NONFICTION BY ABRAHAMS

Tell Freedom. 1954. Faber & Faber 1982 $9.95. ISBN 0-571-11777-5

BRINK, ANDRÉ. 1935–

Born in Orange Free State, South Africa, André Brink is a novelist, short story writer, playwright, critic, and translator. An Afrikaner dissident, he has written a large body of work and has played an important role in modernizing Afrikaans literature.

Brink first attracted international attention with his novel *Looking on Darkness* (1974), which was banned by the South African authorities. The novel tells the story of a colored actor who makes good in England and then returns to South Africa to confront the system of apartheid. Many of his subsequent works have been criticized as overly sensational or sentimental. The best of them, however, such as *Rumors of Rain* (1978), *Chain of Voices* (1982), and *States of Emergency* (1988), are powerful stories about conditions in South Africa.

NOVELS BY BRINK

An Act of Terror. Summit Bks. 1992 $25.00. ISBN 0-671-74858-0. A young couple joins a group plotting to assassinate the State President.
Chain of Voices. Penguin 1983 $9.95. ISBN 0-14-006538-5
A Dry White Season. Viking Penguin 1984 $10.00. ISBN 0-14-006890-2
An Instant in the Wind. Viking Penguin o.p.
Rumors of Rain. Viking Penguin o.p.
States of Emergency. Viking Penguin o.p.

NONFICTION BY BRINK

Bertrand Russell: A Psychobiography of a Moralist. Humanities 1989 $15.00. ISBN 0-391-03605-X. Based on Russell's archives and developments in psychodynamic theory.

BRUTUS, DENNIS. 1924–

The oldest and best-known antiapartheid poet from South Africa, Dennis Brutus, who has been living in exile in Europe and America for many years, is currently professor of English and African literature at the University of Pittsburgh. A sportsman and chairman of the South African Non-Racial Olympic Committee, Brutus led the campaign for the exclusion of segregated South African teams from participation in international sporting competitions during the heyday of apartheid. His poetry is remarkable for its directness of phrasing and its robust physicality, which reflects the violence and urgency of the racial tensions and police brutality in South Africa. He is especially skilled in the subtle use of objective correlatives, which condense his sensual images of the South African situation into universal symbols of perennial human conflicts. For all its concern with racial tension and violence, the poetry of Dennis Brutus is also tender in its treatment of love, hope, and faith in the face of exile and separation from loved ones.

Poetry by Brutus

Airs. Whirlwind Pr. $1.50. ISBN 0-685-25947-1

Airs and Tributes. Ed. by Gil Ott. Whirlwind Pr. 1989 $10.00. ISBN 0-922827-00-1

A Simple Lust. African Writers Ser. Heinemann Ed. 1973 $9.95. ISBN 0-435-90115-X. Selected poems including "Sirens Knuckles Boots," "Letters to Martha," "Poems from Algiers," and "Thoughts Abroad."

Stubborn Hope: Selected Poems of South Africa and a Wider World. African Writers Ser. Heinemann Ed. 1991 $9.95. ISBN 0-435-90208-3. New poems and selections from *China Poems* and *Strains.*

COETZEE, J(ACOBUS) M. 1940–

J. M. Coetzee is among the best-known white South African novelists of his generation. Born in Cape Town, Coetzee was educated as a computer scientist and linguist, receiving his M.A. in 1963 from the University of Cape Town and his Ph.D. from the University of Texas in 1969. Coetzee is a forceful writer who relies heavily on details. The political system of his native country provides the basis for much of his work. Through allegory and fable, he attacks colonialism and demythologizes historical and contemporary myths about colonization. Although his works are generally set in South Africa, they have broad universal appeal. His first novel, *Dusklands* (1974), was followed by *In the Heart of the Country* (1977), *Waiting for Barbarians* (1980), *The Life and Times of Michael K* (1983), for which he was awarded the Booker Prize, and *Foe* (1986).

Novels by Coetzee

Dusklands. Viking Penguin 1985 o.p. Consists of two novellas, *The Vietnam Project* and *The Narrative of Jacobus Coetzee.*

Foe. Viking Penguin 1988 $10.00. ISBN 0-14-011032-1. A complex parable of art and life.

In the Heart of the Country (From the Heart of the Country). 1976. Viking Penguin 1982 $8.95. ISBN 0-14-006228-9. A slender, taut book, it "purports to be a diary of a hysterical spinster on an isolated . . . sheep farm . . . consumed by loneliness . . . and her love/hate relationship with her patriarchal father" (*World Literature Today*).

Life and Times of Michael K. Viking Penguin 1985 $7.95. ISBN 0-14-007448-1. "As in his previous novel, *Waiting for the Barbarians,* Mr. Coetzee's landscapes of suffering are defined by the little-by-little art of moral disclosures . . . his stories might be about everyone and anyplace. At the same time they defy the vice of abstraction; they are engrossed in the minute and the concrete. [He] has rewritten the travail of Huck's insight, but from Nigger Jim's point of view, and set it in a country more terrible . . ." (Cynthia Ozick, *New York Times*).

Waiting for the Barbarians. 1980. Viking Penguin 1982 $5.95. ISBN 0-14-006110-X. A moving portrait of human anguish and nobility.

FUGARD, ATHOL. 1935–

Born in Cape Town and educated at Port Elizabeth Technical College and Cape Town University, Athol Fugard is the leading white South African playwright. After finishing his education, Fugard worked as a seaman and journalist before becoming an actor, director, and playwright. His commitment to the antiapartheid struggle through his plays and other dramatic productions is as long as it is effective in portraying the traumas of racial tensions in the lives of both white and black South Africans. The setting of his plays is contemporary South Africa, but the bleakness and frustrations of life they present, especially for those on the fringes of society, raise the plays to the level of universal human tragedy. Because of their subject, his plays have sometimes met with official opposition. *Blood Knot* (1960), about two coloured brothers, one light-skinned and one dark-skinned, was censored, and some of his other works have only been published abroad.

Fugard has frequently collaborated in his productions with black playwrights and actors, like John Kani and Winston Ntsona, with whom he produced the highly acclaimed and frequently produced plays, *Siswe Bansi Is Dead* (1973) and *Statements* (1972). His work is quite popular in England, and later plays, *Master Harold and the Boys* (1982), *The Road to Mecca* (1984), and *A Place With the Pigs* (1987), have been staged at the National Theatre. Fugard has also written screenplays and a novel, *Tsotsi* (1980).

PLAYS BY FUGARD

Knot and Other Plays. Theatre Comm. 1991 $22.95. ISBN 1-55936-019-4

A Lesson for Aloes. Theatre Comm. 1989 $6.95. ISBN 0-55936-001-1. A searing drama about three victims of psychological and social repression in apartheid society, who insist on surviving.

Marigolds in August and the Guest (with Ross Levenish). Theatre Comm. 1992 $10.95. ISBN 1-55936-059-3

Master Harold & the Boys. Play Ser. Viking Penguin 1984 $5.95. ISBN 0-14-048187-7. A white South African teenager lashes out at his middle-aged black servants.

My Children! My Africa! Theatre Comm. 1990 $16.95. ISBN 0-55936-013-5. Conflict between teacher and student concerning the policy of apartheid.

Statements (with Winston Ntshona and John Kani). Theatre Comm. 1986 $8.95. ISBN 0-930452-61-5. Statements after an arrest under the Immorality Acts.

NOVEL BY FUGARD

Tsotsi. Viking Penguin 1983 $6.95. ISBN 0-14-006772-6. A white man's vision of a black ghetto; a record of a lost period in South Africa's Sophiatown.

GORDIMER, NADINE. 1923– (NOBEL PRIZE 1991)

One of South Africa's best-known authors, Nadine Gordimer, who won the Nobel Prize for Literature in 1991, is a novelist, short story writer, and essayist. Born in Springs, Transvaal, she was educated at a convent school and at the University of the Witwatersrand in Johannesburg. Her first book was *Face to Face* (1949), a collection of short stories.

Although her novels are highly acclaimed, critics generally agree that her short stories are more revealing of her talent. Her dominant theme is South Africa's apartheid policy. She uses her white, middle-class background as the backdrop for many of her stories. Leon Wieseltier, in *Salma-gundi*, has written, "It is not the blacks that Gordimer writes with most authority about, however, but the whites. She is the supreme chronicler of their awakening, or the failure of their awakening." Gordimer's skillful narration of South Africa's political climate vis-à-vis its racial situation is strikingly evident in her *Selected Stories* (1975).

Like her short stories, Gordimer's novels almost always deal with the daily tensions of life in a segregated society. All of her novels, with the exception of *A Guest of Honour* (1970), are set in South Africa. In *A Guest of Honour*, she explores the problems of a newly independent African country through the experiences of a former British administrator.

Much fêted, Gordimer has received numerous awards in addition to the Nobel Prize. These include the Malaparte prize from Italy, the Nelly Sachs prize from Germany, the Scottish Arts Council's Nell Gunn Fellowship, and the French Grand Aigle d'Or.

Novels by Gordimer

Burger's Daughter. 1979. Viking Penguin 1980 $11.00. ISBN 0-13-005593-2. Story about a young woman's slowly evolving identity in the turbulent environment of present-day Africa.

The Conservationist. 1975. Viking Penguin 1983 $10.00. ISBN 0-14-004716-6. A white farmer's struggles with indigenous African beliefs and preservation of African culture.

A Guest of Honour. Viking Penguin 1983 $11.00. ISBN 0-14-003696-2

July's People. 1981. Viking Penguin 1982 $9.00. ISBN 0-14-006140-1. The members of a white liberal family are rescued from terror by their servant, July.

Late Bourgeois World. Viking Penguin 1983 $7.00. ISBN 0-14-005614-9. The childhood of a future black prime minister.

My Son's Story. FS&G 1990 $19.95. ISBN 0-374-21751-3. Follows Sonny and his revolutionary activities.

Something Out There. 1983. Viking Penguin 1986 $8.00. ISBN 0-14-007711-1

A Sport of Nature. 1987. Viking Penguin 1988 $10.00. ISBN 0-14-008470-3. About the life of Hillela, a South African Jew.

A World of Strangers. Viking Penguin 1984 $9.00. ISBN 0-14-001704-6. Toby Hood comes to South Africa to look after his family's publishing firm and begins to shun the liberal politics that his parents support.

Short Story Collections by Gordimer

Crimes of Conscience. Heinemann Ed. 1991 $8.95. ISBN 0-435-90668-2. Betrayal is a dominant theme in these dark, beautiful stories.

Jump and Other Stories. Viking Penguin 1992 $10.00. ISBN 0-14-016534-7. A collection of riveting tales, 16 of which are new.

Selected Stories. 1975. Viking Penguin 1983 $10.00. ISBN 0-14-006737-X. Thirty-one stories arranged in a chronological order, revealing Gordimer's personal and artistic development.

Six Feet of Country. Viking Penguin 1986 $7.00. ISBN 0-14-006559-8. Collection of seven stories set in and near Johannesburg.

A Soldier's Embrace. 1980. Viking Penguin 1982 $8.00. ISBN 0-14-005925-3. Thirteen short stories illuminating the emotional and environmental landscape of Africa.

Nonfiction by Gordimer

The Essential Gesture: Writing, Politics & Places. Viking Penguin 1989 $11.00. ISBN 0-14-012212-5. A collection of powerful essays about the author's turbulent life.

Lifetimes under Apartheid. Knopf 1986 $29.95. ISBN 0-394-55406-X. A spacious volume consisting of photographs accompanied by excerpts.

Three in Bed: Fiction, Morals and Politics. Bennington Chapbooks in Literature Ser. Bennington Coll. 1991 $5.00. ISBN 1-878603-03-5

Book about Gordimer

Wade, Michael. *Modern African Writers: Nadine Gordimer.* St. Mut. 1978 $20.00. ISBN 0-3237-49978-9. An analysis of Gordimer's major novels, with some historical information about each one.

HEAD, BESSIE. 1937–1986

Born in South Africa, Bessie Head wrote from neighboring Botswana, where she lived in exile since 1964. A hallmark of Head's writing, which is set in her adopted country, is unvarnished candor—tradition and customs notwithstanding.

Like her female contemporaries, Head was also deeply concerned about the role of women in African societies. This is an important theme in her writing, and she addressed it with the same frankness and incisiveness as she did other salient issues affecting present-day Africa. In her volume of short stories *The Collector of Treasures* (1977), Head offers fresh insights into the traditional and contemporary status of women in Botswana, reflecting pre- and postindependence influences.

Another of her major concerns is Africa's economic stagnation—a topic she explores in her first novel, *When Rain Clouds Gather* (1969). The protagonist is a South African exile who introduces modern farming techniques to villagers in a remote area of Botswana, despite the opposition of the village chief, a traditionalist. Head's second novel, *Maru* (1972), centers on the delicate subject of caste and color prejudice among particular groups in Botswana.

In Head's semiautobiographical novel, *A Question of Power* (1973), the main character Elizabeth is, like the author, a "colored" South African exile in Botswana. She suffers a nervous breakdown, ". . . and the narrative is actually a description of the events as they unfold within her mind and of the relationship between these internal events and the world outside" (Lloyd W. Brown, *Women Writers of Black Africa*). "Bessie Head depicts African life with a deep personal commitment and a lyrical flair that gives it a delightful tilt into fantasy" (*N.Y. Times Book Review*).

NOVELS BY HEAD

Maru. African Writers Ser. 1972. Heinemann Ed. 1988 $7.95. ISBN 0-435-90718-2

A Question of Power. African Writers Ser. Heinemann Ed. 1974 $8.95. ISBN 0-435-90720-4

Serowe: Village of the Rain-Wind. African Writers Ser. Heinemann Ed. 1981 $9.95. ISBN 0-435-90220-2. Relates the history of a community through the eyes of a thatcher and a school teacher.

When Rain Clouds Gather. African Writers Ser. Heinemann Ed. $8.95. ISBN 0-435-90726-3

NONFICTION BY HEAD

A Woman Alone: Autobiographical Writings. African Writers Ser. Heinemann Ed. 1990 $7.95. ISBN 0-435-90578-3. A posthumous collection of Bessie Head's relatively inaccessible writings.

SHORT STORY COLLECTIONS BY HEAD

The Collector of Treasures. African Writers Ser. Heinemann Ed. 1977 $8.95. ISBN 0-435-90182-6

Tales of Tenderness and Power. African Writers Ser. Heinemann Ed. 1990 $7.95. ISBN 0-435-90597-1. These stories offer a rare insight into African history, culture, and lore.

BOOK ABOUT HEAD

Abrahams, Cecil, ed. *The Tragic Life: Bessie Head & Literature in Southern Africa.* Africa World $29.95. ISBN 0-86543-176-0. Collection of 12 essays.

KUNENE, MAZISI (KUNENE, RAYMOND). 1930–

Born in Durban, South Africa, Mazisi (Raymond) Kunene was educated at the University of Natal, where he earned an M.A. with one of the earliest studies of literature in African languages. He later spent a year at the School of Oriental and African Studies at the University of London, where he continued his African language and literature studies. Although he has published highly competent poetry in English, Kunene is remarkable for his commitment to developing creative writing in his native Zulu language. His *Zulu Poems* (1970) include his original compositions in Zulu, as well as English recreations or translations. In 1979 he produced a copious poem, *Emperor Shaka the Great,* in an effort to introduce the Homeric type of epic into the literary repertoire of his mother-tongue. Kunene is currently a professor of linguistics at the University of California.

Poetry by Kunene

Emperor Shaka the Great. African Writers Ser. Heinemann Ed. 1979 $14.95. ISBN 0-435-90211-3

Zulu Poems. Holmes & Meier 1970 $12.50. ISBN 0-8419-0061-2

LA GUMA, ALEX. 1925–1985.

Born in Cape Town, South Africa, La Guma was a short story writer and novelist. After receiving a high school education, he tried his hand at a wide range of odd jobs before becoming a journalist. The son of James La Guma, a one-time president of the South African Coloured People's Congress, he was imprisoned for his antiapartheid struggles and accused in the notorious treason trials involving Nelson Mandela. After another imprisonment, he was forced to migrate to England in 1966.

La Guma often focuses on his personal experience as a black man and his deep opposition to the South African regime. *A Walk in the Night* (1962), which is set in the slums of Cape Town, pictures the losing struggle to retain fundamental humanity in the face of racial oppression. *And a Threefold Cord* (1964) is also based on life in the ghetto, while *The Stone Country* (1967) is inspired by La Guma's own imprisonment. La Guma's early political activism is reflected in the novel *In the Fog of the Season's End* (1972), which is based on organizing opposition to apartheid. In his fictional worlds, La Guma mirrors the realities of nonwhites in South Africa. Crime and brutality erupt as people keenly aware of their powerlessness confront intolerable situations. There is little sentimentality in his work, although it sometimes contains love and even comedic elements. His writing is concrete and vivid, whether depicting a prison, a shantytown, white suburbs, or a Bantu homeland, as in the novel *Time of the Butcherbird* (1979).

Living in exile since 1966, La Guma was appointed Officer of the Arts and Letters by the French Ministry of Culture in 1984. Less than a year later, in 1985, he died in London.

Novels by La Guma

In the Fog of the Season's End. African Writers Ser. Heinemann Ed. 1972 $49.95. ISBN 0-435-90110-7

Time of the Butcherbird. African Writers Ser. Heinemann Ed. 1989 $8.95. ISBN 0-435-90758-1

SHORT STORY COLLECTION BY LA GUMA

A Walk in the Night and Other Stories. Northwestern U. Pr. 1967 $8.95. ISBN 0-8101-0139-4

BOOK ABOUT LA GUMA

Abrahams, Cecil. *Memories of Home: The writings of Alex La Guma.* Africa World 1992. $29.95. ISBN 0-86543-234-1

MAPANJE, JACK. c.1940?–

Winner of the Rotterdam International Poetry Prize and the PEN Freedom-to-Write award, Mapanje was jailed by Malawian authorities without trial from September 1987 to August 11, 1991—a situation that called international attention to this many-sided genius. A poet, folklorist, editor, and teacher, Mapanje is the founder and editor of *Odi: A Journal of Malawi Literature* and *Kalulu: Journal of Oral Literature.*

POETRY BY MAPANJE

Of Chameleons and Gods. African Writers Ser. Heinemann Ed. 1991 $8.95. ISBN 0-435-91194-5. Large selection of poems in English. Winner of the 1981 BBC Arts and Africa Poetry Award.

MARECHERA, DAMBUDZO. 1952–1987

The writings of this precocious but short-lived literary talent from Zimbabwe have been described as "the work of a tortured genius." His work reflects a passionate concern for Zimbabwe and Africa in general, and brilliantly combines elements of realism and fantasy. His writing is very introspective, with a keen interest in exploring the inner workings of his protagonists. He does not romanticize the African past nor glorify the African personality. Yet, while his work does not seem preoccupied with inequities in African society, it does display a deep disillusionment and cynicism. An element of resignation reveals, on closer examination, an attempt to hide the sensitivity of his characters, whose behavior can be seen as a defense mechanism against the chaos, senselessness, and brutality of life. Marechera's first published work, *The House of Hunger* (1979), received the 1979 Guardian Prize for Fiction, while his posthumously published collection of writings, *The Black Insider and Other Fragments,* was selected for honorable mention by the 1991 Noma Award Committee. In addition to *The House of Hunger,* Marechera also published *Black Sunlight* before his untimely death in 1987.

NOVELS BY MARECHERA

Black Sunlight. African Writers Ser. Heinemann Ed. 1981 $9.95. ISBN 0-435-90237-7

The House of Hunger. African Writers Ser. Heinemann Ed. 1982 repr. of 1978 ed. $9.95. ISBN 0-435-90207-5

WORK BY MARECHERA

The Black Insider and Other Fragments. Boabab Bks. 1991 o.p.

BOOK ABOUT MARECHERA

Veit-Wild, Flora. *Dambudzo Marechera: A Source Book on His Life and Work.* Ed. by Bernth Lindfors. *Documentary Research in African Written Literature Ser.* K. G. Saur 1992 $76.00. ISBN 0-905450-97-3

MOFOLO, THOMAS. 1876–1948

Mofolo is not only the father of literature in his native Sesotho language, but is also widely considered to be the father of modern black South African writing. Educated in Protestant mission schools, Mofolo worked as a teacher in the mission school system and regarded his writings as an instrument for the propagation of the Christian faith among the Sotho-speaking people. He is best known for his ostensibly biographical, but largely fictional, narrative *Chaka* (1925). The novel presents a satanic image of the great Zulu general of that name, reflecting his adherence to traditional Zulu magic. Mofolo also wrote three other works that are deeply rooted in Christian morality. *Moeti Oa Bochabela* (*Traveller of the East*) (1907) presents a romantic journey to the East in a quest for the truth, reminiscent of JOHN BUNYAN's *Pilgrim's Progress*. *L'Ange Déchu* (*The Fallen Angel*), which remains unpublished, was written in reaction against the effusive sentimentality of popular romances. And *Pitseng* (*In the Pot*) is an autobiographical account of Mofolo's own school days.

FICTION BY MOFOLO

Chaka. Tr. Daniel Kunene. *African Writers Ser.* Heinemann Ed. 1981 $9.95. ISBN 0-435-90229-6

The Traveller of the East. Trans. by Ashton East. Kraus 1934 $18.00. ISBN 0-8115-3032-9

MPHAHLELE, ES'KIA (EZEKIEL). 1919–

Born in South Africa, Es'kia Mphahlele left that country in 1957 after the government banned him from teaching because of his active protest against its Bantu education policy. A compassionate and perceptive writer, he is also a respected critic of African literature. Short stories, anthologies, novels, and an autobiography are all part of Mphahlele's repertoire. According to his biographer, Ursula A. Barnett, Mphahlele "has been closely associated with every phase of [contemporary] South African literature and often gave it direction or led the way."

Mphahlele came to the forefront of African writers with the publication of his highly acclaimed autobiography, *Down Second Avenue* (1965), which is also a powerful social commentary on black life in South Africa. Another important work is *The African Image* (1962), a collection of essays that deals specifically with the attempts of black and white writers alike to explain African and Negro life.

Mphahlele's odyssey from Johannesburg took him to several African countries and to Europe before he eventually came to the United States, where he received a Ph.D. from the University of Denver. After teaching for several years at the University of Pennsylvania, he returned to South Africa. Commenting on the problems of writers in exile, he has said: "You have this kind of spiritual, mental ghetto you live in. It's crippling. . . . But you still have the freedom of vision which you would have had in South Africa, and your experiences in exile have also contributed to your growth."

Mphahlele currently teaches at the Center for African Studies at Witwatersrand University, Soweto. Although the government has lifted the ban on some of his works, his first novel, *The Wanderers* (1971), is still on the banned list. Critic Martin Tucker calls the book "a lyric cry of pain for the many rootless black exiles who wander across the African continent searching for a new home." *Chirundu*, Mphahlele's first major work since his return to South Africa, focuses on the rise and fall of the minister of transportation and public works in an imaginary African country.

NOVELS BY MPHAHLELE

Chirundu. L. Hill Bks. 1979 $7.95. ISBN 0-88208-122-5
In Corner B. Northwestern U. Pr. 1967 o.p.

NONFICTION BY MPHAHLELE

Down Second Avenue: Growing up in a South African Ghetto. Faber & Faber 1985 $8.95. ISBN 0-571-09716-2

PATON, ALAN. 1903–

A white South African, Alan Paton writes novels, short stories, essays, and poetry. He was founder and president of the now defunct South African Liberal party. Paton's best-known work is *Cry, the Beloved Country*, published in 1948. Written in simple, cadenced prose, this memorable work explores racial tensions in South Africa while simultaneously advocating universal brotherhood. It has been translated into 20 languages and, ironically, has sold more copies in South Africa than any other book, excluding the Bible. Both the book and the movie based upon it were quite popular in the United States. The story revolves around a Zulu minister's immersion into Johannesburg's underworld as he searches for his son, who is accused of murdering a white man. This novel earned Paton the Anisfield-Wolf and Newspaper Guild of New York awards, among others.

Paton's prolonged interest in race relations stems from his years as a principal in a Johannesburg reform school for African youth. In an effort to stifle, or at least soften, Paton's condemnation of apartheid, the government revoked his passport from 1960 to 1970. However, the racially sensitive novels and numerous essays written after *Cry, the Beloved Country* prove that he is not easily silenced. His biographer, Edward Callan, points out that "[a]ll of Paton's writing, his novels, his short stories, his fiction, his biographies . . . and his . . . autobiography, *Towards the Mountain* (1980), express [his] consistent concern for the freedom, dignity, and worth of individual human beings—a concern that is based, ultimately, on his Christian convictions."

NOVELS BY PATON

Ah, but Your Land Is Beautiful. 1982. Macmillan 1983 $10.95. ISBN 0-684-17830-3
Cry, the Beloved Country. 1948. Buccaneer Bks. 1991 $23.95. ISBN 0-89966-788-0
Too Late the Phalarope. 1953. Macmillan repr. of 1953 ed. $5.95. ISBN 0-684-18500-8. Story of an Afrikaner's affair with a colored woman.

SHORT STORY COLLECTIONS BY PATON

Knocking on the Door. Scribner 1976 o.p. Includes stories from Tales from a Troubled Land, updated with additional verse and short fiction.
Tales from a Troubled Land. 1961. Macmillan ed. 1985 $20.00. ISBN 0-684-15135-9. Written between 1948 and 1953, these tales focus on the theme of human degradation.

NONFICTION BY PATON

The Land and the People of South Africa. HarpC o.p.
Towards the Mountain. 1981. Peter Smith 1988 $19.75. ISBN 0-8446-6328-0

WORK BY PATON

Instrument of Thy Peace. Ballantine 1987 $3.50. ISBN 0-345-35215-7. A book of Lenten meditations prompted by the prayer of St. Francis of Assisi, "Lord, make me an instrument of Thy Peace."

Book about Paton

Callan, Edward. *Alan Paton. Twayne's World Authors Ser.* Macmillan 1982 $19.95. ISBN 0-8057-6512-3. Provides essential background on Paton's life and times, based on Paton's autobiography, *Towards the Mountains.*

TLALI, MIRIAM. 1930–

A widely traveled black woman writer, Miriam Tlali lives in Soweto, and her novels and plays are about conditions in that traumatized black township. Although her first two novels, *Muriel at Metropolitan* (1975) and *Amandla* (1980) were both banned by the South African apartheid regime, she has been able to respond to numerous invitations to lecture and to participate in workshops abroad. In 1978 she attended the International Writers Program in Iowa, and she spent the 1989–90 academic year at Yale University. Tlali's other writings include two collections of short stories—*Mihloti* (1984) and *Soweto Stories* (1989)—and two plays, the latest being *Crimen Injuria*, which was staged at Yale in the spring of 1990.

Novel by Tlali

Muriel at Metropolitan. 1975. *Longman African Classics Ser.* Longman 1987 $9.95. ISBN 0-582-01657-6

CHAPTER 6

Literature of the Indian Subcontinent

Robin Lewis, Sangita Advani, and Priya Joshi

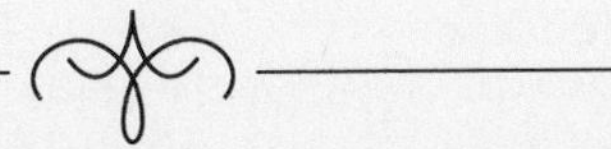

India has been born and reborn scores of times, and it will be reborn again. India is for ever; and India is forever being made.

—Shashi Tharoor, *The Great Indian Novel*

The sprawling landmass of the Indian subcontinent—actually the countries of India, Pakistan, Bangladesh, Nepal, and Sri Lanka—is both a mighty geographical entity and a space in the human mind. Its place in the popular Western imagination is characterized by apparent ambivalence and contradiction. On the one hand, there is the stereotypical image of India, the second most populous country in the world, with its teeming millions and the accompanying associations of poverty and hunger. On the other hand, there is the mystique of India as the womb of the world, the embodiment of traditional Eastern wisdom, a place to seek one's self among gurus and individuals of the likes of Mahatma Gandhi.

A newer and more perplexing image is that of modern India, the world's largest democracy, charting its course of industrialization and technological development. How can the Western perspective of India encompass holy men and Indian rope tricks, and also the established reality of India's nuclear power and its space satellites? Ironically, such seemingly contradictory views point to the only possible answer: the most significant aspect of the history of the Indian subcontinent is its tremendous diversity, reflected in a kaleidoscope of different peoples, cultures, economies, religions, and languages. Indeed, India is a tapestry of such varied threads that to speak only of some, rather than of many, is to speak in half-truths.

A vivid example of this great diversity is the issue of language. Sir George Grierson, a British scholar, spent the first quarter of the twentieth century compiling a monumental linguistic survey of the region, listing a staggering total of 225 principal languages and dialects. Officially, the Indian Constitution recognizes some 15 languages stemming from two separate roots, the Indo-European and the Dravidian. Belonging to the former is Sanskrit, the language of ancient India and its sacred texts, from which the following languages have been derived, much as French and Italian trace their origins to Latin: Hindi, Punjabi, Kashmiri, and Sindhi (the languages of northern India and also of several provinces of Pakistan); Assamese, Bengali—also the main language of Bangladesh—and Oriya (the languages of the eastern region); and Gujarati and Marathi (spoken in the western areas). The languages of southern India, derived from Dravidian roots, are Tamil, with a tradition as old as Sanskrit, and other closely related languages such as Telugu, Kannada, and Malayalam. In addition,

Nepali and its dialects are spoken in Nepal, a mountain kingdom stretching across the Himalayas, while in Pakistan, although Urdu is the official tongue, the majority speak either Sindhi, Punjabi, Pashto, or Baluchi. In the island nation of Sri Lanka (formerly Ceylon), Sinhalese and Tamil are the two major languages. Interestingly enough, it is English—the legacy of more than 200 years of British rule over most of the region—that is the one language commonly spoken and understood by people of all the various areas, making it the subcontinent's unofficial "link language." The subcontinent's potential, from a literary perspective alone, is unprecedented. Contained in this enormous expanse of diverse cultures and peoples is the raw material, the text if you will, of virtually every human experience.

If it is true that the subcontinent is made up of different threads, then it is equally true that these are not isolated strands, but interwoven fibers that give it a vibrant and integrated texture that glories in its variety. This notion of "unity-in-diversity" is a theme that echoes repeatedly through the annals of Indian art, religion, drama, and literature. Perhaps that is why India, to the West, often seems exasperatingly elusive, defying definition. Take the case of the divine love of the god Krishna and the cowherdess Rādhā. What is normally sung in a Hindu temple becomes a poet's love song in the twelfth-century Sanskrit poet Jayadeva's work, the *Gītagovinda*. Even today its verses are enacted through dance, music, and drama, and are also expressed in Indian miniature painting and sculpture. Another case in point is the impact of Islam on Hindu culture—the result was a reformation in medieval Hinduism in the form of the *bhakti* movement, as well as a new religion, Sikhism, which borrowed its central philosophical concepts from both Islam and Hinduism. Other creations of this cultural synthesis were a new language, Urdu, and an exquisite artistic and architectural style that reached its zenith under the Mughal emperors in the sixteenth and seventeenth centuries, giving the world such monuments as the Taj Mahal. The inexorable fact remains that underlying the rich diversity of India is a unifying way of life that transcends the disparities of ethnicity and religion—the unique, indefinable quality, the "Indianness," of a multifaceted but shared heritage.

GENERAL REFERENCE WORKS

The books in this section provide the reader with a general overview of Indian literature from the ancient through the modern periods. They also give the relevant background information about the historical, sociopolitical, religious, and philosophical milieus that gave rise to the literary works.

Alphonso-Karkala, John, and Leena Karkala. *Bibliography of Indo-English Literature: A Checklist of Works by Indian Authors in English 1800–1966*. Nirmala Sadanad 1974 o.p. A well-indexed list subdivided into genres and including bibliographies, reference works, and anthologies.

Dimock, Edward C., Jr., and others. *The Literatures of India: An Introduction*. U. Ch. Pr. 1978 $6.95. ISBN 0-226-15233-2. An invaluable introduction to the history and development of literature in India from the earliest writings to a coda on modern cinema. Includes excerpts from relevant works.

Jain, Sushil Kumar. *Indian Literature in English: An Annotated Bibliography*. 3 vols. Regina Bks. 1967 o.p. Poetry, drama, and fiction each treated by one volume. Includes useful notes and addenda.

Singh, Amritjit, Rajiva Verma, and Irene M. Joshi, eds. *Indian Literature in English, 1827–1979: A Guide to Information Sources.* Gale 1981 $68.00. ISBN 0-8103-1238-7. An invaluable resource, scholarly and well-documented.

ANCIENT INDIAN LITERATURE

The Epics: The Rāmāyana, the Māhabhārata, and the Bhagavad Gītā

The *Rāmāyana*, and the *Māhabhārata*, are two great epic poems of India. The vast storehouse of myths, legends, and moral teaching that comprises the two texts has been reworked over the centuries and has provided the Indian people with the material for artistic productions of every kind, and has colored every aspect of their lives. They have thus given Indian society a stock of more or less common cultural ideals, as well as a treasury of tales and legends known to all. It is this shared inheritance from the epics that is one of the threads that binds together the vastly disparate peoples of India.

The *Rāmāyana*, dated between the second century B.C. and the second century A.D., is traditionally ascribed to Vālmīki, who is considered the first poet of the Sanskrit language. Written in verse, the story is woven around King Rāma and his consort, Sītā, who provide ideal models of behavior, while their story, the *Rāmāyana*, is the central text for the worship of Rāma in Vaishnavism and popular Hinduism.

The *Māhabhārata*, dated between the seventh century B.C. and the fourth century A.D., has an encyclopedic text that centers on a fight for succession to a kingdom between two groups of cousins. To this basic story is added a vast amount of other material—didactic texts (*shastras*), religious and philosophical treatises (the *Bhagavad Gītā*), and unrelated myths and stories.

A relatively late addition to the core of the works of the *Māhabhārata*, the *Bhagavad Gītā* is a religious and philosophical text in the form of a dialogue between Krishna and Arjuna about *dharma*, or man's rightful duty. The *Gītā*, written in verse, is a fundamental text of Hinduism, and it influenced the thought of MAHATMA GANDHI (see Vol. 4) and HENRY DAVID THOREAU (see Vol. 1), among others.

General Reference Works

Embree, Ainslie, ed. *Sources of Indian Tradition. Vol. 1: From the Beginning to 1800.* Col. U. Pr. rev. ed. 1988 $18.00. ISBN 0-231-06651-1. Sourcebook of the philosophies, religions, histories, and politics of the Indian subcontinent dating from 3000 B.C., with useful selections from religious and sacred texts.

Narayan, R. K. *Gods, Demons & Others.* Bantam 1986 $3.50. ISBN 0-553-21240-0. Retelling of the myths and legends that are part of the lore of Ancient India and which appear in various forms in the *Māhabhārata* and the *Rāmāyana.*

O'Flaherty, Wendy Doniger, ed. and trans. *Hindu Myths.* Viking Penguin 1975 $5.95. ISBN 0-14-044306-1. Selection and translation of seventy-five seminal myths from classical Indian sources, with explanatory notes and a bibliography.

THE RĀMĀYANA

Goldman, Robert, trans. *The Rāmāyana of Vālmīki: Balakanda.* Vol. 1 Princeton U. Pr. 1990 $14.95. ISBN 0-691-01485-X. The first volume of an ongoing, scholarly translation of the *Rāmāyana.*

Keshavadas, Sadguru S. *Rāmāyana at a Glance.* S. Asia 1989 $12.50. ISBN 81-208-0545-3. An abridgement of Vālmīki's *Rāmāyana.*

Lal, P., trans. *The Rāmāyana of Vālmīki.* Advent 1981 o.p. Probably the most readable rendering of the epic, presented by a distinguished writer and poet who calls his version a "transcreation" rather than a translation.

Narayan, R. K. *The Rāmāyana of R. K. Narayan: A Shortened Modern Prose Version of the Indian Epic, Suggested by the Tamil Version of Kamban.* Viking Penguin 1977 $7.00. ISBN 0-14-004428-0. A work based on the Tamil version of the epic written by a poet called Kamban in the eleventh century, who, in reinterpreting Vālmīki's Sanskrit text, stuck closely to the original.

Rajagopalachari, C. *Rāmāyana.* Auromere 1979 $6.95. ISBN 0-89744-930-4. Modern prose translation based on the Sanskrit text by Vālmīki.

THE MĀHABHĀRATA

Lal, P. *The Māhabhārata of Vyāsa.* Asia Bk. Corp. 1980 $15.95. ISBN 0-318-37171-5. Condensed from Sanskrit and translated into English.

Narasimhan, Chakravarthi V. *The Māhabhārata.* Col. U. Pr. 1973 $15.00. ISBN 0-231-08321-1. Prose translation of approximately 4,000 verses of the original Sanskrit text that deal with the rivalry and battle between the Pandavas and the Kauravas.

Narayan, R. K. *The Māhabhārata.* S. Asia 1989 $8.00. ISBN 0-81-7094-001-X. Modern prose retelling of *The Māhabhārata* with sketches by the Indian cartoonist R. K. Laxman.

Swami Satyeswarananda, Giri. *The Māhabhārata.* Sanskrit Classics 1986 $40.00. ISBN 1-877854-09-3. Scholarly prose translation from the Sanskrit with illustrations and explanatory notes.

Van Buitenen, J.A.B., ed. and trans. *The Māhabhārata.* 3 vols. U. Ch. Pr. 1973-78 $36.00. ISBN 0-226-84650-4. A complete rendering of the first five books of this massive epic. A scholarly work.

THE BHAGAVAD GĪTĀ (THE SONG OF THE LORD)

Edgerton, Franklin. *The Bhagavad Gītā.* HUP 1944 $7.95. ISBN 0-674-06925-0

Miller, Barbara Stoler, trans. The *Bhagavad Gītā: Krishna's Counsel in Time of War.* Bantam 1991 $9.00. ISBN 0-553-35340-3. Prose translation of the *Gītā* with explanatory notes and a glossary.

Other Ancient Writings

Burton, Richard, trans. and ed. *The Kāma Sūtra of Vātsyāyana: The Classic Hindu Treatise on Love and Social Conduct*.* Viking Penguin 1991 $9.00. ISBN 0-14-019360-X. Famous Hindu treatise attributed to Vātsyāyana, who lived c.300. *Kāma*—the pursuit of love and pleasure—is one of the traditional Hindu ends of man. The *Kāma Sūtra* (*Aphorisms on Love*) yields invaluable information about the social mores and conditions of classical ancient India.

Edgerton, Franklin, ed. *The Panchatantra Reconstructed. Amer. Oriental Ser.* 2 vols. Kraus 1965 repr. of 1924 ed. $56.00. ISBN 0-527-02677-8. A famous collection of didactic animal fables used to teach worldly wisdom to princes. The source of the many similar stories found in the Middle East and Europe.

Hart, George L., III. *The Poems of Ancient Tamil: Their Milieu and Their Sanskrit Counterparts.* U. CA. Pr. 1975 $47.50. ISBN 0-520-02672-1. A sophisticated work for readers who are familiar with the subject.

Ingalls, Daniel H., trans. *Sanskrit Poetry from Vidyākara's "Treasury."* HUP 1968 $22.00. ISBN 0-674-78855-9. A collection of poems from the *Treasury of Well-Turned Verse* compiled by the famous poet Vidyākara in eleventh-century Bengal. Concerned largely with love and nature, the poems also include humorous sketches, poems about gods and heroes, epigrams, panegyrics, and realistic vignettes of village and farm life in ancient India.

Kālidāsa. *The Loom of Time: A Selection of His Plays and Poems.* Trans. by Chandra Rajan. Viking Penguin 1991 $8.95. ISBN 0-14-044538-2. Translations of the work of the classical Sanskrit dramatist Kālidāsa, who has had a profound impact on later writings in India and the West.

______. *The Transport of Love*. Trans. by Leonard Nathan. U. CA Pr. 1976 $7.95. ISBN 0-520-03031-1. A bilingual verse translation of Kālidāsa's exquisite love poem of a minor deity who sends a message to his loved one by a cloud-messenger.

Lal. P., trans. and ed. *Great Sanskrit Plays in Modern Translation*. New Dir. Pr. 1957 $8.95. ISBN 0-8112-0079-5. Modern translations of five Sanskrit plays written between the fourth and ninth centuries. Includes the famous *Shakuntalā* of Kālidāsa which inspired the "Prelude in the Theatre" of Goethe's *Faust*.

______, trans. *Sanskrit Love Lyrics*. Ind-US Inc. 1973 $6.75. ISBN 0-88253-265-0. A selection and translation of some of the finest love poetry in the classical Sanskrit tradition by an erudite scholar and poet.

Miller, Barbara Stoler, trans. *The Hermit and the Love-Thief: Sanskrit Poems of Bhartrihari and Bilhana*. Viking Penguin 1991 $6.95. ISBN 0-14-044584-6. An anthology of selections in the genre of the Sanskrit fragmentary lyric. Includes selections from the *Caurapañcāśikā* (*Fantasies of a Love Thief*), attributed to Bilhana, a poet who lived in the eleventh century.

______. *Love Song of the Dark Lord: Jayadeva's Gītagovinda*. Col. U. Pr. 1977 $14.50. ISBN 0-231-04029-6. Twelfth-century dramatic lyrical poem that focuses on the god Krishna's love for the cowherdess Rādhā, considered to be an allegory of the human soul's love for God. A unique work in Indian literature and a source of religious inspiration in Vaishnavism (the worship of the god Vishnu).

Siegel, Lee. *Fires of Love, Waters of Peace: Passion and Renunciation in Indian Culture*. UH Pr. 1983 $12.50. ISBN 0-8248-0828-2. An introduction to Sanskrit love poetry and religious verse, with translations of selected excerpts from the works of the court poet Amaru and the philosopher Shankara.

Van Buitenen, J.A.B., trans. *Tales of Ancient India*. U. Ch. Pr. 1969 $11.95. ISBN 0-226-84642-4. A selection of popular tales from Sanskrit story collections.

______. *Two Plays of Ancient India*. Col. U. Pr. 1968 o.p. These two ancient plays vividly illustrate the fact that ancient Indian drama represents a highly stylized tradition that achieved exuberant life and rich variety. *The Little Clay Cart* is a humorous tale of romance and villainy. *The Minister's Seal* represents the semihistorical or political play genre of Indian drama.

MEDIEVAL LITERATURE: THE BHAKTI MOVEMENT

A striking feature of medieval India was the great upsurge and spread of devotional or *bhakti* movements that swept across northern India and down the Gangetic plain into Bengal from about the fourteenth through the seventeenth centuries. This popular movement of saint-singers of philosophical and religious songs had begun much earlier (in the fourth to ninth centuries) in the South, with the writings of the Tamil Ālvār saints, then spreading to the Kannada-speaking areas through the works of Basavanna. The late thirteenth century saw it ignite in Maharashtra with an interpretation of the *Bhagavad Gītā* by the saint Jnānesvara; other saints of Maharashtra were Tukarām and Eknath. By the fifteenth century, the movement had spread to the Hindi-speaking areas and the whole of northern India; some of the best-known poets are Kabir, Sūr Dās, and Tulsīdās, and in Bengal, Chandidās, Vidyāpati, and Chaitanya. Two of the most famous women saints were Mīrābai, from Rajasthan, and Lalla, from Kashmir. The saint-teachers who went about making the whole countryside resound with their songs, popular to this day, had a common theme threading through their different philosophies. The first characteristic of the *bhakti* movement was devotion to a personal god, usually a form of Vishnu or Shiva. In addition, there was a belief in monotheism and the equality of all human beings, irrespective of caste, social status, or creed, reflecting the egalitarianism of Islam, with which the *bhakti* movement had also come into contact. The saints, usually ordinary folk, wrote in the accessible vernacular languages rather than in the esoteric Sanskrit of the priests. The *bhakti* movement thus achieved a unique transformation of the older, ritual-bound Hinduism.

Bhattacharya, Deben, trans. *The Love Songs of Chandidās; The Rebel Poet-Priest of Bengal.* Grove Pr. 1970 o.p. In the tradition of other great Bengali poets, Chandidās (c. fifteenth century) wrote of love, focusing on the traditional Bengali interest in Rādhā and Krishna, the great divine lovers of Indian worship and legend.

———. *The Love Songs of Vidyāpati.* Grove Pr. 1963 o.p. Selections from the work of a fourteenth-century Bengali poet. Vidyāpati's songs focus on the love of Krishna and Rādhā, the major love figures of Indian mythology, art, and literature. Contains 100 poems along with 31 plates that show how themes were illustrated in Indian miniature painting.

———. *Songs of the Bards of Bengal.* Grove Pr. 1970 o.p. The name *Baul* refers to a small group of wandering Bengali poets and musicians. In keeping with the *Baul* tradition, which is a revolt against conventional Islam and Hinduism, these troubadour-like songs are iconoclastic yet classical in their lyrics.

Dimock, Edward C., Jr., and Denise Levertov, trans. *In Praise of Krishna: Songs from the Bengali.* U. Ch. Pr. 1981 $8.95. ISBN 0-226-15231-6. Allegorical poems on the love of Rādhā and Krishna, ranging from the twelfth to the seventeenth centuries, including the works of Vidyāpati and great Vaishnava *bhakti* poets such as Chaitanya and Chandidās; illus. by Anju Chaudhurie.

———. *The Thief of Love: Bengali Tales from Court and Village.* U. Ch. Pr. 1975 o.p. A collection of tales that have become part of Bengali folklore.

Hawley, John S. *Sūr Dās: Poet, Singer, Saint.* U. of Wash. Pr. 1984 $25.00. ISBN 0-295-96102-3. An illuminating glimpse into the work of the blind sixteenth-century poet-singer Sūr Dās, who wrote moving devotional songs in praise of Krishna.

Hess, Linda, and Shukdev Singh, trans. *The Bijak of Kabīr.* N. Point Pr. o.p. Kabīr was in many respects the pioneer of Hindi devotional verse, using the vernacular to popularize religious themes from both Hindu and mystical Islamic (Sūfī) traditions. This translation of Kabīr's most authoritative work includes an introduction and notes that place the work in its original context and elucidate its meaning.

Ramanujan, A. K., trans. *Hymns for the Drowning: Poems for Vishnu by Nammālvār.* Princeton U. Pr. 1982 o.p. Eighty-three poems by Nammālvār, celebrated Ālvār saint-poet of the ninth century, in translation from the Tamil. These devotional hymns and love poems are among the earliest *bhakti* texts.

———. *The Interior Landscape: Love Poems from a Classical Tamil Anthology.* Ind. U. Pr. 1967 o.p. Poems from one of the earliest surviving texts of Tamil poetry, the *Ku runtokai,* an anthology of love lyrics probably recorded during the first three centuries A.D. Includes an essay on Tamil poetry.

———. *Poems of Love and War: From the Eight Anthologies and the Ten Songs of Classical Tamil.* Col. U. Pr. 1985 $17.50. ISBN 0-231-05107-7

———. *Speaking of Shiva. Penguin Class. Ser.* 1973 $6.95. ISBN 0-14-044270-7. A collection of *vachanas* or free-verse lyrics written between the tenth and twelfth centuries by four major Kannada poet-saints of the great *bhakti* reform movement. The poems, lyrical expressions of love for the god Shiva, are fiercely monotheistic and have a timeless and universal appeal.

MODERN POETRY

Poetry has been a vital part of the literary tradition in India, in English as well as in the vernacular languages. Prose fiction, and particularly the novel, was to emerge relatively late in Indian letters, finding expression alongside Indian poetry only in the nineteenth century. Urdu poetry, for a number of reasons having to do with the ascendancy of the Mughals and their patronage to the arts, has provided a rich legacy of Urdu verse. While there had been an Islamic presence in the Indian subcontinent since the eighth century, the literary and cultural influence of Islam manifested itself only in the eleventh and twelfth centuries, then flourishing in the thirteenth century, when there was a great influx of Muslims into India. The religious and cultural ideals of the Muslims in India found expression in many languages—Arabic, Persian, Turkish, and the regional Indian languages—but more so in a newly transformed language, Urdu (literally "camp"), a mixture of Hindustani, Persian, and Arabic loanwords. The literature began to develop in the sixteenth century around the courts of Golconda and Bijapur in the Deccan, and later on in Aurangabad, until in the eighteenth century it reached Delhi itself, from where it spread to Lucknow.

The milieu of Urdu literature is that of Muslim court culture and Sūfī religion. The major literary form of the first three centuries was poetry; prose began only in the nineteenth century. The poets pursued many genres: the *qasīda*, a poem praising the ruler or patron; the *hajw*, derogatory verse; the *shahar-āshob*, laments over a destroyed city; the *dastan*, or folk romance tradition that goes back as far as medieval Iran; and the *marsiya*, elegiac verse, often in praise of the martyrdom of Hasan and Husain. The most important genres, however, were the *masnavī*, whose subject matter was very wide and free, and the *ghazal*, a unique blend of love poetry and the mystical experience. Urdu is spoken and written by both Muslims and non-Muslims in modern India; it is the official language of Pakistan. Poetry flourished in the regional languages as well, and the selections below provide the flavor of nineteenth- and twentieth-century Indian poetry.

Anthologies

Ali, Ahmed, ed. and trans. *The Golden Tradition: An Anthology of Urdu Poetry*. Col. U. Pr. 1973 o.p. An anthology of Urdu poetry from the fourteenth to the twentieth centuries. Includes selections from 15 poets of the eighteenth and nineteenth centuries, the most creative period in this literature. An introduction surveys the literary and philosophical background and contains a comparative study of Urdu and English poetic movements.

Faiz, Ahmed Faiz. *Poems by Faiz*. Trans. by Victor Kiernan and Carlo Coppola. Allen & Unwin 1971 o.p. Bilingual edition of the renowned twentieth-century poet's work compiled under the guidance of Faiz. Includes a detailed introduction.

______. *The Rebel's Silhouette*. Trans. by Agha Shahid Ali. Gibbs Smith Pub. 1991 $10.95. ISBN 0-87905-378-X. Collection of Faiz's poems that renders intact their sensuousness and power, along with the poet's irony and compassion.

Ghālib, Mirza Asadullah Khan. *Ghazals of Ghālib: Versions from the Urdu*. Ed. by Aliiaz Ahmad. Bks. Demand repr. of 1971 ed. $51.00. ISBN 0-317-09874-8. Includes both literal translations of Ghālib's couplets as well as lyric transcreations by twentieth-century poets like W. S. Merwin and Adrienne Rich.

Pritchett, Frances W., trans. and ed. *The Romance Tradition in Urdu: Adventures from the Dastan of Amir Hamzah*. Col. U. Pr. 1991 $35.00. ISBN 0-231-07164-7. Translation of excerpts from the romance cycle of Amir Hamzah, which developed over the centuries into the single greatest flowering of Indo-Persian and Urdu romance literature. With scholarly notes and a bibliography.

Russell, Ralph, and Khurshidul Islam. *Three Mughal Poets. Mīr, Mīr Hasan and Saudā*. new ed. ARP 1992 $14.95. ISBN 0-19-562850-0. Three great Urdu poets who lived in the eighteenth century. Saudā's poems are classical in form but satiric in nature. Mīr Hasan, also using classical form, excelled in the *masnavī*, a long narrative poem in rhymed couplets, often telling a love story. His famous poem, "The Enchanting Story," is examined here. Mīr is one of the greatest love poets of world literature. His favorite form, the *ghazal,* is discussed in detail.

Poetry in Regional Languages

Devkota, Laxmiprasad. *Nepali Visions, Nepali Dreams: The Poems of Laxmiprasad Devkota.* Trans. by David Rubin. Col. U. Pr. 1980 $39.00. ISBN 0-231-05014-3. The first English translation of Devkota's complex, vigorous poetry. Includes 45 poems and an extended critical essay.

Kabir, Humayun, ed. *Green and Gold: Stories and Poems from Bengal.* Greenwood repr. of 1970 ed. o.p. Devoted to the work of contemporary Bengali writers and poets.

Mehrotra, A. K., ed. *Twelve Modern Indian Poets.* OUP 1991 o.p. Collection of twelve important modern Indian poets; with insightful introductions to each.

Nirala. *A Season on the Earth: Selected Poems of Nirala.* Trans. by David Rubin. Col. U. Pr. 1977 $40.50. ISBN 0-2310-4160-8. An experimental Hindi poet of the early twentieth century whose work created a genuine renaissance in Hindi literature.

Raina, Trilokinath, ed. and trans. *An Anthology of Modern Kashmiri Verse 1930-1960.* Ind-US Inc. 1974 $12.50. ISBN 0-88253-469-6. Fine selection and translation of modern Kashmiri lyric inspired by the enchanting valleys of Kashmir.

Ramanujan, A. K. and Dharwadker, Vinay, eds. *Modern Indian Poetry: An Anthology.* OUP 1991. ISBN 0-19-562865-9. Containing verse in English translations from fourteen regional languages, this anthology gives a sense of the crowded landscape of modern Indian poetry.

Sen, Samar. *The Complete Poems of Samar Sen.* Trans. by Pritish Nandy. Ind-US Inc. 1975 $4.80. ISBN 0-88253-514-5. Translation by a leading poet of one of the most influential modern Bengali poets, whose literary career spanned a scant ten years.

MODERN FICTION

The epics, romances, fables, and stories of the subcontinent turned for their inspiration and ideas to the vast storehouse of myth and legend preserved in the ancient texts of India. With the arrival of the British, and the introduction of Anglicist education practices in India (c.1835), however, another world of writing was made available to Indian readers: the Western novel, with its focus on the individual and his or her special relationship to the surrounding world. The first crop of Indian novels turned away from classical sources and were generally occupied with social realism (the work of PREMCHAND in Hindi, or RABINDRANATH TAGORE in Bengali, for instance) or political protest (the work of the Bengali writer, Bankimchandra Chatterji is notable here). Most of the formal and stylistic experiments in literature in the early years of the twentieth century were done in the vigorous world of poetry, and it was not until the post-War years that Indian fiction came of age. Experiments in English and the vernacular became more common. A language for the inwardness of the urban individual; a syntax to render the consciousness of rural India; a playfulness and inventiveness with the forms of fiction—all these became a part of modern Indian writing. The selections below from a number of languages provide this flavor.

General Reference Works

Ali, Ahmed. *Twilight in Delhi.* OUP 1985 $13.95. ISBN 0-88253-281-2. An elegy for the dying Muslim culture of Delhi, depicted through the relationships of middle-class

Muslim families. Woven into the novel are fragments of Urdu poetry that highlight the evocative, nostalgic, and melancholic mood of the story.

Anand, Mulk Raj. *Untouchable*. Viking Penguin 1990 $7.95. ISBN 0-14-018395-7. Anand's first and most successful novel, describing an eventful day in the life of a young sweeper from a northern Indian cantonment town.

Anantha Murthy, U. R. *Samskara: A Rite for a Dead Man*. Trans. by A. K. Ramanujan. OUP 1976 $4.95. ISBN 0-19-561079-2. A novel yielding remarkable insights into the workings of a small community of Brahmins in southern India. Considered one of the true masterpieces of modern Indian fiction.

Bandyopadhyaya, Manik. *The Puppet's Tale*. 1936. Trans. by Sachindralal Ghosh. Ind-US Inc. 1968 o.p. This novel, considered the masterpiece of one of the great modern Bengali writers, deals with the clash of traditional and modern values in a Bengali village.

Banerji, Bibhutibhushan. *Pather Panchali*. Asia Bk. Corp. 1987 $10.95. ISBN 0-318-36919-2. A portrayal of Bengali village people and their day-to-day life through the eyes of a small boy and his sister.

Basheer, Vaikom Muhammad. *Me Grandad 'ad an Elephant: Three Stories of Muslim Life in South India*. Trans. by R. E. Asher and A. C. Chandersekaran. Edinburgh U. Pr. 1981 $7.50. ISBN 0-85224-408-8. Of the three stories in this book, Basheer's most lauded is "Me Grandad 'ad an Elephant," a skillfully and intricately constructed story full of humor and wit. An evocative love story as well, it provides insight into an ordinary Kerala Muslim's ideas on life, God, destiny, and human existence.

Bhandari, Mannu. *The Great Feast*. Trans. by Richard Alan Williams. Ind-US Inc. 1981 o.p. A scathing indictment of contemporary Indian politics, revealing how politicians exploit the poor and the downtrodden; as such, it marks a significant departure from the established genres of Hindu fiction.

Chatterjee, Upamanyu. *English, August*. Faber & Faber 1988 o.p. A comic account of one year in the life of a young Indian civil servant in a small provincial town, who is obsessed with women, literature, and soft drugs rather than India's arcane tax laws.

Desani, G. V. *All about H. Hatterr*. Intro. by Anthony Burgess. McPherson & Co. 1986 $10.00. ISBN 0-914232-79-7. A daringly experimental "Joycean" novel, blending Western and Indian narrative forms in a show of stylistic virtuosity.

Deshpande, Shashi. *That Long Silence*. Viking Penguin 1989 o.p. An accomplished portrayal of a suburban housewife trying to erase a "long silence" toward herself and dreams beginning in childhood and continuing through the arid years of her marriage.

Ghosh, Amitav. *The Shadow Lines*. Viking Penguin 1990 $7.95. ISBN 0-14-011835-7. An account of the 1971 India-Pakistan war over Bangladesh seen through the tortured eyes of a love-struck youth.

Holmström, Lakshmi. *The Inner Courtyard: Stories by Indian Women*. Trafalgar 1990 $13.95. ISBN 1-85381-044-4. Short stories by contemporary women writers that capture the conflicts and complexities of experience, technology, modernity, and gender in post-Independence India. Includes a glossary and biographical notes.

Hosain, Attia. *Sunlight on a Broken Column*. Ind-US Inc. 1981 $5.25. ISBN 0-86578-066-8. The troubled years before and after the Partition are viewed through the consciousness of a young Muslim girl who has led a sheltered and affluent life.

Iyengar, K. Srinivasa. *Indian Writing in English*. Apt Bks. 1984 $50.00. ISBN 0-86590-447-2. An encyclopedic volume with bibliographic essays on individual authors and their works; updated to include entries from Indian fiction up to the 1980s.

Jhabvala, Ruth Prawer. *Out of India: Selected Stories*. S & S Trade 1987 $9.00. ISBN 0-671-64221-9. A collection of stories by a writer noted for her engagement with contemporary Indian culture.

Joshi, Arun. *The Foreigner*. Ind-US Inc. 1972 $3.50. ISBN 0-88253-106-9. A novel depicting the problems of post-independence Indian society and the implications of the East-West encounter by an author interested in existential dilemmas and the theme of alienation.

Kali for Women Staff, ed. *Truth Tales: Contemporary Stories by Women Writers of India.* Feminist Pr. 1990 $12.95. ISBN 1-55861-012-X. A collection of short stories compiled by one of the leading feminist groups in India. With notes and a critical introduction.

Malgonkar, Manohar. *Distant Drum.* Ind-US Inc. 1974. ISBN 0-88253-286-3. Two friends who have served together in the British Army meet again in Kashmir—one an officer in the Indian army, the other the commanding officer of a Pakistani regiment.

Manto, Saadat Hasan. *Kingdom's End and Other Stories.* Trans. by Khalid Hasan. Viking Penguin 1989 $7.95. ISBN 0-14-011774-1. Stories by one of the finest short-story writers in Urdu, who turned his satirist's pen to politics, civil life, and religion.

Mukherjee, Meenakshi. *The Twice-born Fiction: Themes and Techniques of the Indian Novel in English.* Heinemann Ed. 1971 o.p. A now-classic analytical study of the development of the Indian novel in English; includes incisive commentary on technique and cultural history and a useful bibliography of Indo-English fiction.

Pillai, Thakazhi Sivasankara. *Chemmeen.* Trans. by Narayana Menon. Ind-US Inc. 1964 $4.00. ISBN 0-88253-066-6. An Indian *Romeo and Juliet* set in a Kerala fishing village; a story of devotion, greed, and sacrifice unleashed by Hindu-Muslim enmity.

Rao, Raja. *Kanthapura.* New Dir. Pr. 1967 $9.95. ISBN 0-8112-8168-6. A fine evocation of the Gandhian age, this is the story of a small southern Indian village caught in the storm of the freedom struggle of the 1930s and completely transformed by it.

Sealy, I. Allan. *The Trotter-nama.* Viking Penguin 1990 o.p. A Rabelaisian family chronicle that spans two hundred years, seven generations, and English and Indian culture in India.

Seth, Vikram. *The Golden Gate: A Novel.* Random 1987 $5.95. ISBN 0-394-75063-2. A story written entirely in Onegin sonnets exploring the possibility of love in the shadows of the Golden Gate Bridge.

Shukla, Srilal. *Raag Darbari, A Novel.* Trans. by Gillian Wright. Viking Penguin 1992. ISBN 0-14-011662-1. An incisively witty Hindi novel hilariously depicting local politics and government machinery in rural India.

Sidhwa, Bapsi. *The Crow Eaters.* Milkweed Ed. 1992 $13.00. ISBN 0-915943-78-6. A brilliant first novel that offers a rare glimpse into the world of the Parsis, one of India's and Pakistan's most influential minority communities.

Singh, Khushwant. *The Train to Pakistan (Mano Majra).* Grove Pr. 1990 $8.95. ISBN 0-8021-3221-9. A moving and action-filled novel about the impact of Partition on a small village on the Indo-Pakistani border.

Tharoor, Shashi. *The Great Indian Novel.* Arcade Pub. Inc. 1992 $10.95. ISBN 1-55970-194-3. A loose parody of the *Māhabhārata*(from which it takes its title) recounting modern Indian history by recasting it in a patchwork from the classical epic.

CHRONOLOGY OF AUTHORS

Tagore, Sir Rabindranath. 1861–1941
Gandhi, Mohandas. 1869–1948
Premchand. 1880–1936
Nehru, Jawaharlal. 1889–1964
Narayan, R. K. 1906–
Sahgal, Nayantara. 1927–
Desai, Anita. 1937–
Rushdie, Salman. 1947–

DESAI, ANITA. 1937–

Anita Desai is one of the finest novelists writing in English today, and her books have achieved a wide readership both in India and in the West. She has lived her life in India's three great cities—Calcutta, Bombay, and Delhi—and has received much acclaim for her writing, beginning with the Royal Society of Literature's Winifred Holtby Memorial Prize in 1978, awarded for her novel *Fire on the Mountain,* (1977). Her works have twice been nominated for Britain's prestigious Booker Prize, and she has also won the coveted Sahitya Akademi Award, given by India's national academy of letters.

Desai's eight novels and numerous short stories have expanded the dimensions of the Indian literary scene by giving voice to a range of characters previously relegated to the margins of Indian fiction: women, children, adolescents, and the elderly. She has also fixed her penetrating eye on the inner lives of the expanding urban middle class, delving deeply into the realms of imagination and fantasy through a variety of techniques relatively new to Indian writing. With its lucid and evocative language and superbly crafted technique, her work has proved to be an inspiration to a new generation of Indian writers.

NOVELS BY DESAI

Baumgartner's Bombay. Viking Penguin 1990 $7.95. ISBN 0-14-013176-0. The story of a German Jew who leaves Hitler's Berlin for Bombay and encounters a city of poverty and violence. Includes stark descriptions of alienation and despair.

Clear Light of Day. 1980. Viking Penguin 1989 $6.95. ISBN 0-14-008670-7. An exquisitely written portrait of a middle-class Hindu family confronting an increasingly problematic world and the breakup of their illusions about themselves.

Fire on the Mountain. 1977. Viking Penguin 1983 $7.95. ISBN 0-14-005347-6. A poignant glimpse into the interior life of a highly accomplished wife and mother who has chosen to retreat from society.

In Custody. 1984. Viking Penguin 1989 $7.95. ISBN 0-14-010868-8. Sad, bitter, funny novel about an impoverished college lecturer who sees a way to escape from the hopelessness of his daily life. Full of the everyday colors and sounds of India, with some truly memorable scenes of comic catastrophe.

SHORT STORY COLLECTION BY DESAI

Games at Twilight. 1978. Viking Penguin 1983 $7.95. ISBN 0-14-005348-4. Eleven short stories, each a delightful miniature encapsulating the unique atmosphere of urban Indian life.

GANDHI, MOHANDAS K(ARAMCHAND). 1869–1948.

[SEE Volume 4.]

NARAYAN, R. K. 1906–

R. K. Narayan is one of the few Indian writers who has captured a wide audience in the United States and Great Britain, as well as in his native India. All of his many novels, gentle social comedies of middle-class life, take place in Malgudi, an imaginary town in southern India that serves as a kind of "golden mean"—neither a large, impersonal city nor an obscure, isolated village—through which Narayan explores the dilemmas of modernization. For example, *The Bachelor of Arts* is the story of a sensitive youth caught in a conflict between Western ideas of love and marriage instilled in him by his education and the still-traditional milieu in which he lives.

Malgudi is a microcosm of modern India, and throughout Narayan's novels, which span more than fifty years of India's growth, we can watch Malgudi's inhabitants evolve in precisely the same way that their hometown does. Narayan's wit and literary skill have made him a favorite with readers all over the world.

NOVELS BY NARAYAN

The Bachelor of Arts. 1937. U. Ch. Pr. 1980 $9.95. ISBN 0-226-56833-4. Explores the dilemma of a young B.A. who faces the world with nothing to do. Includes an introduction by Graham Greene.

The Dark Room. 1938. U. Ch. Pr. 1981 $4.50. ISBN 0-226-56837-7. Explores the predicament of the traditional Hindu wife.

The Financial Expert. 1952. U. Ch. Pr. 1981 $9.95. ISBN 0-226-56841-5. A revealing study of the cash nexus of modern life. Shows the rise and fall of an obscure middleman who ekes out a living by helping illiterate villagers with their loans.

The Guide: A Novel. 1958. Viking Penguin 1988 $5.95. ISBN 0-14-009657-0. Portrays the unwilling transformation of a guide into a half-reluctant and half-purposeful guru, or holy teacher.

The Vendor of Sweets. 1967. Viking Penguin 1983 $5.95. ISBN 0-14-006258-0. Shows how a village is altered by the clash of different generations and values as a street vendor is confronted by the mores of his son, who has just returned from the United States.

NEHRU, JAWAHARLAL. 1889–1964

[SEE Volume 3]

PREMCHAND (pseud. of Dhanpat Rai Srivastava). 1880–1936

Premchand is the greatest figure in twentieth-century Hindi literature. He became one of the leading writers and cultural figures of his generation, achieving considerable fame and recognition late in his career. Shortly before his death, he was chosen as the first president of the Progressive Writers Association, which he had helped found along with Mulk Raj Anand, Ahmed Ali, and others.

Premchand's unique contribution to the creation of an Indian national identity was to bring the lives of poor and low-caste Indians into sharp focus, thereby expanding his readers' conception of what it means to be "Indian" and leading them to realize that these lives are inextricably linked to their own and to India's future.

SHORT STORY COLLECTION BY PREMCHAND

Deliverance & Other Stories. Trans. by David Rubin. Viking Penguin 1989 $7.95. ISBN 0-14-010790-8. Collection of thirty stories, including the classic "The Chess Players," that capture village and small-town India in minute and glittering detail.

NOVELS BY PREMCHAND

The Gift of a Cow: A Translation of the Hindi Novel, Godaan. Trans. by Gordon C. Roadarmel. Ind. U. Pr. 1968 o.p. A classic in Hindi literature. Captures the corruption and cruelty of a village held hostage by its fidelity to the past.

Nirmala. Trans. by David Rubin. S. Asia 1988 $17.50. ISBN 81-7094-030-3. One of Premchand's most popular novels. The story of a woman whose only sin is her failure to accept a husband who would accept her without a dowry.

BOOK ABOUT PREMCHAND

Rai, Amrit. *Premchand, a Life*. People's Pub. 1982 o.p. A critical biography of Premchand's work and the historical period which he chronicled so well. Includes a useful bibliography of the novelist's work.

RUSHDIE, SALMAN. 1947–

Salman Rushdie was born in India, raised in Pakistan, and educated in England, where he now lives. His Rabelaisian skill for telling stories teeming with fantasy and history, and the virtuosity of his style, with its sly transliterations of Indo-English idioms, won him a delighted audience with the publication of *Midnight's Children* in 1980. However, it was the urgency with which he returned to the lands of his birth and childhood to write of a world where politics and the individual are inseparably connected that won him wide acclaim as a brilliant new novelist and intellectual. He manages to stand both inside and outside the world of developing nations and tell their stories. His fantastical retelling of the story of Islam set in a London peopled by immigrants from around the world, *The Satanic Verses* (1988), is his last full-length novel: its publication raised the anger of Muslims in Britain, South Asia, and the Middle East who asked that the novel be banned. In February 1989 Iran's Ayatollah Khomeini decreed a *fatwa* pronouncing the death sentence on him, and Rushdie has since lived in hiding. Subsequently, he offered several published explanations and apologies to Muslims (collected in *Imaginary Homelands*, 1991), and he also wrote a children's story, *Haroun and the Sea of Stories* (1990).

NOVELS BY RUSHDIE

Midnight's Children. 1980. Avon 1982 $5.95. ISBN 0-380-58099-3. Rushdie's best-known work and winner of Great Britain's prestigious Booker Prize in 1981. The story of Saleem Sinai, who was born at the precise moment that India attained her independence.

The Satanic Verses. 1988. Viking Penguin 1989 $19.95. ISBN 0-670-82537-9. Novel of immigrants in London. Considered by its fiercest critics to be a blasphemous attack on the holiest tenets of Islam—the Prophet and the *Quran*—the publication of this work resulted in the 1989 *fatwa* on Rushdie's life.

Shame. 1983. Random 1984 $9.95. ISBN 0-394-72665-0. A satire of the newly independent Pakistan and the elite who corrupt it. Perhaps the most deeply personal of Rushdie's *oeuvre*, it seamlessly blends political drama with fantasy.

WORKS BY RUSHDIE

Imaginary Homelands: Essays and Criticism 1981–1991. Viking Penguin 1991 $24.95. ISBN 0-670-83952-3. A collection of seventy-five essays compiled by Rushdie in the first year of his hiding. Includes such topics as politics, culture, race, literary criticism, book and film reviews, and religion.

SHORT STORIES BY RUSHDIE

Haroun and the Sea of Stories. Viking Penguin 1991 $8.95. ISBN 0-14-015737-9. A contemporary fable filled with riotous verbal pranks.

BOOKS ABOUT RUSHDIE

Brennan, Timothy. *Salman Rushdie and the Third World: Myths of the Nation*. St. Martin 1989 $22.95. ISBN 0-312-03308-7. The most comprehensive critical work on Rushdie to date. Examines his writing in the context of the ex-colonial diaspora of intellectuals from developing nations to the West.

Harrison, James. *Salman Rushdie*. Macmillan 1991 $21.95. ISBN 0-8057-7011-9. Published as part of the Twayne English Author series. Provides useful biographical and critical information and individual readings of *Midnight's Children*, *Shame*, and *The Satanic Verses*.

Maitland, Sara, and Appignanesi, Lisa, eds. *The Rushdie File*. Syracuse U. Pr. 1990 $13.95. ISBN 0-8156-0248-0. Explains the necessity for "an easily accessible document chronicling events from the start of the [publication of *The Satanic Verses*]." Includes material previously printed or spoken on the case.

SAHGAL, NAYANTARA. 1927–

Nayantara Sahgal is one of the most prolific writers in India today. The niece of JAWAHARLAL NEHRU (see Vol. 3) and cousin (and political enemy) of the late Indira Gandhi, Sahgal is known to have insisted, "being Nehru's niece or Madame Pandit's daughter has neither been a help or a hindrance—it has simply been my inheritance and background—but being Mrs. Gandhi's cousin as well as critic is another matter. It has given me a glimpse of how intolerable establishments reduce their critics to non-persons." Much of Sahgal's later fiction has dealt with the politics of post-Independence India and the changes in lifestyles and attitudes that beset the urban elite. Sahgal's sardonic and evocative descriptions of contemporary India and its corrupt politics have won her wide acclaim in India, where she is also well known as a political journalist and civil liberties activist.

Novels by Sahgal

Plans for Departure. Norton 1985 $14.95. ISBN 0-393-02221-8. Set in 1914 in a remote hill town of the Himalayas, this novel explores the lives and conflicts of a European enclave that moves in and out of India but realizes there are fewer and fewer places in the world to move to.

Rich Like Us. New Dir. Pr. 1985 $8.95. ISBN 0-8112-1078-2. Explores the parallel tracks of two very different women, one Indian and the other Cockney English. Set largely in New Delhi, spanning four generations.

A Situation in New Delhi. 1977. Viking Penguin 1988 $6.95. ISBN 0-14-011603-6. An English writer arrives in New Delhi to find the capital in chaos when its leader, Shivraj, dies and his successors begin to destroy what Shivraj had once built.

Storm in Chandigarh. 1969. Viking Penguin 1988 $7.95. ISBN 0-14-011604-4. A political satire of the chaos and machinations following the partition of Punjab into two states with the same capital, Chandigarh.

TAGORE, SIR RABINDRANATH (also Ravindranatha Thakura). 1861–1941 (Nobel Prize 1913)

Rabindranath Tagore, hailed by Mahatma Gandhi (see Vol. 4) as "the Great Sentinel," was one of those versatile men of his age who touched and enriched modern Indian life in many ways. Poet, dramatist, novelist, short-story writer, musical composer, painter, thinker, educator, nationalist freedom fighter, and internationalist—such were the various roles that Tagore played with uniform distinction during his long and fruitful career.

Tagore wrote primarily in Bengali, but it was his own translation into English of his volume of poems entitled *Gitanjali* (*Song-Offerings*) in 1912 that catapulted him to international fame, culminating in his winning the Nobel Prize for Literature in 1913, the first Asian and still the only Indian writer to win this distinction. *Gitanjali,* however, also had the effect of branding Tagore a "mystic," a label he never quite managed to escape, despite his prodigious contributions in many other fields, such as his founding of Shantiniketan, a university based on traditional Indian notions of learning.

Poetry by Tagore

Gitanjali: Collection of Prose Translations Made by the Author from the Original Bengali. 1912. Intro. by William Butler Yeats. Macmillan 1971 $5.95. ISBN 0-02-089630-1. The central theme in the 100-odd pieces in *Gitanjali,* Tagore's finest achievement in English verse, is the poet's mystical and devotional quest. The poems were originally written in Bengali by Tagore and translated into English by him.

Novels by Tagore

The Broken Nest. Trans. by Mary Lago and Supriya Sen. Asia Bk. Corp. 1983 $5.50. ISBN 0-318-37008-8. A novel which vividly dramatizes the clash of traditional and modern values in Calcutta; among Tagore's finest works.

The Home and the World. Trans. Surendranath Tagore. Asia Bk. Corp. 1985 $6.50. ISBN 0-333-91801-0. The powerful story of a young wife who is encouraged by her liberal and intellectual husband to find herself. Set against the backdrop of the early freedom struggle in rural Bengal.

WORKS BY TAGORE

A Tagore Reader. Ed. by Amiya Chakravarty. Beacon Pr. 1966 $18.00. ISBN 0-8070-5971-4. A collection of excerpts from Tagore's works, including letters, travel notes, drama, short stories, poems, criticism, and philosophy; probably the best introduction to Tagore's writing.

BOOKS ABOUT TAGORE

Lago, Mary M. and Ronald Warwick, eds. *Rabindranath Tagore: Perspectives in Times*. Intl Spec. Bk. 1989 $65.00. ISBN 0-333-42871-4. An intelligent and comprehensive overview of Tagore's work by one of his best translators.

Sharma, K. K. *Rabindranath Tagore's Aesthetics*. S. Asia 1988 $12.50. ISBN 81-7017-237-3. A good guide to Tagore's aesthetics, with reference to his poetry and philosophy.

Thompson, Edward J. *Rabindranath Tagore: Poet and Dramatist*. Greenwood 1975 repr. of 1948 ed. $35.00. ISBN 0-8371-8065-1. One of the best evaluations, although somewhat dated, of Tagore's poetry and drama.

CHAPTER 7

Chinese Literature

Frances La Fleur

The moon sinks, a crow caws, and frost
  fills the sky;
Facing river maples and fishermen's
  lights I gloomily doze.
From Cold Mountain Temple outside old
  Soochow's city walls
The tolling midnight bell reaches my
  moored boat.

—CHANG CHI, "Night Anchorage at Maple Bridge"

The favorite tourist destinations in China are often not architectural or natural wonders, but humble spots where a few immortal lines of poetry were written long ago. Maple Bridge outside the city of Soochow is such a place. Sometime during the late eighth century, a melancholy Chang Chi sat aboard a boat moored near it—the story goes that he was on his way home after failing the civil service examination at the capital—and, unable to sleep, composed the poem quoted at the head of this chapter. Now, some 1,200 years later, not only do Chinese flock to the little stone bridge from all over the country and abroad, but so do thousands of Japanese, who have also read this poem in their high school textbooks. It is a very brief lyric containing only four lines, but its evocation of the sights, sounds, and feel of the scene fuse with the poet's emotion to make us feel the beauty and the loneliness. And for those who know something of the history of the place, there is a hint of something more—the temple was named for HAN SHAN, a legendary mad poet-monk who styled himself "Cold Mountain" and supposedly once lived there for a time. For a young man just disappointed in his attempts at a successful government career, perhaps the life of a monk who renounced worldly ambition and spent his life in contemplation and poetry had a special dreamy appeal.

The Chinese are justly proud of their written language and literary heritage, which have formed an unbroken tradition for thousands of years. The earliest archeological writing samples we have, etched on oracle bones and bronze vessels dating from around 1400 B.C. , already show a high level of sophistication, and, in fact, the antecedents of this writing can probably be traced to sites dating back to the fifth millennium B.C.

Though not the earliest world civilization, Chinese culture is striking for its continuity. Whereas modern Egyptians or Iraqis no longer recognize the hieroglyphics or cuneiforms from their precursory civilizations, the Chinese can still recognize many of the characters on the earliest bones, and the language they reflect is essentially that still used today. Not surprisingly, therefore, the Chinese have tended to revere their written language above most other manifestations of culture.

Poetry has always been held in the highest esteem, and it forms one of the five ancient classics, the *BOOK OF SONGS*, compiled in the sixth century B.C. but containing much material that is far older. All educated Chinese were expected to appreciate and to be able to compose poetry, and poetry formed an essential part of the civil service examination that determined entry into the most prestigious careers in government.

The extravagant claim of Ernest Fenollosa (which so inspired the Imagist poet EZRA POUND) (see Vol. 1) that the supposedly pictorial quality of the Chinese character made a marvelous medium for poetry has now been largely dismissed by serious scholars, but it is true that the Chinese classical language does lend itself to lyrical economy of expression. In a traditional verse, there are rarely more than seven monosyllabic words per line, and therefore each noun, verb, and descriptive word must suggest a great deal indirectly. Person, number, and tense are also rarely explicit, tending often to give a quintessential or universal feeling to the poetic images.

Though not as extreme, a similar terseness is also characteristic of the classical language used in other genres, such as prose tales and histories, and, as centuries passed, this language became farther and farther removed from what was actually spoken. Therefore, popular storytellers and actors aiming at a less educated audience adopted a colloquial style in their oral performances that eventually formed the basis for a written literature in the vernacular. In later dynasties (from about the fourteenth century on), learned men also occasionally wrote in this popular style for diversion, producing such lively works as the Robin Hood-like adventures of SHIH's *Outlaws of the Marsh* and the great erotic novel *Golden Lotus* (by WANG SHIH-CHEN); however, they rarely sought public recognition for them, and, if they signed the works at all, they often used pseudonyms. Even TS'AO CHAN, the author of the semiautobiographical novel *The Dream of the Red Chamber*, a work of great psychological subtlety and complexity, felt the need to justify his choice of the vernacular novel form on the grounds that its naturalness of language made it more suitable for his portrayal of a story "true to real life." In general, serious pieces that were intended for a literary person's published collected works were expected to conform to the classical genres, contain elevated sentiments, and be composed in erudite classical language.

But, because the simpler colloquial style was accessible to many more readers, it was promoted by social modernizers after the beginning of the twentieth century as the basis not only for serious modern fiction but also for poetry. Their efforts, coming at a critical time when China was under increasing pressure from the West, proved successful in breaking the 3,000-year stranglehold that the elegant but difficult classical language had exerted on all learned discourse and highbrow literature.

As a consequence of this change of style, and the pronounced Western influence on literature since this time, we now tend to divide Chinese literature into two general periods: traditional, including everything written up until the end of the last imperial dynasty (1912), and modern, covering everything written subsequently, particularly after the so-called May Fourth Movement of 1919, which began as a political protest by university students in Peking against the terms of the Versailles Peace Conference, but which proved to have widespread social and cultural consequences for China as a whole and greatly speeded the pace of the literary revolution.

Though the literary medium changed after 1912, with writers casting more widely for literary inspiration and seeking a broader reading public, something in the message remained the same. Throughout Chinese history, there has always been a strong belief that "literature should convey the Tao"; in other words, it should have a moral. And, more often than not, that moral has been in some way tied to politics, at least since Confucius's disciples interpreted the *Book of Songs* as containing protests against injustices of the Chou dynastic regime and as allegorically expressing models for right conduct and government.

Although there have been various periods of Chinese history when this moral mandate for literature was more honored in the breach (e.g., in the May Fourth era, some of the leading writers initially spurned this idea and promoted individualistic and sentimental writing), it has never been totally forgotten, and most writers even today feel the weight of this "burden." Under the Communist government in mainland China, literature has at times been no more than an instrument of propaganda, glorifying the struggles of the peasants, soldiers, and workers in their fight against the oppression of the privileged. Even in contemporary Taiwan and in mainland China since the somewhat lessened restrictions on artistic expression since the end of the Cultural Revolution, one still finds more didacticism than is common in contemporary Western literature, and a stronger tendency in Chinese readers to look for implicit social or political comment in works by serious writers.

The sweep of Chinese history has seen the rise and fall of many imperial regimes, and with it a succession of literary genres, which, like dynasties, tend eventually to lose their vitality and power. When a dynasty became weak and corrupt, generally popular uprisings occurred and a new leader emerged from among the people to begin the cycle over again. And when a literary genre began to stagnate, Chinese literati in like manner turned for new inspiration to the music and poetry of popular culture for new forms to adopt and refine. As the great literary commentator Wang Kuo-wei (1877–1927) expressed it: "When a literary form has been prevalent for a long time, the sheer number of practitioners will eventually mean the imposition of refinements and restrictions which will make it impossible for even talented writers to express their feelings. So they will turn to another form of literature to free themselves of these restraints. Thus all literary forms must one day decline after a period of flowering." Yet, despite the rise and fall of dynasties, and periods of political division and discord, the Chinese have never lost a sense of themselves as one people unified by culture; and, despite the changing modes of expression and the myriad foreign influences that have bombarded it, there is still a literature with common threads running through it—of a distinctive lyric sensibility, a serious moral underpinning, and a preoccupation more with the mundane than with the metaphysical—that we can call Chinese.

History and Criticism

DeBary, William T. ed. *Sources of Chinese Tradition.* 2 vols. Col. U. Pr. 1960. Vol. 1 $19.50. ISBN 0-231-08602-4. Vol. 2 $18.00. ISBN 0-231-08603-2. Chinese classics well translated, with chronological charts and a helpful introduction.

Fairbank, John K., Edwin O. Reischauer, and Albert M. Craig. *East Asia: Tradition and Transformation.* HM 1989 $50.36. ISBN 0-395-45023-3. Basic text for many college courses on East Asia.

Fitzgerald, Charles P. *China: A Short Cultural History.* Praeger 3 1954 o.p.

Meskill, John. *An Introduction to Chinese Civilization.* Heath 1973 $21.50. ISBN 0-669-73502-7

Tsien, Tsuen-hsuin. *Written on Bamboo and Silk: The Beginnings of Chinese Books and Inscriptions.* U. Chi. Pr. 1962 o.p. Useful for understanding the relation between technological developments and the dissemination of literature.

TRADITIONAL CHINESE LITERATURE

One gauge of the importance of poetry in China throughout its history is the fact that there is no single word for it. Instead, there have been specific terms for each type of verse. However, one of them, *shih,* was the dominant form for so long that it has now become the generic word for poetry.

The earliest poetry of the north reflected in the BOOK OF SONGS was in the *shih* style, based on ancient folk song models. As the borders of the Chinese empire expanded in the Han dynasty (roughly equivalent in time and importance to the Roman Empire), foreign music from Central Asia began to influence Chinese music, and *shih* underwent changes as well. Ballads of the people were collected by the government's Music Bureau, ostensibly to judge the mood of the populace, and so these songs became known as Music Bureau Songs, or *yüeh-fu.* They were polished and imitated by literati, who exploited their dramatic monologues or dialogues, usually in the personae of abandoned wives or lonely soldiers at the battlefront, for artistic and allegorical purposes. The best examples of these are the *Nineteen Ancient Poems* from the later half of the dynasty, whose authorship is uncertain. By the end of the Han dynasty, as the country was breaking up into rival kingdoms, some poets began to forsake the third-person ballad for lyrics in the first person. One of the most influential of these was TS'AO CHIH, son of a Han general who established a hegemony in the north that became the Wei dynasty.

Meanwhile, a rhapsodic style of verse known as *sao* had developed in the Yangtze River basin to the south. This verse, intoned rather than sung, had generally longer lines connected into couplets by a long indrawn sigh. Originally associated with shamanistic ritual courtship of nature gods, this poetry relied on flowery imagery with erotic overtones. The first individually authored long poem in the genre was attributed to an exiled courtier named CH'Ü YÜAN. The *sao* developed into an exuberant rhyme-prose genre, *fu,* which also reached a peak in the Han dynasty. Aimed at a court audience, these sophisticated pieces claimed a moral intent, but their true interest lay in lavish descriptions and verbal magic. YANG HSIUNG was one of the masters of the *fu* genre.

After many years of short-lived dynasties and widespread social unrest, during which time Buddhism imported from India gained a spiritual hold on a people who had lost faith in traditional values, another strong dynasty, the T'ang (618–907), was founded, surpassing even the Han dynasty in power. The cosmopolitan atmosphere fostered in its capital at Ch'ang-an led to another flowering of poetry, which culminated in the regulated verse form, *lü shih,* somewhat like the sonnet in its strict thematic and structural requirements. Two of the greatest practitioners of *lü shih* were WANG WEI, whose imagery created tranquil landscapes symbolic of his Buddhist meditations, and TU FU, who inhabited a much more down-to-earth realm dominated by human joys and sorrows. But, even in the heyday of regulated verse, there were those who balked at its constraints, like LI PO, who infused the freer old-style *shih* with an imaginative boldness that has been termed romantic.

Li Po has also been credited as an early practitioner of the *tz'u* form, a lyric written in irregular meter to conform to the rhythm of a particular tune. Toward the end of the T'ang dynasty and in the following Sung dynasty (960-1279), *tz'u* became the most popular form, and gradually poets moved beyond lyrics of love and parting to more probing and philosophical concerns. A leader in broadening the *tz'u*'s thematic range was the great Sung poet and calligrapher SU TUNG-P'O (SU SHIH), who also wrote many excellent *shih* poems and *fu* rhyme-prose pieces.

Following the *tz'u*, and similar to it in being also a genre based on song words, was the *ch'ü*, which developed simultaneously both in the north, held by the Tartars from 1115 to 1234, and in the Chinese-held south. Begun as street entertainment, and highly vernacular in vocabulary and grammar, it became the basis for song chains with narrative frames and eventually evolved into the lyric drama of the following Yuan dynasty (1280–1368). The greatest such drama was the *Romance of the Western Chamber*, a tragic tale of a woman scorned, which combines passages of great lyric beauty with a lively plot and bawdy humor.

Poetry was still widely written in the last two dynasties, the Ming (1368–1644) and the Ch'ing (1644–1912), but no further major innovations occurred in genre or theme. However, this was the Golden Age of fiction. As early as the Six Dynasties (420-589), short anecdotes on historical and supernatural themes had begun to develop, and, by the T'ang dynasty, these had crystallized into an elegant and sophisticated classical literary form. In the rapidly developing urban centers of the Sung and Yuan dynasties, where street drama flourished, the storyteller's art was gaining great popularity as well, and, by the time of the Ming dynasty, the favorite classical stories were being recast into written vernacular versions. Some writer-compilers, like the clever FENG MENG-LUNG, edited stories in both the literary and the vernacular versions, to cash in on both highbrow and middlebrow publishing markets. As time went by, more and more material from daily life found its way into fiction, and stock types like famous beauties and valiant heroes were superseded by the greedy merchants, brothel madams, wily servants, and petty officials that delighted the broader urban audience.

Cycles of popular tales were also stitched together as long narratives, resulting in the heroic *Romance of the Three Kingdoms*, the picaresque *Journey to the West*, and the lively *Outlaws of the Marsh*. In time this longer fiction developed into a form resembling the Western novel, with such masterpieces as the satirical *The Scholars* by WU CHING-TZU, the sexually explicit *Golden Lotus*, and the tragic family saga *The Dream of the Red Chamber*, which reflect in intimate detail the multifaceted tapestry of late imperial life.

History and Criticism

Arlington, Lewis Charles. *The Chinese Drama from the Earliest Times until Today: A Panoramic Study of the Art in China, Tracing Its Origin and Describing Its Actors (in both) Male and Female Roles, Their Costumes and Make-up, Superstitions and Stage Slang, The Accompanying Music and Musical Instruments Concluding with Synopses of Thirty Chinese Plays*. B. Blom 1966 repr. of 1930 ed. o.p.

Birch, Cyril, ed. *Studies in Chinese Literary Genres*. U. CA Pr. 1975 o.p. Contains 11 essays by leading scholars of Chinese literature.

Birrell, Anne. *Popular Songs and Ballads of Han China*. Unwin Hyman 1988 $39.95. ISBN 0-04-895028-9. Includes folk songs, annotations, and an extensive bibliography.

Bishop, John L., ed. *Studies in Chinese Literature*. HUP 1965 $8.50. ISBN 0-674-84705-9. Eight important essays from the 1950s reprinted from various scholarly journals. Still highly useful.

Chang, K'ang-i Sun. *The Evolution of Chinese Tz'u Poetry: From Late T'ang to Northern Sung*. Princeton U. Pr. 1980 $37.50. ISBN 0-691-06425-3. Concentrates on generic development while attempting a critical literary history. Fully informed by traditional Chinese and western literary scholarship.

______. *Six Dynasties Poetry*. Princeton U. Pr. 1986 $37.50. ISBN 0-691-06669-8. Organized into five chapters on individual poets. Helpful for the general reader; translations sometimes a bit wordy.

Cheng, Francois. *Chinese Poetic Writing*. Trans. by Jerome P. Seaton. Ind. U. Pr. 1982 $35.00. ISBN 0-253-31358-9. *Studies in Chinese Literature and Society Series*. An anthology of T'ang poems with historical and critical annotations.

Chou, Chih-p'ing. *Yüan Hung-tao and the Kung-an School*. Cambridge U. Pr. 1988 $49.95. ISBN 0-521-34207-4. "Trustworthy account of the Kung-an school and a successful effort to place it in historical and literary perspective" (*CLEAR*).

Crump, J. I. *Chinese Theater in the Days of Kublai Khan*. U. of Ariz. Pr. 1991 $30.00. ISBN 0-89264-101-0. Discusses personal lives of Yuan playwrights, physical trappings of stages, backgrounds of plays. Full translations of three dramas. "Colorful, witty, and vibrantly alive" (*Journal of Asian Studies*).

______. *Songs from Xanadu: Studies in Mongol Dynasty Song Poetry (San Ch'u)*. U. of Mich. Pr. 1983 $10.00. ISBN 0-89264-047-2. Analysis of Yuan Dynasty *san-ch'u* poetry, with Chinese texts and English translations of poems discussed.

Davis, A. R., ed. *The Penguin Book of Chinese Verse: Poets Series*. Trans. by Robert Kotewall and Norman L. Smith. Viking Penguin 1975 o.p.

Dolezelova-Velingerova, M., and J. I. Crump, trans. *Ballad of the Hidden Dragon*. NYU Pr. 1971 o.p. One of the earliest examples of the northern ballad-narrative popular in the eleventh century, which was the precursor of Yuan drama.

Feng, Yuan-chun. *An Outline History of Classical Chinese Literature*. Joint Pub. Co. HK 1983 o.p. Updated version of *A Short History of Classical Chinese Literature* (1958). Originally published in Chinese. Includes a bibliography and index.

Frankel, Hans. H. *The Flowering Plum and the Palace Lady: Interpretations of Chinese Poetry*. Yale U. Pr. 1976 $14.00. ISBN 0-300-01889-4. Translation and discussion of poems arranged by theme.

Fung, Sydney S. *Twenty-five T'ang Poets: Index to English Translations*. U. of Wash. Pr. 1984 $75.00. ISBN 0-295-96155-4. An index of 207 volumes published between 1902 and 1981, with approximately 4,000 poems and 12,000 entries of English translation. Foreword by Stephen Owen.

Hanan, Patrick. *The Chinese Short Story: Studies in Dating, Authorship, and Composition*. HUP 1973 $20.00. ISBN 0-674-12525-8. "Amazing erudition and fecundity of interpretive insight . . . Style is very dense" (*Journal of Asian Studies*).

______. *The Chinese Vernacular Story*. HUP 1981 $22.00. ISBN 0-674-12565-7. The most important work on Chinese short fiction.

Hayden, George A., trans. *Crime and Punishment in Medieval Chinese Drama—Three Judge Pao Plays*. HUP 1978 $20.00. ISBN 0-674-17608-1. Objective and scholarly, concerned with generic convention and historical development of morality plays.

Hegel, Robert E. *The Novel in Seventeenth-Century China*. Col. U. Pr. 1981 o.p. "Essential reading for anyone seriously interested in the traditional Chinese novel" (*Ming Studies*).

Hegel, Robert E., and Richard C. Hessney, eds. *Expressions of Self in Chinese Literature*. Col. U. Pr. 1985 $19.00. ISBN 0-231-05829-2. Twelve essays by well-known scholars.

Hightower, James Robert. *Topics in Chinese Literature: Outlines and Bibliographies*. HUP 1962 o.p. A concise and authoritative guide, but bibliography is out of date.

Hsia, Chih-tsing. *The Classic Chinese Novel: A Critical Introduction*. Ind. U. Pr. repr. of 1968 ed. $25.00. ISBN 0-253-17483-X. "For its painstaking research, its impeccable scholarship . . . and its fund of invaluable insights, is a classic in itself" (*Journal of Asian Studies*).

Huang, Chi-ch'ih. *A Research Guide to English Translation of Chinese Verse: Han Dynasty to T'ang Dynasty*. Chinese U. HK 1977 o.p. Gives name of poet, title of poem, original text, and English translation for each entry. Sequence of poems follows the leading Chinese anthology of poetry of this period by Ting Fu-pao. Useful for the specialist and general reader alike.

Hucker, Charles O. *China to 1850: A Short History*. Stanford U. Pr. 1978 $22.50. ISBN 0-8047-0957-2. Useful work by a specialist of Ming Dynasty history.

Levy, Dore. *Chinese Narrative Poetry from the Late Han through T'ang Dynasties*. Duke o.p. "Offers literary theory, comparative criticism and rich cultural history all in one coherent presentation" (*CLEAR*).

Lin, Shuen-fu, and Stephen Owen, eds. *The Vitality of the Lyric Voice: Shih Poetry from the Late Han to T'ang*. Princeton U. Pr. 1986 $57.50. ISBN 0-691-03134-7. Twelve essays on the evolution of *shih* poetry.

Liu, James J. Y. *The Art of Chinese Poetry*. U. Ch. Pr. 1966 $9.95. ISBN 0-226-48687-7. A very useful introduction by a leading scholar of classical poetry.

———. *Chinese Theories of Literature*. U. Ch. Pr. 1979 o.p. Examines the range of Chinese literary criticism using the author's own categories and Western comparisons.

———. *Major Lyricists of the Northern Sung, 960–1126 A.D.* Discusses poems by six important *tz'u* poets who influenced the development of the genre. Useful for the student of classical literature or the serious general reader.

Liu, Tsun-yan, ed. *Chinese Middlebrow Fiction*. U. of Wash. Pr. 1983 o.p. An anthology of popular fiction from the eighteenth, nineteenth, and early twentieth centuries.

Liu, Wu-chi. *An Introduction to Chinese Literature*. Ind. U. Pr. 1990 repr. of 1966 ed. $57.75. ISBN 0-313-26703-0. "On the whole . . . a valuable contribution" (*LJ*). Useful as an introduction for the general reader.

Liu, Wu-chi, and Irving Yucheng Lo, eds. *Sunflower Splendor: Three Thousand Years of Chinese Poetry*. Doubleday 1975; Ind. U. Pr. 1990 $39.95. ISBN 0-253-35580-X. A very comprehensive anthology including some lesser-known pieces and helpful biographical sketches of poets whose works are included.

Lu, Tonglin. *Rose and Lotus: Narrative of Desire in France and China*. State U. NY Pr. 1991 $57.50. ISBN 0-7914-0463-3. Chapters on two French novels and *Dream of the Red Chamber* and *Golden Lotus*. "Confronts the problem of sexuality without apology" (*Journal of Asian Studies*).

Mair, Victor H. *Tunhuang Popular Narratives*. Cambridge U. Pr. 1984 $74.95. ISBN 0-521-24761-6

Miao, Ronald, ed. *Studies in Chinese Poetry and Poetics*. Chinese Materials Ctr. 1978 o.p. Anthology of essays, uneven in quality, but contains useful material.

Nienhauser, William H., Jr., and Stephen H. West, eds. *The Indiana Companion to Traditional Chinese Literature*. Ind. U. Pr. 1985 $75.00. ISBN 0-253-32983-3. A monumental reference work on Chinese literature before 1911, compiled by almost 200 contributors, including more than 500 entries on specific writers, works, genres, styles, and movements, as well as general essays, cross-references, and indexes.

Owen, Stephen. *The Great Age of Chinese Poetry: The High T'ang*. Yale U. Pr. 1980 o.p. Only work of its kind in English. Rather cursory, but a helpful overview.

———. *Poetry of the Early T'ang*. Yale U. Pr. 1977 o.p. The only scholarly treatment available on this transitional period.

———. *Remembrances: The Experience of the Past in Classical Chinese Literature*. HUP 1986 o.p. A comparative perspective. Provocative.

———. *Traditional Chinese Poetry and Poetics: Omen of the World*. U. of Wis. Pr. 1985 $27.50. ISBN 0-299-09420-0. "Ultimately it reveals more of the world of Owen than of the 'omen of the world'" (*Journal of Asian Studies*).

Perng, Ching-hsi. *Double Jeopardy: A Critique of Seven Yuan Courtroom Dramas*. U. of Mich. Pr. 1978 $6.00. ISBN 0-89264-035-9. A close textual study of seven plays. Lively and interesting, intended for the student of Chinese or comparative literature or serious general reader.

Plaks, Andrew, ed. *Chinese Narrative: Critical and Theoretical Essays.* Princeton U. Pr. 1977 $52.50. ISBN 0-691-06328-1. Conference papers by several leading scholars of Chinese narrative theory. Useful for the serious student.

Prusek, Jaroslav. *Chinese History and Literature: Collections of Studies.* Kluwer Ac. 1970 $101.50. ISBN 90-277-0175-X. A useful collection of studies by one of the great Eastern European pioneers in the field of Chinese literature.

Rickett, Adele A., ed. *Chinese Approaches to Literature from Confucius to Liang Ch'i-ch'ao.* Bks. Demand repr. of 1978 ed. $73.40. ISBN 0-8357-6055-3. Uneven, but with some useful essays on classical Chinese literary criticism.

Schafer, E. H. *The Divine Woman: The Dragon Ladies and Rain Maidens in T'ang Literature.* U. CA Pr. 1973 o.p. Useful background on the beliefs behind the frequent allusions to supernatural women in T'ang poetry, with examples translated and analyzed.

———. *Pacing the Void: T'ang Approaches to the Stars.* U. CA Pr. 1977 o.p. Essential reading for anyone truly wishing to understand celestial imagery in T'ang poetry to reconstruct an essential part of the medieval Chinese world view.

———. *The Vermilion Bird: T'ang Images of the South.* U. CA Pr. 1967 $16.95. ISBN 0-520-05463-6. Provides much useful philological and historical background on T'ang poems employing exotic southern imagery.

Schlepp, Wayne. *San-ch'ü: Its Technique and Imagery.* U. of Wis. Pr. 1970 $22.50. ISBN 0-299-05540-X. A study of the dominant verse of the Yuan Dynasty.

Shih, Chung-wen. *The Golden Age of Chinese Drama: Yüan Tsa Chü.* Princeton U. Pr. 1975 o.p. A study of the 171 extant plays of the peak of Chinese drama in the Yuan period (1260–1368).

Shih, Vincent, trans. *The Literary Mind and the Carving of Dragons: A Study of the Thought and Pattern in Chinese Literature.* Coronet Bks. 1983 $63.50. ISBN 962-201-271-X. A full translation of one of the earliest and most important works of Chinese poetic criticism.

Soong, Stephen C., ed. *Song Without Music: Chinese Tz'u Poetry.* U. of Wash. Pr. 1981 o.p. Includes text of each poem in both Chinese and English, plus a discussion of each in English.

Strassberg, Richard E. *The World of K'ung Shang-jen: A Man of Letters in Early Ch'ing China.* Col. U. Pr. 1983 $52.50. ISBN 0-231-05530-7. A biography of the famous Chinese dramatist, with emphasis on his artistic contributions. Includes a scholarly, extensive bibliography.

Wagner, Marsha L. *The Lotus Boat: The Origins of Chinese Tz'u Poetry in T'ang Popular Culture.* Col. U. Pr. 1984 $39.00. ISBN 0-231-04276-0. A study emphasizing the importance of performance in the development of the *tz'u* genre.

Wang, Jing. *The Story of Stone; Intertextuality, Ancient Chinese Stone Lore, and the Stone Symbolism in Dream of the Red Chamber, Water Margin, and the Journey to the West.* Duke 1991 $37.50. ISBN 0-8223-1178-X. "Full of new ideas, good information, and creative insight" (*CLEAR*). Theorizing is a bit labored, otherwise interesting.

Watson, Burton. *Chinese Lyricism.* Col. U. Pr. 1971 o.p. A good overview of the development of the *shih* poetic genre.

———, trans. *Chinese Rhyme-prose.* Col. U. Pr. 1971 o.p. Thirteen poems chronologically arranged from the Han to Six Dynasties. "Generally succeeds in capturing the lushness and exuberance" (*Journal of Asian Studies*).

Yip, Wai-lim. *Chinese Poetry: Major Modes and Genres.* U. CA Pr. 1976 $49.95. ISBN 0-520-02727-2

Yoshikawa, Kojiro. *Five Hundred Years of Chinese Poetry, 1150–1650: The Chin, Yuan, and Ming Dynasties.* Trans. into English by John Timothy Wixted. Princeton U. Pr. 1992 $37.50. ISBN 0-691-06768-6. A work on a little-studied period of Chinese poetry by a major Japanese literary scholar. . . all students in the field will have to take seriously" (*CLEAR*).

Young, David, trans. *Wang Wei, Li Po, Tu Fu, Li Ho: Four T'ang Poets.* Field Translat. Ser. No. 4 1980 o.p.

Yu, Pauline. *The Reading of Imagery in the Chinese Poetic Tradition*. Princeton U. Pr. 1987 $32.50. ISBN 0-691-06682-5. "A sustained investigation of major segments of the Chinese critical tradition and what it has to say about the nature and function of poetic imagery" (*Journal of Asian Studies*).

Collections

Ayling, Alan, and Duncan Mackintosh, eds. and trans. *A Collection of Chinese Lyrics*. Vanderbilt U. Pr. 1967 o.p. "A conscientious labour of love and a pioneering venture in a neglected field" (*TLS*).

———. *Further Collection of Chinese Lyrics*. Vanderbilt U. Pr. 1970 $14.95. ISBN 0-8265-1150-3

Birch, Cyril, ed. and trans. *An Anthology of Chinese Literature*. 2 vols. Grove Pr. 1987. Vol. 1 *From the Earliest Times to the Fourteenth Century*. $17.50. ISBN 0-8021-5038-1. Vol. 2 *From the Fourteenth Century to the Present Day*. $14.95. ISBN 0-8021-5090-X. The first true anthology in English of Chinese literature. [It] is enjoyable, informative, and . . . readable to the student and general reader alike" (*LJ*). With historical and literary commentary.

Birrell, Anne. *Popular Songs and Ballads of Han China*. Unwin Hyman 1988 $39.95. ISBN 0-04-895028-9

Chai, Ch'u, and Winberg Chai, eds. and trans. *A Treasury of Chinese Literature: A New Prose Anthology Including Fiction and Drama*. Hawthorne 1965 o.p. Selected pieces connected by commentary, offering details not easily found elsewhere. An especially valuable section on drama.

Chang, H. C., ed. *Chinese Literature I: Popular Fiction and Drama*. Col. U. Pr. 1982 o.p. An anthology of short stories and excerpts from the best-known plays and novels. Each selection well translated; some annotation.

———. *Chinese Literature II: Nature Poetry*. o.p. Same format as the drama volume, with translations and introductions for some famous landscape poems. A good introduction to the genre for the general reader.

———. *Chinese Literature III: Tales of the Supernatural*. Col. U. Pr. 1984 $32.00. ISBN 0-231-05794-6. Covers a lesser-known aspect of traditional literature. Lively translations with introductions; suitable for the general reader.

Ch'en, C. J. *Poems of Solitude*. Albelar-Schuman 1960 o.p. Translations of poems from the Six Dynasties Period.

Dolby, William, trans. *Eight Chinese Plays—from the 13th Century to the Present*. Col. U. Pr. 1978 $28.00. ISBN 0-231-04488-7. Idiosyncratic choices, but presents new and worthwhile pieces. Intended for the general reader.

Fletcher, W. J. B. *Gems of Chinese Verse and More Gems of Chinese Poetry*. Paragon Hse. 1966 repr. of 1919 ed. bilingual ed. o.p. Includes well-known masterpieces of the T'ang dynasty.

Frodsham, J. D., and Ch'eng Hsi. *An Anthology of Chinese Verse: Han Wei Chin and the Northern and Southern Dynasties*. OUP 1967 o.p. The most comprehensive selection in English of poetry from this period.

Fusek, Lois, trans. *Among the Flowers: A Translation of the Tenth-Century Anthology of Ts'u Lyrics, the Hua Chien Chi*. Col. U. Pr. 1982 o.p. "Fusek's rendition captures elegantly the flavors of both the folk and literary lyrics, written in one of the most confusing periods of Chinese history" (*World Literature Today*).

Graham, A. C., trans. *Poems of the Late T'ang*. Viking Penguin 1977 $6.95. ISBN 0-14-044157-3. "Recommended for undergraduate students of poetry, comparative literature and Far Eastern Studies" (*Choice*).

Kao, Karl, S., ed. *Classical Chinese Tales of the Supernatural and the Fantastic: Selections from the Third to the Tenth Century*. Ind. U. Pr. $27.50. ISBN 0-253-31375-9. Quality of translations varies but a generally "handy collection of representative stories" (*CLEAR*).

Knechtges, David R., ed. and trans. *Selection of Refined Literature*. Princeton U. Pr. 1982 o.p. A complete translation with copious annotation of one of the most important anthologies of Chinese poetry. Volumes I and II are completed. More volumes are forthcoming.

Lu, Lisa, trans. *Romance of the Jade Bracelet and Other Chinese Operas*. Chinese Materials Ctr. 1980 o.p. Intended for a general audience. Translations wander rather far from the originals.

Ma, Y. W., and Joseph S. Lau, ed. *Traditional Chinese Stories: Themes and Variations*. Col. U. Pr. 1991 repr. of 1978 ed. $19.95. ISBN 0-88727-071-9. A major contribution to the body of excellent translations of fiction in readily available anthologies . . . These are translations one can read with confidence and a good measure of enjoyment" (*Journal of Asian Studies*).

McNaughton, L. William, ed. *Chinese Literature: An Anthology from the Earliest Times to the Present Day*. C. E. Tuttle 1974 o.p.

Payne, Robert, ed. *The White Pony: An Anthology of Chinese Poetry from the Earliest Times to the Present Day*. NAL-Dutton 1974 o.p. Quite comprehensive; translations are generally felicitous.

Rexroth, Kenneth, trans. *One Hundred Poems from the Chinese*. New Dir. Pr. 1970 repr. of 1954 ed. $7.95. ISBN 0-8112-0180-5. Felicitous renderings of poems by Tu Fu, Mei Yao-ch'en, Ou-yang Hsiu, Su Tung-p'o, and others. Contains brief notes on authors and poems. Intended for the general reader.

Rexroth, Kenneth, and Ling Chung, trans. and eds. *The Orchid Boat: Women Poets of China*. New Dir. Pr. 1982 $7.95. ISBN 0-8112-0821-4

Roberts, Moss, ed. and trans. *Chinese Fairy Tales and Fantasies*. Pantheon 1980 $14.00. ISBN 0-394-73994-9

CHRONOLOGY OF AUTHORS

The names in this chronology use the Wade-Giles spellings. In the profiles that follow, the pinyin spellings are also given, in brackets, after these Wade-Giles spellings.

Book of Songs. Compiled c.600 B.C.
Ch'ü Yüan. 343?–277 B.C.
Yang Hsiung. 53 B.C.–A.D. 18
Chang Heng. 79–139
Ts'ao Chih. 192–232
Juan Chi. 210–263
Hsi K'ang. 223–262
Lu Chi. 261–303
T'ao Ch'ien. 365–427
Hsieh Ling-yün. 385–433
Hsiao Kang. 505–555
Yü Hsin. 513–581
Meng Hao-jan. 689–740
Wang Ch'ang-ling. 698?–756
Li Po. 701–762
Wang Wei. 701–761
Tu Fu. 719–770
Han Yü. 768–824
Po Chü-i. 772–846
Li Ho. 791–817
Li Shang-yin. 813–858
Wei Chuang. 836–910
Han Shan. fl. early 8th century?
Li Yü. 937–978
Mei Yao-ch'en. 1002–1060
Ou-yang Hsiu. 1007–1072
Wang An-shih. 1021–1086
Su Shih. 1037–1101
Li Ch'ing-chao. 1084–c.1151
Yang Wan-li. 1124–1206
Lu Yu. 1125–1210
Fan Ch'eng-ta. 1126–1193
Kuan Han-ch'ing. c.1220–c.1300
Wang Shih-fu. fl. 13th century
Lo Kuan-chung. c.1330–1400
Kao Ch'i. 1336–1374
Shih Nai-an. fl. before 1400
Wu Ch'eng-en. 1500–1582
Wang Shih-chen. 1526–1590
T'ang Hsien-tzu. 1550–1617
Feng Meng-lung. 1574–1646
Li Yü. 1611–1680?
P'u Sung-ling. 1640–1715
Wu Ching-tzu. 1701–1754
Ts'ao Chan. 1715–1763
Shen Fu. 1763–after 1809?
Liu E. 1857–1909

BOOK OF SONGS (SHIH CHING) [SHI JING]. Compiled c.600 B.C.

This earliest collection of poems has also been called *The Confucian Odes* by EZRA POUND (see Vol. 1), because allegedly it was edited by the great sage Confucius (551–479 B.C.) himself. It is said that he chose these 305 poems from a compilation of more than 3,000 to exhibit the best folk songs, court odes, and dynastic hymns from the feudal principalities of northern China from perhaps as early as 1400 B.C. to his own time.

Whether or not Confucius compiled and worked on the musical accompaniments (for these were originally sung or chanted, not spoken), we do know that he valued them highly and that his disciples firmly believed them to have moral and political significance. At least by the time of the Han dynasty (306 B.C.–A.D. 220) there were commentaries attached to each song, explaining the circumstances of its composition and its moral message. For the past 3,000 years, they were memorized by men aspiring to government service as basic guidelines for statesmanlike conduct.

Looked at objectively without the commentaries, many of them seem to be simple songs reflecting the daily agricultural tasks, courtships and marriages, hunts and battles, and joys and sorrows of ordinary people. However, they all do rhyme in a standard dialect, despite purporting to be from various regions, so it seems likely that at some point they were polished and edited by one hand. Some of the court odes are explicitly political in nature and contain within their concluding lines the reasons for the anonymous poet's discontent or criticism.

Like the "Song of Solomon" in the Bible, which are important for the Hebraic tradition, these songs have been important for Chinese literature because of their status as part of the Confucian canon, and later Chinese poetry is full of allusions to them. But later poetry also owes much to their mode of expression. Typically, the shorter airs are structured in stanzas of perhaps four to six lines, consisting of images from the natural world juxtaposed with straightforward descriptions of emotional human situations. Often the stanzas are repeated, with only slight variations. The juxtaposing of natural images with similar or contrasting human situations became an important model for all later lyric poetry, though the rhythmic and repetitive features altered as poetry later came to be spoken rather than sung. Also very influential on later poetry was the *Songs'* preference for suggestion over clear statement. The images are highly elliptical and impressionistic, with the background of the situation and the speaker only vaguely implied.

Despite all of the generations that have come and gone since these songs were sung, many are as fresh and poignant today as they must have been to their first listeners, speaking as they do about universal human themes:

> In the wilds is a dead doe;
> With white rushes we wrap her.
> There was a girl pining for spring;
> A handsome knight seduced her . . .

TRANSLATIONS OF THE BOOK OF SONGS

The Book of Odes. Trans. by Bernard Karlgren. Museum of Far Eastern Antiquities 1950 o.p. The most scholarly, literal, and annotated translation of the *Odes* in English.

The Book of Songs. Trans. by Arthur Waley. Grove Pr. 1960 o.p.

The Classic Odes. Trans. by James Legge. Hong Kong Univ. Pr. *Chinese Classics Ser.* Vol. 4 1961 o.p. An annotated translation incorporating allegorical interpretations from the Confucian commentaries.

Shih Ching: The Classic Anthology Defined by Confucius. Trans. by Ezra Pound. HUP 1954 $7.95. ISBN 0-674-13397-8. Free and imaginative translations by a modern poet, not literally accurate but highly readable as poetry.

BOOKS ABOUT THE BOOK OF SONGS

Dembo, L. S. *The Confucian Odes of Ezra Pound, A Critical Appraisal.* U. CA Pr. 1963 o.p.

Dobson, W. A. *The Language of the Book of Songs.* Bks. Demand repr. of 1968 ed. $87.80. ISBN 0-317-10173-0

McNaughton, William. *The Book of Songs.* Twayne 1971 o.p. An interesting, lively presentation geared for the general reader.

Wang, C. H. *The Bell and the Drum: A Study of Shih Ching as Formulaic Poetry.* Bks. Demand repr. of 1974 ed. $41.30. ISBN 0-8357-7123-7. An important and somewhat controversial work arguing that the *Odes* were derived from oral formulaic poetry.

CHANG HENG [ZHANG HENG]. 79–139

Chang Heng was a brilliant scientist, scholar, and poet of the later Han dynasty. Born in the area now known as Nanyang Prefecture in Honan Province, he traveled north to the secondary capital of Loyang as a youth and studied at the Imperial Academy. His first government position was in his home area, and it was while serving there that he completed his masterpiece, *The Two Metropolises Rhapsody.* This long poem compares the luxury and wasteful extravagance of the major capital, Ch'ang-an, with the moderation and restraint of Loyang, in order to illustrate Confucian moral virtues. Later he also composed a poem entitled "Southern Capital Rhapsody" about his native area, which was, incidentally, the home of the emperor who had founded the Later Han dynasty.

Chang served the court in many scientific capacities involving astronomy, cartography, and mathematics. His brilliance challenged some powerful court eunuchs who plotted to bring about his disgrace. Deliberating on what to do, he composed the long poem *Contemplating the Cosmos,* in which he debates the merits of remaining in a corrupt world or seeking refuge in philosophical retreat. He ultimately resigned his court position, and, after serving in one more post in what is now central Hopei, he returned home and wrote the poetic piece *Rhapsody on Returning to the Fields,* in which he outlines the joys of life in retirement. He seems to have become restless, however, because he took up another post less than a year later but died shortly thereafter. His rhapsodies are included in the great anthology *Selections of Refined Literature*, compiled by Hsiao T'ung (501–531), which served as the preeminent model for all later poetic writing.

POETRY BY CHANG HENG

Two Chinese Poets: Vignettes of Han Life and Thought. Trans. by E. R. Huges. Greenwood 1977 repr. of 1960 ed. $49.75. ISBN 0-8371-9648-5. Contains his rhapsodies on the two capitals.

CH'Ü YÜAN [QU YUAN]. 343?–277? B.C.

The second great collection of Chinese poetry after the BOOK OF SONGS is the anthology known as the *Ch'u Tz'u*, or *Songs of the South.* The work now extant was compiled by Wang I (fl. 2nd century A.D.), but the most important poems are quite early and represent the other great ancient literary tradition that arose in the south central part of China in the Yangtze River Valley. Central to the volume is the long poem *Encountering Sorrow,* attributed to Ch'ü Yüan. Although a rather shadowy figure, he is important as being the first voice to arise in Chinese literature bearing a name, a lineage, and a keen awareness of his place in time and history. He is also the first to appropriate the traditional elements of his native state of Ch'u to express his own lyric vision, in a long poetic narrative that describes in highly allegorical language his downfall at court and subsequent exile.

It is clear that the main inspiration for his poem, which is structured as a fantastic quest for a goddess to be his mate and takes him soaring as far as the Gate of Heaven, is based on the religious poetry sung by shamans in his native area. But, although he may, in fact, have believed in the realms he describes, the primary function of his imagery is metaphorical; in his quest for a lover, he is expressing his desire to be reunited with his sovereign, who, having been misled by the poet's enemies at court, has ceased to trust him.

Though the poem itself is unclear about his end, legend has it that he ultimately wandered through a wild region to the banks of the Mi-lo, where, clasping a stone to his bosom and reciting another poem entitled "Embracing the Sand," he plunged into the river and drowned. His suicide became a favorite theme of later writers, who well understood what it was like to labor under a despotic ruler who could banish or kill according to his whim. He also became the object of a popular cult, and every year on the anniversary of his death the common people threw special rice cakes into the river to propitiate his spirit.

In addition to *Encountering Sorrow*, he is also credited with composing many other poems in the *Songs of the South* anthology, including the "Nine Songs," which are shaman songs of love to various deities of rivers, clouds, and mountains that he supposedly polished and improved during his exile.

It is impossible to know which, if any, of the poems in the collection are actually his and which are those of his admirers and imitators, but, in any case, this southern style of poetry had a significant impact on later Chinese verse. Unlike the down-to-earth poetry of the north, this poetry is full of dreamlike landscapes with lush imagery and fantastic creatures and is couched in highly flowery and symbolic language. As such it formed the main inspiration for the later lavish descriptions of rhapsodic verse, and for lyric poetry with erotic or supernatural themes.

Poetry by Ch'ü Yüan

Ch'u Tz'u: The Songs of the South: An Ancient Chinese Anthology. Trans. by David Hawkes. Viking Penguin 1985 o.p. A complete and faithful translation of all the poems attributed to Ch'ü Yüan, as well as of the other works in the anthology by later writers.

Li Sao and Other Poems of Ch'u Yuan. Foreign Lang. Pr. China 1955 o.p. Translations of poems attributed to Ch'ü Yüan plus a historical sketch of the poet by the well-known scholar Kuo Mo-jo.

The Nine Songs; A Study of Shamanism in Ancient China. Trans. by Arthur Waley. City Lights 1973 o.p. Includes a study of the religious context of the shamanistic songs traditionally believed to have been polished by Ch'ü Yüan during his exile.

Book about Ch'ü Yüan

Schneider, Laurence A. *A Madman of Ch'u: The Chinese Myth of Loyalty and Dissent*. U. CA Pr. 1980 $45.00. ISBN 0-520-03685-9. Study of the traditional biography of Ch'ü Yüan and its importance for the Chinese political and literary tradition.

FAN CH'ENG-TA [FAN CHENG-DA]. 1126–1193

Fan was a native of Soochow, Kiangsu. He served in a number of important government posts, once acting as special envoy on a diplomatic mission to the court of the Tartars, who at that time held the north of China with their court in Yen (Peking). He was impressed by the longing of the people in the north for liberation from their barbarian invaders, and he wrote a number of poems in a patriotic vein.

Fan is one of the so-called Four Masters of Southern Sung *shih* poetry, and is most famous for a cycle of more than 60 "garden and field" verses written after his retirement to a villa by Stone Lake near his native city. This series describes in a realistic and intimate way the changing of the seasons and the activities of the farmers. Fan took his Confucian principles seriously and felt a genuine concern for the social and economic plight of the common people.

POETRY BY FAN CH'ENG-TA

Five Seasons of a Golden Year, A Chinese Pastoral. Trans. by Gerald Bullett. Chinese U. HK 1980 o.p. Includes notes and calligraphic decorations by Tsui Chi. Bullett's translations present difficulties, but this remains the only complete rendering into English of Fan's rural poem cycle.

Stone Lake: The Poetry of Fan Chengda (1126–1193). Trans. by J. D. Schmidt. Cambridge U. Pr. 1992 $49.95. ISBN 0-521-41782-1

WORK BY FAN CH'ENG-TA

On the Road in Twelfth Century China: The Travel Diaries of Fan Chengda (1126–1193). Trans. by James M. Hargett. Coronet Bks. 1989 $39.50. ISBN 3-515-05375-1. "Major contribution to the study of the topic [of Chinese travel literature]" (*CLEAR*).

BOOK ABOUT FAN CH'ENG-TA

Bullett, Gerald. *The Golden Years of Fan Ch'eng-ta.* Cambridge U. Pr. 1946 o.p. Important study of Fan Ch'eng-ta's work.

FENG MENG-LUNG [FENG MENG-LONG]. 1574–1646

Feng was a frustrated scholar who never passed the high-level metropolitan examinations and therefore could never hold more than a magisterial post in a backward place like Shou-ning in Fukien Province. However, what he lacked in examination skill he made up for in savvy of the Soochow book trade. He realized the potential of the vast urban middlebrow market for stories written in the vernacular, and he published three series of stories, mostly based on earlier sources, which were a great commercial success. He also wrote and edited stories in classical language. His work was cut short by the overthrow of the Ming dynasty, which unfortunately cost him his life; however, his impact on the development of Chinese fiction was great.

Feng's vernacular stories cover all phases of Chinese life—from murders and lawsuits to social comedies and family reunions—in rich and realistic detail, with characters of flesh-and-blood vividness. His sympathies are generally with the poor and defenseless, particularly courageous women from humble backgrounds and maligned singing girls from brothels; money is very often the motivating force behind the twist and turns of plot. His classical stories are somewhat more subtle, exploring mental and psychological motivation more than action and retribution.

SHORT STORY COLLECTIONS BY FENG MENG-LUNG

Chinese Love Stories from "Ching-shih." Trans. by Hua-yuan Li Mowry. Shoe String 1983 $29.50. ISBN 0-208-01920-0. Includes selections from his classical language stories plus an informative introduction. Translations do not necessarily capture the full laconic charm of originals but are still highly enjoyable.

The Courtesan's Jewel Box: Chinese Stories of the Xth-XVIIth Centuries. Trans. by Yang Xianyi and Gladys Yang. Cheng & Tsui 1981 $15.95. ISBN 0-917056-65-5. A popular collection of tales.

Glue and Lacquer; Four Cautionary Tales. Trans. by Harold Acton and Lee Yi-hsieh. Golden Cockerel Pr. 1941 o.p. Foreword by Arthur Waley.

Lazy Dragon: Chinese Stories from the Ming Dynasty. Ed. by Geremie Barmé. Trans. by Yang Xianyi and Gladys Yang. Joint Pub. Co. HK 1981 o.p. All but two are included in the *Courtesan's Jewel Box* collection. Converts original romanization to mainland *pinyin* and adds some footnotes.

Love in a Junk and Other Exotic Tales. Trans. by Harold Acton and Lee Yi-hsieh. Ace Bks. 1931 o.p.

The Perfect Lady by Mistake and Other Stories. Trans. by William Dolby. P. Elek 1976 o.p.

Stories from a Ming Collection. Trans. by Cyril Birch. Grove Pr. 1968 o.p. A standard anthology; highly readable.

Book about Feng Meng-lung

Bishop, John Lyman. *The Colloquial Short Story in China: A Study of the San-yen Collection.* HUP 1956 o.p. A pioneering work.

HAN SHAN. fl. early 8th century?

Han Shan, or "Cold Mountain," was a place and also the sobriquet of a recluse who found refuge within its lofty precincts. But little is actually known about the man to whom the Han Shan collection of poems is attributed, and it appears likely from internal textual evidence that the 300 poems do not all date from the same period. Most likely some are later imitations inspired by Han Shan's style and themes.

Possibly, the historical Han Shan lived in the seventh century and was either a devout layman who made frequent pilgrimages to Buddhist shrines and wilderness areas to meditate or a Buddhist monk. In any case, legends about him abound, and eventually he became an icon of Zen myth, a grinning mad monk oblivious to worldly cares, hiking through his mountains in a tattered robe. His poetry seems quite colloquial compared to most classical T'ang poetry; it ridicules the pursuit of wealth and power, and extolls the beauties of bird songs and misty peaks.

The American poet Gary Synder (see Vol. 1) is greatly attracted to this poet's vision of the spiritual joys of solitude, and, in his translations of Han Shan, he incorporates his own experiences in the wilderness of the Sierra Mountains, where he likes to hike and meditate.

Poetry by Han Shan

Cold Mountain: One Hundred Poems by the T'ang Poet Han Shan. Trans. by Burton Watson. Shambala Pubns. 1992 repr. of 1962 ed. $6.00. ISBN 0-87773-668-5. Reliable and readable renderings from a serious scholar of Chinese literature.

Han Shan in English. Trans. by Paul Kahn. White Pine Pr. 1989 o.p.

The Poetry of Han-shan: A Complete, Annotated Translation of Cold Mountain. Trans. by Robert G. Henricks. State U. NY Pr. 1990 $59.50. ISBN 0-88706-977-0

HAN YÜ [HAN YU]. 768–824

In his own day, Han Yü was hailed as a great innovator in both poetry and the prose essay. He advocated a "return to antiquity"; in prose this meant avoiding ornate parallelism and stilted language in favor of earlier, more natural forms of expression, and in poetry it meant an "opposition poetics" that tried to replace the elegance and wit of court poetry with bold simplicity and serious meaning. Like his predecessor Ch'en Tzu-ang (d. 702), who had turned to Han poets for his models, Han Yü looked back to the days when literature had embodied a forceful moral message; and in a cosmopolitan age when Confucian scholars and officials felt no particular contradiction in practicing Buddhism and Taoism, he was unusual in insisting that Confucian values alone should prevail.

In fact, one of Han Yü's most famous essays, "Memorial on the Bone of the Buddha," took the emperor to task for a great ceremonial event he was planning on the occasion of a religious relic—a bone of the Buddha—being brought to the Imperial Palace. Not mincing words, he reminded the emperor that Buddha was nothing but a long dead barbarian in India who hadn't known the Chinese language, or anything about Chinese ethical principles, or even how to dress appropriately, so it was unseemly to make such a fuss over his decayed and rotten bone, a "filthy and disgusting relic." For his trouble, in 819 the emperor banished Han Yü to exile in the south, but, after Han wrote an abject apology, he was allowed to return to the capital in the following year.

This was just one of many setbacks in Han's life. He had never had an easy time; orphaned at the age of 2, he had been raised by his elder brother in the capital at Ch'ang-an, but that brother and two others all died young. The psychological scars that these untimely deaths left him with are evident in another of his most beloved essays, "Lament for My Nephew Shih-erh Lang," in which he remarks that of all of two generations of the Han family, after his nephew's passing only he himself remained.

However, despite personal loss and lack of any strong political backing from powerful men at court due to his rather modest background, he eventually held several very high government posts, including vice-presidencies of the Ministries of War and Personnel, and metropolitan governor. His fame as a scholar, writer, and teacher also attracted many promising disciples, whom he launched on prestigious careers.

The posthumous fame of Han Yü's essays has somewhat eclipsed his poetic achievements, but he did much to revitalize the *shih* genre, ridding it of clichés and sentimentality, and infusing both its lyric and narrative modes with new rhythms, vivid and sometimes jarring metaphors, and fragments of colorful stories, myths, and supernatural tales to convey his didactic message.

POETRY BY HAN YÜ

Han Yü's Poetische Werke. Trans. by Erwin Von Zach. HUP 1962 o.p.

BOOKS ABOUT HAN YÜ

Hartman, Charles. *Han Yü and the T'ang Search for Unity.* Princeton U. Pr. 1986 $65.00. ISBN 0-691-06665-5. Am ambitious attempt to place Han Yü within a historical and intellectual context. Highly readable, shedding considerable light on his verse. Includes translations of some major works.

Owen, Stephen. *The Poetry of Meng Chiao and Han Yü.* Bks. Demand repr. of 1975 ed. $79.10. ISBN 0-8357-8273-5. Offers many insights and opinions about Han's verse, but translations sometimes a bit insipid.

HSI K'ANG [XI KANG] (also Chi K'ang). 223–262

Hsi K'ang was one of the famed Seven Sages of the Bamboo Grove, a group of thinkers and poets who in the middle of the third century met in a bamboo grove in Shan-yang, near Hsi's home in the north of present-day Honan, to discuss philosophy, drink wine, and write poetry. These men were all great eccentrics, and many anecdotes regarding their antics have survived, but it is probable that some of their "madness" was feigned, in an effort to avoid involvement in the treacherous politics of their day, in which court intrigues often led to swift reprisal and death.

Hsi K'ang, one of the most talented of the Seven Sages, was a man of haughty character who scorned all social niceties and Confucian formalities but upheld an exacting standard in friendship. Besides being a great rhapsodic *fu* writer and poet, he was also a virtuoso on the lute and a keen practitioner of Taoism. Under a large tree in his garden, he set up a forge, where he experimented with alchemy in the hopes of discovering a Taoist elixir of immortality.

Because of his intellectual gifts, he was several times approached about participating in government, but he always refused. When his friend Shan T'ao "compromised his principles" by accepting a high office and even had the effrontery to suggest that Hsi become his assistant, Hsi wrote a famous open letter breaking off relations with him. This letter ridiculed court practices and the hypocrisy of social life. When the Grand Marshall, Duke of Chin read it (shortly before he overthrew the Wei dynasty to set up his own regime), he detected veiled insults aimed at himself, and shortly afterward arrested Hsi K'ang on a trumped-up charge of committing treason against the state. In prison Hsi wrote some sad farewell verses entitled "Dark Desperation," expressing his longing for life and freedom. Although a petition signed by 3,000 students begging for Hsi's release was presented to the court, it was rejected by the duke, and in 262 he was sentenced to death. On his way to the execution grounds, Hsi played his lute and watched the sun set on the faces of his friends and followers. He was 39 years old.

Poetry by Hsi K'ang

Hsi K'ang and His Poetical Essay on the Lute. Trans. by R. H. van Gulik. Sophia Univ. Pr. 1941 o.p. Still useful.

Nonfiction by Hsi K'ang

Philosophy and Argumentation in Third-century China: The Essays of Hsi K'ang. Trans. by Robert G. Henricks. Princeton U. Pr. 1983 $37.50. ISBN 0-691-05378-2. Includes helpful historical background and annotations.

HSIAO KANG [XIAO GANG] (also Emperor Chien-wen). 505–555

Before Hsiao Kang spent a mere two years on the throne of the Liang dynasty, he was for 20 years as crown prince a very active patron of the arts and commissioned a collection of poems entitled *New Songs from the Jade Terrace*, which included some of his own compositions. The 10 sections of the anthology all contain songs about love, from anonymous Han ballads to the highly sophisticated palace-style poems most favored by the crown prince, but it is this latter type which makes up the bulk of the work. And, of these poems, the crown prince's rank among the best.

The subjects of the palace-style poems are women, generally imperial wives but occasionally entertainers, and the dominant theme is abandonment and sexual frustration. Though tame compared to the love poetry of many other cultures, palace-style poetry represents a radical departure from Confucian norms and was able to flourish during the Six Dynasties largely because of governmental instability and large-scale human migrations south to escape incessant warfare. A renaissance of southern culture resulted, more tolerant of playful eroticism and flowery imagery. Even in this period, there were those who championed poetry of moral seriousness (including Hsiao Kang's older brother Hsiao T'ung, who had the anthology *Selection of Refined Literature* compiled), but they are not reflected in the crown prince's anthology.

Palace-style poetry is short on anatomical details of the pining ladies themselves, instead lavishing description on their makeup, hair ornaments, diaphanous gowns, and bedchamber furniture. It is also heavy with allusions to earlier literature and employs much verbal and semantic parallelism within couplets. Though often stereotyped and precious, this poetry occasionally achieves a high level of wit and erotic *double entendre,* and many of its stylistic features persisted well into the T'ang dynasty in court circles.

POETRY BY HSIAO KANG

Yu-t'ai Hsin Yung (New Songs from the Jade Terrace): Anthology of Early Chinese Love Poetry. Trans. by Anne Birrell. Allen & Unwin 1982 o.p. First full translation of the anthology in English. Reflects an effort to challenge the idea that Chinese literature lacks love poetry

BOOK ABOUT HSIAO KANG

Marney, John. *Liang Chien Wen Ti.* G. K. Hall. *Twayne's World Authors Ser.* 1976 o.p. "Primarily a biography . . . framed by an account of the political history of the fifty-five years of Liang rule . . . Views literary theories and practices . . . in a mainly political perspective" (*Journal of Asian Studies*). Includes translations with annotations of 18 of his poems.

HSIEH LING-YÜN [XIE LING-YUN]. 385–433

Hsieh is traditionally credited with being China's first great nature (i.e., "mountains and waters") poet, because much of his mature verse, written near his family's estate in Shih-ning (near modern Shao-hsing, Chekiang), describes the hilly landscape in loving detail. The scenery, however, is often a means, not an end. Hsieh was a believer in the "instantaneous enlightenment" concept of Buddhism, and sometimes during his poetic walks he seems to achieve a mental state in which the landscape is transformed into a mystic vision. One of his great rhapsodic rhyme-prose pieces, "*Fu* on Dwelling in the Mountains," also makes use of lush natural description to discover moral and philosophical lessons—in the purity of snow, the eternity of the river.

Not all of his life was as tranquil as his nature poetry would suggest. Born into one of the powerful aristocratic families that had moved south during the early years of the fourth century, as a young man he anticipated a prominent position in court life. However, he made a strategic mistake in supporting his friend Prince of Lu-ling for the throne, and, when the prince was subsequently murdered, his own life was in peril. He was exiled to a minor magisterial post in Yung-chia, and after about a year he returned home. His time in Yung-chia was one of intense disappointment and spiritual struggle, but it produced a number of fine poems, with themes and imagery borrowed from CH'Ü YÜAN's poems in the *Songs of the South.* It was also during this time that he first began to show a keen interest in the poetic possibilities of his physical surroundings.

No amount of philosophical reflection could completely mitigate the more reckless side of his personality, however. Despite further chances to hold office, his arrogance toward influential people and his neglect of official duties brought him under increasing censure; this was compounded when he staged a small insurrection in 431, resisting another exile to the south. Finally exiled in Canton, he was again arrested on the grounds of fomenting rebellion, and he was publicly executed in 433.

Books about Hsieh Ling-yün

Frodsham, J. D. *The Murmuring Stream: The Life and Works of Hsieh Ling-yün*. 2 vols. Univ. of Malaya Press 1967 o.p. A useful contribution, with many fine translations.

Westbrook, Francis Abeken. *Landscape Description in the Lyric Poetry and "Fuh on Dwelling in the Mountains"* of Shieh Ling-yunn. Yale U. Pr. 1972 o.p.

JUAN CHI [RUAN JI]. 210–263

Like Hsi K'ang, Juan was one of the famous Seven Sages of the Bamboo Grove and the most talented poet among them. He came by his skill naturally, being the son of one of the "Seven Masters of the Chien-an Era." Unfortunately, he had the tragedy to be born into a turbulent era, and he astutely realized that, if he openly resisted the usurpation of the Wei throne by the Grand Marshall of Chin, his whole family would most likely perish, so he instead chose neither to withdraw nor to participate in government, but instead to "act the clown." His strategy succeeded admirably; he died a natural death. On one occasion, in order to avoid a dangerous marriage alliance, he remained drunk for 60 days.

His biography in the official history of the period says this of him: "He had the secret ambition of reforming the age, but having been born in a dangerous era . . . when there were few men of integrity in public life, he was forced to give up a public career and find solace in drink." For a man of his intellect, and physical and personal charm, this must have been a bitter fate. And, in fact, a deep sadness permeates his famous series of 82 poems, "Songs from the Heart."

These poems, which were to have a profound effect on later writers, also betray in their veiled allegorical satire and carefully orchestrated ambiguity a psychological engagement in political and social life, distinguishing him from his friend Hsi K'ang. The complexity of Juan Chi's poetic message served to deepen and broaden the *shih* genre; it is largely thanks to his inspiration that it became the preeminent poetic form for later generations.

Book about Juan Chi

Holzman, Donald. *Poetry and Politics; The Life and Works of Juan Chi (A.D. 210–263)*. Cambridge U. Pr. 1976 o.p. "Not only a masterly contribution to the study of Chinese poetry, but also an original and intriguing inquiry into the intellectual history of the 3rd century" (*Journal of Asian Studies*).

KAO CH'I [GAO QI]. 1336–1374

Kao is widely considered to be the greatest poet of the early Ming dynasty, which is remarkable, given that he only survived seven years into its rule. His talent was very versatile, encompassing all of the major verse forms. In Soochow, near his native city of Ch'ang-chou, he became the acknowledged leader of a group of highly talented and idealistic young men known as the Ten Friends of the Northern Quarter. These young men were distinguished for their scholarly pursuits and also for their unusually passionate interest in all aspects of the martial arts—not only intellectual aspects like military history and tactics, but also hand-to-hand combat, swordsmanship, and horsemanship. They realized that the hated Mongol regime was nearing collapse and desired to play an active role in future events.

Unfortunately for Kao Ch'i and his associates, the rebel leader Chang Shih-ch'eng, who captured the area surrounding Soochow and held sway there for a decade, lost out in 1367 when the Ming forces moved south from their base in Nanking and forced his surrender. Because the Ten Friends had associated with

Chang, and had perhaps, in fact, believed him to be the best hope of China earlier on, they were ever after regarded with suspicion by the Ming regime.

Nevertheless, because of his fame as a man of letters, Kao was called upon to help compile the official history of the fallen Yuan dynasty at the Ming capital in Nanking. Given his ability, all assumed that this first official assignment would launch a prestigious government career. However, when the history was completed and he was summoned by the emperor to serve as an assistant minister, he inexplicably declined the offer and returned to a life of retirement. Perhaps he already felt himself branded as a traitor, and certainly while in Nanking he had had ample opportunity to view the victimization of many others at the hands of this pathologically suspicious emperor.

After returning to Soochow, Kao devoted himself to poetry, writing much of his best work during the next four years. During this time he also became friendly with the new governor of Soochow, and, when he undertook restoration of the prefectural office, Kao wrote a seemingly harmless poem congratulating him. The emperor immediately accused both men of sedition, because formerly Chang Shih-ch'eng had had his chief governmental office on the spot, and therefore, in promoting the restoration, Kao had encouraged the governor to defy the "righteous act of the Ming in destroying the seat of a dangerous rival."

Whether it was actually the poem that sealed Kao's fate or simply that the emperor had been waiting for a pretext to rid himself of a potentially subversive subject, we will probably never know. In any event, the two were publicly executed, and, although the governor was exonerated posthumously a generation later, Kao's name was never cleared. Because he died under a cloud of suspicion, and because the Ming exercised very tight literary censorship, it is a testament to the greatness of his poetry that it has survived at all. Kao's descendants, however, did subject his works to some judicious editing, so that the mysteries surrounding his relations with the Ming regime will probably never be fully known.

BOOK ABOUT KAO CH'I

Mote, Frederick, W. *The Poet Kao Ch'i, 1336–1374.* Princeton U. Pr. 1962 o.p. A meticulously researched and fascinating account of Kao's life and works. Includes fine translations of some of his major works.

KUAN HAN-CH'ING [GUAN HAN-QING]. c.1220–c.1300

Kuan is a founding father of the Yuan drama, or *tsa-chü* form, not only having authored many of the greatest early plays, but also having produced and acted in them. A critic in 1422 praised his works for their lively and natural dialogue, revelation of the many facets of love, and deep understanding of the human heart.

Kuan's knowledge of love was by no means derived vicariously; he boasted of his sexual prowess in a bawdy poem entitled "Not Old—But a Veteran." In a series of clever metaphors derived from slang of his day that termed a rake a "dried pea," he describes the poundings, steamings, stewings, and scorchings he has endured without losing his "hard as brass" constitution.

His libertine morals, and the fact that he was not of the scholar-official class, means that few of the usual biographical sources are available to us for studying his life; much of what we know comes from anecdotal mention in others' writings. All we know from official sources is that he resided south of the Yüan capital of Ta-tu (Peking) and that he was registered on tax roles as a physician.

Whether or not he ever practiced medicine we have no way of knowing. Local legend claims Ch'i-chou (in modern Hopei) as his birthplace, and it seems that his family had been locally prominent there in the days before the successive Tartar and Mongol regimes.

In his own day, Kuan's theatrical genius was already acknowledged: In a 1330 catalog of plays entitled *Ghosts of the Stage*, compiled about 30 years after his death, Kuan is credited with more than 30, and his name is at the top of the list of playwrights of the older generation.

PLAYS BY KUAN HAN-CH'ING

Selected Plays of Guan Hanqing. Trans. by Yang Xianyi and Gladys Yang. Foreign Lang. Pr. HK 1979 o.p.

LI CH'ING-CHAO [LI QING-ZHAO]. 1084–c.1151

There is hardly a Chinese of modest education even today who cannot quote a line or two from one of Li Ch'ing-chao's poems. She is China's most beloved female poet and one of the acknowledged masters of the *tz'u* form. Though only about 50 of her poems remain (and a few of those are of doubtful authenticity), we can see why she has been so greatly admired and why she was a formative influence on later *tz'u* poets, especially HSIN CH'I-CHI. While she perfected a restrained and elegant lyricism, she also undertook daring experiments with rhyme and metrical devices, and wrote thoughtful criticism of her contemporaries' works.

Born into a well-to-do family in Chi-nan (Shantung), Li was brought up in a cultured atmosphere and afforded the luxury of a good education. Her arranged match to a scholar with antiquarian interests proved exceptionally happy, and together the couple compiled a catalog of their considerable collection of *objets d'art*.

Li's blissful existence abruptly ended in 1127 when the Jurchen Tartars overran the north; like many others she and her husband fled south, leaving most of their treasured antiques behind. Illness claimed the life of her husband just two years later, and Li never recovered from the loss. The rest of her life was spent in rather aimless wandering.

Li's extant poems divide rather clearly into two groups: those written during the years of her marriage, when the delicate feelings of a young woman in love predominate, and those of her middle age, when she recalls with poignant intimacy the life she has lost. Some scholars maintain that she married again unhappily late in life, but that remains a matter of controversy. Whether she did or not, it was clearly the past that haunted her melancholy verses.

POETRY BY LI CH'ING-CHAO

The Complete Ci-Poems of Li Qing-zhao: A New English Translation. Trans. by Jiaosheng Wang. U. of Pa. Pr. (Sino-Platonic Papers No. 13) 1989 o.p. "The translations appear to distinguish themselves by emphasizing fidelity rather than creativity" (CLEAR).

Li Ch'ing-chao: Complete Poems. Trans. and edited by Kenneth Rexroth and Ling Chung: New Dir. Pr. 1979 o.p. An attempt to preserve the poetry in English. A good complement to Wang's translation.

BOOK ABOUT LI CH'ING-CHAO

Hu, P'in-ch'ing. *Li Ch'ing-chao*. Twayne *Twayne's World Author Ser.* 1966 o.p.

LI HO [LI HE]. 791–817

Li Ho has gone down in Chinese literary history as the "ghostly genius," and, because the Chinese have always believed that literary style and character are intimately related, the man himself has tended to disappear behind the body of legend that has grown up around him. Only about a generation after the poet's death, LI SHANG-YIN began the myth-making process with his short biographical account, swearing that Li Ho's sister had witnessed a supernatural being dressed in purple and driving a red dragon appear at his deathbed and summon him to Heaven, where the Heavenly Emperor needed him to write verses for his newly constructed White Jade Tower. From stories such as this, we can get some feel for the effects that his poetry produced on imaginative readers.

Li Ho's real story is less fanciful, but no less tragic: He was snatched from life at the tender age of 26, probably from tuberculosis. Though a scion of the T'ang royal family, he was from a minor branch far removed from power and influence, and he grew up in humble circumstances not far from the secondary capital of Loyang. His father had had a modest career in government but died when Li Ho was young, and Li Ho's poems speak frequently of poverty and his anxiety over his widowed mother and younger brother.

Despite these constraints, however, Li Ho fully anticipated a brilliant career. Not only was he extraordinarily gifted, but he also succeeded in winning the patronage of HAN YÜ, an eminent literary man famous for his ability to advance the careers of promising young men.

But fate intervened: Li Ho was denied permission to take the examinations, on the pretext that the first syllable of the word for *metropolitan examination (chin-shih)* had the same sound as the first syllable of his father's name (*Chin-su*). Since it was taboo to speak or write one's father's name, he was declared ineligible. Whether this attack was aimed personally at Li Ho out of simple jealousy, or because he had been too bold in criticizing the government in his satirical ballads, or because some powerful enemy wanted to embarrass Han Yü, is still a matter of controversy. Though Han Yü wrote a forceful essay in Li's defense, the ruling stood, and Li Ho was effectively barred from ever reaching high office.

As the son of a country magistrate who had reached the fifth rank of the bureaucracy, Li Ho was entitled to sit for a selection examination through hereditary privilege. With only that degree, he couldn't expect anything worthy of his talents, but having a mother and brother to consider, he swallowed his pride and took a lowly position in the Court of Imperial Sacrifices as nothing more than a glorified usher.

However, Li Ho's fame as a poet and songwriter gained him many invitations for outings with the aristocracy, and he quickly acquired a taste for high living and expensive women. His poems written in the capital are full of sensuous descriptions of the lifestyles of the rich and the sumptuous chambers of high-class courtesans. His meager income couldn't support such a lifestyle, and after three years, poor and totally discouraged, he resigned his position and returned home. By then he was already suffering from the illness that would eventually take his life, exacerbated no doubt by his deep despair. In one poem he wrote: "I weep in dreams until my hair turns white."

After a short recuperation, Li Ho, like many other young men disappointed in the pursuit of a civil career, decided to try a military route, and he offered his services to General Hsi Shih-mei, who was waging a protracted battle against a rebel army in Shansi. It is not clear how much warfare Li Ho actually witnessed while on the general's staff, but he wrote some very powerful and evocative poems on the terrors, hardships, and loneliness of waging war. Li Ho's military adventure lasted only two years. In 816, weak, emaciated, and plagued by high fevers, he was forced to give up his post and return home, where he died a short time later.

Li Ho has often been called the Chinese BAUDELAIRE, and the comparison is in many ways apt. His poetry has a similar brooding, voluptuousness, and decadent aestheticism, and like Baudelaire, he pioneered a new structuring of verse that relied more on psychological resonances between images than on logical argument. Though he somewhat influenced LI SHANG-YIN's use of symbols, for most of his contemporaries his verse remained a verbally dazzling but disturbing enigma. However, his extraordinary ability to express emotion solely through objective correlative helped to foster the late T'ang and Sung aesthetic ideal of "fusion of emotion and scene." In the twentieth century, his poetry has enjoyed a great resurgence of popularity—in the West and in Japan because of his uncanny affinities with French Symbolist poetry, and in China because he was greatly admired by MAO TSE-TUNG (see also Vol. 3).

POETRY BY LI HO

Goddesses, Ghosts, and Demons; The Collected Poems of Li He (790–816). Trans. by J. D. Frodsham. N. Point Pr. 1983 o.p. A revised version of Frodsham's earlier work geared more to the general reader, with fewer footnotes and a format that separates poems and background notes.

The Poems of Li Ho (791–817). Trans. by J. D. Frodsham. OUP 1970 o.p. Original version of Frodsham's translations of all Li Ho's poems, with extensive annotations, bibliography, and index.

BOOKS ABOUT LI HO

South, Margaret Tudor. *Li Ho: A Scholar-official of the Yüan-ho Period 806–821.* Libraries Board of South Australia 1967 o.p. A study which looks at Li Ho within his social and political context and examines his poetry only for light it sheds on those issues.

Tu, Kuo-ch'ing. *Li Ho.* Twayne 1979 o.p. A general study of Li Ho's life and works with analysis of many of his poems. Introductory in nature, but gives an inkling of Li Ho's extreme moods and sensuality.

LI PO [LI BAI] (also Li Pai). 701–762

For a poet whose name is usually paired with TU FU's, and whose poetry ranks among the best ever written in China, surprisingly little can be definitively stated about Li Po. Early in life he was dubbed the "Banished Immortal" by admirers who argued that his genius was so far above the common herd that surely he was a being from another world exiled for a time on earth. Li Po did everything he could to foster this larger-than-life image, making it hard to separate fact from fiction.

He was probably born in 701 in Central Asia, along the border of what is now Afghanistan and the former Soviet Union, though he spent his boyhood from the age of 5 in southwest China. His family seem to have been traders; they claimed descent from the Li's of Kansu province, which, if true, would make them distant relations of the T'ang royal family.

The T'ang ruling house was of mixed Turkish and Chinese blood, and it is possible that Li Po was not Chinese. Two contemporaries claimed that he could compose in a foreign language, and there are hints in his verse that he was quite familiar with elements of Turkish culture, although that would not have been surprising for someone born in Central Asia in those days regardless of ethnicity. His was a cosmopolitan age, with much activity along the trade routes between China and Persia.

Whatever his origins, Li Po was schooled in Chinese language and culture. Although he became famous for his excessive drinking and un-Confucian behavior, his debauchery did not particularly distinguish him from many of his bona fide Chinese companions, who looked upon drunkenness as a state of sublime receptivity to poetic inspiration. However, it is possible, as Elling Eide has suggested, that a double stigma ("barbarian" and "merchant class") may account for his failure to take the civil service examinations.

Later Chinese scholars claimed that he was too impulsive or lacking in self-discipline to endure the necessary examination preparation, but that contradicts the considerable evidence in his works that he was well read and fond of study. More important, it fails to account for Li Po's own words; he reveals intense disappointment in an allegorical poem entitled "Song of the Heavenly Horse," which seems in many details suspiciously autobiographical:

> The heavenly horse dashed forward.
> He longed for the sovereign's coach.
> With reins let out he could leap and rear
> to tumble the passing clouds,
> But his feet moved in check
> for ten thousand miles,
> And he gazed from afar at the gates
> of the throne.
> He met no horseman like Master Cold Wind
> To employ the scion of vanishing light . . .
> (Trans. by Elling Eide)

It may be that what Li Po lacked was not the appetite for power, but the personality necessary for politics. He was presented to Emperor Hsüan-tsung, who was sufficiently impressed to give him a position in the Hanlin Academy, but he lost it to court intrigues after only a year or two. Then in 755, when the An Lu-shan rebellion rocked the dynasty, he sided with Prince Yung, who was eventually found guilty of treason.

Whatever his personal anguish, Li Po seems to have been completely convincing in the pose of the romantic poet and to have dazzled his contemporaries, who describe his flashing eyes, piercing voice, and poems dashed off at electrifying speed. Tu Fu, for one, held him in considerable awe. Yet there is undoubtedly a complex character behind the flashy façade. Though first struck by the soaring spirit and unbridled imagination of his poems, one eventually discovers that they are actually very intricately patterned, with painstaking attention to rhythm and internal rhyme, and studded with allusions yielding multiple levels of meaning. A very high level of artistry masquerades as effortlessness.

Traditionally, scholars have believed that Li died in late 762, since his kinsman wrote in a preface at that time that he was ailing, and there are no notices dated after that. Legend, however, has it that he actually died from drowning, falling drunk from a boat in a futile effort to embrace a reflection of the moon. Li Po would no doubt prefer the latter story, and it seems an apt metaphor for the life of a man whose reach always seemed to exceed his grasp.

POETRY BY LI PO

Banished Immortal: Poems of Li T'ai-po. Trans. by Sam Hamill. White Pine Pr. 1987 $7.50. ISBN 0-934834-17-2

Bright Moon, Perching Bird: Poems. Wesleyan Univ. Pr. 1987 $30.00. ISBN 0-8195-2143-4. Includes poems by both Li Po and Tu Fu.

I Didn't Notice the Mountain Growing Dark: Poems of Li Pai and Tu Fu. Trans. by Gary Geddes and George Liang. Cormorant Bks. 1988 o.p.

Li Po and Tu Fu. Trans. by Arthur Cooper. Viking Penguin 1973 $6.95. ISBN 0-14-044272-3. Includes very helpful chapters on the poets' backgrounds, T'ang poetry in general, and the distinguishing features of both men's works.

Li Po. Trans. by Elling O. Eide. Anvil Pr. 1983 o.p. Informed by a high level of scholarship and knowledge of the background of his life and times.

The Poet Li Po. Edited by Chia-yee Yung Teng. UH Pr. 1975 $8.00. ISBN 0-8248-0224-1. Chinese text with notes and translation intended for students of the language.

The Works of Li Po the Chinese Poet. Trans. by Shigeyoshi Obata. Paragon Hse. 1966 repr. of 1922 ed. o.p.

Book about Li Po

Waley, Arthur. *The Poetry and Career of Li Po.* Unwin Hyman 1951 $19.95. ISBN 0-04-895012-2. Useful information, but seems to reflect the personality of the author more than the quixotic poet.

LI SHANG-YIN. 813–858

Li Shang-yin was born in Huo-chia, Honan, where his father served as magistrate. His family claimed somewhat questionably to be descended from the same Li clan as the T'ang royal family, but, at any rate, they were of modest means and little influence by the time the poet was born.

Though he passed the metropolitan examinations on his second try and married into a rather rich and influential family, Li's public career was undistinguished under military governors in several different parts of China. This was due partly to bad luck and partly to his impolitic outbursts at unfortunate moments. It is said that, when his name appeared on the list of candidates eligible for appointment, someone remarked, "This man is intolerable—remove him!" By this time his satirical poems had already circulated around the capital. He had too strong a sense of justice for the amoral times in which he lived.

Li's contemporaries admired above all his skillful prose, and he spent a great deal of his career ghost-writing for superiors who lacked his gifts. But it is his poetry that has secured his place in Chinese literary history, and we can now see that his rich imagery and sentimental themes had a considerable impact on later writers.

Like Li Ho, he showed a propensity for dense allusion and symbolic expression, with the result that much of his best poetry is characterized by extreme ambiguity. Chinese commentators have always sought to discover allegory—some have interpreted it as veiled political criticism, others as hints to his patron to better employ his talents, and yet others as love poetry written to forbidden women, such as Taoist nuns and palace ladies. Whatever the initial inspirations may have been, when we read them, we enter a world that James Liu describes as "rich in its sensuous allure, intense in its emotional impact, and profound in its intellectual implications."

Book about Li Shang-yin

Liu, James Y. *The Poetry of Li Shang-yin, Ninth Century Baroque Chinese Poet.* U. Ch. Pr. 1969 o.p. An important and highly readable study that provides translations and explications of 100 of his best poems plus historical essays and critical commentary.

LI YÜ [LI YU] (also Li Hou-chu). 937–978

Though Li Yü's *tz'u* poetry has always been loved, the character of the man has been much maligned. As the last ruler of a short-lived dynasty known as the Southern T'ang, he has been accused of "fiddling while Rome burned." He was never temperamentally suited for imperial duties; he much preferred painting, poetry, calligraphy, and the passivity of Buddhist contemplation to empire building and war. But no matter what his inclinations had been, it would probably have made little difference, because the fate of his dynasty was sealed before he ever took the throne. In 975 his capital fell to the relentless army of the Sung, and he was taken as their captive to Pien-ching (modern Kaifeng, Honan).

Many of Li Yü's idle days of imprisonment were spent writing poetry, and, in fact, the tragedy of his situation inspired some of his most delicate and poignant verses. In his maturity, he seems to have transcended the sort of personal grief that had informed verses on the loss of his beautiful wife and young son and to have embraced the larger futility of human endeavor. Li died on his forty-first birthday after drinking a gift of poisoned wine from the Sung emperor.

POETRY BY LI YÜ

Lyric Poets of the Southern T'ang: Feng Yen-su 903–960 and Li Yü 937–978. Trans. by Daniel Bryant. U. of British Columbia Pr. 1982 o.p. The first full and scholarly translation of these two poets. "Displays the translator's love for his subject . . . as well as his penchant for combating erroneous views both ancient and modern" (*Journal of Asian Studies*).

The Lyrics of Li Yu. Trans. by Stephen Shu-ning Liu. Liu 1973 o.p. Includes some analysis and commentary.

The Poems and Lyrics of Last Lord Lee: A Translation. Trans. by Malcolm Koh Ho Ping and Chandran Nair. Woodrose Pubns. 1975 o.p.

The Poems of Lee Hou-chu. Trans. by Yih-ling Liu and Shahid Suhrawardy. Orient Longman Ltd. India 1948 o.p.

LI YÜ [LI YU]. 1611–1680?

Li Yü, itinerant playwright, led a life that was every bit as colorful as his plays. Having given up on an official career after failing the provincial examinations, he decided to support his large household of concubines and singing girls by entertaining wealthy merchants and mandarins at their residences with his own dramas, performed by his own troupe. Because his girls entertained both on and off the stage, he was accused by Confucian moralists of ruining the morals of the youth from the rich and noble families he visited.

Like the earlier Yuan dynasty playwright KUAN HAN-CH'ING, Li is especially adept at creating female characters, not surprising given the opportunities his lifestyle afforded. His goal is pure entertainment, and therefore his plots have many twists and turns, and his characters, commoners for the most part, are lively and original. Since he has no message in mind, his song lyrics (usually the dramatic climaxes) lack the philosophical depth of playwrights such as T'ANG HSIEN-TZU, although their polish and craft attests to Li's literary skill.

Li was a connoisseur of painting and music as well as literature, and his Mustard Seed Garden in Nanking was the site of the famous painting manuals of the same name, though he did not personally author them. He did, however, pen a number of short stories, and is the alleged author of a notorious pornographic novel. Li wrote at great length on the drama, earning a place as China's most noteworthy traditional critic of the genre.

Novels by Li Yü

The Carnal Prayer Mat. Trans. by Patrick Hanan. Ballantine 1990 $8.95. ISBN 0-345-36508-9. A new translation by a leading expert on traditional Chinese fiction. Includes introduction and notes.

Jou Pu Tuan, The Prayer Mat of Flesh: A Seventeenth Century Exotic Moral Novel. Trans. by Richard Martin. Grove Pr. 1967 o.p.

Works by Li Yü

Li Yü's Twelve Towers. Retold by Nathan Mao. Chinese U. HK 1975 o.p. Takes liberties with the originals omitting verse, repetitions, etc.), but conveys the essence of Li Yü's art.

Silent Operas: Wusheng Xi. Chinese U. HK 1990 o.p.

Books about Li Yü

Chang, Chun-shu. *Crisis and Transformation in Seventeenth-century China: Society, Culture and Modernity in Li Yu's World.* U. of Mich. Pr. 1992 $55.00. ISBN 0-472-10255-9. A useful new study focusing on the cultural and societal influences on Li Yü's work.

Hanan, Patrick. *The Invention of Li Yu.* HUP 1988 $29.95. ISBN 0-674-46425-7. A serious work by an expert in the Chinese narrative field.

Henry, Eric. *Chinese Amusement: The Lively Plays of Li Yü.* Archon Bks. 1980 $35.00. ISBN 0-208-01837-9. Analyzes Li Yü's style, themes, and social context. Contains plot summaries of all plays discussed.

Mao, Nathan K., and Ts'un-yan Liu. *Li Yü.* Twayne 1977 o.p. A biography of the playwright and author, with excerpts from his works.

LIU E (also Liu T'ieh-yün). 1857–1909

Liu E was born near the end of the last imperial dynasty, and in many ways his life and work exemplify the transition from traditional to modern lifestyle and thought. Unfortunately, his pioneering attitudes not only provided rich satiric material for his novel, *Travels of Lao Ts'an*, but also finally resulted in his banishment and premature death.

Liu E had a difficult time finding himself; born into an official's family in Liuho, Kiangsu, he would normally have been expected to study for the civil service examinations and pursue a career like his father's. However, he was a wild youth who preferred playing with neighborhood ruffians to hours of disciplined study. Though as he got older he began to take an interest in more serious subjects, his choices were still rather unconventional and included military science, economics, mathematics, boxing, and flood control. After his father's death, his older brother urged him to make his own living, and he opened a tobacco shop, a very unusual choice, given the traditional disdain of scholar-official families for trade. Unfortunately, his accountant embezzled money, and this venture became the first of many commercial failures.

A spiritual turning point came for Liu E when he traveled to Yangchow and began studying in an esoteric religious society that incorporated Confucian, Buddhist, and Taoist beliefs. His personality seems to have mellowed considerably as a result of his religious conversion, and, from this time on, we begin to see evidence of his growing sense of social responsibility, that is so evident in his later novels. Following his religious training, Liu E tried Chinese medicine, and, when his medical practice failed, he set up a printing house. After initial success he became involved in a lawsuit that forced him once again into bankruptcy. His first real career success came in 1888 when he was able to convince the director general of the Yellow River Conservancy to use him to cope with the flooding of the river near Cheng-chou in Honan. Liu's plan was the excellent result of many years of his study of the subject, and he used unconventional means to carry it out—he discarded his official's robe and personally directed the workmen on foot. He was recommended to the capital, and eventually he became prefect of flood control in Shantung, where he remained for several years and wrote several treatises on river conservancy and mathematics.

Forced to retire for a period of mourning for his mother, Li turned his interest to foreign affairs, and in 1894 he took an examination to enter the Foreign Office in Peking. Convinced that China could prevail against foreign powers only by strengthening her commerce and railways, he launched a series of business and railroad ventures, all of which brought him only the emnity of the conservative government bureaucracy.

It was in Shanghai, engaged in a series of losing enterprises, that Li E wrote his *Travels of Lao Ts'an*. Though it reveals his sad reflections on the harm that human beings do to one another often out of sheer ignorance, it also reveals his curiosity about all aspects of life. In an introduction to the book published in 1925, the great critic HU SHIH praised Liu's skillful handling of the vernacular and his wonderfully realistic descriptions of scenery and music. In the novel's protagonist we can see a self-portrait of the author, with all his quirky disdain for convention and his indignation over the sufferings of ordinary people. He expounds his syncretic religious views and offers some very original ideas about sex, particularly in a second part of the novel, *A Nun from T'aishan*, which is not included in many published editions, but which has been rendered into English by LIN YÜ-T'ANG as a separate work, *Widow, Nun and Courtesan*.

In 1907, as a result of offending several powerful officials in the course of his commercial activities, Liu was charged as a traitor. Though the first charges were subsequently dropped through the intervention of an imperial prince on behalf of Liu's brother-in-law, he was accused again the following year, and, although his family and several friends tried to warn him, he was arrested in July 1908 and banished to Sinkiang. The arduous journey of more than 3,000 miles proved too much for him, and he died shortly after his arrival in his place of exile.

NOVELS BY LIU E

Travels of Lao Can. Trans. by Yang Xianyi and Gladys Yang. China Bks. 1983 o.p. A serviceable translation.

The Travels of Lao Ts'an. Trans. by Harold Shadick. Greenwood 1986 repr. of 1952 ed. $55.00 ISBN 0-313-25164-9. "More than anyone, Shadick succeeds in capturing in English Liu E's riveting descriptions" (*CLEAR*). Includes only the first twenty chapters, with annotations by Shadick.

Widow, Nun and Courtesan. Trans. by Lin Yu-tang. 1951. Greenwood 1971 repr. of 1951 ed. $38.50. ISBN 0-8371-4716-6. Includes the later chapters not translated by Shadick.

LO KUAN-CHUNG [LUO GUAN-ZHONG] (also Lo Pen). c.1330–1400

Very little is known about Lo the man, and even the extent of his participation in the works bearing his name is in some doubt. All we can say for certain is that he lived during the transition from Yuan to Ming dynasties, hailed from T'ai-yuan (in Shansi Province), and spent at least part of his adult life in Hangchow, where he authored three dramas, one of which survives, and worked on two historical narratives that eventually became the famous fiction masterpieces *Outlaws of the Marsh* and *Romance of the Three Kingdoms*.

Traditionally, Lo is given as the first author of the *Romance of the Three Kingdoms,* whereas he is listed as secondary author after SHIH NAI-AN for *Outlaws of the Marsh.* However, it seems probable that he was actually the primary writer of both, basing the first on the historical work *Account of the Three Kingdoms,* about events following the breakup of the Han empire (168–265), and basing the second on storyteller's material compiled by Shih about a legendary band of outlaws active during the reign of Hui-tsung in the Northern Sung (1101–25). Nevertheless, in deference to tradition, *Outlaws of the Marsh* will be discussed under the entry for Shih Nai-an.

Lo's main contribution to Chinese literature in the *Three Kingdoms* epic is in taking incidents recorded in history and long borrowed by the storytelling tradition, and molding them into a coherent chronological narrative. In the process he attempts to sift out the patently false or exaggerated elements while maintaining liveliness and artistic interest. His goal seems to have been to reach a wide reading audience with his lessons, while not pandering to vulgar cravings for Taoist magicians' stunts or Buddhist popular proofs of retribution in the workings of history. Instead, he invites his readers to reflect on how ambition affects different human characters at a time when the stakes are very high—a dynastic title is the prize.

Lo's is a complex vision of reality; his heroes are not rigidly black or white, and virtue is not necessarily rewarded. But his universe is not without laws, and his portrayal of events illustrates the Confucian belief that one's actions determine the outcome of events.

According to a younger contemporary, Lo was a shy and retiring man. Perhaps his personal modesty is mirrored by the style of his great narrative, which is generally lacking in rhetorical flourish, but yet not highly colloquial—a kind of simplified classical Chinese. With his plain style and sober attention to historical fact, the result could have been a dry chronicle, but such was Lo's passion for his subject and his ability to achieve character that generations of Chinese readers have seen the Three Kingdoms period through his eyes and even today admire his heroes and hate his villains.

PROSE FICTION BY LO KUAN-CHUNG

Romance of the Three Kingdoms. Trans. by C. H. Brewitt-Taylor. C. E. Tuttle 1959 o.p. English now sounds a bit dated, but still lively and readable.

LU CHI [LU JI]. 261–303

Lu Chi was from a powerful family that found itself out of favor when the kingdom of Wu, which it had helped found in 229, fell to the Chin. After remaining in retirement at his family's estate in Hua-t'ing (in modern Kiangsu Province) for more than 10 years, Lu Chi reluctantly returned to government in the service of the new dynasty, but he was eventually tempted to join a plot against the emperor in 301 and barely escaped execution. A year later he again took up arms against the regime in another ill-fated coup attempt—this one led by a prince of the ruling house. Ironically, Lu Chi's troops performed so badly in an attack on the capital that the prince doubted his loyalty and had him executed as a traitor, along with his sons and a brother.

More than 100 of Lu Chi's poems survive, but it is for one piece of rhapsodic *fu* that he is remembered. This long prose-poem presents in 131 parallel couplets a systematic analysis of literature itself—initial motivation, the joys and frustrations of the writing process, the requirements of various genres, and the relation of form to content, common literary shortcomings, the ultimate mystery of inspiration, and, finally, literature's uses. This single work exerted a profound influence on all subsequent Chinese literary criticism.

POETRY BY LU CHI

The Art of Letters. Trans. by E. R. Hughes. Pantheon 1951 o.p. Lu's famous long rhapsodic prose-poem on literature, with notes and background.

The Art of Writing: Lu Chi's Wen Fu. Trans. by Sam Hamill. Milkweed Ed. 1991 $6.95. ISBN 0-915943-62-X. A new translation of the famous prose-poem, intended for a general audience.

LU YU [LU YOU]. 1125–1210

Lu Yu was born just two years before the Jurchen Tartars conquered the north, dividing China in two. Though Lu's family lived in Shan-yin (modern Chekiang) in the Chinese-held south, his father instilled in Lu a strong patriotic fervor, which one can see clearly reflected in much of his *shih* poetry. Like FAN CH'ENG-TA and HSIN CH'I-CHI, he longed to see China reunited under a native ruler.

Lu's career looked promising when he passed the examinations in 1153 and 1154, but, because he incurred the wrath of the prime minister, he was barred from taking office until the man's death six years later. At that time he was recalled to the capital of Lin-an (Hangchow) and given an appointment, and he thereby became a colleague of FAN CH'ENG-TA's. But his outspoken views on military policy made him enemies at court, and he ended up serving in a succession of remote provincial posts in Szechuan, Fukien, Kiangsi, and then finally in his native Chekiang. He retired from government in 1190 to his home in Shan-yin.

Lu's disappointments were not limited to his public life; his first marriage to his cousin T'ang Wan also ended in tragedy when his mother forced him to divorce her. One of his best-known *tz'u* poems is thought to have been written on a holiday outing years after the enforced separation, when he and his former wife (both remarried) accidentally met in a garden. She is supposed to have asked her second husband to take some food and wine to Lu Yu, who responded with the poem. Imagined in this context, the verses are moving, particularly the ending lines: "Though our eternal vows remain/Letters of love can be sent—never, never again!"

Despite life's ups and downs, he lived to a ripe old age, grew philosophical in retirement, and left more than 10,000 poems at his death.

POETRY BY LU YU

Living in the Stream: Poems of Lu Yu. Trans. by David M. Gordon. White Pine 1977 o.p.

The Old Man Who Does as He Pleases: Poems and Prose. Trans. by Burton Watson. Col. U. Pr. 1973 o.p.

The Rapier of Lu, Patriot Poet of China. Trans. by Clara M. Candlin. J. Murray 1946 o.p. A biography of the poet with translations of his work.

South China in the Twelfth Century: A Translation of Lu Yu's Travel Diaries. July 3–December 6, 1170. Trans. by Chun-shu Chang and Joan Smythe. Chinese U. HK 1981 o.p. "Outstanding translation of an important Sung source" (*Journal of Asian Studies*).

Translations from Lu Yu. Trans. by David M. Gordon. Juniper Pr. WI 1978 $5.00. ISBN 1-55780-024-3. Supplement to Gordon's original selection of translations.

The Wild Old Man: Poems of Lu Yu. Trans. by David M. Gordon. N. Point Pr. 1984 o.p.

Books about Lu Yu

Duke, Michael. *Lu You.* Twayne. *Twayne's World Authors Ser.* 1977 o.p. Contains a useful introduction, but characterization of poet is a bit vague.

Watson, Burton. *The Old Man Who Does as He Pleases.* Col. U. Pr. 1973 o.p.

MEI YAO-CH'EN [MEI YAO-CHEN]. 1002–1060

Mei is one of the patriarchs of Sung dynasty poetry and a key figure in the revival of Confucianism after the philosophically eclectic T'ang period. Along with one of his lifelong friends, the great statesman Ou-yang Hsiu, Mei greatly admired the views of Han Yü, who had advocated Confucian values and literature with moral seriousness.

In introducing Mei's writings, Ou-yang Hsiu reflected that the crucible of personal pain and disappointment brought out his best poetry, and it does seem that his life's trials contributed to his humanism and concern with larger social injustices. His first wife died young, leaving an infant son who died soon afterward; a daughter by his second wife died four years later. Mei's poems on these sad events are some of the most emotionally direct and moving verses in traditional Chinese literature.

Mei's public career also stagnated at a rather low level, but he numbered among his friends some of the leading figures of his day, including the great reformer Wang An-shih and renaissance man Su Tung-p'o (Su Shih). He impressed his contemporaries as unusually tolerant and humane; his poetry was his outlet for frustrations, pain, and questioning. Though he liked to describe his poetic style as "even and bland," on reflection one senses the originality and depth that gives it its power.

Book about Mei Yao-ch'en

Chaves, Jonathan. *Mei Yao-ch'en and the Development of Early Sung Poetry.* Col. U. Pr. 1976 o.p. A comprehensive study including biography of Mei, comprehensive summary of Sung dynasty poetry, and analysis of Mei's "even and bland" concept.

MENG HAO-JAN [MENG HAO-RAN]. 689–740

Meng Hao-jan is considered to be one of the preeminent nature poets of the Chinese tradition, combining the gentle pastoralism of T'ao Ch'ien and the more ruggedly sublime aspects of Hsieh Ling-yün. He is also regarded more generally as the great poet of the early years of the T'ang poetic renaissance in the generation before Wang Wei and Li Po, and his favorite poetic medium, the five-character regulated verse, was greatly advanced by his skill in combining emotional depth with natural description.

Meng spent most of his life as a recluse in Hsiang-yang (modern Hupei) at his famous Deer Gate Mountain retreat, coming out only once at the age of 40 to take the civil service examinations, which he failed. Following this disappointment, he took a long trip along the Yangtze River, which provided him with much scenic material, and, in the poems that resulted, we can see his mastery of realistic description.

Poetry by Meng Hao-jan

Poetry of Meng Hao-jan. Trans. by James Whipple Miller. Princeton U. Pr. 1972 o.p. Contains a helpful critical introduction.

BOOKS ABOUT MENG HAO-JAN

Frankel, Hans. (trans.) *Biographies of Meng Hao-jan.* U. CA Pr. 1961 o.p. English renditions of Chinese historical sources on the poet's life.

Kroll, Paul W. *Meng Hao-jan.* G. K. Hall. *Twayne's World Authors Ser.* 1981 o.p. "A careful and disciplined work which contains much careful criticism" (*CLEAR*).

OU-YANG HSIU [OU-YANG XIU]. 1007–1072

Ou-yang Hsiu was a political conservative, often at loggerheads with his reformist friend WANG AN-SHIH, but not so straight-laced in his private life, which was criticized by many more puritanical Neo-Confucians of the Sung period.

Born in southwest China in what is now Szechuan, Ou-yang was one of the first "southerners" to be successful at the northern Sung court; recommended by a senior statesman, he was able to receive an appointment in the Imperial Academy not long after passing the civil service examinations. His career subsequently had a number of ups and downs, but, during eight years in the Censorate, he wielded great power. During the times when his political faction was not in the ascendant, he put his talents to other uses: while banished in I-ling (modern Hupei), he wrote a history of the Five Dynasties, and, while in Ch'u-chou (Anhwei), he constructed his famous Drunkard's Pavilion and wrote some of his most memorable essays and poems.

Ou-yang was skilled in all of the major literary genres practiced in his day. His contemporaries compared his *shih* poems to the great LI PO's, his essays rivalled HAN YÜ's, and he especially excelled in *tz'u* lyrics, with his understanding of music and his romantic private life to draw upon for material. There is some evidence that Ou-yang also enjoyed storytelling; at least we can say that a keen appreciation of popular culture and colloquial expression marks his lyrics.

Ou-yang broke new ground with the work he called his "talks on poetry," which offered impressionistic criticism of poets and poems. These initiated a genre that continued in popularity down to the twentieth century.

POETRY BY OU-YANG HSIU

Love and Time: Poems of Ou-yang Hsiu. Trans. by Jerome P. Seaton. Copper Canyon Pr. 1989 $9.00. ISBN 1-55659-024-5. Includes Ou-yang Hsiu's 10-poem West Lake cycle, a set of verses that helped popularize the *ci* form, which has come to typify the poetry of the Song period.

Song of Liang Chou. Trans. by Kenneth Rexroth. Kelly/Winterton Pr. 1981 o.p.

BOOKS ABOUT OU-YANG HSIU

Egan, Ronald C. *The Literary Works of Ou-yang Hsiu 1007–1072.* Cambridge U. Pr. 1984 $84.95. ISBN 0-521-25888-X. A comprehensive approach to Ou-yang's work in four genres: prose, *shih, fu,* and *tz'u.* Immediately conveys the "power and appeal of Ou-yang Hsiu" (*Journal of Asian Studies*).

Liu, James T. *Ou-yang Hsiu: An Eleventh-century neo-Confucianist.* Stanford U. Pr. 1967 $32.50. ISBN 0-8047-0262-4. "A remarkable contribution to the intellectual and political history of the 11th century, sophisticated, well-written, balanced and stimulating" (*Journal of Asian Studies*).

Locke, M. A. *The Early Life of Ou-yang Hsiu and His Relation to the Rise of the Ku-wen Movement of the Sung Dynasty.* 2 vols. U. of London, School of Oriental and African Studies 1951 o.p.

PO CHÜ-I [BAI JU-YI] (also Pai Chü-i). 772–846

Po Chü-i has been beloved for centuries as the "people's poet" because his words are simple and direct and many of his ballads touch on the plight of common people in an age of warfare and social exploitation. It is said that, whenever he wrote a verse, he would read it aloud for an old granny to listen to, and, if she couldn't understand it, he would revise it until she could. Though no doubt apocryphal, the story illustrates the poet's humility of spirit and desire to speak for those who would otherwise not be heard. Po was not above an occasional boast, however, and noted with obvious pride while traveling that he had seen his lyrics copied on the walls of inns and monasteries and had heard them sung by "higher priced" singing girls in the entertainment quarters.

Perhaps it was that instinct for self-promotion, coupled with the seriousness he attached to poetry, which also made him take a different attitude from his contemporaries toward his literary work. While most literary men wrote mainly for others in their immediate social circle, perhaps with a secret hope that someday their works would be collected and passed down, Po took destiny in hand by editing, classifying, and making copies of his own voluminous works, and carefully depositing them in several different places. Thanks to his prodigious efforts, we still have more than 2,800 of his poems to enjoy today.

Probably the most famous poem of all is his long narrative ballad entitled *Lament Everlasting*, which achieved great popularity even in Japan and Korea and has been translated into English many times. It immortalizes the love affair between the Shining Emperor Hsüan-tsung and his concubine Yang Kuei-fei on the eve of the barbarian general An Lu-shan's rebellion in 756, which left the central plains in ruins and tens of thousands dead. Despite Yang Kuei-fei's involvement in the disaster (she had encouraged the emperor to look upon the general as an adopted son and had succeeded in having her incompetent brother installed as chief minister just as An was gaining power), the poet treats her sympathetically, especially her death by strangulation during the emperor's flight from the capital on the difficult mountain road to Szechuan. Although the poem is not particularly innovative technically or imagistically, it tells a gripping story and for that reason is a great rarity in Chinese poetry, which is dominated so much more by lyricism than by narrative plot. One senses the debt in this and Po's several other long narratives to a popular oral tradition.

Po also tried a conscious innovation with his *New Ballads*, a group of 50 satiric poems sharply critical of government policies and social practices. Unfortunately, these didactic pieces did not enjoy the great success that Po had hoped they would and didn't quite live up to his ambitious goal of "saving the world."

Poetry by Po Chü-i

Bai Juyi, 200 Selected Poems. Trans. by Rewi Alley. New World Press NY 1983 o.p.

Lament Everlasting. Trans. by Howard S. Levy. Oriental Bk. Store 1962 o.p.

Translations from Po Chü-i's Collected Works. Trans. by Howard S. Levy. Oriental Bk. Store 1971 o.p. The first two volumes cover old-style poems and regular poems. The second two volumes, done in collaboration with Henry W. Wells, cover Po's poems of middle age and old age. Aimed at the general reader.

The Yüan Chen Variations. Trans. by F. T. Prince. Sheep Meadow 1981 $7.95. ISBN 0-935296-21-2

Books about Po Chü-i

Feifel, Eugene. *Po Chü-i as a Censor: His Memorials Presented to Emperor Hsien-tsung During the Years 808–810*. Mouton 1961 o.p. A classic study, provides good background on T'ang political and economic issues as they relate to the poet's life and times.

Waley, Arthur. *The Life and Times of Po Chü-i.* Allen & Unwin AT 1949 o.p. A sympathetic biographical account, including excellent translations of many of his poems.

P'U SUNG-LING [PU SONG-LING]. 1640–1715

According to the man who wrote P'u's epitaph, on their first meeting, he was expecting someone as brilliant and charming as his stories, only to find an old man who was very precise in his habits and low in his speech, and who found it rather difficult to say what was on his mind. The writer goes on to say, however, that, after knowing P'u a while, he came to appreciate the breadth and depth of his knowledge and the boldness and daring of his ideas.

In his own preface to his *Strange Tales from Make-do Studio*, a work that is now considered one of the great achievements of Chinese fantastic narrative, P'u writes in moving terms what that narrative represents to him, the only vent for his feelings in a world where he feels totally alone and surrounded by poverty and contempt, where he is "a bird terrified by the winter frosts and nestling against the tree which can afford him no warmth." And yet, in his miserable little room with its smoky lamp and table "cold as a sheet of ice," he spins marvelous tales and through them vents his indignation against the arrogance of the rich, the subjugation of women, and the plight of the poor peasants, from whom he was distinguished by education but not by condition.

Though P'u writes in a classical and highly artificial style, studded with literary allusions, there is something disconcertingly modern about his view of the world, with all its cruelties and carefully chosen and subtly realistic detail, and yet illuminated by an unspoken set of very untraditional principles that shines through the supernatural story lines. In P'u's imaginary world, the ideal woman is not a captive, but a bold and independent actor who, unfettered by convention, is free to love a man as her equal. And, although corruption spreads beyond earthly bounds all the way to the underworld, the God of War himself punishes an evil office seeker after his death, so that justice eventually does prevail.

P'u had a hard life and wrote out of his own experience. As the youngest son, he was left with little when family frictions necessitated the division of property, and, having been unsuccessful in the examinations, he was forced to eke out a living as a tutor to various prominent gentry families who treated him as contemptuously as they did their servants. It was only in later years, after his book of tales was completed, that he finally found a comfortable position in a wealthy family who treated him with respect and friendly intimacy. But by that time he was already well into middle age.

It is a great testament to the human imagination that a man in such a setting could weave such unusual tales. Unlike many Chinese writers of fiction P'u did not borrow heavily from tradition, but instead made fairy tales out of real life, where, as Jaroslav Prusek, the great Czech Sinologist has written, "the frontiers between the world of man and the world of other creatures of nature disappeared, . . . and he hinted at something mysterious behind every apparently natural and simple phenomenon, and . . . he flooded the whole of life with an air of inexplicable but unlimited possibilities."

Short Story Collections by P'u Sung-ling

A Queer Cricket: Based on Selected Tales of Liaozhai by Pu Songling. Adapt. by Miao Jie. Zhaohua Pub Hse. 1985 o.p. Popularized versions of some of his stories.

Selected Tales of Liao Zhai. Panda Bks. 1981 o.p.

Selected Translations from Pu Songling's Strange Stories of Liaozhai. Trans. by Mo Ruoqiang, Mo Zunzhong, and Mo Zunjun. Foreign Lang. Pr. HK 1988 o.p.

Strange Stories from a Chinese Studio. Trans. by Herbert A. Giles. Yale U. Pr. rev. ed. 1974 $9.95. ISBN 0-88710-115-1. The classic English translation of selected tales. Some sexually explicit passages edited.

Strange Tales from Make-do Studio. Trans. by Denis C. Mair and Victor H. Mair. Foreign Lang. Pr. HK 1989 $9.95. ISBN 0-8351-2256-5

SHEN FU. 1763–after 1809?

As Lin Yutang has characterized it, *Six Chapters of a Floating Life* is "one of the tenderest accounts of wedded love . . . ever come across in literature." And it is also one of the most delightful examples of the genre of *hsiao p'in* ("little pieces") that flourished in the last years of the Ming and throughout the Ch'ing dynasties—a partly autobiographical little essay that mixes in observations and comments on the art of living, random sketches of scenic places visited, and impressionistic criticism of poems and paintings.

Of the author Shen Fu we know little except what he tells us in the course of the story of his marriage to his cousin Yün—that he was born in November of 1763 near the Ts'ang-lang Pavilion in Soochow into a scholar's family. And we know from other sources that Shen at one time was secretary to a close friend of the brother-in-law of Kao E, the author or editor of the final chapters of *Story of the Stone*, or *Dream of the Red Chamber* (the earlier chapters were written by Ts'ao Chan).

Although there were originally six chapters in Shen's account, we now have only four. These were discovered in 1877 in a secondhand bookshop and published by Yang Yinch'üan, whose brother-in-law remembered having seen the book in his childhood in Soochow. Three of the four extant chapters deal with Shen's betrothal and wedding, the couple's early married life of enjoyment together, their sorrows after Shen's mother became critical of her daughter-in-law, and of Yün's untimely death. The fourth chapter is about various scenic spots that Shen had visited. Apparently the two lost chapters dealt with a trip Shen made to the island of Formosa (Taiwan) and some general reflections on life.

Ultimately, Shen's biography apart from what is revealed in the *Six Chapters* is unimportant, because we get such an intimate feel for his character from his incidental sketches of daily life. Much less studied and self-conscious than a structured autobiography, the *hsiao p'in* genre gives us more a feeling of having glimpsed into an open window of a neighboring house on various occasions, or having overheard someone absent-mindedly talking to himself or to a close friend.

Nonfiction by Shen Fu

Chapters from a Floating Life; The Autobiography of a Chinese Artist. Trans. by Shirley M. Black. OUP 1960 o.p.

Six Chapters of a Floating Life. Trans. by Lin Yutang. Orien 1974 o.p. Has a delightful introduction.

Six Records of a Floating Life. Trans. by Leonard Pratt and Chiang Su-hui. Viking Penguin 1983 $5.95. ISBN 0-14-04429-7. Contains introduction and notes.

SHIH NAI-AN [SHI NAI-AN]. fl. before 1400

Shih Nai-an has traditionally been credited as the primary author of the great fiction narrative *Outlaws of the Marsh*, or *Water Margin*. However, in recent years further research has made it seem increasingly clear that Lo Kuan-chung probably played as important a role in this novel as he did in *Romance of the Three Kingdoms.*

Nothing is known about Shih, but, judging from his name, which means "Patience Temple" and very much resembles the names of known thirteenth-century Buddhist sutra-reciters in Hangchow, chances are he was a master storyteller a generation or two earlier than Lo who authored the primary source from which Lo compiled the novel. Earlier in this century, there was a flurry of scholarly excitement when the alleged genealogy and epitaph of Shi Nai-an were discovered, but upon closer examination they proved to be forgeries. Perhaps someday we will uncover more evidence to clarify the authorship of the novel, but until then we will have to be content with enjoying its lively episodes and characters without knowing who was finally responsible for them.

What we have is a collection of 108 bandit heroes from various conditions and walks of life, who find themselves united against official persecution in the turbulent years of the reign of Emperor Hui-tsung (1101–25). The depiction of their various backgrounds, personal traits, appearances, and experiences is extremely rich and detailed, offering a fascinating glimpse of life "upstairs and downstairs" on the rigid social ladder of late medieval China. We also have vivid and spine-chilling accounts of their various acts of murder, looting, pillage, and general mayhem, usually victimizing only the powerful and tyrannical, and championing the oppressed.

Unlike the *Romance of the Three Kingdoms*, which unfolds chronologically, *Outlaws of the Marsh* is like a continuing banquet, with ensemble actors leaving and returning and their escapades both past and present being gradually revealed. Despite all of the bravado and camaraderie, the novel ends on a rather sad philosophical note of disillusionment and resignation, with the bandits' dreams for a better world unfulfilled and two of the chief characters renouncing lay life for Buddhist devotions. The most enduring value that the novel teaches is *i-ch'i,* or selfless friendship through thick and thin, and for centuries it has stood as the embodiment of popular ideals of humanity.

Prose Fiction by Shih Nai-an

All Men Are Brothers. Trans. by Pearl S. Buck. J. Day Co. 1968 o.p. The classic English translation, intended for the general reader.

Outlaws of the Marsh. 4 vols. Trans. by Sidney Shapiro. China Bks. 1988 $29.95. ISBN 0-8351-2289-1. Highly readable translation with good introduction and notes.

Water Margin. Trans. by J. H. Jackson. Paragon Hse. 1968 o.p.

Book about Shih Nai-an

Irwin, Richard G. *Evolution of a Chinese Novel: Shui Hu Chuan.* HUP 1953 o.p. Some of the author's conclusions now disputed, but still an important and interesting study.

SU SHIH [SU SHI] (also Su Tung-p'o). 1037–1101

If one were to try to find a genius equivalent to Leonardo da Vinci (see Vol. 3) in China, perhaps the first name that would come to mind would be Su Shih's. He seemed to excel at everything he put his hand to, whether it was cooking or painting or public construction. His political career suffered as the Northern Sung dynasty began to disintegrate on the eve of the Tartar invasion, but throughout it all he maintained an amazing equanimity of spirit, and, in every post he served, he seemed to win the love and respect of the common people whom he governed.

When asked by his son the secret of writing well, Su responded that, when one saw tempting goods displayed in the marketplace, the thing that could be deployed to put them at one's disposal was called *money,* and likewise in a literary composition, the thing that could put all of the classical and historical books at one's disposal was called *ideas.* And if anything could be said to distinguish Su's poetry, especially his *tz'u,* it is probably the richness of his thought, which expands the genre from a trivial one concerned primarily with popular sentiments of love to one capable of expressing all his highest philosophical ideals. But it is more than simply his thought that strikes one. Whether he was writing *shih* or *tz'u,* Su Shih's poetry has an unmistakable stamp of exuberance, spontaneity, and abandon that would somehow be impossible for a lesser soul to imitate.

Unfortunately for Su Shih, his exuberance and candor extended to his political writings and discussions, and, as the reformers led by WANG AN-SHIH gained the upper hand, he suffered for his strongly stated opinions. Before his banishment to the southern edge of the empire, the story goes that one night he paced back and forth in his home, put his hands on his ample belly, and asked the women of his household to guess what was in there. One guessed lots of ink, another beautiful writings, but it was the clever concubine who astutely replied, "Your belly is full of unpopular ideas," to which he laughed and nodded assent. Sadly, her guess proved to be only too correct, and she died not long after, following him into exile in the malarial areas of what is now Kwangtung Province. Su Shih himself died soon after the arduous journey back from exile when he was finally pardoned.

Not only was Su famous for his poetry and essays, but he also invented the new art form of painting ink bamboos, and of pen and ink impressionistic sketches which came to be called scholar painting. To this day in the Palace Museum in Taipei one can see his famous *fu* rhyme-prose "On the Red Cliff," written in his own beautiful brushwork.

POETRY BY SU SHIH

The Prose Poetry of Su Tung-p'o; Being Translations into English of the Fu, with Introductory Essays, Notes and Commentaries. Trans. by Cyril LeGros Clark. Paragon Hse. 1964 ed. o.p. With a foreword by the leading Chinese literary scholar Ch'ien Chung-shu.

Su Tung-p'o: Selections of a Sung Dynasty Poet. Trans. by Burton Watson. Col. U. Pr. 1965 o.p. "Mr. Watson has used his considerable talents and wide experience to translate the poetry of Su Tung-p'o with uncommon success and gratifying results" (*Journal of Asian Studies*).

BOOKS ABOUT SU SHIH

Fuller, Michael Anthony. *The Road to East Slope: The Development of Su Shi's Poetic Voice.* Stanford U. Pr. 1990 $42.50. ISBN 0-8047-1587-4. "The first scholarly, book-length study in English of the pre-eminent literary figure" (*CLEAR*).

Lin Yutang. *The Gay Genius: The Life and Times of Su Tung-p'o.* Greenwood repr. of 1971 ed. $35.00. ISBN 0-8371-4715-8. A fascinating account of Su's life for the general reader.

Yang, Vincent. *Nature and Self: A Study of the Poetry of Su Dongpo, with Comparisons to the Poetry of William Wordsworth.* P. Lang Pubs. 1989 $38.50. ISBN 0-8204-0939-1. "Serves as a general introduction to the poetry and thought of Su Shi" (*CLEAR*).

T'ANG HSIEN-TZU [TANG XIAN-ZU]. 1550–1617

T'ang was born in Lin-ch'uan (Kiangsi Province) and passed the provincial examinations at the early age of 20, but, being an impetuous youth, he refused to curry favor with the powerful minister Chang Chü-cheng and therefore could not make further progress until Chang's death in 1852. The following year T'ang went to Peking, passed the metropolitan examination, and was appointed to an advisory post in the Bureau of Sacrifices in the secondary capital of Nanking. He remained there for some years, until his next impolitic move in 1591 when a comet appeared. The Chinese have traditionally believed that unusual astrological phenomena were signs of Heaven's displeasure, and naturally this sighting caused anxiety at court. T'ang promptly sent a memo to the throne in which he lamented the emperor's "twenty wasted years," and in less than a month, he found himself on his way to the southern limits of the empire, to a lowly post as county police officer. He was recalled in 1593 and made a magistrate of Sui-ch'ang (in the hills of Chekiang), which he found pleasant enough duty. However, his laissez-faire approach to government did not sit well with the inspectors sent periodically to assess his performance, and, feeling the pressure, he resigned in 1598.

Returning to his home area, T'ang found a ramshackle old house and restored it, and then turned his energies to playwriting. Within just a few months, he had finished *Peony Pavilion*, and two other plays followed shortly after in 1600 and 1601. He was also active in the theater about 30 miles from Lin-ch'uan in I-huang. This theater was derived from the Hai-yen school of acting (from Chekiang), and, although by this time it had been somewhat eclipsed by the great popularity of the K'un-ch'ü school of southern drama centered near Soochow, T'ang refused to adapt his popular *Peony Pavilion* to the Wu dialect so that the K'un-ch'ü school could perform it. However, an adapted version was produced without his blessing and was quite a success.

Essential to all three of T'ang's plays is a dream motif, for T'ang had a lifelong belief in the importance of dreams, particularly his own. In the *Peony Pavilion*, the heroine falls asleep in her family's garden in spring and dreams of a handsome young scholar making love to her. When she awakes and realizes that in life she has no lover, she languishes and eventually dies. Her grief-stricken parents bury her in the garden, and three years later the young man of her dream actually comes to the spot (although by now it has become a Buddhist temple) and stays there to convalesce from an illness. Her spirit comes to him at night, and the God of the Underworld, moved by her single-minded devotion to this youth, consents to let her return to life. After several complications, all ends happily as in the final scene hero and heroine enter the Imperial Palace for an audience with the emperor.

Though the plot sounds implausible at best, it is the manner in which it is carried out that makes it probably the highest achievement of the Chinese drama. The dream scene of the heroine in the garden has become one of the great scenes of all time. Few well-brought-up girls in China could hope to choose a man of their dreams, or ever give themselves in passion and abandon, with marriages being political alliances between families; thus, this drama resonated particularly with female audiences, who found the idea of love having an existence of its own, regardless of outward circumstances, extremely moving.

The play had appeal for others as well. A great comic wit, T'ang fills the dialogues of some of the supporting characters with clever puns, innuendoes, and apt allusions, and the extremely beautiful and moving lyrics of the arias are seamlessly blended with the lively colloquial language of the rest of the text.

Play by T'ang Hsien-tzu

The Peony Pavilion. Trans. by Cyril Birch. *Chinese Literature in Translation Ser.* Ind. U. Pr. 1980 $35.00. ISBN 0-253-35723-3. "A translation which captures the scope and spirit of . . . one of China's greatest achievements of dramatic and literary art" (*World Literature Today*).

T'AO CH'IEN [TAO QIAN] (also T'ao Yüan-ming). 365–427

The great poetry critic Chung Jung, who lived a generation after T'ao, ranked him as a poet of the second class; nevertheless, his star has been rising ever since, and he is now considered to be one of the finest poets of the entire Chinese lyric tradition. Mainly this is because, in the age in which T'ao lived, ornate and artificial diction was prized in prose and poetry, but in later years, particularly after the great T'ang poetic renaissance, T'ao's natural style and homely themes had a much broader appeal.

Disgusted by office-seeking while still in his early forties, T'ao determined to lead the life of a gentleman farmer in retirement, and he returned to his home area (near modern Kiukiang, in Kiangsi Province), where he devoted the remainder of his life to books, poetry, wine, and the seasonal rounds of farm chores. It is these simple pursuits that he extolls in his poems, and it is this idyllic lifestyle which has earned the admiration and envy of more worldly men and women, who see T'ao as a man whose purity is untouched by vulgar strivings for wealth and power.

Although it is true that his rustic and gentle imagery at times seems to wrap his life in tranquillity and peace, there is also a darker side to T'ao's life, which, if understood, only serves to enhance our appreciation of his artistic achievement. For T'ao was a complex human being living in very difficult times, and his poetry reflects the many dimensions of his life and his desire to conquer his demons.

For one thing, the life T'ao chose was not an easy one; though he had land, he had little money, and at many times was not even well enough off to hire any farm labor. At one point his house burned down, leaving him destitute, and at another time his crop failed and he faced starvation.

T'ao suffered spiritual deprivations as well, which were perhaps harder for him to come to terms with. In many of his poems, we sense the strong possibility of topical allegory, indicating his continuing engagement with the political events of his time, and we also find frequent references to his age, concerns about passing time, and reflections on wasted lives. Whatever philosophical detachment T'ao did achieve, and some of his poems and essays are eloquent testimony to a deep spiritual understanding, came at a high price. Even in some of his most tranquil poems, certain symbolic images—like Southern Mountain and the chrysanthemum (associated with longevity)—give us a richer and rounder view of the poet and his life when we appreciate their multiple levels of meaning.

Poetry by T'ao Ch'ien

The Poems of T'ao Ch'ien. Trans. by Lily Pao-hu Chang and Marjorie Sinclair. UH Pr. 1953 o.p. Intended for the general reader.

The Poetry of T'ao Ch'ien. Trans. and ed. by James R. Hightower. Clarendon Pr. 1970 o.p. Scholarly translations with extensive background and notes.

T'ao the Hermit: Sixty Poems by T'ao Ch'ien. Trans. by William Acker. Thames & Hudson 1952 o.p.

BOOK ABOUT T'AO CH'IEN

Davis, A. R. *T'ao Yüan-ming: His Works and Their Meaning.* 2 vols. Cambridge U. Pr. 1984 $140.00. ISBN 0-521-25347-0. A scholarly and useful study of T'ao's life and poetry.

TS'AO CHAN [CAO ZHAN] (also Ts'ao Hsüeh-ch'in). 1715–1763

Born into a wealthy clan of bondservants to the Manchu imperial family that for three generations had controlled China's textile monopoly in Nanking, Ts'ao Chan spent his childhood and adolescence in a large extended family surrounded by opulence. When Ts'ao was 13, in 1728, the Yung-cheng emperor, suspicious of the Ts'ao family's possible ties to rival claimants of the throne and dissatisfied with their performance in Nanking, confiscated the family property, forcing the family to move to Peking and spend the rest of their lives in greatly reduced circumstances.

Ts'ao Chan, with editorial assistance from his relatives, comforted himself in his lonely middle years by composing the brilliant long novel known as *The Dream of the Red Chamber* (1792) and also as *The Story of the Stone*, which is both a nostalgic recreation of the golden world of his childhood, and a Buddhist and Taoist warning that worldly achievements and material possessions are vain and unenduring.

The last 40 chapters of the 120-chapter novel were written or edited by a second author, Kao O [Gao E], a Manchu nobleman, who more or less followed Ts'ao's original intentions, probably working from rough drafts of Ts'ao's. However, there is some evidence that Ts'ao originally intended the work to end even more starkly and tragically than it does, but that political prudence made it necessary for Kao O to tone down what might have been perceived as criticism of the family's harsh treatment by the emperor.

NOVELS BY TS'AO CHAN

The Dream of the Red Chamber. 3 vols. Trans. by Yang Xianyi and Gladys Yang. Cheng & Tsui 1986 $18.95. ISBN 9971-985-01-2. Serviceable but bland translation.

The Story of the Stone. 5 vols. Trans. by David Hawkes and John Minford. Viking Penguin. Vol. 1 *The Golden Days.* 1974 $11.95. ISBN 0-14-044293-6. Vol. 2 *The Crab-Flower Club.* 1977 $9.95. ISBN 0-14-044326-6. Vol. 3 *The Warning Voice.* 1981 $11.95. ISBN 0-14-044370-3. Vol. 4 *The Debt of Tears.* 1982 $9.95. ISBN 0-14-044371-1. Vol. 5 *The Dreamer Wakes.* 1986 $9.95. ISBN 0-14-044372-X. A superb complete translation into idiomatic English notable for its virtuosity in capturing the distinctions of tone and nuance, in both prose and verse sections. "One of the great translations of this century. No other single book tells us so much about Chinese civilization" (*Bulletin of the School of Oriental and African Studies*).

BOOKS ABOUT TS'AO CHAN

Knoerle, Jeanne. *The Dream of the Red Chamber: A Critical Study.* Ind. U. Pr. 1973 o.p.

Miller, Lucien. *Masks of Fiction in Dream of the Red Chamber: Myth, Mimesis, and Persona.* U. of Ariz. Pr. 1975 o.p. Could serve well as a general introduction. Author claims his study is "mildly revisionist." Fully annotated.

Plaks, Andrew H. *Archetype and Allegory in The Dream of the Red Chamber.* Bks. Demand repr. of 1976 ed. $72.80. ISBN 0-8357-7893-2. Identifies patterns in the novel which author claims underlie all Chinese literature. Provocative, well annotated, intended for serious students.

TS'AO CHIH [CAO ZHI]. 192–232

Legend has painted Ts'ao Chih as the brooding and gifted royal prince, suspected and mistreated by his relatives. Perhaps for the second half of his life this picture is not too far from the truth. After the last Han emperor abdicated the throne, the way was paved for the oldest son of one of his most famous generals, Ts'ao Ts'ao, to become the first Wei emperor. Since Ts'ao Chih, younger brother to the new emperor, had wanted the crown desperately himself and enjoyed the favor of a faction at court, it was hardly surprising that his brother distrusted him and barred him from holding any important political office.

For his first 20 years, while his father had de facto power over the realm but the Han emperor remained on the throne, Ts'ao had lived a rather carefree life, enjoying the banquets, riding and hunting, and other diversions to which his status entitled him. Some of his poems contain lavish descriptions of these entertainments. But he is better known for his poetry of loss and lament, which for the first time in Chinese *shih* poetry seems to give vent to true self-expression rather than writing through the masks of ballad personae. He is also one of the earliest to use distinctive personal imagery; for example, the tumbleweed seems to be a metaphor for his rootless, wandering existence, occasioned by his continually changed estates in various parts of the empire.

Poetry by Ts'ao Chih

Worlds of Dust and Jade. Ed. and trans. by George W. Kent. Philosophical Lib. 1969 o.p. Contains translations of most of Ts'ao's extant poems, with notes and a useful introductory essay on his life and times.

TU FU [DU FU]. 719–770

As Irving Lo has written of him in *Sunflower Splendor*: "Certainly no Chinese writer has mirrored in his work more completely the world he lives in than Tu Fu. Nor has anyone revealed himself with greater passion and candor, or displayed a greater dedication to his craft, or achieved such consummate mastery of his art." Lo's words echo what the Chinese have felt about this writer for more than 10 centuries, for he is revered as the finest poet China has ever produced.

Tu Fu truly is outstanding for his humility, his passion, his social concern, and his extraordinary experimentations with the *shih* form. Though he never passed the official examinations and held only minor posts, he wrote prolifically of his patriotic concern for the nation's welfare and his own search for the most suitable way to be true to himself and to serve society. He had the misfortune of living just as the T'ang dynasty was reeling under the great challenge of the An Lu-shan Rebellion. As a result, he spent some of his best years away from his beloved capital of Ch'ang-an seeking refuge from the incessant warfare and resulting social dislocations in the north. Two of his most moving ballads in the folk style are narrative accounts, one of meeting soldiers on the road, and the other of meeting an abandoned imperial prince on a crossroads near the capital after the emperor and his entourage have fled to the southwest.

Tu Fu's poetry is complex, polished, and emotionally powerful. One of his poems contains the line "If my words don't startle people, I won't rest even in death."

Poetry by Tu Fu

Facing the Snow: Selected Poems of Tu Fu. Trans. by Sam Hamill. White Pine 1991 $10.00. ISBN 0-934834-24-5

I Didn't Notice the Mountain Growing Dark: Poems of Li Pai and Tu Fu. Trans. by Gary Geddes and George Liang. Cormorant Bks. 1988 o.p.

Li Po and Tu Fu. Trans. by Arthur Cooper. Viking Penguin 1973 $6.95. ISBN 0-14-044272-3. Fine translations and lively essays on the poet's background and the characteristics of T'ang poetry.

A Little Primer of Tu Fu. Trans. by David Hawkes. OUP 1967 o.p. Careful paraphrases, translations, and notes along with original Chinese poems. Intended for students of Chinese classical language and literature. With interpretations by Hawkes.

The Selected Poems of Tu Fu. Trans. by David Hinton. New Dir. Pr. 1989 $19.95. ISBN 0-8112-1099-5. A well-annotated book of poems and history.

Thirty-six Poems. Trans. by Kenneth Rexroth and Brice Marden. Wild Carrot. P. Blum ed. 1987 o.p.

Tu Fu: Chinese Greatest Poet. 2 vols. Trans. by William Hung. Russell 1969 o.p. Poems arranged in chronological order and their historical background explained in detail. Reads like a biography. Volume 2 contains additional notes for the serious scholar.

BOOK ABOUT TU FU

Davis, A. R. *Tu Fu.* G. K. Hall. *Twayne's World Authors Ser.* 1971 o.p.

WANG AN-SHIH [WANG AN-SHI]. 1021–1086

Known as one of the Eight T'ang and Sung Masters of Prose, and also one of the greatest *shih* poets of his time, Wang is nevertheless remembered most for the daring political, military, and economic reforms that he put into practice during the reign of Emperor Shen-Tsung (1067–85). His measures were bitterly opposed by some of the greatest minds of his day, including OU-YANG HSIU and SU TUNG-P'O (SU SHIH), and continue to be a subject of controversy among scholars. Wang himself was sure enough of their success after nine years to retire to his estate and leave the running of government to the hands of another of his political faction. But as soon as the emperor died, Wang's party fell from grace, and all his policies were immediately repudiated. He died one year later, a broken man.

Whatever the merits of his government policies, his literary achievements are not in doubt. He was one of the first to realize the greatness of the T'ang poet TU FU, and much of his own greatest work is inspired by Tu Fu's passionate involvement in life and his unsurpassed poetic craftsmanship.

BOOKS ABOUT WANG AN-SHIH

Meskill, John. *Wang An-shih: Practical Reformer?* Heath 1963 o.p. Focuses mainly on his economic policies.

Williamson, Henry R. *Wang An-shih, Chinese Statesman and Educationalist of the Sung Dynasty.* 2 vols. Hyperion Pr. 1989 repr. of 1935 ed. $70.00. ISBN 0-685-02450-4. Includes translations of many of Wang's essays and a discussion of his political reforms.

WANG CH'ANG-LING [WANG CHANG-LING]. 698?–756

Despite the fact that Wang Ch'ang-ling was one of the most celebrated poets of his age, little is known definitively about his life except that he passed the metropolitan examinations in 727 and that he died during the An Lu-shan Rebellion. He may have hailed from the same Wang clan as the other great poet WANG WEI, since we know he came from the region of the capital. He served in the government at the same time as the poet CHANG CHIU-LING, and when Chang fell, he too was exiled to a minor post in the south.

In an anthology compiled during his lifetime in 752, Wang Ch'ang-ling was ranked higher than both LI PO and TU FU. He was especially admired for seven character old-style *shih* poems and his quatrains (half a regulated verse in length, with the same strict requirements). He was also fond of writing ballads of frontier soldiers, although there is no evidence that he ever actually saw military service or traveled as far as the borders himself.

Book about Wang Ch'ang-ling

Lee, Joseph J. *Wang Ch'ang-ling.* G. K. Hall *Twayne's World Authors Ser.* 1982 o.p. Very useful, but sometimes does not clearly separate author and poetic *persona.*

WANG SHIH-CHEN [WANG SHI-ZHEN]. 1526–1590

Many novels of the Ming dynasty were written anonymously, and *The Golden Lotus* is one of them. It has been attributed to Wang Shih-chen, though some modern scholars believe it was written later, in the closing years of the dynasty. The story of its having been penned by Wang Shih-chen has been around at least since the early Ch'ing dynasty, when it was recorded in various anecdotes that Wang wrote the novel as an act of filial piety to avenge his father's death at the hands of minister Yen Shih-fan. Since Yen was addicted to pornography, Wang supposedly poisoned the lower corners of all the pages so that every time Yen moistened his finger to turn one, he would swallow a bit more. This is almost certainly a vicious slander of Wang, but stories so ingenious die hard.

Pearl Buck called *Golden Lotus* "the greatest novel of physical love which China has produced." The *Saturday Review* said, "This extraordinary book . . . plunges the reader into the midst of Chinese society as it existed during the first quarter of the twelfth century . . . when official corruption was rampant and political chaos imminent. It records the amorous exploits and grisly end of a wealthy merchant . . . and the criminal exploits and ghastly death of Golden Lotus, the merchant's Fifth Lady. . . . It records much besides, with a wealth of detail that makes the pages bustle with life; much that will seem strange to today's readers, and much that will seem strangely familiar to them."

However it may strike the modern reader, *Golden Lotus* was certainly the first work of its kind in China. It departs from the earlier narrative tradition of joining episodic fragments together, instead creating an incredibly detailed and realistic world of its own, with lifelike characters in a bourgeois setting, and it surely treats sex more explicitly than even a good many western erotic novels.

Novels by Wang Shih-chen

The Adventurous History of Hsi-men and His Six Wives. Trans. by B. Miall from the German version of F. Kuhn. Putnam Pub. Group 1947 o.p. Somewhat abridged, including numerous erotic passages, but quite readable.

The Golden Lotus: A Translation of the Chinese Novel, Chin P'ing-mei. 4 vols. Trans. by Clement Egerton. Routledge 1972 o.p. Egerton worked from the Chung-chen edition rather than the earlier and fuller Wan-li edition and has deleted some verse passages; nevertheless, a well translated work done in collaboration with the great modern Chinese writer Lao She.

Book about Wang Shih-chen

Carlitz, Katherine. *The Rhetoric of Chin P'ing-mei.* Ind. U. Pr. 1986 $20.00. ISBN 0-253-35009-3. "First appearance of a full-length monograph in English devoted to this interesting and important late-Ming novel" (*Journal of Asian Studies*).

WANG SHIH-FU [WANG SHI-FU]. fl. 13th century

The life story of this famous Chinese playwright, a native of Peking, is unknown. It is thought that he wrote 14 plays, of which only three have survived. One of these is the famous *Romance of the Western Chamber,* actually a five-play cycle based on the T'ang classical short story by Yüan Chen about an illicit love affair between a young girl from a good family and an aspiring young scholar. The original story ends tragically: After the scholar goes off to the capital to take his examinations, he breaks off their affair, leaving her heartbroken. The drama, however, ends on a more upbeat note.

The play's appeal lies almost entirely in its magical poetry, which creates a highly sensual and evocative atmosphere. To borrow the words of David Hawkes, it has "scenes in which one seems almost to brush the glistening dew and to sense the hushed strangeness of a moonlight night." And with these lyric climaxes are juxtaposed scenes of great comic relief from the girl's quick-witted maid, who acts as go-between.

PLAYS BY WANG SHIH-FU

The Moon and the Zither: The Story of the Western Wing. Ed. and trans. by Stephen H. West and Wilt L. Idema. U. CA Pr. 1990 $34.95. ISBN 0-520-06807-6. Excels in presenting the bawdy element, succeeds less well with the lyrical. Well-researched, with much helpful commentary.

The Romance of the Western Chamber. Trans. by S. I. Hsiung. Col. U. Pr. 1968 o.p. Rather bland translation that carefully downplays the erotic, but captures the more sentimental aspects. Helpful critical introduction by the scholar C. T. Hsia.

The Romance of the Western Chamber. Trans. by T. C. Lai and E. Gamarekian. Heinemann Ed. 1979 o.p.

WANG WEI. 701–761

Wang Wei is an exceptionally visual poet, and in reading his descriptions of the play of light over forest and moss, or the reflection of bamboos in a meandering stream, we can easily accept that in his lifetime he was known as much for his paintings as for his verse. In fact, there is some evidence to suggest that he was the first to paint landscapes on long horizontal scrolls, an innovation that brought much greater scope and complexity to Chinese painting. Originally written to accompany such a scroll of unfolding landscapes along the river is a series of poems, the "Wang River Sequence," in which Wang Wei writes of scenes near his country estate in Lan-t'ien (a day's journey in his time from the capital in Ch'ang-an). Unfortunately, though the poems survive, the paintings do not.

Wang Wei had the best pedigree of all of the greatest T'ang poets. His father hailed from the T'ai-yüan (Shensi) Wang clan, one of the most powerful in the capital region, and his mother was a Ts'ui, an equally old and prominent family of accomplished literati. Therefore, it is not surprising that his talents were noticed early and that he passed the highest examinations when he was only 23. His career, however, was not outstanding. He served on and off in a number of modest posts, interspersed with periods of retirement at his beloved estate. What distinguishes Wang is that this failure to rise to high position was probably largely his own choice. While he did not shun the court and politics for the life of a total recluse, he also did not strive. He was a devout Buddhist and seems to have had as strong a pull toward passive contemplation as toward active involvement.

It is his Buddhist inclinations which inspire Wang Wei's poetry; he loves natural imagery as a focus of contemplation, but it is a means for him of reaching integration and harmony with the universe and not merely an end in itself.

POETRY BY WANG WEI

Hiding the Universe. Trans. by Wai-lim Yip. Small Pr. Dist. 1972 o.p.

Laughing Lost in the Mountains: Poems of Wang Wei. Trans. by Tony Barnstone, Willis Barnstone, and Haixin Xu. U. Pr. of New Eng. 1992 $40.00. ISBN 0-87451-563-7. Well-translated book of poems.

Poems of Wang Wei. Trans. by G. W. Robinson. Viking Penguin 1974 $7.95. ISBN 0-14-044296-0. Fine translations and background on Wang's life and times.

The Poetry of Wang Wei: New Translations and Commentary. Trans. and ed. by Pauline Yu. Bks. Demand repr. of 1980 ed. $74.90. ISBN 0-685-44458-9. A scholarly translation, fully annotated. Based on certain precepts of recent phenomenological criticism.

Books about Wang Wei

Wagner, Marsha L. *Wang Wei.* G. K. Hall. *Twayne's World Authors Ser.* 1981 o.p. Can serve as an introduction to his life and works for the general reader.

Walmsley, Lewis C., and Dorothy Walmsley. *Wang Wei, the Painter-Poet.* C. E. Tuttle 1968 o.p. A biographical account intended for the general reader.

WEI CHUANG [WEI ZHUANG]. 836–910

Wei came from an old but impoverished family from the area near the capital of Ch'ang-an. He managed to cultivate his poetic talents only by great personal effort. He lived in turbulent times, witnessing the death throes of the T'ang dynasty, and it was the most dramatic of these episodes that provided the raw material for the great poem that brought him fame.

In 881 a rebel named Huang Ch'ao stormed the capital with 60,000 peasant troups. The emperor fled southwest to Ch'eng-tu (Szechuan), and Huang set himself up as emperor and "Great Exterminator of the T'ang." By the time he was ousted in 883, 80,000 of the capital's inhabitants lay dead, and only 4 government buildings stood, the hundreds of others having been consigned to flames.

Wei, then in his forties, was in the capital for the first horrible year of this carnage. After his escape he traveled to Loyang, where one year later he wrote *Lament of the Lady of Ch'in*, a very long and dramatic political poem, with graphic descriptions of the terrors of Huang and his army. With the writing of this poem, he achieved instant fame.

The T'ang dynasty never fully recovered from this debacle, and Wei lived to see the breakup of the empire and in fact served in a high position in the independent state of Shu set up afterwards in the southwest. It is said that at that time he regretted the gruesome details he had included in *Lament* and refused to let his descendants pass the poem down. For whatever reason, the poem was lost for 1,000 years until a manuscript copy was discovered in the Buddhist caves of Tun-huang in the northwest. After taking up office in the state of Shu, Wei turned his talents to *tz'u* poetry, and more than 50 of his poems can be found in the great anthology *Among the Flowers.*

Poetry by Wei Chuang

The Song-Poetry of Wei Chuang. Trans. by John Timothy Wixted. ASU Ctr. Asian 1979 o.p. (English translations of 48 *tz'u* poems.) Useful introduction.

Book about Wei Chuang

Yates, Robin D. S. *Washing Silk: The Life and Selected Poetry of Wei Chuang.* HUP 1988 $23.00. ISBN 0-674-94775-4. "A modern methodologically informed . . . mutual illumination of history and poetry" (*CLEAR*).

WU CH'ENG-EN [WU CHENG-EN]. 1500–1582

Wu is the reputed author of the great comic-picaresque novel *Journey to the West*, or *Monkey*, as Arthur Waley entitled his translation, which has often been compared for its content and its influence on tradition with *Don Quixote* in European literature. Wu was a native of Huai-an (in Kiangsu), and in the local history published there in 1625 the statement is made about his authorship of the work. However, this was unknown by the general reading public for over 300 years, perhaps partly because Wu died without children to perpetuate his claim to fame.

Though the story of the novel is loosely based on the historical pilgrimage of a Chinese Buddhist monk, Hsüan-tsang, to India in the years 629–645 to obtain Buddhist scriptures, in fact the narrative bears little relation to what actually happened. Instead, it is fabricated from the many popular tales told by storytellers, which over the years embellished the factual chronicles left by Hsüan-tsang with many Chinese beliefs about the monsters and demons of the lands he passed through. The novel teems with humor, invention, and memorable characters, and has been a great favorite with Chinese audiences for centuries. Comic book versions of its stories can be found in Chinatowns all over the world.

NOVELS BY WU CH'ENG-EN

The Journey to the West. 4 vols. Trans. by Anthony C. Yu. U. Ch. Pr. 1977–84 $37.50 ea. ISBNs 0-226-97145-7, 0-226-97146-5, 0-226-97147-3, 0-226-97148-1. "Real tour de force . . . Yu succeeds admirably" (*Journal of Asian Studies*).

Monkey. Trans. by Arthur Waley. Allen & Unwin AT 1942 o.p. Translation of about one third of the novel, omitting much of chapters 13–100. Highly readable.

BOOK ABOUT WU CH'ENG-EN

The Hsi-yu chi: A Study of Antecedents to the Sixteenth-century Chinese Novel. Cambridge U. Pr. 1970 o.p. A highly useful scholarly study for those interested in the evolution of Chinese fiction.

WU CHING-TZU [WU JING-ZI]. 1701–1754

Wu Ching-tzu, like TS'AO CHAN, the author of *The Dream of the Red Chamber*, was a man from a family whose fortunes had declined, and he seems to have been temperamentally unsuited for the disciplined life of study necessary for a successful official career, squandering what small amount of money he did inherit. Timothy Wong, in his study of the author, suggests that the novel *The Scholars* is an apology for Wu's own failure; whatever Wu's motivation, he has bequeathed to us a scathing satire of the scrambling for office in a society obsessed with wealth and social status, juxtaposed with the nobility of the eremetic ideal outlined in the first chapter in the character of Wang Mien, a Yüan dynasty recluse.

The plot of the novel is episodic, following the ups and downs of many candidates for examination and office. The humor is biting, the descriptions of the locales of Nanking, Hangchow, Soochow, and other parts of southeastern China are detailed and fascinating, and the language is fresh and colloquial. Wu paints an unforgettable portrait of late imperial life.

NOVEL BY WU CHING-TZU

The Scholars. Trans. by Yang Xianyi and Gladys Yang. Foreign Lang. Pr. HK 1957 o.p. Complete and generally faithful to the original.

Books about Wu Ching-tzu

Ropp, Paul S. *Dissent in Early Modern China: Ju-lin wai-shih and Ch'ing Social Criticism.* U. of Mich. Pr. 1981 $27.50. ISBN 0-472-10006-8. "First historian's book on that famous novel" (*Journal of Asian Studies*). Ambitious thesis.

Wong, Timothy. *Wu Ching-tzu.* Twayne 1978 o.p. Tries to relate Chinese fiction and satire to world literature.

YANG HSIUNG [YANG XIONG]. 53 B.C.–A.D. 18

Yang Hsiung is famed in Chinese intellectual history for his philosophical and historical writings, but he is equally important in literature as one of the most important figures in the development of the *fu,* or rhyme-prose genre, in which he excelled. Yang's star has always been somewhat eclipsed by a slightly earlier master of *fu* named Su-ma Hsiang-ju, whose literary gifts were undeniably great and whose romantic elopement with a young widow has been the stuff of poetry ever since. Yang has also suffered because of a taint on his character from having served Wang Mang, a man who temporarily took the throne away from the Han dynasty, dividing it into two by his short-lived Hsin dynasty (A.D. 8–23).

However, Yang deserves more credit, for both his theoretical contributions and his writings in the genre. His corpus of *fu* writings is quite diverse, with highly descriptive pieces where the key interest is verbal artistry, as well as more rhetorical poems aimed at persuasion or reprimand. All are sensuously intoxicating in their rhythms and language and reveal the author's rich world of fantasy as much as the scenes of Han court life that he chronicles.

Book about Yang Hsiung

Knechtges, David R. *The Han Rhapsody: A Study of the Fu of Yang Hsiung* (53 B.C.–A.D. 18). Cambridge U. Pr. 1976 o.p. "The merit of Knechtges's study consists in having collected, outlined, and illustrated . . . the views sinology has held on the *fu* genre" (*Journal of Asian Studies*).

YANG WAN-LI. 1124–1206

Yang once said that he loved literature the way other men loved beautiful women, and he spent his life pursuing that love, mainly in his prolific writing of poetry. Though he did pass the metropolitan examinations in 1154, his career was more typical than outstanding. His highest post was Director of the Imperial Library, which he achieved in 1189. Like others of his time, he watched the advance of the Jurchen Tartar armies with unease and advocated a stronger defense against them, as did his contemporaries Lu Yu and Fan Ch'eng-ta.

A native of Chi-chou (Kiangsi), Yang titled himself "The Rustic Man from Sincerity Studio," and he studied the works of other great poets of the Kiangsi school early in his writing career. However, in 1162 he burned his early poems, and by 1178 he felt he had achieved a kind of enlightenment and that he no longer needed to emulate poets of the past. From that time on, he advocated individuality as the key to successful poetic style. He is noted for his extensive use of colloquial language, which some have criticized as vulgar, but others find a part of his rough and honest charm.

Poetry by Yang Wan-li

Heaven My Blanket, Earth My Pillow. Trans. by Jonathan Chaves. Weatherhill 1975 o.p. Yang's colloquial style lends itself to Chaves's American English translations. Contains a short biographical introduction.

BOOK ABOUT YANG WAN-LI

Schmidt, J. D. *Yang Wan-li.* G. K. Hall 1976 o.p. "Serves as a good introduction" (*CLEAR*).

YÜ HSIN [YU XIN]. 513–581

Yü was a great master of three of the most important literary genres of his day—lyric *shih* poetry, ornate parallel prose, and *fu* rhyme-prose. One of his long works in the latter style, *The Lament for the South,* is probably the finest piece of its kind ever written.

Yü belonged to one of the northern clans that took refuge in the south during the Six Dynasties period. By the time Yü was born, they had already been in exile for several generations and had begun to think of themselves as southerners. And a fairly stable new dynasty, the Liang, had been established, with Emperor Wu taking the throne in 502.

Things took an abrupt turn for the worse in 547, when the possibly senile 83-year-old emperor entered into an alliance with a non-Chinese general of a neighboring state, the Eastern Wei, in hopes of annexing its territory. However, the Eastern Wei attacked the wayward general and sent him scurrying to the protection of the Liang, where he quickly felt the Liang's resentment of him. In 548 he attacked their city of Chien-k'ang and held for three years, during which time the kingdom of Liang fell gradually into civil war.

Yü Hsin was in Chien-k'ang when it fell, and his long rhapsody is a lament about the eventual fall of the Liang dynasty. It is written in a highly allegorical and elliptical manner, and therefore has always been considered one of the most difficult of Chinese medieval poems. However, it is a powerful and moving epic, unique in the *fu* genre for its content and its scope.

POETRY BY YÜ HSIN

"The Lament for the South": Yü Hsin's "Ai Chiang-nan fu." Trans. by William T. Graham, Jr. Cambridge U. Pr. 1980 $54.95. ISBN 0-521-22713-5. Includes a detailed literary and historical commentary.

MODERN CHINESE LITERATURE

The history of modern literature in China begins with the confrontation between China and the West. Though trade relations had existed between China and other regions for centuries, it was only after the Opium Wars and the resulting Unequal Treaties in the middle of the nineteenth century that Western missionaries and merchants began flocking there in large numbers.

At that time Western works began to be translated into Chinese, and many of the earliest translated works were scientific, social science, and philosophical texts. The outstanding Lin Shu (1882–1924) rendered 171 works by English, French, and American writers into Chinese, some of which he turned into felicitous classical prose. His works were quite popular and may have influenced the writing of some of the social exposé novels, like *The Travels of Lao Ts'an,* which appears around the turn of the twentieth century. However, these novels still owe at least as much to earlier Chinese novels of social criticism, such as *The Scholars,* as they do to Western models.

People concerned with China's destiny, like the thinker LIANG CH'I-CH'AO, were quick to realize the potential of literature to modernise the ideas of broader segments of the population, and he and several other leading scholars of his day began to experiment with a bold new style of language that mixed the colloquial and the classical, the scientific and the poetical. But it was Sun Yat-sen's 1911 revolution against the imperial regime and the 1919 May Fourth Movement that sped the pace of these literary reforms. Around that time a number of new literary magazines were formed that published writing on both literary and national affairs. One of the leading proponents of "a new language suitable for a new literature" was HU SHIH, recently returned from studying in the United States to teach at Peking University.

More fully modern Chinese fiction was born during the 1920s—a hybrid integrating native Chinese lyricism with Western techniques of social and psychological analysis. From the start two general trends were discernible: one leaning toward romantic self-expression and another favoring didactic social commentary. The divergence became more pronounced with the split between the Nationalists and the Communists after 1927. What essentially had been an urban movement, in both its manifestations, was carried by the Communists to the countryside, where rural themes relevant for the broader masses were advocated. One of the most compelling writers on the misery and ignorance of the countryside was the great LU HSÜN.

After the Communists consolidated their power in 1949, much of what was written in mainland China continued to be geared for party purposes, based on the guidelines set out by Chairman MAO TSE-TUNG (see also Vol. 3) in his "Talks at the Yenan Conference on Literature and Art," promulgated in 1942. Craft was sacrificed for heavy-handed message, and only "realistic" fiction with ideologically correct characters and values was tolerated. Strict censorship on literature coming into China also meant that its writers and readers were isolated from literary developments on the other side of the Bamboo Curtain.

Though restrictions on writers have slackened and tightened periodically, it was only with the economic reforms following the end of the Cultural Revolution (1966–76) that considerable literary experimentation began to take place. First came the "Literature of the Wounded," initiated by writers like LIU HSIN-WU, describing the sufferings endured by intellectuals and others. This trend was followed quickly by others.

After the June Fourth Incident in Tiananmen Square in 1989, yet another crackdown on artistic freedom occurred. However, at the time of this writing there is more communication between mainland China and the outside world than there has been at any time since 1949, and more cross-fertilization by the literatures of the West and Japan, as well as by the other Chinese literatures of Taiwan and Hong Kong, all of which have produced a notable impact on the kinds of fiction and poetry being written.

In Taiwan since 1949, the situation has been different because Western literature has been continuously available, and many of Taiwan's leading writers have been graduates of university foreign literature departments. Therefore, following a rather lean decade in the 1950s when the island was struggling to regain its footing under the Nationalists, the 1960s produced a great many literary experiments with Western-style psychological works, culminating in PAI HSIEN-YUNG'S *Wandering in the Garden, Waking from a Dream.*

During the 1970s, as Taiwan became more prosperous and more critical of the dominant political and artistic influence of the United States, a "nativist" movement got underway that aimed to discover Taiwan's own cultural roots and to address a number of problems brought about by the rapid transition to an industrial society. The writers CH'EN YING-CHEN and HUANG CH'UN-MING were part of this movement.

Hong Kong, long dismissed as a mercenary colony full of cultural philistines, has also shown artistic vitality since the mid-1970s, producing some excellent writers of its own, as well as providing a haven for others from mainland China and Taiwan.

History and Criticism

Anderson, Hugh, trans. *A Wind Across the Grass: Modern Chinese Writing with Fourteen Stories*. Red Rooster Pr. 1985 o.p. Fiction by Han Tzu, Tsung P'u, Wang Hsiao-ying, and others.

Benton, Gregor. *Wild Lilies, Poisonous Weeds: Dissident Voices From People's China*. Pluto Pr. UK 1982 o.p. Includes writings by and interviews with Chinese dissidents. Abridged selections suitable for general readers but less adequate for scholars.

Berninghausen, John, and Ted Huters, eds. *Revolutionary Literature in China: An Anthology*. Bks. Demand 1976 $27.30. ISBN 0-317-30479-8. Spans 1914 to 1966. Includes essays, short stories, and a skit.

Chow, Tse-tsung. *May Fourth Movement: Intellectual Revolution in Modern China*. HUP 1963 $35.50. ISBN 0-674-55750-6. A detailed analysis of the main intellectual currents in China from 1915 to 1923. Chapter 1 on prose particularly relevant.

Contemporary Chinese Women Writers: Volume II. China Bks. 1991 $7.95. ISBN 0-8351-2089-9

Duke, Michael S. *Blooming and Contending: Chinese Literature in the Post-Mao Era*. Ind. U. Pr. 1985 $24.95. ISBN 0-253-31202-7. Essays on the political background of Chinese literature between 1978 and 1981. Rather judgmental; not much analysis.

______, ed. *Contemporary Chinese Literature*. M. E. Sharpe 1985 $39.95. ISBN 0-87332-340-8

Faurot, Jeannette L. *Chinese Fiction from Taiwan: Critical Perspectives*. Bks. Demand repr. of 1980 ed. $73.90. ISBN 0-685-23881-4. Fine selection. Equal emphasis given to nativist and establishment writers.

Gibbs, Donald A., and C. C. Rand. *A Bibliography of Studies and Translations of Modern Chinese Literature, 1918–1942*. HUP 1975 $24.00. ISBN 0-674-07111-5. A comprehensive guide to many English translations of modern Chinese works. Includes references to studies of each author. Needs supplementing with works since 1975.

Goldman, Merle. *China's Intellectuals: Advise & Dissent*. HUP 1981 $22.00. ISBN 0-674-11970-3

______. *Literary Dissent in Communist China*. HUP 1967 $25.50. ISBN 0-674-53625-8. An investigation of the conflict between the Communist party and China's writers in the 1940s and 1950s. "It sheds much light on one aspect of the Chinese situation that has been largely neglected" (*New York Times*).

______, ed. *Modern Chinese Literature in the May Fourth Era: A Social Science Research Council Study*. HUP 1977 $14.95. ISBN 0-674-57911-9. Revised conference papers. Of interest to the serious student.

Grieder, Jerome B. *Intellectuals and the State in Modern China: A Narrative History*. Free Pr. 1981 $29.95. ISBN 0-02-912810-2

Gunn, Edward M., ed. *Unwelcome Muse: Chinese Literature in Shanghai and Peking 1937–1945*. Col. U. Pr. 1980 $43.50. ISBN 0-231-04730-4. A pioneering work on an era that Chinese scholars have tended to shun.

Howard, Roger. *Contemporary Chinese Theatre*. Heinemann Ed. 1978 o.p. Collection of articles from magazines. Includes popular forms useful for the general reader but needs updating.

Hsia, Chih-tsing. *A History of Modern Chinese Fiction*. Yale U. Pr. 1961 o.p. The first serious study in English providing copious translations of actual passages from the works.

Hsu, Vivian Ling, ed. *Born of the Same Roots: Stories of Modern Chinese Women*. Ind. U. Pr. 1981 $29.95. ISBN 0-253-19526-8. Nineteen stories from mainland China and Taiwan. Well translated, intrinsically and sociologically interesting.

Huang, Joe C. *Heroes and Villains in Communist China: The Contemporary Chinese Novel as a Reflection of Life*. Universe 1974 $20.00. ISBN 0-87663-710-1. First full-fledged study of the Communist Chinese novel.

Kinkley, Jeffrey C. *After Mao: Chinese Literature and Society, 1979–1981*. HUP 1985 $14.00. ISBN 0-674-00885-5. "Organized around the theme of literature and society" (*Journal of Asian Studies*). An analysis of popular literature.

Lee, Leo Ou-fan. *The Romantic Generation of Modern Chinese Writers*. HUP 1973 o.p. A pioneering work on seven prominent May Fourth writers.

Liang, Ch'i-ch'ao. *Intellectual Trends in the Ch'ing Period*. Trans. by Immanuel C. Y. Hsu and Benjamin I. Schwartz. HUP 1959 o.p. Useful for understanding the Ch'ing from a Chinese point of view; sheds light on the thinking of Liang.

Lin, Julia C. *Modern Chinese Poetry: An Introduction*. U. of Wash. Pr. 1972 $10.00. ISBN 0-295-95281-4. A selection of twentieth-century poets with extensive commentary.

Link, E. Perry, Jr. *Mandarin Ducks and Butterflies: Popular Fiction in Early Twentieth-century Chinese Cities*. U. CA Pr. 1981 $42.50. ISBN 0-520-04111-9. "Much more than a study of . . . popular fiction. . . . Tells us much about China's urban lifestyle" (*Journal of Asian Studies*).

Lu Hsün. *A Brief History of Chinese Fiction*. Hyperion Conn. 1990 repr. of 1959 ed. $42.00. ISBN 0-88355-065-2. Classic work by a leading modern writer.

Mackerras, Colin. *The Chinese Theatre in Modern Times: From 1840 to the Present Day*. U. of Mass. Pr. 1975 $27.50. ISBN 0-87023-196-0

Martin, Helmut, and Jeffrey Kinkley, eds. *Modern Chinese Writers: Self-Portrayals*. M. E. Sharpe 1992 $55.00. ISBN 0-87332-816-7. Translations by several scholars of writers with their reflections on the creative process. Revealing.

McDougall, Bonnie S. *The Introduction of Western Literary Theories into Modern China 1919–1925*. Centre for East Asian Cultural Studies 1971 o.p. Very useful facts, but interpretations should be approached cautiously.

Nieh, Hualing, ed. *Literature of the Hundred Flowers Period*. 2 vols. Col. U. Pr. 1981. Vol. 1 o.p. Vol. 2 $82.50. ISBN 0-231-05076-3. Fills a gap for western readers regarding literature produced from mid-1956 to mid-1957 in context of political criticism.

Palandri, Angela C. Y. Jung, trans. and ed. *Modern Verse From Taiwan*. Bks. Demand reprt of 1972 ed. $58.50. ISBN 0-318-34903-5.

Pickowicz, Paul. *Marxist Literary Thought In China: The Influence of Ch'ü Ch'iu-pai*. U. CA Pr. 1981 $42.50. ISBN 0-520-04030-9. Fascinating work about a seminal figure in Marxist thought in revolutionary China.

Prusek, Jaroslav. *The Lyrical and the Epic: Studies of Modern Chinese Literature*. Ed. by Leo Ou-fan Lee. Ind. U. Pr. 1980 o.p. "By collecting so many important essays, he [Lee] has offered a fitting commemorative to Prusek" (*Journal of Asian Studies*).

Seven Contemporary Chinese Women Writers. Chinese Lit. Pr. 1982 o.p. Stories by Ju Chih-chüan, Huang Tsung-ying, Tsung P'u, Shen Jung, Chang Chieh, Chang K'ang-k'ang, and Wang An-i.

Tsai, Meishi, comp. *Contemporary Chinese Novels and Short Stories, 1949–1974: An Annotated Bibliography*. HUP 1978 $30.00. ISBN 0-674-16681-7. Gives summaries and vital details including references to translations. Includes a Who's Who and an index by subject matter.

Wang, Te-wei. *Fictional Realism in Twentieth-century China: Mao Dun, Lao She, Shen Congwen*. Col. U. Pr. 1992 $45.00. ISBN 0-231-07656-8. Challenges the traditional view of modern Chinese realism.

Wong, Wang-chi. *Politics and Literature in Shanghai: The Chinese League of Left-Wing Writers, 1930–1936*. St. Martin 1991 $59.95. ISBN 0-7190-2924-4. Useful introduction in English to a less-researched subject.

Yeh, Michelle. *Modern Chinese Poetry: Theory and Practice Since 1917*. Yale U. Pr. 1991 $27.50. ISBN 0-300-04787-8. "First full-length critical study devoted to modern Chinese poetry . . . includes many original translations" (*CLEAR*).

Collections

Cheung, Dominic, ed. and trans. *The Isle Full of Noises: Modern Chinese Poetry from Taiwan*. Col. U. Pr. 1986 $38.50. ISBN 0-231-06402-0. Includes poetry selections of varying quality by 32 poets. No interpretation or analysis.

Chi, Pang-yuan, John L. Deeney, Ho Hsin, and Yü Kwang-chung, eds. *An Anthology of Contemporary Chinese Literature*. 2 Vols. U. Of Wash. Pr. 1976 $50.00. ISBN 0-295-95504-X. Translations generally well done and selection quite representative, except for exclusion of two or three writers at odds with Taiwan government.

Duke, Michael S., ed. *World of Modern Chinese Fiction: Short Stories and Novellas from the People's Republic, Taiwan, and Hong Kong*. M. E. Sharpe 1991 $45.00. ISBN 0-87332-757-8. Presents some interesting modernist fiction as well as more traditionally structured stories.

Finkel, Donald, and Carolyn Kizer, trans. *A Splintered Mirror: Chinese Poetry from the Democracy Movement*. N. Point Pr. 1991 $10.95. ISBN 0-86547-449-4. Poems by Pei Tao, To To, Ku Ch'eng, Mang K'e, Yang Lien, and Shu T'ing from the early 1980s. In some cases, translations excel the originals.

Gunn, Edward M., ed. *Twentieth-century Chinese Drama: An Anthology*. Ind. U. Pr. 1983 $35.00. ISBN 0-253-36109-5. "An anthology of translations of the outcome of the modern encounter between this long history [of drama] and the western theatrical tradition" (*Journal of Asian Studies*).

Hsu, Kai-yu, ed. and trans. *Twentieth-century Chinese Poetry: An Anthology*. Cornell Univ. Pr. repr. of 1963 ed. 1970 o.p. Work of more than 50 poets beautifully translated. Editor gives dates of poets and poems. With biographical and critical introductions.

Hung, Eva. *Contemporary Women Writers: Hong Kong and Taiwan*. Small Pr. Dist. 1990 $9.50. ISBN 962-7255-08-4. "The stories all offer some interesting takes on women in contemporary society" (*CLEAR*). Translations range from excellent to average.

Ing, Nancy, ed. and trans. *Summer Glory: A Collection of Contemporary Chinese Poetry*. Chinese Materials Ctr. 1982 o.p. Poems by 15 contemporary poets. High-quality translations.

______, ed. *Winter Plum: Contemporary Chinese Fiction*. Chinese Materials Ctr. 1982 o.p. Twenty-three stories by different authors active in the 1960s and 1970s in Taiwan.

Isaacs, Harold R., ed. *Straw Sandals: Chinese Stories of Social Realism*. MIT Pr. 1974 o.p. Twenty-three short stories, a play, and a poem, assembled in 1934 with the guidance of two outstanding Chinese writers, Lu Hsün and Mao Tun. Well translated, with biographical information on 16 authors.

Jenner, W. J., ed. and trans. (with Gladys Yang). *Modern Chinese Stories*. OUP 1974 o.p.

Lau, Joseph S. M., ed. (with C. T. Hsia and Leo Ou–fan Lee). *Modern Chinese Stories and Novellas 1919–1949*. Col. U. Pr. 1987. $25.00. ISBN 0-231-04203-5. "Most comprehensive . . . anthology of Republican era fiction available in English" (*Journal of Asian Studies*).

Lau, Joseph S. M., and Timothy A. Ross, eds. *Chinese Stories from Taiwan 1960–1970*. Col. U. Pr. 1976 $50.00. ISBN 0-231-04007-5. Useful and generally faithful to originals.

Lau, Joseph S. M. *The Unbroken Chain: An Anthology of Taiwan Fiction Since 1926*. Ind. U. Pr. 1984 $35.00. ISBN 0-253-36162-1. "Represents a major contribution to the ever-growing corpus of modern Chinese literature in translation" (*World Lit. Today*).

Link, E. Perry, Jr., ed. *Roses and Thorns: The Second Blooming of the Hundred Flowers in Chinese Fiction, 1979–80*. U. CA Pr. 1984 $45.00. ISBN 0-520-04979-9. Intended for the general reader. Twelve short stories. Highly recommended.

______. *Stubborn Weeds: Popular and Controversial Chinese Literature after the Cultural Revolution*. Ind. U. Pr. 1983 $30.00. ISBN 0-253-35512-5. "Comprehensive survey . . . during the 'thaw' . . . consists of short stories, drama, poetry, comic dialogues and clappertales" (*Journal of Asian Studies*).

Siu, Helen F., and Zelda Stern, eds. *Mao's Harvest: Voices from China's New Generation*. OUP 1983 $21.95. ISBN 0-19-503499-6. Works published between 1979 and 1981. Expresses the questions and doubts of young people in China.

Soong, Stephen C., ed. *Trees on the Mountain: An Anthology of New Chinese Writing*. U. of Wash. Pr. 1985 $35.00. ISBN 0-295-96224-0. Recent essays, fiction, poetry, and drama from People's Republic, Taiwan, and Hong Kong.

Yee, Lee. *The New Realism: Writings from China after the Cultural Revolution*. Hippocrene Bks. 1983 $14.95. ISBN 0-88254-810-7. Translations of works selected from various literary magazines in China.

CHRONOLOGY OF AUTHORS

Liang Ch'i-ch'ao. 1873–1929
Lu Hsün. 1881–1936
Hu Shih. 1891–1962
Kuo Mo-jo. 1892–1978
Mao Tse-tung. 1893–1976
Lin Yü-t'ang. 1895–1976
Mao Tun. 1896–1981
Lao She. 1899–1966
Ping Hsin. 1902–1968
Shen Ts'ung-wen. 1902–1988
Feng Hsüeh-feng. 1903–1976
Pa Chin. 1904–
Ting Ling. 1904–1986
Ts'ao Yü. 1905–
Chang T'ien-i. 1906–1985
Hsiao Chun. 1907–1988
Ai Ch'ing. 1910–
Ch'ien Chung-shu. 1910–
Hsiao Hung. 1911–1941
Yang Chiang. 1911–
Ho Ch'i-fang. 1912–1977
Chang Ai-ling. 1921–
Ju Chih-chüan. 1925–
Liu Pin-yen. 1925–
Kao Hsiao-sheng. 1928–
Wang Meng. 1934–
Chang Hsien-liang. 1936–
Chang Chieh. 1937–
Ch'en Ying-chen. 1937–
Pai Hsien-yung. 1937–
Ch'en Jo-hsi. 1938–
Tai Hou-ying. 1938–
Huang Ch'un-ming. 1939–
Chiang Tzu-lung. 1941–
Feng Chi-ts'ai. 1942–
Ku Hua. 1942–
Liu Hsin-wu. 1942–
Ch'eng Nai-shan. 1946–
A-ch'eng. 1949–
Pei Tao. 1949–
Chia P'ing-wa. 1952–
Li Ang. 1952–
Ts'an Hsüeh. 1953–
Chang Hsin-hsin. 1954–
Wang An-i. 1954–
Mo Yen. 1956–

A-CH'ENG [A-CHENG] (pseud. of Chung A'ch'eng). 1949–

A-ch'eng's family was part of China's intellectual and political elite during his childhood in Peking in the 1950s. Both his parents were involved in cinema, his father as a prominent theorist and critic, and his mother as a worker in the Peking Film Studio. But, during the Hundred Flowers Campaign when MAO TSE-TUNG (see also Vol. 3) encouraged intellectuals to offer constructive criticism, A-ch'eng's father brought up government interference in filmmaking, and as a result he was declared a rightist and sent to the countryside for "reform through labor." His family thus fell on hard times. A-ch'eng was asked by his mother to sell his father's books, which he did, but not until he had read them. He devoured the Chinese classic novels and European works by TOLSTOY, DOSTOEVSKY, VICTOR HUGO, and BALZAC.

A-ch'eng's father was restored in the 1960s, and his son was thus able to attend an elite high school. When the Cultural Revolution began in 1966, however, the school shut down along with all the others and A-ch'eng was sent first to Shansi in the northwest and later to Inner Mongolia and the Laotian border, where he helped on a rubber plantation. Life there was harsh, but A-ch'eng discovered that he could get food and tobacco from peasants in exchange for his stories, so he adapted the ones he had read as a child to appeal to their tastes.

Later in the 1970s, A-ch'eng was transferred to the cultural bureaucracy in the capital of Yunnan Province, and in 1979, after the Cultural Revolution ended, a contact he had made in his days in the countryside helped him become an editor of a journal back in Peking. His own fiction was first published in 1984 in *Shanghai Literature,* and he became an overnight sensation. He writes of the experience of intellectual youths sent down to the countryside, and, although his works acknowledge the suffering brought about by failed political policies, his attitude is generally cheerful and fatalistic. He quietly reasserts humane values like friendship and filial piety over impersonal Maoist ones. His father's love of the Taoist philosophical classic *Chuangtzu* is evident in his imagery, and there is also a traditional fairy tale magic to his style that many find reminiscent of the classical T'ang dynasty tales of the supernatural. A-ch'eng traveled to the United States during the late 1980s and is now living in California.

SHORT STORY COLLECTION BY A-CH'ENG

Three Kings: Three Stories from Today's China. Trans. by Bonnie S. McDougall. Collins Harvill 1990 o.p. Has a useful introduction by the translator.

AI CH'ING [AI QING] (pseud. of Chiang Hai-ch'eng). 1910–

Many consider Ai Ch'ing China's greatest living poet. He was born in Chekiang Province, the eldest son in a landed gentry family. His early ambition was to become a painter, and in the late 1920s he went to France to study. There he became interested in poetry, particularly that of WALT WHITMAN (see Vol. 1) and the French symbolists.

Ai Ch'ing returned to China in 1932 and was arrested and jailed shortly after by the police in Shanghai on the grounds that he was "harboring dangerous thoughts." During his three years of imprisonment, he wrote his earliest poetry, much of which was poignant and sentimental, sympathizing with those who had been victimized in the old society.

Following the outbreak of the Sino-Japanese War (1937–45) Ai Ch'ing began to write patriotic verse and became one of the favorite poets of the era. Though much of his writing from the war years now seems transparently propagandistic, the better verses have a command of concrete natural imagery that seems inspired by the classical poet TU FU, also well known for his strong social conscience during turbulent times.

Like many other idealistic young writers, Ai Ch'ing traveled to the Communist base in Yenan in northwest China, where he joined the party in 1941 and attempted to change his style to conform to MAO TSE-TUNG's (see also Vol. 3) new guidelines for revolutionary artistic expression. He volunteered for various party projects among the peasants and experimented with numerous forms of folk songs.

However, although he enjoyed great esteem in the early years after the Communist victory in China, by the mid-1950s he was being criticized for his "lack of political enthusiasm" and "unhealthy bourgeois individualism." He was purged in 1957 and remained totally out of the limelight until 1977. Since the Cultural Revolution Ai Ch'ing has reemerged as a leading figure.

POETRY BY AI CH'ING

The Black Eel. Trans. by Yang Xianyi and Robert C. Friend. China Bks. 1982 o.p.

Selected Poems by Ai Qing. Ed. and trans. by Eugene C. Eoyang. Ind. U. Pr. 1983 o.p. More than 50 poems written from 1936 to 1981. "[Ai Qing's] work is emotional, direct and honest . . . His voice is more collective than individualistic . . . despite the personal vision that informs his poems" (*World Lit. Today*).

CHANG AI-LING [ZHANG AI-LING] (also Eileen Chang). 1921–

Chang Ai-ling comes from a distinguished family that counts the famous statesman Li Hung-chang and official Chang P'ei-lun among its members. She grew up in the Shanghai International Settlement, but, although economically and educationally privileged, she suffered greatly under the tyrannical hand of her father.

She attended college in Hong Kong and remained there until the colony was attacked and occupied by the Japanese in 1942, at which point she returned to Shanghai. She soon began contributing essays to English-language publications, and, in fact, most of her short stories and essays date from the years 1942–45. In Chang Ai-ling's writing, one sees not only traditional Chinese influences but also a debt to her favorite British authors, SOMERSET MAUGHAM (see Vol. 1) and ALDOUS HUXLEY (see Vol. 1). Though lacking Huxley's intellectual breadth or daring experimentation, she shares his dislike of the artificiality of the romantic tradition, which she forsakes for an intense sensuality and rationalism. One also sees an interesting blend of the "strangeness" of the T'ang dynasty tale with elements of the Freudian subconscious.

In 1952 Chang Ai-ling left the mainland of China for Hong Kong, where she wrote two novels, *Rice-sprout Song* (1955) and *Naked Earth* (1956). She arrived in the United States in 1955 and since that time has lived a very secluded life in America.

Many critics of Chinese literature believe her to be among the greatest Chinese writers living today. Her work can have a terrifying power, poised delicately on the surface of what we know to be her characters' submerged world of dark and amoral desires. While she sympathizes with their fight against the cruelty of existence, she never relinquishes her acute moral sense, and this lends a tragic perspective to her vision.

NOVELS BY CHANG AI-LING

Naked Earth. Union Pr. 1956 o.p.
The Rice-sprout Song. Scribner 1955 o.p.
The Rouge of the North. Cassell UK 1967 o.p.

CHANG CHIEH [ZHANG JIE]. 1937–

Chang Chieh's parents separated during the anti-Japanese war, and she was raised by her mother, a teacher, in a village of Liaoning Province in northeast China. Though her passions were music and literature, she was persuaded to study the more practical field of economics, and, upon graduating from People's University of Peking, she got a job in an industrial bureau. Later she was transferred to a film studio, which was much more congenial, allowing her the opportunity to write two film scripts.

Chang Chieh did not take up fiction writing seriously until she was 40 years old, after the fall of the "Gang of Four" that signaled the end of the Cultural Revolution. But her success was almost immediate; in 1978 she won a short story prize for "The Music of the Forests," and later she received the prestigious Mao Tun Literary Prize for her novel *Leaden Wings*.

Her personal life was not happy; she divorced her abusive husband, and this was a social stigma in a society that was still quite traditional in its attitudes. Many of her earlier works center on themes of love and the dilemmas faced by women. In her exposure of male chauvinism and discrimination against women, she showed great courage.

As Chang Chieh has aged, she has begun to tackle a broader range of themes, especially the social problems of nepotism, corruption, excessive bureaucracy, and political hypocrisy. But throughout her career she has been an unswerving Socialist, active in political movements, and committed to seeing China modernize along the lines envisioned by its Communist leaders. Despite poor health, she is mentally tough and often disregards her personal welfare in her zeal to attack and solve the social evils that impede China's progress.

NOVELS BY CHANG CHIEH

Heavy Wings. Trans. by Howard Goldblatt. Grove Pr. 1989 $19.95. ISBN 0-8021-1039-8. A glimpse of a country racked by turmoil.

Leaden Wings. Trans. by Gladys Yang. Virago 1987 o.p. Contains an afterword by the Chinese women's studies scholar Delia Davin.

SHORT STORY COLLECTIONS BY CHANG CHIEH

As Long as Nothing Happens, Nothing Will: Stories. Trans. by Gladys Yang, Deborah J. Leonard, and Zhang Andong. Grove Pr. 1991 $18.95. ISBN 0-8021-1144-0. Chang Chieh brings subtlety as well as anger to her satires.

Love Must Not Be Forgotten. China Bks. 1986 $16.95. ISBN 0-8351-1699-9. Six stories, a novella, and an autobiographical sketch.

CHANG HSIEN-LIANG [ZHANG XIAN-LIANG]. 1936–

Chang was born in Nanking and schooled in Peking. He began work as a teacher in the Gansu Provincial Cadre School in the remote northwest right after graduating from high school in 1955.

Like many other prominent intellectuals, he was declared a Rightist in 1957 and sent to a labor camp in Ning-hsia, only to return home in the 1970s still fired with revolutionary ideals. In his short story collection *Mimosa and Other Stories,* he breaks new ground in his realistic depiction of the cold and hunger that existed in labor camps, such as the one he was sent to, yet he never deviates from Marxist orthodoxy, even at times idealizing and sentimentalizing the brutal life of the countryside and its salutory effects on insufficiently revolutionary individuals.

One often senses Chang's debt to TOLSTOY; some have even joked that certain of his passages read like direct translations from the Russian. But he is also capable of shrewd insights, and he showed courage in tackling the subject of male sexuality in *Half of Man Is Woman* at a time when most writers still considered discussion of sex taboo.

SHORT STORY COLLECTION BY CHANG HSIEN-LIANG

Mimosa and Other Stories. Chinese Lit. Pr. 1985 o.p. Three stories by Chang. Engaging and exhibiting a wider emotional range than many modern works.

NOVELS BY CHANG HSIEN-LIANG

Getting Used to Dying: A Novel. Trans. by Martha Avery. HarpC 1991 $19.95. ISBN 0-06-016521-9. A harrowing account of the effects of repressive government.

Half of Man Is Woman. Trans. by Martha Avery. Ballantine 1991 $4.95. ISBN 0-345-36454-6

CHANG HSIN-HSIN [ZHANG XIN-XIN]. 1954–

Chang is a popular contemporary writer and theatrical director. She was born in Beijing in 1954 and had just completed her primary schooling when the Cultural Revolution broke out in 1966. Like many other young people, she was sent out to the countryside to "learn from the peasants," and she did all kinds of work from farm labor to nursing. She is now the director of Peking's Popular Arts Theater, as well as a writer and a world traveler. During the past several years, she has toured both Europe and the United States.

In addition to her fiction, which is not yet available in English translation, she is famous for the semidocumentary, semifictionalized work that she did in collaboration with her husband, San Yeh. Entitled *Chinese Profiles* or *The Dreams of Our Generation*, it is similar in concept to Studs Terkel's *American Dreams, Lost and Found*, but the oral biographies have been perhaps slightly more fictionalized.

Works by Chang Hsin-hsin

Chinese Profiles. Written with San Yeh. China Bks. 1986 $8.95. ISBN 0-8351-1603-4

The Dreams of Our Generation and Selections from Beijing's People. (Coauthored with San Yeh.) Trans. by Edward Gunn, Donna Jung, and Patricia Farr. Cornell East Asia Pgm. 1986 $7.00. ISBN 0-939657-41-4

CHANG T'IEN-I [ZHANG TIAN-YI] (pseud. of Chang Yuan-ting). 1906–1985

Even compared with other writers of the 1930s, an era that was remarkable in China for the literary talent it produced, Chang T'ien-i stands out as one of the finest short story writers. He is unmatched for his comic wit and his penetrating satire. He spares no group or class in his works, seeing the world, as C. T. Hsia aptly notes, as "filled by snobs and malcontents, abject subordinates and ambitious schemers intent on getting ahead." Though an avowed Marxist and member of the League of Left-Wing Writers, he offers a view of life and society hardly reducible to any simple formula.

Chang was born in Nanking into a prominent family originally hailing from Hunan Province; his mother was a noted poet. A nonconformist in practice as well as theory, he declined his family's support and worked as a government clerk, army officer, reporter, and schoolteacher. No doubt his varied experience provided much of the material for his fiction.

Short Story Collections by Chang T'ien-i

The Big Grey Wolf. Foreign Lang. Pr. (China) 1965 o.p. Fine selection of stories on a variety of Marxist themes.

Big Lin and Little Lin. Foreign Lang. Pr. (China) 1958 o.p.

The Magic Gourd. Trans. by Gladys Yang. Foreign Lang. Pr. (China) 1979 o.p.

Stories of Chinese Young Pioneers. Foreign Lang. Pr. (China) 1954 o.p. Stories focusing on the lives of young Communist party members.

CH'EN JO-HSI [CHEN RO-XI] (pseud of Ch'en Hsiu-mei). 1938–

Ch'en, the daughter of a carpenter, was one of the relatively few native Taiwanese at National Taiwan University at a time when the intellectual life of the island was still dominated by mainland Chinese who had fled there with the Nationalists in 1949. She joined a remarkable group of young writers who published in the magazine *Modern Literature*, in an attempt to be noticed in a field where an older generation was firmly entrenched.

After graduation Ch'en went to the United States, first to take part in the Writers Workshop at the University of Iowa and later to study at Mount Holyoke College and Johns Hopkins University. In 1966 she went with her husband, a young Chinese engineer, to the People's Republic, in time to witness the Cultural Revolution that was just getting underway. They spent seven years there before finally emerging in Hong Kong, shaken by their experiences.

Her experience in China gave Ch'en much new material for her fiction; her short stories provide a unique slant on events there, since she was at the same time an outsider but yet Chinese. Ch'en now makes her home in the United States.

SHORT STORY COLLECTION BY CH'EN JO-HSI

The Execution of Mayor Yin and Other Stories from the Great Proletarian Cultural Revolution. Trans. by Nancy Ing and Howard Goldblatt. Ind. U. Pr. 1978 $9.95. ISBN 0-253-20231-0. Eight stories of bitter irony written following the author's experience in China's Cultural Revolution. Introduction by Simon Leys.

BOOK ABOUT CH'EN JO-HSI

Kao, George. *Two Writers and the Cultural Revolution: Lao She and Chen Jo-hsi.* Chinese U. (HK) 1980 o.p.

CH'EN YING-CHEN [CHEN YING-CHEN]. 1937–

Ch'en Ying-chen is a key figure in the so-called Nativist movement in Taiwan, which began when the native Taiwanese began to challenge the cultural and intellectual dominance of the mainland Chinese who had fled to the island with Chiang Kai-shek after the Communist takeover. Ch'en was a native of Taipei County and a graduate of the Tamkang University's foreign languages department, but he could boast more than the right ethnic background; he also served seven years at the hands of the Taiwanese Garrison Command for subversive activities, a fact that elevated him to heroic near-martyr status.

Ch'en's fiction deals thematically with the plight of the economically and politically disadvantaged native Taiwanese, and also with the empty lip service given their problems by a passive and hypocritical intellectual establishment. He particularly enjoys taking potshots at the comfortable middle class, which he feels will use any means to obtain and to hold on to its financial advantages.

Ch'en eschews traditional narrative techniques, preferring successions of disconnected scenes punctuated by monologues and soliloquies, producing a sort of montage effect. Some have claimed that his technique represents a Brechtian alienation. Certainly he demands the active participation of the reader in searching out meaning, unlike many Chinese authors who tend to spell out their message.

SHORT STORY COLLECTION BY CH'EN YING-CHEN

Exiles at Home: Stories by Ch'en Ying-chen. Trans. by Lucien Miller. U. of Mich. Pr. 1986 o.p.

CH'ENG NAI-SHAN [CHENG NAI-SHAN]. 1946–

Ch'eng Nai-shan is the product of a very Westernized family engaged in banking and commerce. Her native city of Shanghai provides not only the setting and the colorful colloquial language for her stories but also many of the attitudes and habits of her characters, whom it would be difficult to imagine living in a less sophisticated part of China.

Her parents left China with Ch'eng for Hong Kong in 1949 but heeded China's call and returned in 1956. Not long afterward they suffered in the anti-Rightist campaign, and then once again during the Cultural Revolution. When their comfortable house in the old French section of the city was confiscated and their prized furniture and records carted off or destroyed, they were forced to adapt to a much reduced lifestyle in a one-room flat.

Ch'eng's first job after majoring in English at the Shanghai Educational Institute was as a teacher in a slum of the city, but she began writing in 1979, the same year she made the decision to convert to Christianity. (Her short story "In My Heart There Is Room for Thee" deals with this decision in a fictionalized manner.) While her spiritual motivations were no doubt her own, her receptivity to Western religion was probably enhanced by her missionary-educated parents, who had taught her English at home when she was a child.

Ch'eng's fiction is full of the Shanghai characters she knows and loves, running the social gamut from urban poor to Westernized entrepreneurs. She demonstrates that in her city, at least, life is not as simple as the Marxists would like to paint it—between the white of pure communism and the black of capitalism, she draws many, many shades of gray.

NOVELS BY CH'ENG NAI-SHAN

The Blue House. China Bks. 1989 $7.95. ISBN 0-8351-2065-1

The Piano Tuner. Trans. by Britten Dean. China Bks. 1989 $16.95. ISBN 0-8351-2142-9. Describes families surviving the chaos and aftermath of revolution.

CHIA P'ING-WA [JIA PING-WA] (also Chia P'ing-ao). 1952–

Chia was a country boy, born and bred in rural Tanfeng County of Shaansi Province. Like youth all over China, he had his education interrupted during middle school by the Cultural Revolution, and he gave up school for farming.

In 1972 Chia entered the Chinese department of Northwest University in Hsi'an, and after graduation he became the literary editor of the People's Publishing House in Hsi'an and an editor of the Writers Federation literary magazine. He became a professional writer in 1983.

Chia started writing in 1973, first trying poetry and then switching to fiction and nonfiction prose. He has produced a number of short stories and novellas, and in 1991 he came to the United States to accept a prize for his novel *Turbulence.*

NOVELS BY CHIA P'ING-WA

Turbulence: A Novel. Trans. by Howard Goldblatt. La. State U. Pr. 1991 $22.95. ISBN 0-8071-1687-4. Skillfully done.

The Heavenly Hound. Panda Bks. 1991 o.p.

CHIANG TZU-LUNG [JIANG ZI-LONG] (also T'ien Chung). 1941–

There is little in Chiang's early life that would mark him as a future writer. He was born in a village in Ts'ang-hsien County, Hopei Province, and in 1958 he became a worker in the Tianjin Heavy Machinery Factory. He enlisted in the army two years later and did not return to the factory until 1965, where he eventually rose to become workshop vice-director.

Chiang's first fiction was published during his army days, but it was with his 1976 publication of "A Day in the Life of the Machinery and Electricity Bureau Chief" that he first provoked an intense social reaction. Since then, several of his stories have won national awards, and in 1973 he joined the prestigious

Chinese Writers Association—an indication that his national reputation was secured.

Short Story Collection by Chiang Tzu-lung

All the Colours of the Rainbow. Trans. by Wang Mingjie. Panda Bks. 1983 o.p.

CH'IEN CHUNG-SHU [QIAN ZHONG-SHU]. 1910–

Ch'ien was born into a prominent literary family in Wuhsi, Kiangsu Province, in November of 1910. His father, Ch'ien Chi-po (1887–1957), was a respected literary historian and professor. As a youth Ch'ien Chung-shu was blessed with a photographic memory and a great talent for writing Chinese prose and poetry. He also learned foreign languages quickly and excelled in English at the high schools that were affiliated with St. John's University that he attended in Soochow and Wuhsi.

Ch'ien Chung-shu went to Tsinghua University and reportedly held himself aloof from his classmates, thereby earning a reputation for arrogance. However, he did meet his future wife, Yang Chiang, there. After graduating in 1933, he taught at Kuang-hua University in Shanghai and then two years later won a scholarship to Oxford University to study English literature. After getting his B. Lit. degree in 1937, he spent a year in Paris.

When Ch'ien Chung-shu returned to China in 1938, the Sino-Japanese War had already begun. He took a job inland at a university in Kunming, Yunnan Province, and then went on to teach at a number of other places. After the Communist victory in 1949, he returned to Peking to teach at his alma mater. Later he transferred to the Academy of Sciences, where he has been ever since, researching foreign and Chinese literature.

His *Fortress Besieged* (1947) has been called one of the greatest novels produced in modern China, and it has been translated into many languages and made into a serialized television series. Something of his attitude in the novel can be gauged from his preface, which states: "In writing about these people, I did not forget they are human beings, still human beings with the basic nature of hairless, two-legged animals." It is a comic novel, but behind the humor there is always a barb. He began another novel, which he felt was going to be even better than *Fortress*, but the manuscript was lost in the mail during his move back to Peking in 1949 and he never resumed work on it. In recent years Ch'ien has focused on scholarly work in Chinese literature, and he has taken trips abroad to Italy and the United States.

Novel by Ch'ien Chung-shu

Fortress Besieged. Trans. by Jeanne Kelly and Nathan K. Mao. Bks. Demand repr. of 1979 ed. $106.40. ISBN 0-685-20426-X. A comedy of manners on courtship, love, and marriage, with much picaresque humor and insight into the life of the scholar of his day. A bestseller in China after being reprinted in 1980.

Book about Ch'ien Chung-shu

Huters, Theodore. *Qian Zhongshu*. G. K. Hall. *Twayne's World Authors Ser.* 1982 o.p. Excellent study of Ch'ien's life and works, including his literary criticism, essays, and fiction.

FENG CHI-TS'AI [FENG JI-CAI]. 1942–

Feng was born in Tianjin in 1942, one of six children. His father was an entrepreneur and his mother came from a line of scholar-bureaucrats. He led a sheltered youth, and has been described by a friend as having been "a naive, sentimental dreamer who lived in a fantasy world of poetry, painting and music." He was also a mischievous child, talented and creative, but mediocre scholastically.

Feng first wanted to be a painter, and he showed promise, winning a citywide painting competition while he was still in high school. But his height attracted the attention of the coach of the Tianjin Men's Basketball Team, and he ended up playing professional basketball until he resigned because of numerous injuries. He then entered the Tianjin Calligraphy and Painting Society, where he got a job making copies of famous paintings for export, but he hated the work, which lacked any intellectual or artistic challenge.

The Cultural Revolution changed everything for him. One day on the street, he was attacked by Red Guards who cut off his hair, and then his family's home was ransacked and his works of art destroyed. From then on life was difficult, and he and his young wife had to struggle to earn enough money to live on. During this bleak period, he first began to write secretly, moved by the intensity of emotion he felt toward the terror of the events that he was witnessing. Tragically, his manuscripts from this period were lost during the collapse of his house in the great Tangshan earthquake in 1976.

Feng began to publish his fiction in 1977, first sticking to safe historical novels and then in 1979 branching out into contemporary themes. His "Chrysanthemums" won a prize in a 1979 short story competition. He now writes full-time and is vice-chairman of the Tianjin branch of the Chinese Writer's Association.

Short Story Collections by Feng Chi-ts'ai

Chrysanthemums and Other Stories. HarBraceJ 1985 o.p.
The Miraculous Pigtail. Chinese Lit. Pr. 1987 o.p.

Nonfiction by Feng Chi-ts'ai

Voices from the Whirlwind: An Oral History of the Chinese Cultural Revolution. Pantheon 1991 $22.00. ISBN 0-394-58645-X. Fourteen candid and compelling personal reminiscences of the Cultural Revolution.

FENG HSÜEH-FENG [FENG XUE-FENG] (pseud. of Feng Fu-ch'un). 1903–1976

Feng was a well-known essayist and poet. He was also the closest confidant of China's greatest modern writer, Lu Hsün, no mean feat, considering that Lu Hsün was probably as famous for his irascible temper as he was for his brilliant poetry and prose.

Feng was born in Chekiang, and he decided at an early age to become a poet. His first works tended to be lyrical panegyrics to love and nature, but, after he became a member of the Communist party in the late 1920s, his literary talents were put to use writing polemical essays.

He was active politically during the 1930s and participated in the fabled Long March. During the anti-Japanese war, he remained in the Nationalist-held areas, but, after the Communist victory in 1949, he was awarded several prominent positions in the government, including the editorship of the important *Literary Gazette.*

His career was not completely smooth, however. He never totally forgot his early ideas about the importance of spontaneity and individual emotions in literature, and he was denounced in 1954 and again in 1957. He died just after the Cultural Revolution, too soon to see his views of literature espoused by a younger generation of writers.

SHORT STORY COLLECTION BY FENG HSÜEH-FENG

Fables. Trans. by Gladys Yang. Foreign Lang. Pr. (China) 1983 o.p.

HO CH'I-FANG [HE QI-FANG] (pseud. of Ho Yung-fang). 1912–1977

Ho Ch'i-fang was born in Szechuan following Sun Yat-sen's revolution, but he still received a strictly Confucian education. He entered Peking University in 1931 and immediately began publishing poetry; by 1936 he was recognized as a poet of stature. He was strongly attracted to the English and French impressionist and symbolist poets, and his poetry, like theirs, showed an attention to the subtleties of language.

Ho did not participate in the left-wing literary movements of the 1930s but instead remained in Peking, where there was more concern over literary standards than politics. However, in the late 1930s, he did travel to Yenan, and from then on his fate was bound up with Communist policies. His career in post-1949 China had its ups and downs; he clashed with literary bureaucrats in 1959 and 1960 but still managed to serve as vice-director of the Literary Research Institute of Peking University and to remain a leading critic.

WORK BY HO CH'I-FANG

Paths in Dreams: Selected Prose and Poetry of Ho Ch'i-fang. Trans. and ed. by Bonnie S. McDougall. Univ. of Queensland Pr. 1976 o.p. A superb translation, including a short essay about western literary influences on Ho.

HSIAO CHÜN [XIAO JUN] (pseud. of Liu Hung-lin). 1907–1988

Hsiao Chün is regarded as the best modern writer to emerge from Manchuria. Coming from a peasant background, he did not have the advantage of much formal education, but he managed to study Chinese classical literature and a fair amount of Western literature on his own.

In his youth, Hsiao Chün supported himself with various jobs, and then he wandered through the northeast of China, for a time even fighting as a guerilla in Manchuria. During the 1930s in Harbin, he was introduced by a friend to a young woman named HSIAO HUNG, who had escaped there with her lover to avoid an arranged marriage, only to find herself abandoned and pregnant. Hsiao Chün's pity turned to love, and before long they were living a bohemian existence together.

In 1933 they gave away her daughter, sold all they had, and went into debt to travel to the seaside in Tsingtao. There Hsiao Chün completed his novel *Village in August* and Hsiao Hung finished her novella *Fields of Life and Death*. The following year they went to Shanghai, where they were befriended by LU HSÜN. Lu Hsün not only helped Hsiao Chün learn the rudiments of writing but also helped him publish his completed novel, which was an immediate success and a bestseller for years after. Its style was clumsy, but its description of conditions in Manchuria rang true, and its cry for an all-out fight against Japan advanced the Communist cause with the masses of people. Hsiao's novel was by no means totally consistent with Communist ideas, however. He saw the people's resistance to the Japanese as spontaneous rather than orchestrated by the party, and he portrayed the masses as often brutal and ignorant rather than idealized as the Communists tended to do in their propagandist literature.

After the Marco Polo Bridge Incident in 1937, the couple traveled to Wuhan, where they eventually broke up, due partly to strains resulting from Hung's poor health and partly to Hsiao Chün's growing sense of superiority because of the success of his writing. He eventually proceeded on to Yenan alone, where he worked for several years, and then he returned to Manchuria when the party took it over in 1946.

Following the revolution in 1949, Hsiao Chün remained in China, and, although he underwent periods of criticism, notably during the rectification drive in 1948, he lived to a ripe old age.

Novels by Hsiao Chün

A Picture. Foreign Lang. Pr. China 1960 o.p.
Village in August. Greenwood repr. of 1974 ed. o.p.

HSIAO HUNG [XIAO HONG] (pseud. of Chang Nai-ying). 1911–1941

Hsiao Hung was born in 1911 to a landlord family in the Amur (Heilungkiang) Province of Manchuria. By 1929, as a student in the First Girls' High School, she was already a celebrity among her classmates, a "new girl" advocating progressive ideas and introducing the writings of Mao Tun, Ping Hsin, and Hsü Chih-mo to her classmates. In 1930 her parents demanded that she return home for an arranged marriage to the son of a general. She escaped to Peking with her lover, a law student, only to discover that he already had a wife; so she returned to Harbin, alone, pregnant, poverty-stricken, and ill.

A friend introduced her to Hsiao Chün, an aspiring young writer who was also from Manchuria, and soon the two were living a bohemian life together in a run-down hotel. After the birth of her baby, they gave the child away and took what little money they could scrape together to travel to the seaside at Tsingtao, where Hsiao Hung completed her novella *Fields of Life and Death.*

In the following year, 1934, they traveled south to Shanghai and soon became close to the great senior writer Lu Hsün. He was especially fond of Hsiao Hung, not only helping her publish, but also giving her and her lover money and helping to pick out her clothes. However, Lu Hsün died in 1936 and, with the Japanese attack on China in the following year, the young couple decided to flee inland to Wuhan.

In Wuhan their relationship deteriorated. Hsiao Chün was becoming more and more contemptuous of Hsiao Hung, whose work he found inferior to his own, and he was also growing impatient with her poor health, which kept her bedridden much of the time. Hsiao Hung found temporary consolation with another young intellectual, Tuan-mu Hung-liang, but her health worsened and she eventually died of tuberculosis in a hospital in Japanese-occupied Hong Kong.

Novel by Hsiao Hung

The Field of Life and Death and Tales of the Hulan River. Trans. by Howard Goldblatt and Ellen Yeung. Bks. Demand repr. of 1979 ed. $82.50. ISBN 0-8357-6695-0. Clear and accurate translation.

Work by Hsiao Hung

Market Street: A Chinese Woman in Harbin. Trans. by Howard Goldblatt. U. of Wash. Pr. 1986 $17.50. ISBN 0-295-96266-6. Intimate and moving semi-fictionalized glimpse of writer's own life.

Short Story Collection by Hsiao Hung

Selected Stories of Xiao Hong. Trans. by Howard Goldblatt. China Bks. 1982 o.p.

BOOK ABOUT HSIAO HUNG

Goldblatt, Howard. *Hsiao Hung*. G. K. Hall. *Twayne's World Authors Ser.* 1976 o.p. "Not only is it a very readable and fully reliable biography; it is also the first systematic examination . . . of Hsiao Hung's literary career" (*Journal of Asian Studies*).

HU SHIH [HU SHI] (pseud. of Hu Hung-hsing). 1891–1962

Hu Shih is one of the best-known scholars of the twentieth century, a leader in the reformation of literature at the time of the May Fourth Movement. He was born in Chihsi, Anhwei Province, and, because his father died when he was very small, his mother was the most formative influence on him.

At the age of 18, Hu Shih came to the United States to study at Cornell University, and after graduating he attended Columbia University, where he studied for a Ph.D. He returned to China in 1917 and for a number of years taught at various institutions, including Peking University. During this time he strongly advocated the reform of literature, using the colloquial language based on the Mandarin dialect.

From 1938 to 1942, Hu Shih served as ambassador to the United States. He went back to China again in 1946 to become the chancellor of Peking University. When the Nationalist government fell three years later, he fled China for the United States. He lived for several years in retirement in New York City, pursuing his scholarly studies and then serving as the curator of the Gest Oriental Library at Princeton University. He stayed aloof from the furious debate going on at that time in the United States over the "China question." In 1958 he returned to Taiwan at President Chiang Kai-shek's request to take up the post of president of Academia Sinica, where he remained until his death four years later.

NONFICTION BY HU SHIH

China's Own Critics. Commentary by Wei Wang Ching. Hyperion Conn. 1986 repr. of 1931 ed. $22.00. ISBN 0-8305-0006-5

Chinese Renaissance. Paragon Hse. repr. of 1963 ed. o.p.

The Development of the Logical Method in Ancient China. Krishna Pr. $79.95. ISBN 0-87968-524-7

BOOKS ABOUT HU SHIH

Chou, Min-chih. *Hu Shih and Intellectual Choice in Modern China*. U. of Mich. Pr. 1984 $34.50. ISBN 0-472-10039-4

Grieder, Jerome B. *Hu Shih and the Chinese Renaissance: Liberalism in the Chinese Revolution, 1917–1937*. HUP 1970 $38.50. ISBN 0-674-41250-8. An excellent intellectual biography.

Lin, Yü-sheng. *The Crisis of Chinese Consciousness: Radical Antitraditionalism in the May Fourth Era*. U. of Wis. Pr. 1979 $32.50. ISBN 0-299-07410-2. "Provocative and rigorously critical study . . . is interested in the theme of totalistic antitraditionalism and its complex relationship to elements of traditional Chinese thought" (*Journal of Asian Studies*).

HUANG CH'UN-MING [HUANG CHUN-MING]. 1939–

Huang is celebrated as one of Taiwan's "nativist" writers, who delights in depicting local people and events in the small towns and countryside of his island. He was relatively uninterested in the political implications of fiction until the early 1970s, when Taiwan suffered several humiliations on the world stage: The Tiao-yü-t'ai (Senkaku) Islands were returned to Japan, President Nixon visited mainland China, and Taiwan lost its seat in the United Nations.

After these events, Huang began to assert a more militant pride in his birthplace. But he concerns himself even more with social problems brought about by the rapid industrialization of Taiwan society, and with Taiwan's cultural identity, which is threatened by the overwhelming materialistic influences of Japan and the West.

Though Huang is a graduate of Pingtung Normal College in southern Taiwan, he finds making a living from odd jobs more congenial than teaching. A restless man, he rarely stays in any situation more than a year at a time.

SHORT STORY COLLECTION BY HUANG CH'UN-MING

The Drowning of an Old Cat and Other Stories. Ind. U. Pr. 1980 o.p. "The images employed by Hwang Ch'un-ming to characterize the postwar transformation of Taiwan are unforgettably powerful" (*Journal of Asian Studies*).

JU CHIH-CHÜAN [RU ZHI-JUAN]. 1925–

Ju Chih-chüan made her name in 1958 by writing a story called "Lilies." Though on the surface the story appears to be rather innocuous, its writing was actually a courageous act of defiance. It challenged MAO TSE-TUNG'S (see also Vol. 3) literary policy, outlined in 1942, which dictated that fiction should be written in a "bold" proletarian style, not a "graceful and restrained" style smacking of decadent bourgeois values. Ju Chih-chüan's delicate style, therefore, occasioned a national literary controversy, which was finally decided in her favor when Minister of Culture MAO TUN sided with her against her critics.

Following her victory, she continued writing in the same vein, and it is largely due to her efforts that sentiment, family, and motherhood gradually became respectable topics again in China. In 1979 Ju Chih-chüan bucked the trend again, experimenting with a bold "male" style to attack the disastrous agricultural policies of the Great Leap Forward (1958–59). She was one of the first to dare to expose the folly of this failed policy.

Though Ju Chih-chüan has shown extraordinary courage throughout her writing career, her work's international reception is flawed by reliance on political context for true intelligibility. In translation it tends to appear marred by Communist jargon and becomes deceptively mild.

SHORT STORY COLLECTION BY JU CHIH-CHÜAN

Lilies and Other Stories. Panda Bks. 1985 o.p. A representative sample of 10 stories. Translations are a bit awkward at times, but accurate in overall meaning.

KAO HSIAO-SHENG [GAO XIAO-SHENG]. 1928–

Kao was born in the small farming village of Wuchin not too far from the Yangtze River in Kiangsu Province, the son of a farmer of modest means. Unlike many peasants, his father kept a few books at home and encouraged his son to study and develop an appreciation of literature. However, Kao's early years were spent working in the fields beside his parents.

In 1949 Kao participated in political work for the Communist revolutionary cause, and, in the new climate that encouraged men from humble backgrounds like his own, he decided actively to pursue a writing career, feverishly studying and writing at the same time. His early works are rather predictable short stories, plays, and poems extolling the revolutionary changes in the countryside. But by 1956 Kao begins to show definite promise in stories like "Broken Contract," which, though still somewhat immature, reveals his keen eye for observation of the tumultuous changes coming about in rural life, as mirrored in issues of love and marriage. His simple, pithy language has a genuine down-home appeal.

In 1957 Kao and several like-minded comrades formed a literary club called "The Seekers," dedicated to "actively intervening in life to seek out its meaning." Unfortunately, their efforts were nipped in the bud as the political climate changed, and not long after, Kao was labeled a Rightist, sent back to his native county, and subjected to hard labor to remold his thought.

The 20 years that followed were not easy ones for him; with his undesirable political label, he continued to suffer throughout the Cultural Revolution, but from his experiences he gained a more philosophical outlook on life and a clearer understanding of the peasant backbone of China.

Resuming writing after the fall of the Gang of Four, Kao, in his fiction, shows a much greater depth and maturity; his peasant protagonists are not simply sentimentalized as honest and good but are shown also as servile and self-debasing, the result of millennia of disadvantaged status in Chinese society.

During the 10 years after the Cultural Revolution, Kao was quite prolific, producing more than 50 stories that centered on life in the countryside. In the last few years, he has begun to experiment with longer fiction and to include urban characters in his field of vision. He also now tends to avoid pinpointing specific historical circumstances, as if he were consciously aiming at a greater universality.

SHORT STORY COLLECTION BY KAO HSIAO-SHENG

The Broken Betrothal. Chinese Lit. Pr. 1987 $6.95. ISBN 0-8351-2051-1. A wonderful collection of short stories that provides a clear, sometimes harsh picture of the difficult conditions endured by peasants during the Cultural Revolution.

KU HUA [GU HUA] (pseud. of Lo Hung-yü). 1942–

Ku Hua was born in a remote mountain village of Chia-ho County in southern Hunan. He wrote his first published short story in 1962 while working there on a farm. Treasuring the rich folklore of his area, he writes with a strong sense of local color of the peasants and minority hill people.

At his best, Ku can be compared to the great writer of a generation earlier, SHEN TS'UNG-WEN, and some have even compared him to THOMAS HARDY (see Vol. 1). Like these two writers, he does not skirt the issue of sexuality, and for that reason he has occasionally been criticized in the puritanical People's Republic. However, unlike those writers, Ku sometimes gets mired in political jargon and clichés.

Nevertheless, his novel *A Town Called Hibiscus* (1981) is a very moving account of the fortunes of a plucky young country heroine in the dark days of the Cultural Revolution. It won the Mao Tun Prize for Literature and has been highly successful in its movie adaptation as well. It has been translated into more than 10 languages, including English, French, Dutch, German, and Japanese.

NOVEL BY KU HUA

A Town Called Hibiscus. Chinese Lit. Pr. 1981 o.p.

KUO MO-JO [GUO MO-RUO] (pseud. of Kuo K'ai-chen). 1892–1978

Kuo Mo-jo is one of the patriarchs of modern literature, perhaps ranking only after LU HSÜN and MAO TUN in fame in the People's Republic. He was born into a wealthy family in Loshan, Szechuan, and went to Japan to study medicine in

1913. There he developed a passionate interest in literature and was particularly influenced by the poetry of GOETHE, SHELLEY (see Vol. 1), SIR RABINDRANATH TAGORE, and WALT WHITMAN (see Vol. 1). After returning to China, he wrote prodigiously, turning out plays, poems, short stories, and several volumes of autobiography in the years before 1949, in addition to a number of scholarly works and translations from Japanese, English, and German.

Kuo also founded journals and literary societies, the most famous of which was the Creation Society begun in 1921. Though he started out on a quest for beauty in his writing, after the split between the Nationalists and the Communists in 1927, his revolutionary zeal prompted him to develop a proletarian ideal for literature. For his associated left-wing political activities, he was exiled several times to Japan, where he remained until the Sino-Japanese War began in 1937.

After the Communist party assumed power in 1949, Kuo served in a number of prestigious government posts, including vice-chairman of the Chinese People's Political Consultative Conference, chairman of the All-China Federation of Literary and Art Circles, and president of the Academy of Sciences. His writings after becoming a literary bureaucrat were characterized by circumspection and orthodoxy, not revealing any of his earlier preoccupations with literary or humane values that might have conflicted with party policy.

PLAYS BY KUO MO-JO

Chu Yuan; A Play in Five Acts. Trans. by Yang Xian-yi and Gladys Yang. Foreign Lang. Pr. (China) 1953 o.p.

Five Historical Plays. Foreign Lang. Pr. (China) 1984 o.p.

POETRY BY KUO MO-JO

Selected Poems from the Goddesses. Trans. by John Lester and A. C. Barnes. Foreign Lang. Pr. (China) 1958 o.p.

BOOKS ABOUT KUO MO-JO

Prusek, Jaroslav. *Three Sketches of Chinese Literature.* Oriental Inst. in Academia 1969 o.p. Discusses Kuo Mo-jo, Yu Ta-fu, and Mao Tun, three significant shapers of modern Chinese literature.

Roy, David Todd. *Kuo Mo-jo: History of the Formative Years of His Life.* HUP 1978 o.p.

LAO SHE (pseud. of Shu She-yü). 1899–1966

Many look upon Lao She as the wisest, funniest, and most compassionate of modern China's major writers. Certainly he has given us lively, earthy portraits of many flawed but lovable folks struggling to cope with the complexities and frustrations of daily life. His wonderful command of Peking dialect adds a strong sense of local flavor to his works.

Lao She's intimate knowledge of Peking and its inhabitants came naturally. He was born there in 1899, son of a Manchu in the imperial guard who died fighting when the allied army entered the capital during the Boxer Uprising. At the time Lao She was only 2 years old and living with his mother and older siblings in a small lane that was much like many of those about which he would one day write.

Lao She spent some time in England teaching Chinese language, and it was there that he began writing, serializing a novel in 1926 in the *Monthly Magazine of Fiction.* Returning to China, he taught first at Shantung Christian College and then at Shantung University.

During the anti-Japanese war, Lao She worked for the All-China Federation of Literary and Artistic Circles, and, when the war ended, he toured America with the well-known dramatist Ts'ao Yü. He returned to China in 1949 and, after the Communist victory, was active in cultural work.

Lao She is actually a pen name meaning "Always Relinquishing," and it suggests his self-effacing humor and desire to serve others. Tragically, this gentle man was murdered by Red Guards during the Cultural Revolution.

NOVELS BY LAO SHE

Beneath the Red Banner. Trans. by Don J. Cohn. Panda Bks 1982 o.p.

Camel Xiangzi. Ind. U. Pr. 1981 o.p. Lao She's greatest novel, also known in English as *Rickshaw Boy.* Less complete version than *Rickshaw.*

Cat Country: A Satirical Novel of China in the 1930's. Trans. by William A. Lyell, Jr. Ohio St. U. Pr. 1970 o.p.

Ma and Son: A Novel. Trans. by Jean M. James. U. of Hawaii Pr. 1979 o.p. A fine translation.

The Two Mas. Joint Pub. Co. HK 1984 o.p.

The Quest for Love of Lao Lee. Trans. by Helena Kuo. Reynal & Hitchcock 1948 o.p.

Rickshaw: The Novel Lo-t'o Hsiang-tzu. Trans. by Jean M. James UH Pr. 1979 o.p.

SHORT STORY COLLECTION BY LAO SHE

Crescent Moon and Other Stories. Chinese Lit. Pr. 1985 o.p.

PLAY BY LAO SHE

Dragon Beard Ditch: A Play in Three Acts. Foreign Lang. Pr. China 1956 o.p.

BOOKS ABOUT LAO SHE

Kao, George. *Two Writers and the Cultural Revolution: Lao She and Chen Jo-hsi.* U. of Wash. Pr. 1980 o.p.

Vohra, Ranbir. *Lao She and the Chinese Revolution.* HUP 1974 $20.00. ISBN 0-674-51075-5

LI ANG. 1952–

Li Ang was born into an educated family in Lukang, Taiwan. Although her home area had been a key trade center in Ch'ing dynasty times, during the Japanese occupation, its growth had stagnated, with the result that many traditions survived there after having died out elsewhere. This may explain the familiarity with which Li writes about conservative manners and mores in some of her fiction.

However, Li Ang herself is no traditionalist. She published her first fiction piece, "Flower Season," while she was still in high school in 1968, and she was very much caught up in the enthusiasm for existential philosophy and modernist aesthetics sweeping Taiwan at the time. She went on to graduate from the College of Chinese Culture and earn an M.A. in drama at Oregon State University.

She returned to Taiwan to teach at her alma mater and continued her writing. In 1983 her novel *The Butcher's Wife* received the United Newspaper's literary prize and made her famous on both sides of the Taiwan strait. The work is a powerful indictment of male chauvinism and a probing study of the power of sex—as a woman's weapon or as an agent of her self-destruction. Li Ang's depictions are brutal, graphic, and unforgettable.

Novel by Li Ang

The Butcher's Wife. Trans. by Howard Goldblatt and Ellen Yeung. Beacon Pr. 1990 repr. of 1986 ed. $9.95. ISBN 0-8070-8323-2

LIANG CH'I-CH'AO [LIANG QI-CHAO]. 1873–1929

Liang was born in Canton, son of a well-educated farmer and grandson of a man who had obtained a B.A. under the old examination system. Thanks to these two men, Liang received a strong traditional education, and in 1889 he was the youngest of the 100 successful candidates for the second-level degree. His success led to a marriage with the younger sister of the chief examiner. However, he failed the highest level metropolitan examination the following year, and this seems to have caused him to rethink his future.

Liang began reading translations of foreign works and offered himself as a student to the great reformer K'ang Yu-wei, who was then living in Canton. He soon became active in the Peking branch of an organization called the "Reform Club," whose manifesto advocated self-strengthening for China in order to defend itself against imperialistic powers. Liang soon took over its journalistic activities and began writing reformist essays. When the organization was shut down in Peking, he moved to Shanghai.

In 1897 Liang relinquished his responsibilities and traveled to Changsha, Hunan, where he organized a study society to coordinate the political science studies of scholars in the southern provinces. By day he lectured, and by night he wrote.

When K'ang Yu-wei briefly had a chance to try out his policies of reform during the "Hundred Days" of 1898, Liang joined him but ended up having to escape to Japan when the conservative dowager empress, allied with a Manchu military commander, seized the throne from the young Emperor Kuang-hsü, who had supported the reformers.

Many of those who had studied with Liang went on to become leading revolutionaries, but Liang himself never embraced a radical solution. He distrusted the Soviet Union, and he felt that the scholar-official class were the natural leaders of society. Yet he shared certain ideas with the Communists, including the belief that Western movements of social protest were justified and that capitalism was largely responsible for World War I. When China declared war on Germany in 1917 and borrowed heavily from Japan to finance its war effort, Liang quit politics in frustration.

With the growth of Socialist thinking in China during the 1920s, many wanted to abolish everything connected with China's feudal past. However, Liang continued to advocate saving what was worthwhile from China's philosophical and literary heritage, believing that the West was spiritually bankrupt. Thanks to his efforts, some of the neglected ancient philosophers like Mo-tzu were studied anew, and the worth of Buddhism, vernacular literature, and the thought of the Ch'ing period were reevaluated.

Nonfiction by Liang Ch'i-ch'ao

Comments on Journalism. Col. U. Pr. 1953 o.p.

Intellectual Trends in the Ch'ing Period. Trans. by Immanuel C. Y. Hsü. Cambridge U. Pr. 1959 o.p. Includes an introduction and notes.

Books about Liang Ch'i-ch'ao

Chang, Hao. *Liang Ch'i-ch'ao and Intellectual Transition in China 1890–1907*. HUP 1971 o.p. "Less an intellectual biography than a descriptive exposition of the ideas expressed in Liang's writings of the decade 1895–1905" (*Journal of Asian Studies*).

Huang, Philip C. *Liang Ch'i-ch'ao and Modern Chinese Liberalism.* U. of Wash. Pr. 1979 o.p. A survey of Liang's whole career. "Broader in scope [than Chang's book] but less intensive in its treatment" (*Journal of Asian Studies*).

Levenson, Joseph Richmond. *Liang Ch'i-ch'ao and the Mind of Modern China.* U. CA Pr. 1959 o.p. A classic intellectual biography.

LIN YÜ-T'ANG [LIN YUTANG] (pseud. of Lin Ho-le). 1895–1976

Though he was never considered to be a serious original thinker or a leading writer in his native China, Lin Yü-t'ang's role as an essayist and popularizer of things Chinese in the West is worthy of attention. He was a native of Changchow in Amoy, son of a Presbyterian minister, and third-generation Christian. He was brought up in a strict household and prepared for the ministry, and after middle school he was sent to the Protestant College of Amoy. In 1911 he entered the famous St. John's University in Shanghai, and it was during his time there that he became disillusioned with the choice of a religious career and renounced Christianity.

After graduation (with a rather weak academic record), Lin Yü-t'ang became a professor of English at Tsinghua University because his grounding in foreign languages was much stronger than in classical Chinese. In 1919 he decided to pursue further study in the United States, where he spent one year at Harvard University and then went on to France where he worked for the YMCA. He moved to Germany for a term, and at last in 1923 earned a Ph.D. in Leipzig in the field of archaic Chinese phonology.

Lin Yü-t'ang then returned home and tried out various teaching posts, and in 1927 became secretary to the Ministry of Foreign Affairs in the Wuhan government. But politics was not to his liking, and he resigned in the following year.

In 1932 he founded the *Analects Fortnightly,* a magazine of wit and satire that proved to be an instant popular success. Two years later he began another periodical, *This Human World,* which contained short essays. Unfortunately, his satire angered intellectuals on both the Left and the Right, and this was the beginning of his lifelong friction with Chinese literary and academic circles.

In 1936, feeling hostility at home but an increased demand for his writings in the West, Lin Yü-t'ang went to New York City and remained there until 1943, when he went back home to lecture briefly and again became embroiled in controversy. However, in the United States, his essays and ideas were greeted with great enthusiasm.

Early in 1954 he was appointed chancellor of the new Chinese University in Singapore, but, because of a disagreement with the trustees on policy, he and his staff left early in 1955 before the university opened its doors. Not long after this, in New York, he and his wife publicly announced their reconversion to Christianity.

In addition to his many books of essays, Lin Yü-t'ang published a novel, *Moment in Peking,* a saga about a Chinese family spanning the years 1900–38. He also published a number of translations of classical Chinese works, the best of which is perhaps SHEN FU's *Six Chapters of a Floating Life,* the moving autobiographical account of a happy marriage marred by parental disapproval and the tragic early death of the wife.

Lin Yü-t'ang's writings are marked by an appreciation of both Eastern and Western culture, and their sparkling, idiomatic English style has endeared him to thousands of Western readers.

Novel by Lin Yü-t'ang

Moment in Peking. Intl. Spec. Bk. 1980 repr. of 1939 ed. o.p.

Nonfiction by Lin Yü-t'ang

The Best of An Old Friend. Mason/Charter 1975 o.p. Excerpts from his other books.
Between Tears and Laughter. Apt Bks. 1991 $17.95. ISBN 81-207-1270-6
The Importance of Living. Bucaneer Bks. 1991 $31.95. ISBN 0-89966-766-X
My Country and My People. Reynal & Hitchcock 1935 o.p.
Vermilion Gate. Intl. Spec. Bk. 1980 repr. of 1953 ed. o.p.

LIU HSIN-WU [LIU XIN-WU]. 1942–

Liu was born in Ch'eng-tu, Szechuan, but moved to Peking with his parents in 1950, where he spent his formative years. In 1961 he graduated from school and then taught in a high school for 15 years. He began writing fiction for children during the Cultural Revolution, advocating the government-approved ideas of class struggle, active political participation, and loyalty to Maoist principles above ties of friendship or kinship.

It was during the late 1970s, however, that Liu first gained attention with his story "Class Captain," about a teacher in charge of a group of middle-school students. Focusing on the dilemmas facing young people after the tumultuous years of the Cultural Revolution, the story was heralded as one of the first pieces of "scar" or "wound" literature, which detailed the social legacy of those years of violent extremism.

Since at this time the government was advocating a criticism of Cultural Revolution policies in the wake of its new economic reform efforts, Liu's efforts were applauded and he was eventually rewarded with the plum job of editor-in-chief of *People's Literature* in 1986. However, when the relatively liberal Party General Secretary Hu Yao-pang was ousted, and a campaign against "bourgeois liberalism" was launched in 1987, Liu was attacked for allowing a rather sexually explicit short story about Tibet to have appeared in the magazine, and he lost his post. Though reinstated, he was ousted once again in 1990 for his support of the Democracy Movement.

Though Liu has never been particularly innovative in form or technique, and his official sanction has made it necessary for him to tread cautiously in exposing the ills of society, he has nevertheless been a very popular writer in China; his considerable talent for storytelling gives his work a genuine appeal.

As Geremie Barmé has written, "The Velvet Prison [of state-sponsored art] offers the compliant artist all the perks of the modern state—access to the media and literary journals, official recognition, travel . . . and an assured income to go with it—and license to be artistically innovative as long as he does not transgress the borders of orthodoxy." Liu has tried valiantly to accommodate state guidelines while still trying to improve society and further the cause of quality literature. He has found it to be a challenging task.

Short Story Collection by Liu Hsin-wu

Black Walls and Other Stories. Trans. by Michael Duke and others. Chinese U. HK 1990 o.p. The first collection of his short stories to be published in English. Includes his more recent work.

LIU PIN-YEN [LIU BIN-YAN]. 1925–

Liu was born in Kirin in the far northeast. In 1943 he participated in underground work in the Communist party's anti-Japanese campaign in Tianjin, and, after the establishment of the People's Republic, he became an editor of the *China Youth Newspaper.* In 1978 he was sent to the Philosophy Institute of the Academy of Social Sciences, and then in 1979 he became a reporter for the national official newspaper *People's Daily.*

Liu was already in residence as a visiting scholar at Harvard University at the time of The Tiananmen Square incident in June 1989, and his highly critical response to the Chinese government's handling of the Democracy Movement has meant that he has had to remain in the United States. He is best known for his *reportage* literature and has continued his writing in exile.

NONFICTION BY LIU PIN-YEN

China's Crisis, China's Hope. HUP 1990 $22.50. ISBN 0-674-11882-0. Hard-hitting essays on Chinese politics.

A Higher Kind of Loyalty: A Memoir by China's Foremost Journalist. Pantheon 1990 $22.95. ISBN 0-394-57471-0. Liu reflects on the tribulations of his life.

People or Monsters?: And Other Stories and Reportage from China After Mao. Trans. by Perry E. Link. Ind. U. Pr. 1983 $20.00. ISBN 0-253-34329-1. Includes a background introduction by Leo Ou-fan Lee.

"Tell the World": What Happened in China and Why. Pantheon 1989 $18.95. ISBN 0-394-58370-1. Contains Liu's work and that of other exiles after the June Fourth Incident.

LU HSÜN [LU XUN] (pseud. of Chou Shu-jen). 1881–1936

A writer, essayist, translator, poet, and literary theorist and critic, Lu Hsün was born in Chekiang Province of an educated family whose fortunes were in decline. He went to Japan to study Western medicine, but he dropped out of Sendai Medical College in 1906 after seeing news slides of Japanese soldiers decapitating Chinese in Manchuria. He made a decision to cure the "souls" of his countrymen rather than their bodies and chose literature as his medium.

Lu Hsün returned to China in 1909 and watched the progress of the 1911 revolution with dismay. His spirits were raised somewhat in 1917 when the magazine *New Youth* raised the banner of literary revolution. He joined the ranks of the new writers with his short story "Diary of a Madman." Several more stories soon followed, the most famous of which was "The True Story of Ah Q" in the early 1920s.

In 1926, after one of many periodic bouts of depression, Lu Hsün traveled for a while in the south and then settled in Shanghai, where he was greeted as a doyen on the literary scene. However, although many young writers wanted to become his disciples, he had an ambivalent attitude toward them and often became bitter or angry when he disagreed with their theories. The League of Left-Wing Writers was founded in 1930 and promptly took him as their leader. But from the beginning relations were quite strained, and, by the time he died in 1936, he was completely alienated from these men who would later sing his praises.

The extent of Lu Hsün's work and his high standards laid the foundation for modern Chinese literature, and he is still considered to be China's greatest twentieth-century writer in the People's Republic. His stories are satiric, unflinchingly realistic, disturbing, and brilliantly crafted in tone and style. In addition to this rich legacy, he also translated a number of European works of literature and theoretical studies on art and literature into Chinese, and he helped to introduce modern art to China.

Nonfiction by Lu Hsün

A Brief History of Chinese Fiction. Trans. by Yang Xianyi and Gladys Yang. Hyperion Conn. 1990 repr. of 1959 ed. $42.00. ISBN 0-88355-065-2. A well-known work that illuminates Lu Hsün's preferences in traditional literature.

Lu Hsün, Writing for the Revolution: Essays. Red Sun Pubs. 1976 o.p.

Short Story Collections by Lu Hsün

Ah Q and Others: Selected Stories of Lu Hsün. Trans. by Chi-chen Wang. Ayer repr. of 1941 ed. $17.00. ISBN 0-8369-3839-9

The Complete Stories of Lu Xun: Call to Arms: Wandering. Trans. by Gladys Yang. Bks. Demand repr. of 1981 ed. $80.40. ISBN 0-685-23889-X

Dawn Blossoms Plucked at Dusk. Foreign Lang. Pr. China 1976 o.p.

Diary of a Madman and Other Stories. UH Pr. 1990 $40.00. ISBN 0-8248-1278-6

Works by Lu Hsün

Lu Xun, Selected Works. Foreign Lang. Pr. China 1980 o.p.

Masterpieces of Modern Chinese Fiction, 1919–1949. Foreign Lang. Pr. China 1983 o.p.

Wandering. Foreign Lang. Pr. China 1961

Wild Grass. China Bks. 1974 o.p.

Poetry by Lu Hsün

Lu Hsün, Complete Poems: A Translation with Introduction and Annotation. Trans. by David Chen. ASU Ctr. Asian 1988 $10.00. ISBN 0-939252-19-8

Books about Lu Hsün

Chen, Pearl Hsia, and Franklin S. C. Chen. *The Social Thought of Lu Hsün, 1881–1936: A Mirror of the Intellectual Current of Modern China.* Vantage 1976 o.p.

Hsü, Raymond S. W. *The Style of Lu Hsün: Vocabulary and Usage.* Univ. of Hong Kong 1979 o.p. Intended for students of modern Chinese language.

Lee, Leo Ou-fan. *Voices from the Iron House: A Study of Lu Xun.* Ind. U. Pr. 1987 $34.95. ISBN 0-253-36263-6. A good biography and source book.

Lyell, William A. *Lu Hsün's Vision of Reality.* U. CA Pr. 1976 $47.50. ISBN 0-520-02940-2. An analysis of technical and formal aspects of his writing; more useful for the specialist than the general reader.

Wang Shih-ching. *Lu Xun, A Biography.* Trans. by Bonnie S. McDougall and others. Foreign Lang. Pr. China 1984 o.p.

MAO TSE-TUNG [MAO ZE-DONG]. 1893–1976

Mao Tse-tung is, of course, best known as a political leader, having held power in the People's Republic from its founding in 1949 until his death, as president until 1959 and then as chairman of the Communist party. He undertook some of the most radical social experiments in human history, and although he has been dead for many years, he still casts a long shadow over current events in Asia, and his legacy is still hotly debated.

Born into a prosperous peasant family in Hunan Province, Mao first came into contact with revolutionary writings during the decade of the 1910s. He was present at the founding of the Communist party in 1921 and had already risen to prominence by 1935. It was after the heroic Long March, while the Communists were consolidating their power in their northwest base in Yenan, that Mao Tse-tung held his Forum on Literature and Art, which, as Howard L. Boorman has said, "drew a firm line across the page of modern Chinese creative writing and promulgated what has since become, with some later variations, the 'correct' analysis of the literary and aesthetic principles designed to guide the 'progressive' writers and artists of China." Essentially, it was to be a literature shaped by

"Party spirit," designed for the masses (particularly workers, peasants, and soldiers), and written in a bold, simple, and earthy style. There would be no toleration of "art for art's sake," or subjective inspiration, or other bourgeois themes or tendencies. Literature's sole aim would be to serve politics.

One can find many examples of the approved content and style in Mao's own writings. His speeches and essays are strongly colored by his rural roots; one finds an earthy humor and terseness of expression that are reminiscent of many traditional works in the colloquial language.

Mao's poetry is a bit more complicated. Having been educated to some extent in the classical tradition, he has always favored the *tz'u* form for his own verse. And, although he does conform to the time-honored metrical rules, in many ways his poems mark a break with the past in their strong egotism, preference for the present over the past, and desire to conquer nature rather than to live in passive harmony with it. However, his sentimentality and use of imagery still confirm his strong identification with the lyric past, and even many Chinese who disagree with his politics can nevertheless find pleasure in his verses.

NONFICTION BY MAO TSE-TUNG

Chairman Mao Talks to the People: Talks and Letters 1956–1971. Ed. by Stuart Schram. Pantheon 1974 o.p. A fascinating collection of Mao's speeches, writings, and interviews from the early years of the People's Republic through the first part of the Cultural Revolution and the death of Lin Piao. Historically important and filled with lively, entertaining prose.

Mao Zedong's "Talks at the Yan'an Conference on Literature and Art": A Translation of the 1943 Text with Commentary. Trans. by Bonnie S. McDougall. U. of Mich. Pr. 1980 $6.00. ISBN 0-89264-039-1. The key guideline for all literature written under the Communist government in China since 1949. Also sums up the history of revolutionary literature for the 1920s and '30s. Important for an understanding of all subsequent literature in the People's Republic.

Quotations from Chairman Mao. China Bks. 1990 $7.95. ISBN 0-8351-2388-X. New edition of the "Little Red Book," the bible of the Cultural Revolution years. For the full flavor of that era, see the original 1967 Chinese-English edition of the work published by the East Is Red Publishing House, with a foreword by Lin Piao.

Selected Works of Mao Tse-tung. 4 vols. Foreign Lang. Pr. China o.p. Translations of some of Mao's earlier works, authorized by Peking.

The Writings of Mao Zedong, 1949–1976, Vol. 2: January 1956–December 1957. Trans. by Michael Y.M. Kao and John K. Leung. M. E. Sharpe 1991 $95.00. ISBN 0-87332-392-0

POETRY BY MAO TSE-TUNG

Poems of Mao Tse-tung. Trans. by Wong Man. Eastern Horizon Pr. 1966 o.p. Includes annotations and historical background for each of the 24 poems.

Ten More Poems of Mao Tse-tung. Trans. by Wong Man. Eastern Horizon Pr. 1967 o.p. Includes 10 poems not made public in China until 1964. Less annotation than in his earlier book of poems.

Ten Poems and Lyrics by Mao Tse-tung. Trans. by Hui Ming Wang. U. of Mass. Pr. 1975 $15.00. ISBN 0-87023-178-2

BOOKS ABOUT MAO TSE-TUNG

Ch'en, Jerome. *Mao and the Chinese Revolution.* OUP 1967 o.p. One of the standard biographies of Mao. "The poems are translated with an unusual degree of sensitivity for the nuances and subtleties that are characteristic of Chinese poetry" (*SR*).

______, ed. *Mao Papers: Anthology and Bibliography.* OUP 1970 o.p. A useful resource for earlier work on Mao.

Schram, Stuart R. *Mao Tse-tung.* S&S Trade 1967 o.p. A useful biography of Mao up to the beginning of the Cultural Revolution.

MAO TUN [MAO DUN] (pseud. of Shen Yen-ping). 1896–1981

Among those writers sympathetic to the extreme Left, Mao Tun is considered one of the most outstanding. Born in Chekiang Province, he graduated from Hohai Technical School in Nanking and attended a preparatory class at Peking University.

He became an active member in the Literature Study Society founded in 1920, which was attempting to foster a literature to raise people's awareness of social ills, and from then on, for the rest of his life, he devoted himself to this cause. He taught at the People's Girl School established by the Communist party in Shanghai and then served as secretary of the Propaganda Department under the Nationalists in 1925 before the split between them and the Communists. He joined the League of Left-wing Writers in 1930, and during the 1930s he was involved in a number of revolutionary literary and educational projects.

Mao Tun was invited to visit the Soviet Union in 1946, after which he published a volume of his impressions. His strong revolutionary credentials earned him the prestigious post of minister of culture under the Communist government, in which he served from 1949 to 1964.

In addition to his works of fiction, Mao Tun also wrote a large number of essays on literature and life, and several plays, the most famous of which was *Before and After the Ch'ing Ming Festival.*

Novel by Mao Tun

Midnight. Trans. by Hsü Meng-hsiung and A. C. Barnes. Cheng & Tsui 1979 $14.95. ISBN 0-88727-099-9. Mao Tun's best novel, written in 1930–31; a picture of life in Shanghai in 1930.

Short Story Collection by Mao Tun

Spring Silkworms and Other Stories. Trans. by Sidney Shapiro. China Bks. 1980 $9.95. ISBN 0-8351-0615-2. Thirteen short stories dealing primarily with life in the countryside and written between 1930 and 1936.

Book about Mao Tun

Chen, Yu-shih. *Realism and Allegory in the Early Fiction of Mao Tun.* Ind. U. Pr. 1986 $24.95. ISBN 0-253-34950-8. A reappraisal of Mao Tun's early fiction. Raises many interesting questions but "leaves open the question of why one must speak of allegory in fiction that looks realist" (*Journal of Asian Studies*).

MO YEN [MO YAN] (pseud. of Kuan Mo-yeh). 1956–

Mo Yen is a native of Shantung Province. He left school during the Cultural Revolution and returned home, where he worked as a part-time laborer in a linseed oil factory until he enlisted in the People's Liberation Army in 1976. He began writing fiction in 1981, and in 1984 the army transferred him to the Literature Department of the Armed Forces Cultural Academy.

From the first, his fiction contrasted with the majority of party-supported writers choosing rural themes. Mo Yen's vision of the countryside was, as Michael Duke has characterized it, "a nightmarish world of ignorance, poverty, and cruelty, full of suffering, sadness, and misery temporarily relieved by minute doses of kindness, friendship and love."

However, Mo Yen's vision is also more appealing than Duke's quote would lead one to believe, because it is extremely innovative in technique, borrowing much from WILLIAM FAULKNER (see Vol. 1) and written with an imagination that makes his small world of Gaomi County in Shantung Province shimmer like a fairy tale kingdom. It is this magical realism that sets him apart from other writers on predominantly rural themes.

Mo Yen's *Red Sorghum*, while not completely satisfying in structure as a novel, does manage to forge an imaginative connecting link between the almost mythological larger-than-life heroes and villains of the past and the seemingly much diminished real life characters of the present.

SHORT STORY COLLECTION BY MO YEN

Explosions and Other Stories. Ed. and trans. by Janice Wickeri and Duncan Hewitt. Small Pr. Dist. 1991 $10.50. ISBN 0-685-56989-6

NOVEL BY MO YEN

Red Sorghum: A Family Saga. Trans. by Howard Goldblatt. Viking Penguin 1993 $23.00. ISBN 0-670-84402-0. The novel on which the award-winning Chinese movie *Red Sorghum* was based.

PA CHIN [BA JIN] (pseud. of Li Yao-t'ang). 1904–

Pa Chin was born into the wealthy and prominent Li family of Ch'eng-tu, Szechuan, and, for the first 19 years of his life, he lived largely within the confines of its huge mansion, which housed 50 members of his clan and 45 servants. Because his grandfather ruled the family with an iron hand, Pa Chin was forbidden to enter a "modern" school during his grandfather's lifetime. At the age of 21, Pa Chin finally obtained permission to go first to Shanghai and later to Nanking to pursue his studies. He had originally planned to enter Peking University after his graduation from middle school, but he was carried away by the wave of revolution, and, instead, he stayed in Shanghai and became active in the anarchist movement.

But, as the general enthusiasm for anarchism waned during the 1920s and Pa Chin began to feel frustrated in his political work, he decided to leave China for study in Paris. This trip broadened his horizons considerably, and it was while he was abroad that he wrote his first short story, which was accepted for publication back in Shanghai.

After his return to Shanghai, Pa Chin continued to write political pieces and to work on fiction in his spare time. In 1931 he wrote the semiautobiographical *Family*, his masterpiece, which resonated strongly with China's youth, who were struggling to liberate themselves from the yoke of the traditional family system in order to be able to make their own life decisions and marry for love. The novel forms a trilogy with two succeeding novels, *Spring* (1937) and *Autumn* (1940). Together, the three novels are known as *Turbulent Currents*.

Pa Chin continued to write throughout the 1930s and 1940s, moving around from city to city in order to avoid the Japanese. After the end of the war, he returned to Shanghai and wrote *Cold Nights*, his last novel and one of his best. Its atmosphere is depressing, reflecting the struggle for survival during the war years and the increasing corruption of the Nationalist regime.

Pa Chin chose to remain in China after the Communist takeover in 1949, and, until the Hundred Flowers Campaign, when he took too literally MAO TSE-TUNG's (see also Vol. 3) encouragement to criticize and was forced to recant, he lived a relatively peaceful existence. Like many other leading intellectuals, he suffered during the Cultural Revolution. In 1968 his ordeal at the People's Stadium in Shanghai was televised, as he was forced to kneel on broken glass and hear himself denounced as an enemy of Mao. But he survived and has since been "rehabilitated." In the 1980s part of his *Family* saga was made into a television drama.

NOVELS BY PA CHIN

Cold Nights: A Novel by Pa Chin. Trans. by Nathan K. Mao and Liu Ts'un-yan. Chinese U. HK 1978 o.p. The translation has serious deficiencies, but currently the only one available of this important work.

Family. Trans. by Sidney Shapiro. Waveland Pr. 1988 repr. of 1972 ed. $6.50. ISBN 0-88133-373-5. Pa Chin's most popular novel. A largely autobiographical account of painful generation gaps in a large and wealthy family, as China struggled to modernize in the early twentieth century.

Random Thoughts. Trans. by Geremie Barmé. Joint Pub. Co. HK 1984 o.p.

BOOKS ABOUT PA CHIN

Lang, Olga. *Pa Chin and His Writings: Chinese Youth Between Two Revolutions.* HUP 1967 o.p.

Mao, Nathan K. *Pa Chin.* G. K. Hall. *Twayne's World Authors Ser.* 1978 o.p. Contains useful facts, but interpretations should be approached with caution.

PAI HSIEN-YUNG [BAI XIAN-YONG]. 1937–

Son of one of the military leaders of the Nationalist Revolution and high government defense official during the war against Japan, Pai spent much of his youth in wartime Kweilin in southwest China, which has provided much of the material for his subsequent fiction. After the war ended, he resided for a time in Shanghai, and then resettled with his parents in Taiwan when he was of middle-school age. He attended the prestigious National Taiwan University. He published his first short story in September 1958, having just completed his freshman year.

Pai came to the United States in 1963 and since 1965 has taught Chinese at the University of California at Santa Barbara while continuing to publish fiction. His style is among the most polished of any modern writer in Chinese; he depicts his characters with vivid realism, and he often chooses themes that describe the pain of exile, showing the once powerful reduced to humble or humiliating circumstances. Such themes are particularly evident in his highly acclaimed collection of stories, *Wandering in the Garden, Waking from a Dream: Tales of Taipei Characters* (1971), which he dedicates to his parents and "the tumultuous age in which they lived."

With his recent novel *Crystal Boys* (1990), he has become the first modern Chinese writer to explore the theme of homosexuality in a story of gay life in the city of Taipei.

NOVEL BY PAI HSIEN-YUNG

Crystal Boys. Trans. by Howard Goldblatt. Gay Sunshine 1990 $25.00. ISBN 0-940567-10-5. "Goldblatt's translation manages to capture the bittersweet tone" (*World Literature Today*).

SHORT STORY COLLECTION BY PAI HSIEN-YUNG

Wandering in the Garden, Waking from a Dream: Tales of Taipei Characters. Trans. by George Kao. Ind. U. Pr. 1982 o.p. Generally an excellent translation, though more footnotes and more careful use of American slang would be desirable.

PEI TAO [BEI DAO] (Pseud. of Chao Chen-k'ai). 1949–

Pei Tao is best known as a member of the "Misty," or "Obscurantist" School of poetry, so called because many senior poets have looked with a critical eye on these younger poets who sing more of subjective feelings than of politics and use obscure, hard-to-understand images. Begun in the late 1970s, much of this poetry appeared in *Today,* the first underground journal in the People's Republic since 1949. The merits and demerits of the poetry were being widely debated by 1980, and the controversy did not die down for several years. Pei Tao's earlier poems are quite pessimistic, contrasting the small individual with images of immensity, as in traditional landscape paintings; one reviewer, Jane Koepp, has likened his verse to that of the traditional poet LIU TSUNG-YÜAN, who in his exile in the south wrote much poetry with images conveying heaviness and repression.

More recent poetry from Pei Tao's years abroad in Berlin, Oslo, and Stockholm seem slightly more upbeat, hinting that a rebirth may come, may even be imminent—perhaps for art, perhaps for China. In 1990 in Oslo, he and several other exiled writers resurrected the magazine *Today,* where many of his verses have appeared.

In addition to poetry, Pei Tao has also written fiction, much of which appeared in the original incarnation of *Today.* These pieces now seem somewhat dated, because Chinese fiction has changed a good deal in the years since, but they contain hints of the psychological pressures on the young who survived the Cultural Revolution and the forces leading toward the eruption of the Democracy Movement.

POETRY BY PEI TAO

The August Sleepwalker. Trans. by Bonnie S. McDougall. New Dir. Pr. 1990 $16.95. ISBN 0-8112-1131-2. Well-translated book of poems.

Notes from the City of the Sun: Poems by Bei Dao. Ed. and trans. by Bonnie S. McDougall. o.p. Translation is accurate but heavy on interpretation. Original is intentionally obscure. Bei Dao "tried to re-establish literature as an aesthetic medium, a means of emancipating readers without involving them in topical political concerns" (*Journal of Asian Studies*).

Old Snow. Trans. by Bonnie S. McDougall and Chen Maiping. New Dir. Pr. 1991 $16.95. ISBN 0-8112-1182-7. Bilingual collection. "[T]ranslations make Bei Dao's poems easily accessible to readers of English" (*World Literature Today*).

SHORT STORY COLLECTION BY PEI TAO

Waves: Stories. Trans. by Bonnie S. McDougall and Susette Ternent Cooke. New Dir. Pr. 1990 o.p. "Flawlessly translated collection of engrossing prose pieces" (*CLEAR*). Six short stories and a novella dating from the late 1970s and early 1980s.

PING HSIN [BING XIN] (pseud. of Hsieh Wan-ying). 1902–1968

Ping Hsin was born into a scholar-official's family with proud traditions. Her relations with her parents and her brothers were exceptionally close, and this early experience of love seems to permeate many of her later writings. Although born in the south in Minhou, Fukien Province, she spent her youth in the northeast in Yentai (Chefoo), Shantung, which is near the sea. The beauty of the landscape must have made a great impression on her, for in her later work she often makes reference to it.

Ping Hsin graduated from Yenching University (Peking) in 1923 and traveled to the United States, where she pursued an M.A. at Wellesley College. During her years in the United States, she wrote a number of short stories and letters that brought her recognition. She then returned to her alma mater and taught literature until the Sino-Japanese War broke out. During the war she remained in China and became a member of the People's Political Council. However, after the war she spent some time in Japan before making her home permanently in China.

Ping Hsin has penned short stories, poems, and essays. Though she is best known for her fiction, some of her poetry is also of high quality, the more remarkable because, as Julia Lin has pointed out, most of the pioneers in modern Chinese poetry were men. Though her thematic range is admittedly limited, her lyrics have a delicacy and grace that distinguish them. She was much influenced by the Indian poet TAGORE and the form of her verse, like Tagore's, is often brief, with only occasional rhyme for emphasis.

WORK BY PING HSIN

The Photograph. Panda Bks. 1992 o.p.

SHEN TS'UNG-WEN [SHEN CONG-WEN]. 1902–1988

Up to the age of 20, Shen was oblivious to the New Culture movement that was sweeping China. He remained in his home province of Hunan until he came across some books and magazines by new style writers, and then he determined to go to Peking and try a life of literary endeavor himself. But Shen never forgot his rural roots, and later, in a preface to *Border Town*, probably one of his best pieces of fiction, he wrote: "I have an indescribable love for peasants and soldiers. This shows in all my writing, and I have never sought to hide it. I was born and bred in the kind of country town I write about. . . ." This passionate attachment to his backward home region stood him in good stead, and he never seemed to exhaust its creative possibilities for scenic description and character study.

Many have called Shen's fiction pastoral, and it is true that his soldiers, peasants, small shopkeepers, boatmen, and Miao tribesmen have a disarming charm and innocence, even when they are not paragons of virtue. But he is not at all unaware of his country's social ills; it is simply that his nuanced treatment is less blatantly preachy than that of most of his contemporaries. Shen's polished style is extremely popular, and his readers take special delight in his artless Hunanese heroines, most of whom are still protected by youthful innocence or are just on the verge of blossoming into womanhood.

SHORT STORY COLLECTIONS BY SHEN TS'UNG-WEN

The Border Town and Other Stories. Panda Bks. 1981 o.p.

The Chinese Earth. Trans. by Ching Ti and Robert Payne. Col. U. Pr. 1982 $18.50. ISBN 0-231-05485-8. Translations are not always totally reliable but are engagingly literary. Wonderfully diverse material.

BOOK ABOUT SHEN TS'UNG-WEN

Kinkley, Jeffrey C. *The Odyssey of Shen Congwen.* Stanford U. Pr. 1987 $47.50. ISBN 0-8047-1372-3. "The story of Shen's life, his times, his thought, and his art—considered whole" (*CLEAR*).

TAI HOU-YING [DAI HOU-YING]. 1938–

Tai was born in a small town in the province of Anhui and had a difficult childhood after her father, a store manager, was labeled a Rightist for speaking out on economic policy. Her illiterate mother was forced to help keep the family together with her meager earnings as a seamstress. However, Tai was a capable student; she graduated early from East China Normal University in Shanghai and entered the literary arena, being assigned to the Writers' Federation. She married her childhood sweetheart and gave birth to a daughter.

Tragically, she was forced to divorce him a mere six years later during the Cultural Revolution.

In a postscript to her novel *Stones of the Wall*, Tai explains that, for quite a while, being young and impressionable, she went along with the tide of the Cultural Revolution: "In the end, I recognized that all along I had been playing a tragic role in what had seemed to be a comedy. I was a person who although totally deprived of her freedom of thought still believed she was free; a person who showed off her spiritual shackles as if they were a beautiful necklace . . . I then departed from that script and discovered myself."

Before her awakening, Tai had taken part in a committee of inquiry of a poet named Wen Jie (1923–71). Though no wrongdoing was ever proved, he was declared guilty and sent to prison. His wife, humiliated by attacks upon herself after his conviction, committed suicide. Later in 1970 Tai herself was accused of counterrevolutionary activities and sentenced to labor on a farm, where she again met the poet. They fell in love but were denied permission to marry, and further accusations drove Wen Jie to suicide. This incident had a profound impact on Tai, who says she nearly lost her sanity as a result.

In 1979, with the Cultural Revolution behind her, she began teaching literary theory at the University of Shanghai. A student doing a thesis on Wen Jie asked her to write something, and the result was a story entitled "Death of a Poet."

The story launched Tai on a writing career, and her novel *Stones of the Wall* followed in 1980. The protagonists of the novel are teachers and journalists, and each chapter is devoted to one character, who uses an extended monologue that flows like a stream of consciousness to explore a situation or problem in his or her life. Tai's techniques in the novel are a blend of Western stream of consciousness, Freudian analysis, and Chinese drama as created by KUAN HAN-CH'ING. Defending her innovations, Tai writes in her preface that perhaps realism's methods are inadequate to express our age. Certainly, the trends in Chinese fiction in the decade following her novel seem to bear out her observation.

NOVEL BY TAI HOU-YING

Stones of the Wall. Joseph Pub. Co. 1985 o.p.

BOOK ABOUT TAI HOU-YING

Pruyn, Carolyn S. *Humanism in Modern Chinese Literature: The Case of Dai Houying.* Brockmeyer 1988 o.p.

TING LING [DING LING] (pseud. of Chiang Wei). 1904–1986

Ting Ling was born in 1904 in Lingli, Hunan. Her father died when she was very young, and her mother, inspired by the revolutionary ideas of Sun Yat-sen, sent her daughter to Shanghai to a girls' school run by the Communists.

In 1924 Ting Ling moved in with a young writer, Hu Yeh-pin, and later they were joined by SHEN TS'UNG-WEN, forming a *ménage à trois*. In 1928 she shocked literary circles with the publication of *Miss Sophie's Diary*, which revealed the private thoughts of its female protagonists, including their frank admissions of sexual desires.

After her common-law husband Hu Yeh-pin was executed by the Nationalists in 1931, Ting Ling became increasingly radical; she joined the Communist party the following year. She herself then suffered three years of imprisonment by the KMT (Kuomintang) for her political activism, but she eventually made her way to the Communist base in Yenan, where her outspoken criticism of bureaucratic attitudes and male chauvinism brought her into direct conflict with MAO TSE-TUNG (see also Vol. 3).

In 1948 Ting Ling wrote her novel *The Sun Shines Over the Sangkan River*, about the struggle for land reform, which won her the Stalin Prize for Literature in 1951. She had been directly engaged in land reform from 1946 to 1947, and the work reflects her own firsthand experience. It is written in a bold, unadorned revolutionary style. Her dedication was rewarded with chief editorship of the *Literary Gazette*, the party's organ of literary politics.

Ting Ling was denounced in 1955 for her "bourgeois attitudes" and exiled to the northern wastes for 20 years of labor reform. She was finally rehabilitated in the 1970s and proceeded to anger young writers by admonishing them "not to complain so much."

Much of Ting Ling's fiction is admittedly not first-rate, and she has probably received as much notoriety for her flamboyant life as for her literary accomplishments. She has little ear for dialogue and finds it difficult to get into the minds of characters whose backgrounds differ too much from her own. Nevertheless, her work has historical importance, and in recent years has been increasingly studied by feminist scholars outside China.

WORK BY TING LING

I Myself Am a Woman: Selected Writings of Ding Ling. Trans. by Tani E. Barlow and Gary J. Bjorge. Beacon Pr. 1990 $16.00. ISBN 0-8070-6747-4. "Anthology admirably focuses on the complex issues of gender, subjectivity, class, politics, feminism and Marxism in modern Chinese literature as they evolve through the career of a single author" (*CLEAR*).

NOVEL BY TING LING

The Sun Shines Over the Sangkan River. Foreign Lang. Pr. China 1954 o.p.

SHORT STORY COLLECTION BY TING LING

Miss Sophie's Diary and Other Stories. Trans. by William J. F. Jenner. China Bks. 1985 $6.95. ISBN 0-8351-1078-8. "Translation is fluent and idiomatic" (*CLEAR*).

BOOK ABOUT TING LING

Feuerwerker, Yi-tse Mei. *Ding Ling's Fiction*. HUP 1982 $22.00. ISBN 0-674-20765-3. Interesting analysis of her ideological development. Does not claim Ting Ling was necessarily a great writer.

TS'AN HSÜEH [CAN XUE] (pseud. of Teng Hsiao-hua). 1953–

Ts'an Hsüeh was born in Ch'angsha, Hunan, of Communist party activists who married for love and shared the same ideals. However, only four years after her birth, they were declared Rightists and lost their positions at the New Hunan Newspaper office. Her mother was shipped off to a rural commune, where she suffered from illness and malnutrition. Ts'an Hsüeh's maternal grandmother died of starvation in 1961.

Ts'an Hsüeh's education was cut short a few years later by the Cultural Revolution, when she had just finished primary school. For 10 years she worked at various jobs in iron casting, machine fitting, and light industry. In 1978 she met another rusticated youth who had returned to Ch'angsha and had become a carpenter. They married, had a baby, and decided to begin their own tailoring business.

Ts'an Hsüeh began writing fiction during the mid-1980s. Either she accidentally stumbled onto a nonreferential style of writing, or she was actively influenced by Western works in translation; at any rate, she is one of the few Chinese writers to carry out experiments in this direction. As Charlotte Innes writes in her foreword to *Old Floating Cloud*, a book containing two of Ts'an Hsüeh's novellas, "to read Can Xue is . . . like falling asleep over a history book and dreaming a horribly distorted version of what you've just read." Her stories are not allegorical, but there are just enough political phrases sprinkled through them to make one feel that the author's own history and China's destiny are not totally divorced from her surreal world.

One cannot approach Ts'an Hsüeh's works as one would earlier mainland Chinese fiction. Rather than the familiar conventions of Socialist realism, one finds bizarre, morbid, and scatological imagery that may initially repel but that may also fascinate, if seen as an attempt to render symbolically her vision of a revolution degenerated into a nightmare in which humanity's more noble sentiments have been totally debased. Reading Ts'an Hsüeh is a challenge that actively engages the reader in a quest for intelligibility and possible hidden significance.

SHORT STORY COLLECTION BY TS'AN HSÜEH

Dialogues in Paradise. Trans. by Ronald R. Jannsen and Jian Zhang. Northwestern U. Pr. 1989 $19.95. ISBN 0-8101-0830-5. "From the barely readable to the totally non-referential" (*World Literature Today*).

NOVELS BY TS'AN HSÜEH

Old Floating Cloud: Two Novellas. Trans. by Ronald R. Jannsen and Jian Zhang. Northwestern U. Pr. 1991 $32.95. ISBN 0-8101-0974-3. "Like her characters, she seems to be determined, against all odds, to find something worth cherishing and dreaming about" (*World Literature Today*).

TS'AO YÜ [CAO YU] (pseud. of Wan Chia-pao). 1905–

Ts'ao was born into a wealthy family in Hupei Province and already had demonstrated his love for the theater by the time he was in the elite Nankai Middle School in Tianjin, where he was active in dramatics. Later at Tsinghua University he continued to work backstage and to act (even performing once as IBSEN's Nora!), and he immersed himself in Western drama. After graduation he became an instructor in the National Institute of Drama in wartime Chungking, Szechuan.

However, it was in the writing of plays that Ts'ao actually made his greatest contribution. Although modern Chinese theater had been in existence ever since Hung Shen had returned from America in 1921, many of the earliest plays produced in China had tended to be quite didactic in nature. But Ts'ao Yü's plays were something new. Although he borrowed heavily from a wide variety of Western playwrights—from the ancient Greeks to CHEKHOV—his subject matter was thoroughly Chinese, and the people loved it. *Thunderstorm* (1934), produced in 1935 by the Fu Tan Drama Society upon Hung Shen's recommendation, was an immediate box office success. *Sunrise* (1935), *The Wilderness*, *Metamorphosis*, *Peking Man*, and *The Family* followed shortly after, all within the space of a few short years, before the disruptions of the Sino-Japanese War. These works are still among the most popular in the Chinese drama repertoire, and are often produced. In Hong Kong in the 1970s, a Ts'ao Yü Festival was carried out.

As Joseph Lao wrote in his study of Ts'ao Yü, the play *Peking Man* is perhaps his most mature product, in which for the first time he actually utilizes the drama's unique potential for the "art of showing." However, *Thunderstorm* is perhaps his best-known play, depicting a day in the life of the Chao family, when suddenly old secrets are exposed and family unity begins to unravel. It is humid, and a thunderstorm is brewing, both metaphorically and literally.

Ts'ao Yü lived in the United States with the fiction writer LAO SHE from 1946 to 1949 and then returned to China. After the Communist government gained power, he held a number of cultural posts.

PLAYS BY TS'AO YÜ

Peking Man. Trans. by Leslie Nai-kwai Lo, Don Cohn, and Michelle Vosper. Col. U. Pr. 1986 o.p.

Sunrise: A Play in Four Acts. Trans. by A. C. Barnes. Cheng & Tsui 1978 repr. of 1935 ed. $9.95. ISBN 0-917056-73-6

Thunderstorm. Trans. by Liang Tso and A. C. Barnes. Cheng & Tsui 1978 $9.95. ISBN 0-917056-74-4

The Wilderness. Ind. U. Pr. 1980 o.p.

BOOKS ABOUT TS'AO YÜ

Hu, John Y. *Ts'ao Yü*. G. K. Hall. *Twayne's World Authors Ser.* o.p. Interesting biography encompassing most of Ts'ao Yü's life and work.

Lao, Joseph S. M. *Ts'ao Yü*. Hong Kong U. Pr. 1970 o.p. Standard biography.

WANG AN-I [WANG AN-YI]. 1954–

Wang An-i is the only prominent woman writer among the "Seeking Roots" group. Her writing has a distinct Chinese flavor, although one also detects a debt to surrealism and to novels like *One Hundred Years of Solitude*.

The daughter of the fiction writer JU CHIH-CHÜAN, Wang An-i grew up in Shanghai, and, like so many others of her generation, had her education cut short in 1969 when she was sent out to do farm labor on a commune in the very poor and backward northern part of Anhwei Province. In 1972 her fortunes improved when she was relocated to northern Kiangsu to the city of Hsü-chou, where she became part of a cultural troupe. She began to publish short stories in 1976, while she was still away from home.

Wang An-i was allowed to return to Shanghai in 1978, and she found a job as editor of the magazine *Childhood*. Since then her career has been spectacular. In 1980, the year in which she wrote "And the Rain Patters On," she was offered an opportunity for further professional training, and two important stories—"Base of the Wall" and "Lapse of Time"—followed in 1981 and 1982. These stories deal with the subtle psychological changes of characters during the "10 lost years" of the Cultural Revolution.

Wang An-i now claims to be exploring the "deep structure" of Chinese culture, as well as FREUD (see Vols. 3 and 5) and sexuality. She has always claimed that she herself has been driven by "repressed passions," and it is an indication of her intellectual curiosity and honesty that she should probe these forces in her fiction.

Chinese readers admire her "delicate and restrained" style, which may owe something to her mother's early courageous experiments. However, Wang An-i has the potential to surpass her mother's achievements and is considered one of the most promising of the woman fiction writers in China today.

NOVELS BY WANG AN-I

Baotown. Norton 1989 o.p.

Brocade Valley. Trans. by Bonnie S. McDougall and Chen Maiping. New Dir. Pr. 1992 $9.95. ISBN 0-8112-1224-6. The third work in Wang's "love trilogy."

SHORT STORIES BY WANG AN-I

Lapse of Time. China Bks. 1988 $1.99. ISBN 0-8351-2032-5. Stories from the early 1980s. Maxine Hong Kingston has written: "Now that . . . Chinese books are available to American readers, I would recommend *Lapse of Time* as a good place to begin."

Love on a Barren Mountain. Trans. by Eva Hung. Small Pr. Dist. 1991 $8.95. ISBN 962-7255-09-2. A novella written in 1985, exploring extramarital relationships in a repressed society.

WANG MENG. 1934–

Wang is ranked among China's top 12 contemporary writers, and among its technically most innovative and controversial. After being purged as a Rightist at the age of 21, he was sentenced to 5 years of hard labor, followed by indefinite exile to the far northwest in Sinkiang. After 20 years he reappeared in 1979 on the literary scene, and before long he had published "Eyes of the Night," *Bolshevik Salute*, "Butterfly," "Voices of Spring," and "Dreams of the Sea." All of these works came under fire as "Western and modernist," at a time when these terms were far from flattering. But his tremendous creativity spearheaded the rebirth of Chinese literature during the Democracy Wall Movement.

Wang's works all break new ground. "Eyes of the Night" has almost no plot but is rather a study of a character's inner thoughts about the changes in society in the post-Mao era. It is written in the form of a third-person narrative that William Tay describes as an attempt "to render a character's thoughts in his or her own idiom with only the implicit intervention of the narrator." A similar form of narrative monologue is also used in "Voices of Spring."

"Dreams of the Sea" was the first experiment in what came to be called the "flat depiction" method, which "flattened" certain aspects, like character and plot, in order to strengthen powerful lyric emotions. In this type of writing, all becomes subjectified and melded into the feelings of the author. After Wang Meng's initial experiment, it enjoyed a brief vogue among certain writers. With *Bolshevik Salute*, a longer and more complicated work treating the 30 years of history following 1949, we see an early effort to abandon linear, chronological narration, and this technique is also used effectively in "Butterfly."

Wang served as minister of culture from 1986 to 1989. But quite recently, he has again found himself at the center of controversy with a short story entitled "Hard Porridge," which many have read as a thinly veiled allegory of the ineffectual aging Peking leadership in the wake of the disastrous Tiananmen Square incident of 1989.

NOVEL BY WANG MENG

Bolshevik Salute: A Modernist Chinese Novel. Trans. by Wendy Larson. U. of Wash. Pr. 1990 $19.95. ISBN 0-295-96856-7. Closing essay by the translator puts the novel into its historical context.

SHORT STORY COLLECTION BY WANG MENG

The Butterfly and Other Stories. o.p.

YANG CHIANG [YANG JIANG] (pseud. of Yang Chi-k'ang). 1911–

Yang was a student of foreign languages at Tung-wu (Soochow) University and at Tsinghua University in the 1930s. At the latter institution, she met and married her famous husband CH'IEN CHUNG-SHU. She traveled with him to Oxford, returning to China in 1937 just at the outbreak of war with Japan.

Yang was shy and socially retiring, and kept herself out of the limelight entirely until several friends urged her to try writing plays. She proceeded to write four plays during the war period—two comedies, one melodrama, and one tragedy. Her plays are characterized by an unusual degree of ironic detachment and subtle attention to psychology, which drew praise from critics. Audiences loved the comedy.

After 1949 Yang became a professor of English literature at Tsinghua. Later she became a fellow, first in the Institute of Literature and then in the Institute of Foreign Literature. She has translated and done critical studies on several French and Spanish works.

The ordeal that Yang and her husband endured during the Cultural Revolution is the subject of her autobiographical essay, *Six Chapters from My Life "Downunder."* Modeled on SHEN FU's Ch'ing dynasty work, it is similarly a testament to the devotion of a loving couple during times of great physical and spiritual hardship. It is also an allegorical comment on the entire revolutionary process, although low-key and subtle on the surface.

NONFICTION BY YANG CHIANG

Six Chapters from My Life "Downunder." Trans. by Howard Goldblatt. U. of Wash. Pr. 1984 $9.95. ISBN 0-295-96644-0. Reads like an essay, based on the format of the Ch'ing minor classic *Six Chapters from a Floating Life* by Shen Fu.

Six Chapters of Life in a Cadre School: Memoirs from China's Cultural Revolution. Trans. by Chu Djang. Westview 1986 o.p.

CHAPTER 8

Japanese Literature

Dan McLeod and Gale Fox

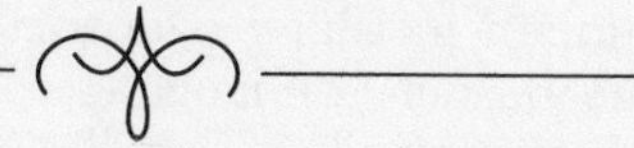

> If man were never to fade away like the dews of Adashino, never to vanish like the smoke over Toribeyama, but lingered on forever in this world, how things would lose their power to move us! The most precious thing in life is its uncertainty.
>
> —YOSHIDA KENKŌ, *Essays in Idleness*

Western literatures tend to reflect Judeo-Christian values that stress permanence. Viewing souls as immortal lends significance to life, and the truth and beauty expressed in Western literatures seem connected with eternal verities. Japanese literature, as suggested by the quotation above from YOSHIDA KENKŌ's fourteenth-century essay, expresses a transitory view of life. Even the forms of classic Japanese literature demonstrate this contrasting world view. The 31-syllable tanka and the 17-syllable haiku are surely the shortest poetic forms for serious poetry in world literature. Yet they are Japan's major poetic forms, perhaps precisely because they are such ideal vehicles for suggesting transient moments of insight and beauty. Furthermore, such short, undeveloped poems lend themselves to a variety of interpretations. Japanese poetry celebrates not the everlasting, but what Kenko claims is "the most precious thing in life . . . uncertainty."

Uncertainty is also a characteristic of traditional, and a good deal of modern, Japanese fiction. Western critics frequently point out the relative formlessness of Japanese narratives, which the Japanese justify as a simple preference for irregular forms over the complex or artificial symmetries of Western plots. The unresolved conclusions of many widely admired Japanese novels have puzzled Western readers. Whether or not *The Tale of Genji* (c.1000), universally acknowledged as the masterpiece of Japanese fiction, is actually completed remains an unanswerable question.

Even the traditional forms of Japanese drama bear only a superficial resemblance to Western theatrical forms. Noh (or Nō) drama, the oldest form, with its masks, chorus, and ritualistic elements, may recall classical Greek drama, and the somewhat later Kabuki theater may remind some of opera, but the seriousness and subtlety of Bunraku, the Japanese puppet theater, has nothing at all in common with the Punch and Judy puppetry of the West.

Because of Japan's long periods of cultural isolation, its literature is more easily categorized into classical and modern than most world literatures, and this chapter follows that division. Classical Japanese literature is usually dated from the eighth century, when the Japanese borrowed and adapted the Chinese writing system and were, for the first time, able to record their oral traditions and begin composing a new written literature. The oldest recorded Japanese literature, the mytho-historic *Kojiki* (Records of Ancient Matters) (c.712) and the large collection of poetry called the *Manyoshu* (The Anthology of Ten Thousand Leaves) (c.759), owe something to ancient Chinese histories and poetry collections, but they are for the most part purely Japanese. Even though some Japanese writers have chosen to write in Chinese from the earliest times to the present, the most significant poetry and fiction—such as the *Kokinshu*, a collection of old and new poems compiled around 905, and the *Tale of Genji* (*Genji monogatari*), written about eight years later—are entirely Japanese in language, themes, and style. This relative freedom from foreign influences is much easier to maintain in island countries such as Japan than in countries with less formidable borders or languages.

The modern literary period is usually dated from about 1868 with the ascension of the Meiji emperor—a little over a decade after Commodore Perry "opened" Japan to the world and ended 200 years of extraordinary isolation. The westernization of Japan has been going on ever since and is the main element in the literature's modernization. While retaining many characteristics of the classical literature, twentieth-century Japanese literature draws on the literatures of Europe and America, just as the translation of Japanese literature into Western languages has influenced writers all over the world.

CLASSICAL JAPANESE LITERATURE

In the chapter's opening epigraph, Kenkō links evaporating dews and drifting smoke to humankind's transitory and uncertain fate. This predisposition to relate human actions and attitudes to natural processes is among the most pervasive characteristics of classical Japanese literature. We find it in the *Kojiki*, where the divine creation of Japan and its imperial family is reflected in myths of the sun goddess and where other origin myths connect natural phenomena like storms and fires to human traits and historical events. We find it also, more intimately expressed, in the Manyoshu. Both works appeared in the eighth century and, along with the *Kaifuso*, a collection of poetry written in Chinese, are the major works of the Ancient Period.

The most important classics of the Heian Period (794–1115) are the *Kokinshu*, (Lady) MURASAKI SHIKIBU's *Tale of Genji*, and SEI SHŌNAGON's *Pillow Book* (*Makura no soshi*) (c.975). Much of Heian literature was written by women, most notably Lady Murasaki, whose *Tale of Genji* (c.1000) is not only the world's first novel but also one of the finest ever written. The *Pillow Book*, whose author was also a lady of the Heian court, is still considered by the Japanese a masterpiece of literary wit and stylistic purity. Part diary, essay, and miscellany, it defies literary classification.

The relatively peaceful Heian period drew to a close in the twelfth century, to be followed by a period of violence and civil strife—Japan's dark ages. Despite the wars that ravaged Kyoto—the site of the aristocrat, elegant Heian culture—this Medieval Period (1185–1600) saw the development of Japan's first great dramatic genre, the austere and ritualistic Noh. Other noteworthy examples of medieval literature are the epiclike *Tale of Heike* (Heiki monogatari) (written down c.fourteenth century) and Kamo no Chomei's *An Account of My Hut* (Hojoki) (1212). Both of these works, and perhaps even the Noh drama, may be viewed as responses to the age's violence. *The Tale of Heike* chronicles the power struggle between the Taira (Heike) and Minamoto (Genji) clans toward the end of the twelfth century, while *An Account of My Hut* reflects the disastrous collapse of Kyoto by fire, earthquake, and civil war. Its author,

Chomei, began his life as a courtier but later took Buddhist vows and retired from the social world. The great poet of the early medieval period was Saigyo (1118–90) who, like Chomei, was a courtier-turned-mendicant monk, sickened by the mindless civil strife. Of these literary developments, perhaps the most significant was the advent of Noh drama, transformed from a simple folk drama by Kanami Kiyotsugu (1333–84) and his son ZEAMI MOTOKIYO (1363–1443) into one of the world's most refined dramatic forms.

While Heian literature dealt mostly with aristocrats and medieval with samurai warriors and Buddhist recluses, the Tokugawa Period (1600–1866) was largely concerned with the bourgeoisie. Samurai and aristocrats continued to support Noh performances, but ordinary city tradespeople enjoyed the more flamboyant Kabuki plays that had developed in the sixteenth century when female dance troupes performed at shrine festivals. The immoral conduct associated with these productions eventually provoked government proscription, and by the time of CHIKAMATSU MONZAEMON (1653–1724), the greatest writer for both Kabuki and Bunraku, only adult males could perform on stage. Chikamatsu's plays are important in world literature as the first genuine tragedies about ordinary people. His contemporary, MATSUO BASHŌ was the greatest of the haiku poets. During the Tokugawa Period, this 17-syllable form largely replaced the 31-syllable waka (also called tanka) as the most important Japanese verse form.

The Tokugawa also saw the development of picaresque fiction, which, even more than Kabuki drama, dealt with ordinary people. Its most celebrated exponent was IHARA SAIKAKU, whose *The Life of an Amorous Man* (*Koshoku ichidai otoko*) recounts the erotic adventures of a young man in a style and milieu entirely different from that of the aristocratic *Tale of Genji*. So popular was it that he followed it with *The Life of an Amorous Woman* (*Koshoku ichidai onna*), which chronicles the decline of a court lady (a heroine every bit as sex-obsessed as the earlier novel's hero) to an ordinary prostitute. Chikamatsu and Saikaku's interest in the plights of ordinary people paved the way for the Japanese interest in realism, one of many Western trends that would trail in the wake of Perry's ships. Their arrival in 1854 marks the beginning of the end for the Tokugawa Period and the start of Japan's modern transformation.

Note: In the bibliographies the editors have followed the Japanese practice of giving a person's surname first. In addition, the reader should be aware that the Japanese also frequently use pen names. This chapter uses the most commonly accepted English versions of an author's name, but the reader is advised that other variations may exist.

History and Criticism: Prose

Kato, Shuichi. *A History of Japanese Literature: The First Thousand Years.* Vol. 1 Trans. by David Chibbet. Kodansha Ltd. Japan 1982 $8.95. ISBN 0-87011-491-3. A lively critical and intellectual history. Begins with discussions of the *Manyoshu* and folk tales and ends with a chapter on Noh.

______. *A History of Japanese Literature: The Years of Isolation.* Vol. 2 Trans. by Rene E. Etiemble. Kodansha Ltd. Japan 1983 $35.00. ISBN 0-87011-568-5. Covers early-seventeenth to mid-nineteenth centuries. Good discussions of haiku, Bunraku, Kabuki, the popular novel, comic haiku, and Kotetsu, Sorai, Hakuseki, Bashō, and Chikamatsu.

Keene, Donald. *Japanese Literature: An Introduction for Western Readers.* Grove Pr. 1955 o.p. A brief but informative work. Basic reading for the beginner.

______. *World within Walls: Japanese Literature of the Pre-Modern Era 1600–1867*. H. Holt & Co. 1976 $22.95. ISBN 0-03-013626-1. Eminently readable either as a whole or as a reference. Part of Keene's monumental critical-history-in-progress.

______. *The Pleasures of Japanese Literature*. Col. U. Pr. 1988 $20.00. ISBN 0-231-06736-4. Essays on traditional Japanese aesthetics, poetry, fiction, and theater. In some ways an update of his now classic *Japanese Literature*.

______. *Travelers of a Hundred Ages*. H. Holt & Co. 1989 $35.00. ISBN 0-8050-0751-2. The most comprehensive commentary in English on the important diary genre. Discusses nearly 80 diaries, Heian through Tokugawa periods.

Konishi, Jin'ichi. *A History of Japanese Literature*. Vol. 1 *The Archaic and Ancient Ages*. Ed. by Earl Miner. Trans. by Aileen Gatten and Nicholas Teele. Princeton U. Pr. 1984 $67.50. ISBN 0-691-06592-6. A complex work, valuable for its emphasis on the interrelations among Chinese, Korean, and Japanese literatures. Part of an exhaustive five-volume study of the classical literature, of which only the first three volumes are translated.

______. *A History of Japanese Literature*. Vol. 2 *The Early Middle Ages*. Ed. by Earl Miner. Trans. by Aileen Gatten. Princeton U. Pr. 1986 $67.50. ISBN 0-691-0055-8. Covers Heian literature.

______. *A History of Japanese Literature*. Vol. 3 *The High Middle Ages*. Ed. by Earl Miner. Trans. by Aileen Gatten and Mark Harbison. Princeton U. Pr. 1991 $74.50. ISBN 0-691-10248-1. Covers the post-Heian literature to the sixteenth century, with chapters on linked poetry (*renga*), poetic diaries (*nikki*), and Noh drama.

LaFleur, William R. *The Karma of Words: Buddhism and the Literary Arts in Medieval Japan*. U. CA Pr. 1983 $12.95. ISBN 0-520-05622-1. Deals with religious themes in Chomei, Zeami, and Bashō and comments on Buddhist style in various arts. Clearly written and influential.

Marks, Alfred H., and Barry D. Bort. *Guide to Japanese Prose. Asian Lit. Bibliography Ser.* G. K. Hall 1984 o.p. Somewhat dated as a bibliography, but useful for its brief histories, plot summaries, and very full annotations.

Miner, Earl, ed. *Principles of Classical Japanese Literature*. Princeton U. Pr. 1985 o.p. Fine essays by the editor, Makoto Ueda, Konishi Jin'ichi, and others on the literature's social implications and structural features.

Miner, Earl, Hiroko Odagiri, and Robert E. Morrel. *The Princeton Companion to Classical Japanese Literature*. Princeton U. Pr. 1985 $59.00. ISBN 0-691-00825-6. An excellent handbook. Contains a brief literary history, chronologies, and short entries on major authors, works, and terms. Extensive chapters on theater and types of literary collections.

Putzer, Edward. *Japanese Literature: A Historical Outline*. Bks. Demand 1973 $69.50. ISBN 0-317-09821-7. A translation and adaptation of *Nihon bungaku (Japanese Literature)* (1960), written by respected Japanese scholars. Mainly valuable now for their literary assessments.

Rimer, J. Thomas. *A Reader's Guide to Japanese Literature: From the Eighth Century to the Present*. Kodansha Ltd. Japan 1988 $14.95. ISBN 0-87011-896-X. Readable summaries and assessments of 20 classical and 30 modern works, with comments on translations and authors.

Ueda, Makoto. *Literary and Art Theories in Japan*. Pr. of Western Reserve Univ. 1967 o.p. Valuable essays on premodern aesthetics and poetics by one of the most respected scholars and interpreters of Japanese literature.

History and Criticism: Drama

Bowers, Faubion. *Japanese Theatre*. Greenwood 1976 repr. of 1952 ed. o.p. A classic work. Includes plot summaries, excerpts, and three kabuki plays. A foreword by Joshua Logan.

Ernst, Earle. *The Kabuki Theatre*. UH Pr. 1974 repr. of 1956 ed. o.p. Often uses Western drama as a point of reference, helpful to the nonspecialist. A standard work.

Fenollosa, Ernest F., and Ezra Pound. *The Classic Noh Theatre of Japan*. Greenwood 1977 repr. of 1959 ed. $45.00. ISBN 0-8371-9580-2. An early study with translations, distinguished by the stature of the authors.

Keene, Donald. *No and Bunraku: Two Forms of Japanese Theatre*. Col. U. Pr. 1990 $37.00. ISBN 0-231-07418-2. An introduction to these forms by the foremost Japanese literature scholar in America.

Kincaid, Zoe. *Kabuki: The Popular Stage of Japan*. Ayer repr. of 1925 ed. $35.50. ISBN 0-405-08703-9. An evocative and entertaining account of the history and performing tradition of Kabuki.

Leiter, Samuel L. *Kabuki Encyclopedia: An English Language Adaptation of Kabuki Jiten*. Greenwood 1979 $55.00. ISBN 0-313-20654-6. Valuable for understanding terminology and for its numerous plot summaries. Includes extremely helpful cross-references and index.

Pronko, Leonard C. *Guide to Japanese Drama. Asian Lit. Bibliography Ser.* G. K. Hall 1984 o.p. A good short history as well as fully annotated bibliographies of criticism and anthologies.

Scott, A. C. *Puppet Theatre of Japan*. C. E. Tuttle 1973 o.p. A brief but useful introduction. Includes summaries of 10 popular plays and a glossary.

History and Criticism: Poetry

Brower, Robert H., and Earl Miner. *Japanese Court Poetry*. Stanford U. Pr. 1961 $55.00. ISBN 0-8047-0536-4. The definitive work on the subject, distinguished by excellent translations and analyses and a detailed history. Includes a helpful glossary and index.

McCullough, Helen Craig. *Brocade by Night: 'Kokiu Wakashu' and the Court Style in Japanese Classical Poetry*. Stanford U. Pr. 1985 $60.00. ISBN 0-8047-1246-8. A survey of the full range of classical Japanese poetry, including what it has drawn from the Chinese.

Miner, Earl. *An Introduction to Japanese Court Poetry*. Stanford U. Pr. 1968 $25.00. ISBN 0-8047-0635-2. The basic book on Japanese verse, 600–1500. Includes valuable information on forms, conventions, and themes, and on the social values they arise from.

______. *Japanese Linked Poetry: An Account with Translations of Renga and Haikai Sequences*. Princeton U. Pr. 1978 $16.95. ISBN 0-691-01368-3. Divided equally between a study of *renga* and *haikai*, which replaced court poetry, and translations of several important poetic sequences.

Ooka, Makoto. *The Colors of Poetry: Essays in Classic Japanese Verse*. Trans. by Takako and Thomas Lento. Katydid Bks. 1991 $19.95. ISBN 0-942668-28-6. Fresh and penetrating studies of Heian waka by a distinguished modern Japanese poet, with a preface by Donald Keene.

Rimer, J. Thomas, and Robert E. Morrell. *Guide to Japanese Poetry. Asian Lit. Bibliography Ser.* G. K. Hall 1984 o.p. A comprehensive introduction. Includes a good short history and detailed annotations of books dealing with all genres.

Collections: Prose

Keene, Donald, ed. *Anthology of Japanese Literature: Earliest Era to Mid-Nineteenth Century*. Grove Pr. 1988 $13.95. ISBN 0-8021-5058-6. Still the basic anthology of premodern Japanese literature, with helpful introductions and good translations.

McCullough, Helen C., ed. and trans. *Classical Japanese Prose*. Stanford U. Pr. 1990 $65.00. ISBN 0-8047-1960-8. A representative collection from the ninth to the seventeenth century. Includes generous selections from every prose form, with good representation of women writers.

Miner, Earl. *Japanese Poetic Diaries*. U. CA Pr. 1969 $10.95. ISBN 0-520-03047-8. An excellent introduction to the *nikki* form, with full translations from Heian times to the twentieth century.

Collections: Drama

Brandon, James R. *Kabuki: Five Classic Plays*. Bks. Demand 1975 $104.80. ISBN 0-7837-2227-3. Excellent translations that capture the genre's vigor and poetic yet colloquial force. The introduction, stage directions, and photographs increase appreciation of the plays.

Keene, Donald, ed. *Twenty Plays of the No Theatre*. Col. U. Pr. 1970 $20.00. ISBN 0-231-03455-5. Still a major modern anthology. Translations, by various contributors, of high literary quality. Includes excellent introductions.

Waley, Arthur. *The No Plays of Japan*. C. E. Tuttle 1976 $12.95. ISBN 0-8048-1198-9. Graceful translations by a major translator of Japanese literature.

Yasuda, Kenneth. *Masterworks of the No Theater*. Trans. by Earl Miner. Ind. U. Pr. 1989 $75.00. ISBN 0-253-36805-7. Splendid translations and thorough commentaries on 18 classic plays. Also includes the translator's own Noh play.

Collections: Poetry

Carter, Steven D., trans. *Traditional Japanese Poetry*. Stanford U. Pr. 1991 $60.00. ISBN 0-8047-1569. A representative selection dating from the earliest times to the twentieth century, with romanticized Japanese texts.

______, trans. *Waiting for the Wind: Thirty-six Poets of Japan's Late Middle Ages*. Col. U. Pr. 1989 $39.00. ISBN 0-231-06854-9. The only anthology of late medieval (1250–(1250–1500) poetry, often neglected by translators. Includes more than 400 selections, with excellent notes and commentaries.

Henderson, Harold G., trans. *An Introduction to Haiku: An Anthology of Poems and Poets from Basho to Shiki*. *Anchor Literary Lib*. Doubleday 1958 $2.50. ISBN 0-385-09376-4. Offers the translator's choice of the poets' best poems. Interspersed with commentary.

Levy, Howard S., trans. *Japan's Best-Loved Poetry Classic: Hyakunin Isshu*. Vol. 1 Oriental Bk. 3rd rev. ed. 1976 o.p. The most widely–known anthology in Japan; includes 100 poems by 100 classical poets.

Rexroth, Kenneth, and Ikuko Atsumi, trans. *Women Poets of Japan (The Burning Heart: Women Poets of Japan)*. New Dir. Pr. 1982 $7.95. ISBN 0-8112-0820-6. Various verse forms from the seventh century to the present. Includes brief biographies of the poets and a concise but helpful survey of women's poetry.

Sato, Hiroaki, and Burton Watson, trans. and eds. *From the Country of Eight Islands*. Col. U. Pr. 1986 $16.00. ISBN 0-231-06395-4. A remarkably complete and diversified anthology of poetry by two distinguished translators. Includes a glossary and brief biographies of major poets.

Anonymously Composed Classics

Chushingura: The Treasure of Loyal Retainers, A Puppet Play. Trans. by Donald Keene. Col. U. Pr. 1971 $40.00. ISBN 0-231-03531-4. First performed in 1748, probably the most popular of Japanese plays. A tale of vendetta, based on an actual event.

Kojiki. Trans. by Donald L. Philippi. Col. U. Pr. 1977 $40.00. ISBN 0-86008-320-9. Completed in 712, Japan's first history and a major source of its mythology. Includes helpful notes and appendixes.

Kokinshu: A Collection of Poems Ancient and Modern. Trans. by Laurel R. Rodd and Mary C. Henkinius. Princeton U. Pr. 1984 $55.00. ISBN 0-691-06593-4. Completed in 905, the *Kokinshu* is the first anthology of court poetry in the *waka* form and the model for many to follow. Its major themes are love and the seasons. The vernacular preface by Ki no Tsurayuki contains the first discussion of Japanese poetics.

Kokin Wakashu. Trans. by Helen Craig McCullough. Stanford U. Pr. 1985 $49.00. ISBN 0-8047-1258-1. Masterful translation with facing romanized Japanese texts. Like the preceding Rodd-Henkinius edition, it provides considerable background on the anthology. Includes translations of the *Tosa Nikki* and the *Shinsen Waka*.

The Manyoshu: The Nippon Gakujutsu Shinkokai Translation of One Thousand Poems. Col. U. Pr. 1969 o.p. Of the more than 4,000 poems in the first extant anthology of Japanese verse, the *Manyoshu* (traditionally dated 759), this edition presents 1,000. The introduction and some attributions of authorship are flawed by prewar biases. However, until the Levy translation is completed (see *The Ten Thousand Leaves*), this is still the standard translation, generally sound in its scholarship.

A Tale of Flowering Fortunes: Annals of Japanese Aristocratic Life in the Heian Period. 2 vols. Trans. by William H. McCullough and Helen C. McCullough. Stanford U. Pr. 1980 o.p. A portrait of an age, rich in detail. Notes and appendices form a fine introduction to the institutions and culture of the time.

The Tale of the Heike: Heike Monogatari. 2 vols. Trans. by Hiroshi Kitagawa and Bruce T. Tsuchida. Col. U. Pr. 1975 $45.00. ISBN 0-86008-189-3. Foreword by Edward G. Seidensticiker. The greatest of the medieval war tales, it depicts the twelfth-century conflict between the Minamoto and Taira clans. Presents the Buddhist notion of life's impermanence and the theme that the proud (the Taira) are bound to fall. Originally transmitted orally, this tale was probably written down in the late fourteenth century.

The Tale of Heike. Trans. by Helen Craig McCullough. Stanford U. Pr. 1988 $65.00. ISBN 0-8047-1418-5. A much more readable translation than that of Kitagawa, Hiroshi, and Tsuchida, but no less scholarly in its introductions, notes, appendices, and glossary.

Tales of Ise: Lyrical Episodes from Tenth-Century Japan (Ise Monogatari). Trans. by Helen C. McCullough. Stanford U. Pr. 1968 $32.50. ISBN 0-8047-0653-0. The subject of this poem-tale, a major source of material for later writers, is the loves of the famous ninth-century poet Ariwara no Narihira. The introduction sets the work in the context of the court culture of its time.

Tales of Times Now Past: Sixty-Two Stories from a Medieval Japanese Collection (Konjaku Monogatari). Trans. by Marian Ury. U. CA Pr. 1979 $10.95. ISBN 0-520-05467-9. These selections from a collection of fables about India, China, and Japan are important examples of the setsuwa (fable) genre. Themes may be either Buddhist or secular.

The Ten Thousand Leaves. Trans. by Ian Hideo Levy. Princeton U. Pr. 1981 $14.95. ISBN 0-691-00029-8. The first five books of a multi-volume translation that will replace the prewar translation of the *Manyoshu* (Ten Thousand Leaves). Honored by a number of prestigious translation prizes.

Yoshitsune: A Fifteenth-Century Japanese Chronicle (Gikeiki). Ed. and trans. by Helen C. McCullough. Stanford U. Pr. 1966 $32.50. ISBN 0-804-0270-5. Set in the same world as *The Tale of the Heike*, this fifteenth-century work deals with the adventures and tragedy of Minamoto no Yoshitsune. It is a good story, well translated, and like *Heike*, a major source of material for later works.

CHRONOLOGY OF AUTHORS

This chronology is given Japanese-style, family names first.

Ki no Tsurayuki. c.868–c.945
The Mother of Fujiwara Michitsuna. d.955
Izumi Shikibu. c.976
Murasaki Shikibu. c.978–c.1030
Sei Shōnagon. fl. late 10th century
Nijō, Lady. b.1257
Kenkō Yoshida. 1283–1352
Zeami. 1363–c.1493
Ihara Saikaku. 1642–1693
Bashō. 1644–1694
Chikamatsu Monzaemon. 1653–1724
Yosa Buson. 1716–1783
Ueda Akinari. 1734–1809
Kobayashi Issa. 1763–1827

BASHŌ (pseud. of Matsuo Munefusa; also Matsuo Bashō). 1644–1694

The greatest of Japan's haiku poets and the greatest poet of his age, Bashō raised the genre from a mediocre entertainment to serious verse and contributed greatly to its poetics. The work of his peak period is characterized by evocations of humankind's ultimate harmony with nature. He traveled widely, recording his journeys in his lyrical poetic diaries. He had numerous disciples, and haiku has remained a vigorous form of poetry to the present.

Poetry by Bashō

A Haiku Journey: Bashō's "The Narrow Road to the Far North" and Selected Haiku. Trans. by Dorothy Britton. Kodansha Ltd. Japan 1975 $5.95. ISBN 0-87011-423-9. Primarily a photographic essay to illustrate Bashō's masterpiece, *Oku no Hosomichi;* the accompanying translation reads well.

The Monkey's Straw Raincoat and Other Poetry of the Bashō School. Trans. by Earl Miner and Hiroko Odagiri. Princeton U. Pr. 1981 $10.40. ISBN 0-8357-3711-X. Primarily a translation of Bashō's *Sarumino*—like *Oku no Hosomichi,* a poetic travel diary. Includes an introduction explaining this genre, helpful annotations, and indexes of terms and poets.

The Narrow Road to the Deep North and Other Travel Sketches. Trans. by Nobuykki Yuasa. Viking Penguin 1967 $6.95. ISBN 0-14-044185-9. Bashō's travel diaries in serviceable translations. Some annotations.

Books about Bashō

Aiken, Robert. *Bashō and His Interpreters: Selected Hokku.* Stanford U. Pr. 1992 $49.50. ISBN 0-8047-1916-0. Presents a wide spectrum of Japanese critical commentary over the last 300 years. Includes new translations of 255 representative haiku.

———. *A Zen Wave: Bashō's Haiku and Zen.* Weatherhill 1979 $9.95. ISBN 0-8348-0137-X. Many fine translations in this study of the religious dimensions of haiku.

Ueda, Makoto. *Matsuo Bashō.* Kodansha Ltd. Japan 1983 $6.50. ISBN 0-87011-553-7. A thorough but readable study of Bashō's life and work. Includes a list of works in English translation, a chronology of Bashō's life, and a map of his journeys.

CHIKAMATSU MONZAEMON. 1653–1724

Widely regarded as the greatest dramatist of the Edo Period, Chikamatsu wrote for both the Kabuki stage and the puppet theater (Bunraku). He gradually abandoned the former because the actors often took liberties with his lines. His plays fall into two major groups, historical and domestic dramas. A dominant theme of the latter, which were sometimes based on contemporary events, is the conflict between duty (*giri*) and human feelings (*ninio*). Some of his finest plays are domestic works, often consisting of the lyrical depiction of ill-fated loves. Chikamatsu's language is rich and reflects his knowledge of the classics, both Japanese and Chinese, and of Buddhism. His plays are still widely read and performed.

Plays by Chikamatsu

Major Plays of Chikamatsu. Trans. by Donald Keene. Col. U. Pr. 1990 $17.50. ISBN 0-231-07414-X. Works for the puppet theater in an excellent translation. Includes an introduction about Chikamatsu, with discussion of puppet theater.

IHARA SAIKAKU (pseud. of Hirayama Togo; also Ibara Saikaku). 1642–1693

A prolific writer of haiku, Saikaku is better known now as a writer of fiction about the life of the townspeople in his native Osaka. His style is marked by detachment, wit, and a satiric tone. A keen observer, Saikaku took as his major themes the search for love and wealth.

Works by Saikaku

Five Women Who Loved Love. Trans. by William T. De Bary. C. E. Tuttle 1955 $9.95. ISBN 0-8048-0184-3. With an introduction and essay that offer helpful studies of Saikaku's life and works.

The Life of an Amorous Man. Trans. by Hamada Kengi. C. E. Tuttle 1963 o.p. Notable as Saikaku's first major work and for its portrayal of the world of courtesans.

The Life of an Amorous Woman and Other Writings. Ed. and trans. by Ivan Morris. New Dir. Pr. 1969 $11.95. ISBN 0-8112-0187-2. Includes a useful introduction and appendixes about the sources of Saikaku's stories, money, and the hierarchy of courtesans. With its indexed notes to the stories, it is an important study of Saikaku's life and time.

Some Final Words of Advice. Trans. by Peter Nosco. C. E. Tuttle 1980 o.p. A posthumously published work revealing the more pessimistic and detached side of Saikaku.

IZUMI SHIKIBU. fl. c.976

One of the most accomplished poets of her time, Izumi is known for the wild course of her love life. In addition to being twice married, she was, in succession, mistress to two princes who were brothers. The younger one, Astumichi, was her true love, and her diary is a fictionalized account of their affair. Little else is known of her life, but she left behind about 1,500 poems, often included in later anthologies.

Work by Izumi

The Izumi Shikibu Diary: A Romance of the Heian Court. Trans. by Edwin A. Cranston. HUP 1969 o.p. Also translated by Earl Miner in *Japanese Poetic Diaries.* Both translations are good, Cranston's the more scholarly in form.

KENKŌ YOSHIDA. c.1283–c.1352

Famous as a poet and essayist, Kenkō obtained a position at court in 1301, but by 1313 he had become a recluse for reasons that are unclear. He was strongly convinced that he was living in an age of decay, and his poetry, which survives in an anthology that he compiled, was in the vein of a conservative school that rejected innovation and urged preservation of past traditions. His *Essays in Idleness* is one of the more important works of classical literature.

Nonfiction by Kenkō

Essays in Idleness: The Tsurezuregusa of Kenkō. Trans. by Donald Keene. Col. U. Pr. 1972 $15.50. ISBN 0-231-18308-4. A collection of essays of greatly varying length on various topics.

KI NO TSURAYUKI. c.868–c.945

Tsurayuki is best known as a poet and as the author of *The Tosa Diary* (935). In both respects he was a pioneer. As a poet, he was the primary compiler of the *Kokinshu* (905), the premier anthology of court poetry. In its vernacular preface, as opposed to the one in Chinese written by another author, he made the first statement about the poetics of verse in Japanese. His diary was the first written in vernacular Japanese by a man in the persona of a woman, a literary landmark because the custom of the time was for men to keep diaries in

Chinese. Tsurayuki was greatly esteemed as a poet and calligrapher in his own time and has been venerated ever since.

Work by Tsurayuki

The Tosa Diary (Tosa Nikki). 935. AMS Pr. repr. of 1912 ed. $11.45. ISBN 0-404-14677-5. An interesting account of life and travel in tenth-century Japan and a moving personal record. Better translations are found in Miner's *Japanese Poetic Diaries* and McCullough's *Classical Japanese Prose.*

KOBAYASHI ISSA (pseud. of Kobayishi Nobuyuki). 1763–1827

An important haiku poet of the Edo Period, Issa wrote in the style of Bashō, but cultivated a particular simplicity of expression and emotion. His was a life of hardship filled with personal tragedies, and yet his writings reveal an unexpected streak of humor. His literary output, not large, is divided between collections of haiku and diaries based either on his travels throughout Japan or events in his family life.

Poetry by Issa

The Dumpling Field: Haiku of Issa. Trans. by Lucien Stryk and Naburo Fujiwara. Ohio U. Pr. 1991 $24.95. ISBN 0-8040-0952-X. The only translation currently in print.

Work by Issa

The Year of My Life: A Translation of Issa's "Oraga Haru." Trans. by Nobuyuki Yuasa. U. CA Pr. o.p. A translation of a major work in which Issa describes the death of a daughter with moving lyricism. Also valuable as one of the few English-language studies of Issa.

THE MOTHER OF FUJIWARA MICHITSUNA. d.955

Although of middling rank, the mother of Fujiwara Michitsuna was said to have been one of the three great beauties of her day. Like most women of her time, her personal name is not known. Her only real joy in married life seems to have been her son; her diary reveals an acerbic personality.

Work by The Mother of Fujiwara Michitsuna

The Gossamer Years: Diary of a Noblewoman of Heian Japan (Kagero Nikki). Trans. by Edward G. Seidensticker. C. E. Tuttle 1974 $12.95. ISBN 0-8048-1123-7. An engrossing work, ably translated. With an introduction analyzing the work and explaining how a noblewoman of the tenth century might have lived.

MURASAKI SHIKIBU (pseud.). c.978–c.1030

Little is known of Murasaki Shikibu's life beyond what she tells in her diary. Even the name by which she is known is a sobriquet. Among her ancestors were men of literary talent. She married and had a daughter but was widowed in 1001. In that same decade, she entered the service of an empress. Her literary reputation may have been a factor in her appointment, and she must have had substantial patronage, because the paper needed for writing a novel was rare and expensive. Her *Tale of Genji* (c.1000) is generally considered the greatest work in Japanese literature. Love would appear to be the main subject, but, in fact, the author probes human frailty, the evanescence of things, and spiritual concerns. Nothing is known of Lady Murasaki's life after 1013.

NOVEL BY MURASAKI

The Tale of Genji. Trans. by Edward G. Seidensticker. Knopf 1978 $24.00. ISBN 0-394-60405-9. A great up-to-date, complete, and felicitous translation, but relatively terse.

The Tale of Genji. Trans. by Arthur Waley. Modern Lib. $16.95. ISBN 0-394-60405-9. A great translation but incomplete and not reflecting modern scholarship; with Waley's rich prose creating an Edwardian setting.

WORK BY MURASAKI

Murasaki Shikibu: Her Diary and Poetic Memoirs. Trans. by Richard Bowring. Princeton U. Pr. 1985 $15.95. ISBN 0-691-01416-7. A brief study of Murasaki's life and well-annotated translation of the works. Helpful appendices and good index.

BOOKS ABOUT MURASAKI

Bowring, Richard. *Murasaki Shikibu: The Tale of Genji.* Cambridge U. Pr. 1988 $27.95. ISBN 0-521-33349-0. An excellent short introduction intended for the general reader.

Field, Norma. *The Splendor of Longing in the Tale of Genji.* Princeton U. Pr. 1987 $55.00. ISBN 0-691-06691-4. Organized around the heroines of the tale; a comprehensive study.

Goff, Janet. *Noh Drama and the Tale of Genji: The Art of Allusion in Fifteen Classical Plays.* Princeton U. Pr. 1991 $39.50. ISBN 0-691-06835-6. The impact of *The Tale of Genji* on medieval drama. Clearly written, but very scholarly.

Pekarik, Andrew, ed. *Ufifune: Love in The Tale of Genji.* Col. U. Pr. 1983 $42.00. ISBN 0-231-04598-0. A consideration of the concluding section of the tale by some of the most distinguished scholars of Heian literature.

Puette, William J. *Guide to The Tale of Genji by Murasaki Shikibu.* C. E. Tuttle 1983 $13.50. ISBN 0-8048-1454-6. Of particular use for its chapter summaries and for the names of characters as given in the Waley and Seidensticker translations.

Shirane, Haruo. *The Bridge of Dreams: A Poetics of The Tale of Genji.* Stanford U. Pr. 1987 $42.50. ISBN 0-8047-1345-6. The most impressive study of the tale in English. Each chapter analyzes a major development in the novel in light of a dominant technique or topic.

NIJŌ, LADY. b.1257

Of good birth, little is known of Lady Nijō's life apart from what she recounts in her diary. It covers the years from 1271, when she was 14 and became a concubine, through her expulsion from court in 1283, to 1306, when she had already turned to a life of religion. She was a keen observer of life, both at the court and elsewhere, and produced a document that depicts aristocratic life giving way to the mores of the rising warrior class.

WORK BY NIJŌ

The Confessions of Lady Nijō. Trans. by Karen Brazell. Stanford U. Pr. 1992 $12.95. ISBN 0-8047-0930-0. A fine translation and commentary that won the National Book Award for translation in 1992.

SEI SHŌNAGON. fl. late 10th century

This woman is known only by her sobriquet at court. She was in the service of an empress, about whom she writes with adulation, but, apart from what she records in *The Pillow Book* (c.975), which is autobiographical, little is known of her life. Her writing does, however, reveal an educated, sensitive, and vivacious woman who held herself in high esteem and was popular at court. Written with wit, *The Pillow Book* includes lists of things that the author liked or disliked, spontaneous observations, anecdotes of court life, and miscellaneous tales, some of her own invention. It is a classic of the *zuihztsu* or miscellany genre.

WORK BY SEI SHŌNAGON

The Pillow Book of Sei Shonagon (*Makura no Zoshi*). Trans. by Ivan Morris. Col. U. Pr. 1991 $12.00. ISBN 0-231-07337-2. A stylish translation. Omits the lists of things, some appendices, and the glossary-index found in the two-volume edition (o.p.), but valuable nonetheless.

UEDA AKINARI. 1734–1809

An adopted child, Ueda ran the family business before he became a full-time writer. In writing *Ugetsu Monogatari,* the gothic tales for which he is probably best known, he drew on both Chinese and Japanese classical traditions and produced a work known for its elegant diction. He was also respected as a waka poet and as a scholar of ancient Japanese literature.

SHORT STORY COLLECTION BY UEDA

Tales of Moonlight and Rain: Japanese Gothic Tales (Ugetsu Monogatari). Trans. by Kengi Hamada. Col. U. Pr. 1971 o.p. An entertaining collection of tales of the supernatural by a master of the genre.

YOSA BUSON (TANIGUCHI BUSON). 1716–1783

Along with BASHŌ and ISSA, Buson was one of the three great haiku poets of the Edo Period. He is equally famous as a painter. His poetry was in the style of Bashō but was distinguished by a particular lyricism and romantic subjectivity. Although more prolific than Bashō, Buson is still underrepresented in English translation.

BOOK ABOUT BUSON

Haiku Master Buson. Trans. by Yuki Sawa and Edith M. Shiller. 1978 o.p. The first and as yet only book in English about Buson. Both a literary and biographical study. Includes both translations of this work and writings about Buson by a disciple.

ZEAMI (pseud. of Yuzakiu Saemon Tayu Motokiyo). 1363–1443

Not only was Zeami a playwright of unparalleled genius and productivity, he was also an actor. About half the currently performed plays in the Japanese Noh repertory are from his hand. Besides composing over 150 plays, he wrote a number of critical works on Noh and its performance. Since his father was the most respected Noh performer of his time, Zeami grew up in the theater and remained with it until he was 59 and entered the priesthood. At 71 he was exiled to Sado Island. Why this happened is uncertain, but we can assume that he was pardoned, because he died in Kyoto. Most Noh plays in English collections are his.

BOOK ABOUT ZEAMI

Hare, Thomas Blenman. *Zeami's Style: The Noh Plays of Zeami Motokiyo.* Stanford U. Pr. 1986 $39.50. ISBN 0-8047-1290-5. Includes a fine biographical chapter followed by detailed analyses of the plays, grouped by themes: old age, women, and war.

MODERN JAPANESE LITERATURE

Modern Japanese literature, despite its basis in traditions, aesthetics, and imagery outside the Western cultural realm, has proven to be marvelously accessible in translation to English readers.

> The tea napkin, as became a young girl, was red, and it impressed one less with its softness than with its freshness, as if the girl's hand were bringing a red flower into bloom.
>
> And one saw a thousand cranes, small and white, start up in flight around her.

This passage from *A Thousand Cranes* (1959), by Nobel laureate KAWABATA YASUNARI, makes no concession to the westernization of Japan that has profoundly influenced modern writers. Yet even the Western reader unfamiliar with things Japanese can respond to the visual detail and evocative juxtaposition of Kawabata's imagery.

The period of deliberate westernization of Japan, dated from the reign of the Meiji emperor in 1868, marks the beginnings of modern Japanese literature. The Meiji era introduced reforms in all aspects of Japanese life: social, industrial, and educational. A newly literate populace was being created even as new literary forms were influencing Japanese writers.

Writer FUTATABEI SHIMEI introduced a work of breakthrough fiction by writing in colloquial Japanese, and MORI ŌGAI, the first Japanese romantic writer, wrote a first-person work that began a major modern literary trend, the autobiographical novel of *shishosetsu*. NATSUME SŌSEKI, SHIMAZAKI TOSON, YOSANO AKIKO, and NAGAI KAFU were also among the first wave who flourished in this time of rapid modernization. Their works are still widely discussed for their responses to Western literary influences.

Kawabata, with TANIZAKI JUN'ICHIRŌ, SHIGA NAOYA, and AKUTAGAWA RYŪNOSUKE, belongs to the era of modern writers who were published before World War II but who subsequently faced the new flood of postwar westernization and felt its increased impact on the forms and themes of their work. These writers were already well-versed in Western literatures, as well as in Chinese and Japanese classics, and their expanded world view lends obvious richness to their works. Not every Japanese writer, of course, welcomed the influences of French, German, and British literary movements. Many writers clung to the traditional aesthetic, or "Japanese spirit," even within new literary forms.

But whether adopting or criticizing Western literary movements, Japanese writers seized the opportunity to compare their works, their traditions, and their aesthetic with those of world literature. Before World War II, a spirit of nationalism and a regime of censorship favored writers who reverted to traditional Japanese themes. After the war, the reassessment of Japan's relationship to Western culture and a new freedom of authorship strengthened the interplay of national and foreign literatures. For example, the works of ABE KŌBŌ, ENDŌ SHŪSAKU, and ARIYOSHI SAWAKO, all writing today, use familiar Western forms. Themes of individualism, which Japanese writers took up in their earliest encounters with the West, emerged with force in writing both by and about women. Not surprising in a culture that produced outstanding poetry and fiction by women writers 1,000 years ago, Japan has a new body of literature, not only written by women, but also focusing on the definition of women in Japanese society. The bibliography lists several excellent anthologies of these works.

Despite these changes, the classical devotion to exquisite detail, the cultural appreciation for suggested ideas, and the device of nature as a character remain woven into every genre of modern Japanese writing. The linguistic characteristics of writing in Japanese and the use of *kakekotoba*, pivot words that permit a mid-sentence or mid-verse change of direction, reflect the classical roots of much of modern Japanese literature.

The influence of the West on modern Japanese literature is now rebounding. With the increasing numbers both of Japanese works in translation and of Westerners becoming fluent in Japanese, poetry and prose of the Western hemisphere already show the evidence of Japanese aesthetics.

History and Criticism

Fowler, Edward. *The Rhetoric of Confession: Shishosetsu in Early Twentieth Century Japanese Fiction*. U. CA Pr. 1988 $37.50. ISBN 0-520-06064-4. A sophisticated analysis of the development of the autobiographical novel.

Gessel, Van C. *Three Modern Novelists: Soseki, Tanizaki, Kawabata*. Kodansha Ltd. Japan 1993 $10.00. ISBN 4-77001-652-2. The writers' private lives and literary careers, in terms of their responses to modernization and their influences on current literature.

Kato, Shuichi. *A History of Japanese Literature*. Vol. 3 *The Modern Years*. Trans. by Don Sanderson. Kodansha Ltd. Japan 1983 $35.00. ISBN 0-87011-569-3. By a highly respected scholar. Rich capsule presentations of major writers' lives and works, in historical context. Includes bibliography of collections in Japanese and individual works in translation.

Keene, Donald. *Dawn to the West: Japanese Literature in the Modern Era*. 2 vols. H. Holt & Co. 1984. Vol. 1 $60.00. ISBN 0-03-062814-8. Vol. 2 $40.00. ISBN 0-03-062816-4. A detailed, authoritative study. Comprehensive, but omits writers still active. Volume 1: fiction; Volume 2: poetry, drama, and criticism.

Kimball, Arthur G. *Crisis in Identity and Contemporary Japanese Novels*. C. E. Tuttle 1972 o.p. Short essays on works, almost all available in translation, by significant postwar writers. Includes "Syllabus: A Suggested Reading Course."

Lewell, John. *Modern Japanese Novelists: A Biographical Dictionary*. Kodansha Ltd. Japan 1992 $29.95. ISBN 4-77001-649-2. Informative essays on more than 60 authors from 1885 to the present. Each entry lists English translations of fiction and criticism with a photograph of the author.

Lippit, Noriko M. *Reality and Fiction in Modern Japanese Literature*. M. E. Sharpe 1979 o.p. Essays on the autobiographical novel, Tanizaki and Akutagawa, Yokomitsu Riichi, Kawabata, and feminist autobiography.

McClellan, Edwin. *Two Japanese Novelists: Soseki and Toson*. Bks. Demand repr. of 1969 ed. $45.00. ISBN 0-317-10055-6. From the preface: "Of all the writers of their time, these two were probably the most influential. Nowhere in the world has the autobiographical novel flourished as it has since Toson's time. . . . [And] had Soseki never lived, there would have been less audacity in Japanese fiction today."

Miyoshi, Masao. *Accomplices of Silence: The Modern Japanese Novel*. U. CA Pr. 1982 $42.50. ISBN 0-520-04609-0. A penetrating study focusing on the Japanese language and the individual as a concept. By a scholar of Western and Japanese literature who emphasizes interrelationships of literary topics, culture, politics, and economics.

Peterson, Gwen Boardman. *The Moon in the Water: Understanding Tanizaki, Kawabata and Mishima*. UH Pr. 1979 o.p. Useful analysis of three widely translated authors, but sometimes idiosyncratic on hidden images and meanings. For the experienced reader.

Rimer, J. Thomas. *Modern Japanese Fiction and Its Traditions: An Introduction*. Bks. Demand repr. of 1978 ed. $85.10. ISBN 0-8357-4287-3. A thought-provoking work that invites readers to understand works of both traditional and modern literature in terms of Japanese literary values.

———. *A Reader's Guide to Japanese Literature*. Kodansha Ltd. Japan 1988 $14.95. ISBN 0-87011-896-X. Presents 30 modern works but also covers classical literature. Includes plot summaries and commentaries for significant writings.

Shinkokai, Kokusai B., comp. *Introduction to Contemporary Japanese Literature: Synopses of Major Works 1956–1970*. Col. U. Pr. 1972 $17.50. ISBN 0-86008-093-5

Ueda, Makoto. *Modern Japanese Poets and the Nature of Literature*. Stanford U. Pr. 1983 $45.00. ISBN 0-8047-1166-6. Covers Masaoka Shiki, Ogiwara Seisensui, Ashikawa Takuboku, Yosano Akiko, Miyazawa Kenji, Takamura Kotaro, Takahashi Shinkichi, and Hagiwara Sakutaro. Includes excerpts of works.

Walker, Janet. *The Japanese Novel of the Meiji Period and the Ideal of Individualism*. Princeton U. Pr. 1979 $45.00. ISBN 0-691-06400-8. Traces the Western theme of individualism through the works of Futabatei, Kitamura Tokoku, Katai, and Shimazaki Toson.

Collections

Gessel, Van C., and Tomone Matsumoto. *The Showa Anthology*. Kodansha Ltd. Japan 1989 $14.95. ISBN 0-87011-922-2. Short fiction by writers active from 1929 through 1984. An excellent selection with biographical and analytical discussions of each writer.

Hibbett, Howard. *Contemporary Japanese Literature: An Anthology of Fiction, Film and Other Writing Since 1945*. Knopf 1977 $19.95. ISBN 0-394-73362-2. Good translations. Includes biographical data for the authors and a critical analysis of their works.

Keene, Donald. *Modern Japanese Literature: From 1868 to the Present Day*. Grove Pr. 1956 $14.95. ISBN 0-8021-5095-0. Translations of poetry, prose, and drama. Introductions present discussions of genre and the relationship between history and literature.

Kobayashi, Takiji. *The Cannery Boat and Other Japanese Short Stories*. Greenwood 1969 repr. of 1933 ed. $35.00. ISBN 0-8371-0133-6. A major anthology of proletarian stories, with many by Kobayashi. Neither great literature nor translations, but important in prewar writing.

Lippit, Noriko Mizuta, and Kyoko Iriye Selden, eds. and trans. *Japanese Women Writers: Twentieth Century Short Fiction*. M. E. Sharpe 1991 $39.95. ISBN 0-87332-193-6. Twelve works providing striking insights into the experiences of modern Japanese women. Includes biographical data on authors.

Mitsios, Helen, ed. *The Best Contemporary Fiction from Japan*. Atlantic Monthly 1992 $10.95. ISBN 0-87113-522-1. Translations, with brief introductions, of very recent Japanese fiction by Haruki Murakami, Eimi Yamada, Banana Yoshimoto, and others. An introduction by Jay McInerney.

Morris, Ivan, ed. *Modern Japanese Stories: An Anthology*. C. E. Tuttle 1977 $14.95. ISBN 0-8048-1226-8. Works from 1910 to 1954, each accompanied by a critical essay. A good general introduction.

Ooka, Makoto, ed. *A Play of Mirrors: Eight Major Poets of Modern Japan*. Katydid Bks. 1987 $21.95. ISBN 0-942668-08-1. The works and biographies of Yoshioka Minoru, Tamura Ryuichi, Iijima Koichi, Tada Chimaku, Tanikawa Shuntaro, Shiraishi Kazuko, Yoshimasu Gozo, and the editor.

Sato, Hiraoki, and Burton Watson, trans. and eds. *From the Country of Eight Islands*. Col. U. Pr. 1986 $16.00. ISBN 0-231-06395-4. A remarkably complete and diversified anthology of poetry by two distinguished translators. Includes a glossary and brief biographies of major poets.

Shiffert, Edith, and Yuki Sawa, trans. *Anthology of Modern Japanese Poetry*. C. E. Tuttle 1971 $9.95. ISBN 0-8048-0672-1. Translations of free verse, tanka, and haiku by Takamura Kotaro, Hagiwara Sakutaro, Muro Saisei, and others, with biographies of the poets.

Takaya, Ted T., trans. *Modern Japanese Drama: An Anthology*. Col. U. Pr. 1980 $50.00. ISBN 0-231-04684-7. Supplies a helpful outline of the development of modern Japanese drama. Has informative footnotes on terms and allusions.

Tanaka, Yukiko, and Elizabeth Hanson, eds. *This Kind of Woman: Ten Stories by Japanese Women Writers, 1960–1976*. Stanford U. Pr. 1982 $35.00. ISBN 0-8047-1130-5. Works by Enchi Fumiko, Oba Minako, Tshushima Yuko, and other outstanding writers. An excellent introduction about each one's presentation of Japanese women.

Tanaka, Yukiko, ed. *To Live and to Write: Selections by Japanese Women Writers, 1913–1938.* Seal Pr. Feminist 1987 $16.95. ISBN 0-931188-44-X. Seven short stories and excerpts from three novels describing women struggling for independence. Good biographical information. Author portraits.

Tanaka, Yukiko, ed. and trans. *Unmapped Territories: New Women's Fiction from Japan.* Women Translation 1991 $10.95. ISBN 1-879679-00-0. Seven pieces of short fiction, written during the 1980s, about Japanese women not living the constrained, traditional roles of wife and mother.

Ueda, Makoto, ed. *The Mother of Dreams and Other Short Stories: Portrayals of Women in Modern Japanese Fiction.* Kodansha Ltd. Japan 1986 $6.95. ISBN 0-87011-926-5. Eighteen stories by sixteen authors reflecting the diversity and changes of women's roles in modern Japan.

CHRONOLOGY OF AUTHORS

This chronology is given Japanese-style, family names first.

Mori Ōgai. 1862–1922
Futabatei Shimei. 1864–1909
Masaoka Shiki. 1867–1902
Natsume Sōseki. 1867–1917
Higuchi Ichiyō. 1872–1896
Shimazaki Tōson. 1872–1943
Yosano Akiko. 1878–1942
Nagai Kafū. 1879–1959
Shiga Naoya. 1883–1971.
Ishikawa Takuboku. 1886–1912
Tanizaki Jun'ichirō. 1886–1965
Kawabata Yasunari. 1889–1972
Akutagawa Ryūnosuke. 1892–1927
Uno Chiyo. 1897–
Ibuse Masuji. 1898–
Yokomitsu Riichi. 1898–1947
Enchi Fumiko. 1905–1986
Inoue Yasushi. 1907–
Dazai Osamu. 1909–1948
Matsumoto Seicho. 1909–
Endō Shūsaku. 1923–
Abe Kōbō. 1924–
Mishima Yukio. 1925–1970
Tachihara Masaaki. 1926–1980
Ariyoshi Sawako. 1931–
Tanikawa Shuntaro. 1931–
Ōe Kenzaburō. 1935–
Tsushima Yuko. 1947–
Murakami Haruki. 1949–

ABE KŌBŌ (pseud. of Abe/Kimifusa). 1924–

Abe Kōbō graduated from the top medical school in Japan but turned to writing and is now the most widely read and translated Japanese author. His surrealistic novel *The Woman in the Dunes* (1964) became a stunningly sensual film, and he has continued to work with director Teshigahara Hiroshi on screenplays; he himself is a successful playwright. His frequent theme in fiction is the loss of personal identity in oppressive, alienating urban life.

NOVELS BY ABE

The Face of Another (Tanin no kao). Trans. by E. Dale Saunders. Kodansha Ltd. Japan 1992 $9.95. ISBN 4-77001-634-4. A man who masks himself to cover his disfigured face consequently takes on a new personality.

The Ruined Map (Moetsukita chizu). Trans. by E. Dale Saunders. Kodansha Ltd. Japan 1993 $12.00. ISBN 4-77001-635-2. A private detective finds his identity beginning to meld with the objective of his investigative search.

The Woman in the Dunes (Suna no onna). Trans. by E. Dale Saunders. Random 1991 $11.00. ISBN 0-679-73378-7. A scientist encounters a village of dune dwellers and is forced to confront his concept of individualism.

AKUTAGAWA RYŪNOSUKE. 1892–1927

Brilliant, sensitive, neurotic, Akutagawa Ryūnosuke left over 100 stories before his suicide at age 35. Feudal fables are often the source for his tales, but Akutagawa also brought his knowledge of several world literatures to enrich his writing. His best-known story, "In a Grove" ("Yabu no naka"), has become a play and was made into the prizewinning movie *Rashōmon* by Kurosawa Akira (see Vol. 3).

Short Story Collection by Akutagawa

Rashomon and Other Stories. Trans. by Takashi Kojima. Liveright 1970 $6.95. ISBN 0-87140-214-9. Six stories, full of surprises.

Novel by Akutagawa

Kappa: A Satire. Trans. by Geoffrey Bowmas. C. E. Tuttle 1971 $9.95. ISBN 0-8048-0994-1. A tale of the mythical creature Kappa who lives in a world opposite to the human. A dark satire revealing the stresses of life in Japan before World War II.

Book about Akutagawa

Yu, Beongcheon. *Akutagawa: An Introduction.* Wayne St. U. Pr. 1972 $9.95. ISBN 0-8143-1467-8. A study of the life, work, and thought of Akutagawa. Includes a chronology, index, and bibliography of stories available in English translation.

ARIYOSHI SAWAKO. 1931–

Ariyoshi Sawako is a novelist concerned with social issues, the position of women among them, although some of her earlier works were less topical. Her recent novels have been bestsellers in Japan.

Novels by Ariyoshi

The River Ki. Trans. by Mildred Tahara. Kodansha Ltd. Japan 1992 $7.95. ISBN 0-87011-514-6. Three generations of women of two families play out their lives in the region defined by the River Ki.

The Twilight Years. Trans. by Mildred Tahara. Kodansha Ltd. Japan 1992 $16.95. ISBN 0-87011-677-0. The story of a woman's sacrifice in caring for her senile father-in-law and other family responsibilities.

DAZAI OSAMU (pseud. of Tsushima Shuji). 1909–1948

Born into a near-aristocratic family whose declining world he depicts in *The Setting Sun* (1947), Dazai had the means to become an accomplished dilettante and rake. Around 1933 he began to think seriously about writing, but his life was complicated by drug addiction, a string of affairs, and two attempts at suicide. The end of the war brought a change in Dazai, and he produced his finest works, even though his own life was ending because of alcoholism and tuberculosis. The darkness of his works reveals his tortured existence, which he ended by suicide.

Novels by Dazai

No Longer Human (Ningen shikkaku). 1948. Trans. by Donald Keene. New Dir. Pr. 1973 $8.95. ISBN 0-8112-0481-2. Dazai's response to the transformation of Japan into a defeated nation. With *The Setting Sun,* considered a masterpiece.

The Setting Sun (Shayo). 1947. Trans. by Donald Keene. New Dir. Pr. 1968 $8.95. ISBN 0-8112-0032-9. The demise of the upper class after World War II.

Nonfiction by Dazai

Return to Tsugaru: Travels of a Purple Tramp. Trans. by James Westerhoven. Kodansha Ltd. Japan 1988 $5.95. ISBN 0-87011-841-2. Dazai's journey home to northern Japan with local description colored by self-deprecating looks inward. Photographs of the region and the people encountered.

Self-Portraits: Tales from the Life of Japan's Great Decadent Romantic. Trans. by Ralph McCarthy. Kodansha Ltd. Japan 1991 $18.95. ISBN 0-87011-779-3. Autobiographical stories presented chronologically. Photographs and commentary accompany the translations.

Book about Dazai

Wolfe, Alan. *Suicidal Narrative in Modern Japan: The Case of Dazai Osamu.* Princeton U. Pr. 1990 $29.95. ISBN 0-691-06774-0. Discussions of Dazai as the last of the autobiographical novelists, the inevitable death of the form, and Dazai's suicide.

ENCHI FUMIKO. 1905–1986

Educated in the classics, Enchi Fumiko began writing plays but turned to fiction. Her novels and short stories often focus on the emotional lives of middle-aged women struggling against the constraints of Japanese society. Enchi's translation into modern Japanese of the Heian Period novel, *The Tale of Genji,* was widely respected. Allusions to *Genji* and the device of imbedding classical elements within the modern story enrich her fiction.

Novels by Enchi

Masks (Onnamen). Trans. by Juliet Winters Carpenter. Random 1983 $11.00. ISBN 0-394-72118-3. The story of the destructive force of jealousy and resentment that cannot be subdued behind a woman's serene countenance.

The Waiting Years (Onnazaka). Trans. by John Bester. Kodansha Ltd. Japan 1980 $5.95. ISBN 0-87011-424-7. Portrays the power of a woman's emotions, repressed during a 40-year marriage.

ENDŌ SHŪSAKU. 1923–

Endō's writing, which has won him many literary prizes, is distinguished by his concern with moral and religious themes. A Roman Catholic, he has often been linked to GRAHAM GREENE (see Vol. 1) because of his preoccupation with issues relating to cultural conflicts.

Novels by Endō

Silence (Chinmoku). Trans. by William Johnson. Taplinger 1980 $7.95. ISBN 0-8008-7186-3. Set in seventeenth-century Japan, a period of persecution of the Christian minority. The story of a Portuguese missionary who can save his followers from torture if he renounces his faith.

Wonderful Fool: A Novel. Trans. by Francis Mathy. HarpC 1983 $13.95. ISBN 0-06-859853-X. About a failed French missionary who sets out for Japan and bumbles his way into adventure. Embodies Endō's ideas of giving love.

FUTABATEI SHIMEI (pseud. of Hasegawa Tatsunosuke). 1864–1909

As a young man, Futabatei Shimei studied Russian literature and later became a prolific translator and essayist. He also tried to develop an appropriate language for literature, which had long been written in a classical style divorced from spoken Japanese. His novel *Ukigumo* (1889), translated as *The Drifting Cloud,* is noted for its pioneering use of colloquial Japanese, realism, and three-dimensional characters. It was the first to focus on the development of character.

NOVEL BY FUTABATEI

Japan's First Modern Novel: Ukigumo of Futabatei Shimei. Trans. and ed. by Marleigh G. Ryan. Greenwood 1983 repr. of 1967 ed. $45.50. ISBN 0-313-24128-7

HIGUCHI ICHIYŌ (pseud. of Higuchi Natsuko). 1872–1896

Ichiyō was the leading woman writer of the Meiji Period and an inspiration to those who followed. She had a limited education and often lived in great poverty but met these obstacles with talent and determination. Best known for her short stories and diary, she also wrote numerous poems. A major theme, personally apt, is that people are denied happiness because of their circumstances in life. Just when others finally recognized her talents, she died of tuberculosis at the age of 24.

BOOK ABOUT ICHIYŌ

Danly, Robert L. *In the Shade of Spring Leaves: The Life of Higuchi Ichiyo, with Nine of Her Best Short Stories.* Norton 1992 $10.95. ISBN 0-393-30913-4. A scholarly yet personal interpretation of Ichiyō's life that quotes heavily and effectively from her diary and the writings of those who knew her.

IBUSE MASUJI. 1898–

The son of middle-class landowners, Ibuse grew up in the country, for which he always retained a special feeling. While a student majoring in French literature, he published his first story and has since won almost every literary prize in Japan. His work is known for its eloquent use of dialect, irony, historical settings, and dry, sometimes dark humor.

NOVEL BY IBUSE

Waves. Trans. by David Aylward and Anthony Liman. Kodansha Ltd. Japan 1986 $17.95. ISBN 0-87011-781-5. Two short novels—one of a highborn samurai, the other of a middle-aged artisan—both characterized by Ibuse's unsentimental sympathy.

WORK BY IBUSE

Black Rain (Kuroi ame). Trans. by John Bester. Kodansha Ltd. Japan 1980 $6.95. ISBN 0-87011-364-X. Based on diaries and interviews with survivors of Hiroshima. A personal story rather than a political reaction, written 20 years after the bombing.

INOUE YASUSHI. 1907–

Inoue Yasushi is considered to be the last of the Japanese masters, heir to the traditions of classical Chinese and Japanese literature. This journalist-turned-novelist writes poetry, historical fiction set in China and old Japan, and novels of modern Japan. His first fiction was published in 1948, and his choice of settings continues to reveal a superb feel for other times, places, and peoples.

WORKS BY INOUE

Lou-lan and Other Stories. Trans. by James T. Araki and Edward Seidensticker. Kodansha Ltd. Japan 1980 $9.95. ISBN 0-87011-389-5. Six stories, mixing ancient and modern perspectives, that illustrate the author's mastery of evoking a historical setting while telling a gripping tale.

Wind and Waves (Futo). Trans. by James T. Araki. UH Pr. 1982 $20.00. ISBN 0-8248-1178-X

ISHIKAWA TAKUBOKU. 1886–1912

Ishikawa's first works were published when he was only 19. The son of a Zen priest, he was fired from a teaching job (one in a string of many professions he tried) for participation in a student strike. In his development from a romantic poet to a naturalist writer to a socialist writer, Ishikawa was associated with several literary movements. Today he is known as a poet and diarist.

Poetry by Ishikawa

Poems to Eat (Kuraubeki shi). Trans. by Carl Sesar. Weatherhill 1992 $24.95. ISBN 0-921062-65-1. A work that reveals Ishikawa's view of poetry as a form of diary.

Work by Ishikawa

Romaji Diary and Sad Toys. Trans. by Seishi Shinoda and Sanford Goldstein. C. E. Tuttle 1985 $12.95. ISBN 0-8048-1494-5. Diaries in which Ishikawa used the Roman alphabet—to keep his innermost feelings safe from prying eyes.

KAWABATA YASUNARI. 1889–1972 (Nobel Prize 1968)

Kawabata Yasunari's first artistic medium was painting, a fact perhaps reflected in his writing's masterful and evocative juxtaposition of imagery. One of Japan's finest novelists, he writes of memories and desires and the intensity of the immediate. His prose is intended to richly suggest more than it declares. For all of his talent and success, Kawabata does not appear to have been a happy man. Knowledgeable in the classics and in Buddhism, he felt a sense of loss and impermanence, as if this world held no particular place for him. Kawabata committed suicide without leaving a word of explanation.

Novels by Kawabata

The Master of Go. Trans. by Edward G. Seidensticker. Putnam Pub. Group 1981 $8.95. ISBN 0-399-50528-8. A fictionalization of a 1938 go match, symbolizing for Kawabata the demise of the aristocratic tradition that sustained Japanese ethics and art until the postwar upheavals.

Snow Country (Yukiguni). 1948. Trans. by Edward G. Seidensticker. Putnam Pub. Group 1981 $8.95. ISBN 0-399-50525-3. First published in installments, with episodes added even after publication in novel form. Tells of the encounter of a Tokyo snob with a hot-spring geisha.

The Sound of the Mountain (Yama no Oto). 1952. Trans. by Edward G. Seidensticker. Putnam Pub. Group 1981 $9.95. ISBN 0-399-50527-X. A richly imagistic story of aging and the premonition of death.

A Thousand Cranes (Sembazuru). 1952. Trans. by Edward G. Seidensticker. Putnam Pub. Group 1981 $7.95. ISBN 0-399-50526-1. A story of lives interconnected by the handing down of tea ceremony utensils.

MASAOKA SHIKI. 1867–1902

The son of a minor samurai, Shiki was educated in Chinese classics and entered the Japanese literature department of Tokyo Imperial University. Shiki and Natsume Sōseki met in 1889 and began a friendship replete with cross-influences on their literary development. Although called "the father of modern haiku," Shiki wrote in several genres and was active in literary criticism. He introduced a new realism and directness into Japanese poetry and prose.

Books about Shiki

Beichman, Janet, *Masaoka Shiki.* Kodansha Ltd. Japan 1986 $5.95. ISBN 0-87011-753-X. A critical discussion of Shiki's diaries and poetry.

Ueda, Makoto. *Modern Japanese Poets and the Nature of Literature.* Stanford U. Pr. 1983 $45.00. ISBN 0-8047-1166-6. Includes some of Shiki's poetry.

MATSUMOTO SEICHO. 1909–

The creator of the social detective story, Seicho is credited with reviving the mystery genre after World War II. He began writing in middle age and has produced over 450 fiction and nonfiction works.

NOVELS BY MATSUMOTO

Inspector Imanishi Investigates. Trans. by Beth Cary. Soho Press 1989 $18.95. ISBN 0-939149-287. Inspector Imanishi, partial to haiku and embarked on a hunt for a murderer, encounters people from every layer of Japanese society.

Points and Lines. Trans. by Yamamoto Makiko and Paul C. Blum. Kodansha Ltd. Japan 1986 $6.95. ISBN 0-87011-456-5. Inspector Mahara senses that what the police call a "love suicide" is really murder.

MISHIMA YUKIO (pseud. of Kimitake Hiraoka). 1925–1970

The son of a Tokyo government official, Mishima Yukio graduated at the head of his class at the Peers' School and found brilliant literary success with his autobiographical novel, *Confessions of a Mask,* published in 1949. Mishima lived and wrote intensely, producing over 30 novels and dozens of plays, essays, and pamphlets; joining the jet set; organizing his own army; practicing bodybuilding and martial arts; singing, modeling, and acting. His literary themes of nationalism, destiny, and purity foreshadowed his death by a public, symbolic, ritualistic samurai-style suicide.

NOVELS BY MISHIMA

Confessions of a Mask, (Kamen no kokuhaku). 1958. Trans. by Meredith Weatherby. New Dir. Pr. 1968 $8.95. ISBN 0-8112-0118-X. A confessional account of Mishima's growing up and self-discovery, important for understanding his life and writings.

Spring Snow (Haru no yuki). Trans. by Michael Gallagher. Random 1990 $12.00. ISBN 0-679-72241-6. About the tragic love of two aristocrats. The first volume of Mishima's tetralogy, *The Sea of Fertility*; subsequent volumes: *Runaway Horses, The Temple of Dawn,* and *The Decay of the Angel.*

The Temple of the Golden Pavilion (Kinkakuji). 1956. Trans. by Ivan Morris. Putnam Pub. Group 1981 $8.95. ISBN 0-399-50488-5. A first-person narration by the historical figure who burned down the exquisite Golden Pavilion of Kyoto.

NONFICTION BY MISHIMA

Sun and Steel (Taiyo to tetsu). 1970. Trans. by John Bester. Kodansha Ltd. Japan 1970 $5.95. ISBN 0-87011-425-5. An autobiographical essay essential for understanding Mishima's evolution from an introverted child to the self-proclaimed conscience of postwar Japan.

BOOKS ABOUT MISHIMA

Nathan, John. *Mishima: A Biography.* Little 1985 $9.95. ISBN 0-316-59846-1. A relatively detached study of Mishima but a valuable source of information.

Scott-Stokes, Henry. *The Life and Death of Yukio Mishima.* FS&G 1974 $10.00. ISBN 0-374-51703-7. Like the Nathan book, a serious study of Mishima, with a somewhat greater emphasis on his literary career and writings.

MORI ŌGAI (pseud. of Mori Rintarō). 1862–1922

Born into a family of physicians, Ōgai had a traditional education in the Chinese classics and was also well read in Japanese, German, and other Western literatures. He studied medicine in Germany for four years. Eventually he became head of the medical division of the Japanese Army Ministry. His literary production, which was often interrupted by official duties, falls into three main groups: 1909–12, semiautobiographical fiction; 1912–16, historical literature; and finally, biography. His *Vita Sexualis* (1972) is a philosophical look at the development of his sexual awareness and the place of sexual desire in life. Although not devoid of humor, this is a serious work that was also intended to chide writers of the naturalist school for their relentless, narrow scrutiny of their own lives. In his historical fiction, Ōgai wrote about real people and real events, researching his subjects carefully and providing notes for readers. He was, however, a superb stylist and engaging storyteller. He was also an able translator. With the exception of his early romantic works, his writing is marked by an austere tone.

Works by Ōgai

The Historical Fiction of Mori Ōgai. Ed. by David Dilworth and J. Thomas Rimer. UH Pr. 1991 repr. of 1977 ed. $16.95. ISBN 0-8248-1366-9

Vita Sexualis. Trans. by Kazuji Ninomiya and Sanford Goldstein. C. E. Tuttle 1972 $8.95. ISBN 0-8048-1048-6

The Wild Geese (Gan). Trans. by Kingo Ochiai and Sanford Goldstein. C. E. Tuttle 1974 $7.95. ISBN 0-8048-1070-2. The traditional melodrama of a woman married off to save her family's fortune, but used to develop the heroine's selfhood. A favorite of the Japanese, made into the film *The Mistress* by Toyoda.

Book about Ōgai

Bowring, Richard John. *Mori Ōgai and the Modernization of Japanese Culture.* Cambridge U. Pr. 1979 $59.95. ISBN 0-521-21319-3. An in-depth study of Ōgai as an individual, writer, and thinker during great cultural flux in Japan. Quotes extensively from Ogai's writings.

MURAKAMI HARUKI, 1949–

Attracted to pop American culture from an early age, Murakami preferred Elvis Presley and KURT VONNEGUT (see Vol. 1) to things Japanese. As a 12-year-old rebel, Murakami turned against his culture and his father, a professor of Japanese literature, and refused to read Japanese works at all for 15 years. With the publication of *Norwegian Wood,* a story of alienation among privileged Tokyo students, the author became a reluctant celebrity. Today Murakami has found his place as a bestselling author of high-tech mythical tales set in postmodern Japan.

Novels by Murakami

Hard-Boiled Wonderland and the End of the World: A Novel. Trans. by Alfred Birnbaum. Kodansha Ltd. Japan 1991 $21.95. ISBN 4-770-01544-5. A futuristic action novel starring a computer-whiz hero.

A Wild Sheep Chase: A Novel (Hitsuji wo meguru boken). Trans. by Alfred Birnbaum. Kodansha Ltd. Japan 1989 $18.95. ISBN 0-87011-905-2. A tale of adventure about the search for a sheep that holds the key to survival.

NAGAI KAFŪ (pseud. of Nagai Sōkichi). 1879–1959

Born into a wealthy family, Nagai Kafū developed an early interest in Edo (feudal Tokyo) Period literature and culture. He disliked formal education and dropped out of school to enjoy popular entertainments, such as Kabuki, and the pleasure quarters, which, in his youth, still retained some of the aura of the preceding age. In his writings, which included novels, essays, and short stories, he revealed a great nostalgia for the vanishing "old" Tokyo, and in his style he looked to the nineteenth century for models. It is fortunate that most of this writing was done before the great Tokyo earthquake of 1923, which put an end to the world he loved.

NOVEL BY KAFŪ

Geisha in Rivalry (Udekurabe). Trans. by Kurt Meissner and Ralph Friedrich. C. E. Tuttle 1963 $5.75. ISBN 0-8048-0204-1. The denizens of the pleasure quarters observed. Loosely plotted, but evocative and sometimes picaresque.

BOOK ABOUT KAFŪ

Seidensticker, Edward G. *Kafu the Scribbler: The Life and Writings of Nagai Kafu, 1879–1959.* U. MI Japan 1990 $13.50. ISBN 0-939512-46-7. Valuable not only as a study but also because almost one-half of the book is made up of translations of works by Kafū, including his highly regarded *River Sumida.*

NATSUME SŌSEKI (pseud. of Natsume Kinnosuke). 1867–1917

Natsume Sōseki's early education included the study of Chinese classics and architecture, but as an English literature major he found his life's work, as well as the friendship of haiku poet MASAOKA SHIKI, an important personal and literary influence. Sōseki's prose, for example, is often interspersed with his own haiku. In 1900 the Japanese government sent Sōseki, who was a professor of English literature, to London, but, poorly funded and isolated, he found his years abroad painful and began to exhibit neurotic behavior. On his return, he shocked society by giving up his teaching position at Tokyo University to write fiction for the *Asahi* newspaper, a profession associated with the world of "entertainers." Despite poor health in the last years of his life, Sōseki continued to write an average of one novel a year.

NOVELS BY SŌSEKI

Botchan. Trans. by Alan Turney. Kodansha Ltd. Japan 1992 $7.00. ISBN 0-87011-367-4. A rollicking story of a young man against the system, revealing Sōseki's concern with alienation.

Kokoro: A Novel by Natsume Sōseki. Trans. by Edwin McClellan. Regnery Gateway 1957 $8.95. ISBN 0-89526-951-1. A novella about a young man whose father is dying and an enigmatic older man. Themes of trust and betrayal, innocence and its loss.

The Miner (*Kofu*). Trans. by Jay Rubin. Stanford U. Pr. 1988 $29.50. ISBN 0-8047-1460-6. A Tokyoite flees from an arranged marriage and becomes a miner.

Sanshirō: A Novel by Natsume Sōseki. Trans. by Jay Rubin. Putnam Pub. Group 1982 $5.95. ISBN 0-399-50613-6. A story about a country boy in Tokyo, an innocent with illusions and ideals bound to be lost to life's realities. With a critical essay by Rubin that analyzes *Sanshirō* and relates it to Sōseki's other writings.

The Three-Cornered World (*Kusamakura*). Trans. by Alan Turney. Putnam Pub. Group 1982 o.p. "An artist is a person who lives in the triangle which remains after the angle we may call common sense has been removed from this four-cornered world" (Sōseki).

BOOK ABOUT SŌSEKI

Doi, Takeo. *The Psychological World of Natsume Sōseki.* Trans. by William Jefferson Tyler. HUP 1976 $20.00. ISBN 0-674-72116-0. By a Japanese psychoanalyst who often uses literary examples in his teaching.

ŌE KENZABURŌ. 1935–

A winner of numerous Japanese literary prizes, Ōe came to manhood during World War II and the occupation. In college he studied JEAN-PAUL SARTRE (see Vols. 2 and 4) and absorbed many popular leftist ideas. These influences appear in his early writings, which often deal with contemporary issues. With the birth of his deformed son, father and son became the new focus of his work. A blend of the personal and the political, rendered by a powerful and poetic imagination, continues to distinguish Ōe's work.

NOVELS BY ŌE

A Personal Matter (Kojin teki no taiken). Trans. by John Nathan. Grove Pr. 1968 $7.95. ISBN 0-9021-5061-6. A semiautobiographical account, in the existential vein, of the author's reaction to the birth of his deformed son.

The Silent Cry (Man'en gannen no futtoboru). Trans. by John Bester. Kodansha Ltd. Japan 1981 $6.95. ISBN 0-87011-466-2. The author's split self, in the form of two brothers, in a hallucinatory visit to their childhood home and a dark past. Also an engrossing mystery.

BOOKS ABOUT ŌE

Wilson, Michiko N. *The Marginal World of Ōe Kenzaburō: Themes and Techniques.* M. E. Sharpe 1986 $39.95. ISBN 0-87332-343-2

SHIGA NAOYA. 1883–1971

Shiga is best known for his short stories and for his confessional mode, writing works about himself and his family and friends, with whom he was often in conflict. Although he lived to be almost 90, he wrote very little from the late thirties on.

NOVEL BY SHIGA

A Dark Night's Passing (An'ya Koro). Trans. by Edwin McClellan. Kodansha Ltd. Japan 1980 $8.95. ISBN 0-87011-362-3. Shiga's only novel and one of his last significant literary works. A major theme is reconciliation.

BOOK ABOUT SHIGA

Sibley, William F. *The Shiga Hero.* U. Ch. Pr. 1979 $21.00. ISBN 0-226-75620-3. Shiga and his works psychoanalyzed. Also contains translations of 10 short stories.

SHIMAZAKI TŌSON (SHIMAZAKI HARUKI). 1872–1943

Poet and novelist Shimazaki Tōson was raised on an old mountain road well-traveled in feudal Japan. As a young man, he lived in Tokyo, then retreated to the northern city of Sendai and lived in Paris during World War I. The poetry of Shimazaki's youth was inspired by the English romanticists. Written in a new, freer style, it set off a movement that eventually liberated Japanese verse from the dominance of tanka and haiku. As a novelist, Shimazaki is perhaps best known for *The Family* (1911), acclaimed as a masterpiece of naturalistic fiction. His complex writing is passionate in its attention to the human dimension of abstract ideological clashes during turbulent historical transitions.

NOVELS BY TŌSON

Before the Dawn, (Yoakemae). Trans. by William E. Naff. UH Pr. 1988 $30.00. ISBN 0-8248-0914-9. A juxtaposition of individual and national responses to the westernization of Japan. Considered one of Tōson's most significant works.

The Family (Ie). 1911. Trans. by Cecilia Segawa Seigle. Col. U. Pr. 1978 $22.50. ISBN 0-86008-254-7. Draws on Tōson's personal experiences. With translator's introduction containing biographical information about Tōson and the extended family depicted.

WORK BY TŌSON

Chikuma River Sketches. Trans. by William Naff. UH Pr. $25.00. ISBN 0-8248-1314-6. Tōson's selection of jottings from his crucial Komoro period, 1899–1905. Also documents the transitional period of Meiji Japan in a rural area.

TACHIHARA MASAAKI. 1926–1980

Son of a Zen priest, Tachihara Masaaki grew up studying the arts of feudal Japan. His works treat the relationship between sensuality and aesthetics, drawing upon the worlds of Noh drama, traditional gardens, and the tea ceremony.

NOVEL BY TACHIHARA

Wind and Stone: A Novel (Yume wa Kareno wo). Trans. by Stephen W. Kohl. Stone Bridge Pr. 1992 $10.95. ISBN 0-9628137-7-X. A story of seduction via aesthetics, as the art and eroticism of a garden designer affects a client.

TANIKAWA SHUNTARO. 1931–

Tanikawa Shuntaro, son of a professor, emerged from the postwar cataclysm to serve as a self-described emblem of optimism. He enjoys a level of popular and financial success accorded to most Western poets only posthumously. Tanikawa writes poetry, often about the theme of the poet on the frontier, face-to-face with boundlessness; children's works; song lyrics; television and movie scripts; and plays. He has also translated Mother Goose rhymes and the comic strip "Peanuts."

POETRY BY TANIKAWA

Floating the River in Melancholy. Trans. by William I. Elliott and Kazuo Kawamura. Prescott St. Pr. 1988 $15.00. ISBN 0-915986-23-X. A bilingual edition of 13 works of poetry including prose poems and linked verse.

TANIZAKI JUN'ICHIRŌ. 1886–1965

A true *Edokko* (child of Tokyo), born in the low-lying merchant areas of the metropolis, Tanizaki lived his later years in the Kansai region and immersed himself in the traditions of the court culture of ancient Japan. He was also widely read in Western literature. A superb storyteller whose characters delight in the sensual, Tanizaki's tales often combine the erotic with details of traditional Japanese arts. He spent three years translating the eleventh-century novel *The Tale of Genji* into modern Japanese.

NOVELS BY TANIZAKI

Diary of a Mad Old Man. 1961. Trans. by Howard Hibbett. Putnam Pub. Group 1981 $10.95. ISBN 0-679-730249. One of Tanizaki's later works, written when he was in his seventies. The story of an ill and impotent old man attracted to his daughter-in-law, and a fine study of old age.

The Key (Kagi). 1957. Trans. by Howard Hibbett. Random 1991 $10.00. ISBN 0-67-73023-0. A middle-aged professor, with an obsessive fear of losing his sexual vigor, and his wife keep diaries.

The Makioka Sisters (Sasame Yuki). 1946–49. Trans. by Edward G. Seidensticker. Putnam Pub. Group 1981 $12.95. ISBN 0-399-50520-2. Widely regarded as Tanizaki's masterpiece. A nostalgic but objective look at the elegant decline of an Osaka merchant family.

Some Prefer Nettles (Tade kuu mushi). 1928. Trans. by Edward G. Seidensticker. Putnam Pub. Group 1981 $8.95. ISBN 0-399-50521-0. The story of a man in a failing marriage who is torn between the allure of the West, as represented by a Eurasian prostitute, and traditional Japan, in the person of his father-in-law's mistress.

Short Story Collection by Tanizaki

A Cat, A Man, and Two Women. Trans. by Paul McCarthy. Kodansha Ltd. Japan 1990 $18.95. ISBN 0-87011-755-6. Three stories about three men, written in three decades. Distinguished by Tanizaki's characteristic graceful writing.

Seven Japanese Tales. Trans. by Howard Hibbett. Putnam Pub. Group 1981 $10.95. ISBN 0-399-50523-7. A collection of major short stories, including the exquisite "A Portrait of Shunkin," written between 1910 and 1959.

Nonfiction by Tanizaki

Childhood Years: A Memoir (Yosho jidai). Trans. by Paul McCarthy. Kodansha Ltd. Japan 1988 $17.95. ISBN 0-87011-863-3. Nostalgia for the Tokyo lost in the great Kanto earthquake of 1923, filtered through the author's acute sense of detail and erotic inclinations.

In Praise of Shadows. Trans. by Thomas Harper and Edward G. Seidensticker. Leete's Island Books 1977 $4.95. ISBN 0-918172-02-0. An essay on Japanese aesthetics that argues for the implicit and unstated over the explicit.

Books about Tanizaki

Ito, Ken K. *Visions of Desire: Tanizaki's Fictional Worlds.* Stanford U. Pr. 1991 $35.00. ISBN 0-8047-1869-5. An in-depth critical assessment of Tanizaki's impact on modern Japanese culture.

TSUSHIMA YUKO. 1947–

First published while a student, Tsushima was immediately well received and continues to write novels and short stories prolifically. Her works are characterized by themes of childhood innocence (from memories of her relationship with her retarded brother) and of the emotional barrenness of family life. Tsushima is the daughter of Dazai Osamu.

Novels by Tsushima

Child of Fortune (Chuji). Trans. by Geraldine Harcourt. Kodansha Ltd. Japan 1992 $6.95. ISBN 4-770-01524-0. A struggle for independence, as the single mother of an adolescent daughter finds herself pregnant again. Rich in images of domestic detail.

Woman Running in the Mountains (Yama wo hashiru onna). Trans. by Geraldine Harcourt. Pantheon 1991 $22.00. ISBN 0-394-58238-1. About a young single woman, pregnant and at war with her family, who finds comfort in motherhood and a nontraditional job. Dream sequences and myths.

UNO CHIYO. 1897–

Born in the Japanese countryside, Uno attended a high school that prohibited the reading of newspapers and magazines. Later, she became a magazine publisher herself, as well as a fashion designer, world traveler, and successful businesswoman. Her unconventional personal life is often the subject of her award-winning fiction.

Novel by Uno

Confessions of Love. Trans. by Phyllis Birnbaum. UH Pr. 1989 $27.00. ISBN 0-8248-1170-4

BOOK ABOUT UNO

Copeland, Rebecca L. *The Sound of the Wind: The Life and Works of Uno Chiyo.* UH Pr. 1992 $28.00. ISBN 0-8248-1409-6. A portrait of the unconventional life of one of Japan's most celebrated women. Includes translations of three works of Uno's short fiction.

YOKOMITSU RIICHI. 1898–1947

During the experimental years of the twenties and thirties, Yokomitsu Riichi played a dynamic role in developing the Japanese novel. With KAWABATA YASUNARI, he was involved in a "neosensualist" literary movement that tried to describe the world through direct sensory impressions rather than through sense interpreted by the mind or emotions. Later, Yokomitsu explored the psychological novel.

SHORT STORY COLLECTION BY YOKOMITSU

Love and Other Stories of Yokomitsu Riichi. Trans. by Dennis Keene. Col. U. Pr. 1979 $12.50. ISBN 0-86008-256-3

BOOK ABOUT YOKOMITSU

Keene, Donald. *Yokomitsu Riichi, Modernist.* Col. U. Pr. 1980 $40.00. ISBN 0-231-04938-2. An analysis of the life and works of one of the most gifted modern Japanese writers.

YOSANO, AKIKO. 1878–1942

Yosano's romantic verse and concern for the welfare of the individual inspired her contemporaries and generations of later poets. While later feminist writers felt the need to abandon their traditional roles in order to write, Yosano felt that her love affair and eventual marriage with her teacher of tanka (Yosano Tekkan), her raising of 11 children, and her life as a homemaker and mother stimulated her creativity.

POETRY BY YOSANO

Tangled Hair: Selected Tanka from Midaregami. Trans. by Sanford Goldstein and Seishi Shinoda. C. E. Tuttle 1987 $9.95. ISBN 0-8048-1522-4. *Midaregami* contains 23 volumes of tanka, bold in their affirmation of sexual passion and self-expression.

CHAPTER 9

Korean Literature

Marshall R. Pihl

Fiction is, in the end, a prose art that takes as its object all things rising out of human interaction; its basic purpose lies in using this art to suggest the joy, anger, sorrow, and pleasure of life.

—O YÔNG-SU, "An Apologia"

For some two millennia, Korean literary creativity has been expressed in a great variety of forms and, indeed, languages. Prior to 1900, Koreans composed in either Korean or Chinese, as was appropriate to the work's purpose and content and the writer's social background. And during the last 100 years, as foreign influence has penetrated Korean culture and as Koreans themselves have spread out into the world (about 5 million now live in 106 countries), their literature has also found its voice in other languages, including Japanese, Russian, French, German, and English.

In spite of such activity, relatively little of Korean literature written before 1900 has been translated into English or European languages. Even less historical and critical writing in foreign languages has addressed the long Korean literary tradition. But as this century ends, a new generation of European and American scholars are building a critical foundation for the study of Korea in all fields.

Like any literature, Korean literature was first oral. It reaches back to the earliest cultures on the Korean peninsula. The appearance of foundation myths, the introduction and growth of Chinese writing, and the emergence of native poetry mark the beginning of the ancient period, which coincides roughly with the Bronze Age. When early states were first taking shape, ruling groups created myths and narrative poetry about their foundings, a means of asserting the group's superiority and establishing civil order. When Chinese writing was first introduced, therefore, it was used to record a history that consisted of foundation myths. As the myths and poems lost their function in the early medieval period, literary composition in Chinese began.

The beginning of the early medieval period (57 B.C.–A.D. 1216) is associated particularly with poetry written in Chinese, which coexisted with a native poetry that borrowed Chinese characters to record Korean songs. (Koreans had no script of their own until 1446.) During this period, oral literature continued to be vigorous, and forms other than foundation narratives became written literature. Folk songs, for example, were recorded and incorporated into the native poetic tradition.

During the Shilla period (57 B.C.–A.D. 935), Chinese was widely used for government recordkeeping and the teaching of Buddhism; in addition, it played a crucial role as a means of self-expression for scholar-officials. Although the Shilla state was ruled by a hereditary royal class, the principal creators and bearers of literature were high-ranking, nonroyal nobility who made their way in life as scribes, using writing for both practical and artistic ends. They strove in particular to mold both Chinese verse and native poetry into an expressive lyric poetry.

"Academic-style" poetry of the Koryô period (918–1392) heralded the arrival of the late medieval period (1216–1600). The "Song of the Scholars," composed about 1216, is the first acknowledged work in this style, which was productive throughout the period. Its practitioners became known as the "newly rising literati." Originally, they served as functionaries in local government, but often the revolt of military officials in 1170, they began to emerge in central political circles. Later, they were leaders in the formation of governments during the Chosôn period (1392–1910). Although Chinese literature was clearly flourishing by the late Koryô, Korean, or native, accomplishment was considerable, too. A compilation made in early Chosôn—the 154-volume *Anthology of Korean Writing* (1478)—handsomely demonstrates the comparable achievements of the two traditions.

One of the most notable achievements of the late medieval period occurred in the mid-fifteenth century when a board of scholars, under royal charge, conducted a phonemic analysis of Korean—the first such analysis of any language. The result was the creation of an alphabet based upon metaphysical concepts and the physiology of the human speech organs: Characters appropriate to each sound. The introduction of that alphabet, called *hangûl* today, altered the course of Korean literature. Starting in 1446, when the script was promulgated, Koreans embarked on a massive program of translation into Korean of major portions of the Confucian and Buddhist Chinese canon. In addition, the scholarly elite composed lengthy Confucian and Buddhist odes in Korean, and the crown prince composed a multivolume prose biography of the historical Buddha, Śākyamuni. It was now possible for the first time in Korean history to record the sounds of the Korean language exactly as uttered, and aristocratic writers took advantage of the new alphabet to record poetry once only performed orally.

A long transitional period, 1600–1919, bridged the late medieval and the modern periods. While Korean fiction in Chinese, such as KIM MAN-JUNG's *A Nine Cloud Dream* (1686–89), remained strong, Korean-language fiction and other narrative prose came into their own in the seventeenth century. In addition to traditional fiction promoting Confucian norms, this period gave rise to the writings of palace memoirs. In them, noble women such as LADY HONG OF HYEGYÔNG PALACE told their side of momentous events that shaped Korea's history. The transitional period, furthermore, saw another flowering of oral literature. These new oral narratives gave voice to contemporary social issues and exerted a decisive influence on fiction written in Korean.

The second half of the transitional period began about 1860, its beginning marked by several events: Ch'oe Che-u's 1863 collection of "seditious" poetry, the growth of a more aware populace, the emergence of the bourgeoisie, and direct expression in literature of dissatisfaction with the medieval ruling system. On the other hand, a modern national consciousness was taking shape as Koreans sensed a need to protect their country from foreign encroachment.

Although in the opening years of the twentieth century there appeared such "enlightenment" literature as the new novel, new-form poetry, and new-wave drama, the period was still transitional. The modern period begins only in the early 1920s. Decisive changes came to writing as a new literary movement arose to force literature written in Chinese from its central position. The Chinese was now thought insufficient as a vehicle for a Korean literature of the new age. Instead, literature was to be based on the spoken Korean language, and its written style was expected to accord with the desideratum, "identity of the spoken and the written."

The new generation of writers that burst forth revolutionized Korean literature, fiction in particular. Key figures included the poets HAN YONG-UN and KIM SO-WÔL along with the notable fiction writers KIM TONG-NI, Hyôn Chin-gôn, and Yôm Sang-sôp. Although traditional fiction still had its audience, these new writers emphasized realism, sought a more coherent use of the language, and showed a preference for the short story. Modern literature fully came into its own during the 1930s, when the leaders of later years—HWANG SUN-WÔN, KANG SHIN-JAE, KIM TONG-NI, O YÔNG-SU, SÔ CHÔNG-JU, and others—had their schooling. And after liberation from Japanese rule in 1945 and the Korean War of 1950–53, yet another generational change brought CHOI IN-HOON, KIM CHI-HA, YI MUN-YÔL, and YUN HEUNG-GIL to the fore. Meanwhile, RICHARD KIM was introducing the Korean experience in the United States, through his novels written in English—an important cultural exchange that continues as more Korean writers are now translated for English-speaking readers.

HISTORY AND CRITICISM

Eckert, Carter, and others. *Korea Old and New, A History*. HUP 1990. ISBN 0-9627713-0-9. The most recent Korean history text. Earlier chapters based on Ki-baik Lee's *New History of Korea*; especially good and original analysis of the late nineteenth and twentieth centuries.

Kim, Han-Kyo. *Studies on Korea: A Scholar's Guide*. UH Pr. 1980 $27.50. ISBN 0-8248-0673-5. Bibliographic essays with an annotated bibliography on Korean history, culture, language, literature, politics, economics, and society.

Lee, Ki-baik. *A New History of Korea*. Trans. by Edward W. Wagner and Edward J. Shultz. HUP 1990 $25.00. ISBN 0-674-61575-1. The standard English history of Korea from earliest times to mid-century; the translation of a Korean standard text.

McCann, David R. *Form and Freedom in Korean Poetry*. E. J. Brill 1988 $20.00. ISBN 90-04-08548-3. The first treatment in English of Korean prosody from a modern perspective. Erases antiquated notions that had earlier dominated the field.

Skillend, William E. *Kodae Sosôl: A Survey of Korean Traditional Style Popular Novels*. Sch. of Oriental & African Studies, U. of London 1968 o.p. The only annotated bibliography in English of Korean traditional popular novels.

COLLECTIONS

Chông, Ch'ôl, Pak Il-lo, and Yun Sôn-do. *Pine River and Lone Peak*. Trans. by Peter H. Lee. UH Pr. 1991 $24.00. ISBN 0-8248-1298-0. Titled after the pen names of three medieval poets.

Chung, Chong-wha, ed. *The Anthology of Modern Korean Poetry*. East-West Pub. 1986 o.p. Anthology of poems by Korean poets born in the 1930s and 1940s.

Kang, Sôk-kyông, Kim Chi-wôn, O Chông-hui. *Words of Farewell: Stories by Korean Women Writers*. Trans. by Bruce and Ju-Chan Fulton. Seal Pr. Feminist 1989 $12.95. ISBN 0-931188-76-8. An excellent translation of stories by three outstanding contemporary Korean women writers who display a wide range of techniques; provides insights into contemporary Korean life.

Kim, Chong-un, trans. *Postwar Korean Short Stories*. UH Pr. 1983 $18.00. ISBN 0-8248-0833-9. Eighteen stories written in the 1950s and 1960s by the key writers of a transitional era.

Kim, Jaihiun J., trans. *Classical Korean Poetry*. Hanshin Pub. 1986 o.p. More than 600 Korean poems, dating from the twelfth century; includes English translation and original Korean texts.

______, trans. *Korean Poetry Today*. Hanshin Pub. 1987 o.p. A 400-page survey of modern verse.

______, trans. *Master Poems from Modern Korea*. Si-sa-yong-o-sa 1980 o.p. Korean poetry of the twentieth century, with an introduction by Kim Jaihiun; includes English translation and original Korean texts.

______, trans. *Master Sijo Poems from Korea*. Si-sa-yong-o-sa 1982 o.p. Poems, both classical and modern, in a form known as *shijo;* includes English translation and original Korean texts.

______, trans. *Traditional Korean Verse since the 1990s*. Hanshin Pub. 1991 o.p. Modern poems in a classic form called *shijo*.

Kim, Jong-gil, trans. *Slow Chrysanthemums*. Anvil Pr. 1987 $9.95. ISBN 0-85646-163-6. Classical Korean poems in Chinese, translated and introduced by a master poet-translator whose publications have spanned more than three decades.

Kim, Uchang, trans. *Selected Poems of Pak Mogwol*. Jain Pub. Co. 1990 $12.00. ISBN 0-89581-920-1. From lyrics to meditations on the plight of the modern Korean, with a sensitive and knowledgeable introduction by the translator.

Lee, Peter H., ed. *Anthology of Korean Literature: From Early Times to the Nineteenth Century*. UH Pr. 1981 $12.95. ISBN 0-8248-0739-1. A wide-ranging, representative survey of traditional Korean literature.

______, ed. *Modern Korean Literature*. UH Pr. 1990 $40.00. ISBN 0-8248-1321-9. An anthology of twentieth-century Korean short stories and poetry, translated from Korean by Korean and American translators.

______, ed. *The Silence of Love*. UH Pr. 1980 $17.95. ISBN 0-8248-0732-4. An anthology of modern verse, from 1900 to the present.

______, trans. *Songs of the Flying Dragons*. HUP 1975 $20.00. ISBN 0-674-82075-4. An erudite, annotated translation of *Yongbi ôch'ôn ka* (1445–47), the first eulogistic ode composed and written in Korean.

Lee, Sung-Il, trans. *The Wind and the Waves: Four Modern Korean Poets*. Jain Pub. Co. 1989 $14.00. ISBN 0-89581-917-1. A sensitive and evocative translation that brings the poetry to life.

McCann, David R., ed. *Black Crane: An Anthology of Korean Literature*. Cornell Univ. Pr. 1977 $7.00. ISBN 0-939657-14-7. Includes traditional and contemporary literature.

Ô, Suk-kwôn. *A Korean Storyteller's Miscellany: The P'aegwan chapki*. Trans. by Peter H. Lee. Princeton U. Pr. 1989 $40.00. ISBN 0-691-06771-6. A collection of notes and jottings by a sixteenth-century Korean scholar that reveal his times and world view; a glimpse into the heart of a lost culture.

O'Rourke, Kevin, trans. *The Cutting Edge: A Selection of Korean Poetry, Ancient and Modern*. Yonsei U. Pr. 1982 o.p. A collection of personal favorites rendered by an established scholar and translator.

______, trans. *Tilting the Jar, Spilling the Moon*. Univ. Pubns. 1988 o.p. A prize-winning collection of verse by Koreans, originally written in Chinese and Korean, from the twelfth century to the present.

Pai, Inez Kong, trans. *The Ever White Mountain: Korean Lyrics in the Classical Sijo Form*. C. E. Tuttle 1965 o.p. A popular collection of Chosôn period (1392–1910) *sijo* verse, providing a view of the riches of traditional Korean culture and art.

Pihl, Marshall R., ed. *Listening to Korea: A Korean Anthology*. Praeger Pubs. 1973 o.p. Translations of essays and short stories on themes and events in Korea's recent past, providing social and cultural insights.

Rutt, Richard, trans. *The Bamboo Grove: An Introduction to Sijo*. U. CA Pr. 1971 o.p. The standard collection of the brief *shijo* form—gathered, annotated, and introduced by the Western pioneer in academic *shijo* studies.

Rutt, Richard, and Kim Chon-un, trans. *Virtuous Women: Three Masterpieces of Traditional Korean Fiction*. Royal Asiatic Soc. Korea Br. 1974 o.p. A unique collection of three major works that are both literature and texts for the study of Korea's society, culture, history, and institutions.

Suh, Ji-moon, trans. *The Rainy Spell and Other Korean Stories*. Onyx 1983 o.p. Articulate translations of 11 stories written between 1920 and 1973.

CHRONOLOGY OF AUTHORS

Kim Man-jung. 1637–1692
Lady Hong of Hyegyông Palace. 1735–1815
Han Yong-un. 1879–1944
Kim So-Wôl. 1902–1934
Kim Tong-ni. 1913–
O Yông-su. 1914–1979
Sô Chông-ju. 1915–
Hwang Sun-wôn. 1915–
Kang Shin-jae. 1924–
Kim, Richard. 1932–
Choi In-hoon. 1936–
Kim Chi-ha. 1941–
Yun Heung-gil. 1942–
Yi Mun-yôl. 1948–

CHOI IN-HOON (Ch'oe In-hun). 1936–

In 1960, only one year after his first publication, Choi In-hoon made an indelible mark on modern Korean fiction with the novel *The Square*, the first work to break the taboo of silence shrouding the internecine horror of the Korean War (1950–53). In *The Square*, which established Choi In-hoon as a major novelist, he addresses the war's origins and presents a protagonist alienated from all Korean society, both the Communist north and the individualistic south.

Though born during the last decade of Japanese rule, Choi In-hoon belonged to a new literary generation whose agenda for their country differed sharply from that of the literary establishment. At the same time, while his tendency toward abstract thinking links him with other young writers, he stands apart because of his insistent concern for external social and political realities. Typically, Choi's alienated characters only with great difficulty adapt to reality's demands.

Novels by Choi In-hoon

The Daily Life of Ku-poh the Novelist. 1970–1971. Trans. by Ki-Chang Hong. Fremont Pr. 1985 o.p. A portrait of a refugee novelist from North Korea who, while living in South Korea, copes with the hardships of life in a divided country.

A Grey Man. 1963. Trans. by Chun Kyung-ja. Pace Intl. Res. 1988. ISBN 0-87296-032-3

The Square. 1960. Trans. by Kevin O'Rourke. Spindlewood 1985 o.p.

HAN YONG-UN. 1879–1944

This stubborn and tough-minded Buddhist monk was not only a leader in the Korean struggle for independence from Japan, but he was also a tender and loving poet whose work continues to stir his people. While he made significant contributions to the development of modern Buddhist thought with his philosophical treatises, he is best known to Koreans for his slim volume of 88 poems, *The Silence of Love*, which has appeared in more than 20 editions since it was first published in 1925. This single work has given rise to more than 90 critical studies.

Among pioneering modern Korean poets, Han Yong-un stands alone, not simply for his detachment from their world but for his peculiar use of poetic diction and style. His basic unit of expression is the sentence, but this "prose," even at its most colloquial, possesses a sensibility and grace that make it poetry. His verse is like intimate speech.

Jaihiun J. Kim, a prolific translator of Korean poetry, characterizes *The Silence of Love* as an encomium to love, "not merely confined to one particular person or thing, but implying something more comprehensive, more profound: love for the country, truth, awakening, liberation from bondage, Buddha's compassion for humanity, in addition to secular love between men and women."

As a boy, Han Yong-un learned classical Chinese at his village school. In keeping with traditional country custom, he was married early, at age 14, but joined partisans in the Tonghak Rebellion of 1896 when he was 18. By 1905, he had taken vows as a Buddhist monk and retreated to a temple in the Sôrak Mountains. It was from there that he gave the world his philosophy and his poetry.

POETRY BY HAN YONG-UN

Meditations of the Lover. 1925. Trans. by Younghill Kang and Frances Keely. Yonsei U. Pr. 1970 o.p. The first English translation of *The Silence of Love*, notable for its translator, Younghill Kang, the first Korean to publish his own autobiography in English (*The Grass Roof*, 1931).

The Silence of Love: Poems by Yong-un Han. 1925. Trans. by Jaihiun J. Kim. Prairie Poet Bks. 1985 $8.00. ISBN 0-938138-52-9. The work of an experienced and well-known translator of Korean poetry.

BOOKS ABOUT HAN YONG-UN

Kim, Young Ho. *Whitman and Han Yong-un*. Soongsil U. Pr. 1987 o.p. Discusses philosophies, themes, and symbols in the poetry of Walt Whitman and Han Yong-un.

Yu, Beongcheon. *Han Yong-un and Yi Kwang-su: Two Pioneers of Modern Korean Literature*. Wayne St. U. Pr. 1992 $26.95. ISBN 0-8143-2354-5. A study of two contrasting contemporaries; "Yu's book should be very informative and stimulating to general readers and at the same time provocative and challenging to specialists" (*Korea Journal*).

LADY HONG OF HYEGYÔNG PALACE. 1735–1815

Of only three extant examples of palace literature by noble women, Lady Hong's memoirs are the most notable. Daughter of the prime minister, Lady Hong was selected as the wife of Crown Prince Sado when she was only 10 and, from that time on, had little or no contact with her own family and friends. In spite of what might seem a redeeming and fortunate situation, her life was made a torment by the madness of her father-in-law, King Yôngjo, who starved her husband to death in a rice chest when Sado was 28. Her son Chôngjo succeeded his grandfather as king in 1776, reigning until 1800.

Lady Hong's single work—variously titled *A Record of Crying Blood, A Record of Sorrow*, and *Reminiscences in Retirement*—is a memoir, started in 1795 and completed in 1805, written to vindicate her husband's tragic death and give a true account of the deaths of her relatives. Like the other two existing palace memoirs, Lady Hong's is written in Korean rather than Chinese, but hers stands apart because she speaks in the first person.

Her translator Yang-hi Choe-Wall has written: "Lady Hong's memoir shows that, as a woman of the court, she held an inferior position. Despite this, her fortitude and extreme devotion to her family, especially under the onslaught of King Yôngjo's growing anger, rank her as an outstanding woman of her time. The crown prince's early death, at the hand of his father, is dealt with in the memoir with the controlled emotion and compassion which permeates the whole of her work. Despite the suffering and tragedy she had to bear, she remained a model of Confucian virtue."

Nonfiction by Lady Hong

Han Joong Nok: Reminiscences in Retirement. 1796–1805. Trans. by Bruce K. Grant and Kim Chin-man. Larchwood Pub. 1980 o.p. Translates entire original text but adds embellishment; uses an elevated English appropriate to the language of Lady Hong.

Memoirs of a Korean Queen. Trans. by Yang-hi Choe-Wall. Routledge Chapman & Hall 1985 $32.50. ISBN 0-7103-0052-2. A sensitive and faithful translation, but covers only about half of the original text.

HWANG SUN-WÔN. 1915–

Hwang Sun-wôn began his literary career as a student poet while studying English at Japan's prestigious Waseda University. By his graduation in 1939, Hwang already had two published poetry collections to his credit—the lyrical *Madly Singing* (1934) and the modernist *Curio* (1936). But in occupied Korea, where the Japanese administration was systematically eliminating open use of the Korean language, his early work was unpublished, a silent apprenticeship.

By the time Hwang regained his public voice, following Korea's liberation from Japan on August 15, 1945, he had fully embarked upon his second stage of artistic development: He had become adept in the short story form, a medium he continued to explore until establishing himself as a novelist in the 1960s.

In the 15 early stories written during World War II and released in *Wild Geese* (1951), already in evidence is the artful balance of humanism and craftsmanship that defines Hwang Sun-wôn's masterful style—a style reflected in more than 100 short stories, 5 novels, and several volumes of poetry since 1930. Hwang Sun-wôn is Korea's most consistently productive writer and also the most widely translated. During the 1980s alone, nearly 1,500 pages of translation appeared.

While Hwang Sun-wôn is representative of his literary generation, his distinct style sets him apart. His sentences—simple, tightly packed, and logically sequential—contrast with the complex, architectural style common among his peers. The impact of Hwang's prose is cumulative, a driving, suspenseful forward movement. Yet, for all his foreshadowing and logical development, Hwang is remarkably unforthcoming with descriptive detail. His economic sentences present only what he deems necessary. He does not paint landscapes or dally with flowers and insects; he is primarily concerned with human beings and their feelings. And this he reveals with careful detail in telling contexts. As a result, the world of a Hwang Sun-wôn story is removed from daily life; it is revealed only insofar as it resonates with the people who populate it. Nearly always a reader senses more than Hwang is telling, darkness and mystery just beyond the light.

Hwang Sun-wôn has been recognized with many prizes and awards, beginning with the Freedom Literary Prize in 1955. Other honors include the National Academy of Arts Award (1961), Order of the Camellia for Civil Merit (1970), and Republic of Korea Literary Award (1983). In addition to being a professor at Kyung Hee University (1955–80), he has served as chairman of the Korean Writers Association and the Korean Novelists Association, president of the National Academy of Arts, and a member of the Advisory Council on State Affairs.

Short Story Collections by Hwang Sun-wôn

The Book of Masks. 1976. Trans. by J. Martin Holman. Readers Intl. 1989 $9.95. ISBN 0-930523-58-X. Arresting stories revealing hidden tensions and suppressed rebellion in Korean life today.

Shadows of a Sound. 1942–1983. Ed. by J. Martin Holman. Mercury Hse. Inc. 1990 $17.95. ISBN 0-916515-65-6. A representative collection of stories, from the bizarre to the sublime.

The Stars and Other Korean Short Stories. 1936–1974. Trans. by Edward W. Poitras. Heinemann Ed. 1980 o.p. The first English anthology of stories, representing five decades of Hwang's work.

Novels by Hwang Sun-wôn

The Moving Castle. 1973. Trans. by Bruce and Ju-chan Fulton. Si-sa-yong-o-sa 1985 o.p. Embodies the spiritual crosscurrents, both traditional and modern, of modern Koreans; a forthright portrait of social, cultural, and psychological strains.

Sunlight, Moonlight. 1964. Trans. by Sol Sun-bong. Si-sa-yong-o-sa 1990 o.p. Hwang's fifth novel, focusing on the mysterious stigma of the *paekchong,* the outcast class of Korea who are hereditary butchers.

Trees on the Cliff. 1960. Trans. by Chang Wang-rok. Larchwood Pub. 1980 o.p. Received the prestigious Korean National Academy of Arts Award; this volume includes two short stories in addition to the novel.

KANG SHIN-JAE. 1924–

Not only were women writers at center stage during the formative years of modern Korean literature, but they have continued to be significant as contemporary literature evolves. Unfortunately, only a few of these writers have book-length English translations, but Kang Shin-jae is one. Since making her writing debut at age 26, she has published more than 25 novels and 30 short story collections, as well as plays and essay collections. Her main characters are frequently women, and much of her early writing explores questions of morality in contemporary male-female relationships. Most recently, however, she has turned her attention to historical fiction. Kang Shin-jae has received the Literary Award for Women and has also been honored with awards from the Korean Literary Association.

Novels by Kang Shin-jae

The Dandelion on the Imjin River. 1962. Trans. by Sôl Soon-bong. Dongsuhmunhaksa 1990 o.p. The gripping story of a Korean family and their courageous daughter in war-torn Seoul under Communist occupation.

The Waves. 1964. Trans. by Tina L. Sallee. Routledge Chapman & Hall 1988 $19.95. ISBN 0-7103-0281-9. Follows the lives of a child and her family through the course of a year in their rural fishing village.

KIM CHI-HA (Kim Yong-il). 1941–

With a name that can be read to mean "underground," Kim Chi-ha during the 1970s and 1980s was a courageous literary figure who symbolized popular resistance to the dictatorial practices of presidents Park Chung Hee and Chun Doo Hwan. He was born in South Chôlla Province, educated in aesthetics at Seoul National University, and began his literary career in 1969 with the publication of "Yellow Earth Road," "Bean Flower," and "The Empty Field" in *Poet* magazine. His first collection was *The Yellow Earth Road* (1970). Although Kim Chi-ha's earlier, shorter poems typically have a "distant tone and express an almost impersonal anger," according to translator David R. McCann, his work of 1970 and after includes longer, satirical allegories such as "The Five Bandits" (1970) and "Groundless Rumors" (1972).

Kim's political activism dates back to his student years in the mid-1960s, but it was "The Five Bandits" that made him a popular spokesperson for the oppressed and a threat to the government. This biting poem—which skewers the sacred public cows of business leaders, national assembly members, government officials, generals, and ministers of state—provoked a chain of events that led to years of imprisonment and even a 1974 death sentence that, in the end, the government did not carry out. The satire was first published in the intellectual magazine *Sasanggye* and then reprinted in the political organ of the leading opposition party. Finally, when a North Korean publication later picked up the poem, the South Korean establishment arrested Kim Chi-ha. In 1981, Kim was recognized by the International Poet's Association with the Outstanding Poet Award.

Poetry by Kim Chi-ha

Cry of the People and Other Poems. Autumn Pr. 1974 o.p. A collection issued by friends and associates when the poet was under threat of execution for his outspoken work.

The Gold Crowned Jesus and Other Writings. Ed. by Chong Sun Kim and Shelly Killen. Bks. Demand 1978 $44.50. ISBN 0-317-26644-6

The Middle Hour: Selected Poems of Kim Chi Ha. Trans. by David R. McCann. E. M. Coleman Ent. 1980 $9.50. ISBN 0-930576-36-5. Prepared in cooperation with the poet and with a preface by the poet Denise Levertov.

KIM MAN-JUNG. 1637–1692

Kim Man-jung's life and work began to attract attention shortly after Korea's liberation from Japanese rule in 1945, when Korean scholars were seeking to substantiate their country's unique cultural heritage. Therefore, were it not for some scholars' assertion that Kim Man-jung wrote his original 1686–89 version of *A Nine Cloud Dream* in the Korean language, he might not be studied or regarded as he is today. In spite of the fact that the oldest surviving version of his novel, dated 1725, is in Chinese and that all Korean versions are demonstrably translations from Chinese, there are those who adduce reasons to support a lost, original Korean text.

Tradition has it that Kim, who never knew his father and naturally esteemed his widowed mother, wrote his novel to console her while he was exiled in the northwest. Her influence over him, both literary and personal, reached back to his childhood. A poor but highly educated woman who enjoyed Chinese literature, she herself tutored Kim Man-jung and his brother in the Chinese classics because they could not afford other schooling. Some critics even assert that Kim's preference for romance literature and concern with the life of women, both evident in *A Nine Cloud Dream*, reflect a home life in which a gentle, educated woman was central.

Novel by Kim Man-jung

A Nine Cloud Dream. 1686–89. Trans. by Richard Rutt. Heinemann Ed. 1980 o.p. A full and faithful translation.

KIM, RICHARD (Kim Ûn-guk). 1932–

Born in Manchuria, raised in Korea, and residing in the United States for the past 30 years, Richard Kim is one of the 5 million Koreans who live in more than 100 countries outside their homeland. As such, his work belongs to a tradition of writing in foreign languages about the Korean experience that is earlier represented by Younghill Kang's English *The Grass Roof* (1931) and Mirok Li's German *The Yalu Flows* (1946). Kim can be considered the first major Korean writer to work in English since the 1930s.

Richard Kim spent his early life among Canadian missionary children in Manchuria, and his mother used to joke that the first words he heard must have been English—"It's a boy!"—because he was born in a missionary hospital. He cannot now recall whether he spoke English and Chinese as a child in Manchuria. The family moved back to Korea in 1948, three years after Korea was liberated from Japanese occupation and rule.

He describes his education as a "total mess," for it was repeatedly interrupted by civil strife and the Korean War. He attended high school and college, erratically, but his formal education ended when he was drafted into the army of the Republic of Korea in October 1950. Because he enjoyed the army, he did not want to accept a scholarship at Vermont's Middlebury College in 1955, but he yielded to the urgings of General Chang To-yông (who later led the 1961 coup d'état that put General Park Chung Hee in power). After studying political science at Middlebury and then literature and writing at Johns Hopkins and the Iowa Writers' Workshop, Kim continued with graduate training at Harvard. In 1963, he embarked on a career of teaching and writing at a number of institutions: "It's amusing that I should be teaching American kids to write in English," he muses.

The first of the trilogy that brought him public notice was *The Martyred* in 1964, a huge success that was soon followed by *The Innocent* in 1968. His favorite book, first published in 1970 and still in print, is *Lost Names*, the story of his childhood in Manchuria and Korea during the Japanese occupation.

NOVELS BY RICHARD KIM

The Innocent. HM 1968 o.p. A tale of adventure based on the military coup d'état that changed Korea at dawn on May 16, 1961; second book in the author's trilogy.

Lost Names. Universe 1988 repr. of 1970 ed. $14.95. ISBN 0-87663-678-4. A fictional memoir of Koreans and Japanese in occupied Korea during the 1930s; third book in the author's trilogy.

The Martyred. Braziller 1964 o.p. The first of Richard Kim's trilogy on the modern Korean experience; "Mr. Kim's book stands out in the great tradition of Job, Dostoevsky, and Albert Camus. . ." (*N. Y. Times*).

KIM SO-WÔL (Kim Chông-shik). 1902–1934

No other modern Korean poet is better known and loved by Koreans than Kim So-wôl, who was born Kim Chông-shik. His lyrical poems, some 250 in all, have appeared in countless editions and today even adorn billboards in Seoul's labyrinthine subway system. He is more translated than any other modern Korean poet, with "Flowers on the Mountains" rendered in at least 17 foreign languages and "Azaleas" in more than 12. One of these widely anthologized poems is usually foreign students' first introduction to Korean poetry. Kim So-wôl's ability to express Korean sensibilities earned him the title "folksong poet," although he hated the term, rejecting such categorization. He was already composing at age 17, and his poetry was first introduced to the public in 1920 in the noted literary journal *Creation*. The bulk of his work appeared by 1926, but then it tapered off sharply. Two years earlier, he had moved to the little town of Namshi in the far north to work in a newspaper branch office near his wife's family. In August and November of 1934, he published a group of 12 poems in

Three Thousand Leagues magazine and then inexplicably killed himself on December 14.

Poetry by Kim So-wôl

The Lamp Burns Low. Trans. by Jaihiun Kim. Seongji sa 1977 o.p. A revision and expansion of a 1973 collection of Kim Jaihiun translations, *Azaleas;* contains 101 poems by Kim So-wôl.

Lost Love. Trans. by Jaihiun Kim. Pan Korea Bk. Corp. 1975 o.p. Includes 99 poems.

Selected Poems of Kim So-wôl. Trans. by Kim Dong-Sung. Sung Moon Gak 1961 o.p. The first complete collection in English, with texts in Korean on facing pages.

KIM TONG-NI. 1913–

Over the past half-century, Kim Tong-ni has written more and has had more written about him than any other living Korean author. He so embodies the history of modern Korean literature that one critic has asserted, "For all the credit we give Europe as our model, modern Korean fiction did not take root for sure until we were given the literature of Kim Tong-ni. What we did before him can be dismissed as practice."

Kim Tong-ni was born in 1913 in Kyôngju, the tradition-conscious capital of the ancient Shilla kingdom, as the third of five children. His oldest brother, distinguished for the ability to read the Chinese classics at age six, went on to become a nationally recognized classical scholar. Tong-ni early learned the meaning of nationalism when his brother, then a sixth-grader, was called in by the Japanese thought police because of his composition entitled "People in White on a Boat without a Sail." The incident created strong resentment in the young Tong-ni, as he began to understand the position of Koreans under the Japanese.

Koreans respond to Kim Tong-ni as the voice of their ethos, as a writer who seeks understanding of what it means to be Korean. Accommodating ethnic materials in a perfectly modern aesthetic, he is anything but a "folk" writer. Two early and still acclaimed stories, "Portrait of a Shaman" (1936) and "Loess Village Story" (1939), demonstrate his ability to be Korean and worldly at the same time. While set in the Korean countryside, these works are invested with a universality that links the national with the shared human experience.

Even in his early works, Kim says, he was trying to express a "humanistic nationalism," which he believed could "overcome cultural barriers and seek identity with universal trends in world literature." It is the universal language of symbols that lets his work, even while heavily laden with local color, reach out to readers beyond Korea's borders.

Even though Kim is particularly well known for "Portrait of a Shaman," he regards it as an "imperfect work." Believing that its theme of the confrontations of Eastern and Western religions could not be handled adequately in the context of a short story, he expanded it into the novel, *Ûlhwa* (1978), which has been translated twice into English, as *Ûlhwa the Shaman* (1979) and as *The Shaman Sorceress* (1988).

Religious belief—whether shamanism, Buddhism, or Christianity—is an undercurrent in nearly all Kim's work. He often speaks of his deep concern about the nihilism of the twentieth century and of so many people's inability to find a new set of principles to counter it. Kim believes his literary mission is "to seek out divinity and identify the relationship between that divinity and humankind."

Kim Tong-ni has long been a prolific writer about literature as well. Since his first critical article, "On the Writer Yi T'ae-jun," appeared in 1937, he has published nearly 100 literary essays. In recent years, he has been devoting increasing attention to critical, rather than creative, writing and has produced such articles as "In What Society is Literature Possible?," "With Humanistic Literature We Can Prevail," "A New Agrarian Literature Is Possible," and "My Literature and Shamanism."

Kim Tong-ni is the recipient of the Freedom Literary Prize (1955), National Academy of Arts Award (1958), Samil Literary Award (1967), Order of the Camellia (1968), Order of the Peony (1970), Seoul City Cultural Prize (1970), and May Sixteenth National Award (1983).

NOVELS BY KIM TONG-NI

The Cross of Shaphan. 1958. Trans. by Sol Sun-bong. Pace Intl. Res. 1983 $25.00. ISBN 0-89209-200-9. A Korean story set against Jewish history of Jesus' time; "I could not write a story about our national tragedy without somehow linking it with light, victory, and hope of salvation" (Kim Tong-ni).

The Shaman Sorceress. 1978. Trans. by Hyun Song Shin and Eugene Chung. Routledge Chapman & Hall 1988 $19.95. ISBN 0-7103-0280-0. The story of Ûlhwa, a shaman, whose son tries to save her from her world of spirits and demigods and convert her to his own Christian beliefs.

O YÔNG-SU. 1914–1979

"I seek affirmation over denial, goodness rather than evil, and beauty before ugliness," said O Yông-su in "An Apologia," an essay that introduced a selection of his work in the multivolume *Collection of Modern Korean Literature* (1967). In a productive career that spanned the three decades from 1949 to 1979, he offered hope to a struggling people who were rebuilding in the wake of the cataclysmic Korean War of 1950–53. In the late 1950s, when much popular fiction was heavy with existentialist gloom, O Yông-su described the same Korean realities but offset them by his glow of human feeling.

Both O Yông-su and his contemporaries recognized that individuals are incapable of changing the external conditions of their lives and that certain forces will conspire to rule their destinies. But, whereas many of his more "realistic" colleagues frequently saw themselves trapped in a dark and absurd hopelessness, O Yông-su believed that hope—the only hope, perhaps—lay in good human relationships. Although, ironically, almost every active relationship in his stories ends in some sort of separation, the reader is still given reason to believe that his characters can have further relationships of equal worth.

SHORT STORY COLLECTION BY O YÔNG-SU

The Good People: Korean Stories by Oh Yông-su. Trans. by Marshall R. Pihl. Heinemann Ed. 1986 $10.00. ISBN 962-225-171-4. Ten stories representative of O Yông-su's celebration of the fundamental human values that he believes carried Koreans through the tumultuous twentieth century.

SÔ CHÔNG-JU. 1915–

Because the tone, imagery, characters, and language of Sô Chông-ju's poetry are deeply colored by his native North Chôlla Province, his countrymen and countrywomen feel him a very "Korean" poet. Though deeply committed to his birthplace, he spent the last five years of the colonial period wandering in Manchuria, where many Koreans were living in self-imposed exile from their homeland.

Sô Chông-ju brings a compelling intensity to his work that lets him convey with equal immediacy the ordinary life of his boyhood, the Buddhist realm of the ancient past, or a passion of today. Translator David R. McCann says of him, "One can look back on the course of his literary career and discover a remarkable parallel to Yeats: the early influence of late-nineteenth-century French poetry; the turning toward a legendary past; the spiritualism; the confrontation with age."

Since 1933, Sô Chông-ju has published some 200 poems and 30 collections. He has been frequently chosen by his colleagues to serve in the leadership of professional literary associations.

Poetry by Sô Chông-ju

Selected Poems of So Chongju. Trans. by David R. McCann. Col. U. Pr. 1989 $38.50. ISBN 0-231-06794-1. Rendered into English by the foremost American poet-translator and scholar of Korean poetic literature.

YI MUN-YÔL. 1948–

Born in the southeastern city of Taegu, Yi Mun-yôl dropped out of high school but was admitted to the College of Education of Seoul National University, only to leave in 1968 before graduating. Upon discharge from the army, he began to work as a reporter for Taegu's *Maeil Shinmun* newspaper. This was a turning point in his life, for it was in a 1977 competition sponsored by the newspaper that he first established himself as a writer.

Immediately, he quit work as a reporter and committed himself to being a writer full time. Before long he rocketed to prominence, producing a critically acclaimed stream of fiction on a wide range of themes. He is known as an incisive observer of the contemporary Korean scene.

Yi Mun-yôl has published nearly 50 works of fiction and some 26 collections. He has been honored with the Writers Today Award, Tongin Literary Prize, Republic of Korea Literature Award, and the prestigious Yi Sang Award for *Our Twisted Hero* (1987).

Novels by Yi Mun-yôl

Hail to the Emperor! 1981. Trans. by Sol Sun-bong. Pace Intl. Res. 1986. ISBN 0-87296-030-7. A man lives his life believing himself ordained by heaven to found a new dynasty and, despite his failure, achieves a greater eminence.

Our Twisted Hero. 1987. Trans. by Kevin O'Rourke. Minumsa Pub. Co. Sth. Korea 1988 o.p. A challenge to the modern age that traces the patterns of the psychology of power: A person's urge to power and the tyrant within.

YUN HEUNG-GIL (Yun Hûng-gil). 1942–

Yun Heung-gil and his peers belong to a distinct generation that is called, variously, the "Liberation Generation" because they were born at about the time of Korea's 1945 release from Japanese domination, the "Hangûl Generation" after the name of the Korean alphabet that had been suppressed prior to liberation, or the "April 19th Generation" after their student-led uprising on that day in 1960, a revolt that toppled the corrupt Syngman Rhee regime. Since they did not know colonialism and were only children during the Korean War, their worldview is distinct from that of their elders, and their writing constitutes an epoch-making departure in Korean literature.

Typical of his peers, Yun Heung-gil questions the value of Korea's rapid industrialization that seems intent on change at any social or cultural cost. He sees Korea's economic "miracle" as a destructive force robbing the people of their native sense, tearing them away from the natural cycles and traditions that assure their identities and give meaning to their lives. With this fear felt worldwide, Yun's stories, while specific to the Korean experience, are at the same time accessible to readers of many other cultures.

Translator Suh Ji-moon sums up Yun's worldview this way: "Yun Heung-gil can see both the large misfortunes and the small but nagging grievances that harass people, and can also perceive the manifold sources of human strength and resiliency that enable them to withstand their fates. His stories, therefore, are not mere chronicles of survival but sincere quests into the problem of how life can be lived at all, and how it can be lived meaningfully."

SHORT STORY COLLECTION BY YUN HEUNG-GIL

The House of Twilight. Ed. by J. Martin Holman. Readers Intl. 1989 $9.95. ISBN 0-930523-60-1. A significant collection, written with humor and sympathy for the ne'er-do-wells and losers of South Korea's get-ahead society.

CHAPTER 10

Southeast Asian Literatures

Carol Mitchell

> The one great social change in Asia that literature documents magnificently is the emergence of the individual writer. This has not come about easily and it is not the same thing as the struggle for individualism that has faltered again and again all over Asia. It is the fact of individual authorship, the idea of the author writing as an individual, that underwent a radical change during the twentieth century. That change has not been uniform and the authors themselves have not always insisted on it. The pressure to conform, to write anonymously or collectively, is still there, but the breakthrough has occurred in most countries.
>
> —WANG GUNGWU, *Society and the Writer*

Because Southeast Asian literatures are an amalgam, the product of centuries of change and contact with outside cultures, readers will find in them both the familiar and the new. Indigenous beliefs, customs, and settings informed precolonial Arabic, Indian, and Chinese literatures. Older, primarily oral, literary techniques blended with genres introduced during colonial rule. And these familiar Western forms were also synthesized with precolonial literatures. In Southeast Asia, an incredible diversity of cultural influences can be seen at once in ancient epics and in contemporary novels.

It must be remembered, too, that this syncretic process was different in each Southeast Asian nation. Traditional oral literatures, often divided between court literature and folk literature, were as varied as the many ethnic groups that produced them; and Buddhism, Hinduism, and Islam—present in all the classical literature of the region—were adapted in varying ways to indigenous beliefs. Truly national literatures, in fact, did not exist until the introduction of Western print technology combined with an expanding educated class.

The lands and islands of Southeast Asia, however, have in turn stimulated Western literature in important ways. Since Europeans began arriving, Western writers have vividly rendered the cultures, landscapes, and people in travelogues, fiction, and ethnography. British writers such as W. SOMERSET MAUGHAM (see Vol. 1), GEORGE ORWELL (see Vol. 1), ANTHONY BURGESS (see Vol. 1), and JOSEPH CONRAD (see Vol. 1) evoked images of Malaysia; the French writers Jean Lartegue and ANDRÉ MALRAUX set novels in Indochina; and Johan Fabricius and Maria Dermout rendered in their work the fabric of the colonial Netherlands. More recently, Paul Theroux, James Clavell, and GRAHAM GREENE (see Vol. 1) have set novels in Southeast Asia. For most of these writers the imaginative focus was the lonely European, thrust into a seemingly untamed world. The themes were colonialism and the conflict between cultures.

The same conflict shows in the work of Southeast Asian writers—not only in theme but also in practice. Censorship has long been common. Colonial governments restricted the number of presses, established review boards, harassed journalists and writers, and, in some cases, jailed outspoken dissident writers. Many of these tactics persist. As a result it is not uncommon for a writer to assume many pseudonyms. Moreover, the allegory, humor, and symbolism in Southeast Asian writers' prose and poetry are often literary devices intended to blind the eye of the government censor.

Contemporary writers lead double lives in another sense, too. Few can support themselves only by writing, so they are teachers, government officers, and journalists. Their perspectives on life are uniquely their own, distilled through a variety of daily work experiences. Yet in the midst of so much difference and even deception, and in the end not surprisingly, a common thread does dominate much of their writing: the struggle to find meaning and identity in the midst of change.

HISTORY AND CRITICISM

Anderson, G. L. *Asian Literature in English: A Guide to Information Sources*. Gale 1981 $68.00. ISBN 0-8103-1362-6. A useful but incomplete and dated source for English-language literature, including translations, in periodicals and monographs.

Brandon, James R. *Theater in Southeast Asia*. HUP 1979 o.p. Survey of contemporary theater.

Christie, C. J. *Preliminary Survey of British Literature on South-East Asia in the Era of Colonial Decline and Decolonisation*. Ctr. Southeast Asian Studies Kyoto Univ. Japan 1986 o.p. An excellent survey defining major themes and demonstrating the strong political and historical content of decolonization on the later period of British writing.

Christie, Clive. *The Quiet American and the Ugly American: Western Literary Perspectives on Indochina in a Decade of Transition, 1950–1960*. Ctr. Southeast Asian Studies Kyoto Univ. Japan 1989 $7.50. ISBN 0-317-018159. Overview of changing literary perceptions.

Davidson, Jeremy H. C. S., and Helen Cordell, eds. *The Short Story in South East Asia: Aspects of a Genre*. School of Oriental & African Studies. U. of London 1982 o.p. A collection of essays examining the evolving short story and its links to western and other literatures.

Herbert, Patricia, and Anthony Milner, eds. *South-East Asia Languages and Literatures: A Select Guide*. UH Pr. 1989 $18.95. ISBN 0-8248-1267-0. An essential guide to the region's history, languages, literatures, and publishing. Includes extensive bibliographic references.

Jenner, Philip N. *Southeast Asia Literature in Translation: A Preliminary Bibliography*. UH Pr. 1973 o.p. The only published guide to translations found in books and journals.

Kintanar, Thelma B. *Self and Society in Southeast Asian Fiction: Thematic Explorations in the Twentieth Century Fiction of Five ASEAN Countries*. Inst. of SE Asian Studies 1988 o.p. Argues that the novel's flexibility and break from traditional forms allow authors to explore new themes of identity, alienation, and class as part of a broader social commitment.

Lim, Patricia. *ASEAN: A Bibliography*. Inst. SE Asian Studies 1984 o.p. Covers regional assessments of literature, journalism, and the arts.

———. ASEAN: *A Bibliography, 1981–1985*. Inst. SE Asian Studies 1986 o.p. Sequel to *ASEAN: A Bibliography* published in 1984.

———. *The Malay World of Southeast Asia: A Select Cultural Bibliography*. Inst. SE Asian Studies 1986 o.p. "Malay World" broadly defined to include all aspects of Malay arts and culture in the countries of Indonesia, Malaysia, the Philippines, Singapore, and Thailand.

Suryadinata, Leo, ed. *The Ethnic Chinese in the ASEAN States: Bibliographical Essays*. Inst. SE Asian Studies 1989 o.p. A broad survey of the impact of Chinese on various aspects of life in Southeast Asia.

Tham, Seong Chee, ed. *Essays on Literature and Society in Southeast Asia: Political and Sociological Perspectives.* Singapore U. Pr. 1981 o.p. Critical accounts of literature as a product of the various Southeast Asian societies.

Van Erven, Eugene. *Playful Revolution: Theatre and Liberation in Asia.* Ind. U. Pr. 1992 o.p. A fascinating look at political theater in the Philippines, Indonesia, and Thailand.

Wang, Gungwu, M. Guerrero, and D. Marr, eds., *Society and the Writer: Essays on Literature in Modern Asia.* Research School of Pacific Studies, Australian National U. 1981 o.p. Focuses on the twentieth century, exploring the extent to which authors and their literature have been instrumental in advancing social change.

Winks, Robin W., and James R. Rush, eds. *Asia in Western Fiction.* UH Pr. 1990 $14.95. ISBN 0-8248-1293-X. A thoughtful look at western writers, visions of "exotic" lands. Covers pulp novelists to masters like Maugham, Conrad, Burgess, Orwell, Greene, and Theroux.

CHRONOLOGY OF AUTHORS

Burmese Literature
Aung San Suu Kyi. 1945–

Indonesian Literature
Alisjahbana, S. Takdir. 1908–
Anwar, Chairil. 1922–1949.
Lubis, Mochtar. 1922–
Toer, Pramoedya Ananta. 1925–
Rendra, W. S. 1935–

Literature of Malaysia, Brunei, and Singapore
Usman Awang. 1929–
Shahnon Ahmad. 1933–
A. Samad Said. 1935–

Philippine Literature
Rizal, José. 1861–1896
Santos, Bienvenido N. 1911–
Joaquin, Nick. 1917–
José, F. Sionil. 1924–

Thai Literature
Sunthorn Phu. 1786–1856.
Khukrit Pramoj. 1911–

Vietnamese Literature
Ho Chi Minh. 1890–1969

BURMESE LITERATURE

The country of Myanmar, formerly Burma, shares mountainous borders with India and Bangladesh on the northwest, China on the north, and Laos and Thailand on the southeast and south. These mountainous areas are home to most of Burma's ethnic minorities: the Shan, Chin, Kachin, and Karen. Burmans, Myanmar's largest ethnic group, reside in the historic heartland, the confluence of the Chindwin and Irrawaddy rivers.

The golden age of Myanmar history followed the establishment of the Pagan dynasty by King Anaw-rahta in the eleventh century. The known literature of this period is prose, found on stone inscriptions, recording deeds of monarchs and others; of poetic works, only indications survived. True literary texts date from the mid-fifteenth century. Poetry then was synonymous with imaginative literature; prose was used only for law, historical chronicles, and interpretations of Buddhist Pali scripts.

In 1724, U Kala produced the *Great Chronicle* (*Maha ya-zawin-gyi*), the first attempt at a comprehensive account of history. The most famous chronicle, *The Glass Palace Chronicle of the Kings of Burma* (*Hman-nan ya-zawin-daw-gyi*) covers Myanmar history through the assumption of British control, ending in 1885.

Three verse forms dominate Burmese literature. The *Maw-gun* form is court poetry exalting the notable deeds of the king. The long *pyo* form, conveying religious themes, narrates an episode from Buddha's life or retells the Indian *jataka* tales. The *yadu* poems, shorter and more structured, are much freer in their subject matter, with many of the best about love. Padei-tha-ya-za, the famous writer of *pyo* and *yadu,* experimented with secular subjects and composed poems depicting village life; he also wrote the first Burmese drama.

By the nineteenth century, poetry became more varied and included more narrative, proselike elements. Drama, once reserved for the court, spread in popularity but declined after the appearance of the first novel in 1904. Early novels, ornately written, offered romance and adventure but were didactic in aim. Also in this century, the publication of literary magazines marked a new era for literature.

After the 1920s short stories and novels changed dramatically in style to relate the stories of peasants and ordinary lives. At the same time, nationalist themes were beginning to appear. Maha Hswei and other novelists depicted the oppressed rising up in revolt. After World War II, realistic fiction examined all aspects of life from the peasant struggling under Japanese occupation in Maung Htin's *NgaBa (NgaBa)* (1947) to the story of prisoners in Ludu U Hla's *Are You All Right?* (*A-lon kaung-gya-ye-la*) (1961). The conflict between traditional and Western cultures is examined in the outstanding novel *Not Out of Hate* (*Mon-ywei-mahu*) (1955) by Ma Ma Lei, Myanmar's leading woman writer.

Poetry remains popular with all of Myanmar society. The humorous, satirical works of Thaw-da Hswei are especially well liked. More recently poetry has been an expressive tool of the Democracy Movement. Since the 1980s, however, strict government censorship and control have sharply curtailed all literary expression.

History and Criticism

Ba Shin, Jean Boisselier, and Alexander B. Griswold. *Essays Offered to G. H. Luce By His Colleagues and Friends in Honour of His Seventy-fifth Birthday*. Aribus Asiae 1966 o.p. Many of the essays touch on aspects of classical and traditional literature.

Bode, Mabel Haynes. *The Pali Literature of Burma*. AMS Pr. repr. of 1909 ed. $15.00. ISBN 0-404-16796-9. An excellent description of the evolution of Pali literature in Burmese society.

Hla Pe. *Burma: Literature, Historiography, Scholarship, Language, Life, and Buddhism*. Inst. SE Asian Studies 1986 $19.75. ISBN 9971-988-00-3. A series of lectures providing insight into Burmese literature and its relation to culture and religion.

Sein, Henneth, and J. A. Withey. *The Great Po Sein: A Chronicle of the Burmese Theater*. Greenwood 1976 $45.00. ISBN 0-8371-8737-0. An account of an actor's life that provides an introduction to Burmese theater during the first half of the twentieth century.

Collections

Gray, James, ed. *Ancient Proverbs and Maxims from Burmese Sources: The Niti Literature of Burma*. AMS Pr. repr. of 1886 ed. $17.50. ISBN 0-404-16822-1. A source of political and ethical wisdom important in Burmese traditional education.

Hla Ludu U. *The Caged Ones*. 1958. Trans. by Sein Tu. Tamarind Pr. 1986 o.p. The stories of political prisoners compiled by one of Burma's best known authors. Won a UNESCO award.

Htin Aung. *Burmese Drama: A Study with Translations of Burmese Plays.* Greenwood 1978 repr. of 1957 ed. $38.50. ISBN 0-313-20381-4. Covers traditional drama through the nineteenth century. Four plays with full translations and extracts from others.

______. *Burmese Folk-tales.* AMS Pr. repr. of 1948 ed. $22.00. ISBN 0-404-16828-0. An excellent collection of 70 tales with an introduction and explanatory notes.

______. *Burmese Monk's Tales.* Col. U. Pr. 1966 o.p. A collection of 59 tales by a famous Burmese monk with 12 additional tales by other monks. Includes an introduction.

Thein Pe Myint. *Selected Stories of Thein Pe Myint.* Trans. by Patricia M. Milne. Cornell SE Asia 1973 o.p. Eight stories written between 1934 and 1951 by the famous writer, journalist, and politician.

Voices from the Jungle: Burmese Youth in Transition. Center for Christian Response to Asian Issues 1989 o.p. A collection of activist statements, stories, and poems voicing a longing for democracy.

AUNG SAN SUU KYI. 1945–

In awarding her the Nobel Peace Prize in 1991, the Norwegian Nobel Committee wrote, "She became the leader of a democratic opposition which employs nonviolent means to resist a regime characterized by brutality. Suu Kyi's struggle is one of the most extraordinary examples of civil courage in Asia in recent decades." As leader of the prodemocracy movement and cofounder of the National League for Democracy, the nation's opposition party, Aung San Suu Kyi has been under house arrest for what Myanmar's leaders call "treasonous" acts after bloody clashes between demonstrators and armed troops in 1988 and 1989.

A scholar and mother, Aung San Suu Kyi had never directly involved herself in politics, yet she was always aware of her identity as the daughter of Aung San, the late Burmese nationalist leader who led the country to independence. During a trip to her homeland, she became aware of deteriorating human rights and the people's cry for democracy. She began her crusade in August 1988 by traveling throughout Burma, calling on the people to help bring democracy to a country governed as a dictatorship since 1962. By introducing the issue of basic human rights, especially the right to choose one's government, Aung San Suu Kyi inspired crowds wherever she went.

Nonfiction by Aung San Suu Kyi

Aung San of Burma: A Biographical Portrait by His Daughter. Kiscadale Pubns. UK 1992 $12.95. ISBN 1-870838-80-7. A personal account of Aung San Suu Kyi's father, a nationalist and founder of Burma.

Freedom from Fear and Other Writings. Viking Penguin 1992 $25.00. ISBN 0685-53849-4. A compilation of essays on human rights by and about Aung San Suu Kyi.

Books about Aung San Suu Kyi

Win, Kanbawza. *Daw Aung San Suu Kyi The Nobel Laureate: A Burmese Perspective.* CPDSK 1992 o.p. A laudatory look at this brave woman's political activities.

CAMBODIAN LITERATURE

Cambodia is bordered by Laos on the north, Vietnam on the east, and Thailand on the west. The Khmer, the predominate ethnic group, constitute 85 percent of the population; other ethnic groups include the Khmer Loeu, Khmer Islam, Chinese, Pear, and tribal minorities. For five centuries, c.800–1300, Cambodia's great kingdom was ruled from the city of Ankor. In the following centuries, Cambodia increasingly came under the control of neighboring kingdoms in Thailand and Vietnam, until in 1863 the French established control.

Early contact with Indian culture and later political domination by Thailand, Vietnam, and France have left their imprint on Cambodia's language and literature. Early written literature was predominantly verse and includes *cpap*, short codes of conduct, and *rioen*, longer epic accounts of history and legends. Two notable epics are *The Poem of Angkor 'Vat* (*Lpoek Angar Vatt*), celebrating the glory of the kingdom, and the Cambodian version of the Ramayana, *Ramakerti*. The Theravada Buddhist religion, which coexisted with earlier animistic beliefs, brought with it such literary texts as the *Jataka* stories and the *Tripitaka*, of which the *Vinayapitaka* and the *Suttapitaka* portions are best known.

Traditional verse forms remained popular into the twentieth century, but the publication of the first newspaper in 1925 opened the doors for new forms of literary expression. The novel was introduced in the 1930s, and by 1975, when all publishing ceased under the Khmer Rouge, nearly one thousand novels had been published. Drama and the short story emerged after 1953. Writers in all genres used Western literary techniques to explore such contemporary issues as women's status, social injustice, and corruption. Today, publishing and creative writing in Cambodia remain extremely limited, but exiled writers are struggling to continue and develop Cambodian literature.

Collections

Carrison, M. P. *Cambodian Folk Stories from the Gatiloke*. C. E. Tuttle 1987 o.p. A collection of humorous tales, animal fables, and trickster tales. With introductory notes to the tales, which were transcribed by a monk in the late nineteenth century.

Chandler, David P. *Favorite Stories from Cambodia*. Heinemann Ed. 1983 o.p. A collection of traditional Cambodian folktales.

Milne, Anthony R., trans. *Mr. Basket-Knife and Other Khmer Folktales*. Allen Unwin AT 1972 o.p. A collection of traditional tales.

Other Work

Jacob, Judith M., trans. *Reamker (Ramakerti): The Cambodia Version of the Ramayana*. Royal Asiatic Society 1986 o.p. Translation includes an introduction and summary of the narrative.

INDONESIAN LITERATURE

Indonesia is a nation of islands, its archipelago extending from south of the Malay Peninsula to New Guinea. Some 350 ethnic groups, each with a different language, culture, and history, give Indonesian culture a rich and varied nature. Although a national Malay-based language unifies the diverse population, regional languages remain important. Primary among them are Javanese, Sundanese, Batak, Balinese, and Toraja.

Indonesian culture is also a synthesis of the indigenous and the foreign. Indian culture—seen in the Sanskrit language, the Hindu and Buddhist religions, an elaborate court system, and the *Ramayana*, the *Mahabharata*, and other literary texts—arrived as early as the fifth century. Islam was introduced in the thirteenth century, and by the fifteenth century had begun to have influence beyond the port cities and trading centers. Today Indonesia is predominantly Muslim, and yet the influences of the earlier cultures are evident in literature, music, the *wayang* shadow puppet plays, and dance. Europeans were first attracted to the famed Spice Islands in the sixteenth century, and in 1799 the Dutch took direct control of Indonesia, ruling until after World War II.

In 1908, increasing government control over Indonesian language and literary development led to the establishment of the Literary Agency (*Balai Pustaka*). By publishing novels and short stories, the Agency encouraged Indonesian authors and contributed to the development of the modern Indonesian novel. Today, the Literary Agency continues to publish but focuses on folklore and regional literatures.

Instituting a publishing outlet, however, did not satisfy all literary unrest. Growing nationalism led the participants at the All Indonesia Youth Conference (1928) to proclaim Indonesian the language of an independent nation, a language that was to provide literary as well as political unity. Nationalist writers seeking independence from the government-controlled Literary Agency established the literary magazine *Pudjangga Baru* (*The New Poet*), and with it a literary movement. Its first editor and primary backer was SUTAN TAKDIR ALISJAHBANA.

Japanese occupation during World War II and the subsequent struggle for independence from the Dutch, led by Sukarno, had a great impact on a generation of writers who have come to be known as the Generation of '45 (*Angkatan '45*). In many respects, the breakdown of Indonesian colonial society enabled young authors like CHAIRIL ANWAR, Idrus, Sitor Situmorang, and PRAMOEDYA ANANTA TOER to depart radically from prewar styles and themes.

Although in Indonesia ideology has always been closely tied to the arts, the debate over the purpose of literature came to dominate all discussions during the 1960s. At the center of the debate was *Lekra,* the Institute of People's Culture, founded in 1950 to promote an "art for the people" that stressed realism. As the government and communist-sponsored groups gained increasing control over the arts, the debate between humanism and social realism polarized writers and social critics.

After the turbulent changes of 1965 and 1966, when Gen. Suharto came to power after an abortive communist coup, young writers and critics proclaimed the birth of a new literary generation, calling themselves the Generation of '66 (*Angkatan '66*). Of this group, MOCHTAR LUBIS, an outspoken critic of *Lekra,* became the editor of a new cultural magazine, *Horison.* Given the absence of strong stylistic or thematic unity, it is doubtful whether the many writers of this period—Ajip Rosidi, W. S. RENDRA, Taufiq Ismail, and others—truly constitute a literary movement.

Many contemporary writers continue to explore social themes. The novels of Nh Dini depict women as enslaved by their daily lives; they are important forces in society, but denied power. The Balinese writer Putu Wijaya has led the return to local, ethnic traditions, using a contemporary style. Wijaya, drawing from his experiences in Rendra's theater workshop and the theater of the absurd, produces novels and dramas blurring the boundaries of reality. Perhaps the most influential of today's authors is Rendra, whose work spans several literary generations.

As in other colonized nations, European authors influenced Indonesian authors. Dutch writers, including MULTATULI, whose biting novel *Max Havelaar* criticized Dutch colonial rule, are part of a long tradition of historical fiction about the colonial period. Contemporary writers shaped by this tradition include Pramoedya Ananta Toer and Y. B. Mangunwijaya.

History and Criticism

Aveling, Harry. *A Thematic History of Indonesian Poetry, 1920 to 1974*. North. Ill. U. Ctr. SE Asian 1974 o.p. Predominant themes and literary conventions of the writers who were instrumental in developing contemporary poetry.

Becker, A. L., ed. *Writing on the Tongue*. Ctr. S&SE Asian 1989 $24.95. ISBN 0-89148-047-1. Six studies of Indonesian, Javanese, and Balinese literature with original texts, translations, and commentaries.

Foulcher, Keith. *Pujangga Baru: Literature and Nationalism in Indonesia, 1933–1942*. Flinders U. 1980 o.p. Surveys the rise of Indonesia's first literary movement.

Foulcher, Keith. *Social Commitment in Literature and the Arts: The Indonesian "Institute of People's Culture" 1950–1965*. Centre of Southeast Asian Studies, Monash U. 1986 o.p. An analysis of the historical and cultural circumstances producing the Institute. Examines the relationship between political commitment and creativity.

Freidus, Alberta Joy. *Sumatran Contributions to the Development of Indonesian Literature, 1920–1942*. UH Pr. 1977 $7.50. ISBN 0-8248-0462-7. Explores reasons behind the disproportionate number of Sumatran writers contributing to the development of Indonesian literature before World War II.

Johns, Anthony H. *Cultural Options and the Role of Tradition: A Collection of Essays on Modern Indonesian and Malaysian Literature*. Faculty of Asian Studies in association with Australian National U. 1979 o.p. Eleven essays primarily focusing on understanding writers and literature as part of society.

Muhammad, Haji Salleh. *Tradition and Change in Contemporary Malay-Indonesian Poetry*. U. Kebangsaan Malaysia 1977 o.p. An analysis of social and political forces, from 1945 to the early 1970s, that influenced contemporary poetry.

Quinn, George. *The Novel in Javanese: Aspects of Its Social and Literary Character*. KITLV Pr. 1992 o.p. The first major effort to examine the development and impact of Javanese novelists on Indonesian literature.

Raffel, Burton. *The Development of Modern Indonesian Poetry*. State U. NY Pr. 1967 o.p. A historical overview analyzing Chairil Anwar, Rivai Apin, Amir Hamzah, Sanusi Pane, Rendra, Sitor Situmorang, and others. Includes translations of the works themselves.

Ras, J. J., and S. O. Robson, eds. *Variation, Transformation and Meaning: Studies on Indonesian Literatures in Honour of A. Teeuw*. Cellar 1992 $23.00. ISBN 90-6718-027-0. A discussion by ten scholars about the wide range of Indonesian literature and its interpretation.

Salmon, Claudine. *Literature in Malay by the Chinese of Indonesia: A Provisional Annotated Bibliography*. Maison des Sciences de l'Homme 1982 o.p. The contributions of Chinese writers to the development of the Indonesian language and literature. Includes an extensive bibliography.

Teeuw, A. *Modern Indonesian Literature*. 2 vols. Martinus Nijhoff 1979 o.p. Comprehensive survey of twentieth-century literature. Includes extensive bibliographies of Indonesian literature, history, and criticism.

Collections

Aveling, Harry. *From Surabaya to Armageddon: Indonesian Short Stories*. Heinemann Ed. 1976 o.p. Stories by Idrus, Pramoedya Ananta Toer, Sitor Situmorang, and others depicting the social upheaval in Indonesia from 1952 to 1965.

Frederick, William H., and John H. McGlynn, eds. and trans. *Reflections on Rebellion: Stories from the Indonesian Upheavals of 1948 and 1965*. Ohio U. Ctr. Intl. 1983 o.p. Stories by Pramoedya Ananta Toer, S. Rukiah Kertapati, and Umar Kayam. With an insightful introduction to the works.

Moor, Cornelia Niekus, ed. *Insulinde: Selected Translations from Dutch Writers of Three Centuries on the Indonesian Archipelago*. UH Pr. 1978 $10.50. ISBN 0-8248-0564-X. Eleven authors serving as an introduction to the range of Dutch colonial writing.

McGlynn, John, ed. *On Foreign Shores: American Images in Indonesian Poetry.* Lontar Foundation 1990 o.p. A collection of poems that shed new light on the familiar.

______, ed. *Walking Westward in the Morning: Seven Contemporary Indonesian Poets.* Lontar Foundation 1990 o.p. An anthology displaying the variety evident in today's poetry while simultaneously revealing a common thread—the author's willingness to examine problems of contemporary society.

Raffel, Burton, ed. *Anthology of Modern Indonesian Poetry.* State U. NY Pr. 1967 $44.50. ISBN 0-87395-024-0. Good representation by New Poets, Generation '45, and Rendra.

Wijaya, Putu. *Bomb: Indonesian Short Stories.* Ed. by Ellen Rafferty and Laurie J. Sears. U. Wis. Ctr. SE Asian 1988 o.p. Eighteen stories blending western perspectives with Balinese culture.

ALISJAHBANA, S. TAKDIR (SUTAN TAKDIR). 1908–

Sutan Takdir Alisjahbana is an important cultural figure in Malaysia, as well as in Indonesia, because of his early and continuing contributions to a contemporary literary language. He began his career as a leader in Indonesia's first literary movement of the 1930s. As the editor of the prominent literary magazine *Pundjangga Baru* (The New Poet), he wrote articles on poetry, language, and culture, and his own poetry, essays, and novels helped shape a creative language.

While an early advocate of Malay-based Indonesian as the national language, Takdir Alisjahbana also argued for learning Dutch and gaining a Western education. In all of his early writings, he linked Indonesian social conditions to literature, which he felt would flourish, like all of an independent Indonesia, with modernization based on a European model: Writers must look forward to a future that incorporates the best of Western society. His controversial essays prompted long replies from those who wanted literature to reignite former glories.

For Takdir Alisjahbana, there is no literary form more representative of the modern than the novel. Unfortunately, his literary works remain untranslated. His most notable novel, *Lajar Terkembang* (With Sails Unfurled), serves as a vehicle to express his polemics. Its characters highlight his Indonesian ideal of being educated, free-thinking, and responsible.

Nonfiction by Alisjahbana

Indonesia: Social and Cultural Revolution. Trans. by Benedict R. Anderson. OUP 1966 o.p. Alisjahbana's views of modernization and the role of culture and language. Written in 1959.

Language Planning for Modernization: The Case of Indonesia and Malaysia. Mouton 1976 $22.75. ISBN 90-279-7712-7. Extends his ideas of the intimate relation of language development to social development.

Values as Integrating Forces in Personality, Society, and Culture: Essay of a New Anthropology. U. of Malaya 1974 o.p. Essential reading for understanding the author's perspectives. Draws from a wide range of reading in philosophy, sociology, and anthropology, concluding that ethics is at the core of personal, social, and cultural life.

ANWAR, CHAIRIL. 1922–1949

Chairil Anwar spent his childhood in Medan, where he was educated at a Dutch school, but in 1940 he was forced to abandon his education when he and his mother moved to Jakarta. Still, Anwar devoted his time to reading poetry and—finding his inspiration in the street life of Jakarta—to writing. Japanese and later Dutch censors prevented him from publishing much of his work.

Chairil Anwar wrote at a time of great social and political upheaval: the Japanese wartime occupation as well as the struggle for independence from the Netherlands. His themes reflect personal and social chaos, their style making a sharp break with the New Poets movement (*Pudjangga Baru*) by using rhythm, alliteration, and repetition. With the admiration of his contemporaries, he became the acknowledged leader of the postwar literary movement, Generation of '45 (*Angkatan '45*).

Although Anwar's output is limited to some 70 poems, many of which had not been published before his death from typhus, he made an enormous impact on modern Indonesian poetry. Perhaps no Indonesian author's writing has received as much attention, both in terms of critical analysis and of an inspiration to later literary movements, especially the Generation of '66 (*Angkatan '66*).

POETRY BY ANWAR

The Complete Poetry and Prose of Chairil Anwar. Ed. and trans. by Burton Raffel. State U. NY Pr. 1970 o.p.

Complete Poems of Chairil Anwar. Ed. and trans. by Liaw Yock Fang and H. B. Yassin. U. Education Pr. 1974 o.p.

Sharp Gravel. Trans. by Donna M. Dickinson. UC Berkely Ctr. SE Asia 1960 o.p.

Voice of the Night: Complete Poetry and Prose of Chairil Anwar. Trans. by Burton Raffel. Ohio U. Pr. 1992 $17.00. ISBN 0-89680-170-5

BOOK ABOUT ANWAR

Oemarjati, Boen S. *Chairil Anwar: The Poet and His Language.* Martinus Nijhoff 1972 o.p. A critical analysis of Anwar's distinctive poetic language.

LUBIS, MOCHTAR. 1922–

A self-educated journalist, Mochtar Lubis is a keen observer of how people respond to fear and stress during war and social upheaval. He gained recognition as the chief editor of the newspaper *Indonesia Raya*, in which he opposed the ideology that held sway through the mid-1960s. After the overthrow of Sukarno, Lubis guided the magazine *Horison* to its position as the voice of contemporary literature and culture.

Frank discussions of social and political life in Indonesia, along with attacks on government hypocrisy and inequities, early earned Lubis the wrath of Sukarno. In 1956 his criticism of the government resulted in imprisonment. Released in 1957, he was under house arrest until 1961 but was shortly rearrested and remained in prison until 1966. During his imprisonment, Lubis says he often thought of the jungles of his youth, where tigers roamed, and these thoughts combined with ideas of great leaders: men and women who may be regarded with awe and fear, but who may also crumble easily. The result was the novel *Tiger!* (1980).

Lubis's works have the power to challenge. Before the 1977 elections, he shocked the nation with an 81-page lecture about modern Indonesian life, castigating its hypocrisy, feudalism, greed, superstition, and indecision. Lubis is the winner of the Gold Medal for Freedom from the International Federation and Press Association and the Magsaysay Award for Journalism in 1958.

SHORT STORY COLLECTION BY LUBIS

The Outlaw and Other Stories. Trans. by J. Lingard. OUP 1988 $8.95. ISBN 0-19-588859-6. Stories written between 1950 and 1970, exploring moral questions in contemporary Indonesian society.

Nonfiction by Lubis

Indonesia: Land Under the Rainbow. OUP 1991 $22.00. ISBN 0-19-588977-0. A journey of national and self-identity in which Lubis says he traveled "into the misty prehistory of Indonesia, . . . through the different stages back to the present."

Indonesian Dilemma. 1977 Trans. by Florence Lamoureux. Rev. ed. of "We Indonesians." G. Brash Ltd. Singapore 1986 $2.50. ISBN 9971-947-35-8. Originally published as *Manusia Indonesia*. Calls on Indonesians to "act in a more humanitarian way" to "bring life again to our people's creative arts and crafts."

Novels by Lubis

Road with No End. Trans. by Anthony Johns. G. Brash Ltd. Singapore 1982 o.p. Story of two men in revolutionary postwar Indonesia—Isa, fearful and impotent, and Hazil, a revolutionary.

Tiger! Trans. by Florence Lamoureux. Select Bks. 1991 o.p. A jungle trip turning into a nightmare of fear, deception, and betrayal for seven villagers being stalked by a tiger.

Twilight in Djakarta. Trans. by Claire Holt. OUP 1983 $8.50. ISBN 0-19-582564-0. A mosaic of images contrasting the corrupt rich with the helpless poor in mid-1950s Jakarta.

RENDRA, W. S. 1935–

An extremely popular writer, actor, and performer in Indonesia and Malaysia, W. S. Rendra is representative of a generation of authors seeking to distance themselves from the earlier ideological polemics of the 1960s. Yet, in doing so, he has not abandoned the tradition of using literature to examine Indonesian society.

Now a devout Muslim, Willibordus Surendra Rendra was born into a Javanese Catholic family. He studied literature at Gadjah Mada University and later spent three years studying at the American Academy of Dramatic Arts in the United States. During his stay, he wrote many of the poems in *Blues for Bonnie*. After returning to Indonesia in 1967, Rendra became interested in theater and set up his own company, adapting foreign plays for Indonesian audiences. He has also drawn on traditional Javanese *wayang* (shadow puppet plays) in his play *The Struggle of the Naga Tribe*.

Rendra's poems are, like the Javanese society he draws from, syncrontic. Combining Christian, Hindu, Islamic, and animistic elements, he emphasizes personal freedom, an assertion for life, and solidarity with common rural people.

Plays by Rendra

The Mastadon and the Condors. Trans. by Harry Aveling. P. Lal 1981 o.p. Represents Rendra's position that writers must reject political involvement. About students organizing to overthrow a military government in a mythical South American country.

State of Emergency. Wild & Wooley 1980 o.p.

The Struggle of the Naga Tribe. Trans. by Max Lane. St. Martin 1980 $20.00. ISBN 0-312-76876-1. Using the *wayang* motif and humor, depicts the struggle against corrupt government; the village versus the city.

Poetry by Rendra

Ballads and Blues: Poems. Trans. by Burton Raffel, Harry Aveling, and Derwent May. OUP 1974 o.p. Most of the poems were written while Rendra was studying in the United States.

BOOK ABOUT RENDRA

Aveling, Harry. *A Thematic History of Indonesian Poetry: 1920–1974.* North. Ill. U. Ctr. SE Asian 1974 o.p. Devotes a significant portion to an examination of Rendra's life and work.

TOER, PRAMOEDYA ANANTA. 1925–

One of Indonesia's most prominent authors, Toer spent most of his adult life in prison; his works have frequently been banned by the government. Toer's first novel, *The Fugitive* (1950), was written during his internment by the Dutch. Toer became a leading figure in the Marxist literary group *Lekra* and was again incarcerated after the 1965 overthrow of Sukarno, joining thousands of other left-wing artists on the prison island of Buru.

The author of over 30 works of fiction and nonfiction, Toer is best known for his Buru tetralogy, which traces the birth of nationalism in Indonesia. Most of the work was composed as narration to fellow prisoners, then later recorded and published after Toer's release in 1979. Although the events of the tetralogy take place in the past, they must be understood in the context of his experiences at Buru. In 1988 Toer received the PEN Freedom-to-Write Award.

NOVELS BY TOER

Awakenings. Viking Penguin 1990 o.p. Presents together the first two novels of the Buru quartet, *This Earth of Mankind* and *Child of All Nations.*

Child of All Nations: A Novel. Trans. by Max Lane. Viking Penguin 1984 o.p. The second book of the Buru tetralogy.

Footsteps: A Novel. Trans. by Max Lane. Viking Penguin 1990 o.p. The third book of the Buru tetralogy.

The Fugitive. Trans. by Willem Samuels. Morrow 1990 $16.95. ISBN 0-688-08698-5

Girl from the Coast. Trans. by Harry Aveling. Select Bks. 1991 o.p.

House of Glass. Trans by Max Lane. Viking Penguin 1992 o.p. The fourth book of the Buru tetralogy.

This Earth of Mankind. Trans. by Max Lane. Morrow 1991 $23.00. ISBN 0-688-09373-6. The first book in the Buru tetralogy.

SHORT STORY COLLECTION BY TOER

Heap of Ashes. Trans. by Harry Aveling. U. of Queensland Pr. 1975 o.p.

LAO LITERATURE

Landlocked, Laos is bordered by China and Burma to the north, Cambodia to the south, and Vietnam to the east. Mountainous terrain in the north isolated the Tai, Hmong, and other ethnic groups from the low-land Lao. Each ethnic group has its own language, but Lao is the predominate language.

While traditional oral tales are as diverse as the people of Laos, only the Lao and Tai possess a written literary culture. As a Buddhist country, religious texts are an important part of literary history, especially the popular *Jataka* stories. A special verse, the *parittam,* is chanted by monks to protect people from danger. Much of the court literature is also verse. Long epic poems of romance and war were sung or chanted to music. The most famous of these is the seventeenth-century *Sin Xay* by Thao Phangkham, but no less important is the Lao version of the *Ramayana, Prah la Prah lam.*

Modern literary efforts can be traced to the rise of nationalism and the widespread introduction of printing in the 1940s. Until the nationalist movement, Lao French-educated intellectuals wrote in French. Breaking with that tradition, Maha Sila Viravong, Phouvong Phimmasone, and Somchine Pierre Nginn pioneered contemporary Lao literature. Using Lao, they wrote popular fiction on traditional themes of romance and war. Later, writers siding with the Lao revolutionary movement, the Lao Patriotic Front, used the short story to convey the struggle of the peasantry.

Contemporary literature necessarily reflects the decades of political turmoil. Much of it is polemic, with writers on both sides, communist and royalist, evoking Buddhism, myths, and ancient tales in support of their ideologies. Still in its infancy is the exile literature of those Lao who came to the United States after the American defeat in Vietnam and the establishment of the Lao People's Democratic Republic. Thousands of Hmong sought refuge in the United States, and, lacking a written culture, they face the task of preserving a rich oral tradition by transcribing and translating their tales.

History and Criticism

Compton, Carol J. *Courting Poetry in Laos: A Textual and Linguistic Analysis.* North. Ill. U. Ctr. SE Asian 1979 o.p. Description of the *lam,* a highly developed form of oral literature that is a major component of Lao performance.

Cordell, Helen. Laos. ABC-CLIO 1991 o.p. Excellent annotated bibliography for literature, also including entries for economics, politics, social life, and customs.

Sahai, Sachchidanand. *The Ramayana in Laos: A Study of the Gvay Dvorahbi.* B. R. Pub. Co. TN 1976 o.p. Introduction and translation of the Lao *Ramayana,* which integrated a number of Lao folk tales and legends.

Collections

Johnson, Charles. *Myths, Legends, and Folk Tales from the Hmong of Laos.* Macalaster College 1985 o.p. A collection of tales including introductory notes on Hmong culture, customs, and beliefs.

Lindell, Kristina, Jan-Ojvind Swahn, and Damrong Tayanin. *Folk Tales from Kammu: A Master Teller's Tales.* St. Mut. 1988 $65.00. ISBN 0-685-32850-3. A series of three books including jokes, fables, and stories from a Khmu storyteller of the Kammu people, who live primarily in northern Laos.

Livo, Norma J., and Dia Cha. *Folk Stories of the Hmong.* Libs. Unl. 1991 $18.50. ISBN 0-87287-854-6. An illustrated introduction to Hmong culture and stories, suitable for juveniles.

Lucas, Alice. *Four Champa Trees.* Voices of Liberty, San Francisco Study Center 1990 o.p. An abridged version of the popular Lao legend.

Rains in the Jungle. Neo Lao Haksat Pub. 1967 o.p. A collection of short stories exemplifying writing from the political left wing.

Vang, Lue, and Judy Lewis. *Grandmother's Path, Grandfather's Path: Hmong Preservation Project, Generation to Generation.* Zellerbach Family Fund 1984 o.p. A collection of folk tales, proverbs, and poetry concluding with a description of Hmong daily life.

LITERATURE OF MALAYSIA, BRUNEI, AND SINGAPORE

The Federation of Malaysia, divided by the South China Sea, includes a portion of the Malay Peninsula and East Malaysia, which comprises the states of Sabah and Sarawak on the island of Borneo. The Malay Peninsula, extending from what is now Thailand, also includes at its tip an island nation now predominately Chinese. Brunei is a small nation between the states of Sarawak and Sabah on Borneo, sharing with Malaysia strong Islamic influences. The similar cultural and social histories of Malaysia, Singapore, and Brunei have led to similar literary histories.

The Malay port of Malacca was the gateway to the Spice Islands and East Asia, bringing Indian, Islamic, and European cultures to the region. European control over the area began in the sixteenth century when the Portuguese arrived and settled in Malacca. After the British gained control in the nineteenth century, foreign laborers from India and China were brought in to work the tin mines and rubber plantations. All of these cultures and peoples continue to play a role in shaping modern Malaysian literature.

Like other aspects of Malay culture, the Malay language has been influenced by Sanskrit, Arabic, and, more recently, English. Today English, Chinese, and Tamil are widely used, but Malay is the official national language of Malaysia and works written in Malay form the corpus of the literature. The Language and Literary Agency (*Dewan Bahasa dan Pustaka*), the nation's largest publisher, oversees the development and promotion of Malay literature.

Sanskrit and Arabic literary traditions are found in early Malay literature and even in modern work. Early transcribers of court poetry commonly used Arabic script, as did some poets and short story writers of the 1950s. Traditional forms of Malay literature include the poetic forms of the *pantun* and the *syair* and the prose form similar to an epic, the *hikayat*. The rhyming quatrain of the *pantun*, often containing internal rhymes and nuances, conveys a message in the final two lines. Its highly structured form continues to be found in contemporary songs and poetry. As tightly structured, but considerably longer and relating history or a story, is the *syair*, whose origin is attributed to Hamzah Fansuri. The *hikayat* is a court-based prose form that relates historical and legendary events. All these traditional forms rely on oral traditions. Even though written, the *hikayat* and *syair* were intended to be recited, not read silently.

With the arrival of the British and the introduction of newspapers and book publishing, new forms of literature came to the peninsula. Influenced by his British employers and departing radically from traditional forms, Munshi Abdullah, or Abdullah bin Abdul-Kadir, related his travels in *Tales of Abdullah's Voyage (Kisah Pelayaran Abdullah)* and wrote his autobiography, *The Hikayat Abdullah* (1849). Besides using Western forms, Munshi Abdullah asserted his personal perspective in discussing Malay politics and society, and his autobiography is commonly used to mark the beginnings of contemporary Malay literature.

Poetry and serialized novels and short stories were regularly published in the Malay press during the 1920s and 1930s. However, not until after World War II, when nationalist writers gathered in Singapore, did the Malay literary movement begin. The young writers who went to Singapore became known as the Generation of '50s Writers (*ASAS '50*), their writing characterized by political commitment and social idealism. Foremost among them were USMAN AWANG, A. SAMAD SAID, and Keris Mas.

Much of Borneo, except for the coastal areas, escaped the influences of Buddhism, Hinduism, and Islam, but, as in Peninsular Malaysia, the literary traditions of Sabah and Sarawak reflect a culturally and linguistically diverse population. Chants, songs, and tales are central to the literatures of the Iban, Penan, Kadazan, Murut, Bajau, and other ethnic groups. For contemporary fiction writers, both historical events and modern society texture their narratives. Increasingly, writers from Sabah and Sarawak are gaining national recognition. Arena Wati, from Sabah, is a leading novelist and short story writer. SHAHNON AMAD, also a fiction writer, explores ethnic tension, the economic and social status of Malays, and rapid development. Chin Kee Onn examines life under the Japanese occupation in her moving novel *MA-RAI-EE* (1981).

In Singapore, with its predominately Chinese population, Chinese-language poetry and novels are published; also, Malay authors maintain close links with writers in Malaysia. However, English is the primary literary language. Notable among English-language writers is Catherine Lim, whose lively stories capture the rapid changes in Singapore society, especially generational conflict. The poems of Edwin Thumbo and Robert Yeo explore the many changes that have taken place in the multi-ethnic society.

Brunei, small and only recently independent from Britain, has established its own Language and Literary Agency (*Brunei*) to further the development of indigenous authors. At the present, few Brunei writers have been translated into English.

History and Criticism

Banks, David J. *From Class to Culture: Social Conscience in Malay Novels Since Independence*. Yale U. SE Asia 1988 $17.00. ISBN 0-938692-29-1. A survey of the development of the Malay novel focusing on the social commentary of their themes.

Brown, Ian, and Rajeswary Ampalavanar. *Malaysia*. ABC-CLIO 1986 $65.00. ISBN 0-903450-23-2. Comprehensive bibliographic guide includes extensive listing of materials on language, literature, and culture.

Hill, Lewis. *A New Checklist of English-Language Fiction Relating to Malaysia, Singapore and Brunei*. Centre for Southeast Asian Studies, Univ. of Hull 1991 o.p. Bibliography of western stories and novels including well-known literary authors and popular series writers.

Mulliner, K., and Lian The-Mulliner. *Historical Dictionary of Singapore*. Scarecrow 1991 $32.50. ISBN 0-8108-2504-X. A useful introduction to important events and people. Includes a bibliography of literature.

Osman, Mohammed Taib bin. *An Introduction to the Development of Modern Malay Language and Literature*. Times Bks. Intl. rev. ed. 1986 o.p. A broad survey of people and events that helped shape contemporary language and literature in Malaysia.

Quah, Stella R., and Jon S. T. Quah. *Singapore*. ABC-CLIO 1988 o.p. Comprehensive guide to publications on Singapore including traditional and contemporary literature.

Sim, Katharine. *More than a Pantun: Understanding Malay Verse*. Times Bks. Intl. 1987 o.p. A simple and appreciative introduction to a popular form of traditional Malay poetry.

Skeat, Walter W. *Malay Magic: An Introduction to the Folklore and Popular Religion of the Malay Peninsula*. Intl. Spec. Bk. 1990 repr. of 1965 ed. $37.50. ISBN 0-7146-2026-2. Classic study examining magical rites connected with nature and social customs, including marriage, birth, funerals, war, and weapons.

Sweeny, Amin. *Authors and Audiences in Traditional Malay Literature*. UC Berkeley Ctr. SE Asia 1980 o.p. About the presentation, consumption, and composition of traditional Malay Literature. Argues against western modes of interpretation.

Tahir, Maimunah Mohammed. *Modern Malay Literary Culture: A Historical Perspective*. Inst. SE Asian Studies 1987 o.p. A survey relating social and political events through the late 1970s to the development of contemporary literature.

Winstedt, Richard. *A History of Classical Malay Literature*. OUP 1969 o.p. Dated in its approach but remains an important survey of precolonial literature.

Collections

Jeyaretnam, Philip. *First Loves*. Times Bks. Intl. 1987 o.p. Prize-winning collection of short stories depicting contemporary Singapore society.

Keris, Mas. *Blood and Tears.* Trans. by Harry Aveling. OUP 1984 o.p. Twenty short stories concerning ordinary people as they react to a rapidly changing society, by a prominent member of the Generation of '50s Writers.

Lim, Catherine. *O Singapore: Stories in Celebration.* Times Bks. Intl. 1989 o.p. Humorous and ironic stories of Singaporeans coming face to face with government directives in their daily lives. Provides a glimpse of modern Singapore.

Lim, Catherine. *Or Else, the Lightning God and Other Stories.* Heinemann Ed. 1980 $5.00. ISBN 0-686-74456-X. Vignettes of the familiar and new in ever-changing Singapore.

Ly, Singko, and Leon Comber, eds. *Modern Malaysian Chinese Stories.* Heinemann Ed. 1967 $5.50. ISBN 0-686-60447-4. The evolution of Malaysian-Chinese literature is reviewed by Han Suyin in an introduction to 13 stories in translation.

Rajendra, Cecil. *Dove on Fire: Poems on Peace, Justice and Ecology.* Wrld. Coun. Churches 1987 $5.75. ISBN 2-8254-0899-9. One of the few examples of English-language dissident writing.

Rubenstein, Carol. *The Honey Tree Song: Poems and Chants of Sarawak Dayaks.* Ohio U. Pr. 1985 $36.95. ISBN 0-8214-0413-X. The oral literature of the Iban, Bidayuh, Melanau, Kelabit, Kayan, Kenyah, and Penan groups of the state of Sarawak.

Salleh, Muhammad Haji. *An Anthology of Contemporary Malaysian Literature.* Dewan Bahasa dan Pustaka 1988 o.p. A collection of short stories, drama, poetry, and criticism in translation. Includes an introduction to postwar literature.

———. *The Travel Journal of Si Tenggang II.* Dewan Bahasa dan Pustaka 1979 o.p. A collection of poems by one of the most prominent poets in Malaysia. First published in Malay in 1975 and awarded the ASEAN Literary Award in 1977.

Thumbo, Edwin, and others. *The Fiction of Singapore.* ASEAN Committee on Culture and Information 1990 o.p. Includes fiction by Chinese, English, Malay, and Tamil writers in translation.

———. *The Poetry of Singapore: Anthology of ASEAN Literature.* 3 vols. ASEAN Committee on Culture & Information 1985 o.p. A collection of Malay, English, and Chinese poetry in English translation, with background introductions.

Thumbo, Edwin, ed. *The Second Tongue: An Anthology of Poetry from Malaysia and Singapore.* Heinemann Ed. 1976 o.p. One of the few collections containing significant English poetry.

Winstedt, Richard. *Malay Proverbs—Bidalan Melayu.* G. Brash Ltd. 1986 o.p. Traditional wisdom and advice, evoking the essential, rural world of the Malays.

A. SAMAD SAID. 1935–

A. Samad Said's novels, poems, short stories, and essays won him the SEA Write Award (Southeast Asia Write Award) in 1979 and the National Writer Award in 1985. This prolific author, English and Malay educated, began his career as part of the Generation of '50s Writers (*ASAS '50*), contributing greatly to the development of Malay literature. He was only 23 when *Salina* (1961) considered a milestone in Malay literature, won first prize in a literary contest. This controversial first novel examines Malay social values and behavior in postwar Singapore through the eyes of a prostitute. It also displays A. Samad Said's talent in capturing colloquial Malay dialog, and, through the urban setting it shares with *Lazy River* (1967), allows him to explore the effects of the rapidly changing Malay world.

For most of his career A. Samad Said has worked as a journalist, writing essays and features; more recently he has been a literary editor.

NOVELS BY A. SAMAD SAID

Lazy River. Trans. by Harry Aveling. Heinemann Ed. 1981 $5.50. ISBN 0-686-79032-4. Set at the end of World War II, as old and young—Malay, Chinese, and Indian—struggle to survive under the Japanese and understand their lives.

Salina. Trans. by Harry Aveling. Dewan Bahasa dan Pustaka 1975 o.p.

Play by A. Samad Said

Lazri Meon: Daerah Zeni. Dewan Bahasa dan Pustaka 1992 o.p. A poetic dramatized adaptation of an earlier novel, in which the main character reflects on his unfinished novel and his fight for freedom.

SHAHNON AHMAD. 1933–

Best known for his short stories and novels, Shahnon Ahmad began translating and writing satirical short stories in 1956 for the Malay literary weekly, *Mastika*. Except for a brief time abroad, when he went to Australia as a researcher and obtained his degree in 1971, Shahnon Ahmad has spent his entire life in the northern part of the Malay Peninsula. After many years in university administration, he was appointed professor of literature at the Science University in Penang.

His novels reflect his deep knowledge of the life of rural Malays in the north who confront the double hardship of inhospitable nature and inequitable society. His most famous novels, *Rope of Ash* and *No Harvest but a Thorn* (1966), portray villagers struggling to survive in the face of human cruelty and harsh nature.

Novels by Shahnon Ahmad

No Harvest but a Thorn. 1966. Trans. by Adibah Amin. OUP 1972 o.p.

Rope of Ash. OUP 1979 o.p.

Srengenge: A Novel from Malaysia. 1973. Trans. by Harry Aveling. Heinemann Ed. 1979 o.p. How villagers living at the foot of Srengenge Mountain perceive the mountain: for hunting, for profit, for religious tranquility.

Short Story Collection by Shahnon Ahmad

Third Notch and Other Stories. Heinemann Ed. 1980 o.p. Stories examining people's reactions to modern forms of oppression and alienation.

Book about Shahnon Ahmad

Hasan, Mohammed Yusof. *Novels of the Troubled Years.* Dewan Bahasa dan Pustaka 1989 o.p. Detailed synopses of Shahnon's many novels, placed in the context of his life and current issues in Malay society.

USMAN AWANG. 1929–

With only a Malay primary education, Usman Awang began his writing career as a proofreader for the Malay newspaper in Singapore. His contributions to the flowering literary movement in 1950s Singapore quickly earned him the reputation as a poet with an intuitive sense of traditional Malay poetic forms, especially the *pantun*. Yet while his poetry is formally traditional, its themes are planted in the contemporary struggles of the oppressed. Above all he is a humanist, and the simplicity of his expression ensures that his concerns about independence, poverty, war, and social change are accessible to all. Although primarily known for his poetry, Usman Awang has also written short stories and plays.

Like many writers in the Generation of '50s Writers who feared reprisals from the British, Usman Awang also wrote under a pseudonym, Tongkat Warrant (Walking Cane Warrant), which refers to his early days in the British police force. After independence he became an activist promoting Malay literature through literary organizations, poetry readings, festivals, and the various magazines published by the Language and Literary Agency. In 1982 Usman Awang was awarded the SEA Write (Southeast Asia Write Award) Award and in

1983 received an honorary doctorate from the University of Malaya as well as the National Literary Award.

POETRY BY USMAN AWANG

Salam Benua: Greetings to the Continent. Dewan Bahasa dan Pustaka 1986 o.p. A bilingual collection of poems, many reflecting thoughts of his visit to the United States.

PLAYS BY USMAN AWANG

Three South East Asian Plays: Si Kabayan by Utuy Sontani, Visitors at Kenny Hill by Usman Awang, Son of Zen by Lee Joo For. Tenggara 1970 o.p. Usman Awang's biting look at contemporary urban Malays.

PHILIPPINE LITERATURE

The Philippines is an archipelagic country of over 7,000 islands. Luzon in the north, Mindanao in the south, and the islands that make up the Visayas are the important centers of commerce, politics, and the arts. The island formation of the Philippines and the mountainous terrain of its larger islands have created a nation of diverse cultures and languages, reflected in the many traditional literatures. The Spanish and English languages, brought by colonizers, also influenced the language and literature of the Philippines.

Tagalog is the predominant Philippine language, especially in Manila and the neighboring provinces. Cebuano, spoken by a large portion of Filipinos, is the language of the Visayas and eastern parts of Mindanao. Ilocano, Hiligaynon, Bikol, Waray, and nearly 70 other indigenous languages are spoken in the highlands or on other islands.

Although the Philippines has an indigenous writing system, the traditional epics, songs, and chants were once transmitted orally. Today many epics, proverbs, and folk tales have been transcribed and translated, but in many parts of the Philippines the oral tradition survives.

Spaniards were the first to introduce Western literary forms. The *pasyon*, a dramatized or chanted narrative poem depicting the death of Christ and performed during the Lenten season, gained popularity in the eighteenth century. At the same time, the *komedya* developed as a popular dramatic form. Drawing from the Spanish ballads celebrating victory over the Moors, the *komedya* was used to show Filipinos the virtues of Christian piety and loyalty. The first half of the nineteenth century saw the rise of the *awit* and *korido*, narrative poems with the same subject matter as the *komedya*. Both were sung or chanted. Francisco Baltazar (popularly known as Baltagas) was a master of the *komedya* and *awit*, with his *Florante at Laura* (1838) considered an *awit* masterpiece. At the end of the nineteenth century, the *komedya* gave way to the *zarzuela* or operetta, a mix of social commentary, music, and romance.

The growth of Philippine nationalism coincided with the introduction of the novel. JOSÉ RIZAL, who wrote two early and influential novels, *Noli Me Tangere* (1887) and *El Filibusterismo* (1891), brought realism into Filipino literature. Writing in Spanish, Rizal reached only an elite audience but greatly influenced later Tagalog and English writers. During the early part of the twentieth century as Tagalog replaced Spanish, writers such as Gabriel Beato Francisco, Valeriano Hernández Peña, Iñigo E. Regalado, and Lope K. Santos combined romance with the social criticism found in Rizal.

During American rule the novel and short story developed rapidly. In 1921, Zoilo M. Galang published the first Philippine novel in English, *A Child of Sorrow*. By the 1930s English-language literature was challenging the vernacular, and the poems and short stories of José Garciá Villa firmly established English as the literary language.

Postwar writers drew inspiration from their native land, but style from American writers: Issues of cultural identity, rural life, and economic inequity were rendered in English. In the 1970s, however, young writers protesting the American domination of Filipino culture returned to their native languages for inspiration. For writers who experienced the political repression of the Marcos regime, language and literature were political as well as artistic expressions. Today, Aida Santos, Joi Barros, Edgar Reyes, and Lahul Bautista are writers seeking to develop literary Tagalog.

Widely read in their homeland, overseas Filipino writers have long had an impact on island Philippine literature. During the 1930s Carlos Bulosan examined the displaced Filipino, and today, BIENVENIDO N. SANTOS examines many of the same themes in his fiction. Ninotchka Rosca, too, has kept her eyes and words focused on the Philippines. Her short stories and novels confront corrupt government and its tortured people. Rosca's most recent novel, *Twice Blessed* (1992), continues the exposé of corrupt power basic to the novels of F. SIONIL JOSÉ.

History and Criticism

Alegre, Edilberto N., and Doreen G. Fernandez. *The Writer and His Milieu: An Oral History of the First Generation of Writers in English*. De La Salle U. Pr. 1984 o.p. Interviews with 14 writers including Leon Guerrero, Arturo B. Rotor, Bienvenido N. Santos, Jose Garcia Villa, and Leopoldo Y. Yabes.

———. *Writers and Their Milieu: An Oral History of Second Generation Writers in English*. De La Salle U. Pr. 1987 o.p. Interviews with writers who began their careers in the 1930s. Includes Francisco Arcellana, N.V.M. Gonzalez, Edilberto K. Tiempo, and Edith L. Tiempo.

Bresnahan, Roger J. *Angels of Vision: Conversations on Philippine Literature*. Cellar 1992 o.p. Discussions with Philippine literary historians and critics.

———. *Conversations with Filipino Writers*. Cellar 1990 $10.75. ISBN 971-10038-0-5. Avoids a banal question-and-answer format to provide insightful conversations about contemporary Philippine literature.

Casper, Leonard. *New Writing from the Philippines: A Critique and Anthology*. Bks. Demand repr. of 1906 ed. $107.30. ISBN 0-317-52002-4. A good introduction to post-World War II literature, including selections by Jose Garcia Villa, Bienvenido Santos, Nick Joaquin, Edith L. Tiempo, N.V.M. Gonzalez, and others.

Galdon, Joseph A., ed. *Essays on the Philippine Novel in English*. Ateneo de Manila U. Pr. 1979 o.p. Nineteen critical reviews of fiction written in English after 1945. Includes four essays on Rizal as a novelist.

Lumbera, Bienvenido. *Revaluation: Essays on Philippine Literature, Cinema, and Popular Culture*. Index Pr. 1984 o.p. Calls for a reassessment of indigenous and anticolonialist cultural production, including folk epics, literature, and comics.

Manuud, Antonio G. *Brown Heritage: Essays on Philippine Cultural Tradition and Literature*. Ateneo de Manila U. Pr. 1967 o.p. An excellent introduction to the social, historical, and cultural background of Philippine literature.

Morajes, Resil B. *Cebuano Literature: A Survey and Bio-Bibliography*. Cellar 1975 $12.50. ISBN 0-686-18663-X. An initial effort to map the terrain of an important literature of the Visayas.

———. *The Origins and Rise of the Filipino Novel: A Generic Study of the Novel Until 1940*. U. of Philippines Pr. 1983 o.p. An excellent study of the rise of the novel, using epics, romances, and biographies to highlight the continuity and change within Filipino narrative tradition.

San Juan, Epifanio, Jr. *Towards a People's Literature: Essays in the Dialectics of Praxis and Contradiction in Philippine Writing.* U. of Philippines Pr. 1985 $10.00. ISBN 0-8248-0904-1. A notable critic argues for a reinterpretation of Philippine literature towards one that accommodates indigenous languages and modes of expression.

Valeros, Florentino B., and Estrellita V. Gruenberg. *Filipino Writers in English.* Cellar 1987 $15.00. ISBN 971-10-0285-X. A biographical and bibliographic guide to Filipino authors.

Collections

Castro, Joveita Ventura, ed. *Epics of the Philippines.* ASEAN Committee on Culture & Information 1983 o.p. Presents the sung or chanted epic literature of the Ifugaos of northern Luzon.

Eugenio, Damiana L. *Awit and Corrido: Philippine Metrical Romances.* U. of Philippines Pr. 1987 $28.00. ISBN 0-8248-1037-7. A detailed look at selected works of what was once the most popular literary form.

Filipina I: Poetry, Drama, Fiction. Cellar 1984 o.p. A collection of works by Women Writers in Media Now, evidencing women's important contributions to current political and social literature.

Majzels, Robert. *The Guerrilla is Like a Poet: An Anthology of Filipino Poetry.* Cormorant Bks. 1988 o.p. Poets committed to fusing art with life, evoking laughter and tears.

Salanga, Alfredo, and Esther M. Pacheco. *Versus: Philippine Protest Poetry, 1983–1986.* U. of Wash. Pr. 1988 $9.95. ISBN 0-295-96599-1. The despair, rage, and hope of a people between the assassination of Benigno Aquino, Jr., and the political uprising that unseated Marcos.

San Juan, Epifanio. *Introduction to Modern Filipino Literature.* Twayne 1974 o.p. Excellent introduction to the development of contemporary Tagalog literature, with an anthology of poetry and fiction and brief introductions to each author.

Villanueva, Marianne. *Ginseng and Other Tales from Manila.* Calyx Bks. 1991 $16.95. ISBN 0-934971-20-X. Stories that frequently deal with the repressive Marcos regime and the sadness the author saw on returning to her homeland.

Other Works

Hagedorn, Jessica. *Dogeaters.* Random 1990 $19.95. ISBN 0-394-57498-2. A young Manila girl's view of corruption and politics in the Philippines, evoking the images of a changing society.

Rosca, Ninotchka. *State of War.* S&S Trade 1990 $9.95. ISBN 0-671-68699-0. The story of generations, politics, and the Philippines in a time of turmoil.

———. *Twice Blessed.* Norton 1992 $19.95. ISBN 0-393-03091-1. A story of corruption and abuse concerning twins who gain power and the presidency through any means possible.

JOAQUIN, NICK. 1917–

Primarily self-educated, Nick Joaquin has earned a reputation as an outstanding journalist, playwright, novelist, short story writer, poet, and biographer. His 1943 essay on the miraculous seventeenth-century Spanish defeat of the Dutch navy, "La Naval de Manila," won him a scholarship to a Dominican monastery. In 1950 he left the seminary, joined an acting troupe, and began his career writing for the leading Manila weekly, *Philippines Free Press*, using the pen name Quijano de Manila (Manila Old-Timer). In 1970 he joined Gregorio Brillantes as co-editor of the *Asian-Philippines Leader* until it was shut down by Marcos in 1972.

Joaquin's essays, biographies, and fiction all demonstrate an understanding of the interplay between the past and the present. His novels and stories juxtapose, as in Filipino society, precolonial religion and values with colonial Catholicism, the moral strictness represented by convent life with American permissiveness. Repeatedly Joaquin demonstrates his belief that Filipinos must ultimately reconcile their multifarious pasts.

In 1991, when the publisher Juan P. Dayan began publishing the weekly *Philippine Graphic*, Joaquin joined a team of dedicated journalists and writers as editor-in-chief. He is the winner of the Palanca Award (1957–58), the Stonehill Award for the Novel (1960), the Republic Cultural Heritage Award (1961), and the National Artist Award (1976).

Nonfiction by Joaquin

The Aquinos of Tarlac: An Essay on History as Three Generations. Cacho Hermanos 1983 o.p. Traces the life of Ninoy Aquino, a member of a powerful family of the Filipino elite.

Book of Sin: From Golden Salakot to Red Hat. Weekly Graphic Pub. 1992 o.p. A portrait of Cardinal Sin which is also a history of the Catholic Church in the Philippines.

Discourses of the Devil's Advocate and Other Controversies. Cacho Hermanos 1983 o.p. Essays on Manila life reprinted from *Philippines Free Press*.

Doy Laurel in Profile: A Philippine Political Odyssey. Makati Trade Times 1985 o.p. A lengthy study of the legislator who was later President Aquino's vice-president, Salvador H. Laurel.

Gloria Diaz and Other Delineations. Natl. Bk. Store Philippines 1977 o.p. Essays on Manila life reprinted from *Philippines Free Press*.

Jaime Ongpin, the Enigma: A Profile of the Filipino as Manager. J. V. Ongpin Institute of Business 1990 o.p. A profile of the businessman-politician.

Language of the Street and Other Essays. Natl. Bk. Store Philippines 1980 o.p. Essays on Manila life reprinted from *Philippines Free Press*.

Manila: Sin City and Other Chronicles. Natl. Bk. Store Philippines 1980 o.p. Essays on Manila life reprinted from *Philippines Free Press*.

Quartet of the Quarter Moon. 1986 o.p. Essays, many of them celebratory, on the 1986 revolt against Marcos.

A Question of Heroes. Natl. Bk. Store Philippines 1981 o.p. A collection of biographical essays documenting heroic contributions to the 1896 revolt.

Reportage on Crime: Thirteen Horror Happenings That Hit the Headlines. Natl. Bk. Store Philippines 1977 o.p. Essays on Manila life reprinted from *Philippines Free Press*.

Reportage on Lovers: A Medley of Factual Romances, Happy or Tragical, Most of Which Made the News. Natl. Bk. Store Philippines 1977 o.p. Essays on Manila life reprinted from *Philippines Free Press*.

Reportage on the Marcoses, 1964–1970. National Media Production Center 1979 o.p. Favorable portraits of the president and his wife, Imelda, before their ouster.

The Seven Ages of Romulo. Filipinas Foundation 1979 o.p. A brief look at Carlos Pena Romulo.

The World of Rafael Salas: Service and Management in the Global Village. Solar Pub. 1987 o.p. A life of Rafael M. Salas, diplomat to the United Nations.

Novels by Joaquin

Cave and Shadows. Natl. Bk. Store Philippines 1982 o.p. Intriguing mystery exploring dichotomies between sacred and profane, illusion and reality, and past and present, set prior to martial law in 1972.

The Woman Who Had Two Navels. 1961 o.p. Probes the question of national identity through the protagonist, Connie Escobar, who develops an illusionary extra navel. Winner of the Stonehill Award.

PLAYS BY JOAQUIN

Portrait of the Artist as Filipino. o.p. Daughters confirm a family tradition when they renounce plans to sell their father's famous painting.

Tropical Baroque: Four Manileño Theatricals. U. of Queensland Pr. 1982 o.p. In addition to *Portrait of the Artist as Filipino,* includes *Tatarin, Fathers and Sons,* and *The Beatas.*

SHORT STORY COLLECTION BY JOAQUIN

Tropical Gothic. U. of Queensland Pr. 1972 o.p. Collection of nine widely read stories, including "The Woman Who Had Two Navels," which eventually was expanded into a novel.

BOOK ABOUT JOAQUIN

San Juan, E., Jr. *Subversions of Desire: Prolegomena to Nick Joaquin.* UH Pr. 1988 o.p. A theoretical analysis of Joaquin's desire and ideology as expressed in his writing.

JOSÉ, F. SIONIL (Francisco Sionil). 1924–

As the owner of the prominent Solidaridad Bookstore, F. Sionil José's literary life extends beyond his prolific output of writings to an avid promotion of literature and books. He is the founder of the Philippine Center of International PEN and former editor-publisher of the influential literary magazine *Solidarity.* He has written, "I left my village in the Central Luzon province of Pangasinan when I was thirteen. My Ilokano forefathers, driven away from their homes in the late nineteenth century by land hunger and Spanish oppression, settled in this village, which they called Cabugawan after the town of Cabugaw in Ilokos Sur, where they came from. It is in this village where I grew up, knew the drudgery of village life, and at the same time learned those solid virtues of industry and thrift which the Ilokansos are noted for."

José is best known for his historical epic of five novels that follow Rosales, a village in Luzon, through a century of Philippine life. In these and other novels, his characters underscore the seemingly endless search for Filipino identity, moral order, and social justice. In exploring the impact of urbanization, he often highlights individual integrity in the face of corruption and evil.

In 1979 José won the Palanca Award and in 1980 the Ramon Magsaysay Award for Journalism, Literature, and Communication Arts.

NOVELS BY JOSÉ

Ermita. Solidaridad Pub. 1988 o.p. About a prostitute, Ermi Rojo, first introduced in the novella *Obsession.*

Mass. Solidaridad Pub. 1979 o.p. The fifth and concluding book of the Rosales series follows Pepe, from the poverty-stricken countryside to Manila's sprawling slum, Tondo, and his transformation into a revolutionary who understands the Filipino people.

My Brother, My Executioner. Cellar 1979 $10.00. ISBN 971-10-0196-9. The third of the Rosales novels set during the Hukbalahap movement of the 1950s, which is symbolized by the conflict between two brothers.

Po-on. Solidaridad Pub. 1984 o.p. The first of the Rosales novels, set in Ilokos in the 1880s. Follows a family fleeing its village to escape Spanish tyranny and a man searching for personal meaning.

The Pretenders. Solidaridad Pub. 1987 o.p. The fourth of the Rosales novels, the story of Antonio Samso, lost and betrayed with nowhere to run.

Three Filipino Women. Random 1992 $22.00. ISBN 0-679-41360-X

Tree. Solidaridad Pub. 1978 o.p. The second of the Rosales novels.

Two Filipino Women. Cellar 1981 $6.50. ISBN 971-10-0113-6. Two novellas, one about a prostitute, the other about a powerful woman who surmounts her small town origins to become a national figure, both searching for a moral order and social justice.

Poetry by José

Questions. Solidaridad Pub. 1988 o.p. Personal expressions that reveal a man seeking to better understand himself.

Short Story Collections by José

Platinum: Ten Filipino Stories. Solidaridad Pub. 1983 o.p. Explores the shallows and depths of the Filipino character with searing honesty.

Waywaya: Eleven Filipino Short Stories. Heinemann Ed. 1980 o.p. Several stories are allegorical reflections on modern Filipino life.

Book about José

Morales, Alfredo T., ed. *F. Sionil José and His Fiction: The Filipino's Journey to Justice and Nationhood.* Vera-Reyes 1989 o.p.

RIZAL, JOSÉ. 1861–1896

José Rizal is regarded as a national hero who died for his country's freedom. Born into an affluent family, Rizal was educated at the best Manila schools and went on to enter the University of Santo Tomas. Unlike many of his fellow students, Rizal was not Spanish, but Filipino, and he quickly "learned to understand better in what sort of world I was. In it there were privileges for some and rules for others, and assuredly the discrimination was not based on capacity." It was while he was studying medicine at the university that Rizal began writing poems and essays.

Beginning in 1882, Rizal attended universities in Madrid, Paris, Heidelberg, and Berlin, where he became involved in the reformist movement and regularly contributed essays to propagandist publications. These writings are powerful indictments against Spain's racial oppression of the Filipinos. While in Europe, Rizal published his most famous works. Published in 1887 and 1891, Rizal's two novels, *The Lost Eden (Noli me tangere)* and its sequel *The Subversive (El filibusterismo)*, mark a transition in history as well as literature. With their vivid depiction of Filipino suffering under colonial rule, they served as one catalyst in the 1896 Philippine Revolution, helping to end Spanish rule and with it an era of Spanish literature. While Rizal was a prolific writer of essays, poetry, and drama, it is as a novelist that he became a model for future generations of writers.

In 1892 Rizal returned to the Philippines, where he founded the reformist organization *La Liga Filipina.* Although he was not a proponent of revolution, Rizal was considered a subversive. He was named as an instigator in the 1896 revolt, which he opposed, and was sentenced to death. His final poem written before his execution, "My Last Farewell," is recognized as an outstanding poetic elegy.

Novels by Rizal

The Lost Eden. 1887. Trans. by Leon M. Guerrero. Greenwood 1968 o.p. Unmasks the hypocrisy of Spanish rule, with Spanish friars as villains and the hero an idealistic and optimistic youth.

The Subversive. 1891. Trans. by Leon M. Guerrero. Norton 1968 o.p. Continues the story of *The Lost Eden,* as the embittered, cynical protagonist seeks violent revolution.

POETRY BY RIZAL

Rizal's Complete Poetical Works: 1869–1896. Trans. by Isidro Escare Abeto. Natl. Bk. Philippines 1976 o.p. Bilingual translations, with annotations giving historical background to each poem.

Complete Poems and Plays of José Rizal. Trans. by Nick Joaquin. Far Eastern U. 1976 o.p. Translated and introduced by the prominent writer and journalist.

NONFICTION BY RIZAL

Political and Historical Writings. National Heroes Commission 1964 o.p. Brings together varied writings that show the range of Rizal's ideas and philosophy.

Rizal's Correspondence with Fellow Reformists (1882–1896). National Heroes Commission 1963 o.p. The complete correspondence, in chronological order, providing samples of Rizal's passionate prose.

The Young Rizal: A Translation of Memorias de un Estudiante de Manila by José Rizal with Translations of Rizal's Early Poems along the Pasig and the Council of the Gods. Trans. by Leon Ma. Guerrero. Essays, plays, and poems charting the growth of a scholar and writer, written when Rizal was only 17.

BOOKS ABOUT RIZAL

Costa, Horacio de la, ed. and trans. *The Trial of Rizal.* Ateneo de Manila U. Pr. 1961 o.p. A transcription of the official Spanish documents.

Craig, Austin. *Lineage, Life, and Labors of Jose Rizal: The Philippine Patriot, a Study of the Growth of Free Ideas in the Transpacific American Territory.* Gordon Pr. 1977 $59.95. ISBN 0-8490-2168-5

Guerrero, Leon M. *The First Filipino: A Biography of José Rizal.* National Heroes Commission 1963 o.p. An encomium for Rizal, written on the centennial of his death.

Hessel, Eugene A. *The Religious Thought of José Rizal.* Cellar 1983 $10.75. ISBN 0-318-01161-1

Ocampo, Ambeth R. *Rizal Without an Overcoat.* Anvil Bks. 1990 o.p. A collection of articles attempting to relate Rizal to the contemporary Philippines.

Yabes, Leopoldo Y., ed. *José Rizal on His Centenary: Being an Attempt at Revaluation of His Significance, by Professors of the University of the Philippines.* U. of Philippines Pr. 1963 o.p. Essays examining Rizal's impact on Philippine society and politics.

SANTOS, BIENVENIDO N. 1911–

The son of Pampango parents who spoke no English, Santos was born in the slums of Tondo, Manila. In 1941, he was sent by the government to the United States to study English. Forced to spend the war years there, Santos did not return to the Philippines until 1946. From 1966 to 1969, Santos was a Fulbright professor of English at the University of Iowa. After this, he returned to the Philippines for one year but now makes his home in the United States.

Santos's fiction draws from his own life experiences. His early stories portray the pain and suffering of living in poverty in the Manila slums. Many of his characters, like Santos, are exiles living in two worlds, the Philippines and the United States. With what has been described as deceptive simplicity, Santos's stories explore the precarious life of Filipinos who have severed their ties with their homeland but return home again and again, often only in their imagination. *Brother, My Brother* (1976), *Villa Magdalena* (1986), and *The Volcano* (1986) question the realities of Philippine economic development and its impact on the people and culture. *The Praying Man* won the Manila Critics Circle National Book Award for fiction in 1983.

Novels by Santos

The Man Who (Thought He) Looked like Robert Taylor. Cellar 1985 $12.50. ISBN 0-317-00355-0

The Praying Man. Cellar 1982 $7.50. ISBN 971-10-0002-4

Villa Magdalena. Cellar 1986 $11.75. ISBN 971-10-0241-8. The story of the once poor but now powerful Medallades, who cannot escape the stench of their former and metaphorical trade, leather.

The Volcano. Cellar 1986 $12.50. ISBN 971-10-0243-4

What the Hell for You Left Your Heart in San Francisco. Cellar 1987 $10.75. ISBN 971-10-0319-8

Poetry by Santos

Distances in Time: Selected Poems. Ateneo de Manila U. Pr. 1983 o.p. His fiction's familiar themes of repudiation, poverty, betrayal, and corruption, condensed to a smaller scale.

Short Story Collections by Santos

Brother, My Brother: A Collection of Stories. Bookmark NY 1976 o.p.

Dwell in the Wilderness: Selected Short Stories (1931–1941). Cellar 1985 $7.50. 971-10-0182-9. Character sketches depicting the life of ordinary Filipinos, written between 1930 and 1941, before Santos came to the United States.

Scent of Apples: A Collection of Stories. U. of Wash. Pr. 1979 $8.95. ISBN 0-295-95695-X. Overseas Filipinos' quest for a home on foreign soil.

THAI LITERATURE

Thailand, known as Siam until 1939, shares a southern border with Malaysia and mountainous northern borders with Laos and Myanmar (Burma). Central Thailand, the nation's cultural, economic, and political center, is home to the ethnically dominant Thai. The Karen, Shan, Lao, White Tai, Black Thai, and Hmong—each with a distinct culture and language—live in northern and northeastern Thailand. Southern Thailand shares its distinct Islamic culture with Malaysia.

Thailand's literature is rich with the variation of local tribal and foreign traditions. Buddhist religious scripts in Pali and the religious language of Hinayana Buddhism dominate Thai religious discourse, and early Thai poetry, known as *suphasit* poetry, shows the influences of these religious writings. Stylistically similar to the Buddhist *jataka* tales, the *suphasit* contain moral instructions and sayings. The Thai *Ramakien,* an epic romance of 70,000 lines written during the reigns of Rama I (1782–1809) and Rama II (1809–24), demonstrates the influence of Indian religion and myth.

As the centralized monarchy of Thailand grew, so did the importance of the court and court arts. Poetry came to dominate, being used in drama, epics, and historical accounts. Best known of the court writers is Sunthorn Phu. Through the years, Thai royalty have also made important contributions to the development of literature. Prince Damrong Rajanubhab was a historian and essayist, and Prince Narit composed songs for *lakhon,* a dance-drama that rose in popularity during the late nineteenth century. Rama VI translated Shakespeare, wrote poetry, and is also credited with establishing a literary club popular with the Thai elite of the 1920s and 1930s. Akatdamkoeng and Mom Luong Bubpha Nimmanhemint (pseudonym Dokmai Sot) are also considered pioneers in the developing Thai literature. Like many writers of the 1920s, 1930s, and early

1940s, Dokmai Sot was conservative in her outlook and criticized modernization's clash with old Thai traditions.

Although never colonized, Thailand felt the impact of increasing contact with the west. As literacy spread beyond the elite, verse gave way to prose and oral traditions gave way to newspapers and books. After World War II, authors strove to give their readers a sense of contemporary society and its issues while retaining didactic themes of wise and moral behavior. Kularb Saipradit (pseudonym Siburapha), a renowned writer in the 1930s, was the mentor of Khamsing Srinawk. Both examine peasant life, but Khamsing surpassed his mentor by breathing life into the villagers and presenting them as complex individuals rather than mere pawns of the elite. In a collection of his stories, *The Politician and Other Stories* (1973), Khamsing dwells on the theme of the walls that separate the urban Thai from the rural Thai and the powerful from the powerless. Similarily, the writer Surasingsamruam Chimphanao (also known as Samruam Singh) has used the countryside to examine the many contrasts in Thai society.

Beginning in the 1960s, and continuing through the 1976 military coup that ended a widening democracy movement, many writers were avowedly socialist in their outlook. This period of great social and political change coincided with an increasing American presence; soldiers, business people, missionaries, academics, and tourists had a considerable impact on Thai society and the arts. While some Thai writers longed for earlier norms, many closely examined the changing society and looked forward. Exploring new social territory, the poet Chitr Phoumisak and the fiction writer Rong Wangsawarn described Bangkok's underworld. Angkhan Kalayaanaphong departed from traditional Thai poetic forms in imagery and style. Writers were not merely observers but actors in the changes, with Suchat Sawatski and Sujit Wongthet, who enjoyed a broad following of students during the 1970s, considered intellectual leaders. Today, KUKRIT PRAMOJ, one of the nation's foremost literary figures, is also a political figure respected for his insights on contemporary Thai society. Indeed, much of contemporary Thai writing has political overtones, both conservative and radical, because no writer has been unaffected by postwar Thailand's political upheavals.

History and Criticism

Anuman Rajadhon. *Essays on Thai Folklore*. Editions Duang Kamol 1969 o.p. Historical insight into Thai customs and thought. Serves as an introduction to aspects of Thai literature.

Bickner, Robert J., Thomas J. Hudak, and Patcharin Peyasantiwong, eds. *Papers from a Conference on Thai Studies in Honor of William J. Gedney*. Ctr. S&SE Asian 1988 $27.95. ISBN 0-89148-030-7. Homage to the famous Thai linguist, containing scholarly essays on language and literature in Thailand, Burma, Cambodia, and Laos.

Phillips, Herbert P. *Modern Thai Literature: With an Ethnographic Interpretation*. UH Pr. 1987 $26.00. ISBN 0-8248-1065-1. A critical analysis of Thai literature as a product of a particular society; includes translations.

Rutnin, Mattani. *Modern Thai Literature: The Process of Modernization and the Transformation of Values*. Thammasat U. Pr. 1988 o.p. Primarily a study of Boonlua Debyasuvarn. Excellent introduction provides background to the development of Thai modern creative literature since the mid-1800s.

———, ed. *The Siamese Theatre: A Collection of Reprints from the Journal of the Siam Society*. Siam Society 1975 o.p. A survey of types of Thai performances, from classical to popular. Includes an introduction to the Thai version of the *Ramayana*.

Wibha Senanan. *The Genesis of the Novel in Thailand.* Thai Watana Panich 1975 o.p. The rise of Thai prose literature and the novel in the early twentieth century, focusing specifically on Si Burapha, Dokmai Sot, and Prince Akatdamkoeng as well as the reading public.

Collections

Anderson, Benedict R. O'G., and Ruchira Mendiones. *In the Mirror: Literature and Politics in the American Era.* Cornell SE Asia 1985 $10.00. ISBN 974-210-389-1. Thirteen short stories from the 1960s and 1970s, accompanied by extensive analysis of themes and social context.

Brun, Viggo. *Sug, the Trickster Who Fooled the Monk: A Northern Thai Tale with Vocabulary.* Curzon UK 1976 o.p. Twenty-seven tales of this popular character. Serves to introduce oral tradition as well as the character of village people.

Ingersoll, Fern S. *Sang Thong: A Dance-Drama from Thailand. Written by King Rama II and the Poets of His Court.* C. E. Tuttle 1973 o.p. *Sang Thong,* The Golden Prince of the Conch Shell, is a widely loved poem that finds its roots in the *jataka* tales. A version notable for its adaptation to the *lakhon nok,* dance-drama tradition.

Khamsong Srinawk. *The Politician and Other Stories.* Trans. by Damnern Garden. OUP 1973 o.p. Short stories depicting tradition in contemporary village society.

Le May, Reginald. *Siamese Tales Old and New: With Some Reflections on the Tales.* Probsthai 1971 repr. of 1930 ed. $7.50. ISBN 0-85382-000-7. Fifteen traditional tales, with an essay on their relation to aspects of Thai culture.

Siburapha. *Behind the Painting and Other Stories.* Trans. by David Smyth. OUP 1990 $12.95. ISBN 0-19-588962-2. Political short stories intended to engage the reader in social action as well as to entertain, by Kularb Saipradit, using the pseudonym Siburapha.

Surasingsaruam Chimphanao. *Voices from the Thai Countryside: The Short Stories of Samruan Singh.* U. Wisc. Ctr. SE Asian 1991 o.p. A collection of political and socially oriented stories by a northern Thai writer. Accompanied by a lengthy introduction.

Other Works

Dokmaisot. *A Secret Past.* Trans. by Ted Strehlow. Cornell SE Asia 1992 $10.00. ISBN 0-87727-126-7. The first translation of this popular novelist whose works portrayed the social problems, in which a young woman comes to terms with her true identity.

Pira Sudham. *Moonsoon Country: Thailand in Transition.* Shire Pr. 1988 o.p. A story covering 25 years highlighting traditional versus modern and the cultural tension between Thai and western cultures.

Tossa, Wajuppa, trans. and ed. *Phadaeng Nang Ai: A Translation of a Thai-Isan Folk Epic in Verse.* Bucknell U. Pr. 1990 $34.50. ISBN 0-8387-5139-3. Set in Isan villages, an epic concerning a tragic love triangle. Reveals a rich literary tradition of Isan.

KHUKRIT PRAMOJ. 1911–

An honored and respected man in Thailand, Khukrit has at various times served as prime minister, deputy finance minister, and member of parliament. He helped to write the 1974 Thai Constitution and is publisher of the newspaper *Siam Rath.* Author of more than 30 books—including 5 novels, travel accounts, satires, and short stories—Khukrit is also an accomplished Thai dancer.

His most famous literary work, *Four Reigns (Sii Phaeaendin),* follows the lives of nobility during the first half of the twentieth century. In it he creates the idealized Thai woman Maeae Phloy, who, being pragmatic, is always loving and forgiving.

As important as his own contributions to Thai literature is Khukrit's support of the intellectual and artistic development of young writers. Suchit Wongthed,

Vasit Dejkunjorn, Prayad S. Naa Khanaad, and Rong Wongsawaan have all, at one time, worked for him. That Khukrit may be more conservative than some of his successors is evident in his novel *Red Bamboo*, which portrays a local communist as somewhat of a social failure.

NOVELS BY KHUKRIT PRAMOJ

Four Reigns. Trans. by Tulachandra. Editions Duang Kamol 1981 o.p. Sweeping historical fiction.

Red Bamboo. Trans. by Phaidaeng. Progress Bookstore 1961 o.p. The story of a Buddhist monk and his childhood friend, now a communist, who tries to lead the monk astray. Inspired by the Don Camillo stories by Giovanni Guareschi.

SUNTHORN PHU. 1786–1856

Born into a commoner's family, Sunthorn Phu spent his youth in the royal palace with his mother, who was a servant. Educated at a monastery, he later became a clerk in the government. Early in his career, however, Sunthorn incurred the wrath of the royalty when he wooed a lady of the court. After a brief imprisonment, he returned to his birthplace in Rayong, where he composed the first of many *nirat*, or narrative poems, depicting a journey far from loved ones.

Returning to Bangkok, Sunthorn Phu won the favor of King Rama II, author of the Thai version of the *Ramayana*, and became a favored court poet. Yet again, though, Sunthorn was stripped of his position when the king's son ascended the throne. Joining the Buddhist priesthood, he composed several *nirat* that described his religious travels. Later, Sunthorn gained favor with other members of the royalty, and under the patronage of Prince Lakhananukhun composed the 52,000-line Thai epic *The Story of Phra Abhai Mani*.

In addition to formal court poetry, Sunthorn composed children's poems. Combining romance, adventure, and humor, they still capture the interest of Thais of all ages.

POETRY BY SUNTHORN PHU

Nirat Muang Klaeng. 1807. Trans. by Prince Prem Purachatra. Natl. Identity Board 1984 o.p. Sunthorn Phu's first travel poem, or *nirat*, based on a trip to eastern Thailand.

The Story of Phra Abhai Mani. Chatra Bks. 1952 o.p. A unique Thai narrative. Fantastic adventures and romance told with a mastery of suspense.

Phra Chai Suriya. P.E.N. International Thailand Center 1986 o.p. A moral tale in *klon* verse form. Accessible to young Thai readers.

VIETNAMESE LITERATURE

Vietnam stretches south from China. Its eastern border is the South China Sea; its western border is shared with Laos and Cambodia. Ethnic Vietnamese make up the majority of the population, but like other Southeast Asian nations, there is great ethnic diversity. The Cham and Khmer live in the south, while nearly 60 linguistic minorities live the mountainous border regions. The long political domination of China, from the second century B.C. until the tenth century A.D., imbued Vietnam with Chinese law, religion, government, literature, and language.

Until the French colonization in the nineteenth century, knowledge of Chinese language and literature restricted writing to an elite class. Vietnamese court literature was thoroughly Chinese in style and themes. The Vietnamese folk expressed themselves in oral tales, riddles, and proverbs, displaying rich and varied influences: origin myths, trickster tales, and Buddhist themes of the futility of material wealth.

During the thirteenth century, the *nom* script gradually came to be used to record Vietnamese oral literatures. Its use spread to a variety of genres and to adaptations from Chinese literature. By the eighteenth century *nom* was commonly used in the *truyen,* or verse novel. One of the most popular *nom* adaptations of ancient Chinese poetry was *Lament of a Soldier's Wife (Chinh phu ngam),* an antiwar narrative poem written in the first half of the eighteenth century, with the best-known adaptation by Doan Thi Diem. Vietnam's greatest narrative poem in *nom* is *The Tale of Kieu (Kim Van Kieu)* by Nguyen Du. This 3,200-line *truyen* is essentially a Chinese romance adapted to include Vietnamese linguistic and folk elements. The success of *The Tale of Kieu* led to an outpouring of narrative poems that continued until the early twentieth century. Perhaps best known of the *nom* poets is Nguyen Khuyen, whose bitter poems express contempt for the foreign rulers.

In the mid-nineteenth century, the romanized alphabet, *quoc ngu,* introduced by missionaries and the French colonial government began to influence literary production. In 1865 the French established the first *quoc ngu* newspaper, with the writer Truong-vinh-Ky in charge. In addition to his contributions to Vietnamese journalism, Truong wrote over 100 books, many of which were important transcriptions of Chinese and *nom* literature into the new romanized script.

The twentieth century ushered in an era of political writing that exists to the present. To counter growing resentment of their colonial rule, in 1917 the French established a literary journal, *South Wind (Nam Phong),* with the aim of promoting French culture. Its editor, Pham Quynh, traditional in his outlook but aware of a changing society, created a journal that provided links between old and new cultures and served as the foundation for contemporary literature. Pham Quynh promoted the publication of essays and translations of French literature, but to further the creation of an indigenous novel, he also encouraged young writers by publishing short stories.

Early Vietnamese romance and travel novels of the 1920s were often didactic, but by the 1930s novelists broke with this tradition to focus on social questions. They described landlords and peasants, beggars and prostitutes. At the same time, The-Lu, nationalist and poet, was at the center of the "new poetry" movement which rejected classical styles in favor of free verse. The formation of the Self-Reliance Literature Group (*Tu Luc Van Doan*) prompted a flowering of Vietnamese literature. In the decade that followed, authors wrote of the struggles of peasants and workers and enjoyed large followings that exist to the present.

After World War II many nationalists and communists went into hiding or were jailed by the French. The writings of jailed intellectuals such as Phan Boi Chau and Ho Chi Minh created a tradition of jail literature. With the 1954 defeat of the French and division of Vietnam by the Geneva Conference, two ideologically different literatures evolved. In the north, writers extolled the virtues of socialism; the work of To Huu, a writer of this period, is indicative of communist revolutionary poetry. In the south, writers had more freedom but were encouraged to espouse the idea that human progress was antithetical to communism. In the south there were also strong nationalist writers like Nguyen Vu, who created novels and plays sympathetic to the *Viet Minh,* the coalition of communists and nationalists originally formed to oppose the Japanese in World War II.

Revolution and war have shaped the literature of more than one generation of Vietnamese writers; these themes remain predominant. The Vietnam War, which involved a half million U.S. troops by 1969, also shaped a generation of American writers, evidenced in the many poems and novels written about Vietnam since the 1960s. Sandra M. Wittman's extensive bibliography, *Writing About Vietnam: A Bibliography of the Literature of the Vietnam Conflict* (1989), enumerates the American literary works produced by a decade's bloody conflict.

History and Criticism

Durand, Maurice M., and Nguyen Tran Huan. *An Introduction to Vietnamese Literature*. Col. U. Pr. 1985 $36.00. ISBN 0-231-05852-7. A chronological survey covering traditional as well as contemporary literature.

Marr, David. *Vietnamese Tradition on Trial, 1920–1945*. U. CA Pr. 1981 $42.50. ISBN 0-520-04180-1. A study of the intellectual milieu of the period. Includes an excellent chapter on language and literacy.

Nguyen, Dinh Tham. *Studies on Vietnamese Language and Literature: A Preliminary Bibliography*. Cornell SE Asia 1992 $15.00. ISBN 0-87727-127-5. A comprehensive guide to western language materials, including translations, literary studies, and folk literature.

Osborne, Milton. *Fear and Fascination in the Tropics: A Reader's Guide to French Fiction on Indochina*. U. Wisc. Ctr. SE Asian 1986 o.p. Highlights the themes found in French fiction about colonial Indochina, with a comparison between these works and Graham Greene's *The Quiet American*.

Vo Phien. *Literature in South Vietnam: 1954–1975*. Trans. by Vo Dinh Mai. Vietnamese Language & Culture Publications 1992 $36.50. ISBN 0-949292-12-5. Authors and their works in South Vietnam during the American war period, beginning with an introduction to the social conditions of southern Vietnam.

Yeager, Jack A. *The Vietnamese Novel in French: A Literary Response to Colonialism*. U. Pr. of New Eng. 1987 $30.00. ISBN 0-87451-382-0. Scholarly study providing background on the Francophone literature of Vietnam, with an insightful analysis of 25 novels.

Collections

Banerian, James, trans. *Vietnamese Short Stories: An Introduction*. Sphinx Pub. 1986 o.p. Eleven short stories with an introduction to each of the ten authors.

Bosley, Keith, ed. and trans. *The War Wife: Vietnamese Poetry*. Allison & Busby 1972 o.p. Includes folk, classical, and contemporary poems.

Huynh Sanh Thong, ed. and trans. *The Heritage of Vietnamese Poetry*. Bks. Demand 1979 o.p. Spans entire history of poetry to the twentieth century; includes brief introduction.

Nguyen Chi Thien. *Flowers from Hell*. Trans. by Huynh Sanh Thong. Yale U. SE Asia 1984 $7.00. ISBN 0-938692-21-6. Collection of poetry by a dissident of the Communist regime.

Thiep Nguyen H., *The General and Other Stories*. OUP 1993 $11.95. ISBN 0-19-588580-5

Nguyen Ngoc Bich, ed. *A Thousand Years of Vietnamese Poetry*. Knopf 1975 o.p. Ancient Chinese scholarly traditions, nationalism, and the agonies of war captured in Vietnamese poetry.

______, ed. *War and Exile: A Vietnamese Anthology*. Vietnamese PEN Abroad, East Coast U.S.A. 1989 o.p. Fiction, essays, and poetry.

Raffel, Burton, trans. *From the Vietnamese: Ten Centuries of Poetry*. October 1968 o.p. An anthology covering the full range of Vietnamese poetic expression.

Vo-Dinh. *The Toad Is the Emperor's Uncle: Animal Folk-Tales from Viet-Nam.* Doubleday 1970 o.p. Eighteen traditional animal tales.

HO CHI MINH. 1890–1969

No writer has influenced Vietnamese thinking more than Ho Chi Minh. Born Nguyen-tat-Thanh in central Vietnam, Ho was the main founder of the Communist party of Indochina in 1930 and was president of the Democratic Republic of Vietnam from 1945 until his death. As the child of nationalist scholars, Ho was instilled with anticolonial sentiment. In 1917, he left for Europe and for the next 24 years divided his time among London, Paris, Moscow, and China.

In Paris, he joined the French Socialist party and later the French Communist party. He organized exiles from French colonies and Vietnamese from overseas into the Intercolonial Union. When he returned to Vietnam in 1941, he founded the independence movement *Viet Minh* and adopted the name Ho Chi Minh, "Enlightened One." During a 1942 visit to China, Ho was arrested on charges of espionage. During his 13-month imprisonment, he composed the poems, written in classical Chinese, that constitute *Prison Diary* (1971). Ho's numerous speeches, letters, and essays are known for their patriotic fervor and have earned him a reputation as one of Vietnam's greatest prose writers.

Work by Ho Chi Minh

On Revolution: Selected Writings, 1920–1966. Westview 1984 repr. of 1967 ed o.p. Introduction by Bernard Fall. The ninety prose writings include the emotional early works, demonstrating Ho Chi Minh's understanding of colonial rule and its human costs.

Poetry by Ho Chi Minh

The Prison Diary of Ho Chi Minh. Trans. by Aileen Palmer. Bantam 1971 o.p. Introduction by Harrison Salisbury.

Reflections from Captivity. Ohio U. Pr. 1978 o.p. Collected with the writings of Phan Boi Chau. Poems addressing the terrible prison conditions and expressing a reverence for life but devoid of broader political themes.

Books about Ho Chi Minh

Halberstam, David. *Ho.* McGraw 1986 $6.60. ISBN 0-07-554223-4. A brief biographical portrait placing the Ho Chi Minh leadership in the context of French colonialism and the struggle for independence.

Lacouture, Jean. *Ho Chi Minh: A Political Biography.* Random 1968 o.p. A detailed portrait of Ho Chi Minh's career through 1966, focusing on the years of struggle for liberation from France.

CHAPTER 11

Greek Literature

Marshall Hurwitz

Even a noble deed will die, if passed over in silence.

—PINDAR, fragment 121

Greek literature from HOMER to the present spans a period of nearly three millenia—six times the length of English literature beginning with CHAUCER (see Vol. 1). Although several elements of continuity exist in this literature, its history conveniently divides into four major divisions: (1) the classical period (the eighth century B.C. to the latter half of the fourth century B.C.); (2) the Hellenistic period (the last quarter of the fourth century B.C. to the fifth century A.D.); (3) the Byzantine period (from the fifth century A.D. to the fifteenth century A.D.); and finally (4) the modern period (from the beginning of the nineteenth century to the present).

CLASSICAL PERIOD

What has come down to us from ancient Greek literature is a fraction of what once existed. The literary remains of that extraordinary culture have been sifted and filtered through many generations of changing taste, and only the more successful or most consistently read works survive. Archeological discoveries have occasionally supplemented our knowledge, but a host of authors and works are known only in the citations of their contemporaries. Homer, for example, had many anonymous antecedents whose works were orally transmitted. Only by comparing Homer with the meager remains of his predecessors can one assess the high degree of sophistication in the two epics that have come down to us in his name. The *Iliad* takes one event in the ninth year of the Trojan War—the conflict between the great hero Achilles and his commander-in-chief Agamemnon over a woman—as a microcosm of the entire war. The *Odyssey* chronicles the adventures of Odysseus on his long-delayed return home from the war and of his triumph over the suitors of his supposed widow, Penelope. Both skillfully lead us through narratives of unforgettable personalities, subtle poetry, and vivid exciting scenes. We have the names of some of Homer's contemporaries who derived from the same oral tradition and wrote about the Trojan War (Arctinus of Miletus, Agias of Troezen, etc.) but only a few fragments or summaries of their works. From the paucity of texts as well as their content, we can conclude that Homer stood out eminently among these bards.

We do have some dactylic hexameter poems, called the *Homeric Hymns*, that in antiquity were believed to be written by Homer—an attribution that probably helped preserve them. These exquisite poems are short narratives about the gods embedded in the context of a prayer to the god. Of HESIOD, also Homer's contemporary, we have only two poems of sure attribution: the *Works and Days* and the *Theogony*. Others are lost.

Our greatest loss, however, is in the area of lyric poetry. Fragments of Archilochus, SAPPHO, Alcaeus, and others tantalize with fleeting images or incomplete poems. In the centuries that followed Homer, these poets created a literature of personal emotion in finely polished gems of poetry unlike Homer's epic narratives or Hesiod's didactic poetry. In choral lyrics they created forms to celebrate weddings (*epithalamia, prothalamia*) and athletic victories (*epinikia*), to lament the dead (*threnoi*), to glorify wine, women, and song (*skolia*), and so forth. Only the remains of PINDAR's odes are extensive enough to let us evaluate firsthand his poetic achievement.

One form of lyric poetry, the dithyramb (a poem dedicated to Dionysus), leads directly into the dramatic form of tragedy. According to the tradition, annual performances of dithyrambs accompanied the Dionysiac festivals. In the sixth century, an actor, Thespis, conceived the idea of having one performer leave the chorus to recite the dialogue, and thus dramatic festivals began. Of the dozens of playwrights whose names we know, the works of only three have been transmitted to us intact—AESCHYLUS, SOPHOCLES, and EURIPIDES. Aeschylus, the oldest of these dramatic poets, presents mythological stories in six of the seven extant plays. He is a poet of ornate language who continued and deepened the stylized Greek theater. Among his innovations was the introduction of a second major actor, an idea that made real interaction possible between characters. Sophocles, whose lifetime spanned the whole fifth century B.C., reduced the importance of the chorus, introduced a third actor, and shifted the focus from religious to more philosophical issues. Euripides, a decade younger, further reduced the role of the chorus and in more realistic language created riveting psychological portraits in Medea, Hippolytus, Pentheus, and others.

"Old Comedy," possibly in imitation of tragedy, was also a festival drama. Our sole representative of this type of comedy, ARISTOPHANES, is full of robust and unrestrained humor. As a social critic and antiwar patriot, he mercilessly makes fun of his contemporary political leaders; sex, religion, class divisions, and literary styles, too, are subjected to his witty barbs. The 11 plays that we have, from a corpus of at least 32, offer an insightful panorama of Athens in the fifth-century B.C.

The fifth century B.C. also witnessed the rise of prose to an art form. Earlier, prose was conceived of as purely functional, to be used for practical matters. Now its use among historians, philosophers, and orators intentionally transcended mere recording; the contemporary Greek audience applauded prose which succeeded in immortalizing thoughts or insights. Helping to create this atmosphere in which prose gained a new respect was the study of rhetoric, promoted by the Sophistic movement.

The impact of this historical and philosophical writing on Western thought, education, and literature has been profound. The fifth-century historians HERODOTUS (see Vol. 3), THUCYDIDES (see Vol. 3), and XENOPHON (see Vols. 3 and 4) laid the foundations for Western secular historiography. Herodotus wrote of the great conflict that initiated the century, the Persian wars. He saw in it a profound clash between Eastern and Western mentalities, between bigness and smallness, between despotism and freedom, and to illustrate his themes, he chose anecdotes and events that helped characterize both individual and national participants. Thucydides' subject was the war that concluded the century as well as the great classical age: the Peloponnesian War. As a general in that war, he gained insight, not only into the battles' military aspects, but also into their political dynamics. His history is a skeptical and critical account of the political forces that shaped the words and deeds of an epoch-ending war. Xenophon, who possessed a less original mind, continues the account of events after Thucydides' history in the *Hellenica*. Moreover, his is a more digressive, or wide-ranging, history. Xenophon writes about his teacher SOCRATES (see Vol. 4) or the Persian king Cyrus, about agriculture, or about an expedition he personally participated in—all in an intelligent, if not brilliant, way.

Socrates is a key figure in the history of Greek philosophy. The thinkers who preceded him (the pre-Socratics) remain to us in fragmentary writings; they were concerned with scientific and metaphysical issues. Socrates, perhaps in response to the Sophists' educational and rhetorical teachings, shifted the focus of philosophy to ethics and politics. He wrote nothing, but his inspiring teaching influenced PLATO (see Vols. 3 and 4) to compose his dialogues, at first representing the teachings of Socrates, but later voicing Plato's own ideas through Socrates' persona. Plato began a school known as the Academy, which spawned brilliant mathematicians and philosophers—including ARISTOTLE (see Vols. 3, 4, and 5), whose lectures covered virtually all phases of human knowledge. He, too, started a school, the Lyceum, in which pupils like THEOPHRASTUS extended his attempts to systematize human knowledge into botanical and psychological spheres.

We have the speeches of some of the great orators of the fifth and fourth centuries B.C., including Antiphon, Andocides, Lysias, and Isaeus. The greatest of these, however, was DEMOSTHENES, who attempted to rouse the Athenians to an awareness of the threat from Macedonia in his *Philippics* and *On the Crown*. Demosthenes' warnings were unsuccessful; Philip of Macedonia eventually defeated the Greeks in 338 B.C. Soon after, Philip's son Alexander conquered the Mediterranean world, changing the whole character of Greek civilization and profoundly affecting Western history and thought.

HELLENISTIC PERIOD

The Hellenistic period is quite different from the classical period that preceded it. Now not only do foreign influences creep into the Greek world view, but many of its writings are produced on foreign soil. In Alexandria, Egypt, the poets THEOCRITUS, Bion, and Moschus developed the conventions of pastoral poetry, and CALLIMACHUS and his disciples refined the elegant short poem. In Rome POLYBIUS (see Vol. 3) wrote a history in straightforward prose, analyzing and describing the rise of Rome as a power in the world. In Judaea and the Jewish diaspora, a whole corpus of Greek literature developed (including the Apocrypha, the pseudepigrapha, PHILO JUDAEUS (see Vol. 4), FLAVIUS JOSEPHUS (see Vols. 3 and 4), and even the New Testament). Besides the revival of old forms, as in the epic *Argonautica* (third century B.C.) by APOLLONIUS RHODIUS, many new forms were created. Comedy underwent a major transformation; instead of the robust critique of political, social, and sexual matters as found in Aristophanes, New Comedy focuses on family relations (the stern father, the irresponsible son, the tricky slave, etc.). Biography and the novel had precursors in the earlier period, but it is in the late Hellenistic times that these forms reached their culmination: biography in PLUTARCH (see Vol. 3) and novels in LONGUS and HELIODORUS. Satire developed out of the earlier Cynic-Stoic diatribes and reached its epitome in the dialogues of LUCIAN. Greek philosophy charted a new course in this period with the birth of Epicureanism and Stoicism and other important movements in the history of Western thought.

BYZANTINE PERIOD

The triumph of Rome in the political sphere and the rise of Christianity in the spiritual realm radically transformed the world, and ancient Greece and its literary products became a prized heritage. The few remains of secular poetry from the Byzantine period are mostly imitative of classical models; it is rather in religious and folk poetry that the period's great literary activity lies. The first outstanding writer, St. Romanos the Melode (d. 556), wrote some 1,000 hymns, of which about 80 survive; St. John of Damascus (675–749) composed hymns that have even come down to survive within English hymnbooks; and Symeon the Mystic (949–1022) wrote passionate but cryptic hymns. In secular poetry, the folk epics stand out. *The Epic of Digenes Akritas*, for example, is a long oral poem about a heroic border guard between Moslem and Christian lands. Originating in the tenth century, it was written down in several versions from the twelfth to the seventeenth centuries.

In prose the significant writers were scholars and historians: PROCOPIUS (see Vol. 3), the secretary of Justinian's general, who recorded the history of Justinian's wars; Michael Psellus (eleventh century), a professor of philosophy who consorted with princes and chronicled their regimes; and Anna Comnena (twelfth century), the woman who wrote a brilliant account of the reign of her father, the Emperor Alexius I.

The fall of Constantinople to the Ottoman Turks in 1453 ended the Byzantine period.

CLASSICAL, HELLENISTIC AND BYZANTINE LITERATURE

History and Criticism

Alsop, Joseph W. *From the Silent Earth: A Report of the Greek Bronze Age*. Greenwood 1981 repr. of 1964 ed. o.p. Introduction by Maurice Bowra.

Bieber, Margaret. *The History of the Greek and Roman Theater*. rev. ed. Princeton U. Pr. 1980 o.p. Indispensable for understanding the appearance of ancient theaters.

Boardman, J., J. Griffin, and O. Murray. *The Oxford History of the Classical World*. OUP 1986 $49.95. ISBN 0-19-872112-9. Treats the political, social and cultural history of the classical world.

Bonner, Robert J. *Aspects of Athenian Democracy*. Russel Sage 1967 repr. of 1933 ed. o.p.

______. *Lawyers and Litigants in Ancient Athens: The Genesis of the Legal Profession*. Ayer repr. of 1927 ed. $20.00. ISBN 0-405-19013-1. Examines the origins of legal practices and their impact on daily life and literature in ancient Greece and Rome.

Bonner, Robert J. and Gertrude S. Smith. *The Administration of Justice from Homer to Aristotle*. 2 vols. AMS Pr. repr. of 1938 ed. $60.00. ISBN 0-404-00650-7

Bowra, Cecil M. *Early Greek Elegists*. Cooper Sq. 1969 repr. of 1938 ed. o.p. Elegiac poetry in Greek history; a series of lectures on Greek elegy.

______. *The Greek Experience*. NAL-Dutton $5.95. ISBN 0-452-00997-9. Greek history and criticism.

Cary, Max. *A History of the Greek World: 323–146 B.C.* Methuen 2nd rev. ed. 1972 repr. of 1951 ed. o.p. Greek civilization to 146 B.C.

Cottrell, Leonard. *The Bull of Minos*. Amereon Ltd. $17.95. ISBN 0-88411-469-4. Introduction to Greek Bronze Age archeology.

de Romilly, J. *A Short History of Greek Literature*. U. Ch. Pr. 1985 $27.00. ISBN 0-226-14311-2. Most reasonable and succinct account of ancient Greek literature currently available in English.

Dickinson, G. Lowes. *The Greek View of Life*. Greenwood repr. of 1958 ed. $35.00. ISBN 0-313-21195-7. Greek civilization to 146 B.C.

Dodds, E. *The Ancient Concept of Progress and Other Essays on Greek Literature and Belief*. OUP 1986 $21.00. ISBN 0-19-814377-X. Essays written around interest in ancient representations of strong personalities in extreme situations.

Dover, Kenneth. *Ancient Greek Literature*. OUP 1980 $14.95. ISBN 0-19-289124-3. A collection of popular essays by such outstanding scholars as Dover, M. L. West, and K. Griffin on different periods of Greek literature.

Eastling, P. E. and B. M. Knox. *Cambridge History of Classical Literature: Greek Literature, Vol. 1*. Cambridge U. Pr. 1985 $110.00. ISBN 0-521-21042-9. Essays by major scholars on authors, movements, and *realia* in classical antiquity.

Ehrenberg, Victor L. *Society and Civilization in Greece and Rome*. HUP 1964 $8.95. ISBN 0-674-81510-6. Social life and customs in Greece and Rome.

Else, Gerald F. *The Origin and Early Form of Greek Tragedy*. HUP 1965 o.p. A history of the Greek tragedy; encompasses a broad view of Greek dramatists and their craft.

Finley, Moses I. *The Ancient Greeks: An Introduction to Their Life and Thought*. Viking Penguin 1987 $9.95. ISBN 0-14-055223-5. A brief history of Greek culture from its beginnings to Roman times.

Flaceliere, Robert. *Love in Ancient Greece*. Trans. by James Cleugh. Greenwood 1973 repr. of 1962 ed. o.p. By a leading French authority, who corrects some popular misconceptions regarding Greek attitudes toward love, sex, and marriage.

Frankel, Hermann. *Early Greek Poetry and Philosophy*. Trans. by James Willis. Irvington 1975 $49.50. ISBN 0-8290-0985-X. An excellent discussion of the literature and the intellectual motifs of Greek authors prior to the fifth century B.C.

Graves, Robert. *The Greek Myths*. Viking Penguin 1992 $16.00. ISBN 0-14-007602-6. An idiosyncratic and amusing presentation of the myths.

Grube, G. M.. *Greek and Roman Critics*. U. of Toronto Pr. repr. of 1968 ed. $96.00. ISBN 0-317-27036-2

Guthrie, W. K. *Greek Philosophers: From Thales to Aristotle*. HarpC $10.00. ISBN 0-06-131008-5. Discusses ancient philosophers and their impact on modern thought.

______. *The Greeks and Their Gods*. Beacon Pr. 1955 $18.95. ISBN 0-8070-5793-2. Religion in the Greek world and their gods.

______. *A History of Greek Philosophy*. 2 vols. Cambridge U. Pr. 1979 $34.95. ISBNs 0-521-29420-1, 0-521-29421-5. Excellent summaries.

______. *Socrates*. Cambridge U. Pr. 1992 $19.95. ISBN 0-521-09667-7

Hadas, Moses. *Ancilla to Classical Reading*. Col. U. Pr. 1961 $17.00. ISBN 0-231-08517-6. A useful companion for the reader of Greek and Latin literature.

Hadas, Moses. *History of Greek Literature*. Col. U. Pr. 1950 $42.00. ISBN 0-231-01767-1. Dedicated to interpreting Greek literature for the twentieth-century audience.

Hamilton, Edith. *The Echo of Greece*. *Norton Lib*. Norton 1964 $7.95. ISBN 0-393-00231-4. A popular interpretation that includes studies of Aristotle, Demosthenes, Alexander the Great, and Menander.

______. *The Greek Way*. Norton 1983 repr. of 1930 ed. $4.95. ISBN 0-393-00230-6. Provides a view of Greek art and thought at the height of Greek achievements.

______. *Mythology*. Little 1942 $9.95. ISBN 0-316-34114-2. A standard retelling of the stories.

Hammond, N. G., and H. H. Scullard, eds. *Oxford Classical Dictionary*. OUP 1970 $45.00 ISBN 0-19-869117-3. An invaluable volume of articles, each with a short bibliography, by experts in all phases of classical scholarship.

Harrison, Jane. *Epilegomena to the Study of Greek Religion, and Themis: A Study of the Social Origins of Greek Religion*. Holmes Pub. 1991 $7.95. ISBN 0-55818-179-2. By a scholar who provoked criticism but also won the admiration of such great scholars as Gilbert Murray, who contributed the "Jane Harrison Memorial Lecture" to this volume.

______. *Prolegomena to the Study of Greek Religion.* Ayer 1976 repr. of 1922 ed. $57.50. ISBN 0-405-07018-7. A scholarly challenge to bring about a consensus about Greek thought in religion.

Harvey, Paul, ed. *Oxford Companion to Classical Literature.* OUP 1989 $45.00. ISBN 0-19-281490-7. A valuable reference work that is comprehensive, concise, and well written.

Havelock, Eric A. *The Literate Revolution in Greece and Its Cultural Consequences.* Princeton U. Pr. 1982 o.p. A discussion of the transformation of literature from an oral to a written form and its significance in early Greece.

Highet, Gilbert. *The Classical Tradition.* OUP 1949 $14.95. ISBN 0-19-500206-7. An admirably rich volume that takes into account the many ways the classical tradition has shaped European and American literature. Scholarly, humanistic, yet never pedantic.

Howatson, M. C. *The Oxford Companion to Classical Literature.* 2nd ed. OUP 1989 $45.00. ISBN 0-19-866121-5. Comprehensive reference source for classical literature.

Huxley, G. L. *Early Sparta.* Biblio Dist. 1972 o.p. A careful study analyzing primary materials about Sparta from 1200 to 490 B.C. (most accounts are Athenian).

Jaeger, Werner. *Paideia: The Ideals of Greek Culture.* 3 vols. Trans. by Gilbert Highet. OUP Vol. 1 1945 $39.95. ISBN 0-19-500399-3. Vol. 2 1943 $39.95. ISBN 0-19-500592-9. Vol. 3 1944 $39.95. ISBN 0-19-500593-7. Brilliant analysis of Greek culture by an eminent authority on intellectual history.

Jones, John. *On Aristotle and Greek Tragedy.* Stanford U. Pr. repr. of 1962 ed. $11.95. ISBN 0-8047-1093-7. An ascerbic discussion dealing with the presence of Greek literary tradition in Western literature.

Kennedy, George. *The Art of Persuasion in Greece.* Bks. Demand repr. of 1963 ed. $94.20. ISBN 0-8357-6027-8. An excellent history of Greek oratory.

Kerenyi, Karoly. *The Religion of the Greeks and Romans.* Greenwood 1973 repr. of 1962 ed. $35.00. ISBN 0-8371-6605-5. Combines Greek and Roman mythology, philology, classic literature, and Jungian psychology. A stimulating view of how the Greeks and Romans faced the absolute.

Kitto, Humphrey D. *Form and Meaning in Drama: A Study of Six Greek Plays and of Hamlet.* Methuen 1979 o.p. A comparison between the style of Greek tragedy and that of Shakespeare's *Hamlet.*

______. *Greek Tragedy: A Literary Study.* Routledge Chapman & Hall 3rd rev. ed. 1966 $15.95. ISBN 0-416-68900-0. A scholarly discussion of intertextual designs in Greek tragedies.

______. *The Greeks.* Peter Smith 1988 $18.50. ISBN 0-8446-6303-4. "Written in [Kitto's] normally graceful, witty, and also opinionated way, it gives a truly wonderful insight into most aspects of ancient Greek civilization" (*LJ*).

Lattimore, Richmond. *The Poetry of Greek Tragedy.* Johns Hopkins 1958 o.p. Penetrating critical study.

______. *Story Patterns in Greek Tragedy.* U. of Mich. Pr. 1964 o.p. Examines characterization and character development in Greek tragedy; covers different types of tragedies.

Lempriere, J. A. *A Classical Dictionary.* 2 vols. Gordon Pr. $600.00. ISBN 0-87968-878-5. Still very useful because of its wealth of anecdotes and literary references.

Lesky, Albin A. *A History of Greek Literature.* T. Y. Crowell 1976 o.p. A superb comprehensive history that discusses in detail all literary genres through the early Christian eras. Full summaries of major works and up-to-date extensive bibliographies.

Lloyd-Jones, Hugh. *The Justice of Zeus.* U. CA Pr. 1971 $12.95. ISBN 0-520-04688-9. Religion in Grecian times; the classical experience.

Luce, T. James, ed. *Ancient Writers: Greece and Rome.* 2 vols. Scribner 1982 $160.00. ISBN 0-684-16595-3. Essays by many respected scholars on the major authors of ancient Greece—some pedantic, others full of insights.

MacKendrick, Paul L. *The Greek Stones Speak: The Story of Archaeology in Greek Lands.* Norton 1983 $24.95. ISBN 0-393-30111-7. A polished study with a wealth of detail; covers over 2,000 years from the era of Homeric legend to Roman occupation.

Marrou, H. I. *History of Education in Antiquity*. U. of Wis. Pr. 1982 $14.95. ISBN 0-299-08814-6. An indispensable, masterful work.

Murray, Gilbert. *History of Ancient Greek Literature*. Continuum 1966 o.p. "Murray combined erudition, imagination, sensitivity, and enthusiasm with an urbane narrative style to make the reading of his book an exciting intellectual adventure" (*LJ*).

———. *The Rise of the Greek Epic*. *Oxford Pap. Ser.* OUP 1934 o.p. A series of lectures given at Harvard University; history and literary criticism of Homer.

Pausanias. *Description of Greece*. 6 vols. Biblo 1897 $150.00. ISBN 0-8196-0144-6. A guidebook for tourists, written in the second century A.D.

Pearson, Lionel. *Popular Ethics in Ancient Greece*. Stanford U. Pr. 1962 $29.50. ISBN 0-8047-0102-4. Covers ethical attitudes of the marketplace and concepts found in Homer, Hesiod, Theognis, Solon, and fifth-century dramatists.

Pendlebury, John D. *The Archeology of Crete*. Biblo $28.00. ISBN 0-8196-0121-7. A firsthand account of the excavation in Crete.

Pickard-Cambridge, A. W. *Dithyramb, Tragedy and Comedy*. 1927. OUP 2nd rev. ed. 1962 o.p. A learned work on the beginnings of Greek drama.

———. *Dramatic Festivals of Athens*. Ed. by J. P. Gould. OUP 1989 $92.50. ISBN 0-19-814258-7. A comprehensive account of the festivals by a foremost scholar.

———. *The Theatre of Dionysus in Athens*. OUP 1946 o.p. A history from the earliest days to the time of the Roman Empire.

Polybius. *The Histories of Polybius, Discoursing of the Warres betwixt the Romanes and Carthaginenses*. Trans. by Christopher Watson. Walter J. Johnson 1969 repr. of 1568 ed. $55.00. ISBN 90-221-0132-0. Records the rapid rise of Rome, as seen by a Greek historian of the second century A.D.

Renault, Mary. *The King Must Die*. Random 1988 $10.00. ISBN 0-394-75104-3. An exciting version of the story of Theseus and Ariadne in Crete.

Reynolds, L., and W. Wilson. *Scribes and Scholars: A Guide to the Transmission of Greek and Latin Literature*. OUP 1991 $89.00. ISBN 0-19-872145-5. A simple introduction for beginners to the field of classical studies—preservations, history of education, and scholarship in ancient times.

Richter, Gisela M. *Sculpture and Sculptors of the Greeks*. Yale U. Pr. 4th ed. 1971 o.p. The standard reference book on Greek sculpture.

Robinson, Charles A., Jr. *Athens in the Age of Pericles*. U. of Okla. Pr. 1971 $57.95. ISBN 0-8061-0935-1. Sharp, revealing, and pertinent comments.

Rose, H. J. *A Handbook of Greek Literature*. NAL-Dutton rev. ed. 1950 o.p. A brief work, excellent for quick reference.

———. *Religion in Greece and Rome*. HarpC o.p. A sophisticated, terse analysis.

Rostovtzeff, Mikhail. *Social and Economic History of the Hellenistic World*. OUP 3 vols. 1986 repr. of 1941 ed. $109.00. ISBN 0-19-814230-7. A definitive study by an eminent historian.

Smith, William, ed. *Dictionary of Greek and Roman Antiquities*. 2 vols. Longwood 1977 repr. of 1890 ed. o.p. All of the Smith dictionaries listed here are valuable reference tools.

———. *Dictionary of Greek and Roman Biography and Mythology*. 3 vols. Ams Pr. repr. of 1890 ed. $245.00. ISBN 0-404-06130-3. Includes a number of biographies and many engravings from wood carvings.

———. *Dictionary of Greek and Roman Geography*. 2 vols. AMS Pr. repr. of 1873 ed. $140.00. ISBN 0-404-06134-6. Classical geography; includes illustrations and maps.

Snell, Bruno. *The Discovery of the Mind in Early Greek Philosophy and Literature*. Dover 1982 $7.50. ISBN 0-486-24264-1. A stimulating view of intellectual history.

———. *Poetry and Society: The Role of Poetry in Ancient Greece*. *Select Bibliographies Repr. Ser.* Ayer repr. of 1961 ed. $14.00. ISBN 0-8369-5965-5. Examines the different facets of poetry within Greek culture and their significance to Grecian society.

Ventris, M., and J. Chadwick. *Documents in Mycenaean Greek*. Cambridge U. Pr. 1974 $160.00. ISBN 0-521-08558-6. Explains how Ventris, a British architect, deciphered one of the last remaining lost languages—that of Homer's heroes—by using clay tablets found in the ruins of King Minos's palace at Knossos, Crete.

Vermeule, Emily T. *Greece in the Bronze Age*. U. Ch. Pr. 1972 $17.95. ISBN 0-226-85354-3. "Professor Vermeule . . . presents a superb, unhackneyed, up-to-date, overall and detailed view of prehistoric Greek mainland civilization, ca. 6500–1100 B.C. . . . Generously documented and illustrated" (*LJ*).

Warner, Rex. *The Stories of the Greeks*. FS&G 1978 o.p. A one-volume edition of the author's three books on the gods, heroes, and wars of ancient Greece: *Men and Gods, Greeks and Trojans*, and *The Vengeance of the Gods*.

Webster, T. B. L. *Studies in Later Greek Comedy*. Greenwood 1981 repr. of 1970 ed. $45.00. ISBN 0-313-23050-1. Discusses comedies produced between the beginning of the fourth century B.C. and the end of the third century B.C.

Whibley, Leonard. *A Companion to Greek Studies*. Folcroft 1979 repr. of 1916 ed. o.p. An older but still useful collection of chapters on different aspects of Greek culture.

Collections—General

Auden, W. H., ed. *The Portable Greek Reader. Viking Portable Lib.* Viking Penguin 1977 $11.00. ISBN 0-14-015039-0. Thematic selections from Homer to Galen; includes a very useful chronological outline of classical Greek civilization.

Edmonds, J. M., trans. *Greek Bucolic Poets: Theocritus, Bion, and Moschus. Loeb Class. Lib.* HUP $15.50. ISBN 0-674-99031-5. Collection of Greek pastoral poetry with discussion.

______. *Greek Elegy, Iambus, and Anacreontea. Loeb Class. Lib.* 2 vols. HUP $15.50 ea. ISBN N/A. Includes works by all of the Greek elegiac and iambic poets from Callinus to Crates.

______. *Greek Lyric. Loeb Class. Lib.* HUP 3 vols. $15.50 ea. Includes works by all of the Greek lyric poets from Eumelus to Timotheus, with the exception of Pindar.

Fowler, Barbara H., ed. *Hellenistic Poetry: An Anthology*. U. of Wis. Pr. 1990 $37.50. ISBN 0-299-12530-0. For undergraduates, as well as the general public; book of poems interpreted.

Gow, Andrew S., and D. L. Page. *The Greek Anthology: Garland of Philip and Other Contemporary Epigrams*. 2 vols. Cambridge U. Pr. 1968 o.p. An admirable anthology, done with sympathy and skill, of an original collection made by Constantius Cephales about 925 A.D. (often called the "Palatine Anthology"). Contains more than 6,000 poems classified according to type and subject and written by 320 authors beginning in the seventh century B.C.

Grant, Michael, ed. *Greek Literature: An Anthology. Penguin Class Ser.* Viking Penguin 1977 $6.95. ISBN 0-14-044323-1. A good anthology of judiciously chosen selections.

Hadas, Moses, trans. and ed. *Three Greek Romances*. Irvington 1964 $29.50. ISBN 0-8290-2405-0. Contains Longus, *Daphnis and Chloe;* Xenophon, *The Ephesian Tale;* and Chrysostom, *Hunters of Euboia.*

Higham, Thomas F., and C. M. Bowra, eds. *Oxford Book of Greek Verse in Translation.* OUP o.p. Comprehensive and skillfully translated.

Jebb, Richard C., ed. *The Attic Orators: Selections from Antiphon, Andocides, Lysias, Isocrates and Isaeus.* 2 vols. Russell Sage 1962 repr. of 1875 ed. o.p. A history and criticism of Greek orations.

Maidment, K. J., and J. O. Burtt, trans. *Minor Attic Orators. Loeb Class Lib.* 2 vols. HUP $15.50 ea. ISBNs 0-674-99340-3, 0-674-99434-5. Includes Antiphon and Andocides; Lycurgus, Dinarchus, Demades, Hyperides.

Murphy, Charles T., Kevin Guinagh, and Whitney J. Oates, eds. *Greek and Roman Classics in Translation.* McKay 1947 o.p. Five complete plays—*Prometheus Bound, Oedipus the King, Hippolytus, The Clouds, The Adelphi*—and selections from many writers.

Collections—Greek Drama

Arnott, Peter D., trans. *Three Greek Plays for the Theatre.* Ind. U. Pr. 1961 o.p. *The Cyclops, Medea,* and *The Frogs,* prepared especially for the actor.

Arrowsmith, William, ed. *Greek Tragedies in New Translations.* 15 vols. OUP 1973–81 o.p. A series of readable translations with an introduction and notes at the back of each volume.

Casson, Lionel, trans. and ed. *Masters of Ancient Comedy: Selections from Aristophanes, Menander, Plautus and Terence.* T. Y. Crowell 1967 o.p. Greek and Latin comedy.

Cooper, Lane, ed. *Fifteen Greek Plays.* Trans. by Gilbert Murray. OUP 1943 o.p. Plays by Aeschylus, Sophocles, Euripides, and Aristophanes translated by Murray and others.

Fitts, Dudley, ed. *Greek Plays in Modern Translation.* H. Holt & Co. 1947 o.p. *The Trojan Women, Agamemnon, Electra, Medea, Hippolytus, Alcestis, King Oedipus, Oedipus at Colonus, Antigone, Prometheus Vinctus, Oresteia.*

Grene, David, and *Richmond Lattimore,* eds. *The Complete Greek Tragedies.* U. Ch. Pr. 1942–60 o.p. The works of Aeschylus, Sophocles, and Euripides.

Hadas, Moses, ed. *Greek Drama.* Bantam 1984 $4.50. ISBN 0-553-21221-4. Contains Aeschylus: *Agamemnon* and *Eumenides;* Sophocles: *Antigone, Oedipus the King,* and *Philoctetes;* Aristophanes: *The Frogs;* Euripides: *Hippolytus, Medea,* and *Trojan Women.*

Havelock, E. A., and Maynard Mack, eds. *Drama Series.* P-H o.p. Individual plays with a good scholarly introduction and commentaries on the bottom of the page.

MacKendrick, Paul L., and Herbert M. Howe, eds. *Classics in Translation.* 2 vols. U. of Wis. Pr. 1959 $14.95 ea. Most translations made for these volumes. Includes Aeschylus, *Agamemnon* (L. MacNeice); Sophocles, *Antigone* (M. F. Neufeld); Euripides, *Medea* (W. R. Agard); Aristophanes, *Frogs* (J. G. Hawthorne).

Oates, Whitney J., and Eugene O'Neill, Jr., eds. *The Complete Greek Drama.* 2 vols. Random 1938 o.p. All the extant tragedies of Aeschylus, Sophocles, and Euripides and the comedies of Aristophanes and Menander, in a variety of translations.

______. *Seven Famous Greek Plays.* Random 1955 $7.95. ISBN 0-394-70125-9. Contains Aeschylus: *Agamemnon* and *Prometheus Bound;* Sophocles: *Oedipus the King* and *Antigone;* Euripides: *Medea* and *Alcestis;* Aristophanes: *The Frogs.*

Reardon, B. P., ed. *Collected Ancient Greek Novels.* U. CA Pr. 1989 $75.00. ISBN 0-520-04303-0. Serious study of oddly neglected literature.

Robinson, Charles A., Jr., ed. *Anthology of Greek Drama. Rinehart Ed.* 2 vols. HarBraceJ repr. of 1949 ed. $14.50. ISBN 0-03-009415-1. Vol. 1: *Agamemnon, Oedipus Rex, Antigone, Medea, Hippolytus, Lysistrata.* Vol. 2: *Prometheus Bound, Choephoroe, Eumenides, Philoctetes, Oedipus at Colonus, The Trojan Women, The Bacchae, The Clouds, The Frogs.*

Trypanis, C. *The Penguin Book of Greek Verse.* Viking Penguin 1988 $9.95. ISBN 0-14-058595-5. A fine collection illustrating the range of Greek poetry from antiquity to the present.

CHRONOLOGY OF AUTHORS

Hesiod. c.700 B.C.
Homer. c.700 B.C.
Sappho. fl. c.610–c.580 B.C.
Aesop. fl. 570 B.C.
Aeschylus. 525–456 B.C.
Pindar. c.518–c.438 B.C.
Sophocles. c.496–406 B.C.
Euripides. c.485–c.406 B.C.
Aristophanes. c.450–c.385 B.C.
Demosthenes. 385?–322 B.C.
Theophrastus. c.371–287 B.C.
Menander. c.342–c.292 B.C.
Theocritus. c.310–c.250 B.C.
Callimachus. c.305–c.240 B.C.
Apollonius Rhodius. 3rd century B.C.
Longinus. c.1st century A.D.
Longus. fl. 2nd or 3rd century A.D.?
Lucian. c.120-c.185?
Heliodorus of Emesa. fl. 220–250

AESCHYLUS. 525–456 B.C.

Aeschylus was born at Eleusis of a noble family. He fought at the Battle of Marathon (490 B.C.), where a small Greek band heroically defeated the invading Persians. At the time of his death in Sicily, Athens was in its golden age. In all of his extant works, his intense love of Greece and Athens finds expression.

Of the nearly 90 plays attributed to him, only 7 survive. These are *The Persians* (produced in 472 B.C.), *Seven against Thebes* (467 B.C.), *The Oresteia* (458 B.C.)—which includes *Agamemnon, Libation Bearers,* and *Eumenides* (or *Furies*)—*Suppliants* (463 B.C.), and *Prometheus Bound* (c.460 B.C.). Six of the seven present mythological stories. The ornate language creates a mood of tragedy and reinforces the already stylized character of the Greek theater.

Aeschylus called his prodigious output "dry scraps from Homer's banquet," because his plots and solemn language are derived from the epic poet. But a more accurate summation of Aeschylus would emphasize his grandeur of mind and spirit and the tragic dignity of his language. Because of his patriotism and belief in divine providence, there is a profound moral order to his plays. Characters such as Clytemnestra, Orestes, and Prometheus personify a great passion or principle. As individuals they conflict with divine will, but, ultimately, justice prevails.

Aeschylus's introduction of the second actor made real theater possible, because the two could address each other and act several roles. His successors imitated his costumes, dances, spectacular effects, long descriptions, choral refrains, invocations, and dialogue. SWINBURNE's (see Vol. 1) enthusiasm for *The Oresteia* sums up all praises of Aeschylus; he called it simply "the greatest achievement of the human mind." Because of his great achievements, Aeschylus might be considered the "father of tragedy."

PLAYS BY AESCHYLUS

Aeschylus I: Oresteia, Agamemnon, the Libation Bearers, the Eumenides. Trans. and ed. by David Grene and Richmond Lattimore. *Complete Greek Tragedies.* U. Ch. Pr. 1969 $7.95. ISBN 0-226-30778-6. Excellent and authoritative modern translations that convey the complexity and the metrics of the originals (also *Aeschylus II*).

Aeschylus II, Four Tragedies: Prometheus Bound, Seven against Thebes, the Persians, the Suppliant Maidens. Trans. by Seth G. Benardete and David Grene. Ed. by David Grene and Richmond Lattimore. *Complete Greek Tragedies* U. Ch. Pr. 1969 $6.95. ISBN 0-226-30779-4

Agamemnon. Ed. by J. D. Denniston and Denys Page. OUP 1987 $19.95. ISBN 0-19-872130-7. Eduard Fraenkel's introduction, critical edition of the Greek text, English translation, and commentary represent the best of modern scholarship on this most difficult and profound play.

The House of Atreus: Adapted from the Oresteia. Ed. by John Lewin. Bks. Demand repr. of 1966 ed. $29.30. ISBN 0-317-41661-8. An adaptation of the trilogy *Agamemnon, The Libation Bearers,* and *The Furies* for contemporary stage presentation. Used by the Minnesota Theater Company for its production at the Tyrone Guthrie Theater in Minneapolis.

The Oresteia. Trans. by David Grene and Wendy D. O'Flaherty. U. Ch. Pr. 1989 $32.50. ISBN 0-226-00771-5

The Persians. Trans. by Janet Lembke and C. John Herington. Ed. by William Arrowsmith. *Greek Tragedy in New Translations.* OUP 1981 $24.95. ISBN 0-19-502777-9

Prometheus Bound. Trans. by James Scully and C. John Herington. Ed. by William Arrowsmith. *Greek Tragedy in New Translations.* OUP 1990 $16.95. ISBN 0-19-506165-9

Seven against Thebes. Trans. by Anthony Hecht and Helen Bacon. *Greek Tragedy in New Translations*. OUP 1991 repr. of 1973 ed. $6.95. ISBN 0-19-507007-0

The Suppliants. Trans. by Janet Lembke. Ed. by William Arrowsmith. *Greek Tragedy in New Translations*. OUP 1975 $19.95. ISBN 0-19-501933-4

Tragedies. 2 vols. Trans. by Herbert Weir Smith. *Loeb Class Lib*. HUP 1922–26 $14.50 ea. ISBNs 0-674-99160-5, 0-674-99161-3. Vol. 1: *The Suppliant Maidens* (c.463 B.C.); *The Persians* (472 B.C.); *Prometheus* (c.460 B.C.); *Seven against Thebes* (467 B.C.). Vol. 2: *Agememnon, The Libation Bearers*, and *Eumenides* (all 458 B.C.); also Fragments.

BOOKS ABOUT AESCHYLUS

Bloom, H., ed. *Aeschylus' The Oresteia. Modern Critical Interpretation Series*. Chelsea Hse. 1988 $29.95. ISBN 0-87754-903-6. A collection of important essays.

Finley, John H., Jr. *Pindar and Aeschylus*. HUP 1955 o.p. A classic study of these two literary giants.

Gagarin, Michael. *Aeschylean Drama*. U. CA Pr. 1976 $32.50. ISBN 0-520-02943-7. A study of ideas and themes.

Goldhill, Simon. *Aeschylus: "The Oresteia."* Cambridge U. Pr. 1993. ISBN 0-521-40293-X

Herington, C. J. *Aeschylus*. Yale U. Pr. 1986 $9.95. ISBN 0-300-03562-4. Excellent introduction to Aeschylus's times, his plays, and the early Athenian theater.

______. *Author of the Prometheus Bound*. U. of Tex. Pr. 1970 o.p. An intelligent discussion of problems in the "Prometheus."

McCall, M., Jr., ed. *Aeschylus: A Collection of Critical Essays*. P-H 1972 o.p.

Rosenmeyer, Thomas G. *The Art of Aeschylus*. U. of CA Pr. 1982 $13.95. ISBN 0-520-04608-0. Focuses on language and character rather than on historical background.

Sheppard, J. T. *Aeschylus and Sophocles: Their Work and Influence*. Cooper Sq. repr. of 1930 ed. o.p. A thorough investigation of the relationship between the modern mind and ancient thought.

Smyth, Herbert W. *Aeschylean Tragedy*. Biblo 1969 repr. of 1924 ed. $23.00. ISBN 0-8196-0235-3. Written by an American authority on Aeschylus.

Solmsen, Friedrich. *Hesiod and Aeschylus*. Ed. by W. R. Connor. Johnson Repr. repr. of 1949 ed. o.p. A sophisticated study of the relationship between the two poets; by a leading Hellenist.

Spatz, Lois. *Aeschylus. Twayne's World Authors Ser*. G. K. Hall 1982 $16.95. ISBN 0-8057-6522-0. Good general introduction to Aeschylus's plays and the period; includes chronology and bibliography.

Thalmann, William G. *Dramatic Art in Aeschylus's Seven Against Thebes*. Yale U. Pr. 1978 $25.00. ISBN 0-300-02219-0

Thomson, George. *Aeschylus and Athens: A Study of Athenian Drama and Democracy*. Haskell 1969 repr. of 1940 ed. $75.00. ISBN 0-8383-0723-X

Winnington-Ingraham, R.P. *Studies in Aeschylus*. Cambridge U. Pr. o.p.

AESOP. c.620 B.C.–c.560 B.C.

Little is known about Aesop, who is said to have composed the animal Fables. It is known that he lived during the second half of the sixth century B.C. and references by ARISTOPHANES and SOCRATES indicate that fables bearing Aesop's name were popular around the end of the fifth century. B.C.

Supposedly, Aesop was a slave, perhaps from the Greek region of Phrygia, who was later given his freedom. Legend places him on the Greek island of Samos, from where he went to the court of King Croesus of Lydia, Greece, and became a valued messenger of the king. On one of his missions to the Greek shrine at Delphi, he supposedly angered the priests with his blasphemous wit and was thrown over a cliff to his death.

There is considerable doubt about how many, if any, of the fables attributed to Aesop were actually written by him. Many of their sources have been traced to earlier literature, suggesting that Aesop was more a collector and a recorder of tales than an original composer of them. The collections known as *Aesop's Fables* were assembled in the second or third century A.D., although the bulk of the material must have evolved several centuries earlier. Versions of the fables were rendered into prose during the Middle Ages.

Short Story Collections by Aesop

Aesop's Fables. Ed. by Ann McGovern. Scholastic Inc. 1990 $2.75. ISBN 0-590-43880-8

Fables of Aesop. Trans. by S. A. Hanford. Viking Penguin 1954 $4.95. ISBN 0-14-044043-7. Collection of 207 very short tales about animals, each one illustrating a moral lesson.

Books about Aesop

Henryson, R. *Moral Fables of Aesop.* U. Notre Dame Pr. 1987

Jacobs, Joseph, ed. *The Fables of Aesop.* Schocken 1966 $8.95. ISBN 0-8052-0138-6. A careful account of the transmission of the fables from antiquity through the Middle Ages to modern times.

Perry, Ben E. *The Ancient Romances: A Literary-Historical Account of Their Origins.* U. CA Pr. 1967 $47.50. ISBN 0-520-01003-5. Places Aesop in the romance tradition.

——— *Studies in the Text History of the Life and Fables of Aesop.* Scholars Pr. 1981 $22.50. ISBN 0-89130-534-3

Perry, Ben E., and Richard M. Dorson, eds. *Aesopica: A Series of Texts Relating to Aesop or Ascribed to Him Closely Connected with the Literary Tradition That Bears His Name.* Vol. 1. Ayer 1980 repr. of 1952 ed. $74.50. ISBN 0-405-13337-5. A valuable source book with ancient testimonies about Aesop.

APOLLONIUS RHODIUS. 3rd century B.C.

This Greek epic poet was a scholar of some note—a fact reflected in his main work, which is based on the legend of the Argonauts, Jason's search for the Golden Fleece. Somewhat pedantic, *The Argonautica* is enlivened by the character of Medea. Virgil used Apollonius as a source for his portrayal of Dido in the *Aeneid.* Apollonius may have been librarian of the great library of Alexandria built by Ptolemy II and certainly studied in Alexandria with Callimachus. His name is derived from his supposed retirement in Rhodes, probably after a literary feud with Callimachus over the relative merits of the long traditional epic as opposed to short, finished poems.

Poetry by Apollonius

The Argonautica. Ed. by W. R. Connor. Trans. by R. C. Seaton. *Loeb Class. Lib.* HUP 1912 $15.50. ISBN 0-674-99001-3. Text and translation recommended.

Voyage of Argo. Trans. by Emil V. Rieu. Viking Penguin 1959 $7.95. ISBN 0-14-044085-2

Book about Apollonius

Beye, Charles R. *Epic and Romance in the Argonautica.* S. Ill. U. Pr. 1982 $29.95. ISBN 0-8093-1020-1. A study of *The Argonautica* as living literature and important history.

ARISTOPHANES. c.450–c.385 B.C.

Aristophanes is the great master of Athenian Old Comedy. In addition to the 11 of his plays that are extant, there are 32 titles and many fragments. Very little is known of his life. Greek drama had reached its peak and was declining when be began to write. His comedies are full of a peculiar mixture of broad political, social, and literary satire; discussions of large ideas; and boisterous vulgarities. His characters are like normal human beings in absurd and preposterous situations. His Greek is exceptionally beautiful, and his idyllic lyrics are delightful.

Edith Hamilton says: "To read Aristophanes is in some sort like reading an Athenian comic paper. All the life of Athens is there: the politics of the day and the politicians; the war party and the anti-war party; pacifism, votes for women, free trade, fiscal reform, complaining taxpayers, educational theories, the current religious and literary talk—everything, in short, that interested the average citizen. All was food for his mockery. He was the speaking picture of the follies and foibles of his day." His sharp barbs were aimed at such targets as SOCRATES (see Vol. 4), EURIPIDES, and AESCHYLUS. Sparing no class, no profession, and no age group, his plays provide insights into the position of women, the contemporaneous literary and political fashions, and class relations in fifth-century Athens, the Athens of Pericles.

PLAYS BY ARISTOPHANES

The Acharnians. Ed. by W. R. Connor. Ayer 1979 repr. of 1909 ed. $27.50. ISBN 0-405-11450-8. An assault on the governmental policies of Athens; precedes *The Knights*, which treats the same subject matter.

The Birds. Ed. by Sommerstein. David Brown 1987 $49.95. ISBN 0-85668-287-X. A fantasy about a kingdom of birds and men in the sky.

The Clouds. Ed. by Kenneth J. Dover. OUP 1989 $24.95. ISBN 0-19-814395-8. Satirizes Socrates by portraying him as a wily sophist who teaches men to cheat others through cunning argument.

Complete Plays. Ed. by Moses Hadas. Bantam 1984 $4.95. ISBN 0-553-21343-1

The Congresswomen (Ecclesiazusae). Trans. by Richmond Lattimore. NAL-Dutton 1970 o.p. Women take control of Athens and put into rule Platonian ethics from Plato's *The Republic;* one of his last extant plays, this work is considered inferior to his earlier works.

The Frogs. Ed. by W. G. Stanford. Focus Info. Gr. 1983 repr. of 1958 ed. $24.95. ISBN 0-317-93972-6. Bacchus, the patron of the stage, descends to Hell in search of Euripides, who is presented as an absurd character.

The Knights. Ed. by William-Alan Landes. Players Pr. 1992 $6.00. ISBN 0-88734-255-8. An acerbic satire of Athenian government and the demogogue Cleon.

Ladies' Day (Thesmopheriazusae). Trans. by Dudley Fitts. HarBraceJ 1959 o.p. "An excellent new adaptation . . . which should receive wide production because of its lively nature." Also lampoons the playwright Euripides.

Lysistrata. Ed. by Jeffrey Henderson. OUP 1990 $22.00. ISBN 0-19-814496-2. A farce in which Athenian women force their husbands to stop warring against each other.

Peace. Ed. by M. Platnauer. Focus Info. Gr. 1981 repr. of 1964 ed. $19.95. ISBN 0-86292-001-9. Deals with the 10-year Athenian war and the political conflict that results.

BOOKS ABOUT ARISTOPHANES

Dearden, C. W. *The Stage of Aristophanes*. Humanities 1976 o.p. Aristophanes' dramatic productions; based largely on the author's thesis.

Dover, Kenneth. *Aristophanic Comedy*. U. CA Pr. 1972 $12.95. ISBN 0-520-02211-4. Useful and detailed analysis of the important characteristics and techniques of Aristophanes' works.

Ehrenberg, Victor. *The People of Aristophanes: A Sociology of Old Attic Comedy*. Porcupine Pr. 2nd rev. ed. repr. of 1951 ed. o.p. A careful study.

Harriott, R. *Aristophanes: Poet and Dramatist*. John Hopkins 1986 $28.00. ISBN 0-8018-3279-9. Suitable for highly specialized students of Greek drama.

Hubbard, Thomas K. *The Mask of Comedy: Aristophanes and the Intertextual Parabasis*. Cornell Univ. Pr. 1991 $35.95. ISBN 0-8014-2564-6

Lord, Louis E. *Aristophanes: His Plays and His Influence*. Cooper Sq. repr. of 1930 ed. $27.50. ISBN 0-8154-0140-X. Scholarly and interesting discussion of the individual plays and of Aristophanes' influence on the art of comedy.

McLeish, Kenneth. *The Theatre of Aristophanes*. Taplinger 1980 o.p.

Murray, Gilbert. *Aristophanes: A Study*. Ayer 1964 repr. of 1933 ed. o.p. Discusses the growth and change of purpose in ideas and thought in Aristophanes' drama.

O'Regan, Daphne. *Rhetoric, Comedy and Violence of Language in Aristophanes' Clouds*. OUP 1992 $39.95. ISBN 0-19-507017-8

Reckford, Kenneth J. *Aristophanes' Old and New Comedy. Vol. 1: Six Essays in Perspective*. U. of NC Pr. 1987 $39.95. ISBN 0-8078-1720-1

Solomos, Alexis. *The Living Aristophanes*. Trans. by Marvin Felheim. U. of Mich. Pr. 1974 o.p. An excellent biography of Aristophanes—his artistic history and life.

Strauss, L. *Socrates and Aristophanes*. U. Ch. Pr. 1980 repr. of 1966 ed. $18.95. ISBN 0-226-77691-3. Contains a bibliography and annotated references.

Whitman, Cedric H. *Aristophanes and the Comic Hero*. HUP 1964 o.p. "This full-fledged, thoroughly documented, sympathetic and sensitive study of the Aristophanic hero and of the nature of Aristophanic comedy is excellent" (*LJ*).

ARISTOTLE. 384–322 B.C.

[SEE Volumes 3, 4, and 5.]

CALLIMACHUS. c.305–c.240 B.C.

At Alexandria Callimachus was appointed by Ptolemy II as bibliographer for the great library; he was also a teacher of APOLLONIUS RHODIUS, and a famous, prolific poet. His beautiful, elegant, and refined epigrams, hymns, elegiacs (the *Aetia* or *Causes*), iambics, and little epic survive in varying degrees of completeness. In his day he was widely admired and later served as a model for CATULLUS and the Roman elegiac poets, especially OVID.

POETRY BY CALLIMACHUS

Aetia, Iambi, Lyric Poems, Minor Epics and Elegiac Poems, Fragments of Epigrams, Fragments of Uncertain Location. Loeb Class. Lib. HUP 1958 $15.50. ISBN 0-674-99463-9

Callimachus: Hymns, Epigrams, Select Fragments. Trans. by S. Lombardo and D. Rayor. Johns Hopkins 1987 $10.95. ISBN 0-8018-3281-0. An exceptional translation.

Hymns and Epigrams. Loeb Class. Lib. HUP 1921 $15.50. ISBN 0-674-99143-5. Contains Lycophron's *Alexandra* and Aratus of Soli's *Phaenomena*.

BOOK ABOUT CALLIMACHUS

Schmiel, Robert. *Callimachus' Hymns One, Two, Five, Six*. Bryn Mawr Commentaries 1984 $6.00. ISBN 0-929524-055

DEMOSTHENES. 385?–322 B.C.

Demosthenes, the magnificent orator, is said to have had to conquer an originally ineffective vocal delivery. After years of private law practice, he delivered the first of his three *Philippics* against Philip of Macedon in 351 B.C. He saw danger to Athens in the tyrannical expansion of the Macedonian state, but his passionate and compelling exhortations did not save the Greeks from defeat at Chaeronea in 338 B.C. Exiled in 324 B.C., he was recalled after the death of Alexander the Great in 323 B.C. Again he tried to organize the Greek resistance but failed and was forced to flee when Athens was taken. He took poison to avoid capture. His speeches are characterized by deep sincerity, prodigious power of verbal suggestion, and intricate structure. His influence on CICERO (see also Vols. 3 and 4) and the Roman rhetoricians was enormous.

WORKS BY DEMOSTHENES

All the Orations of Demosthenes. Trans. by Thomas Leland. AMS Pr. repr. of 1757 ed. $37.50. ISBN 0-404-54113-5

Demosthenes' on the Crown: A Critical Case Study of a Masterpiece of Ancient Oratory. Trans. by J. Keaney. Hermagoras Pr. 1983 repr. of 1967 ed. $9.50. ISBN 0-9611800-1-3

Demosthenes on the Crown. Ed. by Gregory Vlastos. Ayer 1979 repr. of 1901 ed. $27.50. ISBN 0-405-11547-4

Demosthenes' Public Orations. 1912. Trans. by A. W. Pickard-Cambridge. Biblio Dist. 1967 repr. of 1954 ed. o.p. According to the translator, a rendering of "the speeches into such English as a political orator of the present day might use."

Funeral Speech, Erotic Essay, Exordia, and Letters. Ed. by E. H. Warmington. *Loeb Class. Lib.* HUP 1949 $15.50. ISBN 0-674-99412-4. Speeches written for small audiences or introductions to larger speeches.

Private Orations. Trans. by A. T. Murray. *Loeb Class. Lib.* 3 vols. HUP 1936–39 $15.50 ea. ISBNs 0-674-99351-9, 0-674-99381-0, 0-674-99386-1

BOOKS ABOUT DEMOSTHENES

Adams, Charles D. *Demosthenes and His Influence.* Cooper Sq. Pr. repr. of 1930 ed. $25.00. ISBN 0-8154-0001-2. Biography of Demosthenes; examines his writings with regard to their influence on modern European oratory.

Montgomery, H. *The Way to Chaeronea: Foreign Policy, Decision Making, and Political Influence in Demosthenes' Speeches.* OUP 1984 $18.00. ISBN 82-00-06443-3. Discusses the political mind and essays of Demosthenes.

Pearson, Lionel. *The Art of Demosthenes.* Scholars Pr. GA 1982 $23.00. ISBN 0-89130-551-3. Discusses the technique of Demosthenes' oratory; includes an index.

Pickard-Cambridge, A. W. *Demosthenes and the Last Days of Greek Freedom: 384–322 B.C.* Ed. by Gregory Vlastos. Ayer repr. of 1914 ed. $44.00. ISBN 0-405-11566-0

EURIPIDES. c.485–c.406 B.C.

The third of the three great Greek tragedians was born of well-to-do parents in Attica and lived most of his life in Athens. Out of some 92 plays by him, only 19 are extant; the dates of the following plays are known: *Alcestis* (438 B.C.), *Medea* and *Philoctetes* (431 B.C.), *Hippolytus* (428 B.C.), *Hecuba* (c.424 B.C.), *Electra* (417 B.C.), *The Trojan Women* (415 B.C.), *Iphigenia in Tauris* (c.413 B.C.), *Helen* (412 B.C.), *Phoenissae* (after 412 B.C. and before 408 B.C.), *Ion* (c.411 B.C.), *Orestes* (408 B.C.), *Bacchus* and *Iphigenia in Aulis* (c.405 B.C.). The *Rhesus*—if indeed it is genuine—is the earliest.

When Gilbert Murray's translations made the dramatist popular in the early 1900s, readers were impressed by the author's modernity of thought and spirit, and his feeling for human life and problems of pain. Euripides' attitude toward the gods was iconoclastic and rationalistic; toward humans—notably his passionate female characters—deeply sympathetic.

Euripides separated the chorus from the action, the first step toward the complete elimination of the chorus. He used the prologue as an introduction and explanation, and was charged with intemperate use of the "deus ex machina," by which artifice a god is dragged in abruptly at the end to resolve a confusion beyond human powers. He developed the literary devices of reversal, recognition by means of rings and necklaces, substitution of children, and violations of maidens, on all of which New Comedy (see MENANDER) depends. His language is simple and direct, well tuned to the expression of passion. He created some of the most unforgettable psychological portraits.

Despite criticism and satire against him, Euripides did win several prizes for tragedy in his lifetime, and shortly after his death his reputation rose and has never diminished.

Plays by Euripides

Alcestis. Trans. and ed. by William Arrowsmith. *Greek Tragedy in New Translations*. OUP 1989 $6.95. ISBN 0-19-506166-7. A tragedy with strong comic elements dealing with the subordinate position of women.

The Bacchae. Ed. by E. R. Dodds. OUP 1960 $19.95. ISBN 0-19-872125-0

Electra. Ed. by J. D. Denniston. OUP 1973 $19.95. ISBN 0-19-872094-4. Story of revenge and incest.

Euripides I. Ed. by David Grene and Richmond Lattimore. *Complete Greek Tragedies*. U. Ch. Pr. 1955 o.p. Contains *Alcestis, Medea, The Heracleidae,* and *Hippolytus*. An introduction by Lattimore. Various well-known translators in all volumes.

Euripides II. Ed. by David Grene and Richmond Lattimore. *Complete Greek Tragedies*. U. Ch. Pr. 1956 o.p. Contains *The Cyclops, Heracles, Iphigenia in Tauris,* and *Helen*.

Euripides III. Ed. by David Grene and Richmond Lattimore. *Complete Greek Tragedies*. U. Ch. Pr. 1958 o.p. Contains *Hecuba, Andromache, The Trojan Women,* and *Ion*.

Euripides IV. Ed. by David Grene and Richmond Lattimore. *Complete Greek Tragedies*. U. Ch. Pr. 1958 o.p. Contains *Rhesus, The Suppliant Women, Orestes,* and *Iphigenia in Aulis*.

Euripides V. Ed. by David Grene and Richmond Lattimore. *Complete Greek Tragedies*. U. Ch. Pr. 1959 o.p. Contains *Electra, The Phoenician Women,* and *The Bacchae*.

Hippolytus. Trans. by Robert Bagg. Ed. by William Arrowsmith. *Greek Tragedy in New Translations*. OUP 1973 $19.95. ISBN 0-19-501740-4. Deals with the unjust treatment of illegitimate children.

Ion. Trans. by Gilbert Murray. Allen & Unwin 1954 o.p.

Iphigenia at Aulis. Trans. by William Merwin and George Dimock. *Greek Tragedy in New Translations*. OUP 1992 $6.95. ISBN 0-19-507709-1. Story of the sacrifice of a leader's daughter to procure the help of the gods.

Iphigenia in Tauris. Trans. by Richmond Lattimore. Ed. by William Arrowsmith. *Greek Tragedy in New Translations*. OUP 1992 $6.95. ISBN 0-19-507291-X

Medea. Ed. by Alan Elliott. OUP 1969 $12.95. ISBN 0-19-912006-4. About a sharp-tongued heroine who criticizes the treatment of women.

Medea and Hippolytus. Trans. by Sydney Waterlow. AMS Pr. repr. of 1906 ed. $18.50. ISBN 0-404-07905-9

Rhesos. Trans. by Richard E. Braun. Ed. by William Arrowsmith. *Greek Tragedy in New Translations*. OUP 1992 $6.95. ISBN 0-19-507289-8

Ten Plays of Euripides. Trans. by Moses Hadas and John H. McLean. Bantam 1984 $4.95. ISBN 0-553-21363-6. Contains *Alcestis, Medea, Hippolytus, Andromache, Ion, The Trojan Women, Electra, Iphigenia among the Taurians, Bacchants, Iphigenia at Aulis*.

Three Plays of Euripides. Trans. by Paul Roche. Norton 1974 $4.95. ISBN 0-393-09312-3. Contains *Alcestis, Medea,* and *The Bacchae*.

The Trojan Women. Ed. by Barlow. David Brown $49.95. ISBN 0-85668-228-4. Reflects Euripides' outrage over the massacre of Athenians by the inhabitants of Melos.

Works. Trans. by Arthur S. Way. *Loeb Class. Lib.* 4 vols. HUP 1912 $15.50 ea. ISBNs 0-674-99010-2, 0-674-99011-0, 0-674-99012-9, 0-674-99013-7

Books about Euripides

Burian, P., ed. *Directions in Euripidean Criticism: A Collection of Essays*. Duke 1985 $29.95. ISBN 0-8223-0610-7. Volume of essays by a group of distinguished scholars who met at Duke University to discuss diverse issues in Euripidean criticism.

Conacher, D. J. *Euripidean Drama: Myth, Theme and Structure*. Ed. by W. R. Connor. U. of Toronto Pr. 1967 o.p. One chapter on each play; a good summary.

Decharme, Paul. *Euripides and the Spirit of His Dramas*. Trans. by J. Loeb. Assoc. Fac. Pr. 1968 repr. of 1906 ed. o.p. An engaging interpretation of Euripides' works; examines and makes clearer elusive characteristics in the dramas.

Dodds, Eric R. *The Greeks and the Irrational*. U. CA Pr. 1951 $13.95. ISBN 0-520-00327-6. A brilliant analysis of the Dionysian tendencies in Greek letters and thought—particularly relevant to the "Bacchae."

Foley, H. *Ritual Irony: Poetry and Sacrifice in Euripides*. Cornell Univ. Pr. 1985 $32.95. ISBN 0-8014-1692-2. Direct and detailed study of Euripides; provides readers with a good sense of the religious materials employed by Euripides.

Lucas, Frank L. *Euripides and His Influence*. Cooper Sq. Pr. repr. of 1930 ed. $28.50. ISBN 0-8154-0141-8. Euripides' thought, characters, and stage method as applicable for the modern day.

Murray, Gilbert. *Euripides and His Age*. Greenwood 1979 repr. of 1965 ed. $35.00. ISBN 0-313-20989-8. Introduction by H. D. Kitto. Focuses on Euripides in the context of history.

Powell, J. U., and E. A. Barber, eds. *New Chapters in the History of Greek Literature*. Biblo repr. of 1929 ed. $25.00. ISBN 0-8196-0287-6. Ancient Greek writings newly interpreted or recently found.

Vellacott, Philip. *Ironic Drama*. Cambridge U. Pr. 1975 $37.50. ISBN 0-521-20590-5. A reassessment of ironic strategies in Euripides' plays; includes a feminist critique of women characters.

Verrall, Arthur W. *Euripides the Rationalist*. Russell Sage 1967 repr. of 1895 ed. o.p. Explanations for different interpretations by modern readers of Euripides' works.

Whitman, Cedric H. *Euripides and the Full Circle of Myth. Loeb Class. Monographs Ser.* HUP 1974 $13.00. ISBN 0-674-26920-9. Identifies intertextual similarities from personal readings of *Iphigenia in Tauris, Ion,* and *Helen.*

HELIODORUS OF EMESA. fl. 220–250

One of the earliest and longest of the surviving Greek novels, the *Aethiopica* is a romance of two young lovers, Theagenes and Charicleia, set in the fifth century B.C., which shows considerable insight and narrative skill. It was much read by the Byzantines and in the sixteenth and seventeenth centuries was translated into many languages. Almost nothing is known of the author except that he was a native of Emesa in Syria and perhaps later became Bishop of Tricca in Thessaly.

NOVELS BY HELIODORUS

The Aethiopian History. Trans. by Thomas Underdowne. AMS Pr. repr. of 1895 ed. $45.00. ISBN 0-404-51852-4. Introduction by C. Whibley.

Ethiopian Story. Trans. by Walter Lamb. NAL-Dutton 1961 o.p.

HERODOTUS. c.484–c.425 B.C.

[SEE Volume 3.]

HESIOD. c.700 B.C.

The poet Hesiod tells us that his father gave up sea-trading and moved from Ascra to Boeotia, that as he himself tended sheep on Mount Helicon the Muses commanded him to sing of the gods, and that he won a tripod for a funeral song at Chalcis. The poems credited to him with certainty are the *Theogony*, which is an attempt to bring order into the otherwise chaotic material of Greek mythology through genealogies and anecdotes about the gods, and *The Works and Days*, a wise sermon addressed to his brother Perses as a result of a dispute over their dead father's estate. This latter work presents the injustice of the world with mythological examples and memorable images, and concludes with a collection of folk wisdom. Uncertain attributions are the *Shield of Heracles* and the *Catalogue of Women*. Hesiod is a didactic and individualistic poet who is often compared and contrasted with HOMER, as both are representative of early epic style. "Hesiod is earth-bound and dun colored; indeed part of his purpose is to discredit the brilliance and the ideals of heroism glorified in the homeric tradition. But Hesiod too is poetry, though of a different order. . . " (Moses Hadas, *N.Y. Times*).

POETRY BY HESIOD

Hesiod: Theogony, Works and Days. Trans. by Apostolos N. Athanassakis. Johns Hopkins 1983 $9.95. ISBN 0-8018-2998-4. An accurate translation with notes.

Hesiod, Homeric Hymns, Fragments of the Epic Cycle, Homerica. Loeb Class. Lib. HUP $15.50. ISBN 0-674-99063-3. A careful, highly respected, scholarly translation of Hesiod.

Hesiod and Theognis. Trans. by Dorothy Wender. Viking Penguin 1976 $6.95. ISBN 0-14-044283-9

Theogony. Trans. by M. L. West. OUP 1966 $95.00. ISBN 0-19-814169-6. The translator gives a fascinating introduction to the poet.

The Works and Days. Ed. by W. R. Connor. Ayer 1979 repr. of 1932 ed. $17.00. ISBN 0-405-11446-X. A translation in verse, always readable and never strained. An excellent introductory essay with much valuable information about a neglected epic tradition.

Works of Hesiod. Trans. by Thomas Cooke. 2 vols. in 1. AMS Pr. repr. of 1728 ed. $40.00. ISBN 0-404-54170-4

BOOKS ABOUT HESIOD

Burn, Andrew R. *The World of Hesiod.* Ayer 1966 repr. of 1936 ed. $15.00. ISBN 0-405-08332-7. Hesiod in the Middle Ages, c.900–700 B.C.

Hamilton, R. *The Architecture of Hesiodic Poetry.* Johns Hopkins 1989 $25.00. ISBN 0-8018-3819-3. An investigation of the structure of Hesiod's two extant poems—*Theogony* and *Works and Days.*

Lamberton, R. *Hesiod.* Yale U. Pr. 1988 $11.00. ISBN 0-300-04069-5. Presents ancient texts within the perspective of Western humanism with energy and grace.

Pucci, P. *Hesiod and the Language of Poetry.* Bks. Demand repr. of 1977 ed. $43.20. ISBN 0-7837-1109-3. Analyzes Hesiod's writing and questions his beliefs, as represented in the texts.

Solmsen, Friedrich. *Hesiod and Aeschylus.* Ed. by W. R. Connor. Johnson Repr. repr. of 1949 ed. o.p. By a leading classicist and scholar of Hesiod.

Walcott, P. *Hesiod and the Near East.* Verry 1966 o.p. A study of Greece and Near East interaction in the late eighth and early seventh centuries B.C.

HOMER. c.700 B.C.

Greek literature begins with Homer—he was also the first European poet and so is considered the father of European literature. The Greeks believed that both the *Iliad* and the *Odyssey* were composed by the blind bard Homer but were uncertain of his dates or his birthplace. Seven cities claimed him—Athens, Argos, Chios, Colophon, Rhodes, Salamis, and Smyrna. Now it is conjectured that he was an Ionian, probably from Chios, and that he lived around 700 B.C. Scholars have long disputed his authorship of both poems. But, for the present, the urgency of the "Homeric Question" has given way to general agreement that he was the presiding genius behind both epics. Modern experts have shown that these epics could have been recited without a written score or a text to prompt the singer's memory, because he would have relied instead on his stock of formulaic phrases or epithets to keep the narrative flowing. And yet, it must be said that, oral or written, real or imaginary, late or early, Homer remains a mysterious figure wrapped in the mists of the ancient past.

The *Iliad*, considered to be the earlier of the two poems, tells the story of the Trojan War and of its two heroes, Achilles and Hector. The narrative, which begins in the midst of the siege and moves very rapidly toward its tragic conclusion, is often interrupted at a moment of crisis by beautiful similes drawn from nature, farming, and handcrafts. Its language is magnificent and rich and its poetry is at the peak of Western literary tradition.

The *Odyssey*, which may have been written in Homer's old age, recounts the wanderings of Odysseus after the Trojan War and his final homecoming to Ithaca, where he found his wife Penelope still faithful to him. It is a fantastical adventure story with a comic tone and a happy ending. Like the *Iliad*, it is noteworthy for its beautiful poetry, simplicity of statement, dramatic plot and postponement, and nobility of character.

Also attributed to Homer are the *Homeric Hymns*, invocations to such gods as Apollo, Aphrodite, and Hermes. They vary in tone from tender to amusing to erotic, but all are expressed in exquisite Homeric language. They were written in the dactylic hexameter style of Homer; in antiquity they were believed by some to be written by Homer.

Homer was a bible, an oracle, and the repository of all wisdom for the Greeks. His poetry shaped the Greek character and Greek literature from its beginnings. It was the seminal influence on Latin literature and has continued to dominate European vernacular literature even to the present: Hesiod, Pindar, Aeschylus, Sophocles, Euripides, and Plato (see Vols. 3 and 4); Virgil, Horace, and Ovid; Dante; Chaucer (see Vol. 1), Shakespeare (see Vol. 1), and Milton (see Vol. 1); and in our time, Joyce (see Vol. 1) and Kazantzakis. The idea of the hero, of tragedy and comedy, of beginning a story in the middle, dramatic postponement, divine intervention, flashback, and the rich assembly of individual plots and characters—all these fundamentals come from Homer.

Poetry by Homer

THE ILIAD: OLDER VERSIONS

Bryant, William Cullen. *The Iliad.* 1870. o.p. In rhymeless iambic pentameter.

Butler, Samuel. *The Iliad.* 1898 o.p. A prose translation by the author of *Erewhon* and *The Way of All Flesh,* who wanted to rescue Homer's vitality from schoolroom dullness.

Chapman, George, trans. 1616. *The Iliad, The Odyssey, and the Lesser Homerica.* Ed. by Allardyce Nicoll. *Bollingen Ser.* 2 vols. Princeton U. Pr. 1967 o.p. The first English translation of Homer, in rhyming couplets, and the one that inspired Keats. Rather archaic for present-day readers.

Hobbes, Thomas. *Iliads and Odysseys.* AMS Pr. repr. of 1677 ed. $54.50. ISBN 0-404-54188-6. A vigorous version by the famous philosopher.

Lang, Andrew. *The Iliad. Airmont Class. Ser.* Airmont 1966 $2.95. ISBN 0-8049-0115-5. In prose. Written in biblical diction.

Pope, Alexander. *The Iliad.* OUP 1934 o.p. In rhyming couplets of 18 syllables. A literary *tour de force* that remained for many years the standard English version. A great influence on English poetry as well as on the reputation of Homer.

THE ILIAD: MODERN VERSIONS

Fitzgerald, Robert, trans. *The Iliad.* Doubleday 1989 $15.00. ISBN 0-385-05941-0. Fluent, graceful, and eminently readable.

Graves, Robert. *The Anger of Achilles: Homer's Iliad.* o.p. In prose with occasional ballad-like verse. "He is magnificently and unfailingly readable" (Dudley Fitts, *N.Y. Times*).

Lattimore, Richmond, trans. *The Iliad of Homer.* U. Ch. Pr. 1975 $8.95. ISBN 0-226-46940-9. A verse translation in a free six-beat line. The most faithful to Homer of all the modern translations, highly respected for both its accuracy and its poetry.

Murray, Augustus. *The Iliad. Loeb Class. Lib.* 2 vols. HUP $15.50 ea. ISBNs 0-674-99188-5, 0-674-99189-3. In prose, bilingual. A rendering smooth, fluent, and exact.

Richards, Ivor Armstrong. *Iliad: A Shortened Version. Norton Lib.* Norton 1958 $3.95. ISBN 0-393-00101-6. A very readable modern version of strong continuing action, made by cutting many passages and omitting entirely Books 2, 10, 13, and 17.

Rouse, William Henry Denham. *The Iliad*. NAL-Dutton 1950 $4.99. ISBN 0-451-62723-7. In prose. A readable and vigorous rendering.

THE ODYSSEY: OLDER VERSIONS

Bryant, William Cullen. *The Odyssey*. 1871-72 o.p. In blank verse. Rhymeless iambic pentameter similar in excellence to his *Iliad*.

Butler, Samuel. *The Odyssey*. 1900 o.p. In prose. See Butler's *The Iliad*.

Chapman, George. *The Odyssey*. 1616. In all features like Chapman's *Iliad*, except for the use of a line of five accented syllables instead of seven accented syllables.

Cowper, William. *The Odyssey*. 1791 o.p. In Miltonic blank verse, slow and elaborate. Found only in Cowper's collected poetical works.

Pope, Alexander. *Odyssey of Homer*. 2 vols. Ed. by Maynard Mack. Yale U. Pr. 1967 o.p. In rhyming couplets.

THE ODYSSEY: MODERN VERSIONS

Cook, Albert. *The Odyssey*. Norton 1968 $8.95. ISBN 0-393-00744-8. A "literal translation following the original line for line. These lines scan easily and move rapidly, thus reproducing one of the special delights of Homeric style" (Frances D. Lazenby).

Fitzgerald, Robert. *The Odyssey*. Knopf 1992 $20.00. ISBN 0-679-41047-3. A blank-verse translation by an American poet that is now a classic. "One of the great merits of Fitzgerald's book is its rendering of Homer's heroic dignity, his moral force, his religious spirit—and this without loss of narrative, clarity and action" (*N.Y. Times*).

Lattimore, Richmond, trans. *The Odyssey of Homer: A Modern Translation*. HarperC 1975 repr. of 1967 ed. $11.00. ISBN 0-06-090479-8. "Lattimore's [verse] translation . . . is the most eloquent, persuasive and imaginative I have seen. It reads as few translations ever do—as if the poem had been written originally in English, and in language idiomatic, lively, and urgent" (Paul Engle).

Murray, Augustus Taber. *The Odyssey. Loeb Class. Lib.* 2 vols. HUP $15.50 ea. In prose.

Rieu, Emil. *The Odyssey*. Viking Penguin rev. ed 1992 $5.95. ISBN 0-14-044556-0. In prose. An easy, unaffected, and rapid style developed after several experiments and many years. A genuine translation, as is Rieu's *Iliad* (o.p.).

Rouse, W. H. *The Odyssey*. NAL-Dutton 1946 $3.99. ISBN 0-451-62805-5. A prose translation; recommended.

Shaw, T. E. (Lawrence of Arabia). *The Odyssey*. OUP 1932 o.p. Rendered in straightforward, compelling prose and faithful to the intent of the original. Reads better than the other modern translations and comes with a brilliant, eccentric introduction.

HOMERIC HYMNS

These poems are short narratives about the gods, embedded in the context of a prayer to the god. The Homeric Hymn to Apollo, for example, tells the story of Leto's search for a place to give birth and how Artemis and Apollo were born; the Homeric Hymn to Demeter tells how Demeter's daughter was abducted by Hades and the subsequent quest of the mother for the daughter. Other poems tell of Aphrodite's love of mortal man or Hermes' theft of Apollo's cattle and many other such tales. Perhaps the attribution of these songs to Homer helped preserve them.

Athanassakis, Apostolos N. *Homeric Hymns*. Johns Hopkins 1976 $12.00. An attractive, readable translation with notes.

Evelyn-White, H. G. *Ilesiod and the Homeric Hymns. Loeb Class. Lib.* HUP 1914 $12.50. A literal translation in a bilingual edition.

Books about Homer

Arnold, Matthew. *On Translating Homer*. AMS Pr. repr. of 1905 ed. $16.25. ISBN 0-404-00388-5. Presents Arnold's belief that Homer is eminently rapid, plain and direct in expression, simple and direct in idea, and noble.

Austin, Norman. *Archery at the Dark of the Moon: Poetic Problems in Homer's Odyssey.* U. CA Pr. 1975 $45.00. ISBN 0-520-04790-7. A study of Homer and his *Odyssey.*

Bespaloff, R. *On the Iliad. Bollingen Ser.* Princeton U. Pr. 1970 o.p. An engaging analysis showing the relationship of Homer's characters and ethical ideas to the present day.

Beye, Charles R. *The Iliad, the Odyssey, and the Epic Tradition.* Gordian 1976 repr. of 1966 ed. $45.00. ISBN 0-87752-187-5. Discusses the nature of oral poetry; contains information relevant to a critical understanding of the *Iliad* and the *Odyssey* as poetry.

Bloom, Harold, ed. *Homer.* Chelsea Hse. 1986 $29.95. ISBN 0-87754-723-8. Collection of critical essays about Homer.

Bloom, Harold, ed. *Homer's The Odyssey.* Chelsea Hse. 1988 $24.50. ISBN 1-55546-043-7. Contains interesting and thought-provoking essays about Homer's *Odyssey.*

Bowra, C. M. *Tradition and Design in the Iliad.* Greenwood 1977 repr. of 1930 ed. $38.50. ISBN 0-8371-9561-6. Argues that the poem was constructed by one poet using traditional sources and adding new material of his own.

Bradford, Ernle. *Ulysses Found.* HarBraceJ 1964 o.p. About Bradford's lifelong sailing of the Mediterranean in search of Ulysses' route, confirming that Homeric geography "acts as a solid backbone to the poem." "*Ulysses Found* is highly literate, full of wit and wry, a delight from start to finish" (Francis D. Lazenby, *LJ*).

Butler, Samuel. *The Authoress of the Odyssey.* 1897. U. Ch. Pr. 1967 o.p. A heterodox study of the epic arguing that it was written more than two centuries after the *Iliad* and that its author was a young Sicilian woman of Trapan; worth reading.

Camps, W. A. *An Introduction to Homer.* OUP 1980 $13.95. ISBN 0-19-872101-3. Examines the character of Homeric poetry and its effectiveness; also contains notes and elaborations on Homeric poetry.

Carpenter, Rhys. *Folk Tale, Fiction and Saga in the Homeric Epics.* U. CA Pr. 1974 $37.00. ISBN 0-520-02808-2. Analyzes the elements of saga and folk tale in Homer's works.

Clarke, Howard. *The Art of the Odyssey.* P-H 1967 o.p. Five essays intended for readers of Homer in translation. An interesting chapter on the history and problems of English translation.

______. *Homer's Readers: A Historical Introduction to the Iliad and the Odyssey.* U. of Delaware Pr. 1980 $35.00. ISBN 0-87413-150-2. Provides supplementary history to enhance our understanding of Homer's *Iliad* and *Odyssey.*

Cunliffe, Richard J. *A Lexicon of the Homeric Dialect.* U. of Okla. Pr. 1963 $21.95. ISBN 0-8061-1430-4. For English-speaking readers of Homer in the original. A reprint based on the Oxford Classical Text editions; includes all words except, unfortunately, names. Accurate; excellent scholarship.

Edwards, Mark W. *Homer: Poet of the Iliad.* Johns Hopkins 1987 $48.00. ISBN 0-8018-3329-9. Seeks, in the words of its author, "to combine the advantages of a general introduction to Homer and a commentary on the *Iliad.*"

Finley, John H., Jr. *Homer's Odyssey.* HUP 1978 $25.00. ISBN 0-674-40614-1. Interesting essays on various themes and characters.

Finley, Moses I. *The World of Odysseus.* Viking Penguin 1979 $6.95. ISBN 0-14-020570-5. A background book on the ways of the Homeric world for the delight and enlightenment of all readers. Preface by Mark Van Doren.

Gordon, Cyrus H. *Homer and Bible: The Origin and Character of East Mediterranean Literature.* Ventnor 1967 $4.95. ISBN 0-911566-03-1. Explores the connections and interactions of the Mediterranean cultures.

Griffin, J. *Homer.* OUP 1980 $6.95. ISBN 0-19-287532-9. Discusses Homer's literary accomplishments.

Kazantzakis, Nikos. *The Odyssey: A Modern Sequel.* S&S Trade 1969 $14.95. ISBN 0-671-20247-2. The author takes up the story where Homer left off.

Kirk, Geoffrey S. *Homer and the Epic.* Cambridge U. Pr. 1965 $18.95. ISBN 0-521-09356-2. A shortened version of *Songs of Homer.*

Lord, Albert B. *Epic Singers and Oral Tradition.* Cornell Univ. Pr. 1991 $38.95. ISBN 0-8014-2472-0. Collection of 13 essays in which the prevailing theme is that oral-tradition literature can attain a high degree of excellence.

———. *The Singer of Tales*. HUP 1960 $12.95. ISBN 0-671-80881-9. Using the parallel case of Yugoslavian oral epic, explains why Homer may have been an oral poet. A landmark in Homeric studies. Preface by H. Levine.

Michalopoulos, A. *Homer. Twayne's World Authors Ser.* Macmillan 1966 $18.95. ISBN 0-8057-2432-X. Good general introduction to Homer's epics; also contains a discussion of the authorship question.

Mireaux, Emile. *Daily Life in the Time of Homer*. Trans. by Iris Sells. Macmillan 1959 o.p. Good background reading.

Nagler, Michael. *Spontaneity and Tradition: A Study in the Oral Art of Homer*. U. CA Pr. 1975 $32.00. Examines Homer in light of oral tradition.

Nilsson, Martin P. *Homer and Mycenae*. Cooper Sq. Pr. 1968 repr. of 1933 ed. o.p. A compelling theological and anthropological study.

Page, Denys L. *History and the Homeric Iliad*. U. CA Pr. 1976 repr. of 1959 ed. $37.50. ISBN 0-520-03246-2. A heavily annotated and exhaustive study of the preclassical world, based on recent archeological finds.

Parry, Adam, ed. *The Making of Homeric Verse: The Collected Papers of Milman Parry*. OUP 1987 $19.95. ISBN 0-19-520560-X. The papers of Milman Parry, who revolutionized the study of Homer by studying Yugoslavian oral poetry.

Redfield, James M. *Nature and Culture in the Iliad: The Tragedy of Hector*. U. Ch. Pr. 1978 repr. of 1975 ed. o.p. Analyzes the role of Hector in the *Iliad* as a sympathetic and interesting character.

Schein, S. *The Mortal Hero: An Introduction to Homer's Iliad*. U. CA Pr. 1984 $11.95. ISBN 0-520-05626-4. Examines the theme of heroism in the Iliad.

Scott, John A. *The Unity of Homer*. Biblo 1921 $25.00. ISBN 0-8196-0152-7. Views Homer's consistency of style and content.

Stanford, William B. *Ulysses Theme*. U. of Mich. Pr. 1968 o.p. Examines the idea of the traditional hero as found in Homer's work.

Vivante, Paolo. *Homer*. Yale U. Pr. 1985 $30.00. ISBN 0-300-03395-8. Brings to the fore the quality of epiphany and sense of time in Homer.

Wace, Alan J. B., and Frank H. Stubbings, eds. *A Companion to Homer*. Macmillan 1963 o.p. For readers of the Greek originals, but valuable to all. "[T]he publication of this giant in every sense is an important event. The list of 17 contributors resembles a Homeric Who's Who, the contents a Homeric What's What" (*LJ*).

Weil, Simone. *Iliad, or the Poem of Force*. Pendle Hill 1956 $3.00. ISBN 0-87574-091-X. Written by a victim of the Nazi concentration camps who brings her original mind to bear on the meaning of force in the *Iliad*.

Whitman, Cedric H. *Homer and the Heroic Tradition. Norton Lib.* Bobbs 1965 o.p. Chiefly devoted to the *Iliad* (the *Odyssey* is considered in the final chapter). Presents arguments, both historical and contemporary, with objectivity.

Willcock, Malcolm L. *A Companion to the Iliad*. Trans. by Richmond Lattimore. U. Ch. Pr. 1976 o.p. Annotations geared to the English text of Lattimore's translation.

JOSEPHUS, FLAVIUS. 37–95

[SEE Volumes 3 and 4.]

LONGINUS. c.1st century A.D.

"Longinus" is the name given to the author of *On the Sublime* (c. 1st century A.D.), a treatise that defines the characteristics of the lofty style in literature, using HOMER, PLATO (see Vol. 4), and DEMOSTHENES as the chief examples. Translated by Nicolas Boileau in 1674, it greatly influenced literary theory until the early nineteenth century and is of lasting importance as a brilliant critique of classical literature.

WORK BY LONGINUS

On the Sublime (and *On Sublimity*). HUP $15.50. ISBN 0-674-99219-9

LONGUS. fl. 2nd or 3rd century A.D.?

The pastoral *Daphnis and Chloe*, the best of the ancient Greek romances, is attributed to Longus. Nothing is known of his life except what he states in his prologue to the work. His passionate love story of two foundlings raised together by shepherds on Lesbos is sweetly told and has been persistently admired for its bucolic charm.

POETRY BY LONGUS

Daphnis and Chloe (and *Love Romances, Parthenius,* and *Fragments of the Ninus Romance*). Trans. by Moses Hadas. Rev. by J. M. Edmonds. *Loeb Class. Lib.* HUP $15.50. ISBN 0-674-99076-5

BOOKS ABOUT LONGUS

Hagg, Thomas. *The Novel in Antiquity.* U. CA Pr. 1983 $47.50. ISBN 0-520-04923-3. An excellent survey of the whole field.

Heiserman, Arthur. *The Novel before the Novel: Essays and Discussions about the Beginnings of Prose Fiction in the West.* Bks. Demand repr. of 1980 ed. $64.50. ISBN 0-685-23836-9. A useful introduction.

McCulloh, William E. *Longus. World Authors Ser.* Irvington 1970 $17.95. ISBN 0-8057-2540-7. A useful analysis of Longus's work; includes a comprehensive literary discussion of *Daphnis and Chloe.*

Perry, Ben E. *The Ancient Romances: A Literary Historical-Account of Their Origins.* U. CA Pr. 1967 $47.50. ISBN 0-520-01003-5. Places Longus in the context of the romance tradition.

LUCIAN (Lucianus Samosatensis). c. A.D. 120–c.185?

Lucian, the wit and satirist, was a brilliant Greek writer in the time of the Roman Empire. He was born in Samosata, Syria; traveled and lectured in Italy, Asia Minor, and Gaul; and in later life held a government position in Egypt. Of nearly 80 works, the most important and characteristic are his essays, written in dialogue form. "Dialogues of the Gods," which satirizes mythology; "Dialogues of the Dead," which are expositions of human vanity; and "The Sale of Lives," which satirizes various schools of philosophy. He is a good critical source for ancient art and for information about his literary contemporaries. The *True History,* a nonsense fantasy and parody of adventure stories, influenced RABELAIS, SWIFT (see Vol. 1), and VOLTAIRE.

WORKS BY LUCIAN

Dialogues. Loeb Class. Lib. 8 vols. HUP $15.50 ea. ISBNs 0-674-99015-3, 0-674-99060-9, 0-674-99144-3, 0-674-99179-6, 0-674-99333-0, 0-674-99474-4, 0-674-99475-2, 0-674-99476-0

Selected Satires of Lucian. Norton 1968 $10.95. ISBN 0-393-00443-0

Selected Works. Trans. by B. P. Reardon. Macmillan 1965 $5.65. ISBN 0-672-60385-3

True History and Lucius or the Ass. Trans. by Paul Turner. Ind. U. Pr. repr. of 1958 ed. o.p.

The Works of Lucian of Samosata. Trans. by H. W. Fowler and F. G. Fowler. OUP 1905 o.p. A classic translation of Lucian by the authors of the original *Modern English Usage.*

BOOKS ABOUT LUCIAN

Allinson, Francis G. *Lucian, Satirist and Artist.* Cooper Sq. Pr. repr. of 1930 ed. o.p. Examines our debt to Greece and Rome for its literary heritage.

Jebb, Richard C. *Essays and Addresses.* Longwood Pr. 1973 repr. of 1907 ed. o.p. Contains a chapter on Lucian.

Robinson, Christopher. *Lucian and His Influence in Europe.* U. of NC Pr. 1979 $32.50. ISBN 0-8078-1404-0. Identifies the main literary characteristics of Lucian's work and the major strands of his influence on European literature.

Zappala, Michael. *Lucian of Samosata in the Two Hesperias: An Essay in Literary and Cultural Translation.* Scripta 1990 $49.50. ISBN 0-916379-71-X

MENANDER. c.342–c.292 B.C.

The late fourth century B.C. gave rise to New Comedy—a comedy of manners that was more refined and lacked the robustness of Old Comedy. Until the latter part of the nineteenth century, the Greek playwright Menander's plays were known only through adaptations and translations made by the Roman dramatists PLAUTUS and TERENCE, and by the comments of OVID and PLINY (see Vol. 3). Menander wrote approximately 100 plays, and the few extant in the Greek text were found on papyrus rolls in the rubbish heaps of Roman Egypt. However, *The Dyskolos*, the first complete Menander New Comedy to be discovered intact, turned up on papyrus in a private Swiss collection. His comedies are skillfully constructed, his characters well delineated, his diction excellent, and his themes mostly the trials and tribulations of young love with conventional solutions.

Menander was born and died in Athens, presumably a member of the upper class, and studied under the philosopher-scientist THEOPHRASTUS (see also Vol. 4), the successor of ARISTOTLE (see Vols. 3, 4, and 5).

PLAYS BY MENANDER

Comedies. Trans. by Frank G. Allinson. *Loeb Class. Lib.* HUP $15.50. ISBN 0-674-99147-8

The Girl from Samos. Trans. by E. G. Turner. Athlone Pr. 1972 o.p.

Menander: The Principal Fragments. Trans. by Frank G. Allinson. Greenwood 1970 repr. of 1921 ed. $49.75. ISBN 0-8371-4279-2

Plays and Fragments: Menander. Trans. by M. Miller. Viking Penguin 1988 $6.95. ISBN 0-14-044501-3

BOOKS ABOUT MENANDER

Gomme, A. W., and F. H. Sandbach. *Menander: A Commentary.* OUP 1973 $125.00. ISBN 0-19-814197-1. Based on the Oxford Classical Texts of *Dyskolos; Reliquiae Selectae* also edited by Sandbach.

Webster, T. B. *The Birth of Modern Comedy of Manners.* Folcroft 1959 o.p. Origins of Greek comedy of manners.

MOSCHUS. fl. 150 B.C.

[SEE Theocritus in this chapter.]

PHILO JUDAEUS. fl. c. A.D. 1

[SEE Volume 4.]

PINDAR. c.518–c.438 B.C.

The Greek poet Pindar, a Boeotian aristocrat who wrote for aristocrats, lived at Thebes, studied at Athens, and stayed in Sicily at the court of Hieron at Syracuse. His epinicians, choral odes in honor of victors at athletic games, survive almost complete and are divided into four groups, depending upon whether they celebrate victory at the Olympian, Pythian, Nemean, or Isthmian games. Scholars surmise that these are representative of his other poetry—such as hymns, processional songs, and dirges—extant in fragments.

The 44 surviving odes joyfully praise beautiful, brilliant athletes who are like the gods in their moment of triumph. Bold mythological metaphor, dazzling intricacy of language, and metrical complexity together create sublimity of thought and of style. Pindar was famous in his lifetime and later throughout the Hellenistic world, as is attested by the story that Alexander the Great in 335 B.C. ordered the poet's house spared when his army sacked Thebes.

The "Pindaric ode" form used in England in the seventeenth and early eighteenth centuries was based on an incorrect understanding of Pindar's metrical schemes and was characterized by grandiose diction. Abraham Cowley published his *Pindarique Odes* in 1656, and the form was used by DRYDEN (see Vol. 1), POPE (see Vol. 1), SWIFT (see Vol. 1), and others. Cowley's odes were paraphrases rather than translations, according to his preface; he said that "if a man should undertake to translate Pindar word for word, it would be thought that one madman had translated another." Assessing other translations, David Grene in *Poetry* has judged John E. Sandys's prose translation "scholarly and dignified" and the free-verse renderings used by Richmond Lattimore in an effort to suggest Pindar's own meters "clear and lucid, except when Pindar himself is otherwise, and then Mr. Lattimore, like a true translator, reproduces the obscurity of the original by an obscurity transferred to the English." Pindar is considered to be the greatest of the Greek lyric poets.

POETRY BY PINDAR

Odes and Fragments. Trans. by Sir John E. Sandys. *Loeb Class. Lib.* HUP 1915–19 $15.50. ISBN 0-674-99062-5

The Odes of Pindar. Trans. by C. M. Bowra. Viking Penguin 1982 $8.95. ISBN 0-14-044209-X. An adequate version.

Pindar's Odes. Trans. by Roy A. Swanson. Irvington repr. of 1974 ed. $12.95. ISBN 0-8290-0332-0. Includes some famous imitations of Pindar in English.

Pindar's Victory Songs. Trans. by Frank J. Nisetich. Johns Hopkins 1980 $45.00. ISBN 0-8018-2350-1. A very good translation with a useful scholarly introduction.

Songs and Action: Victory Odes of Pindar. Trans. by Kevin Crotty. Johns Hopkins 1982 o.p.

BOOKS ABOUT PINDAR

Bowra, C. M. *Pindar.* Ed. by Basil L. Gildersleeve. OUP 1964 o.p. Indispensable for understanding the difficult poetry of Pindar.

Burton, R. W. B. *Pindar's Pythian Odes.* OUP 1962 o.p. A classic study; essays on interpretation.

Carne-Ross, D. S. *Pindar.* Yale U. Pr. 1985 $27.50. ISBN 0-300-03383-4. Illustrates Pindar's qualities; light on scholarship.

Finley, John H., Jr. *Pindar and Aeschylus.* OUP 1962 o.p. An important study of the relationship between the two poets, who met at Hieron's court in Syracuse.

Nisetich, F. *Pindar and Homer.* Johns Hopkins 1989 $22.00. ISBN 0-8018-3820-7. Clearly written but specialized study that shows how Pindar, the greatest Greek lyric poet, reflects on, echoes, and adapts Homeric epic for his own purposes.

Norwood, Gilbert. *Pindar.* U. CA Pr. 1974 $40.00. ISBN 0-520-01952-0. A scholarly study of the poet and his work.

PLATO. c.429–347 B.C.

[SEE Volumes 3 and 4.]

PLUTARCH. c.46–c.125

[SEE Volume 3.]

POLYBIUS. c.200–c.118 B.C.

[SEE Volume 3.]

PROCOPIUS. c.500–c.565

[SEE Volume 3.]

SAPPHO. fl. c.610–c.580 B.C.

Sappho, whom PLATO (see Vols. 3 and 4) called "the tenth Muse," was the greatest of the early Greek lyric poets. She was born at Mytilene on Lesbos and was a member—perhaps the head—of a group of women who honored the Muses and Aphrodite. Her family was aristocratic; it is said that she was married and had a daughter. Her brilliant love lyrics, marriage songs, and hymns to the gods are written in Aeolic dialect in many meters, one of which is named for her—the Sapphic. Mostly fragments survive of the nine books she is thought to have authored. Her verse is simple and direct, exquisitely passionate and vivid. CATULLUS, OVID, and SWINBURNE (see Vol. 1) were among the many later poets she influenced.

POETRY BY SAPPHO

*Greek Lyrics.*Trans. by D. A. Campbell. *Loeb Class. Lib.* HUP 1982 $15.50. ISBN 0-674-99157-5. Greek text with English translation, superseding Edmonds's erratic translations. Complete, with succinct notes.

*The Love Songs of Sappho.*Trans. by P. Roche. NAL-Dutton 1991 $4.95. ISBN 0-451-52535-3. A well-translated collection of love poems.

The Poems of Sappho. Trans. by J. M. Edmonds. *Loeb Class. Lib.* 3 vols. HUP o.p. Sometimes obscure, but generally faithful translation.

Sappho: A New Translation. Trans. by Mary Barnard. U. CA Pr. 1958 $6.95. ISBN 0-520-01117-1. Competent translation.

Sappho's Lyre: Archaic Lyric and Women Poets of Ancient Greece. Trans. by Diane J. Rayor. U. CA Pr. 1991 $29.95. ISBN 0-520-07335-5. Provides an accurate representation of what Sappho said without imposing her own interpretation or modern emphasis.

BOOKS ABOUT SAPPHO

Bowra, C. M. *Greek Lyric Poetry from Alcman to Simonides.* OUP 1962 o.p. A sensitive critique of Sappho's lyrics and of problems associated with the text.

Burnett, Anne P. *Three Archaic Poets: Archilochus, Alcaeus, Sappho.* HUP 1983 o.p. A close and perceptive reading of fragments, especially good on Sappho.

DeJean, J. *Fictions of Sappho: 1546–1937.* U. Ch. Pr. 1989 $55.00. ISBN 0-226-14135-7. Explores the widely various characterizations of the Greek poet, particularly in France, tracing the interpretations, denial, acceptance, and excusing of homosexual elements in her poems.

Page, Denys L. *Sappho and Alcaeus.* OUP 1955 $36.00. ISBN 0-19-814375-3. Text, translation, and commentary with an introductory essay to the two poets from Lesbos. A distinguished book, required reading for the serious student.

Robinson, David M. *Sappho and Her Influence.* Cooper Sq. repr. of 1930 ed. $28.50. ISBN 0-8154-0195-7. Examines Sappho's influence on female poets.

SOPHOCLES. c.496–406 B.C.

The Greek dramatist Sophocles, born to a wealthy family at Colonus, near Athens, was admired as a boy for his personal beauty and musical skill. He served faithfully as a treasurer and general for Athens when it was expanding its empire and influence. In the dramatic contests, he defeated AESCHYLUS in 468 B.C. for first prize in tragedy, wrote a poem to HERODOTUS (see Vol. 3), and led his chorus and actors in mourning for EURIPIDES just a few months before his own death. He wrote approximately 123 plays, of which 7 tragedies are extant, as well as a fragment of his satiric play, *Ichneutae* (*Hunters*). His plays were produced in the following order: *Ajax* (c.450 B.C.), *Antigone* (441 B.C.), *Oedipus Tyrannus* (c.430 B.C.), *Trachiniae* (c.430 B.C.), *Electra* (between 418 and 410 B.C.), *Philoctetes* (409 B.C.), and *Oedipus at Colonus* (posthumously in 401 B.C.). With Sophocles, Greek tragedy reached its most characteristic form. He added a third actor, made each play independent—that is, not dependent on others in a trilogy—increased the numbers of the chorus, introduced the use of scenery, shifted the focus from religious to more philosophical issues, and brought language and characters, though still majestic, nearer to everyday life. His finely delineated characters are responsible for the tragedy that befalls them, and they accept it heroically. ARISTOTLE (see Vols. 3, 4, and 5) states that Sophocles said he portrayed people as they ought to be; Euripides, as they are. His utter command of tragic speech in the simple grandeur of his choral odes, dialogues, and monologues encourages the English reader to compare him to SHAKESPEARE (see Vol. 1).

PLAYS BY SOPHOCLES

Antigone. Trans. by Michael Townsend. Trans. by Richard E. Braun. Ed. by William Arrowsmith. *Greek Tragedy in New Translations*. OUP 1990 $6.95. ISBN 0-19-506167-5. Tells of Oedipus's daughter Antigone, who is condemned to die because she buries her brother in defiance of King Creon.

The Complete Plays. Trans. by Richard C. Jebb. Ed. by Moses Hadas. Bantam 1982 $3.95. ISBN 0-553-21354-7. A newly revised edition of the famous Jebb translations.

Electra. Trans. by Lewis Theobald and Richard C. Jebb. Macmillan 1950 $1.80. ISBN 0-672-60185-0. Introduction by J. F. Charles. Sophocles' treatment of the Electra legend, in which Electra helps kill her mother to avenge the memory of her father and then marries her brother.

Electra: A Version for the Modern Stage. Trans. by Francis Fergusson. Routledge Chapman & Hall 1938 $3.50. ISBN 0-87830-521-1

Oedipus at Colonus. Trans. by Gilbert Murray and Peter D. Arnott. *Crofts Class. Ser.* Harlan Davidson 1975 $3.50. ISBN 0-88295-107-6. A continuation of the Oedipus legend.

Oedipus the King. Trans. by Robert Bagg. U. of Mass. Pr. 1982 $15.00. ISBN 0-87023-362-9. The tragedy of a doomed prince who unwittingly kills his father and marries his mother.

Oedipus Rex. Ed. by R. D. Dawe. Cambridge U. Pr. 1982 $54.95. ISBN 0-521-24543-5

Sophocles I. U. Ch. Pr. 1969 $6.95. ISBN 0-226-30785-9. Contains *Oedipus the King*, translated by David Grene; *Oedipus at Colonus*, translated by Robert Fitzgerald; *Antigone*, translated by Elizabeth Wyckoff.

Sophocles II. U. Ch. Pr. 1969 $7.95. ISBN 0-226-30786-7. Contains *Ajax*, translated by John Moore; *The Women of Trachis*, translated by Michael Jameson; *Electra* and *Philoctetes*, translated by David Grene.

Three Theban Plays. Trans. by Theodore H. Banks. OUP 1956 $8.95. ISBN 0-19-501059-0. Contains *Antigone*, *Oedipus the King*, and *Oedipus at Colonus*.

Three Tragedies: Antigone, Oedipus the King, and Electra. Trans. by H. D. Kitto. OUP 1962 $7.95. ISBN 0-19-500374-8

Tragedies. 2 vols. Trans. by Francis Storr. *Loeb Class. Lib.* HUP $15.50 ea. Volume 1: *Oedipus the King, Oedipus at Colonus, Antigone*. Volume 2: *Ajax, Electra, Trachinae, Philoctetes*, and a bibliography of editions and translations.

The Tragedies of Sophocles. Trans. by Richard C. Jebb. *Select Bibliographies Repr. Ser.* Ayer repr. of 1904 ed. $19.00. ISBN 0-8369-6811-5

Women of Trachis. Trans. by C. K. Williams and Gregory W. Dickerson. Ed. by William Arrowsmith. *Greek Tragedy in New Translations*. OUP 1978 $19.95. ISBN 0-19-502050-2

BOOKS ABOUT SOPHOCLES

Bates, William N. *Sophocles, Poet and Dramatist*. Ed. by Richmond Lattimore. Russell Sage 1969 repr. of 1940 ed. o.p. Examines Sophocles' life and his lost manuscripts from records; illustrated.

Bloom, Harold, ed. *Sophocles*. Chelsea Hse. 1990 $29.95. ISBN 1-55546-323-1. Collection of critical essays by distinguished scholars that examine Sophocles' works from a variety of perspectives.

Bowra, C. M. *Sophoclean Tragedy*. OUP 1944 o.p. A sensitive and comprehensive study.

Campbell, Lewis. *Tragic Drama in Aeschylus, Sophocles and Shakespeare: An Essay*. Russell Sage 1965 repr. of 1904 ed. o.p. Compares tragic elements of the three playwrights.

Earp, Frank R. *Style of Sophocles*. Russell Sage 1972 repr. of 1944 ed. o.p. An intertextual discussion of Sophocles' writings.

Ehrenberg, Victor. *Sophocles and Pericles*. Humanities 1954 o.p. A description of the friendship between these two great Athenians.

Grene, David. *Reality and the Heroic Pattern: Last Plays of Ibsen, Shakespeare, and Sophocles*. U. Ch. Pr. 1967 o.p. A "basic and lucid study" (*LJ*) by the noted editor of *The Complete Greek Tragedies;* three of ten essays included treat Sophocles' *Ajax, Philoctetes*, and *Oedipus at Colonus*.

Hogan, James C. *A Commentary of the Plays of Sophocles*. S. Ill. U. Pr. 1991 $29.95. ISBN 0-8093-1664-1

Kirkwood, G. M. *A Study of Sophoclean Drama*. Johnson Repr. o.p. An illuminating and important analysis.

Knox, Bernard M. *The Heroic Temper: Studies in Sophoclean Tragedy*. U. CA Pr. 1983 $11.95. ISBN 0-520-04957-8. A perceptive study by a foremost scholar of Sophocles.

Reinhardt, Karl. *Sophocles*. Trans. by Hazel Harvey and David Harvey. B&N Imports 1979 o.p. A classic study. Introduction by Hugh Lloyd-Jones.

Scodel, Ruth. *Sophocles*. G. K. Hall 1980 $17.95. ISBN 0-8057-6578-6. General introduction to Sophocles' work with a valuable discussion of the basic elements of Greek drama.

Segal, Charles. *Tragedy and Civilization: An Interpretation of Sophocles*. HUP 1981 $34.95. ISBN 0-674-90206-8. A significant series of lectures.

Sheppard, J. T. *Aeschylus and Sophocles: Their Work and Influence*. Cooper Sq. repr. of 1930 ed. o.p.

Waldock, Arthur J. *Sophocles the Dramatist*. Cambridge U. Pr. $9.95. ISBN 0-521-09374-0. The author discusses the fundamental conflicts in Sophocles' work and asserts that he is first a dramatist, then a poet.

Webster, T. B. *An Introduction to Sophocles*. 1936. Richard West o.p. An excellent, basic study.

Whitman, Cedric H. *Sophocles: A Study of Heroic Humanism*. HUP 1951 o.p. An analysis of the plays as "literary monuments, social documents . . . philosophical treatises."

Winnington-Ingraham, R. P. *Sophocles: An Interpretation*. Cambridge U. Pr. 1980 o.p. A good introduction to the playwright.

THEOCRITUS. c.310–c.250 B.C.

Regarded as the creator of pastoral poetry, Theocritus was a native of Syracuse and lived in Alexandria. About 30 idylls and a number of his epigrams are extant. His genuine love of the country lends freshness and great beauty to the idylls; his bucolic characters are realistic and alive. He is a master of dramatic presentation, description, and lyrical refinement. He has had many imitators, among them VIRGIL and SPENSER (see Vol. 1). The surviving works of two other Greek pastoral poets are often included with those of Theocritus:

MOSCHUS of Syracuse, who lived in the second century B.C. and Bion, who is best known for his *Lament for Adonis*. The Andrew Lang translation in prose of these three poets is considered an English classic.

POETRY BY THEOCRITUS

The Greek Bucolic Poets. Trans. by J. M. Edmonds. *Loeb Class. Lib.* HUP 1912 $15.50. ISBN 0-674-99031-5. An accurate version; recommended.

Greek Pastoral Poetry: Theocritus, Bion and Moschus. Trans. by A. Holden. Johns Hopkins 1974 o.p.

The Idylls: Theocritus. Trans. by Robert Wells. Viking Penguin 1989 $6.95. ISBN 0-14-044523-4

Idylls of Theocritus. Select Bibliographies Repr. Ser. Ayer repr. of 1919 ed. $24.50. ISBN 0-8369-5688-5.

Poems. Ed. by K. J. Dover. Viking Penguin 1972 o.p. Beautifully produced textual edition and translation with an excellent introduction and commentary by a foremost scholar.

Poems. 2 vols. Trans. by A. S. Gow. Cambridge U. Pr. 1952 $170.00. ISBN 0-521-06616-0. A competent translation.

The Poems of Theocritus. Trans. by Anna Rist. Bks. Demand repr. of 1978 ed. $68.70. ISBN 0-8357-3887-6. Good translations with a useful introduction.

Theocritus. Trans. by Charles S. Calverley. *Select Bibliographies Repr. Ser.* Ayer repr. of 1869 ed. $17.00. ISBN 0-8369-6814-X. Appealing versions by an accomplished Victorian poet-translator.

BOOKS ABOUT THEOCRITUS

Gutzwiller, Kathryn J. *Theocritus' Pastoral Analogies: The Formation of a Genre.* U. of Wis. Pr. 1991 $47.50. ISBN 0-299-12940-3. An analysis of Theocritean pastoral as well as a model for the process by which other genres may have come into being.

Kerlin, Robert T. *Theocritus in English Literature.* Ed. by E. H. Warmington. Folcroft repr. of 1910 ed. o.p.

Rosenmeyer, Thomas G. *The Green Cabinet: Theocritus and the European Pastoral Lyric.* U. CA Pr. 1969 $12.95. ISBN 0-520-02362-5. A literary critique of Theocritus and his later influence.

THEOPHRASTUS. c.371–287 B.C.

This pupil and successor to ARISTOTLE (see Vols. 3, 4, and 5) as head of the Peripatetic school of philosophy wrote on a variety of subjects—botany, metaphysics, physics, and law—but is best known for his *Characters*, 30 satiric sketches of different character types. These were imitated by English writers of the seventeenth century and by La Bruyère in his famous *Caractères*.

WORKS BY THEOPHRASTUS

Characters. Loeb Class. Lib. HUP $15.50. ISBN 0-674-99248-2

Enquiry into Plants, and Minor Works on Odours and Weather Signs. 2 vols. Trans. by Arthur Hort. *Loeb Class. Lib.* HUP 1916 $15.50 ea. ISBNs 0-674-99077-3, 0-674-99088-9. Theophrastus's pre-Linnean works on botany; Greek and English appear on opposite pages.

Menander Plays and Fragments and Theophrastus Characters. Trans. by P. Vellacott. Viking Penguin 1973 o.p.

Moral Characters of Theophrastus. Trans. by Eustace Budgell. AMS Pr. repr. of 1714 ed. $28.00. ISBN 0-404-54147-X

THUCYDIDES. c.470–c.400 B.C.

[SEE Volume 3.]

XENOPHON. c.434?–c.355? B.C.

[SEE Volumes 3 and 4.]

MODERN GREEK LITERATURE

The tensions between tradition and the demands of contemporary society, between classicism and romanticism, and between patriotism and cosmopolitanism have generated the subjects and forms of many great works of art in modern Greece. Modern Greek literature begins with the War of Independence (1821–28), which became a cause for some Europeans and gained fame in English literature through LORD BYRON's (see Vol. 1) participation. After four centuries of Ottoman domination, nationalistic fervor expressed itself first politically and later in a literary renaissance. Two distinct schools arose: one using the *katharevousa* (the written language), imitating European models such as VICTOR HUGO, and producing romantic and patriotic poems (Alexander Soutsos is an example); the other using the *demotiki* (the spoken tongue) and blending the classical and romantic spirit, though adapting some European forms (Dionysios Solomos is an example). Around 1880 a new group arose around Yannis Psycharis in prose and KOSTES PALAMAS in poetry. This school, sometimes called the Parnassians after their French models, aimed at greater objectivity and restraint.

Three giants came to the fore in the first quarter of the twentieth century: ANGELOS SIKELIANOS, CONSTANTINE CAVAFY, and NIKOS KAZANTZAKIS. Sikelianos began under the influence of the Parnassians but grew into a celebrant of Dionysiac rapture in difficult but striking verse. Cavafy, who came from the cosmopolitan city of Alexandria, Egypt, did not start publishing until late in life, producing a small body of sensitive poems mainly about the tragic grandeur of postclassical Greece. The novels of Kazantzakis are well known, not only for their literary quality, but also through their translation into film. Both *Zorba the Greek* (1946) and *The Last Temptation of Christ* (1951), for example, were made into movies reaching a wide American audience. But Kazantzakis, repeatedly nominated for the Nobel Prize, is also a poet who wrote an ambitious epic continuation of the *Odyssey*.

More recent Greek writing includes several strains. Socially conscious writers are represented in the older generation by the Marxist poet Kostas Varnalis and in the present generation by YANNIS RITSOS. These are poets, concerned with political issues and social injustices, whose lives as well as their writings testify to the strength of their convictions. A second strain is the symbolists, such as GEORGE SEFERIS, the first Greek to win the Nobel Prize (1963). Seferis's work shows the influence of T. S. ELIOT (see Vol. 1) (whom he translated into Greek) and the French symbolists, but his voice is distinctive, at once celebrating and recoiling from the void in modern life. Finally, there are the surrealists, central among them ODYSSEUS ELYTIS, Greece's second Nobel laureate (1976). Elytis's poetry is filled with moving evocations of Greek island landscapes, yet often in a framework of difficult surrealistic or incantatory verse. Contemporary Greek literature continues to flourish, with a younger generation of writers building upon earlier literary traditions and experimenting with new forms and themes. Their work represents the latest in a rich and ancient heritage.

History and Criticism

Dimaras, C. T. *History of Modern Greek Literature.* Trans. by Mary P. Gianos. State U. NY Pr. 1973 o.p. Originally published in 1948 and a classic study, but the translation is flawed.

Friar, Kimon, ed. *Modern Greek Poetry: Translation, Introduction, an Essay on Translation, and Notes by Kimon Friar.* IBD Limited 1982 $18.25. ISBN 960-226-243-5. Includes a full introduction and an essay on translating modern Greek.

Gianos, Mary P., ed. *Introduction to Modern Greek Literature.* Irvington 1969 $29.50. ISBN 0-8057-3125-3

Keeley, Edmund, and Peter Bien, eds. *Modern Greek Writers. Princeton Essays in Lit. Ser.* Princeton U. Pr. 1984 $32.50. ISBN 0-691-06586-1. Examines the work of a number of modern Greek writers.

Lambropoulos, V. *Literature as National Institution: Studies in the Politics of Modern Greek Literature.* Princeton U. Pr. 1988 $37.50. ISBN 0-691-06731-7. Explores, with clarity and sophistication, the creation of the canon of modern Greek literature.

Lorenzatos, Zissimos. *The Lost Center and Other Essays in Greek Poetry.* Trans. by Kay Cicellis. *Princeton Essays in Lit. Ser.* Princeton U. Pr. 1980 $32.50. ISBN 0-691-06246-3. A collection of important essays that explore a definition of style through the essay.

Politis, Linos. *A History of Modern Greek Literature.* OUP 1973 o.p. More up-to-date than the history of Dimaras, but lacking some of the elegance of the earlier study.

Sherrard, Philip. *The Marble Threshing Floor. Select Bibliographies Repr. Ser.* Ayer repr. of 1956 ed. $22.00. ISBN 0-8369-5346-0. Analyzes the classical roots of modern Greek writers.

Spencer, Terence J. *Fair Greece, Sad Relic: Literary Philellenism from Shakespeare to Byron.* Hippocrene Bks. 1972 $20.50. ISBN 0-374-97557-4. A survey of literary contacts between England and modern Greece before the nineteenth-century Greek revival in England.

Collections

Barnstone, Willis, ed. *Eighteen Texts: Writings by Contemporary Greek Authors.* HUP 1972 o.p. Published during the rule of the Junta.

Beaton, Roderick. *Folk Poetry of Modern Greece.* Cambridge U. Pr. 1980 $44.95. ISBN 0-521-22853-0. A record of "oral" poetry from Greece, recorded by the author.

Dalven, Rae, ed. *Modern Greek Poetry.* Russell Sage 2nd ed. 1971 repr. of 1949 ed. o.p. Preface by Mark Van Doren.

Gianos, Mary P., ed. *Introduction to Modern Greek Literature.* Irvington repr. of 1969 ed. o.p. Limited to authors born between the years 1850 and 1914. Fiction and drama translated by Gianos, poetry by Kimon Friar.

Keeley, Edmund, and Philip Sherrard, trans. and eds. *Six Poets of Modern Greece.* Knopf 1961 o.p. "The selections stress the burning consciousness these poets share of their heritage. Something almost Delphic broods over the six who project their own personal vision": Cavafy, Sikelianos, Seferis, Antoniou, Elytis, Gatsos.

______. *Voices of Modern Greece: Selected Poems by Cavafy, Sikelianos, Seferis, Elytis, Gatsos.* Princeton U. Pr. rev. ed. 1981 repr. of 1966 ed. $29.95. ISBN 0-691-06473-3. An examination of the works of five major poets of modern Greece.

CHRONOLOGY OF AUTHORS

Makriyannis, John. 1797–1864
Palamas, Kostes. 1859–1943
Cavafy, Constantine P. 1863–1933
Drakopoulou, Theone. 1883–1968
Sikelianos, Angelos. 1884–1951
Kazantzakis, Niko. 1885–1957
Seferis, George. 1900–1971
Ritsos, Yannis. 1909–
Elytis, Odysseus. 1911–
Vakalo, Eleni. 1921–

CAVAFY, CONSTANTINE P. (Konstantinos Petrou Kabaphēs). 1863–1933

Cavafy was born and died in Alexandria, and he has always been closely associated with that city, even though he spent part of his childhood in England and did not settle in Alexandria until 1883. During his lifetime he was considered *the* poet of Alexandria, and today his name is identified primarily with LAWRENCE DURRELL's (see Vol. 1) characterization of him in *The Alexandria Quartet.* He is very much a poet of time and place, but also of a rich, varied language difficult to translate: "As a writer he starts with the ordinary life of his own city, which he knew at all levels from the most to the least reputable. From this, with its complex mixture of West and East, . . . he formed his own outlook on life and sense of values. . . . As a result, his indulgent cynicism, his understanding disillusion, can often bring historical subjects right home today. . . . Cavafy's subtle use of language, his mixture of common speech, officialese, and self-deflating formalisms to produce complex overtones of immediacy, irony, and detachment, are not more than hinted at in the existing translations; but his awareness of life, and his attitudes to it, have a rich place in the modern world" (*Modern World Literature*). Cavafy's work tends to diverge into the erotic—he was one of the first modern poets to deal explicitly with homosexuality—and the historical. Much of his work mingles both the past and the present. His view of life also is essentially tragic. He wrote fewer than 300 lyrics, most of which were distributed privately among friends rather than being published commercially. In recent years he has come to be regarded as one of the finest and most influential modern Greek poets.

POETRY BY CAVAFY

Collected Poems. Trans. by Philip Sherrard. Princeton U. Pr. 1992 $39.50. ISBN 0-691-06984-0. The complete bilingual edition of Cavafy's mature poetry—75 poems.

Complete Poems of Cavafy. HarBraceJ 1976 $10.95. ISBN 0-15-619820-7. Translations that "make genuine poetry, supple, sensitive and civil, as Cavafy's Greek required, and . . . often catch something of his characteristic 'demotic' touches" (*Manchester Guardian*). Useful notes. An excellent introduction by W. H. Auden.

BOOKS ABOUT CAVAFY

Bien, Peter. *Constantine Cavafy. Columbia Essays on Modern Writers Ser.* Col. U. Pr. 1964 o.p.

Jusdanis, Gregory. *The Poetics of Cavafy.* Princeton U. Pr. 1987 $35.00. ISBN 0-691-06720-1

Robinson, Christopher. *C. P. Cavafy. Studies in Modern Greek No. 1.* Caratzas 1990 $25.00 ISBN 0-89241-469-3

DRAKOPOULOU, THEONE (also known as Myrtiotissa). 1883–1968

Born in Constantinople, Theone Drakopoulou was the daughter of the Greek consul stationed there. While a young girl, she moved with her family to Crete, where she later began a career as an actress. Later in life she became a speech professor at the University of Athens.

Although Drakopoulou's literary output included autobiographical prose and translations, it is as a poet that she is best known. Her poetry, which is characterized by a melancholy tone, centers on the themes of despair and disappointment. In addition to such romantic themes, however, Drakopoulou has written poems inspired by Greece's civil war and by the country's liberation from Nazi occupation during World War II. Her 1932 collection of poems, *Gifts of Love,* won an award from the Academy of Athens. Another collection, *Cries* (1939), won her the National Poetry Prize of Greece. A limited number of her poems have been translated into English, including "I Love You" and "Women of Suli."

POETRY BY DRAKOPOULOU

The Penguin Book of Greek Verse. Ed. by C. A. Trypanis. Viking Penguin 1988 $9.95. ISBN 0-14-058595-8. Contains several of Drakopoulou's poems.

Modern Greek Poetry. Ed. by Rae Dalven. IBD Ltd. 1982 $18.25. ISBN 960-226-243-5. Includes a small selection of Drakopoulou's work; contains brief introductions to the poets.

ELYTIS, ODYSSEUS (Odhiseas Alepoudhellis). 1911– (NOBEL PRIZE 1979)

Odysseus Elytis, poet, painter, and translator, was born in Crete and educated in Athens and Paris. Elytis has worked in broadcasting and as an art and literary critic. His pseudonym, Odhiseas Alepoudhellis, is said to combine the three most prevalent themes in his work: Greece, hope, and freedom.

As a young poet, Elytis "turned away from the poetry of the damned . . . the nostalgia of autumnal landscapes foreign to Greece, and embraced the tenets of surrealism as a liberating force" (Friar, *Modern Greek Poetry*). His verse, atmospheric in quality and evocative of the landscape and climate of his island home, is a fusion of Greek myth, history, and nature with a modern twentieth-century consciousness. He is considered to be one of the most powerful contemporary lyric voices in modern Greek literature.

POETRY BY ELYTIS

The Axion Esti. Trans. by Edmund Keeley and George Savidis. *Pitt Poetry Ser.* U. of Pittsburgh Pr. 1979 $8.95. ISBN 0-8229-5318-8. Greek and English on facing pages.

The Sovereign Sun: Selected Poems. Trans. by Kimon Friar. Dufour 1990 $18.95. ISBN 1-85224-120-9. Surrealist poetry based on Greek Aegean Islands landscape; contains an extensive biographical introduction.

KAZANTZAKIS, NIKOS. 1885–1957

This distinguished novelist, poet, and translator was born in Crete and educated in Athens, Germany, Italy, and Paris, where he studied philosophy under HENRI BERGSON (see Vol. 4). He found time to write some 30 novels, plays, and books on philosophy, to serve his government, and to travel widely. He ran the Greek ministry of welfare from 1919 to 1921 and was minister of state briefly in 1945. A political activist, he spent his last years in France and died in Germany.

Kazantzakis's character Zorba has been called "one of the great characters of modern fiction," in a novel that "reflects Greek exhilaration at its best" (*TLS*). A film version of 1965, starring Anthony Quinn, made Kazantzakis widely known in the West. Intensely religious, he imbued his novels with the passion of his own restless spirit, "torn between the active and the contemplative, between the sensual and the aesthetic, between nihilism and commitment" (*Columbia Encyclopedia*). Judas, the hero of *The Last Temptation of Christ* (1951), is asked by Christ to betray him so that he can fulfill his mission through the crucifixion. For this book Kazantzakis was excommunicated from the Greek Orthodox Church. John Ciardi called *The Odyssey: A Modern Sequel* (1938)—Odysseus transformed into a revolutionary saint—"a monument of the age" (*SR*). The reverent fictional biography *Saint Francis* (1953), which follows the historical account closely, is told simply and with a cumulative emotional impact. *The Fratricides*, Kazantzakis's last novel, portrays yet another religious hero, a priest caught between Communists and Royalists in the Greek Civil War. Marc Slonim says that "throughout his work Kazantzakis remained true to the Hellenic tradition: his heroes are harmoniously developed individuals who feel a strong bond with their physical environment; the author's poetic imagination is of the kind that created legends and myths to explain man and the universe" (*N.Y. Times*).

Novels by Kazantzakis

The Fratricides. S&S Trade 1985 o.p.

The Greek Passion. S&S Trade 1953 o.p. A description of Greek peoples and history through myriad characters.

The Last Temptation of Christ. 1951. S&S Trade 1988 $10.95. ISBN 0-671-67257-6. Controversial interpretation of Christ's last days.

Rock Garden. S&S Trade 1963 o.p. One of his earliest novels, telling of a European caught in the Sino-Japanese wars of the 1930s.

Report to Greco. S&S Trade 1975 $12.95. ISBN 0-671-22027-6. Kazantzakis's autobiography, written during the last years of his life.

Saint Francis. 1953. S&S Trade 1971 $10.95. ISBN 0-671-21247-8. Presents a unique view of the famous Catholic saint.

Zorba the Greek. 1946. S&S Trade 1971 $19.95. ISBN 0-671-21132-3. This story of a Greek peasant probes the theme of conflict between the flesh and the spirit.

Poetry by Kazantzakis

The Odyssey: A Modern Sequel. 1938. S&S Trade 1969 $14.95. Takes up the story of Odysseus where Homer left off, "a major achievement" (Moses Hadas, *N.Y. Herald Tribune*).

Works by Kazantzakis

Freedom or Death. S&S Trade 1983 o.p. The Cretans' revolt of 1889 against their Turkish oppressors.

The Saviors of God. Trans. by Kimon Friar. S&S Trade 1969 $10.00. ISBN 0-671-20232-4. Spiritual exercises.

Books about Kazantzakis

Bien, Peter. *Kazantzakis: The Politics of the Spirit.* Princeton U. Pr. 1990 $29.95. ISBN 0-691-06786-4. Intellectual biography that approaches the distinguished (and controversial) writer by describing his struggle with political questions that were in reality aspects of a religious search.

______. *Kazantzakis and Linguistic Revolution in Greek Literature. Princeton Essays in Lit. Ser.* Princeton U. Pr. 1972 o.p. Examines the early career of Kazantzakis—his involvement with demotic writing; explores why demotic writing arose and what forms it took.

______. *Nikos Kazantzakis.* Col. U. Pr. 1972 o.p.

Kazantzakis, Helen. *Nikos Kazantzakis.* S&S Trade 1970 o.p.

______. *Nikos Kazantzakis: A Biography Based on His Letters.* Trans. by Amy Mims. Creative Arts Bks. 1983 repr. of 1968 ed. $12.95. ISBN 0-916870-62-6. "His wife has woven into her text hundreds of his unpublished letters, from those of his school days to the last notes he wrote on his deathbed" (*PW*).

Prevelakis, Pandelis. *Nikos Kazantzakis and His Odyssey.* Trans. by Philip Sherrard. S&S Trade 1961 o.p. Preface by Kimon Friar; a study of the poet and the poems from 1883 to 1957.

MAKRIYANNIS, JOHN. 1797–1864

A hero in the War of Independence, Makriyannis is also one of the greatest figures in modern Greek demotic literature. When he was 32 years old, he taught himself to write in order to record his memoirs, by which he hoped to justify his life and politics in the early years of the new nation. The result was a document of great artistic importance. Makriyannis's manuscript was not published until 1907, 43 years after his death, and the effect on the Greek literary world was enormous. SEFERIS, for example, regarded Makriyannis as the "humblest and also the steadiest" of his teachers.

NONFICTION BY MAKRIYANNIS

Makriyannis: The Memoirs of General Makriyannis, 1797–1864. Trans. by H. A. Lidderdale. OUP o.p.

PALAMAS, KOSTES. 1859–1943

Palamas is the central figure of the New School of Athens and "is a milestone in the history of Greek literature, for his works are the outburst, the catharsis of the long drama of more than 2,000 years, which from the days when the Alexandrian poets ceased to sing had not found the great personality who would give voice to the national sufferings and aspirations, agonies and glories, in the works of full magnitude" (Trypanis, *Medieval and Modern Greek Poetry*).

Born in Patras, Palamas was an erudite, profound, and prolific writer. His complete works include 18 volumes of poetry, fiction, drama, translation, criticism, and articles. Inspired by the cultural and historical legacy of ancient Greece, Byzantium, and the heroic era of 1921, he was influenced by both ancient and contemporary thinkers. Often nominated for the Nobel Prize, Palamas failed to gain during his lifetime the international reputation he deserved.

POETRY BY PALAMAS

The Twelve Words of the Gypsy. Trans. by Theodore Stephanides and George Katsimbalis. U. of Nebr. Pr. 1964 $19.95. ISBN 0-8032-0141-9. An epico-lyric poem of a gypsy musician, who as a "symbol of freedom and art," "develops into the Greek patriot," and finally into the "Hellene, citizen of the world" (Trypanis).

BOOKS ABOUT PALAMAS

Maskaleris, Thanasis. *Kostis Palamas. Twayne's World Authors Ser.* G. K. Hall o.p. A competent biography, examining the author's life with regard to the intellectual and sociopolitical conditions in which he lived.

Stavrou, Theofanis G., and Constantine A. Trypanis. *Kostis Palamas: A Portrait and an Appreciation.* Nostos Bks. 1985 $20.00. ISBN 0-932963-00-5

RITSOS, YANNIS. 1909–

Ritsos, imprisoned by the Greek dictatorship, has repeatedly suffered from his strong revolutionary sentiments: "Haunted by death, driven at times to the edge of madness and suicide, Ritsos throughout his life has been upheld by his obstinate faith in poetry as redemption, and in the revolutionary ideal" (Friar, *Modern Greek Poetry*).

Initially a follower of the demotic tradition, Ritsos went through a phase of militant, doctrinaire poetry. Eventually, however, his work became free of anger and recrimination. In long poems, such as *Romiosyne* (1947), he writes compassionately, celebrating life in an unadorned style. He has produced dozens of volumes of poems, drama, and translations.

POETRY BY RITSOS

Eighteen Short Songs of the Bitter Motherland. Trans. by Amy Mims. Nostos Bks. 1974 o.p. Revelations of the poet and his attachment to Greece.

Exile and Return: Selected Poems. Trans. by Edmund Keeley. Ecco Pr. 1985 $17.50. ISBN 0-88001-017-7. Poems that reflect the author's bitter years of imprisonment.

The Fourth Dimension: Selected Poems of Yannis Ritsos. Trans. by Rae Dalven. Godine 1977 o.p. Examines a few poems selected from each of Ritsos's works; contains a biographical introduction.

Selected Poems. Trans. by Kiman Friar and Kostas Myrsiades. BOA Edns. 1989 $30.00. ISBN 0-918526-66-3. Representative sampling of the full range of Ritsos's abundant poetic production spanning the past 50 years.

SEFERIS, GEORGE (Georgios Sepheriadēs). 1900–1971 (Nobel Prize 1963)

Seferis, who was Greece's ambassador to London in 1961, has done much to integrate the unique Greek heritage with avant-garde European poetry. He is regarded as one of the greatest poets of his time. Born in Smyrna, he moved to Athens at age 14. He studied in Paris at the end of World War I and afterward joined the Greek diplomatic service. "Eminent as he is as a European poet," wrote Rex Warner, "Seferis is preeminently a Greek poet, conscious of the Greek tradition which shaped, and indeed created the tradition of Europe. Throughout the poetry of Seferis one will notice his profound consciousness of the presence of the past and its weight." His themes show a constant awareness of both the dignity and the inevitable sorrow of humanity. His images—the voyage, the search, and the ruins that become alive and yet suggest death—are universal, his treatment of them contemporary. His language has a disciplined power and simplicity. In addition to the *Poems,* selections from his poetry appear in Edmund Keeley and Philip Sherrard's *Six Poets of Modern Greece.* The Royal Swedish Literary Academy awarded Seferis the Nobel Prize "for his eminent lyrical writing, inspired by a deep feeling for the Hellenic world of culture."

Poetry by Seferis

Collected Poems, 1924–1955. Trans. by Philip Sherrard. Princeton U. Pr. 3rd ed. 1981 repr. of 1969 ed. $65.00. ISBN 0-691-06471-7. Bibliography, notes.

Poems. Trans. by Rex Warner. Godine 1979 o.p.

Three Secret Poems. Trans. by Walter Kaiser. HUP 1969 o.p.

Nonfiction by Seferis

A Poet's Journal: Days of 1945–1951. Trans. by Athan Angnostopoulos. HUP 1974 $7.95. ISBN 0-674-68041-3. Introduction by Walter Kaiser.

SIKELIANOS, ANGELOS. 1884–1951

Born on the isle of Lefkas, Sikelianos studied law at Athens but abandoned it without completing his degree. In 1907 he wrote the long poem that established his reputation, *The Visionary,* and also married his first wife, Evelyn Palmer, of Bar Harbor, Maine. He and "Eva" spent much of the next quarter of a century reviving ancient Greek arts and traditions, and even trying to establish a new Delphic religion. During the German occupation of Greece in World War II, Sikelianos helped many people, especially Jews, survive. During that time he wrote and clandestinely circulated his *Akritic Songs,* poems of resistance. Much of his other poetry fuses Christian and pagan elements or recreates a Dionysiac spirit in rapturous, lofty language.

Poetry by Sikelianos

Selected Poems. Trans. by E. Keeley and P. Sherrard. Princeton U. Pr. 1979 o.p. A selection of classical poetry; spans the author's career.

Six Poems from the Greek of Sikelianos and Seferis. Trans. by Lawrence Durrell. Rhodes 1946 o.p.

VAKALO, ELENI (Helen Vakolo). 1921–

Eleni Vakalo was born in Constantinople of Greek parents. After studying archeology at the University of Athens and art history at the Sorbonne in Paris, Vakalo began writing for Greek periodicals in 1949. For many years she served as an art critic for two prominent journals. In 1958 she helped found the School of Decorative Arts with her husband George Vakalo and others, and she has taught art history there.

Vakalo's poetry began appearing in 1945, and she has published 12 volumes of poetry since then. In addition to her poetry, she has translated the work of the modern American poet, MARIANNE MOORE. Like her countrywoman, THEONE DRAKOPOULOU, Vakalo's poetry has its roots in the postwar trauma of the Nazi occupation of Greece and the Greek civil war. Her language is direct and spare, with a deliberate avoidance of luxuriousness and ornateness.

POETRY BY VAKALO

A Book of Women Poets from Antiquity to Now. Ed. by Aliki and Willis Barnstone. Schocken 1992 repr. of 1980 ed. $18.00. ISBN 0-8052-0997-2. Includes several poems by Vakalo. One of the most comprehensive collections of women's poems available in English.

Geneology. Trans. by Paul Merchant. Viking Penguin 1977 o.p. One of Vakalo's few nonsurrealistic collections of poems.

CHAPTER 12

Latin Literature

Fred J. Nichols

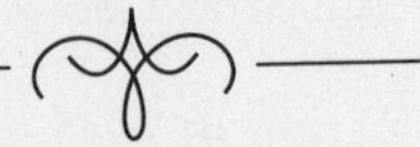

Go, little book, my little tragedy!
God grant thy maker, ere his ending day,
May write some tale of happy poetry!
But, little book, of any poet's lay
Envy of heart here shalt thou not display,
But kiss the steps where pass through ages spacious,
Vergil and Ovid, Homer, Lucan and Statius.

—CHAUCER, *Troilus and Cresseyde*

Latin Literature must always be seen in light of its Greek antecedents and of contemporary Roman history. "Arma virumque cano" ("Of arms and the man I sing"), the opening words of VIRGIL's *The Aeneid,* tell the reader that the poem will comment on HOMER's *Iliad* (the arms) and *Odyssey* (the man). Viewed in another way, however, these words suggest the Roman Empire and the Emperor Augustus. The poem is both the noblest Roman epic and the imperially sanctioned history of Rome.

The early poets Livius Andronicus, Naevius, and Ennius (their works survive only in fragments) adapted Homer and the Greek tragedians in lustrous Latin verse and thereby laid the foundations of the literature. Influenced by Greek New Comedy and native Italian farce, Plautus was a popular playwright when Rome was expanding in the Mediterranean and developing a taste for Hellenic culture. As Greek fashions took firm hold in the second century B.C., particularly in the brilliant circle associated with Scipio Africanus Minor, TERENCE was admired for his polished romantic comedies written after the style of his Greek predecessor MENANDER.

The first century B.C., an era of debilitating civil wars at home and conquest abroad, when Rome had replaced Athens and Alexandria as the political and intellectual center of the Mediterranean world, boasted very great literary artists. CICERO was preeminent as orator, philosopher, and statesman. He translated the eloquence of DEMOSTHENES and the logic of PLATO (see Vol. 4) to Latin letters, which he dominated thereafter. The philosopher EPICURUS (see Vol. 4) was interpreted by LUCRETIUS in his melancholy hexameter poem *De Rerum Natura (On the Nature of the Universe)*. Lucretius's metrical skill and beautiful phrases were imitated by Virgil, HORACE, and CATULLUS. This last celebrated his loves and his hates in a manner suggestive of the Greek Alexandrian poets, who preferred a personal statement in short, elegant verse to the "swollen" epic. Republican Rome ended with the assassination of JULIUS CAESAR (see Vol. 3), himself an intelligent propagandist of his own military acumen in the *Commentaries*.

The Augustan or the Golden Age of Roman literature (c.44 B.C. to A.D. 17) acclaimed the political harmony achieved by the Emperor Augustus after almost a century of civil strife. Its brightest light was Virgil, whose *Aeneid* immortalized the Roman genius for ruling the world with law, establishing the custom of peace, sparing the conquered, subduing the proud. Virgil's friend Horace sang of Roman virtues, such as moderation and patriotism, with technical virtuosity and self-mocking wit. Also at the emperor's court was OVID, whose clever elegiac treatises on love's vagaries and fantastical *Metamorphoses* gently mocked imperial Rome. The elegiac poets TIBULLUS and PROPERTIUS proclaimed their personal—even idiosyncratic—loves.

LIVY's (see Vol. 3) anecdotal histories were to prose what Virgil's epic was to poetry in the Augustan epoch. Writing nearly a century later, TACITUS (see Vol. 3) never shared Livy's optimism. Rather, his *Annals* emphasized the loss of liberty and the resulting moral weakness caused by the absolutism of the Empire. His acute and pessimistic analysis was reminiscent of SALLUST (see Vol. 3), a historian of Cicero's age. And the thread of Tacitus's narrative was taken up again in the fourth century A.D. by AMMIANUS MARCELLINUS (see Vol. 3), who was the last great chronicler of Rome.

In other literary areas, Phaedrus, a Greek freedman attached to Augustus's household, composed beast fables for advice and entertainment. The despotic political climate of the age took its toll of writers. The urbane PETRONIUS, author of *The Satyricon;* SENECA, the Stoic philosopher and mordant playwright; and the epic poet LUCAN all died for political offenses against the emperors. Like Horace before them, PERSIUS and JUVENAL (the most incisive of the three) developed satire as an original Roman genre. Juvenal chafed under the tyranny of the Emperor Domitian, and he suffered for speaking the truth. Others in the first century A.D. (known as the Silver Age of Latin literature) chose not to satirize their own era. QUINTILIAN's manual of rhetoric was a valuable, wise guide to teaching the art of oratory. PLINY'S letters offered a fascinating picture of contemporary Roman life and a tactful account of current politics. SUETONIUS looked back in time to the private lives of the Caesars, and STATIUS wrote of mythological heroes and wars in epic verse. MARTIAL's epigrams could be biting, cruel, and sexually explicit, but their wit and polish made them models of their kind.

APULEIUS, whose engaging prose *Metamorphoses* is more commonly known in English as *The Golden Ass,* flourished in the second century A.D. His was the time of the *pax Romana,* before the collapse of the Empire. Donatus and Servius, the biographer and the commentator of Virgil, recalled the past glories of the Augustan Age. Priscian's grammar became a source book for the Middle Ages, Martianus Capella codified the liberal arts for centuries to come, and Macrobius wrote influential commentaries on Cicero and Virgil.

From the third century onward to the Fall of Rome in the fifth century, Christian doctrine ruled the literary imagination. Tertullian used his training in Roman rhetoric to champion Christianity and was really the first Latin advocate of the new religion. The most classical of all the early apologists was Lactantius, the Christian Cicero. Later, in the fourth century, Prudentius unified classical poetry with Christian thought in his allegory of the soul, which was modeled on Virgil.

The fifth century, dark days for Rome, was illuminated by Christian thinkers. Trained in classical rhetoric, Christian theology, Greek, Hebrew, and with a mastery of Cicero, Virgil, and Horace, St. Jerome made a fresh translation of the scriptures from the original Hebrew and Greek into a literary Latin called the Vulgate, thereby shaping Christian thought and expression for all time. St.

Augustine's knowledge of Latin writers and of Neoplatonism deepened his presentation of Christianity in the seminal *Confessions* and *City of God*.

After the Fall of Rome in the fifth century, Latin continued to be the official language of the West. It survived when Greek was forgotten. Vernacular European authors regarded extant Latin works, especially those of Cicero, Virgil, Horace, and Ovid, as paragons. These models of perfection from antiquity stimulated fertile literary activity, just as the Greek masters had for the Romans centuries earlier. Virgil interpreted Homer and Roman history in sublime Latin verse, and, in turn, fed the genius of DANTE and MILTON (see Vol. 1), the consummate poets of Christianity. Cicero transmitted a Latinate Plato to the church fathers and medieval apologists. These two, and their Greek predecessors, are the pillars of European and American thought and letters.

HISTORY AND CRITICISM

Appian. *Roman History*. 4 vols. Trans. by H. E. White. *Loeb Class. Lib.* HUP $15.50 ea. A fascinating, anecdotal account written by a Greek living in Rome at the time of Antoninus Pius.

Bury, J. B. *A History of the Later Roman Empire: From the Death of Theodosius to the Death of Justinian*. 1889. 2 vols. Dover 1957 $9.95 ea. ISBNs 0-486-20398-0, 0-486-20399-9. The foremost history of the Empire in the fourth, fifth, and sixth centuries.

Carcopino, Jerome. *Daily Life in Ancient Rome: The People and the City at the Height of the Empire*. 1940. Trans. by E. O. Lorimer. Ed. by Henry T. Rowell. Yale U. Pr. 1960 $12.95. ISBN 0-300-00031-6. A standard work.

Cary, M., and H. H. Scullard. *A History of Rome*. St. Martin 1976 $37.35. ISBN 0-312-38395-9. Competent and reliable work.

Christ, Karl. *The Romans: An Introduction to Their History and Civilization*. Trans. by Christopher Holme. U. CA Pr. 1984 $12.95. ISBN 0-520-05634-5. An excellent, clear introduction, with illustrations.

D'Alton, John F. *Roman Literary Theory and Criticism*. 1931. Russell WV 1962 o.p. A valuable outline of the literary canons that influenced Roman writers.

Dudley, Donald R. *The Romans, 850 B.C.–A.D. 337*. Knopf 1970 o.p. Detailed, dense, and thorough, but quite readable.

Duff, John W. *A Literary History of Rome: From the Origins to the Close of the Golden Age*. 1928. Ed. by A. M. Duff. HarpC 1953 o.p. A reset edition of a standard work with a supplementary bibliography of writings that have appeared since 1909. Includes a preliminary study of the origins, language, and character of the Romans, and a history of Latin literature.

______. *A Literary History of Rome in the Silver Age: From Tiberius to Hadrian*. 1927. Ed. by A. M. Duff. Greenwood 1979 repr. of 1964 ed. $47.50. ISBN 0-313-20939-1. An authoritative account.

Fowler, Warde. *The Religious Experience of the Roman People: From the Earliest Times to the Age of Augustus*. 1911. Cooper Sq. 1971 o.p. Respected and authoritative.

Giannelli, Giulio, ed. *The World of Ancient Rome*. Putnam Pub. Group 1967 o.p. An excellent discussion of Roman life by 12 noted classical scholars of Italy, France, and England. "Both text and pictures make this book a welcome companion to all studies in the history, language and literature of Rome" (*LJ*).

Gibbon, Edward. *The Decline and Fall of the Roman Empire*. 1776–88. 3 vols. Random 1977. Vol. 1 $15.95. ISBN 0-394-60401-6. Vol. 2 $16.95. ISBN 0-394-60402-4. Vol. 3 $16.95. ISBN 0-394-60403-2. The classic analysis of Roman history, famous for its incisive observations and impressive prose style.

Griffin, Jasper. *Latin Poets and Roman Life*. U. of NC Pr. 1986 $37.50. ISBN 0-8078-1682-5. A lively and entertaining study of the relationship of literature to its social background.

Hadas, Moses. *A History of Latin Literature*. Col. U. Pr. 1952 $60.00. ISBN 0-231-01848-7. The distinguished classical authority drawing on modern scholarship and newer techniques of analysis and appreciation for his interpretations of the classics.

Hamilton, Edith. *The Roman Way*. Norton 1984 repr. of 1932 ed. $3.95. ISBN 0-393-00232-2. Famous and very readable.

IJsewijn, Jozef. *Companion to Neo-Latin Studies*. Scholars Pr. GA 1990 $54.95. ISBN 1-55540-576-2. A useful introduction to Renaissance Latin Literature.

Johnston, Harold W. *Private Life of the Romans. Select Bibliographies Repr. Ser.* Ayer 1972 repr. of 1903 ed. $32.00. ISBN 0-8369-9915-0. Contains useful background information.

Kennedy, George. *The Art of Rhetoric in the Roman World, 300 B.C.-A.D. 300*. Bks. Demand repr. of 1972 ed. $180.00. ISBN 0-8357-3389-0. A first-rate study of a subject of central importance in Latin literature.

Kenney, E. J., ed. *Latin Literature*. Vol. 2 in *The Cambridge History of Classical Literature*. Cambridge U. Pr. 1983 o.p. Standard and definitive, with full bibliographies.

Konstan, David. *Roman Comedy*. Cornell Univ. Pr. 1983 $29.95. ISBN 0-8014-1531-4. Good critical analysis of key plays in terms of social relations.

Löfstedt, Einar. *Roman Literary Portraits: Aspects of the Literature of the Roman Empire*. Greenwood 1978 repr. of 1958 ed. $38.50. ISBN 0-313-20455-1. Expertly done biographical profiles.

MacKendrick, Paul. *The Mute Stones Speak: The Story of Archaeology in Italy*. Norton 1983 $12.95. ISBN 0-393-30119-2. Fascinating background information.

Nash, Ernest. *Pictorial Dictionary of Ancient Rome*. 2 vols. Hacker 1980 repr. of 1968 ed. $150.00. ISBN 0-87817-265-3. An essential reference work; a systematic pictorial survey of all Roman buildings and monuments, with old etchings, plans, and drawings to document the original appearance of destroyed or altered monuments; thorough bibliography.

Ogilvie, R. M. *Roman Literature and Society*. Viking Penguin 1980 $6.95. ISBN 0-14-022081-X. A brief introductory survey.

Plutarch. *Lives*. 6 vols. Trans. by Thomas North. AMS Pr. repr. of 1896 ed. $270.00. ISBN 0-404-51870-2. Wonderfully entertaining biographies of the elite of antiquity written in graceful English prose.

Putnam, Michael C. *Essays on Latin Lyric, Elegy, and Epic*. Princeton U. Pr. 1982 $50.00. ISBN 0-691-01388-8. Incisive revisionist criticism.

Quinn, Kenneth. *Texts and Contexts: The Roman Writers and Their Audience*. Routledge 1979 o.p. A good introductory survey of major works for the contemporary reader.

Richlin, Amy. *The Garden of Priapus: Sexuality and Aggression in Roman Humor*. OUP 1992 $14.95. ISBN 0-19-506872-6. A thorough approach to an interesting subject.

Rostovtzeff, Mikhail. *Social and Economic History of the Roman Empire*. 2 vols. Ed. by P. M. Frazer. OUP 1957 o.p. Authoritative and widely respected.

Rowell, Henry Thompson. *Rome in the Augustan Age*. U. of Okla. Pr. 1971 repr. of 1962 ed. $10.95. ISBN 0-8061-0956-4. Interesting and authoritative material; excellent index and bibliography.

Sellar, William Young. *The Roman Poets of the Republic*. Biblo 1987 repr. of 1889 ed. $22.00. ISBN 0-8196-0160-8. A well-respected older study.

Sullivan, J. P. *Literature and Politics in the Age of Nero*. Cornell Univ. Pr. 1985 $28.95. ISBN 0-8014-1740-6. Lucid study of the effects of Nero's patronage.

Syme, Ronald. *The Roman Revolution*. OUP 1964 $16.95. ISBN 0-19-881001-6. A sophisticated scholar examines the changeover from republic to monarchy after the death of Caesar in convincing and devastating detail.

Veyne, Paul. *Roman Erotic Elegy: Love, Poetry, and the West*. U. Ch. Pr. 1988 $38.00. ISBN 0-226-85431-0. An influential work.

Wilkinson, L. P. *Golden Latin Artistry*. U. of Okla. Pr. 1986 $16.95. ISBN 0-8061-1943-8. Analyzes Latin literature of the Golden Age with sensitivity and understanding.

Williams, Gordon. *Figures of Thought in Roman Poetry*. Bks. Demand repr. of 1980 ed. $80.40. ISBN 0-8357-3760-8. Described as "about the technique of poetry"; provocative and intelligent.

______. *Tradition and Originality in Roman Poetry*. OUP 1986 $118.00. ISBN 0-19-814347-8. An important seminal study.

Woodman, Tony, and David West, eds. *Poetry and Politics in the Age of Augustus*. Cambridge U. Pr. 1984 $54.95. ISBN 0-521-24553-2. Intelligent essays on Horace, Virgil, Propertius, and Ovid, in the context of the politics of their time.

COLLECTIONS

Davenport, Basil, ed. *The Portable Roman Reader*. *Viking Portable Lib*. Viking Penguin 1977 $8.95. ISBN 0-14-015056-0. An excellent introduction to the most important texts.

Duckworth, George E., ed. *The Complete Roman Drama*. 2 vols. Random 1942 o.p. All the extant comedies of Plautus and Terence and the tragedies of Seneca in a variety of translations.

Grant, Michael, ed. *Latin Literature: An Anthology*. Viking Penguin 1979 $7.95. ISBN 0-14-044389-4. A collection of verse and prose with introductions discussing the authors and their influence.

Harsh, Philip W., ed. *An Anthology of Roman Drama*. HarBraceJ 1960 $14.00. ISBN 0-03-008615-9. A good collection of basic texts.

Nichols, Fred J., trans. and ed. *An Anthology of Neo-Latin Poetry*. Bks. Demand repr. of 1979 ed. $160.00. ISBN 0-8357-8027-9. A selection of Renaissance poetry in Latin ranging from Petrarch to Milton with a critical introduction.

Waddell, Helen, trans. and ed. *More Latin Lyrics: From Virgil to Milton*. Norton 1985 repr. of 1976 ed. $9.95. ISBN 0-393-30232-6. A well translated selection of poems from all periods.

Warmington, E. H., ed. *Minor Latin Poets*. *Loeb Class. Lib*. HUP $15.50. ISBN 0-674-99314-4. Clear prose translations.

Wedeck, Harry E., ed. *Classics of Roman Literature*. Littlefield 1964 o.p. Annotated, with many new translations.

Wender, Dorothea, trans. and ed. *Roman Poetry: From the Republic to the Silver Age*. S. Ill. U. Pr. 1980 $10.95. ISBN 0-8093-1694-3. Lively translations with a good introductory essay.

CHRONOLOGY OF AUTHORS

Terence. c.190 B.C.–159 B.C.
Plautus, Titus Maccius. d. c.184 B.C.
Cicero. 106 B.C.–43 B.C.
Caesar, Julius. 100 B.C.–44 B.C.
Lucretius. c.94 or 99 B.C.–55 B.C.
Catullus. 84? B.C.–54? B.C.
Virgil. 70 B.C.–19 B.C.
Horace. 65 B.C.–8 B.C.
Livy. c.59 B.C.–c.A.D. 17
Propertius. c.50 B.C.–c.16 B.C.
Tibullus. 48? B.C.–19 B.C.
Ovid. 43 B.C.–A.D. 17
Seneca, Lucius Annaeus. c.3 B.C.–A.D. 65
Petronius. d. 65
Persius. 34–62
Quintilian. c.35–c.95
Lucan. 39–65
Martial. 40?–104
Statius, Publius Papinius. c.45–c.96
Tacitus, Cornelius. c.56–c.112
Juvenal. 60?–140?
Pliny the Younger. c.61–c.112
Suetonius. c.69–c.140
Apuleius, Lucius. 114–?

APULEIUS, LUCIUS. 114–?

Apuleius, of African birth, was educated in Carthage and Athens. His most famous work, *The Golden Ass* (c.150), is the tale of a young philosopher who transformed himself not into a bird as he had expected, but into an ass. After many adventures he was rescued by the goddess Isis. The episode of "Cupid and Psyche," told with consummate grace, is the most celebrated section. This romance of the declining Empire influenced the novels of BOCCACCIO, CERVANTES, FIELDING (see Vol. 1), and SMOLLETT (see Vol. 1); Heywood used the theme for a drama and WILLIAM MORRIS (see Vol. 1) used some of the material in *The Earthly Paradise*. Robert Graves's "translation abandons the aureate Latinity of Apuleius for a dry, sharp, plain style—which is itself a small masterpiece of twentieth-century prose" (Kenneth Rexroth, *SR*). The new translation by John Arthur Hanson is authoritative.

WORKS BY APULEIUS

Apologia and Florida. Trans. by H. E. Butler. Greenwood 1970 repr. of 1909 ed. $39.75. ISBN 0-8371-3066-2. A clear and straightforward translation.

The Golden Ass, or Metamorphoses. c. 150. Trans. by Robert Graves. FS&G 1951 $9.95. ISBN 0-374-50532-2

BOOKS ABOUT APULEIUS

Haight, Elizabeth H. *Apuleius and His Influence*. Cooper Sq. 1963 repr. of 1930 ed. $30.00. ISBN 0-8154-0108-6. A standard study.

Neumann, Erich. *Amor and the Psyche: The Psychic Development of the Feminine*. Trans. by Ralph Manheim. Princeton U. Pr. 1956 $8.95. ISBN 0-691-01772-7. A commentary on the tale by Apuleius.

Schlam, Carl C. *The Metamorphoses of Apuleius: On Making an Ass of Oneself*. U. of NC Pr. 1992 $24.95. ISBN 0-8078-2013-X. A witty and intelligent critical analysis.

Tatum, James. *Apuleius and the Golden Ass*. Cornell Univ. Pr. 1979 o.p. An introductory work aimed at the general reader.

CAESAR, JULIUS. 100 B.C.–44 B.C.

[SEE Volume 3]

CATULLUS (Gaius Valerius Catullus). 84? B.C.–54? B.C.

Catullus was born in Verona of a wealthy family, but spent much of his short life in Rome. He moved in fashionable society there and was captivated by a woman he called Lesbia, who has been identified as Clodia, a notorious aristocrat. His 25 poems to her tell the story of his tormented love. These together with his other verse—occasional, satiric, epiclike, and epigrammatic—have been widely imitated. The Latin poets HORACE, VIRGIL, PROPERTIUS, and MARTIAL were all indebted to him, and he has been translated into English by such eminent poets as CAMPION (see Vol. 1), JONSON (see Vol. 1), BYRON (see Vol. 1), and TENNYSON (see Vol. 1). By his successors he was called *doctus* (learned) because of his ideal of technical perfection, development of new literary forms (miniature epic, elegy, and epigram), and erudition.

POETRY BY CATULLUS

Odi et Amo: The Complete Poetry of Catullus. Trans. by Roy A. Swanson. Macmillan 1959 $5.99. ISBN 0-02-418490-X. A very readable translation.

Poems. Trans. by Guy Lee. OUP 1990 $48.00. ISBN 0-19-814743-0. Jaunty and effective translation.

Poems. Trans. by Peter Whigham. U. CA Pr. 1983 $39.95. ISBN 0-520-05082-7. Very free translation.

Works of Catullus and Tibullus. Trans. by F. W. Cornish. *Loeb Class. Lib.* HUP rev. ed. 1935 o.p. A clear prose translation.

Books about Catullus

Garrison, Daniel. *The Student's Catullus.* U. of Okla. Pr. 1991 $12.95. ISBN 0-8061-2354-0. A very useful guide for a newcomer to the poems.

Harrington, Karl P. *Catullus and His Influence.* Cooper Sq. repr. of 1930 ed. $28.50. ISBN 0-8154-0110-8. A fundamental study.

Havelock, Eric Alfred. *The Lyric Genius of Catullus.* Russell WV 1967 repr. of 1939 ed. o.p. A penetrating critical analysis that includes the Latin text of the poems with free translations by the author; bibliography.

Quinn, Kenneth. *The Catullan Revolution.* U. of Mich. Pr. 1971 o.p. An effective critical approach.

______. *Catullus: Poems—A Commentary.* St. Martin 1971 $30.65. ISBN 0-312-12495-3. Quinn examines the literary, political, and social aspects of the poems with passionate interest. All of his studies are good reading.

Small, Stuart G. P. *Catullus: A Reader's Guide to the Poems.* U. Pr. of Amer. 1983 o.p. Straightforward, basic introduction for a reader new to the poems.

Wiseman, T. P. *Catullus and His World: A Reappraisal.* Cambridge U. Pr. 1986 $47.95. ISBN 0-521-31968-4. Vivid and well-informed study of Catullus in the context of his time.

CICERO (Marcus Tullius Cicero). 106 B.C.–43 B.C.

Cicero was Rome's great prose stylist. Of his speeches, 58 are extant, as well as approximately 900 of his letters, many political and philosophical writings, and rhetorical treatises. As a youth he studied law, oratory, Greek literature, and philosophy. He became consul in 63 B.C., uncovered the conspiracy of Catiline, and aroused the people by his famous "Orations against Cataline." His political career was long, stormy, and often inconsistent. When out of favor or banished, he devoted himself to literary composition, writing many revealing letters and such well-known essays as "On Friendship," "On Duties," and "On Old Age," which together with the "Tusculans" and the "Dream of Scipio" have deeply influenced European thought and literature.

During the civil war he sided with Pompey, but after Pompey's decisive defeat at the Battle of Pharsalus in 48 B.C., Cicero became reconciled with Caesar. After Caesar's assassination, Cicero attacked Antony in his *Philippics.* When the Second Triumvirate was established, Antony demanded the head of his enemy. Cicero escaped but was overtaken by soldiers. He died courageously; at Antony's command, his head and hands were displayed over the orators' rostra in Rome. Cicero is one of the subjects of PLUTARCH's *Lives.*

Works by Cicero

Murder Trials. Trans. by Michael Grant. Hippocrene Bks. 1986 $16.95. ISBN 0-88029-075-7. Good translation of fascinating material.

On Duties. Trans. by Miriam T. Griffin and E. M. Atkins. Cambridge U. Pr. 1991 $37.95. ISBN 0-521-34338-0. A fluent and accurate translation.

On Oratory and Orators. Trans. by J. S. Watson. S. Ill. U. Pr. 1986 repr. of 1970 ed. $19.95. ISBN 0-8093-1293-X

On the Commonwealth. c.51 B.C. Trans. by George H. Sabine and Stanley B. Smith. Macmillan 1986 $10.50. ISBN 0-02-404980-8. An introductory translation.

On the Good Life. Trans. by Michael Grant. Viking Penguin 1971 $5.95. ISBN 0-14-044244-8

Philippics. Trans. by D. R. Shackleton Bailey. HUP 1926 $15.50. ISBN 0-674-99208-3. Clear and accurate translation.

Select Letters. Ed. by D. R. Shackleton Bailey. Cambridge U. Pr. 1980 $54.95. ISBN 0-521-29524-6. An excellent study by the foremost authority.

Selected Letters. Trans. by D. R. Shackleton Bailey. *Penguin Class. Ser.* Viking Penguin 1986 $9.95. ISBN 0-14-044458-0. Good translation aimed at nonspecialist.

Selected Political Speeches. Trans. by Michael Grant. Viking Penguin 1977 $6.95. ISBN 0-14-044214-6. Includes some of the most famous orations.

Selected Works. Trans. by Michael Grant. Viking Penguin 1960 $5.95. ISBN 0-14-044099-2. Effective and well-chosen selections.

Works. Loeb Class. Lib. 28 vols. HUP 1912–58 $15.50 ea. Excellent edition.

BOOKS ABOUT CICERO

Gotoff, Harold C. *Cicero's Elegant Style: An Analysis of the Pro Archia.* U. of Ill. Pr. 1979 o.p. Detailed introduction to one of Cicero's most remarkable works for the modern reader.

Mitchell, Thomas N. *Cicero: The Ascending Years.* Yale U. Pr. 1979 o.p.

______. *Cicero: The Senior Statesman.* Yale U. Pr. 1991 $32.50. ISBN 0-300-04779-7. Definitive biography along with the preceding volume.

Petersson, Torsten. *Cicero: A Biography.* Biblo 1920 $25.00. ISBN 0-8196-0119-5. Well-known older study.

Rawson, Elizabeth. *Cicero: A Portrait.* Cornell Univ. Pr. 1983 $39.50. ISBN 0-8014-1628-0

Rolfe, John C. *Cicero and His Influence.* Cooper Sq. repr. of 1930 ed. o.p. An important basic work.

Strachan-Davidson, J. L. *Cicero and the Fall of the Roman Republic.* AMS Pr. repr. of 1894 ed. $30.00. ISBN 0-404-58287-7. A classic analysis.

Wood, Neal. *Cicero's Social and Political Thought.* U. CA Pr. 1991 $45.00. ISBN 0-520-06042-3. Focuses on Cicero's views on natural law and justice, private property, the idea of the state, the theory of the mixed constitution, and the practice of politics.

Wooten, Cecil W. *Cicero's Philippics and Their Demosthenic Model: The Rhetoric of Crisis.* U. of NC Pr. 1983 $27.50. ISBN 0-8078-1558-6. Cicero's response to his Greek models.

HORACE (Quintus Horatius Flaccus). 65 B.C.–8 B.C.

Horace's father was an ambitious "freedman of modest circumstances," who gave his son the best available education. While a student in Athens, Horace met Brutus and fought in the Battle of Philippi. After that defeat he returned to Italy to find his farm confiscated, became a clerk in the civil service, and started writing. Through VIRGIL he met Maecenas, the great patron of literature, who gave him the Sabine farm that Horace celebrated in his poetry. His circumstances improved as his friendship with Maecenas and the Emperor Augustus grew, and the sarcasm and occasional sexual explicitness of the *Epodes* (30 B.C.) and *Satires* (35-30 B.C.) gave way to the more genial and mellow mood of the *Odes* (23–13 B.C.) and *Epistles.* He is acknowledged as one of Rome's greatest poets because of his perfection of verse technique, his candid self-portraiture, urbane wit, sincere patriotism, and sensible commendation of the golden mean. He made the Rome of his day come alive in street scenes, private banquets, love affairs, country weekends, and in personalities great and small, rich and poor. The literary canons set forth in his *Ars Poetica* (13–8 B.C.) dominated literary criticism throughout the Middle Ages and into the eighteenth century. His impeccable and very quotable use of language has been widely admired, and his influence on English letters is extensive. Poetic translations of Horace into English include those by JONSON (see Vol. 1), DRYDEN (see Vol. 1), MILTON (see Vol. 1), CONGREVE (see Vol. 1), and POPE (see Vol. 1).

WORKS BY HORACE

Ars Poetica (The Art of Poetry) (13–8 B.C.). AMS Pr. repr. of 1783 ed. $23.00. ISBN 0-404-54123-2

The Works of Horace. 2 vols. Trans. into English prose by David Watson. Rev. by W. Crakelt. AMS Pr. 1976 repr. of 1792 ed. $87.50. ISBN 0-404-54150-X. An elegant and authoritative translation.

Poetry by Horace

The Essential Horace: Odes, Epodes, Satires and Epistles. Trans. by Burton Raffel. N. Point Pr. 1983 $13.50. ISBN 0-86547-112-6. Foreword and afterword by W. R. Johnston. A very modern translation that often catches the tone.

Horace Talks: The Satires. Trans. by Henry H. Chamberlain. *Select Bibliographies Repr. Ser.* Ayer repr. of 1940 ed. $17.00. ISBN 0-8369-6653-8. "All the elements of Horace's art, both in its spirit and in its form, come to life again in Chamberlain's translation" (E. K. Rand, Preface).

Odes and Epodes: With the Centennial Hymn. Trans. by W. G. Shepherd. Viking Penguin 1983 o.p.

Odes (23–13 B.C.) and *Epodes* (30 B.C.). Trans. by John Marshall. AMS Pr. repr. of 1907 ed. $27.00. ISBN 0-404-07904-0

Satires, Epistles, and Ars Poetica. Trans. by H. Rushton Fairclough. *Loeb Class. Lib.* HUP rev. ed. 1926 $15.50. ISBN 0-674-99214-8. A standard translation; faithful to the original.

Satires (35–30 B.C.) and *Epistles* (20–13 B.C.). Trans. by Smith P. Bovie. U. Ch. Pr. 1959 $14.95. ISBN 0226-06777-7. "Documented and based on a sound text, thorough scholarship, and poetic sensitivity" (*LJ*).

Satires. Trans. by Niall Rudd. U. CA Pr. 1982 o.p. Reliable translation.

Books about Horace

Armstrong, David. *Horace.* Yale U. Pr. 1989 $30.00. ISBN 0-300-04579-4. Intelligent and effective introduction aimed at the general reader.

Commager, Steele. *The Odes of Horace: A Critical Study.* Yale U. Pr. 1962 o.p. "This is good modern criticism, finely calibrated to a classical writer and sustained by firm and conscientious, if somewhat showy, scholarship . . . . it gives us at last a credibly complex picture of a great poet" (*N.Y. Times*).

Davis, Gregson. *Polyhymnia: The Rhetoric of Horatian Lyric Discourse.* U. CA Pr. 1991 $39.95. ISBN 0-520-07077-1. Careful study of style.

Fraenkel, Eduard. *Horace.* OUP 1957 $30.00. ISBN 0-19-814376-1. A basic and comprehensive work by a first-rate scholar that any serious student of Horace must consult.

Perret, Jacques. *Horace.* Trans. by Bertha Humez. NYU Pr. 1964 o.p. Foreword by Jotham Johnson. His "analysis is fresh, wise, perceptive, with excellent insights . . . . The lover of Horace will like this eye-opener; the newcomer will find it a handsome introduction to the poet" (*LJ*).

Porter, David H. *Horace's Poetic Journey: A Reading of Odes 1-3.* Princeton U. Pr. 1987 $40.00. ISBN 0-691-06702-3. Intelligent, lucid criticism of Horace's poetry.

Putnam, Michael C. J. *Artifices of Eternity: Horace's Fourth Book of Odes.* Cornell Univ. Pr. 1986 $28.95. ISBN 0-8014-1856-6. An important study.

Santirocco, Matthew S. *Unity and Design in Horace's Odes.* U. of NC Pr. 1986 $29.95. ISBN 0-8078-1691-4. A detailed critical reading.

Shackleton Bailey, D. R. *Profile of Horace.* HUP 1982 $23.50. ISBN 0-674-71325-7. "He gives us a believable portrait of Horace, but of special importance are his elucidations of the poems" (*Choice*).

Showerman, Grant. *Horace and His Influence.* Cooper Sq. repr. of 1930 ed. $28.50. ISBN 0-8154-0206-6. A careful and detailed study.

Wilkinson, L. P. *Horace and His Lyric Poetry.* Cambridge U. Pr. 1957 o.p. Highly recommended sensitive and scholarly study.

JUVENAL (Decimus Junius Juvenalis). 60?–140?

The 16 *Satires* (c.110–127) of Juvenal, which contain a vivid picture of contemporary Rome under the Empire, have seldom been equaled as biting diatribes. The satire was the only literary form that the Romans did not copy from the Greeks. HORACE merely used it for humorous comment on human folly. Juvenal's invectives in powerful hexameters, exact and epigrammatic, were aimed at lax and luxurious society, tyranny (Domitian's), criminal excesses, and the immorality of women. Juvenal was so sparing of autobiographical detail that we know very little of his life. He was desperately poor at one time and may have been an important magistrate at another.

His influence was great in the Middle Ages; in the seventeenth century he was well translated by DRYDEN (see Vol. 1), and in the eighteenth century he was paraphrased by JOHNSON (see Vol. 1) in his *London* and *The Vanity of Human Wishes*. He inspired in SWIFT (see Vol. 1) the same savage bitterness.

WORKS BY JUVENAL

Satires of Decimus Junius Juvenalis. c.110–127. Trans. by John Dryden. AMS Pr. repr. of 1735 ed. $37.50. ISBN 0-404-54124-0. Translated by Dryden and others.

Satires (and Persius's *Satires*). 1918. Trans. by G. G. Ramsay. *Loeb Class. Lib.* HUP rev. ed. 1950 $15.50. ISBN 0-674-99102-8

Satires. Trans. by Thomas Sheridan. AMS Pr. repr. of 1739 ed. $40.00. ISBN 0-404-54125-9

Sixteen Satires. Trans. by Peter Green. Viking Penguin 1967 $8.95. ISBN 0-14-044194-8

BOOKS ABOUT JUVENAL

Braund, S. H. *Beyond Anger: A Study of Juvenal's Third Book of Satires*. Cambridge U. Pr. 1989 $44.95. ISBN 0-521-35637-7. A very detailed study.

Courtney, E. *A Commentary on the Satires of Juvenal*. Humanities 1980 $110.00. ISBN 0-485-11190-X. Contains a wealth of useful information.

Highet, Gilbert. *Juvenal the Satirist: A Study*. OUP 1954 o.p. For the general reader and the more advanced student.

Jenkyns, Richard. *Three Classical Poets: Sappho, Catullus and Juvenal*. HUP 1982 $29.95. ISBN 0-674-88895-2. Thoughtful, intelligent approach to these three important poets.

LIVY (Titus Livius). c.59 B.C.–C.A.D. 17

[SEE Volume 3.]

LUCAN (Marcus Annaeus Lucanus). 39–65

Grandson of SENECA the Rhetorican and nephew of SENECA the Philosopher (see Vol. 4), Lucan was born in Spain and educated in rhetoric in Rome. He was a favorite at Nero's court until the emperor took offense at his precocious literary talent and prevented him from displaying it in public. Lucan then joined a conspiracy against the monarch and was forced to commit suicide. His epic poem *Bellum Civile (Civil War)*, also called *Pharsalia*, sided with Pompey in his fatal struggle with JULIUS CAESAR (see Vol. 3). His complex rhetorical style was acclaimed in the Middle Ages; DANTE and CHAUCER (see Vol. 1) ranked him high as a poet.

POETRY BY LUCAN

Civil War. Trans. by J. D. Duff. *Loeb Class. Ser.* HUP 1928 $15.50. ISBN 0-674-99242-3

BOOKS ABOUT LUCAN

Ahl, Frederick. *Lucan: An Introduction. Studies in Classical Philology*. Cornell Univ. Pr. 1976 $41.50. ISBN 0-8014-0837-7. A clear and intelligent introductory work.

Johnson, W. R. *Momentary Monsters: Lucan and His Heroes*. Cornell Univ. Pr. 1987 $19.95. ISBN 0-8014-2030-X. Perceptive criticism.

Masters, Jamie. *Poetry and Civil War in Lucan's Bellum Civile*. Cambridge U. Pr. 1992 $59.95. ISBN 0-521-41460-1. Lucan's work expertly analyzed in its political context.

LUCRETIUS (Titus Lucretius Carus). c.94 or 99 B.C.–55 B.C.

Almost nothing is known of Lucretius's life, but legends have attached themselves to him. Donatus said that VIRGIL assumed the toga of manhood the very day Lucretius died (that is, October 15, 55 B.C.); and Jerome stated that the poet was poisoned by a love potion, wrote his *De Rerum Natura* at lucid intervals, and then committed suicide. He may have been one of the Lucretii, an aristocratic Roman family, or a native of Campania who studied Epicureanism in Naples. It is certain, however, that he was a friend or dependent of C. Memmius (who was also the patron of Catullus) to whom the poem is dedicated.

De Rerum Natura (On the Nature of the Universe), Lucretius's only work, written in six books, expounds the philosophy of EPICURUS (see Vol. 4). Because the universe and all things in it are made up of atoms swirling about in different combinations, the human soul perishes with the body. Lucretius was intent on proving this so that he might persuade his audience to give up their fear of death and of punishment in the afterlife and their belief in divine intervention. His exposition of the mechanical nature of the universe shows intensity of thought and feeling and is expressed in beautiful, vivid images. His invocation to Venus in Book I and his denunciation of women and the passion of love in Book IV are famous and their influence enduring.

WORKS BY LUCRETIUS

On the Nature of Things. Trans. by W. H. D. Rouse. *Loeb Class. Lib.* HUP rev. ed. 1975 $15.50. ISBN 0-674-99200-8. Prose translation; highly recommended.

On the Nature of Things, Book Four (De Rerum Natura, IV). Trans. by John Godwin. Aris & Phillips 1986. ISBN 0-85668-308-6. A fluid and faithful prose translation, for the nonspecialist.

On the Nature of the Universe. Trans. by Ronald E. Latham. Viking Penguin 1951 $5.95. ISBN 0-14-044018-6

Lucretius: The Way Things Are. Trans. by Rolfe Humphries. Ind. U. Pr. 1968 $7.95. ISBN 0-253-20125-X. A translation of *On the Nature* in English blank verse.

Lucretius: The Nature of Things. Trans. by Frank O. Copley. Norton 1977 $8.95. ISBN 0-393-09094-9. A clear translation close to the texture of the Latin.

BOOKS ABOUT LUCRETIUS

Bailey, Cyril, ed. *Lucretius: De Rerum Natura*. 3 vols. OUP 1986 $210.00. ISBN 0-19-814405-9. Volume 1: A superb introduction to the poet—his life, philosophy, and poetic technique; Volumes 2 and 3: Latin text with commentary.

De Witt, Norman W. *Epicurus and His Philosophy*. Greenwood 1973 repr. of 1954 ed. $65.00. ISBN 0-8371-6639-X. Clarifies Lucretius's relationship to Epicurus.

Hadzsits, George D. *Lucretius and His Influence*. Cooper Sq. 1963 repr. of 1930 ed. o.p. Valuable for its careful presentation of Lucretius's later influence.

Segal, Charles. *Lucretius on Death and Anxiety: Poetry and Philosophy in De Rerum Natura*. Princeton U. Pr. 1990 $29.95. ISBN 0-691-06826-7. Addresses fears of the process of dying and of nothingness by placing individual death in the context of nature's creative and destructive forces.

Sikes, Edward E. *Lucretius: Poet and Philosopher*. Russell WV 1971 repr. of 1936 ed. o.p. An important critical study of the poet.

MARTIAL (Marcus Valerius Martialis). 40?–104

Martial's 12 books of *Epigrams* were written for the most part in elegiac couplets modeled on OVID and CATULLUS. They show Martial's acute observation of Roman life in the last third of the first century and were written with wit and brevity, often postponing the point or sting until the end. They are frequently insulting and sexually explicit. Not much is known of Martial's life, except that he left his home in Bilbilis, Spain, in 64 to live by his writing and his wits in Rome. He courted the favor of the rich and powerful, was a friend of Seneca, Lucan, Juvenal, and Quintilian, and Pliny the Younger lamented his death. The *Epigrams* have been read and imitated throughout the centuries; one of them was translated as the memorable "I do not love thee, Dr. Fell."

Works by Martial

Epigrams. 80–84. 2 vols. Trans. by Walter C. A. Kerr. *Loeb Class. Lib.* HUP 1919–20 $15.50 ea. ISBNs 0-674-99105-2, 0-674-99106-0

The Epigrams. Trans. by James Michie. Viking Penguin 1988 $6.95. ISBN 0-14-044350-9

Epigrams from Martial: A Verse Translation. Trans. by Barriss Mills. Purdue U. Pr. 1969 $6.75. ISBN 0-911198-16-4. Translations with the verve and liveliness of the originals.

Books about Martial

Nixon, Paul. *Martial and the Modern Epigram*. Cooper Sq. repr. of 1930 ed. $27.50. ISBN 0-8154-0165-5. A good study of the poet's influence on modern works.

Whipple, Thomas K. *Martial and English Epigram from Sir Thomas Wyatt to Ben Jonson*. Phaeton 1970 repr. of 1925 ed. $45.00. ISBN 0-87753-043-2. A classic study.

OVID (Publius Ovidius Naso). 43 B.C.–A.D. 17

Born of an equestrian family in Sulmo, Ovid was educated in rhetoric in Rome but gave it up for poetry. He counted Horace and Propertius among his friends and wrote an elegy on the death of Tibullus. He became the leading poet of Rome but was banished in A.D. 8 by an edict of Augustus to remote Tomis on the Black Sea because of a poem and an indiscretion. Miserable in provincial exile, he died there ten years later.

His brilliant, witty, fertile elegiac poems include *Amores (Loves), Heroides (Heroines)* (c.5 B.C.–A.D. 8), and *Ars Amatoris (The Art of Love)*, but he is perhaps best known for the *Metamorphoses* (c.A.D. 2), a marvelously imaginative compendium of Greek mythology where every story alludes to a change in shape. Ovid was admired and imitated throughout the Middle Ages and Renaissance; Chaucer (see Vol. 1), Spenser (see Vol. 1), Shakespeare, and Jonson (see Vol. 1) knew his works well. His mastery of form, gift for narration, and amusing urbanity are irresistible.

Poetry by Ovid

The Art of Love. c.1 B.C. Trans. by Rolfe Humphries. Ind. U. Pr. 1957 $25.00. ISBN 0-253-10391-6. Lively translation.

The Erotic Poems. Trans. by Peter Green. Viking Penguin 1983 $7.95. ISBN 0-14-044360-6. Good clear translations.

The Fasti. c.A.D. 8. Trans. by James George Frazer. *Loeb Class. Lib.* HUP 1931 $15.50. ISBN 0-674-99279-2. An expert prose translation, expertly annotated.

Heroides (c.5 B.C.–A.D. 8) and *Amores*. Trans. by Daryl Hine. Yale U. Pr. 1991 $27.50. Translation in rhymed couplets.

Heroides (c.5 B.C.–A.D. 8) and *Amores*. Trans. by Grant Showerman. *Loeb Class. Lib.* HUP rev. ed. 1977 $15.50. ISBN 0-674-99045-5. Prose translation, close to the Latin.

Metamorphoses. Trans. by Rolfe Humphries. Ind. U. Pr. 1955 $20.00. ISBN 0-253-33755-0.

Poetry of Exile (*Tristia* and *Ex Ponto*). Trans. by David Slavitt. Johns Hopkins 1990 o.p. A free translation giving the feel of the original.

Tristia (9–12) and *Ex Ponto* (13–17). Trans. by Arthur Leslie Wheeler. *Loeb Class. Lib.* HUP rev. ed. 1985 $15.50. ISBN 0-674-99167-2. Clear and literal prose translation.

Books about Ovid

Ahl, Frederick. *Metaformations: Soundplay and Wordplay in Ovid and the Classical Poets.* Cornell Univ. Pr. 1985 $38.95. ISBN 0-8014-1762-7. Technical but accessible to the general reader.

Boas, Frederick S. *Ovid and the Elizabethans.* Haskell 1970 repr. of 1948 ed. $19.95. ISBN 0-8383-0008-1. Careful study of the poet's influence.

Evans, Harry B. *Publica Carmina: Ovid's Books from Exile.* Bks. Demand repr. of 1983 ed. $55.70. ISBN 0-8357-3799-3. Careful and thorough introduction for the general reader.

Glenn, Edgar M. *The Metamorphoses: Ovid's Roman Games.* U. Pr. of Amer. 1986 $43.75. ISBN 0-8191-5582-9. Aimed at the general reader.

Mack, Sarah. *Ovid.* Yale U. Pr. 1988 $11.00. ISBN 0-300-04295-7. A clear and appreciative introduction for the general reader.

Myerowitz, Molly. *Ovid's Games of Love.* Wayne St. U. Pr. 1985 $32.50. ISBN 0-8143-1746-4. A contemporary critical approach.

Rand, E. K. *Ovid.* Cooper Sq. repr. of 1930 ed. $28.50. ISBN 0-8154-0187-6. Indispensable for understanding Ovid's poetry and his influence on later European literature.

Syme, Ronald. *History in Ovid.* OUP 1979 $59.00. ISBN 0-19-814825-9. A spirited analysis of the historical component of Ovid's poetry.

Verducci, Florence. *Ovid's Toyshop of the Heart: Epistulae Heroidum.* Princeton U. Pr. 1985 $47.50. ISBN 0-691-06638-8. Focuses on depiction of psychological states.

PERSIUS (Aulus Persius Flaccus). 34–62

Persius was a native of Etruria and was educated in Rome, where he became Lucan's friend. He wrote six satires in a somewhat contorted style, which inculcate Stoic morality. His sanity and wit have direct appeal.

Works by Persius

Satires (and Juvenal's *Satires*). Trans. by G. G. Ramsay. *Loeb Class. Lib.* HUP rev. ed. 1950 $15.50. ISBN 0-674-99102-8

The Satires of Persius. Trans. by W. S. Merwin. Assoc. Faculty Pr. 1973 repr. of 1961 ed. o.p. Recommended notes and introduction by W. S. Anderson.

PETRONIUS (Gaius Petronius Arbiter). d. 65

Tacitus (see Vol. 3) called this Roman dandy—the director of entertainments at the Emperor Nero's court—*Arbiter Elegantiae* ("Arbiter of Refined Taste"), and said further that Petronius was in high favor, having been governor of Bithynia and consul, but he was finally denounced by Nero's favorite, Tigellinus, and forced to commit suicide. He is considered to have written *The Satyricon* (c.60), a satiric picaresque romance in prose interspersed with verse which is extant only in fragments. Its subject is Italian low life, and it is characterized by "brilliant wit and riotous obscenity." The chief episode describes the vulgarian-upstart Trimalchio and his banquet for the hero. William Arrowsmith has made a vigorous, appropriately colloquial American English translation. "We savor the satire and the parodies of practically every Greek or Roman literary type, and we see the universal applications behind the catalogue of the vices and excesses of Nero's Rome" (*LJ*).

Works by Petronius

The Satyricon (and Seneca's *Apocolocyntosis*). c.60. Trans. by M. Heseltine and W. H. D. Rouse. *Loeb. Class. Lib.* HUP $15.50. ISBN 0-674-99016-1

The Works of Petronius Arbiter, in Prose and Verse. AMS Pr. repr. of 1736 ed. $34.50. ISBN 0-404-54129-1. A fluent translation.

BOOKS ABOUT PETRONIUS

Bagnani, Gilbert. *Arbiter of Elegance: A Study of the Life and Works of C. Petronius.* U. of Toronto Pr. 1954 o.p. A sound and scholarly work.

Slater, Niall W. *Reading Petronius.* Johns Hopkins 1990 $34.00. ISBN 0-8018-3984-X. A readable and engaging work.

PLAUTUS, TITUS MACCIUS. d. c.184 B.C.

Plautus and TERENCE used stock characters (the young lovers, the clever slave, the irate father) and devices (mistaken identity), but each handled these conventions in his own distinct manner. Plautus was the son of a poor Umbrian farmer who may have fought in the Second Punic War. The playwright Plautus is said to have been a popular actor, true comedian, jovial, tolerant, rough of humor. He not only modeled his plays on the Greek New Comedy, but unhesitatingly inserted long passages translated from the Greek originals. He was the master of comic irony and, as its originator, copied by MOLIÈRE, CORNEILLE, JONSON (see Vol. 1), DRYDEN (see vol. 1), and FIELDING (see Vol. 1). SHAKESPEARE (see Vol. 1) based his *Comedy of Errors* on Plautus's *Menaechmi.* Of more than 100 plays, 21 survive.

PLAYS BY PLAUTUS

Amphitryon and Two Other Plays. Ed. by Lionel Casson. Norton 1971 $8.95. ISBN 0-393-00601-8

The Darker Comedies. Trans. and ed. by James B. Tatum. Johns Hopkins 1983 $11.95. ISBN 0-8018-2901-1. Racy translations intended for performance.

The Menaechmus Twins and Two Other Plays. Trans. by Lionel Casson. Norton 1971 $8.95. ISBN 0-393-00602-6. Contains sprightly, readable translations.

The Pot of Gold and Other Plays. Trans. by E. F. Watling. Viking Penguin 1965 $6.95. ISBN 0-14-044149-2

The Rope and Other Plays. Trans. by E. F. Watling. Viking Penguin 1964 $4.95. ISBN 0-14-044136-0. Good prose translations.

Works. 5 vols. Trans. by Paul Nixon. *Loeb Class. Lib.* HUP 1916–38 $15.50 ea. The best translation for most of the plays, including *Amphitryon; The Comedy of Asses; The Pot of Gold; The Two Vacchises; The Captives; Casina; The Casket Comedy; Curculio; Epicidus; The Two Menaechmuses; The Merchant; The Braggart Warrior; The Haunted House; The Persian; The Little Carthaginatinian; Pseudolus; The Rope; Stichus; Three Bob Day; Truculentus; The Tale of a Travelling Bag* (fragments).

BOOKS ABOUT PLAUTUS

Norwood, Gilbert. *Plautus and Terence.* Cooper Sq. repr. of 1930 ed. $27.50. ISBN 0-8154-0166-3. A clear and thoughtful introduction.

Segal, Erich. *Roman Laughter: The Comedy of Plautus.* OUP 1987 $13.95. ISBN 0-19-504166-6. A knowledgeable and entertaining presentation of Plautus by a famous classicist and novelist.

Slater, Niall W. *Plautus in Performance: The Theatre of the Mind.* Princeton U. Pr. 1987 $15.95. ISBN 0-691-10178-7. An enthusiastic study.

PLINY THE YOUNGER (Gaius Plinius Caecilius Secundus). c.61–c.112

Raised by his uncle Pliny the Elder, who was a scholar and industrious compiler of *Natural History,* Pliny the Younger intended his *Letters* for posterity and polished them with extreme care. He was an orator, statesman, and well-educated man of the world. He wrote with discretion on a variety of subjects, and without the bitterness of his friends Tacitus (see Vol. 3) and Suetonius or the disgust for the social conditions of those troubled times found in the writings of his contemporaries Juvenal and Martial. In the introduction to the Loeb edition, Hutchinson wrote: "Melmoth's translation of Pliny's letters, published in 1746, not only delighted contemporary critics . . . but deservedly ranks as a minor English classic. Apart from its literary excellence, it has the supreme merit of reflecting the spirit of the original. . . . No modern rendering can capture the ease and felicity of Melmoth's; for they came of his living in a world like 'Pliny's own.'"

Works by Pliny the Younger

Fifty Letters. Trans. by A. N. Sherwin-White. OUP 1969 $12.95. ISBN 0-19-912010-2

Letters. 2 vols. Trans. by William Melmoth. Rev. by W. M. L. Hutchinson. *Loeb Class. Lib.* HUP rev. ed. 1969 $15.50 ea. ISBNs 0-674-99061-7, 0-674-99066-8

Book about Pliny the Younger

Sherwin-White, A. N. *Letters of Pliny: A Historical and Social Commentary.* OUP 1986 $125.00. ISBN 0-19-814435-0. Extremely detailed definitive study.

PROPERTIUS (SEXTUS). c.50 B.C.–c.16 B.C.

Propertius was deprived of his Umbrian estate in the confiscation of the civil war. He applied his rhetorical education not to the courts, but to poetry. His first book of elegies to "Cynthia" won him the patronage of Maecenas and established his reputation as a passionate, witty, self-absorbed, and learned poet. The three books that followed invoke Cynthia, but also carry tributes to Maecenas, to Roman greatness, addresses to friends, and antiquarian fragments.

Poetry by Propertius

Elegies. Ed. by G. P. Goold. *Loeb Class. Lib.* HUP 1990 $15.50. ISBN 0-674-99020-X. Literal, readable translations.

Poems. Trans. by J. P. McCulloch. U. CA Pr. 1972 $52.50. ISBN 0-520-02774-4. Translations in a contemporary style.

Propertius. Trans. by H. E. Butler. *Loeb Class. Lib.* HUP 1912 $15.50. ISBN 0-674-99021-8. A careful, scholarly translation.

Books about Propertius

Benediktson, D. Thomas. *Propertius: Modernist Poet of Antiquity.* S. Ill. U. Pr. 1988 $24.95. ISBN 0-8093-1453-3. A careful study of the poet's current appeal.

Papanghelis, Theodore D. *Propertius: A Hellenistic Poet on Love and Death.* Cambridge U. Pr. 1987 $54.95. ISBN 0-521-32314-2. An analysis of the poet in his cultural context.

Stahl, Hans-Peter. *Propertius: Love and War.* U. CA Pr. 1985 $47.50. ISBN 0-520-05166-1. Close reading of individual texts.

QUINTILIAN (Marcus Fabius Quintilianus). c.35–c.95

The *Institutio Oratoria* in 12 books was written by Quintilian, the most famous of the Roman rhetoricians, during his later years. It contains the principles of rhetoric, especially in public speaking, and is a practical treatise on the complete education of a Roman and the best methods used in the Roman schools. It offers, in the tenth book, a famous critique of Greek and Latin authors. Quintilian's ideal orator is a good man skilled in speaking. Quintilian was born in northern Spain but educated in Rome, where he began to teach oratory in 68. He was the first rhetorician to establish a public school and to receive a salary from the state.

WORK BY QUINTILIAN

Institutionis Oratoriae (On the Training of an Orator). 4 vols. Trans. by H. E. Butler. *Loeb Class. Lib.* HUP 1953 $15.50 ea. ISBNs 0-674-99138-9, 0-674-99139-7, 0-674-99140-0, 0-674-99141-9

BOOKS ABOUT QUINTILIAN

Kennedy, George. *Quintilian.* Twayne 1969 o.p. By a leading authority on Roman rhetoric.

Wheelock, Frederic M.*Quintilian as Educator.* Twayne 1974 o.p. A basic and well-done study.

SENECA, LUCIUS ANNAEUS. c.3 B.C.–A.D. 65

Seneca was born in Spain of a wealthy Italian family. His father, LUCIUS ANNAEUS SENECA (see Vol. 4), wrote the well-known *Controversaie (Controversies)* and *Suasoriae (Persuasions),* which are collections of arguments used in rhetorical training, and his nephew LUCAN was the epic poet of the civil war. Educated in rhetoric and philosophy in Rome, he found the Stoic doctrine especially compatible. The younger Seneca became famous as an orator but was exiled by the Emperor Claudius. He was recalled by the Empress Agrippina to become the tutor of her son, the young Nero. After the first five years of Nero's reign, Agrippina was murdered and three years later Octavia, Nero's wife, was exiled. Seneca retired as much as possible from public life and devoted himself to philosophy, writing many treatises at this time. But in 65 he was accused of conspiracy and, by imperial order, committed suicide by opening his veins. He was a Stoic philosopher and met his death with Stoic calm.

Seneca's grisly tragedies fascinated the Renaissance and have been successfully performed in recent years. All ten tragedies are believed genuine, with the exception of *Octavia,* which is now considered to be by a later writer. Translations of the tragedies influenced English dramatists such as JONSON (see Vol. 1), MARLOWE (see Vol. 1), and SHAKESPEARE (see Vol. 1), who all imitated Seneca's scenes of horror and his characters—the ghost, nurse, and villain.

WORKS BY SENECA

Apocolocyntosis (and Petronius's *Satyricon*). Trans. by M. Heseltine and W. H. D. Rouse. *Loeb Class. Lib.* HUP $15.50. ISBN 0-674-99016-1

Letters from a Stoic. Trans. by Robin Campbell. Viking Penguin 1969 $6.95. ISBN 0-14-044210-3

PLAYS BY SENECA

Four Tragedies and Octavia. Trans. by E. F. Watling. Viking Penguin 1966 $7.95. ISBN 0-14-044174-3. Effective blank verse translations.

Seneca: His Tenne Tragedies. 2 vols. Trans. by Thomas Newton. AMS Pr. repr. of 1927 ed. $45.00 ea. ISBN 0-404-52000-6. Foreword by T. S. Eliot. Famous and influential Elizabethan translation.

Seneca's Tragedies. 2 vols. Trans. in prose by Frank Justus Miller. *Loeb Class. Lib.* HUP 1917 $15.50 ea. Volume 1 contains *Hercules Furens; Troades; Medea; Hippolytus; Oedipus.* Volume 2 contains *Agamemnon; Thyestes; Hercules Oetaeus; Phoenissae; Octavia.* Includes comparative analysis, bibliographies, index with identification of mythological and historical characters.

Three Tragedies: Trojan Women, Medea, and Phaedra. Trans. by Frederick M. Ahl. Cornell Univ. Pr. 1986 $41.50. ISBN 0-8014-1664-7. Resonant blank verse translations; contains an excellent introduction.

Tragedies. Trans. by David Slavitt. Johns Hopkins 1992 $38.50. ISBN 0-8018-4308-1. Moving, fluent, and lyric translations.

Troades. Trans. by Elaine Fantham. Princeton U. Pr. 1982 $65.00. ISBN 0-691-03561-X. A prose translation with extensive commentary.

Books about Seneca

Griffin, Miriam T. *Seneca: A Philosopher in Politics*. OUP 1976 o.p. A thoughtful and intelligent work.

Henry, Denis, and Elisabeth Henry. *The Mask of Power: Seneca's Tragedies and Imperial Power*. Bolchazy-Carducci 1985 $22.50. ISBN 0-86516-119-4. A solid introduction for nonspecialists.

Pratt, Norman T. *Seneca's Drama*. U. of NC Pr. 1983 $32.50. ISBN 0-8078-1555-1. An excellent, helpful critical study.

Rosenmeyer, Thomas G. *Senecan Drama and Stoic Cosmology*. U. CA Pr. 1989 $39.95. ISBN 0-520-06445-3. Authoritative criticism.

Segal, Charles. *Language and Desire in Seneca's Phaedra*. Princeton U. Pr. 1986 $37.50. ISBN 0-691-05472-X. An intelligent psychoanalytic reading of the play.

Sørenson, Villy. *Seneca: The Humanist at the Court of Nero*. Trans. by Glyn Jones. U. Ch. Pr. 1984 $25.00. ISBN 0-226-76827-9. A provocative and thoughtful analysis of the man and his works.

STATIUS, PUBLIUS PAPINIUS. c.45–c.96

Born in Naples, the son of a schoolmaster, Statius became prominent in Rome for his verse. He was a favorite in the court of the Emperor Domitian, and his lyric verse includes elegies, odes, and poems in praise of the emperor. The *Thebaid* is an epic in 12 books about the struggle of the two sons of Oedipus to rule Thebes. Only fragments are extant of the unfinished *Achilleid* (*The Story of Achilles*). His *Silvae* are pleasant occasional verses to his friends, his wife, and the emperor. His influence continued through the Middle Ages. Dante regarded him as a Christian; Chaucer (see Vol. 1) imitated his *Thebaid* in *Troilus and Cresseyde* and considered him one of the world's great poets.

Poetry by Statius

Silvae, Thebaid or Thebais, Achilleid. 2 vols. Trans. by J. H. Mozley. *Loeb Class. Lib*. HUP 1928 $15.50 ea. A readable and accurate translation.

Books about Statius

Vessey, David. *Statius and the Thebaid*. Cambridge U. Pr. 1973 o.p. An appreciative analysis and evaluation.

Wise, Boyd A. *The Influence of Statius upon Chaucer*. Phaeton 1967 repr. of 1911 ed. $45.00. ISBN 0-87753-045-9. A standard study of an important influence.

SUETONIUS (Caius Suetonius Tranquillus). c.69–c.140

Suetonius is noted for *The Lives of the Twelve Caesars*, which survives almost intact. Only fragments remain of his much larger collection *Illustrious Men*. He recorded the most minute details of his subjects' lives in a lively, informative style that became a model for many later biographers. The brief period as secretary to the Emperor Hadrian probably gave him access to official archives, so that his background data are authentic, spiced with the gossip of the times.

The 1606 version of Philemon Holland was influential. Rolfe's version "does not lack the qualities of vigor and lightness; on the contrary it is decidedly readable," J. Wright Duff reported in the *Classical Review*. Of the Robert Graves translation, the *Christian Science Monitor* said: "Astonishing truly, that the stiffly framed Latin language that we learn about in our school texts and grammars is capable of such elasticity and color as we find in this reproduction by Mr. Graves."

WORK BY SUETONIUS

The Lives of the Twelve Caesars. 2 vols. Trans. by J. C. Rolfe. *Loeb Class. Lib.* HUP 1914–20 $15.50 ea. ISBNs 0-674-99035-8, 0-674-99042-0

BOOK ABOUT SUETONIUS

Wallace-Hadrill, Andrew. *Suetonius: The Scholar and His Caesars.* Yale U. Pr. 1984 $27.50. ISBN 0-300-03000-2. The first book on Suetonius in English; analyzes him in his social and political context.

TACITUS, CORNELIUS. c.56–c.112

[SEE Volume 3]

TERENCE (Publius Tertentius Afer). c.190 B.C.–159 B.C.

Terence was born in Carthage. As a boy, he was the slave of Terentius Lucanus, a Roman senator, who educated him and set him free. He was an intimate friend of the younger Scipio and of the elegant poet Laelius. They were the gilded youth of Rome, and Terence's plays were undoubtedly written for this inner circle, not for the vulgar crowd. They were adapted from MENANDER and other Greek writers of the New Comedy and, in the main, were written seriously on a high literary plane with careful handling of plot and character. The six comedies are all extant.

PLAYS BY TERENCE

The Brothers. Trans. by Frank O. Copley. Macmillan 1962 $2.15. ISBN 0-672-60311-X

Comedies. 2 vols. Trans. by John Sargeaunt. *Loeb Class. Lib.* HUP 1912 $15.50 ea. Volume 1: *The Lady of Andros, The Self-Tormentor, The Eunuch.* Volume 2: *Phormio, The Mother-in-Law, The Brothers.*

The Comedies of Terence. Trans. by Betty Radice. Viking Penguin 1976 $7.95. ISBN 0-14-044324-X

Eunuch. Trans. by Frank O. Copley. Macmillan 1965 $2.05. ISBN 0-672-60428-0

Phormio. Trans. by Frank O. Copley. Macmillan 1958 $3.50. ISBN 0-672-60286-5. Elegant, witty, and lucid translations.

BOOKS ABOUT TERENCE

Forehand, Walter. *Terence.* Twayne 1985 o.p. An expert introduction.

Goldberg, Sander M. *Understanding Terence.* Princeton U. Pr. 1986 $35.00. ISBN 0-691-03586-5. A thoughtful, intelligent approach for interested readers.

Norwood, Gilbert. *Plautus and Terence.* Cooper Sq. repr. of 1930 ed. $27.50. ISBN 0-8154-0166-3. A clear and thoughtful introductory work.

TIBULLUS (ALBIUS). 48 B.C.?–19 B.C.

Tibullus became the poet laureate of the republican literary circle that had as its leader Messalla Corvinus. The chief inspirations of his elegies were his sentimental longing for rustic simplicity and his amorous longing for two women (whom he called Delia and Nemesis) and a boy (Marathus). Tibullus contributed refinement of form and simplicity of language to Roman elegy. The third book of his collection, containing poems not by Tibullus, includes six love elegies by Sulpicia, the only poems we have by a Roman woman.

POETRY BY TIBULLUS

Works of Catullus and Tibullus with Pervigilium Veneris. Trans. by J. P. Postgate. *Loeb Class. Lib.* HUP rev. ed. 1939 $15.50. A straightforward prose translation.

Book about Tibullus

Putnam, Michael C. *Tibullus: A Commentary.* U. of Okla. Pr. 1979 $13.95. ISBN 0-8061-1560-2. Includes the latest scholarship on the poet; the work of a versatile scholar.

VIRGIL or VERGIL (Publius Vergilius Maro). 70 B.C.–19 B.C.

The reign of Augustus, grandnephew of JULIUS CAESAR (see Vol. 3), who became the first Roman emperor (27 B.C.–A.D. 14), marked the Golden Age of Latin literature. "The writers of the time were moved to celebrate the greatness of Rome, past, present, and to come. The great monument is, of course, Virgil's 'Aeneid,' which links the foundation of Rome to the fall of Troy, traces the ancestry of JULIUS CAESAR (see Vol. 3) to the gods, and makes the greatness of Rome the subject of divine intervention and prophecy" (Basil Davenport).

Virgil was given a good education by his father, a prosperous farmer living near Mantua. After his studies in Rome and Naples, Virgil completed in 37 B.C. *The Eclogues* or *The Bucolics* , which idealized rural life and was modeled on his Greek predecessor THEOCRITUS. At that time Maecenas, a trusted counselor of Augustus, became the poet's patron and was introduced by Virgil to HORACE. *The Georgics* (c.37–29 B.C.), a didactic, realistic treatise on farming in the manner of the Greek poet HESIOD and honoring Maecenas, followed *The Bucolics*; and then Virgil devoted the rest of his life to *The Aeneid* (c.29–19 B.C.). This epic poem, derived from HOMER's *Iliad* and *Odyssey* and drawing on much of Greek and earlier Latin literature, revealed the greatness of the Roman Empire and was written with perfection of technique and tenderness and melancholy of mood. Virgil considered it still in need of polishing and revision at the time of his death and asked his executor to destroy the manuscript, but his order was rescinded by Augustus. Virgil died in Brindisi and was buried in Naples, where his tomb was revered thereafter—St. Paul is said to have wept over it. Master Virgil came to be regarded as a magician and as a prophet of Christianity. And his poetry, particularly *The Aeneid,* was a dominant influence on later European literature. He was DANTE's guide through Hell in the *Divine Comedy*; and in English letters, CHAUCER (see Vol. 1), Surrey, SPENSER (see Vol. 1), MILTON (see Vol. 1), DRYDEN (see Vol. 1), POPE (see Vol. 1), and TENNYSON (see Vol. 1) venerated him.

Poetry by Virgil

The Aeneid. c.29–19 B.C. Trans. by John Dryden. *Airmont Class. Ser.* Airmont 1968 $1.95. ISBN 0-8049-0177-5. Important translation by the great English poet John Dryden.

The Aeneid. c.29–19 B.C. 2 vols. Trans. into Scottish verse by Gawin Douglas. Ed. by George Dundas. AMS Pr. repr. of 1839 ed. $45.00. ISBN 0-404-52775-2. Influential rendering by Douglas, a major Scottish poet.

The Aeneid. c.29–19 B.C. Trans. by Edward F. Taylor. Ed. by Edward M. Forster. AMS Pr. repr. of 1906 ed. $30.00. ISBN 0-404-07903-2

The Aeneid. c.29–19 B.C. Trans. by Patric Dickinson. NAL–Dutton 1961 $2.95. ISBN 0-451-62277-4

The Aeneid. c.29–19 B.C. Trans. by Robert Fitzgerald. Random 1983 $39.95. ISBN 0-394-52827-1. Widely acclaimed translation by Fitzgerald for its skill in capturing the poetic effect of the original.

The Aeneid. c.29–19 B.C. Trans. by Allen Mandelbaum. U. CA Pr. 1981 $13.95. ISBN 0-520-04550-5. Effective and expressive translation.

The Aeneid. c.29–19 B.C. Trans. by David West. *Penguin Class. Ser.* Viking Penguin 1991 $5.95. ISBN 0-14-044457-2

The Eclogues. c.40–37 B.C. Verse trans. by Guy Lee. *Penguin Class. Ser.* Viking Penguin 1984 $5.95. ISBN 0-14-044419-X. A solid translation with good introduction, notes, and bibliography.

The Georgics. c.37–29 B.C. Trans. by L. P. Wilkinson. Viking Penguin 1983 $6.95. ISBN 0-14-044414-9

Works. 2 vols. Trans. by Henry Rushton Fairclough. *Loeb Class. Lib.* HUP 1935 o.p. A standard and concise translation.

BOOKS ABOUT VIRGIL

Alpers, Paul. *The Singer of the Eclogues: A Study of Virgilian Pastoral.* U. CA Pr. 1979 $37.00. ISBN 0-520-03651-4. Introductory; includes a translation.

Cairns, Francis. *Virgil's Augustan Epic.* Cambridge U. Pr. 1989 $54.95. ISBN 0-521-35358-0. Discusses the concepts of divine and human kingship, concord and discord, geography and nationalism.

Camps, W. A. *An Introduction to Virgil's Aeneid.* OUP 1969 $13.95. ISBN 0-19-872024-6. A solid and scholarly study of the poem in its Roman context.

Clausen, Wendell. *Virgil's Aeneid and the Tradition of Hellenistic Poetry.* U. CA Pr. 1987 $35.00. ISBN 0-520-05791-0. Technical but quite engaging analysis.

Cruttwell, Robert W. *Virgil's Mind at Work.* Greenwood 1971 repr. of 1946 ed. $35.00. ISBN 0-8371-4733-6. A useful and careful study.

Di Cesare, Mario. *The Altar and the City: A Reading of Virgil's Aeneid.* Col. U. Pr. 1974 $43.00. ISBN 0-231-03830-5. Thoughtful criticism.

Farrell, Joseph. *Vergil's Georgics and the Traditions of Ancient Epic.* OUP 1991 $35.00. ISBN 0-19-506706-1. An erudite study of the work's relation to its tradition.

Gransden, K. W. *Virgil's Iliad: An Essay on Epic Narrative.* Cambridge U. Pr. 1985 $49.95. ISBN 0-521-24504-4. A close reading of the second half of the *Aeneid.*

Haecker, Theodor. *Virgil: Father of the West.* Trans. by A. Wheen. Johnson Repr. repr. of 1934 ed. $14.00. ISBN 0-384-20705. A famous and influential book.

Henry, Elisabeth. *The Vigour of Prophecy: A Study of Virgil's Aeneid.* S. Ill. U. Pr. 1990 $24.95. ISBN 0-8093-1591-2. A detailed and appreciative analysis.

Johnson, W. R. *Darkness Visible: A Study of Virgil's Aeneid.* U. CA Pr. 1976 $12.95. ISBN 0-520-03848–7. Superb criticism; subtle and wide ranging in its approach.

Leach, Eleanor W. *Virgil's Eclogues: Landscapes of Experience.* Cornell Univ. Pr. 1974 $36.95. ISBN 0-8014-0820-2. A solid and intelligent approach.

Lee, M. Owen. *Death and Rebirth in Virgil's Arcadia.* State U. NY Pr. 1989 $57.50. ISBN 0-7914-0016-6. Introduction for the general reader to early works of the premier Roman poet.

______. *Fathers and Sons in Virgil's Aeneid: Tum Genitor Natum.* State U. NY 1982 $57.50. ISBN 0-87395-402-5. Thoughtfully traces a major theme in Virgil's work.

Lyne, R.O.A.M. *Further Voices in Vergil's Aeneid.* OUP 1987 $69.00. ISBN 0-19-814461-X. Offers extended exegetical analyses of various passages with great forthrightness and clarity.

______. *Words and the Poet: Characteristic Techniques of Style in Vergil's Aeneid.* OUP 1989 $49.95. ISBN 0-19-814896-8. Consistently thoughtful work by Lyne.

Miles, Gary B. *Virgil's Georgics: A New Interpretation.* U. CA Pr. 1980 $40.00. ISBN 0-520-03789-8. A study of the poem's philosophical scope.

O'Hara, James J. *Death and the Optimistic Prophecy in Vergil's Aeneid.* Princeton U. Pr. 1990 $32.50. ISBN 0-691-06815-1. A fluent and informed approach.

Perkell, Christine. *The Poet's Truth: A Study of the Poet in Virgil's Georgics.* U. CA Pr. 1989 $30.00. ISBN 0-520-06323-6. An intelligent critical analysis.

Putnam, Michael C. J. *The Poetry of the Aeneid.* Cornell Univ. Pr. 1988 $11.95. ISBN 0-8014-9518-0. A famous and influential study.

Slavitt, David R. *Virgil.* Yale U. Pr. 1991 $30.00. ISBN 0-300-05101-8. An engaging introduction.

Williams, Gordon. *Technique and Ideas in the Aeneid.* Yale U. Pr. 1985 $15.00. ISBN 0-300-03429-6. An exhaustive, authoritative and important criticism.

CHAPTER 13

Italian Literature

Adelia V. Williams

> The new literature, reconstructed now in the consciousness, freed now from every wrapping whether classical or romantic, the echo now of the life of the day both national and universal, as philosophy, art, history, and criticism—intent on making its content increasingly realistic—not only is called but definitely is "modern literature." In the search for the elements of the real in Italy's life the Italian spirit will create its culture once more, will restore her moral world, will refresh her impressions, will find in her own inner life new sources of inspiration—woman, the family, love, nature, liberty, science, and virtue—and not as brilliant ideas revolving in space around and about her, but as concrete, definite things, become her content.
>
> —FRANCESCO DE SANCTIS, *The History of Italian Literature*

The History of Italian Literature of FRANCESCO DE SANCTIS is still the best introduction to the subject, even though, when it appeared in 1871, united modern Italy had not yet completed its first decade of existence. A literary masterpiece in its own right, it was hailed by BENEDETTO CROCE as the first truly intimate history of Italy as a whole, because "all of Italian life, religious, political, and moral, is represented in it." De Sanctis had been inspired by the critical essays, written mostly in English, of the romantic poet-critic UGO FOSCOLO, who had in turn drawn upon the ideas of GIAMBATTISTA VICO. De Sanctis divided the history of Italian literature into five major overlapping periods. The first began in the late Middle Ages with the earliest significant use of an Italian dialect for literary purposes. During the twelfth and thirteenth centuries, literary centers flourished first in the German imperial court in Sicily, then in St. Francis of Assisi's "sacred Umbria" and the university town of Bologna, and finally in prosperous Florence, where the period quickly culminated in the towering achievement of DANTE'S *Divine Comedy* (c.1308–1321), the great medieval epic that at once took its place among the greatest masterpieces of world literature.

PETRARCH (see also Vol. 4) and BOCCACCIO inaugurated the second period, which extends from the fourteenth through sixteenth centuries, with an abrupt rejection of the cultural world that had been summed up in Dante. The literary masterpieces of this period, which for a long time eclipsed Dante's achievement, are Petrarch's sonnets and songs, Boccaccio's *Decameron* (1348–53), ARIOSTO'S mock epic *Orlando Furioso* (1516–32), MACHIAVELLI'S (see Vols. 3 and 4) *Prince* (1513) and *Mandragola* (1518), and TASSO'S chivalric epic *Jerusalem Delivered* (1581).

The first 200 years of this period of Italian Renaissance humanism—from Petrarch's birth in 1304 to the deaths of ANGELO POLIZIANO and PICO DELLA MIRANDOLA (see Vol. 4) in 1494—were characterized by an extraordinary mood of secular optimism. Educated Italians, studying and imitating classical Latin works, thought of themselves increasingly as citizens not of a politically divided

Italy but rather of an ideal cosmopolitan Republic of Letters with no national boundaries. However, during the same time, most of the other major European countries were completing their political consolidation into powerful nation-states. When France and Spain marched their armies into Italy late in the fifteenth century, Italian optimism abruptly collapsed. Machiavelli witnessed the event; but his desperate plea for Italian unity remained unheeded for another 250 years.

The mood of the third period is perhaps best typified by the wildly adventurous lives of those Italians who fled Italy to seek a measure of freedom and patronage in foreign lands or who, if they remained at home, abandoned themselves to unbridled individualism. On a calmer level of literary activity, this period is one in which content was more and more sacrificed to conventions of fashionable literary form, with rival styles rapidly succeeding one another. The period produced some exceptionally serious figures, like Giambattista Vico, GALILEO GALILEI (see Vols. 4 and 5), and Antonio Muratori, but, for the most part, its mood of estrangement from reality found its most satisfying expression in the universally popular *commedia dell'arte* and enjoyed a final flowering at the close of the century in the marvelous melodramas of Pietro Metastasio.

Although the fourth period began at the close of the eighteenth century with the national theatrical reforms initiated by CARLO GOLDONI and Carlo Gozzi, the great promise of these reforms was fulfilled by GIUSEPPE PARINI and VITTORIO ALFIERI. Their message was simple. If an Italy degraded for centuries under foreign rule was ever to assume a respected place among the modern nations, Italians in large numbers would have to become self-consciously ashamed of the way of life they had accepted. That inspired Ugo Foscolo to review the history of Italian literature from a truly national perspective.

In the last decades of the nineteenth century, the romantic ideal of nationhood faced up to the challenge of political realities. Unification, the new writers found, actually had the effect of bringing Italy down several notches in international standing. As Giuseppe Prezzolini pointed out, "In an Italy divided up into little states and oppressed by foreign nations, Alfieri, Foscolo, Manzoni, and Leopardi had been European voices: in the new united Italy the one real poet, Carducci, found no echo, then or later, in foreign lands."

GIOSUÈ CARDUCCI proved the very opposite in temperament from both Alessandro Manzoni and Francesco De Sanctis. They had tried by literary means to form a united and educated Italian people to accompany national unification. Carducci, on the contrary, was an aristocratic, elitist, classical scholar who despised the novel as a literary genre and who sought to revive a more humanistic approach to literary studies. In 1906, Carducci became the first Italian to be awarded a Nobel Prize for literature. But even the fiction writers of the period felt constrained to reject the romantic idealism of Manzoni and De Sanctis. What such novelists as GIOVANNI VERGA and LUIGI PIRANDELLO preferred was the fashionable scientific positivism and naturalism or realism that already reigned in France and England and much of the rest of Europe.

By the turn of the century, the tension between elitism in poetry and naturalism in fiction had already given rise to a literature of so-called decadence, which soon refracted itself into a colorful spectrum of "isms" that extends into the contemporary period—neobohemianism, futurism, hermeticism, neorealism, and experimentalism. Out of the foment of such "isms," twentieth-century Italian literature has produced a host of literary talents. Since Carducci four other Italians have been awarded the Nobel Prize for literature—GRAZIA DELEDDA, LUIGI PIRANDELLO, SALVATORE QUASIMODO, and EUGENIO

MONTALE. However, contemporary Italian literature shows its greatest promise in its professed experimentalism, which applies to the work of contemporary novelists, playwrights, poets, and even critics.

The postmodern movement in Italy has made contributions to contemporary literature of worldwide impact. This is especially true for avant-garde trends in theater, with the prominence of such figures as DARIO FO and DACIA MARAINI, simultaneously playwrights, producers, and directors. Important postmodern fiction writers are ITALO CALVINO, LEONARDO SCIASCIA, and UMBERTO ECO, who reject Antonio Gramsci's idea of the politically and socially committed novel and individual. Theirs is an antirational, antirealistic approach. Rather than simply holding a mirror to contemporary society, they try to render its complexities and then decode them for the reader's benefit. This is particularly evident in Eco's international best-seller *The Name of the Rose* (1980), a semiotic, medieval detective story with a coded message in need of deciphering.

Finally, Italy has a wealth of contemporary women writers. Grazia Deledda, NATALIA GINZBURG, and ELSA MORANTE paved the way in the first half of the century. Today, Maraini, ORIANA FALLACI, and Rosetta Loy, to name some of the most prominent, treat a wide variety of themes: social issues, domestic concerns, and psychological exploration of the female psyche. The vast corpus of outstanding women's writing has prompted critic Santo Arico to call the phenomenon "a modern Renaissance."

HISTORY AND CRITICISM

Apollonio, Umbro, ed. *Futurist Manifestos*. Viking Penguin 1973 o.p. Solid, scholarly text. Essential for an understanding of the futurist agenda.

Arico, Santo L., ed. *Contemporary Women Writers in Italy: A Modern Renaissance*. U. of Mass. Pr. 1990 $29.50. ISBN 0-87023-710-0. "A serious contribution to the study of Italian women writers" (*Italica*).

Baron, Hans. *Humanistic and Political Literature in Florence and Venice at the Beginning of the Quattrocento: Studies in Criticism and Chronology*. Russell Sage 1968 repr. of 1955 ed. o.p.

Barzini, Luigi. *The Italians*. Peter Smith $22.25. ISBN 0-8446-6146-5. A basic book for understanding Italian culture.

Bernardo, Aldo S., and Anthony L. Pellegrini, eds. *Dante, Petrarch, Boccaccio: Studies in the Italian Trecento in Honor of Charles S. Singleton*. MRTS 1983 $30.00. ISBN 0-86698-061-X. Essays honoring one of the pioneering American Renaissance scholars.

Biasin, Gian-Paolo. *Italian Literary Icons*. Princeton U. Pr. 1985 $37.50. ISBN 0-691-06632-9. "Contemporary Italian studies are now, at long last, beginning to reach an audience extending beyond Italianists" (*Italica*).

______. *Literary Diseases: Theme and Metaphor in the Italian Novel*. U. of Tex. Pr. 1975 $48.90. ISBN 0-8357-7718-9

Burckhardt, Jacob. *The Civilization of the Renaissance in Italy*. Viking Penguin 1990 $9.95. ISBN 0-14-044534-X. An analysis of daily and political life in Renaissance Italy, as well as the thoughts of the period's outstanding minds. A must for understanding the era.

Burke, Peter. *The Historical Anthropology of Early Modern Italy. Essays on Perception and Communication*. Cambridge U. Pr. 1987 $49.50. ISBN 0-521-32041-0. Comments on early sixteenth-century literature, including works by numerous women.

Caesar, Michael, ed. *Writers and Society in Contemporary Italy: A Collection of Essays*. Ed. by Peter Hainsworth. St. Martin 1986 $27.50. ISBN 0-312-89350-7. "This book includes useful bibliographies, of both English and Italian works. . . . The authors considered in detail include theorist and novelist Umberto Eco, poet Andrea Zanzotto, playwright Dario Fo, and activist-writer Leonardo Sciascia" (*Choice*).

Cannon, JoAnn. *Postmodern Italian Fiction: The Crisis of Reason in Calvino, Sciascia, Malerba.* Fairleigh Dickinson $27.50. ISBN 0-8386-3436-3. "Cannon does an admirable job of assessing and situating these works within modern trends of Italian fiction" (*Italica*).

Devoto, Giacomo. *The Languages of Italy.* Trans. by V. Louise Katainen. U. Ch. Pr. 1978 o.p. A study of Italian dialects and modes of expression.

Donadoni, Eugenio. *A History of Italian Literature.* 2 vols. Trans. by Richard Monges. *Gotham Lib.* NYU Pr. 1969 o.p. Used as a textbook in Italian secondary schools.

Foligno, Cesare. *Epochs of Italian Literature.* Assoc. Fac. Pr. 1970 repr. of 1920 ed. o.p. A short overview of the history of Italian literature.

Gatt-Rutter, J. A. *Writers and Politics in Modern Italy.* Holmes & Meier 1978 $15.95. ISBN 0-8419-0413-8. A comparative study by a major critic.

Grillo, Ernesto. *Studies in Modern Italian Literature.* Richard West 1973 repr. of 1930 ed. o.p.

Hainsworth, Peter, Valerio Lucchesi, Christina Roaf, David Robey, and J. R. Woodhouse, eds. *The Languages of Literature in Renaissance Italy.* OUP 1988 $69.00. ISBN 0-19-815832-7. Sixteen essays that "document how Renaissance language and literature compel our critical attention today" (*Italica*).

Haydn, Hiram C. *The Counter-Renaissance.* Peter Smith repr. of 1950 ed. o.p.

Heiney, Donald. *America in Modern Italian Literature.* Rutgers U. Pr. 1965 o.p. Considered the best history of the influence of American writing on such Italian authors as Vittorini, Pavese, Calvino, Soldati, and Silone.

Houston, John P. *The Rhetoric of Poetry in the Renaissance and Seventeenth Century.* La. State U. Pr. 1983 o.p.

Howells, William D. *Modern Italian Poets. Essay Index Repr. Ser.* Ayer 1972 repr. of 1887 ed. $26.50. ISBN 0-8369-7246-5

Jordan, Constance. *Renaissance Feminism: Literary Texts and Political Models.* Cornell Univ. Pr. 1990 $45.00. ISBN 0-8014-2163-2. "A welcome and valuable study" (*Italica*).

Kristeller, Paul O. *Renaissance Thought and Its Sources.* Ed. by Michael Mooney. Col. U. Pr. 1981 $55.00. ISBN 0-231-04512-3. A comprehensive look at this important period in Italian culture, art, and literature.

Lucente, Gregory L. *Beautiful Fables: Self-Consciousness in Italian Narrative from Manzoni to Calvino.* Johns Hopkins 1986 $44.00. ISBN 0-8018-3331-0

McLeod, Addison. *Plays and Players in Modern Italy.* Assoc. Fac. Pr. 1970 repr. of 1912 ed. o.p. Commentary on playwrights such as Butti, Rovetta, Rasi, Bracco, Benelli, and players such as Duse, Borelli, Galli, Salvini, Ruggieri, Falconi, Novelli, and Zacconi.

Migiel, Marilyn, and Juliana Schiesari, eds. *Refiguring Women: Perspectives on Gender and the Italian Renaissance.* Cornell Univ. Pr. 1991 $36.95. ISBN 0-8914-2538-7

Pacifici, Sergio. *A Guide to Contemporary Italian Literature: From Futurism to Neorealism.* S. Ill. U. Pr. 1972 $9.95. ISBN 0-8093-0593-3. A fine look at a variety of important writers, including Moravia, Pratolini, Vittorini, and many contemporary filmmakers.

———. *The Modern Italian Novel: From Pea to Moravia.* S. Ill. U. Pr. 1979 $16.95. ISBN 0-8093-8073-8. A scholarly overview of the century's most enduring novelists.

Praz, Mario. *The Flaming Heart: Essays on Crashaw, Machiavelli and Other Studies from Chaucer to T. S. Eliot.* Peter Smith 1958 $11.75. ISBN 0-8446-1365-7. A comparative study for which the author gained international recognition.

———. *The Romantic Agony.* Trans. by Angus Davidson. OUP 1951 $15.95. ISBN 0-19-281061-8. A major comparative study by a leading literary critic.

Ragusa, Olga, *Narrative and Drama: Essays in Modern Italian Literature from Verga to Pasolini.* Mouton 1976 $40.00. ISBN 90-2793-474-6. Essays collected by a prominent Columbia University scholar.

Riccio, Peter. *Italian Authors of Today. Essay Index Repr. Ser.* Ayer repr. of 1938 ed. $15.00. ISBN 0-8369-1842-8. Treats a number of modern writers, including critics.

Rimanelli, Giose, and Kenneth J. Archity, eds. *Italian Literature: Roots and Branches.* Bks. Demand repr. of 1967 ed. $122.50. ISBN 0-8357-8189-5. Sixteen essays whose topics range from the Middle Ages to the modern period.

Rossetti, Dante Gabriel, trans. *The Early Italian Poets.* U. CA Pr. 1982 $27.50. ISBN 0-520-04468-1. A history and an anthology.

Sandys, John Edwin. *A History of Classical Scholarship.* 3 vols. Hafner 1967 repr. of 1920 ed. o.p. An indispensable work for students of Italian Renaissance humanism.

Springer, Carolyn. *The Marble Wilderness: Ruins and Representation in Italian Romanticism. 1775–1850.* Cambridge U. Pr. 1987 $44.50. ISBN 0-521-33472-1. Discusses the iconography of ruins and its influence on Italian romantic literature.

Symonds, J. A. *Italian Literature: From Ariosto to the Late Renaissance.* Peter Smith o.p. An in-depth study of the Renaissance.

______. *The Renaissance in Italy.* 7 vols. Coronet Bks. 1972 repr. of 1875 ed. $695.00. ISBN 3-487-04145-6. An exhaustive study of the many aspects of the Italian Renaissance.

Thayer, William R. *Italica: Studies in Italian Life and Letters. Essay Index Repr. Ser.* Ayer repr. of 1908 ed. $19.00. ISBN 0-8369-1214-4

Trail, Florence. *A History of Italian Literature.* Haskell 1972 repr. of 1903 ed. $63.95. ISBN 0-8383-1561-5

Valency, Maurice. *In Praise of Love: An Introduction to the Love Poetry of the Renaissance.* Hippocrene Bks. 1976 repr. of 1958 ed. o.p. Troubadour and other traditions of love poetry to the time of Dante.

Venturi, Franco. *Italy and the Enlightenment: Studies in a Cosmopolitan Century.* Ed. by Stuart Woolf. NYU Pr. 1972 o.p. An excellent study of eighteenth-century Italy.

Vittorini, Domenico. *The Age of Dante.* Greenwood 1975 repr. of 1957 ed. o.p. An overview of the Trecento period.

______. *The Modern Italian Novel.* Russell Sage 1967 repr. of 1930 ed. o.p.

Weinberg, Bernard. *A History of Literary Criticism in the Italian Renaissance.* 2 vols. Bks. Demand repr. of 1961 ed. Vol. 1 $160.00. ISBN 0-317-26676-4. Vol. 2 $138.30. ISBN 0-685-10708-6. A compendious two-volume history.

Weiss, Roberto. *Dawn of Humanism in Italy. World History Ser.* Haskell 1970 repr. of 1947 ed. $49.95. ISBN 0-8383-0336-6. A study of the origins of humanistic thought.

West, R., and D. S. Cervigni, eds. *Women's Voices in Italian Literature.* U. of NC Pr. 1989 o.p. Essays considering the emerging voice of Italian female writers.

Whitfield, John H. *A Short History of Italian Literature.* Greenwood 1976 repr. of 1960 ed. $38.50. ISBN 0-8371-8890-3. A narrative survey from Dante to Pirandello.

Wilkins, Ernest H. *A History of Italian Literature.* Ed. by Thomas G. Bergin. HUP rev. ed. 1974 $35.00. ISBN 0-674-39701-0. Of interest to the general reader.

COLLECTIONS

Allen, Beverly, Muriel Kittel, and Jeala Jane Jewell, eds. *The Defiant Muse: Italian Feminist Poems from the Middle Ages to the Present.* Feminist Pr. 1986 $35.00. ISBN 0-935312-48-X. A bilingual anthology with emphasis on the twentieth century.

Bentley, Eric, ed. *The Classic Theatre: Six Italian Plays.* Peter Smith o.p. Contains Machiavelli, *The Mandrake*; Beolco, *Ruzzante Returns from the Wards*; Anon, *The Three Cuckolds*; Gozzi, *The King Stag*; Goldoni, *The Servant of Two Masters* and *Mirandolina.*

Bond, Richard W., ed. *Early Plays from the Italian.* Ayer repr. of 1911 ed. $29.00. ISBN 0-405-08287-8. Includes Ariosto, *Supposes*; Grazzini, *The Bugbears.*

Butler, Arthur J., ed. *The Forerunners of Dante: A Selection from Italian Poetry before 1300.* Gordon Pr. 1977 $59.95. ISBN 0-8490-1857-9. A collection of poetry from the early Middle Ages, including works by saints, troubadors, and works in the courtly tradition.

Caetani, Marguerite, ed. *Anthology of New Italian Writers: Selections from Botteghe Oscure.* Greenwood repr. of 1950 ed. o.p.

Cassirer, Ernst, ed. *Renaissance Philosophy of Man.* U. Ch. Pr. 1956 $12.95. ISBN 0-226-09604-1. Includes Petrarch, *On His Own Ignorance*; Valla, *Dialogue on Free Will*;

Ficino, *Five Questions Concerning the Mind*; Pico della Mirandola, *Oration on the Dignity of Man*; Pompanazzi, *On the Immortality of the Soul*.

De'Lucchi, Lorna, ed. and trans. *An Anthology of Italian Poems: 13th-19th Century*. Biblo repr. of 1922 ed. $28.00. ISBN 0-8196-0198-5. A bilingual edition ranging from St. Francis of Assisi to Giosuè Carducci. Introduction by Cesare Foligno.

Garrett, George, ed. *The Botteghe Oscure Reader*. Wesleyan Univ. Pr. 1974 o.p.

Goldin, Frederick, ed. and trans. *German and Italian Lyrics of the Middle Ages: An Anthology and a History*. Peter Smith o.p. A comprehensive collection and history by an eminent medieval scholar and translator.

Golino, Carlo L., and Salvatore Quasimodo, eds. *Contemporary Italian Poetry: An Anthology*. Greenwood 1977 repr. of 1962 ed. $62.50. ISBN 0-8371-8998-5. A bilingual anthology with useful foreword and preface.

Guercio, Francis M., ed. *Anthology of Contemporary Italian Prose*. Assoc. Fac. Pr. 1970 repr. of 1931 ed. o.p. Short prose pieces by 12 writers, including Luigi Pirandello.

Haller, Herman W. *The Hidden Italy: A Bilingual Edition of Italian Dialect Poetry*. Wayne St. U. Pr. 1986 $45.00. ISBN 0-8143-1802-9. A collection of poetry in regional dialects from the eighteenth century to the present.

Howells, William D. *Modern Italian Poets*. *Essay Index Repr. Ser.* Ayer 1972 repr. of 1887 ed. $26.50. ISBN 0-8369-7246-5

King, Martha, ed. *New Italian Women: A Collection of Short Fiction*. Italica Pr. 1989 $14.95. ISBN 0-934977-16-X. Short stories and excerpts from longer works treating relevant social and human concerns.

Lind, L. R., ed. *Twentieth-Century Italian Poetry: A Bilingual Anthology*. Bobbs 1974 o.p.

Marchione, Margherita, trans. *Twentieth-Century Italian Poetry: A Bilingual Anthology*. Am. Inst. Ital. Stud. 1974 o.p. Nearly 24 modern poets, many untranslated into English, represented here—from Alvaro to Ungaretti. Preface by Charles Angoff.

Painter, William M. *The Palace of Pleasure*. 4 vols. Ed. by Hamish Miles. AMS Pr. repr. of 1929 ed. $240.00. ISBN 0-404-04880-3

Rebay, Luciano, ed. *Italian Poetry: A Selection from St. Francis of Assisi to Salvatore Quasimodo*. Peter Smith o.p. An overview of the major Italian poets from the Middle Ages to modern times.

Rendel, Romilda. *An Anthology of Italian Lyrics from the 13th Century to the Present Day*. Arden Lib. repr. of 1926 ed. o.p.

Smarr, Janet L., trans. *Italian Renaissance Tales*. Solaris Pr. 1983 $13.95. ISBN 0-933760-03-5

Smith, Lawrence R., ed. *The New Italian Poetry, 1945 to the Present: A Bilingual Anthology*. U. CA Pr. 1981 $45.00. ISBN 0-520-03859-2. Includes an excellent introduction and short biographical sketches of each poet.

Spatola, Adriano, and Paul Vangelisti, eds. *Italian Poetry, 1960–1980: From Neo to Post Avant-Garde*. Red Hill Pr. 1982 $15.00. ISBN 0-686-45586-X. A collection of representative Italian poetry.

CHRONOLOGY OF AUTHORS

Cavalcanti, Guido. c.1254–1300
Dante Alighieri. 1265–1321
Petrarch. 1304–1374
Boccaccio, Giovanni. 1313–1375
Alberti, Leon Battista. 1404–1472
Poliziano, Angelo. 1454–1494
Bembo, Pietro. 1470–1547
Ariosto, Ludovico. 1474–1533
Castiglione, Baldassare. 1478–1529
Aretino, Pietro. 1492–1556
Tasso, Torquato. 1544–1595
Bruno, Giordano. 1548–1600
Vico, Giambattista. 1668–1744
Goldoni, Carlo. 1707–1793
Baretti, Giuseppe. 1719–1789
Parini, Giuseppe. 1729–1799
Alfieri, Count Vittorio. 1749–1803
Foscolo, Ugo. 1778–1827
Manzoni, Alessandro. 1785–1873
Belli, Giuseppe Gioacchino. 1791–1863
Leopardi, Giacomo. 1798–1837

De Sanctis, Francesco. 1817–1883
Carducci, Giosuè. 1835–1907
Pascoli, Giovanni. 1835–1912
Verga, Giovanni. 1840–1922
Svevo, Italo. 1861–1928
D'Annunzio, Gabriele. 1863–1938
Croce, Benedetto. 1866–1952
Pirandello, Luigi. 1867–1936
Deledda, Grazia. 1871–1936
Marinetti, Filippo Tommaso. 1875–1944
Papini, Giovanni. 1881–1956
Ungaretti, Giuseppe. 1888–1970
Gramsci, Antonio. 1891–1937
Betti, Ugo. 1892–1953
Lampedusa, Giuseppe Tomasi, Prince of. 1896–1957
Montale, Eugenio. 1896–1981
De Filippo, Eduardo. 1900–1984
Silone, Ignazio. 1900–1978
Quasimodo, Salvatore. 1901–1968
Levi, Carlo. 1902–1975
Buzzati, Dino. 1906–1972
Moravia, Alberto. 1907–1990
Pavese, Cesare. 1908–1950
Vittorini, Elio. 1908–1966
Pratolini, Vasco. 1913–1991
Bassani, Giorgio. 1916–
Ginzburg, Natalia Levi. 1916–1991
Morante, Elsa. 1918–1985
Levi, Primo. 1919–1987
Sciascia, Leonardo. 1921–1989
Pasolini, Pier Paolo. 1922–1975
Calvino, Italo. 1923–1985
Fo, Dario. 1926–
Fallaci, Oriana. 1930–
Eco, Umberto. 1932–
Maraini, Dacia. 1936–

ALBERTI, LEON BATTISTA. 1404–1472

Born in Venice of a Florentine family in exile, Alberti was truly the "universal man" of the Renaissance: a superb gymnast, architect, painter, sculptor, poet, and scholar who wrote treatises, in Latin and Italian, on statics (physics), building, perspective in painting, and mathematics. His most important work in Italian is his dialogue in four books *On the Family* (1436). It treats the education of children, matrimony, acquiring wealth and ensuring family prosperity, virtues and vices, bodily exercise, and the cultivation of friendships. Alberti's Italian prose is fresh and colorful. He could write classical Latin so well that he passed off many of his works as recently discovered ancient originals. He perfected himself as a living work of art, all his abilities cultivated to constitute a harmonious whole.

Works by Alberti

The Albertis of Florence: Leon Battista Alberti's Della Famiglia. 1435–36. Trans. by Guido Guarino. Bucknell U. Pr. 1975 $38.50. ISBN 0-8387-7736-8. Ranks in importance with Machiavelli's *Prince* as a contribution to the founding of modern economic, social, and political sciences.

Dinner Pieces: A Translation of the Intercenales. Trans. by D. Marsh. MRTS 1987 $20.00. ISBN 0-86698-028-8

The Family in Renaissance Florence: A Translation of I Libri Della Famiglia. Trans. by Renee Neu Watkins. U. of SC Pr. 1969 o.p.

Books about Alberti

Gadol, Joan. *Leon Battista Alberti: Universal Man of the Early Renaissance*. U. Ch. Pr. 1969 o.p. A portrait of Alberti's intellectual character.

Jarzombek, Mark. *On Leon Battista Alberti: His Literary and Aesthetic Theories*. MIT Pr. 1989 $22.50. ISBN 0-262-10042-8. Interesting analysis of Alberti's views on art and literature.

ALFIERI, COUNT VITTORIO. 1749–1803

Born in Asti in the Italian Piedmont, Alfieri came into great wealth at age 14. He roamed across Europe, until his meeting with the Princess of Albany, the wife and then the widow of England's Young Pretender, changed his life. Originally, Alfieri wrote in French as well as Italian, but as he became conscious of what he felt was the tragic fate of Italy in the modern world, he devoted himself to perfecting his mastery of the Italian language and to employing it as a national literary prophet. Alfieri came to be seen as the embodiment of a long-suppressed dream of Italian renewal, hailed as such in Italy even before his death, and accepted in that role with great enthusiasm by many in England as well as in the United States. Alfieri saw himself as Italy's fifth greatest poet, after Dante, Petrarch, Ariosto, and Tasso, with two centuries of utter decline that was worse than silence separating him from Tasso. Because of the high austerity of his poetry, many, like Thomas Babington Macaulay (see Vol. 1), saw him instead linked directly to Dante: a return, over the heads of Tasso, Ariosto, and Petrarch, to the fountainhead of Italian poetry. Macaulay accepted the view that Petrarch, the humanist, led Italy astray by departing from Dante's vernacular-directed course. Alfieri wrote almost two dozen tragedies, six comedies, and many sonnets, satires, and odes, including five on American independence. His *Bruto Primo* (1787) was dedicated to George Washington, "the liberator of America." A posthumously published autobiography has gradually come to overshadow his purely literary works as an expression of his presence in Italy's spiritual and literary history.

Plays by Alfieri

Tragedies of Vittorio Alfieri. 2 vols. Trans. by Edgar Alfred Bowring. Greenwood repr. of 1876 ed. o.p. A great improvement over the translation done in 1815 by Charles Lloyd.

Nonfiction by Alfieri

Of Tyranny. 1777. Trans. by Julius A. Molinaro and Beatrice M. Corrigan. U. of Toronto Pr. 1961 o.p. Advocates the assassination of all tyrants as the noble action of a lone hero.

The Prince and the Letters. Trans. by Beatrice M. Corrigan and Julius A. Molinaro. Bks. Demand repr. of 1972 ed. $53.50. ISBN 0-317-10076-9. Argues that poets and writers, as the exponents of freedom, are not only independent from princes, but superior to them.

Book about Alfieri

Betti, Franco. *Vittorio Alfieri. Twayne's World Authors Ser.* G. K. Hall 1984 o.p. A critical and historical biographical narrative, with overviews of Alfieri's works.

ARETINO, PIETRO. 1492–1556

Born in the province of Arezzo, hence "the Aretine," Aretino wrote several comedies, tragedies, satires, and "other works of a scandalous or licentious character." He acquired an international reputation, especially in England, being variously appraised in different periods. Thomas Nashe (see Vol. 1) wrote of him: "It was one of the wittiest knaves God ever made," and Milton (see Vol. 1) spoke of him as "that notorious ribald of Arezzo." Titian (see Vol. 3) was his friend and painted his portrait. He was called the "Scourge of Princes."

Works by Aretino

Dialogues. Trans. by Raymond Rosenthal. Stein & Day 1971 o.p. Mirror Aretino's impetuous personality and the corruption of his times.

Selected Letters. Trans. by George Bull. Viking Penguin 1976 o.p. From Aretino's prodigious correspondence (six volumes 1537–57); most dealing with the flattery of princes, kings, and prelates, soliciting gifts or thanking Aretino for them.

Books about Aretino

Cleugh, James. *The Divine Aretino.* Stein & Day 1964 o.p. An illustrated biography of the half-outlaw, half-connoisseur writer.

Hutton, Edward. *Pietro Aretino: The Scourge of Princes.* Constable 1940 o.p. A biography of this notoriously roguish character.

ARIOSTO, LUDOVICO. 1474–1533

Born in Reggio, Ariosto lived most of his life in Ferrara, enjoying the patronage first of Cardinal Ippolito and then of the cardinal's brother, Alfonso, Duke of Este, who had been his inseparable companion in youth, and who protected him against the wrath of such powerful enemies as Pope Julius II. In addition to his mock epic *Orlando Furioso,* Ariosto wrote many lyric poems in Latin and Italian, 7 satires in *terza rima,* and 5 comedies in unrhymed lines of 11 syllables. His satires were read and imitated by Thomas Wyatt (see Vol. 1), and one of his comedies, *I suppositi,* was translated and adapted into English by George Gascoigne and performed at Gray's Inn in 1566, providing Shakespeare (see Vol. 1) with much of the content and inspiration for his *The Taming of the Shrew.* The mock epic of chivalry *Orlando Furioso,* versions of which appeared in 1516 and 1521 before the definitive edition of 1532, is undoubtedly the "major literary achievement of the Italian Renaissance." Ariosto, Hegel (see Vol. 4) observed, prepared the way for the treatment of chivalry in Cervantes's Don Quixote and Shakespeare's Falstaff, and does so in "the gently veiled humor, the brilliantly disarming ease, the charm, wit, grace, and artful naivete with which he brings on the self-dissolution of all that is in itself essentially fantastical, absurd, or nonsensical." In so doing, Ariosto "highlights and reaffirms all that is truly noble and grand in knighthood, in courage, love and honor." A translation by Sir John Harrington, in English "heroical verse," was published in 1591, but by then Edmund Spenser (see Vol. 1) had already sought to "overgo" Ariosto's great epic in his own *Faerie Queene.* A translation by John Hoole in 1783 was read by Walter Scott (see Vol. 1) and Robert Southey (see Vol. 1), and Byron (see Vol. 1) drew on it—as also on the mock epics of Luigi Pulci and Francesco Berni—for his *Don Juan.*

Poetry by Ariosto

Ariosto's Seven Planets Governing Italie, or His Satyrs. English Experience Ser. Walter J. Johnson 1977 repr. of 1611 ed. $20.00. ISBN 90-221-0770-1. Modeled on Horace's satires.

Orlando Furioso. Trans. by Guido Waldman. *World's Class Ser.* OUP 1983 $14.95. ISBN 0-19-281636-5. "Waldman's complete and very readable prose translation . . . faithfully captures all of the narrative line and much of the magic and majesty of the *Furioso* . . ." (*Choice*).

Books about Ariosto

Ascoli, Albert Russell. *Ariosto's Bitter Harmony: Crisis and Evasion in the Italian Renaissance.* Princeton U. Pr. 1987 $50.00. ISBN 0-691-05479-7. Applies modern literary theory to *Orlando Furioso.*

Griffin, Robert. *Ludovico Ariosto. Twayne's World Authors Ser.* G. K. Hall 1974 o.p. Primarily treats *Orlando Furioso,* but also includes minor works as they reflect on Ariosto's masterpiece.

Javitch, Daniel. *Proclaiming a Classic: The Canonization of the Orlando Furioso.* Princeton U. Pr. 1991 $35.00. ISBN 0-691-06549-7. "Stands as an important contribution to genre criticism and Renaissance cultural studies" (*Italica*).

Marinello, Peter V. *Ariosto and Boiardo: The Origins of Orlando Furioso."* U. of Mo. Pr. 1987 $31.00. ISBN 0-8262-0636-0. "Ranks with the very best Anglo-American works on these poets" (*Italica*).

Rodino, Robert J., and Salvatore DiMaria. *Ludovico Ariosto: An Annotated Bibliography of Criticism, 1956–1980.* U. of Mo. Pr. 1985 $32.00. ISBN 0-8262-0445-7. Updates Giuseppe Fatini's indispensable annotated bibliography for the period 1510–1956.

BARETTI, GIUSEPPE. 1719–1789

An adventurer, Baretti spent many years in England, where he became a close friend of SAMUEL JOHNSON (see Vol. 1), in whose company he mastered English as well as the art of dictionary making. His Italian-English, English-Italian dictionaries remained standard until the twentieth century. Between long periods in England, he edited the notorious Italian magazine, *Frusta Letteraria* (Literary Lash). Inspired by Johnson, he became the first Italian critic to defend SHAKESPEARE (see Vol. 1) against the attacks of VOLTAIRE. Baretti had himself criticized DANTE on grounds similar to those of Voltaire—for having offended classical tastes with his medieval literary barbarism, but, under Johnson's tutelage, Baretti revised his tastes and then wrote in French his famous discourse on Shakespeare and Voltaire, which was first published in London in 1777. In 1769 he had stabbed a man to death in the streets of London in self-defense, and his acquittal was gained through the intervention of his many English friends, including painters, politicians, and actors of the caliber of REYNOLDS (see Vol. 3), Burke, and Garrick, as well as Johnson.

NONFICTION BY BARETTI

A Journey from London to Genoa. St. Mut. 1983 o.p. A lively description in the form of letters of Baretti's return to Italy through Portugal, Spain, and France. (Italian title: *Lettere familiari ai fratelli 1762–3).*

BOOK ABOUT BARETTI

Collison-Morley, Lacy. *Giuseppe Baretti: With an Account of His Literary Friendships and Feuds in Italy and in England in the Days of Dr. Johnson.* Richard West repr. of 1909 ed. o.p. A detailed look at the various periods of Baretti's life and his relationship with such figures as Reynolds, Boswell, and Goldsmith.

BASSANI, GIORGIO. 1916–

The main theme of Giorgio Bassani's novels and short stories, which have earned him wide acclaim outside Italy, has been the advent of anti-Semitism in a provincial Italian city, Ferrara, during World War II. He earlier had a very successful career as an editor with a major publishing house, being credited with helping to bring to public notice TOMASI LAMPEDUSA's *The Leopard.* He also edited a literary magazine and was director of the Italian radio-television network. His first collection of short pieces was *A City on the Plain,* written under the pseudonym Giacomo Marchi. He also published much poetry, in several small volumes, finally collected in 1963. The stories and novels that were to make him famous abroad began to appear in the 1950s. They include *A Prospect of Ferrara* (1960) (five stories), *The Gold Rimmed Spectacles* (1960), and *The Garden of the Finzi-Continis* (1962), Vittorio De Sica's film version of which has become a public television classic.

Novels by Bassani

Behind the Door. 1962. Trans. by William Weaver. HarBraceJ 1976 $6.95. ISBN 0-15-634570-6. Bassani's reflections on his feelings of alienation as a Jew while in high school.

The Garden of the Finzi-Continis. 1962. Trans. by William Weaver. HarBraceJ 1977 $6.95. ISBN 0-15-634570-6. The tragic tale of a wealthy Jewish family during World War II.

The Heron. 1975. HarBraceJ 1986 $5.95. ISBN 0-15-640085-5. A single day of hunting that synthesizes the life of the protagonist, Limentani.

The Smell of Hay. 1972. HarBraceJ 1975 o.p. "Bassani marks the rebirth of his creativity through the importance he now gives life over death" (*Italica*).

Short Story Collection by Bassani

Five Stories of Ferrara. 1960. HarBraceJ 1971 o.p.

Books about Bassani

Radcliff-Umstead, Douglas. *The Exile into Eternity: A Study of the Narrative Writings of Giorgio Bassani.* Fairleigh Dickinson 1987 $29.50. ISBN 0-8386-3296-3. A historical and comprehensive approach to all of Bassani's fiction.

Schneider, Marilyn. *Vengeance and the Victim: History and Symbol in Giorgio Bassani's Fiction.* U. of Minn. Pr. 1986 $39.95. ISBN 0-8166-1512-8. A detailed analysis of the *Five Stories of Ferrara,* as well as Bassani's lesser-known poetry.

BELLI, GIUSEPPE GIOACCHINO. 1791–1863

Author of more than 2,000 sonnets in the modern Roman dialect, Belli produced what has been called a *comédie humaine* that refashions the stories of the Bible, the history of Rome, both ancient and modern, and the actual lives, hopes, fears, prejudices, loves, and hatreds of literally hundreds of typical residents of Rome, including popes and cardinals, ghetto Jews, prostitutes, thieves, and beggars, and the lowest of street people. Frances Trollope, the mother of Anthony Trollope (see Vol. 1), first wrote of Belli's art for English readers.

Poetry by Belli

Sonnets of Giuseppe Belli. Trans. by William Miller. La. State U. Pr. 1981 $22.50. ISBN 0-8071-0762-X.

BEMBO, PIETRO. 1470–1547

This truly "Renaissance man" was the most influential cultural figure of his time. He knew all the men of letters of his age, was a lover of Lucrezia Borgia, and a favorite of Popes Leo X, Clement VII, and Paul II, who finally made him a cardinal in 1539. Bembo wrote in both Latin and Italian, modeling himself on Petrarch (see also Vol. 4). For his important literary work, a dialogue on love entitled *Gli Asolani* (1505), he took inspiration from Plato's (see Vols. 3 and 4) *Symposium,* but modeled his style on Petrarch's Tuscan. Bembo prepared classic editions of Dante and Petrarch and defended their use of Tuscan Italian.

Poetry by Bembo

Gli Asolani. 1505. Trans. by Rudolf B. Gottfried. *Select Bibliographies Repr. Ser.* Ayer repr. of 1954 ed. $18.00. ISBN 0-8369-5941-8

BETTI, UGO. 1892–1953

Born in a small town in Le Marche, Betti was raised primarily by his father, a stern country doctor, because his mother was unwilling to do so. He studied at the classical lyceum, demonstrating an inclination toward literature. For practical reasons, however, his father steered his son toward law school. Betti served in World War I and was taken prisoner by the Germans. His first book of poems, *The Pensive King* (1922), bears witness to the war's stark impact on him. Betti hesitated for a time between returning to his legal career and pursuing his newly found penchant for writing. Deciding to try his hand at both, he served as a judge from the early 1920s through 1943 while also writing poetry, short stories, a novel, and the plays for which he is best known. While clearly influenced by the experimental theater of LUIGI PIRANDELLO, and indeed often viewed as his successor, Betti's outlook was also colored by his years on the bench. He strove to represent reality as more than mere facts, seeking in his work to penetrate human motives, instincts, and truth. In total he wrote 25 plays, which were enormously popular in their day.

PLAYS BY BETTI

Three Plays. Ed. by Gino Rizzo. Hill & Wang 1966 o.p. Includes *The Inquiry* (1944–45), *Goat Island* (1946), and *The Gambler* (1950).

BOOK ABOUT BETTI

Licastro, Emmanuele. *Ugo Betti: An Introduction.* McFarland & Co. 1985 $21.95. ISBN 0-89950-141-9. Considers all of Betti's fictional work: poetry, prose, theater.

BOCCACCIO, GIOVANNI. 1313–1375

Although Boccaccio was actually born in France and raised and educated in Naples (where he wrote his first works under the patronage of the French Angevin ruler), Boccaccio always considered himself a Tuscan, like PETRARCH (see Vols. 2 and 4) and DANTE. After his return to Florence in 1340, he witnessed the outbreak of the great plague, or Black Death, in 1348. This provided the setting for his most famous work, the vernacular prose masterpiece *Il Decamerone (Decameron)* (1353)—a "framed" collection of 100 short stories, told by 10 Florentines who leave plague-infected Florence for the neighboring hill town of Fiesole, the beauty of which is repeatedly described in the tales. Each of the 10 tells a tale a day through a cycle of 10 days. The highly finished work exerted a tremendous influence on all the other modern European literatures even as it established itself as the great classic of Italian fictional prose. Although CHAUCER (see Vol. 1) did not mention Boccaccio's name, his *Canterbury Tales* are clearly modeled on the *Decameron*. Besides the *Decameron*, Boccaccio's Italian works include a short life of Dante and commentaries on the *Divine Comedy*; a prose romance, *Filocolo* (1340); *Filostrato*(1335); *Story of Theseus* (1340–41), his only attempt to write an epic, a work which Chaucer rendered as his "Knight's Tale"; his pastoral romance *L'Ameto* (1341–42); *Amorous Fiametta* (1343–44); *The Nymph of Fiesole* (1340–45); and his last work written in Italian, the gloomy cautionary tale *The Corbaccio* (1355). The *Nymph Song* (1346), as a counterpiece for the *Decameron*, demonstrates that it is possible to read the *Decameron* as an allegory, with the plague representing the "spiritual plague" of medieval Christianity, viewed from the vantage point of Renaissance humanism. Many of the *Decameron* tales are indeed paganized versions of medieval sermons about sin and damnation with the morals reversed. After 1363 Boccaccio concentrated on trying to gain enduring fame by writing, in Latin, a series of "lives" of memorable men and women and a genealogy of the pagan gods.

WORKS BY BOCCACCIO

Amorous Fiametta. 1343–44. Trans. by Bartholomew Young. Greenwood 1970 repr. of 1926 ed. $45.00. ISBN 0-8371-3026-3. Prose narrative.

The Corbaccio. 1355. Trans. by Anthony K. Cassell. U. of Ill. Pr. 1975 o.p. An excellent first translation of this controversial work.

The Decameron. 1348–53. Ed. by Mark Musa and Peter Bondanella. *Norton Critical Eds.* Norton 1977 $15.95. ISBN 0-393-04458-0

Diana's Hunt, Caccia di Diana: Boccaccio's First Fiction. Trans. by Anthony K. Cassell and Victoria Kirkham. U. of Pa. Pr. 1991. $31.95. ISBN 0-8122-8219-1. A short poem that mixes contemporary Neopolitan life with mythological settings.

The Filostrato. 1335. Trans. by Nathaniel E. Griffin and Arthur B. Myrick. Biblo repr. of 1929 ed. $21.00. ISBN 0-8196-0187-X. Served as a model for Chaucer's *Troilus and Criseyde.*

L'Ameto. Trans. by Judith Serafini-Saudi. Garland 1985 o.p. "A much-needed and long-awaited book—greatly enhanced by the translator's own introduction" (*Italica*).

The Nymph of Fiesole. 1340–45. Trans. by Daniel J. Donno. Greenwood 1974 repr. of 1960 ed. o.p. The first Italian idyll, in octaves.

BOOKS ABOUT BOCCACCIO

Bergin, Thomas G. *Boccaccio.* Viking Penguin 1981 o.p. "Learned, lucid, an indispensable volume for students of the Renaissance" (A. Bartlett Giamatti, book jacket).

Chubb, Thomas C. *The Life of Giovanni Boccaccio.* Assoc. Fac. Pr. 1969 repr. of 1930 ed. o.p. One of the early American biographies of Boccaccio.

Mazzotta, Giuseppe. *The World at Play in Boccaccio's* Decameron. Princeton U. Pr. 1986 $40.00. ISBN 0-691-06677-9. "Important and provocative in its interpretive insights for medievalists, Italianists, and comparatists alike" (*Italica*).

Wallace, David. *Chaucer and the Early Writings of Boccaccio.* Boydell & Brewer 1985 $68.00. ISBN 0-85991-186-1. "Among its many virtues are its prose, which is crisp, quick-moving, and full of wit" (*Italica*).

BRUNO, GIORDANO. 1548–1600

This truly cosmopolitan figure of the late Italian Renaissance—often called "the Nolan" after his birthplace near Naples—wandered restlessly across Europe preaching his doctrine of cosmic consciousness and publishing it in dialogues and poetry that read today like volcanic spiritual upheavals. With Tommaso Campanella, author of the utopian *City of the Sun* and a controversial *Defense of Galileo*, Bruno represents the traumatic decline of humanistic philosophy, heralding the birth of modern natural science at the hands of GALILEO (see Vols. 4 and 5) and FRANCIS BACON (see Vols. 1 and 4). His major writings, attacking the Roman Catholic church and celebrating the poetic frenzy of creative geniuses, have inspired writers of a similar temperament down to the days of JAMES JOYCE (see Vol. 1), who drew on Bruno, as well as GIAMBATTISTA VICO, for *Finnegans Wake.*

WORK BY BRUNO

The Heroic Enthusiasts. Gordon Pr. 1976 $59.95. ISBN 0-8490-1947-8. Interprets Bruno's thought as belonging to the occult tradition, based on the text of the pseudo-Hermes Trimegistus.

BOOKS ABOUT BRUNO

Yates, Frances. *Giordano Bruno and the Hermetic Tradition.* U. Ch. Pr. 1990 repr. of 1964 ed. $16.95. ISBN 0-226-95007-7. The relationship of Bruno's metaphysical works to hermetic philosophy.

———. *Lull and Bruno: Collected Essays.* Vol. 1 Routledge Chapman & Hall 1982 $32.50. ISBN 0-7100-0952-6. Essays on the Catalan philosopher and mystic Ramon Lull and Bruno.

BUZZATI, DINO (1906–1972)

Born in Belluno in the Veneto, Buzzati received his law degree from the University of Milan, but never practiced law. Beginning in 1928, he worked as an editor and journalist for the Milanese daily newspaper *Il Corriere della Sera.* His first work of fiction, *Barnabo delle montagne (Barnaby of the Mountains)* (1933), established Buzzati as an inventive writer who evoked the mysteries of ordinary life. Buzzati never linked himself to any literary movement or style, preferring to seek the fantastic and the extraordinary in his often commonplace characters and locales. A talented short story writer, he published most of his short fiction in *Sessanta Racconti* (1958), which was partially translated into English as *Catastrophe.* Here, Buzzati increasingly employs urban settings where machines, instead of quasi-mythical monstrous beings, populate a supernatural world.

SHORT STORY COLLECTION BY BUZZATI

Catastrophe and Other Stories. Trans. by Judith Landry and Cynthia Jolly. Riverrun NY 1982 $9.95. ISBN 0-7145-3914-7

CALVINO, ITALO. 1923–1985

Born in Cuba of Italian parents, Calvino was soon brought to San Remo, near Genoa. After the fall of Mussolini in 1943, he spent some months with a Communist partisan brigade in the mountains and remained a member of the Communist party until 1957 when he left in protest against the Soviet invasion of Hungary. In 1947 he joined the large publishing house of Einaudi—which later published his books—and rose to a top editorial position. His literary sponsors at the start of his career were writers like CESARE PAVESE and ELIO VITTORINI, who were already publishing-house executives. They saw to the publication of Calvino's first novel, *The Path to the Nest of Spiders* (1947), a child's view of an antifascist resistance, which was hailed as one of the main novels of the postwar neorealistic genre. But, even in that work, Calvino showed a tendency to move into a realm of what has since come to be called "magic realism." Thus, in Calvino's short stories, fable alternates with realism, with a tendency toward fusion of the two. Almost total fusion occurs in his three allegorical novels, *The Cloven Viscount* (1959), *The Baron in the Trees* (1959), and *The Nonexistent Knight* (1959). According to SEAMUS HEANEY (see Vol. 1), Calvino's split-level storytelling cycle is a piece of "marvelous binary blarney," and he marvels that Calvino is able to "get away with it" again in *Mr. Palomar,* which Heaney later praised as a "high-wire" performance that gives one a thrilling "sense of the safety net being withdrawn at the end" (*N.Y. Times*).

NOVELS BY CALVINO

The Baron in the Trees. Trans. by Archibald Colquhoun. HarBraceJ 1977 $6.95. ISBN 0-15-610680-9. A fantasy/myth narrated as history.

The Castle of Crossed Destinies. HarBraceJ 1979 $5.95. ISBN 0-15-615455-2. "A most genial idea, and the English version is done by the best modern translator from the Italian" (*Choice*).

Cosmicomics. 1965. Trans. by William Weaver. HarBraceJ 1976 $5.95. ISBN 0-15-622600-6. A novel in which science complements fantasy.

If on a Winter's Night a Traveler. Trans. by William Weaver. HarBraceJ 1982 $7.95. ISBN 0-15-643961-1. A self-conscious novel about reading a novel with this title.

Invisible Cities. 1972. Trans. by William Weaver. HarBraceJ 1978 $7.95. ISBN 0-15-645380-0. Italo Calvino "leaves outer space for a trip through human history, the yearnings and disasters of city life everywhere, and the accumulative pressures of 20th century life" (*PW*).

The Nonexistent Knight and The Cloven Viscount. 1959. Ed. by J. Ferrone and H. Wolff. HarBraceJ 1977 $6.95. ISBN 0-15-665975-1. A fantastic parody of a Renaissance epic, confronting the eternal conflict between good and evil.

The Path to the Nest of Spiders. 1947. Ecco Pr. 1976 $6.95. ISBN 0-88001-189-0. Calvino's first novella.

T Zero. 1967. Trans. by William Weaver. HarBraceJ 1976 $5.95. ISBN 0-15-692400-5. "Calvino does what very few writers can do: he describes imaginary worlds with the most extraordinary precision and beauty" (Gore Vidal, *New York Review of Books*).

Short Story Collections by Calvino

Difficult Loves. Trans. by William Weaver. HarBraceJ 1985 $7.95. ISBN 0-15-626055-7. A collection of short stories covering Calvino's career.

Italian Folktales. Trans. by George Martin. Pantheon 1981 $17.95. ISBN 0-15-145770-0. "Impossible to recommend too highly" (John Gardner, *N.Y. Times*).

Under the Jaguar Sun. Trans. by William Weaver. HarBraceJ 1988 $12.95. ISBN 0-15-192820-7. Taste, hearing, and smell become the driving forces behind Calvino's characters in these three stories.

The Watcher and Other Stories. 1963. Trans. by William Weaver and Archibald Colquhoun. HarBraceJ 1975 $5.95. ISBN 0-15-694952-0. A strong commentary on some voting practices in Italy in the title story.

Work by Calvino

Six Memos for the Next Millenium. Trans. by Patrick Creagh. HUP 1988 $12.95. ISBN 0-674-81040-6. Includes a series of speeches that the late Calvino intended to give as the Charles Eliot Norton lectures at Harvard University in 1985–86.

Books About Calvino

Carter, Albert Howard, III. *Italo Calvino: Metamorphoses of Fantasy.* Bks. Demand repr. of 1987 ed. $50.00. ISBN 0-8357-1780-1. Focuses on fantasy in Calvino's work.

Re, Lucia. *Calvino and The Age of Neorealism: Fables of Estrangement.* Stanford U. Pr. 1990 $35.00. ISBN 0-8047-1650-1. Focuses on Calvino as the early politically committed writer and active partisan in the Italian Resistance during World War II.

CARDUCCI, GIOSUÈ (Joshua). 1835–1907 (Nobel Prize 1906)

When he received Italy's first Nobel Prize for literature in the year before his death, Carducci was not only Italy's leading poet but also its first ranking critic and classical scholar. He has been called the "prophet of Italy in its finest hour," even as Vittorio Alfieri had been prophet of an "Italy yet to be." Carducci celebrated Italy's classical heritage "at the expense of Romanticism and the Church." But he mellowed with age, accepting a constitutional monarchy instead of a republic and showing a fine aesthetic appreciation of Italy's medieval Catholic heritage. His best poems are in his *Rime Nuove* (1887), *Odi Barbare (Barbarian Odes)* (1877–89), and *Rime e ritmi* (1898). The *Odes* were experiments in recovering the quantitative metrical-rhythmical structure of classical poetry for modern Italian. He produced critical studies and scholarly editions of classical Italian as well as Latin and Greek authors.

POETRY BY CARDUCCI

The Best Poems of Joshua Carducci. Trans. by Montgomery Trinidad. A. Classical Coll. Pr. 1979 o.p.

Odi Barbare: Italian Text with English Prose. 1873–89. Trans. by William F. Smith. S. F. Vanni 1950 o.p.

BOOK ABOUT CARDUCCI

Scalia, S. Eugene. *Carducci: His Critics and Translators in England and America, 1881–1932.* S. F. Vanni 1937 $6.50. ISBN 0-913298-59-X

CASTIGLIONE, BALDASSARE. 1478–1529

Castiglione is chiefly known for his prose dialogues titled *The Book of the Courtier,* which passed through more than 40 editions in the century after its original publication in 1528. Written in Italian based on DANTE's Tuscan, it helped to establish Tuscan as the national literary language. The book was destined to be celebrated throughout Europe as a manual of courtly manners, but the attentive reader senses the peculiarly Italian atmosphere that envelops the four main participants in the dialogue as they avoid talking of the political realities that had prompted MACHIAVELLI (see Vols. 3 and 4) to write *The Prince* just a few years before.

WORK BY CASTIGLIONE

The Book of the Courtier. Trans. by George Bull. Viking Penguin 1976 $5.95. ISBN 0-14-044192-1

BOOK ABOUT CASTIGLIONE

Kinney, Arthur F. *Continental Humanist Poetics: Studies in Erasmus, Castiglione, Marguerite de Navarre, Rabelais, and Cervantes.* U. of Mass. Pr. 1989 $37.50. ISBN 0-87023-665-2. Discusses *The Courtier* in the larger scope of European humanism.

CAVALCANTI, GUIDO. c.1254–1300

Guido Cavalcanti's father and his father-in-law, Farinati degli Uberti, were heads of feuding factions in Florence, whose differences were conciliated in part through the marriage of Guido to Beatrice degli Uberti. DANTE made high poetry of these characters in his grand portrayals of Guido's father and father-in-law in the *Inferno.* With his spiritualization of chivalric love, analyzing its psychological depths, Guido Cavalcanti brought to the emergent Italian literary language the last of the important elements necessary for the inspired use Dante would make of it in his *Divine Comedy.* For example, most of Cavalcanti's love songs were addressed to the French woman Mandetta in a role that Beatrice would later play in Dante's poetry. The first translation of Cavalcanti into English was done by the English poet DANTE GABRIEL ROSSETTI (see Vol. 1) in 1861.

POETRY BY CAVALCANTI

The Sonnets and Ballate of Guido Cavalcanti. Trans. by Ezra Pound. Hyperion Conn. 1980 repr. of 1912 ed. $18.00. ISBN 0-88355-834-3. Deeply moving melancholic love poems written mostly in the *dolce stil nuovo.*

Translations. Trans. by Ezra Pound. New Dir. Pr. 1953 o.p. Especially interesting to see how Pound renders Cavalcanti, a poet with very similar tastes and sensibilities.

CELLINI, BENVENUTO. 1500–1571

[SEE Volume 3.]

CROCE, BENEDETTO. 1866–1952

All of Italian literary criticism in the twentieth century, in one way or another, draws on or reflects the influence of the idealist philosopher Benedetto Croce. Born in L'Aquila of a great landowning family and educated at the University of Rome, Croce lived almost his entire life in Naples, raising himself, as a scholar of independent means, to the status of a "cultural institution" of national and then general European importance. He enjoyed an active political career as a senator and minister of education and was fiercely opposed to the Fascist regime. In literature, Croce contributed a major revision of the Italian view of poetry, drawing first on HEGEL (see Vol. 4) and then on the great Italian-Hegelian literary critic FRANCESCO DE SANCTIS for a modernistic view of poetry, distinguishing it from the nonpoetic elements often fused with it. Croce's most influential work is his *Aesthetic as Science of Expression and General Linguistic* (1902), which he brilliantly summarized and updated in *Breviario di estetica* (1913) and in "Aesthetica in nuce," originally written for the fourteenth edition of the *Encyclopaedia Britannica*. In literary criticism, his best works are his studies of the poetry of DANTE and his monographs on ARIOSTO, SHAKESPEARE (see Vol. 1), and CORNEILLE.

NONFICTION BY CROCE

Aesthetic as Science of Expression and General Linguistic. 1902. Trans. by Colin Lyas. Cambridge U. Pr. 1992 $49.95. ISBN 0-521-35216-9. Shows the extent to which Croce was influenced by German idealism.

An Autobiography. Trans. by R. G. Collingwood. *Select Bibliographies Repr. Ser.* Ayer repr. of 1927 ed. $13.00. ISBN 0-8369-5276-6. An indispensable tool for understanding Croce's personality plus the extent of his encyclopedic knowledge.

The Defence of Poetry. Trans. by E. F. Carritt. Folcroft repr. of 1933 ed. o.p.

European Literature in the Nineteenth Century. Studies in Comparative Lit. Haskell 1969 repr. of 1924 ed. $75.00. ISBN 0-8383-0735-3. An example of early comparative literature studies.

Guide to Aesthetics. 1913. Trans. by Patrick Romanell. Regnery Gateway 1979 repr. of 1965 ed. o.p. Emphasizes the concept of art as a "lyrical intuition."

The Philosophy of Giambattista Vico. Trans. by R. G. Collingwood. Russell Sage 1964 repr. of 1913 ed. o.p. Illustrates Croce's vast erudition and his deep philosophical inquiries into the Enlightenment and the Neapolitan philosopher.

Philosophy, Poetry, History: An Anthology of Essays. Trans. by Cecil Sprigge. OUP 1966 o.p. Essays on Croce's philosophical system, in which the influence of German idealism is discernible.

Poetry and Literature: An Introduction to the Criticism and History. Trans. by Giovanni Gullace. S. Ill. U. Pr. 1981 $29.95. ISBN 0-8093-0982-3. Argues that although poetry, as such, does not create ethics or truth, by drawing from the concrete problems of life, it enriches the human personality.

The Poetry of Dante. Trans. by Douglas Ainslie. Appel repr. of 1922 ed. $10.00. ISBN 0-911858-12-1. Croce's well-known study of Dante.

BOOKS ABOUT CROCE

Orsini, Gian N. *Benedetto Croce: Philosopher of Art and Literary Critic*. S. Ill. U. Pr. 1961 o.p. The best book in English on Croce as a literary critic.

Wellek, René. *Four Critics: Croce, Valéry, Lukacs, and Ingarden*. U. of Wash. Pr. 1981 $12.50. ISBN 0-295-95800-6. A comparative study of four modern European critics.

D'ANNUNZIO, GABRIELE. 1863–1938

Born into a patriarchal family of the Abruzzo, D'Annunzio was sent to Prato to master Tuscan Italian. At age 16, under the classicizing influence of GIOSUÈ

Carducci, he published his first poems, *Primo Vere* in 1879. Sent on to Rome, he began to write prose first in the manner of Giovanni Verga, then in that of Joris Karl Huysmans, and finally in that of Nietzsche (see. Vol. 4). In 1896 he had sailed the Aegean with Nietzsche's *Birth of Tragedy* in hand, and upon his return he began to write poems of a manifestly heightened inspiration, especially after the start of his clamorous love affair with the actress Eleanora Duse. His best works of the time include the novel *Il fuoco (The Flame of Life)* (1900); the poems of his *Alcyone* (one of the Pleiades), which are his best; the play *The Dead City* (1898); and his masterpiece *The Daughter of Jorio* (1904), a drama. In the early years of the twentieth century, D'Annunzio had indeed become, as he proclaimed, the "most famous writer in the world." Eager to perform on the world's stage in politics and in war as well as art, he became an ardent nationalist, lost an eye in a wartime flying accident, and then personally led an assault on Fiume in 1919, annexing it to Italy and ruling it like a Roman proconsul for 16 months. His support of Mussolini has prompted some critics to treat him as a progenitor of fascism. He longed to be, but never became, like Shakespeare (see Vol. 1), the national poet and playwright of a great state.

Plays by D'Annunzio

The Daughter of Jorio: A Pastoral Tragedy. 1904. Trans. by Charlotte Porter. Greenwood 1968 repr. of 1907 ed. $44.00. ISBN 0-8371-0005-4

Francesca de Rimini. Trans. by Arthur Symons. Fertig 1989 repr. of 1902 ed. $29.50. ISBN 0-86527-385-5. A tragic drama in verse about Paolo Malatesta and Francesca da Rimini, the lovers made famous by an episode in Dante's *Inferno.*

Work by D'Annunzio

Tales of My Native Town. Trans. by Rafael Mantellini. Greenwood 1968 repr. of 1920 ed. $45.00. ISBN 0-8371-0056-9. Tales that exalt the primitive, mystical, and somewhat pagan traditions of D'Annunzio's native Abruzzi.

Novel by D'Annunzio

The Triumph of Death. 1898. Trans. by G. Harding. Hippocrene Bks. 1990 $9.95. ISBN 0-87052-934-X. A novel strongly influenced by Nietzsche's philosophy.

Books about D'Annunzio

Antongini, Tom. *D'Annunzio. Select Bibliographies Repr. Ser.* Ayer repr. of 1938 ed. $31.00. ISBN 0-8369-6676-7. The first unveiling of the controversial life of D'Annunzio when the poet was still alive.

Gullace, Giovanni. *Gabriele D'Annunzio in France: A Study in Cultural Relations.* Syracuse U. Pr. 1966 $24.95. ISBN 0-8156-2097-7. An intelligent discussion of why "his reputation was greater in France than in Italy. Written in an easy, pleasant style that is a delight" (*LJ*).

Klopp, Charles. *Gabriele D'Annunzio. Twayne's World Authors Ser.* Macmillan 1988 $26.95. ISBN 0-8057-8243-5. "The task of recounting D'Annunzio's *oeuvre* in any format is surely a formidable one, and Klopp has risen to the occasion with wit and verve" (*Italica*).

DANTE ALIGHIERI. 1265–1321

Born in Florence, Dante was the poet destined to give Italy both its greatest literary masterpiece and its national language. As a result of his active, partisan political life, he was permanently banished from his native city in 1302. Almost all that is known about Dante's personal life is derived from his works, especially his imaginative works, so that it is virtually impossible to distinguish his literary portrayals of himself from any life based on so-called nonliterary sources. The works in which he reveals the most about himself are *De Vulgari Eloquentia (On Eloquence in the Vernaculars)* (1304–06), a defense of his decision to write poetry in Italian rather than Latin; *Monarchia (On World Government)* (1310–12), written as a partisan of the claims to "universal empire" of the German imperial house of Hohenstauffen; the famous letter dedicating the *Paradiso* to Can Grande della Scala, the noble ruler of Verona; the *Vita Nuova (New Life)* (1292), a collection of love poems with commentary; *Il Convivio (Banquet)* (1304), an incomplete philosophic treatise; and the *Inferno, Purgatorio,* and *Paradiso* that make up *The Divine Comedy (Divina Commedia)* (1302–21). At the center of these works is *The Divine Comedy,* to the understanding of which the others all contribute. During its time, the work was viewed as an encyclopedia of medieval knowledge, principally philosophy, astrology, and theology. Dante wrote the poem with at least four different "senses" or levels of meaning—the traditional literal, allegorical, moral, and anagogical, or spiritual, senses. On the literal level there is an epic journey: Dante, as the epic hero, journeys to Hell and Purgatory to arrive at the heights of heaven. On the allegorical level it is an epic conflict between the two greatest institutions of the medieval world, the Holy Roman Catholic Church and the Holy Roman Empire. The moral sense of the poem is evident to the reader who seeks in it answers to personal problems or dilemmas. The anagogical sense helps the reader to see how all the other meanings allude to an understanding of God's providential design for all things. Read on the first two levels *The Divine Comedy* qualifies as an epic poem, in the sense of HOMER's *Iliad* and *Odyssey.* Dante succeeded in combining the two types of epic integrally, offering an epic journey on the literal level and an epic conflict on an allegorical level. With his moral and anagogical "senses," Dante raised poetry to levels of meaning usually reserved for moral philosophers and clergy.

As Dante conceived the Christian universe, all of human life on earth amounts to a journey in exile, and his *Divine Comedy* can be read as an exile's epic journey back to God that takes him first of all through Hell, whose inhabitants experience a permanently frustrated longing for God. Coming out of Hell, he "once again sees the stars." But he first must be cleansed or purged of the "stains of sin," on the seven-storied mountain of Purgatory, before he can become what he in fact becomes on its summit: "purified and disposed to rise to the stars." In the last third of *The Divine Comedy*, the *Paradiso*, Dante has the experience of rising directly upward through the heavens, until he is finally "projected into orbit," as it were, by the power of love, to circle inertially forever with "the sun and the other stars." In 1929, T. S. ELIOT (see also Vol. 1) compared Dante to SHAKESPEARE (see Vol. 1): "Take the *Comedy* as a whole, you can compare it to nothing but the *entire* dramatic work of Shakespeare. The comparison of the *Vita Nuova* with the *Sonnets* is another, and interesting, occupation. Dante and Shakespeare divide the modern world between them."

POETRY BY DANTE

Dante's Lyric Poetry. 2 vols. Trans. and ed. by Kenelm Foster and Patrick Boyde. OUP 1967 o.p. Excerpts from such works as the *Convivio* and the *Vita Nuova*.

Dante's Rime. Trans. by Patrick S. Diehl. Princeton U. Pr. 1979 o.p. A collection of poems not included in Dante's major works, and written mainly in his youth.

The Divine Comedy. 1302–21. 3 vols. Trans. by Dorothy L. Sayers. Viking Penguin. Vol. 1 *Inferno (Hell)*. 1950 $5.95. ISBN 0-14-044006-2. Vol. 2 *Purgatorio (Purgatory)*. 1955 $5.95. ISBN 0-14-044046-1. Vol. 3 *Paradiso (Paradise)*. 1962 $6.95. ISBN 0-14-044105-0

Inferno I. Trans. by Anthony K. Cassell, Robert Hollander, and Patrick Creagh. U. of Pa. Pr. 1989 $36.95. ISBN 0-8122-8176-4

Inferno II. Trans. by Rachel Jacoff, William A. Stephany, Patrick Creagh, and Robert Hollander. U. of Pa. Pr. 1989 $25.95. ISBN 0-8122-8177-2

NONFICTION BY DANTE

Il Convivio. 1306–08. Trans. by Christopher Ryan. Anma Libri 1986 o.p. For the most part prose commentaries on poems that are a sort of encyclopedia on medieval culture. A useful companion to *The Divine Comedy* for what it has to say about Dante's decision to use Italian for both the poems and the commentary.

The Literary Criticism of Dante Alighieri. Trans. and ed. by Robert S. Haller. Bks. Demand repr. of 1973 ed. $65.40. ISBN 0-8357-2745-9. "Dante's ideas on poetic art have been culled from his various Italian and Latin works and are brought together . . . in this little book" (*Choice*).

Literature in the Vernacular. c.1302–05. Trans. by Sally Purcell. Carcanet o.p. In defending his decision to use a modified version of his native Florentine dialect to write poetry, Dante provided the first serious Western work of historical philology.

The New Life (and *Il Convivio*). 1292–95. Trans. by Charles E. Norton. Rprt. Serv. repr. of 1985 ed. $39.00. ISBN 0-932051-68-5. *The New Life* is dedicated to Dante's earliest friend Guido Cavalcanti and has been aptly described as the "first autobiographical work in modern literature."

On World Government. 1310–12. Trans. by H. W. Schneider. Bobbs 1957 o.p. An argument to prove that, because of humanity's fallen nature, world peace requires concentration of power in a Roman-imperial-like government, working in harmony with, but not subservient to, the church.

The Portable Dante. Ed. by Paolo Milano. *Viking Portable Lib.* Viking Penguin rev. ed. 1977 $9.95. ISBN 0-14-015032-3. *The Divine Comedy* in its entirety; the complete *Vita Nuova* in Rossetti's version; and a selection from *De Monarchia* and *De Vulgari Eloquentia*, as well as from his *Rhymes* and his *Letters*.

BOOKS ABOUT DANTE

Auerbach, Erich. *Dante: Poet of the Secular World.* Trans. by Ralph Manheim. U. Ch. Pr. 1988 $13.95. ISBN 0-226-03205-1. A classic study, first published in Germany in 1929.

Barolini, Teodolinda. *Dante's Poets: Textuality and Truth in the Comedy.* Princeton U. Pr. 1984 $40.00. ISBN 0-691-06609-4. First published in Florence in 1933. Concise and authoritative, with a critical appraisal of the works.

Bloom, Harold, ed. *Dante.* Chelsea Hse. 1986 $29.95. ISBN 0-87754-665-7. Collection of modern critical essays that assess the works of Dante from a variety of perspectives.

Boitani, Piero. *Chaucer and the Italian Trecento.* Cambridge U. Pr. 1985 $64.95. ISBN 0-521-31350-3. "European scholars . . . describe the 14th century counterpoint between Chaucer in England and Dante, Petrarch and Boccaccio in Italy. . . . Each essay is well footnoted" (*Choice*).

Boyde, Patrick. *Dante, Philomythus and Philosopher: Man in the Cosmos.* Cambridge U. Pr. 1981 $77.50. ISBN 0-521-23598-7

Chiarenza, Marguerite Mills. *The Divine Comedy: Tracing God's Art.* Macmillan 1989 $7.95. ISBN 0-8057-8034-3. Presents a brief but exact review of the historical context of the poem.

Clements, Robert J., ed. *American Critical Essays on "The Divine Comedy."* NYU Pr. 1967 o.p. Sixteen essays for the serious student by such scholars as Erich Auerbach, Thomas G. Bergin, Charles S. Singleton, and the editor.

Croce, Benedetto. *The Poetry of Dante.* Appel repr. of 1922 ed. $10.00. ISBN 0-911858-12-1. A methodical introduction to the *Commedia.*

Di Scipio, Giuseppe. *The Divine Comedy and the Encyclopedia of Arts and Sciences.* Benjamins North Am. 1988 $95.00. ISBN 1-55619-031-X. Essays by leading international experts on the scientific and artistic disciplines that are the sources for Dante's *Commedia*.

Eliot, T. S. *Dante*. Haskell 1974 $75.00. ISBN 0-8383-2060-0. The English poet stresses classical standards in Dante's poetry.

Ellis, Steve. *Dante and English Poetry: Shelley to T. S. Eliot*. Cambridge U. Pr. 1983 $49.95. ISBN 0-521-25126-5. Dante's influence on English poetry of the nineteenth and twentieth centuries.

Fergusson, Francis. *Dante's Drama of the Mind: A Modern Reading of the Purgatorio*. Greenwood 1981 repr. of 1953 ed. $45.00. ISBN 0-313-23034-X. An excellent interpretative study by an extremely intelligent and attentive reader of Dante.

Harrison, Robert Pogue. *The Body of Beatrice*. Johns Hopkins 1988 $32.50. ISBN 0-8018-3680-8. A critical study of the *Vita Nuova*.

Kirkpatrick, R. *Dante's Paradiso and the Limitations of Modern Criticism*. Bks. Demand repr. of 1978 ed. $62.20. ISBN 0-318-34814-4. Shows why Dante must be viewed with a precise historical and intellectual context.

Mazzaro, Jerome. *The Figure of Dante: An Essay on the Vita Nuova*. Bks. Demand repr. of 1981 ed. $45.00. ISBN 0-8357-4671-2. A study of one of Dante's less-studied texts.

Mazzeo, Joseph A. *Medieval Cultural Tradition in Dante's Comedy*. Greenwood 1968 repr. of 1960 ed. o.p. The principles of structure in the *Divine Comedy* and how they relate to the organizing experience of medieval intellectual culture.

Mazzotta, Giuseppe, ed. *Critical Essays on Dante*. Macmillan 1991 $40.00. ISBN 0-8161-8849-1. Contains 21 essays on Dante's *Commedia*; the first and last are by the editor.

Montano, Rocco. *Dante's Thought and Poetry*. Regnery Gateway 1988 $14.95. ISBN 0-89526-771-3. "One of the most important, authoritative voices in Dante criticism" (*Italica*).

Musa, Mark. *Advent at the Gates: Dante's Comedy*. Bks. Demand repr. of 1974 ed. $46.30. ISBN 0-8357-5199-6. An important study by a major Dante critic and translator.

Pelikan, Jaroslav. *Eternal Feminines. Three Theological Allegories in Dante's Paradiso*. Rutgers U. Pr. 1990 $32.00. ISBN 0-8135-1602-1. Has satisfying "good sense and [a] respect for the letter of Dante's poem. Pelikan allows the poet to 'speak for himself' and in the 'languages' of the day" (*Italica*).

Reynolds, Mary T. *Joyce and Dante: The Shaping Imagination*. Princeton U. Pr. 1987 $19.95. ISBN 0-691-10198-1. A look at the modern Irish writer and Dante's influence on him.

Schnapp, Jeffrey T. *The Transfiguration of History at the Center of Dante's Paradise*. Princeton U. Pr. 1986 $40.00. ISBN 0-691-06679-5. "One reaches the last of its relatively few pages with the sense of having traversed a wide and dense critical landscape" (*Italica*).

Schless, Howard. *Chaucer and Dante*. Pilgrim Bks. 1984 $44.95. ISBN 0-937664-59-6. A comparative study of Dante's influence on the English writer.

Sicari, Stephen. *Pound's Epic Ambition: Dante and the Modern World*. State U. NY Pr. 1991 $44.50. ISBN 0-7914-0699-7. Shows how Pound's fragments achieve tentative coherence through the increasingly complex journey of a wandering epic hero.

Took, J. F. *Dante, Lyric Poet and Philosopher: An Introduction to the Minor Works*. OUP 1990 $59.00. ISBN 0-19-815158-6. "A timely and welcome event" (*Italica*).

Toynbee, Paget. *Concise Dictionary of Proper Names and Notable Matters in the Works of Dante*. Phaeton 1968 repr. of 1914 ed. $75.00. ISBN 0-87753-040-8. An important, exhaustive reference work.

DE FILIPPO, EDUARDO. 1900–1984

Eduardo, as he came to be known, started his acting career on the Neapolitan stage at age six. After he and his brother and sister formed their own theater company in the late 1920s, he established himself as Italy's leading comic actor. Before long he was also its best dialect playwright and, after LUIGI PIRANDELLO and UGO BETTI, its best dramatic writer. His well-known plays, most of which were made into successful films, include *Filumena; Marturano*; and *Saturday, Sunday, Monday*.

Plays by De Filippo

Filumena. Trans. by Keith Waterhouse and Willis Hall. Heinemann Ed. 1978 o.p. As in many of De Filippo's plays, characters, themes, and language drawn from the life of Naples.

Saturday, Sunday, Monday. Trans. by Willis Hall and Keith Waterhouse. Heinemann Ed. 1974 $6.50. ISBN 0-435-23201-0

Book about De Filippo

Mignone, Mario B. *Eduardo De Filippo. Twayne's World Authors Ser.* G. K. Hall 1984 o.p. A readable critical biography.

DELEDDA, GRAZIA. 1871–1936 (Nobel Prize 1926)

Among the most honored women writers of modern Italy, Deledda wrote naturalistic or realistic novels, drawing upon her Sardinian background for material. Some critics hold, however, that in Deledda's formula often only the names of places and people serve to evoke a Sardinian atmosphere of strangeness. Her best works—especially *Elias Portolu* (1903), *Cenere* (1904), and *The Mother* (1920)—contain excellent portrayals of women, offering probing analyses of motivations that suggest comparison with Dostoevsky. While her characters are complex, often dominated by an overwhelming sense of destiny and by nature's mythic powers, her narrative structures remain simple and classic.

Novels by Deledda

Cosima. 1937. Trans. by Martha King. Italica Pr. 1988 $10.50. ISBN 0-934977-06-2. Deledda's last work, published posthumously.

The Mother. 1920. Trans. by Mary G. Steegman. Cherokee 1982 repr. of 1923 ed. $15.95. ISBN 0-89783-022-9

DE SANCTIS, FRANCESCO. 1817–1883

The greatest of Italy's literary critics and literary historians, De Sanctis was the first among Europeans and Americans to hold a professorship in comparative literature. A chair in the new field was especially set up for him at the University of Naples in 1871. During the next 40 years, similar chairs were set up at Harvard, Zurich, Lyon, Columbia, and the Sorbonne. His great *History of Italian Literature* (1870) is both an introduction to the subject and a literary masterpiece in its own right. As Giuliano Procacci observed in his *History of the Italian People*, De Sanctis's chief work is "not merely a literary history, but also represents the nearest approach to a general history of Italy that the nineteenth century was able to produce."

Nonfiction by De Sanctis

De Sanctis on Dante. Trans. by Joseph Rossi and Alfred Galpin. U. of Wis. Pr. 1957 o.p. An incomparable model of the "poetic biography" up to Dante's exile.

History of Italian Literature. Trans. by Joan Redfern. Basic repr. of 1931 ed. 1968 o.p. The foundation of modern literary criticism in Italy.

ECO, UMBERTO 1932–

First a semiotician at the University of Bologna, and a leading figure in contemporary Italian culture, Eco brought semiotics to fiction in his first novel,

The Name of the Rose (1980). This unexpected international best-seller employs the techniques of a detective novel along with sophisticated postmodern narrative and verbal conundrums, to recount a series of murders in a medieval monastery. Eco's fascination with the Middle Ages began when he was a student at the University of Torino, where he wrote his doctoral thesis (1954) on St. Thomas Aquinas (see Vol. 4). *The Name of the Rose* (1980) won the Premio Strega and the Premio Anghiar awards in 1981, as well as numerous international awards.

Novels by Eco

Foucault's Pendulum. 1989. Trans. by William Weaver. HarBraceJ 1989 $22.95. ISBN 0-15-132765-3. Three men who scheme to take over the world by computer, with explorations of the Cabala, mysticism, theology, feminism, and pop culture.

The Name of the Rose. 1980. Trans. by William Weaver. HarBraceJ 1983 $29.95. ISBN 0-15-144647-4

Books about Eco

Coletti, Theresa. *Naming the Rose: Eco, Medieval Signs, and Modern Theory.* Cornell Univ. Pr. 1988 $28.95. ISBN 0-8014-2114-4. The ease with which [Coletti] combines medieval and modern is one of the book's greatest strengths" (*Italica*).

Inge, M. Thomas ed. *Naming the Rose: Essays on Eco's "The Name of the Rose."* U. Pr. of Miss. 1988 $30.00. ISBN 0-87805-345-X. "An intelligent, interesting, and eminently worthwhile volume" (*Italica*).

FALLACI, ORIANA. 1930–

A prize-winning novelist and journalist, Fallaci is known primarily for her controversial interviews. She has spoken unabashedly, if not abrasively, with such world figures as Henry Kissinger, Willy Brandt, the Ayatollah Khomeini, Yasir Arafat, the Shah of Iran, Indira Ghandi, and Golda Meir. Her bold, often brilliant, interviewing technique is characterized by brutal frankness, as when she challenged Henry Kissinger to "talk about war."

Nonfiction by Fallaci

Interview With History. HM 1977 $12.70. ISBN 0-395-25223-7. A collection of interviews with major political figures, displaying Fallaci's aggressive, confrontational style.

Novel by Fallaci

Inshallah. Trans. by James Maras. Doubleday 1992 $25.00. ISBN 0-385-41987-2. A war novel about the 400 American and French soldiers killed in the Beirut massacre in 1983. "A masterpiece." (London *Times* Literary Supplement)

FO, DARIO. 1926–

More than a playwright, Dario Fo is a "theatrical activist," a successful comedian who has been performing and writing for radio, television, film, cabaret, and theater for decades. One of Italy's most renowned dramatists, Fo's avant-garde approach is, in fact, a modern renewal of the *commedia dell'arte*. In the late 1960s, he formed the theater company La Nuova Scena (The New Scene), which produced politically committed shows in meeting halls of leftist organizations. One noteworthy example is *Accidental Death of an Anarchist* (1970), which is still performed, its content constantly updated from a radical Marxist standpoint to reflect current events. It was performed in New York City in 1985. In *The Drama Review*, Suzanne Cowan called it "The Throw-Away Theatre of Dario Fo."

PLAYS BY FO

Accidental Death of an Anarchist. 1970. Pluto Pr. 1977 o.p.

We Can't Pay? We Won't Pay! Pluto Pr. 1981 o.p. An excellent example of Fo's "committed theater" (*teatro impegnato*).

FOSCOLO, UGO. 1778–1827

Ugo Foscolo was a truly international literary figure, drawing inspiration from many lands. He translated Laurence Sterne's *A Sentimental Journey*, produced a prose masterpiece in his *Last Letters of Jacopo Ortis* (inspired by GOETHE's *Werther*, but infused with a characteristically Italian romantic patriotism that has no counterpart in Goethe's work), and wrote a poetic masterpiece, *On Sepulchres* (1807), which celebrates the great figures of Italy's past. Of the height of poetic inspiration in this last work, GIOSUÈ CARDUCCI would later say that there is a "fusing together in a single sublime choral harmony the accents of sermon and hymn, elegy and satire, tragedy and epic."

POETRY BY FOSCOLO

On Sepulchres. Trans. by Thomas G. Bergin. Bethany 1971 o.p. Bergin captures "Foscolo's varying moods of anguish and hope and emulates his faultless classical form" (*Choice*).

NONFICTION BY FOSCOLO

Last Letters of Jacopo Ortis. Trans. by Douglas Ulmstead Radcliff. U. of NC Pr. 1970 o.p.

BOOKS ABOUT FOSCOLO

Cambon, Glauco. *Ugo Foscolo: Poet of Exile.* Princeton U. Pr. 1980 $45.00. ISBN 0-691-06424-5

Radcliff-Ulmstead, Douglas. *Ugo Foscolo.* Twayne 1970 o.p. A brief critical introduction to Foscolo's writing.

GALILEI, GALILEO. 1564–1642

[SEE Volumes 4 and 5.]

GINZBURG, NATALIA LEVI. 1916–1991

Born in Palermo, Natalia Ginzburg moved to Turin where her father took a university professorship. She wrote for the Florentine journal *Solaria*, through which she met ELIO VITTORINI and CESARE PAVESE. In 1938 she married the Marxist radical Leone Ginzburg and joined him in his exile as a militant anti-Fascist in a small town in the Abruzzo, an experience mirrored in her first novel, *The Road to the City*. Unlike CARLO LEVI, who wrote warmly of a similar experience in confinement, Ginzburg's professed intention was that every sentence about the villagers "should be like a whipping or a slap." Briefly freed after Mussolini's fall, Leone Ginzburg was seized by the Germans, tortured, and executed in 1944. Natalia Ginzburg's novels dwell on the theme of the family and are autobiographical even when the subject is a historical figure. Deeply rooted in the immediacy of the moment, even when recounted from memory, her antiromantic narratives are generally expressed in the present tense.

NOVELS BY GINZBURG

All Our Yesterdays. 1957. Trans. by Angus Davidson. Arcade Pub. Inc. 1989 $18.95. ISBN 1-559-70026-2. "The late Angus Davidson's 30-year-old translation holds up well and conveys the quality of this writer who is still too little known outside her native Italy."

The City and the House. 1984. Trans. by Dick Davis. Arcade Pub. Inc. 1989 $8.95 ISBN 1-55970-029-7. An epistolary novel written in Ginzburg's typical unassuming and conversational style.

Family. 1977. Trans. by Beryl Stockman. Seaver Bks. 1988 o.p.

Family Sayings. 1963. Trans. by D. M. Low. Arcade Pub Inc. 1989 repr. of 1986 ed. $7.95. ISBN 1-55970-027-0. An affectionate, personal remembrance of the 40-year period before, during, and after fascism, as depicted through small homey objects and seemingly uneventful happenings.

The Little Virtues. 1962. Trans. by Dick Davis. Seaver Bks. 1986 $13.95. ISBN 0-8050-0077-1. Essays derived from experiences during Ginzburg's stay in England with her second husband, Gabriele Baldini, a scholar of English literature.

No Way. Trans. by Sheila Cudahy. HarBraceJ 1974 o.p. The isolation, fragmentation, and loneliness of an upper-middle class family and its friends. Written mainly in the form of letters exchanged among the characters.

The Road to the City. 1942. Trans. by Frances Frenaye. Arcade Pub. Inc. 1990 $16.95. ISBN 1-55970-052-1

Voices in the Evening. 1961. Trans. by D. M. Low. Arcade Pub. Inc. 1989 $16.95. ISBN 1-55970-016-5. Largely autobiographical, like most of Ginzburg's texts.

GOLDONI, CARLO. 1707–1793

Carlo Goldoni, the great Venetian playwright, reformed the Italian theater. In his time, the reigning theatrical genres were the melodrama and the *commedia dell'arte*, the one stressing musicality, the other the antics of familiar "characters" who more often than not improvised their way through a skeletal script. Goldoni's early *Servant of Two Masters* (1745) served to put an end to improvised *commedia dell'arte* by supplying a complete script for masterful actors, but in fact, and hardly ironically, the spirit of the old improvisors lives in modern performances of that comedy. In 1752, Goldoni went to Paris to head the Italian Theater and enjoy the patronage of the royal family, which lasted until the revolution of 1789, after which he lived and died in poverty. He wrote comedies of history, intrigue, and exotic romance, but his plays are comedies of characters and manners. PIRANDELLO praised the latter as Goldoni's triumph. Goldoni had learned from MOLIÈRE and SHAKESPEARE (see Vol. 1), and even MACHIAVELLI (see Vols. 3 and 4), how to set living comic protagonists before his audience; but his genius, said Pirandello, consisted rather in taking subordinate characters—a little housemaid, for instance—and suddenly making her the center of a comedy of her own. Among Goldoni's best plays, are, in Italian, *The Liar* (1750) and *The Fan* (1763); in the Venetian dialect, *The Tyrants*; and in French, *The Beneficent Bear*, which was produced for the marriage of Louis XVI and Marie Antoinette in 1771. This tribute play gave Goldoni the pleasure of seeing a work of his own performed in French on the stage where Molière's plays had triumphed.

PLAYS BY GOLDONI

The Comic Theatre: A Comedy in Three Acts. 1750. U. of Nebr. Pr. repr. of 1969 ed. $31.40. ISBN 0-7837-1894-2. An example of Goldoni's witty, realistic comedic style, which sought to replace the stylized *commedia dell'arte*. Introduction by D. Cheney.

The Liar. 1750. Trans. by Frederick H. Davies. Routledge Chapman & Hall 1963 $3.50. ISBN 0-87830-531-9

Servant of Two Masters. 1745. Trans. by Frederick H. Davies. Theatre Arts Bks. 1961 o.p.

Three Comedies: Mine Hostess, The Boors, The Fan. Trans. by Clifford Bax and others. Greenwood 1979 repr. of 1961 ed. $35.00. ISBN 0-313-21259-7

Books about Goldoni

Kennard, Joseph S. *Goldoni and the Venice of His Time*. Ayer repr. of 1920 ed. o.p. Looks at Goldoni within the context of his thriving native city.

Riedt, Heinz. *Carlo Goldoni*. Trans. by Ursule Molinaro. Continuum 1974 o.p. "This well-informed, stimulating study fills a long-standing void" (*Choice*).

GRAMSCI, ANTONIO. 1891–1937

Born to a poor family in Sardinia, Gramsci had to go to work as a child but still managed to distinguish himself as a bright and promising student. In 1910, after winning a scholarship, he attended the University of Torino, where he was influenced by Benedetto Croce and Francesco De Sanctis. He eventually rejected Croce's idealism, as well as the academic life, for Marxism and politics. His primary interest was the empowerment of the working class. He rose within the Socialist party to the position of secretary of the socialist section of Torino and founded the influential newspaper *L'Ordine Nuovo* (the New Order). In 1921 he cofounded the Italian Communist party and fought against Fascist policy. Elected party secretary in 1924, two years later he was arrested and sent to prison, where he produced much of his writing. He remained incarcerated until his death. Gramsci's writings chronicle the development of his thought on politics, culture, and education.

Nonfiction by Gramsci

Letters from Prison. Trans. by Lynne Lawner. HarpC 1973 o.p. Two editorials from *Ordine Nuovo* and prison notebooks from 1926–37.

The Modern Prince, and Other Writings. Trans. by Louis Marks. Intl. Pubs. 1959 $4.95. ISBN 0-7178-0134-9. Writings on Italian communism.

Books about Gramsci

Adamson, Walter L. *Hegemony and Revolution: A Study of Antonio Gramsci's Political and Cultural Theory*. U. CA Pr. 1980 $12.95. ISBN 0-520-05057-6. A discussion of Gramsci's political and cultural theories.

Dombrowski, Robert S. *Antonio Gramsci*. Twayne 1989 $26.95. ISBN 0-8057-8245-1. A comprehensive biography with discussion of Gramsci's political thought.

LAMPEDUSA, GIUSEPPE TOMASI, PRINCE OF. 1896–1957

A Sicilian intellectual and aristocrat, Lampedusa wrote *The Leopard* (*Il Gattopardo*) (1955–56), one of the classics of twentieth-century European literature. A historical novel, it is based on the life of the author's paternal great-grandfather at the time following the 1830 landing of Garibaldi and his Thousand Red Shirts in Sicily, the liberation of the island from the Bourbon monarchy, and its annexation to the Kingdom of Piedmonte. The novel documents how the elegant traditions of the aristocratic world were supplanted by the coarse values of the shortsighted bourgeoisie. Submitted by the author to a prominent publisher and rejected, *Il Gattopardo* was published posthumously by another publisher following the strong recommendation of Giorgio Bassani. It won the Strega Prize, Italy's most prestigious literary award, and became a world best seller. The director Luchino Visconti adapted the novel for his successful film of the same name.

Novel by Lampedusa

The Leopard. 1955–56. Trans. by Archibald Colquhoun. Pantheon 1991 $12.00. ISBN 0-679-73121-0

LEONARDO DA VINCI. 1452–1519

[SEE Volume 3.]

LEOPARDI, GIACOMO. 1798–1837

Although he is the most purely romantic personality Italian culture can boast of, Leopardi was at the same time thoroughly classical in his approach to literature and, in that sense, antiromantic. Born with a hunchback and other physical deformities, he was extremely sensitive; adoring women, he suffered in despair. Hence, his poetry reveals a most pessimistic outlook. In the judgment of most critics, he is the second lyrical poet of Italy, rivaling PETRARCH (see Vols. 2 and 4) in the musicality of his melancholy songs of love and death, matching ALFIERI in the austerity of his pessimistic passion, and approaching DANTE in his capacity to give poetic expression to a most powerfully experienced sense of an entire universe, in his case a godless universe sublimely devoid of meaning. Leopardi rejected the pedantry and affectation of his contemporaries' poetry, choosing a simple, yet elegant, vocabulary. He is, besides, virtually without a rival in his mastery of philosophic and satiric dialogue and expository prose.

WORKS BY LEOPARDI

Essays, Dialogues and Thoughts of Giacomo Leopardi. Trans. by James Thomson. Ed. by Bertram Dobell. *Lib. of World Lit. Ser.* Hyperion Conn. 1979 repr. of 1905 ed. $27.50. ISBN 0-88355-564-6. Philosophical works expressing Leopardi's cosmic pessimism—his belief in a cosmic nature so relentlessly hostile to humanity that human beings cannot achieve happiness.

A Leopardi Reader. Trans. by Ottavio M. Casale. U. of Ill. Pr. 1981 $29.95. ISBN 0-252-00824-3. "An excellent and welcome edition" (*Choice*).

The Moral Essays: Operette Morali. Trans. by Patrick Creagh. Bks. Demand repr. of 1983 ed. $71.60. ISBN 0-7837-0429-1. Creagh's translation presents itself as prepared "with the cooperation of the Leopardi family."

Pensieri. Trans. by Simone Di Piero. La. State U. Pr. 1981 $22.50. ISBN 0-8071-0885-5. A collection in prose of aphorisms, reflections, and thoughts expressed often in Leopardi's poetry.

BOOKS ABOUT LEOPARDI

Barricelli, Gian Piero. *Giacomo Leopardi.* Twayne 1986 o.p. "Simultaneously shows the poet-philosopher's relevance to the nineteenth century, to our time, and perhaps beyond" (*Italica*).

LEVI, CARLO. 1902–1975

Carlo Levi's book *Christ Stopped at Eboli* (1945) is based on his experience as a doctor "confined" to a small town in southern Italy in the mid-1930s because of his activities against the Fascist regime. Although he was released from confinement before Mussolini fell, he had to hide from the Germans because he was a Jew, and he eventually fled to France. In his book he pictured a peasantry apparently beyond the help of Christianity's God as well as Italy's national government. What comforted the peasants were legendary visions of Robin Hood-like bandits. Noting that Levi had faithfully rendered the fascination of the old bandit myths, Giuseppe Prezzolini praised the whole as a "heartwarming and poetic book . . . greeted with deserved success."

NONFICTION BY CARLO LEVI

Christ Stopped at Eboli. 1945. Trans. by Frances Frenaye. Ed. by Jack Bevan. FS&G 1947 $8.95. ISBN 0-374-50316-8

LEVI, PRIMO. 1919–1987

Born in Torino and a lifelong professional chemist, Primo Levi has the distinction of being the first Jewish-Italian writer to make the twentieth-century European Jewish experience the primary focus of his writing. Captured and deported by the Nazis in 1943, and interned at Auschwitz, his life was spared apparently because of his skill as a chemist. After his release in 1945, Levi began to write about his harrowing experience, tracing it from deportation and internment, to liberation and the survivors' long journey home through Europe. He never removed the number that had been tattooed on his arm so that when strangers asked him what it stood for, they would learn that such an unspeakable event as the Holocaust had truly occurred. More recent works are his chemist's autobiography, *The Periodic Table* (1975); the novel *If Not Now, When?* (1982), which takes its title from the much repeated admonition of Rabbi Hillel; and the philosophical essay *The Drowned and the Saved* (1986). In 1987, Levi committed suicide by hurling himself down the stairwell of his home, the house where he was born.

Nonfiction by Primo Levi

The Drowned and the Saved. 1986. Trans. by Raymond Rosenthal. Random 1989 $18.95. ISBN 0-679-72186-X. A meditation on the Holocaust and death camps as a unique event revealing the extremity of human beings as slaughterers and victims.

Other People's Trades. Trans. by Raymond Rosenthal. S & S Trade 1990 $8.95. ISBN 0-671-70519-9. Haunting short prose pieces that reflect on politics, literature, chemistry, and life.

The Periodic Table. Trans. by Raymond Rosenthal. Schocken 1986. $10.00. ISBN 0-8052-0811-9. Twenty-one pieces, each named after a chemical element, in which Levi draws analogies between the element's properties and personal, social, or political experiences.

The Reawakening. Trans. by Stuart Woolf. Macmillan 1987 $5.95. ISBN 0-02-022370-6. "The lunatic forced journey through Europe of 1945 makes a wonderful tragi-comic pendant" to Levi's earlier work (*The Observer*).

Survival in Auschwitz: The Nazi Assault on Humanity. 1961. Trans. by Stuart Woolf. Macmillan 1987 $5.95. ISBN 0-02-034310-8

Novel by Primo Levi

If Not Now, When? Trans. by William Weaver. Viking Penguin 1986 $18.95. ISBN 0-14-008492-4

Work by Primo Levi

The Mirror Maker. Trans. by Raymond Rosenthal. Schocken 1989 $16.95. ISBN 0-8052-4076-4. Short stories and essays written during Levi's last 20 years.

Book about Primo Levi

Sodi, Risa B. *A Dante of Our Time, Primo Levi and Auschwitz.* P. Lang Pubs. 1990 $36.95. ISBN 0-8204-1219-8. "Always thought-provoking and occasionally eloquent" (*Italica*).

MACHIAVELLI, NICCOLO. 1469–1527

[See Volumes 3 and 4.]

MANZONI, ALESSANDRO. 1785–1873

Born in Milan, the grandson on his mother's side of Cesare Beccaria, world-famous reformer of criminal jurisprudence, Manzoni first established himself as Italy's leading romantic poet, then as its second tragedian, after Vittorio

Alfieri, and finally as its greatest novelist. Although he was raised as a Voltairian rationalist, his major writings date from his "return" to Roman Catholicism. Manzoni's lyric poems, which place him on a par with Petrarch (see Vols. 2 and 4) and Leopardi, include his *Inni Sacri (Sacred Hymns)* (1822), and an ode on the death of Napoleon, *Cinque Maggio* (1821), which Goethe translated into German. Manzoni's historical tragedies, *The Count of Carmagnola* (1820) and *Adelchi* (1822), were influenced by Goethe and Shakespeare (see Vol. 1). But his singular masterpiece, initially inspired by the novels of Sir Walter Scott (see Vol. 1), is *The Betrothed* (1825–27), a historical novel to be ranked with the major works of Dante, Petrarch, Boccaccio, Ariosto, and Machiavelli (see Vols. 3 and 4), and which "has probably had more influence in Italy," as Lacy Collison-Morley said, "than any other novel in any other land." Manzoni painstakingly researched his novel's historical background, and while his plot and characters are fictional, they nonetheless reflect the mores and events of the years of Spanish rule of Lombardy from 1628 to 1630. *The Betrothed* does for modern Italy what Chaucer's (see Vol. 1) tales and Shakespeare's historical plays did for England. Manzoni continued the tradition of literary-linguistic experimentation that began with Dante, while simultaneously providing Italy with a national equivalent of what Homer's epics proved to be for ancient Greece—at once a source of artistic delight and of spiritual education in the broadest sense. Revising his work for its definitive edition of 1840–1842, Manzoni left his native Milan for Dante's Florence, in order to master a form of Italian that would be deeply rooted in the living, local dialect that had produced the greatest Italian masterpieces of the past, while being at the same time fully suited to serve as the "language of newspapers and practical books, of the school and general conversation" for a united modern Italy.

Novel by Manzoni

The Betrothed. 1825–27. Trans. by Bruce Penman. *Penguin Class Ser.* Viking Penguin 1984 $8.95. ISBN 0-14-044274-X

Nonfiction by Manzoni

On the Historical Novel. Trans. by Sandra Bermann. U. of Nebr. Pr. 1984 $20.00. ISBN 0-8032-3084-2. A translation of *Del Romanzo Storico*; includes bibliography and index.

Books about Manzoni

Barricelli, Gian Piero. *Alessandro Manzoni.* Twayne 1976 $17.95. ISBN 0-8057-6251-5. A critical biography and literary overview that dwells especially on Manzoni's later writings.

Wall, Bernard. *Alessandro Manzoni.* Elliots Bks. 1954 $39.50. ISBN 0-686-51343-6. An outstanding biography in English.

MARAINI, DACIA. 1936–

The Florentine Maraini published her first novel, *La Vacanza (The Holiday)*, which treats the theme of contemporary female sexuality, in 1962. The next year she was awarded the Formentor Prize for the novel *L'Era del malessere (The Age of Malaise)*. Later in the decade, she moved almost exclusively to theater, establishing the Teatro di Centocelle in Rome in 1969. Though she resumed prose writing, and also has published numerous collections of poetry, she is best known as one of the most important voices in contemporary Italian theater, a writer, director, and producer. In all of her works, Maraini's protaganists are women, often in conflict with men, who are seeking female solidarity.

NOVELS BY MARAINI

Letters to Marina. 1981. Trans. by Dick Kitto and Elspeth Spottiswood. Crossing Pr. 1988 $24.95. ISBN 0-89594-262-3. A novel advocating female solidarity.

Woman at War. 1975. Trans. by Mara Benetti and Elspeth Spottiswood. Italica Pr. 1989 $14.50. ISBN 0-934977-12-1. An excellent example of Maraini's feminist novel *Donne in guerra.*

MARINETTI, FILIPPO TOMMASO. 1875–1944

Born in Egypt and educated in Paris, Marinetti gained a reputation as a writer in French long before he launched the "futurist movement" with his manifesto of February 20, 1909, in *Le Figaro.* Proclaiming an ideal of "words in liberty," that manifesto elicited high praise from WYNDHAM LEWIS (see Vol. 1), GUILLAUME APOLLINAIRE, EZRA POUND (see Vol. 1), and D. H. LAWRENCE (see Vol. 1), as well as the Italians Aldo Palazzeschi, GIOVANNI PAPINI, and Ardengo Soffici. After his French works were translated into Italian, he was arrested and spent two months in an Italian jail for immorality. Despite the notoriety of his first manifesto, the subsequent *Technical Manifesto* of 1912 epitomizes the essence of futurism: the glorification of war, masculinity, violence, and the machine. As William De Sua correctly wrote: "Of all his works, the *Technical Manifesto* alone should secure his place among such figures as Pablo Picasso, Ezra Pound, Igor Stravinsky, and Guillaume Apollinaire as one of the greatest movers and shapers of modern art."

WORKS BY MARINETTI

Marinetti: Selected Writings. Trans. by R. W. Flint and Arthur A. Coppotelli. FS&G 1972 o.p.

Stung By Salt and War: Creative Texts of the Italian Avant-Gardist F. T. Marinetti. Trans. by Richard J. Pioli. P. Lang Pubs. 1987 $31.50. ISBN 0-8204-0381-4

MICHELANGELO BUONARROTI. 1475–1564

[SEE Volume 3.]

MONTALE, EUGENIO. 1896–1981 (NOBEL PRIZE 1975)

Born in Genoa and largely self-educated, Montale was an infantry officer in World War I and then became a spectator, rather than an activist, during the 20 years of fascism, when he wrote some of his best poetry. He lived in Genoa for his first 30 years, where he started his career as a journalist, and then moved to Florence. There he worked first for a publishing house and then as a reference librarian. Finally, after World War II, he settled down in Milan as literary and music critic and special correspondent for Italy's leading newspaper, *Il corriere della sera.* Montale was much influenced by his readings in Russian, French, and Spanish, as well as by Italian authors, and more particularly by his reading and translating of English and American writers such as SHAKESPEARE (see Vol. 1), HOPKINS (see Vol. 1), HARDY (see Vol. 1), ELIOT (see Vol. 1), MELVILLE (see Vol. 1), TWAIN (see Vol. 1), FAULKNER (see Vol. 1), and O'NEILL (see Vol. 1). As a poet under the influence of GIUSEPPE UNGARETTI, he broke with the traditional poetic style, steeped in formal eloquence, and took the advice of SALVATORE QUASIMODO to write poetry in a style stripped of ornaments so as to allow words to recall their "pristine, evocative meaning." His chief books of poems and essays include *Cuttlefish Bones* (1925), *Occasions* (1939), *The Storm and Other Things* (1956), and *Diary of 1971 and 1972* (1973). When he received the Nobel Prize for literature in 1975, he was hailed as the greatest Italian poet of the twentieth century. His poetry is basically "negative" in spirit, unlike Ungaretti's, which is that of a "Christian poet of sorrow." Yet there is a musicality in the best of Montale's verse that recalls and often matches the hauntingly evocative lyricism of LEOPARDI.

POETRY BY MONTALE

Bones of the Cuttlefish: Selected Poems in Translation. Trans. by Antonino Mazza. Mosaic Pr. OH 1984 o.p. "This translation . . . finally makes available, in a single source, all of the poems of Montale's first, important collection" (*RSI*).

The Butterfly of Dinard. 1956. Trans. by G. Singh. U. Pr. of Ky. 1971 $16.00. ISBN 0-8131-1252-4

Mottetti: Poems of Love: The Motets of Eugenio Montale. Trans. by Dana Gioia. Graywolf 1990 $14.95. ISBN 0-55597-123-7. Provides a bilingual edition of Montale's suite of 20 short poems, originally published in his second collection of verse, *Le occasioni.*

New Poems. Trans. by G. Singh. New Dir. Pr. 1976 $7.95. ISBN 0-8112-0598-3. As in Montale's early poems, these express deep pessimism and the desire for a time and place far away from our tormented age.

Otherwise: Last and First Poems of Eugenio Montale. Trans. by Jonathan Galassi. Random 1984 o.p.

Selected Poems. Ed. by Glauco Cambon. New Dir. Pr. 1966 $8.95. ISBN 0-8112-0119-8. The first American edition of his work in English translation.

The Storm and Other Poems. Trans. by Charles Wright. Oberlin Coll. Pr. 1978 $8.95. ISBN 0-932440-00-2

The Storm and Other Things. Trans. by William Arrowsmith. Norton 1985 o.p.

NONFICTION BY MONTALE

The Second Life of Art: Selected Essays. Trans. and ed. by Jonathan Galassi. Ecco Pr. 1985 $9.50. ISBN 0-912946-85-7. ". . . selections from Montale's writings on art, music, literature, cinema, social issues; on Svevo, Eliot, Pound, Valéry, Ungaretti, Auden, and others, culminating in the 1975 Nobel Prize speech 'Is Poetry Still Possible?'" (*LJ*).

BOOKS ABOUT MONTALE

Becker, Jared. *Eugenio Montale.* Macmillan 1986 $21.95. ISBN 0-8057-6633-2. Sensitive and critical reading of Montale's works, from both a political and sociocultural point of view.

Cambon, Glauco. *Eugenio Montale's Poetry: A Dream in Reason's Presence.* Princeton U. Pr. 1982 $37.50. ISBN 0-691-06520-9. "Cambon benefitted greatly from his long acquaintance with Montale" (*LJ*).

Huffman, Claire De C. L. *Montale and the Occasions of Poetry.* Princeton U. Pr. 1983 $45.00. ISBN 0-691-06562-4. ". . . the author adds a presentation of other critical views followed by her own rebuttals and/or exemplifications, while integrating the poet's own remarks on his work" (*Choice*).

Singh, G. *Eugenio Montale: A Critical Study of His Poetry, Prose, and Criticism.* Bks. Demand repr. of 1973 ed. $58.90. ISBN 0-685-07770-5. Excellent comprehensive study by the well-known translator of Montale's works. Contains some 60 new translations from Montale's poetry.

West, Rebecca J. *Eugenio Montale: Poet on the Edge.* HUP 1981 $20.50. ISBN 0-674-26910-1. A definitive, probing study.

MORANTE, ELSA. 1918–1985

Prolific and highly successful, Elsa Morante distinguished herself as a novelist, short story writer, and poet. The Marxist critic Gyorgy Lukacs hailed Morante's early *House of the Liars* (1948) as "the greatest modern Italian novel," but it was *Arthur's Island* (1957) that brought her international fame and an independent income. Her great financial triumph was, however, *History* (1974), which was the first Italian novel to be marketed with high-pressure promotional advertising, making use of publisher, mass media, and political party resources to push sales up to 600,000 copies in less than six months. Morante married ALBERTO MORAVIA in 1941, and they separated in 1962.

NOVELS BY MORANTE

Aracoeli. Trans. by William Weaver. Random 1984 o.p. A novel strongly influenced by Freudian theory.

History: A Novel. Random 1984 $10.95. ISBN 0-394-72496-8. Set in Rome during World War II and after. Each section of the novel, in which ordinary people lead obscure lives, is introduced by an actual headline of the times' great historical events.

MORAVIA, ALBERTO (pseud. of Alberto Pincherle). 1907–1990

Born in Rome of Jewish-Roman Catholic parents, Moravia was not much affected by the "Fascist racial laws" until Mussolini's fall in 1943 and the consequent German occupation of Rome. Under fascism, Moravia published his first novel, *The Time of Indifference* (1929), at his own expense when he was only 22; yet it was a great success and remains his most characteristic work. He produced nothing to match it until after World War II, when he emerged as the leading Italian neorealist, publishing in rapid order *The Woman of Rome* (1947), *Disobedience* (1948), *The Conformist* (1951), *Ghost at Noon* (1948), *Roman Tales* (1954), and *Two Women* (1957). Many believe the latter is his best novel, telling of the efforts of a shopkeeper and her daughter, raped by Italy's liberators and learning to adapt themselves to the postwar new order. Moravia made a great stir in world literary circles after World War II by announcing his conversion to Roman Catholicism, which had given him solace and protection during the German occupation. Among his more recent publications is *1984*. In 1941 Moravia married ELSA MORANTE. They separated in 1962.

NOVELS BY MORAVIA

The Bitter Honeymoon. 1952. Trans. by Frances Frenaye and others. Woodhill repr. of 1973 ed. o.p.

Bought and Sold. 1970. Trans. by Angus Davidson. FS&G 1973 o.p.

Command, and I Will Obey You. 1967. Woodhill repr. of 1973 ed. o.p. One of Moravia's later essay-novels, in which the protagonist interprets the classical Oedipus myth as a series of tragic events.

Conjugal Love. 1949. Trans. by Angus Davidson. Woodhill repr. of 1973 ed. o.p.

The Fancy Dress Party. 1941. Trans. by Angus Davidson. Woodhill repr. of 1973 ed. o.p.

The Lie. 1965. Woodhill repr. of 1973 ed. o.p. A novel in diary form.

1984. Trans. by William Weaver. FS&G 1983 o.p. "Moravia, 75 has taken his ultimate stand against fanaticism" (*Time*).

Roman Tales. 1954. Woodhill repr. of 1974 ed. o.p. Draws on the language and culture of the Roman working class and poor in order to criticize middle-class conventional values.

Time of Desecration. Trans. by Angus Davidson. FS&G 1980 o.p.

The Time of Indifference. 1928. Trans. by Angus Davidson. Greenwood 1976 repr. of 1953 ed. o.p. Moravia's first novel.

Two: A Phallic Novel. 1970. Trans. by Angus Davidson. FS&G 1972 o.p. Represents the compelling drive for sex as the only possible form of communication in our age.

Two Women. 1957. Trans. by Angus Davidson. Woodhill repr. of 1974 ed. o.p. Adapted by Vittorio De Sica in the award-winning film with Sophia Loren.

The Voyeur. 1985. Trans. by Tim Parks. FS&G 1987 $18.95. ISBN 0-374-28544-6. Story of a 35-year-old intellectual, a professor of French literature, who is locked in Oedipal combat with his aged but still vital father.

The Woman of Rome. 1947. Trans. by Lydia Holland. Woodhill repr. of 1974 ed. o.p. A classic of neorealism.

Short Story Collection by Moravia

The Fetish and Other Stories. 1963. Trans. by Angus Davidson. Greenwood 1976 repr. of 1965 ed. o.p.

Nonfiction by Moravia

The Red Book and the Great Wall: An Impression of Mao's China. 1967. Trans. by Ronald Strom. FS&G 1968 o.p. An intellectual, contemplative travelogue.

Books about Moravia

Cottrell, Jane E. *Alberto Moravia. Lit. and Life Ser.* Continuum 1974 $19.95. ISBN 0-8044-2131-5. Generally superficial study of little value to serious students.

Ross, Joan, and Donald Freed. *Existentialism of Alberto Moravia. Crosscurrents Modern Critiques Ser.* S. Ill. U. Pr. 1972 o.p. "The book should serve as a good introduction to this Italian literary report, with the exception that the writers take their Moravia too seriously" (*Choice*).

PAPINI, GIOVANNI. 1881–1956

With Giuseppe Prezzolini, Papini was a central figure in the pragmatist movement that brought Italy into the mainstream of European culture before World War I. The record of his labors can be read in the journals *Leonardo*, *Regno*, *La Voce*, and *Lacerba*. A restless spirit, his shifts from pragmatism to futurism, from agnosticism to Roman Catholicism, from critical severity to enthusiastic encouragement of new writers, mirror the revolutionary current of his time. His most famous writings include lives of Christ, St. Augustine (see Vol. 4), and Dante, but most characteristic is his world-famous autobiographical novel *The Failure* (1912), which first endeared him to his generation.

Novel by Papini

The Failure. Trans. by Virginia Pope. Greenwood 1972 repr. of 1924 ed. $35.00. ISBN 0-8371-5533-9

PARINI, GIUSEPPE. 1729–1799

Born in Milan, and committed to the priesthood, though without a real vocation, Parini served for many years as a tutor to young aristocrats in several noble Milanese families. Out of that experience, Parini wrote his most famous poem, *The Day* (1763–1804). In that masterful satire, which respects the ideals of the class of people satirized, Parini presented himself as a tutor guiding a young aristocrat through the rituals of living through an entire day. The result is a mirror held up to the servile Italian upper class that had accommodated itself to living almost mindlessly, or hypocritically, under foreign rule, and paying for the comforts of that accommodation with its moral character. There is an all-pervasive irony and compassion that permitted the poet to universalize his characterizations and to produce an exquisitely finished masterpiece that takes the reader out of the atmosphere of Arcadia and Metastasio across the threshold of the Italian *risorgimento* or national revival. The unrhymed lines of 11 syllables are as close as Italian prosody can come to English blank verse.

Poetry by Parini

The Day: Morning, Midday, Evening, Night. 1763–1804. Trans. by Herbert M. Bower. Hyperion Conn. 1977 repr. of 1927 ed. o.p.

PASCOLI, GIOVANNI. 1855–1912

After a youth filled with more than a normal share of personal sorrows, Pascoli, who was born in Romagna and educated at Bologna, went on to become a classical scholar of the first order, eventually succeeding to the chair held by Giosuè Carducci at the University of Bologna. He has been belatedly recognized as Italy's seminal modernist. His best poetry—as in the *Myricae* (1891) and the *Songs of Castelvecchio* (1903)—is Wordsworthian in its disarming surface simplicity but has been correctly characterized as a deliberate retreat into the neutral zone of childlike awareness. His Latin poetry won the leading prizes in Europe, and his studies of Italian authors, especially Leopardi and Dante, help to illuminate his own poetics.

Poetry by Pascoli

Giovanni Pascoli: Convivial Poems. 2 vols. Trans. by Egidio Lunardi and Robert Nugent. Lake Erie Col. Pr. Vol. 1 1979 $12.50. ISBN 0-935518-02-9. Vol. 2 1981 $7.50. ISBN 0-935518-03-7. Called "convivial" because they first appeared in the literary magazine *Il Convito,* these poems are a modern interpretation of historic events and Greek and Roman myths.

PASOLINI, PIER PAOLO. 1922–1975

Born in Bologna, Pasolini spent most of his childhood at his mother's birthplace in Friuli, where he learned the local dialect that he used in his first, last, and best poetry. He became a teacher in a local Communist party chapter, but was accused of blatant immorality in 1949, fired from his job, and expelled from the party. With his mother, he went to Rome, spending much time in the slums, mastering the Roman dialect. His novel *Ragazzi di Vita* (1955), based on his Roman street experience, established him as the leading neorealistic writer of the day. His second neorealistic novel, *A Violent Life* (1959), brought him greater success. Before long, however, he rejected neorealism and began to live for art's sake. Thereafter, except for what he called his "cat-like" nocturnal prowling for homosexual sex or love, Pasolini "did not lose a moment," as Cecelia Ross aptly said, "in his efforts to lay new directions for literature as well as for theater and television." He poured all his talents and energies into his major films, starting with *The Gospel According to St. Matthew* (1964), which sustains the mood of Bach's (see Vol. 3) music, and running through *The Hawks and the Sparrows* (1966), *Oedipus Rex* (1967), *Pigsty, Medea* (1970), and a trilogy made up of *The Decameron* (1970), *Canterbury Tales* (1971), and *Arabian Nights* (1974). Throughout his works, Pasolini explored the culture and language of the outcasts living in the shabby Roman periphery. He was, in fact, murdered in such a setting in a homosexual encounter with a street prostitute. Shortly before he died, Pasolini published a revised and enlarged edition of his dialect poems, *La nuova gioventù* (*The New Youth*) (1975).

Poetry by Pasolini

Lutheran Letters. Trans. by Stuart Hood. Humanities 1983 o.p.

Roman Poems: Bilingual Edition. Trans. by Lawrence Ferlinghetti and Francesca Valente. City Lights 1986 $14.95. ISBN 0-87286-188-0. Poems that reflect the working class life in Italy's capital.

Selected Poems. Trans. by Norman MacAfee and Luciano Martinengo. Riverrun NY 1988 $17.95. ISBN 0-7145-3889-2. ". . . based on a selection Pasolini himself made for an edition in 1970" (N.S. Thompson, *TLS*).

Novel by Pasolini

A Violent Life. Trans. by William Weaver. Pantheon. 1992 repr. of 1959 ed. $12.00. ISBN 0-679-73505-4

Short Story Collection by Pasolini

Roman Nights and Other Stories. Trans. by John Shepley. Marlboro Pr. 1988 $14.95. ISBN 0-910395-19-5. Five narratives about the violent, self-contained world of the boy-urchins of Rome, the hustlers, thieves, and losers who were one minute radiant, the next dead in the dirt.

Nonfiction by Pasolini

Heretical Empiricism. Ed. by Louise K. Barnett. Trans. by Ben Lawton and Louise K. Barnett. Ind. U. Pr. 1988 $39.95. ISBN 0-253-32717-2. Thirty-one essays on language, literature, and film, written from 1964 to 1971.

Books about Pasolini

Allen, Beverly. *Pier Paolo Pasolini: The Poetics of Heresy.* Anma Libri 1982 $46.50. ISBN 0-915838-11-7

Greene, Naomi. *Pier Paolo Pasolini: Cinema as Heresy.* Princeton U. Pr. 1990 $39.95. ISBN 0-691-03148-7. Intelligently explicates the political and social context within which Pasolini became both a leading figure and a significant heretic.

PAVESE, CESARE. 1908–1950

In Torino in his native Piedmont, Pavese studied English and American literature and wrote a dissertation on Walt Whitman (see Vol. 1). He read and translated Defoe (see Vol. 1), Dickens (see Vol. 1), Joyce (see Vol. 1), Dos Passos (see Vol. 1), Stein (see Vol. 1), and Faulkner (see Vol. 1), and his version of Melville's (see Vol. 1) *Moby Dick* is a classic. Except for his book of poems *Lavorare stanca (Work Wearies)* (1936), Pavese's chief works are the novels *The Comrade* (1948), *La Casa in Collina* (*The House on the Hill*) (1949), *Prima che il gallo canti* (*Before the Cock Crows*) (1949), *La bella estate* (*The Beautiful Summer*) (1949), and his last and best, *The Moon and the Bonfire* (1952). During World War II, he was head of the Rome office of the publishing house of Einaudi and, with Elio Vittorini, did much to encourage young writers. Although a member of the Communist party, he had not joined the anti-Fascist resistance. Unhappy in love, unable to believe in Christ, and disappointed with things in postwar Italy, he finally made good on what he had often urged as the finest of "final solutions" for himself, committing suicide after winning the coveted Strega Prize, for *La bella estate*.

Novels by Pavese

Dialogues with Leuco. 1947. Trans. by William Arrowsmith. Eridanos Library 1989 $17.95. ISBN 0-941419-38-X. Retellings of Greek legends, each staged as a dialogue between two classical figures.

Hard Labor. Trans. by William Arrowsmith. Ecco Pr. 1986 repr. of 1979 ed. $9.50. ISBN 0-88001-100-9

Selected Works. Trans. by R. W. Flint. FS&G 1968 o.p. Contains the novels *The Beach, The House on the Hill, Among Women Only,* and *The Devil in the Hills.* "Now there can be no excuse for not reading Pavese, one of the few essential novelists of the mid-twentieth century. The translations and the introductions are admirable" (Susan Sontag).

Nonfiction by Pavese

American Literature: Essays and Opinions. Trans. by Edwin Fussell. U. CA Pr. 1970 o.p. Critical essays collected and published posthumously.

Books about Pavese

Biasini, Gian-Paolo. *Smile of the Gods: A Thematic Study of Cesare Pavese's Work.* Trans. by Yvonne Freccero. Lib. Soc. Sci. 1968 $20.00. ISBN 0-915042-19-3

Lajolo, Davide. *An Absurd Vice: A Biography of Cesare Pavese.* Trans. by Mario Pietralunga and Mark Pietralunga. New Dir. Pr. 1983 $18.50. ISBN 0-8112-0851-6. "Pavese from boyhood, through the fascist era, forever obsessed with his 'absurd vice,' the pull toward death, and finally surrendering with suicide in 1950."

Thompson, Doug. *Cesare Pavese: A Study of the Major Novels and Poems.* Cambridge U. Pr. 1982 $49.50. ISBN 0-521-23602-9

PETRARCH (Francesco Petrarca). 1304–1374

Son of an exiled Florentine notary, Petrarch was born in Arezzo but raised at the papal court in Avignon in southern France. He went to study in Montpellier in 1317 and in Bologna in 1323. Less than a year after he returned to Avignon in 1326, he fell in love with the woman he called Laura in the Italian lyrics that make up his *Rime* or *Canzoniere* (c. 1327). In spite of the fact that, in all probability, Laura was not a real person but an unattainable ideal woman, she is presented more realistically than the conventional feminine image of the Provençal troubadors and of the literature of courtly love and is less ethereal than the angelic woman (*donna angelicata*) of the previous Italian poets. Like Dante, Petrarch turned to the Italian vernacular to express his most intimate feelings; but he did not, like Dante, place any confidence in the notion that writing in Italian could ever bring lasting fame. Although he approved of Dante's decision to give up the living Latin of the church as a medium of literary expression, he believed that a better alternative than the vernacular for serious literature was a revival of classical Latin, so that modern writers could indeed address all educated Europeans, transcending all provincial and national frontiers. Petrarch, first of the great Renaissance humanists, saw himself as looking back upon a thousand years of ignorance of the loftiest human values that the classical civilization of ancient Greece and Rome had cherished, and looking ahead to a bright new era when neglected *humanitas* would again receive its due. For at least two centuries, Petrarch's attitude prevailed, even though it was destined in the long run to fail. What the attitude made possible was, of course, the towering cosmopolitan achievement of Italian humanism and the Italian Renaissance. Among the great Italian humanistic successors of Petrarch in Italy are to be counted Coluccio Salutati, Leonardo Bruni, Lorenzo Valla, Marsilio Ficino, Angelo Poliziano, and Pico della Mirandola (see Vol. 4). Petrarch truly believed that he would enjoy everlasting fame for his works written in Latin. His Latin works are still studied by scholars but little read; whereas his poetry in Italian, in particular his innovation of the sonnet, now indeed called the Petrarchan sonnet, exerted a tremendous influence on the content as well as the form of all subsequent European literature, especially English. Petrarch's vernacular poetry is still a living force of the first order in Italian literature.

WORKS BY PETRARCH

Lord Morley's Tryumphes of Fraunces Petrarcke: The First English Translation of the Trionfi. 1356–74. Ed. by D. D. Carnicelli. HUP 1971 $19.50. ISBN 0-674-53916-1. Successive visions in the poet's dream representing a symbolic history from Earthly Love to Eternity.

Love Rimes of Petrarch. Trans. by Morris Bishop. Greenwood 1980 repr. of 1932 ed. $39.75. ISBN 0-313-22002-6

Petrarch: Selected Sonnets, Odes, Letters. Trans. and ed. by Thomas G. Bergin. *Crofts Class Ser.* Harlan Davidson 1966 o.p. Some poems addressed to friends, others dealing with contemporary issues or religious themes, but most about Laura.

Petrarch the First Modern Scholar and Man of Letters. Trans. and ed. by James H. Robinson and Henry Winchester Rolfe. Greenwood repr. of 1914 ed. o.p. Rich selection of writings, including Petrarch's *Secret.*

Petrarch's Lyric Poems. Trans. and ed. by Robert M. Durling. HUP 1976 $36.00. ISBN 0-674-66345-4. A prose translation.

Petrarch's Secret, Or, The Soul's Conflict with Passion. 1341–45. Trans. by William H. Draper. Hyperion Conn. 1991 repr. of 1911 ed. $24.00. ISBN 0-88355-596-4. Fundamental work for an understanding of Petrarch's inner conflict between his love for Laura and his desire for God, in the form of a dialogue between himself and St. Augustine.

Rime disperse. Trans. by Joseph A. Barber. Garland 1991 $24.00. ISBN 0-8153-0144-8. A collection of various short pieces.

Sonnets and Songs. Trans. by Anna Maria Armi. AMS Pr. repr. of 1946 ed. $67.50. ISBN 0-404-14695-3. A complete translation.

BOOKS ABOUT PETRARCH

Bergin, Thomas G. *Petrarch. Twayne's World Authors Ser.* G. K. Hall o.p. An excellent introduction to the life and works by the eminent Italianist.

Bernardo, Aldo S. *Petrarch, Laura, and the "Triumphs."* State U. NY Pr. 1974 $10.00. ISBN 0-87395-289-8. A brilliant, penetrating study by the eminent Petrarchist on the essentially humanistic inspiration that Laura provided to Petrarch.

Bloom, Harold. *Petrarch.* Chelsea Hse. 1989 $29.95. ISBN 0-55546-308-8. The respected Yale scholar offers a modern look at the Renaissance poet.

Boyle, Marjorie O'Rourke. *Petrarch's Genius: Pentimento and Prophecy.* U. CA Pr. 1991 $34.95 ISBN 0-520-07293-6

Jasenas, Michael. *Petrarch in America.* Pierpont Morgan 1974 o.p. Status of Petrarch studies in the United States.

Petrie, Jennifer. *Petrarch: The Augustan Poets, the Italian Tradition and the "Canzoniere."* Biblio Dist. 1983 o.p. Petrarch viewed within a larger tradition and context.

Scaglione, Aldo. *Francis Petrarch, Six Centuries Later.* U. of NC Pr. 1975 $7.50. ISBN 0-88438-953-7. Outstanding essays by well-known scholars in the United States.

Wilkins, Ernest H. *Studies in the Life and Works of Petrarch.* Medieval Acad. 1977 repr. of 1955 ed. o.p. "Dr. Wilkins is internationally recognized as the great Petrarch scholar of [this century]. . . . highly readable and enjoyable" (*LJ*).

PICO DELLA MIRANDOLA. 1463–1494

[SEE Volume 4.]

PIRANDELLO, LUIGI. 1867–1936 (NOBEL PRIZE 1934)

Born in Sicily, Pirandello attended the universities of Palermo, Rome, and Bonn (where he obtained his doctorate in philology with a thesis on the dialect of his native town, Agrigento) before settling in Rome to teach and write. In 1894, he married a Sicilian girl, Antonietta Portulano, who bore him three children before she went mad and afterwards provided the inspiration for many of his stories and plays. In all, Pirandello wrote 6 novels, some 250 short stories, and about 50 plays. It was a novel, *Il fu Mattia Pascal* (1904), that first brought him fame. Only in 1920, when he was past 50, did he turn seriously to playwriting. His first stage success had been a comedy, *Liolà* (1917), written in the Agrigento dialect. It took its theme, if not its mood, from the *Mandragola* of MACHIAVELLI (see Vols. 3 and 4). In 1921, Pirandello presented his most famous play *Six Characters in Search of an Author.* Here he seeks to confuse his spectators, who are forced into a paradox of reality and illusion when six "characters" search out the actors of a theatrical troupe to play out their inexorable story. The play exemplifies the Pirandellian conflict between art, which is unchanging and constant, and life, which is a continuous succession of mutations. Pirandello deliberately destroyed the traditional boundaries between audience and spectacle, reflecting the relativity and subjectivity of human existence. The play's unconventional format, which resulted in a riot, established Pirandello as Europe's leading avant-garde dramatist.

The main body of Pirandello's plays falls into three overlapping categories, the first exploring the nature of the theater, the second the complexities of personality in the etymological or dramatic sense of the term, and the third rising to dramatic representation of the categorical imperatives of social, religious, and artistic community. Besides the world-famous *Six Characters in Search of an Author* (1918), his best plays in the three categories include *Each in His Own Way* (1924), *It Is So (If You Think So)* (1917), *Henry IV* (1922), *The New Colony* (1925), *Lazarus, As You Desire Me* (1930), and *The Mountain Giants* (1937), written after he had been awarded the Nobel Prize and left incomplete. Pirandello is the forerunner of much modern theater and literature; among the figures who owe their roots to the innovations of Pirandello are BERTOLT BRECHT, JEAN GENET, JEAN-PAUL SARTRE, and SAMUEL BECKETT (see Vol. 1).

PLAYS BY PIRANDELLO

Collected Plays. Trans. by Henry Read and Bruce Penman. Riverrun NY 1986 $10.95. ISBN 0-7145-4110-9. A comprehensive collection of Pirandello's prodigious theatrical output.

Naked Masks: Five Plays. Ed. by Eric Bentley. NAL-Dutton 1957 $7.95. ISBN 0-525-48319-5. Includes *Liolà; It Is So (If You Think So); Henry IV; Six Characters in Search of an Author; Each in His Own Way.*

SHORT STORY COLLECTION BY PIRANDELLO

Better Think Twice about It: And Twelve Other Stories. Short Story Index Repr. Ser. Ayer repr. of 1934 ed. $26.50. ISBN 0-8369-4269-8. Most of Pirandello's short stories deal with the painful absurdities of life. Several later dramatized, since Pirandello found dialogue better satisfied his need to discuss life and its contradictions.

Caps and Bells. 1918. Trans. by John Field and Marion Field. Manyland 1974 $4.00. ISBN 0-87141-048-6. A translation of one of Pirandello's better-known comedies, *Il berretto a sonagli.*

Tales of Madness. Trans. by Giovanni Bussino. Dante U. Am. 1984 $14.50. ISBN 0-937832-26-X

Tales of Suicide. Trans. by Giovanni Bussino. Dante U. Am. 1988 $11.95. ISBN 0-937832-31-6. Twenty stories from Pirandello's *Novelle per un anno.* (1922–36).

NOVEL BY PIRANDELLO

The Notebooks of Serafino Gubbio. 1915. Trans. by C. K. Moncrieff. Hippocrene Bks. 1990 $9.95. ISBN 0-946626-58-8. Published at the eve of World War I, reprinted in 1925 with the title "Notebooks of the Operator Serafino Gubbio."

Nonfiction by Pirandello

Pirandello: On Humor. 1908. Trans. and ed. by Antonio Illiano and Daniel P. Testa. *Studies in Comparative Lit.* U. of NC Pr. 1974 $20.00. ISBN 0-8078-7058-7. "The most complete statement of the Italian playwright's aesthetic. . . . The translation is a lucid reading of a difficult text" (*Choice*).

Work by Pirandello

Tonight We Improvise and "Leonora, Addio." Trans. by J. Douglas Campbell and Leonard G. Sbrocchi. Speedimpex 1987 $10.00. ISBN 0-1691979-2-6. A fine translation of one of Pirandello's most difficult plays and of a short story.

Books about Pirandello

Bishop, Thomas. *Pirandello and the French Theater.* NYU Pr. 1960 o.p. A useful account of Pirandello's lasting influence on French theater. Foreword by Germaine Brée.

Caputi, Anthony. *Pirandello and the Crisis of Modern Consciousness.* U. of Ill. Pr. 1988 $24.95. ISBN 0-252-014468-5. "Lucidly written and intelligently ordered" (*Italica*).

Paolucci, Anne. *Pirandello's Theater: The Recovery of the Modern Stage for Dramatic Art. Crosscurrents Modern Critiques Ser.* S. Ill. U. Pr. 1974 $6.95. ISBN 0-8093-0594-1. An analysis of 14 plays that shows the gradual development of Pirandello's art from Sicilian naturalism to the philosophic bent of the late works.

Radcliff-Umstead, Douglas. *The Mirror of Our Anguish: A Study of Luigi Pirandello's Narrative Works.* Fairleigh Dickinson 1978 $35.00. ISBN 0-8386-1930-4

Ragusa, Olga. *Luigi Pirandello.* Col. U. Pr. 1968 o.p. "If you don't know much about Pirandello, you do well to begin with this book . . . a thorough summing up, a conscientious survey, rich in sympathetic yet shrewd analysis" (Thomas G. Bergin, *World Literature Today*).

Sogliuzzo, A. Richard. *Luigi Pirandello, Director: The Playwright in the Theater.* Scarecrow 1982 $21.00. ISBN 0-8108-1488-9

Starkie, Walter. *Luigi Pirandello, 1867–1936.* U. CA Pr. 1965 o.p. Views Pirandello from a variety of perspectives within the context of European culture: Pirandello the Sicilian, the novelist, the dramatist, etc.

Vittorini, Domenico. *Drama of Lugi Pirandello.* Russell Sage 1969 repr. of 1957 ed. o.p. Foreword by Luigi Pirandello.

POLIZIANO, ANGELO (Politian). 1454–1494

Born Angelo Ambrogini in Tuscany, he was called Poliziano or Politian after the Latin name of his birthplace. At the Medicean court, Lorenzo the Magnificent was his friend and patron, and Luigi Pulci and Pico della Mirandola (see Vol. 4) were close companions. His important works in the vernacular are *La favola di Orfeo* (*The Fable of Orpheus*) (1480), completed in two days, which ranks as the first Italian secular drama, and the *Stanze* (1475–78), written in celebration of a courtly tournament, with brilliant scenes of people and events.

Poetry by Poliziano

The "Stanze" of Angelo Poliziano. Ed. by David Quint. U. of Mass. Pr. 1979 o.p.

Play by Poliziano

A Translation of the Orpheus of Angelo Politian & the Aminta of Torquato Tasso. Greenwood 1986 repr. of 1931 ed. $43.75. ISBN 0-313-25211-4

POLO, MARCO. 1254?–1324?

[See Volume 3.]

PRATOLINI, VASCO. 1913–1991

Pratolini grew up in Florence, which served as the setting for most of his fictional works. Often called Italy's first proletarian novelist, Pratolini was committed to realistic depictions of his working-class childhood and adolescence. He wrote numerous novellas and novels, including the early *Via de' Magazzini* (1942) and *Cronaca Familiare (Family Chronicle)* (1945); his first major success was *Cronache di Poveri Amanti (A Tale of Poor Lovers)* (1947).

Too poor to go beyond elementary school, Pratolini was trained as a typographer but eventually became a self-educated man by assiduously studying the great works of world literature. Though initially drawn to Mussolini's movement, he eventually drifted from the Fascist doctrine. Beginning in 1938, he co-edited the arts journal *Campo di Marte*, subsequently suppressed for its anti-Fascist bias. His 1962 *Two Brothers* was adapted for theater and film, winning that year's Venice Film Festival. In 1967 Pratolini completed the trilogy *An Italian Story*, which continued the themes of his earlier novels. Though mostly silent for the last two decades of his life, he spent those years writing an unfinished novel, *La malatia infantile (Childhood Disease)*.

Novels by Pratolini

Family Chronicle. 1945. Trans. by Martha King. Italica Pr. 1988 ISBN 0-934977-07-0. An autobiographical novel of Pratolini's youth in Florence.

A Tale of Poor Lovers. 1947. Monthly Rev. 1988 repr. of 1949 ed. $7.50. ISBN 0-85345-723-9

QUASIMODO, SALVATORE. 1901–1968 (Nobel Prize 1959)

Born in Sicily and trained as an engineer, Quasimodo was brought into Italian literary circles by his brother-in-law Elio Vittorini, who drew him to Florence and introduced him to Umberto Saba, Eugenio Montale, and other contributors to the modernist journal *Solaria*. In the late 1930s, Quasimodo gave up engineering for journalism and literature, becoming editor in chief of the weekly *Il Tempo* and professor of Italian literature in Milan. His poetic life was divided into a hermetic period that lasted through World War II and a period of open commitment to social-humanistic causes that lasted until his death. To the first period belong the volumes *Waters and Lands* (1930), *Sunken Oboe* (1932), and *Erato and Apollyon* (1936), which together with the "new poems" written after 1936, were collected in *And It Is Suddenly Evening* (1942). The collection is characterized by what has been called Quasimodo's "poetics of the word"—a genuine hermeticism that contrasts with the "bareness" of Montale's effort to strip away ornamentation and with Ungaretti's discursive "imaginings." In creating a "myth of Sicily," Quasimodo sought its roots in the ancient Greek lyric poets and in the Roman poets closest to them, like Catullus and Virgil. That took him into his second poetic period, of disillusionment with his Edenlike mythical image of Sicily, expressed in the volumes *Day after Day* (1947), *Life Is No Dream* (1949), and *The False and True* (1956), followed later by *The Incomparable Land* (1958) and *To Give and to Have* (1966). He was a translator of Ovid, Shakespeare (see Vol. 1), Molière, Ezra Pound (see Vol. 1), and E. E. Cummings (see Vol. 1). When he received the Nobel Prize in 1959, it was especially noted that his best poetry expresses "with classic fire . . . the tragic experience of life in our time."

Poetry by Quasimodo

The Complete Poems of Salvatore Quasimodo. Trans. by Jack Bevan. Schocken 1984 o.p. Quasimodo's poetry from the nostalgic and tender poems about his native Sicily to the period after World War II.

SCIASCIA, LEONARDO. 1921–1989

Born in Sicily, Sciascia was a literary and critical genius as well as a best-selling activist-writer. In the tradition of such Sicilian writers as LUIGI PIRANDELLO and GIUSEPPE DI LAMPEDUSA, he explored in neorealist novels the island's impact on its inhabitants' lives: how they coped with crime, the Mafia, and corruption. His best-known works include *The Day of the Owl, The Sicilian Relatives,* and the collection of short stories *The Wine-Dark Sea.* In his most controversial work, *The Moro Affair,* he implicated Italy's leaders in the 1978 kidnapping and murder of former premier Aldo Moro by the leftist terrorist group, the Red Brigade. Though a long-time Communist, Sciascia eventually left the party to become a member of the Radical party, whose tenets were closer to his own anarchist leanings. As a representative of the party, Sciascia was elected to both the Italian and European Parliaments.

NOVELS BY SCIASCIA

Day of the Owl. Equal Danger. 1961. Godine 1983 $8.95. ISBN 0-87923-516-0. "An absorbing tale in the best tradition of the *roman policier* [that] reveals with cynical clarity the *malaise* that afflicts those engaged in public life" (*Choice*).

Open Doors and Three Novellas. Trans. by Marie Evans, Joseph Farrell, and Sacha Rabinovitch. Knopf 1992 $20.50. ISBN 0-394-58979-3. "Affords a good example of the forensic imagination and artistry of one of the most distinctive voices in twentieth-century European literature." (*NY Times*).

SILONE, IGNAZIO (pseud. of Secondo Tranquilli). 1900–1978

Silone was 15 years old when an earthquake in his native Abruzzi killed his mother and five of his brothers. Before he was 20 he had established himself in Rome as editor of a socialist weekly. In 1921 he went off on the first of many trips to the Soviet Union and became a founding member of the Italian Communist party. Under fascism he hid at first, and then, in 1930, he fled to Switzerland, at which time, however, he also broke with the Communist party. The novels that made him world famous as an anti-Fascist were *Fontamara* (1930) and *Bread and Wine,* the latter first published in English in 1936 and then in 17 other languages as well as in Italian. Silone was virtually unknown in Italy until after World War II, by which time he had undergone a radical spiritual transformation that is explained in a very moving essay, "Emergency Exit," included in Richard Crossman's *The God That Failed* (1950).

BOOKS BY SILONE

Bread and Wine. 1936. Trans. by Harvey Fergusson, Jr. NAL-Dutton $2.95. ISBN 0-451-51757-1

Fontamara. 1930. Trans. by Eric Mosbacher. NAL-Dutton 1981 $7.95. ISBN 0-452-00978-2. Like *Bread and Wine,* treats the theme of southern Italian peasants, their deprivation, their endurance, and the impact of fascism on their lives.

SVEVO, ITALO (pseud. of Ettore Schmitz). 1861–1928

Born in Austrian Trieste of a Jewish Italian-German family, Svevo spoke German fluently and pursued a business career before taking up fiction under a pseudonym that means "Italus the Swabian" or South German. His Italian had indeed something foreign about it, as did the characterizations of heroes and heroines in his novels. His first novel, *A Life* (1893), published at his own expense, and his second, *Senilità (As a Man Grows Older)* (1898), were virtually ignored. Svevo might have despaired had it not been for his friendship with the expatriate Irish novelist JAMES JOYCE (see Vol. 1), with whom he exchanged language lessons in Trieste. Joyce's intervention eventually found a foreign audience for Svevo's third and perhaps best novel, *The Confessions of Zeno* (1923), first published and very well received in France. As Svevo's reputation spread, he was called the Italian PROUST in France, the Italian MUSIL in Germany, and the Italian JOYCE in England. Italian critics now point out that, despite Svevo's foreign success, it was an Italian, EUGENIO MONTALE, who wrote the first significant critical appraisal in 1925. Still, by then Montale had already steeped himself in foreign literatures and could assume a foreign perspective, while more natively rooted Italian critics, including even BENEDETTO CROCE, continued to discount Svevo as a writer writing to be translated.

NOVELS BY SVEVO

As A Man Grows Older. 1898. Trans. by Beryl de Zoete. Sun & Moon Pr. 1991 $11.95. ISBN 1-55713-128-7. An insurance man falls in love with a prostitute and idealizes her persona.

The Confessions of Zeno. 1923. Trans. by Beryl de Zoete. Random 1989 $12.00. ISBN 0-679-72234-3. A novel influenced by Freud in which the protagonist Zeno argues with his psychoanalyst until he discovers the source of his malady to be the Oedipus complex.

SHORT STORY COLLECTION BY SVEVO

Short Sentimental Journey and Other Stories. 1910–28. U. CA Pr. 1967 $21.50. Short stories with masterful psychological portrayals.

WORK BY SVEVO

Further Confessions of Zeno. Trans. by P. N. Furbank. U. CA Pr. 1969 o.p. Contains unfinished works all published posthumously: *The Old Man* (1929), *An Old Man's Confession, Umbertino, A Contract, This Indolence of Mine* (last four items 1949), and the play *Regeneration* (1960).

BOOKS ABOUT SVEVO

Furbank, P. N. *Italo Svevo: The Man and the Writer.* U. CA Pr. 1966 o.p. "A very nearly perfect critical biography" (*N.Y. Times*).

Gatt-Rutter, John. *Italo Svevo: A Double Life.* OUP 1988 $84.00. ISBN 0-19-815848-3. A definitive biography with emphasis on dreams, correspondence, and memorabilia.

Weiss, Beno. *Italo Svevo.* Twayne 1987 $26.95. ISBN 0-8057-6649-9. An important contribution to Svevo studies which combines biography with criticism.

TASSO, TORQUATO. 1544–1595

Few poets have had a more anguished life than Italy's Torquato Tasso, about whom GOETHE wrote his celebrated tragedy *Torquato Tasso.* His great chivalric epic of the Christian crusades is *Jerusalem Delivered* (1575). Tasso, who was a critic before he was a poet, sought to make HOMER and VIRGIL his models and DANTE his source of Christian poetic inspiration, but the resulting epic, as finally published in 1581, is a work of Petrarchan melancholy. Unlike Dante or ARIOSTO, Tasso did not succeed in objectifying a world in the epic manner. In celebrating the deeds of heroes, he remained subjective and lyric. The reason may be, as some have suggested, that he felt Italy was a long way from becoming a significant united nation capable of sustaining a truly epic enterprise in its literature. Forlorn in love, overwhelmed by melancholy, ever suspicious of intrigues against him, Tasso became self-critical to the point of trying to rewrite his epic to placate its severest critics. He traveled much and was several times confined as insane by patrons and friends who loved him. He died in Rome, where he had been summoned to be honored, like Petrarch, with the poet's laurel. Second to *Jerusalem Delivered*, Tasso's most influential literary work has been his pastoral play *Aminta* (1581), which has been performed and highly praised. As in his epic, the poetic voice is lyric. Some modern critics have come to believe that, with his all-pervasive lyricism, Tasso was far ahead of his times.

Works by Tasso

Creation of the World. Trans. by Joseph Tusiani. MRTS 1982 $16.00. ISBN 0-86698-019-9. Notes by Gaetano Cipolla. Poems in seven Cantos, rich in religious fervor and theological doctrine, but poetically inferior, written mainly under the pressure of the Counter Reformation.

Discourses on the Heroic Poem. 1594. Ed. by Mariella Cavalchini and Irene Samuel. OUP 1973 o.p. An excellent translation of an important work of literary history, in which Tasso presented the theory of his own epic, *Gerusalemme Liberata*, and discussed other contemporary critical theories.

Jerusalem Delivered: An English Prose Version. Trans. and ed. by Ralph Nash. Wayne St. U. Pr. 1987 $44.95. ISBN 0-8143-1829-0. "Nash's decision to render Tasso's rhymed octaves in prose is a wise one. . ." because he avoids gross inaccuracies and "a distracting preoccupation with inimitable nuances of Italian style at the expense of the on-going narration" (*Italica*).

Tasso's Dialogues: A Selection, with the Discourse on the Art of the Dialogue. Trans. by Carnes Loard and Dain A. Trafton. U. CA Pr. 1983 $35.00. ISBN 0-520-04464-9. Dialogues that deal with ethical, philosophical, and esthetic questions, written during Tasso's seven-year confinement in the ospedale di Sant'Anna.

Tasso's Jerusalem Delivered. 1575. Bks. Demand repr. of 1962 ed. $147.50. ISBN 0-8357-6669-1. Trans. by Edward Fairfax. Fairfax's translation of 1600 was a major poetic feat with lasting influence: "For Spenser and Fairfax both . . . saw much farther into the Beauties of our Numbers, than those who immediately followed them" (John Dryden).

Books about Tasso

Boulting, William. *Tasso and His Times*. Haskell 1969 repr. of 1907 ed. $75.00. ISBN 0-8383-0915-1. "This scholarly, well-written study of Tasso's life and work constitutes a significant contribution to both Italian and English literary criticism" (*LJ*).

Kates, Judith A. *Tasso and Milton*. Bucknell U. Pr. 1983 $24.50. ISBN 0-8387-5046-X. Explores the friendship between the two men and their mutual influences.

UNGARETTI, GIUSEPPE. 1888–1970

Born in Egypt of Tuscan parents, Ungaretti went to Paris in 1912 to complete his education, attending the lectures of Henri Bergson (see Vol. 4) and forming friendships with distinguished members of the avant-garde, including Picasso (see Vol. 3), Modigliani, and Apollinaire. For a time he was swept up by the futurist movement of Filippo Tommaso Marinetti, affected more by its nationalistic spirit, however, than by the new poetics. A lover of the written word, Ungaretti's aim in poetry was to find a new language that was simple, precise, melodious, and compelling. His World War I experiences in the Italian army inspired his earliest poetry, first in Italian, *Il porto sepolto* (1916), and then in French, *La guerre* (1919). A 1923 edition of the former included a preface by Benito Mussolini. In 1936 Ungaretti left Italy to teach Italian literature in Brazil, out of which grew his subsequently published critical essays on Dante, Petrarch (see also Vol. 4), Vico, and Leopardi, but he returned to Italy in 1942. After Italy's defeat in the war, he received critical attention internationally, spent the year 1964 teaching at Columbia University, and returned to Milan, where he died. *Allegria di naufragi (The Joy of Shipwrecks)* has been the very Leopardian title of a number of editions of his poems. A translator of

Shakespeare (see Vol. 1), Blake (see Vol. 1), Gongora, Racine, and Mallarmé, Ungaretti was for a long time the leading poet of the so-called hermetic school; but, in retrospect, it becomes clear that his chief models for the craft of poetry were Leopardi and Petrarch.

Poetry by Ungaretti

Selected Poems. Trans. by Allen Mandelbaum. Cornell Univ. Pr. 1975 o.p. Ungaretti sees human beings as suffering pilgrims, humble in their vulnerability, yet proud of their intrinsic worth.

Books about Ungaretti

Cambon, Glauco. *Giuseppe Ungaretti.* Col. U. Pr. 1967 $7.50. ISBN 0-231-02957-8. A short essay that looks at the poet's life and poetry.

Cary, Joseph. *Three Modern Italian Poets: Saba, Ungaretti, and Montale.* NYU Pr. 1969 o.p. Discussion of the hermetic movement in modern Italian poetry.

VERGA, GIOVANNI. 1840–1922

A Sicilian, like Leonardo Sciascia and Luigi Pirandello, Verga was educated as a writer in Florence and Milan but drew on Sicily for the subject of his chief novels, plays, and short stories. In 1895 he returned permanently to Catania, his Sicilian birthplace, but by then he had already written his best novels of fictional realism (*verismo*): *Malavoglia (The House by the Medlar Tree)* (1881) and *Mastro-don Gesualdo (Master don Gesualdo)* (1889), the first dealing with a family of poor Sicilian fishermen, the second with the social climbing of a stonemason who has made a fortune. These classic works of realism established Verga as the father of the nineteenth-century Italian novel. In fact, D. H. Lawrence (see Vol. 1) translated several of his novellas, calling him, "the greatest writer of Italian fiction since Manzoni." Of greater international fame has been Verga's novella *Cavalleria Rusticana (Rustic Chivalry)* (1880), which provided the libretto for Mascagni's famous opera.

Novels by Verga

The House by the Medlar Tree. 1881. Trans. by Raymond Rosenthal. U. CA Pr. 1983 $37.50. ISBN 0-520-04850-1. The Rosenthal translation is the first complete version in English and a good one, "conveying [well] the color of the language of the Sicilian fishermen and peasants. . . . A valuable edition" (*Choice*). Introduction by Giovanni Cecchetti.

Little Novels of Sicily. 1925. Trans. by D. H. Lawrence. Greenwood 1975 repr. of 1953 ed. o.p. The best of Verga's tales, with characters that reach a tragic dimension tied to the overwhelming necessities of daily life.

Mastro-don Gesualdo. 1923. Trans. by D. H. Lawrence. Hippocrene Bks. 1985 $5.95. ISBN 0-946626-03-0

Short Story Collections by Verga

Cavalleria Rusticana and Other Stories. 1926. Trans. by D. H. Lawrence. Greenwood 1975 repr. of 1928 ed. o.p.

The She-Wolf and Other Stories. 1880–83. Trans. by Giovanni Cecchetti. U. CA Pr. o.p. Primitive, almost savage characters in a background of poverty and relentless hard labor.

Books about Verga

Bergin, Thomas G. *Giovanni Verga.* Elliots Bks. 1931 $49.50. ISBN 0-686-83557-3

Lucente, Gregory L. *The Narrative of Realism and Myth: Verga, Lawrence, Faulkner and Pavese*. Johns Hopkins 1981 $26.50. ISBN 0-8018-2609-8. A comparative study of four modern Italian, American, and British realist novelists.

VICO, GIAMBATTISTA. 1668–1744

Born in Naples of a relatively poor family, Vico studied privately and became a professor of rhetoric in the prestigious university of his native city. Learned in jurisprudence, philosophy, history, philology, politics, aesthetics, and literary criticism, he anticipated with brilliant insights the thought of the profoundest thinkers of later times, from HERDER (see Vol. 4), KANT (see Vol. 4), and HEGEL (see Vol. 4) down to the modern existentialists. His greatest work is the *Principles of a New Science on the Nature of Nations* (1725), soon to be called simply *The New Science*. "It is generally known," wrote Giuseppe Prezzolini, "that the aesthetics of De Sanctis and Croce have their origin in Vico," while it is "to Croce that we owe the most illuminating expositions of Vico's thought as well as the launching of a series of editions and studies that have given Vico the leading position he deserves in the history of human thought." Vico traced a pattern in the development of all human culture consisting of repeated cycles (*corsi* and *ricorsi*), passing through three phases: theocratic or hieroglyphic, heroic or metaphoric, and human or analytical. More recently, JAMES JOYCE (see Vol. 1) made extensive use of Vico's pattern of cycles for *Finnegans Wake*, challenging his readers to read the work repeatedly, or cyclically, in a Vichean spirit. Long before Joyce, however, Italy's greatest novelist, ALESSANDRO MANZONI, had written an appreciative passage noting how Vico constantly "inspires you with a feeling of having been led to those regions in which alone one may ever hope to find the truth."

NONFICTION BY VICO

The Autobiography of Giambattista Vico. 1725–31. Trans. by Thomas G. Bergin. Cornell Univ. Pr. 1963 $11.95. ISBN 0-8014-9088-X. An excellent introduction.

The New Science of Giambattista Vico. 1725. Trans. by Thomas G. Bergin and Max H. Fisch. Cornell Univ. Pr. 1984 $14.95. ISBN 0-8014-9265-3. "A must for all students of the humanities and social sciences" (*Choice*).

Vico: Selected Writings. Trans. and ed. by Leon Pompa. Cambridge U. Pr. 1982 $44.50. ISBN 0-521-23514-6

BOOKS ABOUT VICO

Caponigri, A. Robert. *Time and Idea: The Theory of History in Giambattista Vico*. U. of Notre Dame Pr. 1968 o.p. A European writer of philosophy who looks at Vico.

Manson, Richard. *The Theory of Knowledge of Giambattista Vico: On the Method of the New Science Concerning the Common Nature of the Nations*. Shoe String 1969 o.p. A study of Vico's greatest work.

Pompa, Leon. *Vico: A Study of the New Science*. Cambridge U. Pr. 1975 $54.95. ISBN 0-521-20584-0. Looks at Vico's *Principi di una scienza nuova*.

Tagliacozzo, Giorgio, ed. *Vico and Marx*. Humanities 1983 o.p. A comparative study by a prominent Vico specialist.

Tagliacozzo, Giorgio, and others. *A Bibliography of Vico in English, 1884–1984*. Philos Document 1986 $24.50. ISBN 0-912632-82-8. The sheer number of entries in this exhaustive bibliography attests to the overwhelming interest in the United States in Vico studies.

VITTORINI, ELIO. 1908–1966

Novelist Elio Vittorini has had a lasting impact on Italian letters that few writers can equal. One of the major exponents of neorealism, with CESARE

PAVESE, Vittorini helped to create Italy's modern "myth of America" between 1930 and 1939 as a means of relieving the anguish of writers constrained, like themselves, to pursue success under Fascist tyranny. Under fascism, Vittorini managed to rise to a position of great power in publishing that enabled him to help literally hundreds of young writers to get their writings published—something he continued to be able to do after the war. What he could not continue to do, however, was to write books as good as he had written under fascism. Martin Seymour-Smith explained this by suggesting, for instance, that Vittorini's *Conversation in Sicily* (1941) is, ironically, his very best book precisely "because the existence of the fascist censorship forced him on to a metaphorical, a more personal plane." Yet, as Giose Rimanelli pointed out, one has finally to face up to the perplexing question of "how the most important books of twentieth-century Italian literature could have been written just by those people in a fascist state."

NOVELS BY VITTORINI

Men and Not Men. Trans. by Sarah Henry. 1987 Marlboro Pr. $16.95. ISBN 0-910395-13-6. A critical view of some social aspects of the contemporary world.

The Red Carnation. 1948. Greenwood 1972 repr. of 1952 ed. o.p. Vittorini's first full-length novel, delineating a link between fascism and violence.

A Vittorini Omnibus: The Twilight of the Elephant and Other Novels. Trans. by Cinina Brescia and others. New Dir. Pr. 1973 $8.95. ISBN 0-8112-0499-5. Three short representative novels: *In Sicily, La Garibaldina*, and the title novel.

Women of Messina. 1949. Trans. by Frances Frenaye and Frances Keene. New Dir. Pr. 1973 $9.50. ISBN 0-8112-0496-0. "Vittorini's own disillusionment in the Communist solution is mirrored in this, his last novel. It is an uneven book but an important one . . ." (*Choice*).

CHAPTER 14

French Literature

Timothy Hampton

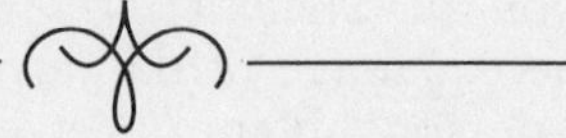

Meaning lies not in the thing you look at, but in your own gaze.
—André Gide, *The Fruits of the Earth*

From the Middle Ages, French literature has held a high place in Western civilization and, from the nineteenth century, has been a principal representative of occidental culture throughout the world. No other literature has held so consistently high the ideal of thought and expression as inseparable; in no other European country has the identification of language, literature, and national identity been as close.

The notion of a specifically French literature arises at the same moment as the notion of a unified France. Throughout the Middle Ages, France existed as a more or less loosely joined collection of small duchies. Its literature was dominated by the lyrics of the itinerant poets and the romances of chivalry, with their tales of knights who wander from court to court. Both forms draw heavily upon traditions and conventions that are international rather than strictly French. With the onset of the sixteenth century, however, the unification of the country under the dynamic young king Francis I was accompanied by the call for the creation of a new, uniquely French literature. Joachim du Bellay's *Défense et Illustration de la Langue Française* (1549), the first of many literary manifestoes in French literary history, called for a new poetry that would break with the country's past and rival the achievements of both classical antiquity and the Italian Renaissance. The remarkable body of lyric poetry produced by du Bellay and his contemporaries, as well as the philosophical meditations of Montaigne and the great verbal exuberance of Rabelais, demonstrates the importance of this conjunction of philosophical reflection, linguistic experimentation, and national identity. Du Bellay's care for the state of the French language illustrates a concern that continues even today in the anxiety about the integrity of French and the intrusion of American English into French life.

In the seventeenth century, linguistic matters were also at the center of the brilliant court of Louis XIV, who helped to establish the French Academy to oversee the language. This development of an academy to "watch over" culture is paralleled, in the realm of ideas, by the rise of Cartesian philosophy. And problems of philosophy, language, and literature are in turn debated in the great theatrical tradition of Corneille, Molière, and Racine, which adorned the Bourbon court.

The rigid formality that marked and made the careers of Molière and Racine at the end of the seventeenth century fell under questioning in the eighteenth century. Voltaire continued to write plays on the established model, but Marivaux added a new dimension with playful recreations of the society around him. It was above all Diderot—particularly in his theoretical essays on theater—who introduced into France and Europe in general the new theater that shunned classical formality and moved toward a more realistic drama. Beaumarchais, at the end of the century, would translate these theories to the stage (*The Barber of Seville, The Marriage of Figaro*) while infusing them with the new rationalist political spirit of the age of revolution.

These new developments are continued in the romantic theater of Hugo, Musset, Vigny, and others, which flourished from about 1815 to 1840. Thereafter, a socially conscious realism took over until the end of the century when neoromanticism and symbolist fantasy began to give way to the extraordinarily rich experiments of the twentieth century—experiments which once again made France the theatrical center of Europe.

A particularly rich moment in French theater came between the two world wars when the theories of Freud (see Vols. 3 and 5), the surrealists' disenchantment with social convention, and a renaissance of the ideal of classical expression came together to produce playwrights like Cocteau, Giraudoux, and Anouilh. The important role played by literary polemic and manifesto, begun with du Bellay and continued in Hugo's preface to *Cromwell,* was taken up again in Artaud's *The Theater and Its Double*, a work whose call for a break with all previous theatrical tradition found analogues in the so-called theater of the absurd (Beckett, Genet, Ionesco, among others).

From the romances of Chrétien de Troyes, through the elegant fables of Mme de La Fayette, to the self-consciously experimental "texts" of the *nouveau roman* school in the 1950s, the French novel has been characterized by psychological nuance and the quest for stylistic perfection. Following Balzac's massive *La Comédie Humaine* in the early nineteenth century (92 novels of more than 100 projected), French novelists turned toward the cultivation of style and structure, toward experimentation with the very forms through which literature represents the world. The romanticism of Balzac and Stendhal gave way to the realism of Flaubert, who combines a concern for social issues with an obsessive attention to aesthetic perfection. Flaubert's social vision was pursued in the naturalism of Zola and in the political novels of the twentieth-century existentialists (Malraux, Sartre, Camus, de Beauvoir), while his aestheticism found its heirs in Gide, Huysmans, and Proust, whose *Remembrance of Things Past* may be both the greatest psychological novel and the most influential apology for the power of art in the history of Europe. In recent years, the phenomenological experiments of the "new novel" (Robbe-Grillet, Butor, Duras, Simon) have been replaced by a more lyrical and imaginative return to storytelling (LeClézio, Tournier).

Lyric poetry is the literary form whose magic comes across least in translation—though French literature has been well served by such superlative translators as Richard Howard, Richard Wilbur, and Louise Varèse. Yet it may be in the domain of poetry that the creative energy of recent French literature finds its most potent expression. After the great flowering of French poetry during the Middle Ages and the Renaissance, the classicism of the seventeenth and eighteenth centuries seemed to stifle the lyric muse. Only with the onset of romanticism, in the powerful voices of Hugo and Lamartine, was vitality restored to the French lyric. The symbolism of Baudelaire, Rimbaud, and Mallarmé broke with the excesses of romantic lyricism, turning attention from politics and national history toward formal experiments and the cultivation of spirituality. The extravagant revolt against tradition brought on by the surrealists (Breton, Aragon, Éluard) spawned a period of poetic discovery that continues to the present, from the "objective" poetry of Ponge to the lyrical celebration of freedom and courage in the work of RENÉ CHAR.

For English-speaking readers of the early and middle twentieth century, French literature often calls to mind a sense of scandal, of provocation and revolt, an image of libertine philosophers and poets at odds with conventional society. In more recent years, this notion of the artist *provocateur* has abated somewhat as the political and philosophical heroes of the two world wars are replaced by writers and critics more closely connected with the world of the university. The newer French intellectual, either as creative writer (CIXOUS, Sollers) or essayist (BARTHES, FOUCAULT, DERRIDA), tends to focus less on heroic existential struggles to find meaning in a godless world and more on the nuances of language itself, on the ways in which language defines and structures the world in which we live. In this new questioning of the modes through which we see and define each other, recent French thought breaks with what precedes it. Yet it also joins a long tradition of philosophical reflection on language and identity that goes back to the Renaissance and is central to the very definition of France itself.

HISTORY AND CRITICISM

Babbitt, Irving. *The Master of Modern French Criticism.* Intro. by Milton Hindus. Greenwood 1977 repr. of 1912 ed. $40.50. ISBN 0-8371-9415-6. A discussion of the most significant of the nineteenth-century critics in which Babbitt, a noted Harvard professor, describes his own critical position.

Barthes, Roland. *S–Z.* Trans. by Richard Miller. Fr. & Eur. 1970 $29.95. ISBN 0-686-53944-3

———. *Writing Degree Zero.* Trans. by Annette Lavers and Colin Smith. FS&G 1977 $9.95. ISBN 0-374-52139-5. Some major works by a very influential contemporary French critic who has proposed a "science of literature" grounded in linguistics.

Bédé, Jean-Albert, and William Edgerton, eds. *Columbia Dictionary of Modern European Literature.* Col. U. Pr. 1980 $163.00. ISBN 0-231-03717-1. Helpful summaries of recent trends in French and other European literatures. Includes brief biographical and critical sketches of leading literary figures.

Blanchot, Maurice. *The Space of Literature.* Trans. by Ann Smock. U. of Nebr. Pr. 1982 $25.00. ISBN 0-8032-1166-X. Challenging philosophical meditations on many major French writers by a critical genius of the contemporary scene.

Bloch, R. Howard. *Etymologies and Genealogies: A Literary Anthropology of the French Middle Ages.* U. Ch. Pr. 1986 $25.00. ISBN 0-226-05981-2. A suggestive interpretation of medieval literature in light of the relationship between language and social institutions.

Cazamian, Louis F. *A History of French Literature.* OUP 1955 o.p. "A comprehensive and thorough account . . . from the earliest times to the present day" (*Manchester Guardian*).

Clark, Priscilla P. *Literary France: The Making of a Culture.* U. CA Pr. 1991 $12.95. ISBN 0-520-07397-5. A sociological study of literary culture in the nineteenth century.

Cobban, Alfred. *A History of Modern France.* 3 vols. Viking Penguin rev. ed. 1961 $6.95–$9.95 ea. ISBNs 0-14-020403-2, 0-14-020525-X, 0-14-020711-2. "The history of France covered here is so interesting and so well told that the book should be purchased by all libraries, large and small" (*LJ*).

Cruickshank, John. ed. *French Literature and Its Background.* 6 vols. OUP 1969–70 o.p. One of the most useful surveys of contemporary French literature.

Culler, Jonathan. *Structuralist Poetics: Structuralism, Linguistics and the Study of Literature.* Cornell Univ. Pr. 1976 $10.95. ISBN 0-8014-9155-X. A very helpful introduction to structuralism in literature, a critical theory that has been broadly influential in recent years, especially in France.

De Jean, Joan, and Nancy Miller, eds. *Displacements: Women, Tradition, Literatures in French.* Johns Hopkins 1990 $45.00. ISBN 0-8018-4070-8. An important collection of feminist essays challenging the traditional male-centered vision of literary history.

Derrida, Jacques. *Dissemination.* Trans. by Barbara Johnson. U. Ch. Pr. 1983 $14.95. ISBN 0-226-14334-1

______. *Of Grammatology.* Trans. by Gayatri C. Spivak. Johns Hopkins 1977 $14.95. ISBN 0-8018-1879-6. Two important and difficult works by a currently influential French philosopher and principal figure in the school of deconstructionism.

Doubrovsky, Serge. *The New Criticism in France.* Trans. by Derek Coltman. U. Ch. Pr. 1973 $20.00. ISBN 0-226-16040-8. A good introduction.

Fox, John. *A Literary History of France.* Ed. by I. D. McFarlane and others. 5 vols. B & N Imports o.p. An overview of French literature, with each period covered by a British authority.

Gay, Peter. *The Party of Humanity: Essays in French Enlightenment.* Norton 1971 repr. of 1964 ed. o.p. A major work on the eighteenth century by an outstanding contemporary historian.

Genette, Gerard. *Figures of Literary Discourse.* Col. U. Pr. 1984 $50.00. ISBN 0-231-04984-6

______. *Narrative Discourse: An Essay in Method.* Trans. by Jane E. Lewin. Cornell Univ. Pr. 1979 $36.95. ISBN 0-8014-1099-1. This book and *Figures of Literary Discourse* are widely read works by a leading French practitioner of the structuralist approach to literature.

Goldmann, Lucien. *Toward a Sociology of the Novel.* Routledge Chapman & Hall 1986 $9.95. ISBN 0-422-76350-0. Collected essays on the novel by a noted Marxist critic.

Harvey, Paul, and Janet E. Heseltine, eds. *The Oxford Companion to French Literature.* OUP 1959 $55.00. ISBN 0-19-866104-5. The most comprehensive one-volume work on French literature.

Hollier, Denis, ed. *A New History of French Literature.* HUP 1989 $49.95. ISBN 0-674-61565-4. A massive and immensely rich collection of essays by scholars from both sides of the Atlantic.

James, Henry. *French Poets and Novelists.* Gordon Pr. 1972 $59.95. ISBN 0-8490-0198-6

Klein, Leonard S. *Encyclopedia of World Literature in the Twentieth Century.* 5 vols. Continuum 1982 $100.00 ea. ISBN 0-8044-3135-3. Contains articles on French and Francophone literatures as well as entries on individual authors and movements.

Kristeva, Julia. *Tales of Love.* Trans. by Leon S. Roudiez. Col. U. Pr. 1989 $16.00. ISBN 0-231-06025-4. A wide-ranging psychoanalytic study including discussions of many French literary texts.

Lancaster, H. Carrington. *A History of French Dramatic Literature in the Seventeenth Century.* 9 vols. Gordian 1966 repr. of 1942 ed. $400.00. ISBN 0-87752-060-7. The major source work on the French theater of the period.

Leupin, Alexandre. *Barbarolexis: Medieval Writing and Sexuality.* Trans. by Kate M. Cooper. HUP 1989 $35.00. ISBN 0-674-06170-5. Good discussions of many masterworks of French medieval literature.

Levin, Harry. *The Gates of Horn: A Study of Five French Realists.* OUP 1986 repr. of 1963 ed. $13.95. ISBN 0-19-500727-1. A rich overview of works by Stendhal, Balzac, Flaubert, Zola, and Proust.

Miller, Nancy K. *Subject to Change: Women's Writing—Feminist Reading.* Col. U. Pr. 1989 $41.00. ISBN 0-231-06660-0. Theoretical reflections on the relationship of feminist criticism and literary tradition.

Nadeau, Maurice. *A History of Surrealism.* Trans. by Richard Howard. HUP 1989 $14.95. ISBN 0-674-40345-2. The origin and history of the surrealist school in literature.

Picon, Gaëtan. *Contemporary French Literature: 1945 and After.* Trans. by Kelvin W. Scott and Graham D. Martin. Continuum 1974 $11.50. ISBN 0-8044-3255-4. "A concise and clear presentation of major trends and authors since 1945" (Douglas Alden, *A Critical Bibliography of French Literature*).

Poulet, Georges. *Studies in Human Time*. Trans. by Elliott Coleman. Greenwood 1979 repr. of 1956 ed. $52.50. ISBN 0-8371-9348-6. Interpretations of French writers from Montaigne to Proust as they are related to the problem of time.

Reid, Joyce M. H., ed. *The Concise Oxford Dictionary of French Literature*. OUP 1985 $29.95. ISBN 0-19-281200-9. Useful for rapid bio-bibliographic information.

Rex, Walter E. *The Attraction of the Contrary: Essays on the Literature of the French Enlightenment*. Cambridge U. Pr. 1987 $64.95. ISBN 0-521-33386-5. An articulate and subtle study linking literary and philosophical issues.

Robbe-Grillet, Alain. *For a New Novel*. Trans. by Richard Howard. Northwestern U. Pr. 1989 $9.95. ISBN 0-8101-0821-6. Critical essays by a leading practitioner of the new novel.

Sarraute, Nathalie. *The Age of Suspicion*. Trans. by Maria Jolas. Braziller 1990 $7.95. ISBN 0-8076-1253-7. Critical essays by a leading practitioner of the new novel.

Stambolian, George, and Elaine Marks, eds. *Homosexualities and French Literature*. Cornell Univ. Pr. 1990 repr. of 1979 ed. $14.95. ISBN 0-8014-9766-3. An important collection of essays which challenge many traditional assumptions about literature and sexuality.

Wilson, Edmund. *Axel's Castle: A Study in the Imaginative Literature of 1870–1930*. Norton 1984 repr. of 1931 ed. $9.95. ISBN 0-393-30194-X. On symbolist writers, Valéry, Proust, Rimbaud, and others. Important and illuminating although some of the author's assumptions have been questioned.

COLLECTIONS

Auster, Paul, ed. *The Random House Book of Twentieth-Century Poetry*. Random 1984 $19.95. ISBN 0-394-71748-1. A beautifully produced and very authoritative collection.

Chiari, Joseph. *Contemporary French Poetry. Essay Index Repr. Ser.* Ayer repr. of 1952 ed. $15.00. ISBN 0-8369-0301-3. Major French poets of the first half of the twentieth century.

Gavronsky, Serge. *Poems and Texts: An Anthology of French Poems*. October 1969 $10.00. ISBN 0-8079-0150-4. Anthology and introduction to six contemporary French poets: Ponge, Frénaud, Bonnefoy, du Bouchet, Roche, and Pleynet.

Giese, Frank S., and Warren F. Wilder, eds. *French Lyric Poetry: An Anthology*. Odyssey Pr. 1965 $7.95. ISBN 0-672-63038-9

Hartley, Anthony, ed. *Penguin Book of French Verse. Penguin Poets Ser.* Viking Penguin 1975 o.p. Includes useful prose translations.

Stanton, Domna, ed. *The Defiant Muse: French Feminist Poems From the Middle Ages to the Present*. Feminist Pr. 1986 $35.00. ISBN 0-935312-46-3. An important collection of a frequently overlooked body of poetry.

THEATER

Cohn R. *From Desire to Godot: Pocket Theater of Postwar Paris*. U. CA Pr. 1987 $32.50. ISBN 0-520-05825-9. A good general overview of French theater in the postwar era.

Esslin, Martin. *The Theatre of the Absurd*. Overlook Pr. rev. ed. 1973 repr. of 1961 ed. $35.00. ISBN 0-87951-005-6. An important guide to the post–World War II theater of the absurd in France and elsewhere.

Grossvogel, David I.. *Twentieth-Century French Drama*. Gordian 1966 repr. of 1961 ed. $50.00. ISBN 0-87752-048-8. A remarkably comprehensive account, with analyses of the best plays of the twentieth century, including most of those by Adamov, Anouilh, Apollinaire, Beckett, Claudel, Cocteau, Giraudoux, Ionesco, Jarry, and Sartre.

Guicharnaud, Jacques, and June Guicharnaud. *Modern French Theatre: From Giraudoux to Genet*. Bks. Demand repr. of 1967 ed. $103.30. ISBN 0-8357-8226-3. An extremely useful guide to the post-World War II theater in France. Includes annotated lists of directors, producers, and performances as well as a bibliography of critical works.

Pronko, Leonard C. *Avant Garde: The Experimental Theater in France.* Greenwood 1978 repr. of 1962 ed. $38.50. ISBN 0-313-20096-3. Excellent analyses of plays by Beckett, Genet, Ionesco, Schéhadé, and others. Good bibliography.

Rodwell, Graham. *French Drama of the Revolutionary Years.* Routledge 1990 $59.95. ISBN 0-415-00808-5. Collection of important but rarely studied works of considerable influence and political importance.

CHRONOLOGY OF AUTHORS AND WORKS

The Song of Roland. 11th century
Tristan and Iseult. c.1160–c.1170
Chrétien de Troyes. c.12th century
Aucassin and Nicolette. 13th century
Romance of the Rose. 13th century
Villon, François. 1431–1465?
Navarre, Marguerite de. 1492–1549
Rabelais, François. 1494–1553?
Ronsard, Pierre de. 1524–1585
Montaigne, Michel Eyquem de. 1533–1592
Corneille, Pierre. 1606–1684
La Rochefoucauld, François, Duc. de. 1613–1680
La Fontaine, Jean de. 1621–1695
Molière. 1622–1673
Sévigné, Mme de. 1626–1696
La Fayette, Marie M. de la Verge, Comtesse de. 1634–1693
Racine, Jean. 1639–1699
Marivaux, Pierre de. 1688–1763
Voltaire. 1694–1778
Diderot, Denis. 1713–1784
Beaumarchais, Pierre A. C. de. 1732–1799
Sade, Comte de. 1740–1814
Laclos, Pierre A. F. C. de. 1741–1803
Staël, Mme de. 1766–1817
Chateaubriand, Francois Rene, Vicomte de. 1768–1848
Stendhal. 1783–1842
Balzac, Honoré de. 1799–1850
Dumas, Alexandre (père). 1802–1870
Hugo, Victor. 1802–1885
Sand, George. 1804–1876
Baudelaire, Charles. 1821–1867
Flaubert, Gustave. 1821–1880
Dumas, Alexandre (fils). 1824–1895
Zola, Émile. 1840–1902
Mallarmé, Stéphane. 1842–1898
France, Anatole. 1844–1924
Verlaine, Paul. 1844–1896
Maupassant, Guy de. 1850–1893
Rimbaud, Arthur. 1854–1891
Rolland, Romain. 1866–1944
Claudel, Paul. 1868–1955
Gide, André. 1869–1951
Proust, Marcel. 1871–1922
Valéry, Paul. 1871–1945
Colette. 1873–1954
Apollinaire, Guillaume. 1880–1918
Giraudoux, Jean. 1882–1944
Mauriac, François. 1885–1970
Romains, Jules. 1885–1972
Perse, Saint-John. 1887–1975
Bernanos, Georges. 1888–1948
Cocteau, Jean. 1889–1963
Celine, Louis-Ferdinand. 1894–1961
Éluard, Paul. 1895–1952
Giono, Jean. 1895–1970
Artaud, Antonin. 1896–1948
Breton, André. 1896–1966
Bataille, Georges. 1897–1962
Ponge, Francis. 1899–1988
Green, Julien. 1900–
Prévert, Jacques. 1900–1977
Saint-Exupéry, Antoine de. 1900–1944
Malraux, André. 1901–1976
Aymé, Marcel. 1902–1967
Sarraute, Nathalie. 1902–
Queneau, Raymond. 1903–1976
Radiquet, Raymond. 1903–1923
Yourcenar, Marguerite. 1903–
Sartre, Jean-Paul. 1905–1980
Beckett, Samuel. 1906–1989
Char, René. 1907–1988
Leduc, Violette. 1907–1971
Beauvoir, Simone de. 1908–1986
Simenon, Georges. 1909–1989
Weil, Simone. 1909–1943
Anouilh, Jean. 1910–
Genet, Jean. 1910–1986
Blanchot, Maurice. 1911–
Ionesco, Eugene. 1912–
Camus, Albert. 1913–1960
Simon, Claude. 1913–
Duras, Marguerite. 1914–
Barthes, Roland. 1915–1980

Pinget, Robert. 1919–
Robbe-Grillet, Alain. 1922–
Bonnefoy, Yves. 1923–
Tournier, Michel. 1924–
Butor, Michel. 1926–
Foucault, Michel. 1926–1984
Cixous, Hélène. 1937–

ANOUILH, JEAN. 1910–

While Paris and most of France were under German occupation, the character of Antigone, from Greek legend, was used symbolically in three new French plays. The most striking, played in modern dress, was Anouilh's. It provided a "rallying point for the aspirations of insurgent youth." His is a distinct and highly original talent. He combines the serious with the fantastic and is "less concerned with making innovations than with returning to a tradition." Anouilh himself groups his works as either *pièces roses*, where the good triumph, or *pièces noires*, where the evil are victorious, in the clash between the symbolic characters prevalent in his drama. His usual themes (said *LJ* in its warm review of *Poor Bitos* [1958]) "are the impossibility of attaining what one once had thought was goodness, the corruptibility of human endeavors, and the pitifulness of the pretenses of those who believe themselves to be distinguished." Anouilh was born in Bordeaux, came to Paris when he was very young, began to study law, then worked for a time in an advertising agency. Always interested in the theater, he became secretary to Louis Jouvet, the famous actor-manager, in 1931, and his first play was produced during the following year.

Anouilh's moving dramatization of the trial of Joan of Arc, *The Lark*, was first presented in New York in 1955 as adapted by Lillian Hellman. About *The Waltz of the Toreadors* (1951), the *New York Times* drama critic Brooks Atkinson said, "Although the manner is antic the substance is melancholy. M. Anouilh and Mr. Richardson (who plays the lead) know how to make a vastly entertaining rumpus of blistering ideas." *Time Remembered* (1942), a romantic love story with satiric overtones and undertones, was Anouilh's first Broadway hit. *Becket*, in which Laurence Olivier and Anthony Quinn exchanged the leading roles, was another in 1960. Though one of France's most internationally famous playwrights, Anouilh's popular success in his own country has come late. It was not until 1971 that one of his plays (*Becket*, in a revival) was first produced at the prestigious *Comédie Française*.

Plays by Anouilh

The Lark. 1953. Trans. by Christopher Fry. OUP 1956 $10.95. ISBN 0-19-500393-4. A satire in which corrupt society spoils an innocent young woman.

Becket. 1959. Trans. by Lucienne Hill. Putnam Pub. Group 1960 $7.95. ISBN 0-399-51354-X. A recreation of the murder of Thomas à Becket, the Archbishop of Canterbury, by his friend, Henry II. Confronts the relationship between honor and power.

Book about Anouilh

McIntyre, H. G. *The Theatre of Jean Anouilh*. B & N Imports 1981 $33.00. ISBN 0-389-20182-0. A good general study.

APOLLINAIRE, GUILLAUME (pseud. of Guillaume de Kostrowitski). 1880–1918

Apollinaire is one of the most widely read and influential of modern French poets. Quintessentially modern, his reputation rests principally on two volumes of poems, *Alcools* (1913) and *Calligrammes* (1918), which broke in both form and content with the traditions of nineteenth-century poetry. Apollinaire introduced free verse, eliminated punctuation, and even wrote poems in the form of pictures to express the dynamism of the new twentieth century. According to René Taupin, "He studied his time like an anthropologist eager to detect in customs and costumes what, for lack of a better word, he called *l'esprit nouveau.*"

His real name was that of his mother, of Polish origin, and he was born either in Rome, where he was baptized, or in Monaco, where he was educated at the Lycée Saint-Charles. In Paris, he wrote novels, short stories, and plays as well as poetry and "developed his erudition in different ways, including the editorship of rare books and responsibilities as censor during World War I. He edited for the Bibliothèque des Curieux erotic books of repute and helped to catalogue the [repository of forbidden books in the] . . . Bibliothèque Nationale." He became the friend of great cubists, including PICASSO (see Vol. 3) and Braque and wrote *The Cubist Painters* (1913), which first defined the nature of cubism. He died in the Spanish-flu epidemic of 1918. Since the end of World War II, there has been increased interest in Apollinaire in both France and the United States.

POETRY BY APOLLINAIRE

Alcools. 1913. Trans. by Anne Hyde Greet. U. CA Pr. 1966 $11.95. ISBN 0-520-00029-3

Caligrammes: Poems of Peace and War. 1918. Trans. by Anne Hyde Greet. U. CA Pr. 1991 $14.95. ISBN 0-520-07390-8

NONFICTION BY APOLLINAIRE

Apollinaire on Art: Essays and Reviews 1902–1918. Trans. by Susan Suleiman. Da Capo 1988 repr. of 1972 ed. $13.95. ISBN 0-306-80312-7. Includes some of the first essays to appreciate the importance of avant-garde art in the early twentieth century.

WORK BY APOLLINAIRE

Selected Writings of Apollinaire. Trans. by Roger Shattuck. New Dir. Pr. rev. ed. 1971 $10.95. ISBN 0-8112-0003-5. A wide ranging collection.

BOOKS ABOUT APOLLINAIRE

Bates, Scott. *Guillaume Apollinaire. Twayne's World Authors Ser.* Macmillan 1989 $26.95. ISBN 0-8057-8246-X. Comprehensive overview of Apollinaire's life and works.

Breunig, LeRoy C. *Guillaume Apollinaire.* Col. U. Pr. 1970 $7.50. ISBN 0-231-02995-0

Mathews, Timothy. *Reading Apollinaire: Theories of Poetic Language.* St. Martin 1988 $55.00. ISBN 0-7190-2220-7. Carefully examines the dilemma of Apollinaire: whether his work explores a common ground of human experience or is a hermetic study of the poet's own self.

Shattuck, Roger. *The Banquet Years: The Origins of the Avant-Garde in France, 1885 to World War One. Essay Index Repr. Ser.* Ayer rev. ed. repr. of 1968 ed. $28.00. ISBN 0-8369-2826-1. A fascinating study of the entire cultural and political context within which Apollinaire and his friends flourished.

Steegmuller, Francis. *Apollinaire: Poet among the Painters. Biography Index Repr. Ser.* Ayer repr. of 1963 ed. $25.00. ISBN 0-8369-8110-3. Discusses Apollinaire's relationship to the visual arts; written by a distinguished scholar and translator.

ARTAUD, ANTONIN. 1896–1948

An early associate of the surrealists, Artaud broke with them to form the "theater of cruelty" in 1932. His goal, set forth in his long essay *The Theater and Its Double* (1938), was to replace the contemporary theater, with its emphasis on psychology, by a theater of myth that would reintroduce the sacred into modern life. Experiments with drugs, coupled with a long history of psychiatric trouble, led to Artaud's commitment to a mental hospital for nine years. He remains a contemporary heir to the nineteenth-century antiestablishment poets and an inspiration to contemporary theoreticians of the theater.

Works by Artaud

Anthology. Ed. Jack Hirschmann. City Lights 1965 $10.95. ISBN 0-87286-000-0. A good introductory collection.

Artaud: Four Texts. Trans. by Clayton Eshelman. Panjandrum 1982 $16.95. ISBN 0-915572-57-5

Collected Works. 6 vols. Trans. by Alastair Hamilton and Victor Corti. Riverrun NY 1993. Vol. 1 $11.95. ISBN 0-7145-0170-0. Vol. 2 $11.95. ISBN 0-7145-0172-7. Vol. 3 $11.95. ISBN 0-7145-0779-2. Vol. 4 $11.95. ISBN 0-7145-0623-0. Vol. 5 $18.95. ISBN 0-7145-3660-1. Vol. 6 $18.95. ISBN 0-7145-3656-3

The Theater and Its Double. Trans. by Mary C. Richards. Grove Pr. $9.95. ISBN 0-8021-5030-6

Books about Artaud

Esslin, Martin. *Antonin Artaud.* Riverrun NY 1992 $8.95. ISBN 0-7145-4204-0. An excellent general study.

Knapp, Bettina L. *Antonin Artaud: Man of Vision.* Swallow 1980 $12.95. ISBN 0-8040-0809-4. A psychologically oriented study.

Sellin, Eric. *Dramatic Concepts of Antonin Artaud.* U. Ch. Pr. 1975 o.p. Helps place Artaud in the history of dramatic theory.

AUCASSIN AND NICOLETTE. 13th century (first half)

The charming romance of Aucassin and Nicolette depicts the love between a French count and a Saracen slave girl. Told with touches of tenderness, irony, and realism, it was written in the dialect of Picardy by an unknown author. Its form is that of a *chante-fable,* alternating passages of heptasyllabic verse and longer passages of prose. The work is one of the best medieval love romances.

Aucassin and Nicolette with other Romances. Trans. and ed. by Eugene Mason. AMS Pr. repr. of 1931 ed. $37.50. ISBN 0-404-07774-9

AYMÉ, MARCEL. 1902–1967

Aymé was one of France's leading humorous writers. He was "insurance broker, bricklayer, journalist, salesman," then—after 1938—a prolific author. His works are imbued with a sense of the ridiculous, counterbalanced by a satirical eye directed toward all forms of snobbishness or pretension. His early works were novels, such as *The Green Mare* (1933), but during World War II he broadened his range to include the essay and theater. Aymé's plays have been hits on the Parisian stage since 1945. His last, *La Convention Belzébir* (1967), in which permits to kill are sold for large sums, satirizes the absurdities of our world.

Novels by Aymé

The Green Mare. 1933. Trans. by Norman Denny. Atheneum 1963 o.p.

Wonderful Farm. HarpC 1951 o.p.

Book about Aymé

Brodin, Dorothy. *Marcel Aymé.* Col. U. Pr. 1968 o.p.

BALZAC, HONORÉ DE. 1799–1850

Balzac is often said to be the greatest of French novelists. His greatness is not only in the richness of his work, which is comparable to that of Dickens, but also in its extent. Even though he died at the age of 51, he left, among other writings, 92 novels (out of more than 100 he had projected), which taken together form what he called *The Human Comedy*. His purpose in this gigantic undertaking, the title of which recalls DANTE's *Divine Comedy*, was to make an inventory of all the vices and virtues of French society in the first half of the nineteenth century and to write a history of the manners and customs of the period. *The Human Comedy* is divided into three parts: Studies of Manners, Philosophic Studies, and Analytic Studies. Studies of Manners is subdivided into Scenes of Private Life, of Provincial Life, of Parisian Life, of Country Life, of Political Life, and of Military Life. It is one of the most ambitious literary plans ever conceived or accomplished; the work contains 2,000 distinctly drawn characters. Balzac was a master observer of social and political mores, as well as a shrewd analyst of economic conditions. A royalist and a Catholic, he deplored both the decadence of the aristocracy and the cynical economic opportunism that he believed characterized the rising middle class in the years after Napoleon's fall. Yet his understanding of society and of human nature was so acute that he was the favorite novelist of KARL MARX (see Vols. 3 and 4), who read his works constantly.

Together, the novels of *The Human Comedy* form a vast fresco, yet each volume is an accessible, self-contained work of art. Among the best known of the novels are *Père Goriot* (*Old Goriot*) (1834), *Cousin Bette* (1846), and *Eugénie Grandet* (1833). Three stories in the Philosophic Studies form an exceptional psychological trilogy: *La Peau de Chagrin* (*The Wild Ass's Skin*) (1831), *Louis Lambert* (1832), and *Séraphita* (1835). *Droll Stories* (1832), written earlier in the vein of RABELAIS, contains 30 stories and does not belong to *The Human Comedy*. "Balzac," wrote ANDRÉ MAUROIS, "was by turns a saint, a criminal, an honest judge, a corrupt judge, a minister, a fop, a harlot, a duchess and always a genius."

NOVELS BY BALZAC

Cousin Bette. 1846. OUP 1992 $4.95. ISBN 0-19-282606-9

Cousin Pons. 1845. Trans. by Herbert J. Hunt. *Penguin Class. Ser.* Viking Penguin 1978 $8.95. ISBN 0-14-044205-7. The story of an eccentric collector and his passion for the objects he loves.

Eugénie Grandet. 1933. Trans. by Sylvia Raphael. OUP 1991 $5.95. ISBN 0-19-282605-0. A story of avarice and oppression in a provincial family.

The Lily of the Valley. 1835. Trans. by May Tomlinson. Carroll & Graf 1989 $9.95. ISBN 0-88184-482-9. A lyrical tale of doomed love between a younger man and an older woman. Set in Balzac's native Touraine.

Lost Illusions. 1837–43. Trans. by Herbert J. Hunt. *Penguin Class. Ser.* Viking Penguin 1976 $7.95. ISBN 0-14-044251-0. The education of a provincial youth who goes to Paris to seek his fortune.

Louis Lambert. 1832. Fr. & Eur. 1968 $10.95. ISBN 0-686-53889-7

Murky Business. 1841. *Penguin Class. Ser.* 1978 $6.95. ISBN 0-14-044271-5

Old Goriot. 1834. Trans. by Marion A. Crawford. Knopf $4.95. ISBN 0-679-40535-6. Often considered Balzac's masterpiece. A tale of paternal love and filial ingratitude in corrupt Parisian society.

Séraphita. 1835. Hippocrene Bks. 1990 $7.95. ISBN 0-87052-612-X

Ursule Mirouet. 1841. Trans. by Donald Adamson. *Penguin Class Ser.* Viking Penguin 1976 $5.95. ISBN 0-14-044316-5. A buried treasure and the ruin of a provincial family after the fall of Napoleon.

The Wild Ass's Skin. 1831. Trans. by Herbert J. Hunt. *Penguin Class. Ser.* Viking Penguin 1977 $6.95. ISBN 0-14-044330-4. An ambitious young man sells his soul for power and pleasure.

Works by Balzac

Balzac: Selected Short Stories. Trans. and ed. by Sylvia Raphael. *Penguin Class. Ser.* Viking Penguin 1977 $6.95. ISBN 0-14-044325-8. Showcases a frequently unappreciated aspect of Balzac's genius—his gift for economy.

Works: With Introduction by George Saintsbury. 10 vols. *Short Story Index Repr. Ser.* Ayer repr. of 1901 ed. $550.00. ISBN 0-8369-3791-0. Valuable for its introduction by a noted British critic.

Books about Balzac

Barthes, Roland. *S–Z.* Trans. by Richard Miller. Fr. & Eur. 1970 $29.95. ISBN 0-686-53945-1. A groundbreaking structuralist analysis. A seminal work of criticism.

Beizer, Janet. *Family Plots: Balzac's Narrative Generation.* Yale U. Pr. 1986 $27.50. ISBN 0-300-03586-1. A psychological study of the relationship between family interactions and narrative form.

Brooks, Peter. *The Melodramatic Imagination: Balzac, Henry James, Melodrama and the Mode of Excess.* Col. U. Pr. 1984 repr. of 1976 ed. $46.50. ISBN 0-231-06006-8. An important analysis of Balzac; realism in light of nineteenth-century melodrama.

Dargan, E. Preston, and Bernard Weinberg. *The Evolution of Balzac's "Comédie Humaine."* Cooper Sq. 1973 repr. of 1942 ed. $33.50. ISBN 0-8154-0452-2

Kanes, Martin. *Critical Essays on Honoré de Balzac.* G.K. Hall 1990 $40.00. ISBN 0-8161-8845-9. Volume of critical essays particularly commendable not only for its scholarly selection of quality texts, but also for the choice of vital and genuinely human literary vignettes.

Maurois, André. *Prometheus: The Life of Balzac.* Carroll & Graf 1983 $11.95. ISBN 0-88184-023-8. A highly readable biography by a well-known French author.

Pasco, Allan H. *Balzacian Montage: Configuring the Comédie Humaine.* U. of Toronto Pr. 1991 $45.00. ISBN 0-8020-2776-8. Argues that Balzac's works are not a collage of different pieces, but a montage to be considered as a whole.

Stowe, William W. *Balzac, James and the Realistic Novel.* Princeton U. Pr. 1986 $32.50. ISBN 0-691-06567-5. Sees Balzac as a precursor of the realist tradition.

Taine, Hippolyte A. *Balzac: A Critical Study.* Haskell 1973 repr. of 1906 ed. $75.00. ISBN 0-8383-1670-0. By a nineteenth-century philosopher. Interesting if curious.

BARTHES, ROLAND. 1915–1980

The writing of Roland Barthes, one of the most influential French critics of his generation, first appeared in the newspaper *Combat.* He taught at universities in Bucharest and Alexandria and subsequently joined the Centre National de Recherche Scientifique in Paris where he did research on symbols and social signs. In 1962 he was named director of studies at the École des Hautes Études and in 1976 to a chair at the Collège de France. His importance as a critic was hailed with the publication in 1953 of his *Le Degré zéro de l'Écriture,* and he became one of the most important of the French New Critics with a strong influence on the *Tel Quel* group. He was a prolific writer, and his other notable works include *Mythologies*—a work in which he applied the principles of structuralism to everyday phenomena—*Eléments de Sémiologie, Système de la Mode, Essais Critiques, Sur Racine, S-Z,* and *Le Plaisir du Texte.* He avoided literary criticism that involved reduction of the meaning of a work to any single statement. Barthes's criticism was wide ranging and cannot be reduced to a single system or method. He was interested not only in structuralist and semiotic approaches to literature, but also in literature and social criticism, psychoanalysis, and theories of "text production." His untimely death in a freak accident—he was run over in a Parisian crosswalk—came when he was at the height of his powers and international influence.

Nonfiction by Barthes

Camera Lucida. 1980. Trans. by Richard Howard. FS&G 1982 $19.95. ISBN 0-374-52134-4. On the relationship between photography, memory, and death.

Critical Essays. 1964. Trans. by Richard Howard. Northwestern U. Pr. 1972 $12.95. ISBN 0-8101-0589-6. Contains many of Barthes's most concise theoretical statements, along with studies of Voltaire, Flaubert, and others.

The Grain of the Voice: Interviews, 1962–1980. 1981. Trans. by Linda Coverdale. U. CA Pr. 1991 $12.95. ISBN 0-520-07737-5. An excellent starting point. Barthes is at his most lucid and fascinating in his interviews.

Michelet. 1954. Trans. by Richard Howard. Hill & Wang 1987 $18.95. ISBN 0-8090-6926-1. A study of the literary dimension of the great historian.

Mythologies. Peter Smith 1983 $21.00. ISBN 0-8446-5982-7. A fascinating and influential application of structuralist literary analysis to phenomena of everyday life.

New Critical Essays. Trans. by Richard Howard. U. CA Pr. 1990 $7.95. ISBN 0-520-07178-6. Analysis of both literary and cultural topics.

The Rustle of Language. 1984. Trans. by Richard Howard. U. CA Pr. 1989 $10.95. ISBN 0-520-06629-4. A posthumous collection of essays on literary and cultural subjects.

Sade-Fourier-Loyola. Trans. by Richard Miller. U. CA Pr. 1989 $9.95. ISBN 0-520-06628-6. Semiological analysis of three marginal authors; helped spark interest in Sade.

Books about Barthes

Culler, Jonathan. *Roland Barthes.* OUP 1983 $25.00. ISBN 0-19-520420-4. An excellent general study.

Lavers, Annette. *Roland Barthes: Structuralism and After.* HUP 1982 $30.50. ISBN 0-674-77721-2

Lombardo, Patrizia. *The Three Paradoxes of Roland Barthes.* Trans. by Jessica Levine. U. of Ga. Pr. 1990 $25.00. ISBN 0-8203-1139-1. By a former student of Barthes. Especially good on his understanding of history.

Thody, Philip. *Roland Barthes: A Conservative Estimate.* U. Ch. Pr. 1984 $7.95. ISBN 0-226-79513-6

BATAILLE, GEORGES. 1897–1962

A central figure in the avant-garde of the World War II era, Bataille sought to outline a literature and philosophy of "transgression" that would define human activity, not through idealism and the realm of the spiritual, but through the material world in its most "debased" forms—violence, excrement, detritus. An avid student of the philosophers Nietzsche (see Vol. 4) and Hegel (see Vol. 4), Bataille earned his living by working at the Bibliothèque Nationale while producing an array of philosophical essays (*The Accursed Share*) (1949), literary meditations (*Literature and Evil*) (1957), and semipornographic novels (*Story of the Eye*) (1928).

Nonfiction by Bataille

The Accursed Share. 1949. 2 vols. Trans. by Robert Hurley. Zone Bks. 1991 $29.95. ISBN 0-942299-20-5. Bataille's philosophical masterpiece on the "economy" of human activity.

Erotism: Death and Sensuality. 1957. Trans. by Mary Dalwood. City Lights repr. of 1986 ed. $12.95. ISBN 0-87286-190-2. A meditation on the erotic through discussions of art, anthropology, and psychology.

Literature and Evil. 1957. Trans. by Alastair Hamilton. M. Boyars Pubs. 1986 $15.00. ISBN 0-7145-0345-2. Studies of Kafka, Brontë, Sade, Blake, and others.

Visions of Excess: Selected Writings 1927–1939. Trans. and ed. by Allan Stoekl. U. of Minn. Pr. 1985 $39.95. ISBN 0-8166-1280-3. A fine selection of Bataille's work, with useful notes. A good place to begin.

Novels by Bataille

L'Abbé C. 1951. Trans. by Philip A. Facey. M. Boyars Pubs. 1988 $9.95. ISBN 0-7145-2848-X. A philosophical novel.

Story of the Eye. Trans. by Joachim Neugroschal. City Lights repr. of 1982 ed. $7.95. ISBN 0-87286-209-7

Book about Bataille

Hollier, Denis. *Against Architecture: The Writings of Georges Bataille.* Trans. by Betsy Wing. MIT Pr. 1992 $14.95. ISBN 0-262-58113-2. An important general study of all aspects of Bataille's work.

BAUDELAIRE, CHARLES. 1821–1867

Baudelaire is probably the most influential European poet of the last two centuries. Born to a bourgeois family, he lived for a while the modish life of a literary dandy on an inheritance from his father, reluctantly joining the "Paris *bohème*" when his fortune ran dry. His literary output was slim, a volume of poems, *Les Fleurs du Mal* (*Flowers of Evil*) (1857); *Paris Spleen* (1869); his prose poems; scattered articles on literature, art and music; some notebooks; and some translations from English. He translated Poe's (see Vol. 1) tales into French, and that writer's love of horror and mystery had a strong influence on Baudelaire's prose writings. Despite his limited output, he is "probably the poet most widely read all over the world" (Enid Starkie).

Baudelaire's poetry is based upon a paradox. He cultivated the image of the dissolute dandy, at odds with society and its morals. His poems celebrate lust, prostitution, drunkenness—decay and decadence in all of its forms. Indeed, *Flowers of Evil* was even tried for obscenity in 1857 and could not be published until three of its most scandalous poems were removed. Yet Baudelaire's poems are characterised by an absolute formal and rhetorical perfection. Even as he praises the sordid and the scandalous, Baudelaire's poetry celebrates the magical power of poetry to transform the world by creating new types of images and sensations. Enid Starkie has said, "At the distance of a century [it is] as if he had written for the present generation with a knowledge of its problems and interests." In addition to his influence as a poet, Baudelaire was one of the first critics to extol artists like Courbet, Corot, and Manet (see Vol. 3) at a time when they were objects of derision.

Poetry by Baudelaire

Les Fleurs du Mal. 1857. Trans. by Richard Howard. Godine 1983 $16.95. ISBN 0-87923-462-8

The Flowers of Evil. Trans. by Edna St. Vincent Millay. New Dir. Pr. rev. ed. 1989 $16.95. ISBN 0-8112-1117-7. A remarkable translation by a distinguished American poet.

Paris Spleen. 1869. Trans. by Louise Varèse. New Dir. Pr. 1970 $5.95. ISBN 0-8112-0007-8

The Parisian Prowler: Le Spleen de Paris. Petits Poèmes en Prose. Trans. by Edward K. Kaplan. U. Ga. Pr. 1990 $19.95. ISBN 0-8203-1162-3. Short prose pieces that serve as complements to—and artistic equals of—the skewed everyday reality of Baudelaire's poems.

The Prose Poems and La Fanfarlo. Trans. by Rosemary Lloyd. OUP 1991 $5.95. ISBN 0-19-282703-0

Selected Poems. Trans. by Geoffrey Wagner. Intro. by Enid Starkie. Grove Pr. 1974 repr. of 1947 ed. $4.95. ISBN 0-8021-5126-4. Bilingual edition.

NONFICTION BY BAUDELAIRE

Baudelaire As a Literary Critic. Trans. by Lois B. Hyslop and Francis E. Hyslop, Jr. Pa. St. U. Pr. 1964 $35.00. ISBN 0-271-73051-X. Reviews and articles on major writers of the nineteenth century.

Baudelaire on Poe: Critical Papers. Trans. by Lois B. Hyslop and Francis E. Hyslop, Jr. Pa. St. U. Pr. 1964 $35.00. ISBN 0-271-73051-X

Intimate Journals. Trans. by Christopher Isherwood. Hyperion Conn. 1985 repr. of 1930 ed. $21.00. ISBN 0-88355-532-8. Introduction by T. S. Eliot.

Letters of Charles Baudelaire to His Mother, 1833–1866. Ed. by Arthur Symons. Ayer repr. of 1927 ed. $22.00. ISBN 0-405-08242-8. A fascinating correspondence between the poet and the most important woman in his life.

The Mirror of Art, Critical Studies. Ed. by Jonathan Mayne. AMS Pr. repr. of 1955 ed. $32.50. ISBN 0-404-16303-3

The Painter of Modern Life and Other Essays. Trans. by Jonathan Mayne. Da Capo 1986 $12.95. ISBN 0-306-80279-1. Includes brilliant and influential discussions of Manet and others.

Selected Letters of Charles Baudelaire: The Conquest of Solitude. Trans. by Rosemary Lloyd. U. Ch. Pr. 1986 $24.95. ISBN 0-226-03928-5. Sensitive translation by a Baudelaire scholar.

Selected Writings on Art and Artists. Trans. by P. E. Charvet. Cambridge U. Pr. 1981 $27.95. ISBN 0-521-28287-X

BOOKS ABOUT BAUDELAIRE

Benjamin, Walter. *Baudelaire: Lyric Poet in the Age of High Capitalism.* Verso 1982 o.p. A fascinating Marxist interpretation by the brilliant German critic. Links Baudelaire's poetry to the rise of the modern city space.

Bersani, Leo. *Baudelaire and Freud.* U. CA Pr. 1978 $32.50. ISBN 0-520-03402-3. An insightful psychological study.

Brombert, Victor. *The Hidden Reader: Stendhal, Balzac, Hugo, Baudelaire, Flaubert.* HUP 1988 $29.95. ISBN 0-674-39012-1. Locates Baudelaire's poetry in the history of new practices of interpretation arising during the nineteenth century.

Burton, Richard D. *Baudelaire in 1859: A Study in the Sources of Poetic Creativity.* Cambridge U. Pr. 1988 $54.95. ISBN 0-521-34577-4

Lloyd, Rosemary. *Baudelaire's Literary Criticism.* Cambridge U. Pr. 1981 $69.95. ISBN 0-521-23552-9

Poulet, Georges. *Exploding Poetry: Baudelaire-Rimbaud.* Trans. by Françoise Meltzer. U. Ch. Pr. 1984 $16.95. ISBN 0-226-67650-1. An insightful phenomenological analysis.

Sartre, Jean-Paul. *Baudelaire.* Trans. by Martin Turnell. New Dir. Pr. 1950 $8.95. ISBN 0-8112-0189-9. Perhaps more interesting for what it says about its famous author than for what it says about Baudelaire.

Starkie, Enid. *Baudelaire.* Paragon Hse. 1988 repr. of 1958 ed. $12.95. ISBN 1-55778-003-X. A good biographical study.

Swinburne, Algernon C. *Les Fleurs du Mal and Other Studies.* Ed. by Edmund Gosse. AMS Pr. repr. of 1913 ed. $22.50. ISBN 0-404-16347-5. Interesting for what it says about Swinburne, as well as for its analysis of Baudelaire.

Turnell, Martin. *Baudelaire: A Study of His Poetry.* New Dir. Pr. 1972 o.p.

BEAUMARCHAIS, PIERRE-AUGUSTIN CARON DE. 1732–1799

The son of a clockmaker, Beaumarchais pursued a number of trades before finding his vocation in the theater. His two masterpieces, *The Barber of Seville* (1775) and *The Marriage of Figaro* (1785), rejuvenated the somewhat dreary, sentimental theater of the time by introducing witty verbal exchanges, sharply drawn characters, and strong satire. The popularity of the two plays led to their being recast in operatic form by ROSSINI (see Vol. 3) and MOZART (see Vol. 3), respectively. In the character of Figaro, the sly playful servant who turns social hierarchy upside down, Beaumarchais gave expression to the new social transformations signaled by the French and American Revolutions.

PLAYS BY BEAUMARCHAIS

The Barber of Seville and The Marriage of Figaro. Trans. by John Wood. Viking Penguin 1964 $5.95. ISBN 0-14-044133-6

BOOK ABOUT BEAUMARCHAIS

Sungolowsky, Joseph. *Beaumarchais. Twayne's World Authors Ser.* G. K. Hall 1974 o.p. A comprehensive overview of Beaumarchais's life and works.

BEAUVOIR, SIMONE DE. 1908–1986

Simone de Beauvoir was among the leading French intellectuals following World War II. She grew up in Paris, received her doctorate in philosophy from the Sorbonne, and taught in *lycées* in Marseilles, Rouen, and Paris until 1943, after which she turned to literature. From her earliest student days she was associated with the writer and philosopher JEAN-PAUL SARTRE (see also Vol. 4). She wrote novels, essays, and plays. Her most important novels include *Le Sang des Autres* (*The Blood of Others*) (1944), *L'Invitée* (*She Came to Stay*) (1943), and *Les Mandarins* (1954). The last novel is a fictional recreation of life in French intellectual circles during the 1940s. Her two-volume essay *The Second Sex* (1949) is one of the leading feminist documents of our time.

Many readers consider her masterpiece to be her multi-volume memoirs. Her *Memoirs of a Dutiful Daughter* (1958) is a fascinating account of her transformation from an obedient middle-class girl to a fiercely independent, nonconformist opponent of bourgeois morality, hypocritical idealism, and second-class citizenship for women. Later volumes in the series include *The Prime of Life* (1960), *Force of Circumstance* (1963), *A Very Easy Death* (1964), and *All Said and Done* (1972).

NONFICTION BY BEAUVOIR

Adieux: A Farewell to Sartre. 1984. Trans. by Patrick O'Brian. Pantheon 1985 $8.95. ISBN 0-394-72898-X. Her poignant goodbye to her longtime companion.

Brigitte Bardot and the Lolita Syndrome. 1960. Ayer 1972 repr. of 1960 ed. $9.50. ISBN 0-405-03912-3

The Ethics of Ambiguity. 1947. Carol Pub. Group 1962 $4.95. ISBN 0-8065-0160-X. Influential moral treatise.

Memoirs of a Dutiful Daughter. 1958. HarpC 1974 repr. of 1959 ed. $12.00. ISBN 0-06-090351-1

The Second Sex. 1949. Trans. by H. M. Parshley. Knopf 1953 $40.00. ISBN 0-394-44415-9

A Very Easy Death. 1964. Pantheon 1985 $11.00. ISBN 0-394-72899-8

BOOKS ABOUT BEAUVOIR

Bair, Deirdre. *Simone de Beauvoir: A Biography.* Summit Bks. 1990 $24.95. ISBN 0-671-60681-6. An exhaustive and very readable portrait.

Marks, Elaine. *Critical Essays on Simone de Beauvoir. Critical Essays Ser.* G. K. Hall 1987 $40.00. ISBN 0-8161-8836-X

Moi, Toril. *Feminist Theory and Simone de Beauvoir.* Blackwell Pubs. 1990 $16.95. ISBN 0-631-17323-4. A sophisticated analysis of de Beauvoir's importance for contemporary philosophy and criticism.

Patterson, Yolanda A. *Simone de Beauvoir and the Demystification of Motherhood.* Univ. Rochester Pr. 1989 o.p. A feminist interpretation.

Wenzel, Helene V., ed. *Simone de Beauvoir: Witness to a Century.* Yale U. Pr. 1987 $15.95. ISBN 0-300-03897-6. A good collection of essays covering many aspects of de Beauvoir's career.

Whitmarsh, Anne. *Simone de Beauvoir and the Limits of Commitment.* Cambridge U. Pr. 1981 $49.95. ISBN 0-521-23669-X

BECKETT, SAMUEL. 1906–1989 (Nobel Prize 1969)

Samuel Beckett, who is most widely known in the United States for his play *Waiting for Godot* (1952), was born in Dublin and educated at Trinity College. He lectured in Paris at the École Normale Supérieure and then at Dublin University. He returned to settle in Paris permanently in 1937 and eventually abandoned English for French in his writing. He is the author of a number of novels: *Murphy* (1938), *Molloy* (1951), *Malone Dies* (1951), *Watt* (1953), and *The Unnamable* (1953). Except for the first work, all of the novels were written in French and translated into English by the author. Beckett shares with Sartre (see also Vol. 4) and Camus an "intense sense of the pervasiveness of misery, solitude, paralysis of will, and above all, the horror of nothingness" (*Manchester Guardian*). Beckett's work is pervaded by a sense of the fragility and potential death of both human feeling and language. It is thus perhaps no accident that his last years were occupied by increasingly brief and inaccessible prose sketches such as *Company* (1980). Other plays of Beckett that have won critical acclaim include *Krapp's Last Tape* (1959), *Endgame* (1958), and *Happy Days* (1960).

Novels by Beckett

Molloy. 1951. Trans. by Samuel Beckett and Patrick Bowles. Grove Pr. 1970 $11.95. ISBN 0-8021-5136-1

Malone Dies. 1951. Trans. by Samuel Beckett. Grove Pr. 1956 $9.95. ISBN 0-8021-5117-5

Murphy. 1938. Grove Pr. 1970 $12.50. ISBN 0-8021-1198-X. The adventures of a working-class eccentric who spends most of his time locked in his darkened room.

The Unnamable. 1953. Grove Pr. 1970 $10.00. ISBN 0-8021-1200-5

Plays by Beckett

Endgame. 1958. Ed. by S. E. Gantarski. Grove Pr. 1993 $35.00. ISBN 0-8021-1089-4

Happy Days. 1960. Grove Pr. 1987 $7.95. ISBN 0-8021-3076-3. A woman, buried to the neck in a mound of dirt, considers the meaning of life.

Krapp's Last Tape and Other Dramatic Pieces. Grove Pr. 1960 $7.95. ISBN 0-8021-5134-5

Waiting for Godot. 1952. Grove Pr. 1987 $6.95. ISBN 0-8021-3034-8. Two hobos wait on a barren plain for a mysterious figure who never arrives. Beckett's masterpiece.

Poetry by Beckett

Collected Poems in English and French. Grove Pr. 1977 $10.00. ISBN 0-8021-1187-4. Stark, diminutive works that reveal an unknown side of Beckett.

Works by Beckett

All Strange Away. Riverrun NY 1991 $5.95. ISBN 0-7145-3858-2

I Can't Go On, I'll Go On: A Samuel Beckett Reader. Grove Pr. 1992 $14.95. ISBN 0-8021-3287-1. Collection of works from all periods of Beckett's long career.

Nonfiction by Beckett

An Examination of James Joyce. Haskell 1974 $75.00. ISBN 0-8383-2025-2. An homage to Beckett's mentor and friend during his early days in Paris.

Proust. 1931. Grove Pr. 1957 $10.95. ISBN 0-8021-5025-X. A rare example of Beckett's criticism.

BOOKS ABOUT BECKETT

Bair, Deirdre. *Samuel Beckett*. S & S Trade 1990 $14.95. ISBN 0-671-69173-2. The basic biography.

Bloom, Harold, ed. *Samuel Beckett's Molloy, Malone Dies, The Unnamable. Modern Critical Interpretations Ser.* Chelsea Hse. 1987 o.p. A good collection of essays on this trilogy of novels.

Esslin, Martin. *Meditations: Essays on Brecht, Beckett and the Media*. Grove Pr. 1980 o.p. By a distinguished student of the modern theater.

Hill, Leslie. *Beckett's Fiction: In Different Words*. Cambridge U. Pr. 1990 $47.50. ISBN 0-521-35645-8. Essay that fully integrates Beckett's prose corpus into poststructuralist criticism.

Kalb, Jonathan. *Beckett in Performance*. Cambridge U. Pr. 1989 $44.95. ISBN 0-521-36549-X. Analysis of the theatrical dimension of Beckett's intensely literary work.

Rabinovitz, Rubin. *The Development of Samuel Beckett's Fiction*. U. of Ill Pr. 1984 $24.95. ISBN 0-252-01095-7. An important study of the author's novels.

Trezise, Thomas. *Into the Breach: Samuel Beckett and the Ends of Literature*. Princeton U. Pr. 1990 $27.50. ISBN 0-691-06789-9. A sophisticated deconstructionist study.

BERNANOS, GEORGES. 1888–1948

A Catholic novelist and essayist, Bernanos was preoccupied in his novels with the theme of the struggle between good and evil within saintly individuals. He traced the unknowing submission of his characters, after some early disappointing experience, to the forces of Satan and the subsequent destruction of their moral selves. His first big success, *Under the Sun of Satan* (1926) deals with such themes. His most famous work is *The Diary of a Country Priest* (1936). Both it and *Mouchette* (1937), a short novel, are set in bleak villages, untouched by the twentieth century. Robert Coles has observed, "In different ways [these books] treat of pride and innocence, those two states of mind and soul that struggle within us for command of whatever destiny we may have in this universe. [They] are suffused with spiritual concerns, but the mystery of Christianity, of salvation and damnation, remains almost austerely beyond analysis or even speculation" (*New Republic*). Both works were made into films by Robert Bresson.

NOVEL BY BERNANOS

The Diary of a Country Priest. 1936. Carroll & Graf 1984 $8.95. ISBN 0-88184-013-0

NONFICTION BY BERNANOS

Last Essays. Greenwood 1968 repr. of 1955 ed. $35.00. ISBN 0-8371-0019-4

BOOKS ABOUT BERNANOS

Cooke, John E. *Georges Bernanos: A Study of Christian Commitment*. Humanities 1981 o.p.

O'Sharkey, Eithne M. *The Role of the Priest in the Novels of Georges Bernanos*. Vantage 1983 o.p.

BLANCHOT, MAURICE. 1911–

Blanchot occupies a unique place in contemporary French letters. Virtually nothing is known of the man or his life. Reclusive in the extreme, refusing to give interviews or even be photographed, he has disappeared behind his dense and difficult body of work. Blanchot's "novels," which feature little plot and less characterization, are experiments in the limits of literature, seeking to break down the barrier between philosophical reflection and narrative prose. His influential critical essays, especially *The Space of Literature* (1955), are strongly influenced by the philosophers Heidegger (see Vol. 4) and Nietzsche (see Vol. 4) and have in turn influenced such contemporary thinkers as Derrida (see Vol. 4) and Foucault (see also Vols. 4 and 5). "Literature," writes Blanchot, "is never there already, it is always being recovered or reinvented."

Novels by Blanchot

Death Sentence. 1948. Trans. by Lydia Davis. Station Hill Pr. 1978 $10.00. ISBN 0-930794-05-2. A woman on her deathbed. An unreal fable about the claim of art to overcome mortality.

The Madness of the Day. (La Folie du Jour). 1973. Trans. by Lydia Davis. Station Hill Pr. 1981 $8.50. ISBN 0-930794-39-7. A brief, enigmatic tale.

Nonfiction by Blanchot

The Space of Literature. 1955. Trans. by Ann Smock. U. of Nebr. Pr. 1982 $25.00. ISBN 0-8032-1166-X. A philosphical meditation on the possibilities of literature through considerations of Kafka, Proust, and others.

The Step Not Beyond. 1973. Trans. by Lycette Nelson. State U. NY Pr. 1992 $34.50. ISBN 0-7914-0907-4. A series of aphorisms and philosophical fragments on death.

Books about Blanchot

Foucault, Michel, and Maurice Blanchot. *Foucault–Blanchot: Maurice Blanchot—The Thought from Outside; Michel Foucault As I Imagine Him.* Trans. by Jeffrey Mehlman. Zone Bks. 1988 $22.95. ISBN 0-942299-02-7. Essays on each other by two of the age's major writers.

Shaviro, Steven. *Passion and Excess: Blanchot, Bataille and Literary Theory.* FL St. U. Pr. 1990 $24.95. ISBN 0-8130-0977-4. An important post-structuralist study.

BONNEFOY, YVES. 1923–

The work of Bonnefoy, a poet, critic, and translator, is philosophical in nature and difficult to penetrate. He has written meditations on the themes of the immobility of matter and the power of language. Influenced by such German philosophers as Hegel (see Vol. 4) and Heidegger (see Vol. 4), his poetry reflects a sense of tragic anguish, often through the use of the implied or the understatement. His principal poetic works include *On the Motion and Immobility of Douve* (1953), a philosophical meditation on the value of language, and *Words in Stone* (1965). He has written essays on art history and poetry in *L'Improbable* and *La Seconde Simplicité.* As a translator, he is well known for his renderings of Shakespeare (see Vol. 1) into French: *Hamlet, Julius Caesar, Henry IV,* and *A Winter's Tale.* "Bonnefoy's work reveals a poet who is difficult, who is primarily heir to the Mallarmé tradition, and who ranks with the foremost poets of his generation" (Germaine Brée).

Works by Bonnefoy

The Act and the Place of Poetry: Selected Essays. Trans. by John T. Naughton. U. Ch. Pr. 1989 $26.95. ISBN 0-226-06449-2. Selection of Bonnefoy's essays, a lecture, and an interview.

Early Poems: 1947–1959. Trans. by Galway Kinnell and Richard Perean. Ohio U. Pr. 1990 $29.95. ISBN 0-8214-0966-2. First English-language translation of the second book of poems of one of France's leading poets.

In the Shadow's Light. Trans. by John T. Naughton. U. Ch. Pr. 1990 $24.95. ISBN 0-226-06447-6. Presents poems that are rooted in a particular personal experience.

Mythologies. 2 vols. Trans. by Wendy Doniger. U. Ch. Pr. 1991 $250.00. ISBN 0-226-06453-0. Collection of articles compiled by Bonnefoy on various aspects of some mythologies written by a group of brilliant and philosophically complex French scholars.

Words in Stone: Pierre Écrite. 1959. Trans. by Susanna Lang. U. of Mass. Pr. 1976 $22.50. ISBN 0-87023-203-7

Books about Bonnefoy

Caws, Mary Ann. *The Inner Theatre of Recent French Poetry: Cendrars, Tzara, Peret, Artaud, Bonnefoy.* Princeton U. Pr. 1972 $32.50. ISBN 0-691-06212-9

______. *Yves Bonnefoy. Twayne's World Authors Ser.* G. K. Hall 1984 o.p. A comprehensive overview of Bonnefoy's life and work.

Naughton, John T. *The Poetics of Yves Bonnefoy.* U. Ch. Pr. 1984 $20.00. ISBN 0-318-39964-4

BRETON, ANDRÉ. 1896–1966

At the time of Breton's death, his novel *Nadja* (1928), about a young dreamer in love with a "hallucinated and ethereal heroine . . . his brightest literary jewel . . . was finally reaching beyond the limited circle of friends and coterie disciples . . . to a new generation of youth" (Anna Balakian, *SR*). Breton, dynamic personage, poet, novelist, philosophical essayist, and art critic, was the father—he was often called the "pope"—of surrealism. From World War I to the 1940s, he was at the forefront of the numerous avant-garde activities that centered in Paris. A prolific producer of pamphlets and manifestoes, he also edited two surrealist periodicals. "Automatic writing," defined by Breton in his *Manifestoes of Surrealism* (1924) as a process "by which one strives to express . . . the genuine functioning of the mind in the absence of all control exercised by reason," was his method of creation. Breton's influence on the art and literature of the twentieth century has been enormous. Picasso (see Vol. 3), Derain, Magritte, Giacometti, Cocteau (see also Vol. 3), Éluard, and Gracq are among the many whose work was affected by his thinking. From 1927 to 1933, he was a member of the Communist party, but thereafter he opposed communism.

Poetry by Breton

Mad Love. 1937. Trans. by Mary Ann Caws. U. of Nebr. Pr. 1987 $22.50. ISBN 0-8032-1200-3. A series of prose poems in praise of passion, written to the author's 16-year-old daughter.

Poems of André Breton: A Bilingual Anthology. Trans. by Jean-Pierre Cauvin and Mary Ann Caws. U. of Tex. Pr. 1982 $35.00. ISBN 0-292-76477-4

Novel by Breton

Nadja. 1928. Trans. by Richard Howard. Grove Pr. 1988 $9.95. ISBN 0-8021-5026-8

Nonfiction by Breton

Communicating Vessels. 1932. Trans. by Mary Ann Caws and Geoffrey Hains. U. of Nebr. Pr. 1990 $20.00. ISBN 0-8032-1218-6. Contains Breton's descriptions of his poetic method.

Manifestoes of Surrealism. 1924. Trans. by Richard Seaver and Helen R. Lane. U. of Mich. Pr. 1969 $14.95. ISBN 0-472-06182-8

What Is Surrealism? Selected Writings. Ed. by Franklin Rosemont. *Studies in Comparative Lit.* Anchor Found. 1991 repr. of 1978 ed. $29.95. ISBN 0-913460-59-1. A wide ranging collection.

Books about Breton

Balakian, Anna. *André Breton: Magus of Surrealism.* Hawkshead Bk. 1971 $20.00. ISBN 0-19-501298-4. Treatment of Breton's role as a cultural leader and spokesperson.

Balakian, Anna, and Rudolf E. Kuenzli, eds. *André Breton Today.* Willis Locker & Owens 1989 $19.95. ISBN 0-930279-16-6. Essays by various authors on different aspects of Breton's work.

Caws, Mary Ann. *André Breton. Twayne's World Authors Ser.* G. K. Hall 1971 o.p.

BUTOR, MICHEL. 1926–

Butor's early education was with the Jesuits, and he subsequently received degrees from the Sorbonne in philosophy. His thesis for his *diplôme d'études supérieures* was *Mathematics and the Idea of Necessity.* He has taught in Egypt, England, and Greece as well as in the United States. He is currently a professor of literature at the University of Geneva. Although technically and intellectually challenging, Butor's work has enjoyed considerable general popularity. *A Change of Heart* (1959) was awarded the Prix Théophraste Renaudot, one of the major French literary prizes, in 1957 and put Butor before the general public. The subject of his novels is consciousness, frequently presented in the form of an interior monologue and described in painstaking detail. *Degrees* (1960) is, according to Leon Roudiez, "a complex novel. . . . Though the story line is usually buried within snatches and bits of dialogue and detail, and though the numerous flashbacks from three points of view occasionally puzzle the reader, the interwoven strands of the book provide a brilliant picture of the perennial schoolboy—and the perennial teacher."

Butor has also written a number of stereoscopies, works on different levels in which the reader must participate actively. His literary and art criticism are contained in *Repertoire I to IV* and *Illustrations I to IV* respectively.

Novels by Butor

Passing Time. 1956. Trans. by Jean Stewart. Riverrun NY 1980 $7.95. ISBN 0-7145-0438-6. Story of a French teacher in a British school.

Mobile: Study for a Representation of the United States. 1962. Trans. by Richard Howard. S & S Trade 1963 o.p.

Nonfiction by Butor

The Spirit of Mediterranean Places. Trans. by Lydia Davis. Marlboro Pr. 1987 $9.00. ISBN 0-910395-17-9. Demonstrates why Butor is widely known in France as an essayist, as well as a novelist.

Books about Butor

McWilliams, Dean. *The Narratives of Michel Butor: The Writer as Janus.* Ohio U. Pr. 1978 $13.00. ISBN 0-8214-0389-3

Spencer, Michael. *Michel Butor. Twayne's World Authors Ser.* G. K. Hall 1974 o.p. A comprehensive overview of Butor's life and works.

Hirsch, Marianne. *Beyond the Single Vision: Henry James, Michel Butor, Uwe Johnson.* Summa Pub. 1981 $16.95. ISBN 0-917786-21-1

CAMUS, ALBERT. 1913–1960 (Nobel Prize 1957)

Albert Camus, the novelist, playwright, and essayist who won the Nobel Prize for literature in 1957, died in 1960 in a car accident near Sens, France. The second youngest man in history to receive the Nobel honor, Camus was also a member of the French Academy.

As one of the leading authors in the French Resistance, he wrote daily outspoken articles in the underground *Combat,* which became an important daily newspaper in France after the war. He was a native of Algeria and lived there until 1940. Though loosely associated with the existentialists, he formulated his own modern brand of stoicism: When confronted with the inevitable absurdities of life, human beings can do nothing but courageously face up to them in full awareness of his situation. This philosophical position is set forth in his essay *The Myth of Sisyphus* (1942). As Camus himself once put it: "The aim is to live lucidly in a world where dispersion is the rule."

His two novels that have had the widest impact are *The Stranger* (1942), a brilliant short work that deals with the theme of the absurd from the social, metaphysical, and religious points of view; and *The Plague* (1947), a defense of the concept of human dignity and a thinly disguised allegory of the French situation during World War II under the German occupation. Since his death, his *Notebooks* have been published.

"Camus was a versatile writer, with a mastery of style almost unique among his contemporaries. 'The last of the heirs of Chateaubriand,' SARTRE (see also Vol. 4) called him. His language is rich in imagery and highly controlled. He was a 'Latin.' . . . 'Every artist, no doubt [he wrote], is in quest of his truth. If he is great, each work brings him closer to it, or, at least, gravitates more closely to that central hidden sun, where all, one day, will be consumed'" (Germaine Brée).

NOVELS BY CAMUS

The Exile and the Kingdom. 1957. Random 1991 $10.00. ISBN 0-679-73385-X. A collection of short stories.

The Fall. 1956. Trans. by Justin O'Brien. Random 1991 $9.00. ISBN 0-679-72022-7. An allegory about human judgment and redemption in which a disillusioned judge tells his story to strangers in an Amsterdam bar.

The Plague. 1947. Trans. by Stuart Gilbert. Random 1991 $10.00. ISBN 0-679-72021-9. An allegorical tale of a doctor's struggle against pestilence in a north African city.

The Stranger. 1942. Trans. by Stuart Gilbert. Random 1954 $2.95. ISBN 0-394-70002-3. An innocent man is condemned for an unintentional crime.

NONFICTION BY CAMUS

The Myth of Sisyphus and Other Essays. 1942. Random 1991 $9.00. ISBN 0-679-733373-6. Contains important existentialist statements on the value of human action.

Notebooks 1935–42. Trans. by Philip Thody. Paragon Hse. 1991 repr. of 1963 ed. $10.95. ISBN 1-55778-412-4. Reflections on Camus's early career.

Notebooks 1942–51. Trans. by Justin O'Brien. Paragon Hse. 1991 repr. of 1965 ed. $10.95. ISBN 1-55778-413-2. The war years and Camus's rise to prominence.

The Rebel: An Essay on Man in Revolt. 1951. Random 1991 $11.00. ISBN 0-679-73384-1. An existentialist manifesto.

Resistance, Rebellion and Death. 1945. Random 1974 $9.00. ISBN 0-394-71966-2. Meditations inspired by the Nazi occupation of France.

BOOKS ABOUT CAMUS

Cruickshank, John. *Albert Camus and the Literature of Revolt.* Greenwood 1978 repr. of 1959 ed. $45.50. ISBN 0-313-20580-9

Ellison, David R. *Understanding Albert Camus.* U. of SC Pr. 1990 $24.95. ISBN 0-87249-705-4. Overview of the development of Camus's major themes and writing style.

Fitch, Brian T. *The Narcissistic Text: A Reading of Camus' Fiction.* U. of Toronto Pr. 1982 $27.50. ISBN 0-8020-2426-2. A sophisticated structural analysis.

Lottman, Herbert. *Albert Camus: A Biography.* Braziller 1981 o.p. The basic biography.

Rhein, Phillip H. *Albert Camus. Twayne's World Authors Ser.* G. K. Hall 1989 $22.95. ISBN 0-8057-8253-2

Showalter, English, Jr. *The Stranger: Humanity and the Absurd.* Macmillan 1989 $20.95. ISBN 0-8057-8022-X

CÉLINE, LOUIS-FERDINAND (pseud. of Louis-Ferdinand Destouches). 1894–1961

Céline, an imaginative, "shocking" writer, horrified his readers in *Journey to the End of Night* (1932) and *Death on the Installment Plan* (1936), which draw upon his experiences as a doctor in the poor neighborhoods of Paris. These novels won him an international readership. Céline's world as portrayed in these books is brutal and violent—a place of filth, perversion, obscenity, perfidy, and crime, but there is "fierce sincerity" in his writing (Bruce Jay Friedman, *NY Times*).

A violent anti-Semite, he was a known collaborationist during the German occupation of France. Fleeing to Denmark after the German collapse, he was imprisoned and later permitted to return to France, mentally unstable and partly paralyzed. His linguistic exuberance recalls a vein of French writing going back through Hugo to Rabelais, and his style has greatly influenced such American writers as Henry Miller (see Vol. 1) and Jack Kerouac (see Vol. 1).

Novels by Céline

Castle to Castle. 1957. Carroll & Graf 1987 $8.95. ISBN 0-88184-360-1. An account of collaborators fleeing the Allies at the end of World War II.

Death on the Installment Plan. 1936. Trans. by Ralph Manheim. New Dir. Pr. 1971 repr. of 1947 ed. $11.95. ISBN 0-8112-0017-5

Guignol's Band. 1944. New Dir. Pr. 1969 $12.95. ISBN 0-8112-0018-3. Set in London during the First World War. Published posthumously.

Journey to the End of the Night. 1932. Trans. by Ralph Manheim. New Dir. Pr. 1983 $10.95. ISBN 0-8112-0847-8. A nightmarish vision of the Parisian underworld.

Book about Céline

Luce, Stanford L. *Céline and His Critics: Scandals and Paradox.* Anma Libri 1986 $46.50. ISBN 0-915838-59-1. Considers the difficulties faced by interpreters of such a controversial author as Céline.

CHAR, RENÉ. 1907–1988

Albert Camus said: "I consider René Char our greatest living poet. . . . This poet of all times speaks immediately to our own. He is in the midst of the fight. He formulates for us both our suffering and our survival." Char speaks in the rhythms of Provence, where he was born and spent much of his life. Influenced early on by surrealism, Char found his major themes while fighting as the leader of a resistance group during World War II. The moral crises and physical suffering of that period find concise expression in his aphoristic prose poems. "To each collapse of proof," writes Char, "the poet responds with a salvo of future."

Poetry by Char

Les Matinaux: The Dawn-Breakers. 1950. Dufour 1992 $18.95. ISBN 1-85224-133-0. One of Char's most important collections.

No Siege Is Absolute. Trans. by Franz Wright. Lost Roads 1983 $5.95. ISBN 0-918786-25-8

Selected Poems of René Char. Trans. by Mary Ann Caws and Tina Jolas. New Dir. Pr. 1992 $19.95. ISBN 0-8112-1191-6. Fine selection and translation of Char's poetry.

BOOKS ABOUT CHAR

Caws, Mary Ann. *The Presence of René Char.* Princeton U. Pr. 1976 $50.00. ISBN 0-691-06305-2. A good study by a major American scholar of Char.

______. *René Char. Twayne's World Authors Ser.* Irvington 1977 $17.95. ISBN 0-8057-6268-X

Lawler, James R. *René Char: The Myth and the Poem.* Princeton U. Pr. 1978 $24.95. ISBN 0-691-06355-9

CHATEAUBRIAND, FRANÇOIS RENÉ, VICOMTE DE. 1768–1848

The work of Chateaubriand, writer and statesman, is a remarkable early example of romanticism in France. In his *Essai Historique, Politique et Moral sur les Révolutions* (1797), he took a stand as a mediator between royalist and revolutionary ideas and as a Rousseauistic freethinker in religion. *Atala, ou les Amours de Deux Sauvages dans le Désert* (1801) is memorable for its lush descriptions of nature and America. The poetic *Génie du Christianisme, ou les Beautés de la Religion Chrétienne* (1802), appealing to the emotions rather than to reason, tried to show that all progress and goodness stemmed from the Christian religion. *René,* a short novel that is largely autobiographical, is taken from this work. Chateaubriand's posthumously published autobiographical *Mémoires d'Outre-tombe* (*Memoirs from Beyond the Grave*) (1849) is considered by many critics to be his masterpiece. A selection under the title *Memoirs of Chateaubriand* was translated and edited by Robert Baldick in 1961 but is currently out of print.

NOVELS BY CHATEAUBRIAND

Atala and *René.* 1801–1802. Trans. by Irving Putter. U. CA Pr. 1952 $10.95. ISBN 0-520-00223-7. Tales of doomed love in the wilderness of North America.

The Natchez: An Indian Tale. 1826. 3 vols. Fertig repr. of 1827 ed. $55.00. ISBN 0-86527-283-2. More passion and exoticism in the Louisiana territory.

BOOKS ABOUT CHATEAUBRIAND

Maurois, André. *Chateaubriand: Poet, Statesman, Lover.* Trans. by Vera Fraser. Greenwood repr. of 1938 ed. o.p. An enjoyable biography.

Porter, Charles A. *Chateaubriand: Composition, Imagination and Poetry.* Anma Libri 1978 $46.50. ISBN 0-915838-37-0

Switzer, Richard. *Chateaubriand. Twayne's World Authors Ser.* Irvington 1971 $17.95. ISBN 0-8057-2208-4

CHRÉTIEN DE TROYES. c.12th century

A French poet about whom practically nothing is known, Chrétien de Troyes lived at the court of Marie de Champagne, daughter of Eleanor of Aquitaine, at Troyes and wrote outstanding Arthurian romances, including *Erec et Enide, Yvain, Lancelot,* and *Perceval.* Chrétien was one of the first to compose after models established by the troubadors of southern France. His romances reflect the milieu of an elegant and sophisticated court society. The unfinished *Perceval, or the Grail* is generally regarded as the earliest work on the theme of the Holy Grail. Chrétien was a gifted storyteller and a master poet. It was he who first took the odd bits and pieces of the Arthurian material and molded them into coherent and individually brilliant works of literary art.

POETRY BY CHRÉTIEN DE TROYES

Arthurian Romances. Trans. by William Kibler and Carleton W. Carroll. Viking Penguin 1991 $7.95. ISBN 0-14-044521-8

Lancelot: The Knight of the Cart. Trans. by Deborah W. Rogers. Col. U. Pr. 1984 $16.00. ISBN 0-231-058-63. A mysterious tale of a knight forced to humiliate himself by riding on a cart.

Perceval: The Story of the Grail. Trans. by Nigel Bryant. Boydell & Brewer 1986 $19.00. ISBN 0-85991-224-8

Yvain, or The Knight with the Lion. Trans. by Ruth H. Cline. U. of Ga. Pr. 1975 $10.00. ISBN 0-8203-0758-0

BOOKS ABOUT CHRÉTIEN DE TROYES

Frappier, Jean. *Chrétien de Troyes: The Man and His Work.* Trans. by Raymond J. Cormier. Ohio U. Pr. 1982 $22.95. ISBN 0-8214-0603-5. A basic study by distinguished medievalist.

Guyer, Foster E. *Chrétien de Troyes: Inventor of the Modern Novel.* AMS Pr. repr. of 1957 ed. $19.50. ISBN 0-404-02965-5

Lacy, Norris J. ed. *The Legacy of Chrétien de Troyes.* Humanities 1988 o.p. Collection of essays about the influence and achievements of Chrétien.

Topsfield, L.T. *Chrétien de Troyes: A Study of the Arthurian Romances.* Cambridge U. Pr. 1981 $74.95. ISBN 0-521-23361-5. A general thematic study.

Vance, Eugene. *From Topic to Tale: Logic and Narrativity in the Middle Ages.* U. of Minn. Pr. 1987 $29.95. ISBN 0-8166-1536-5. A sophisticated poststructuralist analysis focusing on the theme of language.

CIXOUS, HÉLÈNE. 1937–

JACQUES DERRIDA (see Vol. 4) has called Cixous the greatest contemporary French writer. Born in Algeria, Cixous came to Paris, where she is currently professor of English, in 1955. After a dissertation on JOYCE (see Vol. 1), *The Exile of James Joyce* (1968), she began to publish novels, critical essays, and plays, most notably *Le Portrait de Dora* (1976), a feminist retelling of a Freudian case history. She has been an active participant in the development of literary criticism after structuralism and has been a leading figure in the French feminist movement.

NOVEL BY CIXOUS

The Book of Promethea. 1983. Trans. by Betsy Wing. U. of Nebr. Pr. 1991 $29.95. ISBN 0-8032-1443-X. Reflects Cixous's concern with the complexity of love, and whether love can be experienced without the loss of identity of one person in the couple through a passive incorporation into the other.

NONFICTION BY CIXOUS

Coming to Writing and Other Essays. Trans. and ed. by Deborah Jenson. HUP 1991 $24.95. ISBN 0-674-14436-8. A collection of essays that have been especially influential among feminist critics.

The Exile of James Joyce. 1968. Trans. by Sally Purcell. Riverrun NY 1980 o.p. Important political reading of the great Irish novelist.

Newly Born Woman. 1976. Written with Catherine Clément. Trans. by Betsy Wing. U. of Minn. Pr. 1986 $34.95. ISBN 0-8166-1465-2. An important feminist manifesto.

Reading With Clarice Lispector. 1979. Trans. by Verena Conley. U. of Minn. Pr. 1990 $34.95. ISBN 0-8166-1828-3. A poetic meditation on the writing of the Brazilian modernist author.

Readings: The Poetics of Blanchot, Joyce, Kafka, Kleist, Lispector, Tsvetayeva. Trans. by Verena A. Conley. U. of Minn. Pr. 1991 $39.95. ISBN 0-8166-1940-9. Exploring the notion of "feminine writing"—a characteristic attributed by Cixous to certain male writers as well as many female writers.

CLAUDEL, PAUL. 1868–1955

Claudel was a poet, dramatist, essayist, and religious thinker of great power and originality whose works are suffused with his ardent Catholicism. He also had a distinguished career in the French consular and diplomatic service, which enabled him to spend many years abroad in the Far East, North and South America, and Europe. Almost all of Claudel's work embodies an expression of his deep Roman Catholic faith and is an attempt to impress others with its truth. His poetic expression is at once symbolic and lyrical, expressing the joy, beauty, and mystery of existence. Among his most important plays are *The City*, *The Break of Noon*, *The Tidings Brought to Mary* (1912), and *The Satin Slipper* (1928–1939).

Plays by Claudel

Three Plays. Trans. by John Heard. Fertig 1991 repr. of 1945 ed. $35.00. ISBN 0-86527-400-2

Nonfiction by Claudel

Claudel on the Theatre. Trans. by Christine Trollope. U. of Miami Pr. 1972 $12.95. ISBN 0-87024-158-3. A collection of theoretical reflections.

Ways and Crossways. Trans. by Fr. J. O'Conner. *Essay Index Repr. Ser.* Ayer repr. of 1933 ed. $20.00. ISBN 0-8369-0313-7

Books about Claudel

Caranfa, Angelo. *Claudel: Beauty and Grace.* Bucknell U. Pr. 1989 $26.50. ISBN 0-8387-5134-2

Chaigne, Louis. *Paul Claudel: The Man and the Mystic.* Greenwood 1978 repr. of 1961 ed. $45.00. ISBN 0-313-20465-9

Chiari, Joseph. *Poetic Drama of Paul Claudel.* Gordian 1969 repr. of 1954 ed. $50.00. ISBN 0-87752-018-6

Knapp, Bettina L. *Paul Claudel. Lit. and Life Ser.* Continuum 1982 $19.95. ISBN 0-8044-2479-9

COCTEAU, JEAN. 1889–1963

This versatile, sophisticated, eccentric, exuberant poet-dramatist-novelist experimented with almost every literary and artistic form: novels, plays, poems, film scenarios, ballet, criticism, drawing, painting. Prodigal son of a wealthy notary, he became the spokesperson for literary modernism and surrealism. His artist friends and collaborators included PICASSO (see Vol. 3), DIAGHILEV (see Vol. 3), and RILKE. His career is said to have been sparked by Diaghilev's request that he do something "astonishing"; Cocteau became adept at it. Generous and alert for fresh talent, he "launched a number of gifted adolescents like Raymond Radiguet or outlaws like GENET on their paths to fame" (Henri Peyre). Among the nonliterary achievements of this extraordinary man are the decoration of the city hall of Menton and the fisherman's chapel at Villefranche, both on the French Riviera.

Cocteau's greatest success came in theater and film: Francis Fergusson considered him a master of the make-believe; of the glamour and the trickery of the stage. But, as Cocteau explained, he composed his theatrical effects with the rigor of a *symboliste* poet, putting together the words of a small subtle lyric. Sometimes he played with ancient legends, as in *Antigone* (1926) and *Orphée* (1926); sometimes with themes from contemporary fiction or the contemporary theater, as in *The Holy Terrors* (1929), *The Eagle with Two Heads* (1946), and

Intimate Relations (1938). But he always caught the familiar figures in unexpected light, that of his own, unique, poetic intelligence.

NOVEL BY COCTEAU

The Holy Terrors. 1929. New Dir. Pr. 1957 $8.95. ISBN 0-8112-0021-3. A surreal tale of passion and violence between children.

PLAYS BY COCTEAU

The Infernal Machine and Other Plays. Trans. by W. H. Auden, Albert Bermel, E. E. Cummings, Dudley Fitts, Mary Hoeck, and John Savacool. New Dir. Pr. repr. of 1967 ed. $11.95. ISBN 0-8112-0022-1. Includes Cocteau's retelling of the Oedipus myth.

WORKS BY COCTEAU

The Beauty and the Beast: Diary of a Film. 1946. Dover 1972 repr. of 1950 ed. $5.95. ISBN 0-486-22776-6. Cocteau's lyrical reworking of a well-known fairy tale.

Call to Order. 1926. *Studies in French Lit.* Haskell 1974 $75.00. ISBN 0-8383-2056-2

Diary of an Unknown. 1953. Trans. by Jesse Browner. Paragon Hse. 1991 repr. of 1988 ed. $12.95. ISBN 1-55778-466-3. Series of essays from Cocteau's final years that displays the contradictions that hounded the artist throughout his life.

Le Livre Blanc: The White Book. 1928. Trans. by Margaret Crosland. City Lights 1989 $5.95. ISBN 0-87286-238-0

Opium. 1930. Trans. by Margaret Crosland. Dufour 1990 $17.95. ISBN 0-7206-0800-7. Reflections on Cocteau's relationship to narcotics.

Past Tense: The Cocteau Diaries. 2 vols. Trans. by Richard Howard. HarBraceJ 1988. Vol. 1 $8.95. ISBN 0-15-671360-8. Vol. 2 $24.95. ISBN 0-15-171291-3. Fascinating glimpse of one of literature's most self-conscious writers.

Souvenir Portraits: Paris in the Bell Epoque. 1935. Trans. by Jesse Browner. Paragon Hse. 1990 $17.95. ISBN 1-55778-158-3. Evocation of an age by one of its central intellectual and social figures.

BOOKS ABOUT COCTEAU

Emboden, William. *A Visual Art of Jean Cocteau.* Abrams 1990 $49.50. ISBN 0-8109-3153-2. Cocteau as artist of the image—film, drawing, painting.

Knapp, Bettina L. *Jean Cocteau. Twayne's World Authors Ser.* Macmillan 1989 $24.95. ISBN 0-8057-8239-7. Updated edition of a 1970 study in which the author draws on meetings with Cocteau as well as intimate knowledge of his work.

Steegmuller, Francis. *Cocteau: A Biography.* Godine 1986 $15.95. ISBN 0-87923-606-X. Readable portrait by a well-known expert on French literature.

COLETTE (pseud. of Sidonie-Gabrielle Colette). 1873–1954

La grande Colette—romancière, short-story writer, playwright, journalist, editor, actress, dramatic critic, fashion columnist, book reviewer, feature writer, wife and nurse—received the "greatest honor possible for a woman writer in France: the presiding chair in the Goncourt Academy." Her early "Claudine" novels (1900–1903) were published in collaboration with her first husband, the notorious "Willy," pseudonym of Henry Gauthier-Villers, whom she had married at 20 and divorced when she was 33. Under M. Willy's "editorship" she became a master craftsperson. During her varied, active life, reflected in her novels, she became known for her subtle psychological insight and masterly style. The "Claudine" series is taken from her youth, *The Vagabond* (1911) from her days as a music-hall dancer, and *Chéri* (1920) from an affair with a "dissolute" young man. Throughout her works, there runs an awareness of the obstacles faced by women of all ages as they seek to define their identities and find their freedom. GIDE (see also Vol. 1) praised her, and

PROUST wept on reading *Mitsou* (1916). A Grand Officer of the Legion of Honor, she was accorded a formal state funeral and in 1967 Paris named a street in her honor.

NOVELS BY COLETTE

Chéri (and *The Last of Chéri*). 1920–1926. Ballantine 1986 $4.95. ISBN 0-345-34017-5

Gigi, Julie de Carneilhan, Chance Acquaintances. 1941–1944. Trans. by Roger Senhouse and Patrick Fermor. FS&G 1976 o.p. Contains *Gigi,* in which a young woman's charms bring her wealth. Made into a successful film.

My Mother's House (and *Sido*). 1922–1929. Trans. by Una V. Troubridge and Enid McLeod. FS&G $9.95. ISBN 0-374-51218-3

Retreat from Love. 1907. Trans. by Margaret Crosland. HarBraceJ 1980 $5.95. ISBN 0-15-676588-7

The Ripening Seed. 1923. Trans. by Roger Senhouse. FS&G 1975 $7.95. ISBN 0-374-25069-3

The Vagabond. 1911. Trans. by Enid McLeod. Ballantine 1982 $3.95. ISBN 0-345-30061-0. A tale of a dancer who comes to terms with her independence.

SHORT STORY COLLECTION BY COLETTE

The Collected Stories. Ed. by Robert G. Phelps. Trans. by Matthew Ward, Antonia White, and Anne-Marie Callimachi. FS&G 1983 $22.50. ISBN 0-374-12629-1

NONFICTION BY COLETTE

Break of Day. 1928. Trans. by Enid McLeod. FS&G 1975 $6.95. ISBN 0-374-91221-3. A delicate portrait of the author's mother.

Earthly Paradise: An Autobiography of Colette Drawn from Her Lifetime Writings. Ed. by Robert G. Phelps, Herma Briffault, and Derek Coltman. FS&G 1975 o.p.

Letters from Colette. Trans. and ed. by Robert G. Phelps. Ballantine 1983 $2.50. ISBN 0-345-30059-9

BOOKS ABOUT COLETTE

Jouve, Nicole W. *Colette.* Ind. U. Pr. 1987 $29.95. ISBN 0-253-30102-5. Analyzes, among other things, Colette's choice of her father's name for her pen name.

Lottman, Herbert. *Colette: A Life.* Little 1991 $24.95. ISBN 0-316-53361-0. A highly readable biography by an authority on twentieth-century French letters.

CORNEILLE, PIERRE. 1606–1684

Corneille inaugurates the greatest period of French drama. His artistic model and theory of the drama were to be followed by successive generations of dramatists, including RACINE. His plays deal with noble characters in closely defined situations of high moral intensity. After modest success as a writer of complex, baroque comedies, Corneille achieved fame with *Le Cid* (1636–37), adapted from Guillen de Castro's three-day comedy *Las Moceddes del Cid.* It vividly represents the dominant theme of his tragedies: the inner struggle between duty and passion. It also touched off a major debate about the proper rules to follow in writing tragedy. Corneille went on to dominate the French theater of his day with plays that reflect the changing relationships between the aristocracy and the new absolutist state. Some of Corneille's other major tragedies include *Horace* (1640), *Cinna* (1640), and *Polyeuctus* (1643). In his shaping of language and form to his dramatic purposes, Corneille had a great effect on the development of French literature; more specifically, it can be said that he gave form and aim to French neoclassicism. With RACINE and MOLIÈRE, he forms part of the great triumvirate of seventeenth-century French theater.

Plays by Corneille

Le Cid: A Translation in Rhymed Couplets. Trans. by Vincent J. Cheng. U. of Delaware Pr. 1987 $32.50. ISBN 0-87413-294-0

The Cid, Cinna, the Theatrical Illusion. Trans. by John Cairncross. *Penguin Class. Ser.* Viking Penguin 1976 $6.95. ISBN 0-14-044312-6. Contains Corneille's two major early tragedies, along with a delightful comedy of magic and "illusion."

Landmarks of French Classical Drama. Trans. by David Bryer and others. Heinemann Ed. 1991 $14.95. ISBN 0-413-63100-1. Useful collection of important plays.

Rodogune: The French Text with a Facing English Translation. Trans. and ed. by William G. Clubb. U. of Nebr. Pr. 1974 $17.50. ISBN 0-8032-0501-5. A stepmother's power over her two sons.

Books about Corneille

Barneau, Michel, ed. *Pierre Corneille.* MRTS 1989 $10.00. ISBN 0-921984-01-4

Barnwell, H. T. *The Tragic Drama of Corneille and Racine: An Old Parallel Revisited.* OUP 1982 $59.00. ISBN 0-19-815779-7

Schmidt, Josephine A. *If There Are No More Heroes, There Are Heroines: A Feminist Critique of Corneille's Heroines.* U. Pr. of Amer. 1987 o.p. Argues that Corneille's work is dominated by the failure of masculine heroism and the rise of powerful female characters.

Segall, J. B. *Corneille and the Spanish Drama.* Gordon Pr. 1976 $59.95. ISBN 0-8490-1674-6. Connects Corneille to a tradition from which he drew much inspiration.

Turnell, Martin. *The Classical Moment: Studies of Corneille, Molière, and Racine.* Greenwood 1971 repr. of 1948 ed. $45.00. ISBN 0-8371-5803-6

DERRIDA, JACQUES. 1930–

[See Volume 4.]

DESCARTES, RENÉ. 1596–1650

[See Volumes 4 and 5.]

DIDEROT, DENIS. 1713–1784

After about a century and a half of neglect by critics, Diderot is now considered one of the most original minds of the Enlightenment and is ranked along with Montesquieu (see Vol. 3), Voltaire, and Rousseau (see Vol. 3) as one of the prime figures of the period. He was coeditor with D'Alembert of the *Encyclopédie* (1771–76), one of the major intellectual monuments of the eighteenth century, whose purpose was not only to assemble and disseminate knowledge but also to change the way people thought about the general world around them. A philosopher, playwright, novelist, essayist, and literary theoretician, he left behind him works of genius that were appreciated properly only long after his death. *D'Alembert's Dream* (1769) is a statement of his philosophic thought through the experimental form of a dialogue—for he was as interested in literature as in ideas. Perhaps his most engaging satire is *Rameau's Nephew* (1762), a philosophic dialogue in which Diderot examines the problem of morality in a corrupt society, the Paris of his day. His dramatic theories were taken up by later generations in France (starting with Beaumarchais) and influenced ideas about the theater throughout Europe. Diderot's two masterpieces in the novel are *The Nun* (1760), an examination of convent life and female sexuality, and *Jack the Fatalist* (1773), a lively and digressive work somewhat in the manner of Sterne's (see Vol. 1) *Tristram Shandy* that deals with the philosophic problem of individual morality and determinism. His correspondence (particularly with Sophie Volland) provides a valuable portrait of contemporary society. Diderot's *Salons* (1757–81), reviews of painting exhibitions in Paris, are an outstanding example of eighteenth-century art criticism.

Novels by Diderot

Jack the Fatalist and His Master. 1773. Trans. by Wesley D. Camp and others. P. Lang Pubs. 1984 $21.60. ISBN 0-8204-0076-9

The Nun. 1760. Trans. by Leonard W. Tancock. *Penguin Class. Ser.* Viking Penguin 1974 $6.95. ISBN 0-14-044300-2. A young girl is imprisoned in a convent and struggles for her survival.

Nonfiction by Diderot

Diderot, Interpreter of Nature: Selected Writings. Trans. by Jean Stewart and Jonathan Kemp. Hyperion Conn. 1990 repr. of 1937 ed. $35.00. ISBN 0-88355-841-6

Diderot's Early Philosophical Works. Ed. by Margaret Jourdain. AMS Pr. 1972 repr. of 1916 ed. $15.00. ISBN 0-404-08219-X

Diderot's Pictorial Encyclopedia of Trades and Industry. 1765. 2 vols. Ed. by Charles C. Gillispie. Dover 1959 $29.95 ea. ISBNs 0-486-22284-5, 0-486-22284-6

Diderot's Writings on the Theatre. Ed. by F. C. Green. AMS Pr. repr. of 1936 ed. $26.00. ISBN 0-404-60157-X

Encyclopedia: Selections. 1765. Trans. by Nelly S. Hoyt. Macmillan 1965 $8.80. ISBN 0-672-60479-5. The immensely readable compendium of knowledge, written with help from his contemporaries. Many consider it Diderot's masterpiece.

Rameau's Nephew and D'Alembert's Dream. Penguin Class. Ser. Viking Penguin 1976 $6.95. ISBN 0-14-044173-5

Rameau's Nephew and Other Works. 1762. Trans. by Jacques Barzun and Ralph H. Brown. Irvington 1964 $29.50. ISBN 0-672-51089-8

Short Story Collection by Diderot

This is Not a Story and Other Stories. Trans. by P. N. Furbank. U. of Mo. Pr. 1991 $27.50. ISBN 0-8262-0815-0. Witty, often overlooked shorter works.

Books about Diderot

Fellow, Otis. *Diderot. Twayne's World Author Ser.* G. K. Hall 1989 $26.95. ISBN 0-8057-8225-7

Goodman, Dena. *Criticism in Action: Enlightenment Experiments in Political Writing*. Cornell Univ. Pr. 1989 $32.95. ISBN 0-8014-2201-9. Studies the relationship between politics and culture.

Marshall, David. *The Surprising Effects of Sympathy: Marivaux, Diderot, Rousseau and Mary Shelley*. U. Ch. Pr. 1988 $27.50. ISBN 0-226-50710-6. Places Diderot in the context of the psychology of his day.

Vartanian, Aram. *Diderot and Descartes: A Study of Scientific Naturalism in the Enlightenment*. Greenwood 1975 repr. of 1953 ed. $85.80. ISBN 0-317-09015-1. Considers Diderot's relationship to the intellectual currents of his age.

Wilson, Arthur M. *Diderot*. OUP 1972 $45.00. ISBN 0-19-901506-1

DUMAS, ALEXANDRE (père). 1802–1870

After an idle youth, Alexandre Dumas went to Paris and spent some years writing. A volume of short stories and some farces were his only production until 1927, when his play *Henri III* (1829) became a success and made him famous. It was as a storyteller rather than a playwright, however, that Dumas gained enduring success. Perhaps the most broadly popular of French romantic novelists, Dumas published some 1,200 volumes during his lifetime. These were not all written by him, however, but were the works of a body of collaborators known as "Dumas & Co." Some of his best works were plagiarized; for example,

The Three Musketeers (1844) was taken from the *Memoirs of Artagnan* by an eighteenth-century writer, and *The Count of Monte Cristo* (1845) from Penchet's *A Diamond and a Vengeance*. At the end of his life, drained of money and sapped by his work, Dumas left Paris and went to live at his son's villa, where he remained until his death.

NOVELS BY DUMAS (PÈRE)

The Three Musketeers. Trans. by Lowell Bair. Bantam 1984 $5.95. ISBN 0-553-21337-7

The Count of Monte Cristo. 1845. Trans. by David Coward. OUP 1991 $9.95. ISBN 0-19-282715-4

My Memoirs. Ed. and trans. by A. Craig Bell. Greenwood 1975 repr. of 1961 ed. o.p.

BOOKS ABOUT DUMAS (PÈRE)

Maurois, André. *The Titans: A Three-Generation Biography of the Dumas*. Trans. by Gerard Hopkins. Greenwood 1971 repr. of 1957 ed. o.p. Colorful family saga as told by a gifted French writer.

Schopp, Claude. *Alexandre Dumas: Genius of Life*. Watts 1988 $27.50. ISBN 0-531-15093-3. Captivating biography that captures the brio, grandeur, and energy of Dumas's works.

DUMAS, ALEXANDRE (fils). 1824–1895

Dumas (fils), the playwright, was the illegitimate son of Dumas (père), the author of popular historical romances. Although the younger Dumas started writing fiction, he soon moved on to plays. Many of his plays deal with social and domestic problems. The best known is *La Dame aux Camélias* (1852), based on his own novel, and made famous through the opera version by VERDI (see Vol. 3), *La Traviata*, and a motion picture version, *Camille*. Dumas also wrote essays, letters, and speeches, many theorizing about art, morals, politics, and religion.

NOVEL BY DUMAS (FILS)

Camille. 1848. Trans. by Matilde Heron. NAL-Dutton 1972 $4.95. ISBN 0-451-52398-9

PLAY BY DUMAS (FILS)

La Dame aux Camélias. Trans. by David Coward. OUP 1986 $6.95. ISBN 0-19-281736-1

DURAS, MARGUERITE (pseud. of Marguerite Donnadieu). 1914–

Marguerite Duras may well be the most important French writer of our day. Born in Indochina, she went to Paris at the age of 17 and studied at the Sorbonne. During World War II, she joined the Resistance and published her first books. After the liberation, like many intellectuals, she became a member of the Communist party (from which she was expelled in 1955). Her fame in literature dates from *The Sea Wall* (1953)—about white settlers in Vietnam and based loosely on her childhood. Duras has many novels to her credit—all "setting powerful subconscious mechanisms in motion behind a screen of trivia" (*SR*). Seeking meaning and fulfillment, the characters in her novels are sacrificed to the ever-flowing tide of existence, and life is perhaps over before they are fully aware of what has been happening. Associated early on with the "new novelists," Duras's work has taken on a density and power that sets her apart by its obsessive exploration of the dual theme of love and death. In 1959 she wrote her first film scenario, *Hiroshima, Mon Amour*, and has since been involved in a number of other films, including *India Song, Baxter, Vera Baxter, Le Camion* (*The Truck*), and *The Lover*.

Novels by Duras

Destroy, She Said. 1969. Trans. by Barbara Bray. Grove Pr. 1989 $7.95. ISBN 0-8021-5154-X

Four Novels. Trans. by Richard Seaver and others. Grove Pr. 1988 $12.95. ISBN 0-8021-5111-6. Contains *The Square, Moderato Cantabile* (a powerful short novel about adultery and death in a small seaside city), *Ten-Thirty on a Summer Night,* and *The Afternoon of Mr. Andesmas.*

Little Horses of Tarquinia. 1953. Trans. by Peter DuBerg. Riverrun NY 1986 $9.95. ISBN 0-7145-0348-7

The Lover. 1984. Trans. by Barbara Bray. HarpC 1986 $10.00. ISBN 0-06-097040-5. Story of the love affair between a young French woman and an older Indochinese man in prewar Vietnam.

The Ravishing of Lol V. Stein. Trans. by Richard Seaver. Pantheon 1986 $10.00. ISBN 0-394-74304-0. Traces the nervous breakdown of Lol, whose lover left her for another woman.

The Sea Wall. 1953. HarpC 1986 $11.00 ISBN 0-06-097053-7

Whole Days in the Trees. 1953. Trans. by Anita Barrows. Riverrun NY 1984 $11.95. ISBN 0-7145-3854-X

Nonfiction by Duras

The War: A Memoir. 1985. Trans. by Barbara Bray. Pantheon 1986 o.p. A harrowing collection of stories and memories of life in Paris during and after the Nazi occupation.

Works by Duras

Hiroshima, Mon Amour. 1959. Trans. by Richard Seaver. Grove Pr. 1987 $7.95. ISBN 0-8021-3104-2

India Song. 1975. Trans. by Barbara Bray. Grove Pr. 1989 $7.95. ISBN 0-8021-3135-2

Books about Duras

Glassman, Deborah. *Marguerite Duras: Fascinating Vision and Narrative Cure.* Fairleigh Dickinson 1991 $31.50. ISBN 0-8386-3337-4. A critically sophisticated and accessible study of Duras.

Kaivola, Karen. *All Contraries Confounded: The Lyrical Fiction of Virginia Woolf, Djuna Barnes, and Marguerite Duras.* U. of Iowa Pr. 1991 $22.95. ISBN 0-87745-324-1

Selons, Trista. *The Other Woman: Feminism and Femininity in the Works of Marguerite Duras.* Yale U. Pr. 1988 $32.50. ISBN 0-300-04287-6. Considers the relationship between gender and identity in Duras.

Willis, Sharon. *Marguerite Duras: Writing on the Body.* U. of Ill. Pr. 1987 $24.95. ISBN 0-252-01335-2. Sophisticated post-structuralist analysis.

ÉLUARD, PAUL. 1895–1952

"The greatest love poet of the twentieth century," writes Henri Lemaître of Éluard. Raised in a working class suburb, Éluard interrupted his studies to spend two years in a tuberculosis sanitorium, where he read widely in French, German, and American poetry. Associated early with the surrealists, he later fought in the resistance and joined the Communist party. His work combines the dreamlike techniques of surrealism, a political humanism, and an attention to the transforming power of love. Éluard remains one of the contemporary poets most widely read and appreciated in France. "The poet," he wrote, "is he who inspires, much more than he who is inspired."

Poetry by Éluard

Éluard: Selected Poems, Bilingual Edition. Trans. by Gilbert Bowen. Riverrun NY 1988 $10.95. ISBN 0-7145-3995-3. A wide-ranging collection.

Uninterrupted Poetry: Selected Writings of Paul Éluard. Trans. by Andrew Lloyd. Greenwood 1977 repr. of 1975 ed. $45.00. ISBN 0-8371-9779-1

Book about Éluard

Nugent, Robert. *Paul Éluard. Twayne's World Authors Ser.* Irvington 1974 $17.95. ISBN 0-8057-2299-8

FLAUBERT, GUSTAVE. 1821–1880

Flaubert's masterpiece, *Madame Bovary* (1857), is a study of a woman of romantic temperament and upbringing who ruins herself in her thirst for romantic experience. (With the subtitle *Provincial Morals,* it caused a scandal, though Flaubert was declared innocent of offense against public and religious morality in a court case.) *The Sentimental Education* (1869) has a similar theme—with a male protagonist. A novel in quite another vein, intended to shock, was *Salammbô* (1862), a story of sex and violence in ancient Carthage. It leaves "an overwhelming impression" of "nightmarish brutality," even "sadism" (Victor Brombert). A year after Flaubert's death appeared his colossal work, *Bouvard and Pécuchet* (1881), "a precious wilderness of wonderful reading," as H. G. Wells (see Vol. 1) called it. Flaubert was possibly the most painstaking writer in all literature. He wrote slowly and laboriously, and his books followed one another at long intervals. *Madame Bovary* took him 6 years; *Bouvard and Pécuchet* remained unfinished after 13 years of work. His tireless search for the right word and his habit of reading aloud every sentence until its cadence was perfect to the ear have earned for him a reputation as perhaps the greatest stylist of all time. Yet just as he was obsessed with words, with the beauty of aesthetic form, so was Flaubert attentive to the social reality of his day. He prided himself on being a scrupulously objective literary realist who described life as he saw it (in minute detail), but as a serious artist he became involved with his characters: "I am myself Madame Bovary."

Flaubert despised the bourgeoisie and bourgeois thinking, and compiled a witty book of clichés, *The Dictionary of Accepted Ideas* (also published with the title *A Dictionary of Platitudes: Being a Compendium of Conversational Clichés, Blind Beliefs, Fashionable Misconceptions and Fixed Ideas*). His extraordinary style is evident as well in his correspondence. The *Nation* said of his *Selected Letters:* "They are among the finest literary letters in the whole of epistolary literature."

Novels by Flaubert

Bouvard and Pécuchet. 1881. Trans. by A. J. Krailsheimer. *Penguin Class. Ser.* Viking Penguin 1976 $5.95. ISBN 0-14-044320-7

The First Sentimental Education. Trans. by Douglas Garman. U. CA Pr. 1972 $32.50. ISBN 0-520-01967-9

Madame Bovary. 1857. Trans. by Geoffrey Wall. Viking Penguin 1993 $5.95. ISBN 0-14-044526-7

Salammbô. 1862. Trans. by A. J. Krailsheimer. *Penguin Class. Ser.* Viking Penguin 1977 $7.95. ISBN 0-14-044328-2

The Sentimental Education. 1869. Trans. by Robert Baldick. *Penguin Class. Ser.* Viking Penguin 1964 $5.95. ISBN 0-14-044141-7

The Temptation of St. Anthony. Trans. by Kitty Mrosovsky. *Penguin Class. Ser.* Viking Penguin 1983 $6.95. ISBN 0-14-044410-6. Allegorical study of desire and self-denial.

Three Tales. 1877. Trans. by Robert Baldick. *Penguin Class. Ser.* Viking Penguin 1961 $5.95. ISBN 0-14-044106-9. Contains *A Simple Heart,* Flaubert's ironic masterpiece about the devotion of a humble provincial servant to her mistress.

Nonfiction by Flaubert

The Dictionary of Accepted Ideas. Trans. and ed. by Jacques Barzun. New Dir. Pr. rev. ed. 1954 $5.95. ISBN 0-8112-0054-X

Selected Letters. Trans. by Francis Steegmuller. *Biography Index Repr. Ser.* Ayer repr. of 1953 ed. $17.50. ISBN 0-8369-8082-4

The Letters of Gustave Flaubert, 1830–1857. Trans. and ed. by Francis Steegmuller. HUP 1980 $9.95. ISBN 0-674-52637-6. This, and the volume above are collections of letters by a master stylist.

Books about Flaubert

Barnes, Hazel E. *Sartre and Flaubert.* U. Ch. Pr. 1982 $25.00. ISBN 0-226-03720-7. Discusses Flaubert's influence on Sartre.

Brombert, Victor. *The Hidden Reader: Stendhal, Balzac, Hugo, Baudelaire, Flaubert.* HUP 1988 $29.95. ISBN 0-674-39012-1. An insightful analysis of the problems in reading Flaubert.

Culler, Jonathan. *Flaubert: The Uses of Uncertainty.* Cornell Univ. Pr. rev. ed. 1985 $14.95. ISBN 0-8014-9305-6. An important structuralist analysis.

Donato, Eugenio. *The Script of Decadence: Essays on the Fictions of Flaubert and the Poetics of Romanticism.* OUP 1991 $32.50. ISBN 0-19-505724-4. A postmodernist perspective.

Kaplan, Louise. *Female Perversions: The Temptations of Madame Bovary.* Doubleday 1991 $24.95. ISBN 0-385-26233-7. Analyzes major characters in *Madame Bovary* through gender stereotyping and Freudian theories.

Lottman, Herbert. *Flaubert: A Biography.* Little 1989 $24.95. ISBN 0-316-53342-4. Painstakingly reconstructs Flaubert's strange and meticulous life in great detail.

Prendergast, Christopher. *The Order of Mimesis: Balzac, Stendhal, Nerval and Flaubert.* Cambridge U. Pr. 1988 $59.95. ISBN 0-521-23789-0. Presents a comprehensive account of the concept of mimesis and stimulates readers to rethink their own ideas concerning literary representation.

Sartre, Jean-Paul. *The Family Idiot: Gustave Flaubert, 1821–1857.* 4 vols. Trans. by Carol Cosman. U. Ch. Pr. Vol. 1 1981 $25.00. ISBN 0-226-73509-5. Vol. 2 1987 $35.00. ISBN 0-226-73510-9. Vol. 3 1989 $39.95. ISBN 0-226-73516-8. Vol. 4 1991 $34.95. ISBN 0-226-73518-4. Particularly digressive, personal interpretation of important years in Flaubert's life.

Schlossman, Beryl. *The Orient of Style: Modernist Allegories of Conversion.* Duke 1991 $42.50. ISBN 0-8223-1076-7. Contains useful chapter on Flaubert.

Schor, Naomi, and Henry F. Majewski, eds. *Flaubert and Postmodernism.* U. of Nebr. Pr. 1984 $27.50. ISBN 0-8032-414-7. Essays by contemporary critics about the modernity of Flaubert.

Steegmuller, Francis. *Flaubert and Madame Bovary: A Double Portrait.* U. Ch. Pr. 1977 $5.95. ISBN 0-226-77137-7. An important biographical study.

FOUCAULT, MICHEL. 1926–1984

An outstanding philosopher and intellectual figure on the contemporary scene, Foucault has been influential in both philosophy and the recent interpretation of literature. Trained in philosophy and psychology, he was named to a chair at the Collège de France in 1970. He also taught in various departments of French literature as a visiting professor in the United States. Until 1968 he was a major figure in the critical movement known as structuralism, a method of intellectual inquiry based on the idea that all human behavior and achievement arises from an innate ability to organize, or "structure," human experiences. In both *The Order of Things* (1966) and *The Archaeology of Knowledge* (1969) he was interested in the organization of human knowledge and in the transformations of intellectual categories. His influential history of the prison, *Discipline and Punish* (1975), contributed to the study of the relationship of power and various forms of knowledge, as did the several volumes of an unfinished *History of Sexuality* published just before his death.

NONFICTION BY FOUCAULT

The Archaeology of Knowledge. 1969. Trans. by A. M. Sheridan-Smith. Irvington 1972 $29.50. ISBN 0-394-47118-0

Discipline and Punish: The Birth of the Prison. 1975. Trans. by Alan Sheridan. Random 1979 $11.00. ISBN 0-394-72767-3. Fascinating study of penal institutions and practices since the Renaissance. One of the author's most accessible works.

The Foucault Reader. Ed. by Paul Rabinow. Pantheon 1984 $15.00. ISBN 0-394-71340-0. Essays on politics and philosophy, along with interviews.

A History of Sexuality. Trans. by Robert Hurley. Random 1980 $6.95. ISBN 0-394-74026-2

Language, Counter-Memory, Practice: Selected Essays and Interviews. Trans. by Sherry Simon. Ed. by Donald F. Bouchard. Cornell Univ. Pr. 1980 $12.95. ISBN 0-8014-9204-1. Contains several of Foucault's most important essays.

Madness and Civilization: A History of Insanity in the Age of Reason. 1961. Trans. by Richard Howard. Random 1988 $11.00. ISBN 0-679-72110-X. A critique of the Western notion of reason.

The Order of Things: An Archaeology of the Human Sciences. 1966. Random 1973 $10.00. ISBN 0-394-71935-2

BOOKS ABOUT FOUCAULT

Arac, Jonathan, ed. *After Foucault: Humanistic Knowledge, Postmodern Challenges.* Rutgers U. Pr. 1988 $29.00. ISBN 0-8135-1329-4. Nine excellent essays that address the importance of Foucault's work for research in a wide range of humanistic disciplines.

Blanchot, Maurice. *Foucault/Blanchot.* Trans. by Jeffrey Mehlman. Zone Bks. 1988 $22.95. ISBN 0-942299-02-7. The writers Blanchot and Foucault consider each other.

Deleuze, Gilles. *Foucault.* Trans. by Sean Hand. U. of Minn. Pr. 1988 $29.95. ISBN 0-8166-1674-4. A study by a major French philosopher and friend of Foucault.

FRANCE, ANATOLE (pseud. of Anatole-François Thibault). 1844–1924 (NOBEL PRIZE 1921)

Anatole France was the only child of a bookseller. His literary criticism records "the adventures of his soul among masterpieces" and often appears, together with autobiographical elements, under a thin disguise of fiction. Some of the best of this genre are *On Life and Letters* (1911–24), *My Friend's Book* (1885), and *The Opinions of Mr. Jerome Coignard* (1893). *The Crime of Sylvester Bonnard* (1881), France's first success, has enjoyed great popularity. His fiction covers a wide range of subjects and historical periods. Widely respected as the modern heir to the rationalist tradition of VOLTAIRE, he was elected to the French Academy.

NOVELS BY FRANCE

The Gods Will Have Blood. 1912. Trans. by Frederick Davies. *Penguin Class. Ser.* Viking Penguin 1980 $6.95. ISBN 0-14-044352-5. A study of fanaticism set during the French Revolution.

Penguin Island. 1908. Random 1984 $6.95. ISBN 0-394-60516-0. A mocking view of French history in which penguins are mistaken for human beings by a cleric.

NONFICTION BY FRANCE

On Life and Letters. Ed. by Frederic Chapman. *Essay Index Repr. Ser.* Ayer 4 series.

First Series. repr. of 1910 ed. $21.00. ISBN 0-8369-2375-X. *Second Series.* repr. of 1914 ed. $21.50. ISBN 0-8369-2358-8. *Third Series.* repr. of 1924 ed. $22.00. ISBN 0-8369-2359-6. *Fourth Series.* repr. of 1924 ed. $22.00. ISBN 0-8369-2360-X

Short Story Collection by France

Crainquebille. 1901. Trans. by Winifred Stephens. *Short Story Index Repr. Ser.* Ayer 1922 $14.50. ISBN 0-8369-3538-1

Work by France

The Works of Anatole France. 40 vols. Gordon Pr. 1975 $2,700.00. ISBN 0-8490-1329-1

Books about France

Segur, Nicolas. *Conversations with Anatole France.* Gordon Pr. 1977 $59.95. ISBN 0-8490-1673-8

Virtanen, Reino. *Anatole France. Twayne's World Authors Ser.* 1969 o.p. A comprehensive overview of France's life and works.

GENET, JEAN. 1910–1986

Widely considered to be one of France's greatest writers in the period since World War II, Jean Genet has had one of the strangest careers in the history of literature. He was born in Paris, an illegitimate child who never knew his parents. Abandoned to public welfare, he was adopted by a peasant family in the Morvan. At the age of 10, he was sent to a reformatory for stealing. After many years in institutions, he escaped and joined the Foreign Legion but soon deserted. In traveling through Europe, he begged, thieved, smuggled, and was imprisoned in almost every country he visited. He escaped life imprisonment in France in 1948 when the president of the Republic, petitioned by a group of eminent writers and artists, granted him a pardon.

Genet produced his first novel, *Our Lady of the Flowers* (1944), while in prison for theft. It was followed by a series of prose works, including *Miracle of the Rose* (1950) and *The Thief's Journal* (1949), all more or less based on Genet's experiences in the underworld of homosexual prostitutes, thieves, and smugglers. Tom F. Driver (*SR*) called *Miracle of the Rose* "a major achievement of modern literature . . . . Genet transforms experiences of degradation into spiritual exercises and hoodlums into bearers of the majesty of love." Beginning in the early 1950s, Genet turned to the theater, creating plays such as *The Balcony* (1956) and *The Maids* (1948), which have been produced throughout the world. His drama shares many elements with the theater of the absurd. Yet it confronts issues of power and social injustice while avoiding didacticism.

Genet's work has been the subject of two influential critical works by major philosophers. Sartre's (see also Vol. 4) *Saint Genet, Comedian and Martyr* (1952) depicts the writer as an existentialist hero determined to break with social convention. Jacques Derrida's (see Vol. 4) *Glas* (1974)—in many ways a response to Sartre—explores Genet's writing as a system of signs that undermines the notion of identity.

Plays by Genet

The Balcony. 1956. Trans. by Bernard Frechtman. Grove Pr. 1985 $8.95. ISBN 0-8021-5034-9. A brothel forms the backdrop for a tale of illusion and fantasy.

The Blacks: A Clown Story. 1958. Trans. by Bernard Frechtman. Grove Pr. 1988 $8.95. ISBN 0-8021-5028-4. Explores the theme of racism.

Funeral Rites. 1948. Trans. by Bernard Frechtman. Grove Pr. 1987 $9.95. ISBN 0-8021-3087-9

The Maids. 1948. Trans. by Bernard Frechtman. Grove Pr. o.p. An exploration of power and violence in a bourgeois house. Introduction by Jean-Paul Sartre.

The Screens. 1961. Trans. by Bernard Frechtman. Grove Pr. 1987 $7.95. ISBN 0-8021-5158-2

FICTION BY GENET

Our Lady of the Flowers. 1944. Trans. by Bernard Frechtman. Grove Pr. 1987 $8.95. ISBN 0-8021-3013-5. Introduction by Jean-Paul Sartre.

The Thief's Journal. 1949. Trans. by Bernard Frechtman. Grove Pr. 1987 $8.95. ISBN 0-8021-3014-3. Introduction by Jean-Paul Sartre.

Miracle of the Rose. 1950. Trans. by Bernard Frechtman. Grove Pr. 1988 $10.95. ISBN 0-8021-3088-7

BOOKS ABOUT GENET

Choukri, Mohamed. *Jean Genet in Tangier.* Trans. by Paul Bowles. Ecco Pr. 1990 $7.95. ISBN 0-88001-246-3

Derrida, Jacques. *Glas.* Trans. by John P. Leavey and Richard Rand. U. of Nebr. Pr. 1990 repr. of 1974 ed. $80.00. ISBN 0-8032-1667-X. Challenging meditation on Genet and Hegel.

Giles, Jane. *The Cinema of Jean Genet: Un Chant d'Amour. Advances in Semiotics Ser.* Ind. U. Pr. 1991 $29.95. ISBN 0-253-32584-6. Sets forth a shot-by-shot description of Genet's film, including a few stills, as well as an historical introduction to the film and a good general study.

Knapp, Bettina. *Jean Genet. Twayne's World Author Ser.* Macmillan 1989 $26.95. ISBN 0-8057-8240-0. A psychologically based study.

Oswald, Laura. *Jean Genet and the Semiotics of Performance. Advances in Semiotics Ser.* Ind. U. Pr. 1989 $34.95. ISBN 0-253-33152-8. Studies productions of Genet as systems of signs.

Savona, Jeannette L. *Jean Genet.* St. Martin 1990 $11.95. ISBN 0-333-29224-3

GIDE, ANDRÉ. 1869–1951 (NOBEL PRIZE 1947)

Gide, the reflective rebel against bourgeois morality and one of the most important and controversial figures in modern European literature, published his first book anonymously at the age of 18. Gide was born in Paris, the only child of a law professor and a strict Calvinist mother. As a young man, he was an ardent member of the symbolist group, but the style of his later work is more in the tradition of classicism. Much of his work is autobiographical, and the story of his youth and early adult years and the discovery of his own sexual tendencies is related in *Si le grain ne meurt* (*If it die . . .*) (1926). *Corydon* (1923) deals with the question of homosexuality openly. Gide's reflections on life and literature are contained in his *Journals* (1954), which span the years 1889–1949.

He was a founder of the influential *Nouvelle Revue Française,* in which the works of many prominent modern European authors appeared, and he remained a director until 1941. He resigned when the journal passed into the hands of the collaborationists. Gide's sympathies with communism prompted him to travel to Russia, where he found the realities of Soviet life less attractive than he had imagined. His accounts of his disillusionment were published as *Return from the U.S.S.R.* (1937) and *Afterthoughts from the U.S.S.R.* (1938). Always preoccupied with freedom, a champion of the oppressed, a skeptic, he remained an incredibly youthful spirit.

Gide himself classified his fiction into three categories: satirical tales with elements of farce, like *Les Caves du Vatican* (*Lafcadio's Adventures*) (1914), which he termed *soties;* ironic stories narrated in the first person like *The Immoralist* (1902) and *Strait Is the Gate* (1909), which he called *récits;* and a more complex narrative related from a multifaceted point of view, which he called a *roman* (novel). The only example of the last category that he published was *The Counterfeiters* (1926).

Throughout his career, Gide maintained an extensive correspondence with such figures as VALÉRY, CLAUDEL, RILKE, and others.

NOVELS BY GIDE

Amyntas. 1896. Trans. by Richard Howard. Ecco Pr. 1988 $17.00. ISBN 0-88001-166-1

Corydon. 1923. Trans. by Richard Howard. Schoenhof's Foreign Bks. $7.95. ISBN 2-07-038355-0

The Counterfeiters. 1926. Trans. by Dorothy Bussy. Random 1973 $9.00. ISBN 0-394-71842-9

The Immoralist. 1902. Trans. by Richard Howard. Random 1984 $7.95. ISBN 0-394-60500-4. A wealthy intellectual seeks his identity in North Africa.

Lafcadio's Adventures. 1914. Trans. by Dorothy Bussy. Bentley 1980 repr. of 1925 ed. $18.00. ISBN 0-8376-0452-4. An ironic tale of a plot to take over the Vatican in which Gide develops his notion of the "gratuitous act."

Strait Is the Gate. 1909. Trans. by Dorothy Bussy. Bentley 1980 repr. of 1924 ed. $18.00. ISBN 0-8376-0453-2

NONFICTION BY GIDE

Journals of André Gide. 2 vols. Trans. by Justin O'Brien. 1987 repr. of 1947 ed. $14.95 ea. ISBNs 0-8101-0764-3, 0-8101-0765-1. Perhaps Gide's most interesting work. Full of fascinating reflections on life and literature.

Self-Portraits: The Gide-Valéry Letters, 1890–1942. Trans. by June Guicharnaud. Ed. by Robert Mallet. Bks. Demand $86.50. ISBN 0-317-26503-2

BOOKS ABOUT GIDE

Apter, Emily S. *André Gide and the Codes of Homotextuality*. Anma Libri 1987 $46.50. ISBN 0-915838-64-8. Considers the relationship of sexuality to writing in Gide.

Brée, Germaine. *Gide*. Greenwood 1985 repr. of 1963 ed. $57.75. ISBN 0-313-24797-8

Rossi, Vinio. *André Gide*. Col. U. Pr. 1968 $7.50. ISBN 0-231-02960-8

Schlumberger, Jean. *Madeleine and André Gide: The Platonic Marriage of Saint and Homosexual*. Trans. by Richard H. Akeroyd. Portals Pr. 1981 $12.50. ISBN 0-916620-45-X. Study by a noted French intellectual and friend of Gide.

GIONO, JEAN. 1895–1970

Germaine Brée and M. Guiton have written, "When Giono's first novel, *Colline* (*Hill of Destiny*) appeared in 1929, it struck a fresh, new note. . . . After Proust and Gide, Duhamel and Romains, Cocteau and Giraudoux, what could be more restful than a world of wind and sun and simple men who apparently had never heard of psychological analysis, never confronted any social problems, never read any books. . . ." (*An Age of Fiction*). Raised by his shoemaker father in a small town in the south of France, Giono's fiction has its roots in the peasant life of Provence. Horrified by his experiences in World War I, Giono returned to the world of his youth, which became the world of his imagination. After the shock of World War II, his novels seemed to gain in stature. One of his best is *Horseman on the Roof* (1951), his chronicle of the great cholera epidemic of 1838.

NOVELS BY GIONO

Blue Boy. 1932. Trans. by Katherine A. Clarke. N. Point Pr. 1981 repr. of 1946 ed. $9.50. ISBN 0-86547-037-5

Harvest. 1930. Trans. by Henri Fluchère and Geoffrey Myers. N. Point Pr. 1984 repr. of 1930 ed. $9.00. ISBN 0-86547-124-X. Love and redemption in peasant village.
Horseman on the Roof. 1951. Trans. by Jonathan Griffin. N. Point Pr. 1982 repr. of 1954 ed. $12.50. ISBN 0-86547-060-X
Joy of Man's Desiring. 1935. Trans. by Katherine A. Clarke. N. Point Pr. 1980 repr. of 1940 ed. $14.95. ISBN 0-86547-015-4
The Man Who Planted Hope and Grew Happiness. 1954. Friends Nature o.p.
The Man Who Planted Trees. Chelsea Green 1990 $21.95. ISBN 0-930031-35-0
To The Slaughterhouse. 1931. Dufour 1969 $23.00. ISBN 0-7206-3602-7

BOOK ABOUT GIONO

Redfern, Walter D. *The Private World of Jean Giono*. Bks. Demand repr. of 1967 ed. $54.30. ISBN 0-8357-9115-7

GIRAUDOUX, JEAN. 1882–1944

A novelist, playwright, and critic, Giraudoux entered the diplomatic service in 1910 and, with the exception of World War I, pursued that career until his retirement in 1940. He rose from the rank of consular attaché to that of cabinet minister. Giraudoux traveled widely (he was always fascinated by Germany) and had published about 30 titles, most of them novels, before becoming a dramatist at age 46. His first play, *Siegfried* (1922), marks an important watershed in French theater because it turns away from the conventions of naturalism toward a more poetic and intellectually dense drama. Giraudoux's novels are noted for their preciosity of language and their poetic and mythical qualities. His plays are highly stylized and poetic, generally avoiding "psychological realism." They are frequently confrontations of ideas or contrasts of opposing attitudes toward human experience. He was "more interested in ideas than in dramatic action, more interested in conversation than in ideas" (Gassner). Two of Giraudoux's plays won the New York Drama Critics Circle Award: *Ondine* (1939) in 1954 and *Tiger at the Gates* (1935) in 1956.

PLAYS BY GIRAUDOUX

Four Plays. Vol. I. Adapted by Maurice Valency. Hill & Wang 1958 $9.95. ISBN 0-8090-0712-6. Contains *Ondine, The Enchanted, The Madwoman of Chaillot,* and *The Apollo of Bellac*.
Plays. Vol. II. Trans. by Roger Gallert. Boulevard 1967 o.p.
Suzanne and the Pacific. 1921. Trans. by Ben R. Redman. Fertig 1975 repr. of 1923 ed. $40.00. ISBN 0-86527-311-1

BOOKS ABOUT GIRAUDOUX

Body, Jacques. *Jean Giraudoux: The Legend and the Secret*. Trans. by James Norwood. Fairleigh Dickinson 1991 $28.00. ISBN 0-8386-3407-9. Six poetical essays that employ biographical elements to examine different aspects of Giraudoux's work.
Mankin, Paul A. *Precious Irony: The Theatre of Jean Giraudoux. Studies in French Lit.* Mouton 1971 $34.70. ISBN 90-2791-918-6
Raymond, Agnes. *Jean Giraudoux: The Theatre of Victory and Defeat*. U. of Mass. Pr. 1966 $12.95. ISBN 0-87023-013-1

GREEN, JULIEN. 1900–

Julien Green, who writes in French, was born in Paris of American parents. He spent his childhood in France, returning to the United States only to study at the University of Virginia and to serve in both world wars. American life is the background for his two novels, *Mont-Cinère* (1926) and *Moïra* (1950). French provincial life is the setting for *Adrienne Mesurat* (*The Closed Garden*) (1927), and also for *Léviathan* (*The Dark Journey*) (1929). *Each in His Darkness* (1961) is a novel about a Frenchman and his dying uncle in America. In his diary, Julien Green reveals his "sensitive, poetic nature" and provides insights into the obsessive, nightmarish atmosphere of his works as well as into the major conflicts of his life—Catholicism versus Protestantism, and "the struggle between spiritual energy and sensual emotion" (Justin O'Brien, *SR*).

Nonfiction by Green

Diary: Nineteen Twenty-Eight to Nineteen Fifty-Seven. Carroll & Graf 1985 $9.95. ISBN 0-88184-119-6.

God's Fool: The Life of Francis of Assisi. HarpC 1987 $11.00. ISBN 0-06-063464-2

Memories of Evil Days. Ed. by Jean-Pierre Piriou. U. Pr. of Va. 1976 $20.00. ISBN 0-8139-0553-2

Memories of Happy Days. Greenwood repr. of 1942 ed. $45.00. ISBN 0-8371-2310-0

Books about Green

Dunaway, John M. *The Metamorphoses of the Self: The Mystic, the Sensualist, and the Artist in the Works of Julien Green*. U. Pr. of Ky. 1978 o.p.

Kostis, Nicholas. *The Exorcism of Sex and Death in Julien Green's Novels*. Mouton 1973 $20.00. ISBN 90-2792-602-6

HUGO, VICTOR MARIE. 1802–1885

The figure of Victor Hugo dominates the landscape of nineteenth-century French literature. Like a vast colossus he bestrides the century, from the time that it was two years old until the sunset years of the eighties. In the realms of poetry, criticism, drama, and fiction, he left an indelible mark. As a public figure, he offers the prototype for the "committed" intellectuals of our own century.

The revolutionary song of his *Odes et Ballades* (1826) and *Les Orientales* (1829) is alive with music and rich in words and images. *Les Châtiments* (1853) is a collection of invectives directed against Louis Napoleon from Hugo's exile on the island of Guernsey. *La Légende des Siècles* (1859, 1877, and 1883) is a vast poetic vision of world history from the creation to the present and beyond. Hugo's poems are perhaps the greatest of his works, and among the greatest productions of modern literature. It is unfortunate that, of all his work, this part has proved least amenable to translation into English.

In the realm of drama, his *Cromwell* (1827) and *Hernani* (1830) won him notoriety for breaking away from the French neoclassic traditions of the drama. His defense of his aesthetic, the "Preface to Cromwell," is one of the essential documents in the history of criticism.

To English-speaking readers, Hugo is probably best known as the author of *Notre-Dame de Paris* (*The Hunchback of Notre Dame*) (1831) and of *Les Misérables* (1862), an immense tale of human courage and social oppression set in the era of the first Napoleon. Both novels were made into classic motion pictures, and the latter inspired a London and Broadway musical.

When Hugo returned from exile in 1870, at the collapse of the empire of Napoleon III, he was welcomed and propelled into the arena of politics, where he remained a controversial voice to the last. When he died in 1885, all of France went into mourning, as if not an author, but a national hero, had passed from the scene.

Novels by Hugo

The Hunchback of Notre Dame. 1831. P-H 1987 $3.75. ISBN 0-13-448085-6

Les Misérables. Trans. by Norman Denny. Viking Penguin 1982 $8.95. ISBN 0-14-044430-0

Notre-Dame of Paris. Trans. by John Sturrock. Viking Penguin 1978 $5.95. ISBN 0-14-044353-3

Books about Hugo

Brombert, Victor. *Victor Hugo and the Visionary Novel.* HUP 1984 $25.00. ISBN 0-674-93550. A study of the best of Hugo's novels.

Brown, Nathalie B. *Hugo and Dostoevsky.* Ardis Pubs. 1978 o.p. An interesting comparative study.

Guerlac, Suzanne. *The Impersonal Sublime: Hugo, Baudelaire, Lautréamont.* Stanford U. Pr. 1990 $29.50. ISBN 0-8047-1786-9. A poststructuralist, philosophically sophisticated analysis.

Houston, John P. *Victor Hugo. Twayne's World Authors Ser.* G. K. Hall 1974 $22.99. ISBN 0-8057-8238-9

Maurois, André. *Victor Hugo.* Trans. by Gerard Hopkins. Carroll & Graf 1986 $12.95. ISBN 0-88184-211-7. A good, readable biography and evaluative study.

IONESCO, EUGENE. 1912–

Born in Rumania and educated in France, Ionesco first attracted critical notice when *The Chairs* (1952) was produced in New York. Wildly improbable, hilarious, and wholly original, all of his plays combine and contrast the comic and the tragic, the possible and the unlikely. He ranks with Beckett and Brecht as a leading exponent of experimental European theater during the period after World War II.

Ionesco's first play, *The Bald Soprano* (1950)—a farce inspired by the author's attempt to teach himself English—opened to an audience of three persons. Ten years later, his thirteenth play, *Rhinoceros* (1960)—an allegory about social conformity and totalitarianism—opened to a packed house in a national theater under the guidance of no less accomplished a director than Jean-Louis Barrault. Since that time a number of other plays, most notably *Exit the King* (1963) and *Macbett* (1972) have drawn critical acclaim. In recent years Ionesco has also turned his attention to other literary genres, writing essays, stories, and a novel.

Plays by Ionesco

Four Plays. Trans. by Donald M. Allen. Grove Pr. 1988 $8.95. ISBN 0-8021-3079-8. Contains *The Bald Soprano, The Lesson, Jack, or the Submission,* and *The Chairs.*

Killing Game. 1957. Trans. by Helen G. Bishop. Grove Pr. 1989 $2.95. ISBN 0-8021-5047-0

Rhinoceros and Other Plays: The Leader, The Future Is in Eggs. Trans. by Derek Prouse. Grove Pr. 1988 $8.95. ISBN 0-8021-3098-4

Three Plays. Trans. by Donald Watson. Grove Pr. 1988 $8.95. ISBN 0-8021-3101-8. Contains *Amédée, The New Tenant,* and *Victims of Duty.*

Three Plays: Exit the King, The Killer, Macbett. Trans. by Donald Watson and Charles Marowitz. Grove Pr. $12.95. ISBN 0-8021-5110-8

Novel by Ionesco

The Hermit. Trans. by Richard Seaver. Grove Pr. 1987 $7.95. ISBN 0-8050-0178-6. A man withdraws from the world into contemplation.

Works by Ionesco

Fragments of a Journal. 1967. Trans. by Jean Stewart. Paragon Hse. 1990 $16.95. ISBN 1-55-778-390-X

Journeys among the Dead. Trans. by Barbara Wright. Riverrun NY 1984 $5.95. ISBN 0-7145-3956-2

Man with Bags. Trans. by Marie-France Ionesco. Grove Pr. 1977 $3.95. ISBN 0-8021-5166-3

Books about Ionesco

Lamont, Rosette C. *The Two Faces of Ionesco.* Ed. by Rosette C. Lamont and Melvin J. Friedman. Whitston 1978 $15.00. ISBN 0-87875-110-6

Pronko, Leonard C. *Eugene Ionesco.* Col. U. Pr. 1965 $7.50. ISBN 0-231-02681-1

LACLOS, PIERRE AMBROISE FRANÇOIS CHODERLOS DE. 1741–1803

Les Liaisons Dangereuses (1784) by Laclos is, by common agreement, one of the key French novels of the eighteenth century. The fame of Laclos, a military man by profession, rests on this one literary work. A novel of adultery and seduction, the work is structured in the form of a series of letters exchanged by the principal characters as they manipulate and deceive one another. Its brilliant analysis of the strategies and illusions of love and sensuality offers an unparalleled dissection of the relationship between desire and power.

Novel by Laclos

Les Liaisons Dangereuses. 1784. Trans. by P. W. Stone. Knopf 1992 $17.00. ISBN 0-679-41325-1

Book about Laclos

De Jean, Joan. *Literary Fortifications: Rousseau, Laclos, Sade.* Princeton U. Pr. 1984 $47.50. ISBN 0-691-06611-6. A good study that places Laclos in the intellectual context of his age.

LAFAYETTE, MARIE MADELEINE DE LA VERGNE, COMTESSE DE. 1634–1693

La Fayette was married at the age of 21 to an army officer who was many years her senior. After the couple separated, La Fayette became part of the brilliant literary circle that included Mme de Sévigné and La Rochefoucauld. Her great novel, *La Princesse de Clèves* (1678), is a work of acute psychological analysis that focuses on the problem of an extramarital passion that shatters an otherwise apparently happy marriage. La Fayette wrote in an age when women were constrained to conceal their authorship, and for many years it was assumed that much of her work was coauthored by her male "editors." Only recently has the strength and originality of her genius begun to be recognized fully.

Novel by La Fayette

The Princess of Clèves. 1678. Greenwood 1977 repr. of 1951 ed. $38.50. ISBN 0-8371-9729-5

Books about La Fayette

Haig, Stirling. *Madame de La Fayette. Twayne's World Authors Ser.* Irvington 1970 17.95. ISBN 0-8057-2508-3

Kuizenga, Donna. *Narrative Strategies in "La Princesse de Clèves."* French Forum 1976 $9.95. ISBN 0-917058-01-1. A good formalist study.

Willard, Ruth. *Themes and Images in the Fictional Works of Mme de Lafayette.* P. Lang Pubs. 1991 $35.00. ISBN 0-8204-1392-5. Thorough examination of Lafayette's themes and use of imagery.

LA FONTAINE, JEAN DE. 1621–1695

Although he had a degree to practice law, La Fontaine does not seem to have done so but, rather, spent his life in Paris dependent on aristocratic patrons. His principal contribution to literature was his 12 books of *Fables,* to which he devoted 30 years of his life. They were published from 1668 to 1694 and are universally appreciated in France by children and adults alike. In drawing on a tradition of the fable going back to AESOP, La Fontaine created a portrait of human life and French society through the representations of animals. His work is marked by great insight into human moral character, while it preaches the value of the middle road.

SHORT STORY COLLECTIONS BY LA FONTAINE

Fables of La Fontaine. Ed. by Norman Spector. Northwestern U. Pr. 1988 $49.95. ISBN 0-8101-0759-7

Selected Fables. Trans. by Eunice Clark. Dover $4.50. ISBN 0-486-21878-3. Renders La Fontaine's fables as precisely as possible.

Selected Fables. Trans. by James Mitchie. Viking Penguin 1982 $4.95. ISBN 0-14-044376-2

BOOKS ABOUT LA FONTAINE

Guiton, Margaret. *La Fontaine: Poet and Counterpoet.* Brown Bk. 1970 o.p.

Lapp, John C. *Esthetics of Negligence: La Fontaine's Contes.* Cambridge U. Pr. 1971 $44.50. ISBN 0-521-08067-3. Filled with insightful analyses of La Fontaine's style.

Sweetser, Marie-Odile. *La Fontaine. Twayne's World Author Ser.* Macmillan 1987 $22.95. ISBN 0-8057-6639-1. Thorough biography of La Fontaine that takes into account all the most important editions and criticism about him.

Wadsworth, Philip A. *Young La Fontaine.* AMS Pr. 1970 repr. of 1952 ed. $28.00. ISBN 0-404-50729-8

LA ROCHEFOUCAULD, FRANÇOIS, DUC DE. 1613–1680

La Rochefoucauld was one of the great classical French moralists, and his entire literary reputation is based on the small volume *Maxims*, originally published in 1665. La Rochefoucauld pares down the limits of literary expression to the finely balanced measure of a sentence, or a brief paragraph. Carefully, he points out the hypocrisies of humankind. All human behavior—good, evil, or merely ordinary—is, in his eyes, tainted by self-interest. The views expressed in the maxims were the bitter fruit of the author's years as a courtier. When his expectations of favor were at last disappointed, he retired from the royal circle and enjoyed the company and conversation of talented and sympathetic writers such as MME DE SÉVIGNÉ and MME DE LA FAYETTE. His work has been an influence on writers as diverse as NIETZSCHE (see Vol. 4) and BARTHES.

NONFICTION BY LA ROCHEFOUCAULD

The Maxims. Found. Class Reprints 1984 $178.45. ISBN 0-685-08468-X

BOOKS ABOUT LA ROCHEFOUCAULD

Lewis, Philip E. *La Rochefoucauld: The Art of Abstraction.* Cornell Univ. Pr. 1977 o.p. Focuses on Le Rochefoucauld's rhetorical strategies.

Mourgues, Odette de. *Two French Moralists. Major European Authors Ser.* Cambridge U. Pr. 1978 $47.95. ISBN 0-521-21823-3. Useful general analysis comparing La Rochefoucauld and his contemporary La Bruyère.

LEDUC, VIOLETTE. 1907–1971

Violette Leduc had been publishing works of an autobiographical nature in France since 1945. But, aside from the enthusiastic support of SIMONE DE BEAUVOIR, JEAN-PAUL SARTRE (see also Vol. 4), and certain other intellectuals, she had gone unnoticed until the publication of *La Bâtarde* (1964) propelled her to fame—in part, no doubt, for "the candor in the totally uninhibited descriptions of [her] Lesbian loves. . . . This, the story of [her] first forty years, is a courageous confession and a work of art, . . . a weird mixture of burning, naive, lucid, and unadorned sincerity . . . and of poetic inner monologue" (Henri Peyre, *SR*).

NOVELS BY LEDUC

La Bâtarde. Trans. by Derek Coltman. FS&G 1965 o.p.
Mad in Pursuit. 1970. Trans. by Derek Coltman. FS&G 1971 o.p.
The Taxi. 1971. Trans. by Helen Weaver. FS&G 1972 o.p.

BOOK ABOUT LEDUC

Courtivron, Isabelle de. *Violette Leduc. Twayne's World Authors Ser.* G. K. Hall 1985 o.p.

LÉVI-STRAUSS, CLAUDE. 1908–

[SEE Volume 3.]

MALLARMÉ, STÉPHANE. 1842–1898

Mallarmé, along with BAUDELAIRE and RIMBAUD, is a seminal modern poet, and his influence is worldwide. Mallarmé's poetry is difficult to access but extremely rich and rewarding. Realizing early on that a gulf exists between language and the reality it tries to describe, Mallarmé dedicated his life to exploring that gulf, to tracing the ways in which language points to a reality that it can never reach or evoke. His religion was art, to which he dedicated his life, earning his living somewhat shabbily as an English teacher. "Everything in the world," he wrote, "exists to end up in a book." Much of his later life was concerned with working on an unfinished and unfinishable piece entitled *The Book*, that is, the book that would cover and replace the universe. In addition to this impossible task, Mallarmé wrote essays and prose poems. His Thursday afternoon literary salons were a feature of Parisian literary life during the last years of his life, and many of the greatest figures of modern French literature, from GIDE to VALÉRY received their education under Mallarmé's gaze.

POETRY BY MALLARMÉ

Herodias. 1864. Trans. by Clark Mills. AMS Pr. repr. of 1940 ed. $16.50. ISBN 0-404-16329-7
Poems. Trans. by Roger Fry. AMS Pr. repr. of 1937 ed. $32.00. ISBN 0-404-16330-0
Selected Poems. Trans. by C. F. MacIntyre. U. CA Pr. 1957 $9.95. ISBN 0-520-00801-4
Selected Poetry and Prose. Ed. by Mary Ann Caws. New Dir. Pr. 1982 $8.95. ISBN 0-8112-0823-0

WORK BY MALLARMÉ

Selected Letters of Stéphane Mallarmé. Trans. by Rosemary Lloyd. U. Ch. Pr. 1988 $27.50. ISBN 0-226-48841-1. Playful, passionate, and tender letters that reveal both the mature poet and a sensitive, complex human being.

BOOKS ABOUT MALLARMÉ

Bersani, Leo. *The Death of Stéphane Mallarmé.* Cambridge U. Pr. 1982 $27.95. ISBN 0-521-23863-3
Bloom, Harold, ed. *Stéphane Mallarmé.* Chelsea Hse. 1987 o.p. Collection of major articles by French and American critics.
Bowie, Malcolm. *Mallarmé and the Art of Being Difficult.* Cambridge U. Pr. 1982 $39.95. ISBN 0-521-21813-6

Chiari, Joseph. *Symbolism from Poe to Mallarmé: The Growth of a Myth.* Gordian 1970 repr. of 1956 ed. $45.00. ISBN 0-87752-020-8. Foreword by T. S. Eliot.

Cohn, Robert G. *Mallarmé's Prose Poems: A Critical Study.* Cambridge U. Pr. 1987 $44.95. ISBN 0-521-32552-8. Major bilingual edition of Mallarmé's prose poems.

______. *Toward the Poems of Mallarmé.* U. CA Pr. 1965 $10.95. ISBN 0-520-03846-0

Marvick, Louis W. *Mallarmé and the Sublime.* State U. NY Pr. 1986 $19.95. ISBN 0-88706-279-2

Sartre, Jean-Paul. *Mallarmé, or the Poet of Nothingness.* Trans. by Ernest Sturm. Pa. St. U. Pr. 1988 $25.00. ISBN 0-271-00498-3. The philosopher's meditation on Mallarmé as a precursor of existentialism.

MALRAUX, ANDRÉ. 1901–1976

Malraux lived many lives: airplane pilot, explorer, smuggler of art objects, and guerrilla revolutionary in China and Spain. He also served under General de Gaulle in the French Resistance. His literary reputation is based principally on three novels. *Man's Fate* (1933), which won the Prix Goncourt, deals with the Shanghai revolution of 1927. *Days of Wrath* (1936) tells the story of an underground Communist leader in Hitler's Germany. *Man's Hope* (1937), about the civil war in Spain, was made into a stirring film. These novels have little plot. They are crowded with characters and read like firsthand historical testimonies; their heroes are men of action who are passionately devoted to their cause. Though it was Sartre (see also Vol. 4) who was to preach *l'engagement* (involving oneself in the moral struggles of humankind), Malraux "practiced commitment in a much more impressive way. . . . He also expressed the concepts of the 'Absurd' and 'Existentialist Man' well in advance of the time when these terms became part of common parlance" (*NYRB*).

After World War II Malraux combined his literary ambitions with his longstanding interest in art history, producing what many consider his masterpiece, *The Voices of Silence* (1951), a survey of the whole history of art in relation to humanity's religious beliefs and aspirations.

Novels by Malraux

The Conquerors. 1928. Trans. by Stephen Becker. U. Ch. Pr. 1991 $10.95. ISBN 0-226-50290-2. Story of a Bolshevik revolutionary at odds with a European anarchist, based on Malraux's experiences in China during the 1920 revolution.

Days of Wrath. 1936. Trans. by Haakon M. Chevalier. Arden Lib. repr. of 1936 ed. o.p.

Man's Fate. 1933. Trans. by Haakon M. Chevalier. Random 1990 $11.00. ISBN 0-679-72574-1

Man's Hope. 1937. Trans. by Stuart Gilbert and Alastair MacDonald. Random $10.95. ISBN 0-394-60478-4

The Voices of Silence: Man and His Art. 1951. Trans. by Stuart Gilbert. Princeton U. Pr. 1978 repr. of 1953 ed. $80.00. ISBN 0-691-09941-3

Nonfiction by Malraux

Anti-Memoirs. H. Holt & Co. 1990 $13.95. ISBN 0-8050-1409-8. The author's autobiography.

The Walnut Trees of Altenberg. Trans. by A. W. Fielding. U. Ch. Pr. 1991 $11.95. ISBN 0-226-50289-9. A memoir of Malraux's youth.

Books about Malraux

Bevan, David. *André Malraux: Towards the Expression of Transcendence.* U. of Toronto Pr. 1986 $34.95. ISBN 0-7735-0552-0

Bloom, Harold, ed. *André Malraux.* Chelsea Hse. 1988 o.p. Essays on various aspects of Malraux's work.

Frohock, Wilbur M. *André Malraux and the Tragic Imagination.* Stanford U. Pr. 1952 $25.00. ISBN 0-8047-0441-4

Kline, Thomas J. *André Malraux and the Metamorphosis of Death.* Col. U. Pr. 1973 $40.50. ISBN 0-231-03608-6

Wilkinson, David O. *Malraux: An Essay in Political Criticism.* HUP 1967 $18.50. ISBN 0-674-54400-5

MARIVAUX, PIERRE CARLET DE CHAMBLAIN DE. 1688–1763

Marivaux was an outstanding playwright and novelist, noted for his witty plays, which were centered around subtle analyses of the theme of love. Two of the most famous, still performed today in France, are *Le Jeu de l'Amour et du Hasard* (*The Game of Love and Chance*) (1730) and *Les Fausses Confidences* (False Trust) (1737). Marivaux found his home in the literary salons of the day, and his style, termed *marivaudage* and consisting of witty repartee between characters, reflects the delicate nuances of such social existence. Marivaux is also known for two unfinished novels, *La Vie de Marianne* (1731–41), interesting for its depiction of female life in the eighteenth century, and *Le Paysan Parvenu* (The Self-made Peasant) (1735–36), the story of the rise in society of a poor peasant named Jacob.

Plays by Marivaux

Marivaux Plays. Heinemann Ed. 1988 $11.95. ISBN 0-413-18560-5

Seven Comedies. Trans. and ed. by Oscar Mandel and Adrienne Mandel. Irvington 1984 repr. of 1968 ed. $39.00. ISBN 0-686-60850-X. Contains Marivaux's major plays.

Books about Marivaux

Marshall, David. *The Surprising Effects of Sympathy: Marivaux, Diderot, Rousseau and Mary Shelley.* U. Ch. Pr. 1988 $27.50. ISBN 0-226-50710-6. Places Marivaux in the context of the psychology of his day.

Rosbottom, Ronald C. *Marivaux's Novels: Theme and Function in Early Eighteenth-Century Narrative.* Fairleigh Dickinson 1975 $22.50. ISBN 0-8386-1419-1

MAUPASSANT, GUY DE. 1850–1893

A disciple of Gustave Flaubert, Maupassant is one of the most popular writers of the modern short story, of which he published more than 300. He also wrote six novels, including *Bel Ami* (1885) and *Pierre and Jean* (1888). A native of Normandy and a former civil servant, Maupassant demonstrated in his short stories his concern with those two worlds. Among the most famous are "The Necklace" and "Mademoiselle Fifi." His attitude toward bourgeois life was a mixture of contempt and pity, and like his master, Flaubert, Maupassant was a pessimist at heart. Maupassant suffered from mental illness brought on by syphilis, and he died insane at the age of 43.

Short Story Collections by Maupassant

Best Short Stories of Guy de Maupassant. Airmont Class. Ser. Airmont 1968 $2.75. ISBN 0-8049-0161-9

The Dark Side: Tales of Terror and the Supernatural. Trans. by Arnold Kellett. Carroll & Graf 1990 $8.95. ISBN 0-88184-596-5. A collection of chilling tales.

A Day in the Country and Other Stories. Trans. by David Coward. OUP 1990 $5.95. ISBN 0-19-282642-5

Saint Anthony and Other Stories. Trans. by Lafcadio Hearn. Ayer repr. of 1924 ed. $16.00. ISBN 0-14-044243-X

Selected Short Stories. Trans. by Roger Colet. Viking Penguin 1971 $5.95. ISBN 0-14-044243-X. Thirty stories, including "The Jewels" and "A Duel."

Selected Stories. Trans. by Andrew R. MacAndrew. NAL-Dutton 1984 $4.95. ISBN 0-452-00686-4. Twenty-four stories, including "The Necklace" and "A Piece of String."

NOVELS BY MAUPASSANT

Bel Ami. 1885. Trans. by Douglas Parmee. Viking Penguin 1975 $5.95. ISBN 0-14-044315-0

Pierre and Jean. 1888. Trans. by Leonard Tancock. Viking Penguin 1979 $3.95. ISBN 0-14-044358-4. Two brothers dispute an inheritance.

Woman's Life. 1883. Trans. by H. N. Sloman. Viking Penguin 1978 $6.95. ISBN 0-14-044161-1

BOOKS ABOUT MAUPASSANT

Donaldson, Mary C. *A Woman's Revenge: The Chronology of Dispossession in Maupassant's Fiction.* French Forum 1986 $12.95. ISBN 0-917058-65-8. An important feminist study.

Greiman, Algirdas J. *Maupassant: The Semiotics of Text.* Trans. by Paul Perron. Benjamins North Am. 1988 $22.95. ISBN 1-55619-063. A challenging linguistic analysis.

Sullivan, Edward D. *Maupassant the Novelist.* Greenwood 1978 repr. of 1954 ed. $62.50. ISBN 0-313-20497-7. Explores basic themes in each of Maupassant's novels.

MAURIAC, FRANÇOIS. 1885–1970 (NOBEL PRIZE 1952)

François Mauriac started as a poet, publishing his first volume of verse in 1909. It is as a novelist, however, that he is most well known. Most of Mauriac's novels are set in his birthplace, Bordeaux. They reflect his classical culture and his meditation on the gospels and the Catholic contemplative writers. He is a moralist, presenting always the eternal conflict of the world and the flesh against Christian faith and charity: "Every one of his novels is a fresh attempt and an adventure into the unknown, though every one of them ends monotonously with the gift of grace that the novelist insists upon imparting to his sinners" (Henri Peyre). Mauriac is best at describing the anguish of suffering rather than suggesting solutions for human striving. Some of his most successfully drawn characters cannot achieve either earthly happiness or divine salvation. Mauriac resisted the Nazi invaders and the Vichy regime consistently and courageously during World War II. He was elected to the French Academy in 1933 and received the Nobel Prize in 1952.

NOVELS BY MAURIAC

The Desert of Love. 1925. Carroll & Graf 1989 $7.95. ISBN 0-88184-485-3. Describes the love of a father and son for the same woman.

Flesh and Blood. 1920. Carroll & Graf 1989 $8.95. ISBN 0-88184-533-7

Genitrix. 1923. Fr. & Eur. 1964 $9.95. ISBN 0-685-11212-8

La Pharisienne. 1941. Fr. & Eur. $10.95. ISBN 0-685-34299-9. Novel translated in English as *A Woman of the Pharisees.* Depicts the destruction caused by an interfering woman.

Thérèse. 1927. Trans. by Gerard Hopkins. FS&G 1951 o.p. A woman is acquitted of an attempt to poison her husband. Based on an actual trial.

Viper's Tangle. 1932. Carroll & Graf 1987 $8.95. ISBN 0-88184-305-9. Story of a family's miserliness and hypocrisy.

BOOKS ABOUT MAURIAC

Flower, John E., and Bernard C. Swift, eds. *François Mauriac: Visions and Reappraisals.* Berg Pubs. 1989 $44.00. ISBN 0-85496-272-7. Collection of essays by various critics that examine various aspects of Mauriac's work.

Smith, Maxwell A. *François Mauriac. Twayne's World Authors Ser.* Irvington 1970 $17.95. ISBN 0-8057-2604-7. A good, general thematic study.

MOLIÈRE (pseud. of Jean-Baptiste Poquelin). 1622–1673

When asked what was new in the theater, the twentieth-century actor and dramatist Sacha Guitry answered, "Why, Molière!" Molière is by far the most popular of all French playwrights and, indeed, the one who never seems to age. A master of all comic forms, ranging from farce to comedies of the intellect, Molière's brilliant accomplishments as a prolific dramatist were grounded in 12 years of struggles as an actor and as the director of his own theater company in the French provinces. The success of his *Les Précieuses Ridicules* (*The Pretentious Young Ladies*) in 1659 won him the friendship and support of Louis XIV. Molière brought together the intellectual and moral concerns of classical Roman and Greek comedy with the excitement and verbal energy of the Italian *commedia dell'arte*. His theater employs exaggerated and sometimes stock plot situations to explore the forms of human hypocrisy and self-importance. Beneath the laughter provoked by Molière's plays, there is usually a serious underlying reality. His ethical position is one that advocates a middle-of-the-road, practical approach to life. His most important plays include *Les Précieuses Ridicules* (1659), *The School for Wives* (1662), *Tartuffe* (1669), *Don Juan* (1665), *The Misanthrope* (1666), *The Miser* (1668), *The Would-Be Gentleman* (1670), *The Learned Ladies* (1672), and *The Imaginary Invalid* (1673).

Plays by Molière

The Doctor in Spite of Himself and The Bourgeois Gentleman. Trans. by Albert Bermel. Applause Theater Bk. Pubs. 1987 $5.95. ISBN 0-936839-77-5. Two satires on bourgeois pretentiousness.

Don Juan and Other Plays. Trans. by George Gravely and Ian Maclean. OUP 1989 $4.95. ISBN 0-19-282130-X. Includes Molière's telling of the Don Juan legend, his most philosophical play.

Eight Plays by Molière. Amereon Ltd. $22.95. ISBN 0-88411-448-1. Includes the major plays.

The Learned Ladies. Trans. by Richard Wilbur. Dramatists Play 1977 $3.95. ISBN 0-685-81644. Satire on the condition of women.

The Misanthrope and Other Plays. NAL-Dutton 1989 $3.50. ISBN 0-451-51721-0. Includes Molière's greatest meditation on human self-delusion.

One-Act Comedies of Molière. Trans. by Albert Bermel. Applause Theater Bk. Pubs. 1991 $8.95. ISBN 1-55783-109-2. Includes some of the lesser-known plays.

Tartuffe. Trans. by Christopher Hampton. Faber & Faber 1984 $8.50. ISBN 0-571-13358-4. The story of a pious hypocrite who attempts to swindle a Parisian family.

Books about Molière

Bulgakov, Mikhail. *Molière.* Trans. by Mirra Ginsburg. New Dir. Pr. 1986 $17.95. ISBN 0-8112-0956-3. A fictional retelling of Molière's life by the noted Russian novelist who is one of his literary heirs.

Gaines, James F. *Social Structures in Molière's Theatre.* Ohio St. U. Pr. 1984 $36.75. ISBN 0-8142-0358-2. An interesting sociological study.

Gossman, Lionel. *Men and Masks: A Study of Molière.* Johns Hopkins 1969 repr. of 1963 ed. $14.95. ISBN 0-8018-1043-4. An excellent study of the problem of identity in Molière.

Gross, Nathan. *From Gesture to Idea: Aesthetics and Ethics in Molière.* Col. U. Pr. 1982 $39.50. ISBN 0-231-05440-8

Hubert, Judd D. *Molière and the Comedy of Intellect.* U. CA Pr. 1974 $32.50. ISBN 0-520-02520-2

Knutson, Harold C. *The Triumph of Wit: Molière and Restoration Comedy.* Ohio St. U. Pr. 1987 $31.00. ISBN 0-8142-0438-4. Considers Molière's relationship to English theater.

Turnell, Martin. *The Classical Moment: Studies of Corneille, Molière, and Racine.* Greenwood 1971 repr. of 1948 ed. $45.00. ISBN 0-8371-5803-6. A general study of Molière in the context of his time.

MONTAIGNE, MICHEL EYQUEM DE. 1533–1592

Montaigne invented the essay genre, and his *Essays* are a vast compendium of his thoughts, sentiments, reflections, and opinions on all subjects imaginable, from sex to politics. A student of the law, he became counselor to the Parlement of Bordeaux. After attending the royal court in Paris and Rouen, he retired to his property at Montaigne in Périgord in 1571, where he dedicated himself to reading and study in his library tower and to the composition of his *Essays.* Aside from a journey to Italy (of which he kept a detailed diary) and two terms as mayor of Bordeaux, the principal occupation of his mature years was the nurturing of his book, which first appeared in 1580, and of which revised editions appeared in 1588 and 1595. In the *Essays,* Montaigne's thought evolves from stoicism to skepticism and to epicureanism. His lifework offers a vast compendium of the knowledge of the day and gives a fascinating picture of France during the wars of religion that marked the last part of the sixteenth century. But Montaigne's principal topic is himself; he presents in intimate detail the changing matter of his daily existence, his thoughts and his emotions, in an attempt to understand his essential being. In so doing, Montaigne created a mirror for all humankind. He is at once a most individual and universal author.

Works by Montaigne

The Apology for Raymond Sebond. Viking Penguin 1988 $7.95. ISBN 0-14-044493-9. Montaigne's longest and most challenging essay. A skeptic's breviary in which he asks the famous question, "What do I know?" With an introduction by M. A. Screech.

The Complete Works: Essays, Travel Journal, Letters. Trans. by Donald M. Frame. Stanford U. Pr. 1957 o.p. The most accurate and readable modern English translation of Montaigne.

The Essays of Montaigne. 3 vols. Trans. by John Florio. AMS Pr. repr. of 1893 ed. $135.00. ISBN 0-404-51860-5

Books about Montaigne

Bloom, Harold, ed. *Michel de Montaigne's Essays.* Chelsea Hse. 1987 $29.95. ISBN 1-55546-074-7. Contains many articles by principal specialists of Montaigne's work.

Frame, Donald M. *Montaigne: A Biography.* HarBraceJ 1965 o.p.

______. *Montaigne's Discovery of Man: The Humanization of a Humanist.* Greenwood 1983 repr. of 1955 ed. $39.75. ISBN 0-313-24120-1

Friedrich, Hugo. *Montaigne.* Trans. by Dawn Eng. U. CA Pr. 1991 $55.00. ISBN 0-520-06581-6. The best general study of Montaigne. Especially good on the intellectual traditions behind his work.

Henry, Patrick. *Montaigne in Dialogue.* Anma Libri 1988 $46.50. ISBN 0-915838-73-7. A good study of the problem of censorship in Montaigne.

Regosin, Richard. *The Matter of My Book: Montaigne's "Essais" as the Book of the Self.* U. CA Pr. 1977 $35.00. ISBN 0-520-03476-7. A good study of autobiography.

Rider, Frederick. *The Dialectic of Selfhood in Montaigne.* Stanford U. Pr. 1973 $17.50. ISBN 0-8047-0830-4. A phenomenologically oriented study.

Sayce, R. A. *Essays of Montaigne: A Critical Exploration.* Northwestern U. Pr. 1972 o.p. A good introduction.

Schaefer, David. *The Political Philosophy of Montaigne.* Cornell Univ. Pr. 1990 $45.00. ISBN 0-8014-2179-9. A careful reading that places Montaigne in the history of political thought.

Starobinski, Jean. *Montaigne in Motion*. Trans. by Arthur Goldhammer. U. Ch. Pr. 1985 $30.00. ISBN 0-226-77129-6. An important phenomenological reading by a distinguished European scholar. Especially good on the importance of the body in Montaigne's thought.

MONTESQUIEU, CHARLES LOUIS DE SECONDAT, BARON DE LA BREDE ET DE. 1689–1755

[SEE Volume 3.]

NAVARRE, MARGUERITE DE. 1492–1549

Princess of Angoulême, Queen of Navarre, and sister to King Francis I, Marguerite Navarre was in a unique position to contribute to the intellectual and political life of the French Renaissance. She participated actively in state affairs and was celebrated as a patron of the arts, drawing to her court theologians, poets, and scholars who were interested in the new ideas that would forge the Renaissance and Reformation in France. Navarre produced religious dramas and mystical poetry, but her masterpiece is the *Heptameron* (1558), a collection of 72 posthumously published tales, loosely based on BOCCACCIO's *Decameron*. These lively stories of love and adventure frequently focus on the social roles of the sexes and recall the contemporary *querelle des femmes*—the late medieval debate on the status of women. They offer a vivid image of court life during the French Renaissance and a lasting contribution to the literature of feminism.

SHORT STORY COLLECTION BY NAVARRE

The Heptameron. 1558. Trans. by P. A. Chilton. Viking Penguin 1984 $7.95. ISBN 0-14-0443555-X

BOOKS ABOUT NAVARRE

Cholokian, Patricia F. *Rape and Writing in the "Heptameron" of Marguerite de Navarre*. S. Ill. U. Pr. 1991 $34.95. ISBN 0-8093-1708-7. A feminist analysis.

Cottrell, Robert D. *The Grammar of Silence*. Catholic U. of Amer. Pr. 1986 $36.95. ISBN 0-8132-0615-4. Principally devoted to Marguerite's poetry but useful for considering her whole career.

Tetel, Marcel. *Marguerite de Navarre's Heptameron*. Duke 1973 o.p. A good general study.

PASCAL, BLAISE. 1623–1662

[SEE Volume 4.]

PERSE, SAINT-JOHN (pseud. of Alexis Saint-Léger Léger). 1887–1975 (NOBEL PRIZE 1960)

Saint-John Perse managed to combine poetry with diplomacy most of his life. Born on a small family-owned island of Guadeloupe, he became a member of the French diplomatic corps and was permanent secretary of foreign affairs after Briand's death and until the Germans invaded France. He fled to England, then Canada, and, at the request of ARCHIBALD MACLEISH (see Vol. 1), came to the United States to act as consultant on French poetry to the Library of Congress. Manuscripts left behind when he escaped from France were destroyed by the Nazis. He received the Nobel Prize in 1960.

POETRY BY PERSE

Anabasis. 1924. Trans. by T. S. Eliot. HarBraceJ 1970 repr. of 1938 ed. $2.95. ISBN 0-15-607906-0

Birds. 1962. Trans. by Robert Fitzgerald. Princeton U. Pr. 1966 $50.00. ISBN 0-691-09713-5

Collected Poems. Trans. by W. H. Auden. Princeton U. Pr. rev. ed. 1982 $77.50. ISBN 0-691-09949-9. A good selection translated by the great English poet.

Exile and Other Poems. Trans. by Denis Devlin. Princeton U. Pr. 1953 o.p.

Book about Perse

Galand, René. *Saint-John Perse. Twayne's World Authors Ser.* G. K. Hall o.p.

PINGET, ROBERT. 1919–

Before deciding to write professionally, Pinget practiced law in his native city of Geneva and studied painting at the École des Beaux Arts in Paris. He is one of the less accessible of the so-called new novelists and has seemed little interested in attracting a large following. Nevertheless, *The Inquisitory*, awarded the 1962 Prix des Critiques, became a bestseller in France. It is essentially a monologue—a deaf old servant's meandering, half-truthful responses to the terse questions of an interrogator seeking information on a man who has vanished. As the old man speaks, he brings to light all of the vice and corruption of what appears to be a placid provincial town. In 1965 Pinget's *Quelqu'un (Someone)*, about a man's search for a scrap of paper, won the Prix Femina. In addition to his work as a novelist, Pinget has also written a number of plays.

Plays by Pinget

Plays. 2 vols. Trans. by Barbara Wright and Samuel Beckett. Riverrun NY 1981. Vol. 1 $4.95. ISBN 0-7145-0474-2. Vol. 2 $11.95. ISBN 0-7145-0038-0

Short Story Collection by Pinget

Between Fantoine and Agapa. 1951. Trans. by Barbara Wright. Red Dust 1983 $8.95. ISBN 0-87376-040-9. A collection of short stories.

Novels by Pinget

The Apocrypha. 1980. Trans. by Barbara Wright. Red Dust 1987 $12.95. ISBN 0-87376-050-6. Novel whose recurring image is that of a shepherd seated on a rock and gazing out over his flocks.

The Inquisitory. 1962. Trans. by Donald Watson. Riverrun NY 1982 $11.95. ISBN 0-7145-3911-2

Someone. 1965. Trans. by Barbara Wright. Red Dust 1984 $12.95. ISBN 0-87376-043-3

Works by Pinget

Abel and Bela. 1971. Trans. by Barbara Wright. Red Dust 1987 $4.00. ISBN 0-87376-052-2

Baga. 1958. Trans. by John Stevenson. Riverrun NY 1985 repr. of 1967 ed. $7.95. ISBN 0-7145-0099-2

Fable. Trans. by Barbara Wright. Red Dust 1980 $6.95. ISBN 0-87376-036-0

Mahu. 1952. Trans. by A. M. Sheridan-Smith. Riverrun NY 1985 $6.95. ISBN 0-7145-0354-1

Monsieur Song. 1982. Trans. by Barbara Wright. Red Dust 1989 $12.95. ISBN 0-87376-060-3

Passacaglia. 1969. Trans. by Barbara Wright. *New French Writing Ser.* Red Dust 1979 $6.95. ISBN 0-87376-033-6

That Voice. 1975. Trans. by Barbara Wright. Red Dust 1983 $10.95. ISBN 0-87376-041-7

Books about Pinget

Henkels, Robert M., Jr. *Robert Pinget: The Novel as Quest.* U. of Ala. Pr. 1979 o.p.

Mercier, Vivian. *The New Novel: From Queneau to Pinget.* FS&G 1971 o.p. A useful study on Pinget and his contemporaries.

PONGE, FRANCIS. 1899–1988

A poet long unread, Ponge has come into his own since the 1950s with admirers from Sartre (see also Vol. 4) to Sollers. Sartre considered him the poet of existentialism. Yet Ponge's poetry is concerned with the priority of objectivity, with *things* as they exist apart from people. This objectivity has attracted him to writers of the new novel and to the group of semiotic critics centered on the literary review *Tel Quel*. Among his major collections are *Le Parti Pris des Choses* (*The Voice of Things*, 1942), *Le Grand Recueil* (*The Big Collection*, 1961), and *Le Savon* (*Soap*, 1967).

Poetry by Ponge

The Making of the Pré by Francis Ponge. 1971. Trans. by Lee Fahnestock. U. of Mo. Pr. 1982 $16.95. ISBN 0-8262-0381-7

Sun Placed in the Abyss and Other Texts. Trans. by Serge Gavronsky. Sun 1977 o.p.

Vegetation. Trans. by Lee Fahnestock. Red Dust 1987 $4.00. ISBN 0-87376-058-1

The Voice of Things. 1942. Trans. by Beth Archer. McGraw repr. of 1974 ed. o.p.

Books about Ponge

Derrida, Jacques. *Signeponge-Signsponge*. Trans. by Richard Rand. Col. U. Pr. 1985 $40.50. ISBN 0-231-05446-7. A philosophical interpretation.

Sampon, Annette. *Francis Ponge: La Poetique du Figural*. P. Lang Pubs. 1988 $37.00. ISBN 0-8204-0617-1

Sorrell, Martin. *Francis Ponge*. *Twayne's World Authors Ser.* G. K. Hall 1981 o.p.

PRÉVERT, JACQUES. 1900–1977

Prévert's poetry offers an irreverent, childlike view of the everyday world. Employing puns, word games, and jokes, it celebrates the unexpected and pokes fun at the serious or pompous. *Paroles* (1945), his first collection, introduced a freedom of form and an experimentation with spoken language that had been missing from much prewar and wartime poetry. Prévert also played a central role in the history of French cinema, writing several important film scripts, including the classic Marcel Carné film, *Children of Paradise* (1944). He also found the time to compose the lyrics to a number of popular songs, including the jazz standard "Autumn Leaves" ("Les Feuilles Mortes").

Poetry by Prévert

Paroles. 1945. Trans. by Lawrence Ferlinghetti. City Lights 1990 $6.95. ISBN 0-87286-249-6. A translation by a noted American poet.

Words for All Seasons. Trans. by Teo Savory. Unicorn Pr. 1979 $8.95. ISBN 0-87775-122-6. Selected poems.

Books about Prévert

Baker, William E. *Jacques Prévert*. *Twayne's World Authors Ser.* Irvington 1967 $15.95. ISBN 0-685-02667-1

Blakeway, Claire. *Jacques Prévert: Popular French Theater and Cinema*. Fairleigh Dickinson 1989 $36.50. ISBN 0-8386-3309-9. Brings together various aspects of Prévert's work.

PROUST, MARCEL. 1871–1922

Proust is one of the seminal figures in modern literature, matched only in stature by Joyce (see Vol. 1), Woolf (see Vol. 1), Mann, and Kafka. By the last decade of the nineteenth century, the charming and ambitious Proust, born into a wealthy bourgeois family, was already a famous Paris socialite who attended the most fashionable *salons* of the day. The death of his parents in the early years of the twentieth century, coupled with his own increasingly ill health, made of Proust a recluse who confined himself to his cork-lined bedroom on the Boulevard Haussmann. There he concentrated on the composition of his great masterpiece, *Remembrance of Things Past* (1913–27). In recent years, it was discovered that he had already prepared a first draft of the work in the 1890s in *Jean Santeuil,* which was only published posthumously in 1952.

Remembrance of Things Past resists summary. Seeming at turns to be fiction, autobiography, and essay, *Remembrance* is a vast meditation on the relationship between time, memory, and art. In it the narrator, who bears the same first name as the author, attempts to reconstruct his life from early childhood to middle age. In the process, he surveys French society at the turn of the century and describes the eventual decline of the aristocracy in the face of the rising middle class. The process of reconstruction of Marcel's past life is made possible by the psychological device of involuntary memory; according to this theory, all of our past lies hidden within us only to be rediscovered and brought to the surface by some unexpected sense perception. In the final volume of the work, the narrator, who has succeeded in recapturing his past, resolves to preserve it through the *Work of Art,* his novel.

NOVELS BY PROUST

Remembrance of Things Past. 1913–1927. 3 vols. Trans. by C. K. Scott-Moncrieff, Terence Kilmartin, and Andreas Mayor. Random 1981 $75.00. ISBN 0-394-50643-X. The definitive Pléiade edition. Includes: *Swann's Way, Within a Budding Grove, The Guermantes Way, The Cities of the Plain, The Captive, The Fugitive,* and *The Past Recaptured.*

SHORT STORY COLLECTION BY PROUST

Pleasures and Days: And Other Writings. Trans. by Louise Varèse, Gerard Hopkins, and B. Dupee. Fertig 1978 repr. of 1957 ed. $45.00. ISBN 0-86527-293-X. A collection of early sketches.

NONFICTION BY PROUST

Marcel Proust: Selected Letters, Vol. II: 1904–1909. Trans. by Terence Kilmartin. OUP 1989 $35.00. ISBN 0-19-505961-1. Correspondence with many of the great figures of the day.

On Reading Ruskin. Yale U. Pr. 1987 $25.00. ISBN 0-300-03513-6. Proust was an enthusiastic Anglophile who translated some of Ruskin's art criticism. One of the first French appreciations of the great English critic.

Selected Letters, Eighteen Eighty to Nineteen Hundred Three. Trans. by Ralph Mannheim. U. Ch. Pr. 1988 $16.95. ISBN 0-226-68459-8. Written during Proust's youth.

BOOKS ABOUT PROUST

Fowlie, Wallace. *A Reading of Proust.* U. Ch. Pr. 1985 $18.00. ISBN 0-226-25885-8

Goodkin, Richard E. *Around Proust.* Princeton U. Pr. 1991 $37.50. ISBN 0-691-06894-1. Examines Proust's references to Homer, Mallarmé, Racine, and Wagner to enrich the understanding of the novel.

Hayman, Ronald. *Proust: A Biography.* HarpC 1990 $27.50. ISBN 0-06-016438-7. Examines Proust's writings as well as his life to investigate the author's creativity.

Maurois, André. *Proust: Portrait of a Genius.* Carroll & Graf 1984 $10.95. ISBN 0-88184-104-8. A fascinating biography.

Painter, George. *Marcel Proust: A Biography.* 2 vols. Random 1978 $4.95 ea. ISBNs 0-685-04271-5, 0-394-72562-X. The definitive biography.

Peyre, Henri. *Marcel Proust.* Col. U. Pr. 1970 $7.50. ISBN 0-231-03046-7

Poulet, Georges. *Proustian Space*. Trans. by Elliott Coleman. Bks. Demand repr. of 1977 ed. $30.00. ISBN 0-317-41757-6. An important study of a neglected aspect of Proust.

Price, Larkin B., ed. *Marcel Proust: A Critical Panorama*. Bks. Demand repr. of 1973 ed. $75.50. ISBN 0-317-29081-9

Shattuck, Roger. *Marcel Proust. Modern Masters Ser.* Viking Penguin 1974 o.p. A good basic introduction.

Stock, Janet C. *Marcel Proust: A Reference Guide*. G. K. Hall 1991 $47.50. ISBN 0-8161-8987-0. Contains much of the most important criticism of Proust published between 1950 and 1970. Annotated and indexed.

QUENEAU, RAYMOND. 1903–1976

This author of treatises on mathematics and other scholarly works has made his reputation writing comic novels. Queneau (through one of his characters) once defined humor as "an attempt to purge lofty feelings of all the baloney." Roger Shattuck interprets his philosophy: "Life is of course absurd and it is ludicrous to take it seriously; only the comic is serious." Life is so serious to Queneau that only laughter makes it bearable. He has written a play, screenplays, poetry, numerous articles, and many novels, the first of which, *Le Chiendent* (*The Bark Tree*), was published in 1933. In *Exercises in Style* (1947) he tells a simple anecdote 99 different ways.

According to some critics, *The Blue Flowers* (1965) represents Queneau at his best. Its jokes, puns, double-entendres, deceptions, wild events, tricky correspondences, and bawdy language make it a feast of comic riches. The influence of Charlie Chaplin (see Vol. 3), as well as James Joyce (see Vol. 1), is detectable in Queneau's fiction.

Novels by Queneau

The Bark Tree. 1933. Intro. by Barbara Wright. Riverrun NY 1991 $14.95. ISBN 0-7145-0107-7. A comic tale full of jokes, puns, double-entendres, deceptions, and wild events.

The Blue Flowers. 1965. Trans. by Barbara Wright. New Dir. Pr. 1985 $8.95. ISBN 0-8112-0945-8

Exercises in Style. 1947. Trans. by Barbara Wright. New Dir. Pr. 1981 $12.95. ISBN 0-685-03562-X

The Flight of Icarus. 1968. Trans. by Barbara Wright. New Dir. Pr. 1973 $6.95. ISBN 0-8112-0483-9. A magical journey across Paris that employs the techniques of montage and film.

The Last Days. 1936. Trans. by Barbara Wright. Dalkey Arch. 1991 $9.95. ISBN 0-916583-63-5. Tale of three adults facing old age, three students doomed to military service, and one philosopher/waiter central to their destinies.

Pierrot Mon Ami. 1942. Trans. by Barbara Wright. Dalkey Arch. 1989 $20.00. ISBN 0-916583-24-4. Pierrot, a Chaplinesque figure who works at a series of marginal jobs for an amusement park, competes with his friend Paradis for the affections of the owner's daughter.

The Sunday of Life. 1952. Trans. by Barbara Wright. New Dir. Pr. 1977 $5.95. ISBN 0-8112-0645-9

We Always Treat Women Too Well. 1947. Trans. by Barbara Wright. New Dir. Pr. 1981 $6.95. ISBN 0-8112-0792-7

Zazie in the Metro. 1959. Trans. by Barbara Wright. Riverrun NY 1982 $13.95. ISBN 0-7145-3872-8. A hilarious tale of a young girl on the loose.

Poetry by Queneau

Pataphysical Poems. Trans. by Teo Savory. Unicorn Pr. 1985 $25.00. ISBN 0-87775-172-2

Selected Poems. Trans. by Teo Savory. Unicorn Pr. 1971 $6.95. ISBN 0-87775-004-1

Books about Queneau

Guicharnaud, Jacques. *Raymond Queneau.* Col. U. Pr. 1965 o.p.

Hale, Jane A. *The Lyric Encyclopedia of Raymond Queneau.* U. of Mich. Pr. 1990 $32.50. ISBN 0-472-10127-7. Good introductory study of Queneau.

Shorley, Christopher. *Queneau's Fiction: An Introductory Study.* Cambridge U. Pr. 1985 $59.95. ISBN 0-521-30397-4. A good general introduction.

Thiher, Allen. *Raymond Queneau. Twayne's World Author Ser.* Macmillan 1985 $29.95. ISBN 0-8057-6613-8. Provides a careful summary and analysis of each of Queneau's works.

RABELAIS, FRANÇOIS. 1494?–1553?

One of the leading humanist writers of the French Renaissance, Rabelais was at first a Franciscan and then a Benedictine monk, a celebrated physician and professor of anatomy, and later curé of Meudon. The works of Rabelais are filled with life to the overflowing, hence the term "Rabelaisian." His principal protagonists, Gargantua and his son, Pantagruel, are appropriately giants, not only in size, but also in spirit and action. The five books of their adventures are separate works, containing, in different measure, adventures, discussions, farcical scenes, jokes, games, satires, philosophical commentaries, and anything else that a worldly, learned man of genius such as Rabelais could pour into his work. His style is innovative and idiosyncratic, marked by humorous neologisms made up from the learned languages, Greek and Latin, side by side with the most earthy, humble, and rough words of the street and barnyard. His *Gargantua,* published in 1534, satirizes the traditional education of Parisian theologians and, in the Abbé de Thélème episode, recommends a free, hedonistic society of handsome young men and women in contrast to the restrictive life of monasticism. The gigantic scope of Rabelais's work also reflects the Renaissance thirst for encyclopedic knowledge.

Works by Rabelais

The Complete Works of François Rabelais. Trans. by Donald M. Frame. U. CA Pr. 1991 $60.00. ISBN 0-520-06400-3. The first complete translation into English.

Gargantua and Pantagruel. 3 vols. AMS Pr. repr. of 1900 ed. $135.00. ISBN 0-404-51920-2. A vigorous and lively Restoration translation.

Books about Rabelais

Bakhtin, Mikhail. *Rabelais and His World.* Trans. by Helene Iswolsky. Ind. U. Pr. 1984 $39.95. ISBN 0-253-34830-7. Groundbreaking study of Rabelais's relationship to popular culture.

Duval, Edwin M. *The Design of Rabelais' "Pantagruel."* Yale U. Pr. 1991 $28.50. ISBN 0-300-04803-3. A learned and subtle analysis of Rabelais's first book.

Febvre, Lucien. *The Problem of Unbelief in the Sixteenth Century: The Religion of Rabelais.* Trans. by Beatrice Gottlieb. HUP 1982 $12.95. ISBN 0-674-70826-1. An important reappraisal of Rabelais that stresses his religious side.

Schwartz, Jerome. *Irony and Ideology in Rabelais: Structures of Subversion.* Cambridge U. Pr. 1990 $49.50. ISBN 0-521-36520-1. A balanced analysis blending historical background with attention to linguistic features.

Screech, M. A. *Rabelais.* Cornell Univ. Pr. 1980 o.p. A learned commentary.

RACINE, JEAN. 1639–1699

Racine is considered the greatest of French tragic dramatists. If Shakespeare's (see Vol. 1) theater is characterized by exploration and invention, Racine's is defined by restraint and formal perfection. His themes are derived from Greco-Roman, biblical, and oriental sources and are developed in the neoclassic manner: keeping to few characters, observing the "three unities" defined by ARISTOTLE (see Vols. 3, 4, and 5) as essential to tragedy (i. e., unity of time, place, and action), and writing in regular 12-syllable verses called "alexandrines." In contrast to CORNEILLE, whose theater is eminently political and concerned with moral choices, Racine locates tragic intrigue in the conflict of inner emotions. He is a master at exploring the power of erotic passion to transform and pervert the human psyche. As a Jansenist who believed that a person deprived of grace was subject to the tyranny of instincts, Racine was interested in portraying human passions—particularly the passion of love—in a state of crisis. Racine is also one of the greatest of all French poets, and his plays are a challenge to any translator. His major tragedies include *Andromaque* (1667), *Britannicus* (1669), *Bérénice* (1670), *Iphigénie* (1674), and *Phèdre* (1677).

PLAYS BY RACINE

Andromache. 1667. Trans. by Richard Wilbur. HarBraceJ 1984 $6.95. ISBN 0-15-607510-5. An exiled, captive queen seeks to save her defenseless son.

Andromache and Other Plays. Trans. by John Cairncross. *Penguin Class. Ser.* Viking Penguin 1976 $8.95. ISBN 0-14-044195-6

Britannicus; Phaedra; Atalia. Trans. by C. H. Sisson. OUP 1987 $4.95. ISBN 0-19-281758-2. Includes *Atalia,* one of Racine's late experiments in wedding classical tragedy to the stuff of Old Testament history.

Four Greek Plays: Andromache, Iphigenia, Phaedra, Athaliah. Trans. by R. C. Knight. Cambridge U. Pr. 1982 $54.50. ISBN 0-521-24415-3

Phaedra and Other Plays. Trans. by John Cairncross. Viking Penguin 1964 $4.95. ISBN 0-14-044122-0

Phèdre. 1677. Trans. by Margaret Rawlings. NAL-Dutton 1962 $6.95. ISBN 0-525-47099-9. Racine's masterpiece. The passion of a queen for her husband's son.

Three Plays: Phaedra, Andromaque, Britannicus. Trans. by George Dillon. U. Ch. Pr. 1961 $8.00. ISBN 0-226-15077-1

BOOKS ABOUT RACINE

Barthes, Roland. *On Racine.* U. CA Pr. 1992 $12.00. ISBN 0-520-07824-1. A groundbreaking structuralist study.

Goldmann, Lucien. *The Hidden God.* Trans. by Philip Thody. Humanities 1976 o.p. A Marxist analysis. Places Racine in context of religious thought of his day.

Meskell, David. *Racine: A Theatrical Reading.* OUP 1991 $53.00. ISBN 0-19-815161-6. Stresses the performative aspect of Racine's work.

Orlando, Francesco. *Toward a Freudian Theory of Literature.* Trans. by Charmaine Lee. Bks. Demand $58.30. ISBN 0-8357-6622-5. Both a brilliant reading of Racine's *Phaedra* and a psychoanalytic theory of literature. Quite extraordinary.

Turnell, Martin. *Jean Racine: Dramatist.* New Dir. Pr. 1972 $17.75. ISBN 0-8112-0463-4

Weinberg, Bernard. *The Art of Jean Racine.* U. Ch. Pr. 1969 $3.45. ISBN 0-226-88549-6. Stresses the unity of Racine's work.

RADIGUET, RAYMOND. 1903–1923

Radiguet died of typhoid fever at 20, leaving one volume of unpublished poems, *The Devil Within* (1923), and two novels, *Devil in the Flesh* (1923) and *Count d'Orgel's Ball* (1924). He was a close friend of COCTEAU (see also Vol. 3), who said of him: "One is rather appalled by a boy of twenty who publishes the sort of book that can't be written at his age." Radiguet's novels depict the new *mal du siècle* that had broken out during the years following World War I. He combines ingeniously a formal elegance with a licentious content. Radiguet's works deserve reading, both for their inherent excellence and for their influence on Cocteau and others of his generation.

Novels by Radiguet

Count d'Orgel's Ball. 1924. Trans. by Annapaola Cacogni. Marsilio Pubs. 1989 repr. of 1954 ed. $11.00. ISBN 0-941419-30-4. Tale of an intellectual ménage à trois that soon descends into psychological warfare.

Devil in the Flesh. Trans. by A. M. Smith. M. Boyars 1987 repr. of 1968 ed. $7.95. ISBN 0-7145-0193-X

RIMBAUD, (JEAN NICOLAS) ARTHUR. 1854–1891

Rimbaud's life is the stuff of legend. His entire poetic output was produced during adolescence. At 19 he abandoned literature forever. He left France, wandered in many countries, and finally became a trader in Abyssinia. Long an associate of the poet Verlaine, he was once wounded by his friend's pistol, shot during a quarrel. He returned to France to die in 1891.

Roger Shattuck has written in the *New York Review of Books* that Rimbaud's work divides itself "naturally into three parts. There are the poems, highly personal and written in more or less regular verse . . . from 1870 to 1872. Then there is the autobiographical prose work, *A Season in Hell,* thirty intense and loosely connected pages composed in four months beginning April 1873. Passing harsh judgment on his past, Rimbaud appears to bid farewell to the long turbulent relationship with Verlaine and to the 'madness' that Rimbaud had cultivated in order to achieve a new level of living and writing. Thirdly, there is the miscellaneous collection of prose poems called *Illuminations* (probably written 1872–74). In *Illuminations,* he appears finally to make peace with the world and to seek, by name, the order and reason he had scorned earlier." Rimbaud's visionary symbolism is motivated by what he called "the derangement of all senses," that is, the confusion of the traditional meanings attached to both words and actions. For Rimbaud, the poet is a seer whose task is to gaze beneath the surface of reality and express its inner harmony. The poet's mission is magical; it involves nothing less than the reconfiguration of the surface of reality. Rimbaud has fascinated English-speaking poets from Hart Crane (see Vol. 1) and Ezra Pound (see Vol. 1) to the present generation. His influence on European poetry has been enormous.

Poetry by Rimbaud

Complete Works. Trans. by Paul Schmidt. HarpC 1976 $11.00. ISBN 0-06-090490-9

Illuminations. Trans. by Louise Varèse. New Dir. Pr. 1957 $8.95. ISBN 0-8112-0184-8

Rimbaud: Collected Poems. Trans. by Oliver Bernard. Viking Penguin 1987 $6.95. ISBN 0-14-042064-9

A Season in Hell (and *Illuminations*). Trans. by Enid R. Peschel. OUP 1973 $8.95. ISBN 0-19-501760-9

A Season in Hell (and *The Drunken Boat).* Trans. by Louise Varèse. New Dir. Pr. 1961 $5.95. ISBN 0-8112-0185-6

Work by Rimbaud

Complete Works with Selected Letters. Trans. by Wallace Fowlie. U. Ch. Pr. repr. of 1967 ed. $12.95. ISBN 0-226-71973-1

Books about Rimbaud

Ahearn, Edward J. *Rimbaud: Visions and Habitations.* U. CA Pr. 1983 $47.50. ISBN 0-520-04591-2

Blanchard, Marc E. *In Search of the City: Engels, Baudelaire, Rimbaud.* Anma Libri 1985 $37.50. ISBN 0-915838-53-2. Considers utopian aspects in Rimbaud's work.

Bloom, Harold, ed. *Arthur Rimbaud. Modern Critical Views Ser.* Chelsea Hse. 1987 $29.95. ISBN 1-55546-292-8. A collection of essays by various authors.

Hackett, C. A. *Rimbaud: A Critical Introduction.* Cambridge U. Pr. 1981 $47.95. ISBN 0-521-22976-6

Houston, John P. *The Design of Rimbaud's Poetry.* Greenwood 1977 repr. of 1963 ed. $35.00. ISBN 0-8371-9661-2

Miller, Henry. *Time of the Assassins: A Study of Rimbaud.* New Dir. Pr. 1962 $8.95. ISBN 0-8112-0115-5. A highly idiosyncratic interpretation by the well-known novelist.

Perloff, Marjorie. *The Poetics of Indeterminacy.* Princeton U. Pr. 1981 $42.50. ISBN 0-691-06462-8. Places Rimbaud in the history of modernism.

Poulet, Georges. *Exploding Poetry: Baudelaire–Rimbaud.* Trans. by Françoise Meltzer. U. Ch. Pr. 1984 $16.95. ISBN 0-226-67650-1

Ross, Kristin. *The Emergence of Social Space: Rimbaud and the Paris Commune.* U. of Minn. Pr. 1988 $39.95. ISBN 0-8166-1686-8. A new interpretation that stresses the political dimensions of Rimbaud's work.

Starkie, Enid. *Arthur Rimbaud.* New Dir. Pr. rev. ed. 1968 $14.95. ISBN 0-8112-0197-X

ROBBE-GRILLET, ALAIN. 1922–

Robbe-Grillet, generally understood to be the leading practitioner of the French new novel, began his career as an agricultural expert and spent time in Africa and the French Antilles doing research on tropical fruits. With his early novel, *The Erasers* (1953), he established his importance as an avant-garde writer. Generally, he avoids traditional use of character and plot in the novel and places emphasis on the "objectification of things." In *Jealousy* (1957), a romantic triangle is interpreted with utter subjectivity through a "privileged witness," a husband whose suspicions have driven him to the brink. Germaine Brée has written, "His theory was that the writer should thoroughly cover the phenomenology of the object, appealing to the reader to make the act of reading part of the total creative process." He has also applied the use of extremely detailed description in such films as *Last Year at Marienbad* (1961), *L'Immortelle* (1962), and *Trans Europe Express* (1966). Robbe-Grillet has written lucidly on literary theory in his *For a New Novel* (1963).

Novels by Robbe-Grillet

The Erasers. 1953. Trans. by Richard Howard. Grove Pr. 1989 $12.95. ISBN 0-8021-5086-1. A tale of murder and mistaken identity that draws upon the genre of the detective novel.

Jealousy and In the Labyrinth. Trans. by Richard Howard. Grove Pr. 1989 $8.95. ISBN 0-8021-5106-X.

La Maison de Rendez-vous. 1965. Trans. by Richard Howard. Grove Pr. 1987 $8.95. ISBN 0-8021-3017-8

Project for a Revolution in New York. Trans. by Richard Howard. Grove Pr. 1972 $3.95. ISBN 0-8021-5043-8

The Voyeur. 1955. Trans. by Richard Howard. Grove Pr. 1989 $8.95. ISBN 0-8021-3165-4. About a mysterious stranger who may have committed a murder in a small island community.

Nonfiction by Robbe-Grillet

For a New Novel. 1963. Trans. by Richard Howard. Northwestern U. Pr. 1989 $9.95. ISBN 0-8101-0821-6

BOOKS ABOUT ROBBE-GRILLET

Armes, Roy. *The Films of Alain Robbe-Grillet.* Benjamins North Am. 1981 $49.00. ISBN 90-272-1716-5

Leki, Ilona. *Alain Robbe-Grillet. Twayne's World Authors Ser.* G. K. Hall 1983 o.p.

Stoltzfus, Ben. *Alain Robbe-Grillet: The Body of the Text.* Fairleigh Dickinson 1985 $32.50. ISBN 0-8386-3212-2. Concentrates on the second half of the artist's career.

ROLLAND, ROMAIN. 1866–1944 (NOBEL PRIZE 1915)

Rolland was a novelist, playwright, biographer, and critic. Professor of the history of music at the Sorbonne, he wrote a number of books about music and musicians, as well as one on the great ambition of his life, the establishment of a people's theater. *Jean-Christophe* (1904–12) is a fine example of the "biographical" novel, a form of fiction in which the narrative follows exactly the sequence of events in the hero's life. It was the first great novel about a musical genius and contains interesting reflections on music, art, and letters. On completion of *Jean-Christophe,* Rolland was awarded the Grand Prize in Literature by the French Academy (1913) and the Nobel Prize (1915). During World War I, Rolland was an impassionate spokesperson for pacifism, and after the war he became a leader among leftist intellectuals.

NOVEL BY ROLLAND

Jean-Christophe. 1904–12. 3 vols. Trans. by Gilbert Cannan. Fr. & Eur. 1962 $4.50 ea.

NONFICTION BY ROLLAND

Handel. 1916. Johnson Repr. 1990 repr. of 1916 ed. $69.00. ISBN 0-7812-9066-X

I Will Not Rest. Ayer $16.00. ISBN 0-8369-8190-1

Musical Tour through the Land of the Past. 1922. Trans. by B. Miall. *Essay Index Repr. Ser.* Ayer repr. of 1922 ed. $17.00. ISBN 0-8369-0830-9

Life of Ramakrishna. Vedanta Pr. 1952 $4.95. ISBN 0-87481-080-9

Life of Vivekanada. Vedanta Pr. 1987 $4.95. ISBN 0-87481-090-6

WORK BY ROLLAND

Selected Letters of Romain Rolland. Trans. and ed. by Francis Dore and Marie-Laure Prévost. OUP 1990 $12.95. ISBN 0-19-562551-X. Correspondence with many great artists, philosophers, and thinkers.

BOOKS ABOUT ROLLAND

Starr, William T. *Romain Rolland and a World at War.* AMS Pr. repr. of 1956 ed. $27.00. ISBN 0-404-50731-X

Zweig, Stefan. *Romain Rolland: The Man and His Works.* Ayer 1973 repr. of 1921 ed. $24.50. ISBN 0-405-09113-3. A compelling portrait by one of Rolland's greatest contemporaries.

ROMANCE OF THE ROSE. 13th century.

Begun by Guillaume de Lorris around 1230 and continued by Jean de Meun 40 years later, this allegorical poem of some 22,000 octosyllabic lines is one of the masterpieces of the Middle Ages. It tells of the narrator's dream quest to pluck the rose hidden within a castle. The obvious sexual symbolism of the rose is accompanied by the appearance of numerous allegorical figures representing virtues and vices and instructing the narrator as to the path of perfect love. The poem, at once racy and philosophically dense, exercised an important influence on late medieval and Renaissance love poetry.

Romance of the Rose. Trans. by Harry W. Robbins. NAL-Dutton 1962 $13.95. ISBN 0-525-48395-0

ROMAINS, JULES (pseud. of Jules Louis Farigoule). 1885–1972

Romains first appeared in English as a medical researcher, with his scientific work *Eyeless Sight: A Study of Extra-Retinal Vision and the Paroptic Sense* (1923). His first novel, *The Death of a Nobody* (1911), is still considered by many his masterpiece. The serial novel *Men of Good Will* begins in 1933, with its political unrest recalling the sixth of October 1908, six years before World War I, the day on which the first volume opens. The narrative combines imaginary events with historical, and fictitious characters with actual. This epic novel, with its vast canvas and mass of characters, is an expression of the author's "unanimist" conception of life, a theory that defines society through the individual's relation to masses or groups and contends that a group of people with a unanimous emotion (such as goodwill) can develop a mass power superior to any other force. Romains was international president of PEN from 1938 to 1941 and was elected to the French Academy in 1946.

Novels by Romains

The Death of a Nobody. 1911. Trans. by D. MacCarthy and S. Waterlow. Fertig 1977 repr. of 1944 ed. o.p.

Eyeless Sight. 1923. Carol Pub. Group 1978 $4.95. ISBN 0-8065-0632-6

Book about Romains

Boak, Denis. *Jules Romains. Twayne's World Authors Ser.* Macmillan 1974 o.p. An important thematic study.

RONSARD, PIERRE DE. 1524–1585

Ronsard is one of the principal originators of European poetic tradition as it has existed since the Renaissance. Dissatisfied with native French poetic models, and taken with the example of Greek, Latin, and Italian poetry, he set about to make a French poetry that would rival the poetry of the ancients. He was the first to imitate systematically forms such as the ode, the sonnet, the epic, the eclogue, and the elegy. He attracted a circle of sympathetic poets; since the group amounted to seven, they called themselves the *Pléiade*, after the seven-starred constellation. Their professed aim was to build a poetic tradition based on classical (Greek and Roman) or Italian models, instead of medieval French forms. Their manifesto was an essay by Joachim du Bellay called "Défense et illustration de la langue française," the first significant work of French literary criticism.

Of Ronsard's large and varied literary works (including his lyric odes, his *Amours* or love poems addressed to Cassandre, and his *Sonnets pour Hélène*, a new series of love poems), the best known are his sonnets, rich in image and delicate of construction.

Poetry by Ronsard

Poems of Pierre de Ronsard. Ed. by Nicholas Kilmer. U. CA Pr. 1979 $35.00. ISBN 0-520-03078-8

Songs and Sonnets of Pierre de Ronsard. Trans. by Curtis H. Page. Hyperion Conn. 1985 repr. of 1924 ed. $21.00. ISBN 0-88355-604-9. Selections from all periods of the poet's career.

Books about Ronsard

Hanisch, Gertrude S. *Love Elegies of the Renaissance: Marot, Louise Labé and Ronsard.* Anma Libri 1979 $46.50. ISBN 0-915838-24-9. An important comparative study.

Jones, K.R.W. *Pierre de Ronsard. Twayne's World Authors Ser.* Irvington 1970 $17.95. ISBN 0-8057-2778-7

McGowan, Margaret. *Ideal Forms in the Age of Ronsard.* U. CA Pr. 1985 $50.00. ISBN 0-520-04864-4. An evocative study of Ronsard's relationship to the courtly culture of his day.

ROUSSEAU, JEAN JACQUES. 1712–1778

[See Volume 3.]

SADE (DONATIEN ALPHONSE FRANÇOIS), COMTE DE (called Marquis de Sade). 1740–1814

A French novelist and playwright, the Marquis de Sade is largely known for his pathological sexual views and ethical nihilism. Typical of his output is his novel *Justine* (1791), which presents the theme of vice triumphant over virtue and depicts the molestation of a virtuous girl and orgies of sexual perversion in a monastery. Other well-known works of Sade include *Philosophy in the Bedroom* (1795), *Juliette* (1797), and *Aline and Valcourt or The Philosophic Novel* (1795). In recent years, Sade's work, with its curious combination of unbridled sex, violence, and philosophical speculation, has attracted the attention of critics and philosophers of importance.

Novels by Sade

Juliette. Trans. by Austryn Wainhouse. Grove Pr. 1988 $17.95. ISBN 0-8021-3085-2. An introduction by Simone de Beauvoir.

Justine. Trans. by Richard Seaver and Austryn Wainhouse. Grove Pr. 1990 $16.95. ISBN 0-8021-3218-9. Includes *Philosophy in the Bedroom, Éugénie de Franval,* and other writings.

One Hundred Twenty Days of Sodom and Other Writings. Ed. by Austryn Wainhouse and Richard Seaver. Grove Pr. 1987 $16.95. ISBN 0-8021-3012-7

Short Story Collection by Sade

The Gothic Tales of the Marquis de Sade. Trans. by Margaret Crosland. Dufour 1990 $30.00. ISBN 0-7206-0769-8

Books about Sade

Barthes, Roland. *Sade-Fourier-Loyola.* Trans. by Richard Miller. U. CA Pr. 1989 $9.95. ISBN 0-520-06628-6. Analyzes Sade as a philosopher of language.

De Jean, Joan. *Literary Fortifications: Rousseau, Laclos, Sade.* Princeton U. Pr. 1984 $47.50. ISBN 0-691-06611-6. A good contextual study.

LeBrun, Annie. *Sade: A Sudden Abyss.* Trans. by Camille Naish. City Lights 1991 $12.95. ISBN 0-87206-250-X

SAINT-EXUPÉRY, ANTOINE DE. 1900–1944

After escaping death in several accidents while flying as a pilot over the most dangerous sections of the French airmail service in South America, Africa, and the South Atlantic, Saint-Exupéry was reported missing over southern France in 1944. He was mourned as a hero who had caught the imagination of men and women throughout the world. His books are written in beautifully simple poetic prose, exalting courage and heroic hope. He had a rare gift for coining unusual images. *Night Flight* (1931) was introduced by André Gide and was at once proclaimed a masterpiece. *Wind, Sand and Stars* (1939) is a series of tales, interspersed with philosophical reflections on earth as a planet and on the nobility of the common people. *Flight to Arras* (1942) is the author's own account of a hopeless reconnaissance sortie during the tragic days of May 1940.

Novels by Saint-Exupéry

The Little Prince. 1943. Trans. by Katherine Woods. HarBraceJ 1968 $3.95. ISBN 0-15-652820-7

Night Flight. 1931. Trans. by Stuart Gilbert. HarBraceJ 1974 repr. of 1932 ed. $4.95. ISBN 0-15-665605-1

Southern Mail. 1929. Trans. by Curtis Cate. HarBraceJ 1972 repr. of 1929 ed. $4.95. ISBN 0-15-683901-6

Works by Saint-Exupéry

Airman's Odyssey. 1939. Trans. by Lewis Galantiere and Stuart Gilbert. HarBraceJ 1984 $9.95. ISBN 0-15-603733-5. Includes *Wind, Sand and Stars; Night Flight;* and *Flight to Arras*.

Wartime Writings. 1939–1944. Trans. by Noah Purcell. HarBraceJ 1990 $8.95. ISBN 0-685-47700-2

Wind, Sand and Stars. 1939. HarBraceJ 1967 $4.95. ISBN 0-15-697090-2

Nonfiction by Saint-Exupéry

Flight to Arras. 1942. Trans. by Lewis Galantiere. HarBraceJ 1969 repr. of 1942 ed. $5.95. ISBN 0-15-631880-6

Books about Saint-Exupéry

Breaux, Adele. *Saint-Exupéry in America, 1942–1943: A Memoir*. Fairleigh Dickinson 1975 $16.50. ISBN 0-8386-7610-3. Deals with the author's years in exile.

Robinson, Joy M. *Antoine de Saint-Exupéry*. *Twayne's World Authors Ser.* Macmillan 1984 $20.95. ISBN 0-8057-6552-2

SAINT-JOHN PERSE

[See PERSE, SAINT-JOHN]

SAND, GEORGE (pseud. of Amandine-Aurore-Lucie Dupin, Baronne Dudevant). 1804–1876

George Sand began life as Aurore Dupin, the daughter of a count and a dressmaker. Educated both on her aristocratic grandmother's estate and in a Parisian convent, at 18 she married Casimer Dudevant, a provincial gentleman whose rough temperament was the opposite of her own, and from whom she obtained a separation several years later. At 31 she moved to Paris, where she changed her name and plunged into the bohemian world of French romanticism. Frequently dressed in men's clothing, she participated actively in literary debates, cultural events, and even the revolution of 1848. Sand was friend and correspondent with many of the major artists and writers of her age, including Balzac, Flaubert, and Liszt (see Vol. 3). Her love affairs with the poet Musset and the composer Chopin (see Vol. 3) were the stuff of legend, chronicled in her own *Story of My Life* (1855). Sand's immensely popular novels ranged from sentimental stories of wronged women (*Indiana*, 1832), to utopian socialist fictions (her masterpiece is *Consuelo*, 1842), to explorations of pastoral themes written when she retired, late in life, to her estate in Berry (*The Haunted Pool*, 1846). Though frequently dismissed as overblown or too sentimental, Sand's fiction has recently undergone a revaluation, emerging as an influential body of women's writing. As both a writer and an intellectual personality, Sand is a central figure in nineteenth-century French cultural life.

NOVELS BY SAND

Consuelo. 1842. Da Capo 1979 $8.95. ISBN 0-306-80102-7

The Country Waif. 1848. Trans. by Eirene Collis. U. of Nebr. Pr. 1977 $5.95. ISBN 0-8032-0888-X. An important influence on Proust.

Indiana. 1832. Trans. by George B. Ives. Academy Ch. Pubs. 1978 $8.95. ISBN 0-915804-57-6. A love story that takes us from France to the New World.

Marianne. Trans. by Sian Miles. Carroll & Graf 1989 $7.95. ISBN 0-88184-477-2. Tells the story of Marianne Chevreuse, the 25-year-old heroine who embodies many of the ideas for which Sand is known.

Valentine. 1832. Trans. by George B. Ives. Academy Ch. Pubs. 1978 $8.95. ISBN 0-915864-59-2

NONFICTION BY SAND

Winter in Majorca. 1838. Trans. by Robert Graves. Academy Ch. Pubs. 1990 $12.95. ISBN 0-915-864-68-1. Focuses on her relationship with Chopin.

The Intimate Journal. 1926. Trans. by Maria J. Howe. Academy Ch. Pubs. 1978 $8.95. ISBN 0-915864-50-9. Autobiographical reflections.

BOOKS ABOUT SAND

Atwood, William G. *The Lioness and the Little One.* Col. U. Pr. 1986 $38.50. ISBN 231-0492-0. On Sand and Musset.

Datlof, Natalie, et al. *The World of George Sand.* Greenwood Pr. 1991 $45.00. ISBN 0-313-27584-X. A collection of essays by a variety of authors.

Naginski, Isabelle Hoog. *George Sand: Writing for Her Life.* Rutgers U. Pr. 1991 $35.00. ISBN 0-8135-1640-4. Focuses on Sand as a professional woman of letters.

SARRAUTE, NATHALIE. 1902–

Nathalie Sarraute has been an eloquent spokesperson and theorist of the new novel, as well as one of its most talented practitioners. In her essay on the art of fiction, *The Age of Suspicion* (1956), she condemned the techniques used in the novel of the past and took a stand beside ROBBE-GRILLET as a leader of the avant-garde. The novel, she feels, must express "that element of indetermination, of opacity, and mystery that one's own actions always have for the one who lives them." Her works have now become known to an international public. Her ability to render fleeting awareness and the psychological states underlying articulate speech has won both praise and disdain. Janet Flanner has called Sarraute "the only one among the New Novel experimenters who appears finally to have struck her own style—intense, observational, and personal."

Of her novels, *The Golden Fruits* (1963)—about the Paris literary fortunes of an imaginary novel of the same name—is "the most barren of extraneous decor, the most accomplished from the standpoint of her esthetic aims" (*SR*). *Tropisms* (1939), her earliest (very brief) book, contains "all the raw material I have continued to develop in my later works." Her "tropisms," she says, are instinctive "sensations," or even "movements," "produced in us by the presence of others, or by objects from the outside world. [They hide] beneath the most commonplace conversations and the most everyday gestures." She regards her novels as composed of a series of tropisms of varying intensity.

NOVELS BY SARRAUTE

Between Life and Death. 1968. Trans. by Maria Jolas. Riverrun NY 1980 $14.95. ISBN 0-7145-0122-0

Fools Say. Riverrun NY 1989 $9.95. ISBN 0-7145-3751-9

The Golden Fruits. 1963. Trans. by Maria Jolas. Riverrun NY 1980 $9.95. ISBN 0-7145-0259-6

The Planetarium. 1959. Trans. by Maria Jolas. Riverrun NY 1980 $7.95. ISBN 0-7145-0446-0

Portrait of a Man Unknown. 1948. Trans. by Maria Jolas. Braziller 1990 $9.95. ISBN 0-8076-1252-9

Tropisms. 1939. Trans. by Maria Jolas. Braziller 1957 $5.95. ISBN 0-8076-0412-7. A series of short sketches.

Nonfiction by Sarraute

The Age of Suspicion. 1956. Braziller 1990 $7.95. ISBN 0-8076-1253-7

Childhood. 1983. Trans. by Barbara Wright. Braziller 1985 $8.95. ISBN 0-8076-1116-6

Books about Sarraute

Besser, Gretchen R. *Nathalie Sarraute. Twayne's World Authors Ser.* G. K. Hall 1979 o.p. A good general introduction to the author's life and work.

Minogue, Valerie. *Nathalie Sarraute: The War of the Words.* Col. U. Pr. 1981 $24.00 ISBN 0-85224-405-3

Temple, Ruth. *Nathalie Sarraute.* Col. U. Pr. 1968 $7.50. ISBN 0-231-02871-7. One of the first general studies in English.

Watson-Williams, Helen. *The Novels of Nathalie Sarraute.* Humanities 1981 $20.50

SARTRE, JEAN-PAUL. 1905–1980

Sartre is the dominant figure in post-war French intellectual life. A graduate of the prestigious École Normale Supérieure with an *agrégation* in philosophy, Sartre has been a major figure on the literary and philosophical scenes since the late 1930s. Widely known as an atheistic proponent of existentialism, he emphasized the priority of existence over preconceived essences and the importance of human freedom. In his first and best novel, *Nausea* (1938), Sartre contrasted the fluidity of human consciousness with the apparent solidity of external reality and satirized the hypocrisies and pretensions of bourgeois idealism. Sartre's theater is also highly ideological, emphasizing the importance of personal freedom and the commitment of the individual to social and political goals. His first play, *The Flies* (1943), was produced during the German occupation, despite its underlying message of defiance. One of his most popular plays is the one-act *No Exit* (1944), in which the traditional theological concept of hell is redefined in existentialist terms. In *Red Gloves* (*Les Mains Sales*) (1948), Sartre examines the pragmatic implications of the individual involved in political action through the mechanism of the Communist party and a changing historical situation. His highly readable autobiography, *The Words* (1964), tells of his childhood in an idealistic bourgeois Protestant family and of his subsequent rejection of his upbringing. Sartre has also made significant contributions to literary criticism in his 10-volume *Situations* (1947–72) and in works on Baudelaire, Genet, and Flaubert.

Novels by Sartre

The Age of Reason. 1945. Random 1972 $6.95. ISBN 0-394-71838-0. First volume in the trilogy "The Paths of Freedom," which also includes *Troubled Sleep* and *The Reprieve.*

Nausea. 1938. Trans. by Lloyd Alexander. Bentley 1979 repr. of 1949 ed. $14.00. ISBN 0-8376-0443-5

The Reprieve. 1949. Random 1992 $12.00. ISBN 0-679-74078-3

Troubled Sleep. 1949. Random 1972 $9.95. ISBN 0-394-71840-2

The Wall: Intimacy. 1939. Trans. by Lloyd Alexander. New Dir. Pr. 1969 $7.95. ISBN 0-8112-0190-2. Dramatizes the discovery of the meaninglessness of human life.

PLAYS BY SARTRE

The Freud Scenario. Trans. by Quintin Hoare. U. Ch. Pr. 1989 $14.95. ISBN 0-226-73514-1. An unproduced film script about Freud; published posthumously.

No Exit and Three Other Plays. Random 1955 $3.95. ISBN 0-394-70016-3

NONFICTION BY SARTRE

Baudelaire. 1947. Trans. by Martin Turnell. New Dir. Pr. 1950 $8.95. ISBN 0-8112-0189-4. Sartre's insightful study of the great French poet.

Critique of Dialectical Reason. 1960. Trans. by Quintin Hoare. Verso 1991 $49.50. ISBN 0-85091-311-2. Sartre's contribution to Marxist philosophy.

The Family Idiot. 1971. 4 vols. Trans. by Carol Cosman. U. Ch. Pr. Vol. 1 1981 $25.00. ISBN 0-226-73509-5. Vol. 2 1987 $35.00. ISBN 0-226-73510-9. Vol. 3 1989 $39.95. ISBN 0-226-73516-8. Vol. 4 1991 $34.95. ISBN 0-226-73518-4. Sartre's immense and challenging essay on Flaubert; published posthumously.

Saint-Genet: Actor and Martyr. 1952. Pantheon 1983 $11.95. ISBN 0-394-71583-7. Sartre's essay on Jean Genet, whom he sees as the existentialist hero.

What Is Literature and Other Essays. Trans. by Bernard Frechtman and Jeffrey Mehlman. HUP 1988 repr. of 1949 ed. $14.95. ISBN 0-674-95084-4. Sartre's manifesto on the importance of "committed" literature.

The Words. 1964. Random 1981 $8.95. ISBN 0-394-74709-7. The author's autobiography.

BOOKS ABOUT SARTRE

Barnes, Hazel E. *Sartre and Flaubert.* U. Ch. Pr. 1982 $25.00. ISBN 0-226-03720-7

Boschetti, Anna. *The Intellectual Exercise: Sartre and Les Temps Modernes.* Trans. by Richard McCleary. Northwestern U. Pr. 1988 $15.95. ISBN 0-8101-0756-2. Considers Sartre's relationship to the literary journal he helped found.

Brosman, Catherine S. *Jean-Paul Sartre. Twayne's World Author Ser.* Macmillan 1983 $20.95. ISBN 0-8057-6544-1. A good general introduction to Sartre's drama, fiction, and philosophy.

Caws, Peter. *Sartre.* Routledge 1984 $11.95. ISBN 0-7102-0233-4. An interesting philosophical study.

Cohen-Solal, Annie. *Sartre: A Life.* Trans. by Annapaola Cancogni. Pantheon 1988 $12.95. ISBN 0-394-75662-2. A massive, authoritative biography.

Goldthorpe, Rhiannon. *Sartre: Literature and Theory.* Cambridge U. Pr. 1986 $21.95. ISBN 0-521-33878-6. Discusses both the ideas and execution of Sartre's art.

Hollier, Denis. *The Politics of Prose: Essay on Sartre.* Trans. by Jeffrey Mehlman. U. of Minn. Pr. 1987 $14.95. ISBN 0-8106-1510-1. A challenging, poststructuralist study.

Jameson, Fredric. *Sartre: The Origins of a Style.* Col. U. Pr. 1984 repr. of 1961 ed. $50.50. ISBN 0-231-05890-X

SÉVIGNÉ, MME DE (Marie de Rabutin-Chantal, Marquise de Sévigné). 1626–1696

Mme de Sévigné is the great correspondent of French literature. Her letters, written mostly to her daughter from 1648 to 1696, offer both a fascinating depiction of the France of Louis XVI (many of the great of the age are described) and a mine of subtle psychological reflections on human behavior. The portrait they offer of the complex relationship between mother and daughter is compelling, and their style (which influenced many writers, including PROUST) is marked by clarity and elegance.

Nonfiction by Sévigné

Madame de Sévigné: Selected Letters. Ed. by L. W. Tancock. Viking Penguin 1982 $7.95. ISBN 0-14-044405-X

Books about Sévigné

Allentuch, Harriet R. *Madame de Sévigné: A Portrait in Letters.* Greenwood 1978 repr. of 1963 ed. $45.00. ISBN 0-313-20537-X. A selection of letters with comments.

Mossiker, Frances. *Madame de Sévigné: A Life and Letters.* Col. U. Pr. repr. of 1985 ed. $19.50. ISBN 0-231-06153-6. An intriguing portrait of Sévigné in her milieu.

SIMENON, GEORGES. 1909–1989

The prolific Belgian-born writer Georges Simenon produced hundreds of fictional works under his own name and 17 pseudonyms, in addition to more than 70 books about Inspector Maigret, long "the favorite sleuth of highbrow detective-story readers" (*SR*). More than 50 "Simenons" have been made into films. In addition to his mystery stories, he wrote what he called "hard" books, the serious psychological novels numbering well over 100. The autobiographical *Pedigree,* set in his native town of Liege, is perhaps his finest work. The publication of Simenon's intimate memoirs also attracted considerable attention. Simenon himself once said that he would never write a "great novel." Yet Gide called him "a great novelist, perhaps the greatest and truest novelist we have in French literature today," and Thornton Wilder (see Vol. 1) found that Simenon's narrative gift extends "to the tips of his fingers." The following are some of Simenon's novels, exclusive of the Maigret detective stories, that are in print.

Novels by Simenon

The Blue Room. Trans. by Eileen Ellenbogen. HarBraceJ 1978 repr. of 1965 ed. $2.95. ISBN 0-15-613267-2

The Cat. Trans. by Bernard Frechtman. HarBraceJ 1976 $2.95. ISBN 0-15-415549-4

Clockmaker. HarBraceJ 1977 $2.95. ISBN 0-19-618170-3

The Iron Staircase. HarBraceJ 1981 $2.95. ISBN 0-15-645484-X

The Long Exile. Trans. by Eileen Ellenbogen. HarBraceJ 1983 $15.95. ISBN 0-15-152997-3

The Venice Train. Trans. by Alastair Hamilton. HarBraceJ 1983 $3.95. ISBN 0-15-693523-6

Nonfiction by Simenon

Intimate Memoirs. HarBraceJ 1984 $22.95. ISBN 0-15-144892-2

Books about Simenon

Becker, Lucille F. *Georges Simenon. Twayne's World Authors Ser.* G. K. Hall 1977 o.p.

Bresler, Fenton. *The Mystery of Georges Simenon: A Biography.* Madison Bks. 1985 $9.95. ISBN 0-8128-6241-4. An intriguing portrait of the author's turbulent life.

Eskin, Stanley G. *Simenon: A Critical Biography.* McFarland & Co. 1987 $24.95. ISBN 0-89950-281-4. Thorough examination of Simenon's life and work.

Foord, Peter. *Georges Simenon: A Bibliography.* Oak Knoll 1988 $20.00. ISBN 1-871122-03-1

Young, Trudee. *Georges Simenon: A Checklist of His "Maigret" and Other Mystery Novels and Short Stories in French and in English Translations. Author Bibliographies Ser.* Scarecrow 1976 $20.00. ISBN 0-8108-0964-8

SIMON, CLAUDE. 1913– (Nobel Prize 1985)

Claude Simon, whose novels were influenced by both Faulkner (see Vol. 1) and Camus, creates a universe dominated by fatality and pervaded with doom. His heroes are outsiders like Meursault and testify to Simon's leaning toward the philosophy of the absurd. Simon makes great use of the interior monologue and consciously maintains a single point of view in his novels. In *The Flanders Road* (1960), three French POWs in a German camp pass the time by recalling and analyzing incidents, trivial and otherwise, in great detail. The reader receives their memories in a quasi–stream-of-consciousness hodge-podge of confusing scenes and syntax. Of *The Palace* (1962), Henri Peyre wrote: "Nothing happens in this novel, made up of shadowy dialogues and Proustian reminiscences. . . . The chief concern of the novelist, who no longer relates a story or presents images of real people, is to devise a language which may be true to his purely subjective vision."

Novels by Simon

The Acacia. Trans. by Richard Howard. Pantheon 1991 $23.50. ISBN 0-394-58771-5

The Flanders Road. 1960. Trans. by Richard Howard. Riverrun NY 1986 $8.95. ISBN 0-7145-3994-5

Georgics. 1981. Trans. by John Fletcher. Riverrun NY 1991 $29.95. ISBN 0-7145-4089-7. Experimental antiwar novel that thrusts the reader into the midst of blunders and carnage.

The Grass. 1984. Trans. by Richard Howard. Braziller 1986 $8.95. ISBN 0-8076-1156-5

Triptych. Trans. by Helen R. Lane. Riverrun NY 1986 $8.95. ISBN 0-7145-3787-X. Three stories about love and death are tangled together.

The Wind. 1957. Trans. by Richard Howard. Braziller 1986 $8.95. ISBN 0-8076-1155-7

The World about Us. 1975. Trans. by Daniel Weissbort. Ontario Rev. NJ 1983 $14.95. ISBN 0-86538-033-3

Books about Simon

Britton, Celia. *Claude Simon: Writing the Visible.* Cambridge U. Pr. 1987 $54.50. ISBN 0-521-33077-7. Searching and subtle analysis of Simon's writing.

Evans, Michael. *Claude Simon and the Transgressions of Modern Art.* St. Martin 1988 $29.95. ISBN 0-312-01199-7

Fletcher, John. *Claude Simon: And Fiction Now.* M. Boyars 1978 $7.95. ISBN 0-7145-1015-7. One of the first studies in English.

Gould, Karen L. *Claude Simon's Mythic Muse.* Summa Pubns. 1979 $14.95. ISBN 0-917786-48-3. Considers Simon's use of myth and history.

Sarkonak, Ralph. *Understanding Claude Simon.* U. of SC Pr. 1989 $24.95. ISBN 0-87249-669-4. Constitutes a very detailed explication of each of 10 of Simon's major works of fiction.

THE SONG OF ROLAND (Chanson de Roland). End of 11th century

The Song of Roland is the oldest and most famous of the surviving medieval *chansons de geste* or "songs of heroic exploits," a type of narrative poem written during the period extending from the end of the eleventh century to the fourteenth century. The oldest of the seven manuscripts of the text may be consulted at the Bodleian Library at Oxford; the Oxford manuscript consists of 4,002 decasyllabic assonanced verses. The author is unknown but may be the Turoldus referred to at the end of the poem. The poem, considered to be the first great monument of French literature, is based on historical incidents going back to the year 778 when Charlemagne invaded Spain. Versions of the work also exist in other medieval literatures, notably in Basque, Provençal, German, Scandinavian, and Latin.

The Song of Roland. Trans. by Dorothy L. Sayers. *Penguin Class. Ser.* Viking Penguin 1957 $5.95. ISBN 0-14-044075-5

STAËL, MME DE (ANNE-LOUISE-GERMAINE NECKER). 1766–1817.

Germaine de Staël, the daughter of a Swiss banker, was "the first woman of middle-class origins to impress herself, through her own genius, on all the major public events of her time—events political, literary, in every sense revolutionary" (Ellen Moers). Mme de Staël presided over a Paris salon in which the greatest minds of the day met and conversed. Her cosmopolitan liberalism so offended Napoleon that he once forbade her to come within 40 miles of Paris. Mme de Staël's writing helped lay the cultural foundations of French romanticism. Her essay *De l'Allegmagne* (*Of Germany*) (1810) introduced German romantic poetry and philosophy to the French. Her novels depicted strong-willed heroines driven by passion and intellectual curiosity but constrained by social conventions.

Novel by Staël

Corinne or Italy. 1807. Trans. by Isabel Hill. AMS Pr. repr. of 1933 ed. $17.00. ISBN 0-404-54425

Works by Staël

An Extraordinary Woman: Selected Writings of Germaine de Staël. Trans. by Vivian Folkenflik. Col. U. Pr. 1987 $56.00. ISBN 0-231-05586-2. A good selection of both fiction and nonfiction.

Reflections on Suicide. 1812. AMS Pr. repr. of 1813 ed. $24.50. ISBN 0-404-56838-6. A surprisingly modern meditation on a Romantic theme.

Books about Staël

Herold, J. Christopher. *Mistress to an Age: A Life of Mme de Staël.* Greenwood 1975 repr. of 1958 ed. $35.00. ISBN 0-8371-8339-1. A biography stressing de Staël's importance as a broker of ideas.

Levaillant, Maurice. *Passionate Exiles: Madame de Staël and Madame Recamier.* Trans. by Malcolm Barnes. Ayer repr. of 1958 ed. $21.75. ISBN 0-8369-8086-7

Winegarten, Renee. *Madame de Staël.* Berg Pubs. 1987 $25.50. ISBN 0-907582-87-8. Brief yet useful biography that gives a clear outline and discussion of de Staël's ideas on politics and literature.

STENDHAL (pseud. of Henri Beyle). 1783–1842

One of the great French novelists of the nineteenth century, Stendhal describes his unhappy youth with acute sensitivity and intelligence in the autobiography of his early years, *The Life of Henri Brulard*, written in 1835–36 but published in 1890, long after his death. The son of a provincial Grenoble lawyer with aristocratic pretensions and a single-minded passion for money, Stendhal sought to escape very early from this stifling bourgeois environment. With the help of his cousin, he obtained a position in the ministry of war and was sent to Italy, a country in which he lived for a considerable time and which he loved. But he never lost his attachment to Paris, a city to which he returned frequently. His novels, whose heroes reject any form of authority that would repress their sense of individual freedom, are a fascinating amalgam of romantic sensibility and a lucid intelligence characteristic of eighteenth-century rationalism. Stendhal's major novels are novels of alienation, as their initial premise is a hero out of sorts with contemporary society. Stendhal also wrote some 30 volumes of biography, travel, and art and music criticism. For

NIETZSCHE (see Vol. 4), Stendhal was "the last great psychologist" and "the most beautiful accident of my life."

NOVELS BY STENDHAL

The Charterhouse of Parma. 1839. Trans. by M. R. Shaw. Viking Penguin 1958 $5.95. ISBN 0-14-044061-5. A passionate love story set against the backdrop of corrupt aristocratic society in early nineteenth-century Italy.

Lucien Leuwen. 1834–1835. Trans. by L. Varèse. New Dir. Pr. 1950 $5.00. ISBN 0-8112-0388-3. A late, unfinished novel.

The Red and the Black. 1830. Trans. by Lloyd C. Parks. NAL-Dutton 1970 $4.50. ISBN 0-451-51793. The story of Julien Sorel, perhaps the archetypical romantic hero: an ambitious youth from a poor family who seeks to rise in French society through talent and force of will.

NONFICTION BY STENDHAL

Love. 1822. Trans. by Suzanne Sale and Gilbert Sale. Viking Penguin 1975 $6.95. ISBN 0-14-044307-X. A brilliant psychological investigation of romantic love.

Memoirs of a Tourist. 1838. Trans. by A. Seager. Northwestern U. Pr. 1985 $12.95. ISBN 0-8101-0707-4. Stendhal's reflections on his travels, chiefly in Italy.

To the Happy Few: Selected Letters of Stendhal. Trans. by Norman Cameron. Dufour 1986 $15.95. ISBN 0-948166-09-6. Correspondence with both literary and political figures.

SHORT STORY COLLECTION BY STENDHAL

Three Italian Chronicles. Trans. by C. K. Scott-Moncrieff. New Dir. Pr. 1991 $9.95. ISBN 0-8112-1150-9. A retelling of tales from the Italian Renaissance.

BOOKS ABOUT STENDHAL

Alter, Robert, and Carol Cosman. *A Lion for Love: A Critical Biography of Stendhal.* HUP 1986 $10.95. ISBN 0-674-39012-1. A readable and comprehensive biography.

Bloom, Harold, ed. *Stendhal.* Chelsea Hse. 1989 $29.95. ISBN 1-55546-311-8

Haig, Stirling. *Stendhal: The Red and the Black.* Cambridge U. Pr. $7.95. ISBN 0-521-34982-6

Jefferson, Ann. *Reading Realism in Stendhal.* Cambridge U. Pr. 1988 $49.50. ISBN 0-521-26274-7. Considers the question of Stendhal's relationship to the "realist" movement.

May, Gita. *Stendhal and the Age of Napoleon: An Interpretive Biography.* Col. U. Pr. 1977 o.p. Considers Stendhal in his political context.

Prendergast, Christopher. *The Order of Mimesis: Balzac, Stendhal, Nerval and Flaubert.* Cambridge U. Pr. 1988 $19.95. ISBN 0-521-36977-0. An important psychological study.

Strickland, Geoffrey. *Stendhal: The Education of a Novelist.* Cambridge U. Pr. 1974 $47.50. ISBN 0-521-20385-6

Tenenbaum, Elizabeth B. *The Problematic Self: Approaches to Identity in Stendhal, D. H. Lawrence, and Malraux.* HUP 1978 $20.00. ISBN 0-674-70769-9. A comparative study of the self in Stendhal and others.

TOCQUEVILLE, ALEXIS (CHARLES-HENRI MAURICE CLÉREL) DE. 1805–1859

[SEE Volume 3.]

TOURNIER, MICHEL. 1924–

The novelist and essayist Michel Tournier has had a varied career as a producer and director for Radio Television Française, as a journalist, and as director of literary services for the French publishing firm Editions Plon. He was awarded the Grand Prix du Roman by the French Academy in 1967 for his first novel, *Friday*, a takeoff on DEFOE's (see Vol. 1) *Robinson Crusoe*. Tournier's novels are highly complex, revealing a philosophical turn of mind through intricate sets of symbolic allusions. The French title of his second novel, *Le Roi des Aulnes* (1970), is from GOETHE's poem on the Erl-King and has been translated into English as *The Ogre*. The book won Tournier international attention and the Prix Goncourt.

NOVELS BY TOURNIER

Friday. 1967. Trans. by Norman Denny. Pantheon 1985 $7.95. ISBN 0-394-72880-7

Gilles and Jeanne. 1983. Trans. by Alan Sheridan. Grove Pr. 1989 $16.95. ISBN 0-8021-0021-X. Recreates medieval history by exploring the bizarre love of Gilles de Rais for Jeanne d'Arc.

Golden Droplet. Trans. by Barbara Wright. Doubleday 1987 $16.95. ISBN 0-385-23759-6. Follows a 15-year-old Berber shepherd's *rites de passage* as he leaves his Sahara oasis for the Arabic quarters of Marseilles and Paris.

Night. Trans. by Stella Rodway. Bantam 1982 $3.95. ISBN 0-553-27253-5

BOOK ABOUT TOURNIER

Cloonan, William. *Michel Tournier*. *Twayne's World Authors Ser.* G. K. Hall 1985 o.p.

TRISTAN AND ISEULT. c.1160–1170

The story of Tristan and Iseult has held the romantic imagination more strongly perhaps than any other of the medieval legends. There are numerous medieval versions of *Tristan*. The earliest poems of consequence are by Thomas of Britain and by Béroul, a French author. Their poems are known to us only in fragments. Gottfried von Strassburg composed a magnificent version in German; a less-accomplished but undeservedly neglected version was composed in Middle English by a poet named Thomas. In modern times, many poets including MATTHEW ARNOLD (see Vol. 1), A. C. SWINBURNE (see Vol. 1), and ALFRED TENNYSON (see vol. 1) have turned their hands to the theme. The best-known modern version is by RICHARD WAGNER (see Vol. 3), *Tristan and Isolde*, for which he wrote the poetic text (1859) and then the music (1861). His music drama represents the culmination of the view of romantic love as the highest source of human inspiration.

Joseph Bédier's translation of *Tristan and Iseult* (1900) has been for several generations the principal avenue of introduction to the story for French- and English-speaking readers alike. Bédier was a brilliant, learned scholar of medieval French literature, and a brilliant prose stylist in his own right. He took the various fragmentary remains of the Tristan legend and recast them into a version that is part translation into modern French, and part a literary masterpiece in itself.

The Romance of Tristan and Iseult as Retold by Joseph Bédier. Trans. by Hilaire Belloc and Paul Rosenfeld. Random 1965 $5.56. ISBN 0-394-70271-9. Introduction by Padraic Colum.

The Romance of Tristan and Isolt. Trans. by Norman B. Spector. Northwestern U. Pr. 1987 $9.95. ISBN 0-8101-0767-8

BOOKS ABOUT TRISTAN AND ISEULT

Ferrante, Joan M. *The Conflict of Love and Honor: The Medieval Tristan Legend in France, Germany and Italy*. Mouton 1973 $29.35. ISBN 90-2792-604-2. Places the tale in its European context.

Loomis, Gertrude. *Tristan and Isolt: A Study of the Sources of the Romance*. 2 vols. in 1. B. Franklin 1970 o.p.

VALÉRY, PAUL. 1871–1945

Harry T. Moore has written in *Twentieth Century French Literature to World War II*: "Paul Valéry, who published his most important verse between 1917 and 1922, is the greatest French poet the twentieth century has so far produced. . . . Few modern poets . . . have presented richer experience through their verses. Valéry . . . could handle abstractions with a living and always poetic concreteness, and put them into comparable verse-music." He was also a critic and aesthetic theorist, interested in art, architecture, and mathematics. His skepticism, malice, and learning brought him both admiration and hostility. Valéry had been a member of the MALLARMÉ circle in the 1890s and wrote much symbolist poetry at that time, but an unhappy love affair caused him to fall poetically silent (he earned his living as a journalist) until GIDE and others persuaded him, 20 years later, to publish some of his youthful work. He had thought to add a short new poem and instead wrote *La Jeune Parque* (*The Young Fate*) (1917), several hundred lines in length. It won him instant recognition in poetic circles. Several collections of his earlier poems were published in the 1920s, as well as the great *Cimetière Marin* (*Graveyard by the Sea*), a powerful meditation on time and mortality. From then until his death in 1945, he wrote chiefly aesthetic theory, criticism, and an unfinished play about Faust. He helped to revive lively interest in the symbolists and had a pervading influence on French culture generally, though his poetry is not easy for the casual reader. His criticism and aesthetic theory had an important influence on the structuralist critics of the 1960s. He was elected to the French Academy in 1925. His *Collected Works* (1971–75) have been published in expert translations by the Bollingen Foundation.

POETRY BY VALÉRY

Charmes. 1922. Trans. by James L. Brown. Forsan Bks. 1983 $8.75. ISBN 0-9612298-0-2

Collected Works of Paul Valéry. 15 vols. Ed. by Jackson Matthews. *Bollingen Ser.* Princeton U. Pr. 1971–75 $29.95-$52.50 ea.

WORK BY VALÉRY

Selected Writings. New Dir. Pr. 1964 $12.95. ISBN 0-8112-0213-5. Various translators. Includes poetry, essays, dialogues, and critiques.

BOOKS ABOUT VALÉRY

Bloom, Harold, ed. *Paul Valéry*. Chelsea Hse. 1990 $24.95. ISBN 1-55546-315-0. Essays by American and European critics.

Grubbs, Henry A. *Paul Valéry*. *Twayne's World Authors Ser.* Irvington 1968 $17.95. ISBN 0-8051-2920-8

Kluback, William. *Paul Valéry: Philosophical Reflections*. P. Lang Pubs. 1987 $30.50. ISBN 0-8204-0386-5. Monograph on the poet as a philosopher of art.

Lawler, James R. *The Poet as Analyst: Essays on Paul Valéry*. U. CA Pr. 1974 $47.50. ISBN 0-520-02450-8

Mackay, Agnes E. *The Universal Self: A Study of Paul Valéry*. St. Mut. 1982 $45.00. ISBN 0-85335-235-6

Stimpson, Brian. *Paul Valéry and Music: A Study of the Techniques of Composition in Valéry's Poetry*. Cambridge U. Pr. 1984 $64.95. ISBN 0-521-25608-9. Studies an important aspect of Valéry's work.

VERLAINE, PAUL. 1844–1896

The dissolute, erratic leader of the decadents and one of the early symbolists, Verlaine wrote 18 volumes of verse in alternating moods of sensuality and mysticism. He and the Poet RIMBAUD, 10 years younger, wandered throughout Europe together, until their relationship ended when Verlaine shot his companion in Brussels in 1873 and was imprisoned for two years. *Sagesse* (1881), his collection of religious poems of great melodic and emotional beauty, is generally considered his finest volume. In his famous poem *Art Poétique*, Verlaine stressed the primary importance of musicality in poetry over description. MALLARMÉ called the collection in which it appears, *Jadis et Naguère* (1884), "almost continuously a masterpiece . . . disturbing as a demon's work," and described Verlaine's skill as that of a guitarist.

POETRY BY VERLAINE

Baudelaire, Rimbaud and Verlaine: Selected Verse and Prose Poems. Ed. by Joseph M. Bernstein. Carol Pub. Group 1983 $6.95. ISBN 0-8065-0196-0

Confessions of a Poet. Trans. by Joanna Richardson. Hyperion Conn. 1980 repr. of 1950 ed. $22.00. ISBN 0-88355-875-0

Forty Poems. Saifer 1989 $25.00. ISBN 0-87556-697-9

Four French Symbolist Poets: Baudelaire, Rimbaud, Verlaine, Mallarmé. Trans. by Enid R. Peschel. Ohio U. Pr. 1981 o.p.

Poems. Trans. by Jacques Leclerc. Greenwood repr. of 1961 ed. $38.50. ISBN 0-8371-9859-3

Royal Tastes: Erotic Writings of Paul Verlaine. Trans. by Alan Stone. Crown 1984 o.p.

BOOKS ABOUT VERLAINE

Lepelletier, Edmond A. *Paul Verlaine*. AMS Pr. repr. of 1909 ed. $31.45. ISBN 0-404-03968-5

Nicholson, Harold G. *Paul Verlaine*. AMS Pr. repr. of 1921 ed. $27.50. ISBN 0-404-16332-7

Zweig, Stefan. *Paul Verlaine*. Trans. by O. F. Theis. AMS Pr. repr. of 1913 ed. $16.50. ISBN 0-404-16359-9. By the widely read prewar German author.

VILLON, FRANÇOIS (François de Moncorbier). 1431–1465?

Villon is one of the first great French lyric poets and one of the greatest French poets of any age. His "testaments" are mock wills, written in a racy blend of French and underworld slang. Scattered here and there among the ironic items of bequest are exquisite ballads and lyrics, some crystallizing classic themes of medieval literature. Villon's poetry uses traditional forms to create a powerful poetic personality during a period in which poetic individualism was rare. Indeed, his exquisite "Ballad of the Hanged Men" ("Ballade des Pendus") (1489) offers one of the most immediate depictions of death in Western poetry. Moreover, his dissolute life, lived among thieves and prostitutes, makes him a prototype of later decadent or bohemian poets. He was at various times arrested, imprisoned, tortured, and nearly put to death; his final sentence was commuted to exile by King Louis XI on accession to the throne, when he declared amnesties of all sorts, according to the usual practice of the time. It is not known how Villon spent his last years, after his release from prison. Villon's poetry has been translated by ROSSETTI (see Vol. 1), SYNGE (see Vol. 1), and SWINBURNE (see Vol. 1).

POETRY BY VILLON

The Poems of François Villon. Ed. by Galway Kinnell. U. Pr. of New Eng. 1982 $12.95. ISBN 0-87451-236-0. Translated by a noted American poet.

Book of François Villon: The Little Testament and Ballads. Trans. by Algernon C. Swinburne. Branden Pub. Co. $3.95. ISBN 0-8283-1425-X. Translated by the great English symbolist writer.

Books about Villon

Fein, David A. *François Villon and His Reader.* Wayne St. U. Pr. 1989 $28.95. ISBN 0-8143-2131-3. A phenomenological study.

Paris, Gaston. *François Villon.* AMS Pr. repr. of 1901 ed. $21.00. ISBN 0-404-56657. By one of the greatest French specialists of the Middle Ages.

Vitz, Evelyn B. *The Crossroad of Intentions: A Study of Symbolic Expression in the Poetry of François Villon.* Mouton 1974 $28.00. ISBN 90-2792-624-7. A helpful commentary that focuses on the multiple resonances of Villon's vocabulary.

VOLTAIRE (pseud. of François-Marie Arouet). 1694–1778

A leading freethinker of his time and an opponent of political and religious oppression, Voltaire was instrumental in popularizing serious philosophical, religious, and scientific ideas that were frequently derived from liberal thinkers in England, where he lived for two years after his imprisonment in the Bastille. Voltaire's writings are wide ranging: He wrote plays in the neoclassic style, such as *Oedipus* (1718), philosophical essays in a popular vein like *Letters on England* (1734), which has been referred to as the first bomb hurled against the Ancien Régime; and the *Philosophical Dictionary* (1764), a catalog of polemical ideas on a large variety of subjects, particularly religion and philosophy. Voltaire was one of the most prolific letter writers in the entire history of literature, and his correspondence has been published in a French edition of 107 volumes. For the twentieth-century reader, Voltaire is best known for his philosophical tale *Candide* (1759), a masterpiece of satire that is both an attack on the philosophy of metaphysical optimism elaborated earlier in the century by the German philosopher Leibniz (see Vol. 4) and a compendium of the abuses of the Ancien Régime as the author ponders the general problem of evil. Voltaire's unflinching belief in human reason and his easy handling of the language of Enlightenment wit and philosophy led the critic Roland Barthes to dub him "the last happy writer."

Fiction by Voltaire

Candide. 1759. Trans. by John Butt. Viking Penguin 1950 $2.50. ISBN 0-8049-0117-1

Candide and Other Stories. Trans. by Roger Pearson. OUP 1990 $6.95. ISBN 0-19-281730-2

Candide, Zadig and Selected Stories. Trans. by Donald Frame. NAL-Dutton 1989 $2.50. ISBN 0-451-52357-1. In "Zadig," a Persian prince loses his possessions and goes in search of the meaning of life.

Micromegas and Other Stories. Hippocrene Bks. 1990 $6.95. ISBN 0-87052-614-6. Includes some of Voltaire's wittiest writings.

Nonfiction by Voltaire

The Elements of Sir Isaac Newton's Philosophy. 1738. Trans. by John Hanna. Intl. Spec. Bk. 1967 $35.00. ISBN 0-7146-1612-5. A philosophy of science.

Letters Concerning the English Nation. 1734. B. Franklin 1974 repr. of 1926 ed. $19.00. ISBN 0-8337-4467-4. Important letters revealing much about Voltaire's political ideas.

Philosophical Dictionary. 1764. Trans. by Theodore Besterman. *Penguin Class. Ser.* Viking Penguin 1984 $7.95. ISBN 0-14-044257-X

The Philosophy of History. 1765. Carol Pub. Group 1965 $3.45. ISBN 0-8065-0078-6. Important reflections that influenced modern historiographers.

Russia under Peter the Great. 1759. Trans. by M. F. Jenkins. Fairleigh Dickinson 1984 $40.00. ISBN 0-8386-3148-7

Plays by Voltaire

Seven Plays. Trans. by William F. Fleming. Fertig 1988 $45.00. ISBN 0-86527-371-5

Books about Voltaire

Brumfit, J. H. *Voltaire: Historian.* Greenwood 1985 repr. of 1958 ed. o.p. Study of an often neglected side of Voltaire.

Gay, Peter. *Voltaire's Politics: The Poet as Realist.* Yale U. Pr. 1988 $18.00. ISBN 0-300-04095-4. Good study by noted historian.

Morley, John. *Voltaire.* B. Franklin 1973 repr. of 1903 ed. o.p.

Wade, Ira O. *The Intellectual Development of Voltaire.* Bks. Demand repr. of 1969 ed. $160.00. ISBN 0-317-08701-0. A basic general study.

WEIL, SIMONE. 1909–1943

Born in Paris, Weil came from a highly intellectual family. After a brilliant academic career at school and university, she taught philosophy interspersed with periods of hard manual labor on farms and in factories. Throughout her life she combined sophisticated and scholarly interests with an extreme moral intensity and identification with the poor and oppressed. A twentieth-century Pascal (see Vol. 4), this ardently spiritual woman was a social thinker, sensitive to the crises of modern humanity. Jewish by birth, Christian by vocation, and Greek by aesthetic choice, Weil has influenced religious thinking profoundly in the years since her death. "Humility is the root of love," she said as she questioned traditional theologians and held that the apostles had badly interpreted Christ's teaching. Christianity was, she thought, to blame for the heresy of progress. During World War II, Weil starved herself to death, refusing to eat while victims of the war still suffered.

Nonfiction by Weil

Formative Writings. Trans. by Dorothy McFarland. U. of Mass. Pr. 1987 $14.95. ISBN 0-87023-632-6

Iliad, or the Poem of Force. 1953. Pendle Hill 1956 $3.00. ISBN 0-87574-091-X. A controversial interpretation drawing parallels between Homer's poem and modern politics.

Oppression and Liberty. 1955. Trans. by Arthur Wills and John Petrie. U. of Mass. Pr. 1973 $12.95. ISBN 0-87023-251-7

Two Moral Essays: Human Personality and On Human Obligations. Pendle Hill 1981 $3.00. ISBN 0-87574-240-8

Waiting for God. HarpC 1973 $7.95. ISBN 0-06-090295-7

Books about Weil

Blum, Lawrence A., and Victor J. Seidler. *A Truer Liberty: Simone Weil and Marxism.* Routledge 1989 $17.95. ISBN 0-415-90195-2. Considers Weil's leftist leanings.

Coles, Robert. *Simone Weil: A Modern Pilgrimage.* Addison-Wesley 1989 $9.50. ISBN 0-201-07964-X. Reflection of the author by a noted educator.

Fiori, Gabriella. *Simone Weil: An Intellectual Biography.* Trans. by Joseph Berrigan. U. of Ga. Pr. 1989 $34.95. ISBN 0-8203-1102-2. Plumbs into the depths of Weil's thought; relies heavily on interviews with the many people who were touched by her life.

Hellman, John. *Simone Weil: An Introduction to Her Thought.* Humanities 1982 $19.95. ISBN 0-88920-121-8

McFarland, Dorothy T. *Simone Weil. Lit. and Life Ser.* Continuum 1983 $19.95. ISBN 0-8044-2604-X

Winch, Peter. *Simone Weil: The Just Balance.* Cambridge U. Pr. 1989 $15.95. ISBN 0-521-31743-6

YOURCENAR, MARGUERITE (pseud. of Marguerite de Crayencour). 1903–1987

A French novelist, playwright, and essayist born in Belgium, Marguerite Yourcenar was a resident of the United States for many years, living in isolation on a small island off the coast of Maine. Educated at home by wealthy and cultured parents, she had a strong humanistic background, translating the ancient Greek poet Pindar and the poems of the modern Greek Constantine Cavafy. She has translated American Negro spirituals and works of Virginia Woolf (see Vol. 1) and Henry James (see Vol. 1). Her novels include *Alexis* (1929) and *Coup de Grace* (1939). A collection of poems, *Fires,* was published in 1936. She is particularly known for *Hadrian's Memoirs* (1951), a philosophical meditation in the form of a fictional autobiography of the second-century Roman emperor. In Germaine Brée's judgment, "With great erudition and great psychological insight, Marguerite Yourcenar constructed a body of work that is a meditation on the destiny of mankind." In 1981, she became the first woman ever elected to the French Academy.

Novels by Yourcenar

The Abyss. 1968. Trans. by Grace Frick. FS&G 1976 $15.00. ISBN 0-374-51666-9
Alexis. 1929. Trans. by Walter Kaiser. FS&G 1984 $12.95. ISBN 0-374-10263-5
A Coin in Nine Hands. 1934. Trans. by Dori Katz. FS&G 1982 $7.95. ISBN 0-374-51953-6. Story of an assassination attempt of Mussolini.
Coup de Grace. 1939. Trans. by Grace Frick. FS&G 1981 $8.95. ISBN 0-374-51631-6. Story of a Prussian officer who murders the woman he loves.
Fires. 1936. Trans. by Dori Katz. FS&G 1981 $8.95. ISBN 0-374-51748-7
Memoirs of Hadrian. 1951. FS&G 1963 $12.95. ISBN 0-394-50348-6. The reflections of the Roman emperor on the eve of his death.

Nonfiction by Yourcenar

The Dark Brain of Piranesi and Other Essays. Trans. by Richard Howard. FS&G 1984 $8.95. ISBN 0-374-51919-6. Wide ranging essays on art and literature.
Mishima: A Vision of the Void. Trans. by Alberto Manguel. FS&G 1987 $7.95. ISBN 0-374-52061. An interesting study of the Japanese novelist.
That Mighty Sculptor, Time. Trans. by Walter Kaiser. FS&G 1991 $18.95. ISBN 0-374-27358-8. Posthumous collection of essays that reveals Yourcenar's exceptionally wide range of interests.

Book about Yourcenar

Snurr, Georgia H. *Marguerite Yourcenar: A Reader's Guide.* U. Pr. of Amer. 1987 $15.75. ISBN 0-8191-6471-2

ZOLA, ÉMILE. 1840–1902

Zola was the spokesperson for the naturalist novel in France and the leader of a school that championed the infusion of literature with new scientific theories of human development drawn from Charles Darwin (see Vol. 5) and various social philosophers. The theoretical claims for such an approach, which are considered simplistic today, were outlined by Zola in his *Le Roman Expérimental* (*The Experimental Novel*) (1880). He was the author of the series of 20 novels called *The Rougon-Macquart,* in which he attempted to trace scientifically the effects of heredity through five generations of the Rougon and Macquart families. Three of the outstanding volumes are *L'Assommoir* (1877), a study of alcoholism and the working class; *Nana* (1880), a story of a prostitute who is a *femme fatale*; and *Germinal* (1885), a study of a strike at a coal mine. All gave scope to Zola's gift for portraying crowds in turmoil. Today Zola's novels have been appreciated by critics for their epic scope and their visionary and mythical qualities. He continues to be immensely popular with French readers. His newspaper article "J'accuse," written in defense of Alfred Dreyfus, launched Zola into the public limelight and made him the political conscience of his country.

Novels by Zola

L'Assommoir. 1877. *Penguin Class. Ser.* Viking Penguin 1970 $6.95. ISBN 0-14-044231-6

La Bête Humaine. 1890. Trans. by Leonard W. Tancock. *Penguin Class. Ser.* Viking Penguin 1977 $5.95. ISBN 0-14-044327-4. Story of steam locomotive and those affected by its power.

The Debacle. 1892. Trans. by Leonard W. Tancock. *Penguin Class. Ser.* Viking Penguin 1973 $5.95. ISBN 0-14-044280-4

The Earth. 1887. Trans. by Douglas Parmee. *Penguin Class. Ser.* Viking Penguin 1980 $5.95. ISBN 0-14-644327

Germinal. 1885. Trans. by Leonard W. Tancock. *Penguin Class. Ser.* Viking Penguin 1954 $4.50. ISBN 0-14-044-045-3

Masterpiece. 1885. U. of Mich. Pr. 1968 $13.95. ISBN 0-472-06145-3. An ambitious artist seeks to complete his masterpiece. Inspired by Zola's friendship with Manet.

Nana. 1880. Trans. by George Holden. Viking Penguin 1972 $6.95. ISBN 0-14-044263-4

The Sin of Father Mouret. 1875. Trans. by Sandy Petrey. U. of Nebr. Pr. 1983 repr. of 1969 ed. $7.50. ISBN 0-8032-9901-X

Thérèse Raquin. 1867. Trans. by Leonard W. Tancock. *Penguin Class. Ser.* Viking Penguin 1962 $5.95. ISBN 0-14-044120-4. A macabre tale of adultery and murder among the lower classes.

Short Story Collection by Zola

The Attack on the Mill and Other Stories. 1880. Ed. by Douglas Parmee. OUP 1985 $6.95. ISBN 0-19-281599-7

Books about Zola

Bédé, Jean-Albert. *Émile Zola.* Col. U. Pr. 1974 o.p.

Bell, David F. *Models of Power: Politics and Economics in Zola's "Rougon-Macquart."* U. of Nebr. Pr. 1988 $19.95. ISBN 0-8032-1201-1. Demonstrates how Zola associated the political and economic ambitions of Emperor Louis Napoleon with the tumultuous urban renewal of Paris.

Friedman, Lee M. *Zola and the Dreyfus Case.* Haskell 1970 repr. of 1937 ed. $75.00. ISBN 0-8383-0092-8. Focuses on Zola's politics.

Hemmings, F.W.J. *The Life and Times of Zola.* Scribner 1977 o.p. An important contextual study.

Knapp, Bettina L. *Émile Zola.* Continuum 1980 $18.95. ISBN 0-80442482-9

Lethbridge, Robert, and Terry Keefe, eds. *Zola and the Craft of Fiction.* Col. U. Pr. 1990 $45.00. ISBN 0-7185-1312-6. Collected essays about various aspects of Zola's work.

Schor, Naomi. *Zola's Crowds.* Bks. Demand $60.00. ISBN 0-317-42338-X. A good structuralist study.

CHAPTER 15

Spanish Literature

Michael McGaha

The entire complexity of the history of the Spaniards was born magnificently and splendidly, and sometimes painfully, as a consequence of the confrontations and harmony among the peoples of three different religious beliefs. . . . This mixture and coexistence of differently believing peoples, though physically analogous, lent a peculiar shape and appearance to the life and history of the future Spaniards.

—AMÉRICO CASTRO, *The Spaniards*

The saying that geography is destiny is truer of Spain than of most countries. A peninsula jutting out into the Atlantic at the far western extreme of Europe, separated from Africa by only 11 miles of water, Spain is also internally divided into many quarrelsome regions by rugged mountain ranges. Even today strong regionalist and separatist movements exert a powerful centrifugal force that endangers national unity. It is hardly surprising, therefore, that the literature of Spain is for the most part a tragic record of conflicts with enemies both internal and external.

Between the tenth and twelfth centuries, while most of the peninsula was under Muslim rule, Spain could boast of the most advanced civilization in Europe. Though the Christian warlords of the north made sporadic forays into Muslim lands, during most of this period, Muslims coexisted peacefully with Christians and with the large, prosperous, and influential Jewish community. The fruitful interaction of these three groups ultimately produced Spain's distinctive culture, which therefore shares at least as many traits with the peoples of the Middle East as it does with those of Europe. In this atmosphere of tolerant pluralism, Spanish literature was born. The earliest known literary works in Spanish reflect the bilingualism of the Hispanic-Arabic culture. They are refrains, some dating from as early as the eleventh century, to longer poems written in Arabic or Hebrew and are the oldest known lyric poetry in a Romance language.

The epic *The Poem of the Cid*, now believed to have been written in the last quarter of the twelfth century, transforms the eleventh-century mercenary warlord Rodrigo Díaz, whom the great orientalist Reinhardt Dozy described as "more Muslim than Christian," into the embodiment of Castilian Christian values. Nevertheless, the poem portrays the Cid—whose very title is Arabic for *lord*—as at times serving a Muslim ruler, leading a mixed band of Christians and Muslims against a Christian king, and borrowing money from Jews to finance his campaigns.

After the battle of Las Navas de Tolosa (1212), the Christian hordes slowly but steadily advanced southward, and the days of Muslim Spain were numbered. King Alfonso X (1221–84), known as Alfonso the Wise because of his patronage of scholarship and literature, presided over a court where Jewish, Christian, and

Muslim scholars collaborated on translations of Arabic and Hebrew works and on important encyclopedic compendia of history, law, and the sciences. Alfonso's nephew, Don Juan Manuel (1282–1349?), is remembered primarily for his didactic short story collection, *Count Lucanor* (1323–25). This book, inspired largely by Arabic sources, is the first work of prose fiction written in a modern European language.

Ferdinand and Isabella conquered the last Muslim stronghold of Granada in 1492 and in the same year offered the Jews the choice of conversion to Catholicism or expulsion from Spain. Most converted but were never accepted as equals by the Christian population, which continued to discriminate against them; soon they fell prey to the Inquisition's persecution. Most of Spain's leading writers of the Renaissance and Baroque periods—FERNANDO DE ROJAS, MATEO ALEMÁN, ST. TERESA, Fray Luis de León, and probably MIGUEL DE CERVANTES—were either converts from Judaism or their descendants. Their writings reflect the anguished, defensive position this group had to adopt in order to prove themselves as authentic Spaniards.

St. Teresa and ST. JOHN OF THE CROSS—arguably the greatest Catholic mystic writers—flourished in the 1500s, several centuries after mysticism's ascendancy in northern Europe. Curiously, Spain had also produced the major Jewish mystics and some of the leading Sufi mystics in earlier times. The writings of St. Teresa and St. John of the Cross show definite influences of both Jewish and Muslim mysticism, although scholars have still not succeeded in determining exactly how those influences were transmitted to them in a time when most Jewish and Muslim writings were banned in Spain.

During the period known as Spain's Golden Age, roughly from the mid-sixteenth to the mid-seventeenth century, Spanish writers set the tone and style for the rest of European literature, experimenting successively with new types of prose fiction—the romance of chivalry, the pastoral novel, the picaresque novel—before Cervantes at last created in *Don Quijote* (1603–15) the first truly modern novel. The period also produced many of Spain's most brilliant poets, whose work ranged from the serene intellectual Neoplatonism of Fray Luis de León to the fervent lyricism of St. John of the Cross and the tortured eroticism and scathing satiric verse of FRANCISCO DE QUEVEDO.

It was the theater, however, that most captured the public imagination. For over a century scores of prolific playwrights, the best known of whom are LOPE DE VEGA, CALDERÓN DE LA BARCA, and TIRSO DE MOLINA, strove to satisfy the Spanish public's insatiable desire for entertainment. Their dramatic output was unparalleled in the history of the world. Written to appeal to a mass audience, and subject to strict government controls, this theater has long been considered conservative or even reactionary in its support for mainstream values such as Catholicism and the Hapsburg monarchy. Recent studies, however, have begun to reveal that criticism of church, government, and popular views, though necessarily somewhat veiled, was present in much of this drama.

The death in 1700 of Spain's last Hapsburg king—the grotesquely deformed and mentally defective Charles II—eerily symbolized the nation's physical and spiritual exhaustion. The arrival of the Bourbon dynasty ushered in a century of slavish imitation of French fashions in art and literature, to which the resentful masses reacted by exaggerating their conservative anti-intellectualism. The French influence ended only when the outraged populace ousted Napoleon's invading armies from the peninsula, an insurrection since known as the first guerrilla war. The restored reactionary monarchy of Ferdinand VII then effectively stamped out all intellectual activity, especially during the last 10 years (1823–33) of the king's life, known as the "ominous decade." Only after Ferdinand's death did Spain's major writers return from exile in France or England, and with them they brought romanticism. Oddly, the rest of Europe viewed Spain as the romantic land par excellence, yet romanticism reached Spain only when waning in fashion elsewhere.

Spain produced two important poets, Gustavo Adolfo Bécquer and Rosalía de Castro, during the second half of the nineteenth century. The period saw much controversial experimentation in the novel, as writers such as Benito Pérez Galdós, Emilia Pardo Bazán, and Leopoldo Alas struggled to adapt French and English realism and naturalism to Spanish circumstances.

Spain's defeat in the Spanish-American War of 1898, completing the loss of its once far-flung empire, provoked a national crisis of confidence. A group of talented young writers just beginning to publish at that time—including the Basque philosopher Miguel de Unamuno, the Andalusian poet Antonio Machado, and the Levantine essayist Azorín—inevitably turned their attention to the causes, and possible remedies, for Spain's decline. With the detachment of the outlander, they focused affectionate but critical attention on the effects of Castile's hegemonic attempts to suppress regional differences. Collectively known as the Generation of 1898, they were especially preoccupied with Spain's destiny in the world. Could it somehow emerge from a centuries-long isolation to participate fully in the economic and cultural life of modern Europe? Could it do so without sacrificing national identity? What did it really mean to be Spanish?

In 1927 a group of gifted young poets—among whom were Federico García Lorca, Rafael Alberti, Pedro Salinas, and Jorge Guillén—organized an homage to the highly intellectual, hermetic poet Luis de Góngora on the tercentenary of his death. Known as the Generation of 1927, these poets combined surrealism and aestheticism, seeking a pure poetry free of all nonpoetic elements.

The Spanish civil war (1936–39) marked a break in the development of Spanish literature, for many writers were killed, imprisoned, or exiled, and strict censorship effectively silenced those who remained. The Spanish novel entered a period of renewal with the publication of Camilo José Cela's *The Family of Pascual Duarte* in 1942. That novel initiated a movement called *tremendismo,* a style of naturalism focusing on the grotesque and violent that has been continued by Miguel Delibes and Ana María Matute. The mainstream, commercially successful playwright Antonio Buero Vallejo managed indirectly but effectively to protest the Franco dictatorship's repression, while underground playwrights such as Alfonso Sastre voiced even stronger criticisms, though they probably reached a much larger audience outside Spain.

Since Franco's death in 1975, restrictions on free speech have been lifted, and many exiled writers have returned to Spain. Several novelists, such as Juan Goytisolo, Leopoldo Azancot, and Antonio Gala, have found inspiration in Spain's Muslim and Jewish past. Literature has also become less centralized, with regional literatures, especially in Catalan, experiencing a strong revival. Women writers, some writing on feminist themes, are more numerous and prominent than ever. Among these are the novelist and essayist Carmen Martin Gaite, the poet Gloria Fuertes, and the novelist Esther Tusquets. Twenty years is not a long time to recover from a dictator's violent silencing, but the current high achievements of Spain's cinema and plastic arts show how far a cultural rejuvenation has come. In post-Franco literature, voices so individual, varied, and forceful promise an equal vigor.

HISTORY AND CRITICISM

General

Bennassar, Bartolomé. *The Spanish Character: Attitudes and Mentalities from the Sixteenth to the Nineteenth Century.* Trans. by Benjamin Keen. U. CA Pr. 1979 $45.00. ISBN 0-520-03401-5. Spanish culture and its influence on literature from the sixteenth to the nineteenth century.

Benson, Frederick R. *Writers in Arms: The Literary Impact of the Spanish Civil War.* NYU Pr. 1967 o.p. Interweaves literary criticism with political analysis. Helpful chronology, good bibliography.

Bourland, Caroline B. *The Short Story in Spain in the Seventeenth Century, with a Bibliography of the Novella from 1576–1700.* B. Franklin repr. of 1927 ed. o.p. Brief essay on the Italian influence on the Spanish short story in the seventeenth century.

Brenan, Gerald. *The Literature of the Spanish People from Roman Times to the Present Day.* Cambridge U. Pr. 1976 $57.50. ISBN 0-521-04313-1. Highly subjective and sometimes controversial, but always interesting.

Brown, Joan L., ed. *Women Writers of Contemporary Spain.* U. of Delaware Pr. 1991 $39.50. ISBN 0-87413-386-6. Essays by noted scholars introducing works of 13 major women writers of Franco and post-Franco Spain.

Butt, John. *Writers and Politics in Modern Spain. Writers and Politics Ser.* Holmes & Meier 1978 $15.95. ISBN 0-8419-0412-X. History and criticism of twentieth-century Spanish writers.

Chandler, Richard E., and Kessel Schwartz. *A New History of Spanish Literature.* La. State U. Pr. rev. ed. 1991. $45.00. ISBN 0-8071-1699-8. Authoritative volume covering poetry, drama, fiction, and nonfiction with a succinct discussion of Spanish history and culture; appendixes and classified bibliography.

Crow, John A. *Spain: The Root and the Flower.* U. CA Pr. rev. ed. 1985 $45.00. ISBN 0-520-05123-0. Interesting treatment of Spanish culture, particularly during the Golden Age.

Dunn, Peter N. *The Spanish Picaresque Novel. Twayne's World Authors Ser.* G. K. Hall 1979 o.p. Analysis of the genre from *Lazarillo de Tormes* to *Estebanillo González.*

Eoff, Sherman H. *The Modern Spanish Novel: Comparative Essays Examining the Philosophical Impact of Science on Fiction. Gotham Lib.*NYU Pr. 1961 o.p. A study of the modern Spanish philosophical novel through comparisons with works in other European literatures. Compares novelists in light of their common intellectual background.

Green, Otis H. *Spain and the Western Tradition: The Castilian Mind in Literature from El Cid to Calderón.* 4 vols. U. of Wis. Pr. 1969 $9.95 ea. Interprets the essential ideas of Spanish literary texts from the twelfth through the seventeenth centuries. Topics include love, reason, free will, fortune and fate, death, and religion.

Keller, John E., and Richard P. Kinkade. *Iconography in Medieval Spanish Literature.* Ky. U. Pr. 1984 $65.00. ISBN 0-8131-1449-7. History and criticism of Spanish fiction up to the 1500s.

Madariaga, Salvador de. *The Genius of Spain, and Other Essays on Spanish Literature. Essay Index Repr. Ser.* Ayer repr. of 1923 ed. $14.75. ISBN 0-8369-0662-4. Essays on leading writers of the Generation of 1898, relating their work to the Spanish character and to contemporary European literature.

McClelland, I. L. *The Origins of the Romantic Movement in Spain.* Humanities 1975 repr. of 1937 ed. o.p. Explores romantic (broadly defined) tendencies and theories as they apply to the many periods in Spanish literature.

Miller, Beth, ed. *Women in Hispanic Literature: Icons and Fallen Idols.* U. CA Pr. 1983 $42.50. ISBN 0-520-04367-7. An important collection of essays on women authors and on the portrayal of women in Hispanic literature.

Morris, C. B. *A Generation of Spanish Poets, 1920–1936.* Cambridge U. Pr. 1979 $49.50. ISBN 0-521-07381-2. A comprehensive study of this period of transition and change in Spanish poetry.

Northup, George T., and Nelson B. Adams, eds. *An Introduction to Spanish Literature*. U. Ch. Pr. 1960 $3.95. ISBN 0-226-59443-2. An easy-to-read outline of Spanish literature.

Parker, A. A. *The Philosophy of Love in Spanish Literature*. Col. U. Pr. 1985 $15.00. ISBN 0-85224-491-6. Changing attitudes toward love from medieval Courtly Love poetry through the Neo-Stoicism of Quevedo.

Parks, George B., and Ruth Z. Temple, eds. *Romance Literatures. Lit. of the World in Eng. Translation*. 2 vols. Continuum 1970 o.p. Bibliographies of English translations of Spanish, Spanish-American, Portuguese, and Brazilian literatures.

Pattison, Walter T., and Donald W. Bleznick, eds. *Representative Spanish Authors*. 2 vols. OUP 1971. Vol. 1 $24.00. ISBN 0-19-501326-3. Vol. 2 $26.00. ISBN 0-19-501433-2. Selections from Spanish literature from the Middle Ages through the twentieth century. Texts in Spanish but useful introductions to each period and author in English.

Pérez Firmat, Gustavo. *Idle Fictions: The Hispanic Vanguard Novel, 1926-1934*. Duke 1983 $24.75. ISBN 0-8223-0528-3. Interesting study of the phenomenon of the avant-garde novel of the 1920s and 1930s in Spain and Latin America, including an historical overview of its reception.

Post, Chandler R. *Medieval Spanish Allegory*. Gordon Pr. 1984 $90.00. ISBN 0-8490-3235-0. A groundbreaking study of the nature and development of allegory in Spanish literature from the thirteenth through the sixteenth century.

Rivers, Elias L. *Quixotic Scriptures: Essays on the Textuality of Hispanic Literature*. Ind. U. Pr. 1984 $25.00. ISBN 0-253-34761-0. Applies notions from sociolinguistics, speech-act theory, and semiotics to Hispanic literature from its prealphabetic origins through twentieth-century Latin American writings.

Shepard, Sanford. *Lost Lexicon: Secret Meanings in the Vocabulary of Spanish Literature During the Inquisition. Hispanic Studies Collection*. Ediciones 1982 $19.95. ISBN 0-89729-309-6. Fascinating study of the development of a specialized vocabulary by both crypto-Jews and anti-Semites to deal with race and religion as a response to the Inquisition.

Soufas, Teresa S. *Melancholy and the Secular Mind in Spanish Golden Age Literature*. U. of Mo. Pr. 1990 $25.00. ISBN 0-8262-0714-6. Examines melancholy in religion, love, picaresque narrative, and the *conceptista/culteranista* debate. Essential for a comprehensive understanding of Spain's Golden Age.

Stamm, James R. *A Short History of Spanish Literature: Revised and Updated Edition. Gotham Lib*. NYU Pr. 1979 $20.00. ISBN 0-8147-7729-9. Critical analysis of twentieth-century Spanish literature.

Swietlicki, Catherine. *Spanish Christian Cabala: The Works of Luis de León, Santa Teresa de Jesús, and San Juan de la Cruz*. U. of Mo. Pr. 1987 $25.00. ISBN 0-8262-0608-5. Studies adaptation of the Jewish mystical tradition, as well as possible influences of Islamic mysticism, in the works of the three most important Spanish mystics.

Valis, Noel, and Carol Maier, eds. *In the Feminine Mode: Essays on Hispanic Women Writers*. Bucknell U. Pr. 1990 $38.50. ISBN 0-8387-5160-1. Covers peninsular and Latin American literature from various genres and historical periods. "Recommended for college courses in literary criticism as well as for public and college libraries" (*Choice*).

Ward, Philip. *The Oxford Companion to Spanish Literature*. OUP 1978 $55.00. ISBN 0-19-866114-2. Bio-bibliographies and dictionary to Spanish literature.

Drama

Cohen, Walter. *Drama of a Nation: Public Theater in Renaissance England and Spain*. Cornell Univ. Pr. 1985 $47.50. ISBN 0-8014-1793-7. "A pioneering effort on a truly impressive scale . . . admirable for vigorous and exceptionally extensive scholarship and hard thinking" (*Renaissance Quarterly*).

Cook, John A. *Neo-Classic Drama in Spain*. Greenwood 1974 repr. of 1959 ed. $79.50. ISBN 0-8371-7518-6. A well-documented history of the development of neoclassical drama through the failures of romanticism.

Crawford, J. Wickersham. *Spanish Drama before Lope de Vega.* Greenwood 1975 repr. of 1967 ed. o.p. A standard critical work. Traces the development of drama from pre-Encina times to the religious drama, tragedy, and comedy of the late sixteenth century.

______. *The Spanish Pastoral Drama.* Folcroft repr. of 1915 ed. o.p. Pastoral plays from the period before Juan del Encina until the seventeenth century, including those of Lope de Vega and Calderón.

Fiore, Robert L. *Drama and Ethos: Natural Law Ethics in Spanish Golden Age Drama. Studies in Romance Languages.* U. Pr. of Ky. 1975 o.p. Valuable examination of the application of Thomistic precepts in the presentation of ethical problems in Golden Age drama.

Fothergill-Payne, Louise, and Peter Fothergill-Payne, eds. *Parallel Lives: Spanish and English Drama, 1580–1680.* Bucknell U. Pr. 1991 $47.50. ISBN 0-8387-5194-6. An important collection of essays by scholars of English and Spanish theater examining parallels in the development of the classic drama of both nations.

Hesse, Everett W., intro. by. *Approaches to Teaching Spanish Golden Age Drama.* Spanish Lit. Pubns. 1989 $20.00. ISBN 0-938972-14-6. Eight concise essays applying major critical approaches, from the psychological to the deconstructionist, to several frequently studied plays. "A useful guide for selecting plays and methodologies" (*Choice*).

McKendrick, Melveena. *Theatre in Spain: 1490–1700.* Cambridge U. Pr. 1990 $64.95. ISBN 0-521-35592-3. An excellent history of the rise and reign of Spain's national theater in the sixteenth and seventeenth centuries in all its aspects, with particular emphasis on the experimental drama of the sixteenth century before Lope de Vega.

______. *Woman and Society in the Spanish Drama of the Golden Age.* Cambridge U. Pr. 1974 o.p. Study of woman as a character in Spanish drama.

Peers, Edgar A., ed. *Spanish Golden Age in Poetry and Drama.* Phaeton 1974 repr. of 1946 ed. $45.00. ISBN 0-87753-060-2. Essays and lectures on poetry and drama during the Spanish classical period.

Rennert, Hugo A. *The Spanish Stage in the Time of Lope de Vega.* Kraus repr. of 1909 ed. o.p. Discusses major playwrights, the origins of comedy and other types of plays, famous theaters, staging, and notable actors. A classic study.

Shoemaker, William H. *The Multiple Stage in Spain during the Fifteenth and Sixteenth Centuries.* Greenwood 1973 repr. of 1935 ed. $39.75. ISBN 0-8371-5539-8. Stage setting and scenery of classical Spanish theater.

Stoll, Anita K., and Dawn L. Smith, eds. *The Perception of Women in Spanish Theater of the Golden Age.* Bucknell U. Pr. 1991 $42.50. ISBN 0-8387-5189-X. Fourteen essays by American Hispanics examining and evaluating writers' and society's perceptions of women in sixteenth- and seventeenth-century Spain.

Wellwarth, George E. *Spanish Underground Drama.* Pa. St. U. Pr. 1972 $21.50. ISBN 0-271-01154-8. A critical study of Spanish playwrights forced "underground" under the censorship of the Franco regime.

Ziomek, Henryk. *A History of Spanish Golden Age Drama. Studies in Romance Languages.* U. Pr. of Ky. 1984 $25.00. ISBN 0-8131-0158-1. A critical history of Golden Age drama, with special attention to the lesser dramatists who followed the paths of Lope and Calderón.

Fiction

Chandler, Frank W. *Romances of Roguery: The Picaresque Novel in Spain.* Gordon Pr. 1977 $59.95. ISBN 0-8940-2540-0. The social and literary antecedents and the development of the picaresque novel in Spain.

Fox-Lockert, Lucia. *Women Novelists in Spain and Spanish America.* Scarecrow 1979 $27.50. ISBN 0-8108-1270-3. A cursory survey of novels by 22 women writers from the seventeenth century to the present; works analyzed in terms of family, social class, sexuality, and message.

Friedman, Edward H. *The Antiheroine's Voice: Narrative Discourse and Transformations of the Picaresque.* U. of Mo. Pr. 1987 $32.50. ISBN 0-8262-0461-7. Examines "rhetorical manipulation . . . in relation to socio-historical circumstances and feminine concerns [and] provides new and challenging ways of interpreting the entire picaresque genre" (*Hispania*).

Ife, B. W. *Reading and Fiction in Golden Age Spain: A Platonist Critique and Some Picaresque Replies.* Cambridge U. Pr. 1985 $49.50. ISBN 0-521-30375-3. Concerns sixteenth-century attacks on imaginative writing. "Contends that practicing writers were more successful than Neo-Aristotelian theorists in defending fiction from the Platonic attacks" (*Renaissance Quarterly*).

Jones, Margaret E. *Contemporary Spanish Novel, 1939–1975. Twayne's World Authors Ser.* Macmillan 1986 $20.95. ISBN 0-8057-6601-4. An historical overview of the novel in Spain since the civil war.

Labanyi, Jo. *Myth and History in the Contemporary Spanish Novel.* Cambridge U. Pr. 1989 $59.95. ISBN 0-521-24622-9. Studies six novels selected as the most important in post-civil war Spain; four available in English translation.

Landeira, Ricardo. *The Modern Spanish Novel, 1898–1936. Twayne's World Authors Ser.* Macmillan 1985 $30.95. ISBN 0-8057-6603-0. Criticism of twentieth-century Spanish fiction.

Rico, Francisco. *The Spanish Picaresque Novel and the Point of View.* Cambridge U. Pr. 1984 $49.95. ISBN 0-521-25370-5. An important study of *Lazarillo de Tormes* and *Guzmán de Alfarache,* emphasizing the revolutionary nature of narrating the stories of lower-class characters from their own viewpoint.

Spires, Robert C. *Beyond the Metafictional Mode: Directions in the Modern Spanish Novel.* U. Pr. of Ky. 1984 $18.00. ISBN 0-8131-1520-5. Examines selected authors from Cervantes through Martin Gaite to show how fiction has moved beyond the creation of illusion to focus on creation itself.

Thomas, Gareth. *The Novel of the Spanish Civil War, 1936–1975.* Cambridge U. Pr. 1990 $54.95. ISBN 0-521-37158-9. Literature on the civil war and its influence on Spanish fiction.

Thomas, Henry. *Spanish and Portuguese Romances of Chivalry.* Kraus repr. of 1920 ed. $29.00. ISBN 0-527-89700-0. Lectures by Norman MacColl on Spanish and Portuguese fiction.

Poetry

Bergmann, Emilie L. *Art Inscribed: Essays on Ekphrasis in Spanish Golden Age Poetry.* HUP 1979 $20.00. ISBN 0-674-04805-9. An interesting study of the creation of visual images, and of poetry as portrait, in the works of Garcilaso, Lope de Vega, Quevedo, and Góngora.

Cobb, Carl W. *Contemporary Spanish Poetry, 1898–1963. Twayne's World Authors Ser.* G. K. Hall 1976 o.p. Useful introduction to twentieth-century Spanish poetry.

Compton, Linda F. *Andalusian Lyrical Poetry and Old Spanish Love Songs: The "Muwashshah" and Its "Kharja."* o.p. Studies the relationship between the earliest known Spanish poems—the Mozarabic *kharjas*—and the Arabic *muwashshahs* in which they are contained, examining cultural crosscurrents which may have influenced the development of the genre.

Daydí-Tolson, Santiago. *The Post-Civil War Spanish Social Poets. Twayne's World Authors Ser.* G. K. Hall 1984 o.p. An overview of the history of social poetry in post-civil war Spain with special attention to the works of Blas de Otero and Gabriel Celaya.

Debicki, Andrew P. *Poetry of Discovery: The Spanish Generation of 1956–1971.* U. Pr. of Ky. 1982 $22.00. ISBN 0-8131-1461-6. Applies insights taken from the theory of reader-response criticism to elucidate the works of 10 major Spanish poets of the 1950s and 1960s.

Fajardo, Salvador J., and John Wilcox, eds. *After the War: Essays on Recent Spanish Poetry.* Society Sp. & Sp-Am. 1988 $35.00. ISBN 0-89295-055-2

______, eds. *At Home and Beyond: New Essays on Spanish Poets of the Twenties.* Society Sp. & Sp-Am. 1983 $20.00. ISBN 0-89295-022-6. Essays by distinguished critics presenting current critical views of the poetry of the Generation of 1925.

Foster, David W. *The Early Spanish Ballad. Twayne's World Authors Ser.* G. K. Hall o.p. An historical survey of the anonymous Spanish ballads of the fourteenth and fifteenth centuries.

Keller, John E. *Pious Brief Narrative in Medieval Castilian and Galician Verse: From Berceo to Alfonso X. Studies in Romance Languages.* U. Pr. of Ky. 1978 $16.00. ISBN 0-8131-1381-4. Collection of thirteenth-century Christian poetry from Berceo to Alfonso X.

Morris, C. B. *Generation of Spanish Poets, 1920–1936.* Cambridge U. Pr. 1979 $49.50. ISBN 0-521-07381-2. Examination of one of the densest, most varied and rewarding periods in Spanish poetry; bio-bibliographical appendix and a glossary of Spanish terms.

COLLECTIONS

General

Peers, Edgar A. *The Mystics of Spain.* Gordon Pr. 1977 $59.95. ISBN 0-8490-2322-X. Excerpts from the writings of 15 Spanish mystics, translated and introduced by Peers. Study of the evolution of mystical thought from St. Ignatius of Loyola to mysticism after St. Teresa.

Resnick, Seymour, and Jeanne Pasmantier, eds. *Anthology of Spanish Literature in English Translation.* 2 vols. Continuum 1958 o.p. Includes works by many of the authors discussed in this chapter, as well as selections from authors not currently available in English translation.

Salinas, Pedro. *Reality and the Poet in Spanish Poetry.* Trans. by Edith F. Helman. Greenwood 1980 repr. of 1966 ed. $39.75. ISBN 0-313-22436-6. Examines varying attitudes towards reality (reproduction, acceptance, idealization, escape, exaltation, revolt) in poets from the Cid to Espronceda.

Schwartz, Kessel, ed. *Introduction to Modern Spanish Literature.* Irvington 1969 o.p. Contains selections from major works of twentieth-century Spanish literature in translation with a good general introduction and short biographical sketches of the authors.

Drama

Bentley, Eric, ed. *Life Is A Dream and Other Spanish Classics.* Trans. by Roy Campbell. *Eric Bentley's Dramatic Repertoire Series.* Applause Theater Bk. Pubs. 1985 $24.95. ISBN 1-55783-005-3. Spanish classics, including those by Cervantes and Lope de Vega.

Clark, B. H., ed. *Masterpieces of Modern Spanish Drama.* Kraus repr. of 1928 ed. $23.00. ISBN 0-527-17600-1. Plays from contemporary dramatists including José Echegaray, Benito Perez Galdos, and Ángel Guimerà.

Wellwarth, George E., ed. *The New Wave Spanish Drama: An Anthology. Gotham Lib.* NYU Pr. 1970 o.p. Contains J. Ruibal, *The Man and the Fly* and *The Jackass*; J. M. Bellido, *Train to H . . .* and *Bread and Rice, or Geometry in Yellow*; A. M. Ballesteros, *The Hero and the Best of All Possible Worlds*; and Alfonso Sastre, *Sad Are the Eyes of William Tell.*

Poetry

Cannon, Calvin, ed. *Modern Spanish Poems.* Macmillan 1965 o.p.

Crow, John A., ed. *An Anthology of Spanish Poetry: From the Beginnings to the Present Day, Including Both Spain and Spanish America.* La. State U. Pr. 1979 o.p.

Florit, Eugenio, trans. *Spanish Poetry: A Selection from the Cantar de Mío Cid to Miguel Hernández.* Dover 1970 o.p.

Hammer, Louis, and Sara Schyfter, trans. *Recent Poetry of Spain: A Bilingual Anthology.* Sachem Pr. 1983 $24.00. ISBN 0-937584-08-8. A bilingual anthology containing works by 24 poets from Miguel Hernández through the 1970s, with useful bio-bibliographical sketches.

Oliphant, Dave, and others, eds. *New Poetry from a New Spain: The Generation of 1970: A Bilingual Anthology.* Studia Hispanica 1990 $15.95. ISBN 0-934840-15-6

Rivers, Elias L., ed. *Renaissance and Baroque Poetry of Spain.* Waveland Pr. 1988 $12.50. ISBN 0-88133-363-8. Original texts and prose translations, with an excellent introduction and brief bio-bibliographical notes.

Turnbull, Eleanor L., trans. *Contemporary Spanish Poetry: Selections from Ten Poets.* Greenwood repr. of 1945 ed. o.p. Selections from José Morena Villa, Pedro Salinas, Jorge Guillen, Gerardo Diego, Federico García Lorca, Rafael Alberti, Emilio Prados, Vicente Aleixandre, Luis Cernuda, and Manuel Altolaguirre.

CHRONOLOGY OF AUTHORS

The Cid, Poem of. c.1175–1200
Ruiz, Juan. 1283?–1350?
Rojas, Fernando de. 1475?–1541
Teresa of Jesus, St. 1515–1582
John of the Cross, St. 1542–1591
Alemán, Mateo. 1546–1614
Cervantes Saavedra, Miguel de. 1547–1616
The Life of Lazarillo de Tormes. 1554
Góngora y Argote, Luis de. 1561–1627
Vega Carpio, Lope Félix de. 1562–1635
Quevedo y Villegas, Francisco Gómez de. 1580–1645
Tirso de Molina. 1584–1648
Calderón de la Barca, Pedro. 1600–1681
Valera y Alcalá Galiano, Juan. 1827–1905
Bécquer, Gustavo Adolfo. 1836–1870
Castro, Rosalía de. 1837–1885
Pérez Galdós, Benito. 1843–1920
Alas, Leopoldo. 1852–1901
Pardo Bazán, Emilia. 1852–1921
Unamuno y Jugo, Miguel de. 1864–1936
Benavente, Jacinto. 1866–1945
Valle-Inclán, Ramón del. 1866–1936
Baroja y Nessi, Pío. 1872–1956
Machado y Ruiz, Antonio. 1875–1939
Jiménez, Juan Ramón. 1881–1958
Pérez de Ayala, Ramón. 1881–1962
Salinas, Pedro. 1891–1951
Guillén, Jorge. 1893–1984
Aleixandre, Vicente. 1898–1984
García Lorca, Federico. 1898–1936
Alberti, Rafael. 1902–
Hernández, Miguel. 1910–1942
Buero Vallejo, Antonio. 1916–
Cela, Camilo José. 1916–
Delibes, Miguel. 1920–
Matute, Ana María. 1926–
Goytisolo, Juan. 1931–

ALAS, LEOPOLDO (Clarín). 1852–1901

Alas spent most of his life in Oviedo, where he earned his living as a professor of law. In his youth he was greatly influenced by the teachings of Karl C. F. Krause, adopting Krausism's goal of achieving a balance among reason, science, and religion. His love of tolerance and moderation soon brought him into conflict with Spanish reactionaries. The defining characteristic of all his work is its didacticism, evidenced in his passionate striving to improve standards in both the moral and aesthetic realms. Alas first became known as a literary critic. His influential articles were published in *Paliques* (1893) and in the five-volume collection *Solos* (1890–98), and he was among the first to recognize the importance of Galdós's novels. Now widely viewed as the most intelligent, original, cultured, and talented of Spain's naturalistic writers, Alas sought to free naturalism from its excessive materialism and make it compatible with Spanish religion. His two-volume novel *La Regenta,* severely critical of bourgeois life in Oviedo, appeared in 1884. *La Regenta* has been much praised for the brilliant psychological analysis of some of its characters and for its masterful portrayal of provincial life (it has often been compared to FLAUBERT's *Madame Bovary*). Alas is also renowned for his short stories—collected in such volumes as *Pipá* (1886), *El señor* (1893), and *El gallo de Sócrates* (1901)—which are considered the best written in Spanish in the nineteenth century.

NOVEL BY ALAS

La Regenta. Trans. by John Rutherford. U. of Ga. Pr. 1984 $25.00. ISBN 0-8203-0700-9

SHORT STORY COLLECTION BY ALAS

The Moral Tales. Trans. by Kenneth A. Stackhouse. G. Mason Univ. Pr. 1988 $42.75. ISBN 0-913969-12-5. A collection of 20 stories representing Alas's efforts to portray a concept of morality as proof of free will.

BOOK ABOUT ALAS

Valis, Noel M. *The Decadent Vision in Leopoldo Alas.* La. State U. Pr. 1981 $32.50. ISBN 0-8071-0769-7. A valuable study of how Alas internalized the nineteenth-century idea of decadence in his novels *La Regenta* and *Su único hijo.*

ALBERTI, RAFAEL. 1902–

Alberti began his career as a painter, exhibiting his own work in Madrid before age 20. Forced to rest because of poor health, he turned to reading and writing poetry and published his first volume, *Marinero en tierra,* a book of lyrics evoking lost childhood, in 1924. His poetry remained controversial until 1927, when he wrote *Cal y canto* (published in 1929), poems in the Gongorist style dominated by intricate and incongruous images. Alberti said of that volume, "Formal beauty took hold of me until it almost petrified my feelings." Also in 1929 he published the volume considered his most important, *Concerning the Angels,* a difficult, surreal work dealing with the good and bad angels inhabiting modern shattered psyches. At the same time he was becoming active politically, founding a Communist newspaper, *Octubre,* in 1934. His poetry during the 1930s became more political than aesthetic, as for example in *El poeta en la calle.* After fighting on the side of the republic during the civil war, he was forced to flee Spain. Since then he has lived in Argentina and Italy. His poetic imagination, revived by the birth of a daughter in 1941, surfaced in *The Painting* (1945), a series of odes and sonnets addressed to painters. Of *Selected Poems* (1944), *Library Journal* said, "Alberti's tumultuous spiritual pilgrimage is well defined by the selections in this volume." Interspersed are sections of his autobiography, *The Lost Grove* (1942).

POETRY BY ALBERTI

Concerning the Angels. 1929. Ohio U. Pr. 1967 o.p. Poems representing the forces and moods of Alberti's inner nature.

The Other Shore: 100 Poems by Rafael Alberti. Trans. by Paul Martin. Kosmos Edit. SA Mexico 1981 $20.00. ISBN 0-916426-05-X. Poems spanning 31 years of Alberti's writing career.

The Owl's Insomnia: Poems. Trans. by Mark Strand. Atheneum 1973 o.p. A collection of 50 songs and ballads taken from *Sobre los ángeles* (1929), *Sermones y moradas* (1930), and *Retornos de lo vivo lejano* (1952).

NONFICTION BY ALBERTI

The Lost Grove: Autobiography of a Spanish Poet in Exile. Trans. by Gabriel Berns. U. CA Pr. 1977 $37.50. ISBN 0-520-02786-8

BOOK ABOUT ALBERTI

Nantell, Judith. *Rafael Alberti's Poetry of the Thirties: The Poet's Public Voice.* U. of Ga. Pr. 1986 $25.00. ISBN 0-8203-0777-7. Perceptive investigation of Alberti's evolving sociopolitical consciousness.

ALEIXANDRE, VICENTE. 1898–1984 (NOBEL PRIZE 1977)

Poet Vicente Aleixandre was a member of Spain's Generation of 1927. He survived a civil war bomb attack on his house, only to have his work banned by government censors for nearly five years after the war. His early poetry, typified by *Pasión de la tierra* (1935), is hermetic in its surrealism, but his later work, such as *Historia del corazón* (1954), is more accessible and addresses the problems of postwar Spanish society with compassion and human solidarity. As one of the few poets to remain in Spain after the civil war, he was an inspiration to younger poets and encouraged their work.

POETRY BY ALEIXANDRE

A Longing for the Light: Selected Poems of Vicente Aleixandre. Trans. by Lewis Hyde and others. Copper Canyon 1985 $10.00. ISBN 0-914742-89-2. Poems influenced by surrealism and Freudian insight.

Shadow of Paradise: Sombra del Paraiso. Trans. by Hugh A. Harter. U. CA Pr. 1987 $35.00. ISBN 0-520-05599-3. A series of poems reflecting the mood after the Spanish civil war.

BOOK ABOUT ALEIXANDRE

Schwartz, Kessel. *Vicente Aleixandre. Twayne's World Authors Ser.* Irvington 1970 $17.95. ISBN 0-8057-2024-3. A study of the author's life and critical analysis of his work.

ALEMÁN, MATEO. 1546–1614

Mateo Alemán spent much of his life in a kind of picaresque existence, going from the universities of Salamanca and Alcalá to small government jobs to debtor's prison. It was perhaps in a Seville jail that he wrote the *First Part of the Life of the Pícaro Guzmán de Alfarache*, published in Madrid in 1599; the second part, written by an imitator, was published in Lisbon in 1604. Using some formal aspects of LAZARILLO DE TORMES—autobiography, the lower-class hero, his service to several masters, and portraits of diverse classes and characters—Alemán developed the picaresque genre by taking his character, Guzmán, through adulthood, when he becomes a gambler, thief, and beggar. Thus Guzmán contributes to the corruption of society rather than merely being its victim, as is Lazarillo. Guzmán draws a bitter moral lesson from his experiences: Life is cruel, hunger is the rule, and honor cannot be preserved.

NOVEL BY ALEMÁN

The Rogue; or The Life of Guzmán de Alfarache. 1599. 4 vols. Trans. by James Mabbe. Intro. by J. Fitzmaurice-Kelly. AMS Pr. repr. of 1924 ed. $180.00. ISBN 0-404-51970-9

Books about Alemán

McGrady, Donald. *Mateo Alemán. Twayne's World Authors Ser.* Irvington 1968 $17.95. ISBN 0-8057-2028-6. A biographical study of Mateo Alemán and analysis of his picaresque novel *Guzmán de Alfarache.*

Rico, Francisco. *The Spanish Picaresque Novel and the Point of View.* Cambridge U. Pr. 1984 $49.95. ISBN 0-521-25370-5. An important study of *Lazarillo de Tormes* and *Guzmán de Alfarache,* emphasizing the revolutionary nature of narrating the stories of lower-class characters from their own viewpoint.

BAROJA Y NESSI, PÍO. 1872–1956

Pío Baroja, whose works were admired by Ernest Hemingway (see Vol. 1), was one of Spain's foremost twentieth-century novelists. A socially conscious writer whose mission was to expose injustices, Baroja chose as central characters those who live outside society–bohemian vagabonds, anarchists, degenerates, persons from the lower classes, and tormented intellectuals. In *The Restlessness of Shanti Andía* (1911), Baroja uses Basque sailors as protagonists to dramatize his view of life as a constant struggle for survival and to present a shipboard world that functions outside society's laws. In *The Tree of Knowledge* (1911), medical student Andrés Hurtado sees his intelligence as a disease and an incapacitating disgrace. For its treatment of *abulia* (lack of will), Valbuena Prat called this "the novel most typical of the Generation of 1898." Baroja's view that the concepts of beginning and end are human inventions to satisfy unattainable desires for meaning influences the form of his novels, often a series of episodes without cause and effect that end with unresolved problems.

Baroja studied medicine, a discipline reflected in his works by an interest in the pathological. During the 1920s he was popular in the United States, where many of his novels appeared in translation. In 1936 he was elected to the Spanish Academy. Franco later banned all but one of his nearly 100 books, but Baroja continued to live and write, although less assertively, in Spain until his death.

Novels by Baroja

Caesar or Nothing. Trans. by Louis How. Darby Pub. 1976 repr. of 1919 ed. $40.00. ISBN 0-865-27-224-7. Novel about Caesar's examination of his ideals and the final collapse of them.

The Restlessness of Shanti Andía and Other Writings. 1911. Trans. by Anthony Kerrigan. U. of Mich. Pr. 1959 o.p. Sea-action adventure stories.

The Tree of Knowledge. 1911. Trans. by Aubrey F. G. Bell. Fertig 1975 repr. of 1928 ed. o.p. Novel comprised mainly of ideas expressed in conversations.

Book about Baroja

Barrow, Leo L. *Negation in Baroja: A Key to His Novelistic Creativity.* U. of Ariz. Pr. 1971 o.p. Examination of the author's style.

BÉCQUER, GUSTAVO ADOLFO (pseud. of Gustavo Adolfo Domínguez Bastida). 1836–1870

Bécquer was the archetypal romantic poet, devoting his life to poetry and dying at 34 of tuberculosis and the effects of his bohemian life of poverty. *The Rhymes,* published during his lifetime in newspapers and collected by friends in a volume a year after his death, is characterized by subjectivity, musicality, and the traditional romantic themes of love, death, the idealized past, and evocative landscapes. Bécquer uses the metaphor of yearning for an unattainable woman, first an imaginary muse and then a real woman who rejects him, to describe the spiritual quest of the poet for ineffable beauty and inspiration. Bécquer's poetry has been called plastic and painterly for its emphasis on color, light, and architecture. Influences on *The Rhymes* are said to be primarily foreign—Heine, Byron (see Vol. 1), Goethe, Schiller, Musset, and Lamartine. An atmosphere of magic and fantasy pervades the romantic *Legends* (1860–64), which are set in distant places, such as India, and remote times, primarily the Middle Ages. Dámaso Alonso called Bécquer's work the beginning of contemporary poetry, and Bécquer was admired deeply for his lyric poetry by the Generation of 1927: Guillén, Salinas, García Lorca, and Alberti.

Poetry by Bécquer

The Inn of the Cats. Trans. by J. R. Carey. Rogers 1945 o.p.

The Rimas of Gustavo Bécquer. Trans. by Jules Renard. Gordon Pr. 1976 $59.95. ISBN 0-8490-2525-7. Poems about love and death.

Romantic Legends of Spain. Trans. by Cornelia F. Bates and Katharine L. Bates. *Short Story Index Repr. Ser.* Ayer repr. of 1909 ed. $19.50. ISBN 0-8369-4000-8. Short stories set primarily in the Middle Ages.

BENAVENTE, JACINTO. 1866–1945 (Nobel Prize 1922)

Benavente, recipient of the Nobel Prize in 1922, marked the beginning of modern Spanish drama for his break with the melodrama and affectation of the previous style, represented by another Nobel Prize winner, José Echegaray. Benavente called Lope de Vega, Calderón, Shakespeare (see Vol. 1), Ibsen, and Perez Galdós his masters, but beside their works his seem bland and static. He was noted for elegant dialogues, and indeed he used conversation to relate action that takes place offstage. He excelled in the use of social satire, ironic presentations of human weaknesses, and psychological penetration of characters. *The Bonds of Interest* (1907), considered his best play, utilizes puppet figures, which the character Crispín explains are "the same grotesque masks of that Italian *commedia dell'arte,* but not as gay as they were, for in all this time they have thought a great deal." Crispín contrives to secure a financially advantageous marriage for his poverty-stricken master, Leonardo, with Sylvia, daughter of the city's richest man. His thesis that the bonds of money are stronger than those of love seems disproved by the hints of love present in the marriage he finally arranges, but is confirmed in the sequel, which reveals that Leonardo's love waned soon after the marriage.

Plays by Benavente

Four Plays: His Widow's Husband, The Bonds of Interest, The Evil Doers of Good, La Malquerida. Trans. by J. G. Underhill. Fertig 1989 repr. of 1917 ed. $40.00. ISBN 0-86527-386-3. Poems from the author's later period.

Book about Benavente

Peñuelas, Marcelino C. *Jacinto Benavente. Twayne's World Authors Ser.* Irvington 1968 $17.95. ISBN 0-8057-2136-3. A study of the author's life and a critical analysis of his work.

BUERO VALLEJO, ANTONIO. 1916–

Buero Vallejo, Spain's most distinguished playwright of the post-civil war period, served as a medic with the Republicans during the civil war and was imprisoned afterward until 1945. He first came to public attention in 1949 when he won the Lope de Vega prize for *History of a Staircase,* a play often compared to Arthur Miller's (see Vol. 1) *Death of a Salesman* for its tragic portrayal of everyday life. In this play and in others, Buero has renewed the moribund Spanish theater by crafting a new tragic vision to reflect Spain's changed circumstances, but, as Chandler and Schwartz have observed, "for him tragedy . . . involves a sublimation of the human condition with moral and ethical implications, as hope helps revitalize faith and spiritual development." Though postwar censorship made overt criticism of Franco's dictatorship impossible, Buero's plays manage indirectly but effectively to protest Spain's repressive society. *In the Burning Darkness* (1950) is set in a school for the blind, but the characters' physical blindness symbolizes the spiritual blindness of Spanish society. As Martha T. Halsey has noted, several of Buero's plays examine "the role of the intellectual in a repressive society" by focusing on the careers of some of Spain's greatest creative artists: the painter Velázquez in *Las Meninas* (1961), the deaf painter Goya in *The Sleep of Reason* (1971), and the suicidal writer Mariano José de Larra in *The Shot* (1979). *The Foundation* (1974) is an interpretation of Buero's own prison experience. Though written in 1964, *The Double History of Dr. Valmy*, which deals with the use of torture as a political instrument, could not be performed in Spain until 1976, after the death of Franco. In 1986 Buero received Spain's most prestigious literary award, the Cervantes Prize, the first playwright so honored.

Plays by Buero Vallejo

The Shot (La Detonación). 1979. Aris & Phillips UK. ISBN 0-85668-455-4

Three Plays: The Sleep of Reason, The Foundation, and In the Burning Darkness. Trans. by Marion Peter Holt. Trinity U. Pr. 1985 $15.00. ISBN 0-939980-09-6. Plays representing contemporary matters in Spain and in common human experiences.

CALDERÓN DE LA BARCA, PEDRO. 1600–1681

Calderón de la Barca was master of the Spanish stage from Lope de Vega's death until his own, serving as court poet to King Philip IV. While lacking Lope's spontaneity and vitality, he surpassed him in profundity of thought and in depicting interior conflicts in his characters. Much of Calderón's work probes metaphysical questions about free will, predestination, and the brevity of life. In addition, he provided theoretical interpretations of many of the same themes—honor, religion, the monarchy—that were presented dramatically by Lope. His style differs from Lope's in being more condensed, symbolic, and decorative, sharing characteristics of both culteranism and conceptism.

Calderón's piece *Life is a Dream* (c.1635) deals with the same kind of prophecy about an infant that is found in the Oedipus myth. A king, told that his son would step on his head, locks the child away from all contact with the world. When he awakes, he struggles with his instincts for revenge, finally moderating them. *The Mayor of Zalamea* (c.1642) is a reworking of a play by Lope de Vega on the theme of honor. *The Phantom Lady* (1629) is a romantic intrigue, while *Devotion to the Cross* (1633) is an example of the religious play, *auto sacramental,* a form Calderón perfected. He led a comparatively quiet life and after his ordination in 1651 retired from the world, writing only two religious plays a year for the city of Madrid and some plays on mythological themes for the court's entertainment.

Plays by Calderón de la Barca

Beware of Still Waters. Trans. by David Gitlitz. Trinity U. Pr. 1984 o.p. Entertaining theatrical works from the Spanish Baroque era.

Four Comedies by Pedro Calderón de la Barca. Trans. by Kenneth Muir. U. Pr. of Ky. 1980 $26.00. ISBN 0-8131-1409-8. Comedies from Spain's Golden Age.

Life is a Dream. c.1635. Trans. by Edwin Honig. Hill & Wang 1970 o.p.

The Mayor of Zalamea. c.1642. Methuen 1983 o.p.

Three Comedies by Pedro Calderón de la Barca. Trans. by Kenneth Muir and Ann L. MacKenzie. U. Pr. of Ky. 1985 $25.00. ISBN 0-8131-1546-9. Comedies from the early years of Calderón's dramatic career.

BOOKS ABOUT CALDERÓN DE LA BARCA

Greer, Margaret R. *The Play of Power: Mythological Court Dramas of Calderón de la Barca.* Princeton U. Pr. 1990 $39.50. ISBN 0-691-06857-7. Mythology and politics and their influence on seventeenth-century Spain.

Honig, Edwin. *Calderón and the Seizures of Honor.* HUP 1972 $20.50. ISBN 0-674-09075-6. Examines the strong moral imagination theme that pervades Calderón's plays.

Kurtz, Barbara E. *The Play of Allegory in the Autos Sacramentales of Pedro Calderón de la Barca.* Cath. U. Pr. 1991 $34.95. ISBN 0-8132-0733-9. Provokes further research into the rich texture of the *autos sacramentales.*

Maraniss, James E. *On Calderón.* U. of Mo. Pr. 1978 o.p. Compares the works of Calderón and Lope de Vega.

McGaha, Michael D., ed. *Approaches to the Theater of Calderón.* U. Pr. of Amer. 1982 o.p. Critiques of various authors on Calderón's drama.

Sullivan, Henry W. *Calderón in the German Lands and the Low Countries: His Reception and Influence, 1654 to 1980.* Cambridge U. Pr. 1983 $84.95. ISBN 0-521-24902-3. Discusses Calderón's influence on stage history in Germany.

Ter Horst, Robert. *Calderón: The Secular Plays.* U. Pr. of Ky. 1982 $24.00. ISBN 0-8131-1440-3. Critical discussion of Calderón's nonallegorical plays and the use of myth, honor, and history in them.

CASTRO, ROSALÍA DE. 1837–1885

Castro's poetry has still not received the attention it deserves, mainly because she wrote much of it in her native Galician—which she was principally responsible for reviving as a literary language—rather than in Spanish. Gerald Brenan has judged that "had she written in Castilian . . . , she would, I feel sure, be recognized as the greatest woman poet of modern times." Her poetry is always compared to that of her contemporary BÉCQUER for its melancholy lyricism and musicality. Castro was also among the first Spanish poets to use her poetry to draw attention to the plight of the poor.

POETRY BY CASTRO

Poems. Trans. by Anna-Marie Aldaz and Barbara N. Gantt. State U. NY Pr. 1991 $57.50. ISBN 0-7914-0582-6. Includes translations of more than 100 poems, a critical introduction, notes to the translations, and two of the poet's autobiographical prologues.

CELA, CAMILO JOSÉ. 1916– (NOBEL PRIZE 1989)

In Cela's first novel, *The Family of Pascual Duarte* (1942), a condemned criminal relates in letters published after his execution the degrading circumstances that led him to commit a series of brutal murders, including that of a mare, his pet dog, his sister's lover, and his mother. Ironically, he receives the death sentence not for these murders but for killing a local boss. Narrative techniques employed by Cela are epistolary form, stream of consciousness, rupture of chronological sequence, and perspectivism. Cela produced no novel of real literary value after *The Family of Pascual Duarte* until *The Hive* in 1951, a portrait of the sordid world of the lower class of Madrid, and *Mrs. Caldwell Speaks to Her Son* in 1953. In the latter, a mother writing notes to her dead son tries to reconstruct his life as she gradually lapses into insanity and senility:

"Mr. Cela narrates it in a beautiful, stylized way, with a tone of surrealistic casualness and a dash of old-fashioned, good-hearted cynicism" (*New Yorker*). *Journey to the Alcarria* (1948) is a description of Cela's walking tour through Spain in the 1940s.

Novels by Cela

The Family of Pascual Duarte. 1942. Little 1990 $17.95. ISBN 0-316-13432-5
The Hive. 1951. FS&G 1990 $25.00. ISBN 0-374-17155-6
Mrs. Caldwell Speaks to Her Son. 1953. Trans. by J. S. Bernstein. Cornell Univ. Pr. 1990 repr. of 1968 ed. $29.95. ISBN 0-8014-9783-3
San Camilo, 1936: The Eve, Feast, and Octave of St. Camillus of the Year 1936 in Madrid. Trans. by John H. R. Polt. Duke 1991 $49.95. ISBN 0-8223-1179-8. Novel on the reasons and implications of the Spanish civil war.

Nonfiction by Cela

Journey to the Alcarria. Atlantic Monthly 1990 $8.95. ISBN 0-87113-379-2

Book about Cela

McPheeters, D. W. *Camilo José Cela. Twayne's World Authors Ser.* Irvington 1969 $17.95. ISBN 0-8057-2204-1. Author's biographical history, his work, and his influences.

CERVANTES SAAVEDRA, MIGUEL DE. 1547–1616

The son of a poor apothecary-surgeon, Cervantes believed that "two roads lead to wealth and glory, that of letters and that of arms." He first tried that of arms, seeing service with the Spanish-Venetian-papal fleet in the Battle of Lepanto, in which the Turkish invasion of Europe was thwarted. After being captured by Turkish pirates and held for ransom, he returned to Spain, where he attained a post as commissary of the Spanish Armada and tax collector. He was imprisoned when a banker to whom he entrusted government funds went bankrupt.

His first attempts at the road of letters having proved unsuccessful, for he could not compete with Lope de Vega in the theater, he began writing his satiric novel *Don Quijote* in 1603 while still in prison. In the novel, Alonso Quijano, his head turned from excessive reading, can no longer distinguish between everyday reality and that depicted in the novels of romance and chivalry in fashion during his day. Dubbing himself Don Quijote, he sets out on his bony nag, Rocinante, determined to restore justice to the world. He acquires the rotund peasant Sancho Panza as his squire and a barber's basin for a helmet. One of his most famous adventures involves combat with a giant who turns out to be a windmill, thereby originating the expression "to tilt at windmills." His further efforts are equally "quixotic," but he emerges as a tragic figure striving to maintain his illusions. Under his gaze the most basic reality becomes idealized: A homely servant girl becomes a princess, and all whom Don Quijote encounters must swear to her beauty. Part Two, completed in 1615, continues the narrative and introduces philosophic observations on human nature. At the end of Part Two Cervantes has a disillusioned and humbled Don Quijote die as a precaution against imitations of his work. Sancho, however, now shares Don Quijote's faith and will continue his mission.

This first modern novel, dealing with the nature of reality and truth, is said to have been translated into more languages than any other book except the Bible. It appeared in English in 1612–20, French in 1614–18, Italian in 1622–25, German in 1683, and Russian in 1769. Kenneth Rexroth wrote of *Don Quijote*, "Many people, not all of them Spanish, are on record as believing that *Don*

Quijote is the greatest prose fiction ever produced in the Western World. . . . It epitomizes the spiritual world of European man at mid-career as the *Odyssey* and *Iliad* do at his beginnings and *The Brothers Karamazov* does in his decline" (*SR*).

The Exemplary Novels (1613) are short stories with a moral that provided plots for the plays of John Fletcher and Thomas Middleton (see Vol. 1). The *Interludes*, one-act theatrical sketches, represent Cervantes's most successful attempts at writing drama.

NOVEL BY CERVANTES

DON QUIXOTE: EARLY TRANSLATIONS

(Trans. by Thomas Shelton). 1612–20. 4 vols. AMS Pr. repr. of 1896 ed. $40.00 ea. ISBN 0-404-51880-X. The first translation in English; nearly contemporaneous with *Don Quijote*.

(Trans. by Pierre Motteux). 1690. Ed. by John G. Lockhart. 4 vols. Darby Pub. 1983 repr. of 1880 ed. o.p. A version of *Don Quixote* known as "the ribald rendering" because Motteux translated it freely, often in slang, sparing no pains to make it diverting and peppering it with contemporary allusion.

DON QUIXOTE: MODERN TRANSLATIONS

(Trans. by John M. Cohen). Viking Penguin 1951 $5.95. ISBN 0-14-044010-0. A strong translation in modern English that is faithful to the Spanish, by an eminent translator of Spanish literature.

(Trans. by Samuel Putnam). Random 1978 $17.95. ISBN 0-394-60438-5. A translation from the Spanish, with a critical text based on the first editions of 1605 and 1615; includes variant readings, variorum notes, and an introduction by the translator.

(Trans. by Walter Starkie). NAL-Dutton 1965 $6.95. ISBN 0-451-52371-7. "A close translation and, to the average American reader, . . . a bit more stiff in places than that of Putnam. The translation is, however, pleasantly readable and clearly and compactly presented in a single and inexpensive volume. Helpful and excellent introduction and selected bibliography." (*Choice*).

(Trans. by Joseph R. Jones and Kenneth Douglas). *Norton Critical Eds.* Norton 1981 $16.95. ISBN 0-393-09018-3

WORKS BY CERVANTES

The Portable Cervantes. Trans. by Samuel Putnam. *Viking Portable Lib.* Viking Penguin 1977 $9.95. ISBN 0-14-015057-9

Three Exemplary Novels. Trans. by Samuel Putnam. Greenwood 1982 repr. of 1950 ed. $38.50. ISBN 0-313-23346-2. Contains *Rinconete and Cortadillo, Man of Glass*, and *The Colloquy of the Dogs.*

BOOKS ABOUT CERVANTES

Allan, John J. *Don Quixote: Hero or Fool? A Study in Narrative Technique.* U. Press Fla. 1969 $8.00. ISBN 0-8130-0268-0. Critique of *Don Quixote* and the character of the protagonist.

———. *Don Quixote: Hero or Fool? Part II.* U. Press Fla. 1979 $12.00. ISBN 0-8130-0630-9. Clarifies the reader's evolving relationship with the protagonist in the novel.

Canavaggio, Jean. *Cervantes.* Trans. by Joseph R. Jones. Norton 1990 $25.00. ISBN 0-393-02812-7. Examines the life of Cervantes for clues to his work.

Cascardi, Anthony. *The Bounds of Reason: Cervantes, Dostoevsky, Flaubert.* Col. U. Pr. 1986 $44.00. ISBN 0-231-06212-5. Discusses the idea that Cervantes, Flaubert, and Dostoevsky lack skepticism and epistemology in their work.

Drake, Dana B. *Don Quijote, 1894—1970: A Selective and Annotated Bibliography.* Ediciones Vol. 2 1978 $20.00. ISBN 0-89729-186-7. Bibliographies on *Don Quixote.*

Durán, Manuel. *Cervantes. Twayne's World Authors Ser.* G. K. Hall 1974 $20.95. ISBN 0-8057-2206-8. Analysis of the author's life and his literary accomplishments.

Efron, Arthur. *Don Quixote and the Dulcineated World.* Paunch 1985 $12.00. ISBN 0-9602478-6-6. An interesting departure from established approaches to *Don Quixote.*

El Saffar, Ruth. *Beyond Fiction: The Recovery of the Feminine in the Novels of Cervantes.* U. CA Pr. 1984 $37.50. ISBN 0-520-04866-0. Examines the evolution of style and personal psychology of Cervantes through a chronological framework of his work.

______, ed. *Critical Essays on Cervantes.* G. K. Hall 1986 $40.00. ISBN 0-8161-8825-4. Critique of Cervantes's life work.

Flores, Angel, and M. J. Benardete. *Cervantes Across the Centuries: A Quadricentennial Volume.* Gordian 1969 repr. of 1947 ed. $50.00. ISBN 0-87752-036-4. Critical interpretations of *Don Quixote.*

Forcione, Alban K. *Cervantes and the Humanist Vision: A Study of Four Exemplary Novels.* Bks. Demand repr. of 1982 ed. $47.50. ISBN 0-8357-4036-6. Looks at the presence of Erasmism in the novels of Cervantes.

______. *Cervantes, Aristotle, and the Persiles.* Princeton U. Pr. 1970 $55.00. ISBN 0-691-06175-0. Examines the impact of Neo-Aristotelian poetics on Cervantes's *Los trabajos de Persiles y Sigismunda,* a verse romance.

______. *Cervantes' Christian Romance: A Study of* Persiles y Sigismunda. Princeton U. Pr. 1972 $27.00. ISBN 0-691-06213-7. Analyzes *Persiles y Sigismunda* in its historical context; in-depth study of the structure of the text.

Friedman, Edward H. *The Unifying Concept: Approaches to the Structure of Cervantes' Comedias.* Spanish Lit. Pubns. 1981 $18.00. ISBN 0-938972-00-6. Comprehensive study of Cervantes's full-length plays; introduces the idea of "conceptual unity" as the predominant structural agent in his plays.

Gilman, Stephen. *The Novel According to Cervantes.* U. CA Pr. 1989 $30.00. ISBN 0-520-06231-0. Apt illustration of the influence of *Don Quixote* on novel structure; traces the origins of the novel.

Johnson, Carroll B. *Madness and Lust: A Psychoanalytic Approach to Don Quixote.* U. CA Pr. 1983 $42.50. ISBN 0-520-04752-4. Somewhat fantastical study of male midlife crisis: parallels Don Quixote's fictive personality with aging men.

Mancing, Howard. *The Chivalric World of Don Quijote: Style, Structure, and Narrative Technique.* U. of Mo. Pr. 1982 $28.00. ISBN 0-8262-0350-7. Interrelates the nature of archaism and chivalry and examines Don Quixote's concept of his chivalric world.

Martin, Adrienne. *Cervantes and the Burlesque Sonnet.* U. CA Pr. 1991 $40.00. ISBN 0-520-07045-3. Focuses on Cervantes's comic poetry and discusses the place his sonnets occupy within his work and in Spanish literary history.

Nabokov, Vladimir. *Lectures on* Don Quixote. HarBraceJ 1984 $7.95. ISBN 0-15-649540-6. An intense study of the structure of the novel through an analysis of *Don Quixote.*

Nerlich, Michael, and Nicholas Spadaccini, eds. *Cervantes's Exemplary Novellas and the Adventure of Writing.* U. of Minn. Pr. 1990 $14.95. ISBN 0-8166-2014-8. Imaginative text analyzing the novels of Cervantes; examines their reception by German Romanticists.

Percas de Ponseti, Helena. *Cervantes the Writer and the Painter of Don Quijote.* U. of Mo. Pr. 1989 $23.00. ISBN 0-8262-0689-1. Inventive approach that attempts to get at the "voice" of Cervantes; analyzes his paintings to find the reality of the author in *Don Quixote.*

Riley, E. C. *Don Quixote.* Unwin Hyman 1986 $44.95. ISBN 0-04-800009-4. Structured guide to understanding *Don Quixote*; outlines the book's literary and intellectual background.

Robert, Marthe. *The Old and the New: From Don Quixote to Kafka.* Trans. by Carol Cosman. U. CA Pr. 1977 $47.50. ISBN 0-520-02509-1. Innovative study that compares *Don Quixote* to *The Castle* and illuminates the nature of the novel through Cervantes.

Russell, P. E. *Cervantes.* OUP 1985 o.p. Explains the popularity of *Don Quixote* and elucidates why the work is a masterpiece of comic writing.

Weiger, John G. *In the Margins of Cervantes.* U. Pr. of New Eng. 1988 $30.00. ISBN 0-87451-450-9. Extensive interpretation of Cervantes's writings and writing career.

———. *The Individuated Self: Cervantes and the Emergence of the Individual.* Ohio U. Pr. 1979 $15.95. ISBN 0-8214-0396-6. An attempt to interpret *Don Quixote* by examining the psychology of the narrator.

———. *The Substance of Cervantes.* Cambridge U. Pr. 1985 $59.95. ISBN 0-521-30516-0. Revelations of what underlies Cervantes's work and how the author believed he was misunderstood.

Wilson, Diana. *Allegories of Love: Cervantes'* Persiles and Sigismunda. Princeton U. Pr. 1991 $32.50. ISBN 0-691-06854-2. Examines Cervantes's *Persiles and Sigismunda* intertextually; compares it to the rest of his body of literary work.

THE CID, POEM OF. c.1175–1200

The manuscript of *The Poem of the Cid* was transcribed in 1207 by Pedro Abad and lay undiscovered in the monastery of Vicar until 1779. This epic poem recounts in 3,730 lines of verse the character and adventures of a Castilian mercenary warlord, Rodrigo Díaz de Vivar or El Cid (d.1099). While the inspiration of the poem has been attributed to a variety of sources—Germanic, French *chansons de geste,* and Arabic—the Castilian spirit pervades the poem. According to Menéndez Pidal's theory of the gathering of the epic, the songs originated close to the dates of the events related and were transmitted orally through many voices, giving the poem a collective, popular flavor characteristic of much Spanish literature. In the period from 1175 to 1200, a Spaniard, thought to be a Christian living in Muslim territory, integrated the tales to create this manuscript as it now exists.

El Cid, sent into exile by Alfonso VI of León after being accused of withholding some of the tribute money due the king, eventually recaptured the city of Valencia for Castilla, thereby giving the Spaniards access to the Mediterranean. Depicted as a protective father, a loving husband, a loyal vassal, and a servant of God, he remains a human being, rather than becoming a superhuman figure. Although the reality of his deed is somewhat idealized, the Spanish epic is considerably more grounded in reality and history than the *Song of Roland,* for example.

Some of the unique qualities of *The Poem of the Cid* are realism, powerful description, spontaneity, poetic terseness, and vitality. The democratic spirit, respect for the law, political and social consciousness, and religious spirit reflect the Castilian society of the Middle Ages. In his *History of Spanish Literature,* Ticknor wrote, "During the thousand years which elapsed from the time of the decay of Greek and Roman culture, down to the appearance of the *Divina Commedia,* no poetry was produced so original in its tone, or so full of natural feeling, picturesqueness, and energy." The figure and story of Cid have been developed by CORNEILLE (*Le Cid*), HERDER, SOUTHEY (see Vol. 1), HUGO, Heredia, Leconte De Lisle, and Manuel Machado.

The Poem of the Cid. Trans. by W. S. Merwin. NAL-Dutton 1989 $8.95. ISBN 0-452-00915-4

BOOKS ABOUT THE POEM OF THE CID

Christopherson, Merrill G., and Adolfo León. *Cidean Ballads: Ballads about the Great Spanish Hero, El Cid. Comparative Lit. Ser.* Westburg $16.50. ISBN 0-87423-012-8

Fletcher, Richard. *The Quest for El Cid.* Knopf 1990 $24.95. ISBN 0-394-57447-8. Investigative study of Rodrigo Diaz–El Cid.

Smith, Colin. *The Making of the "Poema de Mío Cid."* Cambridge U. Pr. 1983 $59.95. ISBN 0-521-24992-9. Considers the theoretical premise of *El Cid*; substantiates that it was the first Castilian epic poem.

DELIBES, MIGUEL. 1920–

Delibes, one of the most respected novelists in Spain today, is particularly known for his rural novels, in which he views nature with loving but unsentimental eyes. These somewhat pessimistic novels are highly critical of modern industrialized society and full of nostalgia for a simpler, more natural past. *The Hedge* (1969) is a nightmarish tale of a sensitive clerk who is progressively dehumanized by his job and cut off from the rest of humanity by a thick hedge, symbolizing the totalitarian state. *Five Hours with Mario* (1966), which many critics consider Delibes's masterpiece, presents the bitter reflections of a widow as she sits with the corpse of her husband, who has just died after a miserable life of poverty and failure resulting from his defiance of repressive authorities.

Novels by Delibes

Five Hours with Mario. 1966. Trans. by Frances M. López-Morillas. Col. U. Pr. 1988 $29.50. ISBN 0-231-06828-X

The Hedge. 1969. Trans. by Frances M. López-Morillas. Col. U. Pr. 1987 $37.00. ISBN 0-231-05460-2

GARCÍA LORCA, FEDERICO. 1898–1936

García Lorca is perhaps the best known of modern Spanish writers, partly because of his brutal execution outside Granada by Franco's army at the beginning of the civil war, but primarily because of his genius for poetry and drama. In 1928 Lorca published *Gypsy Ballads,* which won him immediate success and is considered one of the most important volumes of poetry of the century. Attracted to the gypsies for their exotic folklore, sexual vitality, and their status as a group on the fringe of Spanish society, Lorca enlarged the gypsy people and their traditions to mythical proportions. Nature takes on human form while reality acquires a dreamlike quality in this powerful transformation of the world into a myth. The verse is colorful, rhythmic, dramatic, symbolic, and suggestive. Lorca visited New York in 1929, experiencing a deep despair about a mechanical and dehumanized society; he saw in blacks the only hope for revitalization of that world. The volume *Poet in New York* (1929) shows the influence of Negro spirituals and the poets Walt Whitman (see Vol. 1) and T. S. Eliot (see Vol. 1).

Although García Lorca was interested in drama throughout his life, he did not produce much of significance until the 1930s. Most important is his trilogy of Spanish rural life, *Blood Wedding* (1933), *Yerma* (1934), and *The House of Bernarda Alba* (1936), all tragedies with women as protagonists. In each play, the fall of the heroine, and of those around her whom she pulls down, is caused by frustrations produced by society. *Blood Wedding* demonstrates the sterility of the traditional code of honor. *Yerma* reveals the emptiness of a traditional marriage in which the woman must bear her husband children to prove her fidelity, and *The House of Bernarda Alba* dramatizes the destructive nature of Bernarda's dictatorial rule over her house, a microcosm of Spain. *The Butterfly's Evil Spell* (1919) is Lorca's first play; *The Shoemaker's Prodigious Wife* (1931) and *Don Perlimplín* (1931) are farces; *The Billy-Club Puppets* (1931) is a puppet play.

Poetry by García Lorca

The Gypsy Ballads of García Lorca. Trans. by Rolfe Humphries. Bks. Demand repr. of 1953 ed. $20.00. ISBN 0-685-23884-8

Lament for the Death of a Bullfighter: And Other Poems. Trans. by A. L. Lloyd. Greenwood 1977 repr. of 1937 ed. $39.75. ISBN 0-8371-9322-2. Poems gauging the distance between the Spanish civil war and the author's early twenties; shows his romantic and classic writing style.

Ode to Walt Whitman and Other Poems. Trans. by Carlos Bauer. City Lights 1988 $6.95. ISBN 0-87286-212-7. Poems based on Garcia Lorca's attraction to America and New York; deals with his homosexuality and torment.

Poem of the Deep Song. Trans. by Carlos Bauer. City Lights 1987 $12.95. ISBN 0-87286-205-4. Beautiful poems about the Andalusian gypsies, the author's homeland, and flamenco dancers.

Poet in New York. Trans. by Ben Belitt. Peter Smith o.p.

Tree of Song. Trans. by Alan Brilliant. Unicorn Pr. 1973 $17.50. ISBN 0-87775-046-7

Plays by García Lorca

Five Plays: Comedies and Tragicomedies. Intro. by Francisco García Lorca. Greenwood 1977 repr. of 1963 ed. $35.00. ISBN 0-8371-9583-7. Encompasses all of García Lorca's comedic plays; includes an introduction and comments by the author's brother.

Four Puppet Plays. The Divan Poems. Sheep Meadow 1990 $11.95. ISBN 0-935296-94-8. Four experimental farces and prose poems written between 1922 and 1934.

Once Five Years Pass and Other Dramatic Works. Trans. by Angel G. Orrios. Station Hill Pr. 1989 $19.95. ISBN 0-88268-070-6. Whimsical collection of plays, drawings, and plot summations that has a somewhat diaristic feeling.

Three Tragedies: Blood Wedding, Yerma, Bernarda Alba. Trans. by James Lujan Graham. Greenwood 1977 repr. of 1955 ed. $48.50. ISBN 0-8371-9578-0

Books about García Lorca

Campbell, Roy. *Lorca: An Appreciation of His Poetry.* Haskell 1971 repr. of 1952 ed. $75.00. ISBN 0-8383-1226-8. Examines García Lorca's role as a political and poetic martyr; juxtaposes his enduring craft with fading polemic poetry.

Gibson, Ian. *Federico García Lorca: A Life.* Pantheon 1990 $29.95. ISBN 0-679-73157-1. An extensive recounting of García Lorca's life and work; includes an especially shattering account of his execution during the Spanish civil war.

Morris, C. Brian. *Cuando Yo Me Muera. Essays in Memory of Federico García Lorca.* U. Pr. of Amer. 1988 o.p. Complete retrospective of García Lorca's literary importance with symposiums and discussions by literary scholars.

Stanton, Edward F. *The Tragic Myth: Lorca and Cante Jondo.* U. Pr. of Ky. 1978 $14.00. ISBN 0-8131-1378-4. An inspired and fantastical study of García Lorca's writing and flamenco music; looks at the Andalusian musical tradition within his work.

Young, Howard T. *Victorious Expression: A Study of Four Contemporary Spanish Poets: Unamuno, Machado, Jiménez and Lorca.* U. of Wis. Pr. 1966 $9.50. ISBN 0-299-03144-6

GÓNGORA Y ARGOTE, LUIS DE. 1561–1627

Born in Córdoba, Luis de Góngora studied for the priesthood there and then served as private chaplain to King Philip III in Madrid. As a member of the court, he became involved in the literary controversy of his day, the antagonism between the exponents of conceptism, led by Quevedo and Gracián, and culteranism, led by Góngora himself. Both schools were manifestations of the baroque spirit, culteranism being characterized by neologism, hyperbaton, and use of metaphors as a poetic substitution for reality, and conceptism relying on conceits and philosophic paradoxes. While Góngora's early poetry consists of relatively simple sonnets, his second period, that of the *Solitudes* (1613), reveals the culteranistic style at its extreme. The *Solitudes* are characterized by pastoral subject matter, artificial language, intricate metaphors, mythological allusions, and musical verse. The French symbolist poets of the late nineteenth century and the Spanish poets of the Generation of 1927 have praised the poetry of Góngora, finding there "delicate imagery, poetic insight, and a heightened awareness of the descriptive capacities of the Spanish language" (Stamm).

Poetry by Góngora

Fourteen Sonnets and Polyphemus. Trans. by Mack Singleton. Hispanic Seminary 1975 o.p.

Poems. Trans. by R. O. Jones. Cambridge U. Pr. 1966 o.p. A representation of the author's more influential works.

Solitudes of Luis de Góngora. Trans. by Gilbert E. Cunningham. Johns Hopkins 1968 o.p.

Books about Góngora

Beverly, John. *Aspects of Góngora's Soledades*. Benjamins North Am. 1980 $32.00. ISBN 90-272-1711-4. Summarizes some of the problems of understanding Góngora's "Soledades."

Dolan, Kathleen H. *Cyclopean Song: Aesthetics of Melancholy in Góngora's Fábula de Polifemo y Galatea*. U. of NC Pr. 1990 $20.00. ISBN 0-8078-9240-8. Studies the allusive meanings of Góngora's poems; examines psychic potency in his imagery using *Polifemo y Galatea* for examples.

Richards, Ruth M. *Concordance to the Sonnets of Góngora*. Hispanic Seminary 1982 o.p. Looks at Góngora's sonnets through a discussion of his writing style; an important aid to analyzing the sonnets.

Woods, M. J. *The Poet and the Natural World in the Age of Góngora*. OUP 1978 o.p. Examines the description of nature in Spanish poetry of the Baroque period and discusses Góngora's contribution to Spain's Golden Age of literature.

GOYTISOLO, JUAN. 1931–

Goytisolo first became known in the United States for his novel *The Young Assassins* (1954), the story of juvenile delinquents corrupted by social conditions during and immediately after the Spanish civil war. His depictions of the spiritual emptiness and moral decay of Spain under the Franco regime led to the censorship of some of his works there, and he moved to Paris in 1957. In 1966 he published *Marks of Identity*, which would eventually form a trilogy with *Count Julian* (1970) and *Juan the Landless* (1975). *Count Julian* is an exile's view of Spain, with Spanish history, literature, and language derisively viewed across the narrow straits of Tangiers for the purpose of destroying them so that they might be reinvented. Formally, it is a "new novel" along the lines of Robbe-Grillet's formulations. *Makbara* (1980), a misogynous novel, also attacks capitalism. *Landscapes after the Battle* (1982), based loosely on the life of Lewis Carroll (see Vol. 1) is, in fact, a self-conscious novel concerned mainly with the problems involved in writing novels.

Novels by Goytisolo

Count Julian. 1970. Trans. by Helen Lane. Consort. Bk. Sales 1990 repr. of 1974 ed. $12.95. ISBN 1-852421-58-4

Juan the Landless. 1975. Consort. Bk. Sales 1991 $14.95. ISBN 1-85242-192-4

Landscapes after the Battle. 1982. Trans. by Helen Lane. Seaver Bks. 1987 $17.95. ISBN 0-8050-0393-2. Offers a skewed tour of Paris street life radiating outward from the neighborhood of the Sentier metro.

Makbara. 1980. Trans. by Helen Lane. Seaver Bks. 1981 o.p.

Marks of Identity. 1966. Consort. Bk. Sales $12.95. ISBN 1-85242-134-7. Explores the themes of exile and expatriation.

BOOK ABOUT GOYTISOLO

Ugarte, Michael. *Trilogy of Treason: An Intertextual Study of Juan Goytisolo.* U. of Mo. Pr. 1982 $22.50. ISBN 0-8262-0353-1. Examines Goytisolo's writing while in Paris, especially his attempt to corrupt, subvert, and reorganize intertextual concerns.

GUILLÉN, JORGE. 1893–1984

Guillén's poetry celebrates this life and things of this world. In *Cántico,* first published in 1928 and then substantially revised numerous times by the poet, he exalts the pure joy of being: "To be, nothing more. And that suffices." This enthusiasm for life was sustained until *Clamor* (three volumes published in 1957, 1960, and 1963), when the brutal realities of the modern world broke into his joyous vision. Even so, Guillén remained optimistic about the future, and in his poem *Goodbye, Goodbye, Europe,* he speaks of escaping the old decaying world to an "innocent new world," a reference to the United States where he taught in universities for many years. Guillén's style is concentrated, economical, disciplined, and polished, showing the influence of classical forms as well as of the gongorist style. His is a "pure poetry" from which he has attempted to remove all nonpoetic elements, such as narrative and anecdote. He has translated PAUL VALÉRY and PAUL CLAUDEL into Spanish.

POETRY BY GUILLÉN

Affirmation: A Bilingual Anthology, 1919—1966. Trans. by Julian Palley. U. of Okla. Pr. 1971 repr. of 1968 ed. $19.95. ISBN 0-8061-0764-2. Representative cross section of Guillén's works from 1919 to 1966.

NONFICTION BY GUILLÉN

Guillén on Guillén: The Poetry and the Poet. Trans. by Anthony L. Geist. Princeton U. Pr. 1979 $12.95. ISBN 0-691-03156-X. Guillén looks at his poetic career and comments on his poems and writing sensibilities.

BOOKS ABOUT GUILLÉN

MacCurdy, C. Grant. *Jorge Guillén. Twayne's World Authors Ser.* G. K. Hall 1981 o.p. A systematic and chronological overview of Guillén's poetry.

Yudin, Florence. *The "Vibrant Silence" in Jorge Guillén's Aire Nuestro. Studies in the Romance Languages and Lit.* U. of NC Pr. 1974 o.p. Scholarly study of Guillén's poeticization of silence; examines his beliefs surrounding all silence in life.

HERNÁNDEZ, MIGUEL. 1910–1942

Little educated, Hernández studiously imitated the style of LUIS DE GÓNGORA in his first volume of poetry, published in 1933. In his best volume, *The Unending Lightning* (1936), he found his own voice, expressing powerful emotion in classical sonnet form. After fighting for the republic during the civil war, Hernández was imprisoned in a concentration camp, where he died of tuberculosis at age 32 in spite of international protests for his freedom. *The Songbook of Absences* (1938–41), written during his years as a political prisoner, is a painful record of his suffering on separation from his wife, his sorrow at the death of his son, and his yearning for the simple country life of his youth.

POETRY BY HERNÁNDEZ

Selected Poems of Miguel Hernández. Trans. by Robert Bly and others. White Pine $10.00. ISBN 0-934834-93-8. Highlights major poems spanning Hernández's poetic career.

The Songbook of Absences. 1938–41. Trans. by Tom Jones. Charioteer 1980 $7.50. ISBN 0-910350-06-X

The Unending Lightning. 1936. Trans. by Edwin Honig. Sheep Meadow 1990 $10.95. ISBN 0-935296-86-7. Short volume of Hernández's Petrarchan love poems.

JIMÉNEZ, JUAN RAMÓN. 1881–1958 (NOBEL PRIZE 1956)

On receiving the Nobel Prize in 1956, Juan Ramón Jiménez was praised for "his lyrical poetry, which constitutes an inspiring example in the Spanish language of spirituality and artistic purity." Jiménez's works have indeed provided inspiration for many younger Spanish poets—FEDERICO GARCÍA LORCA, PEDRO SALINAS, and JORGE GUILLÉN among them—as well as for Latin American poets. His poetic world is both aesthetic and spiritual. Through poetry Jiménez endeavored not only to express his interior reality but also to reach the highest levels of spiritual experience.

Jiménez's early work is marked by a short period of modernism followed by a rejection of it in favor of simpler forms, particularly that of traditional Spanish ballads. The turmoil and anxiety produced by his sea voyage to the United States to marry an American, Zenobia Camprubí, and their return as newlyweds began his second period. That phase was characterized by increasing subjectivity and purification of his poetry, a process furthered by Zenobia, who protected him from intrusions of the world. His use of women to symbolize the objects of his desires to know and experience reveals the influence of GUSTAVO ADOLFO BÉCQUER. In his final stage, he embarked on a mystical search for the absolute. His revelation was that "God desired" and "God desiring" reside within his own soul.

Platero and I (1914), a poignant and charming story in poetic prose about a silver-gray donkey named Platero, is popular with children. Jiménez did not intend it for children exclusively, however, but rather as a celebration of the essence of the child, "a spiritual island fallen from heaven."

POETRY BY JIMÉNEZ

God Desired and Desiring. Trans. by Nicolás De Antonio. Paragon Hse. 1986 $9.95. ISBN 0-913729-23-X. Mystical free verse about God, desire, and love.

Invisible Reality. Trans. by Nicolás De Antonio. Paragon Hse. 1986 $18.95. ISBN 0-913729-34-5. Expansive poems dealing with Jiménez's struggle with God.

Naked Music: Poems of Juan Ramón Jiménez. Trans. by Dennis Maloney. White Pine 1984 o.p.

Platero and I. Trans. by Eloise Roach. U. of Tex. Pr. 1983 $8.95. ISBN 0-292-76479-0

Stories of Life and Death. Trans. by Nicolás De Antonio. Paragon Hse. 1986 $18.95. ISBN 0-913729-21-3. Poems dealing with universal and individual messages in paradoxes, linguistic discourse, and the prosody of poetry.

Three Hundred Poems, 1903—1953. Trans. by Eloise Roach. Intro. by Ricardo Gullón. U. of Tex. Pr. 1962 o.p. A representative collection including poems the poet and his wife considered his best. Selected from the Nobel Prize collection *Libros de Poesía* and from books published between 1903 and 1914.

NONFICTION BY JIMÉNEZ

Time and Space: A Poetic Autobiography. Trans. by Nicolás De Antonio. Paragon Hse. 1988 $18.95. ISBN 0-913729-71-X. Stream-of-consciousness style encompassing the sensibilities of Jiménez's mysticism.

BOOKS ABOUT JIMÉNEZ

Coke-Enguídanos, Mervin. *Word and Work in the Poetry of Juan Ramón Jiménez*. Tamesis Bks. Ltd. 1982 $42.00. ISBN 0-7293-0139-7. Systematic and detailed study of Jiménez's poetry, focusing on both his life and his art.

Olson, Paul R. *Circle of Paradox: Time and Essence in the Poetry of Juan Ramón Jiménez.* Johns Hopkins repr. of 1967 ed. $62.00. ISBN 0-317-28736-2. Considers the symbolic synthesis between time and the essence of change in Jiménez's work; traces forms and themes in his poetry.

Wilcox, John C. *Self and Image in Juan Ramón Jiménez: Modern and Postmodern Readings.* U. of Ill. Pr. 1987 $24.95. ISBN 0-252-01331-X. Interpretations of Jiménez's poetry that examine his literary language.

Young, Howard T. *Juan Ramón Jiménez.* Col. U. Pr. 1967 o.p.

———. *The Line in the Margin: Juan Ramón Jiménez and His Readings in Blake, Shelley and Yeats.* U. of Wis. Pr. 1980 $29.50. ISBN 0-299-07950-3. Emphasizes Jiménez's affinity with the poets Blake, Shelley, and Yeats.

JOHN OF THE CROSS, ST. (Juan de Yepes y Alvarez). 1542–1591

St. John of the Cross represents the pinnacle of Spanish mysticism. In contrast to ST. TERESA's works, which refer frequently to things of this world, St. John's poetry works on a purely spiritual, abstract plane. His poems consist of allegorical descriptions of the journey of his spirit through mortification of earthly appetites, illumination, and purification of the soul to union with God. In his prose commentaries on his own poems he laments the insufficiency of language to communicate his mystical experiences and his interior life.

A disciple of St. Teresa, he became the spiritual director of her convent at Avila in 1572 and was responsible for carrying out many of her rigorous new programs for the Carmelite Order. Objections to his extreme reforms led to a period of imprisonment and torture in Toledo. During this time, according to tradition, he wrote *Spiritual Canticle.* His concentrated symbolic poetry has been studied with enthusiasm by such modern poets as T. S. ELIOT (see Vol. 1), PAUL VALÉRY, and JORGE GUILLÉN.

WORKS BY ST. JOHN OF THE CROSS

Ascent of Mount Carmel. Trans. by Edgar Allison Peers. Gleneida Pub. 1991 $9.95. ISBN 0-8007-3012-7. Exhaustive narrative of the journey of the soul; refers to gospel readings and biblical episodes.

The Collected Works of St. John of the Cross. Trans. by Kieran Kavanaugh and Otilio Rodriguez. ICS Pubns. 1979 $14.95. ISBN 0-9600876-7-2. Retranslation and appended text of verses based on St. John's theological musings.

The Dark Night of the Soul. Doubleday 1959 $7.95. ISBN 0-385-02930-6. Extensive autobiographical ponderings on the relevance of God; develops the idea of a godless existence.

The Living Flame of Love. Trans. by Edgar Allison Peers. Gleneida Pub. 1991 $7.95. ISBN 0-8007-3013-5. Examines St. John's ideas on God and the association with love; introduces sparse historical references to St. John's life.

Spiritual Canticle. Trans. by Edgar Allison Peers. W. T. Taylor 1990 $90.00. ISBN 0-935072-18-7

POETRY BY ST. JOHN OF THE CROSS

Poems of Saint John of the Cross. Trans. by Willis Barnstone. New Dir. Pr. 1972 $5.95. ISBN 0-8112-0449-9

BOOKS ABOUT ST. JOHN OF THE CROSS

Cugno, Alain. *St. John of the Cross: Reflections on Mystical Experience.* Trans. by Barbara Wall. Winston Pr. 1982 o.p.

Frost, Bede. *St. John of the Cross.* Gordon Pr. 1977 $250.00. ISBN 0-8490-2559-1

Hardy, Richard P. *The Search for Nothing: The Life of John of the Cross.* Crossroad NY 1982 $8.95. ISBN 0-8245-0815-7. Realistic portrayal of the life and work of St. John of the Cross.

Icaza, Rosa M. *Stylistic Relationship between Poetry and Prose in the* Cántico Espiritual *of San Juan de la Cruz*. AMS Pr. 1969 repr. of 1957 ed. $21.00. ISBN 0-404-50354-3. Considers direct and symbolic meanings in St. John's *Cantico Espiritual*; reveals different aspects of the prosody in his poetry.

MacDonald, James M. *The Life and Writings of St. John of the Cross*. Gordon Pr. 1977 $250.00. ISBN 0-8490-2164-2

Thompson, Colin P. *The Poet and the Mystic: A Study of the* Cántico Espiritual *of San Juan de la Cruz*. OUP 1977 o.p. Looks at the development of St. John's poetry and theology in the *Cantico Espiritual*; analyzes his achievement from a twentieth-century viewpoint.

THE LIFE OF LAZARILLO DE TORMES. 1554

The composition of *The Life of Lazarillo de Tormes*, published in Burgos, Alcalá, and Antwerp in 1554, has been placed between 1525 and 1550; both the date and the identity of the author remain unknown. The novel gained immediate popularity and is the prototype of the picaresque novel, a genre episodic in form that features the adventures of an antihero, usually young, matching his wits against cruel masters and an indifferent, corrupt society. Among the innovations of *The Life of Lazarillo de Tormes* are the first-person narrative technique, concentration of interest on lower-class figures, and the rejection of chivalric and sentimental literature. Lazarillo, "born in the river Tormes" to a thieving father and a mother of questionable reputation, serves a crafty blind man, a greedy and hypocritical priest, and a starving gentleman striving to keep his appearance of wealth. In each situation the boy must struggle continually for food to stay alive. Lazarillo accepts his fate with resignation, drawing no moral generalizations from his experiences. Fortune, which he naively considers to be good, brings him a marriage with the mistress of the archpriest and a job as a bellringer. The author, however, strips the church, Spain, and human nature in general of its illusions of grandeur, and the next picaresque novel to appear, *Guzmán de Alfarache* by MATEO ALEMÁN, is considerably more bitter in tone and pessimistic in outlook.

The Life of Lazarillo de Tormes. Trans. by J. Gerald Markley. Macmillan 1954 $5.25. ISBN 0-02-376160-1

BOOK ABOUT LAZARILLO DE TORMES

Sieber, Harry. *Language and Society in* La Vida de Lazarillo de Tormes. Johns Hopkins 1979 $20.00. ISBN 0-8018-2121-5

MACHADO Y RUIZ, ANTONIO. 1875–1939

Machado's great love for Castile, nourished during his years as a teacher of French in Soria, is the source of much of his poetry. Rejecting modernism and gongorism, he wrote simple, natural, and spare verses. Sadness and melancholy were his dominant moods, deriving from the somber, barren atmosphere of the Castilian landscape, the death of his young wife in 1912, his own solitary nature, and the pessimism of his generation about Spain. In *Campos de Castilla* (1912), generally considered to mark his poetic height, his themes are lost youth, time, death, religion, and Spain. Machado believed that memory, capable of transforming and reliving experience, is humanity's only defense against time. His preoccupation with the concept of time as a stream carrying man to his end in nothingness may have developed from his study of HENRI BERGSON (see Vol. 4). In *Juan de Mairena* (1936), Machado the poet carries on a dialogue with Machado the philosopher discussing philosophy, metaphysics, and the anguish of existence, topics that characterize him as a member of the Generation of 1898.

POETRY BY MACHADO

Canciones. Trans. by Robert Bly. Coffee Hse. $4.00. ISBN 0-915124-46-7. Machado's poems handled with generous affection.

I Never Wanted Fame. Trans. by Robert Bly. Ally Pr. 1979 $10.00. ISBN 0-915408-20-1

Juan de Mairena: Epigrams, Maxims, Memoranda, and Memoirs of an Apocryphal Professor. Trans. by Ben Belitt. U. CA Pr. 1963 o.p.

The Landscape of Soria. Trans. by Dennis Maloney. White Pine 1985 $4.00. ISBN 0-934834-57-1

Selected Poems. Trans. by Antonio Machado and Alan S. Trueblood. HUP 1982 $14.95. ISBN 0-674-04066-X. Careful analysis of the philosophical underpinnings of Machado's work; detailed preface on the author's life and a comprehensive commentary.

Selected Poems of Antonio Machado: A Dialogue with Time. Trans. by Betty Craige. La. State U. Pr. 1978 $25.00. ISBN 0-8071-0456-0

Times Alone: Selected Poems of Antonio Machado. Trans. by Robert Bly. Wesleyan Univ. Pr. 1983 $14.95. ISBN 0-8195-6081-2. Fifty poems showing the subtlety and expansiveness of Machado's psychic vision.

BOOKS ABOUT MACHADO

Hutman, Norma L. *Machado: A Dialogue with Time—Nature as an Expression of Temporality in the Poetry of Antonio Machado*. Irvington 1969 $29.50. ISBN 0-8290-0186-7. Bibliography on Machado's works and criticism and an index of authors, works, and topics.

Young, Howard T. *Victorious Expression: A Study of Four Contemporary Spanish Poets: Unamuno, Machado, Jiménez and Lorca*. U. of Wis. Pr. 1966 $9.50. ISBN 0-299-03144-6

MATUTE, ANA MARÍA. 1926–

One of Spain's foremost novelists and short story writers of the post-civil war period, Matute is particularly renowned for her loving but unsentimental stories about children and adolescents. Marked by existential anguish and poignant lyricism, these stories often focus on traumatic experiences which lead to a child's sudden awakening to the sordid, cruel, and hypocritical adult world.

NOVEL BY MATUTE

School of the Sun. 1963. Col. U. Pr. 1989 $47.50. ISBN 0-231-06916-2

SHORT STORY COLLECTION BY MATUTE

The Heliotrope Wall and Other Stories. Trans. by Michael S. Doyle. Col. U. Pr. 1989 $34.00. ISBN 0-231-06556-6. Stories of individuals, some from a child's perspective, who exist in a world of their own; "Very Happy" and "Math Notebook" are first-class pieces of short fiction.

BOOK ABOUT MATUTE

Díaz, Janet W. *Ana María Matute. Twayne's World Authors Ser.* Irvington 1971 $17.95. ISBN 0-8290-1753-4. Emphasizes the author's social and political concerns; includes a fascinating description and thematic analysis of Matute's unpublished juvenilia at the Mogar Library of Boston University.

ORTEGA Y GASSET, JOSÉ. 1883–1955

[SEE Volume 4.]

PARDO BAZÁN, EMILIA. 1852–1921

The Countess Emilia Pardo Bazán introduced the French naturalistic movement to Spain with *The Burning Question* (1881). While she recognized the excesses of naturalism in its exclusive concentration on the sordid aspects of life, she saw in it possibilities for directing the Spanish novel to social and political issues. *The Son of the Bondwoman (Los Pasos de Ulloa*, 1886), which deals with the degeneration of an aristocratic family, is naturalistic in subject and in its deterministic conclusion.

Novel by Pardo Bazán

The Son of the Bondwoman. Trans. by E. H. Hearn. Fertig 1976 repr. of 1908 ed. o.p.

Book about Pardo Bazán

Hemingway, Maurice. *Emilia Pardo Bazán: The Making of a Novelist*. Cambridge U. Pr. 1983 $44.50. ISBN 0-521-24466-8. Discusses the influence of "spiritual naturalism" on four of Pardo Bazán's novels characterized by ambiguity and moral complexity.

PÉREZ DE AYALA, RAMÓN. 1881–1962

Pérez de Ayala experimented with a variety of novelistic forms. His controversial novels have been criticized by some as pedantic, nihilistic, and pornographic, while others have praised their intellectual orientation, realistic portrayal of human weaknesses, and frank treatment of sex. *Belarmino and Apolonio* (1921) is a novelistic treatment of the philosophy of perspectivism. At least two versions of an event are narrated, and characters are described from many angles and given more than one name. In *Honeymoon, Bittermoon* (1923) Pérez de Ayala constructed a grotesque, stylized world through skillful use of poetic language, symbol, and caricature, attacking hypocritical prudishness with the story of a young man's initiation into amorous adventures.

Novels by Pérez de Ayala

Belarmino and Apolonio. 1921. Trans. by Murray Baumgarten. U. CA Pr. 1971 $9.95. ISBN 0-520-04958-6

Honeymoon, Bittermoon. 1923. Trans. by Barry Eisenberg. U. CA Pr. 1972 o.p.

Books about Pérez de Ayala

Macklin, John J. *The Window and the Garden: The Modernist Fictions of Ramón Pérez de Ayala*. Society Sp. and Sp-Am. 1988 $30.00. ISBN 0-89295-053-6. Essential work on the fiction of Pérez de Ayala; reevaluates the author's fictions and modernism.

Rand, Marguerite C. *Ramón Pérez de Ayala. Twayne's World Authors Ser.* Irvington 1971 $17.95. ISBN 0-8290-1734-8. Categorizes Peréz de Ayala's novels under three genres: poetry, novels, and nonfictional prose; major novels are summarized, and symbolism is interpreted.

PÉREZ GALDÓS, BENITO. 1843–1920

Pérez Galdós was Spain's outstanding nineteenth-century novelist. In scope, purpose, and achievement he was comparable to Dickens (see Vol. 1) and Balzac, two writers he acknowledged as models. At a time when most Spanish novelists were limited by their regional backgrounds, Galdós possessed the intellect and vision to embrace the Spanish people as a nation. In 1873 he began the *Episodios nacionales* (*National Episodes*), a 46–volume series of historical novels in which he was concerned less with details and facts of history than with their impact on the lives of ordinary people.

His works are sometimes divided into two periods: novels of the first period and contemporary Spanish novels. His early novels, *Doña Perfecta* (1876), *Gloria* (1877), *Marianela* (1878), and *The Family of Leon Roch* (1879), may be characterized as realistic with touches of romanticism. The novels are united by common characters and themes in the manner of Balzac's *Human Comedy*. *Doña Perfecta*is a denunciation of intolerance. *Marianela* explores the irony and tragedy of the destruction of love by scientific progress. *Fortunata and Jacinta*(1886–87), a four-volume masterpiece of the second period, contrasts two women—Jacinta, wife of the wealthy middle-class Juanito Santa Cruz, and Fortunata, his mistress. Both are admirable characters, but it is Fortunata who bears a son, demonstrating the vitality of the lower classes. The character of Maxi reveals Galdós's interest in mental illness and his naturalistic strain.

Born and educated in the Canary Islands, Pérez Galdós studied law briefly and spent most of his adult life in Madrid. His study of lower-class Spanish life and his attempts to improve it led him to the advocacy of more equal distribution of wealth and outspoken opposition to the Catholic church. While always popular with the people, he fared less well in literary circles. In 1889 he sought admission to the Royal Academy, an honor he was refused until 1897, and the Nobel Prize went to a contemporary, José Echegaray, a writer of considerably less talent. Galdós died poor and blind. Although the government refused him a state funeral, the entire Spanish nation mourned him. English translations of his novels now out of print are *The Disinherited Lady* (1881), *Miau* (1888), *Compassion* (1897), and *Tristana*.

NOVELS BY PÉREZ GALDÓS

The Campaign of Maestrazgo. Trans. by Lila W. Guzmán. Hollowbrook 1990 $39.95. ISBN 0-89341-595-2

Fortunata and Jacinta: Two Stories of Married Women. 1886–87. Trans. by Agnes M. Gullón. Viking Penguin 1989 $10.95. ISBN 0-14-043305-8

The Golden Fountain Café. Trans. by Yvette Meller and Walter Rubin. Lat. Am. Lit. Rev. Pr. 1989 $17.95. ISBN 0-935480-36-6. Explores political intrigue and social injustice in the court of Ferdinand VIII; excellent character descriptions and useful notes.

Our Friend Manso. Trans. by Robert H. Russell. Col. U. Pr. 1987 $29.00. ISBN 0-231-06404-7. First-rate translation of a basic title in the nineteenth-century canon; questions the nature of existence, the value of language, and the origins of identity.

Torquemada. Trans. by Frances M. López-Morillas. Col. U. Pr. 1986 $40.50. ISBN 0-231-06228-1. An incomparable portrait of nineteenth-century Spain; realistic, ironic, detailed, and comic.

BOOKS ABOUT PÉREZ GALDÓS

Dendle, Brian J. *Galdós: The Early Historical Novels*. U. of Mo. Pr. 1986 $25.00. ISBN 0-8262-0615-8. Focuses on the 20 historical novels that constitute the first two series of "Episodios nacionales"; a reaction to the social and political turmoil of the period.

Percival, Anthony. *Galdós and His Critics*. U. of Toronto Pr. 1985 $45.00. ISBN 0-8020-5601-6. A compilation and classification of the critical comment on Pérez Galdós's work and life; includes clear summaries, appendix, notes, selected bibliography, and indexes.

Urey, Diane F. *The Novel Histories of Galdós*. Princeton U. Pr. 1989 $35.00. ISBN 0-691-06777-5. Breaks new ground for the better understanding of 46 novels by Pérez Galdós.

QUEVEDO Y VILLEGAS, FRANCISCO GÓMEZ DE. 1580–1645

Born into an aristocratic family and educated in classics at the Universities of Madrid and Alcalá, Quevedo spent much of his adult life in the court of Madrid.

His experiences in the court of the declining Spanish monarchy contributed to his skepticism and bitterness. In *The Swindler* (1626), Don Pablos narrates his picaresque adventures of the most brutal sort, and unlike the naive Lazarillo (see THE LIFE OF LAZARILLO DE TORMES) or the philosophizing Guzmán (see ALEMÁN), this *pícaro* is completely amoral and misanthropic. The language of the work, densely filled with complex puns, jokes, and obscure allusions, amplifies the confusion of the world portrayed. In *Visions* (1627), Quevedo satirized and ridiculed the foibles and defects of people and society. For his nihilism and pessimism he has been compared to SWIFT (see Vol. 1), DOSTOEVSKY, KAFKA, and the twentieth-century existentialists.

NOVELS BY QUEVEDO

Choice Humorous Satirical Works. Trans. by John Stevens. *Lib. of World Lit. Ser.* Hyperion Conn 1991 repr. of 1926 ed. $38.00. ISBN 0-88355-602-2

The Comic Works of Don Francisco de Quevedo. Trans. by John Stevens. AMS Pr. repr. of 1709 ed. o.p.

Two Picaresque Novels. Trans. by Michael Alpert. *Penguin Class. Ser.* Viking Penguin 1969 o.p.

WORK BY QUEVEDO

Dreams and Discourses: Sueños y discursos. Aris & Phillips UK. ISBN 0-85668-352-3

BOOKS ABOUT QUEVEDO

Hoover, L. Elaine. *John Donne and Francisco de Quevedo: Poets of Love and Death.* U. of NC Pr. 1978 $27.50. ISBN 0-8078-7061-7. Discusses the thematic and imagistic manifestations of death in Donne's and Quevedo's love poetry; representative of the Baroque period.

Olivares, Julián. *The Love Poetry of Francisco de Quevedo: An Aesthetic and Existential Study.* Cambridge U. Pr. 1983 $47.95. ISBN 0-521-24362-9. A detailed study and analysis of 70 love sonnets that combine poetics and abstract traditions.

Walters, D. Gareth. *Francisco de Quevedo, Love Poet.* Cath. U. Pr. 1986 o.p. Reflects the struggle between the spiritual and the carnal within the poet.

ROJAS, FERNANDO DE. 1475?–1541

Fernando de Rojas, of Jewish parentage and a convert to Christianity during the Inquisition, is generally considered to have written all but the first act of *Celestina.* This drama, or novel in dialogue, first appeared in 1499 as *The Comedy of Calisto and Melibea,* then in 1502 as *Tragi-Comedy* with five additional acts, and finally in 1519 as *Celestina* in the version now read. While grounded in medieval morality and conventions of courtly love, the work has been designated by Menéndez y Pelayo as marking the birth of the Spanish Renaissance for its tragic lovers Calisto and Melibea, whose passions lead to their own destruction. The work is also known for its use of elegant language, its individualized characters, its glorification of the pleasures of this life, and its emphasis on luck as the law of the universe. Celestina, a worldly wise old schemer who is totally preoccupied with procuring sexual love, once for herself and now for others, is the grand creation of the work. The most important source for the character of Celestina is JUAN RUIZ's *The Book of Good Love*; the influence of BOCCACCIO (through the archpriest of Talavera), as well as Greek and Latin works, may also be detected. Some critics consider *Celestina* to be surpassed in Spanish literature only by CERVANTES's *Don Quijote.*

Play by Rojas

Celestina: A Novel in Dialogue. Trans. by Lesley Byrd Simpson. U. CA Pr. 1955 o.p.

Books about Rojas

Clarke, Dorothy. *Allegory, Decalogue, and Deadly Sins in La Celestina.* Borgo Pr. 1983 repr. of 1968 ed. $25.00. ISBN 0-89370-760-0. Provocative insight into Rojas's masterpiece as an allegory designed to teach the Ten Commandments and the Seven Deadly Sins.

Fothergill-Payne, Louise. *Seneca and Celestina.* Cambridge U. Pr. 1988 $47.95. ISBN 0-521-32212-X. Illustrates how the Spanish Renaissance prose drama *Celestina* is heavily influenced by fifteenth-century Spanish interpretations of Senecan morality.

RUIZ, JUAN. 1283?–1350?

Little is known of the life of Juan Ruiz, often described as Spain's greatest writer of the Middle Ages and likened to Chaucer (see Vol. 1) and Boccaccio. In his term as archpriest of Hita, a small Castilian town east of Madrid, he apparently collected his own verses and songs into book form around 1330 and then revised and expanded it during a term in prison under sentence by the archbishop of Toledo. In the prose introduction to *The Book of Good Love*, Ruiz defined two categories of love: "good love" or the love of God and "crazy love" or carnal love. While avowing that his purpose was to expose the evils of worldly love and to lead his readers to the exclusive love of God, he admitted that his text may provide those who reject divine love with useful knowledge of the other sort of love. Thus the ironic tone of the book, as well as its humorous, satiric, and didactic nature, become apparent in this introduction. Juan Ruiz's self-consciousness as a writer and his awareness of the qualities of his art provide a glimpse of the Renaissance spirit. The primary literary source for *The Book of Good Love* is *Pamphilus and Galatea*, an anonymous twelfth-century play in Latin by a French poet. Américo Castro and others have suggested the possible influence of Arabic models as shown by the work's composite form, ambiguousness, and sensual elements. In its anticlerical attitudes, the book reflects the crisis of faith facing the Catholic church toward the end of the Middle Ages, a crisis complicated in Spain by the necessity of maintaining the religious fervor of the reconquest.

Poetry by Ruiz

The Book of the Archpriest of Hita. Trans. by Mack Singleton. Hispanic Seminary 1975 $7.50. ISBN 0-942260-06-6

The Book of Good Love. Trans. by Mario A. Di Cesare and Rigo Mignani. MRTS $10.00. ISBN 0-87395-048-8

The Book of True Love. Trans. by Saralyn R. Daly. Pa. St. U. Pr. 1978 $29.95. ISBN 0-271-00523-8. The first rhymed translation of the fifteenth-century poem "Libro de buen amor" to be published as a bilingual text.

SALINAS, PEDRO. 1891–1951

Pedro Salinas was one of several modern Spanish poets who sustained themselves in exile with university teaching. After leaving Spain in 1936, Salinas had a distinguished career as a professor at Cambridge, the University of Puerto Rico, Wellesley, and Johns Hopkins University. While Salinas also wrote criticism, essays, drama, and fiction, he is remembered chiefly as a poet. Love is one of his principal subjects, and in *To Live in Pronouns* (1933), his love for a woman is transformed into the quest for spiritual love, which symbolizes his attempt to reconcile the interior and exterior worlds. Salinas regarded love as the power to create a stable inner reality as protection against the chaos of the world. In this treatment of love and his idealization of women he resembled GUSTAVO ADOLFO BÉCQUER and JUAN RAMON JIMÉNEZ, two of his masters. In *El Contemplado (Sea of Puerto Rico)* (1946), he discovered peace through a contemplation of the waters of Puerto Rico. In his final volume, *The Incredible Bomb* (1950), he asserted faith in love against the destruction of the nuclear age.

POETRY BY SALINAS

To Live in Pronouns: Selected Love Poems. 1933. Trans. by Edith Helman and Norma Farber. Norton 1974 o.p.

My Voice Because of You. Trans. by Willis Barnstone. Prologue by Jorge Guillén. State U. NY Pr. 1976 $19.50. ISBN 0-87395-285-5. Contains sensitive, intricate, and passionate love poems and highly artistic rhythms related to Spanish Renaissance and Baroque poetry.

WORK BY SALINAS

Reality and the Poet in Spanish Poetry. Intro. by Jorge Guillén. Greenwood 1980 repr. of 1966 ed. $39.75. ISBN 0-313-22436-6

TERESA OF JESUS, ST. (Teresa de Cepeda y Ahumada) 1515–1582

St. Teresa recorded her extraordinary mystical experiences through metaphor ("the soul is a castle with seven rooms enclosing it") and paradox ("I die because I do not die"). At the same time, her style is simple, clear, and marked by archaisms and illiterate expressions. Personal, rather than literary, she derived her poetry from experience. She was known for her practicality and attention to everyday realities ("the Lord requires works"). She successfully reformed the Carmelite Order, founding 17 convents, against opposition from both ecclesiastical and secular powers. One of her contemporaries called her "a very great woman as regards the things of this world and, as regards the things of the next, greater still." She is one of the saints in GERTRUDE STEIN'S (see Vol. 1) play, *Four Saints in Three Acts.*

WORKS BY ST. TERESA

The Collected Works of St. Teresa of Avila. 3 vols. Trans. by Kieran Kavanagh and Otilio Rodríguez. ICS Pubns. Vol. 1 1976 $7.95. ISBN 0-9600876-2-1. Vol. 2 1980 $9.95. ISBN 0-9600876-6-4. Vol. 3 1985 $7.95. ISBN 0-935216-06-5

The Interior Castle. Trans. by Edgar A. Peers. Doubleday 1972 $9.00. ISBN 0-385-03643-4

The Letters of St. Teresa. 4 vols. Ed. by Cardinal Gasquet. Gordon Pr. 1977 $800.00. ISBN 0-8490-2154-5

The Life of Teresa of Jesus: The Autobiography of St. Teresa of Avila. Trans. by Edgar A. Peers. Doubleday 1991 $12.00. ISBN 0-385-01109-1

Way of Perfection. Trans. by Edgar A. Peers. Doubleday 1991 $9.00. ISBN 0-385-06539-6

BOOKS ABOUT ST. TERESA

Clissold, Stephen. *St. Teresa of Avila.* Winston Pr. 1982 $8.95. ISBN 0-8164-2621-X. Presents the human and heroic figure of St. Teresa against the background of sixteenth-century Spain; includes a firm chronology of the persons, places, and episodes in her life.

Weber, Alison. *Teresa of Avila and the Rhetoric of Femininity.* Princeton U. Pr. 1990 $22.50. ISBN 0-691-06812-7. A valuable study based on St. Teresa's experience as a woman of her age; original and stimulating analysis of her shifting tones and strategies.

Whalen, James. *The Spiritual Teachings of Teresa of Avila and Adrian Van Kaam.* U. Pr. of Amer. 1984 $25.25. ISBN 0-8191-3865-7. Compares St. Teresa's traditional spiritual wisdom with the contemporary formation science of Whalen; a model for studies of other major figures in the history of spirituality.

TIRSO DE MOLINA (Fray Gabriel Téllez). 1584–1648

Tirso de Molina, a priest active in the religious order of La Merced, produced more than 400 plays. Adopting LOPE DE VEGA's principles of dramatic composition, he excelled Lope in character development, most notably in his creation of the Don Juan figure. Although the theme had long been a subject in Spanish folklore and the character had been treated previously by CERVANTES and Lope de Vega, Tirso's play, *The Trickster of Seville* (1630), brought the Don Juan figure to a stature of such figures as Hamlet, Don Quijote, and Faust. Don Juan, who represents complete devotion to worldly pleasures, refuses to repent for his deceptions, seductions, and finally the murder of Don Gonzalo, always maintaining that he still has sufficient time since, according to Roman Catholic doctrine, even a word of repentance on the deathbed suffices to save the sinner from hell. In the most famous scene of the play, he invites the stone statue of Don Gonzalo to supper. The statue comes to life and surprises him with death by poison. Don Juan dies unrepentant and descends into hell for his punishment. The Don Juan theme and figure have been developed by MOLIÈRE, BYRON (see Vol. 1), Zorrilla, SHAW (see Vol. 1), and CAMUS, among many others.

PLAYS BY TIRSO DE MOLINA

Damned for Despair. Trans. by Nicholas G. Round. Aris & Phillips UK 1986 $49.95. ISBN 0-85668-329-9

Don Gil of the Green Breeches. Trans. by Gordon Minter. Aris & Phillips UK o.p.

Trickster of Seville and the Stone Guest. Trans. by Gwynne Edward. Aris & Phillips UK 1986 $49.95. ISBN 0-85668-300-0

BOOK ABOUT TIRSO DE MOLINA

Weinstein, Leo. *Metamorphoses of Don Juan*. AMS Pr. repr. of 1959 ed. $28.00. ISBN 0-404-51828-1

UNAMUNO Y JUGO, MIGUEL DE. 1864–1936

Philosopher, essayist, poet, and novelist, Unamuno was a central figure of the Generation of 1898. His primary concerns were individual destiny, Spain, the nature of human relationships, and renewal of artistic forms. In his major philosophical work, *The Tragic Sense of Life* (1912), Unamuno struggled with his uncertainty about immortality, for him the ultimate problem, since he believed that if man dies completely then nothing in life has meaning. The only possible solution Unamuno saw was a desperate resignation and struggle for an irrational faith that would permit him to live, a solution often compared to KIERKEGAARD's (see Vol. 4) "leap of faith." Man, then, must conduct himself "passionately well" in order to deserve immortal life. Loving other human beings is the key to living well and the only possibility for salvation: The shoemaker who would mourn the death of a client does a religious work. Reevaluating the figure of Don Quijote, Unamuno saw him as a model for the new man who would save the world, for he acts by faith and love rather than by reason. In *The Agony of Christianity* (1925), Unamuno described the struggle to believe and the agony involved in the preservation of Christian faith.

Many of Unamuno's novels exemplify his philosophic and religious ideas. *Mist* (1914), dealing with the theme of immortality, is also an important work for its contributions to the theory of the modern novel. Asserting his autonomy as a character, Augusto Pérez protests to the author of the work about the decision to have him die. *Abel Sánchez* (1917), a novel on the Cain and Abel theme, develops the existentialistic theme of "the other," the theory that envy is self-hatred, and that the envied person inevitably participates in the envy. Unamuno's poetry covers the range of his contradictory ideas and emotions, but it is in the poetry, particularly the verses evoking his homeland written during his exile in France, that the aspect of the author which has been called "the contemplative Unamuno" is found. Rejecting modernism and aestheticism, he subordinated form to ideas in his poetry.

The dictator Primo de Rivera sent Unamuno into exile on the Canary Islands in 1934, but he soon escaped to Paris where he remained until 1930, when he returned to Spain. In 1936 he was placed under house arrest when he spoke against anti-intellectualism, and he died on the final day of that year.

Works by Unamuno

Perplexities and Paradoxes. Trans. by Stuart Gross. Greenwood 1968 repr. of 1945 ed. $35.00. ISBN 0-8371-0253-7

Tragic Sense of Life. 1912. Trans. by J. Crawford Flitch. Dover 1921 $6.95. ISBN 0-486-20257-7

Novels by Unamuno

Abel Sánchez. 1917. Fr. & Eur. $9.95. ISBN 0-8288-2576-9

Three Exemplary Novels. 1920. Trans. by Angel Flores. Intro. by Angel del Rio. Grove Pr. 1987 $7.95. ISBN 0-8021-5153-1

Books about Unamuno

Ellis, Robert Richmond. *The Tragic Pursuit of Being: Unamuno and Sartre*. U. of Ala. Pr. 1988 $19.95. ISBN 0-8173-0385-5. Compares the two writers' life histories, philosophies, theories of literature, and theatrical works.

Marías, Julián. *Miguel de Unamuno*. Trans. by Frances M. López-Morillas. HUP 1970 $7.50. ISBN 0-231-03259-5. Interpretive, probing analysis of Unamuno's novels, poetry, and essays; examines literary and philosophical aspects.

Rudd, Margaret. *The Lone Heretic*. Gordian 1976 repr. of 1963 ed. $50.00. ISBN 0-87752-181-6. Laudable contribution to Unamuno studies; rich in reminiscences of Unamuno's family and friends.

Young, Howard T. *The Victorious Expression: A Study of Four Contemporary Spanish Poets—Unamuno, Machado, Jiménez, and Lorca*. U. of Wis. Pr. 1966 $9.50. ISBN 0-299-03144-6. Very personal but definitive appreciation of each poet's personality; renews the conviction of the timelessness of Spanish poetry.

VALERA Y ALCALÁ GALIANO, JUAN. 1827–1905

A realistic and regional novelist, Valera is best known for his creation of Andalusian atmosphere, sensual themes, and psychological depth. *Pepita Jiménez* (1874), an ironic novel in epistolary form, explores the inner turmoil of Luis, a young seminarian distracted from his religious study by Pepita Jiménez, who is engaged to his own widower father. A moralist concerned with correct behavior, Valera indicated through his conclusion to the novel that Luis's romantically inspired religious faith is hollow and that service to God may take the form of human, as well as spiritual, love. *Doña Luz* (1879) deals with the same themes.

Novels by Valera

Pepita Jiménez. 1874. Trans. by Harriet de Onis. Barron 1965 o.p.

Doña Luz. 1879. Trans. by M. J. Serrano. Fertig 1975 repr. of 1891 ed. $40.00. ISBN 0-86527-239-5

Books about Valera

DeCoster, Cyrus. *Juan Valera. Twayne's World Authors Ser.* Irvington 1974 $17.95. ISBN 0-8057-2919-4. Discusses Valera's aesthetic theory and his peculiar stylistic qualities; also includes plot structures of the main novels, notes and references, and a selected bibliography.

Lott, Robert E. *Language and Psychology in Pepita Jiménez.* U. of Ill. Pr. 1970 o.p. Detailed characterization of Golden Age mystical prose style.

VALLE-INCLÁN, RAMÓN DEL. (Ramón María Valle Peña). 1866–1936

Galician by birth, Madrilenian by adoption, Ramón del Valle-Inclán was Spain's foremost prose stylist of the twentieth century. He is remembered in Spain almost as much for the colorful Bohemian persona he adopted and made famous as for his writings. Valle-Inclán began his career as a decadent aesthete, much influenced by the *fin-de-siècle* French symbolists. The four novels he entitled *Sonatas* (1902–05)—one for each season of the year—recount four erotic episodes in the life of the Marqués de Bradomin, an "ugly, Catholic, sentimental Don Juan." His dramatic trilogy of "barbaric comedies"—*Heraldic Eagle* (1907), *Romance of Wolves* (1908), and *Silver Face* (1922)—powerfully evokes the primitive grandeur of his native Galicia. Long considered unperformable on account of their violence and obscenity, these plays have enjoyed great critical and popular success since Franco's death. *The Lamp of Marvels* (1916) contains Valle's aesthetic philosophy. The last stage of Valle's career was marked by the creation of a new type of novel he christened the *esperpento*: a stylized, dehumanized, highly objective satiric form well suited to express the crisis in values occurring all over Europe immediately after World War I.

Plays by Valle-Inclán

Barbaric Comedies: Silver Face, Heraldic Eagle, and Romance of Wolves. Trans. by Asa Zatz. Eridanos Library 1992 $23.95. ISBN 0-941419-33-9

Nonfiction by Valle-Inclán

The Lamp of Marvels. Trans. by Robert Lima. Lindisfarne Pr. 1986 $8.95. ISBN 0-940262-14-2

Books about Valle-Inclán

Lima, Robert. *Ramón del Valle-Inclán.* Col. U. Pr. 1972 $7.50. ISBN 0-231-03499-7. Examines the content and literary significance of Valle-Inclán's writings; also includes summaries and comments, selected bibliography of Valle-Inclán's principal works, English translations, and criticisms.

———. *Valle-Inclán: The Theater of His Life.* U. of Mo. Pr. 1988 $35.00. ISBN 0-8262-0661-1. Examines aspects of Valle-Inclán's life and his attempt to assimilate them into his work; includes a selected bibliography, notes, index, and appendix.

Lyon, John. *The Theatre of Valle-Inclán.* Cambridge U. Pr. 1984 $54.95. ISBN 0-521-24493-5. Traces the drama's thematic evolution and relates it to contemporary drama; appendixes include Valle-Inclán's dramatic theory and the dates, company, and theater of his plays' first performances.

VEGA CARPIO, LOPE FÉLIX DE. 1562–1635

Lope de Vega was the creator of the national theater in Spain, and his achievements in drama are comparable in many respects to those of Shakespeare (see Vol. 1) in England. Lope embraced all of Spanish life in his drama, combining strands of previous Spanish drama, history, and tradition to produce a drama with both intellectual and popular appeal. A prodigious writer whom CERVANTES called the "monster of nature," Lope is attributed by his biographer with nearly 2,000 plays, 400 religious dramas, and hundreds of pieces of poetry and literature in every form. He was also involved throughout his life in numerous amorous and military adventures and was ordained as a priest in 1614. In his didactic poem *New York Art of Writing Plays* (1609), Lope defined his primary purpose as entertainment of the audience. He recommended a three-act play in which the outcome is withheld until the middle of the third act, when the *dénouement* should be swiftly developed. Maintaining that the possibilities of classical theater had been exhausted, he advocated casting TERENCE and PLAUTUS aside, that is, abandoning the classical unities. His definition of drama was eclectic, admitting combinations of comedy and tragedy, noble and lower-class characters, a variety of verse forms as demanded by different situations, and a wide panoply of themes—national, foreign, mythological, religious, heroic, pastoral, historical, and contemporary. His major strength was the execution of plot; he created no character of the depth or complexity of Shakespeare's major figures. He captured the essence of Spanish character with his treatment of the themes of honor, Catholic faith, the monarchy, and jealousy. In *Peribáñez* (1610?), a lower-class hero is shown to be more honorable than a nobleman. King Henry the Just, a fictional creation, pardons Peribáñez for his revenge killing of the nobleman who contrived to dishonor him by abusing his new bride. In *Fuente Ovejuna*, a play based on an event narrated in the Spanish chronicles, the people resist a cruel overlord, refusing to join the army he tries to mount against King Ferdinand and Queen Isabel. After the overlord interrupts a village wedding, the townspeople of Fuente Ovejuna collectively murder him and finally receive pardon and gratitude from the Catholic kings.

Toward the end of his life Lope lost popularity, but all of Madrid attended his funeral, and his death was mourned throughout Spain. ALBERT CAMUS adapted his play, *The Knight of Olmedo* (1623?), for French-speaking audiences.

PLAYS BY LOPE DE VEGA

Five Plays. Trans. by Jill Booty. Drama Bk. 1961 o.p. Includes *Peribáñez, Fuente Ovejuna, The Dog in the Manger, The Knight of Olmedo,* and *Justice Without Vengeance.*

Four Plays of Lope de Vega. Trans. by John G. Underhill. Hyperion Conn. 1990 repr. of 1936 ed. $37.50. ISBN 0-88355-618-9. Includes *A Certainty for a Doubt; The King, the Greatest Alcalde; The Gardener's Dog;* and *The Sheep Well.*

NOVEL BY LOPE DE VEGA

La Dorotea. Trans. by Alan Trueblood and Edwin Honig. HUP 1985 $32.50. ISBN 0-674-50590-5. Autobiographical novel in dialogue which many critics today consider Lope's masterpiece.

NONFICTION BY LOPE DE VEGA

Acting Is Believing. Trans. by Michael D. McGaha. Trinity U. Pr. 1986 o.p. Lope uses the life of St. Genesius, patron saint of actors, as a pretext for a sustained meditation on the phenomenon of role-playing and its consequences in human life.

BOOKS ABOUT LOPE DE VEGA

Fox, Dian. *Refiguring the Hero: From Peasant to Novel in Lope de Vega and Calderón.* Pa. St. U. Pr. 1991 $29.95. ISBN 0-271-00737-0. Reevaluates the canon of Spanish Golden Age drama within its European context, focusing on the work of Lope de Vega and Pedro Calderón de la Barca.

Larson, Donald R. *The Honor Plays of Lope de Vega*. HUP 1977 $20.00. ISBN 0-674-40628-1. Traces the development of the dramatist through various periods; nine of the eighteen plays listed are discussed individually.

Trueblood, Alan S. *Experience and Artistic Expression in Lope de Vega: The Making of* La Dorotea. HUP 1974 $45.50. ISBN 0-674-27670-1. Traces the development of the experiential material through the ballads, sonnets, and plays to the prose dialogue of *La Dorotea* from 1635.

CHAPTER 16

Portuguese Literature

Noêl W. Ortega

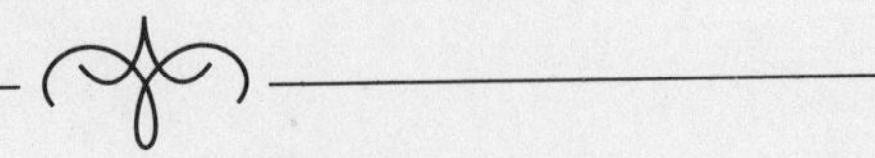

Leave me, all sweet refrains my lip hath made.

—LUÍS VAZ DE CAMÕES, *Sonnet*

Even though Portugal occupies only about one-sixth of the Iberian Peninsula, this small nation of about 10 million people has produced one of the most personal and exhilarating literatures of Europe. Beginning in the Middle Ages, Portugal produced poetry well known for the tenderness of its lyrical verses and the sharpness of its satirical prose. From the 1200s to the early 1400s, the troubadours sang their love poems (*cantigas de amor* and *cantigas de amigo*), which were complaints, or songs of the anguish of lovers' separation. In addition, they produced a caustic and even obscene poetry satirizing the objects of their scorn and contempt (*cantigas de escarnho e maldizer*). About 2,000 of these poems were later compiled in 3 songbooks, or *cancioneiros*.

Portuguese literature remained essentially a literature of poetry until the appearance of the historical chronicles of Fernão Lopes and his successors. These chronicles are important in establishing Portuguese as a major literary language of Europe. This same period saw the emergence of the national theater with Gil Vicente, who wrote 44 plays of religious, allegorical, and comical themes.

With the coming of the Portuguese Renaissance in the sixteenth century and the concomitant interest in classical antiquity and Italian literary forms and ideas, Portugal experienced one of its greatest literary periods. Francisco Sá de Miranda introduced the new metrical forms of the sonnet, the decasyllabic line, *terza rima*, and *ottava rima*. The genius of the period was Luís Vaz de Camões, who used new forms along with traditional Portuguese styles. Both a scholar and a soldier, he captured the spirit of his adventurous nation in the epic poem *Os Lusíadas* (*The Lusiads*) (1572), the highest tribute to the Portuguese spirit and a great literary epic. Camões has inspired and influenced Portuguese writers for centuries. His epic kept the national spirit alive during the Spanish occupation (1580–1640), the struggle for independence, and the fervent patriotism of contemporary Portugal. The leading prose writer of this era is Fernão Mendes Pinto, whose book of travels, *Peregrinação* (1614), relates his adventures in the Far East. Among the mystic writers, Samuel Usque, an exiled Jew, published in Ferrara his *Consolação às Tribulações de Israel* (*Consolations for the Tribulations of Israel*), a religious allegory deploring the persecution and injustices inflicted on the Jewish people. In 1554 Bernardim Ribeiro published his *Menina e Moça* (*As a Young Girl*), a bucolic novel of sentiment that shows the influences of both the pastoral novel and stories of chivalry. A subgenre during this period, unique in European literature, is the Shipwreck Narratives. Some of these tales were collected in the two-volume *Narrativas Trágico-marítimas* published by Bernardo Gomes de Brito.

The eighteenth century was the era of the literary academies and societies. Its greatest poet was Manuel Maria Barbosa du Bocage. The period's talented playwright was António José da Silva, "The Jew" (*O Judeu*), whose comedies for the puppet theater cleverly criticized the Church and the follies of the time, costing him his life at the hands of the Inquisition.

Stemming from the ideals of the French Revolution, Portuguese romanticism is represented by Almeida Garrett and Alexandre Herculano, whose works are immersed in liberty and patriotism. The most prolific Portuguese writer, and a master of the language, is Camilo Castelo Branco, who wrote over 300 works during this period, mainly for the provincial middle class. Toward the end of the nineteenth century, José Maria Eça de Queiróz was the major proponent of realistic fiction. The majority of his novels are social criticisms manifesting his bitter disappointment with Portuguese society. Among the leading poets, Anthero Tarqüínio de Quental was writing philosophical sonnets that were arguably the finest in Europe.

In the early twentieth century, a group of poets founded a magazine called *Orpheu* whose ideologies would continue to influence Portuguese poetry long after its short run of two issues. The group's salient figure was Fernando de Nogueira Pessoa, whose writings are second only to those of Camões. His poems vary in both technique and themes, particularly because he wrote under three different names; each poetic identity possessed a distinct personality and style. Other poets of renown during this period, not readily available in translation, are Mário de Sá-Carneiro, António Botto, Florbela Espanca, José Regio, and Adolfo Casais Monteiro. José Rodrigues Miguéis is a noteworthy neo-realist fiction writer whose work appears in English translation. (Other neo-realists are Aquilino Ribeiro, Miguel Torga, Alves Redol, Ferreira de Castro, Fernando Namora, and Agustina Bessa-Luís.) Many of these writers suffered political harassment and exile during the decades of the Salazarist dictatorship. A major poet who began writing 40 years ago and continues today is Eugenio de Andrade. Since the 1974 revolution, contemporary literature has been a bitter reminder of the years of oppression and the absurdity of the colonial wars. Novelist António Lobo Antunes exemplifies these new writers.

Portugal's literature has not been widely known, but this is changing with the efforts of literary critics such as Audrey F. Bell, an enthusiast of Portuguese belle-lettres who believes that Portuguese literature is the greatest body of work produced by a small country, with the exception of Greece. Finally, Portuguese history and letters are increasingly disseminated, studied, and respected.

GENERAL BIBLIOGRAPHY

Consigliere Pedroso, Zophimo. *Portuguese Folk Tales*. 1882. Trans. by Henriqueta Monteiro. Ayer 1969 repr. of 1882 ed. $10.00. ISBN 0-405-08375-0. Pleasing collection of fairy tales common to Europe but recorded in Portugal.

Ley, Charles D. *Portuguese Voyages, 1498–1663*. Gordon Pr. 1977 $59.95. ISBN 0-8490-2459-5. Selection of passages from letters and travelogues. Includes emotional excerpts from the *Shipwreck Narratives*.

Longland, Jean R. *Selections from Contemporary Portuguese Poetry*. Harvey Pub. Co. 1966 o.p. Reviewers consider the 43 poems by 28 modern poets a good introduction to Portuguese poetry, "a quiet delight . . . faithfully translated . . . [and] finely designed" (*LJ*). Poetry "well chosen and will appeal to both teenagers and adults" (*Commonweal*).

Wohl, Helmut. *Portugal.* Pref. by John Train. Scala Bks. 1983 o.p. General work on Portugal and its culture.

CHRONOLOGY OF AUTHORS

Vicente, Gil. 1465–1537?
Pinto Fernão Mendes. c.1510–1583
Camões, Luís Vaz De. 1524?–1580
Quental, Anthero Tarqüínio De. 1842–1891
Eça De Queiróz, José Maria. 1843–1900
Pessoa, Fernando. 1888–1935
Miguéis, José Rodrigues. 1901–1980
Andrade, Eugénio De. 1923–
Lobo Antunes, Antonio. 1942–

ANDRADE, EUGÉNIO DE. 1923–

Still actively writing today, Eugénio de Andrade is a poet whose work spans more than four decades. His themes and images arise from the four archaic elements (earth, water, air, and fire), all colorfully and vividly entwined.

POETRY BY ANDRADE

Inhabited Heart: The Selected Poems of Eugénio de Andrade. Trans. by Alexis Levitin. Perivale Pr. 1985 $7.95. ISBN 0-912288-24-8. Bilingual edition of 42 poems by one of Portugal's leading comtemporary poets.

CAMÕES, LUÍS VAZ DE (also Luís de Camoens). 1524?–1580

Luís de Camões was Portugal's greatest Renaissance poet, whose profoundly humanistic works have influenced Portuguese literature since their appearance. In 1572 the epic poem *Os Lusíadas* (*The Lusiads*)—Camões's masterpiece and lasting contribution to European literature—was published in Lisbon. By centering on the landmark 1497–98 voyage of Vasco da Gama to India, Camões exalted the Portuguese spirit expressed in history's glorious deeds. Modeled after VIRGIL's *Aeneid*and written in *ottava rima,* the Italian metric form used by ARIOSTO in *Orlando Furioso, Os Lusíadas* is the hallmark of Portuguese classics.

Camões's other poetry (*Rimas*) was published in 1595. In it Camões shows himself to be, in addition to an epic poet, an intensely lyric poet as well.

POETRY BY CAMÕES

Camões: Some Poems. Small Pr. Dist. 1976 o.p.

The Lusiads. 1572. Trans. by William C. Atkinson. Viking Penguin 1975 $8.95. ISBN 0-14-044026-7. The translation by Atkinson is the only prose rendering of the poem.

BOOKS ABOUT CAMÕES

Freitas, William. *Camoens and His Epic.* CA. Inst. Intl. Stud. 1963 o.p. Biographical essay and analysis of allegorical themes in *The Luciads.*

Hart, Henry H. *Luís de Camoens and the Epic of the Lusiads.* U. of Okla. Pr. 1962 o.p. Relates the poet-soldier's story in detail, presents chronological translations of lyrics, describes poet's era and region. Enjoyable and informative.

EÇA DE QUEIRÓZ, JOSÉ MARIA. 1843–1900

Eça de Queiróz was unquestionably Portugal's greatest novelist. Beginning his career in the 1860s as a journalist, he became a constant literary innovator.

He participated in the realist-naturalist revolt against the era's dominant romantics, headed by the poet António Felicano de Castilho. The revolt's two main manifestations were the Coimbra Controversy of 1865 (*A Questão Coimbra*) and the Democratic Speeches at the Lisbon Casino in 1871.

With *The Sin of Father Amaro* (1876) Eça de Queiróz introduced realistic and naturalistic techniques into Portuguese fiction. Set in Leiria, this is a long, tedious novel about provincial life, pettiness, ignorance, and corrupt clergy. Much of its detail comes from Eça's experience in Leiria as a low-level bureaucrat. His second novel, *Cousin Bazílio* (1878), is *Madame Bovary* set in Lisbon. *The Maias* (1888) is his greatest work, a final attempt to create a Portuguese *Human Comedy.* Although critics have focused on Eça's social criticism and protest, he was, as well, an "imaginative, critical, and witty observer of the people" (Guerra da Cal).

Another side of Eça de Queiróz appears in *The Mandarin* (1880), *The Relic* (1886), *The Illustrious House of Ramires* and *The City and the Mountains* (1901). All but the third have humor, fantasy, wit, social criticism, and didactic purposes in common. (Eça, in his preface to *The Mandarin,* maintains that fantasy is the true nature of the Iberian temperament.) The first two books tell the reader that honesty, frankness, hard work, and courage are the keys to happiness and success. *The City and the Mountains* advocates a return of the educated upper class to the soil, to regenerate, in a paternalistic fashion, a national dynamic among the folk. The protagonist of *The Illustrious House of Ramires* ransoms his family's prestige through colonial enterprise. It must be remembered that the last two novels were written after the humiliating ultimatum delivered by Great Britain in 1890, which forced Portugal to give up its claim to the central African territory between Angola and Mozambique.

NOVELS BY EÇA DE QUEIRÓZ

Alves & Co. 1924. Trans. by Robert M. Fedorchek. U. Pr. of Amer. 1988 $14.75. ISBN 0-8191-7157-3. A lesser known early work.

Cousin Bazílio (with the title *Dragon's Teeth*). 1878. Trans. by Mary J. Serrano. Greenwood 1972 repr. of 1899 ed. o.p.

BOOK ABOUT EÇA DE QUEIRÓZ

Coleman, Alexander. *Eça de Queiróz and European Realism.* NYU Pr. 1980 o.p. Summarizes the most important novels and places them within European and Portuguese culture.

LOBO ANTUNES, ANTONIO. 1942–

Lobo Antunes, a psychiatrist and a soldier in the Portuguese colonial wars in Angola, was born in Lisbon. *South of Nowhere,* his second novel, published in 1980, became the center of controversy both because of its daring content and its novel structure. The action is very brief: it lasts only one night. The author tells a silent woman companion his frank impressions about his experience as a medical doctor in the war of liberation against Portuguese colonialism. In some passages the novel makes allusion to *The Lusiads* and its allegorical intentions. It denounces with lucid sarcasm the failure of Portuguese colonization in Africa.

NOVELS BY LOBO ANTUNES

Fado Alexandrino. 1987. Trans. by Gregory Rabassa. Grove Pr. 1990 $24.95. ISBN 0-8021-1299-4. Four veterans of Portugal's colonial wars reminisce about their lives before and during the revolution of 1974.

South of Nowhere. 1980. Trans. by Elizabeth Love. Random 1983 o.p.

MIGUÉIS, JOSÉ RODRIGUES. 1901–1980

Born in Lisbon, Miguéis was part of the neo-realist movement and in many of his works shows the influence of DOSTOEVSKY. Shortly after the publication of his first novel, *Páscoa Feliz* (*Happy Easter*) in 1932, Miguéis went into exile, for many years living in Belgium and Brazil. When he returned years later, he published a number of novels, short stories, and an autobiographical narrative, *Um Homem sorri à morte com meia cara* (*A Man Smiles at Death with Half a Face: An Autobiography of an Illness,* 1959). Miguéis died in 1980 while planning a trip to the United States.

SHORT STORY COLLECTION BY MIGUÉIS

Steerage and Ten Other Stories. Ed. by George Monteiro. Gávea-Brown 1983 $6.00. ISBN 0-943722-06-3. Stories published between 1940 and 1977.

NONFICTION BY MIGUÉIS

A Man Smiles at Death with Half a Face: An Autobiography of an Illness. 1959. Trans. by George Monteiro. U. Pr. of New Eng. 1990 $15.95. ISBN 0-87451-503-3

PESSOA, FERNANDO. 1888–1935

Pessoa remains the poetic genius of twentieth-century Portugal. His creation is such that he has been ranked among the European geniuses of this century: PICASSO (see Vol. 3), STRAVINSKY (see Vol. 3), JOYCE (see Vol. 1), Braque, and Le Corbusier. He was unusual within the Portuguese literary context for having received a British education in Durban, South Africa, where he excelled as a student and as a young English-language poet. He received the Queen Victoria Prize for his entrance exam at the University of Cape Town. Never graduating from a university (he enrolled at the University of Lisbon), he worked for various commercial concerns in Lisbon as a foreign correspondent until his death in 1935.

Pessoa is singular for having written verse not only from his own poetic perspective but also from those of fictitious poets he created. His heteronyms (not to be confused with pseudonyms) were Ricardo Reis, Alberto Caseiro, and Álvaro de Campos. Each poet had a separate life history, and each wrote from a separate philosophical and aesthetic point of view.

POETRY BY PESSOA

The Book of Disquiet. Trans. by Alfred MacAdam. Pantheon 1991 $25.00. ISBN 0-679-40234-9. Fictionalized diary of man who longs to be a father.

The Keeper of Sheep. Trans. by Edward Honig and Susan M. Brown. Sheep Meadow 1986 o.p.

Poems of Fernando Pessoa. Ed. and trans. by Susan M. Brown and Edwin Honig. Ecco Pr. 1986 $19.95 ISBN 0-88001-191-6

The Surprise of Being. Trans. by James Greene and Clara de Azevedo Mafra. Angel Bks. 1987 $25.00. ISBN 0-946162-23-9

NONFICTION BY PESSOA

Always Astonished: Selected Prose. Trans. by Edwin Honig. City Lights 1988 $8.95. ISBN 0-87286-228-3

PINTO, FERNÃO MENDES. c.1510–1583

Very little is known about Pinto's life except what is related in his only work, *Peregrinacão* (translated as *The Travels of Mendes Pinto*). At his death the manuscript for the book passed to Pinto's daughters but was not published until 1614. Pinto left his native Montemoro-Velho for Lisbon, embarking a few years later for the Orient, where he spent almost three decades. He claimed to have been a friend of St. Francis Xavier and, for more than 10 years, a pirate, merchant, and diplomat. While in Asia, he became a Jesuit lay brother for about two years, although he was possibly a Marrano.

NONFICTION BY PINTO

The Travels of Mendes Pinto. 1614. Ed. and trans. by Rebecca D. Catz. U. Ch. Pr. 1989 $49.95. ISBN 0-226-66951-3

QUENTAL, ANTHERO TARQÜÍNIO DE. 1842–1891

Born in the Azores, the poet and essayist Anthero Tarqüínio de Quental became the leader of the rebellious generation of 1870, which openly attacked the reigning romantics in the Coimbra Controversy (*A Questão Coimbra*) and in the Democratic Speeches at the Lisbon Casino. His poetic creation spanned three decades and encompassed romanticism, socialism, rationalism, metaphysical pessimism, and mysticism.

As a philosopher, he opposed positivism and accepted SCHOPENHAUER'S (see Vol. 4) view of the universe, concluding that human beings can unite with God by examining their own egos. God is the Ego of their egos and the Spirit of their spirits.

POETRY COLLECTION BY QUENTAL

Sonnets and Poems of Anthero de Quental. Trans. by Griswold Morley. Gordon Pr. 1973 $59.95. ISBN 0-8490-1088-8. A good collection of early and late poetic works.

VICENTE, GIL. 1465?–1537?

Gil Vicente was the founder of Portuguese theater and a central figure in Spanish literary history. His plays are masterpieces of drama, farce, and allegory, retaining a popularity to the present day.

PLAYS BY VICENTE

Four Plays. Trans. by A. F. Bell. Kraus repr. of 1920 ed. $15.00. ISBN 0-527-93070-9. Four works representing various themes used by Vicente.

CHAPTER 17

German Literature

Boria Sax

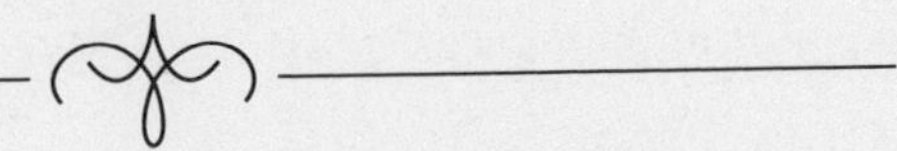

Do not laugh at the child when with his whip and spurs
Brave and mighty he feels on his rocking horse,
For you, you Germans, you too are
Poor in deeds though you've thoughts enough!

Hölderlin, "On the Germans"

The literature of the German-speaking world represents less of a continuous tradition than that of England, France, or perhaps any European nation. This circumstance reflects a history in which cultural activity has been repeatedly disturbed by especially grave political upheavals, economic crises, changes in intellectual opinion, and shifting national boundaries. German identity itself remains highly amorphous. Germany has been the impenetrable frontier of Roman settlement in antiquity, the seat of the mighty Holy Roman Empire in the early Middle Ages, a center of utter devastation in the Thirty Years War (1618–48), a conglomeration of petty kingdoms in the latter seventeenth through early nineteenth centuries, a militaristic world power under Bismarck, and a fanatic enemy of humanistic values under Hitler. Now it has emerged as an economic giant. Accordingly, German culture has been continuously recreated.

The ancient Roman historian TACITUS (see also Vol. 3), in his *Germania* and other works, reports that the German tribes recited songs in praise of their gods and heroes, but none of these compositions have survived. At first, German literature developed very slowly. Through the early Middle Ages we have only a collection of mysterious fragments in the German language, though these often hint at an impressive body of tradition.

Around the beginning of the twelfth century, however, a highly sophisticated literature appeared, with the abruptness that has characterized new developments in German literature ever since. The period produced epic narratives such as *Eric* by HARTMANN VON AUE (c.1180), the anonymous *Nibelungenlied* (c.1200), *Parzifal* by WOLFRAM VON ESCHENBACH (c.1200), *Tristan* by GOTTFRIED VON STRASSBURG (c.1210), as well as lyrics by WALTHER VON DER VOGELWEIDE and many others. Most of the authors of the period were knights, and their inspiration comes largely from the tradition of courtly love, in which poets praised ladies in highly conventionalized, though often sincere, ways.

By the middle of the twelfth century, the traditions of courtly literature had declined almost as abruptly as they appeared, and literature shifted increasingly to the concerns of the emerging middle class. The next two centuries produced some impressive individual works such as *The Plowman from Bohemia* (c.1410) by JOHANNES VON SAAZ (or VON TEPL), but no cohesive literary tradition.

The foundation of modern German literature was established in the early sixteenth century by MARTIN LUTHER (see Vol. 4), also the founder of Protestantism. Through his writings, especially his translation of the Bible (1534), Luther not only helped standardize German but also adapted the language to the expression of abstract ideas.

At the start of the seventeenth century, Martin Opitz wrote a treatise on versification in which he adapted Latin and French forms to the German language. However, what promised to be a literary renaissance in Germany was abruptly cut short by the Thirty Years War. A series of conflicts on German soil involving most great powers of Europe led to a complete economic and social breakdown, in which armies of mercenaries became little more than marauding bands. Entire cities were often massacred, and the horrors of the era were vividly described in the poems of Andreas Gryphius and the novels of Johann (Hans) Jakob Christoffel von Grimmelshausen.

It took Germany about a century to recover its prewar standard of living, and cultural pursuits had to be largely sacrificed to the practical tasks of rebuilding the country's economy. In the mid-eighteenth century Gotthold Ephraim Lessing, the most influential literary figure of the enlightenment in Germany, gave writing a new intellectual sophistication through his critical works.

Just as the renaissance has always been linked primarily with Italy and the enlightenment with France, the romantic movement is most intimately associated with Germany. Most of the characteristic ideas of European romanticism appeared first and remained most prevalent in Germany: the subordination of the intellect to the passions, the prophetic role of the artist, the emulation of folk literature, the awe before the natural world. Throughout the nineteenth century Germany was internationally regarded as the land of romanticism, a view still held by many today. International critics generally designate most German writing from the latter eighteenth and early nineteenth centuries as "romantic," including Goethe and Schiller, while Germans themselves divide this literature into "Storm and Stress" (*Sturm und Drang*), "classicism," and "romanticism."

All of these movements drew much of their inspiration from the works of Johann Gottfried von Herder (see also Vol. 4), who conceived of human cultures as organic, to be understood intuitively through empathy rather than through detached analysis. The Storm and Stress movement (c.1770–85), which included Johann Wolfgang von Goethe's *The Sorrows of Young Werther* (1774) and Friedrich von Schiller's *The Robbers* (1781), sought liberation from the perceived artificiality of social conventions in overpowering emotions. Classicism (c.1785–1832), which included Goethe's *Faust* (1832) and Schiller's later plays, opposed unbridled emotion with the civilizing ideals of harmony, moderation, and restraint. Romanticism, as it is understood in Germany (c.1795–1835), sought a transcendent reality in literature. A rather loose association of authors and literary circles, German romanticism produced an unprecedented diversity of styles. Important representatives include Friedrich Schlegel, Novalis, E.T.A. Hoffmann, and Joseph von Eichendorff. But the poet Friedrich Hölderlin and the dramatist Heinrich von Kleist, who anticipate the spiritual crisis of the twentieth century, elude classification in any movement.

If the term *romantic* is understood a bit more broadly, it may be applied to the dialectic of whimsy and earnestness in the writings of Heinrich Heine or to the delicate lyricism of the country parson Eduard Mörike, indeed to much German writing of the nineteenth century. As the century progressed, however, literature increasingly sought inspiration in the natural sciences rather than in philosophy. Its emphases shifted from inspired reverie to precise description and from lyric poetry to prose. Among the many writers who belong to this realistic tradition are ANNETTE VON DROSTE-HÜLSHOFF, GOTTFRIED KELLER, and THEODOR FONTANE. Naturalistic drama, meanwhile, which endeavored to present events objectively, without sentimentality or moralizing, was anticipated by GEORG BÜCHNER and developed by FRIEDRICH HEBBEL and GERHART HAUPTMANN.

Eventually, an increasing awareness of the limitations of the scientific method began to undermine the realist/naturalist tradition. FRIEDRICH NIETZSCHE (see Vol. 4), whose dramatic rhetoric overwhelmed almost all literary voices of the early twentieth century, regarded science as a symptom of decadence and proclaimed that life could only be justified aesthetically. The reactions against realism took highly divergent forms. A new romanticism emerged in the verse of STEFAN GEORGE, HUGO VON HOFMANNSTHAL, GEORG TRAKL, and RAINER MARIA RILKE, as well as in the novels of HERMANN HESSE. Expressionists like the poet GOTTFRIED BENN challenged traditional ideals of beauty and coherence. The realist tradition was continued by some novelists such as THOMAS MANN, but others such as FRANZ KAFKA experimented with blending presumed objective and psychological perception.

The rise of Hitler to power in 1933 brought an unprecedented exodus of literary figures from Germany, including Mann, Hesse, George, BERTOLT BRECHT, ANNA SEGHERS,and FRANZ WERFEL, among others. Those who returned found a country that was not only in ruins but morally discredited, precipitating a crisis of confidence in inherited traditions entirely characteristic of German literature. Writers as diverse as Mann and Brecht wondered if even cultural monuments were rendered questionable by association with the Third Reich. For many writers who established careers immediately after the war, a traumatic awareness of Auschwitz influenced virtually every work. Such authors include, for example, GÜNTER GRASS, HEINRICH BÖLL, PAUL CELAN, NELLY SACHS, ELIAS CANETTI, FRIEDRICH DÜRRENMATT, CHRISTA WOLF, and MAX FRISCH.

Partly in reaction to Nazism, many writers embraced Marxism. After the war Brecht, Seghers, and STEFAN HEYM offered their enthusiastic support for the ideals of the East German state, while sometimes expressing reservations about the reality. For writers on both sides of the Berlin Wall, erected between East and West Germany in 1961, concern with the Cold War gradually began to eclipse the memory of Nazi crimes. Novelist UWE JOHNSON, who emigrated from East to West Germany, made the contrast between his two homelands his major theme.

The dramatic events of the recent past render evaluation of recent German literature especially difficult. The destruction of the Berlin Wall in 1989, together with the subsequent reunification of East and West Germany, has set off a new round of intense debate on such topics as the German national character and the proper role of literature in society, which may well lead to shifts in critical opinion even greater than those which followed World War II.

BACKGROUND READING

Barraclough, Geoffrey. *The Origins of Modern Germany*. Norton 1984 repr. of 1946 ed. $13.95. ISBN 0-393-30153-2. A clear and detailed presentation of German history from the earliest periods to the middle of the twentieth century. Especially noteworthy chapters on the medieval centuries.

Craig, Gordon. *The Germans.* NAL-Dutton 1991 $10.95. ISBN 0-452-01085-3. A survey of German culture and society, embracing religion, money, literature, education, romanticism, the military, and other topics.

Gay, Peter. *Weimar Culture: The Outsider as Insider.* Greenwood 1981 repr. of 1968 ed. $24.25. ISBN 0-313-22972-4. The society of pre-Hitler Germany, as reflected in everything from poetry to advertising.

Jay, Martin. *The Dialectical Imagination: A History of the Frankfurt School and the Institute of Social Research, 1923-1950.* Little 1973 $14.95. ISBN 0-316-45830-9. The background of such influential theorists as Benjamin, Adorno, Horkheimer, and Marcuse.

Mosse, George L. *The Crisis of German Ideology: Intellectual Origins of the Third Reich.* Schocken 1981 $7.95. ISBN 0-8052-0669-8. A highly detailed study in which the author, without heavy moralizing, tries to reconstruct the roots of Nazi ideology in German culture.

———. *The Nationalization of the Masses: Political Symbolism and Mass Movements in Germany from the Napoleonic Wars through the Third Reich.* Cornell Univ. Pr. 1991 $12.95. ISBN 0-8014-9978-X

Pfeiler, William K. *War and the German Mind.* AMS Pr. repr. of 1941 ed. $19.50. ISBN 0-404-05028-X. Recent reprint of this investigation into the Germans' pre-World War II psychological conditioning. "Pfeiler's extremely fair study will increase our understanding of . . . modern Germany" (*Nation*).

Schorske, Carl E. *Fin-de-Siècle Vienna: Politics and Culture.* Random 1980 $16.95. ISBN 0-394-74478-0

HISTORY AND CRITICISM

Boeschenstein, Hermann. *German Literature in the Nineteenth Century.* St. Martin 1969 $19.95. ISBN 0-312-32585-1

Cernyak-Spatz, Susan E. *German Holocaust Literature.* P. Lang Pubs. 1985 $30.95. ISBN 0-8204-0072-6

Daemmrich, Horst S., and Diether H. Haenicke, eds. *The Challenge of German Literature.* Wayne St. U. Pr. 1971 $34.95. ISBN 8143-1435-X. Contains essays summarizing major trends and periods in German literature.

Demetz, Peter. *Postwar German Literature: A Critical Introduction.* Irvington 1970 $29.75. ISBN 0-8290-0198-0. A survey of the best-known German authors in the decades following World War II.

Francke, Kuno. *History of German Literature as Determined by Social Forces.* AMS Pr. repr. of 1901 ed. $37.50. ISBN 0-404-02545-5. A seminal work by the most distinguished Germanist of the twentieth century.

Fuerst, Norbert. *The Victorian Age of German Literature: Eight Essays.* Pa. St. U. Pr. 1966 $23.50. ISBN 0-271-73107-9. Readably describes the biographical, historical, and philosophical factors affecting the literature of 1820 through 1880.

Gray, Ronald. *The German Tradition in Literature, 1871–1945.* Cambridge U. Pr. 1966 $49.50. ISBN 0-521-05133-9. Analyzes the tradition that flourished in Goethe's time through what the author considers its aberration in the early twentieth century. "[A] wealth of stimulating observations and suggestions" (*LJ*).

Haile, H. G. *The History of Doctor Johann Faustus.* U. of Ill. Pr. 1965 $36.00. ISBN 0-317-09448-3. Describes how the anonymous *Story of Dr. Faustus* (1587) illuminates the beliefs and superstitions of its century.

Hamburger, Michael. *A Proliferation of Prophets: Essays on German Writers from Nietzsche to Brecht.* St. Martin 1984 $22.50. ISBN 0-312-65117-1. Essays on major figures in German literature of the nineteenth and twentieth centuries, with special attention to their shared prophetic aspirations.

Heller, Erich. *In the Age of Prose: Literary and Philosophical Essays.* Cambridge U. Pr. 1984 $47.50. ISBN 0-521-25493-0. Elegant essays by one of the most widely read interpreters of German culture, concentrating on the spiritual crisis of the twentieth century.

Pickering, F. P. *Essays on Medieval German Literature and Iconography.* Cambridge U. Pr. 1980 o.p.

Ritchie, J. M. *German Literature under National Socialism.* B&N Imports 1983 $31.50. ISBN 0-389-20418-8. "A handbook for the study of pre-Nazi, Nazi, and post-Nazi literature. Useful for every level." *(Choice).*

Robinson, J. G. *A History of German Literature.* Ed. by Edna Purdie. William Blackwood & Sons 5th rev. ed. 1902 o.p. A revised edition of a textbook first published in 1902. Though dated in some respects, widely regarded as the most comprehensive and lucid history of German literature in English.

Samuel, Richard, and Thomas R. Hinton. *Expressionism in German Life: Literature and the Theatre.* Saifer 1983 repr. of 1939 ed. $15.00. ISBN 0-87556-308-2

Sax, Boria. *The Romantic Heritage of Marxism: A Study of East German Love Poetry.* P. Lang Pubs. 1987 $34.00. ISBN 0-8204-0487-X. The romantic foundation of the Marxist movement and its reflection in the work of East German poets.

Schrader, Richard J. *God's Handiwork: Images of Women in Early Germanic Literature.* Greenwood 1983 $37.50. ISBN 0-313-23666-6

Silbermann, Marc D. *Literature of the Working World: A Study of the Industrial Novel in East Germany.* P. Lang Pubs. 1977 $23.85. ISBN 3-261-01992-1

Silz, Walter. *Realism and Reality.* AMS Pr. repr. of 1954 ed. $27.00. ISBN 0-404-50911-8. The classic study of the nineteenth century Novelle of German Realism.

Zipes, Jack. *Breaking the Magic Spell: Radical Theories of Folk and Fairy Tales.* Routledge Chapman & Hall 1981 $12.95. ISBN 0-416-01001-6. A survey of the fairy tale as folklore and as a literary form during the era of German romanticism.

COLLECTIONS

Much important German literature is not available in English because of cultural barriers, difficulty of translation, the authors' lack of wide recognition, and other reasons. This deficiency is being partially remedied by a series entitled The German Library, edited by Volkmar Sander and published by Continuum in New York City. The series will eventually cover all periods of German literature in 100 moderately priced volumes; about 35 have appeared so far. Often now, readers who wish to find less well-known German authors in translation must either seek out obscure editions or anthologies like those which follow. Note that these anthologies contain many fine writers who are not profiled in this book, only because of lack of translations. These authors may prove as interesting to the reader as their better-known colleagues.

Blackwell, Jeannine, and Susanne Zantop, eds. *Bitter Healing: German Women Writers from 1700–1830: An Anthology.* U. of Nebr. Pr. 1990 $14.95. ISBN 8032-9909-5. Female German authors, many of whom are currently receiving increased attention.

Engel, Eva L., ed. *German Narrative Prose.* Vol. 1, *The Nineteenth Century.* Berg Pubs. 1987 $19.95. ISBN 0-85496-021-X

Flores, Angel. *An Anthology of German Poetry from Holderlin to Rilke in English Translation.* Peter Smith 1960 o.p.

Forster, Leonard, ed. *The Penguin Book of German Verse.* Viking Penguin 1985 $7.95. ISBN 0-14-05846-X. A comprehensive anthology of German poetry in a bilingual edition, from the earliest fragments to the present.

Francke, Kuno, ed. *German Classics.* 20 vols. AMS Pr. repr. of 1914 ed. $45.00 ea. ISBN 0-404-02600-1. Perhaps the single most comprehensive collection of German literary works currently available in English, despite being somewhat dated.

Hamburger, Michael, ed. *East German Poetry: An Anthology.* Trans. by Gisela Brotherston. Humanities 1979 o.p. An anthology of the poetry written in the early decades of former East Germany, with special emphasis on the dynamism of the generation that emerged in the sixties.

Waidson, H. M., ed. *German Short Stories.* 3 vols. Cambridge U. Pr. 1969 $7.95 ea. ISBN 0-521-06717-0

CHRONOLOGY OF AUTHORS

Hartmann von Aue. c.1160–c.1220
Walther von der Vogelweide. c.1168–1228
Gottfried von Strassburg. 1170?–1210?
Wolfram von Eschenbach. 1170?–1220?
Johannes von Saaz c.1350–c.1414
Brant, Sebastian. 1457?–1521
Sachs, Hans. 1494–1576
Grimmelshausen, Johann Jakob Christoffel von. 1620?–1676
Lessing, Gotthold Ephraim. 1729–1781
Herder, Johann Gottfried von. 1744–1803
Goethe, Johann Wolfgang von. 1749–1832
Schiller, Friedrich von. 1759–1805
Paul, Jean. 1763–1825
Schlegel, August, 1767–1845, and Friedrich Schlegel. 1772–1829
Hölderlin, Friedrich. 1770–1843
Novalis. 1772–1801
Tieck, Ludwig. 1773–1853
Hoffmann, E(rnst) T(heodor) A(madeus). 1776–1822
Kleist, Heinrich von. 1777–1811
Chamisso, Adelbert von. 1781–1838
Grimm, Jacob, 1785–1863, and Wilhelm Grimm. 1786–1859
Eichendorff, Joseph, Freiherr von. 1788–1857
Grillparzer, Franz. 1791–1872
Droste-Hülshoff, Annette von. 1797–1848
Heine, Heinrich. 1797–1856
Mörike, Eduard. 1804–1875
Hoffman, Heinrich. 1809–1894
Büchner, Georg. 1813–1837
Hebbel, Friedrich. 1813–1863
Fontane, Theodor. 1819–1898
Keller, Gottfried. 1819–1890
Busch, Wilhelm. 1832–1908
Hauptmann, Gerhart. 1862–1946
Schnitzler, Arthur. 1862–1931
Wedekind, Frank. 1864–1918
George, Stefan. 1868–1933
Mann, Heinrich. 1871–1950
Hofmannsthal, Hugo von. 1874–1929
Mann, Thomas. 1875–1955
Rilke, Rainer Maria. 1875–1926
Hesse, Hermann. 1877–1962
Döblin, Alfred. 1878–1957
Kaiser, Georg. 1878–1945
Musil, Robert. 1880–1942
Zweig, Stefan. 1881–1942
Kafka, Franz. 1883–1924
Feuchtwanger, Lion. 1884–1958
Benn, Gottfried. 1886–1956
Broch, Hermann. 1886–1951
Trakl, Georg. 1887–1914
Werfel, Franz. 1890–1945
Sachs, Nelly. 1891–1970
Toller, Ernst. 1893–1939
Jünger, Ernst. 1895–
Brecht, Bertolt. 1898–1956
Remarque, Erich Maria. 1898–1970
Seghers, Anna. 1900–1983
Canetti, Elias. 1905–
Frisch, Max. 1911–1991
Heym, Stefan. 1913–
Kirst, Hans Hellmut. 1914–
Weiss, Peter. 1916–1982
Böll, Heinrich. 1917–1985
Celan, Paul. 1920–1970
Borchert, Wolfgang. 1921–1947
Dürrenmatt, Friedrich. 1921–
Bachmann, Ingeborg. 1926–1973
Grass, Günter. 1927–
Lind, Jakov. 1927–
Müller, Heiner. 1929–
Wolf, Christa. 1929–
Bernhard, Thomas. 1931–
Hochhuth, Rolf. 1931–
Johnson, Uwe. 1934–1984
Kirsch, Sarah. 1935–
Biermann, Wolf. 1936–
Handke, Peter. 1942–
Rathenow, Lutz. 1952–

BACHMANN, INGEBORG. 1926–1973

Ingeborg Bachmann was born in the Austrian town of Klagenfurt and moved to Vienna as a young woman to study philosophy. After World War II, she moved to West Berlin, where her first volume of poetry, *Die gestundete Zeit* (On Borrowed Time, 1953), received the prestigious Group 47 prize. Bachmann also published fiction, radio plays, and songs.

Like most writers who experienced the Nazi era, Bachmann often distrusts her society and its institutions. Her rebellion, however, has not taken the form of political activism but of a romantic longing for the absolute. Her verse, notable for its strong rhythms, usually employs traditional forms. She especially excels in describing landscapes.

Poetry by Bachmann

In the Storm of Roses: Selected Poems of Ingeborg Bachmann. Trans. by Mark Anderson. Princeton U. Pr. 1992 $32.50. ISBN 0-632-06672-8. An anthology that won the 1987 Harold Morton Landon Translation Award.

Novel by Bachmann

Malina. 1971. Trans. by Phillip Boehm. Holmes & Meier 1991 $24.95. ISBN 0-8419-1192-4. Lyrical prose, telling of the destruction of a woman in an unhappy love affair and her meeting with her doppelgänger, "Malina."

Short Story Collection by Bachmann

The Thirtieth Year. 1961. Trans. by Michael Bullock. Holmes & Meier 1987 $19.95. ISBN 0-8419-1068-5. Seven tales of human beings who reject their past in the name of absolute ideals.

BENN, GOTTFRIED. 1886–1956

"Benn was a striking figure in his time. . . . He has been a powerful influence on recent younger Germanic poets" (Harry T. Moore). The publication of his first volume of poems, *Morgue*, in 1912, established him as a member of the European avant-garde and an enfant terrible of expressionism. A Berlin physician, Benn brought to his early poems a medically based obsession with the phenomena of physical and mental decay and a radical disillusionment with the bourgeois world.

Work by Benn

Primal Vision, Selected Writings. Trans. by Michael Hamburger and others. M. Boyars Pubs. 1985 $18.00. ISBN 0-7145-2500-6. In addition to poetry, contains Benn's essays, which cover a wide variety of literary, cultural, and anthropological themes.

Book about Benn

Alter, Reinhard. *Gottfried Benn: The Artist and Politics (1910-1934).* P. Lang Pubs. 1976 $26.70. ISBN 3-261-01871-2

BERNHARD, THOMAS. 1931–

Thomas Bernhard was born to Austrian parents in Holland and reared by his mother in the vicinity of Salzburg. Though too young during the war to be acutely aware of politics, his temperament and erratic health did create difficulties for him as he grew up in a society governed by National Socialists. Bernhard finds the alpine landscapes of his native Austria far more harsh than lyrical. The isolation of the characters in his novels is only slightly mitigated by friendship, generally only between men, and never by love, yet many readers feel this lack of sentimentality gives Bernhard's work an epic power.

Novels by Bernhard

Wittgenstein's Nephew: A Friendship. 1982. Knopf 1989 $17.95. ISBN 0-394-56376-X. A fictionalized memoir of Bernhard's relationship with Paul Wittgenstein, whom he met in a hospital.

Woodcutters. 1984. Trans. by David McLintock. Knopf 1988. $15.95. ISBN 0-394-55152-4. A novel based on Bernhard's years as a student in Salzburg, in which the author takes a sardonic view of romantic images of Austria.

BIERMANN, WOLF. 1936–

Wolf Biermann was born in Hamburg to a secular Jewish family affiliated with the communist party. His father was murdered in Auschwitz. After World War II, Biermann settled in East Berlin, where he attempted to work for the socialist ideals of his father. Encouraged by the composer Hans Eisler, he wrote political ballads and songs, in which he criticized not only capitalists but also the bureaucrats in his own land. In 1963 he was forbidden to perform in public and started to emerge as a symbol of new-left opposition to the East German government. His forced expulsion from East Germany in 1973 brought massive protests from literary communities, both in his own country and abroad. Living in exile, Biermann became increasingly disillusioned and eventually repudiated Marxism. In 1992 he received the prestigious Büchner Prize, using the occasion to denounce literary figures who had worked as agents for the East German security police. Despite the naive tone he often adopts in his songs, Biermann is a highly cultivated artist whose craftsmanship has been widely praised.

Poetry by Biermann

Poems and Ballads. Trans. by Steve Gooch. Paul & Co. Pubs. 1977 o.p. Skillfully written, though sometimes propagandistic songs, in which Biermann tries to reconcile his Marxist creed with his criticisms of existing socialism.

BÖLL (or BOELL), HEINRICH. 1917–1985 (Nobel Prize 1972)

Although Böll had won three literary prizes in Germany and had had earlier novels in translation published in the United States (now o.p.), it was not until *Billiards at Half-Past Nine* (1959) that he became established abroad as one of the most important German novelists to have emerged since World War II. *The Clown* (1963), his story of the antihero who cannot make a go of life but continues ruefully to try, is intensely cynical about modern Germany in a lighthearted way. Of a Gauleiter who had "protected" a radical in the Hitler period, who in turn was bound to swear to a "denazification" court that he owed his life to that "swine," Böll writes, "Needless to say he [the Gauleiter] didn't hold his protective hand over everyone, not over Marx the leather merchant and Krupe the Communist. They were murdered. And the Gauleiter is doing all right today. He has a construction business."

Absent without Leave (1964) and *Enter and Exit* are "essential reading for all who care about the contemporary German conscience, consciousness, and literary sensibility" (*SR*). "With his sensitive, tight, allusive prose, shorn of sentimentality, Mr. Böll turns the German soldier into a portrait of every soldier" (*LJ*). *Eighteen Stories,* written over a period of 20 years, "satirizes the indignities and absurdities of making a living in postwar Germany. . . . A shrewd and skillful translation" (*SR*).

The son of Victor Böll, the sculptor, Heinrich was born in Cologne. He was drafted in 1938 shortly after finishing his schooling and served several years in the infantry before his demobilization in 1945. "Böll reminds one of Thomas Mann at his peak as an uncompromising foe of conventionality and political faddism, as well as a writer who in many respects courts the label of 'old-fashioned' by putting narrative ahead of experimentation. Equally unusual is Böll's dedication to literary art, his conviction that it is one of the few contemporary means of free expression" (*N.Y. Times*).

In *The Lost Honor of Katharina Blum* (1974), Böll continues to focus on modern German society and the destructive possibilities latent in it. "What is strong and attractive here, as in Böll's other novels, is the sense of the faint weirdness of daily life in a conformist country. Everything so aspires to order that the very slightest deviation smacks of a disturbing anarchy" (*N.Y. Times*).

In the 1960s and 1970s, Böll became involved in the German peace movement and in the effort to stop the deployment of U.S. nuclear missiles on West German soil. Peter Demetz has said that Böll's "moral commitment, of the absolute sort, actually masks a fundamental disgust with the inevitable politics of small, daily, pragmatic steps. It is all or nothing once again."

Novels by Böll

Adam and the Train. 1949. Trans. by Leila Vennewitz. McGraw 1974 $7.95. ISBN 0-07-006409-1. Bitterly realistic account of the horrors of war.

Billiards at Half-Past Nine. 1959. Peter Smith 1983 $17.75. ISBN 0-8446-6056-6

The Casualty. Norton 1989 $7.95. ISBN 0-393-30599-6

The Clown. 1963. Trans. by Leila Vennewitz. McGraw 1971 $6.95. ISBN 0-07-006420-2. "An engaging and distinguished novel" (*SR*).

Group Portrait with Lady. 1971. Avon 1976 $4.95. ISBN 0-380-00020-2. A cautionary novel against judging people prematurely.

The Lost Honour of Katharina Blum. 1974. Transaction Pubs. 1990 $22.95. ISBN 1-85290-017-2. An indictment of the West German government's antiterrorist measures during the 1970s.

Short Story Collections by Böll

Eighteen Stories. Trans. by Leila Vennewitz. McGraw 1971 $6.95. ISBN 0-07-006416-4

The Stories of Heinrich Böll. Trans. by Leila Vennewitz. McGraw 1987 $9.95. ISBN 0-07-006422-9

Nonfiction by Böll

Irish Journal. 1957. Trans. by Leila Vennewitz. McGraw 1971 $6.95. ISBN 0-07-006415-6. Seventeen sketches of Ireland in the mid–1950s updated with an epilogue. "Böll has an affinity for Ireland and things Irish, a fresh outlook and an uncluttered style" (*PW*).

Book about Böll

Reid, James H. *Heinrich Böll: A German for His Time.* Berg Pubs. 1988 $29.95. ISBN 0-85496-533-5

BONHOEFFER, DIETRICH. 1906–1945

[See Volume 4.]

BORCHERT, WOLFGANG. 1921–1947

Borchert grew up under the Nazi regime. During the war he was imprisoned and even sentenced to death for his "defeatist" attitude. He died at the age of 26, the night before the Hamburg premiere of his great success, *The Outsider* (*The*

Man Outside). Surrealistic in technique, the play concerns the return of a maimed German prisoner of war who finds everything destroyed, all hope shattered, even the symbolic "God" perplexed. The only one who flourishes is the undertaker. The hero's pitiful efforts to make a place for himself end in failure. "If there is one word that could possibly sum up the spirit of *The Outsider*," says Wellwarth in his introduction to *Postwar German Theater*, "it is outrage. The play is . . . a graphic and mercilessly unrestrained excoriation of the sinister and diabolical system that had destroyed Germany so completely, both morally and physically. [It] remains important first because it is an excellent drama itself, the only completed play by one of Germany's greatest modern poetic geniuses; second, because it is the most perfect expression of postwar German youth's disillusionment with the system which had ruined their country and their own best years; and third, because it is the only really successful re-creation of the World War I art form known as Expressionism."

PLAY BY BORCHERT

The Man Outside. 1947. Trans. by A. D. Porter. New Dir. Pr. rev. ed. 1971 $6.95. ISBN 0-8112-0011-6

BRANT (or BRANDT), SEBASTIAN. 1457?–1521

Sebastian Brant was born in Strassburg and studied at Basel, where he became a lecturer. When Basel joined the Swiss Confederacy, he returned to Strassburg and became the town clerk. He was the author of a number of political and religious pamphlets. KATHERINE ANNE PORTER (see Vol. 1) drew on *Das Narrenschiff* (1497) for her novel *Ship of Fools*.

His famous parody of the late medieval period depicts life as a paradise for simpletons. It is a series of rhymed sermons excoriating sin and folly with grotesque satire. The crew of a seabound vessel is made up of 112 fools, each representing a "fashionable foible" of man. In their foolishness, they perish. This was the first book written in German to achieve great international popularity. It was translated into Low German, Latin, French, English, and other languages. A famous early edition of the work was translated by Alexander Barclay in 1509.

POETRY BY BRANT

Ship of Fools. 1497. 2 vols. Trans. by Alexander Barclay. AMS Pr. repr. of 1874 ed. $75.00. ISBN 0-404-01065-2. (with the title *Shyp of Folys of the Worlde*).

BRECHT, BERTOLT. 1898–1956

Eric Bentley has said, "The German avant-garde in drama is Brecht. . . . His work is fresh, vital, and pertinent enough to give a new direction to theatrical history." Brecht left Germany because of Hitler in 1933, and many of his plays, radio scripts, and poems were written against Hitlerism. He was one of the editors of a short-lived anti-Nazi magazine in Moscow (1936–39) and came to the United States in 1941. In 1949 his wife, Helen Weigel, starred successfully in his play *Mother Courage and Her Children* (1941), a Marxist indictment of the economic motives behind internal aggression" (Robert Brustein). Many of Brecht's plays are produced regularly on the U.S. stage. Brecht has also found a large audience as librettist for Kurt Weill's *Threepenny Opera*, an adaptation of John Gay's *Beggar's Opera*. His most ambitious venture in verse drama, *Saint Joan of the Stockyards* (1933), was written in Germany shortly before Hitler came to power.

Brecht was "a playwright with a point of view not only toward society but toward the theater. He saw the stage as a platform for the promulgation of a message. His aim . . . was to 'develop the means of entertainment into an object of instruction and to change certain institutions from places of amusement into organs of public communication'" (*N.Y. Times*). He called himself an epic realist. Howard Taubman has defined the Berlin Epic Theater concept, developed by Brecht and the director Erwin Piscator, in its simplest terms (it involved a good deal more than this and had a tremendous impact on world drama) as a theater "which aims to make one think rather than feel."

On his 1947 American visit, he was summoned to Washington by the House Un-American Activities Committee, before which he testified. He firmly denied that he had ever been a member of the Communist Party. How radical Brecht really was has been the subject of considerable controversy; but, for literary purposes, his politics need only be judged as they contributed to his artistry.

In his final years Brecht experimented with his own theater and company—the Berliner Ensemble—which put on his plays under his direction and which continued after his death with the assistance of his wife. Brecht aspired to create political theater, and it is difficult to evaluate his work in purely aesthetic terms. It is likely that the demise of Marxist governments in Eastern Europe will influence his reputation over the next decade, though the changes are difficult to predict.

Plays by Brecht

Baal, A Man's a Man, and The Elephant Calf. Trans. by Eric Bentley. Grove Pr. 1989 $8.95. ISBN 0-8021-3159-X. Drama from Brecht's early, expressionist phase.

Galileo. 1942. Trans. by Eric Bentley. Grove Pr. 1966 $5.95. ISBN 0-8021-3059-3. Galileo's recanting of his scientific discoveries during the Inquisition. Widely interpreted as a commentary on the relationship of Brecht, represented by Galileo, and the East German government.

The Jewish Wife and Other Short Plays. Trans. by Eric Bentley. Grove Pr. 1965 $5.95. ISBN 0-8021-5098-5. Contains *The Informer, In Search of Justice, The Exception and the Rule, The Measure Taken, The Elephant Calf,* and *Salzburg Dance of Death.*

Jungle of Cities and Other Plays. Trans. by Verschoyle N. Goold. Grove Pr. 1966 $9.95. ISBN 0-8021-5149-3. Contains *Drums in the Night* and *Roundheads and Peakheads.*

Manual of Piety. Trans. by Eric Bentley. Grove Pr. 1992 $9.95. ISBN 0-8021-3245-6

The Mother. 1932. Trans. by Lee Baxandall. Grove Pr. 1989 $8.95. ISBN 0-8021-3160-3. Brecht's dramatic adaptation of Gorky's novel.

Mother Courage and Her Children. 1941. Trans. by Eric Bentley. Grove Pr. 1987 $6.95. ISBN 0-8021-3082-8. Set in the Thirty Years War, a woman acts ruthlessly so she and her family can survive.

Saint Joan of the Stockyards. 1933. Ind. U. Pr. 1970 $25.00. ISBN 0-253-17671-9. A sardonic look at the story of Joan of Arc set in a factory and presented in the style of socialist realism. Portrays Joan as overly zealous and idealistic.

Threepenny Opera. 1928. Trans. by Eric Bentley and Desmond Vesey. Grove Pr. 1964 $5.95. ISBN 0-8021-5039-X

Poetry by Brecht

Bertolt Brecht Poems, 1913–1956. Ed. by John Willett and Ralph Manheim. Heinemann Ed. 1985 $14.95. ISBN 0-413-15210-3. The early poems of Brecht are traditional in form and filled with images of destruction and despair. In his later poems, he sought a maximum simplicity of diction.

Nonfiction by Brecht

Brecht Letters. Trans. by John Willett and Ralph Manheim. Routledge Chapman & Hall 1989 $39.95. ISBN 0-415-90139-1

Brecht on Theatre. Trans. by John Willett. Hill & Wang 1964 $9.95. ISBN 0-8090-0542-5. Especially notable for Brecht's theory of "alienation" or psychic distance between the audience and the play.

BOOKS ABOUT BRECHT

Bentley, Eric. *Brecht Memoir.* Northwestern U Pr. 1990 $19.95 ISBN 0-933826-84-2. Scholarly look at Brecht's life and work.

Gray, Ronald D. *Brecht the Dramatist.* Cambridge U. Pr. 1976 $42.50. ISBN 0-521-20937-4. A balanced, comprehensive discussion of Brecht's life and work concluding that, despite Brecht's artistry, a facile optimism limits the relevance of his drama.

Hayman, Ronald. *Brecht: A Biography.* OUP 1983 $29.95. ISBN 0-19-520434-4

Lyon, James K. *Bertolt Brecht in America.* Princeton U. Pr. 1980 $15.95. ISBN 0-691-01394-2

Rouse, John. *Brecht and the West German Theater.* UMI Res. Collect 1989 $39.95. ISBN 0-8357-2006-3. Analyzes Brecht's work in the context of German politics.

BROCH, HERMANN. 1886–1951

Born in Vienna, this novelist, philosopher, and playwright came to the United States in 1938, was awarded a Guggenheim Fellowship (1941–42), a membership in the American Institute of Arts and Letters (1942), and a Rockefeller Fellowship for Philosophical and Psychological Research at Princeton (1942–44). He had been a mathematician, engineer, and director of a Viennese textile concern. His remarkable prose trilogy describing three stages in the disintegration of modern European society, *The Sleepwalkers* (1932), is "a striking example of a new type of European cultural portraiture in which scientific speculation and poetic imagination are combined to represent the incoherent variety of contemporary experience" (Victor Lange). *The Death of Virgil* (1945), whom Broch regarded "as a prototype of the modern man . . . depicts the last eighteen hours of Virgil's life—an obvious parallel to Joyce's work. . . . Broch's vision of the immanence of death will probably be regarded as his most original contribution to human experience. His evocation of the totality and simultaneity of life is his greatest achievement in literature" (Theodore Ziolkowski).

WORKS BY BROCH

The Death of Virgil. 1945. Trans. by Jean S. Untermeyer. N. Point Pr. 1983 repr. of 1945 ed. $16.95. ISBN 0-86547-115-0. A work combining elements of the novel and essay, which deliberately eludes classification in any genre.

The Sleepwalkers: A Trilogy of Hermann Broch. 1932. Trans. by Edwin Muir. N. Point Pr. 1985 repr. of 1964 ed. $16.95. ISBN 0-86547-200-9. A representation of Prussian society at the end of the nineteenth century, between the old aristocratic order and modernity, like a person between sleep and waking.

BÜCHNER, GEORG. 1813–1837

The life of Georg Büchner was short, intense, and tragic—and extremely significant for the development of modern drama. He started a literary revolution that is continuing still. His three modern plays, *Danton's Death* (1835), *Leonce and Lena* (1850), and *Woyzeck* (1850), were greatly ahead of their time in their penetrating dramatic and psychological treatment. They served as an impetus for contemporary schools of drama as different as Ionesco's Theater of the Absurd and Brecht's Epic Theater. Büchner was particularly modern in his portrayal of isolated individuals, who often talk past one another. He was the first major dramatist to present events in an episodic manner and dispense with logically constructed plots. Alban Berg based the libretto of his opera *Wozzeck* on *Woyzeck*. *Danton's Death,* a powerful drama of the French Revolution, is, like *Woyzeck,* still popular.

Plays by Büchner

Danton's Death. 1835. Trans. by Howard Brenton. TSL Pr. 1983 $4.50. ISBN 0-939858-02-9. Danton, the aesthete, the victim of the revolution he helped create.

Leonce and Lena. 1850. Trans. by Hedwig Rappolt. TSL Pr. 1983 $4.50. ISBN 0-939858-03-7. A tragi-comedy of two bored aristocrats.

Woyzeck. 1850. Trans. by John MacKendrick. Heinemann Ed. 1988 $9.95. ISBN 0-413-38820-4. A play based on the first legal case in which suicide was used as a defense, and a psychological drama in which plot is of relatively minimal importance.

Work by Büchner

The Complete Works and Letters. Continuum 1986 $27.50. ISBN 0-8264-0301-8. Collection of all of Büchner's writings.

Book about Büchner

Grimm, Reinhold. *Love, Lust, and Rebellion: New Approaches to Georg Büchner.* U. of Wis. Pr. 1985 $25.00. ISBN 0-299-09860-5. A thorough review of criticism.

BUSCH, WILHELM. 1832–1908

Wilhelm Busch is, after Grimm, by far the most popular author of books for children in the German language. His *Max and Moritz* (1865), a story of two naughty boys whose pranks finally bring a well-deserved retribution, is reputed to be the best-selling illustrated book in all of literature.

Unlike many authors of books for children, Busch is almost completely without sentimentality or facile optimism. His cartoons and verses, on the contrary, contain social satire far more harsh than that usually found in books for either children or adults. He often sought out the society of animals and children, simply because he found so much corruption among his fellow men and women. But what might have been a very bitter perspective is relieved considerably by the humor with which it is depicted. Busch modernized the fable, a genre that, since Lessing, had been seldom employed in German literature.

Works by Busch

The Genius of Wilhelm Busch. U. CA Pr. 1982 $65.00. ISBN 0-520-03897-5. Includes satire for both adults and children.

German Satirical Writings: Wilhelm Busch and others. Trans. by Wilhelm Lotze and Volkmar Sander. Continuum 1984 $27.50. ISBN 0-8264-0284-4. Includes satire for both adults and children.

Max and Moritz. 1865. Ed. by Arthur H. Klein. Dover 1962 $4.95. ISBN 0-486-20181-3. Complete with Busch's famous illustrations.

CANETTI, ELIAS. 1905– (Nobel Prize 1981)

Born in Bulgaria into a Sephardic Jewish family, Canetti was educated in Germany, Switzerland, and Austria. He holds a Ph.D. from the University of Vienna (1929) and, since 1938, has been a resident of England. Canetti became known first for his novel *Auto-da-Fé* (1938) and for his plays. More recently a good many of his essays have been translated. A dominant theme in his work is the conflict between the attempt at individual self-definition and the autonomous life and driving force of the masses.

Canetti has been awarded the Vienna Prize (1966), the Critics Prize (Germany 1967), the Great Austrian State Prize (1967), the Büchner Prize (1972), the Sachs Prize (1975), the Hebbel Prize (1980), and the Nobel Prize for Literature (1981).

NOVEL BY CANETTI

Auto-da-Fé. 1938. Trans. by D. V. Wedgewood. FS&G 1984 $12.95. ISBN 0-374-51879-3

NONFICTION BY CANETTI

The Conscience of Words. 1975. Trans. by Joachim Neugroschel. FS&G 1984 $8.95. ISBN 0-374-51881-5

Crowds and Power. 1960. Trans. by Carol Stewart. FS&G 1984 $14.95. ISBN 0-374-51820-3. An analysis of the way individuals are submerged in a collective identity, in countries like Nazi Germany.

The Tongue Set Free: Remembrance of a European Childhood. 1977. Trans. by Joachim Neugroschel. FS&G 1983 $9.95. ISBN 0-374-51802-5

The Torch in My Ear. 1980. Trans. by Joachim Neugroschel. FS&G 1983 $9.95. ISBN 0-374-51802-5

CELAN, PAUL. 1920–1970

Paul Celan was born in Czernowitz, Romania, to Jewish parents, who spoke German in the home. His mother and father were both deported to concentration camps during Nazi occupation and killed. Celan managed to hide for some time and then survived the war in a Romanian detention camp. After the war, he worked for a time as an editor and translator; he went to Paris to lecture on German literature. Celan began to receive recognition as a poet with the publication of his volume *Mohn und Gedächtnis* (*Poppy and Memory*) (1952) and continued to publish steadily until his suicide in 1970.

Divided between conflicting loyalties and cultures, Celan created a unique idiom. Despite the traumatic experience of Nazi occupation, he chose to devote himself to the study of German literature. His poetry is one of the most radical attempts to reconstruct the German language and literature in the aftermath of the Holocaust.

POETRY BY CELAN

Poems of Paul Celan. Trans. by Michael Hamburger. Persea Bks. 1989-90 $24.95. ISBN 0-89255-140-2. A selection of poetry from several volumes.

WORK BY CELAN

Collected Prose. Trans. by Katherine Washburn and Margaret Guillemin. Sheep Meadow 1990 $15.95. ISBN 0-935296-92-1

BOOK ABOUT CELAN

Chalfen, Israel. *Paul Celan: A Biography of His Youth.* Trans. by Maximilian Bleyleben. Persea Bks. 1991 $24.95. ISBN 0-89255-162-3. Sheds a pure and painful light on the education of a great twentieth-century poet and the destroyed world that nurtured him.

CHAMISSO, ADELBERT VON (LOUIS CHARLES ADÉLAIDE DE CHAMISSO). 1781–1838

This German romantic writer and naturalist was born in France and forced to flee at the time of the French Revolution. He was a member of the literary circle of Mme. de Staël near Geneva. Some of his verse was set to music by Schumann. He is best known for his humorous tale of *Peter Schlemihl* (1814), the man who sold his shadow to the devil.

NOVEL BY CHAMISSO

Peter Schlemihl: The Shadowless Man. 1814. Telegraph Bks. repr. of 1981 ed. o.p. Introduction by Joseph Jacobs.

NONFICTION BY CHAMISSO

A Voyage Around the World with the Romazov Exploring Expedition in the Years 1815–18. Trans. by Henry Katz. UH Pr. 1986 $32.50. ISBN 0-8248-0983-1. A somewhat romanticized travelogue of what were then considered very exotic lands.

DÖBLIN, ALFRED. 1878–1957

Novelist, playwright, poet, essayist, Alfred Döblin was one of the most prolific writers of his time. He was also a practicing physician in Berlin's working-class district of Alexanderplatz. His novel of this name (1930) is considered his best work, and represents, in its montage technique, Döblin's experimental attitude toward prose writing. Döblin fled the Nazi regime in 1933 and lived for a while in the United States. Later he became a French citizen and a convert to the Roman Catholic Church.

NOVELS BY DÖBLIN

Berlin, Alexanderplatz: The Story of Franz Biberkopf. 1930. Trans. by Eugene Jolas. Continuum 1984 $12.95. ISBN 0-8044-6121-X. The most famous of Döblin's works, recently made into a film by the director Werner Fasbinder. Using modern techniques such as stream of consciousness, tells of a Berlin worker who turns to a life of crime.

Men without Mercy. 1935. Trans. by Phyllis Blewitt. Fertig 1976 repr. of 1937 ed. $48.00. ISBN 0-86527-277-8

Tales of a Long Night. 1956. Trans. by Robert and Rita Kimber. Fromm Intl. Pub. 1984 $18.95. ISBN 0-88064-016-2. A German soldier after the war, confronting unpleasant revelations about his family.

NONFICTION BY DÖBLIN

Karl and Rosa, November 1918: A German Revolution. Trans. by John E. Woods. Fromm Intl. Pub. 1983 $19.95. ISBN 0-88064-010-3. The aborted revolution in Munich, in which Karl Liebknecht and Rosa Luxembourg emerged as martyrs.

DROSTE-HÜLSHOFF, ANNETTE VON. 1797–1848

Annette von Droste-Hülshoff was born in a castle near Munster to an aristocratic Westphalian family. Shy, reclusive, and often troubled by ill health, she led an outwardly uneventful life on her family's estate. Her writing shows an emotional life of much intensity, but without the romantic impulse to self-dramatization. Though attracted by socialist ideals, she remained a devout Catholic, and her religion probably contributes to the serenity that pervades her poetry. She is best known for her novella *Die Judenbuche* (The Beech-Tree of the Jews) (1842), which gives a vivid and detailed portrayal of life among the peasants of Westphalia. Her verse is notable for precise observation of nature.

NOVEL BY DROSTE-HÜLSHOFF

Die Judenbuche: A Bilingual Edition. 1842. Blackwell Pubs. 1989 $15.95. ISBN 0-631-15841-3. Introduction by Peter Foulkes.

BOOKS ABOUT DROSTE-HÜLSHOFF

Guthrie, John. *Annette von Droste-Hülshoff: A Reassessment of Her Life and Writings.* Berg Pubs. 1989 $32.00. ISBN 0-85496-174-7

Morgan, Mary Elizabeth. *Annette von Droste-Hülshoff: A Biography.* P. Lang Pubs. 1984 $26.10. ISBN 0-8204-0036-X

DÜRRENMATT (or DUERRENMATT), FRIEDRICH. 1921–

Dürrenmatt was born near Bern, Switzerland, the son of a Protestant clergyman. He studied philosophy and theology and originally planned to become a painter. "All of a sudden," he has said, "I began to write, and I just had no time to finish my University degree." He has called his first play, *It Is Written* (1947), "a wild story of Anabaptists during the Reformation." When it was first produced in Zurich, it caused a minor theatrical scandal because of its somewhat unorthodox sentiments. *The Marriage of Mr. Mississippi,* his first successful comedy, was produced in Munich in 1952 and, as adapted by Maximillian Slater with the title *Fools are Passing Through,* had a brief off-Broadway production in 1958. With this play he became established as one of the most popular European dramatists writing in German. His seventh play, *The Visit* (1956), which starred Alfred Lunt and Lynn Fontanne on Broadway, received the N.Y. Drama Critics Circle Award in 1959. Brooks Atkinson called it "devastating. A bold, grisly drama of negativism and genius."

In an interview published in *Esquire,* the author was asked what reaction he most preferred his audiences to have to his work. "Fright!" he replied. "That is the modern form of empathy." *The Judge and His Hangman* (1952), his most popular detective story, contrasts human law with cosmic justice.

PLAYS BY DÜRRENMATT

The Physicists. 1962. Trans. by James Kirkup. Grove Pr. 1982 $6.95. ISBN 0-8021-5088-8. After Hiroshima, physicists who find normal life unbearable take refuge in a mental hospital, pretending to be insane.

The Visit. 1956. Trans. by Patrick Bowles. Grove Pr. 1987 $6.95. ISBN 0-8021-3066-6. Dürrenmatt's most popular play, in which a wealthy heiress returns to her hometown to take a terrible revenge against those who wronged her. Explores characteristic themes such as the nature of guilt and complicity.

NOVEL BY DÜRRENMATT

The Judge and His Hangman (and *The Quarry*). 1952, 1953. Godine 1983 $7.95. ISBN 0-87923-437-7. At once a detective thriller and a philosophical exploration of guilt and retribution.

WORK BY DÜRRENMATT

Plays and Essays. Ed. by Volkmar Sander. Continuum 1982 $27.50. ISBN 0-8264-0257-7

BOOK ABOUT DÜRRENMATT

Whitton, Kenneth S. *Dürrenmatt: Reinterpretation in Retrospect.* Berg Pubs. 1990 $45.00. ISBN 0-85496-650-1

EICHENDORFF, JOSEPH, FREIHERR VON. 1788–1857

Born in Silesia, Eichendorff studied in Breslau, Halle, Heidelberg, and Vienna. A devout Roman Catholic, he expresses a serene attitude toward life in all his writings. His poems are beautifully balanced lyrics that embody the romantic and transcendental fashions of his time. Among his novellas, *Memoirs of a Good-for-Nothing* (1821) is especially delightful in its lighthearted spontaneity.

Novel by Eichendorff

Memoirs of a Good-for-Nothing. 1821. Trans. by Leopold von Lowenberg-Wertheim. Riverrun NY 1981 o.p. Follows a good-hearted but naive young man, who wanders out into the world to find love.

Book about Eichendorff

Schwartz, Egon. *Joseph von Eichendorff.* Irvington 1972 $17.95. ISBN 0-8290-1751-8

FEUCHTWANGER, LION (pseud. of J. L. Wetcheek). 1884–1958

Feuchtwanger, novelist and dramatist, was born in Munich, the son of a wealthy Jewish manufacturer. The rise of the Nazis drove him to France, and after the collapse of that country he escaped with great difficulty to Spain; he reached the United States in 1940. A major work is his trilogy on the Jewish historian: *Josephus* (1932), *The Jew of Rome* (1935), and *Josephus and the Emperor* (1942). He was best known in Germany as a dramatist, but his international success was due to his revival of the historical novel written with modern psychological understanding.

Novels by Feuchtwanger

The Oppermanns. 1923. Carroll & Graf 1983 $8.95. ISBN 0-88184-063-7

The Jew Süss. 1925. Carroll & Graf 1984 $18.95. ISBN 0–88184–073–4. A representation of Germany in the eighteenth century, centered on the figure of Joseph Süss-Oppenheimer, a powerful Jewish statesman and banker, who fell victim to political upheavals and was publicly displayed in a cage.

Success. 1930. Carroll & Graf 1984 $10.95. ISBN 0-88184-078-5

Josephus: A Historical Romance. 1932. Macmillan 1973 $12.95. ISBN 0-689-70345-7

Book about Feuchtwanger

Kahn, Lothar. *Insight and Action: The Life and Work of Lion Feuchtwanger.* Fairleigh Dickinson 1976 $28.50. ISBN 0-8386-1314-4

FONTANE, THEODOR. 1819–1898

Fontane's fictional studies of nineteenth-century Berlin society, written in his late maturity, secured him a firm place in literature as a master of the German realist novel; his declared aim was to show "the undistorted reflection of the life we lead." "He introduced his people in spirited conversations at picnics and banquets, and developed a broad and yet intimate perspective of background conditions; he was less interested in plots, and often would make a point by silence" (Ernst Rose). *Effi Briest* (1895), his masterpiece, is a revealing portrait of an individual victimized by outmoded standards. Fontane, on whom Sir Walter Scott (see Vol. 1) had made a deep impression, traveled to England as a journalist and wrote two books based on his experiences: *A Summer in London* (1854) and *Across the Tweed* (1860). He also wrote historical novels, poetry, and dramatic criticism.

Novels by Fontane

Delusions, Confusions, and the Poggenpuhl Family. 1887. Ed. by Peter Demetz. Continuum 1989 $27.50. ISBN 0-8264-0325-5. The portrait of an aristocratic family that has fallen on difficult financial times.

Effi Briest. 1895. Trans. by Douglas Parmee. Viking Penguin 1976 $7.95. ISBN 0-14-044190-5. The consequences of the affair of a young, bored married woman: her lover dead in a duel fought for form, not jealousy.

Jenny Treibel. 1892. Trans. by Ulf Zimmermann. Continuum 1977 $7.50. ISBN 0-8044-6155-4. The revelation of the true values of a middle-class, supposedly idealistic woman when her son wishes to marry a penniless girl.

WORK BY FONTANE

Short Novels and Other Writings. Continuum 1982 $27.50. ISBN 0-8264-0250-X. Foreword by Peter Demetz.

BOOK ABOUT FONTANE

Bance, Alan. *Theodor Fontane: The Major Novels.* Cambridge U. Pr. 1982 $54.50. ISBN 0-521-24532-X

FRISCH, MAX. 1911–1991

Max Frisch was one of the outstanding literary figures in Europe for some 30 years. He was a Swiss architect by profession and a dramatist and novelist by avocation. His important dramatic works, *The Chinese Wall* (1947), *The Firebugs* (1958), and *Andorra* (1961) are out of print. The latter created a sensation in Europe through its portrayal of anti-Semitism. Of his novels, *I'm Not Stiller* (1954) remains his masterpiece.

NOVELS BY FRISCH

Bluebeard. 1982. Trans. by Geoffrey Skelton. HarBraceJ 1984 $3.95. ISBN 0-15-613198-6. A retelling of the fairy tale "Bluebeard" in modern times, in which a man falsely accused of murdering his sixth wife and is acquitted, nevertheless desires punishment and professes guilt.

Gantenbein. 1964. Trans. by Michael Bullock. HarBraceJ 1982 repr. of 1965 ed. $7.95. ISBN 0-15-634407-6. A modernist novel, narrated by a man who pretends to be blind, so others will reveal themselves to him.

Homo Faber. 1957. Trans. by Michael Bullock. HarBraceJ 1971 repr. of 1959 ed. $9.95. ISBN 0-15-642135-6. The life meditation of a "successful" engineer who unknowingly committed incest with his daughter and is trying to understand what went wrong.

I'm Not Stiller. 1954. Random 1958 o.p. An "elaborate and powerful illustration of Kierkegaard's thesis that man's road to freedom lies through self-acceptance. . . . What gives it stature as a novel is Frisch's dissection of the tormented and tormenting relationship between Stiller and his wife." (*N.Y. Herald Tribune*)

Man in the Holocene. 1979. Trans. by Geoffrey Skelton. HarBraceJ 1983 $8.95. ISBN 0-15-682747-6. Nature reclaims the home of an elderly man, whose mental powers decay.

BOOKS ABOUT FRISCH

Probst, Gerhard, and Jay F. Bodine, eds. *Perspectives on Max Frisch.* U. Pr. of KY 1982 $21.00. ISBN 0-8131-1438-1. A collection of essays.

Reschke, Klaus. *Life as a Man: Contemporary Male-Female Relationships in the Novels of Max Frisch.* P. Lang Pubs. 1990 $56.00. ISBN 0-8204-1163-9

GEORGE, STEFAN. 1868–1933

Aristocratic and recondite, George deliberately wrote difficult poetry for those few he believed destined to understand him. Gathered about him was a group of gifted, often physically beautiful young men, the so-called George Kreis (George Circle), to whom he charged the spreading of his ideas. George's poems continue to influence young writers—not so much for their themes as for their austere formal style and perfection of diction, a diction expanded by his vast knowledge of languages, ancient and modern. Many young poets today would aspire to Bithell's praise: "George paints with vowels or plays on them just as a pianist plays on keys; he tangles his construction; he swathes the inner meaning of the poem in a floating veil of symbol."

POETRY BY GEORGE

The Works of Stefan George. Trans. by Olga Marx and Ernst Morwitz. U. of NC Pr. 1974 $32.50. ISBN 0-8078-8078-7. Faithful and readable translations.

GOETHE, JOHANN WOLFGANG VON. 1749–1832

The long career of Goethe embraces an exceptional variety of forms and styles. He began as a young rebel of the school known as Storm and Stress, celebrating a life of passion in his play *Götz von Berlichingen* (1773) and his novel *The Sorrows of Young Werther* (1774), which brought him instant fame. He then settled in Weimar at the invitation of the young Duke Karl August, whose patronage enabled Goethe to pursue a wide range of interests. The emotionalism of his early work gave way to a new classicism, which emphasized order and restraint. Goethe was joined in Weimar by SCHILLER, and the two formed a productive friendship which lasted until Schiller's death. With *Wilhelm Meister*, the final installment of which was published in 1821, Goethe established the novel of education (*Bildungsroman*) as an important genre of German literature. His most important work, however, is probably the poetic drama *Faust* (1832), which he completed and placed in a sealed envelope 5 days before his death (and over 60 years after he had first conceived the project), to be published posthumously.

Goethe also devoted much time to scientific work. With his rediscovery of the intermaxillary bone in human beings, he argued for a closer kinship between people and animals than most of his contemporaries wished to acknowledge. Goethe himself once stated that his greatest achievement was not a work of literature but his theory of colors, with which he opposed the optical work of Newton.

Though we probably know far more about Goethe than about any other major figure of world literature, it is difficult to put his work in perspective. During the late nineteenth and early twentieth centuries, the stature of Goethe and Schiller as the foremost writers in German literature was seldom questioned. As the twentieth century progressed, an increasing number of critics such as E. M. Butler, KARL JASPERS (see Vol. 4), and Erich Heller tempered their admiration of Goethe's poetry with doubts about his contemporary relevance. Richard Friedenthal writes at the end of his biography: "Goethe's stature as one of the masterminds in world literature received early recognition and his fame is undisputed, but he still remains something of an enigma. This is true not only of the world at large . . . but of his own countrymen as well, who have never ceased to worship the great 'Olympian,' while often denigrating and even reviling him, and who finally succeeded in enveloping him in a haze of vague admiration that has little to do with the very earthy and very fascinating person he was."

PLAYS BY GOETHE

Collected Works. Vol. 7 *Early Drama & Prose Plays.* 1770s & 1780s. Ed. by Cyrus Hamlin and Frank Ryder. Trans. by Robert M. Browning. Suhrkamp 1988 $29.50. ISBN 3-518-02564-3

Torquato Tasso. 1790. Trans. by Alan and Sandy Brownjohn. Dufour 1986 $15.95. ISBN 0-946162-19-0. A play from Goethe's classical period, exploring the contrast between the poet and the man of action.

Novels by Goethe

Elective Affinities. 1809. Trans. by Elizabeth Mayer and Louise Bogan. Regnery Gateway 1991 $5.95. ISBN 0-89526-956-2. A philosophical novel exploring the contrast between the impersonal ways of nature and the human demand for fidelity.

The Sufferings of Young Werther. 1873. Trans. by B. W. Morgan. Riverrun NY 1980 $9.95. ISBN 0-7145-0542-0. The work that established Goethe's reputation, in which a sensitive young man kills himself for love.

Wilhelm Meister. 1821. 6 vols. Trans. by H. M. Waidson. Riverrun NY 1982 $7.95 ea. ISBNs 0-7145-3675-X, 0-7145-3699-7, 0-7145-3702-0, 0-7145-3827-2, 0-7145-3838-8, 0-7145-3840-X. Portrait of a naive young man who gradually comes to maturity and accepts a modest but useful position in society.

Poetry by Goethe

Faust, Parts 1 & 2. 1832. Trans. by Louis MacNiece. OUP 1960 $12.95. ISBN 0-19-500410-8. The most intricate, ambitious, and controversial of Goethe's works, concerning a man who makes a pact with the Devil.

Roman Elegies and Other Poems. 1795. Trans. by Michael Hamburger. Black Swan CT 1983 $20.00. ISBN 0-933806-16-3. Contains "The Roman Elegies," love poems to Christina Vulpius, whom Goethe eventually married, that are filled with images of temples, palaces, and gardens of Rome.

Nonfiction by Goethe

The Autobiography of Johann Wolfgang Goethe. 1814. 2 vols. Trans. by John Oxenford. U. Ch. Pr. 1975 $15.00 ea. ISBNs 0-226-30056-0, 0-226-30055-2

Theory of Colors. 1806. MIT Pr. 1970 $13.95. ISBN 0-262-57021-1. A theory, though universally regarded as invalid, that remains interesting as an attempt to place science on a humanistic rather than a mechanistic basis.

Books about Goethe

Bielchowsky, Albert. *Life of Goethe.* 3 vols. Trans. by William A. Cooper. AMS Pr. repr. of 1908 ed. $80.00. ISBN 0-404-00870-4. A highly detailed though somewhat dated biography, complete with illustrations.

Blumenberg, Hans. *Work on Myth.* Trans. by Robert M. Wallace. MIT Pr. 1985 $17.95. ISBN 0-262-52133-4. A difficult but rewarding, and extremely influential, study of the legends of Prometheus and Faust, from their inception to the present; devotes special attention to the literary versions of Goethe.

Friedenthal, Richard. *Goethe: His Life and Times.* World Pub. Co. 1965 o.p. A scholarly yet highly readable biography.

Reed, T. J. *Goethe.* OUP 1984 $6.95. ISBN 0-19-287502-7. A concise introduction to Goethe's life and work.

GOTTFRIED VON STRASSBURG. 1170?–1210?

Little is known about Gottfried von Strassburg, the greatest stylist of the medieval German period. Only one work of his, *Tristan and Isolde* (c.1210), has been preserved (indeed, it may well be the only one he ever wrote), and it is incomplete. Gottfried did not identify himself as the poet, and it is only through later sources that his name is linked with *Tristan.* Internal evidence in *Tristan* suggests that Gottfried stopped working on it around 1210 and it is assumed that he died shortly thereafter. Gottfried based his *Tristan* on the *Tristan* of a Latin poet named Thomas. In his prologue Gottfried makes clear that he is writing a love story for those who truly understand love. He calls those people the "noble hearts" and emphasizes that they are not necessarily noble by birth, but rather in attitude. In *Tristan* Gottfried moves far beyond the conventions of courtly love and examines the phenomenon of love in great detail, so that love assumes an individuality of its own and is viewed as a powerful, independent, mystical force in the world, on a level with religion. Gottfried also presents a view of the poets of his day. In the famous "Literary Excursus," he praises Hartmann von Aue for his clarity of style and criticizes an unnamed poet whom he calls "the companion of the hare, leaping willy-nilly over the word heath." It is generally accepted that Gottfried is taking his colleague Wolfram von Eschenbach to task.

Gottfried, probably a native of Strassburg, was a very learned man, well versed in Latin, French, and German. Unlike his brother poets, Hartmann von Aue and Wolfram von Eschenbach, Gottfried was not a knight, but a member of the urban patrician class. He was urbane, sophisticated, learned—more is not known of this great poet.

Poetry by Gottfried von Strassburg

Tristan. c.1210. Trans. by Arthur T. Hatto. Viking Penguin 1960 $4.95. ISBN 0-14-044098-4

Book about Gottfried von Strassburg

Jackson, William T. *Anatomy of Love: A Study of the Tristan of Gottfried von Strassburg.* Col. U. Pr. 1971 o.p. The emotional and erotic nuances of *Tristan,* in the context of medieval society.

GRASS, GÜNTER. 1927–

The outspoken Günter Grass is Germany's outstanding contemporary writer, its wunderkind. He is a poet, novelist, painter, and sculptor. He won an immediate and enormous audience in Europe and the United States with his first novel, *The Tin Drum* (1959), the "allegorical" story of Oskar Matzerath, who decides at the age of three to stop growing, thereby absolving himself of the responsibility of making adult decisions. He is the rogue, the picaresque outsider, who communicates only by banging his ever-present little drum. The story of Oskar's fantastic progress is a scandalous, sardonic satire of Nazi Germany. In *Cat and Mouse* (1961), Grass again journeys into the realm of the grotesque to tell the story of Joachim Mahlke, another antihero—a youth with an enormous Adam's apple, an outsider because of his peculiarity. In the 1967 German film version of *Cat and Mouse,* Lars Brandt, son of foreign minister Willy Brandt, played the leading role. The Interior Ministry, which subsidized the film, threatened to withdraw its funds because of a scene in which Brandt toys with the Iron Cross, one of Germany's highest wartime decorations. "For Grass, the scene symbolizes young Germany playing on the wreck of Hitler's Reich" (*N.Y. Times*).

The Tin Drum, Cat and Mouse, and *Dog Years* (1963) form a kind of trilogy. *Dog Years,* Grass's most ambitious work, is "the story of an incredible odyssey through the jungle of life in Germany just before, during, and after the Hitler era. . . . Monstrous, magnificent, and unforgettable" (*SR*). It concerns a Jew who creates weird scarecrows—the symbols on which Grass again builds his grimly humorous picture of modern man violating all the standards of decency to which he gives lip service.

In his more recent works it is evident that the former enfant terrible has become more moderate. Grass is now facing up to a new generation of Germans, unburdened by guilt and impatient. Rather than barging ahead, he is now advocating slow, deliberate progress as desirable. In his *Aus dem Tagebuch einer Schnecke* (*From the Diary of a Snail,* 1972), Grass presents the snail as a model worthy of imitation.

Grass was born in Danzig, the son of a grocer, and was once a member of the Hitler Youth; at 16 he was drafted for World War II. Taken prisoner, and released after the war, he became first a farm laborer and stonecutter and eventually a sculptor and stage designer, until writing claimed all his time. He was awarded an honorary doctorate by Harvard University in 1976. Grass makes his home in West Berlin, where since 1983 he has been president of the Academy of Art.

NOVELS BY GRASS

Dog Years. 1963. Fawcett 1986 $4.95. ISBN 0-449-21192-4

The Flounder. 1977. HarBraceJ 1989 $11.95. ISBN 0-15-631935-7. An epic retelling of Grimm's fairy tale "The Fisherman and His Wife," to satirize feminism and to present a broad panorama of modern life.

Headbirths; Or, the Germans Are Dying Out. 1980. Fawcett 1983 $3.95. ISBN 0-449-20057-4

The Meeting at Teltge. 1982. HarBraceJ 1990 $8.95. ISBN 0-15-658575-8. A meeting of German authors after the Thirty Years War, who try, unsuccessfully, to reconstruct German culture.

The Rat. 1988. HarBraceJ 1989 $9.95. ISBN 0-15-675830-X. Contains a melange of fable, history, polemic, diatribe, and jeremiad.

The Tin Drum. 1959. Trans. by Ralph Mannheim. Random 1990 $9.95. ISBN 0-679-72575-X

POETRY BY GRASS

In the Egg and Other Poems. Trans. by Michael Hamburger and Christopher Middleton. HarBraceJ 1977 $5.95. ISBN 0-15-672239-9

BOOKS ABOUT GRASS

Hollington, Michael. *Günter Grass: The Writer in a Pluralist Society.* M. Boyars Pubs. 1980 $16.00. ISBN 0-7145-2678-9

Lawson, Richard H. *Günter Grass. Lit. and Life Ser:* Continuum 1984 $18.95. ISBN 0-8044-2500-0

GRILLPARZER, FRANZ. 1791–1872

Grillparzer was the first Austrian writer to achieve international standing. He was born and lived in a Vienna where music was all important and literature was strictly controlled by the church and the imperial court. His career as a playwright and as a minor government official was beset by difficulty. His plays repeatedly state his personal conviction that to be involved in love or in political power is to invite disaster. He never married his fiancée, though he never released her from their betrothal, and died her lodger.

An ardent patriot, he sought to glorify Austria in his historical plays but met with censorship from Prince Metternich's government. After the failure of his play *Weh Dem, Der Lügt* (*Thou Shalt Not Lie*) in 1838, he permitted no new play to be performed or published, though he continued to write for more than 30 years.

PLAYS BY GRILLPARZER

Hero and Leander: The Waves of the Sea and of Love. 1831. Trans. by Arthur Burkhard. M. S. Rosenberg $6.00. ISBN 0-917324-13-7. A retelling of the ancient romantic legend, emphasizing how Hero is unsuited to her priestly office.

King Ottocar: His Rise and Fall. 1825. Trans. by Arthur Burkhard. M. S. Rosenberg $6.00. ISBN 0-917324-14-5. About a ruthless king of medieval Bohemia, destroyed by hubris, who is replaced by Rudolf I, founder of the Hapsburg dynasty. Sometimes regarded as the national play of Austria.

Medea. 1818. Trans. by Arthur Burkhard. M. S. Rosenberg $6.00. ISBN 0-917324-15-3

Plays on Classic Themes. Trans. by Samuel Solomon. Boulevard 1969 $35.00. ISBN 0-910278-25-3

Sappho. Trans. by Arthur Burkhard. Register Pr. 1953 $5.00. ISBN 0-686-74815-8. The Greek poet as a romantic artist whose purity of feeling is not reciprocated or understood by those around her.

Book about Grillparzer

Yates, Douglas. *Franz Grillparzer: A Critical Biography.* Norwood 1980 repr. of 1946 ed. o.p.

GRIMM, JACOB (LUDWIG KARL), 1785–1863, and WILHELM (KARL) GRIMM. 1786–1859

The Grimm brothers are best known for their collection of German fairy tales, the first edition of which appeared in 1812. They were among the first to value fairy tales as cultural treasures, but, contrary to popular belief, they seldom collected tales from illiterate peasants. The majority of their sources were middle-class women.

While the brothers avowed the principle of exact fidelity to oral traditions, they never recorded stories as faithfully from these traditions as they claimed. Yet the Grimms were major innovators, for simply articulating the principle was enough to usher in the scientific study of folklore.

After the first edition, Jacob, the more reclusive brother, devoted himself almost exclusively to philological studies. The more extroverted brother, Wilhelm, who eventually married one of his story sources, undertook further revision of the fairy tales by himself. A combination of artistic and commercial motivations induced Wilhelm to alter the oral versions with increasing freedom over the six subsequent editions, the last of which was published in 1856.

Both brothers eventually learned well over a score of languages, and they edited many books of myths and legends from around the world. Jacob began the first etymological dictionary of the German language, a massive project that served as a model for later works such as *The Oxford English Dictionary.* In addition, Jacob called attention to the linguistic similarities among Indo-European languages and discovered the law of consonantal shift.

Story Collections by the Grimms

The Complete Grimms' Fairy Tales. 1856. Trans. by Margaret Hunt. Ed. by James Stern. Pantheon 1976 $14.95. ISBN 0-394-70930-6. Does an especially fine job of capturing the earthy charm of the original.

Deutsche Sagen: German Legends. 1816. Ed. by Richard M. Dorson. Ayer repr. of 1891 ed. $37.50. ISBN 0-405-10097-3. The first systematic collection of German legends, in which the Grimm brothers are far more consistently scholarly than in their entertaining treatment of fairy tales.

Short Story Collection by Wilhelm Grimm

Dear Milli. Trans. by Ralph Manheim. FS&G 1988 $16.95. ISBN 0-374-31762-3. A literary tale for children, only recently discovered.

NONFICTION BY JACOB GRIMM

Teutonic Mythology. 1835. 4 vols. Trans. by James S. Stallybrass. Peter Smith 1990 $15.00 ea. ISBN 0-8446-2168-4. A pioneering work on the beliefs of the ancient Germanic tribes that remains highly informative today.

BOOKS ABOUT THE GRIMMS

Bettelheim, Bruno. *Uses of Enchantment: The Meaning and Importance of Fairy Tales*. Random 1989 $10.95. ISBN 0-679-72393-5. An enormously influential psychoanalytic study of fairy tales by the Grimm brothers and others.

Sax, Boria. *The Frog King: On Legends, Fables, Fairy Tales, and Anecdotes of Animals*. Pace Univ. Pr. 1990 $40.95. ISBN 0-944473-01-6. A study of animal tales, with special emphasis on "The Frog King" and other fairy tales by Grimm.

Tatar, Maria. *The Hard Facts of Grimms' Fairy Tales*. Princeton U. Pr. 1987 $9.95. ISBN 0-691-01487-6. Probably the most thorough and balanced discussion of Grimms' fairy tales available in English.

Zipes, Jack. *The Brothers Grimm: From Enchanted Forests to the Modern World*. Routledge Chapman & Hall 1988–89 $35.00. ISBN 0-415-90081-6. Contains an excellent summary of recent research on the Grimm brothers and their tales.

GRIMMELSHAUSEN, JOHANN (HANS) JAKOB CHRISTOFFEL VON. 1620?–1676

A popular didactic novel of the Reformation period, Grimmelshausen's *Simplicissimus* (*Adventures of a Simpleton)* (1669) is largely responsible for establishing the novel as an important genre in German literature. It is an early example of the picaresque genre. The hero of the novel, who shares some of his creator's adventures, is no conventional "fool" reflecting on the follies of mankind, but a real soldier of fortune in the Thirty Years War. The misery he experiences forces him to search for an answer to the riddle of human existence. One of the sequels to *Simplicissimus* is *Landstörtzerin Courasche* (1669), a bawdy, picaresque tale of a woman camp follower in an ugly world, "a symbol of the age and a lively individual [who] comes out on top in any situation with unimpaired self-assurance if not virtue" (*LJ*). *The False Messiah* (1672), in which a thief poses as the Prophet Elijah, "paints an equally grotesque picture of the world" (*SR*). Drawing a parallel between the devastation experienced in Germany during the Thirty Years War and during World War II, GÜNTER GRASS found the work of Grimmelshausen a great source of inspiration. The combination of earnest moralism and cynicism renders the work of Grimmelshausen relatively modern, and it is open to a very wide range of interpretations.

NOVEL BY GRIMMELSHAUSEN

Adventures of a Simpleton. 1669. Trans. by Walter Wallich. Continuum $8.95. ISBN 0-8044-6229-1. A graceful and accurate translation.

HANDKE, PETER. 1942–

An Austrian playwright and novelist, Handke was born in Carinthia. In both his plays and novels, Handke protests against established literary conventions and experiments with new forms: his first production, *Offending the Audience*, had neither characters nor plot. His novels of the 1970s are largely autobiographical. Handke was awarded the Büchner Prize in 1973 and in 1979 refused to accept the Kafka Prize. A graduate of the University of Graz, he has lived in West Berlin and Paris and now makes his home in Salzburg.

Plays by Handke

Kaspar and Other Plays. Trans. by Michael Roloff. FS&G 1970 $8.95. ISBN 0-374-50824-0. Includes *Kaspar, Offending the Audience,* and *Self-Accusation*.

Slow Homecoming. 1979. Trans. by Ralph Manheim. FS&G 1985 $16.95. ISBN 0-374-26635-2.

A Sorrow beyond Dreams. 1972. Trans. by Ralph Manheim. FS&G 1975 o.p. Addresses the suicide of Handke's mother, who survived war and poverty to be crushed by prosperity.

The Weight of the World. 1975. Trans. by Ralph Manheim. FS&G 1984 $16.95. ISBN 0-374-28745-7. A successful official, thinking himself a murderer, is suddenly alienated from everything in his former life.

Book about Handke

Hern, Nicholas. *Peter Handke. Lit. and Life Ser.* Continuum 1972 $18.95. ISBN 0-8044-2380-6. A biography, with discussion of Handke's important works.

HARTMANN VON AUE, c.1160–c.1220

Born in Swabia, Hartmann von Aue is generally credited with having introduced Arthurian romance into German literature. It seems evident that he attended a monastery school and visited France during his youth. He entered service with a lord of Aue to whom he was deeply attached. When his master died, Hartmann joined the crusade of Henry VI in 1197. He wrote epics, love songs, and crusading lyrics, as well as a "Büchlein," a lover's complaint in the form of a debate between the heart and the body. His *Erec* (c.1180) is the first known Arthurian romance in German. It closely follows its French model, the *Eric* of Chrétien de Troyes. Hartmann's *Der Arme Heinrich* and his *Iwein* (c.1190) are famous and influential romances.

In the poem *Gregorius* (c.1195), Hartmann virtually created a new genre, the so-called courtly legend, in which an edifying story is told with all the refinements of courtly style. *Gregorius* is a moral tale of sin and suffering in which penance is followed by reward. The hero is the child of an incestuous union of brother and sister. The boy is abandoned, discovered, raised by monks, becomes a knight-errant, saves a lady in distress, and marries her. Later he discovers that she is his mother. In despair he undertakes a prolonged and bitter expiation. His penance is at last accepted, his virtue recognized, and he is crowned pope. Hartmann's version of the ancient Oedipus legend became the source for Wolfram's *Parzival* and for Thomas Mann's *The Holy Sinner*.

Poetry by Hartmann

Erec. c.1180. Trans. by J. W. Thomas. U. of Nebr. Pr. 1982 $17.95. ISBN 0-8032-4408-8

Gregorius. c. 1195. AMS Pr. repr. of 1955 ed. $27.00. ISBN 0-404-50914-2

Iwein. c. 1190. De Gruyter 1981 $28.00. ISBN 3-11-008540-2

HAUPTMANN, GERHART (JOHANN ROBERT). 1862–1946 (Nobel Prize 1912)

Hauptmann, Germany's outstanding playwright of the naturalist school, was by nature an experimenter. He was a strange mixture: sometimes a revolutionary, as in his greatest play, *The Weavers* (1892); sometimes the compassionate creator, as in *Hannele* (1893), about a beggar girl dreaming of heaven. *The Sunken Bell* (1897), his most famous drama, is an allegorical verse play on the quest for an ideal, similar in theme to Ibsen's *Peer Gynt*. Hauptmann won the Nobel Prize in 1912 and was given an honorary degree by Columbia University in 1932, at which occasion he delivered an oration on Goethe.

Hauptmann is one of the most widely performed German playwrights. He stands as a landmark between the classic and the modern theater. "The heroes of his plays were not from either the ruling class or the bourgeoisie, but almost always from the masses. . . . By 1913, Hauptmann's naturalism was known throughout the world" (*N.Y. Times*).

Hauptmann deserves no less fame as a writer of prose. His earlier works, such as *Thiel the Crossing Keeper* (1888), show him at his strongest in the naturalistic mode. His characters are enslaved by their environment and by their own drives, especially the sex drive. In the *Heretic of Soana* (1918) Hauptmann concentrates on the power of the sexual urge in man in the story of the priest who gave up his church for the love of a woman, but he has moved away from the brooding excesses of naturalism.

Frowned upon by the Nazis for having been a prominent figure under the Republic, which once favored nominating him for the presidency, Hauptmann never spoke out against Nazi tyranny but shook hands with Goebbels and accepted a medal. Yet when he died at his home in the Silesian Mountains, he had been about to move to East Berlin at the invitation of the Soviet Military Government. These events were forgotten or ignored during the 1962 centennial celebrations of his birth in the two Germanys. During the memorial week in Cologne, seven different plays of his were performed—three of them by Cologne's own repertory theater and the others by companies from Munich, Düsseldorf, Hamburg, and Göttingen. In West Germany alone, more than 20 of Hauptmann's plays were presented in theaters throughout the country.

PLAYS BY HAUPTMANN

Three Plays: The Weavers, Hannele, The Beaver Coat. Trans. by Horst Frenz and Miles Waggoner. Waveland Pr. 1991 $8.95. ISBN 0-88133-540-1

HEBBEL, FRIEDRICH. 1813–1863

Hebbel, a North German by birth, lived abroad most of his life. The son of a stonemason and a servant girl, his childhood was passed in dire poverty, and his education was scanty and largely self-achieved. His ties to his early patroness, the novelist Amelia Schoppe, and to Elsie Lensing, a woman some years his senior, caused constant stress; and his later travels, though sponsored in part by the Danish King Christian VIII, were marked by financial difficulties. Only in Vienna, where he married the well-known actress Christine Enghaus, did he settle down to a reasonably peaceful existence.

Hebbel wrote plays, short stories, lyric poems, an epic poem, and a great deal of criticism and dramatic theory. His plays are linked with those of the Viennese FRANZ GRILLPARZER as examples of late classicism.

PLAY BY HEBBEL

Herod and Mariamne. 1850. Trans. by Paul H. Curts. AMS Pr. repr. of 1950 ed. $27.00. ISBN 0-404-50903-7. A portrait of the Biblical child-murderer as a romantic, though ruthless, idealist.

BOOK ABOUT HEBBEL

Flygt, Sten G. *Friedrich Hebbel. Twayne's World Authors Ser.* Irvington 1968 $17.95. ISBN 0-8057-2412-5

HEINE, HEINRICH. 1797–1856

Heinrich Heine is the best-known representative of the political and intellectual movement of the nineteenth century called Young Germany. Son of a

Düsseldorf merchant, Heine's early years were ones of misadventure and failure. Born a Jew, he converted to Christianity in order to receive his law degree from the University of Göttingen in 1825. But his first love did not lie with law, and with the publication of the *Travel Sketches* (1826–31) he became a full-time writer. True to the spirit of the Young Germans, Heine idolized things French and eventually settled in Paris in 1831. There he was active as a journalist and attempted to interpret Germany and events in Germany to his French readers. He never lost his love for Germany, however, and some of his most beautiful poetry reveals the depths of his longing and love for his native land. From 1848 until his death in 1856 he was almost totally paralyzed, but he continued to produce sensitive poetry. The playfulness of his early work, however, gives way to increasingly anguished questioning. Brilliant, mercurial in both poetry and prose, he combined romanticism and sentiment with irony and satire. Abroad, his fame equaled GOETHE's, in part because his work is easy to appreciate with a minimal command of the German language. Many of his poems have been set to music by Schubert, Schumann, and Brahms.

The Bibliothèque Nationale in Paris in 1966 acquired a collection of Heine's manuscripts, which includes "more than 2,500 unpublished pages written by Heinrich Heine and another 2,500 pages of letters to the poet and documents about him" (*N.Y. Times*).

WORK BY HEINE

The Works of Heinrich Heine. 20 vols. Trans. by Charles G. Leland. AMS Pr. repr. of 1906 ed. $20.00 ea. ISBN 0-404-15250-3. A complete set of Heine's published writing.

POETRY BY HEINE

Lyric Poems and Ballads. Trans. by Ernst Feise. U. of Pittsburgh Pr. repr. of 1968 ed. $11.95. ISBN 0-8229-5200-9. The early, melancholy songs of Heine, with their characteristic combination of sharp wit and sentimentality.

Selected Verse. Viking Penguin 1987 $7.95. ISBN 0-14-042098-3. A collection representing the full range of Heine's writing, from playful satires to anguished laments.

NONFICTION BY HEINE

The Romantic School and Other Essays. 1836. Ed. by Volkmar Sander. Continuum 1985 $27.50. ISBN 0-8264-0290-9. Heine's famous essay, a characteristic blend of sarcasm and nostalgia, defining German romanticism as a medieval revival, at once foolish, noble, and endearing.

BOOK ABOUT HEINE

Sammons, Jeffrey L. *Heinrich Heine.* Princeton U. Pr. 1979 $17.95. ISBN 0-691-10081-0. A concise introduction to the life and work of Heine.

HERDER, JOHANN GOTTFRIED VON. 1744–1803

Herder, humanist philosopher, poet, and critic, was born in Mohrungen in East Prussia. He suffered a deprived childhood but managed to attend the University of Königsberg, where he soon abandoned medical studies for theology. It was then that he came under the aegis of KANT (see Vol. 4), an influence that led to Herder's revolutionary approach to history. In his major work, *Reflections on the Philosophy of the History of Mankind* (1784–91), he proclaimed "humanity to be the essence of man's character as well as the irrevocable aim of history" (Ernst Rose). By articulating the idea of different cultures as units that could be understood from without by empathy rather than by analysis, Herder became the foremost theorist of European nationalism.

He called attention to folk genres such as the ballad and the fairy tale, thereby exerting an important influence on romanticism. The work of Herder provided much of the foundation for the developing disciplines of folklore and anthropology.

NONFICTION BY HERDER

Reflections on the Philosophy of the History of Mankind. 1791. U. of Mich. Pr. 1992 $11.60. ISBN 0-8357-7007-9. First formulation of cultural relativism.

Selected Works, 1764–1767; Early Addresses, Essays & Drafts. Pa. St. U. Pr. 1991 $35.00. ISBN 0-271-00712-5. Articulates the idea of a national literature, expressing the collective character and aspirations of an ethnic group.

BOOK ABOUT HERDER

Mayo, Robert S. *Herder and the Beginnings of Comparative Literature.* U. of NC Pr. 1969 o.p. Discusses the vast influence of Herder on both the study and creation of literature.

HESSE, HERMANN. 1877–1962 (NOBEL PRIZE 1946)

When this German novelist, poet, and essayist publicly denounced the savagery and hatred of World War I, he was considered a traitor. He moved to Switzerland where he eventually became a naturalized citizen. He warned of the advent of World War II, predicting that cultureless efficiency would destroy the modern world. His theme is the conflict between the elements of a person's dual nature and the problem of spiritual loneliness. His first novel, *Peter Camenzind*, was published in 1904. His masterpiece, *Death and the Lover* (1930), contrasts a scholarly abbot and his beloved pupil, who leaves the monastery for the adventurous world. *Steppenwolf* (1927), a European best-seller, was published when defeated Germany had begun to plan for another war. It is the story of Haller, who recognizes in himself the blend of the human and wolfish traits of the completely sterile scholarly project. Hesse won the Nobel Prize in 1946. During the 1960s Hesse became a favorite writer of the counter culture, especially in the United States, though his critical reputation has never equaled his popularity.

NOVELS BY HESSE

Demian. 1919. HarpC 1989 $6.95. ISBN 0-06-091652-4. "Portrays a young boy's discovery of the chaos that lies beneath the surface respectability of everyday life" (*SR*).

The Journey to the East. 1932. Trans. by Hilda Rosner. FS&G 1988 $7.95. ISBN 0-374-50036-3. A parable, open to several interpretations, in which the perfect servant turns out to be the teacher.

Magister Ludi: The Glass Bead Game. 1943. Bantam 1982 $4.95. ISBN 0-553-26237-8. A novel of a spiritual elite, cut off from the rest of society to pursue arcane pleasures and mysteries.

Narcissus and Goldmund. 1930. Trans. by Ursule Molinaro. FS&G 1969 $8.95. ISBN 0-374-50684-1. Explores the relationship between spirit and nature, embodied respectively in an ascetic monk named Narcissus and a talented artist named Goldmund, who develop an intense friendship.

Peter Camenzind. 1904. Trans. by Michael Roloff. FS&G 1988 $7.95. ISBN 0-374-50784-8. Lyrical prose, telling of a young man from the countryside who moves to the city, only to return to rural life in the end.

Siddhartha. 1922. Bantam 1982 $3.50. ISBN 0-553-20884-5. A novel inspired by Hesse's travels in India. An Indian prince tries several modes of life, until he finally attains enlightenment.

Steppenwolf. 1927. Bantam 1983 $4.50. ISBN 0-553-27990-4. A fanciful portrait of a charismatic but frustrated intellectual, who undergoes a crisis and has many fantastic adventures.

Wandering. 1927. Trans. by James Wright. FS&G 1972 $5.95. ISBN 0-374-50975-1

Short Story Collections by Hesse

Pictor's Metamorphoses and Other Fantasies. Ed. by Theodore Ziolkowski. FS&G 1983 $9.95. ISBN 0-374-51723-1

Stories of Five Decades. Ed. by Theodore Ziolkowski and Ralph Manheim. Amereon Ltd. repr. of 1973 ed. $20.95. ISBN 0-89190-669-X. Literary fairy tales and parables, which often blend German romanticism, psychoanalysis, and far Eastern religion.

Nonfiction by Hesse

Autobiographical Writings. Trans. by Denver Lindley. Ed. by Theodore Ziolkowski. FS&G 1972 $3.95. ISBN 0-374-50964-6

Books about Hesse

Marrer-Tising, Carlee. *The Reception of Hermann Hesse by Youth in the United States.* P. Lang Pubs. 1982 $74.50. ISBN 3-261-05006-3. How Hesse became a hero of the counter culture.

Mileck, Joseph. *Hermann Hesse: Biography and Bibliography.* 2 vols. U. CA Pr. 1977 $95.00. ISBN 0-520-02756-6

HEYM, STEFAN. 1913–

Stefan Heym is representative of many intellectuals in the former East Germany who found themselves torn between loyalty to the ideals of their state and disdain for the reality. He was born into a secular Jewish family in Chemnitz. As a young man, he went to the United States to escape Hitler, where he worked for a while as a journalist. In 1943 he joined the American army. His first novel, *The Crusaders* (1948), became a best-seller. It was loosely based on his wartime experiences and filled with contempt not only for the Nazi government but for virtually all of German culture. Distressed by the rise of McCarthyism in the United States and by Western tolerance of former Nazi officials, Heym emigrated to East Germany in 1953 and gave his enthusiastic support to the Socialist aspirations of his new homeland. His disillusionment with East Germany was far more gradual and, by his own account, more difficult than that experienced in the United States. In 1976 he protested the forced emigration of singer-songwriter Wolf Biermann from the German Democratic Republic. Two years later he was fined and expelled from the East German Writers' Union for accepting royalties for work published abroad. Though Heym continued to believe that the GDR was the "better-half" of Germany, disillusion with the reality of socialism moved him to turn to his Jewish heritage for inspiration, in novels such as *The King David Report* (1972) and *The Wandering Jew* (1984). In 1992 he became a founding member of the "Committee for Justice," a lobby representing the interests of former East Germans in a newly united Germany.

Novel by Stefan Heym

Collin. 1986. Carol Pub. Group 1992 $12.95. ISBN 0-8184-0300-4. A novel set in an East German hospital, which contrasts the aspirations of East Germans from various generations and professions.

HOCHHUTH, ROLF. 1931–

When *The Deputy*, an epic drama in the manner of SCHILLER, was simultaneously published and performed on stage by Erwin Piscator's company in Berlin in 1963, it created a furor, "almost certainly the largest storm ever raised by a play in the whole history of drama" (Eric Bentley). Reading "like a German doctoral dissertation in verse," (New Republic), it is a searing indictment of Pope Pius XII, "God's deputy" on earth, for not having intervened publicly when Hitler organized and carried out the massacre of six million Jews. A Jesuit priest, the only invented character, reasons with the Pope in the play and in despair "becomes" a Jew and goes off to his death at Auschwitz. "To me," said Hochhuth, "Pius is a symbol, not only for all leaders but for all men . . . who are passive when their brother is deported to death."

The storm raged—with bannings, picketings, and riots in various parts of the world, and countless articles pro and con. Cardinal Spellman and Pope Paul VI were only two of the Catholic churchmen who came to the defense of Pope Pius, the latter on the ground that had the Pope spoken out he "would have been guilty of unleashing on the already tormented world still greater calamities involving innumerable innocent victims."

Unfortunately, this work is no longer in print, nor is Hochhuth's almost equally controversial play *The Soldiers* (1967), in which WINSTON CHURCHILL (see Vol. 3) is accused of being personally responsible for the death of the Polish general Vladislav Sikorski. Hochhuth now lives in Basel, Switzerland.

PLAY BY HOCHHUTH

A German Love Story. 1978. Trans. by John Brownjohn. Little 1980 o.p. The basis for the movie, *A Love in Germany*.

HOFFMANN, E(RNST) T(HEODOR) A(MADEUS). 1776–1822

Hoffmann was among the foremost raconteurs of the late romantic period in Germany. His Gothic influence was felt widely throughout France, England, and America—in the works of Musset, BAUDELAIRE, WALTER SCOTT (see Vol. 1) and POE (see Vol. 1), among others. Offenbach used three of his stories for the opera *Tales of Hoffmann*. Fascinated by the morbid and the grotesque, Hoffmann breathed life into his imaginary world and made it seem quite real. "His writing is . . . plastic, a quality which is conspicuous in his power of endowing with reality the supernatural phantasms of his brain" (J. G. Robertson).

Although he was musically productive in his early years, Hoffmann turned to literature for financial reasons and published his first work, *Weird Tales*, with a preface by JEAN PAUL (RICHTER), in 1814 and 1815. He settled in Berlin, where his literary circle, the Serapionsabende, included CHAMISSO and provided material for *The Serapion Brethren* (1819–21), a collection of stories supposed to have been told by a similar group of friends. The gruesome and chilling *Devil's Elixir* (1815–16), a novel, is interesting for its psychological insights. The tales told by Hoffmann's fictional counterpart, the musician Kreisler, in *Weird Tales*, as well as the novel *Murr the Tomcat* (1820–22), are in part autobiographical.

The greatest influence of Hoffmann has probably been in popular literature. His "Mademoiselle de Seudéri" is often considered the first murder mystery, and Hoffmann also pioneered such genres as horror and science fiction.

Short Story Collections by E.T.A. Hoffmann

The Best Tales of Hoffmann. Ed. by E. F. Bleiler. Dover 1963 $8.95. ISBN 0-486-21793-0. Includes "The Nutcracker" and eight more of Hoffmann's best-known tales.

The Nutcracker. 1819–21. Trans. by C. Andrea. Knopf 1987 $14.95. ISBN 0-394-55384-5. An illustrated edition for children. The story that inspired the ballet by Tschaikovsky, which has become a Christmas classic.

Selected Writings of E.T.A. Hoffmann. 2 vols. U. Ch. Pr. 1969 o.p. Foreword by R. Wellek. A comprehensive selection containing "Mademoiselle de Seudery," "The Golden Pot," and other important works.

The Tales of Hoffmann. Viking Penguin 1982 $5.95. ISBN 0-14-044392-4

Nonfiction by E.T.A. Hoffmann

Selected Letters of E.T.A. Hoffmann. Trans. by Johanna Sahlin. U. Ch. Pr. repr. of 1967 ed. $23.50. ISBN 0-226-34790-7. Highly revealing and entertaining letters, in which Hoffman is alternately earnest, silly, and profound.

Book about E.T.A. Hoffmann

McGlathery, James M. *Mysticism and Sexuality: E.T.A. Hoffmann.* 3 vols. P. Lang Pubs. 1981-84. Vol. 1 $31.60. ISBN 3-261-04927-8. Vol. 2 $31.60. ISBN 3-261-04926-X. Vol. 3 $30.00. ISBN 0-8204-0217-6

HOFFMAN, HEINRICH. 1809–1894

Heinrich Hoffman, a doctor of psychology in Frankfurt, is remembered as the author of a single, short book of moral parables in verse for children, which achieved enormous popularity. When his *Struwwelpeter* (Slovenly Peter) appeared in 1845, the first edition was sold out in a few days. By 1925, when the copyright expired, well over 500 editions had appeared. The book was widely translated and imitated. Mark Twain (see Vol. 1) was so delighted with the book that, despite his poor knowledge of German, he produced a loose translation for his children. The contemporary reader will probably be disturbed by the harsh punishments given to children: a boy who persists in sucking his thumb has the thumb cut off by a tailor, while two children who make fun of a black boy are dipped in chocolate, to be eaten at Christmas. But the style of the book is humorous, and even most children probably knew the punishments were not to be understood literally. That *Struwwelpeter* is not currently in print in the United States shows that the popularity of the book has, in this country at least, finally declined. But several generations were raised on the book, and copies may often be found in libraries and used book stores.

HOFMANNSTHAL, HUGO VON. 1874–1929

Hofmannsthal's plays are all written in verse, and most are modernized adaptations from other dramatists. His masterpiece, *Electra* (1903), was set to music by Richard Strauss (see Vol. 3). Dramas such as *Jedermann* (1911) and *The Tower* (1925, o.p.) showed him to be a serious and responsible social critic: their "deep symbolism is pervaded by an uncanny insight into the demonic forces and potentialities of our century" (*LJ*).

With Max Reinhardt, Hofmannsthal helped to found the Salzburg Festival of music and theater, which is still an annual event. He also collaborated successfully with Strauss, despite their divergent personalities and mutually preferred habit of working at a distance, through the mails. Hofmannsthal wrote the libretti for Strauss's *Der Rosenkavalier, Ariadne auf Naxos,* and *Die Frau ohne Schatten.*

In his poetry, almost all written in his early twenties, Hofmannsthal proved himself to be the most socially sensitive of the Viennese poets of the 1890s. A traditionalist writing in an era of experimentation, he wrote meditations on the theme of transience, noted for their elevated diction and technical perfection.

WORK BY HOFMANNSTHAL

Selected Writings. Bollingen Ser. 3 vols. Princeton U. Pr. 1952-63 $37.50-$50.00 ea. ISBN 0-685-42303-4. Vol. 1 includes tales, novellas, essays, notes on his travels, and the unfinished novel *Andreas.* Vol. 2 includes *Death and the Fool, The Emperor and the Witch, The Little Theater of the World, The Mine at Fauln, The Marriage of Zobeide,* and the prologue to the *Antigone of Sophocles.* Vol. 3 includes three plays and three libretti, chosen to show the range of his theatrical writings.

BOOKS ABOUT HOFMANNSTHAL

Broch, Hermann. *Hugo von Hofmannsthal and His Time: The European Imagination, 1860–1920.* Ed. by Michael P. Steinberg. U. Ch. Pr. 1984 $13.95. ISBN 0-226-07516-8

Hamburger, Martin. *Hofmannsthal: Three Essays.* Princeton U. Pr. 1970 o.p.

HÖLDERLIN, (JOHANN CHRISTIAN) FRIEDRICH. 1770–1843

Only during the last 100 years has Hölderlin come to be recognized as a great lyric poet. Except for his philosophical novel *Hyperion* (1797–99) and translations of two of SOPHOCLES' plays, his works were published by friends after he became hopelessly insane in his thirties. Among his most celebrated works is a play in verse about a pre-Socratic Greek philosopher, entitled *The Death of Empedocles,* which remained incomplete, perhaps because the conception was too ambitious ever to be fully realized.

Hölderlin spent his early life as a private tutor. Hellenic in feeling, his poetry is written in the classical meters or in free verse on Greek themes. Hölderlin knew and wrote of the tragic elements in life, but his poems encompass and transcend these in a vision of ultimate harmony: "He aimed at balance even in his rhythms, matching ascending units with descending ones and uniting many voices in a symphony. . . . He has become a guidepost for moderns" (Ernst Rose).

In Hölderlin's later lyrics, Christopher Middleton has praised "the marvelous balance of energy between disintegration and articulation, plus the mortal conflict of spirit that is going on between these poles."

POETRY BY HÖLDERLIN

Hymns and Fragments. Trans. by Richard Sieburth. Princeton U. Pr. 1984 $40.00. ISBN 0-691-06607-8. Poems written primarily in the intense burst of creativity before Hölderlin became insane.

Hyperion & Selected Poems. Ed. by Eric L. Santer. Continuum 1990 $12.95. ISBN 0-8264-0334-4

Poems and Fragments. Trans. by Michael Hamburger. Cambridge U. Pr. 1980 o.p. The largest selection of his poems available. Includes two fragments of the tragedy *The Death of Empedocles.*

Selected Poems. Dufour 1990 $12.95. ISBN 1-85224-064-4. A representative selection from Hölderlin's poetic works.

BOOKS ABOUT HÖLDERLIN

George, Emery, ed. *Hölderlin Bicentennial Symposium.* Bks. Demand 1970 $88.00. ISBN 0-317-08202-7. A collection of essays on Hölderlin by noted scholars.

Ryan, Thomas E. *Hölderlin's Silence*. P. Lang Pubs. 1988 $44.00. ISBN 0-8204-0551-5. Interprets the silence of Hölderlin's final years as a final rejection of language, the genesis of which is traced throughout his work.

Shelton, Roy C. *The Young Hölderlin*. P. Lang Pubs. 1973 $45.75. ISBN 3-261-00315-4

Unger, Richard. *Hölderlin's Major Poetry: The Dialectics of Unity*. Bks. Demand 1992 $53.40. ISBN 0-317-29903-4

JOHANNES VON SAAZ (or VON TEPL). c.1350–c.1414

Johannes von Saaz was born in the village of Schüttwa and studied at the University of Prague. From 1383 he was town clerk, headmaster, and archepiscopal notary in Saaz. His young wife Margaretta died in 1400, and *The Plowman* (c.1410) is her literary memorial. Written as a legal debate between the plowman as plaintiff and Death as the accused, it forms a perfect miniature play. "This little book in dialogue form is the first really important work of prose literature in the German language," writes M. O'C. Walshe (*Medieval German Literature*). It was the fruit of an early wave of humanism in Bohemia.

Work by Johannes von Saaz

The Plowman from Bohemia. c. 1410. Trans. by Alexander Henderson and Elizabeth Henderson. Continuum 1966 o.p.

JOHNSON, UWE. 1934–1984

One critic summed up Uwe Johnson's vision of Germany this way: "Contemporary Germany is Johnson's all-purpose, modern symbol of confused human motives, social forces that drive people frantic, and frustrations in communication that finally choke men into silence" (Webster Schott, *N.Y. Times*). *The Third Book about Achim* (1961), winner of the $10,000 International Publishers' Prize in 1962, is a novel about divided Germany. It addresses one of the crucial philosophical problems of any age, but particularly the present: What is objective truth? Is there such a thing at all? Johnson's style is difficult: "bewildering time-sequences; abrupt and arbitrary shifts in point of view; shadowy characters; huge, eccentrically punctuated sentences; tortured syntax; esoteric excursions; oceanic digressions" (*SR*). Joachim Remak, in *Harper's*, says, "It is an easy book to dislike at first [but] in the course of the novel all the annoying traits suddenly vanish or become unimportant. For this is a great book; literary award judges can be right."

The novel was a catharsis for Johnson's own personal conflicts: he had reluctantly left his home in East Germany in 1959 in order to have his first novel published without censorship. This first novel, *Speculations about Jacob* (1959), was praised for a style that defies the traditional structure of the novel and indeed of language. In his *Anniversaries* (1970–73), Johnson again treats pressing moral and political issues by having the scene of the novel switch from New York City during the Vietnam War to Mecklenburg, Germany, in the Nazi period. One of the major themes of the book is the failure of liberalism in the United States in the 1960s and in Germany in the 1930s. Johnson's work is consistent, never pedestrian, and sometimes brilliant. In 1971 Johnson received the Büchner Prize.

Novels by Johnson

Anniversaries: From the Life of Gesine Cresspahl. 1970. Trans. by Leila Vennewitz. HarBraceJ 1975 $10.00. ISBN 0-15-107561-1. The story of a woman who works as a translator in New York and tries to reconstruct the turbulent days in Berlin after World War II.

Anniversaries II. 1971. Trans. by Leila Vennewitz and Walter Arndt. HarBraceJ 1987 $29.95. ISBN 0-15-107562-X

Speculations about Jacob. 1959. Trans. by Ursule Molinaro. HarBraceJ 1972 $4.95. ISBN 0-15-684719-1. A murder mystery, involving agents from both East and West Germany, which is never solved but which illustrates the complexity of human contacts across the GDR-FRD border.

BOOK ABOUT JOHNSON

Buolby, Mark. *Uwe Johnson. Lit. and Life Ser.* Continuum 1974 o.p. A basic introduction to Johnson's work.

JÜNGER, ERNST. 1895–

Jünger published his war diary, *The Storm of Steel,* in 1920 at the age of 25. The recipient of the Pour le Mérite, Germany's highest award for bravery in the field, Jünger was lionized by his generation for his celebration of the "purifying" experience of war. His "heroic nihilism" was further articulated in his *War as a Spiritual Experience* (*Der Kampf als Innerer Erlebnis*), published in 1922. His allegorical *On the Marble Cliffs* (1939) is sometimes seen as an attack on Nazism. Nonetheless, Jünger served as an officer in the Reichswehr in Paris during World War II. Since the war he has become involved in the conservation movement, making the defense of nature the subject of his later writing. He remains primarily known for his early works, and his romanticization and aestheticizing of war now elicit much criticism. His recent receipt of a prestigious literary prize was the subject of considerable controversy.

NOVELS BY JÜNGER

Heliopolis. 1949. Trans. by William Eickhorst. Vantage 1987 $14.95. ISBN 0-533-07370-7. A futuristic novel, exploring one relation between individuality and collective endeavor.

The Storm of Steel. 1920. Trans. by B. Creighton. Fertig 1975 repr. of 1929 ed. $45.00. ISBN 0-86527-310-3

KAFKA, FRANZ. 1883–1924

Kafka, a Czech who wrote in German, is now known for his "surpassing originality as an innovator in creative method." Very little of his work was published during his lifetime. The first three uncompleted novels form what Max Brod, his close friend, called a "trilogy of loneliness": "Like every other work, they reflect in a profoundly religious sense the experience of human isolation and the pathos of exclusion." He was born in Prague of middle-class Jewish parents and seems to have suffered early serious personality difficulties as the son of a domineering father. He took a law degree at the German University of Prague, then obtained a position in the workmen's compensation division of the Austrian government. Always neurotic, enigmatic, and obsessed with a sense of inadequacy, failure, and sinfulness, his writing was a quest for fulfillment. He spent several years in sanatoriums and died of tuberculosis in a hospital near Vienna. Before his death he asked Max Brod to burn all his manuscripts. But Brod disregarded this injunction and was responsible for the posthumous publication of Kafka's longer narratives, which have brought him worldwide fame in the past 25 years. The nightmare world of *The Castle* (1926) and *The Trial* (1925), in which the little man is at the mercy of heartless forces that manipulate him without explanation, has become frighteningly relevant to the period of the modern mammoth (or authoritarian) state, in which ordinary citizens find themselves increasingly helpless. This has made his work a major source of inspiration for dissident writers such as Vaclav Havel and Lutz Rathenow in authoritarian regimes of Eastern Europe.

Novels by Kafka

Amerika. 1927. Trans. by Edwin Muir. Schocken 1990 $11.95. ISBN 0-8052-0944-1. Focuses on an inexperienced young man who, having been seduced by a servant girl, is sent to America by his parents and finds himself helpless in the New World.

The Castle. 1926. Schocken 1988 $10.95. ISBN 0-8052-0872-0. Follows a hero making his way through endless layers of bureaucracy, trying to seek entry to a castle.

The Trial. 1925. Knopf rev. ed. 1937 $16.95. ISBN 0-394-44955-X. Portrays a man tried and eventually executed without ever knowing the charges, raising questions about the elusive nature of guilt and innocence.

Short Story Collections by Kafka

The Complete Stories. Ed. by N. N. Glatzer. Schocken 1988 $12.95. ISBN 0-8052-0873-9

The Great Wall of China: Stories and Reflections. 1931. Trans. by Willa Muir and Edwin Muir. Schocken 1987 $7.95. ISBN 0-8052-0419-9

Nonfiction by Kafka

Letters to Milena. Schocken 1987 $5.95. ISBN 0-8052-0427-X

Letters to Felice. Ed. by Jürgen Born and Eric Heller. Trans. by James Stern and Elisabeth Duckworth. Schocken 1987 $17.50. ISBN 0-8052-3500-0. The correspondence with his fiancé.

Letters to Friends, Family, and Editors. Trans. by Richard Winston and Clara Winston. Schocken 1990 $14.95. ISBN 0-8052-0949-2. Contains the famous letter to his father, whom Kafka admires yet finds arbitrary and domineering, the document that probably tells us most about Kafka's psychology.

Letters to Ottla and the Family. Trans. by Richard Winston and Clara Winston. Ed. by N. N. Glatzer. Schocken 1987 $15.95. ISBN 0-8052-3772-0

Parables and Paradoxes. Schocken 1961 $8.95. ISBN 0-8052-0422-9. Striking epigrammatic fragments.

Books about Kafka

Brod, Max. *Franz Kafka: A Biography.* Schocken 1963 $7.50. ISBN 0-8052-0047-9. An intimate biography by Kafka's lifelong friend and literary executor, the man who knew him as well as anyone. "Invaluable to anyone at all interested in the mind of the genius" (Alfred Kazin).

Canetti, Elias. *Kafka's Other Trial: The Letters to Felice.* Trans. by Christopher Middleton. Schocken 1982 $11.95. ISBN 0-8052-3553-1. A critical study of the letters showing how the correspondence and the situation from which it arose greatly inspired Kafka's writings.

Flores, Angel, ed. *The Kafka Problem: An Anthology of Criticism about Franz Kafka.* Gordian 1976 repr. of 1963 ed. $75.00. ISBN 0-87752-204-9. Essays by noted Kafka scholars.

Hayman, Ronald. *Kafka: A Biography.* OUP 1982 $8.95. ISBN 0-19-520411-5. A concise introduction to Kafka.

Pascal, Roy. *Kafka's Narrators: A Study of His Stories and Sketches.* Cambridge U. Pr. 1984 $47.50. ISBN 0-521-24365-3. An examination of Kafka's unique narrative voice.

KAISER, GEORG. 1878–1945

In the "GAS trilogy" *(The Coral, Gas I,* and *Gas II)* Kaiser's fundamental theme, the regeneration of man, is presented in terms of contemporary social conflicts. The cycle of plays encompasses the entire evolution of capitalism within an abstract scheme. In essence it is a morality play.

Kaiser was the leading playwright of German expressionism, and exponent of its meager settings, violent contrasts, and love of the grotesque and shocking—all aimed at arousing in the beholder an intense "awareness of life." His more than 50 plays include every variety of style and subject matter, including social drama, comedy, farce, romance, legend, and history. His characters are types shorn of individual subtleties, embodiments of ideas pure and simple. Kaiser stands as one of the boldest and most fascinating of the older generation of modern dramatists, and his impact on the contemporary theater, both inside and outside Germany, has been considerable. He died in Switzerland.

PLAYS BY KAISER

Plays. 2 vols. Trans. by B. J. Kenworthy. Riverrun NY 1980–82. Vol. 1 $16.95. ISBN 0-7145-0242-1. Vol. 2 $9.95. ISBN 0-7145-3899-X

BOOK ABOUT KAISER

Tyson, Peter. *The Reception of Georg Kaiser.* P. Lang Pubs. 1984 $51.60. ISBN 0-8204-0145-5. An account of the dramatic rise and partial decline of Kaiser's popularity and critical reputation.

KELLER, GOTTFRIED. 1819–1890

This Swiss German-language poet and novelist, born in Zurich, is known for his widely read realistic short stories of Swiss provincial life. *The Saturday Review* wrote of his autobiographical *Green Henry* (1854–55), "The book's instantly captivating quality is the charm with which a quietly sequential life of curiosity and perception is narrated in the pellucid recollection of the mature poet. Keller's eye for the colorful scene and his skill in endowing the concrete particular with something like archetypal significance make him an artist of rare integrity." His best work, *A Village Romeo and Juliet* (1876), "tells of the tragic fate of two youthful lovers who are prevented from making an honest marriage by the sins of their fathers" (Ernst Rose).

SHORT STORY COLLECTIONS BY KELLER

Legends of Long Ago. 1872. Trans. by Charles H. Handchen. *Short Story Index Repr. Ser.* Ayer repr. of 1911 ed. $12.00. ISBN 0-8369-3982-4. Primarily religious legends, centering on the conflict between worldly aspiration and asceticism, retold in a moderately realistic style.

People of Seldwyla (and *Seven Legends*). 1856. Trans. by M. D. Hottinger. *Short Story Index Repr. Ser.* Ayer repr. of 1929 ed. $16.00. ISBN 0-8369-3723-6. Keller's two most famous collections. The first takes a nonsentimental but gentle view of the lives of "typical" Swiss people in his mythical village of Seldwyla. The second pokes gentle fun at the Virgin Mary and other inhabitants of heaven.

Stories. Ed. by Frank Ryder. Continuum 1982 $12.95. ISBN 0-8264-0266-6. Contains "A Village Romeo and Juliet."

NOVELS BY KELLER

Green Henry. 1854–55. Trans. by A. M. Holt. Riverrun NY 1986 $14.95. ISBN 0-7145-0265-0

Martin Salander. 1886. Trans. by Kenneth Halwas. Riverrun NY 1981 $8.95. ISBN 0-7145-0371-1. A novel reflecting Keller's increasing pessimism toward the end of his life, especially about harmony between individual aspirations and social demands. Depicts a trusting young man who repeatedly loses out to those less scrupulous.

KIRSCH, SARAH. 1935–

In contemporary times the phrase "popular poet" may sound like a contradiction, yet Sarah Kirsch comes at least close to meeting that description. After working briefly in a factory and studying biology at the University of Halle, she devoted herself to creative writing at the Johannes R. Becher Institute in Leipzig. Kirsch signed a protest against the expulsion of singer-songwriter Wolf Biermann from East Germany in 1976 and then received permission to emigrate to West Berlin, where she lives today.

Since her first book of poetry *Landaufenhalt* (A Stay in the Country, 1967), Kirsch has gone on to publish many slim volumes of verse, in addition to a few short stories. In a land where both politics and metaphysics are discussed with particular passion, Kirsch has defiantly refused to be drawn into either. A sense of rebelliousness runs through her work, but it generally takes the form of guarding her personal autonomy. Though proudly feminine, she has repudiated any interest in feminist politics. She is openly idiosyncratic yet unpretentious and proud of her individuality.

The poems of Sarah Kirsch are generally meditative and, as she has explained on a number of occasions, are not intended to reveal themselves on the first or second reading. They are poems in which the reader feels that he or she is being treated with friendliness and respect.

Poetry by Kirsch

Conjurations: The Poems of Sarah Kirsch. Ed. by Wayne Kvam. Ohio U. Pr. 1965 $25.95. ISBN 0-8214-0787-2

Nonfiction by Kirsch

The Panther Woman: Five Tales from One Cassette Recorder. Trans. by Marion Faber. U. of Nebr. Pr. 1989 $17.50. ISBN 0-8032-2722-1. Women talking to Sarah Kirsch about their lives, among them a woman who works with big cats in the circus.

KIRST, HANS HELLMUT. 1914–

Kirst drew on his experiences as a soldier and officer in World War II to become "the number one chronicler of the German military mind" (*SR*). He has been a farmer, playwright, and critic and is now one of Germany's most successful novelists; his work has been translated into 24 languages.

Novels by Kirst

The Night of the Long Knives. Fawcett 1977 $11.95. ISBN 0-449-23372-3
Party Games. Ulverscroft 1982 $12.50. ISBN 0-7-089-0880-2

KLEIST, HEINRICH VON. 1777–1811

The plays and stories of Heinrich von Kleist seem particularly modern, in that they show a world in which the individual can no longer rely on the institutions of society, the discoveries of science, or the revelations of religion. Instead, his characters can trust only in their intuition of some higher, though unknowable, providential purpose. At a time when the writers of German classicism counseled moderation and restraint, Kleist excelled in depicting elemental passions. He differed, however, from the writers of both Storm and Stress and romanticism in the austere character of his language and the almost clinical detachment of his narrative prose.

Kleist was born into a distinguished though impoverished Prussian family. In 1799, he broke with family tradition by refusing to pursue a military career. For a while he wished to study natural science, but, in 1801, a reading of Kant (see Vol. 4) precipitated a crisis by convincing him that knowledge was impossible. The rest of his tempestuous life was marked by generally unsuccessful attempts to establish himself in various vocations, including journalism and politics. He achieved some moderate success with his play *Kätchen von Heilbronn* in 1810, but most of his work remained unappreciated. *Prince Friedrich von Homburg,* now his most celebrated play, was not to be discovered and published until 1821, a decade after the author's death by suicide.

The suicide of Kleist brought him the attention that had been denied him in life. He was, almost immediately afterward, recognized as a significant writer, and his reputation has grown steadily ever since. David Luke and Nigel Reeves have written, "It is precisely Kleist's vulnerability and disequilibrium, his desperate challenge to established values and beliefs, that carry him further than Goethe and Schiller across the gap between the eighteenth century and our own age." Despite the great attention now given to the work of Kleist in Germany, he remains largely unknown to the American public. In Japan and Korea, however, in part because of cultural affinities, he is extremely popular.

Plays by Kleist

The Broken Jug. 1808. Trans. by R. Jones. St. Martin 1988 $11.95. ISBN 0-7190-0667-8. A provincial comedy about a petty crime and a corrupt judge, raising questions about the capacity of institutions to assess guilt and innocence.

Plays. Ed. by Walter Hinderer. Continuum 1982 $27.50. ISBN 0-8264-0253-4. A selection of Kleist's most celebrated dramatic works.

Prince Friedrich von Homburg. 1810. Trans. by Frederick and Diana Peters. New Dir. Pr. 1978 $6.95. ISBN 0-8112-0694-7. In the face of death, a young Prussian officer's passage from impetuous heroics to mature courage.

Short Story Collection by Kleist

The Marquise of O and Other Stories. 1810–11. Trans. by David Luke and Nigel Reeves. Viking Penguin 1978 $5.95. ISBN 0-14-044359-2. Tautly written stories of individuals who are driven by passions they cannot explain to those around them.

Books about Kleist

Baker, Joseph O. *The Ethics of Life and Death with Heinrich von Kleist.* P. Lang Pubs. 1992 $35.95. ISBN 0-8204-1687-8. Interprets the suicide of Kleist as the culmination of a search for values that can be traced throughout his work.

Burckhardt, Sigurd. *The Drama of Language: Essays on Goethe and Kleist.* U. of Mich. Pr. $48.70. ISBN 0-8357-6604-7

Dyer, Denys. *The Stories of Kleist: A Critical Study.* Holmes & Meier 1977 $32.50. ISBN 0-8419-0303-4

Ellis, John M. *Kleist's "Prince Friedrich von Homburg": A Critical Study.* U. of Mich. Pr. 1992 $35.00. ISBN 0-317-08876-9

Silz, Walter. *Heinrich von Kleist: Studies in His Works and Literary Character.* Greenwood 1977 repr. of 1962 ed. $35.00. ISBN 0-8371-9796-1

LESSING, GOTTHOLD EPHRAIM. 1729–1781

Lessing, one of the outstanding literary critics of all time, was "the first figure of European stature in modern German literature." The son of a Protestant pastor, he was educated in Meissen and at Leipzig University, then went to Berlin as a journalist in 1749. While employed as secretary to General Tauentzien (1760–65), he devoted his leisure to classical studies. This led to his critical essay *Laocoon*(1776), in which he attempted to clarify certain laws of aesthetic perception by comparing poetry and the visual arts. He fought always for truth and combined a penetrating intellect with shrewd common sense.

He furthered the German theater through his weekly dramatic notes and theories, found mainly in the *Hamburg Dramaturgy* (1769), which he wrote during his connection with the Hamburg National Theater as critic and dramatist (1768–69). His plays include *Miss Sara Sampson* (1755), important as the first German prose tragedy of middle-class life; *Minna von Barnhelm* (1767), his finest comedy and the best of the era; and his noble plea for religious tolerance, *Nathan the Wise*(1779).

Plays by Lessing

Emilia Galotti: A Tragedy in 5 Acts. 1772. Trans. by Edward Dvoretzky. M. S. Rosenberg 1979 $4.00. ISBN 0-917324-17-X. The most tragic and lyrical of Lessing's plays, telling of a young girl who chooses to die for fear she will give in to the seductions of a wealthy and egotistical prince.

Minna von Barnhelm. 1767. Trans. by Kenneth J. Northcott. U. Ch. Pr. 1973 $10.00. ISBN 0-226-473414-4. A gentle satire on the exaggerated, Prussian idea of honor.

Nathan the Wise: A Dramatic Poem in 5 Acts. 1779. Trans. by Bayard Q. Morgan. Continuum 1992 $7.95. ISBN 0-8044-6401-4. A philosophical play set in the era of The Crusades, arguing for mutual tolerance among Jews, Christians, and Moslems.

Nonfiction by Lessing

Laocoon: An Essay on the Limits of Painting and Poetry. 1776. Trans. by Edward A. McCormick. Johns Hopkins 1984 $13.95. ISBN 0-8018-3139-3

Lessing's Theological Writings: Selections in Translation. Trans. by Henry Chadwick. Stanford U. Pr. 1957 $6.95. ISBN 0-8047-0335-3

Books about Lessing

Robertson, John G., ed. *Lessing's Dramatic Theory*. Ayer repr. of 1939 ed. $33.00. ISBN 0-405-08894-9. Lessing's analysis of "the theory of tragedy and the nature of drama." Includes some selections from other Lessing works and from those of European contemporaries.

Wellberry, David E. *Lessing's Laocoon: Semiotics and Aesthetics in the Age of Reason.* Cambridge U. Pr. 1984 $65.00. ISBN 0-521-2594-8. Lessing's distinctions between artistic genres in light of recent theory.

LIND, JAKOV. 1927–

An Austrian Jew whose parents were exterminated during World War II, Lind has translated the bitter memories of his youth into grotesque tales illustrating the horror of the Nazi years. The title story from *Soul of Wood* (1962), actually a short novel, concerns the fate of a paralytic Jewish boy, the son of Nazi victims. He is left on a mountaintop by his guardian, who then vies with others to reclaim the boy for exploitation; all the horrors of Nazism are encountered as events transpire. *Journey through the Night*, another story, describes with black humor the bizarre intellectual game between an admitted cannibal and his proposed victim in a railway compartment. "Lind's stories are fluid, inventive, surrealistic, and fantastic, though based in reality, bitter, and grimly savage. Expert, well-translated nightmares" (*LJ*).

Novels by Lind

Soul of Wood. 1962. Trans. by Ralph Manheim. FS&G 1986 $6.95. ISBN 0-8090-1526-9

The Stove. 1982. Sheep Meadow 1983 $7.95. ISBN 0-935296-27-1

LUTHER, MARTIN. 1483–1546

[See Volume 4.]

MANN, HEINRICH. 1871–1950

Heinrich Mann wrote about artists and poets and voluptuaries, for whom art is a "perverse debauch." His novels set in Germany are usually grotesque caricatures with political implications; those set in Italy tend to be feverish riots of experience in an amoral world. His *Professor Unrat* (1905, o.p.) was made into the famous film *The Blue Angel*. *The Little Town* (1909, o.p.) is perhaps his most benign novel.

Heinrich Mann, like his brother Thomas Mann, fled Nazi Germany and came to the United States. His literary reputation is strongest in Europe. In the United States his reputation is clouded partly by the rancor of his brilliant, hectic prose and partly by his admiration of the former Soviet Union.

Novel by Heinrich Mann

Young Henry of Navarre. 1935. Trans. by Eric Sutton. Overlook Pr. 1986 $14.95. ISBN 0-87951-981-9. A novel set in the late Middle Ages, arguing for religious tolerance.

Book about Heinrich Mann

Hamilton, Nigel. *The Brothers Mann*. U. of Mich. Pr. 1992 $12.40. ISBN 0-8357-8050-3. A comparison of Heinrich and Thomas, as novelists and brothers.

MANN, THOMAS. 1875–1955 (Nobel Prize 1929)

Buddenbrooks (1901), Mann's first novel, was published when he was just 26 years old. An intricate panoramic history of the decline of a German mercantile family not unlike Mann's own, it introduced (in the persons of several family members) what were to be Mann's dominant themes—the isolation of the artist in society, intellectualism versus the life of the emotions and senses, decay and death as sharpeners of life, and the relationship of all these to the political and social climate in which Mann found himself. In *The Magic Mountain* (1924) he studied the fringe world of a tuberculosis sanatorium. The stories *Death in Venice* (1913) and *Mario and the Magician* (1913), about two different varieties of artist, portray with consummate skill and dramatic tension an atmosphere of mounting evil. During the thirties, Mann identified with Goethe, to the point of imitating the latter's mannerisms. His combined worship and emulation of Goethe is reflected in the series of novels *Joseph and His Brothers* (1933) and in *Lotte in Weimar* (1938).

Early in life he claimed to be "unpolitical," even as he produced propagandistic radio broadcasts on behalf of German ambitions during World War I, eventually published under the title *Reflections of a Non-Political Man* (1918). Mann was, however, appalled by the Nazis, and he devoted much of his time to lecturing and writing against the Hitler government.

Mann fled Germany in 1933. He lived the life of an exile in the United States during the period in which his worldwide reputation reached its zenith. His last major work, *Dr. Faustus* (1947), reflected a more distanced relationship to Goethe and to German culture, as he retold the story of Faust and gave it a tragic ending. He left in the McCarthy era for Switzerland and lectured in both zones of Occupied Germany. Both the strengths and limitations of Thomas Mann derive from the tone of ironic detachment that is his trademark.

Novels by Thomas Mann

Buddenbrooks. 1901. Random 1984 $12.95. ISBN 0-394-72637-5

Death in Venice. 1912. Trans. by Erich Heller. McGraw 1970 $5.24. ISBN 0-07-553669-2. A novella based on the poet Stefan George, in which a distinguished author is overpowered by a homosexual infatuation with a young boy.

Dr. Faustus: The Life of the German Composer, Adrian Leverkühn, as Told by a Friend. 1947. Random 1971 $9.95. ISBN 0-394-71297-8

Joseph and His Brothers. 1933. Knopf 1948 $59.50. ISBN 0-394-43132-4. A novelistic retelling of the biblical story of Joseph and his brothers.

Lotte in Weimar: The Beloved Returns. 1938. Trans. by H. Lowe-Porter. U. CA Pr. 1990 $30.00. ISBN 0-520-07006-2 $12.95. ISBN 0-394-43458-7. A novel, moving between adoration and irony, about the aged Goethe, based on a brief encounter between Goethe and the woman who inspired *The Sorrows of Young Werther.* Shows the old patriarch surrounded by obsequious admirers.

The Magic Mountain. 1924. Random 1969 $10.95. ISBN 0-394-70497-5. The story of an ordinary young man, whose extended stay in a resort for victims of tuberculosis gives him opportunities for spiritual cultivation.

Royal Highness. 1909. Random 1983 $7.95. ISBN 0-394-71739-2. A prince, apparently favored by Fortune yet subject to a frustrating isolation from normal life, as a symbol for the artist.

Short Story Collections by Thomas Mann

Nocturnes. 1934. *Short Story Index Repr. Ser.* Ayer repr. of 1934 ed. $9.00. ISBN 0-8369-3728-7

Stories of Three Decades. Random 1979 $9.95. ISBN 0-394-60483-0. Contains a wide range of stories including the novellas *Death in Venice* and *Mario and the Magician.*

Nonfiction by Thomas Mann

Past Masters, and Other Papers. 1933. Trans. by H. T. Lowe-Porter. Ayer repr. of 1933 ed. $15.20. ISBN 0-8369-0674-8. Insightful though sometimes ponderous essays on a variety of literary and philosophical themes; especially concerns German cultural traditions.

Reflections of a Non-Political Man. 1918. Trans. by Walter Morris. Continuum 1987 $35.00. ISBN 0-685-14744-4

Books about Thomas Mann

Bergsten, Gunilla. *Thomas Mann's Doctor Faustus: The Sources and Structure of the Novel.* U. of Mich. Pr. 1992 $63.50. ISBN 0-317-29848-8. Examines the composition of Mann's last major novel, for which he drew on previous versions of the Faust story, including an anonymous chapbook of the late Middle Ages and Goethe's *Faust.*

Feuerlicht, Ignace. *Thomas Mann. Twayne's World Authors Ser.* G. K. Hall 1968 $20.95. ISBN 0-8057-2584-9. Biography that discusses the composition of Mann's major works.

Heller, Erich. *Thomas Mann: The Ironic German.* Regnery Gateway 1979 repr. of 1961 ed. $7.50. ISBN 0-89526-906-6. Discusses Mann's use of irony, both as a literary device and as a philosophic position.

Hollingdale, R. J. *Thomas Mann: A Critical Study.* Bucknell U. Pr. 1971 $25.00. ISBN 0-8387-1004-2

Jonas, Klaus W. *Fifty Years of Thomas Man Studies: A Bibliography of Criticism.* Kraus 1969 repr. of 1955 ed. $28.00. ISBN 0-527-46650-6. An overview of the extensive literature about Mann, intended primarily for the specialist.

Kaufmann, Fritz. *Thomas Mann: The World as Will and Representation.* Cooper Sq. 1973 repr. of 1957 ed. $32.50. ISBN 0-8154-0480-8. Mann's philosophy as a formative element in his art.

Lukacs, Georg. *Essays on Thomas Mann.* Trans. by S. Mitchell. Fertig 1979 repr. of 1965 ed. $35.00. ISBN 0-86527-245-X. Mann as inheritor of the realist tradition.

Stern, Joseph P. *Thomas Mann.* Col. U. Pr. 1967 $7.50. ISBN 0-231-02847-4. A good, concise analysis of Mann's major works and present significance.

Winston, Richard. *Thomas Mann: The Making of an Artist, 1875-1911.* P. Bedrick Bks. 1990 $12.95. ISBN 0-87226-236-7. Afterword by Clara Winston. Discusses the maturation of Mann as an artist and the phenomenon of a near prodigy who appeared middle-aged from the start of his career.

MÖRIKE, EDUARD. 1804–1875

Mörike withdrew from the social and political upheavals of his day to live as a reclusive country parson in his native Swabia. He is best known for his lyric poems which, in their directness, are close to folksongs. He also wrote a novel entitled *Maler Nolten* (*Painter Nolten*) (1832) and many short tales.

The extreme simplicity of his diction and the subtlety of his rhythms render the work of Mörike particularly difficult to translate. Largely for this reason he remains, despite his importance in German literature, little known to the English-speaking public, though his poems are scattered in various anthologies.

Nonfiction by Mörike

Mozart's Journey to Prague. 1855. Trans. by L. Loewenstein-Wertheim. Riverrun NY 1981 $4.50. ISBN 0-7145-0389-4. Mozart as a romantic artist, inspired but awkward in society and inept in practical matters.

Books about Mörike

Adams, Jeffrey, and others. *Critical Essays on Eduard Mörike.* Camden Hse. 1990 $45.00. ISBN 0-938100-75-0. Essays representing a variety of critical perspectives.

Mare, Margaret. *Eduard Mörike: The Man and the Poet.* Greenwood 1973 repr. of 1957 ed. $19.75. ISBN 0-8371-6538-5. A biography with critical comments on the poems and stories.

MÜLLER, HEINER. 1929–

Like many other modern German dramatists—such as Brecht, Weiss, and Peter Hacks—Heiner Müller constantly veers between the poles of authoritarian communism and nihilism. As a young man he served in the German army during World War II. After the defeat of Germany, he became an ardent Marxist and settled in East Berlin. His early plays such as *Der Lohndrücker* (*The Scab*) (1958) were written in the approved style of socialist realism, though the perspective of Müller was often too ardent and too militant for the East German cultural authorities. His later plays such as *Hamlet Machine* (1979) and *Mauser* (1970) express an increasingly bitter disillusionment and despair over the possibility of creating a socialist utopia. Peter Demetz has written that Müller "is the only playwright in the Communist world who, so far, has successfully combined personal allegiance to the past of Socialism with the most challenging exploration of the despair and hate of history, which he shows to be a torture chamber. . . ."

Plays by Müller

Hamlet Machine and Other Texts for the Stage. PAJ Pubns. 1984 $9.95. ISBN 0-933826-45-1

Work by Müller

The Battle: Plays, Prose, Poems. PAJ Pubns. 1989 $19.95. ISBN 1-55554-048-1

MUSIL, ROBERT. 1880–1942

Musil's *Young Törless* (1906) is a novel of troubled adolescence set in a military school, modeled on the one attended by both Musil and RAINER MARIA RILKE. It was his first book and was immediately successful. He then abandoned his studies in engineering, logic, and experimental psychology and turned to writing. He was an officer in the Austrian army in World War I, lived in Berlin until the Nazis came to power, and finally settled in Geneva. He also wrote plays, essays, and short stories.

The Man without Qualities (1930–42), Musil's magnum opus, is a novel about the life and history of prewar Austria. It was unfinished when Musil died, though he had labored over the three-volume work for ten years. Encyclopedic in the manner of PROUST and DOSTOEVSKY, "it is a wonderful and prolonged fireworks display, a well-peopled comedy of ideas" (V. S. Pritchett)—and a critique of contemporary life. It made Musil's largely posthumous reputation. "Musil's whole scheme prophetically describes the bureaucratic condition of our world, and what can only be called the awful, deadly serious, and self-deceptive love affair of one committee for another" (Pritchett).

NOVELS BY MUSIL

The Man without Qualities. 1930. Putnam 1985 $7.95. ISBN 0-399-50152-5
Young Törless. 1906. *Modern Class. Ser.* Pantheon 1982 o.p.

WORK BY MUSIL

Selected Writings. Continuum 1986 $27.50. ISBN 0-8264-0305-6

PLAY BY MUSIL

The Enthusiasts. Trans. by Andrea Simon. Performing Arts 1983 $9.95. ISBN 0-933826-46-X

BOOKS ABOUT MUSIL

Hickman, Hannah. *Robert Musil and the Culture of Vienna.* Open Court 1991 $29.95. ISBN 0-685-47767-3. Summaries and discussions of Musil's fiction that reveal a sound understanding of the complexities of his work.

Luft, David S. *Robert Musil and the Crisis of European Culture, 1880-1942.* U. CA Pr. 1980 $42.50. ISBN 0-520-03852-5

Peters, Frederick G. *Robert Musil, Master of the Hovering Life: A Study of the Major Fiction.* Col. U. Pr. 1978 $47.50. ISBN 0-231-04476-3

THE NIBELUNGENLIED. c.1200

The *Nibelungenlied* is the most powerful and dramatic work of the courtly period. It was also one of the most popular works, and complete or partial versions appear in more than 30 manuscripts. Although the ultimate sources of the epic are to be found in ancient Germanic heroic songs, a medieval German poet, whose identity is still not known and probably never will be, took the matter of these ancient legends and rearranged them. There may be some indirect criticism of the author's contemporaries in the representation of the court of Burgundy, which is dominated by intrigue and gossip.

In the nationalistic nineteenth century, this aspect of the *Nibelungenlied* was overlooked, and instead the warrior ethos of battle and victory at any price was glorified. This outlook persisted through the Third Reich. The reasons for this misunderstanding are complex, and the reader is advised to refer to George Mosse, *The Nationalization of the Masses.* It is only recently that the humane strivings of the *Nibelungen* poet have been recognized and emphasized in scholarship. The tragedy of the *Nibelungen* has attracted the fancy of many German writers and composers. Most noteworthy is FRIEDRICH HEBBEL, who adapted the legend well in his dramatic trilogy *Die Nibelungen*.

Nibelungenlied. Trans. by A. T. Hatto. Penguin 1965 $4.95. ISBN 0-14-0044137-9. The preferred translation, with many excellent appendixes, most noteworthy of which is the "Introduction to a Second Reading."

BOOKS ABOUT THE "NIBELUNGENLIED"

Donington, Robert. *Wagner's "Ring" and Its Symbols.* Faber & Faber 1974 $11.95. ISBN 0-571-04818-8

Shaw, George B. *The Perfect Wagnerite: A Commentary on the Niblung's Ring.* Dover 1966 $4.95. ISBN 0-486-21707-8. An interesting but idiosyncratic work, interpreting the story of the Nibelungs in terms of social and economic movements.

NIETZSCHE, FRIEDRICH (WILHELM). 1844–1900

[SEE Volume 4.]

NOVALIS (pseud. of Friedrich Leopold, Freiherr von Hardenberg). 1772–1801

Novalis, one of the early poets of German romanticism, provided the movement with its best known symbol, the "blue flower," from his fragmentary novel *Heinrich von Ofterdingen* (1802). The blue flower became the symbol for the deep-rooted romantic yearning, the search that would never end. Novalis himself was a Saxon nobleman and a government official who was fated to die young from tuberculosis. His most famous work, *Hymns to the Night*, was written in memory of his fiancée, Sophie von Kuhn, who died in 1797 at the age of 15. His *Hymns* eloquently express his grief and are a unique mixture of religious, mystical feeling and personal sadness. The *Hymns* were composed in 1800 and the death he celebrated struck him a year later.

POETRY BY NOVALIS

Hymns to the Night. Trans. by Dick Higgins. McPherson & Co. 1988 $5.95. ISBN 0-914232-90-8

Pollen and Fragments. Trans. by Arthur Versluis. Phanes Pr. $12.95. ISBN 0-933999-76-3

NOVEL BY NOVALIS

Henry von Ofterdingen. 1802. Trans. by Palmer Hilty. Waveland Pr. 1990 $6.95. ISBN 0-88133-574-6. An excellent translation of a work expressing "Novalis's own ideas and [those of] early German Romanticism in general" (*LJ*). An unfinished novel of the Middle Ages, in which a young man becomes a poet.

BOOKS ABOUT NOVALIS

Dyck, Martin. *Novalis and Mathematics.* AMS Pr. repr. of 1960 ed. $27.00. ISBN 0-404-50927-4

Hannah, Richard W. *The Fichtean Dynamic of Novalis' Poetics.* P. Lang Pubs. 1981 $34.90. ISBN 3-261-04954-5

Hiebel, Friedrich. *Novalis: German Poet, European Thinker, Christian Mystic.* AMS Pr. repr. of 1953 ed. $27.00. ISBN 0-404-50910-X

PAUL, JEAN (pseud. of JEAN PAUL RICHTER). 1763–1825

Jean Paul had to contend with poverty from his childhood through his years as a student of theology in Leipzig. Eventually, however, he attained enormous popularity with novels such as *Quintus Fixlein* (1796), *Siebenkäs* (1796–97),

Titan (1800–03), and *Flegeljahre* (1804–05). He excelled in the description of rural people leading modest lives and emphasized the values of moral integrity and contentment. His manner of ironic detachment anticipates the work of modern novelists such as MUSIL and THOMAS MANN.

NOVELS BY PAUL

Army-Chaplain Schmelzle's Journey to Flätz and *Life of Quintus Fixlein.* 1790. Trans. by Thomas Carlyle. Camden Hse. 1991 $48.00. ISBN 0-938100-89-0. Uses the example of a village schoolmaster to depict the joys of modest lives.

BOOK ABOUT PAUL

Harich, Walther. *Jean Paul.* AMS Pr. repr. of 1925 ed. $49.50. ISBN 0-404-03109-0. A study of Jean Paul from a Marxist perspective.

RATHENOW, LUTZ. 1952–

Lutz Rathenow has become the most widely known writer of the younger generation in what was formerly East Germany, though his publications in that country were confined to a few poems scattered in various magazines. In 1980 he released a collection of stories entitled *Mit dem Schlimmsten wird schon gerechnet* (*Prepared for the Worst*) with a West German publisher against the wishes of the Ministry of Culture. As a result he was arrested but was released after a few weeks, following widespread international protests. He then resisted pressures to emigrate and went on to publish books of stories and plays abroad. During the middle eighties, Rathenow became the most vocal critic of the East German government within literary communities, speaking out frequently in support of the independent peace movement. Since the unification of Germany, he has written widely as a journalist. His book *Berlin Ost* (*East Berlin*)—produced with the photographer Harald Hauswald, first published in 1987, and revised since German unification—describes the texture of daily life in the largest urban center of the former German Democratic Republic. Rathenow's major theme is the conflict between the individual and impersonal institutions and the resulting fears and tensions that pervade normal routines.

WORK BY RATHENOW

Contacts/Kontakte: Poems and Writings of Lutz Rathenow. Trans. and ed. by Boria Sax. Poet's Pr. 1987 o.p. Contains poems and stories smuggled out of East Germany and published in the West that deal largely with the searches, interrogations, and harassment Rathenow experienced.

REMARQUE, ERICH MARIA. 1898–1970

In 1947, after eight successful years in the United States, Remarque became a U.S. citizen. During World War I he was drafted into the German army at the age of 18. After the war he tried various occupations and in his spare time wrote the antimilitaristic *All Quiet on the Western Front* (1929) that became a classic of modern warfare but was condemned as "defeatist" by the Nazis. *The Road Back* (1931) is the sequel. His later novels deal with World War II; they have had greater popularity than critical success.

NOVELS BY REMARQUE

All Quiet on the Western Front. 1929. Fawcett 1987 $4.95. ISBN 0-449-21394-3. A young German soldier in World War I who learns survival skills on the front to no avail.

The Black Obelisk. 1956. Trans. by Denver Lindley. HarBraceJ 1957 $19.95. ISBN 0-15-113181-3

Bobby Deerfield. Fawcett 1978 $1.95. ISBN 0-449-23367-7

Books about Remarque

Barker, Christine, and Rex W. Last. *Erich Maria Remarque.* B&N Imports 1979 $31.50. ISBN 0-06-494066-7. A definitive biography.

Taylor, Harley U., Jr. *Erich Maria Remarque: A Literary and Film Biography.* P. Lang Pubs. 1988 $43.00. ISBN 0-8204-0636-8. Discusses the work of Remarque as it has been used in film.

RILKE, RAINER MARIA. 1875–1926

More than any other modern German writer, Rainer Maria Rilke seems to match our romantic idea of what a poet should be, though, as with many writers, separating artistry from affectation is often difficult. Restless, sensitive, reverent, yet egotistical, Rilke often seems to hover in his poems like a sort of ethereal being. He was born in 1875 to a wealthy family in Prague. After a few years devoted to the study of art and literature, he spent most of his adult life wandering among the European capitals and devoting himself single-mindedly to poetry. His early poems reflect his interest in the visual and plastic arts, as he tries to lose himself in contemplation of objects such as an antique torso of Apollo. His later books of poetry, such as *Duino Elegies* (1923) and *Sonnets to Orpheus* (1923), on the contrary, focus intently on internal realms. The poetry of Rilke is noted, above all, for metaphysical and psychological nuances.

Poetry by Rilke

Duino Elegies. 1923. Trans. by Gary Miranda. Breitenbush Bks. 1981 $8.95. ISBN 0-932576-08-7. Philosophical meditations in free verse, in which the poet considers his relation to God, angels, animals, and death.

Poems from the Book of Hours. 1905. Trans. by Babette Deutsch. New Dir. Pr. 1975 $4.95. ISBN 0-8112-0595-9. Poems addressed primarily to God, with whom the poet carries on an intense though often troubled dialogue.

Sonnets to Orpheus. 1923. Norton 1962 $6.95. ISBN 0-393-00157-1. A series of sonnets, in which the poet is called upon to redeem objects from the limitations of the material world.

Translations from the Poetry of Rainer Maria Rilke. Trans. by M. D. Herter. Norton 1962 $7.95. ISBN 0-393-00156-3. A dual-language edition; for readers with limited German.

Novels by Rilke

The Lay of the Love and Death of Cornet Christopher Rilke. 1906. Trans. by M. D. Herter. Norton 1963 $5.95. ISBN 0-393-00159-8. A poetic novel of the first love and subsequent death in battle of a young officer fighting the Turks in Hungary.

The Notebooks of Malte Laurids Brigge. 1910. Trans. by M. D. Herter. Norton 1964 $7.95. ISBN 0-393-00267-5. A novel of a young man in Paris, who feels called to a poetic vocation yet finds himself unable to create.

Nonfiction by Rilke

Letters. Trans. by M. D. Herter and Jane B. Greene. 2 vols. Norton 1969 $10.95 ea. ISBNs 0-393-00476-7, 0-393-00477-5. Often carefully composed and highly eloquent; may well have been intended as much for posterity as for the recipient.

Letters to a Young Poet. Trans. by Stephen Mitchell. Random 1986 $8.95. ISBN 0-394-74104-8. The thoughts of Rilke on poetry as a calling.

Wartime Letters of Rainer Maria Rilke, 1914–1921. Trans. by M. D. Herter. Norton 1964 $6.95. ISBN 0-393-00160-1. Rilke's account of his traumatic experience of World War I.

Work by Rilke

Prose & Poetry. Continuum 1993 $27.50. ISBN 0-8264-0286-0. A selection of works by Rilke, illustrating various periods and forms.

Books about Rilke

Baron, Frank, ed. *Rilke: The Alchemy of Alienation*. Ed. by Warren R. Maurer and Ernst S. Dick. U. Pr. of KS 1980 $29.95. ISBN 0-7006-0198-8

Bauer, Arnold. *Rainer Maria Rilke. Lit. and Life Ser.* Trans. by Ursula Lamm. Continuum 1972 $18.95. ISBN 0-8044-2025-4

Brodsky, Patricia P. *Rainer Maria Rilke*. G. K. Hall 1988 $26.95. ISBN 0-8057-8226-5. Rilke in the light of recent criticism and research.

Freedman, Ralph. *Rilke: A Biography*. Random 1988 $24.95. ISBN 0-394-52269-9. A life of Rilke; emphasizes single-minded dedication to poetry.

Fuerst, Norbert. *Phases of Rilke*. Haskell 1972 repr. of 1958 ed. $59.95. ISBN 0-8383-1663-8. Rilke's development as a poet, divided into distinct periods.

SACHS, HANS. 1494–1576

The late medieval and sixteenth-century German cities saw the development of a peculiar literature that expressed the taste and interests of the lower and middle bourgeoisie. It is a mixture of the medieval popular genres' ill-digested classical themes and a sharply realistic observation of urban life. Hans Sachs was the most important of those Meistersingers and was as such celebrated in Richard Wagner's (see Vol. 3) opera of that name. Sachs's productivity was enormous: biblical and classical drama takes an important place in it, and he wrote more than 1,000 Lent farces (*Fastnachspiele*). He is best in those earthy farces, which excel in satirical observation of the daily scene.

Work by Hans Sachs

Merry Tales and Three Shrovetide Plays. Trans. by William Leighton. *Lib. of World Lit. Ser.* Hyperion Conn. 1978 repr. of 1910 ed. $23.75. ISBN 0-88355-610-3. Representative works, showing Sachs's versatility and imagination.

SACHS, NELLY. 1891–1970 (Nobel Prize 1966)

Nelly Sachs was born into a secular Jewish family in Berlin. She conceived the ambition to become a writer as a young woman, but her early publications attracted hardly any attention. After the rise to power of Hitler, she witnessed the terrible fate of her fellow Jews. Only the intervention of the Swedish writer Selma Lagerlöf enabled her to leave for Stockholm and escape being sent to a concentration camp. In exile, as she tried to come to terms with the traumatic events of the recent past, she developed the unique poetic idiom for which she is famous. Individual experience hardly seems to exist at all in her poetry, as personal life blends into the mythic story of humanity, especially of her Jewish ancestors. Hans Magnus Enzensberger has written, "The oeuvre of Nelly Sachs is great and mysterious, two attributes that literary criticism has few occasions to apply to poetry these days."

Poetry by Nelly Sachs

O The Chimney. Trans. by Michael Hamburger and others. FS&G 1967 o.p. A selection from several volumes of poetry. Presents Enzensberger's contention that the work of Nelly Sachs is best understood as a whole, rather than through examination of individual poems or volumes in isolation.

The Seeker. Trans. by Ruth Mead, Michael Mead, and Michael Hamburger. FS&G 1970 o.p. A selection of poems taken from many volumes.

SCHILLER, (JOHANN CHRISTOPH) FRIEDRICH VON. 1759–1805

Schiller was the first German dramatist to have his plays translated widely into English. More than 200 such translations were published between 1792 and 1900. Each of his nine dramas is a masterpiece of situation, characterization, subtle psychology, and exalted artistic conception of the dramatic form. *The Robbers* (1781), his first play (prose), was the last of the great works of the German Sturm and Drang period and an immediate success, a rallying cry for the freedom and idealism of youth against the tyranny and hypocrisy that the young Schiller found in the times. *Mary Stuart* (1801), one of the great verse dramas of his "classical" maturity, was "a psychological tragedy in a very modern sense" (J. G. Robertson) and has been the Schiller play most often produced abroad. His themes, usually expressed through historical persons and situations, were freedom, justice, heroism—humanity's noble aspirations.

Schiller's life was a struggle against poverty and, in his last years, tuberculosis. His friendship with Goethe was a rewarding one for both writers and led to Schiller's settling in Weimar. "The German classical age attains its culmination in the friendship of Goethe and Schiller," says Robertson. Together they revitalized German poetry and the German stage: "Schiller's view of life was no calm and dispassionate one like Goethe's. [He] was always a partisan, a champion of high ideas" (Robertson).

Though perhaps the most beloved literary figure of Germany during the nineteenth century, Schiller has often been criticized during the twentieth century for exaggerated pathos and lack of poetic spontaneity. According to Erich Heller, "His work—a lifework of considerable genius, moving single-mindedness, and great moral integrity—is a striking instance of a European catastrophe of the spirit: the invasion and partial disruption of the aesthetic faculty by unemployed religious impulses."

Plays by Schiller

The Bride of Messina, William Tell, and Demetrius. Trans. by Charles E. Passage. Continuum 1962 o.p. Schiller's last, and perhaps most monumental, dramas.

Maiden of Orleans. Trans. by John T. Krumpelman. AMS repr. of 1962 ed. $27.00. ISBN 0-404-50937-1. Shows Joan of Arc, torn between her divine calling and awareness of her human limitations, eventually transcending the latter and becoming "sublime."

Mary Stuart. 1801. Trans. by Joseph Mellish. Applause Theatre Bk. Pubs. 1986 $7.95. ISBN 0-936839-00-7

Plays. Ed. by Walter Hinderer. Continuum 1983 $27.50. ISBN 0-8264-0274-7. A selection of Schiller's best-known plays, spanning the whole of his career.

The Robbers, Wallenstein. Trans. by F. J. Lamport. Viking Penguin 1980 $6.95. ISBN 0-14-044368-1

Wallenstein & Mary Stuart. Ed. by Walter Hinderer. Continuum 1990 $27.50. ISBN 0-8264-0336-0. Two of Schiller's most complex, mature dramas.

William Tell. 1804. Ed. by Kenneth J. Northcott. Trans. by William F. Mainland. U. Ch. Pr. 1973 $9.95. ISBN 0-226-73801-9. The national play of Switzerland.

Books about Schiller

Dewhurst, Kenneth, and Nigel Reeves. *Friedrich Schiller: Medicine, Psychology and Literature, with the First English Edition of His Complete Medical Writings.* U. CA Pr. $52.50. ISBN 0-520-03250-0. Suggests ways in which Schiller's early medical studies may have influenced his literary work.

Thomas, Calvin. *Life and Works of Friedrich Schiller.* AMS Pr. repr. of 1901 ed. $17.50. ISBN 0-404-06369-1. A basic introduction.

SCHLEGEL, AUGUST WILHELM, 1767–1845, and FRIEDRICH SCHLEGEL. 1772–1829

The Schlegel brothers pioneered the study of comparative literature in Germany and laid the theoretical foundations for the romantic movement. August, the elder brother, popularized SHAKESPEARE (see Vol. 1) in Germany by producing a new translation of 17 plays (1797–1801) in collaboration with his wife, Caroline Schlegel, herself an important literary figure. This was to be, for much of the nineteenth century, regarded as the definitive translation, and many critics still consider it, despite some errors, the best version in German. In his *A Course of Lectures on Dramatic Art*, delivered in Berlin and Vienna and published in 1809, August Schlegel explored the distinctions between the "classical" art of ancient Greece and the "romantic" art of the European Middle Ages.

Friedrich was a bit less scholarly but more imaginative than his brother. Prone to bursts of enthusiasm, he articulated many of his most important ideas in short, epigrammatic essays, many of which were published in the Journal *Anthenaem* (1798–1800), which he edited with brother August and LUDWIG TIECK. In one of these, he defined romanticism as a "progressive, universal poetry" that would synthesize all previous literary forms, including not only lyric and narrative prose but also criticism and humor. Friedrich Schlegel attempted to produce such a work with his novel *Lucinde* (1799), written largely for his wife Dorothea Veit Schlegel, the daughter of the philosopher Moses Mendelssohn. Though the novel did not meet with a favorable critical reception, the sort of art Friedrich prophesized was to be created about a century later by authors such as THOMAS MANN. Toward the end of his life, Friedrich turned to the study of Indian culture, and his *Über die Sprache und Weisheit der Indier* (On the Language and Wisdom of the Indians, 1808), is sometimes cited as the beginning of comparative philology.

NONFICTION BY AUGUST WILHELM SCHLEGEL

A Course of Lectures on Dramatic Art. 1809. Trans. by John Black. AMS Pr. repr. of 1846 ed. $29.50. ISBN 0-404-05605-9

NONFICTION BY FRIEDRICH SCHLEGEL

Philosophical Fragments. Trans. by Peter Firchow. U. of Minn. Pr. 1991 $11.95. ISBN 0-8166-1901-8. Contains Friedrich's famous theories of romanticism.

SCHNITZLER, ARTHUR. 1862–1931

Arthur Schnitzler, Viennese playwright, novelist, short story writer, and physician, was a sophisticated writer much in vogue in his time. He chose themes of an erotic, romantic, or social nature, expressed with clarity, irony, and subtle wit. *Reigen*, a series of ten dialogues linking people of various social classes through their physical desire for one another, has been filmed many times as *La Ronde*. As a Jew, Schnitzler was sensitive to the problems of anti-Semitism, which he explored in the play *Professor Bernhardi* (1913), seen in New York in a performance by the Vienna Burgtheater in 1968. Henry Hatfield calls Schnitzler "second only to Hofmannsthal among the Austrian writers of his generation and one of the most underrated of German authors. . . . He combined the naturalist's devotion to fact with the impressionist's interest in nuance; in other words, he told the truth" (*Modern German Literature*).

In his most famous story, *Lieutenant Gustl* (1901), Schnitzler employs the stream-of-consciousness technique in an exposition of the follies and gradual disintegration of society in fin de siècle Vienna. Schnitzler has also been linked with Freud (see Vols. 3 and 5) and is credited with consciously introducing elements of modern psychology into his works.

Works by Schnitzler

Beatrice. 1900. Trans. by Agnes Jacques. AMS Pr. repr. of 1926 ed. $15.00. ISBN 0-404-05612-1

Casanova's Homecoming. 1918. Trans. by Paul Eden and Paul Cedar. AMS Pr. repr. of 1930 ed. $15.00. ISBN 0-404-05619-9. Chronicles Casanova's return to his home city of Venice, where his intrigues and betrayals bring a humiliating end.

Daybreak. 1927. Trans. by William A. Drake. AMS Pr. repr. of 1927 ed. $15.00. ISBN 0-404-05615-6

Dr. Graesler. 1917. Trans. by E. C. Slade. AMS Pr. repr. of 1930 ed. $15.00. ISBN 0-404-05618-0

Fraulein Else. Trans. by Robert A. Simon. AMS Pr. repr. of 1925 ed. $15.00. ISBN 0-404-05611-3

None but the Brave. Trans. by Richard L. Simon. AMS Pr. 1972 repr. of 1926 ed. $15.00. ISBN 0-404-05613-X

Plays and Stories. Ed. by Egon Schwartz. Continuum 1983 $27.50. ISBN 0-8264-0270-4. Literary explorations of the prejudices, misunderstandings and confusions of aristocratic and upper middle-class society in Vienna at around the turn of the century.

Shepherd's Pipe, and Other Stories. Trans. by O. F. Theis. *Short Story Index Repr. Ser.* Ayer repr. of 1922 ed. $11.00. ISBN 0-8369-3732-5. Short, almost epigrammatic narratives, a form in which Schnitzler particularly excelled.

Therese. Trans. by William A. Drake. AMS Pr. 1972 repr. of 1928 ed. $27.50. ISBN 0-404-05617-2

Viennese Idylls. 1913. Trans. by Frederick Eisemann. Ayer repr. of 1913 ed. $16.00. ISBN 0-8369-4226-4

Viennese Novelties. 1908. AMS Pr. repr. of 1931 ed. $31.50. ISBN 0-404-08278-5

Novels by Schnitzler

Little Novels. 1929. Trans. by Eric Sutton. AMS Pr. repr. of 1929 ed. $16.00. ISBN 0-404-08277-7

Rhapsody: A Dream Novel. 1926. Trans. by Otto P. Schinnerer. AMS Pr. repr. of 1927 ed. $15.00. ISBN 0-404-05614-8

Play by Schnitzler

Professor Bernhardi. 1913. Trans. by Hetty Landstone. AMS Pr. repr. of 1928 ed. $15.00. ISBN 0-404-05616-4

Books about Schnitzler

Reichert, Herbert W., and Herman Salinger, eds. *Studies in Arthur Schnitzler.* AMS Pr. repr. of 1963 ed. $27.00. ISBN 0-404-50942-8

Urbach, Reinhard. *Arthur Schnitzler.* Trans. by Donald Daviau. *Lit. and Life Ser.* Continuum 1973 $18.95. ISBN 0-8044-2936-7

SEGHERS, ANNA. 1900–1983.

Anna Seghers was born to a wealthy Jewish family in Mainz. During the twenties she established a modest reputation as a writer committed to social reform. In 1933, when Hitler came to power, Seghers went into exile in France. When France capitulated to the Nazis, she proceeded to Mexico, barely escaping the gestapo. In 1942 she published her novel *The Seventh Cross,* which tells of seven prisoners who attempt to leave a Nazi labor camp and elude the police. It was immediately translated into English and became an international best-seller.

In 1947 she settled in East Berlin, where she was greeted as a national heroine. Seghers began to publish even more prolifically, producing novels and stories in the style of socialist realism. In 1966 she was named president of the East German Writers' Union, an office in which she had considerable influence on cultural policy. She resigned, for personal reasons, in 1978.

Seghers's prose is notable for its epic scope and psychological insight. Her reputation, like that of BRECHT, remains somewhat clouded by unresolved questions of complicity with the Stalinist regime in former East Germany. After the unification of Germany in 1990, archivists uncovered a novel of hers entitled *Der gerechte Richter* (*The Just Judge*), which was critical of the state and which she had deliberately withheld from publication.

NOVEL BY SEGHERS

The Seventh Cross. 1942. Trans. by James A. Galston. Monthly Rev. 1987 $7.50. ISBN 0-85345-712-3

BOOK ABOUT SEGHERS

La Bahn, Kathleen J. *Anna Seghers' Exile Literature: The Mexican Years (1941-1947).* P. Lang Pubs. 1986 $30.50. ISBN 0-8204-0195-1. An account of Seghers's years as an exile, based largely on material in North American archives.

TIECK, LUDWIG. 1773–1853

While many representatives of the romantic movement in Germany led short, troubled lives, often burning themselves out in a period of frenzied creativity, the robust Ludwig Tieck lived to become a patriarch of German letters. He not only wrote in a vast variety of forms, but also acted as a publicist for his more temperamental friends such as Wilhelm Heinrich Wachenroder and NOVALIS. In addition, he helped call attention to the literary value of previously neglected German chapbooks and fairy tales. During his lifetime, Tieck was often celebrated as the successor to GOETHE. Much of his work has now fallen into neglect, and he is remembered above all as the author of literary fairy tales such as "Fair-haired Eckbert" (1797) and the "Runenberg" (1804). These stories convey the sort of terror which the romantic tradition has often associated with insight into the nature of reality. In addition, they anticipate Freudian psychology, particularly with respect to defense mechanisms such as repression.

WORK BY TIECK

The Land of Upside Down. 1811. Trans. by Oscar Mandel. Fairleigh Dickinson 1978 $22.50. ISBN 0-8386-2061-2. The story of Tom Thumb, retold from German folkloric sources.

BOOK ABOUT TIECK

Lillyman, William J. *Reality's Dark Dream: The Narrative Fiction of Ludwig Tieck.* De Gruyter 1979 $37.50. ISBN 3-11007-710-8

TOLLER, ERNST. 1893–1939

A German-Jewish dramatist who fought in World War I, Toller was later imprisoned for trying to stop the war by organizing a strike of the munition workers. For his part in the Bavarian revolution he was exiled by the Nazis and his books were burned. He then came to New York. A radical, he identified strongly with the proletariat. He took his own life in despair following the victory of Franco in Spain and the Munich Pact, perhaps unable to bear the prospect of an inevitable World War II.

Plays by Toller

Seven Plays. Fertig repr. of 1935 ed. $45.00. ISBN 0-86527-399-5. Drama of social protest.

Poetry by Toller

The Swallow Book. 1924. Haskell repr. of 1974 ed. $75.00. ISBN 0-8383-1902-5. Poems in free verse, telling the story of a man in a mental institution whose life comes to center upon a pair of swallows, his only link with the outside world.

Nonfiction by Toller

I Was a German: The Autobiography of Ernst Toller. 1933. AMS Pr. $30.00. ISBN 0-404-16523-0. An account of Toller's boyhood, in which he scorns the pretensions of German nationalism.

Book about Toller

Pittock, Malcolm. *Ernst Toller. Twayne's World Authors Ser.* G. K. Hall 1979 o.p. An introduction to Toller's life and work.

TRAKL, GEORG. 1887–1914

Georg Trakl was born to a family of wealthy industrialists in Salzburg. He proved a poor student and was unable to embark on the professional career his family intended for him. As a young man he grew increasingly morose, indulging heavily in hallucinogenic drugs and alcohol. He apprenticed himself to a pharmacist, a trade that guaranteed him easy access to drugs. In 1912 he received the patronage of Ludwig Flicker, which enabled him to devote much of his time to poetry. Trakl went on to publish two small collections of poems, *Gedichte* (*Poems*) (1913) and *Sebastian im Traum* (*Sebastian in a Dream*) (1914). In 1914 he joined the army. After the battle of Grodek, for which his last and most famous poem is named, Trakl was assigned to look after 90 badly wounded soldiers. Unable to help them, he experienced a mental breakdown. A short while later, he died of an overdose of cocaine, possibly deliberately.

Trakl's poetry is narrow in range, though intense. His verse consists almost entirely of elegies and laments, in which mythic images are held together by slow yet pronounced rhythms. Trakl himself described poetry as an "imperfect penance" for "unabsolved guilt." Rilke wrote in a letter to Erhard Buschbeck, "In the history of the poem Trakl's books are important contributions to the liberation of the poetic image. They seem to have mapped out a new dimension of the spirit and to have disproved that prejudice which judges all poetry only in terms of feeling and content, as if in the direction of lament there were only lament—but here too there is world again."

Poetry by Trakl

Autumn Sonata: Selected Poems of Georg Trakl. Trans. by Daniel Simko. Moyer Bell Limited 1989 $9.95. ISBN 0-918825-94-6. A selection from Trakl's two books of poetry.

Georg Trakl: A Profile. Ed. by Frank Graziano. Trans. by Michael Hamburger and James Wright. Logbridge-Rhodes 1983 $18.00. ISBN 0-937406-28-7. Fine translations from Hamburger, a distinguished German scholar, and Wright, a noted American poet.

WALTHER VON DER VOGELWEIDE. c.1168–1228

Little is known of the life of Walther von der Vogelweide beyond what we can surmise from his poetry. He was born in Austria and spent much of his life wandering as a minstrel among various medieval courts. In 1220 he was granted a fief by the Emperor Friedrich II. Weary of courtly life, Walther resolved to join Friedrich II's crusade of 1227–28, and, since there are no further documents of his life, scholars usually presume that he died on the crusade. His love poems are unusual for their range, both in form and emotion. His political and philosophical lyrics even further surpass the poetic conventions of his day.

Poetry by Walther von der Vogelweide

Songs and Sayings of Walther von der Vogelweide, Minnesanger. Trans. by Frank Bretts. AMS Pr. repr. of 1917 ed. $11.50. ISBN 0-404-14752-6. A selection of representative works by Walther in various forms.

WEDEKIND, FRANK (BENJAMIN FRANKLIN). 1864–1918

This poet-playwright turned actor in order to produce the effect he wanted in his plays. Though as a young writer he associated himself with the naturalists, "Wedekind was not a consistent naturalist," says John Gassner (*Treasury of the Theater*); he was instead an original artist who was not apt to follow fashions ". . . [and who] helped himself to much naturalistic detail to support his personal crusade for frankness about the elemental power of the sexual instinct."

Plays by Wedekind

Lulu Plays and Other Sex Tragedies. 1895. Trans. by Stephen Spender. Riverrun NY 1979 $13.95. ISBN 0-7145-0868-3. Focuses on Lulu, an embodiment of sexuality, who seduces many men and leads them to destruction.

Spring Awakening: A Play. 1908. Trans. by Tom Osborn. Riverrun NY 1979 $8.95. ISBN 7145-0634-6. Explores the values and protected lives of young people, abruptly shattered by awakening sexuality.

WEISS, PETER. 1916–1982

In December 1965 Peter Weiss's *Marat/Sade* (1964), in a presentation by Britain's Royal Shakespeare Company, stormed the Broadway stage, captivating audience and critic alike. The assumption that the play about the murder of Marat by Charlotte Corday might have been one of the many dramatic pieces written by Sade—and enacted by his fellow inmates for "therapeutic" reasons during the Marquis's confinement at Charenton—provided Weiss (who maintained that "every word I put down is political") with his framework for the "confrontation of the revolutionary Marat as the apostle of social improvement and the cynical individualist, the Marquis de Sade" (*N.Y. Times*).

The Investigation (1965), which Weiss considered his best play, was first presented in 20 theaters in East and West Germany; Ingmar Bergman (see Vol. 3) was its Swedish director. It was staged in New York in 1966. Taken almost entirely from the actual proceedings of the 1965 Frankfurt War Crimes Tribunal on Auschwitz, *The Investigation* is a "harrowing but insistently commanding experience" (Walter Kerr, *N.Y. Times*). The audience, in effect, reenacts the role of the original courtroom spectators in this shattering, true account of man's depravity. Weiss received the Büchner Prize in 1982.

PLAY BY WEISS

The Persecution and Assassination of Jean-Paul Marat as Performed by the Inmates of the Asylum of Charenton under the Direction of the Marquis de Sade. 1964. Trans. by Geoffrey Skelton. Atheneum 1978 $6.95. ISBN 0-689-70568-9. Preface by Peter Brook. Includes music examples, biographical note.

BOOK ABOUT WEISS

Best, Otto F. *Peter Weiss.* Trans. by Ursule Molinaro. *Lit. and Life Ser.* Continuum 1976 $18.95. ISBN 0-8044-2038-6

WERFEL, FRANZ. 1890–1945

Born in Prague of Jewish parents, Werfel served in World War I, then lived and wrote in Vienna until driven out by the Nazi occupation of Austria. *And the Bridge Was Love: Memories of a Lifetime*, by his wife, Alma Werfel, in collaboration with E. B. Ashton, is a deeply personal autobiography of a remarkable life in Vienna by the woman who was also married to the composer-conductor Mahler and the architect GROPIUS (see Vol. 3). Werfel escaped to the United States after the fall of France in 1940, where he won international recognition for his fiction. The most popular of Werfel's works was the novel *The Song of Bernadette* (1942), recounting the miraculous vision of the Virgin Mary granted to the young girl who founded Lourdes. Werfel said he wrote the story in honor of his "miraculous" escape from the Nazis but neither affirmed nor denied the miracle at Lourdes.

Werfel also wrote lyrical poetry and drama. His comedy *Jacobowsky and the Colonel* (1944) was successfully produced in New York in 1944. In 1967 the Hamburg Opera presented Giselher Klebe's operatic version of the play at the Metropolitan Opera House in New York.

NOVELS BY WERFEL

Between Heaven and Earth. 1944. Ayer repr. of 1944 ed. $18.00. ISBN 0-8369-2086-4

Class Reunion. Trans. by Whittaker Chambers. Amereon Ltd. $15.95. ISBN 0-88411-718-9

The Forty Days of Musa Dagh. 1934. Carroll & Graf 1983 $9.95. ISBN 0-88184-015-7. Historical novel of the Armenian resistance to the Turks in 1915.

The Song of Bernadette. 1942. St. Martin 1989 $13.95. ISBN 0-312-03429-6

WOLF, CHRISTA. 1929–

Christa Wolf's career has been marked by several abrupt changes that have intrigued and frustrated her readers. As a young girl she was an ardent supporter of the Nazi government, but was later horrified at what the Nazis had done. Much of her writing is marked by a sense of having forfeited her childhood and by a desire to reclaim or reconstruct the past. Her first novel, *The Divided Heaven* (1961), reflected the transfer of her allegiance to her new state of East Germany. It tells of an East German girl whose boyfriend deserts her to emigrate to the West. For a while she considers suicide, but finds solace in the vibrant life around her and in the task of building a socialist society. This was followed, however, by *The Quest for Christa T.* (1968), in which the narrator tries to reconstruct the life of a spirited friend who was driven to suicide by the East German intolerance for individuality. In 1976 Wolf published *Patterns of Childhood*, a fictionalized account of a visit to Landsberg, the town of her childhood, together with her husband and daughter, in which she tries to reconstruct her life growing up in Nazi Germany. Wolf then turned to feminist themes in her novel *Cassandra* (1983), in which she adopts the persona of the

Greek prophetess who foretold the fall of Troy. Her subsequent novels are increasingly free associations, minimally plotted, on a range of social and philosophical themes.

Like many writers, Wolf found herself constantly torn between criticism of the East German society and respect for socialist ideals. During the 1980s the ability to balance conflicting loyalties helped make her the most widely read and discussed writer in the German language. In 1989 and 1990 she angered many people by authoring earnest appeals to the citizens of East Germany to refrain from emigration and resist union with the Federal Republic. After German reunification she published "What Remains" (1991), a manuscript which she had held back over a decade, chronicling her harassment by agents of the secret police. Critic Ulrich Greiner attacked her as an "official poet" of the former German Democratic Republic, while writers like GÜNTER GRASS and LUTZ RATHENOW came to her defense. She remains a highly controversial figure.

NOVELS BY WOLF

Accident: A Day's News. 1990. Trans. by Rick Takvorian and Heike Schwarzbauer. FS&G 1991 $7.95. ISBN 0-374-52254-5. The meditations of the author on the day the Chernoble reactor explodes and her brother undergoes brain surgery.

Cassandra: A Novel and Four Essays. 1983. Trans. by Jan van Heurck. FS&G 1984 $17.45. ISBN 0-374-11956-2

Divided Heaven. 1963. Trans. by Joan Becker. Adlers Foreign Bks. 1976 o.p.

No Place on Earth. 1979. Trans. by Jan van Heurck. FS&G 1982 $11.95. ISBN 0-374-22298-3. An imagined meeting between the playwright Heinrich von Kleist and poet Karonline von Günderrde, both of whom eventually committed suicide.

Patterns of Childhood. Trans. by Ursule Molinaro and Hedwig Rappolt. FS&G 1984 $9.95. ISBN 0-374-51844-0

The Quest for Christa T. 1968. Trans. by Christopher Middleton. FS&G 1979 $9.95. ISBN 0-374-51534-4

SHORT STORY COLLECTION BY WOLF

What Remains and Other Stories. FS&G 1991 $21.95. ISBN 0-374-28888-7

NONFICTION BY WOLF

Selected Essays. Ed. by Alexander Stephan. Trans. by Jan Van Heurck. FS&G 1991 $22.95. ISBN 0-374-12302-0. Contains her theories of "subjective authenticity" in narrative prose.

BOOK ABOUT WOLF

Responses to Christa Wolf: Critical Essays. Ed. by Marilyn S. Fries. Wayne St. U. Pr. 1989 $4.95. ISBN 0-8143-2130-5. Twenty essays by leading Wolf scholars in the United States, Great Britain, and Germany offering diverse critical perspectives.

WOLFRAM VON ESCHENBACH. 1170?–1220?

"I am Wolfram von Eschenbach and I know a little about singing"; thus does perhaps the most unique personality in medieval German literature introduce himself to readers. The second part of the statement is one of the greatest understatements in the realm of literature. He is the author of two unfinished works, *Willehalm* and *Titurel* (both c.1215), and of a few surviving lyrics—all of which show great innovativeness and skill.

He is best known to general audiences as the author of *Parzival,* a Grail romance of more than 24,000 lines. His main source is the incomplete *Perceval, or the Grail* of CHRÉTIEN DE TROYES. Whether Wolfram had another source that supplied him with the end of the tale or whether he provided it himself is not definitely known. Wolfram teases his audience on several occasions by a reference to a mysterious Kyot who supposedly transmitted the tale and who was Wolfram's chief source. Modern scholars have given up the search for Kyot, and most now assume that the completion of the *Parzival* story is by Wolfram himself.

The basic theme of *Parzival* is like that of the other German courtly romances, examining how a person can so arrange his life that he is pleasing to both God and man. As in other tales, the answer lies in compassion. Wolfram's *Parzival* also provided the material used in Wagner's (see Vol. 3) libretto for *Parsifal.*

Poetry by Wolfram von Eschenbach

Parzival of Wolfram von Eschenbach. AMS Pr. repr. of 1951 ed. $18.50. ISBN 0-404-50905-3

Titurel. c.1216. Trans. by Charles E. Passage. Continuum 1985 $25.00. ISBN 0-8044-2181-1. A fragment of a story set in the court of the Holy Grail, with delicate descriptions of awakening love between two young people.

Willehalm. c.1215. Ed. by Karl Lachmann and Dieter Kartschoke. De Gruyter 1968 $28.00. ISBN 3-11-000314-7. An unfinished epic of war between Christians and pagans, notable for its representation of married love and pleas for religious tolerance.

Books about Wolfram von Eschenbach

Green, D. H. *The Art of Recognition in Wolfram's "Parzifal."* Cambridge U. Pr. 1982 $75.00. ISBN 0-521-24500-1

Rachbauer, M. A. *Wolfram von Eschenbach.* AMS Pr. repr. of 1934 ed. $28.00. ISBN 0-404-50224-5. An introduction to the life, times, and poetry of Wolfram.

ZWEIG, STEFAN. 1881–1942

Born in Vienna, the prolific Zweig was a poet in his early years. In the 1920s, he achieved fame with the many biographies he wrote of famous people including Balzac, Dostoevsky, Dickens (see Vol. 1), and Freud (see Vols. 3 and 5). Erasmus (see Vol. 4), with whom he closely identified, was the subject of a longer biography. He also wrote the novellas *Amok* (1922) and *The Royal Game* (1944). As Nazism spread, Zweig, a Jew, fled to the United States and then to Brazil. He hoped to start a new life there, but the haunting memory of Nazism, still undefeated, proved too much for him. He died with his wife in a suicide pact.

Nonfiction by Zweig

Emile Verhaeren. 1910. Trans. by Jethro Bithell. *Select Bibliographies Repr. Ser.* Ayer repr. of 1914 ed. $16.00. ISBN 0-8369-5591-9. A biography of the late nineteenth-century Belgian poet and critic, whose frustrated passion for social reform led to a profound pessimism.

Romain Rolland: The Man and His Works. 1920. Ayer 1973 repr. of 1921 ed. $24.50. ISBN 0-405-09113-3. A biography of the noted French author and musicologist, who was an older contemporary of and something of a model for Zweig.

The World of Yesterday: An Autobiography. 1943. U. of Nebr. Pr. 1964 repr. of 1943 ed. $7.95. ISBN 0-8032-5224-2. Intensely moving and eloquent expression of Zweig's bitter disappointment with the changes that Nazism brought about, especially in the souls of people.

Short Story Collection by Zweig

Passion and Pain. 1938. Trans. by Paul Eden and Paul Cedar. *Short Story Index Repr. Ser.* Ayer repr. of 1925 ed. $15.00. ISBN 0-8369-3882-8. The story of an officer who becomes engaged to a crippled girl out of pity but eventually denies the engagement to his comrades, driving the girl to suicide.

Work by Zweig

Jewish Legends. Trans. by Paul Eden and Paul Cedar. Wiener 1987 $9.95. ISBN 0-910129-59-2

Book about Zweig

Turner, David. *Moral Value and the Human Zoo: The Novellen of Stefan Zweig*. Denali Pr. 1989 $45.00. ISBN 0-85958-476-3. The attempt of Zweig to affirm humanistic values in a Europe filled with chaos and brutality.

CHAPTER 18

Netherlandic Literature

Martinus A. Bakker and Henry J. Baron

The love for one's country is innate to all people.
—JOOST VAN DEN VONDEL, *Gijsbrecht van Amstal*

Dutch is the language of the people living in The Netherlands as well as those living in the part of northern Belgium called Flanders. Only in the spoken form is there a difference between the two versions of the language, neither of which can claim historical authenticity. The "Nederlandse Taalunie" (Netherlands Language Union), an officially appointed body of representatives from both countries, controls spelling and other linguistic interests.

Netherlandic literature began in the twelfth century. The oldest preserved text regarded as genuinely Dutch was discovered in 1932 on the endpaper of a Latin manuscript in the Bodleian Library in Oxford. Only two lines of the complete text are in Dutch:

> Hebban olla uogala nestas bigunnan hinase hic enda thu (Have all birds begun to build nests, except I and you)

This romantic-sounding text probably originated in the area now known as West Flanders. Countless other texts in the form of martial, bridal and burial songs also must have existed without ever having been written down. It is in this context interesting to note that an important episode from the Anglo-Saxon *Beowulf* (eighth century) (see Vol. 1), namely the so-called Hygelac-episode, is located in Friesland, now one of the twelve provinces of The Netherlands, whose inhabitants to this day speak a language in some respects more closely related to English than to Dutch. The Friesians, although Dutch nationals, also pride themselves on a literature of their own. Other well-known Germanic medieval epics, such as the German *Nibelungenlied* and *Gudrun*, also contain materials that may be regarded as early Dutch.

One of the first milestones in Dutch literary history is the work of Heynric (or Hendrik or Henry) van Veldeke (twelfth century), a nobleman and troubadour who lived, as the name indicates, in a hamlet called Veldeke (little field), just south of the present Dutch–Belgian border. Of his *Eneide,* a romance of chivalry and adventure, only the German version has been retained. However, his *Saint Servatius Legend,* dating from 1170, survives in Dutch. In it van Veldeke relates the life and miraculous experiences of the preacher and champion of the faith, Saint Servatius (or Gervase), in a style enjoyable even for present-day readers.

During medieval times, much of Netherlandic literature, like much of the literature of the rest of Europe, was anonymous. The genres in Netherlandic medieval texts are roughly the same as in other West European cultures and are usually divided into the art of the nobility, religious literature, and the art of the Third Estate or the commoners. An example of the first type is the epic poem

Karel ende Elegast (*Charles and Nobleman*). Like many other early Dutch literary works, it was adapted from the French. It describes in colorful lines the obviously largely imaginary chivalrous deeds and adventures of Charles the Great, who ruled the major part of Europe in the eighth century. According to this tale Charles was called by an angel in the middle of the night and, upon his initial hesitation, was ordered three times to go out and burgle the home of his own sister and his brother-in-law, Eggheric. Lying under his brother-in-law's bed Charles overheard Eggheric planning to murder Charles and assume reign of the country.

To the art of the clergy we owe the legend of *Beatrice*, the story of a nun who, although succumbing to worldly pleasures, remained so faithful to Mary that the latter took her place in the convent while Beatrice, for fourteen years, lived a very worldly life. As recently as 1908 this legend was adapted for modern tastes as a play by the poet P. C. Boutens.

From the art of the Third Estate comes the popular animal epic *Reynard the Fox* , a satire on the injustices of feudal society and the greed of the nobility and royalty. Even the often dubious lifestyle of some members of the clergy is not spared by the sharp-witted and merciless fox, the mouthpiece of the writer who, in the first lines, introduces himself as "William who made Madoc."

In the seventeenth century uncertainty about the authors of literary works disappeared with the commencement of the Renaissance. The growing self-confidence of Dutch artists was confirmed and reinforced by Dutch successes in many other areas. The affluence that colonization and industrialization brought was reflected in a wealth of artistic achievement, not least in literature. The focus of cultural activity had by this time shifted from Antwerp to Amsterdam, due to the political subjection of Belgium by Spain. More reinforcement to the self-confidence of the Dutch resulted from the prominence of the sixteenth-century philosopher Erasmus (see Vol. 4) of Rotterdam, and from the work of inventors such as Anthony van Leeuwenhoek, who was instrumental in developing the microscope, and from astronomer Christiaan Huygens, who discovered Saturn's ring and who published his *Brief Demonstration of the Use of the Chronometer for Ascertaining Longitude* in 1658. However, visual art, especially painting, unimpeded by linguistic barriers, did more than literature to put The Netherlands on the international cultural map: the fame of artists such as Rubens (see Vol. 3), Rembrandt (see Vol. 3), and Vermeer may be regarded as proverbial.

Netherlandic writers of the Renaissance and Reformation, though equally deserving, were hindered by the obscurity of the language from achieving international fame. Still, they created works of such high and enduring quality that the era is considered the Golden Age of Netherlandic literature. One example is provided by playwright Joost van den Vondel. Vondel's work is in mobility of diction and richness of descriptive power comparable to Shakespeare's (see Vol. 1), though thematically it is more reminiscent of Milton (see Vol. 1). In 1648 The Netherlands had emerged victorious from a partially religious war, the eighty-year War of Independence against Spain. Thus religious poetry was important and flourishing. Playwrights and poets P. C. Hooft, Gerbrand A. Bredero, and Constantijn Huygens, father of Christiaan, made significant contributions.

The period between this so-called Golden Age and the twentieth century was not as prolific as the seventeenth century, but it did produce classics such as the plays of Pieter Langendijk; the epistolary novels of Betje Wolf; the historical novels of Jacob van Lennep, Bosboom-Tousaint, and Hendrik Conscience; and the anti-colonial novel *Max Havelaar* (1859) by Multatuli. This classic was printed in many languages and was made into a popular movie. As a frame-story, the novel was revolutionary in structure, and it was considered a model of figurative language. It may not have radically influenced the Dutch government's colonial policy immediately, but it may well have done so in a more indirect way; it was even discussed on a parliamentary level, although its literary qualities ultimately outweighed its political message.

Around 1880 a programmatic movement, the Movement of the Eighties, became the fountainhead of a renewed literature. The founders were inspired by contemporary French and German authors, such as the symbolists MALLARMÉ AND VERLAINE, and naturalists like ZOLA. Under these influences, twentieth-century Dutch literature witnessed a remarkable revitalization in both poetry and prose. The writers grouped around the review *Forum* in the 1930s, notably M. ter Braak, Simon Vestdijk, Willem Elsschot, and Edgar du Perron, brought about a profound revolt against formalism and aestheticism, rallying instead around a program for a literature of engagement in social and political life.

Contemporary Netherlandic literature is even now, fifty years after World War II, strongly under the influence of the experiences connected with that war. Increasingly more contemporary Dutch–Flemish writers are being translated. Among these are HARRY MULISCH, whose *The Assault* (1982) has already become a classic and a successful movie, LOUIS PAUL BOON, HUBERT LAMPO, WILLEM FREDERIK HERMANS, HUGO CLAUS, Willem Brakman, MARTIN HART, Cees Nooteboom, and, most recently, Adri van der Heijden.

The Netherlands is a relatively small country. However, it has a unique strategic position, geographically, economically, and culturally, and therefore has, in its own interest, through the ages, conducted an open-border policy. Due to a recent increase in The Netherlands of university programs in English, and to the publication of all kinds of material in English, Netherlandic literature is now becoming more accessible to the English-speaking world.

HISTORY AND CRITICISM

Colledge, Edmund. *Medieval Netherlands Religious Literature.* London Hse. 1965 o.p. Provides useful information to readers who need to know more about the actual contents of a variety of medieval plays and epic poems primarily inspired by the gospels and legendary figures.

———. *Reynard the Fox and Other Medieval Netherlands Secular Literature.* London Hse. 1967 o.p. Concentrates on the immortal story of the fox whose antics are read in numberless languages and formats, explaining that the apparently puerile stories have, in fact, a profound message.

Nieuwenhuys, Robert. *Mirror of the Indies: A History of Dutch Colonial Literature.* Ed. by E. M. Beekman. Trans. by Frans Van Rosevelt. U. of Mass. Pr. 1982 $35.00. ISBN 0-87023-368-8. Discusses the work of authors such as the monumental Multatuli without whose work Dutch literature and cultural history would not have been as varied and rich as it is. A valuable contribution.

Shetter, William Z. *The Netherlands in Perspective.* St. Mut. 1987 $200.00. ISBN 90-6890-070-6. Offers a wide-ranging picture of contemporary Holland describing the various lines along which Dutch society is organized.

Snapper, Johan P., and Thomas F. Shannon. *The Berkeley Conference on Dutch Literature, 1987: New Perspectives on the Modern Period.* U. Pr. of Amer. 1989 $28.00. ISBN 0-8191-7325-8. Contains a variety of papers loosely connected on the basis of their modernity and the views and interpretations of the various presentors.

COLLECTIONS

Beekman, E. M., ed. and tr. *Fugitive Dreams: An Anthology of Dutch Colonial Literature.* U. of Mass. Pr. 1988 $35.00. ISBN 0-87023-575-3. A valuable contribution to the library of Dutch literary works in English translation by an author who specializes in Dutch Colonial literature.

Greshoff, Jan. *Harvest of the Lowlands (An Anthology of Dutch Stories).* Querido 1945 o.p. Very useful for readers who would like to know more about the status and nature of Dutch literature and culture of the first half of this century.

Van Loggem, Manuel. *New Worlds from the Lowlands.* Cross Cult. 1982 $20.00. ISBN 0-89304-053-3. A comprehensive anthology of contemporary fantasy and science fiction in The Netherlands and Flanders.

CHRONOLOGY OF AUTHORS

Reynard the Fox. 12th Century
Hadewijch. c.1200–1250
Bredero, Gerbrand A. 1580–1617
Revius, Jacobus. 1586–1658
Vondel, Joost van den. 1587–1679
Multatuli. 1820–1887
Emants, Marcellus. 1848–1923
Eeden, Frederik van. 1860–1932
Van Schendel, Arthur. 1874–1946
Ellsschot, Willem. 1882–1960
Ostaijen, Paul van. 1896–1928
Vestdijk, Simon. 1898–1971
Alberts, A. 1905–
Boon, Louis Paul. 1912–1979
Haasse, Hella S. 1912–
Schierbeek, Bert. 1918–
Lampo, Hubert. 1920–
Hermans, Willem F. 1921–
Wolkers, Jan. 1925–
Mulisch, Harry. 1927–
Claus, Hugo. 1929–
Ruyslinck, Ward. 1929–
Herzberg, Judith. 1934–
Hart, Martin. 1944–

ALBERTS, A. 1905–

Alberts, who was a civil servant in the Indies before World War II, writes incisive and ironic stories about the contradictory relationships in a colonial situation.

WORK BY ALBERTS

The Islands. Ed. by E. M. Beekman. Trans. by Hans Koning. *Lib. of the Indies Ser.* U. of Mass. Pr. 1983 $22.50. ISBN 0-87023-385-8

BOON, LOUIS PAUL. 1912–1979

Louis Paul Boon was the first Belgian representative of the postwar anti-establishment novelists who have dominated the Dutch literary scene for the last half century. He is best remembered for his eloquent outspokenness in a variety of areas: he started off as an anarchistic communist but gradually mellowed to individualistic socialist; he was openly antireligious; he had revolutionary views on sex which shocked his compatriots and the even more enlightened Dutch so deeply that it took literary critics more than a decade to give him the credit he deserved. Because of his critical attitude, he has been accused of nihilism; viewed from a different perspective, he could be called an idealistic, unconventional reformer. Boon, who began his career as an automobile painter, champions the working class while at the same time giving his novels a wider philosophical scope.

Boon was, moreover, one of the first to experiment with possibilities for a new form of the novel, representing occurrences on three different time levels and mixing historical elements with contemporary and imaginary ones. For his collected works he was nominated by Dutch and Belgian authorities for the Nobel Prize.

NOVEL BY BOON

Chapel Road. Trans. by Adrienne Dixon. Twayne 1972 o.p. The author mercilessly described the evils of society, more particularly Flemish society, of the twentieth century before World War II.

BREDERO, GERBRAND A. 1580–1617

Bredero was the most important comedy writer of the Dutch seventeenth century and one of the most important literary figures overall. His play *The Spanish Brabanter* ridicules the manners of a self-styled nobleman from Antwerp with his Spanish behavior. It is also important for the sharp ear Bredero had for the language and sensibilities of the people.

PLAY BY BREDERO

The Spanish Brabanter. 1617. Trans. by H. David Brumble III. Medieval & Renaissance NY 1982 o.p.

CLAUS, HUGO. 1929–

Claus is a compatriot and kindred spirit to LOUIS PAUL BOON, in spite of seventeen years' difference in age. Claus could also be compared with his Dutch fellow-writer HARRY MULISCH, with whom he shares the postwar, anti-establishment, mildly anarchistic views of so many members of his generation. However, Claus's work is more difficult to characterize than that of either of the two other writers because, first, it is much more diverse and, second, his work underwent a radical change in the course of his writing career. So varied is his artistic production that a consistent theme can hardly be determined. While in Paris, in his early twenties, he explored surrealism, existentialism, and modernism as a member of the Cobra group of experimentalist artists (*Cobra* is an anagram made up from Copenhagen, Brussels, and Amsterdam), and while in Rome he concerned himself with filmmaking and actually produced a film called *Friday* for which he wrote the script himself.

Claus can be regarded as the primary developer of a technique which has become known as intertextuality. Its application in *The Sign of the Hamster* led to accusations of plagiarism, an accusation which many critics rejected because of the recognizability of the references which vary from the classics to the Middle Ages and his own time.

Claus gained recognition as painter, poet, playwright, filmmaker, and writer of classical, psychological, modernist, and experimentalist novels. Moreover, he possesses the ability to adapt his themes and style to the taste of a wide reading public. His latest novel, *The Sorrow of Belgium*, demonstrates his versatility. The book consists of two parts, the first strongly autobiographic, situated in a Roman Catholic boarding school in Belgium, from which Louis, the protagonist, is expelled. The second part describes the experiences of a large number of people, including Louis's mother and father, during and shortly after World War II.

For a play, *Masscheroen*, Claus was charged with blasphemy because he had three naked men represent the holy trinity on the stage. This charge and the possibility of plagiarism identify Claus as a controversial writer, but do not detract from his undeniable artistic talent.

Novels by Claus

The Duck Hunt. Trans. by George Libaire. Random 1955 o.p. Deals with contemporary social evils. Originally translated from the French.

The Sign of the Hamster. Trans. by Paul Claes and others. Leuvense Schrijversaktie 1986 o.p. A collection of poems so full of quotations and references that its publication gave rise to accusations of plagiarism.

The Sorrow of Belgium. Trans. by Arnold J. Pomerans. Pantheon 1990 $24.95. ISBN 0-394-56263-1

Play by Claus

Friday. Trans. by Hugo Claus and Christopher Logue. Davis-Poynter Ltd. 1972 o.p. Deals with the theme of incest which has fascinated Claus for a long time. Constitutes a major contribution to Dutch language drama.

Books about Claus

Four Flemish Poets. Hugo Claus, Gust Gils, Paul Snoek, Hugues C. Pernath. Ed. by Peter Nijmeijer. Transgravity Pr. 1976 o.p. A series of discussions by a variety of critics which constitutes a valuable source of information for students specializing in contemporary Flemish poetry.

Selected Poems 1953–1973 Hugo Claus. Ed. by Theo Hermans. Trans. by Theo Hermans, Paul Brown, and Peter Nijmeijer. Aquila Poetry 1986 o.p. Claus, generally regarded as one of the top ten Dutch–Flemish writers, is presented here as a major poet, primarily of poems in the classical tradition.

EEDEN, FREDERIK VAN. 1860–1932

In his turn-of-the-century novel about a woman's sexual urges, *The Deeps of Deliverance* (1900), the author's handling of the topics of erotic passion, drug abuse, and prostitution reveals his professional training as a psychiatrist. Van Eeden also is a leading figure in the field of Netherlandic literary history: He played an active part in the *Tachtiger-beweging* (The Movement of the Eighties) which marks the beginning of modern Dutch literature. Philosophically, he began as an idealistic reformer.

Van Eeden's influence can be gauged by the fact that, in addition to publishing several outstanding novels, he corresponded and worked extensively with prominent persons in the world of science, such as Arthur Schopenhauer (see Vol. 4), Friedrich Nietsche (see Vol. 4), and Sigmund Freud (see Vols. 3 and 5). He and Upton Sinclair (see Vol. 2) also kept up an exchange of letters. Appreciation for the work of van Eeden is shown by the contributions of these and other world leaders in the *Liber Amicorum* (1930) where van Eeden is presented as a unique and irreplaceable figure.

Novels by Eeden

The Deeps of Deliverance. Trans. by Margaret Robinson. Twayne 1975 o.p.

Paul's Awakening. Trans. by H. S. Lake. Hunter Hse. 1985 $6.95. ISBN 0-86164-156-6. About the death of his son Paul. Like many of his novels, describes the contrast between the world van Eeden dreamed about and persistently believed in, and the real world we live in.

ELSSCHOT, WILLEM (pseud. of Alfons de Ridder). 1882–1960

Willem Elsschot is a classic example of a dilettante turned professional writer. He wrote his stories in his spare time while working as an advertising agent in Antwerp. His profession explains the themes of his most successful stories *Lijmen* (*Soft Soap*) and *Het Been* (*The Leg*), published in 1924 as parts of the same collection of novelettes. Until this time he had never intended to publish anything he wrote and had to be persuaded to do so by the editors of *Nieuw Vlaams Tijdschrift,* a Flemish journal established to specifically promote the cause of Flemish literature and culture.

It is his total lack of interest in anything academic, even literary—he claims never to have read a literary work of art—which lends to Elsschot's work the very fresh and original quality for which it is known. He humorously satirizes the dubious techniques of salespersons in marketing and selling their wares. In addition to his prose works, Elsschot has written some poems which have become a unique part of the Dutch literary heritage.

NOVEL BY ELSSCHOT

Three Novels. British Bk. Ctr. 1965 o.p.

EMANTS, MARCELLUS. 1848-1923

Emants's *A Posthumous Confession,* his best-known novel, is the first-person account of a social misfit who murders his wife. In spite of Emants's awkward style, it created a sensation when it appeared in 1894. To the author's dismay, the public tended to identify him with the protagonist.

Emants's work frequently serves to demonstrate the Dutch involvement in naturalism, a distinction he shares with his better-known fellow novelist and near-contemporary Louis Couperus.

NOVEL BY EMANTS

A Posthumous Confession. 1894. Trans. by J. M. Coetzee. G. K. Hall 1975 o.p.

ERASMUS, DESIDERIUS. 1469-1536

[SEE Vol. 4.]

HAASSE, HELLA S. 1912–

Hella Haasse was born in Batavia, the capital of what was then Dutch East India, now independent Indonesia. It is thus understandable why her first novel, *Oeroeg* (1948), describes the relationship between a Dutch and an Indonesian youth. As the two young men grow up, they gradually become conscious of their ethnic and cultural differences and, in spite of their efforts, nature appears to have destined them to become estranged from each other.

Haasse's greatest impact on the Dutch literary scene occurred when her historical novel *Het woud der verwachting* (*In a Dark Wood Wandering*) (1948) was published. It was translated into English in 1989. This novel became a classic in its own time. In it the author describes the ever-increasing loneliness of the fifteenth-century Romantic poet–prince Charles d'Orleans, pretender to the crown of France, who wrote most of his poems in British and French prisons. In addition to giving a moving report of the life of a person destined to end his life in utter isolation, Hella Haasse succeeds in presenting her main character in a way which allows the reader to identify with him. Charles's life is interwoven with the lives of all the other people he meets in his long and eventful life. Haasse's talent for description and narration and her skill with flashbacks allow her to manage the novel's many characters, constructing a microcosm in which each reader feels 'at home' and meets people with whom he or she can identify.

Novels by Haasse

In a Dark Wood Wandering. Rev. and ed. by Anita Miller from an English translation by Lewis C. Kaplan. Academy Chi. Pubs. 1989 $22.95. ISBN 0-89733-336-5

The Scarlet City. Trans. by Anita Miller. Academy Chi. Pubs. 1990 $12.95. ISBN 0-89733-372-1. Fifteenth- and sixteenth-century Rome. Describes the attempt of the antagonist to discover and analyze his own identity.

HADEWIJCH. c.1200–1250

Hadewijch is one of the most powerful mystical poets in medieval literature. She uses the forms and conventions of courtly love poetry to convey a most intense feeling of rejection and acceptance by the divine lover.

Work by Hadewijch

The Complete Works. Trans. by Columba Hart. Paulist Pr. 1980 o.p.

HART, MARTIN. 1944–

The theme in most of Martin Hart's work (*Martin Hart* is the anglicized version of *Maarten 't Hart*) can be related to the strict views of his religiously conservative parents and the bigoted views of most of the people in his immediate environment. The title of one of his first books is revealing in this respect: *Het Vrome Volk* (The pious people) refers ironically to the people from the village where he grew up, whose false piety he ridicules in one novel after another.

Novel by Hart

Bearers of Bad Tidings. Trans. by J. W. Arriens. Schocken 1979 $13.95. ISBN 0-8052-8176-2. Deacons of the church appear dumb and hypocritical. The butt of Hart's expressions of resentment concerning his own conservative Protestant upbringing.

HERMANS, WILLEM F. 1921–

Hermans's cynicism frequently takes the form of sarcasm, the most obvious characteristic of his many works. This attitude may be explained by a disturbing experience in his youth, when his sister and a cousin committed suicide together upon the invasion of The Netherlands by the Nazis in May of 1940. Much of his condemnation finds an outlet in criticism of society, specifically Dutch society. Since 1973 Hermans has lived in Paris. He continues to publish his novels in Dutch, although he rejects Dutch literary prizes. In spite of, or because of, his negative attitude, he is one of the most widely read authors in The Netherlands.

Hermans's work also protests against life itself: he has been called a nihilist. This philosophy could also be summed up as a belief that war is the natural state of humankind, so that the period between any two given wars cannot be termed peace and is not a state which people really desire. According to Hermans, faith and morality are based on (self)deception. For him, belief in God and heaven is the best example of this form of deception, creating the false impression that somewhere security, harmony, and peace exist. Without this illusion life would become unbearable for most people. The title of Hermans's first novel, *Het Behouden Huis* (*The House of Refuge*) (1951), is a clear reference to heaven as used metaphorically in the Bible and says it all: at the end (of the war) the house referred to is blown up, exposing what it had in fact always been: "a hollow, drafty lump of rock, internally full of decay and filth." As R. P. Meyer puts it in his *Literature of the Low Countries* (1971): "In the work of Hermans chaos always wins, there is never a lasting solution to the absurdity of life."

In its existentialist and often sadistic spirit, as well as its high quality, Hermans's work is reminiscent of SADE, FREUD (see Vols. 3 and 5), and SCHOPENHAUER (see Vol. 4).

NOVEL BY HERMANS

The Dark Room of Damocles. Trans. by Roy Edwards. Heinemann Ed. 1962 o.p. About a typically insignificant man named Henri Osewoudt, arrested and beaten up by German soldiers but unable to prove his innocence to the Dutch Resistance workers, in spite of his heroic deeds.

HERZBERG, JUDITH. 1934–

Judith Herzberg belongs to the group of poets who published in the literary journal *Tirade,* established in 1957 as a reaction to the unemotional style of the preceding literary period. This purpose explains the individualistic character of both the journal and its publications. Herzberg's individuality consists of an ironic style which makes her poems look much simpler than they really are. Upon a closer look the poems prove to be carefully camouflaged expressions of a vulnerable, sensitive spirit poetically reflecting and commenting on human insensitivity. In addition to the publication of several books of poems, Herzberg has been productive in dramatic art, television script-writing, and filmmaking.

POETRY BY HERZBERG

But What. Selected Poems. Trans. by Shirley Kaufman and Judith Herzberg. Oberlin Coll. Pr. 1988 $15.00. ISBN 0-932440-24-X. A selection of poems representative of Herzberg's style and themes dealing primarily with personal experiences in the context of human interrelationships.

Quartet. An Anthology of Dutch and Flemish Poetry by Judith Herzberg. . . . [et al] Wilfion Bks. Scotland 1978 o.p. A useful source for students of contemporary Dutch and Flemish poetry. Illustrates the poet's preference for works that deal with human relations and the misery people can cause one another.

LAMPO, HUBERT. 1920–

Lampo is the major Dutch–Flemish literary exponent of magical realism, which is based on the belief in the collective unconscious, a theory developed by the Swiss psychologist C. G. JUNG (see Vol. 5). Jung's theory identifies the presence of archetypes, "the original pattern or model of all things of the same type." The main characters in Lampo's novels cross borders of time and space which normally separate generations and worlds. His characters are often librarians, archaeologists, or others who are "lost" or out of touch with the here and now, which makes their passing into a different zone plausible.

Quite common in Lampo's novels are variants of the so-called anima or perfect woman, the savior archetype, the witch, the devil, and the Orpheus figure. The latter is, in fact, the main character in *Kasper in de onderwereld* (*Kasper in the Underworld*) (1969), a variation on the Orpheus and Euridice theme in which the harbor area of Rotterdam replaces the "classic" underworld, and Kasper plays a mouth organ instead of a flute. Lampo himself regards this novel as his most successful execution of magical realism. His best-known book is *The Coming of Joachim Stiller* (1974), in which we meet the classical savior type who disappears from the morgue where his body had lain for three days.

NOVELS BY LAMPO

Arthur and the Grail. Sidgwick & Jackson 1988 o.p.
The Coming of Joachim Stiller. Trans. by Emlyn Jones. Twayne 1974 o.p.

MULISCH, HARRY. 1927–

Mulisch's name will go down in history as the writer par excellence of modern myths, and possibly not only in Dutch literary history. Every one of his great novels such as *Het Stenen Bruidsbed* (*The Stone Bridal Bed*) (1959), *Hoogste Tijd* (*High Time*) (1985), and *De Aanslag* (*The Assault*) (1982) is technically based on, or evokes reminiscences of, existing classical myths; at the same time, each work is thematically related to the author's own time and experiences, usually World War II. Every one of the more important characters, excluding the main characters who normally serve as narrators or reporters, is an embodiment or personification of an archetype.

In *The Assault* the various characters not only play completely different roles in the killing of a German officer by members of the Dutch Resistance movement, but they also represent distinct types. The action is also much more than an incident. The protagonist, Anton Steenwijk, spends a lifetime trying to solve the puzzle consisting of the various causes and effects relative to the fatal act. He does this not as a detective but as a normal, thinking human being who is interested in knowing where he came from and where he is headed. The puzzle that presents itself to him is as complex, yet as logical, as the waves created by a passing ship, reverberating indefinitely, even when the ship has disappeared from sight.

Mulisch is, with WOLKERS, HERMANS, and VESTDIJK, one of the most talented novelists of his generation, but he may be expected to outlive all three others because of the classical nature of his work, *classical* here meaning "of primary significance for all people of all times."

NOVELS BY MULISCH

The Stone Bridal Bed. Trans. by Adrienne Dixon. Abelard-Schuman 1962 o.p.

Two Women. Trans. by Els Early. Riverrun NY 1981 $5.95. ISBN 0-7145-3810. Describes the relationship between two lesbian women, adding a cosmological dimension to a phenomenon not normally recognized by most people.

What Poetry Is. Trans. by Claire Nicolas. Cross Cult. 1981 $15.00. ISBN 0-893-04-875-5. Highly personal, though not far-fetched views on a subject in which Mulisch recognizes mythological elements. First published in Dutch in 1978.

Last Call. Trans. by Adrienne Dixon. Viking Penguin 1991 $8.95. ISBN 0-14-015601-1. An excellent example of a novel constituting research in the form of a novel, that is in imaginative form. Deserves more attention than it has received so far.

BOOK ABOUT MULISCH

Hoogenboom, Gerda. *A Study and Translation of Harry Mulisch's "Inspection"*. Canadian Thesis Services 1988 o.p. Available only in microfiche from the Canadian Theses Service at the National Library of Canada in Ottawa. Primarily of interest to students specializing in the work of Mulisch as such.

MULTATULI (pseud. of Eduard Douwes Dekker). 1820-1887

Multatuli is the most important Netherlandic novelist of the nineteenth century. His best-known work is *Max Havelaar* (1860), which was based on his experiences as a government official in the Dutch East Indies. In it, he lambasts the colonial regime for its alleged exploitation and maltreatment of the native population. The book's documentary value is open to question, but in literary and aesthetic terms it was far ahead of its time.

WORKS BY MULTATULI

Max Havelaar: Or the Coffee Auctions of the Dutch Trading Company. 1860. Trans. by Roy Edwards. Intro. by D. H. Lawrence. Afterword by E. M. Beekman. U. of Mass. Pr. 1982 $35.00 ISBN 0-87023-359-9

The Oyster and the Eagle: Selected Aphorisms and Parables. Trans. by E. M. Beekman. U. of Mass. Pr. 1974 $17.50. ISBN 0-87023-123-5. Some of Multatuli's minor writings.

BOOK ABOUT MULTATULI

King, Peter. *Multatuli. Twayne's World Authors Ser.* G. K. Hall o.p.

OSTAIJEN, PAUL VAN. 1896-1928

Van Ostaijen was a Flemish avant-garde writer who led the expressionist movement in Flemish literature. He wrote stories, poems, and criticism.

WORKS BY OSTAIJEN

Feasts of Fear and Agony. 1920. Trans. by H. van Ameyden van Duym. New Dir. Pr. 1976 $5.95. ISBN 0-8112-0600-9

Patriotism, Inc. and Other Tales. Trans. by E. M. Beekman. U. of Mass. Pr. 1971 o.p.

REVIUS, JACOBUS. 1586–1658

This strongly Calvinist poet is noted for his synthesis of the traditions of popular Netherlandic poetry with the forms and conventions developed in Renaissance Italy.

POETRY BY REVIUS

Selected Poems of Jacobus Revius, Dutch Metaphysical Poet. Trans. by Henrietta Ten Harmsel. Wayne St. U. Pr. 1968 o.p.

REYNARD THE FOX. 12th century

The well-known main actors in the collection of stories known as the Reynard cycle are a clever, smooth-talking, unprincipled fox, and his constant adversary, a stupid, coarse-mannered, equally unprincipled wolf named Ysengrim. The tales appear to have originated in the Netherlands, where they became the vehicle for lively comic scenes and sharp satires of the church and the court. Their influence has been worldwide, and parallel versions of the tales may be found in the literature of nations far removed from the Low Countries. There are many other versions of the Reynard cycle than that listed below. Perhaps the most brilliant of them all is the Latin poem *Ysengrimus* by Novardus of Ghent, whose keen-witted verse has been translated into Dutch and German, but not yet into English.

The History of Reynard the Fox. Ed. by N. F. Blake. Trans. by William Caxton. OUP 1970 o.p. An illustrated edition of the text, which became an English classic in the hands of its translator and publisher, the man who brought the art of printing to England.

RUYSLINCK, WARD (pseud. of R.K.M. de Belser). 1929–

Ruyslinck's novels primarily deal with the fate of the sensitive outsider in our mechanized society. In one of his novels *Het Reservaat* (*The Reserve*) (1964), the last specimen of humanity as we know it, i.e. a person with a conscience and a heart in the abstract sense of the word, has been placed in a museum because he had become too maladjusted to function normally in modern society.

Much less pretentious and consequently more convincing is Ruyslinck's moving *Wierook en Tranen* (*Frankincense and Tears*) (1958), which relates the first few days of the Nazi invasion in Belgium as seen through the eyes of two young children. In spite of the fact that Waldo, the little boy, is given thoughts which are clearly the author's, Ruyslinck succeeds in demonstrating that the crimes that are committed, including the rape of a young teen-age girl, are committed not by human beings, but by soldiers, who are themselves victims of the same war. In other words, Ruyslinck succeeds in lifting the action above the immediate—a highly commendable achievement.

NOVEL BY RUYSLINCK

The Depraved Sleepers (and *Golden Ophelia*). Trans. by R. B. Powell and David Smith. G. K. Hall 1978 o.p. An attempt to represent the atmosphere of despondency prevalent after World War II by means of some characters who, for no apparent reason, seem doomed to absolute inactivity and ambitionlessness.

SCHIERBEEK, BERT. 1918–

Schierbeek is one of the most difficult and unconventional of Dutch experimental poets, composing his incantations in a hypnotic prose verse.

WORK BY SCHIERBEEK

Shapes of the Voice. G. K. Hall 1977 o.p. An anthology from his most important work.

SPINOZA, BARUCH (or BENEDICTUS DE). 1632–1677

[SEE Volume 4.]

VAN SCHENDEL, ARTHUR. 1874–1946

Van Schendel's work can be divided into two distinctly different periods: his years in The Netherlands, when he literally romanticized the Italian Middle Ages, and those in Italy, when he made The Netherlands the background for his romanticized theories concerning fate as interpreted by Dutch nineteenth-century Calvinism. The name of the hero of the books with which his name is primarily associated, *Een Zwerver Verliefd* (*The Enamored Wanderer*) (1904) and its sequel *Een Zwerver Verdwaald* (*The Lost Wanderer*) (1907), is "Tamalone." This name is believed to be derived from the English "I am alone," and it describes in a very general way the position of the medieval knight who is hopelessly in love with a noble lady who will forever remain his beloved only in his dreams.

In his *Het Fregatschip Johanna Maria* (*The Johanna Maria*) (1930), the place of the lonely knight is taken by a sail maker on one of the last sailboats before steamships came into use. His dream to own the ship (it has a lady's name!) comes true when there is no longer use for it. Van Schendel's work marks a development without which Dutch literary history would be the poorer.

NOVELS BY VAN SCHENDEL

Grey Birds. Trans. by M. S. Stephens. Routledge 1939 o.p. A novel describing the tragic destruction of a proud family as the result of the unavoidable influence of "fate," here in the form of punishment for "the sins of the fathers" as interpreted on the basis of narrow Calvinistic principles.

The House in Haarlem. Trans. by M. S. Stephens. Routledge 1940 o.p. Explains how even going bankrupt can lead to not only the suicide of the "perpetrator," but even to the punishment and death of a descendant, on the basis of supposedly Calvinistic beliefs.

The Johanna Maria. Trans. by Brian W. Downs. J. Cape 1935 o.p.

John Company. Ed. by E. M. Beekman. Trans. by Fr. van Rosevelt. U. of Mass. Pr. 1983 $25.00. ISBN 0-87023-383-1. Located in seventeenth-century Holland and dealing with the often fateful voyages of the Dutch between the homeland and the Dutch colonies.

The Waterman. Trans. by Neline C. Clegg. Heinemann Ed. 1963 o.p. A bargeman drowns in the water of the canals he knew better than anybody else, the water being the personification of the force that punishes people who try to control powers placed over them by an all-powerful God.

VESTDIJK, SIMON. 1898-1971

Vestdijk is known in The Netherlands as the most erudite and prolific writer of the twentieth century. In addition to more than 50 novels, he published 7 volumes of short stories, 22 books of poetry, 33 collections of essays and critical prose, and a number of nonfiction works on topics varying from astrology to philosophy. A physician, he worked as a ship's doctor before he turned to writing prose full-time. He was one of the first novelists in The Netherlands to make a living solely by writing.

His first several novels were so authentically autobiographical and loaded with topical references that to this day it is possible to make a "Vestdijk-tour" of Harlingen, the village in the province of Friesland where he grew up. A major part of these works is taken up by a narration, i.e. a thorough psychological analysis in literary form, of his youth and puberty. He clearly saw this period of his life as anything but paradisiacal, especially since his personality and talents were often misunderstood and underestimated by the less gifted people in his immediate environment.

More impressive even than his extensive series of so-called psychological novels are his historical novels, which deal with a variety of places and periods—classical Greece, Christ's Palestine, Spain during the Inquisition and the painter El Greco, The Netherlands during its struggle for freedom in the seventeenth century, and impoverished Ireland in the nineteenth century. In these novels, he investigates psychologically the behavior of his protagonists relative to their times and circumstances with convincing results from both a literary and a psychological perspective.

NOVELS BY VESTDIJK

The Garden Where the Brass Band Played. Trans. by A. Brotherton. New Amsterdam Bks. 1989 $18.95. ISBN 0-941533-59-X. The tragic story of the love of the main character, a semi-autobiographic "I," for Trix, the daughter of his music teacher. The music from the band in the park is symbolic of the paradisiac situation where it all begins but which gradually passes away.

Rum Island. Trans. by B. K. Bowes. Calder Pr. 1963 o.p. Conflict between the independent protagonist Anne Bonney, a female pirate who lived in the eighteenth century, and the less imaginative persons in her immediate surroundings of Jamaica.

NONFICTION BY VESTDIJK

The Future of Religion. Trans. by Jacob Faber. Photocopy Ann Arbor Michigan 1989 o.p. Philosophically very interesting but too subjective and unscientific to be taken seriously by systematic theologians.

VONDEL, JOOST VAN DEN. 1587–1679

Vondel could, with some justification, be considered the Shakespeare of the Netherlands because of his output and influence on dramatic art. A contemporary of SHAKESPEARE (see Vol. 1), Vondel was born in Cologne but, as an infant, moved to Amsterdam with his parents where, as soon as he was old enough, he helped his father run a silk stocking shop. To a large extent, Vondel was a self-made man: he taught himself both classical and modern languages, and several of his 32 plays bear witness to the fact that he had a thorough knowledge of classical culture and the Bible as well.

In his best-known historical play, *Gijsbrecht van Amstel* (1637), he describes the siege and consequent destruction of Amsterdam, but moulds it accurately on VIRGIL's report on the fall of Troy in *Aeneas*. In another historical play, *Maria Stuart* (1646), he launches a fierce attack on Queen Elizabeth.

Vondel's parents, being Baptists, had fled from Antwerp to Cologne in order to escape persecution. He adopted the Roman Catholic faith at age 40 and was deeply involved in the religious conflicts between Remonstrants and anti-Remonstrants. It is not surprising, therefore, that his biblical plays far outnumber the historical ones. He regarded his *Jeptha* (1657) as a model classical play, for it fully complied with all the rules of Aristotle: the play has five acts; the first four are followed by a chorus; the unities of time and place are strictly maintained; the lines are written in perfect alexandrines; and Jeptha is the perfect tragic hero, who falls, not because he is basically bad or sinful, but because of evil conquering good, with Jeptha the innocent victim. The tragic death of Jeptha's daughter, owing to a foolish commitment her father had made, is movingly and convincingly told in a style and language which, in contrast to the themes, is more Baroque than Renaissance in character.

On the basis of his sensitive and observant nature, Vondel considered himself called upon to react poetically to a variety of topical occurrences, varying from the beheading of Grand Pensionary van Oldenbarneveld, which Vondel described as a legal murder, to the premature deaths of two of his three children. The phrase *'s Landts oudste en grootste poeet* (the country's oldest and greatest poet) was coined specially on the occasion of Vondel's funeral in 1679 and has continued undisputed after more than three hundred years.

PLAY BY VONDEL

Lucifer. Trans. by Noel Clark. Absolute Class. 1990 o.p. Deals with the fall and banning from heaven of the archangel Lucifer after the creation of man of whom the angel was very jealous. Reminiscent of and comparable to Milton's *Paradise Lost* even though it is in the form of a play.

WOLKERS, JAN. 1925–

Jan Wolkers could serve as the prototype of the group of post–World War II writers who give the impression of having seized the crushing of Nazi power as an opportunity to attempt to cast off the yoke of oppression in all forms and formats. Their protest took the form of rebellion against any form of authority that seemed to restrict their freedom and individuality. In effect they, and more particularly Wolkers, demonstrated against authority in the home (often represented by a supposedly dominant father figure); against the political system (as, for instance, represented by American capitalism and international military involvement); against God and church office-bearers; and finally, against society and social norms in general as these found expression in current views on proper language, morals, and manners.

We thus find that Wolkers's main characters challenge all forms of established, prewar concepts as embodied in selected characters, frequently holding them up for ridicule and caricature. By way of contrast, the author portrays a series of persons who appear to be the victims of the corrupt views of modern society, usually social outcasts such as the immortal Uncle Louis in *Serpentina's Petticoat* (1961) with which Wolkers made his debut and simultaneously established his name. Animals, which almost by definition are also considered innocent, sometimes serve as victims of man's desire for power as well, as in Wolkers's famous *Back to Oegstgeest* (1965).

A unique form of expression of resentment is Wolkers's use of cruelty, as though the writer wishes to vent his anger on anything he can lay his hands on. It is important to note, in this connection, that the negative qualities mentioned above—such as anger, resentment, ridicule, and cruelty—do, in fact, together form the very thin and sometimes transparent shell covering Wolkers's sensitive and vulnerable nature and his religious pursuit of fairness, justice, love, and beauty. In literally demonstrating these commendable qualities, Wolkers is a worthy representative of his generation.

NOVELS BY WOLKERS

Horrible Tango. Trans. by R. R. Symonds. Secker & Warburg UK 1968 o.p. Relates to the relationship between the author and his brother who died young leaving Jan with mixed feelings of sadness, aggression, and guilt.

A Rose of Flesh. Trans. by John Scott. Secker & Warburg UK 1967 o.p. Title refers to a tumor on the body of the main character. The term is typical of the way in which Wolkers protests against "life" and a God who allows such suffering.

Turkish Delight. Trans. by Greta Kilburn. M. Boyars Pubs. 1983 $7.50. ISBN 0-7145-2787-4. One of Wolkers's most popular books. Relates semi-autobiographically to his life as a young artist and a love relationship which came to grief as a result of the young woman's inability to rid herself of an obsession concerning her youth.

FRISIAN LITERATURE

Henry J. Baron

In the early Middle Ages, the kingdom of the Frisians, known as *Magnum Frisia,* comprised much of the Netherlands, Belgium, and Germany. Fiercely independent and insistent on their right to personal freedom, the Frisian people instilled fear into tribes and empires that tried to subjugate them. By 1500, however, the Frisians were controlled by foreign powers, and in 1581, most of their land was incorporated into the Dutch Republic. In 1830 this land, which had become known as Friesland, was given the status of a Dutch province.

Remarkably, while Frisians have lost their political independence, their language and literature have not only survived but flourished. Among Germanic languages, Frisian is the one most closely related to Old English. In the past, this language included North, East, and West Frisian dialects. Today, however, Frisian literature commonly refers only to literature from the province of Friesland in the northern part of the Netherlands.

Frisian literature began around the eighth century with the songs of bards celebrating heroic deeds. Unfortunately, none of these epics still exists. During the medieval period, Frisian literature failed to develop fully, largely due to long periods of political instability. Surviving legal documents from the Middle Ages, however, features poetic qualities in form and thought that provide a glimpse into the nature of early Frisian literature.

Frisian literature as it is known today traces its origins to the seventeenth century with the work of Gysbert Japiks. At that time, the incorporation of Friesland into the Dutch Republic threatened to reduce Frisian to a mere peasant dialect, but Japiks proved with his *Friesche Rymlerye* (Frisian Verse) (1668) that the language could be a rich and versatile instrument for enduring poetry. His musical love lyrics are written with charm, passion, and unpretentiousness, and his dialogues, at their best, are dramatic masterpieces of character portrayal. While Japiks's religious lyrics often lack the spontaneity and wit of his love and nature poetry, they evince emotional depth and power. Noted outside of his own country as well as within, Japiks is known today as the "father of Frisian literature."

In the eighteenth century, no Frisian writers rose to the distinction of Japiks, although C. P. Salverda showed considerable merit. It wasn't until the romantic period of the nineteenth century that the legacy of Japiks was rediscovered and revived and other Frisian authors rose to prominence. During the first half of the century, Harmen Sytstra wrote of the heroic past in old Germanic verse forms, and Eeltsje Halbertsma created popular poetry that stimulated the rise of a rich folk literature in the second half of the century. The work of these writers made many Frisians want to learn to read in their own language. Following in Halbertsma's footsteps were Waling Dykstra and Tsjibbe Gearts van der Meulen, who, through their prose, verse, and comedies, contributed to a rather moralistic but popular Frisian literature in the late nineteenth century. Another writer of the period, Piter Jelles Troelsra, revived romanticism through lyrical verse that celebrated love, nature, and the Frisian homeland.

The twentieth century ushered in a new spirit in Frisian literature when Douwe Kalma challenged younger writers in 1915 to break with the narrow provincialism and didacticism of the past. Yet this break had already been anticipated in the splendid neo-romantic poetry and fiction of Simke Kloosterman, the psychological narratives of Reinder Brolsma, the intensely lyrical and personal verse of Rixt (the pseudonym of H. A. van Dorsen), and the reflective but penetrating poetry of Obe Postma, one of the finest Frisian poets and the first to use free verse in the Frisian language. For his part, Kalma made distinguished contributions in poetry, drama, translation, and literary history and criticism. Other writers who followed Kalma's call to a more artistic and universal expression of the Frisian voice included R. P. Sybesma, an excellent sonneteer; D. H. Kiestra, a talented poet of the soil; D. A. Tamminga, whose unique poetic idiom rendered the people's language into enduring art; and Fedde Schurer, a versatile and popular writer who, in 1946, launched *De Tsjerne*, the literary periodical that monopolized literary opinion in Friesland for more than twenty years.

Since World War II Frisian literature has increasingly reflected the trends in themes and innovative techniques of the western European literary community. Writing has largely broken away from traditional conventions, especially through the leadership of critic, essayist, and novelist Anne Wadman and the poet Jan Wybenga.

During the 1960s, many angry young voices mercilessly attacked the insights and mores of the past. The 1970s, however, saw a shift back toward a more balanced sensibility, most evident in the work of older poets such as Tiny Mulder and Freark Dam, whose vision acknowledges life's pain while affirming its significance, and such younger poets as Daniël Daen and Tsjebbe Hettinga, who have attempted to fuse the abstract and concrete into artistic form.

In fiction, Frisian literature in the last few decades has reached considerable maturity in both style and substance. Many postwar novels reflected the painful trauma of the Nazi occupation. Modern Frisian novels have also reflected the more universal themes and spirit of the twentieth century. The fiction of Ypk fan der Fear (pseudonym of Lipkje Post-Beuckens), Anne Wadman, Durk van der Ploeg, Rink van der Velde, and Trinus Riemersma consistently paint the human condition in somber colors, and their literary landscape is dotted with characters who are trapped and haunted by physical limitations, failed marriages, unfulfilling jobs, or broken relationships. Fan der Fear's novels give sympathetic treatment to tragic heroines alienated from life's mainstream. Wadman probes the layers of society, exposing the emptiness of people's ambitions or the futility of their dreams. Van der Ploeg depicts the plight of characters whose search for significance is invariably doomed by destructive forces from within or without. Van der Velde, Friesland's best-selling and most productive author, portrays rogues and anti-heroes whose fierce independence clashes with all usurpers of freedom and human rights. And Riemersma deals with themes of loneliness, estrangement, and helplessness in an increasingly technological society.

As the quality of Frisian literature has increased in recent years, more and more works have been translated into Dutch and other languages. Only two novels have been published in English so far, however, and neither is a recent work. The first work to be published in English was the popular children's classic *Afke's Ten* (1945) by NYNKE FAN HICHTUM. The second was *The Golden Whip* (1941) by ABE BROUWER. Frisian poets have fared somewhat better, and two bilingual collections of poetry are available.

Thus far, Frisian's status as a minor language has restricted its literature to the narrow confines of its own provincial boundaries. Expanding those boundaries to the English-speaking world would serve well the cause of both Frisian and world literature.

Collections

Jellema, Rod, trans. *Country Fair: Poems from Friesland since 1945*. Eerdmans 1985 o.p.

______. *The Sound That Remains: A Historical Collection of Frisian Poetry*. Eerdmans 1990 $13.95. ISBN 0-8028-0411-X

CHRONOLOGY OF AUTHORS

Fan Hichtum, Nynke. 1860—1939
Brouwer, Abe. 1901—1984

BROUWER, ABE. 1901–1984

Abe Brouwer was raised in the village of Burgumerheide, a pocket of poverty in Friesland. His Christian parents wanted to send him to a theological seminary, but were financially unable to do so because of the expense of raising twelve children. In fact, Abe's education never went beyond the sixth grade. As a young man, Abe left Friesland and went to the Dutch city of Eindhoven where he worked as an orderly in a sanitarium. It was in Eindhoven that he began his first literary efforts. While there, he also began to realize increasingly what his native land meant to him. In 1925, he returned to Friesland and worked with his father as a street paver; but at the same time, he also pursued his avocation as a writer of children's books, poems, plays, and adult novels. From 1955 to 1966 Brouwer again lived outside of Friesland, this time in the Dutch city of Diever, where he acted in the productions of Shakespeare. He retired in the Frisian town of Snits in 1966.

During his life, Brouwer enjoyed the reputation as one of Friesland's most popular folk writers. Though a somewhat careless writer and far from a polished stylist, his stories are fast moving and dramatic, strong in emotional conflicts and vivid in detail. These features characterize the novel *De Gouden Swipe* (*The Golden Whip*), Brouwer's best known work. This novel focuses on the conflict between a father and son and is set against a backdrop of rural life in the early 1900s.

Novel by Brouwer

The Golden Whip. 1941. Trans. by Albert Hyma. Zondervan 1947 o.p.

FAN HICHTUM, NYNKE. 1860–1939

Nynke fan Hichtum was born as Sjoukje Maria Diederika Bokma de Boer in the small Frisian village of Nes. When she became a writer, Sjoukje took the pen name of Nynke in honor of two Nynkes who had enchanted her with their stories when she was a young girl. In 1888 Fan Hichtum married the well-known Frisian statesman, Piter Jelles Troelstra. It was at that time that the author became acquainted with the household of a couple named Marten and Afke through their oldest daughter Hiltsje, who served as a maid in the Troelstra home. Hiltsje was one of ten children, and her family became the inspiration for Fan Hichtum's children's classic *Afke's Ten.* Fan Hichtum adopted Afke, the heroine of the book, as a model for herself. When she sent a copy of the book to her own children, who were attending school in Germany, she wrote this inscription: "In this book of mother love, I have tried to express my own mother love for my two children. May that love warm and comfort you as you read these pages in the foreign land. Your faithful mother, N. van Hichtum."

At the time *Afke's Ten* was written, few children in Friesland could read Frisian, and thus no children's books were published there. As a result, the author wrote her story in Dutch under the title of *Afke's Tiental.* The story was beautifully written and rendered a vividly authentic chronicle of the struggle for survival among the poor. The book quickly became a bestseller, and even made an impact on the Dutch monarch. It was said that Queen Wilhelmina's eyes were opened to the plight of common laborers when the book was read in her presence to her daughter Juliana. The story caught the interest of readers in other lands as well, and the book was translated into twenty-three languages. Ironically, it wasn't until 1956 that it first appeared in the Frisian language. A pioneer in children's literature in Friesland, Nynke fan Hichtum will always be best known for the poignant and endearing *Afke's Ten.*

Novel by Fan Hichtum

Afke's Ten. 1903. Trans. by Marie Kiersted Pidgeon. Viking Penguin 1945 o.p.

CHAPTER 19

Scandinavian Literatures

Susan C. Brantly

> If the purpose of art were to anesthetize, to make us forget life, then a hammer blow to the head would be the simplest and best art.
>
> —Elmer Diktonius, *My Poetry*

This chapter reflects the American usage of the term *Scandinavia,* which denotes not only Denmark, Norway, and Sweden but often Finland, the Faroe Islands, and Iceland as well. These countries, as a whole, refer to themselves as the Nordic countries, reserving the term *Scandinavia* for only Denmark, Norway, and Sweden. The Scandinavian countries included in the American definition do share some cultural traits, and their histories are inextricably intertwined. Their languages, however, show considerable differences. While Danish, Norwegian, and Swedish are mutually intelligible, Faroese and Icelandic cannot be readily understood by the mainland Nordic countries. Finnish belongs to a different language group altogether.

In the early Middle Ages, the Scandinavian countries shared a common mythology and were all participants in the Viking Age. The literary records of this time were uniquely and most thoroughly preserved in the manuscripts of Iceland. The countries were united politically from 1397 to 1520 during the Kalmar Union, which joined the crowns of Denmark, Sweden, and Norway. Shortly after the dissolution of the Kalmar Union came the Reformation, during which all the Scandinavian countries were unified under Lutheranism.

Strife and shifting alliances, however, also have a long history in the region. During the Middle Ages, Iceland, Norway, and Faroes came under the dominion of Denmark. Sweden claimed Finland as its possession, and after the dissolution of the Kalmar Union, Sweden's empire came to include most of the Baltic states. In the centuries that followed the Kalmar Union, these two factions—Denmark on one side, and Sweden on the other—were often at war and the region experienced several shifts in traditional alliances. During the twentieth century, the nation states were formed as they exist today. Only the Faroe Islands are still politically connected to another country—Denmark.

The treasures of the Scandinavian literary tradition are many. Its ballad and folk traditions are exceedingly rich, and the literature of medieval Iceland is perhaps without parallel in Europe. The pearls of the eighteenth century include the Danish dramatist LUDVIG HOLBERG and the Swedish poet Carl Michael Bellman. In the nineteenth century, Scandinavian literature came into its own, and the Danes HANS CHRISTIAN ANDERSEN and SØREN KIERKEGAARD (see Vol. 4) are among the most famous writers from that period. In the latter half of that century, Scandinavia became a literary Mecca, with the Norwegian HENRIK IBSEN and the Swede AUGUST STRINDBERG in the forefront of a host of talented authors. During the twentieth century, Scandinavian literature has continued to flourish, garnering a number of prestigious literary awards, including 14 Nobel Prizes.

HISTORY AND CRITICISM

Andersen, Frank, and John Weinstock, eds. *The Nordic Mind: Current Trends in Scandinavian Literary Criticism*. U. Pr. of Amer. 1987 $33.00. ISBN 0-8191-5692-2. A useful glimpse into Scandinavian methods of literary scholarship.

Bredsdorff, Elias, and others. *Introduction to Scandinavian Literature*. Greenwood 1970 repr. of 1951 ed. $35.00. ISBN 0-8371-2849-8. A standard scholarly overview.

Rossel, Sven. *A History of Scandinavian Literature: 1870 to 1980*. Trans. by Anne C. Ulme. U. of Minn. Pr. 1982 o.p. Necessarily brief entries, but a welcome update of Scandinavian literary history.

Zuck, Virpi, and others. *Dictionary of Scandinavian Literature*. Greenwood 1990 $99.50. ISBN 0-313-21450-6. An extremely useful tool. Includes important bibliographical information.

COLLECTIONS

Alwood, Martin S., ed. *Modern Scandinavian Poetry: The Panorama of Poetry 1900–1975*. New York 1982 o.p. A pleasant way to get an overview of Scandinavian poetry, which can be difficult to find in translation.

Claréus, Ingrid, ed. *Scandinavian Women Writers: An Anthology from the 1880s to the 1890s*. Greenwood 1989 $42.95. ISBN 0-313-25884-8. A worthwhile collection of women's writing spanning a century.

Rossel, Sven, ed. *Scandinavian Ballads*. U. of Wis. Pr. 1982 o.p. Provides a good introduction to Scandinavian ballads, which are difficult to find in translation.

CHRONOLOGY OF AUTHORS

Old Norse-Icelandic Literature

The Poetic Edda. 12th or 13th century
Sturluson, Snorri. 1179–1241
Völsunga Saga. 13th century
Eyrbyggja Saga. c.1230–1280
Laxdaela Saga. c.1250
Njál's Saga. c.1280
Sturlunga Saga. c.1300
Gunnarsson, Gunnar. 1889–1975
Thórdarson, Thorbergur. 1889–1974
Laxness, Halldór Kiljan. 1902–

Danish Literature

Holberg, Ludvig. 1684–1754
Andersen, Hans Christian. 1805–1875
Jacobsen, Jens Peter. 1847–1885
Bang, Herman. 1857–1912
Nexø, Martin Andersen. 1869–1954
Jensen, Johannes V(ilhelm). 1873–1950
Dinesen, Isak. 1885–1962
Munk, Kaj. 1898–1944
Branner, Hans Christian. 1903–1966
Scherfig, Hans. 1905–1979
Hansen, Martin A. 1909–1955
Ditlevsen, Tove. 1918–1976
Andersen, Benny Allen. 1929–
Sørensen, Villy. 1929–
Rifbjerg, Klaus. 1931–
Thorup, Kirsten. 1942–
Nordbrandt, Henrik. 1945–

Faroese Literature

Heinesen, William. 1900–
Jacobsen, Jørgen-Frantz. 1900–1938
Brú, Hedin. 1901–

Finnish Literature

The Kalevala. 1835–1849
Sillanpää, Frans Eemil. 1888–1964
Södergran, Edith. 1892–1923
Schoultz, Solveig von. 1907–
Waltari, Mika Toimi. 1908–1979
Jansson, Tove. 1914–
Carpelan, Bo. 1926–
Kihlman, Christer. 1930–
Saarikoski, Pentti. 1937–

Norwegian Literature
Ibsen, Henrik. 1828–1906
Bjørnson, Bjørnstjerne. 1832–1910
Lie, Jonas. 1833–1908
Skram, Amalie. 1846–1905
Hamsun, Knut. 1859–1952
Rølvaag, Ole Edvart. 1876–1931
Sandel, Cora. 1880–1974
Undset, Sigrid. 1882–1949
Vesaas, Tarjei. 1897–1970
Vik, Bjørg. 1935–
Faldbakken, Knut. 1941–

Swedish Literature
Almqvist, Carl Jonas Love. 1793–1866
Strindberg, August. 1849–1912
Lagerlöf, Selma. 1858–1940
Lagerkvist, Pär. 1891–1974
Moberg, Vilhelm. 1898–1973
Johnson, Eyvind. 1900–1976
Martinson, Harry. 1904–1978
Ekelöf, Gunnar. 1907–1968
Lindgren, Astrid. 1907–
Tranströmer, Tomas. 1931–
Enquist, P(er) O(lov). 1934–
Jersild, P(er) C(hristian). 1935–
Gustafsson, Lars. 1936–

OLD NORSE-ICELANDIC LITERATURE

In medieval times the island nation of Iceland produced a body of literature unsurpassed in Europe in its quality, variety, and sheer quantity. The Icelandic word *saga* is a general term for any fictional or nonfictional prose account, and these narratives embrace several kinds of themes. The Icelandic Family Sagas tell of local events and personalities from the so-called Saga Age (930–1030), although they are not necessarily historically accurate. This particular group of sagas, which includes *Njál's Saga* (c.1280) and *Laxdaela Saga* (c.1250) has received more critical attention than any other. The Legendary Sagas, such as the thirteenth-century *Völsunga Saga* and the fourteenth-century *Hrolf's Saga Kraka,* deal with mythical-heroic figures from Scandinavia's past, whereas the Sagas of the Knights, such as *The Saga of Tristram and Isönd* (1226), consist of Icelandic renderings of the chivalric literature of medieval France and Germany. The so-called contemporary sagas, the foremost of which is the STURLUNGA SAGA (c.1300), deal with events from the twelfth and thirteenth centuries, the age in which most of the sagas were written down. The Sagas of the Kings, which provide accounts of the lives of western Norse rulers, are best known through the translations of SNORRI STURLUSON'S *Heimskringla* (c.1230).

The anonymous works known as the eddic lays, first written down in the thirteenth century, vary in content. Some relate directly to the heroic lays of the eastern and southern Germanic peoples (Goths, Burgundians, Franks), others tell of Nordic mythology, and "The Sayings of the High One" is a collection of aphorisms. Skaldic verse, composed by individual poets from the ninth to fourteenth centuries, is a complex lyric genre that relies on the poet's mastery of metaphor, meter, assonance, and alliteration. Skaldic poems typically recount the lives of famous people, loves past and present, and specific moments in the poet's life. The good *skald* (poet) was a respected craftsperson in medieval Scandinavia, and skaldic verse is often quoted in the prose sagas.

After its extraordinary medieval period, Icelandic literature entered into a fairly sterile period, save for the production of *rimur,* a form of ballad. In the nineteenth century Icelandic letters awoke, influenced by the continental trends of romanticism, realism, and naturalism. Romanticism is represented in the works of Bjarni Thorarensen and Jónas Hallgrímsson. The first modern

Icelandic novel may be said to be Jón Thorodsen's *Lad and Lass* (1850), a depiction of contemporary Icelandic life. Twentieth-century Icelandic fiction culminated in the modernistic novels of HALLDOR KILJAN LAXNESS, who received the Nobel Prize for literature in 1955.

History and Criticism

Andersson, T. M. *The Icelandic Family Saga: An Analytical Reading*. HUP 1967 o.p. One of the most influential scholarly monographs on the subject in this century. Contains useful plot summaries of many sagas.

Brøndsted, Johannes. *The Vikings*. Viking Penguin 1960 $7.95. ISBN 0-14-020459-8. Solid historical background reading.

Clover, Carol. *The Medieval Saga*. Cornell Univ. Pr. 1982 $25.95. ISBN 0-8014-1447-4. Cogent arguments about the origin and narrative of the sagas.

Davidson, H. Ellis. *Gods and Myths of Northern Europe*. Noontide 1986 $7.00. ISBN 0-317-53026-7. The standard scholarly handbook on Nordic mythology.

Einarsson, Stefán. *A History of Icelandic Literature*. Bks. Demand 1957 $105.50. ISBN 0-317-29923-9. Provides a useful overview of modern Icelandic literature.

______. *History of Icelandic Prose Writers*. Kraus repr. of 1940 ed. $26.00. ISBN 0-527-00363-8. Somewhat dated, but one of the few sources in English.

Hallberg, Peter. *The Icelandic Saga*. Trans. by Paul Schach. U. of Nebr. Pr. 1962 o.p. A general overview of the important scholarly questions about the sagas.

______. *Old Icelandic Poetry. Eddic Lay and Skaldic Verse*. Trans. by Paul Schach and Sonja Lindgrenson. U. of Nebr. Pr. 1975 $21.00. ISBN 0-8032-0855-3. Worthwhile introduction to the study of the Old Icelandic poetic genres.

Hollander, Lee. *The Skalds: A Selection of Their Poems with Introduction and Notes*. U. of Mich. Pr. 1968 o.p. A book of interest to all students of medieval poetry, by a master interpreter of the Old Norse skaldic poetic genre.

Jones, Gwyn. *A History of the Vikings*. OUP 1984 repr. of 1968 ed. $13.95. ISBN 0-19-285139-X. Useful historical background from a respected professor of Celtic and Nordic studies.

Collections

Firchow, Evelyn S., ed. *Icelandic Short Stories*. Am. Scandinavian 1975 $14.00. ISBN 0-89067-028-5. Modern Icelandic prose.

Friis, Erik J., ed. *Modern Nordic Plays: Iceland*. Irvington 1982 $16.95. ISBN 0-8290-1163-3. Includes plays by Laxness, Jakobsson, Halldórsson, and Björnsson.

Johnston, George, trans. *Saga of Gisli the Outlaw*. U. of Toronto Pr. 1987 $8.95. ISBN 0-8020-6219-9. An exciting story of a man on the run.

Jones, Gwyn, ed. *Eirik the Red and Other Icelandic Sagas*. OUP 1980 $3.95. ISBN 0-19-281528-8. Includes *Hrafnkel's Saga*, *Gunnlaug Wormtongue*, and *King Hrolf and his Champions*, as well as other short prose pieces.

Magnusson, Magnus, and Hermann Pálsson, trans. *Seven Viking Romances*. Viking Penguin 1986 $8.95. ISBN 0-14-044474-X. Contains a selection of legendary sagas.

______. *The Vinland Sagas*. Viking Penguin 1965 $8.95. ISBN 0-14-044154-9. About the Norse discovery of America.

Magnússon, Sigurdur, trans. *Postwar Poetry of Iceland*. U. of Iowa Pr. 1984 $14.95. ISBN 0-87745-115-X. A general anthology of modern Icelandic poetry.

Pálsson, Hermann, trans. *Hrafnkel's Saga and Other stories*. Viking Penguin 1971 $5.95. ISBN 0-14-044238-3. Contains six other short pieces in addition to *Hrafnkel's Saga*.

______. *The Orkneyinga Saga*. Viking Penguin 1981 $5.95. ISBN 0-14-044383-5. Recounts the history of the earls of Orkney and their relations with the rulers of Norway and Scotland from 900 to 1171. Written c.1200.

EYRBYGGJA SAGA. 1230–1280

This Icelandic family saga tells of the people of the farmstead Eyrr and their enemies. The storytellers' obvious relish for local tradition and ancient customs makes the saga especially valuable for students of early Scandinavian culture.

Eyrbyggja Saga. Trans. by Hermann Pálsson and Paul Edwards. Viking Penguin 1980 $6.95. ISBN 0-14-044530-7

GUNNARSSON, GUNNAR. 1889–1975

Novelist, poet, and dramatist, Gunnarsson was prolific in all the genres he chose, including the short story and historical novel. Like many other Icelandic writers, Gunnarsson spent a period in Copenhagen, returning to Iceland in 1939 and writing in both Danish and Icelandic. He is known as a brilliant interpreter of Icelandic life, particularly that of its humble people, and as a writer of subtle psychological novels of romantic theme. *The Black Cliffs* (1939) is one of these, having to do with a young couple's involvement in a sensational murder case. *The History of the Family at Borg* (1912–14), translated as *Guest the One-Eyed* (1920), and the autobiographical *The Church on the Mountain* (1923–28) are Gunnarsson's best-known works.

NOVEL BY GUNNARSSON

The Black Cliffs. 1939. Trans. by Cecil Wood. U. of Wis. Pr. 1967 $17.50. ISBN 0-299-04471-8

LAXDAELA SAGA. c.1250

Laxdaela Saga follows the course of kinship conflict through several generations, culminating in the death of Kjartan at the hands of his foster-brother Bolli. Many critics have noted similarities between the love intrigue that results in Kjartan's death (Bolli has married Gudrun, who once considered herself promised to Kjartan) and the pattern of the Norse myth of Sigurd and Brynhild, in which Gunnar is married to Brynhild, who was once promised to Sigurd. Brynhild urges her husband Gunnar to slay his former friend and her former lover.

Laxdaela Saga. Trans. by Magnus Magnusson and Hermann Pálsson. Viking Penguin 1988 $5.95. ISBN 0-14-044218-9

LAXNESS, HALLDÓR KILJAN. 1902– (NOBEL PRIZE 1955)

When presenting the 1955 Nobel Prize to Laxness, the Swedish Academy of Letters cited "his vivid writing, which has renewed the Icelandic narrative art." Laxness has been by turns a Catholic convert, a socialist, and a target of the radical press, some of whom accused Laxness of a class ambivalence the *Saturday Review* summarized this way: "Though Laxness came to believe that the novelist's best material is to be found in the proletariat, his rejection of middle-class concerns was never complete, and the ambiguity of his attitude toward the conflict of cultural values accounts for the mixture of humor and pathos that is characteristic of all his novels."

Independent People (1934–35) was a bestseller in this country; *Paradise Reclaimed* (1960), based in part on Laxness's own experiences in the United States, is a novel about a nineteenth-century Icelandic farmer and his travels and experiences, culminating in his conversion to the Mormon church. Laxness owes much to the tradition of the sagas and writes with understated restraint, concentrating almost entirely on external details, from which he extracts the utmost in absurdity. An *Atlantic* writer found that *The Fish Can Sing* (1957), the adventures of a young man in 1900 who wants to be a singer, "simmers with an ironic, disrespectful mirth which gives unexpected dimensions to the themes of lost innocence and the nature of art."

Novels by Laxness

The Atom Station. 1948. Second Chance 1982 repr. of 1948 ed. $16.95. ISBN 0-933256-31-0. A biting satire in which modern Reykjavik is viewed through the eyes of a housemaid from the country.

Independent People: An Epic. 1934–35. Trans. by J. A. Thompson. Greenwood 1976 repr. of 1946 ed. o.p. Documents the struggles of a small farmer against both natural and political obstacles.

Salka Valka. 1931–32. Trans. by F. H. Lyon. Allen Unwin At 1963 o.p. A novel of socialist vision and love set in an Icelandic fishing village.

World Light. 1955. Trans. by Magnus Magnusson. U. of Wis. Pr. 1969 o.p. A tetralogy in which a poor poet tries to maintain his intellectual freedom under oppressive conditions.

Book about Laxness

Hallberg, Peter. *Halldór Laxness*. Trans. by Rory McTurk. Irvington 1971 $15.95. ISBN 0-8057-2516-4. A useful overview of Laxness's life and work.

NJÁL'S SAGA. c.1280

Njál's Saga may well be Iceland's most famous literary work of the Middle Ages. Its author anonymous—a situation typical of Icelandic sagas—the saga tells of events in southern Iceland in the years 960–1015, the period in which the people of Iceland were converted to Christianity. Against this backdrop a conflict between wives accelerates into a tremendous clan feud that eventually involves all of Iceland. The ethical views observed in the story are both heathen and Christian, conflicting in a fateful drama. The author's nuanced characterization is unique in saga literature.

Njál's Saga. Viking Penguin 1960 $6.95. ISBN 0-14-044103-4. The standard translation equipped with a fine introduction and notes; translated by Magnus Magnusson and Hermann Pálsson.

Books about Njál's Saga

Allen, Richard. *Fire and Iron: Critical Approaches to Njál's Saga*. U. of Pittsburgh Pr. 1971 o.p. An important study of the world of *Njál's Saga*.

Lönnroth, Lars. *Njal's Saga: A Critical Approach*. U. CA Pr. 1976 $49.95. ISBN 0-520-02708-6. Contains insights pertinent to the study of all Icelandic sagas.

THE POETIC EDDA. 12th or 13th century

The Poetic Edda (also called *The Elder Edda*, in contrast to *The Prose Edda* of Snorri Sturluson) is a major source of insight into pagan Germanic religious concepts and cosmology. Although recorded in Christian times, the stories are thought to originate in an ancient oral tradition. Serious students of eddic verse will find it useful to consult all available translations of the original Old Icelandic text.

Norse Poems. Trans. by W. H. Auden and Paul Taylor. Humanities 1981 o.p.

The Poetic Edda. Trans. by Lee Hollander. U. of Tex. Pr. 1986 $12.95. ISBN 0-292-76499-5. Scholarly translations, but a bit too stiff.

Poems of the Elder Edda. Trans. by Patricia Terry. U. of Pa. Pr. 1990 $15.95. ISBN 0-8122-8220-5. The most readable translation.

STURLUNGA SAGA. c.1300

The thirteenth century in Iceland was one of great literary production, especially of biographies of kings and nobility. The large collection of accounts entitled *Sturlunga Saga* is so named because of the prominence of the Sturlung family in Icelandic affairs. The heart of this work is Sturla Thórdarson's account of the period 1200–1262, when Iceland lost its independence and came under the power of the king of Norway.

Sturlunga Saga. Trans. by Julia H. McGrew and George Thomas. Irvington 1970–74 o.p.

STURLUSON, SNORRI. 1179–1241

Snorri Sturluson's fame as a historian—his main work is the 16 sagas included in *Heimskringla* (c.1230), a monumental history of Norway from its beginning until 1177—lies both in his critical approach to sources and in his fine, realistic exposition of event and motivation. A similar combination of scholarly and imaginative talent is seen in *The Prose Edda* (c.1220). Intended to be a handbook in skaldic poetry, it preserves invaluable mythological tales that were on the verge of being forgotten even in Sturluson's time. A large part of what we know about Nordic mythology stems from his *Edda*. The bibliography that follows also lists the anonymous *Egil's Saga* (1200–30), which many expert Scandinavian medievalists (e.g., Sigurdur Nordal and Björn M. Olsen) attribute to Sturluson. It is a fascinating account of life in Norway, England, and Iceland and of the poet-warrior Egil, whose skaldic verse is renowned for its unusual emotional and personal qualities. Snorri Sturluson's own life was as eventful as those about whom he wrote. Returning to Iceland from exile in 1239, he again became deeply involved in serious power struggles and was murdered in 1241.

WORKS BY STURLUSON

Egil's Saga. 1200–1230. Trans. by Hermann Pálsson and Paul Edwards. Viking Penguin 1977 $5.95. ISBN 0-14-044321-5

Heimskringla. Trans. by Lee M. Hollander. U. of Tex. Pr. 1991 $19.95. ISBN 0-292-73061-6. An important sourcebook of early Norwegian history.

King Harald's Saga. Trans. by Magnus Magnusson and Hermann Pálsson. Viking Penguin 1976 $6.95. ISBN 0-14-044183-2

The Prose Edda of Snorri Sturluson. Trans. by Jean I. Young. U. CA Pr. 1964 $8.95. ISBN 0-520-01232-1

BOOK ABOUT STURLUSON

Ciklamini, Marlene. *Snorri Sturluson*. Twayne 1978 o.p. A fine overview and a useful bibliography.

THÓRDARSON, THORBERGUR. 1889–1974

Thórdarson was something of a drifter in his youth until he was given a place at the University of Iceland in 1913, where he began to find himself and grew interested in the language and folk culture of Iceland. He devoted himself to "word collecting" for a while, which meant further wandering, but became interested in mysticism and the supernatural, as well as in social problems, all of which became elements in his work. His essays *A Letter to Laura* (1924) created a stir on publication and had an influence on HALLDÓR KILJAN LAXNESS. Many of Thórdarson's works are either biographical or autobiographical and display an irreverent humor and a puckish wit. Perhaps the foremost example of this genre is the six-volume work *The All-Too-Wise* (1940–41), a mixture of tall tales, superstition, and humor posing as the biography of Reverend Arni Thórdarsson.

NOVEL BY THÓRDARSON

In Search of My Beloved. 1938. Trans. by Kenneth G. Chapman. Irvington 1967 o.p. A novella in which a young poet searches for his dream girl, whom he is too shy to approach. Part of an autobiographical novel, *Icelandic Aristocracy* (1938).

VÖLSUNGA SAGA. 13th century

The Saga of the Völsungs is a prose version of the older Sigurd legends preserved in eddic poetry. This ancient story about the ruin of the Völsung chief Sigurd by his wife Gudrun has left its mark on literature for many centuries. The same poetic materials were used in the German *Nibelungenlied.* RICHARD WAGNER (see Vol. 3) drew upon them for his opera cycle *The Ring of the Nibelungs,* and FRIEDRICH HEBBEL used them in his dramatic trilogy *The Nibelungs.* WILLIAM MORRIS (see Vol. 1) made them known to English readers in *The Earthly Paradise* and *Sigurd the Völsung.* THOMAS MANN also treats the theme in his novella "The Blood of the Walsungs."

The Saga of the Volsungs. Trans. by Jesse Byock. U. CA Pr. 1990 $9.95. ISBN 0-520-06904-8

DANISH LITERATURE

A specifically Danish literary tradition begins in the late Middle Ages with Denmark's exceptional ballads. No other European country can boast as many medieval ballads, which began to be recorded in the fifteenth century. The classic collections of ballads were published in the nineteenth century.

The literature of the Baroque in Denmark is not likely to be of interest to the average modern reader since much of it is in Latin or written in complicated verse, impossible to translate. With the coming of the Enlightenment and the eighteenth century, Danish literature began to blossom, culminating in the writings of LUDVIG HOLBERG. Many of Holberg's plays follow the patterns set by MOLIÈRE's comedies and other French classical drama of the seventeenth century. In 1752, the German author Friedrich Klopstock came to Denmark, where he spent the ensuing 19 years. His presence signaled the introduction of a more emotional tone in poetry. Klopstock's foremost Danish disciple was Johannes Ewald, one of Denmark's premier poets whose work has not yet been successfully translated.

Denmark's so-called Golden Age coincides with the early years of the nineteenth century and the romantic movement. The best poet of this period is Axel Oehlenschläger, but because of the usual difficulties of translating poetry, none of the Golden Age poets are well known outside of Denmark. Steen Steensen Blicher, a transitional figure between romanticism and realism, wrote short prose and thus has received some attention. Nicolai Frederik Severin Grundtvig is a dominant cultural figure of late romanticism, who left his mark on Danish theology, politics, and education. He is responsible for the major collection of Danish ballads and was instrumental in reviving an interest in Nordic mythology. The works of both HANS CHRISTIAN ANDERSEN and SØREN KIERKEGAARD (see Vol. 4) can be considered part of a late flowering of romanticism.

In a series of lectures delivered in 1871, the critic Georg Brandes called into being what has later been referred to as the Modern Breakthrough in Scandinavia. Brandes broke with the tenets of romanticism and urged that contemporary literature bring up social problems for debate. The Danish authors of the Modern Breakthrough include JENS PETER JACOBSEN, Karl Gjellerup, and Henrik Pontoppidan. Gjellerup and Pontoppidan shared the Nobel Prize for literature in 1917. The optimism of the Modern Breakthrough gradually turned into the pessimism of the *fin de siècle,* a trend anticipated in the novels of HERMAN BANG.

In the early twentieth century, MARTIN ANDERSEN NEXØ reinvigorated the Danish interest in social realism. Against its prosaic background, ISAK DINESEN blossomed in the 1930s like an exotic flower. However, the German occupation of Denmark during World War II left its mark on Danish letters. After this traumatic national experience, a number of Danish authors turned to existentialism and modernism. Since the late 1960s, a strong group of Danish women writers has emerged, among them KIRSTEN THORUP and Dorrit Willumsen.

History and Criticism

Borum, Paul. *Danish Literature: A Short Critical Survey.* Nordic Bks. 1979 $9.95. ISBN 87-7429-030-4. By an author who is particularly knowledgeable about modern Danish authors.

Mitchell, P. M. *History of Danish Literature.* Am. Scandinavian 1971 $17.50. ISBN 9-89067-034-X. An intelligent overview by one of America's premier experts on Danish literature.

Rossel, Sven H., ed. *A History of Danish Literature.* U. of Nebr. Pr. 1992 $50.00. ISBN 0-8032-3886-X. The most recent and comprehensive overview of Danish literature in English.

Collections

Billeskov-Jansen, F. J., and P. M. Mitchell, eds. *Anthology of Danish Literature.* 2 vols. S. Ill. U. Pr. 1972. Vol. 1 *Middle Ages to Romanticism.* $14.95. ISBN 0-8093-0596-8. Vol. 2 *Realism to the Present.* $15.95. ISBN 0-8093-0597-6. A bilingual anthology that presents the texts in both Danish and English.

Bredsdorff, Elias, ed. and trans. *Contemporary Danish Prose.* Greenwood 1974 repr. of 1958 ed. $35.00. ISBN 0-8371-7358-2. Although a bit dated, provides a nice cross-section of Danish authors.

Christiansen, Inger. *Alphabet.* Trans. by Susanna Nied. Fjord Pr. 1992 $10.95. ISBN 0-940242-61-3. Winner of the American-Scandinavian Foundation Translation Prize in 1982.

Friis, Erik J., ed. *Modern Nordic Plays: Denmark.* Irvington 1982 $16.95. ISBN 0-8290-1164-7. Includes plays by Branner, Olsen, Rifbjerg, and Ronild.

Harder, Uffe. *Paper Houses.* Trans. by Uffe Harder and Alexander Taylor. Curbstone 1983 $4.00. ISBN 0-915306-23-9. The first translation into English of Harder, a surrealistic poet and translator.

Heitman, Annegret, ed. *No Man's Land: An Anthology of Modern Danish Women's Literature.* Dufour 1988 $19.95. ISBN 1-870041-05-4. Contains short pieces by women authors from Dinesen to Willumsen.

Larsen, Marianne. *Selected Poems.* Trans. by Nadia Christensen. Curbstone 1982 $5.00. ISBN 0-915306-29-8. Brilliant poetry and fierce social criticism.

Ober, Kenneth, and P. M. Mitchell, eds. *The Royal Guest: And Other Classical Danish Narrative.* U. Ch. Pr. 1982 $6.95. ISBN 0-226-53214-3. Selections from works by M. Goldschmidt, J. P. Jacobsen, H. Pontoppidan, and H. Bang.

Seeberg, Peter. *The Impostor.* Trans. by Anni Whissen. U. of Nebr. Pr. 1990 $7.95. ISBN 0-8032-9201-5. A modernistic novel that became a cult classic when it appeared.

Sonne, Jørgen. *Flights.* Trans. by Jørgen Sonne and Alexander Taylor. Curbstone 1981 $4.00. ISBN 0-915306-22-0. A writer known for his striking linguistic abilities and mosaic view of the world.

Tafdrup, Pia. *Spring Tide.* Trans. by Anne Born. Dufour 1990 $15.95. ISBN 0-948259-55-8. A collection focusing on the theme of women's passion.

Willumsen, Dorrit. *If It Really Were a Film.* Trans. by Anne M. Rasmussen. Curbstone 1982 $7.95. ISBN 0-915306-35-2. "Willumsen, the 1981 recipient of the Danish Academy's Grand Prize, makes her debut in English with these psychologically suspense-filled short stories" (Choice).

ANDERSEN, BENNY ALLEN. 1929–

A talented jazz pianist, composer, highly popular poet, and writer of short stories, Benny Andersen has also written television plays, children's books, film scripts, and two novels. Andersen's poetry, with its irony, humor, and wordplay, suggests comparison with E. E. CUMMINGS (see Vol. 1). Andersen is a critic of social norms and the large and small brutalities that modern society inflicts on the individual striving for an authentic life; our often bizarre experience is the focus of his intense scrutiny. Andersen's intriguing blend of the humorous and the utterly serious shows an artist intent on shaping values through literature.

POETRY BY BENNY ANDERSEN

Selected Poems. Trans. by Alexander Taylor. Princeton U. Pr. 1975 $8.95. ISBN 0-691-01319-5

SHORT STORY COLLECTIONS BY BENNY ANDERSEN

Selected Stories. Trans. by Donald K. Watkins and others. Curbstone 1983 $7.95. ISBN 0-915306-37-9.

The Pillows. 1965. Curbstone 1983 $7.95. ISBN 0-915306-37-9

BOOK ABOUT BENNY ANDERSEN

Marx, Leonie A. *Benny Andersen: A Critical Study.* Greenwood 1983 $38.50. ISBN 0-313-24168-6. A good overview with a useful bibliography.

ANDERSEN, HANS CHRISTIAN. 1805–1875

The fairy tales for which Andersen is now famous comprise only a small part of his lifework—his novels and travel books were more warmly received by his contemporaries. And in general, during his lifetime his talent was more esteemed in other countries than it was in his native Denmark. CHARLES DICKENS (see Vol. 1), for example, called the Dane "a great writer." Born in Odense, the son of a poor shoemaker, Andersen worked in a factory after his father's death. He soon, however, displayed a talent for poetry and went to Copenhagen to pursue other avenues. His first collection of poems was published in 1830 and a second in 1831. Andersen complained bitterly about the lack of encouragement for his first volume of stories, *Fairy Tales, Told for Children* (1835). In 1843, he began the series called *New Adventures*, the title no longer addressing itself exclusively to children. Other volumes followed until Andersen's death. In his old age, Andersen said, "My fairy tales are written as much for adults as for children. Children understand only the trimmings, and not until they mature will they see and comprehend the whole." That whole was considerable. In Fredrik Böök's words: "There is no longer any doubt that Andersen was born so he could write these fairy tales and stories: they are his contribution to world history."

SHORT STORY COLLECTIONS BY HANS CHRISTIAN ANDERSEN

Eighty Fairy Tales. Trans. by R. P. Keigwin. Pantheon 1982 $11.95. ISBN 0-394-71055-X. An older translation than Conroy and Rossel's.

Tales and Stories by Hans Christian Andersen. Trans. by Patricia Conroy and Sven H. Rossel. U. of Wash. Pr. 1980 $14.95. ISBN 0-295-95936-3. A comprehensive edition edited by scholars.

NONFICTION BY HANS CHRISTIAN ANDERSEN

The Diaries of Hans Christian Andersen. Trans. by Patricia Conroy and Sven Rossel. U. of Wash. Pr. 1990 $45.00. ISBN 0-295-96845-1. A chance to gain insight into the author.

The Story of My Life. 1867. Trans. by Mary B. Howitt. Folcroft o.p.

A Visit to Germany, Italy and Malta 1840–1841. Trans. by Grace Thornton. Dufour 1985 $27.50. ISBN 0-7206-0636-5. One of Andersen's very popular travel chronicles.

BOOKS ABOUT HANS CHRISTIAN ANDERSEN

Böök, Fredrik. *Hans Christian Andersen: A Biography*. Trans. by George C. Schoolfield. Bks. Demand 1962 $71.00. ISBN 0-317-08231-0. An authoritative biography, "persevering in hunting the true Andersen."

Bredsdorff, Elias. *Hans Christian Andersen*. Scribner 1975 o.p. An important work by a Danish scholar.

Gronbech, Bo. *Hans Christian Andersen*. Twayne 1980 o.p. A general overview of Andersen's works and life with a useful bibliography.

BANG, HERMAN. 1857–1912

Herman Bang was both an astute literary critic and a master prose stylist. His style has been described as impressionistic; with a few literary brush strokes, Bang is able to paint sensitive psychological portraits. Bang was not as optimistic as his colleagues about the Modern Breakthrough, the rejection of nineteenth-century perspectives for modern progress. His characters are often gentle individuals crushed by circumstances. Bang's propensity for depicting declining noble families makes him a major precursor of literary decadence and *fin de siècle* pessimism. Although he enjoyed great popularity abroad, particularly in Germany, Bang's success at home in Denmark was hampered by a competition with the critics Georg and Edvard Brandes and the common knowledge that Bang was homosexual. Although several books have been written about Bang in the Scandinavian countries, none have appeared yet in English.

NOVELS BY BANG

Denied a Country. 1906. Trans. by Marie Busch and A. G. Chater. Knopf 1927 o.p. A traveling violinist finds that he has neither homeland nor native tongue.

Ida Brandt. 1896. Trans. by Arthur G. Chater. Knopf 1928 o.p. The moving story of a young woman working in a mental hospital in Copenhagen.

Katinka. 1886. Trans. by Tiina Nunnally. Fjord Pr. 1992 $8.95. ISBN 0-940242-46-X. The heroic struggles of a housewife in a small town.

Tina. 1889. Trans. by Paul Christopherson. Humanities 1984 $18.95. ISBN 0-485-11254-X. A tragic love story during wartime.

BRANNER, HANS CHRISTIAN. 1903–1966

Freudian psychoanalysis, existentialism, and modern humanism are the driving forces in Branner's fine short stories and novels. While the psychological view of human personality presented in Branner seems very simplistic today, his symbolism is intriguing as he describes with great finesse both the erotic awakening of youth and adult sexual relationships. *The Story of Børge* (1942) is one of Branner's best studies of child psychology. *The Riding Master* (1947), his most famous novel, prompted a spirited public reaction by ISAK DINESEN, who found fundamental fault with Branner's concept of humanism.

NOVEL BY BRANNER

The Story of Børge. 1942. Trans. by Kristi Planck. Irvington 1973 $29.50. ISBN 0-8057-3359-0

SHORT STORY COLLECTION BY BRANNER

Two Minutes of Silence: Selected Short Stories. 1944. Trans. by Vera Lindholm Vance. Bks. Demand 1966 $62.20. ISBN 0-8357-6776-0. Includes a detailed bibliography.

BOOK ABOUT BRANNER

Markey, Thomas L. *H. C. Branner*. Twayne 1973 o.p. A general overview of Branner's works and life, plus a useful bibliography.

DINESEN, ISAK (pseud. of Karen Blixen). 1885–1962

In the 1930s, Isak Dinesen was a unique figure in the literature of modern Denmark, quite distant from the trends of social realism which marked the times. From 1914 to 1931 Karen Blixen—her married name, by which she is known in Europe—struggled to maintain a coffee plantation in the British colony of Kenya. The bankruptcy of the farm forced Dinesen to return to Denmark, where she began a new life as a writer. She wrote primarily in a faultless and yet quite personal style of literary English, and she found her most receptive audience not in Denmark, but in the United States.

Dinesen's tales draw on the storytelling tradition of *The Arabian Nights*. BOCCACCIO's *Decameron*, German romanticism, and the English gothic. Setting most of her tales at least 100 years in the past, she peppers her narratives with mistaken identities, masquerades, witches, and strange twists of fate. Adolescent females come to terms with a way of life that would make them feel imprisoned, and the aristocratic, old world order is threatened by the encroachment of the modern world.

Dinesen's dramatized autobiography, *Out of Africa* (1937), and its sequel, *Shadows on the Grass* (1960), portray her life in Africa. These works, written in Dinesen's distinctive elegant prose, are not memoirs in the usual sense. Facts are insignificant as she assesses her African experience; it is the spirit of a primitive and yet noble culture that gives these books their enduring evocative power. HEMINGWAY (see Vol. 1) referred to *Out of Africa* as "the best book about Africa that I ever read." Even though Dinesen's status as a colonial author is problematic, she showed far more respect for African cultures than most of her colonial contemporaries. She perceived an Africa where humanity and nature were still one.

Hollywood's Oscar-winning treatment of Dinesen's life in Africa, also titled *Out of Africa,* bears little resemblance to Dinesen's novel. The Danish film *Babette's Feast,* based on a Dinesen tale, won an Oscar for best foreign film. She is certainly one of Denmark's most popular cultural exports. In 1957 she received an honorary membership in the American Academy and National Institute of Arts and Letters, an honor rarely awarded to nonresidents.

NONFICTION BY DINESEN

Daguerreotypes and Other Essays. 1979. Trans. by P. M. Mitchell and W. D. Paden. U. Ch. Pr. 1984 $9.95. ISBN 0-226-15306-1. Eight essays in which Dinesen describes her views on life, art, and marriage.

Letters from Africa: 1914–1931. 1981. Trans. by Anne Born. U. Ch. Pr. 1984 $10.95. ISBN 0-226-15311-8. A nice complement to Dinesen's African fiction and autobiography.

On Modern Marriage. Trans. by Anne Born. St. Martin 1987 $7.95. ISBN 0-312-01074-5. A recently discovered early essay by Dinesen, which contrasts with her later utterances on women and marriage.

Out of Africa & Shadows on the Grass. 1938 and 1961. Random 1989 $7.95. ISBN 0-679-72475-3. An edition that contains both of Dinesen's books on her life in Kenya.

NOVELS BY DINESEN

The Angelic Avengers. 1944. U. Ch. Pr. 1975 o.p. A Gothic romance that embarrassed Dinesen so much she wrote it under the pseudonym Pierre Andrézel.

Ehrengard. 1963. Random 1975 o.p. A young woman is faced with a dramatic choice.

SHORT STORY COLLECTIONS BY DINESEN

Anecdotes of Destiny. 1958. Random 1985 $7.95. ISBN 0-394-74291-5. Contains five stories.

Carnival: Entertainment and Posthumous Tales. 1977. U. Ch. Pr. 1979 $10.95. ISBN 0-226-15304-5. Eleven more tales, some of which were not published during Dinesen's lifetime.

Last Tales. 1957. Random 1985 $5.95. ISBN 0-394-74292-3. Not Dinesen's last book of tales, contrary to the title.

Seven Gothic Tales. 1934. Random 1985 $6.95. ISBN 0-394-74291-5. Dinesen's first and richest collection of tales.

Winter's Tales. 1942. Random 1961 $8.95. ISBN 0-394-74293-1. Dinesen's most Danish collection of tales, written during the Nazi occupation of Denmark.

BOOKS ABOUT DINESEN

Aiken, Susan Hardy. *Isak Dinesen and the Engendering of Narrative.* U. Ch. Pr. 1990 $19.95. ISBN 0-226-0113-5. A striking feminist study of Dinesen's aesthetics.

Langbaum, Robert. *Isak Dinesen's Art: The Gayety of Vision.* U. Ch. Pr. 1975 $4.95. ISBN 0-226-46871-2. The standard scholarly work on Dinesen as a world literary figure.

Pelensky, Olga Anastasia. *Isak Dinesen: The Life and Imagination of a Seducer.* Ohio U. Pr. 1991 $19.95. ISBN 0-8214-1008-3. Complements, but does not replace, Thurman's standard biography.

Thurman, Judith. *Isak Dinesen: The Life of a Storyteller.* St. Martin 1985 $4.95. ISBN 0-312-90202-6. The standard Dinesen biography.

DITLEVSEN, TOVE. 1918–1976

Ditlevsen grew up in a working-class environment in Copenhagen, an experience that has left a clear stamp on much of her writing. Her novels, generally realistic, revolve around the themes of sexuality, children, and the lives of the poor, and her relentlessly honest depictions have won her a steady following in Denmark.

NOVELS BY DITLEVSEN

Early Spring. 1956. Trans. by Tiina Nunnally. Seal Pr. Feminist 1985 $8.95. ISBN 0-931188-28-8

Faces. 1968. Trans. by Tiina Nunnally. Fjord Pr. 1991 $9.95. ISBN 0-940242-11-7. Lise, an artist, lands in the locked ward of a Copenhagen hospital after a suicide attempt.

Short Story Collection by Ditlevsen

Complete Freedom and Other Stories. Trans. by Jack Brondum. Curbstone 1982 $7.00. ISBN 0-915306-24-7. Received the PEN American-Scandinavian Translation Award.

HANSEN, MARTIN A. 1909–1955

As a critic of the form and content of civilization since the Middle Ages, Martin A. Hansen believed that humanity and morality deteriorated as rationalism and scientism became the guiding lights of European culture. In his childhood, Hansen personally observed the disintegration of rural folk culture when economic and agricultural requirements modernized country life. His participation in the Danish Underground during World War II also greatly increased his sense of the failure of modern times to provide ethical stability. His modernistic prose is highly symbolic and, at times, eludes logical interpretation, but nonetheless his writing delineates its message clearly.

Novels by Hansen

Lucky Kristoffer. 1945. Trans. by John J. Egglishaw. Irvington 1974 $7.50. ISBN 0-8057-3339-6. The ethical chaos of strife-torn sixteenth-century Denmark mirrors modern conflicts.

The Liar. 1950. Trans. by John J. Egglishaw. Twayne 1950 o.p. Written in the form of a schoolteacher's diary; presents a psychological critique of modern times as the teacher experiences a crisis of faith.

Book about Hansen

Ingwersen, Faith, and Niels Ingwersen. *Martin A. Hansen*. Irvington 1976 $17.95. ISBN 0-8057-6259-0. An overview of Hansen's life and work with a useful bibliography.

HOLBERG, LUDVIG. 1684–1754

Holberg, the outstanding genius of the Danish Enlightenment, contributed in the areas of history, philosophy, and literature. His name stands by that of Molière as a master of European comedy. In his own country, 33 comedies created a national repertoire and a theatrical tradition. Holberg's strength in creative writing lay not in extended plot but in the individual scene, the anecdote, the characterization. *Peder Paars* (1719), a mock heroic poem, gave Holberg the framework in which to satirize the government, the church, and the university. The novel *Niels Klim* (1741) likewise reported on human foibles. Students of eighteenth-century European literature will want to seek out translations of Holberg's philosophical writing.

Nonfiction by Holberg

Moral Reflections and Epistles. Trans. by P. M. Mitchell. Dufour 1992 $35.00. ISBN 1-870041-16-X

Selected Essays. Trans. by P. M. Mitchell. Greenwood 1976 repr. of 1955 ed. $38.50. ISBN 0-8371-8970-5

Novel by Holberg

The Journey of Niels Klim to the World Underground. 1741. Ed. by James I. McNelis, Jr. Greenwood 1973 repr. of 1960 ed. o.p. Based on a translation published in London in 1742. Picaresque novel of a man's travels through life.

Plays by Holberg

Four Plays by Holberg. Trans. by Harry Alexander. Kraus repr. of 1946 ed. $26.00. ISBN 0-527-41800-5. Contains *The Masked Ladies, The Fussy Men, The Weathercock,* and *Masquerades*.

Jeppe of the Hill & Other Comedies. Trans. by Sven Rossel and Gerald Arsetsinger. S. Ill. U. Pr. 1990 $19.95. ISBN 0-8093-1481-9. A modern translation of Holberg.

Seven One-Act Plays. Trans. by Henry Alexander. Kraus repr. of 1950 ed. $23.00. ISBN 0-527-41820-X. Contains *The Talkative Barber, The Arabian Powder, The Christmas Party, Diedrich the Temble, The Peasant in Pawn, Sgnarel's Journey to the Land of the Philosophers,* and *The Caged Bridegroom.*

POETRY BY HOLBERG

Peder Paars. 1719. Trans. by Bergliot Stromsoe. Am. Scandinavian 1962 $11.95. ISBN 0-89067-038-2. A mock-heroic poem that gave Holberg the framework in which to satirize the government, the church, and the university.

BOOK ABOUT HOLBERG

Billeskov-Jansen, F. J. *Ludvig Holberg.* Twayne 1974 o.p. A study by a respected Danish scholar. Contains an overview of Holberg's life and work and a useful bibliography.

JACOBSEN, JENS PETER. 1847–1885

Jens Peter Jacobsen, Denmark's foremost novelist of naturalism, expressed in his small body of work his rejection of religion and his enthusiasm for the new doctrine of evolution. In his autobiographical novel *Niels Lyhne* (1880), sometimes called by contemporaries "the bible of atheism," he wrote that "there is no God and man is his prophet." During his troubled life, cut short by tuberculosis, he translated into Danish nearly all the writings of CHARLES DARWIN (see Vols. 1, 3, and 5). His own work—two novels, a book of short stories, and a few poems—strove to "bring into the realm of literature the eternal laws of nature" and to free the concept of nature from the distorted concept of romanticism. The novella *Mogens* (1972) was Jacobsen's first publication; it became famous as an example of the new naturalistic current in literature. In it, life is seen as perceptions of the instant, and people are motivated by natural laws and drives. In *Marie Grubbe* (1876), externally a seventeenth-century historical romance, the life of Marie is determined by her erotic needs; although born into nobility, she finally finds happiness in life as the wife of a coarse stableman. Jacobsen's concern with anxiety and inner torment brings to mind the great nineteenth-century Russian novelists, while his naturalism and interest in psychology are reminiscent of GUSTAVE FLAUBERT. Jacobsen's influence on major European writers who followed him, such as RAINER MARIA RILKE, is well documented.

NOVELS BY JACOBSEN

Marie Grubbe. 1876. Trans. by Hanna Astrup Larsen. Am. Scandinavian 1975 o.p.

Niels Lyhne. 1880. Trans. by Tiina Nunnally. Fjord Pr. 1990 $19.95. ISBN 0-940242-30-3

SHORT STORY COLLECTION BY JACOBSEN

Mogens: And Other Stories. 1872–85. Trans. by Tiina Nunnally. Fjord Pr. 1992 $10.95. ISBN 0-940242-57-5

BOOK ABOUT JACOBSEN

Jensen, Niels L. *Jens Peter Jacobsen.* Twayne 1980 o.p. Well-respected biography; includes a useful bibliography.

JENSEN, JOHANNES V(ILHELM). 1873–1950 (NOBEL PRIZE 1944)

Johannes V. Jensen has had great influence on Danish literature both as a lyric poet and as a novelist. He was born in a village in northwestern Jutland, where his father was a veterinarian and his grandfather a farmer and weaver.

His early short stories, *Himmerland Stories* (1904, 1910), depict this world of his childhood. Jensen studied medicine in Copenhagen but did not become a doctor. His great interest in anthropology and biology was concentrated in the theory of evolution. An optimist, Jensen wrote a series of myths, each portraying the same movement: the present is the culmination of all that has been in the past. This positive Darwinian philosophy permeates the six novels that comprise his epic *The Long Journey* (1908–22).

Novels by Jensen

The Fall of the King. 1901. Trans. by Allen G. Bower. Mermaid Pr. 1992. ISBN 1-880755-06-8. Jensen's most artistically satisfying novel.

The Long Journey. 1908–22. Nobel Prize edition 1945 o.p. A mythical-historical account of the great discoveries of humankind, in six books.

Book about Jensen

Rossel, Sven H. *Johannes V. Jensen*. Twayne 1984 o.p. Focuses on Jensen's early works; includes a useful bibliography.

KIERKEGAARD, SØREN (AABYE). 1813–1855

[See Volume 4.]

MUNK, KAJ (HARALD LEININGER). 1898–1944

Deep religious conviction and love of the heroic, inspired individual were blended in the personality and work of Kaj Munk, perhaps Denmark's most significant dramatist in the twentieth century. As a Lutheran minister he became a magnetic preacher whose political and cultural criticism, ironically, had certain philosophical aspects in common with the antirationalism of contemporary European fascism. In fact, Munk's heroic ideal was humane and Christian. In the spirit of his heroes, Munk persistently and publicly attacked nazism during the occupation of Denmark and was murdered by the Gestapo in 1944. In *Before Cannae* (1943), Hannibal, the ruthless empire builder, is opposed by the humanitarian Fabius. In *He Sits at the Melting Pot* (1938), God endows a man with the strength of love with which to do battle against the power-hungry of this world. *The Word* (1932), Munk's greatest success on the stage, confirms that miracles through faith are possible in modern times.

Plays by Munk

Five Plays. Trans. by R. P. Keigwin. Am. Scandinavian 1964 o.p. Contains *Herod the King, The Word, Cant, He Sits at the Melting Pot,* and *Before Cannae*.

Book about Munk

Harcourt, Melville. *Portraits of Destiny*. Twin Circle 1966 o.p. A look into Munk's very interesting life and literature.

NEXØ, MARTIN ANDERSEN. 1869–1954

Martin Andersen Nexø, the first prominent voice in Danish literature of trade unionism and proletarian solidarity, spent an impoverished youth working at various trades in Copenhagen and on the island of Bornholm. After 1901 he supported himself by writing. A communist and zealous enemy of injustice, he avoided arrest during the Nazi occupation in World War II by fleeing, first to Sweden and then to the Soviet Union. He died in East Germany. *Pelle the Conqueror* (1906–10) and *Ditte* (1917–21) are Nexø's classic proletarian novels. *Pelle* describes the childhood of a poor farm lad and his later activities as a union organizer in Copenhagen; its blend of autobiographical insights, a passion for justice, and epic narrative reminds one of MAXIM GORKY. *Ditte* charts the struggle of a young woman against poverty and cold indifference. Differing rather sharply from *Pelle,* the novel describes the woman's fate in basic moral terms, not as the outcome of political events.

NOVELS BY NEXØ

Ditte: Ditte, Daughter of Man. 1917–21. Trans. by A. G. Chater and Richard Thirsk. Peter Smith 1922 $16.50. ISBN 0-8446-1325-8. Also includes *Girl Alive!* and *Towards the Stars.*

In God's Land. 1929. Trans. by Thomas Seltzer. Peter Smith 1933 o.p.

Pelle the Conqueror. 1906–10. 2 vols. Fjord Pr. Vol. 1 *Childhood.* Trans. by Steven T. Murray. 1989 $9.95. ISBN 0-940242-40-0. Vol. 2 *Apprenticeship.* Trans. by Steven T. Murray and Tiina Nunnally. 1991 $9.95. ISBN 0-940242-48-6. A new, highly readable translation.

BOOK ABOUT NEXØ

Ingwersen, Faith, and Niels Ingwersen. *Quests for a Promised Land: The Works of Martin Andersen Nexø.* Greenwood 1985 $37.95. ISBN 0-313-24469-3. An overview of Nexø's life and work with a useful bibliography.

NORDBRANDT, HENRIK. 1945–

Henrik Nordbrandt's studies of Oriental languages at the University of Copenhagen and the more than 15 years he has lived abroad in Turkey, Greece, and Italy have left a deep mark on his poetry. From his position outside of Danish culture, he has become a sensitive cultural critic. Nordbrandt's poetry, written in the modernist tradition, pits the mysticism and sensuality of the South against the cold rationality of the North. He is also well known for his modern love poetry. Nordbrandt has received numerous prizes for his skillful poetry, among them the Grand Prize from the Danish Academy.

POETRY BY NORDBRANDT

Armenia. 1982. Trans. by Henrik Nordbrandt and Alexander Taylor. Curbstone 1984 $7.95. ISBN 0-915306-41-7

God's House. 1977. Trans. by Henrik Nordbrandt and Alexander Taylor. Curbstone 1979 $4.95. ISBN 0-915306-16-6

Selected Poems. 1981. Trans. by Henrik Nordbrandt and Alexander Taylor. Curbstone 1978 $9.95. ISBN 0-915306-33-6

RIFBJERG, KLAUS. 1931–

The productivity of Rifbjerg has been continuous and extremely prolific: poetry, novels, stories, and plays for the stage as well as for radio and television. Experimenting in all the genres, Rifbjerg deals often with the psychology of the Danish middle classes. He is considered one of the central figures of modernism in Denmark of the 1960s. Since 1967, he has been a member of the Danish Academy.

NOVELS BY RIFBJERG

Anna (I) Anna. 1969. Trans. by Alexander Taylor. Curbstone 1982 $9.95. ISBN 0-915306-30-1. The wife of a diplomat flees her comfortable but trivial life to join a hippie in wandering through central Europe.

Witness to the Future. 1988. Trans. by Steven T. Murray. Fjord Pr. 1987 $8.95. ISBN 0-940242-18-4. Two boys from the 1940s crawl through a cave and end up in the 1980s.

Poetry by Rifbjerg

Selected Poems. Trans. by Alexander Taylor. Curbstone 1985 $5.95. ISBN 0-915306-48-4. The 22 poems show "the range of his poetic voice, sardonic or satiric or witty and displaying compassion for his fellow human beings . . . the finest in lyrics" (*Scandinavian-American Bulletin*).

SCHERFIG, HANS. 1905–1979.

Raised in a privileged upper-middle-class family, Scherfig became a communist at a young age. He was an accomplished painter besides writing a series of highly popular novels. Some of his novels are mysteries, and all share a sense of humor, irony, and a critique of the bourgeoisie establishment. The novels endure, however, because they are highly entertaining.

Novels by Scherfig

The Dead Man. 1937. Trans. by Steven T. Murray. Fjord Pr. 1991 $9.95. ISBN 0-940242-59-1. Scherfig's first novel, poking fun at the bohemian artist circles of Copenhagen in the 1920s and 1930s.

Idealists. 1942. Trans. by Frank Hugus. Fjord Pr. 1991 $9.95. ISBN 0-940242-02-8. A murder mystery and exposé of the abuses of idealism, banned from publication during the German occupation of Denmark.

The Missing Bureaucrat. 1938. Trans. by Frank Hugus. Fjord Pr. 1988 $8.95. ISBN 0-940242-26-5. A satire that exposes the hollow life of a bureaucrat.

Stolen Spring. 1940. Trans. by Frank Hugus. Fjord Pr. 1986 $7.95. ISBN 0-940242-25-7. The mysterious death of a school teacher results in an exposé of a stupefying school system.

SØRENSEN, VILLY. 1929–

Sørensen's education in philosophy provides his readable stories with astonishing depth. He is a master of the short story form. He prefers a Kafkaesque style and is fond of the theme of transition. Sørensen is an active social and literary critic and a member of the Danish Academy.

Nonfiction by Sørensen

Seneca: The Humanist at the Court of Nero. 1976. Trans. by W. Glyn Jones. U. Ch. Pr. 1984 $25.00. ISBN 0-226-76827-9. A monograph on this significant figure from antiquity and his modern implications.

Short Story Collections by Sørensen

Another Metamorphosis and Other Fictions. Trans. by Tiina Nunnally & Steven T. Murray. Fjord Pr. 1992 $15.95. ISBN 0-948259-55-8. Strange and absurd explorations of the human condition.

The Downfall of the Gods. 1982. Trans. by Paula Hostrup-Jessen. U. of Nebr. Pr. 1989 $14.95. ISBN 0-8032-4201-8. A retelling of Old Norse mythological tales.

Harmless Tales. 1955. Trans. by Paula Hostrup-Jessen. Dufour 1992 $17.95. ISBN 1-870041-15-1. Anything but harmless, these tales demonstrate the chaos that perennially breaks into our well-ordered world.

THORUP, KIRSTEN. 1942–

A poet and novelist, Thorup has also written for television. She grew up in the countryside where her father was a bookseller and owned a kiosk. The first of her family to receive a higher education, Thorup often writes of the sense of alienation she has felt as an outsider both in her hometown and in her new academic environment. Thorup's prose is written in a realistic mode with a keen interest in psychology. Her poetry shows modernist influences.

NOVELS BY THORUP

Baby: A Novel. 1973. Trans. by Nadia Christensen and Alexander Taylor. La. State U. Pr. 1980 $18.95. ISBN 0-8071-0772-7. Describes the alienation of people living in the poor section of a city.

Marie. Trans. by Alexander Taylor. Top Stories 1982 $3.00. ISBN 0-917061-11-X

POETRY BY THORUP

Love from Trieste. 1969. Trans. by Nadia Christiansen and Alexander Taylor. Curbstone 1980 $6.00. ISBN 0-915306-20-4. Reflects influences from French absurdism and R. D. Laing's psychology.

FAROESE LITERATURE

The great treasure of Faroese literature is its extremely rich ballad tradition, reaching back to the Middle Ages. Still alive today, this tradition is a rarity in our modern world. More modern Faroese literature has a rather short history. Working in the late nineteenth century, poets such as Fridrikur Petersen, Rasmus Effersöe, and Jóhannes Patursson wrote in a romantic style and succeeded in establishing a more modern vein of Faroese literature. J. H. O. Djurhuus and Christian Matras, early twentieth-century writers, compete in critical opinion for the position of foremost Faroese poet.

The real flowering of modern Faroese literature took place in prose. Hedin Brú, Jørgen-Frantz Jacobsen, and William Heinesen—all born at the turn of the century—have gained international attention for Faroese letters. Jacobsen and Heinesen both write in Danish, which has facilitated the dissemination of their writing to a broader reading public.

In the past few decades, Faroese poetry has shown a strong influence from modernist masters such as T. S. ELIOT (see Vol. 1), Finland's EDITH SÖDERGRAN, and Chile's PABLO NERUDA. Faroese prose tends to bring Faroese traditions to bear on a modern world. For example, Jens Pauli Heinesen has written a novel that seeks to translate the ancient Sigurd myth into modern surroundings.

History and Criticism

Brønner, Hedin. *Three Faroese Novelists: In Appreciation of Jørgen Frantz Jacobsen, William Heinesen, and Hedin Brú.* Irvington 1973 o.p. The primary work on these three famous Faroese novelists.

Jones, W. Glyn. *Faroe and Cosmos.* Newcastle upon Tyne 1974 o.p. A general work by the foremost English scholar of Faroese literature.

Collections

Brønner, Hedin. *Faroese Short Stories.* Irvington 1972 $18.50. ISBN 0-8057-3308-6

West, John F., ed. *Faroese Folktales and Legends.* 1980 o.p.

BRÚ, HEDIN. (pseud. of Hans Jacob Jacobsen) 1901–

Brú studied veterinary medicine in Denmark but as a youth worked on the Faroese fishing fleet. He drew on the fishing experiences for his first novels, which are striking in their realistic depictions of a world never before captured in prose. His best novel is considered to be *The Old Man and His Sons* (1940), which depicts a generational conflict—old ways threatened by a changing world. Brú has also written a number of highly regarded short stories. His decision to write in his native tongue about native themes marks a landmark in Faroese literary history.

Novel by Brú

The Old Man and His Sons. 1949. Trans. by John F. West. Eriksson 1970 $12.95. ISBN 0-8397-8412-0

HEINESEN, WILLIAM. 1900–

As a young man in the Faroe Islands, William Heinesen thought of a profession in art or music. His early poetry from the 1920s—he writes in Danish rather than Faroese—demonstrates keen sensitivity to the powerful sensual contrasts of nature in the Atlantic islands. In the 1930s, his elegiac and ecstatic pantheism had a strong effect on readers' social awareness. Of novels from this period, *Noatun* (1938) has appeared in an English translation in Great Britain. In this novel, the reader meets the vital people of a Faroese settlement bravely surviving storms, sickness, and exploitation as they struggle to establish a *noatun,* or new town. The Faroese people's individualism and sharp beauty are Heinesen's subjects; his strong satire, humor, and imagination have made him one of Denmark's finest prose writers. *The Lost Musicians* (1950) and *The Kingdom of the Earth* (1952) share many of the same characters, created by Heinesen to depict fantastic events in Torshavn a generation or so ago. In Heinesen's rich fantasy is an expression of the antinaturalism and antirealism that also mark the writing of the Danes Isak Dinesen and Martin A. Hansen. It is not necessary to have even heard of the Faroes to enjoy the magic of William Heinesen.

Novels by Heinesen

The Kingdom of The Earth. 1952. Trans. by Hedin Brønner. Irvington 1974 $12.95. ISBN 0-8290-2130-2. A mythical, symbolic narrative.

Lanterna Magica. Trans. by Tiina Nunnally. Fjord Pr. 1987 $7.95. ISBN 0-940242-23-0. A look at the quirky world of a small community in the Faroes.

The Lost Musicians. 1950. Trans. by Erik J. Friis. Hippocrene Bks. 1972 $3.95. ISBN 0-88254-002-5. A humorous look at the attempts to achieve prohibition in the Faroes.

Tower at the Edge of the World. Trans. by Anne Born. U. of Toronto Pr. 1982 $7.95. ISBN 0-906191-64-5. Depicts the Faroes as a place at "the edge of the world."

Short Story Collection by Heinesen

The Winged Darkness and Other Stories by William Heinesen. Trans. by William Heinesen. Irvington 1983 $26.50. ISBN 0-8290-0990-6

Book about Heinesen

Jones, W. Glyn. *William Heinesen.* Twayne 1974 o.p. A general survey of Heinesen's life and work.

JACOBSEN, JØRGEN-FRANTZ. 1900–1938

Jacobsen died at a young age, but during his short life he worked actively toward a greater independence for the Faroese. *Denmark and the Faroes* (1927) is a historical analysis of the relationship between the two countries, and *The Faroes: Countryside and People* (1936) is a journalistic description of life in the Faroes. Jacobsen's primary claim to fame as a literary figure rests on his single novel *Barbara* (1939), which was published posthumously. The novel, based on legend, describes a compelling woman of symbolic stature who exerts terrific power upon those around her. *Barbara* has received international acclaim.

NOVEL BY JACOBSEN

Barbara. 1939. Trans. by Estrid Bannister. Viking Penguin 1948 o.p.

NONFICTION BY JACOBSEN

Denmark and the Faroes. 1927. o.p.
The Faroes. Countryside and People. 1936. o.p.

FINNISH LITERATURE

Because of Finland's long historical relationship with Sweden, Finnish literature encompasses both Finnish-language and Finland-Swedish literature. During the years of Swedish domination, the Finnish-speaking populace served the Swedish-speaking aristocracy that administered the province. When Finland came under Russian rule in 1809, various nationalistic movements were free to take flight. Elias Lönnrot spent many years collecting Finnish folk songs with very ancient roots, compiling them in the work known as *The Kalevala* (1835–1949). Lönnrot's efforts established Finnish as a literary language with great nuance and depth. The great Finland-Swedish poet Johan Ludvig Runeberg helped to define the Finnish national self-image with his romantic poetry. The poem "Our Country" from his famous work *The Tales of Ensign Stål* (1848, 1860) became Finland's national anthem. In the same period, Zacharias Topelius wrote fairy tales and historical novels in a Swedish that captivated the rest of Scandinavia.

Alexis Kivi's novel *Seven Brothers* (1870) is a literary landmark which depicts Finnish rural life in realistic rather than romantic terms. Other prominent early practitioners of Finnish realism include the novelist Juhani Aho and the playwright Minna Canth. The Finland-Swedish author Karl August Tavaststjerna was inspired by the social engagement of the Scandinavian Modern Breakthrough that began in 1871, but eventually turned to decadence and Nietzscheanism. The Finland-Swede Runar Schildt translated his feelings of belonging to a doomed linguistic minority into the literary idiom of decadence.

The Russian Revolution of 1917 and the ensuing Finnish civil war left deep marks upon Finnish literature. The rest of Scandinavia was spared direct involvement in the turbulence which rocked Europe at this time, but Finland's firsthand experience of the chaos created fertile ground for the earliest modernist movement in Scandinavia. The Finland-Swedish modernists included Hagar Olsson, EDITH SÖDERGRAN, Elmer Diktonius, Gunnar Björling, and Rabbe Enckell. The impact this group had on modern Scandinavian poetry has been lasting and profound.

Finnish prose of the twentieth century has shown a strong inclination toward realism and the historical novel, as seen in the works of Nobel Laureate FRANS EEMIL SILLANPÄÄ, MIKA TOIMI WALTARI, and Väinö Linna. On the other hand, poetry since World War II has continued in a modernist vein. The current poet laureate of Swedish-speaking Finland is Lars Huldén, whose wry, irreverent wit is combined with a keen knowledge of language and literary tradition.

History and Criticism

Ahokas, Jaakko. *A History of Finnish Literature.* Mouton 1973 o.p. The main source of information in English.

Collections

Binham, Philip, and Richard Dauenhauer, eds. *Snow in May: An Anthology of Finnish Writing, 1945–1972*. Fairleigh Dickinson 1978 $35.00. ISBN 0-8386-1583-X

Forsström, Tua. *Snow Leopard*. Trans. by David McDuff. Dufour 1991 $15.95. ISBN 1-85224-111-X. A highly acclaimed work by this Finland-Swedish author.

Friis, Erik J., ed. *Modern Nordic Plays: Finland*. Irvington 1972 $16.95. ISBN 0-8290-1162-5. Includes plays by Haavikko, Järner, Manner, and Meri.

Huldén, Lars. *The Chain Dance. Selected Poems*. Trans. by George Schoolfield. Camden Hse. 1991 $56.00. ISBN 0-938100-84-X. Huldén is an entertaining poet and Schoolfield a gifted translator.

Lomas, Herbert, ed. and trans. *Contemporary Finnish Poetry*. Dufour 1991 $21.00. ISBN 1-85224-147-0. A survey of postwar poetry written in the Finnish language.

McDuff, David, trans. and ed. *Ice Around Our Lips: Finland-Swedish Poetry*. Dufour 1989 $16.95. ISBN 1-85224-001-3. Selections from 10 Finland-Swedish poets from the turn of the century to the present.

Parland, Oscar. *The Year of the Bull*. Trans. by Joan Tate. Dufour 1991 $35.00. ISBN 0-7206-0807-4. Autobiographical novel set in 1918 Finland.

Paulaharju, Samuli. *Arctic Twilight: Old Finnish Tales*. Trans. by Allan M. Pitkanen. Finnish Am. Lit. 1982 $15.00. ISBN 0-943478-00-6

Schoolfield, George C., ed. and trans. *Swedo-Finnish Short Stories*. Am. Scandinavian 1974 o.p. Presents a competent and skillful translation of a little-known part of Scandinavian writing.

Simonsuuri, Kirsti, ed. *Enchanting Beasts: An Anthology of Modern Women Poets in Finland*. Dufour 1991 $27.00. ISBN 0-948259-68-X. Contains work from 11 Finnish and Finland-Swedish poets. Recipient of a 1991 Translation Center Award.

CARPELAN, BO. 1926–

Bo Carpelan has long been a highly productive poet, critic, novelist, and author of children's books. Carpelan's poetry follows in the tradition of the early Finland-Swedish modernists. Overall his work evokes the infinite complexities of life.

Novel by Carpelan

Voices at the Late Hour. 1971. Trans. by Irma Martin. U. of Ga. Pr. 1988 $11.95. ISBN 0-8203-1009-3. Describes the outbreak of nuclear war and the reactions of people in the face of impending death.

Poetry by Carpelan

Room without Walls. Trans. by Anne Born. Dufour 1987 $14.95. ISBN 0-948259-08-6. A selection from Carpelan's 14 volumes of verse.

JANSSON, TOVE. 1914–

Tove Jansson has received the Hans Christian Andersen prize for children's literature. The world of the Moomintroll has become internationally famous thanks to her brilliant sense of humor and fabulous illustrations. The delightful Moomintrolls make it through catastrophe after catastrophe through cooperation and plain luck. Although Jansson is best known for her children's books, her adult fiction is equally entertaining.

Children's Fiction by Jansson

Comet in Moominland. Trans. by Elizabeth Portch. FS&G 1990 $12.95. ISBN 0-374-31526-4

Finn Family Moomintroll. FS&G 1990 $3.50. ISBN 0-374-42307-5

Moominsummer Madness. FS&G 1991 $13.95. ISBN 0-374-35039-6

THE KALEVALA. 1835–1849

The Kalevala, the Finnish national epic of three semidivine brothers living in Kaleva, a mythical land of abundance and happiness, was known to scholars as early as 1733 but was ignored until the nineteenth century. The verses were collected by two Finnish physicians, Zacharias Topelius, who published the first fragments in 1822, and Elias Lönnrot, who continued to travel and sift the folk songs chanted to him by rune singers. Lönnrot gave the cycle its present form in 1835–36. His second edition, published in 1849, has remained the definitive version. Rich in mythology and folklore, its influence in all branches of the arts has been great. Jean Sibelius used it in a number of his compositions, and HENRY WADSWORTH LONGFELLOW (see Vol. 1) borrowed its poetic form for *The Song of Hiawatha.*

Kalevala: Epic of the Finnish People. Trans. by Eino Friberg. U. of Ill. Pr. 1989 $39.95. ISBN 951-1-10137-4. The best available translation.

Kalevala: An Epic Poem after Oral Tradition by Elias Lönnrot. Trans. by Keith Bosley. OUP 1989 $12.95. ISBN 0-19-281700-0. A good rendering.

The Kalevala: The Land of Heroes. Trans. by W. F. Kirby. Humanities 1985 $14.95. ISBN 0-485-12048-8. A somewhat dated translation.

The Kalevala: Poems of the Kaleva District. Trans. by Francis Peabody Magoun, Jr. HUP 1963 $12.95. ISBN 0-674-50010-5. A prose translation. Literal, but not artistically satisfying.

KIHLMAN, CHRISTER. 1930–

Kihlman has rebelled against his upper-class background to become the "bad boy" of Finland-Swedish letters. Kihlman finds the material for his novels in the crevices of his own soul and his perceptions of the world around him. Many of his books have caused sensations, such as *The Man Who Trembled* (1971), in which Kihlman confessed his alcoholism and bisexuality. His stylistic mastery and thoughtful treatment of his themes protect his novels from the charge of cheap sensationalism. He is perhaps Finland's most highly regarded contemporary novelist.

NOVELS BY KIHLMAN

All My Sons. 1980. Trans. by Joan Tate. Dufour 1984 $22.00. ISBN 0-7206-0628-4. A controversial autobiographical novel in which Kihlman develops a relationship with a young male prostitute from Buenos Aires.

The Blue Mother. 1963. Trans. by Joan Tate. U. of Nebr. Pr. 1990 $11.95. ISBN 0-8032-7769-5. A semi-autobiographical work, generally considered to be Kihlman's masterpiece.

The Downfall of Gerdt Bladh. Trans. by Joan Tate. Dufour 1990 $25.00. ISBN 0-7206-0747-7. Follows the disintegration of a successful businessman.

SAARIKOSKI, PENTTI. 1937–

A journalist, social critic, satirist, translator, and student of classical languages and literatures, Saarikoski combines classical idioms and everyday speech to achieve a highly individual poetic effect. Saarikoski has also played an important role in Finnish letters by translating many major world authors into Finnish.

POETRY BY SAARIKOSKI

Dances of the Obscure. Trans. by Michael Cole & Karen Kimball. Logbridge-Rhodes 1987 $4.50. ISBN 0-937406-44-9. A brief but interesting visit to Saarikoski's verse.

Poems, 1958–1980. Trans. by Anselm Hollo. Coffee Hse. 1983 $10.00. ISBN 0-915124-76-9. A thorough overview of Saarikoski's production.

SCHOULTZ, SOLVEIG VON. 1907–

Schoultz is both a writer of poetry and of short stories, but she claims the dividing line between the two is thin. Her short stories indeed possess the symbolic depth and verbal precision of a poem. In all her work, her language and style are innovative and distinctive, her contemplations of human existence informed by acceptance and compassion.

Poetry by Schoultz

Snow and Summers. Trans. by Anne Born. Dufour 1990 $16.95. ISBN 0-948259-52-3. A selection of the poet's work spanning five decades.

Short Story Collection by Schoultz

Heartwork: Selected Short Stories. Trans. by Marlaine Delargy. Dufour 1991 $16.95. ISBN 0-948259-50-7. Seven stories that provide a subtle analysis of human relationships.

SILLANPÄÄ, FRANS EEMIL. 1888–1964 (Nobel Prize 1939)

The son of a landless peasant, Sillanpää studied natural science at Helsinki University, but his interest soon shifted to writing. His first novel was published in 1916, and his second, a naturalistic work titled *Meek Heritage* (1919), established him as a major Finnish writer and won him a lifetime pension from the government. His next book to receive international fame was *The Maid Silja* (1931), a story of the Finnish Civil War of 1918. Sillanpää writes of the rural people he knew in his youth, exploring with understanding and sympathy the forces that determine their lives.

Novels by Sillanpää

Meek Heritage. 1919. Eriksson 1972 $5.95. ISBN 0-8397-5782-4. A poor tenant farmer is caught up in the Finnish Civil War on the side of the Reds.

The Maid Silja. 1931. Trans. by Alexander Matson. Cherokee 1984 repr. of 1933 ed. $17.95. ISBN 0-299-03901-3. Follows the fate of a young girl in domestic service, who falls in love, is abandoned, and dies of consumption.

People in the Summer Night: An Epic Suite. 1934. Trans. by Alan Blair. U. of Wis. Pr. 1966 $5.95. ISBN 0-299-03901-3. A single summer night provides the link for a number of human destinies. "Sillanpää is good at capturing the smells, textures, and colors of Finnish country life." (*Choice*)

SÖDERGRAN, EDITH. 1892–1923

Reduced to poverty by the Russian Revolution and dying of tuberculosis, young Edith Södergran made an indelible impact on Swedish-language verse in particular, and modern poetry in general. Still moving today, her poems are powerful, expressionistic evocations of emotions and moods which range from invigoration to resignation. She was the foremost Finland-Swedish modernist and introduced many new poetic devices to Scandinavian poetry.

Poetry by Södergran

Complete Poems. Trans. by David McDuff. Dufour 1984 $25.00. ISBN 0-906897-38-X. Provides a complete overview of Södergran's production but should be compared with other translations.

Love & Solitude: Selected Poems, 1916–1923. Trans. by Stina Katchadourian. Fjord Pr. 1992 $10.95. ISBN 0-940242-14-1. A good rendering of a selection of Södergran's poems.

BOOK ABOUT SÖDERGRAN

Schoolfield, George C. *Edith Södergran: Modernist Poet in Finland.* Greenwood 1984 $37.95. ISBN 0-313-24166-X. A superb study by an expert on Finland-Swedish literature.

WALTARI, MIKA TOIMI. 1908–1979

Born in Helsinki, Waltari went to Paris after receiving a university education. He published his first volume of poetry at 17. At the age of 20, his second novel, *The Great Illusion* (1928), brought him general recognition. Waltari returned to Helsinki from Paris in 1929 and continued to write poems, plays, novels, and fairy tales, a total of 80 texts during the next 20 years. *The Egyptian* (1945), a worldwide success, brought Waltari into prominence in other countries. His three-volume historical novel *From Father to Son* (1942) won the national Literary Prize and was filmed and translated into 14 languages. Unfortunately, 11 English translations of Waltari's work are out of print.

NOVELS BY WALTARI

The Egyptian. 1949. Berkeley 1978 o.p. Historical novel about life in ancient Egypt.

The Etruscan. 1955. Berkeley 1971 o.p. Story detailing life in Italy at the time of the Etruscans.

The Roman. 1964. Berkeley 1966 o.p. As in *The Egyptian* and *The Etruscan*, this historical novel looks at life in ancient Rome.

The Secret of the Kingdom. 1959. Putnam 1961 o.p.

NORWEGIAN LITERATURE

The Norwegians have more reason than the peoples of other Scandinavian countries to claim the Icelandic myths and sagas as part of their own literary tradition. Most of the people who settled Iceland were Norwegians fleeing the tyrannies of King Harald Fair-Hair, and thus Norway figures greatly in the medieval literature about that time. The Icelander SNORRI STURLUSON's *Heimskringla* is a history of the Norwegian kings. Once Norway entered the union with Denmark at the end of the fourteenth century, Denmark became the dominant cultural partner. For a long time, Danish was the official language of the educated classes. Peter Dass's Dano-Norwegian poem, "The Trumpet of Nordland" (1739), is considered an early landmark in Norwegian literature, particularly since its subject is the topography of Norway. The Enlightenment genius LUDVIG HOLBERG was actually born in Norway but is counted as a Danish author because he spent his active literary life in Denmark, writing in Danish and Latin.

In 1814 the union with Denmark was dissolved, and Norway entered into a rather more independent union with Sweden. This political change coincided with a growing wave of romantic nationalism that continued through the mid-nineteenth century. The poet and dramatist Henrik Wergeland spoke out against the Danish tradition in favor of a new Norwegian literature. His chief opponent, the poet Johan Welhaven, argued for a continuation of Danish culture. Peter Christian Asbjørnsen and Jørgen Moe assembled their famous collection of Norwegian folktales at about this time. And Ivar Aasen began the construction of a new national literary language based on Norwegian dialect and in opposition to Dano-Norwegian. The result of Aasen's endeavors is that today Norway has two official languages, *bokmål* (book language) and *nynorsk* (New Norwegian).

The irrepressible Bjørnstjerne Bjørnson, a Nobel laureate of 1903, tried single-handedly to create a Norwegian literary tradition with his tales of country life, poetry, and plays. The groundbreaking dramatist Henrik Ibsen aided this project, but in realistic plays that plumbed both psychology and social injustice in colloquial speech. In her short stories and novels, Camilla Collett anticipated the realism of the late nineteenth-century Scandinavian Modern Breakthrough, which proved to be Norway's Golden Age. It generated a host of superior novelists, such as Jonas Lie, Alexander Kielland, Arne Garborg, and Amalie Skram. The 1890s saw the debut of two major authors: Sigbjørn Obstfelder, a modernist forerunner who had a profound impact on the German poet Rainer Maria Rilke and Knut Hamsun, a major novelist of the twentieth century.

The Norwegian prose tradition has maintained its strength in the twentieth century with the masterful realistic prose of Sigrid Undset, the unusual narrative perspectives of Tarjei Vesaas, the satire of Sigurd Hoel, the keen psychological insights of Danish-born Axel Sandemose, and the subtle psychology of Cora Sandel. A strong younger generation has carried the torch, excelling in several genres: Edvard Hoem in his New Norwegian poetry, novels, and plays; Knut Faldbakken in his striking psychological narratives; Bjørg Vik in her feminist fiction; Herbjørg Wassmo in her modernist prose; and Cecilie Løveid in her experimental narratives.

History and Criticism

Beyer, Harald. *A History of Norwegian Literature*. Trans. by Einar Haugen. Am. Scandinavian 1956 o.p. The standard English handbook.

Lyngstad, Sverre, ed. *Review of National Literature: Norway*. Bagehot Council 1983 $23.00. ISBN 0-918680-17-4. A more up-to-date look at Norwegian letters.

Collections

Asbjørnsen, Peter C., and Jørgen Moe. *Norwegian Folk Tales*. Pantheon 1982 $11.95. ISBN 0-394-71054-1. The best-known forms of Norwegian fairy tales, by the two nineteenth-century collectors Asbjørnsen and Moe.

Carling, Finn. *Under the Evening Sky*. Trans. by Louis A. Muinzer. Dufour 1991 $30.00. ISBN 0-7206-0783-3. A highly entertaining experimental novel.

Christiansen, Reidar T., ed. *Folktales of Norway*. Trans. by Pat S. Iversen. U. Ch. Pr. 1964 $13.95. ISBN 0-226-0510-5. Provides some legends as well as regular fairy tales.

Garton, Janet, and Henning Sehmsdorf, eds. *New Norwegian Plays*. Dufour 1990 $24.00. ISBN 1-870041-11-9. Includes plays by Bjørg Vik, Peder Cappelen, Edvard Hoem, and Cecilie Løveid.

Hanson, Katherine, ed. *An Everyday Story: Norwegian Women's Fiction*. Seal Pr. Feminist 1984 $8.95. ISBN 0-931188-22-9. An excellent sampling of Norwegian women writers from the past 100 years.

Hoem, Edvard. *The Ferry Crossing*. Trans. by Frankie D. Shackleford. Garland 1990 $37.00. ISBN 0-8240-2996-8. Received the American Scandinavian Foundation translation prize.

McFarlane, James, ed. *Slaves of Love and Other Norwegian Short Stories*. OUP 1982 o.p.

Nedreaas, Torborg. 1947. *Nothing Grows by Moonlight*. Trans. by Bibbi Lee. U. of Nebr. Pr. 1987 $15.95. ISBN 0-8032-3313-2. A moving account of a woman, broken by life.

______. *Music from a Blue Well*. 1960. Trans. by Bibbi Lee. U. of Nebr. Pr. 1988 $21.00. ISBN 0-802-3315-9. The story of Herdis, who retreats into a fantasy world.

Obstfelder, Sigbjørn. 1900. *A Priest's Diary*. Trans. by James McFarlane. Dufour 1988 $9.95. ISBN 1-870041-01-1. The final, uncompleted work of one of the major precursors of modernism in Scandinavia.

Wassmo, Herbjørg. 1981. *The House with the Blind Glass Windows*. Trans. by Roseann Lloyd and Allen Simpson. Seal Pr. Feminist 1987 $9.95. ISBN 0-931188-50-4. Young Tora comes to terms with repressed events from her past.

BJØRNSON, BJØRNSTJERNE. 1832–1910 (NOBEL PRIZE 1903)

In his will, Alfred Nobel placed a special emphasis on idealism as an important quality in the work of recipients of the Nobel Prize for Literature. Bjørnstjerne Bjørnson was the consummate idealist, crusading for noble causes all over Europe, but maintaining his sympathy for human failings. Bjørnson's tales of country life were a romantic attempt to capture the Norwegian national character in literature. They were vastly popular in the United States among homesick Norwegian immigrants. When the Modern Breakthrough arrived, Bjørnson began energetically composing plays of social relevance. Although less widely read today, Bjørnson remains a significant figure in Norwegian literary history.

NOVEL BY BJØRNSON

Synnove Solbakken. 1857. Trans. by Julie Sutter. Ayer repr. of 1894 ed. $16.00. ISBN 0-8369-6758-5. A novel-length tale of country life.

PLAYS BY BJØRNSON

Three Comedies. Greenwood 1974 repr. of 1914 ed. $35.00. ISBN 0-8371-7259-4

Three Dramas. Trans. by R. Farquharson Sharp. Greenwood 1974 repr. of 1914 ed. $35.00. ISBN 0-8371-7260-8. Representative social dramas, Bjørnson's most important work.

Three Plays. Trans. by Edwin Bjorkman. Fertig 1989 repr. of 1913 ed. $35.00. ISBN 0-86527-383-9. Includes *The Gauntlet*, *Beyond our Power*, and *The New System*.

SHORT STORY COLLECTIONS BY BJØRNSON

Bridal March & Other Stories. Trans. by Rasmus B. Anderson. Ayer repr. of 1882 ed. $17.00. ISBN 0-8369-3136-X. Tales of country life in Norway.

Captain Mansana & Other Stories. Trans. by Rasmus B. Anderson. Ayer repr. of 1882 ed. $18.00. ISBN 0-8369-3236-6. Tales of country life in Norway.

NONFICTION BY BJØRNSON

Haugen, Eva, and Einar Haugen, eds. *Land of the Free: Bjørnstjerne Bjørnson's America Letters, 1880-1881*. Norwegian-Am. Hist. Assn. 1978 $15.00. ISBN 0-87732-061-6. A collection of special interest to Americans of Norwegian heritage. Bjørnson was a prodigious letter-writer.

FALDBAKKEN, KNUT. 1941–

In his novels, Knut Faldbakken literally pulls no punches. The blow that a male character delivers to his female partner in *The Honeymoon* (1981) generated waves of protest in Norway. Faldbakken is deeply interested in human psychology and relentlessly pursues the outcomes of his characters' natures and circumstances, even to murder and incest. Faldbakken is a brilliant stylist whose explorations of the human soul are always compelling.

NOVELS BY FALDBAKKEN

Adam's Diary. 1978. Trans. by Sverre Lyngstad. U. of Nebr. Pr. 1988 $12.95. ISBN 0-8032-6866-1. An exploration of the complexities of the male role in modern society.

The Honeymoon. 1981. St. Martin 1988 $3.95. ISBN 0-312-91366-4. The psychological trauma of a marital breakup.

Insect Summer. 1972. Trans. by Hall Sutcliffe and Torbjørn Støverud. Dufour 1991 $28.00. ISBN 0-7206-0794-9. About a young boy's passage into adulthood.

The Sleeping Prince. 1971. Trans. by Janet Garton. Dufour 1989 $26.00. ISBN 0-7206-0710-8. Explores the psychological peculiarities of a lonely spinster.

HAMSUN, KNUT. 1859–1952 (NOBEL PRIZE 1920)

The distinction of Knut Hamsun's writing in Norwegian literature is its predominant concern with the individual's immediate emotional life, without reference to social programs or abstract "truths." The very title of Hamsun's first major work, *Hunger* (1899), suggests its theme: the psychic ebb and flow of a brilliant young writer who is actually starving, but who is filled with spontaneity and emotional freedom. Hamsun sharply criticized naturalist writers for the gray superficial reality they described. He made it his goal, by combining art and psychology, to illuminate the mysterious realities of the individual psyche. Yet as a poetic philosopher Hamsun was clearly anti-intellectual. Influences such as AUGUST STRINDBERG, FRIEDRICH NIETZSCHE (see Vol. 4), and Georg Brandes shaped Hamsun's development, but his childhood in the intensely dramatic natural world of northern Norway did as much to create his basic mood. The shifting weather and rich colors of his early home were expressed anew in Hamsun's lyric and often ecstatic prose, in which he created a wide range of imaginative and yet psychologically credible personalities. Both *Pan* (1894) and *Victoria* (1898) are rich in the prose, poetry, eroticism, and pantheism that inspired Hamsun throughout his life. His almost mystical admiration for the spontaneous individual living close to nature led Hamsun to despise industrial society and to mythologize traditional rural Norwegian patriarchal families. Where others saw progressive industrialism, he saw degeneracy: money grubbers and weak conformists. *Growth of the Soil* (1917), which led to Hamsun's Nobel Prize in 1920, is his gospel of the simple life and, by implication, attack on modern civilization. Ironically, Hamsun's visionary and violent love of traditional country life coaxed him in the latter part of his life into a fateful intellectual sympathy with Nazi dogma. Although he was scorned and severely punished by his country's people after World War II, Hamsun's contribution to world literature is great and lasting.

NOVELS BY HAMSUN

Growth of the Soil. 1917. Trans. by W. W. Worster. Random 1972 $7.95. ISBN 0-394-71781-3

Hunger. 1890. Trans. by Robert Bly. FS&G 1967 $9.95. ISBN 0-374-50520-9

Mysteries. 1892. Trans. by Gerry Bothmer. Carroll & Graf 1984 $8.95. ISBN 0-88184-031-9. A singular individual invades the misleadingly peaceful world of a small Norwegian town.

Pan. 1894. Trans. by James W. McFarlane, FS&G 1956 $9.95. ISBN 0-374-50016-9. A celebration of nature and *fin de siècle* psychology.

Victoria. 1898. Trans. by Oliver Stallybrass. Avon 1975 o.p. A tragic love story.

The Wanderer. 1906–09. Trans. by Oliver Stallybrass and Gunvor Stallybrass. FS&G 1975 o.p. A lyrical self-portrait of the author.

Wayfarers. 1927. Trans. by James W. McFarlane. FS&G 1981 $10.95. ISBN 0-374-51592-1. A de-romanticized treatment of the artist.

The Women at the Pump. 1920. Trans. by Gunvor Stallybrass. FS&G 1978 o.p. One of Hamsun's darkest novels.

Short Story Collection by Hamsun

Night Roamers and Other Stories. Trans. by Tiina Nunnally. Fjord Pr. 1991 $9.95. ISBN 0-940242-19-2. A collection of nine stories that Hamsun printed in newspapers, rediscovered and collected in 1988.

Nonfiction by Hamsun

The Cultural Life of Modern America. 1889. Trans. by Barbara C. Morgridge. HUP 1969 o.p. Hamsun's early views on U.S. life and society, rather casually documented but firmly espoused throughout his life, based on his experience in the United States in the 1880s.

Selected Letters: Volume 1, 1878–98. Ed. by Harald Naess and James McFarlane. Dufour 1990 $45.00. ISBN 1-870041-13-5. Interesting reading for the serious Hamsun reader.

Book about Hamsun

Naess, Harald. *Knut Hamsun.* Twayne 1984 o.p. An overview of Hamsun's life and work written by an expert in Norwegian letters. With a useful bibliography.

IBSEN, HENRIK (JOHAN). 1828–1906

Ibsen's career as a dramatist is generally divided into two major phases. In his early phase, Ibsen wrote romantic dramas in verse, most of which have been forgotten by all but Ibsen experts. The culmination of Ibsen's early work is *Brand* (1866) and *Peer Gynt* (1867), companion pieces that explore in turn the uncompromising idealist and the characterless individual. *Brand* and *Peer Gynt* are more dramatic poems than plays, but this has not prevented theater companies from attempting performances—a tremendous technical undertaking.

The second phase of Ibsen's career began with *The Pillars of Society* (1877), the first of his realistic prose plays. The timelessness of the drama from this period—including *A Doll's House* (1879), *Ghosts* (1881), and *An Enemy of the People* (1882)—is attested to by the many Broadway, television, and repertory productions that pay perennial tribute to Ibsen's incisive characterizations of individuals in conflict. Conflict with self rather than social forces best describes Ibsen's next suite of plays: *The Wild Duck* (1884), *Rosmersholm* (1886), *The Lady from the Sea* (1888), and *Hedda Gabler* (1890). *A Doll's House* and *Hedda Gabler* present two equally acute views of the price and value of women's liberation. Ibsen's last plays, *The Master Builder* (1892), *Little Eyolf* (1894), *John Gabriel Borkman* (1896), and *When We Dead Awaken* (1899), generally concern the self-destructive aspects of artistic ambition. The symbolism in these plays makes them more demanding and less well known today. In all his work, Ibsen did not offer simplistic programs for social groups but rather illuminated and probed unique individuals.

Ibsen, together with August Strindberg, is one of the architects of the modern drama. Ibsen's abandonment of verse in drama in order to explore the poetic potential of everyday speech is a landmark in the genre's history. His choice to foreground social problems inspired dramatists like Gerhart Hauptmann, George Bernard Shaw (see Vol. 1), Maxim Gorky, and Bertolt Brecht. Ibsen's mastery of the nuances of language and the symbolic depth he found in a realistic world have inspired poets, novelists, and dramatists alike.

Plays by Ibsen

The Oxford Ibsen. Ed. by James W. McFarlane. 8 vols. OUP 1960–1971. o.p. The source for Ibsen's early plays.

Brand. Trans. by Michael Meyer. Methuen 1967 o.p. A major play that should not be out of print for long. Story of a minister who takes his calling too seriously.

A Doll's House and Other Plays. Trans. by Peter Watts. Viking Penguin 1965 $2.95. ISBN 0-14-044146-8. Includes *League of Youth* and *The Lady from the Sea. A Doll's House* is about an upper middle class housewife who leaves her husband and children.

Ghosts and Other Plays. Trans. by Peter Watts. Viking Penguin 1964 $3.95. ISBN 0-14-044135-2. Includes *Public Enemy* and *When We Dead Awaken. Ghosts* examines the effects a drunk and philanderer has on his family.

Hedda Gabler and Other Plays. Trans. by Una Ellis-Fermor. Viking Penguin 1951 $3.95. ISBN 0-14-044016-X. Includes *Pillars of the Community* and *The Wild Duck.* In *Hedda Gabler,* a woman's jealousy leads to the death of her husband and herself.

The Master Builder and Other Plays. Trans. by Una Ellis-Fermor. Viking Penguin 1959 $4.95. ISBN 0-14-044053-4. Includes *Rosmersholm, Little Eyolf,* and *John Gabriel Borkman. The Master Builder* explores the themes of arrogance and delusion.

Peer Gynt. Trans. by Rolf Fjelde. U. of Minn. Pr. 1980 $11.95. ISBN 0-8166-0915-2. In *Peer Gynt,* a man of little character finds redemption through the love of a woman.

Books about Ibsen

Bryan, George B. *Ibsen Companion: A Dictionary-Guide to the Life, Works, & Critical Reception of Henrik Ibsen.* Greenwood 1984 $65.00. ISBN 0-313-23506-6. A useful tool for the serious student of Ibsen.

Firkins, Ina T. *Henrik Ibsen: A Bibliography of Criticism and Biography, with an Index to Characters.* Folcroft 1973 o.p. An important source of information.

Johnston, Brian. *Text and Supertext in Ibsen's Drama.* Pa. St. U. Pr. 1989 $28.50. ISBN 0-271-00644-7. A new look at Ibsen's plays by an established Ibsen scholar.

Koht, Halvdan. *Life of Ibsen.* Ed. and trans. by Einar Haugen and A. E. Santaniello. Ayer 1971 $33.00. ISBN 0-405-08715-2. The standard English Ibsen biography.

Marker, Fredrick J., and Lise-Lone Marker. *Ibsen's Lively Art: A Performance Study of the Major Plays.* Cambridge U. Pr. 1989 $42.50. ISBN 0-521-26643-2. A source of inspiration for anyone planning the production of an Ibsen play.

Meyer, Michael. *Ibsen, A Biography.* Random 1985 o.p. A colorful and informative look at Ibsen.

McFarlane, James W. *Ibsen & Meaning. Studies, Essays & Prefaces, 1953–1987.* Dufour 1988 $25.00. ISBN 1-870041-07-0. McFarlane is perhaps the world expert on Ibsen.

Northam, John. *Ibsen: A Critical Study.* Cambridge U. Pr. 1973 o.p. A standard scholarly work.

LIE, JONAS. 1833–1908

Lie's first novels in the 1870s were marked by an interest in the supernatural and the subconscious, as well as by their evocation of the northern Norway landscape. The Modern Breakthrough of the 1880s was Lie's realistic phase, when, like other artists of the time, he explored major social questions. In the 1890s, he returned to his earlier interest in the supernatural and the psyche, which at this time coincided with a general European interest in the occult. Lie is remarkable for his narrative innovations, which include an occasionally impressionistic style that inspired Herman Bang. He was a major artistic influence on both his contemporaries and subsequent generations of novelists.

Short Story Collections by Lie

The Seer & Other Norwegian Tales. Trans. by Brian Morton and Richard Trevor. Dufour 1991 $21.00. ISBN 0-948259-65-6. Belongs to the category of Lie's supernatural/psychological fiction.

Weird Tales from the Northern Seas. Ayer repr. of 1893 ed. $14.00. ISBN 0-8369-3024-X. A somewhat dated translation.

BOOK ABOUT LIE

Lyngstad, Sverre. *Jonas Lie.* Irvington 1977 $17.95. ISBN 0-8057-6274-4. Useful overview with bibliography.

RØLVAAG, OLE EDVART. 1876–1931

Norwegian-born Rølvaag emigrated to the United States at age 20 in 1896. Following a college education in Minnesota and Norway, he began the writing and teaching career (at St. Olaf College, Minnesota) that was to bring him fame as an interpreter of the Norwegian-American cultural experience. Rølvaag's understanding of immigrant life on the prairie was the source of novels that have given his name a solid place in both national literatures. His first, highly autobiographical work, *The Third Life of Per Smevik* (1912), was published under the pseudonym Paal Morck. Rølvaag's masterpiece, *Giants in the Earth* (1924–25), is his own translation, with Lincoln Colcord, of the first two of four novels dealing with the family of Per Hansa. *Peder Victorious* (1928) and *Their Fathers' God* (1931) complete the epic, although these two novels are less compelling.

NOVELS BY RØLVAAG

The Boat of Longing: A Novel. 1921. Trans. by Nora O. Solum. Minn. Hist. 1985 $8.95. ISBN 0-83751-184-0. Contrasts life in Norway with the sordidness of the American urban landscape.

Giants in the Earth. 1925. Trans. by Ole Edvart Rølvaag and Lincoln Colcord. HarpC 1991 $6.95. ISBN 0-06-083047-6. Story of a Norwegian pioneer family in the American Midwest in the 1870s.

Peder Victorious: A Tale of the Pioneers Twenty Years Later. 1928. Trans. by Nora O. Solum. U. of Nebr. Pr. 1982 repr. of 1929 ed. $8.50. ISBN 0-8032-8906-5. Continues the story of *Giants in the Earth.*

Pure Gold. Trans. by Sivert Erdahl. Greenwood 1973 repr. of 1930 ed. $38.50. ISBN 0-8371-7070-2

Their Fathers' God. Trans. by Trygve M. Ager. U. of Nebr. Pr. 1983 repr. of 1931 ed. $9.95. ISBN 0-8032-8911-1. With *Giants in the Earth* and *Peder Victorious*, the third volume about life on the American frontier.

The Third Life of Per Smevik. 1912. Trans. by Ella Valborg Tweet and Solveig Zempel. Dillon 1971 o.p.

SHORT STORY COLLECTION BY RØLVAAG

When the Wind Is in the South and Other Stories. Trans. by Solveig Zempel. Augustana Coll. 1985 o.p.

BOOK ABOUT RØLVAAG

Reigstad, Paul. *Rølvaag: His Life and Art.* U. of Nebr. Pr. 1972 $19.95. ISBN 0-8032-0803-0. The standard work on Rølvaag.

SANDEL, CORA (pseud. of Sara Fabricius). 1880–1974

Sandel's best-known work is an autobiographical trilogy—*Alberta and Jacob* (1926), *Alberta and Freedom* (1931), and *Alberta Alone* (1939), which describes with insight and honesty the coming to maturity of a small-town Norwegian girl. Trained as a painter, Sandel has an eye for telling detail. She is also an attentive student of human nature. Sandel's short stories often explore with great sympathy the lives of society's outcasts and underdogs. She is a masterful prose stylist of marvelous delicacy whose work rarely fails to move. Her insight into the psyches of women and artists is especially acute and justly praised.

NOVELS BY SANDEL

Alberta Alone. 1939. Trans. by Elizabeth Rokkan. Ohio U. Pr. 1984 $9.95. ISBN 0-8214-0761-9

Alberta and Freedom. 1931. Trans. by Elizabeth Rokkan. Ohio U. Pr. 1984 $9.95. ISBN 0-8214-0759-7

Alberta and Jacob. 1926. Trans. by Elizabeth Rokkan. Ohio U. Pr. 1984 $15.95. ISBN 0-8214-0756-2

Krane's Cafe: An Interior with Figures. 1945. Trans. by Elizabeth Rokkan. Ohio U. Pr. 1985 $18.00. ISBN 0-8214-0796-1

The Leech. 1958. Trans. by Elizabeth Rokkan. Ohio U. Pr. 1986 $7.95. ISBN 0-8214-0838-0

SHORT STORY COLLECTIONS BY SANDEL

Cora Sandel: Selected Short Stories. Trans. by Barbara Wilson. Seal Pr. Feminist 1985 $8.95. ISBN 0-931188-30-X

The Silken Thread. Trans. by Elizabeth Rokkan. Ohio U. Pr. 1987 $8.95. ISBN 0-8214-0865-8

SKRAM, AMALIE. 1846–1905

Amalie Skram was a scandalous figure at the time of the Modern Breakthrough: not only a divorced woman, but a writer on topics not deemed suitable for a lady. Her hard-hitting naturalism and exposés of social injustice and sexist sexual mores shocked many people. In *Constance Ring* (1885), for example, Skram explores the trauma caused by the societal expectation that women, raised in ignorance and married to men they do not love, should nevertheless become warm sexual partners.

NOVELS BY SKRAM

Constance Ring. 1885. Trans. by Judith Messick and Katherine Hanson. Seal Pr. Feminist 1988 $10.95. ISBN 0-931188-60-1

Under Observation. 1899. Trans. by Judith Messick and Katherine Hanson. Seal Pr. Feminist 1992 $15.95. ISBN 1-879679-03-5. Based on Skram's experiences in a mental hospital.

UNDSET, SIGRID. 1882–1949 (NOBEL PRIZE 1928)

Sigrid Undset was the daughter of archeologist Ingvald Undset. Cultural, autobiographical, and religious topics constitute a large and interesting portion of her fiction, which in Norway is categorized according to the time of action: medieval or modern. *Jenny* (1911), an idealistic and tragic love story, is one of the latter novels. Undset's comprehensive knowledge of medieval Scandinavian culture has its literary monuments in *Kristin Lavransdatter* (1920–22) and *The Master of Hestviken* (1925–27), historical novels that depict life in the Norwegian Middle Ages.

Norwegian criticism of Sigrid Undset's writing centers on her religiosity (she became a conservative, almost reactionary Catholic in Lutheran Norway in the 1920s; she possesses an intensity of belief that is rather naturally expressed in the medieval novels. Yet while she has written religious polemics, the medieval novels are not tendentious. In fact, the central motifs are eroticism, marriage, and family life, in short, the full life of a medieval woman who sees herself in the light of contemporary Christian beliefs. These novels are great, realistic delineations of medieval personalities. During World War II she escaped the German occupation of Norway and fled to America, where she wrote her autobiographical *Happy Times in Norway* (1942).

Novels by Undset

Jenny. 1911. Trans. by W. Emme. Fertig 1975 o.p.

Kristin Lavransdatter. 3 vols. Random 1987 $8.95 ea. Vol. 1 *The Bridal Wreath*. ISBN 0-394-75299-6. Vol. 2 *The Mistress of Husaby*. ISBN 0-394-75293-7. Vol. 3 *The Cross*. ISBN 0-394-75291-0

The Master of Hestviken. 1925–27. Trans. by A. G. Chater. New Amer. Lib. 1978 o.p.

Nonfiction by Undset

Happy Times in Norway. 1942. Trans. by Joran Birkeland. Greenwood 1979 repr. of 1942 ed. $35.00. ISBN 0-313-21267-8

Longest Years. 1934. Trans. by A. G. Chater. Kraus repr. of 1935 ed. $29.00. ISBN 0-527-91500-9. Autobiographical essays.

Stages on the Road. 1933. Trans. by A. G. Chater. Ayer repr. of 1934 ed. $16.50. ISBN 0-8369-1068-0. A collection of essays about her ideas concerning Catholicism and the modern world.

Short Story Collection by Undset

Four Stories. Trans. by Naomi Walford. Greenwood 1978 repr. of 1969 ed. $35.00. ISBN 0-313-20566-3

Books about Undset

Bayerschmidt, Carl F. *Sigrid Undset*. Twayne 1970 o.p. A general overview of Undset's life and work, with a useful bibliography.

Brunsdale, Mitzi. *Sigrid Undset: Chronicler of Norway*. Berg Pubs. 1989 $25.00. ISBN 0-85496-027-9. Undset's world view obviously admired by Brunsdale; nothing new brought to Undset scholarship.

Winsnes, Andreas H. *Sigrid Undset: A Study in Christian*. Realism. Trans. by P. G. Foote. Greenwood 1978 repr. of 1953 ed. $38.50. ISBN 0-8371-4502-3. A standard work on Undset.

VESAAS, TARJEI. 1897–1970

By 1934, when *The Great Cycle* appeared, Tarjei Vesaas has published 11 works. In this novel he clearly showed the enduring qualities of his later work: delicate human portraiture, compelling symbolism and allegory, and constant sensitivity to human beings' universal turmoils of hope, fear, and love. By the end of his life Vesaas had written some 35 works of prose and poetry and had received the Venice Triennial Prize in 1952 and the Nordic Council Prize for literature in 1964. Perhaps his generation's foremost writer of novels and short stories, he wrote of common people in rural Norway who represented humanity at its best and worst. Children and adolescents occupy a special place in Vesaas's writing; in *The Birds* (1957), the reader participates in the inner life of a mentally impaired youth observing the adult world. Vesaas's realism is usually psychological rather than historical, as in *The Seed* (1940), which deals with the hatred, fear, and mass psychosis spawned in a small community by the murder of a girl. It is apparent that the barbarous acts of the killer's lynchers mirror the hideous transformation of decent people in Fascist Europe of the late 1930s.

Novels by Vesaas

The Birds. 1957. Trans. by Torbjorn Stoverud and Michael Barnes. Dufour 1985 $23.00. ISBN 0-7206-0701-9

Bridges. 1966. Trans. by Elizabeth Rokkan. Morrow 1970 o.p.

The Boat in the Evening. 1968. Trans. by Elizabeth Rokkan. Morrow 1972 o.p.

The Great Cycle. 1934. Trans. by Elizabeth Rokkan. U. of Wis. Pr. 1977 $7.95. ISBN 0-299-04494-7

The Ice Palace. Trans. by Elizabeth Rokkan. Sun & Moon CA 1990 $11.95. ISBN 1-55713-094-9. A compelling story told from the perspective of a small girl.

Land of Hidden Fires. 1953. Trans. by Fritz Konig and Jerry Crisp. Wayne St. U. Pr. 1973 o.p.

The Seed and The Spring Night. 1940 and 1954. Trans. by Kenneth Chapman. Am. Scandinavian 1964 o.p.

POETRY BY VESAAS

Selected Poems. Trans. by Anthony Barnett. Small Pr. Dist. 1988 $15.00. ISBN 0-907954-12-X. One hundred poems. "His form is modern and international, free from the musical regularity of the popular ballad, and . . . his themes are mostly the things which gladden his inland heart—the mountains, the snow, and the trees." (Harald Naess)

BOOK ABOUT VESAAS

Chapman, Kenneth C. *Tarjei Vesaas.* Irvington 1970 $17.95. ISBN 0-8057-2948-8. An overview of Vesaas's life and work with a useful bibliography.

VIK, BJØRG. 1935–

As a dramatist and writer of short stories, Vik explores the loneliness, tedium, and materialism of modern life. Although her writing demonstrates a special interest in women's issues, her characters of all ages and sexes share the complex task of living in the modern world and navigating through a minefield of social expectations.

SHORT STORY COLLECTION BY VIK

An Aquarium of Women. 1972. Trans. by Janet Garton. Dufour 1988 $16.95. ISBN 1-870041-04-6. A collection of nine stories which explore how patriarchal culture shapes women's lives.

SWEDISH LITERATURE

The earliest Swedish writings include law codices and the revelations of St. Birgitta from the fourteenth century. Gustav Wasa, the first hereditary monarch of Sweden, who reigned from 1523 to 1560, spearheaded the Lutheran reformation and began building the Swedish Empire; its considerable military influence lasted until the death of Charles XII in 1718. Of note in this period is Georg Stiernhielm's baroque poem *Hercules* (1658), containing a moral lesson for a young prince, an appropriate theme for a poet employed by a superpower.

The development of Swedish letters gained momentum during the reign of Gustav III (1771–92). An enthusiastic patron of the arts, King Gustav tried his hand at both writing and acting—by starring in his own plays. The Gustavian poets include Johan Henrik Kellgren, the Finland-Swede Frans Mikael Franzén, Carl Gustaf af Leopold, and Anna Maria Lenngren. Gustav III even supported a talented, but dissolute, poet and minstrel who has proven to be the enduring genius of this generation: Carl Michael Bellman. Bellman's poetry, which was set to music and brilliantly performed by the poet himself, mixes high and low elements in an exceedingly innovative fashion.

The romantic poets Esaias Tegnér, Per Daniel Amadeus Atterbom, Erik Gustaf Geijer, and Erik Johan Stagnelius followed closely upon the Gustavians. The Swedish literary tradition is founded upon verse, and this was a poetic generation of great talent. Because of the difficulties of translating poetry, however, its figures are not widely known. If more widely translated, Tegnér and Stagnelius would easily have international stature. The renegade of this generation was CARL JONAS LOVE ALMQVIST, whose concern with social issues anticipated the Modern Breakthrough begun in Denmark in the 1870s.

Perhaps because of the exceptional quality of the Swedish romantic poetry, romantic elements held sway over Swedish writing well into the latter half of the nineteenth century. Then in 1879, AUGUST STRINDBERG's realistic novel *The Red Room* swept clean the literary stage, introducing a new type of writing in Sweden. Although Strindberg was the strongest figure of the Swedish Modern Breakthrough, his worthy colleagues included Anne Charlotte Edgren-Leffler, Duchess di Cajanello, and Victoria Benedictsson, who used the pseudonym Ernst Ahlgren.

The 1890s have been called the Golden Age of Swedish literature. The artistic Parnassus of this generation includes the poet Gustaf Fröding and the Nobel laureates Verner von Heidenstam, a poet and novelist, Erik Axel Karlfeldt, a poet, and SELMA LAGERLÖF, a novelist. The common thread uniting this group is an interest in Swedish history and folk traditions. They are often characterized as neo-romantics, but this label does not quite fit Fröding, whose poetry anticipates modernism.

Sweden's twentieth century has been rich. Hjalmar Söderberg is a splendid prose stylist who wrote in the mode of turn-of-the-century pessimism. The negativity of this initial period changed to optimism during the century's second decade, and with a few exceptions, the general literary taste leaned toward the idyll until World War II. The exceptions include PÄR LAGERKVISTand Hjalmar Bergman, both important forerunners of modernism. During the 1930s, the authors such as EYVIND JOHNSON, HARRY MARTINSON, and Artur Lundkvist began turning the tide for modernism, and the 1940s are considered its high point. Also in the 1930s, working-class realism flourished in the hands of such authors as Ivar Lo-Johansson, Jan Fridegård, and Moa Martinson. Recent decades have seen the emergence of an extremely strong group of novelists, including Lars Gyllensten, Sara Lidman, Sven Delblanc, Kerstin Ekman, P. O. ENQUIST, P. C. JERSILD, LARS GUSTAFSSON, and Torgny Lindgren. Sweden's strong poetic tradition still thrives in the work of TOMAS TRANSTRÖMER, Östen Sjöstrand, Elisabet Hermodsson, Göran Palm, and many others. The dramatic arts in Sweden have lived in the shadow of Strindberg, but worthy contributions have been made recently by Lars Norén and P. O. Enquist.

History and Criticism

Gustafson, Alrik. *A History of Swedish Literature*. U. of Minn. Pr. 1961 o.p. An extensive survey including a detailed critical-bibliographic guide and list of Swedish literature in translation to 1961.

Scobbie, Irene, ed. *Aspects of Modern Swedish Literature*. Dufour 1988 $21.00. ISBN 1-870041-02-X. Incisive essays giving an overview of Swedish literature since the 1880s.

Collections

Bly, Robert, ed. and trans. *Friends, You Drank Some Darkness: Three Swedish Poets, Martinson, Ekelöf and Tranströmer*. Beacon Bks. 1975 o.p. Robert Bly, an important American poet and a sensitive interpreter of Scandinavian poetry.

Fridegard, Jan. 3 vols. U. of Nebr. Pr. Trans. by Robert Bjork. Vol. 1 *Land of the Wooden Gods*. 1989 $9.95. ISBN 0-8032-6870-X. Vol. 2 *People of the Dawn*. 1990 $8.95. ISBN

0-8032-6871-8. Vol 3 *Sacrificial Smoke.* 1990 $9.95. ISBN 0-8032-6872-6. An exciting and entertaining trilogy about a Viking Age slave.

Friis, Erik J., ed. *Modern Nordic Plays: Sweden.* Trans. by Harry G. Carlsson and Paul B. Austin. Irvington 1982 $16.95. ISBN 0-8290-1165-X. Plays by Forsell, Fridell, Görling, and Höijer.

Harding, Gunnar, and Stanley Barkan, eds. *Four Contemporary Swedish Poets.* Trans. by Robin Fulton and Anselm Hollo. Cross Cult. 1981 $5.00. ISBN 0-89304-609-4

Lo-Johansson, Ivar. *Breaking Free.* 1933. Trans. by Rochelle Wright. U. of Nebr. Pr. 1990 $42.50. ISBN 0-8032-2891-0. Describes the experiences of the Swedish working class, who worked on farms, not in factories.

______. *Only a Mother.* 1939. Trans. by Robert Bjork. U. of Nebr. Pr. 1991 $45.00. ISBN 0-8032-2882-1. The tragic story of a working-class single mother.

Lundkvist, Artur. 1984. *Journeys in Dream and Imagination.* Trans. by Ann B. Weissmann and Annika Planck. FWEW 1991 $17.95. ISBN 0-941423-67-0. An account of his close brush with death, by a prolific poet, literary critic, and translator of non-Scandinavian literatures.

______. *The Talking Tree. Poems in Prose.* Trans. by Diana Wormuth. Brigham 1982 $9.95. ISBN 0-8425-2099-6. Plays with the limits of genre in one of Lundkvist's favorite hybrids, the prose poem.

Martinson, Moa. *My Mother Gets Married.* 1936. Trans. by Margaret Lacy. Feminist Pr. 1988 $9.95. ISBN 0-935312-81-1. The hard life of a working-class girl in the poor quarter of a city.

______. *Women and Appletrees.* 1933. Trans. by Margaret Lacy. Feminist Pr. 1985 $8.95. ISBN 0-935312-38-2. The destinies of two working-class women.

Sjöstrand, Östen. *Hidden Music: Selected Poems.* Oleander Pr. 1974 $4.95. ISBN 0-902675-35-4. One of Sweden's most important modern poets.

Sonnevi, Göran. *The Economy Spinning Faster and Faster.* Trans. by Robert Bly. Bookslinger 1982 $6.00. ISBN 0-915342-39-1. An important Swedish poet.

Wästberg, Per. *An Anthology of Modern Swedish Literature.* Cross Cult. 1979 $15.00. ISBN 0-89304-701-5. A sampling of modern prose writers such as Jersild, Per Olof Sundman, and Gustafsson.

ALMQVIST, CARL JONAS LOVE. 1793–1866

Almqvist, an erratic genius, was an extremely productive author, writing romantic poetry, polemical essays, novels, and textbooks. Almqvist's ideas about the Swedish peasants and the role of women were advanced for his time and got him into considerable trouble. He spent time in the Swedish countryside trying to create a Rousseauian idyll and even married a woman from the peasant class. When his enthusiasm for that project faded, Almqvist became a school rector in Stockholm but lost the job after his controversial novel *Sara Videbeck* (1839) appeared. Almqvist tried to support himself as a journalist, but finding himself drawn deeper and deeper in debt—and charged with having poisoned a creditor—he fled Sweden. He lived in the United States for some years and died in exile.

Novels by Almqvist

Sara Videbeck–The Chapel. 1839. Trans. by Adolph Benson. Irvington 1972 $6.95. ISBN 0-8057-3354-X. Two of Almqvist's short novels. *Sara Videbeck* examines economic independence for single women, suggesting that men and women would be happier living with each other, instead of getting married.

The Queen's Diadem. 1834. Trans. by Yvonne Sandstroem. Camden Hse. 1991 $49.00. ISBN 0-685-48233-2. One of Almqvist's most intriguing novels, set in the court of Gustav III.

BOOK ABOUT ALMQVIST

Romberg, Bertil. *Carl Jona Love Almqvist.* Twayne 1977 o.p. A good overview of Almqvist's life and works.

BERGMAN, INGMAR. 1918–

[SEE Vol. 3.]

EKELÖF, GUNNAR. 1907–1968

As others have observed, Ekelöf is a poet who deserves much wider recognition: "Ekelöf is a poet of surprising stature, one of the masters of modern poetry, yet little known in America" (*LJ*). Contributing to his obscurity outside Sweden is that few writers of his eminence are more difficult to characterize, for the poetry that began to appear in 1932 was an extremely personal, evolving investigation of human consciousness and culture. For Ekelöf, a twentieth-century mystic, all things, people, and ideas form a complex interdependent unity; the past is in the present, and reality for the poet is his changing inner visions. The strength and genuineness of Ekelöf's often bleak voice won him immense popularity in Sweden as well as almost all Scandinavian literary awards. In his late works, *Diwan over the Prince of Emgión* (1965) and *The Tale of Fatuhmeh* (1966), Ekelöf expertly drew from medieval Greek and Middle Eastern literature to create a mystical and visionary search, while and by means of suffering, for essential human experience.

POETRY BY EKELÖF

Guide to the Underworld. 1967. Trans. by Rika Lesser. U. of Mass. Pr. 1980 $15.00. ISBN 0-87023-306-8. A poetic event of moment in Swedish literature, sensitively rendered.

I Do Best Alone at Night. Trans. by Robert Bly. Charioteer 1977 $7.50. ISBN 0-910350-03-5. A premier American poet interpreting a premier Swedish poet.

A Molna Elegy. 1960. Trans. by Muriel Rukeyser and Leif Sjöberg. Unicorn Pr. 1985 $7.00. ISBN 0-87775-153-6. A poetic experiment with musical structure.

Selected Poems by Gunnar Ekelöf. Trans. by W. H. Auden and Leif Sjöberg. Pantheon 1972 o.p. Taken from two of Ekelöf's last volumes: *Diwan over the Prince of Emgión* (1965) and *The Tale of Fatuhmeh* (1966).

Selected Poems of Gunnar Ekelöf. Trans. by Muriel Rukeyser and Leif Sjöberg. Irvington 1971 $26.50. ISBN 0-8057-5852-6. Selections of his work before 1965. An introduction by the translators, providing fascinating glimpses of a fine lyrical poet whose love of nature and music joined with profound loneliness.

BOOK ABOUT EKELÖF

Sjöberg, Leif. *A Reader's Guide to Gunnar Ekelöf's "A Molna Elegy".* Twayne 1973 o.p. An essential guide for students of Ekelöf.

ENQUIST, P(ER) O(LOV). 1934–

Enquist's writing is characterized by political consciousness and an interest in the past as it affects or reflects the present. During the politicized 1960s, Enquist was a principle practitioner of documentarism, along with Jan Myrdal and Sara Lidman. He is both an important playwright and a novelist.

NOVELS BY ENQUIST

Down Fall. 1985. Trans. by Anna Paterson. Interlink Pub. 1990 $9.95. ISBN 0-7043-0130-X. A love story.

The Legionnaires. 1968. Delacorte 1973 $10.00. ISBN 0-44-04725-0. A controversial documentary novel about Sweden's turning over Baltic refugees to the Soviet Union after World War II.

Plays by Enquist

The Hour of the Lynx. 1981. Trans. by Ross Shideler. Dufour 1991 $21.00. ISBN 0-948259-85-X

The Night of the Tribades: A Play from 1889. 1975. Trans. by Ross Shideler. Dramatists Play 1978 $3.95. ISBN 0-685-08728-X. A drama that engages the difficult personality of August Strindberg.

Book about Enquist

Shideler, Ross. *Per Olov Enquist. A Critical Study.* Greenwood 1984 $37.95. ISBN 0-313-24236-4. An overview of Enquist's work with a useful bibliography.

GUSTAFSSON, LARS. 1936–

Gustafsson's philosophical and linguistic training are central to his work. With his carefully constructed prose, he probes the nature of human knowledge and interpersonal relationships.

Novels by Gustafsson

Bernard Foy's Third Castling. 1986. Trans. by Yvonne L. Sandstroem. New Dir. Pr. 1988 $19.95. ISBN 0-8112-1086-3. A very playful narrative.

The Death of a Beekeeper. 1978. Trans. by Guntram H. Weber and Janet K. Swaffer. New Dir. Pr. 1981 $7.95. ISBN 0-8112-0809-5. A self-contained work and the fifth and final novel in a series known as *Cracks in the Wall.*

Sigismund. 1976. Trans. by John Weinstock. New Dir. Pr. 1985 $7.95. ISBN 0-8112-0924-5. A self-contained work and the fourth novel in the series known as *Cracks in the Wall,* which also includes *Mister Gustafsson Himself, The Wool,* and *The Family Gathering.*

Poetry by Gustafsson

Funeral Music for Freemasons. 1983. Trans. by Yvonne L. Sandstroem. New Dir. Pr. 1987 $9.95. ISBN 0-8112-1018-9

The Stillness of the World Before Bach. 1982. Ed. by Christopher Middleton. New Dir. Pr. 1988 $9.95. ISBN 0-8112-1058-8

Short Story Collections by Gustafsson

Stories of Happy People. 1981. Trans. by Yvonne L. Sandstroem and John Weinstock. New Dir. Pr. 1986 $7.95. ISBN 0-8112-0978-4

The Tennis Players. 1977. Trans. by Yvonne L. Sandstroem. New Dir. Pr. 1983 o.p.

JERSILD, P(ER) C(HRISTIAN). 1935–

Jersild became a doctor of medicine before he turned to literature. He loves telling a good story and does so fluidly and with bizarre humor. Jersild's often absurd and improbable worlds hold up an unflinching mirror to the failings of modern society.

Novels by Jersild

The Animal Doctor. 1973. Trans. by David Mel Paul and Margareta Paul. U. of Nebr. Pr. 1988 $8.95. ISBN 0-8032-7569-2. A middle-aged female veterinarian tries to take on the leaden bureaucracy she works for.

Children's Island. 1976. Trans. by Joan Tate. U. of Nebr. Pr. 1986 $11.50. ISBN 0-8032-7567-6. A 10-year-old boy spends the summer alone in Stockholm.

House of Babel. 1978. Trans. by Joan Tate. U. of Nebr. Pr. 1987 $13.95. ISBN 0-8032-7568-4. A major Swedish bestseller. An exposé of the impersonal Swedish health care system.

A Living Soul. 1980. Trans. by Rika Lesser. Dufour 1989 $19.95. ISBN 1-870041-09-7. Narrated by a brain floating in an aquarium.

JOHNSON, EYVIND (OLOF VERNER). 1900–1976 (NOBEL PRIZE 1974)

Eyvind Johnson came from a working-class rural background but was a voracious reader. During the 1920s, Johnson lived on a shoestring in France and Germany, bringing back with him to 1930s Sweden a knowledge of the experimental writings of MARCEL PROUST, ANDRÉ GIDE, and JAMES JOYCE (see Vol. 1). Johnson's own experimental novels gave central impetus to the Modernist Breakthrough in Sweden. Combining urgent concern for the psychology of the individual with an interest in historical development, he was always a politically engaged writer. It is a pity that none of the works of this major author are in print.

NOVEL BY JOHNSON

The Days of His Grace. 1960. Vanguard 1970 o.p. Set in the empire of Charlemagne. Focuses on young Italians, longing for personal and national freedom, who are overwhelmed by the superior, ruthless force of the totalitarian machine instituted by Charlemagne.

BOOK ABOUT JOHNSON

Orton, Gavin. *Eyvind Johnson.* Twayne 1972 o.p. A good overview of Johnson's life and works.

LAGERKVIST, PÄR (FABIAN). 1891–1974 (NOBEL PRIZE 1951)

In 1913 at the age of 22, Pär Lagerkvist described his goal as a writer: to achieve the classical simplicity and dignity seen in the models of HOMER, classical tragedy, the Old Testament, and the Icelandic saga. In the following 60 years, Lagerkvist realized his early goal in plays and prose of great beauty and terrible immediacy. Man the eternal questioner, man the victim and victimizer, man the pilgrim whose burden is anxiety and uncertainty—these are just a few of the chords struck by Lagerkvist in his internationally recognized work. What was said of *The Holy Land* (1964) is true of all of Lagerkvist's work: "'The Holy Land' rejects all needless words, compels toward a hidden momentous goal, disturbs with cruel symbols, satisfies with symbols. People and things are symbols yet clear to sight and clearly relevant to man" (*Choice*). For many readers, Lagerkvist's most compelling personification is that of *The Dwarf* (1944), who is the evil that lives in all people. There are no easy answers to the questions Lagerkvist poses. His uncertainty concerning the nature of God was expressed in *The Sibyl* (1956), a mystical work that found a particularly enthusiastic audience in the United States.

Lagerkvist was also a groundbreaking poet and an innovator in the theater, advancing techniques he learned from AUGUST STRINDBERG.

NOVELS BY LAGERKVIST

Barabbas. 1950. Trans. by Alan Blair. Random 1989 $7.95. ISBN 0-679-72544-X. Follows the struggle to believe in the man that Christ literally died for.

The Death of Ahasverus. 1962. Trans. by Naomi Walford. Random 1982 o.p. The first novel in a trilogy that includes *Pilgrim at Sea* and *The Holy Land.* An exploration of religious belief that justifies Lagerkvist's description of himself as a religious atheist.

The Dwarf. 1944. Trans. by Alexandra Dick. Hill & Wang 1958 $9.95. ISBN 0-374-52135-2. Set in renaissance Italy.

The Eternal Smile. Trans. by Erik Mesterton and David O'Gorman. Hill & Wang 1971 o.p. A work that poses the question: If God created us, what did he mean by it?

The Holy Land. 1964. Trans. by Naomi Walford. Random 1982 o.p. The last novel in the trilogy that began with *The Death of Ahasverus.*

Pilgrim at Sea. Trans. by Naomi Walford. Random 1982 o.p. The second novel of the trilogy that began with *The Death of Ahasverus.*

The Sibyl. 1956. Trans. by Naomi Walford. Random 1963 $5.95. ISBN 0-394-70240-9. A narrative question mark about the nature of God.

Plays by Lagerkvist

The Man Who Lived His Life Over. 1928. Trans. by Walter Gustafson. Twayne 1971 o.p. Explores whether a person, allowed to relive a life, would be able to correct its mistakes.

Modern Theatre: Seven Plays and an Essay. Trans. by Thomas R. Buckman. U. of Nebr. Pr. 1966 $26.50. ISBN 0-8032-0098-6. A collection that gives a good idea of Lagerkvist's theatrical genius.

Poetry by Lagerkvist

Evening Land: Aftonland. 1953. Trans. by W. H. Auden and Leif Sjöberg. Wayne St. U. Pr. 1975 o.p. His last collection, touched by religious introspection.

Books about Lagerkvist

Sjöberg, Leif. *Pär Lagerkvist.* Col. U. Pr. 1976 $7.50. ISBN 0-231-03103-3. By an expert on modern Swedish poetry.

Spector, Robert D. *Pär Lagerkvist.* Twayne 1973 o.p. Very useful information and bibliography.

White, Ray L. *Pär Lagerkvist in America.* Humanities 1980 o.p. Of special interest to the American reading public.

LAGERLÖF, SELMA (OTTILIANA LOVISA). 1858–1940 (Nobel Prize 1909)

Selma Lagerlöf, winner of the Nobel Prize in 1909, was the first woman to be elected a member of the Swedish Academy. Her first novel, *The Story of Gösta Berling* (1891), assured her position as Sweden's greatest storyteller. She retold the folk tales of her native province, Värmland, in an original and poetic prose. As a woman writer, Lagerlöf early on gained a reputation as a naive purveyor of native traditions, but she herself compared writing a novel to solving a mathematical problem. Her artistry entails making her stories seem simple, but they are told with great attention to symbolism, psychology, and narrative technique. *The Wonderful Adventures of Nils* (1906) is a delightful fantasy written to teach children about Swedish geography, but it has found an international audience. Her third novel and masterpiece, *Jerusalem* (1901–02), the story of farmers from Dalarna who follow their faith to the Holy City, was widely praised for its insights into the lives of peasants searching for a spiritual ideal. During World War II, Lagerlöf helped many German artists and intellectuals escape the Nazis, even donating her gold Nobel Prize medal to a benefit fund to help Finland.

Novels by Lagerlöf

The Changeling. 1915. Trans. by Susanna Stevens. Knopf 1992 $15.00. ISBN 0-679-91035-2. A children's story from the collection *Trolls and People* (1915–21).

From a Swedish Homestead. 1899. Trans. by Jessie Brochner. Ayer repr. of 1901 ed. $22.00. ISBN 0-8369-463-6. The exciting tale of a young man wrenched from insanity by the love of a young girl.

The Further Adventures of Nils. 1907. Skandisk 1992 $12.95. ISBN 0-9615394-4-5. The second volume of *The Wonderful Adventures of Nils.*

Gösta Berling's Saga. 1891. Trans. by Robert Bly. Karlstad 1982 o.p. About cavaliers who make a pact with the devilish Sintram not to do anything sensible for an entire year.

Jerusalem. 1901. Trans. by Jessie Brochner. Greenwood repr. of 1903 ed. $35.50. ISBN 0-8371-3120-0. A moving story of faith in the face of adversity.

The Lowensköld Ring. 1925–28. Trans. by Linda Schenck. Dufour 1991. ISBN 1-870041-14-3. The story of a cursed family.

The Wonderful Adventures of Nils. 1906. Skandisk 1991 $12.95. ISBN 0-9615394-3-7. The story of Nils, shrunk to the size of a thumb by an angry elf, traveling above Sweden on the back of a goose.

SHORT STORY COLLECTIONS BY LAGERLÖF

Christ Legends. Anthroposophic 1990 $10.95. ISBN 0-86315-506-5. A series of legends prompted by the imagery of the Catholic church, which impressed Lagerlöf during a trip to Italy.

The Legend of the Christmas Rose. Holiday 1990 $15.95. ISBN 0-8234-0821-3. Another of Lagerlöf's Christian legends.

BOOK ABOUT LAGERLÖF

Edström, Vivi. *Selma Lagerlöf.* Twayne 1984 o.p. A comprehensive study by one of Sweden's foremost Lagerlöf experts, with a good bibliography.

LINDGREN, ASTRID. 1907–

Lindgren revolutionized children's literature with her boisterous character Pippi Longstocking. Before Lindgren, children's literature sought to teach children adult moral lessons. Pippi revels in the joy of being a child and is constantly misbehaving, to the nervous delight of her playmates Tommy and Annika. She gets through it all with her superhuman strength, her sack of gold, and her adoring friends. Lindgren's books always show a keen appreciation for the world as seen by a child.

CHILDREN'S FICTION BY LINDGREN

The Children of Noisy Village. 1947. Puffin Bks. 1988 $3.95. ISBN 0-14-032609-X. A place where kids are kids.

Mio My Son. 1954. Puffin Bks. 1988 $4.99. ISBN 0-14-032608-1. An unloved foster child finds his kingly father.

Pippi Goes on Board. 1946. Puffin Bks. 1977 $3.95. ISBN 0-14-030959-4. The further adventures of the irrepressible Pippi, who is strong enough to lift her horse and can buy anything she wants with her pirate treasure.

Pippi in the South Seas. 1949. Puffin Bks. 1988 $3.95. ISBN 0-14-032773-8. More of Pippi.

Pippi Longstocking. 1945. Puffin Bks. 1988 $3.95. ISBN 0-14-032772-X. The original work that revolutionized children's literature.

Ronia, the Robber's Daughter. 1981. Puffin Bks. 1985 $3.95. ISBN 0-14-031720-1. Ronia and her friend from the rival robber band trying to settle the differences between the adults.

BOOKS ABOUT LINDGREN

Hurwitz, Johanna. *Astrid Lindgren: Storyteller to the World.* Puffin Bks. 1991 $3.95. ISBN 0-14-032692-8. A biography of Lindgren, suitable for young readers.

MARTINSON, HARRY. 1904–1978 (NOBEL PRIZE 1974)

Martinson was an abandoned child (after his father's death his mother left him and his six sisters and emigrated to America). At a young age, he ran away from his foster parents and went to sea. After returning to Sweden in 1927, ill with tuberculosis and destitute, he came under the care of his future wife, Moa Swartz, who became a well-known author in her own right. Shortly after his first poems appeared, Martinson's reputation as a poet to reckon with was made. Martinson's sense of language is astonishing and his puns sometimes dizzying. He possesses a talent for finding universal significance in a small detail. His novels, even when autobiographical, contain great symbolic depth and his characteristic verbal genius. *The Road* (1948), which tells the story of a tramp, is perhaps the best of them. Martinson was elected to the Swedish Academy in 1949, a notable achievement for a writer with no formal education. His masterpiece is the modern poetic epic *Aniara* (1956), about a spaceship driven off course and left to drift in infinity for eternity. Martinson has been called "the first poet of the space age."

Novels by Martinson

Cape Farewell. 1933. Trans. by Naomi Walford. New York 1934 o.p. Based on Martinson's travels as a sailor.

Flowering Nettle. 1935. Trans. by Naomi Walford. London 1936 o.p. A novel about Martinson's childhood.

The Road. 1948. Trans. by M. A. Michael. London 1955 o.p. A profound novel about the life of a vagabond.

Poetry by Martinson

Aniara. 1956. Trans. by Stephen Klass and Leif Sjöberg. Vekerum 1992 o.p. Martinson's masterpiece.

Wild Bouquet. Nature Poems. Trans. by William J. Smith and Leif Sjöberg. BkMk 1985 $10.95. ISBN 0-933532-48-2. Universal insights derived from the details of nature.

MOBERG, (CARL ARTUR) VILHELM. 1898–1973

The Emigrants (1949) is the first volume of Moberg's internationally famous tetralogy describing the lives of Swedish emigrants in the nineteenth century. *The Last Letter Home* (1959) completes this psychologically penetrating and historically accurate treatment of Swedish settlement in Chisago County, Minnesota. Moberg's strident individualism and enduring empathy with the common people are also seen in *A Time on Earth* (1962), in which the old Swedish-American Albert Carlson assesses his life as death approaches. In Scandinavia, Moberg is famous as a historian and dramatist as well as a novelist. His *History of the Swedish People*(1970–71), of which two volumes were completed when he died in 1973, depicts in characteristically vivid language the life of the common folk—in sharp contrast to that of kings and nobility—throughout Sweden's history.

Novels by Moberg

The Emigrants. 1949. Trans. by Gustaf Lannestock. Warner Bks. 1983 o.p. The first novel in Moberg's immigrant tetralogy. Essential reading for Americans with Swedish heritage.

The Last Letter Home. 1959. Trans. by Gustaf Lannestock. Warner Bks. 1983 o.p. The last novel of the emigrant tetralogy.

The Settlers. 1956. Trans. by Gustaf Lannestock. Warner Bks. 1983 o.p. The third volume of the emigrant tetralogy.

Unto a Good Land. 1952. Trans. by Gustaf Lannestock. Warner Bks. 1983 o.p. The second novel in the emigrant tetralogy.

NONFICTION BY MOBERG

A History of the Swedish People. 1970–71. 2 vols. Trans. by Paul Britten Austin. Dorset Pr. 1989 $24.95 ea. Vol. 1 *From Prehistory to Renaissance*. ISBN 0-88029-312-8. Vol. 2 *From Renaissance to Revolution*. ISBN 0-88029-313-6. A highly readable account of Swedish history.

The Unknown Swedes. 1950. Trans. by Roger McKnight. S. Ill. U. Pr. 1988 $24.50. ISBN 0-8093-1486-X. About Swedish emigration.

BOOK ABOUT MOBERG

Holmes, Philip. *Vilhelm Moberg*. Twayne 1980 o.p. A welcome overview and a useful bibliography.

STRINDBERG, (JOHAN) AUGUST. 1849–1912

The world knows August Strindberg as a dramatist, even though he was also an accomplished novelist, poet, and master of short prose. Among his most performed plays are *The Father* (1887) and *Miss Julie* (1888), both of which date from his early naturalistic period. *The Father* is Strindberg's somewhat defensive response to the growing women's movement. In an age when many authors, led by HENRIK IBSEN, wrote about society's victimization of women, Strindberg created a tragedy in which a family provider has given up his dreams in order to support his wife and child. *Miss Julie* is a play about class differences, in which a woman of noble birth is seduced by a servant. This tragedy has been performed with great effect in cultures where class or racial tensions are acute, such as China, South Africa, and Chicago.

In the 1890s, Strindberg underwent a religious and psychological crisis, documented in his novel *Inferno* (1897). His plays are now often divided into two groups, pre-*Inferno* and post-*Inferno*, marking a shift in style from social realism to metaphysical symbolism. Strindberg's dramatic treatment of his crisis, *To Damascus I* (1898), has been characterized as the first expressionistic play. The anonymous protagonist, making an arduous circular journey, meets characters who appear to be projections of parts of his own psyche. Strindberg's post-*Inferno* masterpiece, however, is *A Dream Play* (1901), which explores the panorama of human life in a series of symbolic, absurd dream sequences. In *The Dance of Death* (1901), Strindberg appears to return to his naturalistic style, yet this intense marital drama contains dark symbolic undercurrents. It was a main inspiration for EDWARD ALBEE's (see Vol. 1) *Who's Afraid of Virginia Woolf?*

Strindberg's prose also shows a wide range. *The Red Room* (1879) was the first realistic novel in Sweden. *The Natives of Hemsö* (1887) is a darkly comic depiction of life in the Stockholm skerries. *By the Open Sea* (1890) presents an intellectual superman whose mental well-being is gradually eroded by the effects of isolation, erotic rejection, and the meanness of the common people. *Inferno* is a compelling portrayal of mental illness from the inside. *The Roofing Ceremony* (1905) is written in a stream-of-consciousness style that anticipates JAMES JOYCE's (see Vol. 1) *Ulysses*.

Strindberg's enormous influence on European and world literature can hardly be exaggerated. He gave important creative impetus to the German expressionist movement, and his work inspired EUGENE O'NEILL (see Vol. 1), TENNESSEE WILLIAMS (see Vol. 1), EUGENE IONESCO, BERTOLT BRECHT, and many others. Strindberg—along with Ibsen, with whom he shared a sort of rivalry affecting both their work—is indeed one of the architects of modern drama.

Novels by Strindberg

By the Open Sea. 1890. Trans. by Mary Sandbach. Viking Penguin 1987 $5.95. ISBN 0-679-72475-3

Inferno: From an Occult Diary. 1897. Trans. by Mary Sandbach. Viking Penguin 1979 $6.95. ISBN 0-14-044364-9

A Madman's Defense. 1895. Trans. by Evert Sprinchorn. U. of Ala. Pr. 1971 $11.25. ISBN 0-8446-3025-X. Strindberg's autobiographical account of his first divorce.

The Roofing Ceremony and The Silver Lake. Trans. by David Mel Paul and Margareta Paul. U. of Nebr. Pr. 1987 $14.95. ISBN 0-8032-4171-2. Advanced stream-of-consciousness prose.

Plays by Strindberg

The Dance of Death. 1901. Trans. by Arvid Paulson. Norton 1976 $5.95. ISBN 0-393-00820-7. A good translation of this important play.

A Dream Play and Four Chamber Plays. Trans. by Walter G. Johnson. Norton 1975 repr. of 1973 ed. $8.95. ISBN 0-393-00791-X. Rendered by a translator who is always scholarly and faithful to the original text. A standard classroom edition.

Plays of Confession and Therapy: To Damascus I, To Damascus II, and To Damascus III. Trans. by Walter G. Johnson. U. of Wash. Pr. 1979 $25.00. ISBN 0-295-95567-8. The world's first expressionistic drama and its sequels.

Pre-Inferno Plays. Trans. by Walter G. Johnson. Norton 1976 $7.95. ISBN 0-393-00834-7. The standard classroom edition of Strindberg's most important naturalistic plays.

Selected Plays. 2 vols. Trans. by Evert Sprinchorn. U. of Minn. Pr. 1986 $12.95 ea. ISBNs 0-8166-1339-9, 0-8166-1338-7. Elegant and performable renderings of a cross section of Strindberg's most important plays.

Strindberg: Five Plays. Trans. by Harry G. Carlson. NAL–Dutton 1984 $5.95. ISBN 0-520-04697-8. A more performable set of translations than Johnson's.

Books about Strindberg

Carlson, Harry G. *Strindberg and the Poetry of Myth*. U. CA Pr. 1982 $37.50. ISBN 0-520-04442-8. Contains important insights into the symbolism of Strindberg's writing.

Lagercrantz, Olof. *August Strindberg*. Trans. by Anselm Hollo. FS&G 1984 $12.95. ISBN 0-374-10685-1. A readable scholarly biography of Strindberg.

Lamm, Martin. *August Strindberg*. Trans. by Harry G. Carlson. Ayer 1971 $25.00. ISBN 0-405-08724-1. A scholarly biography of Strindberg by one of the major Strindberg scholars of all time.

Meyer, Michael. *Strindberg: A Biography*. OUP 1985 $14.95. ISBN 0-19-281995-X. A colorful biography.

Sprinchorn, Evert. *Strindberg as Dramatist*. Yale U. Pr. 1982 $37.50. ISBN 0-300-02731-1. An important study of Strindberg's dramatic art.

Steene, Birgitta. *Greatest Fire: A Study of August Strindberg*. S. Ill. U. Pr. 1973 $6.95. ISBN 0-8093-0548-8. An excellent general survey.

Stockenström, Göran, ed. *Strindberg's Dramaturgy*. U. of Minn. Pr. 1988 $39.95. ISBN 0-8166-1612-4. A collection of essays, by diverse scholars, providing an up-to-date picture of Strindberg scholarship.

SWEDENBORG, EMANUEL. 1688–1772

[See Volume 4.]

TRANSTRÖMER, TOMAS. 1931–

Tranströmer, an occupational psychologist by profession, has regularly published his influential poetry since 1954. His poetic language—admirably reconstructed in the English translations currently available—is the syntax of normal prose and the imagery of everyday life, but often bearing strong symbolism. Basically simple images are wonderfully charged with the power to describe human perceptions of nature and of self.

Poetry by Tranströmer

Baltics. 1974. Oyez 1975 $2.50. ISBN 0-685-56099-6

Selected Poems of Tomas Tranströmer, 1954–1986. Trans. by Robert Hass. Ecco Pr. 1989 $10.95. ISBN 0-88001-113-0. A nice sampling of poems from over 30 years of productivity.

Truth Banners: Poems by Tomas Tranströmer. 1978. Trans. by Robert Bly. Sierra 1980 $9.95. ISBN 0-87156-235-9. Bly's always noteworthy translations.

Tomas Tranströmer: Collected Poems. Trans. by Robin Fulton. Dufour 1988 $17.95. ISBN 1-85224-023-7. The most complete collection by a very good translator.

CHAPTER 20

Russian Literature

Henryk Baran

> "Paul!" called the Countess from behind the screen. "Send me a new novel, will you, but please not the kind they write nowadays."
> "What do you mean, *grand'maman*?"
> "I mean a novel in which the hero does not strangle either his mother or his father, and which describes no drowned bodies. I am terribly scared of drowned bodies."
> "There are no such novels these days. Would you perhaps like some Russian ones?"
> "You don't mean to say there are Russian novels? . . . Send some to me, my dear, send some by all means!"
>
> —ALEKSANDR PUSHKIN, *The Queen of Spades*

One of the great world literatures in the modern era, Russian (East Slavic) literature began by following in the cultural footsteps of Byzantium after the conversion of the Kievan state to Christianity in the tenth century. In the medieval period, the principal genres were religious (saints' lives, sermons) and historical (chronicles). The greatest achievement of medieval Russian verbal art, the unusual, complex, and controversial *Tale of Igor's Campaign*, came toward the end of the twelfth century.

Medieval genres continued to flourish long after the West entered the Renaissance. By the midsixteenth century, resurgent Moscow celebrated its inheritance of both Byzantine and Mongol imperial traditions in a series of monumental textual compilations. The sheer size, ornamental style, and self-assurance of these works mirrored the insular, conservative world view of the Muscovite state.

A decisive cultural shift came with the reforms of Peter the Great in the early 1700s. Under the impact of Western European languages, the lexicon of Russian was significantly enlarged. Poetry changed fundamentally when Mikhail Lomonosov and others established a syllabotonic system of versification that underlies most Russian verse of the nineteenth century and continues to play a key role in the twentieth century. The high genres—the ode, the verse tragedy, the epic poem—prevailed; Lomonosov and Gavril Derzhavin emerged as the two outstanding poets of the eighteenth century, singers of the political and cultural achievements of Peter the Great and, several decades later, Catherine II.

In the early nineteenth century, sharply accelerating foreign influences led to a remarkable coexistence of differing literary schools, aesthetic platforms, and creative methods. Classicism was still present, romanticism had made its appearance, and realism was developing. A Golden Age of poetry—ALEKSANDR PUSHKIN was its greatest figure—held sway into the 1840s, when prose came to the fore for both authors and readers. The literary scene was dominated by fiction writers who were to change European literature as a whole: NIKOLAI

Gogol, Fyodor Dostoyevsky, Leo Tolstoy, Ivan Turgenev, and others. The Russia they depicted—tormented by a cultural tug-of-war between East and West and by the unjust socioeconomic gap between the elite classes and the peasant-serf majority—was familiar to Western readers in pattern, yet exotic and fascinating in particulars. This combination has proved enduringly attractive for readers around the world.

The nineteenth century saw the establishment of a tradition that still sharply differentiates Russian from Western literature. In a society that prohibited normal avenues of political expression, literature and its creators became the voices of society's most urgent concerns. As a result, writers in modern Russia have enjoyed an exceptional degree of influence and a commensurate degree of personal peril. All too often, they have paid the price of commitment with their liberty and their lives.

Poetry again came to the fore during the 1890s. Although important realist or quasi-realist fiction still came from the pens of such new writers as Maxim Gorky and Ivan Bunin, the reading public slowly turned to symbolism. A movement with both Western and Russian roots, philosophical and religious as much as literary, symbolism made art a bridge to the transcendent. Such symbolist masters as Fedor Sologub, Andrei Bely, and Aleksandr Blok brought a new poetic Golden Age. Soon they were joined by members of competing poetic groups, especially the Akmeists (Nikolai Gumilev, Anna Akhmatova, Osip Mandelstam), who advocated the use of concise, clear, and concrete imagery, and the Futurists (Vladimir Mayakovsky and others), who attempted to discard stale and hackneyed poetic styles. By adding new rhythms and enlarging the boundaries of the lexicon, these artists together renewed poetic language. They were willing as well to experiment with content, working in a bold manner that matched the crisis-laden, apocalyptic atmosphere of the pre-World War I period.

During the twentieth century, political events have had a major impact on Russian literature. The October 1917 revolution and subsequent civil war led many writers and poets to leave the country. As a consequence, an émigré literature flourished until 1939 in Germany, France, and several other countries—a literature virtually unknown, until fairly recently, inside the Soviet Union itself.

Initially, the Communist party adopted a neutral attitude toward culture. Still, by the 1920s, patterns of official control over the arts began to emerge. The First Congress of the Union of Soviet Writers (1934) proclaimed socialist realism as the accepted mode of literature, requiring authors to portray Soviet life optimistically. Through alternating periods of political relaxation ("thaws") and tightening, this doctrine remained the dominant form of politically orthodox writing. Only in the period of *glasnost* initiated by former Soviet leader Mikhail Gorbachev in the 1980s was its hollowness finally acknowledged.

Until the dissolution of the Soviet Union in December 1991, literature continued to be buffeted by political trends. Starting in the late 1960s many writers and poets participated in the movements for human rights and freedom of emigration. Prevented from publishing some (or all) of their works, nonconformist authors released them in *samizdat* (the private copying and circulating of unauthorized works) or published them in the West without official sanction. Such acts, and any setting of oneself against party or cultural-establishment norms, frequently brought prison sentences or exile. The departure of many talented figures (Joseph Brodsky, Aleksandr Solzhenitsyn, Vassily Aksyonov, Vladimir Voinovich, and others) for life in the West revitalized the literature of Russia abroad. Only with the removal of political barriers since 1987 has this important stream of talent again flowed into the main body of Russian culture.

In the last two decades, Russian literature has sought to go beyond ideology; to confront the legacy of Soviet history expressed in the country's current political, social, and environmental problems; to capture the reality of both the new urban life and the dying village culture; and to analyze the special problems of women and the many ethnic groups. At the same time, it has striven to experiment with new fictional forms and express new themes through the fantastic and the grotesque, assimilating the experience of both world literature (e.g., Latin America's magical realism) and Russia's own Silver Age, a time of great artistic achievement from the 1890s to 1910s. Today it remains to be seen how Russia's writers—politically engaged, conscious of their historical responsibility, yet grown dependent on the very system they protested—will fare under the unfamiliar freedoms and responsibilities of the post-Soviet life still so economically and politically tenuous.

HISTORY AND CRITICISM

Alexandrova, Vera. *History of Soviet Literature*. Trans. by Mirra Ginsburg. Greenwood 1971 repr. of 1963 ed. $37.50. ISBN 0-8371-6114-2. From Gorky to Yevtushenko, with an epilogue on Solzhenitsyn's *One Day in the Life of Ivan Denisovich;* author a noted figure of the "first wave" emigration.

Andrew, Joe. *Women in Russian Literature. Seventeen Eighty to Eighteen Sixty-Three*. St. Martin 1988 $39.95. ISBN 0-312-01626-3

Auty, R., and D. Obolensky, eds. *Companion to Russian Studies: An Introduction to Russian Language and Literature*. Vol. 2 Cambridge U. Pr. 1981 $21.95. ISBN 0-521-28039-7. An excellent selection of articles (good for beginners and specialists alike) on various aspects of Russian studies.

Avins, Carol. *Border Crossings: The West and Russian Identity in Soviet Literature, 1917–1934*. U. CA Pr. 1983 $37.50. ISBN 0-520-04233-6. Focuses on the "internal change of national identity and self-awareness" (*SEES*); thoroughly researched and well documented.

Baehr, Stephen L. *The Paradise Myth in Eighteenth-Century Russia: Utopian Patterns in Early Secular Russian Literature and Culture*. Stanford U. Pr. 1991 $37.50. ISBN 0-8047-1533-5. A discussion of a key notion in modern Russian culture.

Bakhtin, M. M., and P. N. Medvedev. *The Formal Method in Literary Scholarship: A Critical Introduction to Sociological Poetics*. Trans. by Albert J. Wehrle. HUP 1985 $9.95. ISBN 0-674-30921-9. A critique of Russian Formalism. An important development in the history of criticism during the 1920s.

Baring, Maurice. *An Outline of Russian Literature*. Greenwood 1971 repr. of 1915 ed. $38.50. ISBN 0-8371-4808-1. An early overview, of historical interest.

Barker, Adele M. *The Mother Syndrome in the Russian Folk Imagination*. Slavica 1986 $15.95. ISBN 0-89357-160-1. Analyzes a subject that bears directly on literature and national culture: the complex mother-son relationship in Russian folk and literary tradition.

Berry, Thomas E. *Plots and Characters in Major Russian Fiction*. Vol. 1: *Pushkin, Lermontov, Turgenev, and Tolstoy. Plots and Characters Ser.* Shoe String 1977 $35.00. ISBN 0-208-01584-1

______. *Plots and Characters in Major Russian Fiction*. Vol. 2: *Gogol, Goncharov, and Dostoevski. Plots and Characters Ser.* Shoe String 1978 o.p.

Bethea, David M. *The Shape of Apocalypse in Modern Russian Fiction*. Princeton U. Pr. 1991 $45.00. ISBN 0-691-06746-5. An extensive, insightful discussion of a major theme.

Brodsky, Joseph, and Carl Proffer, eds. *Modern Russian Poets on Poetry: Blok, Mandelstam, Pasternak, Mayakovsky, Gumilev, Tsvetaeva*. Ardis Pubs. 1976 o.p.

Brooks, Jeffrey. *When Russia Learned to Read: Literary and Popular Literature, 1861–1917*. Princeton U. Pr. 1988 $65.00. ISBN 0-691-05450-9. Original and well documented. Covers publishing houses, the cultural marketplace, plots and characters in popular fiction, themes, and other topics.

Brown, Deming. *Soviet Russian Literature since Stalin*. Cambridge U. Pr. 1979 $17.95. ISBN 0-521-29649-8. A detailed history through the 1970s.

Brown, Edward J., ed. *Major Soviet Writers: Essays in Criticism*. OUP 1973 $8.95. ISBN 0-19-501684-X. A fine critical anthology.

———, ed. *Russian Literature since the Revolution*. HUP rev. ed. 1982 $35.00. ISBN 0-674-78203-8. A standard work on the Soviet period.

Brown, William E. *A History of Eighteenth Century Russian Literature*. Ardis Pubs. 1980 o.p. Based on excellent knowledge of both Russian and Western primary texts.

———. *A History of Russian Literature of the Romantic Period*. 4 vols. Ardis Pubs. 1986 $150.00. ISBN 0-88233-938-9. A very detailed treatment, unique in its breadth and depth.

———. *History of Seventeenth Century Russian Literature*. Ardis Pubs. 1980 $10.00. ISBN 0-88233-344-5. The only full English-language discussion of this transitional period.

Chances, Ellen B. *Conformity's Children: An Approach to the Superfluous Man in Russian Literature*. Slavica 1978 o.p. Analyzes a key character type in Russian literature and culture.

Chyzhevskyi, Dmytro. *History of Russian Literature from the Eleventh Century to the End of the Baroque*. Hyperion Conn. 1981 repr. of 1960 ed. $38.50. ISBN 0-8305-0067-7. Very detailed; best reference tool on medieval literature.

Cizevskij, Dmitrij. *History of Nineteenth-Century Russian Literature*. 2 vols. Trans. by Richard N. Porter. Ed. by Serge A. Zenkovsky. Greenwood 1986 repr. $76.50. ISBN 0-313-25274-2. An excellent history; situates Russian developments in a European literary and philosophical context.

Clark, Katerina. *The Soviet Novel: History as Ritual*. U. Ch. Pr. 1985 $11.95. ISBN 0-226-10767-1. A provocative analysis of officially approved fiction.

Clark, Katerina, and Michael Holquist. *Mikhail Bakhtin*. Belknap Pr. 1984 $12.95. ISBN 0-674-57417-6. The first major critical biography of a leading literary theorist and critic.

Clowes, Edith W. *The Revolution of Moral Consciousness: Nietzsche in Russian Literature. 1890–1914*. N. Ill. U. Pr. 1988 $27.50. ISBN 0-87580-139-0. Covers important aspect of Silver Age culture.

Crouch, Martin, and Robert Porter, eds. *Understanding Soviet Politics through Literature*. Unwin Hyman 1984 $16.95. ISBN 0-04-320158-X. A reversal of the usual approach, with provocative results.

Debreczeny, Paul, and Jesse Zeldin, eds. and trans. *Literature and National Identity: Nineteenth-Century Russian Critical Essays*. Bks. Demand repr. of 1970 ed. $55.70. ISBN 0-8357-6193-2. A selection of studies, full and excerpted, by Slavophile-oriented thinkers.

Dreizin, Felix, and David Guaspari. *The Russian Soul and the Jew: Essays in Literary Ethno-Criticism. Studies in Judaism Ser.* U. Pr. of Amer. 1990 $39.50. ISBN 0-8191-7697-4. Relies on psychoanalysis and linguistics in discussing such writers as Dostoevsky, Gogol, Pasternak, and Solzhenitsyn.

Dunham, Vera S. *In Stalin's Time: Middle-Class Values in Soviet Fiction*. Cambridge U. Pr. 1979 $44.50. ISBN 0-521-20949-8. A sociologically based study of orthodox Soviet literature.

Eagle, Herb. *Russian Formalist Film Theory*. Mich. Slavic Pubns. 1981 $10.00. ISBN 0-930042-42-5. A discussion of an important aspect of early twentieth-century structuralism.

Edwards, T. R. *Three Russian Writers and the Irrational: Zamyatin, Pil'nyak, and Bulgakov. Cambridge Studies in Russian Lit. Ser.* Cambridge U. Pr. 1982 $54.95.

ISBN 0-521-23670-3. ". . . well organized, competently written, and intellectually stimulating . . . offers fresh insights . . . and draws broad literary and philosophical parallels" (*Russian Review*).

Eikhenbaum, Boris. *Russian Prose*. Trans. by Ray Parrott. Ardis Pubs. 1985 o.p. Essays by Formalist critics of the 1920s on early nineteenth-century prose.

Erlich, Victor. *Russian Formalism: History-Doctrine*. Yale U. Pr. 1981 3rd ed. $15.00. ISBN 0-300-02635-8. An updated version of a seminal book that introduced the Russian Formalists to the West; important for both history and theory of literature.

______, ed. *Twentieth-Century Russian Literary Criticism*. Bks. Demand repr. of 1975 ed. $85.60. ISBN 0-8357-8356-1. Includes a number of very important studies; the standard text in many academic courses.

Ermolaev, Herman. *Soviet Literary Theories, Nineteen Seventeen to Nineteen Thirty-Four: The Genesis of Socialist Realism*. Hippocrene Bks. 1977 o.p. A detailed treatment of the prelude to official Soviet literary dogma.

Fennell, John, ed. *Nineteenth-Century Russian Literature: Studies of Ten Russian Writers*. U. CA Pr. 1976 $47.50. ISBN 0-520-03203-9. Uneven, but with a great deal of useful information and provocative analysis.

Fennell, John, and Anthony Stokes. *Early Russian Literature*. U. CA Pr. 1974 o.p. A good discussion of various problems in medieval writing.

France, Peter. *Poets of Modern Russia. Cambridge Studies in Russian Lit. Ser.* Cambridge U. Pr. 1983 $18.95. ISBN 0-521-28000-1. "Each chapter . . . becomes a tribute to its poet. . . . it is a book of practical criticism in the best sense" (*SEES*).

Frank, Joseph. *Through the Russian Prism: Essays on Literature and Culture*. Princeton U. Pr. 1990 $32.50. ISBN 0-691-06821-6. A collection of distinguished studies by a leading historian of Russian and world literature.

Frankel, Edith R. *Novy Mir: A Case Study in the Politics of Literature 1952–1958. Cambridge Studies in Russian Lit.* Cambridge U. Pr. 1981 $49.95. ISBN 0-521-23438-7. Contributes to an understanding of post-Stalin culture.

Freeborn, Richard. *The Rise of the Russian Novel: Studies in the Russian Novel from "Eugene Onegin" to "War and Peace"*. Cambridge U. Pr. 1973 $15.95. ISBN 0-521-09738-X. Offers "competent, at times enlightening and provocative précis and criticism" (*SEEJ*).

______. *The Russian Revolutionary Novel: Turgenev to Pasternak. Cambridge Studies in Russian Lit. Ser.* Cambridge U. Pr. 1985 $19.95. ISBN 0-521-31737-1. A thoroughly investigated work; provides excellent analyses of many lesser-known novels.

Friedberg, Maurice. *Russian Culture in the 1980's*. CSI Studies 1985 o.p. By a highly knowledgeable observer of the Soviet cultural landscape.

Garrard, John, ed. *The Russian Novel from Pushkin to Pasternak*. Yale U. Pr. 1983 $40.00. ISBN 0-300-02935-7. Uneven, but some good discussion.

Gasiorowska, Xenia. *The Image of Peter the Great in Russian Fiction*. Bks. Demand repr. of 1979 ed. $55.90. ISBN 0-8357-6795-7. An analysis of an archetype that goes to the roots of modern Russia.

______. *Women in Soviet Fiction, 1917–1964*. U. of Wis. Pr. 1968 o.p. An early study on this subject.

Ginzburg, Lydia. *On Psychological Prose*. Princeton U. Pr. 1991 $49.95. ISBN 0-691-06849-6. "Ginzburg traces developing ideas of personality through French and Russian documentary prose . . . clarifies the work of Russian activists and critics who embodied the transition from romanticism to realism. . . [and deals with] character definition in the 'sociopsychological' novel" (*LJ*).

Glad, John. *Extrapolations from Dystopia: A Critical Study of Soviet Science Fiction*. Kingston Pr. 1981 o.p.

Griffiths, Frederick T., and Stanley Rabinowitz. *Novel Epics: Gogol, Dostoevsky, and National Narrative. Series in Russian Lit. and Theory*. Northwestern U. Pr. 1990 $29.95. ISBN 0-8101-0900-X. A well-received study that seeks to differentiate Russian prose from a broader world context.

Gudzii, Nikolai K. *History of Early Russian Literature*. Hippocrene Bks. 1970 o.p. The standard Soviet textbook on the medieval period; dull but very thorough.

Gumilev, Nikolai. *On Russian Poetry*. Trans. by David Lapeza. *The Prose of the Russian Poets Ser.* Ardis Pubs. 1991 $15.00. ISBN 0-685-46190-4. A distinguished Silver Age poet's views of his contemporaries and of literature.

Gutsche, George J. *Moral Apostasy in Russian Literature*. N. Ill. U. Pr. 1987 $26.00. ISBN 0-87580-118-8. Analyzes six culturally important works, which contain instances of unconventional behavior that have significant moral implications.

Harkins, William E. *Dictionary of Russian Literature*. Greenwood 1971 repr. of 1956 ed. $41.50. ISBN 0-8371-5751-X. Dated, but still has some useful coverage.

Harris, Jane Gary, ed. *Autobiographical Statements in Twentieth-Century Russian Literature*. Princeton U. Pr. 1990 $35.00. ISBN 0-691-06818-6. A collection of articles on autobiographical writing.

Hayward, Max. *Writers in Russia: 1917–1978*. Ed. by Patricia Blake. HarBraceJ 1983 o.p. Stimulating essays by a leading translator and critic.

Hayward, Max, and Leopold Labedz, eds. *Literature and Revolution in Soviet Russia, 1917–1962*. Greenwood 1976 repr. of 1963 ed. $35.00. ISBN 0-8371-8651-X

Heldt, Barbara. *Terrible Perfection: Women and Russian Literature*. MB Ind. U. Pr. repr. of 1987 ed. $25.00. ISBN 0-253-35838-8. An attempt to "introduce feminist theory to Russian literary studies and Russian literary studies to feminist theory" (*SEEJ*); provocative, important.

Hingley, Ronald. *Russian Writers and Society: 1825–1904*. McGraw 1967 o.p. A good introduction to the historical context of nineteenth-century literature.

———. *Russian Writers and Soviet Society, 1917–1978*. Random 1979 o.p. A terse, lucid discussion of the relationships between literature and the state, Communist party, etc.; provides an overview of historical events and figures.

Hosking, Geoffrey. *Beyond Socialist Realism: Soviet Fiction since Ivan Denisovich*. Holmes & Meier 1980 $45.00. ISBN 0-8419-0484-7. Soviet prose since the 1960s; ". . . a major book, one which ought to change our conception of Socialist Realism. . . ." (*SEEJ*).

Ivanits, Linda J. *Russian Folk Belief*. M. E. Sharpe 1988 $39.95. ISBN 0-87332-422-6. A rare English-language survey of the popular imagination in Russia, solidly grounded in Soviet and Western scholarship.

Jakobson, Roman. *Language in Literature*. Ed. by Krystyna Pomorska and Stephen Rudy. HUP 1988 $25.00. ISBN 0-674-51027-5. A selection of studies by leading Slavists. Includes classic studies of Pushkin, Mayakovsky, and Pasternak and expositions of Jakobsonian methods in analysis of poetry and prose.

Jameson, Fredric. *The Prison-House of Language: A Critical Account of Structuralism and Russian Formalism. Princeton Essays in Lit. Ser.* Princeton U. Pr. 1972 $10.95. ISBN 0-691-01316-0. An important controversial assessment of structuralism and formalism from a Marxist perspective.

Janecek, Gerald. *The Look of Russian Literature: Avant-Garde Visual Experiments, 1900–1930*. Princeton U. Pr. 1984 $55.00. ISBN 0-691-06604-3. A detailed survey of Russian avant-garde culture other than the verbal.

Karlinsky, Simon. *Russian Drama from Its Beginnings to the Age of Pushkin*. U. CA Pr. 1985 $47.50. ISBN 0-520-05237-4

Kasack, Wolfgang. *Dictionary of Russian Literature since 1917*. Ed. and rev. by Rebecca Atack. Trans. by Maria Carlson and Jane T. Hedges. Col. U. Pr. 1988 $60.00. ISBN 0-231-05242-1. An indispensable reference work.

Katz, Michael R. *Dreams and the Unconscious in Nineteenth-Century Russian Fiction*. Bks. Demand repr. of 1984 ed. $59.10. ISBN 0-8357-6518-0. Offers illuminating discussions of various authors' use of dreams and dreamlike states in their works.

Kleberg, Lars, and Nils Nilsson, eds. *Theater and Literature in Russia Nineteen Hundred to Nineteen Thirty*. Almqvist & Wiksell SW 1984 o.p. A collection of articles on the critical relationship between the stage and the verbal text in early twentieth-century Russia.

Kropotkin, Peter. *Russian Literature: Ideals and Realities*. Paul & Co. Pubs. 1990 repr. of 1905 ed. $38.95. ISBN 0-921689-85-3. A classic study by a theoretician of Russian anarchism.

LeBlanc, Ronald D. *The Russianization of Gil Blas: A Study in Literary Appropriation.* Slavica 1986 $17.95. ISBN 0-89357-159-8. Discusses the introduction of a major Western literary type into Russian literature.

Lemon, Lee T., and Marion J. Reis, trans. *Russian Formalist Criticism: Four Essays. Regents Critics Ser.* U. of Nebr. Pr. 1965 $4.95. ISBN 0-8032-5460-1. A good sampling of the approach to literature by the "formal" school of the 1920s.

Lenhoff, Gail. *The Martyred Princes Boris and Gleb: A Social-Cultural Study of the Cult and the Texts. UCLA Slavic Studies Ser.* Slavica 1989 $18.95. ISBN 0-89357-204-7. A study of an important medieval cultural-literary tradition.

Levitt, Marcus C. *Russian Literary Politics and the Pushkin Celebration of 1880. Studies of the Harriman Inst. Ser.* Cornell Univ. Pr. 1989 $28.95. ISBN 0-8014-2250-7. Focuses on the meaning attributed to Pushkin by later generations; a most interesting discussion of Dostoevsky's "Pushkin Speech."

Lodge, David. *After Bakhtin: Essays on Fiction and Criticism.* Routledge 1990 $49.95. ISBN 0-415-05037-5. Essays suggesting "that [Bakhtin's] notion of dialog and the poetics of narrative provide more insight into the essence of the novel than the traditional categories of character and plot" (*LJ*).

Loseff, Lev. *On the Beneficence of Censorship: Aesopian Language in Modern Russian Literature.* Trans. by Jane Bobko. Hermitage 1985 $17.00. ISBN 3-87690-211-8. An ironic discussion of the uses (and abuses) of language in the Soviet period.

Lowe, David A. *Russian Writing since Nineteen Fifty-Three: A Critical Survey.* Continuum 1987 $24.50. ISBN 0-8044-2554-X

Lvov-Rogachevsky, V. *A History of Russian Jewish Literature: Including Russian Literature and the Jews.* Trans. by Arthur Levin. Ardis Pubs. 1979 $5.50. ISBN 0-88233-272-4. A classic study, though methodologically old-fashioned; contains a helpful introduction.

Maguire, Robert A. *Red Virgin Soil: Soviet Literature in the 1920's.* Cornell Univ. Pr. 1987 $14.95. ISBN 0-8014-9447-8. An in-depth look at Russian literature in transition.

Markov, Vladimir. *Russian Futurism: A History.* U. CA Pr. 1968 o.p. A magisterial overview of various groups; the best survey of this topic in any language.

Marsh, Rosalind J. *Soviet Fiction since Stalin: Science, Politics and Literature.* B&N Imports 1986 $51.25. ISBN 0-389-20609-1. The author ". . . has mined a great deal of the conformist (and to a lesser extent dissident) literature . . . for the information it yields on the symbiosis between a writer's own preoccupations and conceits and the dominant ideas and myths of "his society" (*SEEJ*).

Masing-Delic, Irene. *Abolishing Death: A Salvation Myth of Russian Twentieth-Century Literature.* Stanford U. Pr. 1992 $39.50. ISBN 0-8047-1935-7. Traces the impact on Russian writers and poets of the idiosyncratic ideas of N. Fyodorov.

Matejka, Ladislav, and Krystyna Pomorska, eds. *Readings in Russian Poetics: Formalist and Structuralist Views.* MIT Pr. 1971 o.p. The best English-language anthology of studies by leading theoreticians; crucial to the history of Russian literary scholarship.

Mathewson, Rufus W., Jr. *The Positive Hero in Russian Literature.* Stanford U. Pr. 1975 $45.00. ISBN 0-8047-0836-3. Traces the transformations of a key character type.

Matich, Olga, and Michael Heim, eds. *The Third Wave: Russian Literature in Emigration.* Ardis Pubs. 1983 $13.50. ISBN 0-88233-783-1. The proceedings of a symposium of émigré writers, Western journalists, and scholars of Russian literature.

McGuire, Patrick L. *Red Stars: Political Aspects of Soviet Science Fiction. Studies in Speculative Fiction Ser.* Bks. Demand repr. of 1985 ed. $44.20. ISBN 0-8357-1579-5.

McMillin, Arnold. *Under Eastern Eyes: The West as Reflected in Recent Russian Emigre Writing.* St. Martin 1991. ISBN 0-312-06809-3

McNally, Raymond T. *Chaadayev and His Friends: An Intellectual History of Peter Chaadayev and His Russian Contemporaries.* Diplomatic IN 1971 o.p. Chaadayev played a major role in shaping Westernization in nineteenth-century Russian culture.

Mihajlov, Mihajlo. *Russian Themes.* FS&G 1968 $2.45. ISBN 0-374-50700-7. Essays by a Yugoslav critic and dissident; somewhat dated, but offers an interesting perspective.

Mirsky, Dimitry S. *Contemporary Russian Literature, 1881–1925.* Kraus 1972 repr. of 1926 ed. $29.00. ISBN 0-527-64000-X. A detailed, superb survey by one contemporary with the Silver Age and early Soviet period. Assessments of writers and works still significant for further study.

———. *History of Russian Literature: From Its Beginnings to 1900.* Ed. by Francis J. Whitfield. Random 1958 $9.00. ISBN 0-394-70720-6. The best one-volume history of the period: accurate, insightful, readable. Contains abridged versions of Mirsky's *History of Russian Literature* and *Contemporary Russian Literature.*

———. *Uncollected Writings on Russian Literature.* Ed. by G. S. Smith. *Modern Russian Lit. & Culture, Studies & Texts Ser.* Berkeley Slavic 1989 $24.00. ISBN 0-933884-68-0. Articles and notes in English and Russian by a top critic of the 1920s and 1930s.

Morson, Gary S., ed. *Literature and History: Theoretical Problems & Russian Case Studies.* Stanford U. Pr. 1986 $39.50. ISBN 0-8047-1302-2. A collection of articles, with a detailed introduction and commentaries by the editor.

Moser, Charles A., ed. *The Cambridge History of Russian Literature.* Cambridge U. Pr. 1989 $85.00. ISBN 0-521-30994-8. ". . . [A] competent, well-written and useful survey . . . a welcome addition to the gallery of histories of Russian literature" (*SEEJ*).

———, ed. *Esthetics as Nightmare: Russian Literary Theory, 1855–1870.* Princeton U. Pr. 1989 $37.50. ISBN 0-691-06763-5. Surveys aesthetic controversies of the post-Belinsky period; fills a gap in the scholarly literature.

Nabokov, Vladimir. *Lectures on Russian Literature.* 1982. Ed. by Fredson Bowers. HarBraceJ $11.95. ISBN 0-15-649591-0. College lectures—characteristically witty, paradoxical, and uneven; best read after a more balanced historical overview.

O'Toole, L. M. *Structure, Style and Interpretation in the Russian Short Story.* Yale U. Pr. 1982 $35.00. ISBN 0-300-02730-3. Methodologically ambitious, if overblown; contains many interesting observations on the texts.

Pachmuss, Temira. *Russian Literature in the Baltic between the World Wars.* Slavica 1988 $24.95. ISBN 0-89357-181-4. Discusses a little-known episode in the history of Russia abroad.

Pomorska, Krystyna. *Jakobsonian Poetics and Slavic Narrative: From Pushkin to Solzhenitsyn.* Ed. by Henryk Baran. *Sound and Meaning: The Roman Jakobson Ser. in Linguistics and Poetics.* Duke 1992 $45.00. ISBN 0-8223-1233-6. Articles on the history and poetics of nineteenth and twentieth century Russian literature; an exposition of Jakobsonian theory.

———. *Russian Formalist Theory and Its Poetic Ambience.* Mouton 1968 $24.00. ISBN 0-686-22536-8. An examination of the relationship between Russian Futurism and Formalist criticism.

Ponomareff, Constantin V. *On the Dark Side of Russian Literature. 1709–1910.* Amer. Univ. Studies XII: Slavic Languages & Lit. P. Lang Pubs. 1987 $37.90. ISBN 0-8204-0503-5. "Ponomareff's contribution to our understanding of the spiritual exhaustion and spiritual laziness of Russian literature—its disagreement with being—is refreshing" (*SEEJ*).

Proffer, Carl R. *The Widows of Russia, Nabokov's Style and Other Essays.* Ardis Pubs. 1987 o.p. Proffer "visited the widows of famous Soviet writers" for a "sharp-eyed, intimate glimpse of the Russian literary world" (*PW*).

———, comp. *Nineteenth-Century Russian Literature in English: A Bibliography of Criticism and Translations.* Ardis Pubs. 1990 $49.50. ISBN 0-88233-943-5

Propp, Vladimir. *Theory and History of Folklore.* Ed. by Anatoly Liberman. Trans. by Ariadna Y. Martin and Richard P. Martin. *Theory & History of Lit. Ser.* U. of Minn. Pr. 1984 $15.95. ISBN 0-8166-1182-3. By a leading folklorist and theoretician whose studies illuminate Russian folklore and structuralist ideas.

Rabinowitz, Stanley, ed. and trans. *The Noise of Change: Russian Literature & the Critics (1891–1917).* Ardis Pubs. 1986 $12.95. ISBN 0-88233-526-X. Critical responses, often little known in the West, in a time of literary transition.

Rancour-Laferriere, Daniel, ed. *Russian Literature and Psychoanalysis. Linguistic and Literary Studies in E. Europe.* Benjamins North Am. 1989 $116.00. ISBN 90-272-

1536-7. Essays by several scholars with varying degrees of commitment to the psychoanalytic method.

Reid, Robert, ed. *Problems of Russian Romanticism*. Ashgate Pub. Co. 1986 $56.95. ISBN 0-566-05029-3. A set of excellent studies by a group of British specialists on romanticism.

Reyfman, Irina. *Vasilii Trediakovsky: The Fool of the "New" Russian Literature*. Stanford U. Pr. 1991 $37.50. ISBN 0-8047-1824-5. Illuminates the formative period of eighteenth-century literature and culture.

Robin, Regine. *Socialist Realism: An Impossible Aesthetic*. Trans. by Catherine Porter. Stanford U. Pr. 1992 $45.00. ISBN 0-8047-1655-2. A theoretical and historical look at socialist realist doctrine.

Rowe, W. W. *Patterns in Russian Literature II: Notes on Classics*. Ardis Pubs. 1988 $29.50. ISBN 0-87501-054-7. A set of essays, most of which focus on individual motifs or stylistic features of such authors as Chekhov, Dostoevsky, Tolstoy, and Turgenev.

Rzhevsky, Nicholas. *Russian Literature and Ideology: Herzen, Dostoevsky, Leontiev, Tolstoy, Fadeyev*. U. of Ill. Pr. 1983 o.p. An important treatment of a major topic in Russian literary and cultural history.

Scherr, Barry P. *Russian Poetry: Meter, Rhythm and Rhyme*. U. CA Pr. 1986 $55.00. ISBN 0-520-05299-4. One of the best treatments in any language of the theory and history of Russian versification.

Segel, Harold B. *Twentieth-Century Russian Drama from Gorky to the Present*. Bks. Demand repr. of 1979 ed. $135.20. ISBN 0-685-20375-1. Although uneven, this is the first attempt at such a survey in English; a valuable resource.

Seyffert, Peter. *Soviet Literary Structuralism: Background, Debate, Issues*. Slavica 1985 $18.95. ISBN 0-89357-140-7. Discusses the new wave in literary scholarship in the Soviet Union since the 1960s.

Shestov, Lev. *Chekhov and Other Essays*. *Ann Arbor Paperbacks Ser.* Bks. Demand repr. of 1966 ed. $58.30. ISBN 0-317-09970-1. Studies by a famous philosopher of the early twentieth century.

Shneidman, N. N. *Soviet Literature in the 1980s: Decade of Transition*. U. of Toronto Pr. $40.00. ISBN 0-8020-5812-4. A sequel to the author's study of the 1970s; "a useful guide to literary trends and controversies" (*SEEJ*).

______. *Soviet Literature in the Nineteen Seventies: Artistic Diversity and Ideological Conformity*. U. of Toronto Pr. 1979 o.p. Focuses on "official" prose; a detailed discussion of the literary, social, and political context.

Sinyavsky, Andrei. *Soviet Civilization: A Cultural History*. Arcade Pub. Inc. 1990 $24.95. ISBN 1-55970-034-3. An illuminating analysis of Soviet society, psychology, and language based heavily on literary works (Mayakovsky, Bulgakov, Blok, Zoshchenko), as well as on personal experiences.

Slonim, Marc. *Soviet Russian Literature: Writers & Problems, 1917–1977*. OUP 1977 2nd ed. $25.00. ISBN 0-19-502151-7. Discusses a variety of topics; slightly dated but still very useful.

Sokolov, Yury M. *Russian Folklore*. Trans. by Catherine R. Smith. Omnigraphics 1971 repr. of 1966 ed. o.p. A standard Soviet textbook; unavoidably ideological but packed with information.

Stacy, Robert H. *Russian Literary Criticism: A Short History*. Syracuse U. Pr. 1974 $9.95. ISBN 0-8156-0108-5. A concise, highly informed overview.

Steiner, Peter. *Russian Formalism: A Metapoetics*. Cornell Univ. Pr. 1984 $36.95. ISBN 0-8014-1710-4. An analysis of Formalist and early structuralist theory. Of special interest to students of criticism.

Stevanovic, Bosiljka, and Vladimir Wertsman, comps. *Free Voices in Russian Literature, 1950s–1980s: A Bio-Bibliographical Guide to over 900 Authors*. *Russica Bib. Ser.* Russica Pubs. 1987 $87.50. ISBN 0-89830-090-8. A major reference tool for unofficial writing.

Struve, Gleb. *Russian Literature under Lenin and Stalin 1917–1953*. U. of Okla. Pr. 1971 $4.95. ISBN 0-8061-1221-2. A very good, detailed discussion of the early Soviet period.

Svirski, Grigory. *A History of Post-War Soviet Writing: The Literature of Moral Opposition.* Trans. by Robert Dessaix and Michael Ulman. Ardis Pubs. 1981 $9.00. ISBN 0-88233-424-7. A Soviet-born and -raised writer looks at a broad range of texts.

Terras, Victor. *Belinskij and Russian Literary Criticism: The Heritage of Organic Aesthetics.* U. of Wis. Pr. 1974 $40.00. ISBN 0-299-06350-X. The influence of a seminal nineteenth-century thinker on Russian critical thought.

———, ed. *Handbook of Russian Literature.* Yale U. Pr. 1990 repr. of 1985 ed. $24.95. ISBN 0-300-04868-8. The best reference work in English. Up-to-date entries by many scholars; bibliographies.

———. *A History of Russian Literature.* Yale U. Pr. 1992 $45.00. ISBN 0-300-04971-4. A sweeping overview by a leading historian; covers both older periods and latest developments.

Thompson, Ewa M. *Russian Formalism and Anglo-American New Criticism: A Comparative Study.* Mouton 1971 $29.35. ISBN 90-2791-845-7. A comparison of two major strains in modern critical thought.

———, ed. *The Search for Self-Definition in Russian Literature.* Rice Univ. 1991 $21.95. ISBN 0-89263-306-9. An important selection of articles.

Todd, William M. *The Familiar Letter as a Literary Genre in the Age of Pushkin.* Bks. Demand repr. of 1976 ed. $62.20. ISBN 0-8357-3690-3. Analysis of a genre; raises questions about historicity of the notion of literature.

———. *Fiction and Society in the Age of Pushkin: Ideology, Institutions, Narrative.* HUP 1986 $25.00. ISBN 0-674-29945-0. Readings of Pushkin's *Eugene Onegin,* Lermontov's *A Hero of Our Time,* and Gogol's *Dead Souls* that demonstrate their "multiple perspectives on the 'cultural plenitude and contradictions of post-Petrine Russia'. . . . a major contribution to interdisciplinary studies" (*LJ*).

———, ed. *Literature and Society in Imperial Russia, 1800–1914.* Stanford U. Pr. 1978 $35.00. ISBN 0-8047-0961-0. Several significant studies on the social context of literature and its institutions.

Trotsky, Leon. *Literature and Revolution.* U. of Mich. Pr. 1960 o.p. A famous work by the Bolshevik leader and Marxist theoretician.

Tynyanov, Yury. *The Problem of Verse Language.* Trans. by Michael Sosa and Brent Harvey. Ardis Pubs. 1981 $6.50. ISBN 0-88233-465-4. A seminal work of Russian structuralism.

Vickery, Walter N. *The Cult of Optimism.* Kraus 1972 repr. of 1963 ed. $23.00. ISBN 0-527-93100-4. A discussion of politically orthodox Soviet literature.

Vogue, E. M. de. *The Russian Novelists.* Haskell 1974 $75.00. ISBN 0-8383-1949-1. A historically significant nineteenth-century overview by a Western critic.

Wachtel, Andrew B. *The Battle for Childhood: Creation of a Russian Myth.* Stanford U. Pr. 1990 $32.50. ISBN 0-8047-1795-8. A book that is ". . . ambitious, consistently intelligent, often provocative, and well written" (*SEEJ*).

Woll, Josephine, and Vladimir Treml. *Soviet Dissident Literature: A Critical Guide.* Macmillan 1983 $29.00. ISBN 0-8161-8626-X. Covers unofficial writing in the Soviet Union.

Zenkovsky, Serge A., and David L. Armbruster, eds. *Guide to the Bibliographies of Russian Literature.* Vanderbuilt U. Pr. 1970 $7.95. ISBN 0-8265-1160-0. Brief, thorough overview of reference tools; somewhat dated.

Zernov, Nicholas. *Three Russian Prophets: Khomiakov, Dostoevsky, Soloviev.* Academic Intl. 1974 repr. of 1944 ed. $18.50. ISBN 0-87569-050-5. A discussion of three major figures in Russian national-religious thought.

Ziolkowski, Margaret. *Hagiography and Modern Russian Literature.* Princeton U. Pr. 1988 $37.50. ISBN 0-691-06737-6. The impact of a major medieval genre in the modern period.

COLLECTIONS

Afanasiev, Aleksandr, ed. *Russian Fairy Tales.* Trans. by Norbert Guterman. *Fairytales & Folklore Lib. Ser.* Pantheon 1976 repr. of 1945 ed. $17.00. ISBN 0-394-73090-9.

Selections from a famous nineteenth-century Russian collection; with an important essay by Roman Jakobson.

______, ed. *Erotic Tales of Old Russia*. Trans. and intro. by Yury Perkov. Berkeley Slavic 1988 $7.95. ISBN 0-933884-59-1. Bilingual volume; includes texts that could not be published in the principal anthology of tales.

Blake, Patricia, and Max Hayward, eds. *Dissonant Voices in Soviet Literature*. Greenwood 1975 repr. of 1962 ed. $24.75. ISBN 0-8371-8109-7. A collection that introduced many authors of the Khrushchev period to Western readers.

Brown, Clarence, ed. *The Portable Twentieth Century Russian Reader*. *Portable Lib. Ser.* Viking Penguin 1985 $9.95. ISBN 0-14-015100-1. Eclectic choices reflect the breadth of twentieth-century Russian literary experience: Zamyatin, Akhmatova, Mandelstam, Pasternak, and others. A new translation of Olesha's *Envy*.

Cooper, Joshua, trans. *The Government Inspector and Other Russian Plays*. Viking Penguin 1991 $8.95. ISBN 0-14-044579-X. Includes works by Gogol, Fonvizin, Griboyedov, Ostrovsky.

Glad, John, and Daniel Weissbort, eds. *Twentieth Century Russian Poetry*. *IA Trans. Ser.* U. of Iowa Pr. 2nd ed. 1992 $42.95. ISBN 0-87745-373-X. Good, up-to-date selections of both authors and texts.

The Golden Age of Soviet Theatre: The Bedbug, Marya, The Dragon. Viking Penguin 1991 $7.95. ISBN 0-14-018407-4. Three major works from the early Soviet period.

Goscilo, Helena, ed. *Balancing Acts: Contemporary Stories by Russian Women*. Ind. U. Pr. 1989 $39.95. ISBN 0-253-31134-9. Works by 15 different authors; ". . . a fine selection of vignettes of a woman's view of Soviet life " (*SEEJ*).

______, ed. *Lives in Transit: A collection of Recent Russian Women's Writing*. Ardis Pubs. 1993 $39.95. ISBN 0-87501-100-4. A forthcoming collection by both established and new writers, offering diverse perspectives on women's issues in present-day Russia.

______, ed. and trans. *Russian and Polish Women's Fiction*. U. of Tenn. Pr. 1985 $38.50. ISBN 0-87049-456-2. Russian texts comprise approximately one-third of of this volume; useful as a tool in courses on women's fiction.

Goscilo, Helena, and Byron Lindsey, eds. *Glasnost: An Anthology of Russian Literature under Gorbachev*. *Contemporary Russian Prose Ser.* Ardis Pubs. 1990 $15.95. ISBN 0-679-73008-7. Although uneven in quality, includes stories by such noted contemporary writers as Lyudmila Petrushevskaya, Tatyana Tolstaya, and Fazil Iskander.

______, eds. *The Wild Beach and Other Stories*. Ardis Pubs. 1992 $39.95. ISBN 0-87501-097-0. Works from the late 1980s; companion volume to the *Glasnost* anthology.

Green, M., and J. Katsell. *The Unknown Russian Theater*. Vol. 1. Ardis Pubs. 1991 $39.95. ISBN 0-88233-554-5. Previously untranslated plays by Gogol, Turgenev, Pisemsky, Ostrovsky, Sollogub.

Grekova, I., ed. *Soviet Women Writing: Fifteen Short Stories*. Abbeville Pr. 1990 $26.95. ISBN 0-89659-882-9. "This well-chosen anthology . . . has its *perestroika* stars (Tatyana Tolstaya, Lyudmila Petrushevskaya) but is more remarkable for a rich selection of works by their predecessors from the late 1970s and early 1980s" (*LJ*).

Hapgood, Isabel F., ed. *Epic Songs of Russia*. Greenwood 1970 repr. of 1886 ed. o.p. Selection of *byliny*; translations dated.

Karlinsky, Simon, and Alfred J. Appel, Jr., eds. *The Bitter Air of Exile: Russian Writers in the West, 1922–1972*. U. CA Pr. 1976 rev. ed. $10.95. ISBN 0-520-02895-3. An important, less-known segment of modern Russian literature.

Kern, Gary, ed. *The Serapion Brothers: A Critical Anthology*. Ardis Pubs. 1975 o.p. About an innovative group of prose writers from the 1920s.

Lawton, Anna, and Herbert Eagle, eds. and trans. *Russian Futurism through Its Manifestos, 1912–1928*. Cornell Univ. Pr. 1988 $44.50. ISBN 0-8014-1883-6. An excellent collection of programmatic documents; clarifies part of the history of the various groups.

Ledkovsky, Marina, ed. *Russia According to Women*. Hermitage 1991 $9.50. ISBN 1-55779-023-X. Covers the Soviet period; the works illustrate different aspects of social life.

Luker, Nicholas, ed. *An anthology of Russian Neo-Realism: The "Znanie" School of Maxim Gorky*. Ardis Pubs. 1982 $10.95. ISBN 0-88233-422-0. Works by Andreyev, Bunin, Kuprin, Artsybashev, and Gorky.

______, ed. *From Furmanov to Sholokhov: An Anthology of the Classics of Socialist Realism*. Ardis Pubs. 1988 text ed. $17.95. ISBN 0-87501-037-7. Texts regarded as exemplars of the officially approved aesthetic doctrine.

Maddock, Mary, trans. *Three Russian Women Poets*. Crossing Pr. 1983 $7.95. ISBN 0-89594-120-1. Poems by Tsvetayeva, Akhmatova, and Akhmadulina.

McLaughlin, Sigrid, ed. and trans. *The Image of Women in Contemporary Soviet Fiction: Selected Short Stories from the U.S.S.R.* St. Martin 1989 $45.00. ISBN 0-312-02823-7. A good selection of stories that reflect traditional attitudes toward women in Russian culture.

Morton, Miriam, ed. *A Harvest of Russian Children's Literature*. U. CA Pr. 1967 $47.50. ISBN 0-520-00886-3

Myers, Alan, trans. *An Age Ago: A Selection of Nineteenth-Century Russian Poetry*. FS&G 1988 $20.00. ISBN 0-374-10442-5. A broad spectrum of poets, figures well known in the West and those unfamiliar. A variety of themes; skillful translation; brief biographies of authors.

Obolensky, Dimitri, ed. *The Heritage of Russian Verse*. Ind. U. Pr. 1976 repr. of 1962 ed. $35.00. ISBN 0-253-32735-0. A standard bilingual anthology; excellent selections; prose translations.

Pachmuss, Temira, ed. and trans. *A Russian Cultural Revival: A Critical Anthology of Russian Emigre Literature before 1939*. U. of Tenn. Pr. 1981 $42.50. ISBN 0-87049-296-9. The first comprehensive anthology of this period that has been translated into English.

______, ed. *Women Writers in Russian Modernism: An Anthology*. U. of Ill. Pr. 1978 $10.95. ISBN 0-252-00700-X

Pomorska, Krystyna, ed. *Fifty Years of Russian Prose: From Pasternak to Solzhenitsyn*. 2 vols. MIT Pr. 1971. Vol. 1 $4.95. ISBN 0-262-66019-9. Vol. 2 $4.95. ISBN 0-262-66020-2. A very broad selection, covering both culturally orthodox and innovative authors; includes a number of minor figures.

Proffer, Carl R., ed. *From Karamzin to Bunin: An Anthology of Russian Short Stories*. Ind. U. Pr. 1969 $13.95. ISBN 0-253-32506-4. Eighteen well-chosen texts; contains helpful commentaries.

______, ed. *Russian Romantic Prose: An Anthology*. Translation Pr. 1979 $17.50. ISBN 0-931556-00-7. A selection of stories by eight writers; good for the nonspecialist reader.

Proffer, Carl, and Ellendea Proffer, eds. *The Ardis Anthology of Russian Futurism*. Ardis Pubs. 1980 $7.50. ISBN 0-686-77801-4. Poems, prose works, manifestoes, scholarly analyses.

______, eds. *Contemporary Russian Prose: An Anthology*. Ardis Pubs. 1982 $14.95. ISBN 0-88233-597-9. Includes Trifonov's *The Exchange*, Sokolov's *A School for Fools*, Aksyonov's *The Steel Bird*.

______, eds. *The Silver Age of Russian Culture: An Anthology*. Ardis Pub. 1975 $5.95. ISBN 0-88233-172-8. Although uneven in its coverage, this anthology captures the "*Zeitgeist*, artistic pungency, and emotional intensity of the period" (*Slavic Review*).

______ et al., eds. *Russian Literature of the Twenties: An Anthology*. Ardis Pubs. 1987 $39.50. ISBN 0-88233-820-X. Prose, poetry, drama, essays, and documents; features Zamyatin's *We*, Mayakovsky's *The Bedbug*, etc.

Raeff, Marc, ed. *Russian Intellectual History: An Anthology*. Humanities repr. of 1966 ed. $22.50. ISBN 0-391-00905-2. Superbly selected readings. An excellent background for the study of Russian literature, with an introduction by Isaiah Berlin.

Reeder, Roberta, ed. and trans. *Russian Folk Lyrics*. Ind. U. Pr. $35.00. ISBN 0-253-34623-1. Russian peasant customs as reflected through a variety of song genres, with an essay by famous folklorist Propp that considers the folk lyric in terms of its original social and historical context.

Reeve, Franklin D., ed. *Contemporary Russian Drama*. Irvington 1968 $39.00. ISBN 0-672-53521-1. Includes Rozov's *Alive Forever*, Pogodin's *Petrarchan Sonner*, Shvartz's *Naked King*, Panova's *It's Been Ages*, Zorkin's *Warsaw Melody*.

______, ed. *Great Soviet Short Stories*. Dell 1990 $5.95. ISBN 0-440-33166-8

Richards, David, ed. *The Penguin Book of Russian Short Stories*. Viking Penguin 1981 $9.95. ISBN 0-14-004816-2. Twenty major writers, from Pushkin to Nabokov and Solzhenitsyn.

Rydel, Christine, ed. and trans. *The Ardis Anthology of Russian Romanticism*. Ardis Pubs. 1984 $18.95. ISBN 0-88233-742-4. Available in On-Demand Printing Series. A broad, comprehensive selection of poems, prose, and criticism from 1810 to 1840.

Scott, H. G., ed. *Problems of Soviet Literature: Reports & Speeches at the First Soviet Writer's Congress by A. Zhdanov, Maxim Gorky, N. Bukharin, K. Radek, A. Stetsky, 1st, Moscow, 1934*. Greenwood 1980 repr. of 1935 ed. $45.00. ISBN 0-313-20998-7. A record of the key session establishing the institutions of literature during the Stalin period.

Smith, Vassar W., ed. and trans. *Pushkin Plus: Lyric Poems of Eight Russian Poets*. Zapizdat Pubns. 1992 $5.95. ISBN 1-880964-02-3. Works by Pushkin, Krylov, Lermontov, Nekrasov, Blok, Sologub, Mandelstam, Yesenin.

Wiener, Leo, ed. *Anthology of Russian Literature from the Earliest Period to the Present*. 2 vols. Gordon Pr. 1976 $150.00. ISBN 0-8490-1436-0

Zenkovsky, Serge, ed. *Medieval Russia's Epics, Chronicles, and Tales*. NAL-Dutton rev. ed. 1974 o.p. An extremely rich anthology of medieval texts; indispensable for understanding Kievan and Muscovite culture.

CHRONOLOGY OF AUTHORS

Karamzin, Nikolai. 1766–1826
Aksakov, Sergei. 1791–1859
Griboyedov, Aleksandr. 1795–1829
Pushkin, Aleksandr. 1799–1837
Tyutchev, Fyodor. 1803–1873
Gogol, Nikolai. 1809–1852
Goncharov, Ivan. 1812–1891
Herzen, Aleksandr. 1812–1870
Lermontov, Mikhail. 1814–1841
Turgenev, Ivan. 1818–1883
Pisemsky, Aleksei. 1820–1881
Dostoyevsky, Fyodor. 1821–1881
Nekrasov, Nikolai. 1821–1878
Ostrovsky, Aleksandr. 1823–1886
Saltykov-Shchedrin, Mikhail. 1826–1889
Chernyshevsky, Nikolai. 1828–1889
Tolstoy, Leo. 1828–1910
Leskov, Nikolai. 1831–1895
Korolenko, Vladimir, 1853–1921
Garshin, Vsevolod. 1855–1888
Chekhov, Anton. 1860–1904
Sologub, Fedor. 1863–1927
Gorky, Maxim. 1868–1936
Hippius (Gippius). 1869–1945
Bunin, Ivan. 1870–1953
Kuprin, Aleksandr. 1870–1938
Andreyev, Leonid. 1871–1919
Bryusov, Valery. 1873–1924
Prishvin, Mikhail. 1873–1954
Kuzmin, Mikhail. 1875–1936
Remizov, Aleksei. 1877–1957
Bely, Andrei. 1880–1934
Blok, Aleksandr. 1880–1921
Chukovsky, Kornei. 1882–1969
Gladkov, Fyodor. 1883–1958
Zamyatin, Yevgeny. 1884–1937
Khlebnikov, Velimir. 1885–1922
Akhmatova, Anna. 1889–1966
Pasternak, Boris. 1890–1960
Bulgakov, Mikhail. 1891–1940
Ehrenburg, Ilya. 1891–1967
Furmanov, Dmitry. 1891–1926
Mandelstam, Osip. 1891–1938
Fedin, Konstantin. 1892–1977
Paustovsky, Konstantin. 1892–1968
Tsvetaeva, Marina. 1892–1941
Mayakovsky, Vladimir. 1893–1930
Babel, Isaac. 1894–1941
Pilnyak, Boris. 1894?–1937?
Tynyanov, Yury. 1894–1943
Esenin, Sergei. 1895–1925
Ivanov, Vsevolod. 1895–1963
Zoshchenko, Mikhail. 1895–1958
Ilf, Ilya. 1897–1937
Kataev, Valentin. 1897–1986
Leonov, Leonid. 1899–
Nabokov, Vladimir. 1899–1977

Olesha, Yury. 1899–1960
Platonov, Andrei. 1899–1951
Berberova, Nina. 1901–
Kaverin, Veniamin. 1902–1989
Petrov, Yevgeny. 1903–1942
Grossman, Vasily. 1905–1964
Panova, Vera. 1905–1973
Sholokhov, Mikhail. 1905–1984
Chukovskaya, Lydia. 1907–
Grekova, Irina. 1907–
Shalamov, Varlam. 1907–1982
Rybakov, Anatoly. 1911–
Simonov, Konstantin. 1915–1979
Galich, Aleksandr. 1918–1977
Solzhenitsyn, Aleksandr. 1918–
Okudzhava, Bulat. 1924–
Soloukhin, Vladimir. 1924–
Sinyavsky, Andrei. 1925–
Strugatsky, Arkady. 1925–
Trifonov, Yury. 1925–1981
Aitmatov, Chingiz. 1928–
Aleshkovsky, Yuz. 1929–
Iskander, Fazil. 1929–
Shukshin, Vasily. 1929–1974
Vladimov, Georgy. 1931–
Aksyonov, Vassily. 1932–
Gorenstein, Friedrich. 1932–
Voinovich, Vladimir. 1932–
Strugatsky, Boris. 1933–
Voznesensky, Andrei. 1933–
Yevtushenko, Yevgeny. 1933–
Gladilin, Anatoly. 1935–
Kushner, Aleksandr. 1936–
Akhmadulina, Bella. 1937–
Bitov, Andrei. 1937–
Rasputin, Valentin. 1937–
Erofeev, Venedikt. 1938 or 1939–
Brodsky, Joseph. 1940–
Dovlatov, Sergei. 1941–1990
Limonov, Edward. 1943–
Sokolov, Sasha. 1943–
Tolstaya, Tatyana. 1951–
Ratushinskaya, Irina. 1954–

AITMATOV, CHINGIZ. 1928–

Aitmatov became well known for his Russian-language prose describing the life of his own Kirghiz people. Although he was a member of the Communist party, his works did not follow the narrow canons of socialist realism. With depth and sensitivity, Aitmatov presented the Kirghiz in the throes of societal change, dealt very broadly with ethical problems, and took up topics that were generally avoided in official Soviet literature. In recent years, he has increasingly criticized Russification and collectivization on traditional Kirghiz society.

NOVELS BY AITMATOV

The Ascent of Mount Fuji (with Kaltai Mukhamedzhanov). FS&G 1975 $4.95. ISBN 0-374-51215-9

The Day Lasts More than a Hundred Years. Trans. by John French. Ind. U. Pr. 1983 $30.00. ISBN 0-253-11595-7. Set in Kazakhstan, the novel draws on legends and history, dealing with both the Kazakh and the Soviet historical past and constructing a science fiction story of the earth's cosmic future.

The Place of the Skull. Grove Pr. 1989 $20.95. ISBN 0-8021-1000-2. A widely discussed novel reminiscent of Bulgakov's *Master and Margarita;* several disparate plot elements, combined with a moral message.

AKHMADULINA, BELLA. 1937–

Akhmadulina is a native of Moscow, a graduate of the Literary Institute. Her poetry initially circulated in *samizdat;* official publication first came in 1955; and her first collection, *The String*, appeared in 1962. Over the years, it was followed by a series of books of verse in the Soviet Union, as well as a major collection, *The Chills* (1968), put out by an émigré publishing house. She was involved in the unofficial collection *Metropol'* (1979).

Akhmadulina is regarded as a major contemporary poet. Her verse is complex, frequently filled with fantastic, surrealist elements, and with colloquialisms, coined words, and obsolete diction. The process of artistic creation and the attendant role of the poet are recurrent subjects.

Poetry by Akhmadulina

The Garden: New and Selected Poetry. Trans. by F. D. Reeve. H. Holt & Co. 1990 $24.95. ISBN 0-8050-1249-4. "Akhmadulina is known for her masterly use of various styles of diction. . . . The translations in this bilingual edition attempt to replicate the vocabulary, meter, and rhyme of the originals, with mixed results" (*LJ*).

AKHMATOVA, ANNA. 1889–1966

Akhmatova began as a creator of simple, yet psychologically deep, lyrics with which she achieved an extraordinary popularity prior to World War I. With her first husband, Nikolai Gumilev, she formed part of the group of poets known as the Acmeists, who, in contrast to the mystically oriented symbolists, sought to make poetry more palpable, more oriented to the material world and human experience. During the Stalin years, she was almost totally barred from literature; her son, a historian, was imprisoned several times. In 1946 Akhmatova and Mikhail Zoshchenko became the target of a public campaign of vilification led by Zhdanov, then culture "boss" and a close associate of Stalin. Her work began to be published again during the 1960s; shortly before her death, she was awarded the Taormina Prize for poetry in Italy and an honorary doctorate from Oxford (the regime permitted her to travel abroad to accept it). During the 1970s and 1980s, a number of important editions of Akhmatova's works appeared, signaling a critical acceptance by the literary establishment that matched the awe with which Russia's readers had always regarded her.

Akhmatova is one of the major figures of twentieth-century Russian poetry. Her themes range from a woman's intimate feelings to the nature of poetic creation and broad issues of Russia's history. In addition to individual lyrics, she has produced two masterpieces: *Requiem* (1935–1940), a cycle of poems which employs Passion motifs to convey people's suffering during the Stalinist terror, and *Poem without a Hero* (1940–66), a complex, highly allusive narrative about Russian literature and culture.

Poetry by Akhmatova

The Complete Poems of Anna Akhmatova. 2 vols. Ed. by Roberta Reeder. Trans. by Judith Hemschemeyer. Zephyr Pr. 1990 $85.00. ISBN 0-939010-13-5. An excellent, book-length introduction and revelatory translator's preface that "make a worthy frame for Akhmatova's glorious poetry, . . . arranged, in exemplary fashion, with respect for choices the poet made in lifetime editions" (*LJ*). Bilingual edition.

Poem without a Hero and Other Poems: A Selection from the Work of Anna Akhmatova. Trans. by Lenore Mayhew and William McNaughton. Oberlin Coll. Pr. 1989 $17.95. ISBN 0-932440-51-7

Poems. Trans. by Lyn Coffin. Norton 1983 $15.50. ISBN 0-393-01567-X. An introduction by Joseph Brodsky.

Selected Poems. Ed. by Walter Arndt. Trans. by Robin Kemball and Carl Proffer. Ardis Pubs. 1976 $12.95. ISBN 0-88233-180-9. Contains over 170 texts; balanced translations.

Selected Poems. Trans. by D. M. Thomas. Viking Penguin 1992 $7.95. ISBN 0-14-018617-4

Selected Poems. Trans. by Richard McKane. Dufour 1988 $18.95. ISBN 1-85224-063-6. A "small anthology with, for the most part, fastidiously accurate prose translations" (*SEEJ*).

Twenty Poems of Anna Akhmatova. Trans. by Jane Kenyon and Vera S. Dunham. Ally Pr. 1985 $6.95. ISBN 0-915408-30-9. An introduction by Jane Kenyon.

NONFICTION BY AKHMATOVA

My Half Century: Selected Prose. Ed. by Ronald Meyer. Trans. by Ronald Meyer, Ronald Peterson, and Sharon Leiter. Ardis Pubs. 1991 $29.95. ISBN 0-87501-063-6. Includes autobiographical writings, reminiscences of friends, Pushkin studies, and a selection of letters.

BOOKS ABOUT AKHMATOVA

Chukovskaya, Lydia. *Conversations with Akhmatova. Vol. 1: 1938–1941*. Trans. by Barry Rubin. FS&G 1992 $22.50. ISBN 0-374-22342-4. Very important memoirs by the poet's lifelong friend; excellent on the social and historical background.

Nayman, Anatoly. *Remembering Anna Akhmatova*. H. Holt & Co. 1991 $29.95. ISBN 0-8050-1408-X. By her literary secretary, also a poet. Nayman "uses her letters and poems, his obscure textual analyses, and short bits of personal conversation" (*LJ*) to evoke her life. Introduction by Brodsky.

AKSAKOV, SERGEI. 1791–1859

A close friend of GOGOL, Aksakov came from the old landholding nobility. His family background became the subject for a series of reminiscences written late in life. Their objective and precise description of the often brutal provincial existence, their insight and honesty about human psychology, as well as their eventful narratives have made them enduring classics of nineteenth-century prose.

NOVELS BY AKSAKOV

A Family Chronicle. St. Mut. 1984 $39.00. ISBN 0-317-42757-1

A Russian Gentleman. Ed. by Edward Crankshaw. Trans. by J. D. Duff. *World's Classics Paperback Ser.* OUP 1982 $9.95. ISBN 0-19-281573-3

A Russian Schoolboy. Trans. by J. D. Duff. *The World's Classics Paperback Ser.* OUP 1983 $9.95. ISBN 0-19-281575-X. An introduction by John Bayley.

Years of Childhood. Trans. by J. D. Duff. *The World's Classics Paperback Ser.* OUP 1983 $10.95. ISBN 0-19-281574-1

AKSYONOV (AKSENOV), VASSILY. 1932–

Aksyonov made his debut during the late 1950s and early 1960s, when he was closely associated with the popular journal *Yunost'* (Youth). His work was distinguished by its contemporary idiom, filled with slang and foreign borrowings, the idiom of the young people whose iconoclasm and social turmoil his prose depicted. During the 1970s, Aksyonov increasingly turned toward the fantastic and the grotesque. Involved in the unofficial *Metropol'* collection, he was exiled in 1980. Since then, he has lived in the United States, where he has published several important works, including *The Island of Crimea*, a political fantasy, and *In Search of Melancholy Baby*, a provocative exploration of contemporary America. During the Gorbachev period, Aksyonov was again published in the Soviet Union, and he is acknowledged as a leading figure in contemporary Russian fiction.

NOVELS BY AKSYONOV

The Burn. 1975. Trans. by Michael Glenny. Random 1985 $18.95. ISBN 0-394-52492-6. ". . . [O]n the whole, Glenny's English is not as loose and colloquial as the author's Russian" (*SEEJ*).

The Island of Crimea. 1983. Trans. by Michael H. Heim. Random 1984 $8.95. ISBN 0-394-72765-7. A fictional investigation of an "alternative" history of twentieth-century Russia; a very good translation.

Our Golden Ironburg. 1972. Trans. by Ronald E. Peterson. Ardis Pubs. 1988 $9.95. ISBN 0-88233-560-X. A loose modernist novel "full of anti-heroes (and an anti-author), straight narration, broken by dreams, forays into the past and nonsensical song lyrics" (*PW*).

Say Cheese! Trans. by Antonina Bouis. Random 1989 $19.95. ISBN 0-394-54363-7. "In this rollicking novel written for his new American audience, Aksyonov . . . describes the bizarre, unequal contest between the Soviet 'Glands' (security organs) and intellectuals . . . (*LJ*).

Nonfiction by Aksyonov

In Search of Melancholy Baby. Trans. by Michael H. Heim and Antonina W. Bouis. Random 1987 $15.95. ISBN 0-394-54364-5. An "exhilarating book" with a "remarkably perceptive . . . grasp of the American character" (*LJ*).

Short Story Collection by Aksyonov

The Destruction of Pompeii and Other Stories. Contemporary Russian Prose Ser. Ardis Pubs. 1991 $9.95. ISBN 0-679-73441-4

Works by Aksyonov

Quest for An Island. PAJ Pubns. 1987 $17.95. ISBN 1-55554-020-1. "The constant in these four stories and two plays, dating from 1967 to 1981 and translated by various hands, is their central voice: a man roughly the author's age much afflicted by what was once dubbed 'existential anguish'" (*LJ*).

Books about Aksyonov

Kustanovich, Konstantin. *The Artist and the Tyrant: Vassily Aksenov's Works in the Brezhnev Era.* Slavica 1992 $17.95. ISBN 0-89357-235-7. A broad, unified view of the writer's work during the period 1963–1979.

Możejko, Edward, ed. *Vasily Pavlovich Aksënov: A Writer in Quest of Himself.* Slavica 1986 $21.95. ISBN 0-89357-141-5. A collection of articles on subjects ranging from early stories to novels published during the early 1980s.

ALESHKOVSKY, YUZ (IOSIF). 1929–

Aleshkovsky, a former prison-camp inmate, enjoyed anonymous fame in the Soviet Union as the author of a celebrated song about Stalin and an obscenely funny novella, *Nikolai Nikolaevich,* which circulated in *samizdat.* Since 1979 he has lived in the United States, where his works have been appearing in Russian and in some English translations. *The Hand* (1980), his second novel, is a monologue by a KGB executioner—a powerful exploration of Soviet history, though slightly boring in its plethora of scatology.

Novels by Aleshkovsky

The Hand. Trans. by Susan Brownsberger. FS&G 1990 $22.95. ISBN 0-374-16770-2. "Aleshkovsky lays bare the bankrupt foundation of the Soviet state and foretells its ultimate demise . . . powerfully prophetic," (*LJ*). An introduction by Joseph Brodsky.

Kangaroo. Trans. by Tamara Glenny. FS&G 1986 $17.95. ISBN 0-374-18068-7

ANDREYEV (ANDREEV), LEONID. 1871–1919

Andreyev became one of the most popular writers of the first decade of the twentieth century because of his ability to combine modernist and realist techniques and his willingness to break taboos of theme. His subjects included sexual problems (e.g., veneral disease) and various abormalities. Such works caused a scandal but won their author a wide following. In the aftermath of 1905, Andreyev dealt with the defeated revolutionaries' moral and psychological dilemmas and with the intelligentsia as a whole, while in *The Tale of the Seven Who Were Hanged* (1909), he produced a stunning condemnation of the death penalty. Andreyev had a talent for depicting the dark, irrational forces in life within existential dilemmas; however, his pessimism and mysticism are sometimes undercut by a blatant tugging on the heartstrings and a lack of personal engagement and authenticity.

WORKS BY ANDREYEV

Little Angel and Other Stories. Dedalus European Fiction Ser. Hippocrene Bks. 1989 $8.95. ISBN 0-946626-42-1

The Red Laugh. Dedalus European Fiction Classics Ser. Hippocrene Bks. 1989 $8.95. ISBN 0-946626-41-3

Visions: Stories and Photographs. Ed. by Olga Andreyev Carlisle. HarBraceJ 1987 $21.95. ISBN 0-15-193900-4. The era of the October Revolution. "Much more than period pieces, . . . skillfully translated by Andreyev's granddaughter, noted journalist and nonfiction author Carlisle" (*PW*).

PLAYS BY ANDREYEV

King Hunger. Trans. by Eugene M. Kayden, Univ. South 1973 $5.95. ISBN 0-685-18783-7

Three Plays: The Black Maskers. The Life of Man. The Sabine Woman. Trans. by C. Meador and F. Scott. Fertig 1989 repr. of 1915 ed. $35.00. ISBN 0-86527-388-X

BOOKS ABOUT ANDREYEV

Davies, Richard. *Leonid Andreyev: Photographs by a Russian Writer: An Undiscovered Portrait of Pre-Revolutionary Russia.* Thames Hudson 1989 $35.00. ISBN 0-500-54143-4

Kaun, Alexander S. *Leonid Andreyev, a Critical Study.* AMS Pr. repr. of 1924 ed. $18.45. ISBN 0-404-03638-4

______. *Leonid Andreyev. Select Bib. Repr. Ser.* Ayer repr. of 1924 ed. $26.50. ISBN 0-8369-5009-7

King, H. H. *Dostoyevsky and Andreyev: Gazers upon the Abyss.* Kraus 1972 repr. of 1936 ed. $18.00. ISBN 0-527-50800-4

Newcombe, Josephine M. *Leonid Andreyev. Lit. and Life Ser.* Continuum 1973 o.p. An introduction intended for readers with no knowledge of this Russian author.

Woodward, James B. *Leonid Andreyev: A Study.* Clarendon Pr. 1972 o.p. A solid attempt to view Andreyev's work as a logical system of thought and Andreyev himself as a philosopher who absorbed the *Weltanschauung* of existential thinkers.

BABEL, ISAAC (ISAAK). 1894–1941

Babel won early success with stories about his native Odessa and about the exploits of the Bolshevik cavalry in the Polish campaign of 1920–21. During the 1930s his output was small, but his talent remained undiminished. He was arrested in May 1939 during the Great Purge, and his manuscripts were confiscated. His exact fate remains unknown. When Babel's reputation was "rehabilitated" in 1956, he was still published only occasionally in the Soviet Union—the very strong Jewish element in his stories, as well as the ambiguous positions he took on war and revolution, made his stories uncomfortable for Soviet authorities.

For a Russian reader, the *Odessa Tales* (1916) are particularly exotic. Their protagonists, members of the city's Jewish underworld, are presented in romantic, epic terms. The Red Cavalry stories are noted for their account of the horrors of war. In both cycles Babel relies on precisely constructed short plots, on paradox of situation and of character response, and on nonstandard, captivating language—be it the combination of Yiddish, slang, and standard

Russian in the *Odessa Tales* or of uneducated Cossack speech and standard Russian in the Red Cavalry cycle. The result of such features is a prose heritage rare in the history of Russian literature.

Short Story Collections by Babel

Benya Krik, The Gangster and Other Stories. Ed. by Avraham Yarmolinsky. Trans. by Bernard G. Guerney. *Masterworks of Modern Jewish Writing Ser.* Wiener Pub. Inc. 1988 repr. of 1969 ed. $4.95. ISBN 0-318-35558-2

Collected Stories. Trans. and ed. by Walter Morison. NAL-Dutton 1974 $9.95. ISBN 0-452-00798-4. Introduction by Lionel Trilling.

Works by Babel

Isaac Babel: The Forgotten Prose. Ed. by N. Stroud. Ardis Pubs. 1978 $12.00. ISBN 0-88233-307-0. Texts of Babel's earliest known writings (1916-1922).

You Must Know Everything. Ed. by Nathalie Babel. Trans. by Max Hayward. Carroll & Graf 1984 $8.95. ISBN 0-88184-027-0. Twenty-five works, well rendered into English.

Books about Babel

Bloom, Harold, ed. *Isaac Babel. Modern Critical Views Ser.* Chelsea Hse. 1987 o.p.

Ehre, Milton. *Isaac Babel. Twayne's World Authors Ser.* Macmillan 1986 $26.95. ISBN 0-8057-6637-5. ". . . [T]his study [of Babel] is free of critical jargon, well written, clear, concise, and effectively organized" (*SEEJ*).

Falen, James E. *Isaac Babel: Russian Master of the Short Story.* Bks. Demand repr. of 1974 ed. $73.90. ISBN 0-685-20454-5. An attempt to discover and interpret major symbolic and mythic patterns in Babel's prose; interesting, although not always persuasive.

Schreurs, Marc. *Procedures of Montage in Isaak Babel's "Red Cavalry". Studies in Slavic Lit. & Poetics.* Humanities 1989 $85.00. ISBN 90-5183-113-7. Applies Sergei Eisenstein's concept of film montage in order to achieve a new reading of Babel's prose cycle.

Sicher, Efraim. *Style and Structure in the Prose of Isaak Babel.* Slavica 1986 $15.95. ISBN 0-89357-163-6. An innovative analysis of the artistic effect of Babel's stories; based on unexpurgated texts and previously unavailable archival sources.

BELY (BIELY), ANDREI (pseud. of Boris Bugayev). 1880–1934

A major "second-wave" symbolist poet, Bely was also a literary critic and theorist and one of the most important figures in twentieth-century Russian fiction. His *Petersburg* (1916–35) is one of the century's great novels. He initially studied science but had begun his literary career even before graduation. His early poetry was shaped by mystical beliefs associated with the concept of the Divine Wisdom (a numinous presence called Sophia), beliefs shared by Aleksandr Blok and other younger symbolist poets. In later years, Bely was deeply affected by the German anthroposophist Rudolf Steiner, whose follower he became in 1912; his writings from that time on bear the imprint of his commitment to Steiner's teachings.

Bely's prose continued the stylistic traditions of Gogol, about whose work he wrote. Brilliantly innovative in language, composition, and subject matter, Bely's fiction had a great impact on early Soviet literature. His novels *St. Petersburg* (1913) and *The Silver Dove* (1910) deal with Russian history in broad cultural perspective, focusing especially on East-West opposition. Another important work, *Kotik Letaev* (1918), anticipated stream-of-consciousness techniques in Western fiction in its depiction of the psyche of a developing infant. His late autobiographical novel, *The Christened Chinaman* (1927), is also highly innovative in its language and three-level narrative.

Novels by Bely

The Christened Chinaman. Trans. by Thomas R. Beyer. Hermitage 1991 $12.00. ISBN 1-55779-042-6

Kotik Letaev. Trans. by Gerald Janecek. Ardis Pubs. 1971 o.p.

Petersburg. Trans. by Robert A. Maguire and John E. Malmstad. *Midland Bks. Ser.* Ind. U. Pr. 1978 $14.95. ISBN 0-253-20219-1. An unabridged and annotated translation, both faithful and readable.

St. Petersburg. Trans. by John Cournos. Grove Pr. 1989 $9.95. ISBN 0-8021-3158-1. A dated, incomplete version by a Silver Age contemporary; reads well.

The Silver Dove. Trans. by George Reavey. Grove Pr. 1974 o.p. "Reavey's translation is for the most part smooth and flowing and sometimes even brilliant" (*SEEJ*).

Short Story Collection by Bely

Complete Short Stories. Ed. by Ronald E. Peterson. Ardis Pubs. 1979 o.p. Bely's short stories make up a minor portion of his writing.

Poetry by Bely

The Dramatic Symphony. Trans. by Roger Keys. Grove Pr. 1989 $8.95. ISBN 0-8021-3122-0. An example of Bely's youthful experimentation.

The First Encounter. Trans. by Gerald Janecek. Princeton U. Pr. 1979 $24.95. ISBN 0-691-06381-8. The first English translation of Bely's poem; good critical apparatus.

Nonfiction by Bely

Reminiscences of Rudolf Steiner (coauthored by Assya Turgenieff and Margarita Voloschin). Adonis Pr. 1990 $15.50. ISBN 0-932776-13-2. An important document of Bely's encounter with anthroposophy, which played a major role in his life and later works.

Selected Essays of Andrey Bely. Trans. by Steven Cassedy. U. CA Pr. 1985 $47.50. ISBN 0-520-05273-0. Six well-translated and well-edited essays from the early 1900s.

Books about Bely

Alexandrov, Vladimir E. *Andrei Bely: The Major Symbolist Fiction. Russian Research Center Studies* HUP 1985 $25.00. ISBN 0-674-03646-8

Elsworth, J. D. *Andrey Bely: A Critical Study of the Novels. Cambridge Studies in Russian Lit. Ser.* Cambridge U. Pr. 1984 $59.95. ISBN 0-521-24724-1. A useful, though uneven study on Bely's novels; is the best on *The Silver Dove* and *St. Petersburg*.

Janecek, Gerald, ed. *Andrey Bely: A Critical Review*. U. Pr. of Ky. 1978 $21.00. ISBN 0-8131-1368-7. First-ever collection of studies on Bely.

Malmstad, John E. *Andrey Bely: Spirit of Symbolism*. Cornell Univ. Pr. 1987 $49.95. ISBN 0-8014-1984-0. "These illuminating essays . . . cover . . . influences (Orthodoxy, Nietzsche, theosophy); experiments in 'musical' prose . . . ; the sound patterning and leitmotifs of the novels . . ." and Bely's work in all genres (*LJ*).

Steinberg, Ada. *Words and Music in the Novels of Andrey Bely. Cambridge Studies in Russian Lit. Ser.* Cambridge U. Pr. 1982 $69.95. ISBN 0-521-23731-9. Covers significant aspects of Bely's craft as a prose writer.

BERBEROVA, NINA. 1901–

Born in pre-Revolutionary St. Petersburg, Berberova emigrated in 1922, living in several European countries before settling in the United States. She wrote frequently for the leading journals and anthologies of the "first wave" of the Russian emigration. *The Italics Are Mine* (1969), her autobiography, is an important record of that period.

Novels by Berberova

The Accompanist. Trans. by Marian Schwartz. Macmillan 1988 $14.95. ISBN 0-689-11989-5

Tattered Cloak and Other Novels. McKay 1991 $20.50. ISBN 0-679-40281-0. "Paris in the Thirties and Forties provides the setting for these six short novels detailing the lives, losses, and loves of Russian émigrés in a style reminiscent of Chekhov" (*LJ*).

Nonfiction by Berberova

The Italics Are Mine. McKay 1992 $29.50. ISBN 0-679-41237-9. An idiosyncratic book, to be treated with caution as a source of information about Russian literature on emigration.

BITOV, ANDREI. 1937–

Although educated as a geologist, Bitov has worked as a professional writer since the early 1960s, publishing a number of collections of fiction and travel notes. His stories often deal with the development of the inner world of an urban protagonist, Monakhov. *Publisher's Weekly* has noted "the kinetic energy of Bitov's episodic, alert, hypersensitive style." Bitov's major work, *The Pushkin House*, had to circulate in *samizdat,* with its final text first appearing in Russian in the United States (1978). This important work represents a striking experiment with the traditions of Russian literature.

Novels by Bitov

A Captive of the Caucasus. Trans. by Susan Brownsberger. FS&G 1992 $23.00. ISBN 0-374-11883-3. "[A] brooding and difficult reflection on ideals, nationhood, and belonging; the creative process; and metaphysics . . ." (*LJ*).

The Pushkin House. Trans. by Susan Brownsberger. FS&G 1987 $22.50. ISBN 0-374-23934-7. "[W]e have to look back to Yuri Olesha and Nabokov for comparably sensitive evocations of the texture and feel of ordinary objects" (*NYT Book Review*).

Short Story Collection by Bitov

Life in Windy Weather: Short Stories. Ed. and trans. by Priscilla Meyer. Ardis Pubs. 1986 $8.95. ISBN 0-88233-692-4. Introduction by Meyer.

BLOK, ALEKSANDR (ALEXANDER). 1880–1921

Blok was one of the most important Russian poets of this century, a lyricist of extraordinary vision and passion whose life and art were closely intertwined. He started to write early. His first collection, *Verses on the Beautiful Lady* (1904), mythologizes his young wife, Lyubov, as the incarnation of a mystical presence, Sophia. Succeeding collections mirror his gradual abandonment of this ideal and his embracing of humankind's tormented existence. The last volume of a trilogy arranged by the poet himself, including the epic *Retribution* (1910–21) and *The Terrible World*, shows Blok at the height of his powers as he explores a welter of interconnected personal, historical, cultural, and philosophical themes. Increasingly in his poetry, as well as in his many essays and plays, Blok gave way to his premonitions of impending apocalyptic events; few of his generation possessed his perception of the cataclysms that the twentieth century would bring; yet his proclamations of doom and avowals of class guilt for the Russian people's suffering found a ready audience.

Blok's best-known work, particularly in the West, is the long poem *The Twelve* (1918), in which a group of revolutionary guardsmen, at once heroes and criminals, with the figure of Christ at their head, marches through darkened newly seized Petersburg. This response to the October Revolution is complex and contradictory, and its changing language and rhythms magnificently reflect the many sources and shifting moods of the poem. Unfortunately, only a relatively small number of Blok's works are available in English.

POETRY BY BLOK

Alexander Blok: Selected Poems. Ed. by Avril Pyman. Pergamon 1972 $130.00. ISBN 0-08-012185-3

The Spirit of Music. Trans. by I. Freiman. *Soviet Lit. in Eng. Trans. Ser.* Hyperion Conn. 1973 repr. of 1946 ed. $15.00. ISBN 0-88355-001-6

The Twelve and Other Poems. Trans. by Anselm Rollo, Gnomon Pr. 1971 o.p.

BOOKS ABOUT BLOK

Chukovsky, Kornei. *Alexander Blok as Man and Poet.* Ed. by Diana Burgin. Trans. by Katherine O'Connor. Ardis Pubs. 1982 o.p. A study by a contemporary and a leading critic.

Mochulsky, Konstantin. *Aleksandr Blok.* Trans. by Doris V. Johnson. Wayne St. U. Pr. 1983 o.p. A major discussion of Blok's writings as a whole, with emphasis on the religious element.

Pirog, Gerald. *Aleksandr Blok's "Ital'janskie Stixi": Confrontation and Disillusionment.* Slavica 1983 $15.95. ISBN 0-89357-095-8. "This is the definitive explication of the *Italian Poems . . ."* (*Poetics Today*).

Pyman, Avril. *Aleksandr Blok: A Biography. Vol. 1: The Distant Thunder. 1880–1908.* OUP 1979 o.p. The first half of a magisterial biography; the single most-important book on the poet in English.

______. *The Life of Aleksandr Blok: A Biography, Vol. 2: The Release of Harmony. 1908–1921.* OUP 1980 o.p. Completes the study of life and works.

Reeve, F. D. *Alexander Blok: Between Image and Idea.* Hippocrene Bks. 1980 o.p.

Sloane, David A. *Aleksandr Blok and the Dynamics of the Lyric Cycle.* Slavica 1989 $19.95. ISBN 0-89357-182-2. Deals with the lyric "trilogy"; analyzes theoretical issues regarding the concept of poetic cycle.

Vickery, Walter N., ed. *Aleksandr Blok Centennial Conference.* Slavica 1984 $26.95. ISBN 0-89357-111-3. Articles covering a wide range of subjects.

Vogel, Lucy, ed. *Alexander Blok: An Anthology of Essays and Memoirs.* Ardis Pubs. 1982 o.p. A good set of critical works, especially by Blok's contemporaries.

BRODSKY, JOSEPH (IOSIF). 1940– (NOBEL PRIZE 1987)

Brodsky's first poems appeared mainly in *Syntax*, a Leningrad underground literary magazine. In 1964 he became the object of international concern after he was tried and sentenced to five years of administrative exile for "parasitism." As a result of intervention by prominent Soviet cultural figures, he was freed in 1965. In 1972, under tremendous pressure from the authorities, he emigrated to the United States, where he has taught at various universities, published a number of poetry collections, and achieved great critical acclaim.

Brodsky is undoubtedly the best contemporary Russian poet, the inheritor of AKHMATOVA's mantle. He has written short lyrics and longer poems and has experimented with various genres and techniques. His concerns are very broad, involving common human experiences frequently informed by nostalgic pessimism. Like Akhmatova, he draws heavily on European culture and literature; while dealing with Russia's problems and concerns, he brings them into a broader historical, experiential purview.

Brodsky has involved himself extensively in U.S. literary life, writing regularly in English-language magazines. In this, he is an exception among "Third-wave" Russian émigrés, but his position is consonant with his poetry's universal themes and concerns. In 1987 Brodsky was awarded the Nobel Prize for literature; in 1991 he was named poet-laureate of the United States—the first poet whose native language was not English to achieve this honor.

Poetry by Brodsky

A Part of Speech. Trans. by Anthony Hecht, George L. Kline, Howard Moss, Alan Myers, David Rigsbee, Barry Rubin, Daniel Weissbort, and Richard Wilbur. FS&G 1980 $15.95. ISBN 0-374-22987-2

Joseph Brodsky: Selected Poems. Trans. by George L. Kline. HarpC 1974 $9.95. ISBN 0-06-010484-8

To Urania. FS&G 1992 $9.00. ISBN 0-374-52333-9. "Brodsky's first collection since *A Part of Speech*[,] . . . this volume contains previously uncollected works dating from 1968 . . . but written mostly in this decade" (*LJ*).

Nonfiction by Brodsky

Less Than One: Selected Essays of Joseph Brodsky. FS&G 1986 $30.00. ISBN 0-374-18503-4. "[N]ot only evinces a supple, witty mastery of the English language, but provides deeply illuminating insights into the Russian literary tradition and political climate and modern poetry and poetics, in addition to compelling autobiographical material" (*LJ*).

Watermark. FS&G 1992 $15.00. ISBN 0-374-14812-0. "In his wayward forays amid canals, streets and cathedrals barnacled with saints, the eternal Venice shimmers through the fog, battered yet resplendent" (*PW*).

Play by Brodsky

Marbles: A Play in Three Acts. Trans. by Alan Myers. FS&G 1990 $25.00. ISBN 0-374-20288-5. A difficult "literary expression of Einstein's relativity theory . . . [with many] allusions to classical literature, history, science, and philosophy" (*LJ*).

Books about Brodsky

Loseff, Lev, and Valentina Polukhina, eds. *Brodsky's Poetics and Aesthetics.* St. Martin 1990 $39.95. ISBN 0-312-04511-5. Papers from a major conference devoted to Brodsky's writings.

Polukhina, Valentina. *Joseph Brodsky: A Poet for Our Time. Cambridge Studies in Russian Lit. Ser.* Cambridge U. Pr. 1989 $54.50. ISBN 0-521-33484-5. The first book-length study of Brodsky in English; very useful, especially on the relationship of Brodsky's verse to a wider European literary context.

BRYUSOV (BRIUSOV), VALERY. 1873–1924

A prolific poet, novelist, critic, and organizer, Bryusov was one of the most important figures of the Silver Age. During the 1890s, thanks largely to him, the new school of symbolism, heavily influenced by French-Belgian developments, came into being in Russia. Of his many collections of verse, the best are *Tertia Vigilia* (1900) and *Stephanos* (1906); they mirror his Western-oriented, aestheticized, literary position.

Bryusov also wrote prose, experimental in both form and theme. His best novel is *The Fiery Angel* (1907–08). Set in Renaissance Germany and reflecting Bryusov's extensive knowledge of the period, it is a first-person account of a soldier-adventurer's love affair with a woman who claims to be a witch. Many of his short stories are fantasy and science fiction.

Novel by Bryusov

The Fiery Angel: A Sixteenth Century Romance. Trans. by Ivor Montagu and Sergei Nalbandov. *Classics of Russian Lit. Ser.* Hyperion Conn. 1992 repr. of 1930 ed. $34.00. ISBN 0-88355-475-5

Short Story Collection by Bryusov

The Republic of the Southern Cross and Other Stories. Classics of Russian Lit. Ser. Hyperion Conn. 1977 repr. of 1919 ed. $15.00. ISBN 0-88355-477-1. Bryusov's ventures into the fantastic, science fiction, and other genres.

Nonfiction by Bryusov

The Diary of Valery Bryusov (1893–1905): With Reminiscences by V. F. Khodasevich and Marina Tsvetaeva. Ed. by Joan D. Grossman. *Documentary Studies in Modern Russian Poetry Ser.* U. CA Pr. 1980 $30.00. ISBN 0-520-03858-4. A very important document for the early history of Russian symbolism.

Book about Bryusov

Rice, Martin. *Valery Briusov and the Rise of Russian Symbolism.* Ardis Pubs. 1975 o.p. Emphasizes Bryusov's role as an organizer, polemicist, and editor; weaker on his poetic achievements.

BULGAKOV, MIKHAIL. 1891–1940

A practicing physician, like Chekhov, Bulgakov became a popular writer and playwright in the comparatively easier political climate of the Soviet Union during the 1920s. The civil war and its internecine horrors became one of his major themes (e.g., in the novel *The White Guard* [1924]), as did the new crazy-quilt Soviet society. His early prose is often satiric, with strong elements of the fantastic and grotesque, but it also contains the themes of guilt and personal responsibility that become so crucial in his later work.

Bulgakov wrote a number of important plays that provoked bitter attacks in the press, and he was shut out of the theater and literature in 1929. Only a direct appeal to Stalin allowed Bulgakov to resume a professional career. Even then, however, some of his important works, such as the novel *Life of Monsieur de Molière* (1933), were rejected by publishing houses and theaters.

Bulgakov's masterpiece, written "for the drawer" over a number of years, and only published decades after his death, is the novel *Master and Margarita* (1966–67). Combining two principal plot lines—Satan's visit to contemporary Moscow and the trial and execution of Jesus in biblical Judaea—the work may be read on many levels, from the purely satiric to the allegorical. It has been acclaimed as one of the most important achievements of twentieth-century Russian fiction.

Today, Bulgakov is celebrated for both his plays and his novels. Several of his plays are public favorites and standard fare in Russian theaters.

Plays by Bulgakov

The Black Snow. Adap. by Keith Dewhurst. *Absolute Classics Ser.* Theatre Comm. 1991 $10.95. ISBN 0-948230-45-2. A dramatization of a 1937 novel about Bulgakov's tragicomic experience with the Moscow Art Theater.

Bulgakov: Six Plays. Trans. by Michael Glenny, William Powell, and Michael Earley. Heinemann Ed. 1991 $13.95. ISBN 0-413-64530-4. An introduction by his biographer, Lesley Milne.

The Early Plays of Mikhail Bulgakov. Ed. by Ellendea Proffer. Trans. by Carl R. Proffer and Ellendea Proffer. Ardis Pubs. 2nd ed. 1992 $14.95. ISBN 0-87501-091-1. Includes *The Days of the Turbins, Zoya's Apartment, Flight, The Crimson Island, A Cabal of Hypocrites* (*Molière*).

Flight and Bliss. Trans. by Mirra Ginsburg. New Dir. Pr. 1985 repr. of 1969 ed. $17.95. ISBN 0-8112-0940-7

Molière. Royal Shakespeare Company PIT Playtext Ser. Heinemann Ed. 1988 $6.95. ISBN 0-413-52320-9

Novels by Bulgakov

Heart of a Dog. 1925. Trans. by Mirra Ginsburg. Grove Pr. 1968 $2.95. ISBN 0-394-17442-9. A wicked satire on the new society, written in 1925 and only recently published in Russia.

The Life of Monsieur de Molière. Trans. by Mirra Ginsburg. *The Revived Modern Classics Ser*. New Dir. Pr. 1986 repr. of 1970 ed. $17.95. ISBN 0-8112-0984-9

The Master and Margarita. Trans. by Diana Burgin and Katherine D. O'Connor. Ardis Pub. 1991 $27.50. ISBN 0-87501-067-9. A translation based on the complete Russian text published by Ardis in 1988.

Master and Margarita. Trans. by Mirra Ginsburg. Grove Pr. 1970 $5.95. ISBN 0-394-17439-9. A splendid, highly readable translation.

The White Guard. Trans. by Michael Glenny. Academy Chi. Pubs. 1987 repr. of 1971 ed. $10.00. ISBN 0-89733-246-6

Short Story Collections by Bulgakov

Diaboliad and Other Stories. Ed. by Carl R. Proffer and Ellendea Proffer. Trans. by Carl R. Proffer. Ardis Pubs. 2nd ed. 1992 $11.95. ISBN 0-87501-090-3. A translation of Bulgakov's own selection of short stories from the mid-1920s.

Mikhail Bulgakov: Selected Works. Ed. by Avril Pyman. Pergamon 1972 $80.00. ISBN 0-08-015506-5

Notes on the Cuff and Other Stories. Trans. by Alison Rice. Ardis Pubs. 1991 $27.50. ISBN 0-87501-057-1. "This book translates several of Bulgakov's early short stories and feuilletons for the first time. . . . His vivid and often humorous sketches of 1920s Moscow bring this era to life" (*LJ*).

Books about Bulgakov

Curtis, J. A. *Bulgakov's Last Decade: The Writer as Hero*. *Cambridge Studies in Russian Lit. Ser*. Cambridge U. Pr. 1987 $54.50. ISBN 0-521-32671-0. "Anyone interested in Bulgakov, including critics, will learn much from Curtis's book. Her writing, moreover, is clear, succinct, and above all sane." (*SEEJ*).

______. *Manuscripts Don't Burn: Mikhail Bulgakov: A Life in Letters and Diaries*. Overlook Pr. 1992 $25.00. ISBN 0-87951-462-0. A rich, well-translated selection; highly readable and useful.

Krugovoy, George. *The Gnostic Novel of Mikhail Bulgakov: Sources and Exegesis*. U. Pr. of Amer. 1991 $52.00. ISBN 0-8191-8288-5

Milne, Lesley. *Mikhail Bulgakov: In Dialogue with Time: A Critical Biography*. Cambridge U. Pr. 1990 $49.50. ISBN 0-521-22728-3. Broad, insightful, and well written; based on new materials.

Natov, Nadine. *Mikhail Bulgakov*. *World Author Ser*. Macmillan 1985 $25.96. ISBN 0-8057-6598-0. "Natov's *Mikhail Bulgakov* may be useful to students looking for a rapid survey" (*SEEJ*).

Pittman, Rita H. *The Writer's Divided Self in Bulgakov's The Master and Margarita*. St. Martin 1991 $45.00. ISBN 0-312-06148-X. ". . . [T]he originality of Dr. Pittman's book lies in a combination of fresh readings and new juxtapositions" (*SEER*).

Proffer, Ellendea. *Bulgakov: Life and Work*. Ardis Pubs. 2nd ed. 1990 $25.00. ISBN 0-88233-199-X. A major study; culmination of 15 years of research and publication of Bulgakov's writings.

BUNIN, IVAN. 1870–1953 (Nobel Prize 1933)

Bunin was little known in the United States until he won the Nobel Prize, the first Russian writer to do so. By then he had decades of extensive literary activity behind him. In the intensely group-oriented literary milieu of turn-of-the-century Russia, Bunin largely remained a loner, working within the realist tradition in prose but enriching it with a powerful lyric element. He traveled abroad a great deal and used exotic locales as settings for many of his works. An outspoken opponent of the Bolsheviks, he emigrated to Paris and ironically, years after his death, he became celebrated in the Soviet Union as a major writer.

Bunin's themes are diverse, ranging from a changing Russia to the universal human experience. Born into an impoverished rural-gentry family, he often wrote about the decline and passing of a way of life. Sometimes his depiction of provincial Russia is elegiac; at other times it is violent and tragic (e.g., the novella *Dry Valley* [1911]). A number of his works, such as the remarkable short story "The Gentleman from San Francisco" (1915), may be read as allegories of human encounter with the transcendent. In later years, Bunin grew increasingly preoccupied with problems of sexual attraction and death, evidenced in his last collection of stories, *Dark Avenues* (1930).

Short Story Collections by Bunin

"The Gentleman from San Francisco" and Other Stories. Trans. by David Richards and Sophie Lund. Viking Penguin 1992 $9.95. ISBN 0-14-018552-6

In a Far Distant Land. Trans. by Robert Bowie. Hermitage 1983 $8.50. ISBN 0-938920-27-8. On the themes of love and death.

Long Ago: Selected Stories. Trans. by David Richards and Sophie Lund. Dufour 1984 $14.95. ISBN 0-946162-11-5

Wolves and Other Love Stories Of Ivan Bunin. Trans. by Mark G. Scott. Borgo Pr. 1989 $25.00. ISBN 0-8095-4066-5. "In 32 brief stories and sketches, most of them written in emigration in Paris . . . Bunin . . . obsessively catalogs varieties of love (or lust) in prerevolutionary Russia" (*LJ*).

Novels by Bunin

Velga. Trans. by Guy Daniels. S. G. Phillips 1970 o.p.

The Village. Trans. by Isabel Hapgood. Fertig 1975 o.p.

Books about Bunin

Connolly, Julian K. *Ivan Bunin. Twayne World Authors Ser.* Macmillan 1982 $22.95. ISBN 0-8057-6513-1. A concise, yet quite full picture of Bunin's development as a writer.

Kryzytski, Serge. *The Works of Ivan Bunin. Slavistic Printings & Reprintings Ser.* Mouton 1971 o.p. A very informative, though somewhat disjointed, study.

Woodward, James B. *Ivan Bunin: A Study of His Fiction.* U. of NC Pr. 1980 $29.95. ISBN 0-8078-1394-X. ". . . [I]n its analysis of specific works, as in its general discussion of Bunin's philosophy, Woodward's study makes an important contribution . . ." (*SEEJ*).

CHEKHOV, ANTON (also TCHEKHOV, TCHEKOV, TCHEKHOFF, CHEHOV). 1860–1904

The greatest of Russian dramatists, Chekhov was also a peerless master of the short story; his influence on world literature in both of these areas is profound. Forced to support himself while he was attending medical school, he began in 1880 to write trivial comic tales for humor magazines. By 1884 the first collection of his stories appeared, and by the end of the decade he was a professional writer.

Chekhov's path to mastery as a dramatist was even more rapid. He moved from one-act plays to four innovative works that are part of the core repertoire of modern world theater: *The Sea Gull* (1896), *Uncle Vanya* (1900), *Three Sisters* (1901), and *The Cherry Orchard* (1904). Chekhov died of tuberculosis at age 44, leaving behind a vast literary heritage, much of which was pioneering in both subject matter and techniques. His themes were drawn from all areas of Russian life; he explored the situations and problems of his characters with both sensitivity and clear-minded hardheadedness, never allowing himself to descend into false pathos. Chekhov showed how tragedies result from human beings' inability to communicate their thoughts and emotions. In this he anticipated a major theme of modern fiction and theater (especially the absurdist). His dramas eschew the conventions of the well-made play and are notable for the complex interrelationships of their elements: The hallmark of Chekhovian theater is a low-keyed network of minor incidents, moods, and words, all typical of ordinary lives, which builds to an almost unbearable emotional intensity.

Although there are numerous English editions of Chekhov, many of his prose tales have not yet been translated. Ronald Hingley's *Oxford Chekhov* series is particularly notable for both its large scope and the high quality of the translations. Constance Garnett's versions are quite reliable, especially in the Norton Critical Editions series. His plays also exist in various English-language versions. However, it is important to distinguish adaptations intended for contemporary stage productions from versions that strictly adhere to the original text.

Short Story Collections by Chekhov

Anton Chekhov's Short Stories. Ed. by Ralph E. Matlaw. Trans. by Constance Garnett. *Norton Critical Ed. Ser.* Norton 1979 $8.95. ISBN 0-393-09002-7. Thirty-four well-selected, beautifully translated works; contains an introduction and a selection of criticism.

Chekhov: The Early Stories: 1883–88. Trans. by Patrick Miles and Harvey Pitcher. Macmillan 1984 $5.95. ISBN 0-02-049390-8

A Doctor's Visit: Short Stories by Anton Chekhov. Bantam 1988 $3.50. ISBN 0-553-21322-9

The Duel and Other Stories. Trans. by Ronald Wilks. Viking Penguin 1984 $4.95. ISBN 0-14-044415-7

The Fiancee and Other Stories. Trans. by Ronald Wilks. Viking Penguin 1986 $5.95. ISBN 0-14-044470-X. Introduction by Wilks.

Five Great Short Stories. Dover 1990 $1.00. ISBN 0-486-26463-7

Forty Stories. Trans. by Robert Payne. Random 1991 $11.00. ISBN 0-679-73375-2

The Kiss and Other Stories. Viking Penguin 1982 $5.95. ISBN 0-14-044336-3

Lady with the Dog. Ed. by Patrick Waddington. *Library of Russian Classics Ser.* Blackwell Pubs. $15.95. ISBN 0-900186-42-9

Late-Blooming Flowers and Other Stories. Carroll & Graf 1984 $8.95. ISBN 0-88184-029-7. With an introduction by I. C. Chertok.

The Princess and Other Stories. Trans. by Ronald Hingley. *The World's Classics Ser.* OUP 1990 $4.95. ISBN 0-19-282662-X. Introduction and notes by Hingley.

The Russian Master and Other Stories. Trans. by Ronald Hingley. *The World's Classics Ser.* OUP 1984 $4.95. ISBN 0-19-281680-2

The Steppe and Other Stories. Trans. by Ronald Hingley. *The World's Classics Ser.* OUP 1991 $4.95. ISBN 0-19-282663-8

Tales of Chekhov. 13 vols. Trans. by Constance Garnett. *The Tales of Chekhov Ser.* Ecco Pr. 1987 $95.00. ISBN 0-88001-175-0. One of the most complete collections of Chekhov's short stories.

Ward Number Six and Other Stories. Trans. by Ronald Hingley. *The World's Classics Ser.* OUP 1988 $4.95. ISBN 0-19-282174-1

Wild Honey. Trans. by Michael Frayn. Heinemann Ed. 1988 $8.95. ISBN 0-413-55160-1

A Woman's Kingdom and Other Stories. Trans. and ed. by Ronald Hingley. *The World's Classics Ser.* OUP 1989 $4.95. ISBN 0-19-282209-8

Plays by Chekhov

The Anniversary. Ed. by William Alan Landes. Trans. by Sergius Ponomarov. Players Pr. 1992 $6.00. ISBN 0-88734-334-1

Anton Chekhov's Plays. Ed. by Eugene K. Bristow. *Norton Critical Ed. Ser.* Norton 1978 $12.95. ISBN 0-393-09163-5. "On the whole, [Bristow's] rendition of Chekhov's major dramas conveys the tone and spirit of the original" (*SEEJ*); contains a good introduction and a selection of criticism on Chekhov.

The Bear. Trans. by Sergius Ponomarov. Ed. by William Alan Landes. *Chekhov Collection Ser.* Players Pr. 1991 $5.00. ISBN 0-88734-317-1. Introduction by Landes.

The Brute and Other Farces: Seven Short Plays. Ed. by Eric Bentley. Trans. by Theodore Hoffman. Applause Theatre Bk. Pubs. 1987 repr. of 1958 ed. $19.95. ISBN 1-55783-003-7. Introduction by Henry Bentley.

Chekhov: Five Major Plays. Trans. by Ronald Hingley. *Bantam Classics Ser.* Bantam 1984 $3.50. ISBN 0-553-21211-7

Chekhov for the Stage: The Sea Gull, Uncle Vanya, The Three Sisters, The Cherry Orchard. Trans. by Milton Ehre. Northwestern U. Pr. 1992 $43.95. ISBN 0-8101-1023-7. Introduction by Ehre.

The Cherry Orchard. Ed. and adap. by David Mamet. Grove Pr. 1987 $8.95. ISBN 0-8021-3002-X

The Cherry Orchard. Trans. by Helen Rappaport. Ed. and adap. by Trevor Griffiths. Faber & Faber 1990 $8.95. ISBN 0-571-14199-4

The Marriage Proposal. Trans. by Sergius Ponomatov. Ed. by William Alan Landes. *Chekhov Collection Ser.* Players Pr. 1990 $5.00. ISBN 0-88734-318-X. Introduction by Landes.

Plays. Trans. by Elisaveta Fen. *Penguin Classics Ser.* Viking Penguin 1959 $4.95. ISBN 0-14-044096-8. All of the major and several of the minor plays.

The Seagull. Adap. by Robert Brustein. *Plays for Performance Ser.* I. R. Dee 1992 $15.95. ISBN 0-929587-89-8

Seagull. Trans. by Michael Frayn. *Methuen Theatre Classics Ser.* Heinemann Ed. 1988 $9.95. ISBN 0-413-42140-6. Introduction by Frayn.

The Sneeze and Other Plays. Trans. by Michael Frayn. *Methuen Theatre Classics Ser.* Heinemann Ed. 1989 $9.95. ISBN 0-413-42490-1. Introduction by Frayn.

Three Sisters. Trans. by Michael Frayn. *Methuen Theatre Classics Ser.* Heinemann Ed. 1988 $9.95. ISBN 0-413-52450-7

Three Sisters. Trans. by Paul Schmidt. *Trans. Ser.* Theatre Comm. 1992 $21.95. ISBN 1-55936-056-9

Uncle Vanya. Trans. by Michael Frayn. *Methuen Theatre Classics Ser.* Heinemann Ed. 1988 $9.95. ISBN 0-413-15950-7

The Wedding. Ed. by A. B. Murphy. *Lib. of Russian Classics Ser.* Blackwell Pubs. $15.95. ISBN 0-900186-48-8

NOVELS BY CHEKHOV

Seven Short Novels. Trans. by Barbara Makanowitzky. Norton 1971 repr. of 1963 ed. $12.95. ISBN 0-393-00552-6. Preface by Gleb Struve.

The Shooting Party: A Novel. U. Ch. Pr. 1987 repr. of 1926 ed. $8.95. ISBN 0-226-10241-6. An introduction by Julian Symons.

WORKS BY CHEKHOV

The Oxford Chekhov. 9 vols. Trans. and ed. by Ronald Hingley. OUP 1964–1980 $49.95 ea. "The edition may stand as a model for the way a major writer ought to be presented to literature readers" (*SEEJ*).

The Portable Chekhov. Ed. by Avrahm Yarmolinsky. *Viking Portable Lib. Ser.* Viking Penguin 1991 $9.95. ISBN 0-14-099707-5

NONFICTION BY CHEKHOV

Anton Chekhov: Literary and Theatrical Reminiscences. Trans. and ed. by Samuel S. Koteliansky. Ayer. 1972 $26.50. ISBN 0-405-08353-X

Anton Chekhov's Life and Thought: Selected Letters and Commentary. Trans. by Simon Karlinsky and Michael Heim. U. CA Pr. 1976 repr. of 1973 ed. $10.95. ISBN 0-520-02684-5. A major edition of the letters.

The Letters of Anton Chekhov. Ed. by Avrahm Yarmolinsky. Viking Penguin 1973 o.p. A major edition.

Letters on the Short Story. Gordon Pr. 1973 $59.95. ISBN 0-8490-0513-2

Life and Letters of Anton Chekhov. Trans. by Samuel S. Koteliansky and Philip Tomlinson. Ayer repr. of 1925 ed. $26.50. ISBN 0-405-08355-6. The first part of a three-volume set.

Notebook of Anton Chekhov. Ecco Pr. 1987 $8.50. ISBN 0-88001-145-9

The Selected Letters of Anton Chekhov. Ed. by Lillian Hellman. Trans. by Sidonie K. Lederer. FS&G 1984 $7.95. ISBN 0-374-51838-6

Books about Chekhov

Barricelli, Jean-Pierre, ed. *Chekhov's Great Plays: A Critical Anthology.* NYU Pr. 1985 $17.50. ISBN 0-8147-1074-3. Essays by leading scholars of literature and theater.

Bill, Valentine T. *Chekhov: The Silent Voice of Freedom. Paperback Ser.* Philos. Lib. 1987 o.p.

Chudakov, A. P. *Chekhov's Poetics.* Trans. by Edwina Cruise and Donald Dragt. Ardis Pubs. 1983 $7.50. ISBN 0-88233-781-5. An analysis by a modern structuralist critic: rigorous, provocative.

Clyman, Toby W., ed. *A Chekhov Companion.* Greenwood 1985 $65.00. ISBN 0-313-23423-X. A good reference work.

De Maegd-Soep, Carolina. *Chekhov and Women: Women in the Life and Work of Chekhov.* Slavica 1987 $17.95. ISBN 0-89357-175-X. Analyzes the many female figures in Chekhov's writings; discusses his personal relationships in depth.

Gottlieb, Vera. *Chekhov in Performance in Russia and Soviet Russia. Theatre in Focus Ser.* Chadwyck-Healey 1984 $100.00. ISBN 0-85964-119-8. Includes 50 slides.

Hahn, Beverly. *Chekhov. Major European Authors Ser.* Cambridge U. Pr. 1979 o.p. "For the reader who has no Russian, Hahn's book represents one of the more comprehensive offerings on Chekhov in recent years" (*SEEJ*).

Hingley, Ronald F. *A Life of Anton Chekhov.* OUP 1989 $12.95. ISBN 0-19-285200-0. A substantial biography by a leading translator and scholar of Chekhov's works.

Jackson, Robert L., ed. *Chekhov: A Collection of Critical Essays.* P-H 1967 o.p.

———, ed. *Reading Chekhov's Text. Ser. in Russian Lit. & Theory.* Northwestern U. Pr. 1992 $44.95. ISBN 0-8101-1080-6. Introduction by Jackson.

Kirk, Irina. *Anton Chekhov. World Authors Ser.* Macmillan 1981 $20.95. ISBN 0-8057-6410-0

Lantz, Kenneth. *Anton Chekhov: A Reference Guide. Reference Guides to Lit. Ser.* Macmillan 1985 $41.00. ISBN 0-8161-8701-0

Meister, Charles W. *Chekhov Criticism, 1880 through 1986.* McFarland & Co. 1988 $35.00. ISBN 0-89950-355-1

Pitcher, Harvey. *The Chekhov Play: A New Interpretation.* U. CA Pr. 1984 $10.95. ISBN 0-520-05311-7

Pritchett, V. S. *Chekhov: A Spirit Set Free.* Random 1988 $17.95. ISBN 0-394-54650-4

Senelik, Lawrence. *Anton Chekhov.* Ed. by Bruce King and Adele King. *Modern Dramatists Ser.* St. Martin 1990 $11.95. ISBN 0-333-30882-4

Simmons, Ernest J. *Chekhov: A Biography.* U. Ch. Pr. 1970 $3.95. ISBN 0-226-75805-2

Troyat, Henri. *Chekhov.* Trans. by Michael H. Heim. Fawcett 1988 $10.95. ISBN 0-449-90281-1. ". . . [T]his book, taken as a whole, ultimately gives us a fine vision of the intelligent and enigmatic figure that was Anton Chekhov" (*SEEJ*).

Watson, Ian. *Chekhov's Journey.* Carroll & Graf 1989 $16.95. ISBN 0-88184-523-X

CHERNYSHEVSKY, NIKOLAI. 1828–1889

Together with Nikolai Dobrolyubov and Dmitry Pisarev, Chernyshevsky was a leading radical thinker of the midnineteenth century. Championing materialism, utilitarianism, and a rather naive idea of social and historical progress, he infused his very influential literary criticism with his social views. His most important philosophical work is *The Anthropological Principle in Philosophy* (1860), in which he argued that social environment determines human behavior and espoused a rational egoism; the treatise became the underpinning of much subsequent radical literature. Chernyshevsky wrote his most famous book, *What Is to Be Done?* (1863), while imprisoned for revolutionary activity. Almost devoid of artistic merit, deliberately unliterary, the novel celebrates female emancipation and the new radical intelligentsia, and offers a vision of a future utopia. Its ideas enormously inspired generations of Russian intellectuals, who regarded it as a major classic. It also has been mercilessly pilloried, first by DOSTOYEVSKY in *Notes from Underground*, and more recently by NABOKOV in *The Gift*.

NONFICTION BY CHERNYSHEVSKY

Belinsky, Chernyshevsky and Dobrolyubov: Selected Criticism. Ed. by Ralph E. Matlaw. Ind. U. Pr. 1976 $5.95. ISBN 0-253-20200-0. Essays by the three great radical critics of the nineteenth century.

NOVELS BY CHERNYSHEVSKY

What Is to be Done? Trans. and ed. by K. Feuer. Ardis Pubs. 1986 $12.95. ISBN 0-87501-017-2

What Is to be Done? Trans. by Michael R. Katz. Cornell Univ. Pr. 1989 $41.95. ISBN 0-8014-1744-9

BOOK ON CHERNYSHEVSKY

Paperno, Irina. *Chernyshevsky and the Age of Realism: A Study in the Semiotics of Behavior.* Standford U. Pr. 1988 $35.00. ISBN 0-8047-1453-3. An important contribution, based on cultural semiotics, on the critic and his time.

CHUKOVSKAYA, LYDIA. 1907–

Daughter of the famous critic KORNEI CHUKOVSKY, Lydia Chukovskaya is a fiction writer and memoirist of note. Her two novels, *Sofia Petrovna* (1965) (also translated as *The Deserted House*) and *Going Under* (1972), dealt with the Stalin period; the former is a splendid portrait of a woman whose psyche gradually dissolves under the impact of the purges. A close friend of ANNA AKHMATOVA, Chukovskaya preserved a detailed account of their encounters, highly important for understanding the poet's biography and views. Chukovskaya became a leading dissident, and was expelled from the Writers' Union in 1974.

NOVELS BY CHUKOVSKAYA

Going Under. Trans. by Peter M. Weston. Times Bks. 1976 o.p.

Sofia Petrovna. Trans. by Aline Werth and Eliza K. Klose. Northwestern U. Pr. 1988 repr. of 1967 ed. $9.95. ISBN 0-8101-0794-5

CHUKOVSKY, KORNEI. 1882–1969

Chukovsky was an extraordinary figure: a critic and memoirist of the Silver Age, a literary scholar and editor, a celebrated children's poet, and a noted translator and theoretician of translation. Especially fine were his translations from English, including renderings of WHITMAN (see Vol. I), TWAIN (see Vol. 1), and CHESTERTON (see Vol. 1).

From Two to Five, first published in 1928 and reissued many times, presents witty, thoughtful observations of children's psychology and verbal creativity, and has been frequently used by linguists. Chukovsky's own verses for children, enormously popular, are among the classics of this genre in Russia.

POETRY BY CHUKOVSKY

The Telephone. Trans. by William J. Smith. Delacorte 1977 $7.95. ISBN 0-440-08532-2. Original poems for children.

NONFICTION BY CHUKOVSKY

The Art of Translation: Kornei Chukovsky's "A High Art". Ed. by Lauren G. Leighton. U. of Tenn. Pr. 1984 o.p. Theoretical and practical problems of the translator's craft.

From Two to Five. Ed. and trans. by Miriam Morton. Univ. of CA Pr. 1963 $10.95. ISBN 0-520-00238-5

BOOK ABOUT CHUKOVSKY

Chukovskaya, Lydia. *To the Memory of Childhood*. Trans. by Eliza K. Klose. Northwestern U. Pr. 1988 $24.95. ISBN 0-8101-0789-9. Not chronological, these "vignettes . . . reveal Chukovsky's powerful affinity for poetry, words and games . . . and his role in . . . pre-Revolutionary Russia" (*PW*).

DOSTOYEVSKY (DOSTOEVSKY, DOSTOEVSKII, DOSTOEVSKI, DOSTOIEVSKY), FYODOR (FEDOR, FEODOR). 1821–1881

One of the most significant figures in modern world literature, Dostoyevsky successfully debuted with *Poor Folk* (1846), a subtle novel about the psychology of the poor and socially insignificant—a major subject throughout his fiction and Russian prose as a whole. In 1849 he and other members of the mildly socialist Petrashevsky Circle were arrested and charged with political crimes; after undergoing a psychologically shattering mock execution, they were sentenced to terms of imprisonment and army service in the ranks. In 1854 Dostoyevsky emerged from a Siberian prison camp, a devout believer in Christianity and Russia. His unconventional views, opposed to both the radical and reactionary attitudes of the time, informed much of his subsequent writing, polemical and fictional. Dostoyevsky's private life during the 1860s was full of vicissitudes, including the deaths of his wife and his brother, struggles with creditors, and a serious gambling addiction. A change for the better came with his second marriage in 1867, which gave him a stable, happy family life. Yet, whatever the private turmoil, this was the start of a period that produced his greatest works, including *Notes from the Underground* (1864), a profound examination of the modern consciousness, and a series of novels ensuring his lasting celebration: *Crime and Punishment* (1866), *The Idiot* (1868), *The Possessed* (also *The Devils*) (1872), and *The Brothers Karamazov* (1880).

During the 1870s, Dostoyevsky drew close to prominent religious figures and to conservative government circles. He wrote a large number of propagandizing pieces on topics ranging from literature to international affairs, often espousing nationalistic, anti-Western views (see especially *A Writer's Diary* [1876–77]). However, his works were popular with a reading public that was often very radical. At the 1880 Pushkin celebrations in Moscow, crowds greeted Dostoyevsky's speech with enthusiasm; the next year saw the same public outpouring of affection at his funeral.

Dostoyevsky's role in modern literature is manifold. Originally influenced by the prose of GOGOL and PUSHKIN, he was a profound innovator, transforming realism and creating a new brand of psychological novel. His works, especially his great novels, operate on a number of levels. In *Crime and Punishment,* a murder mystery becomes the vehicle for examining not only the protagonist's psyche (FREUD [see Vols. 3 and 5] studied Dostoyevsky's startlingly contemporary psychological insights with interest) but also the contemporary family and society, and the most profound philosophical and theological questions about humanity, the world, and the transcendent. He has been treated as a precursor of the existentialists; he has also been interpreted as a religious thinker. Overall, Dostoyevsky was a writer and thinker of such complexity, so open to the clash of ideas, that generations of readers have been able to find in him what they seek.

Almost all of Dostoyevsky's writings are now available in English. Constance Garnett's translations have been a standard; however, they do not always capture the subtleties and flavor of Dostoyevsky's language. David Magarshack's versions of the great novels are somewhat better in this regard and the new translation by Richard Pevear and Larissa Volokhonsky is excellent. The *Norton Critical Editions* are particularly useful: the translations featured in these volumes are updated, with key critical materials appended.

NOVELS BY DOSTOYEVSKY

The Adolescent. 1875. Trans. by Andrew R. MacAndrew. Norton 1981 repr. of 1971 ed. $15.95. ISBN 0-393-00995-5. In the form of a quasimemoir; distills key Dostoyevskian themes. Also known as *The Raw Youth.*

The Brothers Karamazov. 1880. Ed. by Ralph E. Matlaw. Trans. by Constance Garnett. *Critical Ed. Ser.* Norton 1976 $14.95. ISBN 0-393-09214-3. The most complex novel, containing the famous Grand Inquisitor section. Addresses directly evil, grace, salvation; a series of character types that have entered Russian culture.

The Brothers Karamazov. Vintage Classics Ser. Random 1991 $16.00. ISBN 0-679-72925-9

The Brothers Karamazov: A Novel in Four Parts with Epilogue. Trans. by Richard Pevear and Larissa Volokhonsky. N. Point Pr. 1990 $29.95. ISBN 0-86547-422-2. An outstanding contemporary translation that captures the subtlety of Dostoyevsky's style.

Crime and Punishment. 1866. Ed. by George Gibian. *Critical Ed. Ser.* Norton 1989 $11.95. ISBN 0-393-95623-7

Crime and Punishment. Knopf 1992 $24.50. ISBN 0-679-40557-7

Crime and Punishment. Trans. by David McDuff. Viking Penguin 1991 $30.00. ISBN 0-670-83640-0

Crime and Punishment. Knopf 1992 $24.50. ISBN 0-679-40557-7

Crime and Punishment. Trans. by Constance Garnett. Random 1978 $15.00. ISBN 0-394-60450-4. Includes an introduction by Ernest J. Simmons.

The Devils. 1872. Trans. and ed. by Michael R. Katz. *The World's Classics Ser.* OUP 1992 $6.95. ISBN 0-19-281850-3. A great political novel and critique of radicalism. A vision of disintegrating society and of potential totalitarianism. Same as *The Possessed.*

The Double. Trans. by Evelyn Harden. Ardis Pubs. 1985 $9.95. ISBN 0-88233-757-2. Includes both the first and second editions of this important work.

The Gambler. Trans. by Andrew R. MacAndrew. Norton 1981 repr. of 1964 ed. $7.95. ISBN 0-393-00044-3

The Gambler and The Diary of Polina Suslova. Ed. by Edward Wasiolek. Trans. by Victor Terras. U. Ch. Pr. 1973 $12.95. ISBN 0-226-15972-8. An idiomatic translation; contains a perceptive, informative introduction.

The House of the Dead. Trans. by David McDuff. *Penguin Classics Ser.* Viking Penguin 1986 $5.95. ISBN 0-14-044456-4

The Idiot. 1868. Trans. by Constance Garnett. Bantam 1983 $4.50. ISBN 0-553-21352-0. The problem of salvation, beauty, and their role in the world in the context of broken families and a modern Apocalypse.

The Idiot. Ed. by W. J. Leatherbarrow. *The World's Classics Ser.* OUP 1992 $5.95. ISBN 0-19-282604-2

The Idiot. Trans. by David Magarshack. *Penguin Classics Ser.* Viking Penguin 1956 $5.95. ISBN 0-14-044054-2

The Insulted and Injured. 1861. Trans. by Constance Garnett. Greenwood 1975 repr. of 1955 ed. $38.50. ISBN 0-8371-8248-4. A fictional investigation of female psychology.

Netochka Nezvanova. Trans. by Jane Kentish. *Penguin Classics Ser.* Viking Penguin 1986 $5.95. ISBN 0-14-044455-6. Unfinished; reflects the author's interest in female characters.

Notes from Underground and the Double. NAL-Dutton 1991 $5.95. ISBN 0-452-01093-4

Notes from the Underground and the Gambler. Ed. by Jane Kentish and Malcolm Jones. *The World's Classics Ser.* OUP 1992 $5.95. ISBN 0-19-282719-7

The Possessed. Trans. by Constance Garnett. Ed. by Avrahm Yarmolinsky. Random 1978 $7.95. ISBN 0-394-60441-5

The Possessed. Buccaneer Bks. 1989 repr. $49.95. ISBN 0-89966-628-0

Poor Folk. Trans. by Robert Dessaix. Ardis Pubs. 1983 $6.50. ISBN 0-88233-755-6

Short Story Collections by Dostoyevsky

The Best Short Stories of Dostoyevsky. Random 1992 $15.00. ISBN 0-679-60020-5

Great Short Works of Dostoyevsky. HarperC 1968 $7.95. ISBN 0-06-083081-6

Uncle's Dream and Other Stories. Trans. by David McDuff. Viking Penguin 1989 $6.95. ISBN 0-14-044518-8. A fine translation of four works: "Uncle's Dream," "A Weak Heart," "White Nights," and "The Meek Girl"; an introduction by McDuff.

Nonfiction by Dostoyevsky

Complete Letters. 5 Vols. Trans. and ed. by David Lowe. Ardis Pubs. 1988–1991 $35.00 ea. ISBNs 0-88233-897-8, 0-88233-926-5, 0-88233-542-1, 0-88233-543-X, 0-88233-544-8. A masterful series, with admirable translations.

The Notebooks for "The Brothers Karamazov." Ed. by Edward Wasiolek. U. Ch. Pr. 1971 $12.50. ISBN 0-226-15967-1

The Notebooks for "Crime and Punishment." Ed. and trans. by Edward Wasiolek. U. Ch. Pr. 1974 repr. of 1966 ed. $3.95. ISBN 0-226-15960-4

The Notebooks for "The Idiot." Ed. by Edward Wasiolek. Trans. by Katherine Strelsky. U. Ch. Pr. 1973 $2.95. ISBN 0-226-15962-0

The Notebooks for "The Possessed." Ed. by Edward Wasiolek. Trans. by Victor Terras. U. Ch. Pr. 1968 $12.50. ISBN 0-226-15963-9

The Notebooks for "A Raw Youth." Ed. by Edward Wasiolek. Trans. by Victor Terras. U. Ch. Pr. 1969 $15.00. ISBN 0-226-15965-5

Selected Letters of Fyodor Dostoyevsky. Ed. by Joseph Frank and David I. Goldstein. Trans. by Andrew MacAndrew. Rutgers U. Pr. 1987 $29.95. ISBN 0-8135-1185-2. "[A] valuable resource for scholars and admirers of his fiction who don't read Russian . . . (*LJ*).

The Unpublished Dostoyevsky: Diaries and Notebooks 1860–1881. 3 Vols. Trans. and ed. by Carl R. Proffer, David Lapeza and Arline Boyer. Ardis Pubs. 1972–1976 o.p.

The Village of Stepanchikovo and Its Inhabitants. Trans. by Ignat Avsey. Cornell Univ. Pr. 1987 repr. of 1983 ed. $26.95. ISBN 0-8014-2051-2

Winter Notes on Summer Impressions. Trans. by David Patterson. Northwestern U. Pr. 1988 $16.95. ISBN 0-8101-0813-5

A Writer's Diary. 2 Vols. Trans. by Kenneth Lantz. *Studies in Russian Lit. & Theory Ser.* Northwestern U. Pr. 1992 $45.95 ea. ISBN 0-8101-1007-5, 0-8101-1011-3. A new edition of Dostoyevsky's major venture into journalism; diverse subjects; innovative handling of genres.

Books about Dostoyevsky

Bakhtin, Mikhail. *Problems of Dostoevsky's Poetics.* Ed. and trans. by Caryl Emerson. *Theory & History of Lit. Ser.* U. of Minn. Pr. 1984 $39.95. ISBN 0-8166-1227-7. A major contribution to both Dostoyevsky criticism and modern literary theory; a classic. Introduction by Wayne Booth.

Bloom, Harold, ed. *Fyodor Dostoevsky. Modern Critical Views Ser.* Chelsea Hse. 1989 $34.95. ISBN 1-55546-294-4. Introduction by Bloom.

———, ed. *Fyodor Dostoevsky's Brothers Karamazov. Modern Critical Interpretations Ser.* Chelsea Hse. 1987 $29.95. ISBN 1-55546-065-8. Introduction by Bloom.

———, ed. *Fyodor Dostoevsky's Crime and Punishment. Modern Critical Interpretations Ser.* Chelsea Hse. 1987 $24.95. ISBN 1-55546-066-6. Introduction by Bloom.

Catteau, Jacques. *Dostoyevsky and the Process of Literary Creation.* Trans. by Audrey Littlewood. *Cambridge Studies in Russian Lit. Ser.* Cambridge U. Pr. 1989 $75.00. ISBN 0-521-32436-X. ". . . [A] distinguished contribution to Dostoevsky studies . . ." (*SEEJ*).

Cox, Gary. *Tyrant and Victim in Dostoevsky.* Slavica 1984 $13.95. ISBN 0-89357-125-3. Approaches Dostoyevsky's works through a study of the concept of dominance in personal relationships.

Dalton, Elizabeth. *Unconscious Structure in Dostoevsky's "The Idiot": A Study in Literature and Psychoanalysis.* Princeton U. Pr. 1979 $37.50. ISBN 0-691-06364-8. Based on a standard Freudian model; frequently insightful.

Dostoyevsky, Anna. *Dostoyevsky: Reminiscences.* Trans. and ed. by Beatrice Stillman. Liveright 1975 o.p. By Dostoyevsky's second wife. A highly readable account illuminating the later period of his life.

Fanger, Donald. *Dostoevsky and Romantic Realism: A Study of Dostoevsky in Relation to Balzac, Dickens, Gogol.* U. Ch. Pr. 1968 $7.00. ISBN 0-226-23747-8. A study of Dostoyevsky and his literary precursors.

Frank, Joseph. *Dostoevsky: The Seeds of Revolt, 1821–1849.* Princeton U. Pr. 1976 $55.00. ISBN 0-691-06260-9. The first volume of a synthesizing, magisterial study of Dostoyevsky's life and writings.

———. *Dostoevsky: The Stir of Liberation. 1860–1865.* Princeton U. Pr. 1986 $55.00. ISBN 0-691-06652-3. "It is a work of vast erudition and of absorbing interest that can hardly be recommended too highly" (*LJ*).

———. *Dostoevsky: The Years of Ordeal. 1850–1859.* Princeton U. Pr. 1986 $45.00. ISBN 0-691-06576-4. Frank's study "covers a dreary but crucial decade . . . with a total command of available materials, considered with great finesse and insight" (*SEEJ*).

Goldstein, David I. *Dostoyevsky and the Jews.* U. of Tex. Pr. 1981 $20.00. ISBN 0-292-71528-5. Various aspects of Dostoyevsky's strong antipathy; puts his Jewish themes in a broader artistic and ideological framework.

Holquist, Michael. *Dostoevsky and the Novel.* Princeton U. Pr. 1977 $26.50. ISBN 0-691-06342-7. "This is a very ambitious, difficult, irritating, and uneven little book filled with questionable interpretations and genuine insights into Dostoevsky's works" (*Slavic Review*).

Ivanov, Vyacheslav I. *Freedom and the Tragic Life: A Study in Dostoevsky.* Ed. by S. Konovalov. Trans. by Norman Cameron. Hollowbrook 1989 repr. of 1952 ed. $25.00. ISBN 0-89341-554-5. A classic contribution by a symbolist poet and critic; a seminal text in Dostoyevsky criticism.

Jones, Malcolm V. *Dostoyevsky after Bakhtin: Readings in Dostoyevsky's Fantastic Realism.* Cambridge U. Pr. 1990 $39.50. ISBN 0-521-38423-0. A "stimulating journey of discovery, during which Bakhtin's ideas are modified and extended in the light of recent critical theory" (*SEER*).

Kjetsaa, Geir. *Fyodor Dostoyevsky: A Writer's Life.* Trans. by Sigi Hustvedt and David McDuff. Viking Penguin 1987 $24.95. ISBN 0-670-81914-X. "This compact, highly readable biography offers fresh, controversial perspectives on many aspects of Dostoyevsky's life and work" (*PW*).

Leatherbarrow, W. J. *Dostoyevsky: "The Brothers Karamazov". Landmarks of World Lit. Ser.* Cambridge U. Pr. 1992. ISBN 0-521-38424-9

———. *Feodor Dostoevsky: A Reference Guide. Ref. Guide to Lit. Ser.* Macmillan 1990 $40.00. ISBN 0-8161-8941-2

Meyer, Priscilla, and Stephen Rudy, eds. *Dostoevsky and Gogol: Texts and Criticism.* Ardis Pubs. 1979 $11.95. ISBN 0-686-76827-2. Three stories by Gogol and two by Dostoevsky; a selection of criticism dealing with the problems of the two writers' literary relationship.

Miller, Robin F., ed. *Critical Essays on Dostoyevsky. Critical Essays on World Lit. Ser.* G. K. Hall 1986 $40.00. ISBN 0-8161-8828-9

______. *Dostoevsky and The Idiot: Author, Narrator and Reader.* HUP 1981 $25.50. ISBN 0-674-21490-0. A stimulating analysis.

Mochulsky, Konstantin. *Dostoevsky: His Life and Work.* Trans. by Michael A. Minihan. Princeton U. Pr. 1967 $19.95. ISBN 0-691-01299-7. A thorough presentation and analysis of Dostoyevsky's philosophical and theological ideas.

Morson, Gary S. *The Boundaries of Genre: Dostoevsky's "Diary of a Writer" and the Traditions of Literary Utopia.* U. of Tex. Pr. 1981 $25.00. ISBN 0-292-70732-0. A theoretically innovative discussion.

Murav, Harriet. *Holy Foolishness: Dostoevsky's Novels and the Poetics of Cultural Critique.* Stanford U. Pr. 1992 $35.00. ISBN 0-8047-2059-2

Neuville, H. Richmond, Jr. *Monarch Notes on Dostoyevsky's "The Brothers Karamazov".* P-H $3.95. ISBN 0-671-00556-1

Rozanov, Vasily. *Dostoevsky and the Legend of the Grand Inquisitor.* Trans. by Spencer E. Roberts. Cornell Univ. Pr. 1972 $20.00. ISBN 0-8014-0694-3. A classic text of Dostoyevsky criticism from the Silver Age.

Shestov, Lev. *Dostoevsky, Tolstoy and Nietzsche.* Trans. by Bernard Martin and Spencer Roberts. Ohio U. Pr. 1969 o.p. By a noted religious philosopher and critic.

Terras, Victor. *A Karamazov Companion: Commentary on the Genesis, Language, and Style of Dostoevsky's Novel.* U. of Wis. Pr. 1981 $32.50. ISBN 0-299-08310-1. ". . . [T]he perfect guide for a trip through the Karamazov country" (*Slavic Review*).

DOVLATOV, SERGEI. 1941–1990

Dovlatov, who studied at Leningrad University, worked for a while as a journalist in Tallinn, Estonia. His fiction was unpublished in the Soviet Union, but he was active in unofficial literary life and was forced to leave in 1978 for publishing satirical fiction in *samizdat.* After settling in the United States, he cofounded a Russian-language newspaper, worked as a broadcaster for Radio Liberty in New York City, and published both in major Russian émigré publications and in the U.S. press (he wrote short stories for *The New Yorker*). Among his books, known for their irreverent views of Soviet reality, are the autobiographical *The Compromise* (1981) and *Ours* (1983). When Dovlatov died, his works were being reissued and favorably received in Russia.

Novels by Dovlatov

A Foreign Woman. Grove Pr. 1991 $17.95. ISBN 0-8021-1342-7. About Russian émigrés in New York. "Entertaining as well as politically relevant, this novel shows that life is finally what we make it, USSR or USA" (*LJ*).

The Invisible Book: Epilogue. Trans. by Katherine O'Connor. Ardis Pubs. 1979 o.p.

The Zone: A Prison Camp Guard's Story. Trans. by Anne Frydman. Knopf 1985 $14.95. ISBN 0-394-53522-7

Short Story Collections by Dovlatov

The Compromise. Trans. by Anne Frydman. Academy Chi. Pubs. 1990 repr. of 1983 ed. $7.95. ISBN 0-89733-353-5. Eleven stories; the translation is particularly successful.

Ours: A Russian Family Album. Trans. by Anne Frydman. Grove Pr. 1989 o.p. Autobiographical; well translated. "[P]rovides an engaging glimpse of four generations of a Soviet family that suffered relatively little, even under Stalin, and enjoyed considerable upward mobility" (*LJ*).

The Suitcase. Trans. by Antonina W. Bouis. Grove Pr. 1990 $16.95. ISBN 0-8021-1246-3. Linked tales about the circumstances under which the author acquired the eight items he brought with him in his suitcase when he emigrated to the United States.

EHRENBURG (ERENBURG), ILYA. 1891–1967

Extremely widely traveled, Ehrenburg was a versatile if uneven writer, poet, and journalist. Familiar with an extraordinary range of people in Russia and Western Europe, he survived the Stalin era to bear witness to the losses suffered by Russian culture: His memoirs, *People, Years, Life* (1961–65), introduced a younger generation to a host of annihilated and forgotten literary and artistic figures. Of his novels, the first, *Julio Jurenito* (1922), a biting satire of the West, is usually regarded as his best. A later work, *The Thaw* (1954), is his best known. Its cautious yet deliberate deviation from Stalinist norms in literature signaled broader changes in Soviet society. The title became a designation for the immediate post-Stalin period and a generic label for any subsequent moments of liberalization in Soviet life.

NOVELS BY EHRENBURG

Julio Jurenito. 1922. Trans. by Anna Bostok and Yvonne Kapp. Greenwood 1976 o.p.

The Life of the Automobile. Trans. by Joachim Neugroschel. Serpent's Tail UK 1990 $9.95. ISBN 1-852421-30-4

Ninth Wave. Trans. by Tatiana Shebunina and Joseph Castle. Greenwood 1974 repr. of 1955 ed. $69.50. ISBN 0-8371-7672-7

In One Newspaper. Coauthored with Konstantin Simonov. Trans. by Anatol Kagan. Sphinx Pr. 1985 $24.95. ISBN 0-943071-02-X

NONFICTION BY EHRENBURG

Ilya Ehrenburg: Selections from People, Years and Life. Ed. by C. Moody. Pergamon 1972 $115.00. ISBN 0-08-006354-3. A sampler of Ehrenburg's important memoirs.

BOOK ABOUT EHRENBURG

Klimenko, Michael. *Ehrenburg: An Attempt at a Literary Portrait.* P. Lang Pubs. 1990 $57.00. ISBN 0-8204-1122-1. A survey of Ehrenburg's life and works; judged to be "very seriously flawed" (*SEER*).

EROFEEV, VENEDIKT. 1938 or 1939–

Although educated as a philologist, Erofeev held a variety of menial jobs, circulating some of his works in *samizdat.* His reputation rests on the tragifarcical *Moscow-Petushki* (*Moscow to the End of the Line*), written in 1969 and first published in the West in 1977. This text represents a confession by a drunken narrator who recounts a train ride from Moscow to one of its suburbs, in the process mocking a host of shibboleths in Soviet culture. The author interweaves numerous cultural allusions into the sometimes scatological ramblings of the protagonist, and the work may be interpreted as a modern variant on the passion of Christ. The book has been published in the Soviet Union during the period of *glasnost.*

NOVEL BY EROFEEV

Moscow to the End of the Line. 1969. Trans. by William H. Tjalsma. Northwestern U. Pr. 1992 repr. of 1980 ed. $9.95. ISBN 0-8101-1078-4. Introduction by Vera S. Dunham.

ESENIN, SERGEI. 1895–1925

Esenin achieved worldwide notoriety when he married the dancer Isadora Duncan (see Vol. 3) in 1922. His literary reputation has a more substantive basis. Brought up in peasant traditions and initially influenced by the symbolists, his early works are filled with folk and religious themes. After the October Revolution, Esenin's hopes for a new Russia brought to his writing strong messianic expectations. He became leader of a group that emphasized bold, often outrageous imagery as the key to poetry. His works are often rough in both language and imagery, and their contents echo Esenin's bohemian life-style, as in the poetic cycle *Moscow of the Taverns* (1921–24). Even though the authorities and other writers often harshly criticized Esenin, he was very popular with readers. Personal instability, especially his alcoholism, and doubts about his role in the new society led to his suicide by hanging in a Leningrad hotel.

Poetry by Esenin

Confessions of a Hooligan. Trans. by Geoffrey Thurley. Humanities 1973 o.p.

Books about Esenin

Davies, Jessie, ed. and trans. *Esenin: A Biography in Memoirs, Letters, & Documents.* Ardis Pubs. 1982 o.p. "One is hard put to imagine a more effective introduction to Sergei Esenin than this volume" (*Russian Review*).

McVay, Gordon. *Esenin: A Life.* Paragon Hse. 1988 o.p. Both the McVay studies are authoritative and based on extensive archival materials.

______. *Isadora and Esenin.* Ardis Pubs. 1980 $7.50. ISBN 0-88233-338-0. "The value of the book lies in its wealth of documentation and its judicious evaluation of old myths" (*Russian Review*).

FEDIN, KONSTANTIN. 1892–1977

In his early novels, Fedin expressed a certain nostalgia for the passing of the pre-revolutionary way of life. *Cities and Years* (1924) handles this theme by means of deft manipulation of the flow of time. In later works, trying to comply with the dictates of socialist realism, Fedin became more optimistic. *Early Joys* (1946) and *No Ordinary Summer* (1948) falsify history and mythologize Stalin; not surprisingly, their author was awarded the Stalin Prize. During the 1960s, as head of the Union of Soviet Writers and a committed champion of political orthodoxy, Fedin helped to prevent the publication of Solzhenitsyn's *Cancer Ward*, an act condemned by liberal writers and intellectuals.

Novel by Fedin

Cities and Years. 1924. Trans. by Michael Scammell. Northwestern U. Pr. 1992 repr. of 1962 ed. $15.95. ISBN 0-8101-1066-0. Introduction by Scammell.

FURMANOV, DMITRY. 1891–1926

Furmanov earned a place for himself in Soviet literature with *Chapayev* (1923). In part a novel, in part a documentary, this work is based on the author's experiences as a political commissar with the forces of Chapayev, a Bolshevik guerilla leader in the Urals. Furmanov glorified his protagonist as a kind of folk hero, successfully capturing his psychology. The book was subsequently made into a very popular film, which, in turn, sparked a whole series of anecdotes that persisted for decades in Soviet culture.

Novel by Furmanov

Chapayev. Ed. by O. Gorchakov. Trans. by George Kittell and Jeanette Kittell. *Soviet Lit. in Eng. Trans. Ser.* Hyperion Conn. 1973 repr. of 1935 ed. $25.00. ISBN 0-88355-004-0

GALICH, ALEKSANDR (pseud. of GINZBURG). 1918–1977

Galich began as a playwright after World War II; later he also wrote screenplays. During the 1960s and 1970s, along with Bulat Okudzhava and Vladimir Vysotsky, he achieved great fame as one of the most popular unofficial "bards," writing and performing his poem-songs to his own guitar accompaniment. Though they were never published, recordings of his concerts circulated widely on cassette. Galich's modes range from the satirical to the tragic, and he covers such subjects as the fate of Russian writers, the Holocaust, and the situation of Soviet Jews. He was expelled from the Union of Writers in 1971, emigrated to Europe in 1974, traveled widely on concert tours for émigré audiences, and died in Paris in an accident. In recent years, recordings of his songs and collections of the texts have been issued in the Soviet Union.

Work by Galich

Songs and Poems. Trans. by Gerry Smith. Ardis Pubs. 1983 o.p. A good selection of songs and poems by Galich, edited by a leading scholar of the underground Russian "bards."

GARSHIN, VSEVOLOD. 1855–1888

Although his literary output consists of only about 20 short stories, Garshin was a very talented writer, with a great moral sensitivity and compassion for human suffering—qualities that were given a special stimulus by his army experiences during the 1877 war with Turkey. The war is reflected in "Four Days" (1877), a popular story of a wounded soldier who for four days remains on the battlefield next to the putrefying corpse of a Turk.

In spite of his literary reputation, Garshin grew increasingly morbid in his last years and ultimately committed suicide by throwing himself down a staircase. Of his stories, the best are the romantic "Attalea Princeps" (1880), a fable about a palm tree, and "The Red Flower" (1883), about an inmate of an insane asylum and, more broadly, about the problem of evil.

Short Story Collection by Garshin

From the Reminiscences of Private Ivanov, & Other Stories. Trans. by Peter Henry, Liv Tudge,, Donald Rayfield, and Phillip Taylor. Dufour 1988 $30.00. ISBN 0-946162-08-5. Introduction by Peter Henry.

Book about Garshin

Henry, Peter. *A Hamlet of His Time: Vsevolod Garshin. The Man, His Works, and His Milieu*. Willem A. Meeuws 1983 o.p. "This book is one of the most extensive treatments of Garshin in any language . . . complements Edmund Yarwood's *Vsevolod Garshin* . . ." (*SEEJ*).

Yarwood, Edmund. *Vsevolod Garshin. World Authors Ser.* Macmillan 1981 o.p. Contains a well-written, informative introduction; discusses Garshin's debt to, and impact on, other writers.

GLADILIN, ANATOLY. 1935–

Gladilin's first work was published in 1956 in the liberal literary magazine *Yunost'* (*Youth*); numerous books and journal publications followed. His concerns are typical of the "new voices" generation of the 1960s, his heroes usually young men dealing with both personal and ethical problems. Gladilin left the Soviet Union in 1976 after one of his novels was rejected by the censor, circulated in *samizdat,* and published in the West. Since then, he has been very active in émigré literary life. The witty *Moscow Racetrack* was published in Russian in 1983. *The Making and Unmaking of a Soviet Writer* (1979) is an autobiographical account of the pressures of Soviet literary life.

Novel by Gladilin

Moscow Racetrack. Trans. by R. P. Schoenberg and Janet G. Tucker. Ardis Pubs. 1990 $21.50. ISBN 0-87501-064-4. "Penetrating, illuminating, cynical and fascinating . . . [it] is not only the study of a committed gambler's mind. . . . It is also a microcosm of modern Russia" (*NYT Book Review*).

Nonfiction by Gladilin

The Making and Unmaking of a Soviet Writer. Trans. by David Lapeza. Ardis Pubs. 1979 $3.50. ISBN 0-88233-355-0

GLADKOV, FYODOR. 1883–1958

Gladkov began to write after 1922, when he first participated in so-called proletarian literary organizations. *Cement* (1925), his most famous work, deals with the transition from the civil war period to the postwar reconstruction of industry and society. The title refers to a cement plant that, after many obstacles are overcome, is put back into production. Gladkov idealizes and romanticizes the novel's protagonists, yet writes with some vigor and attempt at balance. Over the years, the novel, which became a classic of socialist realism, was revised several times. Responding to prevailing political and literary trends, he made its contents increasingly bloodless.

Gladkov subsequently moved away from the romanticism of *Cement.* His later works include a "five-year plan" novel, *Energy* (1932–38), and a three-volume autobiography.

Novels by Gladkov

Cement: A Novel. Trans. by A. S. Arthur and C. Ashleigh. Continuum 1985 $11.95. ISBN 0-8044-6178-3

Restless Youth. Trans. by R. Parker and V. Scott. *Soviet Lit. in Eng. Trans. Ser.* Hyperion Conn. 1976 repr. of 1958 ed. $21.00. ISBN 0-88355-403-8

GOGOL, NIKOLAI. 1809–1852

A Ukrainian by background, Gogol was one of Russia's greatest writers, unsurpassed in imagination, comic wit, and boldness of fictional design. After trying to establish himself in different professions, he achieved a major success with a volume of stories based on Ukrainian life and folklore, *Evenings on a Farm near Dikanka* (1831–32). Two additional collections were also successful: *Mirgorod* (1835) and *Arabesques* (1835).

During this early period, Gogol was in close contact with various groups of Russian intellectuals and literary figures, including Pushkin. Subsequently, he drew ever closer to the Slavophiles, sharing their belief that Russia's national salvation lay in preserving patriarchal traditions.

His next great success came with the 1836 premiere of the comedy *The Inspector General* (also translated as *The Government Inspector*). Although its satirization of provincial bureaucracy raised a storm of official protest, the play established Gogol as a writer of genius and has remained one of the pillars of

Russian repertoire. Soon afterward he left Russia, from 1836 to 1848, living abroad almost entirely. During this period, he produced several new works, among them "The Overcoat" (1842), perhaps the most influential Russian short story ever written, and the first part of *Dead Souls* (1842).

After 1842 Gogol grew ever more troubled. Certain negative traits began to dominate his personality. A belief in his personal mission to save Russia, faintly present even in some early writings, came to the fore in *Selected Passages from Correspondence with Friends* (1846). The book was derided in Russia. Partly in response to this, Gogol turned toward a fanatical, mystical brand of Christianity and embraced ascetic practices that ruined his health and upset his psychological balance. The combined mental and physical deterioration had a particularly tragic result in February 1852, when he had his servant burn the unpublished manuscripts for the second part of *Dead Souls*. He died shortly afterward.

Generations of readers, writers, and critics have interpreted Gogol in different, often contradictory ways. All of these views find support in his literary heritage, full of enigmas and possibilities. Claimed as a founder of realism, he also has been considered a romantic and was an object of special interest for the symbolists. His early collections are infused with folklore, with its lyric and comic anecdotes of devils, witches, and young lovers. Subsequently, the fantastic is transferred to the cold, bureaucratic world of St. Petersburg, where the demonic assumes a more serious form, acquiring a philosophical dimension. Gogol was a social critic, frequently concerned for the victims of hierarchical inequality ("The Overcoat"), yet he was also the creator of grotesque, puzzling plots that defy rational interpretation ("The Nose" [1836]) and of flawed protagonists who are to a degree responsible for their own misery. Claimed for their own by both liberals and conservatives, he expressed a concern for Russia's future in exceptionally powerful images that have permanently entered the storehouse of national symbols (the galloping troika in *Dead Souls*) and have shaped the Russians' discourse about their culture.

Achieving an equivalent in English for Gogol's rich verbal style has proved difficult. Existing translations are accurate but lack the effervescence of the original.

NOVELS BY GOGOL

Dead Souls. Ed. by George Gibian. *Critical Ed. Ser.* Norton 1986 $14.95. ISBN 0-383-95292-4. Accompanied by a selection of good critical studies.

Dead Souls. Trans. by David Magarshack. *Penguin Classics Ser.* Viking Penguin 1961 $4.95. ISBN 0-14-044113-1

Dead Souls. Buccaneer Bks. 1992 Repr. Lib. Bdg. $17.95. ISBN 0-89966-925-5

Taras Bulba. Amereon Ltd. $13.95. ISBN 0-88411-138-5

SHORT STORY COLLECTIONS BY GOGOL

Arabesques. Trans. by Alexander Tulloch. Ardis Pubs. 1982 $6.00. ISBN 0-88233-436-0

The Complete Tales of Nikolai Gogol. 2 vols. Ed. by Leonard Kent. U. Ch. Pr. 1985 repr. of 1964 ed. Vol. 1 $11.95. ISBN 0-226-30068-4. Vol 2 $12.95. ISBN 0-226-30069-2

Diary of a Madman. Trans. by Ronald Wilks. *Penguin Classics Ser.* Viking Penguin 1973 $4.95. ISBN 0-14-044273-1

Mirgorod: Four Tales. Trans. by David Magarshack. *Funk and W. Bk. Ser.* T. Y. Crowell 1969 o.p.

The Overcoat and Other Short Stories. *Thrift Ed. Ser.* Dover 1992 $1.00. ISBN 0-486-27057-2

The Overcoat and Other Tales of Good & Evil. Trans. by David Magarshack. Bentley 1979 repr. of 1965 ed. $20.00. ISBN 0-8376-0442-7

Plays by Gogol

The Government Inspector. Ed. by Peter Raby. Trans. by Leonid Ignatief. Bks. Demand repr. of 1972 ed. $32.00. ISBN 0-317-28151-8

The Inspector General. NTC Pub. Grp. 1991 $10.95. ISBN 0-8442-4237-3

Inspector and Other Plays. Trans. by Eric Bentley. Applause Theatre Bk. Pubs. 1987 $8.95. ISBN 0-936839-12-0. Introduction by Bentley.

The Theater of Nikolay Gogol. Trans. by Milton Ehre and Fruma Gottschalk. U. Ch. Pr. 1982 $18.50. ISBN 0-226-30064-1. Brings together Gogol's major plays and his main writings about the theater; accurate translations and very helpful annotations.

Nonfiction by Gogol

Hanz Kuechelgarten, Leaving the Theater and Other Works. Ed. by Ronald Meyer. Ardis Pubs. 1990 $27.95. ISBN 0-88233-822-6. An anthology of diverse, previously untranslated Gogol writings, including his first, unsuccessful poem, reviews and essays, and a selection of letters.

Letters of Nikolai Gogol. Ed. by Carl R. Proffer. U. of Mich. Pr. 1967 o.p.

Selected Passages from Correspondence with Friends. Trans. by Jesse Zeldin. Vanderbilt U. Pr. 1969 $14.95. ISBN 0-8265-1126-0. Thirty-two essays, adequately translated; lengthy introduction.

Books about Gogol

Erlich, Victor. *Gogol. Russian & East European Studies Ser.* Yale U. Pr. 1969 o.p. Lively, well written; some gaps; contains an introduction.

Fanger, Donald. *The Creation of Nikolai Gogol.* HUP 1979 $25.50. ISBN 0-674-17565-4. A sophisticated analysis of Gogol's fiction; a major study that seeks "to determine how the Gogolian text has produced the wealth of disparate readings that constitute Gogol scholarship"; "Fanger interprets in rigorous, principled fashion Gogol's work, life, and times" (*Russian Review*).

Frantz, Philip. *Gogol Bibliography.* Ardis Pubs. 1989 $35.00. ISBN 0-88233-809-9

Fusso, Susanne. *Designing "Dead Souls": An Anatomy of Disorder in Gogol.* Stanford U. Pr. 1993 $32.50. ISBN 0-8047-2049-5

Fusso, Susanne, and Priscilla Meyer, eds. *Essays on Gogol: Logos and the Russian Word. Studies in Russian Lit. & Theory Ser.* Northwestern U. Pr. 1992 $34.95. ISBN 0-8101-1009-1

Gippius, V. V. *Gogol.* Ed. and trans. by Robert A. Maguire. *Sources & Trans. Ser. of the Harriman Inst.* Duke 1989 repr. of 1981 ed. $14.95. ISBN 0-8223-0907-6. A classic study by an excellent Russian critic of the early twentieth century.

Grayson, Jane, and Faith Wigzell, eds. *Nikolay Gogol.* St. Martin 1988 $35.00. ISBN 0-312-01696-4

Karlinsky, Simon. *The Sexual Labyrinth of Nikolai Gogol.* HUP 1976 $25.50. ISBN 0-674-80281-0. ". . . [T]his is a major book that once and for all establishes the presence and pervasiveness of Gogol's homosexuality" (*SEEJ*).

Maguire, Robert A., ed. *Gogol from the Twentieth Century: Eleven Essays.* Princeton U. Pr. 1974 $55.00. ISBN 0-691-06268-4. An excellent sampling of studies by various Russian critics; well translated and well annotated.

Nabokov, Vladimir. *Nikolai Gogol.* New Dir. Pr. 1961 $8.95. ISBN 0-8112-0120-1. Idiosyncratic, but an interesting, empathic view by a writer of equal stature.

Peace, Richard. *The Enigma of Gogol. Cambridge Studies in Russian Lit. Ser.* Cambridge U. Pr. 1982 $64.95. ISBN 0-521-23824-2

Rancour-Laferriere, Daniel. *Out from under Gogol's "Overcoat".* Ardis Pubs. 1982 o.p. A psychoanalytic approach.

Setchkarev, Vsevolod. *Gogol: His Life and Works.* Trans. by Robert Kramer, *Gotham Lib. Ser.* NYU Pr. 1965 o.p. A solid life-and-works monograph.

Stilman, Leon. *Gogol.* Ed. by Galina Stilman. Hermitage 1990 $15.00. ISBN 1-55779-035-3. A biographical study.

Trahan, Elizabeth, ed. *Gogol's "Overcoat": An Anthology of Critical Essays.* Ardis Pubs. 1981 $5.00. ISBN 0-686-85662-7. Five major studies, slanted toward an "anti-humanitarian" interpretation of this classic story.

Vinogradov, V. V. *Gogol and the Natural School.* Trans. by D. Ericksen and R. Parrott. Ardis Pubs. 1987 o.p. An early study by a major Russian linguist and literary scholar, situating Gogol's fiction in the context of early realism.

Waszink, P. M. *Such Things Happen in the World: Deixis in Three Short Stories by N. V. Gogol. Studies in Slavic Lit. & Poetics Ser.* Rodopi 1988 $125.00. ISBN 90-5183-026-2. Analyzes the linguistic-logical organization of Gogol's narrative.

Woodward, James B. *Gogol's Dead Souls.* Princeton U. Pr. 1978 $45.00. ISBN 0-691-06360-5. "Woodward studies the text very closely . . . a rich, creative, and unique contribution . . ." (*SEEJ*).

———. *The Symbolic Art of Gogol: Essays on His Short Fiction.* Slavica 1982 $18.95. ISBN 0-89357-093-1. A detailed study of the key stories; an "Outstanding Academic Book" selection for 1982 by *Choice.*

Zeldin, Jesse. *Nikolai Gogol's Quest for Beauty: An Exploration into His Works.* U. Pr. of KS 1978 $25.00. ISBN 0-7006-0173-2. Zeldin claims that there is "a unity in Gogol's perspective unaffected by ideological crises" (*SEEJ*).

GONCHAROV, IVAN. 1812–1891

Born into a wealthy merchant family, Goncharov pursued a career in the civil service, first in the ministry of finance, and later, during more liberal times after 1855, in the censorship department. Most of his life was very placid, troubled only once by an extended sea voyage to Japan, which resulted in a smoothly written travel narrative. *The Frigate Pallas* (1855–57). In his later years, he suffered from paranoia, having become obsessed with the notion that IVAN TURGENEV and such foreign writers as FLAUBERT had plagiarized elements of his last work.

Goncharov's solid reputation as a major realist writer rests, above all, on his second novel, *Oblomov* (1859). The fame of this work derives from its unmatched depiction of human slothfulness and boredom, embodied in the book's likable hero. Oblomov is now a literary and cultural archetype, while the term *Oblomovism* has entered the Russian language, denoting indolence and inertia of epic proportions. Goncharov's other works are of lesser stature. *A Common Story* (1847) is an entertaining *bildungsroman* about a young man's gradual abandonment of his early ideals. *The Precipice* (1869), on which Goncharov worked for almost 20 years, is a massive portrayal of gentry life in the country. Although its antiradical plot is not terribly successful, the book contains a gallery of striking social and psychological types: Particularly memorable are the novel's women.

NOVELS BY GONCHAROV

Oblomov. Trans. by Natalie Duddington. Buccaneer Bks. 1990 $28.95. ISBN 0-89966-685-X

An Ordinary Story. Trans. by Marjorie L. Hoover. Ardis Pubs. 1993 $27.95. ISBN 0-87501-088-1. A new translation that includes the text of the 1966 theatrical adaptation.

The Precipice. Trans. by Laury Magnus and Boris Jakim. Ardis Pubs. 1992 $39.95. ISBN 0-87501-096-2. The first complete translation of Goncharov's ultimate novel.

BOOKS ABOUT GONCHAROV

Ehre, Milton. *Oblomov and His Creator: The Life and Art of Ivan Goncharov.* Princeton U. Pr. 1974 $45.00. ISBN 0-691-06245-5. ". . . [O]riginal, frequently brilliant insights . . . an embarrassment of interpretation" (*SEEJ*).

Setchkarev, Vsevolod. *Ivan Goncharov: His Life and His Works. Colloquium Slavicum Ser.* Humanities 1974 o.p. A "straightforward life-and-works study . . . it can be said to amplify, even though it does not properly outweigh" Ehre's book (*SEEJ*).

GORENSTEIN (GORENSHTEIN), FRIEDRICH. 1932–

Gorenstein, whose father was executed in the 1930s, comes from Kiev. During the period 1952–62, he worked as a miner and an engineer, publishing his first short story in 1964. Most of his early fiction, however, went unpublished, although at the same time he was writing screenplays. Since emigrating and settling in West Germany in 1980, he has published extensively in émigré periodicals. Gorenstein is regarded as a very talented though uneven writer. The novella *The Street of Red Dawns* (1985) and the novel *Expiation* (1984) rank among his best works.

Novel by Gorenstein

Traveling Companions. HarBraceJ 1991 $21.95. ISBN 0-15-191074-X. A "seemingly casual tale [punctuated] with digressions on the perils of ideology, Ukrainian anti-Semitism, sex in literature, his dislike of Russians and much else" (*PW*).

GORKY (GORKI), MAXIM (pseud. of Aleksey Peshkov). 1868–1936

Until the recent collapse of the Soviet state, Gorky was officially viewed as the greatest Russian writer of the twentieth century—an evaluation far above the true measure of his nevertheless considerable talent. Proclaimed the founder of socialist realism, he significantly influenced many Soviet writers as well as others in Europe and in the developing world, and his works were for decades part of the Soviet school curriculum.

His formal education was minimal. From the age of 11, he fended for himself with a variety of jobs. Self-taught, he published his first story, "Makar Chudra," in 1892. His first collection, *Sketches and Stories* (1898), is a romantic celebration of society's strong outcasts—the hobos and the drifters—and helped to popularize such literary protagonists. *Foma Gordeyev* (1899), Gorky's first novel, depicts generational conflict within the Russian bourgeoisie.

A popular public figure on the left, Gorky was often in trouble with the tsarist government. During the 1900s, he was the central figure in the Znanie publishing house, which produced realist prose with a social conscience. Some of his own works were extremely successful. The play *The Lower Depths* (1902), set in a poorhouse and a strong indictment of social injustice, was not only a staple of Soviet theater but also influential in the United States. Eugene O'Neill's (see Vol. 1) *The Iceman Cometh* was influenced by it. The propagandistic, extraordinarily influential novel *Mother* (1906) presents an iconic working-class woman who is transformed into a saint of the Revolution; its optimism in the ultimate triumph of the cause made it a prototype of socialist-realist fiction. During the years prior to 1917, Gorky published a number of autobiographical stories, *All Over Russia* (1912–18) (also *Through Russia*) and his memoirs, *My Childhood* (1913–14), *My Apprenticeship* (1915–16), and *My Universities* (1923). This trilogy shows his art at its best and includes some very lively reminiscences of such writers as Tolstoy and Chekhov.

Although a Bolshevik party member since 1905, Gorky strongly criticized the new regime after the October Revolution: His collected articles from 1917-18, *Untimely Thoughts*, remained unpublished in the Soviet Union until recently. A cultural activist, he helped to save the lives of many writers, artists, and scholars during the cold and hungry years of the civil war. In 1921 he left Russia for Italy but returned permanently a decade later, recognized as the grand old man of Soviet literature. He then worked for Stalin's economic policies and presided over the institutionalization of socialist realism. At his death, he left unfinished a major novel of considerable interest, *The Life of Klim Samgin*, which he had been working on since 1925.

NOVELS BY GORKY

Foma Gordeyev. Greenwood 1974 repr. of 1956 ed. $45.00. ISBN 0-8371-7670-0

The Life of a Useless Man. Trans. by Maura Budberg. Carroll & Graf 1990 $10.95. ISBN 0-88184-647-3

Mother: The Great Revolutionary Novel. Trans. by Isidore Schneider. Carol Pub. Group 1992 $12.95. ISBN 0-8065-0890-6. Introduction by Howard Fast.

SHORT STORY COLLECTIONS BY GORKY

Orloff and His Wife: Tales of the Barefoot Brigade. Trans. by Isabel F. Hapgood. *Short Story Index Repr. Ser.* Ayer 1973 repr. of 1901 ed. $29.00. ISBN 0-8369-4232-9

Outcasts and Other Stories. Short Story Index Repr. Ser. Ayer 1905 $18.00. ISBN 0-8369-3393-1

Selected Short Stories. Beekman Pubs. 1975 $16.95. ISBN 0-8464-0834-1

Selected Stories. Imported Pubns. 1981 $4.00. ISBN 0-8285-2521-8

Stories of the Steppe. Short Story Index Repr. Ser. Ayer 1918 $10.00. ISBN 0-8369-3508-X

Tales of Two Countries. Short Story Index Repr. Ser. Ayer repr. of 1914 ed. $15.00. ISBN 0-8369-3912-3

Twenty-Six and One: And Other Stories. Pref. by Ivan Strannik. *Short Story Index Repr. Ser.* Ayer 1973 repr. of 1902 ed. $15.00. ISBN 0-8369-4233-7

NONFICTION BY GORKY

The Autobiography of Maxim Gorky. 3 vols. in 1. Trans. by Isidore Schneider. Carol Pub. Group 1969 repr. of 1949 ed. $5.95. ISBN 0-8065-0199-5

Culture and the People. Select Bib. Reprint Ser. Ayer repr. of 1939 ed. $19.00. ISBN 0-8369-5373-8

Decadence. Trans. by Veronica Dewey. U. of Nebr. Pr. 1984 repr. of 1927 ed. $8.95. ISBN 0-8032-7012-7. Foreword by Irwin Weil.

Fragments from My Diary. Trans. by Moura Budberg. Viking Penguin 1986 $4.95. ISBN 0-14-044467-X. "The translation is professional . . . the whole work conveying the translator's undisguised respect and admiration for Gorky" (*SEEJ*).

My Apprenticeship. Viking Penguin 1990 $6.95. ISBN 0-14-018284-5

My Childhood. Trans. by Ronald Wilks. *Penguin Classics Ser.* Viking Penguin 1966 $4.95. ISBN 0-14-044178-6

My Universities. Trans. by Ronald Wilks. *Viking Classics Ser.* Viking Penguin 1979 $5.95. ISBN 0-14-044302-9

On Literature. Beekman Pubs. 1975 $22.95. ISBN 0-8464-0684-5. Selection of reminiscences, articles, letters; lively, well translated.

Reminiscences of Tolstoy, Chekhov and Andreev. Humanities 1968 o.p.

Through Russia. Biblio. Dist. 1959 o.p.

Untimely Thoughts. Trans. by Herman Ermolaev. Eriksson 1968 $6.95. ISBN 0-8397-8500-3

PLAYS BY GORKY

Enemies: A Play. 1906. Trans. by Jeremy Brooks and Kitty Hunter-Blair. Viking Penguin 1972 o.p. Features a highly politicized, class-based plot; introduction by Edward Braun.

Gorky: Five Plays. Trans. by Jeremy Brooks and Kitty Hunter-Blair. Heinemann Ed. 1988 $11.95. ISBN 0-413-18110-3. Introduction by Edward Braun.

The Lower Depths and Other Plays. Trans. by Alexander Bakshy and Paul S. Nathan. Yale U. Pr. 1959 $10.00. ISBN 0-300-00100-2

Plays. Imported Pubns. 1975 $6.45. ISBN 0-8285-0980-8

BOOKS ABOUT GORKY

Clowes, Edith W. *Maksim Gorky: A Reference Guide*. Macmillan 1987 $40.00. ISBN 0-8161-8722-3

Hare, Richard. *Maxim Gorky: Romantic Realist and Conservative Revolutionary*. Greenwood 1978 o.p.

Levin, Daniel L. *Stormy Petrel: The Life and Work of Maxim Gorky*. Schocken 1986 $15.95. ISBN 0-8052-0788-0

Scherr, Barry P. *Maxim Gorky*. *World Authors Ser*. Macmillan 1988 $25.95. ISBN 0-8057-6636-7. A very good introduction to the writer.

Wolfe, Bertram D. *The Bridge and the Abyss: The Troubled Friendship of Maxim Gorky and V. I. Lenin*. Greenwood 1983 repr. of 1967 ed. $39.75. ISBN 0-313-23868-5. Wolfe treats Gorky's complex political relationship to Lenin and Russian social democracy.

GREKOVA, IRINA (pseud. of Elena Venttsel). 1907–

A distinguished professional mathematician, Grekova has been publishing short stories and novellas since 1962. She has raised important moral problems: "Ladies' Hairdresser" (1963) depicts a young, charmingly naive protagonist who approaches his first work in the beauty parlor as a creative artist and finds himself persecuted for nonconformism by the management and his colleagues. Grekova's language is witty and polished, and her tales use the perspective of a professional, urban woman—an unusual narrator in Soviet prose.

SHORT STORY COLLECTION BY GREKOVA

Russian Women: Two Stories. Trans. by Lynn Visson. HarbraceJ 1984 o.p. Contains "Ladies' Hairdresser" and "The Hotel Manager"; introduction by Maurice Friedberg.

GRIBOYEDOV (GRIBOEDOV), ALEKSANDR. 1795–1829

Griboyedov, who came from a gentry family, studied at Moscow University at an early age, served in the army during the War of 1812, and became a professional diplomat. He is celebrated for one play, *Woe from Wit* (*The Woes of Wit*), which followed several minor efforts. Completed sometime during the period 1823–24, published with cuts in 1833 and in full only in 1861, the play is a great classic of the Russian stage. It presents a devastatingly funny picture of contemporary, conservative Moscow society, as well as a gallery of unforgettable personalities, including the protagonist, Chatsky (an early "superfluous man"), and his rival, the time-server Molchalin. Written in brilliantly supple and sparkling verse, many of the play's lines have become popular proverbs and sayings.

Griboyedov was quite successful as a diplomat. He served in the Caucasus, negotiated a peace treaty with Persia in 1828, and was promoted to the post of minister to Teheran. There, soon after his arrival in January 1829, he was killed by a mob of fanatics who, incited by a minor incident, stormed the Russian legation.

PLAY BY GRIBOYEDOV

The Woes of Wit. Trans. by Alan Shaw. Hermitage. 1992 $10.00. ISBN 1-55779-043-4. "Alan Shaw . . . eases us into Griboyedov's satiric world, a great deal of manic comic vitality transpires, and the targets of satire are made entirely clear" (Richard Wilbur).

GROSSMAN, VASILY. 1905–1964

Grossman, a graduate in physics and mathematics from Moscow University, worked first as a chemical engineer and became a published writer during the mid-1930s. His early stories and novel deal with such politically orthodox themes as the struggle against the tsarist regime, the civil war, and the building of the new society. Grossman served as a war correspondent during World War II, publishing a series of sketches and stories about his experiences. Along with EHRENBURG, he edited the suppressed documentary volume on the fate of Soviet Jews, *The Black Book*. In 1952 the first part of his new novel, *For the Good of the Cause*, appeared and was sharply criticized for its depiction of the war. The censor rejected another novel, *Forever Flowing* (1955), which was circulated in *samizdat* and published in the West. The secret police confiscated a sequel to *For the Good of the Cause*, the novel *Life and Fate*, in 1961, but a copy was smuggled abroad and published in 1970. Grossman's books were issued in the Soviet Union in the late 1980s and have met with both admiration and, on part of the nationalist right wing, considerable hostility.

NOVELS BY GROSSMAN

Forever Flowing. Trans. by Thomas P. Whitney. HarpC 1986 o.p.

Life and Fate. Trans. by Robert Chandler. HarpC 1986 o.p. "Grossman uses one family's experiences of the months of the Stalingrad campaign to show the entire mad tapestry woven by Stalin and Hitler" (*LJ*).

NONFICTION BY GROSSMAN

The Black Book. Ed. with Ilya Ehrenburg. Holocaust Pubns. 1980 $24.95. ISBN 0-89604-031-3

HERZEN (GERTSEN), ALEKSANDR. 1812–1870

Herzen's primary importance in literature is his role in Russia's political and intellectual history. During the 1830s, with his friend N. Ogaryov, he became the center of a university circle whose members were developing utopian socialist theory. During the 1840s he helped shape the ideas of Russian Westernism. However, he also wrote fiction. His novel *Who Is to Blame?* (1847) presents a woman caught between two men. All three are unable to find a place for themselves in Russian society and, in line with Herzen's ideas about individual dignity and freedom, are responsible for their own unhappiness.

After leaving Russia in 1847, Herzen became active in European revolutionary movements. Their failure produced *From the Other Shore* (1855), a collection of essays and dialogues on historical subjects. But his masterpiece is his memoirs, *My Past and Thoughts*, a unique combination of reminiscences, analyses, and anecdotes on which he worked from 1852 until 1868. Yet another achievement was *The Bell* (*Kolokol*), a weekly publication that Herzen produced for a decade and that had an enormous influence on both government and society in Russia from 1857 to 1861.

Like many radical thinkers of the time (Vissarion Belinsky, NIKOLAY CHERNYSHEVSKY, and others), Herzen combined political and literary interests. Unlike them, however, he never lost his sensitivity of feeling and style, directing his irony at his allies as well as his adversaries. In this he was exceptional in Russian nineteenth-century letters.

NOVEL BY HERZEN

Who Is to Blame? Trans. by Michael R. Katz. Cornell Univ. Pr. 1984 $38.95. ISBN 0-8014-1460-1. An award-winning translation.

NONFICTION BY HERZEN

Childhood, Youth and Exile: My Past and Thoughts. Trans. by J. D. Duff. *The World's Classics Paperbacks Ser.* OUP 1980 $7.95. ISBN 0-19-281505-9. Introduction by Isaiah Berlin.

Ends and Beginnings. Ed. by Aileen Kelly. Trans. by Constance Garnett. *The World's Classics Paperbacks Ser.* OUP 1985 $7.95. ISBN 0-19-281604-7

From the Other Shore, and The Russian People and Socialism. Trans. by Moura Budberg. *Oxford Paperback Bks.* OUP 1979 o.p. Introduction by Isaiah Berlin.

The Memoirs of Alexander Herzen. Trans. by J. D. Duff. Greenwood 1977 repr. of 1923 ed. $45.00. ISBN 0-8371-9319-2. Selections from *My Past and Thoughts.*

My Past and Thoughts. 6 vols. Gordon Pr. 1972 $600.00. ISBN 0-8490-0689-9. A complete edition of the Herzen classic.

My Past and Thoughts: The Memoirs of Alexander Herzen. Ed. by Dwight MacDonald. U. CA Pr. 1981 $49.95. ISBN 0-520-04191-7. Selections.

BOOKS ABOUT HERZEN

Partridge, Monica. *Alexander Herzen 1812–1870. Prominent Figures of Slav Culture Ser.* UNIPUB 1985 $10.00. ISBN 92-3-102255-5

Zimmerman, Judith E. *Midpassage: Alexander Herzen and European Revolution. 1847–1852. Pittsburgh Series in Russian and East European Studies.* U. of Pittsburgh Pr. 1989 $39.95. ISBN 0-8229-3827-8

HIPPIUS (GIPPIUS) (pseud. of Zinaida Merezhkovskaya). 1869–1945

Hippius was a talented and prolific symbolist poet, fiction writer, and critic who conducted a celebrated literary salon in St. Petersburg. Her concerns went beyond the literary: along with her husband, the novelist Dmitry Merezhkovsky, she was a leading figure in the drive among Russian intellectuals at the century's beginning to reexamine the tenets of Russian Orthodoxy. In the case of the Merezhkovskys, this concern led to the development of a private sectarianism based on a belief in the Second Coming of Christ. After the October Revolution, the couple left Russia and organized opposition to the Bolsheviks. Eventually they settled in Paris, where they played a major role in literary and cultural émigré life.

At various levels, Hippius's fiction and verse mirror her philosophical and religious interests. She is a striking poet, is a virtuoso of suggestive images and subtle tonalities, and is also noted for her frequent use of a male persona as lyric "I." Her many diaries and memoirs are an important record of one of the Silver Age's principal figures.

WORKS BY HIPPIUS

Between Paris and St. Petersburg: Selected Diaries of Zinaida Hippius. Ed. by Temira Pachmuss. Bks. Demand repr. of 1975 ed. $86.30. ISBN 0-8357-9664-7. Contains seven different diaries, ranging from the early 1900s to the time of Hippius's emigration after the Bolshevik takeover.

Selected Works of Zinaida Hippius. Ed. and trans. by Temira Pachmuss. Bks. Demand repr. of 1972 ed. $81.80. ISBN 0-317-29016-9. The first full volume of prose works by Hippius to appear in English; contains a good selection of works; a competent translation.

ILF, ILYA (pseud. of Ilya Fainzilberg). 1897–1937, and PETROV, YEVGENY (pseud. of Evgeny Kataev). 1903–1942

The famous collection of Ilf and Petrov created the inimitable rogue and confidence man, Ostap Bender, whose adventures, with their frequent satiric thrusts at Soviet life, have become classics of Russian comic literature. In the first novel, *The Twelve Chairs* (1928), Bender searches for a hoard of jewels concealed in a set of dining-room chairs. In the second, *The Little Golden Calf* (1931), set in the Soviet Union under the first Five-Year Plan, Bender tries hard and fails to become a millionaire. A six-month car trip in 1935–36 through the United States resulted in a witty travelogue. The collaboration was broken by Ilf's untimely death from tuberculosis. Petrov was killed in a plane crash while working as a war correspondent.

Novel by Ilf and Petrov

Little Golden Calf. 1931. Trans. by Charles Malamuth. Continuum 1961 o.p.

Nonfiction by Ilf and Petrov

Little Golden America. Trans. by Charles Malamuth. *Foreign Travelers in Amer. 1810–1935 Ser.* Ayer repr. of 1974 ed. $26.50. ISBN 0-405-05461-0

ISKANDER, FAZIL. 1929–

A native of the Abkhazia region in Georgia, Iskander is a noted Russian novelist. Most of his works are set in his native region and other areas of Georgia. Their first-person narrations and seemingly guileless comic wit allow Iskander to touch on various delicate topics. *The Goatibex Constellation* (1970) is a very funny satire on the Soviet bureaucracy and on Trofim Lysenko's misguided yet once influential (in the Khrushchev period) biological fantasies. Iskander takes a different tack in his second novel, *Sandro from Chegem* (1973), a series of anecdotes about an Abkhazian's life from the 1880s to the 1960s. The protagonist's saga—sometimes witty, sometimes terrifying—allows the author to tell the turbulent story of the Abkhazian people. A small part of this very large work was published in the Soviet Union in the liberal periodical *Novy mir* (*New World*). The complete text appeared first in the West and was reissued in Russia only during the Gorbachev period.

Novels by Iskander

The Goatibex Constellation. Trans. by H. Burlingame. Ardis Pubs. 1982 o.p.
The Gospel according to Chegem. Random 1984 o.p.
Rabbits and Boa Constrictors. Trans. by Ronald E. Peterson, Ardis Pubs. 1989 o.p.
Sandro of Chegem. Trans. by Susan Brownsberger. Random 1983 o.p.

IVANOV, VSEVOLOD. 1895–1963

Ivanov, one of the most interesting Soviet fiction writers of the 1920s, began writing before the October Revolution. His first efforts were encouraged by Gorky. Ivanov's well-known short novel, *Armoured Train 14-69* (1922), about the civil war, uses a number of innovative fiction techniques. The result is a very rich text, though filled with images of violence and cruelty. A prolific writer, Ivanov was a member of the experimentally adventurous Serapion Brotherhood, but after 1930, his highly ornamental style gave way to the more sober practices of socialist realism. Many of Ivanov's works are set in distant regions of the Soviet Union, reflecting his abiding interest in exotic, oriental cultures. A later work by Ivanov, *The Adventures of a Fakir* (1934–35), is autobiographical, very colorful, and quite readable.

Novels by Ivanov

The Adventures of a Fakir. 1934–35. *Soviet Lit. in Eng. Trans. Ser.* Hyperion Conn. 1974 repr. of 1936 ed. $20.35. ISBN 0-88355-172-1

Armoured Train 14-69. 1922. Trans. by Gibson-Cowan and A. T. Grant. Greenwood 1983 repr. of 1933 ed. $39.75. ISBN 0-313-24132-5

KARAMZIN, NIKOLAI. 1766–1826

During 1789–90 Karamzin, a young poet and short-story writer, toured Western Europe. On his return, he distilled his impressions in the form of travel letters, a genre made popular by LAURENCE STERNE (see Vol. 1). *Letters of a Russian Traveler* (1791-1801), in which Karamzin's impressions are woven into a wealth of information about Western European society and culture that he derived from wide reading, became a favorite of readers and was widely imitated.

The most influential prose stylist of the eighteenth century, Karamzin shaped the development of the Russian literary language, introducing many Gallicisms to supplant Slavonic-derived words and idioms and breaking down the classicist canons of isolated language styles. Appointed court historian by Alexander I, he wrote the monumental 12-volume *History of the Russian State* (1818–24)—a model of Russian prose.

NONFICTION BY KARAMZIN

Letters of a Russian Traveler, 1789–1790. Trans. by Florence Jones. *Columbia Slavic Studies.* Greenwood 1976 repr. of 1957 ed. $35.00. ISBN 0-8371-8725-7

Selected Aesthetic Works of Sumarokov and Karamzin. Trans. by Henry M. Nebel, Jr. U. Pr. of Amer. 1982 $12.00. ISBN 0-8191-1910-5. A good selection, ample annotations.

WORK BY KARAMZIN

Selected Prose of N. M. Karamzin. Trans. by Henry M. Nebel, Jr. *Pub. of 18th-Cent. Russian Lit. Ser.* Northwestern U. Pr. 1969 o.p. Good-quality translations; a good selection of fiction and critical essays.

BOOKS ABOUT KARAMZIN

Black, Joseph L. *Nicholas Karamzin and Russian Society in the Nineteenth Century: A Study in Russian Political and Historical Thought.* Bks. Demand repr. of 1975 ed. $70.00. ISBN 0-317-09272-3

______, ed. *Essays on Karamzin: Russian Man of Letters, Political Thinker, Historian, 1766–1826. Slavistic Printings & Repr. Ser.* Mouton 1975 $49.50. ISBN 90-2793-251-4

Cross, A. G. *N. M. Karamzin: A Study of His Literary Career (1783–1803).* S. Ill. U. Pr. 1971 o.p. The most comprehensive study.

Hammarberg, Gita. *From the Idyll to the Novel: Karamzin's Sentimentalist Prose. Cambridge Studies in Russian Lit.* Cambridge U. Pr. 1991 $59.50. ISBN 0-521-38310-2

Pipes, Richard. *Karamzin's Memoir on Ancient and Modern Russia.* Macmillan 1972 $6.95. ISBN 0-689-70157-8. Contains text of Karamzin's famous memorandum, with commentary.

KATAEV (KATAYEV), VALENTIN. 1897–1986

Kataev was a popular novelist during the 1920s, creating comical, parodic works. He wrote an outstanding comic novel, *The Embezzlers* (1927), aiming his wit at corrupt Soviet officials, and an excellent satiric play about the housing shortage, *Squaring the Circle* (1928). In 1932 he published *Time Forward!*, a classic novel of socialist realism, about the construction of a metallurgical plant. Overall, Kataev survived the Stalin years with a minimum of compromise, yet with a fully active professional life. During the 1960s and 1970s, he experimented with semiautobiographical works, playing with time and memory, and paying homage to the many vanished figures of Russian culture.

NOVELS BY KATAEV

The Embezzlers and Envy. Trans. by C. Rougle and T. Berczynski. Ardis Pubs. 1975 o.p. *Envy* is by Yury Olesha.

The Small Farm in the Steppe. Trans. by Anna Bostock. Greenwood 1976 o.p.

Time, Forward! Trans. by Charles Malamuth. Ind. U. Pr. 1976 o.p. Foreword by Edward J. Edward.

NONFICTION BY KATAEV

A Mosaic of Life; or The Magic Horn of Oberon: Memoirs of a Russian Childhood. Trans. by Moura Budberg and Gordon Latta. O'Hara 1976 o.p. Entertaining anecdotes of childhood; good translation.

BOOKS ABOUT KATAEV

Russell, Robert. *Valentin Kataev*. *World Authors Ser*. Macmillan 1981 o.p.

Szarycz, Ireneusz. *Poetics of Valentin Kataev's Prose of the 1960's and 1970's*. *Amer. Univ. Studies Series XII: Slavic Languages and Lit*. P. Lang Pubs. 1989 $35.95. ISBN 0-8204-1081-0

KAVERIN, VENIAMIN (pseud. of Veniamin Zil'ber). 1902–1989

Kaverin, a native of Pskov, began as a member of the Serapion Brotherhood, a loose association of writers united by a belief in art's autonomy and the writer's freedom. His early fiction shows the influence of Western authors: E. T. A. HOFFMAN, EDGAR ALLAN POE (see Vol. 1), ROBERT LOUIS STEVENSON (see Vol. 1). He had a talent for plot and psychological realism. Two of his early novels are particularly noteworthy: *The Troublemaker* (1928) portrays the Leningrad literary milieu, in particular parodying the formalist critics; the pessimistic *The Unknown Artist* (1931) deals with the problem of the artist in the new society. Kaverin's later work, while still confronting important issues, became more conventional and in the 1960s and 1970s turned increasingly philosophical.

NOVEL BY KAVERIN

The Unknown Artist. *Soviet Lit. in Eng. Trans. Ser*. Hyperion Conn. 1973 repr. of 1947 ed. $16.50. ISBN 0-88355-006-7

BOOK ABOUT KAVERIN

Oulanoff, Hongor. *The Prose Fiction of Veniamin A. Kaverin*. Slavica 1976 $14.95. ISBN 0-89357-032-X. An analysis of the works, containing biographical materials; also a bibliography.

KHLEBNIKOV, VELIMIR (VIKTOR). 1885–1922

Khlebnikov, who together with MAYAKOVSKY was a principal figure in the Futurist group, is famous both as a poet and a utopian thinker. He is well known for his radical linguistic theories and experimentation, for his idiosyncratic theories of historical recurrence, and for his nomadic, nonmaterialistic life. His highly complex works, rich in meaning, include a large number of lyric poems, narrative poems, stories, and essays that, over the decades, have influenced many younger poets.

Despite the enormous difficulty of translating Khlebnikov, selections from his writings have appeared in many languages. Paul Schmidt has in progress an English translation of most of his texts, so far well received.

Works by Khlebnikov

Collected Works of Velimir Khlebnikov, Vol. 1: Letters and Theoretical Writings. Ed. by Charlotte Douglas. Trans. by Paul Schmidt. HUP 1987 $35.00. ISBN 0-674-14045-1. Includes a good introductory essay and a chronology.

Collected Works of Velimir Khlebnikov, Vol. 2: Prose, Plays, and Supersagas. Ed. by Ronald Vroon. Trans. by Paul Schmidt. HUP 1989 $39.50. ISBN 0-674-14046-X. Like the previous volume, carefully translated and edited.

The King of Time: Selected Writings of the Russian Futurian. Ed. by Charlotte Douglas. Trans. by Paul Schmidt. HUP 1985 $22.50. ISBN 0-674-50515-8. Selections from the multivolume translation by Schmidt.

Books about Khlebnikov

Cooke, Raymond. *Velimir Khlebnikov: A Critical Study. Cambridge Studies in Russian Lit.* Cambridge U. Pr. 1987 $54.50. ISBN 0-521-32670-2. An in-depth analysis and overview; relies on archival materials as well as published works.

Markov, Vladimir. *The Longer Poems of Velimir Khlebnikov.* Greenwood 1975 o.p. A classic study of an important genre; seminal for introducing the poet to a Western audience.

KOROLENKO, VLADIMIR. 1853–1921

Of mixed Ukrainian-Polish parentage, Korolenko was exiled for political activity to Siberia (1879–84). He then spent a decade in the provincial city of Nizhny Novgorod, where he produced most of his best work.

A major figure among the Populists, Korolenko fought actively against social and political injustices, writing essays about religious persecution, racial discrimination, and other social issues. A fundamental humanism and a belief in human progress also inform his numerous stories and novellas, for example, his famous story "Makar's Dream" (1885). After the October Revolution he was hostile to the Bolshevik government and maintained this attitude until his death.

Korolenko's prose is distinguished by a charming lyricism, an ability to capture natural settings and mood, a talent for depicting common people, and a wonderful sense of humor. His autobiographical *History of My Contemporary* (1922) is perhaps his best work.

Short Story Collections by Korolenko

Birds of Heaven, and Other Stories. Trans. by Clarence A. Manning. *Short Story Index Repr. Ser.* Ayer repr. of 1919 ed. $17.00. ISBN 0-8369-3984-0

The Blind Musician. Gordon Pr. 1973 $34.95. ISBN 0-87968-757-6

Blind Musician. Greenwood 1970 repr. of 1890 ed. $39.75. ISBN 0-8371-4093-5

In a Strange Land. Trans. by Gregory Zilboorg. Greenwood 1975 o.p.

Makar's Dream, and Other Stories. Trans. by Marian Fell. *Short Story Index Repr. Ser.* Ayer repr. of 1916 ed. $17.00. ISBN 0-8369-3951-4

KUPRIN, ALEKSANDR. 1870–1938

Kuprin was a leading figure in the "Znanie" group of realist writers. His education in a military academy and subsequent army service provided the material for many of his early works. The most well known is the short novel *The Duel* (1905), which attacks the brutality of Russian army life. Its subject and high literary qualities made it very popular. Another work that gained wide notoriety through its subject—the life of prostitutes—is *The Pit* (1908–15). In general, Kuprin's forte was the treatment of contemporary social problems; he was less adept at creating plots.

After the October Revolution, Kuprin settled in France. He continued to write, but his humorous works in emigration are not as strong as those of the earlier period. He returned to the Soviet Union shortly before his death.

NOVELS BY KUPRIN

The Duel. Classics of Russian Lit. Ser. Hyperion Conn. 1987 repr. of 1916 ed. $25.00. ISBN 0-88355-491-7

Yama: The Pit. Trans. by Bernard G. Guerney. *Classics of Russian Lit. Ser.* Hyperion Conn. 1977 repr. of 1922 ed. $15.00. ISBN 0-88355-493-3

SHORT STORY COLLECTIONS BY KUPRIN

Gambrinus, and Other Stories. Trans. by Bernard G. Guerney. *Short Story Index Repr. Ser.* Ayer 1925 $13.00. ISBN 0-8369-3627-2

River of Life, and Other Stories. Short Story Index Repr. Ser. Ayer 1916 $18.00. ISBN 0-8369-3006-1

Slav Soul, and Other Stories. Short Story Index Repr. Ser. Ayer repr. of 1916 ed. $17.00. ISBN 0-8369-3844-5

BOOK ABOUT KUPRIN

Luker, Nicholas J.., *Alexander Kuprin. World Authors Ser.* G. K. Hall 1978 o.p. Useful as an overview but too dependent on Soviet scholarship.

KUSHNER, ALEKSANDR. 1936–

Kushner, whose first collection of verse appeared in 1957, is a native of Leningrad, and the city—both its physical topography and cultural-literary terrain—is a principal theme in his poetry. Unlike some other poets of his generation, he writes about life's everyday things and favors simple metaphor and the precise turn of phrase. He also writes poetry for children.

POETRY BY KUSHNER

Apollo in Snow: Selected Poems. Trans. by Paul Graves and Carol Ueland. FS&G 1991 $19.95. ISBN 0-374-10549-9. "Kushner . . . is a deeply cultured yet down-to-earth poet who puts a contemporary spin on classical rhymes and meters" (*PW*).

KUZMIN, MIKHAIL. 1875–1936

Until recently almost unknown to most Soviet readers, Kuzmin occupied an important place in Russian literature of the early twentieth century. An erudite and talented poet and prose writer, personally close to the symbolists, he developed a distinct aesthetic credo, advocating an abandonment of the multilayered "forest of symbols" for an appreciation and celebration of the concrete world of the body and culture. He presented these views in a 1910 article, regarded as a manifesto of Acmeism. In general, Kuzmin's writings reflect his profound immersion in the worlds of literature, art, and philosophy from antiquity to the present. His works often involve a retelling of historical and legendary subjects, as in "The Deed of Alexander of Macedon." Some of his poetic cycles involve a degree of experimentation matched only by MANDELSTAM and AKHMATOVA. Finally, in both prose and poetry, Kuzmin often freely treated the theme of homosexual love (e.g., in the novella *Wings* [1907]), almost alone in Russian literature in this regard.

Major editions of Kuzmin, in Russian and edited by U.S. scholars, appeared in the West during the 1970s and 1980s. In the last several years, some anthologies of his texts have finally been published in Russia.

Works by Kuzmin

Selected Prose and Poetry. Ed. by Michael Green. Ardis Pubs. 1980 $6.50. ISBN 0-88233-418-2. A broad selection, including *Wings.* A good introduction; uneven translation.

LEONOV, LEONID. 1899–

Leonov revived the psychological novel of Dostoevsky, and his early writing shows the influence of the nineteenth-century master. His popular first novel, *The Badgers* (1924), deals with a peasant revolt against Red Army grain collectors during the period of the New Economic Policy. *The Thief* (1927) portrays the psychological traumas of a former civil war hero. During the Stalin period, Leonov produced a number of works generally in accord with the dictates of socialist realism, such as *Soviet River* (1930) (also *River*), but still possessing unusual features and flashes of dissent from the party line. *The Russian Forest* (1953), featuring a conflict between proponents of conservation and of industrialization, offers an interesting commentary on aspects of Stalinism.

Novels by Leonov

The Badgers. Soviet Lit. in Eng. Trans. Ser. Hyperion Conn. 1992 repr. of 1946 ed. $31.00. ISBN 0-88355-008-3

River. Trans. by Liv Tudge. Imported Pubns. 1983 $4.00. ISBN 0-8285-2616-8

The Russian Forest. 2 vols. Imported Pubns. 1976 o.p.

Skutarevsky. 1932. Trans. by Alec Brown. Greenwood 1971 repr. of 1936 ed. $59.75. ISBN 0-8371-5170-8. A Stalin-era novel about a scientist's attempt to adjust to a collectivist society.

Soviet River. Trans. by Ivor Montagu and Sergei Nalbandov. *Soviet Lit. in Eng. Trans. Ser.* Hyperion Conn. 1981 $23.50. ISBN 0-88355-009-1. Introduction by Maxim Gorky.

LERMONTOV, MIKHAIL. 1814–1841

One of Russia's greatest nineteenth-century poets, Lermontov was at first an officer in an elite Guards regiment. Because of the views he expressed in a poem written on the death of Pushkin in 1837, he was arrested, tried, and transferred to the Caucasus. The poem, a passionate condemnation of the St. Petersburg elite for inciting Pushkin's ill-fated confrontation with D'Anthes, brought Lermontov instant fame. He returned to the capital a year later and began to publish regularly; two volumes of poems and the novel *A Hero of Our Time* appeared in 1840. Next year, as punishment for a duel, he was sent again to a line regiment in the Caucasus, where he distinguished himself in battle. In July 1841 he was killed in his last duel, the consequence of his own quarrelsome conduct.

Lermontov was strongly influenced by Byron (see Vol. 1) and Schiller, writing striking confessional poems that presented him in typically romantic defiance toward society. In his final years, he wrote more reflective and philosophical lyrics, as well as longer narrative poems, also derived from Byronic models. The most important of these is *The Demon* (1839), on which he worked for a number of years. The story of a fallen angel's love for a woman, it has provided Russian literature and art with a powerful archetype. Besides poetry, Lermontov also wrote plays and fiction, of which *A Hero of Our Time* is the most important. Made up of several tales by different narrators, the novel centers on Pechorin—a seminal example of the egotistical nineteenth-century "superfluous man," a specifically Russian derivative of the Byronic hero. Both this protagonist and Lermontov's complex narrative technique gave a powerful stimulus to Russian realist fiction.

Poetry by Lermontov

Major Poetical Works. Trans. by Anatoly Liberman. U. of Minn. Pr. 1984 $49.95. ISBN 0-8166-1124-6. This translation is a labor of love; Russian texts are included; an extensive commentary.

Novels by Lermontov

A Hero of Our Time. Trans. by Vladimir Nabokov and Dmitiri Nabokov. Ardis Pubs. 1988 repr. of 1958 ed. $5.95. ISBN 0-87501-049-0. A virtuoso version of the novel.

Vadim. Trans. and ed. by Helena Goscilo. Ardis Pubs. 1983 o.p. Annotated.

Books about Lermontov

Barratt, Andrew, and A. D. Briggs. *A Wicked Irony: The Rhetoric of Lermontov's "A Hero of Our Time".* Intl. Spec. Bk. 1989 $39.95. ISBN 1-85399-020-5

Eikhenbaum, Boris. *Lermontov: An Essay in Literary Historical Evaluation.* Trans. by Ray Parrott and Harry Weber. Ardis Pubs. 1981 $9.95. ISBN 0-88233-705-X. An early work by a leading Formalist scholar, important both for Lermontov and its methodology.

Garrard, John. *Mikhail Lermontov. World Authors Ser.* Macmillan 1982 o.p. An introductory work that is better on biography than textual analysis.

Kelley, Laurence. *Lermontov: Tragedy in the Caucasus.* Braziller 1978 $12.50. ISBN 0-8076-0874-2

Mersereau, John, Jr. *Mikhail Lermontov. Crosscurrents-Modern Critiques Ser.* S. Ill. U. Pr. 1962 o.p.

LESKOV, NIKOLAI. 1831–1895

Leskov, the son of a minor government official, had only a limited formal education, which he supplemented with extensive reading. For a few years, he worked for the estate manager of a wealthy landowner, a job that took him all over Russia and gave him material for his future writings.

In 1860 Leskov became a journalist but soon began to write fiction. His first novel, an attack on the radical intelligentsia, appeared in 1864. Next year he produced his most famous story, "Lady Macbeth of the Mtsensk District" (1865), an account of sexual passion and crime within the merchant class. The novel *The Cathedral Folk* (1872) is a charming, sympathetic depiction of life among the provincial Orthodox clergy, a group generally slighted by writers. During the 1880s and 1890s, Leskov, very close to Tolstoy in his views on religion and art, wrote many didactic parables, often drawing on Byzantine saints' lives and medieval Russian texts. He also wrote a number of brilliant satires on Russian society.

While Leskov ranks among the major fiction writers of the nineteenth century, his reputation among critics oscillated during his lifetime. Yet he has always been widely read and has significantly influenced more recent authors. Remizov, Zamyatin, Zoshchenko, and others have been attracted by his verbal virtuosity, particularly by his narrators' colorful language, filled with colloquialisms, dialect words, and idioms (the *skaz* technique). He was also curiously contemporary in his relative disdain for the realist novel and his interest in such peripheral narrative modes as the memoir, the anecdote, and the ethnographic account.

Novel by Leskov

The Cathedral Folk. Trans. by I. Hapgood. *Classics of Russian Lit. Ser.* Hyperion Conn. 1986 repr. of 1924 ed. $22.00. ISBN 0-88355-488-7

Short Story Collections by Leskov

The Amazon and Other Stories. Trans. by David Magarshack. *Classics of Russian Lit. Ser.* Hyperion Conn. 1987 $10.00. ISBN 0-88355-496-8. Introduction by Magarshack.

The Enchanted Pilgrim and Other Stories. Trans. by David Magarshack. *Classics of Russian Lit. Ser.* Hyperion Conn. 1987 repr. of 1946 ed. $25.00. ISBN 0-88355-497-6

The Enchanted Wanderer. Trans. by A. G. Paschkoff. Dufour 1985 repr. of 1926 ed. $13.95. ISBN 0-948166-04-5. An introduction by Maksim Gorky.

Five Tales. Trans. by Michael Shotton. Dufour 1984 $25.00. ISBN 0-946162-12-3

Lady Macbeth of the Mtsensk District and Other Stories. Trans. by David McDuff. Viking Penguin 1988 $7.95. ISBN 0-14-044491-2. Introduction by McDuff.

The Musk-Ox and Other Tales. Trans. by R. Norman. *Classics of Russian Lit. Ser.* Hyperion Conn. 1987 repr. of 1944 ed. $18.00. ISBN 0-88355-499-2

Satirical Stories of Nikolai Leskov. Ed. and trans. by William B. Edgerton. Pegasus 1969 o.p.

The Sealed Angel and Other Stories by Nikolay Leskov. Trans. by K. A. Lantz. U. of Tenn. Pr. 1984 $29.95. ISBN 0-87049-411-2. "The Sealed Angel" (1873) is an account of a group of Old Believers' devotion to their faith.

The Sentry and Other Tales. Trans. by A. Chamot. *Classics of Russian Lit. Ser.* Hyperion Conn. 1987 repr. of 1922 ed. $22.50. ISBN 0-88355-501-8. Introduction by Edward Garnett.

Nonfiction by Leskov

The Jews in Russia. Ed. and trans. by Harold K. Schefski. Kingston Pr. 1986 $21.00. ISBN 0-940670-29-1. A brochure, commissioned by Petersburg Jewish leaders, which argued in favor of reducing legal restrictions placed on the Jews.

Books about Leskov

Lantz, Kenneth. *Nikolay Leskov. World Authors Ser.* G. K. Hall 1979 o.p. "A useful complement to [McLean's] more comprehensive study" (*SEEJ*).

McLean, Hugh. *Nikolai Leskov: The Man and His Art.* HUP 1977 $45.50. ISBN 0-674-62471-8. An exhaustive, superbly written study.

LIMONOV, EDWARD (pseud. of Eduard Savenko). 1943–

Limonov grew up in Khar'kov and was a member of an unofficial group of artists and writers. In 1975 he emigrated to the United States, where he lived for a few years before moving to France. His early experiences in this country provided the material for *It's Me, Eddie* (1979), which, despite the talented writing, caused an uproar because of the narrator's self-pitying, punklike persona, hatred of American society, and sexual frankness (rare in Russian literature). Two subsequent quasi-autobiographical works followed, covering the protagonist's youth and later experiences in New York. Recently, Limonov, whose art exemplifies what was once despised by the Soviet cultural establishment, is now scandalizing liberals by his espousal of extreme nationalist, right-wing positions and his association with anti-American, quasi-Fascist figures.

Novels by Limonov

His Butler's Story. Trans. by Judson Rosengrant. Grove Pr. 1987 $17.95. ISBN 0-394-55607-0. About a "'servant-philosopher,' [who] impartially mocks Americans and Russians alike as he lives off the fat of capitalism. . . . outrageously peppered with thinly disguised, near-libelous anecdotes of New York and Russian celebrities" (*LJ*).

It's Me, Eddie: A Fictional Memoir. Trans. by S. L. Campbell. Grove Pr. 1987 $7.95. ISBN 0-8021-3007-0

Memoir of a Russian Punk. Trans. by Judson Rosengrant. Grove Pr. 1991 $18.95. ISBN 0-8021-1026-6. ". . . Limonov expertly captures the horrifying boredom of working-class Soviet urban life, and uses just the right hip, offhand tone to describe Eddie's adventures in the demi-world of teenage gangs and small-time hoods" (*PW*).

MANDELSTAM (MANDEL'SHTAM), OSIP. 1891–1938

Mandelstam is ranked as one of the greatest Russian poets of this century, a status not fully attained until rediscovery of his work in the late 1960s. Born into a Jewish merchant family, he was baptized in 1911 but never lost the link with Judaism; at the same time, profoundly steeped in Russian and European culture, he made Russia, its literature, and its fate his primary artistic concern.

His total output is relatively modest. It includes several early and posthumous collections of poetry, numerous essays on Russian and world literature, and experimental masterpieces such as *The Egyptian Stamp* (1927) and *Journey to Armenia* (1932) that obliterate the boundaries between fiction, autobiography, and literary essay. Mandelstam's early works are steeped in literature, as befitted a member of the classically oriented Acmeist group before the October Revolution. He takes up major questions of philosophy and art, frequently quoting from and alluding to earlier poets and writers. The lyricism, suppleness, and classical dignity of works from this period can be broadly appreciated, but a true understanding of the poet's message requires penetration of a complex cultural universe. His later poetry attains an even higher level of artistry, yet becomes simpler. Increasingly, its subject is the poet's own life during the Stalin years and his quest to assert, in literature, the enduring human spirit in the face of totalitarianism.

Mandelstam's creation was inseparable from his life, particularly starting from about 1930. Nonconformist, increasingly isolated within literature and limited in his ability to work professionally, he lived poorly and was subject to persecution. He was arrested and exiled during the early 1930s. In May 1938 he was arrested again, and is said to have died in December of that year in a transit labor camp. His widow Nadezhda and a small group of friends preserved his writings at great personal risk. A number of translators have attempted to convey Mandelstam in English. In general, his prose has fared better at their hands than his poetry.

POETRY BY MANDELSTAM

The Eyesight of Wasps. Trans. by James Greene. Ohio St. U. Pr. 1989 $24.95. ISBN 0-8142-0478-3

Moscow Notebooks. Trans. by Richard McKane and Elizabeth McKane. Dufour 1991 $14.95. ISBN 1-85224-126-8

Osip Mandelstam's Stone. Trans. by Robert Tracy. Bks. Demand repr. of 1981 ed. $69.70. ISBN 0-8357-6930-5

Poems from Mandelstam. Trans. by R. H. Morrison. Fairleigh Dickinson 1990 $26.50. ISBN 0-8386-3382-X. A selection of approximately 80 texts; a supplement to other editions of the poet in English.

Selected Poems. Ed. and trans. by James Greene. Viking Penguin 1992 $7.95. ISBN 0-14-018474-0. Foreword by Nadezhda Mandelstam.

Selected Poems: Bilingual Edition. Trans. by David McDuff. FS&G 1975 $3.95. ISBN 0-374-51162-4. Covers major periods; restrained English versions.

Selected Poems of Osip Mandelstam. Trans. by Clarence Brown and W. S. Merwin. Macmillan 1983 $9.95. ISBN 0-689-11425-7. A collaborative effort by a scholar and an American poet.

Tristia: Poems by Osip Mandelstam. Trans. by Bruce McClelland. Station Hill Pr. 1987 $13.95. ISBN 0-88268-041-2. A complete translation of Mandelstam's second poetic collection.

Nonfiction by Mandelstam

Critical Prose and Letters. Ed. by Jane G. Harris and C. Anthony. Trans. by Jane G. Harris. Ardis Pubs. 2nd ed. 1990 $19.95. ISBN 0-88233-164-7. An award-winning translation; contains notes and index.

Books about Mandelstam

Brown, Clarence. *Mandelstam*. Cambridge U. Pr. 1978 $18.95. ISBN 0-521-29347-2. A thorough biography, with commentary on Mandelstam's writings.

Freidin, Gregory. *A Coat of Many Colors: Osip Mandelstam and His Mythologies of Self-Presentation*. U. CA Pr. 1988 $55.00. ISBN 0-520-05438-5

Harris, Jane G. *Osip Mandelstam*. *World Authors Ser.* Macmillan 1988 $26.95. ISBN 0-8057-8230-3. A concise, readable book; often illuminating on the individual texts.

Koubourlis, Demetrius J., and Stephen M. Parrish, eds. *A Concordance to the Poems of Osip Mandelstam*. *Concordances Ser.* Cornell Univ. Pr. 1974 $60.00. ISBN 0-8014-0806-7. Based on the American edition of the poet, this is an essential tool for the serious scholar.

Mandelstam, Nadezhda. *Hope Abandoned*. Trans. by Max Hayward. Macmillan 1981 $13.95. ISBN 0-689-10549-5. A memoir of Mandelstam's life and epoch by his widow; includes harsh attacks on many personalities in literature and culture.

______. *Hope against Hope*. Macmillan 1976 $13.95. ISBN 0-689-70530-1. Superbly written; a view of the poet and the epoch.

______. *Mozart and Salieri: An Essay on Osip Mandelstam and Poetic Creativity*. Trans. by Robert A. McLean. Ardis Pubs. 1992 $8.95. ISBN 0-88233-035-7. A combination of literary memoir and essay.

Przybylski, Ryszard. *An Essay on the Poetry of Osip Mandelstam: God's Grateful Guest*. Ardis Pubs. $37.50. ISBN 0-87501-013-X. By a Polish critic, an early admirer of Mandelstam's poetry.

Zeeman, Peter. *The Later Poetry of Osip Mandelstam: Text and Context*. *Studies in Slavic Lit. & Poetics Ser.* Humanities 1988 $65.00. ISBN 90-5183-028-9

MAYAKOVSKY, VLADIMIR. 1893–1930

Mayakovsky was one of Russia's most important avant-garde poets. A member of the Futurist group of painters and poets in the century's second decade, he became noted for his flamboyant public appearances, aesthetic iconoclasm, and very real verbal brilliance. Early involvement with the Bolsheviks in 1908 was followed years later by endorsement of the new Soviet government. Mayakovsky placed his talents at the service of the Soviet state, although his dreams for radical cultural changes were rebuffed by the new rulers, most of whom had relatively conservative tastes in literature. During the civil war and the 1920s, Mayakovsky wrote a great deal of agitational verse of varying quality; he also wrote film scenarios and two plays. A notable figure in the Soviet Union, with a considerable international reputation, he was allowed to travel abroad. However, he also drew harsh criticism for his deviation from the increasingly rigid cultural norms. This, combined with problems in his personal life, ultimately led to his suicide at age 36—an event that resounded greatly in Soviet culture.

Mayakovsky was a great innovator in versification, striking in his use of extravagant metaphor and hyperbole. His experiments with rhythm, rhyme, and language affected many poets, and this originality went hand in hand with great lyric talent, often refracted through comic and tragic personas. Among his most important achievements are his long narrative poems, such as *A Cloud in*

Trousers (1915), *War and the World* (1916), and *About That* (1923). Also excellent are his plays, *The Bedbug* (1928) and *The Bathhouse* (1929)—brilliant satires of Soviet philistinism and bureaucracy.

POETRY BY MAYAKOVSKY

The Bedbug and Selected Poetry. Ed. by Patricia Blake. Trans. by Max Hayward and George Reavey. Ind. U. Pr. 1975 $10.95. ISBN 0-253-20189-6

Legends! Early Poems. Trans. by Maria Enzensberger. City Lights 1991 $5.95. ISBN 0-87286-255-0

PLAYS BY MAYAKOVSKY

Complete Plays of Mayakovsky. Trans. by Guy Daniels. S&S Trade 1971 o.p. Introduction by R. Payne.

NONFICTION BY MAYAKOVSKY

How Are Verses Made? Trans. by George Hyde. Intl. Spec. Bk. $14.95. ISBN 1-85399-145-7. An essay highly revealing of Mayakovsky's own creative method.

WORKS BY MAYAKOVSKY

Love Is the Heart of Everything: Correspondence between Vladimir Mayakovsky and Lili Brik 1915–1930. Ed. by Bengt Jangfeldt. Trans. by Julian Graffy. Grove Pr. 1987 o.p. The first complete, well-annotated edition of letters between the poet and his long-time companion Lili Brik; crucial for both his biography and his art.

BOOKS ABOUT MAYAKOVSKY

Barooshian, Vahan D. *Brik and Mayakovsky. Slavistic Printings & Repr. Ser.* Mouton 1978 $39.50. ISBN 90-279-7826-3. Uneven, but the subject matter—the relationship of Mayakovsky to a close friend and mentor—makes the work important.

Brown, Edward J. *Mayakovsky: A Poet in Revolution.* Princeton U. Pr. 1973 $57.50. ISBN 0-691-06255-2. An excellent, thorough analysis of Mayakovsky's life and art.

Leaton, Anne. *Mayakovsky My Love.* Countryman 1984 $13.95. ISBN 0-88150-015-1

Stapanian, Juliette R. *Mayakovsky's Cubo-Futurist Vision.* Rice Univ. 1986 $27.50. ISBN 0-89263-259-3. Interprets "several early lyrics in the context of the contemporary Cubist and Futurist movements in the visual arts . . . remarkably successful" (*SEEJ*).

NABOKOV, VLADIMIR (pseud. "Y. Sirin"). 1899–1977

Nabokov belongs to two literatures, Russian and American. Born into a prominent political family, he emigrated in 1919 and lived in Europe, mostly in Germany, until 1940, when he emigrated to the United States. There he taught in several universities (including Cornell) and not only wrote but also worked professionally in lepidopterology. At age 60, he moved for the last time, settling in Switzerland.

Nabokov's worldwide reputation rests on numerous novels and short stories, both in Russian and English. The former date from his time in Germany and mostly depict life in emigration. The most important of these is *The Gift* (1937–38, 1952), on one level the story of a young writer and his beloved, on another the record of the growth of his artistic talent (culminating in the writing of *The Gift*), and on yet another an appraisal of Russian literature and intellectual history. Of nearly equal weight is *Invitation to a Beheading* (1938), a complex, surrealistic narrative involving a young teacher in a mythical totalitarian world. The English-language novels, written both in America and Switzerland, include the celebrated *Lolita* (1955), *Ada* (1969), and *Look at the Harlequins!* (1974). During this last period, Nabokov also translated (or supervised the translation of) his Russian works, so that a large body of his writings, in authorized versions, is accessible in two languages. In turn, his English-language novels have been translated into Russian (he translated *Lolita* in 1967), finding a large new audience since the Gorbachev era.

A hallmark of Nabokov's art is its deliberate artifice. Nabokov disdained Dostoyevsky and admired Pushkin and Gogol (about whom he wrote a study). Not surprisingly, his own works are full of complex, puzzlelike plots, in which fantasy plays a major role. (Nabokov was himself a chess player, and a chess problem is an appropriate metaphor for many of his narratives.) Literature itself is a prime subject of his fiction: He frequently underscores the artifice of his texts through unreliable narrators, and he fills his novels and stories with literary allusions and quotations, which have proved a fertile ground for scholars—whom he satirizes (but not without sympathy) in his work.

Besides writing fiction, which has made him a major figure in twentieth-century literature, Nabokov also made his mark as a critic and a translator. His annotated prose rendition of Pushkin's "novel in verse" *Eugene Onegin* (1833), though controversial, is a hallmark of Pushkin scholarship.

Work by Nabokov

The Portable Nabokov. Ed. by Page Stegner. *Viking Portable Ser.* Viking Penguin 1978 o.p.

Novels by Nabokov

Ada, or Ardor. Random 1989 $10.95. ISBN 0-685-26529-3
The Annotated Lolita. Random 1991 $19.00. ISBN 0-679-72729-9
Bend Sinister. Vintage Intl. Ser. Random 1990 $9.95. ISBN 0-679-72727-2
Defense. Vintage Intl. Ser. Random 1990 $8.95. ISBN 0-679-72722-1
Despair. Vintage Intl. Ser. Random 1989 $11.00. ISBN 0-679-72343-9
The Enchanter. Random 1991 $9.00. ISBN 0-679-72886-4
Eye. Vintage Intl. Ser. Random 1990 $8.95. ISBN 0-679-72723-X
The Gift. Random 1991 $11.00. ISBN 0-679-72725-6
Glory. Vintage Intl. Ser. Random 1991 $10.00 ISBN 0-679-72724-8
Invitation to a Beheading. Random 1989 $7.95. ISBN 0-679-72531-8
King, Queen, Knave. Vintage Intl. Ser. Random 1989 $8.95. ISBN 0-679-72340-4
Laughter in the Dark. Vintage Intl. Ser. Random 1989 $8.95. ISBN 0-679-72450-8
Laughter in the Dark. New Dir. Pr. 1991 repr. of 1938 ed. $9.95. ISBN 0-8112-1186-X
Lolita. Buccaneer Bks. 1991 $22.95. ISBN 0-89966-860-7
Look at the Harlequins! Vintage Intl. Ser. Random 1990 $9.95. ISBN 0-679-72728-0
Mary. Vintage Intl. Ser. Random 1989 $10.00. ISBN 0-679-72620-9
Pale Fire. Vintage Intl. Ser. Random 1989 $11.00. ISBN 0-679-72342-0
Pnin. Doubleday 1984 $6.95. ISBN 0-385-19116-2
The Real Life of Sebastian Knight. Random 1992 $10.00. ISBN 0-679-72726-4
Strong Opinions. Vintage Intl. Ser. Random 1990 $9.95. ISBN 0-679-72609-8

Short Story Collections by Nabokov

Details of a Sunset and Other Stories. McGraw-Hill Paperback Ser. McGraw 1980 o.p. Thirteen tales of Russian émigré life.
Nabokov's Dozen. Doubleday 1984 $6.95. ISBN 0-385-19117-0
Nabokov's Quartet. Putnam Pub. Group 1983 o.p.
A Russian Beauty and Other Stories. Trans. by Dmitri Nabokov and Simon Karlinsky. McGraw 1974 o.p.
Tyrants Destroyed and Other Stories. McGraw 1981 o.p. Mostly pre-World War II stories.

Nonfiction by Nabokov

Lectures on Don Quixote. HarBraceJ 1984 $7.95. ISBN 0-15-649540-6. Personal vision of the great novel.

Lectures on Literature: British, French and German Writers. HarBraceJ 1980 $19.95. ISBN 0-15-149597-1. Introduction by John Updike. Seven college lectures; a writer's view of fellow writers.

The Letters of Vladimir Nabokov 1940–1977. Ed. by Dmitri Nabokov and Matthew Bruccoli. HarBraceJ 1989 $29.95. ISBN 0-15-164190-0. ". . . [T]he letters are written mainly to publishers, literary friends and editors . . . an intimate, invaluable view of the writer writing" (*PW*).

The Nabokov-Wilson Letters: Correspondence between Vladimir Nabokov and Edmund Wilson, 1940–1971. Ed. by Simon Karlinsky. HarpC 1979 o.p. Approximately 250 letters; fascinating intellectual interaction; well edited and annotated.

Speak, Memory: An Autobiography Revisited. Vintage Intl. Ser. Random 1989 $9.95. ISBN 0-679-72339-0

Transparent Things. Vintage Intl. Ser. Random 1989 $6.95. ISBN 0-679-72541-5

BOOKS ABOUT NABOKOV

Alexandrov, Vladimir E. *Nabokov's Otherworld.* Princeton U. Pr. 1991 $29.95. ISBN 0-691-06866-6. Argues that Nabokov's art is based on "an aesthetic rooted in his intuition of a transcendent realm"; an important achievement.

Barabtarlo, Gennadi. *Phantom of Fact: A Guide to Nabokov's PNIN.* Ardis Pubs. 1989 $37.95. ISBN 0-87501-060-1. "Indispensable to students, teachers, and scholars of Nabokov's writings" (*SEEJ*).

Bloom, Harold, ed. *Vladimir Nabokov's Lolita. Modern Critical Interpretations Ser.* Chelsea Hse. 1987 $24.95. ISBN 1-55546-047-X. Introduction by Bloom.

______, ed. *Vladimir Nabokov. Modern Critical Views Ser.* Chelsea Hse 1987 $34.95. ISBN 1-55546-279-0. Introduction by Bloom.

Boyd, Brian. *Nabokov's Ada: The Place of Consciousness.* Ardis Pubs. 1985 $22.95. ISBN 0-88233-906-0. "Boyd's stunning book is a major contribution of Nabokov scholarship and a delight for all serious students of Nabokov" (*SEEJ*).

______. *Vladimir Nabokov: The American Years.* Princeton U. Pr. 1991 $35.00. ISBN 0-691-06797-X. A "triumphant and definitive biography" (*PW*); the second part of Boyd's exhaustive study of Nabokov's life and art.

______. *Vladimir Nabokov: The Russian Years.* Princeton U. Pr. 1990 $29.95. ISBN 0-691-06794-5. The first volume of a critical biography, "intimate, magisterial, prodigiously researched" (*PW*).

Foster, John B., Jr. *Nabokov's Art of Memory and European Modernism.* Princeton U. Pr. 1993 $29.95. ISBN 0-691-06971-9

Grayson, Jane. *Nabokov Translated: A Comparison of Nabokov's Russian and English Prose. Oxford Modern Languages and Lit. Monographs Ser.* OUP 1977 $55.00. ISBN 0-19-815527-1. "Grayson's book is a rich, well-documented, and often thought-provoking work . . . a major contribution to that central aspect of Nabokov's biography which is the story of his style" (*SEEJ*).

Johnson, D. Barton. *Worlds in Regression: Some Novels of Vladimir Nabokov.* Ardis Pubs. 1985 $9.50. ISBN 0-88233-909-5

Meyer, Priscilla. *Find What the Sailor Has Hidden: Vladmir Nabokov's "Pale Fire".* U. Pr. of New Eng. 1988 $40.00. ISBN 0-8195-5206-2. A detailed exploration of Nabokov's allusions and citations.

Nicol, Charles, and Gennady Barabtarlo, eds. *A Small Alpine Form: Studies in Nabokov's Short Fiction. Ref. Lib. of the Humanities Ser.* Garland 1992. ISBN 0-8153-0857-4

Page, Norman, ed. *Nabokov: The Critical Heritage. Critical Heritage Ser.* Routledge Chapman & Hall 1982 $69.50. ISBN 0-7100-9223-7

Pifer, Ellen. *Nabokov and the Novel.* HUP 1980 $18.95. ISBN 0-674-59840-7. A clear and well-written analysis of seven texts, which argues, in contrast to many critics, for Nabokov's concern with the ethical dimension of the human experience.

Proffer, Carl R. *Keys to Nabokov.* Ardis Pubs. 1990 $39.50. ISBN 0-87501-038-5

Proffer, Ellendea, ed. *Vladimir Nabokov: A Pictorial Biography.* Ardis Pubs. 1991 $39.95. ISBN 0-87501-078-4

Rampton, David. *Vladimir Nabokov: A Critical Study of the Novels. Cambridge Studies in Russian Lit. Ser.* Cambridge U. Pr. 1984 $18.95. ISBN 0-521-27671-3

Rivers, J. E., and Charles Nicol, eds. *Nabokov's Fifth Arc: Nabokov and Others on His Life's Work.* U. of Tex. Pr. 1982 $30.00. ISBN 0-292-75522-8. A collection of critical essays that are frequently excellent.

Roth, Phyllis A., ed. *Critical Essays on Vladimir Nabokov. Critical Essays on American Lit. Ser.* G. K. Hall 1984 $40.00. ISBN 0-8161-8678-2. "This excellent though disparate collection is aimed primarily at the sophisticated American reader with limited or no knowledge of Russian" (*SEEJ*); includes contributions by Western critics and writers, as well as Russian emigré critics.

Rydel, Christine. *A Nabokov Who's Who: A Complete Guide to Characters and Proper Names in the Works of Vladimir Nabokov.* Ardis Pubs. 1993 $49.50. ISBN 0-88233-761-0

Sharpe, Tony. *Vladimir Nabokov. Modern Fiction Ser.* Routledge Chapman & Hall 1992 $10.95. ISBN 0-7131-6575-8

Thibault, Paul J. *Social Semiotics: Text, Meaning, and Nabokov's "Ada". Theory & History of Lit. Ser.* U. of Minn. Pr. 1990 $44.95. ISBN 0-8166-1865-8. Foreword by Wlad Godzich.

Wood, Michael. *Vladimir Nabokov. Contemporary Writers Ser.* Routledge 1988 $8.95. ISBN 0-415-00659-7

NEKRASOV, NIKOLAI. 1821–1878

Nekrasov began to write seriously at an early age after his father, a cruel country squire, refused to support him at the university. A very considerable business ability brought him success in publishing. From 1846 to 1866, he was the co-owner and editor of *The Contemporary,* a journal that in his hands became the leading literary organ in Russia. Later, he achieved a similar success with the journal *Notes of the Fatherland.*

Besides his publishing work, Nekrasov was also a poet. As a principal representative of a realist school influenced by radical critics, he eschewed the aesthetic in favor of the civic, choosing as subjects the problems of contemporary Russian life. Nekrasov's greatest strength was as a satirist. His masterpiece is the vast poem *Who Can Be Happy and Free in Russia?* (written 1863–78), in which a group of peasants wanders through the country in search of a happy man, in the process showing the reader a huge catalog of evils in Russian society. Folklore deeply influenced not only Nekrasov's satires, but also his lyric and narrative poems. Perhaps the most important work showing this trait is his long poem *The Peddlars* (1861), the beginning of which has become a popular song.

Poetry by Nekrasov

Poems. Trans. by Juliet Soskice. *Classics of Russian Lit. Ser.* Hyperion Conn. 1977 repr. of 1929 ed. $15.00. ISBN 0-88355-503-4. Introduction by Lascelles Abercrombie.

Who Can Be Happy and Free in Russia? Trans. by Juliet Soskice. *Classics of Russian Lit. Ser.* Hyperion Conn. 1977 repr. of 1917 ed. $10.00. ISBN 0-88355-505-0. Introduction by David Soskice.

Book about Nekrasov

Chukovsky, Kornei. *The Poet and the Hangman: Nekrasov and Muravyov.* Trans. by R. W. Rotsel. *Ardis Essay Ser.* Ardis Pubs. 1977 $2.95. ISBN 0-88233-218-X

OKUDZHAVA, BULAT. 1924–

Of Georgian and Armenian parents, Okudzhava was born in Moscow, served at the front in World War II (his experiences are reflected in the short novel *So Long, Schoolboy!* [1961]), took a university degree in philology, and taught in a village school. His first book, *Lyrics*, appeared in 1956. Other poetic collections followed. Okudzhava won special renown for his own performances of his verse, in which he accompanied himself on the guitar. Recordings of such songs as "Midnight Trolley" and "The Song of the American Soldier" circulated widely, and he was regarded as a leading unofficial "bard," a spokesman for the post-Stalin generation of urban dwellers. His texts may lack the brutal directness of Vysotsky or the political bite of GALICH, but they employ an elegiac mood, carefully chosen symbols, and unexpected endings that illuminate poignant issues.

Okudzhava's fiction includes a trio of historical novels with political overtones: *A Taste of Liberty* (1969), *Merci, or the Adventures of Shipov* (1971), and *Nocturne* (1979). Although interesting, they do not approach the level of his poetry.

POETRY BY OKUDZHAVA

Sixty-Five Songs; Sixty-Five Pesen. Ed. by Vladimir Frumkin. Ardis Pubs. 1980 $13.50. ISBN 0-88233-638-X

Songs: Bulat Okudzhava. Vol. 2. Ed. by Vladimir Frumkin. Trans. by Tanya Wolfson, Kirsten Painter, and Laura Thompson. Ardis Pubs. 1986 $11.95. ISBN 0-87501-022-9. Bilingual edition.

NOVELS BY OKUDZHAVA

Nocturne: From the Notes of Lt. Amiran Amilakhvari, Retired. Trans. by Antonina W. Bouis. HarpC 1978 o.p.

A Taste of Liberty. Trans. by L. Gruliow. Ardis Pubs. 1986 $9.95. ISBN 0-88233-982-6

OLESHA (OLYESHA), YURY. 1899–1960

Of Polish background, Olesha chose to join the new Soviet state. He became popular in the early 1920s for his satiric verse, but his most important work is fiction, especially the novel *Envy* (1927), which deals with the problems of older intellectuals in accepting the new Soviet society. The play *A List of Benefits* (1931) continues this theme. The novella *The Three Fat Men* (1930), a fairy tale about revolution in an imaginary country, also proved very popular, and Olesha wrote a number of excellent short stories as well. During the Stalin period, his work was essentially suppressed; only after the writer's death was the quasi-autobiographical *No Day without a Line* (1965) put together from his manuscripts.

Although his total output is modest, Olesha is a major modern figure. He was a master of fictional technique, particularly adept at manipulating imagery and at forcing the reader to reexamine personal expectations about the representation of reality in art. The artist's place in contemporary society is one of his major themes, developed in great detail in *Envy*.

NOVEL BY OLESHA

Envy. Trans. by Thomas Berczynski. Ardis Pubs. 1979 $6.95. ISBN 0-88233-091-8

WORKS BY OLESHA

No Day without a Line. Ardis Pubs. 1979 $7.00. ISBN 0-88233-212-0. Literary criticism, memoirs, notes; concise, anecdotal.

Yury Olesha: The Complete Short Stories and The Three Fat Men. Trans. by Aimee Fisher. Ardis Pubs. 1979 $17.50. ISBN 0-88233-213-9

Books about Olesha

Beaujour, Elizabeth K. *The Invisible Land: A Study of the Artistic Imagination of Iurii Olesha*. Col. U. Pr. 1970. $46.00. ISBN 0-231-03428-8

Peppard, Victor. *The Poetics of Yury Olesha. Humanities Monograph Ser.* U. Press Fla. 1989 $19.95. ISBN 0-8130-0950-2. Peppard "presents a convincing case for the presence of carnival elements, 'dialogicality' and estrangement throughout Olesha's work" (*SEEJ*).

OSTROVSKY, ALEKSANDR. 1823–1886

Aleksandr Ostrovsky was the nineteenth century's major playwright, due not only to the generally high quality of his plays but also to their large number (about 50). His work, primarily prose rather than verse, falls into two periods. The first, pre-1861, includes dramas that deal with an area of Russian life Ostrovsky knew quite intimately: the society of merchants and of lower government officials. His treatment of this social sphere was quite varied, for Ostrovsky was at times attracted to and at times disgusted by his characters' milieu, attitudes, and attributes. His masterpiece from this period is *The Storm* (1860), in which social themes provide the background and the motivation for a tragic love story.

After 1861 Ostrovsky devoted himself in part to historical topics and to plots derived from folklore as, for example, in his masterpiece, *The Snow Maiden* (1873). Other plays deal with the gentry in the changed, post-emancipation Russia. Some are staples of the Russian theatrical repertoire.

Plays by Ostrovsky

A Family Affair. Adapted by Nick Dear. *Absolute Classics Ser.* Theatre Comm. 1991 $10.95. ISBN 0-948230-14-2

Plays. Ed. by George R. Noyes. AMS Pr. repr. of 1917 ed. $24.00. ISBN 0-404-04837-4

The Storm. Trans. by David Magarshack. Ardis Pubs. 1988 $5.00. ISBN 0-88233-551-0

Too Clever by Half or The Diary of a Scoundrel. Trans. by Rodney Ackland and Daniel Gerould. Applause Theatre Bk. Pubs. 1988 $7.95. ISBN 1-55783-023-1

Without a Dowry and Other Plays. Ed. and trans. by Norman Henley. Ardis Pubs. 1993 $37.95. ISBN 0-88233-933-8. Most works translated for the first time.

Book about Ostrovsky

Hoover, Marjorie L. *Alexander Ostrovsky. World Authors Ser.* G. K. Hall 1981 o.p. This work "fills the need for an accessible and reasonably competent overview" (*Russian Review*).

PANOVA, VERA. 1905–1973

Panova's first novel, *The Train* (1945), about a hospital train during World War II, won the Stalin Prize. She won two more Stalin prizes for her work but was also criticized at times by the literary establishment. This mixed reputation made less surprising her novel *Span of the Year* (1953), the first work after Stalin's death to violate the canons of official literature. Focusing on the problems of the individual and showing party bureaucrats as fallible, her novel stands as a landmark of the first "thaw." In later years, she wrote finely crafted works about children, such as *Seryozha*, as well as a cycle of tales drawn from medieval Russian history.

Work by Panova

Seryozha: Several Stories from the Life of a Very Small Boy. Trans. by Nicholas Bierkhoff and Ann Krooth. Harvest Pubns. 1988 $10.95. ISBN 0-939074-10-9

PASTERNAK, BORIS. 1890–1960 (NOBEL PRIZE 1958)

Pasternak was acclaimed as a major poet some 30 years before *Doctor Zhivago* (1955) made him world famous. After first pursuing promising careers in music and philosophy, he started to write around 1909 and published his first collection of verse in 1914. His first genuine triumph came with the collection *My Sister, Life* (1917), in which a love affair stimulates a rapturous celebration of nature. The splendid imagery and difficult syntax of this volume are a hallmark of the early Pasternak.

During the 1920s, Pasternak tried to accept the reality of the new society and moved from the lyric to the epic, taking up historical and contemporary subjects. The long poem *The Year 1905* (1926) is an example. While tolerated by the literary establishment, Pasternak turned increasingly in the 1930s to translation rather than original verse. He was a prolific translator; his versions of major Shakespeare plays are the standard texts used in Soviet theaters.

From the start, however, prose was an important focus for Pasternak. The most notable early work is the story "Zhenia's Childhood," written in 1918, which explored a girl's developing consciousness of her surroundings. There is also his artistic and intellectual autobiography *Safe Conduct* (1931). But Pasternak's greatest prose achievement came later: the novel *Doctor Zhivago,* written over a number of years and completed in 1955. Its hero, a physician and poet, confronts the great changes of the early twentieth century—world war, revolution, civil war—and travels a path through life that creates a parallel between his fate and that of Christ. (The theme of preordained sacrifice is strengthened by the cycle of poems included as the last section of the book.) *Doctor Zhivago* was rejected for publication but appeared in 1957 in the West and won its author worldwide acclaim. A Nobel Prize followed in 1958. This led the Soviet authorities to launch a major public campaign against Pasternak and to make his personal life even more difficult. So successful were they that the poet officially turned down the award. After that, he was left in relative peace and died two years later. He was but the first of many writers in the post-Stalin period to challenge the Soviet state.

During the 1970s and 1980s, Pasternak's heritage was cautiously brought into public purview in the Soviet Union. The Gorbachev period saw the removal of all restrictions on his work, and publication of *Doctor Zhivago* followed at long last. Several major editions of Pasternak's writings have appeared.

POETRY BY PASTERNAK

My Sister, Life. Trans. by Mark Rudman and Bohdan Boychuk. Northwestern U. Pr. 1992 repr. of 1989 ed. $12.95. ISBN 0-8101-1090-3. Preface by Rudman.

The Poems of Doctor Zhivago. Ed. and trans. by Donald Davie. Greenwood 1977 repr. of 1965 ed. $38.50. ISBN 0-8371-8294-8

Poems of Boris Pasternak. Trans. by Lydia Pasternak. Unwin Hyman 1984 o.p. The second, expanded edition of an excellent collection; "a sampling of Pasternak's work in an eminently readable and elegant translation" (*SEEJ*).

Second Nature: Forty-Six Poems. Comp. by Andrei Navrozov. Dufour 1990 $34.00. ISBN 0-7206-0751-5

Selected Poems. Trans. by Jon Stallworthy and Peter France. *Twentieth-Century Classics Ser.* Viking Penguin 1992 $7.95. ISBN 0-14-018466-X. Economical, apt translations; a good introduction by Pasternak's son.

NOVELS BY PASTERNAK

Doctor Zhivago. Pantheon 1991 $13.00. ISBN 0-679-73123-7. An introduction by John Bayley.

Safe Conduct. New Dir. Pr. 1958 $9.95. ISBN 0-8112-0135-X. Introduction by B. Deutsch.

WORKS BY PASTERNAK

The Correspondence of Boris Pasternak and Olga Freidenberg, 1910–1954. Ed. and comp. by Elliot Mossman. Trans. by Margaret Wettlin. HarBraceJ 1983 $9.95. ISBN 0-15-622597-2. A moving record of the poet's lengthy exchange with his cousin, a leading classical scholar; an interesting commentary on Soviet society in the Stalin period.

I Remember: Sketch for an Autobiography. Trans. by David Magarshack. HUP 1983 $7.95. ISBN 0-674-43950-3. Pasternak's second autobiography (1957); includes the essay "Translating Shakespeare."

Letters: Summer 1926. (co-authored with Marina Tsvetayeva and Rainer Maria Rilke). Trans. by Margaret Wettlin and Walter Arndt. HarBraceJ 1985 $24.95. ISBN 0-15-150871-2. Very important three-way correspondence among the poets.

The Voice of Prose: Early Prose and Autobiography. Ed. by Christopher Barnes. Grove Pr. 1986 $19.95. ISBN 0-394-55604-6. An excellent anthology of Pasternak's early ventures into prose; a fine translation with notes and introduction by Barnes.

Zhenia's Childhood. Schocken 1987 $5.95. ISBN 0-8052-8129-0

BOOKS ABOUT PASTERNAK

Barnes, Christopher. *Boris Pasternak: A Literary Biography: Volume One: 1890–1928.* Cambridge U. Pr. 1989 $75.00. ISBN 0-521-25957-6. An authoritative new biograhy.

Conquest, Robert. *The Pasternak Affair: Courage of Genius.* Hippocrene Bks. 1979 repr. of 1962 ed. $18.00. ISBN 0-374-91913-5. An account of the circumstances surrounding the Nobel Prize and its aftermath.

Erlich, Victor, ed. *Pasternak: A Collection of Critical Essays. Twentieth Century Views Ser.* P-H 1978 $3.45. ISBN 0-13-652826-0. "This collection offers criticism of high standards" (*Russian Review*).

Fleishman, Lazar. *Boris Pasternak: The Poet and His Politics.* HUP 1990 $37.50. ISBN 0-674-07905-1. An exhaustive, authoritative account of Pasternak's role as a participant in Soviet literary and political life.

______, ed. *Boris Pasternak and His Times.* Berkeley Slavic 1989 $20.00. ISBN 0-933884-56-7. Studies from a major conference on Pasternak, authored by leading specialists.

France, Anna K. *Boris Pasternak's Translations of Shakespeare.* U. CA Pr. 1978 $42.50. ISBN 0-520-03432-5. An illuminating analysis of Pasternak's handling of Shakespearean idiom and its close connection to his original work.

Gladkov, Alexander. *Meetings with Pasternak: A Memoir.* Trans. by Max Hayward. HarBraceJ 1977 o.p.

Ivinskaya, Olga. *A Captive of Time: My Years with Pasternak.* Trans. by Max Hayward. Beekman Pubs. 1979 o.p. A moving account by Pasternak's long-time companion, the prototype of Lara in *Zhivago.*

Livingstone, Angela. *Pasternak: Doctor Zhivago. Landmarks of World Lit.* Cambridge U. Pr. 1989 $22.95. ISBN 0-521-32811-X

Mallac, Guy De. *Boris Pasternak: His Life and Art.* U. of Okla. Pr. 1981 $35.00. ISBN 0-8061-1660-9

Nilsson, Nils A., ed. *Boris Pasternak: Essays. Stockholm Studies in Russian Lit.* Coronet Bks. 1977 $24.00. ISBN 91-22-00086-0. "This volume represents an important part of Pasternak scholarship . . ." (*SEEJ*).

Pasternak, Alexander. *A Vanished Present: The Memoirs of Alexander Pasternak.* Trans. by Ann P. Slater. HarBraceJ 1985 $17.95. ISBN 0-15-193364-2

Pomorska, K. *Themes and Variations in Pasternak's Poetics.* Benjamins North Am. 1975 $20.00. ISBN 0-685-53318-2. Studies on both prose and poetry.

PAUSTOVSKY, KONSTANTIN. 1892–1968

Paustovsky's first story was published in 1912. Over the years, he developed into an extremely fine stylist and was nominated for the Nobel Prize in 1965. He wrote many tales, novels, and plays and managed to escape being totally bound by the straightjacket of socialist realism even during the Stalin era. *Black Gulf* (1932), for example, which deals with the theme of industrialization, is an adventure novel. He is especially known for his short stories, in which a sharp eye for detail combines with depictions of protagonists who escape from reality into dreams. *A Story of a Life* (1947–60), his reminiscences of more than 50 years, is often considered his best work and contains a great deal of interesting material. Paustovsky was very popular during the post-Stalin period and had a great impact on younger writers. In 1966 he made an appeal for the newly convicted Daniel and Andrei Sinyavsky—an action that won him widespread admiration within the Russian intelligentsia.

Novel by Paustovsky

The Black Gulf. 1932. Trans. by Eugenia Schimanskaya. *Soviet Lit. in Eng. Trans. Ser.* Hyperion Conn. 1977 repr. of 1946 ed. $16.00. ISBN 0-88355-411-9

Nonfiction by Paustovsky

A Story of a Life. 1947–1960. Pantheon 1982 $8.95. ISBN 0-394-71014-2

PILNYAK, BORIS (pseud. of Boris Vogau). 1894?–1937?

Pilnyak was a leading and controversial writer of the 1920s. He became very popular after the publication of *The Naked Year* (1921), which deals with the Bolshevik Revolution and its impact on Russia. His subsequent career was marred by several scandals. A 1926 story, "The Tale of the Unextinguished Moon," presented the death of a high-ranking military leader in terms similar to the actual fate of the celebrated army commissar Frunze: All copies of the magazine carrying the story were confiscated. A more dangerous situation arose when the story "Mahogany" (1929) was published in Germany: a campaign of vilification forced Pilnyak from the All-Russian Union of Writers, of which he was chairman. During the 1930s, Pilnyak slowly faded from view. He was arrested during the purges and apparently was shot in 1937.

Pilnyak's great impact on literature came largely from his style. Continuing the ornamental tradition of Bely, he created a literary language that combines epic solemnity with lyricism; draws on folklore; and freely creates complex, often striking or shocking, constructions. The attraction of such techniques was so strong that charges of "Pilnyakism" were leveled against many writers who followed in a similar vein. Pilnyak's works are very carefully crafted and express complex philosophical ideas.

Novels by Pilnyak

Ivan Moscow. 1927. Trans. by A. Schwartzman. *Soviet Lit. in Eng. Trans. Ser.* Hyperion Conn. 1973 repr. of 1935 ed. $15.00. ISBN 0-88355-016-4

The Naked Year. Trans. by Alexander R. Tulloch. Ardis Pubs. 1975 $8.95. ISBN 0-88233-078-0. A faithful, skilled rendition of the very difficult Russian original.

Volga Falls to the Caspian Sea. AMS Pr. repr. of 1931 ed. $15.00. ISBN 0-404-05047-6

Short Story Collections by Pilnyak

Chinese Story and Other Tales. Trans. by Vera T. Reck and Michael Green. U. of Okla. Pr. 1988 $27.95. ISBN 0-8061-2134-3

Mahogany and Other Stories. Ed. and trans. by Vera T. Reck and Michael Green. Ardis Pubs. 1992 $16.95. ISBN 0-87501-104-7. A translation of a major collection; includes a version of the original text of "The Tale of the Unextinguished Moon."

Tales of the Wilderness. Trans. by F. O'Dempsey. *Soviet Lit. in Eng. Trans. Ser.* Hyperion Conn. 1973 repr. of 1925 ed. $18.50. ISBN 0-88355-017-2. Introduction by D. S. Mirsky.

Book about Pilnyak

Browning, Gary. *Boris Pilnyak: Scythian at a Typewriter*. Ardis Pubs. 1985 $32.50. ISBN 0-88233-888-9. A detailed, ground-breaking overview of Pilnyak and his works; "Browning's critical instincts are excellent, his writing very readable, his commitment to scholarly integrity and ideological impartiality gratifying" (*SEEJ*).

PISEMSKY, ALEKSEI. 1820–1881

A provincial, and ridiculed as such by some, Pisemsky was educated in Moscow, where he began to attract attention with his *Sketches of Peasant Life* (1852). In 1858 he became editor of a major literary journal and in the same year published his famous novel *One Thousand Souls*, the story of an ambitious man's unscrupulous rise to power and wealth. He soon produced another notable work: The play *A Bitter Fate* (1859) is a moving tragedy of peasant life. In his art and in many polemic pieces, Pisemsky was a proponent of Slavophile and nationalist ideas. His writings provide a good perspective on this important strain in Russian culture.

Novels by Pisemsky

One Thousand Souls. Trans. by Ivy Litvinov. *Classics of Russian Lit. Ser.* Hyperion Conn. 1989 repr. of 1959 ed. $22.00. ISBN 0-88355-506-9

The Simpleton. Trans. by I. Litvinova. *Classics of Russian Lit. Ser.* Hyperion Conn. 1977 repr. of 1959 ed. $15.00. ISBN 0-88355-508-5

Short Story Collection by Pisemsky

Nina, the Comic Actor and an Old Friend. Trans. by Maya Jenkins. Ardis Pubs. 1988 o.p. "[I]mportant additions to our store of 19th century Russian literature. Pisemsky's brooding romanticism, coupled with his control as a writer, suffers only in comparison with literary giants" (*PW*).

Book about Pisemsky

Moser, Charles A. *Pisemsky: A Provincial Realist*. HUP 1969 $22.50. ISBN 0-674-66975-4. "A pioneering synthesis of available information . . . the first comprehensive, scholarly treatment in any language of that shamefully neglected writer" (*SEEJ*).

PLATONOV, ANDREI (pseud. of Andrei Platonovich Klimentov). 1899–1951

By background an engineer and land-reclamation specialist, for a long time Platonov was remembered mainly as a member of the Pereval group of the 1920s and early 1930s. These were writers who were influenced by the humanist, cultivated ideas of the critic Voronsky. Vehemently attacked for his ideological "mistakes" by the more extreme "proletarian" writers and critics, Platonov was eventually forced to stop publishing. He reemerged during the war, but new attacks once again reduced him to silence. As a result of these persecutions, Russians knew only a portion of his real output.

During the 1970s, Western publication of more works revealed Platonov to be an important figure in modern Russian prose, an artist whose creative flowering came precisely at a time when he was largely barred from Soviet periodicals. His key novels, *Chevengur* (1972) and *The Foundation Pit* (1973), explore the bitter ironies of a land of triumphant socialism—a new Utopia—which systematically deforms language. Profoundly pessimistic, they reveal a man deeply skeptical of attempts to remold human nature and highly sensitive to the dark underside of Stalin's grandiose economic projects.

WORK BY PLATONOV

Andrei Platonov: Collected Works. Trans. by Marion Jordon, Alexei Kiselev, and Anthony Olcott. Ardis Pubs. 1978 o.p. This edition of Platonov is "eminently worth having and make[s] a significant contribution to the body of translated Soviet fiction" (*SEEJ*).

NOVELS BY PLATONOV

Chevengur. Trans. by Anthony Alcott. Ardis Pubs. 1978 $6.50. ISBN 0-88233-310-0. "The availability of this novel marks a publishing milestone . . ." (*SEEJ*).

Fierce, Fine World. Trans. by Laura Beraha. Imported Pubns. 1983 $4.00. ISBN 0-8285-2417-3

BOOKS ABOUT PLATONOV

Seifrid, Thomas. *Andrei Platonov: Uncertainties of Spirit. Studies in Russian Lit. Ser.* Cambridge U. Pr. 1992 $59.95. ISBN 0-521-40522-X

Teskey, Ayleen. *Platonov and Fyodorov: The Influence of Religious Philosophy upon a Soviet Writer.* Humanities 1982 o.p. An analysis of Platonov's major work in the light of a Christian philosophy of collective immortality.

PRISHVIN, MIKHAIL. 1873–1954

By training, Prishvin was a specialist in agronomy. His interests, however, were much broader, encompassing ethnography, folklore, linguistics, and ornithology, all of which benefited from his many travels. His first published work was a collection of stories, *In the Land of Unfrightened Birds* (1907). Its emphasis on nature is characteristic of much of Prishvin's later prose.

Prishvin is distinguished by his rich, colorful language. In this, as well as in his injection of ethnographic concerns into literature, he was close to his contemporary REMIZOV and part of the neorealist strain in early twentieth-century prose.

SHORT STORY COLLECTIONS BY PRISHVIN

The Lake and the Woods: or, Nature's Calendar. Trans. by W. L. Goodman. Greenwood 1975 repr. of 1951 ed. $39.75. ISBN 0-8371-8465-7

Nature's Diary. Nature Lib. Ser. Viking Penguin 1987 $6.95. ISBN 0-14-017003-0. Introduction by John Updike.

PUSHKIN, ALEKSANDR. 1799–1837

Pushkin is acknowledged as the greatest Russian poet—a national poet—unsurpassed in his mastery of diverse genres and in the perfection with which he blends content and form. "Pushkinian simplicity" is a byword in the history of Russian literature.

Born into the gentry, he was educated and made his literary debut in an exclusive school near Petersburg. He was welcomed into the capital's literary society, quickly becoming an intimate of its leading figures, but his rather wild life in Petersburg came to an end in 1820, when his political verses provoked banishment to south Russia. The years of exile were very productive. The exotic, oriental Caucasus, Crimea, and Moldavia stimulated the creation of major works. Equally beneficial was the poet's subsequent confinement to his mother's home in Mikhailovskoye (1824–26), because it kept Pushkin outside the unsuccessful Decembrist revolt in 1825. A new phase in the poet's life began in September 1826 when he was summoned by Emperor Nicholas I, granted a pardon for past offenses, and promised special protection. Yet Pushkin's existence under the eye of his imperial patron and censor proved to be increasingly restrictive. In addition, although his creative genius was in full flower, his personal life was far from happy. In 1831, after a lengthy courtship, Pushkin married the beautiful Nathalie Goncharova. His wife was a success in court circles, and the poet was thrust into the company of people whom he scorned and who, in turn, had little use for him. The final crisis was provoked by Nathalie's friendship with a Frenchman in Russian service, Baron D'Anthès. A series of incidents culminated in a duel between Pushkin and his wife's admirer in January 1837. The poet was seriously wounded and died two days later. At the orders of the authorities, who feared public outrage, he was hastily buried.

Pushkin demonstrated his genius in short lyrics, long narrative poems, plays, and fiction. His lyric verses, especially those of his mature period, are extraordinary in their ease, seemingly effortless control, and universality of thought and feeling. His narrative poems are of various types. Some, such as "The Fountain of Bakhchisaray" (1822), are modeled on BYRON's (see Vol. 1) Eastern tales. *Eugene Onegin* (1823–31), his single greatest creation, is a brilliant, psychologically subtle verse novel about a Petersburg dandy who misses the opportunity for happiness with a girl who loves him. An encyclopedia of Russian life of the time, it helped establish the tradition of realism in literature. His final long poem, *The Bronze Horseman* (1833), deals with the opposition between the rights of the individual and the demands of the state; in this dramatic and majestic work, the conflict, played out on the stage of Russian history, is left unresolved.

Among Pushkin's plays, the SHAKESPEAREAN (see Vol. 1) *Boris Godunov* (1825) is best known in the West due to its operatic version by Modest Mussorgsky, but it yields in depth to a group of extraordinarily concentrated short plays, known collectively as the *Little Tragedies.* These include *Mozart and Salieri* (1830) and "The Stone Guest" (1830), which is based on the Don Juan legend. The poet's prose, which includes the *Tales of Belkin* (1831), *The Queen of Spades* (1833), and *The Captain's Daughter* (1833–36), was extremely important in the development of Russian fiction. It had a major impact on, among others, DOSTOYEVSKY and TOLSTOY. Pushkin also wrote several hundred very lively letters (in the fashion of the time, often intended for a wider audience than the recipient) and many literary essays.

Pushkin's witty, precise, yet melodious writing has presented challenges to translators. VLADIMIR NABOKOV's polemic with Edmund Wilson on how he should be translated is evidence of the very different approaches that may be adopted. Nabokov's own rendition of *Eugene Onegin* is obligatory for anyone with a serious interest in the poet, and the version by Charles Johnston is also quite good. Walter Arndt has been very successful in capturing the rhythms, style, and meaning of many of the poems. Paul Debreczeny's translation of the prose has received very favorable reviews and may now be regarded as a standard.

POETRY BY PUSHKIN

The Bronze Horseman and Other Poems. Trans. by D. M. Thomas. Viking Penguin 1982 o.p. A serious translation endeavor; worth using.

Collected Narrative and Lyrical Poetry. Trans. by Walter Arndt. Ardis Pubs. 1984 $15.95. ISBN 0-88233-826-9. Includes *The Bronze Horseman, The Fountain of Bakhchisaray, The Golden Cockerel, The Gypsies, Poltava,* and other narrative poems and lyrics.

Epigrams and Satirical Verse. Trans. by Cynthia A. Whittaker. Ardis Pubs. 1984 $15.00. ISBN 0-88233-886-2

Eugene Onegin. Trans. by Charles Johnston. Viking Penguin 1978 $12.50. ISBN 0-670-29889-1

Eugene Onegin: A Novel in Verse. 4 vols. Trans. by Vladimir Nabokov. Princeton U. Pr. 1981 repr. of 1975 ed. $180.00. ISBN 0-691-09744-5. Extremely accurate; exhaustive annotations; indispensable to students of Pushkin.

Golden Cockerel and Other Fairy Tales. Trans. by Jessie Wood. Doubleday 1990 $24.95. ISBN 0-385-26252-3

Three Comic Poems. Ed. by William Harkins. Ardis Pubs. 1977 $8.95. ISBN 0-88233-221-X. Includes "Gavriliiada," "Count Nulin," and "The Little House in Kolomna."

SHORT STORY COLLECTIONS BY PUSHKIN

Alexander Pushkin: Complete Prose Fiction. Trans. by Paul Debreczeny. Stanford U. Pr. 1983 $49.50. ISBN 0-8047-1142-9. Accurate, elegant translations by a leading Pushkin scholar; excellent introduction and notes.

The Captain's Daughter and Other Stories. Knopf 1992 $14.50. ISBN 0-679-41331-6

Complete Prose Tales of Pushkin. Norton 1968 $12.95. ISBN 0-393-00465-1

Queen of Spades and Other Stories. Trans. by Rosemary Edmonds. *Penguin Classics Ser.* Viking Penguin 1978 $5.95. ISBN 0-14-044119-0. Includes *The Captain's Daughter* and "Dubrovsky."

Tales of Belkin. Trans. by Gillon Aitken and David Budgen. Dufour 1983 $27.00. ISBN 0-946162-04-2

PLAYS BY PUSHKIN

Boris Godunov. Trans. by Philip L. Barbour. *Columbia Slavic Studies Ser.* Greenwood 1976 repr. of 1953 ed. $38.50. ISBN 0-8371-8522-X

Mozart and Salieri: The Little Tragedies. Trans. by Antony Wood. Dufour 1987 $15.95. ISBN 0-8023-1282-9. "The translation is readable, clear, rhythmical, and largely unstilted" (*SEEJ*).

NONFICTION BY PUSHKIN

The History of Pugachev. Trans. by Earl Sampson. Ardis Pubs. 1983 o.p. Pushkin's late venture into historical investigation and writing.

A Journey to Arzrum. Trans. by Birgitta Ingemanson. Ardis Pubs. 1974 o.p. The account of Pushkin's visit to a Russian army; filled with literary and cultural allusions and asides.

Letters of Alexander Pushkin. 3 vols. in 1. Trans. by J. Thomas Shaw. U. of Wis. Pr. 1967 o.p. The principal source for Pushkin's epistolary in English; well translated and annotated by a leading scholar.

Pushkin on Literature. Ed. and trans. by Tatiana Wolff. Stanford U. Pr. rev. ed. 1986 $49.50. ISBN 0-8047-1322-7. A richly annotated collection of writings on literature, derived from Pushkin's reviews, letters, notes, and diaries.

BOOKS ABOUT PUSHKIN

Bethea, David M., ed. *Pushkin Today.* Ind. U. Pr. 1992 $29.95. ISBN 0-253-31161-6. Perspectives by a group of American specialists; covers various texts and applies diverse modern critical methodologies to Pushkin's biography and art.

Bloom, Harold, ed. *Alexander Pushkin. Modern Critical Views Ser.* Chelsea Hse. 1987 o.p. Introduction by Bloom.

Briggs, A. D. P. *Alexander Pushkin: A Critical Study.* B&N Imports 1983 $40.00. ISBN 0-389-20340-8. Designed primarily for the nonspecialist, concentrates on a reading of several key texts.

Debreczeny, Paul. *The Other Pushkin: A Study of Alexander Pushkin's Prose Fiction.* Stanford U. Pr. 1983 $42.50. ISBN 0-8047-1143-7. A multifaceted analysis of the genre; highly recommended.

Driver, Sam N. *Pushkin: Literature and Social Ideas.* Col. U. Pr. 1989 $33.00. ISBN 0-231-06848-4

Hoisington, Sona S., ed. and trans. *Russian Views of Pushkin's Eugene Onegin.* Contrib. by Walter Arndt. Ind. U. Pr. 1988 $35.00. ISBN 0-253-35067-0. Translations of some key critical studies; contains an excellent introduction on Russian literary criticism.

Kodjak, Andrej. *Pushkin's I. P. Belkin.* Slavica 1979 $10.95. ISBN 0-89357-057-5. A structuralist analysis of the short-story cycle.

Lezhnev, A. *Pushkin's Prose.* Trans. by Roberta Reeder. St. Mut. $45.00. ISBN 0-317-40744-9. An important study from the 1930s.

Mirsky, D. S. *Pushkin. Studies in Russian Lit. & Life.* Haskell 1974 $75.00. ISBN 0-8383-1998-X. Introductory, dated in some respects, but a finely written synthesis.

Sandler, Stephanie. *Distant Pleasures: Alexander Pushkin and the Writing of Exile.* Stanford U. Pr. 1989 $32.50. ISBN 0-8047-1542-4

Shaw, J. Thomas. *Pushkin: A Concordance to the Poetry.* 2 vols. Slavica 1985 $99.95. ISBN 0-89357-130-X. A scholar's indispensable research tool.

Vickery, Walter N. *Alexander Pushkin. Twayne's World Author Ser.* Macmillan rev. ed. 1992. $22.95. ISBN 0-8057-8268-0. ". . . [A]n admirably concise introduction to the life and poetry; every word shows that it is written by a scholar-specialist for a broad audience" (*SEEJ*).

RASPUTIN, VALENTIN. 1937–

Rasputin began to write in 1961, starting with sketches about the Siberian countryside. After the success of the short novel *Money for Maria* (1967), he continued with several other works that made him a leading figure in "village fiction." These included *Farewell to Matyora* (1976), which counterposes the traditional peasant way of life to a new hydroelectric power dam, the symbol of destructive industrialization. Another was *Live and Remember* (1974), the story of a deserter during World War II who tries to return to his wife in Siberia.

Rasputin's accomplished fiction, drawing on folklore and using realistic dialect, emphasizes humanity's struggle against the forces of fate. It is also strongly patriotic. Beginning with the Gorbachev period, he has taken a highly nationalist, right-wing stance, lending his considerable prestige to antireformist, quasi-fascist political groups.

Novels by Rasputin

Farewell to Matyora: A Novel. Trans. by Antonina W. Bouis. Northwestern U. Pr. 1991 repr. of 1979 ed. $12.95. ISBN 0-8101-0997-2. Foreword by Kathleen Parthe.

Live and Remember. Trans. by Antonina W. Bouis. Northwestern U. Pr. 1992 repr. of 1978 ed. $12.95. ISBN 0-8101-1053-9. Foreword by Kathleen Parthe.

Work by Rasputin

Siberia on Fire: Stories and Essays by Valentin Rasputin. Trans. by Gerald Mikkelson and Margaret Winchell. N. Ill. U. Pr. 1989 $30.00. ISBN 0-87580-152-8. "Rasputin's dazzling stories are sophisticated splicings of nonchronological episodes" (*PW*).

Book about Rasputin

Polowy, Teresa. *The Novellas of Valentin Rasputin: Genre, Language and Style. Middlebury Studies in Russian Language & Lit.* P. Lang Pubs. 1989 $42.50. ISBN 0-8204-0643-0

RATUSHINSKAYA, IRINA. 1954–

Born in Odessa, Ratushinskaya received a physics degree at the university, worked as a teacher, and was involved in the human rights movement. In 1980, her request to emigrate from Russia was denied. Two years later, she was arrested for writing and disseminating "anti-Soviet poetry" and was treated very harshly—given a term in a strict-regime camp, to be followed by internal exile. Her brutal camp experiences included solitary confinement, but throughout she continued to write, recording in her poems and diaries the horrors of the Gulag. Ratushinskaya was released in 1986 on the eve of the Reagan-Gorbachev summit in Reykjavik and allowed to go to England, where she now lives.

Poetry by Ratushinskaya

Beyond the Limit. Trans. by Frances P. Brent and Carol Avins. Northwestern U. Pr. 1987 $22.95. ISBN 0-8101-0748-1. Bilingual edition. A cycle of 42 poems composed in 1983–1984 in a Soviet penal camp. "Above all, Ratushinskaya is a witness. This is essential reading for anyone interested in Russian literature or Soviet politics" (*PW*).

Pencil Letter. Random 1989 $9.95. ISBN 0-679-72600-4. Poems written in labor camp, "probably best read as an addendum to her gallant and wrenching memoir of the period" (*LJ*).

Stikhi, Poems, Poèmes. Trans. by Meery Devergnas, Philip Balla, Pamela W. Hadas, Susan Layton, and Ilya Nykin. Hermitage 1984 $8.50. ISBN 0-938920-54-5. Texts in Russian, French, and English, with an introduction by Joseph Brodsky.

Short Story Collection by Ratushinskaya

A Tale of Three Heads. Trans. by Diane N. Ignashev. Hermitage 1986 $7.50. ISBN 0-938920-83-9. Bilingual edition, with an introduction by Ignashev.

Nonfiction by Ratushinskaya

Grey Is the Color of Hope. Trans. by Alyona Kojevnikov. Knopf 1988 $18.95. ISBN 0-394-57140-1. A diary "piercingly beautiful, gripping with its amazing stories of cruelty and survival. . . . A strong, distinctive voice in the swelling chorus of Soviet gulag literature" (*PW*).

Grey Is the Color of Life. Trans. by Alyona Kojevnikov. Random 1989 $8.95. ISBN 0-685-26532-3

In the Beginning. Knopf 1991 $23.00. ISBN 0-394-57141-X. "Most of the memoir concerns Ratushinskaya's hectic life as a dissident in Kiev and Odessa with her husband, Igor Geraschenko, before her arrest. . . . [But it details] Igor's youthful memories as well as her own" (*LJ*).

REMIZOV, ALEKSEI. 1877–1957

A very prolific writer, artist, and calligrapher, Remizov was a paradoxical figure, well known for his love of the grotesque and the comic, in both life and literature. While influenced by symbolism, he maintained a quite personal style in his writing, which over the years moved from realism, albeit with modernist tendencies (as in the novels *The Pond* and *The Clock*, both published in 1908), into an indefinable fictional world of dreams and fantasy. He was fascinated by ethnography and history, particularly Russian, and many of his works are reworkings of medieval and folk texts. A superb stylist, his ornamental prose influenced such writers as Prishvin, Zamyatin, and Pilnyak.

An émigré since the 1920s, Remizov was almost totally ignored in the Soviet Union for decades, but in the Gorbachev period, several collections of his writings were issued. Translations have been appearing for a long time in the West, though these include but a small fraction of his prodigious output. For a translator, Remizov's language—rooted deeply in idiom, dialect, and folkloric or literary allusion—presents a major challenge. Rendering a substantial body of his texts into an English—adequate both semantically and stylistically—is still a task for the future, though the volume by Sona Aronian is a good start.

Works by Remizov

Alexei Remizov: Selected Prose. Ed. by Sona Aronian. Ardis Pubs. 1985 $9.95. ISBN 0-88233-509-X. A comprehensive collection from various periods, with an extensive introduction and a major bibliography of criticism.

The Clock. 1908. Trans. by John Cournos. *Classics of Russian Lit. Ser.* Hyperion Conn. 1977 repr. of 1924 ed. $15.00. ISBN 0-88355-509-3

Fifth Pestilence with the History of the Tinkling Symbol and Sounding Brass: Bound with Ivan Semyonovich Stratilatov. Trans. by Alec Brown. *Classics of Russian Lit. Ser.* Hyperion Conn. 1977 repr. of 1927 ed. $15.00. ISBN 0-88355-511-5. Introduction by Brown.

On a Field Azure. Trans. by Beatrice Scott. *Classics of Russian Lit. Ser.* Hyperion Conn. 1977 repr. of 1946 ed. $10.00. ISBN 0-88355-513-1

Books about Remizov

Slobin, Greta N. *Images of Aleksei Remizov.* Mead Art Mus. 1985 $10.00. ISBN 0-914337-05-X. A useful catalogue of Remizov's visual work.

______. *Remizov's Fictions, 1900–1921.* N. Ill. U. Pr. 1992 $30.00. ISBN 0-87580-158-7. A substantive new study, considering the writer's craft in relation to the broader literary context.

______, ed. *Aleksej Remizov: Approaches to a Protean Writer. UCLA Slavic Studies Ser.* Slavica 1987 $19.95. ISBN 0-89357-167-9. Collection of articles from conference on Remizov.

RYBAKOV, ANATOLY (pseud. of A. Aronov). 1911–

Rybakov grew up and continues to live in Moscow. He worked as a transport engineer, both civilian and military, from 1934 to 1946. After World War II he turned to literature, drawing in part on his previous professional experiences, in the "industrial novel" *The Drivers* (1950), which was awarded the Stalin Prize, and in *Yekaterina Voronina* (1955). He also wrote three short novels about a teenage boy, all narrated by the youthful protagonist.

Rybakov first attracted international attention with *Heavy Sand* (1978), a highly readable novel about a Jewish family in the Soviet Union between 1910 and 1943. The subject was unusual for the time, but Rybakov's handling of it, though honest in many respects, was undercut by subtle, yet unmistakable, political orthodoxy. More recently, he has begun to publish a series of novels about the terror of the Stalin years, starting with *Children of Arbat,* on which he worked from the end of the 1950s until 1982. It was announced for publication twice, in 1966 and in 1978, before finally appearing in 1987. Regarded as a milestone of *glasnost,* it follows a group of young Muscovites to show the effects of the gathering political storm in the 1930s. Rybakov continues to trace the fate of his protagonists—and outline the period's bloody history—in the next novel in the series, *Fear.*

Novels by Rybakov

The Arbat Trilogy, Vol. 2: Fear. Little 1992 $24.95. ISBN 0-316-76377-2

Children of the Arbat. Little 1988 $19.95. ISBN 0-316-76372-1

Heavy Sand. Trans. by Harold Shukman. Viking Penguin 1982 $7.95. ISBN 0-14-005535-5

SALTYKOV-SHCHEDRIN, MIKHAIL (pseud., N. Shchedrin). 1826–1889

The greatest satirist of the nineteenth century, Saltykov served as a government official until the mid-1860s, when he began to devote himself full time to literature. A liberal, interested in Western literature, he suffered the political ups and downs of changing times. While editor of the journal *Notes of the*

Fatherland, he was an influential figure in Russian intellectual life, particularly in its radical wing; at the same time, he had sharp disagreements with other radicals over their social prescriptions for the future.

Much of Saltykov's writing is journalism, too topical to be easily accessible today. His major works, however, continue to be read with great interest. Among these is his magnificent parody on Russian history, *The History of a Town* (1869–70), presented as the chronicle of the town of Foolov (Stupidville). His most important work, however, is a set of stories from the second half of the 1870s about the decline of a gentry family, published as a single text under the title *The Golovlyov Family* (1876). The novel, with its unforgettably materialistic, hypocritical, and fatally flawed hero Porfiry Petrovich, ranks among the great creations of Russian realist prose.

Novels by Saltykov-Shchedrin

The Golovlyov Family. Trans. by Natalie Duddington. *Classics of Russian Lit. Ser.* Hyperion Conn. 1989 repr. of 1954 ed. $31.50. ISBN 0-88355-514-X

The Golovlyov Family. Trans. by Ronald Wilks. Viking Penguin 1988 $6.95. ISBN 0-14-044490-4

The History of a Town; Or, The Chronicle of Foolov. Trans. by Susan Brownsberger. Ardis Pubs. 1982 o.p.

The Pompadours. Trans. by David Magarshack. Ardis Pubs. 1984 $8.95. ISBN 0-88233-744-0. Introduction by Magarshack.

Short Story Collection by Saltykov-Shchedrin

Fables. Trans. by Vera Velkhovsky. *Classics of Russian Lit. Ser.* Hyperion Conn. 1977 repr. of 1931 ed. $15.00. ISBN 0-88355-516-6

SHALAMOV, VARLAM. 1907–1982

Shalamov, a poet and fiction writer, spent about 17 years in the Kolyma camps in Siberia, one of the harshest parts of the Soviet Gulag system. He fixed his experiences and those of other convicts in a cycle of superb short stories that convey the camps' overwhelming horror through terse, often single-episode, plots, dispassionate narration, and irony. Ideally, the Kolyma cycle should be read in conjunction with Solzhenitsyn's *The Gulag Archipelago.* The stories in the first of the two volumes in English translation, *Kolyma Tales,* are stronger than those in the second.

Shalamov's stories were smuggled abroad and first published in the West, in Russian and other languages. Unfortunately, he did not live to see their appearance in the Soviet Union during the Gorbachev period.

Short Story Collections by Shalamov

Graphite. Trans. by John Glad. Norton 1981 $14.95. ISBN 0-393-01476-2

Kolyma Tales. Trans. by John Glad. Norton 1982 o.p.

SHOLOKHOV, MIKHAIL. 1905–1984 (Nobel Prize 1965)

For decades a pillar of the Soviet literary establishment, Sholokhov owes his stature to *And Quiet Flows the Don* (1928–40), a four-volume epic of the life and fate of the Don Cossacks in the Revolution and civil war. Although himself a party member, Sholokhov depicts fairly impartially both sides in the conflict between the Reds and the Whites and shows how his hero, Grigory Melekhov, is driven by background and fate from one camp to the other. This realistic novel captures the exotic Cossack milieu superbly, and the whole works on a scale unseen since Tolstoy's *War and Peace.* Among Sholokhov's later works, *Virgin*

Soil Upturned (1932–60), which deals with the collectivization of agriculture, deserves particular mention; the first volume is far more direct and honest than the much-later second volume.

Over the years, Sholokhov's authorship of *And Quiet Flows the Don* has been questioned, most recently by SOLZHENITSYN, but Sholokhov has had strong defenders in both the Soviet Union and the West. His political stance accounts for part of the anger directed against him. Extremely conservative, Sholokhov made vicious attacks on dissidents and the West and, aside from his concern for environmental issues, was a devoted follower of the party line.

NOVELS BY SHOLOKHOV

And Quiet Flows the Don. Trans. by Stephen Garry. *Vintage Intl. Ser.* Random 1989 $15.00. ISBN 0-679-72521-0. The first two volumes of the four-volume *Quiet Flows the Don.* Contains a number of deletions.

Harvest on the Don. Knopf 1961 o.p. The second volume of *Virgin Soil Upturned.*

WORKS BY SHOLOKHOV

At the Bidding of the Heart: Essays, Sketches, Speeches, Papers. Imported Pubns. 1973 o.p.

Collected Works in Eight Volumes. St. Mut. 1985 $190.00. ISBN 0-317-42830-6

Stories. Imported Pubns. 1975 o.p.

BOOKS ABOUT SHOLOKHOV

Ermolaev, Herman. *Mikhail Sholokhov and His Art.* Princeton U. Pr. 1982 $50.00. ISBN 0-691-07634-0. A thorough life and works by a leading American expert on the writer.

Medvedev, Roi. *Problems in the Literary Biography of Mikhail Sholokhov.* Trans. by A. D. Briggs. Bks. Demand repr. of 1977 ed. $58.80. ISBN 0-317-20597-8. A discussion of Sholokhov's alleged plagiarism.

SHUKSHIN, VASILY. 1929–1974

Shukshin was a popular film actor and director, as well as one of the new generation of "village writers" who celebrate the countryside and search for stable values in the traditional, endangered society of rural Russia. He published a number of popular story collections, plays, and novels that used colloquial language with great effectiveness. Shukshin's most celebrated achievement, however, was the film *Snowball Berry Red,* the story of a former criminal who tries to reform, finds true love, and is killed by his former mates. Shuksin wrote the original story and directed and starred in the film.

SHORT STORY COLLECTIONS BY SHUKSHIN

Roubles in Words, Kopeks in Figures and Other Stories. Trans. by Natasha Ward and David Iliffe. M. Boyars Pubs. 1985 $14.95. ISBN 0-7145-2813-7. Introduction by Yevgeny Yevtushenko; translation occasionally problematic but generally good renderings of Shukshin into English.

Snowball Berry and Other Stories. Ed. by Donald M. Fiene. Trans. by Geoffrey Hosking. Ardis Pubs. 1979 o.p. Twelve works by Shukshin, complemented by good critical essays.

SIMONOV, KONSTANTIN. 1915–1979

Simonov had a long career as a poet, playwright, and novelist. His poetry includes many love lyrics as well as works on historical subjects and on war. He was at his best in fiction, particularly the trilogy dealing with World War II: *Days and Nights* (1943–44), about the battle of Stalingrad; *The Living and the Dead* (1959–71), about Soviet defeats in the first period of the war; and *Soldiers*

Are Not Born (1963–64), also about Stalingrad. Simonov, a leading member of the literary establishment, received the top Soviet prizes.

NOVEL BY SIMONOV

The Living and the Dead. 1959–1971. Trans. by R. Ainsztein. Greenwood 1969 o.p.

PLAY BY SIMONOV

The Whole World Over. Ed., trans., and adap. by Thelma Schnee. Dramatists Play 1990 $4.75. ISBN 0-8222-1248-X. An acting version of an early post-World War II play.

SINYAVSKY, ANDREI (pseud., Abram Terts). 1925–

Using the pseudonym Abram Terts, literary critic Andrei Sinyavsky wrote a number of satiric, often grotesque and surrealistic, prose works, including the short novel *The Trial Begins* (1960) and the essay "On Socialist Realism," a brilliant attack on the cliches of official Soviet literary dogma. In February 1966 he and writer Yuly Daniel were tried in a closed court. In spite of appeals by many writers in Russia and the West, they were sent to the labor camps for maligning the Soviet Union through "hostile" and "slanderous" writings published illegally abroad in the early 1960s. The trial marked the start of confrontations between the authorities and the nascent human-rights movement in the Soviet Union.

After Sinyavsky's emigration to the West in 1973, he became a professor of Russian literature at the Sorbonne and continued to publish, both under his own name and the pseudonym. He was very active in émigré literary life, generally taking a liberal, democratic position and frequently finding himself a target of attacks by more-nationalist figures.

Sinyavsky's newer writings include *A Voice from the Chorus* (1973), a hybrid text in which notes and letters from a penal camp are a vehicle for philosophical and literary meditations, and in which the author's own voice is joined by a multitude of voices of other inmates. His *A Stroll with Pushkin* (1975), a brilliant, joking discussion of Pushkin's art, provoked a storm of criticism both in the Soviet Union and abroad: Sinyavsky has been accused of blaspheming his nation's cultural icon. *Little Jinx* (1980) is a fantasy in which the personalities of both Sinyavsky and Terts are the objects of playful narrative manipulation.

Sinyavsky's varied contributions make him one of the most important figures in contemporary Russian letters. His writings have now been reissued in Russia, where he has recently been awarded an honorary doctorate.

NOVELS BY SINYAVSKY

Goodnight!. Viking Penguin 1989 $22.95. ISBN 0-670-80165-8. A fictional, idiosyncratic version of Sinyavsky's life.

Little Jinx. Trans. by Larry P. Joseph and Rachel May. *Studies in Russian Lit. & Theory Ser.* Northwestern U. Pr. 1992 $19.95. ISBN 0-8101-1016-4. Introduction by Edward J. Brown.

The Makepeace Experiment. Trans. by Manya Harari. Northwestern U. Pr. 1989 repr. of 1965 ed. $10.95. ISBN 0-8101-0838-0. Introduction by Harari.

The Trial Begins. 1960. Trans. by Max Hayward and George Denis. U. CA Pr. 1982 $10.95. ISBN 0-520-04677-3. Introduction by Czeslaw Milosz; bound with "On Socialist Realism."

A Voice from the Chorus. Hippocrene Bks. repr. of 1974 ed. $23.00. ISBN 0-374-97854-9

Short Story Collection by Sinyavsky

Fantastic Stories. Trans. by Max Hayward, Manya Harari, and Ronald Hingley. Northwestern U. Pr. 1986 repr. of 1963 ed. $12.95. ISBN 0-8101-0727-9

Book about Sinyavsky

Lourie, Richard. *Letters to the Future: An Approach to Sinyavsky-Tertz.* Cornell Univ. Pr. 1975 $14.50. ISBN 0-8014-0890-3. Combines biographical and sociohistorical information with commentaries on psychological and literary matters; better for the general reader than the specialist.

SOKOLOV, SASHA (ALEKSANDR). 1943–

Sokolov, who currently lives in the United States, was born in Canada, into a family of Soviet diplomats. After returning to the Soviet Union with his family, he studied journalism at Moscow University and then worked for a couple of newspapers and as a gamekeeper along the Volga River. His first novel, *A School for Fools,* is highly experimental: a powerful first-person account by a schizophrenic adolescent, often involving stream-of-consciousness word play. Sokolov sent the manuscript abroad prior to emigrating from the USSR in 1975, and it was published a year later. His second work, *Between Dog and Wolf* (1980), is a complex, difficult narrative employing extensive manipulation of language and narrative time. Sokolov's third novel, *Palisandriia* (*Astrophobia*) (1985), is a powerful spoof on Soviet society and history, treading not only on official sacred cows (Stalin, Brezhnev, etc.) but also on sexual taboos. Sokolov's works, like those of other writers of the "third wave" of emigration, have recently appeared in the Soviet Union/Russia.

Novels by Sokolov

Astrophobia. Trans. by Michael H. Heim. Grove Pr. 1989 o.p. "A magnificent translation . . . , this novel by a leading avant-garde Russian emigre writer (the next Nabokov?) is a literary parody written with great wit and luxurious verbal texture" (*LJ*).

A School for Fools. Trans. by Carl R. Proffer. FWEW 1988 $9.95. ISBN 0-941423-07-7

SOLOGUB, FEDOR (pseud. of Fyodor Kuzmich Teternikov). 1863–1927

Sologub was a member of the symbolist movement, particularly in its early decadent phase. A schoolteacher and school official for many years, he began to publish in the 1890s. His first novel was *Bad Dreams* (1896), a depiction of a hero struggling against provincial surroundings. He attracted wide attention with his second novel, *The Petty Demon* (1907), in which another provincial town, brilliantly satirized, is the background for the brutish Peredonov's descent into paranoia. This novel, standing at the transition from realist to modernist fiction, has been widely translated and was for a long time the only Sologub work available to Soviet readers. The trilogy *The Created Legend* (1907–13) is an ambitious attempt to lay out in narrative form Sologub's highly integrated, quasi-mythological worldview: very controversial, it was not judged successful.

Sologub also won recognition as a major Silver Age lyric poet, with verse notable for its economy and lyricism. Like much of his prose, it reflects Sologub's pessimistic, dualistic philosophy, which inverts traditional symbols of good and evil. However—moving in its simplicity, power, and authenticity—it is far more successful.

NOVELS BY SOLOGUB

Bad Dreams. Trans. by Vassar Smith. Ardis Pubs. 1978 $5.50. ISBN 0-88233-129-9. "Smith is not only accurate and faithful to the text, but his English rendition reads extremely well . . ." (*SEEJ*).

Created Legend, A Trilogy: Drops of Blood. Vol. 1. Trans. by Samuel Cioran. Ardis Pubs. 1978 $5.00. ISBN 0-88233-131-0. First part of trilogy; mixes lyrical imagery with satire, politics, and science fiction; an excellent translation.

Created Legend, A Trilogy: Queeen Ortruda. Vol. 2. Trans. by Samuel Cioran. Ardis Pubs. 1979 $5.00. ISBN 0-88233-143-4. Continuation of a controversial trilogy.

The Created Legend, A Trilogy: Smoke and Ashes. Vol. 3. Trans. by Samuel Cioran. Ardis Pubs. 1979 $5.00. ISBN 0-88233-145-0. Concludes the trilogy.

The Petty Demon. Trans. by Samuel Cioran. Ardis Pubs. 1983 $10.95. ISBN 0-88233-808-0. A new and readable translation, supplemented by several critical articles; includes textual variants.

SHORT STORY COLLECTION BY SOLOGUB

Sweet-Scented Name and Other Fairy Tales and Stories. Ed. by S. Graham. *Classics of Russian Lit. Ser.* Hyperion Conn. 1977 repr. of 1915 ed. $15.00. ISBN 0-88355-519-0

POETRY BY SOLOGUB

Sologub Twofold: English Verse Translations with Selected Russian Poems of F. K. Sologub. Trans. by Vassar W. Smith. Zapizdat Pubns. 1991 $6.45. ISBN 1-880964-00-7

BOOKS ABOUT SOLOGUB

Greene, Diana. *Insidious Intent: An Interpretation of Fedor Sologub's "The Petty Demon"*. Slavica 1986 $14.95. ISBN 0-89357-158-X. A good discussion of the novel; the first full-length study in English.

Rabinowitz, Stanley J. *Sologub's Literary Children: Keys to a Symbolist's Prose*. Slavica 1980 $13.95. ISBN 0-89357-069-9. Traces a major theme in Sologub's writings.

SOLOUKHIN, VLADIMIR. 1924–

One of the most noted of the "village writers," the prolific Soloukhin started to publish in 1946. His prose celebrates the countryside, both nature and town. A twentieth-century Slavophile, Soloukhin is concerned about the destruction of Russia's cultural monuments, particularly churches and icons, as evidenced in his controversial *Letters from the Russian Museum* (1966). *Vladimir Country Roads* (1953), a lyrical account of a walking trip in central Russia, is one of his best-known works.

NONFICTION BY SOLOUKHIN

Laughter over the Left Shoulder. Trans. by David Martin. Dufour 1990 $36.00. ISBN 0-7206-0798-1. A memoir that "combines the vivid immediacy of a child with the benefit of adult hindsight, intensifying the impact of this celebration of what was best in Russian village life" (*PW*).

Scenes from Russian Life. Trans. by David Martin. Dufour 1989 $34.00. ISBN 0-7206-0712-4. Introduction by Martin.

SOLZHENITSYN, ALEKSANDR. 1918– (NOBEL PRIZE 1970)

Solzhenitsyn achieved fame through works shaped by his experiences during the Stalin years. In February 1945, while in the army, he was arrested for letters written to a friend that were critical of Stalin and was sentenced to eight years' imprisonment. He served his term in various places, including a prison research institute fictionalized in his roman à clef *The First Circle* (1968). Exiled "in perpetuity" in 1953, he taught school in central Asia, overcame stomach cancer (his stay in an oncological clinic is reflected in *Cancer Ward* [1968]), was freed in 1956, and was officially "rehabilitated" a year later.

With this background, Solzhenitsyn became an unmatched chronicler of the Soviet penal system. His novella *One Day in the Life of Ivan Denisovich* (1962), which appeared during Krushchev's anti-Stalin campaign, was the first book to deal honestly with the Soviet "concentration-camp universe" and brought its author instant fame. For a few years, Solzhenitsyn enjoyed some official backing, but subsequently he was stopped from publishing and increasingly harassed. New attacks followed publication in the West of *Cancer Ward* and *The First Circle*; expulsion from the Writers' Union came in 1969. A year later, he was awarded the Nobel Prize for literature (and accepted it, unlike Boris Pasternak). The final episode in his duel with the state came in December 1973 when the first volume of *The Gulag Archipelago* was published in Paris (3 volumes, 1973–75). The appearance of this work, an enormous history and analysis of the camp system, resulted in the author's arrest and expulsion from the Soviet Union in February 1974.

Solzhenitsyn has lived a secluded life in Vermont since 1976, although he has given a number of well-publicized, controversial speeches and interviews concerning Western society, its relationship to the now-defunct Soviet bloc, and the fate of his native land. His most recent nonfiction is *Rebuilding Russia* (1991), published in the Soviet Union itself in an enormous press run. Read in the light of the political cataclysms that have engulfed the Soviet empire, Solzhenitsyn's émigré political writings now appear prophetic. His standing within Russia itself is enormous, and the issue of whether he will return to live there generates major interest.

Because Solzhenitsyn has revised and reissued his earlier works, readers should use newer translations, based on authorized texts. His principal new project is a series of novels (overall title, *The Red Wheel*) dealing with World War I and the Bolsheviks' rise to power. The first of these is *August 1914* (1971); two more installments, *October 1916* and *March 1917*, have appeared in Russian.

Solzhenitsyn follows in the tradition of DOSTOYEVSKY and TOLSTOY, using fiction to examine moral and philosophical concerns. He is a master of language, particularly noted for his picturesque colloquial Russian (including prison-camp slang).

NOVELS BY SOLZHENITSYN

August 1914: The Red Wheel. Trans. by Harry T. Willetts. FS&G 1990 $200.00. ISBN 0-374-10682-7. "This edition . . . contains all of the text from the original, plus additional material written after Solzhenitsyn's exile from the USSR in 1974" (*LJ*).

August 1914: The Red Wheel. Vol. 1. Trans. by Harry T. Willetts. Viking Penguin 1992 $15.00. ISBN 0-14-007122-9

Cancer Ward. Trans. by Nicholas Bethell and David Burg. Random 1989 $10.95. ISBN 0-685-28567-7

The First Circle: A Novel. HarpC 1990 repr. of 1968 ed. $17.00. ISBN 0-06-091683-4

One Day in the Life of Ivan Denisovich. Trans. by Harry T. Willetts. FS&G 1991 $24.95. ISBN 0-374-22643-1

WORKS BY SOLZHENITSYN

Candle in the Wind. Trans. by Keith Armes and Arthur Hudgins. U. of Minn. Pr. 1973 $11.95. ISBN 0-8166-0681-1. Artistically weak but important for its presentation of Solzhenitsyn's ideas.

Detente: Prospects for Democracy and Dictatorship. Issues in Contemporary Civilization Ser. Bks. Demand repr. of 1980 ed. $35.00. ISBN 0-317-20614-1. Criticism of U.S. foreign policy. Also includes a critique of Solzhenitsyn's views.

East and West: The Nobel Lecture on Literature, a World Split Apart, Letter to the Soviet Leaders, and a BBC Interview with Aleksandr I. Solzhenitsyn. HarpC 1980 o.p. Three major polemical statements.

The Gulag Archipelago. Vol. 1. Trans. by Thomas P. Whitney. HarpC 1991 repr. of 1973 ed. $16.00. ISBN 0-06-092102-1. Parts 1 and 2 of the massive chronicle of the Soviet camp system. A fascinating combination of historical analysis, literary craftsmanship, and polemics.

The Gulag Archipelago, Vol. 2: 1918–1956. Trans. by Thomas P. Whitney. HarpC 1992 repr. of 1975 ed. $10.00. ISBN 0-685-52544-9. Parts 3 and 4.

The Gulag Archipelago, Vol. 3: 1918–1956: An Experiment in Literary Investigation. Trans. by Harry T. Willets. HarpC 1992 repr. of 1979 ed. $16.00. ISBN 0-06-092104-8. Parts 5–7.

The Gulag Archipelago Three: Katorga, Exile, Stalin Is No More. Trans. by Harry T. Willetts. HarpC 1979 $4.95. ISBN 0-06-080396-7

The Gulag Archipelago. Ed. by Edward E. Ericson. Trans. by Thomas P. Whitney and Harry T. Willetts. HarpC 1985 $14.95. ISBN 0-06-091280-4. Abridged edition.

Letter to the Soviet Leaders. Trans. by Hilary Sternberg. HarpC 1974 o.p. An early formulation of Solzhenitsyn's views on the future of the Soviet Union, published while he was still living there.

The Mortal Danger: How Misconceptions about Russia Imperil America. HarpC 1986 $9.00. ISBN 0-06-132063-3. A strident criticism of U.S. policy and policy makers.

Nobel Lecture. Trans. by F. D. Reeve. FS&G 1973 o.p.

The Nobel Lecture on Literature. Trans. by Thomas P. Whitney. HarpC 1972 $5.95. ISBN 0-06-013943-9. Solzhenitsyn's lecture emphasizes the moral dimension of literature and authorship.

The Oak and the Calf: A Memoir. Trans. by Harry Willetts. HarpC 1980 $17.45. ISBN 0-06-014014-3. Solzhenitsyn against the Soviet system until his exile; often fascinating, sometimes pretentious.

Prussian Nights: Bilingual Edition. Trans. by Robert Conquest. FS&G 1977 $2.95. ISBN 0-374-51391-0. A weak poem about World War II.

Rebuilding Russia: Toward Some Formulations. Trans. by Alexis Klimoff. FS&G 1991 $14.95. ISBN 0-374-17342-7

Stories and Prose Poems. Trans. by Michael Glenny. FS&G 1971 $8.95. ISBN 0-374-51116-0

Victory Celebrations, Prisoners, and The Love-Girl and the Innocent. FS&G 1986 $12.95. ISBN 0-374-51924-2. The texts of three plays.

Warning to the West. FS&G 1986 $7.95. ISBN 0-374-51334-1. Speeches and interviews 1975–1976, often critical of Western society.

A World Split Apart. HarpC 1988 o.p. Text of the controversial 1978 commencement address at Harvard, a biting critique of Western society and values.

BOOKS ABOUT SOLZHENITSYN

Berman, Ronald, ed. *Solzhenitsyn at Harvard: The Address, Twelve Early Responses, and Six Later Reflections.* Ethics & Public Policy 1980 $9.95. ISBN 0-89633-023-0. A good sample of commentary on Solzhenitsyn's Harvard speech.

Dunlop, John B., Richard Haugh, and Alexis Klimoff, eds. *Aleksandr Solzhenitsyn: Critical Essays and Documentary Materials.* Macmillan 1975 $4.95. ISBN 0-685-52103-6. A very important collection on Solzhenitsyn prior to his exile.

Dunlop, John B., Richard S. Haugh, and Michael Nicholson, eds. *Solzhenitsyn in Exile: Critical Essays and Documentary Materials.* Hoover Inst. Pr. 1985 $19.95. ISBN 0-8179-8051-2. Also a very important, solid anthology.

Feuer, Kathryn B., ed. *Solzhenitsyn: A Collection of Critical Essays.* P-H 1976 o.p. A nice selection of studies, oriented toward literature.

Kelley, Donald R. *The Solzhenitsyn-Sakharov Dialogue: Politics, Society, and the Future. Contributions in Pol. Sci. Ser.* Greenwood repr. of 1982 ed. $42.95. ISBN 0-313-22940-6. Compares the visions of an alternative Soviet Union proposed by the two Nobel Prize winners.

Lakshin, Vladimir. *Solzhenitsyn, Tvardovsky and Novy Mir.* Trans. by Michael Glenny. MIT Pr. 1980 $20.00. ISBN 0-262-12086-0. An account of the early Solzhenitsyn, by a participant in the events surrounding his first publications.

Pontuso, James F. *Solzhenitsyn's Political Thought.* U. Pr. of Va. 1990 $30.00. ISBN 0-8139-1283-0

Scammell, Michael. *Solzhenitsyn: A Biography.* Norton 1986 $14.95. ISBN 0-393-30378-0. The most up-to-date, extensive study of Solzhenitsyn's life and writings.

Siegel, Paul N. *The Great Reversal: Politics and Art in Solzhenitsyn.* Walnut Pub. 1991. ISBN 0-929405-06-4

STRUGATSKY, ARKADY. 1925– and STRUGATSKY, BORIS. 1933–

Popular science-fiction writers, the Strugatsky brothers have used the genre since the 1960s to comment on contemporary society, at times provoking major controversy. *It's Hard to Be a God* (1964) is a dysutopia with commentary on historical theories. *The Snail on the Slope* (1966–68) features a KGB-like organization and an extraordinarily oppressive atmosphere. Pre-*glasnost,* some of the Strugatskys' major works had to be circulated in *samizdat,* but the brothers' situation is now dramatically better.

Novels by Arkady and Boris Strugatsky

Inspector Glebsky's Puzzle. Eagle Pub. Corp. 1988 o.p.

Roadside Picnic. PB 1982 $2.50. ISBN 0-671-45842-6

The Snail on the Slope. Bantam o.p.

The Time Wanderers. Trans. by Antonina W. Bouis. Eagle Pub. Corp. 1987 o.p. Bureaucratic satire that "recalls the work of Stanislaw Lem, but aside from its interesting comment on Soviet imperialism, . . . is a sturdy if unexceptional effort" (*PW*).

Book about Arkady and Boris Strugatsky

Slusser, George E., ed. *Stalkers of the Infinite: The Science Fiction of Arkady and Boris Strugatsky.* Borgo Pr. 1992 $24.95. ISBN 0-8095-4500-4

TOLSTAYA, TATYANA. 1951–

Tatyana Tolstaya—"the most original, tactile, luminous voice in Russian prose today," according to Joseph Brodsky—worked at various publishing jobs after graduating from Leningrad University and appeared on the Moscow literary scene in 1983 with the favorably received story "Loves Me, Loves Me Not." Her first collection, *On the Golden Porch* (1988), proved extremely popular. Soon afterward she came to the United States on the first of a series of visiting university appointments and has plunged actively into cultural life in this country: She writes for the *New York Review of Books,* the *New Republic, The New Yorker,* and other magazines, as well as for publications in Russia. Her forte is the short story, her writing distinguished by exuberance, a talent for description, a comic sensibility, and more than a touch of the surreal. For one reviewer, "the discrepancy between fondest desires and disappointing reality" lies at the core of her writing, which is "a fiction of vast possibility, propelled not by plot, but by a narrative voice that imaginatively conveys the ambiguities of her characters' inner lives" (*Baltimore Morning Sun*). *Sleepwalker in a Fog* (1991) is her second book.

SHORT STORY COLLECTIONS BY TOLSTAYA

On the Golden Porch. Knopf 1989 $17.95. ISBN 0-394-57798-1. "[T]his collection marks Tolstaya as a natural storyteller who sheds fresh light on the contemporary Moscow scene" (*PW*).

Sleepwalker in a Fog: Stories. Knopf 1991 $18.50. ISBN 0-394-58731-6. Eight stories, including "Most Beloved," "Heavenly Flame," and "The Poet and the Muse."

TOLSTOY, LEO (TOLSTOI, LEV). 1828–1910

Tolstoy's life was defined by moral and artistic seeking and by conflict with himself and his surroundings. Of the old nobility, he began by living the usual, dissipated life of a man of his class; however, his inner compulsion for moral self-justification led him in a different direction. In 1851 he became a soldier in the Caucasus and began to publish even while stationed there (*Childhood* [1852] and other works). Even more significant were his experiences during the Crimean War: the siege of Sevastopol provided the background for his sketches of human behavior in battle in the *Sevastopol Stories* (1855–56).

After the war, Tolstoy mixed for a time with St. Petersburg literary society, traveled extensively abroad, and married Sophia Bers. The couple were happy for a long time, with Countess Tolstoy participating actively in her husband's literary and other endeavors. The center of Tolstoy's life became family, which he celebrated in the final section of *War and Peace* (1869). In this great novel, he unfolded the stories of several families in Russia during the Napoleonic period and explored the nature of historical causation and of freedom and necessity. A different note emerged in *Anna Karenina* (1876). Here, too, Tolstoy focused on families but this time emphasized an individual's conflict with society's norms. A period of inner crisis, depression, and thoughts of suicide culminated in Tolstoy's 1879 conversion to a rationalistic form of Christianity in which moral behavior was supremely important. *Confession* (1882) describes this profound transition.

Tolstoy now began to proselytize his new-found faith through fiction, essays, and personal contacts. Between 1880 and 1883, he wrote three major works on religion. A supreme polemicist, he participated in debates on a large number of political and social issues, generally at odds with the government. His advocacy of nonresistance to evil attracted many followers and later had a profound influence on Mahatma Gandhi and, through him, MARTIN LUTHER KING, JR. (see Vol. 4). Tolstoy's stature as a writer and public figure was enormous both within Russia and abroad, greater than that of any other Russian writer. When the Orthodox Church excommunicated him in 1901, a cartoon depicted him as disproportionately larger than his ecclesiastical judges.

Tolstoy's final years were filled with inner torment: Living as he did on a luxurious estate, he felt himself to be a betrayer of his own teachings. He also suffered from disputes with his wife over the disposition of his property, which she wished to safeguard for their children. In 1910, desperately unhappy, the aged writer left his home at Yasnaya Polyana. He did not get far; he caught pneumonia and died of heart failure at a railway station, an event that was headline news throughout the world.

In the course of Tolstoy's career, his art evolved significantly, but it possessed a certain underlying unity. From the beginning, he concentrated on the inner life of human beings, though the manner of his analysis changed. The body of his writing is enormous, encompassing both fiction and a vast amount of theoretical and polemical material. Besides his three great novels—*War and Peace, Anna Karenina*, and *Resurrection* (1899)—he wrote many superb shorter works. Among these, *The Death of Ivan Ilyich* (1886) stands out as a literary masterpiece and fine philosophical text, while the short novel *Hadji Murat* (1904), set in the Caucasus and Russia during the reign of Nicholas I, is a gem of narration and plot construction.

Tolstoy has been translated extensively. The Louise and Aylmer Maude and Constance Garnett translations are institutions (for many works, the only versions available) and are used by different publishers, sometimes in modernized versions. New translations by Rosemary Edmonds, David Magarshack, and Ann Dunigan are also justifiably popular.

Novels by Tolstoy

Anna Karenina. Buccaneer Bks. 1990 $49.95. ISBN 0-89966-672-8

Anna Karenina. Ed. by L. J. Kent and N. Berberova. Trans. by Constance Garnett. Random 1978 $16.95. ISBN 0-394-60448-2

Anna Karenina. Trans. by Louise and Aylmer Maude. *World's Classics Paperback Ser.* OUP 1980 $5.95. ISBN 0-19-281510-5. Introduction by John Bayley.

The Death of Ivan Ilyich. Trans. by Lynn Solotaroff. *Bantam Classics Ser.* Bantam 1981 $2.50. ISBN 0-553-21035-1. Introduction by Ronald Blythe.

The Death of Ivan Ilyich. *Classic Short Stories Ser.* Creative Ed. 1990 $10.95. ISBN 0-88682-298-X

Resurrection. Trans. by Rosemary Edmonds. *Penguin Classics Ser.* Viking Penguin 1966 $5.95. ISBN 0-14-044184-0

War and Peace. Trans. by Constance Garnett. The World's Great Bks. Ser. Time Warner Libraries 1991 $19.95. ISBN 1-879329-02-6

War and Peace. Ed. by Henry Gifford. Trans. by Louise and Aylmer Maude. *The World's Classics Ser.* OUP 1991 $8.95. ISBN 0-19-282780-4

Short Story Collections by Tolstoy

Childhood, "Boyhood" and "Youth". Trans. by Rosemary Edmonds. *Penguin Classics Ser.* Viking Penguin 1964 $5.95. ISBN 0-14-044139-5

Cossacks, Sevastopol, The Invaders and Other Stories. *Short Story Index Repr. Ser.* Ayer repr. of 1899 ed. $32.00. ISBN 0-8369-3416-4

Esarhaddon and Other Tales. *Short Story Index Repr. Ser.* Ayer 1903 $11.00. ISBN 0-8369-3417-2

The Forged Coupon. Trans. by David Patterson. Norton 1985 $12.95. ISBN 0-393-01912-8

Great Short Works of Leo Tolstoy. HarpC 1967 $7.00. ISBN 0-06-083071-9

The Kreutzer Sonata and Other Stories. Trans. by David McDuff. *Penguin Classics Ser.* Viking Penguin 1986 $4.95. ISBN 0-14-044469-6

A Landowner's Morning, Family Happiness, The Devil. Trans. by Kyril Fitzlyon and April Fitzlyon. Salem Hse. Pubs. 1984 $13.95. ISBN 0-7043-2426-1

A Landowner's Morning, Family Happiness, The Devil. Trans. by Kyril Fitzlyon and April Fitzlyon. Interlink Pub. 1990 $11.95. ISBN 0-7043-0117-2

Master and Man and Other Stories. Trans. by Paul Foote. *Penguin Classics Ser.* Viking Penguin 1977 $4.95. ISBN 0-14-044331-2. Includes "Father Sergius" and *Hadji Murat*.

The Raid and Other Stories. Ed. by Louise and Aylmer Maude. *World's Classics Paperback Ser.* OUP 1982 $5.95. ISBN 0-19-281584-9. Introduction by P. N. Furbank.

The Russian Proprietor and Other Stories. Trans. by Nathan H. Dole. *Short Story Index Repr. Ser.* Ayer repr. of 1887 ed. $21.00. ISBN 0-8369-3371-0

The Sebastopol Sketches. Trans. by David McDuff. *Penguin Classics Ser.* Viking Penguin 1986 $5.95. ISBN 0-14-044468-8. Introduction by McDuff.

Tolstoy: Tales of Courage and Conflict. Ed. by Charles Neider. Carroll & Graf 1985 $11.95. ISBN 0-88184-165-X. Thirty-six shorter works arranged chronologically, including "The Death of Ivan Ilyich" and "The Kreutzer Sonata."

Tolstoy's Short Stories. Ed. by Michael Katz. Norton 1990 $9.95. ISBN 0-393-96016-1

NONFICTION BY TOLSTOY

Confession. Trans. by David Patterson. Norton 1984 repr. of 1983 ed. $12.95. ISBN 0-393-01756-7

A Confession and Other Religious Writings. Viking Penguin 1988 $6.95. ISBN 0-14-044473-4. Introduction by Jane Kentish.

Essays and Letters. Trans. by Aylmer Maude. *Select Bib. Ser.* Irvington repr. of 1909 ed. $23.50. ISBN 0-8290-0491-2

I Cannot Be Silent: Selected Non-Fiction by Leo Tolstoy. Ed. by W. Gareth Jones. Intl. Spec. Bk. 1989 $48.00. ISBN 1-85399-022-1. Introduction by Jones.

The Gospel according to Tolstoy. Ed. and trans. by David Patterson. U. of Ala. Pr. 1992. ISBN 0-8173-0590-4

The Kingdom of God Is within You. Trans. by Constance Garnett. U. of Nebr. Pr. 1984 repr. of 1894 ed. $8.50. ISBN 0-8032-9404-2. Foreword by Martin Green.

Last Diaries. Ed. by Robert Kastenbaum. Trans. by Lydia W. Kesich. *Aging & Old Age Ser.* Ayer 1979 repr. of 1960 ed. $23.00. ISBN 0-405-11835-X

Tolstoy: Literary Fragments, Letters and Reminiscences. Ed. by Rene Fullop-Miller. AMS Pr. repr. of 1931 ed. $21.50. ISBN 0-404-06479-5

Tolstoy's Diaries. 2 vols. Ed. and trans. by R. F. Christian. Macmillan 1986 $60.00. ISBN 0-684-18512-1

Tolstoy's Letters. 2 vols. Ed. and trans. by R. F. Christian. *Encore Ed. Ser.* Macmillan 1978 $35.00. ISBN 0-684-15596-6. More than 600 letters from 1845 to 1910; excellent translations; detailed annotations.

Tolstoy on Education. Trans. by Leo Wiener. U. Ch. Pr. 1968 $2.95. ISBN 0-226-80777-0. A selection of essays from the 1860s, with a good introduction; a dated but serviceable translation.

What Is Art? Trans. by Aylmer Maude. Macmillan 1960 $7.00. ISBN 0-672-60221-0. A celebrated exposition of Tolstoy's view of art as a vehicle for humankind's moral transformation.

What Then Must We Do?. Seven Hills Bk. Dists. 1991 $13.95. ISBN 1-870098-33-1. Introduction by Ronald Sampson.

Writings on Civil Disobedience and Nonviolence. Trans. by Aylmer Maude and Ronald Sampson. New Soc. Pubs. 1988 $39.95. ISBN 0-86571-109-7. Introduction by David H. Albert; preface by George Zabelka.

WORKS BY TOLSTOY

Complete Works of Count Tolstoy. 24 vols. Trans. by Leo Wiener. AMS Pr. repr. of 1905 ed. $900.00. ISBN 0-404-06580-5

Father Sergius, and Other Stories and Plays. Short Story Index Repr. Ser. Ayer repr. of 1911 ed. $20.00. ISBN 0-8369-3686-8. Introduction by Aylmer Maude.

The Portable Tolstoy. Ed. by John Bayley. Trans. by Louise Maude, Aylmer Maude, and George L. Kline. *Viking Portable Lib. Ser.* Viking Penguin 1978 $10.95. ISBN 0-14-015091-9. Chronologically arranged; includes "The Kreutzer Sonata" and "The Power of Darkness."

BOOKS ABOUT TOLSTOY

Bayley, John. *Tolstoy and the Novel.* U. Ch. Pr. 1988 $13.95. ISBN 0-226-03960-9. ". . . [F]requently unorthodox interpretations and insights" offered "in an erratic, almost unsystematic manner with little reference to the existing critical literature" (*SEEJ*).

Bloom, Harold, ed. *Leo Tolstoy. Modern Critical Views Ser.* Chelsea Hse. 1986 $34.95. ISBN 0-87754-727-0. Introduction by Bloom.

______, ed. *Leo Tolstoy's Anna Karenina. Modern Critical Interp. Ser.* Chelsea Hse. 1987 $24.95. ISBN 1-55546-077-1. Introduction by Bloom.

______, ed. *Leo Tolstoy's War and Peace. Modern Critical Interp. Ser.* Chelsea Hse. 1987 $24.95. ISBN 1-55546-078-X. Introduction by Bloom.

Chertkov, Vladimir G. *The Last Days of Tolstoy*. Trans. by Nathalie A. Duddington. Kraus 1973 $28.00. ISBN 0-527-16500-X. An account by Tolstoy's chief disciple; one sided but important.

Christian, Reginald F. *Tolstoy: A Critical Introduction*. Cambridge U. Pr. 1970 $19.95. ISBN 0-521-09585-9. Compact, accurate, and well organized.

Diffey, T. J. *Tolstoy's "What Is Art?": An Essay in the Philosophy of Art*. Routledge Chapman & Hall 1986 $39.50. ISBN 0-7099-0891-1

Egan, David R., and Melinda A. Egan. *Leo Tolstoy: An Annotated Bibliography of English-Language Sources to 1978*. Scarecrow 1979 $29.00. ISBN 0-8108-1232-0

Fodor, Alexander. *A Quest for a Non-Violent Russia: The Partnership of Leo Tolstoy and Vladimir Chertkov*. U. Pr. of Amer. 1989 $48.25. ISBN 0-8191-7536-6. Studies the relationship between the writer and his secretary-disciple.

Gifford, Henry. *Tolstoy. Past Masters Ser.* OUP 1982 $14.95. ISBN 0-19-287545-0. An introductory overview of the relationship between Tolstoy's philosophical writings and his imaginative work.

Gustafson, Richard F. *Leo Tolstoy: Resident and Stranger; A Study in Fiction and Theology*. Princeton U. Pr. 1986 $55.00. ISBN 0-691-06674-4. A very sophisticated analysis of the philosophical and theological background of Tolstoy's art and thought.

Jones, Malcolm V., ed. *New Essays on Tolstoy*. Cambridge U. Pr. 1979 $47.95. ISBN 0-521-22091-2. Essays by British scholars; "remarkably intelligent . . . provocative and interesting" (*SEEJ*).

Knowles, A. V., ed. *Tolstoy: The Critical Heritage*. Routledge Chapman & Hall 1978 $69.50. ISBN 0-7100-8947-3. ". . . [T]he material presented offers an interesting panorama of critical opinion, which should prove eminently useful both to the specialist and the general reader" (*SEEJ*).

McLean, Hugh, ed. *In the Shade of the Giant: Essays on Tolstoy*. U. CA Pr. 1989 $35.00. ISBN 0-520-06405-4. ". . . [T]his is an impressive collection of essays, with many useful insights . . ." (*SEEJ*).

Matual, David. *Tolstoy's Translation of the Gospels: A Critical Study*. E Mellen 1992 $69.95. ISBN 0-7734-9502-9

Maude, Aylmer. *The Life of Tolstoy*. 2 vols. OUP 1987 $12.95. ISBN 0-19-282027-3

Pinch, Alan, and Michael Armstrong, eds. *Tolstoy on Education: Tolstoy's Educational Writings, 1861–62*. Fairleigh Dickinson 1982 $40.00. ISBN 0-8386-3121-5

Reaske, Herbert. *Monarch Notes on Tolstoy's Anna Karenina*. P-H $3.95. ISBN 0-671-00571-5

Silbajoris, Rimvydas. *Tolstoy's Aesthetics and His Art*. Slavica 1991 $24.95. ISBN 0-89357-216-0. Argues that there is no discrepancy between Tolstoy's views on art and his practice of it.

Steiner, George. *Tolstoy or Dostoevsky: An Essay in the Old Criticism*. U. Ch. Pr. 1985 $12.95. ISBN 0-226-77226-8. A classic study, focusing on the dichotomy between the two great writers.

Thorlby, Anthony. *Tolstoy: Anna Karenina. Landmarks of World Lit. Ser.* Cambridge U. Pr. 1987 $22.95. ISBN 0-521-32819-5

Tolstaia, Sophia Andreevna. *The Diaries of Sophia Tolstoy*. Ed. by O. A. Golinenko. Trans. by Cathy Porter. Random 1985 $35.00. ISBN 0-394-52818-2. A very useful exposition of family life, conflicts.

Tolstoy, Alexandra L. *Tolstoy: A Life of My Father*. Hippocrene Bks. 1973 repr. of 1953 ed. $29.00. ISBN 0-374-97956-1. Tolstoy's daughter offers a personal view.

Wasiolek, Edward. *Tolstoy's Major Fiction*. U. Ch. Pr. 1981 $6.95. ISBN 0-226-87398-6. A "concise, lucid, and challenging study" (*Slavic Review*).

———, ed. *Critical Essays on Tolstoy. Critical Essays on World Lit. Ser.* G. K. Hall 1986 $40.00. ISBN 0-8161-8827-0

Wilson, A. N. *Tolstoy*. Fawcett 1988 $25.00. ISBN 0-393-02585-3

TRIFONOV, YURY. 1925–1981

The main achievement of Trifonov's three decades in literature is a series of short novels from the late 1960s and 1970s about the Russian intelligentsia: *The Exchange, Preliminary Stocktaking, The Long Goodbye, Another Life, The House on the Embankment,* and *The Old Man.* In them he explores human relationships in the problematic urban existence close to the heart of all ordinary Russian readers: exchange of apartments, competition for careers, money troubles, and so on. The novels are also a longer-term investigation, through flashbacks and reminiscences, of the Stalin period and its disastrous effects on society. *Disappearance,* begun in the 1950s and clearly written "for the drawer" (with no expectations of publication), appeared posthumously. It takes up some of the same themes, such as mass arrests during the period 1937 to 1942, of Trifonov's other works, but much more explicitly.

NOVELS BY TRIFONOV

Disappearance. Trans. by David Lowe. Ardis Pubs. 1991 $23.95. ISBN 0-87501-089-X

SHORT STORY COLLECTION BY TRIFONOV

The Exchange and Other Stories. Trans. by Ronald Meyer. *Contemporary Russian Prose Ser.* Ardis Pubs. 1991 $9.95. ISBN 0-679-73442-2. Introduction by Ellendea Proffer.

BOOK ABOUT TRIFONOV

Kolesnikoff, Nina. *Yury Trifonov: A Critical Study.* Ardis Pubs. 1991 $32.95. ISBN 0-87501-051-2. The first comprehensive treatment of Trifonov in English.

TSVETAEVA (TSVETAYEVA), MARINA. 1892–1941

Tsvetaeva, whose first collection appeared in 1910, ranks among the major twentieth-century Russian poets. Her numerous lyrics and long poems are distinguished by great vigor and passion and an astonishing technical mastery. Her language and rhythms are highly innovative. In subject, her poetry varies greatly, often diarylike but also intensely concerned with the fate of her generation, of Russia, and of Europe. Tsvetaeva did not shy away from controversial topics, often opposing received dogma, be it Soviet or Russian émigré. She frequently subsumed herself in other characters, merging dramatic and lyrical elements. Particularly striking are her long poems *Poem of the Mountain, Poem of the End,* and *Ratcatcher* and her later collections *Craft* (1923) and *After Russia* (1928). After emigrating from the Soviet Union, Tsvetaeva also seriously turned to prose. Drawing on her past, she wrote a number of striking quasi-autobiographical pieces, deeply exploring problems of literary and artistic creation.

Tsvetaeva's husband fought as an officer against the Reds in the Crimea, and she celebrates the White Army in the collection *The Demesne of Swans* (1957). Following the civil war, she led a difficult and isolated existence in Prague and Paris during the twenties and thirties. Her eventual return to the Soviet Union in 1939, largely for family reasons, ended in tragedy; isolated and humiliated by official Soviet literary figures, she committed suicide in 1941. Her work was first republished in the Soviet Union in the 1960s, and the current period has brought a new wave of interest and new editions. As was the case with her writing from the start, poets are a particularly attentive audience.

Poetry by Tsvetaeva

After Russia—Posle Rossii. Ed. and trans. by Michael Naydan. Ardis Pubs. 1992 repr. of 1928 ed. $32.50. ISBN 0-87501-076-8. A bilingual edition of Tsvetaeva's last collection of lyrics.

The Demesne of the Swans—Lebedinyi Stan. Trans. by Robin Kemball. Ardis Pubs. 1993 $15.00. ISBN 0-88233-493-X. Poems on the civil war.

Selected Poems. Trans. by Elaine Feinstein. NAL-Dutton 1987 $12.95. ISBN 0-525-48283-0. "In Feinstein [Tsvetaeva] has found a superb translator and a biographer whose feeling for her subject is evident in every concise line" (*LJ*).

Selected Poems. Trans. by David McDuff. Dufour 1988 $18.95. ISBN 1-85224-025-3

Works by Tsvetaeva

Art in the Light of Conscience: Eight Essays on Poetry by Marina Tsvetaeva. Trans. by Angela Livingstone. HUP 1992 $27.95. ISBN 0-674-04802-4. "[S]he airs gripes about bad criticism and shares her infectious enthusiasm for Russian poetry and poets, including her contemporaries in the Soviet Union. The translation transmits much of the pith of her idiosyncratic prose" (*LJ*).

A Captive Spirit: Selected Prose. Ed. and trans. by J. Marin King. *Prose of the Russian Poets Ser.* Ardis Pubs. 1991 $19.95. ISBN 0-88233-353-4. Experimental prose, accurately translated and well annotated.

Books about Tsvetaeva

Karlinsky, Simon. *Marina Tsvetaeva: The Woman, Her World, and Her Poetry. Cambridge Studies in Russian Lit.* Cambridge U. Pr. 1986 $54.50. ISBN 0-521-25582-1. An excellent overall study by a leading specialist on Tsvetaeva.

Proffer, Ellendea C., ed. *Marina Tsvetaeva: A Pictorial Biography, Eighteen Ninety-Two to Nineteen Forty-One.* Ardis Pubs. 1980 $15.95. ISBN 0-88233-359-3. A wealth of visual material, although poorly organized.

Taubman, Jane A. *A Life through Poetry: Marina Tsvetaeva's Lyric Diary.* Slavica 1989 $17.95. ISBN 0-89357-197-0. Studies the nonnarrative poems as a continuously unfolding diary, a created biography; a careful exploration of biography and myth making.

TURGENEV, IVAN. 1818–1883

Turgenev was the first great Russian novelist to win popularity abroad. Of wealthy aristocratic background, he resided in Western Europe for much of his adult life, receiving honors not only in Russia but also in France and England (Henry James [see Vol. 1] included him in a survey of French novelists). His realistic sketches, first published in the journal *The Contemporary* and later in book form as *Sketches from a Hunter's Album* (1852), were immediately successful and highly influential: they depicted the sufferings of the peasants and helped arouse public opinion concerning the evils of serfdom. The three succeeding novels—*Rudin* (1856), *A Nest of the Gentry* (1859), and *On the Eve* (1860)—helped cement Turgenev's fame and reputation. His best novel, *Fathers and Children* (1862), proved controversial in all quarters, unsentimentally depicting the conflict between radically inclined young people and their more conservative parents. Reacting to the hostile reception, Turgenev permanently abandoned Russia for the West, where he produced his last two novels, *Smoke* (1867), a satire of aristocratic circles, and *Virgin Soil* (1877), about the Populist movement of the 1870s.

Taken together, Turgenev's novels form a literary chronicle of major trends in Russian life during the middle decades of the nineteenth century. Their plots are generally subdued and their protagonists aimless—unsure, "superfluous" men trying to find a role for themselves in society. After the unblinking realism of *Sketches from a Hunter's Album*, the later short works are increasingly nostalgic and resigned, with *Asya* (1858) and *First Love* (1860) superb blends of irony and lyric mood. Tales from the last period of Turgenev's life include strong elements of the fantastic and the poetic, as evidenced by his *Poems in Prose* (originally titled *Senilia*) (1879–83). and show a continually evolving narrative technique.

Turgenev also wrote plays. The most important is *A Month in the Country* (1850), which had an impact on Russian dramatic repertoire and foreshadows certain of CHEKHOV's innovations.

NOVELS BY TURGENEV

Fathers and Children. Knopf 1991 $15.00. ISBN 0-679-40536-4. Introduction by John Bayley.

Fathers and Sons. Ed. and trans. by Richard Freeborn. *The World's Classics Ser.* OUP 1991 $4.95. ISBN 0-19-282256-X

Fathers and Sons. Ed. and trans. by Ralph Matlaw. *Critical Ed. Ser.* Norton 1989 $7.95. ISBN 0-393-95795-0

Fathers and Sons. Trans. by Barbara Makanowitzky. Bantam 1982 $3.50. ISBN 0-553-21259-1. Introduction by Alexandra Tolstoy.

Fathers and Sons. Trans. by Constance Garnett. *Airmont Classics Ser.* Airmont 1967 $1.95. ISBN 0-8049-0129-5. Introduction by R. R. Canon.

Home of the Gentry. Trans. by Richard Freeborn. *Penguin Classics Ser.* Viking Penguin 1970 $6.95. ISBN 0-14-044224-3

Novels of Ivan Turgenev. 15 vols. Trans. by Constance Garnett. AMS Pr. repr. of 1899 ed. $400.00. ISBN 0-404-01900-5

On the Eve. Trans. by Gilbert Gardiner. *Penguin Classics Ser.* Viking Penguin 1950 $4.95. ISBN 0-14-044009-7

Rudin. Trans. by Richard Freeborn. *Penguin Classics Ser.* Viking Penguin 1975 $5.95. ISBN 0-14-044304-5

Smoke. Biblio. Dist. 1965 o.p.

Virgin Soil. Trans. by Constance Garnett. Grove Pr. 1977 o.p. Introduction by Garnett.

SHORT STORY COLLECTIONS BY TURGENEV

Brigadier and Other Stories. Trans. by Isabel F. Hapgood. *Short Story Index Repr. Ser.* Ayer repr. of 1904 ed. $30.00. ISBN 0-8369-4067-9

Desperate Character and Other Stories. Trans. by Constance Garnett. *Short Story Index Repr. Ser.* Ayer repr. of 1917 ed. $16.00. ISBN 0-8369-3688-4

Dream Tales and Prose Poems. Trans. by Constance Garnett. *Short Story Index Repr. Ser.* Ayer repr. of 1897 ed. $20.00. ISBN 0-8369-3273-0

First Love. Ed. by F. G. Gregory. Blackwell Pubs. 1989 $15.95. ISBN 0-631-14384-X

First Love and Other Stories. Ed. and trans. by Richard Freeborn. *The World's Classics Ser.* OUP 1989 $5.95. ISBN 0-19-282591-7

The Jew, and Other Stories. Trans. by Isabel F. Hapgood. *Short Story Index Repr. Ser.* Ayer repr. of 1904 ed. $17.00. ISBN 0-8369-3059-2

Phantoms, and Other Stories. Trans. by Isabel F. Hapgood. *Short Story Index Repr. Ser.* Ayer repr. of 1904 ed. $18.00. ISBN 0-8369-4029-6

Reckless Character, and Other Stories. Trans. by Isabel F. Hapgood. *Short Story Index Repr. Ser.* Ayer repr. of 1904 ed. $20.00. ISBN 0-8369-4066-0

Spring Torrents. Trans. by Leonard Shapiro. *Penguin Classics Ser.* Viking Penguin 1980 $7.95. ISBN 0-14-044369-X

Torrents of Spring, etc. Trans. by Constance Garnett. *Short Story Index Repr. Ser.* Ayer repr. of 1916 ed. $19.00. ISBN 0-8369-3830-5

PLAYS BY TURGENEV

A Month in the Country. Ed. and trans. by Richard Freeborn. *The World's Classics Ser.* OUP 1991 $4.95. ISBN 0-19-282622-0

A Month in the Country. Trans. by Ariadne Nicolaeff. Dramatists Play 1990 $4.75. ISBN 0-8222-0772-9

Three Famous Plays: A Month in the Country; a Provincial Lady; a Poor Gentleman. Trans. by Constance Garnett. *Classics of Russian Lit. Ser.* Hyperion Conn. 1977 repr. of 1951 ed. $15.00. ISBN 0-88355-521-2. Introduction by David Garnett.

Works by Turgenev

The Essential Turgenev. Ed. and trans. by Elizabeth C. Allen. Northwestern U. Pr. $64.95. ISBN 0-8101-1060-1

Letters in Two Volumes. Ed. and trans. by David Lowe. Ardis Pubs. 1983 o.p. A collection of 334 letters; very accurate, though sometimes choppy, translation.

Sketches from a Hunter's Album: The Complete Edition. Trans. by Richard Freeborn. Viking Penguin 1990 $5.95. ISBN 0-14-044522-6. Contains all 25 of Turgenev's pieces.

Turgenev's Letters. Ed. and trans. by A. V. Knowles. Macmillan 1983 $30.00. ISBN 0-684-17867-2. Includes 236 letters; well organized and very readable.

The Vintage Turgenev. 2 vols. Trans. by Harry Stevens. *Russian Lib. Ser.* Random 1960 o.p. Included in volume 1 are *Smoke, Fathers and Sons,* and *First Love*. Volume 2 includes *On the Eye, Rudin, A Quiet Spot,* and *Diary of a Superfluous Man*.

Books about Turgenev

Allen, Elizabeth C. *Beyond Realism: Turgenev's Poetics of Secular Salvation*. Stanford U. Pr. 1992 $35.00. ISBN 0-8047-1873-3

Costlow, Jane T. *Worlds within Worlds: The Novels of Ivan Turgenev*. Princeton U. Pr. 1990 $24.95. ISBN 0-691-06783-X. An attempt to assert the universality of the issues treated in Turgenev's fiction.

Knowles, A. V. *Ivan Turgenev*. *Twayne World Authors Ser.* Macmillan 1988 $20.95. ISBN 0-8057-8241-9

Lowe, David A., ed. *Critical Essays on Ivan Turgenev*. *Critical Essays Ser.* G. K. Hall 1988 $40.00. ISBN 0-8161-8842-4. A selection of translations from the Russian, as well as several recent English-language studies.

Pritchett, V. S. *The Gentle Barbarian: The Life and Work of Ivan Turgenev*. Ecco Pr. 1986 $9.50. ISBN 0-88001-120-3. Often thought provoking on individual works, although contains some weakness in biographical details.

Ripp, Victor. *Turgenev's Russia: From Notes of a Hunter to Fathers and Sons*. Cornell Univ. Pr. 1980 $31.95. ISBN 0-8014-1294-3

Shapiro, Leonard. *Turgenev: His Life and Times*. HUP 1982 $12.50. ISBN 0-674-91297-7. Well written and factually solid; "It will probably be the standard biography of Turgenev in English for some time to come" (*SEEJ*).

Seeley, Frank F. *Turgenev: A Reading of His Fiction*. *Studies in Russian Lit. Ser.* Cambridge U. Pr. 1991 $59.50. ISBN 0-521-36521-X. An extended overview; fills a need unmet by other Turgenev criticism.

Wexford, Jane. *Monarch Notes on Turgenev's Fathers and Sons*. P-H $3.95. ISBN 0-671-00877-3

TYNYANOV, YURY. 1894–1943

Tynyanov, one of the founders of structuralist criticism, made lasting contributions to Pushkin studies, to the theory of verse semantics, and to other fields. His novels tend to embody his theoretical interests. His most important works deal with the oppressive period of Nicholas I's reign. *Death and Diplomacy in Persia* (The Death of Wazir-Mukhtar) (1927–28) is a biographical novel about the celebrated nineteenth-century satirist Aleksandr Griboyedov. Other novels include *Kyukhlya* (1925), about the Decembrist poet Kyukhel'beker, and the unfinished *Pushkin* (1935–37). Among Tynyanov's shorter works, the novella *Second Lieutenant Kije* (1927), set in the time of the temperamental

Emperor Paul I, has achieved the greatest renown and was made into a film in 1934.

NOVELS BY TYNYANOV

Death and Diplomacy in Persia. Trans. by A. Brown. Hyperion Conn. 1974 repr. of 1938 ed. $24.75. ISBN 0-88355-178-0

Lieutenant Kije and Young Vitushishnikov. Trans. by Mirra Ginsburg. Marsilio Pubs. 1991 $17.95. ISBN 0-941419-36-3. "Two glittering novellas . . . satirize the abuses of 18th- and 19th-century czarist regimes, none too obliquely implicating Stalin himself" (*PW*).

TYUTCHEV (TIUTCHEV), FYODOR. 1803–1873

The rather small ouevre of Tyutchev belies his stature as one of the greatest Russian poets of the nineteenth century. He was born into a gentry family, received a superb education in classical and Russian literature, and began to publish verse at an early age. In 1822 he joined the diplomatic service. Appointed to the legation in Munich, he spent more than 20 years in European postings, primarily in Germany. There, he moved extensively in cultural circles and was deeply affected by romanticism. The publication of a group of his poems in 1836 in a journal edited by PUSHKIN brought him serious public attention.

From the mid-1840s, Tyutchev lived in Russia, at times working as a government official. He was a well-known figure in high society, noted for his wit. Besides verse, he also wrote polemic articles on issues of foreign policy, taking a nationalist, imperialist line. A major factor in his life was a long-term love affair, which resulted in some of his finest lyrics.

Besides these and other love poems, Tyutchev is celebrated for his nature poems, in which startling, bold visions of landscapes are interwoven with philosophical themes and the natural and human spheres (in the spirit of romanticism) are paralleled. These works proved particularly interesting to the symbolist poets, who saw in Tyutchev's verse a prototype of and inspiration for their own writings and who did much to bring the poet to the public.

WORK BY TYUTCHEV

Poems and Political Letters of F. I. Tyutchev. Trans. by Jesse Zeldin. U. of Tenn. Pr. 1974 $32.50. ISBN 0-87049-146-6. The largest collection of Tyutchev's work in English, although sometimes inaccurate and carelessly edited.

BOOKS ABOUT TYUTCHEV

Conant, Roger. *The Political Poetry and Ideology of F. I. Tiutchev*. Ardis Pubs. 1983 o.p.

Pratt, Sarah. *Russian Metaphysical Romanticism: The Poetry of Tiutchev and Boratynskii*. Stanford U. Pr. 1984 $35.00. ISBN 0-8047-1188-7

VLADIMOV (pseud. of Volosevich), GEORGY. 1931–

Although he graduated from Leningrad University with a degree in law, Vladimov first worked as a journalist and then turned to literary criticism and fiction. From 1956 to 1959 he worked as an editor at the magazine *Novy Mir*, where he published his first novella, *The Great Ore* (1961), an example of the approved genre of "production novels" but with some ideological ambiguities. He assumed a more public stance in 1967 when he wrote an open letter to the Fourth Congress of Soviet Writers in support of SOLZHENITSYN's struggle against censorship. His *Three Minutes of Silence* (1969), a short novel exploring human beings under stress (it is set on a Soviet fishing trawler), was strongly criticized in the press. By the mid-1970s, Vladimov found himself further at odds with the system. The manuscript of *Faithful Ruslan,* a powerful allegory of Soviet society presented through the eyes of a concentration camp watchdog, was circulating in *samizdat* and was published in West Germany in 1975. Two years later Vladimov resigned from the Writers' Union and came under pressure from the KGB. In 1983, after a letter from Yury Andropov, then head of state and party, he was allowed to emigrate. He settled in West Germany, where for some years he worked as the editor-in-chief of an émigré literary periodical. *Faithful Ruslan* was reissued in the Soviet Union during the Gorbachev period.

NOVELS BY VLADIMOV

Faithful Ruslan. S&S Trade 1979 o.p.
Three Minute's Silence. Trans. by Michael Glenny. Salem Hse. Pubs. 1986 $17.95. ISBN 0-7043-2394-X

VOINOVICH, VLADIMIR. 1932–

The best contemporary Russian satirist, Voinovich served in the Soviet Army and worked for a time at various blue-collar jobs. He published his first story, "We Live Here," in 1961. Describing life on a collective farm, it received immediate acclaim. He got into overt trouble with the authorities when he protested the trial SINYAVSKY and Daniel and SOLZHENITSYN's expulsion from the Writers' Union. Himself barred from publishing in 1974, and increasingly under pressure, Voinovich in 1980 emigrated with his family to West Germany and has since visited and lectured in the United States.

One of Voinovich's best-known works is *The Ivankiad* (1976), a comic account of difficulties in getting an apartment and, more broadly, a description of the anti-individual Soviet bureaucracy. His greatest achievement, *The Life and Extraordinary Adventures of Private Ivan Chonkin* (1976), depicts Soviet society at the start of the German invasion in 1941 and is particularly devastating in rendering the gap between official slogans and reality. The adventures of Chonkin, a peasant-hero in the tradition of CAPEK's Schweik, are continued in *Pretender to the Throne* (1979), a grimmer work that satirizes among other subjects Stalin and the secret police. Voinovich's latest major success is the dystopia *Moscow 2042* (1987), a funny yet frightening vision of a communist society reduced to a nearly animal level; it also contains a devastating parody of SOLZHENITSYN and his Slavophile views. This work, like all of Voinovich's previously banned writings, has now been republished in the Soviet Union.

Part of Voinovich's appeal lies in his ironic narration and skillful rendition of colloquial, often crude speech. He has been well served by his translators; the English-language versions of his works are eminently readable.

NOVELS BY VOINOVICH

The Anti-Soviet Soviet Union. Trans. by Richard Lourie. HarBraceJ 1986 $19.95. ISBN 0-15-107840-8
The Fur Hat. HarBraceJ 1989 $17.95. ISBN 0-15-139100-9
The Ivankiad. Trans. by David Lapeza. Hill & Wang 1977 $7.95. ISBN 0-8090-1544-7
The Life and Extraordinary Adventures of Private Ivan Chonkin. Trans. by Richard Lourie. Bantam 1979 $2.95. ISBN 0-685-59932-9
Moscow, 2042. Trans. by Richard Lourie. HarBraceJ 1987 $16.95. ISBN 0-15-162444-5
Pretender to the Throne: The Further Adventures of Private Ivan Chonkin. Trans. by Richard Lourie. FS&G 1981 $17.95. ISBN 0-374-23715-8

Works by Voinovich

In Plain Russian. Trans. by Richard Lourie. FS&G 1979 o.p. A collection of various short fiction and nonfiction pieces.

VOZNESENSKY, ANDREI. 1933–

Voznesensky initially studied architecture but abandoned it for literature during the late 1950s. His first two collections of verse, *Mosaic* and *Parabola* (both 1960), displayed great energy, verbal virtuosity, and inventiveness—all continuing hallmarks of his writing. During the 1960s, Voznesensky became extremely popular in the Soviet Union. He published several important volumes, including *Antiworlds* (1964) and *Achilles' Heart* (1965). He also made many trips to Western Europe and the United States, achieving wide international recognition. His themes—modern urban life, technology's impact on civilization, artistic freedom—have proved appealing to both Russian and foreign audiences.

Voznesensky was in and out of trouble with the Soviet authorities. Although he enjoyed much more latitude than most writers and received a major government prize for his poetry, he was outspoken on creative freedom and involved in the unofficial *Metropol'* collection. Voznesensky continues to experiment actively, exploring a variety of verbal and visual devices.

Poetry by Voznesensky

An Arrow in the Wall. Ed. by William J. Smith and F. D. Reeve. H. Holt & Co 1988 $10.95. ISBN 0-8050-0784-9. "[A]n instructive review of Voznesensky's career . . . [and] the two recent autobiographical essays add valuable background" (*LJ*). A bilingual edition.

Dogalypse. City Lights 1972 o.p.

Kaligrunes. Trans. by Jack Hirschman. Crosscut Saw 1976 o.p.

Nostalgia for the Present. Doubleday 1978 $4.95. ISBN 0-385-08373-4

YEVTUSHENKO (EVTUSHENKO), YEVGENY. 1933–

Yevtushenko was born in a small junction on the Trans-Siberian Railroad (the subject of his 1956 long poem *Zima Junction*). After Stalin's death in 1953, he emerged as an important poet and spokesman for the younger generation.

In 1961 Yevtushenko published "Babi Yar," which deals with the notorious wartime massacre of Jews in a ravine near Kiev. The poem made Yevtushenko internationally famous, and because it raised the spectre of domestic anti-Semitism, aroused a storm of official opposition. He also created a furor with "Stalin's Heirs" (1962), which raised the spectre of resurgent Stalinism.

Over the years, however, Yevtushenko became part of the Soviet establishment. He seriously damaged his early reputation as a defender of artistic freedom by easily yielding to coercion to write works following the official line. Yet at times he took quite liberal positions at odds with the powers that be. In the Gorbachev period, he became active in political life and has continued to advocate reform, fighting for change within the Writers' Union.

Like Voznesensky, Yevtushenko traveled extensively abroad. His trips inspired many topical, sometimes autobiographical works well received by Western as well as Russian readers: Though exuberant in his verbal style, the poet is quite accessible. But overall, although sometimes quite effective, his writing lacks true depth.

Poetry by Yevtushenko

Almost at the End. Trans. by Antonina Bouis and Albert C. Todd. H. Holt & Co. 1988 $8.95. ISBN 0-8050-0785-7. Features "Fuki," "a meditation in poetry and prose that ranges from childhood war memories to the poet's inability to do more than bear witness to contemporary poverty and injustice" (*LJ*).

Collected Poems. Ed. by Albert Todd. H. Holt & Co 1991 $29.95. ISBN 0-8050-0696-6. "Based on Yevtushenko's own selections from the complete six-volume Russian edition . . . [and] fluently translated by many distinguished poets, among them Richard Wilbur, Stanley Kunitz, and D. M. Thomas" (*LJ*).

Early Poems. Trans. by George Reavey. M. Boyars Pubs. 1989 $12.95. ISBN 0-7145-2896-X

The Face behind the Face. Trans. by Arthur Boyars and Simon Franklin. M. Boyars Pubs. 1990 repr. of 1977 ed. $10.95. ISBN 0-7145-2617-7

The Poetry of Yevgeny Yevtushenko. M. Boyars Pubs. 1981 $8.95. ISBN 0-7145-0482-3. A bilingual edition.

Wild Berries. H. Holt & Co. 1989 $12.95. ISBN 0-8050-1178-1

Nonfiction by Yevtushenko

Fatal Half Measures: The Culture of Democracy in the Soviet Union. Ed. and trans. by Antonina W. Bouis. Little 1991 $21.95. ISBN 0-316-96883-8. "In these selections from his telegrams to Kremlin leaders, speeches, letters, [and] reminiscences, . . . Western readers can share his personal vision of perestroika" (*LJ*).

ZAMYATIN, YEVGENY (ZAMIATIN, EUGENE). 1884–1937

Zamyatin studied at the Polytechnic Institute in St. Petersburg and became a professional naval engineer. His first story appeared in 1908, and he became serious about writing in 1913, when his short novel *A Provincial Tale* (1913) was favorably received. He became part of the neorealist group, which included Remizov and Prishvin. During World War I, he supervised the construction of icebreakers in England for the Russian government. After his return home, he published two satiric works about English life, "The Islanders" (1918) and "The Fisher of Men" (1922).

During the civil war and the early 1920s, Zamyatin published theoretical essays as well as fiction. He played a central role in many cultural activities—as an editor, organizer, and teacher of literary technique—and had an important influence on younger writers, such as Olesha and Ivanov.

Zamyatin's prose after the Revolution involved extensive use of ellipses, color symbolism, and elaborate chains of imagery. It is exemplified in such well-known stories as "Mamai" (1921) and "The Cage" (1922). His best-known work is the novel *We* (1924), a satiric, futuristic tale of a dystopia that was a plausible extrapolation from early twentieth-century social and political trends. The book, which directly influenced George Orwell's (see Vol. 1) *1984,* was published abroad in several translations during the 1920s. In 1927 a shortened Russian version appeared in Prague, and the violent press campaign that followed led to Zamyatin's resignation from a writers' organization and, eventually, to his direct appeal to Stalin for permission to leave the Soviet Union. This being granted in 1931, Zamyatin settled in Paris, where he continued to work until his death. Until *glasnost* he was unpublished and virtually unknown in Russia.

Novel by Zamyatin

We. Trans. by Mirra Ginsburg. Avon 1983 $4.95. ISBN 0-380-63313-2. A very good translation.

SHORT STORY COLLECTION BY ZAMYATIN

The Dragon: Fifteen Stories. Trans. by Mirra Ginsburg. U. Ch. Pr. 1976 $10.00. ISBN 0-226-97867-2

NONFICTION BY ZAMYATIN

A Soviet Heretic: Essays. Ed. and trans. by Mirra Ginsburg. Northwestern U. Pr. 1992 repr. of 1970 ed. $14.95. ISBN 0-8101-1091-1. A comprehensive collection. Contains such key pieces as "On Literature, Revolution, Entropy and Other Matters," "The Psychology of Creative Work," and so forth.

BOOK ABOUT ZAMYATIN

Kern, Gary. *Zamyatin's We: A Collection of Critical Essays.* Ardis Pubs. 1987 $25.00. ISBN 0-88233-804-8

ZOSHCHENKO, MIKHAIL. 1895–1958

Zoshchenko moved with his family from the Ukraine to St. Petersburg in 1904. He volunteered for military service in World War I and spent two years at the front, where his health was permanently damaged by poison gas. During the civil war, he volunteered for the Red Army. Later, he held a succession of jobs, including detective, carpenter, telephone operator, militiaman, and actor.

His first book of stories appeared in 1921 and became extraordinarily popular. However, he came under political pressure in the 1930s because some of his works, such as *Youth Restored* (1933), were too slyly ambiguous to fit the socialist realist model. In 1946, together with AKHMATOVA, he was singled out for an extraordinary attack by culture "boss" Andrei Zhdanov and was expelled from the Union of Soviet Writers. From then on he mostly produced translations.

Zoshchenko was an extremely effective satirist who took his subjects from the paradoxes and incongruities of post-Revolutionary Russian society. He showed that human nature, which the new government was trying to change, would assert itself nonetheless. His language is fascinating. He often chooses lower-class narrators who speak in a mixture of the colloquial and of the new Soviet rhetoric—with highly comic results. During the 1930s, Zoshchenko's fiction began to explore philosophical and theoretical problems. A well-known example is *Before Sunrise*, the first part of which was published in 1943. In it the author analyzes his own psyche, in the process touching on the then-forbidden theories of FREUD (see Vols. 3 and 5). Publication of the complete text of this work did not occur until 1972.

SHORT STORY COLLECTIONS BY ZOSHCHENKO

A Man Is Not a Flea: A Collection of Stories. Trans. by Serge Shishkoff. Ardis Pubs. 1989 o.p. "A most welcome addition to the small body of English-language versions of Zoshchenko's writing" (*SEEJ*).

Nervous People and Other Satires. Ed. by Hugh McLean. Trans. by Maria Gordon and Hugh McLean. Ind. U. Pr. 1975 $12.95. ISBN 0-253-20192-6

Scenes from the Bathhouse: And Other Stories of Communist Russia. Trans. by Sidney Monas. U. of Mich. Pr. 1961 $13.95. ISBN 0-472-06070-8. Introduction by Monas.

Stories of the Nineteen Twenties. Ed. by A. B. Murphy. Blackwell Pubs. 1989 $15.95. ISBN 0-631-14398-X

The Woman Who Could Not Read, and Other Tales. Trans. by E. Fen. *Soviet Lit. in English Trans. Ser.* Hyperion Conn. 1973 repr. of 1940 ed. $15.00. ISBN 0-88355-028-8

The Wonderful Dog and Other Tales. Trans. by E. Fen. *Soviet Lit. in English Trans. Ser.* Hyperion Conn. 1973 repr. of 1942 ed. $15.95. ISBN 0-88355-029-6

Novel by Zoshchenko

Youth Restored. Trans. by Joel Stern. Ardis Pubs. 1984 o.p.

Book about Zoshchenko

Scatton, Linda H. *The Artistic Evolution of Mikhail Zoshchenko: No Laughing Matter. Cambridge Studies in Russian Lit. Ser.* Cambridge U. Pr. 1993. ISBN 0-521-42093-8. First full-length study in English of Zoshchenko's career and political reception of his works in the Soviet Union.

CHAPTER 21

East European Literatures

Vasa D. Mihailovich

O nomen dulce libertatis—O sweet name of liberty.
—CICERO, *Oration against Verres*

All East European literatures have several features in common: They all originated during the process of accepting Christianity and for the purpose of satisfying the needs of the Church; they were directly engaged in the struggle for liberation from various enemies and at various times; they were influenced by the literary developments in the West; they had to struggle against, and in most instances submit to, political dictates in the aftermath of World War II; and they regained their freedom from political dictators in the late 1980s, and the early 1990s. Aside from that, they followed their own timetables of development and the peculiarities of their individual natures. Therefore, it would be a mistake to treat them as a monolithic bloc, despite common historical circumstances, for it is through their uniqueness that each has contributed significantly to world literature.

CHRONOLOGY OF AUTHORS

Albanian Literature
Kadare, Ismail. 1936–

Bulgarian Literature
Botev, Khristo. 1847–1876
Vazov, Ivan. 1850–1921
Pelin, Elin. 1877–1949
Yovkov, Yordan. 1880–1937
Dimitrova, Blaga. 1922–

Byelorussian Literature
Bykaŭ, Vasil. 1924–

Croatian Literature
Šenoa, August. 1838–1881
Krleža, Miroslav. 1893–1981
Marinković, Ranko. 1913–
Parun, Vesna. 1922–
Mihalić, Slavko. 1928–

Czech Literature
Hašek, Jaroslav. 1883–1923
Čapek, Karel. 1890–1938
Seifert, Jaroslav. 1901–1986
Hrabal, Bohumil. 1914–
Holub, Miroslav. 1923–
Škvorecký, Josef. 1924–
Vaculík, Ludvík. 1926–
Kohout, Pavel. 1928–
Kundera, Milan. 1929–
Havel, Václav. 1936–

Estonian Literature
Under, Marie. 1883–1980
Kangro, Bernard. 1910–
Rannit, Aleksis. 1914–1985

Hungarian Literature
Madách Imre. 1823–1864
Petöfi, Sándor. 1823–1849
Jókai, Mór. 1825–1904
Ady, Endre. 1877–1919
Moricz, Szigmond. 1879–1942
Lukács, György. 1885–1971
Lengyel, Jozsef. 1896–1975
Németh, László. 1901–1975
Illyés, Gyula. 1902–1983
József, Attila. 1905–1937
Juhász, Ferenc. 1928–

Lithuanian Literature
Donelaitis, Kristijonas. 1714–1780
Baranauskas, Antanas. 1835–1902
Krėvė, Vincas. 1882–1954
Gliauda, Jurgis. 1906–
Vaičiulaitis, Antanas. 1906–
Landsbergis, Algirdas. 1924–

Macedonian Literature
Koneski, Blaže. 1921–
Janevski, Slavko. 1923–
Stefanovski, Goran. 1952–

Polish Literature
Pasek, Jan Chryzostom. 1630–1701
Fredro, Alexander. 1793–1876
Mickiewicz, Adam Bernard. 1798–1855
Krasiński, Zygmunt. 1812–1859
Prus, Bolesław. 1845–1912
Sienkiewicz, Henryk. 1846–1916
Reymont, Wladyslaw Stanislaw. 1867–1925
Witkiewicz, Stanisław Ignacy. 1885–1939
Tuwim, Julian. 1894–1953
Parandowski, Jan. 1895–1978
Gombrowicz, Witold. 1904–1969
Miłosz, Czesław. 1911–
Dygat, Stanislaw. 1914–
Herling, Gustaw. 1919–
Lem, Stanislaw. 1921–
Różewicz, Tadeusz. 1921–
Białoszewski, Tadeusz. 1922–1984
Borowski, Tadeusz. 1922–1951
Herbert, Zbigniew. 1924–
Konwicki, Tadeusz. 1926–
Mrożek, Sławomir. 1930–
Hlasko, Marek. 1934–1969

Rumanian Literature
Eminescu, Mihail. 1850–1889
Arghezi, Tudor. 1880–1967
Sadoveanu, Mihail. 1880–1961
Rebreanu, Liviu. 1885–1944
Stancu, Zaharia. 1902–1974
Eliade, Mircea. 1907–1986
Dumitriu, Petru. 1924–

Serbian Literature
Njegoš, Petar Petrović. 1813–1851
Dučić, Jovan. 1874–1943
Andrić, Ivo. 1892–1975
Djilas, Milovan. 1911–
Ćosić, Dobrica. 1921–
Popa, Vasko. 1922–1991
Pavlović, Miodrag. 1928–
Pavić, Milorad. 1929–
Kiš, Danilo. 1935–1989

Slovak Literature
Cíger-Hronský, Jozef. 1896–1960
Mňačko, Ladislav. 1919–

Slovenian Literature
Prešeren, France. 1800–1849
Cankar, Ivan. 1876–1918
Župančič, Oton. 1878–1949
Šalamun, Tomaž. 1941–

Ukrainian Literature
Ševčenko, Taras. 1814–1861
Kuliš, Pantelejmon. 1819–1897
Franko, Ivan. 1856–1916
Ukrajinka, Lesja. 1871–1913
Kuliš, Mykola. 1892–1942
Pidmohylny, Valerian. 1901–1941
Honchar, Oleksander. 1918–

ALBANIAN LITERATURE

Whatever possibilities for the development of culture and literature existed in Albania before the sixteenth century, they were dashed by the Turkish conquest and the defeat of Albania's legendary leader Skenderbeg in 1468. The conquest led to the dispersal of spiritual and cultural leaders, mostly to Italy and Sicily, where they wrote in the Roman Catholic tradition for the next 200 years. Almost all writing in this period was of a religious and didactic nature, but there were also dictionaries, encyclopedias, and collections of folk literature. The leading writer was the Calabrian Jeronim de Rada, who collected fragments of Albanian epics to which he added poems of his own, not devoid of a lyrical quality. Similar romantic and patriotic works were written in other Albanian conclaves and colonies in Constantinople, Lebanon, Egypt, Rumania, and the United States.

Writers at home survived mainly because of the help of Roman Catholic missions. Preoccupied with collecting and imitating folk poetry and influenced by Albanian writings abroad, they kept the romantic spirit alive until the national awakening, centered on the League of Prizren, swept Albania in the second half of the nineteenth century. There were also attempts at a historical novel and the crude beginnings of the short story.

The romantic and patriotic spirit in literature lasted until independence was won in 1912. Although romanticism still persisted, writers were exposed to other European trends such as realism and symbolism. Çajupi, Gjergj Fishta, and Fran S. Noli were the leading authors in the first decades of this century. By the 1930s socialist and radical ideas began to influence Albanian writers, especially those from the South, the Tosks. Younger writers were much more influenced by modern European trends than the preceding generation. The most prominent among them was Migjeni (an acronym for Millosh Gjergi Nikolla), whose strong social criticism foreshadowed the literature after World War II.

The last four decades have been difficult for writers. The establishment of a communist state in 1944 forced them to accept socialist realism and strict controls. The elimination of dissidents became the order of the day. Consequently, even though language and style have been enriched, higher quality is still lacking. The lone exception is the poet and novelist ISMAIL KADARE whose novel *The General of the Dead Army* (1963) has been translated and published in more than two dozen countries. The conditions have changed significantly since 1992, when the literary situation became more promising.

Although works by several Albanian writers have been translated into English, unfortunately few are readily available.

History and Criticism

Pipa, Arshi. *Contemporary Albanian Literature*. Col. U. Pr. 1991 $31.55. ISBN 0-88033-202-6. Surveys Albanian literature since World War II, considering both the social realism imposed by the Marxist government and the work of expatriates, particularly the poet Martin Camaj.

Skendi, Stavro. *Albanian and South Slavic Oral Epic Poetry. Amer. Folklore Society Memoirs Ser.* Kraus repr. of 1954 ed. $23.00. ISBN 0-527-01096-0

———. *Albanian National Awakening*, 1878–1912. Bks. Demand repr. of 1967 ed. $114.80. ISBN 0-8357-9492-X

KADARE, ISMAIL. 1936–

Ismail Kadare is the most prominent of contemporary Albanian writers. He has written poetry, short stories, literary criticism, and seven novels. His works have been translated and published in more than two dozen countries. An internationally known figure, he has visited and lectured in many countries. He was also a representative to Albania's People's Assembly. In 1990 Kadare left Albania for Paris where he became openly dissident.

NOVELS BY KADARE

Broken April. 1980. New Amsterdam Bks. 1990 $17.95. ISBN 0-941533-57-3. A short novel dealing with the legendary blood feud in Albania during the 1930s.

Chronicles in Stone. 1971. New Amsterdam Bks. 1987 $19.95. ISBN 0-941533-00-X. A powerful novel set in Kadare's native Gjirokaster.

Doruntine. Trans. by Jon Rothschild. New Amsterdam Bks. 1988 $15.95. ISBN 0-941533-20-4. A brief novel about characters from Albanian folklore.

The General of the Dead Army. 1963. Trans. by Derek Coltman. New Amsterdam Bks. 1991 repr. of 1971 ed. $18.95. ISBN 1-56131-007-7

BULGARIAN LITERATURE

The history of Bulgarian literature goes back to the end of the ninth century, when literary activity was spurred by the disciples of Cyril and Methodius, the two Greek monks chiefly responsible for disseminating Christianity through a written language they had devised based on a Slavic tongue. This brief but intense flourishing laid the foundation of the culture of all Balkan Slavs. The second flourishing occurred in the second half of the fourteenth century, before the country fell to the Turks. During the five-century occupation, little literature was possible. It was not until 1762 that the Bulgarians attempted to regain their literary consciousness, when a monk from the Hilendar monastery on Mount Athos wrote his history of Bulgaria, an attempt to awaken the national consciousness of his enslaved people.

Literary activity in the nineteenth century was closely connected with the struggle for liberation. The best writers of the century, the lyric poet KHRISTO BOTEV and the novelist and poet IVAN VAZOV, drew most of their inspiration from this struggle. But when independence was finally won in 1978, writers satirized the shortcomings of their people, who sometimes proved unworthy of immense sacrifices during the struggle.

At the turn of the century writers began to widen their horizons and to reflect the influence of modern Western literary movements. Foremost among these was Pencho Slaveykov, whose work shows the degree of modernity reached by Bulgarian writers in a relatively short time. Symbolism also attracted some talented poets (Peyo Yavorov and Todor Trayanov), who stayed away from the romantic and realistic themes of the previous generation, while others flirted with expressionism.

All these trends reappeared in the interwar period, resulting in a rich, multifaceted literary activity. In general, short stories and lyric poetry were the most successful genres. Many of the older authors continued to be a factor, but there was also new blood. Among the former, the most significant were the fiction writers ELIN PELIN and YORDAN YOVKOV.

The installment of a communist system in 1944 brought about drastic changes in literature. The dictates of socialist realism resulted in faceless uniformity and atrophy of imagination. Only partial relaxations after 1956 and in the 1960s and 1970s gave young writers a chance to develop their potential, although serious restrictions were still felt. The best writers turned to historical novels, either to escape the present or to compare it with the past. The situation has changed for the better with the removal of the dictatorial regime in the 1990s, leading one hopes to freer expression in literature.

History and Criticism

Manning, Clarence A., and Roman Smal-Stocki. *History of Modern Bulgarian Literature.* Greenwood 1974 repr. of 1960 ed. o.p. A brief survey from the beginnings to the present. Convenient but rather selective and at times unreliable.

Matejic, Mateja. *A Bibliographical Handbook of Bulgarian Authors*. Ed. by Karen L. Black. Slavica 1982 $17.95. ISBN 0-89357-091-5. A very useful and detailed handbook, combining biography with pertinent bibliographic data.

Moser, Charles A. *A History of Bulgarian Literature, 1865-1944*. Mouton 1972 $58.70. ISBN 90-2792-008-7. A detailed treatment of Bulgarian literature, focusing on the literature of the twentieth century. The best history available, with an extensive bibliography.

Slavov, Atanas. *The "Thaw" in Bulgarian Literature. East European Monographs*. East Eur. Quarterly 1981 $42.00. ISBN 0-914710-78-8

Collections

Kirilov, Nikolai, and Frank Kirk, eds. *Introduction to Modern Bulgarian Literature: An Anthology of Short Stories*. Trans. by Marguerite Alexieva. Irvington 1969 $29.50. ISBN 0-8057-3106-7. An extensive anthology of short stories dating from the late nineteenth century. Arranged somewhat haphazardly but provides some notion of modern Bulgarian short fiction. Includes a brief introduction.

Mihailovich, Vasa D., eds. *White Stones and Fir Trees: An Anthology of Contemporary Slavic Literature*. Fairleigh Dickinson 1977 $45.00. ISBN 0-8386-1194-X. A collection of poems and short stories.

BOTEV, KHRISTO. 1847–1876

Although he wrote only about 20 poems, Botev is considered to be the greatest Bulgarian poet of the nineteenth century and with IVAN VAZOV, one of the most significant writers in Bulgarian literature. His fame is enhanced by his work in reawakening the national spirit after nearly five centuries of Turkish occupation. During the struggle for liberation, he was also very active as a journalist. Botev's poetry is impassioned in its call for liberation, combining tender lyricism with epic narration. Yet it also contains a current of philosophical nihilism. Botev's poetic talent, unusual life of modesty combined with persistence, and tragic death in battle at 28 all contribute to his reputation as a national hero and a powerful poet.

POETRY BY BOTEV

Poems. Trans. by Kevin Ireland. Sofia-Press 1982 o.p.

WORK BY BOTEV

Selected Works. Trans. by Petko Drenkov. Sofia-Press 1976 o.p.

DIMITROVA, BLAGA. 1922–

A prolific poet, fiction writer, playwright, and essayist, Dimitrova is one of the most important modern Bulgarian writers. In her numerous books of poetry she has created a world of her own, imbued with a conviction of the poetic Word's power. During the half century of Communist rule, she was also prominent as a keeper of her compatriots' faith in a more just and humane society. For this, as well as for her artistry, she is highly revered today both in her country and abroad.

POETRY BY DIMITROVA

Because the Sea Is Black: Poems of Blaga Dimitrova. Trans. by Niko Boris and Heather McHugh. Wesleyan Univ. Pr. 1989 $22.50. ISBN 0-8195-2166-3. Presents poems of social awareness, especially those focusing on women's issues.

Journey to Oneself. Cassel UK 1969 o.p. A selection of poems.

PELIN, ELIN (pseud. of Dimitŭr Ivanov). 1877–1949

Pelin came from the village to the city to earn his living through literature. The two principal collections of his excellent stories appeared in 1904 and 1911 and brought him fame as the bard of the peasants inhabiting the region around Sofia. In the stories the peasants are presented as strong-willed individuals reluctant to submit to laws made by humans and respectful of the laws of nature. At the same time Pelin did not overlook their negative sides. Pelin also gained renown as a satirist and humorist. After 1922 he wrote relatively little, but he was very critical of socialist realism and dogmatic thinking. He is still considered Bulgaria's best short-story teller.

Short Story Collection By Pelin

Short Stories. Twayne's International Studies and Translations Ser. G. K. Hall o.p. Short works set in the Bulgarian countryside, exploring the intimate human problems of the peasant in his ordinary life.

VAZOV, IVAN. 1850–1921

Vazov dominated the literary scene in Bulgaria at the close of the nineteenth century as a poet, short-story writer, novelist, and playwright. Since then he has been recognized as the patriarch of Bulgarian letters. He lived through the heroic period of his country's liberation from the Turks, chronicled the events of the times, glorified his people's achievements, and agonized over their shortcomings. Through the power of his pen he succeeded in stimulating a sense of nationhood in Bulgarians. He was an unabashed nationalist, using his talents toward the liberation of his people. In addition to his *magnum opus,* the trilogy of which his best work, *Under the Yoke,* is the first part, Vazov wrote several plays which enriched the sparse repertory of the Bulgarian theater. His patriotic poetry and journalistic writings complete the opus of this national bard.

Novel by Vazov

Under the Yoke. Twayne o.p. The most important Bulgarian novel, Vazov's finest work, and a central document of the Bulgarian historical viewpoint. Describes the abortive April 1876 uprising against hopeless odds.

YOVKOV, YORDAN. 1880–1937

Yovkov wrote poems, short stories, novels, and plays. Most of his poetically tinged stories and novels are set in Dobruja, a region lost to Rumania after World War I, where he was a teacher. One of his best works is the novel *The Farmstead at the Frontier* (1934). The best prose craftsman in modern Bulgarian literature, Yovkov filtered the materials provided by real life through his memory to produce extraordinarily delicate small masterpieces. His most characteristic hero is the impractical daydreamer, incapable of dealing with the real world. In the 1930s Yovkov turned to writing for the stage, but fiction remains his most important contribution.

Short Story Collections by Yovkov

The Inn at Antimovo and Legends of Stara Planina. Trans. by John Burnip. Slavica 1990 $14.95. ISBN 0-89357-205-5

Short Stories. Twayne 1965 o.p. Ultimately affirmative stories of the trials and tragedies of life in the Bulgarian countryside.

Book about Yovkov

Mozejko, Edward. *Yordan Yovkov.* Slavica 1984 $9.95. ISBN 0-89357-117-2

BYELORUSSIAN LITERATURE

As is the case of all Slavic literature, the beginnings of Byelorussian literature can be traced to the conversion to Christianity in the eleventh and twelfth centuries. The first literary works were chronicles and other ecclesiastical documents. In the sixteenth century, the Golden Age of Old Byelorussian literature, Francišak Skaryna translated the Bible into Old Byelorussian, and several other writers made their appearance. In the first half of the nineteenth century, the romantic movement revived Byelorussian literature through the works of several capable writers, including Francišak Bahusevič. During this period, the Russians prohibited publication of works in Byelorussian, but the ban was not always enforced.

When the ban was permanently lifted at the beginning of the twentieth century, Byelorussian literature flowered again. This was marked not only by the emergence of several prominent writers, but also by the development of various genres, most notably lyric poetry, the novel, and drama. The two leaders of the literary revival were Jakub Kolas and Janka Kupala. Another prominent writer, Maksim Bahdanovič, transcended the still prevalent romantic realism and introduced neoclassicism, impressionism, and symbolism into Byelorussian poetry. Like their predecessors, all these writers, who gathered in a group called Adradženstva (Renaissance), saw their mission not only in writing literature but also in fighting for a national identity, independence, and even survival.

This struggle continued after World War I, when the Byelorussians found themselves divided between Russia and Poland. An added element was a sharpened ideological difference, which was evident even in the Soviet Union. There, one group, speaking through the journal *Maladniak* (*Saplings*), demanded a stronger ideological commitment and advocated revolutionary romanticism and national communism. Another group, gathered around the journal *Uzvyšča* (*Excelsior*), strove for high literary standards devoid of nonliterary considerations. The differences were resolved through the suppression of versatility and independence during the Stalinist regime, lasting until the mid-1950s. Most Byelorussian writers had to adhere to socialist realism, although some were more adept than others at circumventing it. Despite the limitations, there was a noticeable enhancement of language and style. Not until the break-up of the Soviet Union and the emergence of Byelarus, almost 40 years later, were writers fully free to express themselves. Among the leading contemporary authors, mention should be made of the lyricists Uladzimier Duboŭka and Maksim Tank and the fiction writers Janka Bryl and Vasil Bykaŭ.

History and Criticism

Adamovich, Anthony. *Opposition to Sovietization in Byelorussian Literature, 1917–1957.* Scarecrow 1958 o.p. Foreword by Alexander Dallin. Analyzes literature mainly from 1917 to 1929, the period of enforced conformity to Soviet views. Includes a comprehensive bibliography and short biographies of more than 40 authors.

Bird, Thomas E., ed. *Modern Byelorussian Writing: Essays and Documents.* Queens Coll. Pr. 1976 o.p. A symposium on various aspects of Byelorussian literature in exile.

Collection

Rich, Vera. *Like Water, Like Fire: An Anthology of Byelorussian Poetry from 1828 to the Present Day.* Crane Russak & Co. 1971 o.p. A pioneering anthology of Byelorussian poetry, the first of its kind in English.

BYKAŬ, VASIL. 1924–

A native of a small Byelorussian village, Bykaŭ served in World War II, studied sculpture, and worked as a newspaper editor. His novels, most of which are about soldiers at war, have been translated into many languages. Bykaŭ is one of the most successful among Byelorussian writers today. He gained instant recognition and elicited strong reaction with his novel *The Dead Feel No Pain* (1966). Readers and critics reacted favorably, but the reaction of officials was unfavorable, despite their relative tolerance of his merciless truthfulness. Since then he has written several novels reinforcing his basic theme—the brutality of war and the high price the foot soldier has to pay.

Novels by Bykaŭ

The Ordeal. Trans. by Gordon Clough. NAL–Dutton 1972 o.p. A brief novel about the guerrilla warfare in Byelorussia in World War II.

Pack of Wolves. Trans. by Lynn Solotaroff. T. Y. Crowell 1981 o.p. "A story within a story, this capably translated Russian tale of a postwar search is both stirring and poignant. . ." (*Bulletin of the Center for Children's Books*).

Sign of Misfortune. Trans. by Alan Meyers. Allerton Pr. 1990 $19.95. ISBN 0-89864-049-0. Links the victims of forced collectivization with the enemy in World War II.

CROATIAN LITERATURE

The beginnings of Croatian literature are tied to the ninth-century introduction of Christianity by the Greek brothers Cyril and Methodius. Early literature consisted of prayers, homilies, apocrypha, and hagiographies written in the Glagolitic alphabet of Old Church Slavic, based on a local tongue. The first preserved text dates from around 1100. There were also translations of Greek tales and legends. Vernacular and folk literature infused the Old Church Slavic, so that what had been a language common to all South Slavs gradually acquired its own features. Most of Croatia's early literature has been lost.

The independent Croatian state lasted until 1102, followed by Hungarian, Turkish, and Austrian sovereignty until 1918. However, Croatian literature continued to be written. From the second half of the fifteenth century to the nineteenth century, significant literature flourished in cultural centers along the Adriatic Coast, especially in the Republic of Dubrovnik (Ragusa), which escaped Turkish rule. Writers in this area were influenced by the Italian Renaissance and by Petrarchian poetry. Many poets were educated in Italy and wrote either in Latin or bilingually. Despite the Italian influence, however, the Croatian poets of Dalmatia, notably Marko Marulić, Petar Hektorović, Marin Držić, and Ivan Gundulić, were able to preserve a native color.

As Dubrovnik began to decline, so did its literature. The cultural centers moved northward and inland, where, despite the fighting against the Turks and social instability, new writers gradually emerged, assuring continuity. The Counter-Reformation and the growth of centers like Zagreb brought new, didactic writers such as Andrija Kačić Miošić and Matija Reljković. Toward the middle of the nineteenth century, more accomplished writers around the

Illyrian movement, which advocated the unification of all South Slavs, ushered in romanticism. Their leader, Ljudevit Gaj, reformed the literary language. Romanticists such as Stanko Vraz, Ivan Mažuranić, Petar Preradović, and AUGUST ŠENOA were influenced by the European models but also relied on folk poetry and patriotic fervor.

Romanticism gave way to realism in the second half of the nineteenth century. Changes in rural and urban societies prompted writers—Ante Kovačić, Josip Kozarac, and Vjenceslav Novak among others—to address the issues of the times. As a reaction to realism, at the turn of the century a strong movement called *Moderna* (a term borrowed from Hermann Bahr) appeared. Led by Milan Marjanović and Antun Gustav Matoš, it brought a vigorous cosmopolitan spirit into Croatian literature, giving rise to other capable writers: Silvije Strahimir Kranjčević, Ivo Vojnović, Vladimir Nazor, and Milan Begović. While some of them continued to write after World War I, the interwar period was personified by the towering figure of MIROSLAV KRLEŽA, a prolific Marxist writer. Placing freedom of the arts above his leftist leanings, Krleža led the avant-garde movement and set the literary tone for decades. Among other noteworthy writers were Antun Branko Šimić, Augustin Tin Ujević, and Nikola Šop. Thanks to Krleža, Croatian literature ignored socialist realism after World War II. Today it is marked by freedom of expression, openness to other literatures, and a sophistication derived from the past's rich traditions. RANKO MARINKOVIĆ, Jure Kaštelan, VESNA PARUN, Mirko Božić, and SLAVKO MIHALIĆ lead the long list of accomplished writers.

History and Criticism

Barac, Antun. *A History of Yugoslav Literature*. Mich. Slavic Pubns. 1972 $15.00. ISBN 0-930042-19-0. A reliable general survey, mainly up to 1941.

Eekman, Thomas. *Thirty Years of Yugoslav Literature, 1945–1975*. Mich. Slavic Pubns. 1978 $15.00. ISBN 0-930042-21-2. Complements Barac's history. Filled with facts and cursory analyses of all important authors and works.

Kadic, Ante. *Contemporary Croatian Literature*. Mouton 1964 $16.70. ISBN 90-2791-006-5. Excellent concise introduction.

———. *Essays in South Slavic Literature*. Yale Russian 1988 $18.50. ISBN 0-936586-10-9. Covers Croatian literature primarily.

———. *From Croatian Renaissance to Yugoslav Socialism. Slavistic Printings and Reprintings Ser.* Mouton 1969 o.p. Essays on Croatian literature to the present.

———. *The Tradition of Freedom in Croatian Literature*. Croatian Alliance 1983 o.p.

Lukić, Sveta. *Contemporary Yugoslav Literature: A Sociopolitical Approach*. Ed. by Gertrude J. Robinson. Trans. by Pola Triandis. Bks. Demand repr. of 1972 ed. $74.00. ISBN 0-317-09655-9. A critical analysis by a Marxist revisionist literary critic, especially of the literary scene 1945–68.

Mihailovich, Vasa D., ed. *Modern Slavic Literatures. Lib. of Literary Criticism Ser.* Vol. 2 Continuum 1976 o.p. Contains excerpts from 16 contemporary Croatian authors in the Yugoslav section.

Mihailovich, Vasa D., and Mateja Matejić. *A Comprehensive Bibliography of Yugoslav Literature in English, 1593–1980*. Slavica 1984 $29.95. ISBN 0-89357-136-9. *First Supplement to a Comprehensive Bibliography of Yugoslav Literature in English, 1981-1985*. Slavica 1989 $18.95. ISBN 0-89357-188-1. *Second Supplement to a Comprehensive Bibliography of Yugoslav Literature in English, 1986–1990*. Slavica 1992 $19.95. An all-inclusive bibliography.

Collections

Butler, Thomas. *Monumenta Serbocroatica: A Bilingual Anthology of Serbian and Croatian Texts from the Twelfth to the Nineteenth Century*. Mich. Slavic Pubns. 1980

$15.00. ISBN 0-930042-32-8. An excellent collection of many texts, with introduction, presented in English for the first time.

Lenski, Branko, ed. *Death of a Simple Giant and Other Modern Yugoslav Stories.* Vanguard 1964 o.p. One of the best collections of Yugoslav short stories.

Mihailovich, Vasa D., ed. *Contemporary Yugoslav Poetry. Iowa Translations Ser.* Bks. Demand repr. of 1977 ed. $14.00. ISBN 0-317-42148-4. Introduction by Gertrude G. Champe. The most complete Yugoslav poetry collection in English. Includes 13 Croatian poets.

Mikasinovich, Branko, Dragan Milivojevic, and Vasa D. Mihailovich, eds. *Introduction to Yugoslav Literature. Twayne's International Studies and Translations Ser.* G. K. Hall 1973 o.p. A good collection of writings from the nineteenth and twentieth centuries, including 25 Croatian authors.

KRLEŽA, MIROSLAV. 1893–1981

During his long and fruitful career as a free-lance writer, Miroslav Krleža tried his pen in several genres: poetry, fiction, drama, essays, and literary criticism. He was equally at home in all of them. The constant in all his works is a merciless criticism of bourgeois societies, first in the decomposing Austro-Hungarian empire, then in Yugoslavia between the two world wars. As a consistent Marxist, he saw revolutionary social change as the only way out of the "Pannonian morass," as he called it, yet he also advocated freedom of creativity and the preservation of an artist's dignity. Of his many works, the stories and plays of the Glembay cycle and the multivolume novel *Flags* remain among the most significant achievements not only in Croatian but in all of Yugoslav literature.

Novels by Krleža

On the Edge of Reason. 1938. Trans. by Zora Depolo. Vanguard 1975 o.p. A novel about a Zagreb lawyer's revolt against the trivial, corrupt society.

The Return of Philip Latinowicz. 1932. Trans. by Zora Depolo. Vanguard 1968 o.p. A Proustian elegy about a cosmopolitan painter's return to his provincial town and his difficulties in readjusting to it and regaining his creativity.

Short Story Collection by Krleža

The Cricket beneath the Waterfall and Other Stories. Ed. by Branko Lenski. Vanguard 1972 o.p. Includes the best of Krleža's stories.

MARINKOVIĆ, RANKO. 1913–

Marinković is a native of Dalmatia. Writing in three genres—short stories, novels, and plays—he is a leading contemporary writer whose modest output is offset by its excellence. A well-educated intellectual, Marinković writes often about provincial people, finding in them universal qualities that transcend their intrinsic interest as characters. He developed his interest in playwrighting as a director of the Croatian National Theater and as a professor at the Zagreb Academy of Dramatic Arts, later exerting a strong influence on younger writers.

Plays by Marinković

Five Modern Yugoslav Plays. Ed. by Branko Mikasinovich. Cyrco 1977 o.p. Includes Marinković's best play, *Gloria,* about the conflict between love and the call to serve God.

MIHALIĆ, SLAVKO. 1928–

Slavko Mihalić has published several books of poetry since 1954. In his poems he exhibits neoromantic and intellectual inclinations, attempting to overcome the absurdity of life with an ardent belief in the poet's humanistic role. Writing in an idiom remarkable for its simplicity, precision, and lyrical fluency, he is considered one of Croatia's best contemporary poets.

Poetry by Mihalić

Atlantis: Selected Poems, 1953–1982. Trans. by Charles Simic and Peter Kastmiler. Greenfield Rev. 1984 $5.00. ISBN 0-912678-61-5

PARUN, VESNA. 1922–

A prolific poet, Parun appeared during the modernization of Croatian poetry after World War II, modeling her poetry after prewar avant-garde poets and striking a distinct and resolute chord of nonconformity, almost rebellion. With her numerous books of poems, she insisted on her individuality. In her struggle with literary dictates she has refused to be bullied. Although Parun experienced long periods of public silence, she continued to write, and she has maintained this rebellious attitude throughout her career. In her poetry, Parun is primarily interested in her private world and inner life, but she also protests the dehumanization of modern life and pleads for understanding and tolerance. Her influence on younger Croatian poets has been considerable. She is also well respected abroad.

Poetry by Parun

Selected Poems of Vesna Parun. Ed. and trans. by Dasha Culic Nisula. Green River 1985 $10.00. ISBN 0-940580-33-0. A cross-section of Parun's poetry from the earliest to the latest. Bilingual.

ŠENOA, AUGUST. 1838–1881

The most important fiction writer in Croatian literature of the nineteenth century, Šenoa excelled in the historical novel and is therefore called the Walter Scott of Croatian letters. He is considered the father of modern Croatian literature, having written in multiple genres: poetry, plays, and essays. Although Šenoa wrote novels and stories about contemporary life, he is best remembered for works depicting Croatian history. Most of these novels deal with the capital Zagreb, but also with the peasants' attempts to liberate themselves from foreign domination and better their lives. Moreover, Šenoa drew parallels with the present, instilling in his countrymen and women love for their country and for freedom.

Novel by Šenoa

The Peasant Rebellion. Trans. by Branko Brusar and Matica Iseljenika Hrvatske. 1973 o.p. Šenoa's most important historical novel, about a peasant rebellion in the sixteenth century. Abridged.

CZECH LITERATURE

The first works in Czech literature, written in the fourteenth century, were both religious and secular: hymns, hagiography, epic and lyric poems, drama, and historical and didactic writings. Influenced by Western examples, this activity was interrupted by the Hussite wars, after which an increasingly vernacular literature, especially poetry, began to develop. In the sixteenth century the influence of humanism resulted in the predominance of prose works, culminating in the translation of the Bible. The Thirty Years' War, which resulted in the absorption of Old Bohemia into the Hapsburg empire, put a temporary end to writing in Czech. Only those writers who emigrated continued writing in Czech; among them, Jan Amos Komenský became prominent for his educational and theological works in Latin and Czech.

The national revival did not come until the end of the eighteenth century. One of the first concerns was the renewal of the literary language. Jozef Dobrovský and Jozef Jungmann codified literary Czech, which enabled writers to write in their native language again. Two poets contributed significantly to the resurgence of poetry: Jan Kollar, a Slovak writing in Czech, and Karel Hynek Macha, whose epic poem *Máj* marks the beginning of modern Czech poetry. As the century progressed, the romantic spirit, closely connected with the awakening of national consciousness and with the growing desire to gain independence from Austria, dominated the literary scene.

By the 1890s new realities brought a reaction against romanticism and aligned Czech literature with a more practical and liberal approach regarding the overriding concern of the time—total independence. This movement was inspired by the ideas and writings of Tomáš G. Masaryk, who would later become president of independent Czechoslovakia, and by Jozef Svatopluk Machar and Petr Bezruč. In addition, symbolist lyric poets reflected the increasing influence of Western literature—an influence that has been present in Czech literature from the very beginning.

When independence was finally won in 1918, Czech writers responded to the changed situation in several ways. Some were inspired by the Bolshevik Revolution; others fell under the spell of surrealism; still others wrote novels and short stories with pronounced social overtones. The most famous of these writers did not belong to any of the groups: JAROSLAV HAŠEK, who became world famous for his satirical antiwar and anti-Austrian novel *The Good Soldier Schweik* (1920–23), and KAREL ČAPEK, whose novels, short stories, and plays are also published in many countries. The poet JAROSLAV SEIFERT went through many phases and settled on pure, unaffected poetry of love and everyday life, for which he received the Nobel Prize in 1984. The interwar period was distinguished above all by a sharpened consciousness of many leading writers, some of whom showed distinct leftist leanings.

It was the writers with radical social views who took over when the Communists established their system after 1948. Opponents were silenced or forced into exile. The fluctuation of strict controls and relaxations, however, enabled writers—especially those from the new generation such as the novelists JOSEF ŠKVORECKÝ, LUDVÍK VACULÍK, and MILAN KUNDERA, the poet MIROSLAV HOLUB, and the playwright VÁCLAV HAVEL—to write defiant works of high quality. These writings were terminated by the crushing of the so-called Prague Spring in 1968, and literature fell once again under the strict controls and deadly effects of socialist realism. However, with the country's full independence gained in the early 1990s, the future of Czech literature looks bright again. Havel was elected president in December 1989 and served until 1992.

History and Criticism

Chudoba, F. *Short History of Czech Literature*. Kraus repr. of 1924 ed. $29.00. ISBN 0-527-17000-3. A useful survey of Czech literature up to national independence in 1918, with some translations added.

French, Alfred. *Czech Writers and Politics, 1945–1969. East European Monographs*. East Eur. Quarterly 1982 o.p. Examination of links between literature and politics at various postwar stages.

———. *Poets of Prague: Czech Poetry between the Wars.* OUP 1969 o.p. A perceptive study, with copious citations from translated poetry.

Harkins, William E. *Russian Folk Epos in Czech Literature: 1800–1900.* Greenwood 1971 repr. of 1951 ed. $45.00 ISBN 0-8371-4687-9

Harkins, William E., and Paul I. Trensky, eds. *Czech Literature since 1956: A Symposium.* Bohemica o.p. Ten articles on various topics by leading American scholars.

Kovtun, George J. *Czech and Slovak Literature in English: A Bibliography.* Lib. Congress 1984 o.p. Consult publisher for information. Not an all-inclusive but good bibliography of monographs published from 1832 to 1982.

Liehm, Antonin J. *The Politics of Culture.* Trans. by Peter Kussi. Grove Pr. 1972 o.p. An important collection of interviews with writers involved in the Prague Spring.

Lützow, Francis. *History of Bohemian Literature.* Assoc. Faculty Pr. 1970 repr. of 1899 ed. o.p. An old-fashioned but useful treatment of important writers to 1906. Revised.

Novák, Arne. *Czech Literature.* Trans. by Peter Kussi. Ed. by W. E. Harkins. *Joint Committee on Eastern Europe Publication Ser.* Mich. Slavic Pubns. 1986 $15.00. ISBN 0-930042-64-6

Selver, Paul. *Czechoslovak Literature: An Outline.* Gordon Pr. $175.00. ISBN 0-87968-988-9

Souckova, Milada. *Literary Satellite: Czechoslovak-Russian Literary Relations* U. Ch. Pr. 1970 $12.50. ISBN 0-226-76848-6. A thorough examination of literary relations, mainly 1945–68.

Collections

Busch, Marie, and Otto Pick, eds. *Selected Czech Tales. Short Story Index Repr. Ser.* Ayer repr. of 1925 ed. $15.00. ISBN 0-8369-3669-8. An anthology, mainly of pre-World War I authors.

Harkins, William E. *Czech Prose: An Anthology.* Mich. Slavic Pubns. 1983 $15.00. ISBN 0-930042-51-4. Czech fiction and nonfiction from the early nineteenth century to the founding of the First Czechoslovak Republic in 1918.

Liem, Antonin, and Peter Kussi, eds. *The Writing on the Wall: An Anthology of Czechoslovak Literature Today.* Karz-Cohl Pub. 1983 o.p. Offers access to currently well-known Czech writers; "represents a cross-section of views of Czech life" (*LJ*).

Selver, Paul, trans. *Anthology of Czechoslovak Literature.* Kraus repr. of 1929 ed. o.p. Poetry and fiction of writers before and after World War I.

ČAPEK, KAREL. 1890–1938

Karel Čapek is best known abroad for his plays, but at home he is also revered as an accomplished novelist, short-story writer, essayist, and writer of political articles. His bitingly satirical novel *The War with the Newts* (1936) reveals his understanding of the possible consequences of scientific advance. The novel *Krakatit* (1924), about an explosive that could destroy the world, foreshadows the feared potential of a nuclear disaster. In his numerous short stories he depicts the problems of modern life and common people in a humorous and whimsically philosophical fashion. The plays of Karel Čapek presage the Theater of the Absurd. *R.U.R.* (Rossum's Universal Robots) (1921) was a satire on the machine age. He created the word *robot* (from the Czech noun *robota,* meaning work) for the human-made automatons who in that play took over the world, leaving only one human being alive. *The Insect Comedy* (1921), whose characters *are* insects, is an ironic fantasy on human weakness. *The Makropoulos Secret* (1923), later used as the basis for Leoš Janaček's opera, was an experimental piece that questioned whether immortality is really desirable. All the plays have been produced successfully in New York. Most deal satirically with the modern machine age or with war. Underlying all his work, though, is a faith in humanity, truth, justice, and democracy, which has made him one of the most beloved of all Czech writers.

Novels by Čapek

The Absolute at Large. 1922. Ed. by Lester del Rey. *Science Fiction Ser.* Hyperion Conn. 1989 repr. of 1927 ed. $28.00. ISBN 0-88355-104-7. A novel about an invention releasing the Absolute in the form of a gas.

Krakatit. 1924. *Science Fiction Ser.* Ayer 1975 repr. of 1925 ed. $23.00. ISBN 0-685-51338-6

Three Novels. Trans. by M. Weatherall and R. Weatherall. Catbird Pr. 1990 repr. of 1948 ed. $13.95. ISBN 0-945774-08-7. Contains the trilogy *Hordubal, Meteor,* and *Ordinary Life.*

The War with the Newts. 1936. Trans. by Ewald Osers. Catbird Pr. 1990 $9.95. ISBN 0-945774-10-9. A cautionary science-fiction novel in which artificial creatures threaten to take over the world.

Plays by Čapek

The Makropoulos Secret. 1922. Ed. by Randal C. Burrell. Branden 1992 $3.95. ISBN 0-8283-1447-0

R.U.R. and The Insect Play. 1921. OUP 1961 $9.95. ISBN 0-19-281010-3

Short Story Collections by Čapek

Intimate Things. Essay Index Repr. Ser. Ayer repr. of 1936 ed. $15.00. ISBN 0-8369-0275-0. A collection of early short stories.

Money and Other Stories. 1921. *Short Story Index Repr. Ser.* Ayer repr. of 1930 ed. $18.00. ISBN 0-8369-3293-5. Early stories, foreshadowing the lack of faith in humankind present in Čapek's later works.

Nine Fairy Tales. 1931. Trans. by Dagmar Herrmann. Northwestern U. Pr. 1990 $24.95. ISBN 0-8101-0865-8. Reflects Čapek's brilliant knack for pure storytelling.

Nonfiction by Čapek

The Gardener's Year. U. of Wis. Pr. 1984 repr. of 1929 ed. $14.95. ISBN 0-299-10020-0. Ostensibly for gardeners. Offers musings on meaning and vagaries of life.

President Masaryk Tells His Story. Eastern European Collection Ser. Ayer repr. of 1935 ed. 1970 $25.50. ISBN 0-405-02739-7. Uses Masaryk's own words and beliefs to help create a cult.

Work by Čapek

Toward the Radical Center: A Karel Čapek Reader. Trans. by Peter Kussi. Catbird Pr. 1990 $23.95. ISBN 0-945774-06-0. A good selection from Čapek's works, some hitherto untranslated.

Books about Čapek

Harkins, William E. *Karel Čapek.* Col. U. Pr. 1962 $43.00. ISBN 0-231-02512-2

Masaryk, Thomas G. *On Thought and Life: Conversations with Karel Čapek.* Trans. by M. Weatherall and R. Weatherall. *Essay Index Repr. Ser.* Ayer repr. of 1938 ed. $16.00. ISBN 0-405-02782-6

Matuska, Alexander. *Karel Čapek.* Telegraph Bks. 1983 repr. of 1964 ed. o.p. A critical examination of his works. Bibliography, index.

HAŠEK, JAROSLAV. 1883–1923

Even though Jaroslav Hašek wrote a large number of short stories, his fame rests mainly on his satirical novel *The Good Soldier Schweik* (1920–23), in which he created the fat and cowardly dog-catcher-gone-to-war who personified Czech bitterness toward Austria in World War I. The humorous complications in which Schweik becomes involved derive from Hašek's own experience; his work as a journalist was interrupted by war and, like Schweik, he became a soldier. Eventually he was taken prisoner by the Russians. Later he returned to Prague as a communist to work as a free-lance writer. At his death he had completed only four "Schweik" novels of a projected six. Martin Esslin has said, "Schweik is more than a mere character; he represents a basic human attitude. Schweik defeats the powers that be, the whole universe in its absurdity, not by opposing but by complying with them. . . . In the end the stupidity of the authorities, the idiocy of the law are ruthlessly exposed." The character of Schweik made a tremendous impression on BERTOLT BRECHT, who transformed his name to use him afresh in the play *Schweyk in the Second World War.*

NOVEL BY HAŠEK

The Good Soldier Schweik. 1920–23. Trans. by Cecil Parrott. Viking Penguin 1985 o.p.

HAVEL, VÁCLAV. 1936–

Václav Havel, a skillful practitioner of the Theater of the Absurd, lashes out in his plays at the inability of human beings to communicate, stressing people's difficulties in coping with problems engendered by the machine age. From his early plays on, Havel has protested against the dehumanization of the individual in both the socialist and capitalist systems, advocating the supremacy of the spiritual over the material and of freedom over subjugation. He espouses similar ideas in his eloquent essays, defending humanitarian ideals and human dignity. Because of his sarcastically critical attitude and political dissidence, his plays were not often performed in Czechoslovakia before its independence in the late 1980s, and he was often imprisoned. His political activism in the struggle for independence of his country and for the establishment of democracy earned him the presidency of Czechoslovakia from 1989 to 1992. Havel became well known in the United States and Western Europe, with his essays and other nonfiction widely available in magazines and collections.

PLAYS BY HAVEL

Largo Desolato. Ed. by Tom Stoppard. Grove Pr. 1987 $15.95. ISBN 0-394-55554-6. Paralleling Havel's own life, concerns a nonhero with ambitions to become a national leader.

The Memorandum. 1965. Trans. by Vera Blackwell. Grove Pr. 1981 repr. of 1968 ed. $7.95. ISBN 0-8021-3229-4. Introduction by Tom Stoppard. A work centering on an artificial language.

Temptation. 1986. Trans. by Marie Winn. Grove Pr. 1989 $9.95. ISBN 0-8021-3100-X. About the danger of compromising with any evil.

NONFICTION BY HAVEL

Letters to Olga. 1985. Ed. by Paul Wilson. H. Holt & Co. 1989 $16.95. ISBN 0-8050-0973-6. Essay letters from prison concerning human identity and responsibility.

Long Distance Interrogation. 1986. Knopf 1990 $19.95. ISBN 0-394-58441-4. Autobiographical conversation.

Open Letters: Selected Writings. McKay 1991 $22.00. ISBN 0-679-40027-3. A collection of 25 articles, interviews, and public letters.

Power of the Powerless. M. E. Sharpe 1990 $35.00. ISBN 0-87332-370-X

Václav Havel or Living in Truth. Ed. by Jan Vladislav. Faber & Faber 1986 $10.95. ISBN 0-571-14440-3. Twenty-two essays translated from various languages, published on the occasion of Havel's receiving the Erasmus Prize.

HOLUB, MIROSLAV. 1923–

Holub is a distinguished scientist as well as a poet. The noted British critic A. Alvarez sees Holub's main concern as "the way in which private responses, private anxieties, connect up with the public world of science, technology, and machines."

Poetry by Holub

Although. Grossman 1971 o.p. Introduction by A. Alvarez. Poems from four of Holub's books prior to 1972.

Fly. Trans. by George Theiner and Ewald Osers. Bloodaxe Bks. 1988 $13.95. ISBN 1-85224-018-0. Selection from earlier books.

On the Contrary, and Other Poems. Bloodaxe Bks. 1984 $21.00. ISBN 0-906427-75-4. Reveals the poet's mixture of optimism, irony, and skepticism.

Poems Before and After: Collected English Translations. Trans. by Ian Milner and others. Bloodaxe Bks. 1990 $40.00. ISBN 1-85224-121-7. "No other poet of our time has more vividly and accurately made his poetry both an existentialist microscope and social barometer" (Ian Milner).

Sagital Section: Poems by Miroslav Holub. Field Translat. Ser. Oberlin Coll. Pr. 1980 o.p. Introduction by Charles Simic. A collection of 62 poems, combining "irony, sensitivity and philosophic inquiry" (*Choice*).

Selected Poems. Trans by Ian Milner and George Theiner. Viking Penguin 1967 o.p. A slender cross-section, with a good introduction by A. Alvarez.

The Vanishing Lung Syndrome. Trans. by David Young and Dana Habova. *Field Translat. Ser.* Oberlin Coll. Pr. 1990 $19.95. ISBN 0-932440-53-3. "Clinically observes all kinds of diseases, actual and metaphorical, . . . [resulting in] an intriguing code language governed by mysterious forces just beyond comprehension" (*London Review of Books*).

Nonfiction by Holub

The Dimension of the Present Moment, and Other Essays. Faber & Faber 1991 $9.95. ISBN 0-571-14338-5. Examines his poetry in an attempt to relate it to science.

Works by Holub

Interferon: or, on Theater. Trans. by David Young. *Field Translat. Ser.* Oberlin Coll. Pr. 1982 $10.95. ISBN 0-932440-12-6. Poems and prose, 1979–82. "The unity is both a reflection of earlier tendencies in Holub's work and a culmination of them" (from the Introduction).

The Jingle Bell Principle. Bloodaxe Bks. 1992 $19.95. ISBN 1-85224-123-3.

HRABAL, BOHUMIL. 1914–

Hrabal worked as a lawyer, clerk, railwayman, traveling salesman, steelworker, and laborer before turning to literature in 1962. In his tragic-comic novels and short stories he concentrates on the everyday lives of ordinary people. Thomas Lask says, "Hrabal shows an offbeat, original mind, a fey imagination and a sure hand in constructing his tales" (*N.Y. Times Bk. Review*). Hrabal's novel *Closely Watched Trains* (1965) was made into an internationally successful movie.

Novels by Hrabal

Closely Watched Trains. Writers from Other Europe Ser. 1965. Northwestern U. Pr. 1990 $8.95. ISBN 0-8101-0857-7. Hrabal's postwar classic about a young man's coming of age in German-occupied Czechoslovakia.

I Served the King of England. Trans. by Paul Wilson. HarBraceJ 1989 $17.95. ISBN 0-15-145745-X. The successes and failures of a crooked waiter during the pre-World War II era, the war, and the communist period.

Too Loud a Solitude. Trans. by Michael H. Heim. HarBraceJ 1990 $16.95. ISBN 0-15-190491-X. Life as a series of adventures in a world turned on its head.

KOHOUT, PAVEL. 1928–

At first a staunch supporter of the communist regime, the playwright Pavel Kohout later became an outspoken critic of repressive conditions in the literary life of his home country and, as a consequence, is no longer published there.

Work by Kohout

White Book. Trans. by Alex Page. Braziller 1977 o.p.

KUNDERA, MILAN. 1929–

One of the foremost contemporary Czech writers, Kundera is a novelist, poet, and playwright. His play *The Keeper of the Keys*, produced in Czechoslovakia in 1962, has long been performed in a dozen countries. His first novel, *The Joke* (1967), is a biting satire on the political atmosphere in Czechoslovakia in the 1950s. It tells the story of a young Communist whose life is ruined because of a minor indiscretion: writing a postcard to his girlfriend in which he mocks her political fervor. *The Joke* has been translated into a dozen languages and was made into a film, which Kundera wrote and directed. His novel *Life Is Elsewhere* won the 1973 Prix de Médicis for the best foreign novel.

Kundera has been living in France since 1975. His books, for a long time suppressed in his native country, are once again published. *The Unbearable Lightness of Being* (1984), won him international fame and was a successful English-language film. In this work Kundera moves toward more universal and philosophically tinged themes, thus transforming himself from a political dissident into a writer of international significance.

Novels by Kundera

The Book of Laughter and Forgetting. Trans. by Michael H. Heim. *Writers from the Other Europe Ser.* Knopf 1980 $10.95. Modern intellectuals juxtaposing sex and political systems, following a maxim "Man's fight against might is the fight of memory against forgetting."

Immortality. Trans. by Peter Kussi. Grove Pr. 1991 $21.95. "Out of a story about contemporary neuroses Kundera has fabricated a context in which everything, literally, can be claimed to matter. . . ." (*Time*).

Jacques and His Master. HarpC 1985 $10.00. ISBN 0-06-051222-7

The Joke. HarpC rev. ed. 1992 $25.00. ISBN 0-06-019030-2

Life Is Elsewhere. 1979. Viking Penguin 1986 $8.95. ISBN 0-14-006470-2. The tragedy of a self-deceived poet who dives into sordid politics armed with naive abstractions and a lust for heroism.

The Unbearable Lightness of Being. 1985. Trans. by Michael H. Heim. HarpC 1984 $19.95. ISBN 0-06-015258-3. "[D]emands to be judged not as a work of political or 'dissident' literature, but as a work of art" (*N.Y. Times*).

Short Story Collection by Kundera

Laughable Loves. 1963, 1965. Viking Penguin 1988 $8.95. ISBN 0-14-009691-4. Introduction by Philip Roth. Stories exploring people's diverse responses to the release of suppressed erotic impulses.

Nonfiction by Kundera

The Art of the Novel. 1960. Trans. by Linda Asher and David Bellos. Grove Pr. 1987 $17.95. ISBN 0-8021-0011-2. Includes an important essay on the Czech writer Vladislav Vančura.

SEIFERT, JAROSLAV. 1901–1986 (Nobel Prize 1984)

Seifert published his first book of poetry, *City of Tears*, in 1921 and in the next several decades went through several phases of development. He wrote in an unaffected, down-to-earth style about the everyday concerns and emotions of common people. His early works reflected his interest in the Russian Revolution, dadaism, and surrealism. Later, he rejected Soviet communism and wrote poetry that protested the conquest of his homeland. Married in 1928, Seifert had two children. Throughout the latter part of his life, he lived quietly in a Prague suburb until his death from a heart ailment in 1986.

Poetry by Seifert

The Casting of the Bell. Trans. by Paul Jagasich and Tom O'Grady. *Outstanding Authors Ser*. Spirit That Moves rev. ed. 1983 $15.00. ISBN 0-930370-25-2. A translation that "copies the random arrangement and simple, dignified language of the original" (*TLS*).

Dressed in Light. 1940. Trans. by Paul Jagasich and Tom O'Grady. Seventh Son Pr. 1991 $4.95. ISBN 0-933837-40-2. Written during the Nazi occupation, as a poetic tribute to Prague.

Eight Days: An Elegy for Thomas Garrigue Masaryk. Trans. by Paul Jagasich and Tom O'Grady. Spirit That Moves 1985 $6.00. ISBN 0-930370-28-7. Written in tribute to the first Czech president, Masaryk.

Morový Sloup: The Prague Monument. Trans. by Lyn Coffin. Mich. Slavic Pubns. 1985 o.p. Poems expressing the poet's self-ironic nostalgia about his past.

Mozart in Prague: Thirteen Rondels. Trans. by Paul Jagasich and Tom O'Grady. Spirit That Moves 1985 $6.00. ISBN 0-930370-27-9

The Selected Poetry of Jaroslav Seifert. Trans. by Ewald Osers and George Gibian. Macmillan 1987 $9.95. ISBN 0-02-070760-6

An Umbrella from Picadilly. Trans. by Ewald Osers. Parsons Bks. 1985 o.p.

ŠKVORECKÝ, JOSEF. 1924–

One of the foremost Czech writers of the postwar generation, Škvorecký is the author of five novels and many filmscripts and the translator into Czech of William Faulkner (see Vol. 1), Ernest Hemingway (see Vol. 1), and Dashiell Hammett (see Vol. 1). His first novel, *The Cowards* (1958), took an unorthodox look at the events of May 1945 when Czechoslovakia was liberated from the Nazis. The novel was, in its author's words, a *succès scandale*. In spite of a ban by the party, *The Cowards* circulated underground and exerted a powerful influence on young Czech writers before the political thaw set in. *Miss Silver's Past* was the last of his books to appear in Czechoslovakia, where it was published in 1969. *The Tank Corps*, which should have appeared the same year, was banned. Škvorecký left Czechoslovakia in 1968 and now teaches at the University of Toronto. He also publishes books of Czech émigré writers. In 1980 he received the Neustadt International Prize for Literature.

Novels by Škvorecký

The Bass Saxophone. 1967. Trans. by Káča Polačková-Henley. WSP 1985 $5.95. ISBN 0-671-55681-9. About a young man's failed love affair and obsession with the saxophone amid the political conflicts.

The Cowards. 1958. Trans. by Jeane Nemcová. Ecco Pr. 1980 repr. of 1970 ed. $8.95. ISBN 0-912946-75-X. A compelling novel based on the author's youthful experiences during World War II, attempting to overcome war's grim reality through love and music.

Dvořák in Love. Knopf 1987 $18.95. ISBN 0-317-58073-6. A fictionalized biography of Antonin Dvořák.

The Engineer of Human Souls. 1977. Trans. by Paul Wilson. Knopf 1984 $17.95. ISBN 0-394-50500-X. A satirical novel about the U.S. and Canadian societies.

Miss Silver's Past. 1974. Ecco Pr. 1985 repr. of 1975 ed. $7.50. ISBN 0-88001-074-6. Introduction by Graham Green. Relates "a spellbinding story of moral corruption and political cynicism in the guise of a love story that turns into a murder mystery" (publisher's note).

The Swell Season. Trans. by Paul Wilson. Ecco Pr. 1986 repr. of 1982 ed. $8.50. ISBN 0-88001-090-8. Chronicles the amorous adventures of a high-school student in Nazi-occupied Czechoslovakia.

Talkin' Moscow Blues. Ecco Pr. 1990 $12.95. ISBN 0-88001-231-5

SHORT STORY COLLECTIONS BY ŠKVORECKÝ

End of Lieutenant Boruvka. Norton 1991 o.p. The final series of Boruvka detective stories.

The Mournful Demeanor of Lieutenant Boruvka: Detective Tales. Trans. by Rosemary Kavan and others. Norton 1987 $15.95. ISBN 0-393-02470-9

Return of Lieutenant Boruvka. Norton 1991 $18.95. ISBN 0-393-02928-X. Detective stories.

Sins for Father Knox. Norton 1991 $8.95. ISBN 0-393-307807-5. Tales built on an English priest's application of the Ten Commandments to his love for detective stories.

VACULÍK, LUDVÍK. 1926–

One of the outstanding Czech novelists of the postwar generation, Vaculík has been a shoemaker, teacher, soldier, and journalist. His first novel, *The Busy House*, appeared in 1963. He edited *Literarni Listy* from 1966 until 1968, when it was suppressed by the government. His novel *The Axe*, published in 1966, made Vaculík famous in Czechoslovakia. Neal Ascherson describes this novel as "the story of a lonely farmer who deliberately destroys his own family relationships and friendships to bring socialist collectivization to his village in Moravia and who—through the very challenge that his own integrity offers to the corrupt Stalinist bureaucracy of the new order—is himself destroyed." Among the writers who criticized the Novotny regime at the Writers' Union Congress in 1967, Vaculík was expelled from the party but was readmitted during the Prague Spring of 1968. At this time Vaculík wrote the *Two Thousand Word Manifesto*, which was signed by thousands and which some believe contributed to the Soviet leaders' decision to intervene militarily.

NOVELS BY VACULÍK

The Axe. Trans. by Marian Sling. Okpaku Communications 1973 o.p.

The Guinea Pigs. Trans. by Káča Poláčková-Henley. Northwestern U. Pr. 1986 $9.95. ISBN 0-8101-0726-0. Introduction by Neal Ascherson. Shares likeness with Kafka's "world of meaningless, menacing activity broken into by strokes of atrocity delivered by an authority never named or identified" (Neal Ascherson).

ESTONIAN LITERATURE

The Estonian language is closely related to the Finno-Ugric group of languages. It is not surprising, therefore, that the first important literary work was the epic *Kalevipoeg (The Son of Kalev)*, written from 1857 to 1861, in imitation of the Finnish epic *Kalevala*. The early Estonian literature consists almost entirely of epic and lyric folk poetry. It is estimated that this small nation has produced about 400,000 folk songs. Estonians wrote mostly in Latin until 1525, when the church replaced Latin with Estonian. The publication of

Kalevipoeg signaled the awakening of national consciousness and the rise of romanticism in literature, which prevailed until the end of the nineteenth century. At that time a more realistic trend began to take hold, manifested in the depiction of rural life with social and political overtones. At the same time some authors, who were influenced by the French, introduced symbolism and impressionism. Of greater importance was the emergence of the "Young Estonia" movement, which advocated openness to foreign literatures, stylistic sophistication, and formal excellence. The writers of this movement, for the most part, established the tone of Estonian literature in the interwar period. Gustav Suits and MARIE UNDER, considered the greatest Estonian poets, were leaders in this period. Anton Hansen Tammsaare, with his five-volume novel *Truth and Justice*, and BERNARD KANGRO brought new approaches to Estonian fiction by way of experimentation, symbolism, and psychological probing.

The vicissitudes of Estonian national and political life forced many writers to leave the country, especially after the takeover of Estonia by the Soviet Union and the establishment of a communist state in 1944. In the last few decades two kinds of Estonian literature have existed. The one written at home has been shaped and dictated by the tenets of socialist realism. Although some younger poets have been successful in asserting themselves after some relaxation of controls in the post-Stalin period, very little nonexilic literature rises above the level of propaganda. The best contemporary writers are exiles. The most representative among them are Suits, Under, Kangro, Karl Ristikivi, Ilmar Jaks, Helga Nõu, and ALEKSIS RANNIT. In the 1990s Estonia regained independence from the Soviet Union, and the two literatures became one.

History and Criticism

Rubulis, Aleksis. *Baltic Literature: A Survey of Finnish, Estonian, Latvian, and Lithuanian Literatures*. U. of Notre Dame Pr. 1970 o.p. Brief but very useful survey that "presumes neither to give explicit analyses nor solely to present *chefs-d'oeuvre*" (from the Preface).

Collections

Maas, Selve. *The Moon Painters and Other Estonian Folk Tales*. Viking Penguin 1971 o.p. A good selection of traditional Estonian folk tales, many translated for the first time into English.

Matthews, William Kleesmann, ed. *Anthology of Modern Estonian Poetry*. Greenwood 1977 repr. of 1953 ed. o.p.

KANGRO, BERNARD. 1910–

A poet, prose writer, playwright, literary historian, and critic, Kangro lives and works in Sweden. He has 14 books of poetry and 6 novels to his credit. His poetry is rich, musical, predominantly elegiac, and delusory, while his novels are experimental and psychological.

NOVEL BY KANGRO

Earthbound. Trans. by W. K. Matthews. Estonian Hse. 1951 o.p. An important work.

RANNIT, ALEKSIS. 1914–1985

Rannit published his first book of poems in 1937 and later added five more collections. Because he lived the last three decades of his life in the United States, he is perhaps the best-known Estonian poet in the English-speaking world. He defines poetry as a "dance of syllables . . . the consensually pulsating expression of our spirit . . . a kind of sorcery in which metaphorical thinking blends with authentic reality to create a mythical order."

POETRY BY RANNIT

Cantus Firmus. Trans. by Henry Lyman. Elizabeth Pr. 1978 $50.00. ISBN 0-685-90033-9. Evidences Rannit's striving for perfection; rational analysis in pursuit of the sublime.

Donum Estonicum. Elizabeth Pr. 1976 $16.00. ISBN 0-685-79486-5. A selection of poems reflecting the poet's interest in and knowledge of art.

UNDER, MARIE. 1883–1980

Under, a poet and translator, began publishing poetry in her native country but worked mostly as a free-lance writer in Stockholm upon emigrating there with her husband. The author of more than a dozen collections of poetry from 1917 into the 1950s, she is revered as Estonia's greatest lyric poet. Her poetry is imbued with passion, a joy of life, and a realization of the basic tragedy of human existence. Her later poems are simpler and more direct, dealing primarily with the tragic destiny of her people in the last decades under Soviet domination.

POETRY BY UNDER

Child of Man. Trans. by W. K. Matthews. Estonian Hse. 1955 o.p. Later poetry.

HUNGARIAN LITERATURE

Hungarian literature had its beginnings in the thirteenth century. From then until the early seventeenth century, it manifested itself primarily in such religious works as chronicles and translations of the Bible. Hungarian writers played a very important role in facilitating the conversion to Christianity and in spreading the new religion among the predominantly illiterate populace. Secular literature did not begin to develop until the period of the Enlightenment in the late eighteenth century, when the foundation was laid for the flowering that was to come in the next century. Although literary works were primarily didactic, in tune with the period, there were attempts at a humorous, light-hearted depiction of reality and at the cultivation of national and traditional values as opposed to foreign influences. The first writer of international stature did not appear until the nineteenth century. SÁNDOR PETÖFI, one of the greatest, if not the greatest, of Hungarian poets, wrote patriotic, love, and nature poems inspired to a large degree by folk poetry, which he believed was the only true poetry. His friend János Arany also contributed significantly to the basically romantic literature around the middle of the century, while IMRE MADÁCH wrote dramatic poems of exceptional depth and originality.

Through the nineteenth century, writers came mostly from the ranks of the nobility, while those from lower classes had just begun to make their presence felt. The latter gained full stride early in the twentieth century with the appearance of the revolutionary poet ENDRE ADY, who is still considered the greatest Hungarian poet of this century. The "modern" movement, centered around an influential magazine, *Nyugat* (The West), replaced the stagnant literature of the preceding decades and ushered in a versatile, socially conscious literature on a higher level, open to Western influences. This versatility and high-spirited activity carried over into the interwar period, in which many prewar writers were joined by new voices. The three consummate poets, Mihály Babits, ATTILA JÓZSEF, and GYULA ILLYÉS, raised Hungarian poetry to new heights, while Ferenc Molnár, Lajos Zilahy, and LÁZSLÓ NÉMÉTH brought the Hungarian middle class into a sharper focus with their novels and short stories. Throughout this period, and even after World War II, writers either advocated revolutionary social change or took a more neutral stand, making their art the main modus of existence. The former were aided by the theoretical works of a world-famous Marxist critic, GYÖRGY LUKÁCS, who gradually changed from a liberal to a communist and became the theoretical leader of the writers on the Left. Other writers wrote about the rural life in various regions of Hungary, representing the populist movement that was demanding social reform. In fact, relatively few writers were able to stay out of political and ideological struggles during the 1930s and 1940s, due primarily to a rather volatile political situation in Hungary at that time. This involvement took a terrible toll among writers during and after World War II. Even Lukács was severely criticized at times by the communists for valuing Western literature above that of socialist realism.

After the communist takeover, socialist realism was installed as the official literary method, but it brought forward few worthy results, and writers paid only lip service to it. By the same token, they were not able to fulfill their artistic potential. Nevertheless, new names have entered the literary scene, who along with the established writers provide for a lively literature. Several writers left the country after the events of 1948 and 1956 and continued to write in exile, without repeating their earlier successes. All that has changed, with the country regaining full independence in the late 1980s. There are also Hungarian minority literatures in Rumania, Yugoslavia, and Czechoslovakia; however, they have failed to produce a writer of prominence.

History and Criticism

Czigány, Lóránt. *The Oxford History of Hungarian Literature from the Earliest Times to the Present*. OUP 1984 o.p. The most competent and complete history in English.

Klaniczay, Tibor. *A History of Hungarian Literature*. Intl. Spec. Bk. 1982 $34.95. ISBN 963-13-1542-8. A Marxist-oriented study, with predictable limitations.

Reményi, Joseph. *Hungarian Writers and Literature*. Ed. by August J. Molnar. Rutgers U. Pr. 1964 o.p. Brilliant essays by a knowledgeable observer examining the literature of the nineteenth and twentieth centuries.

Tezla, Albert. *Hungarian Authors: A Bibliographical Handbook*. HUP 1970 $66.00. ISBN 0-674-42650-9. Extension of the author's *An Introductory Bibliography to the Study of Hungarian Literature*and to be used in conjunction with that book.

______. *Introductory Bibliography to the Study of Hungarian Literature*. HUP 1964 $25.50. ISBN 0-674-46350-1

Collections

Duczynszka, Ilona, ed. *The Plough and the Pen: Writing from Hungary, 1930–1956*. Dufour o.p.

Kessler, Jascha, trans. *The Face of Creation: Contemporary Hungarian Poetry*. Coffee Hse. 1988 $11.95. ISBN 0-918273-20-X. Twenty-four poets presented, with Sandor Weores most prominent.

Kirkconnell, Watson, ed. and trans. *Hungarian Helicon*. Szechenyi Society 1985 o.p. One of the best anthologies of epic and other poetry, offering a very thorough cross section.

Tezla, Albert, ed. *Ocean at the Window: Hungarian Prose and Poetry since 1945.* U. of Minn. Pr. 1981 o.p. An extensive anthology of 24 poets and fiction writers since 1945, expertly introduced and translated.

Vajda, Miklos, ed. *Modern Hungarian Poetry.* Col. U. Pr. 1979 $50.00. ISBN 0-231-08370-X. Introduction by Miklos Vajda and William Jay Smith. A competent anthology of 40 poets including Gyula Illyés, Sandor Weores, Laszlo Nagy, and Szabolcs Varady.

ADY, ENDRE. 1877–1919

Considered the greatest Hungarian lyric poet of the twentieth century, Ady introduced new vigor into the stagnant, conventional poetry of the turn of the century. His early poetry was revolutionary in both language and content and offended literary and political conservatives. In his later writings, from before and during World War I, he voices his anguish at social injustice and the carnage of war. Ady wrote poetry dealing with love and religion as well as with social and political themes.

Poetry by Ady

Poems of Endre Ady. Lit. Ser. Hungarian Cultural 1969 $24.00. ISBN 0-914648-00-4

ILLYÉS, GYULA. 1902–1983

A poet, dramatist, novelist, essayist, and translator, Illyés published his first volume of poems in 1928. His published works amount to more than 35 volumes in Hungarian. He was one of the leaders of the populist movement in literature, which attempted to "explore the village" and to write about the squalid condition of the peasantry. His largely autobiographical study of the peasantry, *People of the Puszta,* is considered a classic. Illyés always wrote in the "daily language of simple people," drawing on the wealth and rhythms of the Hungarian language.

Work by Illyés

People of the Puszta. Trans. by G. F. Cushing. Intl. Spec. Bk. 1987 $10.95. ISBN 963-13-0594-5

Book about Illyés

Kabdebo, Thomas, and Paul Tabori, eds. *Tribute to Gyula Illyés: Poems.* Occidental 1968 o.p.

JÓKAI, MÓR (also MÓRICZ, MAURICE). 1825–1904

Mór Jókai, an author of romances who enjoyed great popularity in his day, was a sort of Jules Verne of Hungary who became known throughout Europe. He wrote more than 100 novels. Though weak in characterization, Jókai was a master of suspense and fantastic—sometimes "scientific"—adventure, which took place in exotic settings and was colored by his own exuberant optimism. *The Dark Diamond* (1870) and *The Man with the Golden Touch* (1872, sometimes translated *A Modern Midas*) are his two outstanding tales.

Novels by Jókai

The Dark Diamond. 1870. Trans. by Frances Gerard. Vanous o.p.
The Man with the Golden Touch. 1872. Continuum o.p.

Short Story Collection by Jókai

Tales from Jókai. Trans. by R. Nisbet Bain. *Short Story Index Repr. Ser.* Ayer repr. of 1904 ed. $5.37. ISBN 0-8369-3946-8. Stories from various periods.

JÓZSEF, ATTILA. 1905–1937

A poet, József was born in poverty and remained poor all his life. In his poetry he protested against the conditions of the working class. He was a contributor to the journal *Nyugat* (*The West*). His first collection of poems was *Beggar of Beauty* (1922). In the last years of his life, he became a poet of national and world stature. His best works are the collections of poems *The Bear's Dance* (1934), *There Is No Pardon* (1936–37), the *Last Poems* (1937). József drew on Hungarian folklore, German expressionism, and French surrealism but integrated these materials into his own powerful poetic style. After being held in disrepute by the communist regime during the Zhdanov period, József is now considered the greatest Hungarian poet.

Poetry by József

Perched on Nothing's Branch. Trans. by Peter Hargitai. Apalachee Pr. 1987 ISBN 0-940821-00-1

Works by József

Selected Poems and Texts. Trans. by John Batki. *International Bks.* U. of Iowa Pr. o.p. Samplings of József's poems and essays.

Works of Attila József. Lit. Ser. Hungarian Cultural 1973 $12.00. ISBN 0-914648-01-2. Primarily poems and essays, but includes some other works.

JUHÁSZ, FERENC. 1928–

Juhász's first book of poems, *The Winged Colt* (1947), made his reputation before he was 20. After several works glorifying the new communist regime, Juhász in the early 1950s began to move away from politics and to develop his own original poetic style. The large epic poem *The Prodigal Country,* according to Gomori, introduced a "new epoch in modern Hungarian poetry." Juhász's collection of poems *Battling the White Lamb* (1957) contains *The Boy Changed into a Stag Cries Out at the Gate of Secrets,* which W. H. Auden (see Vol. 1) called "one of the greatest poems written in my time." After being in official disfavor in the late 1950s and early 1960s, Juhász was later tolerated by the regime and allowed to travel abroad. Hungarians consider him the greatest poet of his generation and the heir to Atilla József.

Poetry by Juhász

The Boy Changed into a Stag: Selected Poems, 1949–1967. Trans. by Kenneth McRobbie and Ilona Duczynska. OUP 1970 o.p.

(and Sandor Weores). *Selected Poems.* Trans. by Davis Wevill and Edward Morgan. Peter Smith o.p.

LENGYEL, JOZSEF. 1896–1975

A novelist, memoirist, and short-story writer, Lengyel was an active Communist who, in 1937, was arrested and held in Siberia until 1955. In his writings he describes his experiences of this period and tries to understand the debasement of socialism into Stalinism.

Novels by Lengyel

Acta Sanctorum. Beekman Pubs. o.p. Set in Siberian concentration camps.

Confrontation. Trans. by Anna Novotny. Citadel Pr. 1973 $6.95. ISBN 0-8065-0367-X. About the crimes of Stalinism. Published only in English.

The Judge's Chair. Beekman Pubs. $19.95. ISBN 0-8464-0539-3. About the Hungarian post-World War I revolutionaries.

Prenn Drifting. Beekman Pubs. 1966 $19.95. ISBN 0-8464-0747-7. About a roughneck who evolves into a revolutionary. Combines documentary material with fiction.

The Spell (and *From Beginning to End*). Trans. by Ilona Duczynska. Beekman Pubs. 1964 $17.95. ISBN 0-8464-1466-X. Based on autobiographical material from Lengyel's incarceration in Siberian concentration camps.

LUKÁCS, GYÖRGY (also GEORG, GEORGE). 1885–1971

GEORGE STEINER (see Vol. 1) in *Language and Silence*, calls Lukács "the one major critical talent to have emerged from the gray servitude of the Marxist world." This well-known writer on European literature combines a Marxist-Hegelian concern for the historical process with great artistic sensitivity. Lukács joined the Hungarian Communist party in 1918, serving in its first government until the defeat of Béla Kun. He spent many years in exile, first in Berlin and then, from 1933 to 1945, in Moscow, writing and studying. He later became a professor of aesthetics in Budapest, but after the 1956 revolution he was stripped of influence because of his too-friendly attitude to non-Marxist literatures. Steiner has written: "A Communist by conviction, a dialectical materialist by virtue of his critical method, he has nevertheless kept his eyes resolutely on the past. . . . Despite pressure from his Russian hosts, Lukács gave only perfunctory notice to the much-heralded achievements of 'Soviet Realism.' Instead, he dwelt on the great lineage of eighteenth- and nineteenth-century European poetry and fiction. . . . The critical perspective is rigorously Marxist, but the choice of themes is 'central European' and conservative." Lukács has concentrated mainly on criticism of Russian, French, and German authors and often writes in German. Robert J. Clements (*SR*) has reported that Hungarian young people regard him as somewhat passé.

NONFICTION BY LUKÁCS

Essays on Realism. Trans. by David Fernbach. Ed. by Rodney Livingstone. MIT Pr. 1981 $11.95. ISBN 0-262-62042-1. Marxist interpretations of realistic literature.

Goethe and His Age. Trans. by Robert Anchor. Fertig 1978 repr. of 1968 ed. $35.00. ISBN 0-86527-256-5. Goethe seen as the greatest achievement of the German Enlightenment and a perfect rationalist.

The Historical Novel. 1955. Trans. by Hannah Mitchell and Stanley Mitchell. U. of Nebr. Pr. 1983 repr. of 1937 ed. $10.95. ISBN 0-8032-7910-8. Analysis of the novel of the "great realism," with Balzac and Tolstoy evaluated as the most accomplished realists.

The Meaning of Contemporary Realism. Humanities 1980 $19.95. ISBN 0-85036-250-4. Lukács's disapproval of modern literature's obsession with psychopathology; discusses Thomas Mann, Bertolt Brecht, Joseph Conrad, D. H. Lawrence, and Eugene O'Neill, among others.

Record of a Life: An Autobiographical Sketch. Trans. by Rodney Livingstone. Routledge Chapman & Hall 1983 $14.95. ISBN 0-86091-771-1

Solzhenitsyn. Trans. by William D. Graf. MIT Pr. 1971 $4.95. ISBN 0-262-62021-9. Solzhenitsyn seen from a Marxist critic's point of view.

Theory of the Novel. Trans. by Ann Bostock. MIT Pr. 1971 $9.95. ISBN 0-262-62027-8. Neo-Hegelian treatment of the genre and of the links between aesthetics and history.

BOOKS ABOUT LUKÁCS

Bahr, Ehrhard, and Ruth G. Kunzer. *Georg Lukács. Lit. and Life Ser.* Continuum 1972 $19.95. ISBN 0-8044-2014-9. A brief but useful biography, with numerous references to Lukács's views on literature.

Kiralifalvi, Bela. *The Aesthetics of Gyorgy Lukács.* Princeton U. Pr. 1975 o.p. A systematic but not critical analysis of Lukács's entire aesthetic system.

Meszaros, I. *Lukács' Concept of Dialectics: With Biography, Bibliography and Documents.* Humanities 1972 o.p. Deals concisely with the centrally important concepts in Lukács's work as a whole.

MADÁCH, IMRE. 1823–1864

Madách wrote poems, plays, and essays, with drama his main genre. His play in verse, *The Tragedy of Man,* written in 1859–60 and inspired by MILTON (see Vol. 1), GOETHE, and BYRON (see Vol. 1), is Faustlike in theme. It begins and ends in heaven, and Adam and Eve are its protagonists, with Lucifer battling God for the possession of their souls. *The Tragedy of Man* is still performed on the Hungarian stage as one of that country's great classics. Madách's other plays are tragedies based on Hungarian history and comedies about everyday life under Austrian oppression.

PLAY BY MADÁCH

The Tragedy of Man. 1861. East Eur. Quarterly 1989 $23.50. ISBN 0-88033-169-0

MORICZ, SZIGMOND. 1879–1942

Moricz was a novelist, short-story writer, and playwright associated with the literary journal *Nyugat* (*The West*). In his early works, Moricz described the grim reality of the countryside in a stark, naturalistic manner. His later novels about the upper classes are less forceful than the early ones. Among his best-known novels are *The Torch* (1917) and those of his trilogy *Transylvania* (1922–35). Moricz is generally recognized as Hungary's first modern writer.

NOVEL BY MORICZ

Be Faithful unto Death. Trans. by Susan K. Laszlo. Vanous 1962 o.p. Autobiographical, concentrating on the author's childhood sufferings and on criticism of his participation in the 1918–19 revolution.

NÉMÉTH LÁSZLÓ. 1901–1975

Németh, a philosopher and reformer often characterized as brooding, has written many books on the situation of Hungary in Europe as well as critical works, journalism, and a number of novels. *Revulsion* (1947) is an example of the latter. The sensitive story of a young farm girl, set in the Hungary of the late 1930s, it gives a vivid picture of village and rural life. A novel with an earlier, post-World War I setting, *Guilt* is sharply critical of the upper classes for tolerating, and even causing, class inequities.

NOVEL BY NÉMÉTH

Guilt. Trans. by Gyula Gulyas. Dufour 1966 $22.50. ISBN 0-7206-3845-3. "Vivid accumulation of detail and superb portrayal of character . . . present[s] grimly disillusioned images of the hero in the anonymous modern state" (*The Spectator*).

PETÖFI, SÁNDOR. 1823–1849

Considered the greatest lyric poet of nineteenth-century Hungary, Petöfi takes as the subject for most of his poems the life of Hungarian peasantry. The main themes of his poetry are love and patriotism. He is best known for his poem about peasant life, *Janos the Hero,* and for the "Talpra Magyar," known as the Hungarian "Marseillaise," written during the Hungarian struggle for independence in 1848. Petöfi enlisted in the army in order to take part in this struggle and is believed to have died during the battle of Segesvar in 1849, at the age of 26.

POETRY BY PETÖFI

Sixty Poems. Trans. by Emil Delmar. Kraus repr. of 1948 ed. $12.00. ISBN 0-527-70750-3

WORK BY PETÖFI

Works. Lit. Ser. Hungarian Cultural 1973 $14.90. ISBN 0-914648-04-7. Presents a collection of Petöfi's most important works.

BOOK ABOUT PETÖFI

Tribute to Sándor Petöfi on the 150th Anniversary of His Birth. Intl. Pubng. Serv. 1974 o.p.

LATVIAN LITERATURE

Early Latvian literature consists entirely of folk poetry; more than one million folk songs have been recorded. The Latvians were ruled by the Germans for many centuries, and the first literary works in Latvia were written by the German clergy in the sixteenth century. Latvian literature originated in the second half of the nineteenth century as a result of the national awakening and the drive toward independence. Poems, stories, novels, and plays show the influence of folk literature. The first important work is a novel about the plight of the peasants, *The Time of the Land Surveyors,* written by the brothers Kaudzītes. By the turn of the century, the influence from abroad, especially that of French symbolism, became more noticeable. In the aftermath of the uprising in 1905 against the German landowners, some writers retained their nationalistic fervor while others turned to Marxism.

Among the authors before the independence of 1918, Jānis Rainis stands out. With his philosophically tinged poems and plays, he was the first to draw the attention of the outside world to Latvian literature. Other notables of this period are the poet and fairy tale writer Kārlis Skalbe and the poet Edvards Virza. Most writers in this period, under the influence from abroad, were preoccupied with transforming their legacy of folk literature into a more modern idiom.

After independence, writers either stayed at home or moved to the Soviet Union. The ratio of published books to the population was among the highest in the world. Most of the writers who emigrated to the Soviet Union perished in the purges of the 1930s; at any rate, they failed to produce works of lasting value. The writers at home fared better, although they produced only one outstanding writer, the poet Aleksandrs Čaks, who was able to influence the younger poets with his formal innovations.

The Soviet occupations of 1940 and 1944 brought strict controls and literary dictates. Predictably, few outstanding authors and works have appeared since then, although some younger writers were able to elude the grip of socialist realism by reconciling tradition with contemporaneity. By far the best Latvian literature is written by émigré writers: in Sweden, the poet Veronika Strēlerte, the novelist Andrejs Irbe, and the most important Latvian playwright, Mārtinš Zīverts; in London, the poet Velta Snikere and the novelist Guntis Zarinš; and in the United States, the poets Linards Tauns and Astrīda Ivask and fiction writers Gunars Salinš, Knuts Lesinš, and Anšlāvs Eglītis. Many of these writers were able to rejoin the literary life in Latvia after it regained independence in the early 1990s.

It is indeed unfortunate that very little of Latvian literature is available in English.

History and Criticism

Ekmanis, Rolfs. *Latvian Literature under the Soviets*, 1940-1975. Nordland Pr. 1977 o.p. A scholarly examination of the difficult conditions of Latvian writers in the Soviet Union.

Rubulis, Aleksis. *Baltic Literature: A Survey of Finnish, Estonian, Latvian, and Lithuanian Literatures.* U. of Notre Dame Pr. 1970 o.p. A brief but very useful survey that "presumes neither to give explicit analyses nor solely to present *chefs-d'oeuvre*" (from the Preface).

Straumanis, Alfreds. *Baltic Drama: A Handbook and Bibliography.* Waveland Pr. 1981 $44.95. ISBN 0-917974-63-8. A practical handbook to important dramatic literature in all Baltic literatures.

Collections

Cedrins, Inara (Astrud Ivask), ed. *Contemporary Latvian Poetry. Iowa Translations Ser.* 1984 o.p. Introduction by Juris Silenieks. The best available anthology of Latvian poetry in English.

Straumanis, Alfreds, ed. *Bridge Across the Sea: Seven Baltic Plays.* Waveland Pr. 1983 $23.95. ISBN 0-88133-055-8. Includes Anšlāv Eglītis's *Ferdinand and Sybil* and *Please, Come in, Sir.*

——, ed. *Fire and Night: Five Baltic Plays.* Waveland Pr. 1986 $23.95. ISBN 0-88133-216-X. Includes Janis Rainis's *Fire and Night* and Mārtinš Zīverts's *Power.*

LITHUANIAN LITERATURE

Unfavorable historical and political conditions prevented Lithuanian literature from asserting itself until the late eighteenth century. At that time Kristijonas Donelaitis wrote poems about the pastoral life, reflecting the strong attachment to nature of many Lithuanian writers. Donelaitis's poetry could not inspire other poets because Polish domination was replaced by that of Russia at the beginning of the nineteenth century. The full awakening of national consciousness engendered a strong desire for independence, expressed most eloquently by the romantic poets, especially by those from neighboring Poland. The forerunner of this romantic enthusiasm was Antanas Baranauskas, whose evocation of the past and of the joys of country life exudes optimism. The patriotic zeal of the romantics intensified when the Russians forbade the publication of books in Lithuania after the unsuccessful uprising in 1863. The poet Maironis personifies the patriotic spirit toward the end of the nineteenth century. Other writers, forced to print their books abroad and smuggle them into Lithuania, found their models among Western authors, especially the French symbolists.

The lifting of the ban in 1904 greatly increased literary activity, bringing forth many new names. This process continued after Lithuania finally won its independence in 1918 and between the two world wars. The poet Jonas Aistis blended French modernism with native folkloristic elements. Putinas, who was originally influenced by Russian symbolism, enriched Lithuanian poetry and brought psychological depth to his novels and plays. Vincas Krėvė, perhaps the best Lithuanian fiction writer, found the strength of his heroes in the myths of Lithuania's past. Antanas Vienulis spanned several periods, finally opting for

Soviet Lithuania. In his starkly realistic works, he depicts the everyday life of his countrymen forced to accept the dictates of the mighty. Antanas Vaičiulaitis, a master of impressionistic style, wrote novels and short stories about life in the country, as well as fairy tales. The emotional poetry of Bernardos Brazdžionis displays religious overtones of Catholic mysticism.

Most of these writers emigrated when the Soviets returned in 1944 and continued to write about their homeland. Others blossomed after they had emigrated, mostly to the United States. The most outstanding of them, Henrikas Radauskas, blends fantasy and reality through a sure command of his modernistic poetic idiom. Other noteworthy émigré writers are Jurgis Gliauda, Kazys Braidūnas, Nýka-Niliūnas (pseud. of Alfonsas Čipkus), Antanas Škema, Algirdas Landsbergis, and Kostas Ostrauskas.

The writers who remained, or came later to the fore, in Soviet Lithuania had to work in much harsher conditions and under strict controls. Despite all these difficulties, some authors have succeeded in reconciling their artistic aspirations with the stifling demands of socialist realism. Among those writers are Eduardas Mieželaitis, Juozas Grušas, Justinas Marcinkevičius, Mykolas Sluckis, Icchokas Meras, and Thomas Venclova. Although there has been no work of international acclaim, these writers, especially the younger ones, are at least keeping the hope for a better future alive. Possibilities look much brighter now after Lithuania regained its independence from the Soviet Union in the early 1990s.

History and Criticism

Šilbajoris, Rimvydas. *Perfection of Exile: Fourteen Contemporary Lithuanian Writers.* U. of Okla. Pr. 1970 o.p. Fourteen essays on 14 Lithuanian authors in exile, with a historical survey of Lithuanian literature.

Zobarskas, Stepas. *Lithuanian Short Story: Fifty Years.* Manyland 1977 $12.50. ISBN 0-685-03281-7. Includes 29 stories, most written after 1940. Good introduction by A. Landsbergis.

BARANAUSKAS, ANTANAS. 1835–1902

A Roman Catholic bishop, Baranauskas included creative writing among his other hobbies. *The Forest of Anykščiai* was written in response to the challenge to produce poetry in the Lithuanian language that would measure up to the standards of written Polish. This idyllic work, tracing the history and the demise of a small forest grove, met the challenge in exquisite syllabic verse, melodious and expressive to mirror the complex emotional experience of human beings living in an instinctive harmony with nature.

Poetry by Baranauskas

The Forest of Anykščiai. Trans. by Nadas Rastenis. Lithuanian Days 1970 o.p.

DONELAITIS, KRISTIJONAS. 1714–1780

Author of the first important work in Lithuanian, Donelaitis, a village pastor, wrote very little else. *The Seasons* grew out of his efforts to enlist the services of art in his pastoral work. The long narrative poem surveys the course of the seasons in the life of eighteenth-century Lithuanian peasants "plodding the treadmill of time toward a hoped-for eternity in which their plain country virtue is to meet its just reward" (*Perfection of Exile*).

Poetry by Donelaitis

The Seasons. Trans. by Nadas Rastenis. Lithuanian Days 1967 o.p.

GLIAUDA, JURGIS. 1906–

When the exigencies of exile deprived Gliauda of his profession as a lawyer, he turned to belles lettres and rapidly developed into a prolific novelist, conservative in terms of moral and ethnic values but often experimental in the structure and language of his work. Written in 1945, *House upon the Sand* pictures the "crime and punishment" of a German landowner just before Hitler's empire crumbled.

Novels by Gliauda

House upon the Sand. Trans. by Raphael Sealey and Milton Stark. Manyland 1963 o.p.
Simas. Manyland 1971 $5.00. ISBN 0-87141-042-7
Sonata of Icarus. Trans. by Raphael Sealey. Manyland 1968 $5.00. ISBN 0-87141-024-9. A fictional biography of the Lithuanian composer Čiurlionis.

KRĖVĖ, VINCAS (MICKIEVIČIUS). 1882–1954

The grand old man of Lithuanian letters, Vincas Krėvė laid the foundation for many levels and styles of Lithuanian prose and drama, greatly extending the powers of spoken Lithuanian to function as an effective written medium. *Legends of the Old People of Dainava* (1912) elevated the heroic Lithuanian, using quasi-folkloristic language that approaches high poetry. The historical plays *Šarūnas* (1912) and *Skirgaila* (1925) depict Lithuanian rulers confronted with tremendous moral and intellectual challenges as they struggle to create and then defend a unified Lithuanian nation. *The Herdsman and the Linden Tree* presents some of the best realistic stories Krėvė wrote.

Short Story Collection by Krėvė

The Herdsman and the Linden Tree. Trans. by Baranauskas. Manyland 1964 $3.95. ISBN 0-87141-010-9

LANDSBERGIS, ALGIRDAS. 1924–

Landsbergis began writing in exile, in Germany. His novel *The Journey* (1954) "not so much reflects as refracts the realities of wartime existence as a slave laborer in Germany, passing them through the prism of a young man's consciousness" (*Encyclopedia Lithuanica*). The protagonist is shattered by the loss of home and by the traumatic realization that the entire edifice of civilized Europe is crumbling before his eyes. *Wind in the Willows* (1958), a mystery play, turns to a legend about Saint Casimir, the patron saint of Lithuania. *Five Posts in a Market Place* is a soul-searching play about hopeless guerrilla resistance that imposes crushing burdens of grim heroism on gentle, creative people. For them, peace and freedom have become dreams beyond possibility.

Play by Landsbergis

Five Posts in a Market Place. Manyland 1968 o.p.

Work by Landsbergis

The Last Picnic. Manyland 1977 $4.00. ISBN 0-87141-051-6

VAIČIULAITIS, ANTANAS. 1906–

Educator, diplomat, and writer, Vaičiulaitis stands among the best Lithuanian prose stylists. He is able to register barely perceptible nuances of feeling and to control complex, brooding mental processes in language that is lucid, elegant, and deceptively simple. A gentle lyrical touch, an eye for miniature patterns in nature and in human experience, are blended with a quiet, refined sense of irony and humor. His main novel, *Valentina* (1936), portrays the unfulfilled love of two fragile souls under a dreamy summer sky filled with dark forebodings. *Noon at a Country Inn* contains a number of Vaičiulaitis's best stories, in which human foibles are depicted with loving wit and human tragedy with restrained candor.

Short Story Collection by Vaičiulaitis

Noon at a Country Inn. Manyland 1965 $3.95. ISBN 0-87141-013-3

MACEDONIAN LITERATURE

Macedonian literature originated approximately at the same time as other South Slav literatures but was strongly impeded in its development. Led by Saints Klement and Naum, the Macedonians established South Slavic culture and produced their first literary works after their ninth-century conversion to Christianity by the Greek brothers Cyril and Methodius. However, the rivalry among the Serbs, Bulgarians, and Greeks over their territory, along with centuries-old Turkish occupation, effectively prevented the Macedonians from developing a literature until late in the nineteenth century. Even then foreign supremacy forbade writers from using their native language; with persistence, they were able to write poetry, fiction, and plays, although they could publish only abroad. The most important literature during these centuries of oppression was transmitted orally.

Following World War II, the Macedonians were allowed a separate republic within Yugoslavia and then could publish in their own language. The adoption of a Prilep dialect as an official literary language enabled writers to write in one language, and in a relatively short time, Macedonians produced works that attracted the world's attention. Even though Macedonian literature bypassed entire periods and movements such as romanticism, realism, and symbolism, writers have kept step with modern literary trends, thanks primarily to the brothers Miladinov, Kosta Racin, Blaže Koneski, Slavko Janevski, and Aco Šopov. Racin published the first book of modern Macedonian poetry, *Beli mugri* (*White Dawns*) (1939), and Janevski the first Macedonian novel, *Selo zad sedumte jaseni* (*The Village Beyond the Seven Aspen Trees*) (1952), while the verses of Koneski and Šopov influenced a number of younger poets. Accomplished writers who followed are poets Bogumil Gjuzel, Vlada Urošević, and Radovan Pavlovski; fiction writers Georgi Abadžiev, Yordan Leov, Simon Drakul, and Živko Čingo; and playwrights Kole Čašule and Goran Stefanovski. The vitality of Macedonian literature is exemplified by the annual summer "Struga Poetry Evenings," when writers from all over the world gather at the Lake of Ohrid to celebrate poetry.

History and Criticism

Drugovac, Miodrag. *Contemporary Macedonian Writers.* Macedonian Review 1976 o.p. Very good essays on all important writers.

Eekman, Thomas. *Thirty Years of Yugoslav Literature, 1945–1975*. Mich. Slavic Pubns. 1978 $15.00. ISBN 0-930042-21-2. Facts about and cursory analyses of all important authors and works.

Mihailovich, Vasa D., ed. *Modern Slavic Literatures. Lib. of Literary Criticism Ser.* Vol. 2 Continuum 1976 o.p. Four Macedonian authors included in the Yugoslav section.

Mihailovich, Vasa D., and Mateja Matejić. *A Comprehensive Bibliography of Yugoslav Literature in English, 1593–1980*. Slavica 1984 $29.95. ISBN 0-89357-136-9. *First Supplement to A..., 1981-1985*. Slavica 1989 $18.95. ISBN 0-89337-188-1. *Second Supplement to A..., 1986–1990*. Slavica 1992 $19.95. An all-inclusive bibliography.

Collections

Holton, Milne, ed. *The Big Horse and Other Stories of Modern Macedonia*. U. of Mo. Pr. 1974 o.p. An excellent anthology; includes all leading storytellers.

Holton, Milne, and Graham W. Reed, eds. *Reading the Ashes: An Anthology of the Poetry of Modern Macedonia. Pitt Poetry Ser.* U. of Pittsburgh Pr. o.p. A competently selected and edited anthology of all important poets.

Mihailovich, Vasa D., ed. *Contemporary Yugoslav Poetry. Iowa Translation Ser.* Bks. Demand repr. of 1977 ed. $72.50. ISBN 0-317-42148-4. The most comprehensive Yugoslav poetry collection in English. Includes Macedonian poets.

Mikasinovich, Branko, Dragan Milivojevič, and Vasa D. Mihailovich, eds. *Introduction to Yugoslav Literature. Twayne's International Studies and Translations Ser.* G. K. Hall 1973 o.p. A good collection of writings from the nineteenth and twentieth centuries, including nine Macedonian writers.

Osers, Ewald, trans. *Contemporary Macedonian Poetry*. Forest Bks. 1991 o.p. A wide-ranging selection from 25 poets, exhibiting symbolism, wise-cracking allegory, passion, and lyrical freshness.

JANEVSKI, SLAVKO. 1923–

Janevski was one of the first to publish a book after a Macedonian republic was officially recognized following World War II. At first an *engagée* poet depicting the partisan war in Macedonia, he evolved into a fine, sensitive lyricist with a distinct poetic voice. He is the author of the first Macedonian novel, *Selo zad sedumte jaseni* (*The Village Beyond the Seven Aspen Trees*) (1952), and of essays, travelogues, and screenplays. He is considered a pioneer of modern Macedonian literature.

Poetry by Janevski

The Bandit Wind. Trans. by Charles Simic. Dryad Pr. 1991 $15.95. ISBN 0-931848-76-8. A representative collection of Janevski's poetry translated by one of the best younger American poets. Bilingual.

KONESKI, BLAŽE. 1921–

A major figure in Macedonian culture, Koneski was instrumental in bringing recognition to its literature following World War II. As a linguist he wrote a grammar, history, and dictionary of Macedonian language, enabling all Macedonian writers to share a literary language. He also published one of the first books of poetry. Published steadily since then, his poetry is characterized by fine lyricism, extolling of nature, meditativeness, a delicate balance between emotion and intellect, and a cultivated form. Koneski has also published a book of short stories.

Poetry by Koneski

Pesni-Poems. Trans. by Andrew C. Harvey and Anne Pennington. Makedonska kniga 1981 o.p. A bilingual collection. Excellent translations.

Poems. Trans. by Andrew C. Harvey and Anne Pennington. Andre Deutsch 1979 o.p. Reissue of the above collection.

Poetry. Trans. by Andrew C. Harvey and Anne Pennington. Macedonian P.E.N. Centre 1983 o.p. An expanded version of the above collection.

STEFANOVSKI, GORAN. 1952–

A member of the younger generation of Macedonian writers, Stefanovski has developed into the country's most significant and prolific playwright. While his plays deal with basic modern problems—coping with uncontrollable forces, degraded moral values, and bureaucracy—Stefanovski is also interested in Macedonian history and the current understanding of it. As a professor of dramatic arts who studied abroad, he has been able to apply dramatic techniques that make his plays lively and very contemporary. They are performed and published outside of eastern Europe.

PLAY BY STEFANOVSKI

Hi-Fi and The False Bottom. Trans. by Patricia Marsh Stefanovska. Bookmark 1986 $6.95. ISBN 0-933532-49-0. Two of the best of Stefanovski's plays, in a version used for American performance.

POLISH LITERATURE

In common with the experience of other eastern European countries, the beginnings of Polish literature in the tenth century are tied to the adoption of Christianity. Predominantly religious works—prayers, hymns, the lives of saints, and so on—were written in Latin, with some in the vernacular as well. Although this religious writing flourished from the tenth to the fifteenth centuries, no outstanding literary figure emerged. The first notable Polish writer was Jan Kochanovski, a poet educated in Italy, who wrote elegies in Latin and highly personal lyric poems in Polish. At this time, as Poland exuded political and military strength and economic prosperity, the Renaissance exerted a strong influence on Polish writers, strengthening their national identity. Since Polish culture has always gravitated toward the West, it is no surprise that literature would follow the next development in Western cultural history, that of the baroque. This period, which lasted until the middle of the eighteenth century, gave rise to lyric poetry replete with formalistic innovations and flowery imagery. It is interesting to note that Polish literature does not have medieval epics or abundant folk literature; instead, it developed historical epics and memoirs, which flourished especially during this period, as exemplified by the memoirs of JAN CHRYZOSTOM PASEK.

By the beginning of the eighteenth century, Poland entered a political and economic decline, reflected to some degree in literature. However, despite the loss of the country's independence, literature kept pace with the western European Enlightenment throughout the eighteenth century. The focus shifted toward new ideas, the pursuit of knowledge, and the use of literature for the dissemination of knowledge, as exemplified by the growth of theater. Yet poetry was not neglected, thanks primarily to the greatest poet of the period, Ignacy Krasicki.

Much of Polish literature has been dictated by historical events. When the uprising against the Russians failed in 1831, many writers emigrated, mostly to France. By that time, romanticism, which had reigned in western Europe since the end of the eighteenth century, was already felt in Poland as well. The best

Polish romantic poets—ADAM MICKIEWICZ, Juliusz Slowacki, and Cyprian Norwid—continued to write in the romantic vein abroad, reinforcing, in turn, the romantic spirit of the writers at home. Others who excelled at this time were the playwright ZYGMUNT KRASIŃSKI and Józef Kraszewski, an author of more than 400 novels, most historical. What united these writers, aside from their allegiance to romanticism, was the idea of messianism, which they found in those nations willing to fight for their independence.

Their influence weakened, however, in the second half of the nineteenth century as, again following the general trend of European literature, Polish writers turned toward realism, called "positivism" and "critical realism." In contrast to the predominance of poetry in the romantic period, the realistic period was dominated by the short story and the novel. Under the influence of AUGUSTE COMTE (see Vols. 3 and 4), Hippolyte Taine, JOHN STUART MILL (see Vols. 1, 3, and 4), and CHARLES DARWIN (see Vols. 1 and 5), writers focused on history and on political and social problems. Of the several significant authors, three should be singled out: Eliza Oreszkowa, HENRYK SIENKIEWICZ, and BOLESLAW PRUS. Didactic and hopeful at first, they later turned toward a gloomier reality of social conflicts in both city and village life. Others embraced the biological determinism of naturalism. It is not surprising that poetry did not fare well in these "un-poetic times," as the critic Julian Krzyzanowski called them.

Toward the end of the century, a new movement called "Młoda Polska" (Young Poland) came into being. Paralleling similar movements in other literatures, Young Poland reflected the *fin de siècle* pessimistic mood and the search for artistic innovations manifested in numerous *isms* of the twentieth century's first two decades. The Polish movement was somewhat less pessimistic in that it rejected the utilitarianism of the positivists and demanded a return to former philosophical values and even to romanticism. The constant struggle for independence undoubtedly had something to do with this optimism. It was a dynamic movement, producing a number of spirited writers, including WŁADYSŁAW REYMONT, the recipient of the Nobel Prize in 1924. Their output varied, but their overall impact on Polish literature is unmistakable. Even though the period of the Young Poland closed with the end of World War I, its influence continued to be felt.

The interwar period is characterized by a variety of groups, movements, and approaches to literature. Although many older writers continued to be active, new generations gave the period their own stamp, which is not easily defined because of the high degree of independence of groups and individuals. Poetry again became a dominant genre. The most important group of poets was gathered around the journal *Skamander* and was led by JULIAN TUWIM, one of the most innovative of modern Polish poets. Another group, led by Jan Przyboś, was represented by the Cracow avant-garde.

After the devastation of World War II, additional difficulties arose from the imposition of a communist system in Poland, which led to a division into émigré writers and those who remained at home. A good number chose exile, among them the poet CZESŁAW MIŁOSZ and the playwright SŁAWOMIR MROŻEK. At home there were many excellent writers who tried to salvage their dignity and freedom of creativity. Of these, two leading contemporary poets, TADEUSZ RÓŻEWICZ and Zbigniew Herbert, clearly represent the ultimate survival of Polish literature. It is interesting to note that, unlike other East European authors, the Polish writers in exile and those at home keep in contact and influence each other. After Poland shed the last vestiges of political dependence on the Soviet Union in the late 1980s, Polish literature became free to follow its own course.

History and Criticism

Carpenter, Bogdana. *The Poetic Avant-Garde in Poland, 1918–1939*. U. of Wash. Pr. 1983 $25.00. ISBN 0-295-95996-7. An excellent study of Polish poetry, from Futurism to the new voices shortly before World War II, with numerous citations of poems both in Polish and English.

Coleman, Marion M. *The Polish Land*. Alliance College 1974 o.p. Interesting travelogue containing numerous references to Polish literature.

Ehrlich, Victor, and others, eds. *For Wiktor Weintraub: Essays in Polish Literature, Language and History Presented on the Occasion of His 65th Birthday*. Mouton 1975 $143.35. ISBN 90-2793-346-4. A distinguished collection of scholarly contributions on diverse topics.

Folejewski, Zbigniew, and others, eds. *Studies in Russian and Polish Literature in Honor of Waclaw Lednicki*. Humanities 1962 o.p. The festschrift for one of the leading American Slavic scholars.

Guergelewicz, Mieczyslaw. *Introduction to Polish Versification*. U. of Pa. Pr. 1970 o.p. A useful introductory study.

Kridl, Manfred. *A Survey of Polish Literature and Culture*. Trans. by Olga Scherer-Virski. Col. U. Pr. 1956 o.p. A discussion of Polish literature up to 1939 by a distinguished literary historian.

Krzyzanowski, Julian. *A History of Polish Literature*. Trans. by Doris Ronowicz. St. Mut. 1978 $83.00. ISBN 0-317-56656-3. A competent history, full of information, but lacking the life of Czesław Miłosz's history.

______. *Polish Romantic Literature*. *Essay Index Repr. Ser.* Ayer repr. of 1931 ed. $18.00. ISBN 0-8369-0602-0. An eminent Polish scholar's fundamental examination of a major literary period.

Lednicki, Waclaw. *Russia, Poland and the West: Essay in Literary and Cultural History*. Assoc. Fac. Pr. repr. of 1954 ed. o.p. Erudite and provocative essays by a distinguished scholar.

Levine, Madeline G. *Contemporary Polish Poetry, 1925-1975*. *Twayne's World Authors Ser.* G. K. Hall 1981 o.p. An acclaimed survey by an American scholar.

Maciuszko, Jerzy J. *Polish Short Story in English: A Guide and Critical Bibliography*. Wayne St. U. Pr. 1968 o.p. Comprehensive bibliography of stories published in books and some periodicals from 1884 to 1967, with useful synopses.

Miłosz, Czesław. *The History of Polish Literature*. U. CA Pr. rev. ed. 1983 $42.50. ISBN 0-520-04465-7. A survey of Polish letters and culture from the beginning to modern times by a distinguished modern scholar, the Nobel Prize winner of 1980.

Collections

Carpenter, Bogdana, ed. *Monumenta Polonica*. Mich. Slavic Pubns. 1990 $27.50. ISBN 0-930042-68-9. Bilingual anthology of the first four centuries of Polish poetry, including the Middle Ages, the Renaissance, the baroque era, and the Enlightenment. Intended for general readers as well as for students.

Gillon, Adam, and Ludwik Krzyzanowski, eds. *Introduction to Modern Polish Literature*. Hippocrene Bks. 1981 $6.95. ISBN 0-88254-516-7. Contains poetry and fiction (excerpts) from the last third of the nineteenth century to the mid-twentieth century.

Holton, Milne, and Paul Vangelisti, eds. *The New Polish Poetry: A Bilingual Collection*. *Pitt Poetry Ser.* U. of Pittsburgh Pr. 1978 o.p. A very good selection of 27 post-1956, non-émigré poets.

Miłosz, Czesław. *Postwar Polish Poetry: An Anthology*. U. CA Pr. rev. ed. 1983 $42.00. ISBN 0-520-04475-4. Contains 125 poems by 25 poets, with the emphasis on poetry written after 1956.

Ordon, Edmund, ed. *Ten Contemporary Polish Stories.* Intro. by Olga Virski-Scherer. Greenwood 1974 repr. of 1958 ed. $45.00. ISBN 0-8371-7436-8. An excellently edited anthology, presenting old and new names in artistic translations.

Peterkiewicz, Jerzy, ed. *Five Centuries of Polish Poetry, 1450–1970.* Greenwood 1979 repr. of 1970 ed. $35.00. ISBN 0-313-22014-X. A good, representative selection.

BIAŁOSZEWSKI, TADEUSZ. 1922–1984

Białoszewski, one of the most innovative writers in post–World War II Polish literature, wrote poetry, plays, and autobiographical prose. He had difficulties accepting the norms of socialist realism and spent most of his early career in destitution as a dissident. His first volume of poems, *The Revolution of Things,* appeared in 1956. Deliberately provocative in its use of grotesque imagery, it had a considerable impact. His next book, *Erroneous Emotions* (1961), was radically antipoetic in its choice and use of words and sounds. He published two more collections of poetry plus plays and several books of prose, one of which, *A Memoir of the Warsaw Uprising* (1970), describes the horrors of the ill-fated battle seen through the eyes of the nonheroic civilians. Though an experimenter, Białoszewski contributed to Polish literature primarily by stressing everyday reality in both the material world and human interrelations.

Poetry by Białoszewski

The Revolution of Things. 1956. Trans. by Bogdan Czaykowski and Andrzej Busza. Charioteer 1974 $7.50. ISBN 0-910350-01-9

Nonfiction by Białoszewski

A Memoir of the Warsaw Uprising. 1970. Trans. and ed. by Madeline G. Levine. Northwestern U. Pr. 1991 repr. of 1977 ed. $10.95. ISBN 0-8101-1026-1

BOROWSKI, TADEUSZ. 1922–1951

Borowski finished his secondary schooling in the underground school system of occupied Warsaw and then began to study at the underground Warsaw University. He published a mimeographed volume of poems in 1942. Subsequently, he was arrested by the gestapo and sent to Auschwitz. Although initially he reacted with skepticism to Marxist ideology, he later became a convert and an ardent champion of socialist realism. A combination of personal and ideological factors apparently led to his suicide in 1951.

Short Story Collection by Borowski

This Way for the Gas, Ladies and Gentlemen. Viking Penguin 1976 $8.95. ISBN 0-14-004114-1

DYGAT, STANISLAW. 1914–

Dygat began to publish before 1939. During the war, he was interned for a time in a German concentration camp near Bodensee, an experience that provided him with material for a subsequent antiheroic novel. Among his other novels, *Journey* and *Disneyland* (translated as *Cloak of Illusion*) have been particularly successful.

Novel by Dygat

Cloak of Illusion. Trans. by David Welsh. MIT Pr. 1970 o.p.

FREDRO, ALEXANDER. 1793–1876

Son of a rich landowner, Fredro participated in the 1812 French campaign against Russia as aide-de-camp to Napoleon. Subsequently, disillusioned with the emperor, he departed from the contemporary romantic tradition by consistently debunking the Napoleonic myth. A prolific comedy writer with a classicist outlook, he spent most of his life quietly on his estate. In his plays, which have become a fixture of Polish theater, he exhibits a keen interest in and sensitivity to human beings. *Maidens' Vows* (1832) and *Vengeance* (1833) are among his most amusing works. In another, *Mr. Jowialski,* Fredro created a memorable figure of a teller of fables and proverbs.

Plays by Fredro

The Major Comedies of Alexander Fredro. Trans. by Harold B. Segel. *Columbia Slavic Studies Ser.* Princeton U. Pr. 1969 $57.50. ISBN 0-691-06151-3. Includes *Husband and Wife, Ladies and Hussars, Maidens' Vows, The Vengeance,* and *The Life Amity.*

GOMBROWICZ, WITOLD. 1904–1969

Gombrowicz, son of a wealthy lawyer, studied law at Warsaw University and philosophy and economics in Paris. His first novel, *Ferdydurke,* with its existential themes and a daring use of surrealistic techniques, became a literary sensation in Warsaw. *Yvonne: Princess of Burgundia* (1935), which anticipated many themes of the Theater of the Absurd, was also enormously successful; together with another of his plays, *The Marriage* (1953), it has been staged throughout the world.

During the war, Gombrowicz lived in Argentina. In the postwar period, *Ferdydurke* was at first banned by the Polish authorities (continuing a ban imposed by the Nazis). During the "thaw," it was published in Warsaw in 1957 and its author was hailed as the "greatest living Polish writer" by the critic Sandauer. The ban on Gombrowicz's work was reimposed in 1958. By this time, however, Gombrowicz had achieved a wide reputation in western Europe and the United States. In the sixties, he settled in France.

Novels by Gombrowicz

Cosmos and Pornografia. Grove Pr. 1986 $9.95. ISBN 0-8021-5159-0. The dark side of eroticism (*Cosmos*) and the moral standards in the Polish countryside during World War II (*Pornografia*).

The Marriage. 1953. Northwestern U. Pr. 1986 $9.95. ISBN 0-8101-0725-2

Possessed: Or the Secret of Myslotch. Trans. by J. A. Underwood. M. Boyars Pubs. 1988 $10.95. ISBN 0-7145-2738-6. Gombrowicz's second novel, appearing under a pseudonym, illustrating his early interest in Gothic fiction.

Three Novels: Ferdydurke, Pornografia, and Cosmos. Trans. by Eric Mosbacher and Alisdair Hamilton. Grove Pr. 1978 o.p.

Yvonne: Princess of Burgundia. 1935. Trans. by K. G. Jones and C. Robbins. Grove Pr. o.p.

Nonfiction by Gombrowicz

Diary. 1957–66. 2 vols. Trans. by Lillian Vallee. Northwestern U. Pr. Vol. 1 1988 $29.95. ISBN 0-8101-0714-7. Vol. 2 1989 $29.95. ISBN 0-8101-0716-3. An unorthodox diary, with boundaries between fantasy and reality blurred and facts often reinterpreted to fit the needs of the moment.

A Kind of Testament. 1973. Trans. by Alisdair Hamilton. M. Boyars Pubs. 1982 $8.95. ISBN 0-7145-0916-7. Comments on his own work, showing him as "an exceptional individual . . . whose work, exemplary in so many ways, will continue to be profoundly *perturbing*" (from the introduction by Maurice Nadeau).

Book about Gombrowicz

Thompson, Ewa M. *Witold Gombrowicz. Twayne's World Authors Ser.* G. K. Hall 1979 o.p.

HERBERT, ZBIGNIEW. 1924–

Born in a part of Poland occupied by the Soviet Union, Herbert was forced to move to Warsaw. He began to publish poetry in the late 1940s and has also written plays, primarily for the radio, and essays. A life-long opponent of totalitarianism, Herbert spend several years in the West. His work is marked by moral indignation and the will to act on it, to stand up to forces threatening human dignity. This stance is embodied in his persona and alter-ego, Mr. Cogito, introduced in a book of poems by the same name (1974).

Poetry by Herbert

Report from the Besieged City. Trans. by John Carpenter and Bogdana Carpenter. Ecco Pr. 1986 $8.50. ISBN 0-88001-094-0. Selection of poems, the first Herbert published in an émigré press.

Selected Poems. Trans. by Czesław Miłosz. Intro. by A. Alvarez. Ecco Pr. 1986 $7.50. ISBN 0-88001-099-1. A representative selection of 80 poems.

Nonfiction by Herbert

Still Life with a Bridle. Ecco Pr. 1991 $19.95. ISBN 0-88001-306-0. Cultural essays, many of them on art.

HERLING, GUSTAW (HERLING-GRUDZIŃSKI). 1919–

Herling became known as a literary critic shortly before 1939. During World War II, he was imprisoned for a time in a labor camp in the north of Russia. After the war, he lived in England and finally settled in Naples. *A World Apart* is an excellent work on Stalinist camps. A collection of his short stories appeared in English under the title *The Island.*

Nonfiction by Herling

A World Apart. Trans. by Joseph Marek. Greenwood 1974 repr. of 1951 ed. o.p.

HLASKO, MAREK. 1934–1969

Hlasko began his literary career as a correspondent among workers. His first stories were published in 1955 in literary periodicals; their publication as a single collection under the title *First Step in the Clouds* met with a very favorable reception. He followed up his success with a novella, *The Eighth Day of the Week* (1956). While Hlasko's popularity grew during the Polish "thaw," he faced increasing difficulties with the authorities and defected to the West in 1958. In emigration, his portrayal of life under communism grew harsher; the publication of *The Graveyard* increased the Polish authorities' hostility toward him. He died in Wiesbaden, Germany.

Novels by Hlasko

All Backs Were Turned. Trans. by Tomasz Mirkowicz. Cane Hill Pr. 1991 $8.95. ISBN 0-943433-07-X. Describes a cruel, chauvinistic society of outcasts in which women are the catalysts for men's violence.

The Eighth Day of the Week. Greenwood 1975 $38.50. ISBN 0-8371-7896-7. Not only a brilliant piece of writing . . . also a sociological document of a desperate, nightmarish era" (*Time and Tide*).

The Graveyard. Trans. by Norbert Guterman. Greenwood 1975 repr. of 1959 ed. o.p.

Killing the Second Dog. Trans. by Tomasz Mirkowicz. Cane Hill Pr. 1990 $8.95. ISBN 0-943433-04-5. Set in Israel in the early sixties, follows two Polish immigrants, a writer-actor and a director, neither successful.

KONWICKI, TADEUSZ. 1926–

Konwicki fought as a young man in the resistance movement against the Nazis, an experience that provided him with material for several novels. He later became preoccupied with psychological and philosophical problems of young people and with lyrical reminiscences of his childhood in Lithuania. His strongly anticommunist novel, *The Polish Complex* (1977), was published without the sanction of the authorities.

Novels by Konwicki

Bohin Manor. Trans. by Richard Lourie. FS&G 1990 $19.95. ISBN 0-374-11523-0. An experimental novel in which various techniques render facts relative.

A Dreambook for Our Time. 1963. Trans. by David Welsh. MIT Pr. 1970 o.p. Introduction by Leszak Kolakowski. "A certain dreamlike quality, a gossamer of things long past yet somehow still clinging to life, pervades Konwicki's facile and poetic narration" (SR).

A Minor Apocalypse. Trans. by Richard Lourie. Random 1984 o.p. Ostensibly set in the distant future; depicts the destruction of moral values in contemporary Poland.

Moonrise, Moonset. Trans. by Richard Lourie. FS&G 1987 $19.95. ISBN 0-374-21241-4. A work somewhere between fiction and autobiography.

The Polish Complex. 1977. Trans. by Richard Lourie. FS&G 1982 o.p. Introduction by Joanna Clark.

Nonfiction by Konwicki

New World Avenue and Victory. Trans. by Walter Arndt. FS&G 1991 $24.95. ISBN 0-374-22182-0. Over 50 anecdotal sketches recalling Konwicki's childhood in Polish Lithuania, parents, relatives, and friends.

KRASIŃSKI, ZYGMUNT. 1812–1859

Until World War I, Krasiński was considered, together with Adam Mickiewicz and Slowacki, a national "poet-seer." At present his reputation has been significantly diminished, but he is rightly viewed as a major figure of the romantic period. His best work, the poetic drama *The Undivine Comedy* (1835), deals with the problem of a poet's moral responsibility in a social framework (an important romantic dilemma) and with the problems of revolution. *Iridion* (1836), another poetic drama, is set in third-century Rome.

Poetry by Krasiński

Iridion. Trans. by Florence Noyes. Greenwood 1975 repr. of 1927 ed. o.p.

The Undivine Comedy. Trans. by Harriette E. Kennedy and Zofia Uminska. Greenwood 1976 repr. of 1924 ed. $39.75. ISBN 0-8371-7513-5

Book about Krasiński

Lednicki, Waclaw, ed. *Zygmunt Krasiński, Romantic Universalist: An International Tribute*. Polish Inst. Arts & Sci. 1964 $6.00. ISBN 0-940962-47-0

LEM, STANISLAW. 1921–

Lem is not only Poland's best science fiction writer, but he has also acquired a solid world reputation. A medical graduate of Cracow University, he is at home both in the sciences and in philosophy, and this broad erudition gives his writings genuine depth. He has published extensively, not only fiction, but also theoretical studies. A trend toward increasingly serious philosophical speculation is found in his later works, such as *Solaris* (1961), which was made into an excellent Soviet film.

Novels by Lem

The Cyberiad: Fables for the Cybernetic Age. 1965. HarBraceJ 1985 $7.95. ISBN 0-15-623550-1. A tale about two robots who tinker with writing poetry and arranging the universe, told in a comic style veiling the author's concern about irresponsible science.

Eden. Trans. by E. Heine. HarBraceJ 1989 $19.95. ISBN 0-15-127580-7. A "space parable . . . belong[ing] in a comprehensive science-fiction collection" (*LJ*).

Fiasco. HarBraceJ 1987 $17.95. ISBN 0-15-130640-0. Encounter with an alien world, with resulting misunderstandings and struggles.

His Master's Voice. HarBraceJ 1984 $6.95. ISBN 0-15-640300-5. A typical Lem yarn about his concern for civilization's future in the face of unrestrained technology.

Imaginary Magnitude. Trans. by Marc Heine. HarBraceJ 1985 repr. of 1974 ed. $7.95. ISBN 0-15-644180-2. "The introduction to a five-volume history of 'Bitic' literature (works of non-human authors) gives Lem a chance to examine where the current computer craze can lead" (*LJ*).

Memoirs Found in a Bathtub. 1961. Trans. by Michael Kandel and Christine Rose. HarBraceJ 1986 $7.95. ISBN 0-15-658585-5. A grotesque tale about the gulf between the good intentions and potential disaster of modern science.

A Perfect Vacuum. 1979. Trans. by Michael Kandel. HarBraceJ 1983 $6.95. ISBN 0-15-671686-0. Borders on metafiction.

Return from the Stars. 1961. HarBraceJ 1989 $7.95. ISBN 0-15-676593-4. An oft-repeated concern about the moral responsibility of scientists in their exploration of the unknown.

Solaris. 1961. HarBraceJ 1987 $7.95. ISBN 0-15-683750-1. About the human conquest of a planet covered by an ocean, on which people's subconscious thoughts and feelings become real living creatures.

Short Story Collections by Lem

The Futurological Congress. 1971. Trans. by Michael Kandel. HarBraceJ 1985 repr. of 1975 ed. $7.95. ISBN 0-15-634040-2. Short stories about a character resembling both Munchausen and Gulliver during the exploration of distant galaxies.

More Tales of Pirx the Pilot. Trans. by Louis Iribarne and others. HarBraceJ 1983 repr. of 1982 ed. $6.95. ISBN 0-15-662143-6

The Star Diaries. 1957. Trans. by Michael Kandel. HarBraceJ 1985 $8.95. ISBN 0-15-684905-4. Tales both serious and comic about an explorer of galaxies, reflecting basic problems of human existence. Related to *The Futurological Congress.*

Nonfiction by Lem

The Chain of Chance. 1968. HarBraceJ 1984 $7.95. ISBN 0-15-616500-7. A philosophical essay about the relationship between fantasy and reality.

MICKIEWICZ, ADAM BERNARD. 1798–1855

Mickiewicz was born in Lithuania to the family of a landless lawyer. He received a solid classical education at Wilno University, then the best in Poland. Arrested in 1823 for suspected revolutionary activities, he was exiled to Russia in 1825. His four and a half years there were a period of poetical and social success: He became a friend of Aleksandr Pushkin and a welcome figure in aristocratic salons. In 1829, Mickiewicz left Russia. During the 1831 uprising, he appeared briefly in Prussian Poland and subsequently joined the Great Emigration in Paris, where he was viewed as the spiritual leader of the exiles. During the early 1840s, Mickiewicz became a follower of the Lithuanian mystic

Towiański, a move that finished him as a poet and made him unpopular with most of his fellow exiles. After the outbreak of the Crimean War, his anti-Russian activities brought the poet to Turkey, where he died in late 1855. His remains were transferred to a crypt in Wawel Castle in Cracow in 1890.

Although his education in classical literature left a perceptible trace on his poetic diction, Mickiewicz was both the initiator of the romantic movement and one of its great figures. His literary position was established in 1822 with the publication of a short but striking anthology of poems. His subsequent ballads and historical poems were even finer; however, he reached special heights in his dramatic cycle *Forefathers' Eve* (1823). Mickiewicz's Russian period is distinguished by the creation of sonnets (especially the *Crimean Sonnets* cycle) and of the poem *Konrad Wallenrod* (1826–27).

A period of relative poetic sterility that began after *Konrad Wallenrod* ended in 1832, when Mickiewicz published his *Books of the Polish Nation*, a work in biblical prose that aspired to be the gospel of émigrés and is the clearest example of Polish national messianism. In 1832 Mickiewicz also wrote *Forefathers' Eve, Part III*, which he loosely connected with the earlier dramatic cycle, and in which he considered Poland's relationship with Russia through the prism of an intense personal vision.

Mickiewicz's last masterpiece is *Pan Tadeusz* (1834), which continues the traditions of the epic and to a degree represents a turning away on the poet's part from romanticism. The poem deals with life in Lithuania from 1811 to 1812. A large number of characters, all of whom are basically good, and a wealth of lovingly described details of nature and the country society combine to make *Pan Tadeusz* an extraordinary, if idealized, canvas of everyday life.

POETRY BY MICKIEWICZ

Konrad Wallenrod, and Grazyna. Trans. by Irene Suboczewski. U. Pr. of Amer. 1989 $34.50. ISBN 0-8191-7556-0

Konrad Wallenrod, and Other Writings. Trans. by George R. Noyes. Greenwood 1975 repr. of 1925 ed. o.p.

Pan Tadeusz. 1834. Ed. by Watson Kirkconnell. Polish Inst. Arts & Sci. 1981 o.p.

Poems by Adam Mickiewicz. Ed. by George R. Noyes. Polish Inst. Arts & Sci. 1944 o.p.

BOOKS ABOUT MICKIEWICZ

Gardner, Monica M. *Adam Mickiewicz: The National Poet of Poland. Eastern European Collection Ser.* Ayer 1970–71 repr. of 1911 ed. $19.00. ISBN 0-405-02749-4

Kridl, Manfred, ed. *Adam Mickiewicz, Poet of Poland: A Symposium.* Greenwood 1970 repr. of 1951 ed. $38.50. ISBN 0-8371-2783-1

Weintraub, Wiktor. *Literature as Prophecy: Scholarship and Martinist Poetics in Mickiewicz's Parisian Lectures.* Humanities 1959 o.p.

______. *The Poetry of Adam Mickiewicz.* Humanities 1954 o.p. An excellent, readable survey by an eminent scholar.

MIŁOSZ, CZESŁAW. 1911– (NOBEL PRIZE 1980)

Born in Lithuania, Miłosz published his first volume of poetry in 1933. His next, *Three Winters* (1936), expressed very strongly the "catastrophic" themes current among a number of poets. During World War II he continued his literary activities underground. In 1951 he emigrated from Poland. Miłosz is the author of several prose works, one of which, the well-known study *The Captive Mind* (1953), analyzes East European intellectuals' relationship to Stalinism. He presently teaches at the University of California at Berkeley. In 1978 he received the Neustadt International Prize for Literature, and in 1980 the Nobel Prize.

Poetry by Miłosz

Bells in Winter. Trans. by Lillian Vallee. Ecco Pr. 1978 $15.95. ISBN 0-912946-53-3

The Collected Poems. Ecco Pr. 1990 $14.95. ISBN 0-88001-174-2

Selected Poems. Ecco Pr. rev. ed. 1981 repr. of 1973 ed. o.p. Contains some of Miłosz's best poetry up to 1972.

The Separate Notebooks. Trans. by Robert Haas and others. Ecco Pr. 1986 $12.50. ISBN 0-88001-116-5. A bilingual collection of poems, including the title cycle and poems from the war years.

The World. Arion Pr. 1989 $250.00. ISBN 0-685-30566-X. Illustrated.

Nonfiction by Miłosz

The Captive Mind. Peter Smith 1992 $19.50. ISBN 0-8446-6615-7

Emperor of the Earth: Modes of Eccentric Vision. U. CA Pr. 1977 $35.00. ISBN 0-520-04503-3. Literary essays.

Native Realm: A Search for Self-Definition. 1959. trans. by Catherine S. Leach. U. CA Pr. 1981 $12.95. ISBN 0-520-04474-6. A simultaneous self-definition and examination of his European roots.

Nobel Lecture. FS&G 1981 $5.95. ISBN 0-374-51654-5. Lecture delivered in Stockholm. Bilingual.

Unattainable Earth. Ecco Pr. 1986 $17.95. ISBN 0-88001-098-3. A "fascinating bio-chronology, giving an overview of Miłosz and his world, . . . useful for both literary and social historians. . . . Excellent translations" (*Choice*).

Visions from San Francisco Bay. 1969. Trans. by Richard Lourie. FS&G 1982 $9.95. ISBN 0-374-51763-0. Essays written, in the words of the poet, "to exorcise the evil spirit of contemporary times."

The Witness of Poetry. HUP 1983 $10.95. ISBN 0-674-95382-7. "Provides us with a key to Miłosz's poetic historiosophy, philosophy, and aesthetics" (*The New Criterion*).

Novels by Miłosz

The Issa Valley. 1955. Trans. by Louis Iribarne. FS&G 1982 $12.95. ISBN 0-374-51695-2. Fictional remembrances of the poet's childhood in Lithuania.

The Land of Ulro. 1977. Trans. by Louis Iribarne. FS&G 1985 $9.95. ISBN 0-374-18323-6

The Seizure of Power. Trans. by Celina Wieniewska. FS&G 1982 o.p. A thematic focus on the struggle against political oppression. Winner of the Prix Littéraire Européen.

Book about Miłosz

Nathan, Leonard, and Arthur Quinn. *The Poet's Work: An Introduction to Czesław Miłosz.* HUP 1991 $29.95. ISBN 0-674-68969-0. A study that "will most likely help the average reader understand Miłosz better than more scholarly treatises" (*World Literature Today*).

MROŻEK, SŁAWOMIR. 1930–

Mrożek's plays are well known in eastern Europe, and *Tango* (1964) has been performed throughout the world. It is the story of an intellectual who wants to reform his family but falls prey to his own brother, who establishes a dictatorship. *The Elephant* (1957) is a collection of savage and satiric short stories: "They are all fantastic, yet they reflect, bitterly and wittily, the realities of life behind the Iron Curtain"; Mrożek "has employed the techniques of [George] Orwell (see Vol. 1) and [Franz] Kafka to present contemporary man as terrified and ludicrous. Mrożek's brief fables are grotesque, scathing comments on the new bureaucrats of the People's Democracies" (*Times*, London). Mrożek's work is still performed in Poland, where *Tango* had its sensational first showing in 1966. Mrożek now works and lives, however, in Genoa, Italy.

Plays by Mrożek

Six Plays. Trans. by Nicholas Bethell. Boulevard 1967 o.p. Contains *The Police, The Martyrdom of Peter Ohey, Out at Sea, Charlie, The Party, Enchanted Night.*

Striptease, Tango, Vatzlav: Three Plays. Trans. by Lola Gruenthal and others. Grove Pr. 1986 o.p.

Tango. Trans. by Ralph Manheim and Teresa Dzieduszycka. Grove Pr. 1969 o.p.

Vatzlav. Trans. by Ralph Manheim. Applause Theater Bk. Pubs. 1986 $5.95. ISBN 0-936839-50-3

Short Story Collection by Mrożek

The Elephant. Ed. by Konrad Syrop. Grove Pr. 1985 $6.95. ISBN 0-394-62054-4

PARANDOWSKI, JAN. 1895–1978

Parandowski, whose literary career began in Lwów and continued in Warsaw, was president of the Polish P.E.N. Club. A classicist by education, he concentrated on ancient Greece and Rome in his fiction and essays. His first published novel, *King of Life* (1921), was about Oscar Wilde (see Vol. 1). His series on classical subjects, among which *The Olympic Discus* (1933) is particularly outstanding, is distinguished by an exquisite style that continues Roman, French, and Polish Renaissance tradition in prose. After World War II, Parandowski achieved great success with a prose translation of the *Odyssey.*

Nonfiction by Parandowski

The Olympic Discus. 1933. Trans. by A. M. Malecka and S. A. Walewski. Continuum o.p. Introduction by George Harjan.

Book about Parandowski

Harjan, George. *Jan Parandowski. Twayne's World Authors Ser.* Twayne o.p.

PASEK, JAN CHRYZOSTOM. 1630–1701

Pasek was an adventurer, soldier, and politician. His many activities, typical of a man of his troubled times, provided him with a wealth of material for his memoirs. Pasek's love and mastery of detail, displayed in a rich, witty, and racy colloquial language, have not only given his writings lasting artistic value, but have also made them a source of ideas and idiom for subsequent poets and writers (Słowacki, Sienkiewicz, and others).

Nonfiction by Pasek

Memoirs of Jan C. Pasek. Trans. by Maria Swiecicka. Kosciuszko 1978 $3.00. ISBN 0-917004-15-9. The first part of Pasek's memoirs, describing, among other things, his war experiences in 1656–66. Rises above mere documentation.

Memoirs of the Polish Baroque: The Writings of Jan Chryzostom Pasek, a Squire of the Commonwealth of Poland and Lithuania. Ed. by Catherine S. Leach. U. CA Pr. 1977 $49.95. ISBN 0-520-02752-3. The second part of the memoirs. Deals with his life as a citizen and farmer in 1667–88.

PRUS, BOLESŁAW (pseud. of Aleksander Głowacki). 1845–1912

Prus was by profession an extremely productive and highly influential journalist, who won fame with his *Weekly Chronicles,* short pieces on diverse subjects. His work in fiction began with short stories, usually about the Warsaw poor. His first novel, *The Outpost* (1886), deals with village life, focusing in particular on the mechanism of German settlement in Polish lands. In *The Doll* (1890), Prus creates an enormous rich canvas of Warsaw life, into which he weaves the story of his hero, Wokulski, and his doomed passion for the aristocratic Isabella. His third major novel, *The Pharaoh* (1895–96), is set in eleventh-century B.C. Egypt and deals with the unsuccessful struggle of a young pharaoh against the dominant priestly class.

Novel by Prus

The Doll. Trans. by David Welsh. Polish Inst. Arts & Sci. 1972 $4.50. ISBN 0-686-30918-9

REYMONT, WŁADYSŁAW STANISŁAW. 1867–1925 (Nobel Prize 1924)

Born into a lower middle-class Catholic family, the novelist Reymont had little formal education, but his eventful life as a theater hand and railroad worker provided him with plentiful material for his writing. Although a straightforward realist, he wrote with a lyrical perfection of style. This, combined with sharp psychological insight, placed him in the forefront of Polish fiction until his death. Reymont wrote short stories as well, but he is best known for his novels about Polish life in both rural and urban societies. His magnum opus, *The Peasants* (1902–09), leading to the Nobel Prize in 1924, is a broad panorama of a village caught in internal conflicts of the magnitude of those in classical Greek tragedy. It is characterized, in the words of Per Hallstrom, "by an art so grand, so sure, so powerful, that we may predict a lasting value and rank for it, not only within Polish literature but also within the whole of that branch of imaginative writing which has here been given a distinctive and monumental shape."

Novels by Reymont

The Commedienne. 1896. 1920 o.p. Reymont's first novel, the story of a young woman's pursuit of fame in a theatrical touring company, is drawn from his own experience as a stagehand.

The Peasants. 1902–1909. 1924–1925 o.p. The story of a father and son in love with the same woman.

The Promised Land. 1899. 1927 o.p. A novel about the rise of the Polish textile industry, depicting corruption, greed, mistreatment of workers, and inequality between factory owners and workers.

RÓŻEWICZ, TADEUSZ. 1921–

A soldier in the underground Home Army during the Nazi occupation, Różewicz began to publish immediately after 1945. His first volumes of poetry, *Anxiety* (1947) and *The Red Glove* (1948), made wide use of war material and deliberately sought to destroy literary conventions. In focusing on human beings as essentially alone in the universe, the poet approached the conception of the French existentialists. After 1956 Różewicz turned his attention to the stage, writing plays that basically belong to the Theater of the Absurd. He has also published several collections of short stories and a novel.

Poetry by Różewicz

Conversations with a Prince and Other Poems. Trans. by Adam Czerniawski. Small Pr. Dist. 1982 o.p. Selected poems in which Różewicz expands his moral concerns to encompass all contemporary civilization.

The Survivor and Other Poems. Trans. by Magnus J. Krinski. Bks. Demand repr. of 1976 ed. $46.80. ISBN 0-8357-4202-4. Some of the most representative poems.

Unease. Trans. by Victor Contoski. New Rivers Pr. 1980 $5.00. ISBN 0-89823-013-6. Poems focusing on the horror of war and told in a distinctly new, antipoetic voice that brought the poet instant recognition.

Plays by Różewicz

Marriage Blanc (and *The Hunger Artist Departs*). Trans. by Adam Czerniawski. M. Boyars Pubs. 1983 $13.50. ISBN 0-7145-2776-9

Book About Różewicz

Filipowicz, Halina. *A Laboratory of Impure Forms: The Plays of Tadeusz Różewicz.* Greenwood 1991 $45.00. ISBN 0-313-26805-3. "The first comprehensive examination of the dramatic works of Różewicz and as such will do a great deal to help spread the word about his unique dramaturgy" (*World Literature Today*).

SIENKIEWICZ, HENRYK. 1846–1916 (Nobel Prize 1905)

Far more celebrated than any of his positivist contemporaries, Sienkiewicz began as a journalist and achieved considerable renown with his account of a two-year journey to the United States. Between 1882 and 1888 he wrote three historical novels dealing with political and military events in seventeenth-century Poland: *With Fire and Sword, The Deluge* (1886), and *Fire in the Steppe* (1888, also translated as *Pan Michael*). Although superficial in its analysis of historical events, the trilogy gained enormous popularity both in Poland and in other Slavic countries thanks to Sienkiewicz's masterful use of epic techniques and of the seventeenth-century colloquial idiom. Even more popular, if artistically far weaker, was his *Quo Vadis?* (1896), a novel about Rome in the age of Nero (Sienkiewicz's fame in the West is chiefly based on this work). Another historical novel, *The Teutonic Knights* (1900), deals with the fifteenth-century struggle between Poland-Lithuania and the Teutonic Order. Among his other works is *The Połaniecki Family* (1895), a work that extolled the virtues of philistinism and was sharply attacked by the progressive intelligentsia.

Novels by Sienkiewicz

The Deluge: An Historical Novel of Poland, Sweden, and Russia. 1886. Trans. by W. S. Kuniczak. Hippocrene Bks. 1991 $45.00. ISBN 0-87052-004-0. The second volume of a trilogy, dealing with the Swedish invasion of Poland in 1655–57.

Fire in the Steppe. 1888. Trans. by W. S. Kuniczak. Hippocrene Bks. 1992 $24.95. ISBN 0-87052-005-9. The final volume of a trilogy, dealing with the Turkish invasion of Poland in 1672. Retranslation of *Pan Michael* (the Polish title is *Pan Wolodyjowski*).

Hania. Ayer repr. of 1876 ed. $26.00. ISBN 0-8369-4241-8

Pan Michael: An Historical Novel of Poland, the Ukraine, and Turkey. 1887–88. Trans. by Jeremiah Curtin. Greenwood 1969 repr. of 1898 ed. $69.50. ISBN 0-8371-0227-8. (See *Fire in the Steppe.*)

Quo Vadis? A Narrative of the Time of Nero. 1896. Amereon Ltd. 1980. $28.95. ISBN 0-89190-484-0

With Fire and Sword. Trans. by W. S. Kuniczak. Hippocrene Bks. 1991 $24.95. ISBN 0-87052-974-9. The first part of a trilogy, dealing with the Polish-Cosack war in 1647–51. "To match the original, . . . a monumental masterpiece in modern translation" (*World Literature Today*).

Short Story Collections by Sienkiewicz

Charcoal Sketches, and Other Tales. Trans. by Adam Zamoyski. Dufour 1990 $33.00. ISBN 0-946162-31-X. Stories about political and social evils.

Western Septet: Seven Stories of the American West. Alliance Coll. 1973 o.p. Based on Sienkiewicz's experiences in America.

Books about Sienkiewicz

Coleman, Arthur P., and Marion M. Coleman. *Wanderers Twain: Exploratory Memoir on Helen Modjeska and Henryk Sienkiewicz.* Alliance College 1964 o.p.

Giergielewicz, Mieczyslaw. *Henryk Sienkiewicz. Twayne's World Authors Ser.* Twayne 1968 o.p.

Lednicki, Waclaw. *Henryk Sienkiewicz.* Humanities 1960 o.p. A very good survey.

TUWIM, JULIAN. 1894–1953

A Jew by birth, Tuwim was the major figure of the "Skamander" school and a leading poet of interwar Poland. A marvelous innovator of poetic language, he published not only numerous collections of poetry, but also several encyclopedic works on folklore. His best poem is *Ball at the Opera* (1936), in which he presents an apocalyptic vision of a dictatorship. His most ambitious work, *Polish Flowers,* was written mainly during World War II, in exile in Brazil and the United States.

Poetry by Tuwim

The Dancing Socrates and Other Poems. Twayne 1971 o.p.

WITKIEWICZ, STANISŁAW IGNACY (WITKACY). 1885–1939

Son of an eminent Warsaw art critic, Witkiewicz went through traumatic experiences in Russia during World War I (he served in the Russian army) and the beginning of the Revolution. A prolific writer, he also painted and wrote papers on philosophy. His creative writings consist mainly of novels and dramas (at least 36, of which only 22 have survived). In his plays, Witkiewicz deals with profound social and philosophical problems in a way that makes him a forerunner of the Theater of the Absurd.

Plays by Witkiewicz

Madman and the Nun and the Crazy Locomotive: Three Plays. Applause Theatre Bk. 1988 $8.95. ISBN 0-936839-83-X. Contains the two title plays plus *The Water Hen.*

The Madman and the Nun, and Other Plays. Ed. by C. Durer and Daniel G. Gerould. U. of Wash. Pr. 1968 o.p. Contains the title play, *The Crazy Locomotive, They, The Water Hen, The Shoemakers,* and *The Mother.*

Tropical Madness: Four Plays. Drama Bk. 1973 o.p. Contains *The Pragmatists, Mr. Price or Tropical Madness, Gymbal Wahazar or Along the Cliffs of the Absurd,* and *Metaphysics of a Two-Headed Calf.*

Novel by Witkiewicz

Insatiability: A Novel in Two Parts. Bks. Demand repr. of 1977 ed. $94.10. ISBN 0-8357-9683-3. A dystopian novel presaging the downfall of Western civilization and the coming of totalitarian systems.

Work by Witkiewicz

A Witkacy Reader: The Life and Work of Stanislaw Ignacy Witkiewicz. Trans. by Daniel Gerould. Northwestern U. Pr. 1992 $39.95. ISBN 0-8101-0980-8. The most important works of Witkacy in a handy edition.

RUMANIAN LITERATURE

Although the first written documents in Rumania date back to 1527 and the Bible was translated in 1688, Rumanian literature began to develop only in the nineteenth century, when the Rumanians slowly gained independence from multiple foreign domination. There were numerous writers preceding this period, but few of great importance. The romantic movement, coming mainly from France, enlivened the literary scene, awakening an interest in folk poetry and allowing more accomplished writers to appear. Folk literature, which had been handed down orally for centuries, could now be recorded in a written language that more or less corresponded to the oral form. The first collection of folk poetry was published in 1852 by Vasile Alecsandri, the first Rumanian writer who was exposed to foreign influence, during his study in Paris, and whose works, in turn, were translated into French. His poems and plays, but above all his collections of folk poetry, together with the prose works of Heliade Rădulescu, mark the beginning of modern Rumanian literature.

Rumanian literature came of age in the second half of the nineteenth century with the appearance of some of its great writers in almost all genres. Romanticism gave way to realism, bringing literature more in tune with national and social realities. The best poet of that time, indeed of all Rumanian literature, Mihail Eminescu, published a collection of lyric poems in 1884 about love and death. Meditative and highly pessimistic in mood, they were also sincerely patriotic, with a simplicity derived from folk songs and ballads. With his poetic power and consummate craftsmanship he strongly influenced the further development of Rumanian poetry. One of the best short-story tellers, Ion Creangă, wrote about the bucolic life in his native Moldavia, idealizing the patriotic world of the past.

By the end of the nineteenth century, the French influence, which has always been strong in Rumanian literature, manifested itself in the impact on symbolist poets, especially Alexandru Macedonski, a versatile author who foreshadowed the modernistic tendencies of the twentieth century. Along with these trends there was a sharp turn toward social criticism, best personified by the prolific writer Mihail Sadoveanu, whose keen interest in social problems moved him to the extreme Left and endeared him to the new regime after World War II. Western influences continued to be reflected after World War I in the works of such prominent writers as Ian Barbu, Lucian Blaga, George Bacovia, and perhaps the best poet of the group, Tudor Arghezi, who combined his foreign experiences (in France and Switzerland) with his rich and experimental idiom.

The interwar period also gave rise to a number of new writers unencumbered with the legacies of the prewar past. Perhaps the most prominent among these is the writer and philosopher Mircea Eliade, who lived abroad but published in his own country. Other writers of this group are Zaharia Stancu, a prolific novelist who joined, and achieved a prominent position in, the Communist party, and Liviu Rebreanu, whose novels harrowingly portrayed war and revolution.

Rumanian literature after World War II suffered the same fate as all other East European literatures that have to contend with the dictates of a communist regime. As a result, most writers were unable to rise above mediocrity. However, there are a few writers—the poets Nichita Stanescu, Ion Alexandru, and Marin Sorescu, and the fiction writers Eugen Barnu, Marin Preda, Stefan Banulescu, Petru Dumitriu, and Fanus Neagu—whose talent and originality cannot be denied or contained. There is still a younger generation of promising writers, who hold the future of Rumanian literature in their hands. Their full development, however, is yet to come. After the fall of Ceauçescu's dictatorial regime in 1990, the future looks even more favorable for this new generation.

Collections

Byng, Lucy M., trans. *Roumanian Stories. Short Story Index Repr. Ser.* Ayer repr. of 1921 ed. $18.00. ISBN 0-8369-4004-0. Contains 15 stories of prominent authors, including M. Sadoveany and M. Beza.

Manning, Olivia, ed. *Romanian Short Stories. World's Class. Ser.* OUP 1971 o.p.

ARGHEZI, TUDOR. 1880–1967

Arghezi is widely considered Rumania's most important poet after MIHAIL EMINESCU. Influenced by French *Symbolisme*, Arghezi developed as a modernist but at the same time as a poet of tradition and ancestral continuity, reconciling in his work the most contradictory spiritual and aesthetic tendencies of his age. It was only after World War II that a series of more or less successful translations won him belated recognition in the West. He has also been translated into Italian by Nobel Prize winner SALVATORE QUASIMODO and into Spanish by RAFAEL ALBERTI and PABLO NERUDA.

POETRY BY ARGHEZI

Selected Poems of Tudor Arghezi. Trans. by Brian Swann. Princeton U. Pr. 1976 o.p. A representative selection of the poetry.

DUMITRIU, PETRU. 1924–

This author is the Rumanian novelist probably best known to Americans. Dumitriu's successful early literary career included writing for magazines in Bucharest, winning the Rumanian State Prize for Literature three times, and serving as director of the State Publishing House. In 1960, however, he left Rumania to live in the West, escaping through East Berlin. *Meeting at the Last Judgment* (1962), based on his own experiences, presents a revealing picture of the fear-ridden lives of the Rumanian communist elite. *Incognito* (1962) "reemphasizes the author's earlier theme: the awesome power with which the communists are able to take over a country once the will of its people has been demoralized" (*LJ*). Its sequel, *The Extreme Occident* (1964) shows "the whole of present-day Western Europe as one vast cesspool of aimlessness, desperation, and lost or corrupted values" (*SR*). Dumitriu's books are alive with melodramatic cloak-and-dagger activities, as well as the ideological overtones noted above. He now lives in West Germany.

NOVEL BY DUMITRIU

Incognito. 1962. Trans. by Norman Denny. Melvin McCosh 1964 o.p.

ELIADE, MIRCEA. 1907–1986

Born in Bucharest, Rumania, Mircea Eliade studied at the University of Bucharest and, from 1928 to 1932, at the University of Calcutta with Surendranath Dasgupta. After taking his doctorate in 1933 with a dissertation on yoga, he taught at the University of Bucharest and, after the war, at the Sorbonne in Paris. From 1957, Eliade was a professor of the history of religions at the University of Chicago. He was at the same time a writer of fiction, known and appreciated especially in western Europe, where several of his novels and volumes of short stories appeared in French, German, Spanish, and Portuguese. *Two Tales of the Occult* tries "to relate some yogic techniques, and particularly yogic folklore, to a series of events narrated in the genre of a mystery story." Both *Nights of Serampore* and *The Secret of Dr. Honigberger* evoke the mythical geography and time of India. Mythology, fantasy, and autobiography are skillfully combined in Eliade's tales.

Novels by Eliade

The Old Man and the Bureaucrats. Trans. by Mary P. Stevenson. U. Ch. Pr. $7.95. ISBN 0-226-20410-3. The story of a retired teacher who attempts to trace the subsequent career of one of his pupils in communist Rumania.

Youth Without Youth, and Other Novellas. Trans. by Mac L. Ricketts. Ohio St. U. Pr. 1988 $25.75. ISBN 0-8142-0457-0. Preoccupation with the supernatural permeates these three novellas.

Short Story Collection by Eliade

Tales of the Sacred and the Supernatural. Westminster 1981 $9.95. ISBN 0-664-24391-6

Nonfiction by Eliade

Autobiography Vol. 1: Journey East, Journey West, 1907 to 1937. Trans. by Mac L. Ricketts. U. Ch. Pr. 1990 $15.95. ISBN 0-226-20407-3. Eliade's search for identity and solutions to some basic questions.

EMINESCU, MIHAIL. 1850–1889

Rumanians regard Eminescu as their greatest poet. The richness and suggestive verbal power of his poetry have prompted some to compare him with John Keats (see Vol. 1). His influence was so profound that Rumanian poetry and poetic diction have developed along lines that would have been impossible to predict on the basis of their traditions and achievements up to the mid-nineteenth century. "His use of archaisms, dialectal words, and neologisms, together with skillful metaphor, simile and alliteration, enhanced the expressive power of Rumanian and endowed it with a great richness, while the philosophical nature and profundity of his work gave Rumanian poetry a maturity it hitherto lacked" (*Cassell's Encyclopaedia of World Literature*). The complexity of Eminescu's stylistic imagination makes his poetry extremely hard to translate.

Poetry by Eminescu

The Last Romantic: Mihail Eminescu. Trans. by Roy MacGregor-Hastie. U. of Iowa Pr. 1972 o.p. Part of the European Series of the Translations Collection of UNESCO.

Poems. Gordon Pr. $250.00. ISBN 0-87968-466-6

REBREANU, LIVIU. 1885–1944

The eminent novelist, theater critic, playwright, and essayist Liviu Rebreanu was at the height of his influence in the years between the two world wars. An innovator in Rumanian literature, he is remembered particularly for his portrayals of Rumanian villagers living under hardship, and for his treatment of war and revolution. He wrote many short stories before turning to longer fiction. Of the novels, *Ion* (1920), a vast panorama of Transylvanian village life before World War I, is a "landmark in the history of the Rumanian novel" (*Cassell's Encyclopaedia of World Literature*). *The Forest of the Hanged,* about that war, and *Uprising* (1932), about a peasants' revolt, are his two other important novels.

Novels by Rebreanu

Ion. 1920. Dufour 1965 $30.00. ISBN 0-7206-4650-2

Uprising. 1932. Dufour 1964 $30.00. ISBN 0-7206-9382-9

SADOVEANU, MIHAIL. 1880–1961

Sadoveanu, who wrote more than 120 books, is generally considered to be Rumania's greatest prose writer. His fiction is being published for the first time in this country under a U.S.-Rumanian cultural exchange program. *Tales of War* (1905) was inspired by the people's heroism in the 1877 War of Independence against Turkey. In *Evening Tales* he also writes of the common folk, from innkeepers to gypsies. In *The Mud-Hut Dwellers* (1912), "vivid descriptions of peasant life in nineteenth-century Rumania charm and captivate the reader.... The novel is an affirmation of man, of the joy and love which can be his in spite of his condition" (*Choice*).

NOVELS BY SADOVEANU

Evening Tales. Trans. by E. Farca and L. Marinescu. Irvington 1962 $26.00. ISBN 0-8057-5172-6

The Mud-Hut Dwellers. 1912. Irvington 1964 $22.00. ISBN 0-8057-5195-5

Tales of War. 1905. Irvington 1962 $27.00. ISBN 0-8057-5208-0

STANCU, ZAHARIA. 1902–1974

Stancu began his literary career as a poet. During the 1930s he was active as a journalist and edited such periodicals as *Azi* (Today) and *Lumea romaneasca* (Rumanian World). After World War II he published a cycle of novels that won him official recognition. He was president of the Rumanian Writers' Union from 1965 until his death.

NOVELS BY STANCU

Barefoot. Ed. by Frank Kirk. Irvington 1971 o.p. About a picaresque character in rural Rumania of the past, often speaking for the author himself.

The Gypsy Tribe. Abelard-Schuman 1973 o.p. About a Gypsy in Rumania.

SERBIAN LITERATURE

Serbian literature began shortly after the Serbs' conversion to Christianity in the ninth century. The new alphabet, adapted to a Slavic dialect by the Greek brothers Cyril and Methodius, brought forth church songs, hagiographies, encomiums, and translations of medieval novels. The first original work, the illuminated *Miroslav's Gospel,* dates from the twelfth century. Until the fifteenth century, the prosperous and enlightened Serbian rulers, especially the founder of the Serbian Church, Saint Sava, fostered education and literature, most notably biographies of kings and church leaders. This thriving period came to an end with the Turkish victory at the Kosovo Field in 1389. Afterward, only oral literature was possible, resulting in many epic poems about the glorious past and keeping the national spirit alive during the Turks' centuries of rule. Writers such as WALTER SCOTT (see Vol.1), JOHANN WOLFGANG GOETHE, ALEKSANDR PUSHKIN, and ADAM MICKIEWICZ translated and popularized these epics.

The revival of Serbian literature began in the late eighteenth century, gathering full steam in the nineteenth, with the gradual restoration of national independence. The Serbs who had moved north to Voivodina to escape the Turkish oppression now felt Western influence. Dositej Obradović with didactic works and Vuk Karadžić with the reform of the written language laid the foundation of modern Serbian literature. From then on, the literature made steady progress and to some extent made up for the lost centuries. During the period of romanticism, the best Serbian poet, PETAR PETROVIĆ NJEGOŠ, the

Prince-Bishop of Montenegro, wrote several seminal works, most notably the epic play in verse *Gorski vijenac* (The Mountain Wreath) (1847). He was joined by Branko Radičević, Jovan Jovanović Zmaj, Djura Jakšić, and Laza Kostić, among others. In the second half of the nineteenth century romanticism gave way to realism under the strong influence of French and Russian writers. Milovan Glišić, Laza K. Lazarević, Janko Veselinović, Stevan Sremac, and other realists reflected the rapid changes of their society.

At the turn of the century, modernistic tendencies made their way into Serbian literature, championed by JOVAN DUČIĆ and Milan Rakić, both pupils of French symbolists and Parnassians. Preferring *l'art pour l'art,* they eschewed traditional patriotic and love themes in favor of more complex concerns. Modernism became even more pronounced after World War I, when sophisticated and erudite writers like IVO ANDRIĆ, Miloš Crnjanski, Rastko Petrović, and Momčilo Nastasijević, disillusioned by the horrors of war, embraced expressionism and other *isms.* In the interwar period, writers opened themselves to the world. The period is characterized by bustling activity and a plethora of literary works, though few are of outstanding quality.

After World War II, attempts at socialist realism were soon abandoned. Andrić's novels, with their sweeping portrayal of the diverse peoples of Bosnia, inaugurated the steady rise of literary quality. His high artistry earned him the Nobel Prize in 1961—the only South Slav writer to be so honored. Since 1948 Serbian literature has been free to follow its own course. Many accomplished writers both continue the tradition and follow modern world trends. Several new writers have become internationally known: VASKO POPA, MIODRAG PAVLOVIĆ, and Ivan V. Lalić in poetry; and DOBRICA ĆOSIĆ, Meša Selimović, DANILO KIŠ, and MILORAD PAVIĆ in fiction. At present. Serbian literature is characterized by openness, despite sporadic political restrictions, by sophistication, and by efforts to transcend provincialism.

History and Criticism

Barac, Antun. *A History of Yugoslav Literature.* Mich. Slavic Pubns. 1972 $15.00. ISBN 0-930042-19-0. A general survey, mainly to 1941. A reliable source of basic information.

Eekman, Thomas. *Thirty Years of Yugoslav Literature, 1945–1975.* Mich. Slavic Pubns. 1978 $15.00. ISBN 0-930042-21-2. A survey complementary to Barac's, filled with facts and brief analyses of important authors and works.

Kadic, Ante. *Contemporary Serbian Literature.* Mouton 1964 $16.70. ISBN 90-2791-006-5. A very good introduction.

Koljević, Svetozar. *The Epic in the Making.* OUP 1980 o.p. One of the best treatments of Serbian epic poetry in any language, combining the thorough knowledge of a native scholar with sharp perception.

Lord, Albert B. *The Singer of Tales. Harvard Studies in Comparative Lit.* HUP 1960 $12.95. ISBN 0-674-80881-9. A classic study, based on field-collected South Slav epic songs, of oral epic composition and transmission within a living tradition.

Lukić, Sveta. *Contemporary Yugoslav Literature: A Sociopolitical Approach.* Trans. by Pola Triandis. Ed. by Gertrude J. Robinson. Bks Demand repr. of 1972 ed. $74.00. ISBN 0-317-09655-9. A critical analysis by a Marxist revisionist literary critic, especially of the literary scene from 1945 to 1968.

Mihailovich, Vasa D., ed. *Modern Slavic Literatures. Lib. of Literary Criticism Ser.* Vol. 2. Continuum 1976 o.p. Contains excerpts from 20 Serbian authors in the Yugoslav section.

Mihailovich, Vasa D., and Mateja Matejić. *A Comprehensive Bibliography of Yugoslav Literature in English, 1593–1980.* Slavica 1984 $29.95. ISBN 0-89357-136-9. *First*

Supplement, 1981–1985. Slavica 1989 $18.95. ISBN 0-89357-188-1. *Second Supplement, 1986–1990.* Slavica 1992 $19.95. An all-inclusive bibliography.

Subotić, Dragutin P. *Yugoslav Popular Ballads.* Folcroft 1976 repr. of 1932 ed. o.p. A solid study of mostly Serbian folk poetry, with a treatment of its reception in Germany, France, and English-speaking countries.

Collections

Butler, Thomas. *Monumenta Serbocroatica: A Bilingual Anthology of Serbian and Croatian Texts from the Twelfth to the Nineteenth Century.* Mich. Slavic Pubns. 1979 $15.00. ISBN 0-930042-32-8. An excellent collection; many texts in English for the first time. With introductions.

Dordevic, Mihailo, ed. *Anthology of Serbian Poetry.* Philosophical Lib. 1984 $19.95. ISBN 0-8022-2467-9. A limited but useful anthology of Serbian poetry at the beginning of the twentieth century.

Holton, Milne, and Vasa D. Mihailovich. *Serbian Poetry from the Beginnings to the Present.* Yale Russian 1988 $20.00. ISBN 0-936586-11-7. The most representative anthology, with extensive introductions to periods and poets.

Lenski, Branko, ed. *Death of a Simple Giant and Other Modern Yugoslav Stories.* Vanguard 1964 o.p. One of the best collections of Yugoslav short stories.

Matejić, Mateja, and Dragan Milivojević, eds. *An Anthology of Medieval Serbian Literature in English.* Slavica 1978 $11.95. ISBN 0-89357-055-9. Many medieval pieces offered here in English for the first time.

Mihailovich, Vasa D., ed. *Contemporary Yugoslav Poetry. Iowa Translations Ser.* Bks. Demand repr. of 1977 ed. $72.50. ISBN 0-317-42148-4. Introduction by Gertrude G. Champe. The most complete Yugoslav poetry collection in English, including 14 Serbian poets.

Mikasinovich, Branko, Dragan Milivojević, and Vasa D. Mihailovich, eds. *Introduction to Yugoslav Literature. Twayne's International Studies and Translations Ser.* G. K. Hall o.p. A good collection of writings from the nineteenth and twentieth centuries. Includes 33 Serbian authors.

Pennington, Anne, and Peter Levi, trans. *Marko the Prince: Serbo-Croat Heroic Songs.* St. Martin 1984 $19.95. ISBN 0-312-51537-5. The best selection and translation of Serbo-Croatian epic poems.

ANDRIĆ, IVO. 1892–1975 (Nobel Prize 1961)

Andrić began to write short stories in 1923 and was one of the most respected writers in Yugoslav literature of the interwar period. He gained worldwide acclaim with his postwar novels *The Bridge on the Drina* (1945) and *The Chronicle of Travnik,* which eventually earned him the Nobel Prize in 1961. *The Bridge on the Drina* became the first book in a trilogy, which was followed by *The Bosnian Story* and *The Woman from Sarajevo,* both also published in 1945.

Andrić wrote almost exclusively about his native Bosnia and its people, isolated for centuries in a world of myths, legends, hard life, and unfulfilled aspirations. What interested him most was the mixture of races and religions and their attempts, not always successful, at living together in harmony amid the forces constantly tearing the fragile social fabric apart. Andrić's ability to penetrate the heart and the soul of his characters and his meticulous craftsmanship established his reputation as one of the greatest Yugoslav writers of the twentieth century.

Novels by Andrić

Bosnian Chronicle. 1945. Trans. by Joseph Hitrec. Knopf 1963 o.p. Andrić's second most important novel, about foreign powers' intrigues in nineteenth-century Bosnia. The second title in his trilogy.

The Bridge on the Drina. 1945. Trans. by Lovett Edwards. U. Ch. Pr. 1977 $10.95. ISBN 0-226-02045-2. Introduction by William H. McNeill. The first book in his trilogy, this depicts the struggles of various religious groups over a sixteenth-century bridge, a symbol of permanence.

The Devil's Yard. 1954. Trans. by Kenneth Johnstone. Greenwood 1975 repr. of 1962 ed. $35.00. ISBN 0-8371-8218-2. About an unjustly imprisoned Bosnian in Istanbul and his efforts to retain his dignity.

SHORT STORY COLLECTION BY ANDRIĆ

The Pasha's Concubine and Other Tales. Trans. by Joseph Hitrec. Knopf 1968 o.p. A collection of some of Andrić's best, skillfully translated.

ĆOSIĆ, DOBRICA. 1921–

Dobrica Ćosić participated in World War II as a partisan and afterward wrote a novel about his experiences, *Distant Is the Sun.* Subsequent novels steadily enhanced his reputation as a skillful writer able to transform his engagé subject matter (all Ćosić's novels are politically tinged) into genuine artistic accomplishments. At the same time Ćosić steadily alienated himself from the power structure, to which he himself had contributed, becoming one of the main dissidents among Yugoslav intellectuals. His ambitious tetralogy, *This Land, This Time,* is an apotheosis of the tragic ordeal and eventual triumph of Serbia, a small nation of peasants that "defeated three empires"—the Turkish, Austro-Hungarian, and German—in World War I. His latest series of novels—the first of which, *The Sinner,* appeared in 1985—debunks the myth of infallibility of the Communists before and during World War II, an act that put him again on a collision course with the powers that be, but that also demonstrates his remarkable moral courage.

NOVELS BY ĆOSIĆ

Reach to Eternity. Trans. by Muriel Heppell. HarBraceJ 1980 $14.95. ISBN 0-15-175961-8. The third part of *This Land, This Time.*

South to Destiny. Trans. by Muriel Heppell. HarBraceJ 1981 $19.95. The final installment of *This Land, This Time.*

This Land, This Time. Trans. by Muriel Heppel. 4 vols. HarBraceJ 1983 repr. of 1978 ed. $29.95. ISBN 0-15-690026-2

DJILAS, MILOVAN. 1911–

Milovan Djilas is known as an author of political writings about his experiences as a young communist before and during World War II, as a high functionary after the war, and, finally, as a renegade. His initial ambition, however, was to be a fiction writer, but because of the vicissitudes of his life, he has been able to fulfill that ambition only partly—the few short stories and three volumes of his autobiography, however, reveal all his artistic potential. Ironically, even those few works have been published only in translation into other languages, because he is not allowed to publish in Yugoslavia. In all his works, Djilas cannot get away from his basically political nature, seeing and interpreting everything through the Marxist prism. He has also written a perceptive book on PETAR PETROVIĆ NJEGOŠ.

SHORT STORY COLLECTIONS BY DJILAS

The Leper and Other Stories. Trans. by Lovett Edwards. HarBraceJ 1964 o.p.

The Stone and the Violets. Trans. by Lovett Edwards. HarbraceJ 1972 o.p.

Nonfiction by Djilas

Land Without Justice. 1958. Trans. by Michael B. Petrovich. HarBraceJ 1972 o.p. The author's reminiscences of his country's past.

Montenegro. Trans. by Kenneth Johnstone. HarBraceJ 1963 $9.95. ISBN 0-15-162102-0. An unflinching recollection of the sometimes harsh reality of Montenegro's recent past.

Njegoš: Poet, Prince, Bishop. Trans. by Michael B. Petrovich. HarBraceJ 1966 o.p. A perceptive study of the greatest Serbian poet.

Under the Colors. Trans. by Lovett Edwards. HarBraceJ 1971 o.p. Like *Montenegro,* about the recent past.

DUČIĆ, JOVAN. 1874–1943

Jovan Dučić was a career diplomat and the poet most responsible for the modernization of Serbian poetry at the turn of the century. His poetry was heavily influenced by the French symbolists, but he was able to give it his own touch, that of a sensitive, refined, and highly articulate poet who paid great attention to his craft. In addition to exquisite lyric poems, he wrote poems in prose, erudite travelogues, pseudo-philosophical essays, and historical prose. Often accused of being aloof, pseudo-aristocratic, and posing, he is nevertheless recognized as a master of poetic mood and a consummate craftsman.

Poetry by Dučić

Plave Legende—Blue Legends. Trans. by Vasa D. Mihailovich. Kosovo 1983 o.p. Contains all of Dučić's prose poems, the best in Serbian literature.

KIŠ, DANILO. 1935–1989

Since his first novel in 1963, Danilo Kiš has steadily gained in reputation as one of the most powerful Serbian writers. He "writes in a distinctly personal, lyrical style with a special knack for evoking childhood, or for suggesting the atmosphere of wartime. In modern Serbian literature his novels are conspicuous for their naturalness of expression and purity of expression. Close to the latest currents among the youngest generation of European novelists, Kiš is at the same time faithful to the classic ideals of simplicity and balance" (*Yugoslav Literary Lexicon*).

Novel by Kiš

Hourglass. Trans. by Ralph Manheim. FS&G 1990 $22.95. ISBN 0-374-17287-0. "A subtle and important work asking the universal questions of survival, of what can survive the destructive pressures of time and history" (*World Literature Today*).

Short Story Collections by Kiš

The Encyclopedia of the Dead. Trans. by Michael Heim. FS&G 1989 $17.95. ISBN 0-374-14826-0. Ten short stories in which "the investigation of history and the individual's place in its capriciously unfolding design assume an obsessive dimension" (*World Literature Today*).

A Tomb for Boris Davidovich. Writers from Other Europe Ser. Viking Penguin 1980 $7.95. ISBN 0-14-005452-9. Introduction by Joseph Brodsky. Seven related stories showing "traces of Koestler's *Darkness at Noon* . . . [but with the] special flair . . . [of] someone who is there, *on the other side*" (*The New Leader*).

Nonfiction by Kiš

Garden, Ashes. Trans. by William J. Hannaher. HarBraceJ 1975 $7.95. o.p. Bittersweet memories of childhood and an apotheosis of his father.

NJEGOŠ, PETAR PETROVIĆ. (Prince-Bishop of Montenegro). 1813–1851

Njegoš, the titular head and the spiritual leader of Montenegro, wrote lyrical poetry, epic poems, and plays in verse. He was primarily concerned with helping his people overcome the backwardness imposed on them by historical events, while at the same time warding off the Turkish attacks. His Miltonian epic *The Ray of Microcosm* (1845) expresses his philosophical and religious views, while the verse drama *The Mountain Wreath* (1847) echoes his undying commitment to freedom at all costs. *The Mountain Wreath,* revered as the best work in all South Slavic literature, centers on the Montenegrins' coming to grips with their main dilemma—how to deal with those of their people who have accepted Islam and are siding with the enemy.

Play by Njegoš

The Mountain Wreath. 1847. Trans. by Vasa D. Mihailovich. Charles Schlack, Jr. 1986 o.p. The new translation, adhering to the decasyllabic verse of the original.

Poetry by Njegoš

The Ray of the Microcosm. 1845. Trans. by Žika Rad. Prvulovich. Charles Schlacks, Jr. 1992 o.p.

PAVIĆ, MILORAD. 1929–

Pavić's international success came rather late in his career. He started out as a poet, switched to the short story, and now writes novels almost exclusively. A meditative and erudite author, he strives to merge fantasy and reality in a masterful, controlled, sometimes playful style. Pavić's idiom is thoroughly modern and his mastery of the language brilliant. In his acclaimed, rather complex novels *Dictionary of the Khazars* (1984) and *Landscape Painted with Tea* (1988), he blurs the dividing lines between the past, present, and future, delving into the past to confront problems of the present. With these novels, and others yet to be published in English, he has enjoyed immense international success.

Novels by Pavić

Dictionary of the Khazars. 1984. Trans. by Christina Pribicevic Zoric. Random 1989 $9.95. ISBN 0-679-72461-3. An attempt, in dictionary form, to solve the mysterious disappearance of the mythical Khazar tribe by seeing its people in a contemporary context. In two versions, male and female.

Landscape Painted with Tea. 1988. Trans. by Christina Pribicevic Zoric. Knopf 1990 $21.95. ISBN 0-394-58217-9. A brilliant tour-de-force about a man's search for his identity on two continents.

PAVLOVIĆ, MIODRAG. 1928–

Miodrag Pavlović appeared on the literary scene in the early 1950s. Together with Vasko Popa, Pavlović was most influential in bringing about the modernist revolution in Serbian poetry. His poetry has a strong intellectual ring and a universal scope. It is technically flawless, showing many innovations and striking metaphors. Its language is rich, economical, precise. Like Popa, Pavlović is searching for old myths, which he finds in many quarters, but mostly in medieval Serbian history. Being one of the first to issue a call for regeneration of poetry, away from romanticism or pragmatic utilitarianism, and toward a more disciplined, analytical, and intellectual approach, he has remained remarkably constant in his stance, charting a new course with every new book.

POETRY BY PAVLOVIĆ

The Conquerer in Constantinople. Trans. by Joachim Neugroschel. New Rivers Pr. 1976 $2.00 o.p. Twenty-three poems from the cycle dealing with the Serbs' distant past.

The Slavs Beneath Parnassus. Trans. by Bernard Johnson. New Rivers Pr. 1985 $7.00. ISBN 0-89823-062-4. A comprehensive cross-section of the poet's opus.

POPA, VASKO. 1922–1991

Vasko Popa is the most translated of contemporary Yugoslav poets—his entire poetic opus has been translated into English. He was chiefly responsible for steering Serbian poetry away from stale traditionalism, which came close to being socialist realism, in the early 1950s. His modernism is expressed in terse, aphoristic, elliptical idiom, in beautifully crafted poetic entities that tend to run in cycles, and above all in his efforts to penetrate the essence of the phenomena around him, dead or alive. Popa is a poet's poet, a powerful craftsman of images and metaphors, an incessant seeker of the primeval roots and myths. His eight collections of poems, so far, belong to the most accomplished poetry in all of Yugoslav literature.

POETRY BY POPA

Collected Poems 1943–1976. Trans. by Anne Pennington. Persea Bks. o.p. Introduction by Ted Hughes. The best and most complete collection.

Earth Erect. Trans. by Anne Pennington. Iowa International Writing Program 1973 o.p.

Give Me Back My Rags. Trans. by Charles Simic. Seluzicki Fine Bks. 1985 $9.95. ISBN 0-317-39882-2. A luxurious edition.

Homage to the Lame Wolf: Selected Poems 1956–1975. Trans. by Charles Simic. Oberlin Coll. Pr. 1987 $9.00. ISBN 0-932440-22-3. Presentable selection, superb translation.

The Little Box. Trans. by Charles Simic. Charioteer 1973 $7.50. ISBN 0-910350-09-4. A selection of poems from various books: "I can think of very little recent poetry that is as powerful and complete in its vision" (Charles Simic).

Midnight Sun. Trans. by Branko Mikasinovich. Cross Cult. 1992 $15.00. ISBN 0-89304-963-8. Retranslation of some of Popa's most representative poems.

SLOVAK LITERATURE

If anything was written in Slovak before the eighteenth century, it was not preserved, and not until the 1840s was the written form of the language codified, by L'udovit Stur, with the first works appearing in 1844. The best of the pioneering writers was Janko Král, whose ballads and epic and lyric poems reveal the basic inspiration for Slavic writers: their own folk poetry and the romantic poetry of other Slavic nations. Romanticism prevailed into the 1870s and 1880s. The strongest genre was lyric poetry, and the two poets who helped establish it were Hviezdoslav and Ivan Krasko. Because the romantic movement fostered nationalistic feelings, it overshadowed other movements such as realism: during this period the Slovaks had to resist Hungarian attempts to stifle their aspirations, including writing and publishing in Slovak. The few realists, influenced mainly by Russian writers, are best represented by Martin Kukucin.

The flowering of Slovak literature came after World War I, when the Slovaks were finally able to enjoy full cultural freedom. Writers followed modern European trends, many literary journals were started, and publishing was unfettered. As a result, Slovak writing was enriched in both theme and style, and new, more accomplished writers appeared. By and large, Slovak authors have shared the fate of their Czech compatriots before, during, and after World War

II. In the interwar period, Emil Boleslav Lukac and Jan Smrek were the modernists, Gejza Vamos represented expressionism, while Milo Urban and JOZEF CÍGER-HRONSKÝ were realists who focused on rural Slovakia. Even though there was a strong leftist group before World War II, socialist realism was only minimally successful in Slovak literature after the war and was rejected altogether in the 1960s. Of several promising postwar writers, LADISLAV MŇAČKO has been best received at home and abroad. After 1968, the Slovaks had to submit to strict party controls, an unsavory situation that lasted until the early 1990s, when the new state of Slovakia was established, promising free literary expression and greater artistic achievement.

History and Criticism

Kovtun, George J. *Czech and Slovak Literature in English: A Bibliography*. Lib. of Congress 1984. o.p. Not all-inclusive, but a good bibliography of monographs published from 1832 to 1982.

Selver, Paul. *Czechoslovak Literature: An Outline*. Gordon Pr. 1973 $175.00. ISBN 0-87968-988-9

Součkova, Milada. *Literary Satellite: Czechoslovak-Russian Literary Relations*. U. Ch. Pr. 1970 $12.50. ISBN 0-226-76840-6. A thorough examination of literary relations, mainly between 1945 and 1968.

Collections

Liehm, Antonin, and Peter Kussi, eds. *The Writing on the Wall: An Anthology of Czechoslovak Literature Today*. Karz Cohl 1983 o.p. "Brings to American readers some of the biggest names" (*LJ*).

Selver, Paul, trans. *Anthology of Czechoslovak Literature*. Kraus repr. of 1929 ed. o.p. Poetry and fiction of writers before and after World War I.

CÍGER-HRONSKÝ, JOZEF. 1896–1960

A prominent Slovak fiction writer, Cíger-Hronský depicted in a realistic fashion the village life in Slovakia and the difficulties the peasants experienced coping with the encroaching urban civilization. He was particularly interested in people's relationship to nature, developing his own idea of the natural human. In 1945 Cíger-Hronský emigrated to Argentina where he later died, but his interest in his native land never waned as he continued to use Slovak themes in his works.

NOVEL BY CÍGER-HRONSKÝ

Jozef Mak. Trans. by Andrew Cincura. Slavica 1985 $14.95. ISBN 0-89357-129-6. About a strong peasant who is turned into a weakling by the insensitivity, malice, and greed of others.

MŇAČKO, LADISLAV. 1919–

Mňačko is a leading Slovak communist writer and journalist who has earned the highest literary honors his country could bestow and has received much publicity both for his satirical novel about Czech communist leadership and for his criticism of Czech anti-Semitism and of the Czech pro-Arab position on the Arab-Israeli war. When *The Taste of Power* was published in the United States in August 1967, Mňačko was stripped of his citizenship and the honors he had won and expelled from the Communist party. The book, praised by *Library Journal* as "a work of major significance," exposes "the ironic discrepancies between the public conduct and private motives of . . . [a thinly disguised head of state], a far from attractive yet curiously human figure for whom the taste of power had slowly turned into the taste of gall" (*SR*).

NOVELS BY MŇAČKO

The Seventh Night. NAL-Dutton 1969 o.p. About the 1968 Soviet invasion of Czechoslovakia.

The Taste of Power. Trans. by Paul Stevenson. Praeger Pubs. 1967 o.p.

SLOVENIAN LITERATURE

The Slovenes established their own state in the eighth century, but it was short-lived. Successively ruled by the Franks, the Bavarians, and the Hapsburgs, Slovenia did not recover independence until 1918 and then as a republic within Yugoslavia. The birth of Slovene literature is tied to the acceptance of Christianity, although the first writings were most likely prompted by Irish monks rather than the Greek brothers Cyril and Methodius, who influenced other East European literatures. Cyril and Methodius offered translations of the scriptures in the local tongue, but the first written religious works in Slovenia were in Latin. Of those writings, only a few are preserved, and little else exists before the sixteenth century.

The first book was printed in 1550 during the Protestant Reformation by the leader of the Slovene Protestant church, Primož Trubar, who helped codify a Slovene literary language. His efforts resulted in extensive literary activity, which ended with the defeat of the Reformation. The ensuing Counter-Reformation did relatively little for Slovene literature because the leading intellectuals used German.

The Slovene revival started in the second half of the eighteenth century, stimulated by Austrian Enlightenment policies. Books—mostly didactic and historical but also volumes of poetry—were again published in large numbers, along with literary journals. Romanticism flourished in the revival, aided by the works of Anton Linhart, Valentin Vodnik, FRANCE PREŠEREN, and Jernej Kopitar, a linguist who wrote the first Slovene grammar. Prešeren, the greatest Slovene poet, was the movement's main force.

Romanticism gave way to realism in the second half of the nineteenth century. Writers were inspired by history and by folk narratives, while at the same time portraying everyday life realistically. With leading realists such as Fran Levstik, Josip Stritar, Josip Jurčič, Janko Kersnik, Anton Aškerc, Ivan Tavčar, and IVAN CANKAR, Slovene literature made noticeable advances. Cankar, the greatest Slovene writer of the twentieth century, wrote short stories, novels, and plays, giving substance to the rising modernism movement and setting new standards. Other important modernists were Dragotin Kette, Josip Murn Aleksandrov, and OTON ŽUPANČIČ.

In the interwar period, Slovene writers followed European trends, depicting the conditions in the new state and showing strong leftist leanings. An imposing number of new faces was complemented by an abundance of works. Srečko Kosovel, Prežihov Voranc, and Ciril Kosmač especially wrote lasting poetry and fiction. Most authors continued to write following World War II; after a brief and abortive experiment with socialist realism, they opened up to the world, employing a wide array of approaches. Poetry is now the dominant genre, and poets like Edvard Kocbek, Gregor Strniša, and TOMAŽ ŠALAMUN, despite being different in many respects, have enhanced the reputation of Slovene literature.

History and Criticism

Barac, Antun. *A History of Yugoslav Literature*. Mich. Slavic Pubns. 1972 $15.00. ISBN 0-930042-19-0. A general survey, mainly to 1941. A reliable source of basic information.

Eekman, Thomas. *Thirty Years of Yugoslav Literature, 1945–1975*. Mich. Slavic Pubns. 1978 $15.00. ISBN 0-930042-21-2. A survey complementary to Barac's, filled with facts and brief analyses of important authors and works.

Mihailovich, Vasa D., ed. *Modern Slavic Literatures. Lib. of Literary Criticism Ser.* Vol. 2. Continuum $60.00. ISBN 0-8044-3177-9. Contains excerpts from seven Slovene authors in the Yugoslav section.

______, and Mateja Matejić. *A Comprehensive Bibliography of Yugoslav Literature in English, 1593–1980*. Slavica 1984 $29.95. ISBN 0-89357-136-9. *First Supplement, 1981–1985*. Slavica 1988 $18.95. ISBN 0-89357-188-1. *Second Supplement, 1986–1990*. Slavica 1992 $19.95. An all-inclusive bibliography.

Collections

Lenski, Branko, ed. *Death of a Simple Giant and Other Modern Yugoslav Stories*. Vanguard 1964 o.p. One of the best collections of Yugoslav short stories.

Matthews, William, and Anton Slodnjak, eds. *The Parnassus of a Small Nation: An Anthology of Slovene Lyrics*. Calder Pr. 1957 o.p. The best collection of Slovene poetry in English.

Mihailovich, Vasa D., ed. *Contemporary Yugoslav Poetry. Iowa Translations Ser.* Bks. Demand repr. of 1977 ed. $72.50. ISBN 0-317-42148-4. Introduction by Gertrude G. Champe. The most complete Yugoslav poetry collection in English, including nine Slovene poets.

Mikasinovich, Branko, Dragan Milivojević, and Vasa D. Mihailovich, eds. *Introduction to Yugoslav Literature. Twayne's International Studies and Translations Ser.* G. K. Hall 1973 o.p. A good collection of writings from the nineteenth and twentieth centuries. Includes 13 Slovene authors.

CANKAR, IVAN. 1876–1918

Prolific and one of the best Slovene writers, Cankar excelled in poetry, short stories, novels, plays, and essays. His first, and only, book of poetry, *Erotica*, was well received by the critics and readers but also bought up and destroyed by the bishop because of its "lascivious" nature. Later he turned to fiction, writing exquisite vignette-stories and successful plays. What earned him the reputation of a great writer as well as wide popularity was, among other things, a humanitarian approach to society's problems, a deep understanding of the little people and their lives, a willingness to stand up for his beliefs, and hope despite sometimes desperate conditions. Cankar also supported the idea of a common destiny for all South Slavs. Through a successful fusion of subject matter and style and the power of rhythmic language, he influenced many younger writers and lifted Slovene literature out of its provincial obscurity.

SHORT STORY COLLECTIONS BY CANKAR

Dream Visions and Other Selected Stories. 1917. Trans. by Anton Druzina. Slovenian Research Center of America 1982 o.p. One of the best collections, skillfully translated and artfully illustrated, of stories written shortly before Cankar's death.

My Life and Other Sketches. Trans. by Elza Jereb and Alasdair MacKinnon. Državna založba Slovenije 1971 o.p. Contains 26 of Cankar's best stories.

Novels by Cankar

The Bailiff Yerney and His Rights. 1907. Trans. by Sidonie Yeras and H. C. Sewel Grant. Rodker 1930 o.p. One of Cankar's most powerful stories about the denial of a downtrodden servant's basic rights.

The Ward of Our Lady of Mercy. 1904. Trans. by Henry Leeming. Državna založba Slovenije 1976 o.p. Another masterful novella revealing Cankar's compassion and deep understanding of human interrelationships.

PREŠEREN, FRANCE. 1800–1849

France Prešeren was the first Slovenian to write poetry approaching world literary standards, and he is still the nation's greatest poet. He excelled in lyric verses, as well as in epic, meditative, narrative, satirical, and epigrammatic poetry. Most of his early work speaks of unhappy love. His "Garland of Sonnets" is devoted in its entirety to the unrequited love of a wealthy girl who marries a German. Prešeren's greatest work is the epic *Baptism at the Savica*, reaching back to pagan times when the Slovenes were converted to Christianity. Prešeren spent most of his life unhappy and died young, yet he endured all personal disappointments stoically and with dignity. His many achievements, especially his formal artistry, are all the more remarkable since there was no poetic tradition to speak of before him.

Poetry by Prešeren

The Baptism on the Savica. Trans. by Henry R. Cooper, Jr. Slovene Studies 1985 o.p. A skillful, knowledgeable translation.

Selection of Poems. Edited by W. K. Matthews and A. Slodnjak. Blackwell Pubs. 1954 o.p.

Book About Prešeren

Cooper, Henry R., Jr. *France Prešeren*. Twayne 1981 o.p. The best monograph on Prešeren in English by a young scholar of Slovene literature.

ŠALAMUN, TOMAŽ. 1941–

Šalamun is undoubtedly the most outstanding among the younger Slovene poets. What sets him apart from many other talented contemporaries is his iconoclastic attitude, rare in his nation but very much like that of younger poets elsewhere. In his numerous collections since 1966, he is unconventional, daring, innovative, at times irreverent, but always urging a reevaluation of established values. His poetic world is unlike any other in Slovene letters, and he has never wavered from an intent to be different. At the same time, he has artistic power that supports his claim for originality. He has been widely translated.

Poetry by Šalamun

Painted Desert: Poems. Trans. by Michael Biggins and others. Ed. by Richard Seehus. Poetry Miscellany 1991 o.p.

The Selected Poems of Tomaž Šalamun. Trans. by Charles Simic and others. Ecco Pr. 1988 $17.50. ISBN 0-88001-160-2. A representative selection, translated by the author together with Simic and other poets.

Snow. Trans. by Anselm Hollo and others. Coffee Hse. 1973 o.p. A random selection of poems.

Turbines. 1975. Trans. by Anselm Hollo and others. Windhover Pr. 1973 o.p.

ŽUPANČIČ, OTON. 1878–1949

The most important Slovenian poet after FRANCE PREŠEREN, Oton Župančič was a member of the modernist movement at the beginning of the twentieth century. After several collections from 1899 to 1920, he did not publish another until 1945. The reasons for his long silence, in addition to purely personal ones, were disillusionment and pessimism concerning his country's future. His poetry consists of love and patriotic poems, ballads, and romances on folk themes. His last collection extols the partisan struggle in World War II. A strong individualist, he was less involved in group and patriotic activities than some of his friends, yet his patriotic fervor was no less pronounced. Also, as an accomplished translator familiar with several literatures, he had a cosmopolitan outlook and was open to Western influences. Župančič in addition wrote a successful play.

POETRY BY ŽUPANČIČ

A Selection of Poems. Ed. by Janko Lavrin. Državna založba Slovenije o.p. An excellent translation of Župančič's most important poetry.

UKRAINIAN LITERATURE

The history of Ukrainian literature goes back to the eleventh century when, during the Kievan Rus, the Ukrainians converted to Christianity and began to write religious literature, notably vitae and chronicles, in Church Slavic, a written language common to all early Slavs. Parallel to these works were epic and lyric songs in oral form, the most outstanding of which is the *Tale of Ihor's Campaign* (the epic is also claimed by the Russians). This remarkable work depicts in a highly poetic fashion a military expedition of one of the early Kievan princes against the nomadic tribes. After the Kievan Rus was destroyed by the Mongols and the Ukrainians were incorporated into the Polish-Lithuanian state, literary activity was confined to copying old books and translating the Bible into Ukrainian. In the sixteenth and seventeenth centuries, poetry and drama began to develop. After 1654, however, when the Ukraine was absorbed into the Russian empire and writing in Ukrainian was banned, some Ukrainian writers chose to write in Russian. It was not until 1798 that publishing in Ukrainian was restored, beginning with *Eneyida*, a syllabo-tonic verse imitation of VIRGIL by Ivan Kotlyarevski. For the next century or so Ukrainian writers had to cope with severe restrictions on their use of Ukrainian, but they still managed to produce several great authors: the poet TARAS ŠEVČENKO, the novelist IVAN FRANKO, and the playwrights LESJA UKRAJINKA and MYKOLA KULIŠ, By then the romantic movement, which had dominated Ukrainian literature for most of the century, gave way to realism and, at the turn of the century, to modernistic tendencies. In the first two decades of the twentieth century, several notable writers reflected the modern Western trends of symbolism, futurism, and neoclassicism, while other authors experimented with expressionism, impressionism, and other movements.

This lively activity continued in the first decade after the Bolshevik Revolution. At first the Ukrainians were encouraged to develop their culture, which resulted in sort of a national and cultural revival. Many prewar writers continued their work while new faces also appeared. The most influential group was that of VAPLITE (Free Academy of Proletarian Literature), which, enjoying the support of the regime, was trying to uphold high literary standards and to look for models in the West, not in Russia. However, the activity was brought to a tragic halt in the 1930s, as many authors were purged or liquidated. As in all other literatures in the so-called socialist camp, writers had to accept strict controls and socialist realism was the only valid literary method. Very little good literature was produced at this time. After the ravages of World War II, which were especially devastating in the Ukraine, Ukrainian literature continued to exist under restrictive conditions although, during the various periods of relaxation since Stalin's death, writers were able to write somewhat more freely. More important, talented new writers have made Ukrainian literature of the last three or so decades artistically more accomplished and colorful. Perhaps the most prominent of these new faces is the novelist OLEKSANDER HONCHAR, who excelled in his war novels. Among younger writers, the poets Ivan Drach and Vasyl Symonenko should be singled out.

Two other aspects of contemporary Ukrainian literature are worth mentioning: the dissent in the Ukraine manifested primarily through underground publishing (*samvydav*) and the literary activity of numerous émigré writers, gathered mostly in West Germany, Canada, and the United States. Although neither of these phenomena has produced literature of high order, both are indicative of the unsettled conditions under which the Ukrainian writers have to work, as they have done practically throughout their history. In 1991 Ukraine gained independence for the first time in centuries, and this development bodes well for the future of Ukrainian literature.

History and Criticism

Čyževskyj, Dmytro. *A History of Ukrainian Literature from the 11th to the End of the 19th Century*. Trans. by D. Ferguson. Ukrainian Arts Sci. 1975 $30.00. ISBN 0-87287-170-3. A seminal, thorough history by one of the leading Slavic scholars.

Grabowicz, George G. *Toward a History of Ukrainian Literature*. HUP 1981 $5.00. ISBN 0-674-89676-9. A critical examination of Čyževskyj's *A History of Ukrainian Literature*, with the goal of an alternative and more accurate and functional history.

Luckyj, George S. *Literary Politics in the Soviet Ukraine 1917–1934. Select Bibliographies Repr. Ser.* Duke 1990 $37.50. ISBN 0-8223-1081-3. Deals with literary organizations, their histories and conflicts.

Manning, Clarence A. *Ukrainian Literature: Studies of the Leading Authors. Essay Index Repr. Ser.* Ayer repr. of 1944 ed. $18.00. ISBN 0-8369-2244-1. Brief portraits of the major Ukrainian literary figures.

Collections

Andrusyshen, C. H., and Watson Kirkconnell, trans. *The Ukrainian Poets, 1189–1962*. U. of Toronto Pr. 1963 o.p. The best anthology of Ukrainian poetry in English, including almost a hundred poets, with critical introductions.

Luckyj, George S., ed. *Modern Ukrainian Short Stories*. Ukrainian Arts Sci. 1973 o.p.

Zenkovsky, Serge A., ed. *Medieval Russia's Epics, Chronicles, and Tales*. NAL-Dutton rev. ed. 1974 o.p. An excellent collection of medieval texts, many hitherto unavailable in English.

FRANKO, IVAN. 1856–1916

Franko, a prolific Galician Ukrainian writer, scholar, and journalist, was a master of several genres; his works also show an extraordinary variety of themes. His earliest published works include a series of romantic historical novels and a group of naturalistic portrayals of the conflict of nascent industrialism and labor in the Ukraine. Other works depict the social disintegration of the gentry and the attempts of the new intelligentsia to supplant it. He is perhaps best known for his epic verses, especially the great epic *Moses* (1905), in which he expounds his philosophy of the nation and the role of the charismatic personality.

POETRY BY FRANKO

Fox Mykyta. Trans. by Bohdan Melnyk. Tundra Bks. 1978 o.p. A satirical poem with modernistic tendencies, despite Franko's misgivings about modernism.

Ivan Franko: The Poet of the Western Ukraine, Selected Poems. Trans. by Percival Cundy. Greenwood repr. of 1948 ed. o.p. A representative selection, the only one in English.

HONCHAR, OLEKSANDER. 1918–

Honchar writes short stories and novels. His novels deal with World War II and with life in the former Soviet Union. In his early works he subscribed to the tenets of socialist realism, but later, especially in his novel *The Cathedral* (1968), he employed bolder themes of Ukrainian spiritual values and yearning for freedom. He is adept at describing nature and is a precise stylist in the Ukrainian literary language. Lately he has become involved in the struggle for human rights in Ukraine.

NOVEL BY HONCHAR

Shore of Love. Imported Pubns. 1980 o.p.

KULIŠ, MYKOLA. 1892–1942

Kuliš was an outstanding Soviet Ukrainian dramatist. He first wrote in the vein of ethnographic realism, but went on to compose highly original ethnographic plays. The *Sonata Pathetique* is a vivid representation of the Revolution of 1917, which is allegorically presented as an expressive and profoundly tragic sonata. The play was staged by the two leading theaters in Russia, but its presentation was not allowed on the Ukrainian stage.

PLAY BY MYKOLA KULIŠ

Sonata Pathetique. Trans. by George S. N. Luckyj and Moira Luckyj. Ukrainian Acad. 1975 o.p. Introduction by Ralph Lindheim.

KULIŠ, PANTELEJMON (also KULISH). 1819–1897

Kuliš, a scholar as well as a novelist, in *The Black Council* gives a vivid picture of the different levels of society in seventeenth-century Ukraine. His theme is the need for people to be motivated by high ideals as they engage in the "struggle of truth with injustice."

NOVEL BY PANTELEJMON KULIŠ

The Black Council. Trans. and abr. by George S. N. Luckyj and Moira Luckyj. Ukrainian Acad. 1973 o.p. Introduction by Romana Bahrij Pikulyk.

BOOK ABOUT PANTELEJMON KULIŠ

Luckyj, George S. *Pantelejmon Kuliš: A Sketch of His Life and Times.* East European Quarterly 1983 $42.00. ISBN 0-88033-016-3. Examines Kuliš's life in order to analyze his works. A "sketch" because necessary material is unavailable.

PIDMOHYLNY, VALERIAN. 1901–1941

Pidmohylny, a member of the literary group "The Link," wrote short stories and novels on existentialist themes. His last novel, *A Little Touch of Drama,* published in 1930, shows the influence of French writers such as GUY DE MAUPASSANT. In his earlier works he experimented with impressionistic psychological stories and with literary expressionism. Although he was not politically involved, he was arrested and eventually perished in a concentration camp.

NOVEL BY PIDMOHYLNY

A Little Touch of Drama. Ukrainian Classics in Translation Ser. Trans. by George S. Luckyj and Moira Luckyj. Ukrainian Arts Sci. 1972 o.p.

ŠEVČENKO, TARAS (also SHEVCHENKO). 1814–1861

Ševčenko is the outstanding Ukrainian romantic poet, creator of the Ukrainian literary language and symbol of the national movement. He was born a serf and educated in St. Petersburg to serve as a portraitist and artist. His freedom was purchased in 1838 by several of his admirers. Ševčenko's first eight poems were collected in *The Bandura Player.* The publication of this collection in 1840 was a literary sensation. This collection was followed in the next three years by *The Haidamaks* and a series of poems based strongly on folk-song rhythms. The writings composed after his return to the Ukraine in 1843 included strong invectives against serfdom and the baneful role that Russians played in Ukrainian history.

For a decade after 1847 Ševčenko was exiled to Central Asia for his participation in the Sts. Cyril and Methodius Society. This clandestine organization advocated the union of all Slavs on the basis of independence and equality. During his exile he wrote several lyrics and novelettes. The poems of the last four years of his life, including *Neofity* and *Mariya,* are built on strongly religious themes.

POETRY BY ŠEVČENKO

The Poetical Works of Taras Shevchenko. Trans. by C. H. Andrusyshen and Watson Kirkconnell. U. of Toronto Pr. 1964 $32.50. ISBN 0-8020-3114-5. A good collection by two veteran interpreters of Ukrainian poetry.

BOOKS ABOUT ŠEVČENKO

Grabowicz, George G. *The Poet as Mythmaker: A Study of Symbolic Meaning in Taras Ševčenko.* HUP 1982 $14.00. ISBN 0-674-67852-4. A reexamination of Ševčenko from Grabowicz's belief that many critics are "uninterested in systematic symbolic analysis and relentlessly trim Ševčenko to their various extra-literary needs."

Luckyj, George G. *Ševčenko and the Critics, 1861–1980.* Bks. Demand repr. of 1980 ed. $139.40. ISBN 0-8357-4731-X. An excellent compendium of critical texts, intended primarily for university students.

UKRAJINKA, LESJA (pseud. of Larysa Petrivna Kvitka, née Kosač). 1871–1913

Ukrajinka was a modernist poet at the end of the nineteenth century and the beginning of the twentieth century. Her earliest works were lyric patriotic poems with exotic themes and motifs borrowed from remote times and places. After experimenting in prose drama, she wrote a great number of dramatic poems, the genre for which she is most famous. Her best work, the dramatic poem *A Forest Song* (1912), is based on Ukrainian folklore, as are many of her other works. Her main themes were love for her country and love of freedom.

WORK BY UKRAJINKA

Spirit of Flame: A Collection of the Works of Lesya Ukrainka. Trans. by Percival Cundy. Greenwood 1971 repr. of 1950 ed. $47.50. ISBN 0-8371-5990-3. Foreword by Clarence A. Manning. A representative selection of poetry and other works.

BOOK ABOUT UKRAJINKA

Bida, Constantine. *Lesya Ukrainka: Life and Works.* Trans. by Vera Rich. U. of Toronto Pr. 1968 o.p. Contains selections from her work.

CHAPTER 22

Latin American Literatures

David William Foster

> . . . we should feel that our patrimony is the universe; we should essay all themes, and we cannot limit ourselves to purely Argentine subjects in order to be Argentine; for either being Argentine is an inescapable act of fate—and in that case we shall be so in all events—or being Argentine is a mere affectation, a mask.
>
> I believe that if we surrender ourselves to that voluntary dream which is artistic creation, we shall be Argentine and we shall also be good or tolerable writers.
>
> —JORGE LUIS BORGES, *El Escritor Argentino y la Tradición*

The literatures of Latin America (Central and South America) are derived primarily from two languages—Spanish and Portuguese. Two fundamental concerns affect the establishment of parameters for Spanish American literature: the chronological beginning of a specific Spanish American cultural production and the precise geographical boundaries of that production. The following facts demonstrate the geographical problem. Approximately one-half of what was once part of the Mexican nation became U.S. territory in the mid-1800s; approximately 20 million native speakers of Spanish reside within the territorial United States, with a literary production in Spanish among Chicanos/Mexican Americans, Neoricans (i.e., Puerto Ricans on the continental mainland), Cuban Americans, and others of Latin American descent. A further complication is the fact that the Caribbean as a geographical designation is only partly Hispanic: Cuba, Puerto Rico, the Dominican Republic, and portions of Mexico, Colombia, and Venezuela. Latin American literature, of course, also includes the non-Spanish literature of Brazil, a Portuguese-speaking country. (See the separate section for Brazilian literature in this chapter.) While Spanish language authors from the Caribbean are included in this chapter, the Caribbean as a regional entity is included elsewhere in this volume. (See Chapter 24.) That chapter focuses on the English and French literary heritage of the Caribbean region.

Another dimension of this question is the tragic fact that much of Spanish American literature has been an exilic production, whether an exile for political, social, economic, or cultural and professional reasons, or whether a permanent exile or a phenomenon of multiple residencies. Although exile has in some cases meant adopting the language of another culture (e.g., the case of the Argentine William Henry Hudson), it has more often meant the creative compromises imposed by distance from one's native soil. A complementary problem is internal exile: a silenced production or a clandestine one, perhaps not published during the author's lifetime.

The Nobel Prize winner GABRIEL GARCÍA MÁRQUEZ, for example, wrote *One Hundred Years of Solitude* (1967) in exile, and he has essentially lived outside of

Colombia for the past 40 years. PABLO NERUDA, also a Nobel Prize winner, spent many periods outside of Chile, in part because of diplomatic assignments, but also because of political persecution. The Guatemalan Nobel Prize winner MIGUEL ANGEL ASTURIAS wrote most of his major novels in Argentina. HORACIO QUIROGA lived so much of his life in Argentina that he is more often identified with its literature than with that of his native Uruguay. JULIO CORTÁZAR left Argentina for Paris in the 1950s, where he remained until his death in the 1980s; only sporadically did he return to Argentina in later years, and some critics have underscored the "de-Argentinization" of his literary language. The Mexican MARIANO AZUELA had to publish his most famous novel, *The Underdogs* (1915), in Texas because of his criticism of revolutionary fervor. Peru's CÉSAR VALLEJO spent the last half of his life in European exile, during which some of his most important poetry was written, and where he fought and died in the Spanish Civil War. Cuba's REINALDO ARENAS, who spent part of his life in Castro's concentration camps for "sexual deviants," was able to complete his major novelistic cycle after seeking exile in New York. Peru's MARIO VARGAS LLOSA, Cuba's GUILLERMO CABRERA INFANTE, Chile's ARIEL DORFMAN, and Argentina's MANUEL PUIG are all principal novelists of contemporary Latin America who have lived, written, published, and, in the case of Puig, died in exile. And, finally, Paraguay's AUGUSTO ROA BASTOS, who has lived almost his entire adult life outside his native country, is a paradigm of the exiled contemporary Latin American writer. Exile in its many forms, therefore, must be recognized as one of the most salient characteristics of Latin American literature.

Indeed, the peculiar geographical and political circumstances of Spanish American writing produce a number of its notable features: the diversity of the Spanish language; the writers' international perspectives, which may or may not meld with cultural nationalism (especially noticeable in the case of Mexico); the emphasis on sociopolitical commitments; awareness of the historical dimensions of cultural production; and the recurring image of literature as a mediating force in human affairs. Mexico and Puerto Rico, however, are exceptions to this panorama. Mexico has experienced institutional continuity since the nation's reorganization following the 1910 revolution, and Puerto Rico is a part of the United States. Yet one notes the uneasy confluence of the Mexican and the Mexican American (e.g., MIGUEL MÉNDEZ-M.) and the stateside experience of some Puerto Ricans as, in fact, a wrenching exile (e.g., RENÉ MARQUÉS).

The chronological boundaries of Spanish American writing are no more absolute than its physical ones. One could insist that Spanish American literature begins with the national republics established as part of the independence movement (principally 1810–30) that separated Spanish America from Spain. Such a determination, however, is not without problems: Cuba did not achieve independence from Spain until 1898, and Puerto Rico stands little chance of achieving nationhood anytime soon, despite its euphemistic status as an Associated Free State. Unquestionably, though, an identifiable Puerto Rican literature exists, and to speak of a Cuban literature only after 1900 makes no intuitive sense at all.

Moreover, a significant cultural production in Spanish America dates from the landing of the conquistadores and the arrival of permanent colonists, due largely to the learnedness of the Spanish officers and priests and to the vigorous and cultured colonial courts. Lima, Mexico City, Bogotá, Asunción, Córdoba, San Juan, and La Habana were all centers of refined arts and letters well over a century before the English settlers to the north moved beyond hornbooks and divinity schools. While it is true that much of the cultural production of the sixteenth and seventeenth centuries is literally a "translation" of imperial baroque culture to the Americas, there is an early native production that significantly surpasses Spain's cultural activity. The Mexican nun JUANA INÉS DE LA CRUZ exemplifies this native genius and is in many ways a starting point for a resistant, autochthonous Spanish American culture.

Yet temporal points such as these can never entirely fix the origins of Spanish American literature or of a peculiarly American consciousness, for a telling reason—the permanence of pre-Columbian indigenous cultures. These cultures have deeply marked Spanish American literature in many ways: the distinctive American dialects of Spanish influenced by pre-Colombian languages; the mestizo cultures formed in vast areas of the continent; and writers' recurring imperative to assess the complex relationships among native cultures, the Hispanic conquest, and the resulting demographic constellations. Writers whose work prominently explores this complexity include Peru's JOSÉ MARÍA ARGUEDAS, Mexico's CARLOS FUENTES and JUAN RULFO, Chile's PABLO NERUDA, and Guatemala's MIGUEL ANGEL ASTURIAS.

Finally, there is the role played by immigrant culture, particularly the blacks in the Caribbean and the Italians and Jews in the River Platte. Black culture extends throughout most of Latin America, the result of the massive importation of African slaves for agriculture and mining. While Brazil's black cultural roots are legendary, virtually no area of Caribbean culture is untouched by profound and vigorous black contributions. The Cuban poet and activist NICOLÁS GUILLÉN is perhaps the most prominent representative of this dominant cultural component. Nonblack writers like ALEJO CARPENTIER, SEVERO SARDUY, and GUILLERMO CABRERA INFANTE have also dealt with black history in the Caribbean.

Peru's ISAAC GOLDEMBERG and Mexico's JOSÉ EMILIO PACHECO are only two of many Spanish American writers of Jewish origins, but it is in Buenos Aires that Italian and Jewish cultural strands are simply overwhelming. The unique urban culture produced by this Latin American melting pot is particularly present in an author like ROBERTO ARLT, and JORGE LUIS BORGES is famous for his interest in Jewish culture. Argentine writers as diverse as EDUARDO MALLEA, ADOLFO BIOY CASARES (in his collaborations with Borges and in his own fiction), and MANUEL PUIG have dealt with aspects of Buenos Aires's notably Italianate urban society. To the extent that the city's rich identity sprang from the massive immigration that began around 1880, one could suggest that a characteristic Argentine culture does not begin until a full 70 years or more after independence.

An additional dimension of Latin American literature directly flows from the foregoing: its definition is almost exclusively in urban terms, with only a nostalgic or archeological nod toward historically rural societies. Even Argentines who embrace the Gaucho motifs of JOSÉ HERNÁNDEZ's pseudo-epic have little more than a superficial knowledge of the social realities behind those motifs; most are second-generation immigrants, and authentic Gaucho society had disappeared long before their forebears arrived in Argentina. Mexico, too, may seem an exception that is not. Although rural motifs have been dominant in Mexican writing, that country now has one of the world's true megalopolises, and Mexico City threatens to draw all of the country into its urban vortex. For some writers, the rural versus the urban is paired with the subaltern versus the hegemonic, the authentic versus the imperial. Urban culture manifests its many complex faces in GUILLERMO CABRERA INFANTE, MARIO VARGAS LLOSA, MANUEL PUIG, JULIO CORTÁZAR, JOSÉ DONOSO, and ENRIQUE MEDINA, who both describe in detail the features of urban life and see in those features signs of larger social issues involving linguistics, class, and ethnicity.

Spanish American literature, like that of all colonized societies, only with difficulty gauges its international valuation: Is its identity enmeshed with subjugation? Often only those writers who have adapted cosmopolitan models seem to be prized; often only those who have something tropically exotic about them attract interest. Such judgments could be disheartening reinforcements of Latin America's historical repressions. What is heartening now is the quantity and variety of Spanish American literature available in translation. Readers may read widely, for many reasons, and for themselves.

HISTORY AND CRITICISM

Aldrich, Earl M., Jr. *Modern Short Story in Peru.* U. of Wis. Pr. 1966 $25.00. ISBN 0-299-03960-9. Chronological development and maturation of Peruvian short stories.

Anderson-Imbert, Enrique. *Spanish American Literature: A History.* 2 vols. Trans. by John V. Falconieri. Wayne St. U. Pr. 1969 $24.95. ISBN 0-685-05331-8. An extraordinarily complete study by an Argentine writer of "keen critical abilities" (*LJ*).

Brotherston, Gordon. *The Emergence of the Latin American Novel.* Cambridge U. Pr. 1979 $32.50. ISBN 0-521-21478-5. A general introduction, including Brazil, and chapters on Arguedas, Asturias, Carpentier, Cortázar, García Márquez, Onetti, Rulfo, and Vargas Llosa.

______. *Latin American Poetry.* Cambridge U. Pr. 1975 $39.50. ISBN 0-521-09944-7. An excellent historical introduction.

Brushwood, John S. *Genteel Barbarism: Experiments in Analysis of Nineteenth Century Spanish-American Novels.* U. of Nebr. Pr. 1981 $23.50. ISBN 0-8032-1165-1. An analysis of nineteenth-century fiction from Spanish America.

______. *Mexico in Its Novel: A Nation's Search for Identity. Texas Pan-Amer. Ser.* U. of Tex. Pr. 1966 $8.95. ISBN 0-292-70070-9. The best reference source for the field.

Burgess, Ronald D. *The New Dramatists of Mexico, 1967–85.* U. Pr. of Ky. 1991 $22.00. ISBN 0-8131-1727-5. A carefully documented historical study of the problems and issues facing the recent generation of dramatists in Mexico.

DeCosta, Miriam, ed. *Blacks in Hispanic Literature: Critical Essays.* Assoc. Fac. Pr. 1976 o.p. An informative overview of an important topic.

Donosa, José. *The Bloom in Spanish American Literature: A Personal History.* Trans. by Gregory Kolovakos. Col. U. Pr. 1977 o.p. A highly personal view of recent literature by one of its most original and idiosyncratic voices. Introduction by Ronald Christ.

Fernández Moreno, César, Julio Ortega, and Ivan A. Schulman, eds. *Latin America in Its Literature.* Trans. by Mary G. Berg. Holmes & Meier 1980 $54.50. ISBN 0-685-02332-X. A good background in social and literary history for recent developments in literature.

Foster, David William. *Alternate Voices in the Contemporary Latin American Narrative.* U. of Mo. Pr. 1985 $23.00. ISBN 0-8262-0481-3. Covers various forms of Latin American writing outside of principal categories in traditional Western literary histories.

______. *Currents in the Contemporary Argentine Novel: Arlt, Mallea, Sábato, and Cortázar.* U. of Mo. Pr. 1975 o.p. An outline history of the Argentine novel in first chapter. Includes a substantial bibliography.

______. *Gay and Lesbian Themes in Latin American Writing.* U. of Tex. Pr. 1991 $27.50. ISBN 0-292-77646-2. An examination of key texts in order to establish a tradition of Latin American writing on homoerotic issues.

______, comp. *A Dictionary of Contemporary Latin American Authors.* ASU Lat. Am. St. 1982 $9.55. ISBN 0-87918-051-X. Entries on significant Spanish- and French-language writers prepared by specialists in the national literatures.

______, ed. *Handbook of Latin American Literature.* Garland 1988 $60.00. ISBN 0-8240-8559-0. Authoritative essays on each of the national literatures, Hispanic literature in the United States, film, and paraliterature.

———. *Studies in the Contemporary Spanish-American Short Story.* U. of Mo. Pr. 1979 $18.00. ISBN 0-8262-0279-9. Structuralist analyses of stories by Benedetti, Borges, Cabrera Infante, Cortázar, García Márquez, and Rulfo in the vein of recent European criticism.

Foster, David William, and Virginia R. Foster, eds. *Modern Latin American Literature.* 2 vols. *Lib. of Literary Criticism Ser.* Continuum 1975 $120.00. ISBN 0-8044-3139-6. Selections from reviews and critical articles on works by twentieth-century Latin American authors, including Brazilian writers; an excellent reference book.

Franco, Jean. *Introduction to Spanish American Literature.* Cambridge U. Pr. 1969 o.p. A comprehensive, relatively difficult history of Spanish American literature beginning with colonial times.

———. *Plotting Women: Gender and Representation in Mexico.* Col. U. Pr. 1989 $31.50. ISBN 0-231-06422-5. An important contribution to third-world gender studies and to Mexican cultural history generally, focusing on prominent female intellectuals and writers from the colonial period to the present.

———. *Spanish American Literature since Independence.* B&N Imports 1973 o.p. Examines the most important literary currents in Latin America.

Freudenthal, Juan R., Jeffrey Katz, and Patricia M. Freudenthal. *Index to Anthologies of Latin American Literature in English Translation.* G. K. Hall 1977 o.p. In addition to indexing 116 anthologies, provides bibliographies for further reading in history, criticism, and essay.

Gallagher, D. P., and Nathan Milton. *Modern Latin American Literature.* OUP 1973 $3.95. ISBN 0-19-888071-5

González Echevarría, Roberto. *The Voice of the Masters: Writing and Authority in Modern Latin American Literature.* U. of Tex. Pr. 1985 $8.95. ISBN 0-292-78709-X. Examines major texts in terms of the relationship between language and authority and of competing ideologies of culture and writing.

Guibert, Rita, ed. *Seven Voices: Pablo Neruda, Jorge Luis Borges, Miguel Angel Asturias, Octavio Paz, Julio Cortázar, Gabriel García Márquez, Guillermo Cabrera Infante.* Knopf 1972 o.p. Interviews with Pablo Neruda, Jorge Luis Borges, Miguel Angel Asturias, Octavio Paz, Julio Cortázar, Gabriel García Márquez, and Guillermo Cabrera Infante; a very good reference source.

Handbook of Latin American Studies. 51 vols. U. Press Fla. Vols. 1–14, 22, 24, 27–40 1935–78 $35.00 ea. Hippocrene Bks. Vols. 15–21, 25–26 1949–60 o.p. U. of Tex. Pr. Vols. 41–51 1980–92 $65.00 ea. An annual comprehensive, critical bibliography, begun in 1935 by Harvard University Press. Now reorganized into two volumes—social sciences and humanities—published in alternate years. Thorough section on translations of literary works.

Harss, Luis, and Barbara Dohmann. *Into the Mainstream: Conversations with Latin American Writers.* HarpC 1967 o.p. Valuable reference source that discusses Carpentier, Asturias, Borges, Cortázar, Guimarães Rosa, Onetti, Rulfo, Fuentes, García Márquez, and Vargas Llosa.

Jackson, Richard L. *Black Writers in Latin America.* Bks. Demand repr. of 1979 ed. $59.50. ISBN 0-8357-7301-9. Examines self-awareness of black writers and their place in Latin American literature and society.

Kadir, Djelal. *Questing Fictions: Latin America's Family Romance.* U. of Minn. Pr. 1986 $39.95. ISBN 0-8166-1516-0. A study of the so-called family romance in fiction, in which sociohistorical issues are cast in terms of the typically dysfunctional family nucleus.

Langford, Walter M. *The Mexican Novel Comes of Age.* U. of Notre Dame Pr. 1971 $18.95. ISBN 0-8290-2401-8. A useful study of modern Mexican novelists.

Lindstrom, Naomi. *Jewish Issues in Argentine Literature: from Gerchunoff to Szichman.* U. of Mo. Pr. 1989 $24.00. ISBN 0-8262-0708-1. Begins with an historical essay on Jewish intellectuals in Argentina to 1976; analyzes novels and collections of poetry; concludes with Jewish Argentine writing 1976–88.

———. *Woman's Voice in Latin American Literature.* Three Continents 1990 $26.00. ISBN 0-89410-295-8. Essays on principal women writers examining strategies for expression of feminine consciousness.

Lyday, Leon F., and George W. Woodyard, eds. *Dramatists in Revolt.* U. of Tex. Pr. 1976 o.p. A collection of essays on key Latin American (including Brazilian) dramatists.

MacAdam, Alfred J. *Modern Latin American Narratives: The Dreams of Reason.* U. Ch. Pr. 1977 $15.00. ISBN 0-226-49993-6. Examines major texts in terms of thesis that contemporary Latin American writing is fundamentally satirical.

McMurray, George R. *Spanish American Writing Since 1941: A Critical Survey.* Continuum 1987 $24.50. ISBN 0-8044-2623-6. A solid survey of major movements, genres, and works. Inadequate representation of women authors but useful nevertheless.

Magnarelli, Sharon. *The Lost Rib: Female Characters in the Spanish-American Novel.* Bucknell U. Pr. 1985 $38.50. ISBN 0-8387-5074-5. Attempts to explain the almost total absence of memorable female protagonists in the Spanish-American novel through careful analysis of female characters in works spanning 100 years; all but one novel written by men.

Martin, Gerald. *Journeys through the Labyrinth: Latin American Fiction in the Twentieth Century.* Routledge Chapman & Hall 1989 $65.00. ISBN 0-86091-238-8. A useful survey of major categories of narrative forms, with a good representation of marginal phenomena.

Marting, Diane E., ed. *Spanish American Women Writers: A Bio-Bibliographical Source Book.* Greenwood 1990 $85.00. ISBN 0-313-25194-0. An encyclopedia of entries on over 50 major women writers with excellent characterizations of their works and bibliographical information.

Menton, Seymour. *Magic Realism Rediscovered, 1917–1981.* Art Alliance 1983 $35.00. ISBN 0-87982-038-1. The source of a much-used term often applied to Latin American fiction.

———. *Prose Fiction of the Cuban Revolution. Latin Amer. Monographs.* Bks. Demand repr. of 1975 ed. $94.70. ISBN 0-8357-7713-8. A record and classification of the more than 200 volumes of novels and short stories published in Cuba between 1959 and 1975.

Miller, Yvette, and Charles Tatum, eds. *Latin American Women Writers: Yesterday and Today.* Lat. Am. Lit. Rev. Pr. 1977 $12.50. ISBN 0-935480-56-0. A collection of papers on women.

Muñoz, Braulio. *Sons of the Wind: The Search for Identity in Spanish American Indian Literature.* Rutgers U. Pr. 1982 o.p. Presents issues of cultural unity in Spanish America and attempts to gauge the effects of a hegemony of mestizo culture.

Peden, Margaret S., ed. *The Latin American Short Story: A Critical History. Twayne's Critical History of the Modern Short Story Ser.* Macmillan 1983 $22.95. ISBN 0-8057-9351-8. A series of detailed studies on the short story.

Schwartz, Kessel. *A New History of Spanish American Fiction.* 2 vols. U. Pr. of Miami 1972 $18.95 ea. A superficial coverage of major authors and texts.

Schwartz, Ronald. *Nomads, Exiles, and Emigrés: The Rebirth of the Latin American Narrative, 1960–80.* Scarecrow 1980 $20.00. ISBN 0-8108-1389-9. General introduction with useful bibliographies.

Shaw, Bradley A. *Latin American Literature in English, 1975–1978.* Center for Inter-Amer. Relations 1979 o.p. Supplements in the following volume.

———. *Latin American Literature in English Translation*: An Annotated Bibliography. NYU Pr. 1976 $17.75. A good reference source.

Sommer, Doris. *Foundational Fictions: The National Romances of Latin America.* U. CA Pr. 1991 $45.00. ISBN 0-520-07110-7. Explicates the relationships, in important nineteenth-century fictional texts, among family romances, feminine images, and national consciousness and identity. A brilliant analysis.

Souza, Raymond D. *Major Cuban Novelists: Innovation and Tradition.* U. of Mo. Pr. 1976 o.p. Carpentier, Lezama Lima, and Cabrera Infante.

Stabb, Martin S. *In Quest of Identity.* U. of NC Pr. 1967 o.p. An excellent analysis of major essayists who use the form to define Latin American identity.

Stimson, Frederick S. *The New Schools of Spanish American Poetry.* Castalia Pub. 1970 o.p. A general survey dividing poets into "schools," with each division focusing on a key figure.

Terry, Edward D., ed. *Artists and Writers in the Evolution of Latin America.* U. of Ala. Pr. 1969 o.p. Critical essays on Miguel Angel Asturias, Euclydes da Cunha, social protest in the Spanish American novel, art and life in Mexico, José Mariátegui, and Chilean politics.

Tittler, Jonathan. *Narrative Irony in the Contemporary Spanish-American Novel.* Cornell Univ. Pr. 1984 $29.95. ISBN 0-8014-1574-8. Examines irony as the motivating principle of a range of current major fiction. Of note is the concept of "narrative irony" as a dimension of structurally complex and highly self-conscious texts.

Williams, Raymond L. *The Colombian Novel, 1844–1987.* U. of Tex. Pr. 1991 $32.50. ISBN 0-292-75542-2. A solid survey of the development of this significant national production.

Zea, Leopoldo. *The Latin American Mind.* Trans. by James H. Abbott and Lowell Dunham. U. of Okla. Pr. 1970 o.p. Traces the rise of positivism as the aftermath of romanticism; an important work by an eminent Mexican philosopher.

COLLECTIONS

Agosin, Marjorie, ed. *Landscapes of a New Land: Fiction by Latin American Women.* White Pine 1989 $19.00. ISBN 0-934834-88-1. Contemporary fiction.

______, ed. *Secret Weavers, Stories of the Fantastic by Women of Argentina and Chile.* White Pine 1991 $14.00. ISBN 1-877727-15-6. Collection of more than 40 stories by Latin American women that demonstrate that magic realism is a shared response to the region's landscape and history rather than the exclusive property of male writers like Borges and García Márquez.

Bierhorst, John, ed. and trans. *Black Rainbow: Legends of the Incas and Myths of Ancient Peru.* FS&G 1976 o.p. Ethnographically-based materials.

______, ed. and trans. *The Mythology of Mexico and Central America.* Morrow 1992 $9.95. ISBN 0-688-11280-3. Presents a well-documented look at the gods and heroes of Mexico and Central America and discusses the influences these myths have had on the modern cultural and political life of the region.

______, ed. and trans. *The Mythology of South America.* Morrow 1991 $9.00. ISBN 0-688-10739-7. Concentrates on the themes and motifs of the principal myths, the variants of them among the tribes, and on legends unique to individual tribes of South America.

Blackwell, Alice Stone, trans. *Some Spanish-American Poets.* Biblo 1968 repr. of 1937 ed. $24.00. ISBN 0-8196-0217-5. Selections by poets from 19 Spanish American countries.

Brotherston, Gordon. *Images of the New World: The American Continent Portrayed in Native Texts.* Thames Hudson 1982 o.p. Writing by authors of indigenous roots.

Caistor, Nick, ed. *The Faber Book of Contemporary Latin American Short Stories.* Faber & Faber 1991 $10.95. ISBN 0-571-15359-3

Colecchia, Francesca, and Julio Matas, trans. *Selected Latin American One-Act Plays. Pitt Latin-Amer. Ser.* U. of Pittsburgh Pr. 1974 $12.95. ISBN 0-8229-5241-6

Craig, George D., ed. *The Modernist Trend in Spanish American Poetry: A Collection of Representative Poems of the Modernist Movement.* Gordon Pr. 1977 $59.95. ISBN 0-8490-2273-8. Major texts of late nineteenth-century poetry.

Cranfill, Thomas M., ed. *The Muse in Mexico: A Mid-Century Miscellany.* U. of Tex. Pr. 1959 $12.50. ISBN 0-292-73310-0. Poetry, fiction, photographs, and drawings.

Erro-Peralta, Nora, and Caridad Silva-Núñez, eds. *Beyond the Border: A New Age in Latin American Women's Fiction.* Cleis Pr. 1991 $24.95. ISBN 0-939416-42-5. Includes works by Isabel Allende, Elena Poniatwoska, Luisa Valenzuela, and other writers from Cuba, the Dominican Republic, Brazil, Puerto Rico, Peru, Mexico, Argentina, Uruguay, Venezuela, and Costa Rica.

Flores, Angel, and Harriet Anderson. *Masterpieces of Latin American Literature.* 2 vols. Macmillan o.p. Excellent introduction to each author and bibliographies.

Franco, Jean, ed. *Spanish Short Stories.* Viking Penguin 1966 $6.95. ISBN 0-14-002500-6. The majority of these stories are by Spanish Americans, including Onetti, Martínez Moreno, Rulfo, and Benedetti.

Frank, Waldo, ed. *Tales from the Argentine.* Trans. by Anita Brenner. *Short Story Index Repr. Ser.* Gordon Pr. 1977 $59.95. ISBN 0-8490-2728-4. Stories by Ricardo Güiraldes, Lucio Vicente López, Leopoldo Lugones, Roberto J. Payró, Horacio Quiroga, and Domingo Faustino Sarmiento.

Fremantel, Anne, ed. *Latin-American Literature Today.* NAL-Dutton 1977 o.p. Includes a number of less well known authors.

Garfield, Evelyn Picon, ed. *Women's Fiction from Latin America: Selections from Twelve Contemporary Authors.* Wayne St. U. Pr. 1988 $39.95. ISBN 0-8143-1858-4. Short stories and fictional fragments.

Howes, Barbara, ed. *Eye of the Heart: Short Stories from Latin America.* Avon 1990 $10.95. ISBN 0-380-70942-2. An excellent selection of 42 short stories by Latin American authors; includes six Brazilian writers.

Jones, Willis Knapp. *Spanish-American Literature in Translation.* 2 vols. Continuum o.p. An extensive collection.

______, trans. *Men and Angels: Three South American Comedies.* S. Ill. U. Pr. 1970 o.p. Contains J. F. C. Barthes and C. S. Damel, *The Quack Doctor*; J. M. Rivarola Matto, *The Fate of Chipí González*; M. Frank, *The Man of the Century.* Three samples of commercial theater.

Kalechofsky, Roberta, ed. *Echad: An Anthology of Latin American Jewish Writings.* Micah Pubns. 1984 $11.95. ISBN 0-916288-06-4. Poems, a play, fiction, and essays by 24 writers from 12 countries.

Lewald, H. Ernest, ed. *The Web: Stories by Argentine Women.* Three Continents 1983 $26.00. ISBN 0-89410-085-8. Contemporary stories.

Leyland, Winston, ed. *My Deep Dark Pain Is Love: A Collection of Latin American Gay Fiction.* Gay Sunshine 1983 $20.00. ISBN 0-91734-202-X. Gay works by men.

______, ed. *Now the Volcano: An Anthology of Latin American Gay Literature.* Gay Sunshine 1983 $25.00. ISBN 0-917342-02-X. Fiction and poetry by men, with emphasis on Brazil.

Luby, Barry J., and Wayne H. Finke, eds. *Anthology of Contemporary Latin American Literature, 1960–1984.* Farleigh Dickinson 1986 $45.00. ISBN 0-8386-3255-6. Unusual gathering of prose and poetry pieces by established literary figures.

Luzuriaga, Gerado, and Robert S. Rudder, eds. and trans. *Modern One-Act Plays from Latin America.* UCLA Lat. Am. Ctr. 1974 o.p. Modern one-act plays.

Mancini, Pat M., ed. *Contemporary Latin American Short Stories.* Fawcett 1979 $1.95. ISBN 0-449-30844-8. Miscellany of contemporary short stories.

Manguel, Alberto, ed. *Other Fires: Short Fiction by Latin American Women.* Crown 1985 $9.95. ISBN 0-517-55870-X. Remarkable collection representing cultures and countries that evolved separately.

Marzán, Julio, ed. *Inventing a Word: An Anthology of Twentieth Century Puerto Rican Poetry.* Col. U. Pr. 1980 $39.00. ISBN 0-231-05010-0. A good introduction to the complicated thrust of Puerto Rican poetry today.

Meyer, Doris, and Margarite Fernández Olmos, eds. *Introductory Essays. Contemporary Woman Authors of Latin America Ser.* Vol. 1 Brooklyn Coll. Pr. 1984 $9.50. ISBN 0-930888-20-0. A valuable introduction to a flourishing area of Latin American literature.

______. *New Translations. Contemporary Woman Authors of Latin America Ser.* Vol. 2 Brooklyn Coll. Pr. 1984 $12.50. ISBN 0-930888-21-9. A collection of writing by Latin American women.

Oliver, William I., ed. and trans. *Voices of Change in the Spanish American Theater: An Anthology.* U. of Tex. Pr. 1971 $20.00. ISBN 0-292-70123-3. Contains E. Carballido, *Loose on the Lions*; G. Gambaro, *The Camp*; C. Maggi, *The Library*; E. Buenaventura, *On the Right Hand of God the Father*; L. J. Hernández, *The Mullato's Orgy*; S.

Vodanovic, *Viña and Three Beach Plays*, all of which represent the changing culture of Spanish America.

Partnoy, Alicia, ed. *You Can't Drown the Fire: Latin American Women Writing in Exile*. Cleis Pr. 1988 $24.95. ISBN 0-939416-16-6. Essays, fiction, poetry, and correspondence by women from eight politically oppressive Latin American countries.

Paschke, Barbara, and David Volpendesta, eds. *Clamor of Innocence: Central American Short Stories*. City Lights 1988 $9.95. ISBN 0-87286-227-5. Contemporary stories.

Paz, Octavio, ed. *An Anthology of Mexican Poetry*. Trans. by Samuel Beckett. Riverrun NY 1991 $13.95. ISBN 0-7145-0086-0. Paz chose the poems and wrote a historical introduction for this important collection.

Rodríguez Monegal, Emir, ed. *The Borzoi Anthology of Latin American Literature*. 2 vols. Knopf 1977 $19.95 ea. ISBNs 0-394-73301-0, 0-394-73366-5. Especially important for the more recent period and for its coverage of Brazil.

Santos, Rosario, ed. *And We Sold the Rain: Contemporary Fiction from Central America*. FWEW 1988 $18.95. ISBN 0-941423-16-6. Short stories from Costa Rica, Guatemala, El Salvador, Panama, Honduras, and Nicaragua that powerfully evoke life in these countries.

Tipton, David, ed. *Peru: The New Poetry*. Red Dust 1977 $10.95. ISBN 0-87376-024-7. Peruvian poetry by authors born between 1922 and 1947.

White, Steven F., ed. and trans. *Poets of Nicaragua: A Bilingual Anthology, 1918–1979*. Unicorn Pr. 1982 $29.95. ISBN 0-87775-132-3. Thirteen poets.

Wieser, Nora J., ed. and trans. *Open to the Sun: A Bilingual Anthology of Latin American Women Poets*. Perivale Pr. 1980 o.p. Includes some newer poets in addition to the famous figures from the early part of the twentieth century.

CHRONOLOGY OF AUTHORS

Cruz, Sor Júana Inés de la. 1648–1695
Sarmiento, Domingo Faustino. 1811–1888
Hernández, José. 1834–1866
Martí, José. 1853–1895
Darío, Rubén. 1867–1916
Azuela, Mariano. 1873–1952
Quiroga, Horacio. 1878–1937
Rivera, José Eustasio. 1888–1928
Mistral, Gabriela. 1889–1957
Vallejo, César. 1892–1938
Huidobro, Vicente. 1893–1948
Asturias, Miguel Angel. 1899–1974
Borges, Jorge Luis. 1899–1986
Arlt, Roberto. 1900–1942
Gorostiza, José. 1901–1973
Guillén, Nicolas. 1902–1989
Mallea, Eduardo. 1903–1983
Carpentier, Alejo. 1904–1980
Neruda, Pablo. 1904–1973
Yáñez, Agustin. 1904–1980
Onetti, Juan Carlos. 1909–
Arguedas, José María. 1911–1969
Sábato, Ernesto. 1911–
Bioy Casares, Adolfo. 1914–
Cortázar, Julio. 1914–1984
Parra, Nicanor. 1914–
Paz, Octavio. 1914–
Roa Bastos, Augusto. 1917–
Arreola, Juan José. 1918–
Rulfo, Juan. 1918–1986
Marqués, René. 1919–1979
Garro, Elena. 1920–
Carballido, Emilio. 1925–
Cardenal, Ernesto. 1925–
Castellanos, Rosario. 1925–1974
Donoso, José. 1925–
Wolff, Egon. 1926–
García Márquez, Gabriel. 1928–
Cabrera Infante, Guillermo. 1929–
Fuentes, Carlos. 1929–
Lihn, Enrique. 1929–
Méndez-M., Miguel. 1930–
Padilla, Heberto. 1932–
Puig, Manuel. 1932–1991
Sánchez, Luis Rafael. 1932–
Dalton, Roque. 1935–1975
Pizarnik, Alejandra. 1936–1972
Vargas Llosa, Mario. 1936–
Medina, Enrique. 1937–
Sarduy, Severo. 1937–
Valenzuela, Luisa. 1938–
Pacheco, José Emilio. 1939–
Aridjis, Homero. 1940–
Skármeta, Antonio. 1940–

Allende, Isabel. 1942–
Arenas, Reinaldo. 1943–1990
Dorfman, Ariel. 1943–
Goldemberg, Isaac. 1945–
Zapata, Luis. 1951–

ALLENDE, ISABEL. 1942– Chile

As second cousin of fallen Chilean president Salvador Allende, Isabel Allende attracted immediate interest when she appeared on the U.S. literary scene in the mid-1980s. On its own merits, though, *The House of the Spirits* (1982; English translation 1985) is a superb novel. Four generations of Chilean women—female descendants of an oligarchic family—provide a unifying thread and feminine consciousness for a fictional history of a Latin American society. Often compared to Colombia's GABRIEL GARCÍA MÁRQUEZ, whose *One Hundred Years of Solitude* is something of a Marxist fictional history of Latin America, Allende skillfully constructs a novel in which one generation of women pass on to the next a legacy of survival strategies and profound human understanding within oppressive social structures. Allende's combination of the personal and the political in the person of the youngest women unmistakably evokes Allende's socialist government, the subsequent military overthrow and neofascist dictatorship, and resistance to tyranny. The names of all four women are synonyms of the Spanish word for clarity and thus figure the clairvoyance, with its accompanying problems and triumphs, that keeps the narrative going for over 400 pages.

Allende's fiction after *The House of the Spirits*, both novels and short stories, is weaker but remains commercially successful in English translation. Some of its elements reinforce U.S. myths about Latin America, especially the questionable concept of a subaltern feminist solidarity. This matriarchy, captured in the person of Eva Luna, who gives her name to one novel and a collection of short stories, threatens to usurp the legendary patriarchy. Nevertheless, along with Argentina's LUISA VALENZUELA, Allende remains the most prominent Latin American woman writer on the U.S. literary scene, and the critical response to her writing has indeed been impressive. Allende, who lives a good part of the time in the United States, is much in demand for cultural forums and academic programs.

NOVELS BY ALLENDE

Eva Luna. Trans. by Margaret Sayers. Knopf 1988 $18.95. ISBN 0-394-57273-4. An orphan girl and a young man driven from Germany by his family meet and fall in love during their efforts to support a guerrilla movement fighting against a regime of dictators.

The House of Spirits. Trans. by Magda Bogin. Knopf 1985 $24.50. ISBN 0-394-53907-9

Of Love and Shadows. Trans. by Margaret S. Peden. Bantam 1988 $5.95. ISBN 0-553-27360-4. A soap-opera novel concerning love and resistance to the Pinochet dictatorship.

SHORT STORY COLLECTION BY ALLENDE

The Stories of Eva Luna. Trans. by Margaret Sayers Peden. Macmillan 1991 $18.95. ISBN 0-689-12102-4. Eponymous heroine of *Eva Luna* returns as the narrator of 23 tales.

BOOK ABOUT ALLENDE

Hart, Patricia. *Narrative Magic in the Fiction of Isabel Allende*. Farleigh Dickinson 1989 $34.50. ISBN 0-8386-3351-X

ARENAS, REINALDO. 1943–1990 Cuba

The novel *The Ill-fated Peregrinations of Fray Servando* recreates in a poetic style, in which time, space, and character move on multiple planes of fantasy and reality, the life of Fray Servando Teresa de Mier, a Mexican priest famous for his hatred of the Spaniards. Mier denied even that the Spaniards had brought Christianity to the New World. Arenas begins with a letter to the friar: "Ever since I discovered you in an execrable history of Spanish literature, described as the friar who had traveled over the whole of Europe on foot having improbable adventures; I have tried to find out more about you." In a meditation on the nature of fiction, Arenas discovers that he and Servando are the same person, and author and character become one.

Novels by Arenas

The Doorman. Trans. by Dolores M. Koch. Grove Pr. 1991 $16.95. ISBN 0-8021-1109-2. A Cuban refugee as a doorman in a luxury apartment building in Manhattan.

Farewell to the Sea. Trans. by Andrew Hurley. Viking Penguin 1987 $7.95. ISBN 0-14-006636-5. Focuses on cultural repression in Castro's Cuba.

Graveyard of the Angels. Trans. by Alfred A. MacAdam. Avon 1987 $3.95. ISBN 0-380-75075-9. Story of a mulatto woman and her white lover in Old Havana.

The Ill-Fated Peregrinations of Fray Servando. Trans. by Andrew Hurley. Avon 1987 $7.95. ISBN 0-380-75074-0

Old Rosa: A Novel in Two Stories. Trans. by Ann T. Slater and Andrew Hurley. Grove Pr. 1989 $16.95. ISBN 0-8021-1092-4. An autobiographical novel of personal and sexual identity.

The Palace of the White Skunks. Trans. by Andrew Hurley. Viking Penguin 1991 o.p. Centers on the pre-Castro bourgeoisie.

Singing from the Well. Trans. by Andrew Hurley. Viking Penguin 1988 $7.95. ISBN 0-14-009444-X. Uses childhood to dramatize repressive Cuban society.

ARGUEDAS, JOSÉ MARIÁ. 1911–1969 Peru

Arguedas was an ethnologist and teacher and the product of a rural Peruvian world in which Indian and white were inextricably mingled yet lived separately, with disastrous psychological results for both. In his prose he created a fusion of the two worlds, which is at the same time a disguised symbolic autobiography, using language that combined elements of Spanish and Quechua syntax in an effort to express this complex reality. He was the son of a rural judge and lawyer. The problems created by a disrupted and difficult childhood were exacerbated by the cultural tensions of his society, and he finally committed suicide.

Novels by Arguedas

Deep Rivers. 1958. Trans. by Frances H. Barraclough. U. of Tex. Pr. 1978 $10.95. ISBN 0-292-71533-1. About conflict between indigenous and Hispanic-Catholic culture.

Yawar Fiesta. 1941. Trans. by Frances H. Barraclough. U. of Tex. Pr. 1985 $22.50. ISBN 0-292-71601-3. Portrays the social relations between the various classes and races in the Peruvian highland town of Puquio in the 1930s.

ARIDJIS, HOMERO. 1940– Mexico

Like most Latin American writers, Aridjis has had to resort to journalism for financial support while creating a body of poetry that becomes more impressive with each volume. His is basically a poetry of the search for love and the love relationship, and through this relationship, of the search for value and meaning. Love and poetry thus become almost interchangeable, since poetry is also a unique source of knowledge. *Exaltation of Light* extends this approach to other areas of human experience, and to the everpresent Aztec past, so that the Mexican experience becomes a metaphor for humankind's pursuit of life. Aridjis enjoys current prominence as an important environmental spokesperson in Mexico City, a city of enormous ecological problems.

POETRY BY ARIDJIS

Exaltation of Light. Trans. by Eliot Weinberger. BOA Edns. 1981 $20.00. ISBN 0-918526-29-9

ARLT, ROBERTO. 1900–1942 Argentina

Arlt is acknowledged as a seminal figure in the development of the theater and novel in Argentina; in his treatment of madness and the uncertainties of external reality; and in his use of shifting point of view and internal monologue. The seven madmen in the book of that title organize a secret society to be financed by a chain of brothels, with the purpose of changing society. At the same time, each of them pursues his own special fixation. Against this background, the protagonist pursues his own existential search for meaning. Arlt's work is a perceptive comment both on the role of the individual in modern society and society's destructive effects on that individual. Arlt is one of Argentina's first major urban writers, with a special focus on the immigrant petite bourgeoisie.

NOVEL BY ARLT

The Seven Madmen. Trans. by Naomi Lindstrom. Godine 1984 o.p.

ARREOLA, JUAN JOSÉ. 1918– Mexico

Confabulario and Other Inventions is a collection of Arreola's short stories, satiric sketches, and fables published from 1941 to 1961 in several separate volumes. One section comprises his *Bestiary*, 26 fables and allegories, each developing the human qualities and foibles of a particular beast. Arreola is an extraordinarily versatile author, and his tales range from sheer fantasy, through ironic social criticism, to occasional, although rare, realism. *The Fair* is a collage of dialogic voices providing a vision of a town. No subject escapes Arreola's pointedly satiric pen in his witty, compact, phantasmagorical stories.

SHORT STORY COLLECTIONS BY ARREOLA

Confabulario and Other Inventions, 1941–1961. Trans. by George D. Shade. U. of Tex. Pr. 1974 repr. of 1964 ed. $14.95. ISBN 0-29273-196-5

The Fair. Trans. by John Upton. U. of Tex. Pr. 1977 $12.95. ISBN 0-292-73417-9

ASTURIAS, MIGUEL ANGEL. 1899–1974 (NOBEL PRIZE 1967) Guatemala

Novelist, playwright, poet, translator, and diplomat, Asturias won the Nobel Prize "for his highly colored writing rooted in national individuality and Indian tradition." His first novel, *El Señor Presidente*, a fictional account of the sordid, terror-ridden period of violence and human degradation under the Guatemalan dictator Estrada Cabrera, was completed in 1932 but not published until 1946 for political reasons. It was pioneering in its use of surrealistic structures and Indian myth as integrated parts of the novel's structure. *Mulata* (1963) uses a Guatemalan version of the legend of Faust as a point of departure for Asturias's inventive use of Indian myth.

Asturias, who during his first stay in Paris associated with the surrealists André Bretón and Paul Eluard, described his process of writing as "automatic." He stated that "What I obtain from automatic writing is the mating or juxtaposition of words which, as the Indians say, have never met before." In 1966, Asturias received the Lenin Peace Prize for writings that "expose American intervention against the Guatemalan people."

Following the 1954 uprising, Asturias was deprived of his citizenship by the new government and lived in exile for eight years. In 1967, on the election of President Julio César Méndez Montenegro, he was restored to his country's diplomatic services as ambassador to Paris and continued to publish. "My work," he said, "will continue to reflect the voice of the peoples, gathering their myths and popular beliefs and at the same time seeking to give birth to a universal consciousness of Latin American problems."

Novels by Asturias.

El Señor Presidente. 1946. Trans. by Frances Partridge. Macmillan 1975 $9.95. ISBN 0-689-70521-2

Mulata. 1963. Avon 1982 o.p.

Men of Maize. Trans. by Gerald Martin. Routledge Chapman & Hall 1988 $19.95. ISBN 0-86091-190-X. Explores corn-god myths.

Nonfiction by Asturias

Guatemalan Sociology. Trans. by Maureen Ahern. ASU Lat. Am. St. 1977 $7.95. ISBN 0-87918-037-4. A sociological treatise on the destruction of Indian culture.

AZUELA, MARIANO. 1873–1952 Mexico

After receiving his degree in medicine, Azuela returned to poor districts to practice, a manifestation of his lifelong concern for the *pueblo* of Mexico. During the Mexican Revolution, Azuela joined the forces of Francisco Villa, becoming director of public education in Jalisco under the Villa government. When that government fell, he served as doctor to Villa's men during their retreat northward. From these experiences came his novel *The Underdogs*, which he published in installments in a newspaper after fleeing to Texas in 1915. That novel, which has been called an "epic poem in prose of the Mexican Revolution" (Torres-Rioseco), deals with the revolution from the point of view of the humble soldiers, examining the circumstances that keep them in poverty, the brutality of the fighting, and the opportunism and betrayal of the revolution. An admirer of Émile Zola, Azuela stressed the effect of environment on character in many of his novels.

Novels by Azuela

Two Novels of Mexico: The Flies and The Bosses. Trans. by Lesley B. Simpson. U. CA Pr. 1956 $9.95. ISBN 0-520-00053-6. Satirical sketches of the Mexican Revolution.

The Underdogs. Trans. by E. Munguía, Jr. Buccaneer Bks. $17.95. ISBN 0-89966-515-2

Books about Azuela

Leal, Luis. *Mariano Azuela*. *Twayne's World Authors Ser.* G. K. Hall 1971 o.p. Comprehensive analysis of Azuela's work.

Robe, Stanley L. *Azuela and the Mexican Underdogs*. U. CA Pr. 1979 $45.00. ISBN 0-520-03293-4. An examination of Azuela's experiences and how they shaped his writing.

BIOY CASARES, ADOLFO. 1914– Argentina

Bioy Casares has collaborated with JORGE LUIS BORGES on a number of works, including their *Anthology of Fantastic Literature* (1940), a documentation of the development of Spanish American suprarealism, and *Six Problems for Don Isidro Parodi* (1981), a playful and inventive variation on the theme of the detective who cannot visit the scene of the crime; in this case, he is imprisoned. Bioy Casares's numerous works are characterized by intelligence and a sense of playful fantasy. *The Invention of Morel* (1953), about which Borges stated in his prologue that Bioy Casares has disproven Ortega's theory that no new subject matter exists for the novel, concerns a scientist's illusions about immortality. *Asleep in the Sun* is in the form of a letter from a mental hospital; its tale is so bizarre that ultimately the recipient (and the reader) are left to wonder if, in fact, the puzzle has any solution or whether it is not, like much of Bioy Casares's and Borges's work, an inside joke between author and reader.

NOVELS BY BIOY CASARES

Asleep in the Sun. Trans. by Suzanne Jill Levine. Persea Bks. 1978 $8.95. ISBN 0-89255-030-9

The Diary of the War of the Pig. Trans. by Donald Yates and Gregory Woodruff. NAL-Dutton 1988 o.p. A tale of fanatical social repression; centers on gerontophobia.

A Plan for Escape. 1945. Trans. by Suzanne Jill Levine. Graywolf 1988 $7.50. ISBN 1-55597-107-5. First paperback edition of Bioy Casares' blackly comic novel.

SHORT STORY COLLECTIONS BY BIOY CASARES

Chronicles of Bustos Domecq. (coauthored with Jorge Luis Borges). Trans. by Norman T. Di Giovanni. NAL-Dutton 1979 o.p. A series of parodies of detective fiction.

The Invention of Morel and Other Stories. 1953. Trans. by Ruth L. Simms. U. of Tex. Pr. 1985 $9.95. ISBN 0-292-73840-4

Six Problems for Don Isidro Parodi. (coauthored with Jorge Luis Borges). 1981. Trans. by Norman T. Di Giovanni. NAL-Dutton 1983 o.p.

BORGES, JORGE LUIS. 1899–1986 Argentina

Born in Buenos Aires, Borges was educated by an English governess and studied in Europe. He returned to Buenos Aires in 1921, where he helped to found several avant-garde literary periodicals. In 1955, after the fall of Juan Perón, whom he vigorously opposed, he was appointed director of the Argentine National Library. With SAMUEL BECKETT he won the $10,000 International Publishers Prize in 1961, thus establishing himself as one of the most prominent writers in the world. He regularly taught and lectured throughout the United States and Europe. His ideas have been a profound influence on writers throughout the Western world and on the most recent developments in literary and critical theory.

Borges was a writer of massive international culture, and his work reflects this, as well as his sense of literature—and life—as a combination of game and puzzle. He regarded all of people's endeavors to understand an incomprehensible world as fiction; hence, his fiction is metaphysical and based on an "esthetics of the intellect," in his words. Some critics have called him a mystic of the intellect. A prolific writer of essays, short stories—they are sometimes difficult to distinguish—and poetry, Borges's concerns are perhaps clearest in his stories, which Jean Franco described as follows: "Each of his story collections to which he gave the name *'ficciones'*—*Ficciones* (1944), *El Aleph* (1949), *"Dreamtigers"* (1960)—is a masterpiece, whose deceptively limpid surface constantly knots the reader into problems. Saturated with literary references, often as near to essay as the conventional idea of short story, the *'ficciones'* nevertheless challenge print culture at a very deep level and perhaps even suggest its impossibility." A central image in Borges's work is the labyrinth, a mental and poetic construct, "a universe in miniature," which human beings build and therefore believe they control but which nevertheless traps them. In spite of Borges's belief that people cannot understand the chaotic world, in his writing he continually attempted to do so, and much of his work deals with people's efforts to find the center of the labyrinth, symbolic of achieving understanding of their place in a mysterious universe. In such later works as *The Gold of the Tigers* he wrote of his lifelong descent into blindness and what this had done to his perceptions of the world around him and himself as a writer. He died in Geneva in 1986.

Nonfiction by Borges

An Introduction to American Literature. Trans. by L. Clark Keatine and others. Bks. Demand repr. of 1971 ed. $27.90. ISBN 0-685-20786-2. An introduction to American Literature—Borges's personal preferences.

Other Inquisitions, 1937–1952. Trans. by Ruth L. Simms. U. of Tex. Pr. 1964 $12.95. ISBN 0-292-76002-7. Essays on intellectual, philosophical, and literary themes.

Seven Nights. Trans. by Eliot Weinberger. New Dir. Pr. 1984 $14.00. ISBN 0-8112-0904-0. A series of lectures on major literary figures.

Short Story Collections by Borges

The Book of Fantasy. (coauthored with Adolf Bioy Casares and Silvina Bullrich). Carroll & Graf 1990 $10.95. ISBN 0-88184-656-2

Chronicles of Bustos Domecq. (coauthored with Adolfo Bioy Casares). Trans. by Norman Thomas di Giovanni. NAL-Dutton 1979 o.p. A series of parodies of detective fiction.

Ficciones. Trans. by Anthony Kerrigan. Grove Pr. 1987 $6.95. ISBN 0-8021-3030-5

Poetry by Borges

In Praise of Darkness. Trans. by Norman Thomas di Giovanni. NAL-Dutton 1974 $5.95. ISBN 0-525-03635-0. Poems highlighting motif of blindness.

Works by Borges

The Aleph and Other Stories, 1933–1969. Trans. by Norman Thomas di Giovanni in collaboration with the author. NAL-Dutton 1979 $8.95. ISBN 0-52547-539-7. Parodic fiction, plus important autobiographic essays.

The Book of Sand. Trans. by Norman Thomas di Giovanni. Transaction Pubs. repr. of 1979 ed. $22.95. ISBN 0-85290-022-9

Dreamtigers. Trans. by Mildred Boyer and Harold Morland. U. of Tex. Pr. 1984 $14.95. ISBN 0-292-73217-1. "A collection of miscellaneous poems, stories, anecdotes, essays, vignettes, all [of] which add up to [a] psychic portrait of the author" (*LJ*).

Evaristo Carriego: A Book about Old-time Buenos Aires. Trans. by Norman Thomas di Giovanni and Susan Ashe. NAL-Dutton 1984 $8.95. ISBN 0-525-48085-4

Labyrinths: Selected Short Stories and Other Writings. Ed. by Donald A. Yates and James E. Irby. New Dir. Pr. 1969 $9.95. ISBN 0-8112-0012-4. Contains 22 "fictions," 120 essays, and 8 parables. Essays include "The Argentine Writer and Tradition," "The Fearful Sphere of Pascal," and "Kafka and His Precursors." The parables concern classic literary works and various philosophical problems.

A Personal Anthology. Trans. by Anthony Kerrigan, Alastair Reid, and others. Grove Pr. 1967 $8.95. ISBN 0-8021-3077-1. "Composed of twenty-eight prose pieces (stories, essays, parables) and twenty poems, . . . translated admirably into English" (*SR*). "Both a delight for Borges fans and an introduction for Borges tyros . . . splendidly displays [Borges's] various facets" (*New Yorker*).

BOOKS ABOUT BORGES

Aizenberg, Edna. *The Aleph Weaver: Biblical, Kabbalistic and Judaic Elements in Borges.* Scripta 1984 $25.00. ISBN 0-916379-12-4. Traces the response that Borges has had to Judaism and to the body of cultural documents it has produced.

Alazraki, Jaime. *Borges and the Kabbalah and Other Essays on His Fiction and Poetry.* Cambridge U. Pr. 1988 $44.95. ISBN 0-521-30684-1. Critical essays that fill in some of the glaring gaps in research on Borges.

———, ed. *Critical Essays on Jorge Luis Borges.* G. K. Hall 1987 $40.00. ISBN 0-8161-8829-7. A sampling of the best criticism on Borges written in English from a U.S. perspective.

Balderston, Daniel. *The Literary Universe of Jorge Luis Borges: An Index to References and Allusions to Persons, Title, and Places in His Writings.* Greenwood 1986 $49.95. ISBN 0-313-25083-9. Comprehensive labor of literary love that provides the location in Borges's works of allusions to people, titles, and places.

Bell-Villada, Gene H. *Borges and His Fiction: A Guide to His Mind and Art.* U. of NC Pr. 1981 $29.95. ISBN 0-8078-1458-X. Discusses Borges's influence on and contribution to Hispanic and Western literature.

Cheselka, Paul. *The Poetry and Poetics of Jorge Luis Borges.* P. Lang Pubs. 1988 $36.95. ISBN 0-8204-0318-0. Discusses Borges's poetic theory and thematic content, with considerable attention devoted to the poet's obsession with revising individual texts and altering the makeup of the various collections.

Cortínez, Carlos, ed. *Borges the Poet.* U. of Ark. Pr. 1986 $15.00. ISBN 0-938626-48-5. Collection of papers on many aspects of Borges's poetry: themes, motifs, imagery, language, as well as its influence and poetics.

Di Giovanni, Norman Thomas. *Borges on Writing.* NAL-Dutton 1973 o.p. Insightful analysis on the influence of Borges's literary prose.

Friedman, Mary Lusky. *The Emperor's Kites: A Morphology of Borges' Tales.* Duke 1987 $22.50. ISBN 0-8223-0712-X. Discusses Borges's fiction and its dependence on a single paradigm.

Kushigian, Julia Alexis. *Orientalism in the Hispanic Literary Tradition: In Dialogue with Borges, Paz, and Sarduy.* U. of NM Pr. 1991 $29.95. ISBN 0-8263-1314-0. Documents Oriental influences and the intermingling of East and West in Borges's poetry.

Merrell, Floyd. *Unthinking Thinking: Jorge Luis Borges, Mathematics, and the New Physics.* Purdue U. Pr. 1991 $29.50. ISBN 1-55753-011-4. Reveals how early twentieth-century and contemporary mathematics and physics participated in Borges's narrative design.

Rodríguez-Luis, Julio. *The Contemporary Praxis of the Fantastic: Borges and Cortázar.* Garland 1991 $19.00. ISBN 0-8153-0101-4. Explores the ways in which many tales by Jorge Luis Borges and Julio Cortázar can be said to be fantastic, eventually arriving at a sensible definition that can be applied to postmodern Spanish American texts.

Rodríguez Monegal, Emir. *Jorge Luis Borges: A Literary Biography.* Paragon Hse. 1987 $10.95. ISBN 0-913729-98-1. Biography of both the author's personal and private lives.

Sorrentino, Fernando. *Seven Conversations with Jorge Luis Borges.* Whitston Pub. 1981 $18.50. ISBN 0-87875-214-5. Provides an insightful look at Borges.

Stabb, Martin S. *Borges Revisited.* Macmillan 1991 $24.95. ISBN 0-8057-8263-X. A general overview of Borges's literary production.

CABRERA INFANTE, GUILLERMO. 1929– Cuba

Three Trapped Tigers, winner of the Barcelona Seix Barral Prize in 1964, takes Havana nightlife before the revolution as a symbol of the decadence of the Batista regime. The protagonists are singers, musicians, aristocrats, and intellectuals who live off an American-supported and -dominated entertainment world. The triumph of the novel is in its language, a combination of "Spanglish" and the daily idiom of the Cuban subworld. In his puns and wordplay (the title in Spanish is a tongue twister), Cabrera Infante demonstrates the debt to his acknowledged masters: LEWIS CARROLL (see Vol. 1), NABOKOV, and JOYCE (see Vol. 1). At the same time, however, he attempts to free Cuban language and literature from constricting foreign influence. *Infante's Inferno* (1984), again a punning title—the original is *La Habana para un infante difunto*, still another pun—is a parody of novels about the writing of novels; at the same time, it is a lament for the author's lost Havana and a search for identity in a world where all anchors have been torn loose. In 1965, Cabrera Infante defected from Cuba to England, where he now resides.

NOVELS BY CABRERA INFANTE

Infante's Inferno. Trans. by Suzanne Jill Levine and Guillermo Cabrera Infante. Avon 1985 $4.95. ISBN 0-380-69965-6

View of Dawn in the Tropics. Trans. by Suzanne Jill Levine. HarpC 1978 o.p. A series of vignettes constituting an alternate version of Cuban history.

CARBALLIDO, EMILIO. 1925– Mexico

Carballido is known primarily as a playwright and one of the leaders of a movement that revitalized Mexican theater during the 1950s and 1960s. Previously, Mexican theater had been derivative of European models. Carballido is responsible for breaking from the traditional realistic drama and introducing a surrealistic, fantastic world (one to which the Mexican novel had already turned) into the theater. At the same time, Carballido probes the nature of reality and of human responsibility. The play *Theseus*, included in the volume *The Golden Thread* (1957), is a twentieth-century version of the Greek myth, in which Theseus takes full responsibility for his actions, willfully neglecting to put up the white sail of victory on his return from killing the minotaur so that his father will hurl himself from the Parthenon and he will become king. *The Clockmaker from Cordoba* is a wryly comic vision of the fallibility of justice and the weakness of humankind. Like all Carballido's work, ultimately it expresses an abiding faith in a weak but essentially striving humanity.

PLAYS BY CARBALLIDO

The Golden Thread and Other Plays. 1957. Trans. by Margaret S. Peden. *Texas Pan-Amer. Ser.* U. of Tex. Pr. 1970 $11.95. ISBN 0-292-70039-3

NOVEL BY CARBALLIDO

The Norther. 1958. Trans. by Margaret S. Peden. Bks. Demand repr. of 1968 ed. $26.30. ISBN 0-8357-7753-7. A novel about human relationships.

BOOK ABOUT CARBALLIDO

Peden, Margaret S. *Emilio Carballido*. *Twayne's World Authors Ser.* G. K. Hall 1980 o.p. Presents a general overview of Carballido's literary production.

CARDENAL, ERNESTO. 1925– Nicaragua

An ordained priest who lives in Solentiname, a community that he founded, and a member of the Nicaraguan cabinet, Cardenal is Latin America's best known exponent of what might be called the literature of the theology of liberation. His poetry is the expression of tension between his faith and a strongly rooted sense of reality and the need for drastic change. Influenced heavily by THOMAS MERTON (see Vol. 4), by his residence in the Trappist community of Gethsemane, Kentucky, by English and American poetry, Christianity, and the fact of social injustice, Cardenal consciously writes antirhetorical and often didactic poetry. Frequently, he uses other sources: newspapers, Native American texts, and so on, just as the masses at Solentiname use nontraditional sources as subjects for discussion. *Zero Hour* (1980) details the existence of tyranny in America; the *Psalms* (1981) are a rewriting of the biblical Psalms of David for a modern world. *The Gospel in Solentiname* (1982) is a collection of dialogues or commentaries on the Gospels. Cardenal served as minister of culture in the government organized after the 1979 ouster of Anastasio Somoza in Nicaragua.

POETRY BY CARDENAL

Apocalypse and Other Poems. Ed. by Robert Pring-Mill and Donald D. Walsh. New Dir. Pr. 1977 $7.95. ISBN 0-8112-0662-9. A collection of poems on socio-religious themes.

Flights of Victory. Trans. by Marc Zimmerman. Bks. Demand repr. of 1985 ed. $41.60. ISBN 0-8357-4058-7. Poems reflecting the experience of the Nicaraguan Revolution.

From Nicaragua with Love: Poems 1979–1986. Trans. by Jonathan Cohen. City Lights o.p. Poems from the period after the Nicaraguan Revolution.

The Gospel in Solentiname. 4 vols. Trans. by Donald D. Walsh. Orbis Bks. 1982 o.p. Series of reactions to gospel lessons.

Homage to the American Indians. Trans. by Carlos Altschul and Monique Altschul. Bks. Demand repr. of 1973 ed. $30.80. ISBN 0-317-09702-4. Studies of Pre-Columbian Amerindian cultures.

Nicaraguan New Time. Trans. by Dinah Livingstone. Paul & Co. Pubs. 1990 $7.95. ISBN 1-85172-027-8

Psalms. Crossroad NY 1981 o.p.

With Walker in Nicaragua and Other Early Poems. Trans. by Jonathan Cohen. Wesleyan U. Pr. 1984 $12.95. ISBN 0-8195-5123-6. Early poems of Cardenal.

Zero Hour and Other Documentary Poems. Trans. by Donald D. Walsh. New Dir. Pr. 1980 $6.95. ISBN 0-685-03565-4. A collection of poems that document reality.

NONFICTION BY CARDENAL

In Cuba. Trans. by Donald D. Walsh. New Dir. Pr. 1974 $9.95. ISBN 0-8112-0538-X. Deals with the virtues and defects of Castro's Cuba.

CARPENTIER, ALEJO. 1904–1980 Cuba

Carpentier was director of Cuba's National Press, which published many millions of volumes in an ambitious program, and for some years was Cuba's ambassador to France. A composer and musicologist, he consciously applied the principles of musical composition in much of his work. Imprisoned for political activity in 1928, he escaped with the aid of Robert Desnos, a French surrealist poet, to Paris, where he joined the literary circle of surrealists Louis Aragon, Tristan Tzara, and PAUL ELUARD. Surrealism influenced his style and, according to Carpentier, helped him to see "aspects of American life he had not previously seen, in their telluric, epic, and poetic contexts." Carpentier articulated a theory of marvelous reality, "lo real maravilloso," with an almost surrealistic sense of the relationship among unrelated or antithetical elements, often from distinct ethnic and cultural backgrounds. *The Lost Steps* (1953) takes the form of a diary of a Cuban musician and intellectual who seeks escape from civilization during his trip to a remote Amazon village in search of native musical instruments. The three short stories "The Road to Santiago," "Journey to the Seed," and "Similar to Night," and the novel *The Pursuit*, printed in *The War of Time* (1958) (the title is an allusion to a line from LOPE DE VEGA defining a man as "a soldier in the war of time"), present time as subjective rather than historical, and capable of remarkable personal variations. *The Kingdom of This World* (1949) deals with the period of Henri Christophe and the slave revolts in

Haiti. Its circular structure presents the inevitable recurrence of tyranny and the need for eternal struggle against it. *Reasons of State* (1976) is another notable addition to the gallery of Latin American fictional portraits of dictators; it uses Carpentier's love for baroque style and parody to raise complex questions about the nature of revolution.

Novels by Carpentier

The Chase. Trans. by Alfred MacAdam. FS&G 1990 $17.95. ISBN 0-374-52239-1

Concierto Barroco. Trans. by Asa Zatz. Coun. Oak Bks. 1988 $7.95. ISBN 0-933031-12-2. An eighteenth-century nameless Mexican nobleman and his Cuban servant, Filomeno, journey from the New World to the Old.

Explosion in a Cathedral. Trans. by John Sturrock. FS&G 1989 $11.95. ISBN 0-374-52198-0. A novel about the order in the natural chaos.

The Harp and the Shadow. Trans. by Thomas Christensen and Carol Christensen. Mercury Hse. Inc. 1990 $16.95. ISBN 0-916515-71-0. Presents—in an introspective first-person account—the life of Christopher Columbus.

The Kingdom of This World. Trans. by Harriet De Onis. FS&G 1989 $8.95. ISBN 0-374-52197-2

The Lost Steps. Trans. by Harriet De Onis. FS&G 1989 $9.95. ISBN 0-374-52199-9

Reasons of State. 1976. Trans. by Frances Partridge. Writers & Readers 1981 $4.95. ISBN 0-904613-52-6. A bitterly satiric treatment of a Latin American dictator.

Short Story Collection by Carpentier

The War of Time. 1958. Trans. by Frances Partridge. Knopf 1971 o.p.

Books about Carpentier

González Echeverría, Roberto. *Alejo Carpentier: The Pilgrim at Home.* U. of Tex. Pr. rev. ed. 1990 $14.95. ISBN 0-292-70417-8. A major critical study that covers the life and work of the late, great Cuban novelist.

Janney, Frank. *Alejo Carpentier and His Early Works.* Boydell & Brewer 1981 $40.00. ISBN 0-7293-0062-5.

CASTELLANOS, ROSARIO. 1925–1974 — Mexico

Castellanos always enjoyed a comfortable middle-class existence; yet she early emerged in her writing as an eloquent spokesperson for the feminist movements that began to gain currency in the 1950s. Moreover, Castellanos moved beyond feminist concerns of her own class to speak for marginal or subaltern Mexican women, most significantly for the indigenous women whom the culture had mythified, stereotyped, or simply overlooked. Castellanos was especially successful in thematizing the multi-leveled, conflictual relationships between indigenous and middle-class women. *The Nine Guardians* (1957) is autobiographical in nature, drawing on childhood memories of Castellanos's contacts in southeast Mexico, near the Guatemalan border, with indigenous society. Other novels deal in complex and innovative ways with the roles of indigenous culture and of women in contemporary Mexican society. Castellanos published numerous volumes of poetry, and her drama *The Eternal Feminine* (1975; included in *A Rosario Castellanos Reader*) is considered one of the most innovative and influential feminist texts in Latin American literature. Castellanos, who also produced a steady output of perceptive essays, was Mexico's ambassador to Israel when she died accidentally of electrocution.

Works by Castellanos

Another Way to Be: Selected Works by Rosario Castellanos. Trans. by Myralyn F. Allgood. U. of Ga. Pr. 1990 $25.00. ISBN 0-8203-1222-3. Provides a generous sampling of

Castellanos's poetry, fiction, and essays that draw deeply upon her experience as a white, Mexican female in Chiapas.

A Rosario Castellanos Reader. Trans. by Maureen Ahern and others. U. of Tex. Pr. 1988 $29.95. ISBN 0-292-77039-1. A collection of poems, short stories, essays, and a play.

POETRY BY CASTELLANOS

Meditation on the Threshold: A Bilingual Anthology of Poetry. Trans. by Julian Palley. Biling. Rev-Pr. 1988 $10.00. ISBN 0-91695-080-8. A selection of Castellanos's feminist-based poetry.

BOOK ABOUT CASTELLANOS

Bonifaz Caballero, Oscar. Remembering Rosario: A Personal Glimpse into the Life and Works of Rosario Castellanos. Trans. by Myralyn F. Allgood. Scripta 1990 $27.50. ISBN 0-916379-72-8. Presents an overview of Castellanos's writing.

CORTÁZAR, JULIO. 1914–1984 Argentina

Cortázar's view that fantasy and reality, the rational and the irrational, exist on both intersecting and identical planes produced his formal experiments with the novel and short story, experiments always in the spirit of philosophical and literary play. His short stories explore from fresh perspectives interchanging identities and intersecting levels of reality and time. *Blow-Up* provided the director MICHAELANGELO ANTONIONI (see Vol. 3) with the point of departure for his film of that title. In *Cronopios and Famas* (1962), Cortázar created a world filled with imaginary beings who represent the magic of everyday life, the *cronopios,* while *famas* are those seeing only conventional reality. This perception of the comic pervades all of Cortázar's work, giving it its special tone.

The Winners (1960) uses the classic structure of a voyage with travelers of widely different origins to ask metaphysical questions about human relationships and the purpose of the voyage, representing life. The protagonist of *Hopscotch* (1963), in quest of reality (the heaven or home of a hopscotch game), tries to liberate himself from the restrictions imposed by time, language, and social conventions. The novel has alternative structures from which the reader may choose. "I was trying," the author wrote, "to break the habits of readers—not just for the sake of breaking them, but to make the reader free. . . . Space and time are left completely by the wayside. There are moments in it when the reader will not know when or where the action is taking place." *Sixty-two: A Model Kit,* literally translated as *A Model to Be Put Together* (1968), continues the theoretical lines developed in *Hopscotch.* It is an attempt to replace routine psychologizing with alternative modes of presenting inner realities. *A Manual for Manuel* (1973) explores the relationship of dream to fiction and to reality, always with a sense of the comic absurdity of existence and of its underlying tragedy. Cortázar left Argentina permanently in the 1950s during the Peronist regime. While he supported revolutionary movements in general, he insisted on remaining an independent intellectual.

SHORT STORY COLLECTIONS BY CORTÁZAR

Blow Up and Other Stories. Trans. by Paul Blackburn. Pantheon 1985 $10.00. ISBN 0-394-72881-5

A Certain Lucas. Trans. by Gregory Rabassa. Knopf 1984 $12.95. ISBN 0-394-50723-1. Explores politics and interpersonal relationships.

We Love Glenda So Much and Other Stories. Trans. by Gregory Rabassa. Random 1984 $14.95. ISBN 0-394-72297-3

NOVELS BY CORTÁZAR

Hopscotch. Trans. by Gregory Rabassa. Pantheon 1987 $15.95. ISBN 0-394-75284-8

The Winners. Trans. by Elaine Kerrigan. Pantheon 1984 o.p. Satire about Argentinian class relations.

NONFICTION BY CORTÁZAR

Nicaraguan Sketches. Trans. by Kathleen Weaver. Norton 1989 $15.95. ISBN 0-393-02764-3. Skillfully translated posthumous collection of essays based on a clandestine visit Cortázar took to Nicaragua in 1976.

BOOKS ABOUT CORTÁZAR

Alazraki, Jaime, and Ivar Ivask, eds. *The Final Island: The Fiction of Julio Cortázar.* U. of Okla. Pr. 1978 $22.95. ISBN 0-8061-1436-3. Essays that analyze and interpret Cortázar's fiction.

Boldy, Stephen. *The Novels of Julio Cortázar.* Cambridge U. Pr. 1980 $44.95. ISBN 0-521-23097-7. Criticism and interpretation of Cortázar's novels.

Brody, Robert. *Julio Cortázar: Rayuela.* Boydell & Brewer 1976 o.p. Provides a general introduction to Cortázar's *Hopscotch.*

CRUZ, SOR JUANA INÉS DE LA. 1648–1695 Mexico

Born Juana de Asbaje in a small town, this Mexican author became a nun in 1669, probably because her illegitimate birth removed her from consideration for marriage to someone worthy of her. A misfit in a restrictive colonial society that mistrusted such intense intellectual curiosity in a woman, Asbaje was the finest lyric poet and one of the most interesting dramatists of the Spanish American colonial period. Despite the opposition of the ecclesiastical hierarchy, she carried out scientific experiments and became the confidante of nobility and a correspondent of intellectuals throughout Spanish America. *A Woman of Genius (Respuesta a Sor Filotea)* is an extraordinary document of the intellectual history of a woman who would not be defeated by her circumstances. Ultimately, she sold her books and devoted herself to caring for the sick and poor; she died of an illness contracted while nursing during an outbreak of the plague.

WORK BY CRUZ

A Woman of Genius: The Intellectual Autobiography of Sor Juana Inés de la Cruz. Trans. by Margaret S. Peden. Lime Rock Pr. 1982 $37.50. ISBN 0-915998-14-9. With an introduction by Margaret S. Peden.

DALTON, ROQUE. 1935–1975 El Salvador

Dalton is almost an icon of revolutionary poetry in Latin America because of his eloquent melding of political activism, armed revolutionary struggle, and the testimonial role of literature. Certainly he is one of his generation's most-read poets. In line with much contemporary poetry and with Latin America's "antipoetry" movement (that is, antigrandiloquence and anti–Great Poet), Dalton seeks to avoid sentimentality and abstractions and to ground his expression in the concrete reality of his own life. Dalton's political commitments forced him to live most of his adult life in exile. In a tragic chapter of the liberation movement, Dalton was accused of counterrevolutionary activities and executed by his own comrades. He is the only Salvadoran writer to attract international attention, with poems translated into numerous languages. His declaration "I came to revolution by way / of poetry" captures an important unifying sentiment of the 1960s and early 1970s in Latin America.

POETRY BY DALTON

Clandestine Poems. Trans. by Jack Hirschman. Curbstone 1990 repr. of 1984 ed. $7.95. ISBN 0-915306-91-3. Presents a series of poems reflecting political insights.

Clandestine Poems—Poemas clandestinos: Bilingual Edition. Trans. by Jack Hirschman. New Amer. Pr. 1984 $7.00. ISBN 0-942638-07-7

Poems. Trans. by Richard Schaaf. Curbstone 1984 $13.50. ISBN 0-915306-45-X. Poems focusing on the struggle for freedom.

Poetry and Militancy in Latin America. Trans. by Arlene Scully and James Scully. Curbstone 1982 $4.00. ISBN 0-915306-26-3. Contains poems expressive of the El Salvadorian people.

DARÍO, RUBÉN (pseud. of Félix Rubén García Sarmiento). 1867–1916 Nicaragua

Darío, a Nicaraguan who traveled widely in the Spanish-speaking world, was the greatest poet of the modernist movement and profoundly influenced twentieth-century poetry in Spanish. *Azul (Azure)* (1888), a volume in three parts consisting of stories, poetic prose, and poetry, is still strongly romantic but also shows Darío's assimilation of French Parnassianism and symbolism. Darío strove for artistic refinement, elegance of expression, and the renovation of poetic language and form. He invented daring neologisms and verse forms, but also renewed forgotten techniques. Initially, his was the world of swans, centaurs, and doves, of art for art's sake. With his *Profane Prose* (1896), he distinguished himself as the true leader of the modernist movement. The title itself reveals his desire to alter the use of the language, for the contents are neither prose nor profane, but rather elegant, aristocratic verse. Here Darío experimented with combinations of rhythms, sounds, accents, and meter, treating such exotic themes as peacocks and princesses with erotic and pagan tones. His next volume, *Songs of Life and Hope* (1905), which contains some of his best verse, shows a turn away from evasion of reality toward meditative introspection on life and death, commitment to the concept of a Spanish America united in a search for freedom, and an intense preoccupation about the power of the United States, as revealed in *To Roosevelt*.

POETRY BY DARÍO

Eleven Poems of Rubén Darío: Bilingual Edition. Trans. by Thomas Walsh and Salomon De la Selva. Gordon Pr. 1977 $59.95. ISBN 0-8490-1758-0

Selected Poems of Rubén Darío. Trans. by Lysander Kemp. U. of Tex. Pr. 1988 repr. of 1965 ed. $6.95. ISBN 0-292-77615-2. A collection of modernist poems.

BOOKS ABOUT DARÍO

Ellis, Keith. *Critical Approaches to Rubén Darío*. U. of Toronto Pr. 1975 o.p. Various critical approaches to Darío's poetry.

DONOSO, JOSÉ. 1925– Chile

Donoso has been compared to HENRY JAMES (see Vol. 1) for his psychological penetration of characters and to WILLIAM FAULKNER (see Vol. 1) for novelistic technique. His obsessive subject is the decay of the Chilean bourgeoisie, but he vigorously rejects anything reminiscent of traditional realism or the portrayal of regional customs. In *This Sunday* (1966), he focuses on a family's activities on Sundays in order to view the boredom, passions, and misery of Chilean bourgeois society and its servants. *The Obscene Bird of Night* (1970) deals with the decline of feudal society through the story of a landholding family in a kaleidoscopic vision of decay and outrageous behavior.

Novels by Donoso

Curfew. Trans. by Alfred MacAdam. Grove Pr. 1989 $10.95. ISBN 1-55584-448-0. Explores the effects of a country under dictatorship.

The Obscene Bird of Night. 1970. Trans. by Leonard Mades. Godine 1979 repr. of 1973 ed. $12.95. ISBN 0-87923-191-2. Explores the dark side of the imagination.

This Sunday. Trans. by Lorraine O'Grady Freeman. Knopf 1967 o.p.

Nonfiction by Donoso

The Boom in Spanish-American Literature: A Personal History. Trans. by Gregory Rabassa. Col. U. Pr. 1977 o.p. Chronicles the exodus of Latin American writers.

Book about Donoso

McMurray, George R. *José Donoso. Twayne's World Authors Ser.* G. K. Hall 1979 o.p. A useful general introduction to Donoso's themes and critical reputation.

DORFMAN, ARIEL. 1943– Chile

Born in Argentina of Jewish refugee parents, Dorfman spent part of his childhood in Manhattan and is thoroughly bilingual. A resident of Holland since being exiled from Chile in 1973 by the military government, Dorfman is a vociferous critic of U.S. economic and political involvement in Latin America. In *The Emperor's Old Clothes,* he saw cultural imperialism in unexpected facets of American society. *Widows* is a parable of military dictatorship. Its setting in Greece after World War II does not hide the fact that it is an extended metaphor for the present Chilean situation. It deals with the problem of the *desaparecidos,* those who have been kidnapped by government agents and simply vanished. The novel was refused publication in General Pinochet's Chile.

Novels by Dorfman

The Last Song of Manuel Sendero. Trans. by George R. Shivers and Ariel Dorfman. Viking Penguin 1988 $8.95. ISBN 0-14-008896-2. About a Chilean social revolutionary.

Mascara. Viking Penguin 1989 $7.95. ISBN 0-14-011253-7. An allegorical novel about loveless society and masked emotions.

Widows. Trans. by Stephen Kessler. Viking Penguin 1989 $8.95. ISBN 0-14-011659-1

Nonfiction by Dorfman

The Emperor's Old Clothes: What the Lone Ranger, Babar, and Other Innocent Heroes Do to Our Minds. Trans. by Clark Hansen. Pantheon 1983 $9.95. ISBN 0-394-71486-5

How to Read Donald Duck: Imperialist Ideology in the Disney Comics. (coauthored with Armand Mattelart). Trans. by David Kunzle. Intl. General 1984 $10.95. ISBN 0-88477-023-0. Considers cultural imperialism and children's literature.

Some Write to the Future: Essays on Contemporary Latin American Fiction. Trans. by George Shivers. Duke 1991 $12.95. ISBN 0-8223-1269-7. Essays on contemporary Latin American literature.

Short Story Collection by Dorfman

My House Is on Fire. Trans. by George Shivers. Viking Penguin 1991 $7.95. ISBN 0-14-014728-4. Stories of political resistance.

Poetry by Dorfman

Last Waltz in Santiago and Other Poems of Exile and Disappearance. Trans. by Edith Grossman and Ariel Dorfman. Viking Penguin 1988 $8.95. ISBN 0-14-058608-3. Poems on twin motifs of exile and political disappearance.

PLAY BY DORFMAN

Death and the Maiden. Viking Penguin 1992 $7.00. ISBN 0-14-048238-5. A compelling drama about the abuses of a Latin American military regime. Focuses on themes of the domination and abuse of women by men, and whether such crimes can, or should, ever be forgiven.

FUENTES, CARLOS. 1929– Mexico

The most famous Mexican novelist of the twentieth century is probably Carlos Fuentes, also an essayist, journalist, film writer, and diplomat. Fuentes was educated as a child in the United States and is bilingual, which has often allowed him to serve there as an eloquent spokesperson for Mexican culture. All of Fuentes's works demonstrate his primary concern, the interpretation of Mexican culture and history. He finds Mexico's search for identity particularly difficult due to its beginning with the annihilation of the Indians. The protagonist of *Where the Air Is Clear* (1959), described by Fuentes as "a synthesis of the Mexican present," is the whole of Mexico City, and a panorama of post-revolutionary Mexican life is presented through a wide range of characters from various classes and professions. *The Death of Artemio Cruz* (1962), which made an international reputation for Fuentes, narrates a dying man's reflections on the crucial decisions of his life as vitality and energy drain from him; its progression from present to past provides a unique perspective on both the individual and the historical process. At the appearance of *A Change of Skin* (1968) in English, Robert J. Clements described it as a "great book . . . incorporating every technique of the contemporary novel . . . bursting in energy, capacious in content, gripping in evocation, and humanitarian in its universal tolerance" (*SR*). There are other threads to Fuentes's fiction, however; the theme of doubling of personality and consciousness allied to the persistence of the past, as in *Aura* (1962), or the deliberate parody of spy fiction in *The Hydra Head* (1978). *Terra Nostra* (1975) is a massive effort to capture the multiple strands of history, European and American, that have gone to make up the complexities of Mexico; like all Fuentes's work, it struggles to unravel the significance and the forms in which the past shapes the present. *Christopher Unborn* (1989) is an apocalyptic, distopian vision of the postmodern, postindustrialist Mexican millenium.

NOVELS BY FUENTES

Aura. Trans. by Lysander Kemp. FS&G 1986 $9.95. ISBN 0-374-51171-3

The Campaign. Trans. by Alfred MacAdam. FS&G 1991 $22.95. ISBN 0-374-118828-0. Chronicles Latin America's wars of independence in the early nineteenth century.

A Change of Skin. 1968. Trans. by Sam Hileman. FS&G 1986 $14.95. ISBN 0-374-51427-5

Christopher Unborn. Trans. by Alfred MacAdam. FS&G 1989 $75.00. ISBN 0-374-12335-7

The Death of Artemio Cruz. 1962. Trans. by Alfred MacAdam. FS&G 1991 $30.00. ISBN 0-374-13559-2

Distant Relations. Trans. by Margaret S. Peden. FS&G 1982 $11.95. ISBN 0-374-14082-0

The Good Conscience. Trans. by Sam Hileman. FS&G 1987 $7.95. ISBN 0-374-50736-8. Focuses on the provincial Mexican petite bourgeoisie.

The Hydra Head. 1978. Trans. by Margaret S. Peden. FS&G 1986 $8.95. ISBN 0-374-17397-4

The Old Gringo. Trans. by Margaret S. Peden. HarpC 1986 $10.00. ISBN 0-06-097063-4. A novel about Ambrose Bierce and the Mexican Revolution of 1910.

Terra Nostra. 1975. Trans. by Margaret S. Peden. FS&G 1987 $19.95. ISBN 0-374-51750-9

Where the Air is Clear. 1959. Trans. by Sam Hileman. FS&G 1988 $11.95. ISBN 0-374-50919-0

Short Story Collections by Fuentes

Burnt Water. Trans. by Margaret S. Peden. FS&G 1986 $10.95. ISBN 0-374-51988-9. Contains Fuentes's early stories.

Constancia and Other Stories for Virgins. Trans. by Thomas Christensen. FS&G 1990. $19.95. ISBN 0-374-12886-3. Title story is narrated by an elderly American doctor who, while bemoaning his own mortality, learns in a Poe-like twist that he has been married to the ghost of a Russian emigrée who died in the Spanish Civil War 49 years earlier.

Nonfiction by Fuentes

Don Quixote, or the Critique of Reading. U. TX Inst. Lat. Am. Stud. 1976. $2.00. ISBN 0-86728-015-8. Essays on motif of Don Quixote in fiction.

Myself with Others; Selected Essays. FS&G 1988 $19.95. ISBN 0-374-21750-5. Autobiographical musings and literary essays from the Mexican novelist that explore the roots of his own work both in Europe and in Latin America.

Books about Fuentes

Brody, Robert, and Charles Rossman, eds. *Carlos Fuentes: A Critical View.* U. of Tex. Pr. 1982 o.p. A collection of essays and reviews that assess Fuentes's major works and evaluate his critical reputation.

Durán, Gloria. *The Archetypes of Carlos Fuentes: From Witch to Androgyne.* Shoe String 1980 o.p. Explores the significance of puppets and dolls in Fuentes's fiction.

Faris, Wendy B. *Carlos Fuentes.* Continuum 1983 $19.95. ISBN 0-8044-2193-5. General study and introduction to Fuentes's life and works; a good source for the general reader and student.

GARCÍA MÁRQUEZ, GABRIEL. 1928– (Nobel Prize 1982) Colombia

García Márquez has created a fictional world out of his memories in a town named Macondo, which is the setting for most of his novels and short stories. Earlier story collections like *Leaf Storm* (1955) and *No One Writes to the Colonel* (1961) had already examined the dust and rain and boredom of this cultural and economic backwater, but the publication of *One Hundred Years of Solitude* (1967) caused a literary sensation. An epic novel covering a one-hundred-year cycle of the town's existence, it traces its founding by José Arcadio Buendía with an incestuous relationship through its destruction by a cyclone. The magical style mingles the fantastic, mythical, and commonplace on multiple levels. The tone and structure have a number of biblical parallels. Although much of the novel is comic, its characters are finally tragic for their self-imposed isolation and destruction. With this work García Márquez established himself internationally as a major novelist and was awarded the Nobel Prize in 1982.

He is not, however, a one-book novelist. *In Evil Hour* (1978) is a chilling portrait of the stagnation, broken only by violence, of a provincial dead end. *The Autumn of the Patriarch* (1976) is a portrait of a mythical dictator who assumes the characteristics, and some of the historical details, of a series of Latin American tyrants, but with a fine sense of irony. *Chronicle of a Death Foretold* (1980) presents from the inside the disastrous consequences of the male code of honor in Hispanic society, and many of García Márquez's short stories are brilliantly imaginative parables of a world that threatens logic and reason. *The General in His Labyrinth* (1990) is the deathbed story of a disillusioned Simón Bolívar, who said that "to govern America is to plow the sea."

NOVELS BY GARCÍA MÁRQUEZ

The Autumn of the Patriarch. Trans. by Gregory Rabassa. Avon 1977 $4.95. ISBN 0-380-01774-1

Chronicle of a Death Foretold. Trans. by Gregory Rabassa. Knopf 1983 $18.95. ISBN 0-394-53074-8

Collected Novellas. HarpC 1990 $22.95. ISBN 0-06-016384-4. Three psychologically provocative novellas that involve the turmoil of violent death in small, lethargic Colombian villages.

The General in His Labyrinth. Trans. by Edith Grossman. Knopf 1990 $19.95. ISBN 0-394-58258-6

In Evil Hour. Trans. by Gregory Rabassa. Avon 1980 $4.95. ISBN 0-380-52167-9. Explores the power of gossip and secrets.

Love in the Time of Cholera. Trans. by Edith Grossman. Knopf 1988 $18.95. ISBN 0-394-56161-9. Story of an unrequited love that survives 51 years.

One Hundred Years of Solitude. Trans. by Gregory Rabassa. Avon 1976 $5.95. ISBN 0-380-01503-X

The Story of a Shipwrecked Sailor. Trans. by Randolph Hogan. Knopf 1986 $13.95. ISBN 0-394-54810-8. Hallucinatory tale of a sailor washed off his boat.

SHORT STORY COLLECTIONS BY GARCÍA MÁRQUEZ

Collected Stories. Trans. by Gregory Rabassa and S. J. Bernstein. HarpC 1985 $11.00. ISBN 0-06-091306-1

Innocent Erendira and Other Stories. Trans. by Gregory Rabassa. HarpC 1979 $10.00. ISBN 0-06-090701-0. Stories illuminating the author's literary hindsight.

Leaf Storm, and Other Stories. Trans. by Gregory Rabassa. Borgo Pr. 1991 $20.00. ISBN 0-8095-9053-0

No One Writes to the Colonel and Other Stories. Trans. by J. S. Bernstein. HarpC 1979 $10.00. ISBN 0-06-090700-2. Stories of social and physical isolation.

NONFICTION BY GARCÍA MÁRQUEZ

Clandestine in Chile: The Adventures of Miguel Littin. Trans. by Asa Zatz. H. Holt & Co. 1987 $13.95. ISBN 0-8050-0322-3. Documentary on the Chilean filmmaker Miguel Littin.

BOOKS ABOUT GARCÍA MÁRQUEZ

Bell-Villada, Gene H. *García Márquez: The Man and His Work.* U. of NC Pr. 1990 $12.95. ISBN 0-8078-14264-8. A scholarly examination of the life and works of García Márquez.

Bloom, Harold, ed. *Gabriel García Márquez.* Chelsea Hse. 1989 $34.95. ISBN 1-55546-297-9. A selection of critical works on García Márquez.

McGuirk, Bernard, and Richard Cardwell, eds. *Gabriel García Márquez: New Readings.* Cambridge U. Pr. 1987 $49.95. ISBN 0-521-32836-5. Extends criticism of Márquez's work to English-speaking readers and shows the range of theoretical approaches to the author's short stories and novels.

McMurray, George R., ed. *Critical Essays on Gabriel García Márquez.* Macmillan 1987 $40.00. ISBN 0-8161-8834-3. A good representative selection of reviews and articles on the Colombian master of myth and magical realism.

Minta, Stephen. *García Márquez, Writer of Colombia.* HarpC 1987 o.p. An overview of Márquez within a political and literary context.

Oberhelman, Harley D., comp. *Gabriel García Márquez: A Study of the Short Fiction.* Macmillan 1991 $21.95. ISBN 0-8057-8333-4. Explores Faulkner's influence on Márquez's fiction.

Ortega, Julio, and Claudia Elliott, eds. *Gabriel García Márquez and the Powers of Fiction.* U. of Tex. Pr. 1988 $16.95. ISBN 0-292-72740-2. Five critical essays on García Márquez by a variety of authors.

Palencia-Roth, Michael. *Myth and the Modern Novel: García Márquez, Mann, and Joyce.* Garland 1987 $52.00. ISBN 0-824-08432-2. Explores the use of myth in Márquez's writing.

Williams, Raymond L. *Gabriel García Márquez.* Macmillan 1984 $20.95. ISBN 0-8057-6597-2. A study of García Márquez's life and work.

Wood, Michael. *García Márquez: One Hundred Years of Solitude.* Cambridge U. Pr. 1990 $27.95. ISBN 0-521-32823-3. Critical analysis of the author's well-known novel.

GARRO, ELENA. 1920– Mexico

Best known as a dramatist, Elena Garro won the important Premio Xavier Villaurrutia in 1963 for the novel *Recollections of Things to Come.* The interior world of the characters' memories of life in Ixtepec during the Cristero Rebellion of 1926–28 is narrated dramatically in poetic prose that makes considerable use of Aztec mythology in its creation of a myth of Mexican women. A choreographer, script writer, and journalist, Elena Garro was at one time married to the Mexican poet OCTAVIO PAZ.

NOVEL BY GARRO

Recollections of Things to Come. 1962. Trans. by Ruth L. Simms. *Texas Pan-Amer. Ser.* U. of Tex. Pr. 1986 repr. of 1969 ed. $12.95. ISBN 0-292-77032-4

GOLDEMBERG, ISAAC. 1945– Peru

Among the many shifts in Latin American literature during the past few years, one of the most important has been the emergence of a group of writers who chronicle the Jewish immigrant experience. For Goldemberg's characters, growing up as Jews in Peru has been an experience of sorrow and desolation laced with humor. His work is a fascinating document and a source of constant surprises, as in the need to develop a daily idiom built on elements from Spanish, Yiddish, and Quechua, in an effort to harmonize the triple tradition of these cultures.

NOVELS BY GOLDEMBERG

The Fragmented Life of Don Jacobo Lerner. Trans. by Robert S. Picciotto. Persea Bks. 1985 repr. of 1976 ed. $8.95. ISBN 0-89255-003-1. Follows an itinerant Jewish peddler in Peru.

Play by Play. Trans. by Hardie St. Martin. Persea Bks. 1985 $13.95. ISBN 0-89255-092-9. The intersection of two Peruvian social realities: the Jewish community and professional soccer.

POETRY BY GOLDEMBERG

Hombre de Paso, Just Passing Through. Trans. by Isaac Goldemberg and David Ungar. Ediciones Norte 1981 $9.00. ISBN 0-910061-07-6

GOROSTIZA, JOSÉ. 1901–1973 Mexico

Death without End (1939), a complex, metaphysical volume, has been called "the most important Mexican poem to appear up to that time in his generation" (Enrique Anderson Imbert). Utilizing ironic contrast with great power, the poem expresses humankind's unavailing effort to find order and permanence; its central metaphor is the water, symbol of the poet, of humanity, and of all matter, which is momentarily given form by the glass (intelligence and language), but which may be spilled and run into nothingness and chaos, what Margaret S. Peden has called "the paradox of form in formlessness" (Handbook of Latin American Studies).

POETRY BY GOROSTIZA

Death without End. 1939. Trans. by Laura Villaseñor. U. of Tex. Pr. 1969 $15.00. ISBN 0-87959-057-2

GUILLÉN, NICOLAS. 1902–1989 Cuba

Guillén, one of the leaders of the Afro-Antillean school of poetry, was inspired by popular dance, ballads, song rhythms, and speech patterns, all of which show a heavy African influence. In his first volumes, *Motives of Sound* (1930) and *Sóngoro Cosongo* (1931), meaning is communicated primarily through sound, and many poems are in regional popular dialect. Much of his subsequent poetry reflects his profound social commitment: *West Indies Limited* (1934) opposes imperialism, and *Spain* (1937) expresses his support for the republic during the Spanish civil war. *Tengo* (1964) deals with the Cuban Revolution in a tone aimed at a popular audience. All Guillén's work is an intense effort to relate poetry to the culture of the Cuban people and to political and social protest.

POETRY BY GUILLÉN

The Daily Daily. Trans. by Vera Kutzinski. U. CA Pr. 1989 $30.00. ISBN 0-520-06218-3

The Great Zoo and Other Poems. Trans. by Robert Márquez. Monthly Rev. 1973 $8.00. ISBN 0-85345-287-3

Man-making Words. Trans. by Robert Márquez and David Arthur McMurray. U. of Mass. Pr. 1972 o.p.

Tengo. 1964. Trans., by Richard J. Carr. Broadside Pr. 1974 $7.25. ISBN 0-910296-28-6. With an introduction by José Antonio Portuondo.

BOOK ABOUT GUILLÉN

Ellis, Keith. *Cuba's Nicolas Guillén: Poetry and Ideology.* U. of Toronto Pr. 1983 $13.95. ISBN 0-8020-6605-4

HERNÁNDEZ, JOSÉ. 1834–1866 Argentina

The Gaucho Martín Fierro (1872) is a lyric epic poem written in praise of the gaucho way of life at a time when gauchos were looked on as curiosities or nuisances by the European-dominated Buenos Aires society and were being swallowed by industrial and agricultural progress and manipulated by contending political parties. Hernández's primary purpose was to inform people about the vanishing culture of the gaucho; although the first part of the poem portrays the rebellion against society's mistreatment of the gaucho and its restrictions on his freedom to roam as he saw fit, the second part has a more didactic tone and urges a reconciliation, but one which necessarily involves the gaucho's acceptance of landowner hegemony. This poem became the voice of the gaucho, but it has also been adopted by all Argentines as an important part of their national tradition.

POETRY BY HERNÁNDEZ

The Gaucho Martín Fierro. Trans. by Norman Mangouni. Schol. Facsimiles 1974 repr. of 1872 ed. $50.00. ISBN 0-8201-1133-3

HUIDOBRO, VICENTE. 1893–1948 Chile

Virtually unknown in the United States, Huidobro was one of the most important innovators in Latin America poetry of the early twentieth century and an important theoretician of the new art. He lived in Europe for many years, specifically in Paris from 1916 to 1926, where he wrote poetry in French and participated in French poetic movements. He proclaimed himself the inventor of the school that he called Creationism, which he considered the foundation of a new way of conceiving art. For Huidobro the mission of the poet was the creation of new poetic realities. Art was totally free and the poem was free of both its poet-creator and the circumstances in which it was created. Huidobro tended to exaggerate and became a center of polemics, but he was one of the first to announce such important avant-garde concepts. His creative work is startling because of the novelty of the metaphors and the formal and verbal experimentation.

POETRY BY HUIDOBRO

Altazor. Trans. by Eliot Weinberger. Graywolf 1988 $8.50. ISBN 0-55597-106-7. A vast vanguard poem of the poet as God.

LIHN, ENRIQUE. 1929– Chile

Lihn is a difficult poet because his sources lie in various traditions of modern Chilean poetry, especially NERUDA and PARRA, while he rejects traditionalism. He is in the line of neorealism and antipoetry, but is unwilling to settle into schools or a school. His *Poesía de Paso* received the Cuban Casa de las Americas Prize in 1966. He says of his own work, "my poetry postulates, instead of discontinuity, the coherence [delirious, in the best of cases] of a continuous discourse, it tries to become a reflection, it rambles; and although it may integrate linguistic elements of the most diverse origins, signs of a traumatic relation with *Literature* prevail."

POETRY BY LIHN

The Dark Room and Other Poems. Ed. by Patricio C. Lerzundi. Trans. by Jonathan Cohen and others. New Dir. Pr. 1978 $8.95. ISBN 0-8112-0676-9

MALLEA, EDUARDO. 1903–1983 Argentina

Mallea was associated with Argentina's avant-garde from the late 1920s and for 15 years greatly influenced Argentine letters in his position as literary director of the newspaper *La Nación*. *History of an Argentine Passion*, a spiritual and intellectual autobiography, has been widely read throughout Latin America. His view of the world basically existentialist, Mallea is concerned with people's loneliness, lack of communication, and alienation. He utilizes stream-of-consciousness techniques and disjunctures of chronological time to portray inner realities. Mallea names as literary influences BLAKE (see Vol. 1), RIMBAUD, KIERKEGAARD (see also Vol. 4), UNAMUNO Y JUGO, KAFKA, JOYCE (see Vol. 1), and PROUST, and he was among the first to introduce the techniques of these European novelists to Argentina. Mallea won the Buenos Aires Municipal Prize for prose in 1935 and the National Prize for literature in 1937.

NONFICTION BY MALLEA

History of an Argentine Passion. Trans. by Yvette E. Miller and Myron Lichtblau. Lat. Am. Lit. Rev. Pr. 1983 $13.95. ISBN 0-935480-10-2

MARQUÉS, RENÉ. 1919–1979 Puerto Rico

Marqués is the most important of the Puerto Rican dramatists who in the 1950s and 1960s created a theater that revealed a surge in Puerto Rican pride and ethnic identity. His early work is heavily naturalistic, but in later plays he made extensive use of unorthodox time sequences and imaginative lighting to create a symbolic portrait of what he considered his island's problems. In his essays, Marqués examined the identity of the Puerto Rican as he saw it, against the backdrop of a dreaded cultural and linguistic assimilation with the United States.

NOVEL BY MARQUÉS

The Look. Trans. by Charles Pilditch. Senda Nueva 1983 $11.95. ISBN 0-918454-29-8. Marqués's attempt at a gay novel, about a Puerto Rican outsider.

MARTÍ, JOSÉ. 1853–1895 Cuba

Martí is a symbol of Cuban independence, for he campaigned throughout his life for its liberation and finally died in the war against Spain. He was also an important literary figure and one of the founders of modernism. Rejecting the elaborate aestheticism of many modernists, he wrote in a simpler style based largely on folk poetry, as in *Ismaelillo* and *Versos Sencillos*, and much of his poetry deals with the struggle for freedom and his political and emotional exile from his homeland. He was also an accomplished prose stylist in a much more intricate fashion and influenced the later development of the short story and essay. His writings, now collected, many of which were originally published in newspapers, are essential for an understanding of the Spanish American independence process.

NONFICTION BY MARTÍ

Inside the Monster: Writings on the United States and American Imperialism. Trans. by Elinor Randall. Monthly Rev. 1977 $16.50. ISBN 0-85345-359-4

Martí on the U.S.A. Trans. by Luis A. Baralt. S. Ill. U. Pr. 1966 o.p.

On Art and Literature: Critical Writings. Trans. by Elinor Randall. Monthly Rev. 1982 $18.00. ISBN 0-85345-589-9

On Education: Articles on Educational Theory and Pedagogy, and Writings for Children from "The Age of Gold." Trans. by Elinor Randall. Monthly Rev. 1979 $14.00. ISBN 0-85345-483-3

Our America: Writings on Latin America and the Struggle for Cuban Independence. Trans. by Elinor Randall. Monthly Rev. 1978 $16.50. ISBN 0-85345-414-0. The opening essay is Martí's most famous.

Political Parties and Elections in the United States. Trans. by Elinor Randall. Temple U. Pr. 1989 $24.95. ISBN 0-87722-604-0. English translation of eight reports written for publication in Latin American newspapers by Martí while he was living in exile in the United States.

POETRY BY MARTÍ

Major Poems. Trans. by Elinor Randall. Ed. by Philip S. Foner. Holmes & Meier 1982 $27.50. ISBN 0-8419-0761-7

BOOKS ABOUT MARTÍ

Abel, Christopher, and Nissa Torrents, eds. *José Martí: Revolutionary Democrat.* Duke 1986 $32.50. ISBN 0-8223-0679-4. Discusses the significance of Martí in a nonpartisan, dispassionate manner.

González, Edward, ed. *José Martí and the Cuban Revolution Retraced.* UCLA Lat. Am. Ctr. 1986 $9.50. ISBN 0-87903-062-3. Essays on Martí within the context of the Cuban Revolution.

Turton, Peter. *José Martí: Architect of Cuba's Freedom.* Humanities 1986 $39.95. ISBN 0-86232-510-2. Analysis of Martí as paragon of Cuban struggle for independence from Spain and the United States.

MEDINA, ENRIQUE. 1937– Argentina

Probably no other fiction writer in Latin America can match Medina for the directness and violence of his portrayals of the authoritarian social structure underlying Argentina and the whole region. Medina, who has published over 20 novels and collections of stories and newspaper writings sees himself as a direct heir of Céline and Bukowski. Virtually all of his works were banned during recent military dictatorships in Argentina, but the country's return to democracy in 1983 has not significantly altered Medina's commitment to unmasking moral, political, and social hypocrisy. Medina spent much of his youth in a combined orphanage and reform school, placed there by his working-class mother when she could no longer care for him. His first, largely autobiographical novel, *The Tombs,* focuses on a juvenile reformatory as an efficient institution for inculcating the dynamics of tyranny and the violence it breeds. The frequent accusations leveled against Medina of sloppy writing and an obsession with the seamiest realms of human existence may contain an element of truth, but they are arguably beside the point: Medina specifically promotes an unadorned discourse freed from poeticizing impulses and the disingenuous ideologies of the oppressors. Whether a narrative voice, however confident, can reveal the naked truth of life is an interesting problem, but the fact remains that Medina's writing, especially his weekly newspaper columns, have exercised an enormous impact during dark days in Argentina. *The Duke*, about a prizefighter turned death squad agent, is one such work. Medina's writing stands in stark contrast to that of Latin American writers who have provided foreign readers with benign magical realist fantasies.

Works by Medina

The Duke: Memories and Anti-Memories of a Participant in the Repression. Trans. by David William Foster. Humanities 1985 o.p.

The Tombs. Trans. by David William Foster. Garland o.p.

MÉNDEZ-M., MIGUEL. 1930– Mexico/United States

Born in Bisbee, Arizona, an old mining town near the Mexican border, Méndez-M. is emblematic of the bilingual, bicultural Mexican-American writer. Although he has mostly lived in the United States, Méndez-M. is an autodidact who has chosen to write exclusively in Spanish. Before devoting himself full-time to writing, he worked in construction and as a farm laborer. He is now a faculty member of the University of Arizona. With this history, and by writing in Spanish, Méndez-M. has played a crucial role in maintaining the ethnic consciousness begun in the 1960s and renovating a Chicano literary tradition. He writes trenchantly about Mexican Americans' harsh conditions of survival in an inhospitable landscape, as well as about their social marginalization, imposed by the dominant Anglo society. He includes both those Mexicans who became "Americans" with the 1848 Treaty of Guadalupe, which made half of Mexico part of the United States, and those who have been drawn to the states as cheap labor. *Pilgrims in Aztlán* (1974) is a powerful portrait of these people and arguably the most important Chicano novel yet written. Aztlán is the legendary name for the Southwest formerly within Mexico, a mythicohistorical realm separate from both the United States and Mexico. *The Dream of Santa María de las Piedras* (1986) is a densely allegorical novel. Narrated by the voices of old men in a rural, lost Sonoran Desert village, it recounts the alternately fantastic and hellish journey of a young townsman who seeks his fortune in the United States.

NOVELS BY MÉNDEZ-M.

The Dream of Santa María de las Piedras. 1986. Trans. by David William Foster. Biling. Rev-Pr. 1989 $19.00. ISBN 0-916950-98-0

Pilgrims in Aztlán. 1974. Trans. by David William Foster. Biling. Rev-Pr. 1992 $20.00. ISBN 0-927534-22-3

MISTRAL, GABRIELA (pseud. of Lucila Godoy y Alcayaga). 1889–1957 (NOBEL PRIZE 1945) Chile

Gabriela Mistral's pen name was formed from those of Frederic Mistral, a Provençal poet, and GABRIELE D'ANNUNZIO, the Italian poet and patriot. Her first major collection of poetry was published in the United States in 1922 under the title *Desolación*. The sonnets of this volume, among her very best, evoke her passion for a young lover and her anguish at his suicide. Critics consider her collection *Tala (Felling of Trees)*, published in Buenos Aires in 1938, her best work. Mistral's translated collections are now out of print in the United States.

Anti-imperialism and a feminist rebellion against a masculine society are among the main themes of Mistral's poetry, but love—physical, religious, humanitarian, and maternal—was her primary subject; an unhappy personal life provided the source of much of her poetic drive. Much of Mistral's time and energy was dedicated to the children of the world; she was an energetic spokesperson for them and was responsible for the foundation of schools throughout Latin America. On the invitation of the Mexican government, she reorganized that country's school system in the 1920s, and she represented Chile in various posts at the League of Nations, the United Nations, and as a member of the consular service. She was one of Eleanor Roosevelt's many friends in the international community of women's issues.

POETRY BY MISTRAL

Selected Poems. Trans. by Langston Hughes. Ind. U. Pr. 1957 o.p.

Selected Poems of Gabriela Mistral. Trans. and ed. by Doris Dana. Johns Hopkins 1971 o.p.

BOOKS ABOUT MISTRAL

Arce de Vázquez, Margot. *Gabriela Mistral: The Poet and Her Work*. NYU Pr. 1964 o.p. An affectionate catalogue of Mistral's achievements as well as a brief biographical sketch; useful introduction for the general reader.

Gazarian-Gautier, Marie-Lise. *Gabriela Mistral*. Franciscan Pr. 1974 o.p. A profound and perceptive biography written by one of her students.

Taylor, Martin C. *Gabriela Mistral's Religious Sensibility*. U. CA Pr. 1968 o.p. A study of Jewish and Christian religious imagery in Mistral, with particular attention to such resonant symbols as trees, wood, blood, water, and wine.

NERUDA, PABLO (pseud. of Neftalí Ricardo Reyes). 1904–1973 (NOBEL PRIZE 1971) Chile

Neruda's poetry moved through a variety of periods and styles, beginning with the youthful romanticism of *Crepusculary* (1919), which shows the seeds of his later social commitment. In *Twenty Poems of Love and a Song of Despair* (1924), his tone becomes more despairing, a mood amplified in *The Attempt of Infinite Man*, an experiment with the avant-garde expressing the painful confrontation with human limits. The three hermetic volumes of *Residence on Earth* (1933) are surrealistic in style and subject matter, characterized by twisted syntax, audacious metaphors, and truncated phrases that express the chaos of the modern mind and an ontological despair. The *Canto General*

(1950) is an effort to capture the epic tone of Latin America's history; highly political in large part, it contains some of the poet's finest work, as in his single greatest work, *The Heights of Machu Picchu* (1945). In later work Neruda ranged from experiments with "conversational" poetry in *Extravagaria* (1958) to lyric autobiography to the rapturous contemplation of the natural world's wonders. In volumes such as *Spain in the Heart* and *Intimate Letter to Millions*, his verse becomes less hermetic, more accessible, and particularly more political.

In 1927 Neruda entered Chile's diplomatic corps, and after an unpleasant tour in the Orient, he became consul to Barcelona and then moved to Madrid in 1935. He devoted himself to the cause of the Spanish republic, and its destruction by Franco's forces led him into political activism and a conversion to communism. He saw as his mission the education of the proletariat, and the pessimism of his early period changed to optimism about humankind's solidarity and the future of communism. Neruda remained an international figure throughout his life, as well as an important force in Chilean politics. His extraordinary poetic talent and his active social role made him a legendary and symbolic figure for intellectuals, students, and artists from all of Latin America. "The tension, the repression, the drama of our position in Latin America doesn't permit us the luxury of being uncommitted," he said. Neruda won the Nobel Prize in 1971 "for poetry that, with the action of an elemental force, brings alive a continent's destiny and dreams." He died in Chile shortly after the coup d'état that deposed President Allende in 1973, and this coincidence gave a renewed resonance to his name in the opposition to the dictatorship of General Pinochet.

Poetry by Neruda

Art of Birds. Trans. by Jack Schmitt. U. of Tex. Pr. 1985. $19.95. ISBN 0-292-70371-6. Shows Neruda's love for the natural world in its beauty, grace, and mystery.

The Book of Questions. Trans. by William O'Daly. Copper Canyon 1991 $19.00. ISBN 1-55659-040-7. Contains 74 poems and 316 playful questions about death, nature, and rebirth.

Canto General. 1950. Trans. by Jack Schmitt. U. CA Pr. 1991 $35.00. ISBN 0-520-05433-4

The Captain's Verses. 1952. Trans. by Donald D. Walsh. New Dir. Pr. 1972 $6.95. ISBN 0-8112-0457-X. Collection of poetry.

Extravagaria. 1958. Trans. by Alastair Reid. FS&G 1974 o.p. Bilingual edition.

Five Decades: Poems 1925–1970. 1974. Trans. by Ben Bellit. Grove Pr. 1987 $14.50. ISBN 0-8021-3035-6. Anthology of Neruda's poetry.

Fully Empowered. Trans. by Alastair Reid. FS&G 1976 o.p. Poems based on the elements of nature.

The Heights of Macchu Picchu. Trans. by Nathaniel Tarn. FS&G 1967 $9.95. ISBN 0-374-50658-5. Bilingual edition.

The House in the Sand. 1966. Trans. by Dennis Maloney and Clark Zlotchew. Milkweed Ed. 1990 $14.95. ISBN 0-915943-49-2. Bilingual edition of Neruda's 1966 book of prose poems, set in his beloved Isla Negra.

Incitement to Nixonicide. Trans. by Steve Kowit. Fr. & Eur. $27.50. ISBN 0-9600306-3-8. Poems against Nixon and the U.S. overthrow of Allende.

Late and Posthumous Poems, 1968–1974. Trans. by Ben Belitt. Grove Pr. 1989 $11.95. ISBN 0-8021-3145-X. Includes 14 poems from *The Sea and the Bells* as well as 86 gathered from 8 other collections.

Let the Railsplitter Awake and Other Poems. Trans. by Waldeen Intl. Pubs. Co. 1989 $4.95. ISBN 0-7178-0668-5. Polemic poems and revolutionary hymns for the worker.

One Hundred Love Sonnets: Cien sonetos de amor. Trans. by Stephen Tapscott. U. of Tex. Pr. 1986 $22.50. ISBN 0-292-76029-9. Captures the lyrical vision and language of Neruda in its English translation with great accuracy and preserves the rhythm of the original Spanish.

Residence on Earth and Other Poems. Trans. by Donald D. Walsh. New Dir. Pr. 1973 $11.95. ISBN 0-8112-0467-7

The Sea and the Bells. Trans. by William O'Daly. Copper Canyon 1988 $10.00. ISBN 1-55659-019-9. Focuses on nature as a catalyst to the spirit's rejuvenation.

Selected Odes of Pablo Neruda. Trans. by Margaret S. Peden. U. CA Pr. 1990 $40.00. ISBN 0-520-05944-1. Collection of Neruda's odes on quotidian motifs.

Selected Poems. Trans. by Ben Belitt. Grove Pr. 1989. $10.95. ISBN 0-8021-5102-7. Covers the whole field of Neruda's achievements.

A Separate Rose. Trans. by William O'Daly. Copper Canyon 1985 $9.00. ISBN 0-914742-88-4. Collection of poetry that attempts to unravel both the ancient silence and mystery of Easter Island and the human condition of Neruda's contemporary world.

Spain in the Heart. Trans. by Richard Schaaf. Floricanto Pr. 1992 $29.95. ISBN 0-685-38357-1

Still Another Day. Trans. by William O'Daly. Copper Canyon 1984 $75.00. ISBN 0-914742-78-7. Collection of poetry.

The Stones of Chile. Trans. by Dennis Maloney. White Pine 1987 $10.00. ISBN 0-934834-01-6. Poems of geographic contemplation; keynote of the collection is the primal howl of marine sounds that issues from the stark infertile coastline of Chile.

Stones of the Sky. Trans. by James Nolan. Copper Canyon 1987 $15.00. ISBN 1-55659-006-7. Thirty poems that redirect Neruda's amorous, telluric, and quotidian predilections toward rocks and gems.

Three Spanish American Poets: Pellicer, Neruda, Andrade. Trans. by Lloyd Mallan. Gordon Pr. 1977 $59.95. ISBN 0-8490-2747-0. Anthology that includes Neruda.

Twenty Love Poems and a Song of Despair. 1924. Trans. by W. S. Merwin. Viking Penguin 1976 $4.95. ISBN 0-14-042205-6

Winter Garden. Trans. by William O'Daly. Copper Canyon 1986 $15.00. ISBN 0-914742-99-X. Elegantly timeless and fresh poems, showing a poet torn between the joys of solitude and his sense of duty as a spokesperson for humanity.

The Yellow Heart. Trans. by William O'Daly. Copper Canyon 1990 $17.00. ISBN 0-55659-028-8. Poems that present Neruda's usual themes and symbols, yet have a lighter feel to them; published posthumously.

NONFICTION BY NERUDA

Isla Negra: a Notebook. Trans. by Alastair Reid. FS&G 1982 $14.95. ISBN 0-374-51734-7. Poetic autobiographic entries about Neruda's birthplace, rootlessness, travel, and search for identity.

Memoirs. Trans. by Hardie St. Martin. Viking Penguin 1978 $7.95. ISBN 0-14-004661-5. Autobiographic descriptions of Neruda's aging as both a man and a poet.

Passions and Impressions. Trans. by Margaret S. Peden. FS&G 1984 $10.95. ISBN 0-374-51811-4. Poetical, social, and political essays that encompass Neruda's life's work.

Toward the Splendid City: Nobel Lecture. FS&G 1974 $4.95. ISBN 0-374-27850-4. Neruda's lecture upon receiving the Nobel Prize.

Windows that Open Inward: Images of Chile. Trans. by Alastair Reid. White Pine 1984 $25.00. ISBN 0-934834-51-2. Writing on Chilean motifs.

BOOKS ABOUT NERUDA

Agosin, Marjorie. *Pablo Neruda*. Twayne 1986 o.p. Good introduction to Neruda's life and works that identifies the major influences on his poetry.

Anderson, David G. *On Elevating the Commonplace: a Structuralist Analysis of the "Odas" of Pablo Neruda*. Albatross 1987 o.p. Examines Neruda's "Odas" in historical context.

Bizarro, Salvatore. *Pablo Neruda: All Poets the Poet*. Scarecrow 1979 $20.00. ISBN 0-8108-1189-8. Study of the evolution of the poet as interpreter of realism.

Bloom, Harold, ed. *Pablo Neruda*. Chelsea Hse. 1989 $34.95. ISBN 1-55546-298-7. Useful collection of modern critical essays that discuss Neruda's poetry from a variety of critical perspectives.

De Costa, René. *The Poetry of Pablo Neruda*. HUP 1979 $19.95. ISBN 0-674-67980-6. Describes and evaluates the reception of each of Neruda's published works.

Riess, Frank. *The Word and the Stone; Language and Imagery in Neruda's* Canto General. OUP 1972 o.p. Studies the themes and imagery in the *Canto General.*

Santí, Enrico. *Pablo Neruda: The Politics of Prophecy*. Cornell Univ. Pr. 1982 o.p. A critical understanding of Neruda's poetic career from his early prophetic poems to the later polemic ones.

Teitelboim, Volodia. *Neruda: An Intimate Biography*. U. of Tex. Pr. 1992 $17.95. ISBN 0-292-78124-5. Biography of Neruda by another Chilean poet, Neruda's close friend and political associate.

ONETTI, JUAN CARLOS. 1909– Uruguay

Onetti's subject is the decay and materialism of the modern world, but he presents it in a dense, indirect prose style that creates a world often bordering on nightmare. The narrator of *A Brief Life* (1950), creates a number of other existences for himself to escape the boredom and limits, symbolized by his wife's mastectomy, of his own. Ultimately, the created worlds take over supposed reality. *The Shipyard* (1961), generally considered his best novel, demonstrates the central character's inability to control his life in an absurd existence. Onetti's characters never cease trying to create meaning, but they flounder helplessly in a world that is beyond their efforts at control.

Novels by Onetti

Body Snatcher. Trans. by Alfred MacAdam. Pantheon 1991 $23.00. ISBN 0-679-40178-4. An existential novel of personal truth.

A Brief Life. 1950. Trans. by Hortense Carpentier. Viking Penguin 1976 o.p.

Short Story Collection by Onetti

Goodbyes and Other Stories. Trans. by Daniel Balderston. U. of Tex. Pr. 1990 $22.50. ISBN 0-292-72743-7. Collection of 10 tales of alienation and despair.

Book about Onetti

Kadir, Djelal. *Juan Carlos Onetti. Twayne's World Authors Ser.* G. K. Hall 1977 o.p. Concentrates on Onetti as a novelist and elaborates on all of his works.

PACHECO, JOSÉ EMILIO. 1939– Mexico

Pacheco, one of Mexico's ablest critics, is also a poet of extraordinarily formal and thematic diversity, preoccupied with the struggle to express social concerns while maintaining artistic integrity. Originally preoccupied with metaphysical concerns, he sees humankind caught in time between poles of a destructive flow; people are trapped in a permanent present as time, somehow, passes. In his questioning of every aspect of existence, even poetry, the poet creates a sense of harmony within flux. Pacheco's writing has also brought a Jewish note to Mexican letters.

Poetry by Pacheco

Don't Ask Me How the Time Goes By: Poems, 1964–1968. Trans. by Alastair Reid. Col. U. Pr. 1978 $42.00. ISBN 0-231-04284-1. Includes poems that pertain to the act of writing, travel, and Mexico.

Selected Poems. Trans. by Thomas Hoeksema and others. New Dir. Pr. 1987 $23.95. ISBN 0-8112-1021-9. Collection of Pacheco's poetry in which earth, air, fire, and water all conspire, in time, to bring everything to nothing.

SHORT STORY COLLECTION BY PACHECO

Battles in the Desert and Other Stories. Trans. by Katherine Silver. New Dir. Pr. 1987 $19.95. ISBN 0-8112-1019-7. Title story is rich in references to a post–World War II Mexico City seen through the misty eyes of a lovesick adolescent.

PADILLA, HEBERTO. 1932– Cuba

Padilla held a number of bureaucratic, educational, and journalistic positions under the government of Fidel Castro. His outspokenness in cultural affairs caused considerable tension and his collection of poems *Fuera del Juego* won an important Cuban prize but was judged antirevolutionary. Now an exile in the United States, he was the protagonist in the notorious "Padilla Affair," and was accused of subversive activities, causing an international protest. In 1980 he was permitted to leave Cuba. Padilla's poetry is anchored in the real world and tends to satirize abstract theorizing. The poems collected below mark his imprisonment, as well as his taste for Eliot and the breadth of his literary interests.

POETRY BY PADILLA

Legacies: Selected Poems. Trans. by Alastair Reid and Andrew Hurley. FS&G 1982 $9.95. ISBN 0-374-51736-3. Poems moved with narrative and descriptive devices, encompassing a large selection of his work.

NONFICTION BY PADILLA

Heroes Are Grazing in My Garden. Trans. by Andrew Hurley. FS&G 1984 o.p. Chronicles Padilla's political experiences in Cuba.

Self-Portrait of the Other: A Memoir. Trans. by Alexander Coleman. FS&G 1990 $19.95. ISBN 0-374-26086-9. Spans Padilla's career, from his ardent early support of the revolution to his subsequent imprisonment and ostracism by the Castro regime.

PARRA, NICANOR. 1914– Chile

In an effort to transform poetry, Parra invented what he calls the "antipoem," which, he says, "returns poetry to its roots." He uses elements commonly considered ugly or antipoetic, ordinary objects and commonplace language, with a sardonic humor and an unexpected angle of vision. His work is comparable to that of the American Beat poets of the 1950s in its nonpoetic flat tone, direct statement, black humor, and violence, and he intends his poetry as an affront to society. At the same time, he works within a Chilean popular tradition, which gives his work a distinctly original flavor. Parra has also served as a professor of theoretical physics at the University of Chile and is an accomplished folk musician. PABLO NERUDA called him "one of the great names in the literature of our language."

POETRY BY PARRA

Antipoems: New and Selected. Trans. by Lawrence Ferlinghetti and others. New Dir. Pr. 1985 $19.95. ISBN 0-8112-0959-8

Emergency Poems. Trans. by Miller Williams. New Dir. Pr. 1972 $8.75. ISBN 0-8112-0340-9. Second book of Parra's poems; theme shifts from poetical to satirical.

Sermons and Homilies of the Christ of Elqui. Trans. by Sandra Reyes. U. Mo. Pr. 1984 $13.50. ISBN 0-8262-0451-1. Characterization of Christ of Elqui; mixes realism with absurdity in poetic form.

PAZ, OCTAVIO. 1914– (NOBEL PRIZE 1990) Mexico

Octavio Paz's poetic roots are in romanticism and such neoromantics as D. H. LAWRENCE (see Vol. 1), but he has been profoundly influenced by Mexican Indian mythology and oriental religious philosophy, particularly Tantric Buddhism. The latter influence came about while he was serving as Mexico's ambassador to India (1962–68), when he resigned to protest the government's treatment of students demonstrating prior to the Olympic Games in Mexico City. He conceives of poetry as a way of transcending barriers of world, time, and individual self. Through poetry he seeks to achieve a state of innocence and a euphoria of the senses bordering on the mystical, and he expresses anguish when language fails him. Much of Paz's poetry is erotic, with women being the vehicle across the abyss to "the other side of the river," where union with universal consciousness is possible. This element in his poetic vision has of late left him open to acerbic feminist readings.

Paz constantly experiments with form in an effort to break down the traditional forms of poetry; several of his long major works are circular and have coexisting variant readings, and *Renga* is a collaborative poem by poets in four languages. Poetry for Paz is necessarily in conflict with society because of its potential for transmuting and reforming it, and the poetic imagination is a valuable tool for understanding society. His essays on the Mexican character, history, and traditions, such as *The Labyrinth of Solitude* (1950) and *The Other Mexico* (1969), are fundamental to understanding Mexican society. He has also written extensively on aesthetics, poetics, and the nature of language and poetry.

POETRY BY PAZ

Alternating Current. Trans. by Helen R. Lane. Arcade Pub. Inc. 1991 $9.95. ISBN 1-55970-136-6. Poems that explore literary theory, Mexican fiction, Oriental theory, and drugs.

The Collected Poems 1957–1987. Trans. by Eliot Weinberger. New Dir. Pr. 1987 $37.50. ISBN 0-8112-1037-5. Contains in bilingual format all the poetry that Paz has written since 1957, including his premier long poem, "Sunstone," and "A Tree Within."

Configurations. Trans. by G. Aroul and others. New Dir. Pr. 1971 $7.95. ISBN 0-8112-0150-3

Conjunctions and Disjunctions. Trans. by Helen R. Lane. Arcade Pub. Inc. 1991 $8.95. ISBN 1-55970-137-4. Poems that formalize Paz's ideas about grammar in essay form.

A Draft of Shadows and Other Poems. 1978. Trans. by Eliot Weinberger. New Dir. Pr. 1979 $8.95. ISBN 0-8112-0738-2. Poems filled with volcanic rage toward Mexico's poverty-stricken countryside.

Eagle or Sun? 1973. Trans. by Eliot Weinberger. New Dir. Pr. 1976 $8.50. ISBN 0-8112-0622-X.

Early Poems. 1935–1955. Trans. by Muriel Rukeyser. New Dir. Pr. rev. ed. 1973 $7.95. ISBN 0-8112-0478-2. Considers the growth of Paz's work over 20 years.

Selected Poems of Octavio Paz. Trans. by G. Aroul and others. New Dir. Pr. 1984 $8.95. ISBN 0-8112-0899-0. Comprehensive selection showing the range of Paz's poetic work.

Sunstone—Piedra de sol. Trans. by Eliot Weinberger. New Dir. Pr. 1991 repr. of 1963 ed. $18.95. ISBN 0-8112-1197-5. Poetry on the sunstone motif.

A Tree Within. Trans. by Eliot Weinberger. New Dir. Pr. 1988 $9.95. ISBN 0-8112-1071-5. Poems dedicated to Miro, Balthus, and Duchamp; a meditation on love and death in a prophetic sense.

NONFICTION BY PAZ

The Bow and the Lyre: The Poem. The Poetic Revelation. Poetry and History. Trans. by Ruth L. Simms. U. of Tex. Pr. 1987 $12.95. ISBN 0-292-70764-9. Fine translation that explains Paz's view of the essence and significance of poetry.

Convergences: Essays on Art and Literature. Trans. by Helen R. Lane. HarBraceJ 1987 $19.95. ISBN 0-15-122585-0. Selected essays conveying ideas of language and perceptions.

In Search of the Present. Trans. by Anthony Stanton. HarBraceJ 1991 $8.95. ISBN 0-15-644556-5. Novel Prize acceptance speech for the Swedish Academy of Letters.

The Labyrinth of Solitude. The Other Mexico, Return to the Labyrinth of Solitude, Mexico and the U.S.A., the Philanthropic Ogre. Trans. by Lysander Kemp. Grove Pr. 1989 $11.95. ISBN 0-8021-5042-X

Marcel Duchamp: Appearance Stripped Bare. Trans. by Rachel Phillips and Donald Gardner. Arcade Pub. Inc. 1991 $9.95. ISBN 1-55970-138-2. Essays on Marcel Duchamp.

The Monkey Grammarian. Trans. by Helen R. Lane. Arcade Pub. Inc. 1991 $9.95. ISBN 1-55970-135-8. Free-verse composition on the origins of language through the landscape of Mexico.

On Poets and Others. Trans. by Michael Schmidt. Seaver Bks. 1986 $18.95. ISBN 0-8050-0003-8. Real and directed essays on Frost, Whitman, Williams, Sartre, Baudelaire, and others.

One Earth, Four or Five Worlds: Reflections on Contemporary History. Trans. by Helen R. Lane. HarBraceJ 1986 $5.95. ISBN 0-15-668746-1. Essays that comment on the tangled cultural and political history of his country, his continent, and the looming forces of the superpowers beyond.

One Word to the Other. Latitudes Pr. 1991 $7.00. ISBN 0-318-41819-3

Rufino Tamayo: Myth and Magic. Trans. by Rachel Phillips. S. R. Guggenheim 1979 $12.95. ISBN 0-89207-019-6. Tamayo's eightieth birthday retrospective at the Guggenheim Museum.

Siren and the Seashell: And Other Essays on Poets and Poetry by Octavio Paz. U. of Tex. Pr. 1991 $9.95. ISBN 0-292-77652-7. Deciphers and analyzes other poets' works; companion to *The Bow and the Lyre.*

Sor Juana: Or, the Traps of Faith. Trans. by Margaret S. Peden. HUP 1988 $29.95. ISBN 0-674-82105-X. Massive study on the Mexican nun and poet, Sor Juana, and Mexican colonial culture.

BOOKS ABOUT PAZ

Chantikian, Kosrof, ed. *Octavio Paz: Homage to the Poet.* KOSMOS. 1981 $20.00. ISBN 0-916426-03-3. Examines Paz's craft and personality by interweaving essays by Paz with those of friends.

Chiles, Frances. *Octavio Paz: The Mythic Dimension.* P. Lang. Pubs. 1987 $44.00. ISBN 0-8204-0079-3. Scholarly study of myth and mythmaking in Paz's poetry that concentrates on the archetypal themes and symbols in his work.

Wilson, Jason. *Octavio Paz.* Cambridge U. Pr. 1979 $34.50. ISBN 0-521-22306-7. Study of Paz's life and works that examines the poet's themes and techniques for the general reader.

PIZARNIK, ALEJANDRA. 1936–1972 Argentina

The daughter of Polish-Jewish immigrants, Pizarnik suffered throughout her life from severe depression and committed suicide one weekend on leave from the psychiatric hospital where she was institutionalized. Pizarnik spent several years in Paris in contact with the European poetic vanguard and toward the end of her life held a Guggenheim Foundation award. Her poetry portrays the life of Latin American women as a bodily dismemberment by a multiply oppressive and repressive patriarchy. It sparked interest alone for the intensity with which it chronicles the obsessions of a feminine *poète maudit.* Concomitantly, Pizarnik's poetry assumed a clandestine and iconic dimension because the bulk of her mature output coincided with the military regimes in Argentine. For some, her work is a symbol of the destruction of the individual by neo-Fascist tyranny. Although Pizarnik mostly wrote highly charged poetic vignettes, leading her to be compared with SYLVIA PLATH (see Vol. 1), she also wrote outstanding prose poems, culminating in *The Bloody Countess* (1971). This is a chilly recreation of the nefarious Hungarian noblewoman, Erzbet Báthory, who was accused in the seventeenth century of torturing to death 600 maidens; and it is a work whose interest overlaps, if only obliquely, with the significant lesbian dimension of Pizarnik's writing.

WORK BY PIZARNIK

Alejandra Pizarnik: A Profile. Trans. by María Rosa Fort and Suzanne Jill Levine. Logbridge-Rhodes 1987 $18.00. ISBN 0-937406-37-6. Collection of Pizarnik's poetry, prose, and personal diaries, with enlightening commentaries about the poet that provide a complete and interesting vision of the artist's life, friendships, and obsessions.

PUIG, MANUEL. 1932–1991 Argentina

Puig is fascinated by the variety and richness, and at the same time, by the stultifying effects of pop culture. Most of his novels are technically parodies of some form of pop art while they portray the spiritual emptiness of the characters who are affected by these forms. *Betrayed by Rita Hayworth* (1968) is an innovative novel narrating through a variety of techniques the story of a young Argentine boy who lives vicariously through the movies. Puig uses the phenomenon of compulsive movie-going as a symbol for alienation and escape from reality. *Heartbreak Tango* (1969) evokes the spiritual emptiness of the Argentine provincial life in the 1930s and the vulgarity of popular music and the soap opera; *The Buenos Aires Affair* (1972) uses the form of the detective novel to parody pop fiction. *Kiss of the Spider Woman* (1979) examines political and sexual liberation in novelistic techniques that reject traditional dialogue in favor of various other kinds of texts, and in *Blood of Unrequited Love*, a man and a woman relive an old but passionate affair in the Brazilian backlands. *Eternal Curse on the Reader of These Pages* (1981) is a novelty for Puig in that it consists entirely of dialogue, plus an epilogue in letters. Less obviously parodic and more elliptical, with less reliance on the machinery of pop culture, it demonstrates his constant search for a new form for his novels. Puig, who always rejected the category of "homosexual writer," may nevertheless be Latin America's best example of a contemporary gay sensibility in his generally countercultural artistic stance.

NOVELS BY PUIG

Betrayed by Rita Hayworth. 1968. Trans. by Suzanne J. Levine. Random 1981 o.p.

Blood of Unrequited Love. Trans. by Jan L. Grayson. Random 1984 $9.95. ISBN 0-394-72440-2

The Buenos Aires Affair: A Detective Novel. 1972. Trans. by Suzanne J. Levine. Random 1980 o.p.

Eternal Curse on the Reader of These Pages. 1981. Random 1982 o.p.

Heartbreak Tango. 1969. Trans. by Suzanne J. Levine. Viking Penguin 1991 $8.95. ISBN 0-14-015346-2

Kiss of the Spider Woman. 1979. Trans. by Thomas Colchie. Random 1991 $10.00. ISBN 0-679-72449-4

Tropical Night Falling. Trans. by Suzanne J. Levine. S & S Trade 1991 $9.00. ISBN 0-671-67996-1. Tells the story of two old sisters who live in Rio, both of whom at first seem to be living utterly vicarious lives.

BOOK ABOUT PUIG

Kerr, Lucille. *Suspended Fictions: Reading Novels by Manuel Puig*. U. of Ill. Pr. 1987 $29.95. ISBN 0-252-01329-8. First book-length study of Puig that insists that his novels both uphold and caricature popular forms on which they are based.

QUIROGA, HORACIO. 1878–1937 Argentina

One of the fathers of the Spanish American short story, Quiroga participated extensively in the modernist movement in Montevideo and later lived in the tropical province of Misiones. Although best known as the author of stories about the jungle that reveal the dangers at every step, he also wrote imaginative fantastic tales among the best of their kind in an area that has produced a great number of such authors. His work, like his life (he eventually committed suicide), is filled with violent tragedy and a sense of foreboding.

SHORT STORY COLLECTIONS BY QUIROGA

The Decapitated Chicken and Other Stories. Trans. by Margaret S. Peden. *Texas Pan-Amer. Ser.* U. of Tex. Pr. 1976 $8.95. ISBN 0-292-71541-2. Short stories that explore elements of tragedy and violence.

The Exiles and Other Stories. Trans. by David J. Danielson. U. of Tex. Pr. 1987 $17.95. ISBN 0-292-72050-5. Contains 13 stories that convey the despair, the hope, and the fear that grip Quiroga's South American characters.

RIVERA, JOSÉ EUSTASIO. 1888–1928 Colombia

After the publication of a book of romantic sonnets entitled *The Promised Land* (1921), Rivera wrote *The Vortex* (1924), the prototype of the Latin American jungle novel. Rejecting the traditional romantic view of the jungle as magnificent landscape peopled by innocent natives, Rivera presented a cannabilistic, terrifying green trap that closes on the protagonist. The narrator is Arturo Cova, a persona of Rivera, whose memoirs relate his seduction of a young girl, their escape into the jungle, crime and corruption in the rubber industry, and the extreme violence that results when people's instincts are unchecked by civilization. Based on historical data, personal observation, and travel logs, *The Vortex* grew out of the conflict Rivera saw between literary presentations of the jungle and his own experiences of it. Rivera died of diseases contracted in the jungle in the course of his work as member of a commission appointed to settle a boundary dispute between Colombia and Venezuela.

NOVEL BY RIVERA

The Vortex. 1924. Trans. by James K. Earl. Fertig 1979 repr. of 1935 ed. o.p.

ROA BASTOS, AUGUSTO. 1917– Paraguay

To say that Roa Bastos is the paradigm of the Latin American writer in exile would be no exaggeration. After spending 25 years in Buenos Aires following an abortive conspiracy in the 1940s to overthrow a dictatorship, Roa accepted a teaching position at the Université de Toulouse-Le Mirail, from which he is now retired. In the mid-1980s, he accepted an offer of Spanish citizenship, resigned to his never again living in his native country. Roa Bastos's complex fiction is the attempt to record the "inner" history of Paraguay and to record the many silenced voices: those of the indigenous population (including those who speak the Guarani language, which dominates in Paraguay's bilingual and bicultural society); the original independence fighters and their revolutionary offspring; the marginalized artist who is forced to live, if not an actual exile, an interior exile; and those decent men and women whose very decency exposes them to exploitation and oppression. Roa Bastos's novel *Son of Man* is his effort to create such an inner history. Passages in an almost biblical style create a panoramic transition between vignettes in which Christ figures represent the injustices of Paraguayan society and its victims' sacrifices. *I, the Supreme* (1974) is the first-person narrative of José Gaspar Rodríguez de Francia, the Enlightenment-inspired Paraguayan strongman of the mid-1800s who sought to create an autochthonous utopia in the Paraguayan heartland. Francia fought against the overwhelming odds of international forces desiring to thwart Paraguay's political independence and to appropriate its natural resources, and Roa Bastos portrays him as a tragic figure. In the novel, he is caught between, on the one hand, the historical necessities of brutal dictatorship and the inevitable destiny of the young South American republics, and, on the other, the profoundly seductive chimeras of sociocultural independence.

Novels by Roa Bastos

I, the Supreme. 1974. Trans. by Helen Lane. Knopf 1986 $18.95. ISBN 0-394-58535-9

Son of Man. 1960. Trans. by Rachel Caffyn. Monthly Rev. 1988 $24.00. ISBN 0-85345-767-0

Books about Roa Bastos

Foster, David William. *Augusto Roa Bastos*. Twayne 1978 o.p. A general overview of Roa Bastos's literary production.

RULFO, JUAN. 1918–1986 Mexico

Rulfo's collection of short stories, *The Burning Plain* (1953), deals in harsh, colloquial language with the poor peasants of remote areas of the province of Jalisco—their traditions, problems, and passions. His only published novel, *Pedro Páramo* (1955), also based on rural life, treats the theme of the *cacique* or boss of a town. The structure of the novel, influenced in part by Faulkner (see Vol. 1), involves the juxtaposition and transposition of pieces of narrative, monologue, dialogue, and poetic prose. Rulfo's uncompromising vision of the harsh injustices of rural life effectively brought to an end the Mexican postrevolutionary mythification of rural society.

Novel by Rulfo

Pedro Páramo. 1955. Trans. by Lysander Kemp. Grove Pr. 1990 $7.95. ISBN 0-8021-3216-2

Short Story Collection by Rulfo

The Burning Plain and Other Stories. 1953. Trans. by George D. Schade. *Texas Pan-Amer. Ser.* U. of Tex. Pr. 1967 $8.95. ISBN 0-29270132-2

SÁBATO, ERNESTO. 1911– Argentina

Sábato's protagonists in his three major novels are all obsessive neurotics trapped in a society that went wrong centuries ago. *On Heroes and Tombs* (1981) analyzes the phenomenon of Peronism and the social conditions that caused it, but it is also an anguished examination of what Sábato preceives to be the basic errors of Argentine society from its beginnings. The complex plot integrates the tyranny of Perón with that of Rosas a century earlier. Its principal characters counterpoint the decadence of the old aristocracy with the potential for change of the descendants of the European immigrants. One entire major section is devoted to a schizophrenic episode by a protagonist-villain, Fernando Vidal Olmos, who may also be seen as hero. Sábato is also a prolific and provocative essayist. Although he was written little in recent years, he enjoyed a renewed prominence in the mid-1980s as chair of the presidential commission on disappeared persons during the 1976–83 military dictatorship.

NOVELS BY SÁBATO

On Heroes and Tombs. 1981. Trans. by Helen R. Lane. Ballantine 1988 $5.99. ISBN 0-345-34928-8

The Tunnel. Trans. by Margaret S. Peden. Ballantine 1991 $5.99. ISBN 0-345-37377-4. A novel of existential conflict in contemporary Argentine society.

NONFICTION BY SÁBATO

The Writer in the Catastrophe of Our Time. Trans. by Asa Zatz. Coun. Oak Bks. 1990 $9.95. ISBN 0-933031-24-6. Sábato's writings on the place of the writer in contemporary society.

SÁNCHEZ, LUIS RAFAEL. 1932– Puerto Rico

The bulk of Sánchez's works have been published outside of Puerto Rico; nevertheless, he remains the island's most important contemporary author and one of its most controversial. In a key essay, he defends a "poetics of the filthy," by which he means everything that is authentic about Puerto Rican life but that is ignored or vilified by those who want to assimilate Puerto Rico into alienating North American society. His most famous novel, *Macho Camacho's Beat* (1976), originally published in Argentina, is a scathing indictment of the senseless fragmentation of Puerto Rican life as seen in the urban setting of San Juan. Sánchez's irreverant comedy builds on the silly lyrics of a popular song (the beat of the title), which he develops as a synthesis of life in a "country" that is neither independent nor really a significant part of American society. Sánchez has written a number of widely respected plays on the tragicomic texture of Puerto Rican life, and his fiction in general is noted for its treatment and incorporation of popular culture materials.

NOVELS BY SANCHEZ

Macho Camacho's Beat. 1976. Trans. by Gregory Rabassa. Pantheon 1980 o.p.

SARDUY, SEVERO. 1937– Cuba

Sarduy has written primarily in exile and under the aegis of contemporary French intellectual and cultural movements. His essays are dense speculations about the complex structure of contemporary culture, a line of inquiry that forms the basis of his highly wrought fiction. He explores individuals and situations as the intersection of multiple levels of cultural formation enacted (unconsciously by the characters) in even the most menial actions and events. Stripped down to their narrative core, Sarduy's novels typically deal with the quotidian, but the quotidian figured in a richly textured language that is as difficult to read as his cultural formations are to understand. Moreover, Sarduy has been especially audacious both in depicting taboo (panerotic sexualism, homosexuality, transvestism, and transgressive "gender bending" in general) and in demonstrating taboo's irrelevance to daily life. In Sarduy's vision, the lines drawn between taboo and transgression, the conventional and the deviant, are not real. In one sense, Sarduy's writing is quintessentially Cuban in themes and tone, while at the same time one of the best examples of Latin American late modernism.

NOVEL BY SARDUY

Maitreya. 1978. Trans. by Suzanne Jill Levine. Ediciones Norte 1987 $9.50. ISBN 0-910061-31-9. Complex novel that takes place in the Cuba of the early 1960s and in Tibet after the Chinese invasion in 1950.

NONFICTION BY SARDUY

Written on a Body. Trans. by Carol Maier. Lumen Inc. 1989 $9.95. ISBN 0-930829-04-2. Essays on contemporary cultural themes relating to the body.

POETRY BY SARDUY

For Voice. Trans. by Philip Barnard. Lat. Am. Lit. Rev. Pr. 1985 $12.95. ISBN 0-935480-20-X. Celebrates the creativity of language itself and its multiplicity of significances.

BOOKS ABOUT SARDUY

Kushigian, Julia A. *Orientalism in the Hispanic Literary Tradition: In Dialogue with Borges, Paz, and Sarduy.* U. of NM Pr. 1991 $29.95. ISBN 0-8263-1314-0. Documents Oriental influences and the intermingling of East and West from the Middle Ages to the present in Sarduy's writing.

Montero, Oscar. *The Name Game: The Semiotic Intertext of* De donde son los cantantes. U. of NC Pr. 1988 $20.00. ISBN 0-8078-9236-X. Extensive dissertation concerning characterization and theme in Sarduy's writing; a companion to *De dondo son los cantantes.*

SARMIENTO, DOMINGO FAUSTINO. 1811–1888 Argentina

Born into a humble family, Sarmiento became president of the Argentine republic in 1868. He was a driving force in the effort to Europeanize Argentina and in the struggle against the rural power elite. His reputation in literature is based on *Civilization and Barbarism: Life of Juan Facundo Quiroga* (1845), a combination of essay and history that often approaches the novel in its handling of imaginative narrative. Demonstrating the barbaric actions of both Juan Manuel de Rosas, the dictatorial governor of Argentina, and the gaucho Facundo in *Tiger of the Pampas* (o.p.), Sarmiento advocated the civilizing influences of education and economic progress. His ambivalent feelings and romantic view of the gaucho led him to create a mythical character rather than a historical figure. The narratives and sketches in *Travels* (1849) have been described as "a virtual novel" (Anderson Imbert) for their imaginative quality.

NONFICTION BY SARMIENTO

Life in the Argentine Republic in the Days of the Tyrants, or Civilization and Barbarism. 1845. Trans. by Marty T. Mann. Hafner 1970 $10.95. ISBN 0-02-851650-8. Sarmiento's exposition of his famous binarism, civilization versus barbarism.

Sarmiento's Travels in the United States in 1847. Trans. by M. A. Rockland. Bks. Demand 1970 $88.20. ISBN 0-8357-39525-7. Journal entries in which Sarmiento compares the United States to Argentina; includes general descriptions, travel incidents, and a diary of expenses.

BOOK ABOUT SARMIENTO

Katra, William H. *Domingo F. Sarmiento: Public Writer (Between 1839 and 1852).* ASU Lat. Am. St. 1985 $15.15. ISBN 0-87918-061-7. Ideological analysis of Sarmiento as a public figure and writer.

SKÁRMETA, ANTONIO. 1940– Chile

Skármeta is another of the Chileans profoundly affected by his country's political travail; since 1975, he has lived in Berlin. *The Insurrection* is a novel of the Nicaraguan Revolution just before Somoza's fall; it captures the intensity and extremes of a moment that transforms a whole society. The novel has been translated into seven languages and was made into an award-winning film in Europe. *Chileno!* was written for adolescents, drawing on Skármeta's own experience of exile.

NOVELS BY SKÁRMETA

Burning Patience. Trans. by Katherine Silver. Pantheon 1987 $10.95. ISBN 0-394-55576-7. Humorous novel in which an unschooled but enthusiastic island boy obtains a job at the local post office delivering mail to a sole client—Pablo Neruda, the famous Chilean poet and diplomat.

Chileno! Trans. by Hortense Carpentier. Morrow 1979 o.p.

The Insurrection. Trans. by Paula Sharp. Ediciones Norte 1983 $12.00. ISBN 0-910061-13-0

VALENZUELA, LUISA. 1938– Argentina

Luisa Valenzuela is one of the many women who have emerged as major voices in Latin American fiction. Her elliptic metaphoric pieces broaden the definitions of short story and novel. *Strange Things Happen Here* (1977) is close to an allegory of the Argentine political situation, but it shuns conventional realism to blur reality in a hallucinatory style. JULIO CORTÁZAR said of Valenzuela that she lucidly charts "the seldom-chosen course of a woman deeply anchored in her condition, conscious of discriminations that are still horrible all over our continent, but, at the same time, filled with joy in life that permits her to surmount both the elementary stages of protest and an overestimation of women in order to put herself on a perfectly equal footing with any literature—masculine or not."

NOVELS BY VALENZUELA

Blame. 1992. S&S Trade 1992 $20.00. ISBN 0-671-68764-6. Probing novel about an Argentinian novelist haunted by the woman who he has brutally murdered.

He Who Searches. Trans. by Helen Lane. Delrey Arch. 1987 repr. of 1979 ed. $8.00. ISBN 0-916583-20-1. A narrative of political torture and repression from a feminist perspective.

The Lizard's Tail. Trans. by Gregory Rabassa. FS&G 1992 repr. of 1983 ed. $14.99. ISBN 1-85242-112-6. A political and fantastic novel on the career of Lopez Rega.

Strange Things Happen Here. 1977. HarBraceJ 1979 o.p.

SHORT STORY COLLECTION BY VALENZUELA

Other Weapons. Trans. by Deborah Bonner. Ediciones Norte 1985 $10.00. ISBN 0-910061-22-X. Collection of short stories with feminist and political themes.

VALLEJO, CÉSAR. 1892–1938 Peru

Primarily a poet and one of Latin America's finest of the twentieth century, Vallejo also wrote several novels and plays with a strong social content. His situation as a mestizo of part Indian blood, his humble social background, and the political and social discrimination to which he was subjected because of these factors, created the profound psychological tensions and alienation from society that mark his work. His work is permeated with a sense of the dignity of the oppressed Indian and a spirit of rebellion. In his first volume, *The Black Heralds* (1918), he used the techniques of symbolism to express bitterness at his suffering and condition of isolation. *Trilce* (1922) is one of the most original works of modern poetry, with an innovative syntax and structure that transcend normal logical rules to express the poet's feeling of solitude and the helplessness of oppressed peoples. After the publication of *Trilce,* Vallejo moved to Paris, where he lived in poverty and was harshly treated because of his political opinions. In poetry of a simpler structure and form, his posthumously published *Human Poems* (1939) and *Spain, Let This Cup Pass from Me* (1939) reveal his anguish over the Spanish civil war and his sense of solidarity with combatants for peace and freedom.

Poetry by Vallejo

The Black Heralds. 1918. Trans. by Kathleen Ross and Richard Schaaf. Lat. Am. Lit. Rev. Pr. 1990 $12.95. ISBN 0-935480-43-9

The Complete Posthumous Poetry. Trans. by Clayton Eshelman and José R. Barcia. U. CA Pr. 1979 $14.95. ISBN 0–520–04099–6

Poemas Humanos: Human Poems. 1939. Trans. by Clayton Eshelman. Grove Pr. 1969 o.p.

Selected Poems of César Vallejo. Trans. by R. H. Hays. Sachem Pr. 1981 $13.50. ISBN 0-937584-01-0. Poems that focus on family, God, savagery, and compassion; the finest of Vallejo's surrealistic work.

Songs of Home. Trans. by Kathleen Ross and Richard Schaaf. Ziesing Bros. 1981 $3.25. ISBN 0-917488-05-9

Spain, Let This Cup Pass from Me. 1939. Trans. by Alvaro Cardoña-Hine. Invisible-Red Hill 1972 $4.00. ISBN 0-88031-049-9

Trilce. 1922. Trans. by Rebecca Seiferle. Sheep Meadow 1992 $12.95. ISBN 1-878818-12-0

Novel by Vallejo

Tungsten: A Novel. Trans. by Robert Mezey. Syracuse U. Pr. 1988 $24.95. ISBN 0-8156-0226-X. Scantily camouflaged Marxist denunciation of North American capitalism and its rampant destruction.

Nonfiction by Vallejo

Autopsy on Surrealism. Trans. by Richard Schaaf. Curbstone 1982 o.p. An essay on surrealism.

The Mayakovsky Case. Trans. by Richard Schaaf. Curbstone 1982 $4.00. ISBN 0-915306-31-X. Analysis of the Russian poet.

VARGAS LLOSA, MARIO. 1936– Peru

Vargas Llosa, who received his doctorate from the University of Madrid and has lived in London and Paris, now resides in Peru. In addition to novels, he has also written extensively on the modern novel, especially the works of García Márquez and Flaubert, and recently premiered two successful plays. Vargas Llosa's first novel, *The City and the Dogs (The Time of the Hero)* (1966), brought both scandal and fame to its author. A thousand copies were ceremoniously burned in Peru, where Vargas Llosa was denounced as an enemy of the state, but the novel was published in Spain to high critical acclaim.

The Green House (1968), based on memories of experiences in the jungle, contains five interrelated stories fragmented through the five parts of the novel and covering a span of 45 years. Space, time, character, and action are broken and juxtaposed in a marvelous display of novelistic technique. Implicit are critiques of Peru's religious and military establishments. In *Conversation in the Cathedral* (1969), *La Catedral* being a bar, Vargas Llosa used the conversation between the son of a wealthy man and his father's mulatto chauffeur as a base for a series of juxtaposed pieces of other conversations, again exposing a corrupt society and revealing humanity's weaknesses and desperate condition.

Captain Pantoja and the Special Service (1973) is Vargas Llosa's first openly comic novel, but it also uses overlapping simultaneous plots and a sardonic approach to the role of the military in Latin American public (and private) life. The humor does not hide the dark underside of a jungle where the unexpected is always waiting. *Aunt Julia and the Scriptwriter* (1977) is openly autobiographical, dealing in barely disguised form with his first marriage. It again uses a favorite technique of juxtaposing two distinct narrative threads to satirize the commercialism and hypocrisy of society. In *The War of the End of the World* (1984), Vargas Llosa used a popular messianic revolt in the Brazilian backlands at the turn of the century to explore relations between fiction and so-called reality, one of his favorite critical themes. This may well be the first major novel on Brazil by a Spanish American writer.

NOVELS BY VARGAS LLOSA

Aunt Julia and the Scriptwriter. 1977. Trans. by Helen R. Lane. Avon 1985 $9.95. ISBN 0-380-70046-8

Captain Pantoja and the Special Service. 1973. FS&G 1990 $8.95. ISBN 0-374-52236-7

Conversation in the Cathedral. 1969. Trans. by Gregory Rabassa. FS&G 1984 $14.95. ISBN 0-374-51815-7

Green House. Trans. by Gregory Rabassa. FS&G 1985 $14.95. ISBN 0-374-51888-2

The War of the End of the World. 1984. Trans. by Helen R. Lane. Avon 1985 $11.95. ISBN 0-380-69987-7

SHORT STORY COLLECTION BY VARGAS LLOSA

The Cubs and Other Stories. Trans. by Gregory Kolovakos and Ronald Christ. FS&G 1989 $6.95. ISBN 0-374-52194-8. Short fiction from the two Spanish collections, *Los Jefes* (1965) and *Los Cachorros* (1967).

BOOKS ABOUT VARGAS LLOSA

Rossman, Charles, and Alan Warren Friedman, eds. *Mario Vargas Llosa: A Collection of Critical Essays*. U. of Tex. Pr. 1978 o.p. Critical essays of Vargas Llosa's work and personality by various writers.

Williams, Raymond Leslie. *Mario Vargas Llosa*. Continuum 1987 $15.95. ISBN 0-8044-2978-2. Provides the specialist and nonspecialist with highly readable overviews and introductions to Vargas Llosa's writings.

WOLFF, EGON. 1926– Chile

After working as a chemical engineer, Wolff began writing plays in 1958. He is one of a group of playwrights who developed their work with the support of Chilean university theaters. His plays most often deal with the demise of the guilt-ridden middle class, but he has abandoned overt realism in favor of a series of dramatic images that resist reduction to a simplistic message. *Paper Flowers*, which, in the translator's words, portrays the "destruction of a bourgeoisie indifferent to its surrounding social problems," is also a chilling portrait of a psychopathic personality and an investigation of the dynamics of human relationships.

PLAY BY WOLFF

Paper Flowers: A Play in Six Scenes. Trans. by Margaret S. Peden. U. of Mo. Pr. 1971 o.p.

YÁÑEZ, AGUSTIN. 1904–1980 Mexico

An important figure in Mexican public life, Yáñez served as governor of his state of Jalisco, professor at the National University, and secretary of public education. Although not well known outside Mexico, he was a founder of the contemporary novel, and his *The Edge of the Storm*, published in 1947, has been termed by Walter M. Langford the single most important work in the history of the Mexican novel. Influenced by Dos Passos (see Vol. 1), Aldous Huxley (see Vol. 1), and James Joyce (see Vol. 1), Yáñez brought the Mexican novel into the twentieth century in the areas of narrative technique and psychological penetration. *The Edge of the Storm* is the first of a trilogy, now including *The Prodigal Land* and *The Lean Lands* (1962).

Books by Yáñez

The Edge of the Storm. 1947. Trans. by Ethel Brinton. *Texas Pan-Amer. Ser.* U. of Tex. Pr. 1963 $12.95. ISBN 0-292-70131-4

The Lean Lands. 1962. Trans. by Ethel Brinton. *Texas Pan-Amer. Ser.* U. of Tex. Pr. 1968 o.p.

ZAPATA, LUIS. 1951– Mexico

Zapata's professional training is in medieval French literature, but he has made a major contribution to Mexican literature during the past decade in writing openly gay fiction. *Adonis García* (1979), still his most famous novel, is the picaresque chronicle of a solidly bourgeois but rebellious Mexican youth, who leaves his family and, in order to survive, turns to street prostitution in Mexico City. However, once in the city, the confluence of wealthy, jaded Mexicans, creative and intellectual Bohemians, and adventurous tourists transforms García. No longer a male prostitute who does not consider himself a homosexual, he achieves the beginnings of a gay identity—a process that is central in Zapata's subsequent writings. Zapata brings to his narratives an excellent sense of the transformations taking place in Mexico (whose capital is often viewed as paradigmatically postmodern). He explores the intersection of popular culture and outmoded bourgeois ideologies and has an accurate ear for the capital's many expressive cadences, including the speech of the millions of newly immigrant provincials. Because of both his commitment to countercultural discourses and his multi-leveled urban settings, Zapata is a key figure in contemporary Mexican fiction and, along with Puig, one of Latin America's most prominent gay writers.

Novel by Zapata

Adonis Garcia: A Picaresque Novel. 1979. Trans. by E. A. Lacey. Gay Sunshine 1981 $20.00. ISBN 0-917342-79-8

BRAZILIAN LITERATURE

As a consequence of linguistic and geographical factors, it has always been difficult to integrate Brazil with Spanish America. While Spanish and Portuguese may be mutually intelligible languages, sufficient differences exist, especially regarding everyday speech and writing, to underscore how the two languages have diverged. The fact that most of Brazil's nearly 200 million inhabitants are concentrated on the Atlantic coast has led some to speak of Brazil as the Chile of South America's east coast. Brazil's vast stretches of harsh and sparsely inhabited interior only serve to accentuate its geographic separation from the rest of the subcontinent. Only to the south is there anything approximating bilingual and bicultural frontiers, the former especially evident with the Spanish of Uruguay and the latter with the indigenous populations of Peru, Bolivia, Paraguay, and Northern Argentina.

For several decades early in the eighteenth century, during the French occupation of the Iberian peninsula, Brazil served as the imperial court of the Portuguese empire. After the withdrawal of the imperial court, Brazil existed as an autonomous monarchy until the establishment of the Republic in 1880. The transition from monarchy to republic provided Brazil's metropolitan centers, especially Rio de Janeiro, with a level of cultural splendor and artistic stimulation outstripping most of South America. It is also, not coincidentally, the creative period of the continent's first writer of international stature, MACHADA DE ASSIS, the founder of the Brazilian Academy of Letters. Moreover, Machado was a mulatto, a fact that speaks volumes to the cultural synchretism that has always characterized Brazil. Like most of the rest of Latin America, Brazil early imported blacks as slaves, but for a number of complex socioeconomic reasons, blacks have played a more sustained role in Brazilian cultural life than they have in Spanish America. And like the Andean area, Brazil has had, particularly in the south, an important ingredient of indigenous culture, while like Argentina, it has had a strong component of immigrants, with Italians and Jews particularly notable in cultural production. In the twentieth century, Japanese immigrants have attained prominence, so much so that there are more native speakers of Japanese in Brazil than all of the indigenous languages put together, although the Japanese Brazilians, while culturally active, have yet to make a major impact in literature.

Perhaps the most significant cultural event in Brazilian history was the *Semana de Arte Moderna* (Week of Modern Art), held in São Paolo in early 1922. In the spirit of New York's famous 1913 Armory Show, it showcased the most vital components of international modernism and its national manifestations. Many of the most important names of Brazilian literature were associated with *Modernismo,* with MÁRIO DE ANDRADE the most prominent. (In Brazil, the term *Modernismo* has roughly the same semantic scope as *Modernism* in Anglo-American and European culture. The Spanish cognate, however, refers to an adaptation of, among other things, French Parnassianism and Symbolism, during the period approximately 1880–1910.) *Modernismo,* among other things, affirmed Brazilian cultural independence (based ironically on the assimilation of the European vanguard) and represented a definitive break with Portuguese models. Most important, *Modernismo* affirmed Brazilian linguistic autonomy. The Spanish American vanguard also asserted its liberation from Peninsular Spanish (the young Borges was particularly prominent in this regard), but it was the Portuguese of Brazil that carried such efforts to their extreme. Efforts to underscore the differences between Portuguese and the continent's hegemonic Spanish characterized a linguistic renovation that resulted in the enormous development of Brazilian literature since the 1920s.

Although Brazil has experienced two periods of dictatorship (the 1930–50 Vargas fascism and the neo-Fascist military tyranny 1964–85) that have left a decisive cultural imprint, Brazilian cultural production has remained vigorous through the century. The poet OSWALDO DE ANDRADE, the social historian GILBERTO FREYRE, and the novelist DARCY RIBEIRO (the latter also a highly influential cultural anthropologist) have continued EUCLYDES DE CUNHA'S efforts to interpret the country's social phenomena. Women writers such as RAQUEL DE QUEIRÓS, CLARICE LISPECTOR, and LYGIA TELLES (Lispector attaining an international feminist reputation) have focused on the public and private lives of women. IVAN ANGELO, IGNACIO BRANDÃO, JOÃO UBALDO RIBEIRO, and MÁRCIO SOUZA are part of the countercultural or resistance writing that emerged under the recent military regimes. And MOACYR SCLIAR represents a specifically Jewish consciousness. The prolific novelist JORGE AMADO may be denounced by many cultural historians and literary critics—for his exotic sentimentalizing of Brazilian life, for his binarism of devilish whites and vitalistic blacks, and for his romantic socialism—but he successfully promotes one prominent view of Brazil's African heritage as well as a determined resistance to the homogenizing internationalism so prevalent in Brazil's urban centers. Finally, both GRACILIANO RAMOS and JOÃO GUIMARÃES ROSA deserve mention for their dedication to fictional interpretations of the isolated and marginalized backlands so often lost from urban view. Ramos wrote as a socialist realist about everyday emptiness, or *Barren Lives* (1938), while Rosa chose more poetic registers that many critics associated with the magical realism of the 1960s. Before Rosa's death many believed that his work, emphasizing the rich texture of Brazilian life and demonstrating the strength and sophistication of Portuguese as a literary language, merited the Nobel Prize.

Brazilian literary production equals in volume and quality that of all of Spanish America. The number of English translations available rivals those of Argentina and Mexico put together, attesting to the prominence Brazil enjoys in Latin American literature, though it has not yet received the quantity of critical study it deserves.

History and Criticism

Coutinho, Alfranio. *An Introduction to Literature in Brazil*. Trans. by Gregory Rabassa. Col. U. Pr. 1969 o.p. Standard introduction to Brazilian literature.

Foster, David William, and Roberto Reis, comps. *A Dictionary of Contemporary Brazilian Authors*. ASU Lat. Am. St. 1982 $9.55. ISBN 0-87918-051-X. Entries on significant Brazilian writers.

Goldberg, Isaac. *Brazilian Literature. Essay Index Repr. Ser.* Roth Pub. Inc. 1978 $24.50. ISBN 0-8486-3019-X. Essays on major Brazilian writers. Introduction by J. D. Ford.

Hulet, Claude L. *Brazilian Literature*. 3 vols. Georgetown U. Pr. 1974–75 $8.95 ea. ISBN 0-685-01897-0. Survey history of Brazilian literature with anthology.

Martins, Wilson. *The Modernist Idea: A Critical Survey of Brazilian Writing in the Twentieth Century*. Trans. by Jack E. Tomlins. Greenwood 1979 repr. of 1970 ed. $38.50. ISBN 0-313-20811-5. Major analysis of Brazilian modernism.

Moog, Clodomir V. *An Interpretation of Brazilian Literature*. Trans. by John Knox. Greenwood repr. of 1951 ed. o.p. General introduction to Brazilian literature.

Patai, Daphne. *Myth and Ideology in Contemporary Brazilian Fiction*. Fairleigh Dickinson 1983 $35.00. ISBN 0-8386-3132-0. Major interpretation of contemporary Brazilian novel.

Putnam, Samuel. *Marvelous Journey: A Survey of Four Centuries of Brazilian Writing*. Hippocrene Bks. 1971 repr. of 1948 ed. $20.50. ISBN 0-374-96703-2. Survey of important literary figures.

Stern, Irwin. *Dictionary of Brazilian Literature*. Greenwood 1988 $67.00. ISBN 0-313-24932-6. Includes 300 entries in English on the most significant writers, literary schools, and cultural movements in the twentieth century.

Veríssimo, Érico. *Brazilian Literature: An Outline*. Greenwood 1970 repr. of 1945 ed. $39.75. ISBN 0-8371-2319-4. Survey history of Brazilian literature.

Collections

Bishop, Elizabeth, ed. *An Anthology of Twentieth Century Brazilian Poetry*. Trans by Paul Blackburn. U. Pr. of New Eng. 1972 $16.95. ISBN 0-8195-6023-5. Selections with biographical introductions from 14 poets.

Brasil, Emanuel, and William J. Smith, eds. *Brazilian Poetry (1950–1980)*. Bks. Demand repr. of 1983 ed. $53.20. ISBN 0-7837-0209-4. Excellent collection of poems spanning three decades.

Grossman, William L., ed. *Modern Brazilian Short Stories*. U. CA Pr. 1974 o.p. Short stories written during Brazil's modernist period, a literary revival beginning in 1922.

Pontiero, G., ed. *An Anthology of Brazilian Modernist Poetry*. Franklin Bks. 1969 $110.00. ISBN 0-08-013326-6. Large collection of poetry including many of Brazil's most important modern poets.

CHRONOLOGY OF AUTHORS

Alencar, José de. 1829–1877
Machado de Assis, Joaquim Maria. 1839–1908
Cunha, Euclydes da. 1866–1909
Bandeira, Manuel. 1886–1968
Andrade, Oswald de. 1890–1954
Ramos, Graciliano. 1892–1953
Andrade, Mário de. 1893–1945
Freyre, Gilberto de Mello. 1900–1987
Veríssimo, Érico. 1905–1975
Rosa, João Guimarães. 1908–1967
Queirós, Raquel de. 1910–
Amado, Jorge. 1912–
Ribeiro, Darcy. 1922–
Telles, Lygia Fagundes. 1923–
Lispector, Clarice. 1924–1977
Ângelo, Ivan. 1936–
Brandão, Ignácio de Loyola. 1936–
Scliar, Moacyr. 1937–
Ribeiro, João Ubaldo. 1940–
Souza, Márcio. 1946–

ALENCAR, JOSÉ DE. 1829–1877

José de Alencar is Brazil's greatest romantic novelist and its best exponent of Indianism and regionalism. Born in Ceará on May 1, 1829, Alencar did his early schooling in Rio de Janeiro. In 1850, he graduated from law school in São Paulo and then went on to practice law in Rio while teaching business law at the Instituto Comercial. Alencar adored his people and his native land. His profound love for anything Brazilian inspired much of his work, including the descriptive embellishments found in his poem-like novels *Iracema* (1865) and *The Guarani* (1857). *Iracema,* the only work available in translation, is the love story of an Indian princess and a Portuguese officer. Its theme of two races uniting to form a new American people is also found in other works by Alencar.

NOVEL BY ALENCAR

Iracema. The Honey Lips, a Legend of Brazil. Trans. by Isabel Burton. Gordon Pr. 1976 $59.95. ISBN 0-8490-2076-X. The title of this novel is an anagram for America.

AMADO, JORGE. 1912–

Elected to the Brazilian Academy of Letters, Jorge Amado possesses a talent for storytelling as well as a deep concern for social and economic justice. For some critics, his early works suffer from his politics: Fred Ellison wrote, "He reacted violently at times, and some of his books have been marred by extreme partisanship to the left." Currently, critics more commonly express reservations concerning Amado's sentimentality and erotico-mythic stereotyping. In the works represented in English translation, however, his literary merits prevail. *The Violent Land* (1942) chronicles the development of Brazilian territory and struggles for its resources, memorializing the deeds of those who built the country. *Gabriela, Clove and Cinnamon* (1958), which achieved critical and popular success in both Brazil and the United States, is even less political, relating a sensual love story of a Syrian bar owner and his beautiful cook whose skin is the color of the spices that enliven her food. *Home Is the Sailor* (1962) concerns Captain Vasco Moscoso de Aragão, a comic figure in the tradition of Don Quijote, who poses as a retired sea captain and must suddenly command a ship in an emergency. In *Doña Flor and Her Two Husbands* (1966), Amado introduced the folk culture of shamans and Yorube gods who resuscitate Doña Flor's first husband during her marriage to the second. The protagonists of *Shepherds of the Night* (1964) are Bahia's poor, and "Amado has given us a deeply moving and funny picture of life in the slums" (*Nation*).

NOVELS BY AMADO

Captains of the Sands. 1937. Trans. by Gregory Rabassa. Avon 1988 $7.95. ISBN 0-380-89718-0. "Captains" are a gang of abandoned children who live in a waterfront warehouse and survive by robbing the rich.

Doña Flor and Her Two Husbands. 1966. Trans. by Harriet de Onis. Avon 1977 $10.00. ISBN 0-380-75469-X

Gabriela, Clove and Cinnamon. 1958. Trans. by James L. Taylor and William L. Grossman. Avon 1988 $11.00. ISBN 0-380-75470-3

Home Is the Sailor. 1962. Trans. by Harriet de Onis. Avon 1988 $7.95. ISBN 0-380-75474-6

Jubiaba. 1935. Trans. by Margaret A. Neves. Avon 1989 $7.95. ISBN 0-380-75479-7. Black culture in Bahia.

Pen, Sword and Camisole. Trans. by Helen R. Lane. Avon 1989 $7.95. ISBN 0-380-75480-0. Literary politics in Brazil and the military establishment.

Sea of Death. 1936. Trans. by Gregory Rabassa. Avon 1989 $7.95. ISBN 0-380-75478-9. Novel that represents the mysteries of sailors and the sea.

Shepherds of the Night. 1964. Trans. by Harriet De Onis. Avon 1988 $7.95. ISBN 0-380-75471-1

Showdown. Trans. by Gregory Rabassa. Bantam 1989 $18.95. ISBN 0-553-05174-1. Frontier violence in the cacao plantations.

The Swallow and the Tom Cat: A Love Story. Trans. by Barbara S. Merello. Delacorte 1982 o.p. An allegory, told as a children's story, of personal and cultural identity.

Tent of Miracles. 1969. Trans. by Barbara Shelby. Avon 1988 $10.00. ISBN 0-380-75472-X. Exposes violence and racism directed against Brazilian blacks.

Tereza Batista: Home from the Wars. 1977. Trans. by Barbara S. Merello. Avon 1988 $9.95. ISBN 0-380-75468-1. A black Bahian prostitute as protagonist.

Tieta. Trans. by Barbara S. Merello. Avon 1988 $9.95. ISBN 0-380-75477-0. A prostitute becomes a madam; set in São Paulo and northeast Brazil.

The Two Deaths of Quincas Wateryell: A Tall Tale. Trans. by Barbara S. Merello. Avon 1988 $5.95. ISBN 0-380-75476-2. Centers on a middle-class man turned social outcast.

The Violent Land. 1942. Trans. by Samuel Putnam. Avon 1988 $7.95. ISBN 0-380-75475-4

BOOKS ABOUT AMADO

Chamberlain, Bobby J. *Jorge Amado.* Twayne 1990 $25.95. ISBN 0-8057-8261-3. General overview of Amado's literary production.

Ellison, Fred P. *Brazil's New Novel; Four Northeastern Masters: José Lins do Rego, Jorge Amado, Graciliano Ramos, Rachel de Queiroz.* U. CA Pr. 1965 o.p. Includes detailed analysis of novels by Amado.

ANDRADE, MÁRIO DE. 1893–1945

Mário de Andrade, born in São Paulo, was one of the founders of the modernist movement of Brazil. His purpose was to review the Brazilian language and to awaken his countrypeople to the need for social change. He wrote one of the most important works in twentieth-century Brazilian poetry and a large volume of literary, music, and art criticism. His novel *Macunaíma* (1928) is one of the masterworks of Brazilian literature—"inventive, blessedly unsentimental" (*Kirkus Review*). It is considered by some critics a precursor of

Latin American magical realism in its highly creative portrayal of the irresolvable conflicts between native and European rural and urban cultures.

NOVELS BY ANDRADE

Fraulein. Trans. by Margaret Hollingworth. Gordon Pr. 1977 $59.95. ISBN 0-8490-1864-1. About a proper German governess in a Brazilian patriarchal family.

Macunaíma. 1928. Trans. by E. A. Goodland. U. of Pittsburgh Pr. 1988 $34.95. ISBN 8-5702-8007-6

POETRY BY ANDRADE

Hallucinated City. Trans. by Jack E. Tomlins. Vanderbilt U. Pr. 1968 $7.95. ISBN 0-8265-1113-9. Collection of poetry inaugurating Brazilian modernism.

ANDRADE, OSWALD DE. 1890–1954

Together with MÁRIO DE ANDRADE, Oswald de Andrade is one of the initiators of Brazilian modernism. As a young man studying and traveling in Europe, Andrade became interested in the avant garde, especially the futurist movement. Back in Brazil he helped organize the Modern Art Week in São Paulo and published his manifesto, *Pau Brasil* (1925). This manifesto proposed a new Brazilian poetry that would influence Europe as Europe has influenced Brazilian literature. Andrade's poems are short, at times ironic, evocations of diverse topics such as nature, landscapes, cities, streets, and various incidents of Brazilian history. He also wrote novels such as *Marco Zero* (1943) (a trilogy), *The Condemned, Sentimental Memoirs of John Seaborne* (1924), and *Seraphim Grosse Pointe* (1934).

NOVELS BY ANDRADE

Sentimental Memoirs of John Seaborne. Trans. by Albert Bork and Ralph Niebuhr. Nefertiti 1979 o.p. Strongly satirizes Brazilian society of the 1920s and parodies the language of the day.

Seraphim Grosse Pointe. Trans. by Kenneth Jackson and Albert Bork. Nefertiti 1979 o.p. Virulently mocks the Brazilian bourgeoisie of the post–World War I era.

ÂNGELO, IVAN. 1936–

Ivan Ângelo was born in Minas Gerais, Brazil. He is a journalist and the managing editor of an influential evening daily in São Paulo. *The Celebration* (1976) is a controversial novel of modern Brazil under censorship in the 1970s and a winner of the Brazilian Publisher's Prize.

NOVELS BY ÂNGELO

The Celebration. 1976. Trans. by Thomas Colchie. Avon 1982 o.p.

The Tower of Glass. Trans. by Ellen Watson. Avon 1986 $3.95. ISBN 0-380-89607-9

BANDEIRA, MANUEL. 1886–1968

Born in Recife, Manuel Bandeira was raised in Rio de Janeiro and Ceará. Bandeira began to write poetry at an early age. In 1917 he selected some of his poems and published them under the title *A Cinza das horas*, which became an instant success. From that point he dedicated his life to the poetic art and published a sizable amount of verse. His verses display vague romantic overtones and are often touched with irony, melancholy, and tragic humor. At times his verse also contains small biographical sketches. In his work, Bandeira used traditionally rhymed verse as well as the unrhymed freer forms advocated by the bards of the modernist movement.

Poetry by Bandeira

This Earth, That Sky: Poems by Manuel Bandeira. Trans. by Candace Slater. U. CA Pr. 1989 $35.00. ISBN 0-520-06090-3. Contains more than 100 poems with a good critical overview for readers.

BRANDÃO, IGNÁCIO DE LOYOLA. 1936–

Brandão was born in the state of São Paulo, Brazil. He started his career in journalism at a very young age writing movie reviews in his hometown. Later he moved to São Paulo where he worked for the major newspapers and wrote several novels. *Zero* was finished in 1969 but was only published five years later in Italy, followed by its publication in Brazil in 1975. Although the book was received with critical acclaim and given literary prizes, it was banned in 1976 by the Ministry of Justice. The censorship was lifted in 1979, and soon after *Zero* became a bestseller. *And Still the Earth* (1982) is often mentioned as a modern Orwellian novel in the manner of *1984*. The author presents a dystopian vision of the future in Brazil: the destruction of the natural environment; the scarcity of water; the crowds in the city oppressed by the brutality of an omnipotent government that controls every one of its subjects.

Books by Brandão

And Still the Earth. 1982. Trans. by Ellen Watson. Avon 1985 o.p.
Zero. 1975. Trans. by Ellen Watson. Avon 1983 o.p.

CUNHA, EUCLYDES DA. 1866–1909

Cunha accompanied Brazilian government forces on a series of four military expeditions in 1896–97 to put down a rebellion started by a religious fanatic, Antonio the Counsellor, who had proclaimed himself the Messiah. *Rebellion in the Backlands* (1902), Cunha's account of the battles, originally published as newspaper stories, is an inquiry into the condition of the Brazilian people, embellished with descriptions of landscape and living conditions. The work has been described as "the first literary work in Brazil . . . to face Brazilian social problems adequately and with imagination" (Seymour-Smith). The book may be marred for the modern reader by its doctrine of racial superiority and an overly complex style. Cunha is the protagonist of Vargas Llosa's *The War of the End of the World.*

Nonfiction by Cunha

Rebellion in the Backlands. 1902. Trans. by Samuel Putnam. U. Ch. Pr. 1957 repr. of 1944 ed. $18.95. ISBN 0-226-12444-4

FREYRE, GILBERTO DE MELLO. 1900–1987

Gilberto Freyre, winner of the 1967 Aspen Award for outstanding contribution to the humanities, has been influential in changing the way Brazilians see themselves and their country. By relating Brazilian history to modern life and by demonstrating how the Portuguese, blacks, and Indians have mingled to form a unique culture and a great nation, Freyre has destroyed the nation's inferiority complex. Alexander Coleman wrote of *The Masters and the Slaves* (1933), "His is a Proustian history, a rich web of counterpoint between formative cultural factors and psychological and biological predisposition, all made living once again within the reconstituted 'tone' of the period." Freyre, whose sophisticated writings have had a pervasive influence on modern Brazilian fiction, termed his *Mother and Son* a "semi-novel." The political and social currents of late nineteenth-century Brazil move against the portrait in the foreground of an overbearing mother and her effeminate son destined for the priesthood: "There is a special charm in this book, in its combination of the earthy and the spiritual, of warmth and intellectuality" (*SR*).

A popular public figure in Brazil, Freyre has served as a member of Brazil's U.N. delegation and in its Chamber of Deputies. In 1967, Columbia University, where he once taught, appointed him to a panel to consider the problems of cities and city planning.

NONFICTION BY FREYRE

The Mansions and the Shanties: The Making of Modern Brazil. 1936. Trans. by Harriet De Onis. Greenwood 1980 $48.50. ISBN 0-313-22148-0. Sociological analysis of feudalism and slavery.

The Masters and the Slaves: A Study in the Development of Brazilian Civilization. Trans. by Samuel Putnam. U. CA Pr. 1986 $17.95. ISBN 0-520-05665-5

Order and Progress: Brazil from Monarchy to Republic. Trans. by Rod Horton. Greenwood 1980 $48.50. ISBN 0-313-22363-7. Social history of Brazil.

LISPECTOR, CLARICE. 1924–1977

Clarice Lispector was born in the Ukraine and was taken to Brazil as a young child. She was a law student, editor, translator, and newswriter, who traveled widely, spending eight years in the United States.

Family Ties (1960) is a collection of short stories revealing Lispector's existentialist view of life and demonstrating that even family ties and social relationships are temporary. Although tied to each other and to the outside world, the characters are finally totally alone and separate. Lispector received praise from American critics for *The Apple in the Dark* (1967), a novel about a guilt-ridden man's search for the ultimate knowledge (Eve's apple), which he believes will bring him hope: "Lispector is a superb writer, an artist of vivid imagination and sensitivity, with a glorious feeling for language and its uses" (*SR*). Lispector's books are being translated into various languages in Europe, especially in France, where the critic HÉLÈNE CIXOUS is one of her great admirers and a promoter of her works.

NOVELS BY LISPECTOR

The Apple in the Dark. Trans. by Gregory Rabassa. U. of Tex. Pr. 1986 $12.95. ISBN 0-292-70392-9

An Apprenticeship or the Book of Delights. Trans. by Richard A. Mazzara and Lorri A. Parris. U. of Tex. Pr. 1986 $18.95. ISBN 0-292-79030-9. Existential novel of human solitude.

Family Ties. Trans. by Giovanni Pontiero. U. of Tex. Pr. 1984 $8.95. ISBN 0-292-72448-9

The Hour of the Star. Trans. by Giovanni Pontiero. New Dir. Pr. 1992 $8.95. ISBN 0-8112-1190-8. The isolation and death of a provincial girl in São Paulo.

Near to the Wild Heart. Trans. by Giovanni Pontiero. New Dir. Pr. 1990 $17.95. ISBN 0-8112-1139-8. A feminist novel on conventionalism versus personal authenticity.

The Passion According to G.H. Trans. by Ronald W. Sousa. U. of Minn. Pr. 1988 $24.95. ISBN 0-8166-1771-2. A novel of existential agony and nausea.

The Stream of Life. Trans. by Elizabeth Lowe and Earl Fitz. U. of Minn. Pr. 1989 $24.95. ISBN 0-8166-1781-3. Novel that is as much an extended metaphor for the act of writing as it is the lyrical, plotless monologue of the unnamed female protagonist's awareness of self-realization.

Short Story Collections by Lispector

The Foreign Legion. Trans. by Giovanni Pontiero. New Dir. Pr. 1992 $10.95. ISBN 0-8112-1189-4. Exemplifies Lispector's obsession with language and character development.

Soulstorm: Stories. Trans. by Alexis Levitin. New Dir. Pr. 1989 $19.95. ISBN 0-8112-1090-1. Sixteen stories that offer glimpses into moments of psychological dawning—when a certain juxtaposition of events allows an individual a clearer view of the way things really are.

Books about Lispector

Cixous, Hélène. *Reading with Clarice Lispector.* U. of Minn. Pr. 1990 $39.95. ISBN 0-8166-1828-3. Major feminist analysis of Lispector.

Fitz, Earl E. *Clarice Lispector.* Twayne 1985 o.p. Examines Lispector's obsession with language and her membership in Brazil's modernist movement.

MACHADO DE ASSIS, JOAQUIM MARIA. 1839–1908

Machado de Assis's achievement in both the novel and poetry make him Brazil's paradigm of a writer. His novels are characterized "by a psychological insight as well as a broad view of social conditions in Brazil and the world. The seriousness of the realistic view is highlighted with ironic humor" (*SR*). Beginning as a romantic, Assis developed a style that embraced realism, naturalism, and symbolism. *Epitaph for a Small Winner* (1881) reveals his essential pessimism, as the only consolation for Bras Cubas is that he has not passed on his misery to any offspring. About his writing in *Dom Casmurro* (1900), it was said "No satirist, not even Swift, is less merciful in his exposure of the pretentiousness and the hypocrisy that lurk in the average good man and woman" (*New Republic*).

Born in the slums of Rio de Janeiro, Machado de Assis was orphaned early in life. He advanced from typesetter to proofreader and finally to journalist before entering the Brazilian civil service. He was the author of nine novels, more than 200 short stories, opera libretti, drama, and lyric poetry.

Novels by Machado de Assis

Counselor Ayres Memorial. Trans. by Helen Caldwell. U. CA Pr. 1973 $32.50. ISBN 0-520-2227-0. Concerns the psychological dimensions of love.

Dom Casmurro. 1900. Trans. by Helen Caldwell. FS&G 1991 $12.00. ISBN 0-374-52303-7

Epitaph for a Small Winner. 1881. Trans. by William Grossman. Avon 1977 o.p.

Esau and Jacob. Trans. by Helen Caldwell. U. CA Pr. 1965 $22.50. ISBN 0-520-00788-3. A Castor-Pollax novel of differing sociopolitical ideologies.

Helena. Trans. by Helen Caldwell. U. CA. Pr. 1984 $32.50. ISBN 0-520-04812-1. Sardonic parody of romantic motif of incest.

Short Story Collection by Machado de Assis

The Devil's Church and Other Stories. Trans. by Jack Schmitt and Lorie Ishimatsu. U. of Tex. Pr. 1977 $7.95. ISBN 0-292-71542-0. Short stories that revolve around the idea of horror, social satire, and psychological realism.

Books about Machado de Assis

Caldwell, Helen. *Machado de Assis; The Brazilian Master and His Novels.* U. CA Pr. 1970 o.p. Detailed analysis of Machado de Assis's major place in contemporary fiction.

Dixon, Paul B. *Retired Dreams*: Dom Casmurro, *Myth and Modernity.* Purdue U. Pr. 1989 $10.95. ISBN 0-911198-98-9. Detailed study of Machado de Assis's novel *Dom Casmurro.*

Gledson, John. *The Deceptive Realism of Machado de Assis: A Dissenting Interpretation of* Dom Casmurro. Fracis Cairns 1984 o.p. A view of the society to which Machado de Assis belonged; discusses Machado's aim in *Dom Casmurro.*

Nunes, Maria Luisa. *The Craft of an Absolute Winner: Characterization and Narratology in the Novels of Machado de Assis.* Greenwood 1983 $37.50. ISBN 0-313-23631-3. History of Machado de Assis's life and career; questions the origins of his genius for characterization.

QUEIRÓS, RAQUEL DE. 1910–

Raquel de Queirós gained national recognition at age 20 with her first novel *The Year Fifteen* (1930), which won the Graça Aranha Foundation Prize. A realistic account of the 1915 drought in the Brazilian Northeast, the novel also reveals the immaturity of the author as an artist. In *The Three Marias* (1939), however, Queirós triumphed artistically. Although demonstrating women's subordinate and degrading roles in an unsympathetic society, the novel at the same time reveals the author's compassion for men's predicaments as well. Fred Ellison wrote of her work, "Simplicity, sobriety, and directness are characteristic of her writing, but are most highly refined in *The Three Marias*. . . . And as an artist, one of the most gifted of the present generation, she has been able to give beautiful form to her tragic inspiring vision."

NOVELS BY QUEIRÓS

Dora, Doralina. 1975. Trans. by Dorothy Scott Loos. Avon 1984 $4.50. ISBN 0-380-84822-8. About repressive rural Brazilian society; feminist in scope.

The Three Marias. 1939. Trans. by Fred Ellison. U. of Tex. Pr. 1985 o.p.

BOOK ABOUT QUEIRÓS

Ellison, Fred P. *Brazil's New Novel; Four Northeastern Masters: José Lins do Rego, Jorge Amado, Graciliano Ramos, Rachel de Queiroz.* U. CA Pr. 1965 o.p. Includes detailed analysis of novels by Queirós.

RAMOS, GRACILIANO. 1892–1953

Ramos was one of many leftist intellectuals purged by President Getúlio Vargas's government during the 1930s. *Barren Lives* (1938) examines the psychology of poverty during the drought in the interior of northeastern Brazil. The novel is narrated through the minds of several members of a family who, due to their lack of education and primitive natures, rarely communicate verbally. Of Ramos's technical accomplishments, Morton Zabel wrote in *The Nation*, "Graciliano Ramos is notable among the contemporary Brazilian writers for a severity of style, an accuracy of social and moral observation, and an intensity of tragic sensibility which derive as much from fidelity to native experience as from the stylists—PROUST, JOYCE (see Vol. 1), and, more relevantly, CÉLINE—whom his American publisher mentions as models."

NOVEL BY RAMOS

Barren Lives. 1938. Trans. by Ralph E. Dimmick. *Texas Pan-Amer. Ser.* U. of Tex. Pr. 1965 $12.95. ISBN 0-292-73172-8

BOOK ABOUT RAMOS

Ellison, Fred P. *Brazil's New Novel; Four Northeastern Masters: José Lins do Rego, Jorge Amado, Graciliano Ramos, Rachel de Queiroz.* U. CA Pr. 1965 o.p. Includes detailed analysis of novels by Ramos.

RIBEIRO, DARCY. 1922–

Darcy Ribeiro was born in Minas Gerais, Brazil, in 1922. World-renowned anthropologist, minister of education, and personal adviser to President Goulart, Ribeiro lived in exile after the military coup of 1964. Since his return to Brazil, he has added another dimension to his image of Renaissance man—educator, distinguished statesman, lieutenant governor of Rio de Janeiro, anthropologist, and now a man of letters.

Maíra (1978) is the most acclaimed of his novels, with translations in French, German, Spanish, and Italian. The novel's major character is Isaías, a young Amazon Indian who attends a Catholic seminary in Rome and returns to his tribe to become its chieftain. Alma, a young white woman in search of her own spiritual fulfillment, joins a group of missionaries that work among the Maírum, Isaías's people. Their stories of return and of discovery, respectively, become a metaphor for the irreconcilable conflict between the rich and complex culture of the Indians and the modern technological Western civilization. *Maíra* is an elegy of a culture that is disappearing.

Book by Darcy Ribeiro

Maíra. 1978. *Lib. of Contemporary World Lit.* Random 1983 o.p.

RIBEIRO, JOÃO UBALDO. 1940–

João Ubaldo Ribeiro was born in the northeastern state of Bahia, Brazil. He has an M.A. degree in political science, but has been mostly involved in journalism. He lives on his native island of Itaparica, near Salvador, where he is the editor in chief of the *Tribuna da Bahia.* He writes weekly columns for *Istoé* magazine, as well as fiction. *Vivo o Povo Brasileiro* (1971), his last novel, was well received by the critics and public alike. *Sergeant Getúlio* (1971) is like an epic journey through the *sertões,* the backlands of Euclydes da Cunha's classic account. Getúlio, a police officer, is a prototype of the antihero of the Brazilian Northeast—a brutish, cruel man guided by a primitive sense of honor: "Overriding in violence . . . is the memorable portrait of the hero-narrator" (*Chicago Tribune*). "Getúlio will offend everyone and yet take most readers prisoner and carry them all the way to the explosive conclusion of his journey" (*Los Angeles Times*).

Novels by João Ubaldo Ribeiro

An Invincible Memory. Trans. by the author. HarpC 1989 $25.00. ISBN 0-060-15622-8. A panoramic family saga illuminating 400 years of Brazilian society.

Sergeant Getúlio. 1971. Fwd. by Jorge Amada. Avon 1984 o.p.

ROSA, JOÃO GUIMARÃES. 1908–1967

Many critics consider João Guimarães Rosa to have been the best Brazilian novelist since Machado de Assis. *The Devil to Pay in the Backlands* (1956) is a Faustian quest for self-knowledge and identity with a northeastern bandit, Riobaldo, as protagonist. "But," as Emir Rodríguez Monegal pointed out, "this is a modern morality tale, and therefore not a simple one, so Rosa's angel and his devil are not always clearly distinguishable." The devil in fact turns out to be Riobaldo's unconscious and submerged instincts. A *New York Times* reviewer wrote of the novel, "He entrances the readers with the beauty and grandeur of these backlands. But his descriptions of outer nature are always subordinate to a poignant inner realism, which remains local in flavor while presenting the elemental contrasts of human nature everywhere." The artistic achievement of the novel was defined in the *Times Literary Supplement*: "To the Brazilian public *Big Backlands: Narrow Paths* [the literal translation of the title] was remarkable above all because it signified a linguistic revolution. The language was compounded from archaic Portuguese, from dialects and neologisms."

Rosa was a country doctor in his native state. He took part in the revolution and civil war of 1930–32, then embarked on a diplomatic career, serving in Hamburg, Bogotá, and Paris. He was elected to the Brazilian Academy of Letters in 1963 but postponed his investiture until 1967 "because he feared 'the emotion of the moment'" (*N.Y. Times*). A few days after the induction, he died unexpectedly from a heart attack.

NOVEL BY ROSA

The Devil to Pay in the Backlands. 1956. Trans. by James L. Taylor and Harriet de Onis. Knopf o.p.

SCLIAR, MOACYR. 1937–

Scliar was born and still lives in Rio Grande do Sul, Brazil. A physician since 1962, Scliar started his career as a writer telling stories about his experiences as a young doctor. He is a prolific writer and has produced more than 10 novels, many of which have won literary prizes. He studied at the Yiddish College in Porto Alegre and went to a Catholic school for his secondary studies. This childhood experience provided the imaginative background for many of his stories. His writing has much of what he called "his Jewishness": "As much as possible I live in peace with my Jewishness. I have extracted from it what it has of the best: fantasy, ethical substance, and above all, humor" (*Escrever & Viver*). *The Centaur in the Garden* is a story about a centaur who is Brazilian and Jewish, a fantasy of the half-horse, half-human child who grows into adulthood in search of his identity.

NOVELS BY SCLIAR

The Centaur in the Garden. Trans. by Margaret A. Neves. Ballantine 1987 $3.95. ISBN 0-345-35194-0

The Gods of Raquel. Trans. by Eloah F. Giacomelli. Ballantine 1987 $3.50. ISBN 0-345-35357-9. Fantastic and personal vision of the conflicts of humanity and religion in novel form.

Max and the Cats. Trans. by Eloah Giacomelli. Ballantine 1990 $7.95. ISBN 0-345-36707-3. A boy's perspective of Nazi Germany and Jewish refugees in Brazil.

Strange Nation of Rafael Mandies. Trans. by Eloah F. Giacomelli. Ballantine 1988 $4.95. ISBN 0-345-34861-3. One catastrophic day in the life of a Brazilian businessman.

SHORT STORY COLLECTION BY SCLIAR

Enigmatic Eye. Trans. by Eloah F. Giacomelli. Ballantine 1989 $5.95. ISBN 0-345-35969-0. Provides a clear idea of Scliar's plot development and characterization techniques.

SOUZA, MÁRCIO. 1946–

Souza was born in the northern state of Amazonas, Brazil. He studied social sciences at the University of São Paulo in the South. It was during that period that Souza decided to write about his native region, the Amazon, feeling that very little was known about its history and culture. *The Emperor of the Amazon*, his first novel, was an extraordinary bestseller and was well received in France and in the United States. It is about the adventures of a latter-day conquistador in the heart of the jungle, involved by accident in a mock epic tale of conquest and revolution. *Mad Maria* (1980) is a novel set again in the Amazon region, with a group of people determined to cut a railroad through the forest.

Novels by Souza

Emperor of the Amazon. Trans. by Thomas Colchie. Avon 1980 $2.95. ISBN 0-380-76240-4

Mad Maria. 1980. Trans. by Thomas Colchie. Avon 1985 $4.95. ISBN 0-380-89871-3

The Order of the Day: An Unidentified Flying Opus. Trans. by Thomas Colchie. Avon 1986 $4.50. ISBN 0-380-89765-2. A fictionalized biography of Alberto Santos Domant, Brazilian aviation pioneer.

Nonfiction by Souza

Rain on Fire: The Murder of Chico Mendes and the End of the Amazon. Doubleday 1990 $18.95. ISBN 0-385-41384-X. A documentary account of the murder of the passionate ecologist Chico Mendes.

TELLES, LYGIA FAGUNDES. 1923–

Telles was born in São Paulo and spent most of her childhood in the small towns of the state. She holds degrees in law and physical education and started publishing in the 1940s when she was very young. Since then, she has published three novels, a half dozen novellas, and seven short-story collections. In 1969 she was awarded the Cannes Prix International des Femmes for her short story "Before the Green Masquerade." In 1973, *The Girl in the Photograph* won her various literary prizes. Today, she is considered one of the finest women writers in Brazil and is one of the few women elected to the Brazilian Academy of Letters.

Novel by Telles

The Girl in the Photograph. 1973. Avon 1982 o.p.

Short Story Collection by Telles

Tigrela: And Other Stories. Trans. by Margaret A. Neves. Avon 1986 $3.95. ISBN 0-380-89627-3. Stories of political and social satire meshed with supernatural circumstances.

VERÍSSIMO, ÉRICO. 1905–1975

The most versatile novelist of the Generation of 1930, Érico Veríssimo, was born in the southern Brazilian state of Rio Grande do Sul, where he spent most of his youth. Veríssimo began to publish short stories in the magazine *Madrugada* and later, while manager of the magazine *Revista do Globo,* he selected and translated English prose. In 1932 he published a series of short stories under the title *Fantoches.* His first novel *Clarissa,* was published in 1933 and was followed by a dozen more. Veríssimo's interests also extended to children's literature, and he published ten books in that genre. All of Veríssimo's works display clear messages of peace, justice, and brotherhood. He strongly believed that humanity will succeed and achieve happiness through self-development and love.

Novels by Veríssimo

Consider the Lilies of the Field. Trans. by Jean N. Karnoff. Greenwood 1969 repr. of 1947 ed. $38.50. ISBN 0-8371-2320-8. Concerned with lives that are drawn together in everyday events and personal tragedies.

Rest is Silence. Trans. by L. C. Kaplan. Greenwood 1969 repr. of 1946 ed. $38.50. ISBN 0-8371-2318-6. Reflects the cultural environment of gaucho life; employs uncomplicated, direct, and conversational language.

Time and the Wind. Trans. by L. L. Barrett. Greenwood 1970 repr. of 1951 ed. $38.50. ISBN 0-8371-2111-6. Epic historical trilogy that traces two hundred years in the history of a gaucho family in Rio Grande do Sul.

CHAPTER 23

Canadian Literature

Robert L. Ross

> To say that you must read your own literature to know who you are, to avoid being a sort of cultural moron, is not the same as saying that you should read nothing else, though the "internationalist" or Canada Last opponents of this notion sometimes think it is. A reader cannot live by Canlit alone, and it is a disservice to Canlit to try it. . . . The study of Canadian literature ought to be comparative, as should the study of any literature; it is by contrast that distinctive patterns show up most strongly. To know ourselves, we must know our own literature; to know ourselves accurately, we need to know it as part of literature as a whole.
>
> — MARGARET ATWOOD, *Survival*

Like so much of the writing by former members of the once-powerful British Empire, the literature of Canada has had to shape its own identity, to overcome its second-class status, and to prove both at home and abroad that it has something distinctive to say. That has been accomplished. For Canadian literature in English no longer falls into vague categories like "literature of the Dominions" or "Commonwealth literature." Nor is it now a minor appendage to what once was considered the real writing in English: that is, literature from Great Britain. Finally, Canadian literature today speaks to its own people, to its southern neighbors, and to those overseas; and it no longer speaks in hesitant tones but forthrightly about the human condition. (It should be noted at this point that Canada has also produced an impressive literature in French, but this discussion is limited to English-language writing.)

What MARGARET ATWOOD—an internationally admired writer herself—has to say (in the introductory quote) about the place of Canadian literature in the larger picture precludes any tendency toward provincialism. Along this line, one of the interesting developments in recent years has been the Canadian interchange of writers and writing from the other so-called settler countries—New Zealand, Australia, and South Africa. Canadian readers and critics have also shown a lively interest in the postcolonial writing from India, Africa, and other areas. As well, modern Canadian writing shows numerous international influences. While earlier Canadian authors drew primarily from Britain for literary forms, contemporary writers have looked to sources as diverse as the writing from the southern United States—such as the work of WILLIAM FAULKNER (see Vol. 1)—or the writing of Latin America—in particular, at the fictional innovations of GABRIEL GARCÍA MÁRQUEZ. All of this crossing of boundaries enriches the writers and their work, and in turn enriches the readers.

That Canadian literature is vital and meaningful to those at home and to those far beyond the country's borders should not be surprising. First, the physical Canada—which some have called a collection of regions rather than a country—knows no limits: The gentle maritime states along the Atlantic Ocean; the cosmopolitan cities like Toronto; the all-but-empty prairies dotted with sometimes dreary towns and solitary farms; the Rocky Mountains, their grandeur nearly untouched by settlement; and the Far North, vast and inhospitable. Place has always been central to Canadian literature, beginning perhaps with SUSANNA MOODIE, the colonial writer whose account of pioneer life, *Roughing It in the Bush*, expresses the love-hate relationship that Canadians often felt—and perhaps at times still do—toward their unrelenting northern land. But later writers have come to grips with this dichotomy. MARGARET LAURENCE, for example, sees the prairies as a life-giving force rather than an enemy. The poets, too, have found beauty and meaning in a geography and climate that once seemed a formidable barrier to the survival of the human spirit.

Second, Canadian literature draws life and gains significance from its blend of peoples. A character in one of MAVIS GALLANT's short stories recalls that while growing up in the Anglo-Saxon Canada of another time, she was led to believe that God was an Englishman. After all, many of the early settlers were Loyalists to the British Crown who made their way north after the American Revolution, and a residue of their thinking lingered. Following World War II, however, the composition of the people changed. Ironically, some of them were already there, such as the natives, the Chinese, and the French, but the dominant society of Anglo-Saxon origin had long tended to ignore them. This is no longer the case. For Canada has not only proclaimed itself a multicultural society; it is one. The varied makeup of the country's 23 million inhabitants—many of them recent immigrants from all parts of the world—cannot help but create a vital literature that reflects the tensions such a society undergoes.

Further, while the writers in English once were mainly of Anglo-Saxon origin, they are now joined by a major Jewish figure, MORDECAI RICHLER; a Sri Lankan immigrant, MICHAEL ONDAATJE; and a Parsee from Bombay, ROHINTON MISTRY. The voices of native peoples, whose oral tradition comprised Canada's first literature, have also taken up the English language to express their particular concerns. The recent anthology *Canadian Native Literature in English*, edited by Daniel David Moses and Terry Goldie, attests to the abundance and the quality of this writing.

Canadian literature has also been well served by its critics and scholars. Unlike in Australia, for example, there does not appear to be a chasm between the academy and the literary world. For one thing, many writers teach in the universities and write criticism as well as poetry, fiction, or drama. Considering that Canada has produced one of the most influential international critics, Northrop Frye, the practice of criticism and scholarship is a respected one. In general, critical writing in Canada avoids provincialism and internal squabbling, reaching instead toward the international view for which Atwood calls. In addition, extensive bibliographical material has been and continues to be compiled, several journals devoted to Canadian literature are published, detailed and sound histories have been written, and well-edited volumes of major writers' works remain in print. Inexpensive paperback editions of contemporary books are also easily accessible. The pivotal role that the critical and publishing apparatus plays in the development of a literature cannot be overestimated.

One of Canada's highly regarded writers, TIMOTHY FINDLEY,made an apt observation about the present state of Canadian literature: "I think this is the moment when it is going to happen, when identity will blossom for individuals and people will suddenly realize, My god, we have writers; we don't need 'Canadian' writers, we have writers."

HISTORY AND CRITICISM

Atwood, Margaret. *Survival: A Thematic Guide to Canadian Literature.* Anansi 1991 $8.95. ISBN 0-88784-613-0. Witty, informative guide to significant patterns in Canadian literature.

Benson, Eugene, and L. W. Connolly, eds. *The Oxford Companion to Canadian Theatre.* OUP 1989 $59.95. ISBN 0-19-540672-9. Alphabetical entries including genres, information on theaters and theater companies, biography, criticism, and discussion of major authors and plays.

Davidson, Arnold E., ed. *Studies on Canadian Literature: Introductory and Critical Essays.* Modern Lang. 1990 $37.00. ISBN 0-87352-199-4. An essential book on a wide range of topics, including criticism, individual writers, writing in English and French, and native writing.

Frye, Northrop. *The Bush Garden: Essays on the Canadian Imagination.* Anansi 1991 $12.95. ISBN 0-88784-620-3. An important critic's insights, written over a period of 30 years, into varied aspects of Canadian literature and its development.

Gibson, Graeme. *Eleven Canadian Novelists.* Anansi 1991 $12.95. ISBN 0-88784-712-9. Interviews with novelists, including Atwood, Laurence, Munro, Findley, and Richler.

Goldie, Terry. *Fear and Temptation: The Image of the Indigene in Canadian, Australian, and New Zealand Literatures.* McGill CN 1989 $32.95. ISBN 0-7735-0691-8. Examines 350 texts to show how white writers have treated native people in their work.

Hancock, Geoff. *Canadian Writers at Work.* OUP 1987 $19.95. ISBN 0-19-540638-9. Interviews with novelists, including Gallant, Kroetsch, Munro, Atwood, and Hodgins.

Klinck, Carl F., ed. *Literary History of Canada: Canadian Literature in English.* 3 vols. U. of Toronto Pr. 1976. Vols. 1 and 2 o.p. Vol. 3 $16.95. ISBN 0-8020-6378-4. In volume 3, literary developments from 1945 through 1972; in volumes 1–2, Canadian literature from its beginnings.

Lecker, Robert, and others, eds. *Canadian Writers and Their Works: Fiction Series.* ECW Pr. $45.00 ea. Vol. 1 1983 ISBN 0-920802-45-1. Vol. 2 1989 ISBN 1-55022-046-2. Vol. 3 1988 ISBN 0-920763-74-X. Vol. 4 1990 ISBN 1-55022-052-7. Vol. 5 1990 ISBN 1-55022-027-6. Vol. 6 1985 ISBN 0-920802-86-9. Vol. 7 1985 ISBN 0-920802-88-5. Vol. 8 1989 ISBN 1-55022-032-2. Vol. 9 1987 ISBN 0-92763-79-0. Vol. 10 1987 ISBN 0-920763-85-5. Essays on form, context, and development of major Canadian fiction writers; four or five writers in each volume.

______. *Canadian Writers and Their Works: Poetry Series.* ECW Pr. $45.00 ea. Vol. 1 1987 ISBN 0-920763-69-3. Vol. 2 1982 ISBN 0-920802-46-X. Vol. 3 1987 ISBN 0-920763-19-7. Vol. 4 1990 ISBN 1-55022-021-7. Vol. 5 1985 ISBN 0-920802-90-7. Vol. 6 1988 ISBN 1-55022-007-1. Vol. 7 1990 ISBN 1-55022-057-8. Vol. 8 1991 ISBN 1-55022-063-2. Vol. 9 1984 ISBN 0-920802-47-8. Vol. 10 1991 ISBN 1-55022-069-1. Essays on form, context, and development of major Canadian poets; four or five writers in each volume.

Moss, John, ed. *The Canadian Novel: A Critical Anthology.* U of NC Pr. 1980-85. Vol. 1 *Here and Now* $17.95. ISBN 0-920053-06-8. Vol. 2 *Beginnings* $17.95. ISBN 0-920053-15-7. Vol. 3 *Modern Times* $12.95. ISBN 0-919601-90-1. Vol. 4 *Present Tense* $17.95. ISBN 0-919601-67-7. Collections of essays focusing on the history and development of the Canadian novel, with emphasis on major writers.

______, ed. *Future Indicative: Literary Theory and Canadian Literature.* U. of Ottawa Pr. 1987 $39.95. ISBN 0-7766-0185-7. Essays on ways Canadian literature has been subjected to critical theory and on future critical methodology.

New, W. H. *A History of Canadian Literature.* New Amsterdam Bks. 1989 $30.00. ISBN 0-941533-54-9. A readable and comprehensive survey of Canadian literary development from precontact native writing to contemporary work.

______, ed. *Literary History of Canada: Canadian Literature in English*, Vol. 4. U. of Toronto Pr. 1990 $60.00. ISBN 0-8020-5685-7. Surveys literary development from 1972 to 1984, focusing on poetry, drama, fiction, and nonfiction.

Petrone, Penny. *Native Literature in Canada: From the Oral Tradition to the Present.* OUP 1990 $16.95. ISBN 0-19-540796-2. Traces the development of native writing, with specific discussions of major writers.

Ross, Malcolm. *Impossible Sum of Our Tradition.* McClelland and Stewart CN 1986 $19.95. ISBN 0-7710-7726-2. Stresses how Canada has discovered a sense of identity through its literature.

Stouck, David. *Major Canadian Authors.* U. of Nebr. Pr. rev. ed. 1988 $23.95. ISBN 0-8032-4195-X. Focuses on the work of 18 writers from the nineteenth and twentieth centuries; includes bibliographies.

Toye, William, gen. ed. *The Oxford Companion to Canadian Literature.* OUP 1983 $45.00. ISBN 0-19-540283-9. Valuable information on varied literary subjects, including writers, genres, history, movements, and places.

COLLECTIONS

Atwood, Margaret, and Robert Weaver. *Oxford Book of Canadian Short Stories in English.* OUP 1988 $14.95. ISBN 0-19-540597-8. Contains a varied and representative selection of short fiction.

Brown, Russell, and others, eds. *An Anthology of Canadian Literature in English.* rev. and abridged ed. OUP 1990 $24.95. ISBN 0-19-540785-7. Provides basic texts from the eighteenth century to the present day, with detailed introductory material.

Moses, Daniel David, and Terry Goldie, eds. *An Anthology of Canadian Native Literature in English.* OUP 1992 $19.95. ISBN 0-19-540819-5. An extensive collection ranging from traditional songs to contemporary poetry, fiction, and nonfiction.

New, W. H., ed. *Canadian Short Fiction.* P-H 1986 $18.95. ISBN 0-13-113820-0. An anthology offering a wide variety of short stories.

Sullivan, Rosemary, ed. *Poetry by Canadian Women.* OUP 1989 $19.95. ISBN 0-19-540688-5. Provides a wide variety of poetry without political bias.

Weaver, Robert, and William Toye, eds. *Oxford Anthology of Canadian Literature.* OUP rev. ed. 1985 $24.00. ISBN 0-19-540376-2. Provides representative selections from the colonial period through the present day.

CHRONOLOGY OF AUTHORS

Haliburton, Thomas Chandler. 1796–1865
Moodie, Susanna. 1803–1885
Roberts, Charles G. 1860–1943
Carman, Bliss. 1861–1929
Scott, Duncan Campbell. 1862–1947
Pratt, E(dwin) J(ohn). 1882–1964
Leacock, Stephen. 1896–1944
Callaghan, Morley. 1903–1990
Birney, Earle. 1904–
Ross, Sinclair. 1908–
Klein, A(braham) M(oses). 1909–1972
Lowry, Malcolm. 1909–1957
Layton, Irving. 1912–
Davies, Robertson. 1913–
Waddington, Miriam. 1917–
Purdy, Al. 1918–
Gallant, Mavis. 1922–
Laurence, Margaret. 1926–1987
Kroetsch, Robert. 1927–
Hood, Hugh. 1928–
Findley, Timothy. 1930–
Macpherson, Jay. 1931–
Munro, Alice. 1931–
Richler, Mordecai. 1931–
Joe, Rita. 1932–
Cohen, Leonard. 1934–
Wiebe, Rudy. 1934–
Hodgins, Jack. 1938–
Atwood, Margaret. 1939–
Ondaatje, Michael. 1943–
Mistry, Rohinton. 1952–

ATWOOD, MARGARET. 1939–

A critic, editor, poet, and fiction writer of international reputation, Margaret Atwood is one of the most significant voices in Canadian literature. The publication of her first full-length book of poems, *The Circle Game* (1966), gained critical attention for its lean, unconventional verse. *The Journals of Susanna Moodie*(1970) is an innovative collection of poems that takes as its narrator the convention-bound colonialist of the title. *Procedures from Underground* (1970) relies on native Indian mythology for its particular vision. With *Power Politics* (1971), Atwood established herself as a feminist poet through her exploration of the destructive and alienating aspects of sexual relationships.

Toward the end of the 1960s, Atwood shifted from poetry to fiction. Her novels, with the exception of *Life before Man* (1979), feature a female protagonist who, because of various circumstances, must radically reassess her life. In *Lady Oracle* (1976), the heroine decides to stage her death in order to escape into a new life; *Surfacing* (1972) is the story of a woman who sets out to find her botanist father in the Quebec bush and instead discovers a new perspective on the union of nature and humanity. In 1986 Atwood departed from the form of her earlier novels to depict in *The Handmaid's Tale* (1985) a feminist dystopia in a futuristic theocracy called the Republic of Gilead. This cautionary tale, set in what was formerly Boston, parallels the Puritan era in American history. A *bildungsroman* followed, *Cat's Eye* (1989), which tells the story of a girl's childhood in Canada, her attempts to find herself as a young woman, her success as an artist, then her struggle to redefine herself as a middle-aged woman.

Atwood, a remarkably complex and forever-changing writer, has reached throughout her career in varied directions for form and subject matter. The daughter of an entomologist, Margaret Atwood was born in Ottawa and grew up in northern Ontario and Quebec. She received a B.A. from the University of Toronto and an M.A. from Radcliffe.

POETRY BY ATWOOD

The Circle Game. 1966. Anansi 1978 $4.95. ISBN 0-88784-070-1

The Journals of Susanna Moodie: Poems. 1970 OUP 1970 $10.00. ISBN 0-19-540169-7

Power Politics. Anansi 1971 $4.95. ISBN 0-88784-020-5

Selected Poems 1966-1984. OUP 1990 $19.95. ISBN 0-19-540808-X. Best-known and representative poems from previous collections.

NOVELS BY ATWOOD

Bodily Harm. 1981. Bantam 1983 $4.95. ISBN 0-553-27455-4. Traces the inner journey of Rennie Wilford, while recounting her adventures as a journalist visiting Caribbean islands.

Cat's Eye. 1988. Doubleday 1989 $18.95. ISBN 0-385-26007-5

The Edible Woman. 1969. Warner Bks. 1989 $4.95. ISBN 0-446-31498-6. The relations between the sexes through the metaphor of a consumer society in which men view women as commodities.

The Handmaid's Tale. 1985. Fawcett 1986 $5.95. ISBN 0-449-21260-2

Lady Oracle. 1976. Fawcett 1987 $5.95. ISBN 0-449-21376-5

Life before Man. 1979. Fawcett 1987 $4.95. ISBN 0-449-21377-3. A realistic novel about urban infidelity and the moral conditions of the late 1970s.

Surfacing. 1972. Fawcett 1987 $4.95. ISBN 0-449-21375-7

BOOKS ABOUT ATWOOD

Carrington, Ildiko de Papp. *Margaret Atwood and Her Works (Fiction). Canadian Writers Ser.* ECW Pr. 1987 $9.95. ISBN 0-920763-25-1. Provides biographical material, a survey of the works, and bibliographies.

Mallinson, Jean. *Margaret Atwood and Her Works (Poetry). Canadian Writers Ser.* ECW Pr. 1984 o.p. Focuses on Atwood's poetry, tracing its pattern of self-dramatization.

Rigney, Barbara Hill. *Margaret Atwood.* B&N Imports 1987 $38.50. ISBN 0-389-20742-X. Stresses Atwood's political and moral dimension, suggesting she is a radical humanist.

Van Spanckeren, Kathryn, and Jan Garden Castro, eds. *Margaret Atwood: Vision and Forms.* S. Ill. U. Pr. 1988 $29.95. ISBN 0-8093-1408-8. Essays examining major concerns in Atwood's work—feminism, ecology, the Gothic, and U.S.–Canadian relations.

BIRNEY, (ALFRED) EARLE. 1904–

Earle Birney was born in Calgary, Alberta, and raised in rural Alberta and British Columbia. To earn money for college, Birney held a variety of manual jobs before enrolling at the University of British Columbia in 1922. Clearly, both his studies and his experience in the labor force gave to his poetry a wide variety of themes and situations. After receiving his Ph.D. in 1938, Birney accepted a position at the University of Toronto, where he worked until he joined the army in 1942. After serving as a personnel officer during the war, he obtained a professorship in medieval literature at the University of British Columbia, a post from which he retired in 1965.

Earle Birney's poetry has received recognition both in Canada and abroad. He is credited with introducing into Canadian poetry a metrics based on everyday speech rather than on artificial cadences. His visual poems are considered the forerunners of concrete poetry and his experiments with sound the forerunners of sound poetry in Canada. Since publishing his first book of poems, *David and Other Poems*, in 1942, Birney has published 15 more volumes of verse, two novels, and several books of critical writing; in *The Cow Jumped over the Moon* (1972), he talks about the composition of his own poetry.

POETRY BY BIRNEY

Ghost in the Wheels: Selected Poems, 1920–1976. McClelland & Stewart CN 1977 $12.95. ISBN 0-7710-1408-2. Representative poems from Birney's long career.

BOOK ABOUT BIRNEY

Aichinger, Peter. *Earle Birney and His Works. Canadian Writers Ser.* ECW Pr. 1984 $9.95. ISBN 0-920802-79-6. Provides biographical information and a thorough introduction to the poetry.

CALLAGHAN, MORLEY. 1903–1990

A master of the short story and author of several excellent novels, Morley Callaghan has long been a writer of international reputation. Callaghan was born and raised in Toronto, educated at St. Michael's College, University of Toronto, and Osgoode Hall Law school. Working as a reporter for the *Toronto Daily Star*, he met ERNEST HEMINGWAY (see Vol. 1), who was also working with the newspaper. In 1929, the same year as his first volume of short stories, *Native Argosy*, was published, Callaghan traveled to Paris, where he became reacquainted with Hemingway and met JAMES JOYCE and F. SCOTT FITZGERALD (see Vol. 1). *That Summer in Paris* (1963) contains Callaghan's memoirs of his experiences with these famous expatriates.

Morley Callaghan is renowned for the clarity and economy of his prose. While Callaghan's work appears forthright and uncomplicated, each of the novels focuses on a character who faces a crisis. How this turning point is handled determines the direction the character's life will take. Callaghan, who was a devout Catholic, saw himself as a moralist as well as one who gave "shape and form to human experience." While some critics may question the merit of Callaghan's novels, they generally agree that his short stories will endure.

Novels by Callaghan

The Loved and the Lost. 1951. Stoddart 1989 $6.95. ISBN 0-7715-9296-5. A story of misunderstood love ruined finally by doubt and suspicion.

Such Is My Beloved. 1934. McClelland & Stewart CN 1989 $5.95. ISBN 0-7710-9955-X. What happens to an idealistic young priest who attempts to reform prostitutes.

That Summer in Paris. 1963. Stoddart 1986 $5.95. ISBN 0-7715-9270-1 o.p.

Short Story Collections by Callaghan

The Lost and Found Stories of Morley Callaghan. 1985. HarpC 1986 $7.95. ISBN 0-00-223121-2. Previously uncollected stories.

Morley Callaghan's Stories. 1959. Stoddart 1986 $5.95. ISBN 0-7715-9247-7. Collection of Callaghan's best-known short works.

Book about Callaghan

Boire, Gary. *Morley Callaghan and His Works. Canadian Writers Ser.* ECW Pr. 1990 $9.95. ISBN 1-55022-029-2. Provides biographical material and a study of major themes in the fiction.

CARMAN, BLISS. 1861–1929

A first cousin of Charles G. Roberts (see Vol. 1) and a distant relation of Ralph Waldo Emerson (see Vol. 1), Carman was born in Fredericton, New Brunswick, and educated at the Universities of New Brunswick, Oxford, Edinburgh, and Harvard. Always a restless and emotionally unstable man, Carman attempted a fitful career as a journalist in New York before devoting himself fully to poetry. In 1921, he embarked on a poetry-reading tour across Canada. This proved so successful that by its completion Carman was hailed as Canada's unofficial poet laureate.

Enormously popular in his day, Carman produced more than 50 chapbooks and books of poetry, most of it heavily influenced by William Wordsworth (see Vol. 1), Emerson, and the Pre-Raphaelites. His most important verse was produced in collaboration with his friend Richard Hovey: The resulting "Vagabondia" series eventually ran to four volumes—*Songs from Vagabondia* (1894), *Last Songs from Vagabondia* (1900), *Echoes from Vagabondia*, and *More Songs from Vagabondia* (1896).

Bliss Carman's best poetry reflects his sincere joy in nature and the affirmation of a divine presence, which its cyclical rhythms suggest. He is at his weakest when a growing interest in transcendentalism and a rather vague form of pantheism mired his poems in abstractions and repetitiveness.

Poetry by Carman

Windflower: Selected Poems of Bliss Carman. Ed. by Raymond Souster and Douglas Lochhead. Tecumseh 1986 $25.95. ISBN 0-919662-06-4. A collection of Carman's representative poems.

WORKS BY CARMAN

Letters of Bliss Carman. Ed. by H. Pearson Gunday. McGill CN 1981 $35.00. ISBN 0-7735-0364. Varied correspondence that reflects the poet's life.

BOOKS ABOUT CARMAN

Lynch, Gerald, ed. *Bliss Carman: A Reappraisal.* U. of Ottawa Pr. 1990 $24.95. ISBN 0-7766-0286-1. Essays examining various aspects of Carman's career and attempting to place him in Canadian literature.

Miller, Muriel. *Bliss Carman: Quest and Revolt.* Jesperson 1985 $36.00. ISBN 0-920502-62-8. An excellent study of this intriguing figure and his work.

COHEN, LEONARD. 1934–

Leonard Cohen should properly be described as an artist rather than a poet or prose writer. Born and raised in the affluent Westmount district of Montreal, Cohen graduated from McGill in 1955 and for a short time attended graduate school at Columbia. With the decision to become a professional writer, he returned to Montreal. In 1963 he became an expatriate, and lived intermittently on the Greek island of Hydra, in California, New York, and occasionally Montreal.

Throughout the 1960s, Cohen's verse, both as song and poetry, became extremely popular. His "Suzanne" was one of the most-recorded songs of the decade. Always a poet whose work reflected the attitudes of society's nonconformists, Cohen successively identified with the Beat Generation of the 1950s, the rhetoricians of protest of the mid-1960s, and the more meditative disillusionment of the 1970s.

Cohen's best-known work, *Beautiful Losers* (1966), is a dazzling novel that is an abstraction of all searches for a lost innocence. In *Death of a Lady's Man* (1978), one of Cohen's collections of poetry, his preoccupation with the duality of beauty and decadence is once again explored.

NOVEL BY COHEN

Beautiful Losers. 1966. McClelland & Stewart CN 1991 $6.95. ISBN 0-7710-9875-8

POETRY BY COHEN

Book of Mercy. McClelland & Stewart CN 1984 $14.95. ISBN 0-7710-2206-9. Poetry that points toward some forms of spiritual regeneration.

Death of a Lady's Man. McClelland & Stewart CN 1978 $19.95. ISBN 0-7710-2177-1

The Energy of Slaves. McClelland & Stewart CN 1972 $12.95. ISBN 0-7710-2204-2. Poems on the themes of nihilism, suicide, and artistic burnout.

BOOKS ABOUT COHEN

Hutcheon, Linda. *Leonard Cohen and His Works (Fiction).* ECW Pr. 1989 $9.95. ISBN 0-920763-86-3. A thorough study of Cohen's fiction from a thematic standpoint, with biographical details.

———. *Leonard Cohen and His Works (Poetry).* ECW Pr. 1991 $9.95. ISBN 1-55022-074-8. Examines the themes and techniques of Cohen's poetry.

DAVIES, ROBERTSON. 1913–

Novelist, playwright, and journalist, Robertson Davies is one of Canada's best-known writers internationally. He grew up in Kingston, Ontario, where he later attended Queen's University. In 1938 he received a B.Litt. from Oxford, and then joined the Old Vic Theatre Company. Returning to Canada in 1940, he served as editor of the influential publication *Saturday Night* until 1942. For the next 20 years he was editor of the *Peterborough Examiner* in Ontario, where he wrote the Samuel Marchbanks Sketches. From 1953 to 1971 he served on the board of the Stratford Festival. In 1963 Davies became the first master of Massey College, a graduate college at the University of Toronto.

In the 1970s Davies published the *Deptford Trilogy—Fifth Business* (1970), *The Manticore* (1972), and *World of Wonders* (1975)—a series of novels relying heavily on CARL JUNG's (see Vol. 5) theory of archetypes. This trilogy stands in contrast to Davies's earlier novels, which are largely comedies of manners: The *Salterton Trilogy—Tempest Tost* (1951), *Leaven of Malice* (1954), and *A Mixture of Frailties* (1958). Here Davies explores the pettiness and pretensions of small-town Canadian life. Beginning in 1981, Davies published the *Cornish Trilogy: The Rebel Angels* (1981), *What's Bred in the Bone* (1985), and *The Lyre of Orpheus* (1988). These novels, with their academic setting, reveal Davies's awareness of Canada's intellectual and artistic sophistication. Sometimes accused of being a colonial lackey and looking down on his native land through his fiction, Davies presents in this trilogy a positive impression of Canadian life, as he depicts homegrown artists, writers, intellectuals, and patrons of the arts.

NOVELS BY DAVIES

Fifth Business. 1970. Viking Penguin 1977 $5.95. ISBN 0-14-004387-X
Leaven of Malice. 1954. Viking Penguin 1980 $4.95. ISBN 0-14-005433-2
The Lyre of Orpheus. 1988. Viking Penguin 1989 $19.95. ISBN 0-670-82416-X
The Manticore. 1972. Viking Penguin 1977 $5.95. ISBN 0-14-004388-8
A Mixture of Frailties. 1958. Viking Penguin 1980 $4.95. ISBN 0-14-005432-4
Murther and Walking Spirits. Viking Penguin 1991 $21.95. ISBN 0-670-84189-7. A narrative in which the central character revisits his ancestors.
The Rebel Angels. 1981. Viking Penguin 1983 $9.95. ISBN 0-14-006271-8
Tempest-Tost. 1951. Viking Penguin 1980 $4.95. ISBN 0-14-005431-6
What's Bred in the Bone. 1985. Viking Penguin 1986 $8.95. ISBN 0-14-009711-2
World of Wonders. 1975. Viking Penguin 1977 $6.95. ISBN 0-14-004389-6

BOOKS ABOUT DAVIES

Cameron, Elspeth, ed. *Robertson Davies: An Appreciation.* Broadview Pr. 1991 $16.95. ISBN 0-921149-81-6. Essays taking various approaches to Davies's fiction and other work.

Davis, J. Madison, ed. *Conversations with Robertson Davies.* U. of Miss. Pr. 1989 $32.50. ISBN 0-87805-383-2. A collection of 28 interviews recorded between 1963 and 1988.

Peterman, Michael. *Robertson Davies.* Macmillan 1986 $22.95. ISBN 0-8057-6629-4. A biography and commentary on Davies's fiction, drama, and humorous writing, stressing the Canadian cultural background.

FINDLEY, TIMOTHY. 1930–

A native of Toronto, novelist and playwright Timothy Findley initially embarked upon an acting career. In its first season (1953), Findley worked for the Canadian Stratford Festival and later, after study at London's Central School of Speech and Drama, he toured Britain, Europe, and the United States as a contract player. While performing in *The Matchmaker,* by THORNTON WILDER (see Vol. 1), Findley was encouraged by the playwright to write fiction. Influenced by film techniques, Findley's first novel, *The Last of the Crazy People* (1967) is a penetrating look at a family of "emotional cripples" from a child's perspective. With his character Hooker, Findley captures "the irrational logic of a child's mind, while avoiding the pitfall of treating childhood sentimentally" (*Journal of Canadian Studies*). *The Butterfly Plague* followed in 1969. *The Wars*

(1978), Findley's most successful novel, has been translated into numerous languages and was made into a film. In *The Wars*, "the device of a story-within-a-story is used to illustrate how a personality transcends elemental forces even while being destroyed by them, and how the value of past experience is a function of the skill with which we recreate it imaginatively, transcending the chaos of time and history" (*Canadian Literature*). In 1981 *Famous Last Words* was published. This fictionalization of *Hugh Selwyn Mauberley*, by EZRA POUND (see Vol. 1), a work that was already a "fictional fact," examines fascism. In *Not Wanted on the Voyage* (1984), Findley rewrites the story of Noah's Ark by giving voices to women, children, workers, animals, and folklore creatures, all of whom question Noah's authority. The novel turns into a parable that seems to challenge imperialism, eugenics, fascism, and any other force that endangers human survival. Again repeating an earlier text, Findley turns to Thomas Mann's *Death in Venice* to write *The Telling of Lies* (1986). This novel draws parallels between World War II atrocities and contemporary North America, which Findley sees as a metaphoric concentration camp.

NOVELS BY FINDLEY

The Butterfly Plague. 1969. Viking Penguin 1990 $6.95. ISBN 0-14-013395
Famous Last Words. 1981. Stoddart 1981 $12.95. ISBN 0-7720-1362-4
The Last of the Crazy People. 1967. Viking Penguin 1983 $6.95. ISBN 0-14-006846-5
Not Wanted on the Voyage. 1984. Dell 1987 $4.95. ISBN 0-440-36499-X
The Telling of Lies. 1986. Delacorte 1988 $7.95. ISBN 0-440-55001-7
The Wars. 1978. Stoddart 1989 $12.00. ISBN 0-7737-2364

SHORT STORY COLLECTIONS BY FINDLEY

Dinner along the Amazon. 1984. Viking Penguin 1990 $6.95. ISBN 0-14-014599-0. Stories that develop Findley's obsession with what he sees as a morally corrupt society.
Stones. 1988. Delacorte 1990 $9.95. ISBN 0-385-30002-6. Stories on the recurrent theme of how war affects its survivors.

GALLANT, MAVIS (DE TRAFFORD YOUNG). 1922–

Born in Montreal, Mavis Gallant grew up in Canada and the United States. In 1950 she settled in France, but she still retains ties to Canada. Although bilingual from childhood and thoroughly involved in French culture, Gallant writes fiction only in English. Her first stories appeared in *The New Yorker*, where she continues to publish. She has written two novels, *Green Water, Green Sky* (1959) and *A Fairly Good Time* (1970), both of them character studies about alienation. The short story and novella, however, are the vehicles that best display her talent. Her short fiction has been collected over the years since 1956 in a number of volumes. *Overhead in a Balloon* (1985) contains stories about France, *Home Truths* (1981) stories about Canada, and *The Pegnitz Junction* (1973) stories about German fascism.

Urbane in tone, elegantly chiseled in style, Gallant's stories focus primarily on character. Whether Canadians or French—at home or abroad, or world wanderers of all nationalities—the people she writes about suffer from alienation in an uncaring society, exile within their own experience. Gallant's finely tuned dialogue reflects the inability to overcome the loss these characters face, for they find it impossible to express fully or directly what they feel so strongly. Yet, in spite of separation from their physical and spiritual homeland as well as from other humans in the same predicament, the characters manage to survive. They appear to accept the statement at the conclusion of one of

Gallant's most brilliant stories, "The Ice Wagon Going Down the Street" from *Home Truths:* "Everything works out, somehow or other."

Novels by Gallant

A Fairly Good Time. 1970. Macmillan 1983 $9.95. ISBN 0-7715-9775-4
Green Water, Green Sky. 1959. Macmillan 1983 $7.95. ISBN 0-7715-9774-6

Short Story Collections by Gallant

The End of the World and Other Stories. McClelland & Stewart CN 1974 $4.95. ISBN 0-7710-919-5
From the Fifteenth District. 1974. Stoddart 1986 $4.95. ISBN 0-7715-9250-7
Home Truths. 1981. Stoddart 1986 $5.95. ISBN 0-7715-9267-1
In Transit. 1988. Viking Penguin 1989 $6.95. ISBN 0-14-010917-X
My Heart Is Broken. 1964. General 1981 $4.95. ISBN 0-7736-7020-3
The Other Paris. 1956. Macmillan 1986 $8.95. ISBN 0-7715-9738-X
Overhead in a Balloon. 1985. Stoddart 1989 $6.95. ISBN 0-7715-9961-7
The Pegnitz Junction. 1973. Stoddart 1988 $5.95. ISBN 0-7715-9543-3

Book about Gallant

Grant, Judith Skelton. *Mavis Gallant and Her Works*. ECW Pr. 1989 $9.95. ISBN 1-55022-033-0. Surveys Gallant's fiction to discover its major themes and technique; with biographical information.

HALIBURTON, THOMAS CHANDLER. 1796–1865

Although he died before Canada achieved Confederation in 1867, Thomas Chandler Haliburton's depiction of prefederation Nova Scotia has given him a prominent place in Canàdian literature. Born in Windsor, Nova Scotia, he was the son of Connecticut and Rhode Island Loyalists. In 1826 he was made a member of Nova Scotia's provincial assembly, a post he held until his appointment as a circuit judge in 1829. At this point a confirmed Burkean-Tory, Haliburton began writing satiric sketches for the *Nova Scotian*. Encouraged by their local popularity, he had them published as *The Clockmaker, or, The Sayings and Doings of Samuel Slick of Slickville* (1836), which became the first Canadian bestseller. *The Clockmaker* follows the adventures of Sam Slick, an unscrupulous Connecticut peddler. An uneasy embodiment of Yankee shrewdness and Tory-Loyalist principles, Sam Slick instantly became an international comic hero whose travels were eventually chronicled in seven volumes. Haliburton was reportedly called "the father of American humor" by Artemus Ward, and his work is often considered an influence on Mark Twain (see Vol. 1).

In 1841, Haliburton was appointed to the Supreme Court of Nova Scotia; 15 years later he moved to England, where he held a seat in the House of Commons. Oxford University awarded him an honorary degree for his literary accomplishments, making Haliburton the first writer from a Commonwealth country to receive such recognition.

Works by Haliburton

The Clockmaker, or, The Sayings and Doings of Samuel Slick of Slickville. 1836. McClelland & Stewart CN 1965 $5.95. ISBN 0-7710-9106-0
The Letters of Thomas Chandler Haliburton. Ed. by Richard Davies. U. of Toronto Pr. 1988 $45.00. ISBN 0-8020-2628. A close view of Haliburton and his times.
The Old Judge, or, Life in a Colony. 1849. Tecumseh 1978 $9.95. ISBN 0-919662-69-2. Presents a detailed picture of colonial Nova Scotian life.

BOOK ABOUT HALIBURTON

McMullin, Stanley. *Thomas Chandler Haliburton and His Works.* ECW Pr. 1989 $9.95. ISBN 1-55022-0470. A thorough introduction and analysis of Haliburton's writing, placing it in the Canadian colonial era.

HODGINS, JACK. 1938–

Jack Hodgins grew up in a logging town on northern Vancouver Island, a remote area he has described as separate from all the rest of Canada, including its literary traditions. In order to shape fiction about this region with its scattered, lonely towns and often eccentric inhabitants, Hodgins has drawn on various traditions in addition to the Canadian, such as the Gothic techniques employed by WILLIAM FAULKNER (see Vol. 1) and the magic realism of Latin American writers. Hodgins remains on Vancouver Island, where he teaches English at the University of Victoria.

Hodgins's first novel, *The Invention of the World* (1977), uses contemporary characters to re-create the mythic birth of Donal Keneally, who led Irish villagers to establish a colony in western Canada. The next novel is also reminiscent of GABRIEL GARCÍA MÁRQUEZ's *One Hundred Years of Solitude*; in *The Resurrection of Joseph Bourne, or, A Word or Two on Those Port Annie Miracles*(1980), a tidal wave washes ashore in western Canada a ship from Peru and a "Peruvian seabird." This odd occurrence sets off a series of bizarre events that the locals accept without question. *The Honorary Patron* (1987) continues the saga of northern Canada's lonely reaches; this time the central character returns to the area after a long absence and brings about peculiar happenings. Hodgins has also published two volumes of short stories in the same mode as the novels.

NOVELS BY HODGINS

The Honorary Patron. 1987. McClelland & Stewart CN 1989 $6.95. ISBN 0-7710-4190
The Invention of the World. 1977. Stoddart 1985 $5.95. ISBN 0-7715-9252-3
The Resurrection of Joseph Bourne, or, A Word or Two on Those Port Annie Miracles. 1980. Stoddart 1990 $6.95. ISBN 0-7715-9959-5

SHORT STORY COLLECTIONS BY HODGINS

The Barclay Family Theatre. 1981. Macmillan 1983 $9.95. ISBN 0-7715-9765-7
Spit Delaney's Island. 1976. Stoddart 1986 $4.95. ISBN 0-7715-9268-X

BOOK ABOUT HODGINS

Jeffrey, David. *Jack Hodgins and His Works.* ECW Pr. 1989 $9.95. ISBN 0-920763-89-8. Examines Hodgins's metafictional techniques, explores his themes, and relates his work to the Canadian tradition.

HOOD, HUGH. 1928–

While he is best known as a writer of short stories, Hugh Hood's fourth novel, *You Can't Get There from Here* (1972), exhibits his usual skill at characterization, and a concern with descriptive prose, dialogue, and ironic humor. Hood's humor features universal themes and a strong moral tone, the latter being a product of the author's Roman Catholic sensibility. *You Can't Get There from Here* is a satirical look at multinational corporations and philanthropists who descend on third world countries.

His several collections of short stories include *August Nights*, *Flying a Red Kite* (1962), and *None Genuine without This Signature*. The subject matter of these stories "shapes a chronicle of our age," and their "didactic impulse" and "moral vision" reflect what Hood himself calls "the primal guarantee of the actual, the authentic certificate of its existence which God provides, the signature in the heart of the existent." The first volume in Hood's proposed cycle of 12 novels appeared in 1975: *The Swing in the Garden*. It was followed by *A New Athens* (1977), *Reservoir Ravine* (1979), *Black and White Keys* (1982), *The Scenic Art* (1984), *The Motor Boys in Ottawa* (1986), and *Tony's Book* (1988). Under the collective title of *The New Age*, these novels trace through a character named Matthew Goderich the connected histories of a man and a family from 1880 to 2000.

Hood was born in Toronto and received his B.A., M.A., and Ph.D. from the University. He teaches at the University of Montreal.

Novels by Hood

Black and White Keys. 1982. General 1985 $4.95. ISBN 0-7736-7101-3
The Motor Boys in Ottawa. Stoddart 1986 $14.95. ISBN 0-7737-5080-0
A New Athens. 1977. General 1984 $4.95. ISBN 0-7736-7082-3
Reservoir Ravine. 1979. General 1985 $4.95. ISBN 0-7736-7100-5
The Swing in the Garden. 1975. General 1984 $4.95. ISBN 0-7736-7083-1
Tony's Book. Stoddart 1988 $14.95. ISBN 0-7737-5208-0
You Can't Get There from Here. 1972. General 1983 $3.95. ISBN 0-7736-7065-3

Short Story Collections by Hood

August Nights. Stoddart 1985 $14.95. ISBN 0-7737-5046-0
Flying a Red Kite. 1962. Porcupine's Quill rev. ed. 1987 $12.95. ISBN 0-88984-110-1
None Genuine without This Signature. ECW Pr. 1980 $7.95. ISBN 0-920802-10-9

Book about Hood

Garebian, Keith. *Hugh Hood and His Works*. ECW Pr. 1984 $9.95. ISBN 0-920802-77-X. Excellent overview of Hood's life and fiction, including analysis of theme and technique.

JOE, RITA. 1932–

A member of the Micmac nation, Rita Joe is one of the best-known native writers. Born in Nova Scotia, where she now lives on the Eskasoni Reserve in Cape Breton, Joe won the Nova Scotia Writers Federation competition in 1974. Later she said that winning the prize made her think that other native writers would say: "If she can do it so can I." She has commented that "the stroke of a Native pen does wonders, especially for the coming generation." Deeply involved in education, Joe works not only with native children but speaks as well to a wide range of audiences on native culture, stressing its importance, development, and preservation.

Her first book, *Poems of Rita Joe*, appeared in 1978 and contains 26 poems. While Micmac translations accompany some of these poems, there are no translations in her second book, *Song of Eskasoni: More Poems of Rita Joe* (1988), which makes full use of Micmac lines and phrases along with the English. Marked by simplicity and directness, Joe's poetry expresses her solution to the problems of Indian-white relations: to rely on "the power of love and understanding."

Poetry by Rita Joe

Lnu and Indians We're Called: Poems of Rita Joe. Ragweed 1991 $8.95. ISBN 0-921556-22-5

Song of Eskasoni: More Poems of Rita Joe. 1988. Ragweed 1989 $9.95. ISBN 0-921556-22-5

KLEIN, A(BRAHAM) M(OSES). 1909–1972

Ludwig Lewisohn wrote in the foreword to A. M. Klein's first book of poems, *Hath Not a Jew . . .*, that Klein was "the first contributor of authentic Jewish poetry to the English language." Indeed, Klein's impact on the Canadian literary scene, with his open exploration of Jewishness, paved the way for later Jewish writers such as Irving Layton, LEONARD COHEN, MORDECAI RICHLER, MIRIAM WADDINGTON, and Adele Wiseman.

Born in the Ukraine, Abraham Moses Klein left at the age of one with his parents for Montreal, where he remained for the rest of his life. A brilliant student of orthodox background, he resisted family pressure to become a rabbi and enrolled at McGill University in 1926. In 1933 he graduated from the law school at the University of Montreal and established a practice. Deeply involved with the Jewish community, Klein early exhibited a commitment to the Zionist movement. From 1936 to 1937 he edited *The Canadian Zionist* and from 1939 to 1954 he held the editorship of *The Canadian Jewish Chronicle*.

Most of Klein's work reveals his debt to JAMES JOYCE (see Vol. 1). His reliance upon Joycean allusions, multilingual puns, and complex metaphors is especially prevalent in *The Rocking Chair* (1948), considered by many to contain Klein's finest verse. These poems are somewhat of a departure from his earlier work, exemplified in *Poems* (1944), which is more traditional in theme and technique. Klein also wrote some short stories and a highly successful novel, *The Second Scroll* (1951).

POETRY BY KLEIN

A. M. Klein: Complete Poems. Ed. by Zailig Pollock. U. of Toronto Pr. 1990 $125.00. ISBN 0-8020-5802-7. Poems from 1926 to 1934 (Part 1) and from 1937 to 1955 (Part 2).

SHORT STORY COLLECTION BY KLEIN

A. M. Klein: Short Stories. Ed. by M. W. Steinberg. U. of Toronto Pr. 1983 $40.00. ISBN 0-8020-5598-2. Collection of short stories written over a lifetime, many concerning the Jewish experience in Canada.

NOVEL BY KLEIN

The Second Scroll. 1951. McClelland & Stewart CN 1961 $4.95. ISBN 0-7710-9315-2. Follows the search by a young Canadian for his uncle after World War II.

BOOK ABOUT KLEIN

Golfman, Noreen. *A. M. Klein and His Works.* ECW Pr. 1990 $9.95. ISBN 1-55022-024-1. A thorough introduction to Klein's poetry and fiction, with biographical materials.

KROETSCH, ROBERT. 1927–

Robert Kroetsch was born in Heisler, Alberta, and received his B.A. from the University of Alberta. In 1954 he studied creative writing at McGill University under Hugh MacLennan. He obtained a Ph.D. in creative writing from the University of Iowa in 1961. For 14 years Kroetsch taught English at the State University of New York in Binghamton. He is currently a professor of English at the University of Manitoba.

With the trilogy *The Words of My Roaring* (1966), *The Studhorse Man* (1969), and *Gone Indian* (1973), Kroetsch departed from realism to experiment with a surreal or fabulous approach to literature. An updated version of HOMER'S

Odyssey, The Studhorse Man chronicles a loner's search for the perfect mare to produce the ultimate breed of horses. *Badlands* (1975), Kroetsch's fifth novel, is a kind of postmodern *Huckleberry Finn* narrated in the form of notes written by a paleontologist rafting through the Alberta Badlands. *Alibi* (1983) is a mythic tale of the quest for the perfect spa, a novel that operates in a more realistic vein than Kroetsch's earlier fiction.

Novels by Kroetsch

Alibi. 1983. General 1984 $4.95. ISBN 0-7736-7084-X

The Studhorse Man. 1969. Random 1988 $8.95. ISBN 0-394-22049-8

What the Crow Said. 1978. General 1983 $3.95. ISBN 0-7736-7060-2. An attempt, heavily influenced by South American magic realism, to capture western Canadian experience and history.

Poetry by Kroetsch

The Completed Field Notes: The Long Poems of Robert Kroetsch. McClelland & Stewart CN 1989 $16.95. ISBN 0-7710-4506-9. A collection of highly experimental poems.

Books about Kroetsch

Munton, Ann. *Robert Kroetsch and His Works*. ECW Pr. 1991 $9.95. ISBN 1-55022-072-1. Examines Kroetsch's poetry and fiction, focusing in particular on his experimentation.

Thomas, Peter. *Robert Kroetsch*. Douglas & McIntyre CN 1980 $6.95. ISBN 0-88894-263-X. Introduction to Kroetsch's writing.

LAURENCE, (JEAN) MARGARET (WEMYSS). 1926–1987

Born and raised in the plains town of Neepawa, Manitoba, Margaret Laurence graduated from United College in Winnipeg and worked first as a reporter. After her marriage, she traveled with her engineer husband to Somalia and Ghana. Her first novel, *This Side Jordan* (1960), is set in Ghana and focuses on how British imperialism affected Africans in the postcolonial era. The narrative tells the story of a teacher, Nathaniel Amegbe, who embodies the conflict between past and present, between African and British values.

Yet it was Laurence's birthplace, fictionalized as Manawaka, that became the setting for her major works. In all these novels, the female protagonists see life as a quest, sometimes joyful but inevitably alienating. The novels also address another kind of colonialism: That of male dominance over women. *The Stone Angel* (1964), Laurence's best-known work, tells the story of Hagar Shipley, an old woman who, like King Lear, must come to terms with her own life. Both *A Jest of God* (1966), about an unmarried schoolteacher, and *The Fire-Dwellers* (1969), about a middle-aged housewife, focus on women who battle a life-denying, self-imposed isolation. *A Bird in the House* (1970), eight interconnected stories set in Manawaka, follow a central character through a 10-year period beginning in the mid-1930s. Laurence's final and most complex novel, *The Diviners* (1974), is preoccupied with the meaning of an individual's heritage. The heroine, Morag, and her Métis lover, Jules, both discover that the past has bequeathed to them the strength to resist society's attempts to mold or to reject those they consider outsiders.

Acknowledged as Canada's most widely read novelist, Margaret Laurence gained her popularity primarily from her powerful ability to create memorable characters. David Stouck has written that "Margaret Laurence's fictions stand out for their unforgettable portraits of women wrestling with their personal demons, striving through self-examination to find meaningful patterns to their lives."

NOVELS BY LAURENCE

A Bird in the House. 1970. McClelland & Stewart CN 1989 $4.95. ISBN 0-7710-9985-1
The Diviners. 1974. McClelland & Stewart CN 1988 $5.95. ISBN 0-7710-9986-X
The Fire-Dwellers. 1969. McClelland & Stewart CN 1988 $4.95. ISBN 0-7710-9987-8
A Jest of God. 1966. McClelland & Stewart CN 1988 $4.95. ISBN 0-7710-9988-6
The Stone Angel. 1964. McClelland & Stewart CN 1988 $4.95. ISBN 0-7710-9989-4
This Side Jordan. 1960. McClelland & Stewart CN 1989 $6.95. ISBN 0-7710-9967-3

WORK BY LAURENCE

Dance on the Earth. McClelland & Stewart CN 1989 $26.95. ISBN 0-7710-47-46-0. Memoir that offers insights into the writer's life; published posthumously.

BOOKS ABOUT LAURENCE

Kertzer, J. W. *Margaret Laurence and Her Works.* ECW Pr. 1987 $9.95. ISBN 0-920763-28-6. Discusses fiction, especially narrative voice, and places the work in the Canadian literary tradition; with biographical background.

Morley, Patricia. *Margaret Laurence: The Long Journey Home.* McGill CN 1991 $14.95. ISBN 0-7735-0856-2. Treats Laurence's writing as a "psychic journey towards inner freedom and spiritual maturity."

Verduyn, Christl, ed. *Margaret Laurence: An Appreciation.* Broadview Pr. 1988 $24.95. ISBN 0-921149-18-2. Articles taking various critical approaches; includes updated biography and bibliography.

LAYTON, IRVING. 1912–

Irving Layton was born in Romania in 1912; a year later he and his parents arrived in Montreal. Educated in the same city, he received his B.Sc. in agriculture from Macdonald College and an M.A. in political economy from McGill University. Throughout his career Layton has been writer-in-residence at several Canadian universities. Easily the most controversial Canadian poet, he was professor of English at Toronto's York University, a post from which he retired in 1978.

Layton's verse has been variously described as dazzling, vulgar, sexist, and hyperbolic, yet Layton has always redeemed himself by the integrity with which he approaches his craft. His poetry avoids sentimentality, often centering on decidedly unpoetic, mundane images. Layton is a self-proclaimed "public exhibitionist," and his frank, bawdy verse and antagonist persona have tended to alienate him from both intellectual circles and the general public. Layton has published 40 or so volumes of poetry, some with outrageous titles such as *The Gucci Bag* (1983), *For My Brother Jesus* (1976), and *Droppings from Heaven* (1979). Much of his work is in print, a testament to his continuing popularity, and supports his declaration that the "poet has a public function as a prophet."

POETRY BY LAYTON

Droppings from Heaven. McClelland & Stewart CN 1979 $19.95. ISBN 0-7710-4945-5
For My Brother Jesus. McClelland & Stewart CN 1976 $10.95. ISBN 0-7710-4847-5
The Gucci Bag. McClelland & Stewart CN 1983 $12.95. ISBN 0-7710-4917-X
The Uncollected Poems 1936–1959. Mosaic Pr. OH 1977 $150.00. ISBN 0-88962-042-3
The Unwavering Eye: Selected Poems 1969–1975. McClelland & Stewart CN 1975 $14.95. ISBN 0-7710-4843

Book about Layton

Mayne, Seymour. *Irving Layton: The Poet and His Critics.* McGraw 1986 $10.95. ISBN 0-07-549285-7. Examines Layton's stormy poetic career, focusing on the reception of his work.

LEACOCK, STEPHEN (BUTLER). 1869–1944

Born in Swanmore, England, Stephen Leacock was one of 11 children of an unsuccessful farmer and an ambitious mother, a woman to whom Leacock no doubt owed his energetic and status-conscious nature. In 1891, while teaching at the prestigious Upper Canada College in Toronto, Leacock obtained a modern language degree from the University of Toronto. In 1903, after receiving a Ph.D. in political economy from the University of Chicago, he joined the staff of McGill University, Montreal, as professor of politics and economics. Leacock's career as a humorist began when he had some comic pieces published as *Literary Lapses* in 1910. This successful book was followed by two more books of comic sketches, *Nonsense Novels* (1911) and *Sunshine Sketches of a Little Town* (1912), which is now considered his best book. Leacock continued this frantic literary output for the remainder of his career, producing more than 30 books of humor as well as biographies and social commentaries. The Stephen Leacock Medal for Humour was established after his death to honor annually an outstanding Canadian humorist.

Works by Leacock

Arcadian Adventures with the Idle Rich. 1914. McClelland & Stewart CN 1989 $5.95. ISBN 0-7710-9966-6. Sketches of city life based on his experiences in Montreal.
Literary Lapses. 1910. McClelland & Stewart CN 1989 $4.95. ISBN 0-7710-9983-5
Nonsense Novels. 1911. McClelland & Stewart CN 1963 $4.95. ISBN 0-7710-9135-4
Sunshine Sketches of a Little Town. 1912. McClelland & Stewart CN 1989 $5.95. ISBN 0-7710-9984-3

Books about Leacock

Curry, Ralph. *Stephen Leacock and His Works.* ECW Pr. 1988 $9.95. ISBN 0-920763-76-6. Examines Leacock's humorous writing in light of its historical setting; with biographical information.

Lynch, Gerald. *Stephen Leacock: Humor and Humanity.* McGill CN 1988 $34.95. ISBN 0-7735-0652-7. A detailed study of Leacock's humor, relating it to Canadian history and identity.

LOWRY, MALCOLM. 1909–1957

Born and raised in an upper-middle-class British family, Malcolm Lowry did not come to Canada until 1939, and then as a "remittance man" who received regular payments from his father in England. For the next 15 years, Lowry and his wife lived in a beach cabin near Vancouver, where he completed most of his major work. Three years after leaving Canada, Lowry died by what the English coroner called "misadventure," which could be an apt description of a life plagued by emotional problems and alcoholism.

Lowry is known mainly for a single novel, *Under the Volcano* (1947), which is set in Mexico and based in part on his experiences in Cuernavaca in 1936–37. The novel depicts the final day in the lives of a drunken British ex-consul and his estranged wife, drinking, eating, and arguing. As the day comes to a close, the police shoot the ex-consul and a horse tramples his wife to death. This plot summary does little justice to the complexity of the novel, which has been described as "one of the great books of this century because of the beauty of its language, the power and importance of its subject—the fall of mankind and the destruction of this world, and the strength of its intricate yet supple structure."

Lowry planned a series of novels with the collective title of *The Voyage That Never Ends. Under the Volcano* is the only one completed in his lifetime. Three of the unfinished works were issued posthumously: *Lunar Caustic* (1963), *Dark as the Grave Wherein my Friend is Laid* (1968), and *October Ferry to Gabriola* (1970). A book of short stories, *Hear us O Lord from heaven thy dwelling place*, appeared in 1961. These eight highly experimental stories are arranged to represent a metaphysical journey, the structure coinciding with Lowry's obsession with "the voyage that never ends."

NOVELS BY LOWRY

October Ferry to Gabriola. 1970. Ed. by Earle Birney and Margerie Lowry. Douglas & McIntyre CN 1988 $10.95. ISBN 0-88894-592-2. The story of a couple on a voyage in search of a new home.

Ultramarine. 1933. Viking Penguin rev. ed. 1974 $9.95. ISBN 0-14-003475-7. A symbolic account of a young man at sea for the first time, who accepts the need to set out on a lifelong voyage.

Under the Volcano. 1947. Carroll & Graf 1984 $8.95. ISBN 0-88184-258-3

SHORT STORY COLLECTION BY LOWRY

Hear us O Lord from heaven thy dwelling place. 1961. Douglas & McIntyre CN 1987 $10.95. ISBN 0-88894-539-6

BOOKS ABOUT LOWRY

Bareham, Tony. *Malcolm Lowry.* St. Martin 1989 $24.00. ISBN 0-312-02445-2. Provides an introduction to Lowry's work and a close reading of *Under the Volcano.*

Day, Douglas. *Malcolm Lowry: A Biography.* OUP 1973 $9.95. ISBN 0-19-503523-2. Full biography, taking a Freudian approach to the fiction; excellent discussion of *Under the Volcano.*

Dodson, Daniel B. *Malcolm Lowry.* Col. U. Pr. 1971 $7.50. ISBN 0-231-03244-7. Includes a short but useful discussion of Lowry's work, *Under the Volcano.*

MACPHERSON, JAY. 1931–

Although her literary production has been small, Jay Macpherson has proved to be an excellent and influential poet. Born in England, she moved with her mother and brother to Newfoundland in 1940. She attended university in Ottawa and Toronto, where she received a Ph.D. in English literature in 1964. In 1957, Oxford University Press published what subsequently became her best-known work, *The Boatman* (1957), winner of the Governor General's Award. *Poems Twice Told* (1981) reprints *The Boatman* and *Welcoming Disaster* (1974) in one volume. Heavily influenced by the eminent Canadian critic Northrop Frye, Macpherson is at the hub of the mythopoeic school that sprang from Frye's literary theory. She is a professor of English at Victoria College, University of Toronto.

POETRY BY MACPHERSON

Poems Twice Told: Containing The Boatman and *Welcoming Disaster.* OUP 1981 $9.95. ISBN 0-19-540379-7

MISTRY, ROHINTON. 1952–

An immigrant to Canada in 1975, Rohinton Mistry was born in Bombay, India. He is a member of the Parsee religious community, whose roots lie in the Zoroastrian tradition of ancient Persia. That a significant number of critics consider Mistry one of Canada's most promising young writers attests to the multicultural society that is developing there.

While working in a bank and taking English and philosophy courses at the University of Toronto, Mistry began writing short stories about Parsee life in Bombay—recording a world in sharp contrast to the predominantly Anglo-Saxon settlement in the cold northern climate where he was living. Mistry received several prizes for these stories, and in 1987 a collection of them appeared, *Tales from Firozsha Baaq*. The linked stories, their events overlapping and the characters reappearing, take place in a Bombay apartment house. While the social and religious fabric of the closely knit Parsee community emerges as a central theme, the idea of immigration and separation from the community hovers over the stories. That changing pattern is drawn more completely in Mistry's novel, *Such a Long Journey* (1991). Again centered on a Parsee family in a Bombay apartment building, the novel traces a son's rebellion against traditions he finds both reassuring and stultifying; at the same time, that once static way of life may be vanishing in the face of modernity. Perhaps Mistry will move on next to the immigrant experience, a promising theme in Canadian literature and all international literature in English. His work is comparable to that of the Pakistani writer Bapsi Sidhwa, now a citizen of the United States; also a Parsee, she has written several novels in English about life in this minority religious community.

Filled with gentle comedy, meticulous attention to detail, a close rendering of Indian English, and intimate glimpses into Parsee life and religious practice, Mistry's fiction returns to what might be considered old-fashioned storytelling.

Novel by Mistry

Such a Long Journey. McClelland & Stewart CN 1991 $26.95. ISBN 0-7710-6058-0

Short Story Collection by Mistry

Tales from Firozsha Baaq. Viking Penguin 1987 $12.95. ISBN 0-14-009777-5

MOODIE, SUSANNA (STRICKLAND). 1803–1885

Susanna Moodie, born in Suffolk, England, was the youngest of five daughters, four of whom became writers of fiction and poetry. (Moodie's elder sister, Catharine Parr Traill, a lesser-known British colonial author, wrote *The Backwoods of Canada*). Before immigrating to Canada, in 1832, Moodie penned numerous poems and stories, all heavily didactic and decidedly second-rate. However, once she had settled in Upper Canada (now Ontario) with her husband, John Dunbar Moodie, the harsh life of the settler provoked a more realistic literary response. Her autobiographical *Roughing It in the Bush*, published in 1852, is a series of sketches stitched into a larger narrative. It is a book expressing the hopes and defeat, the pride and the anger the early settlers felt toward their new home, the Canadian bush. A sequel, *Life in the Clearings versus the Bush*, appeared in 1853. Throughout her life Susanna Moodie's literary output continued to be prolific. Yet it is the frank and colorful quality of *Roughing It* that has placed her in the forefront of early Canadian writers.

Nonfiction by Moodie

Life in the Clearings versus the Bush. 1853. McClelland & Stewart CN 1989 $6.95. ISBN 0-7710-9976-2

Roughing It in the Bush. 1852. McClelland & Stewart CN $8.95. ISBN 0-7710-9975-4

WORK BY MOODIE

Susanna Moodie: Letters of a Lifetime. Ed. by Carl Ballstadt and others. U. of Toronto Pr. 1985 $35.00. ISBN 0-8020-2580-3. Provides insights into the life and thinking of this intriguing colonial figure.

BOOK ABOUT MOODIE

Shields, Carol. *Susanna Moodie: Voice and Vision.* Borealis Pr. 1977 $9.95. ISBN 0-919594-46-8. Examines Moodie's life and writing in relation to her place in the development of Canadian identity.

MUNRO, ALICE (LAIDLAW). 1931–

In 1968 when Alice Munro received the distinguished Governor General's Award for her first book of short stories, *Dance of the Happy Shades,* Canadian newspapers referred to her as a "shy housewife" and a "mother of three." Since then she has established herself as an internationally recognized writer whose urbane fiction about women had already discredited those patronizing labels. Born in southwestern Ontario, Munro has lived in various parts of western Canada, but she sets most of her fiction in her home region, where she now lives. Prior to the appearance of *Dance of the Happy Shades,* Munro had already published 11 of the 15 stories in the book. This continues to be her pattern, with many of the stories appearing first in *The New Yorker.*

The themes that run through this first book have to do with a girl's discovery of the boundaries women face, awareness of the female body, and the forming of female consciousness. Her second book, *Lives of Girls and Women* (1971), relates Del Jordan's growth from childhood to adolescence through eight connected stories. Each one, told by an older Del, focuses on a significant experience in her young life. The female narrators in *Something I've Been Meaning to Tell You* (1974) seek a language to understand their private worlds and to discover their places in the larger world. In another text, *Who Do You Think You Are?* (1978), Munro continues her questioning of women's roles. *The Moons of Jupiter* (1982) and *The Progress of Love* (1986) focus, as well, on sexual politics but in new ways, for in these books the protagonists are older and look less to the past than to the future. The stories in *Friend of My Youth* (1990) are concerned for the most part with male-female relationships—the difficulties, the rewards, the prices sometimes paid.

Although local in setting and seemingly small in scope, Munro's fiction thrives on what might appear to be its limitations. Her adroit use of language and subtle development of character, along with a skilled narrative technique that avoids the experimental, allow the fictions to record the commonplace while revealing a larger consciousness.

SHORT STORY COLLECTIONS BY MUNRO

The Beggar Maid or Who Do You Think You Are? 1978. Viking Penguin 1984 $6.95. ISBN 0-14-006011-1

Dance of the Happy Shades. 1968. McGraw 1988 $5.95. ISBN 0-07-549717-4

Friend of My Youth. Knopf 1990 $18.95. ISBN 0-394-58442-2

Lives of Girls and Women. 1971. NAL-Dutton 1989 $7.95. ISBN 0-452-25975-4

The Moons of Jupiter. 1982. Random 1991 $10.00. ISBN 0-679-73270-5

The Progress of Love. Knopf 1986 $16.95. ISBN 0-394-55272-5

Something I've Been Meaning to Tell You. NAL-Dutton 1984 $9.95. ISBN 0-452-26021-3

Books about Munro

Dahlie, Hallvard. *Alice Munro and Her Works.* ECW Pr. 1984 $9.95. ISBN 0-920802-69-9. Overview of Munro's fiction, examining its themes and technique; with biographical information.

Martin, W. R. *Alice Munro: Paradox and Parallel.* U. Alta Pr. 1989 $14.95. ISBN 0-888640116-8. Discussion of narrative techniques, themes, and patterns of language, with analysis of most stories in Munro's first six collections.

ONDAATJE, MICHAEL. 1943–

Michael Ondaatje has published several volumes of poetry, including *There's a Trick with a Knife I'm Learning to Do*, which consists of selections from earlier books, *The Dainty Monsters* (1967) and *Rat Jelly* (1973). Much of his poetry addresses the crossing of cultural boundaries. Ondaatje was born in Ceylon (now Sri Lanka) and moved to Canada in 1962. He earned a B.A. from the University of Toronto and an M.A. from Queen's University, Kingston, and teaches English at York University.

Ondaatje's fiction and other works that defy classification by genre have also gained widespread attention. A writer quite unconcerned with typical Canadian themes, he focuses on the bizarre, which he renders through surreal, innovative techniques. For example, in *The Collected Works of Billy the Kid* (1970), Ondaatje toys with various literary genres—drama, interviews, lyrics—to relate the life of that legendary figure. In *Coming through Slaughter* (1982), supposedly the biography of jazz musician Charles "Buddy" Bolden, Ondaatje uses Bolden's life to illustrate the artistic dichotomy of creativity and destruction. *Running in the Family* (1982) is a fictionalized account of Ondaatje's Ceylonese ancestors. *In the Skin of a Lion* (1987) dramatizes the heroic efforts of workers who construct skyscrapers. Always in his writing, according to *An Anthology of Canadian Literature in English*, "destruction is as commonplace as creation and hate as available as love; his is a vision of lives lived in extremes."

Novels by Ondaatje

Coming through Slaughter. General 1982 $5.95. ISBN 0-7736-1177-0

In the Skin of a Lion. McClelland & Stewart CN 1987 $22.50. ISBN 0-7710-6887-5

Running in the Family. McClelland & Stewart CN 1982 $22.95. ISBN 0-7710-6885-0

Poetry by Ondaatje

The Collected Works of Billy the Kid. Anansi 1970 $16.95. ISBN 0-88784-118-X

The Dainty Monsters. 1967. Coach Hse. CN 1974 $12.95. ISBN 0-88910-014-4

Rat Jelly. Coach Hse. CN 1973 $12.95. ISBN 0-88910-107-8

There's a Trick with a Knife I'm Learning to Do: Poems 1963–1978. McClelland & Stewart CN 1979 $11.95. ISBN 0-7710-6882-4

Books about Ondaatje

Mundwiler, Leslie. *Michael Ondaatje: Word, Image, Imagination.* Talon Pr. 1984 $11.95. ISBN 0-88922-216-9. Thorough study of Ondaatje's work, stressing his use of language and his imaginative responses to experience.

Waldman, Nell. *Michael Ondaatje and His Works.* ECW Pr. 1991 $9.95. ISBN 1-55022-061-6. Overview of Ondaatje's work: theme, technique, concerns; includes biographical information.

PRATT, E(DWIN) J(OHN). 1882–1964

E. J. Pratt is considered to be the poet who initiated the Canadian modernist movement. Yet, unlike his literary contemporaries, Pratt was attracted to the convention of epic poetry: *Brébeuf and His Brethren* (1940) and *Towards the Last Spike* (1952) are impressive examples of this style and are also ambitious attempts to forge a national mythology through verse.

Edwin John Pratt was born at Western Bay, Newfoundland. As he grew up in this desolate coastal town, Pratt's association with the sea impressed him with an image that would later reverberate throughout his poetry. Although trained as a Methodist minister, Pratt evidently experienced a crisis of faith following his studies in philosophy and psychology at the University of Toronto, where he received a Ph.D. in theology. In 1920, largely because of his promise as a poet, he was given an English professorship at Victoria College, University of Toronto, a post from which he retired in 1953.

Pratt's verse is aptly described by E. K. Brown as the "work of an experimenter who is continuing to clutch at a tradition although that tradition is actually stifling him."

POETRY BY PRATT

E. J. Pratt: Complete Poems. 2 vols. Ed. by Sandra Diawa and R. G. Moyles. U. of Toronto Pr. 1988 $80.00. ISBN 0-8020-5775-6

WORK BY PRATT

E. J. Pratt on His Life and Poetry. Ed. by Susan Gingell. U. of Toronto Pr. 1984 $13.95. ISBN 0-8020-6567-8. Contains autobiographical and critical writing by Pratt.

BOOK ABOUT PRATT

Buitenhuis, Peter. *E. J. Pratt and His Works.* ECW Pr. 1986 $9.95. ISBN 0-920763-23-5. Overview of Pratt's work, providing analysis of major poems; with biographical material.

PURDY, AL. 1918–

The author of 30 or so volumes of poetry, Al Purdy is admired for "his fascination with observed detail and his rhythmic skill with laconic idiom," in the words of W. H. New. In 1978, *Being Alive* offered a selection of Purdy's best work from the previous 25 years, and in 1986 *Collected Poems: 1956–1986* appeared, with 250 poems out of the 700 he had published. Although a prolific poet, Purdy is also a stern critic of his own work.

Born in a small town on the eastern end of Lake Ontario, Purdy has remained in that area most of his life. From what he called a "Bush land scrub land," he has drawn the inspiration and subject matter for much of his poetry. His extensive travels are reflected in his poetry, as in the 1984 volume *Piling Blood.* Showing his continuing development as a writer, the poems in *A Woman on the Shore* (1990) are more intense than much of his earlier work.

W. H. New, the author of *A History of Canadian Literature*, has called Purdy "a representative voice of the multiple identity that is modern Canada."

POETRY BY PURDY

Being Alive. McClelland & Stewart CN 1978 $9.95. ISBN 0-7710-7207-4
Collected Poems: 1956–1986. McClelland & Stewart CN 1986 $29.95. ISBN 0-7710-7215-5
Piling Blood. McClelland & Stewart CN 1984 $12.95. ISBN 0-7710-7213-9
A Woman on the Shore. McClelland & Stewart CN 1990 $9.95. ISBN 0-7710-7217-1

BOOK ABOUT PURDY

MacKendrick, Louis K. *Al Purdy and His Works.* ECW Pr. 1990 $9.95. ISBN 0-55022-058-6. An excellent introduction to Purdy's poetry and analysis of major poems; with biographical material.

RICHLER, MORDECAI. 1931–

A consummate and caustic novelist, Mordecai Richler is one of the Montreal Jewish writers whose work has gained both critical attention and a strong public following. Born in Montreal at the onset of the Depression, Richler reflects in his best work, in a wry and engaging manner, his experiences in the Jewish ghettos around St. Urbain Street. Richler left Sir George Williams College without obtaining a degree, to travel to Europe and begin a writing career. After a sojourn in Canada, he became an expatriate writer in England, returning to Montreal in 1972.

Richler has been described as "the loser's advocate," an author who can elicit sympathy for unsympathetic characters. One of the more famous of these creations is Duddy Kravitz, hero of *The Apprenticeship of Duddy Kravitz* (1959). An amoral trickster, Duddy schemes his way out of the Jewish ghetto to become a landowner. A pivotal work, later a film, *Duddy Kravitz* paved the way for novels with similar themes. *Saint Urbain's Horseman* (1971) is a superb, ironic examination of Jake Hersch, who must come to terms with his dual (Canadian and Jewish) heritage. *Joshua Then and Now* (1980) has as its protagonist Joshua Shapiro, a man who must confront the mistakes of the past and present in order to evaluate what has become the prevalent theme in Richler's fiction: the question of moral responsibility.

Novels by Richler

The Apprenticeship of Duddy Kravitz. 1959. Viking Penguin 1990 $5.95. ISBN 0-14-002179-5

The Incomparable Atuk. 1963. McClelland & Stewart CN 1989 $5.95. ISBN 0-7710-9973-8. A satiric narrative on faddish nationalism. (Published in the United States as *Stick Your Neck Out*.)

Joshua Then and Now. 1980. McClelland & Stewart CN 1989 $5.95. ISBN 0-7710-9864-2

Saint Urbain's Horseman. 1971. McClelland & Stewart CN 1989 $5.95. ISBN 0-7710-9974-6

Solomon Gursky Was Here. Viking Penguin 1989 $26.95. ISBN 0-670-82526-3. A Canadian generational novel.

Son of a Smaller Hero. 1955. McClelland & Stewart CN 1989 $5.95. ISBN 0-7710-9970-3. Narrates a young Jew's struggle to free himself of family restrictions and provincial Canadian society.

Nonfiction by Richler

The Great Comic Book Heroes and Other Essays. McClelland & Stewart CN 1978 $4.95. ISBN 0-7710-9268-7. Selections of Richler's freelance journalism on various topics.

The Street. 1969. Viking Penguin 1985 $9.95. ISBN 0-14-007666-2. Contains autobiographical sketches about Richler's youth.

Book about Richler

McSweeney, Kerry. *Mordecai Richler and His Works*. ECW Pr. $9.95. ISBN 0-920802-67-2. Examines Richler's fiction and journalism, stressing his satire; with biographical information.

ROBERTS, CHARLES G. 1860–1943

Roberts is considered by many to be the dean of Canadian poetry. His English-Loyalist background and close contact with the untamed Canada of the Confederation combined to provide a rich source for his creative writing. A cousin of the writer Bliss Carman, Roberts was born in Douglas, New

Brunswick. While pursuing a degree, Roberts began writing poetry. This early productivity yielded three books of verse. The first of these, *Orion* (1990), garnered the praise of MATTHEW ARNOLD (see Vol. 1).

A prolific writer, Roberts was an outspoken supporter of Canadian literature; however, this did not prevent the Confederation poet from spending a sizable portion of his life in New York and later London (from 1895 to 1925). Apart from his influential poetry, with its presentation of divinely ordered nature, Roberts produced a highly successful series of animal stories, tales that portrayed the violence involved in survival and avoided the moral tone often associated with such works. Roberts also wrote several adult romances that invariably feature the English/French tension in eighteenth-century Canada. Roberts was knighted in 1935.

POETRY BY ROBERTS

The Collected Poems of Sir Charles G. D. Roberts: A Critical Edition. Ed. by Desmond Pacey and Graham Adams. Wombat 1985 $49.50. ISBN 0-9690828-3-5.

NOVEL BY ROBERTS

The Heart of the Ancient Wood. 1900. McClelland & Stewart CN 1974 o.p. A romance in which the heroine gives up the lure of the wild for human companionship.

ROSS, SINCLAIR. 1908–

Born and reared on the prairies of Saskatchewan, Ross has spent his life working in Canadian banks. It may have been these experiences that led him to write about the isolation of farm families and the hardships of farmers during the Depression—both of which lend his work an air of desolation. Introducing Sinclair's collection of short fiction *The Lamp at Noon* (1968), MARGARET LAURENCE notes that, in the stories, "the farms stand far apart. . . . The human community is, for most of the time, reduced to its smallest unit, one family. The isolation is virtually complete." No matter how bleak the circumstances, however, the characters survive, even if they are often trapped between the poles of despair and hope.

Ross has also published four novels, but his reputation rests on his first one, *As for Me and My House* (1941). Although it did not receive much attention when it appeared, it is now firmly established as a Canadian classic. Spare yet richly textured, the narrative recounts the relationship between a disillusioned minister and his wife, whose diary serves as the vehicle for the tale. *A Whir of Gold* (1970), concerned with city life in Canada, and *Sawbones Memorial* (1974), about Canadian small-town life, lack the power of the first book. Ross is considered one of the first Canadian writers to employ modernist techniques, such as a restricted third-person point of view, the unreliable narrator, and multiple points of view.

NOVELS BY ROSS

As for Me and My House. 1941. McClelland & Stewart CN 1989 $5.95. ISBN 0-7710-9997-5

Sawbones Memorial. 1974. McClelland & Stewart CN 1978 $4.95. ISBN 0-7710-9262-8

A Whir of Gold. McClelland & Stewart CN 1970 $15.95. ISBN 0-7710-7745-9

SHORT STORY COLLECTIONS BY ROSS

The Lamp at Noon and Other Stories. 1968. McClelland & Stewart CN 1988 $5.95. ISBN 0-7710-9996-7

The Race and Other Stories. Ed. by Lorraine McMullen. OUP 1982 o.p. Stories previously published plus new stories.

Books about Ross

Moss, John, ed. *Sinclair Ross: A Reappraisal.* U. of Ottawa Pr. 1991 $19.95. ISBN 0-7766-0329-9. Essays examining Ross's work in light of current views of his substantial accomplishment.

Ross, Morton. *Sinclair Ross and His Works.* ECW Pr. 1990 $9.95. ISBN 1-55022-056-X. Provides an introduction to Ross's work, examining major themes; with biographical information.

SCOTT, DUNCAN CAMPBELL. 1862–1947

Born in Ottawa, Duncan Campbell Scott was the son of a Methodist minister. On joining the civil service, Scott became a clerk and later commissioner to the Indian tribes of the James Bay Region. It was in these positions that Scott gained a firsthand knowledge of Canada's native peoples, a knowledge reflected in much of his verse. Eventually, Scott was made deputy minister of Indian affairs, a post from which he retired in 1932. Good collections of Scott's poetry, now out of print, may be found in *Selected Poems of Duncan Campbell Scott* or *Duncan Campbell Scott: Selected Poetry.*

Scott is a fine example of a Confederation poet, one who was influenced by both nineteenth-century British and American thought but at the same time developed a commitment to the presentation of his native land and its people. Scott also published two collections of short stories: *In the Village of Viger* (1896) and *The Witching of Elspie* (1923). While the latter book is out of print, an excellent edition of his selected stories is available.

Poetry by Scott

Powassan's Drum: Selected Poems of Duncan Campbell Scott. Ed. by Raymond Souster and Douglas Lochhead. Tecumseh 1986 $23.95. ISBN 0-919662-10-2

Selected Poetry of Duncan Campbell Scott. Ed. by Glenn Clever. Tecumseh 1974 $8.95. ISBN 0-919662-52-8

Short Story Collections by Scott

In the Village of Viger and Other Stories. McClelland & Stewart CN 1973 $4.95. ISBN 0-7710-9192-3

Selected Stories of Duncan Campbell Scott. Ed. by Glenn Clever. U. of Ontario Pr. 1987 $13.95. ISBN 0-7766-0183-0

Book about Scott

Dragland, Stan, ed. *Duncan Campbell Scott: A Book of Criticism.* Tecumseh 1974 $8.95. ISBN 0-919662-51-X. A collection of essays on Scott's work, taking a number of critical approaches.

WADDINGTON, MIRIAM (DWORKIN). 1917–

Growing up in Winnipeg's Russian Jewish immigrant community, Miriam Waddington early on experienced a mixture of European traditions and Canadian life. After she earned degrees from the University of Toronto and the University of Pennsylvania, she became a social worker in Montreal. During this period she published poetry that expressed her anger over social conditions. In 1960, Waddington left social work and earned an M.A. in English. She taught at York University from 1964 until her retirement, in 1983.

Waddington's poetry and short fiction are informed by her being both a Jew and a woman. Although her work conveys a sense of loss and a feeling of displacement, the despair "is always mitigated, for she retains threads of traditions that still anchor her, memories that keep her company, and an ironic sense of humor," according to *An Anthology of Canadian Literature*.

POETRY BY WADDINGTON

Collected Poems. OUP 1986 $24.95. ISBN 0-19-540535-8. Poems from her previously published separate volumes.

SHORT STORY COLLECTION BY WADDINGTON

Summer at Lonely Beach: Selected Short Stories. Mosaic Pr. OH 1982 $17.95. ISBN 0-88962-157-8. Collection of Waddington's best-known stories.

WIEBE, RUDY. 1934–

A firm belief in the redemptive possibilities of history dominates Rudy Wiebe's fiction. His characters search for community, for a spiritual collective informed and strengthened by historical consciousness. This attempt to unite the present and the past stems from Wiebe's Mennonite religious background. Central to the Mennonite belief is the rejection of loyalty to contemporary and worldly government; personal commitment belongs, instead, to the religious community, with its hard-earned historical heritage as a nonconformist movement. Wiebe was born in a northern Saskatchewan farming community; in 1947 the family moved to Alberta, and he completed his education at the University of Alberta, where he teaches.

Wiebe's first novel, *Peace Shall Destroy Many* (1962), addresses pacifism, a belief central to Mennonites. The novel's hero faces a moral quandary when forced to choose between religious convictions and Canadian nationalistic fervor during World War II. While *The Blue Mountains of China* (1970) records Mennonite history, *The Temptations of Big Bear* (1973) examines the destruction of Indian culture in white Canada, and *The Scorched-Wood People* (1977) takes up the plight of the Metis—those with mixed blood; all three novels focus on minorities who must struggle to maintain their sense of community. Ideas repugnant to the Mennonite sensibility, violence and self-destruction, figure in *The Mad Trapper* (1980), which recounts the hunt for a man whose isolation has driven him into madness. In 1980 Wiebe's short stories were collected in *The Angel of the Tar Sands and Other Stories*. Stylistically, Wiebe gives little ground to the reader, for his fiction is characterized by difficult dialects, a web of details, and a dense style.

NOVELS BY WIEBE

The Blue Mountains of China. 1970. McClelland & Stewart CN 1989 $6.95. ISBN 0-7710-9208-3

The Mad Trapper. McClelland & Stewart CN 1980 $16.95. ISBN 0-7710-8976-7

Peace Shall Destroy Many. 1962. McClelland & Stewart CN 1989 $6.95. ISBN 0-7710-9182-6

The Scorched-Wood People. McClelland & Stewart CN 1977 $6.95. ISBN 0-7710-9294-6

The Temptations of Big Bear. 1973. McClelland & Stewart CN 1975 $6.95. ISBN 0-7710-9222-9

SHORT STORY COLLECTION BY WIEBE

The Angel of the Tar Sands and Other Stories. 1980. McClelland & Stewart CN 1982 $5.95. ISBN 0-7710-9308-X

Book about Wiebe

Whaley, Susan. *Rudy Wiebe and His Works.* ECW Pr. 1986 $9.95. ISBN 0-920763-26-X. A helpful introduction to the complex works, examining technique, themes, and historical emphasis; with biographical material.

CHAPTER 24

Literature of the Caribbean

Ruby S. Ramraj

Three million people
And our several territories,
Africa England America Portugal and Spain
India and France China Syria
Black brown yellow pink and cream . . .
All these and more you wish
To fix in one quick-drying definition.
—MERVYN MORRIS, "To a West Indian Definer"

Caribbean literature, although barely known in the United States a decade ago, is now widely read there, as well as in many other countries around the world. This rich and complex literature is a product of a number of islands and, by extension, neighboring shores that represent a variety of ethnic and cultural strands—English, African, Dutch, French, East Indian, Portuguese, and Hispanic—and is inevitably shaped by its history of imperialism, colonialism, and discrimination. Exile, voluntary or forced, is a central fact of much Caribbean literature; many Caribbean authors are immigrants from Asia, while others have emigrated from the West Indies to England, Australia, Canada, or other nations. The nostalgia for African roots and the clear sense of cultural identity have led to the publication of a number of studies and collections that include both African and Caribbean authors. Many Caribbean writers deal with the commonality of background and situation, despite national, regional, or even linguistic differences.

The literature of the Caribbean reflects great diversity; although English and, to a lesser degree, French are the dominant languages, there are also many regional *patois,* or folk languages, that are vehicles for literary expression, much like the Scot dialect in Great Britain. Lamentably, little of this non-English material has been translated, so that Haitian literature, for example, is almost totally inaccessible to the non-French reading public. Writers of international importance such as the Martinican poet and dramatist Aime Cesaire and the Guyanese poet Leon-Gontran Damas, among the founders of the important Negritude movement, are unavailable in English. Even important English-language texts are soon out of print, although Heinemann's series of Caribbean writers is a healthy step toward remedying the situation.

It was not until the very end of the nineteenth century that the French- and English-speaking Caribbean began to produce a literature that was not simply the product of transplanted Londoners or Parisians. Shortly after 1900, writers of black and white ancestry alike began to describe the Caribbean experience as something distinct from the European tradition. At present, there is a flourishing literature of considerable diversity in the Caribbean that is encouraged by increasing government sponsorship, university creative writing workshops and courses, and a new interest among readers in international and postcolonial literatures.

HISTORY AND CRITICISM

Benitez-Rojo, Antonio. *The Repeating Island: The Caribbean*. Duke 1992 $45.00. ISBN 0-8223-1225-5. Argues that, despite the Caribbean's disorder of geography, language, and politics, a repeating order exists.

Brown, Lloyd W. *West Indian Poetry*. Heinemann Ed. 1984 o.p. Provides a historical survey of major and minor English-speaking Caribbean poets.

Cartey, Wilfred. *Whispers from the Caribbean: I Going Away, I Going Home*. U. CA Pr. 1991 $43.00. ISBN 0-934934-35-5. Examines approximately 70 novels by 26 Caribbean authors.

Cudjoe, Selwyn R. *Caribbean Women Writers: Essays from the First International Conference*. U. of Mass. Pr. 1990 $14.95. ISBN 0-87023-732-2. Essays based on papers given at the conference on major and minor women writers.

______. *Resistance and Caribbean Literature*. Ohio U. Pr. 1980 o.p. Discusses the impact of political and social conditions in the Caribbean on writers like Lamming and Reid.

Dance, Daryl Cumber, ed. *Fifty Caribbean Writers: A Bio-Bibliographical Critical Sourcebook*. Greenwood 1986 $75.00. ISBN 0-313-23939-8. Studies of important Caribbean authors with biographical, critical, and bibliographic information.

Dathorne, O. R. *Dark Ancestor: The Literature of the Black Man in the Caribbean*. La. State U. Pr. 1981 $37.50. ISBN 0-8071-0757-3. Examines the plight of the African people and their attempts to express this in writing. Scope is so wide that there is little sustained critical analysis of works.

Davies, Carole Boyce, and Elaine Savory Fido. *Out of the Kumbla: Caribbean Women and Literature*. Africa World 1990 $15.95. ISBN 0-86543-043-8. Provides a comprehensive overview of the Caribbean's cultural context as well as a commentary on how its literature developed.

Gilkes, Michael. *The West Indian Novel. Twayne's World Authors Ser.* G. K. Hall 1981 o.p. Discusses the preoccupation of major Caribbean writers like Mittelholzer and Reid with issues such as class structure, racial mixture, politics, and colonialism.

Harris, Wilson. *The Womb of Space: The Cross-cultural Imagination*. Greenwood 1983 $37.50. ISBN 0-313-23774-3. Emphasizes the importance of the imagination to writers in transcending the traditional and creating new patterns and myths.

Herdeck, Donald E., ed. *Caribbean Writers: A Bio-Bibliographical Critical Encyclopedia*. Three Continents 1979 $70.00. ISBN 0-914478-74-5. Useful sourcebook on Caribbean writers.

James, Louis, ed. *The Islands in Between: Essays in West Indian Literature*. OUP 1968 o.p. One of the earliest books on Caribbean writers with a useful introduction by the author and essays by various critics on major writers including Mais and Walcott.

King, Bruce. *West Indian Literature*. Shoe String 1980 o.p. Essays on the historical background, Mittelholzer, Selvon, Lamming, Walcott, Naipaul, Harris, Braithwaite, and Rhys.

Nelson, Emmanuel S., ed. *Reworlding: The Literature of the Indian Diaspora*. Greenwood 1992 $45.00. ISBN 0-313-27794-X. Essays on writers of East Indian origin from the Caribbean and elsewhere, including Naipaul, Selvon, and Bissoondath.

Ormerod, Beverley. *An Introduction to the French Caribbean*. Heinemann Ed. 1985 $12.50. ISBN 0-435-91839-7. Offers a concise understanding of the French Antilles through a thorough examination of sex novels of the most prominent writers from Haiti, Guadeloupe, and Martinique.

Ramchand, Kenneth. *The West Indian Novel and Its Background*. Heinemann Ed. 1984 o.p. A seminal work that traces the history of Caribbean writing from its beginning in 1903 to 1970.

COLLECTIONS

Dathorne, O. R. *Caribbean Narrative*. Heinemann Ed. 1966 o.p. A collection of stories by major and minor writers with a useful introduction by the author.

______. *Caribbean Verse: An Anthology*. Heinemann Ed. 1967 o.p. One of the earliest and most widely read anthologies, with several representative poems from a variety of poets.

D'Costa, Jean, and Barbara Lalla, eds. *Voices in Exile: Jamaican Texts of the Eighteenth and Nineteenth Centuries*. U. of Ala. Pr. 1989 $24.50. ISBN 0-8173-0382-0. Collection that provides a linguistic history of the origin and development of the unique Jamaican Creole.

Echevarria, Roberto G., ed. *Hispanic Caribbean Literature: Special Issue*. Lat. Am. Lit. Rev. Pr. 1980 $16.00. ISBN 0-685-07677-6. Important collection of Spanish-based Caribbean literature reflecting a variety of genres.

Fenwick, M. J., ed. *Writers of the Caribbean and Central America: A Bibliography*. 2 vols. Garland 1992 $200.00. ISBN 0-8240-4010-4. Includes writers from 42 different countries.

Gordon, R., ed. *The Literature of the West Indies*. 20 vols. Gordon Pr. 1977 $50.00 ea. ISBN 0-8490-2171-5. Comprehensive collection of Caribbean literature.

______, ed. *Novels of the Caribbean*. 20 vols. Gordon Pr. 1977 $50.00 ea. ISBN 0-8490-2363-7

Jekyll, Walter. *Jamaica Song and Story*. AMS Pr. repr. of 1907 ed. o.p. Features a wide variety of popular songs, folk tales, and stories from Jamaica. Introduction by Alice Werner.

Lewis, Theresa, ed. *Caribbean Folk Legends*. Africa World 1990 $19.95. ISBN 0-86543-158-2. Interesting collection of folk tales and legends from the Caribbean region.

Lomax, Alan, and Raoul Abdul, eds. *3000 Years of Black Poetry: An Anthology*. Dodd 1984 o.p. Poems by blacks around the world, starting with an early traditional song and ending with poems by Derek Walcott and Langston Hughes.

McFarlane, John E. *A Treasury of Jamaican Poetry*. Gordon Pr. 1977 $59.95. ISBN 0-8490-2760-8. A selection of poems by major and minor poets by this early Jamaican poet.

______. *Voices from Summerland: An Anthology of Jamaican Poetry*. Gordon Pr. 1977 $59.95. ISBN 0-8490-2802-7. This collection of early Jamaican poetry is a reprint of the 1929 edition, which was privately printed by the author.

Ramchand, Kenneth, ed. *West Indian Narrative: An Introductory Anthology*. Humanities 1966 o.p. Contains extracts from the works of lesser known and major writers such as Lamming, Selvon, Naipaul, and Harris.

Salkey, Andrew, ed. *West Indian Stories*. Faber & Faber 1968 o.p. A selection of twenty-five colorful and moving stories by writers such as Mais, Reid, and Selvon.

Sander, Reinhard W., ed. *From Trinidad: An Anthology of Early West Indian Writing*. Holmes & Meier 1979 $45.00. ISBN 0-8419-0352-2. Collection of short fiction, poetry, and articles by early Trinidadian writers like Gomes and Mendes, showing their influence on the established Caribbean writers of today.

Shapiro, Norman R., ed. *Negritude: Black Poetry from Africa and the Caribbean*. October 1970 $8.95. ISBN 0-8079-0164-4. Fifty-one poems by twenty Caribbean poets.

Sherlock, Philip M. *West Indian Folk Tales*. OUP 1988 $6.95. ISBN 0-19-274127-6. A collection of popular folk tales including Anansi and Tiger stories.

Sherlock, Philip M., and Helen Sherlock. *Ears and Tales and Commonsense: More Stories from the Caribbean*. HarpC 1974 o.p. A collection of more traditional, but lesser known stories from this region.

Underwood, Edna. *The Poets of Haiti*. Gordon Pr. 1977 repr. of 1934 ed. $34.95. ISBN 0-8490-2449-8

Wolkstein, Diane, ed. *The Magic Orange Tree and Other Haitian Folktales*. Schocken 1987 repr. of 1978 ed. $14.95. ISBN 0-8052-0650-7. Includes drawings, a short introduction, and a song section in English and Creole.

CHRONOLOGY OF AUTHORS

De Lisser, Herbert George. 1878–1944
Rhys, Jean. 1890–1979
Mais, Roger. 1905–1955
Roumain, Jacques. 1907–1944
Mittelholzer, Edgar. 1909–1965
Gomes, Albert M. 1911–1978
Reid, V(ictor) S(tafford). 1913–
Harris, Wilson. 1921–
Selvon, Samuel. 1923–
Lamming, George. 1927–
Salkey, Andrew. 1928–
Braithwaite, Edward Kamau. 1930–
Walcott, Derek. 1930–
Anthony, Michael. 1932–
Naipaul, V(idiadhar) S(urajprasad). 1932–
Clarke, Austin. 1934–
Kincaid, Jamaica. 1949–
Bissoondath, Neil. 1955–

ANTHONY, MICHAEL. 1932– Trinidad

Anthony, a novelist and historian, avoids the social and the polemic in his novels; his work is a skillful recreation of the rural experiences of his youth in a style that avoids the excesses of political commitment and of avant-gardism. *The Year in San Fernando* (1965) is an ironic, first-person narrative of a twelve-year-old boy's experiences of a year in the city. Anthony's novels, such as *The Games Were Coming* (1963) and *Green Days by the River* (1967), focus more on problems in human relationships among friends, family members, and lovers than on problems of exile or identity. His historical works, especially his history of Trinidad, reveal a careful, sensitive historian.

Novels by Anthony

All That Glitters. 1981. Heinemann Ed. 1983 $7.95. ISBN 0-435-98034-3. A sympathetic portrayal of relationships among young adults, with two forceful female characters.
The Games Were Coming. 1963. Heinemann Ed. 1977 $7.95. ISBN 0-435-98033-5
Green Days by the River. 1967. Heinemann Ed. 1973 $7.95. ISBN 0-435-98030-0
Streets of Conflict. Andre Deutsch 1976 o.p. Examines the relationship between a man and woman during student riots in Brazil.
The Year in San Fernando. 1965. Heinemann Ed. 1970 $7.95. ISBN 0-435-98031-9

Short Story Collection by Anthony

Sandra Street and Other Stories. Heinemann Ed. 1973 o.p. His first collection of stories, centering on the lives of children and young adults.

Nonfiction by Anthony

Bright Road to El Dorado. Nelson 1982 o.p. A valuable historical portrait of the Caribbean region.
Profile Trinidad: A Historical Survey from the Discovery to 1900. Macmillan 1975 o.p. A readable and informative history of Trinidad from its discovery in 1492 to 1900.

ARENAS, REINALDO. 1943-1990 (Cuba)

[See Chapter 22]

BISSOONDATH, NEIL. 1955– Trinidad

Considered both a West Indian and a Canadian writer, Bissoondath began his literary career as a short-story writer. His first book, *Digging Up the Mountains* (1985), is a collection of short stories relating the experiences of immigrants in

Toronto as they combat feelings of nostalgia and marginality and try to adapt to their new home. He returns to this theme of placelessness in the novel *A Casual Brutality* (1988), in which the protagonist feels alienated in both Toronto and Casquemada. His most recent novel, *The Innocence of Age* (1992), is set in Toronto and is a departure from these themes. Here, defying the current appropriation of voice debate, he uses a Canadian Caucasian father and son to describe the difficulties in parent-child relationships, especially evident in communication between fathers and sons. As a relatively new writer, Bissoondath has received some critical attention, but as yet there is no book-length study of his work.

SHORT STORIES BY BISSOONDATH

Digging Up the Mountains. Macmillan 1985 $4.95. ISBN 0-7715-9246-9

On the Eve of Uncertain Tomorrows. Crown 1991 $18.95. ISBN 0-517-58233-3. A collection of short stories dealing with the feeling of rootlessness among immigrants from the Caribbean, Latin America, and the Far East.

NOVELS BY BISSOONDATH

A Casual Brutality. Macmillan 1988 $22.95. ISBN 0-7715-9646-4

The Innocence of Age. Random 1992 o.p.

BRAITHWAITE, EDWARD KAMAU. 1930– Barbados

Born in Bridgetown, Barbados, Edward Braithwaite attended Cambridge University in England. As a writer, he has been influenced by his life in Barbados, his experiences in England, and his long residence in Ghana, where he taught early in his career. Since the 1960s, he has been a historian at the University of the West Indies where, in 1983, he was appointed professor of social and cultural history. Braithwaite is vitally interested in the cultural transmission of ideas from Africa to the Caribbean. His scholarly publications include books on folk culture and on the Creole society of Jamaica. In Braithwaite's poetry, there is little of the personal agonizing characteristic of the poetry of DEREK WALCOTT; instead, his poems focus on community and tribal concerns and the spiritual growth of the black man. His poetry makes extensive use of dialect and of the fusion-tension between European and African sources, and it is strongly influenced by African oral communication. He has also used the blues, flavored by African oral tradition, and island music and speech rhythms to express the oppression of the Caribbean people. He appears to regard poetry as a vehicle for communicating an emerging synthetic culture. The result is a vigorous, ironic poetic idiom. Described by some as one of the finest living poets in the Western hemisphere, his major achievement is *The Arrivants: A New World Trilogy* (1973).

POETRY BY BRAITHWAITE

The Arrivants: A New World Trilogy. OUP 1973 $8.95. ISBN 0-19-911103-0. Comprising *Rights of Passage, Masks,* and *Islands,* this is Braithwaite's major achievement as a poet. A rich and complex evocation of black heritage.

Masks. OUP 1968 o.p. Second of *The Arrivants* trilogy. An imaginative account of the black man's journey to the New World and his search for roots in Africa.

Mother Poem. OUP 1977 $10.95. ISBN 0-19-211859-5. Here Barbados is seen as the mother figure dominating his work.

Other Exiles. OUP 1975 o.p. A collection of miscellaneous poems.

Rights of Passage. OUP 1967 o.p. The author's first book of poetry, and the first of a trilogy called *The Arrivants.*

Sun Poem. OUP 1982 $11.95. ISBN 0-19-211945-1. A companion volume to *Mother Poem,* in which the poet examines the masculine world of Barbados.

Third World Poems. Longman 1983 o.p. His latest collection of poems, dealing with national and ethnic identity.

NONFICTION BY BRAITHWAITE

The Development of Creole Society in Jamaica 1770–1820. OUP 1971 o.p. Focuses on the growth of Creole society and the impact of colonialism.

Folk Culture of the Slaves in Jamaica. New Beacon 1970 o.p. Discusses the historical and social development of the slaves brought to the Caribbean.

CABRERA INFANTE, GUILLERMO. 1929– (Cuba)

[See Chapter 22]

CARPENTIER, ALEJO. 1904–1980 (Cuba)

[See Chapter 22]

CLARKE, AUSTIN. 1934– Barbados

Clarke's novels and short stories focus primarily on the problems associated with colonialism and exile. His first novel, *Survivors of the Crossing* (1964), deals with the difficulties a black peasant worker faces when he attempts to revolt against the white establishment. Several of Clarke's short stories and his later novels set in Toronto, *The Meeting Point* (1967), *Storm of Fortune* (1973), and *The Bigger Light* (1975), focus on Barbadians in exile in Canada and the United States who suffer cultural alienation and loss of identity in their adopted homes. *Growing Up Stupid Under the Union Jack* (1980) is a comic look at the colonial's acceptance of British culture and standards.

NOVELS BY CLARKE

The Bigger Light. Little 1975 o.p.

Growing Up Stupid Under the Union Jack. McClelland 1980 $24.95. ISBN 0-7710-2131-3

The Meeting Point. 1967. Little 1972 o.p.

Proud Empires. 1986. Viking Penguin 1988 $19.95. ISBN 0-670-81756-2. Story of a young boy who becomes aware of corruption and treachery in the social and political life of Barbados.

Storm of Fortune. Little 1973 o.p.

The Survivors of the Crossing. McClelland 1964 o.p.

SHORT STORY COLLECTION BY CLARKE

Nine Men Who Laughed. 1985. Viking Penguin 1986 $12.95. ISBN 0-14-008560-2. Satiric stories about emigrants to Canada.

DELISSER, HERBERT GEORGE. 1878–1944 Jamaica

Of mixed Portuguese, Jewish, and African ancestry, DeLisser was a journalist and a prominent conservative member of the white society in Jamaica. In spite of his racial biases and conservative ideas, he writes accurately about Jamaican society. Some of his novels are historical romances like *The White Witch of Rosehall* (1929), while others can be termed novels of social realism. In *Jane's Career* (1914), his best-known early novel, DeLisser's sympathetic portrayal of Jane, the black girl who emancipates herself economically after a series of predictable dilemmas, shows his awareness of the problems of a wide spectrum of his society. His concern with the theme of miscegenation springs partly from his personal experiences as a person of mixed ancestry and from his awareness of the social and political realities of his time. Though he wrote over twenty novels of varying quality, he is considered first and foremost as a journalist.

NOVELS BY DELISSER

Jane's Career. 1914. Heinemann Ed. 1972 o.p.

Morgan's Daughter. 1931. Macmillan 1984 o.p. Story of an illegitimate mulatto woman whose love for an English scoundrel makes her a partner in his crimes.

The White Witch of Rosehall. 1929. Macmillan 1984 o.p.

GOMES, ALBERT M. 1911–1978 Trinidad

Of Portuguese ancestry, Gomes studied in Port of Spain and New York. Active in politics and the union movement, he also wrote poetry, novels, and an autobiography. In 1931 he launched the literary magazine *The Beacon,* which created a literary tradition for Trinidad and the West Indies. Gomes's political career led to service on the city council and terms as deputy mayor of Port of Spain and in the government of Trinidad and Tobago. After the collapse of the Federation of the West Indies in 1962, Gomes settled in England. His poetry is formally traditional and tends towards abstract intellectualism.

NOVEL BY GOMES

All Papa's Children. Three Continents 1978 o.p. Recounts the life and experiences of a Portuguese family in a predominantly African-Asian community.

NONFICTION BY GOMES

Through a Maze of Colour. Key Caribbean Pubs. o.p. A controversial autobiographical work recounting the author's turbulent political life and his awareness of the racial and social politics of Trinidad.

GUILLÉN, NICOLÁS. 1902– (Cuba)

[See Chapter 22]

HARRIS, WILSON. 1921– Guyana

Harris started his literary career as a poet but turned to writing novels when he left Guyana for Great Britain in 1959. His interest in the coexistence of people of different races and cultures is reflected in the wide, imaginative scope of his works and in his themes of the unity of humankind and the connection among peoples throughout the ages. Avoiding the realistic and chronological in his works, Harris employs more complex and intricate structures, with allusions to other works of literature and mythology. His novels deal typically with metaphoric voyages of self-discovery, often through the Guyanese hinterland or upriver as in *Palace of the Peacock* (1960). The heroes of *Da Silva da Silva's Cultivated Wilderness and Genesis of the Clowns* (1977) both live in London and use the city as a base for the inner exploration of their multiethnic antecedents. Harris sees a relationship between words as the raw material of literature and colors as the material of art; he attempts to use language as a painter uses paints, in layers or shocking contrasts. Harris has received several awards, including a Guggenheim Fellowship in 1973.

NOVELS BY HARRIS

The Angel at the Gate. Faber & Faber 1982 $15.95. ISBN 0-571-11929-8. Uses the metaphor of painting to explore the theme of resurrection.

Ascent to Omai. Faber & Faber 1970 o.p. The protagonist, Victor, experiences a sense of loss and alienation.

Da Silva da Silva's Cultivated Wilderness and Genesis of the Clowns. Faber & Faber 1977 $6.95. ISBN 0-571-10819-9

The Eye of the Scarecrow. Faber & Faber 1965 o.p. Pursues the theme of loss through the consciousness of the character Idiot Nameless.

Palace of the Peacock. Faber & Faber 1960 $6.95. ISBN 0-571-08930-5

The Whole Armour and The Secret Ladder. Faber & Faber 1963 o.p. Explores different aspects of Guyana's people and history using biblical and classical mythology.

Nonfiction by Harris

The Womb of Space: The Cross-Cultural Imagination. Greenwood 1983 $37.50. ISBN 0-313-23774-3. Emphasizes the importance of the imagination in transcending the traditional and in creating new patterns and myths.

Books about Harris

Drake, Sandra E. *Wilson Harris and the Modern Tradition: A New Architecture of the World.* Greenwood 1986 $29.95. ISBN 0-313-24783-8. Scholarly, technical, and detailed study of Harris's fiction, appropriate for graduate students in English.

Gilkes, Michael. *Wilson Harris and the Caribbean Novel.* Longman 1975 o.p. Examines Harris's use of symbols and images.

Maes-Jelinek, Hena. *Wilson Harris.* Twayne 1982 o.p. Views Harris as one of the foremost writers of the twentieth century. Defends the complexity and unconventionality of many of his novels.

KINCAID, JAMAICA. 1949– Antigua

Kincaid came to the United States in 1966 as a free-lance writer and is now on staff at the *New Yorker.* Her first volume of stories, *At the Bottom of the River* (1983), depicts men and women alienated from each other by conflict, physical separation, or death. The story "My Mother" vividly describes the painful separation between mother and daughter; and the stories in *Annie John* (1985) clearly reveal that the world of the past cannot be recaptured. Kincaid's poetic use of language and everyday images allows the reader to experience ordinary events with a new and heightened sensitivity. Kincaid is a relatively new writer whose works are beginning to receive critical attention.

Short Story Collections by Kincaid

Annie John. FS&G 1985 $8.95. ISBN 0-374-10521-9

At the Bottom of the River. FS&G 1983 $9.95. ISBN 0-374-10660-0

LAMMING, GEORGE. 1927– Barbados

Born in Carrington Village, Barbados, Lamming taught in Trinidad and Venezuela before going to England in 1950. In England, he worked in a factory and also hosted a book program for the BBC West Indian Service while pursuing his writing.

Lamming's works are a panorama of West Indian history with a strong sense of nationalism. *In the Castle of My Skin* (1953) is at least partially autobiographical in its presentation of the protagonist's growing sense of individuality and his consequent estrangement from the village and folk community. The subsequent exile of this protagonist is told in *The Emigrants* (1954), his return is the focus in *Of Age and Innocence* (1958), and the reclamation of his heritage is the major theme in *Season of Adventure* (1960). His novels focus on the social and economic changes taking place in the Caribbean, and he uses his protagonists as mouthpieces for his own ideas.

NOVELS BY LAMMING

The Emigrants. 1954. Schocken 1987 $14.95. ISBN 0-8052-8037-5
In the Castle of My Skin. 1953. U. of Mich. Pr. 1991 repr. of 1953 ed. $37.50. ISBN 0-472-09468-8. A novel of the black colonial experience.
Natives of My Person. U. of Mich. Pr. 1992 repr. of 1972 ed. $37.50. ISBN 0-472-09467-X
Of Age and Innocence. 1958. Schocken 1987 $13.95. ISBN 0-8052-8095-2
Season of Adventure. 1960. Schocken 1979 o.p.

BOOK ABOUT LAMMING

Paquet, Sandra Pouchet. *The Novels of George Lamming.* Heinemann Ed. 1982 o.p. Examines the political symbols inherent in Lamming's novels, but gives little comment on the literary aspects of his work.

MAIS, ROGER. 1905–1955 Jamaica

Mais spoke for the dispossessed black community of Jamaica. His novel *The Hills Were Joyful Together* (1953) is a devastating portrait of degradation and violence that uses a complicated symbolic structure. Set in a tenement yard in Kingston, the work focuses on a multitude of characters and their struggle merely to exist. In 1952, Mais left Jamaica, perhaps because of the negative reaction to the social voice in his work. The works published after he left his native country continue his preoccupation with the social constrictions of his time, and they show a growing tension between the concept of the artist's duty and the notion of the individual artistic conscience.

NOVELS BY MAIS

Black Lightning. 1955. Heinemann Ed. 1983 repr. of 1955 ed. $8.95. ISBN 0-435-98584-1. Story of a man struggling to find self-sufficiency after becoming blind.
Brother Man. 1954. Heinemann Ed. 1974 $8.95. ISBN 0-435-98585-X. This optimistic novel focuses on Brother Man and his generosity that binds together a community.
The Hills Were Joyful Together. 1953. Heinemann Ed. 1981 $9.95. ISBN 0-435-98586-8

BOOK ABOUT MAIS

D'Costa, Jean. *Roger Mais.* Longman 1978 o.p. An insightful account of Mais's social background, with sound critical evaluation of the novels.

MARQUÉS, RENE. 1919–1979 (Puerto Rico)

[See Chapter 22]

MARTÍ, JOSÉ. 1853–1895 (Cuba)

[See Chapter 22]

MITTELHOLZER, EDGAR. 1909–1965 Guyana

Of mixed Swiss and Creole heritage, Mittelholzer decided at an early age to become a writer. His works represent the personal struggle between a sense of identification with European culture and a sense of identity as a West Indian. He was the first writer of his generation to emigrate from the West Indies and attempt a career as a serious novelist in England. In his relatively short life, Mittelholzer published 22 novels, as well as other works. *Corentyne Thunder* (1941) is a traditionally written novel, but it deals with the spiritual schizophrenia of a protagonist torn between two conflicting loyalties. *A Morning at the Office* (1950) is a coldly objective view of the absurdities of a tightly organized hierarchical colonial society. His Kaywana trilogy—*Children of Kaywana* (1952), *The Harrowing of Hubertus* (1954), and *Kaywana Blood* (1958)—an imaginative account of a proud, violent family—is considered his finest work. Near the end of his life, his works were increasingly concerned with isolation, disintegration, and suicide. Mittelholzer was the first West Indian writer to be awarded the Guggenheim Fellowship for Creative Writing (1952). He burned himself to death in a field in Surrey, England, in 1965.

NOVELS BY MITTELHOLZER

Children of Kaywana. 1952. New English Library 1972 o.p.
Corentyne Thunder. 1941. Heinemann Ed. 1970 $8.95. ISBN 0-435-98593-0
The Harrowing of Hubertus. 1954. Four Square 1962 o.p.
Kaywana Blood. 1958. Fawcett 1971 o.p.
A Morning at the Office. 1950. Heinemann Ed. 1974 o.p.
My Bones and My Flute. 1955. Longman 1982 o.p. A chilling story of the supernatural, set in Guyana.

NAIPAUL, V(IDIADHAR) S(URAJPRASAD). 1932– Trinidad

Born in Trinidad of Hindu parents, V. S. Naipaul was educated at Oxford University and has lived in Great Britain since 1950. With an exile's sensibility, Naipaul's writing is concerned with both the West Indies of his childhood and his strong identification with India. It focuses on personal and political freedom, the function of the writer and the nature of sexuality, and is characterized by clarity, subtlety, and detached irony of tone. "A particular delight of Mr. Naipaul's writing is the dialogue. The West Indian idiom in his hands is full of color and a rich Elizabethan disregard for conventional correctness" (*TLS*). The *New York Herald Tribune* wrote of his beguiling, warmly humorous *Mystic Masseur* (1957): "The characterizations are vivid and witty. Human truths are revealed, and we are entertained." The novel *Miguel Street* (1959) describes the aberrant lives of a mean street in Port of Spain, Trinidad. *A House for Mr. Biswas* (1961), his most well-known work, solidified his reputation as a novelist. It tells the tragicomic story of the search for independence and identity of a Brahmin Indian living in Trinidad.

Naipaul's work, even when he appears to be analyzing a picturesque character, is really an analysis of the entire society of Trinidad. *The Middle Passage* (1962) extends this analysis of the social order to other areas of the West Indies—Surinam, Martinique, Jamaica, and Guyana—and finds that "the present character of the regions he visited express their history as colonial territories built on slave labor." Naipaul's work also deals with other parts of the world as well. In *An Area of Darkness* (1964), he expresses with sympathy and insight his observations on a trip to India, where he saw the loftiest of human values contrasted with the meanest physical suffering. His novel *A Bend in the River* (1979), set in a new African nation, depicts the difficulties ordinary people face during times of political upheaval. *A Turn in the South* (1989) is a sensitive portrayal of the American South.

Naipaul's works have elicited polarized responses, yet he is regarded by many as one of the best writers of our time, and he is a perennial nominee for the Nobel Prize in Literature. Irving Howe makes this observation of his works: "For sheer abundance of talent there can hardly be a writer alive who surpasses V. S. Naipaul."

NOVELS BY NAIPAUL

A Bend in the River. 1979. Peter Smith 1992 $19.50. ISBN 0-8446-6631-9

The Enigma of Arrival. Random 1988 repr. of 1987 ed. $6.95. ISBN 0-394-75760-2. Set in the countryside, this novel explores the process of change and decay in a rural community.

Guerrillas. 1975. Random 1990 $10.95. ISBN 0-679-73174-1. A bleak novel that recounts the sense of futility haunting the main characters.

A House for Mr. Biswas. 1961. Random 1984 $9.95. ISBN 0-394-72050-4

Miguel Street. 1959. Heinemann Ed. 1974 $7.95. ISBN 0-435-98645-7

The Mystic Masseur. 1957. Viking Penguin 1977 $10.00. ISBN 0-14-002156-6

NONFICTION BY NAIPAUL

Among the Believers: An Islamic Journey. 1981. Random 1982 $14.00. ISBN 0-394-71195-5. An account of Naipaul's experiences in the Islamic world.

An Area of Darkness. 1964. Random 1981 o.p.

India: A Wounded Civilization. 1976. Random 1977 $10.00. ISBN 0-394-72463-1. A searching and honest portrayal of Naipaul's ancestral land.

The Middle Passage. 1962. Random 1981 o.p.

The Return of Eva Peron. 1980. Random 1981 o.p. Selection of reviews and articles about the well-known Argentinian.

A Turn in the South. Random 1990 $11.00. ISBN 0-679-72488-5

BOOKS ABOUT NAIPAUL

Boxill, Anthony. *V. S. Naipaul's Fiction: In Quest of the Enemy.* York Pr. 1983 o.p. Explores the theme of the enemy in Naipaul's early and later novels.

Cudjoe, Selwyn R. *V. S. Naipaul: A Materialist Reading.* U. of Mass. Pr. 1988 $14.95. ISBN 0-87023-620-2. Naipaul considers himself rootless, but this work examines his place in the literary and historical tradition of the Caribbean.

Hamner, Robert D., ed. *Critical Perspectives on V. S. Naipaul.* Three Continents 1977 $25.00. ISBN 0-914478-17-6. A useful collection of essays.

______. *V. S. Naipaul.* Twayne 1973 o.p. An introductory study assessing Naipaul's place in contemporary writing.

Hughes, Peter. *V. S. Naipaul.* Routledge 1988 $6.95. ISBN 0-415-00654-6. Study of Naipaul's life and works for the general reader; puts particular emphasis on Naipaul's West Indian themes.

King, Bruce. *V. S. Naipaul.* Archon 1979 o.p. An insightful study of Naipaul's background and major works.

McSweeney, Kerry. *Four Contemporary Novelists: Angus Wilson, Brian Moore, John Fowles, V. S. Naipaul.* McGill-Queen's U. Pr. 1983 $34.95. ISBN 0-7735-0399-4. Discusses the entire canon of Naipaul's works, from the earliest to the most recent.

Morris, Robert K. *Paradox of Order: Some Perspectives.* U. of Mo. Pr. 1975 o.p. Discusses the interaction of chaos and order in Naipaul's fiction.

Sudha, Rai. *V. S. Naipaul: A Study in Expatriate Sensibility.* IND-US 1982 $12.00. ISBN 0-86578-143-5. Examines Naipaul's colonial past and explores the themes of exile and colonialism in his works.

Theroux, Paul. *V. S. Naipaul: An Introduction to His Work.* Africana 1972 o.p. First booklength study of Naipaul's novels, focusing on his major themes.

Thorpe, Michael. *V. S. Naipaul.* Longman 1976 o.p. Short introductory study of Naipaul's life and major works..

Walsh, William. *V. S. Naipaul.* Oliver and Boyd 1973 o.p. Examines Naipaul's growth as a writer and the complexity of his art.

White, Landeg. *V. S. Naipaul: A Critical Introduction.* Macmillan 1975 o.p. Focuses on the autobiographical basis of most of Naipaul's works.

PADILLA, HEBERTO. 1932– (Cuba)

[See Chapter 22]

REID, V(ICTOR) S(TAFFORD). 1913– Jamaica

Reid's historical novel *New Day* (1949) is based on the Morant Bay Uprising of 1865 and deals with armed resistance to oppression, showing a certain ambivalence towards this resistance. The book employs an interesting use of dialect and skillful contrast of two time levels. The novel *The Leopard* (1958), which presents an African protagonist during the Mau Mau Rebellion in Kenya, is clearly allegorical, but its lyric character and understanding of the African circumstances have been much praised. Both revolts were connected to the inequalities of colonial structures, and Reid's themes show his awareness of the similarity of the colonial experience.

Novels by Reid

The Leopard. 1958. Heinemann Ed. 1980 $7.95. ISBN 0-435-98660-0
New Day. 1949. Chatham Bkseller 1972 o.p.

Nonfiction by Reid

The Horse of the Morning: A Life of Norman Washington Manley. Caribbean Authors 1985 o.p. A well-written biography of Manley, one of Jamaica's most respected, but controversial, prime ministers.

RHYS, JEAN. 1890–1979 Dominica

Born in Dominica and educated in England, Rhys brings to her fiction an awareness of the problems associated with life in these two seemingly different worlds. The daughter of a Welsh doctor and a Creole mother, Rhys was sent to England at age 16 to attend school. Shortly afterward, her father died, leaving her penniless. After working at a variety of jobs, she married a Dutch journalist, Max Hamer, and moved to Paris, where she met a number of writers and artists. Of those, the writer Ford Maddox Ford (see Vol. 1) encouraged her to pursue her own writing.

The protagonists of Rhys's works are often described as lonely, placeless individuals who feel lost and exiled in the worlds of both Europe and the West Indies. Her first work, *The Left Bank and Other Stories* (1927), reveals her skill as an artist and her insight into the plight of the disadvantaged. Her best known novel, *Wide Sargasso Sea* (1966), is a retelling of the story of the first Mrs. Rochester of Charlotte Bronte's (see Vol. 1) *Jane Eyre,* whose childhood is shaken by racial and cultural conflicts which strain her spirituality and sanity. Rhys's writing has been acclaimed for its complexity, its innovation in narrative techniques, and its incisive portrayal of displaced, alienated individuals.

Novels by Rhys

Good Morning, Midnight. 1939. Norton 1986 $7.95. ISBN 0-393-02375-3. A stream of consciousness novel focusing on the cruelty in the relationship of the two main characters.
Wide Sargasso Sea. 1966. Viking Penguin 1992 $8.95. ISBN 0-393-30880-4

Short Stories by Rhys

The Left Bank and Other Stories. 1927. Ayer Co Pub repr. $21.95. ISBN 0-8369-3698-1

Nonfiction by Rhys

Smile, Please: An Unfinished Autobiography. 1979. Viking Penguin 1982 o.p. Rather than a continuous account of Rhys's life, this presents glimpses of the past through vignettes revealing the close link between her life and work.

BOOKS ABOUT RHYS

James, Louis, *Jean Rhys.* Longman 1978 o.p.

Nebeker, Helen E. *Jean Rhys, Woman in Passage: A Critical Study of the Novels of Jean Rhys.* Eden Pr. 1981 o.p. Focuses on the effect of myth and Victorian patriarchy on the social and sexual relationships of Rhys's fictional characters.

Staley, Thomas. *Jean Rhys: A Critical Study.* Macmillan 1979 o.p. A study of Rhys's life and work emphasizing her craft. Compares her novels to those of Virginia Woolf.

Wolfe, Peter. *Jean Rhys.* Twayne 1980 o.p. An introductory study of Rhys's works focusing on their structure and major themes.

ROUMAIN, JACQUES. 1907–1944 — Haiti

Jacques Roumain was one of an educated group of young people who were interested in the revindication of national folkways and culture, centered around the foundation of the publication *La Revue Indigene* in 1927. Their experience generated a movement of social protest as well as literary nationalism in Haiti. Poet and author of ethnological studies, Roumain also wrote a number of novels. His posthumous novel *The Masters of the Dew* (1978) is a powerful, realistic vision of life in a peasant community. The rhythm of Creolized French, the language of the people, and their culture permeate the novel.

NOVEL BY ROUMAIN

The Masters of the Dew. 1978. Trans. by Langston Hughes and Mercer Cook. Heinemann Ed. 1978 $9.95. ISBN 0-435-98745-3

SALKEY, ANDREW. 1928– — Jamaica

Born in Panama and educated in Jamaica and London, Salkey is an important critic and anthologist who uses African folk tales and variegated West Indian popular culture, such as cultism, as sources for his novels and short stories. His first novel, *A Quality of Violence* (1959), focuses on life in rural Jamaica. His later novels portray urban, middle-class protagonists unable to relate to others because of racial, cultural, or class differences. Salkey is also a poet and a writer of travel literature. As a writer, he attempts to forge a distinctive West Indian personality out of the diversity of the various ethnic sources.

NOVEL BY SALKEY

A Quality of Violence. 1959. New Beacon 1978 o.p.

SHORT STORY COLLECTION BY SALKEY

West Indian Stories. 1960. Faber & Faber 1968 o.p. Twenty-five stories with a unique Caribbean flavor.

POETRY BY SALKEY

Away. Schocken 1980 o.p. A collection of recent poems.

In the Hills Where Her Dreams Live. 1979. Black Scholar Pr. 1981 o.p. A collection of poems written between 1973 and 1979.

SÁNCHEZ, LUIS RAFAEL. 1932– (Puerto Rico)

[See Chapter 22]

SARDUY, SEVERO. 1937– (Cuba)

[See Chapter 22]

SELVON, SAMUEL. 1923– Trinidad

Largely self-educated, Selvon was first a poet, later a journalist, and then a professional writer. In 1946 he became an editor at the *Guardian Weekly* in Trinidad. He left for England in 1950, where he wrote and published his first novel, *A Brighter Sun* (1952). This novel depicts the struggle of the protagonist, a newly married Indian peasant, to adapt to life in a suburban area. In *Turn Again Tiger* (1958), a sequel to his highly successful first novel, the protagonist of *A Brighter Sun* returns to his community with a deeper sense of place. Both novels explore his relations to his origins and the various layers of Trinidadian society. *Moses Ascending* (1975) is a humorous satire on the situation of the West Indian in London. Although his roots are in the nineteenth-century novel, Selvon has created a personal literary language out of the fusion of standard English with Creole folk language, just as he has joined the techniques of European fiction to the West Indian rhythms. Though he now lives in Calgary, Canada, Selvon continues to write about West Indians with humor and sensitivity and tries to communicate his view that all West Indians—in spite of racial diversity—have a common identity.

NOVELS BY SELVON

A Brighter Sun. 1952. Dearborn Trade $9.95. ISBN 0-582-64265-5

The Lonely Londoners. 1956. TSAR 1991 $10.95. ISBN 0-920661-16-5. Humorous and affectionate story of Caribbean immigrants in London.

Moses Ascending. 1975. Heinemann Ed. 1984 repr. of 1975 ed. $7.95. ISBN 0-435-98952-9

Moses Migrating. Three Continents 1992 $20.00. ISBN 0-89410-715-1. A comic, often satirical story of the title character's return to the Caribbean from London.

Turn Again Tiger. 1958. Heinemann Ed. 1980 $8.95. ISBN 0-435-98780-1

WORK BY SELVON

Foreday Morning: Selected Prose 1946–1986. Longman 1989 $11.89. ISBN 0-582-03982-7. A collection of selected prose pieces on various topics.

BOOK ABOUT SELVON

Nasta, Susheila, ed. *Critical Perspectives on Sam Selvon*. Three Continents 1988 $25.95. ISBN 0-89410-239-7. Contains articles by Selvon and interviews with him. Also includes several critical essays.

WALCOTT, DEREK. 1930– (NOBEL PRIZE 1992) Saint Lucia

Walcott, a prolific author of prose, plays, and poetry, studied at the University of the West Indies and has lived extensively in Great Britain and the United States. Although his childhood on the island of Saint Lucia is apparent in his work, he is less rooted in popular language and folklore and rejects a simplistic nostalgia. Unlike many other West Indian writers, Walcott attempts to incorporate both the European and African traditions in his work: He is an individual trying to locate his own place and the place of the Caribbean citizen in a complex world. Much of Walcott's writing contains vivid images of nostalgia for the distant island along with a sense of isolation and alienation. His volume of poetry *Sea Grapes* (1976) is a disenchanted warning against self-aggrandizing political leaders. The long narrative poem *Another Life* (1973) is a picturesque gallery of scenes of Caribbean life, but it also presents life as an odyssey, a perpetual search for change and growth. In *Midsummer* (1984), Walcott's many sonnet-like lyrical poems return to themes that constantly preoccupy him—exile, permanence, and the power of the imagination to transcend these conflicting feelings. One of the most distinguished writers of the West Indies,

Walcott has been awarded many honors and fellowships, including the prestigious Nobel Prize for Literature which he received in 1992, the first West Indian writer to be so honored.

POETRY BY WALCOTT

Another Life. 1973. Three Continents 1982 o.p.

The Fortunate Traveller. FS&G 1982 $8.95. ISBN 0-374-51744-4. These poems reveal a longing for the Caribbean and a concern for the lot of the world's poor.

Midsummer. FS&G 1984 $7.95. ISBN 0-374-51863-7

Sea Grapes. FS&G 1976 o.p.

The Star-Apple Kingdom. FS&G 1979 $7.95. ISBN 0-374-51532-8. A collection of poems using middle-aged protagonists whose attitude toward life is bleak and often cynical.

PLAYS BY WALCOTT

Dream on Monkey Mountain and Other Plays. FS&G 1970 $12.95. ISBN 0-374-50860-7. Established Walcott as a dramatist. These plays use historical and fictional characters as heroes, and employ West Indian music.

The Joker of Seville and O Babylon: Two Plays. FS&G 1978 $15.00. ISBN 0-374-17998-0. These plays take the more conventional form of the Broadway musical.

Remembrance and Pantomime. FS&G 1980 $7.95. ISBN 0-374-51569-7. Avoiding a musical format, Walcott explores the cultural and psychological aspects of colonialism.

Three Plays: The Last Carnival; Beef, No Chicken; A Branch of the Blue Nile. FS&G 1985 $9.95. ISBN 0-374-51883-1. Plays of a somewhat lighter vein than those in previous collections.

BOOKS ABOUT WALCOTT

Baugh, Edward. *Derek Walcott*. Longman 1978 o.p. A study of Walcott's work, focusing on word use and images in his poems.

Hamner, Robert D. *Derek Walcott*. Twayne 1981 o.p. Suggests that Walcott's vision is more positive than it first appears in his work.

Hill, Errol. *Derek Walcott*. Macmillan 1984 o.p. A study of Walcott's poems and plays by a renowned Caribbean dramatist.

CHAPTER 25

Australian Literature

Robert L. Ross

> We take pleasure in the Australianity of our literature. We like it; though we must never again accept it as a sole test.
>
> — R. D. FITZGERALD, *Nationalism and Internationalism*

British settlers came to the continent of Australia in 1788. The First Fleet carried shiploads of male and female convicts to serve sentences for crimes ranging from murder to minor theft, upper-class men appointed by the government to oversee the colony's establishment, and military personnel to keep order. The land, approximately the size of the United States, had been the home for 40,000 years of a roaming native people. Although long called Aboriginals—a term that has stuck—by the British, the racially mixed descendants of the once-sizable native population now prefer to be called Koori.

An elaborate oral tradition existed in Australia before European settlement, but it was largely ignored until after 1960. Until then, Australian literature consisted mainly of writing by Anglo-Celtic settlers and their descendants. This body of literature grew rapidly as the nineteenth century progressed, with the transportation of convicts ceasing in the 1840s and free settlers starting to arrive. During this period, writing from the colony was not considered seriously, for the real literature remained that from England. Journals and diaries, marveling at the oddities of the antipodes, appeared first and were intended mainly for a British audience. Then novels and poetry, often in the same vein of reportage and amazement, were written by the new settlers or visitors and were usually published in England.

By the end of the nineteenth century, however, a surge of nationalism had overtaken Australia, and the literature started to reflect this change. The most influential publication to promote a nationalistic literature was *The Bulletin,* a newspaper whose "red page" published poetry and fiction that remained faithful to the Australian landscape and its people. Although some plays were written and produced, the theater continued to be a bastion of British and world drama, showing little interest in developing a national drama. So fiction and poetry dominated until after World War II.

The fiction of this period mainly adhered to the tenets of social realism. Its primary purpose was to record Australian life, especially life in the bush, and to celebrate the courage of those who fought against the hardships endemic to so inhospitable a land. The poetry performed the same task, or it followed the forms of English romanticism and focused on nature. Some of the work, fiction especially, did gain an international audience, but chiefly as a result of curiosity about this faraway place, of which little was known until after 1945. The emphasis in Australia continued to be on British writing, for Australian work was considered "colonial" at home as well as abroad. In truth, much of the

Australian literature of this era, ranging from the late nineteenth century until after World War II, retains more historical than literary interest. Of course, there were exceptions, such as JOSEPH FURPHY'S *Such Is Life* (1903), HENRY HANDEL RICHARDSON'S trilogy, *The Fortunes of Richard Mahony* (1917–29), and CHRISTINA STEAD'S fiction; however, none of this work was widely known in Australia until after the war, and both Richardson and Stead were expatriates.

In spite of the nationalistic tone of Australian literature, not all writers agreed that their work should constitute nothing more than an accurate picture of Australian life. The argument over "nationalism" and "internationalism" may have started in 1856, when Frederick Sinnett published what is usually considered the first piece of criticism on Australian literature. In his "The Fiction Fields of Australia," appearing in the *Journal of Australasia*, he said: "We may remark that most Australian stories are *too* Australian, and, instead of human life, we have only local 'manners and customs' portrayed in them." On one side, there were those who insisted that a work's "Australianness" be its major criterion; on the other side, critics and writers thought the literature should move into the mainstream of world writing. Through the years, the argument raged and sometimes was taken to extremes, all of which makes Australian literary history a fascinating account.

As should be the case, the literature itself settled the argument. In the 1930s and early 1940s, poets like JAMES MCAULEY, KENNETH SLESSOR, and JUDITH WRIGHT were emerging, their work no longer handling Australian materials in the traditional manner. In 1939 PATRICK WHITE published, albeit in England and the United States, his first novel, *Happy Valley*. Although set in rural Australia, as so many novels before it had been, this work brought something new to the country's fiction; even so, it was at first generally rejected by Australian critics. White, who went on to receive the Nobel Prize for literature in 1973, observed, in his now much-quoted essay "The Prodigal Son" (*Australian Letters*, 1958), that the Australian novel need "not necessarily [be] the dreary dun-coloured offspring of journalistic realism."

White and those who followed him, as well as a few writers in the past, did indeed prove otherwise. The poets, many of them heavily influenced after 1945 by American poetry, also moved away from the long-established traditions of Australian verse. And at last Australia started to develop a drama of its own; Ray Lawler's *Summer of the Seventeenth Doll* (1957) is usually credited as the turning point in a dramatic literature that continues to flourish.

As the twentieth century draws to a close, Australian literature has taken on a vibrance that is both distinctive and universal. No longer a minor colonial appendage to the literature of England, it has come into its own. And the charge that the literary heritage belongs solely to Anglo-Celtic writers is no longer valid. Since the 1960s, Aboriginal writers have made their voices heard in an impressive body of English-language writing. In part these poems, plays, novels, and autobiographies protest a long suppression and serve as a rallying cry to bring the people together. At the same time, some of the writers are striving to restore the lost Koori heritage. After the war, the majority Anglo-Celtic white population of Australia accepted, sometimes reluctantly, thousands of European refugees, followed later by Asian immigrants. These voices are now being heard in English-language writing. Their work, perhaps erroneously, is sometimes set apart by its own practitioners as "migrant" literature. Are not all Australian writers "migrants," except for the descendants of those who have inhabited the continent for 40,000 years?

All things considered, such distinctions are really not relevant. For Australian writers have developed a literature that lends identity to the people of their country, whether they consider themselves Anglo-Celtic, Koori, or migrant. The writers have also made an impressive contribution to the ever-growing body of international literature in English.

HISTORY AND CRITICISM

Elliott, Brian. *The Jindyworobaks.* U. of Queensland Pr. 1980 $17.95. ISBN 07-0221-29-70. A thorough exploration, through poetry and criticism, of the nationalist movement that flourished in the 1930s.

Goodwin, Ken. *A History of Australian Literature.* Macmillan 1986 $19.95. ISBN 0-312-01135-0. A readable and comprehensive introduction to Australian literature, especially contemporary.

Green, H. M. *A History of Australian Literature.* 2 vols. Rev. by Dorothy Green. Angus & Robertson AT 1984. Vol. 1 $50.00. ISBN 0-20713-825-7. Vol. 2 $40.00. ISBN 0-20714-255-6. Charts Australian literature's development from 1788 to 1950, covering all forms of literature.

Gunew, Sneja, and Kateryna O. Longley, eds. *Striking Chords: Multicultural Literary Interpretations.* Allen Unwin AT 1992 $19.95. ISBN 1-86373-089-3. Offers 33 essays by non-Anglo-Celtic, non-Aboriginal writers and critics on all aspects of multicultural (or migrant) writing.

Healy, J. J. *Literature and the Aborigine in Australia, 1770–1975.* U. of Queensland Pr. rev. ed. 1989 $29.95. ISBN 0-7022-2150-3. The moral, aesthetic, and historical factors in the works of European Australians who attempt to come to grips with the Aborigine.

Hergenhan, Laurie, ed. *The Penguin New Literary History of Australia.* Viking Penguin 1988 $19.99. ISBN 0-14-007514-3. Various critics on culture, Aboriginal literature, language, humor, war literature, children's literature, and genres.

Holloway, Peter, ed. *Contemporary Australian Drama: Perspectives since 1955.* Currency Pr. AT 1987 $36.00. ISBN 0-86819-108-6. General developments in the Australian theater and on major writers since 1950, with bibliographies.

Hughes, Robert. *The Fatal Shore: The Epic of Australia's Founding.* Knopf 1987 $24.95. ISBN 0-394-50668-5. History of Australia's convict settlement that provides background for understanding the literature.

Kirkby, Joan, ed. *The American Model: Influence and Independence in Australian Poetry.* Hale & Iremonger 1982 $29.95. ISBN 0-90809-482-5. Addresses the effect of American poetry on Australian writers through essays by American and Australian poets.

Kramer, Leonie, ed. *The Oxford History of Australian Literature.* OUP 1981 $35.00. ISBN 0-19554-335-1. Comprehensive guide to the fiction, drama, and poetry of Australia, with bibliography and biographies.

McAuley, James. *Map of Australian Verse.* OUP 1975 $22.50. ISBN 0-19550-474-7. Critical, biographical, and historical information about Australia's major poets, with samples of their work.

McLaren, John. *Australian Literature: An Historical Introduction.* Longman Cheshire 1989 $26.99. ISBN 0-582-71279-3. Comprehensive account of Australian literature that discusses Aboriginal legends and traces contemporary movements.

Narogin, Mudrooroo. *Writing from the Fringe: A Study of Modern Aboriginal Literature.* Hyland Hse. AT 1989 $19.95. ISBN 0-94706-255-6. Traces Aboriginal writing from its conciliatory period to its activist period.

Ross, Robert L. *Australian Literary Criticism—1945–1988.* Garland 1989 $45.00. ISBN 0-8240-1510-X. Covers development of postwar criticism on all aspects of Australian literature, both in Australia and abroad.

Shoemaker, Adam. *Black Words, White Page: Aboriginal Literature 1929-1988.* U. of Queensland Pr. 1989 $29.95. ISBN 0-7022-2149-X. Surveys the development of writing by Aboriginals, focusing on major writers, socio-political contexts, and reception.

Walker, Shirley, ed. *Who Is She? Images of Women in Australian Fiction.* St. Martin 1983 $29.95. ISBN 0-312-87015-9. Excellent collection of essays in feminist criticism in relation to Australian fiction.

Wilde, William H., Joy Hooton, and Barry Andrews, eds. *The Oxford Companion to Australian Literature.* OUP 1985 $62.00. ISBN 0-19-554233-9. A comprehensive guide covering individual writers, development of genres, literary movements, and cultural events.

COLLECTIONS

Bail, Murray, ed. *The Faber Book of Contemporary Australian Short Stories.* Faber & Faber 1988 $25.00. ISBN 0-571-14763-1. Offers 32 stories by 24 writers from the post-World War II period.

Daniel, Helen. *Liars: Australian New Novelists.* Viking Penguin 1988 $8.95. ISBN 0-14-009788-0. Examines narrative and stylistic trends in the work of Peter Carey, Elizabeth Jolley, and others.

Davis, Jack, and others. *Paperbark: A Collection of Black Australian Writings.* U. of Queensland Pr. 1990 $16.95. ISBN 0-7022-2180-5. A work of 36 Aboriginal and Islander writers: transcriptions of oral literature, fiction, poetry, song, drama, polemic.

Gilbert, Kevin, ed. *Black Australia: An Anthology of Aboriginal Poetry.* Viking Penguin 1988 $12.95. ISBN 0-14-011126-3. Poems by over 40 poets, providing a wide sampling of Aboriginal concerns in political context.

Goodwin, Ken, and Alan Lawson, eds. *Macmillan Anthology of Australian Literature.* Intl. Spec. Bk. 1990 $69.95. ISBN 0-685-47246-9. Representative collection of Australian writing from its beginnings to contemporary times, arranged thematically.

Hergenhan, Laurie, ed. *The Australian Short Story: An Anthology from the 1890s to the 1980s.* U. of Queensland Pr. 1986 $17.95. ISBN 0-70221-787-5. Selection of classic and contemporary short fiction, with biographical and bibliographical materials.

Jordan, Richard D., and Peter Pierce, eds. *The Poet's Discovery: Nineteenth-Century Australia in Verse.* Melbourne U. Pr. AT 1990 $22.95. ISBN 05-2284-40-22. Extensive collection of poems by known and unknown poets, on a great variety of subjects.

Tranter, John, and Philip Mead, eds. *The Penguin Book of Modern Australian Poetry.* Viking Penguin 1991 $19.95. ISBN 0-14058-649-0. Edited by two major poets and offering a rich sampling of contemporary poetry.

CHRONOLOGY OF AUTHORS

Furphy, Joseph. 1843–1912
Richardson, Henry Handel. 1870–1946
Franklin, Miles (Stella Maria). 1879–1954
Boyd, Martin. 1893–1972
Shute, Nevil. 1899–1960
Slessor, Kenneth. 1901–1971
Herbert, Xavier. 1901–1984
Stead, Christina. 1902–1983
Hope, A. D. 1907–
White, Patrick. 1912–1990
Wright, Judith. 1915–
McAuley, James. 1917–1976
Anderson, Jessica. c.1920s–
Jolley, Elizabeth. 1923–
Astley, Thea. 1925–
Hazzard, Shirley. 1931–
Malouf, David. 1934–
Keneally, Thomas. 1935–
Stow, Randolph. 1935–
Murray, Les. 1938–
Narogin, Mudrooroo. 1939–
Williamson, David. 1942–
Carey, Peter. 1943–

ANDERSON, JESSICA. c.1920s–

Except for a few years spent in London, Jessica Anderson has lived mainly in Sydney. This cosmopolitan city has been the setting for much of her work, including her first novel, *An Ordinary Lunacy* (1963), which satirizes Sydney society. *The Last Man's Head* (1970) appeared next; on one level it is a detective novel, but its psychological approach and moral vision lend it depth. Anderson's birthplace, Brisbane, figures in her third novel, *The Commandant* (1975), which contains a vivid account of the Moreton Bay (former name of Brisbane) penal settlement in the early nineteenth century. The historically based story focuses in part on how women fare in such a place—the role of women in society being a recurrent theme in Anderson's work. Her best-known book is *Tirra Lirra by the River* (1978), which retraces the life of a 70-year-old bedridden woman, Nora Roche. Through exploring her memory, Nora attempts to rediscover pivotal events in her life, to make some sense of what has happened, and to accept her present state. *The Impersonators* (1980) examines a Sydney family and the way money affects the family members' outward lives, making them—especially the women—"impersonators." Anderson's final novel (she has announced that she is "retiring" from writing), *Taking Shelter* (1989), again examines Sydney society, this time in contemporary terms as the characters deal with their sexuality in the age of AIDS. The "shelter" for which they are searching is essentially love in all its forms—another recurrent theme in Anderson's fiction.

Although Anderson did not begin to write novels until after she was 40 or so, she has established herself as a major figure both in Australia and abroad. Noted for varied and exact characterization, spare narrative strategies, lyrical style, subtle irony, and truthfully rendered dialogue, Anderson has made skillful use of the society she knows best to observe and delineate basic human conflicts. In order to survive, in order to achieve identity—Anderson seems to be saying—individuals must discover and assert their true selves. That is, they must learn *not* to be "impersonators." Many critics compare her books, which have been called "novels of manners," with those of HENRY JAMES (see Vol. 1), an influence Anderson acknowledged in an interview: "I adapted some of his work for radio, and he is so good, he is so sound, that nobody could adapt his work without learning something about construction."

NOVELS BY ANDERSON

The Commandant. 1975. Viking Penguin 1988 $9.99. ISBN 0-14-005910-5

The Impersonators (U.S. title: *The Only Daughter*). 1980. Viking Penguin 1986 $6.95. ISBN 0-14-006333-1

The Last Man's Head. 1970. Viking Penguin 1987 $11.99. ISBN 0-14-0102884-4

An Ordinary Lunacy. 1963. Viking Penguin 1987 $6.95. ISBN 0-14-009707-4

Taking Shelter. 1989. Viking Penguin 1990 $17.95. ISBN 0-670-82950-1

Tirra Lirra by the River. 1978. Viking Penguin 1991 $6.95. ISBN 0-14-099705-9

SHORT STORY COLLECTION BY ANDERSON

Stories from the Warm Zone and Sydney Stories. 1987. Viking Penguin 1990 $6.95. ISBN 0-14-009708-2. Stories set in Brisbane ("the warm zone") during the 1920s or in contemporary Sydney.

BOOK ABOUT ANDERSON

Barry, Elaine. *Fabricating the Self: The Fictions of Jessica Anderson.* U. of Queensland Pr. 1992 $29.95. Points out that Anderson's work escapes easy classifications such as "national," "political," or "feminist."

ASTLEY, THEA. 1925–

Australia's tropical state of Queensland, where Thea Astley was born and grew up, serves as the setting for most of her fiction. Sometimes called "the deep North" to show the likeness to the American South, this vast region is noted for its conservatism, parochialism, exotic landscape, and scant population. Queenslanders are fiercely independent—and, in Astley's version of their lives, a bit quirky. In spite of the close fictional ties to her roots, Astley is far from a parochial or local-color writer. In a writing career that has spanned 35 years, she has produced 12 novels, a book of short fiction, and numerous uncollected essays and short stories.

Although the fiction has ranged in subject matter from the lives of country schoolteachers to colonial savagery against Aborigines, the work is unified by a single theme: the individual's quest for spiritual fulfillment. For Astley the greatest work of art emerges as personal salvation, so that the process of fiction and the personal quest become intertwined. This quality that distinguishes her writing long prevented a widespread acceptance by Australian critics and readers, who found the work's vision too dark, its treatment of the human condition harsh and bitterly ironic. Some of Astley's characters—her "misfits," as she calls them—may get glimpses of the sought-after spiritual "center" but are denied full entrance into it. The style also met with resistance, often criticized for its experimentation with the boundaries of language.

Even without a wide critical or popular reception, Astley's books have received numerous literary prizes in Australia: the Miles Franklin Award three times; Australian Society of Literature's Gold Medal; and Book of the Year, *The Age* (a Melbourne newspaper). In 1989 she received the Patrick White Prize, which is given each year to an Australian writer who has made a notable contribution to the country's literature but has not received full recognition. During the 1980s Astley's fiction started to get favorable attention in the United States and Canada, and she is one of the handful of Australian novelists who are published regularly, reviewed favorably, and read widely in North America. Whether as a result or not, her work now receives more acclaim in Australia. In fact, a recent advertisement in the national newspaper, the *Australian,* calls her "Australia's most important contemporary novelist."

NOVELS BY ASTLEY

The Acolyte. 1972. Viking Penguin 1990 $6.95. ISBN 0-14-011784-9. Examines the artist in a postcolonial society, through the career of an Australian composer.

Beachmasters. 1985. Viking Penguin 1988 $6.95. ISBN 0-14-010946-3. Traces a revolution on a South Sea island, in its personal and political contexts.

A Boat Load of Home Folk. 1968. Viking Penguin 1983 $4.95. ISBN 0-14-006743-4. Tourists on a tropical island facing a hurricane, both within and without.

A Descant for Gossips. 1960. U. of Queensland Pr. 1986 $12.95. ISBN 0-7022-1843-X. Small-town malice destroys the relation between two teachers and the life of an isolated young girl.

Girl with a Monkey. 1958. Viking Penguin 1987 $5.95. ISBN 0-14-009881-X. Reveals the drab life of a country schoolteacher in Australia, as she escapes from an unrewarding romance.

An Item from the Late News. 1982. Viking Penguin 1984 $5.95. ISBN 0-14-006948-8. A misfit clashing with the parochial values of a small town.

It's Raining in Mango. 1987. Viking Penguin 1988 $6.95. ISBN 0-14-011403-3. A family history of several generations of northern Queenslanders.

A Kindness Cup. 1974. Viking Penguin 1989 $6.95. ISBN 0-14-011780-6. Retells a historical event in which settlers drove Aborigines off a cliff.

Reaching Tin River. 1990. Viking Penguin 1991 $8.95. ISBN 0-14-014897-3. A woman's quest for her own and Australia's center.

The Slow Natives. 1965. Viking Penguin 1990 $12.99. ISBN 01-4013-41-15. Examines family life, especially the relation between parent and child.

Vanishing Points. Putnam Pub. Group 1992 $21.95. ISBN 0-399-13770-X. Two linked novellas, "The Genteel Poverty Bus Company" and "Inventing the Weather," with tourism as their metaphor.

The Well Dressed Explorer. 1962. Viking Penguin 1988 $6.95. ISBN 0-14-009882-8. A comic biography of a Sydney journalist who is finally destroyed by his personal illusions.

Short Story Collection by Astley

Hunting the Wild Pineapple. 1979. Viking Penguin 1981 $3.95. ISBN 0-14-005843-5. Eight stories about the oddities of northern Queensland life.

BOYD, MARTIN. 1893–1972

Martin Boyd's major novels take Australia and Europe as settings to record the bihemispheric lives of those who until after World War II considered themselves "Anglo-Australians," rather than just plain Australians, and spent more time at "home" in England than in their birthplace. Boyd started publishing in 1925, his first four novels appearing under pseudonyms. Six additional novels, published under his own name in the 1930s and in 1940, enjoyed modest success, but it was not until 1946, with the publication of *Lucinda Brayford*, that Boyd received international attention. A substantial work, *Lucinda Brayford* records the mundane life of the title character, who grows up in Melbourne as an aristocratic Anglo-Australian, then moves to London, where she is just a "colonial." Although the book can be read as a social history that goes past the Second World War, its heroine also embodies Boyd's idea of the aristocratic principle. Through clinging to this concept, Lucinda, in spite of a ruined marriage and other defeats, manages to attain a kind of victory, in part spiritual and in part personal.

Boyd's greatest achievement is the *Langton Quartet*, which appeared between 1952 and 1962: *The Cardboard Crown* (1952), *A Difficult Young Man* (1955), *Outbreak of Love* (1957), and *When Blackbirds Sing* (1962). Returning to the same autobiographical material that served so well in *Lucinda Brayford*, Boyd traces 80 years in the history of the Langtons, a thinly disguised version of his own Anglo-Australian family. The novels offer memorable characters and a strong evocation of time and place; they show the gradual disintegration of the Langtons as they forsake their aristocratic ideals for those of a modern bourgeois society.

The *Langton Quartet* received attention in Australia and abroad, but even that soon faded. When Boyd died in genteel poverty in Italy, he and his work were largely forgotten. By then Australians shunned the prefix "Anglo," striving instead in their fiction to establish a national identity separate from Great Britain. In recent years, however, there has been a revival of interest in *Lucinda Brayford* and the *Langton Quartet*, with international paperback editions appearing. Because of his archaic social attitudes and literary style, Boyd is not a fashionable novelist by modern standards. Yet he does accurately record an important part of the colonial experience.

Novels by Boyd

The Cardboard Crown. 1952. Viking Penguin 1986 $4.95. ISBN 0-14-006904-6
A Difficult Young Man. 1955. Viking Penguin 1986 $4.95. ISBN 0-14-006906-2

Lucinda Brayford. 1946. Viking Penguin 1985 $5.95. ISBN 0-14-007231-4
Outbreak of Love. 1957. Viking Penguin 1984 $9.99. ISBN 0-14-007229-2
When Blackbirds Sing. 1962. Viking Penguin 1984 $5.95. ISBN 14-006905-4

BOOK ABOUT BOYD

Niall, Brenda. *Martin Boyd: A Life*. Melbourne U. Pr. AT 1988 $39.95. ISBN 0-522-84268-2. Considers Boyd and his work as more complex than most realize and provides a sympathetic and intelligent biography.

CAREY, PETER. 1943–

Born in Bacchus Marsh, a country town in the southern state of Victoria, Peter Carey has put his Australian background to good use. Still, even though he consistently writes about Australia, he is far from a regionalist. His writing is marked by its wit, flights of imagination, clear style, solid characterization, and rich texture. He brings to all his fiction a cosmopolitan quality and metaphysical dimension that has led critics to compare his work with that of JORGE LUIS BORGES and GABRIEL GARCÍA MÁRQUEZ. When asked about the debt to Borges, Carey replied: "It is there, it cannot *not* be there." His first volume of short fiction, *The Fat Man in History* (1974), with its original and unrealistic use of Australian materials, gained immediate acclaim in Australia. One critic noted that Carey at last fills "a vacancy in the Sophisticated Fantasy Section of the Short Story Industry." A second book of stories, *War Crimes* (1979), was equally well received and won an important Australian literary award.

In 1982 his first novel, *Bliss*, appeared. At this time Carey was balancing his writing career with the operation of an advertising agency in Sydney, and his books were not generally known outside of Australia. When *Illywhacker* was published, in 1985, followed by British and American editions, he began to receive international attention. This novel, whose title employs an Australian slang word for con artist, retells Australian history and looks into the nation's future, stressing all the while the lies that constitute the national myth; the work was short-listed for the British Booker Prize. Carey's next novel, *Oscar and Lucinda* (1988), did receive that prestigious prize, and his reputation as an Australian writer with international stature was firmly established. In 1989 he moved to New York, where he still lives, teaching part time at New York University and writing. Even though *The Tax Inspector* (1992) was written in New York, it continues Carey's exploration of the Australian myth and its effect on the individual. Yet all of Carey's work transcends the Australian experience.

NOVELS BY CAREY

Bliss. 1982. HarpC 1992 $10.00. ISBN 0-06-091355. Records Harry Joy's three deaths and resurrections while exploring society's shortcomings and possibilities.

Illywhacker. 1985. HarpC 1992 $10.00. ISBN 0-06-091331-2. Picaresque novel of the adventures of a con artist through Australian history.

Oscar and Lucinda. 1988. HarpC 1992 $11.00. ISBN 0-06-091592-7. Gambling as a metaphor to explore relations between native and settler Australians.

The Tax Inspector. Knopf 1992 $21.00. ISBN 0-679-40434-1. A satirical look at a bizarre family whose car agency is under investigation by the tax collector in Sydney.

SHORT STORY COLLECTIONS BY CAREY

The Fat Man in History. 1974. U. of Queensland Pr. 1991 $7.95. ISBN 0-7022-0900-7. Collection of stories set in Australia, each with a surrealistic twist.

War Crimes. 1979. U. of Queensland Pr. 1991 $7.95. ISBN 0-7022-1649-6. Short stories set in Australia, some futuristic, all far removed from reality.

FRANKLIN, MILES (STELLA MARIA). 1879–1954

Miles Franklin was born and reared on farms in remote parts of New South Wales. These early experiences of a family struggling against an inhospitable land served as the basis for her first and best-known novel, *My Brilliant Career* (1901). The story of Sybylla Melvyn and her fantastic adventures in colonial Australia was made into a successful film, which brought about a revival of interest in Franklin and her long-forgotten novel; the interest, however, has been directed more toward her feminism than her literary work. Immediately after *My Brilliant Career,* Franklin wrote *My Career Goes Bung* (1946), which follows Sybylla's experiences as a successful author. Both of these novels foretell Franklin's lifelong revolt against the roles open to women.

Through her literary and feminist contacts after the success of *My Brilliant Career,* Franklin found work as a freelance writer in Sydney before going to the United States in 1905, where she remained for nine years. In Chicago, she engaged in social work and suffragist activity for the National Women's Trade Union League. In 1927, she returned permanently to Australia, where she continued to write. Under the pseudonym "Brent of Bin Bin," she published six novels depicting Australian bush life, but they were never particularly successful. It has been pointed out that by the 1930s Australian fiction was changing, taking up new topics and moving away from realistic accounts of colonial life.

Franklin's tireless promotion of Australian writing through her criticism and active involvement in literary circles, along with her feminist activities, make her an important figure in Australian literature, even though much of her work is of more historical significance than literary. Following her death in 1954, the Miles Franklin Award for Fiction was instituted, to be given to a novelist whose work authentically represents Australian life.

Novels by Franklin

All That Swagger. 1936. Sirius 1984 $9.95. ISBN 0-20-7149-98-4. Sweeping tale of pioneer life during the colonial period.

My Brilliant Career. 1901. Angus & Robertson AT 1991 $7.95. ISBN 0-20-7158-18-5

My Career Goes Bung. 1946. Angus & Robertson AT 1991 $7.95. ISBN 0-20-7158-18-5

FURPHY, JOSEPH. 1843–1912

When Furphy died in 1912, his major work, *Such Is Life* (1903), had met with little success. It was not until the 1940s that Australians discovered this masterpiece, and soon it was brought back into print, along with his two other novels—parts that had been excised from *Such Is Life,* on its original publication: *Rigby's Romance* and *The Buln-Buln and the Brolga.* Since then Furphy, sometimes called Australia's Mark Twain (see Vol. 1), has been granted a secure place in Australian literature. He is often credited with turning Australian literature away from realistic and romantic accounts of life in the bush toward a more metaphysical bent. Furphy's own announcement at the completion of his novel serves best to describe it: "I have just finished writing a full-sized novel, title, *Such Is Life,* scene, Riverina and Northern Vic; temper, democratic; bias, offensively Australian."

Born to Irish immigrants in an Australian farming area, Furphy at various times worked as a laborer, spent time on the goldfields, and drove a team of oxen. He was not formally educated but a voracious reader. Once he settled in a town in Victoria to work at his brother's foundry, he started contributing items to the famous newspaper *The Bulletin* and wrote *Such Is Life.*

NOVEL BY FURPHY

Such Is Life. 1903. Angus & Robertson AT 1987 $8.95. ISBN 0-20-7158-19-3

WORK BY FURPHY

Joseph Furphy. Ed. by John Barnes. U. of Queensland Pr. 1981 $17.95. ISBN 0-70-2216-12-7. Contains text of *Such Is Life* and other writings.

BOOK ABOUT FURPHY

Barnes, John. *The Order of Things: A Life of Joseph Furphy.* OUP 1990 $39.95. ISBN 0-19-5531-87-6. Illuminates the life as well as the work of Furphy, focusing on the philosophy inculcated in *Such Is Life.*

HAZZARD, SHIRLEY. 1931–

Shirley Hazzard left Australia in the late 1940s and is now a citizen of the United States. She lives in New York and is married to the noted scholar of French literature and culture Francis Steegmuller. Widely regarded in both countries and in Europe, Hazzard might best be considered an "international" novelist, who happened to be born and reared in Australia and who happens to live in the United States. Hazzard's major work, *The Transit of Venus* (1980), makes use of her Australian background, as well as her European and American experiences. This highly complex novel follows a group of sophisticated characters from all parts of the world—expatriates, scientists, artists, government officials, hangers-on—in their quest for personal fulfillment. They are metaphorical exiles in search of a home, of a paradise, a paradise sometimes discovered through love and through art but more often elusive or lost.

Hazzard has called modern society a "no-man's land," adding that "one of the greatest challenges faced by contemporary novelists is an unprecedented loss of geographical, and, to some extent, national and even social, sense of belonging." Formerly serving on the United Nations headquarters staff, Hazzard relies on those experiences in *People in Glass Houses* (1967), a series of stories connected by recurrent figures who work for a global organization and are captives of its mammoth bureaucracy. Without real homes, the characters struggle in their glass prisons (the office buildings) to retain their dignity and to assert their humanity. The inability to love dominates the stories in *Cliffs of Fall* (1963), each one depicting people adrift in hotels, pensions, cafes, and railway stations. Separation and desolation loom over *The Evening of the Holiday* (1966), which focuses on the end of an affair between a half-English, half-Italian woman and a Sicilian. Neither have the inner resources to rescue their love from its transitory nature. *The Bay of Noon* (1970) focuses again on a search for paradise, its setting also in Italy. But even when it is possible to find such a place, as these characters do, their spiritual vacuum eventually leaves them at a loss. Often compared with the work of JANE AUSTEN (see Vol. 1) and HENRY JAMES (see Vol. 1), Hazzard's writing possesses an elegant and mannered quality. Its narrative technique is subtle, its language finely sculptured, its insights resonant, and its wedding of artistry and theme perfectly blended.

NOVELS BY HAZZARD

The Bay of Noon. 1970. Viking Penguin 1988 $6.95. ISBN 0-14-010450-X
The Evening of the Holiday. 1966. Viking Penguin 1988 $3.50. ISBN 0-14-010451-8
The Transit of Venus. 1980. Viking Penguin 1990 $8.95. ISBN 0-14-010747-9

Short Story Collections by Hazzard

Cliffs of Fall. 1963. Viking Penguin 1988 $6.95. ISBN 0-14-010449-6
People in Glass Houses. 1967. Viking Penguin 1988 $6.95. ISBN 0-14-010452-6

HERBERT, XAVIER. 1901–1984

Long a strident critic of the Australians—both in person and in his fiction—Xavier Herbert still emerges as one of the most purely Australian writers in the contemporary period. He was loudly anti-British and anti-American, and at times appeared to be anti-Australian. Yet he believed firmly in his native land's possibilities while weeping over its shortcomings—which he thought to include unjust treatment of the Aborigines, destruction of the environment for profit, toadying to foreign interests, and pursuit of mindless pleasure. On the other hand, he admired the natural wisdom of the Aborigines and their spiritual relationship to the land. And he admired those independent Australians who lived in the bush far from the seductive cities with their foreign interests and pretentious society. His first novel, *Capricornia* (1938), addresses these concerns as it unfolds a complex story of Aborigines and sometimes crude, sometimes comic, but generally decent white Australians in the vast but sparsely settled Northern Territory (Herbert's Capricornia). The novel is also distinguished by its unromanticized, knowledgeable, and fair treatment of Aborigines, a quality not always present in earlier Australian fiction.

In 1976 a large cast of characters from the territory of Capricornia appeared again, this time in Herbert's massive novel (1,468 pages), *Poor Fellow My Country*. More pessimistic and disillusioned in tone than the earlier work, this book depicts the experiences of a prominent rancher in the territory during the late 1930s and through World War II. Often thought to be Herbert's persona, the articulate, opinionated, and—in some views—bigoted hero is surrounded by a host of characters, whites and Aborigines, whose stories unfold in a skillfully structured and controlled narrative.

In spite of the didacticism that flows through Herbert's work, it manages not to dominate. For Herbert is, above all else, a great storyteller. Although sometimes given to ponderous prose, he overcomes this obstacle most of the time and remains deft at characterization, exact in his replication of Australian speech, and splendid in evoking the landscape of his beloved Capricornia. By the time of Herbert's death, his always shaky reputation had begun to decline, many considering him an old-fashioned, nationalistic, social realist. Currently, though, his work, especially *Capricornia,* is being reevaluated and reclaimed in Australia, a revival that may spread abroad, where Herbert had never made many inroads.

Novels by Herbert

Capricornia. 1938. HarpC 1990 $16.95. ISBN 0-20717024-X
Poor Fellow My Country. 1976. Angus & Robertson AT 1980 $35.00. ISBN 07-3220035-0
Soldiers Women. 1961. Angus & Robertson AT 1987 $11.95. ISBN 0-006-54244-1. A sensitive portrayal of women in wartime, emphasizing the tricks of human destiny and the meaning of sexuality.

Nonfiction by Herbert

Disturbing Element. 1963. Angus & Robertson AT 1987 $11.95. ISBN 0-006-54237-6. Tells about growing up in the frontier society of western Australia and his decision to be a writer.

Work by Herbert

Xavier Herbert. Ed. by Frances de Groen and Peter Pierce. U. of Queensland Pr. 1992. Selections from *Capricornia* and *Poor Fellow My Country*, along with other writing, including letters.

HOPE, A. D. 1907–

One of the best-known Australian poets outside his own country, A. D. Hope did not publish his first book of poetry until he was nearly 50. Born in New South Wales, the son of a Presbyterian minister, Hope attended school and college in Australia, then did graduate work at Oxford. On his return to Australia, in the midst of the Depression, he taught in high school and in universities, becoming professor of English at Australian National University in 1951.

He exhibits in his work qualities alien to most Australian poetry, for he rarely writes about the landscape, the people, and the day-to-day concerns of his native country. Instead, his poems rely on world mythology, found in sources as diverse as the Bible and the literature of ancient Greece and Rome, the Italian Renaissance, and the Elizabethan period. His work reveals an obsession with the individual's capacity to rise above the mundane. It is "the poet's trade," Hope wrote in one of his poems, to remake and reshape world myths to help modern humankind validate its existence rather than sink into cynicism. It has been said that he considers the poet's work as "sacred." The poetry, coming out of what turned into a lengthy poetic career in spite of its late beginning, is immensely sophisticated, erudite, witty, cosmopolitan, and highly literary in nature. Long a vocal enemy of free verse and lyricism, Hope has always written in formal structure.

He has published, in addition to his 12 books of poetry, 2 verse plays and 7 incisive books of criticism, ranging in subject matter from poetic theory to D. H. Lawrence (see Vol. 1) to *Beowulf* (see Vol. 1). Even though he has often been accused of being un-Australian in his poetry, Hope has been a tireless champion of the country's literature; it is the subject of much of his critical writing, which has contributed immeasurably to the development of Australian literary criticism.

Poetry by Hope

Collected Poems. Angus & Robertson AT 1986 $9.95. ISBN 0-207-13545-2. Offers a wide selection of Hope's best-known poems, from 1930 to 1970.

Nonfiction by Hope

The New Cratylus. 1979 o.p. A complete statement on his views of poetry and its process, in part theoretical and in part personal.

JOLLEY, ELIZABETH. 1923–

Something of a literary phenomenon in Australia, Elizabeth Jolley published her first book of short stories, *Five Acre Virgin and Other Stories*, in 1976, and her first novel, *Palomino*, in 1980. Both were brought out by a small regional press. But by the end of the 1980s she had produced an amazing amount of work, which rapidly gained her fame and admiration in Australia and abroad. That she is celebrated as a brilliant new Australian novelist seems a bit ironic. After all, she is English by birth, coming in 1959 at the age of 36 to the isolated western Australian city of Perth with her husband—a librarian—and her family. Still, she sets most of her work in and around Perth, and her Australian characters ring true, even if some Australian critics have perhaps correctly noted that Jolley's view of Australia and its people is that of an outside observer.

During Jolley's first 15 or so years in Perth, she began writing but remained unpublished, and worked at odd jobs such as nursing, housecleaning, and farming. These experiences she put to good use, for many of her characters engage in similar occupations. For instance, one of her delightful early novels, *The Newspaper of Claremont Street* (1981), follows a cleaning lady on her daily rounds. Jolley's nursing experience shows up in *Mr. Scobie's Riddle* (1982), which takes place in a nursing home and displays an admirable understanding of both patients and staff. Two of her novels, *The Well* (1986) and *Palomino* (1980), are set on isolated farms, both depicting relationships between two women caught in a state of isolation. Jolley also relies on her English background, especially her work as a nurse during World War II, the subject of *My Father's Moon* (1989). *Miss Peabody's Inheritance* (1983), one of Jolley's most interesting novels, combines the Australian and British experiences as it reveals the ironic relationship between a lonely, pathetic Englishwoman and an Australian woman she thinks lives a life of adventure and glamour. The writer also figures in Jolley's work, as in the novel *Foxybaby* (1985), whose peculiar events unfold—or are imagined or dreamed—in a remote summer institute for writers at which the central character is a featured guest.

However well the plot of a Jolley novel may be summarized, the retelling hardly does it justice. For Jolley is not so much a storyteller as a fabulist. A nurse is not just a nurse, a housekeeper not just a housekeeper, two women on a farm not just two women: Always there intrudes the Gothic element, the bizarre, the strange twists, the quirky narrative structure, elements of the macabre, the irony. The theme of personal isolation and dislocation dominates Jolley's fiction—that theme so central to many postcolonial writers. Possibly one of the fascinations Jolley's work holds for the reader lies in its ambiguity.

Novels by Jolley

Cabin Fever. Viking Penguin 1990 $29.99. ISBN 0-67-08315-57. The plight of Vera Wright, the central character of *My Father's Moon,* struggling as an unwed mother; set in England.

Foxybaby. 1985. Viking Penguin 1986 $5.95. ISBN 0-14-008380-4

Milk and Honey. 1984. Persea Bks. 1986 $8.95. ISBN 0–89255–103–8. Experiences of a European immigrant family in Australia who isolate themselves from what they consider a country without culture or heritage.

Miss Peabody's Inheritance. 1983. Viking Penguin 1985 $6.95. ISBN 0-14-007743-X

Mr. Scobie's Riddle. 1982. Viking Penguin 1984 $6.95. ISBN 0-14-007490-2

My Father's Moon. 1989. HarpC 1990 $8.95. ISBN 0-06-091659-1

The Newspaper of Claremont Street. 1981. Viking Penguin 1988 $6.95. ISBN 0-14-008582-3

Palomino. 1980. U. of Queensland Pr. 1984 $13.95. ISBN 0-70-2219-48-7

The Sugar Mother. 1988. HarpC 1989 $7.95. ISBN 0-06-091588-9. Tells of a man's domination by two women.

The Well. 1986. Viking Penguin 1987 $6.95. ISBN 0-14-008901-2

Short Story Collections by Jolley

Five Acre Virgin and Other Stories. 1976. Fremantle ACP AT 1989 $12.95. ISBN 0-94-92064-90. Foreshadow of what is to come in Jolley's writing.

The Traveling Entertainer and Other Stories. 1979. Fremantle ACP AT 1989 $12.95. ISBN 0-90-9144-21-4. Early but typical Jolley stories, with twists of plot and character.

Woman in a Lampshade. 1983. Viking Penguin 1986 $6.95. ISBN 0-14-008418-5. Witty, ironic tales, with the usual eccentric characters in odd situations.

KENEALLY, THOMAS. 1935–

The author of 19 novels since 1964, Thomas Keneally emerges as Australia's most prolific, varied, and popular contemporary novelist. His books range in subject matter from Australia's convict days to war-ravaged Eritrea in Africa. Their locales move from realistic depictions of the American South during the Civil War to similarly convincing pictures of colonial Australia. The sometimes historical characters include figures as diverse as Joan of Arc and the negotiators of the Armistice at the end of World War I. His fiction is also forthright, coherent, and well plotted; and the books often make the best-selling lists both in Australia and overseas. But this vast output, variety, readability, and literary success has made some critics suspicious. After all, how can someone so prolific, so widespread in his concerns, so enjoyable to read, and so well received by the general public be considered a serious writer? (Needless to say, not all 19 novels have attained equal success, and the forgettable ones have gone out of print.) In 1982 Keneally received the distinguished British literary award, the Booker Prize, for *Schindler's Ark*.

Keneally has been dismissed as a mere chronicler of current happenings or, even worse, a historical novelist; and he has been accused of externalizing his characters. The best of his books, however, re-create the texture of things past or present and establish the reality of the people who act out these events. But the characters are more than adept actors on a well-set stage. They are ultimately attempting to come to terms with themselves, and are seeking their personal salvation. To an extent, then, Keneally tells—in different garb, place, and time—the same story over and again. The most succinct description of this impressive body of work came from Keneally himself when he defined the past as "a parable about the present."

Born in New South Wales, Keneally studied for the Catholic priesthood but did not take orders. That background figures heavily in his work. Since 1970 he has devoted himself to writing, with some part-time teaching assignments. He now spends considerable time in the United States.

NOVELS BY KENEALLY

Blood Red, Sister Rose. 1974. Hodder 1991 $12.95. ISBN 0-34-03659-43. Subtitled in its American edition *A Novel of the Maid of Orleans*.

Bring Larks and Heroes. 1967. Viking Penguin 1988 $6.95. ISBN 0-14-010929-3. Both an authentic picture of convict life and a universal portrayal of suffering, the quest for salvation, and human destiny.

The Chant of Jimmie Blacksmith. 1972. Viking Penguin 1983 $6.95. ISBN 0-14-006973-9. Based on the story of an Aboriginal who murders several white settlers during the colonial period.

The Confederates. 1979. Hodder 1988 $12.95. ISBN 03-40431-03-2. Depicts the battles and personal struggles of the American Civil War.

Flying Hero Class. 1991. Warner Bks. 1992 $10.99. ISBN 0-446-39347-9. Depicts the hijacking of a plane by terrorists, focusing on an Aboriginal dance troupe and their white manager.

Gossip from the Forest. 1975. HarBraceJ 1985 $6.95. ISBN 0-15-636469-7. Imagines what the major figures did and thought during the signing of the World War I armistice.

The Playmaker. 1987. Hodder 1988 $12.95. ISBN 03-40422-63-7. The production of a play during the convict period in Australia; based on historical fact.

Schindler's Ark. 1982. (U.S. title: *Schindler's List*). Viking Penguin 1983 $8.95. ISBN 0-14-006784-1. The story of an actual German industrialist who saved Jews from the gas chambers.

To Asmara. 1989. Warner Bks. 1990 $10.95. ISBN 0-446-39171-9. The outward actions and personal struggles of an Australian reporter's visit to war-torn Eritrea.

Three Cheers for the Paraclete. 1968. Viking Penguin 1988 $12.99. ISBN 0-14-0030-99-9. Records a priest's difficulties with his superiors.

McAULEY, JAMES. 1917–1976

From the beginning of his poetic career, and as a critic and the editor-founder of *Quadrant*—a conservative journal of opinion and the arts—James McAuley injected an influential conservative element into the Australian literary scene. He was also a professor of English at the University of Tasmania.

During the 1940s he attempted to weaken the nationalist Jindyworobak and avant-garde Angry Penguin movements with arguments for formal control in poetry. In *Quadrant,* he wrote: "Subtlety, complexity and balance are all on the side of traditional verse. It provides the best combination of freedom and order." A religious Catholic, in his prose writings he emerges a staunch advocate for what he considered traditional values in opposition to secularism and Communism. The finely executed poetry—much of it based on classical mythology—is far less didactic. By examining the past, it looks askance at the weaknesses of modern civilization and affirms what McAuley considered was the unchanging nature of spiritual and moral conditions. Many see McAuley as an enemy of modernism, a view that has dampened the reception of his work in recent years. The editor of the 1988 collection *James McAuley: Poetry, Essays and Personal Commentary* argues for a more complex view of the poet and his eight volumes of verse, and sets out to place him in an international context.

Work by McAuley

James McAuley: Poetry, Essays and Personal Commentary. Ed. by Leonie Kramer. U. of Queensland Pr. 1988 $17.95. ISBN 0-70221-925-8

MALOUF, DAVID. 1934–

David Malouf's fiction and poetry has gained a wide audience both in Australia and overseas. His first volume of poetry, *Bicycle and Other Poems,* appeared in 1970, and his first novel, *Johnno,* in 1975. A bildungsroman, *Johnno* is based on Malouf's childhood in Brisbane during World War II. Not only does the novel provide a sensitive picture of a boy growing into maturity, but it captures time and place with immense effectiveness—that is, the provincial, tropical city of Brisbane threatened by Japanese invasion while being overrun with U.S. soldiers. Malouf's second novel, *An Imaginary Life* (1978), moves far away from Australia and the twentieth century as it tells the story of the Roman poet Ovid during the last years of his life, in exile.

What may be his finest novel so far, *Harland's Half Acre* (1984), traces the development of an Australian painter who gains an international reputation. The exquisitely structured narrative balances the ordinary life with the artistic life, and at the same time examines the condition of the artist in a postcolonial society. In an interview, Malouf said that fiction gives "a life to people who are living inside what comes to be called history but who don't appear on the page of any history." This statement aptly describes *The Great World* (1990), the story of ordinary Australian soldiers held prisoners in Japanese-occupied Singapore and Malaysia during World War II. Malouf has also published four novellas and a play, and he wrote the libretto for the opera *Voss,* based on the novel by Patrick White. The novellas demonstrate further the wide spectrum of Malouf's fiction. For example, *Child's Play* (1981), based on fact, documents the actions of an Italian terrorist as he prepares to assassinate a great writer, while *Fly Away Peter* (1981) tells the story of an Australian who fights in World War I, juxtaposing the peaceful Queensland landscape where the central character watched birds against the horror of the trenches.

Like the fiction, Malouf's poetry ranges widely in themes and embraces both his Australian and European experiences. Urbane in tone, versatile in subject matter, original in execution, finely tuned stylistically, Malouf's work extends a view of the past and present that he defined in an interview: "Simply not seeing the world as separate events . . . but seeing the world as an evolving, fluid process."

NOVELS BY MALOUF

The Great World. 1990. Pantheon 1991 $21.50. ISBN 0-679-40176-8
Harland's Half Acre. 1984. Viking Penguin 1985 $11.99. ISBN 01-400746-94
An Imaginary Life. 1978. Braziller 1985 $6.95. ISBN 0-8076-1114-X
Johnno. 1975. Viking Penguin 1990 $12.99. ISBN 01-400425-63

NOVELLAS BY MALOUF

Child's Play. 1981. Viking Penguin 1990 $12.99. ISBN 01-400701-68
Fly Away Peter. 1981. Viking Penguin 1985 $11.99. ISBN 01-4007015-X

POETRY BY MALOUF

Selected Poems. 1980. Angus & Robertson AT 1981 $7.95. ISBN 02-071410-88. A variety of poems collected from his earlier books of poetry.

BOOK ABOUT MALOUF

Neilsen, Phillip. *Imagined Lives: A Study of David Malouf*. U. of Queensland Pr. 1990 $29.95. ISBN 07-0222-27-47. A thematic approach to the novels, the fictional techniques used, and the relationship between Malouf's poetry and fiction.

MURRAY, LES. 1938–

Born on a dairy farm in rural New South Wales, Les Murray has emerged, since he started publishing in the 1960s, as one of Australia's major poets. His dozen or so volumes of poetry cover a wide range of topics and draw for the most part from the Australian experience. He has, however, gained an appreciative audience overseas. Formerly a translator, Murray decided in 1971 to become what he called "a flagrant full-time poet." Since then he has supported himself as a poet, critic, and anthologist; his major accomplishment in the latter field is *The New Oxford Book of Australian Verse* (1986).

Murray's work—some of it in free verse, some formal—is rooted deeply in the dairy-farming country on the Australian coast where he grew up and now lives. His poetry celebrates the simplicity of rural life and the people whose values stem from the land, and warns modern society against shunning such values. Sometimes witty and often homely in subject matter, the poetry displays an adventurous handling of language, carries religious overtones, and offers a well-grounded philosophical basis.

POETRY BY MURRAY

The Daylight Moon and Other Poems. Persea Bks. 1988 $9.95. ISBN 0-89255-138-0. Collection of newer poems.
The Vernacular Republic. Persea Bks. 1982 $8.95. ISBN 0-89255-063-5. Collection of poems focusing on the common people and their lives.

WORK BY MURRAY

The New Oxford Book of Australian Verse. OUP 1986 $39.95. ISBN 0-89255-125-9. A broad representation of Australian poetry.

NAROGIN, MUDROOROO. 1939–

Originally publishing under the name Colin Johnson, this Aboriginal writer took a tribal name in 1988, Mudrooroo Narogin. The most widely known and generally considered the foremost Aboriginal writer, Narogin published his first novel, *Wild Cat Falling,* in 1965; it was also the first novel to be published by an Aboriginal writer in Australia. Although fiction remains his major achievement, Narogin also publishes poetry, which is distinctive mainly because it draws from Aboriginal tradition and mythology. He publishes extensively about Aboriginal literature as well and often employs postmodern theory; this criticism is in part a manifesto for the cause of Aboriginal writing.

Born in Western Australia and reared in a Catholic orphanage, Narogin as a young man moved to the more cosmopolitan Melbourne, where he worked in the state's civil service and began writing. Both *Wild Cat Falling* (1965) and the novel that followed, *Long Live Sandawara* (1979), are conventional in structure and deal with alienated Aboriginal heroes living on the fringes of society. The first novel records the trials of a young Aboriginal adrift and isolated in an uncaring white world. His reaction is to attack, and eventually he faces arrest on a charge of attempted murder. While he awaits the police, he talks with a wise old Aborigine, who restores his sense of identity and purpose. *Long Live Sandawara* narrates the struggles of a young and idealistic Aborigine who attempts unsuccessfully to establish a resistance group in the Western Australian city of Perth. Taking its title and central image from the legendary Aboriginal figure of Sandawara, who had resisted white settlement, the novel ends on a positive note in spite of the hero's immediate failure. Narogin's most successful novel is *Doctor Wooreddy's Prescription for Enduring the Ending of the World* (1983). In a highly original way, the book relates the history of Tasmania during the nineteenth century, when the white settlers extinguished, at first through casual slaughter and later through neglect, all the Aborigines living on the Tasmanian island, off the southern coast of Australia. The work sidesteps the pitfalls of direct blame or bitterness, but tells the horrible story through an imaginative and at times fantastic re-creation of the precontact Aboriginal world and the devastation of that Eden by white settlers, including whalers, convicts, and an actual missionary much involved in the final stages of the tragedy.

In 1988, the year Australia celebrated 200 years of white settlement, Narogin published a new version of his first novel, this one called *Doin Wildcat: A Novel "Koori" Script as Constructed by Mudrooroo Narogin.* One critic noted that when the 1965 text and the 1988 text are placed side by side, "we see the way *Doin Wildcat* absorbs the Aboriginality he has been exploring and the postmodernism he has been exploiting and doing so inside the Aboriginal vernacular . . . , [and] then we begin to understand Narogin and *Doin Wildcat* as speaking to the coming together after a long struggle of a writer, a culture, a people, a body of work." Narogin has taken a long journey in his fiction from the cliché of alienation in the first novels to the absorption of Aboriginality in the book that came almost 25 years later.

NOVELS BY NAROGIN

(AS COLIN JOHNSON)

Doctor Wooreddy's Prescription for Enduring the Ending of the World. 1983. Ballantine 1983 $3.95. ISBN 0-345-36342-6

Long Live Sandawara. 1979. Hyland Hse. AT 1987 $12.95. ISBN 09-470620-17

Wild Cat Falling. 1965. Angus & Robertson AT 1987 $8.95. ISBN 02-071439-35

(AS MUDROOROO NAROGIN)

Doin Wildcat. 1988. Hyland Hse. AT 1988 $19.95. ISBN 09-470624-59

RICHARDSON, HENRY HANDEL (pseud. of Ethel Florence Lindesay Richardson). 1870–1946

An expatriate writer, Henry Handel Richardson wrote one of Australia's classic works, *The Fortunes of Richard Mahony* (1917–1929). The three novels that make up this trilogy, *Australia Felix* (1917), *The Way Home* (1925), and *Ultima Thule* (1929), unfold the saga of Richard Mahony, a character loosely based on Richardson's physician-father. The trilogy is often labeled—not always in a complimentary manner—as "naturalistic," a literary form not currently popular. In recent years, however, readers have begun to approach it in different ways. For example, feminist critics have called attention to the novels' strong women, who provide the strength for the new nation. The trilogy has also been examined as an incisive psychological study of failure revealed through the complex character of Mahony. The novels are so rich in texture that they can also be read as late nineteenth- and early twentieth-century social history, depicting as they do day-to-day life in the goldmining town of Balaraat and the colonial city of Melbourne.

Richardson was born in Melbourne, but after her father's death her nearly destitute mother took up the duties of postmistress in a country town. At the age of 13, Richardson became a boarder at the Presbyterian Ladies' College in Melbourne. The experiences there she later used as the basis for *The Getting of Wisdom* (1910), which was turned into a highly successful film that helped to revive interest in Richardson's work. After graduating from this preparatory school, she received a musical scholarship to provide for further training in Leipzig; her mother had hopes of a career for her daughter as a concert pianist. Later Richardson would use her experiences in Germany as the basis of her first novel, *Maurice Guest* (1908). Instead of pursuing a concert career, however, Richardson married a Scottish professor of German and settled in London, remaining there and in the English countryside until her death. She returned to Australia only once or twice after her departure as a young girl; but in her imagination she must have gone back many times. In recognition of her literary achievements, Richardson was awarded the Australian Gold Medal and the King George Jubilee Medal.

NOVELS BY RICHARDSON

The Fortunes of Richard Mahony. 1917–29. Viking Penguin 1982 $14.95. ISBN 0-14-00613-98

The Getting of Wisdom. 1910. Mandarin 1990 $10.95. ISBN 1-86-3300-57-0

BOOK ABOUT RICHARDSON

McLeod, Karen. *Henry Handel Richardson.* Cambridge U. Pr. 1985 $55.00. ISBN 0-52-1130-30-44. Argues that Richardson deserves higher regard as a writer, for her depiction of human relationships.

SHUTE, NEVIL (pseud. of Nevil Shute Norway). 1899–1960

Born in London, Nevil Shute earned a degree in engineering at Oxford, and then established an aircraft construction company. In 1938, he sold his company interests to become a full-time writer. He emigrated with his family to Australia in 1950 to a farm in Langwarin, Victoria. Nevil Shute was a prolific writer who explored widely disparate themes and situations. *In the Wet* is a wry account of the Queen of England's decision to move from Britain to progressive Australia. In *On the Beach* (1957), Australia became the last refuge for a world ravaged by nuclear war. Shute's hugely successful *A Town Like Alice* (1950) is the story of an Australian soldier and a woman who survive a Japanese death march during World War II. Internationally respected, Shute's work has also found an appreciative audience in the popular market.

Novels by Shute

The Breaking Wave. 1955. Ballantine 1988 $3.50. ISBN 0-345-32173-1

The Chequer Board. 1947. Ballantine 1988 $3.50. ISBN 0-345-00743-3

Most Secret. 1945. Ballantine 1988 $3.95. ISBN 0-345-00709-3

On the Beach. 1957. Ballantine 1983 $3.95. ISBN 0-345-31148-5. In Australia the survivors of a nuclear war wait for the end of human life.

The Rainbow and the Rose. 1958. Ballantine 1988 $2.95. ISBN 0-345-32251-7

A Town like Alice. 1950. Ballantine 1987 $3.95. ISBN 0-345-35374-9

SLESSOR, KENNETH. 1901–1971

Variously called Australia's first modern poet, the father of modern Australian poetry, and "the master craftsman of them all," Kenneth Slessor continues to be admired in Australia and abroad for a comparatively small body of work. Yet one of his critics, Herbert C. Jaffa, has said that "some of [Slessor's] poems are among the most important written in English in modern literature." His work has been praised for its startling images, for its melding of the emotional and intellectual, for its brilliant language, and for the control it exercises over the poetic process. Slessor drew from his Australian experience for the most part, but lent that experience a universality not always present in the country's earlier poetry. Two of his poems, which many readers consider examples of Australia's finest poetry, are frequently anthologized: "Five Bells," an elegy for a friend, and "Beach Burial," a chilling and unforgettable reminder of the horrors of war.

Except for light verse, Slessor wrote no poetry for the last 25 years of his life. Born in Australia, he was a journalist by profession and spent most of his life in Sydney, where he worked on newspapers in various positions, including a distinguished tenure as a book reviewer. In World War II he served as an overseas correspondent for a Sydney newspaper. The dispatches and diary of his experiences have been collected in *The War Diaries*. Through his work as an editor and critic, along with his active involvement in literary circles, Slessor exerted a strong and lasting influence during a critical juncture in the development of Australian literature.

Works by Slessor

Kenneth Slessor. Ed. by Dennis Haskell. U. of Queensland Pr. 1991 Collection of Slessor's poetry, newspaper articles, letters, and other writings.

The War Diaries of Kenneth Slessor. Ed. by Clement Semmler. Intl. Spec. Bk. 1988 $44.95. ISBN 0-7022-2076-0

BOOK ABOUT SLESSOR

Dutton, Geoffrey. *Kenneth Slessor: A Biography*. Viking Penguin 1991 $30.00. ISBN 0-670-83268-5. A well-researched, well-written account of the poet and his work.

STEAD, CHRISTINA. 1902–1983

Although Christina Stead often castigated feminists and ridiculed the whole feminist movement, her novels focus heavily on the limited roles open for women, the social expectations that control their lives, and the economic forces that subdue them. That Stead's work enjoys a wide acceptance internationally depends in large part on feminist critics and readers. The book considered her masterpiece, *The Man Who Loved Children* (1940), appears on reading lists in feminist studies courses the world over. This is not to say that Stead's work has no appeal for men, who have been some of her most devoted supporters and critics.

In her mid-20s, Stead left her native Australia for England, where she married an American writer and political activist, William Blake. For the next 40 years she and Blake lived in Europe and the United States; at one point Stead worked as a script writer in Hollywood. Over the years she published several novels, which met with little success. In 1965, however, she received at last the acclaim she deserved, when an American publisher reissued the 1940 novel, *The Man Who Loved Children*. (1940) The rediscovery of this book brought international attention, even in her native country, which had long ignored her and had even banned one of her novels, *Letty Fox* (1946), as pornographic. Stead's other long out-of-print books also became available. Soon after this turning point in Stead's fortunes, her husband died and she wrote little more. Some previously unpublished and some new work appeared, but none of it reached the level of the earlier fiction. After the loss of the man she had once called "my home," Stead returned to Australia for the first time and eventually settled there. She died in Sydney, the city of her birth.

Except for *Seven Poor Men of Sydney* (1934), an impressionistic account of Sydney life, and the first half of her *bildungsroman, For Love Alone* (1944), none of the fiction is set in Australia. Once the stifling early life of the central character of *For Love Alone* has been fully documented, the novel moves to her adventures in London. One of Stead's less widely known early works is *House of All Nations* (1938), which deals with international banking and finance. *Letty Fox: Her Luck* uses an American setting to chronicle the life of a promiscuous young woman who rebels against her set role. But it is *The Man Who Loved Children* on which Stead's reputation rests. Set in Baltimore and the surrounding area, this account of Samuel Clemens Pollit and his effect on his family was praised by the American poet RANDALL JARRELL (see Vol. 1) as containing a "frightening power of remembrance." The book most frequently discussed, *The Man Who Loved Children* has been interpreted—to name but a few approaches—from Freudian, Marxist, feminist, autobiographical, mythical, Gothic, and sexual standpoints. Whatever the perspective taken on her work, Stead—an Australian writer only by accident of birth—belongs to the highest rank of international writers in English.

NOVELS BY STEAD

For Love Alone. 1944. Sirius 1987 $12.95. ISBN 0-20-71581-69
House of All Nations. 1938. Sirius 1988 $19.95. ISBN 0-20-71602-87
Letty Fox: Her Luck. 1946. Imprint 1991 $16.95. ISBN 0-20-71663-82
The Man Who Loved Children. 1940. Viking Penguin 1985 $15.99. ISBN 0-14-01818-22

Seven Poor Men of Sydney. 1934. Angus & Robertson AT $9.95. ISBN 0-20-71404-64

BOOKS ABOUT STEAD

Lidoff, Joan. *Christina Stead*. Continuum 1982 $18.95. ISBN 0-8044-2520-5. Concentrates on *The Man Who Loved Children* and *For Love Alone*, using a feminist approach.

Williams, Chris. *Christina Stead—a Life of Letters*. McPhee Gribble 1989 $24.99. ISBN 0-8691-4046-9. First biography of Stead, relying on many unpublished materials; well-written and researched.

STOW, RANDOLPH. 1935–

Born in Western Australia and educated at the university there, Stow wrote his first novels while he was an undergraduate. He has lived in England since 1966. His third novel, *To the Islands* (1958), received Australia's distinguished Miles Franklin Award for Fiction, a high honor for so young a writer. The novel unfolds the surreal saga of Herriot, a disillusioned missionary whose loss of faith compels him to embark on a pilgrimage of self-discovery through the desert to the Aboriginal islands of the dead. The desert landscape also serves as the setting for *Tourmaline* (1963), a fable in which a water diviner comes to a drought-ridden settlement promising water but discovering gold. *The Merry-Go-Round in the Sea* (1965) relies much less on the allusive symbolism characteristic of Stow's other work; instead, it records a boy's transition to adolescence against the background of a remote settlement on the far side of Australia. In *The Visitants* (1979) Stow fictionalizes his experiences as an assistant to the government anthropologist of Papua, New Guinea, but this metaphysical adventure in the tropics has little to do with autobiography. *Suburbs of Hell* (1984) reveals a series of brutal, motiveless murders that take place in an English village. Also set in England and making use of British myth, *The Girl Green as Elderflower* (1980) traces the recuperation of a man who has experienced strange things in his past.

Stow's work is widely admired, both in Australia and abroad, for the expression of Taoist philosophy, a heightened artistry, an extended use of symbolism, and surreal qualities, even as it handles mainly Australian materials. Critics consider Stow an important influence on younger writers who have followed him in breaking away from the realistic molds that long constricted Australian fiction.

NOVELS BY STOW

The Girl Green as Elderflower. 1980 o.p.
The Merry-Go-Round in the Sea. 1965. Viking Penguin 1968 $11.99. ISBN 0-1400-2835-8
Suburbs of Hell. 1984 o.p.
To the Islands. 1958 o.p.
Tourmaline: A Novel. 1963. Viking Penguin 1984 $7.95. ISBN 0-1400-7032-X
Visitants: A Novel. 1979 o.p.

BOOK ABOUT STOW

Hassall, Anthony J. *Strange Country: A Study of Randolph Stow*. U. of Queensland Pr. 1986 $29.95. ISBN 0-702222-73-9. Stow as a metaphysical novelist more interested in his characters' spiritual relations than in their personal ones.

WHITE, PATRICK. 1912–1990 (NOBEL PRIZE 1973)

Patricia Morely, one of Patrick White's early critics, wrote that "Out of tension and the many selves came the work that made White the greatest novelist writing in English in the twentieth century." While some might disagree with this assessment, no one could truthfully argue with White's great achievement. His twelve novels, written over nearly 50 years, focus again and again on spiritual longing. White sifts the human race into one part practical, the other impractical. The practical people settle into a life of doing, and the impractical ones—the visionaries—reach for a life of being. But in human terms even the visionaries fail to satisfy their longing for spiritual understanding. Their quest is never complete, for the novels maintain a nervous, unsettled energy, failing in their open endings to reach the completeness of understanding for which they strive so hard. White's writing style is cohesive with this central theme of the movement toward being. Although the stylistic elements have been criticized, especially the tortured syntax, they must be accepted and appreciated as inseparable from which is being said. For White's language struggles, too, and sometimes fails, along with the characters and their actions. Finally, the novels are not all solemnity but record as well the comic side of the irrational and illogical world in which men and women are placed to seek some sort of meaning.

A fifth-generation Australian from a wealthy landowning family, White was educated in England, served in World War II, and then settled in Sydney, where he wrote his major novels. Always fascinated by the theater, he also wrote several plays, but they never met with the success his fiction has and have not been produced outside Australia.

White's initial reputation was made in the United States and Europe, where his work first received publication. Few Australian critics recognized the greatness of these novels, which would alter the face of Australian literature. Although most of White's work is set in Australia, he handled the traditional materials in new ways, turning away from the realistic tradition of Australian fiction and moving into metaphysical realms. Once White received the Nobel Prize, the first writer of the British Commonwealth to be so honored, the resistance in Australia toward his work largely faded. Yet he remains an international figure. His work has been translated into many languages, and the abundant criticism that continues to appear comes from all parts of the world.

White's first novel, *Happy Valley* (1939), unmasks the frustration and spiritual desolation of a bush town's inhabitants. Perhaps his weakest work was published next, *The Living and the Dead* (1941), set in pre-World War II London. The novel many consider one of his best, *The Aunt's Story* (1948), chronicles the desolation of Theodora Goodman, an Australian woman whose quest carries her from her native land to Europe and America. *The Tree of Man* (1955), published seven years later, reveals the outwardly mundane lives of an ordinary Australian farm couple, while examining the possibilities of their inner being. *Voss* (1957), which some consider White's greatest work, reverses the myth of heroism as it traces the explorations of a German in the Australian desert. *Riders in the Chariot* (1961) reveals the outer and inner lives of the four visionaries who ride in the chariot: A half-mad daughter of a once-aristocratic family, an Aboriginal painter, a washerwoman, and a Jewish refugee. Two brothers figure in *The Solid Mandala* (1966), one a visionary, the other a practical and doomed man. In *The Vivisector* (1970), an Australian painter, whose art records his spiritual quest, is portrayed. *The Eye of the Storm* (1973), one of White's most sophisticated novels, centers on the deathbed of Elizabeth Hunter. *A Fringe of Leaves* (1976), set in Australia's colonial period, tells the story of Ellen Roxburgh, whose capture by Aborigines deepens her understanding. Three figures in one dominate *The Twyborn Affair* (1979); this story of Eddie, who as a transvestite becomes Eudoxia in his early life and Eadie in his maturity, holds one of White's most original treatments of his recurrent themes. His final novel, *Memoirs of Many in One, by Alex Xenophon Demirjian Gray* (1986), is a reprise of the themes and characters White explored for half a century.

Novels by White

The Aunt's Story. 1948. Viking Penguin 1963 $9.95. ISBN 0-14004-14-51
The Eye of the Storm. 1973. Viking Penguin 1975 $10.99. ISBN 0-14-003963-5
A Fringe of Leaves. 1976. Viking Penguin 1984 $8.95. ISBN 0-14-004409-4
Happy Valley. Viking Penguin 1939 o.p.
The Living and the Dead. 1941. AMS Pr. 1991 $28.50. ISBN 0-404-15240-6
Memoirs of Many in One, by Alex Xenophon Demirjian Gray. 1986. Viking Penguin 1988 $6.95. ISBN 0-14-009426-1.
Riders in the Chariot. 1961. Viking Penguin 1985 $8.95. ISBN 0-14-002185-X
The Solid Mandala. Viking Penguin 1966 $11.95. ISBN 0-14-002975-3
The Tree of Man. 1955. Viking Penguin 1963 $9.95. ISBN 0-1400-16-75-0
The Twyborn Affair. 1979 o.p.
The Vivisector. 1970. Viking Penguin 1986 $6.95. ISBN 0-14-003693-8
Voss. 1957. Viking Penguin $9.95. ISBN 0-14-001438-1

Short Story Collections by White

The Burnt Ones. 1964. Viking Penguin 1966 $14.99. ISBN 0-14-002776-9. Contains one of White's best-known short stories, "Down at the Dump."
The Cockatoos, Shorter Novels and Stories. 1974. Viking Penguin 1978 $12.95. ISBN 0-14-004463-9. Six rather long works, set in Australia and abroad.
Three Uneasy Pieces. Pascoe Pub. AT 1987 $7.95. ISBN 0-94-708713-3. White's last published fiction, reflecting on a life of art.

Plays by White

Big Toys. 1978 o.p. Examines greed, sex, and corruption in contemporary Sydney.
Collected Plays. 1965. Currency Pr. 1985 $19.95. Contains *Ham Funeral, The Season at Sarsaparilla, A Cheery Soul, Night on Bald Mountain.*
Netherwood. Currency Pr. AT 1983 $8.95. ISBN 0-86-819071-3. Reveals the peculiar happenings in a large Australian country manor.
The Night of the Prowler, Short Story and Screenplay. 1978 o.p. Focuses on violence in contemporary life.
Signal Driver. Currency Pr. AT 1983 $11.95. ISBN 0-86-819068-3. Two people waiting all their lives for a metaphysical bus to take them to their ill-defined destination.

Work by White

Flaws in the Glass: A Self-Portrait. 1981. Viking Penguin 1983 $6.95. ISBN 0-14-006293-9. An honest examination of White's childhood, friends, enemies, writing, and "sexual ambivalence."

Books about White

Bliss, Carolyn. *Patrick White's Fiction: The Paradox of Fortunate Failure*. St. Martin 1986 $25.00. ISBN 0-312-59805. Argues that the failures expressed in the characters' lives sometimes lead to redemption.
Edgecombe, Rodney Stenning. *Vision and Style in Patrick White: A Study of Five Novels*. U. of Ala. Pr. 1989 $24.50. ISBN 0-8173-0407-X. Concentrates on five novels, *Voss, Riders in the Chariot, The Solid Mandala, The Vivisector,* and *The Eye of the Storm.*
Marr, David. 1991. *Patrick White: A Life*. Knopf 1992 $30.00. ISBN 0-394-57435-4. An authorized but unvarnished account of White as a person and an artist.
Tacey, David. *Patrick White: Fiction and the Unconscious*. OUP 1988 $42.50. ISBN 0-19-554867-1. An argument, based on Jungian ideas, that White's unconscious mind dominates his fiction.

Wolfe, Peter, ed. *Critical Essays on Patrick White*. G. K. Hall 1990 $40.00. ISBN 0-8161-8846-7. Includes essays by White, famous reviews of his books, and articles on various aspects of his work.

WILLIAMSON, DAVID. 1942–

The author of 15 plays, as well as numerous screen and television scripts, David Williamson is certainly Australia's most prolific playwright. He is also the country's most popular dramatist and the one best known abroad. Finally, most critics and general theatergoers would agree that he is the best playwright Australia has produced so far. Although his screenplays move into areas outside Australia, the plays remain fixed in his native land. Always well received in Australia, they have also been successful in Europe and the United States. Williamson's greatest achievement, then, lies in the way he makes universal that experience peculiar to Australians.

Born in a small town near Melbourne, Williamson did not appear destined for a theatrical career. While majoring in engineering in college, he began writing for campus productions, and soon turned to a career as a playwright.

Not particularly experimental, each play is marked by firm structure, exact sense of place, vivid language, satire, and comedy. These elements cohere to reveal believable characters facing often ordinary conflicts. Their responses are sometimes mundane and muddled, and rarely does a resolution take place. Among his works of the 1970s, *The Removalists* (1971) uses techniques of theater of cruelty. The plot revolves around police violence against individuals as a metaphor for gratuitous violence in society. *Don's Party* (1971) reveals the public and personal frustrations of a group of professional men and women at an election day party. In *The Coming of Stork*, a group of educated, urban young men and women seek their places in the social structure. The adverse role the Vietnam War played in Australian society is depicted in *Jugglers Three*, while *What If You Died Tomorrow* dramatizes the effect of fame on marriage and family relationships. Later plays include *Travelling North* (1980), *The Perfectionist* (1982), *Sons of Cain* (1985), *Emerald City* (1987), and *Top Silk* (1990).

Williamson has addressed a number of themes, many relevant to Australian society and to cultures in other parts of the world. Yet his plays are never didactic; they entertain first, and then challenge the viewer. Insisting that his work is naturalistic, Williamson does indeed create a very real picture of life. Always, though, the reality is tempered by comedy and by a sympathetic attitude toward the characters inhabiting the imaginary world of the stage—a world in which viewers at times see themselves and their own foibles exposed.

PLAYS BY WILLIAMSON

The Club (U.S.title, *Players*). Currency Pr. AT 1978 $11.95. ISBN 08-681901-36. Reveals behind-the-game politics in a Melbourne football club.

Collected Plays. Currency Pr. 1986 $19.95. ISBN 08-681911-08. Includes many of Williamson's earlier plays.

The Department. 1974. Currency Pr. AT 1988 o.p. Records a departmental meeting in a technical college, stressing compromise and personal ambition.

Emerald City. 1987. Applause Theatre Bk. Pubs. 1991 $7.95. ISBN 1-55783-055-X. Depicts an artist who faces the moral choice between making money and preserving his integrity.

The Perfectionist. Currency Pr. AT 1983 $11.95. ISBN 08-681906-91. Examines the hypocrisy that often occurs in marriage, through a focus on an Australian professor and his wife.

Sons of Cain. 1985. Currency Pr. AT 1988 $11.95. ISBN 08-681917-95. Addresses corruption in high places and the media's refusal to expose it, in a play about newspaper people.

Top Silk. Currency Pr. AT 1990 $11.95. ISBN 08-68192-63-5. Portrays successful parents whose son is a potential dropout, revealing divisions between public and private life.

Travelling North. Currency Pr. AT 1980 $11.95. ISBN 08-681927-08. A story of a couple who remarry in old age and leave grown but dependent children to fend for themselves.

Book about Williamson

Kiernan, Brian. *David Williamson—a Writer's Career.* Heinemann Ed. 1990 $45.95. ISBN 0-85561-357-2. Chronicles Williamson's personal life along with his development as a writer.

WRIGHT, JUDITH. 1915–

Born and reared in the pastoral country of New South Wales, Judith Wright returned to this area during World War II, after attending the University of Sydney and traveling in Europe. It was a significant homecoming, for she rediscovered her heritage and put that rediscovery into poetry. She wrote about the beautiful region known as New England, those who peopled it—both the descendants of white settlers and the Aborigines. Her first book, *The Moving Image*, appeared in 1946, and was enthusiastically received, the poems admired for their lyricism and honesty. Like other writers emerging at this time, she employed Australian materials in a new way, no longer seeing them in a literal sense. Wright continued to publish poetry for the next 30 years, 14 or so volumes in all, as well as making important contributions as a critic and anthologist. Although her early poems are still admired, often anthologized in Australia and abroad, the later work has faded.

Turning away from poetry in recent years, Wright has written extensively about the environment and the treatment of Aboriginals, and has also become an articulate public defender of these causes. Her book about white Australia's destruction of Aborigines, *The Cry for the Dead* (1981), stresses the vacuum that the disappearing Aboriginal culture has left both in nature and Australian society, and reveals the guilt felt by white Australians aware of the genocide practiced by earlier generations.

Even though Bruce Bennett, one of Wright's critics, admits that her poetry has gone "off the boil," he sees this as "a temporary phenomenon" and believes that the "informing ecological vision so deeply rooted in her work since her first book of poems, *The Moving Image*, is ever more urgently relevant."

Poetry by Wright

Collected Poems. Angus & Robertson AT 1982 $8.95. ISBN 0-207-13219-4. An excellent selection of Wright's poetry, including the best-known works.

Works by Wright

The Cry for the Dead. OUP 1981 $32.50. ISBN 0-19-554296-7

Generations of Men. OUP 1965 $16.95. ISBN 0-19-550295-7. An autobiographical work that records Wright's family history, going back to the early settlement of Australia.

Book about Wright

Walker, Shirley. *Flame and Shadow.* U. of Queensland Pr. 1991 $29.95. ISBN 07-0222-3522. A thorough study of Wright's work that stresses the lyrical qualities of the poetry.

CHAPTER 26

New Zealand Literature

Robert L. Ross

> Here we discover what we ought always to have known, that for New Zealand literature the way out is the way in; and that what is most exclusively ours is what is "embrac'd and open to most men."
>
> —ALLEN CURNOW, "New Zealand Literature: The Case for a Working Definition"

New Zealand poet and critic Allen Curnow places his country's literature in an international context as he seeks a "working definition" for this significant body of novels, plays, poetry, and essays that belongs to the larger body of writing in English. Curnow disputes the idea sometimes still held in countries of the former British Commonwealth; that is, their literature is somehow inferior to the writing from Great Britian and the United States; it is good enough for home consumption but not good enough for attention in other parts of the world. Further, he sees New Zealand writers both drawing from and contributing to world literature. Certainly, Curnow suggests, the writing bears the stamp of New Zealand—as is the case with any country's literature; but at the same time it reaches outward to make a statement about the human condition that crosses national borders.

New Zealand took its place in the international literary arena before the other settler countries, Canada and Australia, at least in part because of KATHERINE MANSFIELD's reputation in the early twentieth century. Again fortunate, New Zealand can claim one of the English language's greatest contemporary novelists, JANET FRAME, whose work has received acclaim wherever English is read. Although Frame sometimes sets her work in other parts of the world, it always returns to her New Zealand experience, making this remote nation of two tiny islands a focal point, the locus for her way of seeing life.

Settled first a thousand or so years ago by Polynesians, the islands that came to be known as New Zealand are spectacularly beautiful, green, and fertile. The British colonists who started arriving in the nineteenth century found the countryside reminded them of England—a major attraction, indeed, for the homesick settlers thousands of miles away from another "emerald isle." As the years passed, its inhabitants sometimes called their land "God's Own Country," a label that has been shortened to "Godzone." Never a convict colony like Australia and a land more hospitable to settlement than its neighboring enclave of British settlers, New Zealand has always maintained a stronger British influence in its customs, attitudes, and language. Perhaps what some have called this lingering colonial mentality hindered the development of an original literature. This may have been true before World War II, but in the years following—that period known widely as the postcolonial era—New Zealand writers have shaken off the vestiges of colonialism, have often strongly insisted that New Zealanders form their own identity.

Much of the prewar writing, the fiction and drama realistic in nature, the poetry romantic in tone, celebrated the pioneer experience or attempted to capture the landscape. And in so doing, the literature tended to suggest that it was the work of visitors, not people of European descent who had been on the land for several generations. Those who had lived there much longer, the Maoris, were simply ignored. In the postwar period, however, that has changed dramatically. Contemporary New Zealand writers, especially the legion of poets, have attempted to come to grips with the physical isolation that often evolves into a metaphorical isolation. Carrying this idea to its logical conclusion, the writers seek to establish a New Zealand identity, which they believe will come about in large part from the country's artists. But the effort will not always be an easy one. For many fiction writers of European descent have been quick to point out what they see as the society's smugness and provinciality, and the unintentional but often cruel outcome of such thinking; for example, this sort of indictment remains central to the novels of MAURICE GEE and often figures in Janet Frame's work. On the other hand, English-language writers of Polynesian descent frequently examine the inherent European prejudice toward those with different skin colors and world views.

Indeed, another major change in the postcolonial era has been the emergence of Maori writers, as well as those from the surrounding islands. In a sense these peoples had been colonized on a tertiary level; their culture, language, and customs were irretrievably altered by the subjects of the British Crown who arrived uninvited, took over, and stayed on. Writers of Maori descent, like WITI IHIMAERA, KERI HULME, and PATRICIA GRACE, and a Samoan writer like ALBERT WENDT, have started to revise the received history of imperalism—and are doing so in English, the language of the colonizers. The awareness they bring to those New Zealanders of European descent is immeasurable. Likewise, these writers join the once colonized people around the world who give fuller meaning to Salman Rushdie's words: "The Empire writes back."

C. K. Stead, in the introduction to his collection of essays on New Zealand literature, said: "When I considered the body of work discussed in this book, and all the work not discussed that might have been, I have to conclude that this country has produced good literature far in excess of statistical probability." New Zealand's population is around 3.5 million. Stead, a distinguished poet and novelist himself, is absolutely right.

HISTORY AND CRITICISM

Alpers, Antony. *The World of the Polynesians Seen through Their Myths and Legends, Poetry and Art*. OUP 1987 $11.95. ISBN 0-19-558142-3. Excellent source for background on the developing literature of the islands.

Evans, Patrick. *The Penguin History of New Zealand Literature*. Viking Penguin 1990 $24.95. ISBN 0-14-011371-1. Discusses major writers; places the literature within the context of cultural history, publishing, and the literary relationship with other English-speaking countries.

Gadd, Bernard, ed. *Other Voices: New Writers and Writing in New Zealand*. Brick Row 1989 $19.95. ISBN 0-908595-45-X. Focuses on nonestablished writers' work; varied, sometimes uneven, but always interesting.

Harcourt, Peter. *A Dramatic Appearance: New Zealand Theatre*. Playmarket 1978 $20.00. ISBN 0-456024-10-7. Chronicles the development of New Zealand theater from 1920 to 1970, focusing on all aspects—playwrights and their work, theater companies, reception, and changes over half a century.

Jones, Lawrence. *Barbed Wire and Mirrors: Essays on New Zealand Prose.* Intl. Spec. Bk. 1990 $36.95. ISBN 0-908569-53-X. A collection of Jones's reviews and articles that provide an incisive look at the way New Zealand fiction is developing.

McGregor, Graham, and Mark Williams, eds. *Dirty Silence: Aspects of Language and Literature in New Zealand.* OUP 1991 $29.95. ISBN 0-19-558227-6. Collection of essays focusing on various aspects of Maori writing, culture, and language.

Simms, Norman. *Silence and Invisibility: A Study of the Literature of the Pacific, Australia, and New Zealand.* Three Continents 1986 $26.00. ISBN 0-89410-362-8. Surveys the writing in this region and draws some comparisons.

______. *Writers from the South Pacific.* Three Continents 1991 $35.00. ISBN 0-89410-594-9. Provides an overview; a good source for reference in an area on which little material is available.

Stead, C. K. *In the Glass Case: Essays on New Zealand Literature.* OUP 1981 o.p. A collection of essays and reviews by a distinguished New Zealand critic, poet, and fiction writer.

Sturm, Terry, ed. *The Oxford History of New Zealand Literature in English.* OUP 1991 $79.95. ISBN 0-19-558211-X. A comprehensive and scholarly work that contains chapters on Maori literature, nonfiction, fiction, drama, poetry, children's literature, popular fiction, and publishing.

Subramini. *South Pacific Literature: From Myth to Fabulation.* Inst. of Pacific Studies, U. of the South Pacific 1985 o.p. Surveys the writing from the South Pacific islands.

Williams, Mark. *Leaving the Highway: Six Contemporary New Zealand Novelists.* OUP 1991 $29.95. ISBN 1-86940-044-5. Critical studies of Frame, Stead, Hulme, Ihimaera, Wedde, and Gee, with general introduction and conclusion.

COLLECTIONS

Davis, Susan, and Russell Haley, eds. *Penguin Book of Contemporary New Zealand Short Stories.* Viking Penguin 1989 $29.95. ISBN 0-14-011007-0. A representative collection of short stories, a popular form in New Zealand, from both new and established writers.

Evans, Miriama, Harvey McQueen, and Ian Wedde, eds. *Penguin Book of Contemporary New Zealand Poetry.* Viking Penguin 1989 $29.95. ISBN 0-14-058592-3. An excellent collection that stresses "plurality" and includes new and established writers and poems in many forms, showing the active and evolving state of New Zealand poetry.

Gadd, Bernard, ed. *Other Voices: New Writers and Writing in New Zealand.* Brick Row 1989 $19.95. ISBN 0-908595-45-X. Focuses on nonestablished writers' work; varied, sometimes uneven, but always interesting.

Manhire, Bill. *Six by Six.* Victoria U. Pr. 1989 $34.95. ISBN 0-86473-087-X. Includes six stories each by K. Mansfield, F. Sargeson, M. Duggan, J. Frame, P. Grace, and O. Marshall.

O'Sullivan, Vincent, ed. *An Anthology of Twentieth-Century New Zealand Poetry.* OUP 1970 $25.95. ISBN 0-19-558163-6. Still the standard work, although fairly traditional in approach.

Petrie, Barbara. *Kiwi and Emu: Anthology of Contemporary Poetry by Australian and New Zealand Women.* St. Mut. 1990 $105.00. ISBN 0-947333-05-3. Recent and varied poems by 34 Australians and 24 New Zealanders.

CHRONOLOGY OF AUTHORS

Mansfield, Katherine. 1888–1923
Sargeson, Frank. 1903–1982
Brasch, Charles Orwell. 1909–1973
Curnow, Allen. 1911–
Frame, Janet. 1924–
Baxter, James Keir. 1926–1972
Gee, Maurice. 1931–
Grace, Patricia. 1937–

Wendt, Albert. 1939–
Ihimaera, Witi. 1944–
Hulme, Keri. 1947–

BAXTER, JAMES KEIR. 1926–1972

Considered New Zealand's most significant poet, James K. Baxter has also been called "one of the most remarkable English-language poets of the mid-twentieth century" by the critic Charles Doyle. Born into an educated family in New Zealand, he spent most of his life there and became a much-loved and respected figure in his homeland. Starting out as something of a boy prodigy in the field of poetry, Baxter went on to face alcoholism, then to convert to Catholicism. In his last years, some considered him a saint as he wandered around New Zealand "barefoot, long-bearded, patched and baggy."

Baxter published his first poetry in 1944, followed by numerous other volumes of poems; his work appeared as well in chapbooks, broadsides, and pamphlets. He also wrote 20 or so plays—many of them produced successfully—4 books of literary commentary and criticism, numerous religious essays, and fiction. His *Collected Poems* runs 688 pages, but most of his work in other genres is out of print.

Believing strongly in the poet's vocation, in the poet as "prophet," Baxter was also a skilled artist. His work, which is characterized by a technical conservatism and an adherence to formality, also reflects his familiarity with a wide range of poets, including the English romantics, Greek and Latin poets, and modernists like Yeats (see Vol. 1), Hopkins (see Vol. 1), and Hardy (see Vol. 1),

Poetry by Baxter

Collected Poems. OUP 1988 $35.95. ISBN 0-19-558193-8

Book About Baxter

McKay, Frank. *The Life of James K. Baxter.* OUP 1990 $39.95. ISBN 0-19-558134-2. A thorough, scholarly, and even account of Baxter's fascinating life, and a sound discussion of his poetic accomplishment.

BRASCH, CHARLES ORWELL. 1909–1973

As a literary figure, Charles Brasch has double significance for New Zealand. In addition to his accomplishment as a poet, he was the founding editor of *Landfall.* This enormously influential journal still provides a forum for New Zealand writers, publishing both their work and criticism on it.

Born into a prosperous family, Brasch left New Zealand at age 17 to study history at St. John's College, Oxford. After extensive travel in Europe and the Near East, he returned to New Zealand. There, against his father's wishes, he decided to become a poet rather than a businessman. He established a reputation, both as a poet who wrote about his country in an inventive way and as an editor who helped to lift New Zealand literature above its colonial status. While much of his work is currently out of print, certain of the poems appear in standard anthologies.

Moving from romanticism to modernism in technique as his career progressed, Brasch used his New Zealand experience as a metaphor for a sense of personal isolation and alienation. The less-developed and rugged South Island of New Zealand often served as his landscape, which symbolized his sense of "rootlessness, exile, spiritual impoverishment," living on "an immature island nation" whose settlers of European descent did not feel at home. His work, sometimes elegiac in nature, expresses the strong desire to belong to this remote place, where "distance looks our way." Finally, Brasch's poetry extends beyond his ocean islands to make a dramatic statement on modern humankind's distance from the spiritual center.

POETRY BY BRASCH

Home Ground. Caxton 1974 o.p. Representative work that shows both his preoccupations and his technical ability.

WORK BY BRASCH

Universal Dance: Selection from the Critical Prose Writings. Ed. by J. L. Watson. U. of Otago Pr. 1981 o.p. Contains a representative sampling of the writer's work on a number of literary and artistic topics.

CURNOW, ALLEN. 1911–

Born and educated in New Zealand, Allen Curnow worked as a journalist before he started teaching in the English Department of Auckland University. He is highly regarded in New Zealand and abroad both as a poet and editor. In particular, he demonstrated his critical acumen in the influential introductions to the pioneering anthologies of New Zealand poetry that he edited, *A Book of New Zealand Verse: 1923–45* (1945, enlarged edition 1951) and *The Penguin Book of New Zealand Verse* (1960). These introductions, along with numerous articles and reviews on poetry, appear in a 1987 collection of his criticism, *Look Back Harder*.

According to C. K. Stead, Curnow's work is preoccupied with the conflict between "imagination" and "rational will." In Curnow's discussion of New Zealand poetry, he stresses the necessity of reality "prior to the poem"; he follows this precept in his own work, which most often finds its reality in the New Zealand landscape or in the places where he has traveled. But Curnow himself is a modernist poet, his work complex and intelligent, full of metaphysical conceits and allusions to literary works. His fondness for linguistic oddities shows that his disciplined and finely tuned technique does not foreclose on flexibility and invention. Although he has never gained the widespread popularity of a writer like JAMES K. BAXTER, most critics consider Curnow's work as some of New Zealand's best.

POETRY BY CURNOW

Continuum: New and Later Poems 1972–1988. Auckland U. Pr. 1988 o.p. Representative work that shows Curnow's refinement of technique and continuing development.

Selected Poems (1940–1989). Viking Penguin 1990 $49.95. ISBN 0-14-058639-3. Curnow's major work from half a century that demonstrates his poetic accomplishment.

WORK BY CURNOW

Look Back Harder: Critical Writings of Allen Curnow 1935–84. Ed. by Peter Simpson. Auckland U. Pr. 1987 o.p.

FRAME, JANET. 1924–

Janet Frame is not only New Zealand's best-known contemporary writer but also is one of the most original novelists writing in English anywhere in the world.

In 1982 the first volume of her autobiography *To the Is-Land*, appeared, followed in 1984 by *An Angel at My Table* and a year later by *The Envoy from*

Mirror City. On the one hand, these books record her life: growing up in a poor family on the South Island of New Zealand; attending the University of Otago; spending several years in a mental hospital after being mistakenly diagnosed as schizophrenic, undergoing shock treatments, then narrowly escaping a lobotomy; recovering from those experiences and concentrating on writing, traveling extensively, and establishing an international reputation. On the other hand, the autobiography focuses less on the reality of Frame's life than on the world of the imagination—what she calls "mirror city" and considers the source of her writing. The autobiography has been made into a successful film, *An Angel at My Table*.

Her first short story collection, *The Lagoon*, appeared in 1951. Since 1957 she has published 11 novels, 2 more collections of short stories, *The Reservoir* (1963) and *Snowman, Snowman* (1963), and a volume of poetry, *The Pocket Mirror* (1967). Her reputation, however, rests on the novels. The first one, *Owls Do Cry* (1957), thought to be largely autobiographical, traces the disintegration of a poor New Zealand family. In *Faces in the Water* (1961), Frame makes use of her own mental hospital experiences to create a terrifying picture of day-to-day life in such an institution. The next three novels move away from personal experience and toward the material derived from the author's "mirror city": *The Edge of the Alphabet* (1962), about language and how it affects its users; *Scented Gardens for the Blind* (1963), a story of the failure of human communication; and *A State of Siege* (1966), about a retired teacher. On one level, Frame's next novel, *Yellow Flowers in the Antipodean Room* (1969), unfolds realistically, as it tells the story of a man, mistakenly pronounced dead, whose return to life offends the people around him. *Intensive Care* (1970) imagines a family suffering in a fantasy world of eugenic ruthlessness, and *Daughter Buffalo* (1972) returns to Frame's obsessive concern with loneliness. *Living in the Maniototo* (1979) recounts the misadventures of a novelist, while *The Carpathians* (1988) looks toward the end of the world.

While Frame sets her work for the most part in New Zealand, she also makes use of her travels, so Baltimore, London, and Berkeley have also served as settings. At times the fiction takes a straightforward tone, especially when Frame exercises her considerable comic and satiric powers. In other instances, the work falls into poetry and sometimes near-indecipherable musings. A trickster with narrative and characters, Frame often leads the reader astray. However, she writes with consummate skill, in language that, in her words, "touches like a branding iron."

Novels by Frame

The Adaptable Man. 1965. Braziller 1982 $9.95. ISBN 0-8076-1285-5
The Carpathians. Braziller 1988 $17.50. ISBN 0-8076-1205-7
Daughter Buffalo. 1972. Braziller 1992 $8.95. ISBN 0-8076-1284-7
The Edge of the Alphabet. 1962. Braziller 1982 $8.95. ISBN 0-8076-1270-7
Faces in the Water. 1961. Braziller 1982 $8.95. ISBN 0-8076-0957-9
Intensive Care. 1970. Random 1987 o.p.
Living in the Maniototo. Braziller 1979 $7.95. ISBN 0-8076-0958-7
Owls Do Cry. 1957. Braziller 1982 $7.95. ISBN 0-8076-0956-0
Scented Gardens for the Blind. 1963. Braziller 1980 $4.95. ISBN 0-8076-0985-4
A State of Siege. 1966. Braziller 1981 $4.95. ISBN 0-8076-0986-2
Yellow Flowers in the Antipodean Room. Braziller 1969 o.p. Originally titled *The Rainbirds*.

NONFICTION BY FRAME

An Autobiography: To the Is-Land; An Angel at My Table; Envoy from Mirror City. Braziller 1991 $17.50. ISBN 0-8076-1259-6

SHORT STORY COLLECTION BY FRAME

The Lagoon and Other Stories. 1951. Random 1990 o.p.

GEE, MAURICE. 1931–

After working for several years as a schoolteacher and a librarian, Maurice Gee, a native New Zealander, became a full-time writer in 1976. Highly regarded in his own country, he has established an overseas reputation as well for his fiction about contemporary New Zealand life, even though his work consistently indicts what Gee considers the ugly, provincial side of that life.

He started publishing short stories in the late 1950s, and his first novel, *The Big Season*, appeared in 1962, followed by *A Special Flower* in 1965. Since then he has written several more novels, short stories, and numerous well-received children's books. His third novel, *In My Father's Den* (1972), tells the story of a murder and its solution, but the book rises above detective fiction in its handling of the personal consequences of smug, small-town and suburban attitudes. Gee's greatest accomplishment is his trilogy about a New Zealand family, the Plumbs: *Plumb* (1978), *Meg* (1982), and *Sole Survivor* (1983). In these novels, Gee again addresses the concerns that dominate his earlier fiction—family life and its complex dynamics, conformity and nonconformity, the individual's relationship to the community. Covering a span of time from the late nineteenth century to the 1980s, the trilogy encompasses not only the history of the Plumb family but also much of New Zealand history. While the trilogy does not exactly close on a pessimistic note, it stresses the debasement of a New Zealand vision that Gee sees moving away from the heroic toward the materialistic.

NOVELS BY GEE

In My Father's Den. 1972. OUP 1984 $15.95. ISBN 0-19-558111-3
Meg. 1982. Viking Penguin 1984 $10.95. ISBN 0-14-006712-4
Plumb. 1978. Viking Penguin 1991 $19.95. ISBN 0-14-014932-5
Sole Survivor. 1983. Viking Penguin 1984 $10.95. ISBN 0-14-006700-0

SHORT STORY COLLECTION BY GEE

Collected Stories. Viking Penguin 1986 $14.95. ISBN 0-14-008804-0. A representative gathering of Gee's short fiction.

GRACE, PATRICIA. 1937–

Born in Wellington, New Zealand, Patricia Grace is of Maori descent. One of the first Maori writers in English to gain widespread recognition, Grace has become a force in the promotion and development of writing by those with Maori backgrounds. In 1989 she received an honorary doctorate in literature from Victoria University, Wellington.

Much of Grace's fiction depicts Maori life in conflict with the world of the Pakeha (the Maori term for New Zealanders of European descent). The style that frames the complex conflicts between a dominant and a subordinate culture is deceptively simple. Her dialogue carries the cadence and structure of Maori English, in contrast to what Grace calls in one story "Pakehafied" talking. Her method blends with the narratives themselves, which speak for the often silent world of the colonized Maoris, whose way of life has been irretrievably altered by the European settlers. Grace portrays Maori women suffering from the demands and traditions of their own society, as well as from those of the Pakeha world; she also celebrates the sustaining role of women in the Maori community.

The title story of Grace's second collection of short fiction, *The Dream Sleepers* (1980), in many ways typifies her writing as it describes the lives of Maori children whose mothers clean office buildings at night. The book most widely known is *Electric City and Other Stories* (1987), a depiction of Maori survival in urban society. Grace's two novels are *Mutuwhenua: The Moon Sleeps* (1978), which examines the difficulties faced when a Maori woman marries a Pakeha, and *Potiki* (1986), a highly complex work that links Maori and Christian mythology. A major theme in Grace's work is that of departure from the security of family, and adjustment to a new way of life that makes return impossible.

Novels by Grace

Mutuwhenua: The Moon Sleeps. 1978. Viking Penguin 1986 $13.95. ISBN 0-14-008945-4
Potiki. Viking Penguin 1986 $27.95. ISBN 0-670-81055-X

Short Story Collections by Grace

The Dream Sleepers. 1980. Viking Penguin 1986 $12.95. ISBN 0-14-008946-2
Electric City and Other Stories. Viking Penguin 1987 $12.95. ISBN 0-14-010511-9
Selected Stories. Viking Penguin 1990 $19.95. ISBN 0-14-014518-4
Waiariki. 1975. Viking Penguin 1986 $12.95. ISBN 0-14-008947-0

HULME, KERI. 1947–

Keri Hulme had been writing for several years, little known outside New Zealand feminist and Maori literary circles. Then, during the mid-1980s, she gained international attention for her novel *The Bone People*: In 1984 she received the Mobil Pegasus Award for Maori Writers and the New Zealand Book of the Year Award for fiction, and, in the following year, the distinguished Booker-McConnel Prize, Britain's highest literary honor.

Hulme, who was born in Christchurch, is of Maori descent on her mother's side; her father was an Englishman from Lancashire. Studying for a law degree but not completing it, she worked at various jobs before settling down to write full time.

The Bone People (1984) remains Hulme's major work so far. Almost impossible to describe in a coherent way, the novel is a sprawling and puzzling story about a relationship between a strange child, a powerful woman named Kerewin who reluctantly takes him in, and the child's father, who treats him brutally. According to the critic Margery Fee, the implausible yet metaphoric and sophisticated structure of the text sets out "to rework the old stories that govern the way New Zealanders—both Maori (indigenous New Zealanders) and Pakeha (New Zealanders of European origin)—think about their country."

Hulme has also published two books of short stories about Maori life, *Lost Possessions* (1985) and *Te Kaihau: The Windeater* (1986); the short fiction, too, incorporates the intentionally chaotic and often bombastic style that dominates *The Bone People*. She has written two volumes of free verse as well, *The Silences Between (Moeraki Conversations)* (1982) and *Strands* (1992).

Hulme has received extensive attention from international critics who see her, as Margery Fee says, in the forefront of the "postcolonial discursive formation evolving worldwide"—that is, writers who have set out to reinvent the history of imperialism.

Novel by Hulme

The Bone People. La. State U. Pr. 1985 $19.95. ISBN 0-8071-1284-4

Short Story Collections by Hulme

Lost Possessions. Victoria U. Pr. 1985 o.p.
Te Kaihau: The Windeater. Victoria U. Pr. 1986 o.p.

Poetry by Hulme

Strands. OUP 1992 $13.95. ISBN 1-86940-068-2

IHIMAERA, WITI. 1944–

Born in the countryside of New Zealand into a Maori family of Mormons, Witi Ihimaera is not only a major writer but a diplomat as well. He began his career in the foreign service in 1976 and served, among other posts, as New Zealand consul-general in New York. After completing a B.A. in English, Ihimaera worked as a journalist in New Zealand and, describing himself as a "compulsive storyteller," started writing fiction. In 1982 he coedited an anthology of Maori writing, *Into the World of Light*, and continues to be a champion of literature in English by Maoris.

In retrospect, Ihimaera describes his first collection of short stories, *Pounamu, Pounamu* (1972), as *Songs of Innocence*; this subtitle applies as well to his two early novels, *Tangi* (1973) and *Whanau* (1974). These three books are filled with romantic images of a childhood spent in the security of the extended Maori family, offering what Ihimaera calls a "landscape of the heart." But in 1975 winds of change swept the Maori community as political awareness grew. Reflecting that change, the collection of Ihimaera's short fiction that appeared in 1976, *The New Net Goes Fishing*, moves out of the earlier work's Eden into a violent and disruptive world. *Dear Miss Mansfield* (1989), a group of stories about Maori life, uses the postmodernist technique of rewriting or responding to an earlier text—in this instance, some of the short fiction by New Zealand's most famous writer, Katherine Mansfield. Described as a contentious work, *The Matriarch* (1986) marks a dramatic departure from Ihimaera's earlier novels. Here the sweet memories of childhood have been discarded for a confrontational view of the Maori role in modern society.

To a degree, a survey of Ihimaera's work is also a survey of the changing attitudes in New Zealand society on the part of both the Maoris (indigenous New Zealanders) and the Pakehas (New Zealanders of European descent), as they at last confront openly and honestly the legacy of imperialism to which they are heirs.

Novels by Ihimaera

The Matriarch. 1986. Picador 1988 o.p.
Tangi. 1973. Heinemann Ed. 1990 repr. of 1973 ed. $9.95. ISBN 0-7900-0045-8
Whanau. 1974. Octopus 1973 o.p.

Short Story Collections by Ihimaera

Dear Miss Mansfield: Tribute to Kathleen Mansfield Beauchamp. Viking Penguin 1989 $29.95. ISBN 0-670-82624-3
The New Net Goes Fishing. Octopus 1977 o.p.
Pounamu, Pounamu. Octopus 1972 o.p.

BOOKS ABOUT IHIMAERA

Corballis, Richard, and Simon Garrett. *Introducing Witi Ihimaera*. Longman Paul 1982 o.p. A Detailed discussion of short stories, with emphasis on Ihimaera's narrative construction.

Ojinmah, Umelo Reubens. *Witi Ihimaera and the Bicultural Vision*. U. of Otago Pr. 1990 o.p. Compares Ihimaera's work with that of the African writer Chinua Achebe.

MANSFIELD, KATHERINE. 1888–1923

A world figure more than a New Zealand writer, Katherine Mansfield is one of the first writers from the once flourishing British Empire to forge an international reputation. Mansfield's real name is Kathleen Mansfield Beauchamp. Like her name, her life and work created a series of doubles. Born into a wealthy New Zealand family, she spent most of her life in Europe, yet some of her best fiction is set in her homeland. A disciplined artist who experienced intense periods of creativity, she was plagued with depression and illness. As a writer she understood perfectly the subtleties and complexities of human relationships and revealed them truthfully in her fiction; yet, in her own life, she was unable to maintain satisfactory relationships with friends, family, or her husband, John Middleton Murry, the British-born editor and writer.

Whatever the sometimes troubling state of Mansfield's short and unhappy life, the work she left behind constituted a brilliant accomplishment: a body of short fiction unparalleled in its ability to penetrate the core of human experience. The innovative techniques she employed so unobtrusively have been credited with altering the form of the short story in English, and her influence on other writers in English can only be called immense. How her continued success has affected the development of New Zealand literature remains an open question. As was the case with many writers from the pre-World War II British Commonwealth, Mansfield gained her initial reputation abroad, then in her homeland. Today she is treated as a national treasure in New Zealand; her childhood home is a museum.

During her lifetime, Mansfield published five volumes of fiction. *In a German Pension* (1911) appeared first and contains stories set in Europe. *Prelude* (1918), *Je ne parle pas français* (1920), and *Bliss and Other Stories* (1920), the next three volumes, continued in this vein. In *The Garden Party and Other Stories* (1922), she returned to her New Zealand childhood for much of the material she transforms into lasting fiction. The title story, considered one of her finest and often anthologized, unfolds events that lead to a young girl's loss of innocence—a frequent enough theme in literature but one that Mansfield handles both subtly and explosively. Three more volumes were published posthumously, *The Dove's Nest and Other Stories* (1923), *Something Childish and Other Stories* (1924), and *The Aloe* (1930), all edited by Murry.

SHORT STORY COLLECTION BY MANSFIELD

The Short Stories of Katherine Mansfield. Ecco Pr. 1983 repr. of 1920 ed. $15.95. ISBN 0-8804-025-8. A huge volume–688 pages–containing all the stories.

WORK BY MANSFIELD

The Collected Letters of Katherine Mansfield, Volume II: 1918–September 1919. Ed. by Vincent O'Sullivan and Margaret Scott. OUP 1987 $34.00. ISBN 0-19-812614-X. An absorbing collection (by a self-described "compulsive letter writer") of many of Mansfield's letters to Murry and others.

Journal of Katherine Mansfield. Ecco Pr. 1983 $6.95. ISBN 0-88001-023-1. Covers a broad range of matters that interested Mansfield, especially the writing of her contemporaries.

Katherine Mansfield: Selected Letters. Ed. by Vincent O'Sullivan. OUP 1989 $39.95. ISBN 0-19-818592-8. A collection of unpublished letters supporting one critic's observation that Mansfield's letters are in a sense the novel she never published.

BOOKS ABOUT MANSFIELD

Alpers, Antony. *The Life of Katherine Mansfield.* Viking Penguin 1980 o.p. Remains the best biography of Mansfield, interpreting the work generally from a biographical standpoint.

Kobler, Jasper F. *Katherine Mansfield.* Macmillan 1990 $20.95. ISBN 0-8057-8325-3. Focuses on technique and theme; provides sound analyses of individual stories.

Meyers, Jeffrey. *Katherine Mansfield: A Biography.* New Dir. Pr. 1980 $10.50. ISBN 0-8112-0834-6. An insightful look into Mansfield's life, which the biographer relates to her art.

SARGESON, FRANK. 1903–1982

Frank Sargeson won international recognition as a writer whose work reflects a strong New Zealand sensibility. Born and raised in Hamilton, he trained as a lawyer. Seeking to escape the puritanical restraints of his family, he traveled to England but returned two years later, in 1928. Sargeson's first book, *Conversation with My Uncle and Other Sketches*, appeared in 1936. The writer continued to publish throughout his life, including novels and plays, as well as autobiography and criticism, but his short stories remain his major accomplishment. The fact that much of his work is out of print may suggest the changing fashions in literary tastes. Still, Sargeson is an important figure in New Zealand literature. Contemporary criticism tends to see his work not merely as a realistic depiction of New Zealand life but as a fictional process preoccupied with identity: "gender identity, national identity, economic identity, social identity, and cultural identity," in the words of Lydia Wevers.

SHORT STORY COLLECTION BY SARGESON

Stories of Frank Sargeson. Viking Penguin 1986 $19.95. ISBN 0-14-006068-5. A substantial and representative collection of Sargeson's stories, covering his long career.

WENDT, ALBERT. 1939–

The best-known writer from the South Pacific, Albert Wendt was born into a Samoan family. He left Samoa in 1952 to attend a high school in New Zealand as a scholarship student. He later received an M.A. in history from Victoria University in Wellington. After teaching at universities in Fiji and Samoa, Wendt now holds a professorship of Pacific studies at Auckland University.

Wendt is the product of two cultures—the Samoan of his childhood and the European of his education. This inevitable clash of values figures in Wendt's first novel, *Sons for the Return Home* (1973), which recounts a doomed love affair between a Samoan man and a woman of European descent. The narrative also reveals how the young man feels torn between two cultural poles. Wendt's next novel, *Pouliuli* (1976), takes Samoan life as its subject. Sometimes called a South Pacific version of *King Lear*, the story follows the trials of an aged chief who tests those around him. Wendt's novel receiving the most attention is *Leaves of the Banyan Tree* (1979), a saga of Samoan family life that moves through several decades until the post-independence period.

Flying-Fox in a Freedom Tree and *The Birth and Death of the Miracle Man*, Wendt's two collections of short stories, take up aspects of Samoan life—its traditions, its clashes with European culture, and its disintegration. In these stories Wendt rewrites old myths to show how tradition can instruct the present. Wendt has also published poetry, *Inside Us the Dead* (1976) and *Shaman of Visions* (1984), which incorporates the tropical beauty of Samoa and its oral traditions. He also has compiled several anthologies, including collections of poetry from Fiji, Western Samoa, the New Hebrides, and the Solomons.

Novels by Wendt

Leaves of the Banyan Tree. 1979. Viking Penguin 1981 $15.95. ISBN 0-14-005473-1
Pouliuli. 1976. Viking Penguin 1987 $9.95. ISBN 0-14-008109-7
Sons for the Return Home. 1973. Viking Penguin 1987 $12.95. ISBN 0-14-009680-9

Short Story Collections by Wendt

The Birth and Death of the Miracle Man. 1986. Viking Penguin $12.95. ISBN 0-14-008109-7
Flying-Fox in a Freedom Tree and Other Stories. 1974. Viking Penguin 1988 $10.95. ISBN 0-14-010221-3

Poetry by Wendt

Shaman of Visions. Auckland U. Pr. 1984 o.p.

CHAPTER 27

Comparative Literature

Helane Levine-Keating

> [The categories of comparative literature] can be aptly symbolized by the elements of ancient chemistry: air, water, earth, and fire. Air, which unifies the whole living world, suggests overall literary relations. Water represents literary movements. As streams of water are the classical image for the flux of time, studies of movements have to consider the chronological sequence of cultural events. Artistic moods and intellectual modes develop and progress as a river grows from a trickle at its source to a torrent at its mouth. Earth is the only solid element that assumes durable forms; it signifies, therefore, literary genres. And, to complete our analogy, fire illustrates the theme and motif, the translucent soul of every literary product.
>
> —FRANÇOIS JOST, *Introduction to Comparative Literature*

Considering the age of some of the great works of world literature, whether the work of HOMER, DANTE ALIGHIERI, or WILLIAM SHAKESPEARE (see Vol. 1), the comparative approach to literature is a relatively new phenomenon. The term *ilittérature comparée*was probably first used in the early nineteenth century in France. That it quickly became well known is evidenced by the many studies of European literatures that bore it in their titles during the 1820s through the 1840s. Several decades later, similar studies began to appear in Great Britain, Italy, and Germany. The first chair of comparative literature was established in 1861 at the University of Naples, and in 1871, Francesco de Sanctis began teaching "letteratura comparata" based on the premise that "literature constitutes a whole." Today departments of comparative literature are common in universities everywhere.

Comparative literature involves the study of literature that transcends national borders as well as the study of literature's interrelationships with other arts and areas of thought. It emerged in the West from the growing recognition that international and universal literary forces played important roles in the formation of national literatures. Scholars interested in this type of research have developed methods for examining the transnational dimensions of literary works and have agreed on standards for determining valid comparisons. While Western literature was originally the basis for comparative studies, scholars today draw on the literature of all cultures and nations. One challenge they face in interpreting the literature of vastly different cultures is determining whether the concepts and assumptions of one culture are valid tools for literary analysis in another.

In comparative literature, there are seven ways of comparing works from different cultures and written in different languages or dialects. One method of comparison focuses on the sharing of a common theme, type, or motif. For example, a scholar might compare the way the Cain and Abel theme is treated by authors of different cultures and literary epochs. The theme may appear in different genres or forms. The comparative literature scholar might then examine individual literary texts in order to understand the evolution of the treatments and the meaning of parallels and contrasts the texts reveal.

Another method of comparison centers on the study of works sharing characteristics of a literary movement, epoch, period, generation, or trend. The study of Western romanticism in late eighteenth- and early nineteenth-century German, French, and British literature and mid-nineteenth-century American literature, for instance, has been a fruitful one for comparatists.

A third comparative approach is the study of the relationship between literature and other arts or areas of knowledge. Exploring the connections between literature and art, music, myth, anthropology, psychology, science, religion, or philosophy offers considerable insight into literature. For example, the common ground that literature and psychology share makes them practically inseparable, for in attempting to understand literature we are always bringing psychology to bear. Psychology informs our study of the structure and content of a literary work, the imagination that generated its form, and the human behavior it describes. Comparatists who focus on the psychological dimensions of literature embrace the views of different theorists, for example, SIGMUND FREUD (see Vols. 3 and 5), CARL JUNG (see Vol. 5), JACQUES LACAN (see Vol. 5), or Nancy Chodorow.

Many comparative literature scholars are drawn to yet another approach, the study of influence and imitation. This study takes several forms: the resemblances between two or more works, authors, or national literatures, the influence of one author on a writer or writers in other countries, the influence of a group of writers on another, and, finally, the reception of a work or literary movement in another country. The French poet CHARLES BAUDELAIRE (1821–67) translated the American author EDGAR ALLAN POE (1809–49) (see Vol. 1), and comparatists have traced Poe's influence in aspects of Baudelaire's often macabre imagery. Baudelaire himself influenced the French symbolist poets and the German writer STEFAN GEORGE. Resemblances between literary works can arise, however, even when an author is unfamiliar with the work of the other author if, for example, both have been subject to the same historical forces. An East European contemporary of the Austrian writer FRANZ KAFKA (1883–1924), for instance, might not have read Kafka's fiction—most of which was published posthumously—but might produce works noticeably similar to Kafka's works, due to the writers' similar political or social backgrounds.

The study of genres—the ode, the ballad, the sonnet, the short story, the epic, the essay, and so forth—is another approach. A genre may not exist forever, may not exist in all cultures and civilizations, may reflect a particular historical period or a stage, may take several forms (such as the Italian and Elizabethan sonnets), and may evolve over time. Generally, there are four categories of genre study: the attempt to establish and define genres, the history of specific genres, the interpretation of literary works in terms of genre, and the theory of genre itself.

Finally, in order to study comparative literature, comparatists must rely on translations when they are not conversant in the language of the works they are studying. The art of translation and the task of the translator are crucial to transnational comparative literature: A translator can distort the original work, contributing an alien point of view; on the other hand, translators can bring a whole literary movement to a country, as did the Elizabethan translators who introduced the Italian Renaissance to England. The problems of translating poetry—involving imitating, altering, or abandoning the poem's rhyme, rhyme scheme, or meter, as well as capturing the poem's cadence, diction, lyricism, and imagery—have plagued literary translators for centuries. In the famous poem "On First Looking into Chapman's Homer" (1816) by the English romantic JOHN KEATS (1795–1821) (see Vol. 1), Keats praises not only HOMER's transforming poetry, but also Chapman's translation of it: "Yet did I never breathe its [Homer's realm's] pure serene / Till I heard Chapman speak out loud and bold: / Then felt I like some watcher of the skies / When a new planet swims into his ken." Without Chapman, Homer would have been lost to Keats, and Keats's poem, perhaps, lost to us.

The synthesis of these various approaches and methodologies forms the discipline of comparative literature. Studied in universities all over the world, it encourages multiculturalism, diversity, the study of foreign languages, and interdisciplinary learning. The International Comparative Literature Association holds yearly conferences and has also launched a series of works examining aspects of comparative literary history. In today's global village, the comparative approach to world literature offers intellectual challenge as well as innovative and needed research.

HISTORY AND PRINCIPLES OF COMPARATIVE LITERATURE

The following bibliography includes most of the major texts that describe the history and principles of comparative literature. These texts present a thorough introduction to the discipline's various approaches and its evolution in countries throughout the world. Many also include helpful bibliographies of their own.

Alridge, A. Owen. *Comparative Literature: Matter and Method*. U. of Ill. Pr. 1969 o.p. Seventeen essays by leading comparatists grouped under criticism and theory, movements, themes, genres, and literary relations (including history of ideas, influence studies, cross-cultural relations, and others); introduction to each section.

Clements, Robert J. *Comparative Literature as Academic Discipline: A Statement of Principles, Praxis, Standards*. Bks. Demand repr. of 1978 ed. $95.20. ISBN 0-8357-7549-6. Reviews definitions of comparative literature and methods of training students; practical guidelines for research, course planning, and teaching.

Corstius, Jan Brandt. *Introduction to the Study of Comparative Literature*. Random 1968 o.p. Dated but still valuable elementary introduction; period-by-period examination of Western literary criticism, demonstrating a common heritage.

Friedrich, Werner. *Outline of Comparative Literature from Dante Alighieri to Eugene O'Neill*. Johnson Repr. 1970 repr. of 1959 ed. o.p "A supranational, truly comparative history of literature, stressing influences, parallels and contrasts" (Stallknecht and Frenz, *Comparative Literature*); groundbreaking and visionary when first published, now somewhat dated.

______. *The Challenge of Comparative Literature, and Other Addresses*. U. of NC Pr. 1970 $19.95. ISBN 0-8078-7051-X. A history of comparative literature since World War II, with Part One examining the discipline in general and Part Two offering specific studies.

Jefferson, Ann, and David Robey, eds. *Modern Literary Theory: A Comparative Introduction*. B & N Imports 1984 o.p. A first-rate collection of essays by British scholars that examines both current and older schools of criticism and interpretive approaches; indexes of concepts, an excellent bibliography; highly recommended.

Jost, François. *Introduction to Comparative Literature*. Pegasus 1974 o.p. A very good introduction to study of influences, movements, genres, and motifs; excellent bibliography up to 1974.

Nichols, Stephen G., Jr., and Richard B. Vowles, eds. *Comparatists at Work: Studies in Comparative Literature*. Blaisdale 1968 o.p. An excellent comparative "sampler," including essays by Rene Wellek, Claudio Guillen, Harry Levin, and W. Bernard Fleischmann; text analyses, critical theory, history of ideas, literature and other arts.

Prawer, S. S. *Comparative Literary Studies: An Introduction*. B & N Imports 1973 o.p. A learned, exhaustive, and readable outline and critical examination of methods and theory; integrates others' work with his own keen evaluations and judgments.

Shaffer, E. S., ed. *Comparative Criticism: A Yearbook*. 4 vols. Cambridge U. Pr. 1979-82 $37.50–$49.50 ea. ISBNs 0-521-22296-6, 0-521-22756-9, 0-521-23276-7, 0-521-24578-8. A valuable collection of essays, mainly by British comparatists: "Our intention . . . is to explore the notion of literary canon as it relates to the present situation within literary studies in Britain" (Preface).

Stallknecht, Newton P., and Horst Frenz, eds. *Comparative Literature: Method and Perspective*. S. Ill. U. Pr. rev. ed. 1973 o.p. Twelve essays on the history and methods of comparative literature by prominent professionals; important insights into the assumptions underlying the discipline, although portions dated.

Weisstein, Ulrich, *Comparative Literature and Literary Theory: Survey and Introduction*. Trans. by William Riggan. Ind. U. Pr. 1974 o.p An astute, in-depth examination of the basic approaches; excellent appendixes on the discipline's prehistory and history and on the problems of compiling comparative bibliographies.

Wellek, Rene. *Discriminations: Further Concepts of Criticism*. Bks. Demand repr. of 1970 ed. $103.30. ISBN 0-8357-8097-X. A major study by one of the most influential scholars in the field, accessible to the general reader and beginning students; stands on its own but a sequel to *Concepts of Criticism*, also highly recommended.

Wellek, Rene, and Austin Warren. *Theory of Literature*. HarBraceJ 1964 $9.95. ISBN 0-15-689084-4. A rigorous, seminal work containing numerous outline-like essays; discusses many aspects of literary theory within a general rather than a historical framework; can be forbidding to an inexperienced reader.

THEMES AND MOTIFS

Analyzing themes and motifs is a very broad, multifaceted approach to comparative literature. The following bibliography, while by no means exhaustive, covers a good range of the spectrum. It includes excellent studies of many common literary themes, such as the narratives of Cain and Abel, Narcissus, Faust, Don Juan, Ulysses, Antigone, Christ, and Joan of Arc. Other studies focus on archetypal images or motifs like the double or second self and the descent to the underworld. Several texts offer studies of archetypal patterns such as the quest or the conflict of generations.

Bloom, Harold, ed. *Joan of Arc*. Chelsea Hse. 1992 $34.95 ISBN 0-7910-1015-5. Essays examining the Joan of Arc theme in the works of Shakespeare, Schiller, Shaw, Anouilh, and others.

______, ed. *Odysseus/Ulysses*. Chelsea Hse. 1991 $34.95. ISBN 0-7910-0924-6. Essays by well-known authors examining the Ulysses theme in the work of Homer, Sophocles, Dante, Shakespeare, Tennyson, Joyce, and Kazantzakis.

Bodkin, Maud. *Archetypal Patterns in Poetry: Psychological Studies of the Imagination*. AMS Pr. 1934 $26.50. ISBN 0-404-14004-1. A classic Jungian study of archetypes in the works of Shakespeare, Coleridge, Virgil, Dante, Milton, Homer, Woolf, Lawrence, and Eliot, among others.

Crook, Eugene J., ed. *Fearful Symmetry: Doubles and Doubling in Literature and Film*. U. Press Fla. 1981 $10.95. ISBN 0-8130-0723-2. Far-ranging essays using innovative approaches to study the double motif.

Damiani, Bruno, and Barbara Mujica. *Et in Arcadia Ego: Essays on Death in the Pastoral Novel*. U. Pr. of Amer. 1990 $19.50. ISBN 0-8191-7773-3. Examines the treatment of death in major pastoral novels of Great Britain and continental Europe, finding links between love and death.

Ditsky, John. *The Onstage Christ: Studies in the Persistence of a Theme.* Rowman 1980 $40.00. ISBN 0-389-20059-X. Examines patterns of "Christ-presence"—as sacrificial victim, teacher, benefactor, or redeemer—in 13 modern plays.

Frontain, Raymond-Jean, and Jan Wojcic, eds. *Old Testament Women in Western Literature.* Univ. Central AR Pr. 1991 $28.95 ISBN 0-944436-12-9. A comparative study of such figures as Eve, Rachel, and Dinah as they appear in literature from Dante to the present.

Keppler, C.F. *The Literature of the Second Self.* Bks. Demand 1972 $63.80. ISBN 0-317-51984-0. A study of the various forms, for example, twin brother, tempter, beloved, of the *doppelgänger* in various literary works.

Matthews, Honor. *The Primal Curse: The Myth of Cain and Abel in the Theatre.* Schocken 1967 o.p. An interesting study of the treatment of the myth in Shakespeare, Chapman, Beckett, Camus, Sartre, Ibsen, Pinter, and Strindberg.

Miller, Karl. *Doubles: Studies in Literary History.* OUP 1987 $14.95. ISBN 0-19-282047-8. Focuses on such writers as Poe, Dickens, Dostoevsky, Wharton, Plath, Lowell, Bellow, and Mailer to examine more recent manifestations of human duality.

Pratt, Annis. *Archetypal Patterns in Women's Fiction.* Bks Demand repr. of 1981 ed. $57.50. ISBN 0-8357-5719-6. Focuses on dominant and recurrent motifs, for example, the Demeter/Kore and Ishtar/Tammuz rebirth myths, Arthurian grail narratives, and symbols from witchcraft.

Quinones, Ricardo J. *The Changes of Cain: Violence and the Lost Brother in Cain and Abel Literature.* Princeton U. Pr. 1991 $24.95. ISBN 0-691-06883-6. Examines this "master metaphor" in Byron, Conrad, Hesse, Melville, Unamuno, Steinbeck, and others.

Smeed, John William. *Don Juan: Variation on a Theme.* Routledge 1990 $39.95. ISBN 0-415-00750-X. Examines the Don Juan story and its alterations in Hoffman, Strauss, Molière, Byron, Pushkin, Shaw, Anouilh, and Frisch.

______. *Faust in Literature.* Greenwood 1987 $62.50. ISBN 0-313-25657-8. Examines the significance of the Faust legend and traces its presence and evolution in literature.

Smith, Evans Lansing. *Rape and Revelation: The Descent to the Underworld of Modernism.* U. Pr. of Amer. 1990 $35.50. ISBN 0-8191-7644-3. An insightful look into the myth of descent into the underworld in Strindberg, Yeats, Conrad, Eliot, Lawrence, Mann, Lowry, Pynchon, and Broch.

Stanford, William Bedell. *The Ulysses Theme: A Study in the Adaptability of a Traditional Hero.* B & N Imports 1964 o.p. A survey of the variation in the characterization of Ulysses since Homer, with chapters on Greek and Latin sources, modern developments, and the wider mythological implications.

Steiner, George. *Antigones: How the Antigone Legend Has Endured in Western Literature, Art, and Thought.* OUP 1984 $9.95. ISBN 0-19-281934-8. A consideration of some of the principal interpretations of the Antigone motif in all genres of literature as well as in opera, ballet, film, and art.

Zweig, Paul. *The Heresy of Self-Love: A Study of Subversive Individualism.* Princeton U. Pr. 1980 $10.95. ISBN 0-691-01371-3. The recurrent theme of Narcissus as it appears in literature and culture from the second century A.D. to the present.

LITERARY MOVEMENTS

The following texts explore many of the major literary movements, epochs, and trends. Focusing on classicism, romanticism, naturalism, realism, symbolism, surrealism, modernism, and postmodernism, these studies offer a variety of points of view, concentrating predominantly on European, North American, and South American authors.

Auerbach, Erich. *Mimesis: The Representation of Reality in Western Literature.* Princeton U. Pr. 1953 $14.95. ISBN 0-691-01269-5. An excellent examination of European literature from Homer to Virginia Woolf, offering a penetrating analysis of postclassical literature.

Baker, Carlos. *The Echoing Green: Romanticism, Modernism, and the Phenomena of Transference in Poetry.* Princeton U. Pr. 1984 $45.00. ISBN 0-691-06595-0. An examination of the influence of the English romantics on Yeats, Frost, Auden, and other modernists.

Balakian, Anna. *Surrealism: The Road to the Absolute.* U. Ch. Pr. 1987 $13.95. ISBN 0-226-03560-3. A thorough and accessible introduction to surrealism in literature, focusing on Lautréamont, Saint-Pol-Roux, Apollinaire, Reverdy, and Breton, with reproductions of contemporary surrealist paintings.

______ . *The Symbolist Movement: A Critical Appraisal.* NYU Pr. 1977 $17.50. ISBN 0-81147-0994-X. An exploration by a major comparatist of symbolism in European literature, including the symbolist theater, with a focus on Baudelaire, Verlaine, and Mallarmé.

Becker, George Joseph. *Master European Realists of the Nineteenth Century.* Continuum 1982 o.p. Examines major realists such as Flaubert, the Goncourt brothers, Zola, Tolstoy, Dostoevsky, Chekhov, and Galdós.

______ . *Realism in Modern Literature.* Continuum 1980 o.p An examination of the climate and definition of nineteenth-century realism, showing its importance in the development of modern fiction; includes an overview of major realistic writers since the 1850s.

Bradbury, Malcolm. *The Modern World: Ten Great Writers.* Viking Penguin 1990 $8.95. ISBN 0-14-011484-X. A provocative look at Woolf, Kafka, Proust, Mann, Joyce, Eliot, Conrad, Ibsen, Pirandello, and Dostoevsky.

Bradbury, Malcolm, and James McFarlane, eds. *Modernism: 1890–1930.* Viking Penguin 1978 $7.95. ISBN 0-14-021933-1. A comprehensive history and analysis of the modernist movement in European literature; extensive bibliographical material, biographies of major figures.

Cantor, Norman F., and Mindy Cantor. *Twentieth-Century Culture: Modernism to Deconstruction.* P. Lang Pubs. 1988 $39.95. ISBN 0-685-22743-X. Modernism in all aspects of culture, with chapters focusing on literature and the arts, psychology and politics, structuralism, deconstruction, and postmodernism.

Fowlie, Wallace. *Age of Surrealism.* Ind. U. Pr. 1966 o.p Traces the growth of surrealism in the work of Lautréamont, Rimbaud, Mallarmé, Apollinaire, Breton, Cocteau, Éluard, and Picasso.

Hamburger, Michael. *The Truth of Poetry: Tensions in Modern Poetry from Baudelaire to the Nineteen-Sixties.* HarBraceJ 1969 o.p. Places the start of modern poetry with Baudelaire; examines its nature, function, and historical and political contexts.

Hedges, Inez. *Languages of Revolt: Dada and Surrealist Literature and Film.* Duke 1983 o.p. A new understanding of dadaism and surrealism using insights provided by semiotics, psychoanalysis, linguistics, and Russian formalism; focuses on Breton, Ernst, Artaud, Buñuel, Mon, Cortázar, and Roche.

Mellor, Anne K., ed. *Romanticism and Feminism.* Ind. U. Pr. 1988 $12.95. ISBN 0-253-20462-3. Fascinating essays focusing on the silencing of the female, portrayals of women, and women writers' responses in the romantic era.

Nalbantian, Suzanne. *The Seeds of Decadence in the Late Nineteenth-Century Novel: A Crisis in Values.* St. Martin 1984 $29.95. ISBN 0-312-70925-0. A comparative study of the characteristics of decadence in Dostoevsky, James, Zola, Hardy, and Conrad.

______ . *The Symbol of the Soul from Holderlin to Yeats: A Study in Metonymy.* Col. U. Pr. 1977 $37.00. ISBN 0-231-04148-9. Examines the soul as a symbolic device in the poetry of Yeats, Holderlin, Shelley, Keats, Baudelaire, the symbolists, and the postsymbolists.

Praz, Mario. *The Romantic Agony.* OUP 1951 $15.95. ISBN 0-19-28106-8. A classic study of romanticism's major themes and their portrayal by various writers.

Quinones, Ricardo J. *Mapping Literary Modernism: Time and Development.* Princeton U. Pr. 1985 $40.00. ISBN 0-691-06636-1. Explores the cultural confrontation between two formative epochs, the Renaissance and the modern era, showing how literary modernists challenged the Renaissance's ethical and dynamic sense of time.

Robinson, Jeffrey Cane. *The Current of Romantic Passion*. U. of Wis. Pr. 1991 $16.95. ISBN 0-299-12964-0. A fascinating study of the notion of romanticism and the nature of passion in literature of the period.

Ross, Marlon B. *The Contours of Masculine Desire: Romanticism and the Rise of Women's Poetry*. OUP 1990 $42.50. ISBN 0-19-505791-0. A groundbreaking examination of the traditional works of romanticism, with a new look at the often neglected writing of women poets of the period.

Sussman, Henry. *Afterimages of Modernity: Structure and Indifference in Twentieth-Century Literature*. Johns Hopkins 1990 $34.00. ISBN 0-8018-3887-8. Focuses on structure as concept and formal device in Joyce, Kafka, Beckett, Adorno, Wittgenstein, and Bernhard to show that modernism's innovation is generated by the disfiguration of structure.

Symons, Arthur. *The Symbolist Movement in Literature*. AMP Pr. 1980 repr. of 1899 ed. $17.50. ISBN 0-404-16348-3. The classic introduction to French symbolists for English and American audiences; essays on Rimbaud, Verlaine, Mallarmé, Balzac, Flaubert, and Baudelaire; introduction by Richard Ellman.

Vernon, John. *Money and Fiction: Literary Realism in the Nineteenth and Early Twentieth Centuries*. Cornell Univ. Pr. 1984 o.p. An original argument that the recurrent theme of money is a key to the nineteenth-century novel; examines such types as the miser and the poor person who becomes a gentleman or a lady in British, American, and European novels.

Wilson, Edmund. *Axel's Castle: A Study in the Imaginative Literature of 1870–1930*. Macmillan 1991 repr. of 1931 ed. $12.95. ISBN 0-02-012871-1. An important study of the development of symbolism and its "fusion or conflict with Naturalism" (Wilson) as seen in Yeats, Joyce, Eliot, Stein, Proust, and Valéry.

INTERRELATIONS IN LITERATURE

The potential for studying interrelations between literature and other disciplines is vast. The books listed below explore connections between literature and other important areas of knowledge, such as Art, Music, and Literature; Myth and Literature; Philosophy and Literature; Politics and Literature; Psychoanalysis and Literature; Religion and Literature; and Science and Literature.

General

Barricelli, Jean-Pierre, and Joseph Gibaldi, eds. *Interrelations of Literature*. Modern Lang. 1982 $16.50. ISBN 0-87352-091-2. Essays covering such areas as literature and philosophy, literature and politics, literature and myth, and so forth, with a thorough bibliography for each essay.

Art, Music, and Literature

Bowen, Zack R. *Musical Allusion in the Works of James Joyce: Early Poetry Through Ulysses*. SUNY Pr. 1974 $49.50. ISBN 0-87395-248-0

DiGaetani, John L. *Richard Wagner and the Modern British Novel*. Fairleigh Dickinson 1978 $22.50. ISBN 0-8386-1955-X. Examines Wagner's influence on the works of Conrad, Lawrence, Forster, Woolf, and Joyce.

Hollander, John. *The Untuning of the Sky: Ideas of Music in English Poetry, 1500–1700*. Princeton U. Pr. 1961 o.p. A critical survey of music-related English poetry from Chaucer to Dryden.

Kerman, Joseph. *Opera as Drama*. U. CA Pr. rev. ed. 1988 $30.00 ISBN 0-520-06273-6. One of the most captivating books on opera to date.

Kramer, Lawrence. *Music and Poetry: The Nineteenth Century and After*. U. CA Pr. 1984 $14.95. ISBN 0-520-05884-4

Maritain, Jacques. *Creative Intuition in Art and Poetry*. Princeton U. Pr. 1952 $60.00. ISBN 0-691-09789-5. Examines the indissoluble relationship between art and poetry, concentrating on the role of the intellect and intuition in creativity.

Steiner, Wendy. *Pictures of Romance: Form against Context in Painting and Literature*. U. Ch. Pr. 1988 $13.95. ISBN 0-226-77229-2. Analyzes how pictures tell stories and the frequent references to paintings and the visual arts in the literary romance.

Wallace, Robert K. *Emily Brontë and Beethoven: Romantic Equilibrium in Fiction and Music*. U. of Ga. Pr. 1986 $30.00. ISBN 0-8203-0813-7. Draws unexpected parallels between Brontë and Beethoven, using romanticism as the comparative lens.

______. *Jane Austen and Mozart: Classical Equilibrium in Fiction and Music*. U. of Ga. Pr. 1983 $32.50. ISBN 0-8203-0671-1. An interesting and original study pairing an unlikely couple, Austen and Mozart, in the context of classicism.

Watts, Emily. *Ernest Hemingway and the Arts*. Bks. Demand repr. of 1971 ed. $49.30. ISBN 0-685-15286-3

Myth and Literature

Feder, Lillian. *Ancient Myth in Modern Poetry*. Princeton U. Pr. 1972 $16.95. ISBN 0-691-01336-5. An excellent examination of the way myth functions as an aesthetic device in the poetry of Yeats, Pound, Eliot, and Auden.

Frye, Northrop. *Fables of Identity: Studies in Poetic Mythology*. HarBraceJ 1963 $8.95. ISBN 0-15-629730-2. Essays exploring the archetypal structure of a variety of authors, including Homer, Spenser, Twain, Shakespeare, Milton, Blake, Dickinson, and Joyce.

______. *Northrop Frye. Myth and Metaphor: Selected Essays, 1974–1988*. U. Pr. of Va. 1992 $14.95. ISBN 0-8139-1369-1. Twenty-four dazzling essays published just before Frye's death.

______. *Spiritus Mundi: Essays on Literature, Myth, and Society*. Ind. U. Pr. 1976 $9.95. ISBN 0-253-20289-2. Essays on Milton, Blake, Yeats, and Wallace Stevens.

Vickery, John, ed. *Myth and Literature: Contemporary Theory and Practice*. Bks. Demand 1966 $100.80. ISBN 0-317-42112-3. First-rate essays by well-known critics on archetypal criticism, mythopoeia, and the presence of myth in literature.

Philosophy and Literature

Barrett, William. *Irrational Man: A Study in Existential Philosophy*. Doubleday 1958 $9.95. ISBN 0-385-03138-6. A study of the foremost existentialists—Kierkegaard, Nietzsche, Heidegger, and Sartre—and authors from Dostoevsky to Beckett.

Nussbaum, Martha C. *Love's Knowledge: Essays on Philosophy and Literature*. OUP 1990 $15.95. ISBN 0-19-507485-8. Interdisciplinary essays that draw on the classics, modern comparative literature, and philosophy.

Scholes, Robert. *Protocols of Reading*. Yale U. Pr. 1989 $22.50. ISBN 0-300-04513-1. Presents a series of associatively linked arguments and examples that attempt to determine the ethical-political demands that weigh upon every experience of reading.

Politics and Literature

Des Pres, Terrence. *Praises and Dispraises: Poetry and Politics, the Twentieth Century*. Viking Penguin 1989 $8.95. ISBN 0-14-012760-7. Posits that poetry must go beyond the private into the political, using the works of Yeats (Ireland), Brecht (Germany), Breytenback (South Africa), Adrienne Rich and Thomas McGrath (United States) as examples.

Eagleton, Terry, Frederic Jameson, and Edward W. Said. *Nationalism, Colonialism, and Literature*. U. of Minn. Pr. 1990 $9.95. ISBN 0-8166-1863-1. Essays analyzing the role of cultural production in comprehending the aftermath of colonization, especially in Ireland.

Gordimer, Nadine. *The Essential Gesture: Writing, Politics, Places.* Viking Penguin 1989 $11.00. ISBN 0-14-012212-5. An excellent collection by the 1991 Nobel Prize winner, reflecting on the relationship between politics and art and the importance of place.

Howe, Irving. *Politics and the Novel.* NAL–Dutton 1957 $9.95. ISBN 0-452-00844-1. Analyzes the political ideology informing the novels of Stendhal, Dostoevsky, Conrad, Turgenev, James, Hawthorne, Malraux, Koestler, and others.

Michie, Helena. *Sororophobia: Differences among Women in Literature and Culture.* OUP 1992 $29.95. ISBN 0-19-507387-8. How women's differences have been textually represented in such cultural contexts as African-American mulatto novels, Victorian mainstream fiction, lesbian communities, and country music.

Newey, Vincent, and Ann Thompson. *Literature and Nationalism.* Rowman 1991 $49.50. ISBN 0-389-20954-6. Essays exploring the interrelations of drama and nationalism in the times of Shakespeare and Yeats.

Showalter, Elaine. *Sexual Anarchy: Gender and Culture at the Fin de Siècle.* Viking Penguin 1990 $9.95. ISBN 0-14-011587-0. Compares feminist images in late nineteenth-century women's writing with values expressed in contemporary literature and film.

Psychoanalysis and Literature

Edel, Leon. *The Modern Psychological Novel.* Peter Smith 1955 $11.25. ISBN 0-8446-2020-3. An important analysis, covering many novelists.

Felman, Shoshana, ed. *Literature and Psychoanalysis: The Question of Reading: Otherwise.* Johns Hopkins 1982 $42.50. ISBN 0-8018-02754-X. Essays influenced by French psychoanalytic theory, containing readings of writers from Dante to Derrida.

Holland, Norman N. *Holland's Guide to Psychoanalytic Psychology and Literature-and-Psychology.* OUP 1990 $10.95. ISBN 0-19-506280-9. A short, very accessible guide to the immense field of psychoanalysis and literature, broken into the subcategories of psychology.

Rogers, Robert. *A Psychoanalytic Study of the Double in Literature.* Wayne St. U. Pr. 1970 o.p. A Freudian examination of the double's various forms in Melville's *Billy Budd* and *Pierre*, Shakespeare's *Othello,* and Kafka's stories, among others.

Ruitenbeck, Hendrik M., ed. *Psychoanalysis and Literature.* Dutton 1964 o.p. Excellent essays by major psychoanalysts and literary critics, including Ernest Jones, Marie Bonaparte, Kenneth Burke, Norman Holland, Lionel Trilling, and Heinz Kohut.

Ryan, Judith. *The Vanishing Subject: Early Psychology and Literary Modernism.* U. Ch. Pr. 1991 $29.95. ISBN 0-226-73226-6. The impact on 15 authors of the late nineteenth-century idea that consciousness is separate from the notion of self.

Religion and Literature

Alter, Robert. *The Art of Biblical Narrative.* Basic Bks. 1983 $11.95. ISBN 0-465-00427-X

Frye, Northrop. *The Great Code: The Bible and Literature.* HarBraceJ 1982 $8.95. ISBN 0-15-636480-8. Discusses the Bible as encyclopedic epic and its immense influence on literature.

Gunn, Giles, ed. *Literature and Religion.* HarpC 1971 o.p Critical essays outlining the nature and goal of the study of religion and literature.

Steiner, George. *Real Presences.* U. Ch. Pr. 1989 $11.95. ISBN 0-226-77234-9. An argument that a transcendent reality is necessary for the creation of literature and art and grounds all human communication.

Science and Literature

Hayles, N. Katherine, ed. *Chaos and Order: Complex Dynamics in Literature and Science.* U. Ch. Pr. 1991 $14.95. ISBN 0-226-32144-4. Fourteen theorists examine the new paradigm of chaotics and its significance in literary and cultural studies.

Huxley, Aldous. *Literature and Science*. Ox Bow 1991 repr. of 1963 ed. $25.00. ISBN 0-918024-84-6. A study by the famous novelist of the relationship between science and literature, showing how scientific knowledge is used.

Levine, George. *Darwin and the Novelists: Patterns of Science in Victorian Fiction*. U. Ch. Pr. 1988 $16.95. ISBN 0-226-47574-3. Investigates the impact of Darwin and natural theology on nineteenth-century British fiction.

Turner, Frederick. *Natural Classicism: Essays on Literature and Science*. U. Pr. of Va. 1991 $14.94. ISBN 0-8139-1391-8. Examines the interconnectedness of nature and human endeavor; tries to integrate literature, art, music, biology, psychology, anthropology, linguistics, and aesthetics.

INTERNATIONAL INFLUENCES

Although studies of international influences exist in different languages and focus on a variety of nationalities, the following bibliography reflects a tendency in the discipline to focus on Western literature. Comparatists are beginning, however, to move beyond the boundaries of the West, and as the global village shrinks, new and exciting studies are appearing.

Clements, Patricia. *Baudelaire and the English Tradition: Canonization of the Subversive*. Princeton U. Pr. 1985 $55.00. ISBN 0-691-06649-3. An excellent study tracing Baudelaire's influence on British writers, showing his importance in the development of modernism.

Magnus, Laurie. *English Literature in Its Foreign Relations, 1300 to 1800*. Ayer 1968 repr. of 1927 ed. $20.00. ISBN 0-405-08775-6. Examines the foreign influences on Chaucer, Spenser, Shakespeare, Milton, and Dryden, drawing on the Bible, Ovid, Molière, Racine, and other sources.

Sheppard, John Tresidder. *Aeschylus and Sophocles: Their Work and Influence*. Cooper Sq. 1963 o.p. Attributes the common conception of tragedy in such authors as Horace, Dante, Shakespeare, and Racine to Aeschylus and Sophocles.

Simms, Norman Toby. *Points of Contact: A Study of the Interplay and Intersection of Traditional and Non-Traditional Literatures, Cultures, and Mentalities*. Pace Univ. Pr. 1990 $37.50. ISBN 0-944473-04-0. Examines Western civilization's prejudice against oral literary traditions; introduces the rich oral cultures of the South Pacific, New Guinea, and New Zealand.

TRANSLATION

Bassnett-McGuire, Susan. *Translation Studies*. Routledge 1991 $14.95. ISBN 0-415-06528-3. A general introduction to translation theory; excellent.

Brower, Reuben, *Mirror on Mirror: Translation, Imitation, Parody. Studies in Comparative Lit.* HUP 1974 $18.50. ISBN 0-674-57645-4. An interesting collection of essays but diffuse.

Kelly, Louis. *The True Interpreter*. Blackwell Pubs. 1979 o.p. A good history of translation in the West.

Lefevre, Andre. *Translating Literature: The German Tradition from Luther to Rosenzweig*. Humanities 1977 o.p. A collection of historically important texts, from Martin Luther to Walter Benjamin, some of which have never before been translated into English.

Matthiessen, F. O. *Translation, An Elizabethan Art*. Rprt Serv. 1992 $79.00. ISBN 0-7812-7034-0. A classic study showing how the Renaissance came to England, focusing on the Elizabethan era.

Newmark, Peter. *Approaches to Translation: Aspects of Translation*. Pergamon 1980 o.p. Linguistic research in translation theory.

Nida, Eugene A., and C. R. Taber, eds. *The Theory and Practice of Translation*. Am. Bible 1974 $18.75. ISBN 90-04-06550-4. An older but very valuable introduction to translation theory among linguistic and anthropological lines; uses the Bible, as well as narratives from West African culture, as material.

Savory, Theodore. *The Art of Translation*. Jonathan Cape 1968 o.p. A layperson's introduction to translation theory that is impressionistic, but fun and good nonetheless.

Schulte, Hans and Gerhart Teuscher. *The Art of Literary Translation*. U. Pr. of Amer. 1991 $48.50. ISBN 0-8191-7839-4. Essays addressing the art and role in society of the translator and his or her contributions.

Schulte, Rainer, and John Biguenet, eds. *Theories of Translation: An Anthology of Essays from Dryden to Derrida*. U. Ch. Pr. 1991 $12.95. ISBN 0-226-04871-3. An important collection, spanning centuries and cultures, that addresses the question of whether literary translation is feasible.

Steiner, George. *After Babel: Aspects of Language and Translation*. OUP 2nd. ed. 1993 $12.95. ISBN 0-19-212300-9. One of the great works on translation, a monument to the subject; argues that everything pertaining to the use of language is translation; anecdotal, filled with examples.

Wills, Wolfram. *The Science of Translation: Theoretical and Applicative Aspects*. Benjamins North Am. 1982 o.p. Methodical, rigorous introduction to translation theory on linguistic grounds.

Zuber, O. *The Languages of Theatre: Problems in the Translation and Transposition of Drama*. Pergamon 1980 o.p. The first study on the various ways of translating for the theater and of getting translated plays produced; full of information; a valuable collection of essays.

Name Index

In addition to authors of books, this index includes the names of persons mentioned in introductory essays, section introductions, biographical profiles, general bibliographic entries, and "Books about" sections. Throughout, however, persons mentioned only in passing—to indicate friendships, relationships, and so on—are generally not indexed. Editors, translators, and compilers are not indexed unless there is no specific author given for the work in question. Writers of the introductions, forewords, afterwords, and similar parts of works are not indexed. The names of individuals who are represented by separate biographical profiles appear in boldface, as do the page numbers on which their profiles appear.

Title Index

Titles of all books discussed in *The Reader's Adviser* are indexed here, except broad generic titles such as "Complete Works," "Selections," "Poems," "Correspondence." Also omitted is any title written by a profiled author that also includes that author's full name or last name as part of the title, such as *The Works of Horace* or *Horace Talks: The Satires*. The only exception to this is Shakespeare (Volume 1), where *all* works by and about him are indexed. To locate all titles by and about a profiled author, the user should refer to the Name Index for the author's primary listing (given in boldface). In general, subtitles are omitted unless two or more works have the same main title, or the main title consists of an author's full or last name (e.g., *Simone de Beauvoir: A Biography* and *Simone de Beauvoir: Witness to a Century*). When two or more works by different authors have the same title, the authors' last names will appear in parentheses following the title.

Subject Index

This index provides detailed, multiple-approach access to the subject content of the volume. Arrangement is alphabetical. The names of profiled, main-entry authors are not included in this index; the reader is reminded to use the Name Index to locate these individuals. For additional information, the reader should refer to the detailed Table of Contents at the front of the volume.